ENCYCLOPEDIA OF RELIGION

SECOND EDITION

ENCYCLOPEDIA OF RELIGION

SECOND EDITION

5

ETERNITY
•
GOD

LINDSAY JONES
EDITOR IN CHIEF

MACMILLAN REFERENCE USA
An imprint of Thomson Gale, a part of The Thomson Corporation

THOMSON
GALE

Detroit • New York • San Francisco • San Diego • New Haven, Conn. • Waterville, Maine • London • Munich

THOMSON
GALE

Encyclopedia of Religion, Second Edition

Lindsay Jones, Editor in Chief

For more information, contact
Macmillan Reference USA
An imprint of Thomson Gale
27500 Drake Rd.
Farmington, Hills, MI 48331-3535
Or you can visit our Internet site at
http://www.gale.com

LIBRARY OF CONGRESS CATALOGING-IN-PUBLICATION DATA

Encyclopedia of religion / Lindsay Jones, editor in chief.— 2nd ed.
p. cm.
Includes bibliographical references and index.
ISBN 0-02-865733-0 (SET HARDCOVER : ALK. PAPER) —
ISBN 0-02-865734-9 (V. 1) — ISBN 0-02-865735-7 (v. 2) —
ISBN 0-02-865736-5 (v. 3) — ISBN 0-02-865737-3 (v. 4) —
ISBN 0-02-865738-1 (v. 5) — ISBN 0-02-865739-X (v. 6) —
ISBN 0-02-865740-3 (v. 7) — ISBN 0-02-865741-1 (v. 8) —
ISBN 0-02-865742-X (v. 9) — ISBN 0-02-865743-8 (v. 10)
— ISBN 0-02-865980-5 (v. 11) — ISBN 0-02-865981-3 (v. 12) — ISBN 0-02-865982-1 (v. 13) — ISBN 0-02-865983-X (v. 14) — ISBN 0-02-865984-8 (v. 15)
1. RELIGION—ENCYCLOPEDIAS. I. JONES, LINDSAY, 1954-

BL31.E46 2005
200'.3—dc22 2004017052

This title is also available as an e-book.
ISBN 0-02-865997-X
Contact your Thomson Gale representative for ordering information.

Printed in the United States of America
10 9 8 7 6 5 4 3 2 1

EDITORS AND CONSULTANTS

Editor in Chief

Lindsay Jones
Associate Professor, Department of Comparative Studies, Ohio State University

Board Members

Davíd Carrasco
Neil Rudenstine Professor of Study of Latin America, Divinity School and Department of Anthropology, Harvard University

Giovanni Casadio
Professor of History of Religions, Dipartimento di Scienze dell'Antichità, Università degli Studi di Salerno

Wendy Doniger
Mircea Eliade Distinguished Service Professor of the History of Religions, University of Chicago

Gary L. Ebersole
Professor of History and Religious Studies, and Director, UMKC Center for Religious Studies, University of Missouri—Kansas City

Janet Gyatso
Hershey Professor of Buddhist Studies, The Divinity School, Harvard University

Charles Hallisey
Associate Professor, Department of Languages and Cultures of Asia and Program in Religious Studies, University of Wisconsin—Madison

Charles H. Long
Professor of History of Religions, Emeritus, and Former Director of Research Center for Black Studies, University of California, Santa Barbara

Mary N. MacDonald
Professor, History of Religions, Le Moyne College (Syracuse, New York)

Dale B. Martin
Professor of Religious Studies, and Chair, Department of Religious Studies, Yale University

Azim Nanji
Professor and Director, The Institute of Ismaili Studies, London

Jacob Olupona
Professor, African American and African Studies Program, University of California, Davis

Michael Swartz
Professor of Hebrew and Religious Studies, Ohio State University

Inés Talamantez
Associate Professor, Religious Studies Department, University of California, Santa Barbara

Consultants

Gregory D. Alles
Associate Professor of Religious Studies, McDaniel College
Study of Religion

Sigma Ankrava
Professor, Department of Literary and Cultural Studies, Faculty of Modern Languages, University of Latvia
Baltic Religion and Slavic Religion

Diane Apostolos-Cappadona
Center for Muslim–Christian Understanding and Liberal Studies Program, Georgetown University
Art and Religion

Diane Bell
Professor of Anthropology and Women's Studies, George Washington University
Australian Indigenous Religions

Kees W. Bolle
Professor Emeritus of History, University of California, Los Angeles, and Fellow, Netherlands Institute for Advanced Studies in the Humanities and Social Sciences
History of Religions

Mark Csikszentmihalyi
Associate Professor in the Department of East Asian Languages and Literature and the Program in Religious Studies, University of Wisconsin—Madison
Chinese Religions

Richard A. Gardner
Faculty of Comparative Culture, Sophia University
Humor and Religion

John A. Grim
Professor of Religion, Bucknell University and Co-Coordinator,

Harvard Forum on Religion and Ecology
Ecology and Religion

JOSEPH HARRIS
Francis Lee Higginson Professor of English Literature and Professor of Folklore, Harvard University
Germanic Religions

URSULA KING
Professor Emerita, Senior Research Fellow and Associate Member of the Institute for Advanced Studies, University of Bristol, England, and Professorial Research Associate, Centre for Gender and Religions Research, School of Oriental and African Studies, University of London
Gender and Religion

DAVID MORGAN
Duesenberg Professor of Christianity and the Arts, and Professor of Humanities and Art History, Valparaiso University
Color Inserts and Essays

JOSEPH F. NAGY
Professor, Department of English, University of California, Los Angeles
Celtic Religion

MATTHEW OJO
Obafemi Awolowo University
African Religions

JUHA PENTIKÄINEN
Professor of Comparative Religion, The University of Helsinki, Member of Academia Scientiarum Fennica, Finland
Arctic Religions and Uralic Religions

TED PETERS
Professor of Systematic Theology, Pacific Lutheran Theological Seminary and the Center for Theology and the Natural Sciences at the Graduate Theological Union, Berkeley, California
Science and Religion

FRANK E. REYNOLDS
Professor of the History of Religions and Buddhist Studies in the Divinity School and the Department of South Asian Languages and Civilizations, Emeritus, University of Chicago
History of Religions

GONZALO RUBIO
Assistant Professor, Department of Classics and Ancient Mediterranean Studies and Department of History and Religious Studies, Pennsylvania State University
Ancient Near Eastern Religions

SUSAN SERED
Director of Research, Religion, Health and Healing Initiative, Center for the Study of World Religions, Harvard University, and Senior Research Associate, Center for Women's Health and Human Rights, Suffolk University
Healing, Medicine, and Religion

LAWRENCE E. SULLIVAN
Professor, Department of Theology, University of Notre Dame
History of Religions

WINNIFRED FALLERS SULLIVAN
Dean of Students and Senior Lecturer in the Anthropology and Sociology of Religion, University of Chicago
Law and Religion

TOD SWANSON
Associate Professor of Religious Studies, and Director, Center for Latin American Studies, Arizona State University
South American Religions

MARY EVELYN TUCKER
Professor of Religion, Bucknell University, Founder and Coordinator, Harvard Forum on Religion and Ecology, Research Fellow, Harvard Yenching Institute, Research Associate, Harvard Reischauer Institute of Japanese Studies
Ecology and Religion

HUGH URBAN
Associate Professor, Department of Comparative Studies, Ohio State University
Politics and Religion

CATHERINE WESSINGER
Professor of the History of Religions and Women's Studies, Loyola University New Orleans
New Religious Movements

ROBERT A. YELLE
Mellon Postdoctoral Fellow, University of Toronto
Law and Religion

ERIC ZIOLKOWSKI
Charles A. Dana Professor of Religious Studies, Lafayette College
Literature and Religion

ABBREVIATIONS AND SYMBOLS USED IN THIS WORK

abbr. abbreviated; abbreviation
abr. abridged; abridgment
AD *anno Domini,* in the year of the (our) Lord
Afrik. Afrikaans
AH *anno Hegirae,* in the year of the Hijrah
Akk. Akkadian
Ala. Alabama
Alb. Albanian
Am. *Amos*
AM *ante meridiem,* before noon
amend. amended; amendment
annot. annotated; annotation
Ap. *Apocalypse*
Apn. *Apocryphon*
app. appendix
Arab. Arabic
ʿArakh. *ʿArakhin*
Aram. Aramaic
Ariz. Arizona
Ark. Arkansas
Arm. Armenian
art. article (pl., arts.)
AS Anglo-Saxon
Asm. Mos. *Assumption of Moses*
Assyr. Assyrian
A.S.S.R. Autonomous Soviet Socialist Republic
Av. Avestan
ʿA.Z. *ʿAvodah zarah*
b. born
Bab. Babylonian
Ban. Bantu
1 Bar. *1 Baruch*
2 Bar. *2 Baruch*
3 Bar. *3 Baruch*
4 Bar. *4 Baruch*
B.B. *Bavaʾ batraʾ*
BBC British Broadcasting Corporation
BC before Christ
BCE before the common era
B.D. Bachelor of Divinity
Beits. *Beitsah*
Bekh. *Bekhorot*
Beng. Bengali
Ber. *Berakhot*
Berb. Berber
Bik. *Bikkurim*
bk. book (pl., bks.)
B.M. *Bavaʾ metsiʿaʾ*
BP before the present
B.Q. *Bavaʾ qammaʾ*
Brāh. *Brāhmaṇa*
Bret. Breton
B.T. Babylonian Talmud
Bulg. Bulgarian
Burm. Burmese
c. *circa,* about, approximately
Calif. California
Can. Canaanite
Catal. Catalan
CE of the common era
Celt. Celtic
cf. *confer,* compare
Chald. Chaldean
chap. chapter (pl., chaps.)
Chin. Chinese
C.H.M. Community of the Holy Myrrhbearers
1 Chr. *1 Chronicles*
2 Chr. *2 Chronicles*
Ch. Slav. Church Slavic
cm centimeters
col. column (pl., cols.)
Col. *Colossians*
Colo. Colorado
comp. compiler (pl., comps.)
Conn. Connecticut
cont. continued
Copt. Coptic
1 Cor. *1 Corinthians*
2 Cor. *2 Corinthians*
corr. corrected
C.S.P. Congregatio Sancti Pauli, Congregation of Saint Paul (Paulists)
d. died
D Deuteronomic (source of the Pentateuch)
Dan. Danish
D.B. Divinitatis Baccalaureus, Bachelor of Divinity
D.C. District of Columbia
D.D. Divinitatis Doctor, Doctor of Divinity
Del. Delaware
Dem. *Demaʾi*
dim. diminutive
diss. dissertation
Dn. *Daniel*
D.Phil. Doctor of Philosophy
Dt. *Deuteronomy*
Du. Dutch
E Elohist (source of the Pentateuch)
Eccl. *Ecclesiastes*
ed. editor (pl., eds.); edition; edited by

ʿEduy. *ʿEduyyot*
e.g. *exempli gratia,* for example
Egyp. Egyptian
1 En. *1 Enoch*
2 En. *2 Enoch*
3 En. *3 Enoch*
Eng. English
enl. enlarged
Eph. *Ephesians*
ʿEruv. *ʿEruvin*
1 Esd. *1 Esdras*
2 Esd. *2 Esdras*
3 Esd. *3 Esdras*
4 Esd. *4 Esdras*
esp. especially
Est. Estonian
Est. *Esther*
et al. *et alii,* and others
etc. *et cetera,* and so forth
Eth. Ethiopic
EV English version
Ex. *Exodus*
exp. expanded
Ez. *Ezekiel*
Ezr. *Ezra*
2 Ezr. *2 Ezra*
4 Ezr. *4 Ezra*
f. feminine; and following (pl., ff.)
fasc. fascicle (pl., fascs.)
fig. figure (pl., figs.)
Finn. Finnish
fl. *floruit,* flourished
Fla. Florida
Fr. French
frag. fragment
ft. feet
Ga. Georgia
Gal. *Galatians*
Gaul. Gaulish
Ger. German
Giṭ. *Giṭṭin*
Gn. *Genesis*
Gr. Greek
Ḥag. *Ḥagigah*
Ḥal. *Ḥallah*
Hau. Hausa
Hb. *Habakkuk*
Heb. Hebrew
Heb. *Hebrews*
Hg. *Haggai*
Hitt. Hittite
Hor. *Horayot*
Hos. *Hosea*
Ḥul. *Ḥullin*
Hung. Hungarian
ibid. *ibidem,* in the same place (as the one immediately preceding)
Icel. Icelandic
i.e. *id est,* that is
IE Indo-European
Ill. Illinois
Ind. Indiana
intro. introduction
Ir. Gael. Irish Gaelic
Iran. Iranian
Is. *Isaiah*
Ital. Italian
J Yahvist (source of the Pentateuch)
Jas. *James*
Jav. Javanese
Jb. *Job*
Jdt. *Judith*
Jer. *Jeremiah*
Jgs. *Judges*
Jl. *Joel*
Jn. *John*
1 Jn. *1 John*
2 Jn. *2 John*
3 Jn. *3 John*
Jon. *Jonah*
Jos. *Joshua*
Jpn. Japanese
JPS Jewish Publication Society translation (1985) of the Hebrew Bible
J.T. Jerusalem Talmud
Jub. *Jubilees*
Kans. Kansas
Kel. *Kelim*
Ker. *Keritot*
Ket. *Ketubbot*
1 Kgs. *1 Kings*
2 Kgs. *2 Kings*
Khois. Khoisan
Kil. *Kilʾayim*
km kilometers
Kor. Korean
Ky. Kentucky
l. line (pl., ll.)
La. Louisiana
Lam. *Lamentations*
Lat. Latin
Latv. Latvian
L. en Th. Licencié en Théologie, Licentiate in Theology
L. ès L. Licencié ès Lettres, Licentiate in Literature
Let. Jer. *Letter of Jeremiah*
lit. literally
Lith. Lithuanian
Lk. *Luke*
LL Late Latin
LL.D. Legum Doctor, Doctor of Laws
Lv. *Leviticus*
m meters
m. masculine
M.A. Master of Arts
Ma ʿas. *Maʿaserot*
Ma ʿas. Sh. *Maʿ aser sheni*
Mak. *Makkot*
Makh. *Makhshirin*
Mal. *Malachi*
Mar. Marathi
Mass. Massachusetts
1 Mc. *1 Maccabees*
2 Mc. *2 Maccabees*
3 Mc. *3 Maccabees*
4 Mc. *4 Maccabees*
Md. Maryland
M.D. Medicinae Doctor, Doctor of Medicine
ME Middle English
Meg. *Megillah*
Me ʿil. *Meʿilah*
Men. *Menaḥot*
MHG Middle High German
mi. miles
Mi. *Micah*
Mich. Michigan
Mid. *Middot*
Minn. Minnesota
Miq. *Miqvaʾot*
MIran. Middle Iranian
Miss. Mississippi
Mk. *Mark*
Mo. Missouri
Moʿed Q. *Moʿed qaṭan*
Mont. Montana
MPers. Middle Persian
MS. *manuscriptum,* manuscript (pl., MSS)
Mt. *Matthew*
MT Masoretic text
n. note
Na. *Nahum*
Nah. Nahuatl
Naz. *Nazir*
N.B. *nota bene,* take careful note
N.C. North Carolina
n.d. no date
N.Dak. North Dakota
NEB New English Bible
Nebr. Nebraska

Ned. *Nedarim*
Neg. *Nega'im*
Neh. *Nehemiah*
Nev. Nevada
N.H. New Hampshire
Nid. *Niddah*
N.J. New Jersey
Nm. *Numbers*
N.Mex. New Mexico
no. number (pl., nos.)
Nor. Norwegian
n.p. no place
n.s. new series
N.Y. New York
Ob. *Obadiah*
O.Cist. Ordo Cisterciencium, Order of Cîteaux (Cistercians)
OCS Old Church Slavonic
OE Old English
O.F.M. Ordo Fratrum Minorum, Order of Friars Minor (Franciscans)
OFr. Old French
Ohal. *Ohalot*
OHG Old High German
OIr. Old Irish
OIran. Old Iranian
Okla. Oklahoma
ON Old Norse
O.P. Ordo Praedicatorum, Order of Preachers (Dominicans)
OPers. Old Persian
op. cit. *opere citato,* in the work cited
OPrus. Old Prussian
Oreg. Oregon
'Orl. *'Orlah*
O.S.B. Ordo Sancti Benedicti, Order of Saint Benedict (Benedictines)
p. page (pl., pp.)
P Priestly (source of the Pentateuch)
Pa. Pennsylvania
Pahl. Pahlavi
Par. *Parah*
para. paragraph (pl., paras.)
Pers. Persian
Pes. *Pesahim*
Ph.D. Philosophiae Doctor, Doctor of Philosophy
Phil. *Philippians*
Phlm. *Philemon*
Phoen. Phoenician
pl. plural; plate (pl., pls.)
PM *post meridiem,* after noon
Pol. Polish
pop. population
Port. Portuguese
Prv. *Proverbs*
Ps. *Psalms*
Ps. 151 *Psalm 151*
Ps. Sol. *Psalms of Solomon*
pt. part (pl., pts.)
1Pt. *1 Peter*
2 Pt. *2 Peter*
Pth. Parthian
Q hypothetical source of the synoptic Gospels
Qid. *Qiddushin*
Qin. *Qinnim*
r. reigned; ruled
Rab. *Rabbah*
rev. revised
R. ha-Sh. *Ro'sh ha-shanah*
R.I. Rhode Island
Rom. Romanian
Rom. *Romans*
R.S.C.J. Societas Sacratissimi Cordis Jesu, Religious of the Sacred Heart
RSV Revised Standard Version of the Bible
Ru. *Ruth*
Rus. Russian
Rv. *Revelation*
Rv. Ezr. *Revelation of Ezra*
San. *Sanhedrin*
S.C. South Carolina
Scot. Gael. Scottish Gaelic
S.Dak. South Dakota
sec. section (pl., secs.)
Sem. Semitic
ser. series
sg. singular
Sg. *Song of Songs*
Sg. of 3 *Prayer of Azariah and the Song of the Three Young Men*
Shab. *Shabbat*
Shav. *Shavu'ot*
Sheq. *Sheqalim*
Sib. Or. *Sibylline Oracles*
Sind. Sindhi
Sinh. Sinhala
Sir. *Ben Sira*
S.J. Societas Jesu, Society of Jesus (Jesuits)
Skt. Sanskrit
1 Sm. *1 Samuel*
2 Sm. *2 Samuel*
Sogd. Sogdian
Soṭ. *Soṭah*
sp. species (pl., spp.)
Span. Spanish
sq. square
S.S.R. Soviet Socialist Republic
st. stanza (pl., ss.)
S.T.M. Sacrae Theologiae Magister, Master of Sacred Theology
Suk. *Sukkah*
Sum. Sumerian
supp. supplement; supplementary
Sus. *Susanna*
s.v. *sub verbo,* under the word (pl., s.v.v.)
Swed. Swedish
Syr. Syriac
Syr. Men. *Syriac Menander*
Ta' an. *Ta'anit*
Tam. Tamil
Tam. *Tamid*
Tb. *Tobit*
T.D. *Taishō shinshū daizōkyō,* edited by Takakusu Junjirō et al. (Tokyo,1922–1934)
Tem. *Temurah*
Tenn. Tennessee
Ter. Terumot
Ṭev. Y. *Ṭevul yom*
Tex. Texas
Th.D. Theologicae Doctor, Doctor of Theology
1 Thes. *1 Thessalonians*
2 Thes. *2 Thessalonians*
Thrac. Thracian
Ti. *Titus*
Tib. Tibetan
1 Tm. *1 Timothy*
2 Tm. *2 Timothy*
T. of 12 *Testaments of the Twelve Patriarchs*
Ṭoh. *ṭohorot*
Tong. Tongan
trans. translator, translators; translated by; translation
Turk. Turkish
Ukr. Ukrainian
Upan. *Upaniṣad*
U.S. United States
U.S.S.R. Union of Soviet Socialist Republics
Uqts. *Uqtsin*
v. verse (pl., vv.)
Va. Virginia
var. variant; variation
Viet. Vietnamese

viz. *videlicet,* namely
vol. volume (pl., vols.)
Vt. Vermont
Wash. Washington
Wel. Welsh
Wis. Wisconsin
Wis. *Wisdom of Solomon*
W.Va. West Virginia
Wyo. Wyoming

Yad. *Yadayim*
Yev. *Yevamot*
Yi. Yiddish
Yor. Yoruba
Zav. *Zavim*
Zec. *Zechariah*
Zep. *Zephaniah*
Zev. *Zevaḥim*

* hypothetical
? uncertain; possibly; perhaps
° degrees
+ plus
– minus
= equals; is equivalent to
× by; multiplied by
→ yields

E
CONTINUED

ETERNITY is the condition or attribute of divine life by which it relates with equal immediacy and potency to all times. The notion emerges at the point of contact of three distinct religious concerns. The oldest of these is the question of the state of life after death, especially in light of the continuing presence of the dead among the living as acknowledged in the various forms of the cult of the dead. A later-developing speculative concern is the question about divine creation, especially when creative power is seen as the production in a divine mind of a world of ideas, a *logos* or paradigm made present in this world as in an image. Finally, there is the concern with contemplative or mystical experience, especially when regarded as a way of partaking of the divine life within the conditions of present existence. Reflection on these themes converges upon the notion of a dimension of life that is "vertically" related to the "horizontal" flowing of time, that transcends time without being apart from it.

Because eternity touches each and every time, it is easily confused with the closely related concept of what "always was, is, and will be," or, in a word, the everlasting. But in its own proper concept, the eternal only "is"; only in the present tense can it be said to be or act in any way. Exempted from all having-been and going-to-be, eternity is familiarly defined as timelessness, in distinction from the everlasting (sometimes also called the sempiternal). The everlasting antecedes and outlasts everything that begins and ends in time, but because it is just as much given over to being partly past, partly future as are things that come to be and perish, it is therefore just as much in time. Eternity, on the other hand, does not transcend finite spans of time extensively, but intensively. It draws the multiplicity of times into a unity no longer mediated by relations of precedence and posteriority and therefore, at least in this specific sense, no longer timelike.

Yet it oversimplifies to call eternity timelessness. Though eternity excludes pastness and futurity, it remains correct to speak of it as presence, which after all is one of the three fundamental determinations of time. In the Platonic tradition, which gave the concept its classical development and passed it on through Muslim and Christian theology

CLOCKWISE FROM TOP LEFT CORNER. Colossus of Ramses II at the Temple of Amun in Karnak, Egypt. *[©Gian Berto Vanni/Corbis]*; Coptic ceremonial fan depicting Ethiopian saints. *[©Werner Forman/Art Resource, N.Y.]*; Reverse of an early-fourth-century BCE Etruscan bronze mirror showing the mythical seer Calchas dressed as an haruspex and examining an animal liver. Museo Gregoriano Profano, Vatican Museums. *[©Scala/Art Resource, N.Y.]*; Twelfth-century mosaic of Jesus as Pantocrator. Duomo di Cefalu, Sicily. *[©Adam Woolfitt/Corbis]*; Glazed pottery eagle from second- to third-century CE Italy. Museo Ostiense, Ostia. *[©Erich Lessing/Art Resource, N.Y.]* .

to modern European philosophy, the present tense retains its temporal sense in affirmations concerning eternity. In this way the Western notion of eternity differs from some Buddhist accounts of *nirvāṇa,* into which not just pastness and futurity but presence as well are dissolved. Platonic eternity by contrast is a paradigmatic presence, and the present in time is its partial but authentic image.

The present is called the "now." Latin metaphysics spoke therefore of eternity as *nunc stans,* a "standing now," and of time as *nunc fluens,* a "flowing now." Since the now of time, which is always experienced as having a certain duration, converges under logical analysis toward the limiting concept of the instantaneous, the dimensionless moment of transition, the problem arises whether the eternal Now is itself a kind of frozen instant, a durationless simplicity about which no experiences of life in time are instructive. Remarkably, the single feature most vividly affirmed of eternity by its classic expositors is that it is life, and not just life but divine life, "a god, manifesting himself as he is," as the third-century CE Neoplatonist mystic Plotinus says in one place (see the following). How does one incorporate a religious discourse in which eternity is divine life into the stark conceptual analyses of pure metaphysics, which seem to lead to a static, almost mathematical abstraction?

The synthesis of logical, psychological, and theological analyses into a rigorous conception of eternity is proprietary to the Platonic philosophical tradition, and is in many ways the single-handed achievement of Plotinus. There are rather complete analogies to the concept in some of the Upaniṣads in India, but in Asia one finds in the main only partial parallels; the metaphysical cake that is the complex Western idea is there cut apart in different ways, so to speak. Pending the outcome of more penetrating philosophical study than the Asian texts have so far received from Western translators and historians, the story of eternity remains at present the story of the Plotinian synthesis, its sources and its influences. The discussion that follows reflects this situation. It reviews, in decreasing detail (1) the classic Platonic conception of eternity as Plotinus understands it, (2) the place of this conception in its own, mainly European, spiritual history, and (3) those points in Indian and Asian philosophy where search for analogous intuitions most plausibly might begin.

PLATONIC ETERNITY IN PLOTINUS. In the Platonic tradition, eternity and time are regularly considered together. They make up in fact a single topic, in the old literary sense of the Greek term *topos* ("place"), where it refers to a particular place in a canonical text. The discussion of eternity invariably proceeds among Platonists as a meditation on the place in the *Timaeus* of Plato where eternity is described as "abiding in unity" and time as an "eternal image of eternity, moving according to number" (37d). At a minimum, this passage imposes the idea that eternity and time are in some respect comparable to one another. But Neoplatonism makes a stronger claim for a vision of eternity and time as extremes of a continuum. Life itself, the interior life of the soul, bridges the gap according to Plotinus, and this makes possible an account of the experience of eternity itself.

In some ways it is an extremely familiar experience. Consider reading a book that one finds completely compelling, that draws one along in apparently inexhaustible attentiveness and interest. Hours can pass unregistered; it can be shocking to discover how much time has passed, and how meaningless that fact seems compared with the inner composure and vividness of the interval. Any activity that is intensely self-collected, full of purposiveness and power, can generate this effect—not just intellectual but also aesthetic, even physical activity such as dancing or athletics.

Experiences of this kind are a threshold for the pure experience of eternity, contemplation. It is important to notice that they are not without duration, indeed they are rich in inner activity and movement. One experiences something like time in them, but a time that arises more than passes, that gives rather than takes. An inexhaustible power seems to well up within oneself. When, as is inevitable, the spell is broken, one speaks of having fallen away from that power, not of the power itself having lapsed.

Plotinus calls this power the life of the Mind, and in order to express its inexhaustibility says that it is infinite, limitless. In earlier Greek philosophy, to be infinite was to be indefinite, without form or intelligibility, wholly a negative condition. Plotinus too portrays the intelligible world of Platonic Ideas as finite, formally and structurally. But grasped within the living Mind that is its origin and substrate, it is limitlessly vivacious, a world "boiling with life" (6.7.12). The living and dynamic quality of eternal Mind is as central a theme in Plotinus as its simplicity and composure, and is expressed in a remarkable passage where he says that "its nature is to become other in every way," accomplished in a "wandering" (*planē,* as of the planets) within itself that is like a ceaseless adventure on the "plain of truth" (6.7.13).

For the soul that awakens to this presence of mind, the experience is like a homecoming, a coming into oneself rather than a journey to another self or state of existence. The old Platonic image of this movement as an *anamnēsis,* an unforgetting, depended on the Orphic mythical theme of the preexistence of the soul and was therefore easily understood to be a recollection from elsewhere and elsewhen, so to speak. But in Plotinus *anamnēsis* is altogether what it is in Augustine also, an interior conversion of the soul completed in contemplative immediacy—conversion both in the sense of a turning, from distracting cares to tranquil insight, and of a transformation, from the condition of life that is soul to that of pure intellectual apprehension or Mind.

Because the condition of the life of the soul is time, humans fall away from presence of mind in a recurrent downward movement that makes one's encounter with eternity multiple and episodic. Yet, "if you look attentively at it again, you will find it as it was" (3.7.5). In that contemplation one will be one's self again, self-possessed and self-contained, puzzled by the vulnerability to scatteredness and confusion into which the soul falls in time. A traditional term for the self-possession of eternal life is *stasis,* still used in English, and especially in the familiar complaint that the eternity of Greek metaphysics is "static." This is a fundamental misunderstanding.

Stasis means "staying, standing rather than falling, holding together rather than lapsing into dispersion." One can get the sense of eternal stasis best from the English word *homeostasis,* as used in biology to name the dynamic composure that the very diverse movements of metabolism and organic activity maintain within a living system. The simplicity and unity of eternal life is that of a homeostasis, a self-enveloping completion that is at the same time the space for an unlimited enjoyment of activity, purpose, and power.

"Hence," Plotinus writes, "eternity is a majestic thing, and thought declares it identical with the god." He goes on: "Eternity could be well described as a god proclaiming and manifesting himself as he is, that is, as being which is unshakeable and self-identical and always as it is, and firmly grounded in life." From this follows the definition: Eternity is "life that is here and now endless because it is total and expends nothing of itself" (3.7.5).

Familiar in the Latin West through the paraphrase of Boethius, "interminabilis vitae tota simul et perfecta possessio" ("the all-at-once total and perfect possession of endless life," *The Consolation of Philosophy* 5.6), the Plotinian experience of eternity marks the divine life as a presence and opens the route of human approach to this life through contemplative mysticism.

HISTORICAL BACKGROUND AND CONSEQUENCE. The Greek term that translates as "eternity" in Plato and Plotinus is *aiōn,* and this has given many students of the history of the notion pause. *Aiōn* survives in English in the Latinized spelling *aeon,* and here retains much of its original meaning. *Aiōn* means "life, span of life, lifetime; epoch, aeon." While it never suggests duration simply on the level of measure or standard interval, even the Homeric places where it comes closest to meaning "inner life force" include strongly the suggestion of power to perdure, of life reaching out to take up its proper span of time. It seems a very timelike term, not only because of its connotation of span or duration, but because beginning, middle, and end belong so much to the kind of totality or completion it expresses still in English.

The term first occurs in surviving fragments of early Greek philosophy in the fifth-century BCE writer Heraclitus, in the gnome "*Aiōn* is a child playing a board game; the kingly power is a child's" (Heraclitus, B52). The translation "eternity" is clearly inadmissible; those translators who instead supply "time" have good cause. Heraclitus's theme is the spontaneity and immanence of the laws or patterns manifest in the give-and-take of natural processes; the intelligibility of constant change is not outside nature like a god, but the cosmos is in and by itself an "Everliving Fire, flaring up by measure, dying down by measure" (B30). Under the control of this ruling image, *aiōn* again means a form of completion embracing birth and death and the process that weaves them together.

It is not at all clear to what degree Plato distinguishes between the adjectival form *aiōnios,* "eternal," and another term *aïdios,* "everlasting." Because in fact he inclines to the (false) etymology that takes *aiōn* from *aei ōn,* "always being," he gives place to the very confusion the Neoplatonists are most concerned to prevent. In the very text in *Timaeus* that becomes decisive, he says of *aiōn* that "its nature is everlasting [*aïdios*]" (37d).

Among consequences of this situation is a protracted controversy among the Hellenistic Platonists of the centuries around the beginning of the common era concerning what is called "the eternity of the world." The question was whether, as Aristotle argues in the *Metaphysics* (12.6), the world is everlasting and has no beginning in time or whether, as *Timaeus* would suggest if its mythical form were given substantive import, the world began to be at some definite time. Alexandrian Jewish and later Christian Platonists tended to join the argument on the latter side, partly through their effort to coordinate the story in *Timaeus* with that of *Genesis.* It should be clear that once the rigorous nontemporal concept of eternity had been established, it was a mistake to call this question the question of the "eternity" of the world, but only Augustine (*Confessions* 11) diagnoses the category mistake with full philosophical precision.

The antecedents of the Neoplatonic conception of eternity lie not in the lexicography of the term's classical philosophical usage, but in the associations it takes on through the constant interaction of Platonic image and argument with popular religious consciousness. This includes first of all the concern with immortality and afterlife, the context for talk of the eternal life of the soul. Because this concern is profoundly rooted in the archaic, mythological sensibility and its experience of the structure that Mircea Eliade has called "eternal return," it made available the notion of another time, a transcending and divine time that could intersect with mundane time, embedding life in a dimension that surpasses birth and death. The eternity that can be abstracted from this archaic experience is an eternal past more than the eternal present of the proper concept; fundamental imaginative possibilities were appropriated from this origin. The mediating religious context was in large measure the emergence of the mystery religions in the Greco-Roman world, among them the mysteries of baptism and of table blessing central to Christianity.

Aiōn in the New Testament is principally an apocalyptic term, qualified as "this aeon" as against "the aeon to come" (synoptic Gospels, Paul). It shares with the rest of the apocalyptic scenario a Persian, Zoroastrian background, and in a few Pauline or deutero-Pauline places (e.g., *Col.* 1:26, *Eph.* 3:9) seems to be personified in the sense of an equation of Aion with Zurwān, an equation that sets the stage for the florid multiplication of such personified aions in the gnostic literature of the second century CE. Though there has been speculation that this kind of connection between Mediterranean and Near Eastern symbolism contributed to the emergence of the novel Neoplatonic sense of *aiōn,* it seems preferable to portray this as a digression.

A richer question is whether "eternal life" in the *Gospel of John* is consonant with the radical Platonic idea, or already on common ground with it. The predominance of present-tense statements by the glorified Son in that text ("Before Abraham was, I am," *Jn.* 8:58, et al.), its transformation of apocalyptic into realized eschatology, and its eucharist of epiphany and participation ("He who eats my flesh and drinks my blood abides in me, and I in him," *Jn.* 6:56) made it possible for Christian Neoplatonism of the Augustinian type to embrace the strict nontemporal eternity without sensing any violence in its interpretation of scripture.

The story of the appropriation of Plotinian contemplative mysticism by later Christian and Muslim theology defeats summary. Suffice it to say that the Neoplatonic system was adapted to biblical monotheism with considerable penetration and accuracy, especially by Augustine and the Latin tradition through Boethius and Bonaventure, by the apophatic tradition from Dionysius the Areopagite through John Scottus Eriugena to Meister Eckhart, and by Ṣūfī philosophy. The close connection between the theoretical role of eternity as an attribute or name of God and its experiential richness as an element of contemplative spirituality remained characteristic of these traditions.

A certain purely logical interest in the eternity/time contrast, detectable already in Boethius (responding more to Porphyry than Plotinus) and Thomas Aquinas, was amplified by the new mathematical spirit of the metaphysics of the seventeenth century, resulting in the reduction of eternal presence to a kind of schematic simplicity illustrated particularly clearly in the system of Spinoza. The effect was to dissociate the speculative notion from its experiential basis, producing in the end the degraded conception of eternity as lifeless stasis or logical tenselessness that has been the target of complaint in historicist, existentialist, and process theologies of the past century.

ETERNITY IN NON-WESTERN THOUGHT. It is a commonplace that the religious themes of afterlife, divine creation, and the nature of the soul are drawn together in different patterns by non-Western traditions. The Buddha is represented as holding that speculation on none of these furthers one toward enlightenment. It is no surprise to find that a concept like eternity, which emerges at the intersection of these themes in Platonism and then becomes influential precisely through its adaptability to biblical theology, does not always have strict analogies in other religious discourse.

The exegetical and hermeneutical complications that derive from this situation have not always been registered in the translations of non-Western sources. Only some preliminary pointers about other treatments of eternity are here appropriate.

The striking parallels that are being discovered between Neoplatonism and Vedānta philosophy appear to hold also in the case of eternity. The Sanskrit *nitya* can be translated "eternity" with some confidence already in Upaniṣads, especially at the point where "immortality," *amṛta,* is pressed beyond the popular image of outliving death, or life after death, to the radical notion of *mokṣa,* "liberation," deliverance from the cycle of birth and death itself. The fundamental conception in the Upaniṣads that the authentic self, the *ātman,* gathered into its own interior unity from the levels of psychic life, is one with *brahman,* the universal spirit, is developed in ways that regularly parallel the account of the authentic self on the level of the *Nous,* or divine Mind, in Plotinus. It is less clear, however, whether the eternal present, self-consolidated beyond all passage through birth and death, is to be found in the Vedas.

Buddhism presents a much more complex situation. The negative assessment of timelike continuity and the rejection of substantiality and causality that are frequent in Buddhist philosophy lead to descriptions of enlightenment that often have a Platonic ring. In Buddhism, the parallels are particularly pronounced in the meditative traditions that emphasize "sudden enlightenment," where the unconditioned and spontaneous quality of transcendental insight (Skt., *prajñā*) is stressed. In the Mahāyāna Pure Land tradition, the paradisical Sukhāvatī ("land of bliss") of the Buddha Amitābha is sometimes developed in ways reminiscent of the Platonic world of ideal presences, pervaded by divine mentality. If there is an authentic parallel here to the notion of eternity, this will have to be tested by careful analysis of the account of temporal presence itself, for it is this that is ascribed to eternity by Platonism, and in turn made the image of eternity and mark of authentic being for life in time. In those radical portrayals of *nirvāṇa* as release from all forms of temporal conditioning, not just pastness and futurity, but presence itself sometimes seems to be denied of awakened mind.

A focal problem in the search for analogy to eternity in Chinese thought is the proper account of the first line of the *Dao de jing,* often translated, "The Dao that can be spoken is not the eternal Dao [*chang dao*]." "Eternal" may overtranslate *chang;* the core meaning is closer to "steadfast," "constant," "abiding." The parallel seems strongest to *aiōn* at the stage it had reached in Heraclitus. It needs study whether the idealization found in the Vedānta or late Platonic pattern is appropriate for interpretation of this text.

Special wariness should be reserved for the use of the phrase "eternal life" in describing prephilosophical doctrines of immortality and afterlife, or "eternal return" for the transcendental relation of divine life to mundane in the experience of cyclical time that is fundamental in myth-using cultures. Most commonly what is meant by "eternal" in this context is "perpetual" or "everlasting." Whether the primordial time of beginnings, the transcendent past of divine creative action, is a predecessor of the eternal present is a separate question that needs careful consideration. While the proper notion of eternity may be very near the surface in Egypt, it is much less likely to exist in the preliterate cultures for which the cycle of death and rebirth is a naturalistic image more than a philosophical idealization.

See Also Anamnēsis; Plotinus; Sacred Time.

Bibliography

The concept of eternity is still most accessible from primary sources, notably the treatise "On Eternity and Time" of Plotinus, *Enneads* 3.7.45, in *Plotinus,* translated by A. Hilary Armstrong, "Loeb Classical Library," vol. 3 (Cambridge, Mass., 1966), and book 11 of the *Confessions* of Augustine, for which there are many suitable editions. An instructive summary of the concept in the full technical development it received in medieval theology can be found in the article by Adolf Darlap and Joseph de Finance, "Eternity," in *Sacramentum Mundi,* edited by Karl Rahner (New York, 1968), vol. 2. Mircea Eliade's *Cosmos and History: The Myth of Eternal Return* (New York, 1954) remains a standard introduction to the role of a transcending divine time in the religious experience of myth-using cultures. A very helpful account of eternity is incorporated into a sketch of the history of the idea of immortality in the ancient Near East and Christian Europe by John S. Dunne, *The City of the Gods* (Notre Dame, Ind., 1978). The classic exposition of the interior experience of eternity in Western mysticism is Bonaventure's "The Soul's Journey into God," in *Bonaventure,* edited and translated by Ewert Cousins (New York, 1978). For eternity in Indian thought, the edition of *The Principal Upaniṣads* by Sarvepalli Radhakrishnan (New York, 1953) is especially useful, both for its extensive introduction and its very rich annotations, which include frequent citation of Western parallels.

New Sources

Ashton, John. *The Quest for Paradise: Heaven and Eternity in the World's Myths and Religions.* San Francisco, 2001.

Bernstein, Alan. *The Formation of Hell: Death and Retribution in the Ancient and Early Christian Worlds.* Ithaca, N.Y., 1993.

Dales, Richard. *Medieval Discussions of the Eternity of the World.* New York, 1990.

Futch, Michael. "Leibniz on Plenitude, Infinity, and the Eternity of the World." *British Journal for the History of Philosophy* 10 (November 2002): 541–561.

Padgett, Alan. *God, Eternity, and the Nature of Time.* New York, 1992.

Rouner, Leroy, ed. *If I Should Die.* Notre Dame, Ind., 2001.

Russell, Jeffrey Burton. "Goodness, Gracious(ness) Great Balls of Fire: Visions of Eternity Just Aren't What They Used to Be." *Christian History* 70 (2001): 38–42.

Walter, Tony. *The Eclipse of Eternity: A Sociology of the Afterlife.* Basingstoke, U.K., 1996.

Peter Manchester (1987)
Revised Bibliography

ETHICAL CULTURE, a movement dedicated to the ethical improvement of society and the ethical growth of the individual, was inaugurated with the founding of the New York Society for Ethical Culture in May 1876 by Felix Adler and a group of his Jewish supporters. Adler was the son of Rabbi Samuel Adler of New York's Temple Emanu-El, and he was expected to succeed his father in this cathedral pulpit of American Reform Judaism. But having been exposed in German universities to nineteenth-century science, Kantian philosophy, and historical criticism of religion, he came to reject theism and the finality of Jewish theology even in its most liberal form. His new faith consisted of a passionate belief in the inviolability and power of the moral law and the duty to apply it to society, especially to the problems of industrialization, urbanization, and the working poor.

What initially began as a Sunday lecture movement, somewhat patterned after the Independent Church movement and free religious societies such as those of O. B. Frothingham, grew under Adler's leadership to become a vital organization spearheading social reforms and social reconstruction. Adler's personal magnetism drew a membership of well more than one thousand to the society by the early 1880s, mostly but not exclusively people of Jewish origin. He also attracted ethically idealistic and socially committed people of liberal Christian background whom he helped groom to be leaders of other Ethical Culture societies. The Ethical Culture movement took on a national flavor as Adler's apprentices organized new societies in other cities: William M. Salter, Chicago, 1883; S. Burns Weston, Philadelphia, 1885; Walter L. Sheldon, Saint Louis, 1886. The American societies federated as a national organization in 1889, the American Ethical Union, and over the years, new societies springing up in urban and suburban areas across the country (Brooklyn, Westchester County, Washington, Baltimore, Pittsburgh, Los Angeles, Cleveland, Essex County, N.J.) were added to its roster. By 1930, membership in American Ethical Culture societies numbered about thirty-five hundred, and by the mid-1980s, membership in the more than twenty societies totaled approximately five thousand. (The largest society remains the New York branch, at about one thousand.)

Ethical Culture became truly international in scope in the 1890s. The London Ethical Society had been founded in 1886, with such distinguished thinkers participating as Bernard Bosanquet, Edward Caird, and Leslie Stephen, and British interest had been spurred when Stanton Coit, another Adler apprentice, arrived in 1887 and led London's South Place Chapel into the Ethical Culture movement. Coit subsequently created a British Ethical Union in 1896. The movement reached Germany, where a society was founded in Berlin in 1892, and societies also appeared in France, Austria, Italy, Switzerland, and Japan in this new decade. The various societies, each with its own nuanced organizational goals and ethical approaches, were in contact and quite cognizant of each other's activities. At a Zurich meeting in 1896 they created an international confederation, the International Ethical Union, which kept member organizations in touch with each other and which also convened world congresses devoted to specific themes, such as those in London (1908) and the Hague (1912). In the wake of World War II the union became moribund, but in 1952 humanist organizations joined with Ethical Culture societies led by the American Ethical Union to found the International Humanist and Ethical Union with member groups in North and Latin America, Europe, Africa, Asia, and Australia.

Whether or not Ethical Culture is judged a religion depends on one's definition of *religion* and one's inclination either to use or not use the word to designate an ethical humanist posture. Felix Adler did regard Ethical Culture to be a religion and in his later years tried to work out a metaphysic to express it. Still, he adamantly insisted that Ethical Culture embraced all in ethical fellowship regardless of diverse approaches and different names given to the quest for meaning in life. This openness has clearly persisted to this day. Nonetheless, the societies do assume the guise of a religious organization to some extent. (In the United States, many are incorporated as "religious and educational" institutions in their respective states.) A weekly meeting is usually held on Sunday morning or evening (in Germany, during the weekdays), consisting of music, an inspirational reading, and a major address on a topical issue, usually with an eye to its ethical implications. There are no symbols or ritual acts, although the English societies tend to be a bit more ceremonial. Ethical leaders officiate at life-cycle events such as marriage and funerals; they come individually from a variety of social and intellectual backgrounds and may have previous religious affiliations. There is no Ethical Culture seminary, but each prospective leader undertakes a personally tailored training program administered by the Leadership Training Committee of the American Ethical Union.

No established Ethical Culture ideology exists, although general principles certainly have been articulated. To a large extent, Adler's early motto, "Not the creed, but the deed," still serves as the unifying theoretical orientation of Ethical Culture, although with a deepened and richer meaning than Adler himself provided. Members are free to believe what they wish on all issues, including religion, but they generally subscribe to the following ideals: (1) the intrinsic worth of each human being, (2) the importance of seeking ethical principles as a guide to all aspects of life, and (3) the need to work for the material and spiritual betterment of society and humanity.

This last commitment to applied social ethics rather than to any theoretical formulation of an ethical approach has been the quintessential characteristic of Ethical Culture from its inception. In this regard, the Ethical Culture movement, particularly in the United States, has been quite successful, far beyond its limited membership. Its leaders in the first four to five decades—Adler, Salter, Weston, Coit, John L. Elliott, Alfred Martin, David Muzzey, Henry Newman, Algernon D. Black, among others—were actively involved in most of the progressive causes of social welfare and reform. They and their societies were pioneers in the areas of education for young and old, tenement reforms, settlement work, legal aid societies, boys' clubs, good government clubs, and visiting nursing associations. Many of their ventures—free kindergarten (1877), district visiting nursing (1877), the Neighborhood Guild (1886), the Bureau of Justice (1888), the Arts High School (1913)—served as models for similar undertakings by urban communities. In more recent decades, Ethical Culture, while not a leader as it once was, has nevertheless been involved with significant programs supporting liberal social causes, such as prison reform, drug rehabilitation, the right to abortion. The movement has also sponsored journals of popular and scholarly nature to reflect on the ethical domain as it relates to public policy and philosophy: *Ethical Record* (1888); *International Journal of Ethics* (1890); *Ethical Addresses* (1895); *The Standard* (1914); *Ethical Outlook* (1956); *Ethical Forum* (1965).

See Also Adler, Felix; Morality and Religion.

Bibliography

The most comprehensive one-volume history of Ethical Culture is Howard B. Radest's *Toward Common Ground: The Story of the Ethical Societies in the United States* (New York, 1969), which deals with the origins and evolution of the movement through the 1960s. Although written by an insider, the book is not unwilling to take a critical look at the movement and its leaders. My book *From Reform Judaism to Ethical Culture: The Religious Evolution of Felix Adler* (Cincinnati, 1979) gives a detailed institutional history of the founding of the New York Society for Ethical Culture and forwards a careful analysis of Adler's early ideological postures. Important evaluations of the meaning of Ethical Culture can be found in Horace L. Friess's *Felix Adler and Ethical Culture* (New York, 1981), which traces the development of Adler's own thinking on the subject, from initial conceptions to mature reformulations. Robert S. Guttchen's *Felix Adler* (New York, 1974) analyzes Adler's concept of human worth, which remains vital to Ethical Culture's own self-understanding. Another important analysis of Ethical Culture has been made by David S. Muzzey in *Ethics as a Religion*, 2d ed. (New York, 1967). A second-generation leader in the movement, and distinguished professor of American history, Muzzey argues for the religious nature of Ethical Culture. The book contains a brief, useful epilogue on the founding of the movement by Adler.

Benny Kraut (1987)

ETHICS See BUDDHIST ETHICS; CHRISTIAN ETHICS; JEWISH THOUGHT AND PHILOSOPHY, *ARTICLE ON* JEWISH ETHICAL LITERATURE; MORALITY AND RELIGION

ETHIOPIAN CHURCH. The Ethiopian or Abyssinian church, on the Horn of Africa, is one of the five so-called monophysite Christian churches that reject the Council of Chalcedon (451) and its formula of faith. The church does not call itself monophysite but rather Tāwaḥedo (Unionite; also spelled Tewahedo), a word expressing the union in Christ of the human and divine natures, to distinguish itself from the Eastern Orthodox churches, which accept the formulas accepted at Chalcedon. For the Tāwaḥedo Orthodox Church of Ethiopia, both Nestorius and Eutyches are heretics. Although formally under the jurisdiction of the Coptic church of Alexandria until 1950, the Ethiopian Orthodox church has managed to retain its indigenous language, literature, art, and music. It expects its faithful to practice circumcision, observe the food prescriptions set forth in the Hebrew scriptures (Old Testament), and honor Saturday as the Sabbath. The church has its own liturgy, including an horologion that contains the daily offices (initially for each of the twenty-four hours of the day), a missal of over fourteen anaphoras, the Deggwā (an antiphonary for each day of the year), doxologies (various collections of *nagś* hymns), and homiliaries in honor of the angels, saints, and martyrs. The most innovative aspect of this church is the provision in the Deggwā for the chanting of *qenē* (poetic hymns) in the liturgy. There are several types of *qenē* varying in number of lines from two to eleven, which one of the clergy usually improvises during the service in keeping with the spirit of *Psalms* 149:1, "Sing unto the Lord a new song."

Until the Ethiopian revolution of 1974, the Ethiopian Orthodox Church (the population of which was at least sixteen million in the early twenty-first century, according to the World Council of Churches) had been a national church defended by the political leader of the country. The monarch's reign had to be legitimized by the church at a religious ceremony where the new king swore allegiance to the church and committed himself to defend the Christian kingdom.

Early History. Historians disagree in assigning a date to the introduction of Christianity into Ethiopia, depending upon which Ethiopian king they think first adopted the faith. The conversion of the monarch, however, is a poor indication of the date of that introduction because not only was he by no means among the country's first converts, but also because until about 960, the monarchy changed hands so frequently that the ruler was not as consistently Christian as were certain segments of the population. We should also be wary of using the local tradition that the Ethiopian eunuch Qinā qis (*Acts* 8:26–39) was martyred teaching Christianity in Ethiopia as evidence of the country's conversion. However, we do know that Adulis, the famous port of Ethiopia, and Aksum, the capital, were frequented by Christian traders from the Hellenistic world since the early history of Christianity. Some of these settled there, forming Christian communities and attracting to their religion those with whom they interacted daily.

Ethiopia officially joined the Christian world when Frumentius was consecrated its first bishop by Athanasius of Alexandria in about 347. The contemporary historian Rufinus (*Ecclesiastical History* 1.9) tells us how this came about. A certain ship was attacked while calling on one of the Ethiopian ports. Of the voyagers, only two Syrian boys from Tyre (modern-day south Lebanon), Frumentius and Aedesius, escaped death. The boys were taken to the palace, where the king made Frumentius his secretary and Aedesius his cupbearer. Frumentius used his influence in the palace to facilitate the building of an oratory by the Christians in the city. This center was also used as a school where children, even those from non-Christian families, came to receive religious instruction. As soon as the two foreigners received their freedom, Frumentius went to Alexandria to ask the archbishop there to consecrate a bishop for the Christians in Ethiopia. Athanasius thereupon chose Frumentius to be the bishop of Aksum. Rufinus says that he received this story "from the mouth of Aedesius himself," who became a priest in Tyre. Even though Rufinus, like some other historians, calls the country India, there is no doubt that the story deals with Ethiopia. A letter from the Arian emperor, Constantius II (r. 337–361), to the rulers of Ethiopia, Ezana (ʿĒzānā) and Sazana, concerning Frumentius is extant in Athanasius's *Apology to Constantine* (*Patrologia Graeca,* ed. by J.-P. Migne, 25. 636–637). From Ezana's rule to the middle of the twentieth century, the head of the Ethiopian church remained a Copt. It was only in the twentieth century that an Ethiopian, Bāsleyos (1951–1970), was consecrated patriarch. It must be noted, however, that the Coptic metropolitan was in charge primarily of spiritual and theological matters. The administration of other church affairs was the responsibility of a native official with the title of *ʿaqqābē saʿāt* and subsequently *echagē.*

Medieval Period. The Ethiopian church took many significant steps forward between the fourth and the seventh century. It vigorously translated a great deal of Christian literature from Greek. This included the Old Testament from the Septuagint and the New Testament from the Lucianic recension (the Greek Bible revised by Lucian of Antioch, d. 312) used in the Syrian church. The Ethiopian Bible of eighty-one books includes the *Book of Jubilees* and the *Book of Enoch,* two books that have been preserved in their entirety only in Ethiopic. The *Synodicon* (a collection of canon law), the *Didascalia Apostolorum* (a church order), the *Testament of Our Lord,* and the *Qalēmenṭos* (an apocalyptic writing ascribed to Clement of Rome) are also part of the Ethiopian canonical scriptures. The number of churches and monasteries also grew quickly. Traveling through Ethiopian territories in the sixth century, a Greek monk, Cosmas Indicopleustes, was impressed to see churches everywhere.

It has been suggested that the *Rule of Pachomius* and the theological writings of the Fathers in the *Qērelos* (including writings from Cyril of Alexandria, Epiphanius, et al.) were brought to Ethiopia by the so-called Nine Saints who came from the Hellenistic or Mediterranean world, including Egypt, in the sixth or seventh century. But any of the many travelers and anchorites (such as Abbā Yoḥannes Kamā) who came to Ethiopia much earlier than the Nine Saints might have brought them along with several other works. Our historical knowledge about the Nine Saints is not firmly based even though they are highly revered in the church as the founders of monasticism in Ethiopia.

Unfortunately for the faithful, the young church suffered encroachment and harassment by Islam, starting in the eighth century. Locally, too, a vassal queen of one of the provinces, Gudit, revolted and devastated the Christian civilization, paving the way for another dynasty, the Zāgwē (1137–1270).

The Zāgwē kings were more interested in religion than in politics. Many of them were priests as well as rulers, and the last four of the dynasty are, in fact, among the saints of the church. The building of the several rock-hewn churches in Lāstā (central Ethiopia) is ascribed to them. The so-called Solomonic dynasty, which was to overthrow them, would boast of its alleged descendance from Solomon of Israel, while the Zāgwē attempted to reproduce the holy places in their own land, calling their capital Roha (after Edessa), their river Yordanos (after Jordan), and so on.

In 1270 the clergy, led by Takla Hāymānot, the founder of the Monastery of Dabra Libanos (in Shewa), and Iyyasus Moʾa, the founder of the Monastery of Ḥayq Esṭifānos (in Amhara), collaborated with Yekunno Amlāk to overthrow the Zāgwē and to found the Solomonic dynasty. Although the Solomonic kings did not always observe the church's teaching, it was nonetheless during this period that indigenous religious literature flourished, and Christianity spread into the south and west through the efforts of the monks of Dabra Libanos of Shewa, the twelve *neburāna ed*, chosen by the metropolitan according to the number of the apostles.

RELIGIOUS CONTROVERSIES. Late in the medieval period and afterward, religious controversies arose because of objections by some to the tradition of undue reverence for the Cross, icons of the Madonna and Child, and the king. We hear of these disputes during the reign of Yāqbeʾa Ṣeyon (r. 1285–1294), and they appear again in the days of Sayfa Arʿada (r. 1344–1372). The controversies became serious during the reign of Zarʾa Yāʿeqob (1434–1468), when an anchorite, Esṭifānos, succeeded in attracting to his teaching of rejection of the tradition many monks who, like him, refused to be shaken by the dreadful persecution that ensued. Another controversy, this time involving the Coptic church also, centered around the Sabbath observance of Saturday in addition to Sunday. Several monasteries, led by the monk Ēwosṭātēwos (d. 1369), successfully defied the decree of the king and the Coptic metropolitan that sought to abolish the practice of observing the first Sabbath (Saturday). But the most serious controversy dealt with the concept of the unity and trinity of God. The church taught that each being in the Trinity (three suns with one light) has a form or image, *malkeʿ*, which must look like that of a human because humans were created in God's image (*Gen.* 1:27). The heretics, followers of Zamikāʾēl, while admitting that God has an image, refused to define a form, quoting *John* 1:18—"No one has seen God." They also maintained a different theology of the unity and trinity of God (one sun with three attributes—disc, light, and heat). Another dispute developed when some monasteries objected to the use of the Deggwā in the liturgy; this intricate collection of antiphonary hymns recommends dancing while chanting during service (*Ps.* 150:4). The number of canonical books and the inclusion of the pseudepigrapha and the pseudoapostolic writings in the canon were also challenged.

RELIGIOUS CIVIL WAR OF THE SIXTEENTH CENTURY. The chronic skirmishes between the Christians and the Muslims in Ethiopia took a different form in the sixteenth century when the latter, led by Imām Ahmad ibn Ibrāhīm al-Ghāzī (or Ahmad Grāñ), sought and received help from the Turks. By this time also the astounding wealth of the individual churches in solid gold, silver, and precious clothes had become an irresistible booty and the *grāñ* sacked the monasteries and burned the churches of the empire for about fifteen years (1527–1542). The Christians turned to Portugal for help. The army of the imām collapsed when he was killed in early 1543. But it was about this time that the Cushitic people the Galla, who call themselves Oromo, migrated into Ethiopia en masse, destroying a great part of the Christian heritage that had escaped the *grāñ's* devastation.

THE JESUITS' ENTERPRISE. The Portuguese came to help the church in its war against Islam with the assumption that the lost flock, the church of Ethiopia, would come back to the Roman Catholic Church. The Ethiopians, however, were never ready to abandon their faith. The pressure of the Jesuits, however, which started with missionaries sent by Pope Julius III (1487–1555), continued until the seventeenth century, when they succeeded in converting Emperor Suseneyos (r. 1607–1632) to Catholicism. In 1626 a Catholic patriarch, Alphonsus Mendez, came from Rome, and the emperor issued a decree that his subjects should follow his own example. However, the sweeping change that Mendez attempted to introduce into the age-old religious traditions of the nation met with stiff resistance. Led by the monastic leaders, tens of thousands of the faithful were martyred. The Catholic missionaries were finally asked to leave, and the emperor was assassinated, even though he had abdicated the throne to his son Fāsiladas (r. 1632–1667). Fāsiladas was magnanimous with the Jesuits despite the fact that they had attempted to overthrow him by courting one of his brothers.

Even though the Jesuits left, the controversy stemming from their theology of the two natures of Christ continues to the present, taking a local character and creating schism in the Ethiopian church. Overtly, this controversy is centered on the theological significance of qebʾat, *unction* (*Acts* 10:38), and bakwr, *first-born* (*Rom.* 8:29), when applied to Christ the Messiah, the only Son of God. But those who raised these questions were clearly attempting to show the monophysites the implication of a theology of one nature in Christ, by drawing their attention to the distinct presence of the human nature in him and its inferior position vis-à-vis his divinity. For one group, the Kārroch, or Tāwaḥedo (the Unionists of Tegrāy), whose position the church has held officially since 1878, *unction* means the union of divinity with humanity: Christ, who is the ointment and the anointed, became the natural Son of God in his humanity through this union. For the Qebatoch (unctionists of Gonder and Gojam), *unction* means that Christ in his humanity became the natural Son of God through the unction of the Holy Spirit: God the Father is the anointer, the Son the anointed, and the Holy Spirit the ointment. The third group, the Ṣaggoch (adoptionists of Shewa), who are accused of tending toward Catholicism, believe that Christ in his humanity became the Son of God by grace through the unction of the Holy Spirit either in Mary's womb at the Annunciation or at the baptism. They call the occasion when he became the Son of God by grace a third birth for Christ, in relation to the eternal birth from the Father and the temporal birth from Mary, hence the heresy of the three births condemned at the Council of Boru Meda in Welo (central Ethiopia) in 1878. The Ṣaggoch vehemently oppose the notion that Christ became the natural Son of God in his humanity. They are, however, in the minority.

THE CHURCH OUTSIDE AFRICA. Designed to express its spiritual message and to perform the services in the local culture, the Ethiopian church is strictly local and national. In its history it has not engaged in any missionary activities beyond the frontiers that political leaders claimed to be territories of their ancestors. King Kālēb's expedition to Najrān (southern Arabia) in about 525, to rescue the Christians from the persecution of a Jewish ruler and to reorganize the Christian communities there, may not be considered sustained activity by the church outside Ethiopia. Even the Ethiopian churches in the Holy Land could not be exceptions to this historical fact, since they were built to serve Ethiopian nationals who visited the holy places in Palestine and Egypt. Ethiopian monastic communities have lived in Jerusalem since the Middle Ages, and they were Ethiopia's main window to the outside world. In modern times, there were also Ethiopian churches in the former British Somaliland, Kenya, and the Sudan, but they too were serving Ethiopian nationals, refugees who fled the 1936 to 1941 Italian occupation of Ethiopia.

In the 1950s the Ethiopian church was faced with a most unusual challenge. The local church was called upon to respond to the need for cultural and racial identity of the oppressed black people in Africa and the Americas. Churches with the term *Abyssinian* as part of their name started to emerge in these continents. Although the historical link between the Ethiopian church and these churches is lacking, and the Ethiopian church was not economically, educationally, and politically up to the challenge, delegates consisting of clergy were sent from Ethiopia to East Africa (still under British rule), the Caribbean region, and North America. The inevitable problems were how to attract the middle class to an African church and how to adapt the culturally alien church services to English-speaking communities in Africa and the Americas, not to mention the question of rebaptism. The compromise reached was to retain some parts of the liturgy in Geʿez and conduct the rest in English. This compromise was not only unsatisfactory to both the church authorities and congregations, but it also meant training the clergy, Ethiopians and non-Ethiopians alike, in Geʿez and English. In spite of several problems, the church is gaining strength, especially in the West Indies and the Caribbean (e.g., Jamaica, Guyana, Trinidad, and Tobago). The number of the faithful in the United States (New York, Washington, D.C., and Los Angeles) grew because of the influx of Ethiopian refugees fleeing the military Marxist repression that started with the overthrow of the monarchy in 1974.

In 1987 Ethiopia officially became the People's Democratic Republic of Ethiopia, but a rebel movement later overthrew the government and with it centuries of Amharic rule. Eritrea declared its independence from Ethiopia following a UN-sponsored referendum in 1993, and the Orthodox Church of Eritrea broke away from the Ethiopian Church. In 1991 the patriarch of Ethiopia, Abune Merkorios, accused of collaboration with the communist authorities, was removed by the Holy Synod. Merkorios was replaced by Abune Paulos in 1992. Paulos is recognized as the patriarch by the Holy Synod of the Ethiopian Orthodox Tāwaḥedo Church inside Ethiopia. Merkorios went into exile in Kenya and is upheld as patriarch by the Holy Synod in Exile. Efforts continue to avert a permanent schism of the church.

SEE ALSO Aksumite Religion.

BIBLIOGRAPHY

For the history of both the church and the country, Jean Doresse's *Ethiopia* (London, 1959) is a good introduction even though it lacks annotation to the sources. Carlo Conti Rossini's *Storia d'Etiopia*, vol. 1, *Dalle origini all' avvento della dinastia Salomonide* (Bergamo, Italy, 1928), remains the standard reference for the early history. Unfortunately, however, this book too has neither adequate annotation to sources nor a bibliography. An index for it has been prepared by Edward Ullendorff in *Rassegna di studi etiopici* 18 (1962): 97–141.

The only book that examines many aspects of the Ethiopian Bible is Edward Ullendorff's *Ethiopia and the Bible* (London, 1968). This book also contains an excellent bibliography. See also Roger W. Cowley's *The Traditional Interpretation of the Apocalypse of St. John in the Ethiopian Orthodox Church* (Cambridge, U.K., 1983). The introduction to this work offers more than the title suggests. The history of Geʿez (Ethiopic) literature has been ably surveyed in Enrico Cerulli's *La letteratura etiopica*, 3d ed. (Florence, Italy, 1968). Ernst Hammerschmidt's *Studies in the Ethiopic Anaphoras* (Berlin, 1961) summarizes the different studies of the anaphoras in one small volume. For an English version of the anaphoras themselves, see Marcos Daoud and Marsie Hazen's *The Liturgy of the Ethiopian Church* (Cairo, 1959). The most comprehensive study thus far on *qenē* hymns is Anton Schall's *Zur äthiopischen Verskunst* (Wiesbaden, Germany, 1961).

The period of the Zāgwē dynasty and the rock-hewn churches of Lāstā are well treated in Georg Gerster's *Churches in Rock* (London, 1970), with many large and impressive photographs and an adequate bibliography. The history of the church from the beginning of the Solomonic dynasty to the Islamic invasion of the sixteenth century has been uniquely treated in Taddesse Tamrat's *Church and State in Ethiopia, 1270–1527* (Oxford, 1972). Francisco Alvarez's *Narrative of the Portuguese Embassy to Abyssinia during the Years 1520–1527,* translated by Lord Stanley of Alderley (London, 1881), is a rare description of church and secular life immediately before the war with the *grāññ.* The translation was revised by C. F. Beckingham and G. W. B. Huntingford and published under the title *The Prester John of the Indies,* 2 vols. (Cambridge, U.K., 1961).

Some of the sources for the religious controversies of the late medieval period were edited and translated in Enrico Cerulli's *Il libro etiopico dei miracoli di Maria e le sue fonti nelle letterature del medio evo latino* (Rome, 1943) and *Scritti teologici etiopici dei secoli XVI–XVII,* 2 vols., "Studi e testi," no. 198 (Rome, 1958).

The unique source for the destruction of the churches by the forces of the *grāññ* in the sixteenth century is Futūḥ al-Ḥabashah, composed by ʿArab Faqīh, the chronicler of the imām, edited and translated in René Basset's *Histoire de la conquête de l'Abyssinie (seizième siècle) par Chihab ed-Din Aḥmed ben ʿAbd el-Qâder surnommé Arab-Faqih,* 2 vols. (Paris, 1898–1901). The Portuguese, too, have left invaluable though sometimes exaggerated and conflicting reports of the campaign. See *The Portuguese Expedition to Abyssinia in 1541–1543, as Narrated by Castanhoso, with Some Letters, the Short Account of Bermudez, and Certain Extracts from Correa* (London, 1902).

The best work on the religious controversies that started in the seventeenth century is Friedrich Heyer's *Die Kirche Äthiopiens: Eine Bestandsaufnahme* (Berlin and New York, 1971). The history of the religious controversy caused particularly by the Portuguese has been ably and succinctly presented in Germa Ḅeshah and Merid Wolde Aregay's *The Question of the Union of the Churches in Luso-Ethiopian Relations (1500–1632)* (Lisbon, 1964). See also Donald Crummey's *Priests and Politicians: Protestant and Catholic Missions in Orthodox Ethiopia, 1830–1868* (Oxford, 1972). The book has an excellent bibliography with useful comments on some of the works.

Questions about the church that are of interest to Western Christians are answered in *The Teaching of the Abyssinian Church as Set forth by the Doctors of the Same,* translated from Amharic, the vernacular of Ethiopia, by A. F. Matthew (London, 1936). See also Harry Middleton Hyatt's *The Church of Abyssinia* (London, 1928). This work describes in detail the religious practices of the church.

Kirsten Pedersen's *The History of the Ethiopian Community in the Holy Land from the Time of Emperor Tewodros II till 1974* (Jerusalem, 1983) is a result of several years of study of the original and secondary sources on the subject. The minor mistakes pertaining to modern history of Ethiopia do not in any way minimize the usefulness of this work. The major English sources on all aspects of the church are surveyed in Jon Bonk's *An Annotated and Classified Bibliography of English Literature Pertaining to the Ethiopian Orthodox Church* (Metuchen, N.J., 1984).

GETATCHEW HAILE (1987)

ETHNOASTRONOMY.

This article is limited to discussion of the ethnoastronomies of native South America because of their primary importance in the development of this area of study.

PATTERNS. In the ethnographic literature on indigenous South American Indian populations, there is a considerable body of evidence attesting to the importance of ethnoastronomical beliefs. These beliefs, expressed with varying degrees of emphasis in mythology and ritual, bear witness to longstanding traditions of astronomical observations undertaken for a variety of purposes, ranging from the construction of precise calendar systems to the production of symbols and metaphors for expressing enduring relationships that characterize interactions between men and women, social groups, humans and animals, and so forth. While there are no universally shared astronomical symbols, several recurrent thematic patterns emerge from a comparative study of the ways in which different groupings of celestial bodies are interrelated in the mythology and ritualism of the Andean and Tropical Forest (Amazonian and Orinocoan) religious traditions.

Sun and Moon. A clear expression of the notion of the thematic patterning of relations in an astronomical mode is found in a number of origin myths, especially those in which the origin of humans is thought to have occurred virtually simultaneously with their separation into different—but complementary—kinship or social categories (e.g., siblings, spouses, clans, or moieties). The Apinagé of the Araguaya River of Brazil hold that Sun created the two moieties and localized one (the Kolti moiety) in his own northern half of the circular villages while leaving the other (the Kolre) with his sister, Moon, in the south. The Apinagé held ceremonies directed to Sun during the planting and harvesting periods, while they invoked Moon to help the crops mature (Nimuendajú, 1967, p. 164). The pairing of Sun and Moon as, respectively, brother and sister is also found among the Tapirapé (Wagley, 1940, p. 256) and the Conibo (*Handbook of South American Indians,* 1948, p. 595; hereafter referred to as *H. S. A. I.*). Among the Chiriguano (H. S. A. I., 1948, pp. 483–484), the Kogi (Reichel-Dolmatoff, 1982, p. 178), and the Inca, Sun and Moon are simultaneously brother and sister and husband and wife. For the Xerente, who once occupied several villages southeast of the Apinagé along the Tocantins River, Sun and Moon are "companions" (i. e., neither siblings nor spouses), although each is associated with one of the two moieties. Sun, who is referred to by all Xerente regardless of their moiety affiliation as "Our Creator," communicated with the Siptato moiety through a group of intermediaries, including Venus, Jupiter, the Belt of Orion, and k Orionis; the intermediaries between Moon and the people of the Sdakra moiety are Mars, Carrion Vultures, and Seven Stars (probably the Pleiades; Nimuendajú, 1942, pp. 84–85). Through the association of Sun and Moon with linked pairs of complementary, yet often asymmetric and hierarchical, social categories (e.g., husband and wife, brother and sister, and the moieties), astronomical phenomena are made to participate in the process of classifying human society on the basis of fundamental dichotomies and processes (e.g., alliance and reproduction) that occur throughout the natural world. The relations between Sun and Moon serve as the "charter" for cosmic and social order throughout the succession of the generations. Yet just as inevitably as social order is established and maintained within each society by rules governing relations among different groups of people, the rules are forever being broken and the right order of things momentarily threatened. The inevitability of disorder arising from the violation of rules and prohibitions has its celestial reminder in the spots besmirching the face of the full moon. Throughout the mythological traditions of the tropical forest, the spots on the moon are commonly associated with incestuous relations, especially between brothers and sisters. In a typical example of this theme, the Záparoan-speaking tribes of the Marañón, Napo, and Pastaza rivers say that Moon was formerly a man who, in the dark of night, had sexual intercourse with his sister. In order to identify her lover, the girl one night smeared his face with genipa (a blue-black vegetable dye). Out of shame, the man went away to the sky and became the moon, his genipa-covered face being reexposed to the Záparo every month (*H. S. A. I.,* 1948, p. 649; cf. Roth, 1908–1909, p. 255; Wagley, 1940, p. 256). Asocial (incestuous) sexual relations may generally be compared with unproductive sexual encounters, which are everywhere signaled by menstruation. Among the contemporary Quechua of the Peruvian highlands, Sun (Inti) is male and Moon (Killa) is female; menses is referred to as *killa chayamushan* ("moon coming, or arriving"). Sun and Moon are also often associated with brightly colored birds or with the plumage of such birds. For example, the Trumai and the Paresí (*H. S. A. I.,* 1948, pp. 348, 360) say that Sun is a ball or headdress of red parrot feathers, while they identify Moon as a collection of yellow feathers. In the Záparo myth discussed above, the wife of the incestuous man who became the moon was herself simultaneously transformed into a night bird. And in a congeries of these various bird images and relations, the Tapirapé of central Brazil, west of the Araguaya River, say that Moon was the sister of Sun and that the latter wears a headdress of red parrot feathers. Sun is said to have slapped Moon's face with his genipa-covered hand because of her sexual misbehavior. Moon was married to a culture hero who divided all birds into two groups. Among the Tapirapé, the two men's moities are subdivided into three age grades, each of which carries the name of a bird (Wagley, 1940, p. 256).

The Milky Way. Aside from the sun and the moon, one other celestial phenomenon is important throughout the ethnoastronomies of South America: the Milky Way. The Milky Way serves as a means for organizing and orienting the celestial sphere in the spatial, temporal, and mythological dimensions. The Quechua-speakers of the Peruvian Andes refer to the Milky Way as a river *(mayu)* composed of two branches. The branches originate in the north within the cosmic sea that encircles the earth. Water is taken into the Milky Way, and the two branches separate, flowing away from each other toward the south, where they collide in the heavens near the Southern Cross. The foam *(posuqu)* stirred up by their collision is seen in the bright clouds of the southern Milky Way from the Southern Triangle to the False Cross in Carina. The two branches of the celestial river alternately rise, pass through the zenith, and set; one branch, when it stands in the zenith, passes from the northeast to the southwest, while the other branch passes from the northwest through the zenith to the southeast (Urton, 1981, pp. 54–63). The Barasana, a Tucanoan-speaking group on the Vaupés River in Colombia, conceive of the Milky Way as divided into two "star paths"; one, called New Path, is oriented southeast-northwest, while the other, Old Path, is oriented northeast-southwest. New Path and Old Path are the sites of most of the constellations recognized by the Barasana (Hugh-Jones, 1982, p. 182). For the Desána, another Tucanoan-speaking group of the Vaupés region, the Milky Way, as a single construct, is likened to a river, a trail in the forest, an immense cortege of people, a cast-off snake skin, and a fertilizing stream of semen. In a dualistic image focusing on its cyclical, alternating axes, the Milky Way is imagined as two huge snakes: the starry, luminous part is a rainbow boa, a male principle; the dark part is an anaconda, a female principle. The shifting of the Milky Way, seen as a swinging motion made by the two snakes, punctuates the cycle of fertilizing forces emanating from the sky (Reichel-Dolmatoff, 1982, pp. 170–171). Using metaphors of human sexuality that recall the menstrual cycle of the moon, the Barasana, like the Desána, conceive of the Milky Way as participating in a cycle of fertilizing forces. The connection between the principle of fertility, the Milky Way, and the flow of menses is occasioned by the comparison of the menstrual and seasonal cycles. The rainy season is the menstrual period of the sky, which is personified by Woman Shaman, a creator who has a gourd of wax identified with the Pleiades, which are called Star Thing and are the principal aspect of the New Path of the Milky Way. The gourd is Woman Shaman's vagina; the wax, her menstrual blood; and the melting of the wax, her menstrual period, which is compared, as an internal, rejuvenating "skin change," to the rainy season, which begins in the Vaupés in April, as the stars of the Pleiades set. In Barasana cosmology, the internal skin change of Woman Shaman, associated with Star Thing (the gourd of melting wax), is contrasted with the external skin change of the constellation called Caterpillar Jaguar (Scorpius), which stands opposed to, and alternates with, Star Thing (Hugh-Jones, 1982, pp. 196–197).

Bright-star and dark-cloud constellations. Data from the Barasana and Desána introduce a final and far more complex recurrent theme, one that forms perhaps the core of ethnoastronomical symbolism among South American Indian societies. This theme concerns groups of interrelated metaphorical images built up out of animals, anthropomorphic beings, and constellations stretched along the bright path or paths of the Milky Way. The theme of animals and humans as constellations concerns a group of celestial phenomena located principally along, or within, the path of the Milky Way. In order to understand many of the references discussed below, it is necessary to see the Milky Way as visually composed of two distinct but interconnected elements: first, it appears in its overall form as a wide, bright band of stars; and second, it contains several dark spots and streaks formed by fixed clouds of interstellar dust that cut through the central path. Both of these galactic phenomena, the bright band of stars against the dark background of the night sky and the dark clouds cutting through the bright path of stars, are recognized as named celestial constructs in South American ethnoastronomical traditions. When viewed as a path, the Milky Way is often considered to be a road along which animals, humans, and spirits move. The Indians of Guiana refer to the Milky Way as both the "path of the tapir" and the path that is walked upon by a group of people bearing white clay, the type used for making pottery (Roth, 1908–1909, p. 260). The Chiriguano (H. S. A. I., 1948, p. 483) know the Milky Way as the "path of the rhea"; they identify the head of the rhea either with the Southern Cross or with the Coalsack, the dark spot at the foot of the Southern Cross. The Amahuaca say that the Milky Way is the trail or path of the sun, formed when a jaguar dragged a manatee across the sky. For the Trumai, the Milky Way is like a drum containing animals; it is the road to the afterworld and the abode of jaguars *(H. S. A. I.,* 1948, p. 348). Finally, the Tapirapé see in the Milky Way the "path of the shamans," by which shamans travel to the sky to visit celestial bodies (Wagley, 1940, p. 257). That many of the characters who move along the celestial path (or river) are animals reinforces the observation that the most common identifications of the dark clouds that cut through the Milky Way are with animals, birds, or fish. As mentioned earlier, among the Quechua of the central Andes, the Milky Way is seen as two interconnected branches of a river. Within the river, in the southern skies, are several animals, each identified as one of the dark clouds *(yana phuyu)*; these include a snake, a toad, a tinamou, a mother llama with her baby, and a fox that pursues the llamas (Urton, 1981, p. 170). The pursuit of a herbivore by a carnivore, as in the pursuit of the llamas by the fox, is a common element in the South American ethnoastronomical symbolism of the dark spots. Within the tropical forest, however, the carnivore is most often a jaguar rather than a fox. For instance, the Paresí and Conibo see a jaguar pursuing a deer in some dark spots in the southern Milky Way (*H. S. A. I.*, 1948, pp. 360, 595). Certain tribes of Guiana see, in the same general area, a tapir being chased by a dog, which in turn is pursued by a jaguar (Roth, 1908–1909, p. 260). The Tukuna locate the bodies of a jaguar and an anteater in dark clouds in the southern skies near the constellation of Centaurus; the two animals are locked in a nightly struggle, although in a Tukuna myth that describes a similar fight the anteater defeats the jaguar, rips open his stomach, and sucks out his liver (Nimuendajú, 1952, p. 143). The Campa say that a dark streak near Antares (in the constellation of Scorpius) is a digging stick and that the Coalsack below the Southern Cross is a bees' nest (Weiss, 1972, p. 160). The Múra, however, see in the Coalsack a manatee carrying a fisherman on its back (*H. S. A. I.*, 1948, p. 265). As is clear from the illustrations above, the identification of the dark clouds of the Milky Way with animals is a widely shared feature in South American Indian ethnoastronomies. Although the specific animals vary from tradition to tradition (as one would expect, given that the various ethnoastronomical data derive from societies in widely differing environmental settings), it is reasonable to suppose that the animals may be identified and interrelated according to similar classificatory principles and symbolic interests as one moves from one society to the next. That this may be so, in at least one respect, is suggested by the fact that the ethnographic literature contains several references to the belief that there is a conceived (if not perceived) relationship between an animal's reproductive cycle and the first appearance of that animal's celestial counterpart in the early morning skies (Urton, 1981, pp. 176–189). In addition, there are suggestions that the rising of the celestial representation of an animal or bird serves as an indication that the season to hunt the terrestrial version of that same animal or bird has arrived (Roth, 1908–1909, p. 261). These data suggest that in the process of establishing local calendar systems there is considered to be a temporal correlation between the appearance of a particular dark-cloud animal and the biological periodicity of, or the cycles of human activity in the exploitation of, its terrestrial counterpart.

Classification and Symbolism. Such a purely calendrically oriented interpretation of the significance of the animals located in the dark spots of the Milky Way should be augmented by two other considerations, one classificatory, the other symbolic. In relation to the former, the animals of the Milky Way may represent those forms considered to be classificatorily "prototypical," the most representative members of particular classes of animals. Alternatively, they may represent "marked" animals, ones that do not fit comfortably into a single class but that rather bridge two or more classes. That one or the other of these considerations may be significant in Quechua astronomy is suggested by the fact that the sequence of animals that stretches along, and within, the Milky Way includes a reptile (snake), an amphibian (toad), a bird (tinamou), a herbivorous mammal (llama), and a carnivorous mammal (fox). The classificatory significance of these life forms would therefore rest not only on the particular characteristics of each individual animal in turn but also on the relations between and among the various types as they are projected into the sky in a particular sequence (i.e., from a reptile to a mammal). Another classificatory factor that may be important throughout the various ethnoastronomical traditions is a consideration of the color of the animals in question. That is, many of the animals have either a dull, dark coloring (e.g., fox, deer, anteater), or else they are spotted or mottled (e.g., tinamou, toad, anaconda, rainbow boa, jaguar). The dark spots along the "body" of the Milky Way recall the dark or mottled coloring of the terrestrial animals.

In this regard, there may also be a conceptual similarity between the dark spots of the Milky Way and the spots on the moon. The latter, as mentioned earlier, are typically associated with asocial (e.g., incestuous) relationships.

Mythic oppositions. The symbolic significance of the dark-cloud animals will vary considerably from one ethnoastronomical tradition to another and can be understood only on the basis of a careful consideration of the particular characteristics of the celestial animals as they are portrayed in the mythology of each culture. In considering the mythological descriptions of celestial phenomena, however, it is essential first to turn to the material referring to those constellations that are composed of clusters or groupings of stars, since the mythological data for stellar constellations are more abundant, and explicit, than those for the dark spots of the Milky Way. The principal stellar constellations recognized in South American ethnoastronomies are, for the most part, also located near or within the Milky Way; these include the Pleiades, the Hyades, the Belt (and Sword) of Orion, Scorpius, the Southern Cross, and α and β Centauri. By far the richest ethnoastronomical material concerns the Pleiades, a small cluster of some six to ten stars (visible with the naked eye) in the constellation of Taurus. The Pleiades are referred to in a variety of ways, many of which emphasize the visual appearance of this cluster of stars as a group or "bunch" of things. In the tropical forest, the Pleiades are variously referred to as bees, wasps, a handful of flour spilled on the ground, parrots, white down, a bunch of flowers, and so forth (Lévi-Strauss, 1969, p. 222). Claude Lévi-Strauss pointed out an important principle in Tropical Forest ethnoastronomies when he argued that the Pleiades are typically classed together with, while at the same time opposed to, the nearby constellation of the Belt and Sword of Orion. The latter is referred to as a tortoise shell, a bird, a stick, and a leg (or a one-legged man; Lévi-Strauss, 1969, pp. 222–223; cf. Reichel-Dolmatoff, 1982, pp. 173–174). Lévi-Strauss's argument is that the Pleiades and Orion are diachronically associated, since they rise within a few days of each other, but that they are synchronically opposed, since the Pleiades represent, or are in the category of, the continuous, whereas Orion is in that of the discontinuous. For the Pleiades and Orion, respectively, he notes that "we have names that boil down to collective terms describing a chance distribution of . . . related elements: and on the other, analytical terms describing a systematic arrangement of clearly individualized elements" (Lévi-Strauss, 1969, pp. 222–223; cf. 1973, pp. 268–270). Throughout South America, it can be shown that the Pleiades are contrasted in various ways with other nearby star groupings (e.g., Orion and the Hyades), whereas, on another level, they are grouped together with these same nearby stars and contrasted with other constellations (e.g., Coma Berenices, Corvus, Scorpius, the Southern Cross, and α and β Centauri). These two groupings of stars are contrasted or deemed complementary in terms of their symbolic characteristics, and they are coincidental or alternating in terms of the phasing of the dates of their rising and setting (cf. Hugh-Jones, 1982; Zuidema, 1982; Wilbert, 1975). The questions to be addressed with regard to these observations are "On what bases are the Pleiades contrasted with other, nearby constellations?" and "On what bases are the Pleiades grouped together with these nearby constellations and contrasted with another, more distant group of constellations?" I suggest that the first question may be approached primarily through a consideration of the mythological data referring to social relations and social organization, whereas the second question can best be addressed on the basis of data referring to meteorological, seasonal, and, ultimately, economic concerns. As for the contrast between the Pleiades, the Hyades, and Orion, there are several myths that mention these three constellations in related mythological contexts. For instance, among certain Carib-speaking tribes there are myths of a woman (the Pleiades) who cuts off her husband's leg (Orion's Belt and Sword) and runs away with a tapir (the Hyades; Jara and Magaña, 1983, p. 125; cf. Roth, 1908–1909, p. 262). The Amahuaca of eastern Peru say that the V-shaped Hyades represent the jaw of a caiman that bit off the leg of a man who mistook it for a canoe; the leg is seen in the Pleiades, while Orion's Belt and Sword represent the man's brother holding the lance with which he killed the caiman (cf. Reichel-Dolmatoff, 1982, pp. 173–174). The Campa see in the Pleiades a Campa man and his family; the man's brother-in-law is the Belt and Sword of Orion. They also say that Orion is a Campa man who is being pursued by a warrior wasp and has received an arrow in his leg (Weiss, 1972, p. 160). The various myths that deal with the Pleiades, the Hyades, and Orion are centered on animals and people (or their body parts) who are related by ties of blood or, more commonly, marriage. In many cases, there are also characters present who are implicated in the violation of these kinship and marriage ties (e.g., the tapir who seduces and runs away with a man's wife). In this regard, it should be recalled that among the Xerente, who practice moiety exogamy, the belt of Orion and k Orionis are related to one moiety, while Seven Stars (the Pleiades?) are related to the other (Nimuendajú, 1942, pp. 25, 85). In addition to the "local" contrast between the Pleiades and the neighboring constellations of the Hyades and Orion, there are several references to the contrast between the Pleiades and constellations farther removed. In Barasana cosmology, the Pleiades (Star Thing) are associated with the dry season and opposed to Scorpius (Caterpillar Jaguar), which is associated with the wet season (Hugh-Jones, 1982, p. 197). The Pleiades and Scorpius are similarly opposed, and each is related to either the dry or the wet season, or to planting or harvest, in the cosmology of the Quechua (Urton, 1981, pp. 122–125) and the Chiriguano (*H. S. A. I.*, 1948, p. 483). Similar examples of the opposition of the Pleiades to other constellations (e.g., Corvus and Coma Berenices) appear in the timing of fishing cycles (Lévi-Strauss, 1978, pp. 36–40), honey availability (Lévi-Strauss, 1973, pp. 57–58, 268–272, 282–285), or both fishing cycles and honey availability (Lévi-Strauss, 1973, p. 114). The evening rising and setting of the Pleiades (which occur at different times of the year) are associated by the Barasana and the Desána with the fruiting periods of trees (Hugh-Jones, 1982, p. 190; Reichel-Dolmatoff, 1982, p. 173). R. Tom Zuidema has shown that the critical dates in the Inca calendar system, a system that coordinated political, ritual, and agricultural events throughout the year, were determined by the times of the rising, setting, and the upper and lower culminations of the Pleiades in opposition to the Southern Cross and α and β Centauri. In Inca and contemporary Quechua astronomy, the Pleiades represent (among other things) a storehouse; the Southern Cross is important, as it stands just above the dark-cloud constellation of the tinamou; and α and β Centauri are the eyes of the dark-cloud constellation of the llama (Zuidema, 1982, pp. 221–224; Urton, 1981, pp. 181–188).

Mythic similarities. While particular contrasts between (1) the Pleiades, the Hyades, and Orion and (2) the Southern Cross, α and β Centauri, Corvus, Coma Berenices, and Scorpius vary over different parts of South America, the temporal relations between the two groups of constellations represent essentially similar seasonal oppositions regardless of which particular members of the two sets are contrasted. In terms of their celestial locations, the constellations in group 1 are located between right ascension three to six hours, while those of group 2 are between right ascension twelve to sixteen hours. Therefore, the members of one group will rise as the members of the other set. This temporal opposition, and its attendant symbolic and mythological associations, is one other important feature shared by the ethnoastronomies of South American Indians. Although the various Indian tribes of South America are situated in extremely diverse environmental regions, from the dense tropical forests of the Amazon and Orinoco basins to the high Andean mountains along the western side of the continent, there are a number of similarities in the ethnoastronomical traditions of these various groups. One source of similarities may lie in the fact that these cultures are all located within the tropics (see Aveni, 1981): the Amazon River is roughly coincident with the line of the equator. But beyond the similarities that are encountered in the observational phenomena viewed by these cultures, there are perhaps more fundamental similarities in the way in which the celestial bodies are described and interrelated in their mythological and religious traditions. There are fundamental principles that give meaning and coherence to ethnoastronomical beliefs concerning the sun and the moon, the Milky Way, and the two types of constellations. These are the same conceptual foundations that ground the various religious traditions. These basic premises revolve around relations between and among men and women, humans and animals, and beings on earth and those in the sky.

BIBLIOGRAPHY

For excellent discussions of naked-eye observational astronomy in the Americas, see Anthony F. Aveni's *Skywatchers* (Austin, Tex., 2001), and Stephen M. Fabian's *Patterns in the Sky: An Introduction to Ethnoastronomy* (Prospect Heights, Ill., 2001). Separate ethnographic descriptions, many of which include ethnoastronomical material for a variety of Tropical Forest tribes, can be found in *The Tropical Forest Tribes,* vol. 3 of the *Handbook of South American Indians,* edited by Julian H. Steward (Washington, D.C., 1948). Collections of Tropical Forest Indian myths are included in the following three books by the French anthropologist Claude Lévi-Strauss: *The Raw and the Cooked* (New York, 1969), *From Honey to Ashes* (New York, 1973), and *The Origin of Table Manners* (New York, 1978), all translated by John Weightman and Doreen Weightman. An excellent resource for Amazonian and Andean mythological and cosmological traditions is Lawrence E. Sullivan's, *Icanchu's Drum: An Orientation to Meaning in South American Religions* (New York and London, 1988). The ethnoastronomies of various tribes in northeastern South America are described in Fabiola Jara and Edmundo Magaña's "Astronomy of the Coastal Caribs of Surinam," *L'homme* 23 (1983): 111–133; Walter E. Roth's "An Inquiry into the Animism and Folklore of the Guiana Indians," in the *Thirtieth Annual Report of the Bureau of American Ethnology* (Washington, D.C., 1908–1909); and Johannes Wilbert's "Eschatology in a Participatory Universe: Destinies of the Soul among the Warao Indians of Venezuela," in *Death and the Afterlife in Pre-Columbian America,* edited by Elizabeth P. Benson (Washington, D.C., 1975). Ethnoastronomies of the Indians of the Colombian rain forest are discussed in Stephen Hugh-Jones's "The Pleiades and Scorpius in Barasana Cosmology" and in Gerardo Reichel-Dolmatoff's "Astronomical Models of Social Behavior among Some Indians of Colombia," both of which can be found in *Ethnoastronomy and Archaeoastronomy in the American Tropics,* edited by Anthony F. Aveni and Gary Urton (New York, 1982). The ethnoastronomies of Tropical Forest tribes in eastern Peru are discussed in Gerald Weiss's "Campa Cosmology," *Ethnology* 11 (April 1972): 157–172 and in Peter Roe's *The Cosmic Zygote: Cosmology in the Amazon Basin* (New Brunswick, N.J., 1982). Some of the best descriptions of the astronomy and cosmology of the tribes of the southern Amazon basin are to be found in three works by Curt Nimuendajú: *The Sherente,* translated by Robert H. Lowie (Los Angeles, 1942); *The Tukuna,* translated by William D. Hohenthal, edited by Robert H. Lowie (Berkeley, Calif., 1952); and *The Apinayé,* translated by Robert H. Lowie, edited by John M. Cooper and Robert H. Lowie (Oosterhout, The Netherlands, 1967). Additional valuable discussions of southern Amazonian ethnoastronomy are to be found in Charles Wagley's "World View of the Tapirape Indians," *Journal of American Folklore* 53 (1940): 252–260 and Stephen M. Fabian, *Space-Time of the Bororo of Brazil* (Gainesville, Fla., 1992). For descriptions and analyses of Inca and contemporary Quechua ethnoastronomy, see R. Tom Zuidema's article "Catachillay: The Role of the Pleiades and of the Southern Cross and α and β Centauri in the Calendar of the Incas," in *Ethnoastronomy and Archaeoastronomy in the American Tropics,* mentioned above; and my book, *At the Crossroads of the Earth and the Sky: An Andean Cosmology* (Austin, Tex., 1981). For an example of astronomic configurations in the religious life of hunters, see Otto Zerries's "Sternbilder als Audruck Jägerischer Geisteshaltung in Südamerika," *Paideuma* 5 (1952): 220–235.

Gary Urton (1987 and 2005)

ETHNOLOGY SEE ANTRHOPOLOGY, ETHNOLOGY, AND RELIGION

ETHOLOGY OF RELIGION.

Human ethology is the biological study of human behavior. It emphasizes the notion that both the behavior of humankind and its physiological basis have evolved phylogenetically and should be studied as an aspect of evolution. Ethology overlaps other disciplines such as sociobiology, behavioral ecology, evolutionary psychology, human anthropology, and even consciousness studies, which in part employ similar strategies of research.

HISTORY OF ETHOLOGY. The historical roots of ethology can be traced to Charles Darwin's theory of evolution. In his book *The Expression of the Emotions in Man and Animals* (1872) Darwin recognized that the role of instinct is just as important for the survival of the species as the adaptation of morphological structures in the course of their phylogenetic histories. During the following decades, however, the Darwinian approach continued to be disregarded. Instead, a scientific school with roots in psychology dominated the study of animal and human behavior. This behaviorism was based on the premise that psychology should be regarded as the science of behavior, rather than the science of mental life. Proceeding from the assumption that behavior is a product of learning, American behaviorists focused on the study of observable behavior and the ascertainable or contrived circumstances of its occurrence. As a result, behaviorists were successful in all kinds of research with regard to general laws of learning, but failed to take evolutionary approaches into account. Until the 1970s most behaviorists and sociologists were convinced that the behavior of humans and animals was mainly a product of their environment and education.

Within the scientific climate at that time, anthropology and the study of religions developed approaches of cultural relativism that considered human culture as phenomena upon which the biological heritage had no influence. This opinion first came into question when the experienced historian of religions Karl Meuli (1891–1968) was able to prove that religions as distinct from one another as the religions of ancient Greece, imperial Rome, recent arctic hunter-gatherers, and probably even prehistoric hunters, shared similar ritual customs. This observation was unintelligible from an environmental point of view. In spite of the prevailing paradigm, Meuli concluded that these similar manifestations of sacrificial practices must originate in an innate behavior pattern acquired during human evolution.

From a biological standpoint, the final impulses for the revision of the extremely environmentally oriented approaches came from zoologists like Konrad Lorenz (1903–1989) and Nikolaas Tinbergen (1907–1988). During the 1940s and 1950s, Tinbergen and Lorenz focused on the investigation of instinctive behavior in the animal's natural habitat, its meaning seen from an evolutionary point of view, and its physiological and genetic foundation. At the same time they assumed that similar action patterns had been developed to serve as social signals or releasers for appropriate behavior, not only among animal species but among humans as well. As a result, the study of human ethology attempted to apply ethological methods and the evolutionary perspective to psychological, sociological and, finally, even religious phenomena.

During the following decades the German zoologist Irenäus Eibl-Eibesfeldt (1928–) and others contributed to this new discipline by studying expressive movements with signal functions. These behavior patterns are usually incorporated into more complex behavioral events for which the term *ritual* was introduced by Julian Huxley (1887–1975). As for the origin of behavioral patterns, a distinction can be made between phylogenetically evolved, culturally acquired, and individually invented signals. The criteria of homology are applicable to phylogenetically acquired, as well as to culturally acquired, signals. Expressive behavior and ritual behavior both serve the function of communication. As far as religions are concerned, two important remarks have to be taken into account: first, expressive behavior does not necessarily mean that a message is consciously intended; second, originally functional acts can change their function from goal-directed acts into symbolic acts, so that, in the end, even elaborate displays mainly serve the function of social bonding.

STRATEGIES OF INTERACTION. Darwin had already pointed out that a number of facial and bodily expressions are inherent to humankind. Evidence could be derived from studying the expressive behavior of those born blind and deaf, who were deprived of visual and auditory knowledge regarding the facial expressions of their fellow humans and who, nevertheless, exhibited the usual patterns of smiling, laughing, and crying. Besides such ontogenetic studies, cross-cultural documentation of human behavior and primate comparison confirm the assumption that certain human behavior patterns are the result of phylogenetic adaptations.

Eibl-Eibesfeldt's cross-cultural documentation contains many examples of universals in human behavior, which of course only occur in a very generalized form and may vary considerably from culture to culture. The display of the genitals, for example, originates in the sexual behavior of primates, in which erection of the penis expresses not only a willingness for sexual intercourse but also masculine power and vigor. Contrarily, the display of the female breasts is supposed to have an appeasing effect, while the act of raising the arm and showing the palm of one's hand is usually taken as a gesture of defense. All these gestures serve as signals that safely trigger certain responses from the recipient and are universally understood, even if not acted out but manifested in objects of art. The phallic sculpture, therefore, must be understood as a threatening object warding off enemies or evil forces. Phallic figures and signs are frequently used in a religious context to mark tribal territory or serve as a protective guardian of a house or temple. A similar gesture can be observed in patterns of female behavior. The obscene display of the vulva provokes a fear reaction and demonstrates superiority and dominance. At the same time, this threatening gesture of the female is combined with an encouragement for sexual intercourse, having an appeasing effect on the possible aggressor. As a result, the obscene female idols, amulets, and pendants that frequently occur in various cultures and religions can be understood as bearers of might, with the capability of protecting the owner from harm.

Unfortunately, ethological signs and figures are sometimes difficult to decipher or to encode. As human ethology has been able to prove, these behavioral signals are often portrayed in a devious manner. This form of communication media developed its own traditions, and the manner in which an object is portrayed will probably modify during history. Pictures will change into signs after several generations, signs into mere patterns. In human ethology, art history, the history of religions, and related fields of research, scholars have analyzed the historical development of symbols and patterns in pagan art and have achieved remarkable results. For example, Otto König's documentation of the patterns on the boats of Mediterranean fishermen exemplifies the change of the image of the protective "staring eye" from representation into an abstract symbol, and Karl von den Steinen (1855–1929) was able to explain the meaning of Marquesan tattoos by tracing them back to former portrayals of the skulls of the deceased.

Not only expressive behavior, but also the more complex rituals, serve the function of communication. In ritual, acts are fused into longer sequences that support strategies of social interaction. A functional equivalent of these ritualized sequences of action is language, where verbalized behavior takes the place of expressive gesture.

Ritualized human behavior as observed in greeting rituals and feasts usually displays a certain structure characterized by three successive stages: the opening phase, the phase of interaction, and the phase of parting. Each of these three phases is characterized by a set of verbal and nonverbal behavior patterns that not only correlates with a specific functional aspect of the phase, but also appears in repetition to deliver the same message through different channels and in different forms.

Toward an Ethology (Anthropology) of Religion. Any behavior pattern is adaptive in the sense that it contributes to the reproductive success or to the survival of the individual, the group, or the species. In that sense, as the historian of ancient religions Walter Burkert (1931–) points out, well-adapted religious activities promote the success of a culture. He refers explicitly to the results of human ethology when tracing rituals and other activities within the scope of religious behavior to their supposed biological origins. Several basic elements of religious practice and thought, and, in particular, sacrifice, have to be seen as being inherited from the animal world, where they may contribute to the survival of the individual or the group in dangerous situations.

The anthropologist Marvin Harris (1927–2001) raises the question of whether or not religious behavior should be understood as the result of the adaptation of a culture to its specific ecological niche. For example, Harris describes the Aztec religion, with its focus on human sacrifice and religious cannibalism. Because population growth and the depleted condition of the natural fauna led to a lack of animal foods, it is assumed that the Aztecs pursued a strategy of religious cannibalism to achieve the necessary amount of proteins, vitamins, and minerals. Their religious beliefs, therefore, reflected the importance of a high-protein diet and the lack of natural resources in their habitat. The occurrence of rites of passage, especially seen in male initiation, can also be traced to biological roots. A low-protein diet makes prolonged nursing a necessity. This, however, results in a postpartum sex taboo that leads to polygyny. The resulting mother-child households, together with prolonged nursing, lead to an intensive bonding between mother and child and, finally, to cross-sex identification. Severe male initiation ceremonies that include circumcision or other forms of ritual torture and mind control are then required to break the prepubescent identity in order to allow for later identification with fathers and other males.

A different concern with issues of function and structure shaped the work of the anthropologist Roy Rappaport (1926–1997). As Rappaport points out, ritual and language have coevolved, with ritual providing a necessary counteraction to language-created problems that may otherwise lead to social disorder and violence. Ritual contains self-referential messages that supply information about the size, density, or strength of the group, and similarly serve the purpose of competition by supplying information about the social status and psychophysical characteristics of the participants. By participating in ritual, in which invariable words and actions recur, men and women assume wider commitments—the so-called ultimate sacred postulates—which are forged at a deeper level of the psyche. Even if these postulates are ideally untestable and have no immediate consequences, they cannot be questioned and hold a key position in the governing hierarchy of ideas. Rituals, therefore, as religion's main components, form the concepts that people consider to be religious, and therefore they have been central in the adaptation of the human species as part of a larger ecological whole.

While Burkert, Rappaport, and Harris mostly refer to the adaptive values of religious behavior and thought, the Indologist Frits Staal focuses on the analysis of ritual and mantra by adopting an ethological approach in order to explain the origin of religion. Far from sharing the common scholarly opinion that ritual is a symbolic representation of what people believe, he emphasizes that rituals have to be understood without reference to their supposed religious background. Staal's careful investigation and documentation of

Vedic rituals result in the statement that rituals are pure activity without any meaning or goal, in which only faultless execution in accordance with the rules counts. Staal draws the conclusion that the origins of religion lie deep in inborn behavior patterns. Religions, which do not necessarily have doctrines and beliefs, originate in ritualization as observed in animal behavior. Only later does ritual become religious in the Western and monotheistic sense of the word, when provided with a religious interpretation that includes doctrine and the belief in an afterlife.

For the anthropologist Weston La Barre (1911–1996) religion is the result of the adaptation of human beings to their ecological niche and is shaped by both biological and cultural evolution. In particular, human biology with neoteny (i.e., the persistence of larval features in adult animals) and the resulting need for domestication leads to psychological responses that establish the basis for the capacity and the propensity for magic and religion in men. Belief in God, therefore, is the result of male-fantasized omnipotence as acquired by being locked into a lifelong phallic paranoid state. When vatic personalities, such as priests and their more primitive counterparts, shamans, speak with the voice of God, it is nothing but an expression of the self, deprived of its psychosexual maturity.

According to La Barre, religion first emerged when an early shaman, as depicted in the Stone Age cave of Les Trois Frères, proclaimed to have magic power over game and, after his death, became the supernatural helper of later shamans and, finally, the master of animals. Shaped by Paleolithic belief, shamans persisted as gods into protohistoric and historic times, where they were transformed to suit the needs of an agricultural society. In discovering the human nature of their gods, the Greeks resecularized their nature deities into mere heroes, while the Hebrews sacralized their patriarchal sheikhs and shamans into a moral and spiritual god, who, due to the influence of Greek crisis cults, developed into the Christian God.

Although ethological approaches to the study of religions have helped to gain insight into the ways multiple cultural systems are related to the biology of the human species, heavy criticism has been heaped upon an approach that is accused of being materialistic and nonhistoric—and of working with unnecessary complex and nonverifiable models of social dynamics. The assumed structural parallels of religions with biology, consciousness studies, and linguistics suggest a scientific character that aims at a natural truth underlying conventional scholarly results. As the anthropologist and scholar of religions Benson Saler (1930–) points out, the reference to universals existing in all cultures leads to definitions of universal categories that are so vague and abstract they are nearly useless and, furthermore, contradict the archaeological and anthropological records. The stress on universals, therefore, runs the risk of deflecting attention from the characteristics of a given religion that make it a solitary system of conceptions and deeds acquired throughout the course of history. According to the historians Carlo Ginzburg (1939–) and Jean-Pierre Vernant (1914–), the specific history of a society and its religion shapes the spiritual universe of a people and modifies certain psychological attitudes, which have retroactive effects on religious behavior and thought.

Anthropological approaches stressing the results of ethological research are undoubtedly of great value as starting points for new and interesting inquiries, but in abandoning the historical method such approaches partially miss the goal of ethology. Because the emphasis of ethology has been based on the notion that the behavior of humans and its manifestations in religion have evolved throughout history, ethological inquiry must consider the historical circumstances under which the custom in question developed. To make matters perfectly clear, the theory of evolution has made biology into a historical science. Methodologically speaking, the descriptive techniques used by both ethologists and historians of religions are now fairly sophisticated, and they should be put to use by scholars surveying the religious behavior of closely defined groups. Comparative studies can be a fertile source of ideas and data if they avoid the implication that one group of people is just like another, and instead provide principles whose applicability to the religion under question can be assessed. Finally, the basic scientific issues of ethological research have to be taken into account, as there are questions of causation, ontogeny, function, and evolution (history). It would be desirable to include not only ethological theory and terminology, but also ethological method, especially in small-scale research. Such an approach would surely lead to remarkable results in future research.

See Also Ecology and Religion; Evolution; Prehistoric Religions; Sociobiology and Evolutionary Psychology.

Bibliography

Bronkhorst, Johannes. "Asceticism, Religion, and Biological Evolution." *Method and Theory in the Study of Religion* 13 (2001): 374–418.

Burkert, Walter. *Homo necans: Interpretationen altgriechischer Opferriten und Mythen.* Berlin and New York, 1972. Translated by Peter Bing as *Homo Necans: The Anthropology of Ancient Greek Sacrificial Ritual and Myth* (Berkeley, 1983).

Burkert, Walter. *Creation of the Sacred: Tracks of Biology in Early Religions.* Cambridge, Mass., 1996.

Eibl-Eibesfeldt, Irenäus. *Die Biologie des menschlichen Verhaltens: Grundriss der Humanethologie.* Munich, 1984.

Ginzburg, Carlo. *Miti, emblemi, spie: Morfologia e storia.* Turin, Italy, 1986. Translated by John and Anne Tedeschi as *Clues, Myths, and the Historical Method* (Baltimore, 1989).

Ginzburg, Carlo. *Storia notturna: Una decifrazione del sabba.* Turin, Italy, 1989. Translated by Raymond Rosenthal as *Ecstasies: Deciphering the Witches' Sabbath* (New York, 1991).

Harris, Marvin. *Culture, People, Nature: An Introduction to General Anthropology.* New York, 1975. 7th ed., 1997.

Harris, Marvin. *Cannibals and Kings: The Origins of Culture.* New York, 1977.

Hinde, Robert A. *Ethology: Its Nature and Relations with Other Sciences.* New York and Oxford 1982.

König, Otto. *Kultur und Verhaltensforschung: Einführung in die Kulturethologie.* Munich, 1970.

La Barre, Weston. *The Ghost Dance: Origins of Religion.* New York, 1970.

Lévêque, Pierre. *Bêtes, dieux, et hommes: L'imaginaire des premières religions.* Paris, 1985.

Lorenz, Konrad. *Über tierisches und menschliches Verhalten: Aus dem Werdegang der Verhaltenslehre.* Munich, 1965.

Meuli, Karl. "Griechische Opferbräuche." In *Phyllobolia* (Festschrift Peter von der Mühll), pp. 185–288. Basel, Switzerland, 1946; reprinted in Karl Meuli, *Gesammelte Schriften,* vol. 2, pp. 907–1021 (Basel, Switzerland, and Stuttgart, Germany, 1975).

Meuli, Karl. "An Karl Schefold." In *Gestalt und Geschichte* (Festschrift Karl Schefold zu seinem sechzigsten Geburtstag am 26. January 1965), pp. 159–161. Bern, Switzerland, 1967; reprinted in Karl Meuli, *Gesammelte Schriften,* vol. 2, pp. 1083–1092 (Basel, Switzerland, and Stuttgart, Germany, 1975).

Müller, Hans-Peter. "Religion als Teil der Natur des Menschen." *Archiv fur Religionsgeschichte* 5 (2003): 227–242.

Rappaport, Roy. *Ritual and Religion in the Making of Humanity.* Cambridge, UK, 1999.

Saler, Benson. "Biology and Religion." *Method and Theory in the Study of Religion* 11 (1999): 386–394.

Staal, Frits. *Rules without Meaning: Ritual, Mantras, and the Human Sciences.* New York, 1989.

Vernant, Jean-Pierre. *Les origines de la pensée grecque.* Paris, 1962. English translation: *The Origins of Greek Thought.* Ithaca, N.Y., 1982.

Wunn, Ina. "Beginning of Religion." *Numen* 47 (2000): 417–452.

INA WUNN (2005)

ETRUSCAN RELIGION.

Between the beginning of the eighth century BCE and the end of the fifth century BCE, Etruria was the dominant power in central Italy. The Etruscans had built up profitable commercial relations with the Phoenicians and the Greeks, established on the island of Pithecusa (modern Ischia) in Campania, then on the mainland in the town of Cumae around 750 BCE. This wealth and these relations allowed them to develop a much more advanced level of civilization than other peoples of the region. One indication of this is that Rome was under the rule of Etruscan kings between 616 and 509 BCE. Yet it is not this image of a military and political power that the Romans retained concerning their northern neighbors; as the historian Livy remarked at the time of Emperor Augustus, they were "the people most dedicated to matters of religion" (Livy 5.1.6). Thus the Romans saw the Etruscans' intense religious nature as their distinctive characteristic.

SOURCES OF INFORMATION ON THE ETRUSCAN RELIGION. This appreciative judgment concerning Etruscan religion might appear surprising in that the Etruscan religion seems to be simply a rather ordinary polytheism with gods like those in the Greek or Roman pantheon. This is the picture that comes through from the majority of the existing sources.

These sources are restricted. Apart from divination, a subject this article will return to, Greek and Latin writers give few details, and Etruscan literature that could provide this information has not survived. As for Etruscan inscriptions, they make a limited contribution. The majority are epitaphs, which yield only the name of the deceased, while the votive plaques placed in temples reveal only the name of the divinity to which they were dedicated. Admittedly, some longer documentary sources are available, which could be of greater interest concerning the subject, but the continued inability to understand the language means that they are only partially understood. This is the case with the two longest extant Etruscan texts: the Capua Tile, a terra-cotta plaque bearing three hundred legible words, and the Liber Linteus (Linen book) of Zagreb, a text of twelve hundred words. The story of the latter's survival is amazing. It was written in ink, as was the practice in ancient Italy, on a linen cloth that was taken to Egypt, where it was cut into strips and used as the wrapping for a mummy now preserved at the Zagreb Museum. These texts are both ritual calendars, in any case.

Some archaeological finds exist. Even with these, however, what can be deduced remains limited. The results of excavations of many Etruscan temples are known, and they confirm the statement of the Roman architect Vitruvius that the Etruscans were responsible for the spread of the "Tuscan temple" that, in contrast to the Greek temple from which it took its inspiration, was raised on a high podium, dominating the town the god protected. However, it is impossible to be certain that, as Latin authors claim, the main city temples were dedicated to triads (groups of three gods). Only certain temples at Veii (Portonaccio), Orvieto (Belvedere), or Marzabotto (temple C) demonstrate evidence of a triple structure. It is not impossible that the idea of triadic temples was inferred from the Roman Capitol built by the Etruscan kings (the Tarquins), where Jupiter was flanked by two goddesses, Juno and Minerva.

There remains an extensive amount of iconography on tomb or vase paintings, statues, stone and terracotta reliefs, and engravings on bronze mirrors. From its beginnings, however, Etruscan art was suffused with Hellenic influence. Often, Etruscan documents portray scenes from Greek mythology. Nonetheless, this has one advantage: these Etruscan documents provide the names of the gods corresponding to their Greek equivalents, using the process of interpretation that consists of identifying a Greek god with the local god whose functions are most similar.

THE ETRUSCAN PANTHEON. In this way, scholars have some idea of the Etruscan pantheon. It included a heavenly chief god, analogous to the Greek Zeus or the Latin Jupiter, whom they called Tin or Tinia, which means "the shining day" (like the names Zeus and Jupiter). Just as with the Greek Zeus, this god is portrayed as a majestic bearded figure armed with thunderbolts. This Tinia is associated with a female consort, Uni, identified with the Greek Hera or the Latin Juno (whose name is perhaps related). Other female divinities are known, sometimes with names of Greek origin, such as Phersipnai, who is the Etruscan equivalent of the Greek Persephone. She appears enthroned at the side of her husband Aita (an Etruscan transcription of the Greek god of the underworld, Hades) in paintings on the tomb of the Orcus at Tarquinia and the Golini tomb at Orvieto. Another underworld divinity, Vei, has a purely Etruscan name, however. This name, which must be part of the name of the town of Veii, remains obscure. This is not the case with another indigenous underworld goddess, Culsu, who is depicted on the sarcophagus of Hasti Afunei at Chiusi as placed at the entrance of the underworld. She is its guardian, and the Etruscan word *culs,* meaning "gate," derives from her name. The indigenous name Lasa is given to a series of minor female deities with various names who appear to be associated with more important goddesses, such as Achavisur, Alpanu, and Zipna, and who can be seen on mirrors assisting Turan, the goddess of love, the equivalent of Aphrodite, in getting dressed. The Etruscans also recognized a powerful chthonic goddess, Cel ati; the two parts of her name mean "earth" and "mother." She is a "Mother Earth," analogous to the Greek Demeter and the Latin Terra Mater. Mention should also be made of Menerva, derived from the Latin Minerva, goddess of the intellect (*mens*).

Among the male gods is a god of water, Nethuns, and a god of the forest, Selvans, corresponding, respectively, to the Latin equivalents Neptune and Silvanus. Other gods with Latin equivalents include Satre, corresponding to Saturn; Velchans, corresponding to Vulcan (Volcanus); Vetis, corresponding to Jupiter of the night and the underworld, Vediovis. On the other hand, Apulu, a Greek name, is the god Apollo, whom the Etruscans adopted under this name along with his myths. The *Apollo of Veii* statue from the end of the sixth century BCE in the temple of Portonaccio shows him fighting with Hercules in the episode of the capture of the Cerynian hind. Yet many other gods have local names. Several are the equivalents of figures in the Greek pantheon, including Turms, portrayed as the messenger of the gods Hermes; Sethlans as the blacksmith god Hephaistos; Usil as the sun god Helios, with rays coming from his head; and Fufluns as the god of the wine, Dionysos (and sometimes given the epithet Pachie, a transcription of the name Bacchus). However, several gods had no Greek equivalents. This is the case with Suris, who seems to have been an infernal and war god, like the mysterious Pater Soranus of Mount Soracte in Capena, in the territory of the Sabines, to which the name seems related.

This list shows Greek religious influence. Certain gods, such as Apollo, were borrowed from the Greeks, whereas on another level the success of the hero Hercules, whom they called Hercle, is noteworthy. A large number of statues and statuettes, evidence of his cult, have been found in Etruria. One should also be aware of the deities with Latin or Italic equivalents, including Nethuns, Selvans, Velchans, Vetis, Menerva, and certainly Uni and Satre, who bear names that may be explained as derived from Italic forms (and not the other way around). This shows that the Etruscan religion was formed in the same mold as the religions of the other peoples of the peninsula in prehistoric Italy at the end of the second and the beginning of the first millennium BCE.

THE PERSISTENT ORIGINALITY OF THE ETRUSCAN RELIGION: THE VISION OF THE UNDERWORLD. This does not, however, mean that the Etruscan religion is not original. Leaving aside divination, Etruria made its mark on what it borrowed from others. This can be seen most obviously in their portrayal of the underworld, where Greek influence is evident. The sacred books dealing with these matters were called the Books of Acheron, after the underworld river in Greek mythology, from which the Etruscans took the infernal boatman Charon. But Charon, who is called Charun, appeared on tomb paintings brandishing a huge hammer with which he made ready to strike those who were about to die, an element not found in the Greek original. More generally, the Etruscans created an entire demonology that was perhaps inspired by certain Greek pieces (such as the depiction of the underworld by Polygnotus in the Cnidian Lesche at Delphi) but that, starting from the first paintings, such as the Tomb of the Blue Demons at Tarquinia from the fifth century BCE, certainly underwent considerable development. Another male demon is Tuchulcha, depicted with a hooked beak and pointed ears with two snakes rising on his head. Female demons also exist. They are often depicted on funerary urns to indicate that the person shown alongside is going to die. In particular, the female demon Vanth is a winged woman, bare-breasted or even completely naked, brandishing a torch, sometimes with snakes, at other times with a roll of parchment on which the fate of the deceased was written.

ETRUSCAN WOMEN AND RELIGION. It is true that the Etruscans were original in one aspect in which their civilization differed from those of Greece and Rome; that is, the accepted position of women in society. The Etruscan woman enjoyed much greater freedom than her Greek and Roman sisters. She can be seen lying alongside her husband on the same banqueting couch. This would have been unthinkable in Greece, where the banquet was an entirely male affair and only prostitutes were present, with lawful wives remaining in the *gynaeceum.* One might therefore expect that Etruscan women would occupy a privileged religious position.

However, this is not apparent in the evidence. Women are more often found in classical roles without particularly high status, such as mourners who, on the fifth-century BCE funerary reliefs at Chiusi, are seen weeping at the scene of the laying out of the dead. Maybe there were female priestesses, but the only definite instance involves a bacchante, who is depicted lying on the lid of a fine marble sarcophagus at Tarquinia holding a thyrsus and a vase with handles with a doe beside her. This woman appears in a religious role on the fringes of the official religion of the city.

However, the restricted role played by women in what the sources reveal concerning Etruscan religion need not be at variance with real life. Even if Etruscan women had more rights than Greek or Roman women, one must be careful not to overrate their social role. One should not take at face value what Greek and Latin writers say about Etruscan women. As peoples who had been the Etruscans' enemies, they were inclined to be critical of them. Thus, the liberty, at least in a relative sense, that the Etruscans allowed their women might be taken by these writers as loose living. They also tended to exaggerate everything they said about them, stating that they gave themselves shamelessly to lovemaking with anyone at all during banquets. The same exaggeration occurred in the religious sphere. Whereas Roman tradition holds that Tanaquil, the wife of L. Tarquinius Priscus, was an expert in divination and interpreted the omens from which her husband and the young Servius Tullius benefited, this is more a matter of Roman imagination than Etruscan reality. The haruspices known from the epigraphic or literary sources are exclusively men.

PROPHETS OF THE ETRUSCAN RELIGION AND THE *ETRUSCA DISCIPLINA*. Even so, there is one sphere in which the Etruscans developed their own myths, and these reveal what is truly original about Etruscan religion and why the Romans considered them the most religious of peoples. They had created what the Romans called *Etrusca disciplina*, using the Latin word *disciplina* to mean a "science." In their case it is a religious science centered around divination and rituals. The Etruscans did not view this *Etrusca disciplina* as the work of human beings. It was the result of a revelation given by gods to human beings at the beginning of their national history. This revelation, committed to writing, was the basis for the Etruscan religious sacred books.

Several competing traditions existed. The most famous was from Tarquinia. According to this version, the *Etrusca disciplina* was owed to a divine child called Tages. As a newborn, he was discovered by a plowman on the outskirts of the town. He had obviously been born from the earth, and no sooner had he been born than he began to speak and issue a revelation. He set out the basic principles of religious science, which those present eagerly committed to writing. Then he disappeared as mysteriously as he had appeared.

The story seems ridiculous, and Cicero, who relates it in his treatise *On Divination*, is openly contemptuous. As a good Roman he did not believe the gods could intervene directly in human affairs and rejected mythology as puerile stories. But the legend may be analyzed in terms of standard motifs. There is the autochthonous myth, in which a being is described as earthborn, produced like a plant. This is how the Athenians described their origins. This motif is coupled with the combination of old man and infant, fusing in one person the physical characteristics of infancy and the wisdom of old age. These are standard legendary motifs; what is interesting is that, in the Etruscan case, they are not used for the tale of a hero or the story of the origin of a people but to establish the founding myth of the national religious science. This proves its importance to the Etruscans.

THE HARUSPICES. The revelation issued by Tages (or by Vegoia) gave rise to an entire sacred literature, the "Etruscan books," which set out the substance of the national religious science that Latin writers frequently describe. This means that, for once, scholars are relatively well informed. These books were the mark of the specialists of the Etruscan discipline, the haruspices. These haruspices—whose name originally applied to one of their specialities, the inspection of the liver of sacrificial victims, but then took on a more general meaning—could be recognized by their distinctive dress. They wore a tapering, pointed hat. Sometimes this hat is seen on sarcophagi on top of a kind of folded sheet, which is in fact a linen book (like the one from the Zagreb mummy). This was the particular mark of the haruspex of the dead, who carried out his duties wearing this headgear while consulting his books.

These haruspices, at least in Etruria, were high-ranking individuals. Thus Cicero tells that one of his Etruscan friends, Caecina, was an expert in the national religious science and belonged to one of the most important Tuscan aristocratic families. Haruspices considered the Etruscan discipline as their exclusive possession and handed down the books from one generation to the next, fathers taking care to instruct their sons in their use. This instruction was deadly serious, conveying the scientific aspect, at least to ancient eyes, of the Etruscan discipline. Etruscan haruspicy, concerned with ritual or even with divination, did not allow itself to be guided by what the Greeks called *mania*, the god entering the body and soul of the person acting as the intermediary between the gods and human beings. Etruscan haruspicy studied the phenomena set before it with the help of the classifications laid down in its books. This required seriousness, the exact opposite of the trances of soothsayers possessed by divine inspiration. A famous fifth-century BCE mirror from Vulci shows Calchas, the soothsayer of the Greek army at Troy, as an Etruscan haruspex examining the liver of a victim. He is bent over the organ, which he is studying carefully, looking at the slightest variations in shape, texture, and color. It is quite correct to talk of a science, the term for the rigorous deductive method based upon detailed observation by which the haruspex formed his opinions. The Etruscan discipline even involved experimental science. Far from becoming a closed corpus, fixed once and for all by the initial revelation of Tages, Etruscan sacred literature was enhanced by observations of haruspices of later times. Cicero says they noted in their books new phenomena they observed and thus managed to enlarge upon the basic principles contained in the religious literature handed down to them.

THE SACRED BOOKS OF THE ETRUSCAN RELIGION. According to Cicero, Etruscan religious literature was divided into three kinds of books: the books of thunderbolts, the books of haruspicy, and the books of rituals. The extensive role of divination is clear, since the first two categories were dedicated to it. The *libri fulgurales* dealt with divination by thunderbolt and lightning, or brontoscopy; and the *libri haruspicini* with divination by inspecting the livers of sacrificial animals, or hepatoscopy; whereas in the *libri rituales* certain other kinds of divination are also considered, such as omens.

The books of thunderbolts. The Etruscans were not the first to be interested in thunderbolts; the phenomenon has always seemed to be of divine origin. In observing them, the haruspices demonstrated their analytical abilities. Seneca, in his *Natural Questions*, and Pliny the Elder, in his *Natural History*, drawing on Etruscan sources, show the fine distinctions the Etruscans made, establishing minute, generally complex classifications, distinguishing thunderbolts by their color, their shape, and the effect they had when they hit the ground. This theory of thunderbolts gave rise to a vision of the way the world worked. The Etruscans maintained that the principal god Tinia had three kinds of thunderbolts. The first, the most benevolent, was used to issue warnings; he used this on his own authority. The effects of the second were more serious; it brought only misfortune. However, the god could only hurl this on the advice of a council of twelve deities, six gods and six goddesses. The third left nothing untouched and changed the way the world was organized. Tinia only used this on the instructions of mysterious divinities—masters of destiny—gods said to be hidden or superior, whose names, numbers, and gender remained unknown.

The Etruscans did not consider the workings of the world the result of the whims of a god, however, even the chief god Tinia. Even he was subject to a destiny more powerful than he. This idea was developed in certain *libri rituales*, the books called *fatales*, concerning *fatum* (destiny). For the Etruscans the history of the world did not unfold by chance but was divided into a certain number of *saecula* (a period of varying length, calculated according to the lifespan of the longest living individual of a particular generation, so *saecula* could consist of 123 or 119 years). Each nation was entitled to a given number of *saecula*, ten in the case of the Etruscans, after which it would disappear, its destiny fulfilled.

The Books of Haruspicy. The *libri haruspicini* dealt with another classical kind of divination, hepatoscopy, which was particularly well known among the ancient peoples of the Middle East and based upon the study of the livers of animals offered to the gods in the central cult ceremony, the bloody sacrifice. Scholars are relatively well informed on Etruscan hepatoscopy. In 1877, in a field near Piacenza in Emilia, a bronze model liver was discovered. Subsequently known as the Liver of Piacenza, it had a box diagram on its surface, each section marked with the name of a god. This model liver was used to teach young haruspices. Thus they learned a particular interpretative grid, which they then used as a gauge for the actual livers they examined. If they found a particular feature in one of the boxes in the diagnostic diagram, they knew the god named in that box had sent this sign and needed to be placated.

The Liver of Piacenza allows still further understanding of the Etruscan religious system. The apparently unsystematic arrangement of boxes on the surface of the liver is in fact amenable to a certain organization. The two halves of the organ are separated by the anatomical division, the *incisura umbilicalis*. The right side, which literary sources call the *pars familiaris*, with neatly arranged square boxes, contains the heavenly gods, such as Tinia, who are relatively benign. In contrast, the left side, which sources describe as *pars hostilis*, arranged in a circle, has the names of infernal gods, such as Vetis, or unsettling gods, such as Satre or Selvans. Above all, the circumference of the organ has a series of sixteen boxes in a band around the object. This ties in with a detail known from elsewhere: Etruscan haruspices divided the vault of heaven into sixteen sectors according to the cardinal points, beginning from the quadrant going from north to west.

This allows an understanding of the theoretical basis of Etruscan hepatoscopy. By reproducing the sky with the abodes of the gods who live there, the liver is a microcosm reflecting the macrocosm of the universe, whose workings the gods oversee. It logically follows that the gods imprint in the microcosm signs that correspond to their actions in the macrocosm. And it is not a matter of indifference that these signs are passed down to the human race using the liver of a sacrificial animal.

According to a thorough analysis of the portion given to the human beings and the portion given to the gods in Greece by Jean-Pierre Vernant and Marcel Detienne and a group of their pupils, published in *La cuisine du sacrifice* in Paris in 1979, the liver reverts to the gods, to whom it is conveyed, when burned upon the altar. Considered by the ancients as the life center of the animal, it reverts by right to the immortal gods, masters of the life of every living creature. Yet if, as this work has emphasized, the Greek sacrifice in this way stresses the difference between the gods and human beings, in the Etruscan sacrifice it was their association, the exchange effected between them, that was considered crucial. The Etruscan sacrifice was defined by ancient authors as consultative: the consultation, involving the examination of the liver by the haruspex, was considered a fundamental part of the ceremony. What mattered to the Etruscans above all was the examination performed on the liver by the haruspex. The organ became the place of exchange between human beings and the gods, and the divinatory signs the gods placed there were their responses to the offering made.

The books of rituals. The third category of books, the books of rituals, is not a single whole. These books discuss divination as regards omens and destiny, the subject of the subcategory *libri fatales*. Nevertheless, rituals are also a significant subject for a religion that regarded the exact performance of ceremonies of vital importance, the slightest error potentially provoking the anger of the gods and leading to disaster. Many Etruscan rituals were brought to Rome. The foundation rite that Romulus is said to have followed when he founded Rome in 753 BCE is universally considered of

Etruscan origin. Romulus invited specialists from Etruria, who explained to him how to draw the sacred boundary of the city, the *pomerium*, by digging the *sulcus primigenius*, the first furrow, with the help of a plow pulled by a white bull and a white cow.

These books also describe other rituals. The subcategory called the Books of Acheron describes certain sacrifices offered for the dead, who it was believed were thus able to become actual gods, called *dei animales*, where *animales* means "created from a soul" (*anima* means "soul" in Latin). The process was simply ritual: it was sufficient to sacrifice certain animals and offer their blood to certain deities. This may seem childish; however, compared to the specifically Roman religion, which said nothing concerning human prospects after death, the Etruscan religion had an infinitely richer view of the future of human beings in the afterlife.

ROME AND ETRUSCAN HARUSPICY. Far from disappearing after the Roman conquest between 396 BCE, the date of the fall of the first Etruscan city, Veii, and 264 BCE, when the last remaining independent city, Volsinii, fell, this aspect of Etruscan religion continued to exist in a world that had now become a Roman one. The Romans were impressed by the practical benefits of the Etruscan discipline.

An ancient state could not be secular. One of its most important tasks was to ensure good relations between the city and the gods. If human beings were to blame for some misdeed or some oversight on their part, what was called the *pax deorum* (peace of the gods)—that is, the harmonious state of relations between the gods and the city—was broken. The gods showed their anger, which risked turning into the worst of disasters, visible in terms of events that indicated a break in the natural order of things, omens, and the outbreak of the supernatural in the normal course of existence. Faced with such signs, it was vital that the city understand what it had done wrong and what action should be taken. Confronted by such divine signs, Roman religion, in terms of its national heritage, was powerless. Faced with disasters, such as earthquakes or epidemics, heavenly signs, such as comets or hailstorms, or even mere curious happenings, such as the birth of a hermaphrodite child or a sheep with two heads, it was necessary to consult the Etruscan haruspices, who would discover in their books what needed to be done.

Rome was not slow to employ the skills of Etruscan specialists in matters of rituals and divination. Probably from the time they had completed the conquest, the Senate organized the Order of Sixty Haruspices, drawn from young nobles of various Etruscan cities, who could be consulted as soon as some event seemed to require the use of the Etruscan discipline.

THE SPREAD OF HARUSPICY IN THE ROMAN EMPIRE. In these circumstances the integration of Etruria into the Roman sphere, far from signaling the disappearance of the Etruscan discipline, enabled new expansion. Individuals also took advantage of the knowledge of the Etruscan soothsayers for their own personal needs. Some important people had their own haruspex in their retinue: Spurinna, Caesar's haruspex, unsuccessfully warned him of the danger on the Ides of March. Many generals were accompanied by a haruspex, and subsequent emperors had their own specialized staff for Etruscan divination.

These were important figures. Spurinna belonged to one of the most important Etruscan aristocratic families, and an imperial haruspex like Umbricius Melior, who in turn served Galba, Otho, and Vespasian, was important enough for the town of Tarentum to be honored by his patronage. Yet not all haruspices were such highfliers. Many were poor scoundrels trading on public gullibility. Cato, in his treatise on agriculture, warned the steward of the ideal farm he described to be wary of the haruspices who roamed the countryside. A number of Latin authors, including Cicero, the comic playwright Plautus, and the philosopher-poet Lucretius, denounced low-grade haruspices as nothing more than charlatans. This did not prevent them from flourishing; inscriptions indicate their presence throughout the Roman Empire.

HARUSPICES AND THE DEFENSE OF TRADITIONAL ROMAN RELIGION. Henceforth the Etruscan religious tradition no longer seemed like a foreign body differing from the national Roman tradition, the *mos maiorum*, as the Romans called their ancestral traditions. Etruscan religion was fully integrated into the heart of Roman religion and had an officially recognized place. It even seemed to be a key element. For Emperor Claudius, who reorganized the ancient collegium of sixty haruspices in 47 CE, it represented the the most distinguished part of traditional Roman religion.

Claudius justified his actions by the need to combat "foreign superstitions," namely all those religious systems not part of traditional Greco-Roman paganism, including the developing Christian religion. The old Etruscan tradition was called upon to play its part in the defense of the *mos maiorum*, and the place held by haruspicy in the religious functions of the Roman res publica meant that at times haruspices were effectively in the forefront of the struggle against the Christians. Thus, the Great Persecution of Diocletian, decreed in 303 CE, the gravest crisis the young religion had faced, was embarked upon following an incident, reported by the Christian writer Lactantius, in which haruspices played a key part. Lactantius stated that Christian slaves present at the celebration of an imperial sacrifice disrupted it, causing the anger of the gods. Consequently Diocletian decided to persecute the Christians.

DEVELOPMENT OF ETRUSCAN RELIGIOUS TRADITION UNDER THE EMPIRE. It would be misleading, however, to see in the attitude of the haruspices toward new religions, and particularly in their hostility to Christianity, nothing more than narrow-minded conservatism. On the contrary, it is notable that the knowledge of the development of Etruscan beliefs during this period demonstrates the haruspices' adaptability to contemporary expectations—including, if need be, features borrowed from their rivals. An amazing text, preserved in the Byzantine lexicon the *Suda*, presents a supposedly Etruscan account of creation, which is simply a copy of the biblical story in *Genesis*. As noted, the Etruscan discipline was not closed and inward-looking. The scant evidence of its later condition shows that it evolved and adopted ideas that would have originally been totally alien in the early days, such as the idea of the world being created by God. The Etruscan tradition contained within it an ability to adapt, which other forms of Greco-Roman religion did not possess.

ETRUSCAN RELIGION AND THE DEFENSE OF ROMAN PAGANISM. The main explanation of the genuine revival enjoyed by the Etruscan religious tradition in the late days of the Roman Empire is that, compared to other religions, it appeared firmly rooted in the most authentic Roman tradition. In an age when, as that great defender of traditional Roman religion in fourth-century Rome, the senator Symmachus, remarked, all religions were considered of equal value in approaching the ineffable mystery of God, the Etruscan tradition retained an enormous advantage over the others. It seemed to be from Italy and thus something with which the Romans should urgently reconnect. This is stated in a letter from a pagan priest, Longinianus, to Augustine, who had asked him about his beliefs. This has been preserved in the letters of the bishop of Hippo. In the letter, Longinianus outlined a theory of revelation, explaining that every part of the world has its own particular prophet and that for Italy this prophet had been Tages, the child-prophet of Tarquinia, to whom the Romans should turn back as a matter of urgency. Here is the trump card of the Etruscan religious tradition: it could put forward prophetic figures, like those required in Judeo-Christian traditions, and it was based upon sacred books setting out the teachings of these prophets. With Tages and the sacred Etruscan books as part of their national heritage, the Romans had no need of the Bible or of a prophet born in a remote corner of Judaea.

These aspects of Etruscan religious tradition ensured that it played a part in the task of defending ancient religion, which occupied philosophers at the end of paganism. A Roman writer of the second half of the third century, Cornelius Labeo, put it forward in his writings, notably in a treatise in which he described the doctrine of the transformation of the souls of the dead into gods, as mentioned in the Books of Acheron. His works have not survived, but they had some influence because this Etruscan doctrine is one of the pagan doctrines concerning the afterlife that Christian writers felt it necessary to attack.

Nonetheless this intellectual volte-face was unable to prevent the imminent disappearance of the last vestiges of the Etruscan religion. These vestiges were closely bound to traditional Roman religion, and they were even, because of the place given to haruspicy in the official religion, bound up with the position of the ancestral religion in the workings of the res publica. As soon as the Empire abandoned these religious practices and, with the edicts of Theodosius in 391 and 392 CE, banned public celebration of the pagan cult, the old Etruscan tradition, which was too directly bound up with the official cult, was doomed to die out. Whereas one can hear echoes in Proclos, the "last pagan" who ran the school of philosophy at Athens between 430 and 485 CE, and even later in the work of John the Lydian, who in the time of Justinian was interested in the ancient religious customs of Etruria in that last outpost of Rome, Byzantium, they were nothing more than nostalgia for a past long gone.

SEE ALSO Divination; Portents and Prodigies.

BIBLIOGRAPHY

General Works on Etruscan Religion

Dumézil, Georges. "La religion des Étrusques." In *La religion romaine archaïque*, pp. 593–600. Paris, 1966. Mainly based upon literary sources.

Gaultier, Françoise, and Dominique Briquel, eds. *Les Étrusques, les plus religieux des hommes: Actes du colloque international Galeries nationales du Grand Palais, 17–18–19 November 1992.* XXes rencontres de l'École du Louve. Paris, 1997. Completely in French with contributions by the leading Etruscologists, the proceedings of a conference dealing with research on the Etruscan religion. Extensive bibliography.

Grenier, Albert. *Les religions étrusque et romaine.* Series Mana, vol. 3. Paris, 1948. Good description of Greek and Latin sources.

Jannot, Jean-René. *Devins, dieux, et démons: Regards sur la religion de l'Étrurie antique.* Paris, 1998. Well-informed survey with extensive iconography.

Maggiani, Adriano, and Erika Simon. "Il pensiero scientifico e religioso." In *Gli Etruschi: Una nuova immagine*, edited by Mauro Cristofani et al., pp. 139–168. Florence, 1984. Brief discussion but well informed, with a good iconography.

Pfiffig, Ambros Josef. *Religio Etrusca.* Graz, Austria, 1975. In German, a complete work with an analysis of archaeological and iconographical data.

Capua Tile and Linen Book of Zagreb

Cristofani, Mauro. *Tabula Capuana, un calendario festivo di età arcaica.* Florence, 1995. Work by one of the greatest Etruscologists, dealing with the meaning of the Capua Tile.

Pallottino, Massimo. "Il contenuto della mummia di Zagabria." *Studi Etruschi* 11 (1937): 203–237. Reprinted in *Saggi di antichità*, vol. 2, *Documenti per la storia della civiltà etrusca*, pp. 547–588. Rome, 1979. An old article but one of the best introductions to the contents of the Linen Book of Zagreb.

Etruscan Temples

Banti, Luisa. "Il culto del cosidetto 'tempio di Apollo' a Veii e il problema delle triadi etrusco-italiche." *Studi Etruschi* 17 (1943): 187–201. An old article but helpful on the subject of triads.

Colonna, Giovanni. "Tarquinio Prisco e il tempio di Giove Capitolino." *Parola del Passato* 36 (1981): 41–59. On the exceptional nature of the temple of Jupiter Capitolinus in Rome.

Colonna, Giovanni, ed. *Santuari d'Etruria.* Milan, 1985. Catalog of an exhibition in Arezzo in 1985 with a survey of the main Etruscan temple excavations and the corpus of archaeological data.

Prayon, Friedhelm. "Deorum sedes: Sull'orientamento dei templi etrusco-italici." In *Miscellanea etrusca e italica in onore di*

Massimo Pallottino, pp. 1285–1295. Archeologia Classica 43. Rome, 1991. On the orientation of Etruscan temples.

Studies on Etruscan Gods

Ackerman, Hans Christoph, and Jean-Robert Gisler, eds. *Lexicon Iconographicon Mythologiae Classicae.* 8 vols. Zurich, 1981–1997. Articles dedicated to the various Etruscan divinities. Two index volumes were published in 1999.

Berti, Fede, ed. *Dioniso, culti, e mistero.* Comacchio, Italy, 1991. Proceedings of a conference dealing with the Dionysiac cult, notably in Etruria.

Capdeville, Gérard. "*Velchans (?)." In *Volcanus, recherches comparatistes sur les origines du culte de Vulcain,* pp. 289–409. Rome, 1995. In the context of a study of the Roman god Vulcan, introduction of data on the Etruscan Velchans that shows it is not possible to draw any firm conclusions.

Rallo, Antonia. *Lasa, iconografia e esegesi.* Florence, 1974. Study on the Etruscan Lasa, regarded as the equivalent of Greek nymphs.

Etruscan Demonology

Krauskopf, Ingrid. *Todesdämonen und Totengötter im vorhellenistischen Etrurien, Kontinuität und Wandel.* Florence, 1987. Study of the different Etruscan demons and their origins (predates the discovery of the Tomb of the Blue Demons in Tarquinia).

Roncalli, Francesco. "Iconographie funéraire et topographie de l'au-delà en Étrurie." In *Les Étrusques, les plus religieux des hommes,* pp. 37–54. Paris, 1997. Study of the Tomb of the Blue Demons.

Ruyt, Franz de. *Charun, démon étrusque de la mort.* Rome, 1934. Complete iconographical study of the Etruscan Charun.

Etruscan Women

Amann, Petra. *Die Etruskerin, Geschlechterverhältnis und Stellung der Frau im frühen Etrurien (9.–5. Jh. v. Chr.).* Vienna, 2000. Comprehensive study, well documented archaeologically, on the position of women in Etruscan society in the archaic period.

Rallo, Antonia, ed. *Le donne in Etruria.* Rome, 1989. Collection devoted to the place of women in Etruscan society.

Etruscan Discipline

Bouché-Leclercq, Auguste. *Histoire de la divination dans l'antiquité.* 4 vols. New York, 1975; reprint, Grenoble, France, 2003. Survey of divination practices in the world of classical antiquity. Good analysis of types of divination.

Thulin, Carl Olof. *Die etruskische Disciplin.* 2 vols. Göteborg, Sweden, 1906–1909. Old but fundamental work.

Weinstock, Stefan. "*Libri fulgurales.*" In *Papers of the British School at Rome,* vol. 19, pp. 122–153. London, 1951.

Attitude of Greek and Latin Authors to Etruscan Divination

Guillaumont, François. *Philosophe et augure: Recherches sur la théorie cicéronienne de la divination.* Brussels, 1984. Attitude of Cicero to Etruscan divination.

Guittard, Charles. *La divination dans le monde étrusco-italique.* In *Suppléments à Caesarodunum,* vol. 1, Suppl. 52. Tours, 1985.

Guittard, Charles. *La divination dans le monde étrusco-italique.* In *Suppléments à Caesarodunum,* vol. 2, Suppl. 54. Tours, 1986.

Guittard, Charles. *La divination dans le monde étrusco-italique.* In *Suppléments à Caesarodunum,* vol. 3, Suppl. 56. Tours, 1986.

Guittard, Charles. *La divination dans le monde étrusco-italique.* In *Suppléments à Caesarodunum,* vol. 4, *Les auteurs du Siècle d'Auguste et l'Etrusca disciplina,* part I, Suppl. 61. Tours, 1991.

Guittard, Charles. *La divination dans le monde étrusco-italique.* In *Suppléments à Caesarodunum,* vol. 5, *Les auteurs du Siècle d'Auguste et l'Etrusca disciplina,* part. II, Suppl. 63. Tours, 1993.

Guittard, Charles. *La divination dans le monde étrusco-italique.* In *Suppléments à Caesarodunum,* vol. 6, *Les écrivains et l'Etrusca disciplina de Claude à Trajan,* Suppl. 64. Tours, 1995.

Guittard, Charles. *La divination dans le monde étrusco-italique.* In *Suppléments à Caesarodunum,* vol. 7, *Les écrivains du IIe siècle et l'Etrusca disciplina,* Suppl. 65. Tours, 1996.

Guittard, Charles. *La divination dans le monde étrusco-italique.* In *Suppléments à Caesarodunum,* vol. 8, *Les écrivains du troisième siècle et l'Etrusca disciplina,* Suppl. 66. Tours, 1999.

Guittard volumes present a systematic investigation of the attitude of Greek and Latin authors to Etruscan divination, with articles by different contributors.

The Liver of Piacenza

Maggiani, Adriano. "Qualche osservazione sul fegato di Piacenza." *Studi Etruschi* 50 (1982): 53–88. Fundamental study with new readings of inscriptions.

Meer, L. Bouke van der. *The Bronze Liver of Piacenza: Analysis of a Polytheistic Structure.* Amsterdam, 1987. Analysis of the evidence according to principles different from those adopted by Maggiani.

Omens and Gods Formed from a Soul

Bloch, Raymond. *Les prodiges dans l'Antiquité classique: Grèce, Étrurie, et Rome.* Paris, 1963.

Briquel, Dominique. "Regards étrusques sur l'au-delà." In *La mort, les morts, et l'au-delà dans le monde romain,* edited by François Hinard, pp. 263–277. Caen, France, 1985.

Haruspices in Republican Rome

MacBain, Bruce. *Prodigy and Expiation: A Study in Religion and Politics in Republican Rome.* Brussels, 1982. Fundamental work on the official haruspicy in Rome during the Republic.

Rawson, Elizabeth. "Caesar and the *Etrusca Disciplina.*" *Journal of Roman Studies* 68 (1978): 132–152.

Position of Haruspicy in Imperial Rome

Briquel, Dominique. *Chrétiens et haruspices: La religion étrusque, dernier rempart du paganisme romain.* Paris, 1997. Relations between those ancient Romans representing traditional Etruscan religion and Christians.

Mastandrea, Paolo. *Un neoplatonico latino, Cornelio Labeone.* Leiden, 1979. Role of Cornelius Labeo in the revival of Etruscan discipline.

Montero, Santiago. *Politica y adivinación en el Bajo Imperio Romano: Emperadores y harúspices.* Brussels, 1991. Systematic examination of evidence regarding late haruspicy.

DOMINIQUE BRIQUEL (2005)
Translated from French by Paul Ellis

EUCHARIST. The Eucharist, also known as the Mass, Communion service, Lord's Supper, and Divine Liturgy, among other names, is the central act of Christian worship, practiced by almost all denominations of Christians. Though varying in form from the very austere to the very elaborate, the Eucharist has as its essential elements the breaking and sharing of bread and the pouring and sharing of wine (in some Protestant churches, unfermented grape juice) among the worshipers in commemoration of the actions of Jesus Christ on the eve of his death.

The word *eucharist* is taken from the Greek *eucharistia,* which means "thanksgiving" or "gratitude" and which was used by the early Christians for the Hebrew *berakhah,* meaning "a blessing" such as a table grace. When Christians adopted the word from the Greek into other languages, the meaning was narrowed to the specific designation of the ritual of the bread and wine.

HISTORY. The ritual attributed to Jesus by the writers of the New Testament is portrayed as a Jewish Passover seder meal in which Jesus reinterprets the symbolism of the traditional celebration (Paul in *1 Cor.* 11:23–26, *Mk.* 14:22–25, *Mt.* 26:26–29, and *Lk.* 22:14–20). Passover commemorates the liberation of the Hebrews from slavery in Egypt, which was the first step in their becoming a people in covenant with God. It is celebrated to this day by a lengthy ceremonial meal with prescribed foods, in which the story of the deliverance is symbolically reenacted (see *Ex.* 12:1–28). Selecting from the many symbolic foods customary in his time, Jesus takes only the unleavened bread (the bread of emergency or affliction) and the wine. The tradition of the early witnesses is that Jesus asks the traditional questions about the meaning of the ritual and answers, first about the bread he is breaking, "This is my body, broken for you," and then about the wine, "This is my blood, the blood of the covenant, which is to be poured out for many." It is clear that Jesus refers to his death and is interpreting the significance of that death in terms of the symbolism of the Exodus story and the Passover ritual. He invites the disciples to repeat the action frequently and thus enter into his death and the outcome of that death. By placing his death in the context of Passover, Jesus interprets it as a liberation bringing his followers into community as one people in covenant with God (see *1 Cor.* 11:17–34).

In the earliest Christian times, Eucharist was celebrated rather spontaneously as part of an ordinary meal for which the local followers of Jesus were gathered in his name in a private home. By the second century it is clear that there were strong efforts to regulate it under the authority and supervision of the local church leaders known as bishops. By the fourth century, Eucharist was celebrated with great pomp and ceremony in public buildings, and the meal was no longer in evidence. At that time, solemn processions emphasized the role of a clergy arrayed in special vestments. The form of the celebration included several readings from the Bible, prayers, chants, a homily, and the great prayer of thanksgiving, in the course of which the words and actions of Jesus at his farewell supper were recited, followed by the distribution of the consecrated bread and wine to the participants.

The Orthodox and other Eastern churches retained this general format with some variations. The liturgy of the Western churches, however, went through a long period of accretion and elaboration of secondary symbolism which obscured the meaning of the action and tended to leave the congregation passive spectators of what the clergy were doing. During the Middle Ages there also emerged the private Mass, a Eucharist celebrated by a priest without a congregation of worshipers present.

The sixteenth-century reformers took action to strip away all accretions and elements that did not seem to be in accord with the text of the Bible. Zwingli and Calvin were more radical in this than Luther. The Roman Catholic church also instituted extensive reforms of the rite in the sixteenth century, leaving a uniform pattern later known as the Tridentine Mass. This, however, was very substantially revised after the Second Vatican Council (1962–1965), allowing more spontaneity and congregational participation as well as offering more variety.

THEOLOGY. Eucharist is understood by all Christians to commemorate the saving death and resurrection of Jesus, and to mediate communion with God and community among the worshipers. Beyond this basic concept, the theology of the Eucharist varies very widely among the Christian denominations and has often been a cause of bitter dispute between them.

Both Orthodox and Roman Catholic Christians understand the presence of Christ very concretely, taking seriously the so-called words of institution, "This is my body . . . this is my blood." However, the Orthodox insist that while there is an actual change in the bread and wine that justifies these words, the manner of the change is a mystery not to be analyzed or explained rationally. Since medieval times Catholic Christians have attempted to give an intellectually satisfying explanation, focusing on the notion of a transubstantiation of bread and wine. While the eucharistic theology of the various Protestant churches varies widely, they are united in finding a theology of transubstantiation not in harmony with their interpretation of scripture.

The meaning and effect of the Eucharist have also been discussed in Catholic theology under the term *real presence.* This emphasizes that the presence of Christ mediated by the bread and wine is prior to the faith of the congregation. Protestant theology has generally rejected the term *real presence* as one liable to superstitious interpretation.

Orthodox and Catholic Christians also agree on an interpretation of the Eucharist in terms of sacrifice; that is, a renewed offering by Christ himself of his immolation in death. Again, there have been determined efforts in the Catholic theological tradition to give intellectually satisfying explanations of this, while Orthodox theology tends to tolerate a variety of explanations at the same time as it insists on fidelity to the words of the liturgy itself. Protestants believe the theology of sacrifice lacks biblical foundation and doctrinal validity, and prefer to emphasize the role of the Eucharist as a memorial.

It is paradoxical that the Eucharist is the sacrament of unity for Christians yet is a sign and cause of disunity among denominations. In general denominations exclude others from their eucharistic table, usually on account of theological differences. Contemporary initiatives reflect attempts to reconcile some of these differences and to experiment cautiously with "intercommunion" among the churches. Such initiatives appear to be far more extensive among laity than in the official legislation of the churches.

See Also Beverages; Bread; Food; Leaven; Passover.

Bibliography

The texts of the eucharistic celebrations of the various Western churches are given in *Liturgies of the Western Church,* selected and introduced by Bard Thompson (1961; reprint, Philadelphia, 1980). An account of the Orthodox Divine Liturgy and its theology is given in Alexander Schmemann's *Introduction to Liturgical Theology* (London, 1966). A description of the early Christians' Eucharist and eucharistic theology, with identification of sources, is presented in *The Eucharist of the Early Christians,* by Willy Rordorf and others (New York, 1978). More specifically concerned with the theology of the Eucharist are Joseph M. Powers's *Eucharistic Theology* (New York, 1967), from a Catholic perspective, and Geoffrey Wainwright's *Eucharist and Eschatology* (1971; reprint, New York, 1981), from a Protestant, particularly a Methodist, perspective. A discussion of the social implications of eucharistic celebration can be found in my book, *The Eucharist and the Hunger of the World* (New York, 1976).

Monika K. Hellwig (1987)

EUCLID (c. 300 BCE) was a Greek mathematician. Plato described mathematics as a discipline that turns one's gaze from the Becoming of the sensible world to the Being of the intelligible. The great value of mathematics is to prepare the mind for the apprehension of pure ideas. After Plato's death, geometry flourished among his students. One of the few details known about Euclid's life is that he studied under Plato's followers. Subsequently he founded the great school of mathematics at Alexandria, Egypt. He wrote on mathematics, optics, and astronomy.

Euclid's *Elements* is the most influential work in all of mathematics. Though other "Elements" were produced before Euclid, his work organized and completed that of his predecessors, who are now known chiefly by reference. As the letters (Gr., *stoikheia;* "elements") of the alphabet are to language, so are the *Elements* to mathematics, wrote the Neoplatonist Proclus in the fifth century CE. The analogy is apt. In thirteen books Euclid goes from the most elementary definitions and assumptions about points, lines, and angles all the way to the geometry of solids, and he includes a theory of the proportions of magnitudes, number theory, and geometric algebra. His procedure epitomized the axiomatic-deductive method and became a paradigm for philosophical and scientific reasoning. The greatest works in the history of astronomy imitate the *Elements:* Ptolemy's *Almagest* (c. 150 CE), Copernicus's *De revolutionibus* (1543), and Newton's *Principia* (1686). There is no greater example of Euclid's influence in philosophy than Spinoza's *Ethics* (1675), which scrupulously reproduced Euclid's method of definitions, axioms, and propositions.

The *Elements* became the elementary introduction to mathematics in Hellenistic civilization. Translated into Arabic in the ninth century and into Latin in the thirteenth, it became the foundation of Islamic, medieval, and Renaissance mathematics. It standardized the body of mathematical knowledge well into the twentieth century. The *Elements* was not translated into Sanskrit until the 1720s, though there is evidence of some prior knowledge. The Chinese may have known Euclid in the thirteenth century, but it did not affect the development of their mathematics until 1607, when the Jesuit Matteo Ricci produced a highly praised translation of the first six books of the *Elements* as part of the Jesuit missionary strategy in China. The use of the *Elements* as *the* textbook of mathematics over millennia is the source of the often repeated claim that, second only to the Bible, the *Elements* is the most widely circulated book in human history.

Euclid's religious significance can be seen in two ways. First, Euclid fulfilled the value Plato saw in mathematics. Euclid's masterpiece remains the enduring testament of the human capacity to construct a transparently intelligible system of relations grounded in logic and capable of extension to the physical world, though not derived from it. He demonstrates with lucid brevity how reason can successfully operate with purely intelligible objects such as points, lines, and triangles, and discover new and unforeseen truths with them. Such exercise frees the mind from the appearances of the senses and initiates it into an intellectual realm that Plato referred to as the realm of Being. In Neoplatonism such exercise had a paramount spiritual value. Augustine of Hippo, in his *Soliloquies* (386), written the year before his baptism, esteemed mathematics as a preparation for the soul's ascent to God. The mind perceives necessary truths first in mathematics and is then prepared to pursue eternal, divine truth. Having tasted the sweetness and splendor of truth in mathematics and the liberal arts, the mind actively seeks the divine. A millennium later, the Christian mystic Nicholas of Cusa wrote in his *Of Learned Ignorance* (1440) that the most fitting approach to knowledge of divine things is through symbols. Therefore he uses mathematical images because of their "indestructible certitude" (bk. 1, chap. 11).

Second, Euclid's geometry implicitly defined the nature of space for Western civilizations up to the nineteenth century. That "a straight line is drawn between two points," Euclid's first postulate, is also a statement about the space that makes it possible. Conceptions of space have religious repercussions because they involve matters of orientation. Isaac

Newton (1642–1727) reified Euclidean space in his physics. He identified absolute space and absolute time, which together constitute the ultimate frame of reference for cosmic phenomena, with God's ubiquity and eternity. Euclid's fifth postulate stipulated the conditions under which straight lines intersect, and, by implication, when they are parallel. To his continuing credit, Euclid presented the conditions as assumptions. For millennia mathematicians tried unsuccessfully to prove them. But, because Euclid's postulates were only assumptions, other conditions were possible. Thus in the nineteenth century Nikolai Lobachevskii, Farkas Bolyai, and G. F. B. Riemann were inspired to develop non-Euclidean geometries. These were crucial to Einstein's theories of special and general relativity (1905, 1913) and, hence, to the present cosmology, wherein a straight line cannot be drawn between two points. The conclusion that space and time are inseparable in the mathematical and physical theories of the nineteenth and twentieth centuries owes its existence to the force of the Euclidean tradition.

BIBLIOGRAPHY

The classic English translation of the *Elements* is Thomas L. Heath's *The Thirteen Books of Euclid's Elements,* 2d ed. (New York, 1956). It includes an introduction to Euclid's place in the history of mathematics and a thorough commentary on the text. A more recent account of Euclid and his achievement, as well as the history of the *Elements,* with comprehensive bibliographies, is found in Ivor Bulmer-Thomas's "Euclid" and John Murdoch's "Euclid: Transmission of the *Elements,*" in the *Dictionary of Scientific Biography* (New York, 1970–1980). A discussion of the historical and philosophical antecedents to Euclid and how his methods incorporate Platonic and Aristotelian developments in the philosophy of mathematics is provided in Edward A. Maziarz and Thomas Greenwood's *Greek Mathematical Philosophy* (New York, 1968). The importance of mathematics in the education of the philosopher is addressed in Werner Jaeger's *Paideia: The Ideals of Greek Culture,* 3 vols., translated by Gilbert Highet (Oxford, 1939–1944).

New Sources

Gray, Jeremy. *Ideas of Space: Euclidean, Non-Euclidean, and Relativistic.* New York, 1989.

Lloyd, G.E.R.. *The Ambitions of Curiosity: Understanding the World in Ancient Greece and China.* New York, 2002.

Mlodinow, Leonard. *Euclid's Window: The Story of Geometry from Parallel Lines to Hyperspace.* New York, 2001.

MICHAEL A. KERZE (1987)
Revised Bibliography

EUGENICS. The term *eugenics,* from the Greek meaning "good birth," was coined by British scientist Francis Galton (1822–1911). As Galton defined it in *Essays in Eugenics* (1909), eugenics is "the study of agencies under social control which may improve or impair the racial qualities of future generations" (p. 81). Eugenics seeks to improve the human gene pool by encouraging reproduction among "desirable" members of society (positive eugenics) and by discouraging reproduction among the "undesirable" (negative eugenics).

THE ORIGINS OF EUGENICS. Influenced by his cousin Charles Darwin's theory of evolution by natural selection, Galton researched the ancestry of eminent men in Great Britain and believed that the characteristics that led to their success—especially disposition and cognitive ability—were inherited. Environment might have had some influence, but for Galton heredity was central to an individual's traits and personality.

In addition to believing that talent and character could be inherited, Galton recognized that society was interfering with natural selection. Though evolution by Darwinian natural selection had produced humanity, developed society was drastically altering its course. In nature, natural selection eliminated the weak and the sick, allowing only the swift and strong to survive. In civilized societies, however, weak and "feebleminded" persons were cared for and provided for through charities, government programs, and religious groups, so that natural selection was no longer operating on humanity. Galton believed that if nothing were done, society would suffer the deleterious effects of having "fit" traits diluted by "unfit" traits.

Consequently, Galton believed that civilized human society ought to take control of its own breeding practices by encouraging eugenic behavior that promoted the future health of society. He suggested that, much as farmers breed only the best livestock, humans should promote reproduction among only the best of the human stock. Only then would the human race be able to maintain its level of civilization and prevent the regression of humanity toward greater feeblemindedness and greater physical weakness. Galton's solution to the problem was to encourage individuals in the upper classes—whose success Galton attributed to inherited traits—to have more children.

After 1900, when the work of the Austrian monk Gregor Mendel (1822–1884) was rediscovered, the true impact of heredity permeated both the scientific community and society, and eugenics seemed to gain momentum. In his experiments with pea plants, Mendel had shown how individual characteristics such as pea color and plant height were inherited according to a regular pattern. Eugenicists applied Mendel's results to human trait inheritance, assuming that intelligence, attitude, and other complex human behaviors were the result of a clear-cut pattern of inheritance. Examining an individual's pedigree, then, could yield powerful clues about what traits that individual's offspring might inherit.

Building on this apparently solid scientific foundation, eugenic scientists in both the United Kingdom and the United States attempted to persuade governments and society to embrace eugenic measures. Established in 1910 by Charles Davenport (1866–1944), the Eugenics Records Office in Cold Spring Harbor, New York, served as the central clearinghouse for family pedigree information and eugenic research in the United States. Davenport and his colleague Harry H. Laughlin (1880–1943), superintendent of the Eugenics Records Office, developed pedigree surveys and trained fieldworkers to gather family pedigree information for hundreds of individuals. Based on their examination of such pedigrees, Davenport and Laughlin became convinced that the nation's gene pool faced threats on two fronts. Internally, "feebleminded" individuals were outbreeding the graduates of Ivy League universities, lowering the overall intelligence of the gene pool. Externally, waves of new immigrants from eastern and southern Europe threatened to overtake the Anglo-Saxon stock in the United States. Both problems were "dysgenic" because they caused a decline in the quality breeding population, so urgent action was required to prevent the further deterioration of society.

In dealing with the dysgenic effects of immigration, the Eugenics Records Office was influential in convincing the U.S. Congress to pass restrictive new laws. Psychologist Henry H. Goddard (1886–1957) had performed intelligence tests on immigrants at Ellis Island that seemed to support the eugenic argument that immigrants were of lower intelligence than native stock. Using Goddard's research as well as his own, Laughlin testified before Congress that the waves of immigrants from southern and eastern Europe were diluting the "purity" of older American immigrant populations from northern Europe, as well as costing taxpayers millions of dollars in social services. Heavily influenced by the eugenicists' arguments, Congress passed the Immigration Act of 1924, which set immigration quotas based on the 1890 census. Consequently, immigrants of "eugenic" stock from northern and western Europe were admitted in larger numbers than the "dysgenic" stock from southern and eastern Europe.

In addition to its work with the U.S. Congress, the Eugenics Records Office provided model sterilization laws for states trying to implement "negative" eugenic measures. Scientists and fieldworkers from the Eugenics Records Office offered expert testimony in sterilization and institutionalization cases for those who had been diagnosed with a range of inherited "defects," such as alcoholism, pauperism, criminality, feeblemindedness, and insanity. Yet even before the coordinated efforts by the Eugenics Records Office, states began passing eugenic sterilization laws, beginning with Indiana in 1907. Other states soon followed, including California in 1909. In 1913 and 1917, amendments to the California law expanded the state's power to involuntarily sterilize the "feebleminded," certain prisoners, and criminals with more than three convictions.

In 1927, the U.S. Supreme Court heard an appeal by a seventeen-year-old woman from Virginia named Carrie Buck. Buck, along with her mother Emma, had been labeled "feebleminded" and placed under the care of the Virginia Colony for Epileptics and Feebleminded. After the unmarried Carrie Buck gave birth to a baby girl who was diagnosed as "feebleminded" at eight months of age, the superintendent of the institution ordered her sterilization under a new Virginia law. The case was appealed to the Supreme Court, who, having heard testimony in favor of sterilization from eugenic experts including Laughlin, ruled that the state of Virginia did indeed have the constitutional right to involuntarily sterilize Carrie Buck. In the majority opinion (*Buck v. Bell* 274 U.S. 200, 1927), Justice Oliver Wendell Holmes argued that the public good demanded that action be taken to sterilize Carrie Buck, because "three generations of imbeciles are enough."

The Supreme Court ruling in *Buck v. Bell* allowed states to continue forcibly sterilizing and institutionalizing those deemed unfit for reproduction. California had involuntarily sterilized nearly twenty thousand individuals by the time its sterilization law was overturned in 1951, more than had been sterilized in any other state. All told, over sixty thousand people in thirty-three states were sterilized for a variety of inherited "defects."

In Germany, the eugenics movement (*Rassenhygiene*) gained momentum as the Nazis rose to power and passed forced sterilization laws beginning in 1933. Nazi scientists and politicians approvingly cited the American experiment with eugenics, particularly in California, in their arguments for broader powers in determining who should be sterilized. When the horrors of the Nazi regime's racial hygiene program were fully revealed, eugenics programs in the United States and elsewhere were largely discredited. Some have argued, however, that though state-sponsored eugenics is now roundly condemned, eugenic attitudes persist in less overt forms.

RELIGION AND EUGENICS. Galton recognized the potential power of eugenic ideals and the necessary conditions for their acceptance. He wrote in 1909 in his *Memories of My Life*, "I take Eugenics very seriously, feeling that its principles ought to become one of the dominant motives in a civilized nation, much as if they were one of its religious tenets" (p. 322). The success of eugenics lay not only in its ability to present pertinent information in support of eugenics, but also in its ability to influence one's entire way of living. Thus, the eugenicists appealed not only to the science behind their efforts but also to religious sensibilities by providing an ultimate explanation for an individual's existence: responsibility to the future of the gene pool. Eugenics required an attitude of individual submission, an ethical orientation toward the greater good. To many scientists who argued for eugenic measures, religion motivated ethical behavior better than any other social phenomenon. Hence, eugenicists went to great lengths in analyzing and appropriating religion for eugenic ends.

Davenport grounded religious belief on the apparent science of eugenics in a lecture he delivered in 1916, "Eugenics as a Religion." Noting that every proper religion has its own statement of belief, Davenport proceeded to annunciate a twelve-point creed to serve as the basis for the new religion of eugenics. For Davenport, believing in eugenics meant believing that one is the "trustee" of one's genetic material; that one believes in the power of pedigree over environment; that one should have four to six offspring; that immigration should be limited to weed out the "socially unfit"; and that one is responsible ultimately to the race. Davenport's eugenic religion required that one be responsible both to one's genetic past and to society's genetic future. Along with Davenport's creed, the American Eugenics Society provided *A Eugenics Catechism* (1926) in question-and-answer form. The catechism assured readers that eugenics was not antagonistic to the Bible, for eugenics was concerned with the well-being of the totality of humanity. The catechism also promised immortality through one's genetic inheritance, passed on from generation to generation.

Likewise, Paul Popenoe and Roswell Johnson's *Applied Eugenics* (1933) gave immortality a firm grounding in scientific knowledge. In a passage describing the long line of human descent, Popenoe and Johnson argue that one's genetic makeup is immortal because genes, as the factors that determine who one is, can be passed on to innumerable generations. The authors argue that immortality is no longer merely hope but a real possibility. Even as the body dies, the genes that contain the information to produce the body live on in one's offspring. Popenoe and Johnson conclude, "To the eugenist, life everlasting is something more than a figure of speech or a theological concept—it is as much a reality as the beat of a heart, the growth of muscles, or the activity of the mind" (p. 41). Popenoe and Johnson go so far as to argue that one passes on one's soul from generation to generation by the propagation of the genetic material; religion has but speculated about the nature of the soul and its immortality, but eugenic science has proven their relationship. According to eugenics, then, an individual passes on his or her very soul to his or her offspring. As Davenport had argued in his creed, the proper attitude is one of submission to the greater good of society and to the precious inheritance of genetic material.

Popenoe and Johnson devote an entire chapter to the subject of eugenics and its relationship to religion. Interestingly, Popenoe and Johnson begin by asserting that "natural selection favors the altruistic and ethical individual because he is more likely to leave children to carry on his endowment and his attitude" than the merely selfish, shortsighted individual. As Galton had first observed, modern society has interfered with the operation of Darwinian natural selection. But unlike Galton, Popenoe and Johnson see the problem not only in society's failure to eliminate the weak and unintelligent, but also in its failure to rid itself of selfish and shortsighted individuals. They argue that selfishness creates problems for eugenicists since eugenics is based on placing the good of the race ahead of the good of the individual. Thus, the eugenics movement requires a structure for encouraging altruism and selflessness, a structure provided by religion.

For Popenoe and Johnson, science can offer religion a solid basis for ethics, one amenable to eugenic ideals, as well as present a rational explanation for the immortality of the soul. Religion need not retreat from the field of ethics; instead, religion should reexamine its ethical groundings. Dogmatic moral injunctions are no longer tenable in a eugenic world. Popenoe and Johnson conclude that the success of eugenics depends on the individual placing the present and future good of humanity above the good of the individual. Though many societal organizations foster selfless giving, the church is the most effective at encouraging altruism. Religion and the church can be a driving force behind eugenic change if they will but base their ethical systems on a science.

The "Report and Program of the Eugenics Society of the United States of America" (1925) pointed to the central role that religion had played in fostering both dysgenic and eugenic attitudes. Still, the society wondered whether the social value of religion could be used to further eugenic ends. No doubt, religion influenced dysgenic behavior by encouraging charity and providing social services. But like Popenoe and Johnson, both of whom sat on the Eugenics Society's advisory council, the society recognized religion's potential to influence individual behavior toward eugenic ends. The Eugenics Society concluded that if further research showed that religion were in fact primarily dysgenic, then eugenics had to devise a means of using religion's moral authority while altering its message.

One way in which the Eugenics Society encouraged religious engagement with eugenic principles was by sponsoring a sermon contest for clergy. Submissions were judged according to their ability to present eugenic ideals in clear and coherent fashion. Most did so by interpreting religious teachings in light of eugenic ideals. One sermon claimed that the Bible was a book of eugenics because it chronicled the lineages of important leaders and prophets. Jesus was seen as the product of the highest religious and moral stock of priestly and prophetic individuals. Another sermon claimed it a sin to bring feebleminded and diseased children into the world. Finally, one sermon argued that Jesus endorsed eugenics in saying that it would have been better if Judas had never been born (*Mt.* 26:24; *Mk.* 14:21). In this view, eugenics could be a crucial tool in bringing about the ordered society of which Jesus seemingly spoke.

Because marriage was an important focus of eugenic measures, some clergy took the initiative to aid the eugenic movement by enforcing a version of "negative" eugenics. In 1912, W. T. Sumner, the dean of the Episcopal Cathedral of Chicago, announced that he would not marry couples who failed to produce a physician's certificate of good health, a move endorsed by two hundred clergy. The hope was that the clergy would aid eugenicists by preventing unprofitable unions that would pass on undesirable traits.

Eugenic scientists embraced religious language even as they critiqued the dysgenic impact of various religions. Still, they recognized religion's unequalled social power in influencing individual behavior and in urging action. Even as they criticized the dysgenic effects of unconditional religious charity and threatened to take over the entire field of ethics, eugenicists urged religion to incorporate scientific analyses into its ethical systems and embrace eugenic ideals.

EUGENICS IN RECENT HISTORY. Interest in the history of the eugenics movement has increased markedly since the 1980s as new genetic technologies have been developed and as the Human Genome Project has completed the map of human DNA. Prenatal screening for genetic disorders, along with the legalization of abortion in the United States and the United Kingdom, has increased the debate over the social consequences of genetic knowledge. Debates have swirled around the proper use of such new technologies and the social consequences of their availability. Key concerns include the difference between notions of treatment versus notions of improvement. For example, if it becomes possible, should the genes for Tay-Sachs disease or cystic fibrosis be removed from the gene pool? Would such action constitute eugenic improvement or disease prevention?

The history of eugenics has also been invoked in debates surrounding the connection between intelligence and race. Richard J. Herrnstein and Charles Murray's *The Bell Curve* (1994) worries about the dysgenic effects of variable breeding rates because, the authors argue, racial groups with lower intelligence levels are reproducing at a higher rate than races with higher IQs. Critics of *The Bell Curve* assert a more environmental explanation for variations in intelligence and argue that genetics are not decisive in determining an individual's intelligence.

Other scholars have maintained that the use of new genetic technologies tends to support existing social hierarchies and vested economic interests. They worry that economic interests will determine for whom and for what purpose genetic technologies will be used, which will in turn reinforce social stratification as those unable to afford genetic enhancements are left behind. If the means for enhancement are available, some argue, parents will demand that such technology be used. In this case, consumer demand, not government control, will drive a new eugenics based on the desire for "designer babies." Though they recognize the eugenic dangers, a number of theologians and ethicists have endorsed certain forms of genetic research because of their potential to relieve human suffering. For them, the promise of healing offered by genetic therapies outweighs the concerns over the misuse of new technologies and new therapies.

BIBLIOGRAPHY

Allen, Garland E. "The Eugenics Records Office at Cold Spring Harbor, 1910–1940: An Essay in Institutional History." *Osiris* 2 (1986): 225–264.

American Eugenics Society. *A Eugenics Catechism.* New Haven, Conn., 1926.

Carlson, Elof Axel. *The Unfit: A History of a Bad Idea.* Cold Spring Harbor, N.Y., 2001. Traces the broad history of the idea of certain people as "undesirable" in connecting previous eugenic impulses with the eugenics movement in the twentieth century and the emerging issues raised by the genetic technologies of the twenty-first century.

Davenport, Charles. *Heredity in Relation to Eugenics.* New York, 1911. Contains Davenport's research on trait inheritance and proposes a number of eugenic measures that were successfully implemented with Davenport's aid.

Duster, Troy. *Backdoor to Eugenics.* 2d ed. New York, 2003. A sociologist's exploration of the potential for eugenics in social and economic policies.

Galton, Francis. *Inquiries into Human Faculty and its Development.* London, 1883. Chronicles Galton's proposals for eugenic measures.

Galton, Francis. *Memories of My Life.* 3d ed. London, 1909.

Galton, Francis. *Essays in Eugenics.* New York, 1909.

Herrnstein, Richard J., and Charles Murray. *The Bell Curve: Intelligence and Class Structure in American Life.* New York, 1994.

Kevles, Daniel J. *In the Name of Eugenics: Genetics and the Uses of Human Heredity.* Cambridge, Mass., 1995. The most comprehensive history of eugenics in the United States and the United Kingdom, connecting the early twentieth-century eugenics movement with subsequent developments in genetics and with debates over the role of genetics in human behavior and intelligence.

Larson, Edward J. *Sex, Race, and Science: Eugenics in the Deep South.* Baltimore, Md., 1995.

Paul, Diane B. *Controlling Human Heredity: 1865 to the Present.* Atlantic Highlands, N.J., 1995. Provides a good introduction to eugenics, examining its appeal to scientists and intellectuals.

Popenoe, Paul, and Roswell Johnson. *Applied Eugenics.* 2d ed. New York, 1933. Two leading American eugenicists explore the wide-ranging implications of eugenics for society.

NATHAN J. HALLANGER (2005)

EUHEMERUS AND EUHEMERISM.

Euhemerus, a Greek (c. 340–260 BCE), achieved fame as the result of an imaginative story he wrote that speaks, in a certain fashion, about the origins of divinities. After his death, Euhemerus's name became identified with a special, widely discussed and disputed way of interpreting religion. Euhemerism had an impact for many centuries. Even today, no one dealing with the history of scholarship of religion will leave Euhemerus unmentioned. Very little is known about Euhemerus himself. What is known is precisely what tradition has made him: the originator of *euhemerism,* an elucidation of religion that explains the gods as elevated images of historical individuals whose acts were beneficial to those around them.

The term *euhemerism* came to refer to a method of empirical explanation applied to the accounts of gods found in sacred traditions. Indeed, Aristotle, the first great Greek thinker with an empirical sense of inquiry, was part of the generation that preceded Euhemerus. There is no reason to believe that Euhemerus was an empiricist or that he shared Aristotle's analytical views concerning traditional religion. Euhemerus's turn of mind went elsewhere. In Euhemerus's day, well before Strabo (c. 63 BCE–c. 24 CE), geography was far from the accurate discipline it would become. Traveling, however, was a most attractive topic, and travel stories were told everywhere, from China to the shores of the Mediterranean. Euhemerus achieved renown in his own time as the teller of a travel story.

The title of a novelette Euhemerus wrote has come down to us as *Hiera Anagraphē*, a title that is usually rendered as "Treatise on Sacred Matters." It is not known whether this title was given by Euhemerus himself or by someone later, nor is it known whether this title renders Euhemerus's own intentions. In fact, a real impediment to modern access to Euhemerus is the fact that no version of the text he wrote exists. (The understanding of *hiera* as "sacred" might be misleading; one might just as well translate the title as "treatise on religious matters.") All that exists are summaries of much later date. The two most extensive writings about Euhemerus come from the Christian apologist Lactantius (c. 260–340 CE) and, earlier, Diodorus Siculus (died after 21 BCE), who wrote a world history and is one of our best sources for the history of antiquity.

Hiera Anagraphē tells of a voyage to an island in the east called Panchaia, from which—according to the story—on clear days India could be seen. On this island stood a golden pillar with a golden engraving on it. The pillar recounted the life of Zeus, and also of the rulers of Panchaia before him: his father, Kronos, and his grandfather, Ouranos. Zeus, according to this story, traveled through the world, and wherever he went the worship of the gods became established. But Zeus and the kings before him were rulers who bestowed benefits on the inhabitants of Panchaia. The people came to worship them as gods. In other words, Zeus, his father, and his grandfather were royal rulers who were made gods because of their acts on behalf of human beings.

What Euhemerus wrote differs considerably from older, didactic traditions, such as that of Xenophanes of Colophon (sixth century BCE), who is known for his emphasis on the difference between gods and men: "But the mortals think that the gods are born and dress, speak and look just like they themselves do," (Diels and Kranz, 1934, fragment 14), and "there is only one single God, the supreme among gods and people, unlike the people both in appearance and in thought," (Diels and Kranz, 1934, fragment 23).

Euhemerus wrote as a storyteller. Storytelling can be a way of conveying the sacred, of speaking about the sacred, which we find in virtually all places and all times. Yet Euhemerus's narrative came to be viewed as an early attempt to find some rational basis of religion, and its author came to be seen as a sort of rationalist explainer. From the time of the early church fathers on, certain trends in Western thought caused theologians and other scholars to approach Euhemerus as if he were a critic or debunker of the gods. Nevertheless, euhemerism lost little of its prestige. The French scholar Abbé Banier (1673–1741) used it eagerly in his work *La mythologie et les fables expliqués par l'histoire* (Mythology and fables explained by history). From the age of the Enlightenment onward, scholars, among them many a classicist, looked upon Euhemerus as a debunker whose work represented a rational critique of religion. This element of "desacralization" was admired by some and regretted by others—but both sides of that argument were missing the boat. Few of Euhemerus's contemporaries were likely to have felt Euhemerus as a critical force. Greek religion was imparted primarily in storytelling.

The classical historian Truesdell S. Brown quite rightly stressed a simple fact many of his peers had overlooked: the Greek gods were unlike the God of the Bible (and of the Qurʾān, the holy book of the third Abrahamic tradition). Brown emphasized that the entire known Greek religious heritage consists in stories (that is, myths), whereas the vast majority of biblical writings, apart from notable exceptions like the *Psalms*, present themselves neither as unmythical, or as history. Moreover, the Greeks did not have "holy scripture" or "church dogma."

The Germanist and historian of religions Jan de Vries was more in keeping with certain of his colleagues when he called Euhemerus "a clear example of the triviality to which the fourth century sank in explaining the gods." Joseph Fontenrose, a classicist, by contrast, lauded Euhemerus for his "rationalism" and for the position that mere people are at the root of divinity. These positions of De Vries and Fontenrose nicely exemplify those disagreements regarding Euhemerus wherein both sides miss the point that matters by missing the storytelling structure of the religion of the Greeks.

Augustine of Hippo (354–430) accomplished a fateful reunderstanding of Euhemerus (as did many of the early Christian thinkers). Augustine was familiar with Euhemerus's ideas, and for him they only indicate that the "pagans" themselves were of the opinion that their gods were mere people. Moreover, Augustine was convinced that those individuals who were elevated to divinity gained that status as a result of their stupendous evil—and this inversion, we can see, is precisely the opposite of what Euhemerus said. This *Euhemerismus inversus* of the early Christians had great persistence. Since the nineteenth century (when most missionary societies were established), many a missionary has held the opinion that "pagan" gods are demons. This opinion is an offshoot of those early Christian theologies.

Among more "secular" scholars, it is remarkable that a number have taken Euhemerus very seriously as a rationalist, and some have even developed theories that resemble his supposed rational reductionism. The theory of "animism" proposed by E. B. Tylor (1832–1917) lingers to this day—for example, in the writings of journalists who need a shorthand label ("animist") to identify the religions of peoples in remote parts of the world, peoples who once would have been called "savage," "pagan," or "primitive." Tylor's theory concerns the origin of religion and displays a mechanical cause-and-effect rationalism, which many thought they saw (and liked) in Euhemerus.

Turning away from rationalizing and theorizing about the origins of religion, one can confront the fact of the extraordinary importance of storytelling. The medieval world, Christianized as it was, told stories and performed plays in which Jesus, Joseph, and Mary, and of course the devil, spoke with one another. And, of course, there were songs. And institutions or authorities did not condemn storytelling and songs.

It remains true that most of the time in most of the world the myths of each religious tradition have been *stories.* Certainly in Greece and in antiquity in general, doctrines of "faith" were inconceivable. The sloppy habit of equating *religion* with *faith* is a modern deviation, a by-product of Christian church history; *faith* cannot be translated, for example, into the languages of classical India or China.

SEE ALSO Animism and Animatism; Apotheosis; Atheism; Deity; Fetishism; Hellenistic Religions; Manism; Utopia.

BIBLIOGRAPHY

Bolle, Kees W. "In Defense of Euhemerus." In *Myth and Law among the Indo-Europeans: Studies in Indo-European Comparative Mythology,* edited by Jaan Puhvel, pp. 19–38. Berkeley, 1970.

Brown, Truesdell S. "Euhemerus and the Historians." *Harvard Theological Review* 39 (1946): 259–274.

Diels, Hermann, and Walther Kranz, eds. *Die Fragmente der Vorsokratiker.* 6th ed. Berlin, 1952.

Ferguson, John. *Utopias of the Classical World.* London and Ithaca, N.Y., 1975.

Fontenrose, Joseph. *Python: A Study of Delphic Myth and Its Origins.* Berkeley, 1959.

Manuel, Frank A. *The Eighteenth Century Confronts the Gods.* Cambridge, Mass., 1959.

Puhvel, Jaan. *Comparative Mythology.* Baltimore, 1987.

Vallauri, Giovanna. *Origine e diffusione dell'evemerismo nel pensiero classico.* Torino, Italy, 1960.

Vries, Jan de. *Perspectives in the History of Religions.* Translated by Kees W. Bolle. Berkeley, 1967.

Winiarczyk, Marek, ed. *Euhemeri Messenii reliquiae.* Leipzig and Stuttgart, Germany, 1991. Contains the fragments, testimonies, and a full bibliography on Euhemerus.

KEES W. BOLLE (2005)

EUSEBIUS (c. 260/70–c. 339), a Christian bishop of Caesarea in Palestine from 314, was a leading early Christian historian, exegete, and apologist. A disciple of Pamphilus at Caesarea, Eusebius wrote a life of his master and called himself "of Pamphilus." He traced his intellectual descent to Origen, and with Pamphilus wrote a defense of Origen against the theological and personal criticisms current during the persecution of 303–313. Little is known of Eusebius's early life, but it seems clear that he wrote his *Historia ecclesiastica* (History of the church) at Caesarea during the persecution, possibly though not certainly after composing at a slightly earlier date a first draft of it as well as a first draft of his *Chronicon* (Chronicle). At the end of the persecution, in spite of occasional slanders concerning apostasy spread by his enemies, he became bishop of Caesarea. During this time he continued to update his *Historia* and composed other significant works, such as the *Demonstratio evangelica* and *Praeparatio evangelica.* He gradually became involved in the Arian controversy; his defense of a traditional subordinationist Christology partly resembling Origen's was criticized by many fellow bishops. Indeed, a synod held at Antioch in 324 or 325 condemned him and a few others, though he was given the right of later appeal. At the synod held at Nicaea Eusebius set forth the local creed of Caesarea but accepted the Alexandrian term *homoousios* ("of the same substance"), which transformed the creed's meaning. Thereafter he helped drive the pro-Nicene bishop Eustathius out of Antioch, acted as a judge when Athanasius was brought before several synods, and attacked Marcellus of Ancyra as a Sabellian. At the celebration of Constantine's thirtieth anniversary Eusebius delivered a panegyric on the emperor and his divinely inspired deeds. Similar themes appear in his *Life of Constantine,* written after 337. Eusebius died before the synod of Antioch in 341.

Eusebius is known less for his deeds than for his multitudinous writings, some of which are lost. Constant revision and the transfer of materials from one work to another make his development as a writer difficult to assess. He was an exegete, an apologist, a historian, and a panegyrist, but his various roles cannot be completely separated.

As exegete he followed the example of Origen in his textual criticism and made some use of the latter's works in his commentaries on *Isaiah* and *Psalms.* In addition, he produced "canons" for finding gospel parallels and wrote an introduction to theology (*General Elementary Introduction,* of which parts survive in his *Eclogae propheticae*). Biblical exegesis recurs throughout the *Demonstratio,* primarily in regard to Old Testament prophecies of Christ and the church.

Eusebius's apologetic is implicit throughout the *Historia* and explicit in the *Praeparatio* (sages and seers anticipated Christianity, although inadequately), the treatise *Against Hierocles* (Christ superior to Apollonius of Tyana, a first-century wonder-worker), and the twenty-five lost books against the Neoplatonist philosopher Porphyry, who had written against Christians and criticized Origen. A treatise that survived only in a Syriac version is titled *On the Theophany;* it combines materials from other books.

As historian, Eusebius is best known for his ten books on the history of the church from its divine origin to Constantine's defeat of the pagan emperor Licinius in 324. The work does not discuss the later conflicts over Arianism, Melitianism, and Donatism, or the synods of 324 and 325. A late edition deletes Eusebius's expectation that Constantine's son Crispus would be the emperor's heir; the deletion must have been made after Crispus's execution in 326. The main sources of the *Historia* lay in the church archives and libraries at Caesarea and Jerusalem, where there was no documentation for the churches of the West or for many churches of the East. Eusebius seems to have known little about the church of Antioch and had the good sense to refuse translation there in about 330. His strong emphasis on Alexandrian Christianity results from his love for the school of Origen.

Eusebius's panegyrics usually start from his own experiences. Thus his work *The Martyrs of Palestine* (two editions) was based largely on his own acquaintance with the persecution in 303–313; he visited Egypt perhaps in 312, where he witnessed mass executions of Christians. He praised also other martyrs (especially of Gaul), the benefactors who rebuilt the ruined church at Tyre, and above all the emperor Constantine as the divinely appointed champion of Christianity.

It may be that Eusebius's major contribution was as librarian or bibliographer. To him is owed the collections of Origen's letters and the stories of "ancient martyrdoms." The *Chronicon, Historia, Praeparatio,* and *Demonstratio* are essentially collections of collections or even source books without very full annotation. In other words, his materials may be more important than what he did with them. Although one has to watch for deletions, misconceptions, and other errors, Eusebius does not usually falsify his materials, but his changing attitudes have left strange juxtapositions in the text of the *Historia.*

He was conciliatory toward pagan philosophy and politics but hostile toward pagan religion, in which he could see a main cause of the Great Persecution. In this regard he was aligned with Origen, but he underestimated the ultimate force of the newer Alexandrian theology and its preference for orthodoxy over the harmony that Eusebius, like Constantine, had supported. During his lifetime he enjoyed good fortune. He was in imperial favor at least during his last decade, and by 340 his opponent Eustathius was dead, Athanasius in exile, and Marcellus about to be deposed. The question of his supposed Arianism has agitated historians of doctrine for centuries, but it cannot be answered without greater knowledge of the theology of the early fourth century.

His place in the history of Christian learning and literature was high during his lifetime and continued so for centuries. Those who wrote the history of the Eastern church in the fifth and sixth centuries invariably refered to his work as basic and irrefutable. Less innovative or skilled in philosophy than Origen, he was more concerned with tradition, and this concern led him to an exegesis often more sober and literal. It was this concern, also, that led to his search for early Christian documents. Perhaps he succeeded to the headship of Origen's school at Caesarea. It is possible that the lost life of Eusebius by his successor Acacius resembled the panegyric that a disciple, probably Gregory Thaumaturgus, addressed to Origen. If so, there must have been significant differences. A disciple of Eusebius would have insisted on the importance of history, not philosophical theology, as the key to exegesis and apologetics.

BIBLIOGRAPHY

Most of Eusebius's works have been critically edited by Ivar A. Heikel and others in *Eusebius Werke: Die griechischen christlichen Schriftsteller der ersten drei Jahrhunderte* (Berlin, 1902–1975). Most important in this collection is the three-volume *Kirchengeschichte,* edited by Eduard Schwartz (Leipzig, 1908). Other texts can be located through Johannes Quasten's *Patrology,* vol. 3 (Utrecht and Westminster, Md., 1960), pp. 309–345. Quasten also takes note of the modern literature. Important secondary sources include Glenn F. Chesnut's *The First Christian Histories* (Paris, 1977), Pierre Nautin's *Origène: Sa vie et son œuvre* (Paris, 1977), Robert M. Grant's *Eusebius as Church Historian* (Oxford, 1980), and Timothy D. Barnes's *Constantine and Eusebius* (Cambridge, Mass., and London, 1981).

ROBERT M. GRANT (1987)

EUTYCHES (c. 378–454), was the archimandrite and founder of the monophysite heresy. Eutyches was born in Constantinople and was archimandrite of a monastery near there. As sponsor of the eunuch Chrysaphius, Eutyches was very influential in the imperial court. Chrysaphius was one of the more powerful counselors of the emperor Theodosius II.

Eutyches was the originator of an extreme form of monophysitism that came to be called Eutychianism. In reaction to the separationist Christology of Nestorius (who accepted two distinct natures in Christ), Eutyches concluded that there was in Christ a single nature. When Theodoret of Cyrrhus wrote the *Eranistes* against Eutyches' opinions, Flavian, the patriarch of Constantinople (446–449), sent Eutyches to the Council of Constantinople (448) for judgment.

Eutyches appeared at the council but refused to accept the existence of two natures in Christ and was on that account condemned and deposed. Flavian's successor on the throne of Constantinople, Cyril, was, however, sympathetic to Eutyches' teaching, which corresponded to the general framework of the teaching of the Alexandrian school, rather than that of the Antiochene school. Because Cyril assumed that Flavian was a representative of the Antiochene school, he opposed the measures taken against Eutyches. Cyril promoted the convocation of a synod that later became known as the Robber Synod (449), which restored Eutyches and condemned and deposed Eusebius of Dorylaeum—who also opposed the heresy of Nestorius—as well as Flavian. Despite this, and on account of the loss of imperial favor because of the death of Theodosius II (450), Eutyches was expelled from his monastery. The new emperors, Pulcheria and her consort Marcian, convoked an ecumenical council at Chalcedon in 451, which denounced the Robber Synod, excommunicated Dioscorus (patriarch of Alexandria who had presided over the synod), restored the expelled bishops, and condemned Nestorianism, as well as Eutyches along with his teachings.

Eutyches believed that after the union of the divine and the human in Christ, there were no longer two natures but one, and this one nature was a mingling of the two. After this blending, only the divine nature remained, because the human nature was absorbed by the divine. The Council of Chalcedon, by contrast, affirmed that within Christ there are united, without confusion or division, two natures that are wholly God and wholly human.

BIBLIOGRAPHY

The texts of Eutyches' *Confessions of Faith* and several of his letters can be found, along with notes and commentary, in Eduard Schwartz's *Der Prozess des Eutyches* (Munich, 1929). See also W. H. C. Frend's *The Rise of the Monophysite Movement* (Cambridge, U.K., 1979), which includes sources and a bibliography.

THEODORE ZISSIS (1987)
Translated from Greek by Philip M. McGhee

EVAGRIOS OF PONTUS

EVAGRIOS OF PONTUS (345–399), also known as Evagrios Pontikos; Greek theologian and mystic. Evagrios was surnamed Pontikos because he was a native of Pontus, in Asia Minor. He was born to a prosperous, educated family. His father was a *chorepiskopos,* a bishop, of an area adjacent to the family estates of Basil of Caesarea. Evagrios studied under Basil, who ordained him a reader. When Basil died in 379, Evagrios became a disciple of Gregory of Nazianzus, who ordained him deacon and took him under his aegis. Under the Cappadocian fathers, Evagrios became a skilled theologian. Directly or indirectly influenced by the thought of Origen and Gregory of Nyssa, he viewed Hellenism as an enrichment rather than as a corruption of Christianity.

When Gregory of Nazianzus moved to Constantinople as patriarch, Evagrios was invited along. There he participated in the deliberations of the Council of Constantinople (381), which brought the Arian controversy to an end and established the Nicene Creed in its final form. The young deacon impressed many in the council with his brilliant mind and skillful debating.

When Evagrios fell in love with a married woman, he decided to leave the capital and seek peace and salvation in the monastic life. He traveled to centers of monasticism in Egypt and Palestine, where he was the guest of Melania, the Roman aristocrat who ran a hospice on the Mount of Olives for Christian pilgrims. He also became acquainted with Rufinus, who had founded a monastery near the Mount of Olives. Later he moved to Egypt, where he spent two years in the mountains of Nitria and fourteen in the nearby Desert of the Cells (a settlement where six hundred anchorites lived). In Egypt, he came under the influence of the Macarii monks, known as the Makroi Adelphoi (Long Brothers), champions of Origenism. Early in his life among the Egyptian monks he encountered their hostility. They did not like "the cultured Greek living in their midst." Still the Desert Fathers exerted a significant influence on Evagrios's spirituality. He was to live among these monks until his death.

Evagrios was a prolific author of theological and ascetic essays, biblical commentaries, and letters. Some of his writings survive in the original Greek but most have survived only in Syriac, Armenian, or Latin translations. His writings reveal his indebtedness to Origen, the Desert and the Cappadocian fathers (Gregory of Nyssa in particular), and his concern with mystical and ascetic theology.

Among some fourteen authentic works by Evagrios is a trilogy: the *Praktikos,* the *Gnostikos,* and the *Kefalaia gnostika.* The first is a comprehensive exposition of his ascetic philosophy in short chapters intended for simple monks; the second is a continuation of the *Praktikos* for educated monks; and the third, the most important, known also as the *Problemata gnostika,* develops his cosmological, anthropological, and philosophical thought. It is here that Origen's influence on Evagrios is most apparent. This work was used for Evagrios's condemnation by the Second Council of Constantinople (553). Evagrios's most important essay, known as "Chapters on Prayer," is preserved in its original Greek under the name of Nilus of Ancyra.

Evagrios is acknowledged as an important spiritual influence on Christian spirituality and Islamic Sufism. He influenced Maximos the Confessor, Dionysius the Areopagite, and John of Klimakos (John Climacus) and became the forerunner of the hesychasts of later Byzantium. Through Rufinus and John Cassian, Evagrios's ascetic and mystical theology influenced John Scottus Eriugena as well as Bernard of Clairvaux and other Cistercian mystics.

BIBLIOGRAPHY

Primary Sources

Evagrios's works (including fragments) in their original Greek can be found in *Patrologia Graeca,* edited by J.-P. Migne, vols. 40 and 79 (Paris, 1858–1860)—in volume 79, s.v. *Nilus Ancyranus*—and in *Nonnenspiegel und Mönchsspiegel des Euagrios Pontikos,* edited by Hugo Gressmann (Leipzig, 1913). Sources in other languages include *The Praktikos: Chapters on Prayer,* translated and edited by John Eudes Bamberger (Spencer, Mass., 1970); *The Ecclesiastical History* by Socrates Scholasticus (London, 1884), bk. 4, pt. 23; *Evagriana Syriaca: Textes inédits du British Museum et de la Vatican,* edited and translated by Joseph Muyldermans (Louvain, 1952); and *The Lausiac History* by Palladios, edited and translated by Robert T. Meyer (Westminster, Md., 1965).

Secondary Sources

Works about Evagrios and the milieu in which he flourished include Ioustinou I. Mouseskou's *Euagrios ho Pontikos* (Athens, 1937); Hrothrd Glotobdky's "Euagrios ho Pontikos," in *Ethikē kai threskeutikē enkyklopaideia,* vol. 5 (Athens, 1964); and Derwas J. Chitty's *The Desert a City* (Crestwood, N.Y., 1977).

DEMETRIOS J. CONSTANTELOS (1987)

EVANGELICAL AND FUNDAMENTAL CHRISTIANITY. The term *evangelicalism* usually refers to a largely Protestant movement that emphasizes:

(1) the Bible as authoritative and reliable;

(2) eternal salvation as possible only by regeneration (being "born again"), involving personal trust in Christ and in his atoning work;

(3) a spiritually transformed life marked by moral conduct and personal devotion, such as Bible reading and prayer; and

(4) zeal for evangelism and missions.

Among Lutherans the term *evangelical* has long had a more general usage, roughly equivalent to *Protestant,* and some neo-orthodox theologians have used the term in its broad sense of "gospel believer." In the Spanish-speaking world, the term *evangélico* roughly parallels the Lutheran usage, referring in general to non-Catholic Christian groups of any stripe, although historically most *evangélicos* have in fact been evangelicals as more narrowly defined above. In the English-speaking world, evangelical designates a distinct movement that emerged from the religious awakenings of the eighteenth century and that by the early nineteenth century had taken clear shape in the United States, in England and the British Empire, and in many mission fields.

Fundamentalism is a subspecies of evangelicalism. The term originated in the United States in 1920 and referred to evangelicals who considered it a chief Christian duty to combat uncompromisingly "modernist" theology and certain secularizing cultural trends. Organized militancy was the feature that most clearly distinguished fundamentalists from other evangelicals. Fundamentalism originated as primarily an American phenomenon, although it has British and British Empire counterparts, is paralleled by some militant groups in other traditions, and has been exported worldwide through missions.

Whereas *fundamentalism* and *fundamentalist* continue to be useful terms for historians, they are less useful as terms descriptive of any particular group, in part because the term has become so pejorative in Western culture that only the extreme right wing of evangelicalism would welcome being labeled as such. In addition, the distinction between fundamentalist and evangelical is not always an easy one to make, and what can be said of fundamentalists can often be said, at least in part, of some (even most) evangelicals. Nevertheless, the term is applied with some usefulness to the more theologically and culturally conservative wing of evangelicalism, although the precise parameters of that wing are open to conjecture.

The two characteristics by which fundamentalists are most easily recognized represent both an engagement with Western culture and a rejection of it. Fundamentalists challenge Western culture in an organized, militant battle over secularizing cultural trends even as they appropriate the latest advances in technology and technique in an evangelistic struggle for human hearts. In an attempt to nurture their constituents, especially their children, within their own subculture, fundamentalists withdraw from Western culture into communities and institutions of their own creation that often parallel the communities and institutions of secular culture. Both evangelicalism and fundamentalism are complex coalitions reflecting the convergences of a number of traditions.

EMERGENCE OF EVANGELICALISM. Although evangelicalism is largely an Anglo-American phenomenon, its origins give it ties with European Protestantism. The central evangelical doctrines, especially the sole authority of the Bible and the necessity of personal trust in Christ, reflect Reformation teachings. Seventeenth-century Puritanism solidly implanted these emphases in a part of the British Protestant psyche, especially in the North American colonies. In the eighteenth century this heritage merged with parallel trends in continental pietism. The influence of the Moravians on John Wesley (1703–1791) best exemplifies this convergence. Wesley's Methodist movement in the mid-eighteenth century was part of a wider series of awakenings and Pietist renewal movements appearing in Protestant countries from the late seventeenth century through much of the nineteenth century. In England the awakenings were manifested in Methodism, in evangelical renewals among nonconformists, and in the rise of a notable evangelical party in the Church of England. By the mid-nineteenth century, evangelicalism was the most typical form of Protestantism in Great Britain.

In the United States, evangelicalism was even more influential. Evangelical religion had fewer well-established competitors than in the Old World. The rise of the United States as a new nation and the rise of evangelicalism coincided, so the religion often assumed a quasi-official status. Evangelical emphasis on voluntary acceptance of Christianity also was well matched to American ideas of individual freedom.

The character of American evangelicalism began to take shape during the Great Awakening of the eighteenth century. This movement, really a series of revivals throughout the middle decades of the century, brought together several movements. These included New England Puritanism, continental Pietism, revivalist Presbyterianism, Baptist anti-establishment democratic impulses, the Calvinist revivalism of the Englishman George Whitefield (1714–1770), and Methodism (which surpassed all the others after the Revolutionary era). During the first half of the nineteenth century, evangelicalism developed a strong populist base and became by far the most common form of Protestantism in the United States. Evangelicalism had many denominational varieties but tended to blend Calvinist and Methodist theologies, to emphasize conversion experiences evidenced by lives freed from barroom vices, to vigorously promote revivals and missions, and to view the church as a voluntary association of believers founded on the authority of the Bible alone.

By the early nineteenth century evangelicals in Great Britain and the United States had established a formidable network of nonsectarian "voluntary societies" to promote their causes. Of these the various missionary societies, founded around the beginning of the century, were the most prominent, providing, together with denominational agencies, the home support for the most massive worldwide missionary effort ever seen. Home missionary endeavors were comparably vigorous, supported by a host of agencies for promoting evangelism, founding Sunday schools, distributing Bibles and religious tracts, establishing schools and colleges, and bringing the gospel to various needy groups. Revivalism spearheaded such efforts, exemplified best in the extensive campaigns of Charles Finney (1792–1875) both in the United States and in England. These mission and evangelistic efforts were accompanied by campaigns, organized by voluntary societies, for charity and social reform. On both sides of the Atlantic evangelicals played leading roles in combating slavery; in Great Britain, especially under the leadership of William Wilberforce (1759–1833), they were influential in bringing about its abolition throughout the empire. Evangelicals promoted other reforms, including Sabbatarian and temperance legislation, prison reform, and the establishment of private charities. Such reforming spirit was usually part of a postmillennial vision of steady spiritual and moral progress leading to a millennial age of the triumph of the gospel throughout the world, after which Christ himself would return. When linked in the popular mind with notions of the progress achievable through science, the focus brought by romanticism to the possibilities inherent in individuals, and the manifest destiny of the Anglo-Saxon race on the North American continent, this evangelical vision lent itself to a triumphalist view of what could be achieved by Americans in the New World. The downside of this heady brew of evangelicalism and patriotism was at times a nativist impulse that fed both racism and anti-Catholicism.

The Loss of Cultural Dominance. In the latter half of the nineteenth century, the vigorous evangelicalism that had grown so successfully in the early industrial era found itself in a new world. The concentrated new industrialism and the massively crowded cities tended to overwhelm the individualistic and voluntaristic evangelical programs. Conceptions of dominating the culture became more difficult to maintain. Evangelicals accordingly increasingly stressed those aspects of their message that involved personal commitment to Christ and personal holiness rather than social programs, although aspirations to be a major moral influence on the culture never entirely disappeared. The evangelicalism of Dwight L. Moody (1837–1899) exemplified this trend. Moody, like Finney before him, had great successes in both the United States and Great Britain. He omitted entirely, however, Finney's postmillennial emphasis on social reform, stressing instead the importance of rescuing the perishing from the sinking ship that was the condemned world. This increasing sense of evangelical alienation from Anglo-American culture was reflected in Moody's premillennialism and in the growth of premillennialism among most of the newer evangelical movements of the day. Premillennialists looked to the second coming of Christ as the only cure for the world's social and political woes. New emphasis on personal holiness, notably exemplified in the rise of the Keswick holiness movement in Britain after 1875, reflected similar tendencies. Keswick teaching, which spread widely among American evangelical and later fundamentalist followers of Moody, stressed personal victory over sin, personal witnessing about the gospel, and support of missions as chief among Christian duties. Keswick was only one of several new holiness movements that flourished among evangelicals in the mid- and late nineteenth century. Most of these movements had generic ties with Methodism and Wesley's teachings concerning Christian perfection. Some holiness groups, most notably the Salvation Army, founded in England in 1865, combined their evangelism with extensive charitable work among the needy. Others among an emerging number of holiness denominations emphasized more the personal experience of being filled by the Holy Spirit. Such emphasis in heightened forms was apparent in the rise in the United States after 1900 of Pentecostalism, which also brought separate denominations and almost exclusive emphasis on intense personal spiritual experience. By the early twentieth century, evangelicalism was thus subdivided into a variety of camps on questions of personal holiness and the nature of spiritual experience.

Equally important during this same era, from the later decades of the nineteenth century to World War I, was that evangelicals found themselves in a new world intellectually. Darwinism became the focal symbol of a many-faceted revolution in assumptions dominating the culture. Some of the early debates over Darwinism left an impression, damaging to evangelicalism, that modern science and biblical Christianity were inherently opposed. A deeper issue, however, was a broader revolution in conceptions of reality and truth. Rather than seeing truth as fixed and absolute, Western people were more and more viewing it as a changing function of human cultural evolution. Religion, in such a view, was not absolute truth revealed by the deity but the record of developing human conceptions about God and morality. Such conceptions were devastating when applied to the Bible, which in the higher criticism of the late nineteenth century often was regarded as simply the record of Hebrew religious experience.

The widespread evangelical consensus was shaken to its foundations. The absolute authority of the Bible as the source of the doctrine of salvation was widely questioned, even within the churches. Moral absolutes based on Scripture were also questioned; again the questioning was often from within the churches. The result was a profound split in most of the denominations that had been at the center of the mid-nineteenth-century evangelical alliance. Liberals, sometimes called "modernists" in the early twentieth century, adjusted Christian doctrine to fit the temper of the times. God's revelation of his kingdom was not so much in startling supernatural interventions as in working through the best in the natural processes of the growth of civilization and morality. Essentially, Christianity was not so much a doctrine of eternal salvation for another world as a divine revelation of a humane way of life for this world. Sometimes liberals advocated a "social gospel," based on the progressive politics of the early twentieth century, to replace the individualism of older evangelicalism's conceptions of salvation. Many traditionalist evangelicals, on the other hand, resisted these trends toward more naturalistic, relativistic, and modern conceptions of the heart of the gospel, continuing rather to preach traditional evangelical doctrine of a miraculous Bible whose revelation centered on describing the means of divine rescue from sin, death, and hell.

THE RISE OF FUNDAMENTALISM. Fundamentalism arose in this context. It combined an organized militant defense of most traditional evangelical doctrines with some of the revivalist evangelical innovations of the nineteenth century. The most important of these innovations, eventually accepted by most fundamentalists, was the elaborate system of biblical interpretation known as *dispensationalism.* Dispensationalism was a version of the premillennialism popularized among revivalists in the late nineteenth century. Originated in England especially by the Plymouth Brethren leader John Nelson Darby (1800–1882), dispensationalism was developed and promoted in the United States principally by Bible teacher associates of Moody, such as Reuben A. Torrey (1856–1928), James M. Gray (1851–1935), and C. I. Scofield (1843–1921), editor of the famous dispensationalist *Scofield Reference Bible,* published in 1909.

Dispensationalism is a systematic scheme for interpreting all of history on the basis of the Bible, following the principle of "literal where possible"; biblical prophecies, especially, are taken to refer to real historical events. This approach yields a rather detailed account of all human history, which is divided into seven dispensations, or eras, of differing relationships between God and humanity (such as the Dispensation of Innocence in Eden or the Dispensation of Law, from Moses to Christ). The last of these eras is the millennium, which will be preceded by the personal return of Jesus, the secret "rapture" of believers who are to "meet him in the air," a seven-year period of wars among those who remain on earth (resulting in the victory of Christ), the conversion of the Jews, and the establishment of a kingdom in Jerusalem, where Jesus will reign for exactly one thousand years before the Last Judgment. Such exact interpretations of prophecy committed dispensationalists firmly to a view of the Bible as divinely inspired and without error in any detail. The "inerrancy" of Scripture in scientific and historical detail accordingly became the key test of faith for fundamentalists. This doctrine, while not entirely novel in the history of the church, was also given a new and especially forceful articulation by nondispensationalist Presbyterian traditionalists at Princeton Theological Seminary, especially Benjamin B. Warfield (1851–1921), who for a time was allied with dispensationalists in battles against liberal theology and higher criticism of the Bible.

The other major innovation widely accepted by fundamentalists was the Keswick holiness teaching. The same groups of Bible teachers who taught dispensationalism widely promoted Keswick doctrine as well. These leaders established regular summer Bible conferences and, more important, founded a network of Bible institutes for training lay workers in evangelism. These institutes, together with local churches and agencies directly promoting revivalism, such as those of Billy Sunday (1862–1935), provided the principal institutional base for fundamentalism.

Fundamentalism was also a mood as much as a set of doctrines and institutions. It was a mood of militancy in opposition to modernist theology and to some of the relativistic cultural changes that modernism embraced. This militancy provided the basis for a wider antimodernist coalition that emerged as a distinct movement in the United States during the 1920s. The immediate occasion for the appearance of fundamentalism was the sense of cultural crisis that gripped the United States after World War I. Reflecting this mood, fundamentalism gave focus to the anxieties of Protestant traditionalists. This focus was directed first of all against the modernists in major denominations, most notably the major Baptist and Presbyterian churches in the northern United States. Especially in the years from 1920 to 1925, fundamentalists led major efforts to expel such liberals from their denominations, but these efforts met with little success. The other focus was American culture itself. The United States seemed to many evangelicals to have lost its Christian and biblical moorings. World War I precipitated this sense of alarm, for the war sped up a revolution in morals that, despite the rearguard action of Prohibition legislation, replaced Victorian evangelical standards with the public morals of the Jazz Age. The international crisis also generated fears of social upheaval at home, particularly alarm about the rise of bolshevism and atheism in the United States during the "red scare" of 1919 and 1920. Many Protestants also remained concerned about the social and moral impact of the immense immigration of the preceding half century and were antagonistic to the spread of Roman Catholic influences.

Fundamentalists saw all these factors as signs of the end of a Bible-based civilization in the United States. Their chief social anxieties, however, centered on the question of evolution. During the war, extreme propaganda had convinced most Americans that Germany, the homeland of the Reformation, had lapsed into barbarism. The same thing might happen in the United States. The "will to power" philosophy of Friedrich Nietzsche (1844–1900), said the propagandists, had destroyed German morals. Fundamentalists contended that this was an evolutionary philosophy and that evolutionary and relativistic ideas had long been incorporated into German theology, now taught by liberals in America's churches. Under the leadership of William Jennings Bryan (1860–1925), fundamentalists campaigned to bring the

United States back to the Bible by banning the teaching of biological evolution in public schools. This crusade brought organized fundamentalism into the American South, where homegrown Protestant antimodernist tendencies had been strong since the Civil War. The fundamentalist antievolution campaign reached its peak in the 1925 trial of John Scopes (1900–1970) in Dayton, Tennessee, for teaching biological evolution in a high school. At the highly publicized proceedings, Bryan debated the lawyer Clarence Darrow (1857–1938) concerning the authenticity of biblical miracles. Bryan was ridiculed in the world press, and his death shortly after the trial signaled the beginning of a decline of early fundamentalist efforts to control American culture. During the late 1920s the strength of fundamentalist efforts to purge major northern denominations also declined dramatically. During this era organized fundamentalism had some branches in Canada and some relatively small counterparts in Great Britain.

In the United States, fundamentalism was only the prominent fighting edge of the larger evangelical movement. During the decades from 1925 to 1945 the public press paid less attention to fundamentalist complaints, but the movement itself was regrouping rather than retreating. During this time fundamentalism developed a firmer institutional base, especially in independent local churches and in some smaller denominations, although considerable numbers of fundamentalists remained in major denominations. The revivalist heritage of the movement was especially apparent in this era, as it turned its strongest efforts toward winning the United States through evangelization. In addition to traditional means for evangelization, fundamentalists developed effective radio ministries. Particularly prominent was Charles E. Fuller's (1887–1968) *Old-Fashioned Revival Hour,* which by 1942 had a larger audience than any other radio program in the United States.

Fundamentalist evangelicals also founded new sorts of ministries, such as Youth for Christ, begun in 1942, which soon had hundreds of chapters across the country. Bible institutes, such as Moody Bible Institute in Chicago and the Bible Institute of Los Angeles, remained important centers for the movement, training and sending out evangelists and missionaries, conducting Bible conferences, establishing effective radio ministries, and publishing many books and periodicals.

THE NEW EVANGELICALS. A sharp tension was developing in the fundamentalist-evangelical movement that survived the controversies of the 1920s. This tension led eventually to a deep split between "fundamentalists" and "evangelicals." The fundamentalists kept in the forefront the militancy that had characterized the movement in the 1920s. Furthermore, they followed the logic of their military metaphors by adding ecclesiastical separatism as a test of true commitment. This separatist stance sometimes also reflected the influence of dispensationalism, which taught that the Bible prophesied the decline and apostasy of the major churches during the present era.

Another element in the generation that had been raised on the fundamentalist controversies of the 1920s sought to bring the movement back toward a broader evangelicalism. Without rejecting entirely their fundamentalist heritage, they nonetheless softened the militancy and often moved away from dispensationalism. Repudiating separatism as a test of the faith, they especially emphasized positive evangelism. By the early 1940s a distinct movement with these emphases was apparent, signaled by the founding of the National Association of Evangelicals (NAE) in 1942. In contrast to the smaller, militantly separatist American Council of Christian Churches, founded in 1941 by the fundamentalist Carl McIntire (1906–2002), the NAE included Pentecostal and holiness denominations as well as individual members who remained in major American denominations.

Following World War II, some younger leaders, notably Harold John Ockenga (1905–1985), Carl F. H. Henry (1913–2003), and Edward J. Carnell (1919–1967), organized a "neoevangelical" movement with the explicit purpose of moderating and broadening fundamentalist evangelicalism. Joined by Fuller, they organized the Fuller Theological Seminary in Pasadena, California, in 1947. Their efforts were vastly aided by the emergence of Billy Graham as America's leading evangelist after 1949. This group in 1956 also founded *Christianity Today* to provide a solid periodical base for the movement.

The final break in the fundamentalist-evangelical movement came with Graham's New York crusade in 1957. Graham accepted the cooperation of some prominent liberal church leaders. Separatist fundamentalists such as Bob Jones Sr. (1883–1968), founder of Bob Jones University; John R. Rice (1895–1980), editor of the influential *Sword of the Lord;* and McIntire anathematized Graham and the neoevangelicals as traitors from within. Neoevangelicals in turn soon ceased altogether to call themselves fundamentalists, preferring the designation "evangelical."

In the meantime, Graham's crusade in Great Britain in 1954 set off a small flurry of ecclesiastical debate known as the "fundamentalist controversy" in England. This designation confused the terminological issue, since in England the friends of Graham, rather than just his more conservative enemies, were called fundamentalists. (British parlance of the era often lacked the distinction between fundamentalist and evangelical that developed in the United States after the late 1950s.) In any case conservative evangelicalism remained a factor in British church life, especially in the evangelical party in the Church of England. Influenced considerably by the long-standing university ministry of the Inter-Varsity Fellowship, and less a product of the sensational promotional competitions that characterized American revivalism, British evangelicalism was often more sophisticated and less militant than its American counterparts and played an important role in the intellectual leadership of the international movement. Throughout the English-speaking world there are also counterparts to the more strictly fundamentalist, holiness, and Pentecostal groups found in the United States.

THE REEMERGENCE OF EVANGELICALISM IN THE PUBLIC EYE. Evangelicalism was indeed a widespread international phenomenon, even if its Anglo-American manifestations provided its most focused identity as a distinct movement. The Pietist varieties of worldwide Protestantism were scarcely distinguishable from Anglo-American evangelicalism. Moreover, nearly two centuries of massive missionary efforts had planted evangelical communities in most of the nations of the world. The sense of identity of an international evangelicalism was evidenced in world conferences, notably the 1966 World Congress on Evangelism in Berlin and the 1974 International Congress on World Evangelization in Lausanne, Switzerland. Such gatherings were initially organized primarily by Anglo-American friends of Graham, but they also marked the emergence among evangelicals of significant voices and leadership from developing nations. The Lausanne congress, for instance, included over two thousand participants from 150 countries. Traditional evangelical emphases on the reliability and authority of Scripture and on the urgency for world evangelization were apparent, but so was emphasis on the necessity of social and political concern for aiding the poor and victims of injustice.

In the United States, in the meantime, evangelicalism reemerged on the public scene with renewed vigor. During the 1970s the American media suddenly discovered that evangelicalism was a major force in American life. Evangelicalism had in fact been growing steadily for many years, so the numbers of evangelicals had grown to at least forty or fifty million, whereas other Protestants and Roman Catholics were declining in numbers. Once evangelicals were discovered, they became conspicuous in the media, boasting many sports and entertainment stars. Being "born again" suddenly became a political asset, evidenced in 1976 by the victorious presidential campaign of Jimmy Carter, and evangelicalism was reckoned as a powerful if mysterious political force.

The discovery of evangelicalism reflected not only real growth and change in the movement but also the power of a concept. Numerous strands in American religious life were now viewed as part of a more or less unified "evangelicalism." Such a perception was at once helpful and deceptive. It was helpful in pointing to a large phenomenon: Christians who shared fundamental evangelical beliefs. It was deceptive, however, in its implication that their movement was more unified than it actually was. Certainly evangelicalism as a movement that could claim forty or fifty million adherents was much larger than the consciously organized evangelical movement that had grown out of fundamentalist evangelicalism and that was led by associates of Graham. For instance, black evangelicals, including most of black Protestantism, had little to do with that fundamentalist evangelicalism, even though most of their beliefs and emphases were closely parallel. The same was true, but to a lesser degree, of much of the Southern Baptist Convention, the largest of American evangelical groups. Most holiness denominations and evangelical Methodists were only tangentially related to the organized fundamentalist evangelical movement. So also were most Pentecostals and charismatics, who sponsored some of the largest television ministries and set the tone for much of the evangelical resurgence. Peace churches were generally evangelical in doctrine but preserved a heritage distinct from fundamentalist evangelicalism. Confessional denominations, such as the Missouri Synod Lutheran and the Christian Reformed Church, were close allies of evangelicals but always kept enough distance to preserve distinct doctrinal heritages.

Many evangelicals were in major American denominations, such as Baptist, Presbyterian, Methodist, Disciples of Christ, or Episcopal, but might be as much shaped by the distinctiveness of their denomination's history as by a conscious evangelical identity. Others in such denominations might identify closely with the doctrines and emphases of a parachurch evangelistic agency, such as Campus Crusade, founded by Bill Bright in 1951. Such variety within evangelicalism, compounded by many denominational and regional differences, suggests that generalization about the movement is hazardous.

Such hazards are especially great concerning evangelicals' political stances. Whereas one important strand of nineteenth-century American evangelicalism was politically progressive and reformist, in the twentieth century most fundamentalist evangelicals and other white evangelicals were politically conservative. After the 1960s, however, more variety reappeared, especially among spokespersons of the sort who hold conferences and issue declarations. Evangelical voices have been heard across the spectrum of political options, although most of the evangelical constituency is at least moderately conservative.

THE CONTINUING IMPACT OF FUNDAMENTALIST EVANGELICALS. Most hard-line fundamentalists went their separate ways after about 1950, reorganizing themselves loosely in a number of fellowships or smaller denominations. The largest fellowship was the Baptist Bible Fellowship, founded by fundamentalists who split with the volatile Texas fundamentalist F. Frank Norris. By the early 1980s this fellowship claimed to represent two to three million members. During this era some local fundamentalist pastors built huge churches, claiming both membership and Sunday school attendance of over ten thousand each by the 1970s. Prominent among these were Jack Hyles's First Baptist Church of Hammond, Indiana, Lee Roberson's Highland Park Baptist Church in Chattanooga, Tennessee, and Jerry Falwell's Thomas Road Baptist Church in Lynchburg, Virginia. Typically, such ministries were structured as small, individually run empires, including branch chapels, a college, publications, radio and television broadcasts, missionary work, and specialized ministries. The total number of members of strictly separatist fundamentalist churches in the United States by 1980 was perhaps around five million, although the number of evangelicals leaning toward fundamentalism was probably much greater. Moreover, such militant fundamentalism spread throughout the English-speaking world, and active missions carried its doctrines to every nation where Christian missions were permitted.

Soul winning and church growth are the fundamentalist's first concerns, as they are for most evangelicals. In addition, extreme militancy against theological liberalism led many fundamentalists to emphasize separation even from other evangelicals, especially neoevangelicals, charismatics, and members of large groups, such as the Southern Baptist Convention. The question of separation also divided fundamentalists among themselves. Some fundamentalist leaders, especially those associated with Bob Jones University, advocated "second-degree separation"—that is, separation even from fellow fundamentalists who are not strict fundamentalists. In the 1970s, for instance, Bob Jones III attacked the noted fundamentalist evangelist Rice for publishing materials by Southern Baptists in his widely read paper the *Sword of the Lord.*

Most fundamentalists are militant dispensationalists, usually claiming that the signs of the times indicate that within a few years the dramatic events surrounding the return of Christ will bring the present era to a violent end. The dispensationalist heritage has made most fundamentalist evangelicals sympathetic to the state of Israel, whose existence as a nation is viewed as the fulfillment of prophecy and a key trigger of end-time events. Dispensationalists also take literally the biblical promises of blessing to countries that support Israel. This sympathy by large numbers of evangelicals has had a considerable impact on American foreign policy. During the 1970s, dispensationalist prophetic views attracted wide interest, as indicated by the popularity of Hal Lindsey's book *The Late Great Planet Earth* (1970), of which some ten million copies were printed during the decade. The graphic dispensationalist vision for the end times continued to attract interest far beyond the fundamentalist or even evangelical communities. The pastor and author Tim LaHaye's *Left Behind* series of novels, essentially a fictionalization of the events described earlier by Lindsey and any number of dispensational prophecy teachers, became phenomenal best-sellers in the 1990s and early 2000s. The books regularly debuted at number one on the *New York Times* best-seller list, and over forty million copies (fifty million counting the graphic novels and children's versions) had been sold by 2003.

Until the later 1970s most separatist fundamentalists were not active politically. Some prominent fundamentalist leaders, such as McIntire and Billy James Hargis, were in the forefront of anticommunist crusades during the decades following World War II, but such activists probably did not represent the majority of the movement. Fundamentalists emerged as a considerable force in American political life with the formation of the Moral Majority in 1979. This political coalition of fundamentalists and some other political conservatives was led by Falwell and benefited from his large television ministry. Some strict fundamentalists condemned such efforts because they involved cooperation with Roman Catholics, Orthodox Jews, neoevangelicals, and other alleged apostates.

Nonetheless, the Moral Majority brought together several long-standing fundamentalist concerns with political issues of the time. Most evangelicals and almost all fundamentalists, for instance, had long held conservative views on the role of women, on the family, and on questions related to sexuality. Sparked by the legalization of abortion in 1973, the women's movement and the proposed Equal Rights Amendment, legislation proposing increased rights for homosexuals, and general permissiveness, many fundamentalist and conservative evangelicals expressed alarm. The Moral Majority focused such sentiments and organized them politically. Reaching a constituency well beyond fundamentalists and fundamentalist evangelicals, its program included endorsement of American conservative political ideals: smaller government, larger military, patriotism, and freedom for businesses. Fundamentalists, supported by the Moral Majority, also successfully revived the antievolution crusade, introducing legislation into a number of states that would require the teaching of fundamentalist "creation science" (arguments that the earth is no more than ten thousand years old) whenever biological evolution is taught in public schools.

Perhaps the closest parallel to such late-twentieth-century American political fundamentalism was the militant Protestantism in Northern Ireland led by Ian Paisley. Paisley, an avowed fundamentalist with connections to American leaders such as Jones and McIntire, mixed conservative Protestantism with aggressive political anti-Catholicism. The long history of the Irish conflict, however, has given Irish fundamentalism a character more violent than its American counterparts. A far more genteel political action movement with some evangelical leadership was England's Festival of Light, an organization prominent in the 1970s and 1980s in its efforts to maintain public decency, particularly in matters concerning sexuality. In general, evangelicalism in Great Britain was less political and less confrontational than in the United States, put relatively more emphasis on evangelism and missions, operated more through traditional denominations, and was a much less influential force in the culture at large.

In the United States the organized political coalitions of the Christian Right had their greatest influence in the period from 1980 to 1994. Contributors to the Republican electoral victory of Ronald Reagan in 1980, they were nonetheless frustrated by the mainstream positions of Reagan on cultural issues. In 1988 the television evangelist Pat Robertson entered the Republican presidential primaries and gained considerable early attention by mobilizing approximately 10 percent of the Republican vote in the states where he ran. Robertson's Christian Coalition reached its greatest strength in the 1990s, when conservative Christians were instrumental in electing a strongly Republican House of Representatives led by the outspoken Speaker of the House, Newt Gingrich. Despite these advances, conservative Christians continued to find most of their political goals frustrated. Perhaps most important, the Christian Coalition marked the consolidation of a culturally conservative wing of evangelicalism solidly entrenched in the Republican Party. By the 1990s, conservative politics were taken for granted in many of the largest evangelical and fundamentalist churches and organizations, although there were always exceptions.

A high-water mark for fundamentalist-leaning evangelicals in church life was the 1990s, when they completed a long campaign to take over control of the central agencies and theological seminaries of the Southern Baptist Convention, the nation's largest Protestant denomination, essentially winning the kind of denominational battle they had been losing since the early twentieth century. Although some Southern Baptist leaders resisted following the lead of what they considered "Yankee-based evangelicalism," they now found themselves fighting over issues such as inerrancy, battles that had been fought among fundamentalists and evangelicals in the North and the West several decades previous. In response to losing control of key institutions, Southern Baptist moderates took advantage of the decentralized Baptist polity to form their own organizations.

The influence of Pentecostal and charismatic models of church life is another key development within Western evangelicalism after 1970. If fundamentalist militancy set the tone for much of evangelicalism in the era from the 1920s through the 1960s, the charismatic and Pentecostal churches set the tone after that. This is especially true in styles of worship and methods of ministry. The 1960s created an atmosphere in which visionary evangelical pastors began experimenting with new ways of reaching out to the broader culture. Many churches initially developed during this period became megachurches, pulling in thousands every Sunday and spawning virtual denominations of like-minded churches around the country and the world. Churches such as Calvary Chapel and the Vineyard in southern California or Willow Creek in the suburbs of Chicago, whereas conservative theologically, managed to engage the mainstream of American culture and influenced countless other evangelical churches in the process. By 2003, for example, there were over 825 Calvary Chapels in the United States with another 210 around the world. Over 7,200 churches around the world were at least loosely affiliated with Willow Creek. Typically, these churches use contemporary or Pentecostal styles of worship, highly value lay leadership and small group ministries, and are led by low-key but charismatic and visionary individuals who often have little to no advanced training. Willow Creek has pioneered "seeker" oriented services that use drama, contemporary music, video, and sermons focused on common life problems to attract people who might be alienated by more traditional service styles. With churches like these leading the way, the number of evangelicals in the United States, although difficult to pinpoint with accuracy, remains high. Polls conducted in the late 1990s reveal that, whereas 13 percent of the U.S. population self-identify as either fundamentalist or evangelical, 33 percent of the U.S. population are members of or attend conservative Protestant denominations that theologically, at least, fall within the evangelical camp.

In addition, evangelicalism in all its forms became one of the West's leading cultural exports as North American missions came to dominate the world missionary movement. By the end of the twentieth century, as liberal Christians either lost the missionary impulse or transferred it to social welfare agencies, such as the Peace Corps, evangelicals took over the missionary enterprise. Fundamentalists and evangelicals founded "faith missions" by the score in the late nineteenth century and early twentieth century. These agencies, modeled on J. Hudson Taylor's (1832–1905) influential China Inland Mission (1865), refused to pay salaries or to raise funds in any overt fashion. Influenced by Keswick piety, which promoted slogans such as "Let go and let God," the new missions professed to rely solely on God to supply recruits and the necessary funds. After enduring some difficult times, they learned to supplement faith in God with aggressive publicity within the evangelical community. By midcentury many of these agencies had high profiles in the evangelical community and routinely attracted some of the most committed evangelical young people. By the end of the twentieth century, roughly 90 percent of American foreign missionaries were evangelical. American missionary efforts helped spark the huge growth of evangelical Protestantism in Latin America and Africa. Aided largely by the massive growth of Pentecostal and charismatic churches, whose adherents number in the hundreds of millions worldwide, most of worldwide Protestantism developed a distinctly evangelical character.

SEE ALSO Christian Social Movements; Millenarianism, overview article; Modernism, article on Christian Modernism; Pentecostal and Charismatic Christianity; Protestantism.

BIBLIOGRAPHY

Ammerman, Nancy Tatom. *Bible Believers: Fundamentalists in the Modern World.* New Brunswick, N.J., 1987.

Ariel, Yaakov. *On Behalf of Israel: American Fundamentalist Attitudes toward Jews, Judaism, and Zionism, 1865–1945.* Brooklyn, N.Y., 1991.

Bays, Daniel H., and Grant Wacker, eds. *The Foreign Missionary Enterprise at Home: Explorations in North American Cultural History.* Tuscaloosa, Ala., 2003.

Beale, David O. *In Pursuit of Purity: American Fundamentalism since 1850.* Greenville, S.C., 1986.

Bebbington, David W. *Evangelicalism in Modern Britain: A History from the 1730s to the 1980s.* London and Boston, 1989.

Bendroth, Margaret Lamberts. *Fundamentalism and Gender, 1875 to the Present.* New Haven, Conn., 1993.

Blumhofer, Edith L. *Aimee Semple McPherson: Everybody's Sister.* Grand Rapids, Mich., 1993.

Blumhofer, Edith L. *Restoring the Faith: The Assemblies of God, Pentecostalism, and American Culture.* Urbana, Ill., 1993.

Boyer, Paul S. *When Time Shall Be No More: Prophecy Belief in Modern American Culture.* Cambridge, Mass., 1992.

Brekus, Catherine A. *Strangers and Pilgrims: Female Preaching in America, 1740–1845.* Chapel Hill, N.C., 1998.

Brereton, Virginia Lieson. *Training God's Army: The American Bible School, 1880–1940.* Bloomington, Ind., 1990.

Carpenter, Joel A. *Revive Us Again: The Reawakening of American Fundamentalism.* New York, 1997.

Carwardine, Richard J. *Evangelicals and Politics in Antebellum America.* New Haven, Conn., 1993.

Dayton, Donald W., and Robert K. Johnston, eds. *The Variety of American Evangelicalism.* Knoxville, Tenn., 1991.

DeBerg, Betty A. *Ungodly Women: Gender and the First Wave of American Fundamentalism.* Minneapolis, Minn., 1990.

Dieter, Melvin Easterday. *The Holiness Revival of the Nineteenth Century.* Lanham, Md., 1996.

Emerson, Michael O., and Christian Smith. *Divided by Faith: Evangelical Religion and the Problem of Race in America.* New York, 2000.

Griffith, R. Marie. *God's Daughters: Evangelical Women and the Power of Submission.* Berkeley, Calif., 1997.

Hankins, Barry. *Uneasy in Babylon: Southern Baptist Conservatives and American Culture.* Tuscaloosa, Ala., 2002.

Harrell, David Edwin, Jr. *Oral Roberts: An American Life.* San Francisco, 1987.

Hart, D. G. *Defending the Faith: J. Gresham Machen and the Crisis of Conservative Protestantism in Modern America.* Baltimore, Md., 1994.

Hatch, Nathan O. *The Democratization of American Christianity.* New Haven, Conn., 1989.

Heyrman, Christine Leigh. *Southern Cross: The Beginnings of the Bible Belt.* Chapel Hill, N.C., 1997.

Hill, Patricia R. *The World Their Household: The American Woman's Foreign Mission Movement and Cultural Transformation, 1870–1920.* Ann Arbor, Mich., 1984.

Hughes, Richard T., ed. *The Primitive Church in the Modern World.* Urbana, Ill., 1995.

Hutchison, William R. *Errand to the World: American Protestant Thought and Foreign Missions.* Chicago, 1987.

Larson, Edward J. *Summer for the Gods: The Scopes Trial and America's Continuing Debate over Science and Religion.* New York, 1997.

Long, Kathryn Teresa. *The Revival of 1857–58: Interpreting an American Religious Awakening.* New York, 1998.

Loveland, Anne C. *American Evangelicals and the U.S. Military: 1942–1993.* Baton Rouge, La., 1996.

Marsden, George M. *Fundamentalism and American Culture: The Shaping of Twentieth Century Evangelicalism 1870–1925.* New York, 1980.

Marsden, George M. *Reforming Fundamentalism: Fuller Seminary and the New Evangelicalism.* Grand Rapids, Mich., 1987.

Marsden, George M. *Jonathan Edwards: A Life.* New Haven, Conn., 2003.

Martin, William C. *With God on Our Side: The Rise of the Religious Right in America.* New York, 1996.

Marty, Martin E., and R. Scott Appleby, eds. *Fundamentalisms Comprehended.* Chicago, 1995.

Miller, Donald E. *Reinventing American Protestantism: Christianity in the New Millennium.* Berkeley, Calif., 1997.

Noll, Mark A. *A History of Christianity in the United States and Canada.* Grand Rapids, Mich., 1992.

Noll, Mark A. *America's God: From Jonathan Edwards to Abraham Lincoln.* New York, 2002.

Noll, Mark A., ed. *Religion and American Politics: From the Colonial Period to the 1980s.* New York, 1990.

Numbers, Ronald L. *The Creationists.* New York, 1992.

Sandeen, Ernest R. *The Roots of Fundamentalism: British and American Millenarianism, 1800–1930.* Chicago, 1970.

Smith, Christian. *American Evangelicalism: Embattled and Thriving.* Chicago, 1998.

Smith, Christian. *Christian America? What Evangelicals Really Want.* Berkeley, Calif., 2000.

Stout, Harry S. *The Divine Dramatist: George Whitefield and the Rise of Modern Evangelicalism.* Grand Rapids, Mich., 1991.

Sweet, Leonard I. "The Evangelical Tradition in America." In *The Evangelical Tradition in America,* edited by Leonard I. Sweet, pp. 1–86. Macon, Ga., 1984. Provides a thorough bibliography of sources through the early 1980s.

Wacker, Grant. *Heaven Below: Early Pentecostals and American Culture.* Cambridge, Mass., 2001.

Walls, Andrew F. *The Missionary Movement in Christian History: Studies in the Transmission of Faith.* Maryknoll, N.Y., 1996.

Wigger, John H. *Taking Heaven by Storm: Methodism and the Rise of Popular Christianity in America.* New York, 1998.

George M. Marsden (1987 and 2005)
William L. Svelmoe (2005)

EVANGELIZATION See MISSIONS, *ARTICLE ON* MISSIONARY ACTIVITY

EVANS, ARTHUR (1851–1941) was an English archaeologist who excavated the ruins of Knossos in Crete, center of an early civilization he called Minoan. Son of Sir John Evans, a wealthy Victorian polymath and active amateur archaeologist, Arthur Evans began his work in 1899 at Knossos, which established his fame and for which he was knighted in 1911. Seeking evidence for an early system of writing, Evans uncovered an inscribed clay tablet in his first week of excavation and soon amassed a large archive written in two syllabic scripts now known as Linear A and Linear B. (The latter was deciphered as an early form of Greek by Michael Ventris and John Chadwick in 1952.) The treasures of the palace at Knossos, which Evans named for the legendary King Minos, included many objects that he interpreted as possessing religious significance. In the palace, a building of great size and complex plan, images of bulls' horns, the motif of the double ax, and depictions of young men and women performing acrobatic feats with bulls furnished attractive parallels with Greek legend: *labrus* means "ax," so that *labyrinthos* suggests "the place of the ax," to which, according to legend, seven young men and seven young women were sent from Athens each year to encounter the Minotaur. Evans interpreted the double ax as symbolizing, or marking the presence of, the Cretan Zeus, a deity of quite different type from the Indo-European sky god of the same name with whom he became identified. The Cretan Zeus died and was reborn in an annual cycle. Also important in Minoan religion was the association of trees and pillars as cult objects, a theme Evans discussed in works published in 1900, in the earliest days of the excavation, and in 1931.

Evans faced the usual difficulties of interpreting religious objects in the absence of verbal evidence. (The Linear B tablets, which proved to be records of tribute paid and other stocktaking records, have added very little.) In the manner of his day, Evans was an evolutionist and comparatist, and he drew heavily on the folklore and practice of other cultures. Evaluations of his interpretations vary, but in the field of Greek religion, as in other branches of classical studies, his importance rests on the abundance of material he excavated and assiduously published.

BIBLIOGRAPHY

Evans's views on Minoan-Mycenaean religion are to be found in *The Mycenaean Tree and Pillar Cult and Its Mediterranean Relations* (London, 1901) and *The Earlier Religion of Greece in the Light of Cretan Discoveries* (London, 1931); the latter was Evans's Frazer Lecture for 1931 at the University of Cambridge. The full account of the Knossos excavation is contained in *The Palace of Minos,* 4 vols. in 6 (London, 1921–1935).

New Sources

Harrington, Spencer P M. "Saving Knossos: The Struggle to Preserve a Landmark of Europe's First Great Civilization." *Archaeology* 52, no. 1 (January-February 1999): 30–40.

MacGillivray, J. A. *Minotaur: Sir Arthur Evans and the Archaeology of the Minoan Myth.* New York, 2000.

A. W. H. ADKINS (1987)
Revised Bibliography

EVANS-PRITCHARD, E. E. (1902–1973), was an English anthropologist. Edward Evan Evans-Pritchard was the son of a clergyman of the Church of England. He took a degree in history at the University of Oxford and in 1927 a doctorate in anthropology at the University of London, where he was supervised by C. G. Seligman. His thesis was based on field research undertaken from 1926 to 1930 among the Azande of the Sudan. He carried out research among the Nuer, another Sudanese people, intermittently between 1930 and 1935 and also for brief periods among the Anuak, the Luo, and other East African peoples. During World War II he worked at intervals, when free from military service, among the bedouin of Cyrenaica. In 1944 he joined the Roman Catholic church. He taught at the University of London, Fuad I University in Cairo, Cambridge University, and finally Oxford, where in 1946 he succeeded A. R. Radcliffe-Brown as professor of social anthropology. He retired in 1970, was knighted in 1971, and died in Oxford in September 1973.

Evans-Pritchard's work in religion is unique. It is based on brilliant, sensitive, and meticulous field research, on his mastery of languages (he was fluent in Arabic, Zande, and Nuer), and on his deep knowledge and understanding of the work of his predecessors, in particular those sociologists (Durkheim et al.) associated with *L'année sociologique.* Most of his writings on religion fall into one of four main categories: works on the Azande, the Nuer, the Sanusi, and comparative and theoretical topics.

Each piece of Evans-Pritchard's research and writing is based on certain central problems in anthropology, although never limited to them in a narrow sense. His work among the Azande, a cluster of kingdoms of the southwestern Sudan, led to the publication of *Witchcraft, Oracles, and Magic among the Azande* (1937), perhaps the outstanding work of anthropology published in this century. It is concerned essentially with questions asked, although hardly answered in any convincing manner, by Lucien Lévy-Bruhl in his writings on "primitive" and "scientific" modes of thought. The questions as to whether there are differences between these two modes of thought and, if so, what they are and how they might function in social contexts are basic to anthropology, and Evans-Pritchard's discussion of them has changed the nature of anthropological inquiry. He writes about Zande notions of magic, witchcraft, and divination, that is, their notions of natural and supernatural causation and interference in people's everyday lives. He shows that Zande ideas are rational and systematic; given certain premises of knowledge they are closed and self-perpetuating, and they are not held in isolation but are consistent with forms of authority and power found in Zande society. This is essentially a study of rationality and corrects all earlier views about the "irrationality" of so-called primitive peoples. Later Evans-Pritchard published an immense number of Zande texts, in both Zande and English, with commentaries. This work is probably the greatest single corpus of the myths and tales of an African culture that has yet been published and confirms one of his strongest beliefs: that "primitive" texts are not quaint "folkloristic" stories but are as worthy of careful analysis as those of literate cultures.

Evans-Pritchard's *Nuer Religion* (1956) is the final volume of a trilogy on the Nuer of the southern Sudan (the others are *The Nuer,* 1940, and *Kinship and Marriage among the Nuer,* 1951). In this book he presents Nuer religious thought and ritual as a system of theology that has a subtlety and profundity comparable to those of literate cultures. Here he takes up another basic problem raised by Lévy-Bruhl, that of "mystical participation" between human beings and what in ethnocentric terms are called the supernatural and the natural. This problem is examined within the context of a series of related aspects of Nuer religion: conceptions of God, spirits, the soul, and ghosts; symbolism; sin and sacrifice; and priesthood and prophecy. Because of Evans-Pritchard's great skill in unfolding the complexity of Nuer religious thought, never since has it been possible for scholars of comparative religion to dismiss a nonliterate religion as "primitive" or as a form of "animism." Throughout this work, as in that on the Azande, Evans-Pritchard stresses what he considered to be the central problem of anthropology, that of translation—not the simple problem of translation of words and phrases in a narrow linguistic sense, but the far more complex question of translation of one culture's experience into the terms of another's.

Evans-Pritchard's other "ethnographic" work on religion is rather different, taking as its basic problem the relationship between prophets (a topic raised earlier in his work on the Nuer) and forms of religious and political authority as exemplified in the history of the Muslim Sanusi order in Cyrenaica (*The Sanusi of Cyrenaica,* 1951). Here he was able to use written records as well as his own field research, and he produces a model account of religious history and change.

Evans-Pritchard's last achievement in the study of religion is his many critical writings on the history of the anthropology of religion, of which the best known is *Theories of Primitive Religion* (1965). It is a superb and sophisticated study of the relations between thought, ideology, and society.

The influence of E. E. Evans-Pritchard's writings in the anthropological study of religion has been immense. There has been little later analysis made of modes of thought, systems of causation, witch beliefs, sacrifice, notions of sin, and ritual symbolism that has not been influenced by, if not based upon, his work. In addition, much recent research on the philosophy of knowledge has leaned heavily on his book on the Azande. Evans-Pritchard's influence upon younger anthropologists has been great. The anthropological, historical, and comparative study of religions owes more to him than to any other anthropologist.

Bibliography

The main works of Evans-Pritchard are cited in the article. The most insightful view of his work, in the form of an obituary, is by T. O. Beidelman, "Sir Edward Evan Evans-Pritchard, 1902–1973: An Appreciation," *Anthropos* 69 (1974): 553–567. Beidelman is also the editor of *A Bibliography of the Writings of E. E. Evans-Pritchard* (London, 1974). Mary Douglas's *Edward Evans-Pritchard* (New York, 1980) is a fuller but rather uneven account.

New Sources

Burton, John W. *An Introduction to Evans-Pritchard.* Fribourg, Switzerland, 1992.

John Middleton (1987)
Revised Bibliography

EVE, or, in Hebrew, Ḥavvah; the first woman in the creation narratives of the Hebrew Bible, according to which she was formed from one of the ribs of Adam, the first man (*Gn.* 2:21–23). In this account the creator god wished for Adam to have a mate and so brought all the beasts of the fold and birds of the sky before him to see what he would call each one (*Gn.* 2:19). However, among these creatures the man found no one to be his companion (*Gn.* 2:20). Accordingly, this episode is not solely an etiology of the primal naming of all creatures by the male ancestor of the human race but an account of how this man *(ish)* found no helpmeet until a woman was formed from one of his ribs, whom he named "woman" (*ishshah; Gn.* 2:23). This account is juxtaposed with a comment that serves etiologically to establish the social institution of marriage wherein a male leaves his father and mother and cleaves to his wife so that they become "one flesh" together (*Gn.* 2:24). The matrimonial union is thus a reunion of a primordial situation when the woman was, literally and figuratively, flesh of man's flesh.

Such a version of the origin of the woman, as a special creation from Adam's body, stands in marked contrast to the creation tradition found in *Genesis* 1:27b, where there is a hint that the primordial person *(adam)* was in fact an androgyne. Alternatively, this latter half-verse may have been concerned with correcting a tradition of an originally lone male by the statement that both male and female were simultaneously created as the first "Adam."

This mythic image of a male as the source of all human life (*Gn.* 2:21–22) reflects a male fantasy of self-sufficiency. The subsequent narrative introduces a more realistic perspective. Thus, after the woman has succumbed to the wiles of the snake, eaten of the tree of the knowledge of good and evil, and shared it with her husband, she is acknowledged as a source of new life—albeit with negative overtones, since the narrative stresses the punishment of pain that must be borne by Adam's mate and all her female descendants during pregnancy and childbirth. In token of her role as human genetrix, the man gave to the woman a new name: she was thenceforth called Eve—"for she was the mother of all life" (*Gn.* 2:19).

This new name, *Eve* (Heb., *Ḥavvah*), is in fact a pun on the noun for "life" (Heb., *ḥay*), since both *ḥavvah* and *ḥay* allude to old Semitic words (in Aramaic, Phoenician, and Arabic) for "serpent," as the ancient rabbis noted. Another intriguing cross-cultural pun should be recalled, insofar as it may also underlie the key motifs of the biblical narrative. Thus, in a Sumerian myth it is told that when Enki had a pain in his rib, Ninhursaga caused Nin-ti ("woman of the rib") to be created from him. Strikingly, the Sumerian logogram *ti* (in the goddess's name) stands for both "rib" and "life."

According to one rabbinic *midrash,* Eve was taken from the thirteenth rib of Adam's right side after Lilith, his first wife, had left him (*Pirqei de-Rabbi Eliʿezer* 20). Other legends emphasize Eve's susceptibility to guile and persuasion. Christian traditions use the episode of Eve to encourage the submission of women to their husbands (cf. *2 Cor.* 11:3, *1 Tm.* 2:22–25). Several church fathers typologically compared Eve with Mary, the "new Eve" and mother of Jesus: the sinfulness and disobedience of the former were specifically contrasted with the latter. The temptation motif and the banishment of Eve and Adam are frequently found in medieval Jewish and Christian illuminated manuscripts and in Persian iconography. The theme is also found in medieval morality plays and in the apocalyptic tract *Life of Adam and Eve.*

SEE ALSO Adam; Lilith.

BIBLIOGRAPHY

Ginzberg, Louis. *The Legends of the Jews* (1909–1938). 7 vols. Translated by Henrietta Szold et al. Reprint, Philadelphia, 1937–1966. See the index, s.v. *Eve.*

Mangenot, Eugène. "Eve." In *Dictionnaire de théologie catholique,* vol. 5, cols. 1640–1655. Paris, 1913.

Speiser, E. A. "Genesis." *Anchor Bible,* vol. 1. Garden City, N.Y., 1964.

MICHAEL FISHBANE (1987)

EVIL. If there is one human experience ruled by myth, it is certainly that of evil. One can understand why: the two major forms of this experience—moral evil and physical evil—both contain an enigmatic element in whose shadows the difference between them tends to vanish.

On the one hand, it is only at the conclusion of a thoroughgoing critique of mythical representations that moral evil could be conceived of as the product of a free act involving human responsibility alone. Social blame, interiorized as guilt, is in fact a response to an existential quality that was initially represented as a stain infecting the human heart as if from outside. And even when this quasi-magical representation of a contamination by an external or superior power is replaced by the feeling of a sin of which we are the authors, we can feel that we have been seduced by overwhelming powers. Moreover, each of us finds evil already present in the world; no one initiates evil but everyone has the feeling of belonging to a history of evil more ancient than any individual evil act. This strange experience of passivity, which is at the very heart of evildoing, makes us feel ourselves to be the victims in the very act that makes us guilty.

On the other hand, it is also only at the conclusion of a comparable critique of mythical representations that physical evil is recognized as the effect of natural causes of a physical, biological, and even social nature: sickness, which often takes the form of great epidemics ravaging entire populations, simultaneously attacks each person in the very depths of his existence by making him suffer and is spontaneously experienced as an aggression, at once external and internal, coming from maleficent powers that are easily confused with those that seduce the human heart and persuade it to do evil. Moreover, the sort of fate that seems to lead the sick and aging to the threshold of death tends to make mortality the very emblem of the human condition. From this, it is easy to take the next step and consider suffering and death as punishments. Do not guilt and mortality constitute the same enigma?

The persistence of mythical representations of evil can be explained by a third phenomenon, namely the extraordinary way in which guilt and suffering remain intertwined with a stage of development in which the human mind believes it has freed itself from the realm of mythical representations. To declare someone guilty is to declare that person deserving of punishment. And punishment is, in its turn, a suffering, both physical and moral, inflicted by someone other than the guilty party. Punishment, as suffering, therefore bridges the gap between the evil committed and the evil suffered. This same boundary is crossed in the other direction by the fact that a major cause of suffering lies in the violence that human beings exercise on one another. In fact, to do evil is always, directly or indirectly, to make someone else suffer. This mutual overlapping of evil done and evil suffered prevents the two major forms of evil from ever being entirely separate and, in particular, from ever being entirely stripped of their enigmatic character. An essential opaqueness in the human condition is therefore bound up with the experience of evil, which is continually carried back to its darkness, its obscurity, by the exercise of violence, always unjust, and of punishment, even when it is held to be just.

This invincible connection of moral evil and physical evil is expressed on the level of language in the specific "language game" designated by the general term *lamentation.* Lamentation, indeed, is not confined to the moanings rising up from the abyss of suffering, announcing the coming of death. It encompasses the guilty and the victims, for the guilty suffer twice over, first by blame, which states their unworthiness, and then by punishment, which holds them under the reign of violence. With lamentation, the experience of evil becomes heard. The cry becomes a voice, the voice of the undivided enigma of evil. Lamentation forms a bridge between the evil committed or suffered and the myth. And indeed it connects suffering to language only by joining a question to its moaning. "Why evil?" "Why do children die?" "Why me?" In turning itself into a question, lamentation itself appeals to myth.

MYTHS OF EVIL. How does myth reply to the enigma of evil? It provides the first explanatory schema available to humanity. Myth replies to "why?" with "because"—which claims to fulfill the request for sense that is the mediation of lamentation. We shall discuss, in conclusion, why this claim is doomed to fail. But first we must discuss the power of myth.

Before stressing the fantastic, legendary, and even delirious side of myths, three features must be noted that define myth, at least provisionally, as an appropriate response to the "why?" that rises up from lamentation. The first characteristic of myth is to state an order indivisibly uniting ethos and cosmos. By encompassing in a single configuration celestial and terrestial phenomena, inanimate and animate nature, seasons and festivals, labors and days, myth offers a privileged framework of thought within which to link together moral evil and physical evil, guilt and mortality, violence and punishment: in short, a framework that preserves, in its answer, the unity of the enigma of evil as a question.

Next, the ambivalence of the sacred, as Rudolf Otto describes it, confers upon myth the power of taking on both the dark and the luminous sides of human existence. Many myths point to a primordial sphere of existence that can be said to be beyond good and evil. Finally, myth incorporates our fragmentary experience of evil within great narratives of origin, as Mircea Eliade has stressed in his many works on this topic. By recounting how the world began, myth recounts how the human condition reached the wretched and miserable form that we know it to take. Theogony, cosmogony, and anthropogenesis therefore form a single narrative chain that scans the "great time" of origin. Order, ambivalence, and omnitemporality are thus the major features of myth, owing to which the mythical explanation can claim to provide an all-encompassing framework for evil.

This is all we can say about myth in general, however, without running the risk of applying to one precise category of myth characters belonging solely to another. This is not to imply that we must cease to speak of myth in general: the case of myths of evil is exemplary in this respect. It appears, in fact, that myth, considered as a type of discourse, draws a certain unity from the place it assumes in a hierarchy of levels of discourse that can be organized according to stages of increasing rationality. Myth constitutes in this regard the lowest level, coming before wisdom and gnosis, which leads to the threshold of the rationalizing theodicies of philosophy and theology. One must be aware, however, that the ordering principle thus alleged is the offshoot of a certain idea of reason that was, in the West, born with philosophy itself. A purely comparativist approach could never assume unreservedly this "prejudice of reason." On the other hand, if we bracket it completely—and doubtless this must be the case in a purely descriptive history of religions—then we expose ourselves to the inverse danger, which is that the universe of myths will splinter into an infinite number of parts.

It is precisely this feature that prevails in the case of myths of evil when we bracket, at least for a while, the question of the place of myth in an ordered series of levels of discourse. Order, ambivalence, and omnitemporality then appear only as inconsequential abstract and formal elements in relation to the explanatory schemas that mythical thought has produced throughout space and time. Nowhere else as much as in the area of the explanation of evil does myth reveal itself to be this vast field of experimentation, which is unfolded in the literature of the ancient Near East, India, and the Far East. In this immense laboratory everything occurs as if there were no conceivable solution that had not been tried at one point or another as a reply to the enigma of evil. It is precisely here that the myth forms the great matrix in which are rooted the sapiential, Gnostic, and properly speculative modes of the great discourse proffered by humankind in the space opened up by lamentation between the cry and utter silence. In this sense, myth remains the schema for all subsequent speculation. The question then arises whether, outside any hierarchical order of discourses, this great phantasmagoria of evil lends itself to some typology that will not do violence to its proliferating diversity.

A prudent reply is needed to this methodological question: on the one hand, myths of evil lend themselves to classification by virtue of their narrative character, mentioned above as the third general feature of the mythical universe. Narratives of origin are presented as dramas recounting how evil began; it is therefore possible to apply a structural analysis to them that reduces them to a relatively limited number of ideal types, in Max Weber's sense—that is, of paradigms constructed by comparative science midway between the clearly transcendental *a priori* and empirical proliferation. The ideal types are those of an exemplary story, organizing segments of action, characters, fortunate and unfortunate events, as in the great epics that take place in our time, after the beginning.

The proliferation of myths can thus be mastered to a relative degree by a typology of dramatic paradigms. On the other hand, individual myths contain so many inconsistent elements, which convey a desperate attempt to explain the unexplainable in order to give an account of what is inscrutable, that they prove to be in large part hostile to all classification. At the most they present "family resemblances" that cause a number of overlaps between types of myth. There is no myth that, in some way or other, does not coincide with another myth. In this way we are prevented from working out a table of the strict play of differences and combinations among myths. In *The Symbolism of Evil*, I proposed a typology limited to the ancient Near East and to archaic Greece, that is, to the cultural memory of the European. (I shall discuss below a vaster typology that will take into account Indian and Buddhist mythology.)

The ancient Near East and Archaic Greece. The restricted typology of *The Symbolism of Evil* verifies the two opposing characteristics mentioned above. On the one hand, the attempt to classify myths in terms of a limited number of paradigms is relatively successful; on the other, the overlapping that occurs shows that every paradigm implies in some aspect or another a very different paradigm.

For a static analysis of the myths of evil, the myths of the cultural sphere considered can be divided fairly easily into four great paradigms.

1. In the myths of chaos, illustrated most strikingly by the Sumerian-Akkadian theogonic myths but also by the Homeric and Hesiodic theogonies, the origin of evil that strikes humans is included within the larger narrative of the final victory of order over chaos in the common genesis of the gods, the cosmos, and humanity. The great creation epic, *Enuma elish,* makes the appearance of man the final act in a drama that begins with the generation of the gods. One can truly speak in this connection of an epical ontogenesis to describe this sort of total narrative. As regards evil in particular, it is noteworthy that chaos precedes order and that the principle of evil is coextensive here with the generation of the divine. The poem does not hesitate to characterize as evil the hates, the plotting, and the murders that mark not only the primitive struggles among the most ancient gods but also the victory of the younger gods—Marduk, for example, in the Babylonian version of the myth.

Evil therefore precedes humankind, who finds it already present and merely continues it. Evil, in other words, belongs to the very origin of all things; it is what has been overcome in setting up the world as it now is, but it, too, contributed to this state of affairs. This is why order is precarious and its genesis must continually be reenacted by cultic rites. If, in this family of myths, the fall is mentioned, it is never in the sense of the unprecedented emergence of an evil that would be simply "human, all too human," but as an episode in the drama of creation. In the same way, the failure of the quest for immortality, recounted in the famous *Epic of Gilgamesh,* is tied up with the jealousy of the gods, who trace out the boundary between the sphere of mortals and that of immortals by an act of violence placed beyond good and evil.

2. An evil god and a tragic vision of existence are depicted in the second paradigm of evil in European culture. Here, evil is in a way shared by humankind and gods. It calls, on the one hand, for a figure with the stature of a hero, possessing higher qualities than ordinary men but who commits a grave error, which can be said to be neither the effect of mere ignorance, in the Socratic sense, nor the result of a deliberately bad choice, in the Hebraic sense. Moreover, the overwhelming error that precipitates his fall is deplored by the tragic chorus and by the hero himself as a blindness that has crept over him as a result of the jealousy of the gods; thus the hubris of the tragic hero is at once the cause and the effect of the wickedness belonging to the plane of the divinities. Aeschylus's *Prometheus Bound* is the frightening document of this tragic theology and this tragic anthropology in which the hero in a sense cooperates in a loss, the origin of which is superhuman. It is important to note that the tragic myth produced a spectacle, rather than a speculation, a spectacle that makes the spectators participate in the tragic drama through the catharsis of the emotions of terror and pity.

3. The third type is illustrated by Archaic Orphic myths, which are continued in Platonism and Neoplatonism. This can be termed the myth of the exiled soul, imprisoned in a foreign body. It assumes a radical distinction between a soul, akin to the gods, and a body, perceived as a prison or a tomb. Life itself appears as a punishment, possibly for some fault committed in a previous life. Evil is therefore identified with incarnation itself and even, in certain Far Eastern mythologies, with reincarnation. The model of the body-as-prison, extended by that of the repetition of reincarnations, is further darkened by the model of infernal punishment, as if life in the body were the image of hell. Life is then a death, which calls for a death that will be true life. Only through purification, at once ethical, ritual, and meditative, can the soul be delivered from this quagmire of bodily existence, which itself mirrors hell. In a sense, this myth alone can properly be termed a myth of the fall, for the incarnation itself marks the loss of an infinitely superior condition and so a loss of height, of altitude, which is precisely what the word *fall* signifies.

4. Compared with these three paradigms, the biblical myth of paradise lost differs in three ways. First, the Adamic myth is purely anthropological, excluding any drama of creation in which evil would originally be included: creation is good, very good; humankind alone initiates evil, although tempted, to be sure, by the serpent (an important feature discussed below); but the serpent too is a creature. Next, evil is clearly ethical, in the sense that it results from an act of disobedience. It therefore cannot be a matter of hubris, which like disobedience would represent a blindness sent down by jealous gods, although "Second Isaiah" does not hesitate, after the difficulties of exile, to make his confession in the form of God's own self-presentation, as in prophesy: "I form light and create darkness, I make weal and create war, I am the Lord, who does all these things" (*Is.* 45:7). Finally, evil is not the result of the fall of the soul into a body; it consists of a gap, a deviation of humankind as a whole, of the flesh, which is unaware of the body-soul dualism.

The Adamic myth is therefore anthropological in the strongest sense of the term, to the extent that Adam is Man, neither a Titan nor a captive soul but the ancestor of all humankind, of the same nature as all the generations springing from him. If the Adamic myth nevertheless deserves the title of myth, this is inasmuch as the narrative in which it consists is incommensurate to the historical time in which the exemplary adventure of the people of Israel takes place. The myth elevates to the level of exemplary and universal history the penitential experience of one particular people, the Jewish people. All the later speculations about the supernatural perfection of Adam before the Fall are adventitious interpretations that profoundly alter the original meaning; they tend to make Adam a superior being and so foreign to our own condition. Hence the confusion over the idea of the Fall.

The intention of the Adamic myth is to separate the origin of evil from that of good, in other words, to posit a radical origin of evil distinct from the more primordial origin of the goodness of all created things; humanity commences evil but does not commence creation. However, it is in the form of a story that the myth accounts for this catastrophe at the heart of the goodness of creation; the passage from innocence to sin is narrated as something that took place. That is why the explanation given here of the origin of evil is not yet elevated to the plane of speculation, as will later happen with the dogma of original sin, but remains an etiological myth involving legendary characters and fabulous events.

With respect to its structure, the myth takes on the form of a twofold conflict: on the one hand, that between the central figure, Adam, and the Adversary, represented by the serpent, who will later become the Devil, and on the other hand, that between the two halves of a split figure, Adam and Eve. From this complex configuration the Adamic myth receives an enigmatic depth, the second pair adding a subtle psychological dimension and an internal density that would not have been attained by the confrontation between Man and his Other alone. In this way the myth universalizes the penitential experience of the Jewish people, but the concrete universal that it forges remains caught up in the gangue of the narrative and the symbolic.

The protohistorical myth is the only vehicle for a speculation akin to sapiential literature. In order to state the discordance between a creation that is fundamentally good and a historical condition that is already bad, the myth has no other resources than to concentrate the origin of evil in a single instant, in a leap, even if it stretches out this instant in a drama that takes time, introduces a series of events, and involves several characters. In this way the myth reflects in its very structure, in which the concentrated instant and the extended drama confront one another, the structure of the phenomenon of evil as such, which at one and the same time commences with each evil act and continues an immemorial tradition.

The etiological character of the myth is further reinforced by the narrative of the maledictions that ensue, following the initial act of disobedience: every human dimension—language, work, institutions, sexuality—is stamped with the twofold mark of being destined for the good and inclined toward evil. The power of naming all beings is so deeply perverted that we no longer recognize it except in reference to the division of speech into different tongues. Work ceases to be a sort of peaceful gardening and becomes hard labor that places man in a hostile relation to nature. The nakedness of innocence is replaced by the shame that casts the shadow of concealment over all aspects of communication. The pain of childbirth tarnishes the joy of procreation; death itself is afflicted by the malediction of the awareness of its immanence. In short, what the myth recounts is how it happened that human beings are obliged to suffer the rule of hardship as we know it in our present condition. The myth's "method" is always the same: stretching out in the time of a narrated drama the paradoxical—because simultaneous—aspects of the present human condition.

This is the restricted typology that we can construct in the limited sphere of the archaic state of the European. Before attempting to move into other cultural spheres, it is important to do justice to the contrary aspect stressed above concerning the level of the typology of myths of evil: the paradigms, we said, are not simply distinct from one another in the sense of Weberian ideal types but they overlap with one another to such an extent that we can discover in each one some aspect that lends it a family resemblance to the others. The danger of the structural approach we have followed up to now lies in giving an exaggerated cohesiveness to narratives of origin that also possess a composite, paradoxical, even extravagant character, well suited to the heuristic function of myth, when myth is considered as a thought experiment that unfolds in the region of the collective imagination. This is why the static analysis of myths, governed by the search for and the description of ideal types, must be completed by the addition of a dynamic approach to myths, attentive to the internal discordances that make them overlap in places and in this way outline a vast narrative and symbolic cycle.

If we take the Adamic myth as a point of reference, we find in it the muted echo of all the others and vice versa. We can therefore speak of a tragic aspect in the Adamic myth, expressed in the deep and shadowy psychology of temptation. There is a sort of fatalistic side of the ethical confession of sins. But there is also an irreducible remainder of the theogonic combat, which can be seen in the figure of the serpent and in other biblical figures related to the primordial chaos. What is more, the essentially ethical affirmation of God's saintliness can never entirely rid us of the suspicion that God is somehow beyond good and evil and that for this very reason he sends evil as well as good.

This is why later speculation will continually return to what is at once an unthinkable and an invincible possibility, namely that the deity has a dark and terrible side, in which something of the tragic vision and also something of the myth of chaos is preserved and even reaffirmed. If this admission shows itself to be so persistent it is precisely because the human experience of evil itself contains the admission that, in positing the existence of evil, humankind discovers the other side of evil, namely that it has always existed, in a paradoxical exteriority that, as stated above, relates sin to suffering within the undivided mystery of iniquity. The acknowledgment of a nonhuman source of evil is what continually gives new life to theogony and to tragedy alongside an ethical vision of the world.

The same thing should be said with respect to the typological distance between the Adamic myth and the myth of the exiled soul. It is not by sheer chance that, under the influence of Platonism and of Neoplatonism, the Adamic myth has almost fused with the myth of the Fall. There was most likely in the original myth a tendency that led it to confuse the quasi-external character of evil as already present with the body, understood as the sole root of evil. In the same way, the Babylonian exile provided the model of banishment, which continues with that of the expulsion from the garden of paradise. The symbols of captivity and of exodus that underlie the Adamic myth thus lend themselves to contamination by the symbolism, coming from another source, of a fallen "soul." Elevating the figure of Adam above the condition of ordinary mortals doubtless facilitated the reinterpretation of the myth of disobedience in terms of a myth of the Fall: when Adam is represented as a sort of superman endowed with all knowledge, beatitude, and immortality, his degradation could be represented in no other way than as a fall.

This play of overlappings could be considered from the perspective of each of the four myths that structure the symbolic imagination in the Western world: there is no myth of chaos that, at one moment or another, does not include the confession of sins by a repentant sinner; there is no tragic myth that does not admit the deep fault tied to a hubris for which humankind recognizes itself to be guilty. And would the fall of the soul be such a misfortune if humankind did not contribute to it at least through consent?

Hindu and Buddhist mythologies. The division into four great paradigms that we apply to the vast—although restricted—domain of Semitic archaism and Hellenic archaism, which, together, structure the cultural memory of the West, itself constitutes only a restricted typology. What happens when Westerners attempt to extend their vision to a wider field? Does the typology offer the same features of relative order and of multiple overlappings when we try to pass from the restricted form to a generalized form? For anyone who undertakes the perilous task of incorporating into his or her own vision the universes of thought that entertain complex relations of distance and proximity with one's own cultural memory, two warnings should be taken into consideration: first, it is senseless to seek to be exhaustive; there is no Archimedes point from which one could attempt to raise the totality of mythical universes. We must always confine ourselves to limited incursions into the regions that we intuitively suspect will contain treasures likely to enrich our cultural memory, and from this results the unavoidably selective nature of the itinerary of these incursions.

Second, we must give up the hope of any simple taxonomy, such as a distribution into monisms, dualisms, and mixed forms of these. These distinctions are practically useless on the mythical level itself, assuming they have a less debatable validity on the level of more speculative discourse. The two examples we have chosen, Hindu mythology and Buddhist mythology, taking into account the first warning, also raise issues related to the second warning: Hindu mythology perhaps more than Buddhist mythology confronts us with a profusion of explanatory frameworks requiring a taxonomical refinement that challenges any classificatory principle. Buddhist mythology, perhaps more than Hindu mythology, shows us how the same "solution" can oscillate among several planes of expression, from the level of legend and folklore to that of a metaphysical speculation. This profusion and this variation of levels constitute fearsome challenges for any attempt at typology.

If we admit that theodicy is not restricted to monotheism but forms the touchstone of all religions, when the existential need to explain suffering and moral evil is brought to the level of language, then we can seek and find theodicies in all of them. If, moreover, we admit that Vedantic Hinduism, in which the problem of evil is dismissed rather than resolved by a refined speculation on the relation between suffering and ignorance, is not the same as all systems placed under the vast heading of Hinduism, we can, following Wendy Doniger O'Flaherty in *The Origins of Evil in Hindu Mythology* (Berkeley, 1976), class the expression of theodicies on the clearly mythological level as Puranic Hinduism. These figurative and narrative theodicies lend themselves to a certain classification of different conceptual attitudes toward evil, a classification that struggles with the proliferation of myths to the point of succumbing under their weight.

O'Flaherty, our guide through this labyrinth, observes that four characters can assume the role of the villain in the drama: mortals, fate, demons, and gods. The first type of myth, which recalls the Adamic myth, seems surprising if one considers the doctrine of *karman*, according to which our present experience is the direct result of the good or bad actions of previous existences to be the Indian solution to the problem of evil. Neither gods nor demons are then to blame, and even blame itself is obliterated by the recognition of an eternal cycle in which everything is justified and finds its recompense. The paradox lies in the fact that the feeling generated by rumination on past faults opens the way for all sorts of speculation on the moral responsibility of humankind for the origin of evil, nuanced by the attitude that human beings are always as much victim as guilty party (as we see in the myths of the loss of a golden age).

After all, the very doctrine of *karman* posits that the links in the endless chain of evil are our desires and our sins; Buddhism takes this as its starting point. The paradox, however, is reversed when a primordial fall is evoked; then it is fate rather than humankind that is to blame. This forms a second cycle of myths, where we see God or a god create evil as a positive element in the universe, whether he acts as a willing or unwilling instrument of fate or whether he himself decides that evil must come to be. Logical thought tends to see a contradiction here between being constrained or deciding freely to create an ambivalent universe; Hindu thought, however, moves effortlessly between what ultimately appears to be two variants of a *dharma* that abolishes the distinction between what is and what ought to be.

The opposite is no less true: it is because a doctrine like that of *karman* proves to be emotionally unsatisfactory in certain ways while remaining valid in the eyes of the wise that mythology continually reworks the variants, producing new divergences. It is then not surprising that mythical speculation turns toward gods and demons. Myths placing guilt on the shoulders of gods or demons proliferate, all the more so as ethical and cosmic dualism, illustrated in its purest and most coherent form by Manichaeism, was never victorious in India: the ambiguous nature of the demons, and even of the gods, served to thwart this clear and radical distinction. India prefered to struggle with the paradox of superhuman entities, which are almost all of the same nature and which are distinguished and opposed to another only by their combat. Those who always win are gods, but because their adversaries are never really eliminated, the kinship of the gods and the demons always resurfaces.

Here the guide we have chosen to follow remarks with irony that as a consequence of these reversals the gods reputed to be good are more wicked than we might expect and that the demons reputed to be evil prove to be good demons. This gives rise to a reflection on the demonic as such, in which power overrides benevolence, thus verifying the extent to which myths operate as depth probes sounding the ambivalence of the human condition itself, while on the surface they seem to operate as explanations. By recounting our origins, where we come from, myths describe in a symbolic way what we are: the paradox of the good demon and that of the evil god are not merely playful fantasies but the privileged means of unraveling the tangled skein of passions belonging to the human heart. When the myth tells, for example, how the gods corrupted the demons, something is said about the hidden perversity of the "higher" part of ourselves. When the myth recounts the birth of death, it touches the secret thread of our fright in the face of death, a fright that in fact closely links together evil and death and confronts death as a personified demon.

The fact that myths are indifferent to logical coherence is attested to by another cycle of myths, characteristic of *bhakti* spirituality, where we see a god create evil (for example, a fallacious heresy) for the good of humanity, a lesser malediction freeing a graver one. The cycle is then complete: submitted to this stringent economy, humankind is carried back to the problem of its own evil, as in the theory of *karman.* This cycle, however, is considerably vaster than that of the restricted typology with which we began. It is also more loosely knit. And it is truly in the mythic theodicies of India that we see verified the notion suggested at the beginning of this article, namely that the mythical world is an immense laboratory in which all imaginable solutions are tried.

This acceptance of multiplicity by the same culture confirms one of the conclusions arrived at by our restricted typology (restricted to the archaic Semitic and Greek worlds)—namely, that in every myth, owing to its own incoherence, we discover a sketch in miniature that another myth will develop on a much larger scale. The feature that has not received sufficient attention, however, has to do with the difference in level that allows us to go beyond a lower truth (for example, the struggle between gods and demons or the corruption of demons and mortals by the gods) by means of a higher truth (for example, *karman*), which, far from eliminating the prior truth, confirms it in its subordinate place. This is what Buddhism forcefully demonstrates.

Buddhism poses a singular problem for any careful investigation, not only with respect to the multitude of mythical figures of evil, but also to the oscillation between different levels of discourse. On the one hand, indeed, no religion has gone so far toward a speculation stripped of any narrative or figurative element on behalf of a doctrine of inner illumination. On the other hand, Buddhism seldom appears in a form completely cut off from popular beliefs and from their characteristic demonology, especially in the cultural universes previously shaped by Hinduism. What is more, Buddhism has generated within its own midst, if not a new demonology, at least a mythical figure of evil, Māra, somewhat comparable to Satan in late Judaism and in early Christianity. Buddhism reinforces in this respect the hypothesis according to which one can speak of the origin of evil only by way of myths. At the same time it appears to constitute a counterexample to this hypothesis, because mythology seems at first to be so incompatible with the purified form of spirituality characteristic of Buddhism. It is, to be sure, in the Pali canon and not in the Mahāyāna documents that T. O. Ling, in his *Buddhism and the Mythology of Evil* (London, 1962), finds the most striking illustration of this phenomenon, which at first sight seems paradoxical.

To begin with, one must admit that a wide gap exists between pure Buddhist doctrine and popular mythologies concerning the origin of evil. The latter are characterized basically by the radically external nature they attribute to demonic powers, represented as threatening, terrifying, devouring creatures. In addition, as is not the case in Iranian dualism, these demons form a swarm in which it is difficult to distinguish the forces of evil from the forces of good. Finally, the principal resource of humans in defending themselves against these external forces is an action itself turned toward the outside, whether this is a propitiatory sacrifice, an invocation addressed to higher powers or the manipulation of hostile forces through magical actions, or even the constraint that is supposed to be exerted on the gods by self-mortification.

On the other hand, if, following T. R. V. Murti in *The Central Philosophy of Buddhism* (London, 1955), we take as our criterion for Buddhism the "philosophical" section of the canon, that is the Abhidhamma Pitaka and, more precisely, Buddhaghosa's *Visuddhimagga* (Path of Purification), which in the Theravāda school is at once its conclusion and compendium, then we are correct in speaking of a Buddhism without mythology, as Ling does. The thinking behind this radical position is easy to understand. In the first place, the doctrine is entirely directed toward the purely mental conditions of the evils of existence. These conditions are analyzed, catalogued, and hierarchized with the most extraordinary care; they are also submitted to an exploration of the "dependent origination" of the lines of interdependence, which allows the sources of evil to be tracked down in their deepest hiding places. What the analysis exposes are not external forces but, basically, ignorance, which itself results from false views of the world, generated in their turn by an overestimation of the self. Popular demonologies are precisely the crudest sort of expression of these false points of view.

The second reason for incompatibility with mythology is that the analysis itself, in certain schools, is confined to scholasticism, due to the subtlety of its distinctions and derivations, and is placed in the service of a wisdom aimed at establishing a state of emptiness, a void. This state is entirely separate from the familiar realities of everyday existence and wholly unrelated to the fantastic creatures produced by desire and, even more so, by fear. Demons vanish along with all external reality as a result of the purifying meditation that deserves the name of enlightenment.

And yet, it is not simply a matter of making concessions to popular beliefs if the Pali canon assigns a place in its teachings to the Evil One and gives him the name of Māra. This entity can be termed mythical due to his resemblance to the demons of popular belief and, more precisely, due to his personification of original evil. Ling confirms here the earlier analysis of Ernst W. Windisch in *Māra und Buddha* (Leipzig, 1895). According to both of them, this figure is finally not foreign to the central core of Buddhism to the extent that it is part of the very experience of the Buddha's enlightenment, as a force that threatens, attacks, and seeks to distract the individual from contemplation—a force that the wise person must address, confront, and finally conquer.

Specialists in this field argue whether this confrontation with the threat of distraction is characteristic only of the first stage in the spiritual adventure or whether it is present up to the end; they argue whether the proliferation of legends that attribute to this figure of evil the status of a demon result from subsequent contamination by the surrounding demonologies or whether they develop a mythical core inherent in the pure doctrine. The essential point is that the figure of Māra in its barest signification is the product of Buddhism. Ignorance driven out by knowledge; shadows dissipated by that enlightenment, are experienced as an inner adversity that is spontaneously personified in the figure of an adversary. As is not the case in popular demonology, however, Māra is personified by a single figure, symbolizing the internal enemy, namely the adversary of meditation.

If Buddhism seems to confirm in such a paradoxical fashion the thesis that one can speak only in mythical terms of the origin of evil, this is because the source of evil, however much it may be interiorized, retains a certain hostile nature that calls for a figurative approximation in terms of externality. Expressed in external terms, the myth gives a symbolic expression to the interior experience of evil.

BEYOND MYTH? Myth, however, is not alone in using language to deal with the enigma of evil. I mentioned above that there exists a hierarchy of different levels of discourse within which myth takes its place. We can go beyond myth in two directions, that of theodicy and that of wisdom. These two paths often intersect but they conform to two distinct series of requirements.

The path of theodicy. Theodicy replies to a demand for rational coherence. This requirement stems from lamentation itself, inasmuch as it carries within it an interrogation: "Why? Why must my child die? Why must there be suffering and death? How long, O Lord?" But it also stems from myth itself, inasmuch as it brings the reply of a vaster and more ancient order than the miserable condition of humankind. This reply, however, suffers at once from an excess and from a defect: an excess resulting from a proliferation that staggers the imagination (the mythical world, Lévi-Strauss observes, is a world that is too full); its defect is due to the mutual incompatibility of myths, to their internal contradictions, and, finally, to their narrative form itself: to tell a story is not to explain. Rationalization has taken a number of different forms: in India, this involves the grand speculations on *karman,* on the degrees of being, on the order of things placed beyond good and evil. In Buddhism, this concerns speculation on the tie between ignorance and suffering and, above all, on the tie between wisdom, which I shall discuss below, and suffering. In Greece, myth was surpassed by philosophy, which essentially separates the question of origin in the sense of foundation from the question of the beginning in the sense of theogonies and genealogies. By virtue of this fundamental clarification, Plato prefers to say that God is the cause of good alone rather than to say, along with myth, that the gods are bad or that they are beyond good and evil.

In the Christian sphere, rationalization takes place within theology, mainly at the time of the confrontation with gnosis, which is still no more than a rationalized myth, and in connection with an overall hellenization of speculation. In this regard, the doctrine of original sin in Augustine offers at once the features of an antignosis as a result of what its conceptual framework borrows from Neoplatonism (being, nothingness, substance, etc.) and the features of a quasi gnosis, and hence of a rationalized myth, due to the way it mixes together the legal model of individual guilt and a biological model of contamination at birth and of hereditary transmission. This is why such rationalization was continued beyond this quasi gnosis in onto-theologies to which we owe the theodicies as such, in Leibniz and, finally, in Hegel. To these theodicies we owe, if not a solution to the enigma of evil, at least the transformation of the enigma into a problem, namely whether or not we can maintain the following three propositions at once: God is all-powerful. God is absolutely good. Evil exists. This is not the place, however, to weigh the success or failure of rational theodicies.

The path of Wisdom. Assuming that a coherent reply could be given to the enigma that has been raised in this way to the level of a rational problem, there could still be no exclusive means for explaining it. The question of evil, indeed, is not simply "Why does evil exist?" but also "Why is evil greater than humans can bear?" and, along with this, "Why this particular evil? Why must my child die? Why me?" The question is also posed, then, to wisdom.

It is Wisdom's task first to develop an argument on the basis of this personal and intimate question that myth does not treat, since it invokes an order that does not concern individual suffering. Wisdom thus forces myth to shift levels. It must not simply tell of the origin in such a way as to explain how the human condition reached its present miserable state; it must also justify the distribution of good and evil to every individual. Myth recounts a story, Wisdom argues. It is in this sense that we see the *Book of Job* question explanation in terms of retribution in the name of the just man who suffers. If the *Book of Job* occupies a primary place in world literature, it does so first because it is a classic of Wisdom's argumentative mode. But it is so because of the enigmatic and even perhaps deliberately ambiguous character of its conclusion. The final theophany gives no direct reply to Job's personal suffering, and speculation must be made in more than one direction. The vision of a creator whose designs are unfathomable may suggest either consolation that has to be deferred until the eschaton, or that Job's complaint is displaced, even set aside, in the eyes of God, the master of good and evil, or that perhaps the complaint has to stand one of the purificatory tests to which Wisdom, itself grafted on a certain *docta ignorantia,* must submit so that Job can love God "for nought" in response to Satan's wager at the beginning of the tale.

This final suggestion reveals the second function of Wisdom, which is no longer to develop arguments or even to accuse God but to transform, practically and emotionally, the nature of the desire that is at the base of the request for explanation. To transform desire practically means to leave behind the question of origins, toward which myth stubbornly carries speculative thought, and to substitute for it the question of the future and the end of evil. For practice, evil is simply what should not but does exist, hence what must be combated. This practical attitude concerns principally that immense share of suffering resulting from violence, that is, from the evil that humans inflict on their fellows. To transform desire emotionally is to give up any consolation, at least for oneself, by giving up the complaint itself. It is perhaps at this point that Job's wisdom coincides with that of Buddhism. Whatever can be said of this meeting of two such remote traditions of wisdom, it is only at this point that myth can be surpassed. But it is not easy to give up the question "why?" to which myth attempts—and fails—to reply.

SEE ALSO Chaos; Devils; Fall, The; Myth; Sin and Guilt; Suffering; Theodicy; Wisdom.

BIBLIOGRAPHY

Davis, Stephen T., ed. *Encountering Evil; Live Options in Theodicy.* Edinburgh, 1981.

Ling, T. O. *Buddhism and the Mythology of Evil.* London, 1962.

Murti, T. R. V. *The Central Philosophy of Buddhism.* 2d ed. London, 1955.

O'Flaherty, Wendy Doniger. *The Origins of Evil in Hindu Mythology.* Berkeley, 1976.

Ricoeur, Paul. *The Symbolism of Evil.* Boston, 1967.

Windisch, Ernst W. *Māra und Buddha.* Leipzig, 1895.

New Sources

Adams, Marilyn McCord. *Horrendous Evils and the Goodness of God.* Ithaca, N. Y., 1999.

Adams, Marilyn McCord, and Robert Merrihew Adams, ed. *The Problem of Evil.* New York, 1990.

Card, Claudia. *The Atrocity Paradigm.* New York, 2002.

Copjec, Joan, ed. *Radical Evil.* New York, 1996.

Geddis, Jennifer. *Evil after Postmodernism: Histories, Narratives, and Ethics.* New York, 2001.

Lara, Maria Pia. *Rethinking Evil: Contemporary Perspectives.* Berkeley, 2001.

Matthewes, Charles T. *Evil and the Augustinian Tradition.* New York, 2001.

Morrow, Lance. *Evil: An Investigation.* New York, 2003.

Rorty, Amélie Oksenberg. *The Many Faces of Evil: Historical Perspectives.* New York, 2001.

Swinburne, Ricjard. *Providence and the Problem of Evil.* New York, 1998.

PAUL RICOEUR **(1987)**
Revised Bibliography

EVOLA, JULIUS. Giulio Cesare Andrea Evola (Julius; 1898–1974) was a cultural, religious-historical, philosophical, esoteric, and political author. Evola was born in Rome, most likely to Sicilian aristocracy, and was raised Catholic. He came under the early spiritual influence of Arthur Rimbaud (1854–1891), Friedrich Nietzsche (1844–1900), Carlo Michelstaedter (1887–1910), and Otto Weininger (1880–1903). After returning from service in Word War I, Evola experienced an existential crisis, which almost ended in suicide. According to his own statement, he was rescued by a sentence from the Buddhist Pali canon. Psychological experiments under the influence of ether led Evola to a transcendental experience of his self (Ego), which transformed him completely. He experienced his self as all-comprising and identical with the highest spiritual power in the universe. During this time he became friends with the futurist Giovanni Papini (1881–1956), who interested Evola in the Eastern wisdom teachings and the mystic Meister Eckhart (c. 1260–1328), whose extreme clarity always remained a model for Evola. Evola was also well acquainted with the futurist theorist and author Filippo Tommaso Marinetti (1876–1944), who might even have introduced him to Benito Mussolini.

Soon, however, Evola turned towards Dadaism and became friends with its main proponent, Tristan Tzara (1896–1963). Due to the quality of his paintings, poetry, and writings on the theory of modern art, Evola is considered the main representative of Italian Dadaism. He saw art as flowing from a "higher consciousness." All of Evola's work is incidentally characterized by his effort to elevate mere human existence to a supramundane level and to concentrate on transcendental principles. This concentration is marked, however, by a militantly active aspect, which drove the contemplative into the background.

In 1922 Evola abandoned his artistic activities, and in the same year, when he was just twenty-four, he completed a translation of the *Dao de jing,* influenced by idealist philosophy; he completely revised this translation in 1959. Evola dedicated himself subsequently to the construction of his own philosophical system, which he called "magical idealism," after Novalis (Friedrich von Hardenberg, 1772–1801). Based upon German idealism (mainly Friedrich Schelling, J. G. Fichte, and Novalis) and complemented by his own transcendent "ego experiences," as well as teachings from the Far East, Evola eventually formulated the notion of an "absolute self," related to the idea of the Hindu *ātman.* He postulated the "absolute self" as being free from all spiritual or material constraints, wherein freedom, power, and realization form a unity.

In 1926 Evola abandoned his extensive philosophical studies because he was searching for an actual breakthrough to transcendent "initiatic" levels. He had already formed close contacts with Ultra, an independent theosophical group in Rome, through which he got to know the most important Italian scholar of Asian religions, Giuseppe Tucci (1894–1984). He also came into contact with Tantrism, which he studied intensively, drawn by its practical emphasis and promise of direct transcendental experiences. Evola soon entered into correspondence with John Woodroffe (Arthur Avalon; 1865–1936), who had brought Kuṇḍalinī Yoga and Tantrism to the West. Evola's *L'Uomo come Potenza* (Man as power, 1925) followed. Although still having a strong Western philosophical tendency, this work was based on Woodroffe's research and translations from Sanskrit sources, and it thus became the first work to make Tantrism known in Italy.

At that time, through René Guénon (1886–1951), Evola received his first exposure to Integral Tradition, according to which all fundamental religions and cultures are said to arise out of a primordial tradition of transcendent origin. From 1927 to 1929, he led the magical-initiatory Group of Ur, in which both esotericists and representatives of general Italian spiritual life, including Emilio Servadio (1904–1995), the "father of Italian psychoanalysis," participated anonymously. The goal was complete human self-transformation and integration into transcendental regions by way of an experimental path, which Evola called *initiation*; the Daoist *wei wu wei* (nonintentional doing) was a precondition for effective magical actions. The group's magazine published, besides its own reports, first Italian translations of the ancient Mithraic *Apathanathismos*, as well as excerpts from Avalon's texts, the Buddhist Pali canon, the biography of the Tibetan Mi la ras pa, the Chinese *Tract of the Golden Flower*, and an article by the French Orientalist Paul Masson-Oursel (1882–1956). After the Group of Ur disbanded, Evola founded the political and literary journal *La Torre*, which published, among others, an article by Paul Tillich (1886–1965) about the demonic and several excerpts from writings by Johann Jakob Bachofen (1815–1887). However, because of its uncompromising positions, *La Torre* had to cease publication at the behest of Mussolini after only ten issues.

Evola's acquaintance with the then most important Italian philosophers, Benedetto Croce (1866–1952) and Giovanni Gentile (1875–1944), led to a collaboration on the *Enciclopedia Italiana.* In the 1930s Evola busied himself intensely with alchemy, a critical analysis of the then prevailing esoteric groups, and the myth of the Holy Grail. His underlying traditional philosophy did not see historical-cultural development as advancement, but rather as decay, a view that reflected Indian and ancient teachings on the cosmic cycles, at the "gloomy" end of which, known as the *kaliyuga*, people live today.

At the same time, Evola traveled throughout Europe to meet with representatives of political views that corresponded to his own sacral-holistic, antiliberalist, and antidemocratic ideas, including the revolutionary conservative Edgar Julius Jung (1894–1934), who was later murdered by the Nazis, the Catholic monarchist Karl Anton Prinz Rohan (1898–1975), and the founder of Romania's Iron Guard, Corneliu Codreanu (1899–1938). During his visit to Romania in 1937, Evola met Mircea Eliade (1907–1986), who belonged to the Iron Guard. Evola and Eliade had corresponded since the second half of the 1920s, but only several of Evola's and none of Eliade's letters have survived because Evola destroyed letters he received after answering them. Evola wrote five contributions for the German cultural journal *Antaios*, published by Ernst Jünger (1895–1998) and Eliade between 1960 and 1970. Evola's influence on Eliade is undeniable, even if Eliade cannot be regarded as belonging to the Integral Tradition school of thought. The parallels to Evola are particularly evident in Eliade's early alchemic works. After World War II, Evola introduced Eliade to Italian publishers and translated some of his works. Evola was also acquainted with Angelo Brelich (1913–1977), who published two articles (one about Jupiter and the Roman idea of state) in 1937 and 1940 in *Diorama Filosofico*, Evola's cultural supplement to the *Regime Fascista* magazine. The article on Jupiter and Rome testifies to Evola's great interest in Roman religion, which formed the spiritual foundation of the *Imperium Romanum*, which Evola hoped to see reestablished. Letters from Evola preserved in the archives of the great historian of religion Raffaele Pettazzoni (1883–1959) and the mythologist Karl Kerényi (1897–1973) show that he was also in contact with them.

Before and during World War II, Evola concentrated intensely on Buddhism, which he described as a path to spiritual freedom that maintained its validity even in modern times. Evola almost exclusively referred to the Pali canon, and he pointed out that the historical Buddha was a member of the warrior caste. Evola rejected the widespread teaching of modern Mahāyāna Buddhism, which sets peacefulness and universal love in the foreground, instead of clear initiatory knowledge through asceticism and exercise. Nevertheless, Anagarika Govinda (1898–1985), who was the first Westerner to receive the title of lama, praised Evola's work.

In 1940 Evola wrote an article for the magazine *Asiatica*, published by Tucci. This work was later continued in the subsequent renowned journal *East and West*, which Tucci also managed. Another well-known Orientalist with whom

Evola had been closely connected since his youth was Pio Filippani-Ronconi (b. 1920) who taught at the University of Naples. A close friendship on the basis of common esoteric interests connected Evola with the Egyptologist Boris de Rachewiltz (1926–1997). He was also well acquainted with the historian and researcher of ancient Roman religion, Franz Altheim (1898–1976).

Evola's ambivalent attitude towards fascism, which he hoped would lead Italy back to a heathen-sacral *Imperium Romanum*, but which lacked any transcendent basis, led him closer to National Socialism, and in particular to the *Schutzstaffeln* (SS), which he considered a fighting spiritual order, at least in the beginning. However, by 1938 he was denounced as a "reactionary Roman and visionary" in an SS document, which led to an order that Evola's behavior was to be observed. Starting in the mid-1930s, Evola was heavily involved with questions of race, and he hoped that official recognition and influence would result from this work. After all, Mussolini had expressed positive thoughts about Evola's theses of "spiritual" racism, with which he wanted to oppose the "material-biologic" racism of Hitler's Germany. When American troops marched into Rome in 1944, Evola fled to Vienna, where he suffered a severe spinal injury in a bomb attack in 1945. He was confined to a wheelchair for the rest of his life.

After spending three years in hospitals and sanatoriums, Evola returned to Rome in 1948. In 1951 he was accused of being a "spiritual instigator" of secret neo-fascist terror groups and arrested. Following six months of investigative lockup, he was acquitted. Evola's political tendencies changed thereafter more and more into what he called "apolitia," by which he meant a firm spiritual-political position far above daily politics. He also became more heavily involved with Zen Buddhism, which he made widely known in Italy, especially after he began publishing other Zen Buddhist authors. In his last years of life he translated the first volume of *Essays in Zen Buddhism* by D.T. Suzuki, for which he also wrote the introduction. The other two volumes of these *Essays* appeared later on in the book series *Orizzonti dello spirito*, which Evola had founded and for which he selected works from Avalon, Eliade, Tucci, Scholem, and Lu K'uan Yu, among others.

Evola's efforts in popularizing Asian religions helped improve the European image of Asia at a time when a positive view of Asia was not customary. However, his quest was not scientific, although he remained as true to original sources as was possible at the time. For him, as in the case of his esoteric writings, his work in comparative religion was more about revealing paths that could extract modern humans from rampant materialism and lead them to spiritual freedom. Therefore, Evola's religious-historical works examine only selected aspects corresponding to this quest, and they are unsuitable as surveys. This can be seen most clearly in Evola's handling of Hinduism, where he highlighted only the warrior and ascetic aspects of the *Bhagavadgītā*. The same is true for Islam. Despite this intentional one-sidedness, his books are still appreciated in Orientalist circles, and such experts as Jean Varenne, Filippani-Ronconi, or Silvio Vietta have written forewords to new editions of his works. Academic circles have become increasingly interested in Evola, as evidenced by the numerous books, essays, conference proceedings, and dissertations written about him, and the many translations of his writings.

Although he was never a party member, Evola's involvement with fascism, National Socialism, and racism continues to make him an extremely controversial figure. Controversy has also resulted from the numerous anti-Semitic comments that he made, mainly in the fascist daily press, and from the introduction he wrote in 1937 for the Italian version of the forged *Protocols of the Elders of Zion*. Evola saw in Judaism the modern materialist and economic dominance that he fought against, although he highly valued Orthodox and qabbalistic Judaism.

Evola passed away in 1974. He had expressly refused a Catholic burial, and his ashes were scattered in a crevasse of Monte Rosa.

Bibliography

Evola's writings comprise more than twenty books, approximately one hundred important essays, and some one thousand newspaper and journal articles, of which practically all have been published in various volumes and collected works. Evola was also an extraordinarily industrious translator. The most readily available bibliography, although not the most recent, is Renato del Ponte, "Julius Evola: Una bibliografia 1920–1994," in *Futuro Presente* 6 (1995): 28–70. The definitive editions of Evola's books are published by Gianfranco de Turris, the head of the Fondazione Julius Evola in Rome, in the Opere di Julius Evola series with Edizioni Mediterranee in Rome. His religious-historical works include *La Tradizione Ermetica: Nei suoi Simboli, nella sua Dottrina e nella sua "Arte Regia"* (Bari, Italy, 1931), which describes alchemy as a spiritual discipline on the basis of numerous original sources; this book was used and valued by C. G. Jung, and it was translated by E. E. Rehmus as *The Hermetic Tradition: Symbols and Teachings of the Royal Art* (Rochester, Vt., 1995). *Rivolta contro il mondo moderno* (Milan, 1934), which is considered Evola's main work, gives an overview of his general weltanschauung, which is based on Guénon's Integral Tradition. This work was positively evaluated by both Mircea Eliade and Ananda K. Coomaraswamy, the latter publishing a chapter in 1940 in English. This entire work was translated by Guido Stucco as *Revolt against the Modern World: Politics, Religion, and Social Order of the Kali Yuga* (Rochester, Vt., 1995). Evola's *La Dottrina del Risveglio* (Bari, Italy, 1943), translated by H. E. Musson as *The Doctrine of Awakening: The Attainment of Self-Mastery according to the Earliest Buddhist Texts* (London, 1951; reprint, Rochester, Vt., 1996), describes ancient Buddhism as an initiatory path. *Lo Yoga della Potenza* (Milan, 1949), translated by Guido Stucco as *The Yoga of Power: Tantra, Shakti, and the Secret Way* (Rochester, Vt., 1992), is a complete revision of Evola's first Tantra book, *L'uomo come potenza*, and is much more based on Avalon's writings than the original *L'uomo come potenza*, which had a strong Western philosophical bent. *Metafisica del Sesso* (Rome, 1958), translated as *The Metaphysics of Sex* (New York, 1983), describes the connections between religion, esotericism, and sexuality, whereby Evola sees sex as the only remaining force that lets modern humans perceive transcendental planes. Evola's autobiography, *Il Cammino del Cinabro* (Milan, 1963), largely ignores his private life and is useful mostly as an annotated autobibliography.

Periodicals that published Evola's works include *Ur* (Rome, 1927–1928) and *Krur* (Rome, 1929), both of which were reprinted in Rome in heavily revised three-volume editions in 1955 and 1971 under the title *Introduzione alla Magia quale Scienza dell'Io*. An English edition of the first 1927 volume is available as *Introduction into Magic* (Rochester, Vt., 2000).

Studi Evoliani, published by Gianfranco de Turris, was inaugurated in 1998; though an erratic sequence, it contains extensive essays on Evola. Despite the many books, articles, and dissertations written about Evola, many aspects of his life and work remain unexplored due to the great variety of special fields involved, and there is still no comprehensive biography about him. The following are recommended.

Bonvecchio, Claudio, Richard Drake, Joscelyn Godwin, et al. *Julius Evola: un pensiero per la fine del millennio*. Rome, 2001. A volume of lectures held in Milan in 1998 on the occasion of Evola's 100th birthday.

Boutin, Christophe. *Politique et tradition: Julius Evola dans le siècle (1898–1974)*. Paris, 1992. The most comprehensive work on Evola to date, it mainly discusses his political influence.

Consolato, Sandro. *Julius Evola e il Buddhismo*. Borzano, Italy, 1995. A sympathetic work explaining Evola's approach to Buddhism.

del Ponte, Renato. *Evola e il magico "Gruppo di Ur."* Borzano, Italy, 1994. A work that tries to shed light on the historical and personal background of the Group of Ur.

de Turris, Gianfranco, ed. *Testimonianze su Evola*. Rome, 1973; rev. ed., 1985. Various authors' personal memories of Evola written in honour of his seventy-fifth birthday.

di Dario, Beniamino M. *La via romana al Divino: Julius Evola e la religione romana*. Padua, Italy, 2001. Discusses Evola's perceptions of Roman religion, with heathen sacrality and the imperial idea as central themes.

di Vona, Piero. *Evola, Guénon, di Giorgio*. Borzano, Italy, 1993. The author, a Spinoza specialist at the University of Naples, describes the complex relationships between René Guénon and his two Italian disciples, Evola and di Giorgio.

Fraquelli, Marco. *Il filosofo proibito: Tradizione e reazione nell'opera di Julius Evola*. Milan, 1994. Discusses Evola's danger for democracy and the value of enlightenment.

Germinario, Francesco. *Razza del Sangue, razza dello Spirito: Julius Evola, l'antisemitismo, e il nazionalsocialismo, 1930–1943*. Turin, Italy, 2001. A critical but well-documented work on Evola's racist and anti-Semitic writings.

Guyot-Jeannin, Arnaud, ed. *Julius Evola*. Lausanne, Switzerland, 1997. A collection exploring various aspects of Evola; includes an interesting appendix with various documentary opinions on Evola.

Hansen, H. T. "Julius Evola's Political Endeavors." Preface to *Men among the Ruins: Post-War Reflections of a Radical Traditionalist* by Julius Evola, pp. 1–104. Rochester, Vt., 2001. Currently the most comprehensive English-language work on Evola; it strives to uncover Evola's most important intellectual sources.

Rossi, Marco. "Julius Evola and the Independent Theosophical Association of Rome." *Theosophical History* 6, no. 3 (1996–1997): 107–114.

Sheehan, Thomas. "Diventare Dio: Julius Evola and the Metaphysics of Fascism." *Stanford Italian Review* 6, nos. 1–2 (1986): 279–292. A critical survey of Evola's political ideas.

Spineto, Natale. "Mircea Eliade and Traditionalism." *ARIES* 1, no. 1 (2001): 62–87. A well-documented study about Eliade, which mainly shows how he integrated the influences of traditionalist authors, Evola included, without being a traditionalist himself.

HANS THOMAS HAKL (2005)
Translated from German by Marvin C. Sterling

EVOLUTION

This entry consists of the following articles:

EVOLUTION: THE CONTROVERSY WITH CREATIONISM

Perhaps no topic evokes a greater visceral reaction among both scientific and religious communities than that of the treatment of Darwinian evolution in Western society. On the one hand, scientists realize that this model of how the observed complexity of the living world likely arose seems, at this point in its history, almost self-evident. On the other hand, the media attention engendered by the vocal elements in opposition, whether motivated by creationism or intelligent design, pushes the churchgoing public to think that evolution (and by extension all of science) and religion are "at war." This caricature of the relationship is not only misleading but also mistaken. Ian Barbour, in his seminal work "Religion and Science" (1997) has shown convincingly that the warfare or conflict mode is one of four archetypes for the relationship between science and religion. In fact, the conflict mode represents the reaction of the extremes in both fields. In order to understand the true nature of this conversation as well as the specific positions taken by Darwinists and creationists, it is necessary to review both the science and the history of biological evolution.

DARWIN AND HIS TIMES. It is important to place Charles Darwin within the framework of both the English society of the nineteenth century and the scientific culture of western Europe and the United States during that time. Darwin was a product of the British intellectual class in every sense of the word. His father and his grandfather were both physicians. In addition, Erasmus Darwin, his paternal grandfather, was among those naturalists (now called biologists) who, at the end of the eighteenth century, challenged the notion that species were "fixed," that they existed in the same form in which they were originally created. Thus the concept of species changing over time was a part of Charles Darwin's personal history.

Darwin's voyage on the HMS *Beagle* from 1831 to 1836 became the means by which the Cambridge-educated student cemented his interest in biology and severed his path toward the theological training to which he seemed destined. He returned to England with his notebooks full of observations but with the ideas that would become his major work still unformed. By 1838 his interaction with the London society of naturalists resulted in the first formulations of his model.

After the voyage, Darwin did not leave England again. His marriage to Emma Wedgewood in 1839 and their life together at Down House in Kent were the stage for the remainder of his life. From that place, in the setting of a country squire and consummate Victorian intellectual, Darwin published the works through which he is known.

At Down House, perhaps taking one of his famous meditative strolls along the Sandwalk, Darwin decided to publish his book *On the Origin of Species by Means of Natural Selection.* His work on this had been ongoing since his return to England on the *Beagle.* The final stimulus to publication was a paper by Alfred Wallace, a young naturalist working in the Far East. The similarity of their conclusions led Darwin to finally complete his book for release in November 1859. *Origin of Species* was released in a total of six editions, all overseen by Darwin. The sixth, published in 1872, was his last. Darwin died in 1882.

The Darwinian Model. Darwin's great contribution was to provide a physical explanation for the observed complexity of the living world. Rather than assume that all things were created in the form in which they now occur (preformationism), he posited that everything arose by descent with modification from a common ancestor. The driving force of this, he proposed, was natural selection. His choice of terms for this force was not accidental. In fact, he was referring by comparison to the commonly understood agricultural practices of his day, by which desired traits of plants or animals were selected artificially by breeding. He argued that, in a similar fashion, favorable traits are selected in the natural world and that this selection results in the complexity of species.

John Maynard Smith put forward a convenient statement of the Darwinian model in 1991:

1. Population of entities (units of evolution) exist with three properties: (a) multiplication (one can give rise to two), (b) variation (not all entities are alike), and (c) heredity (like usually begets like during multiplication).
2. Differences between entities influence the likelihood of surviving and reproducing. That is, the differences influence their fitness.
3. The population changes over time (evolves) in the presence of selective forces.
4. The entities come to possess traits that increase their fitness. (Smith, 1991, p. 27)

It is important to note the emphasis on reproductive fitness in this model. When Darwin used the term *fitness* in *Origin of Species,* he meant it in this sense. That is, those traits that increase the likelihood of the organism reproducing are defined as making the organism more fit. In trying to clarify his meaning about this in subsequent editions, Darwin eventually came to rely on a phrase penned by Herbert Spencer, his contemporary and one of the great figures of Victorian England. In chapter three of the sixth edition of *Origin of Species,* Darwin wrote: "I have called this principle, by which each slight variation, if useful, is preserved, by the term Natural Selection, in order to mark its relation to man's power of selection. But the expression often used by Mr. Herbert Spencer, of the Survival of the Fittest, is more accurate, and is sometimes equally convenient" (1872, p. 32).

The image of "nature red in tooth and claw," to use Alfred, Lord Tennyson's oft-quoted line (*In Memoriam,* 1850, verse LVI), comes from a misreading of this epithet from Spencer. Nonetheless, it is true that Darwin's model does propose that some individuals are less reproductively fit than others and that this will inevitably entail the die-off of species. It is from this consequence of his model that the theodicy problem arises. Darwin was keenly aware of the theological impact of his own physical interpretations. He wrote in an 1860 letter to the American naturalist Asa Gray that he had trouble reconciling a loving God with some of what he observed in nature. In particular, referencing a species of wasp who lays her eggs in the living body of a caterpillar, whose flesh is then used as nourishment for the wasp's offspring, Darwin wrote, "I cannot persuade myself that a beneficent and omnipotent God would have designedly created the *Ichneumonidae* with the express intention of their feeding within the living bodies of Caterpillars, or that a cat should play with mice" (Darwin, 1860).

This theological challenge became a part of the catalyst that led to the reaction against the Darwinian model in a minority of Christian communities in the United States. The larger issue, as discussed below, is that of the completely materialistic interpretation of nature that scientific descendants of Darwin make, especially in the modern era.

The Modern Synthesis: Neo-Darwinism and Twentieth-Century Biology. The decade from 1859 to 1869 saw three scientific achievements that, nearly one hundred years later, were intimately related in the modern paradigms of biology. The first was the publication of Darwin's masterwork in November 1859. During this time Gregor Mendel, an Augustinian monk working in Brün (now Brno), Austria, developed a quantitative understanding of inheritance. He presented his work to the Brün Academy of Sciences in 1868 and published it in the academy's journal a year later. In 1869 Johann Fredriech Miescher, a Swiss chemist working at the time in Tübingen, isolated a substance from white blood cells found on used bandages. He named this material nuclein. It is now known as DNA.

In the nineteenth century, no one had any idea that these three events were related in any way. Certainly both Mendel and Miescher, as active scientists, were aware of Darwin's work and the implications of his model. However, virtually no scientist of the day even read Mendel's paper or appreciated the shift it signaled. In addition, no one could foresee that the genes whose behavior Mendel described and whose variants were the selectable traits Darwin's model relied upon would be found to be sequences of nitrogenous bases making up the structure of Miescher's nuclein.

In 1942 Julian Huxley, the grandson of Thomas Huxley, Darwin's champion, published *Evolution: The Modern Synthesis.* Huxley proposed that the Darwinian model, which had been relatively neglected by biologists (although popular with social scientists), could now be "rescued" by linking it with Mendelian genetics. Mendel of course had been rediscovered at the beginning of the twentieth century, when his experiments were repeated and shown to coincide with the behavior of cells as observed by more powerful microscopes than were available in the 1860s. The power of genetics was evident in the impressive data produced with model organisms such as the fruit fly. In addition, the field of biochemistry added to this new formulation with a search for what the chemical nature of the gene might be.

The search culminated in 1942 with the discovery by Oswald Avery and his colleagues that DNA was indeed the genetic material. Although it took another ten years for this idea to be accepted completely, the stage was now set for a full statement of what has come to be called the neo-Darwinian synthesis. This formulation includes the following features:

- Genes: information in the form of the linear array of bases that make up the DNA molecules of chromosomes.
- The traits of an organism (phenotype): direct expression of the information found in the genes (genotype).
- Variations: result of subtle differences in this information (changes in base pairs).
- Changes in genes: mutational events that occur in a "random" way. Random here means that it is not possible to predict which nitrogenous base changes within the DNA. However, the nature of the change is predictable, given the mutagenic stimulus.
- A population of entities: will have variations in traits that are the result of mutational events (genetic drift).

In this new world of biology, the variant genes are acted upon by natural selection. Variants with a greater likelihood of allowing the organism to reproduce and pass these traits on to the next generation have a positive selective advantage and are said to be more fit.

ENCOUNTERS BETWEEN EVOLUTION AND THEOLOGY. Immediately after the publication of Darwin's book there was a theological reaction within the Abrahamic religions, mainly the Protestant Christian denominations. At first glance it would seem that the problem was with the challenge to the *Genesis* account of creation. However, it must be understood that the fixity of species had also been assumed by science as well. After all, the eighteenth-century Swedish naturalist Carl von Linné (Carolus Linnaeus), whose taxonomic classification system is still used in the early twenty-first century, assumed that the species he was describing in his work had existed in their present forms since the beginning. Even in Darwin's day this was the predominant model for many biologists, although challenges had already been mounted before 1859. Therefore, while this issue was a problem for theology, it was also a problem for many scientists as well.

A larger theological issue concerned the explanation itself. Darwin consciously wrote his book with earlier models in mind, especially the natural theology of William Paley. In 1802 the Reverend Paley published his view of the origin of life's complexity in a volume called *Natural Theology; or, Evidences for the Existence and Attributes of the Deity, Collected from the Appearances of Nature.* In this book Paley presented his famous watch and watchmaker metaphor. This theistic use of nature ultimately led the modern evolutionary biologist Richard Dawkins to title his challenge to theism *The Blind Watchmaker* (1986).

Darwin, in response to Paley's model of an interventionist God creating all things at the beginning, offered instead a naturalistic and materialistic explanation: descent with modification from a common ancestor through the nonsupernatural force of natural selection. While this model does not assume the absence of a God, it certainly does not invoke God's action in any direct way in its presentation. Darwin was not unaware of the effect his model had among theologians and religious communities. In fact, in the second edition of *Origin of Species* he added the following statement, somewhat in his own defense:

> I see no reason why the views given in this volume should shock the religious feelings of any one. It is satisfactory, as showing how transient such impressions are, to remember that the greatest discovery ever made by man, namely, the law of the attraction of gravity, was also attacked by Leibnitz, "as subversive of natural, and inferentially of revealed, religion." (p. 239)

Darwin's view of the transience of the problem is certainly touching in light of the debate that still seems to rage in some circles over his "volume." Nonetheless, in this short and somewhat disingenuous statement he was attempting to make the case for two ideas: the need for science to be seen as not in contradistinction to religion, and the need for theology-religion to take into account the latest scientific advances.

In spite of Darwin's position that there was no threat to religion, the interpreters of his model had other ideas. Thomas Huxley, one of Darwin's chief defenders, saw the evolutionary model as something that went beyond the biology it described. He called for the development of a social philosophy, akin to and as a substitute for religion, based on the Darwinian principles. For Huxley, the highest goals and values of humanity could be seen as the continuing evolution of the human species. Herbert Spencer also used Darwinian principals to develop a philosophical and political framework but wanted to apply the survival of the fittest model to the evolution of social systems. Finally, Francis Galton, Darwin's first cousin, used the model to advocate for the purposeful direction of the evolution of humans, a process he called eugenics.

Among theologians of the time there were some who tried to cling to the strict interpretative view of creation as described in *Genesis,* which was not at odds with the model of many naturalists of the day. Others took the new model to heart and attempted to make theological sense out of this new view of the living world. Those theologians who embraced the new idea were already, in some sense, committed to a new kind of biblical criticism that was beginning to supplant literalism among some of the more liberal Christian thinkers. This movement, rather than Darwinian evolution per se, gave rise to the fundamentalists.

THE FUNDAMENTALISTS. It is commonly assumed that antievolutionism is synonymous with Christian fundamentalism. While many Christians who identify with fundamentalism are antievolutionist, the origins of this strain of Christian thought did not include this tenet. When the General Assembly of the Presbyterian Church met in 1910 to approve those beliefs that would be considered fundamental to being a Christian, the following five were adopted:

1. the inerrancy of the Scriptures in their original documents;
2. the deity of Jesus Christ, including the virgin birth;
3. substitutionary atonement;
4. the physical resurrection of Christ;
5. the miracle-working power of Jesus Christ.

Nowhere in this list is there any reference to Darwinian evolution. In fact some of the theologians involved in the formulation of these basic tenets accepted evolution although they were still believing Christians. Thus, at its very foundations, fundamentalism was not antievolution.

How is it then that the modern understanding of a fundamentalist includes this anti-Darwinian posture? Certainly over the years since the establishment of these basic tenets of belief as essential some things have changed. The first fundamental is the inerrancy of Scripture. As originally argued, this tenet was directed against the liberal Protestant theologians who were coming to rely more and more on historical methods of criticism in biblical hermeneutics. The reaction was not against the scientific enterprise itself. The first fundamental deals with the divine authority of Scripture, juxtaposed against the view that these writings were but the historical works of humans. The intent was to defend the purity of the teaching against internal disagreement within the Christian community, as opposed to direct challenges from science.

The move from this position to one that espouses the literal meaning of *Genesis* as a description of how creation actually took place is a matter of only a few steps. In the face of the growing social movement of secular humanism, itself a spin-off of the scientific enterprise, it is not surprising that some elements of the fundamentalist community began to react against the Darwinian model itself. What developed from this reaction is the theological stance called biblical creationism, which rejects the scientific models completely and relies upon Scripture as the sole source for understanding how the natural world arose.

SCIENTIFIC CREATIONISM. A visit to the Institute for Creation Research (ICR) in the foothills east of San Diego, California, is quite instructive. It is clear that this is a facility that celebrates rather than rejects science. The founding members, such as Duane Guish (biochemistry) and Henry Morris (geology) are trained in science, not theology. One is surrounded by evidence that scientific instruments and techniques are employed in their work. And yet their interpretation of their investigations is given one and only one direction: scientific support of the creation story as given in the *Book of Genesis.*

The ICR founder and president, John Morris, posted the following introduction to their mission on the institute's website:

> Our world, our church, our schools, our society, need the truth of creation more than ever. We see the wrong thinking of evolution having produced devastating results in every realm. Our passion at the Institute for Creation Research is to see science return to its rightful God-glorifying position, and see creation recognized as a strength by the body of Christ; supporting Scripture, answering questions, satisfying doubts and removing road blocks to the Gospel. The Institute for Creation Research Graduate School exists to train students in scientific research and teaching skills, preparing effective warriors for the faith.

Morris and others see themselves as scientists whose duty is to correct the errors of the recent past and allow science to resume its "correct" relationship with religion as support for the truths revealed in Scripture. They are not theologians, nor do they pretend to any theological insights whatsoever. Their focus is on the instruments and methods of science and how these can be brought to bear on the questions related to the natural world as seen through the words of *Genesis.* They apply the term *young earth creationism* to their view of the world, and they support six principles:

1. *Creatio ex nihilo* by divine action, without any subsequent development. Everything was created as it exists now.
2. Mutation and natural selection cannot explain the subsequent development of all living things. This is a rejec-

tion of the idea that gradual change (variations) can confer selective advantages that lead to new species.

3. Speciation does not occur. That is, changes happen within a species (within a "kind" in their usage), but new species do not develop from preexisting species.
4. There is no descent from a common ancestor. With respect to human origins in particular, this rejects the notion that humans and other primates have an ancestral link.
5. The geology of the earth is a result of catastrophism rather than evolution. In particular, much of what is seen can be explained by positing a great flood, as described in *Genesis.*
6. The earth is less than ten thousand years old.

All of these principles—especially the last one, with its rejection of all modern dating techniques as inherently flawed—put the scientific creationists in complete disagreement with any natural scientists and with most mainstream theologians. This then raises one of the principle ironies of scientific creationism. Its proponents embrace the methodology of science but reject the standard interpretation of those results. To say that their science is influenced by their religious belief is perhaps self-evident from the conclusions they draw. However, a careful reading of their literature reveals that they take themselves to be scientists and that their argument is with what they view as the incorrect interpretations of the data. This of course leads them into dangerous waters, both scientifically and theologically. For instance, the young earth creationists cannot deny the geological data that leads to the 4.5-billion-year age of the earth. Rather, they argue that God created the earth to have the "appearance" of age, when in reality it is only ten thousand years old. In *Finding Darwin's God* (1999) Kenneth Miller, a Brown University cellular biologist, argues that this is incorrect from the standpoints of both science and theology. He writes that their rejection of evolution leads them to characterize God as a "schemer, trickster, even a charlatan" (Miller, 1999, p. 80).

In the end, the controversy is not really between science and faith but between one kind of science and another. True, creation science assumes that the *Genesis* story is the literal description of the origin of the natural world. However, it contends that science would also agree with this if only it sharpened its interpretive powers and admitted the errors of the Darwinian model.

Intelligent Design. The controversy between creationism and evolution has spilled over into society, mainly in the form of debates about what should or should not be included in the educational curriculum taught in elementary and secondary schools. The classic case of the so-called Scopes monkey trial in 1925 was just the beginning of these questions. Even into the twenty-first century, school boards are constantly beset with requests to include "both sides" of the story in any curriculum discussing the origins and subsequent development of the natural world. As such, even the word *evolution* becomes suspect as soon as such deliberations are opened. The antiscientific and, perhaps, anti-intellectual position of biblical literalism can usually be set aside as not appropriate to be taught in the same course of study as the methods of science. Even scientific creationism, with its appeal to those very methods, cannot make the cut as "science" in most school board meetings or courtrooms. However, the new contender for attention is neither of these, but rather the intelligent design movement. Intelligent design is best understood as the contention that the living world has features that can only be explained by the action of an intelligent designer. For instance, Michael Behe, in *Darwin's Black Box* (1996), argues that there are examples of cellular function that could not have arisen as the result of gradual mutational change under the pressure of natural selection. He calls such features "irreducibly complex" and gives a list of six examples from his understanding of the biochemistry of living systems. Of course, his position eventually devolves into a "god of the gaps" argument. In this sense, as soon as an explanation for what appears to be irreducibly complex is presented with a naturalistic basis, his designer disappears from the scene. However, this is not the only issue at stake in this discussion. William Dembski, in *Intelligent Design* (1999) and *No Free Lunch* (2002), takes aim at the philosophical underpinnings of the modern scientific method. He proposes the concept of "specified complexity" to describe features of living systems that infer design. At issue for Dembski is not so much the god of the gaps problem, but rather what he believes to be an insufficiency within the scientific enterprise itself. He argues that science by definition is opaque to the idea of purpose or design. This goes back to the original Aristotelian-Thomistic uses of teleology as the fourth or final cause of a thing. The problem here is that the philosophical assumptions of modern science derive from those post-Cartesian thinkers who rejected teleological explanations as a part of their methodology. On the one hand, this allowed for a more objective approach to understanding nature, opening the way for the experimentalists. On the other hand, the philosophical analogy imbedded in Aquinas's fifth way of understanding God, the so-called argument from design, seemed no longer valid. Dembski and the intelligent design movement push for a fundamental shift in the philosophy of science. In this way they are distinct from the scientific creationists. They are modern scientists in every sense of the word. However, they would argue that a model of origin and complexification for the living world must include a recognition of purpose, and through this a sense that some features require the action of a designer. Therefore these features would be characterized as specified or irreducible complexity. There is no challenge to current science from the notion of irreducible complexity in itself, in the sense that the properties of complex systems are not explainable as the sum of the parts. This is, in fact, the hallmark of the move to networks and complexity analysis in biology. However, when this complexity is seen to be "specified" by a designer with intent, the issue is joined. The need for a designer then leads to the question of who this designer might be and necessarily becomes a theological problem, not a scientific one. Most commentators prefer to see intelligent design as just another form of scientific creationism. However, a closer reading of advocates such as Behe and Dembski reveals some distinct differences. Those most closely associated with the scientific arguments for intelligent design are not in any sense rejecting evidence for the age of the earth or other features of the geological record. The scientific creationists accept the methodology of science as given, with its reductionism in place, but have a different interpretation of the data based of course on their view of the *Genesis* description. Nonetheless, both movements fall within the same anti-Darwinian camp. As such, the conversations that concern curriculum focus on the inclusion of intelligent design rather than scientific creationism in the science classroom.

THEISTIC EVOLUTION. Given the fireworks surrounding the media reporting of creationism-evolution discussions, it is no wonder that the general public, and indeed a fair portion of the scientific community, believe it is one or the other; one is either a Darwinian or a Christian. However, for the majority of both theologians and scientists, the truth lies in between these two artificial extremes.

To see this middle position clearly, it is necessary to understand the nature of the scientific enterprise and its self-imposed limits. Science restricts its investigations to the collection of data and the building of physical models of explanation for natural phenomena. It is never the function of science to say that certain data prove or disprove the existence of God. However, it is natural for a scientist, once having derived a model such as Darwin's, to speculate on its meaning beyond the data itself. While this is normal, the scientist is at that point engaging in philosophy or even theology. The confusion arises when a particular scientist or scientific commentator attempts to make the data apply directly to the philosophical point. Thus Daniel Dennett, in *Darwin's Dangerous Idea* (1995), argued that Darwinian evolution "proves" that God does not exist.

The result of this confusion has been the polarized view that many have of these issues. A more reasonable understanding of the possible positions is in John Haught's *God after Darwin* (2000) and Michael Ruse's *Can a Darwinian Be a Christian?* (2001). Theistic evolution is not one position but rather a group of related positions. Theistic evolution accepts the facts leading up to and supporting the Darwinian model and concludes that this model is the most likely explanation for those facts. However, theistic evolution also accepts the idea of divine action in all of creation and sees the Darwinian model as one way in which divine action might have operated.

For the theistic evolutionist there is no inconsistency in this stance. It is a combination of scientific understanding and faith. Haught, as a theologian, argues that theology must respond to the facts of evolution with introspection. The theodicy issue that Darwin saw as a part of his model must be encountered, Haught proposes, with a full acceptance of the evolutionary history of the world.

CONCLUSION. Modern biology relies upon the neo-Darwinian model as a central paradigm of the discipline. While modifications are proposed to the structure of the model, nothing appears in the early twenty-first century to be a rejection of the model in the sense that the scientific creationists wish to see. As a result, the so-called controversy between science and theology that this represents must be thought of as a conversation waiting to be explored.

BIBLIOGRAPHY

Behe, Michael J. *Darwin's Black Box: The Biochemical Challenge to Evolution.* New York, 1996. Behe is a biochemist who takes the position that certain features of living systems are "irreducibly complex" and require the intervention of an intelligent designer.

Darwin, Charles. *Letter to Asa Gray,* 1860. Quoted by Stephen Jay Gould in "Nonmoral Nature," available from http://www.stephenjaygould.org/library/gould_nonmoral.html.

Darwin, Charles, *The Origin of Species by Means of Natural Selection.* 1859 (first edition). References here are to the *Encyclopedia Britannica* re-publication of the sixth and final edition.

Dawkins, Richard. *The Blind Watchmaker.* New York, 1986.

Dawkins, Richard. *Climbing Mount Improbable.* New York, 1996. Written for lay audiences by an evolutionary biologist and champion of the Darwinian model.

Dembski, William A. *Intelligent Design.* Downer's Grove, Ill., 1999.

Dembski, William A. *No Free Lunch: Why Specified Complexity Cannot Be Purchased without Intelligence.* Lanham, Md., 2002. Dembski is a mathematician and philosopher. Some of the material in these two books is not easily approachable, but the overviews presented represent the gist of the intelligent design movement.

Dennett, Daniel C. *Darwin's Dangerous Idea.* New York, 1995.

Haught, John F. *God after Darwin: A Theology of Evolution.* Boulder, Colo., 2000. Haught is a Georgetown University theologian who defends the theistic evolution stance.

Huxley, Julian. *Evolution: The Modern Synthesis.* London, 1942.

Institute for Creation Science. "Introduction to ICR." Available from http://www.icr.org/abouticr/intro.htm.

Miller, Kenneth R. *Finding Darwin's God: A Scientist's Search for Common Ground between God and Evolution.* New York, 1999. An explanation of the evolutionary model and a critique of various antievolutionist views. Written by a scientist for a lay audience.

Morris, Henry M. *A History of Modern Creationism.* San Diego, Calif., 1984. A discussion of scientific creationism by the founder and president of the Institution for Creation Research.

Paley, William. *Natural Theology; or, Evidences for the Existence and Attributes of the Deity, Collected from the Appearances of Nature.* London, 1802.

Peters, Ted, and Martinez Hewlett. *Evolution from Creation to New Creation.* Nashville, Tenn., 2003. A survey and critique of all of the positions by a theologian and a biological scientist, this work in the end supports theistic evolution.

Ruse, Michael. *Taking Darwin Seriously.* Amherst, N.Y., 1998.

Ruse, Michael. *Can a Darwinian Be a Christian? The Relationship between Science and Religion.* Cambridge, U.K., 2001. Two important books by one of the most important commentators on evolution and the debate with theology. Accessible to the lay person.

Smith, John Maynard. In *Symbiosis as a Source of Evolutionary Innovation: Speciation and Morphogenesis,* edited by L. Margulis and R. Fester. Cambridge, Mass., 1991.

MARTINEZ HEWLETT (2005)

EVOLUTION: EVOLUTIONISM

Evolutionism is a term commonly employed to designate a number of similar, usually nineteenth-century anthropological theories that attempt to account for the genesis and development of religion. Although the term *evolutionism* could be used to describe a collection of theologians such as Pierre Teilhard De Chardin (1881–1955) and others belonging to the school of theistic evolution, this article will focus strictly on the uses of the term within the development of anthropological science.

Evolutionist theories of religion's origin hold in common a presupposed "psychic unity of mankind"; that is, they assume that all human groups are possessed of a more or less common developmental pattern (though the shape of this pattern differs from theorist to theorist) and that therefore significant clues as to how religion originated—and in turn as to what religion essentially is—can be detected through a study of the religious lives of the world's "primitive" peoples. If evolutionist assumptions are correct, it should follow that commonalities displayed among groups at each level of development will reveal, when set in diachronic order, a necessary "psychic history" of the human race.

INFLUENCES ON EVOLUTIONIST THOUGHT. Evolutionist anthropological theories represent one manifestation of the nineteenth century's enthusiasm for developmental schemata that find their bases in what might loosely be called a philosophy of history. This philosophy of history declares that human development is rectilinear and progressive and that the mind tends necessarily toward greater and greater rationality and complexity. The idea of progress, especially in its component notion that history is unidirectional and proceeds by way of identifiable stages, is older certainly than the beginning of the nineteenth century. Indeed, one may speculate that there is a nascent "evolutionism" at work already in the Pauline formulation that, with the appearance of Christ, an age of grace supplanted and rendered obsolete an earlier age of law. (To trace "scientific" evolutionism's origins to the beginnings of Christian historiography provides some insight regarding the apologetic purposes that evolutionist thinking seems always to serve.) But for convenience one may point to the philosophical work of G. W. F. Hegel (1770–1831) as having planted the seed that led, by the nineteenth century's close, to the full flowering of the evolutionist creed among those who considered themselves the first truly scientific investigators of the phenomenon of humans.

In his *Phenomenology of Spirit* (1807), Hegel launched a revolution in thinking about the human past. Put simply, the Hegelian system declares that history (by which Hegel and his followers mean the history of the world as a whole) reveals the progressive manifestation of *Geist* (spirit) in the world: a process that leads eventually to spirit's self-actualization and to human self-understanding. History, according to Hegel, propels itself forward through a dynamic process, within which each successive age "resolves and synthesizes" the antagonisms of earlier eras. Each historical period therefore not only results from what has gone before, but also in some sense contains within itself the self-understanding of earlier eras. Locating anthropological evolutionism's foundation in Hegelian philosophy may therefore help one comprehend what amounts to a "genetic obsession" on the parts of the participants in the debates that raged during the late nineteenth century, debates that had as their crux a question concerning what constitutes the essential—that is, the originary—form of religious consciousness. To identify this originary form would be to uncover an essential element of human beings, for it was generally held among evolutionist theorists that religious belief was the distinguishing characteristic setting the human apart from the animal. This endeavor may seem odd given much of the later history of scientific anthropology, but it makes sense when placed within the context of a fledgling scientific discipline that had not yet weaned itself of philosophical anthropology.

More directly influential than Hegelian philosophy upon the development of scientific anthropological evolutionism, however, is the work of Herbert Spencer (1820–1903), the English polymath and, with the Frenchman Auguste Comte (1798–1957), cofounder of the discipline of sociology. Even before Charles Darwin's *On the Origin of Species by Means of Natural Selection* (1859) revolutionized biological science, Spencer had landed on evolution as the principle that accounts for all change, whether inorganic, organic, or mental (if one may so characterize the quality that separates the development of human societies and individuals from mere organic growth). In his essay "Progress: Its Law and Cause" (1857), Spencer first gave voice to what may be called the essential element of anthropological evolutionist dogma:

> The advance from the simple to the complex, through a process of successive differentiations, is seen . . . in the evolution of Humanity, whether contemplated in the civilized individual, or in the aggregate of races; it is seen in the evolution of Society in respect alike of its political, its religious, and its economical organization; and it is seen in the evolution of all those endless concrete and abstract products of human activity. (Spencer, 1914, p. 35)

Having thus laid the theoretical groundwork for his never-to-be-completed "natural history of society," Spencer nevertheless managed to construct the first systematic sociology of religion in English, one of the tasks undertaken in his three-volume *Principles of Sociology* (1876–1896). In this work he identifies the origin of religion (which, Spencer says, supplanted an aboriginal atheism) in what he perceives to be the universal practice among primitive peoples of worshipping the ghosts of their ancestors. He then goes on to trace the further evolution of religious consciousness through polytheism and monotheism. According to Spencer, religion culminates in agnosticism—a metaphysical position girded by the "positivist" epistemological principles that are the earmarks of the scientific age and of the scientific historiography, epitomized in Spencerian sociology—that helps to inaugurate this new era of human development. That Spencer considered agnosticism a genuinely religious position bears noting insofar as one may be tempted to see the work of Spencer and other evolutionists as antagonistic toward religion. It is nearer the case to say that at least some of these thinkers sought, among other agendas, to defend what they found to be the "spiritual maturity" of the age of science to which they belonged.

TYLOR AND HIS CRITICS. Among theorists of religion, E. B. Tylor (1832–1917) perhaps best deserves to be called an "evolutionist." Tylor's work, more than that of any other scholar, invites one to identify evolutionism with British "armchair" anthropology of the late nineteenth century. Influences on Tylor include Spencer (whose "ghost theory" of the origin of religion closely resembles the animistic hypothesis forwarded by Tylor) and F. Max Müller (1823–1900), the German-English philologist whose etymological investigations helped inspire Tylor's researches into the *Urgrund* (primeval ground of being) of religious consciousness.

Before proceeding to a description of the theory of religion's origin advanced by Tylor, one should note what is perhaps the most significant characteristic of Tylor's (and indeed of other evolutionist theorists') manner of thinking about religion. It goes without saying that "religion" is, for these writers, at root one thing. But beyond this it is worth emphasizing that in this framework religion is essentially of an intellectual or cognitive kind. Evolutionist theories of religious development proffer histories of religions within which religion is single-mindedly construed as belief; the affective dimensions of religious experience are simply elided or are written off as so much superstructure.

This intellectualist approach to anthropological research is clearly seen in Tylor's famous "minimum definition of Religion" as "belief in Spiritual Beings." Tylor's intellectualism—and that of his contemporaries—has been harshly derided and largely superseded by twentieth-century anthropologists. And yet this at least ought to be said in its favor: for all their concern to distinguish between modern, Western rationality and the "primitive" mentality of "savage" or "low" races, it is yet the case that the nineteenth-century initiators of anthropological discourse were the first Europeans to conceive of the human race as a single entity; they were the first, that is, to accord to "savages" human minds. Though they were termed "primitive," the religions of "low races" were recognized as religions. (It is clearly a part of Tylor's purpose to put the lie to what he considered the slanderous reports of missionaries and adventurers concerning the godlessness of the tribal peoples they encountered.) Moreover, in so doing, the evolutionists—who, through their examinations of "primitive" people, hoped to uncover keys to human nature per se—helped overturn the privileged position of the European scientific observer, no matter how far such an outcome may have been from their intention. Certainly the work of Tylor and others, especially James G. Frazer (1854–1941), was instrumental in revolutionizing classical studies and thus in altering forever the picture of antiquity, and hence of the West's own intellectual heritage.

Tylor's name has come to be identified with the term *animism* or, as he also called it, "the doctrine of souls." He first proposed this as the most rudimentary stage of religious belief in a paper titled "The Religion of Savages," published in the *Fortnightly Review* in 1866. Tylor's monumental influence upon succeeding generations of students of religion can be measured by the fact that, although Tylor's theory of religion's origin has long since been discredited, the term *animism* is still widely used to describe the religious beliefs of those peoples who have as yet resisted conversion to one or another of the "great" missionary religions. In articulating the concept and the conceptual basis of animism, however, Tylor did not mean to describe an obsolescent form of religious consciousness but rather to identify the constant center or core of religious belief. The following passage, extracted from Tylor's masterwork *Primitive Culture* (1871), both points up the universality of animistic belief and identifies the conceptual maneuver responsible for engendering the animistic hypothesis:

> At the lowest levels of culture of which we have clear knowledge, the notion of a ghost-soul animating man while in the body, and appearing in dream and vision out of the body, is found deeply ingrained. . . . Among races within the limits of savagery, the general doctrine of souls is found worked out with remarkable breadth and consistency. The souls of animals are recognized by a natural extension from the theory of human souls; the souls of trees and plants follow in some vague partial way; and the souls of inanimate objects expand the general category to its extremest boundary. . . . Far on into civilization, men still act as though in some half-meant way they believed in souls or ghosts of objects. (Quoted in Waardenburg, 1973, pp. 216–217)

Tylor's doctrine of "survivals"—that is, his claim that, although they may over the course of time lose much or even most of their original meanings, elements of the primitive worldview perdure within and continue to exercise influence upon the mindsets of more advanced cultures—is also hinted at in the foregoing passage. For Tylor, as for perhaps the latest of his heritors, Sigmund Freud (1856–1939), the child is truly father to the man. Both of these thinkers depended, whether consciously or not, upon the Hegelian principle that ontogeny recapitulates phylogeny. For Tylor, as well as decades later for Freud, the investigation of the mental life of primitive races provided insight into the psychic infancy of humankind and so to the inevitable hurdles that must be overcome in order for the human species to achieve psychic adulthood.

Within British anthropological circles, criticism of Tylor's animistic hypothesis came from two corners. The first of Tylor's critics was the Scottish folklorist Andrew Lang (1844–1912). Though Lang's constructive contributions to anthropological science were minimal, he dealt a devastating blow to the notion that animism represented the earliest stage of religious consciousness. In his book *Myth, Ritual, and Religion* (1887), he pointed to the overwhelming evidence of what he termed "high gods" among many of those peoples who until then had been characterized by anthropologists as being too primitive to be able to conceptualize so abstractly as to arrive at any notion resembling that of an omnipotent, creative deity. Though Lang turned his attention toward other interests during the remainder of his career, his critique of Tylor laid the foundation for the massive researches into the topic of "primitive monotheism" that were later conducted by Wilhelm Schmidt (1868–1954).

The second blow to the animistic hypothesis was struck by R. R. Marett (1866–1943), Tylor's disciple, biographer, and successor to the position of reader in social anthropology at Oxford University. In an essay titled "Preanimistic Religion" published in the journal *Folklore* in 1900, Marett, drawing on the ethnographic data compiled in Melanesia by the Anglican missionary R. H. Codrington, advanced the claim that animism had been preceded by a pre-animistic stage of religious consciousness characterized by belief in an impersonal force or power that invests persons and objects, rendering them sacred. Marett, borrowing from the Melanesian vocabulary supplied by Codrington, termed this "electric" force *mana.* In accord with the evolutionist principles outlined earlier, belief in mana possesses, for Marett, both diachronic and ontological priority. One hears an echo of Tylor in Marett's proposition, in the article "Mana" that he contributed to James Hastings's *Encyclopaedia of Religion and Ethics,* that mana and taboo (which Marett conceives of as mana's "negative" complement) together constitute "a minimum definition of the magico-religious"

While neither Lang nor Marett disavowed evolutionist principles, it is worth noting that the criticisms leveled against Tylor by these writers eventually had the effect of helping to undermine the cogency of evolutionist explanations of the origin and development of religion, insofar as the work of each served to invite anthropologists to a closer examination of actual ethnographic data.

FURTHER HISTORY OF EVOLUTIONIST THEORIES. The early twentieth century saw the demise of "armchair" approaches to anthropological research as anthropologists began to conduct detailed, long-term studies of tribal peoples within the contexts of these peoples' actual habitats. One effect of this focus on field research was the production, especially during the middle decades of the twentieth century and within the Anglo-American anthropological tradition, of great numbers of immensely detailed monographs on the day-to-day lives of primitive societies. The quest for a comprehensive and systematic natural history of humankind was gradually abandoned.

This abandonment undoubtedly found one of its sources in an awakening to the theoretical inadequacies of the evolutionist approach to human culture. It began to become clear to anthropological researchers that the systematic theoreticians of humankind's development employed, in their search for the unvarying laws underlying what they perceived to be the relentless progress of human societies toward ever more complex and rational forms, a logic that was wholly circular. In the mere designation of some societies as "primitive" and others as "advanced" a host of culturally engendered presuppositions were employed, and a host of significant theoretical questions were begged. Another inadequacy of evolutionist thinking that began forcibly to strike the notice of scholars of religion was the fact that this mode of explanation ignores the trading of cultural elements, which so evidently has always figured importantly in the change, and especially the complexification, of human societies. (It should be noted that few evolutionists adhered strictly to a doctrine of absolute rectilinear evolution. Spencer admitted the possibility that racial differences accounted for the multiple and apparently irreconcilable directions taken by different cultures, and even the archevolutionist Tylor, in his early work, proposed "diffusionist" explanations for the puzzling appearance of "high" cultures among the Indians of Mesoamerica.) This insight alone was responsible for the instigation of what one may loosely term a school of thought regarding the origins and development of religious phenomena: that of the so-called diffusionists.

Twentieth-century anthropological science also saw the interest in religion as an (or the) essential element in the life of human societies fall out of fashion. From the 1920s through the 1960s, many anthropologists, especially those who received training in England or the United States, focused their attention on kinship relations, economic arrangements, and the like—aspects of society, that is, that they considered more tractable to the "hard," objective studies they were intent upon pursuing. (There were of course exceptions to this trend—E. E. Evans-Pritchard [1902–1973] and Raymond Firth [1901–2002] stand as two of the more important—but even these scientists concentrated their efforts on conducting meticulous examinations of the religious lives of particular societies.) It may not be too inaccurate to generalize to the effect that the nineteenth-century obsession with origins (as a concomitant of the grandiose quest to discover the foundational design of human progress) was replaced in the twentieth century, at least among Anglophone anthropologists, by an obsession with "objectivity."

But to generalize in this manner is dangerous insofar as it ignores, first, the continuing influence of evolutionist anthropological theory on continental anthropological science, and second, the powerful, hardly diminishing influence of evolutionist theory upon Western culture generally. Though there is too little space in this brief treatment to do more than mention them, one may list Émile Durkheim (1858–1917) and Lucien Lévy-Bruhl (1857–1939) as among the continental heritors of evolutionist theory. The debate concerning the nature of "primitive" as opposed to "civilized" (or rational) forms of mentation that was refueled by Lévy-Bruhl continues, though in different, structuralist guise, even in the early twenty-first century.

Though his work represents what many consider a dead end in terms of a continuing influence on anthropological thought, James G. Frazer (1854–1941) produced what must count as the single most imposing monument of evolutionist theory, *The Golden Bough* (1890), which in its third edition (1911–1915) ran to twelve volumes. Not only the most prolix of evolutionist theorists, Frazer was also the most doctrinaire, convinced that human culture's development is governed by unvarying natural laws and that the human race has evolved, mentally and physically, in uniform fashion. Frazer's temper was utterly intellectualist; his evolutionary scheme, which posits the successive replacement of an aboriginal magical mode of thought by first a religious and then a scientific mode, finds its basis in Frazer's conviction that human culture's development is effected as later generations of human beings awaken to the errors and the resultant practical inefficacy of their predecessors' worldviews. (A reading of *The Golden Bough* prompted Ludwig Wittgenstein's [1889–1951] trenchant remark to the effect that, when Frazer reports on a primitive European peasant woman pulling a doll from beneath her skirt during a fertility rite, he seems to think that she is making some sort of mistake and actually believes the puppet to be a child.)

The influence of Frazer's work on later anthropological theory has been negligible, aside perhaps from the significant impact it had on classical studies. Yet Frazer's *Golden Bough* rates as one of the century's most celebrated books because of its profound effect on the literary and artistic dimensions of Western culture, and because of its formative influence on psychoanalytic theory, which with Marxism (itself utterly dependent upon evolutionist assumptions regarding history) stands as a ruling ideology of the twentieth century. Though the axioms of the psychoanalytic model for understanding the human mind and its cultural products probably owe more to evolutionist biology and its philosophical antecedents than they do to British anthropological theory, it is nevertheless the case that the work of Freud (especially his late work) drew heavily upon that of Frazer. Frazer's *Totemism and Exogamy* (1910) was a direct influence upon Freud's *Totem and Taboo* (1918). The latter, *The Future of an Illusion* (1928), and *Civilization and Its Discontents* (1930) constitute Freud's contribution to evolutionist theory. Seeking to demonstrate the logical coincidence of the behavior of neurotics with the "obsessional" practices of primitive peoples, Freud aimed to map a theory of culture whose purposes are both descriptive and prophylactic, insofar as (in the manner of clinical psychoanalytic method) to understand past conflicts that live on within an unconscious realm—whence they continue to exert control over human destiny—is to take a sure step toward resolving these conflicts and thereby achieving psychic health or emotional (and by implication political) maturity. It may need no pointing out that Freud identifies the coming of the race's adulthood with the waning of religious belief.

Freud's influence on anthropological science during the middle decades of the twentieth century was minimal, but Freudian-based anthropological theory seemed to experience a rejuvenescence in the late twentieth century, as Melford E. Spiro's *Oedipus in the Trobriands* (1982) demonstrates. As for the medical import of Freud's program for human destiny, it again is instructive to observe that evolutionist theory has consistently coupled a descriptive aim with an apologetic and heuristic intention. This has remained true of evolutionism from its modern origins in the thought of Hegel and Spencer down through its modern embodiments both in Marxist historiography and political practice and in Freudian theory and psychoanalytic technique.

Modern Perspectives: Sociobiology and Evolutionary Psychology. The application of the neo-Darwinian model prevalent in modern biology to the evolution of human behaviors and social structures was brought to the fore with the publication of *Sociobiology* by Edward O. Wilson of Harvard in 1975. Wilson's observations of behavior among the social insects became the focal point of his theoretical approach to understanding the origin and evolution of human institutions. At the heart of this theory is the assumption that human behaviors at both the individual and group levels must confer a reproductive advantage if they are to be preserved over evolutionary time. Furthermore, it is assumed that, in order for selection to take place (in the Darwinian sense), such behaviors must in fact be genetically determined. It is only fair to say that Wilson, contrary to his most vocal critics, is not as strict a reductionist or genetic determinist as this sounds. Nevertheless the use of Darwinian principles for understanding the origins and continued existence of human behaviors flows naturally out of Wilson's approach.

Religion was not discussed per se in Wilson's 1975 book. However, in his later book *Consilience* (1998) he devotes an entire chapter to the origins of ethics and religion. He subscribes to the same kind of primitive-origin hypothesis as did Tylor and Frazer. Wilson argues that the development of religious instincts is encoded in the genes and that such genetic material conferred a reproductive survival advantage on those groups who exhibited it. He suggests that tribal religious systems served to unify those groups that employed them, and that such systems spring from the inevitable result of the human brain's genetic evolution.

The Darwinian approach taken by Wilson and others to understanding the origins of human behavior finds even greater application in the emerging field of evolutionary psychology. Led by Leda Cosmides and John Tooby at the University of California, Santa Barbara, this field attempts to derive Darwinian models for the origins of all human behaviors.

One of the principle tenets of evolutionary psychology is that the current form of the human brain took shape during a period called the environment of evolutionary adaptation, or EEA. While most place this era in the late Pleistocene, the EEA is really thought of as a composite of selective pressures that served the adaptation of humans' present brain structure. It is thought that during this period of evolutionary history those physical components of human brains that resulted in specific behaviors conferring reproductive advantage or fitness were under selective pressure. In this view, the origins of religious impulse would also be accounted for as a product of the EEA.

The physical nature of the religious experience has been investigated by neuroscience. A number of investigators have reported that the religious impulse could be located to the temporal lobe of the brain. In these studies the link to religious feelings and brain structure go hand in hand with the idea that the adaptation of the brain includes the origin of religion per se.

The work of sociobiology and evolutionary psychology has been critiqued by several evolutionary biologists, including Stephen Jay Gould (1941–2002). Their argument is that the research agenda of both fields is entirely too reductionistic and deterministic. Gould in particular took issue with the conclusions of evolutionary psychology, writing that "the chief strategy proposed for identifying adaptation is untestable and therefore unscientific" (quoted in Rose and Rose, 2000, p. 120).

Nonetheless in this modern version of evolutionism one sees the same process as that which motivated Spencer, Tylor, and Frazer in the nineteenth century and the early twentieth century. The motivation to give an anthropological and even materialist explanation for the occurrence of religions persists in the early twenty-first century.

See Also Animism and Animatism; Durkheim, Émile; Dynamism; Freud, Sigmund; Kulturkreiselehre; Lévy-Bruhl, Lucien; Müller, F. Max; Power; Schmidt, Wilhelm; Structuralism; Supreme Beings; Teilhard de Chardin, Pierre.

Bibliography

A good introduction for the layperson to the impact on Western thought of various ideas of history is R. G. Collingwood's *The Idea of History* (Oxford, 1946). Good surveys of the evolutionist movement in anthropology (and its decline) are Eric J. Sharpe's *Comparative Religion: A History* (London, 1975) and Jan de Vries's *The Study of Religion: A Historical Approach* (New York, 1967). E. E. Evans-Pritchard's insightful and amusing critique of "intellectualist" theories of religion, among which he includes the evolutionist mode, is in his *Theories of Primitive Religion* (Oxford, 1965). Edward O. Wilson's *Consilience* (New York, 1998) is easily accessible for most readers; see also his *Sociobiology* (Cambridge, Mass., 1975). A collection of essays critical of evolutionary psychology is contained in Hilary Rose and Stephen Rose, *Alas, Poor Darwin* (New York, 2000), including Stephen Jay Gould's "More Things in Heaven and Earth," cited above. See also G. W. F. Hegel, *Phenomenology of Spirit* (New York, 1977); Herbert Spencer, *Essays: Scientific, Political, and Speculative* (New York, 1914) and *Principles of Sociology* (Westport, Conn., 1975); E. B. Tylor, "The Religion of Savages," *Fortnightly Review* (1866) and *Primitive Culture* (London, 1871); Jacques Waardenburg, *Classical Approaches to the Study of Religion*, vol. 1, *Introduction and Anthology* (The Hague, 1973); R. R. Marett, "Preanimistic Religion," *Folklore* (1900) and "Mana," in *Encyclopaedia of Religion and Ethics*, edited by James Hastings; Andrew Lang, *Myth, Ritual, and Religion* (London, 1887); James G. Frazer, *Totemism and Exogamy* (London, 1910) and *The Golden Bough*, 3d ed. (1911–1915); Sigmund Freud, *Totem and Taboo* (New York, 1918), *The Future of an Illusion* (New York, 1928), and *Civilization and Its Discontents* (New York, 1930); and Melford E. Spiro, *Oedipus in the Trobriands* (Chicago, 1982).

James Waller (1987)
Mary Edwardsen (1987)
Martinez Hewlett (2005)

EVOLUTION: EVOLUTIONARY ETHICS

Evolutionary ethics attempts to use the biological theory of evolution as a foundation for ethics. As such, its history is closely linked with the development and popularization of evolutionary theories starting in the nineteenth century. To a large extent, the history of evolutionary ethics is associated with efforts to find alternatives to religion as a foundation for moral law. The growth of industrialism, the establishment of German biblical criticism, and the rise of science all contributed to growing secularism during the middle of the nineteenth century. Like other attempts to extend an understanding of biological evolution to the human situation, evolutionary ethics has been highly controversial. Although various evolutionary ethics were proposed throughout Western countries, its greatest popularity was in the Anglo-American world. The history of evolutionary ethics is divided into three phases, the initial Darwin and Spencer period, an early-twentieth-century period, and a contemporary period.

Initial Period: Darwin and Spencer. When Charles Darwin published his *Origin of Species* in 1859, he avoided discussion of human evolution as well as the implications of his theory for an understanding of human society. He was fully aware, however, that others would immediately extend his theory to cover human evolution and that the implications of his work would be discussed. In his *Descent of Man* (1871) Darwin tackled these issues directly. Of central concern to him was the "moral faculty," the possession of which he considered the most important difference between humans and all other "lower animals."

Darwin's theory of evolution attempted to understand the origin of contemporary animal and plant life in naturalistic terms, that is, without reference to any supernatural causes. Since humans, according to his theory, were considered to have had a natural origin, Darwin approached the problem of the origin of the moral faculty as he did other physical and mental traits. His general approach in trying to understand the origin of complex traits, such as the human eye, was to depict them as part of a continuum—instead of focusing on their unique or unusual aspects, he depicted them as part of a series. In the case of the eye, for example, he constructed a series of traits starting with simple, light-sensitive cells on the skin of a primitive organism and ended with the highly complex vertebrate eye. This allowed him to illustrate how, over time, a trait could change by small increments from one end of a spectrum to the other, from simple to complex. He used this approach with the moral faculty and claimed that it was the natural development of the intellectual capacity of social animals.

Any social animal, according to Darwin, that attained an intelligence that was close to human intelligence would develop a moral faculty. He explained the moral faculty in the following manner: With increased intelligence, early humans attained the capacity for various sentiments (e.g., courage, sympathy), and these gave advantages to the group. Groups with these sentiments survived better than those without them. Over time, one of these sentiments evolved into a moral sense that helped consolidate the group and gave it increased survival value. Darwin was aware of the ethnographic literature of his day, which suggested that all human groups had sets of ethical beliefs, and he felt that in time people would understand the adaptive value of these beliefs. Darwin did not attempt to justify moral beliefs by reference to their origin. He was primarily concerned with how they came about.

In contrast, Darwin's contemporary Herbert Spencer sought justification for ethical positions. Spencer elaborated an ethical theory that he believed had evolved from nature, and he argued that his system was natural and prescriptive. In his *Social Statics* (1851) Spencer derived a basic principle for ethics: "Every man has freedom to do all that he wills, provided he infringes not the equal freedom of any other man" (p. 121). This principle allowed individuals to seek what gave them pleasure, and in his later *Principles of Ethics* (1879–1893) he elaborated an evolutionary philosophy to explain how seeking pleasure (and avoiding pain) drove the evolutionary process in biology and psychology and was therefore a natural principle on which to base ethics.

Spencer's evolutionary ethics was more Lamarckian than Darwinian. That is, he did not stress the adaptive value of the moral sentiment but rather emphasized the inheritance of acquired characteristics and thought of nature as moving to a predetermined goal. For Spencer, a natural process was moving human evolution toward a state where duty became pleasure, mutual aid replaced competition, and the greatest possible individual freedom existed.

Contemporaries did not always carefully distinguish between Darwin's ideas and those of Spencer. And numerous supporters of evolutionary ethics combined ideas in new and novel combinations. Consequently, evolutionary ethics varied considerably. In the United States, John Fiske emerged as the most energetic supporter of evolutionary ethics. Fiske was an admirer of Spencer, but he believed that evolutionary ideas opened up the path to a new, reborn Christianity. Fiske's religious orientation was somewhat unusual in the evolutionary ethics tradition. Leslie Stephen in England was more Darwinian, and he believed that evolution provided the foundation for an agnostic, liberal morality. Other important supporters of evolutionary ethics were Woods Hutchinson in the United States and Benjamin Kidd in Britain.

Evolutionary ethics had support, but also a number of critics. Two of the period's major evolutionists, Thomas Henry Huxley and Alfred Russel Wallace, were strongly opposed to the position and wrote critical works arguing against it. Huxley, citing David Hume, argued that describing what "is" does not give one the authority to proscribe what "ought" to be (the famous IS/OUGHT distinction). Wallace took a quite different approach in his critique and was drawn to a spiritualist view of moral thought. He rejected both Darwin's and Spencer's positions on ethics and contended that evolutionary biology could not provide a foundation for ethics.

Of greater importance, the philosophic community was nearly unanimous in its rejection of evolutionary ethics. The leading figure at the time in ethics, Henry Sidgwick of Cambridge University, dismissed evolutionary ethics in his major work, *Methods of Ethics* (1874). He wrote that the justification of evolutionary ethics depended upon one of two arguments. The first, going from a description of a moral belief to a belief in its validity, he rejected because he contended that such an argument merely tells about a custom and is of no value to ethics. The second specifies a hypothetical "natural state" of humans and society and goes on to use that state as a foundation for ethics. He rejected it because he felt it was a confused position; any impulse, desire, or tendency can be considered "natural." How can one deem a particular one significantly natural without some prior justification? According to Sidgwick, ethics is a systematic examination of beliefs about what is right or wrong, with the goal of constructing a rational system of moral ideas. From his perspective, evolutionary ethics was not an ethical system but merely a discussion of how ethical systems may have come into being or a discussion of various held beliefs. It was not to be taken seriously as constructive ethics.

In the early part of the twentieth century, Sidgwick's condemnation of evolutionary ethics was repeated and extended by the Cambridge philosopher G. E. Moore. His arguments are the ones most often cited in criticism of evolutionary ethics. In his *Principia Ethica* (1903), Moore rejected evolutionary ethics along with other forms of naturalistic ethics, all of which he claimed were based on the "naturalistic fallacy." He meant by this that attempts to explain the "good" by reference to some property were not valid. The "good" is a simple notion that cannot be defined as pleasure or an evolutionary adaptation. Moore's critique was aimed at more than just evolutionary ethics, and his writings served to redirect ethical writing. American philosophers were no more accepting of evolutionary ethics than the English. William James and John Dewey, both sympathetic to and influenced by evolutionary ideas, rejected evolutionary ethics.

Early-Twentieth-Century Period. Evolutionary ethics entered a new phase in the early twentieth century due to changes in evolutionary science itself and the extension of evolutionary ideas into a broad worldview. The most outspoken supporter was Julian Huxley, grandson of Thomas Henry Huxley (who had been so critical of the position in the previous century). Julian Huxley is famous for being one of the architects of the Modern Synthesis, the neo-Darwinian theory that stressed Darwin's original insight that natural selection of small random variations were the central driving force in evolution. The new theory built on the dramatic new genetic understanding of variation as well as careful work in natural history on geographic variation. Huxley played a key role in synthesizing this knowledge and in popularizing it. Equally important, Huxley believed that the new evolutionary theory provided a foundation for a new humanist philosophy that had important implications for social policy and ethical thought. He elaborated on his version of evolutionary ethics in his Romanes Lecture in 1943.

At the heart of Huxley's argument was his contention that evolution was a progressive process with three different stages: cosmic, biological, and psychosocial. The process of evolution had led to the emergence of humans, the highest and most advanced species, one capable of cultural evolution and ultimately of a sense of moral obligation. To explain the origin of moral obligation, Huxley made reference to psychology, in particular Sigmund Freud's concept of the superego, an internalized authority that allows one's sense of guilt to repress aggression and that is the source of one's senses of "wrong" and of "duty." Moral obligation evolved over time, as did human ethical standards, the ethics accepted by social groups. Huxley argued that the direction of moral progress was toward greater human fulfillment and the realization of values that had "intrinsic worth" (rather than adaptive worth). Only a society that respected individual rights, stressed education, encouraged responsibility, and promoted the arts could realize those goals.

Huxley's scientific humanism enjoyed a limited popularity with the general public in the decades after World War II, as did the writings of C. H. Waddington, who argued along similar lines in his 1960 book *The Ethical Animal.* Waddington departed from Huxley, however, in emphasizing that the "good" in evolutionary ethics had to be viewed in terms of what furthers human evolution. Their version of evolutionary ethics rested on a new and widely accepted theory of evolution, but the old criticisms raised by Sidgwick and Moore remained. Moreover the philosophy community by this time had moved onto other approaches to ethics. Some, like Charles Stevenson, stressed language; others followed A. J. Ayer and his logical positivism, which tended to dismiss ethics as merely expressions of feeling and not having any truth value. None of these newer approaches to ethics accepted evolutionary ethics, and by the 1970s the position had few supporters.

Contemporary Period: Evolutionary Ethics after 1975. With the appearance of Edward O. Wilson's *Sociobiology* in 1975, a new chapter in the history of evolutionary ethics began. Wilson's text synthesized research on the Modern Synthesis with population biology and animal behavior. The central argument of the book is that behavior should be regarded as adaptive and can be understand best from an evolutionary perspective, not just animal behavior but human behavior as well. *Sociobiology* had a short section on ethics, and in it Wilson claimed that the time had come for ethics to be removed temporarily from the domain of philosophy and moved into biology. The study of the biological basis of social behavior promised, according to Wilson, to provide a new Darwinian foundation for ethics and for an understanding of social sciences and humanities.

Wilson followed up his suggestion with his Pulitzer Prize–winning book *On Human Nature* (1978), in which he elaborated on his evolutionary understanding of ethics. Unlike Darwin, who had relied on a view of group selection to explain the origin of the moral sentiment, Wilson built on the work of William Hamilton, who argued for understanding "altruistic behavior" as an activity that can promote passage of a greater number of an individual's genes to the next generation. Hamilton, in a set of classic papers in 1964, showed that an "altruistic act" can have selective value if it leads to the survival and reproduction of near relatives with whom one shares common genes. Because a person shares half of his or her genes with a sibling and an eighth with a cousin, if a person acts in a manner that sacrifices his or her life but that more than doubles the reproductive rate of a sibling, then copies of that person's genes will increase in the next generation. From an evolutionary perspective, an individual passing on his or her genes is of central value. The individual who passes on genes has a greater impact on the next generation than one who does not. Hamilton's ideas were popularized by Richard Dawkins in his *The Selfish Gene* (1976), which argues that all supposed selfish acts are ultimately selfish in a genetic sense.

Wilson used Hamilton to explain how an action that "appears" altruistic, that helps another at one's expense, in the long run can work for its carrier's "benefit" and therefore have a selective value. But what actions "ought" one take? Here Wilson also utilized the central, modern evolutionary principle, the survival and reproduction of genes. He argued that what promotes survival and reproduction of the gene pool is "good" and what negatively affects it is "bad." Atomic warfare, from this perspective, is bad. Wilson in fact derived an entire set of "good" actions and "bad" actions based on their effects on the gene pool. Ultimately, Wilson concluded, science will provide a more powerful mythology than religion, and humans will be able to construct meaningful and moral lives from a totally secular perspective.

Although a few biologists and other intellectuals, particularly evolutionary psychologists, have embraced this new evolutionary ethics, the position has drawn considerable criticism. Philosophers and historians have noted that the new ethics, which draws on evolutionary theory, although up-to-date in its biology, suffers from the same flaws that were first raised by Sidgwick and other early critics. The emphasis on genes and their survival has also raised the question of how deterministic the view is. After all, if people do not have any free will to make decisions, if people are hardwired to act in certain ways, how can one claim that actions are "good?" Wilson has grappled with the issue and argued that genes and culture interact, but that individuals have "tendencies" that predispose them in certain ways. Others see culture as more independent. Richard Alexander, an animal behaviorist, argued that evolutionary analysis can reveal quite a lot about the origin and development of laws and ethical opinions but cannot reveal which ones are "right." Such views undercut the value of evolutionary ethics, because they underscore its inadequacy of providing a guide for action.

As with the earlier versions of evolutionary ethics, supporters of modern theories of evolutionary ethics have made little headway toward gaining acceptance. Evolutionary ethics has long had an attraction for some. It serves as an essential subject for worldviews based on evolution and has provided a secular foundation for moral beliefs. Unfortunately, it has suffered from a set of serious philosophical flaws, and it has failed to meet the challenges posed by philosophers.

See Also Ethology of Religion; Sociobiology and Evolutionary Psychology, article on Sociobiology of Religion; Spencer, Herbert.

Bibliography

Breuer, Georg. *Sociobiology and the Human Dimension.* Cambridge, U.K., 1982. A perceptive discussion of the debate over sociobiology.

Darwin, Charles. *The Descent of Man.* London, 1871.

Dawkins, Richard. *The Selfish Gene.* New York, 1976.

Degler, Carl N. *In Search of Human Nature: The Decline and Revival of Darwinism in American Social Thought.* New York, 1991. A review of the impact of Darwinism on theories of human nature.

Farber, Paul Lawrence. *The Temptations of Evolutionary Ethics.* Berkeley, Calif., 1994. A history from Darwin to Edward O. Wilson.

Flew, Anthony. *Evolutionary Ethics.* London, 1967. A philosophical critique of the position.

Huxley, Thomas, and Julian Huxley. *Touchstone for Ethics, 1893–1943.* New York, 1947. Contains Thomas Huxley's critique of evolutionary ethics and Julian Huxley's defense.

Kitcher, Philip. *Vaulting Ambition: Sociobiology and the Quest for Human Nature.* Cambridge, Mass., 1985. An extensive critique of the attempt to understand human nature through sociobiology.

Midgley, Mary. *Evolution as a Religion: Strange Hopes and Stranger Fears.* London, 1985. A perceptive discussion of the attempt to understand ethical issues from a biological perspective.

Moore, G. E. *Principia Ethica.* Cambridge, U.K., 1903.

Murphy, Jeffrie G.. *Evolution, Morality, and the Meaning of Life.* Totowa, N.J., 1982. A good general discussion of the issues.

Quillian, William F., Jr. *The Moral Theory of Evolutionary Naturalism.* New Haven, Conn., 1945. A careful philosophical analysis of the central argument.

Quinton, Anthony. "Ethics and the Theory of Evolution." In *Biology and Personality: Frontier Problems in Science, Philosophy, and Religion,* edited by Ian T. Ramsey. Oxford, 1965, pp, 107–131. A discussion of the philosophical problems with evolutionary ethics.

Richards, Robert J. *Darwin and the Emergence of Evolutionary Theories of Mind and Behavior.* Chicago, 1987. A good background work for the subject, and a spirited defense.

Rottschaefer, William A. *The Biology and Psychology of Moral Agency.* New York, 1998. An interesting attempt to solve some of the philosophical issues that surround evolutionary ethics.

Ruse, Michael. *Taking Darwin Seriously: A Naturalistic Approach to Philosophy.* New York, 1986. A modified version of evolutionary ethics.

Schilcher, Florian von, and Neil Tennant. *Philosophy, Evolution, and Human Nature.* London, 1984. A careful analysis of the central issues.

Sidgwick, Henry. *The Methods of Ethics.* London, 1901. An extended discussion and critique of evolutionary ethics.

Spencer, Herbert. *Social Statics.* London, 1851.

Spencer, Herbert. *Principles of Ethics.* 1879–1893. 2 volumes.

Waddington, C. H. *The Ethical Animal.* London, 1960.

Williams, Cora M. *A Review of the Systems of Ethics Founded on the Theory of Evolution.* London, 1893. A discussion of the early major statements of evolutionary ethics.

Wilson, Edward O. *Sociobiology.* Cambridge, Mass., 1975.

Wilson, Edward O. *On Human Nature.* Cambridge, Mass., 1978. Wilson's major work on evolutionary ethics.

Paul Lawrence Farber (2005)

EXCOMMUNICATION.

To excommunicate means "to cut off from communion" or "to exclude from fellowship in a community." In a Christian setting, the term *excommunication* also applies to exclusion from Holy Communion, or the Eucharist.

Historically, religious practice admitted some form of putting a person outside the community. Any community claims the right to protect itself against nonconforming members who may threaten the common welfare. In a religious setting this right has often been reinforced by the belief that the sanction affects one's standing before God, inasmuch as it entails being cut off from the community of the saved. In religious traditions in which nonconformity was punishable by death, excommunication was introduced as a mitigation of the death penalty. In medieval Christendom and during the early years of the Reformation, excommunicated persons were turned over to civil authorities, who could inflict the death penalty upon them.

With the shift in modern times to considering religious affiliation a matter of free choice, doubts have been expressed about the meaning and value of excommunication. Although practiced less frequently today, some current examples include the *ḥerem* in Orthodox Judaism, "shunning" among some traditional Christian bodies, withdrawal of membership by congregation-based communities, and "excommunication" as practiced by Mormons, Roman Catholics, and some other mainline Christian churches.

In the Western Christian tradition, excommunication is seen as based on practice reflected in scripture, especially Paul (see, for example, *1 Cor.* 5:1–13, *2 Cor.* 2:5–11, *2 Thes.* 3:14–15). Theoretical justification is taken from the command to bind and loose (*Mt.* 18:15–18). This same passage supplies key elements of procedure, including advance warning and attempts to lead the delinquent to conversion.

Early Christian practice mixed liturgical excommunications, which were part of the nonrepeatable public penitential practices, with disciplinary ones that could culminate in a person being declared anathema. In the thirteenth century Innocent III specified excommunication as a disciplinary penalty distinct from other punishments, characterizing it as specifically medicinal, intended to heal the delinquent. The number of crimes for which excommunication could be incurred increased steadily through the eighteenth century, but a marked reduction in their number began with the reforms of Pius IX in 1869 and continued with the promulgation of the Code of Canon Law in 1917.

As a medicinal, or healing, penalty, excommunication under Roman Catholic law may be incurred only if a serious sin has been committed, or if the person is obstinate in a position after being given formal warnings and time to repent. Reflecting medieval and later developments, some excommunications are automatic (*latae sententiae*), incurred by committing a specified act, such as abortion or physically striking the pope. Other excommunications are imposed (*ferendae sententiae*) after an administrative or judicial investigation. Excommunication must always be lifted as soon as the delinquent repents and seeks peace with the church.

A distinction used to be drawn between major excommunications, which cut a person off from all participation in community life, and minor ones, which prohibited participation in the sacraments, especially the Eucharist. Current canon law has dropped this distinction, although the 1917 code did characterize some excommunicates as *vitandi,* with whom contact must be completely avoided. Under the 1917 code all others were *tolerati,* and contact with them could be permitted.

An excommunicated person loses basic rights in the church, but not the effects of baptism, which can never be lost. In the revision of the code carried out after Vatican II the effects of excommunication were clarified, and the distinction of *vitandi* and *tolerati* was dropped. Instead, all are treated as *tolerati* so far as the effects are concerned. These depend on whether the excommunication was imposed by a public declaration or sentence of condemnation, or was incurred automatically but without much public notice.

Generally, a person who is excommunicated is denied any role in administering the sacraments, especially the Eucharist. He or she may not receive any of the sacraments or administer sacramentals, such as burials, and is forbidden to exercise any church offices or functions. If the penalty has been declared or imposed by a sentence, any liturgical actions the excommunicate attempts are to be suspended until he or she leaves; the excommunicate loses any offices or other functions in the church; and may make no claim for income or other benefits from the church.

Under the reform of the law, automatic excommunication can be incurred in only six instances, including abortion. It may be imposed for a limited number of other crimes against faith, the Eucharist, or the seal of the confessional in the sacrament of penance. If imposed by a sentence or public declaration, excommunication can be lifted only by a public authority in the church, usually the local diocesan bishop. Otherwise, it can be lifted by a priest during the sacrament of penance, but unlike the 1917 code the revised rules require that in all cases the bishop be contacted afterward for the reconciliation to remain in effect.

BIBLIOGRAPHY

Recommended studies of early Christian practice are Kenneth Helm's *Eucharist and Excommunication: A Study in Early Christian Doctrine and Discipline* (Frankfurt, 1973) and John E. Lynch's "The Limits of *Communio* in the Pre-Constantinian Church," *Jurist* 36 (1976): 159–190. For historical background and detailed commentary on Roman Catholic canon law through the 1917 Code of Canon Law, see Francis Edward Hyland's *Excommunication: Its Nature, Historical Development and Effects* (Washington, D. C., 1928), and for an overview of efforts to reform Roman Catholic law on this subject, see Thomas J. Green's "Future of Penal Law in the Church," *Jurist* 35 (1975): 212–275, which includes a bibliography. Both the *Dictionnaire de droit canonique* (Paris, 1953) and the *Lexikon für Theologie und Kirche,* 2d ed. (Freiburg, 1957–1968), offer extensive articles, under the terms *Excommunication* and *Bann,* respectively.

JAMES H. PROVOST (1987)

EXEGESIS SEE BIBLICAL EXEGESIS; HERMENEUTICS; TAFSĪR

EXILE. Often prompted by historical conditions, the concept of exile appears in various religious traditions as a symbol of separation, alienation, and that which is unredeemed.

IN JUDAISM. With the Babylonian invasion of Judah and the subsequent destruction of the Jerusalem Temple in 587/6 BCE, the concept of exile (Heb., *golah* or *galut*) came to reflect both a historical reality and a communal perception. Forced into exile in Babylonia, members of the upper classes found themselves uprooted from their national and spiritual homeland. Literally, then, the term *exile* came to describe the forced dispersion of the Jewish people and their subjugation under alien rule. Although according to Jewish tradition (*Jer* 29:10) the Babylonian exile was only seventy years in duration, the destruction of the Second Temple in 70 CE and the triumph of Rome caused a national uprootedness that lasted for almost two thousand years. Historically, one can thus maintain that the exile of the Jewish people from the land of Israel began in the sixth century BCE and came to an end in 1948 with the establishment of the state of Israel and the restoration of Jewish political independence.

Metaphorically, however, the term *exile* was and is still used as a symbol of alienation, reflecting the Jews' separation from the land of Israel, from the Torah by which God commanded them to live, from God, and from the non-Jew and the non-Jewish world in general.

To the biblical prophets, exile was a symbol of divine retribution. As Isaiah makes clear (44:9–20), in worshiping other deities, the people of Israel revealed a lack of fidelity to their God and to the covenant that God had established with them. Their punishment, then, was the destruction of their spiritual center, Jerusalem, as well as of the Temple in which sacrifices were offered, and the forced removal of many from the land that had been promised to them. At the same time, however, exile became a symbol of judgment. Those who remained religiously faithful, becoming, in Isaiah's words, God's "suffering servants" (43:10), would reap the rewards of righteousness and ultimately be redeemed.

According to the prophet Ezekiel (14:3ff., 21:31ff.), exile was a trial through which God tested Israel's faithfulness to God and God's teachings. It was also a symbol of Israel's election, with the Babylonians, and later the Romans and all those under whose rule the Jewish people were subjugated, acting as instruments of a divine schema through which, as Isaiah writes, God's "faithful remnant" (27:31ff.) would be redeemed. Exile thus became a metaphor of separation not only from God but also from righteousness. As such, it was associated with a pre-messianic, pre-redemptive era. In exile, as John Bright maintains, one was to purge oneself of sin in order to prepare for the future, to "return," that is, to remember that God, the Creator of the world, chose Israel to be God's people. Obeying the divine commandments given to them was therefore a way out of exile both historically and spiritually. On a historical level, the Jewish people would be led back to the Land of Israel, with the Temple rebuilt and political independence restored, while on a spiritual level, as Isaiah writes (51:6), the righteous would attain eternal salvation.

Throughout the Middle Ages, the concept of exile gave theological significance to the continued political, social, and economic oppression of the Jewish people. The tenth-century philosopher Sa'adyah Gaon, in his *Book of Beliefs and Opinions*, emphasized the importance of exile as a trial and as a means of purification, while according to an anonymous contemporary, exile, as a divine gift and a "blessing of Abraham," served as a mark of Israel's election. According to this view, exile was not a punishment for sin but an opportunity given by God to bring God's teachings to all of humanity. After fifteen hundred years of Jewish settlement in Spain, characterized by a social, economic, and political integration unknown elsewhere in the medieval world, King Ferdinand and Queen Isabella's edict of expulsion in 1492, left generations of Spanish Jewry feeling doubly exiled. As Jane Gerber notes, the exiles and their descendents viewed Spain as a second Jerusalem. Their expulsion, therefore, "was as keenly lamented as was exile from the Holy Land," leading to "both a new dynamism and a heightened sense of despair."

To many medieval Jewish mystics, exile took on additional significance as a metaphor describing on the divine level what historically had befallen the Jewish people. One finds in the thirteenth-century *Zohar*, for example, the claim that with the destruction of the Second Temple both the Jewish people and the tenth emanation of God, identified as *shekhinah* (God's visible presence in the world), went into exile. Thus, the separation of the Jewish people from the Land of Israel became mirrored in the alienation of God from a part of Godself. This idea is reiterated and broadened in the writings of the sixteenth-century mystic Isaac Luria (1534–1572), in which the exile of the *shekhinah* is said to reflect the exile or "fall" of humanity as a whole into the domination of demonic powers.

Finally, on a psychological level, the concept of exile served to reinforce the national self-consciousness among a people who no longer shared a common culture, language, or land. Exclusion from non-Jewish society, coupled with a Jewish liturgy and calendar that reinforced the notion of the Land of Israel as home, underscored the alien nature of the Jew in the non-Jewish world. After the seventeenth century, however, as European emancipation came to afford growing numbers of Jews the opportunity to participate more fully in non-Jewish society, many began to feel that the Diaspora did not necessarily have to be equated with exile. One sees this most clearly in the writings of nineteenth-century religious reformers who, insisting that Jews were members of a religious community but not of a specific nation, maintained that it was possible for Jews to view any country as home.

Since 1948, it is debatable whether Jews choosing to live outside the state of Israel historically are still in exile. Yet one can argue, as does Arthur Hertzberg in *Being Jewish in America,* that on a psychological level the concept of exile remains a compelling symbol. Hertzberg maintains that even in the United States, where Jews have gained great acceptance and freedom, the Jew continues to be an alien. As an externally and internally imposed sense of self-identification, exile thus reflects the conviction of many Jews that the Diaspora can never truly be seen as "home."

IN CHRISTIANITY. The metaphor of exile appears in Christianity in two separate ways: first, as that reflecting the historical and spiritual conditions under which the Jewish people have lived since the fall of the Second Temple, and second, as descriptive of life in this world as opposed to life in the kingdom of heaven.

Like their Jewish contemporaries, the Fathers of the early church attached theological significance to the destruction of the Jerusalem Temple in 70 CE. They maintained, however, that its destruction was not caused by sinfulness in general but by one particular sin, namely the rejection by most of the Jewish community in Palestine of Jesus as the Messiah for whom they had been waiting. Thus, the historical exile of the Jewish people was seen to mirror the spiritual exile—or alienation—of the Jews from God. To "return" in the Christian sense came to imply not only repentance but also acknowledgement of Jesus as savior.

In the New Testament *Gospel of John,* one sees that which is usually identified as a more Gnostic understanding of exile. Jesus here identifies himself as one who is "not of the world." Those who are "of the world," he says (*Jn.* 17:16), are those who have not acknowledged that he is the Christ (Messiah), sent by his father, the one true God, in order to redeem his people. To be "not of the world," he continues, is to be with God in the Divine spiritual kingdom, possible even before death. Exile thus functions here as an individual rather than a collective metaphor of alienation or separation from God. Not surprisingly, John's understanding of "return," rooted in an individual declaration of faith, is also personal in nature.

IN GNOSTICISM. The concept of exile comes to play a central role in a number of early Gnostic texts. Set within a dualistic framework of spirit versus matter, light versus darkness, goodness versus evil, exile again functions as a symbol of alienation. Here, however, it is not a particular people that are said to be in exile or the nonbeliever per se but the human soul. Belonging to the spiritual realm of light but trapped in the world of matter or darkness, it depends upon the "saving knowledge" of the Gnostic to begin its journey home.

The *Apocryphon of John,* written probably in the late second century CE, the third-century *Gospel of Thomas,* and the fourth-century *Pistis Sophia* are among several Gnostic Christian texts that depict Jesus as having been sent down to earth to impart this saving knowledge to others. Reminding his listeners of their heavenly origin, he tells them that the soul can be set free only through this insight, or *gnōsis.* To be in exile is to be unredeemed, ignorant of one's origins and of the nature of the human soul. In these and other texts, knowledge thus becomes the necessary key to salvation.

Yet having attained this knowledge, the Gnostic cannot help but experience life in this world as "alien." Hans Jonas maintains that this experience serves as the primary symbol not just of Christian Gnosticism but of other forms of gnosticism as well. Life in this world is depicted as a descent into darkness and captivity, a life of exile for which, as the Mandaeans claimed, the only "day of escape" is death. As a metaphor, then, exile takes on personal rather than communal significance, reflecting the experience of the Gnostic who, alienated from and in revolt against the cosmos, longs to return home.

Among the Isma'iliyah, an Islamic movement of radical Shi'ah founded in the late third century AH (ninth century CE), one again finds the concept of exile serving as a central symbol of alienation. Here, it is the imam who leads the gnostic away from the world of darkness. Possessing the esoteric knowledge of the soul's true spiritual birth, the imam offers this knowledge to his disciple as a "salvatory revelation." Having attained this revelation, the disciple is freed from exile and reborn as a "being of light."

THE ISHRĀQĪYAH. Revealing the influences of Zoroastrianism, Gnosticism, Persian mysticism, and Neoplatonism, the illuminative philosophy of the twelfth-century thinker Shihāb al-Dīn Yaḥyá Suhrawardī (Shihāb al-Dīn Yaḥyá ibn Ḥabash ibn Amīrak Abū al-Futūḥ Suhrawardī; AH 549–587/1170–1208 CE) uses exile as a symbol of ignorance of one's true spiritual nature and of reality in general. "Home," in the Ishrāqī school, is metaphorically identified with the world of light, while exile is described as entrapment within the realm of darkness. In order to journey homeward, the Ishrāqīyun need to move beyond rational inquiry to the imaginal world and illumination *(ishrāq).* Only then can the souls of the Ishrāqīyah attain mystical union with the inner divine presence, experiencing an ecstatic separation from the physical body and an anticipation of death. Thus to journey out of exile is to overcome the separation of the soul from the divine and to become inflamed by what Henry Corbin labels the "divine fire."

Suhrawardī's understanding of exile is developed most fully in his *Recital of the Western Exile,* a spiritual autobiography that describes the struggles of the "man of light" to free himself from darkness. Associating ignorance with the West and illumination with the East, Suhrawardī begins his tale with the exile of the soul to the western city of Kairouan. Forgetting his origins and eventually taken captive, the man of light slowly comes to an awareness of his true identity and sets out on the long journey home. Thought at first he is forced to return to the West, he is finally set free. Stripped of the "fetters of matter," his soul becomes possessed by an angel who helps it return to its celestial condition. Thus beginning its heavenly ascent, it leaves the world of exile forever.

IN CONTEMPORARY TIBETAN BUDDHISM. Forced to live in exile since 1959, the XIV Dalai Lama, religious and secular head of Tibet, along with well over 100,000 Tibetan refugees, have sought refuge in India, in the Himalayan town of Dharamsala. With the Chinese military annexation of Tibet, the systematic attempt to destroy Tibet's religion, and the massive influx of ethnic Chinese, Tibetan Buddhists have lost their land, temples, monasteries, and most of their religious leaders. Consequently, they also risk losing their identity.

Recognizing the difficulty of returning to Tibet as a free people, the Dalai Lama has created in Dharamsala a Tibetan Government in Exile. In an effort to rebuild the refugees' shattered lives, it features new governmental departments of Education, Rehabilitation, Information, and Security, as well as new Offices of Religious and Economic Affairs. It also features a monastery built in 1968 and a temple built in 1970, leading to what the Dalai Lama has described as a "thriving monastic community of over six thousand strong." The Library of Tibetan Works and Archives opened in Dharamsala in the late 1960s. Housing over forty thousand original Tibetan volumes and involved in published English language and Tibetan books, it has become a world-wide center of Buddhist research and study.

In an effort to preserve the religion and culture of the six million Tibetan Buddhists that he represents, while promoting world peace through nonviolence, the Dalai Lama has devoted himself to building a strong Tibetan community in exile. He also has engaged in dialogue with political and religious leaders throughout the world.

Among them has been a group of rabbis and Jewish scholars first invited to meet with the Dalai Lama in 1989, the same year that he was awarded the Nobel Peace Prize. According to Rodger Kamenetz, "in the Dalai Lama's eyes, and to many of the Tibetans, Jews are survival experts. The idea that Jewish history, with all its traumas, is relevant to another exiled people was inspiring." So was the Jewish observance of home rituals; the preservation and renewal of religious culture and tradition; and most importantly, the Jewish emphasis on remembrance, including the memory of exile.

For over four decades, Tibetan Buddhists have experienced exile as a political and geographical reality. Yet despite the longing of exiled Tibetan Buddhists to return to their home, holy spaces are primarily symbolic in the Buddhist imagination. Since ultimately, they come from an individual's inner spiritual power, they can be transported. Thus Tibet in-and-of-itself is not as central to Tibetan Buddhism as Jerusalem is to Judaism. Nor, for that matter, is the concept of physical exile. Nonetheless, ongoing attempts by the Dalai Lama to free Tibet from Chinese control and to keep Tibetan Buddhism alive, even in exile, have helped differentiate Tibetan Buddhism from other forms of Buddhist belief and practice. So have the efforts by hundreds of resident scholars and monks at the Tibetan Library in Dharamsala to preserve and help translate original Tibetan manuscripts, including rare ones smuggled out of Tibet over the past forty years.

SEE ALSO Buddhism, article on Buddhism in Tibet; Buddhism, Schools of, article on Tibetan and Mongolian Buddhism; Dalai Lama; Gnosticism; Ishraqiyah; Shekhinah; Soul.

BIBLIOGRAPHY

Excellent summaries of the early historical development of the concept of exile in Judaism can be found in John Bright's *A History of Israel,* 3d ed., (Philadelphia, 1981), and William F. Albright's essay on "The Biblical Period" in *The Jews,* vol. 1, edited by Louis Finkelstein (Philadelphia, 1949), pp. 3–69. For insight into why Spanish Jewry came to feel a sense of being doubly exiled, see Jane Gerber's *The Jews of Spain: A History of the Sephardic Experience* (New York, 1992). For a discussion of the significance of exile in medieval Jewish mysticism, see Gershom Scholem's *Major Trends in Jewish Mysticism* (1941; New York, 1961), especially lectures two, six, and seven. Michael A. Meyer's *The Origins of the Modern Jew* (Detroit, 1967), provides insight into the relationship between European emancipation and the later Jewish reevaluation of exile as a meaningful theological symbol. Finally, Arthur Hertzberg reflects at length on the concept of exile in the American Jewish imagination in his *Being Jewish in America: The Modern Experience* (New York, 1979), and more recently, in his autobiographical *A Jew in America: My Life and a People's Struggle for Identity* (San Francisco, 2002).

The best study of exile as metaphor in Christian and Hellenistic Gnosticism remains Hans Jonas's second revised edition of *The Gnostic Religion* (Boston, 1963). For a comparison between these ideas and those found in the New Testament *Gospel of John,* see James M. Robinson's "Gnosticism and the New Testament," in *Gnosis: Festschrift fur Hans Jonas,* edited by Barbara Aland (Göttingen, West Germany, 1978), pp. 125–157. Bernard Lewis's *The Origins of Ismailism* (1940; New York, 1975) provides a good overview of this concept among the Isma'iliyah, while Henry Corbin's *En Islam iranien: Aspects spirituals et philosophiques,* vol. 2, (Paris, 1971) and *Spiritual Body and Celestial Earth* (Princeton, 1977) offer cogent accounts of exile as metaphor in Suhrawardī's theosophy of light.

For a lengthy discussion of exile as symbol and reality in contemporary Tibetan Buddhism, see Bstan dzin rgya mtsho, Dalai Lama XIV, *Freedom in Exile: The Autobiography of the Dalai Lama* (New York, 1990). Detailed descriptions of meetings between the Dalai Lama and Jewish leaders can be found in Rodger Kamenetz's *The Jew in the Lotus: A Poet's Rediscovery of Jewish Identity in Buddhist India* (San Francisco, 1994).

ELLEN M. UMANSKY (1987 AND 2005)

EXISTENTIALISM is a type of philosophy difficult to define because it does not have any agreed body of doctrine;

it is rather a way of doing philosophy in which life and thought are closely related to each other. Thus, while some existentialists have been theists and others atheists, they have arrived at their different results by rather similar processes of thought. The existentialist who believes in God does so not as a result of intellectual demonstration—he or she is more likely to say that the attempts to prove God's existence are a waste of time, or even harmful—but on the grounds of passionate inward conviction; likewise the atheistic existentialist rejects God not because of being persuaded by argument but because the very idea of God poses a threat to the freedom and autonomy of the human being, and so to the integrity of humanity. But if such nonrational factors are allowed their say, is it not a departure from philosophy altogether? Perhaps not, if one thinks that reason has become so ambitious that it ceases to perceive its own limitations and so becomes misleading. The all-embracing rational system of Hegel provoked not only Kierkegaard's existentialism but also the skepticism of the left-wing Hegelians and neo-Kantian positivism. The existentialists of the twentieth century emerged about the same time as the logical positivists, and both groups shared doubts about the omnicompetence of reason. The existentialist would still claim to be a philosopher, in the sense of a thinker, but, in Kierkegaard's expression, an "existing thinker," that is, a thinker who is always involved in the reality being thought about, so that the thinker cannot take up the purely objective attitude of a spectator; also, the thinker is always on the way from one matter to another, so that as long as the thinker exists he or she never has a complete picture. So existentialism stands opposed to all those grand metaphysical systems that profess to give a comprehensive and objective account of all that is. Significantly, Kierkegaard titles two of his most important writings *Philosophical Fragments* and *Concluding Unscientific Postscript,* and these titles implicitly contrast his work with that of philosophers who aim at a comprehensive system.

Though some earlier writers, such as Blaise Pascal (1623–1662), who criticized the theistic proofs and contrasted the God of the philosophers with the living God of Abraham, Isaac, and Jacob, have been seen in retrospect as forerunners of existentialism, the movement belongs essentially to the nineteenth and twentieth centuries. Søren Kierkegaard (1813–1855) is usually regarded as its founder. His philosophy is inextricably entangled with his struggle over what it means to become a Christian. Friedrich Nietzsche (1844–1900) is in many ways at the opposite extreme from Kierkegaard, but his proclamation of the death of God was just as passionate as Kierkegaard's fascination with the God-man paradox. Some Russian thinkers of the same period showed similar existentialist tendencies, notably Fyodor Dostoevsky (1821–1881) and Vladimir Solov'ev (1853–1900). All of these profoundly influenced the existentialists of the twentieth century, among whom may be counted Miguel de Unamuno (1864–1936), Karl Jaspers (1883–1969), Martin Heidegger (1889–1976), and Jean-Paul Sartre (1905–1980), though it should be noted that the term *existentialist* had, in popular usage, become so widely applied and covered so many differences that most of the philosophers mentioned were unwilling to accept it. The Jewish thinker Martin Buber (1878–1965) had existentialist affinities but criticized the individualism of the typical existentialist. Nevertheless, all the philosophers mentioned above share a number of "family resemblances" that make them existentialists in a broad sense.

It is sometimes suggested that existentialism is a thing of the past, that it was a phenomenon called into being by the specific events of the times in which these thinkers lived but that humanity has now moved into new times with new problems. Up to a point, this may be true. The very fact that the existentialist is an *existing* thinker means that he or she has a concrete relation to the events of his or her own time. Yet there are some characteristics of the human condition that seem to belong to all times or to recur at different times, and some of the insights of the existential philosophers into what it means to be human have a permanent value and are likely to provoke new thought and new investigations in the future.

Some Distinguishing Characteristics. As the name implies, existentialism is a philosophy of existence. It should be noted, however, that the word *existence* is used in a restricted sense. In ordinary speech, one says that stars exist, trees exist, cows exist, men and women exist, and so on of everything that has a place in the spatiotemporal world. The existentialist restricts the term to the human existent. By doing this, there is no intention to suggest that stars, trees, cows and the like are unreal. The existentialist only wants to draw attention to the fact that their being is quite different from the being of a human person. When an existentialist speaks of a human being as "existing," he or she is taking the word in what may be supposed to be the original etymological sense of "standing out." Stars and the like have their being simply by lying around, so to speak. Their nature or essence is already given to them. The human being exists actively, by standing out or emerging through the decisions and acts that make this person the unique being that he or she is. In Sartre's famous definition, *existence* means that the human person begins as nothing, and only afterward does that being become something and form its essence through its chosen policies of action.

Although existentialists use the word *existence* in the sense just explained, it retains something of its traditional meaning. In the history of philosophy, existence (referring to the fact *that* something is) has usually been contrasted with essence (referring to *what* something is or the basic properties of that thing). Philosophies of essence (Platonism is the great example) concentrate attention on the universal properties of things, properties which remain the same in all circumstances and at all times. These universals are amenable to the operations of thinking, so that the essentialist tends to end up as an idealist, holding that thought and reality coincide. The philosopher of existence, on the other hand, concentrates attention on the concrete, individually existing reality, but this has a particularity and contingency that make it much more resistant to the systematizing tendencies of thought, so that, for such a thinker, reality does not conform to thought, and there are always loose ends that refuse to be accommodated in some tidy intellectual construction.

It should be noticed too that the existentialist finds room for dimensions of human existence other than thinking. For several centuries, Western philosophy has been deeply influenced by Descartes's famous pronouncement, "I think, therefore I am." The existentialist would claim that this accords too much preeminence to thinking. Humans are also beings who experience emotion, and these emotions are not just transient inner moods but rather ways of relating to the world and becoming aware of some of its properties that do not reveal themselves to rational observation. Equally important is the will. One learns about the world not just by beholding it and reflecting upon it but rather by acting in it and encountering its resistances.

It follows from this that existentialism is also a philosophy of the subject. Kierkegaard declared that truth is subjectivity. At first sight, this seems a subversive statement, one which might even imply the abolition of truth. But what Kierkegaard meant was that the most important truths of life are not to be achieved by observation and cannot be set down in textbooks to be looked up when required. They are the kind of truths that can be won only through inward and perhaps painful appropriation. The truths of religion are the most obvious case—they cannot be learned from books of theology but only by following the way of faith that is one with the truth and the life (*John* 14:6).

IMPLICATIONS FOR RELIGION. The existentialist recognition of the distinctiveness of human existence as over against the world of nature, together with the claim that the truth of human existence is to be reached by the way of subjectivity, is significant for the philosophy of religion. The tendency in modern times has been to treat the human person as one more natural phenomenon, to be understood objectively through human sciences which model their methods on that of the natural sciences. Existentialists, however, believe that human nature can be understood only from the inside, as it were, through one's own participation in it. The phenomenological analysis of consciousness, developed by Husserl, has been adopted by existentialist philosophers, but long before Husserl similar methods were being used, for instance, by Kierkegaard in *The Concept of Anxiety*.

One obvious result of the application of such methods of inquiry to the human person is the claim that freedom is essential to being human. Decision, conscience, and responsibility are major themes in existentialist writers, in opposition to the determinism or near-determinism characteristic of supposedly scientific views of humanity. Perhaps it would not be going too far to say that freedom is the supreme value among the existentialists. Human existence is said to be "authentic" when the individual freely chooses who and what he or she will become. The freedom to choose and decide is, of course, never absolute. The human being is finite, inserted at a given position in space and time and therefore subject to all the constraints and influences that operate at that point. Thus one's freedom is always threatened. One may simply reflect the values of one's culture, without ever deciding one's relation to those values, or one may be caught up in the race for money or pleasure, though these may be inimical to the development of one's finest potentialities.

Thus all human existence is lived in the tension between finitude and freedom. This tension can also be expressed as that between freedom (the areas that are still open for choice) and facticity (those elements in existence which are simply given and reduce the area of free decision). It is because of this tension that freedom is always accompanied by anxiety. Existentialists, from Kierkegaard on, have laid great stress on anxiety as a basic emotion or state of mind which illuminates the human condition. In the case of Kierkegaard and other Christian existentialists, the experience of anxiety may predispose toward the life of faith by awakening the need for salvation; but among atheistic existentialists, anxiety points rather to despair, for the inner contradiction in the human being is taken to be incapable of resolution, so that human existence is always on the verge of absurdity. Part of human finitude is the fact that existence will in any case come to an end in death. But here too there are differences in interpretation. Heidegger believes that the fact of death, by closing off the future of existence, makes it possible to achieve a unifying and meaningful pattern in that existence. Sartre, on the other hand, thinks that death, by canceling out all achievement, is the ultimate indication of the absurdity of existence.

The criticism is sometimes made that there is something morbid in the existentialists' preoccupation with anxiety and death, and this criticism also impinges on those Christian theologians who have used these ideas to urge the need for faith and dependence on God. But it should be noted that there is another and more affirmative side to existentialism. Many writers of the school speak also of "transcendence," and by this they do not mean the transcendence of God, as commonly understood in theology, but the transcendence of the human existent moving constantly beyond itself into new situations. Those who stress transcendence believe that the goal of human life is to realize more and more one's authentic possibilities. Whereas the early Heidegger believed that this is to be achieved by human effort, by a steady "resoluteness" in the face of facticity and death, Christian writers such as Gabriel Marcel have thought of human transcendence as a transcendence toward God, and have taught that this is to be achieved not just through human effort but through the assistance of divine grace.

Most existentialists have had a bias toward individualism. This was true of Kierkegaard, who was alarmed by the tendencies toward collectivism in Hegel's philosophy. It is also true of Sartre, who depicts interpersonal relations as essentially frustrating. On the other hand, Marcel claims that a relation to others is essential to an authentic human existence, while Heidegger sees "being-with-others" as an inescapable dimension of the human being. Critics of existentialism have reckoned its individualism as a defect, on the ground that it prevents the development of a political philosophy, but others have praised the stress on the individual as a defense of human freedom in face of the totalitarian pretensions of the modern state. Nietzsche and Heidegger have both sought to go beyond the biography of the individual to the outlines of a philosophy of history. In this, they oppose the so-called scientific history that seeks to establish objective facts. Nietzsche speaks scornfully of the "antiquarian" type of historian who seeks to reconstruct the past. He prefers the "monumental" historian who goes to some great creative event of the past in order to discover its power and to learn its lessons for the present and future. Heidegger likewise is uninterested in the history that confines itself to the analysis of past events. History, he claims, is oriented to the future. The historian goes to the past only in order to learn about such authentic possibilities of human existence as may be repeatable in the present. This view of history was very influential for Rudolf Bultmann's existential interpretation of the "saving events" of the New Testament, an interpretation succinctly expressed as "making Christ's cross one's own."

The stress on human freedom together with the bias toward individualism raises the question of the significance of existentialism for ethics. The existentialist has no use for an ethic of law, for the requirement of a universal law ignores the unique individual and conforms everyone to the same pattern. So one finds Kierkegaard defending Abraham's decision to sacrifice Isaac, for although this meant the "suspension" of ethics, only so could Abraham be true to his own self and be "authentic." Similary Nietzsche is found claiming that the "superman" must create his own values to supersede traditional values, while Heidegger claims that what is ordinarily called "conscience" is only the voice of the mediocre values of society and that the true conscience is the deep inward summons of the authentic self. In each case, the value of an action is judged not by its content but by the intensity and freedom with which it is done. Such an ethic is too formless for human society and represents an overreaction against the cramping restraints of legalism. Nevertheless, this extremely permissive ethic has seemed to some Christian thinkers to be compatible with Jesus' teaching that love rather than law must guide one's conduct, and it is reflected in the various types of "situation ethics" that flourished for a short time.

Finally, although existentialism turns away from the attempt to formulate any detailed and inclusive metaphysic, its adherents seem to find it impossible to avoid assenting to some ontology or theory of being. Kierkegaard and other Christian existentialists assume (but do not seek to prove) a theistic view of the world as the setting of human existence; Sartre is frankly dualistic in opposing the free but fragile being of humankind (the *pour soi)* to the massive unintelligent being (the *en soi)* of the physical world; there are mystical elements both in Heidegger's talk of "being" and Jaspers's of "transcendence." Existentialist theologians have also found that the reconstruction of Christian theology in terms of human possibilities is inadequate and needs the supplementation of a theistic philosophy.

Bibliography

An introduction to existentialism is provided in my book *Existentialism* (Baltimore, 1973). Major existentialist texts include Søren Kierkegaard's *Philosophical Fragments,* translated by David F. Swenson (Princeton, N. J., 1936); Martin Heidegger's *Being and Time,* translated by me and Edward Robinson (New York, 1962); Jean-Paul Sartre's *Being and Nothingness,* translated by Hazel E. Barnes (New York, 1956); and Fritz Buri's *Theology of Existence,* translated by Harold H. Oliver and Gerhard Onder (Greenwood, S.C., 1965).

New Sources

Cotkin, George. *Existential America.* Baltimore, 2003.

Fulton, Ann. *Apostles of Sartre: Existentialists in America, 1945–1963.* Evanston, Ill., 1999.

Hardwick, Charley. *Events of Grace: Naturalism, Existentialism, and Theology.* New York, 1996.

Low, Douglas Beck. *The Existential Dialogue of Marx and Merleau Ponty.* New York, 1987.

Murdoch, Iris, and Peter Conradi, eds. *Existentialists and Mystics: Writings on Philosophy and Literature.* London, 1998.

Pattison, George. *Anxious Angels: A Retrospective View of Religious Existentialism.* New York, 1999.

Solomon, Robert. *From Rationalism to Existentialism: The Existentialists and Their Nineteenth-Century Backgrounds.* Lanham, Md., 1992.

John Macquarrie (1987)
Revised Bibliography

EXORCISM.

The English word *exorcism* derives from the Greek *exorkizein,* a compound of *ex* (out) plus *horkizein* (to cause to swear, or to bind by an oath). Whereas in Greek the word sometimes is used simply as a more intensive form of the root, meaning "to adjure," English derivatives usually designate a "swearing out" of invasive spiritual forces from the body in a formal rite of expulsion. Thus exorcism cannot fully be understood without reference to the concept of spirit possession, the state that it redresses.

The spirits to be exorcised most commonly are conceived either as demons or as restless ghosts. These evil spirits penetrate into the bodies of their victims and completely control, or at least strongly influence, their actions. Possessing spirits may also cause physical illness by interfering with the body's normal physiological processes or mental illness by affecting the will, intellect, and emotions. Yet in many cultures, spirit possession is diagnosed only retrospectively. That is, the victim often must display abnormal behavior for some time before friends and family diagnose her as possessed by a spirit. Both cross-culturally and transhistorically, spirit possession afflicts women more often than men. This pattern has been the subject of much discussion among specialists who study the phenomenon.

The forms and prevalence of exorcism within a given culture are intimately related to the question of how the invading spirits are conceived. In certain contexts, possession by neutral or beneficent spirits is highly valued, and in these settings exorcisms are unlikely to be an important constituent of the local culture. Within other religious contexts, however, spirit possession is understood as the work of evil spirits or demons dedicated to the downfall of humanity, and exorcism thus is viewed as a vitally important form of healing. Lastly, many cultures, both historically and worldwide, consider possessing spirits to be the ghosts of the dead. Responses to possession in these cases may involve ambivalent attitudes toward the invading spirit. Communities invariably wish to heal the victim through exorcism but also may feel compassion toward the dead spirit that has invaded the living. Moreover witnesses to exorcisms of ghosts frequently use the occasion to interrogate the spirit about the details of the afterlife.

Exorcisms vary widely. Whereas some rites are purely verbal formulae, many employ objects, gestures, and actions thought to be of particular power against invasive spirits. In some contexts, exorcism may be accomplished simply through the charismatic power of a particularly powerful or righteous individual. Many cultures use dance and music as essential elements of exorcism rituals. In this article, the word *exorcism* may refer either to the procedure itself or to its end result, the liberation from spirits that it accomplishes.

CHRISTIAN EXORCISM. From its origins, Christianity has included a strong belief in spirit possession by demons, understood as primordial forces of evil and followers of the devil. Thus exorcism has a long history within Christianity, particularly (though not exclusively) among Catholics. These traditions continue to the modern day.

In the New Testament. The Greek verb *exorkizein* appears only once in the New Testament, in *Matthew* 26:63, where the high priest "adjures" Jesus to reveal whether he is the Christ. Yet the action of expelling demons frequently does appear in the New Testament canon. Exorcism is among Jesus' favorite miracles in the Synoptic tradition, comprised of the *Gospels of Mark, Matthew,* and *Luke,* yet no exorcisms appear in the latest gospel, *John.* The *Acts of the Apostles,* by the same author as the *Gospel of Luke,* also recounts exorcisms by Jesus' followers after his death and employs the noun *exorkistes* to refer to some Jews who attempt to cast out demons using Jesus' name (*Lk.* 19:13). Indeed in respect to exorcism, the emerging Jesus Movement was much in accord with developments in other Jewish sects of the period, many of which had begun to place a greater emphasis upon exorcisms and charismatic forms of healing than had been the case in earlier Jewish tradition.

In the earliest gospel, *Mark,* an exorcism is Jesus' first miracle:

> And immediately there was in their synagogue a man with an unclean spirit; and he cried out, "What have you to do with us, Jesus of Nazareth? Have you come to destroy us? I know who you are, the Holy One of God." But Jesus rebuked him, saying, "Be silent and come out of him!" And the unclean spirit, convulsing him and crying with a loud voice, came out of him. (*Mk.* 1:23–26)

Mark subsequently presents Jesus as famed for his exorcism ability, pairing this miracle with Jesus' eloquence in preaching as his two main sources of appeal throughout his travels in Galilee (*Mk.* 1:39). Mark's gospel thus uses exorcism as a way of demonstrating Jesus' uncanny power as a complement to his teaching: Jesus is shown as battling against malign spiritual forces both physically and pedagogically.

The most complete account of exorcism is that of the Gerasene demoniac, recounted in all three synoptic gospels (*Mk.* 5:1–20; *Mt.* 8:28–34; *Lk.* 8:26–39). The tale concerns Jesus' encounter with a man possessed by a multitude of evil spirits. The man was living in the cemetery on the edge of a city—among the tombs of the dead—because his disordered state of mind and superhuman strength rendered him unfit for the society of the living. Jesus interviews the spirits inside the man, which speak through his mouth, and elicits their collective name, Legion. Jesus then commands the spirits to depart from the man but gives them permission to enter into a herd of pigs foraging nearby. The possessed pigs then plunge themselves into the sea and drown, prompting the local herdsmen to flee and tell the story throughout the city. A group of people then come out to Jesus and ask him to leave. The passage reveals much about conceptions of possession and exorcism in this time period, including the disruption of identity and of bodily control characteristic of demoniacs; the importance of learning the demons' names in order to gain power over them; and Jesus' charismatic use of a simple verbal command to accomplish the expulsion. However, the conclusion of the tale suggests that Jesus' action is regarded with considerable fear and ambivalence by the local community.

The Synoptic Gospels report that during his lifetime Jesus empowered his disciples to cast out demons as well. Yet upon occasion this power failed them, as in the case of a dumb and deaf spirit that had entered a child, tormenting him with convulsions. After the disciples proved unable to heal the boy, Jesus successfully completed the task through prayer and fasting (*Mt.* 9:17; *Mt.* 16; *Lk.* 9:40). Jesus' followers continued to perform exorcisms after his death. The *Acts of the Apostles* describes several cases accomplished through a noteworthy diversity of means. Paul exorcises a slave girl through a verbal rebuke similar to those used by Jesus (*Acts* 16:18), but Peter heals the possessed simply by having them gather in his shadow (*Acts* 5:16). Paul also exorcises spirits through handkerchiefs impregnated with his power of supernatural healing (*Acts* 19:11–12). Simply invoking the name of Jesus was considered a powerful method of exorcism, one even employed by non-Christians, according to *Acts.* Chapter nineteen describes some Jews in Ephesus who attempt to cast out demons in Jesus' name, though without success.

Late antiquity and the Middle Ages. As in Jesus' own early career, exorcism was an important element in winning new converts for the early generations of the Jesus Movement. The second-century Christian apologist Justin Martyr characterized exorcism as a particularly impressive gift among Christians, noting that any demon, no matter how powerful, became submissive when conjured in Jesus' name. Indeed exorcism became a competitive arena in which Roman Christians claimed triumph over Jewish and pagan rivals, suggesting that their conjurations of demons were more efficacious than any other form of healing. Peter Brown has shown in "The Rise and Function of the Holy Man in Late Antiquity" (1982) that the essential mark of the early Christian holy person was his or her charismatic ability to exorcise, and Christian saints became closely associated with this activity. Thus when a little girl in fourth-century Syria wished to parody a monk in order to entertain her companions, she did so by pretending to exorcise them with all due solemnity.

With the Christian community growing in numbers, the church began to require the exorcism both of adult converts and of infants at baptism. The earliest Catholic baptismal liturgy incorporated exorcisms; one function of godparents, in cases of infant baptism, was to answer for the child when the exorcist asked, "Do you renounce the devil and all his works?" In consequence of this development, by the third century a designated exorcist was required in every Christian community. Documents from this time period make note of a formal order of exorcists that constituted a lowly step on the ecclesiastical hierarchy. The Fourth Council of Carthage in 398 CE is the first surviving text to prescribe the rite of ordination for an exorcist: "When an Exorcist is Ordained: Let him accept from the hand of the priest the little book in which the exorcisms are written, and let the priest say to him, 'Take this and memorize it, and may you have the power of laying on hands upon an energumen, whether baptized or a catechumen'" (Caciola, 2003, p. 229).

As Christianity spread into northern Europe and became a dominant institution in the medieval west, exorcism practices continued to evolve. Whereas the order of exorcists slowly declined in importance and eventually disappeared from view, descriptions of exorcisms performed by saints vastly increased. Medieval hagiographies frequently mention exorcisms performed during their subjects' lifetimes as well as postmortem exorcisms accomplished by the saints' relics or tombs. This development accelerated after the twelfth century, when accounts of demonic possession saw an exponential increase in hagiographical texts. Bernard of Clairvaux (1090–1153 CE), for example, was credited with many personal exorcisms, whereas Hildegard of Bingen (1098–1179 CE) provided detailed advice on how to exorcise a possessed woman in one of her letters. Some of the best surviving accounts of exorcisms during this time period are set at saints' tombs, and certain shrines became known as centers of exorcistic healing. The arm relic of John Gualbert of Florence (999–1073 CE), for example, was famed for its exorcistic properties, and the miracle accounts recorded at his shrine in the later Middle Ages include a number of healings of the possessed. In some cases, families traveled considerable distances for an exorcism of a relative, vowing particular devotion to the saint if he or she provided aid to the possessed at the end of the pilgrimage.

Exorcisms by living saints or their relics were not the only means of casting out demons, however. Medieval people also employed a number of other techniques, often in a somewhat improvisational manner. Friends, family, and religious professionals might try to cast out the demon through prayer and fasting; by showing the demoniac religious paintings; by placing relics or books of Scripture on the victim's head or body; through anointing with holy water, holy oil, or blessed salt; or by giving the demoniac a consecrated Eucharistic wafer.

Medieval popular culture included its own notions of spirit possession and of appropriate remedies as well. Many contemporary texts attest to the northern European belief that demons could invade dead bodies, animate them, and use them for nefarious purposes. In such cases, the preferred solution to the problem was to destroy the corpse as fully as possible. In Mediterranean regions, the spirits that possessed the living were often identified as ghosts rather than as demons. As for cures, the possessed sometimes were immersed in a running body of water as a form of cure. In some areas local men made names for themselves as secular exorcists and healers, each with his own unique formula, rhyming jingles, and other procedures. Thus medieval cultures held diverse notions of spirit possession and exorcism in addition to purely ecclesiastical definitions.

The emergence of a liturgical rite in the fifteenth century. The fifteenth century marked an important turning point in the history of exorcism within the Catholic Church. At this time, as Caciola (2003) has shown, the church began to use formal scripted, liturgical exorcisms, numerous examples of which are preserved in manuscripts. The change likely stemmed from a desire on the part of the Catholic hierarchy to standardize practices of exorcism at a time when the number of reported possessions remained high. In so doing the church also arrogated control over the process of exorcism to the ecclesiastical hierarchy rather than allowing decentralized and improvised practices of exorcism to persist.

Liturgical exorcisms are a species of *clamor,* a family of ritual forms that cry out to God for aid against oppressors. Other examples of this kind of ritual include excommunications, humiliations, and maledictions. These exorcisms also are intimately related to the baptismal liturgy, repeating verbal formulations from the baptismal rite as well as other elements, such as the blessing of salt and water. A third textual precedent for these rites is Jewish conjurations, particularly the inclusion of exhaustive compendia of the names of God. Indeed liturgical exorcisms are rife with lists of all kinds: those that recount events from the life of Jesus; that call upon the aid of all the saints and the hierarchy of angels; that cast the demon forth from each body part; and that imagine vivid apocalyptic scenarios of demonic defeat and eternal torment. Several manuscripts of exorcism suggest the use of demonic language in order to gain control over the possessing spirit, incorporating brief spells composed of unintelligible words that are said to have been personally composed by the devil. After conjuring the demon in its own language, the exorcist may then proceed to inquire into its precise status, its reason for invading the victim, and its requirements for a successful expulsion. The following quotation from a manuscript held in Munich gives a sense of how a typical liturgical exorcism begins:

> Take the head of the possessed person in your left hand and place your right thumb in the possessed person's mouth, saying the following words in both ears: ABRE MONTE ABRYA ABREMONTE CONSACRAMENTARIA SYPAR YPAR YTUMBA OPOTE ALACENT ALAPHIE. Then hold him firmly and say these conjurations: I conjure you, evil spirits, by the terrible name of God Agla. . . . I also conjure you by the great name Pneumaton and by the name Ysiton, that you ascend to the tongue and give me a laugh. If they do not respond, then know that they are mute spirits. The exorcist should diligently discover and require whether it is incubi, or succubi, or even dragons that possesses the obsessed person; whether they are attendants of Pluto, or servants of Satan, or disciples of Astaroth; if they are from the east or the west; from noonday or evening; from the air, earth, water, fire, or whatever kind of spirit. (Caciola, pp. 248–249)

It was believed that once the demon was made to answer questions about itself (either through use of the demonic language or through some other constraint) it would be easier to exorcise.

The liturgy continues with insults to the demon, commands for it to depart, and prayers for divine aid, as well as Bible readings interspersed with lists of body parts, saints, angels, and the names of God. Throughout the rite, the exorcist is frequently directed to make the sign of the cross over the victim or to sprinkle him or her with holy water. The rite usually concludes with a prayer of thanksgiving and a plea for future protection against similar attacks. This basic template was to persist as the basis for the liturgy of exorcism for centuries.

The Reformation and beyond. The Reformation period saw a notable increase in demonological phenomena, most notably the witch hunts that came to a peak in this time period. Whereas the reformers accepted the possibility of demonic possession, they nevertheless opened a vigorous debate over the efficacy of liturgical exorcism as a remedy. Protestant texts satirized the splashing of holy water and frequent crossing of demoniacs performed by Catholic exorcists, deriding them alternately as "superstition," "empty rituals," or "magic." Yet beneath this general atmosphere of rejection lay a diversity of attitudes toward exorcism. Some reformers, like John Calvin (1509–1564) and Ulrich Zwingli (1484–1531), rejected all ritual exorcism; others, however, were less radical in their approaches. Martin Luther (1483–1546), for example, defended the use of traditional rites of exorcism during infant baptisms, deeming them a kind of prayer on behalf of the infant for divine protection. Most Protestant groups eschewed liturgies of exorcism for adults but did not reject simpler forms of exorcism through prayer and fasting, viewing them as acceptable pleas for divine aid against possessing demons.

Among Catholics, belief in the benefits of ritual exorcism continued to flourish unabated. Many elements of the liturgy that was formulated in the fifteenth century were codified in 1614 in the official Roman Ritual. Also during this time period, plural possessions and group exorcisms became a common Catholic form of the phenomenon, usually in a convent setting. The most famous case is the 1634 account of possessed nuns of Loudon studied by Michel de Certeau in *The Possession at Loudon* (1996), but plural possessions also occurred in Spain, Italy, the Low Countries, and France from the mid–sixteenth century through the early seventeenth century.

Some possession cases became closely bound up with the witchcraft persecutions; demonological literature taught that witches could send demons to possess their enemies. The priest of Loudon, Urbain Grandier (1590?–1634), ultimately was convicted of having bewitched the nuns. For this crime, he paid with his life. Likewise the eighteenth-century Puritan witchcraft trials in Salem, Massachusetts, originated with charges that the witches had caused their young accusers to be possessed.

A significant aspect of exorcism in this time period is the degree to which spectacular cases of possession and exorcism entered into public discourse and became causes célèbres. Due to the spread of print technology, for the first time such events could be widely known about and discussed. The publicity provided by pamphlets and broadsides, combined with the fractious confessional politics of the day, made exorcism a vehicle of Catholic polemic against Protestants and Jews. This dynamic was first noted by Daniel Pickering Walker in *Unclean Spirits* (1981). Thus Nicole Obry, a young Catholic woman who became possessed in 1565 and was publicly exorcised in the city of Laon, regaled the vast crowds attending the event in the voice of her possessing demon, which confessed that it was close friends with the Huguenots (preferring them even to the Jews) and that it sustained the greatest torment when young Nicole was given the Eucharist. Here insults to other religious traditions were combined with an endorsement of the Catholic doctrine of transubstantiation.

Nicole's case was widely copied, most notably in the subsequent generation by the famous demoniac Marthe Brossier (1573–16??). Protestant groups were unable to engage in widespread counterpropaganda, however, because they rejected exorcism for the most part. In England, the Protestant minister John Darrell became famed in the 1590s for exorcisms achieved through prayer and fasting, but the accounts of these cases lack the explicitly propagandistic elements of the Catholic cases. In a slightly different polemical vein, a sixteenth-century Catholic exorcist conjured the demons afflicting a group of young Roman girls who had been converted from Judaism. These demons explained their presence as the result of a curse laid upon the girls by their fathers who, angry at the loss of their children, summoned forth demons to possess them.

Exorcism declined in Europe during the eighteenth century, though it never entirely disappeared. Indeed professional exorcists like German Johann Joseph Gassner (1727–1779) continued to appear. Among the educated classes, however, symptoms that traditionally had led to a diagnosis of demonic possession increasingly came to be regarded as indicators of natural pathologies like hysteria, epilepsy, or melancholia. Although naturalistic diagnoses for "possessed behaviors" had been available since the twelfth century, the eighteenth century saw a more definitive shift in favor of medical epistemologies. In consequence exorcism was less frequently indicated as a cure.

The contemporary Christian Churches. Perhaps the best-known modern image of the rite of exorcism derives from the 1973 film *The Exorcist*, based on the 1971 novel of the same title by William Peter Blatty (b. 1928). Though the account is fictionalized, Blatty's story of a demonically possessed little girl was based upon a 1949 case of prolonged exorcism of a young Lutheran boy by a Catholic priest. The film spurred a revival of interest in exorcism in the United States, and Catholic bishops began receiving more and more requests for the procedure. Only a small proportion of such requests were granted because twentieth-century Catholic officials regard genuine demonic possession as an extremely rare phenomenon that is easily confounded with natural mental disturbances. In recognition of this stance, the Vatican in 1999 updated the ritual of exorcism for the first time since 1614, advising consultation with doctors and psychologists in order to rule out organic pathologies; however, the twenty-seven-page exorcism ritual was left largely intact.

Whereas the Catholic hierarchy preaches restraint in regard to exorcism, certain Catholic communities reject this stance along with many other features of the modern church. The most active Catholic exorcists of the late twentieth century belonged to conservative groups that rejected the reforms of the Second Vatican Council (1962–1965), especially the abandonment of the Latin Tridentine Mass. These exorcists contended that the new Mass left the faithful unprotected against demonic attack and believed that as a result of Vatican II, the number of possessions had increased exponentially.

Some modern American Protestant groups have become interested in possession and exorcism as well. The beginnings of modern Pentecostalism in the early twentieth century fostered a broad, interdenominational movement of Christian charismatics who placed direct spiritual interventions at the center of their theology. Some modern charismatics practice exorcism or "deliverance," as documented by Michael Cuneo in *American Exorcism*. Although deliverances can take many different forms according to the individual practitioner, the majority are simple prayer sessions for the victim's relief. The most extensive deliverances include a clairvoyant discernment of spirits, in which a specialist intuits what type of demon is afflicting the individual: a demon of lust, stubbornness, greed, or other sin. In rare cases, the demon may be identified as an entity of "intergenerational evil," an inherited demon dedicated to afflicting a particular bloodline; such a diagnosis is particularly likely when the individual requesting deliverance has a family history involving violence or mental illness. More formal rites of deliverance often begin with a binding of the devil, in which the indwelling demon is adjured, in the name of Jesus, to remain calm and desist from thrashing about inside the victim. Next is the prayer phase, which may be accompanied by fasting and a laying on of hands. As with Catholic traditionalists who practice exorcism, Protestant charismatics interested in deliverance tend to be social conservatives opposed to the increasing theological liberalism of the mainline churches.

JUDAISM. Judaism does not have a strongly attested focus on spirit possession and exorcism before the middle of the sixteenth century. At that time belief in possession by reincarnate spirits of the dead began to emerge in the Sephardic Jewish community of Safed in the Galilee. These ideas eventually were disseminated to eastern European Jewish communities, becoming particularly vigorous among eighteenth- and nineteenth-century Hasidic groups. The most familiar term for the possessing spirit, *dybbuk*, came into use only in the late seventeenth century, but it is employed by scholars of Judaism to refer to possession by a ghost even in earlier epochs.

Early history. The earliest account of an exorcism in Jewish tradition is *1 Samuel* 16:14–23. The text recounts how after the spirit of YHWH departed from King Saul, an evil spirit began to torment him. Saul's counselors suggest that music may be able to soothe his affliction, and David is brought to him to play the lyre. The sweet strains of the music succeed in exorcising the spirit from Saul whenever he feels invaded by its presence.

This is the sole account of spirit possession and exorcism in the Hebrew Bible. By the Second Temple period, however, the invasions of demons and forms of spiritual healing had become more prominent within Judaism. These phenomena were central features of the career of Jesus, for instance, as he traveled through the Jewish communities of first-century Palestine. The Qumran texts likewise place significant emphasis upon demonic attacks and human counterattacks, often in the form of protective spells, whereas scattered tales in rabbinic literature recount exorcisms by particularly righteous Jewish teachers.

Surviving bits of material culture testify to the contemporary interest in exorcism as well, particularly a number of bowls inscribed with Aramaic exorcisms that utilize a legalistic language of divorcing the spirit. Josephus (37–c. 100 CE) provides a story about contemporary Jewish exorcism techniques that he ascribes to traditions originating with King Solomon. According to this author, an exorcist named Eleazar gained fame for the efficacy of his cures and even was called upon to demonstrate his prowess before the emperor Vespasian (9–79 CE) along with all his court and army. Eleazar's secret was to draw the demons out from the possessed person's body by employing a certain root, discovered by Solomon, which was encased in a ring. By holding the ring to a demoniac's nose, he allowed that person to inhale the scent of the root, then he extracted the demon from the victim's body through the nostrils.

Accounts of exorcism are rare in medieval Jewish sources, although—as attested in the articles collected by Matt Goldish in *Spirit Possession in Judaism* (2003)—many scholars believe that the practice itself persisted. Medieval Catholic exorcisms include elements drawn from Jewish tradition, such as the use of lists of the names of God and the acronym AGLA (for *Atah Gibbor Le-ʿolam Adonai*, "You are mighty forever, my Lord"). This interreligious borrowing may suggest that Jewish exorcism traditions remained in common use. An early-sixteenth-century compilation of Jewish magical and exorcism texts, the *Shoshan Yesod ha-ʿOlam*, testifies to a vigorous tradition of spiritual healing; the book likely incorporates many older traditions that are not attested in surviving earlier literature. The exorcisms here are liturgical in character, involving verbal conjurations of demons and commands to depart. One formula adjures the demon, by the seventy-two names of God, to reveal its own name and parentage, then requires it to depart from the human body and enter into a flask that the exorcist is directed to have handy.

The emergence of dybbuk possession in the sixteenth century. In the sixteenth century spirit possession underwent a significant resurgence and evolution within Jewish thought. Beginning with the case of a young boy in the 1540s, the Galilean village of Safed became the epicenter of a new series of sensational possessions and exorcisms, several of which were associated with the circle of the qabbalist Rabbi Isaac Luria (1534–1572). Not only was possession suddenly a renewed topic of reportage, but the terms in which it was envisioned seem to have shifted. Whereas earlier Jewish attestations of exorcism usually refer to the possessing spirit as a demon, the cases in Safed (which in the early twenty-first century have received sustained treatment from Jeffrey H. Chajes in *Between Worlds* [2003]) constitute the first detailed descriptions of possessing spirits conceived as transmigratory souls of the dead.

Already in the late fourteenth century, Spanish qabbalistic literature had begun to explore the notion of *ʿibbur*, "pregnancy," as a form of spirit possession. The term was used to designate the invasion of a living human being by the transmigrating spirit of a deceased person, thus suggesting the coexistence of two souls within a single body. The sixteenth-century Safedian qabbalists expanded upon this tradition significantly. Although *ʿibbur* could involve either benign or maleficent dead spirits, the concern here is with the latter.

The qabbalists explained that the soul of a sinful person might not be permitted to enter into Gehenna directly upon death but instead would wander, disembodied and subject to beatings from angels of destruction. Seeking refuge from the angels, such a spirit would seek to enter into a physical body—either animal or human—for shelter; human bodies could be made vulnerable to such invasion through certain sins. Exorcism of the spirit should ideally be conducted in the presence of witnesses, a *minyan* of ten men. Because the ritual did not follow an invariant form, elements such as extensive suffumigation of the victim with strong incense, the blowing of the *shofar* (ram's horn) into the possessed's ear, and invocation of the names of God were used to force the *dybbuk* to reveal its own name and background. Once the identity of the spirit was established, the exorcist might converse with it, asking questions about its own former life and sins as well as seeking information about the afterlife. The *dybbuk* was often adjured to exit the victim by the big toe, lest the victim choke if it left via the throat. After the departure, the victim was to be given a protective amulet to wear to fend off further spiritual infestations. Texts recounting famous exorcisms served hagiographic functions, glorifying the rabbi who performed a successful expulsion. This is true not only of sixteenth-century Safed but of the later history of the *dybbuk* phenomenon as well.

It is notable that, in cases of *dybbuk* possession, the compassion of rabbinic exorcists was directed not only toward the possessed victim but also toward the possessing spirit. Because the latter was conceived as human, it too merited a degree of concern and healing. Thus even as the exorcist cast the demon out from the body it possessed, he often sought to discover how to help the *dybbuk* achieve *tikkun*, or rectification. If the spirit were permitted to enter Gehenna, it could then find rest and cease tormenting other living beings. This sympathetic feature of Jewish *dybbuk* exorcism could not find a counterpart in earlier Jewish traditions or in Christian traditions, which conceive of the possessing spirits as unredeemable and demonic.

Later developments. The *ʿibbur* form of possession appeared in 1575 in Ferrara, Italy, where the spirit possessing a Jewish woman claimed it was the ghost of a recently executed Christian. Scholars are divided as to whether this and subsequent Italian cases resulted from a dissemination of Lurianic notions of possession and exorcism or arose from other contingencies. In the seventeenth century the Italian rabbi

Moses Zacuto (1625–1697) became well known as an exorcist, engaging the topic repeatedly in his correspondence.

By the eighteenth and nineteenth centuries *dybbuk* possession had become common in eastern European Hasidic communities; the term *dybbuk* is first attested in a Yiddish pamphlet published around 1680 in Volhynia. Sholom Anski's (1863–1920) 1910s play *The Dybbuk;* or, *Between Two Worlds,* which is set in a Hasidic context, popularized and romanticized the notion of ghostly possession. Like Blatty's *The Exorcist,* the story ultimately may have influenced the course of the religious phenomenon on the ground. Cases of *dybbuk* possession reminiscent of Anski's narrative have been reported in modern Israel and have begun to be studied by modern folklorists and anthropologists.

COMPETING EXORCISM FORMS IN EGYPT. In modern Islamic Egypt, spirit possession may be managed by one of two means: through Qur'anic healing or participation in a *zār* cult. Islamic demonology is extensive, and the choice of which form of healing to pursue is in part a reflection of how the inhabiting spirit is identified.

Zār. *Zār,* a relatively recent invention dating only to the 1870s, is a form of participatory ritual group healing found in several East African countries. Dominated by women, *zār* cults involve regular meetings at which participants dance to drumming with the goal of entering into individual trance states. Islamic authorities in Egypt often denounce *zār* as a vulgar superstition held by women too ignorant to realize that their actions are un-Islamic. Participants, however, regard the meetings as fully compatible with Islamic tradition.

Strictly speaking, the *zār* cult is not a complete form of exorcism but rather a recurrent form of pacification. The goal of the ceremony is to learn to coexist with the spirit, or *zār* master, by temporarily lessening the intensity of the spirit's hold upon the individual. As documented by Gerda Sengers in *Women and Demons* (2003), the beginning of involvement with *zār* is customarily a private initiation ceremony paid for by the possessed victim and attended by friends, family, and other women who are possessed. After an opening prayer drawn from the Qur'ān, several different drum bands perform in sequence; their purpose is to get the participants dancing and help spur the onset of a trance. The new "*zār* bride," dressed in a long white tunic, is led by the *kudya,* a *zār* specialist who has assisted in the diagnosis of the victim's illness and identification of her invading spirit, or *zār* master. These may be of several kinds, including (among others) Gado, master of the toilet; the atheist *zār* master known as the Red Sultan; the Sultan of the Sea, who affects the brains; and even Christian *zār* masters. (The latter are easily identified because they make their victims desire alcohol, which normally is forbidden to Muslims but allowed to those possessed by Christian *zār* masters at *zār* ceremonies.) *Zār* masters often have negative qualities and cause distress or illness, but they are distinct from the more purely evil Islamic demons and devils known as *jinn* and *shayatin.*

Participants in the *zār* dance not with one another but with their individual *zār* masters. Thus the action, while collective, is not truly communal. After the private *zār* ceremony—sponsored by the family of the new initiate—the initiate will likely join a regular public *zār* group or *hadrah.* The *hadrah* meets regularly, usually on a weekly basis, and each participant contributes funds to pay for the drummers and to support the *kudra.* The repetition of the dance ritual each week keeps the *zār* master quiet within the victim, allowing her to pursue her normal life in all other ways.

Qur'anic healing. Qur'anic healing is a true exorcism that definitively drives out the invasive spirits, which in this case are often *jinn* or *shayatin,* though they can be *zār* masters as well. The healing usually is conducted by a *sheik* who specializes in Qur'anic exorcism on the grounds of a mosque, perhaps in an upstairs room or other chamber; as with *zār* ceremonies, these usually are group meetings with several possessed persons in attendance at once. Paticipants are segregated by sex, either by some form of barrier or by designating different days of the week for gatherings of men and of women. Nevertheless in Egypt—as in other parts of the world—spirit possession tends to afflict women more often than men. Qur'anic healers consider themselves as a more orthodox alternative to the *zār* cult, which they tend to deride as superstitious, corrupt, and anti-Islamic.

The rite begins with a rapid sequence of prayers, recited either by the *sheik* himself, one of his assistants, or the whole group. As the prayers go on, some of the possessed are likely to become excited and to begin writhing and crying out. At this point the assistants direct their prayers more loudly and forcefully at that individual; they may strike her with a stick while repeatedly shouting at the *jinn* to get out immediately. Eventually the exorcist or his assistant conjures the demon, asking its name, other details of its identity, and its reasons for possessing the victim. One may be possessed by a *jinn* for a variety of offenses, including such sins as hitting a cat. If the demon turns out not to be Muslim, it is given the chance to convert. The spirit is then required to enter into the possessed person's finger and to indicate its presence there by lifting that digit. The exorcist then pricks that finger with a needle, drawing a drop of blood and forcing the spirit out with it. After the rite, the victim is often counseled to adopt a higher level of piety in everyday life by, for example, dressing more modestly or praying more often.

REGIONALISM ON THE INDIAN SUBCONTINENT. The linguistic and cultural diversity of the Indian subcontinent is paralleled by a wide degree of variance in exorcism practices. Certain spirit possession beliefs are widespread in India, such as the frequency with which ghosts as well as demons possess the living; the predominance of women among the possessed; the belief that possession may sometimes be caused by another person's act of sorcery; and the retrospective diagnosis of the onset of possession as occurring at a moment when the victim was alone and felt a sudden fear. Regional variations in possession beliefs—and especially in exorcism techniques—however, are legion. Indeed even within a single locale there may be several different exorcism techniques in play.

North India: The Balaji temple. The North Indian town of Mehndipur, Rajasthan, is home to the Balaji temple, dedicated to the monkey god Hanumān. The latter deity is an apt choice for a divine exorcist, for he is a heroic figure drawn from the epic *Rāmāyaṇa*, which recounts his devoted service to Rāma during a protracted battle with the Sri Lankan demon Rāvaṇa. The Balaji temple is famed throughout Rajasthan and neighboring states for its successful exorcisms, attracting the possessed from as far away as Delhi. Indeed the Balaji temple has long been a popular pilgrimage destination: it invariably is filled with supplicants come to ask the monkey god for release from possessing spirits of the dead, from demons of the Hindu pantheon, and even sometimes from Muslim *jinn*.

Exorcisms performed at the temple are collective in character. Together caregivers and temple priests intone prayers to Hanumān, with the goal of initiating the victims into an altered state of consciousness or trance *(peshi)*. Though the latter often involves convulsions, loud shrieking, and other extreme behaviors, *peshi* is held to be a prerequisite for healing. Victims may return to the temple for several successive days before achieving *peshi*, but once the catharsis of trance is achieved and then exited, the victim is likely to be considered on the road to complete healing. The process may be swift or slow, depending on the number and nature of the possessing spirits. After the exorcism, the newly healed individual may report having received from Hanumān a protective spirit, or *dut*, to help guard against future attacks.

South India. In South India, possession most frequently afflicts new, young brides; the spirit usually (though not invariably) is described as the ghost of a young man. Thus the possession state frequently has a sexual aspect that is explicitly articulated within the local understanding of these events. The ghosts or *peys* that afflict the victims often died unmarried; indeed a common reason for becoming this type of restless, possessing spirit is suicide because of unfulfilled love. These lonely ghosts of the untimely dead may become attracted to a lovely young bride with a still-fresh scent of sexual initiation about her and try to "catch" or possess her, often gaining entry through the woman's hair. Afterward the spirit becomes jealous and impels the woman to reject the sexual advances of her husband: this act often is the initiating event in a diagnosis of possession.

The exorcism ritual used to cure such afflictions usually involves a controlled, benign counterpossession. Here exorcists are specialists in dance techniques that enable them to enter into a state of trance, during which they incarnate a female deity like Kālī or Ankalaparamecuvari. The rite is known as "dancing the goddess." Because these deities are of superior power to the possessing ghost or demon, once the medium has become voluntarily possessed, the incarnate goddess is able to drive out the *pey* through a combination of supernatural threats and material sacrifices. The negotiation between the two possessed individuals may consume many hours, with the goddess-exorcist demanding that the *pey* leave and hurling insults at it and the ghost attempting to retain hold of the possessed woman and requiring various gifts or sacrifices before agreeing to exit. The exorcists who "dance the goddess" may resort to physical violence against the *pey*, beating the possessed or pulling her hair in order to convince the spirit inside that it must acquiesce and depart. This form of exorcism conceives of the struggle for healing as properly a battle between supernatural beings—the ghost versus the goddess—who nonetheless act through and on human bodies. The long hours of music, the dance, the confrontation between the two possessing personalities, and the ultimate triumph of the goddess-exorcist provides healing for the possessed victim as well as entertainment for the local village.

This counterpossession model of exorcism is supplemented by local practices with a more restricted geographic range. In the South Arcot District of Tamil Nadu, for instance, exorcisms sometimes are conducted by troupes of musicians known as *pampaikkarar*. The exorcism in this instance begins with a singer attempting to lure the possessed woman into a state of trance, after which the ghost who is possessing her may be interviewed. The details of its biography, death story, and the circumstances surrounding its possession of the victim are elicited; indeed the ghost is encouraged to explain its restlessness and its desires. As the music continues into the night, it is not uncommon for bystanders to dance the goddess, thus combining the better-known ritual with the more localized practice.

After the possessing spirit and its grievances have been identified, the musicians negotiate with it, promising a sacrifice in return for its pledge to depart. The spirit is asked to identify the specific lock of the victim's hair in which it resides; this tress is then tied into a knot over the protestations of the *pey*, which may complain that the action is painful. Afterward the sacrifice, a chicken, is offered, with its severed head being placed in the victim's mouth. This action shocks and frightens the *pey* and represents the beginnings of the actual expulsion. The possessed is then handed a large stone, said to represent "the weight of the *pey's* desire," and is herded toward the nearest tamarind tree. After the possessed person reaches the tree, the rock is laid at its roots, and the knotted lock of hair that contains the spirit is cut from the possessed woman's head and nailed to the trunk. Following this the exorcism is complete and the victim is considered healed. The culminating actions of the exorcism have been interpreted by Isabelle Nabokov in her article "Expel the Lover, Recover the Wife" (1997) as representing the final "divorce" of the lonely ghost from its victim and its "remarriage" to the tamarind tree, understood as a female entity in Tamil culture. When the *pey's* desire is given to the tamarind and the *pey* is severed from the woman and united with the tree, the affections of the lonely ghost are thereby redirected to a nonhuman object.

Scholarly Interpretations of Exorcism. Exorcism has long attracted attention from academics, thus becoming a category of scholarly analysis as well as of religious practice. The comments below identify some major strands in the interpretation of exorcism emanating from within the disciplines of anthropology, psychology, and history. Many of these analyses have tried to address the question of why women predominate in reports of possession and exorcism.

Anthropology. In the late nineteenth century and early twentieth century, the foundational literature of cultural anthropology gave prominent place to divergent cultural conceptualizations of spirits, their capabilities, and human responses to them. This focus was characteristic of the early anthropological approach to so-called "folk" religions, viewed as largely indistinguishable from culture, in contradistinction to "historical" religions, based on scriptural canons and textual precedents. Thus the anthropological literature on spirit possession and exorcism has a long and complex history within the discipline.

A well-known modern anthropological analysis of spirit possession and exorcism is I. M. Lewis's important 1971 work, *Ecstatic Religion.* Lewis was struck by the frequency with which socially marginal groups, particularly young women, were involuntarily overtaken by spirits, a phenomenon he termed "peripheral possession." He further noted that, while in a state of possession, the women often gained prestige and were able to act in more assertive ways than was the case in their regular daily lives. Thus they might openly critique their husbands or relatives, shirk household duties, or act in ways deemed immodest or inappropriate for their cultural settings. Lewis suggested that the reason for women's predominance among the spirit possessed in nearly all cultures is related to a covert desire for status enhancement. Women's possessing spirits allowed them to articulate resentments and desires that they normally would have had to suppress while simultaneously permitting them to disavow personal responsibility for their transgressive actions. This dynamic only reached its fullest expression, however, in the process of exorcism, which in many cultures takes the form of bargaining with the spirits to depart. The spirit may demand a series of concessions before agreeing to leave, often in the form of material gifts of direct benefit to the possessed woman: a feast, new clothes, or some other special treat.

Many scholars have suggested alternatives to Lewis's analysis or raised critiques to his approach. Bruce Kapferer, in his 1983 study of exorcism in Sri Lanka, *A Celebration of Demons,* argued that Lewis overvalued individual motivations and self-determination and undervalued broader cultural forces that symbolically align women with the sphere of the demonic and the unclean. Other scholars, including Janice Boddy in her review article "Spirit Possession Revisited" (1994), have called for a reframing of the question that moves "beyond instrumentality" to discuss broader notions of gender, body, and social organization that mitigate a narrowly functionalist view. Others, like Isabelle Nabokov (1997), have vigorously disputed the notion that exorcism acts to advance the interests of marginal groups, interpreting its symbolism as, rather, a means of asserting the hegemony of dominant cultural values. Nevertheless Lewis's "social deprivation analysis" remains a dominant influence in anthropological studies of exorcism. Lewis renewed his analysis in a follow-up study published in 1986, *Religion in Context*; this work in turn was reissued in an expanded edition in 1996.

Psychology. The interest of psychologists in possession and exorcism originates with Sigmund Freud, who in the 1920s wrote about the seventeenth-century case of the painter Christopher Haizmann. (A translation of this work is in Brian Levack, *Possession and Exorcism* [1992].) Regarding accounts of Haizmann's possession as descriptions of a "demonological neurosis," Freud presented an elaborate interpretation centered on Haizmann's depression due to the death of a close relative, whom Freud assumes to be Haizmann's father. The devil, Freud writes, entered into a contract with Haizmann in which he agreed to serve as the painter's father figure for a term of nine years. Freud argues that the use of the number nine in relation to a span of time reveals Haizmann's adhesion to a feminine aspect in relation to his father, indeed "a long-repressed phantasy of pregnancy" (nine being the number of months of gestation), combined with a strong castration anxiety (Levack, 1992, p. 90). Haizmann's eventual release through exorcisms and a pilgrimage to a shrine to the Virgin Mary signal Haizmann's salutary turn toward another substitute parent, the mother. Through maternal intervention, Haizmann is sufficiently healed to enter into a religious order, thus finding a more appropriate father substitute in these "fathers of the church."

Nevertheless Freud's interest in these phenomena set the stage for further psychohistorical and ethnopsychological investigations into possession and exorcism. Understandings of spirit possession as a culturally constructed idiom for expressing repressed or illicit desires, as forms of wish fulfillment, as involving supernatural parent or lover substitutes, or as representative of sexual anxieties and identity disturbances are now a significant component of the scholarly literature. Once again the predominance of young women among the possessed has proven particularly provocative to scholars because the notion of physical penetration by a spirit, often conceived as male, lends itself both to a psychosexual analysis and also potentially to a diagnosis of disturbed gender identity.

Exorcisms have been regarded as having therapeutic value in part because they are couched in the same idiom as the patient's own expression of neurosis while nonetheless orchestrating the same kind of emotional buildup and catharsis that underlay Freud's early psychoanalyses. The emphasis upon social reintegration that is central to many exorcism rites has been seen as a cipher for the reintegration of the individual sufferer's psychic or sexual self: "the expulsion of the masculine and the resumption of an unfragmented conventional sexual identity," according to Lyndal Roper in

Oedipus and the Devil (Roper, 1994, p. 191). Conversely, the psychological commonplace of "exorcising inner demons" forces a convergence between religious and psychoanalytic idioms. Exorcism and therapy are thereby defined as different terms for the same healing process.

History. Historians have turned their attention to spirit possession and exorcism relatively recently as part of the movement toward cultural history (sometimes called history of mentalities). Whereas the dominant anthropological and psychological interpretations of exorcism focus upon the victim's experiences and desires, the leading historians working on this problem emphasize the societal power relations deployed in the performance of exorcism. (Indeed Freud's psychoanalysis of Haizmann has been sharply criticized by Eric Midelfort in his article "Catholic and Lutheran Reactions to Demon Possession in the Late Seventeenth Century" [Levack, 1992] as anachronistic and individually overdetermined, with too little consideration given to the structure of the contextual society.) Thus the focus of historians has been less on the person who is the object of the exorcism and more on the ways practices of exorcism fuel larger social processes. It has been seen then as either a dynamic or a static social force, depending on the context.

An example of exorcism's potential to propel change is provided by the many scholars who have elucidated its value as a catalyst for conversion. These historians have pointed out how successful public exorcisms can be instrumental in recruiting new believers to the religion of the exorcising group. The rite often seems to have functioned in this way when practiced within a context of intense competition among rival religious systems. As a visible, materially enacted battle with supernatural referents, exorcism easily can become a testing ground for the power of one deity, doctrine, or practice over another. In other cases, however, exorcism may be used to reaffirm a potentially threatened continuity with the past. Thus as noted above the fifteenth-century rise of liturgical exorcism has been shown to be linked to a broader struggle on the part of the Catholic hierarchy to reaffirm its traditional authority at a moment of significant instability and stress. Here innovation in the performance of exorcism acted to reinforce the institutional prerogatives of the Catholic Church.

Perhaps the most elegant historical study of exorcism has been penned by the French social theorist Michel de Certeau. The author's article "Language Altered: The Sorcerer's Speech" in *The Writing of History* (1988) focuses on the ways in which early modern exorcists reasserted the hegemony of written traditions by turning to them for neat categorizations of the untidy, real-life possession cases unfolding before them. Certeau begins by noting that a diagnosis of possession was usually applied to a woman soon after she manifested a "disturbance of discourse." No longer an individual, well-bounded subject, the possessed woman was viewed as displaced from herself. The invading spirit disrupted the continuity of the victim's selfhood by speaking through her mouth: her lips and tongue pronounced the spirit's sentiments and experiences. Thus for Certeau, the speech of the possessed woman was a logical paradox that existed outside normally comprehensible speech patterns. The speaking entity was both male and female, mortal and immortal, powerless and powerful, the victim and the Other.

The processes of exorcism and conjuration of the spirit, Certeau suggests, were a means of resolving this logical paradox by identifying the indwelling spirit. Thus the first goal of an exorcism always was to categorize the speech of the victim as the discourse of a specific, indwelling demon known in advance from exorcistic and demonological literature: Beelzebub, Asmodeus, Leviathan. Through this process, the exorcism transformed the garbled speech of the possessed woman into the recognizable voice of a well-known demon. Naming the demon in turn gave the exorcist power over it: the conjuration could then proceed as a series of conversations between the exorcist and the indwelling demon. Hence the exorcist only can gain mastery by identifying the speech of the victim with a specific demonic name, but in the process the possessed woman's identity is occluded. Exorcism is an assertion of power, Certeau suggests, insofar as it superimposes traditional categorizations over the creative potential of a paradox. It thus acts as a potent tool of social control.

SEE ALSO Biblical Literature, article on New Testament; Christianity, overview article; Christianity and Judaism; Dybbuk; Egyptian Religion, overview article; Jesus Movement; Judaism, overview article; Qurʾān, overview article.

BIBLIOGRAPHY

Boddy, Janice. *Wombs and Alien Spirits: Women, Men, and the Zar Cult in Northern Sudan.* Madison, Wis., 1989. An exploration of the role of fertility and gender roles in Sudanese spirit possession and the *zār* cult.

Boddy, Janice. "Spirit Possession Revisited: Beyond Instrumentality." *Annual Review of Anthropology* 23 (1994): 407–434. An excellent review essay of the major anthropological literature and interpretations.

Bourgignon, Erika, ed. *Religion, Altered States of Consciousness, and Social Change.* Columbus, Ohio, 1973. A classic collection of articles with an interdisciplinary perspective.

Brown, Peter. "Sorcery, Demons, and the Rise of Christianity." In *Witchcraft Confessions and Accusations*, edited by Mary Douglas, pp. 17–45. London, 1970. The relationship between exorcism and the expansion of the early Christian Church.

Brown, Peter. "The Rise and Function of the Holy Man in Late Antiquity." In *Society and the Holy in Late Antiquity*, pp. 103–152. Berkeley, Calif., and Los Angeles, 1982. How successful exorcisms functioned to cement the saintly reputations of holy men in late antiquity.

Brown, Peter. "Town Village and Holy Man: The Case of Syria." In *Society and the Holy in Late Antiquity*, pp. 153–165. Berkeley, Calif., and Los Angeles, 1982. Expands upon the previous article with a more specific geographical focus.

Caciola, Nancy. "Wraiths, Revenants, and Ritual in Medieval Culture." *Past and Present* 152 (1996): 3–45. A study of the medieval popular-culture belief that demons can possess and move dead bodies.

Caciola, Nancy. "Spirits Seeking Bodies: Death, Possession, and Communal Memory in the Middle Ages." In *The Place of the Dead: Death and Remembrance in Late Medieval and Early Modern Europe*, edited by Bruce Gordon and Peter Marshall, pp. 66–86. Cambridge, U.K., 2000. An exploration of stories of possession by ghosts in medieval popular culture.

Caciola, Nancy. *Discerning Spirits: Divine and Demonic Possession in the Middle Ages.* Ithaca, N.Y., 2003. A study of medieval spirit possession, both benign and malign; chapter five explores the history of exorcism and gives detailed descriptions of the rite.

Certeau, Michel de. "Language Altered: The Sorcerer's Speech." In *The Writing of History*, translated by Tom Conley, pp. 244–268. New York, 1988. A close study of the process of categorizing spirit possession through the qualification of the possessed woman's speech as demonic.

Certeau, Michel de. "What Freud Makes of History: 'A Seventeenth-Century Demonological Neurosis.'" In *The Writing of History*, translated by Tom Conley, pp. 287–307. New York, 1988. A historian meditates on Freud's discussion of Haizmann.

Certeau, Michel de. *The Possession at Loudon.* Translated by Michael Smith. Chicago, 1996. Closely examines the famous case of plural possession among the nuns of Loudon in the seventeenth century.

Chajes, Jeffrey H. "Judgements Sweetened: Possession and Exorcism in Early Modern Jewish Culture." *Journal of Early Modern History* 1– 2 (1997): 124–169. A general discussion of early modern Jewish belief in possession by ghosts.

Chajes, Jeffrey H. *Between Worlds: Dybbuks, Exorcists, and Early Modern Judaism.* Philadelphia, 2003. A detailed study of the history of Jewish possession and exorcism with emphasis on the shift toward *dybbuk* possession in the sixteenth century; chapter three presents Jewish technologies of exorcism.

Crapanzano, Vincent, and Vivian Garrison. *Case Studies in Spirit Possession.* New York, 1977. A classic collection of anthropological articles.

Csordas, Thomas. *The Sacred Self: A Cultural Phenomenology of Charismatic Healing.* Berkeley, Calif., and Los Angeles, 1994. Discussion of Catholic Pentecostal faith healing.

Cuneo, Michael. *American Exorcism: Expelling Demons in the Land of Plenty.* New York, 2001. Investigation into the relationship between contemporary American popular culture images of exorcism and the rising demand for real-life exorcisms.

Dyer, Graham. *The Divine and the Demonic: Supernatural Affliction and Its Treatment in North India.* London, 2003. A general study of supernatural illness and healing in India with focus on the psychology of the emotions involved in these processes; discussion of the Balaji temple.

Goldish, Matt, ed. *Spirit Possession in Judaism: Cases and Contexts from the Middle Ages to the Present.* Detroit, Mich., 2003. This excellent collection brings together contributions from most of the modern scholars working on this topic.

Kakar, Sudhir. *Shamans, Mystics, and Doctors.* Delhi, India, 1981. A psychoanalytic approach to Indian religion with discussion of the Balaji temple.

Kapferer, Bruce. *A Celebration of Demons: Exorcism and the Aesthetics of Healing in Sri Lanka.* Bloomington, Ind., 1983. Detailed exposition of exorcism ceremonies in Sri Lanka with attention to notions of gender and impurity in Sinhalese ideas about possession.

Levack, Brian, ed. *Possession and Exorcism.* New York, 1992. A wonderful sampling that includes Freud's study of Haizmann and a number of other foundational articles.

Levi, Giovanni. *Inheriting Power: The Story of an Exorcist.* Translated by Lydia G. Cochrane. Chicago, 1988. The story of an unlicensed, popular exorcist in early modern Italy.

Lewis, I. M. *Ecstatic Religion: An Anthropoloigical Study of Spirit Possession and Shamanism.* Harmondsworth, U.K., 1971. A classic in the anthropological study of possession with particular attention to gender issues and "social deprivation" analysis.

Lewis, I. M. *Religion in Context: Cults and Charisma.* 2d ed. Cambridge, U.K., 1996. An extension of the positions advanced in the previous work with more range.

Mageo, Jeannette, and Alan Howard. *Spirits in Culture, History, and Mind.* New York and London, 1996. Focuses on possession in the cultures of various Pacific islands.

Midelfort, Eric. *A History of Madness in Sixteenth-Century Germany.* Palo Alto, Calif., 1999. Discusses early modern European concepts of madness, spirit possession, and folly.

Nabokov, Isabelle. "Expel the Lover, Recover the Wife: Symbolic Analysis of a South Indian Exorcism." *Journal of the Royal Anthropological Institute* 3, no. 2 (1997): 297–316. A fascinating case study of a local exorcism ritual.

Obeyesekere, Gananath. "The Idiom of Demonic Possession: A Case Study." *Social Science and Medicine* 4, no. 1 (1970): 97–111. A psychoanalytic approach to Indian spirit possession.

Patai, Raphael. "Exorcism and Xenoglossia among the Safed Kabbalists." *Journal of American Folklore* 91, no. 361 (1978): 823–833. Close reading of a case studies in early modern Jewish exorcism with particular focus on the process of verifying the possessing ghost's identity.

Roper, Lyndal. *Oedipus and the Devil: Witchcraft, Sexuality, and Religion in Early Modern Europe.* London, 1994. Covers a broad array of topics, including exorcism.

Sengers, Gerda. *Women and Demons: Cult Healing in Islamic Egypt.* Leiden, Netherlands, 2003. A detailed study of the *zār* cult and Qurʾanic healing based on fieldwork in Cairo, Egypt.

Sluhovsky, Moshe. "The Devil in the Convent." *American Historical Review* 107, no. 5 (2002): 1379–1411. A close study of plural possessions in early modern Europe.

Tambiah, Stanley. "The Magical Power of Words." In *Culture, Thought, and Social Action: An Anthropological Perspective.* Cambridge, Mass., 1985. An important discussion of mantras and "demonic language" in Sri Lankan exorcisms.

Walker, Daniel Pickering. *Unclean Spirits: Possession and Exorcism in France and England in the Late Sixteenth and Early Seventeenth Centuries.* Philadelphia 1981. Focuses on the uses of public exorcisms for purposes of interreligious propaganda.

Wooley, Reginald. *Exorcism and the Healing of the Sick.* London, 1932. How possession relates to illness in the Christian tradition.

NANCY CACIOLA (2005)

EXPERIENCE, RELIGIOUS

SEE RELIGIOUS EXPERIENCE

EXPIATION

SEE ATONEMENT; CONFESSION OF SINS

EXPULSION.

Expulsion can be harmful but also beneficial, depending on the purposes toward which it is directed. Associated concepts are alienation, banishment, excommunication, exile, exorcism, expurgation, purification, repentance, scapegoating, defilement, and cleansing. Greeks, Romans, and Indians practiced expulsion as a means of exerting social control over individuals or groups over millennia. Against that cultural background, religious communities adopted and adapted expulsion to their own purposes and provided some of the most dramatic instances of one or another form of expulsion.

The story in the book of *Genesis* in the Hebrew Bible of Yahweh sending Adam and Eve from the Garden of Eden as punishment for their disobedience of his commands is an archetypal story of expulsion that is widely known, particularly in the West. One widespread and persistent interpretation of the story asserts that ever since that momentous expulsion humans have been estranged and alienated from their proper relationship with the divine. Religious communities often seek to provide means to restore the relationship, sometimes through rituals, sometimes through recommended ethical behaviors, sometimes through doctrines said to articulate the proper understanding of the divine-human relationship to which intellectual assent by believers is required.

Further narratives abound in the literature of many other religions indicating that similar experiences occur within their residual memories of the realm of human relations as individuals are estranged from and by other individuals. Humans also experience alienation from themselves and from their feelings and thoughts, sometimes referred to as "self-alienation." This underscores the necessity to attend to spiritual and psychological dimensions to provide a rounded account of expulsion.

Being alienated from family, friends, communities, organizations, and nations happens as a result of beliefs, actions, and even attitudes that run counter to prevailing norms. Although sometimes voluntary, when for principled reasons a person goes into exile, more often it is a punishment imposed by others. Think of Alexandr Solzhenitsyn, banished by Soviet Union in the 1970s for his books criticizing communism. In Solzhenitsyn's case the demise of the communist regime in the early 1990s enabled him to return to his beloved country freed from the dictatorial power that had expelled him.

EXILE. A person can be excommunicated from a community for denying beliefs held to be central to that community or for actions judged unacceptable by the community. In such instances a prescribed path is sometimes offered to enable the excommunicant to return to the community. Instances of such banishment and subsequent restoration are in the histories of such groups as the Amish, the Mennonites, and the Hutterites. Expulsion from such groups is often the penalty for some member becoming too "modernistic" in belief or action. A return is sometimes achieved by the person's renouncing or recanting her or his offending beliefs or practices. In such instances the power and authority of the community and its traditions is affirmed first by the expulsion and then by its allowing the offender to return on terms the community establishes. Temporary expulsion is a form of ostracizing a person or group for a time of chastisement.

Thus a person can either voluntarily enter into exile to protest a turn of events within a community, often a nation in which a person has held a position of leadership, or one can be banished and thereby become an exile. In the instance of voluntary exile a person makes a principled move aimed at calling attention to, and seeking allies to oppose, whatever is objectionable. In either case, if the situation changes in the community or nation, the person in exile sometimes returns, even triumphantly. A prominent historical instance of this is the case of Martin Luther (1483–1546), who was declared a heretic by the Roman Catholic Church after the Diet of Worms in 1521 and simultaneously was declared an outlaw by the Holy Roman Empire. However, Luther was protected by Prince Frederick the Wise against any move Emperor Charles might have made to enforce the death penalty pronounced against him.

After two years in hiding, Luther returned to Wittenberg, the university city in which he had written his critique of many of the central beliefs and practices of papal Roman Catholicism. That Luther made this return and lived there until his death in 1546 demonstrates that the power and control of both the pope and the Holy Roman emperor were insufficient to make Luther's expulsion effective. He freely moved about in those Germanic territories in which he lived. His banishment by and from Catholicism had no practical consequences for him in that Luther defied both church and Empire and lived to tell the story. In addition, his actions and thoughts led to the emergence of a new interpretation of Christianity called Protestantism.

BANISHMENT. Expulsion is neither voluntary, as exile sometimes is, nor is there usually any possibility of return, as excommunication sometimes offers. Expulsion is a decision made by people holding power to enforce the judgment against a person or group based on a claim that the larger community will be improved or enhanced by ridding itself of those objectionable or corrupting people. Such a draconian judgment leaves those expelled without the support of a society or institution. Thus expulsion is synonymous with irreversible banishment. It is one of the cruelest acts that can be perpetrated against humans, for it is a deliberate cutting off of individuals or groups from the social, economic, spiritual, and other resources of the expelling community. It is a sentence of "social death."

The ideology of expulsion rests upon two bases. First, those who hold sufficient power to impose expulsion typically regard themselves as the sole authentic power center of the institutions over which they rule or within which they hold authority. Any opponents who are perceived to hold views antithetical to those held by the rulers are regarded as threats to the established status quo, and thus as dangerous. This justifies the decisions to rid the institution, the community, or the nation of the purported threat. "Away with them," is the response. Second, those who impose the expulsion reduce those who are victims in some way or another to either a real or virtual subhuman characterization. This attitude dehumanizes those who thereby become "others" and both allows and legitimizes cruelty and banishment of those "heretics" or infidels. Sometimes such practices are forms of creating a scapegoat, which is the practice of identifying an innocent person, group, or even animal to bear the guilt and blame that rightly belongs to others (cf. *Lv.* 16 in the Hebrew Bible). Scapegoating is the false accusation of an offense that results in the persecution or even murder of those so accused.

One of the most widely known instances of a collective expulsion is that of Jews being driven from Spain in 1492, ironically the date that also marks the voyage of exploration of Christopher Columbus. The notorious Tomás de Torquemada (1420–1498) persuaded King Ferdinand and Queen Isabella to expel the Jews. He argued that the Catholic faith was in peril due to the corrupting presence and influence of the false converts from Judaism (and from Islam as well) who were called *conversos* or, even more insultingly, *marranos*, the Hebrew word for pig. This dogmatic and literalistic perspective insisted on one and only one interpretation of Christianity. It overruled any vestige of Christian charity and forced a major eastward movement of Jews. In the twentieth century the Holocaust perpetrated by Nazi Germany focused its horrendous persecution and extermination upon the Jews in many European countries. The goal was the annihilation of all Jews everywhere. This is quantitatively one of the most radical instances of expulsion and destruction in history.

The powerful residual memory of this expulsion contributed significantly to the idea of Jewish immigration to the "promised land" of Zion. In the nineteenth century some Jewish thinkers, such as Theodor Herzl (1860–1904), developed the ideology of Zionism. The combination of the Holocaust and Zionism propelled the migration of Jews from many nations to Palestine and the creation of the State of Israel in the twentieth century.

PURIFICATION. There are, however, other considerations pertaining to expulsion. The eminent twentieth-century historian of religions Mircea Eliade notes that expulsion is not always a negative or reactive matter, at least in connotation. Rather, he convincingly demonstrates that in many cultures and religious traditions expulsion is a rite of purification incorporated into rituals of regeneration. He observes that "demons, diseases, and sins" are all subject to expulsion by ritual actions and that they are regarded as evils that must be expelled in order for the cleansing to be complete (Eliade, 1959). If one recognizes these "expulsions" as having contemporary analogues, this positive connotation takes on a deeper resonance. For example, in the practice of scientific medicine, prescriptions of certain medicines are precisely meant to expel symptoms and the disease they manifest. Further, certain surgical interventions are designed to remove diseased organs or intrusive growths that are compromising the health of a person's body.

Confession of sins is a prominent dimension of certain modern religious practices. Confession leads to repentance and, in some traditions, to the requirement that the penitent person engage in certain actions designed to purge the sins that have been confessed. This is a kind of expulsion that is accomplished in the combination of confession and penance.

The idea of demons still awakens deep anxiety and even fear in large numbers of people. "Demon possession" is a diagnosis not confined to persons but also applied to physical places, such as buildings and homes. The depth of this sensitivity gives rise in some traditions to the practice of exorcism. Two definitions of *exorcise* are to expel (an evil spirit) by, or as if by, incantation, command, or prayer; and to free from evil spirits or malign influences. Popular culture bears witness to the power of the ideas of demon possession and exorcism through both the novel and the movie from the 1970s entitled *The Exorcist*. The extraordinary longevity of both book and movie and the remarkable breadth of their popularity demonstrate that demons still occupy a lively place in the contemporary human imagination.

Thus, if diseases, sins, and demons are regarded as realities in the lives of humans from antiquity until the twenty-first century, then means for expelling them—and thereby purifying and regenerating their hosts—will also predictably be of widespread interest and concern. Such instances of expulsion are valued and sought after.

Finally, another form of expulsion is manifest in the act of expurgation that aims to remove or expel objectionable material from a book or magazine or some other word-based medium before it can be published. This, like exorcism, aims to cleanse or purify a text of some kind or other as targeted material. In text-based religious traditions great care is expended by designated guardians who comb earlier editions to identify any items that need expurgation to ensure that new editions of the sacred writings are as accurate and error-free as possible. This practice demonstrates another instance of expelling what is objectionable and unwanted by participants in a community who are committed to living in conformity with the pure words of their texts.

In the contemporary world, formal religious expulsion, or even expurgation, is comparatively rare, in large measure owing to the heterogeneity of modern societies. People are less confined to participation in only one social, or even religious, grouping. Thus the power of expulsion is reduced to a degree. But informal and powerful instances of ostracizing or banning people still persist in some communities. To the extent that such practices are employed under any circumstances, they serve to demonstrate that expulsion resonates, even in the contemporary world, as a tool of imposing conformity of beliefs, attitudes, and actions.

See Also Excommunication; Fall, The; Scapegoat.

Bibliography

Dumont, Louis. *Homo Hierarchicus: An Essay on the Caste System.* Rev. ed. Translated by Mark Sainsbury. Chicago, 1980.

Eliade, Mircea. *Cosmos and History: The Myth of the Eternal Return.* Translated from French by Willard R. Trask. New York, 1959. Rev. ed. published as *The Myth of the Eternal Return; or, Cosmos and History.* Princeton, N.J., 1971.

Frazer, James George. *The Scapegoat.* Part 6 of *The Golden Bough: A Study in Magic and Religion,* 3d ed., rev. and enl. London, 1913.

Girard, René. *Violence and the Sacred.* Translated by Patrick Gregory. Baltimore, 1977.

James B. Wiggins (2005)

EYE.

EYE. The eye is one of the most widespread symbols in all religious representation. As the active organ of visual perception, it is closely linked with light. Without light, the eye could neither see nor discern clearly. It is therefore only natural that in most cultures the eye is the symbol of intellectual perception and the discovery of truth. The eye knows because it sees. As early as the fifth century BCE, Democrites thought that certain images exist already in the body and that they emerge from the gaze of certain persons. Pliny the Elder explained that the small image inscribed in the pupil is a sort of miniature soul (*Natural History* 21.12.51). Similarly, the Bambara of West Africa say that the image perceived by the eye is, in fact, the double of the object or being that is seen: "Man's world is his eye." Thus the eye is often considered the mirror of the soul, the body's window, which reveals each person's deep thoughts by means of his gaze. As the mirror of the interior, the eye is the place where the mysterious life of the soul is glimpsed. In seeking to discover the reality behind the physical appearances it perceives, the eye becomes the locus of inner revelation. The expression "His eyes were opened" means that a rational or religious truth has been unveiled.

According to the symbolic conception of man as microcosm, which is found in the most ancient cultures, the eye is likened to the sun. Like the luminous star, it sees all, shines, and sparkles. Its glances are rays that pierce like arrows. Among the Semang, the Boshiman, and the Fuegians, the sun is the eye of the supreme god. This isomorphism of the eye and the sun reveals moral and religious values according to which all vision introduces clairvoyance, justice, and righteousness. Just as the sun illuminates by projecting its light everywhere, the eye seeks to discover and see everything, even faults and crimes. It thus becomes the emblem of a superior being who punishes and takes vengeance. To be all-seeing is to become omnipotent. Such valorization of the eye sometimes leads to its sacrificial oblation, which results in a supernatural second sight that replaces and sublimates simple, corporeal vision. This second sight is like the inner eye, or the "eye of the heart," so common among mystics who perceive the divine light.

The Eye as Divine Attribute. In Egypt, as in the most ancient cultures of the eastern Mediterranean Basin, the presence of a symbolic eye signifies the power of the supreme divinity to see and know everything. Thus "the eye of Horus" appears on the stelae of Memphis, and eyes are engraved on a Cretan ring in the Ashmolean Museum (Oxford University), the symbol of an anonymous divinity who looks at and listens to men. The sacerdotal myths and traditions of ancient Egypt testify that the eye has a solar nature and is the fiery source of light and knowledge. Re, the sun god, is endowed with a burning eye and appears in the form of a rearing cobra with dilated eyes. In the cult of Harmerti, Re and Thoth are the two eyes of Horus, the god of the sky. One Harmerti story relates the struggle between Horus and Seth; Seth pokes out the eye of Horus, who is later cured by Thoth. The healed, healthy eye is the *oudjat* eye that shines in the dark and vanquishes death. *The Book of Going Forth by Day* (17.29ff.) recapitulates that mythical episode in a formula that is said to the dead person by the one playing the role of Thoth: "I restore to the eye the fullness it possessed on the day of the fight between the two adversaries." This means that light and darkness, life and death, are reconciled in the beyond. This *oudjat* eye was painted on the inner sides of the coffin, on each side of the head, and an inscription affirmed that they were hereafter the eyes by which the dead person would see in the afterlife and which would permit him to follow the spectacle of the exterior world while remaining in his tomb. The *oudjat* eye was provided for the dead person "in order that he be animated by it" (Pyramid Texts 578). This is why Horus's eye made an excellent amulet.

At Tell Brak in eastern Syria, the excavation of a sanctuary going back to 2500 BCE has revealed the worship of a divinity with a thousand eyes. In this temple consecrated to Inanna (Ishtar), hundreds of statuettes with multiple eyes have been found, votive offerings or apotropaic images attesting that the eye was the emblem of that all-seeing and omnipresent feminine divinity. Analogous finds have been made at Ur, Lagash, and Mari. Inanna's brother Shamash is the sun god, whose eye sees everything and who knows the most secret thoughts. He can reward or punish deliberately. In Babylon, Shamash was invoked before every divination, for he was the one who wrote the signs in the entrails of sacrificial victims. Without his help, the diviner could not see them.

The Indo-European world attached the same value to the eye as to the sun and to the gods, that is, the quality of being able to see everything. In the *Ṛgveda,* the god Sūrya, son of Dyaus, is called "the eye of the sky" (10.37.2) and "the eye of Mithra and of Varuna" (1.115.1, 7.61.1, 10.37.1). He sees from afar and everywhere, and spies on the whole world. Varuṇa, the celestial god, is described as *sahasrāta,* god of a thousand eyes, for he sees everything. According to the hymn of Puruṣa (*Ṛgveda* 10.90), the sun was born from the eye of the cosmic giant Puruṣa so that at death, when a man's soul and body return to the cosmic primordial man, his eye will go back to the sun. It is understandable why, in the *Bhagavadgītā* as well as in certain Upaniṣads, eyes are identified with the two celestial lights, the sun and moon, which are the eyes of Viśvakarman, the divine architect with multiple eyes who ordained everything. The Tamil caste of the Kammalans, who claim to descend from him, have as their main task painting the eyes of divine statues according to a ritual as sacred as that of the *oudjat* eye, the eye of Horus, in Egypt. In Iranian tradition, the sun is also the eye of Ahura Mazdā (*Yasna* 1.11), whereas in the tenth *Yasht* of the Avesta, Mithra is called the "master of vast plains who has a thousand ears and ten thousand eyes," thus assimilating him to the sun.

For the Greeks, the gods "with piercing gaze" saw everything belonging to the past, present, and future in a single, unified vision. This *panopteia* is the very mark of their divinity. Thus there is Kronos, who has four eyes, two in front and two in back; Zeus, whose "vast gaze" pierces through to the most secret things (Hesiod, *Works and Days* 240, 265); Apollo, the solar god, who sees everything (*Iliad* 3.277, *Odyssey* 11.109); and Dionysos, whose Bacchic hymn repeats that he "shines like a star with his eye of fire that darts its rays over the whole earth" (Diodorus of Sicily, 1.11.3). All the Greek gods cast a sovereign and pure gaze on man. The gaze of Athena Glaukopis shines and fascinates; the eye she fixes on her enemies is "a sharp one, an eye of bronze." When Achilles, driven by rage, tries to kill Agamemnon, Athena seizes him by his hair and forces him to look at her. The hero cries out, "It is terrifying to see the light of your eyes" (*Iliad* 1.200), for the light in her eyes is the light of reason. In Greek poetry, the image of the eye or the pupil is used to mark the quality of a person and the affection one feels for him: "Where is the eye of my beloved Amphiaraos, this hero who was both a seer and a valiant warrior?" (Pindar, *Olympian Odes* 6.16.7). The Greek religious experience consisted primarily of a vision. Since Homeric times, an indissoluble relationship has existed between knowing and seeing: knowledge is based on sight, on an optical intuition. In his *Metaphysics,* Aristotle speaks of that joy of seeing, which makes a better basis for knowing than any other perception. The joy of sensitive contemplation is the climax of the initiation into the great mysteries of Eleusis, the *epopteia,* and the very source of all philosophy, repeats Plato (*Timaeus* 47a). For the knowledge of truth rests on a vision that moves upward from tangible realities to timeless and eternal things: "Holy is the man who has the gods before his eyes" (scholium on Pindar, *Pythian Odes* 4.151b).

The Germanic and Celtic worlds also valued the magical power of the eye. Óðinn (Odin), god of war and magic, is a one-eyed god, for he voluntarily gave an eye in payment to the sorcerer-giant Mímir, or Memory. In return, Óðinn was permitted to drink every day at the spring of knowledge and thus to learn the science of the runes. The loss of an eye is therefore the means of acquiring superior vision and the supernatural powers that flow from it. After the Vanir killed Mímir, Óðinn practiced divination by interrogating the head, which he succeeded in preserving (*Ynglingasaga* 4, 7). This theme of knowledge acquired as a result of blindness—even ocular mutilation—is found elsewhere in other Indo-European traditions. Thus, the Greek diviner Tiresias attains the ability to see the future by becoming blind; Oedipus learns the will of the gods by blinding himself; and the blind king Dhṛtarāṣṭra in the *Mahābhārata* has special powers. Blindness, or voluntary mutilation of the eyes, becomes the sign of the superior sight possessed by the druids and the diviners. Indeed, this quasi-magical power of the eye is found again in Celtic myths. The god Lugh keeps only one eye open. He makes a tour of the enemies' camp, hopping and singing in an act similar to Óðinn's during the battle between the Æsir and the Vanir. The same attitude is found in the Celtic hero Cú Chulainn, who, when seized by furor, closes one eye and enlarges the other, or sometimes swallows one eye and places the other on his cheek to frighten his adversary. Many Gallic coins show a hero's head with an eye disproportionately enlarged.

Other myths also valorize the magical power of the one-eyed person, as if the reduction of vision to a single eye increased the intensity of the gaze. Thus a glance from Medusa's single eye petrifies anyone who crosses its path, for it is the glance of death that leads to Hades. To overcome it, Perseus must first escape the other two Gorgons and hide the one eye they share between them. He conquers Medusa only by making use of Athena's mirror, which allows him to see the monster without being seen by her.

THE EVIL EYE AND MAGIC. The belief in the unlucky influence of the evil eye is universal. It rests on a valorization of the gaze reputed to be harmful because the eye is abnormal (eyes of different colors, double pupils, squinting); such a gaze magically reveals the malevolent intention of the soul whose window the eye is. The evil eye, cast for vengeance or out of envy, is an invisible threat against which one must protect oneself with countermagic, as, for example, in this Babylonian incantation: "Take the eye, attach its feet to a bush in the desert, then take the eye and break it like a pottery vase!" In Egypt it was common practice to bear apotropaic names, wear amulets, and recite formulas. In the Roman world, fear of the *fascinum* was constant. Many mosaics have as a central motif a dangerous eye pierced by an arrow, surrounded by animals, and defended by an owl (the bird of evil omen) perched on its eyelid. Against this danger, people resorted to amulets picturing an eye or a phallus. Eyes were even painted on the prows of boats.

Ever since the time of the apostle Paul (*Gal.* 3:1), Christian preachers never ceased to raise their voices, in vain, against the belief in the evil eye. Some rituals of the Greek Orthodox church as found in the *Mikron Euchologion* contain a formula for exorcism against *baskania* ("witchcraft") similar to that found in certain Babylonian curses. The same belief is found in pre-Islamic Arabia and in the Muslim world. Muḥammad himself recited incantations to preserve his grandson from the evil eye, reviving the formulas that Abraham made use of in order to protect Ishmael and Isaac, the legend says. One Arabic proverb states that "the evil eye empties houses and fills tombs." The eye frequently occurs in the magical preparations of certain African ethnic groups as well as in the Eastern Orthodox world, where the eyes of the figures in icons were poked out and crushed and then made into a magical powder.

Religious and Mystical Values of the Eye. The word *eye* recurs 675 times in the Hebrew scriptures (Old Testament) and 137 times in the New Testament; this indicates the richness of its symbolic meanings. It designates, first, the organ of vision fashioned by the creator for the good of man (*Ps.* 94:9, *Prv.* 20:12), for "it is a joy for the eye to see the sun" (*Eccl.* 11:7). But the eye is also a privileged organ of knowledge that scripture always associates with the characteristics of the wise and learned: for example, Balaam, the diviner whose eye is closed to the terrestrial realities that surround him but is open to the hidden and the invisible once he meets the All-Powerful (*Nm.* 23–24). The Targum Yerushalmi makes Balaam a one-eyed seer, thus taking up again the theme of a second sight superior to normal corporeal vision. Symbolically, the eye designates the consciousness of man that Yahveh opens to the knowledge of his law and therefore of good and evil (*Dt.* 29:3, *Is.* 6:10). For Yahveh sees all (*Ps.* 14:2); he is the witnessing God from whom nothing escapes (*Ps.* 139:7–8). This ability to see all is an essential characteristic of his transcendent sovereignty, and the divine eye is the administrator of justice: before it the just man can find grace (*Dt.* 31:29, *Jb.* 11:4). But it is also the paternal eye of Providence, "who turns toward those who fear him" (*Ps.* 33;18), like Nehemiah praying night and day for the people of Israel (*Neh.* 1:6, *Lv.* 16:2, *Nm.* 4:20).

But however great his desire, man may not see God face to face (*Ps.* 42:3), for no one can see Yahveh without dying (Ex. 19:21, *Lv.* 16:2, *Nm.* 4:20). Even Moses saw only the back of the glory of God (*Ex.* 33:20–23). If some prophets have had a vision of divine glory, it is in a fugitive and symbolic fashion, through a cloud or in human shape. Thus Zachariah (c. 520 BCE) saw Yahveh put before the high priest "a single stone decorated with seven eyes," symbol of God's vigilant presence in his temple. They are the seven planets, or seven divine eyes that sweep over the earth without resting. Likewise Ezekiel, in his vision of the chariot evoking Yahveh's throne, sees wheels whose rims are decorated with open eyes (*Ez.* 1:18), signs of Yahveh's omniscience.

Although, as the apostle John says, "No one has ever seen God" (*1 Jn.* 4:12), Jesus promised the pure in heart that they shall see God (*Mt.* 5:8). This beatitude makes of the eye a symbol of inner purity (*Mt.* 6:22–23); otherwise the eye, as the opportunity for scandal, ought to be plucked out and thrown far away. Early Christian preaching insists on the opposition between the eyes of flesh and those of the spirit; in Paul's case, physical blinding symbolically preceded the opening of the eyes of the heart (*Acts* 9:18). Furthermore, the function of the Son is to render visible his Father: "Whoever sees me has seen the Father," says Jesus to Philip (*Jn.* 14:9). But at the end of time, full vision will be given to everyone and "man's eyes will contemplate the glory of God just as he is" (*1 Jn.* 3:2). Gnosticism especially retains the Pauline theme of "the eye of the heart," an image already frequent in the writings of the Greek philosophers and the Hebrew rabbis. For the gnostic, "the eye is the inner light to the man of light" (*Gospel of Thomas,* logion 24), and the prototype of the man of light is "the eye of light" *(Sophia of Jesus Christ).*

In numerous philosophical and religious traditions, the inner eye allows access to wisdom. Plotinus explains that the eye of the soul dazzled by the light of understanding is fixed on pure transparency; the soul therefore sees the light found at the interior of his own gaze, and the eye of understanding contemplates the light of *nous* by participating in the very light of this sun-spirit (*Enneads* 5.3[17].28). Recalling that the wise man is he who sees and that the fool is blind, Philo Judaeus explained that formerly the prophets were called "seers" (*1 Sm.* 9:8). For him, wisdom is not only what is obtained by the vision of the inner eye, just as light is perceived by the carnal eye; but wisdom also sees itself, and this is the splendor of God, who, in opening the soul's eye to wisdom, shows himself to man (*De migratione Abraham* 38).

In Hinduism, the god Śiva is endowed with a third eye, the frontal eye that gives him a unifying vision. His look of fire expresses the pureness of the present without any other temporal dimension, as well as the simultaneity of beings and events, which he reduces to ashes in revelation of the all. Likewise Buddha, the "awakened one," received inner enlightenment through the celestial eye, which permitted him to see the life of all beings simultaneously and gave him the knowledge of the chain of the fundamental forces of existence as well as its previous forms. This eye of wisdom, *prajñācakṣus,* is found at the limit of unity and multiplicity, of emptiness and creation; it permits the wise man to grasp them simultaneously. The organ of inner vision, it is the very sign of Buddhist wisdom.

But the inner eye is the organ of wisdom only because it is capable of actually experiencing the divine. Every revelation presents itself as a veil that has been pulled back before the gaze of religious man, for whom the beatific vision and the contemplation of God are the very essence of eternal life. The eye of the heart is thus a frequent theme in spiritual and mystical literature. Just as the eye can neither see nor discern its object without light, so the soul cannot contemplate God without the light of faith, which alone opens the eyes of the heart. "Man must therefore become entirely eye"; such is the teaching of the Desert Fathers reiterated by Symeon the New Theologian (*Hymns of the Divine Loves* 45), for the soul's eye, relieved of carnal passions, can perceive the divine light that opens up on the heavens. Following Origen and his theory of spiritual senses, Gregory of Nyssa, Augustine, Bernard of Clairvaux, and all the Fathers state that it is God who, by opening the heart's eye, makes one see. Meister Eckhart again picks up this teaching *(Sermons)*, and Teresa of Ávila specifies that what we know otherwise than by faith, the soul recognizes at sight, although not by eyesight. Leon Bloy writes in his *Journal* (June 6, 1894) that "we must turn our eyes inward" in order to speak our desire for a vision of truth, for the carnal eye only allows us to see "in enigma and as in a mirror." The eye of the heart is therefore man seeing God and, at the same time, God looking at man; it is the instrument of enlightenment and inner unification: "We shall find the pearl of the kingdom of heaven inside our hearts if we first purify the eye of our spirit" (Philotheus of Sinai, *Forty Chapters on Spiritual Sobriety* 23).

SEE ALSO Sun; Visions.

BIBLIOGRAPHY

Bleeker, C. Jouco. *The Sacred Bridge.* Leiden, 1963.

Boyer, Régis. *La religion des anciens scandinaves.* Paris, 1981.

Crawford, O. G. S. *The Eye Goddess.* London, 1957.

Durand, Gilbert. *Les structures anthropologiques de l'imaginaire.* 3d ed. Paris, 1969.

Hocart, Arthur M. "The Mechanism of the Evil Eye." *Folk-Lore* 49 (June 1938): 156–157.

Pettazzoni, Raffaele. *The All-Knowing God.* Translated by H. J. Rose. London, 1956.

Seligman, Siegfried. *Der böse Blick.* Berlin, 1910.

Vries, Jan de. *Altgermanische Religionsgeschichte.* 2d ed. 2 vols. Berlin, 1956–1957.

Vries, Jan de. *Keltische Religion.* Stuttgart, 1961.

MICHEL MESLIN (1987)
Translated from French by Kristine Anderson

EZEKIEL (sixth century BCE), or, in Hebrew, Yeḥezqe'l, was a Hebrew prophet. A hereditary priest, Ezekiel is known primarily from the biblical book of prophecy named after him that contains first-person reports of revelations made to him. For example, the opening verse of *Ezekiel* reads: "In the thirtieth year, in the fourth month, on the fifth of the month, when I was among the exiles on the Chebar canal [in the vicinity of the Babylonian city of Nippur], the heavens opened and I saw a divine vision" (a description of God's majesty borne on the divine "chariot" follows). The time of his prophesying is fixed by some fifteen dates scattered through the book, which, apart from the obscure first one cited above, belong to the era of "our exile"—that is, the exile of King Jehoiachin of Judah, his courtiers, and his administrative staff, in 597 BCE); it may be inferred that Ezekiel was among those deported to Babylon with the king. The dates fall between 593 and 571, all within the reign of the Babylonian king Nebuchadrezzar II (605–562), who is mentioned several times in the book as a world conqueror. No references to events subsequent to the reign of that king are made, nor does the editorial work on the book necessitate assumption of later hands, so that its contents—internally consistent though literarily varied—may be considered the record of a single author's career. The only personal details given of Ezekiel's life are his priestly descent and the death of his wife in exile. That the enigmatic "thirtieth year" of the opening verse (cited above) alludes to the prophet's age at the start of his vocation is an unsupported guess that goes back at least as far as Origen.

Two determinants of the prophet's outlook stand out in his prophecies: his priesthood and his exile. The former is reflected in his schooling in the full range of Israel's literary traditions (legal, prophetic, historiographic), his manner of expression (echoing the Priestly writings of the Pentateuch), and his preoccupations (the Temple, God's holiness, offenses against his worship). The response to exile is reflected in Ezekiel's anguish and rage at what he perceives as God's rejection of his apostate people. Ezekiel's prophecy is characterized by a leaning toward systematization; he propounds doctrines permeated by a severe logic that centers on the injury Israel inflicted on the majesty of God and its reparation rather than on the piteous situation of the people. The *Book of Ezekiel* may be divided into three sections:

- Chapters 1–24 are composed mostly of dooms against Jerusalem that date before its fall in 587/6 BCE. (Chapter 33 is an appendix related to this section.)
- Chapters 34–48 contain prophecies of the restoration of Israel, composed, presumably, after the city's fall. The first six of these chapters are rhapsodic, the latter nine legislative.
- Chapters 25–32 link the two main divisions in the form of prophecies against Israel's neighbors, settling accounts with them for their exploitation of, or participation in the collapse of Judah.

No other prophetic book shows so thorough a working through of principles in its arrangement, pointing to the hand of this prophet.

MAIN THEMES OF EZEKIEL'S PROPHECY. The chief burden of Ezekiel's pre-586 prophecies (chaps. 2–24) was that Jerusalem was inevitably doomed to destruction by Nebuchadrezzar. This contradicted the mood both of the exiles and of the homelanders, among whom prophets of good tidings were at work (chap. 13). Patriotism, faith in the security offered by God's presence in the Jerusalem Temple, and the encouragement by Egypt of anti-Babylonian forces in Judah combined to rouse the people's hopes, indeed their expectation that subjection to Babylonia was ephemeral; that the exiles would shortly return home; and that resistance to the overlord, supported by Egypt, would be successful. Like Jeremiah, his contemporary in Jerusalem, Ezekiel regarded such hopes as illusory; worse, they revealed spiritual obtuseness in their blindness to the divine purpose realizing itself in Judah's plight. As Jeremiah and Ezekiel saw it, the people's idolatrous infidelity to their covenant with God, reaching back to the beginnings of their history and peaking during the reign of King Manasseh of Judah (*2 Kgs.* 21), had finally outrun God's patience. And alongside apostasy was the corruption of the social order (idolatry and immorality were bound together in the minds of biblical authors): the oppression of the governed by their rulers, the trampling of the poor, the unfortunate, and the aliens by the people at large, until not one righteous person could be found in Jerusalem to stem the onset of God's retributive fury (*Ez.* 22). Another form of infidelity to God that Ezekiel denounced with particular vehemence was the resort of Judah's kings to Egypt for help against Mesopotamian powers (Assyria, Babylonia), instead of trusting in divine protection. These offenses are set out in bills of indictment ending in sentences of doom: God had resolved to abandon his Temple (desecrated by the people) and to deliver his city and land to be ravaged by the Babylonians (chaps. 8–11, 16, 23). In listing the evidences of Jerusalem's guilt and stressing the unavoidability of its fall, Ezekiel sought to disabuse his fellow exiles of their misplaced hopes, turn their minds to consider their evil ways, and lead them to repentance. (Because his dooms are addressed rhetorically to Jerusalem, it has been thought that they were intended to dissuade the Judahite court from pursuing its rebellious policy against Babylonia, but their emphatic unconditionality could hardly serve that end.)

Ezekiel conveyed his messages in deeds as well as words, making much use of dramatic and symbolic acts. He arrayed toy siege works against a representation of Jerusalem drawn on a brick; he lay on his side eating scant siege rations for many days; carrying an exile's pack on his shoulder, he acted out the clandestine flight of the king from the fallen city; he repressed his sighs of mourning for his dead wife to presage the stupefaction of those who would live through the coming carnage (chaps. 4–5, 12, 24)—all these and more. No prophet went to such lengths to impress his audience because none was so convinced of their imperviousness to his message (chaps. 2–3). Still, although at his commissioning he was forewarned of his audience's adamant hostility, in actuality he became the cynosure of exiles in his hometown, Tel Abib: indeed, he complains that they flock to him as to an entertainment but fail to act on his admonitions (chap. 33).

To the exiles he addressed calls for repentance. For their conversion he propounded the doctrine of the eternal availability of divine forgiveness, thus countering the despair that was bound to follow on acceptance of his interpretation of events. For if Israel indeed lay under a generations-long accumulation of guilt—Ezekiel once went so far as to describe Jerusalem as congenitally depraved (*Ez.* 16:3–45)—so overwhelming it caused God to forsake his Temple and his land, what future had they to look forward to? Ezekiel met despair with the twin doctrines of the moral autonomy of each generation—that is, the nonbequeathal of guilt from fathers to sons and God's ever-readiness to accept the penitent wicked. God judges each according to his own ways, not those of his ancestors, and he judges him as he is now, not as he was yesterday. Hence each generation may hope for reconciliation with God, and anyone can unburden himself of a guilty past by renouncing it and turning a new leaf. God does not desire the death of the wicked person but his or her repentance, so that they may live (chaps. 18, 33).

As Jerusalem suffered under the protracted siege that was to end in its fall (in 587/6), Ezekiel began to deliver his oracles against foreign nations; the first is dated in 587, the last in 585 (except for an appendix dated to 571, in chap. 29). Judah's small neighbors, formerly co-rebels with it, abandoned it in the crisis. Some gloated over its fall; Edom seized the occasion to appropriate some of Judah's territory. These countries are denounced for their hubris and their show of contempt toward their downfallen neighbor, and their own ruin is predicted (chaps. 25–28). On the other hand, Egypt, which had encouraged Judah to revolt, is condemned to temporary exile and permanent degradation for having proven to be a "reedy staff" in the hour of need, collapsing when Judah leaned on it (chaps. 29–32). When God punishes his own so ruthlessly, the perfidy and contemptuousness of their neighbors will not be ignored. Some of the most vivid passages in the book occur in these prophecies: a unique list of the Phoenecian trade (Tyre's imports and exports and the nations with which it traded); a mythical depiction of the king of Tyre as the denizen of Paradise, expelled from it for his sin; and a picture of the underworld realm of the dead receiving Pharaoh and his defeated army.

The fall of Jerusalem gave rise to a new concern: the only nation on earth that acknowledged the one true God (however imperfectly) had suffered a crushing defeat on the field and the cream of its population had, for a second time, been deported. However justified these punishments were in terms of Israel's covenant with God, to the world they could only signify the humiliation of Israel's God—or so at least Ezekiel portrayed it in chapter 36. The extreme measures taken to punish Israel for flouting God (in Ezekiel's words, for "profaning God's name") resulted in a still greater "profanation": the nations pointed to the exiles and jeered, "These are the Lord's people and from his land they have come forth!" It followed as an ironbound consequence that God must now vindicate his authority by restoring Israel to its homeland and so redeem his reputation. This key idea of chapter 36 is the motive of the rhapsodic restoration prophecies of chapters 34–39. All is done for the greater glory of God: Israel's "dry bones" are vivified and the miraculously re-created people are gathered into their land; the former two kingdoms (Israel and Judah) are united under the rule of a new David; the land is blessed with peace and unprecedented fertility. The crowning transformation is in the very nature of the Israelites: their "heart of stone" will be replaced with a "heart of flesh." God's spirit will animate them to observe his laws effortlessly, thus averting forever the recurrence of the terrible cycle of sin, punishment, exile, and profanation of God's name among humans. Moreover, because the restoration of Israel will not be for their sake, but for the sake of God's name (reputation), it will not depend on Israel's taking the initiative to reform itself but will happen at God's initiative. Israel's self-recrimination and remorse over its evil past will follow, not precede, its salvation (chap. 36). To impress his sovereignty finally on the minds of all, God will, after restoring Israel, engineer an attack on them by the barbarian Gog of Magog. Attracted by the prospect of plundering the prospering, undefended cities of Israel, Gog and the armies mustered from the far north under his banner will descend on them, only to be miraculously routed and massacred. Then all will realize that the misfortune that befell Israel was punishment for their sins (not a sign of God's weakness!), and their restoration, a "sanctification of God's name" in the sight of all humankind (chaps. 38–39).

The last major section of the book is legislative and prescriptive: a unique series of revisions of certain Israelite institutions designed to maintain the sanctity of the Temple precinct. The section consists of a vision of the future Temple climaxed by God's return to it (chaps. 41–43:12), and instructions for righting past misconduct in relation to it so that it would never again be abandoned (chaps. 43:13–48).

The future Temple is envisaged as laid out with a well-defined gradation of sacred areas, access to which is rigorously controlled in accordance with grades of personal holiness. The corps of Temple servants is restructured, with a sharp division between priests and nonpriests, the latter being strictly excluded from access to the highest grades of holy space. The role that the future king (archaically entitled "chief") is to play in worship is so defined as to prevent him, a layman, from trespassing on the areas of highest sanctity (as preexilic kings were accustomed to do), while at the same time making allowances for his superior dignity. New periodic sacrifices of purgation are instituted to keep the inevitable contamination of the sanctuary by the natural impurities and inadvertencies of the people from accumulating dangerously. Finally, the land is redistributed among the ingathered population, archaically defined as the twelve tribes, with boundaries derived from the ancient idea of the promised "land of Canaan" rather than from the actual boundaries of the land under the monarchy. The disposition of the tribes is such as to isolate the Temple from contact with the profane by cordons of sacred personnel surrounding it. God will dwell forever in his holy city, renamed accordingly *YHVH Shammah,* "The Lord is there" (replacing *Yerushalayim,* "Jerusalem").

LATER INFLUENCES. In later times, Ezekiel's justification of the collapse of Israel influenced the revision of the old history of the monarchy (the *Book of Kings*) undertaken under Persian rule embodied in the *Book of Chronicles.* The Chronicler's story of the conduct of the last Judahite kings (from Manasseh on) shows the effect of Ezekiel's doctrines with particular clarity. On the other hand, Ezekiel's rhapsodic descriptions of restoration were far removed from the modest dimensions and achievements of returned exiles. And their mood of repentance (surely owing at least in part to Ezekiel's teachings) kindled in them a resolve to adhere scrupulously to the ancient covenant laws of Moses rather than to Ezekiel's newfangled revisions (which anyway supposed a very different geodemographic reality from that of the postexilic community). Ezekiel had to give way before Moses, and his program was relegated to messianic utopia. His vision of the divine "chariot" (chaps. 7, 10) was to play a decisive role in Jewish mystical experience from Second Temple times onward.

BIBLIOGRAPHY

A number of commentaries on *Ezekiel* may be consulted, among which the following, listed chronologically, are recommended.

Herrmann, Johannes. *Ezechiel, übersetzt und erklärt.* Kommentar zum Alten Testament. Leipzig, 1924.

Cooke, G. A. *A Critical and Exegetical Commentary on the Book of Ezekiel.* 2 vols. New York, 1937.

Fohrer, Georg. *Ezechiel.* Handbuch zum Alten Testament, vol. 13. Tübingen, 1955.

Eichrodt, Walther. *Der Prophet Hesekiel.* Das Alte Testament Deutsch. Göttingen, 1965–1966. Translated into English as *Ezekiel: A Commentary,* "Old Testament Library" (Philadelphia, 1970).

Wevers, John W. *Ezekiel.* Century Bible, n.s., pt. 1, vol. 26. London, 1969.

Zimmerli, Walther. *Ezechiel (1–48).* 2 vols. Biblischer Kommentar Alter Testament, vol. 13, nos. 1–2. Neunkirchen, 1969. Translated into English in two parts: *Ezekiel 1,* by R. E. Clements (Philadelphia, 1979), and *Ezekiel 2,* by James D. Martin (Philadelphia, 1983).

Greenberg, Moshe. *Ezekiel 1–20.* Anchor Bible, vol. 22. Garden City, N.Y., 1983.

For general surveys, consult Walther Zimmerli's "The Message of the Prophet Ezekiel," *Interpretation* 23 (1969): 131–157, and my own article "Ezekiel" in the *Encyclopaedia Judaica* (Jerusalem, 1971). Bernhard Lang's *Ezechiel: Der Prophet und das Buch,* "Erträge der Forschung," no. 153 (Darmstadt, 1981), is a good review of modern scholarship on Ezekiel. The influence of Ezekiel on Jewish mysticism is treated in David J. Halperin's *The Merkabah in Rabbinic Literature,* "American Oriental Series," no. 62 (New Haven, 1980).

New Sources

Biggs, Charles R. *The Book of Ezekiel.* Epworth Commentaries. London, 1996.

Block, Daniel Isaac. *The Book of Ezekiel.* New International Commentary on the Old Testament. Grand Rapids, Mich., 1997.

Eynde, Sabine M. L. van den. "Interpreting 'Can These Bones Come Back to Life?' in *Ezekiel* 37:3: The Technique of Hiding Knowledge." *Old Testament Essays* 14 (2001): 153–165.

Vawter, Bruce, and Leslie J. Hoppe. *A New Heart: A Commentary on the Book of Ezekiel.* International Theological Commentary. Grand Rapids, Mich., and Edinburgh, 1991.

Wright, Christopher J. H. *The Message of Ezekiel: A New Heart and a New Spirit.* Bible Speaks Today. Leicester and Downers Grove, Ill, 2001.

MOSHE GREENBERG (1987)
Revised Bibliography

EZRA (late fifth and early fourth centuries BCE) was known for his restoration of the Law of Moses in the postexilic period and is generally regarded as the founder of Judaism.

LITERARY SOURCES. The account of Ezra's activity is contained in *Ezra* and in *Nehemiah* 8–9. The history covered by *Ezra* is a continuation from *2 Chronicles* and is probably by the same author. It begins with the edict of Cyrus (538 BCE), which permitted the return of exiles from Babylonia to their homeland and the chance to rebuild the Temple. Using some independent sources whose chronology is not clearly understood, the author attempts to trace the history of the Jerusalem community down to the time of Ezra (Heb., 'Ezra'), which begins only in chapter 7. Within chapters 7 to 9 there is a first-person narration by Ezra, often considered to be a separate source, "the memoirs of Ezra," although it cannot easily be separated from its context in 7:1–26 and chapter 10, where Ezra is referred to in the third person. It appears to have been composed after the style of the so-called Nehemiah memoirs.

On the basis of the Greek version (*1 Esd.*) it appears that *Nehemiah* 8 originally followed and was a part of *Ezra*, so that the climax of the history was Ezra's reading of the law book to the Jerusalem community. A later editor who wanted to make the activity of Ezra and Nehemiah appear contemporary transposed this part of the history to its present position. *Nehemiah* 9, the prayer of confession of Ezra, also fits badly as a continuation of chapter 8 and is a later addition. At any rate the biblical portrait of Ezra is not a contemporary record but, in my view, is Hellenistic in date and must be used with caution in any historical reconstruction of the period.

BIBLICAL TRADITION. Ezra's introduction, in *Ezra* 7:1–5, identifies him as a priest and gives him a pedigree back to Aaron. But he is especially known as "the scribe of the law of God." The account indicates that he was given a special commission by the Persian king, Artaxerxes, to promulgate the Law of Moses not only in Judah but in the whole of Syria-Palestine. He also received considerable monetary support for the cult in Jerusalem. Ezra set out from Babylon with five thousand companions and great treasure and arrived in Jerusalem safely five months later. Shortly after he returned to Jerusalem he discovered that many Jews had intermarried with non-Jews, and after much soul-searching he set about to dissolve all the mixed marriages. In the second year after his arrival, in the seventh month, at Sukkot, Ezra brought forth the Law and read it to the people in a great public ceremony (*Neh.* 8). This is now followed (in *Neh.* 9) by a fast on the twenty-fourth day of the seventh month, in which Ezra leads the people in a great confession of sins and a covenant renewal (*Neh.* 10) by which the people commit themselves to the support of the sanctuary, the observance of the Sabbath, and other laws of the Torah.

There are various layers in the biblical tradition concerning Ezra. The one that identifies Ezra as the scribe who brought the Law to the restored community in Jerusalem is clearly the oldest tradition. Many scholars believe that this tradition reflects the introduction of the Pentateuch into, and its formal acceptance by, the Jewish community in Jerusalem. For this reason the figure of Ezra represents a new era in which the community stands under the Law and its interpreters and becomes, in this view, a religion "of the book," so that it is often regarded as the beginning of Judaism. However, any notion of a radical discontinuity with the religion of the Jews in the late monarchy or exilic periods is quite unwarranted, because the Pentateuch itself embodies much from these periods.

Nevertheless, the mission of Ezra is now seen in the Bible through the eyes of the Chronicler, who considered his presentation of the Law as the climax of his history, and later Judaism did much to further enhance the significance of this event. Already within the biblical account the later levels of the Ezra tradition that portray him as a judge and reformer (*Ezr.* 9–10), or as an intercessor and covenant mediator (*Neh.* 9–10), cast him more and more in the image of a second Moses.

HISTORICAL PROBLEMS. The exact dating of Ezra's activity within the Persian period and especially his relationship to his near contemporary Nehemiah have long been matters of disagreement among scholars. The *Book of Ezra* dates the beginning of Ezra's activity to the seventh year, and Nehemiah to the twentieth year, of Artaxerxes. If these dates refer to the same king, then Ezra would be prior to Nehemiah, as the present biblical tradition suggests. But there is reason to believe that Ezra should be dated to the reign of Artaxerxes II (404–359 BCE) which would put him about 397 BCE, well after Nehemiah. Ezra's return seems to presuppose a revitalized Jerusalem community with protective walls (*Ezr.* 9:9), while Nehemiah seems to know nothing of the large band of exiles that returned with Ezra. It also seems most unlikely that Ezra waited thirteen years after his arrival before promulgating his law if this was his primary commission. Another possibility is to view Ezra as coming during Nehemiah's second term of office, in the thirty-seventh year of Artaxerxes I, but this involves a textual emendation for which there is little justification.

Another area of debate is how to understand the law book that Ezra brought to Jerusalem from the Babylonian exile. Was it a particular part of the Pentateuch, such as the so-called Priestly code, or was it a more complete form of the Torah, much as it is today? And just exactly what was the nature of Ezra's commission from the Persian court and the scope of his authority? The way in which one answers these questions greatly affects one's understanding of the history of the restoration and the development and interpretation of the Pentateuch.

THE APOCALYPSE OF EZRA. Also known as *4 Ezra,* the *Apocalypse of Ezra* is a Jewish work of about 100 CE that presents Ezra (also called Salathiel) as a prophet who experiences dreams and visions of an apocalyptic nature in the thirtieth year after the destruction of Jerusalem. In addition, just like Moses he hears the voice of God speaking from a thornbush and then withdraws from the people for forty days to receive a revelation from God. This revelation includes not only the Law of Moses that had been lost in the destruction of Jerusalem but also the complete twenty-four books of the Hebrew scriptures and seventy secret books for the "wise." Like Moses, Ezra also experienced an assumption to heaven.

How this earlier Ezra the prophet was thought to relate to the later Ezra the scribe is problematic. The common element is Ezra's association with the Law of Moses and his portrayal as a second Moses. This seems to have been carried to the point where in one form of the tradition, Ezra, like Moses, never got back to the land of Palestine. This extracanonical form of the tradition received great elaboration in the medieval period.

EZRA IN JUDAISM, CHRISTIANITY, AND ISLAM. The Jewish *aggadah* regarded Ezra with great honor. He was not just a priest but the high priest and a second Moses. He was especially revered for restoring the Law of Moses, which had been forgotten, and for establishing the regular public reading of the Law. He is also credited with setting up schools for the study of the Law. The law that Ezra brought to the people was not only the written Law of Moses but included the unwritten law as well. In addition, he is also credited with writing parts of *Chronicles* and the *Book of Psalms* and is identified by some as the prophet Malachi.

Following *4 Ezra* early Christian authors regarded Ezra as a prophet who under inspiration recovered all the ancient scriptures that had been destroyed by the Babylonian invasion—not just the Law of Moses. Some extracanonical works such as *Enoch* are also attributed to his prophetic recollection. Whether there were two Ezras, the prophet and the priest-scribe, or just one was a matter of debate.

The Qurʾān contains only one curious remark about Ezra, that the Jews believed him to be the son of God (*sūrah* 9:30). The basis for this statement is not clear and not reflected in any extant Jewish source.

BIBLIOGRAPHY

The many literary and historical problems associated with Ezra make the literature on this subject enormous and controversial. For the historical reconstructions of the times of Ezra and Nehemiah one should compare the histories of John Bright, *A History of Israel,* 3d ed. (Philadelphia, 1981); Siegfried Herrmann, *Geschichte Israels in alttestamentlicher Zeit,* 2d ed. (Munich, 1973), translated by John Bowden as *A History of Israel in Old Testament Times,* 2d ed. (Philadelphia, 1981); and Peter R. Ackroyd, *Israel under Babylon and Persia* (London, 1970).

For a treatment of Ezra's place in the religion of Israel and especially his relationship to the Law, compare the very influential but somewhat controversial treatment by Yeḥezkel Kaufmann, *Toledot ha-emunah ha-Yisreʾelit,* vol. 4 (Tel Aviv, 1956), translated by Clarence W. Efroymson as *History of the Religion of Israel,* vol. 4, *From the Babylonian Captivity to the End of Prophecy* (New York, 1977), with the work of J. G. Vink et al., *The Priestly Code and Seven Other Studies,* "Oudtestamentische Studien," vol. 15 (Leiden, 1969).

Very helpful on matters of literary composition, text, and versions is the commentary by Jacob M. Myers in *Ezra, Nehemiah,* vol. 14 of the Anchor Bible (Garden City, N.Y., 1965).

For a review of recent scholarship and a comprehensive bibliography, see the article "Esra/Esraschriften" by Magne Saebo, in *Theologische Realenzyklopädie,* vol. 10 (New York, 1982).

New Sources

Bedford, Peter Ross. "Diaspora: Homeland Relations in Ezra-Nehemiah." *Vetus Testamentum* 52 (2002): 147–165.

Esler, Philip F. "Ezra-Nehemiah as a Narrative of (Re-invented) Israelite Identity." *Biblical Interpretation* 11 (2003): 413–426.

Janzen, David. "The 'Mission' of Ezra and the Persian-Period Temple Community." *Journal of Biblical Literature* 119 (2000): 619–643.

Japhet, Sara. "Composition and Chronology in the Book of Ezra-Nehemiah." In *Second Temple Studies: Community in the Persian Period,* edited by Tamara C. Eskenazi and Kent H. Richards, vol. 2, pp. 189–216. Sheffield, 1994.

Pfann, Stephen J. "The Aramaic Text and Language of Daniel and Ezra in the Light of Some Manuscripts from Qumran." *Textus* 16 (1991): 127–137.

JOHN VAN SETERS (1987)
Revised Bibliography

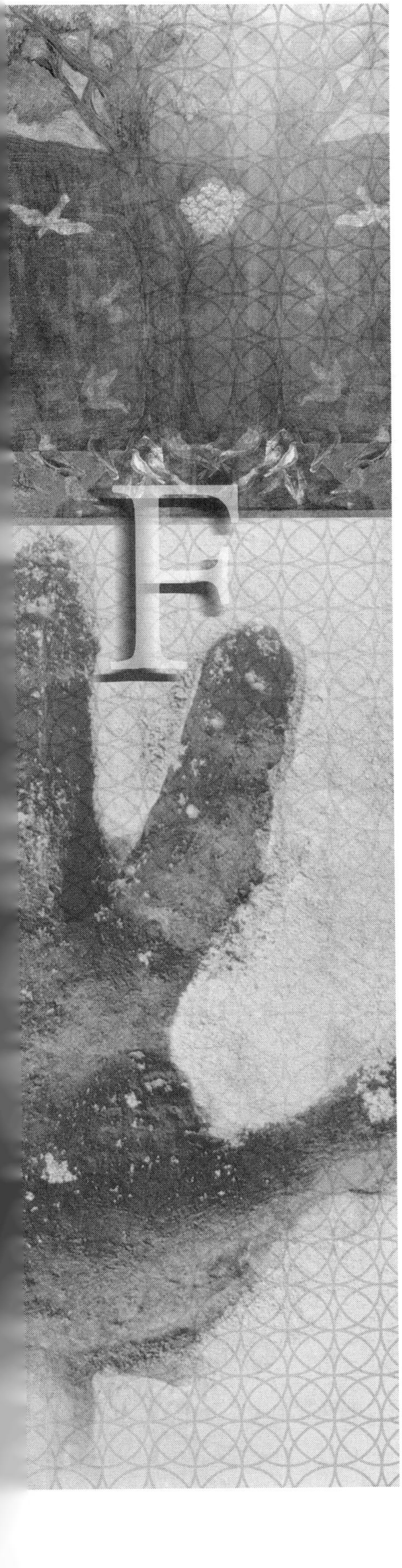

F

FACKENHEIM, EMIL (1916–2003) is best known for his sustained commitment to refashion Judaism in the shadow of the Nazi holocaust. He was born in Halle, Germany, on June 22, 1916. In 1935 he moved to Berlin where he entered the rabbinical program at the *Hochschule für die Wissenschaft des Judentums*; he also began a degree in philosophy at the University of Halle. Fackenheim's academic career in Germany was interrupted by *Kristallnacht* and internment for several months in Sachsenhausen. In the spring of 1940 he fled to Aberdeen, Scotland, and matriculated in a degree program in philosophy at the university. A year later Fackenheim and other refugees were interred in camps and then dispersed throughout the British Empire.

Fackenheim traveled by ship to Canada, spent months in a camp in Sherbrooke, Ontario, and was eventually released, whereupon he went directly to the University of Toronto and was accepted into the doctoral program in philosophy. Fackenheim received his degree in 1945 with a dissertation on medieval Arabic philosophy and its classical antecedents. From 1943 to 1948 he served as rabbi for congregation Anshe Shalom in Hamilton, Ontario. Invited to teach philosophy at the University of Toronto in 1948, he remained there until 1983, when he retired as University Professor. He and his family then immigrated to Israel in 1983. He taught at the Institute for Contemporary Jewry at the Hebrew University of Jerusalem for several years. Fackenheim died in Jerusalem on September 19, 2003.

FACKENHEIM'S 614TH COMMANDMENT. In the postwar period Fackenheim pursued two intellectual interests. First, he began a philosophical examination of faith and reason from Kant (1724–1804) to Kierkegaard (1813–1855), with special attention to Hegel (1770–1831). Second, he explored the role of revelation in modern culture, in particular dealing with Jewish faith, autonomy, the challenge of naturalism and secularism, and the defense of revelation in the thought of Martin Buber (1878–1965) and Franz Rosenzweig (1886–1929).

Until 1966 Fackenheim largely avoided dealing with the Nazi assault on Jews and Judaism and the atrocities of the death camps. On March 26, 1967, at a symposium titled

---

CLOCKWISE FROM TOP LEFT CORNER. Stone relief of the Buddha's footprints on a pillar at the Great Stupa in Sāñcī, India. *[©Adam Woolfit/Corbis]*; *Saint Francis Preaching to the Birds* by Giotto di Bondone (c. 1267–1337). S. Francesco, Assisi, Italy. *[©Scala/Art Resource, N.Y.]*; The hand of Fāṭima, an Islamic good luck symbol. *[©Bernard and Catherine Desjeux/Corbis]*; Fifteenth- to sixteenth-century bronze of Atropos, Greek goddess of fate. Kunsthistorisches Museum, Vienna. *[©Erich Lessing/Art Resource, N.Y.]*; Thirteenth-century French painting of God creating the universe. *[©Bettmann/Corbis]* .

"Jewish Values in the Post–Holocaust Future," convened by the American Jewish Committee and organized by the editor of its journal *Judaism*, Steven Schwarzschild, Fackenheim first formulated and presented his imperative for authentic Jewish response to the Holocaust, what he called the 614th commandment: "The authentic Jew of today is forbidden to hand Hitler yet another, posthumous victory." He elaborated the reasoning that led to this imperative and its hermeneutical content in "Jewish Faith and the Holocaust," which appeared in *Commentary* and, in a slightly different form, in the introduction to his collection of essays, *Quest for Past and Future* (1968). His argument appeared in its most developed form in the third chapter of *God's Presence in History*, published in 1970 and based on his 1968 Deems Lectures at New York University.

In these central writings, Fackenheim argues that although no intellectual response—historical, political, theological, or psychological—to the evil of Auschwitz is satisfactory, an existential response is necessary. But neither philosophy nor theology is capable of framing what a genuine response should be. One can and must turn to actual lived experience, during and after the event, to grasp how Jews have responded and hence how one ought to respond. Such ongoing Jewish life, Fackenheim claims, can be interpreted as a response to a sense of necessity, and this necessity takes the shape of a duty to oppose all that Nazism sought to accomplish in its hatred of Jews and Judaism and in its rejection of human dignity. Although for secular Jews, such a duty has no ground but is accepted as forceful without one, for believing Jews, the only ground that is possible is the voice of a commanding God. Hence for them, it has the status of a divine command, alongside but not superseding the other, traditional 613 biblical commandments. It is, in his famous formulation, a 614th commandment.

Fackenheim's route to this imperative of resistance to Nazi purposes capitalized on several crucial insights. One was that after Auschwitz, as he put it, even Hegel would not be a Hegelian, that is, that Auschwitz was a case of evil for evil's sake and was therefore inassimilable into any prior conceptual system. Even the most systematic philosophic thought was historically situated and was ruptured by the horrors of the death camps. The second was his commitment to existential–dialectical thinking about the human condition and to its hermeneutical character. The third was the recognition that although Auschwitz threatened all prior systems, ways of life, and beliefs, Judaism must and could survive exposure to it. The work of Elie Wiesel (b. 1928) and Wiesel himself, a survivor and a novelist, confirmed this hope and this realization.

To Mend the World. In the 1970s Fackenheim's thought extended the lines of thinking summarized above. On the one hand, he applied this framework to a variety of themes—most notably to the State of Israel, its reestablishment and defense, but also to the belief in God, the relationship between Jews and Christians, and the necessity of struggling against all attempts to diminish human dignity and the value of human life (see essays collected in his *The Jewish Return Into History* and selections in Morgan [ed.], *The Jewish Thought of Emil Fackenheim*). On the other hand, he turned to important philosophical problems with his existential and hermeneutical argument. The crucial one had to do with the possibility of performing the imperative of resistance or, as one might put it, the possibility of confronting the radical threat of rupture and not giving way to total despair. This was to become the central problem of the book he always took to be his magnum opus, *To Mend the World*, first published in 1982. In the earlier period, culminating in 1970, Fackenheim had argued from the necessity of the commandment or imperative to its possibility, either on Kantian grounds, that duty entails the freedom to perform it, or on Rosenzweigian grounds, that along with the commandments that God grants in an act of grace, he also gives humankind out of the same love the freedom to perform them. By the late 1970s Fackenheim had come to see how both responses failed to respect the victims of the Nazi horrors. In the crucial chapter of *To Mend the World*, he systematically and dialectically explores the agency of evil and its victims, in order to arrive at a moment of lucid understanding that grasps the whole of horror and reacts in opposition to it with surprise, and he confirms this intellectual grasp with an emblematic case of a victim of the atrocities who both sees clearly what she is being subjected to, what the evil is, and senses a duty to oppose it in her life. This episode constitutes an ontological ground of resistance. Judaism, through the idea of a cosmic rupture and a human act that respects and yet opposes it, what is called in the Jewish mystical tradition (*Qabbalah*) *tikkun olam*, provides philosophy with a concept essential to grasp this moment of horrified surprise and recovery from it, the possibility of genuine post-Holocaust life. *To Mend the World* proceeds to apply these lessons in three domains—philosophy, Christianity, and Jewish existence—in each case locating an emblematic case of *tikkun* (mending or repair) that respects the evil of Auschwitz as a total and unqualified rupture and yet finds a route to hope and recovery.

In the last two decades of his life, Fackenheim once more extended the lines of this argument: with a book on the Bible and how it ought to be read by Jews and Christians, together, in a post–Holocaust world (*The Jewish Bible after the Holocaust*, 1990); with a survey of Jewish belief and practice of Jews in the 1980s (*What Is Judaism?*, 1987); and with a number of essays on the State of Israel as a paradigmatically genuine response to the Nazi assault, that is, as a unique blending of religious purposes and secular self-reliance, combining a commitment to a homeland for Jews against the most extreme assault and to its defense.

Fackenheim's philosophical commitments were deeply immersed in existential and concrete realities, most notably the historicity of philosophical and religious thought, the hermeneutical and situated character of human existence, and the unprecedented evil of Nazis and the death camps.

Auschwitz led him to expose philosophy, culture, and religion unconditionally to historical refutation; yet his deepest yearnings were to find continued hope and to avoid despair, to appreciate the necessity of Jewish life and the defense of human value and dignity. These dispositions, however, were what one might call "rationally defended yearnings" and hence necessities (duties and obligations) only in a deeply contextual sense. In this respect, Fackenheim bears some similarity to the contemporary Anglo-American philosophers such as Charles Taylor, Hilary Putnam, Richard Rorty, and even the French philosopher Emmanuel Levinas (1906–1955), although except for Levinas, the motivation for Fackenheim's philosophical and theological work was the experience of Auschwitz and not theoretical considerations. In this respect, in the twentieth century, his thought is distinctive and significant and in Jewish life and thought virtually unique.

BIBLIOGRAPHY

Fackenheim, Emil L. "Jewish Faith and the Holocaust." *Commentary* 46 (1968): 30-36.

Fackenheim, Emil L. *God's Presence in History.* New York, 1970.

Fackenheim, Emil L. *Quest for Past and Future* (1968). Boston, 1970.

Fackenheim, Emil L. *What Is Judaism?* New York, 1987.

Fackenheim, Emil L. *To Mend the World* (1982). 3d ed. Bloomington, Ind., 1994.

Fackenheim, Emil L. *The Jewish Bible after the Holocaust.* Bloomington, Ind., 1990.

Greenspan, Louis, and Graeme Nicholson, eds. *Fackenheim: German Philosophy & Jewish Thought.* Toronto, Canada, 1992.

Morgan, Michael L., ed. *The Jewish Thought of Emil Fackenheim.* Detroit, Mich., 1987.

Morgan, Michael L., ed. *Emil Fackenheim: Jewish Philosophers and Jewish Philosophy.* Bloomington, Ind., 1996.

Morgan, Michael L. *Beyond Auschwitz: Post–Holocaust Jewish Thought in America.* New York, 2001.

MICHAEL L. MORGAN (2005)

FA-HSIEN SEE FAXIAN

FAIRIES.

FAIRIES. *Fay,* the old word for "fairy," is thought to come from the Latin *fata,* which signifies the Fates, supernatural women who appear beside the cradle of a newborn infant to decide its future. The fairies invited to Sleeping Beauty's christening are an echo of this belief. During the Middle Ages *fairy* meant the state of enchantment and the land of enchanted beings as well as those who live in it.

Fairies are found under various names in many countries, but they are more typical of Europe and Asia than of the Americas and Africa. To some extent their social organization reflects the world of humans. In *Irish Fairy and Folk Tales* (1893) the poet William Butler Yeats distinguished between trooping fairies and solitary fairies. The trooping fairies appear in medieval Arthurian legend and romance and are most popular in the literature of Elizabethan England; since that time stories about them have ceased to be written. They are handsome, aristocratic, and beautifully dressed, and they take part in the Fairy Ride. Like their human counterparts, they hunt and hawk, trotting in procession behind their king and queen, who ride white horses decorated with silver bells. Their fairy realm, which is centered on their royal court, is noted for the excellence of its music, dancing, and feasting as well as for the beauty of its women. The Irish Tuatha Dé Danann ("people of the goddess Danu") are trooping fairies; they are immortal and live in Tír na n'Og, the Land of Youth.

The nonaristocratic, solitary fairies are described as ugly and often ominous and ill-natured. Some are engaged in trade, like the Irish leprechaun shoemaker, who is quite harmless. A third category of fairy comprises those who live in family groups. They work the land, hold their own markets, and visit human fairs.

Nature fairies are spirits of streams, lakes, and trees. The Russian *rusalki* are water nymphs, who take the form of young maidens. Dryads are tree spirits. So are oak men; hence there is a saying, "Fairy folks are in old oaks." In England, hawthorn is haunted by the fairies, especially if it grows near fairy hills, and the Gooseberry Wife, in the form of a great hairy caterpillar, stands guard over the fruit bushes.

Tutelary fairies, the family guardians and domestic spirits, look after the fortunes of a particular household. The Scottish MacLeods on the island of Skye were given a fairy flag by their supernatural guardian. Germans call their house spirit *der Kobold* ("gnome"), an unreliable creature whose name survives in the modern *cobalt.* (German miners called this slightly magnetic element after the famous sprite because they found it tiresome and difficult to use.) Danes have their *nis;* the French their *esprit follet;* the Spaniards their *duende;* and the Faeroese Islanders, in the North Atlantic, their *niagruisar.*

Russians call their domestic spirits *domovois,* after *dom* ("house"). Legend says that these creatures were rebellious spirits who opposed God and so were thrown down from heaven, falling on people's roofs and into their yards. They are amiable and live in the warmth near the hearth. Because it is considered important to please the *domovoi,* peasants leave egg pancakes for him on the threshing floor. When a peasant family moves, they put a piece of bread beside the stove in hopes that the *domovoi* will come with them. In his autobiography *Childhood* (1913), the Russian writer Maxim Gorky describes how his family moved from their house: His grandmother took an old shoe, held it under the stove, and called to the household spirit, asking him to ride in the shoe and bring the family good luck in their new home.

English brownies are also associated with the hearth. They are active at night and do work that the servants have neglected: cleaning and drawing water for the house, tending farm animals, reaping, mowing, threshing, and churning butter. Families can leave food, such as a bowl of cream or little cakes spread with honey for the brownies, but direct gifts, such as money or clothes, will drive the spirit away.

Domestic spirits can be very tiresome. A folktale well known all over Europe tells of a farmer so bothered by the pranks of a boggart (or mischievous brownie) that he decides to move. The family packs their household belongings and loads the cart. As they are leaving, a voice from inside the milk churn says, "Yes, we're moving!" It is the boggart. The family gives up and decides to stay, for what would be the point of moving if the creature was coming too? In other versions of the story the boggart immigrates with the family to the United States.

The most tragic tutelary fairy is the banshee, an Irish and Highland Scottish spirit of death. The word means a woman (*ban*) of the fairy folk (*sídh,* pronounced "shee"). This apparition materializes when someone is about to die. In Scotland the banshee is seen washing the doomed person's graveclothes or bloodstained garmets and can be heard wailing and lamenting, her eyes red with tears. Mélusine, daughter of the fairy Pressina, became the banshee of the house of Lusignan in France. When the family was wiped out and its castle fell to the crown, she appeared, foretelling the deaths of the kings of France.

Some supernatural creatures are closely associated with a particular historical era or geographic area. The gnomes of Europe, for example, were a product of the ancient Hermetic and Neoplatonic doctrine from which medieval medicine and science derived. According to medieval thought, all mortal creatures are a blend of earth, air, fire, and water, and the four elemental beings are gnomes (who inhabit the earth), sylphs (who inhabit the air), salamanders (who inhabit fire), and nereids (who inhabit water). The *Oxford English Dictionary* suggests that the word *gnome* is an elision of the Latin *genomus* ("earth dweller"). Paracelsus (1493–1541), the Swiss physician and alchemist, provides in his *De nymphus* the first description of gnomes as elemental beings of the earth. According to tradition, gnomes live underground and are treasure guardians. Also known as dwarfs, they are skilled metalworkers, supplying medieval knights with armor and weapons that they themselves forge. They are also often associated with mines.

The knockers are said to live in the tin mines of England's Cornwall. They are friendly creatures and will knock on the mine walls to indicate veins of ore. An anti-Semitic legend claims that they were the ghosts of Jews who had been sent to work the mines as a punishment for taking part in the Crucifixion. Richard, earl of Cornwall (1200–1272), is said to have put the Jews to work in the Cornish tin mines, and Robert Hunt, in his *Popular Romances of the West of England* (1865), claims that the tin mines were farmed out to the Jews in the thirteenth century. But Jewish merchants had very little connection with the tin trade, and no evidence supports these improbable suggestions.

Pixies are another group of fairies belonging to English west-country tradition. They are found in Somerset, Devonshire, and Cornwall. Anna Eliza Bray first brought them to the attention of the public in a series of letters to the poet Robert Southey that were published under the title *The Borders of the Tavy and the Tamar* (1836). The chief characteristic of pixies is that they mislead travelers; as recently as 1961, a woman claimed to have been misled by pixies in a wood near Budleigh Salterton. Local tradition says that pixies are the souls of those who died before Christ was born or of unbaptized children.

Closely related to the pixie and its habit of leading travelers astray is the will-o'-the-wisp (Fr., *le feu follet;* Ger., *das Irrlicht*), also called jack-o'-lantern or *ignis fatuus* ("foolish fire"). This sprite appears in the folklore of many countries and is often an omen of death. In England the will-o'-the-wisp is also identified with the mischievous sprite Puck, or Robin Goodfellow. Traditional legends about this spirit who lures folks to their death in the bog may be an attempt to account for marsh gas, which emanates from rotting organic matter and is ghostly in appearance.

Other malevolent spirits are also linked with the environment. The malicious yarthkins of Lincolnshire, England, another damp area, disappeared when the fens were drained.

The English *goblin,* or *hobgoblin,* is a generic term for evil spirits. It is difficult to distinguish between goblins and imps, however. Originally *imp* referred to an offshoot or a cutting, but in its sense as a supernatural creature it means a small demon, an offshoot of Satan. In England the Puritans thought all fairy creatures were devils, and thus the preacher John Bunyan, in his famous book *Pilgrim's Progress* (1678), numbers the hobgoblin and the "foul fiend" among the forces of evil to be resisted.

Elves reached England from Norse mythology, where they were known as *huldre* folk, closely resembling fairies. The girl elves are very beautiful but they are hollow behind and have long cow's tails. Trolls are another Norse group of supernatural beings. Originally they were thought of as giant ogres, but in later Swedish and Danish tradition they become dwarfs who live in hills and caverns. Like the German dwarfs, they are fine craftsmen and treasure guardians, noted for their stupidity. In the Shetland Islands, north of Scotland, where Scandinavian influence is strong, these beings are called *trows.*

Not all mischievous, supernatural creatures are of ancient origin. The gremlin, a supernatural being who causes trouble for pilots and aircrews, dates from World War I. An explanation for human error, flight fatigue, and high-altitude pressures, the gremlin may originate from the Old English word *gremian* ("to vex").

The relationships that fairies enjoy with human beings has varied considerably. Some can be very helpful; such helpfulness is said to be how the MacCrimmons, the most distinguished Scottish pipers, learned their skill. As mentioned, guardian spirits look after the families in their care, and brownies do household chores. But they become malevolent if badly treated—or simply disappear. Anybody who spies on them is severely punished.

In folk tradition human beings are sometimes abducted by the fairies. Thomas the Rhymer (Thomas of Erceldoune), the poet and prophet, lived in thirteenth-century England. His tale is told in *The Ballad of True Thomas* and by Sir Walter Scott in *Minstrelsy of the Scottish Border* (1802). Legend says that Thomas received the gift of prophecy from the Queen of Elfland, who loved him and took him away to live with her for seven years.

Stories of fairy brides are common and usually end in tragedy. The lovely creature marries a mortal and imposes some taboo on him. When it is broken, the fairy bride returns to fairyland, deserting her husband and children. Seal-maidens and swan-maidens are usually captured against their will by the theft of their skin or feathers. As soon as they can retrieve the stolen item, they escape.

When a mortal visits fairyland, the result is often equally tragic. The visitor cannot escape and becomes the victim of the supernatural passage of time, whereby one day represents hundreds of years. King Herla was able to return home with his knights, but when they dismounted they crumbled into dust because they had been away for three hundred years.

Although fairies lead independent lives, there are many examples of their dependence on mortals. Narratives tell of midwives summoned to help a fairy in labor and of fairies anxious to possess human children. Stories of the theft of babies continue from the Middle Ages to the present time. Typically the fairies steal an unbaptized child and leave an ugly fairy baby in its place. If the changeling is surprised, it will speak, revealing its true identity; then it can be driven away. Various methods may be used to trick the spirit, such as serving him beer brewed in eggshells. In German tradition the creature would exclaim, "I am as old as the forests of Bohemia, and I've never seen beer brewed in an eggshell before."

These legends conceal much human suffering and cruelty to children. Malformed babies were put over a fire in order to pressure the fairies into returning the supposedly stolen child. Such cases have been recorded as late as the early twentieth century in Ireland. Until recently it was thought that a defect in a child resulted from a defect in the parents. Basically, changelings were sickly, backward, or deformed children. Simple people, unwilling to accept that such a child could be theirs, maintained that the fairies had stolen the real baby and left this wretched thing in its place.

Belief in fairies thus has an aetiologic function: It provides an explanation for mysterious objects and events that are otherwise not understood. The remains of earlier civilizations, which puzzled the uneducated in days gone by, are another obvious example. The ancient Pictish areas of Scotland contain the remains of brochs, round, hill-shaped farmhouses with stone walls and a turf covering. These structures are often referred to as fairy knowes. Burial mounds have also been linked with fairyland. Sudden, disabling illness, such as that caused by a stroke, was traditionally considered to be the result of an elf shot, a wound from one of the flint arrows that are found in low-lying areas, and many Anglo-Saxon charms meant to protect against such attacks have been preserved. Various other illnesses whose origin seemed puzzling centuries ago, such as a slipped disk, rheumatism, and anything that deforms the body, were attributed to invisible blows from the little creatures. Paralysis, skin disease, wasting illnesses such as tuberculosis, and animal disorders such as swine fever and brucellosis have all been blamed on the fairies.

Unusual topographical features are also sometimes attributed to fairies. Those curious, dark green circles that appear on grassy lawns and meadows, often surrounded by a circle of mushrooms, are known as fairy rings, and it is considered very unlucky to damage them in any way. They are in fact caused by *Marasmius oreades,* a type of fungus, but people believe that they are spots where the fairies dance.

Sometimes supernatural origins are attributed to exceptionally large or beautiful objects. There are various stories of a cup stolen from the fairies. The "Luck of Eden Hall" in Cumberland, England, is a lovely green glass goblet, a talisman that was supposed to preserve the Eden family's fortunes. Legend says that the goblet was snatched from the fairies by a servant; if it broke, the family would be destroyed. Eden Hall was pulled down in 1934, but the "Luck" is preserved in the Victoria and Albert Museum in London.

In the thirteenth-century Church of Saint Mary at Frensham in Surrey, England, stands a huge caldron, measuring one yard across. Local tradition says that it was borrowed from the fairies who lived on nearby Borough Hill and was never returned. Probably it was employed in parish feasts and celebrations and then this early usage was forgotten.

Sightings and eyewitness accounts of fairies are common. A striking example was provided by Robert Kirk (1644–1692), a folklorist who became the subject of a fairy tale. Kirk was a Gaelic scholar and a minister of the Scottish church. Evidently his parishioners disapproved of his researches in the supernatural, for when he died and his body was found lying beside a fairy knowe, rumor said that he was living with the fairies inside it. This legend is recorded by Scott in his *Letters on Demonology and Witchcraft* (1830). Kirk's own account of fairy beliefs in the Scottish Highlands, *The Secret Commonwealth of Elves, Fauns and Fairies,* was not published until 1815, long after his death. The brilliant and eccentric English painter and poet William Blake (1757–1827) claimed to have seen a fairy funeral. The body, he said, was laid out on a rose leaf and carried in procession by creatures the size and color of grasshoppers.

In Ireland, places once associated with fairies are pointed out and treated with great respect. To interfere with them is thought to bring bad luck. More than once new roads have been rerouted for such a reason. Recently a fairy bush was cut down in front of a Dutch-owned factory in Limerick. Dutch workmen performed the task because local workers refused. When the works closed not long after and well over a thousand jobs were lost, the disaster was blamed on the removal of the fairy bush.

Traditionally, the fairies dress in green. Green is their color, and even today, many people regard it as unlucky and will not wear it, although they no longer remember the reason.

Various theories have been put forward to explain the origins of the fairies. A British tradition suggests that fairies represent memories of an ancient Stone Age race. When the Celts arrived in England from central Europe in about 500 BCE, the earlier inhabitants were driven back into the hills and hid in caves. They lived underground and were so adept at hiding in the woods that they seemed to be invisible. The popular belief that iron provides protection from the fairies is in line with this view, for the Celts possessed iron weapons, whereas the earlier inhabitants used objects of bronze or stone. The many stories of fairies' borrowings and thefts also lend weight to this theory, for it was thought that these earlier inhabitants borrowed grain and implements, and one can easily imagine a conquered people in hiding, creeping anxiously about to see what they could steal or borrow from their conquerors.

Another view suggests that fairies originated as memories of ancient pagan gods and heroes. They are small in stature because their significance has been reduced. Still another theory sees fairies as personified spirits of nature. Modern supporters of this argument believe that spirits fertilize plants and care for flowers. But this explanation excludes other types of fairy, such as the family guardians and the fairy communities with their elaborate social organization. A fourth suggestion is that the fairies are ghosts. Certainly there are many connections between fairies and the realm of the dead: They live in burial mounds, and many are obviously ghosts and are described as such. None of these theories is entirely adequate, and the answer may well lie in a blend of them all, coupled with the natural desire to find an explanation for puzzling phenomena throughout the world.

SEE ALSO Celtic Religion; Demons; Germanic Religion.

BIBLIOGRAPHY

Briggs, K. M. *The Anatomy of Puck.* London, 1959. An examination of fairy beliefs among Shakespeare's contemporaries and successors.

Briggs, K. M. *The Fairies in Tradition and Literature.* London, 1967. Provides an account of fairy traditions, traffic between humans and fairies, and the literary use of these beliefs.

Croker, Thomas Crofton. *Fairy Legends and Traditions of the South of Ireland.* 3 vols. London, 1825–1828. This work was enthusiastically received by the public of its day. Jacob and Wilhelm Grimm translated it into German, and Sir Walter Scott corresponded with the author. It remains a valuable contribution to the development of folklore studies.

Gardner, Edward L. *Fairies.* London, 1945. A book that claims to present photographs of real fairies.

Hunt, Robert. *Popular Romances of the West of England.* 2 vols. London, 1865. The fruits of a ten-month walking tour in Cornwall during 1829, when the author collected, as he put it, "every existing tale of its ancient people."

Keightley, Thomas. *The Fairy Mythology* (1828). 2 vols. in 1. New York, 1968. An early study of comparative folklore by an Irish writer with an interest in oral tradition.

Sikes, Wirt. *British Goblins.* London, 1880. A collection of Welsh material assembled by the U.S. consul for Wales.

New Sources

Brasey, Edouard. *Fées et elfs: l'universe féerique.* Paris, 1999.

Doulet, Jean-Michel. *Quand les démons enlaivent les enfants: les changelins: étude d'une figure mythique.* Paris, 2002.

Letcher, Andy. "The Scouring of the Shire: Fairies, Trolls and Pixies in Eco-Protest Culture." *Folklore* 112 (October 2001): 147–161.

Mack, Carol K., and Dinah Mack. *A Field Guide to Demons, Fairies, Fallen Angels, and Other Subversive Spirits.* New York, 1998.

Purkiss, Diane. *Troublesome Things: A History of Fairies and Fairy Stories.* London, 2000.

Silver, Carole G. *Strange and Secret Peoples: Faeries and Victorian Consciousness.* New York, 1999.

Wilby, Emma. "The Witch's Familiar and the Fairy in Early Modern England and Scotland." *Folklore* 111 (October 2000): 283–305.

VENETIA NEWALL (1987)
Revised Bibliography

FAITH, in probably the best-known definition of it, is "the assurance of things hoped for, the conviction of things not seen." Although this definition itself comes from the Christian scriptures, specifically from the anonymous epistle to the Hebrews in the New Testament, it can, *mutatis mutandis,* be applied across a broad spectrum of religions and religious traditions. Whether or not the term *faith* appears in those traditions is, at least in part, a matter of how various terms are translated into modern Western languages. More importantly, however, *faith* is used, even in Judaism and Christianity (where it has been the most successfully domesticated), to cover an entire cluster of concepts that are related to one another but are by no means identical. If there is truth in the contention that *faith* is the abstract term with which to describe that attitude of the human mind and spirit of which prayer is the concrete expression, then one or more of these concepts may probably be said to play some part in every religious tradition, and in that sense at least, "faith" may likewise be said to appear there. Hence an enumeration of these discrete concepts, each of them in some way a synonym for *faith,* may serve to provide, if not a logical definition, then at any rate a cumulative description, of it.

FAITH-AS-FAITHFULNESS. In its most fundamental meaning, faith has been defined as faithfulness, and as such, it has been taken as an attribute both of the divine and of believers in the divine. The Latin adjective *pius,* for example, was used in Vergil's *Aeneid* to describe *pius Aeneas* or *pius Achates,* but it also appeared there in such a phrase as *pia numina* to characterize the reciprocal fidelity that the gods manifested in their dealings with human beings; something of both senses, presumably, attached to the word when it became a standard part of the official title of the Roman emperor, most familiarly in the case of Antoninus Pius (r. 138–161 CE). *Pius* went on having both meanings also in postclassical Latin, as the usage of the "Dies Irae" attests. The reciprocity implied in the concept of faith when predicated of human social relations, where (as in the notion of "keeping faith" with someone) "faith" has become almost synonymous with "loyalty," has carried over likewise into its use for the divine-human relation. Wherever the gods were said to promise something in that relation, *faith* would seem to be an appropriate term for their keeping or fulfilling the promise. Conversely—and much more customarily—it was the appropriate term for the loyalty or "fealty" (that English word is indeed derived, via medieval French, from the Latin *fidelitas*) that the gods in turn rightly expected of mortals. In those religions in which the initiates received a mark on their body as a sign of their special bond with the divine, these marks have often been seen as a pledge and a reminder to those who wore them that they were expected to remain faithful to the terms of that special bond. The consequences of a breach of faith-as-faithfulness formed the basis for practices of discipline, punishment, and in most traditions possible reinstatement, though only after a period of purgation and testing (see "The Community of Faith," below). Even where the other connotations of "faith" discussed below have appeared to predominate, this emphasis on faith-as-faithfulness, both divine and human, has never been absent, pertaining as it does to the very concept of adhering to the practices, structures, obligations, or beliefs of any particular way of having faith. When it has been divorced from some or all of those other connotations, however, faith-as-faithfulness could all too easily be reduced to the formalism and external propriety that the prophets and critics in many religious traditions have attacked.

FAITH-AS-OBEDIENCE. Faith as faithfulness has expressed itself not only in loyalty but in obedience, yet obedience has meant even more than faithfulness. The precise content of such obedience has varied enormously with the content of what was perceived to have been the divine will or law. Obedience, therefore, carried both liturgical and moral connotations. An imperative to reenact, periodically or once in a lifetime, the acts of the divine model required the obedient and meticulous observance of the demands that those acts had placed upon the believer. Initiation into the faith involved learning the specific methods of such ritual observance, with rites of passage frequently serving as the occasion for such learning. Where the divine will was conceived of as having laid down rules not only for ritual actions but for ethics, the obedience of faith meant moral behavior in conformity with divine commands; thus in Hinduism, *dharma* as moral law required righteous conduct. Ordinarily there was no explicit antithesis between ethics and ritual action, which together were the content of authentic obedience, often enjoined in the same gnomic saying or story. But the declaration of the prophet Samuel in the Hebrew scriptures, "Has the Lord as great delight in burnt offerings and sacrifices, as in obeying the voice of the Lord? Behold, to obey is better than sacrifice, and to hearken than the fat of rams" (*1 Sm.* 15:22), articulated the awareness, which other religions have shared with Judaism, that faith-as-obedience was above all a compliance with the moral imperative. Presupposed in those words was the belief, central to Judaism, that the moral imperative had been made known in the historical revelation of the word of God to Moses, and through him to the people of Israel. But they have been no less applicable in those religious and philosophical traditions that have emphasized the inner imperative of conscience rather than the outer imperative of law as the norm of ethical action: Here, too, faith has been above all obedience, in Immanuel Kant's formula, "the recognition of all our duties as divine commands." Even where faith has been defined primarily as trust or as worship or as creed (see below), obedience was inevitably a constitutive element of it.

FAITH AND WORKS. The definition of faith as obedience, and yet as somehow not reducible to obedience, points to the perennial and unavoidable problem of the relation between faith and works. On the one hand, even the most theocentric versions of faith have found themselves obliged to assert, often in self-defense against the charge that they were severing the moral nerve, that they were in fact reinforcing ethics precisely by their emphasis on its vertical dimension: It has been a universal conviction of believers, across religious boundaries, that "faith without works is dead." On the other hand, those religious systems that have appeared to outsiders, whether critical or friendly, to equate faith and works and to be indifferent to any considerations except the "purely" moral ones prove, upon closer examination, to have been no less sensitive to the dialectic between works and faith. Especially since the Enlightenment, Western critics of traditional supernaturalism have taken Confucianism as the ideal of a religion that eschewed metaphysical subtleties to concentrate on the one thing needful, and they have either criticized traditional Western religions for not conforming to that ideal or reinterpreted them in accordance with it. For in the *Analects* Confucius repeatedly professed ignorance about the mysteries of "Heaven" and avoided discussing the miraculous phenomena in which conventional faith had sought manifestations of supernatural power; even the question of personal immortality did not admit of a clear and definite answer. Rather, he concentrated his attention on works of piety and of service to others, preferring generosity to greed and virtue to success. All of this Confucius (like many other religious teachers) called "the way," but it is an unwarranted modern reductionism to see in this attitude a moralistic preoccupation with works alone, at the expense of "faith." For "Heaven," which he said had "infused the virtue that is in me," was the authentic source of the works themselves, as well as the ultimate foundation for the serenity that made the works possible. The faith of Confucius may have been less detailed than that of some teachers in its information about the ontological status of "Heaven" and similar speculative questions, but he knew and expressed a confidence in its providential care as the basis for the works with which he and his disciples were to serve the will of "Heaven."

Faith-as-Trust. Such a confidence in the providential care of "Heaven" underlies the definition of faith-as-trust. In the classic formulation of Martin Luther, "to 'have a god' is nothing else than to trust and believe him with our whole heart," because "it is the trust and faith of the heart alone that makes both God and an idol" (*Large Catechism*). Many of the conventional metaphors for the divine in various traditions, from "rock" and "mountain" to "mother" or "father," have served as representations of the conviction that "the trust and faith of the heart" could appropriately be vested in such an object, and that the divine object would prove worthy of human trust. Conventional practices like divination and prayer may likewise be read as expressions of the belief that the divine will—if it could once be known, or perhaps even if it was mysterious and ultimately unknowable—deserved trust. The historic triad of faith, hope, and love (best known from the New Testament, but paralleled elsewhere) has made it necessary for expositors to clarify the distinction between faith and hope as they were both applied to the expectation of future blessings. However, the definition of faith-as-trust has been a way of focusing such expectation on the reliability of divine providence in both prosperity and failure: For good or ill, the ways of the divine will could be counted on, even though the details of their specific intent might not be discernible at any given moment. Such faith-as-trust even in the inscrutable goodness of the divine order presupposed a pattern of divine guidance in the past, which made it safe to conclude that there would be a continuity of such guidance into the future. Historically as well as psychologically, therefore, it is difficult to conceive of faith-as-trust in the absence of such a pattern, be it the outcome of the individual's own cumulative autobiography or of the history of the community to which the individual has come to belong (or of both). Once established on the basis of this pattern of divine guidance, faith-as-trust has implied that the vicissitudes of the moment could not, or at any rate should not, undermine the confidence that ultimately the object of that trust would be vindicated. As Johann Wolfgang von Goethe said in his autobiography, *Dichtung und Wahrheit,* "Faith is a profound sense of security in regard to both the present and the future; and this assurance springs from confidence." In the choruses of the Greek tragedians or in the reflections of the Muslim mystics or in the discourses of Job, the ambiguities and difficulties of such confidence in the face of concrete reality have served to deepen the understanding of trust and to transform Pollyanna-like optimism into mature faith-as-trust.

Faith-as-Dependence. This combination of mystery and reliability in the divine will, even after that will has made itself known, has introduced into the definition of faith the element of dependence and submission. For if obedience to the divine will was the completion of the circle of faith in the moral realm, dependence on the divine will was the way faith-as-trust affirmed the relation of human weakness to divine power. In those traditions in which the divine has been seen as creator and/or preserver, faith-as-dependence has been, in the first instance, an affirmation of the origin and derivation of humanity and of its world; in those traditions that have tended not to distinguish as sharply between "being" as applied to the divine and as applied to human beings, dependence has been the basis for identifying the locations of both the divine and the human within the "great chain of Being"; in those traditions that have emphasized the recurrence of patterns known to be embedded within the very structure of the cosmos, dependence has made it possible for the community and its individual members to participate, through myth and ritual, in such patterns; and in those traditions that have interpreted human history as the arena in which the will and way of the divine could above all be discerned, dependence has employed the recitation of the decisive events in that history to reinforce the sovereignty of God as the one who was active and knowable within, but always transcendent over, such saving and revelatory events. Thus in Islam (a term that is commonly translated into English as "submission," but that might perhaps as well be translated as "dependence"), the saying of the Qurʾān, "God causes whom he wills to err, and whom he wills he guides; and you shall assuredly be called to account for your doings," gave voice to the Prophet's conviction that the believer must depend on the divine will regardless of circumstances, but that such dependence did not preclude human accountability. In Islam, the Five Pillars of Faith were the specific moral and cultic duties for which every Muslim believer would be held accountable, yet the first two Pillars (the recitation of faith in the oneness of God and the daily prayers) were declarations of the paradoxical affirmation that God was not dependent on creatures or their performance of these duties but would be sovereign regardless. That paradox has been central to the definition of faith-as-dependence in many religious traditions, with theories ranging all the way from thoroughgoing determinism to apparent moralism (for example, to use the terms familiar to the Western tradition, all the way from Calvinism to Pelagianism) as efforts to come to terms with both poles of a dialectical truth.

Faith-as-Experience. In one way or another, each of these definitions of faith has been derived from faith-as-experience. For even the most transcendent notions of the mystery of the divine will have, by their very act of affirming the mysteriousness of that mystery, laid claim to an experience in which the individual believer or the community tradition has caught a glimpse of just how mysterious the divine could be. Although mystics and prophets—and, following their lead, historians and philosophers of religion—have often spoken of such experiences in isolation from the continuum of human consciousness, that is not, of course, how they have actually occurred. From the biographies of seers and saints it is obvious that these experiences often came in response and in reaction to specific moments of exaltation or depression, in feverish intensity or in the excitement and release of love and death. That inseparability of faith-as-experience from all the other experiences of life has persuaded some observers of the phenomenon to see it as in fact the sublimation and "supernatural" reinterpretation of an essentially "natural" event. Ludwig Feuerbach, both as historian and as philosopher, penetrated deeply into this aspect of faith-as-experience; and Freudian psychology has been especially successful in explaining religious experience in its relation to the totality and complexity of how the human mind has attempted to cope with all the data of its experience. But in opposition to the reductionism that has frequently been represented as the only acceptable conclusion from this quality of faith-as-experience, the philosophical interpretation of religion, systematized perhaps most effectively by Rudolf Otto, has sought to identify what was distinct about this experience even if it was not separate from other experience. Otto's formulation, which has since become all but canonical, is "the experience of the Holy." He called it "a category of interpretation and valuation peculiar to the sphere of religion," and declared that "there is no religion in which it does not live as the real innermost core, and without it no religion would be worthy of the name." Yet precisely because faith's experience of the holy has upon further reflection come to include the recognition of its inherent ineffability, the language of faith has drawn upon other experience—aesthetic, moral, intellectual—to be able to speak about the unspeakable at all.

The Community of Faith. In the sacred literatures of religious faith, faith-as-experience has often been described in highly individualistic terms: How the poet or prophet has come to know the holy in personal experience has dominated how he or she has described that experience for others, so that they in turn, one at a time, might also come to share in such an experience and duplicate it for themselves. Individualism of that kind underlay, for example, the recurring definition of religion as "what one does with one's solitariness." Except for passing moments of intense mystical rapture, however, such individualism has been shown to be illusory. And except for occasional glossolalia, the very language in which the individual has spoken about faith-as-experience has been derived from the history of the community, even when that language has been aimed against the present corruption of the community or when it has been directed toward the founding of a new and purer community. When examined in its total context, moreover, it becomes apparent that the individualized experience of faith has repeatedly taken place during or after corporate worship: The setting of the private vision has often been the temple itself; or when the vision has come in the solitude of the desert or in the privacy of the soul, it has come as a consequence of participation in the ritual of the temple or as a response to instruction in the lore of the community's tradition. Just as the distinction between the experience of faith and general human experience has engaged the interest of psychologists of religion, so sociologists of religion have probed the connection (in the formulas of Joachim Wach) between "religion and natural groups," as well as then the "specifically religious organization of society." The community of faith, as coextensive with the family or tribe, has conferred its authority on that social organization in marriage, war, and commerce, and has derived its sanctions from it in turn. Then exclusion from the believing community was identical with ostracism from the natural community. But with the more sophisticated identification of the specific nature of faith has come a distinction between the two, often through the emergence of an *ecclesiola in ecclesia* as a more precisely delineated community of faith or (using a pejorative word in a nonpejorative sense) a "sect."

Faith and Worship. The community of faith has always been a community of worship; in fact, worship has been far more explicitly a part of its definition than has faith. Western observers of "primitive" societies have sometimes been prevented from recognizing this, either (as in the case of some Christian missionaries) by too particularistic an understanding of worship or (as in the case of some modern anthropologists) by too reductionistic an understanding of ritual. One of the most important scholarly sources for the new and deeper recognition of faith-as-worship has been the investigation of the interrelation between myth and ritual: Myth came to be read as the validation, in the deeds of the ancients or of the gods, of what the ritual now enjoined upon believers; and ritual acquired a new dimension by being understood as not merely outward ceremonial performed *ex opere operato* but as the repetition in the believers' actions of what the myth recited in words about the divine actions that had made the world and founded the community. Amid an infinite variety of ritual forms and liturgical prescriptions, therefore, worship has defined "faith." For example, the fourth and last of the Four Noble Truths of Buddhism as formulated by Gautama Buddha himself was the recognition of the methods by which the believer could overcome the inner yearning for pleasure out of which the misery of *dukkha* sprang. Similarly, the eighth and last part of the Eightfold Path of Buddhism consisted in proper meditation, which was inseparable from the first seven. Methodologically, the task of discovering the specifics of the faith expressing itself in a particular worship ritual continues to challenge the ingenuity of historians of religion, as is manifested by their disputes over the meaning of (to cite an example present in several traditions) the ritual of circumcision. Even the widely shared assumption that the ritual antedated the myth, which in turn antedated the theological explanation of both, must be modified by the repeatedly attested rise of new rituals out of the composition of the myth or after the adoption of the theological doctrine. Yet in the absence of any verifiable statistical data it does seem a safe generalization to suggest that, even more than faith-as-obedience to a moral imperative or commandment, faith-as-worship has defined faith for most of the human race through most of its history. Even the term *orthodoxy,* which has acquired the meaning "right doctrine" in most of the languages where it appears and which carries that meaning also when it is used in a secular sense for political or literary theories, really means "right worship," as the Russian translation of the word, *pravoslavie* ("the right way to celebrate"), demonstrates.

FAITH-AS-CREDO. Yet *orthodoxy* does mean primarily "right doctrine" now, and one of the definitions of "faith" is "credo" (which is the Latin for "I believe"). Because so much of the history and interpretation of world religions has been the work of Christian thinkers trained in the doctrinal theology of the several Christian churches, early scholarship in "comparative religion" regularly consisted of a review, doctrine by doctrine, of what the various religions were perceived as having taught. As often as not, such reviews were organized according to the schema of categories devised by Thomistic or orthodox Lutheran and Reformed systematic theologians, even, for example, in so sensitive a treatment as Karl Friedrich Nägelsbach's *Homeric Theology* (1840) and *Post-Homeric Theology* (1857). The artificiality and arbitrariness of imposing these categories from the outside on literary and religious traditions having an integrity of their own led later generations of scholars to employ greater caution in claiming to have discovered "doctrinal" meanings (in the sense in which Christian theology spoke of "doctrines") in non-Christian religions, even sometimes in postbiblical Judaism. Significantly, however, one outcome of the tensions that have arisen between various of those religions and modern thought (see "Faith and Knowledge" below) has been the development, within the traditions themselves and at the hands of their own faithful devotees, of something very like systematic doctrinal theology, which has included comparative judgments about their relation to other traditions and their "doctrines." As already suggested, nevertheless, the definition of faith-as-credo has been especially prominent in Western and Christian thought.

In medieval usage, for example, the Latin word *fides* must commonly be translated as "*the* faith" rather than simply as "faith," because it referred in the first instance to the content of what was believed (*fides quae creditur*) rather than to the act of believing (*fides qua creditur*), and specifically to one of the orthodox creeds of the church, generally the Apostles' Creed or the Nicene Creed; once defined, orthodox doctrines were binding *de fide,* by the authority of the faith. To "have faith," then, meant first of all to "hold *the* faith" as this had been laid down in the apostolic "deposit of faith" and legislated by church fathers, councils, and popes. And even the repudiation of the medieval system by the Protestant Reformation, a major plank of which was Luther's elevation of faith-as-trust over the Roman Catholic faith-as-credo, still retained, and in some ways even intensified, the insistence on right doctrine, a knowledge of which and an assent to which were the necessary presupposition for a correct faith-as-trust.

FAITH AND TRADITION. Acceptance of a "deposit of faith" has implied some notion of tradition as that which has been *traditum,* first "handed down" and then "handed on." Although the thinkers of the eighteenth-century Enlightenment drew a sharp distinction between "traditionary religion" and "natural religion," vastly preferring the latter to the former, it was in fact only the former that was to be found in the history of religion; eventually even the "natural religion" of the Enlightenment acquired a certain traditional content and was transmitted from one generation to the next by way of an intellectual tradition. "Traditionary religion," therefore, has defined itself and its faith on the basis of received tradition. The myth of how holy things have happened; the ritual of how holy acts were to be performed; the rules of conduct by which the faithful were expected to guide their lives; the structure through which the holy community was founded and governed; the doctrine by which the community gave an account of the myth and ritual—all these expressions of faith have been the subject and the content of the holy tradition. In all those religions that have ascribed normative status to a holy book, the question of faith-as-tradition has taken a special form, as they have sought to deal with the question of the relation between the revelation in the book, as given once and for all, and the continuing revelation in the tradition. Reformers in each of those groups have drawn an antithesis between the purity of the original scripture and the accretions of later tradition, which needed to be expunged, while defenders of tradition have posited a continuity between the scripture and the tradition, sometimes by characterizing them as "two sources of revelation" but sometimes by describing the ongoing tradition as the process through which the properly validated authorities had gradually made explicit the content of the faith already implicit in scripture. Thus a twentieth-century Russian Orthodox thinker, Vladimir Lossky, defined tradition as "the life of the Holy Spirit in the Church, communicating to each member of the Body of Christ the faculty of hearing, of receiving, of knowing the Truth in the Light which belongs to it, and not according to the natural light of human reason." By setting faith into the framework of such a theory of tradition, Lossky and his counterparts in other faiths (who could have used much of the same language, substituting other proper names) have sought to combine the static view of tradition as a "deposit of the faith" in the past with a dynamic view of tradition as "living faith" in the present and future.

FAITH AND KNOWLEDGE. Whether it has been interpreted as a second channel of revelation for faith or as the development of a truth already implicitly present in the original deposit of faith, tradition has been a way of knowing the truth. Faith, therefore, has been taken to be a species of knowledge, differing from ordinary knowledge by its superior claims: An arcane character, a transcendent content, privileged channels of communication, or divine certainty (or all of the above). So long as such claims remained publicly uncontested, faith could stand as objectively sure, even when subjectively the individual believer might question or doubt it. There is no reason to suppose that such existential questioning and doubting have ever been absent from the experience of faith, and plenty of reason to find evidence of their presence in the artifacts and literary remains of various religious faiths from the past. What has made the situation of religious faith in the present unique, however, is the gravity and the universality of the tension between faith and knowledge. One by one, each of the world faiths has been obliged to confront the competing truth claims not only of other faiths, as it had perhaps done before, but of other forms of knowledge that seemed to render any faith-as-knowledge, regardless of which faith was involved, superfluous or absurd. The identification of faith with accounts of miracles and similar wondrous events that a later generation has found to be, quite literally, incredible has undermined the authority of the faith itself. Orthodox methods of harmonizing away contradictions in the authoritative tradition through allegory or a theory of multiple meanings have not been able to withstand the pressures of the historical method of dealing with the tradition. The discovery or invention of alternate means of dealing with those crises of life and needs of society for which faith had served as the divinely prescribed cure relegated it to a secondary status as a superstitious nostrum still needed only by those who did not know any better. When Immanuel Kant said in his *Critique of Pure Reason* (1781) that he had "found it necessary to deny *knowledge* of God, freedom, and immortality in order to find a place for *faith*," he was speaking for believers in many traditions who have salvaged faith by making it invulnerable to the claims and counterclaims of knowledge; but in so doing, they have also brought into question most of the other functions of faith. At the same time, the very challenge of knowledge to faith has produced a clearer understanding both of faith's relation to other aspects of human experience and of its distinctive meaning and power.

SEE ALSO Doubt and Belief; Knowledge and Ignorance; Obedience; Orthopraxy; Physics and Religion; Tradition.

BIBLIOGRAPHY

Eliade, Mircea. *Patterns in Comparative Religion.* New York, 1958.

Feuerbach, Ludwig. *The Essence of Christianity.* Translated by George Eliot. London, 1854.

Freud, Sigmund. *The Future of an Illusion.* London, 1928.

Heiler, Friedrich. *Prayer: A Study in the History and Psychology of Religion.* Oxford, 1932.

Hügel, Friedrich von. *The Mystical Element of Religion.* 2 vols. London, 1961.

James, William. *The Varieties of Religious Experience.* New York, 1902.

Lossky, Vladimir. *In the Image and Likeness of God.* Scarsdale, N.Y., 1974.

Otto, Rudolf. *The Idea of the Holy.* New York, 1928.

Smith, Wilfred Cantwell. *Faith and Belief.* Princeton, N.J, 1979.

Söderblom, Nathan. *The Living God: Basal Forms of Personal Religion.* Oxford, 1933.

Wach, Joachim. *Sociology of Religion.* Chicago, 1944.

JAROSLAV PELIKAN (1987)

FAKHR AL-DĪN AL-RĀZĪ

SEE RĀZĪ, FAKHR AL-DĪN AL-

FALL, THE.

The concept of the fall appears in myths, traditions, and religions of a great many peoples and presents a number of interrelated themes of primary importance in the history of religious thought. In general, the fall is to be thought of as an accident that arose after the creation or genesis of the world bearing consequences for the present human condition; this accident explains a new situation in the world that is recognized as a decline or degradation when contrasted to the original state of humankind and the cosmos. This fundamental conception of the fall takes different forms in different cultures and religions.

PERSPECTIVES ON MYTHS OF THE FALL. The theme of the fall may be considered from the perspective of (1) historical time and its unfolding; (2) theogony; (3) cosmogony; and (4) anthropogony, which encompasses the creation of humanity and its present condition.

Historical time. Considered temporally, the fall takes place between *Urzeit* and *Endzeit,* between the beginning and the end of creation. Within historical time, it is very close to the beginnings of time conceived as a golden age in contrast to which the fall and its consequences represent a break or degradation. This temporal and historical conception of the fall can be found in various popular traditions as well as myths of the golden age and paradise lost.

Theogony. The theogonic aspect of the fall deals with the degradation of the divine and is found in the numerous myths concerning the origin of the gods, of their victory over chaos, or of the victory of the more recent forces of divinity over older ones. Coextensive with the creation, the fall as presented in theogony implies the identification of evil and chaos on the one hand and of salvation and creation on the other. This conception of the fall is found especially in Sumero-Akkadian theogonic myths that recount the victory of order over preexisting chaos; it is found also in the Egyptian myth of the battle between Seth and Horus. Strictly speaking, these theogonic myths are not true myths of the fall, but two of their recurrent themes justify their inclusion in a typology of myths of the fall. First, they emphasize the ritual celebration of the maintenance of the creation and cosmic order, as in the festival of Akitu in Babylon. Second, they present, through a variety of mythologies, the theme of the degradation of divinity that results from the fall of some portion of the divine substance into matter, body, or darkness. This theme is central to the three most important forms of religious dualism: Orphism, Gnosticism, and Manichaeism.

Cosmogony. From the perspective of cosmogony, the fall is seen as an accident occurring after the genesis of the world that affects cosmic forces and explains the present condition of earth or the universe. Myths that tell of the progressive degradation of the universe and its destruction and recreation in successive cosmic cycles exemplify this cosmogonic view of the fall. The flood is an important example of this type of fall, and numerous myths of the flood are found among religious traditions of the world.

Anthropogony. Anthropogony, however, offers the most important perspective on the fall. From this perspective, the contemporary human condition—a condition of degradation in contrast to that of the golden age of humanity—is explained as the consequence of a fall, a tragic event that bursts into human history. Around this event are clustered those myths and symbols that seek to explain the origins of illness and death and the tragic nature of the human condition after the fall.

From these four perspectives, it is possible to develop a typology through which the myriad myths of the fall in cultures throughout the world become comprehensible. Furthermore, these perspectives illuminate the fundamental aspect of the concept of the fall and the inherent meaning that emerges from these myths: The present human condition is explained by the accident that occurred after creation and ended the golden age.

Myths of the fall clearly show three essential elements: (1) the concept of a golden age in the beginning, (2) the accident that is a break or degradation of original harmony, (3) the explanation of the present human condition. From these three elements, it is possible to trace a historico-phenomenological picture of the traditions dealing with the fall. One final remark needs to be added, however, before proceeding to an analysis of this picture. An understanding of the complexity of the problems related to the concept of the fall must not lose sight of the intimate relationship of this concept with the problem of evil; any conception of the fall has implications concerning the origins of evil, as well as intimations of a possible overcoming of evil through a recovery of the state that existed previous to the fall. Thus a philosophical and ethical dimension is grafted onto, and is coextensive with, the idea of the fall and forms an important part of a hermeneutical approach that tries to come to terms with its relationship to guilt or fault. The scope of this article, however, does not permit an envisage of these other aspects of the fall.

ARCHAIC RELIGIONS AND ORAL TRADITIONS. The myth of an earthly paradise, where humans are immortal, is an integral part of cosmogony and descriptions of the world's beginning in many cultures. That primordial person enjoys a bliss and freedom that it lost as the result of a fall is the dominant theme of this myth, a theme offering many variations.

The Jorai cosmogony of the autochthonous peoples of Indochina gives an idyllic description of original humanity. Living with the god Oi Adei, humankind enjoyed a deathless existence in a paradise where one could fly like a bird and talk with plants and animals, where bundles of wicker grew on trees and shovels turned over the earth by themselves. Man had only to feed his tools; but he got drunk and did not do so, and the tools revolted. In the Sre cosmogony of Indochina, humans had no need to work in the earthly paradise, because the god Ong Ndu had made them immortal; but when the primordial couple refused the god's command to dive into a well, they were punished for their disobedience by suffering, old age, and death.

The cosmogonies of Bantu speakers from the Mayombe region north of the Kongo River, the cradle of the old Kongo civilization, contain significant stories of the fall. In the Yombe tradition, humankind's golden age was brought to an end by Nzondo, a spirit whose magic also created the Zaire River after a flood. Nzondo drove people from their original home, dispersing them over the earth and setting in motion the chain of disasters that have since befallen the race.

In a Dogon myth from Mali, heaven and earth were originally very close to each other. But God separated them and made men mortal, after being disturbed by the noise of the women crushing millet. Similarly, in a myth from Cameroon and Burkina Faso (Upper Volta), the vault of heaven was originally within humanity's reach, but when a woman who touched the vault with a load of wood she was carrying on her head asked God to move it out of her way, he moved it so far that he abandoned humankind to death. These myths tell of a paradise lost; but they also stress the theme of God's rejection of a disobedient humankind, of his consigning humanity to death as punishment for a variety of sins, that is, for violating a divine prohibition, for lying or theft, for domestic rivalries, for lack of charity. Death is explained as divine punishment prompted by human disobedience. Similar myths are found among the Diola in Senegal, the Nupe in Nigeria, the Bena Kanioka in Zaire, and the Anyi in the Ivory Coast.

Myths of the fall as fate, though less frequently encountered than those of the fall as punishment, are also significant in sub-Saharan Africa. These myths involve an archetypal badly delivered message—a divine message of immortality that reaches humanity either too late or in abridged or altered form. Here, the original separation of heaven and earth replaces the earthly paradise where God and humans live together; from heaven, God sends messages to people on earth. In a Tsonga myth, a chameleon carries the message of eternal life, while the giant lizard Galagala carries the message of death. The lizard, moving faster, arrives first, and humanity so becomes mortal. In a Bete version of the same myth, from the Ivory Coast, the lizard advises the chameleon to walk slowly. Animals are always the messengers in these myths, and the message of mortality always arrives first. Other myths emphasize the change and deterioration of the message in the course of its transmission; myths of this sort are found among the Mossi in Burkina Faso, the Ashanti in Ghana, the Kabiye in Togo, and the Kikuyu in Kenya.

In Australia, the Aranda regard their totem ancestors as the heroic forgers of civilizations who gave form to the countryside, who allotted individual lives to humans by creating separate embryos, who lived in a mythical golden age where they were untouched by the woes of contemporary humankind. These totem ancestors were immortal, and those among them who apparently died in battle in fact went to heaven, where they became *tjurungas*, sacred beings who were powerful and creative, traveling to and fro above or below the earth.

Exhausted when they completed their creative work, and seized by an overwhelming lassitude, these mythical ancestors sank into the earth. But before they disappeared they laid down, by some of their actions, the rudiments of death; thus, the first people knew both death and the pains of the human condition. The myth of the magpie Urbura explains the permanence of death. When the first mortal tried to leave his tomb, Urbura struck at him with her claws, thrust a spear through his neck, and nailed him to the ground, establishing forever humanity's mortal condition.

Common to myths of the fall and to nostalgia for a lost golden age is the view that the original human condition was a condition of paradise. Heaven lay close to the earth, and people could go there merely by climbing a mountain, a tree, a ladder, or a vine (Eliade, 1960). Enjoying the friendship of both the gods and the animals—and speaking their language—man enjoyed a life that was immortal, free, spontaneous, and perfectly happy.

That this paradise was lost as the result of the fall is a second commonly held view. Often, the fall is an accident, as in Australia, where myths of the Aranda tribe merely record it. In various African traditions the accident is equated with sleep: The god had asked humans to remain awake through the night to await a message from him, but when it arrived they were asleep. If sleep is understood as a symbol for death, the accident of sleep explains both the precarious human condition and the establishment of death.

The fall may also result from human failings. Once again, the most important documentation is found in sub-Saharan Africa. A Maasai myth known in both Africa and Madagascar tells of a package that humans were given by God but forbidden to open; driven by curiosity, they opened it and let loose sickness and death. The divine prohibition takes other forms in other traditions. In a Pygmy story of central Africa, it is against looking at something; in a story of the Luba in the Democratic Republic of the Congo, it forbids the eating of certain fruits; in a Lozi myth found in the Democratic Republic of the Congo and Malawi, it prohibits the taking of wild game.

Sometimes humanity's fault is best understood anthropologically, as in myths describing theft or lying, or those that stress lack of charity, or the race's capacity for domestic violence, as in a Chiga myth from Uganda. The curiosity of the primordial couple who aspire to the secrets of the gods is a frequent mythical theme in Africa, where myths of the fall also emphasize the cohesiveness of individual and group (Thomas, 1982, pp. 32–48).

ANCIENT CIVILIZATIONS. Important approaches to the theme of the fall are found in the great civilizations of antiquity. This section examines those myths and traditions found in the civilizations of Egypt, Sumer and Babylonia, ancient India, ancient Iran, and ancient Greece.

Egypt. Egyptian religious thought also shows an awareness of a golden age existing at the beginning. The study of archaic texts has prompted the hypothesis that this age was thought to have had two stages, the first of which was *Urzeit,* primordial time before the creation. The idea of a primordial time is expressed by such formulas as "that did not yet exist" (*nhprt*) or, in the wording of Pyramid Texts 1040 and 1043, "When the heavens did not yet exist . . . there existed neither death nor disorder." In contrast to this mythic primordial time is the time that follows it, the time of creation and of creator gods such as Re and Osiris (Otto, 1969, pp. 96–99).

Whatever the validity of this hypothesis, the time of creation, the *Schöpfungszeit,* was definitely considered a golden age. A variety of texts make it possible to assert this interpretation with certainty. "Law was established in their time. Justice (Maat) came down from heaven to earth in their age and united herself with those on the earth. There was an abundance on the earth; stomachs were full, and there was no lean year in the Two Lands. Wall did not collapse, thorn did not prick in the time of the primeval Gods" (Kákosy, 1964, p. 206). An inscription from the temple of Idfu speaks in the same way: "There was no sin on the earth. The crocodile did not seize prey, the serpent did not bite in the age of the primeval Gods." This golden age is depicted in other temple inscriptions and is found again in the Coffin Texts; it is, in fact, a very ancient doctrine in which myths of a golden age and fall are tied to the problem of death.

Three great Egyptian cosmogonies explain the creation of the world. In the Memphis theology, the word of the god Ptah created all things; at Heliopolis, the creation takes place with Re-Atum's separation of heaven and earth; at Hermopolis Magna, the creator is the god Thoth, who fashions an egg from which the sun, organizer of the cosmos, emerges. The Memphis theology makes it clear that, by putting the cosmos, the gods, and the gods' images and cults in place, Ptah established a definitive cosmic order in which Maat, the principle of order, replaced disorder (Pyramid Text 265.1775b).

The myth of the celestial cow, a myth of archaic origin, although known from a text of the New Kingdom, is the most important witness to the Egyptian doctrine of the fall. It tells of insults hurled by humans at the god Re (variously called "silver-boned Re," "golden-limbed Re," "Re of the lapis lazuli hair") and of Re's attempt to determine their punishment in a secret council of the gods held in the Nun, or primordial chaos. From his throne, Re glared fixedly at the rebellious humans, as the gods had advised; immediately, his eye became the goddess Hathor, henceforth called Sekhmet, the Powerful; she organized a massacre of the rebels as they fled into the desert. Re, however, preferred to save remaining humankind; ordering that pomegranates be brought to him, he extracted their juice, and at dawn carried the juice to the flooded area of humanity's impending extermination. There he determined to spare the human race; but he also withdrew to the highest place in heaven, and sat on the back of Nut, the vault of heaven transformed into a cow, assigning to Thoth the role of scribe and the task of civilizing humanity.

The *Book of Going Forth by Day* is another witness to the Egyptian doctrine of the fall. Chapter 17, alluding to Re's enemies, declares: "I was All when I was in the Nun, and I am Re. . . . When Re first appeared as king of all that he had created, when the uprisings of Shu did not yet exist, he was on the hill that is at Hermopolis and at that time the children of the fall at Hermopolis were delivered over to him." To this passage, which tells of the revolt against Re, correspond the lines at the beginning of chapter 175, which speak of the disorder created by the children of Nut: "O Thoth, what is to be done with the children of Nut? They have fomented war, they have provoked quarrels, they have caused disorder, they have massacred. . . . They have brought low that which was great in all that I created. Show strength, Thoth, says Atum. . . . Shorten their years, cut off their months. For they have secretly destroyed all that you created."

From such texts, it is clear that pharaonic Egypt was acquainted very early with a doctrine of a golden age, an age followed by the fall that explains the *Jetztzeit,* the present human condition of death and degradation. Nevertheless, the Egyptian theology that viewed royalty as a divine continuation of Maat, the cosmic and moral order, had a paramount influence on three thousand years of Egyptian history under the pharaohs and the Ptolemies, and although each great historic era ended in a period of disorder, the disorder itself gave rise to the reestablishment of Egyptian society under renewed pharaonic rule. Life and survival were inseparable in Egypt, and the optimism running throughout Egyptian culture is made obvious by the absence of traditions dealing with great cosmic disasters such as the flood.

There was also, however, a darker side to Egyptian thought, one that does relate that evil, incarnate in the god Seth, existed before the creation of humans. Hence some Egyptologists interpret the verses quoted above from chapter 175 of the *Book of Going Forth by Day,* referring to the children of Nut, as an allusion to a quarrel among the gods and evidence of a primordial sin that stood at the origin of the fall.

Sumer and Babylonia. The numerous Mesopotamian traditions dealing with the origins of the gods, the cosmos, and humanity go back to the Sumerian period, well before the third millennium BCE, and become completely intermixed over time with Sumerian, Akkadian, and Babylonian myths. Thus, it is possible to present these traditions coherently by selecting characteristic examples from these three groups of myths.

Samuel Noah Kramer (1981) finds the first document of the Golden Age in the Sumerian story called *Emmer-kai and the Lord of Aratta.* The story speaks of "an earlier time," before the fall, when humankind lived in peace and harmony, without fear and without rival. During that time, before the creation of snake or scorpion, hyena or lion, wolf or wild dog, all peoples of the universe worshiped the same god, Enlil. But the gods brought about humankind's fall when Enki cast an evil spell and stole Enlil's empire.

The creation poem *Enuma elish,* which dates from 1100 BCE but actually goes back to the first Babylonian dynasty at the beginning of the second millennium, relates the genesis of the gods before it describes the genesis of the world or humanity, and shows that strife and murder existed among the gods from the moment of their creation. The younger gods banded together against their mother, Tiamat; they behaved riotously and spread fear throughout the dwelling places on high. The goddess Ea caused the god Apsu—who would himself have murdered the other gods, had his scheme not been betrayed—to fall into a deep sleep, then undressed him to take away his strength, and finally put him to death. The Atrahasis myth, dating from the reign of the Babylonian king Ammisadaqa (1646–1626 BCE), gives another version of these events, in which the gods declared war on Enlil and gathered in arms before his temple for the decisive battle.

In these two myths, evil is coextensive with the first generation of the gods, and disorder begins in the divine world itself when the younger gods kill their mother, Tiamat (who in any case had planned to murder them). From this perspective, the gods are responsible for evil, and order appears among them only with the advent of the god Marduk, the principle of an ordered divine world. Hence, humans simply find evil in the world; they are not the cause of it.

Both the Atrahasis myth and the poem *Enuma elish* show that the gods created humans with the intention of imposing burdensome tasks upon them: food gathering, the building of waterways, dikes, canals, and so forth. In the Atrahasis text, the god Weilu is killed by the other gods, who then mix his flesh and blood with clay to make humankind, upon whom they immediately impose the gods' "basket" (i.e., workload); in a story dating from the seventeenth century BCE and found in a bilingual text from the reign of King Tiglath-pileser I (1114–1076 BCE), An, Enlil, and Enki kill the Alla gods and from their blood create humankind, which they also charge with tasks previously borne by the gods.

In these texts, and in many others that echo them, it is clear that Mesopotamian thought saw the human condition as one of total subordination to the gods, who were absolute masters of the world. This dualistic thought presents a humanity fashioned both from the blood of a murdered god and from mere clay, a humanity knowing no primordial fall but only a destiny of submission to the gods and subordination to divine power. The gods reserve a deathless, happy life for themselves, imposing on humanity a precarious existence that ends in death, itself a divine decision. The dead lead only a shadowy existence in the realm of the god Nergal.

Two ancient texts provide Akkadian and Babylonian versions of the Mesopotamian flood. The earlier, dating from the beginning of the third millennium, was found on a Sumerian tablet unearthed in the ruins of Nippur; the other is found in tablet 11 of the *Epic of Gilgamesh.*

The Sumerian tablet describes the creation of the world and humans and the building of the first cities, including Eridu and Shuruppak. The rather fragmentary story of the flood tells of how the gods decided upon a deluge, from which only the pious king Ziusudra was spared. After the disaster, Ziusudra sacrificed an ox and a sheep to the sun god Utu and thereby reconciled the gods and humankind.

In the Babylonian version, from the *Epic of Gilgamesh,* the man saved from the flood was Utanapishtim, to whom the gods gave immortality. After the flood, the quarrel that had divided the gods started up again, and Enlil, the lord of earth and sky who had been the cause of the flood, wanted to destroy its sole survivor; but Ea and Ishtar, protectors of humankind, intervened and Utanapishtim was saved.

In neither version of the flood does the question of human responsibility for the cosmic disaster arise; as in Mesopotamian stories of humanity's creation, the stories of the flood deal only with theogony and with quarrels of the gods. The Atrahasis myth does indicate the gods' motive for the flood—the noise and disturbance produced by the ever-increasing number of humans—but this motive is analogous to that behind the gods' first quarrel. Thus, whatever the reason for the gods' displeasure with humanity, the human failings that appear at the time of the fall are simply part of a divinely ordained chaos. In the final analysis, myths of the fall in Sumero-Babylonian thought are intimately tied to theogonic and cosmogonic myths in which the fall, like everything else that happens, results from the will of the gods.

Ancient India. In India, which has experienced its past far more through myths than through historical interpretation of actual past events, the most important documents of mythic history are the Purāṇas, or "ancient tales." One part of the speculations of the *Vāyu Purāṇa* treats the four *yuga*s, or ages, of the world. The present age, the fourth *yuga,* is called the *kaliyuga.* The first age, named *kṛtayuga* or *satyayuga,* is described in the *Vāyu Purāṇa* as a golden age when Prajapati created all things from a superabundance of light and intelligence.

During this *yuga,* a perfect age that lasted four thousand years (plus an additional four hundred for its dawn and dusk), all creatures lived in a state of spiritual perfection, doing as they pleased, free from heat and cold, fatigue and suffering, ignorant alike of justice and injustice. Possessing similar forms, their pleasures, their life span, and their ever-youthful bodies ensured a life of abundant happiness, joy, and light, knowing neither classes nor different ways of being. Whatever was sought after by the spirit sprang from the earth, and all enjoyed truth, forbearance, satisfaction, and contentment.

The *Vāyu Purāṇa* does not describe a fall, but simply a decline, from this golden age. The second age, *tretāyuga,* was still, at its beginning, part of the golden age; beings still lived without suffering, joyous and satisfied. With time, however, they became greedy; they laid waste the fruit trees and the honey that had fed them in ease. Afflicted now by wind, heat, and cold, people built houses, then villages and cities. Now too rains came, bringing streams, rivers, and rank vegetation. Humans were divided into four classes: *brāhmaṇa, kṣatriya, vaiśya,* and *śūdra;* and, because humans no longer fulfilled their duties, the *brāhmaṇa*s assigned specific functions to each class. The *brāhmaṇa*s were to make sacrifices on behalf of others, to read the Veda, to receive offerings; the *kṣatriya*s were to exercise power, make war, and dispense justice; the *vaiśya*s were to raise livestock or practice agriculture or commerce; the *śūdra*s were to practice the various trades. The *brāhmaṇa*s likewise introduced and named the four stages of life: first, the quest for knowledge, followed by domestic life, the retreat into the forest, and, finally, renunciation.

It is clear from the *Vāyu Purāṇa* that by the end of the second *yuga* the conditions of humanity and the cosmos were such that the golden age had been lost, the victim not of a fall in the usual sense but of a progressive decline, and of the negative effects of time. As differences appeared among them, humans lost their original vitality, turning to passion, vice, and greed, and ceasing to carry out their duties faithfully. The *Vāyu Purāṇa* emphasizes the role of human responsibility in this cosmic and social decline.

From the sixth century BCE on, the idea of *karman,* specific to Hindu religious thought, was used to explain the decline of the human condition. Linked to the idea of *sāṃsara,* the incessant whirlpool of rebirths, the ethical idea of *karman,* gradually replacing older Vedic ritual notions, placed the human soul under the necessity of being reborn in animal, human, or divine forms. Thus humanity by its actions was made responsible for its decline and for the repercussions of that decline in the cosmos. Holding humankind accountable for his position in the universe, the law of the *karman* became a law of just retribution for actions.

The Indian idea of the flood, of "cosmic disaster," appears within a cyclical conception of time—a conception analogous to the idea of the *karman* involving the periodic destruction and rebirth of the cosmos. The oldest of numerous Indian versions of a cosmic fall in the form of a flood is that of the *Śatapatha Brāhmaṇa* 1.8.1; it presents the story of Manu, the first man and the survivor of the flood, in a typically Vedic context. Warned of the flood by a fish, Manu takes the fish under his protection and then is saved by it as the waters rise and carry away all other creatures. Left alone, Manu offers the *pāka* sacrifice, and, after a year, a woman—his daughter, called Iḍā, the offering—is born; through her Manu will create his posterity, the renewed humanity.

Ancient Iran. The Avesta preserves ancient Iran's memories of the golden age that existed in the beginning, during the reign of the first king, Yima (*Vendidad* 2.1–20, *Yasna* 9.4–5, *Yashts* 9.9, 13.130, 15.15, 17.29, 19.32). According to *Yasna* 9.4, Yima, the good shepherd, the most glorious of mortals ever born, looked benevolently on all creatures; his reign was one with neither drought nor heat nor cold, when food was always plentiful, and when people and animals lived without want or old age or death. The *Vendidad* (2.7) says that Ahura Mazdā brought Yima the two implements symbolizing a prosperous reign, a golden seal and a sword encrusted with gold. Yima also asked for a thousand-year reign of immortality in the world created by the Lord. For three hundred years after the creation, the world filled up with humans and animals; then Yima, advancing in the path of the sun, smote the earth with his seal and pierced it with his sword, and the earth increased in size by a third; he did this again after six hundred winters, and again the earth became a third larger; when he had repeated this act yet again, the earth was enlarged to three times its original surface (*Vendidad* 2.7, 2.8–9, 2.10–11, 2.17–19). Thus ends the story of the paradise of Yima, a paradise that in a Pahlavi text, the *Dēnkard* 8.1.24, is compared to the highest heaven.

The Avestan text *Yashts* 19.34–38 describes the fall that marked the end of this felicity. When Yima began to take pleasure in false and deceitful speech, the *khvarenah*—the celestial light, the mark of divinity, the sign of the elect and of power—at once abandoned him. He thus lost the three marks of glory associated with the *khvarenah,* the marks of the priest, the warrior, and the agriculturalist-herdsman. Seen in the context of Indo-Iranian thought, the loss of these marks represents the loss of the three great Aryan functions of sovereignty, power, and fecundity. Confounded and distraught, Yima fell to earth and became mortal.

The cause of the fall, the "lie against the truth," is stressed in *Yashts* 19.34; this lie deprived Yima of his aura of light and delivered him over defenseless to the Evil Spirit, who hounded him with demons and forced him to flee. Yima actually made two mistakes: The first was "the lie and the error," or *druj,* condemned by the entire Mazdean tradition and still decried in Manichaeism, for Mani taught that lying and deceit constitute the evil that resides in matter and darkness; the second mistake was the offense to God caused by pride (Widengren, 1968, p. 72). Because, in this very ancient myth, Yima is the archetype of the cosmic king who holds sovereignty over the gods and humans, the king of the three functions that correspond to the three classes of society, his fall will mark both the cosmos and the human condition.

Describing Yima's meeting with Ahura Mazdā, *Vendidad* 2.21–22 mentions hard winters of bitter cold and heavy snow; in *Bundahishn* 7, there is a story of what appears to be a flood; and al-Masʿūdī (d. 957) relates how, according to one tradition, the flood came during Yima's time. In the nineteenth century, scholars such as C. P. Tiele, François Lenormant, and A. V. Rydberg saw an allusion to the flood in this evidence; but early in the twentieth century, Nathan Söderblom, in a lengthy discussion of the question, showed that it is impossible to know whether the devastating winters mentioned in these passages were considered part of a real past before they came to symbolize the end of the world later incorporated into Mazdean eschatology. Söderblom leaned toward a strictly eschatological meaning of the myth of the *vara* of Yima and the winter of Mahrkuska; more recently, Geo Widengren has observed that in the few traces of a flood linked to the myth of Yima two different themes have been combined: one of the golden age of Yima, the other of a period when the more fortunate of humankind took refuge in the *vara* because winters threatened their existence (Widengren, 1968, pp. 70–71). Going over the evidence once again, Mary Boyce still finds the narrative of the *vara* of Yima puzzling; but she argues that, because the editing of the *Vendidad* in the Parthian period is comparatively recent, the Avestan story very probably was contaminated by the Mesopotamian and biblical stories of the cosmic flood (Boyce, 1975, pp. 92–96).

Ancient Greece. The term *golden age* (Gr., *chruseon genos*) comes from the ancient Greek world. In *Works and Days,* Hesiod provided the myth of the Golden Age to which later Greek and Latin poets would return again and again, a myth of five races of humans to which correspond five ages of the world: ages of gold, silver, and bronze, of heroes, and, finally, of iron. Created when Kronos reigned in the heavens, the race of gold lived as gods on the earth, perfectly happy and secure, sheltered from all woe, fatigue, pain, or illness. The earth gave forth abundantly all things that people desired, and although this first race of humans was not immortal, its death was a mere going to sleep. This age of paradise, when humans enjoyed the blessing and friendship of the gods, ended with the fall of Kronos; then Zeus made benevolent gods of these first humans.

Plato elaborated on the conditions of this golden age in the *Politics* (271c,d–272a); in that age, he says, the gods were responsible for different parts of the cosmos, and demons served as shepherds for the various species and groups of animals; the earth's climate was always temperate, and everything was designed to serve men, who lived on fruit picked from trees. There were neither cities nor even women or children, because they were reborn from the earth without any memory of earlier lives.

Horace, Vergil, and Ovid later take up this theme, adapting it to the legendary history of Rome; thus Kronos will become Saturn and Latium will have the name Ansonia during the golden age—a time when, according to the Latin poets, springtime was perpetual, and, because lying and theft did not yet exist, houses had no doors.

Four races will follow that of the golden age. Extremely slow in coming to maturity, the silver race will lose the qualities of life that characterized the previous age. Although created by the Olympian gods, the people of this race could not refrain from foolish excesses, even refusing to sacrifice to the gods, and Zeus buried them, transforming them into the spirits of the underworld. He then created the fearless and warlike race of bronze, a race so given to violence that it destroyed itself and was followed in its turn by the race of heroes, heroes who founded famous cities, fought beneath the walls of Troy and Thebes, and ended their days in the Isles of the Blessed. At last came the present race of humans, the race of iron, whose ephemeral and vulnerable existence is plagued by illness and want.

The myth of the races of humans, which recalls the Indian myth of the four *yugas*, is, like it, a myth of decline rather than fall; like the text of the *Vāyu Purāṇa,* the Hesiodic text emphasizes progressive degeneration. Gradually humanity loses the virtues and qualities of the primordial period; its strength and endurance diminish, and finally it loses the longevity of the first age. Recent analyses of this myth have also laid stress on the evil pointed out by Hesiod: human pride, the hubris that makes humans refuse to sacrifice to the gods and to defy *dike* ("justice").

In his *Theogony,* Hesiod describes the triumph of an ordered world over chaos and proclaims the sovereign power of Zeus, who imposes himself upon both the universe and the other Olympian gods, to whom he distributes functions and privileges. In *Works and Days,* before recounting the myth of the races of humankind, he tells the story of Pandora, the first woman, created by Zeus's command to bring punishment upon the human race. All the Olympians joined in making this special gift to humans. Zeus sent her to the naive Epimetheus, who was seduced by her beauty and married her.

At pains to stress how humans had originally enjoyed the earth free from troubles, weariness, or illness, Hesiod now relates that Pandora had barely arrived on earth when she was devoured by curiosity to learn the contents of the vase she had brought with her and lifted its lid, thus sending throughout the world all the present and future afflictions and woes of humankind, leaving only hope at the bottom of the vase when she replaced the lid. Henceforth, innumerable miseries will plague humanity, and thus, Hesiod concludes, none can escape the plan of Zeus (*Works and Days* 90–102, 105). In the myth of Pandora, the themes of hubris and fate come together, and the description of the fall shows the fundamental link between divine will and human fate.

Orpheus seems to be a figure of the archaic religious type that, in certain traditions, is thrown back to the earliest time; he stands in sharp contrast to the Olympian gods. Hesiod's theogony and cosmogony oppose an ordered world upon which Zeus has at last imposed himself to an earlier, primordial chaos; Orphic theogony, on the other hand, presents a primordial Eros, or Protogonos ("firstborn"), or Phanes ("light"), that itself creates night, Ouranos, Kronos, Zeus, and, finally, Dionysos.

Orphic anthropogony, in sources that date from later antiquity, recounts the myth of a Dionysos torn apart and cut to pieces by the Titans, who then divided the dead god among themselves and ate him. Zeus hurled lightning bolts at them as a punishment and killed them; he then created the present race of humans from their ashes. Thus, humans possess both the evil nature of the Titans and the divine nature of Dionysos whom the Titans had assimilated by eating him. The Neoplatonist Proclus talks of three races of humans: the race of gold ruled by Phanes, the god of the beginning of things; the silver race over which Kronos was lord; and the Titanic race, created by Zeus from limbs of Titans whom he had punished for their crime. Plato himself had already referred to this race, Titanic in origin, who likewise refused to obey both laws and parents, refused to abide by oaths, and despised the gods. Both Diodorus Siculus and Firmicus Maternus repeat these basic elements of the Orphic myth; and the dualism of Orphic anthropogony, in which the story of the Titans is presented as an etiological myth accounting for the present human condition, has been further confirmed by the discovery, in 1962, of the fourth-century Dervani Papyrus.

Orphism explains the human condition through the dualistic myth of the exiled soul. Humankind is composed of a divine soul, daughter of heaven, and of an evil, Titanic nature; the tragedy of his condition comes from this mixture, itself the outcome of an earlier, prehuman crime. Evil is the legacy of an event that stands at the origin of the mixed human nature; it originates in the murder of Dionysos, but that murder signifies both the death of the god and the participation of his slayers in his divine nature. The original sin, the sin of the fall, is murder, and with the murder of Dionysos the soul experiences a brutal descent into a body that becomes its prison (see Ricoeur, 1960, pp. 264–279).

The myth of Deukalion and Pyrrha presents the Greek version of the flood, but the fragmentary Greek texts do not give Zeus's reasons for suppressing humankind. However, as Roman mythology disappeared, it absorbed Greek mythology (a phenomenon discussed by Georges Dumézil, *La religion romaine archaïque,* 2d ed., Paris, 1974, pp. 63–75), and it is therefore legitimate to seek Zeus's reasons in Roman mythology, especially in Ovid's *Metamorphoses,* which provides a fuller account of the Greek version of the flood (*Metamorphoses* 1.230, 7.352–356). Taking up the Hesiodic theme of the ages of the world, Ovid emphasizes that humans were progressively perverted by crime and lust. Zeus, before humanity's destruction, visited Lycaon, king of Arcadia, who served him a feast of human flesh; outraged and at the end of his patience, Zeus swept away all creatures, cities, almost the whole of earth itself, in the flood. Only one couple, Deukalion and his wife, Pyrrha, were saved, and from them Zeus re-created the race.

WORLD RELIGIONS. Each of the world religions discussed in this section—Gnosticism and Manichaeism, and the three great monotheisms, Judaism, Christianity, and Islam—lend great richness to the concept of the fall.

Gnosticism and Manichaeism. From the second century CE onward, Gnosticism, a religious movement composed of a number of different sects, came to maturity throughout the Mediterranean world and in the Near East. The central element of Gnostic metaphysical speculation is a dualistic doctrine according to which humanity possesses a divine spark that, although originating from on high, has fallen into matter, into body, which holds it prisoner in the lower world. The myth of the fall, therefore, is an integral part of Gnostic teaching. Each Gnostic sect offered salvation through its specific creed and rites of initiation into these dualistic mysteries. These constituted its particular gnosis. Understood only by adherents who were gradually initiated into it, the gnosis brought about an identity of the initiate with the means of his salvation and with divine substance.

Because it claims to possess the most perfect gnosis, Manichaeism holds a special place in the spectrum of gnostic thought. Its founder, Mani (216–276), taught that, as the transmitter of the gnosis, he was the greatest of the prophets and the ultimate revelation, sent by the Holy Spirit, after the trials and failures of his predecessors—most notably Zarathushtra, the Buddha, and Jesus—to establish the church of the end of time, the church of light, and to provide the definitive revelation that would enlighten all people. According to Mani, the soul, a spark detached from divine light and held prisoner by matter, must tear itself away from the darkness of the body in order to return to the realm of light where it had originated.

The Manichaean gnosis offers the clearest conception of the beginning, the middle, and the end, the three divisions of time. In the beginning, there existed two radically opposed natures, darkness and light, eternal and unborn principles. These two natures created two earths, two different realms. The realm of light is located on high, in a city of incomparable beauty, in the house of the Father of Greatness; the breath of the spirit breathes life and light throughout this realm, where all things exude blessing and peace. But beneath this realm, and separated from it by an impregnable border, lies the realm of darkness, the domain of matter and of demons, a realm governed by the Prince of Lies. Obviously, the Manichaean gnosis presents the golden age within a context of radical gnostic dualism.

In other forms of gnosis, dualism appears against a monistic background, because the world on high—everlasting, immutable, and incorruptible—is held to have existed before the lower world. Indeed, many gnostic writings speak of the Pleroma, of the world on high in all its plenitude, emanating from a being that is the source of all things. The gnostic Pleroma is the union of the Aeons that emanate from the All and constitute, with the First Father, the harmonious universe of peace and light.

The symbol of the fall is omnipresent in gnostic texts; indeed, the precosmic fall of a portion of the divine principle is the underlying reason for the genesis of the cosmos and humanity (Jonas, 1963). In the different metaphysical speculations that explain this fall, it is generally held that the divine principle descended voluntarily, and that guilt came into being as the Aeons turned toward the lower world. Turning toward matter by a burning desire to know it, the soul then sank into it and was swallowed up. Hence, the fall that gave birth to the cosmos also imprisoned the soul in matter.

In Gnostic writings, important groups of symbols suggesting captivity describe the tragic fate of this dualistic, imprisoned soul. One group of symbols suggests pain or danger: violence, fear, and the wounds and bites of animals; another suggests the soul's forgetfulness: torpor, sleep, death, darkness, drunkenness, lack of conscience, ignorance. As a snake's bite causes an infection that debilitates the body, so the poison of darkness causes an infection of the soul that makes it lose awareness of its divine origin. In a frequently used image, the soul falls asleep in matter, and the gnostic message strives to awaken it; hence, gnosticism attaches great importance to its call. Also characteristic of gnostic writings are the images used by Valentinus when describing the behavior of Sophia ("wisdom") after she had fallen into error. The youngest Aeon of the Pleroma, Sophia was the cause of her own fall, through the passion that carried her away—the origin of a fall that brought about the lower world of the Demiurge, who created the material world.

A true religious genius endowed with uncommon imagination, Mani brought together a number of Eastern cosmogonic myths and from them produced a synthesis in which the entire range of dualistic cosmogony, soteriology, and eschatology is included.

In the beginning, Mani taught, the Prince of Darkness, jealous and envious of the Father, hurled a war cry against the realm of light, signaling the beginning of a gigantic cosmic conflict. Primordial Man, the first emanation of the Father, marched against the forces of darkness, but he was wounded and defeated and fell among the archons (cosmic rulers). This was the fall, the moment when the living soul, the divine portion of Primordial Man, was engulfed by darkness; it was also the beginning of the second division of time, the middle, when divinity fell into matter and humanity's mixed nature became fixed. Henceforth, salvation became an imperious necessity. The liberation of Primordial Man from this fallen state is the prototype of the salvation of each soul; and the second emanation of the Father, the Living Spirit (also called the Friend of Light or the Great Architect), extends his right hand to Primordial Man and leads him back to the realm of light. But the fall has permanent consequences, because a part of the light remains captive in the lower realm.

The first moment of middle time, the moment of the fall, is followed by the moment of the creation and the freeing of another part of light, as part of the punishment of the archons. The Living Spirit chained down the archons and cut them to pieces; from their skins he made the vault of heaven, from their bones the mountains, from their flesh and excrement the earth, and from the light taken from them he created the sun, moon, and stars. When a Third Messenger descended from on high in the form of a luminous virgin, the semen of the archons excited by this apparition fell on the earth and produced trees and vegetation. Animals were next created, and finally the first couple was born, the work of demons. This couple was Adam and Eve, creatures of mixed nature whose posterity nonetheless carried with it the greater part of light.

The third moment of middle time is the moment of the messengers of the gnosis, the moment of true and divine hypostasis brought about by the fourth emanation of the Father, Jesus the Splendid, a transcendent, cosmic being, fifth Greatness of the Realm, the life and salvation of humanity. Messengers of the gnosis have followed one after another from Sethel, the son of Adam, to Jesus (here considered as a historical figure), who both announced and sent the final messenger, Mani. Hence, everything was made ready for the third division of time, the end, when all things will become as they had been at the beginning, and the total separation of the realms of darkness and light will be reestablished.

The Eastern myths of the fall brought together by Mani constitute one great myth of the fall and redemption of the divine soul. Each human soul is part of the divine soul that is partly imprisoned in bodies, partly in plants, trees, and earth; in all its imprisoned parts, that divine soul is the soul of the world and the third representation of Jesus, *Jesus patibilis.* In the great Manichaean myth of the fall is found the gnostic myth of the exiled soul; but, in contrast to most gnostic creeds, in Manichaeism the soul is not responsible for its fall and exile in the body, because that exile is a part of a greater, cosmic fall of light. To this cosmic myth of the fall corresponds the cosmic salvation by a gnosis accessible to individual souls in a church that is both the location and the means of individual salvation, a church charged with proclaiming the message of the fall and issuing the call to salvation, as well as awakening human souls and initiating them into the dualistic mysteries.

Judaism. Central to the biblical message is the view that the creation of humankind and the cosmos is the work of a unique and transcendent God who freely willed and effected a creation that also marks the beginning of time.

Two different stories of the creation are given in *Genesis.* The Bible opens with the so-called sacerdotal account of the creation, "the work of six days" (*Gn.* 1:1–31, 2:1–3). In this cosmogony, primordial chaos is replaced by order through the creative power of God's word. The sacerdotal account emphasizes the transcendence of the creator God and presents his creative activity in an order of ascending importance; although the creation of the world and of animal and vegetable life are all deemed "good," the crowning work in the beginning is the creation of humankind.

The second, so-called Yahvistic, creation story (*Gn.* 2:4–25) does not talk of the creation of the earth and sky but rather of a desert made fertile by Yahveh; it stresses God's action, his fashioning the first man from clay and breathing the breath of life into his nostrils. It is in the Yahvistic story that God plants a garden in Eden, where humans are the creatures of unequaled importance, the rest of creation being made in relation to them. Together, the two stories of creation provide genetic explanations of important aspects of the human condition; in both, huamity occupies a privileged position in creation. The biblical stories stress that humanity is free and not controlled by fate.

In Hebrew, the word *gan*—*paradeisos* in Greek (related to the Iranian *paridaida*)—designates the place where, according to *Genesis* 2:8, God placed humanity. The Yahvistic creation story speaks of an arid land on which Yahveh caused rain to fall, after which he took man and placed him in the garden of Eden, created especially for him. This paradise appears as an oasis in the Oriental desert, although its name is linked by some scholars to the Sumerian word *edin,* for which several Assyrologists read "plain" or "countryside." The word *paradeisos* adopted by the Greek Bible denotes the pleasure gardens and royal hunting lands of Iran and Asia Minor. For the Greek reader the word suggests a garden of fruits and fruit trees. Certainly the biblical garden is the archetype of all regions of luxuriant vegetation (*Gn.* 13:10, *Is.* 51:3, *Ez.* 31:8).

The text of *Genesis* 2:10–14, which mentions the four rivers flowing out of Eden, is clearly intended to locate the garden symbolically at the center of the cosmos; a story in Mesopotamian mythology also places a divine residence at the source of rivers. The biblical text seeks to establish a relationship between a divine garden and a human earth, thereby emphasizing the marvelous fertility of humanity's first home. The garden of Eden is also characterized by the presence of two special trees—the tree of life and the tree of the knowledge of good and evil (*Gn.* 2:16–17). The tree of life is part of a larger Mesopotamian group of symbols, known through a number of texts. The tree of the knowledge of good and evil, however, has no parallel in any other ancient text; it is specific to the Yahvistic story of creation and stresses the relationship between life and obedience to God.

Adam and Eve enjoy a life of paradise in the garden, living together in harmony and at peace with the animals, as in Mesopotamian myths of the golden age. Both the Yahvistic and the sacerdotal text stress the privileged situation of humans in Eden—their intimacy with God, their hope of immortality, suggested by the tree of life—and evoke the harmony that exists there, seen in humanity's relations with the rest of creation and its life of ease. The presence in Eden of the tree of the knowledge of good and evil shows that obedience to God is essential to maintaining this privileged situation. The biblical text emphasizes considerations that are absent in all other myths of the golden age—considerations of freedom, of moral choice in the face of good and evil. Through a choice of its own, humanity decides its standing before God and at the same time the direction of its destiny.

The testing of humanity in Eden is related to the problem of human freedom. In mythical language, *Genesis* 2–3 describes the situation of humans in the world and in the face of God. The garden of Eden is the place where humanity lives in easy familiarity with God, but it is also the symbolic microcosm where its has been given mastery, and where it enjoys the free use of all other created things; thus the conquest and humanization of the world will become the condition of its vocation. The prohibition against eating from the tree of knowledge belongs to another order, for it deals with the basic human appreciation of the value of earthly things and of the human situation before God (*Gn.* 3:5–6). It will bring about humankind's fall from paradise.

The story of Eden stresses the primordial couple's disobedience to God and their expulsion from the garden, and it emphasizes that they lost the privileged status of Eden for themselves and for their descendants. Thus, their sin is presented as the prototype of that part of human sin that is universal. The essence of hubris is the desire to be like God; when this desire becomes action, the fall takes place and ushers in the woes of humankind. The Yahvistic document asserts both directly and symbolically that human experience of evil had an absolute beginning, a beginning that coincides with the beginning of human history, the history of freedom. Although the first exercise of that freedom resulted in disaster, through it humanity inaugurated the drama of choice that gives particular significance to human life and its relationship to God. Subsequent biblical books and apocryphal texts repeatedly return to these lessons of the fall (*Ez.* 28; *Dt.* 30:15–20; *Prv.* 3:2, 3:22, 6:15, 10:25; *Sir.* 37:3; *Wis.* 1:13–14, 10:1–2).

The editors of chapters 4–11 of *Genesis* saw in the fall of humanity in Eden not only the loss of paradise and the transformation of the human condition but also the source of a whole series of evils that subsequently beset humankind. Thus, at each stage in the rise of civilization and the institutionalization of the social developments that formed human lives in antiquity, the biblical text notes humanity's corruption, variously described as fratricidal war, polygamy, desert warfare, or the division of nations and tongues (*Gn.* 4:8, 4:19, 4:23–24, 11:5–9). Since the fall, evil is born in the hearts of humans and always remains at the heart of history, an inevitable force in human affairs.

The most important biblical event having the characteristics of a universal fall is the flood (*Gn.* 6:5–8:14). The story of Noah in the Bible reinforces elements of the *Epic of Gilgamesh,* but its editors have taken over and reinterpreted Mesopotamian themes in order to transform them into an episode in sacred history and to show the progressive degeneration of humanity that justifies the flood. In both its Yahvistic and its sacerdotal forms, the biblical story is very different from the Mesopotamian one. The latter sees in the flood simply the decree of gods annoyed with a despised humanity. In the Bible, the memory of the flood serves as the prototype of God's judgment against a sinful humankind; the human situation as a responsible being is stressed, and humanity is not abandoned to the blows of blind destiny. In this myth of the universal fall, a new alliance is foreseen, in which *Urzeit* leads to *Endzeit.*

Genesis 6:1–4 contains the story of the *benei Elohim* who take the daughters of humans as wives. This unusual text presupposes an oral tradition and possibly other written texts. It appears as a preface to the flood and may be interpreted as further evidence of the sins that will provoke the flood, but it is also the starting point for numerous speculations about the fall of the angels. The rabbinical interpretation has seen in the *benei Elohim,* "the sons of God," angels who sinned with the daughters of humans and were for that reason shut up in the depths of the earth; at the last judgment, they will be thrown into the fire.

Christianity. Allusions to humanity's fall appear throughout the New Testament, although the Gospels speak of it only in *Matthew* 19:4–6, *Mark* 10:6–8, and *John* 3:5 and 8:41–44. It was Paul who was especially interested in the relationship between the fall and sin. In chapters 1–3 of *Romans,* he asserts that no one can escape the domination of sin, and in chapter 7 he gives a lengthy description of the human condition in the earthly paradise, where as yet humans knew neither covetousness nor death, and contrasts this with the actual condition to which they have been reduced by sin and death. He asserts that the actual human condition comes from the first sin, the sin of Adam and Eve in the earthly paradise (*Rom.* 7:13–15); and in *1 Corinthians* 15:21–22, he opposes the first Adam, the author of death, to Christ, the second Adam, the author of life. In general, Paul sees in the story of Eden not only humanity's hereditary punishment of suffering and death but also its hereditary fallen state, a state of sin transmitted to all humankind.

Islam. The Qur'ān demonstrates the importance Islam attaches to the idea of God the creator, the all-powerful. God is the creator (*al-khāliq*), the creator par excellence (*al-khallāq*); all things are created by virtue of the divine resolution that precedes their appearance. The Qur'ān describes a God who creates through his word, a word that is creative, eternal, and ever present (*sūrahs* 11:9 and 41:8–11).

God created humankind and called it *khalīfah,* vicar or viceroy (2:28). Adam, *khalīfat Allāh,* vicar of a God who had placed him at the center of the world, is the preeminent creature, although, made of mud and clay, it owes everything to God (15:26). Many verses of the Qur'ān stress the preeminent dignity of humanity; even the angels must bow down before humankind (2:32), and when the evil angel Iblīs refuses to do so, God damns him and Iblīs falls, followed by other angels (15:26–35, 17:63–67). The continuing work of creation is also stressed by the Qurʾān; because every person is made by God, the activity of God the creator is permanent.

God put Adam and his wife in the midst of a garden where they could take fruit from the trees, but he forbade them to approach one tree, under pain of falling among sinners (2:33). But the demon made Adam and his wife sin by eating fruit from that tree and thereby caused their expulsion from the place where God had placed them. God said to them, "Leave the garden. You are now enemies one of another, and on earth you will have only brief enjoyment, and brief lives" (2:34). The episodes in the Qurʾān concerning Adam are reminiscent of *Genesis:* his creation out of earth, his title of vicar, his temptation, fall, and expulsion from paradise. Only the episode of Iblīs is not found in the Bible.

Sūrah 7 mentions the story of the fall and punishment (7:21–24). Here it is the demon who suggests that humans break the divine prohibition in order to obtain immortality. After Adam has sinned, God declares that henceforth men born of the first couple will be enemies one of another (2:34, 7:23, 20:21), and the Qurʾān relates the first fratricidal struggle, between two unnamed sons of Adam whom later Muslim authors call Qābīl and Hābīl.

Noah appears in the Qurʾān as a great prophet who opposes unbelievers (11:27–36, 23:23–26). He receives from God the command to build an ark in order to survive the flood; but, contrary to *Genesis,* which stresses the universal character of the flood, the Qurʾān appears to restrict divine punishment to Noah's own people, who had become impious. The Qurʾān treats their punishment as both a warning and a sign.

CONCLUSION. Reflection on the fall is a constant preoccupation of *homo religiosus.* In his "nostalgia for beginnings," he turns instinctively toward a primordial, sacred history, where he finds a golden age that corresponds to what humankind must have been in the beginning. He sees that humanity's present situation no longer corresponds to that of the golden age, and he strives to explain the accident that has taken place and the consequences of that accident, of that break with primordial harmony.

This article has sought to present the theme of the fall as it appears in the religious thought of the greater part of humankind, although it has been necessary to limit the discussion of myths of the fall to those that describe the fall in relation to a supposed golden age—an age that has haunted human memory—and that locates humanity's fall and its present condition between *Urzeit* and *Endzeit.* Most of this article's attention was given to myths of the human fall; but, when pertinent, myths of a cosmic fall, or of the fall of lesser deities, have also been considered.

Nostalgia for the beginning of things is clearly a permanent feature of humankind's collective memory, and representation of a golden age provides the archetype through which that nostalgia is repeatedly expressed. As can be seen by the study of various peoples and cultures, peoples everywhere sought to explain their present condition through the contrast it provides to their supposed primordial condition; in light of that contrast, they have also classified and interpreted their mythical, historical, and symbolic heritage and related these to sacred history.

SEE ALSO Ages of the World; Death; Evil; Flood, The; Gardens; Golden Age; Paradise.

BIBLIOGRAPHY

Baumann, Hermann. *Schöpfung und Urzeit des Menschen im Mythos der afrikanischen Völker.* Berlin, 1936.

Boyce, Mary. *A History of Zoroastrianism,* vol. 1. Leiden, 1975.

Dexinger, Ferdinand. *Sturz der Göttersöhne oder Engel vor der Sintflut.* Vienna, 1966.

Eliade, Mircea. *Patterns in Comparative Religion.* New York, 1958.

Eliade, Mircea. "Nostalgia for Paradise in the Primitive Traditions." In his *Myths, Dreams and Mysteries.* New York, 1960.

Feldmann, Joseph. *Paradies und Sündenfall.* Münster, 1913.

Frazer, James G. *Folklore in the Old Testament.* 3 vols. London, 1919.

Jonas, Hans. *The Gnostic Religion.* 2d rev. ed. Boston, 1963.

Kákosy, L. "Ideas about the Fallen State of the World in Egyptian Religion: Decline of the Golden Age." *Acta Orientalia* (Budapest) 17 (1964): 205–216.

Kramer, Samuel Noah. *History Begins at Sumer* (1957). 3d ed. Philadelphia, 1981.

Lambert, W. G., and A. R. Millard. *Atra-Hasis: The Babylonian Story of the Flood.* Oxford, 1968.

Otto, Eberhard. "Das goldene Zeitalter in einem aegyptischen Text." In his *Religions en Egypte hellénistique et romaine.* Paris, 1969.

Ricoeur, Paul. *La symbolique du mal.* 2 vols. Paris, 1960. Translated as *The Symbolism of Evil* (Boston, 1967).

Söderblom, Nathan. *La vie future d'apres le mazdéisme à la lumière des croyances parallèles dans les autres religions.* Paris, 1901.

Thomas, Louis-Vincent. *La mort africaine.* Paris, 1982.

Widengren, Geo. *Les religions de l'Iran.* Paris, 1968.

New Sources

Blocher, Henri. *Original Sin: Illuminating the Riddle.* New Studies in Biblical Theology. Downers Grove, Ill., 2001.

Clatworthy, Jonathan. "Let the Fall Down: The Environmental Implications of the Doctrine of the Fall." *Ecotheology* 4 (January 1998): 27–35.

Korsmeyer, Jerry. *Evolution and Eden: Balancing Original Sin and Contemporary Science.* New York, 1998.

Linzey, Andrew. "Unfinished Creation: The Moral and Theological Significance of the Fall." *Ecotheology* 4 (January 1998): 20–27.

Minois, Georges. *Les origines du mal: une histroie du péché originel.* Paris, 2002.

Norman, Andrew. "Regress and the Doctrine of Epistemic Original Sin." *Philosophy Quarterly* 47 (October 1997): 477–495.

Rees, G. "The Anxiety of Inheritance: Reinhold Niebuhr and the Literal Truth of Original Sin." *Journal of Religious Ethics* 31 (spring 2003): 75–100.

Suchocki, Marjorie. *The Fall to Violence: Original Sin in Relational Theology.* New York, 1994.

Wetzel, James. "Moral Personality, Perversity, and Original Sin." *Journal of Religious Ethics* 23 (spring 1995): 3–26.

Williams, Patricia. *Doing without Adam and Eve: Sociobiology and Original Sin.* Minneapolis, 2001.

JULIEN RIES (1987)
Translated from French by Jeffrey Haight and Annie S. Mahler
Revised Bibliography

FALSAFAH. The term *falsafah* is the Arabized loan word from the Greek *philosophia,* "love of wisdom," and hence in its general sense simply means "philosophy." It is, however, also used (as it will be in this account) in a more specific sense as an abbreviation of the expression *al-falsafah al-islāmīyah,* "Islamic philosophy." Similarly, the general Arabic word for "philosophers," *falāsifah* (sg., *faylasūf),* is used more specifically as an abbreviation for the expression *al-falāsifah al-islāmīyūn,* "the Islamic philosophers."

Because for many Muslims, past and present, *falsafah* remains at best doctrinally suspect, the sense in which it will be referred to here as "Islamic" requires clarification. This term, as applied to *falsafah* and *falāsifah,* will first of all be used in a broad cultural sense, for *falsafah* was developed within an Islamic cultural milieu by men whose culture was Islamic. This cultural use of the term *Islamic* is implicit in medieval Arabic usage. Thus, for example, one famous intellectual who condemned some of the *falāsifah* as "infidels" nonetheless referred to them as "Islamic," while another included among the Islamic philosophers the Christians of Baghdad who wrote in Arabic. This latter example calls for a narrowing of the sense in which *Islamic* will be used, however, for in addition to being "Islamic" in the cultural sense, the *falāsifah* were "Islamic" in that they regarded themselves as Muslims, claiming that their conceptions of God and the world were consistent with the Qur'anic view. Most of them attempted to demonstrate the harmony between their respective philosophies and Islamic revelation, and whether such attempts proved convincing or not, they represent a characteristic feature of *falsafah.*

It should be stressed that while the *falāsifah* were theists, they were not theologians. For a proper understanding of *falsafah,* it must be distinguished from *kalām,* Islamic speculative theology. Both disciplines used reason in formulating their respective conceptions of God and his creation, but they differed in approach and motivation. The starting point of *kalām* was revelation. Reason was used in defending the revealed word and in interpreting the natural order in conformity with a Qur'anic view of creation. With *falsafah,* the starting point was reason; the motivation, the quest after "the true nature of things." The *falāsifah* maintained that this quest led them to a demonstrative proof of the existence of a first cause of the universe, which they claimed was identical with the God of the Qur'ān—a claim contested by the Islamic theologians, particularly those who followed the school of *kalām* of al-Ash'arī (d. 935). At issue between *falsafah* and *kalām* was not the question of God's existence; rather, the question was the nature of God.

Another difference between them was historical. *Kalām* antedated *falsafah*; its beginnings are traceable to the period of the Umayyad caliphate (AH 41–132/661–750 CE) and more definitely, to the second half of the eighth century. Moreover, it arose out of religious and political conflicts within Islam. Although subject to foreign influences, particularly Greek thought, *kalām*'s modes of argument and perspectives remained to a great extent indigenous. *Falsafah,* on the other hand, was the direct result of a concerted effort to translate Greek science and philosophy into Arabic beginning early in the ninth century. The first Islamic philosopher, al-Kindī, it should be noted, died around 870.

Falsafah was thus rooted in Greek philosophy, or more accurately, Greek philosophy in its translated form. The *falāsifah* regarded themselves not only as guardians of the truths arrived at by the ancient Greek philosophers but also as participants in a continuous quest after truth: As al-Kindī expressed it, the attainment of truth is difficult and requires the cooperative efforts of generations past and present. Thus, the *falāsifah* did not simply accept ideas they received through the translations. They criticized, selected, and rejected; they made distinctions, refined and remolded concepts to formulate their own philosophies. But the conceptual building blocks, so to speak, of these philosophies remained Greek.

THE TRANSLATION MOVEMENT. Although there are indications that some translations of Greek scientific works were made in the period of the Umayyad caliphate, the translation movement properly speaking took place during the caliphate of the Abbasids, who came to power in 750. Translations were undertaken sporadically just after the establishment of Abbasid rule but flourished in the ninth and tenth centuries. The ruler who gave this movement its real impetus was the caliph al-Ma'mūn, who ruled from 813 to 833, and his active sponsorship of the translation of Greek philosophy and science into Arabic was continued by his successors and by families attached to the caliphal court. The *Bayt al-Ḥikmah* (House of Wisdom), a center for scientific activity and translations that al-Ma'mūn built in Baghdad, symbolized this Abbasid sponsorship of the translation movement.

The motives for this concern with translations were varied. There were practical considerations, such as the need for medical and astronomical knowledge. There was also the probable motive of prestige: The Byzantines could boast of the Greek philosophical and scientific tradition, and the Abbasids likewise wanted to avail themselves of the intellectual treasures of the ancients. This was also a period of intellectual ferment and genuine interest in learning, and scholars were available to undertake the task of translation. In particular, within the Abbasid realm and close to the heart of their empire were the Syriac-speaking people, a culture within a culture who were themselves partly Hellenized. The utilization of this rich intellectual resource by the intelligent leaders of the Islamic state seemed natural.

Apart from the Syriac-speaking scholars, who were mostly Nestorian and Jacobite Christians, there were scholars in the north Syrian city of Harran who also undertook translations. The Harranians adhered to the Sabian sect, a religion that included star worship but also had a Greek philosophical base. Among the Christian scholars, there were two traditions of scholarship. One was the tradition of the medical and philosophical school of Alexandria; members of this school seem to have moved in the Umayyad period to Antioch and then in the Abbasid period to Harran and finally to Baghdad. The other tradition was that of the medical school and hospital of the Nestorians of Jundīshāpūr in Persia. Originally a camp for Roman captives built in the third century CE by the Sasanid emperor Shāpūr I, Jundīshāpūr became a refuge for Nestorians after the deposition of their patriarch, Nestorius, at the Council of Ephesus in 431. The school flourished in Sasanid times, and although little is known about it in the Umayyad period, it became prominent under the Abbasids as well; from 765 to 870, its Bakhtīshūʿ family provided court physicians for the caliphs.

Among the early translators, mention must be made of Yaḥyā ibn al-Biṭrīq (d. 830?); Astat (Eustathius), about whom very little is known, but who made a translation of Aristotle's *Metaphysics,* a work known to al-Kindī; and Ibn Naʿīmah al-Ḥimṣī (d. 835), who translated the very influential if apocryphal *Theology of Aristotle.* The best-known and most influential of the translators was the Nestorian physician and scholar Ḥunayn ibn Isḥāq (d. 873), who was known for his translations of medical works but who was responsible for translating logical and philosophical treatises as well. Unlike earlier and some later scholars, Ḥunayn knew Greek; he followed a system of collating Greek manuscripts before translating and undertook revision of earlier translations from the Syriac. He worked with a team of other translators, who included his son Isḥāq, his nephew Ḥubaysh, and ʿIsā ibn Yaḥyā. Among the Harranians the most important translator was Thābit ibn Qurrah (d. 901), who also wrote a commentary on Aristotle's *Physics.* Later translators included Qusṭā ibn Lūqā (d. 912?), also noted for his treatise *The Difference between Soul and Spirit,* Abū ʿUthmān Saʿīd al-Dimashqī (d. 900), the logician Abū Bishr Mattā (d. 940), Yaḥyā ibn ʿAdī (d. 974), Ibn Zurʿah (d. 1008), and Ibn al-Khammār (d. 1020).

The three ancient philosophers who conditioned the rise and development of *falsafah* were Plato, Aristotle, and Plotinus. As with medieval western Europe, Aristotle was the most authoritative figure; his influence lay in the realms of logic, physics, and metaphysics. Plato, whose thought was known largely through the expositions of others, particularly the translated works of the physician Galen, had his greatest influence on the political philosophy of the *falāsifah.* Plotinus was likewise known indirectly, through two main works, the Neoplatonic *Theology of Aristotle,* a paraphrase of books 4, 5, and 6 of the *Enneads,* and the work based on Proclus known in Arabic as *Fī maḥḍ al-khayr* (On the pure good), which was translated into medieval Latin as the *Liber de causis.*

A substantial body of commentary, particularly on Aristotle, was also translated. Thus such commentators as Themistius, Simplicius, and Alexander of Aphrodisias were influential in the development of *falsafah.* There was knowledge of pre-Socratic philosophy and late Stoic philosophy and logic, and the translations also included a body of medical works, particularly those of Galen, and mathematical and scientific works such as Euclid's *Elements* and Ptolemy's *Almagest.*

AL-KINDĪ AND AL-RĀZĪ. The philosophical venture in medieval Islam was pioneered in different ways by two remarkable thinkers, Abū Yūsuf Yaʿqūb al-Kindī and the physician-philosopher Abū Bakr al-Rāzī (d. 926). Their philosophies, particularly in their doctrines on the world's creation and the nature of the Creator, differed radically from the thought of the major philosophers who succeeded them. As *falāsifah,* they were atypical; moreover, they differed radically from each other.

Ironically, al-Kindī was atypical because his philosophy conformed with fundamental, generally accepted Muslim beliefs. Thus he argued vigorously and at great length to prove that the world was created ex nihilo and at a finite moment of time in the past relative to the present. He also upheld the doctrine of bodily resurrection. At the same time, his writings were thoroughly philosophical in approach and spirit. "We must not," he insisted, "be ashamed of deeming truth good and of acquiring truth from wherever it comes, even if it comes from races remote from us and nations different from us" (*Rāsa'il al-Kindī al-falsafīyah,* ed. M. A. A. Abū Rīdah, Cairo, 1950, p. 103). Al-Kindī was born around the year 800 in Kufa. Little is known about his education except that he was associated with Christian translators and the caliphs who sponsored the translation movement. He alights on the philosophical scene quite unexpectedly, yet with full confidence, betraying none of the hesitancy of the novice. Like the Islamic philosophers who succeeded him, he was also a physician and a scientist, and the range of his learning was encyclopedic.

Of his numerous writings, only a few treatises, philosophical and scientific, have survived. Fortunately, these include the very important work *On First Philosophy,* a relatively long treatise consisting of four chapters. In the first, al-Kindī offers an introduction to philosophy, which he defines as "knowledge of things in their true nature, to the extent of man's capability." The chapter is also a justification and promotion of its pursuit: Philosophy's ultimate concern, he argues, is the quest after "the True One," the supreme good, the cause of all things.

The chapters that follow constitute a remarkable piece of vigorous, sustained argument. Most of the second chapter is devoted to proving the creation of the world ex nihilo at a distant but finite past. The argument rests on a basic premise, the impossibility of an infinite magnitude. Al-Kindī begins by arguing that an infinite body is impossible. If one supposes the existence of such a body, he maintains, then theoretically it is possible to remove from it a finite part. What remains would also be infinite, but less than the original infinite by the amount of the finite body removed. The consequence would then be the existence of two unequal infinities, amounting, for al-Kindī, to a contradiction. But if a body must be finite, he then tries to show, time and motion must also be finite. The temporal existence of the world could not then go back to infinity; it must have a temporal beginning. Moreover, he argues, creation in time cannot simply mean that a static world (and hence a world outside time) was put into motion at some past finite moment relative to the present. A body by definition, he argues, must be in motion; a static world is a contradiction in terms. Hence not only did the world begin at a finite moment in the past, but it came into being out of nothing.

Having proved the doctrine of creation ex nihilo to his own satisfaction, al-Kindī then offers a proof for the existence of God, "the True One," and an investigation of the nature of this oneness. The Neoplatonic influences on this part of the treatise are very manifest, particularly in al-Kindī's exposition of the nature of divine oneness. The proof for God's existence is a causal one, based, however, on the phenomenon of plurality and unity in the world. The proof, given in a short version and a lengthy one, is quite elaborate. The fundamental point al-Kindī makes is that the unity that one experiences in things and that is the cause of plurality does not belong essentially to things; it is a derivative, accidental unity. He then argues that it must derive ultimately from a being who is essentially one and the only being who is essentially one. This is the True One who bestows accidental unities on things. The giver of this unity is the giver of existence.

In this and other treatises, al-Kindī also makes statements about prophecy and the nature of revelation. These are not detailed statements, but the ones concerning prophecy are suggestive of the kind of developed theories encountered later on in the thought of al-Fārābī and Ibn Sīnā (Avicenna). Thus, anticipating Ibn Sīnā, al-Kindī argues that prophetic knowledge is received "instantaneously," requiring neither intellectual exertion on the part of the prophet nor the disciplines of mathematics and logic. In conformity with generally accepted Islamic belief, al-Kindī maintains that the inimitability of the Qur'ān lies in the excellence of its literary expression, in the way it conveys divine truths directly and succinctly.

Although al-Kindī had followers, notably al-Sarakhsī (d. 899), properly speaking it cannot be said that he founded a school of philosophical thought. The same is true of the major *faylasūf* to succeed him, al-Rāzī. Abū Bakr Zakarīyā' al-Rāzī (Rhazes), one of the foremost physicians of medieval times, was born in 865 in the Persian town of Rayy, and he practiced medicine there as well as in Baghdad. Very few of his philosophical works have survived, and consequently, much of his philosophical thought has to be reconstructed from medieval Islamic accounts that are, for the most part, highly critical of his ideas.

In his cosmogony, al-Rāzī was greatly influenced by Plato's *Timaeus*. The world, he holds, was created at a finite moment in time, but not out of nothing. As with Plato, creation for al-Rāzī means the imposing of order on disorder. He subscribes to the doctrine of the five eternal principles: atomic matter, space, time, the world soul, and the Creator. The atoms, flitting about in disorder, are given order by God at a moment in time. The now-organized atoms allow the world soul to join matter and to become individuated by it, forming individual living beings. Just as this ordering of the atoms, that is, creation, came about at a finite moment of time in the past, the order will cease at a finite moment of time in the future when the five eternal principles revert to their original state. Al-Rāzī offers discussions of atomic matter, absolute space, and absolute time that are scientific in spirit and approach. But when it comes to explaining ultimates, namely, the reason for the world's creation, he resorts to myth, and his philosophy is noted for its myth of creation.

For al-Rāzī, creation poses two related questions: Why is it that the world was created at one particular moment of time and not at any other, and why was the world created at all? In answering the first, al-Rāzī holds that it is precisely because all the moments of time are similar that God's choice of one moment rather than another was utterly free. If the moments of time were not similar, then his choice of one moment rather than another would have been determined by "a giver of preponderance" (*murajjiḥ*) outside him. Hence it is because the Creator's will is utterly free that he arbitrarily chooses one moment for his creation to take place. It is in his answer to the second question that al-Rāzī provides his famous myth.

The world soul became infatuated with matter and sought union with it. To achieve this union, the soul endeavored to give disorganized matter form. Matter, however, resisted this forming activity of the soul, leaving the latter in sorrow. God, being powerful and compassionate, then intervened to help the soul and introduced form, order to the material atoms; in other words, he created the world. In creating humankind, God endowed humans with reason, an emanation of his very essence, so that the soul would awake from its bodily slumber and seek a return to its original eternal existence. This, for al-Rāzī, is salvation. At some finite moment in the future, all people's souls, awakened by philosophy, will shun their bodies. The individual souls then will reunite with the eternal world soul, and the atoms will resume their chaotic state for eternity.

Salvation, as defined by al-Rāzī, is possible only through philosophy. He thus maintains that there is no need for prophets. All people are capable of pursuing truth through reason. The fact that many do not pursue this rational course is not due to inability, but to willful choice. He further argues that it would also be unjust for the Creator to favor either one individual or one nation with prophethood. The mistaken belief that God has favored individuals and nations with prophets has caused nothing but strife, so that, al-Rāzī maintains, for the most part wars are caused by religion. If to this is added that al-Rāzī also subscribed to a theory of the transmigration of souls, one can see why his ideas did not find favor within Islam. Nonetheless, he helped the fermentation of philosophical ideas, and the responses to his philosophy constitute a body of intense argument, philosophical and theological.

Apart from the intrinsic interest of their philosophies, both al-Kindī and al-Rāzī showed in their respective ways how philosophizing is possible within medieval Islam, and thus they prepared the ground for the flowering of *falsafah* in medieval Islam.

Al-Fārābī and Ibn Sīnā. In the tenth and early eleventh centuries, Islamic philosophical thought was dominated by two intellectual giants, al-Fārābī (d. 950) and Ibn Sīnā (d. 1037). Their philosophies have much in common, but remain quite distinct. Al-Fārābī, born shortly after 870 in Transoxania, studied and taught in Baghdad until 942. He studied logic with the Nestorian logician Yuḥannā ibn Haylān (d. 910) and was associated with Abū Bishr Mattā ibn Yūnus, who was another renowned Nestorian logician. He also studied Arabic grammar with Ibn al-Sarrāj (d. 929), a leading grammarian of the period. In 942, for reasons not fully known, he left Baghdad for Syria, and he seems to have lived the remaining years of his life in relative seclusion in Damascus, where he died.

The foremost logician of his time, al-Fārābī wrote commentaries on Aristotle's *Organon* and on other works of Aristotle and other Greek writers. He was medieval Islam's greatest musical theorist and musicologist and is reputed to have been a skilled instrumentalist. He developed a Neoplatonic emanative scheme that greatly influenced the development of emanative systems by his Islamic successors. But perhaps above all else, he was the founder of a Platonic theory of the state that was adopted (with variations) by the major *falāsifah* who succeeded him. It should be noted, however, that his philosophical writings pose problems of dating and raise the question of whether they always reflect his real views.

For al-Fārābī, the world is an eternal emanation from God, forming a hierarchically ordered series of existents with the closest to him being the highest in rank. This highest existent is a first intelligence, overflowing directly from God. From it the emanative process continues in the form of dyads: The intelligence undergoes two acts of cognition, an act of knowing God and an act of self-knowledge, from which in turn proceed two existents, a second intelligence and a body—the outermost body of the universe. The second intelligence undergoes a similar act of knowing God and knowing itself, resulting in the emanation of a third intelligence and the sphere of the fixed stars. Successive intelligences repeat this cognitive process, causing the existence of the spheres of the planets, the sun, the moon, and finally, from the last of the intelligences, the Active Intellect, which is this world, the world of generation and corruption.

This entire cosmic order is rational and harmonious, with each sphere governed by an intelligence. Humanity in the world of generation and corruption, endowed with reason and free will, must actualize its potentialities and attain the highest good, happiness. This is achieved when in their way of life people emulate the rational cosmic order, but they can only do this in the society of others. Hence they must strive to form a society that is itself in tune with the rational cosmic order, a hierarchical society ruled by reason, where the various ranks actualize their potentialities in harmony.

In order to achieve this ideal political order, which al-Fārābī refers to as "virtuous," its first ruler must be both a philosopher and a prophet, an individual who receives the revealed law. Because this law is received from the Active Intellect in the form of images that symbolize universal philosophical knowledge or represent particular examples of it, revelation is the "imitation" of philosophy, a copy of it in images and symbols that the nonphilosopher can understand. Revelation and philosophy are thus in total harmony. Another necessary condition for achieving a virtuous political regime, however, is that the philosopher-ruler must be endowed with exceptional practical powers, for it is necessary to persuade, lead, and educate a majority of citizens incapable of philosophical understanding. In fact, the philosopher-ruler must not address the nonphilosophical majority in philosophical language.

Al-Fārābī's political philosophy is comprehensive, detailed, and subtle. It includes, for example, detailed discussion of the existence of nonvirtuous states, the majority of which he characterizes as "ignorant" because they are led by people who are ignorant of the true nature of happiness. While his view is certainly Platonic in its essentials, one meets in al-Fārābī a tendency toward universalism that is less perceptible in Plato. Thus al-Fārābī does not speak only of the virtuous "city" but also of a desirable nation consisting of virtuous "cities" and of a desirable world consisting of virtuous "nations." He also maintains that inasmuch as people in different parts of the world differ in language and in their symbols, it is quite possible that the differences among religions are merely differences in symbols, not in what is being symbolized.

It was on the foundations laid by al-Fārābī in logic, metaphysics, and political theory that his successor, the renowned Ibn Sīnā, built his imposing philosophical system. Born in 980 near Bukhara and largely self-taught, Ibn Sīnā was one of medieval Islam's leading physicians, an astronomer, and a scientist. He held positions as court physician, sometimes as vizier as well, in various Persian principalities until his death in 1037.

Of his numerous writings, mostly in Arabic, but some in Persian, two in particular were very influential in Europe, namely, the encyclopedic *Al-qānūn fī al-ṭibb* (Canon of medicine) and his major philosophical work, the voluminous *Al-shifāʾ* (Healing). His writings include short mystical narratives and treatises where the language of symbolism is used. This mysticism, encountered in his writings, is not inconsistent with his "rationalism." The mystic's journey to God is the journey of the rational soul to the ultimate source of all reason. God, for Ibn Sīnā, is pure mind *(ʿaql maḥḍ).*

Ibn Sīnā's philosophical system is "rationalist." He maintains that in addition to the self-evident first principles of logic, not dependent on one's sense perception of the external world, there are self-evident intuitive concepts, also not dependent on sense experience. These intuitive concepts include the "existent," the "thing," and the "necessary," the last with its correlates, the "possible" and the "impossible." A rational consideration of these concepts is sufficient to yield a demonstration of God's existence. In itself, an "existent" is either necessary or only possible. If it is necessary in itself, Ibn Sīnā then tries to show, it must be the only such existent, devoid of multiplicity and uncaused. If it is only possible in itself, he then argues, it must be necessitated by another existent, the latter by yet another, and so on, forming a chain that must be finite, having as its beginning the existent necessary in itself. Hence each alternative affirms the existent necessary in itself, which is God.

But what does it mean to say that every existent other than God is in itself only possible? This is the distinction on which Ibn Sīnā's philosophy rests, the distinction between the quiddity or essence of the possible and its existence. From what a thing is, one cannot infer that it exists, because existence is not included in the definition of the possible existent. The quiddity considered in itself excludes not only existence, but unity and plurality, particularity and universality. From this concept of the quiddity considered in itself, Ibn Sīnā develops a theory of universals (where universality is something added to the quiddity as such) that is of intrinsic philosophical interest and one that had great influence on medieval Latin thought.

Although the existent, other than God, is in itself only possible, it is necessitated by another. Ibn Sīnā uses this concept of the possible in itself but necessary through another to transform al-Fārābī's dyadic emanative scheme into a triadic system. God, the existent necessary in himself, undergoes an eternal act of self-knowledge that necessitates the existence of a first intelligence, an existent in itself only possible, but necessary through another. This intelligence then undergoes three acts of cognition: knowledge of God, knowledge of itself as a necessitated being, and knowledge of itself as a possible being. These three acts produce three other existents respectively: another intelligence, a soul, and a body, the outermost body of the universe. This process is repeated by each successive intellect, giving existence to the various heavenly spheres, each with its soul and intelligence, until from the last of the celestial intelligences, the Active Intellect, the world of generation and corruption emanates.

The human rational soul, an emanation from the Active Intellect, is immaterial, becomes individuated when it joins the body, and retains its individuality as an immortal soul when it separates from the body after death. Good souls, untarnished by having succumbed in their earthly existence to animal passions, live an eternal life of bliss contemplating the celestial intelligences and God; bad souls live an eternal life of misery, being deprived from such contemplation yet forever seeking it. All theoretical knowledge is received from the Active Intellect. This knowledge consists of primary intelligibles, which are the self-evident logical truths and primitive concepts received by all people without the need of experience and learning. It also consists of the secondary intelligibles (received only by those capable of abstract thought), namely, deductions from the primary intelligible as well as more complex concepts. Normally the reception of these intelligibles from the Active Intellect requires preparatory activities of the soul such as sensation, memory, imagination, and cogitation and the learning processes associated with them. Only the prophets do not require these preparatory activities of the soul; they receive all or most of the secondary intelligibles directly and instantaneously, and this theoretical knowledge is then translated through the prophet's imaginative faculty into symbols and images that the nonphilosopher can understand. These constitute the revealed word, which is in total harmony with philosophy, and here Ibn Sīnā embraces al-Fārābī's doctrine that religion is the "imitation" of philosophy.

Ibn Sīnā thus believes in the oneness of God, the prophethood of Muḥammad, and the individual immortality of the soul. His philosophical interpretations of these beliefs, however, were found unacceptable by his chief critic, al-Ghazālī.

AL-GHAZĀLĪ'S CRITIQUE OF THE FALĀSIFAH. *Falsafah,* as represented by al-Fārābī and Ibn Sīnā, received its most severe rational criticism at the hands of Islam's great religious thinker, the lawyer, Ashʿarī theologian, and mystic Abū Ḥāmid al-Ghazālī (d. 1111). Tension between *kalām* and *falsafah* had existed prior to al-Ghazālī's critique of the *falāsifah,* although it was expressed in reciprocal, but on the whole, muted criticism. Underlying this tension were differences in starting point and ethos, which crystallized in irreconcilable metaphysical outlooks.

Kalām in its Ashʿarī form was atomic in its theory of matter and occasionalist in its interpretation of causal sequences. Accordingly, the temporal and transient conglomerates of atoms forming the physical world were not seen to interact causally with each other in reality. Causal efficacy resided with God; what appear as natural causes and effects are in reality concomitant events created directly by God. The uniform order of nature has no intrinsic necessity but is arbitrarily decreed by the divine will; the divine act is not the outcome of any necessity within the divine nature. Causal action proceeds only from a living, willing, powerful agent, not as the necessary consequence of an existent's nature or essence. By contrast, al-Fārābī and Ibn Sīnā embraced the Aristotelian theory of matter as potentially infinitely divisible. Moreover, Ibn Sīnā maintains quite explicitly that the world proceeds from God as the necessitated effect of God, the supreme cause of all other existents, and this doctrine seems implicit in al-Fārābī's emanative scheme as well. God, in his essence an eternally active, changeless cause, necessarily produces an eternal effect—the world.

It is the conflict between these two worldviews that al-Ghazālī makes explicit in his attack on philosophy. Between 1091 and 1095, while teaching Islamic law in Baghdad, he made a systematic study of *falsafah,* particularly that of Ibn Sīnā. It should be emphasized that al-Ghazālī was greatly impressed by Ibn Sīnā's logic and wrote a number of works explaining this logic to his fellow theologians and lawyers, urging them to adopt it. He considered this discipline doctrinally neutral, a mere tool of knowledge, nothing more, a view that he expresses in one of the four introductions to his incisive critique of al-Fārābī and Ibn Sīnā, *Tahāfut al-falāsifah* (The incoherence of the philosophers). In these introductions he asserts that his concern is only with those philosophical theories that contravene religious principle and that he will show how, contrary to their own claims, the *falāsifah* have failed to demonstrate such theories. Moreover, he states that in this work he will not adopt any particular doctrinal position, his task being only to refute, and it is true that in the *Tahāfut,* for the sake of arguing against the *falāsifah,* al-Ghazālī sometimes adopts non-Ashʿarī views. It can be shown, however, that for the most part the premises underlying his attack on *falsafah* remain Ashʿarī.

Al-Ghazālī directs logical arguments against twenty philosophical theories, seventeen of which he regards as heretical innovations and three as utter Islamic unbelief. His method is to present the opponents' position clearly, object to it, raise possible objections to his objection, answer these, and so on, until he is satisfied that the theory in question has been refuted. Thus, before condemning these theories, he strives to show on rational grounds either that they have been unproven or that they are outright inconsistent. The three theories he condemns as utterly irreligious are those of the world's pre-eternity, Ibn Sīnā's theory that God knows the particulars in the world of generation and corruption only in a universal way (which means that he does not know every individual in the terrestrial world), and the doctrine of the soul's individual immortality, which denies bodily resurrection.

The most detailed of his discussions is the first, in which he attacks the theory of the world's pre-eternity. The main thrust of his attack is that such a theory is based on the unproven premise that God's acts proceed by necessity, a premise that, in effect, denies the divine attribute of will. Further, Ibn Sīnā's theory that God knows terrestrial individuals only in a universal way is unproven and contrary to the Qurʾanic pronouncements that God knows all things. The denial of bodily resurrection is also a denial of divine power, al-Ghazālī argues; bodily resurrection is not logically impossible, and what is logically possible is within God's power.

In the Seventeenth Discussion of the *Tahāfut,* al-Ghazālī argues for the possibility of certain kinds of miracles that are rejected as impossible by the *falāsifah,* who base their rejection on a theory of natural, necessary causal connection. Al-Ghazālī first tries to show that this theory is provable neither logically nor empirically—observation shows only concomitance, not necessary causal connection. In this he voices the Ashʿarī position that all change is caused directly by God and then suggests another possible causal theory, modifying the philosophers' theory to allow the possibility of the miracles the philosophers reject. In the *Tahāfut,* he declares that both these theories are possible, but in his *Iqtiṣād fī al-iʿtiqād* (Moderation in belief), the theological work that complements the *Tahāfut,* he reaffirms the Ashʿarī occasionalist position as the only true one.

Al-Ghazālī's attack on *falsafah* put it on the defensive, more so than it had hitherto been. At the same time, his attack made *falsafah* better known, because in order to refute the *falāsifah,* al-Ghazālī had to explain them to the nonphilosophers. In the same way, he legitimized and popularized the study of Ibn Sīnā's logic, and this had the effect of making Greek modes of thinking accessible to the more traditional Muslims. Finally, his criticism evoked replies, the most important of which came from Islamic Spain.

Falsafah in Islamic Spain. In the intellectual history of Islamic Spain, or al-Andalus, as the Arabs called it, *falsafah* was a latecomer. A lone Andalusian *faylasūf,* Ibn Masarrah (d. 931), appeared relatively early, but he was a shadowy figure who made no real philosophical impact. The first major Andalusian *faylasūf* was Ibn Bājjah (Avempace, d. 1138), and he was followed by two major thinkers, Ibn Ṭufayl (d. 1185) and Ibn Rushd (Averroës) (d. 1198), the greatest of the Andalusian *falāsifah.* The late flowering of *falsafah* in Spain was partly due to its geographic remoteness from the centers where the translation movement took place. Scientific and philosophical ideas, however, did travel from the Islamic East to Spain, stimulating a very significant scientific and philosophical movement.

A number of Ibn Bājjah's philosophical treatises have survived, including his *Tadbīr al-mutawaḥḥid* (Governance of the solitary), a major work in the tradition of al-Fārābī's metaphysical and political thought. It expands on a theme that appears in al-Fārābī almost in passing, namely that of the philosopher in a corrupt political state. Al-Fārābī had stated that such a philosopher should immigrate to a virtuous city, but that if no such city existed at the time, the philosopher would be "a stranger in the world, live poorly in it, death for him being better than life" (al-Fārābī, *Fuṣūl muntazaʿah,* ed. F. M. Najjār, Beirut, 1971, p. 95). Ibn Bājjah, however, argues that if no virtuous city exists at the time, the philosopher must be isolated from society, associating with others only to ensure survival, and must be devoted to inner intellectual and moral growth. Ibn Bājjah discusses psychology, epistemology, ethics, and metaphysics as he outlines the path the solitary philosopher must pursue to attain the highest good, the state of union with the Active Intellect. The philosopher's isolation, Ibn Bājjah admits, is "essentially" an evil, because one by nature is a social or political animal. Under the circumstances of the philosopher's having to live in a corrupt political regime, however, such isolation becomes "accidentally" a good.

Most of the writings of Ibn Bājjah's successor, Ibn Ṭufayl, physician, astronomer, and administrator at the court of the Almohad (al-Muwaḥḥid) dynasty then ruling al-Andalus, are lost. The notable exception is his masterly philosophical story, *Ḥayy ibn Yaqẓān,* written as an answer to a friend (real or fictitious) who asks Ibn Ṭufayl to divulge to him the secrets of Ibn Sīnā's mystical philosophy. In the introduction, which includes criticisms of al-Fārābī, al-Ghazālī, and Ibn Bājjah, Ibn Ṭufayl answers, in effect, that because the mystical experience is ineffable, he can only suggest to his friend the sort of thing its pursuit involves by narrating the story of Ḥayy.

Ḥayy ibn Yaqẓān (literally, "the living, son of the awake") is the name of the story's hero. In a lush equatorial island, uninhabited by humans, a baby boy, Ḥayy, comes on the scene. (The author gives two possible explanations for his being there.) A deer that had lost its young discovers the infant, suckles him, and rears him. Ḥayy then undergoes a process of self-education, learning how to clothe himself and fend for himself, but he continues to live with his mother, the deer. She eventually dies, and in his anguish, Ḥayy tries to bring her back to life by dissecting her, only to realize then that his real mother was spirit, not the material body that died. At this point his education takes a reflective turn: Through observation and rational thought, he discovers that every event must have a cause, that an actual infinity of causes is impossible, and hence that there must be one cause of all existents, which is God. He now seeks knowledge of God, and through contemplation, asceticism, and spiritual exercises he achieves his goal: direct experiences of the divine and of the emanative chain of being descending from him. Meanwhile, on a nearby island, a community ruled by the revealed law, which is a replica of philosophical truth, there are two brothers named Salāmān and Absāl (or Āsāl) who have different attitudes toward scriptural language. Salāmān and the rest of the community accept it literally, being incapable of comprehending its inner meaning. Absāl, on the other hand, pursues its inner meaning. Finding no one on the island who understands his quest, he seeks seclusion on a deserted island, which turns out to be Ḥayy's abode. The two meet. Absāl teaches Ḥayy language and discovers that Ḥayy is an unusual philosophical mystic who, unaided, has attained the highest truth, of which Absāl's own religion gives symbolic expression. For his part, Ḥayy recognizes Absāl's religion to be true and believes in its prophet. Both return to Absāl's island, where Ḥayy endeavors to teach some of its religious citizens the inner meaning of their religion. In this he fails because they are incapable of understanding him. He then adjures them to forget everything he has told them and to continue to take their religion literally. He and Absāl leave for their deserted island to live their mystical existence to the end of their days.

This story, amenable to a variety of interpretations, gives dramatic illustration of two of al-Fārābī's principles: that religion is the "imitation" of philosophy, and that the nonphilosopher ought not be addressed in philosophical language.

It was Ibn Ṭufayl who introduced Ibn Rushd to the Almohad court. Born in 1126 in Cordova, Ibn Rushd was the son and grandson of noted Islamic judges. Trained in medicine, philosophy, and Islamic law, this most Aristotelian of the *falāsifah* was a noted Islamic lawyer and, according to medieval accounts, an authority on Arabic poetry. In 1169 he was appointed judge in Seville and in 1171, chief judge of Cordova. He then became attached to the Almohad court, serving its philosophical ruler Abū Yaʿqūb until the latter's death in 1184, and then his son, al-Manṣūr, for another ten years. Largely because of the opposition of conservative religious scholars, as it seems, al-Manṣūr exiled Ibn Rushd in 1194 but reinstated him soon afterward. The philosopher died in the service of this monarch in 1198.

Ibn Rushd is noted in the history of philosophy for his substantial body of commentaries, largely on Aristotle but also on other thinkers. These commentaries had great impact on medieval Latin philosophy as well as the philosophy of the Italian Renaissance. Although Ibn Rushd never set out to formulate a philosophical system of his own, from his commentaries, and perhaps more so from his philosophical reply to al-Ghazālī's criticism of *falsafah,* an Aristotelian philosophical view emerges, informed by Ibn Rushd's individual insights and stamped by his personality. The view is powerful and compelling.

Al-Ghazālī's attack on *falsafah* in his *Tahāfut,* although logically incisive, was theologically motivated. Moreover, his condemnation of al-Fārābī and Ibn Sīnā as "infidels" was a pronouncement in terms of Islamic law. Thus Ibn Rushd's reply to al-Ghazālī encompasses the legal, the theological, and the philosophical. The legal and theological replies are embodied in two main works that are relatively short, namely, the *Faṣl al-maqāl* (Decisive treatise) and the *Kashf ʿan manāhij al-adillah* (Expositions of the methods of proof); the philosophical reply to al-Ghazālī's *Tahāfut* is the *Tahāfut al-Tahāfut* (Incoherence of *The Incoherence*), a much larger book.

In the *Faṣl,* Ibn Rushd raises the general question of whether Islamic law commands, allows, or prohibits the study of philosophy. He answers that the law commands its study but that this command is incumbent only on the one class of scholars, the demonstrative class (i.e. scholars who understand and use Aristotle's demonstrative method in acquiring knowledge), capable of understanding philosophy; nonphilosophers must not pursue it. Ibn Rushd's position is essentially that of al-Fārābī, but it is now couched in Islamic legal language. The *Faṣl* also includes a theory of scriptural interpretation and a defense of the *falāsifah*'s three doctrines against al-Ghazālī's charge that they were irreligious. The *Kashf* complements the *Faṣl* but offers more specific criticisms of Ashʿarī theological principles.

In the *Tahāfut al-Tahāfut,* Ibn Rushd quotes almost all of al-Ghazālī's *Tahāfut,* commenting on it paragraph by paragraph. Although his main criticisms are directed against al-Ghazālī, at times he criticizes Ibn Sīnā, particularly for his Neoplatonism. Ibn Rushd's *Tahāfut* is a sober work of criticism that tracks down ambiguities, draws distinctions, reformulates positions, corrects misunderstandings, and offers analyses. It reasserts and defends an Aristotelian causal view, arguing incessantly against the Ashʿarī conception of divine causality and against their denial of natural causes.

Ibn Rushd's writings on the hereafter, however, pose the question of what he actually believes on this matter. His "technical" discussions of the question of the soul's immortality—whether in his commentaries on Aristotle or in those parts of the *Tahāfut* where he is highly critical of Ibn Sīnā's doctrine of the soul's individual immortality—leave no room for a theory of the soul's individual immortality, to say nothing of a doctrine of bodily resurrection. In the *Kashf,* however, he affirms a doctrine of individual immortality, whether this is confined to the soul or involves bodily resurrection. Again, at the end of the *Tahāfut* (where the discussion is not technical) he seems to affirm a doctrine of bodily resurrection. The indications are that in these conflicting statements he is practicing what he preaches as a follower of al-Fārābī's political thinking. In other words, he is addressing the philosophers philosophically and the nonphilosophers in language they can understand. He also seems to be protecting himself against charges of unbelief.

Falsafah did not end with Ibn Rushd. But the period from al-Kindī to Ibn Rushd witnessed some of its greatest practitioners and established a rich philosophical tradition on which later Islamic thinkers, men of originality and genius, were to build and enrich *falsafah* even more. The majority of these thinkers came from Persia and were in a real sense the spiritual descendants of Ibn Sīnā. But some came from other parts of the Islamic world—Spain and North Africa, for example.

Persia became noted for its mystical philosophy of illumination, *al-ishrāq.* The founder of this tradition was al-Suhrawardī (d. 1191), a contemporary of Ibn Rushd. The basic idea of his philosophy is that reality consists of light of varying degrees of intensity. Light, which for al-Suhrawardī is neither material nor definable, proceeds from the Light of lights (*nūr al-anwār*), God. Its emanation and diffusion at various levels constitute the created world. In this metaphysics of light and illumination, he harks back to the old religions of Persia. He is also noted for criticizing the Aristotelians for their rejection of the Platonic doctrine of eternal forms. From the thirteenth century onward, al-Suhrawardī was succeeded by a series of Persian philosophers who either adopted his doctrine of *al-ishrāq* or, such as the philosopher-scientist Nāṣir al-Dīn al-Ṭūsī (d. 1274), were greatly influenced by it. Those who adopted it included such leading thinkers as Mīr Dāmād (d. 1631), Mullā Ṣadrā (d. 1640), and the latter's commentator, Sabzawārī (d. 1866), to name but a few.

Of al-Suhrawardī's successors, Mullā Ṣadrā is generally recognized as the most important and most original. Although he adopted al-Suhrawardī's metaphysics of illumination, he disagreed with him on a basic idea concerning the relation of essence to existence. Al- Suhrawardī had argued for the priority of essence over existence. Mullā Ṣadrā maintained the reverse, arguing for the priority and "primacy of existence" *(aṣālat al-wujūd).* By "existence," he meant real existence as distinct from the static concept of existence in the mind. Real existence is grasped intuitively, the act of intuiting it being itself part of the flow of existence. The key idea governing his whole philosophy is that of existence as a dynamic process. This manifests itself in his theories of motion and time. Motion is not simply the rotation of forms over a static substratum, but is inherent in the substratum itself. Similarly, time is not merely the measure of motion: Physical body has an inherent time dimension. There is an ever upward moving process of existence (imperceptible to humans) that is irreversible, a manifestation of God's ceaseless creative impulse.

In Western Islam, philosophical mystical thought attained its heights with two thirteenth-century thinkers, both from Murcia, Spain. The first was the great philosophical mystic Ibn al-ʿArabī (d. 1240), noted for his doctrine of the unity of being *(waḥdat al-wujūd),* which exerted a very great influence on Persian mystical thought. The second was Ibn Sabʿīn (d. 1270), a mystic-philosopher who expounded a doctrine of the unity of being in terms of Aristotle's concept of form. A much more empirical approach is encountered in the thought of the Tunisian-born historian-philosopher Ibn Khaldūn, one of Islam's most original minds. He served various Islamic rulers as ambassador, envoy, and chief judge. Combining a thorough legal, theological, and philosophical education with firsthand experience in politics, he utilized this background to write his universal history, best noted for its *muqaddimah* ("prolegomena"). It is in this *muqaddimah* that he sets forth his conception of history as a science concerned with the causal explanation for the rise, decline, and fall of civilizations and that he probed the rise and development of social institutions. In doing this, he realized, in effect, a philosophy of history.

Both Ibn Khaldūn and Mullā Ṣadrā in their very different ways are examples of philosophers who broadened the dimensions of *falsafah.* They certainly made advances over the thought of their predecessors. But these were advances within a rich philosophical tradition whose first foundation stone was laid in the ninth century by al-Kindī.

SEE ALSO Ishrāqīyah; Kalām.

BIBLIOGRAPHY

General Histories

Corbin, Henry. *Histoire de la philosophie islamique.* Paris, 1964.

Fakhry, Majid. *A History of Islamic Philosophy.* Rev. ed. New York, 1983.

Sharif, M. M., ed. *A History of Muslim Philosophy,* vol. 1. Wiesbaden, 1963.

Collections of Studies

Anawati, Georges C. *Études de philosophie musulmane.* Paris, 1974.

Hourani, G. F., ed. *Essays on Islamic Philosophy and Science.* Albany, N.Y., 1975.

Marmura, M. E., ed. *Islamic Theology and Philosophy: Studies in Honor of G. F. Hourani.* Albany, N.Y., 1984.

Morewedge, Parvis, ed. *Islamic Philosophical Theology.* Albany, N.Y., 1979.

Morewedge, Parvis, ed. *Islamic Philosophy and Mysticism.* Delmar, N.Y., 1981.

Stern, S. M., Albert Hourani, and Vivian Brown, eds. *Islamic Philosophy and the Classical Tradition.* Columbia, S.C., 1972.

Walzer, Richard. *Greek into Arabic: Essays on Islamic Philosophy.* Cambridge, Mass., 1962.

Translations

Fārābī, al-. *Alfarabi's Philosophy of Plato and Aristotle.* Translated by Muhsin Mahdi. New York, 1962.

Fārābī, al-. *Al-Farabi's Commentary and Short Treatise on Aristotle's De Interpretatione.* Translated by F. W. Zimmerman. London, 1981.

Hyman, Alfred, and James J. Walsh, eds. *Philosophy in the Middle Ages: The Christian, Islamic and Jewish Traditions.* New York, 1967. Includes translations of al-Fārābī, Avicenna, al-Ghazālī, and Averroës (pp. 20–235).

Ibn Rushd (Averroës). *Tahāfut al-Tahāfut.* Translated by S. Van Den Bergh as *The Incoherence of the Incoherence.* London, 1953.

Ibn Sīnā (Avicenna). *Avicenna's Philosophy.* Translated by Fazlur Rahman. London, 1952.

Ibn Sīnā. *The Life of Ibn Sīnā.* Edited and translated by William E. Gohlman. New York, 1967.

Kindī, al-. *Al-Kindī's Metaphysics.* Translated by Alfred L. Ivry. New York, 1963.

Lerner, Ralph, and Muhsin Madhi, eds. *Medieval Political Philosophy: A Source Book.* New York, 1963. Includes translations of al-Fārābī, Avicenna, Ibn Bājjah, Ibn Ṭufayl, and Averroës (pp. 21–190).

MICHAEL E. MARMURA (1987)

FALSIFICATION SEE DOUBT AND BELIEF; LOGICAL POSITIVISM

FALUN GONG.

Falun Gong, also known as Falun Dafa, is a Chinese spiritual movement founded in 1992 by Li Hongzhi (1951–). Although most Western scholars would classify it as a "new religious movement," Li and his followers understand Falun Gong not as a religion but as a "cultivation system," based on principles of *qigong* that are widely accepted in China. Falun Gong rapidly became very popular in China, attracting millions of followers in the years immediately after its founding. For complex reasons, Falun Gong soon ran afoul of the Chinese state, and a massive protest in Beijing by Falun Gong practitioners against media censure at the end of April 1999 led to a harsh crackdown by the Chinese government on the grounds that Falun Gong was a dangerous "heterodox sect."

***QIGONG* AND THE *QIGONG* BOOM.** To understand the rise and popularity of Falun Gong, it is essential to understand the rise and popularity of *qigong.* In Chinese, *qi* means "vital breath" or "energy" and refers to a force existing in nature that can be harnessed for a variety of purposes. *Gong* means "skill" or "technique," and the two characters together mean "the cultivation of *qi* energy." *Qigong* practice includes a variety of techniques, some stressing physical movement, some stressing meditation or visualization. The goal of practice is self-healing, stress reduction, and the cultivation of supernormal powers.

The practices and principles of *qigong* are drawn from traditional Chinese medicine, folk healing, martial arts, and popular religion, many varieties of which have claimed magical healing powers. These practices did not, however, exist as a coherent whole prior to the Communist revolution of 1949, nor did the notion of *qigong* exist as such. Ironically, given the state's later opposition, *qigong* was created and nurtured by the Chinese government in the 1950s as part of an effort to preserve traditional Chinese medical practices in the face of a massive importation of Western medicine. The goal of those who "invented" *qigong* in the 1950s was to separate pure *qigong* technique from its traditional spiritual underpinnings so as to preserve the scientific benefits of *qigong* while discarding its dangerous and "superstitious" wrappings. The first "consumers" of *qigong* were high-level cadres of the Chinese government, who practiced *qigong* in sanatoria run by the Chinese traditional medical establishment.

After the death of Mao Zedong in 1976, *qigong* became a mass phenomenon in the freer, less politically charged atmosphere of post-Mao China. One important element of this transformation was the emergence of charismatic *qigong* masters who in the late 1970s and early 1980s took *qigong* out of the sanatoria and into the public parks of urban China, where *qigong* was taught to any and all who were interested. As the popularity of *qigong* grew, masters sought larger venues, even renting sports stadiums at the height of the boom and selling tickets to eager followers. The credibility of *qigong* was enhanced by the "discovery" by well-known Chinese scientists that *qi* was a material substance and that the development of supernormal powers based on the mastery of *qi* had a scientific foundation.

Encouraged by the scientific endorsement of the reality of *qi* and *qigong,* the Chinese government lent its support to the *qigong* movement. From a practical point of view, mass practice of *qigong* promised to improve the health of the Chinese people and reduce demands on the health care system at a time when the leadership hoped to economize by shrinking its investment in public health. In addition, after the failure of Mao's Cultural Revolution (1966–1976), the post-Mao Chinese leadership sought legitimacy as much in Chinese nationalism as in Marxism-Leninism, and the government was pleased that many Chinese people were becoming reacquainted with China's traditional culture through their practice of *qigong,* which *qigong* masters linked to China's rich cultural heritage. China's leaders were equally proud to tout *qigong* to the world as China's contribution to modern science—yet another manifestation of post-Mao Chinese nationalism. At the same time, China's leaders sought to regulate *qigong,* and to this end set up the Chinese Qigong Scientific Research Association in April 1986.

Over the course of the 1980s and 1990s, China went wild for *qigong* in what was known as the "*qigong* boom." Hundreds of millions of people participated, and thousands of articles on *qigong* appeared in official media, as well as in newly created journals and newspapers wholly devoted to *qigong.* Hundreds of *qigong* masters competed for public attention. The most visible symbol of the *qigong* boom was the appearance of nationwide networks of *qigong* practitioners, all of whom were organized around charismatic *qigong* masters, who gave lecture tours, appeared on television, and published and sold books and cassettes. Chinese interest in *qigong* had become a mass movement, which began to take on the character of a new religious movement. Masters, in their explanations of the workings of *qigong,* began to elaborate theories that went beyond the technical aspects of *qigong* practice and the achievement of physical well-being; they linked *qigong* to morality, spirituality, the meaning of life, and the meaning of the universe. In addition, *qigong* practitioners began to fall into trances, experience visions, and suffer "possession," and a widespread enthusiasm for the pursuit of supernormal powers through *qigong* practice signaled the embrace of *qigong* as a force capable of altering ordinary reality.

Li Hongzhi and Falun Gong. Li Hongzhi and Falun Gong emerged as part of the *qigong* boom. Both were initially embraced as part of the movement, and Falun Gong was welcomed into the Qigong Scientific Research Association, which sponsored and helped to organize many of Li's activities between 1992 and 1994. Notable among those activities were fifty-four major lectures given throughout China to a total audience of some twenty thousand. Like other masters, Li published books of his teachings, which achieved such success that he was soon able to offer his lectures free of charge.

Still, if Li Hongzhi and Falun Gong owed their initial success to their kinship with other *qigong* masters and schools, there was something different about Li Hongzhi. Li condemned other *qigong* schools for their crass materialism, in effect accusing them of fraud. More fundamentally, he reproached the entire *qigong* establishment for an unhealthy obsession with healing and supernormal powers, which came, in his view, at the expense of a deeper spiritual orientation. To Li, Falun Gong was *qigong* taken to a higher plane. Falun Gong, he claimed, could heal illnesses and confer supernormal powers, but the more important objective was to arrive at a physical transformation of the body and a fundamental transformation of one's understanding of the composition of the universe and one's role therein. These transformations were to be effected through Falun Gong practice, which, like other styles of *qigong,* included physical movements, but which also accorded an importance to scripture (i.e., Li Hongzhi's writings). This emphasis on the master's writings was unusual in the context of the *qigong* movement. Unlike other *qigong* schools, Falun Gong also stressed the miraculous, godlike powers of Li Hongzhi (i.e., the ability to assure the health and welfare of all of his followers at all times) in a way that differed from other *qigong* schools.

Li's teachings are an eclectic mixture of Buddhism, Daoism, popular religion, and "scientism." His theology draws largely on Buddhism, and he calls on followers to sever all "attachments," be they to meat, alcohol, medicines, material possessions, or other human beings. Practitioners are to be compassionate to all, but such compassion should not engender attachments that detract from salvation. Li frequently evokes the traditional Buddhist concept of karma—the notion, linked to reincarnation, that the merits and demerits of one's present life will be reflected in one's status at the moment of rebirth in a future life. The "scientistic" cast of Li Hongzhi's message is reflected in its conception of karma, which in Falun Gong literature has a material basis: karma is a black substance present in the body, which can be transformed by suffering and virtuous practice into a white substance. The transformation, according to Li, occurs at the molecular level and accounts scientifically for the improved health of Falun Gong practitioners. Indeed, the promise of improved health has been the primary attraction of Falun Gong for many practitioners, who consider disease a form of karma to be eliminated through suffering and cultivation. Most Falun Gong practitioners avoid doctors, hospitals, and medication.

Another aspect of Li's teachings concerns world destruction and renewal. He argues that the world has been destroyed and re-created eighty-one times, and that signs indicate that another cycle of world destruction and renewal is imminent. Li drew these ideas from traditional strains of Chinese apocalyptic thinking, found especially in popularized versions of Daoism and Buddhism. Interestingly, Li did not stress this teaching prior to the Chinese government's suppression of Falun Gong.

Li argues furthermore that truth *(zhen),* benevolence *(shan),* and forbearance *(ren),* the three cardinal principles of

Falun Gong practice, are in fact the forces that make up the physical universe. Falun Gong practitioners achieve oneness with cosmic reality in cultivating truth, benevolence, and forbearance in their personal lives. Rather than present scientific arguments to illustrate his contentions, Li claims to have transcended science and thus to understand all of reality from another, higher level. His writings are full of scientific (or parascientific) references (his reflections on the proper understanding of gravity, for example), which his followers take as seriously as the rest of his writings.

Falun Gong practice is simple, albeit time-consuming. The exercises, described in the book *China Falun Gong* (1993), are to be performed on a daily basis if possible, alone or with other practitioners. The more important aspect of Falun Gong practice is the reading and rereading of Li Hongzhi's most important work, *Zhuan Falun* (The revolving wheel of the Buddhist law), first published in Chinese in 1995. This work is held to be the source of all truth; many practitioners report having read it in a single sitting and having experienced an immediate revelation. In China prior to the suppression of Falun Gong, a nationwide network of practice centers brought practitioners together on a regular basis, which allowed for the rapid diffusion of the Falun Gong message to interested parties. The centers offered no worship services, however, and Li Hongzhi forbids anyone to speak in his place; all "teaching" is thus carried out via books or video and audio recordings, or via other materials made available on the Falun Gong websites.

This same basic structure has been copied on a smaller scale outside of China. Many followers exercise daily and meet weekly with other practitioners to read Li Hongzhi's works and to exchange experiences. Large "experience-sharing conferences" are an important part of the North American Falun Gong experience. These are regional events, held on a rotating basis in cities where there are significant numbers of Falun Gong practitioners. Such events add witness statements to the Falun Gong repertoire of exercises and reading of scripture; practitioners deliver prepared statements of their experience before and after coming to know Falun Gong. Li Hongzhi frequently appears at such events, the only occasions at which ordinary members can see the master.

Chinese practitioners in North America are in general highly educated and reasonably wealthy, in part because American and Canadian immigration procedures attempt to filter out the poorly educated and those who are likely to become wards of the state. In China, Falun Gong, like *qigong,* appealed to a broad range of the population—rich and poor, educated and uneducated, powerful and powerless, urban and rural, women and men, as well as members of the Communist Party.

FALUN GONG'S CONFLICT WITH THE CHINESE GOVERNMENT. In his pre-1999 writings, Li Hongzhi appears to be nationalistic and patriotic, but largely apolitical. Nevertheless, while other *qigong* leaders took care to cast their message in such a way as to avoid conflict with the authorities, Li seems to have worried little about the response his writings might evoke. *Zhuan Falun,* for example, teems with references to spirit possession, the destruction and re-creation of the word, extraterrestrial interference in the affairs of humankind—in short, a host of references unlikely to please Communist authorities.

As a nationwide mass movement organized around a charismatic leader who largely ignored the Chinese Communist Party, Falun Gong represented a potential threat, but as such it was not much different from other *qigong* schools. What distinguished Falun Gong as an organization was its propensity to react quickly and vigorously to perceived slights from the media, a practice that rapidly became "political," since most media outlets in China are little more than mouthpieces for the government. Sources hostile to Falun Gong report more than three hundred such instances, beginning in the summer of 1996, none of which were violent and all of which essentially demanded that "erroneous" information about Falun Gong be corrected. Falun Gong practitioners later likened their protests to those of Mahatma Gandhi in India or Martin Luther King Jr. in the United States. But China has little tradition of civil rights demonstrations, and actions such as surrounding the state-owned and state-run Beijing television station, which Falun Gong practitioners did in May 1998, were perceived as audacious, if not seditious, in the Chinese setting.

Criticism of Falun Gong in the official media suggested that the movement had detractors in high places. Indeed, official opinion about Falun Gong, and about the *qigong* movement in general, was divided. At various points during the *qigong* boom, some critics expressed concern that *qigong* and Falun Gong were little more than a return to "feudal superstition" and that organizations built on such foundations were not to be trusted. It was probably due to such criticisms that Li Hongzhi decided to leave China for the United States in 1996, roughly the same time that Falun Gong "protests" began in China. Subsequently, problems over Falun Gong's continued recognition as an "official" *qigong* organization signaled that the Chinese government was particularly worried about Falun Gong.

The Falun Gong encirclement of Communist Party headquarters in Beijing in 1999 was sparked by a media affair in the neighboring city of Tianjin, and should thus be understood as a continuation of previous protests. The huge demonstration on April 29, 1999, when some ten thousand practitioners surrounded party headquarters at Zhongnanhai, was surely designed to draw the attention of the authorities to the ongoing criticism of Falun Gong in the media. The demonstration may even have been intended to suggest the power of Falun Gong (it was the largest protest China had experienced since the student democracy movement of 1989), and it apparently came as a complete surprise to China's leadership.

If Li Hongzhi expected the Chinese authorities to back down, he must have been sorely disappointed, for the state responded to the demonstration with a fierce campaign against Falun Gong. Laws passed during the summer and fall of 1999 defined Falun Gong as a "heterodox sect" and authorized confiscation of Falun Gong books, recordings, and other paraphernalia. Consistent with their tradition of protest, Falun Gong practitioners—encouraged, one assumes, by the Falun Gong leadership—sought out Chinese authorities at all levels, insisting that Falun Gong was benevolent. The most visible of these Falun Gong protesters were the practitioners who demonstrated in Beijing's Tiananmen Square, in essence demanding a confrontation with the authorities in China's central political space. Confrontation ensued, as the state arrested, imprisoned, and tortured tens of thousands of Falun Gong practitioners beginning in the fall of 1999.

After the campaign against Falun Gong, Li Hongzhi's message began to change. Li largely disappeared from circulation between the spring of 1999 and the fall of 2000. When he reemerged, delivering impromptu addresses at experience-sharing conferences in North America and Europe, he emphasized the apocalyptic aspects of his discourse in ways he had not done prior to April 1999. He began, for example, to depict the suppression of the Falun Gong movement in China as a part of a "final trial," and he seemed to promise that those who martyred themselves to the cause would receive instant "consummation" or enlightenment, the final completion of their cultivation efforts.

Falun Gong practitioners outside of China began to organize during this period, both to ensure that the truth about Falun Gong and about the suppression reach China, and to bring pressure on Western governments to condemn the actions of the Chinese state. These efforts, particularly those addressed to Western governments, achieved considerable success. However, an important moment in this conflict was the alleged self-immolation of a number of Falun Gong practitioners in Tiananmen Square in late January 2001. Although doubts persist as to the identity of those who set themselves on fire (Falun Gong practitioners insist that the event was staged by Chinese authorities), the incident marked an important public relations victory for the Chinese government within China. Many Chinese who had remained neutral to that point came to share the authorities' view that Falun Gong was indeed a dangerous heterodox sect. The Chinese authorities succeeded in suppressing Falun Gong, as well as other *qigong* schools, within China, but at great cost in terms of the regime's international prestige and the loss of money and energy that could have been more usefully invested elsewhere.

SEE ALSO Chinese Religion; New Religious Movements, overview article.

BIBLIOGRAPHY

Despeux, Catherine. "Le *Qigong*: Une expression de la modernité chinoise." In *En suivant la voie royale: Mélanges offerts en hommage à Léon Vandermeersch,* edited by Jacques Gernet and Marc Kalinowski, pp. 267–281. Paris, 1997.

Li Hongzhi. *Falun Gong,* rev. ed. (English version). Hong Kong, 1998. Originally published as *China Falun Gong* in 1993. Available from http://www.falundafa.org/eng/books.htm.

Li Hongzhi. *Zhuan Falun.* 2d ed. Hong Kong, 1998. Original Chinese edition published in 1995. Available from http://www.falundafa.org/eng/books.htm.

Madsen, Richard. "Understanding Falun Gong." *Current History* 99 (2000): 243–247.

Nova Religio 6, no. 2 (2003). An entire issue devoted to Falun Gong.

Ownby, David. "A History for Falun Gong: Popular Religion and the Chinese State since the Ming Dynasty." *Nova Religio* 6, no. 2 (2003): 223–243.

Palmer, David. "The Doctrine of Li Hongzhi." *China Perspectives* 35 (2001): 14–23.

Penny, Benjamin. "Falun Gong, Prophesy, and Apocalypse." *East Asian History* 23 (2002): 149–168.

Tong, James. "An Organizational Analysis of the Falun Gong: Structure, Communications, Financing." *China Quarterly* 171 (2002): 636–660.

Vermander, Benoît. "Looking at China Through the Mirror of Falun Gong." *China Perspectives* 35 (2001): 4–13.

Wong, John. *The Mystery of Falun Gong: Its Rise and Fall in China.* EAI Background Brief, no. 39. Singapore, 1999.

Zhu Xiaoyang and Benjamin Penny, eds. "The *Qigong* Boom." *Chinese Sociology and Anthropology* 27, no. 1 (1994).

DAVID OWNBY (2005)

FAMILY is vitally important to most religious traditions in two closely interconnected ways: Various ritual processes enacted by, to, and for the family help to create and sustain it as well as give it meaning, and it functions as an important symbol of deity. Historically and cross-culturally, family in various forms has (until the late twentieth century in postindustrialized cultures) been so basic to human existence as to be a universal symbol of ultimacy.

DEFINITION. Exactly what constitutes family is not always clear. Some scholars equate family with household, another imprecise construct that variously includes all permanent members such as servants or else excludes unrelated householders. Further confusion results because most anthropologists posit two basic kinds of family: the nuclear family, consisting of mother, father, and unmarried children, and the extended family, typically including mother, father, all unmarried children, and one or more sons with their wives and children. Numerous complicated variations exist, including different polygynous arrangements in which two or more cowives live under the same roof. A few domestic groupings, such as those of the Nayar of India, whose men never live with their wives, defy all categories. Nonetheless, family, in some variant, is considered universal.

Also confusing is the fact that all married people simultaneously belong to two different families. Family as seat of origination stresses ties of blood, whereas family as affiliation emphasizes bonds of marriage. To keep separate these two different kinds of family, some anthropologists designate the first as "kin" and the second as "family." Kin are those who share common ancestors, as do mother and child (in contrast to mother and father, who do not). Strictly speaking, although family incorporates kin, the reverse is not true because, excepting incestuous marriages, spouses usually are not blood relatives.

Consequently, family is basically a reconciliation of many different opposites: female and male, life and death, ascendants and descendants, kin and affines (relatives by marriage), biology and culture, freedom and servitude, corporation and individuality. The differing ways in which family contains these opposites represent diverse systems of order in which family roles are valued according to accepted local religiocultural belief and custom. Valuation of all members is almost never equal; therefore, family as a whole embodies and symbolizes order of a particular sort—hierarchy.

In its entirety this "natural" order of human relationships, presumed to have evolved out of earlier hominid bands of approximately thirty, has frequently been deified, with members typically reflecting family as experienced in a particular culture. Thus Kwoiam, the warrior hero of Mabuiag, an island off New Guinea, lives with his mother, her brother and sister, and his sister's son in a matrilineal "family" (technically, a kin system) that omits the father. Very different is the Homeric extended patriarchal family of Zeus and Hera, which includes variously begotten offspring. The smaller nuclear family is symbolized in various cultures, as for example the Egyptian Osiris, Isis, and Horus; the holy family of Christianity consisting of Joseph (or God the Father), Mary, and Jesus; and the holy triad of the Yurak Samoyed: Nyebye-haha, the mother deity; Wesako-haha, her spouse; and Nyu-haha, their son. Curious variants appear in the enneads (triple triads) so characteristic of dynastic Egypt.

In its smallest possible configuration (apart from the single individual sometimes defined as family in the post-industrialized West)—as husband and wife—family appears in almost all mythologies. Universally, tales of the *hieros gamos* tell of the sacred marriage of Heaven and Earth from whom humanity springs, as illustrated by the Zuni Awitelin-tsita, the fourfold-containing Mother Earth, and Apoyan Ta ʾChu, the all-covering Father Sky. Often such etiological stories of how the world came to be tell how one or more of the children produced by the union separate the pair, often forcibly, to form the realms of earth and sky. Such is the case in the Vedic account of Dyaus and Pṛthivī.

ANCESTORS. Probably no members so fully embody both the ritual and the symbolic significance of the traditional extended family as do ancestors. From the Paleolithic period to the present, many cultures have venerated ancestors to varying degrees, although Herbert Spencer's theory that ancestor worship stands behind all religious practice has been generally discarded. For example, almost all Native American tribes believe that spirits of tribal ancestors return to earth to warn, protect, and instruct the living, although only specially trained shamans are capable of seeing them.

Babylonian mythology and artifacts incorporate important motifs of ancestor veneration. The failed attempt of the hero Gilgamesh to escape mortality by visiting his ancestor Utanapishtim, the Babylonian Noah who did escape it, indicates the salvific role hoped for from ancestors. Between the third millennium BCE or earlier, when sacrifices were offered to the departed kings Shulgi and Gudea, and about 2500 BCE, when Grimalsin of the second dynasty of Ur appears to have been deified while still living, two other important themes emerge: Ancestor worship by actual descendants tends to merge with homage paid by a whole people to departed rulers or "fathers." Thus, in many cultures ancestors function variously as objects of domestic and state devotion, a situation that became pronounced in the Roman Empire. Attribution of divine ancestry has been common for kings, as notably in post-Meiji Restoration Japan, where the emperor was officially proclaimed a direct descendant of the sun goddess Amaterasu Ōmikami. Such ancestry has even been assigned to whole peoples, as repeatedly shown in epic poetry.

So important are the honored ancestors in cultures such as those in China, Japan after Chinese contact (seventh century CE), and areas of Aryan influence, particularly India and Rome, that the traditional family often seems to exist more for their sake than for that of the living. This point indicates one theme present in the traditional family, its orientation toward death. Furthermore, because typically in these cultures ancestors collectively overpower and stifle the individuality now common in the Western world, ancestor veneration also highlights a second important theme: Family as corporate entity strongly opposes the individuality of its members.

Emphasis on ancestors indicates that family is not only the matrix within which an individual enters life but also the means by which he (less commonly she) achieves a kind of immortality. Paradoxically, this denial of death that leads to ancestor veneration makes the family a kind of perpetual cult of the dead enacted by the living.

CHILDREN. In contrast to dead family members, who are almost universally venerated, children are often treated ambivalently. Though desired in the abstract for perpetuating the family, children may be abused or even denied life, as in the ancient classical world. Hippocrates illustrates this point when he asks, "Which children should be raised?" The essentially universal theme of infanticide is clearly present in the biblical stories of Isaac and Moses, who were saved. To this day the practice continues sporadically for girls in parts of India and China, as historically had been the case almost worldwide.

The countertheme of life orientation surfaces most strongly in connection with those newborns elected to survive. Yet even here the tension of opposites is strained, for only some attain family membership. Commonly thought of as "natural," family construction is actually often highly artificial.

Birth, mating, and death, the three natural methods of creating, maintaining, and pruning families, are simultaneously both biological and socioreligious events. Successful delivery of a live baby does not guarantee the existence of a new family member. In many cultures, once a child is born (notably, in patriarchal Hellenic Greece or even contemporary China or India), the father must determine whether or not to keep it. Then it must be incorporated into the family. The contemporary Islamic Malays illustrate one variant of this once nearly universal practice: First, the father whispers into the infant's ear the Islamic call to prayer; next, a specially selected person touches certain objects to the baby's lips to guard against future lying and gossiping; then, forty-four days later, the father buries the placenta beneath a coconut palm seedling. These and other birth rituals help place the child in its familial and socioreligious context. Thus a new family member is "created" only in the most superficial way by its actual birth. Subsequent actions of family members, often other than the mother, bring the child fully into family life.

As a symbol of deity, the divine child appears in various traditions. Archaeological finds such as vase paintings and figurines depicting infancy themes and rituals place this concept at least as far back as the Neolithic and Chalcolithic periods (c. 7000–3500 BCE) in Old Europe (roughly, southeastern Europe from Czechoslovakia to the Aegean). Motifs of birth and maturing of the infant later took shape mythically and cultically in many variations that recount the passion of the young god of vegetation. Representative is the cult of the infant Dionysos, originally Boeotian and Cretan but subsequently almost universal in Greece, in which the infant Dionysos-Zagreus is dismembered. According to myth, the Titans lured the child with rattles, knucklebones, a top, a ball, and a mirror, then cut him to pieces, cooked him, and devoured him. In some versions he is resurrected by the earth mother, Rhea. This death and resurrection theme, common to the complex of images central to agrarian religion, finds in the child (or alternatively in the seed) an appropriate image of renewal.

Worship of the divine child was originally shared by or even predominantly directed to the mother goddess, as in the case of Ishtar, Astarte, and Cybele, whose son-consorts were of secondary importance. With time, however, the child, originally of either sex as suggested by numerous Sumerian female Marduks, ceases to be merely the child or sacrificial consort and becomes more and more an object of veneration in its own right. Christianity epitomizes this process whereby the divine child eclipses its mother.

In a very different form, images of the divine child as divine hero are also common in Native American mythology. This pattern is typified by the Haida story of Shining Heavens. One day a Haida woman was digging on the beach. Hearing a cry from a cockle shell, she uncovered it and found the baby Shining Heavens. She took him home and soon discovered his supernatural power, manifested in his ability to grow up almost immediately. This common motif of the wonder child who grows almost instantly from baby to strong youth or man is also illustrated by the Siouan Young Rabbit and the Algonquian Blood-Clot Boy. Sometimes the child-hero even makes plans in the womb, as do the Iroquoian twins Good Mind and Evil Mind. Such "unnatural" capabilities illustrate the power of godhead to transcend nature.

Such capability is even more apparent in the Vallabha and Caitanya sects of Hinduism, in which worship of the cowherd Kṛṣṇa as the divine child has been popular from at least 900 CE. In the spontaneity of his laughter, pranks, dancing, disobedience, and play, the child Kṛṣṇa symbolizes the unconditional nature of divinity. In such activity, engaged in for no purpose beyond sheer joy, the play of the child metaphorically expresses an aspect of divinity less easily rendered by "adult" personifications.

MOTHERS. So important is a woman's role as mother in most societies that the biblical Hebrews, for example, insisted that a wife who failed to bear children was obligated to provide her husband with a concubine (*Gn.* 16:2). According to popular Islamic tradition, the main duty of a woman is to obey and serve her husband respectfully; her second duty is to give him male heirs. In traditional China with its strong Confucian ethic, life was meaningless without sons. Without sons, a wife could count on a second wife essentially replacing her.

Theorists assume that the discovery of stockbreeding and planting taught humans about male reproductive capability. That means that for only about twelve thousand of the million years of hominid existence have humans understood paternity and reckoned male as well as female lineage. Thus was the ancient mother-child kin tie challenged by the familial tie. The nineteenth-century belief in mother right, espoused by J. J. Bachofen, Robert Stephen Briffault, Henry Maine, and others, whereby women were thought to have held social and political power during a prepatriarchal era, has long been invalidated; but current scholarship makes indisputable the existence of a practice of prehistoric mother worship in Europe and Asia Minor.

Material evidence in the form of large numbers of "Venuses," often with exaggerated secondary sex characteristics and pregnant bellies, as exemplified by the well-known Venus of Willendorf, firmly roots the idea of divine motherhood in the Upper Paleolithic period in Eurasia (c. 22,000 BCE). By the time of the Neolithic and Chalcolithic periods (c. 7000–3500 BCE) in Old Europe and the Near East, the Great Mother, with her accumulated Paleolithic traits, is well established in the variant forms that generally characterize her in agricultural societies around the world. (In patrilineal totemic and patriarchal nomadic cultures she figures less prominently, as an adjunct to the dominant sky god.) Under various names she appears almost universally wherever agriculture develops—as Ishtar (Babylon and Assyria); Astarte (Canaan); Isis (Egypt); Cybele (Phrygia); Rhea, Gaia (pre-Hellenic Greece); Pṛthivī (Vedic India); Di (ancient China); Pachamama (Inca); and so on.

In cultures such as those of Old Europe, pre-Hellenistic Greece, and pre-Vedic India (Harappa, Mohenjo-Daro), which were not dominated by nomadic pastoral peoples, motherhood is typically aligned with a concept seemingly opposed to it—that of virginity. But this belief reflects the archaic notion that birth results from parthenogenesis, an understandable belief for those unaware of the male role. Far from being a moralistic concept, as it subsequently became in patrilineal and patriarchal cultures, it originally reflected an understanding of woman as creator and powerful figure in her own right.

Earth and related vegetal phenomena such as grains are not the only natural elements associated with motherhood. Water, the medium from which humans originally emerge onto land, also functions this way, as with the ancient Mexican goddess of the waters, Chalchiuhtlicue, and the water mother common to the ancient Karelians and other Finno-Ugric peoples. Sometimes, as with the Japanese sun goddess Amaterasu, or the pre-Islamic mother of the heavens Allat, or the Egyptian sky goddess Nut, the traditional association of earth with motherhood and of sky with fatherhood are reversed; consequently, the predominant associations do not always hold, as when the concept "down," normally affiliated with earth and motherhood, attaches to a male chthonic deity. The variant son-consorts of the mother goddess, such as Adonis and Tammuz, reflect this phenomenon.

Various interconnected processes particularly affect the ways motherhood is represented in divinity and vice versa. Specialization tends to separate qualities originally mixed together in a single great goddess figure into different embodying images, as exemplified by the goddesses of the Homeric pantheon. Artemis and Aphrodite, for example, both lose their original fullness of personality to become mainly associated with the hunt and with erotic love, respectively. In this way motherhood, especially in Western cultures dominated by monotheism, has typically been strictly separated from all other potential and actual attributes of womanhood. Thus hunting, wisdom, sex, and war, all attributes of the undifferentiated goddess, come to appear totally divorced from each other.

A related process polarizes "good" and "bad" qualities into beneficient and terrible goddesses. Such terrible mothers of death and destruction as the Hindu Kālī, the Aztec Tlamatecuhtli, and the Greek Medusa typify this process. Such splitting dichotomizes the originally unified cycle of birth and death, in which Mother Earth gives birth (often quite literally, as in the Greek story of Erichthonius and in the many Native American myths that portray humanity emerging from the womb of the Earth) and later takes back her dead for burial (as in the Pueblo belief that Shipapu, the underworld, is also the womb of the earth goddess, Natya Ha ʾAtse.) With polarization come goddesses of the underearth realm such as the Greek Persephone and the dread Sumero-Akkadian Ereshkigal, who are separate from beneficent counterparts such as Demeter and Ishtar.

In a variant process the single goddess multiplies, usually into a triad, as in the case of the Scandinavian Norns, the Greek Fates, or the strange *matres* and *matrones* figures from the Celtic and Germanic provinces of the Roman Empire. Such trinitarian representations often involve different stages of motherhood, as in various ubiquitous virgin-mother-crone triads (the Hindu Pārvatī, Durgā, and Umā and the Celtic Macha, Morríghan, and Badhbh, for example).

FATHERS. Next to ancestors and frequently amalgamated with them conceptually, fathers hold the greatest power in traditional patriarchal families, whether or not their fatherhood is biological. This paradox is logical when fatherhood is divided into three categories: The genetic father fertilizes the ovum; the genitor contributes to the child's growth in the womb, as when the Holy Ghost causes Mary to conceive through her ear; and the social father, known as the *pater,* dominates family life. Whether as genetic father, adoptive father, or maternal uncle, the *pater* supplies the child's social position.

In a patrifocal extended family the *pater,* as oldest living father in a direct line of descent, firmly heads the family hierarchy. This pattern was thoroughly worked out in the Roman family, where patriarchal power was so complete that, until he died, the father retained limitless authority over unmarried daughters and grown sons and their children. A married daughter customarily joined the household of her husband and so came under the authority of his father. Such extreme paternal power distinguished the Roman father from fathers in other societies in degree, but not in kind.

In contrast to motherhood, which results from pregnancy and childbirth, fatherhood is not immediately self-evident. Nor can fatherhood be as readily represented in images. Development and evolution of the concept are consequently less certain and less easy to follow. Almost everywhere, the most archaic manifestation of divine fatherhood is the "high god" located in the sky. Typically this "father" is originally a creator whose traits include goodness, age (eternity), and remoteness from the world of human affairs. So transcendent is he that he often abdicates his role of creator, handing it over to a successor-demiurge. Consequently, he is seldom reverenced in cult and may even disappear entirely. Representative examples are the Australian All-Father deities Baiame, worshiped by the Kamilaroi, and Bunjil (of the Kulin tribes); the Andamanese Puluga; numerous African father gods such as Nzambi of the Bantu-speaking peoples and Nyan Kupon of the Tshis. Existence of a sky god of this sort is evident from Neolithic times on and may well go back to Paleolithic times, but hard material evidence to prove it is currently insufficient. Aside from images suggesting the bull-roarers universally associated with father gods, no images comparable to the Paleolithic Venuses have been discovered.

The fatherhood of such archaic deities is often less specifically biological than creative, as reflected by the terms *Bawai* and *Apap,* applied respectively by the African Chawai and Teso, which convey the fatherhood of God relative to creation. In this sense the supreme being is a "father" whether or not he creates in the well-known *hieros gamos* of Mother Earth and Father Sky or through powers entirely his, as Baiami does.

By contrast, in many less archaic mythological and ritualized conceptions, divine fatherhood is unmistakably biological. Here the archaic mating of Mother Earth and Father Sky, originally an abstract description of creation, becomes far more concrete. The sovereign father is typically eclipsed by his son, as is the Greek Ouranos by Kronos, the Australian Baiami by Grogoragally, the Tiv Awondo by the Sun. Thus, one theme typically connected to divine fatherhood in most mythologies is the generational conflict of fathers and sons. As the archaic father god recedes, the son who replaces him, even as he himself achieves fatherhood, seldom attains the stature of his own progenitor. This is indicated by his characteristic shift from sky god variously to solar or weather god (as when the weather god Zeus replaces Kronos) or agricultural deity (as when the Babylonian Marduk, both a solar and a vegetation deity, eventually supplants the Sumerian great triad of sky gods Anu, Enlil, and Ea), all of which lack the majestic connotations universally ascribed to the sky.

Particularly in the Chalcolithic cultures of the Near East (e.g., Sumer, Babylonia), where worship of the Paleolithic goddess developed strongly into the historic period, this shift is apparent. Here earth as mother, rather than sky as father, typically symbolizes the supreme being, rendering fatherhood a less exalted concept. The god is father solely as fecundator, being more often lover than spouse. Such vegetation gods as Adonis, Tammuz, and their myriad counterparts function this way.

In marked contrast to this biological, often chthonic, fatherhood is the refinement of sky-oriented fatherhood apparent in the monotheistic religions—Judaism, Christianity, and Islam—and in dualistic Zoroastrianism, all of which developed out of patriarchal nomadic herding societies that retained more of the archaic religion than did their matrilineal agricultural counterparts. The biblical Yahveh, for example, is thought to have emerged from the celestial West Semitic deity known as Ya, Yami, or Yahu.

One of the attributes frequently credited to father-gods in almost all patriarchal cultures is that of giving birth: The biblical God creates life without aid from a female deity; Zeus produces Athena from his brow and gestates Dionysos in his thigh; the Scandinavian giant Ymir and the Aboriginal Australian Great Father, Kakora, both give birth from their armpits; and the Egyptian Khepri variously spits and masturbates to produce Shu and Tefnut, respectively.

In ritual, too, fathers often mimic the maternal role. Particularly among various Australian Aboriginal groups, initiation rites for boys, frequently reveal the fathers of a tribe functioning as male mothers, as they ritually mimic menstruation and "giving birth" to the young male initiates. Such sexual crossing over introduces into the concept of fatherhood several conflicting themes. Variously, fatherhood is as self-contained as motherhood in its parthenogenetic form; or it projects a "maternal" nurturing quality far different from the remoteness of the archaic sky god; or sometimes it deemphasizes sexual differentiation by blurring, a theme explicit in fertility figures such as Marduk, whose sex changes. These are just some of the ways in which concepts of fatherhood and divine fathers have developed their complexity worldwide.

SIBLINGS. Symbolically, relationships between siblings are almost as central to religion and mythology as those between parents and children. This is partly because brothers and sisters are frequently also spouses, like Zeus and Hera, especially in creation myths, making the theme of incest a common universal mythologem. Almost universally, cross twins (those of opposite sex) are believed to have been the first humans from whom all others descend.

The first couple of the ancient Egyptian ennead were the twins Shu and Tefnut; the second were the brother and sister Geb and Nut, the father and mother of the Osirian gods. The Vedic twins Yama and Yami and the Norse Askr and Embla functioned similarly.

Some idea of the possible meanings of sibling "marriage," whether of twins or not, is evident from the Japanese myth of Amaterasu Ōmikami, the Heaven-Illuminating Goddess, and her brother Susano-o no Mikoto, the Valiant-Swift-Impetuous Hero. The rule of the universe was divided between these two: The realm of light, including heaven and earth, was presided over wisely by the sun goddess, while the ocean and the domain of hidden things was ruled widely by her stormy brother. In consequence of her brother's evil behavior, Amaterasu hid in a cave, plunging the entire world into darkness. When she emerged, light triumphed over dark, and her brother was banished to a remote region.

Most variants of this rivalry show the siblings as two brothers, often twins, as in the ancient Persian Zoroastrian myth of the twins Ōhrmazd ("light") and Ahriman ("darkness") or in the Iroquoian myth of Ioskeha, the creator and preserver, and Tawiskara, the deadly winter god. Unlike the Iroquoian pair, however, the Persian dyad, representing the principles of good and evil, respectively, set the stage for a dualistic system of thought in which both principles are equal.

Often sibling rivalry incorporates the theme of fratricide, as in the case of the Egyptian Seth who kills Osiris or the Greek brothers Ismenos and Kaanthos through whom fratricide was first introduced into the world. This common theme dramatizes the invidious distinction most cultures make between elder brothers and all other children. An Australian creation myth about two brothers traveling together at the beginning of time vividly dramatizes this distinction. When the elder brother desires a wife, he operates on his sibling, making him into a woman. The younger brother-turned-wife simply continues in the subordinate position he had occupied all along, making clear the equivalent impotence of younger brothers and wives.

All these sibling tales ring changes on certain important familial themes. Battling twins represent identity altering into difference; fighting sisters and brothers depict familial opposition; cohabiting sisters and brothers embody familial unity; and battling brothers symbolize the struggle between equality and hierarchy, as brotherhood gives way to the rights of the elder brother, the patriarch-to-be.

SERVANTS. Of all the traditional family members, none so emphasizes the way family functions as both example and symbol of a hierarchical order as does the servant, the hired or enslaved person contributing to family life and economics in both agrarian and commercial settings. Particularly in its most extreme form, as slavery, servitude emphasizes the hierarchical nature of the traditional family. In ancient Hawaiian culture, for instance, one outcast social group, the *kauwa,* were designated to serve the chiefs and touch them directly. They alone were exempt from the *kapu* ("taboo") that prohibited touching the chiefs on pain of death. Yet these *kauwa* were themselves untouchable: It was not proper to eat with them or sleep close to them. At the death of their masters, they were buried alive, often as sacrificial atonement for *kapu* violations committed by others. While extreme, this example, like others involving Indian untouchable servants, American black slaves, and Middle Eastern eunuchs, clearly embodies the themes of scapegoating, sacrifice, and hierarchy common to families in general.

Certain religious traditions overtly take up the themes implicit in servitude, stressing them as positive rather than negative attributes, as in the cases of Hanuman, the perfect Hindu servant, and Christ, understood as fulfilling the promise of the servant poems of "Second Isaiah." Others simply portray servitude as an institution as natural to divinity as to humanity: In Japanese mythology, for example, the fox functions as the messenger of the god of harvests, Inari, much as Hermes serves the Greek Olympians. Among the Haida of the Northwest Coast, Old-Woman-under-the-Fire serves as messenger of the supernaturals, going between this world and that of the spirits. Servitude, exemplifying a humility appropriate to worshipers, characterizes many traditions; thus the Vedic Hindus feel like slaves in the presence of Varuṇa (*Ṛgveda* 1.25.1).

SEE ALSO Ancestors; Child; Deus Otiosus; Domestic Observances; Goddess Worship; Hieros Gamos; Home; Sky; Supreme Beings; Twins; Virgin Goddess.

BIBLIOGRAPHY

Besides canonical scriptures, the most useful primary texts for students of the family are the ancient religio-legal codes developed by most literate cultures. Representative is the *Institutes of Hindu Law, or The Ordinances of Menu, according to the Gloss of Culluca; Comprising the Indian System of Duties, Religious and Civil,* translated from the original Sanskrit by William Jones (1794; 2d ed., London, 1876); the ordinances cover a wide range of family-related topics, including divorce, remarriage, status of wives, and the like. An excellent compendium of various issues of concern to contemporary students of family is the Spring 1977 issue of *Daedalus,* which ranges from articles on specific cultures to family policy issues in the United States to the study of the history of the family.

Of the hundreds of recent works on family studies, *Household and Family in Past Time,* edited by Peter Laslett with the assistance of Richard Wall (Cambridge, 1972), is most representative of the controversial demographic approach. In this work Laslett presents his provocative, ground-breaking argument that the nuclear family preceded the industrial revolution and hence was causative rather than resultant. Also representative of the new demographic scholarship on family is Michael Mitterauer and Reinhard Seider's *The European Family: Patriarchy to Partnership from the Middle Ages to the Present* (Chicago, 1977). For those who wish to pursue the historical aspects of family in depth, particularly by looking at small numbers of people in very precisely documented areas, the *Journal of Family History* (Worcester, Mass., 1796–) presents the most recent work.

Among numerous excellent sources of information on the mother goddess, two stand out for their lucidity: E. O. James's *The Cult of the Mother-Goddess: An Archaeological and Documentary Study* (New York, 1959) and Marija Gimbutas's *The Goddesses and Gods of Old Europe, 6500–3500 B.C.: Myths and Cult Images* (Berkeley, Calif., 1982). Somewhat more difficult to trace for lack of early material evidence and fewer books devoted exclusively to the subject is the concept of the father god. Helpful sources include E. O. James's *The Worship of the Sky-God: A Comparative Study in Semitic and Indo-European Religion* (London, 1963); Wilhelm Schmidt's *The Origin and Growth of Religion: Facts and Theories* (1931; New York, 1972), considered by many the *locus classicus* for its topic; and Mircea Eliade's *Patterns in Comparative Religion* (New York, 1958), in which see especially chapter 2, "The Sky and Sky Gods," and chapter 3, "The Sun and Sun-Worship." A helpful discussion of Kṛṣṇa as divine child appears in David Kinsley's *The Sword and the Flute: Kali and Kṛṣṇa, Dark Visions of the Terrible and the Sublime in Hindu Mythology* (Berkeley, 1975). Much useful information on siblings appears in Donald J. Ward's *The Divine Twins: An Indo-European Myth in Germanic Tradition* (Berkeley, Calif., 1968).

New Sources

The *Histoire de la famille,* edited by André Burguière, Christiane Klapisch-Zuber, Marin Segalen and Françoise Zonabend (Paris, 1986), is the basic work of reference. It contains historical chapters on Mediterranean antiquity, European Middle Ages and ancient Asia as well as anthropological surveys on family in today's Western and Eastern world. The three prefaces by an historian such as Georges Duby and two anthropologists such as Claude Lévi-Strauss and Jack Goody are very inspiring from the methodological point of view.

The well-organized bibliographies and the ample indexes are very helpful. Among the classics, N. D. Fustel de Coulanges, *La cité antique* (Paris, 1872) and Edward Westermarck, *A Short History of Marriage* (London, 1926) are still worth reading as well as various essays on society and religion by Talcott Parsons. Philip Ariès, *L'enfant et la vie familiale sous l'ancien régime* (Paris, 1960); J. L. Flandrin, *Familles. Parenté, maison, sexualité dans l'ancienne société* (Paris, 1976); and Lawrence Stone, *The Family, Sex and Marriage in England 1500–1800* (London, 1977) have been innovating historical studies. *The Development of the Family and Marriage in Europe* (Cambridge, U.K., 1983) and *The Oriental, the Ancient and the Primitive. Systems of Marriage and the Family in Pre-industrial Societies of Eurasia* (Cambridge, U.K., 1990) by Jack Goody are provoking comparative surveys of pre-modern family institutions throughout the world who challenge many traditional assumptions.

Günther Kehrer, "Familie" in *Handbuch religionswissenschaftlicher Grundbegriffe,* vol. 2, edited by H. Cancik, B. Gladigow and M. Laubscher (Stuttgart, Germany, 1990), pp. 404–414 is one of the very few accounts of the relationship between family and religion, written from the perspective of social scientific studies. Marzio Barbagli, "Famiglia. 1. Sociologia," in *Enciclopedia delle scienze sociali,* vol. 3 (Rome, 1993), is particularly useful for his ample bibliography.

For religions (especially religions of the Book) in the contemporary situations of American families, see the site of the "Religion, Culture, and Family Project," directed by Don Browning at the University of Chicago Divinity School (http://divinity.uchicago.edu/family/index.html), which addresses marriage, sex, and family issues from a range of theological, historical, legal, biblical, and cultural perspectives.

KATHRYN ALLEN RABUZZI (1987)
Revised Bibliography

FAMILY, THE. The religious movement that calls itself "the Family" (though it has also been called the Children of God since its inception) began in the 1960s as the ministry of a particular family and the related musical evangelism called Teens for Christ. Positioning itself in radical opposition to the mainstream churches, which it scorned as worldly "churchianity," it rapidly recruited young adults from the 1960s counterculture and spread beyond its origins in the United States to establish communes around the world. Its visibility made it a target both for secularists aligned with the psychotherapy movement and for some conventional Christians who assumed its unusually high levels of member commitment were caused by brainwashing. Thus, members of the Family were the first victims of forcible "deprogramming," and over a period of years fully six hundred of the group's children were seized by authorities, inadvertently traumatized by their captivity, then returned after the legal basis for holding them proved spurious. The Family remains an intriguing challenge for scholars and social scientists, because it claims to be authentically Christian yet rejects the standard denominations' limits on erotic and spiritual communion, practicing a form of free love and professing to communicate on a regular basis with Jesus and with deceased persons.

ORIGINS. David Brandt Berg, founder of the Family and variously called Moses David or Father David, was the grandson of John Lincoln Brandt, a leader in the Disciples of Christ, and the son of Virginia Brandt Berg, a radio evangelist and faith healer in the Christian and Missionary Alliance, part of the Holiness movement. After serving as a minister of the Christian and Missionary Alliance in Arizona, Father David worked for a decade in the Soul Clinic, a Pentecostal movement. A break with the Soul Clinic and a "Warning Prophecy" channeled by his mother at the end of 1967 delivered Berg and his family to Huntington Beach, near Los Angeles, where they encountered the hippie movement.

A cultural historian might say the Family was an amalgam of the Holiness movement and the hippie movement, both of which stressed intense, intimate spiritual experiences. However, this analysis may be too facile, because not all the new recruits could be described as hippies and much of the religious inspiration came from the personal experiences of Father David rather than merely reflecting his denominational background. For example, from its formative period in California, the Family has always been profoundly millenarian, yet Father David had no connections to Adventism, and his Holiness tradition was not millenarian. Possibly inspired by the quite different millenarian quality of the hippie movement and the revolutionary anarchism of the associated New Left, Father David studied the books of *Daniel* and *Revelation* to develop his own perspective on the imminence of the apocalypse.

Soon Father David's growing movement was staging colorful public protests, marching in red robes while pounding seven-foot staves on the ground in tempo with shouts of "Woe!" or arguing with ministers of conventional churches during their sermons. A few horrified parents sought the aid of Ted Patrick and other deprogrammers to rescue their sons and daughters from the group, thereby giving birth to the American anticult movement. In 1970 Father David flew to Israel for a temporary visit (his subsequent whereabouts were usually secret, but outside the United States), and his followers began moving first into Europe and then across Asia and Latin America. The highly committed membership living in communes and supporting themselves entirely through missionary work and donations reached ten thousand in 1983 and remained at about that level through the remainder of the twentieth century.

THE LAW OF LOVE. After a celibate period during its formation, the Family developed a theology that endorsed giving erotic satisfaction to other people and sharing sexual experiences beyond marriage with the consent of all parties. In 1969, in a tract called "Scriptural, Revolutionary Love-Making," Father David argued that the biblical *Song of Solomon* was sacred instruction for sexual intercourse. From other parts of the Bible (for example, *Matt.* 22:36–40; *Gal.* 5:14, 22–23; *Titus* 1:15) he derived the Law of Love: that any harmless sexual act can be good if performed in God's love and with the agreement of those people involved. In 1974, while living in Tenerife in the Canary Islands, Father David developed a new method of witnessing for Jesus, called "flirty-fishing" or "Ffing," in which women of the group offered themselves sexually to selected nonmember men as samples of the Lord's love.

Over the next few years this practice spread to many, but by no means all, of the far-flung communes and became a significant part of the group's relationship with the surrounding world (in some geographic areas more than others) before being abandoned in 1987. Some former members claim they were sexually exploited during this period, but their testimonies are somewhat lacking in detail, and the central organization has generally had difficulty imposing policies on the highly dispersed local groups except through example and exhortation. Interviews by social scientists with women who had engaged in flirty-fishing reveal a variety of relationships with the men involved, and many of them seem to have been sincere supporters of the group. By one internal estimate, 200,000 men received flirty-fishing, but only a vanishingly small fraction became committed members afterward.

In the 1990s, strict rules were instituted to limit sexual contact outside the Family and, at times, even outside the particular communal group. Perhaps in compensation for these limitations, insiders were encouraged to share erotically beyond the married dyad. A questionnaire was administered to 1,025 members of the Family in 1997, based on items from the General Social Survey that had earlier been administrated to a random sample of American adults. One battery of items inquired about various sexual relationships, including, "What about a married person having sexual relations with someone other than his or her husband or wife?" (Bainbridge, 2002, p. 125). Of American adults, 78 percent said this would always be wrong, compared with only 1 percent of members of the Family.

Ritual, in the conventional sense of the term, is almost completely absent in the Family, except for giving thanks at meals and occasional spontaneous communion experiences within a home (in spontaneous communion somebody will, on impulse, suggest passing a cup of wine with prayers). Ritual's function is taken by various forms of emotional sharing among members, including not only eroticism but also an extensive repertoire of member-created music, a vast internal literature provided by the central organization, and (since the death of Father David in 1994) a remarkable flood of explicit communications that members believe they receive directly from the supernatural.

SPIRITUAL COMMUNICATION. During the years he led the Family, Father David claimed to be in constant communication both with Jesus and with lesser spirit guides. The core leadership who lived with him accepted these claims and fully expected to receive his gift of prophecy after his passing. To their surprise, at first they had difficulty receiving messages from the spirit world, but prayer, experimentation, and patience eventually prevailed.

In general, established religious organizations discourage their membership from engaging in direct communication with the supernatural, reserving this function either for the priesthood or for ancient prophets of bygone days. The Family, however, encouraged all members to receive prophecies. The 1997 survey of members found that 95 percent "received prophecy, visions, or messages from the spirit world" (Bainbridge, 2002, p. 81). Interviews with members revealed that individuals mean a great variety of things by *prophecy*—all the way from literally seeing and hearing the voice of Jesus or a deceased relative to a vague intuitive sense of communion or guidance.

Members frequently write up the prophetic messages they receive and send them to the central organization, which is called World Services. It publishes selected examples within the group. Some of these messages ostensibly come from recently deceased loved ones, who report they are extremely happy in the afterlife, which grieving believers find quite comforting. Remarkably, other messages have been entire posthumous works of literature attributed to deceased authors of the past, including William Shakespeare, C. S. Lewis, and Sir Walter Scott.

THE END-TIME. The Family believes that the world has entered the end-time, and members frequently compare biblical passages with the latest news, identifying what may be signs and portents of the coming end. Although for a time they speculated about whether the antichrist might possibly establish his world government around 1985 or 1986, they have never confidently set a date, and they do not accept early Adventist traditions that it is possible to deduce the date through close analysis of the Bible. The group's image of the millennium and the paradise to follow is quite detailed, asserting, for example, that the holy city, New Jerusalem, will be a pyramid fifteen hundred miles along each edge. According to the beliefs of the group, all true members and others who sincerely accepted Jesus as their savior will be resurrected in spiritual bodies, enjoying all the pleasures of the flesh but suffering no sin.

For the first quarter century of its existence, the Family expected the consummation of the end-time at any moment. When members first began having children, they did not imagine the children would have the time to grow up. As the years passed, they began educating the children at home rather than enter schools operated by the detested "system." Second-generation adult respondents to the 1997 survey reported, on average, a total of ten years of home schooling but only one year of schooling outside the home, and 63 percent said they had never attended a non-Family school. This survey also revealed that only 3 percent of members have full-time jobs, other than their missionary work with the Family, and thus the overwhelming majority look toward the future not in terms of a secular career but in terms of saving souls in preparation for the end-time.

Over the years the Family has been able to maintain what sociologists call high tension with the surrounding sociocultural environment, living apart from the institutions of secular society and estranged from the conventional churches. It has done so by periodically launching revivals it calls revolutions and by refusing to compromise with the ambient culture. By placing high demands on membership, it sustains commitment but makes it difficult for people to join. The scholars and social scientists who have followed the Family over its history agree that it entered the twenty-first century facing some difficulty in keeping second-generation members as they enter adulthood and in preventing local schisms. The cultural milieu in which it was formed, California of the late 1960s, is long past, but comparable recruitment episodes may arise in one or more of the roughly ninety nations in which the Family's missionaries are seeking to save souls. Thus it is impossible to predict how much longer the Family will be able to sustain its revolutionary ministry.

There is no evidence that members of the Family consider that the continued existence of the sinful world contradicts their millenarian prophecies. Rather, the sin and misery of life on earth prove to them that each person must urgently accept Jesus. They note that the world does end for the thousands of people who die every day, and they stress that each person should not waste a single day further. In their worldwide ministry they tend to measure success in terms of the many people who kneel in prayer with them to let Jesus into their hearts, not in terms of recruits to Family membership. Social scientists have found the Family to be a veritable treasure trove of research challenges, and it will be interesting to see whether historians and theologians also benefit by studying this radical movement over the coming decades.

SEE ALSO Jesus Movement.

BIBLIOGRAPHY

Bainbridge, William Sims. *The Sociology of Religious Movements.* New York, 1997. This general text on religious movements contains a chapter about the Family based on interviews and observation.

Bainbridge, William Sims. *The Endtime Family: Children of God.* Albany, N.Y., 2002. A study of the contemporary group largely based on a questionnaire completed by 1,025 members.

Chancellor, James D. *Life in the Family: An Oral History of the Children of God.* Syracuse, N.Y., 2000. A scholarly study based on interviews and extensive observation.

Davis, Rex, and James T. Richardson. "The Organization and Functioning of the Children of God." *Sociological Analysis* 37 (1976): 321–339. An early examination of the group by social scientists.

Lewis, James R., and J. Gordon Melton, eds. *Sex, Slander, and Salvation: Investigating the Family/Children of God.* Stanford, Calif., 1994. A collection of essays by scholars from various academic disciplines.

Patrick, Ted, with Tom Dulak. *Let Our Children Go!* New York, 1976. A book by the professional deprogrammer who first tried to deconvert members.

Van Zandt, David E. *Living in the Children of God.* Princeton, N.J., 1991. An early descriptive account.

Wallis, Roy. *Salvation and Protest.* New York, 1979. This book contains a section on the early group.

Williams, Miriam. *Heaven's Harlots: My Fifteen Years as a Sacred Prostitute in the Children of God Cult.* New York, 1998. A personal memoir, apparently packaged by the publisher to emphasize controversial aspects.

WILLIAM SIMS BAINBRIDGE (2005)

FANGSHI

FANGSHI. The *fangshi* ("specialists in occult prescriptions"), also called "magicians" and "recipe masters," and later known as *daoshi* ("specialists in the Way") were important contributors to the development of religious Daoism. They were experimental philosophers and occult technicians who, in the course of their observations of nature and search for physical immortality, created a body of prescientific knowledge that formed the basis of Chinese medicine, pharmacology, chemistry, astrology, divination, and physiological alchemy. A major part of this knowledge was later incorporated into the Daoist religion.

The origin and precise meaning of the term *fangshi* are far from certain; but they may have developed from the *wu*, shamans or sorcerers who were involved in mediating between the human and spiritual realms from the earliest times in Chinese court and village life. By the second century BCE the term was used to refer to a group of practitioners of various esoteric arts who were generally outside the literati mainstream. These practitioners apparently maintained their own texts and lore and transmitted their knowledge from master to disciple, yet they have never been regarded as constituting a distinct philosophical school. This is perhaps due to the fact that, while early historians respected their arcane skills, they did not hold them in very high regard and only recorded events in which these abilities were used to strive for political power. The *fangshi* were most influential in China during a period of roughly six hundred years beginning in the third century BCE.

While in later times they came from various areas on the periphery of the empire, the *fangshi* were first associated with the coastal states of Qi and Yan (now Shantung), and it is here in about 330 BCE that we hear of them encouraging local rulers to set out to sea in search of the holy immortals (*xian*) who possessed the potions of immortality. Though their exact relationship to the Naturalist school first systematized by Zou Yan (340–270 BCE) remains unclear, we know that they took the ideas of this school as the philosophical basis for their observations of nature and their various experimental techniques. According to this Naturalist philosophy, all phenomena are infused by one of the Five Phases (*wuxing*) of Energy (*qi*), namely, Earth, Fire, Water, Wood, and Metal. Phenomena infused with the same phase of energy influence and resonate with one another, and these phases themselves spontaneously transform according to their own inherent laws, and so influence all things from the succession of seasons to the succession of dynasties.

When the first emperor of China, Qin Shihuangdi, united the country in 221 BCE, *fangshi* from Qi and Yan flocked to his court. Their influence there is clearly attested to by the historical records. The emperor believed that he had come to power because the energetic phase of water had gained ascendancy in the world, and so he adopted water as the symbol of his reign. He also sent expeditions to search for Penglai, the Isle of the Immortals, and was himself devoted to the quest for immortality.

In the succeeding century and a half, the cult of immortality flourished, and its principal proponents, the *fangshi*, were influential among the ruling elite. Their power reached its zenith under Han Wudi (140–87 BCE), who appointed a number of them court officials when they promised to contact the immortals and to provide him with their secrets of avoiding death. On the advice of these specialists in occult prescriptions, the emperor undertook expeditions both to the eastern seacoast and to the sacred Kunlun mountains in the west in quest of these secrets. He also reinstated ancient sacrifices to the spirits, the most important of which were the *feng* and *shan* sacrifices on Mount Tai. According to the *fangshi*, the *feng* and *shan* sacrifices had last been performed by their patron and ancestor, the Yellow Emperor (Huangdi), who thereupon had achieved immortality. The ultimate failure of these endeavors was discouraging to Emperor Wu, and after his reign the influence of these esoteric masters declined considerably on a national scale.

On the local level, however, the *fangshi* were still powerful at the courts of a number of vassal states. The most notable was the state of Huainan, whose ruler, Liu An, was sponsor and editor of the important philosophical compendium the *Huainanzi*. Liu An died in 122 BCE after his presumed rebellion was discovered by imperial authorities, but according to legend, the *fangshi* gave him and his family a potion of immortality and they all ascended to heaven to live forever. It is interesting to note that rulers of several other vassal states in which the specialists in occult prescriptions were influential during the next two centuries also plotted (unsuccessful) rebellions and that a number of them were associated with Wang Mang, who seized the reins of the empire for fifteen years early in the first century CE.

The surviving records show the *fangshi* to have been involved in a wide range of experiments aimed at lengthening life and avoiding death. Their experimentation with transmuting cinnabar to mercury and gold in the search for the potion of eternal life is regarded as the origin of Chinese alchemy and chemistry. Their creation of various plant and animal compounds for health and longevity is the basis of the long Chinese pharmacological and medical traditions. Their respiratory and gymnastic techniques, methods of dietary hygiene, and various "bedroom arts" are among the earliest examples of physiological alchemy. The *fangshi* were also adept at shamanistic trance and at contacting and influencing spirits and demons. Mantic practices were also an important aspect of their tradition. Some of the large cache of medical and divinatory texts excavated at Mawang dui in 1973 are likely representative of *fangshi* writings.

Ultimately a large part of the knowledge and practices of the *fangshi* found their way into the Daoist religion. Their occult practices and philosophies included breath cultivation and a cosmology of the Dao that are also the hallmarks of the famous foundational works of the Daoist religion, *Laozi* and *Zhuang Zi*, as well as some lesser known texts such as "Inward Training" (*Nei-yeh*), a fourth century BCE poetic work included in the *Guan Zi* that contains the oldest extant Chinese discussion of meditation and its results. The *fangshi* maintained their own independent learning centers throughout the Han dynasty and their lore and practices formed the foundations of the organized Daoist religion that coalesced around a few charismatic *fangshi* leaders between 140 and 184 CE. The oldest source of religious Daoism, the *Taiping jing*, is said to have been authored by *fangshi* and was presented to the imperial court by one in 140 CE. They also wrote a collection of now lost subaltern commentaries on the Confucian classics, the *Zhanwei* ("Wei Apochrypha") that were also transmitted outside government sanctioned circles. Because the rise of Daoism as a religious and political force during the second century CE took place largely outside the purview of the official historians who are our main sources, the precise role of the *fangshi* in the beginnings of the Daoist religion is difficult to clarify. However scholars have been able to identify textual influences between Han dynasty *fangshi* works and the later Shang qing ("Highest Clarity") and Lingbao ("Numinous Treasure") Schools of Religious Daoism.

SEE ALSO Alchemy, article on Chinese Alchemy; Daoism, overview article; Liu An; Xian; Yinyang Wuxing.

BIBLIOGRAPHY

There are three Western-language sources devoted exclusively to the *fangshi*. Ngo Van Xuyet's *Divination, magie et politique dans la Chine ancienne* (Paris, 1976) contains an accurate translation of all the *fangshi* biographies in the *History of the Latter Han* (*Hou Han shu*) as well as excellent supporting material including a detailed discussion of the historical context of the biographies and appendices on the various esoteric techniques of the *fangshi*. Kenneth J. DeWoskin has published one article and one book on the *fangshi*. "A Source Guide to the Lives and Techniques of Han and Six Dynasties *Fangshi*," *Society for the Study of Chinese Religion Bulletin* 9 (1981): 79–105, is a valuable list of biographical sources and makes an important attempt to define the *fangshi* and delineate their activities. Many of the biographies listed in this article, and all of those translated in Ngo's work, are translated by DeWoskin in *Doctors, Diviners, and Magicians of Ancient China: Biographies of Fangshi* (New York, 1983), which also contains a useful introduction. This work is the most comprehensive to date in the West but unfortunately fails to deal with the very thorny problem of the role of the *fangshi* in the rise of the Daoist religion.

Information on the *fangshi* can be found in a number of other works, the most valuable of which is Yu Yingshi's "Life and

Immortality in the Mind of Han China," *Harvard Journal of Asiatic Studies* 25 (1964–1965): 80–122. Anna K. Seidel's superb study *La divinisation de Lao-tseu dans le daoïsme des Han* (Paris, 1969) contains some useful information on the *fangshi* and their relationship to the Yellow Emperor and to the Huang-Lao Daoists. The activities of the *fangshi* under Qin Shihuangdi and Emperor Wu of the Han can be found in Burton Watson's translation of Ssu-ma Qien's *Shih chi, Records of the Grand Historian of China*, vol. 2 (New York, 1963), pp. 13–69. There are also scattered references to the *fangshi* in Joseph Needham's *Science and Civilization in China* (Cambridge, U.K., 1956–1976), especially volume 2, which contains an excellent discussion of the school of Naturalists, and volume 5, part 3, which discusses alchemy. Finally there is a detailed discussion of the practices and texts of the *fangshi* along with a meticulous translation of medical writings that likely derived from them in Donald Harper, *Early Chinese Medical Literature: The Mawangdui Medical Manuscripts* (London, 1998).

There are now several excellent sources for the relationship between the *fangshi* and the organized Daoist religion. Solid overviews can be found in two general histories of Daoism, Isabelle Robinet's *Daoism: Growth of a Religion* (Stanford, 1997) and Livia Kohn's *Daoism and Chinese Culture* (Boston, 2001). Toshiaki Yamada's "Longevity Techniques and the Compilation of the *Lingbao wufuxu*" in Kohn's edited collection *Daoist Meditation and Longevity Techniques* (Ann Arbor, 1989), pp. 99–123, is a superb textual study of the links between this religious Daoist work and the *fangshi*. There are also a number of notable articles in the masterful *Handbook of Daoism* edited by Kohn (Leiden, 2000): Robinet's "Shangqing–Highest Clarity," pp. 196–224, an overview of this important Daoist school in which she traces its roots back to the Han dynasty *fangshi*; Yamada's "The Lingbao School," pp. 225–255, which demonstrates the influence of the *fangshi* on the development of this second major school of religious Daoism; Fabrizio Pregadio's "Elixirs and Alchemy," pp. 165–195, which argues that the roots of inner and outer alchemy can be found in *fangshi* practices and texts; and Mark Csikszentmihalyi's "Han Cosmology and Mantic Practices," pp. 53–73, an analysis of the divination practices and texts of the Han dynasty *fangshi* and how they were transmitted. Finally, for a discussion of early Daoist meditation and its origins, see Harold D. Roth, *Original Dao: Inward Training and the Foundations of Daoist Mysticism* (New York, 1999).

HAROLD D. ROTH (1987 AND 2005)

FĀRĀBĪ, AL-. Abū Naṣr Muḥammad ibn Muḥammad ibn Tarkhān ibn Awzalagh al-Fārābī (258–339? AH/870–950? CE) was a Hellenized Muslim-Arabic philosopher *(faylasūf)*, known in the Islamic tradition as the "Second Teacher" (second to Aristotle); in Latin, al-Fārābī was called Avennasar or Alfarabius. His Arabic biographers called him the first great logician; modern scholars have declared him the chief political philosopher of Islam and the founder of Islamic Neoplatonism. More than one hundred works are attributed to him, not all of which have survived.

While the details of his life are unclear, with the historical accuracy of many later biographical accounts suspect, the following reconstruction has a reasonable degree of certainty. Al-Fārābī was of Turkish origin, born in Fārāb in Transoxiana; he studied logic in Abbasid Baghdad under Nestorian Christian scholars Yuḥannā ibn Ḥaylān (d. 910) and the prominent translator of Aristotle into Arabic, Abū Bishr Mattā (d. 940); his most famous student, too, was a Christian, the Jacobite Yaḥyā ibn ʿAdī (d. 974), another important translator and logician. After having crossed the age of seventy, he left for Syria and attached himself to the court of the Shīʿī ruler, the Hamdanid Sayf al-Dawla; his writings do show some Shīʿī leanings. After having traveled to Aleppo and Egypt, he finally returned to Damascus, where he died.

There seem to be good reasons why al-Fārābī enjoyed the prestigious stature of the "Second Teacher" after Aristotle, for in the history of Hellenized philosophy in Islam, he is the first system-builder and one with a heightened sense of curricular organization and rigor. Thus the various elements of his philosophical discourses constitute a coherent body of thought in which every identifiable proper part seems to be related to every other. This monumental synthesis was carried out in an Aristotelian manner but supplemented, modified, and controlled by a peculiar brand of Platonism, Neoplatonism, and Islamism. One of his celebrated works, *Iḥṣāʾ al-ʿUlūm* (Enumeration of the sciences), that was also known to medieval Europe in its Latin translation, contains a comprehensive didactic account of the hierarchical relationship he saw between different kinds of sciences—rational, linguistic, theological, and juridical—and their subdivisions, establishing the precise order in which they should be studied.

It is a testimony to the integrative power of al-Fārābī's system that in his works different branches of philosophy begin to display inherent interconnections that are both unexpected and, to a good degree, original in their construction. For example, his theory of prophecy, revelation, and religion is inextricably linked to and makes sense only in the fuller context of his logic and philosophy of language on the one hand, and epistemology and metaphysics on the other, and all of this is related to his psychology and philosophy of mind. But then, quite unexpectedly, his discourses on metaphysics are largely to be found not in isolated treatises on this subject, but in his political writings, in particular *al-Madīna al-Fāḍila* (The virtuous city) and *al-Siyāsa al-Madaniyya* (Civil polity). Likewise, he hardly dedicates separated treatises to psychology and philosophy of mind; his discussions on these disciplines are again to be found in his political works. Does it mean that political writings form the core of al-Fārābī's system? The answer to this question cannot be straightforward.

The complexity arises because al-Fārābī's system has multiple cores at once, each core having been worked with equally uncompromising forensic diligence. Logic forms one of these cores, where he surpassed Syriac logicians by going beyond the traditionally limited number of Aristotle's specific logical works they read and commented upon, and pioneering the study of the entire range of Aristotle's logical treatises, a corpus known as the *Organon*, as well as *Rhetorics* and *Poetics*. This is a major event in the history of philosophy. Apart from his epitomes of and commentaries on Aristotle's individual logical texts, al-Fārābī also wrote his own *Kitāb al-Ḥurūf* (Book of letters) and *Kitāb al-Alfaẓ al-Musta'mala fi'l-Manṭiq* (Book of utterances employed in logic), both of which concern logic and its relationship with language. Given this, these two books can also be considered discourses in linguistic philosophy. Here it would seem that al-Fārābī is trying to reduce all else in his philosophical universe to logical-linguistic problems. And it is this reductionism that makes logic one of the core components of his system.

But on both historical and philosophical grounds, al-Fārābī's discourses on prophecy and religion can legitimately be considered yet another core of his system. For if all true philosophers bear the onus of communicating their philosophy to the masses, as al-Fārābī believes, following Plato; and if attainment of happiness through the establishment of a just civil society is the very aim of philosophy, and—speaking metaphysically and psychology as he does in his *Taḥṣīl al-Sa'āda* (Attainment of happiness)—human happiness ultimately consists in the soul's assimilation with the "agent intellect" *(al-'aql al-fa''al)*, being the supreme and the last in the hierarchy of four intellects that he posits in a Neoplatonic vein; then by virtue of his own doctrine, the ideal philosopher and the true prophet receiving revelation become practically identical. Indeed in the *Taḥṣīl* al-Fārābī does argue for the real and conceptual identity of the philosopher and the lawgiver (that is, the prophet), and so writing about philosophy and reason—which was al-Fārābī's fundamental trade—was effectively writing about prophecy and religion.

While neither consistent nor neat on this issue, al-Fārābī says repeatedly that true prophet is an ideal philosopher—for true prophecy, like the religion that it generates, is the symbolization and imitation of those very truths that are known demonstratively and discursively to the philosopher. This symbolization of philosophical truths is accomplished by the prophet through his supremely keen imaginative faculty that has *muḥākāh* (mimesis) as one of its functions. By means of *muḥākāh*, the prophet is able to represent objects with the images of other objects and to depict even immaterial realities. In this way philosophical truths, imaginatively symbolized, are communicated to the members of the general public who thereby receive abstract intelligibles from the prophet in a concrete form that they are able to grasp non-philosophically.

Historically too, al-Fārābī's concern with prophecy and religion can be considered a core of his system, with every other element of his thought appearing to be anchored in this concern and reduced to it. For it would seem that he was engaged fundamentally in addressing what happened to be a historical contingency—namely, Islam's encounter with Hellenism. The phenomenon of Islamic religion had become too massive to be ignored by him; he took it seriously and took it upon himself to give it an all-embracing philosophical respectability, while at the same time creating a niche for Hellenistic rational philosophy in an Arabic-Islamic milieu. Indeed, it is al-Fārābī who established the classical tradition of Arabic philosophers' attitude to revelation. It has been observed that his interest in types of rationality, modes of discourse, hierarchy of intellects, imagination, poetics, and the relations between ordinary and philosophical language all reflect that very core concern with revelation.

And yet it is possible to identify many other cores in al-Fārābī's philosophical world, and this only shows the richness, range, intricacy, and coherence of the system he built and the intellectual control that guided this grand task.

BIBLIOGRAPHY

Though highly simplified, Majid Fakhry's monograph, *Al-Fārābī, Founder of Islamic Neoplatonism* (Oxford, 2002), is a good single-volume introduction to different aspects of the philosopher's system. It also has a useful updated bibliography which lists all modern editions of al-Fārābī's texts as well as translations of his texts into modern European languages; also specified are Arabic sources and a selection of secondary works. Ian Netton's *Al-Fārābī and His School* (London, 1992) is a crisply written general work which clarifies many hitherto obscure areas of al-Fārābī's thought.

For al-Fārābī's contributions to the formal aspects of logic, F. W. Zimmerman's introduction in his translations of *Al-Fārābī's Commentary and Short Treatise on Aristotle's De Interpretatione* (London, 1981) is still the most rigorous piece of work in this field, learned and reliable. Readers with specialized interests should also look at the studies of Charles Butterworth, D. M. Dunlop, and Muhsin Mahdi. But for the non-expert, Deborah Black's chapter on al-Fārābī in *Routledge History of Islamic Philosophy*, edited by Seyyed H. Nasr and Oliver Leaman (London, 1996) is another readable, solid, brief but comprehensive survey.

S. NOMANUL HAQ (2005)

FAREL, GUILLAUME (1489–1565), was an early Protestant reformer of western Switzerland. Born in Gap in the Alps of southeastern France of a poor but noble family, Farel studied in Paris and there came under the influence of the Christian humanist Jacques Lefèvre. Through Lefèvre, Farel was introduced to Paul's epistles and to the doctrine of justification by faith alone. Lefèvre and his students left Paris for Meaux, where they had the support of Bishop Briçonnet, a mild reformer and also a student of Lefèvre, and of Marguerite of Navarre. Farel and others were authorized to preach in the surrounding territory. Neither Briçonnet nor Lefèvre saw a need to renounce Catholicism, and Farel's ideas and preaching were soon forbidden as too radical.

After leaving Meaux, Farel became acquainted with most of the leading reformers. In 1526 he settled in Aigle under the control of Bern, taking part in that city's religious reformation, and in 1529 he introduced the Reformation to Neuchâtel. In 1532 he visited the Waldensians and was present at the synod when they adopted the principles of the Protestant Reformation and began their alignment with Reformed Protestantism.

Farel's most significant work for the future of Protestantism took place in Geneva, which he first visited in 1532. Opposition to the Reformation was strong, but Farel persisted under the protection of Bern. Geneva came to a full acceptance of the Reformation on Sunday, May 21, 1536.

Expelled, along with Calvin, in 1538 from Geneva, Farel returned to Neuchâtel and devoted the last twenty-seven years of his life to building up this church. He continued his preaching missions in neighboring territories almost to the time of his death in 1565. It remained for Calvin, whom Farel had compelled to serve the Reformation in Geneva, to make that city the center of Reformed Protestantism.

Farel's primary contribution was that of a preacher and advocate of the Reformation. He was an intense man of passionate conviction and a powerful preacher who commanded the attention of audiences and elicited opposition as well as conviction. He is best known for his work in Geneva and the support he gave to Calvin until the latter's death. As a writer, he left 350 to 400 letters that, together with those of other reformers, played an important part in the Reformation. He was also the author of various polemical and practical tracts. His liturgy, "The Manner Observed in Preaching When the People Are Assembled to Hear the Word of God," was, according to Bard Thompson in his *Liturgies of the Western Church,* the "first manual of evangelical worship in the French language." Farel's best and most important work was *Sommaire: C'est une brieve declaration d'aucuns lieux fort nécessaires a un chacun chrestien pour mettre sa confiance en Dieu et a ayder son prochain,* the first summary of the evangelical faith in the French language. It was published in six editions during Farel's lifetime; the last was corrected and completed in conformity with Calvinist theology.

Bibliography

Guillaume Farel, 1489–1565: Biographie nouvelle écrite d'après les documents originaux (Paris, 1930) is an outstanding volume published by a committee of Farel scholars with many collaborators. Two English translations of lives of Farel by nineteenth-century biographers are available: Melchior Kirchhofer's *The Life of William Farel, the Swiss Reformer* (London, 1837) and Frances A. Bevan's *William Farel,* 5th ed. (London, 1880). An extended account of Farel's work can be found in Philip Schaff's *History of the Christian Church,* vol. 7, *Modern Christianity: The German Reformation and the Swiss Reformation* (1910; reprint, Grand Rapids, Mich., 1974) and in Williston Walker's biography, *John Calvin: The Organizer of Reformed Calvinism, 1509–1564* (1906; reprint, New York, 1969).

JOHN H. LEITH (1987)

FASTI (from *fasti dies,* "the divinely authorized days") were the calendars of the ancient Romans. They are the only known form of a graphical representation of all days of the year from the ancient Mediterranean world. By usually displaying twelve columns of the days of the single months, the *fasti* offered the standard pattern for Christian calendars from late antiquity and ultimately for all representations of the Julian and Gregorian calendars. The listing of the days was organized by the recurring letters A to H (for a continuous week of eight days) at the beginning of every entry. The main information concerned the juridical character of the day, especially indicating whether it was *fas* (right) to open processes in front of the Roman praetor or not (*nefas*). The terminologically divine sanction had other consequences, too: The *comitia,* the Roman legislative body of the people, could not meet on *dies nefasti*; and, probably at the beginning of the third century BCE, a special class of *dies comitiales* that could not be used for the opening of legal cases but could be used for the holding of assemblies was established.

The distribution of days in the known late republican calendars was obviously the outcome of different political and juridical practices; at least from the second century BCE onwards the regulation as a whole was attributed to the codifications of the mid-fifth century (Twelve tables). Religious traditions, too, were integrated: *feriae,* a special class of days given to the gods as property (and hence free from every mundane activity) were marked in a particular way; that is, as *dies nefasti* whose violation made piacular sacrifices necessary (marked by the letters *NP* and abbreviations of the festival names). Obviously, the featuring of this type of religious information helped to enhance the legitimacy of the rigid systematization of temporal rules when published from within the college of the pontiffs (*pontifices,* priests), who formed an important body for the development of legal ruling and procedural guidelines during the early and middle republic. An important tradition attributed the publication to Gnaeus Flavius, probably aedile in 304 BCE and scribe of the pontifical college.

Scholars of Roman religion took a particular interest in the list of the *feriae* as transmitted by early imperial *fasti,* and they postulated a regal "calendar of Numa" as its ultimate source (Theodor Mommsen, 1817–1903). Hence, the *fasti* gained the status of the single most important source for early Roman history (Georg Wissowa, 1859–1931). Yet, even if the list contained some very old traditions, it is not possible to read it as a coherent archaic system. A large number of festivals for Mars and the dedications of the former festivals of the full moon, the *(e)idus,* point to a complex history.

The legal and political institutions regulated by the *fasti* gradually fell into disuse under the Empire. Two developments, however, gave them high importance as a visual medium. Within the growing interest in a systematic reconstruction of Rome's past during the third and second centuries BCE, the *fasti* were discovered as a medium for a display of historical achievements. When shortly after 179 BCE Marcus Fulvius Nobilior, assisted by the poet Ennius, dedicated a painted calendar to the temple of Hercules and the Muses, the temporal pattern of the year was used to add the dates of the dedications of other temples, usually events caused and financed by successful warfare. Days of iterated disaster, too, could be memorized, thereby rendering the year into a temporal "mnemotope." Additionally, a list of the highest Roman magistrates, including the consuls used in dating ("eponyms"), was added. This practice was frequently imitated, hence the term *fasti* was used for many lists of magistrates. Not infrequently, such lists could be enlarged to short chronicles by the addition of important dated events (e.g., the *Fasti Ostienses*). Whereas the text of the calendar—even if displayed in middle Italian townships—is cautiously restricted to events in the city of Rome, the lists could present (or add) local magistrates and connect local history with the history of the hegemonial city of Rome.

The dictatorship of Caesar, his divinization, and the religious restoration under Augustus witnessed a second development. A new class of *feriae* was born: festivals celebrating imperial victories and dynastic events. Without clear assignation of a divine owner, these days were given the status of *feriae* and meticulously documented in the *fasti*. Suddenly the ordinary medium of temporal coordination, the calendar (recently reformed by C. Iulius Caesar), was an indicator of recent political developments. Within a few years, the fashion of producing calendars in the form of large (and expensive) marble inscriptions spread over Rome and the center of Italy, even reaching to Taormina (Sicily), an area practicing an alternative form of lunar time-reckoning. The earliest known (and fragmentarily transmitted) marble calendar stems from the grove of Dea Dia, the sanctuary of the priesthoods of the Arval Brethren, reorganized by Octavianus/Augustus around 30 BCE and in particular dedicated to the cult and welfare of Roman emperors. Soon copies were to be found on public places or in the assembly halls of voluntary associations. Probably without larger practical usage (papyrus calendars must have been widespread), such inscriptions demonstrated loyalty to the emperor and his political as well as religious program.

The new interest in the calendar was not restricted to stonemasons. Parallel to the spread of inscribed *fasti*, commentaries on the *fasti* were written. The antiquarian interest of late republican writers like Marcus Terentius Varro (116–27 BCE) in the institution of the Roman year was intensified. Varro, who pursued the initial stage of a political career, entertained vast historical interest, paying particular attention to the history of language and literature. Although philosophical originality is denied to his eclecticism, even his main antiquarian work, the *Antiquitates rerum humanarum et divinarum*, is controlled by an academic-skeptical outlook. Human society (as the title indicates) precedes its religious institutions, and festivals, like the notion of specific gods and their worship, arise under specific and partly reconstructable historical circumstances. These premises are reflected in Varro's etymological dealing with the calendar in his *De lingua Latina 6*.

It is noteworthy that the versified commentary of Publius Ovidius Naso (43 BCE –17 CE) explicitly declared the same interest that could be detected in the temporal pattern of the spread of inscriptional *fasti*. The emperor is shown as an inseparable part of Roman history and religion; his (extraconstitutional) power is naturalized by his integration into the cosmic scheme of the rising and setting of stars that is part of Ovid's poetic project and easily linked to the traditional calendar by the Julian reform. At the same time, the calendrical scheme offers a convenient pattern for a description of Roman ritual, of those festivals and temples that form the visible part of Roman religion. From Varro's *Antiquitates rerum humanarum et divinarum* and Verrius Flaccus's lexicon on the "meaning of words" down to Macrobius's fifth-century *Saturnalia* dialogue, this pattern remained attractive for the historical or nostalgic description of contemporary or past religion. Ovid himself, who finally ended up in exile, stresses the contemporary commemorative and entertaining functioning of urban festivals. Augustus, to whom the first edition (in 4 CE or shortly before) was dedicated, gets his due share of attention and praise. Yet, Ovid deliberately stops his poem by the end of June—that is, before dealing with the dynastically named and festival-laden months of Iulius and Augustus. It is rather in the epic *Metamorphoses* (fifteen books), published a few years later, that Ovid gives a teleological account of universal and Roman history leading down to Caesar's divinization.

Even if the fashion of epigraphic *fasti* was restricted to the early Principate, the graphical form of the *fasti* remained attractive for wall paintings, as well as for luxury book calendars. The Chronograph of 354 CE forms an ensemble of lists and chronicles around the kernel of contemporary *fasti*, still featuring the pagan festivals and dynastic anniversaries of the mid-fourth century. At the same time, processes that de facto and de jure replaced traditional holidays by attributing the characteristics of *feriae* to Christian festivals continued and renewed the *fasti*. The Jewish-Christian week of seven days, already marked in a calendar of Augustan times as the astrological week of the seven planets, replaced the Roman nundinal week of eight days by the second half of the fourth century. Even if it was difficult to graphically insert the complex determination of the festival of Easter into a calendar intended to be in use for a couple of years, the "birthdays" (*dies natales*) of martyrs and other saints, commemorated on the fixed days of the Julian calendar by the Western church, could easily slip into the graphical (and mental) pattern of the Roman calendar.

SEE ALSO Calendars, overview article; Roman Religion, article on The Early Period.

BIBLIOGRAPHY

Barchiesi, Alessandro. *Il poeta e il principe: Ovidio e il discorso Augusteo.* Rome, 1994. Translated as *The Poet and the Prince: Ovid and Augustine Discourse* (Berkeley, 1997).

Degrassi, Attilio. *Inscriptiones Italiae,* vol. 13, fasc. 2. Rome, 1963.

Feeney, Denis. *Literature and Religion at Rome: Cultures, Contexts, and Beliefs.* Cambridge, U.K., 1998.

Frazer, James George, ed. and trans. *Publii Ovidii Nasonis Fastorum libri sex: The Fasti of Ovid.* 5 vols. London, 1929.

Lehmann, Yves. *Varron théologien et philosophe romain.* Brussels, 1997.

Michels, Agnes. *The Calendar of the Roman Republic.* Princeton, 1967.

Pfaff-Reydellet. Maud. *Le princeps dans les Fastes d'Ovide.* Stuttgart, Germany, 2004.

Porte, Danielle. *L'Étiologie religieuse dans les Fastes d'Ovide.* Paris, 1985.

Radke, Gerhard. *Fasti Romani: Betrachtungen zur Frühgeschichte des römischen Kalenders.* Münster, Germany, 1990.

Rüpke, Jörg. *Kalender und Öffentlichkeit: Die Geschichte der Repräsentation und religiösen Qualifikation von Zeit in Rom.* Berlin, 1995.

Salzman, Michele Renee. *On Roman Time: The Codex-Calendar of 354 and the Rhythms of Urban Life in Late Antiquity.* Berkeley, 1990.

Scullard, H. H. *Festivals and Ceremonies of the Roman Republic.* London, 1981.

Vidman, Ladislav. *Fasti Ostienses.* 2d ed. Prague, 1982.

JOHN SCHEID (1987)
JÖRG RÜPKE (2005)
Translated from French by Matthew J. O'Connell

FASTING, that is, complete or partial abstinence from nourishment, is an almost universal phenomenon within both Eastern and Western cultures. Although fasting has been and continues to be subscribed to for a variety of reasons, the present article deals with it as a phenomenon evoked for religious reasons, that is, by ideals or beliefs that consider it a necessary or advantageous practice leading to the initiation or maintenance of contact with divinity, or some supranatural or transcendent being.

Although the origins of fasting as a moral or religious discipline are obscure, the custom or practice of fasting is attested in many ancient cultures. The fact that it was in some cultures connected with rites of mourning has led some scholars to equate its origins with the custom whereby friends and relatives leave with the dead the food and drink that they (the living) would normally consume, so that the deceased might have nourishment in an afterlife.

Others consider fasting in earlier cultures to have arisen as a result of the discovery that it could induce a state of susceptibility to visions and dreams and hence give the practitioner direct access to a spiritual world. As such it became for some a discipline creating the proper state necessary for some degree of participation in divinity. It gradually became an integral part of a purity ritual with definite religious intent. In some of the more archaic religions fasting became part of the discipline ensuring both a defense against taboo powers and a means of obtaining *mana,* or sacred power.

Within certain Greco-Roman philosophical schools and religious fellowships (e.g., the Pythagorean), fasting, as one aspect of asceticism, was closely aligned to the belief that humanity had originally experienced a primordial state of perfection that was forfeited by a transgression. Through various ascetic practices such as fasting, poverty, and so forth, the individual could be restored to a state where communication and union with the divine was again made possible. Hence, in various religious traditions a return to a primordial state of innocence or bliss triggered a number of ascetical practices deemed necessary or advantageous in bringing about such return. For such groups the basic underlying assumption was that fasting was in some way conducive to initiating or maintaining contact with some divine power or powers. In some religious groups (for example, Judaism, Christianity, and Islam) fasting gradually became a standard way of expressing devotion and worship to a specific divine being.

Although it is difficult to pinpoint a specific rationale or motivation for an individual's or a group's fasting, in most cultures that ascribe to it at least three motivations are easily discernible: (1) preliminary to or preparatory for an important event or time in an individual's or a people's life; (2) as an act of penitence or purification; or (3) as an act of supplication.

PREPARATORY FASTING. In addition to the basic underlying assumption that fasting is an essential preparation for divine revelation or for some type of communing with the spiritual (what is above or beyond the natural for humans), many cultures believe that fasting is a prelude to important times in a person's life. It purifies or prepares the person (or group) for greater receptivity in communion with the spiritual. In the Greco-Roman mystery religions, for example, fasting was deemed an aid to enlightenment by a deity, and an initiate into most of these religions had to abstain from all or certain specified foods and drink in order to receive knowledge of the mysteries of the specific religion.

Within some of the mystery cults, fasting was incorporated as part of the ritual preparation for the incubation sleep that, by means of dreams, was to provide answers to specific questions and needs of the person. Dreams and visions were viewed as media through which spiritual or divine revelations were made manifest. Philostratus (c. 170–c. 245 CE), for example, presents the view that since the soul was influenced by diet, only by frugal living and the avoidance of meat and drink could the soul receive unconfused dreams (*Life of Apollonius* 2.37). Both Greek philosophers (e.g., Pythagoreans and Neoplatonists) and Hebrew prophets believed that fasting could produce trancelike states through which revelations would occur. Plutarch narrates how the priests of ancient Egypt abstained from meat and wine in order to receive and interpret divine revelations (*Isis and Osiris* 5–6), and Iamblichus tells how the prophetess fasted three days prior to giving an oracle (*Egyptian Mysteries* 3.7).

Among the Eastern traditions Hindu and Jain ascetics fasted while on pilgrimage and in preparation for certain festivals. Within classical Chinese religious practice, *chai,* or ritual fasting, preceded the time of sacrifices. By contrast, later Chinese religious thought, particularly Daoism, taught that "fasting of the heart" (*xinzhai*), rather than bodily fasting, was more beneficial to arriving at "the Way" (*dao*). Confucianism followed the practice of Confucius in approving fasting as preparation for those times set aside for worship of ancestral spirits. Although the Buddha taught moderation rather than excessive fasting, many Buddhist monks and nuns adhered to the custom of eating only one meal per day, in the forenoon, and they were obliged to fast on days of new and full moon. Among modern-day Buddhists it is more common to fast and confess one's sins four times per month.

Within the Judaic tradition only one day of fasting was imposed by Mosaic law, Yom Kippur, the Day of Atonement (*Lv.* 16:29–34), but four additional days were added after the Babylonian exile (*Zec.* 8:19) to commemorate days on which disasters had occurred. The Hebrew scriptures set fasting within the context of being vigilant in the service of Yahveh (e.g., *Lv.* 16:29ff.; *Jgs.* 20:26), and it was considered important as a preliminary to prophecy (e.g., Moses fasted forty days on Sinai; Elijah fasted forty days as he journeyed to Horeb). Judaism allowed for individual voluntary fasts, and there is evidence that Mondays and Thursdays were set aside by some Jewish communities as special days of fasting. According to Tacitus, fasting had become so characteristic of the Jews of the first century that Augustus could boast that he fasted more seriously than a Jew (*Histories* 5.4).

Although formalized fasting was spoken against in the New Testament (*Mt.* 6:16–6:18), it eventually became the favorite ascetic practice of the desert dwellers and monastic men and women who saw it as a necessary measure to free the soul from worldly attachments and desires. Within the Christian tradition there gradually developed seasonal fasts such as the Lenten one of forty days preparatory to Easter; Rogation Days in spring in supplication for good crops; and Ember Days, days of prayer and fasting during each of the four seasons of the year. There were also weekly fasts on Wednesdays and Fridays and fasts prior to solemn occasions celebrating important moments in people's lives (e.g., baptism, ordination to priesthood, admission to knighthood, and reception of the Eucharist).

In the Islamic tradition Muslims continue to observe the ninth month, Ramaḍān, as one of rigorous fasting (*ṣawm*), during which days no liquid or food is allowed between dawn and sunset, as stipulated in the Qurʾān (2:180ff.). Some of the stricter Muslim groups fast each Monday and Thursday, and the Qurʾān recommends fasting as a penance during a pilgrimage, three days going and seven returning (2:193). Ṣūfīs recommend additional fasting for the purpose of communing with the divine, and the Shīʿī Muslims require fasting as one of the ways of commemorating the martyrdom of ʿAlī, the son-in-law of the Prophet, and his two sons.

Basic to the beliefs of many Native American tribes was the view that fasting was efficacious for receiving guidance from the Great Spirit. Generally, a brave was sent off into the wilderness on a fast in quest of such guidance, which was usually revealed through a personal vision. The young man's vision was often viewed as necessary for his future success in life, indicating a personal relationship between himself and his guardian spirit. Lakota braves, for example, were advised in their search for a vision of Wakantanka, the supreme being, to "walk in remote places, crying to Wakantanka, and neither eat nor drink for four days." Within many of the tribes there was a period of ritual fasting prior to a boy's reaching puberty and a girl's first menstrual period, considered times of growth into adulthood. In New South Wales, Australia, boys had to fast for two days at their *bora* ceremonies. In the Aztec culture the ritual training required of one who aspired to become a sacrificing priest included fasting as one form of abstinence. While fasting was often viewed as a disciplinary measure that would strengthen the body and character of the individual, prolonged fasting and other austerities were also undergone so that the individual might see or hear the guardian spirit who would remain with him or her for life.

FASTING AS PENANCE OR PURIFICATION. Ancient Egyptian and Babylonian customs included ritualized fasting as a form of penance that accompanied other expressions of sorrow for wrongdoing. Like people of later times, these nations viewed fasting as meritorious in atoning for faults and sins and thus turning away the wrath of the gods. In the *Book of Jonah,* for example, the Assyrians are depicted as covered with sackcloth, weeping, fasting, and praying to God for forgiveness (*Jon.* 3:5ff.).

For the Jews, fasting was an outward expression of inner penitence, and on various occasions a general fast was proclaimed as a public recognition of the sin of the people (*1 Sm.* 14:24, *1 Kgs.* 21:9, *Jer.* 36:9). Yom Kippur, the Day of Atonement, is such a day of fasting and praying for forgiveness of sins. But fasting is also viewed as a means of orienting the human spirit to something or someone greater. According to Philo Judaeus (25 BCE–50 CE), the Therapeutae, a group of Jewish contemplatives living in community, fasted as a means of purifying the spirit so that it could turn itself to more spiritual activities such as reading and study (*On the Contemplative Life*). The Essenes, a Jewish group who followed their "righteous teacher" into the wilderness at Qumran (c. 135 BCE–70 CE), in their *Manual of Discipline* prescribed fasting as one of the ways of purification, of preparing for the coming of the "end of days."

Although fasting as a means of atonement and purification is evident in other traditions, it was among the Christians that fasting became a predominant feature. Already in the first and second centuries it began to appear as one of the many ascetic practices that became widespread in the Middle Ages. With the rapid growth of ascetic movements that incorporated Greek dualism into their thought patterns, fasting became an important means of ridding the body of its attachment to material possessions and pleasures, thus freeing the person for attaining the higher good, the love for and imitation of Christ. The prevailing notion was that whereas food in moderation was a necessary good for maintaining health, abstention from food was particularly effective in controlling the balance between body and spirit. Like the Pythagoreans with their elaborate taboos on food (sixth to fourth century BCE), the early Christians saw such ascetic practices as fasting, praying, and almsgiving as means of reducing or eliminating the tension between the earthbound body and the divine, spiritual soul. Although it is true that for some individuals or groups fasting became an end in itself rather than a means to an end, most monastic manuals or rules warn the monastics to avoid excessive fasting, which could bring harm to both body and soul. Though the practice of fasting varied in different countries, most Christian manuals of instruction and worship began to regulate more strictly the times for obligatory fasts (cf. *Didachē* 7ff.; Justin Martyr, *1 Apology* 61). But it was with the growth of monastic communities in the fourth century that fasts began to be more universal.

Modern-day Christian denominations display a considerable diversity of opinion and practice in regard to fasting. For most Protestant denominations, except for some of the more evangelically oriented groups, fasting is left to the discretion of the individual. Although within the Roman Catholic and Greek Orthodox churches prescriptions still govern both individual and corporate practices, rigid fasting practices have been abolished. Roman Catholics still practice partial fasting and abstinence from meat on Ash Wednesday and Good Friday. Within the Greek Orthodox church fasting is usually one of the acts of purification preparing one for participation in the liturgical mysteries.

Although Buddhists generally favor restraint in taking food, and many consider fasting a non-Buddhist practice, it is listed as one of the thirteen Buddhist practices that can serve as an aid to leading a happy life, a means of purification (*dhutanga*). Therefore, many Buddhist monks have the custom of eating only one meal a day, often eating only from the alms bowl and declining a second helping. For other Buddhists enlightenment was considered more easily attainable by renunciation of wrong ideas and views rather than by fasting. Within Jainism there is the belief that certain ascetic practices, like fasting, are purificatory in that they can remove the accumulation of *karman* that weighs down the life-monad. Fasting could therefore carry people upward along the path to liberation from *karman*. Within the Islamic tradition fasting is viewed as one of the "good works," one of the recognized duties of the devout Muslim, and is considered efficacious in pardoning an individual from all past sins (Tibrīzī, *Mishkāt al-maṣābīh* 7.7.1).

Within some of the Native American tribes, the practice of fasting was considered conducive to purifying the body prior to some great feat or challenge. The Cherokee Indians believed that prior to slaying an eagle the individual had to undergo a long period of prayer and fasting that purified the body, strengthening it for the necessary combat. Siouan-speaking Indians believed that before both hunting and war the body had to be purified through fasting for these noble tasks. Among the Incas, fasting from salt, chili peppers, meat, or *chicha* (beer made from maize) was one of the ways of preparing the body for an important event and also for a public form of penance.

FASTING AS SUPPLICATION. Although it is difficult in many instances to distinguish clearly between fasting as a means of penitence and fasting as a means of supplication, within certain traditions the latter has widespread usage. Within Judaism, for example, fasting was one way of "bending the ear of Yahveh," of asking God to turn to the Jews in mercy and grant them the favor requested. Ahab, for example, fasted to avert the disaster predicted by Elijah (*1 Kgs.* 21:27–29, cf. *Nm.* 1:4, *2 Chr.* 20:3, *Jer.* 36:9). Because penitence and supplication were often dual motivational forces for fasting within Judaism, fasting emerged as both conciliatory and supplicatory. As in the Christian and Islamic traditions, the Jewish notion of fasting reflected an attitude of interior sorrow and conversion of heart. Within the Christian ascetic circles, fasting was viewed as one of the more meritorious acts, which exorcised demons and demonic temptation from the individual's consciousness. Therefore, fasting emerged within Christianity as a potent force in calling down God's mercy and aid in ridding the individual of temptations against "the world, the flesh, and the devil." Fasting was a means of calling God to the struggling Christians' side in order to be both strength and encouragement in the battle against sin. In the Qurʾān fasting as supplication to God is considered of merit only if one also abandons false words and deeds. Otherwise, God pays no heed to the supplication (see, e.g., *sūrah* 2:26).

Within other groups fasting was also viewed as meritorious in obtaining rewards from higher powers. In the Intichiuma ceremonies of the tribes in central Australia fasting was practiced to assure an increase in the totem food supply. Young Jain girls fasted as one means of requesting the higher power to give them a good husband and a happy married life. Fasting frequently accompanied or preceded the dance rituals of certain tribes who prayed for a renewal of fertility and a productive harvest from the earth (e.g., the Dakota Sun Dance; the Cheyenne New Life Lodge; the Ponca Sacred Dance, or Mystery Dance).

In summary, from earliest records to contemporary society, fasting has been a common religious practice, serving as both a prelude to and a means of deepening the experience of transcendence of the material or bodily state. The voluntary abstinence from nourishment has been for many an ideal means of expressing human dependence on a higher power, or a liberation from those things that stifle aspirations toward a "higher" form of existence. Fasting has often served as a sign and symbol of the human conversion toward something beyond the everyday, a turning toward the spiritual, the transcendent, the Great Spirit, God, and so on. In modern times the therapeutic value of fasting has been adopted as a good health practice that has often taken on the aspect of religious ritual.

SEE ALSO Asceticism; Ṣawm.

BIBLIOGRAPHY

Brandon, S. G. F., ed. *A Dictionary of Comparative Religion.* London, 1970.

MacCulloch, J. A., and A. J. Maclean. "Fasting." In *Encyclopaedia of Religion and Ethics,* edited by James Hastings, vol. 5. Edinburgh, 1912.

MacDermot, Violet. *The Cult of the Seer in the Ancient Middle East.* London, 1971.

Rogers, Eric N. *Fasting: The Phenomenon of Self-Denial.* Nashville, 1976.

Ryan, Thomas. *Fasting Rediscovered: A Guide to Health and Wholeness for Your Body-Spirit.* New York, 1981.

Underhill, Ruth M. *Red Man's America: A History of Indians in the United States.* Rev. ed. Chicago, 1971.

Wakefield, Gordon S., ed. *The Westminster Dictionary of Christian Spirituality.* London, 1983.

New Sources

Berghuis, Kent D. "A Biblical Perspective on Fasting." *Bibliotheca Sacra* 629 (2001): 86–103.

Diamond, Eliezer. *Holy Men and Hunger Artists: Fasting and Asceticism in Rabbinic Culture.* Oxford and New York, 2004.

Kaushik, Jai Narain. *Fasts of the Hindus around the Week: Background Stories, Ways of Performance and Their Importance.* Delhi, 1992.

Lambert, David. "Fasting as a Penitential Rite: A Biblical Phenomenon?" *Harvard Theological Review* 96 (2003): 477–512.

Shaw, Teresa Marie. *The Burden of the Flesh: Fasting and Sexuality in Early Christianity.* Minneapolis, 1998.

Siebenbrunner, Barbara. *Die Problematik der kirchlichen Fasten- und Abstinenzgesetzgebung: eine Untersuchung zu dem im Zuge des zweiten Vatikanischen Konzils erfolgten Wandel.* Frankfurt am Main and New York, 2001.

Stökl, Daniel Johannes. "Whose Fast Is It? The Ember Day of September and Yom Kippur." In *The Ways That Never Parted: Jews and Christians in Late Antiquity and the Early Middle Ages,* edited by Adam H. Becker and Annette Yoshiko Reed, pp. 259–282. Tübingen, 2003.

ROSEMARY RADER (1987)
Revised Bibliography

FATE.

Derived from the Latin *fatum* (something spoken, a prophetic declaration, an oracle, a divine determination), the term *fate* denotes the idea that everything in human lives, in society, and in the world itself takes place according to a set, immutable pattern. *Fatalism* is the term for the submission by human beings to fate in resignation. Fate and fatalism should not be confused with the idea of determinism propagated by nineteenth-century philosophical positivism, which was convinced that science was on its way to uncovering that law of all cause and effect relationships in the world. The assumption of determinism was that a complete set of scientific laws was within reach of the human mind, and that all these would reside in the public domain and be transparent to inquiring reason. By contrast, the notion of fate, in whatever variation, language, or shade of meaning it occurs, always retains a basic element of mystery. Fate may be in the hands of some powerful, superhuman being; it may be superior to the gods; it may be accessible to some select individuals. But, in contrast with philosophical determinism, not only is a certain knowledge possible vis-à-vis fate, but so is a certain "negotiation" with, or even a staving off of, fate's decrees.

There are no religious traditions in which a notion of fate is supreme, exclusive, and all-powerful. Furthermore, the effort to define fate in a universally valid way cannot go much further than the formal lines drawn above. Only in psychological terms can generalizations be added. The more problematic, and at the same time more fascinating, issues arise when one confronts the variety of notions about fate in cultures and historical eras.

PSYCHOLOGICAL OBSERVATIONS. In the intellectual mood of the modern age, it is natural to think of the notion of fate first of all in psychological terms. Some remarks can certainly be made here, although they do not help a great deal in understanding fate in the ways in which it is presented in specific religious contexts.

The idea that fear is a root cause of all religions was already proposed in antiquity, and through the ages thinkers have tried to revive the idea, though with little success. With respect to fate and fatalism, however, the function of a psychological ambivalence in many human situations seems hard to deny. Especially in the case of fatalism—that is, the full surrender to fate—an attitude of defeat is in evidence in the belief that the future is as inevitable and fixed as the past. One's acts become acts of a higher power, and Sigmund Freud's observation concerning a death wish as the ultimate motivation may be fully applicable in many instances. Such ambivalence consists of the renunciation of one's own reason (hence also of one's own responsibility) and the hypothesis of a rational coherence of events in another order.

Examples of a grisly sort of fatalism became familiar in the twentieth century. During World War II the suicidal Japanese torpedo attacks and the suicides in SS (Schutzstaffel) quarters during Adolf Hitler's regime occurred in response to a notion of destiny *(Schicksal)* supposedly far beyond the value of individual human lives. Well known are the endeavors to inculcate soldiers in the Nazi years in Germany with fatalism—in the dubious certainty that this was an ancient Germanic warrior stance. In the 1980s, religiously inspired suicidal attacks on targets conceived as threats to Islam, especially in the cause of Shīʿah, became an almost regular feature in the Middle East, and many more suicidal missions have been undertaken in various areas of the Middle East, not only among traditionally different factions within Islam, but particularly against the State of Israel. It is important to look at these phenomena as instances of fatalism. Indeed, there are many phenomena in the present world that have far more than a superficial resemblance to "fatalism." Wars have devastated the lives of soldiers and civilians in Korea, Vietnam, many African nations, and Iraq, where fatalism came to reign supreme, leaving soldiers and citizens with inner, indeed fatal, devastation, even when they survived. One should not dismiss such matters from an inquiry into "fate," for one needs the reminder that cults of fate can revive much more easily than one may imagine. An example, if not of fatalism per se, then of tendencies in this direction in the modern West, began after World War II with the wave of astrology in general literature, as a rubric in most newspapers, and, perhaps more basically, as a way of filling up the empty space of an underlying uncertainty.

The cluster of fear, escape from fear, and dismissal of one's responsibility as a fundamental cause in the formation of certain conceptions of religion and fate is suggested both in the recent past and in ancient civilizations. The fear of rulers, wild animals, foes, disease, and many things under the rubric *nature* has had its influence on the formulation of religious ideas, even in the earliest times. Samuel Noah Kramer translated a few expressive lines from a Sumerian poet who obviously had meditated on some golden age as a time that contrasted with a fateful present. Characteristically, he thought of that age as one without fear:

> Once upon a time, there was no snake, There was no scorpion, There was no hyena, there was no lion, There was no wild dog, no wolf, There was no fear, no terror, Man had no rival. (Kramer, 1963, p. 262)

It would be wrong to conclude that the idea of fate could be fully explained as a projection of basic human fears or uncertainties. The most striking fact militating against this explanation is that certain periods and cultures that knew many fears and reasons for fear have little to tell us of fatalism.

EARLIEST EXPRESSION IN AGRICULTURAL CULTURES. There is no evidence of any religiously central preoccupation with fate in cultures preceding the earliest civilizations based on the cultivation of cereals, nor is there any special religiously significant place provided for notions of fate in hunting cultures. One looks in vain for a significant role or clear expression of "fate" in truly archaic or preliterate societies in general. Everything points to the relative comfort of a grain- or rice-producing culture as a minimum condition for a religious articulation concerning fate. At the same time, it seems obvious that the chance of crop failures by itself does not create a notion or cult of fate.

DIFFUSION OF ASTROLOGY. One complex of a fatalistic type, though certainly not among the earliest ones, has clearly passed beyond the borders of its land of origin and through many different language areas as well, and that is astrology. Two reasons may be given for its spread

First, it is possible to look upon endeavors to relate celestial observations to the course of human destinies as a special modification, under certain historical conditions, of the macrocosmic-microcosmic correspondence that seems to occur with the structure of human religious symbolization everywhere. In a sense, astrology is not an altogether new phenomenon but rather a transplantation within a common matrix when it appears and is diffused in late antiquity, grafted onto existing cosmogonic and cosmological traditions.

Although astronomical calculation had risen to great heights in ancient Babylon, full-blown astrological systems were first produced in the Greek language of the Hellenistic period. Nevertheless, it is important to realize that astronomy in early antiquity was not what would today be called an exact science, distinct from religion and the humanities. Details such as the linkage of the five classical planets plus the sun and the moon to different celestial spheres were accepted in all parts of the world that had any contact with the ancient Middle East. In all probability, this diffusion of ideas began well before the Hellenistic Age. Cosmological ideas among Siberian tribes, as well as architectonic expressions as far east as the Borobudur temple on Java, show the powerful influence of discoveries from the ancient Middle East. This leads to the second reason that astrology passed so easily from one cultural area to others that were on a lower level of civilization than Mesopotamia.

From the outset—from the earliest appearance of astronomical and mathematical tables in Babylon—formulas tracing and predicting the course of the heavenly bodies had never taken the form of a scientific enterprise in isolation. In the ancient Middle East this science was presented together with the invocations of deities—the clay tablets and other writings with astronomical and calendar data frequently show religious symbols at the same time. In Siberian and Mongolian shamanism, the shaman, the person with expert knowledge and experience of the traffic between this world and the other world, travels in his or her ecstatic journey from earth to heaven passing through the heavenly spheres in between, each as a rule represented by notches in the very real pole the shaman ascends; all the while the shaman is narrating to the community's people, who witness the events, what is happening from heaven to heaven. In India, the Vedic texts make frequent use of calendrical numbers, of months or days in the year, and equate them with ingredients necessary for traditional sacrifices and other rituals.

Thus each religious system did what was natural to it; rather than adding "scientific" information to its body of traditional lore, each appropriated the new discoveries as further revelations of religious reality and inserted them in the religious tradition as was fitting. That human life was intrinsically and harmoniously related to the cosmos was beyond doubt. The ground was well prepared for the waves of astrological influences that followed. As a result, the line separating astronomy from astrology is not easy to draw in the ancient and classical worlds. Astrology was accepted as a way to gain knowledge of details in the general macro-microcosmic harmony. It became possible to ascertain the relation of a person to the course of the heavenly bodies on the basis of the time of that person's birth and the celestial sign under which the birth had taken place. In principle, it became possible also to alter destiny. It is not difficult to see that astrology functions by and large in the same way in very different religious traditions and cultural areas. In Hinduism, the astrologer's counsel is taken very seriously—for example to determine the appropriate day for a wedding ceremony. In the world of Judaism and Christianity, astrology cannot boast of such integration in the religious tradition. The Greek philosophers were generally critical of astrology, and that tradition continued and was reinforced under the influence of the biblical tradition. Setting store by astrology's expertise was obviously not in harmony with God's supreme judgment and his power over human destiny. Nevertheless, wherever astrology functions, it remains based on the same principles of ancient science, and in that respect we may speak of a certain sameness, a homogeneity in the astrological complex throughout history.

Ancient and Classical Concerns. Wherever there are clear references to fate in religious documents, the expressions demonstrate immediately that one cannot speak of fate as a single concept. The assumptions and inquiries commonly used in logic, psychology, or sociology do not suffice. Within the history of religions, statements should depend on a clear recognition of the intentions shown by the traditions being investigated. It is beyond the scope of this entry to survey all religions, yet a number of different tendencies within their symbolic contexts can be indicated. The following points present some strands and specific meanings of *fate.* Without exaggerating their importance, they do point to "moments," in the sense of elements that are constituents of well-delineated notions of fate.

Fate that is relatively independent within a religious tradition. Not only moderns who consider themselves secularized, and in some manner "objective" in their views of religious traditions, but also the ancients, among them the Greeks and Romans, have had difficulty defining *fate.* The religious documents themselves show ambivalence. The documents show, however, that such ambivalence is not mere intellectual uncertainty but often an intentional compromise of distinct views, each of which is unassailable. In the case of fate, such necessary ambiguity is much easier to fathom than it is in most other symbolic complexes (e.g., sacrifices or forms of worship).

In the *Theogony,* Hesiod (eighth century BCE) collected and tried to classify ancient and even some pre-Homeric traditions. The Moirai, the goddesses of fate, together with some others, are called by Hesiod daughters of Night (*Theogony* 211–225), although he immediately adds that they punish transgressions by both men and the gods (217–222). When Zeus, king of the gods, has firmly established his rule, the role of the Moirai (together with the Horae, that is, the three goddesses Eunomia, Dikē, and Eirene) is that of dispensers of good and evil. In the new context they function as goddesses of fate, and they are also called the honored daughters of Zeus. The ambivalence, therefore, of their descent from Night and also from the supreme god, whose veneration is certainly the major theme of Hesiod's work, cannot be satisfactorily explained as a conflict of different traditions. It is, of course, possible that such supposed separate traditions existed, but then the major problem still remains: how did such very different pedigrees for the representations of fate come about? The ambivalence is no doubt likely to be related to the nature of fate: on the one hand, there exists an origin of darkness, if not of uncanny supreme independence; on the other, the central god cannot be depicted as subordinate to fate but must be seen as, in fact, generating it.

In the famous epics of the classical traditions, we find this view confirmed in detail. Homer (eighth century BCE) presents a series of dramatic scenes in *Iliad* 16 that establish the case of a purposeful ambivalence. Under the guidance of Patroclus, the Danaans win a mighty victory over the Trojans. Patroclus kills several heroes in succession. Then the Trojan warrior Sarpedon attempts to turn the battle and attacks Patroclus, only to meet with death by his opponent's spear. However, before this fight ensues, Zeus looks down on the battlefield. He has good reason to be concerned, for Sarpedon is his son. Zeus asks his wife Hera whether he should remove Sarpedon from the scene of battle and thus preserve his life, or allow him to be killed. Hera answers with a moving argument: Mortals are doomed by fate. At the same time, however, Zeus can do as he pleases, though once he takes action to save his son, every one of the gods might do the same for a son in battle, for each one loves his son. The best thing, she concludes, is to let Sarpedon be killed by Patroclus, then let him be sent back to his homeland in Lycia, where his family and friends can conduct a proper funeral. In this argument, a highpoint in the religion of the Olympians, Zeus remains supreme; yet in perfect harmony with his supremacy, fate is accepted.

The Roman poet Vergil (70–19 BCE) brings fate even closer to the supreme god in the story of Dido and Aeneas in the fourth chapter of the *Aeneid.* Aeneas, who according to Jupiter's plans must go to Italy to lay the foundations of the Roman state, is delayed in his journey by the charms of the love-stricken Dido. Juno, Jupiter's consort, contrives to have the two marry to make the relationship legal. But Venus counsels Juno to inquire into Jupiter's plans. Jupiter, thus alerted, sends Mercury to Aeneas to remind him of his real goal: to establish rule over Italy. Thematically less subtle than Homer, Vergil leaves no doubt concerning the supremacy over destiny of the king of the gods. Even Venus, known for her truly fateful power, here victimizing Aeneas as much as Dido, is no match for Jupiter's determination of fate.

This purposeful ambivalence has early roots in the classical world. The classicist William Chase Greene, who studied the subject of fate extensively, attributes much to human dependence on nature, expressed in Greece in the figure of Mother Earth, Gaia. Was she, on whom everything depended, identified with fate? Greene touches the heart of the matter in summaries of earlier classicists (notably Jane E. Harrison) and in his own study of texts by explaining that Gaia's way is the way of *Dikē*. *Dikē* (justice, but also judgment or punishment) is a term akin to fate, although the documents do not allow an unambiguous identification. Often the texts also speak of Themis as a goddess; she is "the right tradition" and also "the right dispensation." It is true that she is sometimes identified with Gaia (earth [the Titan goddess Gaia-Themis is the mother of Prometheus]). However, in the myths this goddess is not a supreme deity but rather the guardian of ancient sacred customs when their solidity is shaken.

Comparable to Themis, or right tradition, *dharma* in Hinduism occurs as a divinity, the god Dharma. Typically, however, this god is not identified with any supreme deity; rather, he occurs in legends and myths as the embodied reminder of what should be done. In the epic *Mahābhārata,* the hero Yudhiṣṭhira is also known as Dharmarāja. He is the son of the god Dharma, and his name implies his justness as a ruler. This heroic character has been divinized and enjoys a cult in a number of minor popular traditions in South India. However, the complexity of these cults also involves other divine and divinized characters who play significant roles in myth and ritual. Although *dharma* (the maintenance of right tradition) and a hero/god are drawn together, this popular tradition also refrains from identifying any notion of fate with a divine power.

Much earlier, in the period of the Vedas and in Brahmanism (from c. 1200 to 600 BCE, but also in later texts), we find the term *ṛta.* It may be rendered as "truth," and in that sense it is commonly used in later times. Nevertheless, its earliest meaning, never completely lost later on, is closer to "cosmic balance." *Ṛta* is the power or function that preserves the world in its proper order. Its kinship to the generic term *fate* is evident, but this case is also preserved in its own mystery. Two deities, Mitra and Varuṇa, are called the guardians of *ṛta* in the Vedic texts, but not its owners. No deity appropriates it, owns it, or is identical with it.

In Greece, the Moirai (fate) personified in three goddesses, are sometimes called by individual names: Clotho, who spins the thread of life; Lachesis, who measures it; and Atropos, who cuts it off. The symbolism of weaving is eloquent: a tapestry of life is created and by itself does not imply the design of a superior deity. Homer, as we have seen, does not identify Zeus with fate, but he speaks in several places of one single Moira, whose decisions are irrevocable and to whom even the gods are subjected. Moira's inscrutable nature is not evil; indeed, a wholly evil deity does not occur in Homer, unless it be the goddess Atē (the Romans called her Discordia), but her role is not significant within the structure of classical Greek religion.

The act of weaving (not only cloth but also baskets) has been a source of symbolism concerning fate in many times and places. Urðr (Urd) in Old Norse literature is a personification of fate: a female figure, seated at a source under the world tree, determining destiny. Her name is related to the verb *verða,* akin to Latin *vertere* ("to turn," including the turning and twisting of the thread of destiny). Norse mythology has much to say about fate, including the inevitable destruction of the world (Ragnarǫk). Conceivably, the sources for this mythology, which for the most part are very late, show a certain obsession with destiny under the impact of changes brought about by Christianity.

In Germanic heroic poetry the role of goddesses of fate is largely played by the valkyries, nine in number. They are servants of Óðinn (Odin), and their name indicates their activity in war. In ancient Norse there are the three *valkyrja,* who are associated respectively with the past, the present, and the future, and whose name refers explicitly to their task of determining who will be slain in battle. According to the sagas, Óðinn will employ the valkyries in the final battle before Ragnarǫk. Thus, in the Germanic world, one detects a certain, no doubt purposeful, ambiguity regarding fate: those who determine fate are somehow independent and even beyond the gods, and nevertheless their activity jibes with the supreme god's will.

In Sanskrit literature, the most common word for fate is *daiva,* an adjectival form of *deva* (god). It is "the divine" in a most general sense, for it refers to what is beyond human beings and human ken. A term that took on far greater significance in the sphere of fate in Indian religious history is *karman,* which owes its principal force to the context in which it first occurs in Vedic sacrificial texts. Vedic sacrificial proceedings, the heart of early Indian religious life as we know it from the texts, are acts that by definition could not be in vain; a ritual was an act (*karman*) par excellence. While it is difficult to define the purpose of those acts, this is a modern reader's problem. The texts agree that all power (and in fact everything that one might want to cover with the word *religion*) was concentrated in the act performed, whether by gods or people, the act that could not miss the mark.

In later Vedic texts (the Upaniṣads), in the Indian epics, and in Yoga literature, the term *karman* absorbs the meaning of the manner in which life is determined by previous acts, or acts in a previous existence. In Buddhism, *karman* becomes the term used for the law of causality determining the cycle of *saṃsāra,* that is, the continuous flow of all finite existences. This meaning of *karman* has become dominant in virtually all Indian religious tradition. this notion, in spite of its philosophical contexts and subtleties, can obviously be understood as an expression of fate and fatalism. The religious center, however, from which its meaning derives, is not immutable destiny itself, but the access in human existence toward *mokṣa* or *nirvāṇa;* that is, freedom from bondage to the law of *karman.* Notably, certain Indian religious traditions with archaic Indian roots, such as the *bhakti* cults of the south, are relatively unaffected by ideas concerning the law of *karman.* The loving devotion (*bhakti*) to a gracious god or goddess is so central and so strongly supported by ancient local temple traditions as to make theories concerning laws of causality recede in significance.

Fate beyond the gods. In the Mediterranean world in late antiquity, notions of fate did not disappear, yet new views began to prevail, at least in certain circles, and ancient notions began to be understood in a modified way. The new mood is the same as that which provided a ready acceptance of astrological data and Gnosticism. Tyche in Greece and Fortuna in Rome are goddesses who enjoyed worship, though their names do not seem to indicate much more than "chance," "fortune," and "good luck." Fortuna was invoked under several names, for example, Annonaria (referring to her function of providing food), Muliebris (womanhood), Primigenia (she who is first born, the original one), and Virilis (she who is strong and masculine). Her greatest sanctuary was in Praeneste, the oldest part of which was built in approximately 200 BCE. Fortuna came to be identified with Tyche (fate, or chance) and was a tutelary deity of the state in Hellenistic times. Her cult became very popular.

It is true that earlier times had deities of fate whose names did not seem personal in the strict sense of the word. *Moira* and *daiva* are examples. The Greek term *anankē* may also be mentioned here. *Anankē* does not denote a deity but is a general world for "necessity," yet necessity of a more than physical nature; it is seen as the antithesis to freedom (and forms an important subject for Plato in, for example, his *Timaeus*). The term *anankē* preserved its mysterious, dreadful meaning throughout Greek history. Rather different, *Moira* was fate personified from the earliest times, in spite of the clear, abstract etymology of the word. The name *Moira* is related to a verb of which the participial form *heimarmenē* meant, and continued to mean in later times, "fate" proper. The term *heimarmenē* is a feminine past participle form of a verb meaning "to attribute" or "allot," and hence the meaning "what has been allotted" seems clear—if it were not for the unexpected feminine form. The relationship to Moira is not transparent. By contrast, the personification in the Hellenistic period of other feminine deities such as Fortuna is quite distinct. Fortuna's veneration is symptomatic of a certain obsession with chance and fate. Typically, the Roman poet and philosopher Lucretius (c. 96–55 BCE) begins his work *De rerum natura* (The way things are) with an invocation of Venus, the classical goddess of love, who in that capacity is closely associated with chance and fate. It is she who embodies control over all things, but Lucretius's poem makes a strong case for chance (and in doing so does not conceal the author's critique of all established religion).

Specific epithets for several goddesses who enjoyed worship at the time, including Venus, all refer to the same fundamental concern with chance or fate. The epithets for Fortuna all amount to a transparent naming of the mysterious power that determines the course of nature and history. The great classical gods seem to recede to the background. In roughly the same period, and well into the Middle Ages, during the time in which Indian influences extended into Southeast Asia, the god Kāma ("love," in the sense of erotic love) came to be much celebrated.

Autonomous fate and divinities holding fate in their power. The eventual victory of Christianity over the Hellenistic religions signifies a change in the religious occupation with fate. The idea of "fate" or "chance" as an independent or supreme force in the universe became a major enemy for many Christians. One might even argue that a prevailing mood shifted from one extreme to another. Later Western philosophers, such as Barukh Spinoza (1632–1677) and David Hume (1711–1776), still found it necessary to go to great lengths to refute Lucretius's rational reflections on chance. Generally, the Abrahamic religions—Judaism, Christianity, and Islam—looked askance at every semblance of a fate that could be ascertained apart from God.

Martin Luther (1483–1546) dismissed all the serious claims of astrology, since it had "neither principle nor proofs" (*Tischreden* 3.2834b, Weimar ed., 1914). The predestination of John Calvin (1509–1564) is often mistaken for a form of determinism or fatalism, but it is in fact something very different, and Calvin took great pains, with all the philosophical means at his disposal, to explain ultimate human destiny as God's decision, made within the mystery of God's eternity, inaccessible to the inquiring mind of human beings (*Institutes* 3.21–23, 1559 ed.). In contrast to the biblically rooted religions, it is striking that in Hinduism, which was not affected by these historical religious developments, astrology continued to flourish unabated, integrated into the Hindu religious structures themselves.

Before the emergence of the religion of Israel, there occured in Mesopotamia eloquent depictions of fate held in a god's hands. The Akkadian creation epic known as *Enuma elish,* written down about 1000 BCE but much older in origin, tells of the "tablets of fate" given to Marduk, the leading warrior and king of the gods. The presentation of these tablets is the seal of his sovereignty. He may be said to determine fate. At the same time, religious practice in the Middle East was multifarious, and a dogmatic definition of *god* and *fate* is not given. Among the terms for fate are the early Sumerian *me* or *mu* and the Akkadian *shimtu* (pl., *shimatu*). *Shimatu* (destinies) can somehow be manipulated; this is literally true according to the documents. The tablet of destinies (*tupshimati*) is a cuneiform tablet; it controls the world, and the myths tell us that it could change hands. A lesser god, Anzu, once stole the tablet, thus endangering the order of the universe. Although the *Enuma elish* has destiny firmly planted in Marduk's power, another text (the *Exaltation of Inanna*) tells of the goddess Inanna hanging the *mes* (destinies) on her head like jewels. On one occasion, Inanna tricked Enki (the Sumerian name of Ea, Marduk's father, who had formerly held fate in his power) into handing over the destinies.

One cannot do justice to the Babylonian notions concerning fate by explaining them, because of the highly developed art of divination, as a central item in a world of magic; divination was not a mere superstition but rather an attempt to understand and control reality (Buccellati, 1982). Furthermore, Mesopotamia never developed a cult of fate. The Mesopotamian notion of fate can perhaps best be seen as parallel to the notion of necessity (*anankē*) in Plato, and there is no reason to oppose the art of gaining knowledge of the laws controlling the universe to Greek philosophy as if the former were more "primitive" than the latter. In any event, a divine autonomy over destiny is a prevailing theme in ancient Mesopotamia, and this certainly differs from Plato's tendency to oppose *anankē* to God's *nous* (mind) that created the world and human beings.

Historical continuations may be difficult to demonstrate in detail, yet in the Middle East the world of Islam seems to have preserved a number of very ancient ideas concerning destiny. These ideas found their way into the text of the Qurʾān. Specific terms are set in human life: sex, happiness, misery, the amount of one's sustenance, and the time of death (a point especially emphasized for soldiers). Qurʾān 9:51 states that nothing will happen to a man but what God has written down for him. Fate in God's hands here seems to come close to determinism, although it is just as likely, as in Calvin's predestination, that it was more of a stimulus to truly trust God. Certainly, as in the ancient Middle East of many centuries earlier, rational lucidity is not the issue. In Islamic teachings, beginning with the Qurʾān, rewards and punishments in this world as well as in the hereafter are far more significant, and their logic is not always immediately evident. In the history of Islam, theologians and lawyers have struggled with problems that have arisen from the text. Unjustly, many outsiders looking at Islam have considered all Muslims fatalists. God, the almighty, is at the same time the compassionate one. The religious "inconsistency" here in the handling of fate is no more conducive to a monolithic conceptualization than representations of fate elsewhere.

In the Hebrew Bible, the tendency is to associate fate with the will of God. Joseph and Daniel are the outstanding examples of dream readers, but their stories make it clear that they can look into the future through their art only under the inspiration of God. A complementary story of a man interested in necromancy who is not presented as a man of God is that of Saul consulting a woman of Endor, who conjures up the ghost of the dead Samuel (*1 Sm.* 28:8–25).

The problem of fate beyond God or gods. The theme of a destiny that is in harmony with a supreme divinity or ultimately dependent on that divinity's will is widespread and has many variations, yet some periods have also seen inroads on this general rule. The clearest examples come from situations of great intellectual concern and from an overflow of mystical craving. The conception of a god can "dry up," as it were; it can become a pale, rational reflection in the history of a tradition. In the expression of great mystics, such a development can be translated into a frightening reality, a horror that is too great to be endured. It would be overly simple to suggest that the conceptualization of the idea of God causes mysticism, but as a historical factor there is little doubt that it plays a role. In both Jewish and Christian mysticism certain stark phrases and terms, though they certainly do not sum up the whole of the mystic's vision, may be understood in part as reactions to a world of abstract propositions. Among these are the *deus absconditus;* certain metaphorical, not to say euphemistic, names in early Spanish Qabbalah, especially *Ein Sof;* "the dark night of the soul" of John of the Cross (1542–1591); and "the abyss of the deity" of Johannes Tauler (1300–1361). In the history of Buddhism, the tenacious process of negation in the meditations of Nāgārjuna (second century CE) may also serve as an example. In all these cases traditional concepts are forced to yield to a higher reality, a vision the tradition supposedly intended but had not disclosed hitherto. In the history of Islamic mysticism such use and interpretation of and reaction to traditional concepts have often led to open conflict and to the seer's condemnation and execution, as in the famous case of al-Ḥallāj (d. 922).

There is a compelling reason to relate these trends in heterogeneous forms of mysticism to the subject of fate: in all instances something higher and more powerful than what tradition allowed or was capable of understanding is posited as absolute. The term *fate* falls short of this highest element, which is often called ineffable. And yet, in intellectual circles that are not (or not necessarily) inclined toward mysticism, the desire to point to and name the power beyond what the tradition tolerates does occur. The Christian theologian Paul Tillich spoke of a "God who is Being itself," who as such would transcend "God who is *a* being." Tillich intended this idea as a bulwark against any fatefulness of the sort that he thought threatened Greek religion in the form of a fate above Zeus, and he made his case with the help of the mystic vocabulary concerning God as ground and abyss of every being. In late antiquity, Gnostic doctrines of salvation show patterns that bear striking resemblances to a fate beyond God. The traditional image of God is rejected as in fact inferior to the real God, who is truly supreme, and who is the source of salvation. The person's self is instructed to consider itself ultimately as alien to the world as is the real, truly transcendent God. Thus, here also, something is posited beyond that which the tradition had declared supreme, and this something higher is that which really determines the world.

OTHER THEMES OF FATE. What follows are points pertaining to some pronounced "moments" in expressions of fate.

Greece and Rome. Practical, down-to-earth ways of handling fate occur nowhere so markedly as in ancient Roman religion. "Signs" are read to interpret the uncertainties of life, signs that are very common, such as sneezes or twitches of the eyelids, or signs that are completely beyond human reach, such as celestial phenomena or the flights of birds. Messages (*omina*) can be deduced from all such signs. As a rule, one has already set out on an enterprise, and then the signs are observed, and precisely this custom preserves a practical human freedom. There seems to have existed a great certainty that the interpretations were of use to the actions undertaken. The Roman situation differs considerably from that of the Greeks, who exhibit a much more encompassing interest in the drama of the future. The Greek oracles, such as the renowned oracle at Delphi, did not provide "yes" or "no" answers to an inquiry; rather, each oracular event was itself a mystery in need of interpretation. All major trends in Greece show a good deal of respect for the nature of fate, and nothing that might resemble a trivialization. Quite strikingly, Plato, in his last work, *Laws,* conceives a heavy penalty for those who are of the opinion that the gods can be caused to change their minds (10.909a). From the perspective not only of the Greeks, but of most traditions with explicit concerns for fate, the Roman customs may perhaps seem trivial.

China. The practicality in conceptions of fate in China differs markedly from ancient Roman customs. On a wider scale of comparison, the religions of China seem generally much less concerned with theory and very much down-to-earth. This difference is visible in expressions touching on fate and fatalism. Typically, the philosopher Wang Chong (probably first century CE) compared the significance of a person to that of a flea or louse in the folds of the garment of the universe. In neo-Daoist literature, expressions with a fatalistic ring occasionally occur. The *Liezi,* written in the third century CE, contains a dialogue between Effort and Fate. At a moment when Fate seems all-powerful, Fate's reply to the question of whether the way things are is indeed under its control is surprising: "Since I am called Fate, how can I have control?. . .All things come naturally and of themselves. How should I know anything about them?" (6.1a). Dao, the Way, shows its force in preventing Fate itself from reaching sovereignty. In Confucian tradition, strict fatalism is difficult to detect. In ordinary life, however, Confucian scholars have, as a rule, declined to instruct anyone who did not give them the respect they deserved, thereby leaving unwise decision-makers to their own "fate." This practical "fatalism" is clearly only a by-product; it does not tell us much about the essentials of Confucius and Confucianism.

Iran. The singular place of ancient Iran in the general history of religions is also reflected in ideas concerning fate. Zoroastrianism conceived of a set period of duration for the world. In the end, the forces of good would triumph over those of evil. Human life has its significance on the stage of this world drama. Both good and evil ultimately follow the course of destiny. In later Zoroastrian orthodoxy, fate was often identified with time; a system approaching determinism developed. In effect, all power of Ahriman or Angra Mainyu (the evil spirit), as well as of Ōhrmazd, or Ahura Mazdā (the wise lord), was thus dissipated. This later period is commonly referred to as Zurvanism, after Zurwān, in whom Infinite Time is personalized and mythologized. (Zurvanites were the predominant sect in Iran in the third century BCE.) The identification of fate and time has no prototype in other or earlier Iranian religion. One later text, known as the *Epistle of Tonsar* (probably from the end of the sixth century BCE) condemns both people who trust exclusively in their own efforts and people who entrust themselves exclusively to fate. Manichaeism was strongly affected by Zoroastrian thought in its ideas about time, fate, good, and evil. In its turn, Manichaeism influenced the teachings of Gnostic and Christian traditions, in particular from the third to the seventh centuries.

Zurwān (time) is a late development from the ancient Iranian tradition of the Avesta. The great original opponents, Ōhrmazd and Ahriman, were the two antipodes of heaven, Ōhrmazd being the absolute good one, and Ahriman the absolute evil one. In Avesta mythology, all gods and people will eventually participate in a final battle between the two parties, but the good will triumph. When in the course of time the religion of the Avesta became the established religion, new transformations occurred. One such transformation amounts to the "heresy" of Zurwān (Puhvel, 1987). What is most striking is that Zurwān is transformed into the father of both Ahura Mazdā and Ahriman, which would seem to justify the designation of "heresy."

The travel of destinies. A subject that does not always get the attention it deserves is the movement of ideas over wide areas, often as a result of conquest. The death of Alexander in 323 BCE is normally seen as the beginning of the Hellenistic Age. Not only did Greek become the major language of communication from Egypt to Rome, in a manner of speaking "Greek" also became the language of the world—in the sense that a world of ideas, of communication, opened up and endured for a long time. Eventually both the Islamic East and the Christian West came to lean on Greek ideas. And without the rediscovery of the Greek thinkers—a rediscovery made by the Islamic world—history might have taken a very different course. The Renaissance, for example, would have been unthinkable.

The end of the Hellenistic Age is generally set at 31 BCE, with the end of the Roman Republic and the ascension of Emperor Augustus (27 BCE). History, especially political history, sets its signposts explicitly, but the flow of ideas is a different matter.

Fate, as we have seen, is a notion that can emerge anywhere. However, it is always the context that gives it its special touch. Traveling ideas can have a great impact. It is striking that during the first several centuries of the common era, ideas touching on fate seem to have traveled frequently and over considerable distances. It was a period in which Greek philosophical ideas—from Aristotle and Plato, the Stoics, Epicureans, Skeptics, Cynics—moved from country to country. The influence of Plotinus (third century CE), the greatest of the Neoplatonists, crossed borders—as he himself did. Plotinus eventually settled in Rome, where he taught and was eminent in intellectual life. This was the time of the early Christians, who also had ideas about fate, most of them rejecting it, for it would belittle the almightiness of God. Nevertheless, there was much ongoing discussion of the subject.

When the religion of the Avesta became the established religion (under the Sassanian rulers from the third to the seventh centuries CE), new manifestations occurred. One of these was the "heresy" in which Zurwān becomes the father of Ōhrmazd and Ahriman. This is precisely the "solution" that came to appeal to many further west; for example, in Greece and Rome. Particularly striking in this regard are the references to Zoroaster, especially in Gnostic texts. The tendency to understand time as the all-devourer became an obsession in various circles. In art, time becomes a monster, gruesome to behold.

The world of ideas is endlessly fascinating. Neoplatonism did not merely survive, but flourished. But even though the thought of Plato and Plotinus survived, much of the argument of this period is lost to us. The religious turmoil of that time is no longer easy to fathom. Nevertheless, that turmoil was considerable. Quite rightly, Gregory Shaw begins his book *Theurgy and the Soul: The Neoplatonism of Iamblichus* (1995) with a moving description of the agitation of Greek peasants when the temples that guaranteed their lives and their crops were being ruined.

Fates of nations and empires. National fate should not be left unmentioned, since it cannot be separated from the subject of religion. China's "mandate of heaven" was interwoven with the religious mandate of kingship. And it was thought to determine China's, and indeed the entire world's, lot. We have seen above that Jupiter decided the founding of Rome. In modern history, manifest destiny, the American doctrine that gained great popularity in the nineteenth-century age of nationalism, held that it was the duty and fate of the Anglo-Saxon nations, particularly the United States, to dominate the Western hemisphere. Closely related to manifest destiny is the appeal of the British poet Rudyard Kipling in his poem "The White Man's Burden" (1899), which calls on the "white man" to persevere through hardships in his heroic efforts to protect, instruct, and lead to a truly civilized existence his "new-caught, sullen peoples / Half devil and half child." Equally fraught with pseudo-religious pathos is the *Schicksal* verbiage indulged in by the leaders of Nazi Germany.

TENACITY OF NOTIONS OF FATE. The complexity of notions of fate and their varying frames of reference should not prevent us from observing the force of certain underlying ideas over very long periods of time. Faithful to his theistic inheritance, the mathematician Isaac Newton (1642–1727) interpreted his astronomical observations and calculations in terms of God's design. A Japanese religious movement, Tenrikyō (which came about late in the nineteenth century), is in most ways eclectic and has freely borrowed from theistic systems, but its ideas concerning fate are in perfect harmony with prevailing and popular Buddhist ideas of *karman.*

In moments of crisis that hit the individual, the charm of astrology tends to disappear, and earlier ideas of fate reemerge. This is not altogether surprising, as astrology was never accepted in the dominant Western religious traditions. Everything points to the remarkable religious tenacity of deep-seated convictions touching on fate, destiny, chance, and related problems. Even when certain conservative religious phenomena submerge or change, as for instance when funeral ceremonies are replaced by other means of disposing of the dead, basic assumptions about fate and images of fate seem hard to repress in social and private life. When occupying German authorities forced Jewish professors to step down, students in Amsterdam published in November 1940 a farewell message concluding: "In this heavy trial brought on you, we implore the Almighty to support you, Him in Whose hands your and our destiny lies, and whose decisions rule the course of existence for all of us." As in the case with other symbolisms, individuals do not make up their own novel ideas about fate. Instead, old ideas dominant in cultures come to the surface from time to time. They may appear new and striking, yet on closer scrutiny they are like irrepressible sounds made when old strings vibrate anew.

SEE ALSO Astrology; Chance; Fortuna; Free Will and Determinism; Free Will and Predestination; Oracles; Webs and Nets.

BIBLIOGRAPHY

Armstrong, A. H., trans. *Plotinus, with an English Translation.* 7 vols. Cambridge, Mass., 1978–1988.

Bayet, Jean. *Histoire politique et psychologique de la religion romaine.* 2d ed. Paris, 1969. This volume is of special importance for placing dealings with fate in their ordinary life surroundings.

Bianchi, Ugo. *Dios Aisa: Destino, uomini, e divinità nell'epos, nelle teogonie e nel culto dei Greci.* Rome, 1953. Discusses fate in the Greek tradition.

Bianchi, Ugo. *Zaman i Ohrmazd: Lo Zoroastrismo nelle sue origini e nella sua essenza.* Torino, Italy, 1958. A classic critique of Zaehner and the Uppsala school.

Bianchi, Ugo. *The History of Religions.* Leiden, 1975. One of the most "matter of fact" introductions to the study of religious phenomena.

Bottéro, Jean. *The Birth of God: The Bible and the Historian.* Translated by Kees W. Bolle. University Park, Pa., 2000.

Boyce, Mary. *A History of Zoroastrianism.* 3 vols. (Vol. 3 by Boyce and Frantz Grenet). London, 1975–. This work is of special use for an inquiry into fate because of its treatment of Zurvanism.

Buccellati, Giorgio. *A Primer of Ancient Mesopotamian Religion.* Malibu, Calif., 1982. Pays special attention to a nonreductionistic interpretation of fate and to magic relating to fate.

David, Madeleine. *Les dieux et le destin en Babylonie.* Paris, 1949. A philologically based study, written with great philosophical sensitivity.

de Bary, William Theodore, and Irene Bloom, with Wing-tsit Chan et al. *Sources of Chinese Tradition.* 2d ed. New York, 1999. Contains important documents, especially in part 3, showing notions of fate in specific settings.

Dietrich, Bernard Clive. *Death, Fate, and the Gods: The Development of a Religious Idea in Greek Popular Belief and in Homer.* London, 1965.

Doniger O'Flaherty, Wendy, ed. *Karma and Rebirth in Classical Indian Traditions.* Berkeley, 1980. The work contains excellent studies by specialists on the subject in India that is most relevant to the concept of *karman.*

Eliade, Mircea. *Shamanism: Archaic Techniques of Ecstasy.* Rev. and enl. ed., translated by Willard R. Trask. New York, 1964. Fundamental to an understanding of the transformation and diffusion of ancient Middle Eastern ideas to nonliterate cultures.

Gonda, Jan. *Die Religionen Indiens.* 2 vols. Stuttgart, Germany, 1960–1963. Includes information concerning astronomical and astrological ideas in India.

Grant, Robert M. *Gnosticism: A Source Book of Heretical Writings from the Early Christian Period.* New York, 1961. This is the most convenient collection of Gnostic texts, with helpful indexes.

Greene, William C. *Moira: Fate, Good, and Evil in Greek Thought.* Cambridge, Mass., 1944. An exhaustive study of fate in Greece.

Hadas, Moses, trans. *The Stoic Philosophy of Seneca: Essays and Letters.* New York, 1958.

Humphries, Rolfe, trans. *The Way Things Are: The "De rerum natura" of Titus Lucretius Carus.* Bloomington, Ind., 1968. The best translation of the most famous text on chance and related topics.

Jonas, Robert Hans. *The Gnostic Religion: The Message of the Alien God and the Beginnings of Christianity.* 2d ed. Boston, 1963. Interprets the world of late antiquity in which ideas and cults of fate flourished.

Kramer, Samuel Noah. *The Sumerians: Their History, Culture, and Character.* Chicago, 1963. Presents a sober yet vivid account of the earliest civilization, including its views of fate.

Lanzi, Silvia. *Theos Anaitios: Storia della teodicea da Omero ad Agostino.* Rome, 2000.

Long, A. A. *Hellenistic Philosophy: Stoics, Epicureans, Sceptics.* 2d ed. Berkeley and Los Angeles, 1986.

Long, A. A., and D. N. Sedley. *The Hellenistic Philosophers,* vol. 1, *Translations of the Principal Sources, with Philosophical Commentary;* vol. 2, *Greek and Latin Texts with Notes and Bibliography.* Cambridge, U.K., 1987.

Magris, Aldo. *L'idea di destino nel pensiero antico.* 2 vols. Udine, Italy, 1984–1985. The most encompassing study of destiny in ancient Greece.

Needham, Joseph. *Science and Civilization in China,* vol. 2, *History of Scientific Thought.* Cambridge, U.K., 1956. Deals with scientific thought on a large scale and presents astronomical and astrological ideas in China.

Neugebauer, Otto. *The Exact Sciences in Antiquity.* 2d ed. Providence, R.I., 1957. The basic work on early science and astronomy, from which astrological systems derived.

Nilsson, Martin P. *Geschichte der griechischen Religion.* 2 vols., 3d ed. Munich, 1961–1967.

Pingree, David, trans. and ed. *The Yavanajātaka of Sphujidhvaja.* 2 vols. Cambridge, Mass., 1978. One of several Indian texts on astronomy translated by Pingree.

Puhvel, Jaan. *Comparative Mythology.* Baltimore, 1987.

Ringgren, Helmer. *Fatalism in Persian Epics.* Uppsala, Sweden, 1952. Discusses fate and fortune in Iran from Zoroastrianism to Islam.

Ringgren, Helmer, ed. *Fatalistic Beliefs in Religion, Folklore, and Literature.* Stockholm, 1967. Contains essays by specialists on religion, folklore, and literature.

Rist, J. M. *Plotinus: The Road to Reality.* Cambridge, UK, 1967.

Rist, J. M. *Stoic Philosophy.* Cambridge, UK, 1969.

Rist, J. M. *Human Value: A Study in Ancient Philosophical Ethics.* Leiden, 1982.

Runia, David T., ed. *Plotinus amid Gnostics and Christians.* Amsterdam, 1984. Lectures by A. P. Bos, A. H. Armstrong, R. Ferwerda, and Th. G. Sinnige.

Shaw, Gregory. *Theurgy and the Soul: The Neoplatonism of Iamblichus.* University Park, Pa., 1995. Perhaps one of the most enlightening books on the Christianization of the world.

Wallis, Richard T., and Jay Bregman, eds. *Neoplatonism and Gnosticism.* Albany, N.Y., 1992. This volume contains, among other things: "Dualism: Platonic, Gnostic, and Christian" by A. H. Armstrong; "Synesius, the Hermetica and Gnosis" by Jay Bregman; "Plotinus's Anti-Gnostic Polemic" and "Porphyry's *Against the Christians*" by Christos Evangeliou; and "Theurgic Tendencies against Gnosticism and Iamblichus's Conception of Theurgy" by Birger A. Pearson.

Yang, C. K. *Religion in Chinese Society: A Study of Contemporary Social Functions of Religion and Some of Their Historical Factors.* Berkeley, 1961. Devotes special attention to Chinese attitudes toward fate in social life.

Zaehner, Robert Charles. *Zurvan: A Zoroastrian Dilemma.* Oxford, 1955. A seminal work.

KEES W. BOLLE (1987 AND 2005)

FATHER DIVINE. The Harlem-based minister known as Father Divine (1879–1965) became famous during the Great Depression for feeding the hungry and drawing thousands of disciples (white as well as black) who venerated him as God on earth. A short, balding man of great energy and charisma, Divine promoted racial integration in his Peace Mission movement at a time when nearly all American congregations were segregated. He summed up his religious crusade for social justice, saying, "If God cannot prepare a heaven here for you, you are not going anywhere."

Born George Baker in Rockville, Maryland, in 1879, Divine grew up in a southern black farm-laborer's family. As a young man he traveled through the South preaching to poor blacks. Citing *1 Corinthians* 3:16, "the spirit of God dwelleth in you," he declared that all people were godly and so deserved equal rights and dignity. But after several arrests and detention in an insane asylum, Divine left the Jim Crow South and, in 1915, settled in New York City, then emerging as a center of African American culture amid an influx of migrants from the rural South.

In 1919, Baker, calling himself the Reverend M. J. Divine, relocated to Sayville, Long Island. Living with a few followers who pooled their funds, he distributed books on New Thought, such as Robert Collier's multivolume works, *The Book of Life* (1925), *The Secret of Gold* (1927), and *The Life Magnet* (1928), which taught that everyone could achieve earthly success by visualizing positive images and tapping an inner spiritual power. Disciples also strived for unity with God by renouncing carnal temptations such as tobacco, alcohol, drugs, and sexual relations.

As Divine's communal movement continued to prosper after the onset of the Great Depression in late 1929, his free Sunday banquets attracted blacks from Harlem and Newark, plus a growing minority of whites. These interracial gatherings, though, led to "Father's" arrest in 1931 for "disturbing the peace," and he was convicted the following June after a blatantly racist trial. Yet even before the verdict was overturned in January 1933, Divine found his messianic aura enhanced when, three days after sentencing and censuring Divine, the judge suddenly died. Relocating to Harlem, Divine presided over a burgeoning movement called the Peace Mission, which was clustered in northern ghettos but also featured predominantly white branches in California and other states.

Divine's Peace Mission became a melting pot of the discontented. A majority of Divine's followers were poor black women, often widowed or divorced, and generally from the lowest strata of ghetto society. But others, men and women, held well-paying jobs and were highly educated, including a substantial minority of affluent whites who were drawn to Divine out of idealism or spiritual seeking. In New York and New Jersey, states that contained the heart of Divine's support, the following was 85 to 90 percent black. In states farther west the proportion of blacks in the movement often dropped sharply, but almost never fell below a third of the disciples in any Peace Mission center.

Estimates of the total Peace Mission membership during the 1930s varied sharply. At its peak in the mid-1930s, the movement had perhaps ten thousand hard-core followers who believed fervently in Father Divine's divinity, gave their possessions to the Peace Mission, and lived in one of the more than 150 movement centers. This conservative count excludes many ghetto residents who disdained notions of Father Divine's godhood yet admired his leadership as a philanthropist and champion of racial equality.

Divine pioneered in the growing struggle for equal rights and opportunity. He encouraged integration of "light and dark complected" followers (the words *Negro* and *colored* were forbidden) and used whites as secret emissaries to circumvent restrictive housing covenants and acquire homes, hotels, and beach fronts for his followers in northern white neighborhoods. The Peace Mission proved the vitality of cooperative enterprise by becoming the largest landowner in Harlem and operating businesses with an estimated value of $15 million. In January 1936 the Peace Mission's "Righteous Government Convention" in Harlem called for the abolition of segregation, lynching, and capital punishment, and also urged an expanded government commitment to end unemployment, poverty, and hunger.

After 1940 the Peace Mission sharply declined in numbers and influence as the return of prosperity lessened its philanthropic appeal, and it evolved from a mass movement to a formal sect featuring a half-dozen incorporated churches. In 1942 Divine left Harlem for Philadelphia, and four years later he announced a "spiritual" marriage to a 21-year-old white disciple, Edna Rose Ritchings, thereafter known as Mother Divine. When Father Divine died in September 1965 after a long illness, disciples were stunned and saddened, but not to the point of mass desertion. He had been largely out of public view for several years, during which time Mother Divine had prepared followers for the day when "Father will not be with us personally."

Since the late 1950s Mother Divine and her secretarial staff have administered the Peace Mission from a 72-acre estate called Woodmont, outside Philadelphia. Although the Peace Mission's membership has dwindled to perhaps a few hundred and most of its properties have been sold off, disciples still save a place for "Father" at their banquet tables. They pay special homage to Woodmont's Shrine to Life, a structure designed by Mother Divine: it surrounds a red marble crypt that holds the body of Father Divine. Followers believe that "Father" did not die, but rather cast off his mortal body in order to rule the universe through his spirit.

See Also New Thought Movement.

Bibliography

Two early biographies that emphasize sensational or allegedly scandalous aspects of Father Divine's ministry are John Hoshor, *God in a Rolls-Royce; The Rise of Father Divine: Madman, Menace, or Messiah* (New York, 1936); and Robert A. Parker, *Incredible Messiah: The Deification of Father Divine* (Boston, 1937). Robert Weisbrot's *Father Divine and the Struggle for Racial Equality* (Urbana, Ill., 1983) focuses on Divine's vanguard activism for racial justice; the volume contains an annotated listing of primary and secondary sources for further study (pp. 224–232). Jill Watts's *God, Harlem U.S.A.: The Father Divine Story* (Berkeley and Los Angeles, 1992) sheds new light on Divine's origins and highlights the role of New Thought in his religious leadership.

Robert Weisbrot (2005)

FĀṬIMAH BINT MUḤAMMAD

FĀṬIMAH BINT MUḤAMMAD (d. 11 AH/633 CE) was the youngest and best-known daughter of the prophet Muḥammad and his first wife Khadījah. His bloodline continues exclusively through her.

BIOGRAPHICAL DETAILS. The sources give Fāṭimah's date of birth as falling between 609 and 614 CE. She is described as having been greatly beloved of Muḥammad, and in turn was completely devoted to him. Her mother Khadījah's death while Fāṭimah was still very young filled her with great grief. She shared her father's travails during his years of persecution in Mecca before the emigration (*hijrah*) to Medina in 622 CE.

Shortly after the *hijrah*, two close associates of the Prophet, Abū Bakr and ʿUmar (who later became the first and second caliph), asked for Fāṭimah's hand in marriage. Muḥammad refused both of them, and instead encouraged his cousin ʿAlī, despite his greatly impoverished circumstances, to propose marriage to his daughter. ʿAlī, at the Prophet's behest, sold his shield and thereby obtained a sum of roughly 480 *dirhams* to offer as the bridal gift. Fāṭimah was between fifteen and twenty-one and ʿAlī twenty-five years of age at the time of marriage. A modest wedding feast was arranged and the couple moved into a home close to the Prophet's residence. They lived in grinding poverty, especially for the first several years of their marriage; the sources depict them as often having very little to eat. To earn a meager living, ʿAlī would draw water from the wells and water other people's lands, and Fāṭimah did all the housework herself, being unable to afford servants. Despite this, Fāṭimah is well-known for her highly charitable disposition, and before her marriage had tended to the *ahl al-Ṣuffah* (people of the bench), a group of destitute Muslims who took refuge in the Prophet's mosque in Medina.

The two famous sons of Fāṭimah and ʿAlī, al-Ḥasan and al-Ḥusayn, were born within the first four years of their marriage. A third son, Muḥassin (or Muḥsin), was stillborn. Two daughters followed, Umm Kulthūm and Zaynab, who were named after Fāṭimah's elder sisters.

There was apparently friction between Fāṭimah and ʿAlī, and she would complain to her father about the latter's harshness to her. Muḥammad is said to have been distressed by this lack of conjugal harmony and intervened on such occasions to effect a reconciliation between the sparring couple. A serious rift threatened to erupt between the couple when ʿAlī began to actively consider taking a second wife. The Prophet came to the defense of Fāṭimah and forbade ʿAlī from contracting a second marriage unless he were to divorce her first. Muḥammad's affection for his daughter was codified in a *ḥadīth* he uttered on this occasion: "Fāṭimah is a part of me and whoever offends her offends me." ʿAlī was thus dissuaded from taking a second consort. This event is sometimes invoked to point to the Prophet's preference for monogamy over polygamy, in the absence of extenuating circumstances.

Both the Sunnīs and the Shīʿah venerate Fāṭimah greatly as the beloved daughter of the Prophet, through whom his descendants are traced. She is one of the five members of the Prophet's family (*ahl al-bayt*; literally "family of the house [of the Prophet]"), which includes additionally, besides Muḥammad, ʿAlī and their two sons, al-Ḥasan and al-Ḥusayn. The term *ahl al-bayt* is a highly charged term, particularly for the Shīʿah. It occurs in a significant verse in the Qurʾān (33:33), which states, "O People of the House, God wishes only to remove from you uncleanliness." To whom precisely *ahl al-bayt* refers has remained unresolved to this day. Many Sunnī commentators have understood this verse to include not only the five members indicated above but also all the Prophet's wives. But Shīʿī commentators, and a number of pro-ʿAlid Sunnī exegetes, have interpreted *ahl al-bayt* as referring only to the five members, and have stressed the Qurʾanically mandated privileged status thereby accruing to them. An "occasion of revelation" is frequently recounted in connection with this verse, which further anchors this circumscribed meaning of *ahl al-bayt*. The sources relate that during an event that has come to be known as *al-mubāhalah* (mutual adjuration), the Prophet gathered ʿAlī, Fāṭimah, al-Ḥasan, and al-Ḥusayn under a cloak before a Christian delegation from Najrān as a proof of his prophethood, according to one version. "The family of the cloak" (*ahl al-kisāʾ*), as they are referred to after this incident, tends to become conflated with *ahl al-bayt* in Shīʿī exegetical works in particular.

Another *ḥadīth*, known as the *ḥadīth al-thaqalayn* (the Prophet's statement regarding the two weighty [things]), underscores the high status of the *ahl al-bayt* and is recorded in both Sunnī and Shīʿī standard *ḥadīth* compilations. In this report, Muḥammad says, "Indeed, I am leaving behind two weighty [things] among you: the Book of God and my kindred, the *ahl al-bayt*."

The family of the Prophet is greatly revered by both Sunnīs and Shīʿah alike—although among the Shīʿah, allegiance to the *ahl al-bayt* becomes a religious tenet. Both Sunnī and Shīʿī sources attest to the special bond of affection and closeness that existed between Muḥammad and Fāṭimah in particular. She is said to have closely resembled him in appearance and manner. Fāṭimah's usual epithet, *al-Zahrāʾ*, means "the radiant one." It is worthy of note that the most famous and oldest institution of higher learning in the Islamic world, al-Azhar (masculine form of al-Zahrāʾ) in Cairo, Egypt, is named after her. This mosque-university was built in 969 CE by the Ismāʿīlī dynasty from North Africa, known, once again after Fāṭimah, as the Fāṭimids.

Fāṭimah died in 633, about four to six months after her father. ʿAlī prepared her body for burial, and she was laid to rest in the family cemetery of Baqīʿ al-Gharqad in Medina.

THE CULT OF FĀṬIMAH The cult of Fāṭimah grew as the Shīʿah became more confirmed in their oppositional role to the majoritarian Sunnīs. As the former progressively came to stress over time that legitimate and just leadership of the Muslim polity could only be exercised by a descendant of Fāṭimah and ʿAlī, her status, as the only daughter of the Prophet to produce heirs who lived into adulthood and thus continue his line, grew accordingly. In Shīʿī sources, Fāṭimah, in addition to al-Zahrāʾ, is given eight other names: al-Baṭūl (the Chaste/Virgin), al-Ṣiddīqah (the Truthful), al-Ṭāhirah (the Pure), al-Mubārakah (the Blessed), al-Zakīyah (the Pure), al-Raḍīyah (the One Contented [with God's pleasure]), al-Marḍiyah (One with whom [God is] pleased), al-Muḥaddathah (the One Spoken to [by angels]), and Umm Muḥammad/Umm Abīhā (Mother of Muḥammad/Mother of Her Father). The last epithet invokes the memory of the occulted Twelfth Imām in Imāmī or Twelver Shīʿī belief, whose name was Muḥammad, like the Prophet of Islam. In this sense, Fāṭimah is the "mother" of her distant descendant, and thus "of her father" who bears the same name.

In Shīʿī hagiography, the name *Fāṭimah* itself is glossed as "One who was weaned [by God from the Fire];" those who love her will also be saved from it. Fāṭimah is the Pure and Chaste one because she was not subject to the blood of menstruation and parturition on account of having been created from the waters of paradise. The Qurʾanic verse (33:33) cited above is taken by the Shīʿah as a proof-text attesting to Fāṭimah's *ʿismah,* or "[moral] impeccability" or "sinlessness" (and that of other members of the family of the Prophet as well). Fāṭimah is moreover believed to have been entrusted with a special "scroll," known as *Maṣḥaf Fāṭimah,* brought to her by Gabriel to console her on the death of her father. The cult of Fāṭimah has been likened to the cult of the Virgin Mary in Roman Catholicism; there are indeed many parallels to be observed. Like Mary, she is virginal, despite being a wife and mother; and she is a tragic yet powerful female figure, eliciting the greatest loyalty from those devoted to her. The Shīʿah often refer to Fāṭimah as Maryam al-Kubrá (the Greater Mary).

BIBLIOGRAPHY

Bill, James A., and John Alden Williams. *Roman Catholics and Shiʿi Muslims: Prayer, Passion, and Politics.* Chapel Hill, N.C., 2002. See pages 28–29 and 52–55.

McAuliffe, Jane Dammen. "Chosen of All Women: Mary and Fatimah in Qurʾanic Exegesis." *Islamochristiana* 7 (1981): 19–28.

Momen, Moojan. *Introduction to Shiʿi Islam: The History and Doctrines of Twelver Shiʿism.* New Haven, 1985.

Vaglieri, Laura Veccia. "Fāṭimah." In *The Encyclopaedia of Islam.* New ed. Edited by H. A. R. Gibb et al., vol. 2, pp. 841–850. Leiden and London, 1960.

ASMA AFSARUDDIN (2005)

FA-TSANG SEE FAZANG

FAUST.

In sixteenth-century Europe, Faust was reviled as a godless man who, as a consequence of making a pact with the Devil, met a gruesome yet appropriate fate. By the nineteenth century, he had become the archetypal Romantic hero; the term *Faustian,* coined by Oswald Spengler (1880–1936), was taken as a positive epithet to describe those tormented, defiant individuals who strive for more than is humanly possible. Whether condemned or condoned, Faust is the protagonist of an enduring story that embodies fundamental religious and philosophical questions about humanity's place in the universe, the nature of good and evil, and the limitations of human knowledge.

THE HISTORICAL FAUST. Between 1507 and 1540, numerous references appear in German diaries, letters, and records to an unsavory character with the last name of Faust. The picture that emerges is of a fairly well educated man: He may have been the Johann Faust listed in the matriculation records of the University of Heidelberg for 1509, or he may have been the Georg Faust who received a hostile reception at the University of Erfurt. In any event, he traveled extensively, and he was viewed with a mixture of fear and contempt by his contemporaries, who describe him variously as a magician, a necromancer, a charlatan, an astrologer, an alchemist, a braggart, a sodomite, a gourmand, and a drunkard. His evil reputation, enhanced by his boast of having made a pact with the Devil, is confirmed by references to his expulsion from various cities. According to contemporary accounts, Faust died mysteriously. Philipp Melanchthon (1497–1560) says he was strangled by the Devil in a rural inn in Württemberg on the day their pact fell due.

ORIGIN OF THE FAUST LEGEND. The development of the Faust legend began in 1540, shortly after contemporary references to his activities ceased. The legend, a by-product of the Reformation, originated in Lutheran circles as a reaction against Roman Catholicism and Renaissance magic and science. It illustrates the anti-intellectual strain within the Christian tradition that has erupted periodically in campaigns of censorship and denunciations of "forbidden" knowledge. Faust became a convenient symbol of deviant religious, scientific, and philosophical thought. He was identified with several of the most controversial thinkers of the sixteenth century: Paracelsus, Trithemius, and Agrippa.

LITERARY TREATMENT OF THE FAUST LEGEND. The earliest printed collection of Faust stories, known as the *Spies Faustbuch,* was published by Johann Spies at Frankfurt in 1587. Enormously popular, it was reprinted eighteen times in the next ten years. Before the end of the century, translations appeared in English, Dutch, and French. The German text went through several revisions, the last of which, republished frequently in the eighteenth century, was probably known to Goethe.

The basic story presents Faust as a scholar whose intellectual arrogance prompts him to abandon the legitimate study of theology for the forbidden science of magic. In return for a specified number of years of power and knowledge,

Faust sells his soul to the Devil. He performs astonishing magical feats, conjures up the dead, flies over the earth, and eventually captivates the most beautiful woman in the world, Helen of Troy, by whom he has a son. When the pact expires, he is carried off to Hell.

The two most famous literary treatments of the story are Christopher Marlowe's *The Tragicall History of Doctor Faustus* (1604) and Goethe's *Faust* (1808, 1832). Marlowe based his play on the English *Faustbook.* His version of the story is in the tradition of morality plays, but he adds the specifically Protestant theme that Faust's damnation was due to his despairing fatalism and his refusal to accept justification by faith.

The first recorded performance of Marlowe's play was in Graz, Austria, by a company of English players. The play became a staple of German puppet theater, where it was seen by both Lessing and Goethe as children. As adults, both used the Faust story in plays of their own. Faust's defiant attempt to transcend the limits of human existence appealed to both men and fit in with the repudiation of Enlightenment rationalism that characterized the *Sturm und Drang* movement to which they belonged.

Only fragments of Lessing's proposed Faust dramas exist, but Goethe's two-part drama is considered the greatest work of Germany's greatest poet. By emphasizing the tragic elements only hinted at in earlier versions and by making them the source of Faust's salvation rather than his damnation, Goethe transformed the story of a venal, vainglorious magician into that of an inspiring, tragic hero. In Goethe's drama, God has the last word in the prologue: Striving and error go hand in hand ("Es irrt der Mensch, solang' er strebt"), but only those who dare to cultivate the divine spark within can hope to be saved ("Ein guter Mensch in seinem dunkel Drange / Ist sich des rechten Weges wohl bewusst").

The Faust story continued to be popular throughout the nineteenth and twentieth centuries. Among the many authors attracted to the legend were Lenau, Klinger, Chamisso, Grillparzer, Heine, de Nerval, Valéry, and Mann. Most of them, however, rejected Goethe's optimistic conclusion and stressed instead the danger inherent in Faust's insatiable thirst for knowledge.

BIBLIOGRAPHY

In *The Sources of the Faust Tradition* (Oxford, 1936), P. M. Palmer and R. P. More discuss the background to the Faust tradition and print many of the sources, together with the English *Faustbook* of 1592, several early Faust dramas and puppet plays, and the fragments of Lessing's Faust dramas. Another important book on the tradition's development is Frank Baron's *Doctor Faustus: From History to Legend* (Munich, 1978). E. M. Butler has made a wide-ranging study of the Faust legend in three books: *The Myth of the Magus* (Cambridge, U.K., 1948), *Ritual Magic* (Cambridge, U.K., 1949), and *The Fortunes of Faust* (Cambridge, U.K., 1952). Geneviève Bianquis surveys the literature in *Faust à travers quatre siècles,* 2d rev. ed. (Aubier, 1955). Lily B. Campbell discusses Marlowe's *Doctor Faustus* in the context of Reformation theology in "Dr. Faustus: A Case of Conscience," *Publications of the Modern Language Association of America* 67 (March 1952): 219–239.

New Sources

Grim, William E. *The Faust Legend in Music and Literature.* Lewiston, N.Y., 1992.

Mahal, Günther. *Faust und Frankfurt: Anstösse, Reaktionen, Verknüpfungen, Reibungen.* Frankfurt am Main, 1994.

Werres, Peter. *Doctor Faustus: Archetypal Subtext at the Millennium.* Morgantown, W. Va.,1999.

Wutrich, Timothy. *Prometheus and Faust: The Promethean Revolt in Drama from Classical Antiquity to Goethe.* Westport, Conn., 1995.

Ziolkowski, Theodore. *The Sin of Knowledge: Ancient Themes and Modern Variations.* Princeton, 2000.

ALLISON COUDERT (1987)
Revised Bibliography

FAXIAN (fl. 399–418), Chinese Buddhist monk, translator, and the earliest successful Chinese Buddhist pilgrim to India. Faxian's family name was Gong; he was born in Wuyang in Pingyang Prefecture (in Shanxi province). After being fully ordained at the age of twenty, Faxian recognized that the Buddhist monastic rules (the Vinaya) available in China at the time were incomplete and confused and thus vowed to journey to India to search for Vinaya texts. After years of preparation he organized a party of five monks, who left Chang'an in 399 and passed out of China through Qiangui, Zhangye and Dunhuang (all in northwestern China). From Dunhuang they proceeded along the southern marches of the Tarim basin to the central Asian kingdoms of Shan-shan, Agni, and Khotan, where they watched the religious procession of the Buddha's image. From there they traveled to Chakarka, crossed the Pamirs and Agzi, and finally arrived at the kingdom of Uḍḍiyāna in North India, via Darada and the Indus River valley. So long and arduous was their journey that it took three years for the Chinese pilgrims to reach North India from China.

Faxian spent a summer retreat in Uḍḍiyāna then traveled to the south, passed through Suvastu, Gandhara, Takṣaśīla (Taxila), and arrived at Puruṣapura. There, three members of the mission decided to return to China. Faxian and the others continued the journey, traveling to Hilo and paying homage to the Buddha's shadow at Nagārhara. They crossed over the Lesser Snow Mountain, where Huijing, one of the three members of the party, died. Faxian then traveled to Lakki, where he had the summer retreat in 403, after which he went on to Mathura via Harana and Uccha. He passed the summer retreat in 404 at Śaṃkāśya. Turning southeastward, he then passed through Kanyakubja (Kanauj), Vaiśākha, the Jetavana grove at Śrāvastī, and the birthplace of the Buddha at the Lumbinī near Kapilavastu on the Indo-Nepal border. From there he traveled eastward to Rāmagrāma, Kuśinagara, Vaiśālī, and finally arrived at Pāṭaliputra, the capital of Magadha kingdom. After a short stay at the city, Faxian went to the southeast. In Rājagṛha he performed a rite of worship at the top of Gṛdhrakūta. He worshiped the bodhi tree at Bodh Gayā, visited other places nearby, and returned to Pāṭaliputra. From there he went westward, made a pilgrimage to Vārāṇasī, the Mṛgadava, or the Deer Park at Sarnath, and concluded the trip with a visit to Kauśāmbi.

Between the years 405 and 407, Faxian stayed at the Mahāyāna monastery of Pāṭaliputra, concentrating on the study of the Sanskrit language and Buddhist scriptures. From the monastery, he obtained a collection of the widely observed monastic discipline of the Mahāsāṃghika school. He also obtained a condensed version of the monastic rules according to the Sarvāstivāda school along with several other texts, including the *Saṃyuktābhidharma-hṛdaya Śāstra* in six thousand verses, the *Mahāparinirvāṇa Sūtra* in two thousand five hundred verses, the *Vaipulya-parinirvāṇa Sūtra* in five thousand verses, and the Abhidharma collection of the Mahāsāṃghika school. Although most of these texts seem to have been copied by Faxian himself, at least one was presented to him by a lay Buddhist named Jialuo at the Mahāyāna monastery as a token of appreciation for Faxian's journey to India.

After the completion of his study at Pāṭaliputra, Daozheng, the other remaining member of the mission, declared his intention to stay in India permanently, leaving Faxian alone to complete his mission. In 407 he left Pāṭaliputra for Tāmraliptī via Champa. He remained at Tāmraliptī for two years (408–409), after which he traveled to Sri Lanka. He stayed on the island for two years, made pilgrimages to the holy places, and attended lectures delivered by an Indian monk. He also obtained additional scriptures there, including the Vinaya of the Mahīśāsaka school, the *Dīrghāgama*, the *Saṃyuktāgama*, and the *Zazang jing*, none of which was available in China. In 411 he embarked on a merchant ship and sailed for home with the Sanskrit manuscripts he had collected during the trip. Ninety days later, after being blown off course by a typhoon, the ship arrived at the kingdom of Yavadvipa (South Sumatra island). The monk remained on the island for five months, then embarked on another ship for Guangzhou (Canton). A month into the voyage another typhoon disrupted the journey. After nearly ninety days the ship landed at a place that the travelers later discovered was Laoshan in Zhangguang prefecture (Shandong Peninsula). The year was 412. Eventually, Faxian went to Jiankang (Nanjing) and began to translate the Sanskrit texts he had collected in India and Sri Lanka. He had traveled to approximately thirty kingdoms in fifteen years, and was the first Chinese Buddhist monk to successfully journey to India and return with Buddhist scriptures.

In 416, Faxian was asked by his colleagues to write an autobiographical account of his journey. The resulting chronicle, known as *Foguo ji* (A record of the Buddhist countries), is an important historical and religious document for South Asian history and for the Buddhist tradition. Five of Faxian's translations are extant. All of them have been translated jointly by Faxian and Buddhabhadra (d. 429), an Indian Buddhist missionary. Two of these translations are of the Vinaya of the Mahāsāṃghika school (T.D. nos. 1425 and 1427), two are Mahāyāna scriptures (T.D. nos. 376 and 745), and one is a Hīnayāna scripture (T.D. no. 7). According to one catalog, a translation bearing the title *Za ebitan xinlun* in thirteen fascicles is also ascribed to him and Buddhabhadra, but the book has been lost. Two other Sanskrit texts brought back to China by Faxian have been translated into Chinese by Buddhajīva (T.D. no. 1421) and Guṇabhadra (T.D. no. 99) respectively. Faxian continued to translate until the time of his death in 418 at the Xin Monastery of Jingzhou (in Hubei province). His successful journey to India and his search for an authentic tradition of Buddhism remained a source of inspiration for later generations of Chinese Buddhists.

SEE ALSO Pilgrimage, article on Buddhist Pilgrimage in South and Southeast Asia.

BIBLIOGRAPHY

The earliest translation of Faxian's autobiographical account is the *Foé Koué Ki, ou Relation des royaumes bouddhiques: Voyages dans la tartarie, dans l'Afghanistan et dans l'Inde*, translated by Jean Pierre Abel Rémusat et al. (Paris, 1836). The French text was translated into English with additional notes by J. W. Laidley under the title *The Pilgrimage of Fa Hian* (Calcutta, 1848). James Legge's translation, *A Record of Buddhistic Kingdoms* (1886; reprint, New York, 1965), still stands as a useful reference and is easily available. H. A. Giles's retranslation, *The Travel of Fa-hsien, 399–414 A.D.* (1923; reprint, London, 1959), is good. Li Yung-hsi's version, *A Record of the Buddhist Countries* (Beijing, 1957), is the most recent and readable translation. Faxian's biography in the *Gaoseng zhuan* has been translated by Robert Shih in his *Biographies des moines éminents (Kao seng tchouan) de Houei-kiao* (Louvain, 1968), pp. 108–115. A study of his translations and writing is found in Prabodh Chandra Bagchi's *Le canon bouddhique en Chine*, vol. 1 (Paris, 1927), pp. 347–348.

New Sources

Giles, Herbert, trans. "From Record of the Buddhistic Kingdoms, a Chinese Pilgrim in Ceylon." In *Classical Chinese Literature: An Anthology of Translations.* Volume 1: *From Antiquity to the Tang Dynasty*, edited by John Minford and Joseph Lau, pp. 599–605. New York, 2000.

Hazra, Kanai Lal. *Buddhism in India as Described by the Chinese Pilgrims AD 399–689.* New Delhi, 1983.

Liu, Xinru. *Ancient India and Ancient China: Trade and Religious Exchanges, A.D. 1–600.* New Delhi, 1988.

Liu, Xinru. *The Silk Road: Overland Trade and Cultural Interactions in Eurasia.* Washington D.C., 1998.

Rongxi, Li, and Albert A. Dalia, trans. *Lives of Great Monks and Nuns.* Berkeley, 2002.

JAN YÜN-HUA (1987)
Revised Bibliography

FAZANG (643–712), also known as Xianshou; third patriarch and systematizer of the Huayan school, a Chinese Buddhist tradition centered around exegesis of the *Avataṃsaka Sūtra.* His surname, Kang, indicates that his family was originally from Samarkand in Central Asia. Fazang was a son of Mi, a high-ranking army officer in the Tang dynasty. When he was sixteen years old he burned off one of his fingers as an offering to the Buddha before an Aśoka stupa in which relics of the Buddha were enshrined. After seeking without success for a satisfactory teacher, he entered Mount Taibei, where he studied Mahāyāna Buddhism in seclusion. Some years later, hearing that his parents were ill, he returned home to Chang'an, where Zhiyan (later reckoned the second Huayan patriarch) was lecturing on the *Huayan jing (Mahāvaipulya-buddhagaṇḍavyūha Sūtra)* at the Yunhua Si. Yan Zhaoyin, Fazang's biographer, described the meeting of these two as a "smooth acceptance, like pouring water into a vessel, a harmonious condition compared to mingling milk and water." Subsequent to this encounter, Fazang became Zhiyan's disciple.

In 668, when his master Zhiyan passed away, Fazang was still a layman. When he was twenty-eight, Empress Wu Zetian built a new temple named Taiyuan Si in memory of her mother, Yongguo. It was at this time that Fazang was ordained and became a monk at this temple, probably at the empress's request. In 684, he met Divākara, a monk from middle India, at Xitaiyuan Si and studied Śīlabhadra's and Jñānaprabha's *jiaopan* (classification of Buddhist teachings). The next year he joined with Divākara for the translation of that portion of the *Gaṇḍavyūha* (an independent sūtra comprising the last chapter of the *Huayan jing*) that was missing from Buddhabhadra's translation of the text. He also frequently assisted such excellent translators as Devaprajñā, Śikṣānanda, and Yijing.

Fazang is best known as the systematizer and propagator of Huayan Buddhism; he is said to have given more than thirty lectures on the *Huayan jing.* His principal works are (1) *Huayan jing zhigui* (The essential meaning of the *Huayan jing;* T.D. no. 1871); (2) *Huayan wujiao zhang* (Outline of the Huayan Five Teachings Doctrine; T.D. no. 1866); (3) *Huayan jing tanxuan ji* (Plumbing the profound import of the *Huayan jing;* T.D. no. 1733); (4) *Dasheng qixinlun yiji* (A commentary on the *Awakening of Faith;* T.D. no. 1846); (5) *Panruoxin jing lüeshu* (A brief commentary on the *Prajñāpāramitāhṛdaya Sūtra;* T.D. no. 1712); (6) *Rulengqie xinxuan yi* (The essential meaning of the *Laṅkāvatāra Sūtra;* T.D. no. 1790); (7) *Fanwan jing pusa jieben shu* (A commentary on the bodhisattva precepts in the *Brahmajāla Sūtra;* T.D. no. 1813); and (8) *Huayan jing chuanji* (On the tradition of study of the *Huayan jing;* T.D. no. 2073).

According to legend, Fazang was a miracle worker who sought merit for the people. One of his miracles allegedly caused both Emperor Zhongzong and his successor Ruizong to receive the *bodhisattva* precepts and provide government support to establish five temples for the propagation of Huayan Buddhism. When Fazang died in November of 712, the emperor Xuanzong bestowed upon him the honorary title of Hongluqing, director of palace ceremonies.

Fazang is credited with three major advances in Huayan doctrine. The first is his classification of Buddhist teachings in "five grades and ten qualities." Through this classification Fazang tried to show that Huayan Buddhism should be regarded as the acme of Buddhist teachings, superior even to the Faxiang (Yogācāra) school newly imported by Xuanzang. The second achievement is his advocacy of a doctrine known as *sanxing tongyiyi* ("the original way of explaining the doctrine of the three kinds of existence"). Using this theory, he insisted that ultimate truth and deluded consciousness are not mutually exclusive and that consequently even deluded consciousness can penetrate into the very root of truth. Fazang's third achievement is his clarification of the ultimate modality of *pratītya-samutpāda* ("dependent origination"). That is to say, Fazang elaborated upon Zhiyan's philosophy of *fajie yuanqi* ("*pratītya-samutpāda* in the True Realm") so as to emphasize that matter was no different from the truth *(lishi wu'ai).* According to Fazang, when seen from the viewpoint of the Buddha, all phenomena not only depend upon each other but also enter into each other infinitely *(shishi wu'ai).*

SEE ALSO Huayan.

BIBLIOGRAPHY

Chan, Wing-tsit. *A Source Book in Chinese Philosophy.* Princeton, 1963. Pages 406–424 include a brief survey of Huayan thought and translations of the *Jinshizi zhang* (complete), attributed to Fazang, and two chapters from his *Huayan yihai bomen.*

Kamata Shigeo. *Chūgoku kegonshisōshi kenkyū.* Tokyo, 1965. In the chapter entitled "Bushūōchō ni okeru kegon shisō no keisei" the author discusses the political and intellectual background of Fazang's thought.

Kimura Kiyotaka. "Hōzō no kegon kyōgaku." *Risō* 606 (1983): 64–86. Treats the role of Fazang's understanding of *pratītya-samutpāda* in the history of the development of Huayan thought.

Yoshizu Yoshihide. "Hōzōden no kenkyū." *Komazawa daigaku bukkyōgakubu kenkyū kiyō* 37 (1983): 168–193. The most recent and comprehensive study of the life of Fazang.

New Sources

Hartshorne, Charles. "Sankara, Nagarjuna, and Fazang, with Some Western Analogues." In *Interpreting Across Boundaries: New Essays in Comparative Philosophy,* edited by Gerald James Larson and Eliot Deutsch, pp. 98–115. Princeton, 1988.

Shim, Jae-ryong. "Faith and Practice in Huayan Buddhism: A Critique of Fazang (643–712) by Li T'ung-hsuan (646–740)." In *Buddhist and Taoist Practice in Medieval Chinese Society,* edited by David W. Chappell, pp. 109–124. Honolulu, 1987.

Wright, Dale. "The 'Thought of Enlightenment' in Fazang's Huayan Buddhism." *Eastern Buddhist* 33, no. 2 (2001): 97–106.

KIMURA KIYOTAKA (1987)
Revised Bibliography

FEASTING SEE FOOD; SEASONAL CEREMONIES; WORSHIP AND DEVOTIONAL LIFE

FEET are multivalent symbols. In some mythologies the rays of the sun—as depicted, for example, in the figure of the swastika—are likened to feet. C. G. Jung finds the foot frequently phallic in significance; others believe it is sometimes a symbol of the soul, an idea rarely directly substantiated but indirectly confirmed when lameness is taken to symbolize some defect of the spirit, as in the cases of Hephaistos, Wieland the blacksmith, Mani, and Oedipus.

The heel of the foot is both suitable for and vulnerable to attack; it may dispatch a serpent or it may be the locus of a fatal wound (Achilles, Sigurd, and Kṛṣṇa). In the Hebrew scriptures, Jacob grasps Esau's heel in order to defeat him. In Celtic legend, Gwydion masters Arianrhod by grasping her foot.

Feet are also vulnerable because of their contact with the earth. Vital and sacred forces can be drained away through them. For this reason, the Aztec ruler Moctezuma II was carried on the shoulders of noblemen, and members of the royal family in Uganda were carried on the shoulders of men of the Buffalo clan. An emperor of Japan, it is said, would have been deprived of his office had his feet ever touched the earth. The Irish hero Oisín, who had lived in the Land of Youth for three hundred years, could remain young upon revisiting the land of his birth only if he did not touch his feet to the ground.

The foot is also a symbol of humility because it touches and is besmirched by the dust of the earth. Victory and subjection are represented by the conqueror placing his foot on the neck of the vanquished or using him as a footstool. Worshipers all over the ancient world removed their shoes before entering sanctuaries and temples, as Muslims, Hindus, and Jains do today before entering places of worship. Foot washing has commonly served as part of rites of purification.

Foot washing as an act of hospitality was also widespread throughout the ancient world. The Christian ritual of foot washing was derived from this practice, and especially from Jesus' washing his disciples' feet (*Jn.* 13:5). As such, the ritual does not focus on cleansing but on humility, and on the Christian ideals of willing service and penitence.

Footprints of divine or holy figures may symbolize the way to the truth, or the salvation offered by them. Footprints of both Viṣṇu and the Buddha appear all over India. Such physical evidence of the earthly presence of divinity is a way of picturing what is wholly transcendent. This is probably the intended symbolism in depictions of Christ's ascension, found especially in eleventh-century English art, where only the feet and part of the legs show at the top of the picture. On a carved medieval bench-end from Launcells in Cornwall, the feet of Christ are seen vanishing into clouds while footprints are left on a rock. Similarily, pilgrims to Palestine can see footprints in the Church of the Ascension on the Mount of Olives.

BIBLIOGRAPHY

There is no really adequate discussion of feet as a religious symbol. James G. Frazer in *The Golden Bough,* 3d ed., rev. & enl. (London, 1911–1915), discusses the taboo against touching the feet to the ground, but he focuses on the loss of power and on the earth as the agency of loss rather than on feet. For a more convenient and up-to-date source, see *The New Golden Bough,* the one-volume abridgment by Theodor H. Gaster (New York, 1959). On foot washing, see G. A. Frank Knight's article "Feet-Washing," in the *Encyclopaedia of Religion and Ethics,* edited by James Hastings, vol. 5 (Edinburgh, 1912), which discusses both secular and religious customs in great detail. Concerning Hephaistos and the "magical or shamanic lameness," consult *Hephaïstos, ou La légende du magicien* by Marie Delcourt (Paris, 1957).

ELAINE MAGALIS (1987)

FEINSTEIN, MOSHE (1895–1986), was an American Orthodox rabbi and Jewish legal authority. Born to a rabbinical family in Uzda, Belorussia, Feinstein prepared for a career in the rabbinate under the tutelage of his father, David Feinstein, and subsequently as a student in the leading Talmudic academies of that region. Upon his arrival in the United States in 1937, Feinstein became dean of the Talmudic academy Metivta Tiferet Jerusalem in New York, a position that he held until his death. He played a prominent role in both the Union of Orthodox Rabbis and Agudat Yisraʾel, the world movement of Orthodox Jewry.

Feinstein enjoyed worldwide recognition by Orthodox rabbis and laity alike as a leading interpreter and decisor of Jewish law. His *responsa* (legal decisions) have been published in a work entitled *Iggerot Mosheh* (Letters of Moshe). Students of Jewish law have enthusiastically hailed the appearance of *Iggerot Mosheh* because it offers a Jewish legal perspective on numerous issues relating to contemporary scientific, technological, and sociological developments. The topics Feinstein covers include heart transplants, autopsies, brain death, experimentation with live human tissue, intrauterine devices, the use of electric blankets and transistor microphones on the Sabbath, adoption, life insurance, labor unions, and sex manuals. Thus, the subject matter of *Iggerot Mosheh* dramatizes Feinstein's concern to use the technical capability of Jewish law to address ongoing changes in social reality.

Moreover, a number of Feinstein's rulings reflect a creative and bold flexibility, particularly in the realm of Jewish family law. In one controversial decision, Feinstein permitted, with qualification, artificial insemination even from a donor other than the husband. In a series of rulings regarding the status of a marriage solemnized in either a civil or non-Orthodox ceremony, Feinstein permitted the subsequent remarriage of either spouse without the prior granting of a *get,* a Jewish writ of divorce.

It would be inaccurate, however, to characterize Feinstein as a liberal interpreter of Jewish law. A staunchly traditionalist work, the *Iggerot Mosheh* contains numerous rulings of a conservative nature as well. In the final analysis, then, the Jewish legal process as reflected in the *Iggerot Mosheh* demonstrates both receptivity and resistance to changing sociocultural circumstances. Feinstein's profound and encyclopedic grasp of Jewish law and his legal creativity were coupled with an outstanding reputation for personal piety and selflessness. It is because of these qualities that his halakhic rulings are considered authoritative by a wide cross-section of Orthodox Jewry.

See Also Agudat Yisra'el.

Bibliography

Eisenstadt, Benzion. *Sefer dorot ha-Aḥaronim.* Brooklyn, N.Y., 1940. See volume 2, pages 191–192.

Kirschenbaum, Aaron. "Rabbi Moshe Feinstein's Responsa: A Major Halakhic Event." *Judaism* 15 (Summer 1966): 364–373.

Rackman, Emanuel. "Halakhic Progress: Rabbi Moshe Feinstein's *Igrot Moshe* on *Even Ha-Ezer.*" *Judaism* 13 (Summer 1964): 365–373.

Rand, Oscar Z., ed. *Toledot anshei shem.* New York, 1950. See page 98.

New Sources

Rosner, Fred. "Rabbi Moshe Feinstein's Influence on Medical Halacha." *Journal of Halacha and Contemporary Society* 20 (1990): 47–75.

Rod M. Glogower (1987)
Revised Bibliography

FEMININE SACRALITY.

FEMININE SACRALITY. Attributing gender to manifestations of sacred power in the world is a longstanding human practice. Such manifestations generally are said to be "feminine" when they function in ways analogous to women's most common modes of physiological or cultural activity. Hence that which contains, as in a womb, is often considered feminine, particularly if the containment can be perceived as gestation (e.g., the gestation of seeds in the earth). That which nurtures by providing food and shelter or spiritual sustenance, as a mother offers milk and refuge to her child, may also be considered feminine. That which changes may be feminine, especially if it changes periodically, as a woman's body changes through its monthly cycle, swells in pregnancy, or replaces childhood smoothness with the fullness of maturity and later with the flaccidity of old age. Similarly, that which works changes on materials outside itself may be feminine, just as a woman's care changes her infant into a self-sufficient child or a woman's processing changes raw materials into food and clothing.

Feminine symbols and divinities were especially prominent in religious systems of ancient cultures, and they have remained important in certain Asian cultures and among small-scale agricultural and hunting peoples. Although overshadowed in the West for many centuries by male deities and imagery, they have undergone a renaissance in Neopagan, feminist spirituality, and environmentalist movements.

Feminine Sacrality in Nature. Perhaps the best-known and most frequently cited forms of feminine sacrality are those connected with that portion of the world at large that produces and reproduces itself without human intervention. Many peoples have experienced this "natural" world as a constellation of powers and realities that both limit humans and open human opportunities. Often such powers and realties in nature are perceived as female. In fact, the entire natural realm may be experienced as female; people in modern Western cultures acknowledge such an experience when they speak of "Mother Nature." But the experience of the "feminine" in nature is more commonly restricted to certain sectors.

The earth. "According to [alchemist] Basilus Valentinius, the earth . . . is not a dead body but is inhabited by a spirit that is its life and soul. All created things, minerals included, draw their strength from the earth spirit. This spirit is life, . . . and it gives nourishment to all the living things it shelters in its womb" (Jung, 1968, p. 342). Throughout history many peoples have taught that the earth is a living organism and the source of all other life that inhabits its surface and crevices. As such, it is the ultimate womb and mother of all.

A poet of ancient India celebrated the earth as "the mistress of that which was and shall be" and declared that "the earth is the mother, and I the earth's son." She is the "womb of all," pouring forth milk for her offspring (*Atharvaveda* 12.1.1, 10, 12, 43). A poet of ancient Greece sang to the earth as "mother of all things, feeding upon her soil all that exists"(Homeric *Hymn to Earth*). The Oglala of the upper Great Plains in North America were solemnly taught: "For the Earth is your Grandmother and Mother and she is sacred. Every step that is taken upon her should be as a prayer" (Brown, 1953, pp. 5–6). Thus they prayed, "O you, Grandmother, from whom all things come, and O You, Mother Earth, who bear and nourish all fruits, behold us and listen" (Brown, 1953, p. 133).

When represented iconographically, the earth takes the form of a buxom, mature woman. Hindu temple sculptors have portrayed her in this way when illustrating the story of her rescue by a great boar that dives in pursuit after a demon carries her to the bottom of the ocean; she clings demurely to the boar's tusk as he rises from the waters. This boar is a form of Viṣṇu, great Lord of cosmic order. The earth also appears beside Viṣṇu in temple images as his consort the goddess Bhū, "She Who Becomes." Buddhist art offers a more revealing portrayal in scenes where the Buddha-to-be calls the earth to witness to his generosity as he strives to repel the attack of Māra, the god of death and desire. Here, the goddess appears as torso only, rising from the ground. The lower portion of her body—her "womb"—must be understood as the earth itself, of which the anthropomorphic torso is just a temporary projection. The earth goddess Gaia of ancient Greece was similarly portrayed as torso only.

The earth's motherhood is often understood quite literally. Across the world, myths have asserted that humans and other beings first emerged from a womb within the earth's depths. Bronislaw Malinowski's famed 1948 Trobriand Island studies found that residents of each village traced their ancestry to a sister and a brother who emerged from a nearby hole in the ground. In West Africa, the Ashanti likewise claimed that their ancestors first came from holes in the earth. Among native peoples of North America, 120 versions of human emergence from the earth have been recorded. The Oglala tell how their people were initially tricked into leaving the earth womb as the result of a conspiracy between Inktomi, the trickster Spider, and Anukite, the double-faced Deer Woman. The two enticed the people to the surface with gifts of meat and clothing and a promise of unending plenty. Then winter came, the buffalo grew scarce, and the people could no longer find their way back into the cave womb. In the Southwest the Navajo and Pueblo peoples developed complex emergence myths describing how the people evolved into higher and higher levels of refinement as they ascended through a series of wombs before exiting onto the earth's surface.

How are earth's offspring first engendered? The earth need not have a partner to help her produce her children. The Trobriand myths cited above make no mention of a genitor who fertilizes their great genetrix. According to Malinowski, Trobrianders themselves did not believe that children came through sexual fertilization. Like the earth from which they ascended, Trobriand women received departed ancestral spirits into their wombs and returned these spirits to life as children. Hence both earth and women accomplished a form of parthenogenesis (virgin birth).

In many cultures, however, the earth is paired with a male fecundator, usually Sky Father. Before the known world is created, she and he are a single entity, locked together in a lasting embrace. Then the embrace is broken, and earth and sky separate, allowing light and motion to enter the intervening realm. Sometimes this separation is voluntary, as in the long cosmogonic cycle of the North American Zuni, where Earth Mother pushes Sky Father away after she becomes pregnant. Often, however, the separation is forced. In a version of this myth told by the Arawa tribe of New Zealand, the children of the primeval parents Ranga and Papa separate their parents because they have grown weary of the darkness. After several fruitless attempts, the son—Tanemahuta, "father of forests" (a great tree)—shoves them apart. In the Mediterranean world the act becomes still more violent; according to the version retold by the Greek poet Hesiod, the primeval mother and father, Gaia and Ouranos, separate after their son Kronos castrates his father with a sickle.

If the earth is a sacred mother, it follows that the act of tilling her is also potentially an act of violence. The violence implicit in gardening is vividly acknowledged in a myth from the island of Ceram in Indonesia. A pubescent maiden named Hainuwele is slain and dismembered as her people perform a spiral dance. When planted, her body parts yield the yams that are the islanders' chief staple food and gardening product. Because her murder brings death into the world, the violence that brings the yams also costs Hainuwele's people the paradisal life that they had known before.

Reluctance to violate the earth and seize her products can also be seen in a frequently cited speech by the American Indian prophet Smohalla. Told that his people should become farmers, Smohalla responded: "You ask me to plough the ground. Shall I take a knife and tear my mother's breast? Then when I die she will not take my bosom to rest. You ask me to dig for stone. Shall I dig under her skin for her bones? Then when I die I cannot enter her body to be born again. You ask me to cut grass and make hay and sell it and be rich like white men. But how dare I cut off my mother's hair?" (Mooney, 1896, p. 721).

The cave as earth womb. If humans are children of earth, born from a womb in her depths, the significance of caves in religious belief and practice becomes apparent. Often a people identifies some cave within its ancestral territory as its own place of origin. For example, the Oglala say their ancestors emerged at Wind Cave in the Black Hills of South Dakota. The belief that caves are the original earth wombs may have been responsible for the great cave sanctuaries of Paleolithic times in Europe. Sections that bear splendid paintings of animals and the hunt are all hard to reach and are located at a distance from the entrance. Some scholars have argued that these caverns may have been utilized for another sort of "birthing" from the earth—namely rituals of initiation—such as those that often feature a symbolic "return to the womb." In this case the return would have been literal, as initiates worked their way back into the bowels of the earth from which their ancestors had ascended.

Another sort of return to the earth mother is accomplished when humans encounter death. The land of the dead is often located in a cavern beneath the earth. In the Latin epic *Aeneid,* the hero Aeneas descends to the land of the dead via a cave at Cumae, west of present-day Naples. The Greeks similarly located their Erebus or Tartarus in a subterranean region, as did the Hebrews their She'ol. Muslim texts portray the underworld as the huge fiery crater Jahannam, into which the unrighteous are thrown after judgment. Dante borrowed from such concepts when he portrayed his Inferno as a fiery pit whose nadir is deep within the earth's bowels.

The classical Mediterranean underworlds described above are not explicitly defined as female. Nor do females alone rule them; in Greek and Roman sources a goddess (Greek, Persephone; Latin, Proserpina) shares the throne of the dead with her consort (Greek, Hades; Latin, Pluto). In ancient Sumeria, however, the netherworld's queen was a lone goddess, the dread widow Ereshkigal. Similarly, the Germanic goddess Hel was her underworld's sole ruler. In Japan the counterpart was the primeval ancestress Izanagi, who became the first being to die (after giving birth to fire). Among the Maori of New Zealand, the ruler of the dead was Hine-nui-te-po (great goddess of darkness), a former dawn maiden who fled in shame to the underworld after learning that her husband was also her father.

Alternatively, a dread female guards the underworld's entrance; she is often less a woman than a female monster. Perhaps the most interesting example is a figure prominent in myth and ritual of the island of Malekula in the archipelago of Vanuatu. Malekulans say the wind blows the released soul across the waters of death. On the farther side, by the underworld's entrance, the soul encounters the monstrous female Le-hev-hev. Before her on the sand is the design of a maze or labyrinth, half of which she erases as the soul approaches. The soul must restore the missing half of the drawing in order to enter the land of the dead. If the soul fails, the guardian devours it. Mastery of this labyrinth thus becomes a central feature of Malekulan initiation rites.

Feminine sacrality and water. Note that the Malekulan myth perceives the journey of death not only as a passage into a female underworld but also as a voyage that crosses water. Water appears often in stories of human descents to and emergences from subterranean regions. The Greek who entered the underworld land of the dead had to cross the river Styx. Called by Hesiod the "awful goddess hated by the other gods," the Styx was a branch of the ocean stream that coiled around the world (*Theogony* 12.775–778). According to Plato, a soul returning to the earth for rebirth had to cross and drink from another river, Lethe, the stream of forgetfulness (*Republic* 10.620). In some regions of rural Europe, even during the twentieth century, the souls of children were said to emerge not only from caves but also from grottoes, pools, and springs. Versions of the Native American emergence myth replace the usual cave of emergence with a lake, or a subterranean flood drives the people to the surface.

Waters are not merely an amniotic presence within the earth womb; in many cosmogonic accounts they also become the very matrix from which the earth is born. Even the resolutely male-centered Judeo-Christian Creation myth acknowledges their presence: in the beginning the spirit of God hovers upon the face of the waters. In the ancient Near East, where this account originated, other stories of the world's origin depict a process of evolution from primeval waters. According to the Babylonian creation epic *Enuma Elish*, waters alone existed in the beginning. The sweet and potable waters called Apsu that now lie beneath the earth were then commingled with the primal sea Tiamat. As the two lay together, early generations of the gods were born, culminating in the lord Ea. Then Apsu plotted to kill his children, because their clamor disturbed him. But Ea overcame Apsu and established a dwelling place for himself upon Apsu's waters. Thus the first separation of waters occurred. The second followed after Tiamat, angered by the loss of her consort, gave birth to an army of monsters that attacked her divine children. The latter then found a new hero, Ea's son Marduk. Following a ferocious battle, Marduk slew Tiamat and split her body in a second separation of waters. Half of that body was cast upward to become the waters of the sky. A gap in the text prevents an understanding of what became of the other half, but presumably it transformed into rivers and oceans, whereas Ea's dwelling, the land, was extended as homes for other gods were added. Finally, humankind was created to serve the gods in their new shrines.

According to one Hindu version of the cosmogony, the world's source is a giant male who sleeps upon a serpent in primal waters. A lotus or tree grows from his navel; both are symbols of the cosmos. Alternatively, an egg is born from the waters and then breaks apart, its two halves evolving into heaven and earth. In the Finnish epic *Kalevala* a bird lays the cosmic egg on a knee that the Mother of Waters raises to give the bird a place to build her nest.

Waters preceding the earth's birth become even more explicitly amniotic in "earth diver" myths common in Siberia and on the west coast of North America. In a gesture reminiscent of sexual intercourse, a male animal dives beneath the waters to secure a few scrapings of soil that will become the germ of the land. The land is then stretched out from a central point, just as an embryo grows from its navel. Often the diver in such stories is a duck or a turtle. The boar who rescues the earth and takes her as consort in the Hindu story cited earlier is an alternative form of the Siberian earth diver transplanted onto Indian soil.

Just as waters that give birth to the earth or nourish nascent life beneath its surface are often female, so also are waters flowing over the earth's surface. India is the preeminent land of sacred female watercourses; all of its rivers are goddesses, the first of them being Gangā Mātā (Mother Ganges). Female deities guarded rivers in China, above all in the South. Especially prominent in ancient times, they often had dragonlike characteristics. In ancient Mexico all rivers belonged to the goddess Chalchiuhtlicue (jade skirt). The face of the Mediterranean world was dotted by springs, pools, and streams inhabited by water nymphs or dryads. Similar lesser female deities connected to local waters are found across Eurasia. Sometimes, like the little mermaid of Hans Christian Andersen's celebrated folktale, they venture forth on the earth seeking human lovers or husbands. The child born of such a liaison may become a great king or hero.

Mounds, rocks, and mountains. Rivers are not the only manifestation of the feminine upon the earth's surface; any protuberance or extension of the earth may be viewed as a special concentration of the feminine. Mounds are often associated with the feminine sacred and honored as earth navels—places where the earth first rose above the waters. The famous omphalos (navel) at Delphi, where the Pythia sat to receive visions of the future, was such a mound; appropriately, like the mound itself and the earth from which it erupted, the priestess-seer of the oracle was also female. Rocks may also manifest female power. In village shrines of South India small rocks or heaps of stones are icons for the *ammas,* local goddesses who protect the villages. When the goddess Cybele was moved to Rome from her initial home in Anatolia, she traveled in the form of a sacred black stone. Again, a mountain or volcano may be the visible form of a goddess or her dwelling place or birthplace—a good example is the Hawaiian volcano Kilauea, venerated as home of the goddess Pele.

Vegetation. In the varied mythologies of the world, sacred plants and vegetation deities have been both male and female. Nonetheless, plants are conspicuously connected to both the earth and the waters and often linked with female powers. Popular images of a goddess who is a source of life and fertility may show her seated under a tree or clinging to a branch with her hand, or her body becomes the tree's trunk while its branches rise from her shoulders. Female spirits often haunt trees. Herbs too may be female: a hymn of India's *Yajur Veda* exclaims: "O herbs! Oh, you who are mothers! I hail you as goddesses!" (4.2.6). Sacred plants that grow in swamps are often female; India's lotus, closely associated with Lakṣmī, goddess of prosperity, is an excellent example.

Staple food plants too are sometimes manifestations, gifts, or transformations of feminine sacred powers. This concept was mentioned above in the myth of the murdered maiden Hainuwele—the yam is the transformed maiden. In North America a similar story is told about the origin of corn, which many Native Americans revered as Corn Mother. According to one version of Corn Mother's story, the slain goddess was killed and dragged along the ground to fertilize the land where corn would emerge. An alternative version claims the goddess gave the corn and its rites to the husband who pursued her after she ran away from home.

Lady of the animals. Given the central role of the earth and waters in crop production, it is not surprising that forms of feminine sacrality are often prominent among peoples who practice gardening and agriculture. Except for the earth mother, honored widely among all people who depend on her products, important feminine powers are found less often among hunting peoples. Occasionally, however, a goddess appears among the category of deities known as "lords of animals." Such deities control the supply of animals essential to the hunting economy, either by creating them, corralling and releasing them to produce scarcity and abundance, or restoring them to life after they have been slain. One such lady of animals is the ill-tempered Sedna of Inuit (Eskimo) legends. Deprived of her fingers and drowned by her father, this once-human maiden tends the seals at the bottom of the ocean. Misdeeds of the Eskimo foul her hair, which she cannot comb for lack of fingers. She then becomes angry and withholds the seals, releasing them only after a shaman descends to comb her matted hair. A far more positive figure is the White Buffalo Calf Woman of the Oglala Lakota. Appearing either as a white buffalo or as a beautiful young woman, this deity brought the sacred pipe to the Lakota and taught them how to summon the Great Spirit with it. She is a prototype not only of the buffalo but also of Oglala women, who were initiated at puberty by a rite in which they imitated movements of a buffalo cow.

Darkness, night, and moon. The earth's dark crevices are often perceived as the womb of an awesome feminine power, and by extension darkness of any kind may be perceived as female. Hence night becomes a female deity, often of awesome power—according to the Greek epic *Iliad,* even Zeus, king of the gods, dared not displease Night. Night may replace the waters as preformal matrix in accounts of the birth of the cosmos. An Orphic myth recounts how Night laid a silver egg in the womb of Darkness. Eros, or desire, was born from that egg and set the universe in motion. In most mythologies of the world, however, Night is relegated to the background of dramatic action; her principal luminary, the moon, receives far more attention.

The moon is most simply perceived as a complement to the sun—as spouse, lover, or sibling. As the gentler of the two lights, the moon is often, but not always, the female partner. Myths of marriage between the sun and the moon are legion, as are etiological accounts explaining why they do not travel the sky at the same time. The most common cause of their separation is some kind of falling-out. An African myth reports, for example, that the moon tired of the sun and took a lover after she had borne many children (the stars) with her husband. The sun then divided his possessions with her and drove her and her children away from his home. A similar myth of the Oglala tells how Moon and Sun were assigned to separate realms after the woman Face usurped the Moon's place beside her husband at a banquet.

Perhaps because she is so often a prototypical spouse, or perhaps because her body swells periodically, the moon is closely linked to pregnancy and childbirth. Lunar goddesses often preside over childbirth or protect married women during their childbearing years. Examples include Juno, a powerful goddess of ancient Italy who became queen of the Roman pantheon, and Mama Quilla, sister and wife and second in command to Inti, the sun god of the Inca Empire. In many areas of the world, mothers hold newborn babies up to the light of the moon, believing that this act brings blessings upon the children. Even when portrayed as a masculine power, the moon retains its connection with childbearing; many peoples tell tales of women made pregnant by moonbeams.

The moon is also cyclic, and the connection between lunar and menstrual cycles has often been noted. The Mbuti (Pygmy) peoples of Africa call menstrual blood *matu* (moon maiden), while the Iroquois of North America have maintained that all menstrual periods occur when the moon is new. Both the association with childbearing and this link to the menstrual cycle seem to generate a special bond between the moon and pubescent women. The Ceramese story of Hainuwele—the maiden whose murder results in the first yams (see above)—has a striking variant in which a rape precedes the murder and the murdered maiden becomes the moon. In this version an ugly rash-covered sun man named Tuwale seeks to marry the maiden, here called Rabia. After he passes harsh tests that her parents set to dissuade him, the parents allow the wedding but place a dead pig in the marriage bed instead of their daughter. The angry Tuwale pursues his fleeing bride and claims her so violently that he pounds her into the ground and no one can free her. As she sinks into the earth, she asks her parents to perform a three-day funeral ritual for her, substituting a dead pig for her missing body. On the third night, she says, she will reappear, shining down upon them as a light from heaven.

The myth of Rabia points to a third important aspect of lunar sacrality, its ties to cycles of death and regeneration. The moon constantly dies and is as constantly reborn. Thus the moon may be a source of immortality, or the home of a goddess who possesses some life-sustaining nectar. The Chinese say, for example, that the moon goddess Ch'ang-o was once a woman who stole the elixir of immortality from her husband; she then fled to the moon to escape her husband's anger. Women and children honored this goddess in one of China's three great annual festivals.

Finally, lunar cycles mark off the passage of time and help to weave the tapestry that is human history. The moon is linked to goddesses who determine human fate, such as the Greek Moirai or the Germanic Norns. Like the moon herself, such goddesses are often portrayed as spinners and weavers; two of the Norns spin and twist the thread of life, while the third cuts it off. Lunar goddesses of fate are commonly portrayed in triple form, corresponding to the waxing, full, and waning moon, as well as to past, present, and future or to youth, adulthood, and old age.

Sun and fire. In its journeys through the sky, the sun has also woven human time and cosmic rhythms. The sun may therefore also be a weaver, as in Japanese tales of Amaterasu, one of the rare female solar divinities to become the focus of a significant cult. Amaterasu was the ancestress of Japan's imperial lineage; a priestess from the imperial family still serves her shrine at Ise. According to the chronicles *Kojiki* and *Nihongi,* Amaterasu emerged from the right eye of the primal ancestor Izanami as he cleansed himself in a river after an abortive attempt to rescue his consort Izanagi from the land of the dead. Amaterasu's most famous myth describes how she fled from the earth and hid in a cave, from which she was coaxed by the sight of her own shining reflection in a mirror. She hid after her obstreperous brother Susano-o polluted her sacred weaving hall by heaving into it a piebald colt skinned backward. One weaving maiden startled by this stabbed her genitals with a shuttle and died (according to one version of the story, Amaterasu herself was this maiden).

Like the sun, fire is usually understood to be a masculine power, but there are some noteworthy exceptions. In the ancient Mediterranean world, the hearth fire was a goddess (Greek, Hestia; Roman, Vesta). In ancient Rome this goddess had a special temple at which a perpetual fire burned. Priestesses who tended this fire had to remain celibate—to lose one's virginity (and hence pollute the vestal fire) brought a penalty of death. The hearth fire was also a goddess among the Ainu people of Japan. This Old Goddess of the Hearth, named Fuji like Japan's most famous volcano, was not only a means of cooking and the source of a family's warmth but also a psychopomp, guiding souls of the dead back to the land of spirits from which they had come. Another apparent connection between the fire of the hearth and volcanic fire is found in one of the many Polynesian tales about the trickster Maui. Maui steals fire for the use of humankind from his ancestress Mahui-ike, who lives in the underworld and hoards the fire in her fingernails. Fire likewise emerges from a tellurian woman's body in the Japanese story (cited above) of the ancestress Izanagi, who dies as she gives birth to her fiery son.

FEMININE SACRALITY IN CULTURE. In his massive study of feminine symbols and divinities titled *The Great Mother* (1963), the Jungian psychologist Erich Neumann points to two fundamental aspects of feminine power that such symbols and divinities manifest. On the one hand, feminine power is source, giving rise to the multiple forms of life, whereas on the other hand it is process, an agent of growth and transformation. Both aspects of the feminine can be recognized in the natural manifestations described in the preceding section. But it is the second, the transformative, that becomes most prominent in the modes of feminine sacrality associated with cultural activities and institutions. For the production of culture itself is a process of transformation: that which comes to humans "raw" from the natural realm is "cooked" and made fit for human consumption.

Feminine sacrality can enter at virtually any point in this transformative process. In rituals of initiation, for example, where initiates must leave one mode of human existence and enter another, the transition may be accomplished by passing them through the womb of a female power. The postulated relationship between this practice and the cave sanctuaries of western Europe were noted above. Both men and women may evoke feminine powers in rituals of this sort, although the ways in which they utilize them are likely to differ.

Gardening, weaving, baking and cooking, and pottery. However, certain transformative processes seem so inherently female that some cultures assign them usually or solely to women. The underlying premise here seems to be that the women who bear life and nurture it into growth are better attuned than men to the powers that achieve these transformations. Hence they are better qualified to channel such powers.

Gardening is perhaps the simplest example of a process in which women work with a power construed as feminine to capture a segment of the wild natural world and tame it for human appropriation. In some societies only women practice gardening, especially if other activities, such as hunting, give men alternative economic functions. Among the North American Iroquois, for example, not only were women responsible for all practical functions of gardening, but they also summoned and supervised all calendrical rites connected to gardening and "owned" all of the songs with themes related to food crops. Weaving is another transformative skill often located within the special province of women. Celestial powers that mark off time, such as the moon and the sun, are regarded as spinners and weavers of human destiny. The women who shape human destiny on earth by bearing and nurturing children may appropriately be accounted mistresses of spinning and weaving. Indeed, the two processes may influence each other. Thus people of rural Sweden once believed that if a woman who had just finished weaving rode away carrying a stick she had stuck in her web, she would conceive a child of the same sex as the first person or animal she met. If her husband cut her web from its loom quickly and efficiently, his horses would deliver foals with ease. The power of the weaver's web to alter the world around it also explains the many weaving enchantresses of the world's folklore.

Cooking and baking also tap the transformative powers characteristic of feminine sacrality and of women. A striking illustration is found in the Navajo Kinaaldá ceremony, which completes a girl's transition to adulthood after the appearance of her menses. During the ceremony the girl impersonates and becomes Changing Woman, a complex mythical being who empowers all growth and transformation in the cosmos. As a focal act of the long and taxing ritual, the girl and the women who sponsor her prepare an enormous corn cake. It is then baked in a pit in the earth for an entire night, during which time the girl and her helpers must not fall asleep. The cake is cut on the following day, and the girl hands out pieces to guests at the ceremony. Because many aspects of the ceremony test the girl's ability to function as a woman, it seems appropriate to assume that the cake is also a test. It tests her ability, as representative of Changing Woman, to take the corn that is sacred to the Navajo and change it into food.

The story of Changing Woman's own Kinaaldá asserts that the cake represents Mother Earth. The cake is, in fact, born of the earth, a product of the corn and the pit in which it is cooked. Transformative powers of cooking and baking are often linked to the earth, for the various pots, cauldrons, and ovens in which these processes are accomplished are made of the clay or iron that constitute the earth's own substance. Thus pots, cauldrons, and ovens are doubly feminine, both as extensions of the earth and as sources of nourishment. It is no wonder then that pottery making is sometimes restricted to women, as it is among the Pueblo peoples of North America. Nor is it surprising that pots can substitute for the earth or earth goddesses in myths and rituals. A story of the Dinka in East Africa recounts how the Creator grew the first humans to full size in a pot after he had made them—the pot clearly represents the earth womb. Pots are often used as movable images of goddesses during various rites and festivals of India.

Spiritual transformations. The province of the feminine sacred is not restricted to material transformations. Processes of spiritual growth and transformation may also tap powers perceived as feminine.

Institutions offering spiritual nourishment and the promise of renewed life are often described through feminine metaphors. The Christian Church has been called the mother of Christ's flock, nourishing his children with her milk. Such maternal imagery is partly an extension of the metaphor in the New Testament *Letter to the Ephesians* (5:23–32) portraying the church as a "wife" of Christ. For Jews, the life-giving bride is not the community itself but the radiant Sabbath that arrives to restore it each week. "Come, my friend, to meet the bride; Let us welcome in the Sabbath" begins the sixteenth-century song *Lecha Dodi* by Solomon Alkabets, still sung at Friday evening Sabbath services. Nor is this concept of the Sabbath bride merely a literary image; during medieval times in Europe, Jewish qabbalists dressed in their best clothes on the Sabbath eve and went to the fields to welcome the incoming beloved.

Alternatively, the knowledge, insight, or wisdom that brings spiritual maturation may be assigned feminine gender and portrayed iconographically by female images. In Hindu India the goddess Sarasvatī is the patron of knowledge, honored especially by scholars and students. For Buddhists of the Mahāyāna tradition, also Indian in origin, the term for liberating insight *(prajñā)* was likewise feminine; its ultimate form *prajñāpāramitā* (perfection of wisdom) is called the "Mother of Buddhas" and is represented iconographically as a goddess. In writings of Hellenistic Judaism and of Greek Orthodox Christianity, Sophia, saving Wisdom, was at times identified as the female aspect of an androgynous God.

The compassionate figure who intervenes to aid the needy struggler for salvation may likewise be female. The bodhisattva Kuan-yin of Pure Land Buddhist sects in China is an especially interesting example, because her prototype, the Indian Avalokiteśvara, was male. This personification of the Mahāyāna virtue of compassion came to escort the faithful to paradise at the hour of death. But he or she also offered other, lesser, varieties of salvation by extinguishing fires, stilling waves, calming storms, freeing those condemned to prison or slavery or execution, disarming enemies, blinding demons, even bringing healthy babies to imploring women. Roman Catholic and Eastern Orthodox Christians are familiar with the compassionate intervening female in the form of the Virgin Mary.

The Terrible Side of the Feminine Sacred. Concepts of the earth as feminine power also include a more daunting aspect. The power who brings forth life also reabsorbs it into herself as the dread goddess who rules the subterranean land of the dead. Moreover, the terrible aspect of certain female deities is not merely a product of association with the bowels of a feminine earth; rather it is the other side of the processes of growth and transformation that so many female deities represent. Life and growth inevitably entail death and decay, while misdirected spiritual striving readily deteriorates into madness.

Perhaps the most infamous of the deadly goddesses is Kālī, the awesome Black Goddess of India, born from the wrath of her demon-slaying mother Durgā. Kālī's teeth are fangs; her tongue lolls out of her devouring mouth like that of a wild dog or tiger. One of her many hands brandishes an upraised sword, another lifts a bowl of blood made from the sliced-off cap of a human skull. Kālī wears a necklace of human heads and a skirt of lopped-off human arms; sometimes she stands, squats, or dances on the corpse of her consort, the great Lord Śiva. Kālī is time and death, but also life, and may be adored as a loving mother. She is also the illusion inherent in life's pleasures, so affirming her for what she is can sustain her worshiper on a liberating path.

Still more gruesome than Kālī was a trio that reflected the horrors implicit in the Aztec cult of war and human sacrifice. To recognize their role as the terrible side of the same process that generates life, one must understand the Aztec presuppositions that human sacrifice was necessary to replenish the swiftly waning vitality of the cosmos and that war was also essential to provide victims for the sacrifice. Coatlicue (snake skirt) was mother to the war god Huitzilopochtli. She wears a skirt of writhing snakes, from which she derives her name; her hands are the heads of serpents; her feet have the claws of a predatory bird. She is headless and twin spurts of blood gush from her neck into the mouths of waiting rattlesnakes. Closely related to Coatlicue is Cihuacoatl (snake woman), said to "preside over and personify the collective hunger of the gods for human victims" (Brundage, 1979, p. 170). She was also sometimes called the war god's mother, for she incited the wars over which Huitzilopochtli presided. In Aztec iconography the lower jaw of Cihuacoatl's gaping mouth is that of a bare human skeleton. Her clothes and body are the chalky white of a heap of bleached bones. She prowls at night, braying and screaming insanely; on her back is the knife of sacrifice, swaddled like an Aztec baby. The knife is a transformation of the third terrible goddess, Itzpapalotl (obsidian knife butterfly). This knife is one of the fragments into which this goddess shattered after antagonistic gods cast her into a fire. She wears a skirt fringed with knives and has the wings and tail of a bird; similarly, her hands and feet have a predatory bird's sharp talons.

Cihuacoatl sometimes was said to change into a beautiful young woman. She would seduce men, who withered and died after they had intercourse with her. She has counterparts in the sirens and seducers recurring in folk songs and legends throughout the world—the seduction that lures men to death or madness is a common characteristic of the awful feminine sacred. Dreadful female powers may also be patrons of witches, like Hekate, the triple-headed goddess of ancient Greece. In the dark of the night, Hekate prowled the world with a pack of bitches, hunting souls to take to her friend Persephone, queen of the dead.

Feminine Sacrality in Women. This same ambiguity of response to feminine sacrality—the recognition that it holds both constructive and destructive potential—is found in conceptions of the sacrality of ordinary women. Women themselves have been viewed as repositories of creative and transformative power throughout human history and within a wide variety of cultural contexts. This concept is inherent in the belief that women are better attuned than men to transformative procedures, such as weaving and cooking. The next section explores further this concept of feminine powers linking women to other aspects of the cosmos. This section examines two different ways in which women's sacrality has been imagined.

According to one prominent conception, women are sacred under specific physiological circumstances: sacred power resides in the condition rather than in the woman. For example, menstruation and childbirth often render a woman taboo and dangerous, because she produces blood, an extremely potent substance. Pregnancy may likewise bring danger: in rural Taiwan a pregnant woman is a threat to brides and children. Virginity evokes purity, and virgins may be essential to certain ritual roles, such as cutting the sacred tree during the Lakota sun dance or tending the vestal fire in ancient Rome. Menopause may endow women with magical or healing powers; hence older women are subject to accusations of witchcraft but are also often solicited for special ritual functions.

A different conception of women's sacrality perceives women as repositories of a single power that they manifest and channel throughout their lives. But this power becomes alternatively beneficent or destructive depending on whether or not it is properly disciplined. For example, all women of Tamil Nadu in South India are understood to be vehicles for *śakti,* a natural energy essential to all action and prosperity. A married woman who controls her *śakti* via faithfulness to her husband is extremely auspicious. Considered a living incarnation of Lakṣmī, the goddess of good fortune, she blesses her family not only while she is alive but even after her death. More capricious but still beneficent is the virgin female who is not yet married—her *śakti* is an unrealized potential. Negative and potentially dangerous figures are widows, unmarried mothers, barren women, and women who die in pregnancy and childbirth. The awesome power of a disciplined *śakti* is most dramatically displayed in the Tamil epic

Cilappatikāram. The faithful wife Kannagi, widowed by miscarried justice, destroys not only the king responsible for her suffering but also his capital city Madurai. No matter how conceived, women's sacrality is often said to be prior to powers that men hold or channel. A myth acknowledging this priority has been recorded in regions of the world as disparate as Africa, Australia, and Tierra del Fuego. Once upon a time, it asserts, women had control of the sacred symbols and rituals. One day, however, the men stole these symbols and rituals (according to some versions, because women were abusing their power). An Australian version of the story points to the counterbalancing reserve of sacrality that compensates the women for their loss. When the Djanggawul sisters realize what has happened, they say: "We know everything. We have really lost nothing, for we remember it all, and we can let them have that small part. For aren't we still sacred, even if we have lost the bags? Haven't we still our uteri?" (Berndt, 1953, pp. 40–41).

FEMININE SACRALITY AS UNIFYING POWER WITH MULTIPLE MANIFESTATIONS. While surveying the wide variety of forms through which feminine sacrality has been manifested, it is important to remember that the powers called "sacred" and "feminine" are not always related to these forms in the same way. People who speak of the earth as their sacred mother sometimes intend this statement quite literally: the earth itself is the awesome power that sustains them. But they may also refer to a generative and transformative power that resides within the earth. The same is true of other manifestations. The moon may be a deity, discrete and specific to the ever-changing orb that paces the night sky. Or a deity may show herself or himself through the moon. This distinction between manifestation and power is reflected in the common assertion that the moon—or mountain, cave, or spring—is the deity's "home." Such an assertion leaves open the possibility that the deity will have another home, or possibly many homes—that is to say, the power that is the deity may have many modes of manifestation. In fact, many of the great goddesses not explored in this article represent powers of birth, transformation, and death that show themselves in many different ways. The celebrated goddesses of the ancient Near East were all multiple-mode deities of this order. The Egyptian Isis, for example, was the deified throne, which in turn extended and concentrated the power of the earth. But she was also known as the "mother of stars," or Night, and her tears produced the Nile's annual and fructifying flood. She could bring life out of death—and did so when she awoke her dead husband Osiris and secured from him the child Horus. Yet she was also death, as is shown by her title "queen of the west"—west being the direction of the underworld. Isis even became the compassionate savior who bestows wisdom and immortality upon the faithful when the Greeks and Romans converted her cult into a mystery religion. Changing Woman of the Navajo, Durgā of India—even the Virgin Mary of Christianity—all are feminine powers with multiple modes of expression.

In some cases even the deity herself is understood to be a form of some more abstract energy that she shares with other manifestations. South India's multiple goddesses—Durgā, her extension Kālī, the many village "mothers"—are all modes of *śakti,* which, as demonstrated, is also manifested in ordinary women and in all forces of increase and prosperity. This inherently female energy may in turn be located within some overarching schema that juxtaposes it against a complementary energy identified as male. The Chinese concept of yin and yang is a classic example: yin predominates in everything that is dark, shaded, cool, wet, waning, bending, earthy, and female; whereas yang is bright, hot, dry, waxing, stubborn, aggressive, heavenly, and male. Despite the high level of abstraction that has generated these concepts, one recognizes in yin several components that have been associated with feminine sacrality in many eras and cultures: the earth, the dark, the waters, the changing, and the dying.

More frequently the concept of a common power remains unarticulated; only the network of symbols clustered together in myth or ritual reveals the presumption that they somehow share a common essence. Earth/waters/moon/women/root crops is one such cluster, often found in horticultural societies, that links together the sources and manifestations of growth and transformation. But the complex need not be the same in all cultures. The ethnographer Joseph Bastien (2001) has studied a complex in Andean Bolivia that clusters women, river, wind, and rats—all powers sharing the capacity to flow or erode, and therefore bring about change.

CONTEMPORARY FEMININE SACRALITY. Many beliefs and customs cited above have faded as the people who have carried them slip under the influence of modern secular culture. Some, however, have gained new prominence as the result of twentieth-century movements grounded in political or countercultural protest. During the later years of British colonial rule in India, for example, nationalists striving to rouse Hindus to resistance did so by evoking ancient images of land-linked goddesses and *śakti.* India was a goddess, they taught, a once-generous and loving mother currently battered and starved by oppressive rulers. Nonetheless, *śakti* newly awakening in the world could empower Mother India's progeny to free her and restore her. One by-product of such rhetoric has been a revival of Hindu interest in female deities, female symbols, and holy women.

In English-speaking countries of the Western world, renewed interest in female sacred imagery has been largely a product of three separate but intertwined movements: contemporary paganism, especially the several strands of Wicca ("wise one"; also called "the Craft"); the closely related "feminist spirituality" movement; and the environmental or "green" movement. The first documented coven of the movement called Wicca began meeting in England in 1948 under the leadership of occult enthusiast Gerald Gardener. Gardener claimed he was reviving pre-Christian ritual traditions that had been preserved in secret over the centuries by lineages of practitioners who, during the Middle Ages, had been burned as witches. Intended to bring worldly benefit and healing, these ancient rituals drew on sacred powers grounded in the natural realm. Central to these were a horned god and an awesome goddess said to have been worshiped since Paleolithic times, as well as assignment of priestly roles to women. Portrayals of the goddess reflected ideas current in popular and academic literature of the time. She manifested in three modes (maiden, mother, and crone), was immanent in all nature, and had special links to earth and moon, fertility and transformation. Certain Wiccan traditions emerging after Gardener's further emphasized roles of both the goddess and of women—so-called Dianic Wiccans honor the goddess alone and initiate only women into their covens.

The feminist spirituality movement is an offshoot of a critique of patriarchy in religion that began among woman theologians in the late 1960s and the 1970s. Although some feminist theologians chose to work for change within traditional religious frameworks, others aligned themselves with Wiccans in embracing feminine symbols and constructions of deity. Proponents of feminist spirituality seek to empower women, to help them draw on their own strengths and value their own bodies, and to turn women's energies toward working for a more humane and sustainable world. In doing so they have drawn on many ideas and images described in this essay: images of female deity immanent in the world and natural processes; mythic images of divine maidens, mothers, and crones that reveal different modes of female potentiality; and positive values placed on transformation, nurture, and interdependence.

Many contemporary pagans and proponents of feminist spirituality strongly support environmental movements, asserting that their beliefs promote reverence for nature and resistance to earth's exploitation. An important link between these groups and environmentalists has been the "Gaia hypothesis," first published in *Gaia: A New Look at Life on Earth* (1979) by the scientific writer James Lovelock. Lovelock argues that earth and the natural environment should be viewed as a single massive organism, which he calls Gaia, the ancient Greek name for the goddess Earth. To Lovelock, the image of earth as goddess is a metaphor meant to change attitudes toward the matrix in which humans live. Neopagans and spiritual feminists sometimes interpret his image more literally, however.

But this need not be the case, for precise nuances of belief within such movements vary widely. Goddesses may be understood literally as powerful sacred beings external to humans, as powers of growth and transformation surging within the world and humans, and as metaphors for human potentiality. Some groups honor the Wiccan threefold goddess and address her by Celtic or classic names; some may study and call upon female figures from all the world's mythologies; or some may say that, in the end, all goddesses are one. All assert that imageries of feminine sacrality affirm life, connection, the female body, sexuality, and change; that they aid in dealing with death; that they promote creativity and respect for nature; and that they counteract exploitation not only of nature but also throughout human society.

SEE ALSO Durgā Hinduism; Earth; Gender and Religion; Lady of the Animals; Lotus; Moon; Mountains; Phallus and Vagina; Sexuality; Shabbat; Stones; Textiles; Water; Webs and Nets; Wisdom.

BIBLIOGRAPHY

A path-breaking comparative study of female sacrality still of value is the Jungian psychologist Erich Neumann's *The Great Mother,* 2d ed., translated by Ralph Manheim (New York, 1963; reprint, Princeton, N.J., 1972). Especially valuable are its many photographic plates. Neumann's data are embedded in a controversial theory of the evolution of human consciousness, and readers using his work must remain critically alert. Many fine studies of goddesses and goddess mythology supplement Neumann's work. Useful essay collections are James J. Preston, ed., *Mother Worship* (Chapel Hill, N.C., 1982); Carl Olson, ed., *The Book of the Goddess, Past and Present* (New York, 1983); and John Stratton Hawley and Donna M. Wulff, eds., *Devī: Goddesses of India* (Berkeley, Calif., 1996). Valuable single-author works are Lotte Motz, *The Faces of the Goddess* (New York and Oxford, 1997); David R. Kinsley, *The Goddesses' Mirror* (Albany, N.Y., 1989); and Kinsley, *Hindu Goddesses* (Berkeley, Calif., 1986).

Mircea Eliade's *Patterns in Comparative Religion,* translated by Rosemary Sheed (New York, 1958), cites many valuable examples of earth, waters, moon, vegetation, and gardening symbolisms; his *Birth and Rebirth* (London, 1958), issued in the United States as *Rites and Symbols of Initiation* (New York, 1958; reprint, New York, 1975), offers significant insight into the role of feminine symbolism in initiation. Charles H. Long's *Alpha: The Myths of Creation* (New York, 1963) furnishes fine examples of world parent, earth diver, and emergence myths. For a helpful survey of the latter in North America, see also Erminie Wheeler-Vogelin and Remedios W. Moore's "The Emergence Myth in North America," in *Studies in Folklore,* edited by W. Edson Richmond, pp. 69–91 (Bloomington, Ind., 1957). Sam D. Gill's *Mother Earth: An American Story* (Chicago, 1987) challenges the idea that Mother Earth is an ancient Native American conceptualization. See also C. G. Jung, *Psychology and Alchemy,* vol. 12 of *Collected Works* (Princeton, N.J., 1968), and Bronislaw Malinowski, *Magic, Science, and Religion* (Garden City, N.Y., 1948).

A valuable resource for the study of goddesses who produce food crops from their bodies is Gudmund Hatt's "The Corn Mother in America and Indonesia," *Anthropos* 46 (1951): 853–914. The original collection of variations on the Hainuwele motif is Adolf E. Jensen's *Hainuwele* (Frankfurt am Main, 1939). Although highly specialized, Steven G. Darian's *The Ganges in Myth and History* (Honolulu, Hawai'i, 1978) and Edward H. Shafter's *The Divine Woman* (Berkeley, Calif., 1973) furnish interesting views of water-related female deities in India and China; see also Diana L. Eck's "Gangā: The Goddess Ganges in Hindu Sacred Geography" in Hawley and Wulff (1996), cited above.

A good twentieth-century study of Indian village goddesses is Richard Brubaker, *The Ambivalent Mistress: A Study of South Indian Village Goddesses and Their Religious Meaning* (Ph.D. diss., University of Chicago, 1978, microform). For the White Buffalo Calf Woman of the Oglala, see Black Elk, *The Sacred Pipe,* edited by Joseph Epes Brown (Norman, Okla., 1953); a broader survey of female powers among the Oglala is Marla N. Powers's *Oglala Women* (Chicago, 1986). See also James Mooney, *The Ghost Dance Religion and the Sioux Outbreak of 1890,* Annual Report of the Bureau of American Ethnography, 14: 2 (Washington, D.C., 1896).

Materials on the transformative powers manifested through women's cultural activities remain sparse. But see K. R. V. Wikman's *Die Magie des Webens und des Webstuhls im Schwedieschen Volksglauben* (Turku, Finland, 1920). The original source on the Navajo puberty ritual for girls is Charlotte Johnson Frisbee's *Kinaaldá* (Middletown, Conn., 1967). Neumann's *The Great Mother* (see above) is a comprehensive source on the role of feminine powers in spiritual transformations. But see also Joanna R. Macy's "Perfection of Wisdom," in *Beyond Androcentrism,* edited by Rita M. Gross, pp. 315–334 (Missoula, Mont., 1977); the same volume includes an intriguing essay on the transformative powers of Sedna, the Inuit mistress of animals.

A readable account of the goddess Kālī is Kinsley's *The Sword and the Flute* (Berkeley, Calif., 1975); Burr C. Brundage offers a compact and fascinating sketch of the terrifying Aztec goddesses in *The Fifth Sun* (Austin, Tex., 1979). For the monster Le-hev-hev, see John W. Layard's *Stone Men of Malekula* (London, 1942).

For the sacrality of women's physiological states, see Rita M. Gross's *Exclusion and Participation: The Role of Women in Aboriginal Australian Religion* (Ph.D. diss., University of Chicago, 1975, microform). A summary of Gross's principal argument is in *Unspoken Worlds,* edited by Nancy A. Falk and Rita M. Gross, 3d ed., pp. 301–310 (Belmont, Calif., 2001). The same volume includes Joseph W. Bastien's "Rosinta, Rats, and the River," pp. 243–252, on the women/river/wind complex of the Bolivian Kallawaya, and Inés M. Talamentes's "The Presence of Isanaklesh," pp. 290–301, with materials on the Apache Isanaklesh, a counterpart of the Navajo Changing Woman. Carolyn Niethammer's *Daughters of the Earth* (New York, 1977) offers examples of responses to menstruation, childbirth, and postmenopausal women among Native Americans. Emily M. Ahern's "The Power and Pollution of Chinese Women," in *Women in Chinese Society,* edited by Margery Wolf and Roxanne Witke (Stanford, Calif., 1975), also documents perceptions of menstruation and childbirth. Excellent information on the concept of *śakti* is in Susan S. Wadley, ed., *The Powers of Tamil Women* (Syracuse, N.Y., 1980). For the myth of Australian women's prior power, see Ronald M. Berndt, *Djanggawul* (New York, 1953).

Two essays by Nancy A. Falk address the contemporary resurgence of feminine sacrality among Hindus: "*Śakti* Ascending," in *Religion in Modern India,* edited by Robert D. Baird, pp. 298–334 (New Delhi, 1995), and "Mata, Land, and Line," in *Invoking Goddesses,* edited by Nilima Chitgopekar, pp. 140–164 (New Delhi, 2002). See also Ronald M. Berndt, *Djanggawul* (New York, 1953). Materials on Wicca and feminist spirituality are legion. A meticulous reconstruction of Wiccan history and antecedents in Britain is in Ronald Hutton's *The Triumph of the Moon* (Oxford, 1999); an American counterpart of broader reach is Margot Adler's *Drawing down the Moon,* 2d ed. (Boston, 1986). Perhaps the most famed writing from within Wicca is the San Francisco priestess Starhawk's *The Spiral Dance* (San Francisco, 1979). For a Wiccan approach to deity, see Monica Sjöö and Barbara Mor, *The Great Cosmic Mother* (San Francisco, 1987). Carol Christ's essay "Why Women Need the Goddess" was of major importance in launching the feminist spirituality movement; it is easiest to find in Carol P. Christ and Judith Plaskow's anthology, *Womanspirit Rising* (San Francisco, 1992). A good example of more recent writing on Wicca-linked feminist spirituality is Melissa Raphael, *Thealogy and Embodiment* (Sheffield, U.K., 1996). For an approach by feminists working within the Christian tradition, see Charlotte Caron, *To Make and Make Again* (New York, 1993). James Lovelock first published his Gaia hypothesis in *Gaia: A New Look at Life on Earth* (Oxford, 1979).

NANCY AUER FALK (1987 AND 2005)

FEMINISM

This entry consists of the following articles:

FEMINISM, GENDER STUDIES, AND RELIGION
FRENCH FEMINISTS ON RELIGION

FEMINISM: FEMINISM, GENDER STUDIES, AND RELIGION

Very few academic fields have remained untouched by the emergence of feminist and gender theory as critical tools for reflecting on, and challenging, the legitimacy of regnant epistemologies. The study of religions is no exception, although it has been slower than other fields to incorporate the insights of contemporary feminist and gender discourses. This entry provides a brief survey of the development of feminism and gender theory and their place within the field of religious studies, and also discusses their critique of traditional methodologies and concepts within the context of the (predominantly Western) study of religious traditions.

FEMINISM AND GENDER STUDIES: AN OVERVIEW. As with many terms, defining *feminism* presents an immediate difficulty, as it suggests a homogeneity that is belied both by the history of its development and the diversity of its articulations and forms. The multiplicity of feminisms that together constitute feminism—whether early suffrage campaigns, discursive analyses of gender hierarchies, or lesbian activism, for example—indicates subtle differences of emphasis and context. Most feminisms are concerned, nonetheless, with promoting political and theoretical programs that address the secondary status of women. In this entry, the term *feminism* will be deployed to refer to a broad set of common themes and concepts, however differently expressed, that articulate a critical analysis of gender relations at meta-theoretical and empirical levels. Feminist theory, as the intellectual conduit of a diversity of feminisms, engages with an array of concerns, all of which reflect an accumulated fund of knowledge and experience that is situated in an ongoing teleological and etiological analysis of gender inequalities and identities in all social and cultural arenas. The possibility of conceptual and political transformation is thus at the heart of feminist practices, theories, and methodologies.

It is common to discuss the development of feminism in terms of the three main "waves." First wave feminism, from the mid-1850s to the publication of Simone de Beauvoir's ground-breaking book *The Second Sex* in 1949, was characterized by materialist debates and political activism concerning universal suffrage, women's rights to self-determination, access to higher education, and ownership of property. Second wave feminism refers to the reemergence of feminist political activism and literature in the late 1960s. It was largely defined by its liberal agenda; its vision of female solidarity; political interventions in the spheres of reproduction and sexuality, employment, and cultural representation; and theorization of patriarchy. It was during the second wave that feminist theory emerged as a field of cultural critique and began to make its presence felt in a wide variety of academic disciplines. These decades saw the establishment of a large number of women's studies departments, an innovation that sought to address the absence of women in the androcentric intellectual history of most academic fields by developing women-focused syllabi and research programs.

While many of the concerns of the second wave continue to be important, feminist activity in the late twentieth and early twenty-first centuries is referred to as third wave feminism, or *post-feminism.* It marks both a self-reflexive turn and a mature phase in feminist theorizing as it seeks to critique the previously hegemonic assumptions of the second wave. This stage registers a shift in the common preoccupations that have informed many of the debates between feminists. Most notably, third-wave feminists have moved away from the denunciation of gender inequalities towards the theorization of discursive, dialogic constructions of gender. In addition, influenced by poststructural, postcolonial, and queer theories of identity formation, third wave feminists advocate the rejection of oversimplistic and essentialist descriptions of female and male identity. This includes a sustained examination of hegemonic representations of masculinity, and a more nuanced understanding of the often significant differences between men and women in the contexts of class, ethnicity, sexuality, and economic status. In academic circles, the focus has shifted from women's studies to gender studies.

Feminist Theory, Gender Theory, and the Study of Religions. The emergence of the feminist study of religious traditions has paralleled the three-wave pattern of feminism's development. Much pioneering feminist scholarship in the 1960s and 1970s was concerned with mapping women's lives and experiences within religious traditions in order to render them analytically visible. In addition, feminist scholars challenged the androcentrism of the field's epistemological foundations and outlined alternative methodologies. The early emphasis on women contributed to the tendency of methodological and epistemological evaluation by feminist scholars to be rather narrowly focused. While it was crucial for identifying the unique place of female expression within religious traditions, it was marginalized in broader methodological debates. Feminist scholars therefore developed multiple critiques of the history of religious studies and, from the 1980s onwards, gender theory was increasingly applied not only to the analysis of religious phenomena but also to the disciplinary paradigms that sought to understand them. Feminist and gender theory began to be articulated in terms of offering the possibility of a paradigm shift, one that would generate conceptual change and renewal within the discipline and provide a necessary corrective to its androcentric foundations (see King, 1995, pp. 1–38). Accordingly, gender-critical scholarship has since been conceived of as a supplementary discourse.

For Jacques Derrida, a supplement is something "added on," seemingly deliberately, to a prior term in order to address an omission within it, although it appears to be exterior and secondary to the primary term it supplements. Derrida, however, argues against the metaphysical logic that places the supplement in a secondary or derivative position. He suggests that if the supplement is necessary to compensate for the absence it reveals in a prior term, then it is not so much an external extra as a necessary constituent of the term it supplements: "The *supplément* is neither a plus nor a minus, neither an outside nor the complement of an inside, neither accident nor essence" (Derrida, 1981, p. 43). An example of supplementarity that provides a useful parallel for understanding the role of feminist and gender theory in the study of religions is the emergence of the field of "women's history." As Joan Scott has argued, "there is a troubling ambiguity inherent in the project of women's history for it is at once an innocuous supplement to, and a radical replacement for, established history" (Scott, 1991, p. 49). As the study of women is added to the discipline of history it also occasions its rewriting. Gender theory, applied to the study of religions, similarly attends to the exclusion of female and non-elite male perspectives at the level of data gathering and analysis, and, further, queries the epistemological and conceptual formulations that enable such exclusion in the first place. Feminist interventions have thus insisted on the implementation of a series of critical adjustments to traditional concepts and theories in the study of religion's methodological paradigms.

Feminist and Gender Theory: Transforming Methodologies. June O'Connor, in her influential article "The Epistemological Significance of Feminist Research in Religion" (1995), usefully summarizes the epistemological framework of feminist and gender theory in the context of the study of religions. She identifies five moments that define the contours of feminist research (p. 46):

1. Application of a hermeneutics of suspicion that recognizes the androcentric content and context of sources;

2. Attention to the retrieval of the religious history of women, alongside other marginalized groups;
3. Critique and transformation of established concepts, particularly universal and androcentric notions of human subjectivity;
4. Rejection of exclusionary modes of scholarship;
5. Self-reflexive scrutiny of assumptions and ideological commitments in order to avoid the assertion of new orthodoxies.

These steps constitute the basis for the critical transformation, by feminist discourses, of the epistemological grounds of the study of religions, a task that has been taken up vigorously.

Feminist scholars have identified central androcentric biases in the formulation of core disciplinary questions that were, historically, defined from the perspective of predominantly white, educated men. It is for this reason that feminists have been quick to criticize the textual bias of traditional studies for unthinkingly replicating elite, male perspectives and rendering the participation of women in religious traditions as either invisible, or as defined only in androcentric terms. Moreover, categories like *homo religiosus* and the insider/outsider debates have been censured for further enacting the marginalization of women. Rosalind Shaw argues, for example, that the *homo religiosus,* as representative of a religious collective, is generally "undifferentiated by gender, race, class or age, or defined explicitly as male" (1995, p. 67). The insider/outsider formulation also falls down on its failure to account for the "outsider" status of women within their own religious traditions. From the perspective of feminist analyses then, the main consequence of biased, androcentric scholarship has been the production of distorted, partial scholarly accounts that contain serious deficiencies at the basic level of data-collection and interpretation, as well as in the subsequent development of theoretical paradigms (see Gross, 1974, p. 7).

Randi Warne points out, however, that the partiality of traditional epistemological models is not solved by simply adding the study of women to existing scholarship: "Women were not simply 'omitted' through a[n] . . . act of scholarly absent-mindedness; women were excluded from . . . scholarship, as from 'significant' subject matter, as from positions of authority and power, when the basic ideas, definitions, principles and facts were being formulated" (2001, p. 150). A key feminist strategy for confronting gender bias has thus been to revisit traditional methodological debates and to propose critical adjustments to their fundamental premises. Grace Jantzen, for example, in her book *Becoming Divine* (1998), has argued that the traditional philosophy of religion, and Western thought more generally, has wielded theoretical categories that are considered neutral—for example, rationality, objectivity, truth, and God—but which are undeniably biased towards male values, authorizing masculine master-discourses at the expense of female perspectives. A first step in confronting this bias and correcting its glaring lacunae has been to undertake what Jantzen calls "a radical deconstruction of both religion and secularism to make evident their unacknowledged dependence on alterities of race, gender, and sexuality" (Jantzen, 1998, p. 2). Subsequently, Jantzen seeks to develop alternative epistemologies that celebrate difference, acknowledge the subjective basis of knowledge production, and promote a variety of new models from a feminist perspective, including an emphasis on metaphors of natality and human flourishing as foundational principles.

Feminists have also challenged the conceptual assumptions of the phenomenology of religion, particularly its claim to undertake disinterested observation of religious phenomena and to replicate scientific empiricism at the methodological level. Given the feminist critique of the androcentric nature of the traditional study of religions, the claim of methodological disinterestedness is both demonstrably false and theoretically naive. Although the attempt to justify such a methodology on the grounds of the autonomy of disciplinary boundaries is understandable, feminism's metatheoretical orientation suggests, instead, a fluidity of critical perspectives and the benefits of multidisciplinarity.

Related to the rejection of "disinterested" research and the rigid policing of disciplinary boundaries has been the development, by feminist scholars of religion, of a cooperative relationship with feminist theology. There are two main reasons for this: firstly, feminist theology, with its emphasis on the primacy of female experience for assessing the validity of religious doctrines and authority, offers both an academic method and a social vision with regard to the position of women within religious traditions; secondly, the hermeneutic orientations of many feminist theologians provide a promising and well-trodden pathway for the analysis and critique of patriarchal religious symbols, narratives, and discourses. Importantly, the affiliation with feminist theology has occurred at a time when many scholars of religious studies have made a concerted effort to delineate between their own nonconfessional, secular approach and the confessional stance of Christian theology. As feminist scholars of religion have sought to make connections with feminist theologians, they have called into question both the clarity of disciplinary boundaries and the purportedly secular orientation of religious studies.

Some scholars of religion have criticized the tendency of feminist scholars to reduce religious phenomena to their interrelation with cultural forms such as gender and class. Feminists have replied to the charge of reductionism by arguing that the acknowledgment of the social and political constitution of religious phenomena is a vital frame of reference for adequately theorizing difference in religious contexts. As Shaw has noted:

> Attempting to understand a woman's experience of religion in terms of (not just "in the context of") her position within a male-dominated religious tradition is reductionist only if we have severed "religion" from

> "power" in the first place. On the contrary, it would be a "reduction"—in the rather different sense of a diminished and distorted representation of her experience—to bracket off "male dominance" and "gender asymmetry" as a mere biographical backdrop to, but not really part of, the experiences which she calls "religious." (Shaw, 1995, p. 70)

Feminism and gender studies offer innovative epistemological tools for scholarly reflection on the processes and politics of academic knowledge production, as well as for the understanding of religious phenomena. They insist on conceptual transformation in order to account for the fluid, heterogeneous, and polymorphic dimensions of religious expressions, and further maintain that the topography of religious studies must be mapped within a cultural arena that accounts for, and acknowledges, the contradictions and contexts that attend cultural symbolizations. The breadth and depth of feminist scholarship in the study of religions holds out the promise of a much-needed paradigm shift, one that is slowly, but surely, being realized.

See Also Gender and Religion, overview article and article on History of Study.

Bibliography

Anderson, Pamela Sue. *A Feminist Philosophy of Religion: The Rationality and Myths of Religious Belief.* Oxford, 1998. Anderson queries traditional empirical realist accounts of theistic belief in the philosophy of religion and offers an analysis of the theoretical devices that exclude women. She develops a revisionist program using feminist frameworks and epistemologies that challenge traditional assumptions of sex and gender, and seeks to broaden the fundamental propositions of the philosophy of religion.

Anderson, Pamela Sue, and Beverley Clack, eds. *Feminist Philosophy of Religion: Critical Readings.* London and New York, 2003. The first collection of key readings on the feminist philosophy of religion. It offers an introductory overview of the different types of feminist philosophies of religion, and considers some of the important religious concepts that are addressed by poststructuralist and psychoanalytical approaches. It includes essays from leading thinkers in the field, including Grace Jantzen, Alison Jasper, and Janet Martin Soskice.

Butler, Judith P. *Gender Trouble: Feminism and the Subversion of Identity.* London and New York, 1990; reprint, 1999. A now classic study of gender theory and one of the most influential books in the field. It addresses the limits of French feminist theory for interrogating gender ontologies, proposing instead to understand gender construction in terms of parody and performativity. In the 1999 tenth-anniversary edition, Butler addresses the critical response to her original arguments and the ways her thinking has been adjusted as a result. Although its language is dense and often difficult, it is ultimately rewarding and is compulsory reading for anyone working with gender theory.

Butler, Judith P., and Joan W. Scott, eds. *Feminists Theorize the Political.* New York and London, 1992. A rich collection of work by leading feminist scholars that addresses the relevance of poststructuralism to feminist politics. It affirms the importance of feminist theorizing for the transformation of gender relations and understandings and provides a useful overview of contemporary feminist debates operating at the metatheoretical level.

Castelli, Elizabeth A., and Rosamond C. Rodman, eds. *Women, Gender, Religion: A Reader.* New York and Basingstoke, U.K., 2001. This interdisciplinary and multitraditional volume highlights the contributions that different disciplinary approaches offer feminist and gender-theoretical studies of religion. It demonstrates the theoretical richness of contemporary debates in the field and includes contributions from Mieke Bal, Donna J. Haraway, Nancy Jay, Patricia Jeffery, Aihwa Ong, Oyèrónkẹ́ Oyěwùmí, and Judith Plaskow, among others. A useful reader for the classroom.

Derrida, Jacques. *Positions.* Translated by Alan Bass. London, 1981.

Flax, Jane. *Thinking Fragments: Psychoanalysis, Feminism, and Postmodernism in the Contemporary West.* Berkeley, Los Angeles, and Oxford, 1990. Flax offers a wide-ranging and careful critique of psychoanalytic, feminist, and postmodern theory, examining the relations between them and evaluating the ways in which each set of theories succeeds in coming to terms with the crises of truth, knowledge, self, and power in contemporary Western culture. An essential text for thinking through the role of theory in humanities research.

Franzmann, Majella. *Women and Religion.* New York and Oxford, 2000. *Women and Religion* is aimed at undergraduate students of religious studies and is an accessible and serious introduction to the process of studying and listening to women's accounts of their own religious experiences. It discusses women's roles, positions, and experiences within five religious traditions: Buddhism, Christianity, Islam, Hinduism, and Judaism. The topics that are covered include the widespread marginalization of women in the context of mainstream religious texts, rituals, and codes of law; women's experiences within less orthodox religious contexts; women's independent forms of religious expression; and women's creative reimaginations of older forms of religion.

Garry, Ann, and Marilyn Pearsall, eds. *Women, Knowledge, and Reality: Explorations in Feminist Philosophy.* 2d ed. London and New York, 1996. A broadly useful collection of twenty-five essays by well-known feminist scholars that addresses key issues in feminist philosophizing, including epistemology, metaphysics, mind-body dichotomies, gender and language, gender and race, and postmodern perspectives. It also offers a window into some of the most prominent controversies in feminist theory and philosophy.

Gross, Rita M., ed. *Beyond Androcentrism: New Essays on Women and Religion.* Missoula, Mont., 1974. A classic collection of essays dealing with methodological issues in the study of women and religion.

Jantzen, Grace. *Becoming Divine: Towards a Feminist Philosophy of Religion.* Manchester, U.K., 1998. A compelling and groundbreaking revision of the field of the philosophy of religion. Jantzen proposes a lucid and timely critique of the core preoccupations and epistemological assumptions of the field and sketches alternative philosophical models based on ideas about gender, desire, community, and justice. Drawing on the critical thought of key continental thinkers like Derrida and Luce Irigaray, she further proposes an imaginative concept of the divine that challenges traditional dualistic thought and emphasizes process and becoming as a model of divinity. A substantial, solidly argued, and scholarly book, not aimed at beginners.

Juschka, Darlene M., ed. *Feminism in the Study of Religion: A Reader.* London and New York, 2001. A useful anthology of the feminist theories that have been influential in the development of the feminist study of religion. The selected readings provide a wide range of perspectives and include the work of religious studies scholars, as well as scholars from other disciplines, such as Nancy Chodorow and Judith Butler. The book shows how debates about feminism within the study of religion have been influenced by broader theoretical discussions and offers an excellent overview of the range and breadth of feminist theorizing.

King, Ursula, ed. *Religion and Gender.* Oxford and Cambridge, Mass., 1995. The standard textbook for the field of gender theory and the study of religion. The book brings together an international group of scholars, provides a systematic overview of the new theoretical and critical perspectives that gender theory offers religious studies and offers a comprehensive discussion of important methodological and hermeneutical issues. King's introduction provides a thorough and systematic outline of key developments and interventions in the field.

King, Ursula, and Tina Beattie, eds. *Gender, Religion, and Diversity: Cross-Cultural Perspectives.* London and New York, 2004. An essential collection of twenty articles that provides a timely follow-up to King's well-received volume *Religion and Gender.* It is particularly useful for its assessment of the impact of postcolonial, queer, and gay and lesbian theories on feminist theory in the study of religions. Contributors include Melissa Raphael, Rita M. Gross, Morny Joy, and Diane Treacy-Cole. A key volume for advanced undergraduate and postgraduate teaching.

Morgan, Sue. "Feminist Approaches." In *Approaches to the Study of Religions,* edited by Peter Connolly, pp. 42–72. London and New York, 1999. A comprehensive overview of the history and context of feminist approaches to the study of religions, including a helpful discussion of the relationship of these approaches to feminist theology.

O'Connor, June. "The Epistemological Significance of Feminist Research in Religion." In *Religion and Gender,* edited by Ursula King, pp. 45–63. Oxford and Cambridge, Mass., 1995.

Scott, Joan W. "Gender: A Useful Category of Historical Analysis." In *Coming to Terms: Feminism, Theory, Politics,* edited by Elizabeth Weed, pp. 81–100. London and New York, 1989.

Scott, Joan W. "Women's History." In *New Perspectives on Historical Writing,* edited by Peter Burke, pp. 42–66. Cambridge, U.K., 1991.

Segal, Lynne. *Why Feminism? Gender, Psychology, Politics.* Cambridge, U.K., 1999. Surveys the shifts in feminist thought since its emergence in the 1960s. Segal examines critically the significance of feminism for cultural theorizing, its controversial relationship with psychoanalysis, the influence of queer theory, and some of the contentious efforts to address issues of masculinity in gender theory. An important and well-timed assessment of the status and influence of feminist inquiry.

Shaw, Rosalind. "Feminist Anthropology and the Gendering of Religious Studies." In *Religion and Gender,* edited by Ursula King, pp. 65–76. Oxford and Cambridge, Mass., 1995.

Tong, Rosemary. *Feminist Thought: A More Comprehensive Introduction.* 2d ed. Oxford, 1998. Tong provides a substantial and thorough summary of twentieth-century feminist thought, including the liberal, radical (libertarian and cultural), and Marxist-socialist schools of feminism, and psychoanalytic, existentialist, and postmodern approaches to questions of gender.

Warne, Randi. "Engendering the Study of Religions." In *Feminism in the Study of Religion: A Reader,* edited by Darlene M. Juschka, pp. 147–156. London and New York, 2001.

SîAN HAWTHORNE (2005)

FEMINISM: FRENCH FEMINISTS ON RELIGION

French feminism, understood here to refer to a variety of feminisms of sexual difference that have evolved in France since 1968, has become increasingly influential in religious studies in the late twentieth century and the early twenty-first century. While the term *French feminism* has been criticized widely as a construct of Anglophone academic feminists—a construct that ignores the majority of movements for women's rights in France—it has nevertheless become entrenched in common parlance in the English-speaking world, and the "French feminist" movement is widely understood to include such theorists as Hélène Cixous, Catherine Clément, Luce Irigaray, Julia Kristeva, and Monique Wittig. Unlike many Anglo-American feminists, these French thinkers are less concerned with liberal projects such as equal rights for women than with articulating the problematic of sexual difference that they perceive as fundamental to all forms of cultural expression in the West. The "French feminists," while representing diverse perspectives on this problematic, can be seen to be engaged in an ongoing conversation based on a set of shared premises that each adopts or critiques to varying degrees.

Although all of the French feminists are at least somewhat critical of the work of the French psychoanalytic theorist Jacques Lacan, most are influenced by his theories of subject formation and gender construction (the notable exception to this being Monique Wittig, who rejects psychoanalytic feminism as inherently apolitical). Central to much French feminist theory is the Lacanian view that the subject is linguistically constructed and that the earliest forays into language position the subject within an Oedipal, paternal order (governed by what Lacan calls the "Law of the Father" and symbolized by the phallus). Further, the French feminists tend to follow Lacan in seeing both gender and sexuality as effects of the sociolinguistic foundations of subjectivity. Where most differ from Lacan is in their view that the "phallocentric" Law of the Father is not the only possible social order and that feminist interventions in the linguistic and symbolic structures of both Western and non-Western cultures might open a path to a new, postpatriarchal world.

Additionally most of the French feminist theorists are influenced by the deconstructive literary-critical methodology and the philosophical thought of Jacques Derrida—although again not without reservations. Of particular significance is Derrida's strategy of examining texts for the hidden meanings that both supplement and challenge any explicit signification as well as his claim that the Western philosophical and theological traditions have organized reality into opposing and hierarchically ordered binaries (e.g., presence/absence, good/evil, spirit/body, writing/speech), with man/woman serving as the paradigmatic example. Derrida's notion of *différance*, an unending play of differing and deferring that both underlies and disrupts the "logocentric" production of univocal meaning, is also useful, as is his view that "woman" is the privileged site of *différance* (although this latter notion is also seen as somewhat problematic).

Beginning from their various understandings of these two thinkers then—and further influenced by such figures as Ferdinand de Saussure, Louis Althusser, Emmanuel Levinas, Roland Barthes, and Claude Lévi-Strauss—the French feminists have articulated a profoundly important body of philosophical and critical thought about the role of sexual difference in the Western tradition, and their work has many implications for the study of religion. The religious discourses of the West emerge as key instances of the "phallogocentrism" of Western thought (that is, of the central role occupied by the phallus and the written word), with the Jewish and Christian Father-God appearing as a symbol with even more power than those marshaled by the state to found a repressive model of subjectivity. The exclusive maleness of the Trinitarian divinity—God conceived as Father, Son, and Holy Spirit—is seen as paradigmatic of the "logic of the same" that the French feminists, and many other French theorists of the late twentieth century and early twenty-first century, trace from Plato through Hegel. This model of God comes under censure both for its eclipsing of the central importance of the mother in the process of (re)producing life and for its underwriting of a patriarchal model of the subject that reduces the feminine to the inferior "other" of the masculine. However, French feminist religious thought is as noteworthy for its constructive impulses as for its critique of established religions and is characterized, especially in later works, by attempts to imagine new ways of being religious that would allow the repressed feminine to find expression.

In this context French feminists have explored such areas of interest as the necessity for honoring (and sacralizing) mother-daughter genealogies; the relationship between divinity and subjectivity; the affinity of women for mysticism; the nature of Jewish and Christian notions of defilement and sin; and the resources offered to Western feminists by non-Western religious traditions. What follows below is merely a suggestion, in somewhat arbitrary order, of the ways these themes find expression in the work of the French feminists, based primarily on the ways in which their work has been taken up by feminist scholars of religion. Further it should be noted that many aspects of French feminist theory that have no direct bearing on religion have found such wide acceptance in religious studies that the French feminists, especially Julia Kristeva and Luce Irigaray, are frequently referenced in feminist religious scholarship.

Maternity and Mother-Daughter Genealogies. The issue of the erasure of mothers and daughters from the religious traditions of the West—and the necessity for reworking those traditions in ways that allow maternity to emerge as sacred in its own right—has generated much comment from the French feminists, and their thought in this area has in turn sparked much interest from feminist scholars of religion. In her 1987 "Stabat Mater" and *In the Beginning Was Love*, for example, Julia Kristeva offered a psychoanalytic reading of maternity intended to undermine what she saw as the phallocentrism of Lacan's theory of subject formation, a reading that has implications for patriarchal understandings of Christianity as well. In questioning the primacy accorded to the father by Lacan, Kristeva also challenges the appropriation of the Virgin Mary within the Catholic and Orthodox traditions, arguing that that appropriation erases the bodily nature of motherhood and domesticates maternity within a patriarchal order. For Kristeva, the bond between mother and infant is the precursor of the infant's ability to relate to an Other, so that maternal love is the necessary condition of Christian agape.

Although Luce Irigaray too is very much influenced by psychoanalytic methods, she tends to approach her discussion of motherhood genealogically, sifting through the myths of the Western tradition for lost images of sacred mothers and daughters. In such essays as "The Forgotten Mystery of Female Ancestry" (1994), for example, she explores the story of Demeter and Persephone for what it has to tell the modern world about the ways the mother-daughter relationship, seen by Irigaray as the paradigmatic relationship between women, has been co-opted and subverted by patriarchy and argues that the re-sacralization of such relationships is essential to establishing social justice for women.This approach has not been uniformly welcomed by feminist scholars of religion, many of whom see it as yet another attempt to reclaim or reimagine goddess traditions that fail to intervene effectively in the male-centeredness of the Western religious traditions. Alternatively then in "When the Gods Are Born" (1991), Irigaray turns to Friedrich Nietzsche to show how the maternal function is appropriated both by the Greek gods Apollo and Dionysos, with whom Nietzsche was so fascinated, and by Nietzsche himself in his quest for a revaluation of all values. Behind this metaphorization of motherhood, Irigaray claims, lies a betrayal of the body that is all too often repeated in Christian thinking about embodiment, although in her view it need not be.

SUBJECTIVITY AND DIVINITY. In *Speculum of the Other Woman* (1985) Irigaray examined psychoanalytic and philosophical theories of subjectivity to mount a critique of what she saw as the implicit masculinity of the Western subject. Although she paid little attention in that text to religion, her argument that Freudian and Platonic conceptions of knowledge function to render true sexual difference invisible was quickly taken up by feminist scholars of religion who saw in it a valuable resource for intervening in the patriarchal legacy of the Christian and Jewish traditions. In a subsequent and widely cited essay, "Divine Women" in *Sexes and Genealogies* (1993), Irigaray returned to this theme to assert the importance for women of a feminine conception of divinity. Borrowing from Ludwig Feuerbach's claim that God is the idealized expression of "man's" potential, Irigaray suggested that the Father-God of Christianity could only perform this function for men and that women need a feminine divine to ground the specifically feminine mode of subjectivity that she envisions.

In spite of her many theoretical differences from Irigaray, Monique Wittig implicitly follows this same line of reasoning in her radical lesbian interventions in the mythic and religious imagery of the West. Wittig rejects the psychoanalytic foundations of Irigaray's project, and yet she too wants to reimagine divinity in a feminine mode, as is clear in such novels as *Les Guérillères* (1971), in which, for example, the Eve of the *Genesis* creation myth emerges as a superhuman solar goddess who willingly eats the forbidden fruit to gain divine knowledge, and *The Lesbian Body* (1975), in which the biblical *Song of Solomon* is reworked as a hymn of divinized love for another woman. In both of these texts Wittig creatively appropriates masculine gods from a wide range of religious traditions of the world to recast them as goddesses who then function as idealized images of the power of women to free themselves from masculine oppression and to become autonomous subjects in their own right.

WOMEN AND MYSTICISM. The importance of mystical religious experience as an expression of repressed elements of Western culture has long been a favorite theme of Catherine Clément. For Clément, who is strongly influenced by Lacanian psychoanalytic theory, every culture necessarily excludes from representation certain aspects of its own experience, and Western culture, with its demand for rationality, tends to exclude the nonrational. Because women have historically been excluded from full participation in society, they have borne the burden of representing these excluded, nonrepresentable elements. In *The Newly Born Woman* (cowritten with Hélène Cixous, 1986) it is primarily the witch and the hysteric who capture Clément's attention in this context, but in such later books as *Syncope: The Philosophy of Rapture* (1994) and *The Feminine and the Sacred* (cowritten with Julia Kristeva, 2001), Clément increasingly offers Asian mystics, especially practitioners of Tantric and other forms of Yoga, as examples of the marginal figures who haunt and destabilize the masculine social order but do not have the power to overturn it. For Clément, these figures represent a privileged relationship to the sacred, outside of the confines of any form of organized religion.

Irigaray too has expressed interest in female mystical experience; indeed the essay "La Mystérique" in *Speculum* was one of her first interrogations of religious experience. In this essay she argued that mysticism was properly feminine because of its preference for embodied modes of knowledge over reason. She also suggested that in Christianity the relationship of mystic to God is essentially specular—that is, that the mystic attempts to obliterate her own imperfect identity in order to mirror divine perfection. In this way, for Irigaray, the role of the female mystic echoes the role of women in patriarchal society, where women are expected to mirror men's selves to them to sustain the masculine illusion of self-sufficiency. Since *I Love to You* (1996), however, Irigaray has increasingly turned her attention to Yoga and to a lyrical appreciation of the importance, especially for women, of cultivating the breath, which she sees as having the power to undo such binaries as inside/outside, matter/spirit, and the like. In *Between East and West: From Singularity to Community* (2002) she offers her most extended consideration of the discipline of Yoga, contrasting it with Christian mysticism and suggesting that it might provide a key to rethinking the patriarchal religious traditions of the West.

DEFILEMENT AND SIN. Kristeva is widely known, both within and outside the context of religious studies, for her theorization of abjection—the quality of repulsiveness that haunts human experience of bodily fluids, seen as waste products with the power to defile whomever they touch. First elaborated in her *Powers of Horror: An Essay on Abjection* (1982), Kristeva's interest in the abject is clearly related to her interest in the effacement of the maternal body in Western culture; as she sees it, the mother's body must be abjected, or cast away, if the subject is to enter into the symbolic order of language. To the great interest of many scholars of religion, Kristeva has developed some of the religious implications of this theory in her psychoanalytic reading of the Levitical prohibitions in *Powers of Horror* and in the later "Reading the Bible" in *New Maladies of the Soul* (1995) and has linked the sacrificial logic of Judaism and Christianity with the primal matricide that she sees, pace Sigmund Freud, as underlying both culture and the individual subject.

Hélène Cixous's approach to the problem of sin is intimately bound up with her notion of *écriture feminine*, a feminine practice of writing that reaches beyond what she sees as a masculine fear of otherness to enable new modes of relationship between self and other. For Cixous, writing is, or has the potential to become, a process that instantiates both the feminine (otherwise lost in the patriarchal order of Western culture) and God. This is so because writing participates in what Cixous calls the feminine economy, in which the self gives with no thought of return. To illustrate this notion,

Cixous has at several points taken up the *Genesis* creation story, reworking it so that it reveals the feminine economy underlying Eve's eating of the apple. For Cixous, that is, Eve eats the apple not in spite of the prohibition against doing so but precisely because of that prohibition; in choosing the pleasure of taking the fruit into herself over obedience to divine law, Eve enacts the economy that risks the loss of self to open the self up to the other. Eve is also exemplary of Cixous's notion, articulated in "Grace and Innocence: Heinrich von Kleist" (1991), that the only innocence worth having is a second innocence that comes after knowledge and guilt, after paradise is lost. For Cixous, in other words, the possibility of relationship with the other is of paramount importance, and the law that punishes Eve for pursuing that possibility is itself the source of "sin."

NON-WESTERN RESOURCES. As suggested above, several of the French feminists are especially noteworthy for their interest in what they see as the resources offered by non-Western religious traditions. In *Les Guérillères* and *The Lesbian Body*, for example, Wittig has mined Hindu and Buddhist mythologies as well as those of ancient Africa and Mesoamerica both for potentially feminist forms of religious worship and for goddesses, such as Kālī and the Aztec solar goddess Cihuacoatl, who represent the fierce, self-sustaining qualities of women, qualities that would help bring into being the radical lesbian culture that Wittig envisioned. As is the case when she invokes various figures from Judaism and Christianity, she freely appropriates from Asian traditions to suit her own purposes rather than to shed any light on those traditions as they are practiced.

Clément's consideration of non-Western traditions is arguably more respectful, although she has been criticized by some scholars for being overly romantic in her appreciation of those traditions. As noted above, *Syncope* reveals a fascination with Tantra and other forms of Yoga, practices that produce moments of rapture that, for Clément, are among the deepest expressions of both the sacred and the feminine. In the novel *Theo's Odyssey* (1999) too she explores such diverse traditions as Hinduism, Zen Buddhism, and African tribal religions to show what she sees as the healing power of ecstatic experience, a power linked in the narrative of the novel to being able both to mourn and to recapture the lost feminine.

It is in the work of Irigaray, perhaps, that the most dramatic turning to the East emerges. In such texts as "Practical Teachings: Love—Between Passion and Civility" in *I Love to You*, *The Age of the Breath* (1999), and *Between East and West*, Irigaray elaborates the value of Yogic discipline, specifically cultivation of the breath, for feminist religious practice. Here the breath is seen as paradigmatic of what Irigaray refers to as the "sensible transcendental," that is, the breath is both transcendent (of each individual's limitations) and immanent (in the body). Thus learning to practice the art of breathing offers a path out of the binaries of self/other, body/spirit, immanent/transcendent that haunt Western thought and underlie the repression of the feminine and the oppression of women.

FRENCH FEMINISM AND RELIGION: THE POSSIBILITIES. In its multifaceted approach to the problematic of sexual difference, French feminist thought is clearly a valuable resource for the study of religion. Indeed many of the themes sketched out above have yet to be extensively mined by feminist scholars of religion, and the work of only two of the thinkers discussed—Irigaray and Kristeva—has found wide acceptance in religious studies. Clearly though Clément, Cixous, and Wittig also have much to offer in the domain of religious thought, and it is certain that a further investigation of their work will shed light on the place of women in the patriarchal religious traditions of the West.

SEE ALSO Gender and Religion, overview article and article on History of Study; Goddess Worship; Mary.

BIBLIOGRAPHY

Cixous, Hélène. *"Coming to Writing" and Other Essays.* Edited by Deborah Jenson, translated by Sarah Cornell et al. Cambridge, Mass., 1991. This volume includes essays in which Cixous articulates her fascination with God, links the divine with the feminine and with writing, and explores the *Genesis* myth of Eve and the apple.

Cixous, Hélène. "Grace and Innocence: Heinrich von Kleist." In *Readings: The Poetics of Blanchot, Joyce, Kafka, Kleist, Lispector, and Tsvetayeva.* Edited and translated by Verena Andermatt Conley. Minneapolis, 1991. This essay explores the dramatic work of Kleist as a pretext for raising questions about the nature of grace and innocence in political as well as theological contexts.

Cixous, Hélène, and Catherine Clément. *The Newly Born Woman.* Translated by Betsy Wing. Minneapolis, 1986. This is the first major work of both authors to be translated into English, and it introduces themes that are essential to understanding their subsequent writings.

Clément, Catherine. *Syncope: The Philosophy of Rapture.* Translated by Sally O'Driscoll and Deirdre M. Mahoney. Minneapolis, 1994. Throughout the essays of this collection, Clément draws on the mystical elements of both Western and Eastern religious traditions to elaborate her affinity for the kinds of nonrational experiences often repressed in Western culture.

Clément, Catherine. *Theo's Odyssey.* Translated by Steve Cox and Ros Schwartz. New York, 1999.

Clément, Catherine, and Julia Kristeva. *The Feminine and the Sacred.* Translated by Jane Marie Todd. New York, 2001. This volume consists of a collection of e-mailed and faxed letters in which Clément and Kristeva explore the relationship between women and the sacred and consider whether there exists a specifically feminine form of the sacred.

Duchen, Clare. *Feminism in France: From May '68 to Mitterand.* London, 1986. This book offers a comprehensive overview of the development and intellectual context of French feminism.

Grosz, Elizabeth. *Sexual Subversions: Three French Feminists.* Sydney, 1989. Although not concerned solely with religious themes, this book is a helpful introduction to the work of Julia Kristeva, Luce Irigaray, and Michèle Le Dœuff and elaborates themes that bear on their religious thought.

Irigaray, Luce. *Speculum of the Other Woman.* Translated by Gillian C. Gill. Ithaca, N.Y., 1985. This is Irigaray's first major work to be translated into English, and its deconstructive critique of what she calls the "phallogocentrism" of Western thought lays the groundwork for her subsequent writings.

Irigaray, Luce. "When the Gods Are Born." In *Marine Lover of Friedrich Nietzsche*, pp. 121–190; translated by Gillian C. Gill. New York, 1991. This essay explores the ways Nietzsche's suppression of the feminine echoes that found in Christianity.

Irigaray, Luce. *Sexes and Genealogies.* Translated by Gillian C. Gill. New York, 1993. Included here are several important essays exemplifying Irigaray's early religious thought.

Irigaray, Luce. "Equal to Whom?" Translated by Robert Mazzola. In *The Essential Difference*, edited by Naomi Schor and Elizabeth Weed, pp. 59–76. Bloomington, Ind., 1994. This often referenced essay represents Irigaray's response to the feminist theological project of Elisabeth Schüssler Fiorenza.

Irigaray, Luce. "The Forgotten Mystery of Female Ancestry." *In Thinking the Difference: For a Peaceful Revolution*, pp. 89–113. New York, 1994. In this essay Irigaray argues for the necessity of resacralizing mother-daughter genealogies.

Irigaray, Luce. *I Love to You.* Translated by Alison Martin. New York, 1996.

Irigaray, Luce. *The Age of the Breath.* Rüsselsheim, Germany, 1999. Irigaray develops her emerging emphasis on the sacred power of the breath.

Irigaray, Luce. *Between East and West: From Singularity to Community.* Translated by Stephen Pluháček. New York, 2002. In this book Irigaray presents a meditation on the importance of the breath in Asian religious disciplines and suggests that the Yogic tradition offers resources for Western feminist religious practice.

Joy, Morny, Kathleen O'Grady, and Judith L. Poxon, eds. *French Feminists on Religion: A Reader.* London, 2002. This volume consists of a selection of important excerpts from the writings of the French feminists on a variety of religious and theological themes. It includes a foreword by Catherine Clément.

Joy, Morny, Kathleen O'Grady, and Judith L. Poxon, eds. *Religion in French Feminist Thought: Critical Perspectives.* London, 2003. This volume contains thirteen scholarly essays on aspects of the religious thought of the French feminists. It includes an introductory essay by Luce Irigaray.

Kim, C. W. Maggie, Susan M. St. Ville, and Susan M. Simonaitis, eds. *Transfigurations: Theology and the French Feminists.* Minneapolis, 1993. This is an important early collection of scholarly papers on the emerging significance of French feminist thought for religious studies.

Kristeva, Julia. *Powers of Horror: An Essay on Abjection.* Translated by Leon S. Roudiez. New York, 1982. In this early work Kristeva offers an extended exploration of her concept of abjection, a concept that has been influential among feminist scholars in religious studies.

Kristeva, Julia. *In the Beginning Was Love: Psychoanalysis and Faith.* Translated by Arthur Goldhammer. New York, 1987. As the title suggests, the essays in this volume explore aspects of the relationship between religious belief and psychoanalysis; in "Credence-Credit," Kristeva links Christian agape with the love between a mother and an infant.

Kristeva, Julia. "Stabat Mater." In *Tales of Love*, pp. 234–263. Translated by Leon S. Roudiez. New York, 1987. This widely cited essay offers a poetic and scholarly meditation on motherhood, focusing in particular on the appropriation of the Virgin Mary in the Catholic and Orthodox traditions of Christianity.

Kristeva, Julia. "Reading the Bible." In *New Maladies of the Soul*, pp. 115–126. Translated by Ross Guberman. New York, 1995. This essay offers a good example of Kristeva's psychoanalytic reading of sacred texts. Here she applies her earlier work on abjection to *Leviticus* and demonstrates that the subject in the Hebrew Scriptures can be understood only in relation to the Other.

Wittig, Monique. *Les Guérillères.* Translated by David Le Vay. New York, 1971. In this early novel Wittig offers her vision of Eve as a heroine who acts alone, without the company of Adam, to win essential knowledge for women. Wittig also invokes a number of warlike solar goddesses from ancient religious traditions around the world.

Wittig, Monique. *The Lesbian Body.* Translated by David Le Vay. New York, 1975. Although not concerned primarily with religious themes, this novel nevertheless illustrates how Wittig reworks patriarchal religious figurations from a wide variety of traditions in her attempt to construct a lesbian imaginary.

Wittig, Monique. *The Straight Mind and Other Essays.* Boston, 1992. This is a collection of essays in which Wittig articulates her understanding of feminism and challenges aspects of the projects of other French feminist theorists.

JUDITH L. POXON (2005)

FEMINIST THEOLOGY

This entry consists of the following articles:

AN OVERVIEW
CHRISTIAN FEMINIST THEOLOGY

FEMINIST THEOLOGY: AN OVERVIEW

Theology, as rational exploration of the nature and traits of God or deity, is central to Christianity. While other religions, by definition, include some theological assumptions, exploring the nature of deity does not have the same prestige or importance in any other religion, including the other monotheistic religions. Therefore, it is sometimes claimed that explicit and deliberate attention to theology by adherents of other religions is more an imitation of Christianity than an indigenous pursuit. For Buddhism and other nontheistic religions, the term is especially awkward, and some commentators refuse to use the term even if they wish to do critical and constructive reflections on their traditions. Nevertheless, by extension, many non-Christians do use the term for their own reflective work.

Feminist theology originated among Christians in late 1960s and early 1970s, though Jewish feminist commentators quickly joined the discussion. But while Christian feminist theologians took up questions about the implications of feminism for traditional concepts of deity as a major concern, feminists in many other traditions bracketed the question of language and imagery of deity, claiming that other issues, such as women's status under religious law, were much more pressing for women.

When discussing feminist theologies other than Christian feminist theology, the term *feminism* is equally problematic. In much of the world, the term has extremely negative connotations; people think it means an anti-men and anti-family movement that imposes Western values on other cultures. (This assessment of feminism tends to be promoted by religious conservatives who do not want women in their traditions to take a critical stance vis-à-vis the tradition.) Therefore, most people avoid the term, even if the work they are doing would qualify as feminist according to the Western use of the term. The term *feminist* implies taking a critical and constructive approach that centers on questions of women's well-being and agency to a religious tradition. Such critical and constructive tasks can involve changing or reinterpreting the tradition when it is found that women's well-being is compromised by traditional teachings and practices. The practice of feminist theology can also involve highlighting aspects of a tradition that have been largely neglected, but that do promote women's well-being. However, scholarship that simply provides more information about women's religious lives without invoking any critical perspectives does not qualify as feminist theology.

Feminist theologies generally take up two separate but interrelated tasks (these same tasks are also major topics in Christian feminist theology). Feminist reflection within a religious tradition is usually first sparked by women's resentment of their secondary and peripheral status in all the world's major religious traditions. This discovery leads to many explorations. The history of the tradition is reexamined to search out forgotten but more inspiring role models for women; sometimes this research leads to the conclusion that the religion actually had feminist values originally, but that these values gradually eroded under the weight of convention and tradition. The scriptures are examined anew to see if the traditional patriarchal interpretations are the only possible interpretations; many feminist interpreters of their scriptures claim that the scriptures do promote women's dignity, equality, and well-being, but that traditionalists have focused on a few passages, often taken out of context, that seem to promote male dominance. Rituals and liturgies are studied to see if they can be practiced in ways that are more inclusive of women. Sometimes this involves advocating the actual presence of women in the ritual spaces that were formerly closed to them. Sometimes it involves changing liturgical language to be gender-neutral and gender-inclusive. Sometimes it involves creating new rituals that meet women's religious needs more adequately. Finally, religious institutions are critiqued. Are women kept out of leadership roles? Is study of their tradition difficult for them? Do the laws and customs favor men over women? Feminists find traditional institutional set-ups quite inadequate if one defines the purpose of religious institutions as promoting the well-being of women equally with that of men.

Such questions are all part of the first agenda for feminist theology—reforming the tradition so that it serves women's needs more adequately. However, feminist theological reflection does not always take up the second, more comprehensive and challenging task. Is the whole religious worldview implicated in the male dominance of the tradition and in its typical disregard for women's well-being? This question is extremely threatening to many religious people, regardless of their specific religious tradition, because a positive answer would involve rethinking the most fundamental assumptions of the tradition. Nevertheless, some feminist theologians have explored this question. One notable example is the critique of the assumed maleness of the deity, which has been made mainly by Jewish and Christian feminist theologians. Lurking behind the assumed maleness of the deity, some feminist theologians have also found questionable assumptions about the relationship between the deity and the world, as well as about many other basic theological issues. This question has not been raised so thoroughly in other religious traditions, though some feminists have questioned some basic Buddhist assumptions. The *guru* or religious teacher is usually male, raising the question of whether this practice limits Buddhist women in the same way the maleness of the deity is claimed to limit Jewish and Christian women? Would women *gurus* highlight teachings and practices that have been largely downplayed by male *gurus*? How helpful is the strong feminine imagery prevalent in some forms of Buddhism for women?

FEMINIST THEOLOGY IN JUDAISM AND ISLAM. Judaism and Islam are similar to each other in many ways. Both are strictly monotheistic and often use male imagery and language for the deity. Both value religious law over theology and pride themselves on providing a comprehensive overarching way of life for their followers. Both regard the sexes as complementary; each sex has its distinctive sphere, and it is often claimed that these separate spheres are of equal value. Both regard public religious observance as a male preserve and see women's roles as being centered in home and family. Both look extremely male-dominated by standard feminist assessments.

There have been strong women's movements in both traditions, but the movements are quite different, in part because the Jewish feminist movement is quite critical of the tradition, whereas Muslim women's movements often seek to educate women about rights they have under Muslim law that are often not fully observed. These differences are also due to the fact that the Jewish women's movement is centered in North America, where feminism is part of the culture, whereas Muslims must constantly deal with the accusation that any attempts to critique or reform Muslim practices surrounding gender are inappropriate forms of "westernization" and should be resisted.

Jewish feminist theology takes the form of both an attempt to include women in all aspects of traditional Judaism from which they have previously been excluded and an attempt to radically rethink the basic categories of Judaism, such as God, Torah, and Israel. Women have been ordained as rabbis in all forms of Judaism, except the Orthodox movement. Jewish education for women and girls has grown exponentially since the 1960s, with the result that women insist on participating equally in the synagogue roles for which they are trained, and many women have taken on the obligations of daily prayer that are required only of men. But such egalitarian reforms do not go far enough, according to some Jewish feminists, who argue that Jewish theology must be entirely reconceptualized. For example, in addition to insisting that female imagery and language of deity is appropriate, many wish to challenge traditional images of the deity as a ruler with power over humanity and develop partnership models of the relationship between deity and humanity.

Muslims, both feminist and nonfeminist, insist that Islam improved the status of women over what it had been in pre-Islamic Arabia. Muslims also insist, correctly, that Islam gave women rights that women in Christian and Western countries have obtained only recently, even if these rights may seem inadequate from a contemporary feminist point of view. Many Muslims also insist that the primary problem for women is lack of education, not lack of rights. Women may not know what rights they have under Islamic law, and local customs have often eroded whatever rights they have. Some Muslim feminists have shown that many traditional beliefs about women's inferiority have no basis in genuine Muslim thought. The customs that feminists find most problematic, such as female circumcision, honor killings, and even veiling, have no basis in the Qurʾān, though modest dress is required for both women and men. However, the traditional practices of sexual segregation and the requirement of separate spheres for women and men have not been challenged consistently. Traditional theology and concepts of God have not been subjected to feminist analysis.

FEMINIST THEOLOGY IN HINDUISM AND BUDDHISM. The agenda for feminist theology has been largely determined by its Western and Christian practitioners. Some of their concerns merge well into the Hindu and Buddhist contexts, but others find no parallels in Hinduism and Buddhism. Generally, concerns about male-dominated religious institutions and women's access to prestigious religious practices are central to feminist critiques of these traditions. However, many of the more theological issues involving claims about the deity simply do not translate into Hindu or Buddhist contexts.

Hinduism, an umbrella term for extremely varied religious beliefs and practices in India, is as formally male-dominated as religion could possibly be. However, feminist commentators frequently point out that there are the formal law codes on the one hand, and there is religion as it is actually practiced on the other. In India, the former are usually more stringent than the latter. For example, women should not study the Sanskrit Vedas, but they do; a son is needed to light the parent's funeral pyre, but in the absence of a son, daughters sometimes light the fire. Especially in the twentieth century, most areas formerly closed to women were at least formally opened to them. Nowadays, Sanskrit learning is largely accessible to women, and some *gurūs* have transmitted their lineages to women disciples, who now hold positions of the highest religious authority. Additionally, offsetting the male dominance of much public religious practice, Hindu women have always had a rich repertoire of rituals for women led by women. The problem of the male deity does not exist in Hinduism, not because there are no male deities, but because there are also numerous female deities, many of them fierce and strong. Hinduism is largely a theistic religion, but it traditionally includes an almost unlimited number of ways to imagine deity. For all these reasons, as well as a general Asian reluctance to use the term *feminism,* there has been little feminist theology, per se, in the Hindu context, and few organized movements to improve women's status in religion. Nevertheless, women are quietly doing virtually everything religiously in Hinduism, at least in some places.

For Buddhism, the situation is somewhat different. Because of Buddhism's growing popularity in the West, it has encountered more direct feminist critiques and reconstructions. There is also a worldwide Buddhist women's movement. Its agenda is restoring the *bhikkhunī* (nuns) ordination in places where it has been lost and improving the education and status of nuns everywhere, but it also addresses women's concerns more generally. Buddhist teachings are remarkably gender-neutral and gender-free, probably more so than those of any other religion. That is because all Buddhist teachings point to the ultimate irrelevance of gender and to the fact that, like all phenomena, gender lacks substantial reality and is, in that sense, illusory. Buddhism is also a nontheistic religion, so the problem of the male deity does not exist. The plentiful anthropomorphic imagery found in Mahāyāna and Vajrayāna Buddhism features many prominent and popular female representations, as well as male ones. The problem in Buddhism has been its institutional setup, which historically has been extremely male-dominated and much more favorable to men than to women. Thus, Buddhist feminists primarily point to this internal contradiction within Buddhism rather than suggesting profound changes in its worldview. Regarding institutional reforms, progress in Asia is slow, but things are definitely changing. In North America, which in many ways can take a fresh start, the situation is different. Many of the best-known Western teachers of Buddhism are women, as are about half the senior teachers. However, most of these women teachers do not explicitly deal with feminist issues.

FEMINIST THEOLOGY IN EAST ASIAN RELIGIONS. The major religions of East Asia—Confucianism and Daoism—are religions under stress due to the influence of missionaries and other Western critics of Chinese religion, as well as to the hostility of the Chinese Communist government to religion in any form. Consequently, there has been little feminist analysis or reconceptualization of these religions. A few Western-educated Chinese scholars have compared the teachings of these religions with the claims of modern feminism and have found much room for dialogue between Daoism and feminism, but less consonance between Confucianism and feminism. It remains to be seen if these religions regain their former influence, but Daoism in particular does seem to be making a comeback and is also attracting non-Chinese followers. If they do make a comeback, these religions will also undoubtedly receive more attention from feminist theologians.

CONCLUSION. *Feminist theology* may or may not be an appropriate term for the feminist analysis that is done in nonmonotheistic or nontheistic contexts. But it is important to recognize that critical and constructive work regarding gender has been done and is appropriate in those religious contexts. Too often in North American theological and academic studies of religion, the process of Christian theologizing is thoroughly discussed, whereas other religious traditions are presented only as static, completed systems of thought. The term *theology* does acknowledge that all religious traditions are changing and responding to current issues, including those brought about by the various feminist critiques of male-dominated religions and societies.

However, feminist theologies in the various religions are much more complex and nuanced than could be indicated within the limits of this short article. It is also important to note that even though several major religions have been discussed, many others, including all the world's indigenous traditions, have been omitted from this short survey.

SEE ALSO Dialogue of Religions; Feminism, article on Feminism, Gender Studies, and Religion; Gender and Religion, overview article, and article on History of Study; Religious Diversity; Theology, articles on Christian Theology, Comparative Theology.

BIBLIOGRAPHY

Three anthologies give systematic accounts of feminist theology in various religions: Paula M. Cooey, William R. Eakin, and Jay B. McDaniel, *After Patriarchy: Feminist Transformations of the World Religions* (Maryknoll, N.Y., 1991); Arvind Sharma and Katherine K. Young, *Feminism and World Religions* (Albany, 1999); and Arvind Sharma and Katherine K. Young, *Her Voice, Her Faith: Women Speak on World Religions* (Boulder, Colo., 2003). Two other anthologies have collected religious views on topics important to feminists: Daniel C. Maguire, ed., *Sacred Rights: The Case for Abortion and Contraception in World Religions* (Oxford, 2003), and Patricia Beattie Young, Mary E. Hunt, and Radhika Balakrishnan, eds., *Good Sex: Feminist Perspectives from the World's Religions* (New Brunswick, N.J., 2001). For an overview of feminist issues in the world's religions see Rita M. Gross, *Feminism and Religion: An Introduction* (Boston, 1996). The most important feminist analyses of Judaism include, in the order of their publication, Blu Greenberg, *On Women and Judaism: A View from Tradition* (Philadelphia, 1981); Judith Plaskow, *Standing Again at Sinai: Judaism from a Feminist Perspective* (San Francisco, 1990); and Rachel Adler, *Engendering Judaism: An Inclusive Theology and Ethics* (Boston, 1998). Many books on women and Islam have appeared, but most of them are descriptive rather than analytical. More analytical discussions include Barbara Freyer Stowasser's *Women in the Qur'an: Traditions and Interpretations* (Oxford, 1994) and Fatima Mernissi's *The Veil and the Male Elite: A Feminist Interpretation of Women's Rights in Islam* (Reading, Mass., 1991). For a gripping autobiographical account, *The Hidden Face of Eve: Women in the Arab World* (Boston, 1980), by the well-known feminist activist Nawal el Saadawi, is recommended. Finally, the anthology *Progressive Muslims: On Justice, Gender, and Pluralism* (Oxford, 2003), edited by Omid Safi, includes a section on gender issues in Islam. Many fine anthropological accounts on Hindu women have appeared, so that earlier generalizations about Hindu women are no longer relevant or appropriate. Nevertheless, there are few explicitly feminist analyses of Hinduism. One of the few such books is Alf Hiltebeital and Kathleen M. Erndl, *Is the Goddess a Feminist?: The Politics of South Asian Goddesses* (Sheffield, U.K., 2000). The most thorough feminist analysis of Buddhism is Rita M. Gross, *Buddhism after Patriarchy: A Feminist History, Analysis, and Reconstruction of Buddhism* (Albany, 1993). Three anthologies on women and Buddhism also offer useful feminist perspectives: Marianne Dresser, ed., *Buddhist Women on the Edge: Contemporary Perspectives from the Western Frontier* (Berkeley, 1996); Lenore Friedman and Susan Moon, eds., *Being Bodies: Buddhist Women on the Paradox of Embodiment* (Boston, 1997); and Karma Lekshe Tsomo, *Innovative Buddhist Women, Swimming against the Stream* (Richmond, U.K., 2000).

RITA M. GROSS (2005)

FEMINIST THEOLOGY: CHRISTIAN FEMINIST THEOLOGY

Christianity's encounter with feminism might be one of the most significant revolutions ever to happen within the Christian tradition, rivaling the impact of the early councils or the reformation in its implications for the future of Christian belief and practice. Although feminism continues to be marginalized, ignored, or condemned by many Christians, its effects are felt across the whole spectrum of contemporary Christianity.

Feminist theology emerged in the United States during the 1960s when so-called second wave feminism was making an impact on academic ideas as well as on western politics and culture. European feminists have made their own distinctive contribution. In the last forty years, feminist theology has become a global movement representing a wide range of cultural, political, and religious perspectives. The Ecumenical Association of Third-World Theologians (EATWOT) has provided a significant forum for the development of feminist theologies in engagement with a wide range of women's concerns and experiences from all five continents.

However, it is also true that women have been doing theology since the early church, and the task of feminist theologians is as much about retrieving the neglected voices of women of the past as it is about formulating new theological symbols and values for the present and the future. *The*

Woman's Bible, a critique of Christianity produced in the 1890s by American suffragist Elizabeth Cady Stanton (1815–1902), is regarded as an important founding moment in Christian feminism. Today, feminist theological reflection includes academic scholarship as well as literature, music, liturgy, and a range of insights drawn from the exploration of women's experiences in many different contexts. Although feminist theology is not simply another form of liberation theology, its challenge to the oppression and exploitation of women gives it a strongly liberationist perspective.

The publication of Valerie Saiving's article in 1960, "The Human Situation: A Feminine View" (Saiving, 1992), has with hindsight been recognized as a key event in the contemporary development of feminist theology. Saiving asked the extent to which Christian concepts of sin (pride, ambition, self-centeredness) are influenced by masculine perspectives so that they do not reflect feminine sins (self-denigration, triviality, lack of focus). Feminist theology thus began to question much of what had gone before, not only in terms of women's place in the church, but more generally in terms of the gendering of theological ideas and in the implicit and explicit privileging of the masculine over the feminine at every level of Christian doctrine and practice.

The encounter between feminism and theology was given added impetus by the Second Vatican Council (1962–1965), which encouraged Roman Catholics to enter into a positive engagement with the non-Catholic world. Pioneers such as Rosemary Radford Ruether, Mary Daly, and Elizabeth Johnson were Catholics working in the initially optimistic climate that followed the council. Daly's 1968 book, *The Church and the Second Sex*, offered a hard-hitting feminist critique of Christian misogyny, but still expressed hope that the church could be transformed. Later editions include disclaimers in which Daly makes clear her subsequent rejection of Christianity as irredeemably patriarchal (Daly, 1985). Daphne Hampson has come to the same conclusion about the impossibility of reconciliation between feminism and the Christian tradition (Hampson, 1996).

Nevertheless, feminist theology brings together academics, activists, and believers from all denominations, men as well as women, who believe that the Christian faith, however problematic, can be transformed and continues to offer a message of hope for the world. While it is impossible to do justice to the full range of feminist theological reflection in a short survey, this is an overview of general trends and significant developments in a field of study that is constantly evolving as new perspectives emerge.

WOMEN'S EXPERIENCE. In 1983, Ruether defined "the critical principle of feminist theology" as "the promotion of the full humanity of women" (Ruether, 1992, p. 18). This definition has inspired a process of theological reflection that begins with women's experience, in recognition of the fact that theology has been almost exclusively informed by the experiences of men. Although theology as a discipline is concerned with reflection upon the nature of God as revealed in scripture, the natural law, and the prayerful use of human reason (described by St. Anselm as "faith seeking understanding"), feminists point out the extent to which theological knowledge is shaped by the cultural context and bodily specificity of the theologian, including his or her gendered embodiment. Strictly speaking, therefore, the appeal to women's experience need not be seen as an attempt to construct a theory of God from the starting point of woman but rather as a corrective to the androcentrism of existing theological discourse. If Christianity recognizes the ultimate mystery and unspeakability of God, it also believes that it can and, indeed, must speak of God in the language and concepts of human embodiment because it believes that God is supremely and (for some) uniquely and exclusively revealed in the human person of Jesus Christ and in the Bible. If male and female are both made in the image of God (*Gen.* 1:27), then the human understanding of God requires the theological participation of both sexes. To bring women's perspectives into theology is not simply to "add women and stir," but to introduce a catalyst capable of initiating radical transformation.

Nevertheless, the appeal to women's experience has been criticized by some feminists and by some antagonistic to feminism. An early and significant critique came from those who argued that the work of theologians such as Ruether and Daly was premised on the experience of white Western women, and that the category of "woman" did not reflect the plurality and diversity of women's experiences in different contexts. As a result, feminist theology now embraces a wide range of perspectives and methods. In seeking to express both a relationship to and a distance from Western feminism, these diverse theologies use a variety of names, including, among others, womanist theology (arising out of the experiences of black North American women), *dalit* women's theology (which explores the situation of low-caste Christian women in India), concerned African women's theology (primarily focusing on the encounter between African culture, Christianity, and feminism), *minjung* feminist theology (Korean women's theology from the perspective of the poor and the marginalized), and *mujerista* theology (informed by the experiences of Hispanic-American women) (King, 1994). This plurality means that methods and sources extend far beyond those regarded as theological in the strictly academic sense, including, among others, oral traditions, literature, art, biography, and autobiography.

While these theologies are often based on a liberal or liberationist approach, since the early 1990s a growing number of feminist theologians have adopted a postmodernist perspective informed by the deconstructive and poststructuralist approaches of secular feminist theory, and by the work of critical theorists such as Jacques Derrida, Michel Foucault, Luce Irigaray, and Julia Kristeva (Chopp and Davaney, 1997; Kim, St. Ville, and Simonaitis, 1993). From this perspective, the appeal to women's experience is problematized by the recognition that all experience is socially constructed and linguistically mediated, and it is argued that feminist theology needs to concern itself with the analysis of theological language and symbolism. Although this approach has gained some currency, there has been considerable debate over the extent to which political concerns for justice become marginalized if feminist theology aligns itself too closely with theory at the expense of practice. As Janet Martin Soskice notes, "Feminism in theology may lack the theoretical framework of some of its sister subjects, but its prospect for reaching millions of lives, including those of the world's poorest women, is immense" (Soskice in Soskice and Lipton, 2003, p. 8).

Another critique of the appeal to experience comes from those who argue that theological reflection cannot begin with the individual subject but must take the form of a prayerful encounter with the revelation of God. From this perspective, while it is right to criticize excessive androcentrism as a failing in the theological tradition, the corrective is not to introduce another foundational form of gendered subjectivity but to rediscover the importance of doing theology in a space of communication between human awareness and divine revelation within the context of the Christian community (Martin, 1994). Feminists such as Linda Woodhead and Susan Parsons have raised similar concerns, arguing that feminist theology risks the sacrifice of a vital transcendent perspective of faith and hope in favor of a more modernist and individualistic rhetoric of women's liberation (Woodhead, 1997; Parsons, 2000).

Theological Language. Potentially the most challenging aspect of feminist theology is its questioning of Christian concepts of God. At one level, this involves the recognition that theological language is almost exclusively masculine, with God being referred to in concepts associated with fatherhood and maleness, and never with images that evoke maternal feminine characteristics. Although the idea of referring to God as "mother" or "she" is anathema to many modern Christians, theological language was in the past much more fluid in terms of gender, frequently referring to God, Christ, and the Holy Spirit in maternal metaphors and symbols. Feminist theologians whose work is informed by critical theory reject the appeal to inclusive language as masking rather than resolving the problem of androcentrism. They would argue that symbols and language must be deconstructed in order to identify the dynamics of power, dissimulation, and ideological manipulation that are encoded within the structures, values, and relationships of theological narratives.

The critique of masculine theological language also challenges the privileging of the Father-Son relationship between God and Jesus Christ, and the representation of the relationship among the three persons of the Trinity, perceived as masculine. Catherine Mowry LaCugna, in *God for Us*, argues that western theology constructed its doctrine of the Trinity around a hierarchy of relationships that in turn lends justification to social hierarchies based on submission to patriarchal authority figures. She seeks the reclamation of a more interpersonal understanding of the Trinity through an appeal to pre-Nicene theology, particularly that of the Cappadocians, arguing that the doctrine of the Trinity is practical and has radical social implications (LaCugna, 1992). Elizabeth Johnson, in her influential book *She Who Is*, argues that the mystery of God as Trinity can only be expressed through a rich plurality of images and associations, including both male and female terms (Johnson 1992).

While these constitute feminist refigurations of, rather than departures from, traditional theology, some radical feminist theologians (sometimes referred to in the feminized form as thealogians) would associate the Judeo-Christian tradition with the triumph of patriarchal monotheism over the more matriarchal goddess religions. They would advocate the reclamation of goddess worship and symbolism as a resource for women's spirituality. While for some this entails the transformation rather than the rejection of Christianity, including the reclamation of the Virgin Mary as the goddess of the Christian tradition, others would see it as a form of post-Christian feminist spirituality that liberates women from the constraints of patriarchal religion (Baring and Cashford, 1991).

The Bible. Feminist biblical criticism has in its short history exhibited a dynamic and innovative capacity for scriptural interpretation, discovering in the biblical narratives a multifaceted resource for the critique of patriarchy and for the reclamation of women's stories of redemption. Feminist hermeneutics entail the recognition that the meaning of a text depends both upon the context in which it was written and the context in which it is interpreted. To consciously read the Bible as a woman and to resist dominant, androcentric readings is to discover previously unrecognized challenges and meanings. This also involves the acknowledgment that the authors of scripture were male and that the Bible, like every other text, is situated within particular cultural and historical contexts that reflect the perspectives of its authors. The quest for revelation thus becomes a struggle with the text, and a resistance to authoritative readings that justify the subordination or oppression of women. Elisabeth Schüssler Fiorenza pioneered a hermeneutical approach that seeks to reclaim the lives of the women around Jesus and in the early church, arguing that the first Christian communities were radically egalitarian and that women shared roles of discipleship and leadership with their male counterparts (Schüssler Fiorenza, 1994a and 1994b). No less influential is the rhetorical criticism and exegesis of Phyllis Trible, whose readings of the Hebrew scriptures challenge existing orthodoxies, particularly with regard to the construction of sexual hierarchies through an appeal to the story of *Genesis* 2–3 (Trible, 1978).

The participation of women from many different cultural perspectives also brings rich new insights to biblical interpretation (King, 1994, pp. 183–242). The Womanist theologian, Delores Williams, proposes a reading of the story of Hagar in *Genesis* 16-21 as one in which Hagar, the Egyptian slave woman persecuted and sexually exploited in the patriarchal household of Abraham, reflects the experiences of black women in the United States (Williams, 1993). The women disciples of Jesus and those who feature in the Pauline letters have been the focus of extensive feminist study, as have the Pauline injunctions on marriage and on women's behavior in church.

While all feminist biblical criticism is to some extent deconstructive, in recent years there has been a significant shift in some feminist approaches to the Bible, through the adoption of a more theoretical linguistic approach to the study of texts. This includes asking to what extent women in ancient literature are in fact ciphers employed by male writers rather than reliable historical accounts. From this perspective, the attempt to reconstruct women's histories from biblical and early Christian texts becomes a more challenging task than has previously been recognized (Clark, 1998).

EMBODIMENT, SEXUALITY, AND NATURE. The position of the female body in Christian worship, language, and ethics is a central concern of feminist theology (Isherwood and Stuart 1998). Again, the ways in which this is addressed vary widely according to different theological perspectives and contexts. For some, the belief that God became incarnate in Jesus Christ raises a fundamental question about the place of the female body in the doctrine of salvation, summarized in Ruether's question, "Can a male savior save women?" (Ruether, 1992). For Ruether, the answer is dependent upon the recognition that Christ's maleness is a contingency of his humanity, and does not have doctrinal significance. Sarah Coakley analyzes the representation of sexuality and the body in Christian texts to show the ambiguity and inherent instability of theological concepts of gender (Coakley, 2002). Others explore the significance of the Virgin Mary as one who bodily participated in the incarnation in a way that has redemptive significance for the female body (Beattie, 2002).

Related to questions about the masculinity of Christ are questions about the role of the female body in relation to Christian symbols and sacraments. Given the relationship between the shedding of Christ's blood, the doctrine of salvation, and the doctrine of the Eucharist, some women theologians ask what symbolic associations might be discovered between the body of Christ and the body of women in terms of their capacity to nurture, to bleed, and to give new life. From an anthropological perspective, Nancy Jay's work has been influential in exploring the relationship between religious concepts of sacrifice and taboos against women priests associated with fears of menstruation and childbirth (Jay, 1992). Bynum has shown that there was a close association between female embodiment and the body of Christ in medieval women's devotions, based on the belief that the divinity of Christ derived from God the Father, but his humanity derived from the female flesh of his mother (Bynum, 1992).

Another area of widespread concern to feminist theologians is the question of female sexuality, which has almost universally been portrayed in negative terms in Christian writings. While obedient and chaste women modeled on the Virgin Mary have been seen as worthy exemplars of Christian womanhood, female sexuality associated with Eve, temptation, sin, and death has been viewed with fear and condemnation. Christian feminists seek the celebration of sexuality in general and female sexuality in particular as a God-given dimension of human embodiment. For some, this includes the affirmation of lesbian sexuality and its capacity to express Christian love and friendship between women (Stuart, 1995). For others, the primary concern is the extent to which women and children continue to be victims of sexual violence and abuse, both with regard to the ongoing problem of domestic violence and to the burgeoning problem of the global sex trade (King, 1994, pp. 105–79).

Questions about the theological significance of the female body open into wider concerns regarding Christian attitudes toward nature, given the long-standing association between female embodiment and nature. Women's theologies are thus often deeply influenced by the arguments and ideas of eco-feminism, seeking a way beyond modern attitudes of domination and exploitation in order to rediscover a sense of the goodness of creation and the interdependence of the relationship between humankind and the natural world (McFague, 1993).

At a time when many secular academics regard the whole pursuit of theology as moribund or anachronistic, it is in the field of feminist studies that this discipline continues to develop with vitality and intellectual vigor, exposing the extent to which the practices and methods of Christian scholarship have been intellectually limited by the unacknowledged biases of patriarchy and androcentrism. To say this is not to dismiss the legitimate criticisms that have been made of some feminist arguments, nor is it to deny that feminists too bring their own ideological presuppositions and cultural assumptions to their task. Feminist theologians face complex challenges, not least in accommodating the perspectives of those women who resist some or all of their claims because they still find in traditional forms of Christianity a deep source of meaning and inspiration. The challenge is to sustain a sense of the Christian community as inclusive, interactive, and mutually responsible for the creation of a materially significant culture of redemptive hope, while continuing to work for the transformation of a tradition that is also associated with a long and tragic history of violence, sexual oppression, and abusive power relations, which have been both sanctioned and challenged by the Christian understanding of God.

SEE ALSO Androcentrism; Biblical Exegesis, article on Christian Views; Ecology and Religion; Feminine Sacrality; Feminism, article on French Feminists on Religion; Gaia; Gender and Religion, overview article, articles on Gender and Christianity, History of Study; Gender Roles; God; Goddess Worship; Gynocentrism; Human Body, article on Human Bodies, Religion, and Gender; Liberation Theology; Mary; Patriarchy and Matriarchy; Priesthood; Sexuality; Stanton, Elizabeth Cady; Thealogy; Virgin Goddess; Women's Studies in Religion.

Bibliography

Baring, Anne, and Jules Cashford. *The Myth of the Goddess: Evolution of an Image.* London, 1991. The authors offer an in-depth study of goddess myths and religions that they argue have been repressed or annihilated by Judeo-Christian patriarchal monotheism.

Beattie, Tina. *God's Mother, Eve's Advocate: A Marian Narrative of Women's Salvation.* London and New York, 2002. Beattie reads the texts of the early church and recent Catholic theology in engagement with Luce Irigaray and other critical theorists, to argue for the symbolic reclamation of Eve and Mary in the Christian story.

Bynum, Caroline Walker. *Fragmentation and Redemption: Essays on Gender and the Human Body in Medieval Religion.* New York, 1992. Bynum's study of medieval attitudes towards gender and the body in the writings of Christian mystics, saints, and theologians has proved an enduring resource for feminist scholarship.

Chopp, Rebecca S., and Sheila Greeve Davaney, eds. *Horizons in Feminist Theology: Identity, Tradition, and Norms.* Minneapolis, 1997. Chopp and Davaney bring together a range of feminist theologians in essays that explore the significance of feminist theory for feminist theology. For a debate concerning the relevance and the limitations of this approach, see also Emily R. Neil et al., "Roundtable Discussion: From Generation to Generation. Horizons in Feminist Theology or Reinventing the Wheel?" in *The Journal of Feminist Studies in Religion* 15, no. 1 (1999): 102–138.

Clark, Elizabeth A. "The Lady Vanishes: Dilemmas of a Feminist Historian after the 'Linguistic Turn'" *Church History* 67, no. 1 (1998): 1–31. Clark's article is informative for those seeking to understand the problematic relationship between poststructuralist and deconstructive approaches to language, and the feminist retrievals of early Christian women's histories.

Coakley, Sarah. *Powers and Submission: Spirituality, Philosophy, and Gender.* Oxford, and Malden, Mass., 2002. Coakley brings a finely honed feminist sensibility to her reading of the Christian tradition in these wide-ranging essays analyzing western philosophy and theology.

Daly, Mary. *The Church and the Second Sex.* Boston, 1985. First published in 1968, reissued in 1975 with an autobiographical preface and feminist postchristian introduction, and in 1985 with a new archaic afterword; the various versions of this book offer an insight into one woman's journey from radical Catholic theologian to controversial post-Christian feminist.

Hampson, Daphne. *After Christianity.* London, 1996. Hampson argues that Christianity is neither true nor moral and must be rejected as a false patriarchal myth to allow for new ways of conceptualizing God that more truthfully reflect the experiences and spiritual ideals of people today.

Isherwood, Lisa, and Elizabeth Stuart. *Introducing Body Theology.* Sheffield, U.K., 1998. This book provides a good survey of feminist concerns regarding the theological representation of the relationship between the body, sexuality, and spirituality.

Jay, Nancy. *Throughout Your Generations Forever: Sacrifice, Religion, and Paternity.* Chicago, 1992. Jay's interdisciplinary study of sacrifice leads her to argue that blood sacrifice is a means of establishing and sustaining patriarchal social structures that allow paternal lineage to transcend the maternal relationship established by childbirth and motherhood.

Johnson, Elizabeth A. *She Who Is: The Mystery of God in Feminist Theological Discourse.* New York, 1992. Johnson offers a feminist re-evaluation of the Christian doctrine of the Trinity in a careful reading of the Catholic tradition and its influential thinkers such as Thomas Aquinas and Karl Rahner.

Kim, C.W. Maggie, Susan M. St. Ville, and Susan M. Simonaitis, eds. *Transfigurations: Theology & The French Feminists.* Minneapolis, 1993. This edited collection of essays offers a critical engagement with feminist theology from the perspective of French feminism.

King, Ursula, ed. *Feminist Theology from the Third World: A Reader.* London and Maryknoll, N.Y., 1994. King's selection of feminist theological writings from around the world gives a sense of the range of hopes and struggles that informs Christian women in their engagement with feminism and of the methods and perspectives that shape their work.

LaCugna, Catherine Mowry. *God for Us: The Trinity and Christian Life.* San Francisco, 1992. LaCugna interprets the doctrine of the Trinity as having far-reaching practical implications for human relationships, through the ways in which theology understands the action of God in the world.

Martin, Francis. *The Feminist Question: Feminist Theology in the Light of Christian Tradition.* (Edinburgh, 1994). While Martin acknowledges the importance of feminist theology, he is critical of its foundationalism in appealing to the individual experiencing subject as the source of theological knowledge.

McFague, Sallie. *The Body of God: An Ecological Theology.* Minneapolis, 1993. Using the idea of the universe as a metaphor for the body of God, McFague seeks the transformation of Christian attitudes to the body and creation. Although her work has been criticized by some scholars for its misreading of the Christian tradition, she remains an influential resource for feminist environmental theology.

Parsons, Susan Frank. "Accounting for Hope: Feminist Theology as Fundamental Theology" in *Challenging Women's Orthodoxies in the Context of Faith.* Aldershot, U.K., 2003. Parsons criticizes the work of some feminist theologians, particularly Ruether and Fiorenza, for a nihilistic tendency in which the hope of the Christian faith in God is negated in favor of a politicized approach that fails to recognize its own collusion in perpetuating modern forms of power and control.

Ruether, Rosemary Radford. *Sexism and God-Talk: Towards a Feminist Theology.* London, 1992; first published, 1983. One of the pioneering books of feminist theology, Ruether's work, although sometimes criticized for its liberal orientation, remains highly influential for a new generation of feminist scholars.

Saiving, Valerie. "The Human Situation: A Feminine View," first published 1960. In *Womanspirit Rising: A Feminist Reader in Religion,* edited by Carol P. Christ and Judith Plaskow. San Francisco, 1992. Saiving's essay is widely recognized as a pioneering analysis of the gendering of sin in the Christian tradition.

Schüssler Fiorenza, Elisabeth. *In Memory of Her: A Feminist Theological Reconstruction of Christian Origins,* second edition, first published 1983. London, 1994a. Although her historical interpretation of women in the early Church has been criticized, Schüssler Fiorenza's work remains an important resource for feminist biblical hermeneutics.

Schüssler Fiorenza, Elisabeth, ed. *Searching the Scriptures,* Volumes 1 and 2. New York and London, 1994b. This two-volume edited collection provides an excellent insight into the methods, approaches, and concerns of feminist biblical scholars.

Soskice, Janet Martin and Diana Lipton, eds. *Feminism & Theology.* Oxford, 2003. This anthology of writings by Jewish and Christian women reflects the ways in which the encounter between feminism and theology is explored in literature, historical studies, theological reflection, and biblical studies.

Stuart, Elizabeth. *Just Good Friends: Towards a Lesbian and Gay Theology of Relationships.* London, 1995. Stuart asks what it would mean for the church to accept gays and lesbians as equal in the eyes of God, and what heterosexuals might learn from this acceptance.

Trible, Phyllis. *God and the Rhetoric of Sexuality.* Minneapolis, 1978. Trible's acclaimed study of the Hebrew scriptures, including her vastly influential re-reading of the story of *Genesis* 1–3, continues to be an important resource for feminist biblical criticism.

Trible, Phyllis. *Texts of Terror: Literary-Feminist Readings of Biblical Narratives.* London and Minneapolis, 2003; first published 1984. Trible analyzes some of the most problematic texts of the Hebrew scriptures in their representation of violence against women and shows how they can be read as a divine protest against rather than an endorsement of such violence.

Williams, Delores S. *Sisters in the Wilderness: The Challenge of Womanist God-Talk.* Maryknoll, N.Y., 1993. Williams presents a Womanist theology in which she examines the doctrines and values of Christianity from the perspective of black American women's experiences, including their history of slavery and sexual and economic exploitation.

Woodhead, Linda. "Spiritualising the Sacred: A Critique of Feminist Theology." In *Modern Theology* 13, no. 2. (April 1997). Woodhead offers a critique of feminist theology for failing to represent the true interests of women through its conformity to modern individualistic ideas of spirituality and its neglect of traditional theological methods materially rooted in communal practices of faithfulness and prayer.

TINA BEATTIE (2005)

FÉNELON, FRANÇOIS (1651–1715), was a French philosopher, theologian, and educator, and Roman Catholic archbishop of Cambrai. Born in the Château de Fénelon in Périgord, François de Salignac de la Mothe Fénelon, an aristocrat by birth and upbringing, spent the first years of his education at home. After the death of his father in 1663, he was sent to study with the Jesuits at the University of Cahors; then, in 1665, he went to Paris, where he studied philosophy and theology at the College of Le Plessis. Finally, probably in 1672, he entered the Seminary of Saint-Sulpice to prepare for the priesthood.

Ordained at the age of twenty-four, Fénelon worked in the parish of Saint-Sulpice from 1675 to 1678. In 1678 he became superior of the Convent of New Catholics (a position he held until 1689), where he strengthened the faith of young women recently converted to the Catholic church. In August 1689 Louis XIV chose him to be private tutor to his grandson, the duke of Burgundy, a post Fénelon held until 1699. In 1693 he was elected a member of the French Academy and in 1695 was nominated archbishop of Cambrai. Fénelon spent the final years of his life as a successful administrator and zealous bishop.

Fénelon's writings concern pedagogy, literature, politics, philosophy, and theology. In his *Traité de l'éducation des filles* (1687), for example, foreshadowing Rousseau's *Émile,* one finds his educational philosophy. His literary ability and political ideas are felicitously woven together in his *Les aventures de Télémaque* (1699), a mythological novel written for the instruction of the dauphin. Here allegory dissimulates the real import of his views. Fénelon depicts the confused ideal of a monarchy at once absolute, aristocratic, and urbane, while condemning indirectly the despotic and bellicose reign of Louis XIV. The views expressed in this novel redounded inevitably to his discredit in the eyes of the king and his loss of favor at court.

It is the controversy over quietism, however, that has weighed most heavily on the memory of Fénelon, making it difficult to give an objective assessment of him. His undulating and generous nature had made him adopt the principle of the "dévotion idéale" professed by Madame Guyon (1648–1717), a mystic Fénelon had met and befriended in 1688: The soul, completely absorbed by the love of God, becomes indifferent to everything, even its own life and salvation. Feeling obliged, however, to justify himself before the public, Fénelon formally disowned the excesses and consequences of quietism in his *L'explication des maximes des saints sur la vie intérieure* (1697). Nevertheless, in 1699 the Holy See decided to condemn twenty-three propositions extracted from this book.

Yet, with his aristocratic cast of mind and his poetic makeup, Fénelon exercised a strong influence on his contemporaries and left a mark on the history of spirituality. Original insofar as he adopted a scale of values that was personal to him, he provided a philosophical justification for his attitude toward spiritual matters by establishing as the basis of his spiritual system two notions directly connected with each other: pure love and indifference, the latter being the psychological state in which pure love is born.

Fénelon's life and works witness to the more human and subtle exigencies of French spirituality. He was aware of his own defects yet was too deeply committed to the world to have the courage to deny it. His troubled and sublime spirit needed more the experience of God and less the life of the intellect; more freedom for the soul, more spontaneity, and less dedication to the rewards of piety.

SEE ALSO Quietism.

BIBLIOGRAPHY

There have been numerous editions of Fénelon's *Œuvres complètes:* Paris, 1810; Versailles, 1820–1830; Paris, 1835; Paris, 1851–1852; and Paris, 1854. For general information about Fénelon, the following two biographies are still useful: Paul Janet's *Fénelon* (Paris, 1892) and Élie Carcassonne's *Fénelon* (Paris, 1946). Janet's book has been translated into English and edited, with introduction, notes, and index, by Victor Leuliette as *Fénelon: His Life and Works* (Port Washington, N.Y., 1970). See also Carcassonne's *État présent des travaux sur Fénelon* (Paris, 1939). For informative articles on Fénelon, see A. Largent's "Fénelon," *Dictionnaire de théologie catholique,* vol. 5 (Paris, 1924), and Louis Cognet's "Fénelon," *Dictionnaire de spiritualité ascétique et mystique,* vol. 5 (Paris, 1964).

E. GERHARD CARROLL (1987)

FERGHUS MAC ROICH. Tradition has it that Ferghus mac Roich was king of the Ulaidh, or Ulstermen, but was driven from his throne by Conchobhar mac Nessa, the king of Ulster, during the momentous events related by the epic *Táin Bó Cuailnge* (The cattle raid of Cuailnge) and other tales. Ferghus went into exile to Cruachain, the court of Ailill and Medhbh of Connacht, and this is why he and his companions were in the Connacht camp when Ailill and Medhbh made their famous incursion into Ulster. An alternative, and probably secondary, explanation for his absence from Ulster is provided by the Old Irish tale *Longes mac nUislenn* (The exile of the sons of Uisliu), which is really the story of the tragic heroine Deirdre: acting on Conchobhar's behalf, Ferghus offers to the Sons of Uisliu safe conduct back from their exile in Scotland, and when Conchobhar slays them despite these assurances, Ferghus wreaks carnage at Emhain Mhacha, capital of the Ulstermen, before going into exile himself.

Both elements of his name suggest physical power: *Ferghus* is a compound word meaning "manly vigor, excellence" and *Roich* (originally disyllabic *Roïch*) is the genitive of *ro-ech* ("great horse"). His virility was proverbial and measured in heptads: he ate seven times as much as an ordinary man and had the strength of seven hundred men; his nose, mouth, and penis were seven fingers in length, and his scrotum as large as a sack of flour; finally, he needed seven women to satisfy him when separated from his wife Flidhais, a goddess who ruled over the beasts of the forest. This is reminiscent of the description of Indra in the *Ṛgveda* (6.46.3) as *sahasramuṣka* ("with the thousand testicles"), an epithet which, as Georges Dumézil remarks, alludes to the *supervirilité* which all peoples freely attribute to warriors and warrior gods (*Heur et malheur du guerrier,* Paris, 1969, p. 64). As late as the nineteenth century the famous Lia Fáil, the standing stone at Tara which in early times was reputed to cry out on contact with the man destined to be king, was known to local people as *bod Fhearghusa* ("the phallus of Ferghus"). It is particularly appropriate, therefore, that the much-mated Medhbh, queen and goddess of sovereignty, whose sexual capacity is a commonplace of the early literature, should have cuckolded her husband Ailill with Ferghus, as recounted in *Táin Bó Cuailnge.*

Ferghus had a famous sword called Caladhbholg (the Irish counterpart of the Welsh Caledvwlch, later to become the Excalibur of Arthurian romance), and with it he lopped off the tops of three hills in the province of Midhe when in the grip of his battle rage. According to T. F. O'Rahilly, this is the lightning sword of the great otherworld deity with whom he identifies Ferghus and other mythic-heroic figures (*Early Irish History and Mythology,* Dublin, 1946, p. 68). In several archaic genealogical poems a number of tributary peoples in the province of Munster are assigned descent from Ferghus, and it is clear that the substance of the tradition embodied in the Ulster saga of *Táin Bó Cuailnge* was already familiar in the southern province in the early seventh century. The name *Ferghus* is borne by several pseudohistorical kings of Emhain Mhacha (the royal center of the province of Ulster), and one of these, Ferghus mac Leide, who is the hero of a submarine adventure, is very probably a doublet of Ferghus mac Roich.

BIBLIOGRAPHY

Further information on Ferghus can be found in Rudolf Thurneysen's *Die irische Helden- und Königsage bis zum siebzehnten Jahrhundert,* 2 vols. (Halle, 1921), the classic study of *Táin Bó Cuailnge.*

PROINSIAS MAC CANA (1987 AND 2005)

FESTIVALS SEE SEASONAL CEREMONIES; WORSHIP AND DEVOTIONAL LIFE

FESTSCHRIFTEN. *Festschrift* or *Festgabe* (plural, *Festschriften, Festgaben*) is the German word for a collection of articles written in honor of a scholar or high-ranking person (poet, politician, etc.) on the occasion of an anniversary (birth, award of doctorate, term of service, or death) or other important event, usually written by colleagues, pupils, or friends of the honoree. A list of publications may also be part of a Festschrift, as well as unpublished articles by the honored person. In addition, it has become customary to provide a picture of the honoree as the frontispiece of the volume. The first German Festschriften were published in the 1840s. Subsequently, the German word was taken over into other languages, although these also developed their own words or expressions for this academic genre: English *Studies in hono(u)r of;* French *Mélanges* or *Hommage;* Italian *Studi in onore di* or *Omaggio*; Russian *Sbornik statej,* etc. While Festschriften for the anniversaries of such institutions as universities or cities may also contribute to academic discussion, this is not necessarily the case with Festschriften for anniversaries of such societies as fire brigades or sports clubs, which became very popular in German-speaking countries. An example of this nonacademic type of commemorative collection would be the Festschrift produced in 1882 for the twentieth anniversary of the *Mitteldeutsche Pferdezucht-Verein* (Central German Horse-Breeding Association).

Hence, the genre of Festschriften is a typical product of nineteenth-century German *Gelehrtenkultur* (culture of the educated), with its peculiar social structure and habits, that took on new characteristics after having been introduced into academic milieus outside Germany and Austria. After World War II, particularly in the 1960s, Festschriften lost much of their former prestige and were often regarded as old-fashioned, but this trend was reversed in the 1990s. Once again it became very fashionable to present Festschriften to older scholars—in fact, to precisely those scholars who had been most opposed to this academic custom when they were students.

Festschriften as Historical Sources. The academic merit of this particular genre is an open question. When the historian Theodor Mommsen received a Festschrift on the occasion of his sixtieth birthday in 1877, he said it would take him months to disprove the nonsense that had been said. Because a Festschrift is an occasion to honor rather than critique, to which friends rather than academic enemies are invited to contribute, and because articles are not usually peer-reviewed, these collections are of mixed academic quality. On the other hand, Festschriften gained a status of their own within academic debate as an appropriate tool in order to call attention to the research of a particular person—at times ironically known only through the Festschrift—and to expand on his or her theories, apply them to other fields, or discuss them in a friendly atmosphere. Festschriften are thus important resources for historians of science because they reflect the contemporary discourse on a given subject and the influence of certain theories on subsequent generations of scholars. In addition, from an anthropological perspective Festschriften tell a lot about the "family relations" within the academic community: Who contributes to a given volume and who does not? Although contingencies are involved in the selection of authors, the field of religious studies—particularly in such small academic communities as those of Germany, the Netherlands, or France—can be described and analyzed according to the names of the contributors to Festschriften.

Examples. Not all major scholars in the broad field of religious studies received Festschriften. In fact, so many lacked a respective volume that the absence of a Festschrift should not be interpreted to their discredit. Eminent scholars in the field who did not receive Festschriften include Johann Jakob Bachofen, Auguste Comte, Henry Corbin, Wilhelm Dilthey, Émile Durkheim, Sir James George Frazer, Jane Ellen Harrison, Lucien Lévy-Bruhl, Bronislaw Malinowski, Robert Ranulph Marett, Marcel Mauss, J. H. Mead, Friedrich Max Müller, Raffaele Pettazoni, Friedrich Schleiermacher, William Ramsey Smith, Nathan Söderblom, Ernst Troeltsch, Victor Turner, and Joachim Wach. Judging from extant Festschriften, however, one can easily find examples of the characteristics mentioned earlier. A Festschrift tells something about the transition of theories from one generation to another; to name but one example, Robin Horton edited a Festschrift for E. E. Evans-Pritchard (1973). That Festschriften may serve as instruments comparable to conference proceedings for putting themes on the scholarly agenda may be exemplified with Gershom Scholem (1967), Carsten Colpe (1991 and 1994), or Antoine Faivre (2001).

When scholars receive more than one Festschrift on different occasions, a comparison of these collections may illuminate progress or changes of interest in their research. The work and impact of Carl Gustav Jung, for instance, is reflected in the five Festschriften dedicated to him between 1935 and 1975, from his sixtieth to his hundredth birthday. The 1945 Festschrift, published as volume 12 of the *Eranos-Jahrbücher,* may be read as an attempt to cope psychologically with the catastrophe of the Second World War. The preface to the volume, written by O. Fröbe-Kapteyn, spoke of an "archetypal situation of transition between ending and beginning, death and rebirth on all fields." Explicitly harking back to the "psychological universe" of the "wisdom of the endlessly gifted antiquity," W. Wili's *Geleitwort* (foreword) presented Jung's archetypal theory as a cure for the "epidemic of sadism" that swept over Germany and its concentration camps, as well as the east and Europe, "as apocalyptic riders," against the "soul-pestilences" of the twentieth century, and against the "terrible force of the neuroses of the politically leading persons." Other Festschriften listed in the collection below likewise reflect their *Zeitgeist* both with regard to the cultural context and the particular scholarly fashions of the time.

See Also Encyclopedias; Reference Works.

Bibliography

A Collection of Major Festschriften

The following overview is intended to provide the reader with examples of the characteristics of Festschriften discussed in the article. It focuses on important figures in the history of religion and well-known contemporary scholars. The honorees are listed in alphabetical order.

Carsten Colpe received two Festschriften: Elsas, Christoph, and Hans G. Kippenberg, eds. *Loyalitätskonflikte in der Religionsgeschichte. Festschrift für Carsten Colpe* (Würzburg, Germany, 1991); and Elsas, Christoph et al., eds. *Tradition und Translation. Zum Problem der interkulturellen Übersetzbarkeit religiöser Phänomene. Festschrift für Carsten Colpe zum 65. Geburtstag* (Berlin and New York, 1994). Mircea Eliade's Festschrift is a rigorous collection of a few articles from a large pool of interested authors: Kitagawa, Joseph M., and Charles H. Long, eds. *Myths and Symbols: Studies in Honor of Mircea Eliade* (Chicago and London, 1969). Edward E. Evans-Pritchard received two Festschriften: Cunnison, Ian, and Wendy James, eds. *Essays in Sudan Ethnography, Presented to Sir Edward Evans-Pritchard* (London, 1972); and

Horton, Robin, and Ruth Finnegan, eds. *Modes of Thought: Essays on Thinking in Western and Non-Western Societies. Collection dedicated to Sir Edward Evans-Pritchard* (London, 1973). The voluminous Festschrift for Antoine Faivre fostered the study of Western esotericism: Caron, Richard, Joscelyn Godwin, Wouter J. Hanegraaff, and Jean-Louis Vieillard-Baron, eds. *Ésotérisme, Gnoses et Imaginaire symbolique. Mélanges offerts à Antoine Faivre* (Leuven, Belgium, 2001). Among the major Festschriften for Sigmund Freud is Alexander, Franz, ed. *Freud in der Gegenwart. Ein Vortragszyklus der Universitäten Frankfurt und Heidelberg zum 100. Geburtstag* (Frankfurt am Main, Germany, 1957). A Festschrift for Friedrich Heiler that clearly reflects his theological agenda was edited by Christel Matthias Schröder: *In Deo omnia unum. Eine Sammlung von Aufsätzen, Friedrich Heiler zum 50. Geburtstage dargebracht* (Munich, Germany, 1942). Karl Hoheisel was also honored with a Festschrift: Hutter, Manfred, et al., eds. *Hairesis. Festschrift für Karl Hoheisel zum 65. Geburtstag* (Münster, Germany, 2002).

William James received two important Festschriften: *Essays, Philosophical and Psychological, in Honor of William James . . . , by His Colleagues at Columbia University* (New York, 1908); and Kallen, Horace Meyer, ed. *In Commemoration of William James, 1842–1942* (New York, 1942). The five Festschriften for C. G. Jung are: Alm, Ivar et al., eds. *Die kulturelle Bedeutung der komplexen Psychologie. Festschrift zum 60. Geburtstag von Carl Gustav Jung* (Berlin, 1935); Fröbe-Kapteyn, Olga, ed. *Studien zum Problem des Archetypischen. Festgabe für C. G. Jung zum siebzigsten Geburtstag 26.7.1945* (Zürich, Switzerland, 1945); Fröbe-Kapteyn, Olga, ed. *Aus der Welt der Urbilder. Sonderband für Carl Gustav Jung zum 75. Geburtstag, 26.7.1950* (Zürich, Switzerland, 1950); C.-G.-Jung-Institut Zürich, ed. *Studien zur analytischen Psychologie Carl Gustav Jungs. Festschrift zum 80. Geburtstag von C. G. Jung.* 2 vols. (Zürich, Switzerland, 1955); Dieckmann, Hans, et al., eds. *Aspekte analytischer Psychologie. Zum 100. Geburtstag von Carl Gustav Jung 1875–1975* (Basel, Switzerland, 1975).

Among the important recent Festschriften is one for Hans G. Kippenberg: Luchesi, Brigitte, and Kocku von Stuckrad, eds. *Religion im kulturellen Diskurs. Festschrift für Hans G. Kippenberg zu seinem 65. Geburtstag / Religion in Cultural Discourse. Essays in Honor of Hans G. Kippenberg on the Occasion of His 65th Birthday* (Berlin and New York, 2004); and one for E. Thomas Lawson: Light, Timothy, and Brian C. Wilson, eds. *Religion as a Human Capacity: A Festschrift in Honor of E. Thomas Lawson* (Leiden, Netherlands, 2004). Gerardus van der Leeuw received a Festschrift that reflected a strong theological commitment: Kooiman, W. J., et al., eds. *Pro regno–pro santuario. Een bundle studies en bijdragen bij de 60. verjaardag van Prof. Dr. Gerardus van der Leeuw* (Nijkerk, Netherlands, 1950). Of interest for religious studies is also a Festschrift for Karl Löwith: Braun, Hermann, and Manfred Riedel, eds. *Natur und Geschichte. Karl Löwith zum 70. Geburtstag* (Stuttgart, Germany, 1967); and one for Johann Maier: Merklein, Helmut, et al., eds. *Bibel in jüdischer und christlicher Tradition. Festschrift für Johann Maier zum 60. Geburtstag* (Frankfurt am Main, Germany, 1993). Gustav Mensching's Festschrift was edited by Rudolf Thomas: *Religion und Religionen. Festschrift für Gustav Mensching zu seinem 65. Geburtstag, dargebracht von Freunden und Kollegen* (Bonn, Germany, 1967).

A typical example of a nineteenth-century Festschrift is that for Theodor Mommsen: *Commentationes philologae in honorem Theodori Mommseni scripserunt amici* (Berlin, 1877). The Festschriften for Rudolf Otto include Frick, Heinrich, ed. *Rudolf-Otto-Festgruß. Aufsätze eines Kollegenkreises zu Rudolf Ottos 60. Geburtstag* (Gotha, Germany, 1931); Frick, Heinrich, ed. *Rudolf-Otto-Ehrung.* 3 vols. (Berlin, 1940); and Benz, Ernst, ed. *Rudolf Otto's Bedeutung für die Religionswissenschaft und die Theologie heute. Zur 100-Jahrfeier seines Geburtstags, 25.9.1969* (Leiden, Netherlands, 1971). Heinrich Rickert also received a Festschrift: Faust, August, ed. *Festgabe für Heinrich Rickert zum 70. Geburtstag* (Buhl, Germany, 1933). Kurt Rudolph's Festschrift influenced the study of Gnosis and Gnosticism: Preißler, Holger, and Hubert Seiwert, eds. *Gnosisforschung und Religionsgeschichte. Festschrift für Kurt Rudolph zum 65. Geburtstag* (Marburg, Germany, 1994).

An important Festschrift for Gershom Scholem was edited by Ephraim E. Urbach and others: *Studies in Mysticism and Religion, Presented to Gershom G. Scholem on His 70th Birthday by Pupils, Colleagues and Friends.* 2 vols. (Jerusalem, 1967). Georg Simmel was honored with a more personal Festschrift: Gassen, Kurt, and Michael Landmann, eds. *Buch des Dankes an Georg Simmel. Briefe, Erinnerungen, Bibliographie. Zu seinem 100. Geburtstag am 1.3.1958* (Berlin, 1958). Edward B. Tylor received a Festschrift late in his career: Balfour, Henry, et al., eds. *Anthropological Essays Presented to Edward Burnett Tylor in Honour of His 75th Birthday, 2.10.1907.* (Oxford, 1907). Max Weber received several Festschriften: Palyi, Melchior, ed. *Hauptprobleme der Soziologie. Erinnerungsgabe für Max Weber.* 2 vols. (Munich, Germany, 1923; König, René, and Johannes Winckelmann, eds. *Max Weber zum Gedächtnis. Materialien und Dokumente zur Bewertung von Werk und Persönlichkeit* (Cologne, Germany, 1963); and Englisch, Karl et al., eds. *Max Weber Gedächtnisschrift der Ludwig-Maximilians-Universität München zur 100. Wiederkehr seines Geburtstags* (Berlin, 1966).

Reference Works about Festschriften

Leistner, Otto. *Internationale Bibliographie der Festschriften / International bibliography of Festschriften.* Osnabrück, Germany, 1976. This resource provides a German and English index of names and subjects.

For the period after 1983, the *Internationale Jahresbibliographie der Festschriften IJBF / International Annual Bibliography of Festschriften,* published by K. G. Saur in Munich, Germany, is the major reference tool. This interdisciplinary database with information about 20,300 international Festschriften and 450,000 contributions is available on CD-ROM and online through some university networks. About a thousand Festschriften comprising twelve thousand articles are added to the indexed references each year. The *IJBF* focuses on European Festschriften in the area of the humanities.

KOCKU VON STUCKRAD (2005)

FETISHISM. The *Oxford English Dictionary* (1893–1897) defines *fetishism* as the "superstition of which . . . the characteristic feature" is "an inanimate object worshipped by savages on account of its supposed inherent magical powers, or as being animated by a spirit." This fetish is distinguished from an idol "in that it is worshipped in its own character, not as the image, symbol, or occasional residence of the deity." The only problem with this definition is that neither fetishism nor the fetish exists as such. There are indeed material objects believed to be imbued with force or power, the nature of which varies with object and culture, and that are used with the intention of achieving particular ends. Consider the list offered by Mesquitela Lima:

> diviners' implements (i.e., the figurines contained in the diviner's basket, most of which are carved from any one of a variety of materials); figurines sculpted in clay or in termite secretion; small dried trees or even parts of a tree, such as roots, twigs, leaves, branches, and fruit; coarsely sculpted tree trunks; small dolls clothed in net; miniature musical instruments or miniature agricultural or hunting implements; a large number of figurines carved in wood, bone, or ivory in the shape of human beings, animals or even abstract forms; horns, nails, or claws, or bits of human or animal skin; small tortoise shells; sacred rocks or minerals; crucifixes, medals, or images used in Christian cults; philters or magic substances and medicines. (Lima, 1987, p. 315)

However, these objects and their use by no means constitute a system or the entirety of any culture's religious practices and beliefs. Moreover Wyatt MacGaffey, in his analysis of Kongo religious practices surrounding what have been considered the exemplary fetish objects known as *minkisi,* has demonstrated the inadequacy of any notion of fetish that entails the personification of material cultic objects. Supplementing Marcel Mauss's dismissal of the ethnographic significance of "fetishism" as "nothing but an immense misunderstanding between two civilizations, the African and the European" (Mauss, 1905–1906, p. 309), MacGaffey placed the ethnographic data against the characteristic components of the fetish as determined by William Pietz, whose analysis of discourses about fetishism is the standard against which contemporary discussions of this topic take their measure (MacGaffey, 1994a). Pietz delineated the four primary attributes of the fetish as:

1. irreducibly material and not representing an immaterial, elsewhere located spirit,
2. fixing previously heterogeneous elements (e.g., an object and a place) into a novel identity,
3. embodying the problem of the nonuniversality of value, and though separate from the body,
4. functioning at times as though it were in control of it. (MacGaffey 1994a; cf. Pietz 1985, 1987, 1988, 1993)

In his studies MacGaffey finds fundamental disjunctions between Kongo *minkisi* and the fetish so defined.

Consequently this article will focus on how the signifier *fetishism* has come to delineate a discursive space in which the often misrecognized attempt is made to mediate difference(s) by means of material objects (or persons). Simultaneous epistemic and value crises are often provoked by persistent contact with otherness. An inadequacy of extant categories and a disproportion of ascribed values distinguish this ongoing encounter and are met by both avowal and disavowal of that difference. The threatened party finds the ever-deferred resolution of these dilemmas by displacing the recognition of difference upon an object that in its material opacity embodies even as it screens the ambiguity. Correspondingly, ambivalent affect is directed at, even as significance is affixed to, the object. Thus localized and materialized, otherness can be marked and mastered while the marking individual or group's identity is rendered the norm. The seemingly incommensurable differences between European and non-European, colonizer and colonized, capitalist and worker, male and female are articulated during contact in terms of oppositions, including religion and nonreligion, science and superstition (the absence of science), rationality and irrationality, spirit and matter, necessity and accident, subject and object, order and chaos, culture and nature, human and animal, public and private.

Since its emergence in the contact zone of European-African encounter, no other signifier in the history of the study of religions has been appropriated by so many secular discourses. This article will follow how fetishism has traversed from mercantile encounter to rationalist anthropology to philosophy to positivist sociology to political economy to sexology to psychoanalysis to aesthetics to postcolonial analysis. During its journey "fetishism" functioned as a camera obscura, projecting an inverted picture of Euro-America upon the screen of a number of persistent others, including the non-Euro-American, the woman, the Jew, and the insane.

The Invention of Fetishism. While the term *fetishism (fétichisme)* was coined in 1760 by Charles de Brosses in his *Du culte des dieux fétiches* (The cult of the fetish gods), the purported practices and beliefs to which the term referred as well as the family of Portuguese words related to *feiticaria* or witchcraft from which it emerged had long been in circulation. Indeed the philological genealogy of *fetishism* in many ways anticipated the series of oppositions the term would eventually mediate. *Feiticaria* finds its roots in the Latin *facticius* (manufactured), which also had the occasional pejorative connotation of artifice or something factitious (without an original). In medieval Christian discourse such objects were associated with the manufactured amulets, images, and potions employed for witchcraft (as opposed to the talismans, remedies, relics, and other sacramental objects given legitimacy by the church) and, in medieval Portuguese, came to be known as *feitiços. Feitiços* were distinguished from *idolos* as witchcraft was from idolatry or more generally as magic was distinguished from those religions—Christianity, Judaism, Islam, and paganism or idolatry—that could found an orderly society. An additional distinction was that *feitiços* were concerned with material bodies rather than souls. In contradistinction to such magical objects, the object of idol worship was the immaterial demon or false god that the idol represented and who acted upon the soul of the worshiper.

As the Portuguese developed a trade zone along the west coast of Africa from what is now Senegal to Angola, *feitiço* rather than *idolo* came to be the dominant Portuguese ascription of the "religious" practices of the cultures encountered in this series of spaces. As trade grew the related pidgin term *fetisso* became affixed by all involved parties to sacramental objects, traded commodities, political emblems, medical preparations, and women's ornaments that circulated among the various populations who peopled these areas of cross-cultural exchange. The travel accounts of sixteenth- and seventeenth-century European traders, Protestant Dutch and English as well as Catholic Portuguese and French, frequently referred to material objects held to be endowed by the African populations with magical powers or animated by spirits. Attribution of religious value by Africans to a wide range of material objects was correlated with their apparent inability to recognize the proper value of the commodities involved in trade with the Europeans as well as their inability to maintain proper distinctions between public and private, male and female, animal and human. Ironically the same anecdotes that illustrated the moral depravity of fetishists depicted anarchic polities ruled exclusively by the principle of interest—projecting upon the other the forces and values that shaped European society. Moreover that the Africans were said to arbitrarily associate these *fetissos* with the accomplishment of some desired end appeared to confirm the European assumption of the Africans' allegedly deficient mental abilities.

By the eighteenth century, as the *fetisso* began its migration from the exclusive reserve of travel literature to the emergent rationalist critique of clericalism and superstition, it was rechristened as the *fétiche* (fetish). The scene shifted from the zone of contact where Europe fashioned itself against its non-European other to the emerging zone where the secular fashioned itself against its religious other. Anecdotes from those travelogues, especially Willem Bosman's *A New and Accurate Description of the Coast of Guinea* (1704) and its analogy of fetish worship with Roman Catholicism, became illustrations of the irrationality and immoral consequences of ascribing supernatural or teleological qualities to material objects rather than recognizing physical and mechanical causality.

Just after mid-century a new term to describe and generalize fetish worship, *fetishism*, emerged with the publication of Charles de Brosses's *Cult of the Fetish Gods*. Fetishism would become the zero degree of the Enlightenment taxonomy of its other, religion. Rather than sui generis, African fetish worship became only the foremost surviving variant of a variety of worldwide practices relating to cult objects: from the biblical Urim and Thummim to Egyptian obelisks to Native American manitous. Fetishism was distinguished from polytheistic idolatry and provided a deeper wedge for cracking open the theological monopoly on the definition of religious origins. From the privilege ascribed to theistic belief and the human-divine relation, a discourse emerged in Bernard Fontanelle and David Hume that located the source of religion in faulty epistemology, childlike intellects, imagination, fear, and desire. Where natural causality would be, there were the gods. With de Brosses, a stage of human and religious development that preceded polytheism was recognized. Neither beliefs in invisible beings nor amorphous nature initiated that development, rather the forces behind the gratification of human desires or the realization of human fears lay in supernaturally endowed "material, terrestrial entities": fetishes (Brosses, 1988, p. 11).

Although in the wake of Brosses's work the primitivity and primordiality of fetishism became a truism, its material and magical dimensions, in contrast to the spiritual and social dimensions of polytheism and the three monotheisms of Christianity, Judaism, and Islam, led to the question whether fetishism indeed represented the original religion or was instead the stage preceding religion. Complicating the theological and philosophical questions over the relationship between the material and the spiritual were the demands of colonialism (and later imperialism). Indigenous religion was a fundamental tool for maintaining control of the colonized. Consequently, as David Chidester argues, "fetish worship" would be characterized as a religion, not as a consequence of "prolonged exposure, increased familiarity, acquired linguistic competence, intercultural dialogue, or participant observation," but as a result of Europeans achieving political and economic control of the particular region (Chidester, 1996, pp. 16–17). The Europeans did not perceive themselves as supplanting some other legitimate sovereign entity, rather European control was imposed upon an anarchic situation ruled by arbitrariness, irrationality, and desire. On a more fundamental level the distinction between order and disorder represented the distinction between the human, defined as the *zoon politikon* (political animal), and the nonhuman, pictured as the demonic or savage that found its confirmation in the distinction between religion and fetishism since, as Ludwig Feuerbach, drawing upon René Descartes and Thomas Hobbes (and before them John Calvin), asserted in the opening of his *Essence of Christianity,* "Religion has its basis in the essential difference between man and the brute" (Feuerbach, 1989, p. 1).

CONTACT, CONQUEST, AND CRISIS: FETISHISM AND THE HUMAN SCIENCES. As a consequence of its delineation and appropriation by French philosophes, fetishism disseminated throughout European philosophic discourse. In his *Religion within the Limits of Reason Alone* (1793) Immanuel Kant analogized clericalism to fetishism in order to distinguish between true moral religion and false religion, between autonomy and heteronomy. Such labeling allowed Kant to discredit his opponents, render them "irrational," without ascribing either evil intent or demonism to them.

> Now the man who does make use of actions, as means, which in themselves contain nothing pleasing to God

> (i.e., nothing moral), in order to earn thereby immediate divine approval of himself and there with the attainment of his desires, labors under the illusion that he possesses an art of bringing about a supernatural effect through wholly natural means. Such attempts we are wont to entitle sorcery. But (since this term carries with it the attendant concept of commerce with the evil principle, whereas the above mentioned attempt can be conceived to be undertaken, through misunderstanding, with good moral intent) we desire to use in place of it the word fetishism, familiar in other connections. (Kant, 1960, p. 165)

By extending materiality from particular objects to all means, fetishism, or "fetish-faith," came to extend beyond the borders of Africa to encompass everything in the realm of religion—including, in a clear allusion to Moses Mendelssohn's *Jerusalem* (1783), the Jews—except for "purely moral" religion (Kant, 1960, p. 181–182).

G. W. F. Hegel, by contrast, limited the extent of fetishism to sub-Saharan Africa, where it came to exemplify the historical development or lack thereof of a continent and its peoples. Fetishism was emblematic of the African character, which

> is difficult to comprehend, because it is so totally different from our own culture, and so remote and alien in relation to our own mode of consciousness. We must forget all the categories which are fundamental to our own spiritual life, i.e. the forms under which we normally subsume the data which confront us; the difficulty here is that our customary preconceptions will still inevitably intrude in all out deliberations. (Hegel, 1975, p. 176)

The people characterized by fetishism were outside history and substantial objectivity, outside God and morality; they were ruled by caprice, by the arbitrary rule of the individual projected outward onto a misrecognized natural form. This religion of "sensuous arbitrariness" was the lowest form of religion, immediate religion. If religion it was: "A fetish of this kind has no independent existence as an object of religion, and even less as a work of art. It is merely an artifact which expresses the arbitrary will of its creator, and which always remains in his hands" (Hegel, 1975, pp. 190, 181). This debasement of consciousness mirrored the debasement of social life: fetishism was one with cannibalism and slavery. Fetishism embodied the origin that future development would disavow; it was the threshold moment when humanity separated itself from bare life, from animal nature.

Though Samuel Taylor Coleridge analogized fetishism with vulgar empiricism, the proponent of scientific positivism Auguste Comte would determine it to be the first developmental stage of human intelligence and world history. In his *Course in Positive Philosophy* (1830–1842) Comte posited three universal stages of human development—theology, metaphysics, and science (scientific positivism)—with the first, the age of theology, itself assuming a triadic structure: fetishism, polytheism, monotheism. For Comte, in the stage of fetishism "primitive man" endows all external objects with agency and therefore rises above sheer animal inertia. While Comte later reevaluated "fetishism," or rather "pure fetishism," as a necessary component of his new positivist religion of humanity, his implicitly (r)evolutionary scheme was most influential. While the primacy he ascribed to fetishism as the first religion (evolving from a primal atheism) was asserted by John Lubbock in his *Origin of Civilisation and the Primitive Condition of Man* (1870) and by representatives of the German school of ethnopsychology (*Völkerpsychologie*) among others, its primordial status was contested by animism, animatism, totemism, *Urmonotheismus* (primal monotheism), and other claimants.

In the 1840s Brosses's work not only influenced Comte's positivist musings, it was also picked up and excerpted by the young Karl Marx, who was in the midst of an extensive ethnographic reading program that also included other discussions of fetishism by Karl Böttiger and Benjamin Constant. These early studies of what Marx called "the religion of sensuous desire" were soon relocated from the colonial periphery to a metropole itself divided into secular and religious spheres as well as into exploiting capitalist and exploited proletariat classes. Marx began his analysis of value in contemporary capitalism in the first volume of *Capital* with a discussion of the fetishism of commodities: that which was viewed as most primitive came to characterize the seat of civilization, and that which was viewed as the most secular of activities—political economy—was unveiled as the religion of everyday life. In a dialectically materialist appropriation of Feuerbach's theory of religion, the value borne by the fetishized commodity was the culmination of the alienation and objectification of human labor. In contrast to Marx's earlier construction, fetishism, as the fetishism of commodities, is directed at "a thing which transcends sensuousness." With the circulation of commodities, "the definite social relation between men themselves . . . assumes here, for them, the fantastic form of a relation between things" (Marx, 1977, pp. 163, 165). As in the fetishism described in his early readings, Marx analogizes, "The products of the human brain appear as autonomous figures endowed with a life of their own, which enter into relations both with each other and with the human race" (Marx, 1977, p. 165). Even as it expropriates use value from the fetishist other, capital reproduces the misrecognitions that it ascribes to that other.

Just as the fetish had come to figure and facilitate the debasement of social life—whether in the form of slavery according to Hegel or proletarianization for Marx—and of society-sustaining morality, so it became associated with the fears of degeneration that haunted the Europeans of the last decades of the nineteenth century. In a France that was experiencing a decline in both its colonial reach and its European position, the perceived source of the threatening physical and moral debilitation and consequent devirilization and depopulation, of cultural crises of national, sexual, and gender difference, was sexual perversion. The psychiatrist Alfred Binet

(1887) gave the cause of individual and national decay a name: fetishism. Like the people under French colonial domination, French men were seeking the satisfaction of their sensuous desires not by the real (here: "natural" acts of genital sexuality) but by fixing their attention upon objects (or body parts) whose value accrued from some past accidental encounter. Fetishism was characteristic of a perverse predisposition, just as Hegel had suggested that the fetishistic behavior of Africans was inherent to their character. Yet even as the fetish was displaced from the religious to the sexual, Binet felt compelled to analogize different levels of fetishism with those other religious stages with which fetishism had previously been contrasted, polytheism and monotheism. He compared normal love, which is composed of a myriad of fetishistic excitations, with polytheism and fetishism, previously associated with the base of the pyramid of religious forms, in its most singular and perverted form with monotheism, the pinnacle. In a world gone upside down, the civilized were going native. Within four years after the publication of Binet's 1887 "Le fétichisme dans l'amour" (Fetishism in Love), the authoritative compendia of sexual pathology, Richard Krafft-Ebing's *Psychopathis Sexualis* declared fetishism the general form of sexual pathology.

Unlike totemism, fetishism came under Sigmund Freud's scrutiny in his analyses of sexuality and not of the genesis of religion. Instead of the perception of fetishism as the sign of a crisis of difference, the degeneration feared by the French medical community, such a crisis was its source: the little boy's encounter with sexual difference disrupting his narcissistic enjoyment of an undifferentiated, self-contained world. According to Freud, the discovery that women do not have penises leads the little boy to fear for his own. Fetishistic object choice—a symbolic substitute for the mother's (nonexistent) penis—is one way by which the boy mediates his desire to elide difference (and its feared causes and consequences) with the actuality of that difference; the mother's castration is both disavowed and affirmed. With the crisis surmounted, the boy not only assumes a gendered and sexualized identity, he is inserted into the social order.

As psychoanalytic and materialist analyses interpenetrated, most influentially with Walter Benjamin's criticism of the work of art and the political symbol in which "traces of the fetishist" are at play in the object's "aura" and "authenticity," the discourse of fetishism became a prime weapon in the critical armory of cultural studies (Benjamin, 1969, p. 244). With the later admixture of postcolonial analysis to the phantasmagoric study of fetishism, what went around came around. The discourses about the colonized and dominated other, including those about the (non)religion of fetishism, were recognized as themselves fetishistic attempts to mediate the possibly incompatible differences between social and cultural forms. The cultural analyst Homi Bhabha read the racial stereotype in its multiple and contradictory shapes of colonial discourse in terms of fetishism. As extended by Jay Geller and others, such as Anne McClintock, the colonial stereotype often entailed the Euro-Americans' discursive fixation upon a part of the other's body. The fixated-upon body part was often one that had been subjected to some discipline, practice, or technique: the circumcised penis, the bound foot, tattooed skin. This overvalued mark or member uncannily conjoined the natural and the cultural. This ambiguous conjunction of two (culturally) differentiated orders of being contributed to both the fascination and the horror evoked by such body techniques. Further, through such corporeal metonymies, discourses in which historical difference was naturalized as race and in which natural difference was figured by sex combined to construct the ethnic, gender, and sexual identity of the other. These fetishistic constructs provided symbolic substitutes for and objectified representations of the otherness—both the indigenous heterogeneous populations of modern Euro-American society and the different peoples contacted in colonial expansion—which undermined the narcissistic phantasy of Euro-American wholeness, of autonomy and dominance.

In sum, fetishism has come to signify the apotropaically monumentalized negotiations at the internal and external borders of culture. That is, it signifies the stuff that helps one think (or more likely misrecognize) the alienations, ambiguities, and contradictions that make up everyday life.

See Also Transculturation and Religion.

Bibliography

Benjamin, Walter. "The Work of Art in the Age of Mechanical Reproduction." In *Illuminations*, edited by Hannah Arendt, pp. 217–251. New York, 1969.

Bhabha, Homi K. "The Other Question: Stereotype, Discrimination, and the Discourse of Colonialism." In *The Location of Culture*, pp. 66–84. New York, 1994.

Binet, Alfred. "Le fétichisme dans l'amour." *Revue philosophique de la France et de l'étranger* 24 (1887): 143–167, 252–274.

Bosman, Willem. *A New and Accurate Description of the Coast of Guinea* (1704). London, 1967.

Brosses, Charles de. *Du culte des dieux fétiches* (1760). Paris, 1988.

Chidester, David. *Savage Systems: Colonialism and Comparative Religion in Southern Africa* Charlottesville, Va., 1996.

Comte, Auguste. *The Positive Philosophy* (1830). New York, 1974.

Feuerbach, Ludwig. *The Essence of Christianity* (1843), translated by George Eliot. Buffalo, N.Y., 1989.

Freud, Sigmund. *Three Essays on the Theory of Sexuality* (1905). In *The Standard Edition of the Complete Psychological Works of Sigmund Freud*, vol. 7, translated by James Strachey, pp. 123–243. London, 1953–1972.

Freud, Sigmund. "Fetishism" (1927). In *The Standard Edition of the Complete Psychological Works of Sigmund Freud*, vol. 21, translated by James Strachey, pp. 149–157. London, 1953–1972.

Geller, Jay. "*Judenzopf/ Chinesenzopf*: Of Jews and Queues." *positions* 2 (1994): 500–537.

Hegel, Georg Wilhelm Friedrich. In *Lectures on the Philosophy of World History, Introduction, Reason in History* (1830). Translated by H. B. Nisbet. Cambridge, U.K., 1975.

Hegel, Georg Wilhelm Friedrich. *Lectures on the Philosophy of Religion* (1824–1831). Edited by Peter C. Hodgson. Berkeley, Calif., 1988.

Kant, Immanuel. *Religion within the Limits of Reason Alone* (1793). New York, 1960.

Lima, Mesquitela. "Fetishism." In *The Encyclopedia of Religion*, vol. 5, edited by Mircea Eliade, pp. 314–317. New York, 1987.

Lubbock, John. *The Origin of Civilisation and the Primitive Condition of Man.* London, 1870.

MacGaffey, Wyatt. "African Objects and the Idea of Fetish." *RES* 25 (1994a): 123–131.

MacGaffey, Wyatt. "Dialogues of the Deaf: Europeans on the Atlantic Coast of Africa." In *Implicit Understandings: Observing, Reporting, and Reflecting on the Encounters between Europeans and Other Peoples in the Early Modern Era*, edited by Stuart B. Schwartz, pp. 249–267. Cambridge, U.K., 1994b.

Marx, Karl. *Capital: A Critique of Political Economy.* Vol. 1: *The Process of Capitalist Production* (1867). New York, 1977.

Mauss, Marcel. Review of R. E. Dennett, *At the Back of the Black Man's Mind. L'année sociologique* 10 (1905–1906): 305–311.

Mauss, Marcel. "L'art et le myth d'après M. Wundt." *Revue philosophique de la France et de l'étranger* 66 (1908): 48–78.

McClintock, Anne. *Imperial Leather: Race, Gender, and Sexuality in the Colonial Contest.* New York, 1995.

Nye, Robert A. "The Medical Origins of Sexual Fetisism." In *Fetishism as Cultural Discourse*, edited by Emily Apter and William Pietz, pp. 13–30. Ithaca, N.Y., 1993.

Pietz, William. "The Problem of the Fetish, I–IIIa." *RES* 9, 13, 16 (1985, 1987, 1988): 5–17, 23–46, 105–124.

Pietz, William. "Fetishism and Materialism: The Limits of Theory in Marx." In *Fetishism as Cultural Discourse*, edited by Emily Apter and William Pietz, pp. 119–151. Ithaca, N.Y., 1993.

JAY GELLER (2005)

FEUERBACH, LUDWIG (1804–1872), German humanistic philosopher of religion and influential spokesman for the Young Hegelians. Born into a gifted Bavarian family, Ludwig Andreas Feuerbach studied theology at the University of Heidelberg before transferring to Berlin, where he became an enthusiastic convert to Hegelianism. In 1828 he completed his doctoral work at the University of Erlangen, where he remained as a docent until he was denied tenure, having been identified as the author of the anonymously published book *Thoughts on Death and Immortality.* In it he argued that the Christian doctrine of personal immortality was a form of egoism incompatible with a belief in the Absolute as infinite love. The book was especially offensive because of the sarcastic epigrams about pietistic Christianity appended to the text. Never again was he offered an academic position.

In 1837 Feuerbach married Bertha Löw, and the income from a porcelain factory of which she was part owner supported him until it went bankrupt in 1860. Although in the early 1830s he contributed to the principal journal of the Young Hegelians, the *Hallische Jahrbücher für deutsche Wissenschaft und Kunst,* he shunned political activity and, except for a brief appearance in the Frankfurt Assembly in 1848, lived in studious seclusion in Bruckberg. He became famous in the early 1840s for his atheistic interpretation of religion in *The Essence of Christianity* (1841), as well as for his attacks on Hegelian philosophy in two monographs, *Vorläufige Thesen zur Reform der Philosophie* and *Grundsätze der Philosophie der Zukunft,* which influenced the young Karl Marx. Although Feuerbach returned again and again to the interpretation of religion, his later writings were relatively ignored. He maintained a prolific correspondence with friends all over Europe and America, and when the porcelain factory went bankrupt, he and his wife were sustained by the generosity of friends. When the social democratic press reported that he had suffered a stroke in 1870, contributions poured in from Europe and the United States. He died in Nuremberg in 1872.

Feuerbach's *Essence of Christianity* can best be understood against the background of his two fundamental criticisms of Hegel's speculative idealism. The first was of Hegel's basic tendency to treat abstract predicates—reason, thought, consciousness, and being—as entities. For example, having established that thought was of the essence of humanity, Hegel then transformed this predicate into a metaphysical entity, a subject. Thus whatever truth there was in Hegel's thought could be appropriated by inverting once again the subject and the predicate, so as to make thinking and consciousness the predicates of existing individuals. The second criticism of Hegel concerned his preoccupation with thought in contrast to the actual sensuous existence of human beings. Hegel, together with classical philosophy generally, believed that the ultimate criteria of the real is its capability of being thought. For Feuerbach, the real is that which offers resistance to the entire sensuous being of the person—to sight, feeling, even love. Consequently, human existence is existence with others—it is communal.

Feuerbach's inversion of Hegel's basic metaphysical vision informs *The Essence of Christianity.* If Hegel regarded nature and history as the self-objectification of the Absolute, Feuerbach regarded God, the Absolute, as the reification of the essential predicates of human existence: reason, feeling, and love. The idea of God is the idea of the species characteristics of humankind involuntarily and unconsciously projected as an object of thought and worship. God is, so to speak, an acoustical illusion of consciousness. Hence the history of religions, of which Christianity is the culmination, is the childlike, collective dream of humanity in which it worships and contemplates its own essential nature. Just as Hegel argued that the Absolute must become reconciled with its alienated objectifications (the finite), so too Feuerbach argued that human well-being depends on the reappropriation of the real content contained in the alienated idea of God. The inner meaning of Christian theology is anthropology.

The first part of *The Essence of Christianity* attempts to show that all the major Christian doctrines—especially those of God and the incarnation—can best be understood as anthropology. The second part is more negative, seeking to establish that Christian theology is full of contradictions if these human predicates are attributed to a single, metaphysical being.

Feuerbach's book is still regarded by many as one of the seminal works of the nineteenth century and the first comprehensive projection theory of religion. Religion is not dismissed merely as superstitious belief, but seen as a necessary stage in the development of human self-consciousness. Moreover, the book is the first systematic attempt to develop a body of principles for interpreting Christian doctrine in its entirety. Christian doctrines are profound insights when taken as anthropological truths, but a mass of contradictions when taken as objective theological propositions.

Feuerbach modified his theory of religion in a small book, *The Essence of Religion* (1845), which in turn was amplified in *Lectures on the Essence of Religion* (1848). In these books he emphasized the role of external nature in the development of the religious consciousness, as well as the causal role played by wishes, needs, instincts, and desires. The basic drive of the self to preserve and develop all its powers (*Egoismus*) is said to be the hidden subjective cause of religion, while nature, falsified by the imagination, is said to be its objective ground.

Feuerbach stated that his first and last thoughts were about religion, and he turned to it once again in *Theogonie,* first published in 1857 and again, with a slightly altered title, in 1866. This work attempts to explain morality, culture, and religion in terms of a basic drive for happiness (*Glückseligkeitstrieb*), with arguments drawn from classical Greek, Hebraic, and early Christian sources. The gods are said to be the reified wishes of humankind. Since all wishes are fraught with a haunting sense of their contingency and possible failure, the imagination seizes upon the idea of a being that is not subject to limitation and death. Although Feuerbach regarded this book as his finest, it has generally been ignored.

BIBLIOGRAPHY

A new critical edition of Feuerbach's works, *Gesammelte Werke,* 20 vols. (Berlin, 1967–), is under the editorship of Werner Schuffenhauer; indispensable for serious scholarship, it contains the textual variations of all editions of Feuerbach's major works. It supplants Wilhelm Bolin and Friedrich Jodl's edition, *Sämtliche Werke,* 10 vols. (Stuttgart, 1903–1911), which was reissued in facsimile in 1960–1964 under the editorship of H.-M. Sass. In the facsimile edition, two more volumes were added. The eleventh contains a photographic facsimile of Feuerbach's inauguration dissertation of 1828 (in Latin), his *Thoughts on Death and Immortality* (1830), and an extensive bibliography of all works on Feuerbach in German between 1833 and 1961. The twelve (double) volumes contain Sass's expanded edition of Bolin's *Selected Correspondence from and to Ludwig Feuerbach,* together with some of Bolin's memoirs.

Six of Feuerbach's works have been translated into English: (1) *Thoughts on Death and Immortality,* translated with introduction and notes by James A. Massey (Berkeley, 1980); (2) *The Essence of Christianity,* the famous translation by George Eliot of the second German edition (New York, 1957); (3) *The Essence of Faith According to Luther,* translated with a brief but suggestive introduction by Melvin Cherno (New York, 1967); (4) *Principles of the Philosophy of the Future* (Indianapolis, 1966), which contains a long introduction by the translator, Manfred H. Vogel, exploring Feuerbach's philosophy of religion and his relationship to Hegel; (5) *Lectures on the Essence of Religion* (New York, 1967), a translation by Ralph Manheim based on the Bolin-Jodl version of 1908 and not the text Feuerbach himself published; and (6) *The Essence of Religion* (New York, 1873), an abridged edition translated by Alexander Loos, long out of print.

There are four scholarly treatments of Feuerbach in English: Van A. Harvey, *Feuerbach and the Interpretation of Religion,* (Cambridge, 1995); Larry Johnston, *Between Transcendence and Nihilism,* (New York, 1995); Marx W. Wartofsky, *Feuerbach* (New York, 1977); and Charles A. Wilson *Feuerbach and the Search for Otherness,* (New York, 1989). A useful introduction is Eugene Kamenka's *The Philosophy of Ludwig Feuerbach* (New York, 1970). There are many important books about Feuerbach in German. Still indispensable is Simon Rawidowicz's *Ludwig Feuerbachs Philosophie: Ursprung und Schicksal* (1931; reprint, Berlin, 1964). Also recommended is Michael von Gagern, *Ludwig Feuerbach. Philosophie und Religionskritik* (Munich and Salzburg, 1970).

VAN A. HARVEY (1987 AND 2005)

FICHTE, JOHANN GOTTLIEB (1762–1814), was a German Idealist philosopher and religious thinker. Usually remembered mainly for his part in the development of German Idealism from Kant to Hegel and for his contribution to the rise of German national consciousness, Fichte is also an important figure in European religious thought at the end of the Enlightenment. Born in Rammenau (Lausitz), he enrolled in the University of Jena as a student of theology when he was eighteen. During his studies and a subsequent period as a private tutor in Zurich, he was apparently unacquainted with Kant's philosophy and seems to have been a determinist who admired Spinoza. Returning to Leipzig in 1790, he began a study of Kant that led to his conversion to Kantian practical philosophy. His fragmentary "Aphorismen über Religion und Deismus," written at this time, reveals his concern with the tension between simple Christian piety and philosophical speculation.

A fateful turn in Fichte's life and career came in 1791, when he traveled to Königsberg to meet Kant. Hoping to attract the master's attention, Fichte set out to write his own letter of introduction in the form of a Kantian-style "critique of revelation." When financial hardship cut short his stay in Königsberg, Fichte asked Kant for a loan to finance his return to Leipzig but got instead an offer to arrange publication of Fichte's manuscript with Kant's own publisher. Delayed for a time by the Prussian state censor, Fichte's *Attempt at a Critique of All Revelation* made its debut at the Leipzig Easter Fair in 1792 under puzzling circumstances. The publisher, perhaps deliberately, omitted both the author's name and his signed preface. The book was widely assumed to be Kant's long-awaited work on religion and received laudatory reviews in the leading journals. When Kant announced the true authorship, Fichte became an important philosopher virtually overnight. The book appeared in a revised second edition the following year, with Fichte's name on the title page, and in 1794 he was appointed to a chair of philosophy in Jena.

Like Kant's *Religion within the Limits of Reason Alone* (published a year later), Fichte's *Critique of All Revelation* argues that a valid revelation must conform to the moral law, which is purely an internal concern of reason. Fichte maintains that a revelation in external nature is nevertheless possible because some people are so enmeshed in the sensuous that God can advance the moral law only by presenting it in sensuous terms. When Fichte published his own Idealist system in 1794, titled *Wissenschaftslehre* (Science of knowledge), he abandoned his explicit dependence on Kant's philosophy while claiming to remain loyal to its fundamental aims. By giving up the Kantian "thing-in-itself" (*Ding an sich*), Fichte overcomes the duality of theoretical and practical, deriving all knowing from the activity of the transcendental ego (*das Ich*). He thereby inaugurates the transformation of Kant's critical philosophy, which culminates in the absolute Idealism of Schelling and Hegel. Fichte's essay on the divine governance of the world, published in 1798, led to the famous Atheism Controversy, which resulted in the loss of his position in Jena and his move to Berlin. Fichte's religious position at this time could be more accurately described as ethical pantheism than as atheism, for he equated the human inner sense of the moral law with God's governance of the world. Convicted of teaching "atheism," he was dismissed from the University of Jena in 1799.

During the last period of his life in Berlin, Fichte developed his political and economic views in the *Speeches to the German Nation,* while continuing to revise and develop his *Wissenschaftslehre* in lectures and in print. Ironically, the man who lost his position for being an atheist moved in an increasingly mystical and theosophical direction in his later years.

Fichte died in 1814 of a fever caught from his wife, who was nursing victims of an epidemic. His writings exerted a continuing influence not only on philosophers but also on theologians, including Friedrich Schleiermacher. Fichte stands as a Janus figure between the religious rationalism of the Enlightenment, which he embraced in his youth, and the new currents of Idealist and Romantic thought, to which he contributed original impulses.

BIBLIOGRAPHY

Works by Fichte

The standard and most accessible edition of Fichte's works is *Johann Gottlieb Fichte's sämmtliche Werke,* 8 vols., edited by J. H. Fichte (1845–1846; reprint, Berlin 1971); the writings on religion make up volume 5. A critical edition is being published as the *J. G. Fichte-Gesamtausgabe der Bayerischen Akademie der Wissenschaften,* edited by Reinhard Lauth and Hans Jacob (Stuttgart, 1964–). I have translated *Versuch einer Kritik aller Offenbarung,* 2d ed. (Königsberg, 1793), as *Attempt at a Critique of All Revelation* (Cambridge, 1978), with an introduction and a bibliography of primary and secondary works.

Works about Fichte

An insightful discussion of Fichte's importance for Christian thought is contained in volume 4 of Emanuel Hirsch's *Geschichte der neuern evangelischen Theologie,* 5 vols. (Gütersloh, 1949). Wolfgang Ritzel traces the development of Fichte's religious thought through his entire career in *Fichtes Religionsphilosophie,* "Forschungen zur Kirchen- und Geistesgeschichte," vol. 5 (Stuttgart, 1956).

Garrett Green (1987)

FICINO, MARSILIO

FICINO, MARSILIO (1433–1499), was the most eminent philosopher of the Renaissance. Ficino employed Neoplatonism, the characteristic form of Renaissance philosophy, as a support for Christianity. Cosimo de' Medici, impressed with Ficino's precosity, gave him the opportunity to learn Greek and presented him with his country house at Florence, the Villa Careggi, where Ficino presided over his "Platonic academy."

Ficino edited the complete works of Plato, translated Plato's *Dialogues,* wrote a commentary on the *Symposium,* and edited and translated various works of Neoplatonists such as Plotinus (the *Enneads*), Proclus, Iamblichus, Porphyry, and Dionysius the Areopagite. He also translated from Greek to Latin various second- and third-century mystical and gnostic texts (*Poimandres*) ascribed to Hermes Trismegistos.

In 1473, after an extended period of melancholy, Ficino became a priest. His own best-known works are *On the Christian Religion* and *Platonic Theology,* the latter an elaborate statement of his Christianized Neoplatonic philosophy. Ficino's "pious philosophy" or "learned religion" presupposed an epistemology of poesy and faith. Divine poetry and allegory serve as a veil for true religion, for the rhapsodic and the mystical express religious truth, which cannot be expressed by simple intellectual formulas. A religious syncretist and universalist, Ficino believed that truth has been transmitted through a long tradition from the ancient philosophers and that wisdom has been revealed in many forms. Plato and the Neoplatonists, he believed, encompassed in their thought all the elements of the "ancient philosophy of the gentiles." Ficino envisioned everything within the cosmos as a great hierarchy of being. The One (God) is the absolute and uncontradicted original essence prior to the plurality of finite things, the ultimate unity of all things. The lesser orders are brought into being by emanations proceeding from the One. The way of ascent to the eternal One moves from bodies, through qualities, souls, and heavenly intelligences, with humanity at the center of this great chain of being, for humans are bound to the world of matter by their bodies and linked to the realm of the spirit by their souls. Humanity is assured of its own divinity, since God is immanent in humans through emanation. Ficino added a Christian patina to this Neoplatonic theodicy by identifying the demiurge, or intermediary, between the One and the subdivided spiritual and material world with the divine Logos, Christ, through whom the world was made and who "became flesh and dwelt among us." The church through dogma and sacrament keeps its people in touch with the spiritual world. Someday the immortal human soul, freed from the prison house of the body, will enjoy the beatific vision of God without mediation.

All parts of the universe, Ficino taught in his treatise *On Light,* are held together by bonds of sympathetic love. The highest form of love, Platonic love, moves the true lover to love another for the sake of God. This love guides humanity in its choice of good over evil and of the beautiful over the unlovely. Ficino's close association of goodness and truth with beauty appealed to the aesthetic sense of the Renaissance and influenced literature and art as well as philosophy and theology.

BIBLIOGRAPHY

Ficino's works have been published as *Opera omnia* (1576), 2 vols. (Turin, 1959), and *Supplementum Ficinianum,* 2 vols., edited by Paul O. Kristeller (Florence, 1937). See also *The Letters of Marsilio Ficino,* 3 vols. (London, 1975–1981). On his thought, the most comprehensive study available in English is Kristeller's *The Philosophy of Marsilio Ficino* (1943; reprint, Gloucester, Mass., 1964). For a brief introduction to his thought, one may turn to Kristeller's *Eight Philosophers of the Italian Renaissance* (Stanford, Calif., 1964), pp. 37–53, and *The Renaissance Philosophy of Man,* edited by Ernst Cassirer et al. (Chicago, 1948), pp. 185–212. For the larger picture of Neoplatonism and its influence, see Nesca A. Robb's *Neoplatonism of the Italian Renaissance* (1935; reprint, New York, 1968).

LEWIS W. SPITZ (1987)

FICTION

This entry consists of the following articles:

FICTION: HISTORY OF THE NOVEL

The novel has long been considered a literary form existing apart from religion, even if religion as social and moral fact may enter into the lives of its characters from time to time. The belief that the novel, our term for a lengthy work of fiction in prose, is solely the product of the period currently (if unhappily) labeled "Early Modern" has helped to sustain the belief that the novel is a triumphantly modern and secular form of literature. We dwell on authorship and prose style, but ignore earlier problematic points of development, including the eventual advent of the author as an individual "maker" instead of inspired recipient of divine information (see Finkelberg, 1998); in modern literature departments we rarely pause to inquire into the rise of prose itself as a significant and perhaps intrinsically democratic medium (see Goldhill, 2002).

THE HISTORY OF THE NOVEL AND ITS HISTORIANS.

Claude de Saumaise. The English history of the novel, born in the eighteenth century and placing its conception and birth in that century, flew in the face of another history composed by scholars on the Continent. The noted scholar and political theorist Claude de Saumaise (Claudius Salmasius; 1588–1653) in 1640 proposes a line of transmission in succinct prefatory essays to his edition of the Greek text of Achilles Tatius's novel, here presented as *Erotikon, sive de Clitophontis et Levkippes Amoribus* (Erotic stories, or the Loves of Kleitophon and Leukippe). In his dedicatory *Praefatio* and the address *Ad Lectorem* (To the reader) Salmasius tacitly picks up a suggestion made by Miguel de Cervantes (1547–1616), when the Spanish novelist's unnamed frame-narrator of *Don Quixote* describes the finding of the mysterious manuscript written in Arabic by Cide Hamete Benengeli, for which he must find a (Muslim) Arab-speaking translator, although officially there are no such persons left in Spain after the ethnic cleansing of the Catholic kings. (The initial act of censorship is massacre and expulsion.) Salmasius proposes that the novel's origins lie in the East, "The Persians first affected this kind of amorous literature. . . . You will not find it hard to believe that of old they introduced the beginning [*originem*] of Milesian fables in Asia [i.e., Asia Minor] which they ruled. Certainly they gave to the Arabs the fashion of this same kind of writing and the genius for it. The Arabs then transmitted it to the Spanish. From the Spanish we Gauls in turn took it, and from them indeed it also went elsewhere."

Salmasius traces a clear line of transmission: antique fiction comes from the Persians into Asia Minor and thence into Greek and Roman writings; modern European prose fiction derives from Arabic fiction already influenced by Persians and Greeks and then transmitted through the Moors to Spain and thence to the rest of Europe.

Pierre-Daniel Huet. A few years after Salmasius succinctly propounded this theory, Bishop Pierre-Daniel Huet (1630–1721) wrote his *Traité de l'origine des romans.* This important work was first published in 1670 as a preface to

Zayde, a novel about an Oriental woman written by a woman, though issued under the name of a male writer (Segrais). Huet's treatise (in the form of a letter to Segrais, a respectable male-male discussion) was soon reprinted and amplified as a book. Huet argues that in composing histories of this kind of writing we have stuck too close to home, "It is neither in Provence nor in Spain, as many believe, that we must hope to find the first beginnings of this agreeable amusement of good idle folk [*cet agréable amusement des honnestes paresseux*]; we must go to seek them in the most distant countries and in the most remote antiquity."

Huet's history makes the novel an arena of cultural anxiety and contestation. By 1674 Nicolas Boileau (1636–1711) was forced to take into account the implications of Huet's *Traité*. Boileau initiated the brilliant strategy of attacking the novel not only as a feminine and effeminating kind of literature, but also as a "bourgeois" form. For Huet, the novel existed before such modern social or literary classifications, springing as it does from the deep past and from diverse sources in folk traditions and various aristocratic cultures. It was an international—one could say "multicultural"—form of literature. The English definers of the novel tradition were trying to wrest the form from Huet and from contamination by the alien. Their strategy entails ignoring Continental fiction almost entirely at least, until after the "rise" of the novels of Daniel Defoe (1660–1731), Samuel Richardson (1689–1761), and Henry Fielding (1707–1754) ensured the establishment of the "new" form as of English growth. Such a story of the novel has been freshly established in Ian Watt's *The Rise of the Novel: Studies in Defoe, Richardson, and Fielding* (1957). In this English-manufactured account, only *Don Quixote* of all Continental works is allowed a place. Unlike Salmasius and Huet, English claimants to the invention of the novel do not see in *Don Quixote* a tribute to the Oriental sources of this literature, but rather a handy repudiation of all Continental forms of novelistic fiction. *Don Quixote* becomes an honorary British fiction, a herald of the realistic and commonsensical novel that remained for the English to invent and perfect. (Too bad for Cervantes that such an account made it necessary to suppress all reference to his last work, *Persiles y Sigismunda*, a prose romance manifesting the devices and tropes that Cervantes is supposed to have killed off.)

Development of the term *novel*. The word *novel* is a relatively modern invention; in the sixteenth and seventeenth centuries the term was in use but functioning much like our term *novella*, referring to a short fiction. A long fiction in prose, like long fictions in poetic narration, was termed a *romance*; the word *romance* indicated simply and basically a work written in the vernacular (one of the romance languages, such as French, Italian, or Spanish) and had no negative significance—save to those who disliked all made-up stories. To this day, Continental languages have stubbornly adhered to the basic terms *il romanzo* (Italian), *le roman* (French), and *der roman* (German). For the English the term became suspect by the mid-eighteenth century, and the term *history* was more generally employed to describe a full-length work of prose fiction, for example, Fielding's *The History of Tom Jones, a Foundling*. This influenced Continental usage; see, for example, Antoine-François Prévost d'Exiles's (1697–1763) *L'Histoire d'une Grecque moderne*.

Ancient Novels. We must admit, along with Huet, that the novel in the West has much longer and less certainly "Western" roots. Certain prose fictions by authors writing in Greek and Latin from about the first century BCE to the third century CE continued to influence Western literature both in the Byzantine regions and in Roman Europe. Their influence was renewed in the Age of Print; some of these novels were among the earliest fictional works to be printed, such as *Asinus aureus* (The golden ass) by the second-century author known as Apuleius (c. 124–c. 170), first printed in 1469. Many of these works, rendered familiar to readers of the Renaissance, acted as decided influences on the development of new fictions in the vernacular, including novelists writing in English in the eighteenth century and later. The influence of *Aithiopika*, to take but one example, can be seen not only in the *Arcadia* by Sir Philip Sidney (1554–1586), but also in Cervantes' *Persiles y Sigismunda*, and in Richardson's *Clarissa*.

What were these early Western novels? We must be leery of writing stories of "origins" at least in the sense of finding an exact terminus. We do not know when the first of the Greek stories of love and adventures (such as used to be called "Greek romances") was written. Possibly the earliest of those surviving in full is Chariton of Aphrodisias' (first or second century CE) *Chaireas and Kallirhoe*, which some wish to date as early as 50 BCE, though others would put it as late as the second century. One piece of literary evidence indicates that there were a number of such novels in existence by the early first century CE. If we accept the standard equation of Petronius the author with Petronius Arbiter, his work on the *Satyricon* was finished by the date of his enforced death in 66 CE. This novel plays with the tropes of the Greek novels: with wandering lovers separated, much roaming from place to place, impediments resulting from offenses committed against the gods, the temporary enslavement of the central characters, a sea journey and shipwreck, and so on. If Petronius is able to treat the material of the novel as well known and to play thus with it, the genre must have been fully established by the mid-first century, though the best of the surviving examples come to us from the second and third centuries.

Latin novels. Only two major novels in Latin have come down to us. Petronius' *Satyricon*, if early in the temporal sequence, is ultrasophisticated and its fragmentary state adds to a sophistication in montage creatively imitated by writers like François Rabelais (1483–1553), Laurence Sterne (1713–1768), and James Joyce (1882–1941). Apuleius' *Metamorphoses* has an ascertained author and a fairly clear date (c. 160 CE). Shorter works in Latin include the late *Ephemeris Belli Troiani* (Diary of the Trojan War), presented as a found manuscript by an invented narrator "Dictys Cretensis" or "Dictys of Crete" (traditionally, all Cretans are liars). There were many other fictions, now lost; Apuleius wrote a second novel that—sadly—has not come down to us. Apuleius' extant novel is based on the Greek novel *Onos* (The ass), which was once attributed (wrongly, we now think) to Lucian of Samosata (c. 120–c. 190), who is, however, certainly the author of that fine parodic work of science fiction, known as *Vera Historia* (True story; c. 170 CE).

Greek novels. There are many more extant examples of ancient novels in Greek, including the novella *Chion of Heraklea* (c. 100 CE), which demonstrates that the classical world had already invented epistolary narrative. There are five works of substantial length; one, *Ephesiaka* (The Ephesian story; c. 150 CE) by Xenophon of Ephesus (dates unknown), may be partly a paraphrase. The other four are complete texts (given a few cruxes and some missing sentences): *Chaireas and Kallirhoe* by Chariton; *Kleitophon and Leukippe* (c. 150 CE) by Achilles Tatius; *Daphnis and Chloe* (c. 200 CE) by Longus; and *Aithiopika* (The Ethiopian story) by Heliodorus of Emesa (date uncertain; estimates have ranged from the second to the late fourth century, but it is most tempting to believe it belongs to the period of rule of the African emperor Septimius Severus (r. 193–211 CE). All these have named authors (though whether these are the genuine names of the writers has been challenged) and all are referred to in varying titles, sometimes naming the heroine alone: Achilles' *Leukippe* and Heliodorus's *Charikleia.*

The dating of these works is vexed, and we should be warned by the errors of great scholars of the past such as Erwin Rohde (1845–1898) not to put too much faith into our own current temporal schemata. Scholars used to be attracted to the late classical self-definition of the period of the "Second Sophistic," in which rhetorical play of a kind partly associated with the East (including Alexandria) enjoyed a recrudescence in new works. Plays of ideas and words, an understanding of how to interpret and describe works of visual art, clever and unexpected uses of literary allusions, and a self-conscious stance in relation to the literary tradition—all mark works of the Second Sophistic. These qualities, however, can be found outside the second-century temporal zone.

The term *Second Sophistic* was coined in reference to a presumed "First Sophistic," the period of the late fifth and early fourth century BCE, in which rhetoricians had flourished in Athens. "Sophists" were repudiated as pseudo-wise and dangerous by Socrates (c. 469–399 BCE) and Plato (c. 428–348 BCE). Sophists, Plato believed, pervert the truth with ingenious twisting of words and undermine aristocracy by the employment of verbal techniques that they could make available to anyone who pays. Proponents of the Second Sophistic consciously reversed Plato, declaring there is value in this *préciosité.*

The Sophists were often foreign to Athens—men such as Gorgias of Leontini, who came to Athens as an ambassador in 427 BCE, or Hippodamos of Miletus (fifth century BCE), one of the foreigners who brought the scientific spirit of Ionia to the marketplace of Athens. Dangerous if attractive representatives of alien cultures were introducing moral relativism, disrespecting tradition, and undermining the independent city-state, the polis. The democratizing of power through rhetoric probably did herald the end of an idealized enclosed and aristocratically controlled polis. After the polis had been fundamentally altered in the Hellenistic age and then subsumed into the Roman Empire, gentlemen from different regions shared a common educational syllabus, including training in rhetoric. Athens had become a kind of university where wealthy young males from various parts of the Roman Empire could meet, instilling in themselves the Hellenic—or Hellenistic—sense of the beautiful and true. The writers of our novels arose out of this colonial matrix, sharing something of the culture of the center. Yet, they were capable of going beyond the Hellenistic- and Roman-adapted mental world. By and before the second century CE writers and readers were evidently interested in finding ways of understanding and assimilating influences that did not emanate from Rome or Athens as Rome interpreted it. By this time the Hebrew scriptures had become available in the Greek Septuagint to non-Jewish readers. Christianity was becoming a force to be reckoned with, though it was only one of many strange religions. Christian, Jewish, and "pagan" authors sought new narrative forms, visible to us in works like the Apocrypha, the Gospels, and the *Acts;* some recent studies attend to the relation between Christian writings and the early novels (e.g., Thomas, 2003). Christian imagination found expression in a number of works, including the Greek *Poimen* (*The Shepherd of Hermas*), a sometimes novelistic text that once had practically canonical standing). *Recognitiones* (Recognitions; c. 150–250), the Latin Christian novel, has as its narrator Clement, the future second pope; here, he is a young man, who becomes a convert and a member of the circle around Saint Peter (d. c. 64 CE) during the conflict with Simon Magus.

There is at least one Jewish novel, aside from works like *Judith* and *Daniel. Joseph and Asenath* perhaps existed in the first century BCE, if rewritten later, so as to convey a Christian perspective. The Egyptian heroine Asenath, based on a personage crisply alluded to in *Genesis* 41:50, is the center of the story. Amusingly, she is at first utterly contemptuous of Joseph (her future husband), seeing him as an alien fortune-teller who (she has heard) lay with his mistress. (She will be converted to Joseph and to Judaism.)

Cultural variety of novelists. One thing is as clear to us as it evidently was to Huet: the authors of the Greek novels were not Hellenes from the mainland of Greece. These authors came from the conquered eastern areas of the Roman Empire. They were Syrians like Lucian and Heliodorus (who came from a town in modern Iraq), or they came from inland Asia Minor like Chariton or from the intellectually and materially rich coastal region, like Xenophon of Ephesus and Longus, who appears to be from the Lesbos he describes. Petronius alone has the credentials of a man of the center of Italy, a genuine Roman citizen, but Apuleius, in marked contrast, is a North African, a Berber from Numidia who after much travel settles in Carthage.

The same pattern of diverse authorship appears when we consider the novels in Greek that exist only in fragments or in paraphrase. Substantial pieces of a number of these have been found, though the fullest account of some can be gathered only from the paraphrases prepared by Photios (c. 820–891), Patriarch of Constantinople, who composed a sort of reader's diary. Called *Bibliotheke*, it gives a fairly full account of the books he liked including novels, offering not only his opinion of style and substance, but also detailed plot summaries. His commentary and paraphrase gives us a fairly full if muffled rendition of Iamblichos' (second century CE) *Babyloniaka* (The Babylonian story) or Antonius Diogenes' *Apista hyper Thulen* (Wonders beyond Thule). Exact dates for these works and others surviving in fragments are not known; see the scholarly edition of *Ancient Greek Novels* by Susan Stephens and John J. Winkler (1995).

Photios provides manuscript sources of about six pages' worth each of *Semiramis and Nisus* (a love story set in an exotic past with historical characters, perhaps written as early as 100 BCE) and of *Metiochos and Parthenope* (c. 150 CE), a story surviving in fragmentary papyrus emanating from the Fayum in Egypt. The novels were certainly read in Egypt—but we know from the evidence of expensive mosaic illustrations that a wealthy house owner in Syrian Antioch wanted to surround himself with images from these two novels. Despite disdainful assumptions on the part of some that these early novels could have been perused only by women and the semiliterate, evidence indicates a wide readership, socially and geographically, definitely including wealthy males, that was able to pay not only for full-length manuscript copies, but even for costly artwork illustrating the stories.

Different styles of Greek novels. A strange work that has recently come in its fragmentary way to light is *Phoinikika* (The Phoenician story; first published in 1972) by Lollianos. The discovery of this lively comic novel put an end to our earlier theory that only Latin novelists penned realistic, sexually explicit, and comic works of fiction, whereas the Greek novelists were romantic and sentimental. It is more likely that the authors choosing to write in Latin took up forms and comic styles from works in Greek, and it is probable that works in Latin of a more romantic style are now lost to us. Other works of Greek fiction that have come into view include *Herpyllis*, whose surviving passage deals with a storm at sea, a trope beloved of novelists; *Sesonchosis*, with Egyptian characters and themes; and *Chione*, about a heroine whose name could be translated as "Snow White" (Stephens and Winkler, 1995).

THE DEEP TRADITION: FICTIONS OF BABYLON, SYRIA AND ELSEWHERE. It is apparent from the previously mentioned titles that the Greek novels are interested in dealing with material related to various regions that were not Roman. Nor should the resort to Babylon, Phoenicia, the Assyria of Ninus, or the Egypt of Pharaoh Sesonchosis be thought of as mere "exoticism." Readers and writers alike came from these regions. A matter capable of future examination is the possible influence on the novel of literatures of even more ancient cultures than those that we customarily mean in referring to "antiquity"—a passé label. When Renaissance scholars first seriously published commentaries on these fictional texts, they lacked almost completely any real information (aside from Hebrew scripture and the Apocrypha) about the literature of Babylon, Assyria, and Egypt. Slowly, more is coming come to light.

Consider, for example, the incursion of *Gilgamesh* on our literary studies in the late twentieth century. This epic is not an action-epic like the *Iliad* or *Aeneid*, nor a story of wandering, discovery, loss, and restoration like the *Odyssey* (which, however, can strike one as having some Egyptian strands). *Gilgamesh* begins as an action story but becomes a story of love, death, grief, and loss—of coming to terms with something that will not allow a victory. The central character in his coming to grips with the hard fact of death and bereavement becomes a hero of the interior life. *Gilgamesh* might guard us against rash suppositions about regularly progressive development, of the sort that Friedrich Nietzsche (1844–1900) negatively imagines in *The Birth of Tragedy* (1871), when he propounds an original fall from the Dionysiac perfection of ancient theater to the degenerate rationalism and individualism signaled in Socrates and the works of the ancient novelists, in which a sublime communal experience has been exchanged for individual self-consciousness and emotional self-attention.

Our desire for linear progression leads us to render literary history in a rather simplistic mode: first there was the folktale, then there was the epic, reflecting national and group consciousness shaped by an aristocratic class; then, in a new development (progressive or degenerative, according to taste), the epic action became the story of an unimportant individual, and the action turned inward, toward consciousness and what Johann Christoph Friedrich von Schiller (1759–1805) termed the "sentimental," away from the first "naive" strength. Poetry gave place to prose, and action to sentiment, as we move (sadly, perhaps) from Homer (eighth century BCE) to Henry James (1843–1916). So attractive is this line of progress or regress that we are unwilling to notice how this plotline can be changed. At any moment, what we call "folk" material can reenter the picture and refresh the narrative—as with the advent of the folk tales of Jacob Grimm (1785–1863) and Wilhelm Grimm (1786–1859). Poetic narrative can reassume the telling elsewhere associated with prose fiction as in *Evgeny Onegin* (1823–1831) by Aleksandr Pushkin (1799–1837).

One text that challenges the paradigm is the Cretan narrative poem *Erotókritos*. This heroic love story is a narrative poem written by a Venetian Cretan Vitzéntzos Kornáros (seventeenth century). Kornáros's work, drawing on the material of novels, is also epic and nationalistic, a defense not only of Greek Orthodox personages against the Ottomans, but also of Cretan identity. This novel-based literary work of an individual Renaissance artificer becomes for Cretans their genuine national epic. It folds itself back into folklore and folk motif, with many tellings and popular, even homemade, graphic depictions of the hero and heroine, into at least the twentieth century. *Erotókritos* challenges many of our assumptions, as it seems in so many ways to go "backward"—from novel back to epic and then back to folktale. But our surprised impression of an almost unnatural reversal arises from our adaptation of a linear notion of a "progress" and certain staid, if recent assumptions about absolute divisions between literary culture and popular culture.

Eastern and African influences on the novel. If we question our linear representations of such "histories," we may be willing to admit into the novel written and not just folkloric "influence" from non-Hellenic sources, as Huet divined. It is tantalizing to know that Babylonians of Chaldea had libraries (destroyed by Sennacherib [c. 704–681]) and that the Assyrians followed suit, with libraries of books in clay tablets open to the public. The Chaldeans invented systems and discovered much mathematical knowledge, including geometrical figures; when the Greeks fell in love with geometry as a training for the mind, they were really imbibing the discoveries of Mesopotamia, as transmitted through the cultures of coastal Asia Minor. Much of what we call "literature" could have followed a similar route.

Punic Carthage had philosophies, a priesthood, and a library—all was wrecked by the invading Romans, save for one useful treatise on agriculture. Yet, it seems hard to believe that so much thought could altogether disappear; and elements of Phoenician and more particularly Carthaginian thought and style may be lurking in a number of texts, invisible to us. By contrast we can now pick out the bright red thread of Egyptian thinking, style, and concerns. Since the late nineteenth century we have possessed a collection of classic Egyptian fiction, and poetic stories like *The Story of Sinuhe* or *The Shipwrecked Sailor* seem strongly related not only to some biblical material, but also to many elements in our own fiction. More saliently visible is the influence of the Egyptian religion. The story of Isis (Isis/Osiris) is everywhere alluded to in the ancient novels, and Isis worship forms an extensive part of Apuleius' *Metamorphoses.* The other and older central Egyptian religious story, that of the solar boat in its journey through the underworld during the twelve hours of darkness, was elaborated by Egyptian thinkers and artists, so that it becomes the basic story of all ordeals—and of all twelve-step programs.

The Egyptians are strongly attracted to stories of an ordeal (of Isis, or of the solar voyager) that develops through multiple sequent phases. A number of the "Gnostic gospels," written around the same time as our novel texts, betray decided signs of Egyptian influence, especially in the love of progressions through the twelve stages. Dante Alighieri's (1265–1321) *Inferno* and the *Purgatorio* both have an ultimately Egyptian ancestry. Journeying is important to the Egyptian ordeal, loss of self, loneliness in the midst of an unmarked world momentarily completely alien, and the encounter with the monster or the monstrous. Yet, in "classic" Egyptian fiction of the two millennia BCE, redemption seems almost always possible, as does some new negotiation of the relation between authority and its subject, as between divine and human.

When we look at the longest and most sophisticated of our Greek and Latin "early" and "Western" novels, *Metamorphoses* and *Aithiopika,* we can see that the writers are very conscious of the possibilities of multicultural narratives. Different traditions are signaled in the introduction of different kinds of story within the main or frame story. We meet characters of varying national or ethnic identities. People establish relations who have no original familial or even ethnic connection with each other. A young Sicilian woman, once in the power of the Persian Great King, develops a friendship with the Persian queen, and on returning to her native Sicily urges the queen "write to me often." A chatty young Athenian walks on the banks of the Nile with an elderly Egyptian priest and hears the story of the trials of an Ethiopian family. A blond young Greek male from Attica, sentenced to the harshness of the Roman games in Corinth, is spared and consoled by the ministrations of an Egyptian priest and becomes fully a convert to the Egyptian religion of Isis.

Poetry, drama, folk tale and the novel. Traditional or "classical" Hellenic stories are mixed in with new styles and materials from other sources. As examples of the interweaving of different forms of narrative, we may take Heliodorus' inclusion of the "Phaidra and Hippolytus" kind of story told by a young and somewhat silly if good-natured Athenian young man who is the Hippolytus of his tale; we can note how his story contrasts with the story about himself told by the dignified Egyptian priest Kalasiris, a story that has some resonance with the early Christian semifictional *The Shepherd of Hermas.* In *Metamorphoses* Apuleius sets within with his hero's comically painful autobiography a miniature epic-cum-love elegy, the charming and puzzling story of "Eros and Psyche," and then includes sex stories both grim and ribald, told with a twist, and set in a heavily marked social context, the sort of thing medieval writers were to call *fabliau.* Folk material of magic, ghosts, and werewolves mingles with reference to elegantly written literature, and realistic observation of behavior exchanges places with magical transformation, as in *realismo magico.* We do not here forget the presence of alien and oppressive power. Apuleius strikingly describes the way the brutal soldier piles his weapons on top of his dunnage so as to strike terror in the hearts of the ordinary people. Perhaps Apuleius is the first to employ the word *terror* in such an ideologically critical manner. Certainly, he is aware throughout the entire novel of the accoutrements of power used by an oppressive ruler and daily encountered by the vanquished.

Novel and Political Resistance. The novels of the first centuries CE reflect a tacit resistance to Roman (or Greco-Roman) domination, a search for an imaginative home free of the oppressive dominion of the present. It may have been prudence that dictated that most of these novelists should give their works a historical setting, in an era safely past, customarily when Persia was the ruler of the world. (Persians could be safely criticized.) The political implications of ancient novels have been underemphasized. This may be because of our own allegiance to Rome and our reluctance to realize that its presence could be felt—not only in Judea but elsewhere—as an unjust weight. We do not customarily hear in school, for instance, about the overt expressions of revulsion against Roman rule, as in 88 BCE when the people of Ephesus, with the assistance of the king of Pontus, Mithradates VI Eupator (120–63 BCE), revolted against the Romans, first overthrowing Roman statues and then massacring the Italians found in the region. (Freedom was short lived; the Romans inevitably exacted a strong penalty.) If analyzed, almost every one of these novels is capable of bearing an interpretation of resistance to imposed power. The theme of resistance is strongest in *Chion of Heraklea*, where the student-hero becomes a tyrannicide. Less overtly, the theme of resistance also becomes clear at the end of Chariton's novel *Chaireas and Kallirhoe*, when Chaireas invites all those of his fellow warriors, hitherto living among the Persians and fighting for the Great King of Persia, to join him in coming to Sicily, here imagined as a land of the free (book 8, cap. 2). The hero is willing to include his former enemies, Egyptian fighting men, as well as the Greeks, but only with their own free will; each person is to be asked individually: "*hina monon tous hekontas paralabomen*" (so that we take up only those who are willing).

Slavery and choice. "Choice" is at the center of the morality pursued or invented by the novels—of all kinds. Aristotle notably gave great weight to choice, but only a few people (educated free males) in his view had the power of real choice. Slaves represent human entities who are not persons and absolutely lack choice. In the novels, however, most of the central characters experience enslavement and degradation—in a sense it is true to say that all the central characters are both rulers and slaves. The characters, however low their circumstances, are never without significance, and never, even in enslavement, without the concept of choice—which is proclaimed and presented through their attention to their own inner lives. This is a monumental, not to say monstrous, departure from the classical ordering of the social world. In the novel the individual matters most. The definition of a set cannot be the ultimate measure of a person. A personage is first of all a person—and not first of all, slave or free, Greek or Egyptian, or even male or female. Barriers between civilized and barbarian are set aside. The identity we now call "racial," the difference between "black" and "white" persons, becomes in *Aithiopika* a gigantic conundrum; the heroine proves to be both "black" and "white." Whether Heliodorus' Charikleia is Greek or Ethiopian is less important than that she is Charikleia.

Individual life. These novels consistently show the life of the individual as central; the individual casts off, overtly or secretly, the restrictions of familial authority, arranged marriage, and custom. Individuality encompasses an inner life. From this individual inner life spring new apprehensions of morality, new orderings of society, and new religious insights. New perceptions and actions may be deeply spiritual, but the central religion is no longer the religion of the state. Public religious ceremonies indeed figure—often as a means for the lovers to lay eyes on each other—but the most loved deity has intercourse with the individual spirit, as Isis makes herself known to asinine Lucius. Epic must not put the individual at the center; the heroic individual, like an Aeneas, is simply and grandly at the service of his clan or nation, and the enticements of a Dido must be got over. It cannot be possible for Aeneas to have a new revelation as to how to live. In the novels, individuals constantly make new cultural adjustments and experience new revelations.

Women and freedom. Another great change from the traditional Greco-Roman view of things is the installation of the female at the center of the story. Many of the Greek novels were called simply by the name of the heroine: *Kallirhoe*, *Leukippe*, and *Charikleia*.

The story of courtship in the Greek novels sets aside the reality of marriage in most parts of the empire. Traditionally, a good Greek marriage consisted of the union of a young girl of fifteen or so—who had nothing to say in the matter—with a man of about thirty. The two were not equal and were not meant to be so. Love as a practical affection was supposed to grow between a married pair, though given the limitations of the female and her patent inferiority, the role of the erotic was to be limited in marriage; in illegitimate heterosexual connections, the desirable female (slave or freedwoman) was usually a prostitute, well below the male in class, and not officially important. When the Greeks—especially the Athenians—of the classical period wrote about what we recognize as romantic love (e.g., in the *Symposium*), they treat the homosexual connection of an older man (the lover) with a youth (the beloved). (Or, in the poems of Sappho [late seventh century BCE], the pull of an older woman toward a nubile girl.)

As David Konstan points out, the traditional Greek equation of love is always unequal, the relation asymmetrical; thus, the novels make a great leap in boldly imagining courtship between equals. The hero and heroine in any of the new novels are both young and near in age, and each is both lover and beloved. There is no division between agent and patient. The two have chosen to love each other—despite their families. The woman consistently has a choice about what she or even they will do, and both display intelligence and courage (and sometimes dull-wittedness and timidity). This equal couple escapes the confines of family and city, roaming through the world. In the course of their wanderings they make friends who are by all traditional standards unsuitable (in any case, it is traditionally unsuitable for the woman to have friends outside of home, her *oikos*). The rule of the household, the rule of the polis, and the rule of the empire are all challenged in this representation, which offers a new definition of what freedom might mean.

Hero and heroine together overthrow the "citizen" as an ideal. Love takes them away from convention and into discovery. They are not unguided, for there is a tutelary deity, perhaps several; the deity presiding over many of these novels, however, is a female god: Artemis, Aphrodite, or Isis. (Ephesus, the center of the worship of powerful Artemis, "Diana of the Ephesians," figures incessantly in the novel as locale and reference.) The novels can be seen as explorations of the relation with the goddess rather than with the god. The goddess endorses freedom, love, experience, and searching. The goddess also implicitly endorses the significance of both the physical life of the body (which must include death) and the life of consciousness. The goddess recurs in modern novels as much as in ancient ones, and may be lurking in surprising haunts; one critic (Brown, 2004) convincingly traces the pattern of Celtic myth and the role of the fierce Celtic mother goddess Mor Rigan in *Mrs. Dalloway* (1922) by Virginia Woolf (1882–1941).

Religion and the Novel in the West. Unlike tragedy, comedy, or epic, the novel has traditionally been supposed to have arisen without religious affiliation. That view was challenged by some twentieth-century scholars, most notably by Karl Kerényi in *Die Griechish-Orientalische Romanliteratur in Religionsgeschichtlicher Beleuchtung* (1927) and by Reinhold Merkelbach in *Roman und Mysterium in der Antike* (1962).

Kerényi emphasizes the connection between novelistic and Christian perceptions; the central character(s) of the ancient novel imitates on the human level the trials of a divine being. Merkelbach proposes that the early novels embody and encode a mystery ritual, a sequence of experiences initiated ultimately by the divine power. Merkelbach considers that these Greek and Latin novels present to us and their readers the actual images and practices of the mystery cults and are close to the religions of Demeter and Isis. The characters, like the mystery initiates, undergo tests and trials—being beaten, imprisoned, and even left for dead; they eventually encounter various important figures of consolation and enlightenment, including the shepherd or herdsman and the fisherman. From a near-death or seeming death (*Scheintod*) they are resurrected to new life.

Merkelbach applies his discovery only to the ancient novels, but it can be applied to novels beyond this temporal range. The novel, if we look at the templates suggested by the ancient novels, embodies a sequence of experiences that not only the character, but also the reader follows in a sequence of initiation. These "tropes of the novel" take the reader through a participatory ritual. It is the reader as well as the character who undergoes the shock and excitement of entering the new, being cut off from past life at an initial critical moment, and crossing a borderland of marsh or muddy margins. The reader vicariously undergoes a kind of baptism, walks the labyrinth, gazes on enigmatic images demanding interpretation and understanding, descends into the abyss, and is resurrected. The hidden pattern of initiatory ritual and enlightenment within each novel makes it possible for us to read novels, which would otherwise fly apart under the pressure of their novelty, becoming abstract kaleidoscopes of words, or mere journalism. The goddess presides over this new life, this metamorphosis and grappling with the phenomenal—*phainomena symbola*, to use a term from the opening of *Aithiopika*.

That the "goddess" presides can be explained in another fashion. Under the sign of the male we have placed the creation of what is abstract and enduring: a philosophy, a law, and a work of art—monuments more lasting than bronze. The sphere of the female is more lowly; women create what is temporary and consumed: cakes, fabric, and babies. The novel is the only form that consistently summons the goddess because it is the form that centrally deals with the sacredness of daily transitory and physical life. It respects the fundamental equality of all human beings and their relation both to the animal and spiritual worlds. The novel never ignores the perishable and transient things such as food, lovemaking, dreams, conversation, fabric, babies.

Plato opposed the changeable, and even Aristotle saw our love of change as a weakness, but the novel gives over the search for steadfast rest and permanence, celebrating the capacity to change. Every novel could really bear the title of Apuleius' *Metamorphoses*, because all characters are metamorphosing—Elizabeth Bennet, Anna Karenina, or Gregor Samsa. And all are journeying, through space and time. The title *Journey to the West* could apply to all—the journey to enlightenment is simultaneously a journey toward sunset and the grave.

Religion and the Novel in the East. Both Chinese and Japanese fiction display qualities and patterns remarkably similar to those found in Western novels. The orderly disorder of birth/death, muddying, eating, contemplating images, plunging into the depths and arising—all these ritual experiences can be found. There is perpetual contestation between the political public male-ordered world and the world of private experience.

The earliest collection of poems in Chinese literature may be read as personal lyrics of love and longing, or as coded references to political affairs. The personal can be set against the ideal of order—even the ideal of political order, so central to Chinese thinking and endorsed by Confucianism. Rebellion is a topic, as in the fourteenth-century *Outlaws of the Marsh*, where we follow the individual lives of bandit-heroes, who dwell on the muddy margins. One of them, Song Jiang, is given three heavenly books by the goddess-like Mystic Queen of the Ninth Heaven, who exhorts him to remember justice and bring peace to the people. In the sixteenth-century classic known as *Journey to the West*, a complex narrative of a pilgrimage from China to the borders of India to find the original Buddhist scriptures and bring them to China, the heroes are often aided by a divine female, the *bodhisattva* Guanyin, who gave them their assignment. By contrast with the refreshment of her rare presence, monasteries encountered en route seem abodes of greed and inertia, masculinity without heart and without spirit. Spiritual life develops in the lived life. The insertion of Monkey, the famous mischief-making hero, reinstates the body and the life of desire in a story that both supports and questions Buddhism itself, as it also questions the Dao that supplies so many of this narrative's fascinating systems of contrasts and affinities. At the end of the novel, the importance of "sacred text" becomes subtly ironic—the truth is within, so a blank page is as good as any other. This strange ending also suggests that the real story is always about to be—that the religious truth can be encountered only in the experience of seeking it.

In the high flowering of the Chinese novel, the feminine moves to a central place, countering both the worldly orderliness of Confucianism and the sense-rejecting purity of Buddhism. One of the greatest of the world's novels is *Hong Lou Meng* (*Dream of the Red Chamber*, or *Story of the Stone*) by Cao Xueqin (c. 1715–1763). Generations have marveled at and wept over the complex and fated loves of Bao-yu and Dai-yu. Divine discontent has never been more subtly or powerfully revealed in a novel teeming with multifaceted characters and taking time to deal with many developments over half a lifetime. Its only rival in representing the subtleties of consciousness in relation to love and loss is the great Japanese novel *Genji Monogatori* (*The Tale of Genji*), written at the turn of the eleventh century by a woman author called Murasaki Shikibu (late tenth to early eleventh century). In both of these novels, love is at the center, love and the yearning of desire, which is constantly faced by the great fact of Death. In contemplating loss and absence, the soul stirs. Individual life is experienced in a world full of social, financial, and moral complexity, with much bustle and comedy, as well as beautiful and ugly objects; yet, amid the welter of experience the spirit knows an inalienable loneliness, sharpened by the metamorphoses demanded by living. The quest for love can awaken and enlighten the spirit, but is not soothing.

These Eastern novels have extraordinarily fine and subtle endings, endings that dramatically make the reader experience that what is desired cannot be grasped; it is the experience of the desire that educates the soul and continually kills and gives rebirth to the self. The self, too, is something not capable of being fully known, even to the self. These are religious revelations, but they cannot be precisely squared with Dao or Buddhism, however much is to be learned from these. What is most approachable is the feminine deity, the goddess of compassion and of the senses, who makes constant change bearable. There is in both Western and Eastern novels an allusion to something that endorses our eagerness to live—and not only to live but to satisfy curiosity and to undergo change in ourselves—which means living through perpetual dying (and very dangerous that may be). In living our lives and in reading a novel we pursue a mystery that lies deeper than any plot.

CONCLUSION. The novel is really a religiously developed form. It quietly sets itself in opposition to political and religious conventions and traditions to plunge itself and its reader into a closer apprehension of the sacredness that imbues the individual person and the world. It may at times appear dismissive of what is called religion, or it may appear fascinated by religions, but it is not orthodox and will never yield humbly to orthodox authority—even when an author tries to do so. The novel is secular—secular in the original sense, having to do with the *saeclum*, that is, with *time*. Novels, more than any other form, show the individual dealing with experience in time—including not only biological time, but also a particular social and political era (historical or imaginary). The novel pays heed to the importance of time and space, in which the phenomena of matter manifest themselves. It draws on each reader's bodily and temporal experience; the smell of jasmine or urine, the feeling of spring rain, and the taste of honey are supplied by the reader's sensuous knowledge. The novel exhibits characters living with the biological body amid a welter of detail and necessities (including food and money). To live so realistically is not to be subordinated to things, but to have an arena for spiritual experiment, and the novel displays consciousness itself as a major experiment, in harmony with the expedient that is each individual novel.

BIBLIOGRAPHY

Anderson, Graham. *Ancient Fiction: The Novel in the Graeco-Roman World.* London, 1984.

Brown, Keith. "An Offering to the Goddess." *Times Literary Supplement,* June 18, 2004, pp. 14–16.

Burkert, Walter. *The Orientalizing Revolution: Near Eastern Influence on Greek Culture in the Early Archaic Age.* Cambridge, Mass., 1992.

Cohen, David. *Law, Sexuality, and Society: The Enforcement of Morals in Classical Athens.* Cambridge, U.K., 1991.

Doody, Margaret. *The True Story of the Novel.* New Brunswick, N.J., 1996.

Finkelberg, Margalit. *The Birth of Literary Fiction in Ancient Greece.* Oxford, 1998.

Goldhill, Simon. *The Invention of Prose.* Oxford, 2002.

Harrison, S. J. *Apuleius: A Latin Sophist.* Oxford, 2000.

Henrichs, Albert. *Die "Phoinikika" des Lollianos.* Bonn, 1972.

Hermas. *Le Pasteur.* Edited and translated by Robert Joly. Paris, 1968.

Kerényi, Karl. *Die Griechisch-Orientalische Romanliteratur in Religionsgeschichtlicher Beleuchtung* (1927). 2d ed. Darmstadt, Germany, 1962.

Konstan, David. *Sexual Symmetry: Love in the Ancient Novel and Related Genres.* Princeton, N.J., 1994

Merkelbach, Reinhold. *Roman und Mysterium in der Antike.* Munich, 1962.

Morgan, J. R., and Richard Stoneman. *Greek Fiction: The Greek Novel in Context.* London, 1994.

Photius I. *Bibliothèque.* Edited and translated by René Henry. 11 vols. Paris, 1959–1991.

Reardon, Bryan P., ed. *Collected Ancient Greek Novels.* Berkeley, Calif., 1989.

Rohde, Erwin. *Der griechische Roman und seine Vorlaufer.* Hildesheim, Germany, 1876.

Stephens, Susan, and John J. Winkler. *Ancient Greek Novels.* Princeton, N.J., 1995.

Tatum, James, ed. *The Search for the Ancient Novel.* Baltimore, 1994.

Thomas, Christine M. *The Acts of Peter, Gospel Literature, and the Ancient Novel: Rewriting the Past.* Oxford, 2003.

Watt, Ian P. *The Rise of the Novel: Studies in Defoe, Richardson, and Fielding.* Berkeley, Calif., 1957.

MARGARET ANNE DOODY (2005)

FICTION: THE WESTERN NOVEL AND RELIGION

While a foremost contemporary American writer of fiction asserts that "the literary artist, to achieve full effectiveness, must assume a religious state of mind" (Updike, p. 239), there is no denying that the novel is a genre of literary art that rarely takes religion as its obvious and principal theme. Among the more prominent twentieth-century theorists of the novel, one viewed it as "the epic of a world that has been abandoned by God" (Lukács, p. 88), and another considered it the genre in which "the absolute past" of the gods, demigods, and heroes is "contemporized" and "brought low, represented on a plane equal with contemporary life, in an everyday environment, in the low language of contemporaneity" (Bakhtin, p. 21).

Some books that read like novels do overtly take religion as their theme, but they are better described as works of edification—although they may possess grace of style or persuasive power, their inspiration is not artistic but propagandist. A true novel, even in modest categories of this genre, seeks to show the human being in society; any teaching that may be inherent in it, or any moral conclusion it may point to, is secondary to this artistic impulse. The great novelists frequently write on themes that have religious implications, but these are approached indirectly and shown in action or reflection rather than direct admonition. To form any notion of the connection between the novel and religion, we must look below the surface of the work of art, and we must not expect wholehearted assent to any version of orthodoxy.

This is not to set the novel at odds with religion, if we accept the latter word in terms of its derivation as implying the careful consideration of forces, laws, ideas, or ideals that are sufficiently powerful to inspire awe or devotion. The novel seeks to show the human being, confused and fallible, meeting the complexities of life, among which are likely to be those elements describable as numinous. If, indeed, humans are naturally religious, the novel cannot avoid religion, though its principal theme will continue to be the human being.

Although it is actually an ancient genre (Doody, 1996), the novel in its most recognizable current form developed in the seventeenth century as a successor to the epic, which dealt with humans as heroic beings, and the romance, which was free of any necessity for its characters to obey the broad laws of probability, or for stated causes to bring their usual consequences. Conditioned by the Renaissance and strongly influenced by the Reformation, the modern novel required that a story should be, in broad terms, probable, and its characters believable in terms of common experience. The novel was expected to be a story about what most readers would accept as real life, and as ideas of real life are inseparably associated with what human beings, at any period of history, are inclined to take for granted without much reflection, the novel became a mirror of society, and thus a mirror of the nature of the era for which it was written. Although the novel does not seek to avoid issues that are properly religious, its principal energy in this area is better described as moral.

The morality put forward by Western novelists may be reduced to a number of broad precepts. "God is not mocked: for whatsoever a man soweth, that shall he also reap" (*Gal.* 6:7); "Vengeance is mine, I will repay, saith the Lord" (*Rom.* 12:19); "The dog is turned to his own vomit again; and the sow that was washed to her wallowing in the mire" (*2 Pet.* 2:22); "For if a man think himself to be something, when he is nothing, he deceiveth himself" (*Gal.* 6:3). These are but a few of the more minatory precepts found in the Bible that underlie scores of novels. That these general laws may be seen at work in daily life, in the uttermost variety of circumstances, and that they are psychological truths, makes them natural guides of the novelist, who must be, like any artist, an undeluded observer. The novelist may deal with these grim truths humorously, and some of the most truly religious novels are seen by the world as funny books, but their underlying morality is far from funny.

This encyclopedia treats the history of the novel in a separate entry, but it is useful here to begin with *Don Quixote* (pt. 1, 1605; pt. 2, 1615), by Miguel de Cervantes, often spoken of as the first truly modern novel. Its story is of the fortunes of a Spanish gentleman whose wits have been turned by reading old books of romance and chivalry. He equips himself absurdly as a knight and rides forth in search of adventures, and in a rambling and sometimes coarse and perfunctory tale he is mocked, beaten, and humiliated until, on his deathbed, he understands the folly of his delusion.

The book is often read superficially, or not read at all, by many people who are nevertheless aware of it, as the story is familiar from stage, film, and operatic adaptations, and as the word *quixotic*, meaning "actuated by impracticable ideals of honor," is in common use. A careful reading of the novel reveals the mainspring of the book's extraordinary power. It is the first instance in popular literature of the profoundly religious theme of victory plucked from defeat, which has strong Christian implications. The Don, who is courteous and chivalrous toward those who abuse or mock him, and who is ready to help the distressed and attack tyranny or cruelty at whatever cost to himself, is manifestly a greater person than the dull-witted peasants and cruel nobles who torment and despise him. Many readers love him because his folly is Christlike—his victory is not of this world.

The theme is repeated in countless novels, including a lineage of works in which the quixotic protagonist undergoes a discernible process of "sanctification" that runs counter to the more oft-discussed secularizing tendency of modern literature. Three of the most notable examples are Henry Fielding's *Joseph Andrews* (1742), Fyodor Dostoevsky's *The Idiot* (1869), and Graham Greene's *Monsignor Quixote* (1982), with their respective depictions of Parson Adams, Prince Myshkin, and Father Quixote. In these novels, the modes of living, acting, and speaking as a good-natured man (Adams), a holy fool (Myshkin), or a Roman Catholic priest struggling with faith and doubt (Father Quixote) reflect different aspects of the Christian ideal, though they also call to mind the mad delusion of Cervantes's hero by virtue of their discrepancy with the predominantly profane or secular currents of the modern West (Ziolkowski, 1991).

Among the greatest literary adaptations of the Quixote theme is Charles Dickens's *Pickwick Papers*. The titular hero, whom we first meet as a foolish and almost buffoonlike character, is deepened by an unjust imprisonment to a point where he is truly aware of the misery that is part of the society in which he lives. It is of importance to our theme that Mr. Pickwick is dependent on his valet, Sam Weller, as Don Quixote is dependent on his peasant squire, Sancho Panza, for a measure of common sense and practical wisdom that saves him from disaster. Faith, hope, charity, justice, and fortitude are exemplified in the masters, but without the prudence and temperance of the servants they would be lost. A character who possessed all the seven great virtues would never do as the hero of a novel, but when a hero who has most of them is complemented by a helper and server who has what he or she lacks, great and magical fiction may result.

As the mighty virtues appear in numerous, though often disguised, forms in great novels, so also do the capital sins. To provide an equivalent for each suggests a list that inevitably means the exclusion of many others equally cogent. When we think of pride, however, we remember how brilliantly it is deployed in Dickens's *Domby and Son* (1846); wrath recalls Dostoevsky's *The Brothers Karamazov* (1880) and Herman Melville's *Moby Dick* (1851); envy is the mainspring of Honoré de Balzac's *La cousine Bette* (1846); lust has many exemplars, some of them presenting the vice in a refined form, as in Samuel Richardson's *Clarissa Harlowe* (1747), and others explicit, as in John Cleland's *Fanny Hill* (1748–1749); gluttony is a less popular theme, though drunkenness, which might be regarded as one of its forms, is very common and is explored in Émile Zola's *L'Assommoir* (1877); avarice is popular, and Balzac's *Le cousin Pons* (1847) shows it in the guise of the collector's mania, linked in Sylvain Pons with a greed that exemplifies gluttony in the guise of gourmandise (the gourmet's refinement of the uglier word); sloth recalls Ivan Goncharov's *Oblomov* (1857), in which that sin is explored to its depth. This list is certainly not meant to be definitive, and the Seven Deadly Sins do not include cruelty, of which Dickens affords many examples, nor stupidity, which Gustave Flaubert displays subtly in *Madame Bovary* (1857), nor snobbery, which, though hardly a sin, is a deep preoccupation of the bourgeois world and has never been more searchingly anatomized than in Marcel Proust's *À la recherche du temps perdu* (1913–1927). Virtually any attribute, when exaggerated, may become a vice, and in some circumstances vice may take on the color of virtue. This makes heavy work for the moralist but is the delight of the novelist, who thrives on delicate distinctions and on that *enantiodromia*, or tendency of attributes and emotions to run into their opposites, which is familiar in psychology.

The novel has proved effective in depicting what, from the traditional Jewish or Christian perspectives, would be ultimate acts of human evil: rebellion against God through an effort to be God's equal (cf. the biblical tale of Babel), and the human conversion of life in this world to a hell on earth. The preeminent example of the first theme is Mary Shelley's *Frankenstein* (1818), which represents the effort of a scientist to, in effect, usurp God's role as creator and conqueror of death. To affirm the jointly Hellenic and Hebrew roots of this theme, Shelley dubbed her titular protagonist "the Modern Prometheus" and included in her narrative explicit references to the rebellious Satan of John Milton's *Paradise Lost. Frankenstein* crystallized a distinctly Gothic dimension of early nineteenth-century Romanticism, some of whose exponents displayed an irrepressible fascination with medieval legends about the Devil (Mephistopheles) and lore of the demonic. In the twentieth century, in contrast, the theme that emerged of the human-made, terrestrial inferno, where countless innocents suffer and perish, was an immediate outgrowth of historical reality. The theme is thus chiefly exemplified in novels by actual survivors of the pogroms, the "concentration-camp universe," the gulag, and other forms of genocide that marked the century. Elie Wiesel's *La Nuit* (1958) and Jerzy Kosinski's *The Painted Bird* (1965) are among the most haunting novelistic testimonies to the horrors of the Nazi Holocaust, while Aleksandr Solzhenitsyn's *The First Circle* (1968) and his multivolume *The Gulag Archipelago, 1918–1956: An Experiment in Literary Investigation* (1973–1978) expose unforgettably the infernal dimensions of the Soviet slave-labor camps. As memory is the capacity that is *sine qua non* for any novelist, and perhaps especially for those who record atrocities, the novels of Toni Morrison have represented most poignantly the abomination of human slavery and its psychological and spiritual legacies in America.

When novelists choose churches and churchmen as their theme, they frequently dwell on faults that are undeniable, but paint an ungenerous picture of the whole. This is particularly the case when the sort of religion portrayed is of the evangelistic, nonsacramental kind. In such religion, popular opinion expects that the evangelist or the parson will exemplify in himself the virtues he urges on others; in Sinclair Lewis's term, he is a Professional Good Man. His failure to be wholly good makes diverting reading, for hypocrisy provides livelier fiction than virtue. In Lewis's *Elmer Gantry* (1927), all the shams of vulgar religiosity are exposed, and its appeal to naive and unreflective people held up to ridicule. Set likewise during the first half of the twentieth century, but focusing upon a particular African American family against the bleak backdrop of a racist, segregated America, James Baldwin's *Go Tell It on the Mountain* (1953) presents the deacon Gabriel Grimes as the quintessential religious hypocrite. Having once thought himself divinely promised to father a saintly lineage, Gabriel espouses a harshly moralistic brand of Pentecostalism while mistreating his own family (especially his good stepson John, the novel's central protagonist) and concealing his own past moral lapses, most notably his having fathered another son out of wedlock and then abandoned him and the mother.

A variant depiction of the religious life as it is lived by well-intentioned but not spiritually gifted priests is to be found in the novels of Anthony Trollope. In *The Warden* (1855), the principal character, the Reverend Septimus Harding, is a good man, but timid and weak, and his dilemma when he is accused of holding a sinecure is a choice between Christian precept and the way of the world; obedient to public opinion, he resigns his wardenship. In its sequel, *Barchester Towers* (1857), we meet the warden's son-in-law, Archdeacon Grantly, who dearly longs to succeed his father as bishop, for he is a man of strong worldly ambition; but in the first chapter of the book Grantly must decide whether he desires the bishopric at the cost of his father's life. His decision is made in terms of his faith rather than his ambition. The scene in which he prays for forgiveness at his father's bedside is moving and finely realized. Not a crumb of religiosity or false sentiment is to be found in it. Grantly is no saint, but he is a man of principle.

In the same fine novel we meet the bishop's chaplain, Mr. Slope, who cloaks inordinate ambition under evangelistic piety, and the Reverend Dr. Vesey Stanhope, who draws his salary as a clergyman but lives a fashionable life in Italy, leaving his work to curates. Trollope parades before us a wide variety of clergy, some of whom are saved from moral ignominy by the fact that the Church of England, through its catholicism, separates the priestly function from the man who discharges it (though abuse of this distinction is frowned upon). But such characters as Mr. Harding, the warden; the Reverend Francis Arabin, an exemplar of the scholar-priest and intellectual; and the Reverend Josiah Crawley, in whom his creator combines pride with humility, manliness with weakness, and acute conscience with bitter prejudice, redeem Trollope's clergy and emphasize his very English, very Victorian conviction that a clergyman is not required to be a saint but should unquestionably be a man of principle and a gentleman. This is a long way from Elmer Gantry, who was neither.

No discussion of this subject can escape some consideration of the part the intellectual and artistic character of the novelist plays in his depiction of religion, and its influence on his characters. All generalizations are suspect, but it may be stated broadly that the temperament that makes a writer a novelist is unlikely to be friendly to orthodoxy, and that the Manichaean struggle between darkness and light is more friendly to the novelist's purpose (the depiction of the human being in society) than is an unwavering adherence to a creed. Inevitably, there are important exceptions. Calvinist predestination is the mainspring of James Hogg's fine *The Private Memoirs and Confessions of a Justified Sinner* (1824). There is no mistaking the Roman Catholic thought behind all the work of James Joyce, Graham Greene, and Anthony Burgess, or the monolithic Russian Orthodoxy that informs the novels of Solzhenitsyn. Likewise the novels of Chaim Potok are thoroughly saturated by the world of Orthodox Judaism in modern urban America, highlighting the tensions between the everyday, worldly Orthodoxy and a more stringent form of Hasidism.

More often, however, the theme of Don Quixote is repeated: the good man or woman exhibits, and is betrayed by, weaknesses, but the forces that oppose him or her—which are more likely to be stupidity, conventionality, and self-seeking than determined evil—succeed in the short view. It is the reader who understands and appreciates the goodness of the hero, and whereas in a work of inferior artistic merit this may simply flatter the reader's ego, in a great novel it may leave readers with a larger vision of life and an appreciation of the weight of religious feeling that they did not have before.

Good novelists manage this by indirect means; the aim of such novelists is not to teach but to entertain, and thus to persuade. Their chief purpose, from which they stray at their peril as artists, is to depict life as they see it, and whatever they touch will be colored by their own temperament. The temperament of the artist is not unwaveringly noble—wholeness of spirit, not perfection, is the artist's aim. Many novelists, of whom Sinclair Lewis may serve as an example, are disappointed idealists, angry with life because it does not conform to the best they can conceive, and their strictures on religion, as on other great themes, are apt to be bitter. The calm observation of Trollope is a rarer gift.

Examples could be cited to the point of weariness, without achieving very much. Let it suffice to say that a turbulent and tormented spirit such as Dostoevsky will not see religion as it is seen by a stronger, more deeply and often more narrowly moral writer such as Tolstoy. Neither exhibits the philosophical, ironic, but finally positive spirit of Thomas

Mann. To look for what is called "real life" in the novels of these and countless others is to search for something definable only in vague terms. Vladimir Nabokov once described a fictional masterpiece as an "original world" that is unlikely to fit the reader's own world. Serious readers enter such an original world as they encounter any work of art—in search of enlargement and enlightenment. If the novel has this effect, the reader's concept of "real life" has been changed.

Serious readers, however, are not a majority, nor are serious writers. We must beware of the critical error that tries to define art solely in terms of the best. Below the level of greatness are innumerable novels that cannot be dismissed as having no merit; they may be lesser works of art, or on a level below that, or they may be widely popular and thus, in some measure, influential. The best-seller should not be brushed aside simply because many people like it; its very popularity is a strong clue to what a multitude of people will accept as a depiction of the human being in society, and therefore as an indication of what those people believe society to be. Even more than what these readers believe to be true, popular literature displays what they wish were true, about religion as well as many other things. Thus, having appeared at a time when idealistic discussions of social and economic "globalization" are persistently defied by the realities of international conflicts or tensions that are often rooted in religious differences, Catherine Clément's international best-seller *Le Voyage de Théo* (1997) tells of a boy taken on a tour of the world's religions, traveling literally from one continent to the next, and arriving finally at the simple morale that one should be at peace with God, whatever one conceives God to be. In one sense, *Le Voyage de Théo* seeks to exploit the same function that numerous profounder novels have fulfilled in illuminating forms of religious life largely unfamiliar to "mainstream" Western readers. The portrayals of Brahmanic and Buddhist asceticism in Hermann Hesse's *Siddhartha. Eine indische Dichtung* (1922), and of Chippewa traditions in the novels of Louise Erdrich, are but two examples that come immediately to mind.

What many readers seem to wish is that religion should not obtrude into a novel, either directly or in some awareness of the numinous. Writers who ignore their wish feel the lash of their resentment. Aldous Huxley, who seemed to a large and eager group of readers to be the perfection of the cynicism of the period following World War I, astonished and displeased them when, in 1936, he published *Eyeless in Gaza*, in which the voice of the moralist and explorer of faith that had been earlier evident in *Brave New World* (1932) could no longer be ignored. A similar experience befell Evelyn Waugh, whose works, being both witty and funny (for the two are not interchangeable terms), had secured him a delighted following of readers who, although they knew him to be a Roman Catholic, did not appreciate how determinedly Catholic he was until 1945, when *Brideshead Revisited* demanded that Catholic orthodoxy be taken with the uttermost seriousness. The deathbed repentance of the earl of Marchmain was ridiculed by those critics who could not bring themselves to believe that it might be true. That the wit, the funnyman, should also be religious was unbearable to multitudes of religious illiterates, many of them critics.

It is significant that when Huxley revealed the quester beneath the cynic he was forty, and that when Waugh forced his readers to face an embarrassing fact he was forty-two. Both men had reached the midpoint in life, when radical psychological change presents problems that can no longer be dismissed or dissembled before the artist's audience. The lives of virtually all novelists of the serious sort reveal some such alteration in the thrust of their work. If not religion in some readily identifiable form, the religious spirit of awe and a moral conviction asserts itself and shows in the work that is most characteristic.

In fiction on the most popular level, that of the best-seller, religion or the trappings of religion may be used (not necessarily cynically) by an author to induce in readers an impression that they are thinking about and weighing serious problems. The familiar tale of the priest who falls in love lies beneath many plots, an example of which is *The Thorn Birds* (1977), by Colleen McCullough, hailed as admirable and even profound by innumerable readers. The priest cannot deny his love, for to do so would be to reject something necessary to his wholeness. In time, as a cardinal, he receives his unacknowledged son into the priesthood.

There may lie beneath McCullough's book, and others like it, something that should not be ignored: Christianity has never wholly accepted human sexuality as a potentially noble part of the human makeup. Such books are a protest against that attitude, a demand that religion include sexuality and the distinctively feminine element in the human spirit as it shows itself in both sexes. The conflict between a high feminine spirit and a torturing, wholly masculine morality is finely explored in Nathaniel Hawthorne's *The Scarlet Letter* (1850); Hester Prynne's greatness is opposed to the orthodoxy of her secret lover, the Reverend Arthur Dimmesdale, and there can be no doubt which spirit is the more truly religious.

Innumerable books have dealt with this question in a manner that may have been the best possible to their authors but that can only be called slight and, in some cases, cynically frivolous. An early example is *The Monk* (1796), the immensely popular novel by Matthew Gregory Lewis, in which the externals of Catholicism are exploited in a tale of nymphomania, murder, magic, and unappeasable lust. Unquestionably it is lively reading, but its notions of numinosity reach no higher than scenes of the Inquisition and a trumpery pact with the Devil. (For a fine example of the theme of the pact with the Devil, one may turn to Thomas Mann's *Dr. Faustus*, 1947.) Lewis's Gothic shocker is mentioned here because it is the forerunner of many such tales in which religion serves indecency in the manner Shakespeare describes as "to have honey a sauce to sugar" (*As You Like It*, 3.3.26–27). But they are popular, and it cannot be denied that they represent what religion means to many people. Victor Hugo's *Notre-Dame de Paris* (1831) offers an artistically superior example. Eugène Marie-Joseph Sue's *Le Juif errant* (1844–1845) is a lesser work in which the supposed unscrupulous intellectualism of the Jesuits is exploited.

Some reference must be made to the large category of books that make use of the occult as part of the paraphernalia of their stories, employing a romantic Satanism to produce an atmosphere of evil and decadence. Two works of Joris-Karl Huysmans have been admired: *À rebours* (1884), in which Catholicism is embraced as a remedy against a blighting pessimism, and *Là-bas* (1891), in which the hero searches for a consoling faith through the path of black magic. On a lower level of artistic achievement is the long-lived romance by Bram Stoker, *Dracula* (1897), in which the popular theme of vampirism is the mainspring of the action (among today's popularizers of this theme, the foremost is undoubtedly Anne Rice). These books are relevant to any discussion of religion and the novel inasmuch as they are evidence of a yearning in a large reading public for something to balance the apparent spiritual barrenness of the world that has emerged from the industrial, scientific, and technological revolution. That the public responds to the negative spirit of black magic rather than to something more hopeful is not surprising. Where religion loses its force, superstition is quick to supplant it, and it would need a strong new religious impulse or revelation to reverse that movement.

It is not surprising that when religion appears in this class of literature it is usually Catholicism, Orthodoxy, or Jewish mysticism (Qabbalah) that accommodate naive or unevolved religious feeling more sympathetically than Protestantism. The reformed versions of Christianity in their eagerness to banish superstition appear sometimes to have banished any sense of the numinous along with it, and it may be argued that the human being cannot live comfortably without some elements of belief that a stern moralist would class as superstitious. The human psyche cannot relate wholly toward the positive and the light side of life; it must have some balancing element of the dark, the unknown, and the fearful.

It is because of this unrecognized pull toward the numinous in its dark side that it is so difficult, even for a great literary artist, to portray a wholly good and admirable character. Dickens's villains have a power not found in his good men and women, and the great artist usually provides a balance, as he does in *The Old Curiosity Shop* (1841), where the innocent and saintly Little Nell is opposed to the grotesque villainy of the dwarf Quilp. This opposition provides the tension that gives the novel life and would slacken if Nell had things too much her own way. In *The Brothers Karamazov* (1880), Dostoevsky cannot, by his finest art, make the saintly Alyosha as real to us as the man divided between his good and evil, his brother Ivan. Modern human beings are aware of this tension as a demanding element in their own lives and respond to it in fiction.

When Tolstoy wrote *War and Peace* (1868) and *Anna Karenina* (1878), his powerful depiction of this tension made him a literary artist of the highest achievement, yet when he was impelled later to write works determinedly improving in tone, that splendor did not survive. But we must sympathize with Tolstoy's deep conviction that art should be religious in its impulse and make religious feeling at its highest available to a public neither devout nor philosophical. This is a conviction recognizable in many novels of the first rank.

In vast areas of popular literature a defensible, if sometimes crude, morality asserts itself, greatly to the satisfaction of its readers. In Westerns, the Good Guy—and the values he stands for—triumphs over the Bad Guy, who is corrupt, cruel, and frequently cynical in his attitude toward women. For the Bad Guy to win in the struggle would topple the myth of worthiness and decency that readers of Westerns value. The same simple morality informs much science fiction and fantasy literature (e.g., C. S. Lewis's "Space Trilogy" [1938–1945] and his "Chronicles of Narnia" [1950–1956], with their overarching Christian cosmology), and even J. K. Rowling's wildly popular Harry Potter novels of alternate worlds and sorcery.

This is significant. In the words of G. K. Chesterton, "men's basic assumptions and everlasting energies are to be found in penny dreadfuls and halfpenny novelettes" (*Heretics*, 1905). Great numbers of readers of detective stories are, without ever defining their attitude, devoted to the morality of "Vengeance is mine, I will repay, saith the Lord," or the bleaker law of *Exodus* 21:23–24: "If any mischief follow then thou shalt give life for life, eye for eye, tooth for tooth, hand for hand, foot for foot." Who is the instrument of the Lord's vengeance, who brings the murderer or the thief to his just reward? The Great Detective, of course. Be he the cold reasoning-machine Sherlock Holmes; the man of pity, Chesterton's own Father Brown; the high-born, donnish Peter Wimsey, or the immobile, intellectual Nero Wolfe; he—or she, as in the cases, say, of Agatha Christie's Miss Marple or Sara Paretsky's V. I. Warshawski—is always the figure recognizable from medieval religious drama, sometimes called Divine Correction. He or she is the restorer of balance, the dispenser of justice, working on behalf of a higher authority.

The same pattern is observable in the spy story, which is the main rival of the detective novel. However attractive or extenuating may be the temptations that make the spy betray his country, and however plodding, weary, disillusioned, and dowdy the spy-catcher may be, in the end the betrayer of the highest values must be found and brought to some sort of justice. Often the tone is cynical; often the secret service is represented as no more than a game; but behind every game lies the desire to win, and thereby to establish or reaffirm some superiority. What superiority? That of an overriding morality.

How far is morality from religion? To the novelist it sometimes looks like the religion that people profess who wish to ignore God—or keep him behind a veil as being too grand for common concerns. It may be the religion of people who find an ever-present God embarrassing company, because they are aware that they cannot live always on the heights, and they do not believe that God understands their insufficiencies. But to support a system of morality without some reference to numinous values is uphill work for a philosopher, and beyond the scope of even a highly intelligent general reader.

The novel, at its best, is a work of literary art and a form of entertainment at all levels, concerned with human beings in every aspect of their lives, including, but not necessarily approving, their religious life. That its connection with religion should be, in the main, through morality rather than through faith or revelation should therefore surprise no one. Whatever pinnacles it may achieve in morality or philosophy, its character remains secular.

Bibliography

Many books of criticism that deal with the novel make passing reference to religious concerns when these are relevant, but not all critics are even-handed in their treatment of religion, and some of them seem almost to be religious illiterates, who either stand in foolish awe of what they have not examined or ignorantly decry it. The reader who wishes to pursue the train of thought suggested in the preceding entry might well reread the novels mentioned, with special attention to their religious implication. The following list confines itself to those critical works cited in the article:

Bakhtin, M. M. *The Dialogic Imagination: Four Essays.* Edited by Michael Holquist. Translated by Caryl Emerson and Michael Holquist. Austin, Tex., 1981.

Doody, Margaret Anne. *The True Story of the Novel.* New Brunswick, N.J., 1996.

Lukács, Georg. *The Theory of the Novel: A Historico-Philosophical Essay on the Forms of Great Epic Literature.* Translated by Anna Bostock. Cambridge, Mass., 1971.

Updike, John. "Religion and Literature." In *The Religion Factor: An Introduction to How Religion Matters,* edited by William Scott Green and Jacob Neusner. Louisville, Ky., 1996.

Ziolkowski, Eric. *The Sanctification of Don Quixote: From Hidalgo to Priest.* University Park, Pa., 1991.

Robertson Davies (1987)
Eric Ziolkowski (2005)

FICTION: LATIN AMERICAN FICTION AND RELIGION

As in most places in the world where different cultures and religions have come together as the result of political conquests, in Latin America, fiction, religion and history are inseparably connected. In *The Invention of America: An Inquiry into the Historical Nature of the New World and the Meaning of History* (1961), Edmundo O'Gorman makes substantiated claims that the New World was already an invention in the European imagination before 1492. Early documents about the conquest and colonization of the Americas tell the story of such invention and of the theological conflicts caused in Western Christian thought by the encounter of a New World different from the known world of Europe, Asia and Africa. The zeal of evangelization, which accompanied political and economic expansion, resulted in theological schisms within the Church that lasted for centuries, vestiges of which can be seen today in the figure of revolutionary priests such as Camilo Torres and Ernesto Cardenal, Liberation Theology and, in various forms, in nineteenth and twentieth century Latin American literary discourses. Christian theology, Judeo-Christian messianic literature, and medieval legends and myths colored the way Europeans perceived the New World. Even Christopher Columbus, who believed he had arrived in India, also claimed in his fourth diary to have found the entrance to Paradise: a claim that the Postmodern Argentinean writer, Abel Posse, humorously engages in his novel *Los perros del paraíso* (1983). Augusto Roa Bastos, in *Vigilia del Almirante* (1992), and Alejo Carpentier, in *El arpa y la sombra* (1979), return to the figure of Columbus to question foundational *truths* in the history of the New World.

In an attempt to understand native religions, and as a vehicle for teaching Christian faith, Humanist Christian missionaries in the New World established analogies between indigenous religions and Christianity. Even as late as the eighteenth century the association was made between Christ's Apostle Thomas and Viracocha, the white deity of the Incas, and between Thomas and the Aztec wind god Quetzacoatl. Christian theology, fused with pre-Columbian and African myths, and infused with Erasmus's theological treaties on human liberty, dignity, and pure spirituality (*De libero arbitrio,* 1524), created the conditions for the emergence of messianic movements of different religious and political orders. Some announced an apocalyptic second-coming of Christ colored by indigenous New World and African religions; others longed for political messiahs. Alejo Carpentier's novel *The Kingdom of This World* (1957), and Gabriel García Márquez's *One Hundred Years of Solitude* (*Cian años de soledad,* 1967), find in these religious prophesies a metaphor for a cosmic revolution that, like the Arawak and the Quiché Maya deity Huracán, destroys an old order of things. The already archetypal image in Latin America of the cosmic wind of destruction and creation (*Popol Vuh*), brings together in these two novels the Judeo-Christian story of the Flood, the Christian prophesies of a Judgement Day, as well as the Maya-Quiché stories in the *Popol Vuh* about the gods' destruction of their first creation. In his monumental 1981 novel *The War of the End of the World (La guerra del fin del mundo),* Mario Vargas Llosa records the tragic destruction of one such movement in the hinterlands of Bahia, Brazil. The novel is based on Euclides da Cunha's accounts in his 1903 Brazilian Classic *Rebellion in the Backlands (Os sertoes),* about the war the Republic of Brazil waged against Canudos and its messianic spiritual leader. Both texts are meditations on religious and political fanaticisms in Latin America.

Sixteenth-century political and religious conflicts have attracted the attention of twentieth-century Latin American writers. The writers often return to the foundational texts of this period in order to explore the conflictive religious thoughts that participate in the formation of Latin American cultures, and the imprints those thoughts left in local memories and in those cultures. Mario Vargas Llosa's novel, *El hablador* (1987) is the story of a modern Peruvian of Jewish and Christian background who becomes involved in the life of an Amazonian tribe. He eventually becomes an itinerant tribal storyteller who blends into the traditional tribal tales he narrates, Western literature and Judeo-Christian myths. The novel is a metaphor for the religious and cultural syncretism that has taken place in Latin America.

An example of the religious exchanges that have attracted writers in Latin America, especially in the second half of the twentieth century, is the apparition in Mexico of the dark-skinned Virgin of Guadalupe in 1531, to an Indian man, Juan Diego. This is the single most important religious event for modern Mexico, as she is a symbol of national identity and religious consciousness. Guadalupe served as an icon for the Mexican war of independence, for the Chicano movements in the 1970s, and for the Zapatista movement in the 1990s. What is of interest for contemporary Mexican writers is the fact that, as Jacques Lafaye points out, the Christian Virgin of Guadalupe appeared at the same site, in *Tepeyac,* where the Aztec mother goddess Tonantzin was worshipped prior to the arrival of the Spanish. Like other contemporary Latin American writers, Mexican fictional literature dwells on the significance of such syncretisms in modern Mexico. Carlos Fuentes's work places a special emphasis on the relationship between pre-Colombian religions and modern Mexico. In his novel, *La región más transparente* (1958), his novella, *Aura* (1964), and in his short story, "Chac Mool," Fuentes explores the duality of a pre-Colombian realm masked by modern Mexican culture. In *Aura,* we find a contemporary Mexican historian, and in "Chac Mool," a modern day collectionist of pre-Colombian art, both drawn into a mythical Aztec-Maya cyclical time of death and renewal. Fuentes is interested in exploring the religious ambiguities of modern Mexico in relationship to the concepts of death and sacrifice. Based on the Aztec notion that time is a living entity rejuvenated through sacrifice, Fuentes establishes a contrast between the Christian veneration of Christ's sacrifice for the salvation of humanity and the Aztec veneration of sacrificial death as a mode of collective salvation. Syncretism, as a literary trope, can be found in Mexican literature as far back as the seventeenth century when Sor Juana Inés de la Cruz, a Mexican nun and a major writer of the Baroque period, made the association in her play *El divino Narciso* between Christ, the Classical figure of Narcissus—who through metamorphosis transcends his humanity—and the Aztec God of the Seeds, who is reborn after death.

The image of a self-sacrificial crucified Christ and the idea of redemption through death appear frequently in Latin American fiction as a literary trope for social inequality and political injustice. However, the Brazilian writer Clarisse Lispector offers a different metaphor for the *Christi* sacrifice remembered in the Christian rite of the Eucharist. Clarisse's 1964 novel, *The Passion according to G.H.,* represents an allegorical communion between an artist, the writer, and the very origins of life, through the self-sacrificial act of ingesting a roach. Lispector metaphorically associates the ingested insect, which represents a lower but primal form of life in contemporary urban society, with the sacred Egyptian beetle, also a symbol of life and rejuvenation. In another Brazilian Classic, *Grande Sertão: Veredas* (1958), João Guimarães Rosa explores the universal struggle between good and evil, from the syncretic gaze of Christian theology and Asian thought, while at the same time proposing that the act of writing is an alchemical search for a higher truth that can only be intimated through imagination. In *Grande Sertão: Veredas,* the hinterland of Brazil is the stage for the universal battle between good and evil. At the end of the novel, good and evil destroy each other, resulting in a state of nothingness, a *nonada* that reduces humanity's universal saga to the ritual act of memory, and to a repetitive imaginary act of recovery through fiction. Guimarães Rosas's novel also records, reconstructs, and reinvents a way of thinking in the hinterlands, characterized by the fusion of indigenous, African and Christian religions.

AFRICAN RELIGIONS IN LATIN AMERICAN FICTION. Ritual allows its participants to experience and be a part of the source of creation. In Latin American fiction, writers often turn to the representation of ritual in order to record the importance of African traditions in the development of Latin American cultures. The Cuban writer Alejo Carpentier proposes in *The Kingdom of this World,* that the unwavering faith in the African *loas* in Haitian Vodou is what gave Haitian slaves the will power and spiritual strength to defeat the French and to gain independence. Twentieth-century Caribbean and Brazilian fiction demystify the demonic image that African religions have endured since the sixteenth century, while recording the drama of African gods in an American context, colored by Christian and Classical myths.

Caribbean and Brazilian writers may refer to a given *orisha* or *loa,* with the name of a saint, a religious characteristic or a symbol without referring directly to the deity. For example, terms like *red, sun, fire* and *double ax,* may refer to the *orisha Shango,* while images of yellow, copper, cinnamon, honey and fresh waters, may refer to *Oshun.* Jorge Amado's title for his novel, *Gabriela, Clove, and Cinnamon,* alerts the reader to the association in the text between Gabriela and the *orixá Oshun.* African languages also survived in the Caribbean and in Brazil due to their ritual importance, and to the fact that ritual words that define religious concepts, like *ashe* or in Cuba *aché,* do not find exact correspondences in Western thought. The presence of these words in Latin American vernacular languages and in fiction, disrupts, but also enriches the dominance of Western traditions in Latin America by slowly inscribing in them different ways of conceiving life, humanity, and the divine.

African religious thought conceives the cosmos as a dynamic play of forces in which human beings are also players; therefore, through a ritual process of give-and-take, sacrifice, divination, and offerings, human beings can control those forces. This is also the dynamic realm of the *orixás,* which the Brazilian writer Jorge Amado represents in his novels, always in the syncretic cultural setting of Salvador, Bahia. In *Donna Flor and Her Two Husbands,* Amado constructs an invisible realm of popular African traditions and beliefs that coexist in Brazilian society with Christianity in a cultural and religious dynamic interchange. This is a process Fernando Ortiz calls *transculturation* (in Bronislaw Malinowski's introduction to Ortiz's *Cuban Counterpoint, Tobacco and Sugar,* 1940, 1995) to differentiate it from the concept of syncretism.

In Cuba, Lydia Cabrera's work carved out a sacred space in Cuban studies and literature for the religious Afro-Cuban concept of *monte,* meaning jungle, forest, mount, countryside and backyard, as the space where the dynamic forces of the cosmos are at play; where the give-and-take between human beings and natural forces takes place. In her short stories and fables, from *Cuentos negros de Cuba* in 1936 to *Ayapá. Cuentos de Jicotea* in 1971, *monte* is the creole Olympus where the drama of the Afro Cuban deities takes place, mirroring the strengths and weakness, desires, longings, faith and politics of creole society.

A unique representation of African religions and of a greater African consciousness in the Americas can be found in the 1984 novel by the Colombian writer Manuel Zapata Olivella, *Changó el gran Putas.* The novel turns to sixteenth-century Latin American history in order to reinvent America from the gaze of African thought. Here the history of America, including slavery, is the providential design of *Shango,* the ancestral Yoruba *orisha*-king of Ọ̀yọ́, lord of lightning, thunder and fire, whose American counterparts in Zapata's novel are the Aztec wind-god Quetzacoatl, and the Supreme Fire-Father Sun, Inti, of the Incas. Zapata's choice for choosing Shango as the Supreme African Patriarch, is based on the historical fact that Shango is one of the most important African deities in the New World (Bascom, *Shango in the New World,* 1972): a cultural African and African American hero and deity, whose strengths and powers are always balanced by his human-like weaknesses.

In order to place the act of writing within an African tradition from which to retell the same, but different, story of the Americas from the gaze of a triethnic writer, Zapata follows the structure of African ritual recitations and Afro-Caribbean rituals. The novel begins with the act of summoning African and Afro-Indo-American ancestors and *orishas.* As we find in Zapata's novel, in Afro-Caribbean rituals Legba, or Elegua in Cuba, lord of the crossroads, doors, roads and the Word, is the first one and the last one to speak in all rituals. From a postmodern perspective the novel questions and breaks away from the strictures of literary genres and Western epistemology, and also resists the hegemony of Western thought in Latin American literature and history. It also brings together as one Bantu and Yoruba traditions with Haitian Vodou, in which, significantly, Legba is associated with Christ, in order to propose a greater African, Afro-Indo-American consciousness conceived in Zapata's novel from the gaze of African religious thought. Zapata also collapses the conceptual and rhetorical differences between fiction and religion by claiming that he wrote this novel under the spiritual guidance of Ifá: a system of divination of African Yoruba tradition brought to the New World by African slaves that serves as a spiritual guide to those who follow it. In and through Ifá the natural divine forces speak to humans through a system of letters or figures made by the position in which cowrie shells or kola nuts thrown by the priest or *Babalawo* fall on the divining table. Each position forms an *Odu,* or road, of positive or negative outcomes. There are numerous anecdotes with each *Odu* that the *Babalawo* recites as part of the divining process. The anecdotes related to Ifá constitute a sacred oral tradition in Africa. In the Caribbean, the anecdotes of Ifá, and those of a similar divining system known as *Diloggun,* form a written corpus of religious literature (known in Cuba as *Pataki)* that records the survival of an ancestral African consciousness in America. This consciousness is what Zapata defines in his novel as *Muntu.* As in Zapata's novel, the drama of the African deities in Latin American fiction provides a record of African religious traditions, while at the same time recording and retelling the greater story of the Indo-African experience in America.

BIBLIOGRAPHY

Arnone, Robert, Stephen Franz, and Kimberly Morse Cordova. "Religion in Latin America." In *Understanding Contemporary Latin America,* edited by Richard Hillman. Boulder, Colo., 2001.

Barnet, Miguel. *La fuente viva.* La Habana, Cuba, 1983.

Batallón, Marcel. *Erasmo y España.* Vol. 2. Mexico, 1990. A comprehensive study on the influence Desiderus Erasmus's theological thought had in the Spanish Church and in Spanish Humanism. Here Batallón also discusses the passage of Erasmian theology to Spanish America.

Bascom, William. "Two Forms of Afro-Cuban Divination." In *Acculturation in the Americas,* edited by Sol Tax. Chicago, 1952.

Castellanos, Jorge, and Isabel Castellanos. *Cultura afrocubana* (Vol. 4). Miami, 1992. A comprehensive study of four volumes, covering the relationship of Afro Cuban religions and culture with literature and art (Vol. 4), and with languages (Vol. 3).

Cuervo Hewitt, Julia. *Aché: Presencia africana. Tradiciones Yoruba Lucumí en la narrativa cubuana.* New York, 1988.

Deive, Carlos Esteban. *Vodú y magia en Santo Domingo.* Santo Domingo, Dominican Republic, 1975. A study of Vodou as it is practiced in the Dominican Republic, its history and imprints in Dominican literature and art.

Demangles, Leslie. *The Faces of the Gods: Vodou and Roman Catholicism in Haiti.* Chapel Hill, N. C., 1992.

Eliade, Mircea. *The Vanishing God.* Chicago, 1972.

Fernández Olmos, Margarite, and Lizabeth Parvisini-Gebert. *Creole Religions of the Caribbean.* New York, 2003.

Gerbi, Antonello. *The Dispute of the New World: the History of a Polemic (1750–1900),* Pittsburgh, 1973.

Jahn, Janheinz. *Muntu: African Culture and the Western World.* New York, 1990.

Lafaye, Jacques. *Quetzalcóatl y Guadalupe. La formación de la conciencia nacional en México.* Mexico, 1995 (translated from the French: *Quetzalcóatl et Guadalupe. La formation de la consciente nationale au Mexique.* Paris, 1974).

Linsay, Arturo, ed. *Santería Aesthetics in Contemporary Latin American Art.* Washington, D.C., 1996.

Lópe-Calvo, Ignacio. *Religión y militarismo en la obra de Marcos Aguinis 1963–2000.* New York, 2002. A study of Aguinis's work of fiction and the writer's representation of Judaism and the Jewish experience in Argentina.

Phelan, John Leddy. *The Millennial Kingdom of the Franciscans in the New World: A Study of the Writings of Gerónimo de Mendieta (1525–1604).* Berkeley, Calif., 1956, 1970.

Stanley, Porter, Michael Hayes, and David Tombs, eds. *Faith in the Millennium.* Sheffield, U.K., 2001. Numerous papers by different authors that include theological perspectives in Latin America, theology and literature, millenary movements past and present, theology of liberation, art, religion syncretism, and literature.

Verger, Pierre Fatumbi. *Orixás.* Bahia and São Paulo, Brazil, 1981.

JULIA CUERVO HEWITT (2005)

FICTION: CHINESE FICTION AND RELIGION

This essay examines five genres or subgenres of Chinese fiction, namely the *zhiguai*, *chuanqi*, *bianwen*, vernacular short story, and vernacular novel (premodern and modern). Each genre contains works that have themes or structures with religious dimensions. Readership and religious functions of later fictional works will also be mentioned, although these aspects of early works should not be neglected.

ZHIGUAI. The birth of what is usually rendered as Chinese prose fiction (*xiaoshuo*) remains a subject of debate. In defining Chinese fiction in a strict sense, most literary historians trace its origin to the *zhiguai* (records of anomalies), fictional narratives in classical language, in the Six Dynasties period (220–589 CE). These narratives are characterized by an outlook and context rooted in the supernatural world replete with themes such as immortality, the afterlife, the causal relation between merit and punishment, magic, shamanism, and alchemical theories and procedures. In composing these tales, many authors assumed the serious mission of proving the actual existence of the supernatural. Whether or not they succeeded in convincing their readers, this intent along with the general subject matter constitutes the religious dimensions in *zhiguai* tales. Definitive examples in the genre like the *Soushen ji* (In search of the supernatural) of Gan Bao (fl. 320) all represent this tendency.

Zhiguai narratives with religious dimensions can be divided into the modes of *fangshi* magicians, Daoist, and Buddhist. Some *zhiguai* collections of the Six Dynasties, especially the early ones, were perhaps composed by *fangshi* magicians. They are reminiscences of *fangshi* magicians, diviners, and healers as well as of their erudition and expertise.

Zhiguai anthologies of mainly Buddhist and Daoist origins were apparently put together by those who maintained and practiced the religious faith shown in the works represented. The most explicit are the collections focusing on biographies of Daoist immortals (*xian*) and Buddhist miracle tales. Narratives belonging to the Daoist mode tell of ascension, meditation, and autonomy, all laying claim to the Daoist authority. They emerged predominantly out of the immortality cult and the alchemical practices common to popular Daoism.

Regarding the Buddhist mode, these Buddhist miracle tales are largely of the following three general types: (1) accounts of divine intervention and supernatural power in times of need, usually wielded by Avalokiteśvara (Guanyin); (2) illustrations of piety and sincere belief, often through descriptions of the inexorable workings of the law of karmic retribution; and (3) remarkable deeds of monks or laypeople, serving to demonstrate their high spiritual attainments.

Zhiguai tales stress communication between humans and supernatural beings. Whether it is a man's union with a female deity or a human's sojourn in the immortal territory, the stories invariably embody a state of transcendence for which Daoist practitioners yearn. One of the motifs is communication between the living and the dead. Still many *zhiguai* stories are about retributive phenomena.

CHUANQI. *Chuanqi* (transmission of the extraordinary) as a genre refers to fictional narratives in the classical language, longer than *zhiguai*, that emerged during the Tang dynasty (618–907 CE). Tang *chuanqi* tales were overwhelmed by a curiosity about traffic with the transcendent world of gods, immortals, and numinous beings or with the world beyond the grave. Compared to the Six Dynasties *zhiguai*, what distinguishes Tang *chuanqi* lies not so much in what kinds of supernatural themes are presented in a tale, as in how they are represented. With its particular narrative method and polished style, the concern of *chuanqi* is mainly on human motivations and on the exemplary side of human nature. In other words, the supernatural tends to be less arbitrary and arrogant but more benevolent and accessible in its relationship with humans. Their sympathy lies with those who have withdrawn from the official life or shown a tendency to a religious life.

While half of the *chuanqi* tales are determined by the theme of the supernatural, the other favorite subject is love, which is sometimes amalgamated with religious elements. In terms of depiction of supernatural beings, *chuanqi* brought several innovations. First, supernatural beings could become psychologically complex and sympathetic. The common topoi in *chuanqi* tales include the predestined marriage made in heaven, in which the romance with a nonhuman woman was particularly suited to the *chuanqi*'s combination of the emotional with the extraordinary. In some tales black magic transforms humans into beasts, including the self-motivated transformation of Daoists and Buddhists. Some tales present the process of alchemical formation as a psychological trial of dangerous experiences. Dragon lore in Tang *chuanqi* highlights human involvement in the dragon family. Some tales are about the predestination or revelation of a person's future, likely because of the belief given by the Buddhist doctrine of karmic retribution. Some tales narrate new kinds of oddity involved in dream phenomena and put into service essentially the Daoist-Buddhist ideas concerning the illusory nature of life and the vanity of striving after worldly gain. A great number of tales provide ideal knight errantry that possesses supernatural and fantastic elements, with the Daoist propensity to having the *xia* (swordsman) hero or heroine retire from the human world after his or her mission is accomplished. And again many tales tell of communication with ghosts.

Although the *zhiguai* from the Six Dynasties and *chuanqi* from the Tang are the most well known, later collections of *zhiguai* and *chuanqi* are also numerous. Some of them, such as Hong Mai's (1123–1202) *Yijian zhi* (Records of the listener), have been used extensively by historians of Chinese religion as a source book for delineating religious beliefs and ritual practice at that time. In the Qing dynasty (1644–1911) *Liaozhai zhiyi* (Strange tales from make-do studio) by Pu Songling (1640–1715) is the most celebrated collection of supernatural tales in the entire canon in the Chinese tradition, which alone contains almost five hundred stories. It is viewed as the pinnacle of the *zhiguai* and *chuanqi* traditions. *Liaozhai zhiyi* is especially famous for the depiction of female ghosts and fox spirits.

Bianwen. *Bianwen* (transformation texts) of the Tang dynasty and the Five Dynasties periods (907–960 CE) from the Dunhuang caves are narratives written in semicolloquial Chinese in a prosimetric style. These texts, as a type of storytelling, were performed, intending to represent a miraculous event for the purpose of enlightening the audience with Buddhist teachings. Transformation texts are believed to have been used in combination with visual images for performances in Buddhist temples or in certain ritual services. The performers of these transformations were professional entertainers, and the copyists of the extant manuscripts were mostly lay students studying a largely secular curriculum in schools run by Buddhist monasteries.

Some transformation texts with Buddhist subject matter excel in conjuring vast *maṇḍalas* of fantastic beings, divinities, or demons surrounding the central Buddha and vistas of other worlds. *Bianwen* have their roots in Buddhist literature, though the genre quickly became a secular form of entertainment, adopting Chinese historical and contemporary themes. As an example of the Buddhist influence on Chinese thought and writing, *bianwen* stimulated Chinese fiction with many new forms and themes (prosimetric form, greater extension, and relinquishment of the claim that verifiable historical facts are being recorded) and provided an immeasurable variety of stories and figures.

Vernacular Short Stories. Chinese vernacular fiction has its origins in the professional storytelling of the Song (960–1279) and Yuan (1206–1368) periods. Scholars debate what the precise categories of storytelling are in Song records. There were at least two schools of storytelling, among four or six, related to religious phenomena: first, *xiaoshuo* or short stories that included such supernatural themes as ghosts and marvels, and second, Buddhist scriptural narration, monastic tales, and scriptural parodies. In the Yuan, professional storytelling *xiaoshuo* is divided into eight classes. Of the eight, three are primarily concerned with religious themes: spirits and demons, sorcery, and gods and immortals. All these types of the Song-Yuan storytelling continued to appear in later written stories.

With this background in mind, *huaben* should be considered next. *Huaben,* or the vernacular story, refers to a short story from the Song to the Qing dynasties that is written in the vernacular. Many *huaben* stories dealt with the lives of the middle to lower classes, focusing on down-to-earth concerns like preservation of family or lineage and the quest for worldly success. Some, however, treated Daoist and Buddhist themes, emphasizing the emptiness of mundane glory as well as the happiness of reclusion and transcendence.

The development of vernacular stories can be divided into three periods. In the early period (the Yuan and early Ming dynasties, up to 1450), the themes of these early stories include demons, ghosts, and religion. The demon stories normally tell how a young man encounters an animal spirit or a ghost in the guise of a young girl, makes love to her, discovers his danger, and calls an exorcist, usually a Daoist master, to subdue her.

One distinctive story type of the middle period (mid–Ming dynasty, 1400–1575) pertains to the Buddhist stories. They tell of priests, their deaths, and sometimes their reincarnations, combining themes involving the priesthood with that of karmic causation. The stories are concerned above all with the priest's vow of chastity and the temptations to which he is subjected, but they also possess a certain religious meaning. The stories of the middle period are either Buddhist in inspiration or reveal a down-to-earth morality that inevitably links deeds to punishments.

The stories of the late period (after 1550) were written by literati who often fused Confucian principles with popular religious ideas. Many stories in the "Three Words" (*sanyan*), three forty-piece collections of stories compiled by Feng Menglong (1574–1646), have a strong Buddhist flavor. A representative *sanyan* story has its plot building on Buddhist beliefs, its narrative furnished with Buddhist lore, and its conclusion engaging the mediation of Buddhist deities or the attainment of buddhahood.

Among storywriters of this period, Langxian's stories stress reclusion and religious beliefs. They are devoted to

Daoist themes, such as the attainment of immortality, more than any previous stories. Yet the Daoism of Langxian's works was not a rigid doctrine but one of the sentimental and artistic.

Confucian literati also described religious phenomena in their short stories. Ling Mengchu (1580–1644) in *Paian jingqi* (Slapping the table in amazement) and in *Erke paian jingqi* (Slapping the table in amazement, second collection), two collections of stories commonly known as "Two Slappings" (*erpai*), described many religious people and motifs. These stories are ultimately related to the typical example of the *Shanshu* (morality books).

VERNACULAR NOVELS. *Zhanghui xiaoshuo,* a term that is used for full-length vernacular fiction, from premodern times, is customarily translated as "vernacular novel." When *novel* is used in the premodern Chinese context, however, it does not imply a secular literary genre. Nor does it necessarily project humans in society as the novel in the Western counterpart.

Lu Xun (1881–1936), in his pioneering *Zhongguo xiaoshuo shilue* (Brief history of Chinese fiction), defines *shenmo xiaoshuo* (novels of gods and demons) as a subgenre with religious or supernatural subject matters. There are over one hundred extant novels in this category. But religious or supernatural elements are not limited to these novels. Any novel without a religious or supernatural element would be rare. The Buddhist imagery and its underlying ideology in Chinese novels are obvious. Among the most important Buddhist motifs in Chinese novels are karmic retribution, rebirth, heavens and hells, miraculous transformations and manifestations, and illusion and dream. In many novels the theme, plot, structure, mode of expression, psychological conflicts, and finale are shaped by Buddhist epistemic-soteriological models, especially by the quest for enlightenment as prescribed by the Chinese Mahāyāna tradition.

Honglou meng (Dream of the red chamber; or, The story of the stone) by Cao Xueqin (1715?–1763 or 1764) is the universally acknowledged masterpiece in the Chinese novel. The relationship between Bao-yu and his cousin, Dai-yu, can be interpreted as the narrative enactment of their karmic reciprocity, origin, and destiny. The novel shows the Buddhist complication of desire, as exemplified by Bao-yu's long journey to the Gates of Emptiness. *The Story of the Stone* deals with important Buddhist images of dreams and mirrors. It also represents the paradox of Mahāyāna Buddhism: only in the world of suffering can one find deliverance. That a full-length novel centers its plot on the protagonist's desire for liberation from his emotional sufferings and on his final determination to become a monk has few precedents. While the affirmation of the Buddhist view of reality is but one side of the novel, its success lies in the author's masterful translation of the mythic and religious into the aesthetic and realistic. *The Story of the Stone* in this light can be read as a book of enlightenment through love.

Besides *The Story of the Stone*, Dong Yue's (1620–1686) *Xiyou bu* (Supplement to journey to the west) manifests Buddhist psychology. In *Jin Ping Mei* (Plum in the golden vase) and *Xingshi yinyuan zhuan* (The bonds of matrimony; or, Marriage destines to awaken the world), the Buddhist vision based on merit-making and karmic retribution is apparent. One type of Buddhist novel is the hagiographical fictional work, such as *Qiantang hu yin Jidian Chanshi yulu* (The recorded sayings of the recluse from Qiantang Lake, the Chan master Crazy Ji; 1569).

Most Chinese novels begin with an account of the initial cosmogony. In these novels this familiar Chinese creation myth is immediately followed by an embodiment of the general patterns in specific mythical-historical processes. This pattern of cosmogony is of Daoist character. Indeed Daoism provides the Chinese novel with a soteriologic and narrative structure. In many novels the heroes (or heroines) usually have divine origins (*chushen*) in heaven or paradise, and because of their own mistakes they are banished to or reborn in the human world to experience suffering, redemption, and self-cultivation (*xiuxing*) and to accumulate merits by rescuing other sentient beings, saving the world, or subduing demons. After they accomplish their mundane missions, they return to their primordial heavenly positions or reattain immortality. All works of "fiction of gods and demons" and many other novels share this pattern of development. While *The Story of the Stone* can be read undoubtedly as a profound Buddhist allegory, the same novel can also be read as a Daoist myth in which the male and female protagonists as heavenly immortal beings are banished to the human world to repay their debts of love. After they fulfill their long-cherished wish of falling in love with each other as an experience of the vicissitudes of life, they have no other way but to return to their origins.

In *Shuihu zhuan* (Outlaws of the marsh; or, Water margin) the 108 bandits are 108 stars who are released by accident. They finally vanish in the world because of their redemption and accomplishment. The same sort of Daoist frame of previous origins is present in the Ming novel *Pingyao zhuan* (The quelling of demons), Luo Maodeng's (fl. 1597) *Sanbao taijian xiyang ji tongsu yanyi* (Journey to the western ocean), Li Baichuan's (c. 1720–after 1762) *Lüye xianzong* (Trials of immortals in the green wilds), and Li Ruzhen's (c. 1763–1830) *Jinghua yuan* (Flowers in the mirror) and is used more ironically in Wu Jingzi's (1701–1754) *Rulin waishi* (The scholars). Even for the historical novel *Sanguo yanyi* (Romance of the three kingdoms; c. 1400–1500), its antecedent *Sanguozhi pinghua* (Stories from the records of the three kingdoms; c. 1321–1323) still retains this supernatural episode. In a majority of erotic novels, toward the end the protagonists forgo their practice and attain immortality, centering on the Daoist art of love and pursuit of longevity. Of course one of the best-known Daoist novels is *Fengshen yanyi* (Investiture of the gods). Despite Buddhist influence, this novel exhibits the most explicit Daoist framework and elements by changing a historical novel into a "novel of gods and demons." The Daoists participate in the transition between the Shang and the Zhou from the beginning to the end. The war between the two Daoist sects in the novel represents a hierarchical struggle in Daoism: the official Daoism and folk Daoism. In fact the wars launched in the human world are envisioned as part of the divine cosmogonic process, that is, the "investiture of the gods."

Some novels even have the flavor of popular or sectarian religion. Pan Jingruo's *Sanjiao kaimi guizheng yanyi* (The romance of the three teachings clearing up the deluded and returning them to the true way; 1612–1620) reveals the mentality behind morality books, a lay religious movement. The moral motif of the novel was also stimulated by the Religion of the Three Teachings, a syncretic popular religious sect founded by Lin Zhao'en (1517–1598). Liu E's (1857–1909) *Laocan youji* (The travels of Laocan; 1907) intends to show the author's religious vision based on the Taigu school, an esoteric philosophy-turned-religious society with a syncretic creed, that embodied elements from Confucianism, Buddhism, Daoism, and probably even Manichaeism. Episodes in the novel, especially in chapters eight to eleven, which constitute the central part of the twenty-chapter work, were modeled after the Taigu school and its main figures, including a Taigu version of worldly paradise, a religious vision and cosmology of the Taigu school, the transcendental realm of this sectarian movement with its cultivation arts, and its prophetic faith in and eschatological problems with history and Chinese culture as well as its political criticism.

The religious novel par excellence is *Xiyou ji* (Journey to the west; or, Monkey), which is attributed to Wu Cheng'en (c. 1500–1582). Religious themes and rhetoric permeate the entire work. *Journey to the West* contains many references to *yinyang* and five-phases (*wuxing*) terminology, *Yijing* (Classic of change) and alchemical lore, and various other Daoist, Buddhist, and Confucian ideas and practices. For more than three centuries the principal concern of criticism on the novel has been to decipher the allegory by separating the narrative surface into moral, religious, and philosophical meanings. While the novel can be read as a tale of travel and adventure or Confucian rectification of the mind and moral self-cultivation, it can also be read as a religious allegory. The immense appropriation of the teaching from the Three Religions (*sanjiao*) is what makes *Journey to the West* a unique text in the history of the Chinese novel. On the Buddhist side, *Journey to the West* consistently projects a distinctly Buddhist worldview. There are countless allusions to Buddhist concepts and legends structured in the narrative. Although there may be no systematic discourse of one particular Buddhist doctrine in the narrative, certain themes and figures, such as karmic laws, merit making, Buddha's mercy, and the paradoxical connection between mind and buddhahood, do receive consistent development. Viewing the text this way, *Journey to the West* can be read as a story of Buddhist *karma* and redemption or enlightenment.

The story of *Journey to the West* raises a rather perplexing phenomenon, that is, that the narrative provides astonishingly few details traceable to specific Buddhist sources, although its story is built on the historical pilgrimage undertaken by Xuanzang (596–664 CE), one of the most famous Buddhist personalities in Chinese history. It is rather noteworthy how extensively the Daoist themes and rhetoric appear in every part of the work. In the novel Daoist elements function not merely as means of providing commentary on incidents and characters in the narrative but often as an aid to disclose the true nature of the fellow pilgrims, to help characterize their essential relationships, and to evolve the narrative action itself. Moreover *Journey to the West* on the whole presents a complete process of internal alchemical cultivation, both the cultivation of nature (*xinggong*) and cultivation of life (*minggong*), including various stages in a proper sequence. Besides the Buddhist notion of salvation or enlightenment and the neo-Confucian rectification of the mind, the author now adds immortality as the distinctive goal of the pilgrimage.

Religious functions. Many authors, editors, and publishers of novels intended their works to be read as religious scriptures, and many readers accepted this claim. In this light *Journey to the West* is one of the three most important Daoist texts for adepts to study in their self-cultivation as a modern Quanzhen (Complete Perfection) Daoist asserts. Indeed many Chinese novels serve as religious texts, namely, morality books. Certain novels and morality books were printed together as two parts of the same work, making the former the exemplar and the latter the tenet. Many temples have printed and issued several novels as morality books or religious texts. There are always some messages at the end of these novels encouraging distributing these novels as merit making. Thus the readers, with their shared value and understanding of the devotional intent of the novels, constituted a religious community by disseminating and receiving these devotional novels in the same temples.

Some of these novels were not only devotional in nature but also revelatory as well. They have their origins in a context of religious revelations. At some point of their transmission, the novels may have been associated with a personage or group with techniques of revelation, such as spirit possession, shamanism, and spirit writing. In this case perhaps either the patron deities of the cults revealed the text or the mediums that the deities possessed "delivered" the text in spirit writing of planchette séances (*fuji*). The appendixes at the end of *Dongyou ji* (Journey to the east) reveal that it was obviously an output of the planchette spirit writing. New novels, such as *Dongming baoji* (A precious record of the mysteries of outlying realms), were uttered by the deities through this technique of spirit writing.

The novels that functioned as vehicles for their protagonists' cults can also affirm these cults' existence. Thus it may well be that a proselytizing purpose probably underlies at least some "novels of gods and demons." For example, *Romance of the Three Kingdoms* has had an enormous impact on secret societies, and its character Lord Guan (Guan Yu) was deified as a universal god in Chinese religion. With respect to *Journey to the West,* Monkey exerts its influence on folk religion, making the Monkey cult in southeast China and Hong Kong one of the most popular cults. Many popular deities are drawn from *Investiture of the Gods* as well. Sometimes the influence of popular novels has had imprints on the monastic attitude toward the saints or deities. And some novels themselves were even canonized by the Buddhist or Daoist institutions.

Many novels, such as *Plum in the Golden Vase,* provide vivid pictures of Daoist and Buddhist rites. More important the novel has had a closer affinity with religious ritual. The ritual appendix found at the end of *Beiyou ji* (Journey to the north) stipulates the rules of worship. The readership was thus anticipated not to read the novel passively but to actively perform rites in honor of the novel's protagonist, God Perfect Warrior. In Jiangxi province in the early twenty-first century a Daoist ritual called "Breaking the Yellow River Trap" is directly from a battle described in chapter fifty of *Investiture of the Gods.*

Martial arts novels. *Wuxia xiaoshuo* or martial arts novels as a genre of popular fiction emerged in the popular urban press of the 1920s and 1930s and was later produced in the 1950s in Hong Kong and Taiwan (also encompassing the genre's thematic predecessors in earlier literature). In the 1920s and 1930s Huanzhulouzhu (1902–1961), in *Shushan jianxia zhuan* (Swordsmen of the mountains of Shu), narrates amazing tales of flying swordsmen, monsters, and magical combat largely drawn from Buddhist, Daoist, and popular religious fantasies. The "New School" of martial arts novels since the 1950s, represented by Liang Yusheng (Chen Wentong; 1922–), Jin Yong (Zha Liangyong; 1924–), and Gu Long (Xiong Yaohua; 1936–1985), inherits religious fantasies as the central plots and structures. But these novels also explore the religious meanings and truth behind martial arts, especially in Jin Yong's novels.

Modern fiction. Foreign cultural influences are particularly noticeable in fiction by and for the intelligentsia in the wake of the vernacular literature movement and the May Fourth New Culture movement. Influenced by the Enlightenment spirit, most modern Chinese fiction writers maintained an antireligion attitude. Given the Western cultural impact, however, some writers more or less tended to borrow Christianity in their fictional works. To most of the May Fourth writers, such as Lu Xun (1881–1936), Guo Moruo (1892–1978), and Mao Dun (Shen Yanbing; 1896–1981), Christ's teachings and lifestyle epitomize a spiritual force that can guide the individual in his or her pursuit of wholeness. Thus, in the minds of these writers, the individual should not adhere to Christ through religious faith but must follow his teachings in a basically humanistic fashion. Besides, Buddhism also exerted certain influence on modern fiction. As China was devastated by civil wars, foreign encroachment, and internal corruption, authors such as Fei Ming (Feng Wenbing; 1901–1967) accepted the Buddhist philosophy and acknowledged the imperfectness of this world and the sadness of human life; others like Yu Dafu (1896–1945) were pessimistic romantics, taking refuge in the *nirvāṇa* of love. Among modern Chinese fiction writers, Xu Dishan (1893–1941) had a strong interest in religion, including Buddhism and Christianity. What distinguished Xu Dishan from his contemporaries was his concern with the basic religious experience of charity or love and endeavor, which manifests in nearly all his stories to show its pervasive presence in human lives.

The decades from the 1990s onward saw a revival of interest in folklore and awareness of religion in Chinese fiction. Jia Pingwa (1952–), in his short stories, particularly the collection *Taibai* (1991), demonstrates a return to the classical tale tradition and its fascination in mystical and numinous phenomena, including religious magic. Gao Xingjian (1940–), the 2000 Nobel literature laureate, is more outstanding in this respect in his quest for individual spiritual freedom. In his best-known epic novel *Lingshan* (Soul mountain, 1990), Gao Xingjian makes manifest his sincere pursuit of religious values. Much of *Soul Mountain* explores or imagines a Chinese tradition counter to the orthodoxy and gives a reference to Daoism, which provides a moral baseline and cultural ground. It marks not only the first Chinese winner of the Nobel Prize for literature but also the fading of scorn for religion among most modern Chinese intellectuals and their literature, including fiction.

Bibliography

Adkins, Curtis Peter. "The Supernatural in T'ang Ch'uan-Ch'i Tales: An Archetypal View." Ph.D. diss., Ohio State University, 1976.

Berling, Judith A. "Religion and Popular Culture: The Management of Moral Capital in *The Romance of the Three Teachings.*" In *Popular Culture in Late Imperial China,* edited by David Johnson, Andrew J. Nathan, and Evelyn S. Rawski, pp. 188–218. Berkeley, Calif., 1985.

Bokenkamp, Stephen R. "The Peach Flower Font and the Grotto Passage." *Journal of the American Oriental Society* 106 (1986): 65–77.

Campany, Robert Ford. *Strange Writing: Anomaly Accounts in Early Medieval China.* Albany, N.Y., 1996.

Cedzich, Ursula-Angelika. "The Cult of the Wu-t'ung/Wu-hsien in History and Fiction: The Religious Roots of the *Journey to the South.*" In *Ritual and Scripture in Chinese Popular Religion: Five Studies,* edited by David Johnson, pp. 137–218. Berkeley, Calif., 1995.

Chang, H. C. "General Introduction." In *Chinese Literature,* vol. 3: *Tales of the Supernatural,* edited by H. C. Chang. New York, 1984.

Despeux, Catherine. "Les lectures alchemiques du *His-yu chi.*" In *Religion und Philosophie in Ostasien: Festschrift für Hans Steininger zum 65. Geburtstag,* edited by Gert Naundorf, Karl-Heinz Pohl, and Hans-Hermann Schmidt, pp. 61–75. Würzburg, Germany, 1985.

DeWoskin, Kenneth J. "The Six Dynasties *Chih-kuai* and the Birth of Fiction." In *Chinese Narrative: Critical and Theoreti-*

cal Essays, edited by Andrew H. Plaks, pp. 21–52. Princeton, N.J., 1977.

Dudbridge, Glen. *Religious Experience and Lay Society in T'ang China: A Reading of Tai Fu's Kuang-i chi.* Cambridge, U.K., 1995.

Eichhorn, Werner. "Bemerkungen über einen Daoistischen Roman." In *Studia Sino-mongolica: Festschrift für Herbert Franke*, edited by Wolfgang Bauer, pp. 353–361. Wiesbaden, Germany, 1979.

Éliasberg, Danielle. *Le roman du pourfendeur de démons: Traduction annotée et commentaries.* Vol. 4. Paris, 1976.

Gjertson, Donald E. "The Early Chinese Buddhist Miracle Tale: A Preliminary Survey." *Journal of the American Oriental Society* 101, no. 3 (1981): 287–301.

Hanan, Patrick. *The Chinese Vernacular Story.* Cambridge, Mass., 1981.

Kao, Karl S. Y. "Introduction." In *Classical Chinese Tales of the Supernatural and the Fantastic: Selections from the Third to the Tenth Century*, edited by Karl S. Y. Kao, pp. 1–51. Bloomington, Ind., 1985.

Kominami Ichirō. *Chūgoku no shinwa to monoratari: Ko shōsetsushi no tenkai* (Chinese mythology and stories: On the history of ancient fiction). Tokyo, 1984.

Lauwaert, Françoise. "Comptes des dieux, calculs des hommes: Essai sur la notion de rétribution dans les contes en langue vulgaire du 17ème siècle." *T'oung Pao* 76, nos. 1–3 (1990): 62–94.

Li, Fengmao. *Xu Xun yu Sa Shoujian: Deng Zhimo Daojiao xiaoshuo yanjiu* (Xu Xun and Sa Shoujian: Studies in Deng Zhimo's Daoist novels). Taipei, 1997.

Li, Qiancheng. *Fictions of Enlightenment: Journey to the West, Tower of Myriad Mirrors, and Dream of the Red Chamber.* Honolulu, 2004.

Liu Ts'un-jen. *Buddhist and Taoist Influences on Chinese Novels*, vol. 1: *The Authorship of the Feng Shen Yen I.* Wiesbaden, Germany, 1962.

Liu Ts'un-jen. "Quanzhen jiao he xiaoshuo *Xiyou ji*" (Quanzhen Daoism and the novel *Journey to the West*). In *Hefeng tang wenji* (Collected works of the harmonious hall), edited by Liu Ts'un-jen, vol. 3, pp. 1319–1391. Shanghai, 1991.

Liu, Xiaolian. *The Odyssey of the Buddhist Mind: The Allegory of the Later "Journey to the West."* Lanham, Md., 1994.

Mair, Victor H. "The Narrative Revolution in Chinese Literature: Ontological Presuppositions." *Chinese Literature: Essays, Articles, Reviews* 5, nos. 1–2 (1983): 1–28.

Mair, Victor H. "The Contributions of T'ang and Five Dynasties Transformation Texts (*Pien-Wen*) to Later Chinese Popular Literature." *Sino-Platonic Papers* 12 (1989): 1–71.

Mair, Victor H. *T'ang Transformation Texts: A Study of the Buddhist Contribution to the Rise of Vernacular Fiction and Drama in China.* Cambridge, Mass., 1989.

Maspero, Henri. "Un text Daoiste sur l'orient roman." In *Études historiques*, edited by Henri Maspero, pp. 93–108. Paris, 1950.

Robinson, Lewis Stewart. *Double-Edged Sword: Christianity and Twentieth Century Chinese Fiction.* Hong Kong, 1986.

Sawada Mizuho. *Bukkyō to Chūgoku bungaku* (Buddhism and Chinese literature). Tokyo, 1975.

Schipper, Kristofer Marinus. *L'empereur Wou des Han dans la légende taoïste: Han Wou-ti nei-tchouan.* Paris, 1965.

Seaman, Gary. "Introduction." In *Journey to the North: An Ethnohistorical Analysis and Annotated Translation of the Chinese Folk Novel Pei-yu chi*, pp. 1–39. Berkeley, Calif., 1987.

Shahar, Meir. *Crazy Ji: Chinese Religion and Popular Literature.* Cambridge, Mass., 1998.

Wang, Yao. "Xiaoshuo yu fangshu" (Fiction and magic). In *Zhonggu wenxueshi lunji* (Essays on the history of medieval Chinese literature), pp. 85–110. Shanghai, 1956.

Yu, Anthony C. "'Rest, Rest, Perturbed Spirit!' Ghosts in Traditional Chinese Prose Fiction." *Harvard Journal of Asiatic Studies* 47, no. 2 (1987): 397–434.

Yu, Anthony C. *Yu Guofan Xi you ji lun ji* (Essays by Anthony C. Yu on *Journey to the West*). Taipei, 1989. Contains the Chinese translation of the articles originally in English on *Journey to the West.*

Yu, Anthony C. *Rereading the Stone: Desire and the Making of Fiction in Dream of the Red Chamber.* Princeton, N.J., 1997.

Yu, Anthony C., trans. and ed. *The Journey to the West.* 4 vols. Chicago, 1977–1983.

Zhang, Longxi. "Revolutionary as Christ: The Unrecognized Savior in Lu Xun's Works." *Christianity and Literature* 45, no. 1 (1995): 81–93.

RICHARD G. WANG (2005)

FICTION: JAPANESE FICTION AND RELIGION

Like its Western counterpart, modern Japanese fiction is predominantly secular. Despite the ostensibly heavy Buddhist overtone in premodern Japanese literature, modern Japanese fiction reflects the rapid westernization and modernization brought on by the Meiji Restoration (1868) and betrays a deliberate break from the premodern when literature was at times used as a vehicle for conveying Buddhist thoughts and teachings. Modern Japanese fiction, in its predominantly introspective mode, can be seen as an extended quest for a god that is not there rather than a testimony of religious faith. Ichirō in Natsume Sōseki's (1867–1916) *The Wayfarer* (*Kōjin*, 1912–1913) is the prime example of the frustrated spiritual quest of a modern intellectual. In a moment of existential angst, he proclaims that the three choices open to him are "religion, suicide, and madness" and proceeds to hover in a state of mental breakdown, knowing in fact that religion as a choice was foreclosed to him. Another character who personifies the futile quest for solace in religion is Sōsuke in Sōseki's *The Gate* (*Mon*, 1910) who, in a moment of intense guilt and spiritual exhaustion, knocks in vain at the closed gate of a Buddhist temple. It is as if the modern ego is told to look somewhere else for spiritual redemption, if such an option exists at all.

To recognize the difficult and elusive relationship between religion and modern Japanese fiction from the onset is not to deny the relevance of a religious quest in writers ranging from Kitamura Tōkuku (1868–1894) to Kunikida

Doppo (1871–1908) in the Meiji era (1868–1912), from Arishima Takeo (1878–1923) to Miyazawa Kenji (1896–1933) in the Taisho era (1912–1926), and from Endo Shūsaku (1923–1996) to Sono Ayako (b. 1931) in the Shōwa (1926–1988) and Heisei (1988–) eras. In the following sections, we will examine some representative works in the different eras and explore the following aspects: the intellectual and spiritual reaction generated by the encounter between a pantheistic mode of religion (Shintoism and the legendary gods in the *Kojiki* [712]) and a monotheistic mode; the interpretation and exploitation of Buddhist imagery and shamanism; and the intersection between religion and modern Japanese fiction.

MEIJI ERA. The Japanese government lifted the ban on Christianity in 1873, and many Meiji writers absorbed the influence of Christianity in various degrees as part of the drive for "Enlightenment and Civilization" (*bunmei kaika*). Among them, Kitamura Tōkoku, Shimazaki Tōson (1872–1943), Kunikida Doppo, and Tayama Katai (1871–1930), all Christian converts in their youth, contributed significantly to the Meiji literary movements of Romanticism and Naturalism. Tōkoku was baptized by Iwamoto Yoshiharu (1863–1942), the founder and editor of *Jogaku Zasshi*, a women's magazine whose goals and contents were defined by his Christian faith and idealism. While Tōkoku kept his Christian faith throughout his short life, shifting from Presbyterianism to Quakerism, he was soon disenchanted with Iwamoto's moralistic and utilitarian view of literature and religion. In 1893, along with Tōson, Hoshino Tenchi (1862–1950, also a Christian convert), Hirata Tokuboku (1873–1943), and Togawa Shūkotsu (1870–1939), Tōkoku separated from *Jogaku Zasshi* and founded *Bungakukai*, one of the most influential literary magazines in the Meiji era. *Bungakukai* carried a terse announcement that summed up the break between literature and Christianity: "Literature is literature and religion is religion. *Bungakukai* is made up of a group of people with literary aspirations; they are not necessarily religious adherents. Furthermore, it is not limited to Christians or to Christian beliefs" (Brownstein, 1980, p. 335).

Disappointment with the external trappings of the church led Tōkoku toward a more internal form of Christianity, and his spiritual quest is evident in his essays and poetry. In "Essay on the Inner Life" (*Naibu seimei ron*, 1893), he argues that "The great difference between the cultures of the East and West is that in one there is a religion which preaches life and in the other there is not" (Mathy, 1964, p. 102). Perhaps in reaction to centuries of feudalism marked by an underevaluation of the individual and an overevaluation of society, Tōkoku celebrates love (*rabu*) in "The Pessimistic Poet and Womanhood" (*Ensei shika to josei*, 1892): "Love is the secret to life. Only after love came into being did human society exist" (quoted in Keene, 1987, p. 195). But above all else, Christianity provides Tōkoku with a language for a new poetics. He defines "inspiration" as an aspect of the Divine (*shin*), and, in Tōkoku's view, as one enters the Divine, language and self dissolve into a state of the sublime (Brownstein, 1990). Thus, Christianity provides a context and language for Tōkoku and his contemporaries to define spiritual freedom, love, and aesthetic and poetic ideals crucial to Japanese Romanticism.

Kunikida Doppo was a leading voice in Naturalism (*shizen shūgi*, 1906–1910), a literary movement marked by an intense inward search for the individual in the form of the confessional novel (*watakushi shōsetsu*). Unlike Tōson in *Spring* (*Haru*, 1908) and Tayama Katai in *The Quilt* (*Futon*, 1907), who wallow in their own sins and confessions, Doppo considers his role as a poet to be a heaven-sent mission. "I am to a be a poet of God," Doppo declared, and one of his famous poems begins: "Freedom is found in the mountains and forests./ As I recite this verse I feel my blood dance./ Ah, freedom is found in the mountains and forests behind" (1897) (quoted in Keene, p. 231). Like many of his contemporaries, Doppo experienced some ambivalence with his adopted faith, and his works betray not so much the influence of a monotheistic culture as the romantic notion that he is an instrument through which the splendor of God's creation is conveyed. He says that the aim of his work is "to describe with my pen all that my independent soul has been able to learn, observe, and feel" (1893) (quoted in Keene, p. 233).

Like Tōkoku, Doppo is under the heavy influence of the English Romantic poets, and his fiction is a testimony of the magnificence of nature. "Old Gen" (*Gen-oji*, 1897) captures a Wordsworthian stormy sea, while "Unforgettable People" (*Wasureenu hibito*, 1899) resembles a painted scroll of impressionistic scenery in which human existence is marked by its insignificance and randomness. In his later works, such as "The Bamboo Fence" (*Take no kido*, 1908), Doppo shows a great capacity to understand human suffering and despair.

In the historical context of scientific and social enlightenment and technological advancement after 350 years of feudalism and isolation, the Nietzschean modern man in Sōseki's fiction remains skeptical of religion, and the rational physician/scientist in Mori Ōgai's (1862–1922) fiction (e.g. *Kompira*, 1909) doubts yet fears the power of folk religious practices. These texts are moral inquiries into the soul of the modern individual: What becomes of him or her when the whirlwind of change brought on by modernization creates a spiritual vacuum in which old Confucian morality and feudal order are swept away while a new morality and a new faith is not in sight? What happens when the individual commits a grave sin? Unlike Dostoevsky, for whom, according to R. B. Blackmur, "a true rebirth, a great conversion, can come only after a great sin" (quoted in Irving Howe, *Politics and the Novel*, 2d ed. [New York, 1987], pp. 55–56), Sōseki knows no such religious assurances, so he would eliminate his protagonists before they commit a potential crime—for example, Takayanagi in *The Autumn Wind* (*Nowaki*, 1905)—or condemn the sinner to face the dark abyss of his guilt and choose death—for example, Sensei in *Kokoro* (1914).

Izumi Kyōka (1873–1939) explores the religious imagination from a purely aesthetic angle by tabbing into a twilight zone populated by divine beings, ghosts, and monsters in his fiction, including *The Holy Man of Mount Kōya* (*Kōya hirjiri*, 1900). If a religious imagination is marked by an ability to envision a world other than that which one inhabits, then the twilight world in Kyōka's fiction expresses that imagination most eloquently. In "The Taste of Twilight" (*Tasogare no aji*, 1900), Kyōka speaks of a "twilight" aesthetics in which day meets night and engenders a subtle dimension beyond ordinary sensations, an otherworldliness in which modern individuals come in contact with their innermost being and experiences a sense of wonder and mystery.

TAISHŌ ERA. Arishima Takeo received his early education in a mission school, attended Sapporo Agricultural College (founded by the Christian educator William Clark), lodged with Nitobe Inazō (a renowned Japanese Quaker), and became a close friend to a disciple of the samurai-Christian preacher and pacifist Uchimura Kanzō. An intensely spiritual and sincere Bible-reading Protestant Christian, Arishima eventually bent under the puritanical and austere ideals he imposed on his life, and his encounter with the poetry of Walt Whitman made him long for individual liberation and personal independence. *A Certain Woman* (*Aru onna*, 1919) is "an attack on conventional Christians" (Strong, 1978, p. 18) and an exploration of human nature in the raw. True to his Protestant upbringing, Arishima shows a moral imagination that is strictly confined to a puritanical dimension; after the rejection of Christianity, the fate that awaits his heroine is moral and physical degeneration, sin, and death: "She was not a woman any longer, only a nameless, grotesque, animal contorted with suffering" (p. 380). Like the protagonist in *The Descendants of Cain* (*Kain no matsue*, 1917), there is no atonement after the fall.

In the broad canon of Japanese fiction, perhaps Miyazawa Kenji possesses the most creative religious imagination. As Giles Gunn pointed out, if "what typifies religious man's experience of the sacred, of that which he takes to be of the essence of life, is its 'otherness,' its differentiation (though not necessarily alienation) from his own mode of being" (1975, p. 107), then Miyazawa's poetry and tales reveal a special ability to access this "otherness." A devout Buddhist of the Nichiren sect who recites the *Lotus Sūtra* daily, Miyazawa wrote tales (often featuring animals and nature and written in the guise of "children's stories") that are meditations on birth, suffering, sorrow, death, and rebirth. The mysterious "A Stem of Lilies" (*Yomata no yuri*, posthumous) is itself a Buddhist fable, while the description of dying in "The Bears of Nametoko" (*Nametoko no kuma,* posthumous) explores the dimension of "otherness" when death bodies forth in life. Embedded in Miyazawa's tales is poetry whose piercing beauty introduces an epiphanic moment of wonder and amazement, as in the following from "The First Deer Dance" (*Shishi-odori no hajimari*, 1921): "Now the sun's behind its back,/See the leafy alder tree/Like a mirror crack/ And shatter in a million lights" (in *Once and Forever*, translated by John Bester, 1997, p. 54). Miyazawa's indebtedness to Christianity is also evident in the description of a transcendental world in his famous *The Night of the Milky Way Express* (*Gingatetsudō no yoru*, posthumous) and the nighthawk's transfiguration and ascension to heaven in "The Nighthawk Star" (*Yodaka no hoshi*, posthumous). Miyazawa also alludes to Japanese folklore, legends, myths, and ethnographical studies to create a cosmology distinguished by its structural beauty and integrity as a profound alternative reality.

SHŌWA AND HEISEI ERAS. The atrocity and calamity of the Fifteen Years' War (1931–1945), ending in the nuclear destruction of Hiroshima and Nagasaki, stirred up feelings of guilt, incomprehension, and pain, compelling a whole generation of writers to embark on soul-searching literary journeys to understand what Ibuse Masuji, in "The Crazy Iris" (*Kakitsubata*, 1951), called a "crazy age." The list of Christian writers is substantial, ranging from the famous and prolific Endo Shūsaku, Ariyoshi Sawako (1931–1984), Inoue Hisashi (b. 1934), Miura Ayako (b. 1922), and Sono Ayako, to the serious and contemplative Shimao Toshio (1917–1986) and Shiina Rinzō (1911–1973) (Gessel, 1982, pp. 437–457). Some writers handle religious themes and issues directly in their works, while some refer to Christianity only at an oblique angle. Some texts are hopeful and optimistic (Shiina) while others have a darker shade of sin and guilt (Shimao). Endo Shūsaku is most forthright about his identity as a Catholic author and consistently thematizes Japanese church history in his fiction, earning himself the appellation of the "Graham Greene of the East." Francis Mathy points out that Endo contrasts a pantheistic Japanese world that is "insensitive to God, sin and even to death" to the monotheistic Christian world of the West that affirms the judgment and salvation of a supreme being. In some texts, Christianity is swallowed up or transformed in the metaphorical swamp that is Japan—for example, *Yellow Man* (*Kiiroi hito*, 1955), *Silence* (*Chinmoku*, 1966)—while in others, such as *Wonderful Fool* (*Obakasan*, 1959), Christ-like characters appear to lift others out of the non-Christian mud swamp (Mathy, 1992). Endo's description of Christ in *A Life of Jesus* (*Iesu no shōgai*, 1973) is a sad figure to whom "a yellow man" can relate to, much like the earthy figure of the Virgin Mary in "Fumie," whom illiterate Japanese peasants worship. Despite his tremendous output as a writer on religious themes, many of Endo's works use church history as a pretext for telling exotic tales with the suggestion of a distorted form of Orientalism and are wanting in theological or spiritual depth.

Among Catholic writers in the Shōwa era, Sono Ayako is noteworthy for the spiritual strength, humanity, and sincerity in her work. Sono received seventeen years of Catholic education at the Sacred Heart Girls School and College, and the strength of her faith is revealed in her boldness in creating intelligent, humane, yet fundamentally questioning characters who challenge the certitude of a divine order. In doing so, she posits a world of incertitude in which believers and nonbelievers alike have to struggle to make sense of suffering and death that often elude understanding. In *Watcher from the Shore* (*Kami no yogoreta te*, 1979–1980), Dr. Nobeji, a gynecologist whose work in artificial insemination, delivery, and abortion forces him to confront life-or-death decisions daily, finds himself struggling to understand the will of God. Without providing comforting answers to moral issues raised in the novel but adhering to a sympathetic treatment of the protagonist's incertitude, Sono forces the reader to reflect upon faith and moral judgment in an imperfect world. Sono's tremendous output in fiction and essays is a continuous quest of the place of humanity in the larger scheme of God.

Among modern Japanese writers, Mishima Yukio (1925–1970) uses various religious thoughts and iconography most lavishly in his stories. Yet the frequent evocation of religion is for the most part a pretext to summon a remote and exotic other world that provides an alien and fantastical setting for the fermentation of his aesthetic theories. The biblical iconography of the Madonna, Sodom and St. Sebastian in *The Confessions of a Mask* (*Kamen no kokuhaku*, 1949) sets up a triadic tension among the purity of spirit, the corruption of flesh, and martyrdom as the ultimate vision of beauty in Mishima's aesthetic world. The references to sacred space in *The Temple of the Golden Pavilion* (*Kinkakuji*, 1956) and the three holy shrines of Kumano in "Acts of Worship" (*Mikumano mode*, 1965) are instances in which famous Buddhist and Shintō sites are borrowed as convenient locales for the protagonists to confront their hopeless search for an ever elusive beauty and the all too nagging presence of their selfishness, desires, and physical ugliness or deterioration. The Buddhist idea of reincarnation, so prominent a plot mechanism in his tetralogy *The Sea of Fertility* (*Hōyū no umi*, 1965–1970), is no more than a device for him to indulge in the longing of eternal youth and a beautiful death, a destiny privileged to his chosen casts of iconic references, ranging from the sailor in *The Sailor who Fell from Grace with the Sea* (*Gogo no eikō*, 1963) to Joan of Arc and St. Sebastian in *The Confessions of a Mask*, and Kiyoaki and his reincarnated selves in *The Sea of Fertility*. To his credit, Mishima's references to Christian, Buddhist, and Shintō thoughts and iconography are articulate and serve as points of interest to the student of religious practices and tradition, most impressive of which being the reference to the five signs of angelic decay in his last novel *The Decay of the Angel* (*Tennin gosui*, 1970). Yet the final negation in his last novel of the tenet of suffering and rebirth in Buddhist thought—ideas that underlie the construction of the tetralogy—testifies the nihilistic view of a man who is tired of exploiting popular religious beliefs as an excuse for horror and extravagance, and has left not a trace of serious engagement in a dialogue of literature and religion.

Non-Christian Japanese writers also explore religious imagery for various purposes in their texts. Abe Kōbō's (1924–1993) vision of an apocalypse and a surviving ark of humanity in *The Ark Sakura* (*Hakobune no sakura*, 1984) transforms his fiction into a continuous quest of existential meaning in a world without God. Enchi Fumiko (1905–1986) explores the world of shamanism and spiritual possession in a number of her novels, including *Masks* (*Onnamen*, 1958) and *A Tale of False Fortunes* (*Namamiko monogatari*, 1965), a theme that ostensibly links her fiction to the phantoms and rituals of the Heian past. However, Enchi's spiritual world is not meant to be a space for philosophical or religious contemplation but a device that effectively ties her to the legacy of the literary past and an excuse to explore the psychology of her female characters. Nakagami Kenji (1946–1992) wades even deeper into the spiritual realm in such novels as *The Immortal* (*Fushi*, 1984) and *Gravity's Capital* (*Jûryoku no miyako*, 1981) by setting his fiction in the sacred spaces of Kumano and linking his texts, linguistically and temporally, to the world of the mythical gods in *Kojiki*. Yet Nakagami uses the spiritual realm fundamentally to create a postmodern space of multiple realities in order to address political and social problems of the discrimination of the *burakumin*. In that sense, religious imagery is a convenient pretext for Abe, Enchi, and Nakagami to examine existential, feminist, and political issues, while their writings remain fundamentally secular.

In the contemporary literary scene, when the novel has to compete with other forms of more readily consumable media stimulation, a few writers continue to grapple with religious and spiritual issues. Kaga Otohiko (b. 1929), a medical doctor who practiced psychiatry and taught psychology, wrote novels and essays about World War II, including *Riding the East Wind: A Novel of War and Peace* (*Ikari no nai fune*, 1982), and death row inmates (*Love and Light on the Brink of Death; Letters from Death Row* [*Shi no fuchi no ai to hikari*, 1992]) as a means to understand humanity and come to terms with his faith. Suga Atsuko (1929–1998) wrote stories and essays that capture the lives of Catholic saints with great persuasion. A simple metaphor in "The Life of St. Katalina" (*Shiena no seijo: sei Katalina den*, 1957) helps to illuminate the connection between Japanese fiction and religion: "Prepare a secret little chamber in your soul, and enter the chamber when it is ready. Find yourself, and find God" (*Suga Atsuko zenshū*, 8: 187). If the quest for divine understanding can be undertaken by way of a quest for the self, then the majority of Japanese fiction, itself a continuous process of introspection and reflection, is very close to a spiritual and religious quest, despite its predominant secular nature.

Religion intersects with modern Japanese fiction in various ways and serves, on the one hand, as a channel for a new poetics, a romantic quest for individual liberation, and moral inquiries, and on the other hand, as a pretext for generating exotic modern tales. There is no master narrative that governs the relationship between religion and modern Japanese fiction, but perhaps the following scene of mass cremation in Ibuse Masuji's *Black Rain* (*Kuroi ame*, 1966), a novel about the aftermath of the atomic bombing of Hiroshima, expresses most eloquently the place of religion in modern

Japanese fiction. As the protagonist Shigematsu wanders among the mounds of dead bodies, the only expression that comes to him, an atheist who survived the atomic bomb and finds himself acting as a surrogate priest to offer prayers for the dead, are words from the Buddhist "Sermon on Mortality": "Sooner or later, on this day or the morrow, to me or to my neighbor. . . . So shall the rosy cheeks or morning yield to the skull of eventide. One breath from the wind of change, and the bright eyes shall be closed" (*Black Rain,* 1988, p. 277). Religion intersects with modern Japanese fiction most intimately in addressing the spiritual need to understand the mystery and inscrutability of life and death, and a larger force that exists beyond humanity.

Bibliography

Most criticism that deals with modern Japanese fiction does not touch upon religious issues, so the reader who wishes to make further religious inquiries might prefer to read the works of fiction mentioned with special attention to their religious implications. Those who wish to pursue the study of Christianity and Japanese fiction are advised to read the articles by Brownstein, Mathy, and Gessel quoted in the article. Further adventures in reading will include exploring the works of the list of Japanese Christian authors quoted in the article as well as the following works of fiction: Natsume Sōseki, *Ten Nights of Dream* (*Yume juya,* 1908) (deals with "other worlds"); *And Then* (*Sore kara,* 1909) (a near religious quest of love and beauty by an atheist); Akutagawa Ryūnosuke, "The Man from the West" (*Saihō no hito,* 1927) (an attempt to understand the relevance of Christ); "Death of a Martyr" (*Hōkyōjin no shi,* 1918) (a dramatic account of the life of a saint); Shiga Naoyo, "At Kinosaki" (*Kinosaki ni te,* 1917) (a meditation on life and death); *A Dark Night's Passing* (*An'ya kōro,* 1921–1937) (note especially the divine revelation in nature towards the end of the novel).

Some of the most thought-provoking and valuable studies on religion and literature do not mention Japanese fiction at all but provide important background in exploring modernity, literature, and religion. These include:

Gunn, Giles. *The Interpretation of Otherness: Literature, Religion, and the American Imagination.* New York, 1975.

Keene, Donald. *Dawn to the West: Japanese Literature in the Modern Era.* New York, 1987.

Strong, Kenneth. Introduction to *A Certain Woman,* by Takeo Arishima. Tokyo, 1978.

Journal Articles

Brownstein, Michael. "*Jogaku Zasshi* and the Founding of Bungakukai." *Monumenta Nipponica* 35, no. 3 (1980): 319–336.

Brownstein, Michael. "Tōkoku at Matsushima." *Monumenta Nipponica* 45, no. 3 (1990): 285–302.

Gessel, Van C. "Voices in the Wilderness: Japanese Christian Authors." *Monumenta Nipponica* 37, no. 4 (1982): 437–457.

Hagiwara Takao. "Innocence and the Other World: The Tale of Miyazawa Kenji." *Monumenta Nipponica* 47, no. 2 (1992): 241–263.

Hagiwara Takao. "The Bodhisattva Ideal and the Idea of Innocence in Miyazawa Kenji's Life and Literature." *Journal of the Association of Teachers of Japanese* 27 (April 1993): 35–56.

Mathy, Francis. "Kitamura Tōkoku Essays on the Inner Life." *Monumenta Nipponica* 19, nos. 1/2 (1964): 66–110.

Mathy, Francis. "Shūsaku Endo: Japanese Catholic Novelist." *America* 167, no. 3 (1992): 66–71.

Nakamura Mariko. "Novelists of Integrity: Nogami Yaeko and Kaga Otohiko." *Japanese Studies* 20, no. 2 (2000): 141–157.

Sono Ayako. "Drifting in Outer Space." Translated by Robert Epp. *Japan Christian Quarterly: An Independent Journal of Christian Thought and Opinion* 38 (1972): 206–215.

ANGELA YIU (2005)

FICTION: SOUTHEAST ASIAN FICTION AND RELIGION

The term *Southeast Asia* was coined during World War II to refer to the part of the continent of Asia that lies south of China and east of India. The region can be divided into two sections.

There are the "mainland" states: Myanmar (Burma), Thailand, Laos, Cambodia, and Vietnam. The distinct cultures of these states remain strongly influenced by Theravāda Buddhism and elements of South Asian religious traditions. In addition, Vietnam has been strongly influenced by Chinese culture, including Taoism, Confucianism, and Mahāyāna Buddhism.

Below the latitude of approximately seven degrees north of the equator as marked on the Malay Peninsula are the "island" states of Malaysia, Singapore, Indonesia, Brunei, and the Philippines. Although the cultures of these states also accepted the influence of Hinduism and Buddhism, from the thirteenth century CE onward they were strongly influenced by the spread of Islam. The northern part of the Philippines was converted to Catholicism after 1535.

TRADITIONAL RELIGIOUS NARRATIVES. The traditional narrative literature of both parts of the region can be divided into two levels. There is the mass of folk literature, which varies from one country to another, and often extensively within each country as well. Being oral literature, this is not available to historical inspection. There is also the written literature produced in the various courts and religious centers; records of some of this, but only a small amount, has survived. From the religious perspective, this written literature dealt in different ways with the stories of the past lives of the Buddha, known as the *jataka* tales, and with the two Indian epics, the *Rāmāyaṇa* and the *Mahābhārata.*

Cambodia was the site of the earliest kingdom in Southeast Asia, called Funan (first century CE). As the area developed with a variety of religious influences through the Angkor period, it came to incorporate areas that are now known as Laos, Thailand, and parts of Burma and Vietnam. Around the ninth century the Burmans settled in the area known today as Myanmar, where they came into contact with earlier settlers, the Pyu, whose ancient cities attest to the influence of Hinduism and Buddhism. By the mid-eleventh century the pagan dynasty was founded, ushering in a golden age of art and the popularization of Theravāda Buddhism, a trend also occurring in Angkor, whose glory would finally be eclipsed in the fourteenth and fifteenth centuries by the Thai kingdom of Ayutthaya, itself destroyed by the Burmese in 1767.

In Myanmar palm leaf manuscripts were used for religious, grammatical, literary, historical, legal, and other major texts. The earliest surviving examples of prose, which date from the twelfth century, took the form of folding paper books that included illustrated scenes from the life of the Buddha and the *jataka* stories. Some similar manuscripts were probably also used in Cambodia, Thailand, and Laos. In Myanmar 8 of the 10 greater *jataka,* and all 537 minor *jataka,* were translated by two monks during the second half of the eighteenth century.

The first recorded prose text in Thailand is the aristocratic Phya Lithai's *Trai Phum* (Sermon on the Three Worlds; 1345). The sermon contains many illustrative stories on Buddhist cosmology; its teachings also served to legitimate the role of the Buddhist king *(cakkavatti).* Although there are no remaining *jataka* tales to be found in island Southeast Asia, the stories are included on the wall sculptures of the great eighth-century central Javanese shrine, the Borobodur, and were presumably common at that time.

Both mainland and island Southeast Asian countries developed their own versions of the two epics. The *Rāmāyaṇa* has its parallels in the Cambodian *Ramakerti,* the Lao *Phra Lak Phra Lam,* and the Thai *Ramakian.* These are not translations but are distinctive retellings of the story that vary in significant ways from the Indian original. For example, Thailand's *Ramakian* includes a remarkable infusion of Buddhist elements.

In Java the earliest surviving narrative poem is the *Kakawin Rāmāyaṇa,* which is considered by later generations to be the first and finest classical Javanese narrative poem. It was probably written during the second half of the ninth century. The whole of the *Mahābhārata* and the *Rāmāyaṇa* was rendered into Old Javanese *parwa* (prose texts), beginning a century later (i.e., after 1000 CE). These texts were later transferred to Bali and preserved there, following the fall of Majapahit, the major inland Javanese kingdom, after 1350.

The stories of the *Rāmāyaṇa* and the *Mahābhārata* were not only read; they were also appreciated by cultivated audiences in the forms of religious architecture, as well as in dance and shadow-puppet theater (*wayang*). Scholars have divided the repertory of the puppet theater into four cycles: (1) those with animistic themes, (2) stories of Arjuna taken from the *Rāmāyaṇa,* (3) stories based on the *Rāmāyaṇa,* and (4) the majority, stories from the *Mahābhārata.*

The earliest prose fiction from Vietnam, *Linh-nam trich quai,* is a collection of fables written in Chinese and dating from the fifteenth century. The collection reveals a mixture of animistic beliefs and Chinese influence and includes the Daoist theme of mortals forming relationships with immortals. There are also records of storytelling in the vernacular for entertainment at palace gatherings during the Tran dynasty (1225–1400). This Chinese style of literature at the court and in the government bureaucracy was ultimately transformed by an indigenous rich narrative to produce a uniquely Vietnamese style of fiction by the eighteenth and nineteenth centuries, when prose began to acquire more importance as a literary medium.

Traditional Islamic Narrative Literature. Unlike Java and Bali, all surviving texts in Malay are written in an adaptation of the Arabic script and therefore date from after the coming of Islam to the peninsula. There are still many surviving manuscripts based on the stories from the two Indian epics, but they have all been modified to give them a superficial Muslim flavor. For example, the *Hikayat Seri Rama* (The Story of Seri Rama), last copied before 1590, begins with references to Allah and Adam, the first prophet.

There are five types of Muslim narratives in traditional Malay literature. Some deal with the life of the Prophet Muhammad, from his archetypal existence (*Hikayat Nur Muhammad),* to his life and miracles (*Hikayat Isra'* and *Mikraj*), and to his death (*Hikayat Nabi Wafat*). Also included in this first category are works that deal with members of the prophet's own family (e.g., the *Hikayat Nabi Mengajar Anaknya Fatimah,* describing the Prophet's instructions on the duties of women, as given to his daughter Fāṭimah). There are further chronicles about the other great prophets of Allāh, such as Joseph, Moses, Solomon, and Zachariah. (A major anthology of these stories is the *Qisas al-Anbiya.*) The stories of the "Companions" of the Prophet Muḥammad include not only his close disciples (*Hikayat Abu Bakar* and *Hikayat al-Mu'minin Umar*), but also his son-in-law, ʿAlī, and ʿAlī's two sons who were later martyred, Ḥasan and Ḥusayn (e.g., *Hikayat Ali Kahwin,* on the marriage of Ali). This is a strong indication of the importance of Shiite influences in early Malayan Islam. Works in the next category, chronicles of the great warriors of Islam, present some of the great commanders during the time of Muḥammad (*Hikayat Muḥammad Hanifiyah*), but also include Alexander the Great (*Hikayat Iskandar Dzulkarnain*) and the Yemeni warrior Saif al-Lizan (*Hikayat Saif al-Lizan*). The devout men and women whose lives are described are variously ascetics and mystics, kings and judges. The *Hikayat Ibrahim ibn Adham* tells of a king who renounces his throne to devote himself to a life of prayer; the *Hikayat Raja Jumjumah* tells of an evil king who was restored to life by the Prophet Jesus and thereafter committed himself to constant contemplation.

It is important to note that although all these narratives—Hindu, Buddhist, and Muslim—may, from one perspective, be considered imaginative works, they are definitely not considered as "fictional" (in the sense of "untrue") by those who do, or did, believe in the sacred stories they tell.

The Emergence of Modern Genres. Modern narrative fiction proposes an imagined personal description by a named author of contemporary society and the complexities of psychological description. Such writing was a product of Western influence, which began in the late sixteenth century but made its real impact following the nineteenth century. The consequent vast changes in social and economic structures, and the attendant human problems and situations, were represented to readers through the spread of printing and mass literacy. Such writing often combined with other preexisting factors, including religious literary influences and oral folktale traditions. While much "modern" writing has a secular emphasis, religious themes are also still to be seen in literary works produced throughout the region. Some writings are critical of traditional practices. Others occasionally still use major characters from both of the traditional Indian epics as a device to indirectly criticize political corruption, social inequity, or the loss of traditional values.

The Mainland Buddhist States. In Burma the first presses were established during the 1800s by Christian missionaries who pioneered a translation and printing of the Bible. British colonial rule began in 1862 and with it the gradual development of modern Burmese prose fiction influenced by British literature. Religious themes, sometimes critical of Buddhism, occur in Myanmar's modern fiction. Thein Pe Myint's novel *Tet Hpon-gyi* (Modern Monk; 1937) criticized corruption in the Buddhist Sangha, causing a great uproar among the monks. Zaw-gyi's memorable short story "Thu maya" (His Spouse, 1960) involves a husband who decides to enter monkhood in order to avoid family responsibilities. Ne Win Myint's short story "Thadun" (1995) is a political satire based on one of the crucial events in the Buddha's growth toward Enlightenment. Despite considerable state censorship, Myanmar has a vibrant contemporary literary culture.

Modern fiction appeared in Thailand from the 1880s, written largely by young male aristocrats who had studied abroad. One of the first published short stories was Krom Luang Phichit Prichakon's popular and controversial "Sanuk nuk" (Fun Thinking; 1885). Set in a famous Bangkok temple, the story describes an imaginary conversation between four young Buddhist monks about their futures and the pragmatic advantages and disadvantages of remaining a monk. Further episodes were banned. With a growing educated middle class, women also became interested in the art of prose fiction. From the 1930s socially concerned fiction with its ethnographic quality became part of the literary landscape that included Thai Buddhist culture. Khammaan Khonkhai's popular 1978 ethnographic novel *The Teachers of Mad Dog Swamp* reveals the village cycle of Buddhist rituals as a backdrop to the struggles of the protagonist Piya. Having received his university education in Bangkok while living in a *wat* (temple or monastery), Piya returns to the countryside as a young idealistic teacher. He is spurred into action against the politicians and business elite who are illegally logging the area and have lost their sense of Buddhist morality. Writers of the American era (1965–1973), like Si Dao Ruang (Wanna Thappananon) in "Mother of Waters, Thaokae Bak, and a Dog" (1977) and Sujit Wongthet in "Second Nature" (1967), criticize the commercialization of Buddhist festivals. Si Dao Ruang has a cycle of stories including "Sita Puts Out the Fire" (1984), which relocates characters from the *Rāmāyaṇa* within the modern urban setting of Bangkok.

Laos and Cambodia lag behind the other countries of Southeast Asia in the development of prose fiction. Both countries were colonized in the mid-1800s by the French, who delayed the introduction of printing presses and public education until the early 1900s. In Cambodia traditionalist monks resisted the printing of Khmer script since hand-copied manuscripts were considered sacred. Their objections were overcome by Venerables Chuon Nath (1883–1969) and Huot Tath (1891–1975), who enabled the printing of a variety of Khmer texts. In fact, most of the early fiction writers were educated monks. The journal *Kambuja Suriya* (1926) of the Buddhist Institute, established by the French, was the first to publish modern novels in serialized form.

Early prose writers, such as Rim Kin in *Sophat* (1938) and Nou Kan in *Tun Jhin* (1947), were naturally influenced by Cambodian religion. The cultural milieu for their fiction includes magic, ghosts, sages, Hindu deities, Buddhist monks, and pagoda schools. In her novella *Gu san mitt min drust mitt* (1947), Sou Seth, the first woman writer of modern prose, develops a complex love story in which the male protagonist renounces secular life to become a monk. Nhok Them in *Kulap pailin* (1943) and Kim Hak in *Dik Danle Sap* (1941) make use of the Buddhist themes of impermanence, karma, and self-determination. In *Dik Danle Sap* a corrupt former monk is finally discredited when his moneymaking meditation scam is discovered. Because of the lingering impact of the Pol Pot era (1975–1979) in Cambodia and government control over literature in Laos, both countries are still struggling to establish strong modern literary traditions.

Vietnam. The development of the modern novel and short story in Vietnam began in 1862 with French colonial control. The influence of the Chinese-language based literati slowly waned as the French modernized the Vietnamese language by employing a romanized script, *quoc-ngu*, originally developed by the French Jesuit Alexandre de Rhodes (1591–1660) in 1651. *Quoc-ngu* was popularized by Vietnamese Roman Catholic writers at the end of the eighteenth century. The most famous of these, Paulus Cua (1834–1907), is credited with developing modern Vietnamese prose. Some of the first publications of prose were collections of tales: *Truyen giai buon* (Stories to Dispel Sadness; 1880) and *Truyen giai buon cuon sau* (More Stories to Dispel Sadness; 1885). The popularity of tales continued throughout the modern period, for example, Nguyen Dong Chi's *Kho tang truyen co tich Viet-nam* (Treasury of Ancient Vietnamese Stories; 1958). Many of these tales show Chinese and Buddhist influence. *Su-tich 18 ong la-han* (Story of the Eighteen Arahats), for example, tells of eighteen thieves who renounce their profession, commit suicide, and become arahats (enlightened monks). Other stories relay the deeds of various bodhisattvas including Kuan-yin or are reminiscent of stories in the *Dhammapada.*

With modernization, the spread of education, and a growing middle class, both male and female writers experimenting with prose fiction emerged from all social levels. From the early 1900s until 1975 writers split over the aesthetics of literature as art for society's sake or art for art's sake. After 1975 social realism became the officially stipulated style for literature until the *Doi Moi* (renovation) policy implemented in 1986, which allowed for greater freedom of expression.

The most internationally well-known Buddhist fiction writer and poet of this modern period is Thich Nhat Hanh, a Thien Buddhist monk who was exiled from Vietnam in 1966, having been banned from participating in antiviolence protests. *The Stone Boy and Other Stories* (1996) is a collection of his short fiction that incorporates tales of monks, bodhisattvas, compassion, and loving kindness in the Vietnamese Buddhist tradition. Among the many *Doi Moi* era writers, two should be mentioned. Nguyen Huy Tiep, a master of the psychological tale, is considered by some to be a postmodernist writer because of his narrative approach to storytelling. In *The General Retires and Other Stories* (1992) and his other fiction themes include decadent Confucianism and Buddhism in a society that seems to have lost its moral compass. Duong Thu Huong lyrically explores the spiritual malaise of failed political ideology in many of her novels, including *Novel without a Name* (1995).

Malaysia and Indonesia. Despite sharing a common language, Indonesian/Malay, and a common religion, Islam, the island regions between the British and the Dutch were divided during the early nineteenth century, leading to the development of two distinctly different modern literary traditions. Both of these owe their origins to the rise of popular printing presses. In Malaya and Singapore the presses had strong connections to the Middle East and frequently published translations of Arabic stories. In an increasingly plural society (Malay, Chinese, and Indian) being a Muslim was seen as part of the definition of being a Malay. In the Dutch East Indies the presses belonged to Chinese and Eurasian settlers; after 1908 the colonial government also established its own publishing house, Balai Pustaka, to promote a modernizing and secular literacy. Islam has, therefore, played a more obvious role in Indonesian literature than in Malay.

Hikayat Faridah Hanum (1925), by Syed Sheikh bin Ahmad Al-Hadi (1867–1934), is often considered the first modern Malay novel, even though it is entirely set in the Middle East. A love story, the novel promotes female emancipation and Islamic reformism in general and criticizes more traditional Muslim figures wherever possible. Following the consolidation of prose in the 1950s, Malay literature was caught up into the Islamic revival movement of the 1970s and a serious prolonged debate about the nature of a "Muslim literature" followed. The main spokesman was Shahnon Ahmad. Shahnon highlighted the natural place of Islam at the heart of rural Malay life and the importance of its morality in maintaining a moral society.

For a long time Islam seemed marginal to modern Indonesian fiction. One exception was the pre–World War II author Haji Abdul Malik Karim Amrullah. His first novel *Di bawah lindungan Ka'abah* (Beneath the Protection of the Ka'abah; 1938) tells of a young man forbidden to marry his true love because of local custom, who flees to Mecca and finds refuge there and eventually death. The later novel *Tuan Direktur* (The Director; 1939) contrasts the material values of the businessman with the simple piety of the villager Pak Yasin. After the war *Atheis* (The Atheist; 1949), by Achdiat Karta Mihardja, explores the spiritual struggles of a young West Javanese man, raised in a repressive and superstitious Islam, that arise when he is confronted with the secularism, rationalism, and self-centered life styles of the capital, Jakarta. The debate about a Muslim literature began in Indonesia only in the mid-1980s and had a much greater influence on poetry than on prose. With the continuing increasing importance of Islam in Indonesian public life, however, a new genre has arisen since 1998: Islamic youth literature. These stories focus on the daily lives of young Muslims and are written in an unselfconscious contemporary Indonesian. A major author in this field is Helvy Tiana Rose. In *Segenggam Gumam,* a collection of her essays published in 2003, she argues that an Islamic literature should be written by a pious Muslim, that it should be informed by a serious knowledge of the teachings of the faith, and that it should encourage readers to dedicate themselves to God and the Muslim community.

Philippines. Before Spanish influence, prose narratives in the Philippines consisted largely of origin myths, hero tales, fables, and legends. The native syllabary, possibly influenced by an Indic script, was replaced by the Roman alphabet introduced by the Spaniards in 1565. As the number of Christianized Filipinos grew, old manuscripts on perishable material were left to disintegrate or were destroyed by missionaries "who believed the indigenous pagan culture was the handicraft of the devil himself" (Lumbera and Lumbera, 1982, p. 3). Resistance to the colonizers or isolation from them allowed for some survival of indigenous literary forms during a period when Christianity spread rapidly under the influence of the Spanish friars.

Filipino literature during the 333 years of Spanish rule was "predominantly religious and moral in character and tone" (San Juan, 1974, p. 4). Ladino writers began to compose in mixed Tagalog and Spanish. The power of the Catholic Church grew to such an extent that all literature had to be approved for publication. In 1856 the Permanent Commission of Censors was established, which included four religious members out of a total of nine.

During the late 1800s the *Ilustrados* of the Propaganda movement emerged in response to this repression. One of them, the great novelist José Rizal (1861–1896), whose literary brilliance would continue to inspire writers throughout the modern period, exposed the sexual misdeeds and the political intrigues of the powerful Catholic friars in his *Noli Me Tangere* (1887) and its sequel *El Filibusterismo* (1891). Realizing that their campaign for reform was failing, these reformist writers shifted from Spanish to Tagalog in the hope of reaching a wider audience. Their nationalistic attempts, which did establish the beginning of a self-conscious Filipino literature, would be further frustrated by the American colonization of the area from 1898 to 1945, an age when the short-story genre would fully develop and women would also become accomplished writers.

The cultural landscape of Catholic influence, with its resonant church bells and solemn rituals, forms part of the aesthetic setting for many romantic or socially critical stories and novels during the modern and contemporary periods, from Paz Marquez Benitez's (1894–1983) "Dead Stars" (1925) to Cristina Pantoja Hidalgo's (1944–) "The Painting" (1993). The appetites of the friars who abetted Spanish colonial oppression are a theme taken up by the next generation of socially critical authors now writing in Tagalog. These include Gabriel Beato Francisco (1850–1935), in his trilogy *Fulgencia Galbillo* (1907), *Capitan Bensio* (1907), and *Alfaro* (1909), and Iñigo Ed. Regalado (1888–1976), with his anticlerical and anticolonial discourse in *Madaling-Araw* (1909). In contrast, Faustino Aguilar (1882–1955) focuses on the subjective blindness of Filipino religious belief in his novel *Pinaglahuan* (1907). The popular novelist Lazaro M. Francisco (1898–1980) in his last two novels, *Maganda Pa Ang Daigdig* (1956) and its sequel *Daluyong* (1962), portrays a progressive priest whose humanity illustrates the positive role religion can play in society. The theme of "priest as social reformist" is also expressed in Paulino Lim's political novel *Requiem for a Rebel Priest* (1996).

SEE ALSO Burmese Religion; Lao Religion; Mahābhārata; Rāmāyaṇa; Southeast Asian Religions, article on Mainland Cultures; Thai Religion; Vietnamese Religion.

BIBLIOGRAPHY

Achdiat Karta Mihardja. *Atheis.* Translated by R. J. Maguire. St. Lucia, Australia, 1972.

Amilah Ab. Rahman and Nor Azmah Shehidan, eds. *People on the Bridge: An Anthology of ASEAN Short Stories.* Kuala Lumpur, 2001.

Aveling, H. *Shahnon Ahmad: Islam, Power, and Gender.* Bangi, Philippines, 2000.

A. Wahab Ali. *The Emergence of the Novel in Modern Indonesian and Malaysian Literature: A Comparative Study.* Kuala Lumpur, 1991.

Duong Thu Huong. *Novel without a Name.* Translated by Phan Huy Duong and Nina McPherson. New York, 1995.

Duranf, M. Maurice, and Nguyen Tran Huan. *An Introduction to Vietnamese Literature.* Translated by D. M. Hawke. New York, 1985.

Francia, Luis H., ed. *Brown River, White Ocean: An Anthology of Twentieth-Century Philippine Literature in English.* New Brunswick, N.J., 1993.

Khonkhai, Khammaan. *The Teachers of Mad Dog Swamp.* Translated by Gehan Wijeyewardene. St. Lucia, Australia, 1982.

Harun Mat Piah et al. *Traditional Malay Literature.* Translated by Harry Aveling. Kuala Lumpur, 2002.

Herbert, Patricia, and Anthony Milner, eds. *South-east Asia Languages and Literatures: A Select Guide.* Honolulu, 1989.

Lumbera, Bienvenido, and Cynthia Nograles Lumbera, eds. *Philippine Literature: A History and Anthology.* Manila, 1982.

Nguyen Huy Thiep. *The General Retires and Other Stories.* Translated by Greg Lockart. Singapore, 1992.

Reynolds, Frank E., and Mani B. Reynolds, trans. *Three Worlds According to King Ruang: A Thai Buddhist Cosmology.* Berkeley, Calif., 1982.

Rizal, José. *Noli Me Tangere.* Edited by Raul L. Locsin. Translated by Ma. Soledad Lacson-Locsin. Manila, 1995.

Thich Nhat Hanh, Vo-Dinh Mai, and Mobi Warren. *The Stone Boy and Other Stories.* Berkeley, Calif., 1996.

San Juan, E., Jr., ed. *Introduction to Modern Pilipino Literature.* New York, 1974.

Yamada, Teri Shaffer, ed. *Virtual Lotus: Modern Fiction of Southeast Asia.* Ann Arbor, Mich., 2002.

HARRY AVELING (2005)
TERI SHAFFER YAMADA (2005)

FICTION: AUSTRALIAN FICTION AND RELIGION

Evidence of indigenous habitation of Australia dates back some forty or fifty thousand years before European settlement. As Mudrooroo (previously Colin Johnson, b. 1939) noted in *The Indigenous Literature of Australia,* Aboriginal oral literature contains accounts of the wanderings of the creative ancestors who shaped the land and people, but the most sacred aspects of these stories were reserved for initiates. As the white Australian governments of the nineteenth and twentieth centuries discouraged Aboriginal communities from following their cultural and religious practices, many sacred secret stories were lost. Other, more public, stories often suffered in translation from Aboriginal languages, their mythological dimensions reduced to the status of fairy tales or simplistic creation stories for children.

INDIGENOUS FICTION AND RELIGION. Aboriginal people were introduced to the Roman alphabet by the British following their landing at Sydney Cove in 1788. Christian missionaries were zealous educators, and their influence has been seen in the "strong current of Christianity" that runs through Aboriginal writing (Mudrooroo, 1997, p. 10). The first acknowledged Aboriginal writer, David Unaipon (1873–

1967), was raised on a Christian mission and wove biblical values and classical allusions into traditional Ngarrindjeri stories in his booklet *Native Legends* (c. 1929). European Australians, including Ronald and Catherine Berndt and T. G. H. Strehlow, compiled major collections of oral Aboriginal literature.

White children were introduced to indigenous characters and mythology by white writers, most notably novelist Patricia Wrightson (b. 1921) in *The Rocks of Honey* (1960) and the Wirrun Trilogy (1977–1981). Although Wrightson tried to dispel the white blindness that denied Aboriginals their human dignity, and although she was scrupulous in her research, indicating where she had invented material, this aspect of her work has since polarized opinion: did it hasten white appreciation of Aboriginal spirituality, or did it obscure the nature of that spirituality?

In 1964, against a background of increasing demands for justice and Aboriginal land rights, Kath Walker (later Oodgeroo Noonuccal, 1920–1993) published a book of poetry, *We Are Going*, now credited as the beginning of a new phase of Aboriginal writing, one which spoke directly to white Australians. Much contemporary Aboriginal writing is concerned with retrieving and reclaiming the past and with establishing individual and communal identity, as demonstrated by the popularity of the autobiographical and biographical forms. The first indigenous novel to be published, *Karobran* (1978) by Monica Clare (1924–1973), was based on the author's experiences growing up in welfare institutions and white foster homes.

The disintegration of Aboriginal community life because of (and despite) white intervention, the physical and emotional illnesses caused by disregard of sacred rituals, the saving power of the old ways, and the critical importance of the land to the health of the community and the individual are all played out in Kim Scott's novel, *True Country* (1993). In his story of Billy, a part-Aboriginal schoolteacher who is posted to a remote settlement in the far north of Australia, Scott (b. 1957) casts an unflinching eye over the corrupt behavior of both whites and Aborigines who ignore the presence of the sacred and refuse to honor their obligations. There is a suggestion that, for Aboriginals and whites alike, Christianity might survive if the concept of God were to change, if God were to be thought of "as a great spirit, a creator spirit, an artist. A creative force behind the world, living in the world, and giving ceremony and the land." "Maybe," Scott's sympathetic white Catholic priest says, "they, we, will end up with a new God here, some sort of major spirit from the Dreaming or whatever, who named everything and us—or should I say the Aborigines?—and created this special relationship. People, creation, the land" (Scott, 1993, p. 221). Billy's own moment of understanding, his acceptance into the Aboriginal spirit community and the true country, comes as he nearly drowns, swallowed by the snake-like river, the Rainbow Serpent, the Aboriginal figure of divinity. In this spiritual rebirth the abiding presence of the law, the unity of nature and spirit, and the possibility of hope are affirmed.

Postsettlement Religion and Fiction. Since the arrival of the Europeans, Christianity has been the dominant religious influence in Australia, although the number of Australians claiming to be Christian declined throughout the twentieth century. In the 2001 census 68 percent of the population claimed Christian affiliation, but church surveys suggest that only around 20 percent of these people attend religious services. The fastest-growing religions in Australia between 1996 and 2001, according to the census, were Buddhism, Hinduism, and Islam, but they accounted for only 3.9 percent of the population. Much of their growth has been the result of immigration from Southeast Asia and the Middle East.

The Australian attitude to Christianity is ambivalent, stemming from the origins of the colony as a penal settlement where the church was expected to enforce good order among the inhabitants. The brutality of the penal system was graphically illustrated in the novel *For the Term of His Natural Life* (1874) by Marcus Clarke (1846–1881). Early writers such as Clarke, Joseph Furphy (1843–1912) and Henry Lawson (1869–1922) had no sympathy for institutionalized Christianity in their fiction, praising instead Christlike behavior among the convicts, settlers, and bushmen who were battling to survive. The concept of mutual support among men became enshrined as a quasi-religious nationalist creed known as mateship, which has been cited as evidence of widespread Australian adherence to Christ's teaching of love for one's neighbor. Attempts by some theologians in the late 1970s and the mid-1980s to use mateship as the foundation of a specifically Australian Christianity failed, however, because the concept is fundamentally secular and is vulnerable to misuse by sexist, racist, and anti-intellectual interests.

Historically, the Christian churches did little to win the minds of Australians. In 1977 Richard Campbell complained of the lack of "a substantial and continuous intellectual tradition" in Australian religion, noting the absence of great theological colleges, the reliance on imported theologians, and the emphasis on vocational training, rather than "intellectual critique of the church's language about God" (p. 179). In the late 1970s, theologians, tired of making do with a derivative European religion, turned to literature and the arts to find ways to address God in the vernacular. Two of the pioneering commentators, Dorothy Green (1915–1991) and Veronica Brady (b. 1929), were practicing literary critics.

Although a body of novels addresses the experience of growing up within a restrictive religious tradition—Catholic, Greek Orthodox, fundamentalist, Jewish—these works have been overlooked in discussions about Australian theology. Also overlooked have been books by internationally oriented novelists such as Morris West (1916–1999), whose Vatican trilogy was published 1959 and 1990, and Colleen McCullough (b. 1937), author of *The Thorn Birds* (1977), and works of Holocaust and refugee literature, including *Schindler's Ark* (1982) by Thomas Keneally (b. 1935).

Of most interest have been "literary" writers and works set in Australia that have been seen to comment on the nature of God and the individual's relationship with God, the individual's behavior towards others, and the role of nature as an agent of redemption and as a sign of God's presence. At the heart of these works has been the wish to demonstrate the continuing relevance of Christianity, or, at least, to find a way of expressing the sacred within the context of a (post-) Christian culture.

RELATING TO GOD. In 1976 Dorothy Green detected the presence of religion and religious feeling in the work of most important Australian novelists in the nineteenth and twentieth centuries, even "amongst those who would describe themselves as atheist, agnostic or indifferent" (p. 9). She was able to come to such a generous assessment because she was looking for evidence of adherence to the second Great Commandment, that is, "Thou shalt love thy neighbour as thyself" (*Matt.* 12:31).

Had she concentrated exclusively on a literary preoccupation with the nature of God, or even on works that bore witness to the first Great Commandment, "Thou shalt love the Lord thy God with all thy heart, with all thy soul and with all thy mind . . ." (*Matt.* 12:30), the result would have been different, for few Australian writers have been prepared to engage directly with God across a body of work. Green argued for Martin Boyd (1893–1972) as the author who most completely represented the fusion of the two commandments, an author who believed that "the Christian story corresponds with man's experience on earth" (p. 25). Boyd, however, spent most of his adult life in Europe, and although his novels comprising the Langton tetralogy (published between 1952 and 1962) used Australian material, his ongoing influence on Australian theological thinking has been negligible compared with that of Patrick White.

It is Patrick White (1912–1990) whom Christian commentators most often regard as Australia's preeminent religious author, although White wrote (in a letter dated August 15, 1985) that he could not see himself as a "true Christian. My faith is put together out of bits and pieces. I am a *believer*, but not the kind most 'Christians' would accept" (Marr, 1994, p. 604). White did not write novels for the benefit of theologians. Claims, for example, that his novel *Voss*, about an ill-fated desert expedition by a German explorer, represents the archetypal Australian Christian parable of suffering and redemption are at odds with White's own description of Voss as a "megalomaniac explorer" with "delusions of divinity" (September 11, 1956, Marr, 1994, p. 107). White does not comfort his readers but challenges them, as he wrote on May 10, 1970: "I suppose what I am increasingly intent on trying to do in my books is to give professed unbelievers glimpses of their own unprofessed faith. I believe most people have a religious faith, but are afraid that by admitting it they will forfeit their right to be considered intellectuals" (Marr, 1994, p. 363).

While the academy has been unable to deny the intellectual scope of White's writing, some of its members mistrust religious readings of his works. Ambiguity is one of White's strengths and also a reminder that any article on religious themes in literature is entirely subjective. This can be illustrated by a key scene from White's *The Tree of Man* in which the old man, Stan Parker, cornered by a young evangelist who is pressing him as to whether he believes in God, points to a gob of his own spittle "glittering intensely and personally on the ground": "'That is God,' he said" (p. 476). The scene has been read both as proof that Stan has moved to agnostic secularism and as verification that he has achieved illumination.

The most thorough exploration of religious elements in White's novels *The Tree of Man* (1955), *Voss* (1957), *Riders in the Chariot* (1961), and *The Solid Mandala* (1966) can be found in Peter Beatson's *The Eye in the Mandala* (1977). Beatson argues that to make sense of White's work, it is necessary to accept the presence of a Hidden God behind the material world. White's characters, through "their emotional responses and the assumptions of their cultures," try to comprehend the nature of the Hidden God. But although they always fall short of the truth, this is not to say that God is completely remote from his creation: on the contrary, "every encounter in the human and natural worlds is potentially a moment of dialogue between the individual and God. . . . Union with the Hidden God is not achieved in White's novels by withdrawal from the things of the senses, but by acquiescence to all the conditions of the fallen world in which man finds himself" (pp. 9–10).

RELATING TO OTHER PEOPLE. Christ-figures are generally absent in Australian literature, despite the remarkable presence of Mordecai ben Moshe Himmelfarb, Patrick White's Orthodox Jewish post-Holocaust refugee in *Riders in the Chariot.* Blamed for Christ's crucifixion, he is himself "crucified" by his Australian workmates; he dies on Good Friday and is given a Christian burial: White's point is that all men are the same and all faiths are one.

Himmelfarb, like other characters who might evince Christlike attributes, is not complete in himself: he cannot be redeemed until he learns to accept and give love. In Australian literature the way to God is usually not through excessive penance and self-purification, but through loyalty, compassion, and loving kindness. This is seen clearly, for instance, in the fiction of Thea Astley (b. 1925).

Astley is usually depicted as a social satirist, but she was raised a Catholic and has been a consistent critic of the institutional church, most often Catholic, but of any denomination that demands mindless adherence from its followers. In her early books she criticized the church hierarchy for its pomposity and insincerity, implying, as she did in her first novel, *Girl with a Monkey* (1958), that true spiritual experience was to be had not at a mass rally with an unctuous bishop but with a small group gathered with a Franciscan priest in a community dance hall amidst tropical undergrowth, where humanity and nature come together to partake of the eternal mystery, the transcendent made immanent in the mass. Her later books, including *Vanishing Points* (1992), attack the patriarchal restrictions of church leadership.

The most sympathetic characters in her novella "Inventing the Weather" (in *Vanishing Points*) are three elderly nuns who, against the wishes of the church, are living with and working for a remote Aboriginal community. Above the kitchen sink is a wall plaque that reads: "Where there is no love, put love and there you will find love" (p. 182). In Astley's fiction love is the paramount virtue. Love is not necessarily found in the church (the pettiness and legalism of the church crushes the vocations of the most humane religious in *The Slow Natives* [1965] and *A Boat Load of Home Folk* [1968]) but is more likely seen in transactions between fallible human beings in acts of kindness. Astley is critical of those who seek individual salvation, removing themselves from the responsibilities of daily life: in her books the divine is found through community.

Despite Astley's use of Catholic imagery, her critique of religion, and her passionate commitment to issues of social justice, her work has been ignored in discussions about developing an Australian theology. She is not alone in this, however, as the writings of other women, including Elizabeth Jolley (b. 1923), Helen Garner (b. 1942), and Marion Halligan (b. 1940), who also value the practice of *caritas* over individual salvation, are similarly ignored, except by exponents of feminist theology. It would seem that because their work fails to reproduce certain "sacred" stereotypes, they are thought to have nothing to contribute to religion in Australia.

NATURE AND THE SACRED. The first European settlers found themselves in an alien landscape that could not be captured in conventional language and imagery. European expressions of Christianity were similarly inadequate in a place where nature seemed superior—and indifferent—to human beings. The gradual shift over time, in both theology and literature, from depicting the country as hostile wilderness to sacred site is a measure of people's increasing spiritual at-homeness.

Veronica Brady, in her treatment of Clarke's *For the Term of His Natural Life*, notes how the novel, "like many substantial works of Australian fiction, echoes the psalms and the prophets of the Old Testament" in its awareness of the sheer power of nature (1981, p. 5). And there is a thread in Australian theology that posits the wilderness, most often figured as the desert, as a place representing humanity's fall from grace, a place of suffering that may purify the individual pilgrim. More recently, and perhaps under the influence of Aboriginal spirituality, the desert is seen as a repository of the sacred, a site where, freed from the distractions of the everyday, one might encounter God. Reverence has been afforded novels that use a desert setting (White's *Voss*, Randolph Stow's *To the Islands* [1958], Thomas Keneally's *Woman of the Inner Sea* [1992]), but until Tim Winton (b. 1960) started writing novels set in riverside Perth and coastal Western Australia, little attention was paid to spiritual readings of the moist or settled areas.

It was Winton's overwhelmingly popular saga, *Cloudstreet* (1991), set between the 1940s and 1960s, that caused theologians to look seriously at the playing out of religious values among suburban families. Commentators such as Michael Goonan have picked up on the way in which Winton likens the house on Cloud Street, the home of two battling families, the Pickles and the Lambs, to the Australian continent, a "vast indoors," a "big emptiness" that almost paralyses them "with spaces and surfaces that yield nothing to them" (Winton, p. 41). As Goonan notes, a crucial question underlies the text of *Cloudstreet*: whether it is possible for non-Aboriginal Australians to belong to the land. For Goonan, resolution comes when the key characters follow the advice of the enigmatic Aboriginal man who appears at crucial moments in the story, most often urging them to return to the house at Cloudstreet, not to sell it, impressing upon the Lambs and the Pickles the importance of family. It is as though Winton is opening up the possibility for spiritual healing of white Australians, should they be prepared to acknowledge key aspects of Aboriginal culture and spirituality, the centrality of land and community.

In his tribute to the Western Australian coastline, *Land's Edge*, Winton has written that "everything that lives is holy and somehow integrated" (p. 50). Other writers might be less forthright in speaking of their beliefs, but, nevertheless, their work can refresh the religious imagination and realize the hope of reconciliation.

BIBLIOGRAPHY

Astley, Thea. *Vanishing Points.* Port Melbourne, Australia, 1992.

Beatson, Peter. *The Eye in the Mandala. Patrick White: A Vision of Man and God.* Sydney, 1977. An enlightening study of White's novels up to and including *The Eye of the Storm* (1973), revealing the somewhat unorthodox Christianity that underlies White's artistic universe. Beatson respects the texts and refrains from twisting them to fit his own theories.

Brady, Veronica. *A Crucible of Prophets: Australians and the Question of God.* Sydney, 1981. A groundbreaking study of the way nineteenth- and twentieth-century Australian male novelists address questions about God in their work.

Brown, Cavan. *Pilgrim through This Barren Land.* Sutherland, New South Wales, 1991. Uses the journals of the early European explorers and nineteenth- and twentieth-century literature to flesh out a desert-based Australian spirituality.

Campbell, Richard. "The Character of Australian Religion." *Meanjin* 36, no. 2 (July 1977): 178–188.

Clare, Monica. *Karobran: The Story of an Aboriginal Girl.* Chippendale, New South Wales, 1978.

Goonan, Michael. *A Community of Exiles: Exploring Australian Spirituality.* Homebush, New South Wales, 1996. Discusses Tim Winton's *Cloudstreet* and Tom Keneally's *Woman of the Inner Sea* in relation to the Jewish experience of exile in the stories of Tobit and Esther.

Green, Dorothy. "Sheep or Goats? Some Religious Ideas in Australian Literature." *St Mark's Review* (June 1976): 3–29.

Heiss, Anita M. *Dhuuluu-Yala (to talk straight): Publishing Indigenous Literature.* Canberra, 2003.

Lindsay, Elaine. *Rewriting God: Spirituality in Contemporary Australian Women's Fiction.* Amsterdam and Atlanta, Ga., 2000. Critiques desert spirituality and develops an alternative women's spirituality with reference to the fictions of Thea Astley, Elizabeth Jolley, and Barbara Hanrahan.

Marr, David, ed. *Patrick White Letters.* Milsons Point, New South Wales, 1994.

Mudrooroo. *The Indigenous Literature of Australia—Milli Milli Wangka.* South Melbourne, Australia, 1997.

Murray, John. "Inheriting the Land? Some Literary and Ethical Issues in the Use of Indigenous Material by an Australian Children's Writer, 1960–1990." In *Religion Literature and the Arts Conference Proceedings 1994*, edited by Michael Griffith and Ross Keating, pp. 279–288. Sydney, 1995.

Rossiter, Richard, and Lyn Jacobs, eds. *Reading Tim Winton.* Pymble, New South Wales, 1993. Includes an article by Yvonne Miels, "Singing the Great Creator: The Spiritual in Tim Winton's Novels," pp. 29–44.

Scott, Kim. *True Country.* South Fremantle, Western Australia, 1993.

Thompson, Roger C. *Religion in Australia: A History.* South Melbourne, Australia, 1994.

Webby, Elizabeth, ed. *The Cambridge Companion to Australian Literature.* Cambridge, U.K., 2000.

White, Patrick. *The Tree of Man.* London, 1955; reprint, Harmondsworth, Victoria, 1967.

Wilde, William H, Joy Hooton, and Barry Andrews, eds. *The Oxford Companion to Australian Literature.* Oxford, 1985; reprint, 1986.

Winton, Tim. *Cloudstreet.* Melbourne, 1991; reprint, Ringwood, Victoria, 1998.

Winton, Tim. *Land's Edge.* Sydney, 1993; reprint, 1998.

ELAINE LINDSAY (2005)

FICTION: OCEANIC FICTION AND RELIGION

Oceania names the lands of the South Central Pacific. It is an area bounded to the west by the east coast of Australia, to the north by Hawai'i, to the east by Easter Island (Rapanui), and to the south by New Zealand (Aotearoa). Spanish explorers had charted Pacific Islands in the early seventeenth century, and James Cook discovered parts of New Zealand in 1769 and both Hawai'i and the east coast of Australia in 1788. However, oral narrative began in Oceania long before there was any contact with European culture.

In Australia two migrant groups existed—one arriving some 70,000 years ago, almost certainly from Indonesia, and the other about 50,000 years ago, most likely from southern China. Modern Aborigines are the descendents of these groups, although precise lines of descent cannot be drawn. Nor is it known how Aboriginal religious practices derive from the migrants. Yet it is correct to speak of Aboriginal religions, not religion. It was the arrival of the European culture that changed the perception of the indigenous population and made its beliefs and cultures appear more homogeneous than they likely were. The first narratives on the continent take the form of song cycles, which are not well translated by either the term *fiction* or *poetry.*

With the exception of Easter Island, which was reached from South America, the Pacific Islands were settled by Asians. Between two and three thousands years ago, migrants used Melanesia as a base and branched out from there to Fiji and Tahiti. The Hawaiian islands appear to have been settled by Polynesians, who set out from Tahiti about 1,600 years ago. In New Zealand migrants started to arrive some 1,500 years ago from Melanesia, and by 1300 CE a significant Polynesian settlement appears to have been in place. Hawai'i and New Zealand share legends of gods and goddesses that originated in Tahiti. Stories of Maui, who fished for islands, and Tawhaki, who visited the heavens, can be found on many islands. The notions of *mana* and *tabu*—on which so much twentieth-century speculation about religion depends—derive from Polynesia and influence the stories told about the spirit world. Unlike the polytheistic islanders, the Aborigines follow totemic religious practices. Yet, on neither side of the Tasman Sea is it possible to recover a pristine sense of beliefs before European colonization. With the European settlers came Christianity. The first Anglican service in Australia was held in 1788. Not until 1814 did Samuel Marsden (1764–1838) establish a mission in New Zealand, whereas missionaries arrived in Hawai'i in 1820, following a royal decree for the natives to give up paganism. Throughout Oceania, narrative fiction followed only on Christian settlement.

RELIGIOUS NARRATIVE FICTION. A narrative fiction oriented to religious themes began in Australia in 1838 with John Curtis's *Shipwreck of the Stirling Castle.* It turns on the tale of Elisa Fraser, shipwrecked on K'gari (now Fraser Island) in 1836. Mrs. Fraser's faith—like that of the Children of Israel (and like Jesus in the wilderness)—is put to the test. Her story is retold by Patrick White in *A Fringe of Leaves* (1976) but with the female character, Ellen Roxburgh, who has lost her faith in the Christian God and is supported solely by a faith in life itself.

Aboriginal religion appears briefly in James Tucker's *Ralph Rashleigh* (1845?) but is quickly dismissed as infantile, a matter of warriors' ghosts. Tucker's character Rashleigh is aware that the Aborigines regard certain sites as sacred but interprets their awe simply as fear of supernatural beings. About the same time, Charles Rowcraft's novel *The Bushranger of Van Dieman's Land* (1846) at least admits—albeit somewhat patronizingly—that the black people have souls. Not until White's *The Tree of Man* (1955) and *Voss* (1957) is there an authentic sense that Aborigines discern a true spirit in the land. Randolph Stow, especially in *To the Islands* (1958), casts Aboriginal spirituality as superior to imported

Christian beliefs. The character Stephen Heriot, a sixty-seven-year-old missionary, loses his faith and with the help of an Aboriginal guide gains a visionary understanding of the Kimberlies. His spirit eventually merges with that of the land.

Returning to the nineteenth century, Christian moralism is strongly felt in the stories of Mary Vidal collected in *Tales for the Bush* (1845). As with Curtis's Elisa Fraser, the perspective is female. However, now decency rather than survival is the pressing concern. Christianity reveals itself mainly in the need to keep the working people honest and the Sabbath holy. A stronger evangelical current is felt in Caroline Leakey's *The Broad Arrow* (1859), which, like *Ralph Rashleigh*, is set in Tasmania. The heroine is sentenced to life imprisonment there, becomes a "fallen woman," and then finally repents. In the mid-twentieth century there is still interest in the Hobart of convict times, although it is characteristic of the times that Hal Porter's novel *The Tilted Cross* (1961) appeals to Christianity for its symbolism rather than for its spiritual discipline. Throughout the nineteenth century and well after, Australia is represented as a dangerous place for inexperienced Europeans, and more often than not, the land punishes their innocence. Thus there are many stories of children lost in the bush, the best known of which remains Marcus Clarke's "Pretty Dick" (1869). The poor boy dies in the unforgiving landscape, but when at story's end the reader is informed "God had taken him home," the narrator's tone is hardly comforting.

A skeptical attitude toward religion, combined with an anticlerical attitude, gain force in the late nineteenth century. Both can be felt in *The Bulletin* in the 1890s, the magazine's heyday. Only among Catholic writers are clerics at all well regarded; elsewhere, it is remembered that the established Church was rarely a friend of the poor. The Victorian era continues to attract contemporary novelists. In *Oscar and Lucinda* (1988), Peter Carey shows an Anglican minister of that time who, like Pascal but with rather less spirit, regards the religious life as a bet on the existence of God. It is more indicative of the late-twentieth than the nineteenth century, however, that when Oscar dies he begs forgiveness for his part in the death of Aborigines.

Two geographical figures largely organize the plane of religious experience in Australian fiction: the island and the desert. Neither is simple. If the island can be a site of suffering (as it is for Curtis and White), it can also be a metaphor for death transfigured by native understanding (as it is for Stow). It can also be a new Eden. So it is in Martin Boyd's *Nuns in Jeopardy* (1940) and Thea Astley's *Girl with a Monkey* (1958). In *Voss* and *To the Islands*, the desert is a metaphor for a spiritual quest, whereas for Kim Scott in *True Country* (1993), the Outback stands for the sacred. In the middle of this plane of religious experience, a variety of figures can be found: White's Stan and Amy Parker in *The Tree of Man* as a new Adam and Eve; a sense of the divine in the landscape in Elizabeth Jolley's *Palomino* (1980), as well as a folding of the notion of pilgrimage in her *Mr. Scobie's Riddle* (1983); and a discernment of vocation in David Malouf's *Remembering Babylon* (1995).

Denominational and Religious Influences. Of the Christian denominations, the Catholics have spent most time exploring the institutional dimension of religion in Australia. Thomas Keneally's *Three Cheers for the Paraclete* (1968) is set in a seminary and casts a comic eye on ecclesial politics and theological niceties. In New Zealand, Elizabeth Smither also attends to post-Vatican II perplexities in her story "Sister Felicity and Sister Perpetua" (1994). A novelist of ideas, the Australian Morris West has gone the furthest in Church politics in his "Vatican series": *The Shoes of the Fisherman* (1963), *The Clowns of God* (1981) and *Lazarus* (1990). Gerard Windsor examines an Australian salesman in Ireland hawking religious accessories in his novella *That Fierce Virgin* (1988) and hints at mystical depths older than Christianity. The theme of Catholic childhood, often guilt-ridden, has received ample treatment in twentieth-century Australian fiction. Gerald Murnane's *Tamarisk Row* (1974) and *A Lifetime on Clouds* (1976) represent the strain at its most enduring.

Predominantly Christian since settlement, Australia also has sizable—and growing—numbers of Buddhists and Muslims. Yet, of the non-Christian faiths, only Judaism figures to any extent in Australian fiction. It does so significantly in White's fiction, beginning in *The Living and the Dead* (1941), and then with more force in *Riders in the Chariot* (1961), *The Solid Mandala* (1966) and *The Eye of the Storm* (1973). In *Riders in the Chariot*, Judaism and Christianity are confronted when Mordecai Himmelfarb, maker of bicycle lamps and a Jewish mystic, is crucified on a jacaranda tree in Sydney. Keneally's *Schindler's Ark* (1982) tells the story of Oskar Schindler who risks his life to help Polish Jews. Could a new religion be formed in the New World? Nevil Shute considers the possibility in *Round the Bend* (1951), in which a Malayan aircraft mechanic becomes the leader of a new religious movement. In *The Fortunes of Richard Mahoney* (1930), Henry Handel Richardson shows a grieving hero succumbing to spiritualism, and Kylie Tennant casts a wry eye on Southwell Vaughan-Quilter of the Order of Human Brotherhood in her novel *Ride on Stranger* (1943). Helen Garner's *Cosmo Cosmolino* (1992) treats New Age spirituality in the character of Maxine who shares a house in Carlton, Melbourne, with a fundamentalist, a skeptic, and a visiting angel. Garner is not the only Pacific writer interested in divine messengers: New Zealander Elizabeth Knox has an angel as a central character in her novel *The Vintner's Luck* (1999).

Patrick White saw Puritanism as a flaw in the Australian character. More so than in Australia, though, a strong strain of twentieth-century New Zealand fiction has been a diagnosis of and rebellion against a narrow-minded and unimaginative religious conservatism. It too is identified as Puritanism, although, as for White, the word indicates a belated Victorian prudery, loosely regarded as required for progress, rather than the fierce religious impulse of the early New Englanders. Jane Mander is the first to treat the theme in her *The Story of a New Zealand River* (1920), and Frank Sargeson approaches it in his early short stories, "A Good Boy" (1936) and "Good Samaritan" (1936), as well as in the novel *I Saw in My Dream* (1949). Joy Cowley's story "God Loves You, Miss Rosewater" (1978) should also be mentioned for its amused look at puritan sexuality. However, Maurice Gee provides the most pointed critique of the dolorous world, beginning with *In My Father's Den* (1972) and then in his "Plumb trilogy," especially the first volume, *Plumb* (1978).

RELIGIOUS THEMES. Religious themes appear from time to time in other works by New Zealand writers. Sargeson's story "Tod" (1938) poignantly evokes the human need to call on God. Allusions to Maori myths can be found in Witi Ihimaera's *Tangi* (1973), Kerri Hulme's *The Bone People* (1983) and Patricia Grace's *Potiki* (1986). Note should also be made of Apirana Taylor's story "Carving up the Cross" (1990), which examines an artist's thwarted desire to combine Maori and Christian symbols. Michael Brown examines the transmigration of souls in his *The Weaver's Apprentice* (1986), whereas Vincent O'Sullivan observes a French nun who works among the poor in *Believers to the Bright Coast* (1998). As in Australia, a consciousness of a spirit in the land surfaces from time to time. Sargeson's story "Gods Live in Woods" (1943) is an instance, whereas Roderick Finlayson's story "Wi Gets the Gospel" (1937) sympathetically notes the loss of *mana* from the land for Mauris Ihimaera's story "The Greenstone Patu" (1977) identifies a powerful spirit in a *patu* (hand club). Special mention should be made of *Tales of the Tikongs* (1983), stories by the Tongan writer Epeli Hau'ofa that examine the ways in which the Bible has saturated the local culture.

Missionary activity in Hawai'i is the focus of Ruth Eleanor McKee's *The Lord's Anointed* (1934), a novel that stirred up controversy among descendents of the original missionaries. Jonathan and Constancy Williams are missionaries who came to the island in 1820; they exist side by side with historical characters and serve to highlight the hardships of daily life. Constancy relates in her diary that she feigned her conversion when smitten by Jonathan. *The Return of Lono* (1956) is O. A. Bushnell's historical novel about James Cook's last voyage to Hawai'i. John Forrest, the narrator, is the medium in which tensions between the faith exemplified by William Bligh and enlightened reason embodied in Cook are played out partly, if unknowingly, within himself. Without the slightest trace of original sin, the natives have nonetheless fallen victim to local priestcraft, he thinks. Hawai'i is at once a horrible place, filled with cruel gods and terrible injustices, and a paradise of graceful, generous people, an Eden that is soon to be lost by dint of the very presence of the white man. A clash between ancient Hawaiian spirituality and contemporary values is explored through the character of Mark Hull in John Dominis Holt's novel *Waimea Summer* (1976).

SEE ALSO Christianity, article on Christianity in Australia and New Zealand; Cosmology, article on Oceanic Cosmologies; Oceanic Religions, overview article and article on Missionary Movements.

BIBLIOGRAPHY

Charlesworth, Max. *Religious Inventions: Four Essays.* Cambridge, U.K., 1997. Study of Aboriginal religions in chapter 2.

Hogan, Michael. *The Sectarian Strand: Religion in Australian History.* Ringwood, Australia, 1987. History of religion in Australia.

Lindsay, Elaine. "Not the Desert Experience: Spirituality in Australian Women's Fiction." In *Religion, Literature, and the Arts,* edited by Michael Griffith and Ross Keating, pp. 239–51. Sydney, Australia, 1994. Australian women's fiction and religion.

Scott, Jamie S., ed. *"And the Birds Began to Sing": Religion and Literature in Post-Colonial Cultures.* Cross-Cultures: Readings in Post/Colonial Literatures in English, vol. 22. Atlanta, Ga., 1996. Chapters on New Zealand and Tongan fiction.

Strum, Terry, ed. *The Oxford History of New Zealand Literature in English.* 2d ed. Auckland, New Zealand, 1998. Excellent chapter by Lawrence Jones on the New Zealand novel.

Swain, Tony, and Garry Trompf. *The Religions of Oceania.* New York, 1995. Anthropological study of Oceanic religions.

Sumida, Stephen H. *And the View from the Shore: Literary Traditions of Hawai'i.* Seattle, Wash., 1991. Study of fiction in Hawai'i.

Williams, Mark, ed. *The Source of the Song: New Zealand Writers on Catholicism.* Wellington, New Zealand, 1995.

KEVIN HART (2005)

FICTION: AFRICAN FICTION AND RELIGION

Although storytelling is a universal human activity, the term "African fiction" refers to a European genre of storytelling—comprised of secular novels and short stories—that Africans have adopted and adapted to represent continental African realities in the wake of nineteenth- and twentieth-century European colonialism and post-colonialism. The genre will provide a unifying thread throughout the many oral and written traditions in African as well as European languages.

Although an ancient practice in Africa, as witnessed in pharaonic Egypt, writing in African languages began in Muslim and Christian missionary activity, some of which dates back to pre-modern times, as is the case for Geez or Amharic in Ethiopia. Other African languages such as Sesuto, Xhosa, Zulu, and Yoruba, began in nineteenth- and twentieth-century Euro-Christian missionary schools and feature allegorical novels inspired by Bunyan's *Pilgrim's Progress.* But the tension between Euro-Christianity and African tradition is apparent in the Yoruba novels of Fagunwa (Nigeria), such as *The Forest of a Thousand Daemons,* in which references to a Christian God are imposed on Yoruba mythology. Modern Muslim missionary activity gave rise to Arabic script literatures in languages such as Wolof, Swahili, and Hausa. European-language writing in French, English, and Portuguese is a result of modern colonialism.

African writers of fiction use the genre to enter into dialogue with African and European religious traditions alike. Drawing on oral myths, epics and tales, these writers oppose representations of Africa found in European fiction, as well as in European governmental, missionary, and commercial reports. In the process African writers also rewrite and rework oral traditions.

African oral traditions reflect hierarchies of power in ways parallel to European fiction. At the top of the hierarchy are such works as ceremonial ritual religious poems or the great Dogon cosmogonic myth, according to which the universe originates from a single seed. Next are the great chanted epics such as the Malian epic of Sundiata or the Mwindo epic, which feature shamanic heroes, founders of their society. The great oral praise songs for outstanding men and women are formal lyrics that use epic materials. On a more common level are occupational poems, sung to accompany an activity such as farming, fishing, hunting or smithing. Even these lower forms recall religious functions of individuals or callings.

Short narrative tales may use mythic and epic materials more informally to explain the origins of a people, the founding of a dynasty, or the nature of divine beings, as well as phenomena such as the behavior of certain animals or the origins of geographic details. However, the genre is derivative rather than authoritative, drawing on chanted epics and ceremonial ritual religious poems, praise and occupational poetry. The narrative tale has a more realistic bent. A prominent theme is that of the trickster-hero, who succeeds through cleverness rather than through morality. Recalling the Yoruba (Nigeria) god Eshu-Elegba, the hero may be human or an animal such as the hare (source of the African American Br'er Rabbit), the hyena or the spider. In such tales, might or cleverness makes right and the outcome is not always moral. Shorter forms that one finds frequently used in African fiction are proverbs ("the palm oil with which words are eaten"), epigrams and riddles.

Written African fiction draws on this tradition in many ways in terms of characters, themes, motifs, and formal structures. In terms of religion, most significant is a "vitalist" ontology according to which being is a dynamic vital force that pervades everything much like a fluid as opposed to a collection of static, discrete entities. Hence Western distinctions between human, animal and divine, or the living and the dead do not necessarily apply. Because of vital force human beings have totemic relationships with animals with which they share the force of being. For example, the epic hero Sundiata draws totemically on the power of the buffalo through his mother, Sogolon, and on the power of the lion, which bears a totemic relationship with his male ancestors. In this way, departed ancestors exercise their force through the living.

In the epic, such ontology is portrayed in an unproblematic synthesis with Islam. For example, Sundiata's male ancestors trace their lineage back to Bilali Bounama, a servant of the Prophet Muḥammad.

A second religiously important structure that pervades African literature, as Mohammadou Kane has observed, is the initiatory journey, usually presented in three stages: a hero leaves home as a child, goes on a series of adventures and returns as an adult. The epic of Sundiata is an example. The young Sundiata, who after a long period of lameness stands up to walk, must go into exile and face a series of trials, which he overcomes. Then he returns home to found the empire of Mali. This outcome is never in doubt from the day that Sundiata's father sacrifices a red bull and lets its blood soak into the ground. Yet, all is seen as in the hands of the "Almighty." As the family griot, Gnankouman Doua, observes, "The Almighty has his mysteries . . . The silk-cotton tree emerges from a tiny seed" (Kane, p. 16).

That such traditional African elements are portrayed in an unproblematic synthesis with Islam is a witness to the fact of the gradual infiltration of Islam, which was adapted by various groups of society, usually merchants first, then the ruling classes, and finally the people at large. Works such as *Sundiata* reveal ways in which ruling classes gradually combined Islamic and pre-Islamic elements to build the foundation of their power. A similar approach may be seen in the European Renaissance when the French *rex christianissimus* traced his lineage to Hector; the Catholic Hapsburg emperors, and to Jason and the Golden Fleece.

One also finds a relatively syncretistic harmony in autobiographical works such as the Guinean Camara Laye's *The Dark Child* or the Nigerian Wole Soyinka's *Ake.* Although not syncretistic, African language allegorical novels in the tradition of Bunyan's *Pilgrim's Progress* are pre-modern in that they assume a classic religious orthodoxy.

Modern and post-modern African fiction tends to portray fault lines and conflict such as in the Nigerian Fagunwa's Yoruba novel mentioned above or the Kenyan Ngugi wa Thiongo's bitingly satirical Gikuyu, *Devil on the Cross.*

Eschewing heroes, African fiction, like its European models, foregrounds main characters in what Northrop Frye (*Anatomy of Criticism*) calls the "low mimetic" and "ironic modes." Frye defines these modes not according to the morality of the main character but rather according to his or her "power of action" (Frye, p. 33). As opposed to a Sundiata, who is invincible, the "low mimetic" mode represents characters less powerful than other people or their environment. Characters in the "ironic mode" are inferior to the reader in either power or intelligence, and often the brunt of comedy.

The question of power is particularly pertinent to Africans, for whom colonialism created new and problematic conflicts between the ideal, moral, and practical aspects of religious experience, calling into question the traditional hierarchies and values implied in the oral tradition. For the most part, African fiction in which religion is a significant theme works out issues of colonial and post-colonial (dis)empowerment, and features not only inter-religious tensions but also conflicts between religion and secular forces often imperfectly understood. On the one hand is a traditional religious mentality according to which religion accounts for an approach to visible and invisible reality that does not observe the Western distinction between natural and supernatural. As Robin Horton observes in *Patterns of Thought in Africa and the West*, such traditional religion provided ways to explain, control and predict events in the visible universe as well as establish communion with an invisible being or beings. On the other hand is a purely secular mentality according to which events unfold due to impersonal political, social, and psychological forces unleashed by the European conquest and occupation.

Novels leading up to African independences in the 1960s underscore such tensions, but retain a faith in a possible future for the continent and for the world. In the Senegalese Cheikh Hamidou Kane's *Ambiguous Adventure* the lure of European technology causes the complicity between Islam and traditional political power to break down. In another time the royal and spiritually gifted Samba Diallo may have been left to pursue a path of spiritual greatness in the hands of his Ṣūfī spiritual director Tierno or become a kind of priest/king. His family decides instead to tear him away from the ascetic discipline of renunciation and send him to Europe on a kind of "initiatory journey" to learn how "better to join wood to wood" (Kane, p. 29), so as to bring his people into the modern world. The experiment fails, however. Once in Europe Samba Diallo decides to study philosophy, and on his return home is killed by his spiritual director. This death, however, brings Samba Diallo into a Ṣūfī mystical communion with God. Even though Samba Diallo's death marks the failure of his initiation into the ways of secular Europe, this death may also be considered an extreme form of world renunciation, in which the young man's spiritual vocation is fulfilled.

Although renunciation of this world has always been commonplace in mystical traditions, the split between a European technological material world and Islamic spirituality reflects a limited orientalist view of Islam that overlooks medieval Muslim scientific and technological advances and prowess. It also plays into theses of Negritude that try to rehabilitate orientalist dichotomies in calling for a "universal civilization" that combines spiritual, intuitive and rhythmical "Black" culture in harmony with nature, on the one hand, with analytic and technological "White" culture, on the other.

In works such as the novel *God's Bits of Wood* and the short-story collection *Tribal Scars*, the Senegalese writer Ousmane Sembène eschews the sentimentality of Negritude. Mystical Islam is portrayed as ineffective and its clergy accused of complicity with colonial rule and patriarchal exploitation of women. For Sembène, the only way out of the colonial impasse is through a Marxist-inspired collective political action of the working classes. In *God's Bits of Wood*, it is only in a railroad workers strike that dignity is regained. For example, learning to act collectively without hatred, the brutish, stammering Tiémoko is released to sing the epic of Sundiata. Formerly sacred royal power is now in the hands of secular working people.

While French West African fiction is presented in the terms of concepts of universal pretensions such as Islam, Marxism and Negritude, the novels of the Nigerian Chinua Achebe (*Things Fall Apart*; *Arrow of God*) and the Cameroonian Mongo Beti (*The Poor Christ of Bomba*; *King Lazarus*) and Ferdinand Oyono (*Houseboy*; *Old Man and the Medal*) are more local in scope, in that theirs is a context of forest people such as the Ibo, who live in loose federations or small chiefdoms. These novels denounce the abuses not so much of Christianity as the Christian mission enterprise, which is seen as a source of European violence and conquest. Behind the missionaries come the merchants and the military. Church, hospital, schools and prisons are seen as European institutions in complicity with one another. In *Things Fall Apart*, the missionary prepares the way for the colonial administrator. In *The Poor Christ of Bomba*, the R. P. Drumont who cannot manage to reform the sexual mores of his converts sadly realizes that his efforts result in softening up his "faithful" for exploitation in the colonial labor force.

In these novels Christian conversion is seen to be based on misunderstandings and to yield ludicrous harmful results. King Lazarus converts on his deathbed only to get well and have to face a diplomatic crisis, as he must now choose only one among his many wives. In *Old Man and the Medal*, Meka, who has converted to Christianity and given up his lands to the Catholic mission, embarks on what turns out to be a mock initiatory journey from his community to the administrative center of the Whites. He finds himself standing in the middle of a stadium in a chalk-drawn circle under the hot sun, in ill-fitting shoes and having a strong urge to urinate as he waits for the French colonial administrator to pin a medal on him for his contributions to the community. In such a time of trial only the memory of the pain he endured at his circumcision gives him the courage to withstand heat and burning pain. The true meaning of this medal is revealed when later, Meka is brutally beaten and thrown into jail by the police, who do not recognize him. Here too he resorts to his totemic relations with panthers to muster up the necessary strength.

In both cases, the caricatural evocation of traditional religion is tragi-comic, revealing the comical ineffectiveness of the tradition in the new setting of colonialism. On his return home, Meka is chastened and cynical about his Christian faith and relation with the whites. But his "initiation" leaves him with little new knowledge except for a relief to be back among the grasses and animals of his home. Here unlike the West African novels, there is no faith in an overarching scheme of things. There is also an unremitting satirical criticism implied of African traditions. The indulgent humor of the narrator, who laughs with as well as at the characters, leaves the reader with the conviction of the inherent dignity and resilience of African people.

In all of these works the narrative voice often plays against sliding conceptions of the distinction between the secular and the sacred. In *Things Fall Apart* and in *Houseboy*, child converts whom Christians believe that God has touched are in fact fleeing abusive fathers. In Achebe's novels the fact that Europeans trample sacred forests and kill sacred animals with impunity is taken to be a sign of divine intervention. In fiction such as this, even where there is an implied criticism of African tradition, the overriding message is that the abuse of European colonialism must stop, so that Africans may regroup and take charge of their own fate.

Post-colonial fiction is marked by a turn toward an African audience to address African problems. The multiple consciousness of several sides to a story is taken to new heights with a dialogical representation of reality from an even more complex, pluralistic perspective. Fama, the last of the royal line of Doumbouya in the Ivórian Ahmadou Kourouma's *Suns of Independence* also sets off on a tripartite journey. He leaves the capital for a funeral in Togobala, a seedy village that is all that remains of his family's ancient capital, and he returns home only to be thrown into prison. This tripartite structure, inspired by the initiatory journey is a failure, but can be seen from three equally valid perspectives. The Doumbouya decadence is (1) an eschatological sign of Muslim last days; (2) the result of disrespect for the ancient fetishes; (3) or a secular working out of post-colonial corruption. But no matter how the sequence of events is explained, there is an overriding angry irony at the corruption of contemporary society. Kourouma's novel, *Allah n'est pas obligé*, is even angrier, as he portrays an Africa sinking deeper into crisis under the eyes of an indifferent God. The latter is among what Lilyan Kesteloot calls novels of chaos, novels written in despair of a spectacle of an Africa racked by such corruption, famine and genocide that it seems to be without a God. One bears in mind the Rwanda writers' project, in which several African writers such as Boubacar Boris Diop (Senegal) or Véronique Tadjo (Ivory Coast) committed themselves to write about the genocide in that country. One can also contrast Ngugi wa Thiong'o's *Devil on the Cross*, which brutally satirizes Christianity, to his earlier novels such as *The River Between*, which portrays the protagonist Waiyake (Kenyatta) as a Christ figure.

A dialogical pluralism similar to Kourouma's may be found in the Nigerian Buchi Emechetta's *Joys of Motherhood*. In this book the protagonist, Nnu Ego, lives out a miserable existence that may be seen as the result of a combination of traditional patriarchy and European colonial exploitation which leave women particularly vulnerable. On the other hand, Nnu Ego's sorry fate may be consistently explained down to its smallest details as the unremitting curse of her *chi*, who in a previous life was forced to be buried alive at her husband's funeral.

Dialogical pluralism of Kourouma and Emechetta is but an extreme example of the tendency of African fiction to call into question constructions, not only of Christianity and Islam, but also of anthropological accounts of local religions. Through devices of irony and comedy the main characters belong yet do not belong to European and African religious traditions. In this respect, one should mention V. Y. Mudimbe's *Entre les Eaux*, in which the priest, Pierre Landu fails to bring together Christianity and Marxism. He is an example of what Wim van Binsbergen calls "Central African clerical intellectualism," an intellectualism of a certain category of Catholic clerics who have little to do with traditional African religion.

Other fiction of the 1970s, 1980s, and 1990s continues this trend toward pluralism, emphasizing intrareligious more than interreligious difference, especially with reference to Islam. In response to Islamic fundamentalism, postmodern fiction from Northern Africa (always a cross-roads of many cultures and religions) reaches back to Islamic traditional means of interpretation in the *ḥadīth* to reveal the suppressed voices of the religion. Novelists such as the Moroccans Driss Chraïbi (*La Mère du Printemps*), and Fatima Mernissi (*Le Harem politique*), the Algerian Assia Djebar (*Loin de la Médine*), and the Egyptian Nawal El Sadaawi (*God Dies by the Nile*) question Islamic patriarchy and oppose such concepts as *jihad* (holy war, but also self-discipline) and *itjihād* (interpretation).

The Somalian novelist Nuruddin Farah goes even further than most of the fiction writers here. In *Maps* he criticizes not Islamic practices or traditions but the internal morality of the religion itself and its nefarious effects on Somalian society, although he falls more into the main line in his *Close Sesame*, which emphasizes the gap between ideal Islam and the way it is played out in society.

One sees a similar process in South Africa, where a novel such as Rayda Jacob's *Confessions of a Gambler* portrays a freer, postmodern Islam in the person of the protagonist, an emancipated Capetonian Islamic woman who gambles. Writers such as Zoë Wicomb (*You Can't Get Lost in Cape Town*; and *David's Story*) and Zakes Mda (*The Madonna of Excelsior*), on the other hand, criticize hypocrisy of the abusive Christianity brought by the Dutch Calvinist settlers. These settlers claim South Africa as a land promised to them by God, and are portrayed in Afrikaner novels such as André Brink's *A Dry White Season*.

BIBLIOGRAPHY

Primary Sources

Achebe, Chinua. *Things Fall Apart*. London, 1958.

Achebe, Chinua. *Arrow of God*. London, 1964.

Beti, Mongo. *Le Roi miraculé: chronique des Essazam* Paris, 1958. Translated by Peter Green under the title *King Lazarus*. London, 1960.

Beti, Mongo. *Le Pauvre Chris de Bomba*. Paris, 1976. Translated by Gerald Moore under the title *The Poor Christ of Bomba*. London, 1971.

Brink, André. *A Dry White Season*. New York, 1980.

Chraïbi, Driss. *La Mère du Printemps* (*L'Oum-er-Bia*). Paris, 1982. Translated by Hugh A. Harter under the title *Mother Spring*. Washington D.C., 1989.

Diebuyck, Daniel, and Kahombo C. Mateene, trans. and eds. *The Mwindo Epic from the Banyanga (Congo Republic)*. Berkeley, Calif., 1969.

Djebar, Assia. *Loin de la Médine*. Paris, 1991.

Emechetta, Buchi. *The Joys of Motherhood*. London, 1979.

Fagunwa, D.O. *The Forest of a Thousand Daemons*. Translated by Wole Soyinka. London, 1968.

Farah, Nuruddin. *Maps*. New York, 1986.

Farah, Nuruddin. *Close Sesame*. Saint Paul, Minn., 1992.

Jacob, Rayda. *Confessions of a Gambler*. Cape Town, South Africa, 2003.

Kane, Cheikh Hamidou. *Aventure Ambiguë*. Paris, 1961. Translated by Katherine Woods under the title *Ambiguous Adventure*. 1962. New York, 1969.

Kourouma, Ahmadou. *Les Soleils des Indépendance*. Montréal, 1968. Translated by Adrian Adams under the title *The Suns of Independence*. London, 1981.

Kourouma, Ahmadou. *Allah n'est pas oblige*. Paris, 2000.

Laye, Camara. *L'Enfant noir*. Paris, 1953. Translated by James Kirkup and Ernest Jones under the title, *The Dark Child*. Introduction by Philippe Thoby-Marcellin. New York, 1954.

Mda, Zakes. *The Madonna of Excelsior*. Oxford, 2002.

Mernissi, Fatima. *Le Harem politique: Le Prophète et les Femmes*. Paris, 1987.

Mudimbe, V. Y. *Entre les Eaux*. Paris, 1973.

Niane, D. T. *Soundjata ou L'épopée mandingue*. Paris, 1960.Translated by G. D. Pickett under the title *Sundiata: An Epic of Old Mali*. London, 1965.

Ngugi wa Thiong. *The River Between*. London, 1965.

Ngugi wa Thiong. *Devil on the Cross*. London, 1982.

Oyono, Ferdinand. *Une Vie de Boy*. Paris, 1956. Translated by John Reed under the title *Houseboy*. London 1966.

Oyono, Ferdinand. *Le vieux nègre et la médaille*. Paris, 1956. Translated by John Reed under the title *Old Man and the Medal*. London, 1969.

El Sadaawi, Nawal. *God Dies by the Nile*. 1974. London, 1985.

Sembène, Ousmane. *Les Bouts de Bois de Dieu*. Paris, 1960. Translated by Francis Price under the title *God's Bits of Wood*. New York, 1962.

Sembène, Ousmane. *Voltaïque. La noire de. . .nouvelles*. Paris, 1971. Translated by Len Ortzen under the title *Tribal Scars and Other Stories*. London, 1973.

Soyinka, Wole. *Ake: The Years of Childhood*. London, 1981.

Wicomb, Zoë. *You Can't Get Lost in Cape Town*. London, 1987.

Wicomb, Zoë. *David's Story*. New York, 2000.

Criticism and General Studies

Bâ, Hampaté. *Aspects de la civilization africaine*. Paris, 1972.

Battestini, Simon P. X. "Muslim Influences on West African Literature and Culture." *Journal of Muslim Minority Affairs* 7 (July 1986): 2, 476–502.

Finnegan, Ruth. *Oral Literature in Africa*. Oxford, 1970.

Frye, Northrop. *Anatomy of Criticism: Four Essays*. Princeton, N.J., 1957.

Gérard, Albert. *African Language Literatures: An Introduction to the Literary History of Sub-Saharan Africa*. Washington, D.C, 1980.

Gérard, Albert. *European-Language Writing in Sub-Saharan Africa*. 2 vols. Budapest, Hungary, 1986.

Griaule, Marcel. *Conversations with Ogotemmêli*. London, 1948.

Harrow, Ken, ed. *Faces of Islam in African Literature. Studies in African Literature: New Series*. Portsmouth, N.H., 1991.

Harrow, Ken, ed. *The Marabout and the Muse: New Approaches to Islam in African Literature*. Portsmouth, N.H., 1996. These two books edited by Ken Harrow constitute an indispensable introduction to the relation between Islam and African literature. The more than thirty individual articles cannot be listed here.

Horton, Robin. *Patterns of Thought in Africa and the West: Essays on Magic, Religion and Science*. Cambridge, U.K., 1993.

Hutcheon, Linda. *A Poetics of Postmodernism*. London, 1988.

Johnson, Lemuel A. "Cross and Consciousness: The Failure of Orthodoxy in African and Afro-Hispanic Literature." *Studies in Afro-Hispanic Literature* 2 (1978): 53–89.

Kane, Mohammadou. *Roman et traditions*. Dakar, Senegal, 1984.

Kesteloot, Lilyan. *Histoire de la Littérature Négro-Africaine*. Paris, 2001.

Killam, Douglas, and Ruth Rowe. *The Companion to African Literatures*. Bloomington, Ind., 2000.

Mazrui, Ali. *The Africans: A Triple Heritage*. London, 1986.

Obiechina, Emmanuel. *Culture, Tradition and Society in the West African Novel*. New York, 1975.

Okpewho, Isidore. *African Oral Literature: Backgrounds, Character, and Continuity*. Bloomington, Ind., 1992.

Soyinka, Wole. *Myth, Literature and the African World*. London, 1976.

Tempels, Placide. *La Philosophie bantoue*. Paris, 1949. Translated into English under the title *Bantu Philosophy*. Paris, 1969. A good presentation of the ontological concept of "vital force," in spite of its missionary intentions.

Zell, Hans M., Carol Bundy and Virginia Coulon, eds. *A New Reader's Guide to African Literature*. New York, 1983.

GEORGE JOSEPH (2005)

FICTION: NATIVE AMERICAN FICTION AND RELIGION

Given the many geographical, cultural, and spiritual differences among indigenous peoples in North America, compiling a historical narrative of religious themes in American Indian fiction is a complicated enterprise. Native groups do share common traditions of oral storytelling and episodes of contact with waves of colonizing Europeans. Themes that manifest themselves in this fiction include colonialism and postcolonialism, identity and alienation, the loss of land, relocation, memory, healing, religious freedom, the repatriation of sacred objects and skeletal remains, experience with missionaries and boarding schools, cultural continuity, and community building. Native authors are politically and historically conscious, and, in a very real sense, their characters are struggling to survive in the modern world.

Native spirituality encompasses many traditions of belief, from Laguna creation stories to Ojibwa trickster tales, from the Sun Dance to the Ghost Dance, from puberty ceremonies to vision quests to peyote ceremonies at the Native American Church. Native religions embody worldviews without explicit creeds and principles. Vine Deloria Jr. defines tribal religions as "complexes of attitudes, beliefs, and practices fine-tuned to harmonize with the lands on which the people live" (1994, p. 70). "Every factor of human experience is seen in a religious light as part of the meaning of life," Deloria continues (p. 195). This further complicates the analysis of religious themes in American Indian literature, for spirituality pervades every aspect of the work. Further, works of fiction in English by Indian authors are inherently postcontact narratives and thus also address experiences with Christianity. As Kimberly Blaeser notes, much of Native literature compares Native beliefs to Christianity, rhetorically critiques Christianity, or focuses on the Christian/Native religious conflict (1994, p. 16). For many peoples, becoming Christian did not mean giving up tribal beliefs and customs. Often, the most favorable aspects of each religion have been combined in a syncretic or hybrid manner, and sometimes these religious variations cause irreparable rifts in communities and families. Since the 1970s, however, there has been a resurgence of traditional tribal practices.

The Roots of Storytelling. That American Indians are competent storytellers is no surprise: entire histories and mythologies have long been passed on through story. Prayers, chants, and songs performed during ceremonies are also part of this tradition. LaVonne Ruoff writes, "Because sacred oral literature is so closely interwoven into the fabric of traditional Indian religious life, it is difficult to distinguish between literature and religion" (1990, pp. 141–142). Oral storytelling provides not only pleasure to an audience, but it often passes on knowledge, history, culture, and rules for living. Stories teach "abstract notions of behavior, cosmology, and ways of seeing or thinking about things" (Beck et al., 1995, p. 59). In Pueblo culture, explains writer Leslie Marmon Silko, no distinctions are made "between types of story—historical, sacred, plain gossip" (1996, p. 53). There are as many oral traditions as there are indigenous groups. Pomo author Greg Sarris points out that "it is as impossible to generalize about 'oral discourse' as it is about 'culture'" (1993, p. 47). "Storytelling is a communal act," writes Joseph Epes Brown (2001, p. 54). As it is the nature of oral tradition to take audience and circumstance into account for each telling, the storyteller can appeal to changing pities and fears—and incorporate contemporary elements.

In his essay "The Native Voice in American Literature," Kiowa writer N. Scott Momaday writes that the "unconditional belief in the efficacy of language" resides "at the heart of the American Indian oral tradition" (1997, p. 15). Creek scholar Craig Womack concurs: "Native artistry is not pure aesthetics, or art for art's sake: as often as not Indian writers are trying to *invoke* as much as *evoke.* The idea behind ceremonial chant is that language, spoken in the appropriate ritual contexts, will actually cause a change in the physical universe" (1999, pp. 16–17). The same can be said for contemporary American Indian writing. With the introduction of the written word, storytelling was transformed, but orality was never abandoned. Oral tradition continues to inform Native expression, whether in poetry or the European form of the novel.

Early American Indian Fiction. In many ways, Native novelists have followed the trends of Euro-American literature. In the late 1800s when Anglo- and African American women took up the sentimental plot, often for political purposes, Native women did the same. Three examples are S. Alice Callahan's *Wynema: A Child of the Forest* (1891), Zitkala-Sa's *American Indian Stories* (1921), and Mourning Dove's *Co-ge-wea* (1927), all of which address the "Indian problem." Other important early writers include John Joseph Mathews, an Osage writer whose novels include *Wah'kon-tah: The Osage and the White Man's Road* (1932) and *Sundown* (1934), and Lakota author Ella Cara Deloria, whose novel *Waterlily* was written in 1944 (but not published until 1988). In general, early Native authors were concerned with Euro-American contact, missionaries, and loss of land and language and culture. At the same time, they were working against the mainstream notion that their people would indeed become extinct.

The first known published work of fiction by a Native woman is *Wynema* by Callahan, a mixed-blood Muscogee (or Creek). Written in 1891 for a non-Native audience, the book was out of print until 1997. Like much early Native fiction, *Wynema* addresses the impact of colonization and missionization. Unfortunately, Callahan does not provide much description of traditional Creek culture (and, in fact, never mentions the word *Creek* in the text), a move that Susan Bernardin describes as an effort to write "a generic Indian story" that is "putatively pantribal" (2001, p. 4). However, Womack faults Callahan for "purposefully, not accidentally, misrepresenting culture" (1999, p. 115). He calls *Wynema* "a document of Christian supremicism and assimilation" (1999, p. 107). Callahan's most detailed ethnographic passage describes the green corn ceremony, which is practiced in this community even after the adoption of Christianity. There is also a funeral scene that combines Creek and Christian rituals. But, for the most part, Creek culture is completely negated by Methodism. The novel follows Wynema Harjo, a full-blood Muscogee woman who befriends Genevieve Weir, a Methodist teacher from Alabama, the place from which the Muscogees were removed on the Trail of Tears in 1830. Genevieve eventually marries the local Methodist minister, Gerald Keithly, while Wynema marries Genevieve's brother Robin. In many ways, Genevieve is the novel's heroine, for it is she who must overcome stereotypes and develop as a character. Although Genevieve begins as a model Indian reformer, Gerald points out that acculturation is reciprocal. *Wynema*'s domestic plot is infused with social commentary from the two young women, who often combine suffragist concerns with Indian affairs. At the end of the novel, Callahan shifts her focus from the plots at hand to a wider view of current events in Indian Country. The final two chapters give voice to Lakota rebels and Chikena, a sole survivor of the massacre of Wounded Knee in 1890. When a missionary tells one of the rebels, "Place yourselves in a submissive attitude and the government will protect you," he replies, "peace is not the watchword of the oppressed" (Callahan, 1997, pp. 80, 82). The reader is left with a vision of this very recent horrific carnage at the hands of the U. S. government and a critical voice on the doctrine of Christian submission.

D'Arcy McNickle's novel *The Surrounded* appeared in 1936 and was reprinted in the 1970s. Like other works of this era, *The Surrounded* is told in the mode of social realism. As McNickle explains in an epigraph, the title for the book is taken from the name of his Montana setting, *Sniél-emen,* or "Mountains of the Surrounded," referring to the proximity of the settlers. The story follows the homecoming of Archilde Leon, a mixed-blood whose mother Catherine is Salish and father Max is Spanish. While his mother practices mostly traditional Salish religion, which includes public confession and whipping, Archilde's father is Catholic. Enacting modes of oral tradition, McNickle recounts three versions of how the Salish compelled the Jesuit missionaries to come to them. Father Grepilloux, who is characterized as a good-hearted man, tells Max Leon, "It was inevitable that a new age would come" (McNickle, 1994, p. 108). Archilde has learned the Catholic traditions and plays violin at the church. His nephews attend the mission school. In a crucial scene, Archilde recalls seeing a cross in the sky while at boarding school (p. 103). When he notices that a bird does not recognize the cross as a "sign" from God, Archilde begins to question the authority of the Catholic Church. After having a series of dreams, Archilde's mother renounces her baptism. In her dreaming, Catherine goes to white heaven, but there are no Indians there. She goes to Indian heaven, but they will not accept baptized Indians. Although the novel ends with uncertainty, Archilde's own doubts about Christianity remain constant. As Laird Christensen points out, McNickle's novel questions Christianity's impact on the "cosmology, values, and economy" of this Salish community. In particular, the "Christian concept of eternal judgment [acts] as a wedge that forces the Salish out of traditional patterns of relating to family, society, and ultimately the more-than-human world" (1999, pp. 2–3). McNickle's second novel, *Wind from an Enemy Sky,* was published in 1978.

THE NATIVE AMERICAN RENAISSANCE. The beginning of what Kenneth Lincoln has called the Native American Renaissance is marked by the 1968 publication of *House Made of Dawn,* for which N. Scott Momaday won the Pulitzer Prize in 1969. Momaday's novel begins with Abel's return home to his grandfather in Walatawa, New Mexico, after serving in the Korean War. Abel's grandfather Francisco is a tribal elder and a sacristan of the Catholic Church in this Pueblo. Soon after Abel's return, which coincides with the Feast of Santiago, he sleeps with Mrs. Angela Grace St. John, a white woman who comes to Walatawa for its healing waters, and he murders the albino man who is to represent the figure of Santiago during the festivities. The novel follows Abel to Los Angeles, where seven years later he lies in a ditch with broken hands. During a vision quest of sorts, he thinks about his childhood and his time in the city, which includes sermons by Reverend Tosamah, a Native preacher whose grandmother attended the last Kiowa Sun Dance. Abel once again returns home, and his grandfather dies seven days later. After preparing Francisco's body in the traditional way, Abel goes to town to inform the priest, then joins the Jemez dawn runners on the mesa.

Many critics have discussed the religious strains in *House Made of Dawn.* Kenneth Lincoln, for example, has argued that the murder of the albino is a reversal of the biblical murder of Abel. Harold S. McAllister contends that Angela St. John represents the Virgin Mary and shows Abel "the way to salvation" (1974, p. 115). Not all critics focus on the Catholicism in the novel, however. Robert Nelson focuses on the role of place in Abel's healing process, a relationship inherent to Pueblo spirituality. Susan Scarberry-Garcia discusses "Abel's illness in relation to Navajo theories of disease and his restoration in light of both Navajo song texts and Navajo, Kiowa, and Pueblo ritual patterns" (1990, p. 86). Bernard Hirsch describes Reverend Tosamah, a Priest of the Sun and Coyote figure, as "a priest whose saving message, because he has divorced his religion from his everyday life, has an ironic as well as a revelatory dimension" (1983, p. 319). Momaday's fiction also includes *The Ancient Child* (1989).

Leslie Marmon Silko's *Ceremony* (1977) offers a more overt affirmation of Pueblo mythology over Christian dogma. Incorporating traditions of oral culture, Silko begins *Ceremony* with a poem about Thought-Woman, who in Laguna cosmology created the world. The novel traces World War II veteran Tayo as he returns to his home in Laguna Pueblo. Like Momaday's Abel, Tayo is alienated and in need of healing. He feels responsible for the death of his cousin Rocky during the war. Because he cursed the rain that made Rocky's injury worse, Tayo is certain to have caused the drought that plagues Laguna. Suffering from postwar trauma, Tayo participates in a healing ceremony arranged by his grandmother. When Ku'oosh, the local shaman, cannot heal him, Tayo is taken to Gallup to see Betonie, a Navajo who uses a hybrid method of healing. In the mountains, Tayo encounters Ts'eh, a seemingly mythical woman reminiscent of Yellow Woman, who helps Tayo recover his uncle's lost cattle.

Silko's novel focuses on the necessity of achieving balance in the world, of remembering the stories and knowing one's place in them, and of recognizing the relationships between all things, as Robert Nelson proposes. Much *Ceremony* scholarship focuses on aspects of Native spirituality—healing rituals, medicine wheels, witchery, star maps, and the function Ts'eh (see Lincoln, 1983, and Mitchell, 1979). Some critics have focused on the religious syncretism or hybridity in the novel (see Gianferrari, 1999). Jace Weaver points to the importance of community as religious practice in the novel—and that "Tayo is able to achieve wholeness only in re-membering himself in the collective" (1997, p. 134). That sense of community, of working toward communal values, is an outward manifestation of traditional beliefs. One of Silko's short stories, "The Man to Send Rainclouds" (1981), also takes up the conflict between Christianity and Laguna spirituality. Silko's other novels include *Almanac of the Dead* (1991) and *Gardens in the Dunes* (1999).

Other novels published in the 1970s include James Welch's *Winter in the Blood* (1974) and *The Death of Jim Loney* (1979), and Gerald Vizenor's *Darkness in Saint Louis Bearheart* (1978).

THE 1980S AND BEYOND. The 1980s saw a proliferation of American Indian novelists, Louise Erdrich included. Erdrich's first novel *Love Medicine* (1984, revised in 1993)—and later *The Beet Queen* (1986), *Tracks* (1988), *Tales of Burning Love* (1990), *The Bingo Palace* (1994), *The Antelope Wife* (1998), *The Last Report of the Miracles at Little No Horse* (2001), and *The Master Butcher's Singing Club* (2002)—follow certain Ojibwa, German, and mixed-blood families in North Dakota from historical times to the present. Throughout these novels, Erdrich also chronicles the relationship between the Ojibwa and the missionary Jesuits near the fictional town of Argus. *Love Medicine* is told through the voices of multiple narrators and spans fifty years, 1934 to 1984. The novel begins "the morning before Easter Sunday" when June Morrissey decides to walk home from Williston, North Dakota (1993, p. 1). A blizzard unexpectedly begins, and June dies in the snow: "June walked over it like water and came home" (p. 7).

Louis Owens has called June "the feminine Christ-figure resurrected as trickster" (1992, p. 196). Kimberly Blaeser agrees: "By intermingling the symbolism from both religions in June's story, Erdrich seems to challenge not only the exclusiveness of religious myths, but also the exclusive nature of religious ideas themselves" (1994, p. 28). During the remainder of the novel, the community works on coming to terms with June's death. Among the numerous plot lines is Marie Lazarre's experience with Sister Leopolda at the Sacred Heart Convent in 1934. Marie's back is scalded and her hand stabbed by Sister Leopolda, who is trying to save young Marie from the "Dark One." "Christ has marked me," Marie says ironically (p. 60). Marie describes the sisters as *windigos*, half-starved creatures from Chippewa lore, again in a combination of religious imagery (see Jaskoski, 2000). Sister Leopolda is in fact Pauline Puyat, Marie's own mother, which is revealed in *Tracks*. Traditional Ojibwa religion does not go unscathed, however. The love medicine of the title, which Lipsha Morrissey creates to reunite Marie and Nector Kashpaw, ends up choking Nector to death. When Nector Kashpaw had once yelled his prayers at Mass, Lipsha agreed that "God's being going deaf" for years, or that maybe Chippewas "just don't speak its language" (pp. 235–236). Critic Dennis Walsh discusses this "spiritual failure of Catholicism" in the novel (2001, p. 125). Two later chapters also carry enormous religious significance. In "Crown of Thorns," alcoholism is just that for Gordie Kashpaw. In "Resurrection," Marie reclaims her Ojibwa spirituality by speaking the language and preparing to pass down Nector's ceremonial pipe to Lipsha. In *Love Medicine*, Erdrich enacts what Patricia Riley calls "mythological synergy," a move beyond religious syncretism that offers a counternarrative to the story of the vanishing Indian and ensures the survival of her mixed-blood characters (2000, p. 14). Erdrich certainly questions the beneficence of Catholicism throughout her work. In a 2001 interview, Erdrich explains, "Missionary work is essentially tragic. Those who enter the field from the religious side often do so out of love, and out of love they destroy the essence of the people they love."

Like many contemporary Native novels, Greg Sarris's *Grand Avenue: A Novel in Stories* (1994) takes place off the reservation, which for Sarris is Santa Rosa, California, where families of Pomo descent have relocated. The Pomos have created an "in-town reservation" (Sarris, 1994, p. 198). By transporting traditional ceremonies and familial ties to the city, Sarris offers a different type of narrative. He highlights the traditional as a reclaiming of what has been lost to missionizing and time. Sarris's focus on community and the need for healing in a displaced locale makes *Grand Avenue* what Jace Weaver calls a "communitist" text. The character Nellie Copaz (based on Mabel McKay, a renowned Pomo basketweaver and medicine woman who helped raise Sarris) demonstrates the delicate balance between surviving in the city and preserving tradition. Nellie is the firmest believer in communal values and is sought in times of illness. The two strongest cultural practices in this novel are traditional basketmaking and healing, which are both performed by Nellie.

In the chapter "Waiting for the Green Frog" Nellie recalls hearing the singing frog near her shed on ancestral land. The frog is not specific to tribal lands, for he follows Nellie wherever she moves, including Santa Rosa. Mary Mackie argues that "the green frogs serve as predictors of change, foretellers of a new healer, and the continuance of Pomo culture" (2001, p. 216). Nellie's medical instruments are a combination of the traditional and the modern: "the old canoe basket, the flint piece, a tobacco pipe from a mail order catalog, and a cocoon rattle" (Sarris, 1994, p. 78). When Nellie teaches young Alice Goode how to make baskets, she is performing an act of healing. Nellie also tells Alice how and where to collect the materials, making connections to geographical and ancestral space. Although Alice is often quiet during these lessons, Nellie tells stories. In the last scene, Alice is visited by the green frog, signaling her future as a healer. Even in the direst of circumstances, Sarris imagines the continuity of Pomo traditions. Sarris's second novel, *Watermelon Nights*, which follows many of the same families, was published in 1998.

American Indian fiction has grown dramatically in recent decades. Novels published in the 1980s include Paula Gunn Allen's *The Woman Who Owned the Shadows* (1983), Janet Campbell Hale's *The Jailing of Cecilia Capture* (1985), James Welch's *Fools Crow* (1986), Michael Dorris's *A Yellow Raft in Blue Water* (1987), and Anna Lee Walters's *Ghost Singer* (1988). Novels of the 1990s include James Welch's *The Indian Lawyer* (1990); Linda Hogan's *Mean Spirit* (1990), *Solar Storms* (1995), and *Power* (1998); Gerald Vizenor's *Dead Voices* (1992); Louis Owens's *The Sharpest Sight* (1992) and *Bone Game* (1994); Ray Young Bear's *Black Eagle Child* (1992) and *Remnants of the First Earth* (1996); Betty Louise Bell's *Faces in the Moon* (1994); Susan Power's *Grass Dancer* (1994); Adrian C. Louis's *Skins* (1995); Sherman Alexie's *Reservation Blues* (1995) and *Indian Killer* (1996); and Diane Glancy's *Pushing the Bear* (1996). Novels of the first decade of the twenty-first century include James Welch's *The Heartsong of Charging Elk* (2000), LeAnne Howe's *Shell Shaker* (2001), and Adrian C. Louis's *Bone and Juice* (2001). Short story collections include Anna Lee Walters's *Sun Is Not Merciful* (1985); Adrian Louis's *Wild Indians and Other Creatures* (1992); Sherman Alexie's *Lone Ranger and Tonto Fistfight in Heaven* (1993), *The Toughest Indian in the World* (2000), and *Ten Little Indians* (2003); N. Scott Momaday's *In the Bear's House* (1999); and Susan Power's *Roofwalker* (2003).

SEE ALSO North American Indian Religions, article on Mythic Themes; Poetry, article on Native American Poetry and Religion.

BIBLIOGRAPHY

Bacon, Katie. "An Emissary of the Between-World." Interview with Louise Erdrich. *Atlantic* (January 17, 2001). Available from: www.theatlantic.com/unbound/interviews/int2001-01-17.htm.

Beck, Peggy V., Anna Lee Walters, and Nia Francisco. *The Sacred: Ways of Knowledge, Sources of Life.* Tsaile, Ariz., 1977; reprint, 1995.

Bernardin, Susan. "On the Meeting Grounds of Sentiment: S. Alice Callahan's *Wynema: A Child of the Forest.*" *American Transcendental Quarterly* 15, no. 3 (2001): 209–224.

Blaeser, Kimberly M. "Pagans Rewriting the Bible: Heterodoxy and the Representation of Spirituality in Native American Literature." *Ariel* 25, no. 1 (1994): 12–32.

Brown, Joseph Epes. *Teaching Spirits: Understanding Native American Religious Traditions.* New York, 2001.

Callahan, S. Alice. *Wynema: A Child of the Forest* (1891). Lincoln, Neb., 1997.

Chavkin, Allan, ed. *Leslie Marmon Silko's* Ceremony: *A Casebook.* New York, 2002.

Christensen, Laird. "'Not Exactly Like Heaven': Theological Imperialism in *The Surrounded.*" *Studies in American Indian Literatures* 11, no. 1 (1999): 2–16.

Deloria, Vine, Jr. *God Is Red: A Native View of Religion.* Golden, Colo., 1994.

Erdrich, Louise. *Love Medicine.* New York, 1984; rev. ed., 1993.

Gianferrari, Maria Christina. "Hybrid Voices/Hybrid Texts: A Study of Syncretism in the Works of Samson Occom, Handsome Lake, Leslie Marmon Silko, and Louise Erdrich." Ph.D. diss., State University of New York, Stony Brook, 1999.

Jaskoski, Helen. "From the Time Immemorial: Native American Traditions in Contemporary Short Fiction." In *Louise Erdrich's* Love Medicine*: A Casebook,* edited by Hertha D. Sweet Wong, pp. 27–34. New York, 2000.

Jaskoski, Helen, ed. *Early Native American Writing: New Critical Essays.* New York, 1996.

Lincoln, Kenneth. *Native American Renaissance.* Berkeley, 1983.

Mackie, Mary Margaret. "The Art That Will Not Die: The Story-Telling of Greg Sarris and Thomas King." Ph.D. diss., University of Oklahoma, 2001.

McAllister, Harold S. "Incarnate Grace and the Paths of Salvation in *House Made of Dawn.*" *South Dakota Review* 12, no. 4 (1974): 115–125.

McNickle, D'Arcy. *The Surrounded.* New York, 1936; reprint, Albuquerque, 1994.

Mitchell, Carol. "*Ceremony* as Ritual." *American Indian Quarterly* 5 (1979): 27–35.

Momaday, N. Scott. *House Made of Dawn.* New York, 1968; reprint, 1999.

Momaday, N. Scott. *Man Made of Words.* New York, 1997.

Nelson, Robert M. *Place and Vision: The Function of Landscape in Native American Fiction.* New York, 1993.

Owens, Louis. "The Red Road to Nowhere: D'Arcy McNickle's *The Surrounded* and 'The Hungry Generations.'" *American Indian Quarterly* 13, no. 3 (1989): 239–248.

Owens, Louis. *Other Destinies: Understanding the American Indian Novel.* Norman, Okla., 1992.

Purdy, John Lloyd. *Word Ways: The Novels of D'Arcy McNickle.* Tucson, Ariz., 1990.

Purdy, John Lloyd, ed. *The Legacy of D'Arcy McNickle: Writer, Historian, Activist.* Norman, Okla., 1996.

Riley, Patricia. "There Is No Limit to this Dust: The Refusal of Sacrifice in Louise Erdrich's *Love Medicine.*" *Studies in American Indian Literatures* 12, no. 2 (2000): 13–23.

Ruoff, A. LaVonne Brown. *American Indian Literatures: An Introduction, Bibliographic Review, and Selected Bibliography.* New York, 1990.

Sarris, Greg. *Keeping Slug Woman Alive: A Holistic Approach to American Indian Texts.* Berkeley, 1993.

Sarris, Greg. *Grand Avenue: A Novel in Stories.* New York, 1994.

Scarberry-Garcia, Susan. *Landmarks of Healing: A Study of House Made of Dawn.* Albuquerque, 1990.

Silko, Leslie Marmon. *Ceremony.* New York, 1977; reprint, 1986.

Silko, Leslie Marmon. *Yellow Woman and a Beauty of the Spirit.* New York, 1996.

Velie, Alan R. *Four American Indian Literary Masters: N. Scott Momaday, James Welch, Leslie Marmon Silko, and Gerald Vizenor.* Norman, Okla., 1982.

Walsh, Dennis. "Catholicism in Louise Erdrich's *Love Medicine* and *Tracks.*" *American Indian Culture and Research Journal* 25, no. 2 (2001): 107–127.

Weaver, Jace. *That the People Might Live: Native American Literatures and Native American Community.* New York, 1997.

Womack, Craig S. *Red on Red: Native American Literary Separatism.* Minneapolis, 1999.

Wong, Hertha D. Sweet, ed. *Louise Erdrich's* Love Medicine*: A Casebook.* New York, 2000.

LAURA FURLAN SZANTO (2005)

FIDES. The Roman goddess Fides is the personification of an idea that in itself is secular: the idea of "confidence" (*fides*) and, especially (in a more derivative sense of *fides*), the "good faith" or "trustworthiness" that inspires confidence. Fides made her appearance in the Roman pantheon in the third century CE, about 250, when a temple was dedicated to her by A. Atilius Calatinus. This temple stood on the Capitol, directly next to the temple of Jupiter. But there must have been an earlier sanctuary of Fides (tradition says the cult was established by Numa, the second king of Rome), and the temple built by Calatinus was probably erected on the same site.

The site of the temple of Fides, next to that of Jupiter, is indicative of her origin, for everything points to her having emerged from the supreme deity by a process of hypostatization. In this light, it is easy to understand why Jupiter is guarantor, not only with Fides but also with Dius Fidius, of the observance of oaths and compacts (*federa*). In fact, Dius Fidius, as "patron of good faith," is a first, archaic hypostatization of Jupiter. He is the god of oaths taken *sub divo,* that is, "in the open air." His temple, open to the sky, was located on the Quirinal, where it was situated on the *Capitolium vetus* ("old Capitol," or place of headship), next to the *sacellum Iovis, Iunonis, Minervae* ("chapel of Jupiter, Juno, Minerva"). Fides, for her part, appears in the wake of Jupiter Capitolinus. Her powers are broader and more flexible than those of Dius Fidius and include in particular the guaranteeing both of secrets and of the virtue (the interior disposition) of trustworthiness.

The goddess was honored by a special ritual: Each year some *flamines* (priests) journeyed to her temple in solemn fashion, riding in a covered cart. The sacrificing priest—the *flamen* of Jupiter—celebrated the cult with his right hand wrapped in a piece of white material. The right hand was shielded in this way because it was considered as consecrated when used to swear fidelity. For this reason it was liable to the wrath of heaven if the fidelity was violated. Mucius Scaevola, who lost his right hand after swearing a false oath, is a mythical illustration of this belief. The rite of the veiled hand is also attested in Umbria in connection with the god Fisu Sakio, who closely resembles Dius Fidius. At Rome, too, it was the *fidius* aspect of Jupiter that was honored in this way in the person of Fides.

The temple of Fides stood on the *area Capitolina* (the level top of the Capitoline Hill), probably right against its southern edge. Its importance was considerable, because the goddess was patroness of all agreements entered into with a gesture of the right hand. From her commanding position, visible from many points in Rome, she also stood as guarantor of political accords and economic contracts; she encouraged the trustworthiness of citizens toward one another as well as that of the Roman people toward other nations. Her religious function was to procure confidence, credit, and hence often, albeit indirectly, wealth for her trustworthy disciples. (Her temple stood immediately next to that of Ops, a goddess of fertility and plenty.)

The cult of the goddess Fides, suspended during a good part of the first century BCE, was probably restored by the emperor Augustus. Treaties and military documents were posted on the wall of her temple at least until the end of the first century CE. The many representations of Fides on coins minted after that date show that her influence extended well beyond the first century of the common era.

BIBLIOGRAPHY

Dumézil, Georges. "Credo et fides." In his *Idées romaines,* pp. 48–59. Paris, 1969.

Freyburger, Gérard. "Vénus et Fides." In *Hommages à Robert Schilling,* edited by Hubert Zehnacker and Gustave Hentz, pp. 101–108. Paris, 1983.

Lombardi, Luigi. *Dalla "fides" alla "bona fides."* Milan, 1961. See especially pages 147–162.

Piccaluga, Giulia. "Fides nella religione romana di età imperiale." In *Aufstieg und Niedergang der römischen Welt,* vol. 2.17.2, pp. 703–735. Berlin and New York, 1981.

New Sources

Carcaterra, Antonio. "Dea fides e fides. Storia di una laicizzazione." *Studia et Documenta Historiae Iuris* 50 (1984): 199–234.

Freyburger, Gérard. *Fides. Étude sémantique et religieuse depuis les origines jusqu'à l'époque augustéenne.* Paris, 1986.

Freyburger, Gérard. "La fides civique." In *Antiquité et Citoyenneté. Actes du Colloque International tenu à Besançon les 3, 4 et 5 novembre 1999,* edited by Stéphane Ratti, pp. 341–347. Paris, 2002.

Ramelli, Ilaria. *Studi su Fides. Premessa alle traduzioni di Eduard Fraenkel, Richard Heinze, Pierre Boyancé.* Madrid, 2002.

Reusser, Christoph. *Der Fidestempel auf dem Kapitol in Rom und seine Ausstattung.* Rome, 1993.

GÉRARD FREYBURGER (1987)
Translated from French by Matthew J. O'Connell
Revised Bibliography

FILARET OF MOSCOW (1782–1867) was a metropolitan of Moscow and Russian Orthodox church leader.

Filaret was born into the clerical "caste." He became a monk in 1808 and was ordained a priest in the following year. By 1812 he was rector of the Saint Petersburg Theological Academy. He became archbishop of Moscow (1821), then metropolitan of Moscow (1826); he served in the latter office until he died. Meanwhile Filaret had become a member of the Holy Synod (1819), the governing body of the Russian Orthodox church. Whether active participant or (from 1842) estranged consultant, he was to dominate its work for almost half a century. In the process he was able to demonstrate that the church need not be as subservient to the state as successive lay procurators-general of the synod expected it to be.

Filaret was barred from participation in the deliberations of the synod after 1842 largely because of the ban imposed on a privately circulated translation of the Old Testament. This translation was held suspect for two reasons: It was made from the Hebrew, rather than the Septuagint (considered normative by the Orthodox church), and it was made into modern Russian. Filaret had early been a proponent of exactly such a translation, and he had participated in the Russian Bible Society's work on the New Testament and *Psalms* (published 1818–1823). This work, discouraged after 1824, was not resumed until 1858. The publication of a complete (and, until the late twentieth century, standard) Russian translation of the Bible was begun in the year after Filaret's death. But it was associated with his name.

Filaret also supported the pioneer translation into Russian of patristic literature. This translation had an impact far beyond the boundaries of those academic centers in which it was undertaken. The freshly uncovered wisdom of the Fathers was to inform and transmute the thought, even the piety, of the Russian church and to rescue it from its previous "Babylonian captivity" to Western theological patterns. Filaret himself was prominent among the beneficiaries of this rescue operation.

Filaret gave much thought to the reform of theological schooling and stressed that Russian Orthodox scholarship should "develop its own models in the true spirit of the apostolic church." He produced a standard text, *Longer Catechism* (1823, revised 1839), to help the clergy with its work. Of more lasting importance were his carefully considered sermons, which mark him as an exceptionally subtle theologian, always willing to have his personal and profound experience tempered by Orthodox tradition.

Filaret's posthumous publications include a vast range of memoranda, opinions, and correspondence. They show him to have been a statesman as well as a hierarch of the church. They also demonstrate his curious mixture of determined liberalism with cautious conservatism. He was ill at ease with "democratic principles." But whatever his limitations in the secular sphere, he reinvigorated the Russian church at every level of its life and, in the fullest sense, reoriented it.

Bibliography

A rich Russian-language bibliography is provided in Georgii V. Florovskii's *Puti russkogo bogosloviia* (Paris, 1937). Among Filaret's variously collected works should be mentioned his sermons: *Slova i rechi*, 7th ed., 5 vols. (Moscow, 1873–1885). Some of these appeared in English translation as *Select Sermons by the Late Metropolitan of Moscow, Philaret* (London, 1873). Others appeared in French, notably those translated by A. Serpinet as *Choix de sermons et discours de son Eminence Mgr Philarète*, 3 vols. (Paris, 1866). Less revealing is Filaret's *Longer Catechism*, translated by R. W. Blackmore in *The Doctrine of the Russian Church* (1845; Willits, Calif., 1973). No full-length study of Filaret has appeared in English aside from R. L. Nichol's dissertation on him, "Metropolitan Filaret of Moscow and the Awakening of Orthodoxy" (University of Washington, 1972).

Sergei Hackel (1987)

FILLMORE, CHARLES AND MYRTLE. Myrtle (Mary Caroline) Page Fillmore (1845–1931) and Charles Sherlock Fillmore (1854–1948), a married couple, were the founders of Unity, the largest and most distinctly Christian movement in the New Thought tradition. They are the most notable students of New Thought's founder, Emma Curtis Hopkins (1849–1925). From its inception, Charles Fillmore was the leader of the movement and the primary force in the development of Unity's theological system and institutional structures. Although less visible than her husband, Myrtle Fillmore was equally important to the emergence and early expansion of the movement, with the healing of her tuberculosis in 1888 precipitating the movement's founding.

Myrtle was born in Pagetown, Ohio, the eighth of nine children. Her parents were prominent members of the local Methodist Episcopal Church. Unity biographical literature describes her as "not robust" and at times "seriously ill," but also "active and enthusiastic." Before entering college, she worked briefly as a newspaper writer. In 1868, after a year of study at Oberlin College, she was licensed as a teacher and began a career as a teacher in Clinton, Missouri. In an effort to maintain her fragile health, a result of suffering from both tuberculosis and malaria, in 1874 she relocated to Denison, Texas, where she established a private school.

Charles was born on a Chippewa reservation near Saint Cloud, Minnesota, the oldest of two sons. He had little contact with his father, who separated from the family when he was seven. Charles remained close to his mother until her death in 1931. Although his mother was a devout Episcopalian, she and her sons seldom attended church services. At the age of ten, Charles suffered a severe hip injury, which disabled him for two years and resulted in permanent damage to his right leg. As a result of his physical challenges and the necessity of finding employment to support the household, Charles's formal education ended when he was fourteen, although he did receive tutoring throughout his teens from Caroline Taylor, a graduate of Oberlin College. His studies with Taylor included readings in philosophy and theology. In 1874 Charles left Saint Cloud for the frontier town of Caddo in what is now Oklahoma. Shortly after his arrival he moved to Denison and took a job with the Missouri, Kansas, and Texas Railroad.

Myrtle and Charles met in Denison in 1876 and were married in Clinton, Missouri, in 1881. From 1881 to 1884, the Fillmores resided in Pueblo, Colorado, where Charles Fillmore was a real-estate partner with Charles Small, the husband of Alethea Brooks Small (1848–1906), who later played an important role in the founding of Divine Science. Following opportunities in the West's volatile real-estate market, the Fillmores moved to Omaha, Nebraska, and after a brief residency there they moved to Kansas City, Missouri. It was there that they founded Unity in 1889.

Before beginning their religious work, the couple had pursued livelihoods common to persons living in the nineteenth-century Midwest. Myrtle had been a teacher, and prior to his real estate career, Charles had held jobs as a printer's assistant, railroad freight inspector, mule-team driver, insurance salesperson, and assayer. They were active in the temperance movement, attended Methodist and Episcopal churches, and were exposed to Spiritualism and perhaps Theosophy. They had three sons—Lowell (1882–1975), Rickert (1884–1965), and Royal (1889–1923), each of whom was active in the Unity movement, with Lowell succeeding his father as president of Unity School of Christianity.

In 1886, at the same time the Kansas City real-estate market was beginning to decline, Myrtle experienced a flare-up of her tuberculosis. Seeking relief, she and Charles attended a lecture by E. B. Weeks, a mental healer from Chicago. Charles was not impressed with the lecture, but Myrtle was, specifically by Weeks's statement, "I am a child of God and therefore I do not inherit sickness." Using the statement as a healing affirmation and applying other mental healing techniques, Myrtle recovered, pronouncing herself healed in 1888. During this time, she also began to pray with others, who reported healings as a result. Myrtle's healing and her assistance in the healings of others awakened Charles's interest, and he began to practice mental healing rituals himself. His health improved and denominational histories report that his hip became stronger and his right leg began to lengthen.

As a result of their healings, the Fillmores became interested in the emerging mental healing movement, which was then identified as "Christian Science" (used in a generic sense) but would, by the turn of the century, be called New Thought, to distinguish it from the religion of Mary Baker Eddy (1821–1910). Their interest brought them into contact with Emma Curtis Hopkins, with whom they studied in Chicago and through correspondence from Kansas City. The Fillmores were ordained by Hopkins as ministers in 1891. Hopkins was the single most important influence on the Fillmores' religious development prior to their founding of Unity. Her impact is evident in the Fillmores' teachings (especially Charles's idealistic theology) and the organizational strategies they used in the early years of the Unity movement.

In 1889 (the year Unity recognizes as its founding), the Fillmores embarked on their first organizational endeavor, the publication of *Modern Thought*, a periodical "devoted to the spiritualization of humanity from an independent standpoint." The following year, Myrtle's healing talents led to the formation of a prayer ministry, the Society of Silent Help (later renamed Silent Unity). The success of *Modern Thought* (later absorbed into *Unity* magazine) and the Society of Silent Help served as the impetus for the emergence of Unity as a denomination.

Unity histories report that the couple did not desire to establish a religion, but in 1903 they formed a religious organization, the Unity Society of Practical Christianity, and they were members of the first group of ordained Unity ministers in 1906 (W. G. Haseltine, the president of the board of the Unity Society, performed the ordination). In 1914, they incorporated Unity School of Christianity, which continues to the present as the movement's most representative institution.

Myrtle's role in the leadership of Unity began to decline as the movement became more institutionalized. She left the office of editor of Unity's children's magazine, *Wee Wisdom*, in 1907, and in 1916 she relinquished her post as director of Silent Unity. In her later years her primary activities consisted of correspondence with Unity followers and assistance to Charles. Myrtle died in 1931, the year of the couple's fiftieth wedding anniversary.

In 1933 Charles married Cora Dedrick, who had been his secretary. He gradually relinquished control of the movement to his sons, especially Lowell, who succeeded him as president of Unity School. Charles and Cora traveled extensively, and he spent considerable time in California. He continued to lecture and write until the last few years of his life. His thirteen books are still printed and distributed by Unity School.

SEE ALSO Hopkins, Emma Curtis; New Thought Movement; Unity.

BIBLIOGRAPHY

Bach, Marcus. *The Unity Way*. Unity Village, Mo., 1982.

D'Andrade, Hugh. *Charles Fillmore: Herald of the New Age*. New York, 1974.

deChant, Dell. "Myrtle Fillmore and Her Daughters: An Observation and Analysis of the Role of Women in Unity." In *Women's Leadership in Marginal Religions: Explorations Outside the Mainstream*, edited by Catherine Wessinger, pp. 102–124. Urbana, Ill., 1993.

Freeman, James Dillet. *The Story of Unity*. Unity Village, Mo., 1954.

Teener, James W. "Unity School of Christianity." Ph.D. diss. University of Chicago, 1942.

Vahle, Neal. *Torch-Bearer to Light the Way: The Life of Myrtle Fillmore.* Mill Valley, Calif., 1996.

Witherspoon, Thomas E. *Myrtle Fillmore: Mother of Unity.* Unity Village, Mo., 1977.

DELL DECHANT (2005)
GAIL M. HARLEY (2005)

FILM AND RELIGION. While the academic study of "film and religion" as a subfield within religious studies has only come of age since the late 1980s, the connection between film and religion is as old as film itself. As film theorist André Bazin once put it, "The cinema has always been interested in God" (Bazin, 1997, p. 61). Indeed, if one accepts the now-standard origin of cinema to begin with the Lumière brothers' first public screening for a paying audience in December 1895, then the first decade of cinema saw at least a half dozen filmed versions of the life and passion of Jesus Christ, including those made by the inventors of film themselves, Thomas Edison and Louis Lumière. The figure of Jesus Christ has continued to be a popular topic for film and a touchstone for cinematic controversy throughout the twentieth century, with such directors as Sidney Olcott, D. W. Griffith, Cecil B. DeMille, George Stevens, Pier Paolo Pasolini, Norman Jewison, Martin Scorsese, and Mel Gibson offering various theological perspectives. Jesus is not the only religious figure to appear on screen, however, and religious issues, practices, characters, and conflicts are presented on a frequent basis in films around the world. The first half of this entry will thus offer a global survey of examples of films since the mid-1980s that deal with matters of interest to religious studies.

It is not only the content of film that connects film and religion, for as a number of critics have observed, one can find religious interests and implications in the formal style of film, as well as in the cinematic experience of viewing film. As another early film critic and director, Jean Epstein, once said, "I would even go so far as to say that the cinema is polytheistic and theogonic" (Abel, 1988, p. 317). Film, and the experience of viewing film, may be religious in and of itself, creating its own gods, goddesses, and myths, and film does not merely represent or reflect an already established religion. So, while not mutually exclusive categories, film studies and religion studies can be usefully divided into three key approaches, and the second half of this entry will examine the various scholarly responses to the connections between film and religion: religion in film, religion as film, and the cinematic experience and ritual.

RELIGIONS AND CINEMAS AROUND THE WORLD. While an all-inclusive list would be impossible to include here, there are a number of international filmmakers since 1985 (approximately since the entry on film was written for the first edition of *The Encyclopedia of Religion*) who have dealt with religious issues in myriad ways. Many films in world cinema that touch on religious themes often do so by presenting religion in conflict. The most common conflicts arise when older religious values are challenged by the social, political, economic, and religious realities of modern life, especially in a postcolonial environment. There is conflict when, due to modern life and the aftereffects of colonialism, religious people from differing traditions are placed side by side and forced to get along (or not). And conflict arises when individual gender, sexual, and ethnic identities meet socioreligious identities. This list is in no way comprehensive, but is intended to display the number of directions that the study of film and religion can go in without treading across the same territory of previous studies. There is little or no critical literature from a religious studies standpoint in English on the films mentioned in this entry, and these films are mentioned precisely for this reason, to show the breadth of possible subject matter for religious studies scholars interested in film.

East Asian cinema has seen the development of several movements since the 1970s, as filmmakers have experimented with new styles and modes of production. In the wake of Akira Kurosawa and Yasujiro Ozu, Japan has continued to be a prominent producer of films dealing with key religious themes. Toshihiro Tenma's *Kyosono Tanjo* (Many happy returns, 1993) explores new religious movements in Japan; Hirokazu Koreeda's *Maborosi* (1995) utilizes a "Zen aesthetic"; and two films produced in 1989 examine the life of the Zen Buddhist tea master Rikyu: Kei Kumai's *Sen no Rikyu* and Hiroshi Teshigahara's *Rikyu.* Also vibrant in Japan is the work of anime writers and directors, including Hayao Miyazaki's *Princess Mononoke* (1997) and *Spirited Away* (2001), Hideaki Anno's two *Neon Genesis Evangelion* films (1997), and Katsuhiro Ôtomo's *Akira* (1988). Ôtomo also wrote the screenplay for *Metropolis* (2001), directed by Taro Rin. A number of Korean directors have infused Buddhism into their films, including Bae Yong-gyun in *Why Has the Bodhidharma Left for the East?* (1989), Im Kwon-Taek in *Sopyonje* (1993) and *Come Come Come Upward* (1989), and Chang Sonu in *Passage to Buddha* (1993).

China's New Cinema movement has had a huge impact on the international film scene since the mid-1980s, occasionally incorporating Daoist and Confucian elements. Daoist issues arise in Chinese director Chen Kaige's *King of the Children* (1987), while critiques of Confucian ethics are seen in Zhang Yimou's *Ju Dou* (1990). In Bangladesh, Tareque Masud's *Matir Moina* (The clay bird, 2002) tells the story of the emergence of the nation of Bangladesh, offering a sympathetic yet critical look at Islam in the midst of the move toward political independence.

Notable films with religious interests from New Zealand include the work of Jane Campion: *Angel at My Table* (1990), *The Piano* (1993), and *Holy Smoke* (1999). Cross-cultural conflicts between Maoris, whites, and others get taken up in Lee Tamahori's *Once Were Warriors* (1994) and Gregor Nicholas's *Broken English* (1996). In Australia, films such as Nicholas Parsons's *Dead Heart* (1996) and Tracey Moffatt's *Nice Coloured Girls* (1987) deal with Christian-

Aboriginal cultural conflicts. From another standpoint, David MacDougall's ethnographic films of Aboriginal culture, such as *Transfer of Power* (1986), offer intriguing examinations of cultural differences, and MacDougall has been prolifically thinking through the issues of visual representation in his films and writings.

South Asian cinema, because of its enormity (Mumbai's yearly production dwarfs Hollywood's) and because mythological themes are so intertwined in Indian cultures, is almost impossible to classify. Indian film history is steeped in mythological themes and stories of Hindu saints, and today's *masala* films often incorporate many of these narratives, weaving them into song and dance routines, domestic drama, and action-adventure sequences. Some films with themes of interest to the religious studies scholar might include the *Mahābhārata* retelling in Arjun Sagnani's *Agni Varsha* (2002), the postcolonial religion/cricket epic *Lagaan* (2001) by Ashutosh Gowariker, and the Muslim-Hindu religious conflicts dealt with in Kamal Haasan's *Hey Ram* (2000), Khalid Mohamed's *Fiza* (2000), and Deepa Mehta's *Earth* (1998). Films about the Indian diaspora and consequent cross-cultural challenges figure prominently in newer Indian films; important among these are the story of a wedding in Sooraj R. Barjatya's *Hum Aapke Hain Koun* (Who am I to you? 1994) and Subhash Ghai's coming of age story, *Pardes* (Abroad, 1997). And apart from Western filmmakers looking at Tibetan Buddhism, including Jean-Jacques Annaud's *Seven Years in Tibet* (1997) and Martin Scorsese's *Kundun* (1997), former Tibetan monk Khyentse Norbu made *The Cup* (1999), a prime film for teaching religious studies, as it deconstructs an exoticizing gaze.

The most productive site in western Asia for film production is Iran, where the films of Abbas Kiarostami (e.g., *A Taste of Cherry* [1997], *The Wind Will Carry Us* [1999]); Mohsen Makhmalbaf (e.g., *A Moment of Innocence* [1996], *The Gabbeh* [1996], *The Silence* [1998]); Majid Majidi (e.g., *Children of Heaven* [1997], *The Color of Paradise* [1999]); and Jafar Panahi (e.g., *The Mirror* [1997], *The Circle* [2000]), among others, all reflect everyday life in postrevolutionary Iran. Faced with heavy censorship, Iranian filmmakers have continued to produce some of the most critically acclaimed films in the world. While the religious studies scholar may wish to see more explicit images of Islam, there are a number of ways to read these highly allegorical films that point toward a Persian-Islamic worldview. And while Islam may not always be present, these films are peopled with Muslims, and it is crucial, as always, not to confuse an essentialist term like *Islam* for the people who actually practice the religion.

Toward the Mediterranean, films from Israel have shown the conflicts between gender and religion (as in Amos Gitai's *Kadosh* [1999]), sexuality and religion (as in Sandi Simcha Dubowski's *Trembling Before G-d* [2001]), and between the orthodox and the secular, with a good dose of Qabbalah (as in Yossi Somer's *The Dybbuk of the Holy Apple Field* [1998]). In Palestine, Elia Suleiman's *Divine Intervention* (2001) portrays conflicts through the mixing of theology and politics.

The continent of Africa has experienced a strong increase in film production since the 1970s, with films confronting postcolonial situations that pit the traditional against the modern; in sub-Saharan Africa this often includes the conflict between Christianity and indigenous beliefs and practice. Egypt is the "Hollywood of the Arab World" and has garnered the attention of the international film world, especially since Youssef Chahine's *Destiny,* a film set in twelfth-century Islamic Andalusia, was nominated for the Golden Palm at the Cannes Film Festival in 1997. Other Egyptian standouts dealing with religious-political conflicts include Daoud Abdel Sayed's *Land of Fear* (1999) and Atef Hetata's *Closed Doors* (1999).

Elsewhere in Africa, examples of the modern-traditional debate with reference to Islamic, Christian, and indigenous religions include Drissa Toure's *Haramuya* (1995) and Dani Kouyaté's *Keita: Heritage of the Griot* (1994), both from Burkina Faso; Amadou Thior's *Almodou* (2000) from Senegal; Nouri Bouzid's *Bezness* (1992) from Tunisia; and Saddiq Balewa's *Kasarmu Ce* (The land is ours, 1994) from Nigeria. Perhaps the best-known and most prolific filmmaker in Africa is Ousmane Sembene from Senegal, whose many films include *Guelwaar* (1992), which offers a critique of interreligious conflict. Like Sembene, director Med Hondo of Mauritania self-consciously makes films that offer an alternative aesthetic to that of Western filmmaking; one example is *Sarraounia* (1986), about a warrior-queen who leads her people in the challenges posed by the colonizing French. In western Africa, there has been a boom in film production through new, inexpensive video technologies that are used to produce "videofilms" that have a mass appeal, many of which are produced by Pentecostal religious groups. The African diaspora is the topic of many films produced in and out of Africa, and can be seen, for example, in such films as Julie Dash's *Daughters of the Dust* (1991), Felix de Rooy's *Desiree* (1984), and Haile Gerima's many films, especially *Sankofa* (1993), as well as a number of Latin American films discussed below.

In southeastern Europe, in the midst of decades of political upheaval, film production has been strong. Of particular note is Milcho Manchevski's *Before the Rain* (1994), which tells of Orthodox Christian and Muslim communities and their conflicts in the former Yugoslavia. Romany/Gypsy cultures are seen in a number of productions, including the great Bosnian director Emir Kusturica's *Time of the Gypsies* (1989) and Tony Gatlif's *Latcho Drom* (1993) and *Gadja Dilo* (1997), the former created without any dialogue, only music and movement.

The works of western European directors have been well-traversed by religion scholars, and are only mentioned in passing here. In many ways inspired by former countrymen Carl Theodor Dreyer and Søren Kierkegaard, Danish filmmaking has consistently returned to existentially religious themes. Such films include Thomas Vinterberg's *Celebration* (1998), Roy Andersson's *Songs from the Second Floor* (2000), and the works of Lars von Trier, especially *The Kingdom* (1994, 1997), *Breaking the Waves* (1996), and *Dancer in the Dark* (2000). In Poland, the late Krzysztof Kieslowski's religiously inspired films include the *Three Colors* trilogy (1993–1994), *Decalogue* (1988), and the posthumous project eventually directed by Thomas Tykwer, *Heaven* (2002). In Spain, Julio Medem shies away from depicting religion explicitly, yet his style evokes a mystical aura in ways akin to the magic seen through early film theory, especially in *Tierra* (1996), *Lovers of the Arctic Circle* (1998), and *Sex and Lucia* (2001). And Pedro Almodóvar, as a descendant of Luis Buñuel's surrealism and Roman Catholic satire, continues to utilize critical, yet not unsympathetic, portrayals of nuns and the institution of the church in such films as *Matador* (1986), *Live Flesh* (1997), and *All about My Mother* (1999). A number of French films through the 1990s updated the existentialist quest for meaning in life, notably Benoît Jacquot's *School of Flesh* (1998) and Danièle Dubroux's *Diary of a Seducer* (1996), while the cross-cultural clashes of suburban Paris are seen in Mathieu Kassovitz's *Hate* (1995).

Themes of religion in Central and South America have tended be critical of Roman Catholicism, or have delved into the hybrid religions of Afro-Catholic mixings. Cuba has been a fertile site for film production since the 1959 revolution, with Santerian practices showing up, for example, in Gloria Rolando's *Oggún* (1991), Tomás Gutiérrez Alea's *Guantamamera* (1994), and Humberto Solás's *Honey for Oshun* (2001). Films from Mexico include critiques of Roman Catholicism in Carlos Carrera's *Crime of Father Amaro* (2002) and Nicolás Echevarría's *Cabeza de Vaca* (1991). In Brazil, Tania Cypriano's documentary *Odô yá! Life with AIDS* (1997) portrays the importance of Candomblé in education about AIDS, and her short, *Ex-Voto* (1990), is a devotional expression to the patron saint of Brazil. One of the masters of Brazilian Cinema Novo is filmmaker Nelson Pereira dos Santos, whose many films include *Jubiata* (1987), which deals with interracial, interclass issues with a strong dose of Afro-Brazilian religious practice. Vodoun is probably the most slighted religion in the history of film, but can be seen in a somewhat objective light in Maya Deren's posthumously produced documentary *Divine Horsemen* (1985) and Alberto Venzago's documentary *Mounted by the Gods* (2000).

Independent filmmakers in the United States continue to weave religious themes into their works, often improvising on ancient myths and mythic structures, and examining the ways narratives construct the communal and personal identities of Americans. Of note in this regard are the films of Jim Jarmusch (e.g., *Dead Man* [1995], *Ghost Dog* [1999]); Hal Hartley (e.g., *Henry Fool* [1997], *The Book of Life* [1998], *No Such Thing* [2001]); and John Sayles (e.g., *City of Hope* [1991], *Lone Star* [1996], *Limbo* [1999]). The annual Sundance Film Festival gives evidence to the continued presence of religious interests among young filmmakers, and religious matters have been taken up, for example, in Sarah Rogacki's debut, *Rhythm of the Saints* (2002); Jonathan Kesselman's comedy, *The Hebrew Hammer* (2002); Larry Fessenden's mythic *Wendigo* (2001); and Greg Watkins's relationship comedy, *A Sign from God* (2000). Intriguing insights into the spirituality of rave culture can be seen in Greg Harrison's *Groove* (2000) and Jon Reiss's documentary, *Better Living through Circuitry* (1999).

In Canada, Egyptian-born director Atom Egoyan, whose films include *Calendar* (1993), *Exotica* (1994), *The Sweet Hereafter* (1997), and *Ararat* (2002), continually plays with the ambiguous relation between historical time and memory—specifically in reference to loss, tragedy, and the possibilities of redemption—in ways inherent to the medium of film. The mature works of David Cronenberg, including *Crash* (1996), *eXistenZ* (1999), and *Spider* (2002), deal with issues of identity and relationships in ways that probe the depths of what it is to be human, developing existential questions in a postmodern age.

SCHOLARLY APPROACHES TO FILM AND RELIGION. There are three key scholarly approaches to the relationship between film and religion. The first might be called "religion *in* film," a way of analyzing the religious dimensions of film by focusing primarily on its narrative content. "Film *as* religion" is the second key approach, and is based on formal parallels between the aesthetic styles of film and religious practices. Finally, there is an interest in "cinematic experience and ritual," where a focus on spectatorship and its relation to ritual takes precedence. These categories often overlap in individual studies, and are charted here for heuristic reasons. The key question that divides these approaches seems to revolve around the location of meaning: Is religious meaning found in the subject matter of the film, in the aesthetic form of the film, or in the experience of viewing the film?

Religion in film. Whether a film plot is based on a messiah, a saint, a bodhisattva, a pilgrimage, a reenactment of a sacred text, or whether religious performances are displayed in documentary film, religion shows up in film on a regular basis. This way of thinking about the relation between film and religion seems to be the most apparent to the textual and narrative bias of most religious studies, and it has therefore become the most prominent method of examining the relationship. As with so much of the study of religion itself, a vast majority of these studies have been based in Christian theology and display a Euro-American outlook.

P. Adams Sitney's contribution to the 1987 *Encyclopedia of Religion* ("Cinema and Religion") came along at the end of what might be called the first wave of religion-in-film criticism, a loose canon of publications roughly extending from the 1960s to the late 1980s. Book-length studies during this period typically offered broad approaches, and they often worked from the standpoint of existential theology: film could be religiously instructive because it taught about the human condition, providing stories and images that struggled for meaning. John R. May should be credited as the key person in the development of the interdisciplinary field—especially for amassing and publishing the work of other scholars interested in the topic—as a legitimate focus of study within religious studies.

As most of the publications in this first wave made clear, the connection between film and religion was primarily to be found in European cinema, particularly in the work of directors such as Pier Paolo Passolini, Carl Theodor Dreyer, Robert Bresson, and Ingmar Bergman (Japanese directors Yasujiro Ozu and Akira Kurosawa were the two key non-Westerners). Relevant U.S. productions included work by D. W. Griffith and Cecil B. DeMille in the early years of cinema, with Alfred Hitchcock adding a few flourishes mid-century, and George Lucas, Stanley Kubrick, and Martin Scorsese providing a religious flavor to film in the 1960s to 1990s. During this period, religion-in-film scholars tended to shy away from popular films, choosing instead to focus on what would later be called "art house" films. This probably does not reflect an elitist attitude on the part of this first wave of scholars so much as it reflects the struggle they faced in getting others in the academy take their work seriously. After all, who could argue against the seriousness with which Bergman or Kurosawa portrayed religious matters?

The study of film and religion became solidified through the decade of the 1990s, as evidenced by the upsurge of publications in the field, the establishment of a program unit on film and religion within the American Academy of Religion, and the launch of the online *Journal of Religion and Film.* In many ways reacting to the earlier paradigm that found film and religion only in "serious" art house films, the 1990s witnessed the next wave of film and religion criticism, which self-consciously took popular Hollywood film as its primary focus. Biblical scholars and theologians began to take a second look at popular culture, and found a wealth of resources in film, particularly in popular film. Christian theologians reworked Reinhold Niebuhr's and Paul Tillich's thoughts on the relation between Christianity and culture, and decided that there must be an engagement with culture, with film being one of the cultural expressions par excellence in modern life. The prevalence of the ideas of Tillich and Niebuhr in film and religion studies, a half-century after their writing, attest to these theologians' keen insights in relating religion and culture, though it probably also attests to the need for new theories of culture, since the culture of the first half of the twentieth century looks less and less like that of the twenty-first.

This second wave is also marked by a number of explicitly Christian theological studies, in contrast to the tendency to use existentially universal language evident in many of the first-wave publications. Studies through the 1990s include the relation of film to Christian, and occasionally Jewish, understandings of the Bible; the relation of film to doctrines of Christian theology; and a plethora of works on Christ figures in film. While there are a variety of interests indicated in these works, they can be seen collectively through their examination of popular film, by their chiefly Christian theological orientation, and ultimately by the ways they see religion in film, paying scant attention to the specificities of the medium or the role of spectatorship.

Since the mid-1990s there have been several attempts at historicizing, categorizing, and hence legitimizing the subfield. One of the more influential and useful schemas for the approach to religion in film is found in Joel W. Martin and Conrad E. Ostwalt's edited volume *Screening the Sacred* (1995). In the introduction, Martin lays out three ways of viewing film from a religious studies standpoint: theological criticism, mythological criticism, and ideological criticism. Not meant to be exclusive categories, Martin points toward a "future" synthesis of these modes, implying that such a synthesis has not yet occurred. A wide variety of films can be included under the three categories, yet the actual studies within the book itself all primarily function from the understanding that religious meaning is found within the film story or characters. Following on these categories, in *Film as Religion* (2003) John Lyden rightly notes that most film and religion studies are either too theological or too ideological: the former remains bound by presuppositions as to what constitutes "religion" (i.e., Christianity), and the latter tends to be so focused on critiquing the power structures that it neglects some of the more positive understandings of religion. Lyden goes on to develop a more nuanced approach that draws heavily on the myth and ritual theories of Clifford Geertz, supplemented by the theories of Wendy Doniger and Jonathan Z. Smith. By investigating "religion as film," Lyden's work crosses over into the second category of film and religion approaches.

Religion as film. Early film theorists, chiefly because of the visual prominence of silent film, emphatically stressed formalist understandings of cinema. They argued about the psychological and social effects that the medium of film has on its audience due to its rearranging of "normal" space and time through cinematography, mise-en-scène, and editing. In the 1920s in France, film theorists (in particular, Louis Delluc, Jean Epstein, and Léon Moussinac) developed the idea of *photogenie,* the cinematic transformation of reality through the technological properties inherent in the form of film itself. Because of its emphasis on the formal properties of filmmaking, much of this early film theory did not depend on narrative film, and indeed often triumphed nonlinear, nonnarrative films. Thus, through the camera's ability to slow down or speed up "real time," or to juxtapose images in ways that display new relations, or to zoom in on particular segments of visual reality, the world itself is reconfigured and viewers are given a brand new outlook, a new "world-view." Representation became a means for knowledge, "revealing" the truth of the world in an altogether new form. And even though debates eventually emerged between the realists and antirealists in film theory, both arguments have implications for a religious view of film form.

From a religious studies perspective, what is interesting about film's capacity to rearrange the "world-as-it-is" is the frequent use of religious language to justify the theory. Epstein has already been quoted as seeing the theogonic properties of cinema, and others spoke of cinema as "revelation," as "magic," and as a "miracle." Recapping many of these ideas in her book *Savage Theory* (2000), Rachel Moore argues that early film theorists and filmmakers (especially Walter Benjamin, Sergei Eisenstein, Vachel Lindsay, Siegfried Kracauer, and Bazin) saw in film a potential re-enchantment of a modern world that had lost language's expressive ability (explicated in Ferdinand de Saussure's account of the arbitrariness of the sign) and that experienced a general mode of alienation due to industrialized, modern life. In the early 1960s, avant-garde filmmaker Stan Brakhage would continue this language, expressing the religious possibilities of film form in his quasi-manifesto "Metaphors on Vision" (1963). For Brakhage, film artists are "essentially preoccupied by and deal imagistically with—birth, sex, death, and the search for God" (Mast, Cohen, and Braudy, 1992, p. 72).

Later, director and screenwriter Paul Schrader's 1972 *Transcendental Style in Film* examined the "aesthetics of sparseness" in the films of Ozu, Bresson, and Dreyer. Even though these directors had differing religious backgrounds, Schrader sees them each using a filmic style that emerges through pared-down filmmaking techniques, including austere cinematography, unexpressive acting, and light-handed editing. Thus, the properties specific to filmmaking itself allow access to the transcendental; a long take of a close-up of an expressionless face, no matter whose face it is, can evoke an experience of transcendence.

From another angle, the religious dimension to film form and style can also be seen in relation to the contemplative emphasis of various religious traditions, and here film becomes a new medium in a long list of visual media, from icons to yantras to *thangka* paintings, designed to facilitate meditation. Francisca Cho, for example, discusses the relation of Korean Buddhist films to a "cultic mode" of viewing heavily dependent on the aesthetic choices made in the making of film (see Cho in Plate and Jasper, 1999). And as with each of the examples given here regarding "film as religion," Cho's cultic mode of viewing film implicitly suggests that meaning cannot simply be found in the film form, for there must also be an audience that views the edited juxtapositions, the austere lighting, or the slow movement of actors.

The cinematic experience and ritual. Apart from the formal style, the plot, and the characters of film, there is also the cinematic experience—the reception of film—which is a critical point of interrogation for the scholar of religion. While theorists of film and religion continually mention the importance of audience reception, very little work has been done in this area. Scholars often theorize about the effect of editing, for example, but seldom do they do any ethnographic work to find out how audiences actually do react. More complicated still would be a study that gauged the responses to a particular film in varying locations, times, and cultures, thereby reorienting the location of the meaning of film to the cinematic event.

The religious implications of film reception are most obvious when the experience is understood and analyzed in terms of ritual; this is not to say that every screening of every film is a ritual, for that would make both terms meaningless, but that the cinematic experience can become a ritual. We can see this when viewers perform *pūja* (devotional offerings) before screenings of mythological films in South Asian theaters; when young people in the United States, wearing specific clothes, line up for a "midnight mass" on Saturday night to watch *The Rocky Horror Picture Show* again and again; or when films are televised, and family and friends in North America gather in living rooms to watch the annual broadcast of *It's a Wonderful Life* at Christmas, *King of Kings* at Easter, or *The Wizard of Oz* in July. In these ritualized performances, the religious content of the film is beside the point. Rather, what is crucial is the way these activities occur at special "set apart" times (often in seasonal cycles) and in special places (whether the living room of the family home or in the film theater) in which there is an emphasis on a communal experience and on the aesthetics of seeing and listening (and usually eating as well), and on interacting with other viewers and with the film. Whatever else a ritual is, it certainly aims to be an activity that promotes attentiveness and sensual focus, and film form enables just that.

In this approach to the relation of film and religion, social-scientific approaches become prominent, and such newer fields as media studies and cultural studies offer useful methodologies. Nonetheless, communications and media studies, even when discussing the ritual dimensions of audiovisual media, usually neglect film and spend most of their time evaluating audience reception of television shows and news media. The work of Stewart Hoover, Lynn Schofield Clark, and Eric Rothenbuhler, among others, has offered interesting studies on the ritualized reception of media (mostly television and news media), analyzing many of the parallels between ritual and media, and the methods of these scholars can be useful to film and religion studies. Perhaps the most vital new field that provides a "third term" in linking film and religion is that of visual-culture studies, which combines the formalist interests typical of the humanities with the reception interests typical of the social sciences. Inherent is also an interest in the cross-cultural dimensions to visuality, to see the cinematic experience located within particular cultures, at particular times, paying attention also to the gendered, ethnic, sexual, and religious differences of the activity of seeing. Thus, visual culture offers a way to think through all three of the approaches to film and religion listed here.

CONCLUSIONS AND FUTURES. The subfield of film and religion has gradually gained acceptance in religious studies, and prominent theorists of religion now regularly incorporate discussion of films into their analyses of myth, ritual, and other aspects of religion. Alongside this development are newer modes of religious inquiry that utilize material and visual artifacts as primary evidence, rather than "illustration," of religious belief and practice. As part of a broader movement within religious studies that is increasingly paying attention to visual- and material-culture studies (and concomitantly emphasizing religious practice rather than merely belief), film and religion studies can continue to play a vital role in the shaping of religious studies and not merely be an appendage to the discipline. Along these lines there are two key directions that the field is beginning to take (and will likely keep elaborating on). First, film and religion studies is moving beyond the Christian-Hollywood matrix and displaying the varieties of global religious experiences and traditions as mediated through film. Second, religious approaches to film are helping to point out the constructed nature of vision by making links between visual representation and the creation of socioreligious, worlds with all their attendant myths, ideologies, and practices.

Because postmodern, postcolonial life consists of multicultural and interreligious encounters on a regular basis, there is an obvious need to branch out beyond the Hollywood centrism evident in a majority of film-and-religion studies in the past. Films made outside of Hollywood do not conform to the same aesthetic standards that capitalist, industrial film relies upon, and by looking at films made in South America, Africa, and Asia, for example, and through attention to film form and reception, the student of film and religion begins to see the ways other worlds are visually constructed, not excluding religious worlds.

In so doing, the religious studies scholar may begin to develop what might be called an "ethics of vision" that is attentive to the differences in cultures, races, classes, genders, sexualities, and a host of other identity factors. Seeing is an activity that humans learn how to do; it is not an innate ability. Among other factors, this sensual activity is shaped by visual technologies such as film, television, video games, and the Internet, as well as ever more powerful telescopes and microscopes. Thus, by moving beyond the search for religious characters in film, scholars can look at the larger religious questions involved in the social construction of reality through visual terms.

Finally, as Sitney ended his 1987 *Encyclopedia of Religion* entry with a nod to avant-garde film, so will this entry. There remains much promise for religious studies in the avant-garde films of Stan Brakhage, Maya Deren, Kenneth Anger, and Hollis Frampton, among others, and it should not be too easily overlooked. While there is often a strong religious content, albeit obscure, in avant-garde works, there is a religious dimension to the formal style of these films that is perhaps more important. Sitney's own study of the avant-garde, *Visionary Film* (2002), is now in its third edition, and his analysis highlights many engaging relations between film and religion. While avant-garde films remain difficult to watch, they nonetheless help to point out the constructed nature of vision itself. As Brakhage put it in "Metaphors on Vision": "Suppose the Vision of the saint and the artist to be an increased ability to see—vision" (Mast, Cohen, Braudy, 1992, p. 71).

SEE ALSO Art and Religion; Media and Religion; Niebuhr, Reinhold; Popular Culture; Tillich, Paul Johannes; Visual Culture and Religion.

BIBLIOGRAPHY

Early film theorists considered issues of religion on a regular basis. For a good critical study of early film theory and the quasi-religious language that the theorists used see Rachel O. Moore, *Savage Theory: Cinema as Modern Magic* (Durham, N.C., 2000). Useful anthologies on film theory include Richard Abel, ed., *French Film Theory and Criticism: A History/Anthology, 1907–1939,* 2 vols. (Princeton, 1988) and, more broadly, Gerald Mast, Marshall Cohen, and Leo Braudy, eds., *Film Theory and Criticism: Introductory Readings,* 4th ed. (New York and Oxford, 1992) and Bill Nichols's *Movies and Methods,* 2 vols. (Berkeley, 1976–1985). See also André Bazin's article "Cinema and Theology" in *Bazin at Work: Major Essays & Reviews from the Forties & Fifties,* edited by Bert Cardullo and translated by Cardullo and Alain Piette (New York, 1997), pp. 61–72.

There have been few studies of religion and film outside Christianity and outside European and North American productions. Occasional articles in edited collections, such as John May's *New Image of Religious Film* (Kansas City, Mo., 1997) and several of the chapters in S. Brent Plate and David Jasper's *Imag(in)ing Otherness: Filmic Visions of Living Together* (Atlanta and Oxford, 1999), as well as Plate's *Representing Religion in World Cinema: Filmmaking, Mythmaking, and Culture Making* (New York, 2003), deal with non-Christian, non-Hollywood films. *The Journal of Religion and Film,* available from http://cid.unomaha.edu/~wwwjrf, has also published a number of articles dealing with world cinema.

Significant among the first wave of "religion in film" studies dealing with broad, existentially religious themes are Neil Hurley's *Theology through Film* (New York, 1970), Ernest Ferlita and John May's *Film Odyssey: The Art of Film as Search for Meaning* (New York, 1976), and Ronald Holloway's *Beyond the Image: Approaches to the Religious Dimension in the Cinema* (Geneva, 1977). Some of the second wave of studies that turned toward popular film yet retained a broad understanding of religion can be seen in Joel Martin and Conrad Ostwalt's edited *Screening the Sacred: Religion, Myth, and Ideology in Popular American Film* (Boulder, Colo., 1995) and Margaret Miles's *Seeing and Believing: Religion and Values in the Movies* (Boston, 1996). The second wave also includes many works dealing explicitly with Christian theology, including Clive Marsh and Gaye Ortiz's edited *Explorations in Theology and Film: Movies and Meaning* (Malden, Mass., 1998), and an overabundance of books dealing specifically with images of Jesus and "Christ figures" on screen, including Roy Kinnard and Tim Davis's *Divine Images: A History of Jesus on the Screen* (New York, 1992), Lloyd Baugh's *Imaging the Divine: Jesus and Christ-Figures in Film* (Kansas City, Mo., 1997), and Christopher Deacy's *Screen Christologies: Redemption and the Medium of Film* (Cardiff, UK, 2001). There are also many works dealing with relations of the Bible to film, such as Robert Jewett's *Saint Paul at the Movies: The Apostle's Dialogue with American Culture* (Louisville, Ky., 1993), Bernard Brandon Scott's *Hollywood Dreams and Biblical Stories* (Minneapolis, 1994), George Aichele and Richard Walsh's edited *Screening Scripture: Intertextual Connections between Scripture and Film* (Harrisburg, Pa., 2002), and Erin Runions's *How Hysterical: Identification and Resistance in the Bible and Film* (New York, 2003). For an updated theory (beyond Tillich and Niebuhr) of the relations of Christianity to culture, see Kathryn Tanner's *Theories of Culture: A New Agenda for Theology* (Minneapolis, 1997).

For overviews of some of the studies dealing with religion in film, see chapter 1 of John C. Lyden's *Film as Religion: Myths, Morals, and Rituals* (New York, 2003) and Steve Nolan's "The Books of the Films" in *Literature and Theology* 12, no. 1 (1998): 1–15.

Studies focusing on "religion as film" come from a variety of perspectives, including Lyden's religious studies orientation in *Film as Religion.* For a film studies perspective see Paul Schrader's *Transcendental Style in Film: Ozu, Bresson, Dreyer* (Berkeley, 1972) and P. Adams Sitney's *Visionary Film: The American Avant-Garde, 1943–2000,* 3d ed. (Oxford, 2002). Many of the early film theorists took this approach as well; see the sources listed above.

Scholarly work relating the "cinematic experience" to religion and ritual is still in its early stages, but see, for example, the work coming out of the social sciences, such as Patrick Kinkade and Michael Katovich's essay "Toward a Sociology of Cult Films: Reading *Rocky Horror*" in *Sociological Quarterly* 33, no. 2 (1992): 191–209. Paul Nathanson's *Over the Rainbow: The Wizard of Oz as a Secular Myth of America* (Albany, N.Y., 1991) and several of the articles in Plate's *Representing Religion in World Cinema* deal with the religious reception of films. Film and religion are usefully brought together by the use of such third terms as cultural studies, media studies, or visual culture. From a media studies perspective, see Eric Rothenbuhler's *Ritual Communication: From Everyday Conversation to Mediated Ceremony* (Thousand Oaks, Calif., 1998) and Stewart Hoover and Lynn Schofield Clark's edited *Practicing Religion in the Age of Media: Explorations in Media, Religion, and Culture* (New York, 2002). David Morgan, while not dealing with moving images, nonetheless develops useful methods for seeing the relations between religion and visual culture, particularly in his *Visual Piety: A History and Theory of Popular Religious Images* (Berkeley, 1998).

S. Brent Plate (2005)

FINNISH RELIGIONS. The scope of what is covered by the phrase Finnish religion(s) varies according to the different meanings of Finn, Finnish, and Finland geographically, linguistically, and historically.

Finland is, with Iceland, the world's most northerly country. Its location on the Gulf Stream allows for the economic diversity that supports its population, which has been quite small throughout history and totaled around 5.2 million in 2004.

Despite the fact that Finland is less Arctic than parallel territories in Russia, Canada, and the United States, being only partly under permafrost, the north is crucial in the religions of the Sami (ca. 8,000 in Finland) and Finns, the two indigenous peoples of Northern Europe. The Latin word *fenni,* first found in Tacitus's *Germania* (98 CE), comes from Germanic speakers who defined their northern and eastern neighbors as Finns. Tacitus describes barbarian people somewhere in the northeastern Baltic region, living "in unparalleled squalor and poverty." As the nomadic *fenni* lifestyle differed from that of the Germanic peoples, who lived a more settled existence, the term *Finn* might have referred to the way of life these people followed. Thus, the word *fenni* may have encompassed the ancestors of both Finnish and Sami speakers, who shared a common "Lapp" nomadic way of life. Old Norse sagas and chronicles by Saxo Grammaticus and Adam von Bremen make a distinction between two types of Finns, those who were settled down and the nomads known as *Scridfinni.*

The word *Finn* (Finnish, *suomalainen*) means citizen of Finland, an independent country since 1917. Despite joining the European Union in 1995, increased international activity, and a trend toward multiculturalism, Finland today is more monocultural than a century ago; the 2004 census reveals a population that is over 90 percent Finnish *(suomi),* around 6 percent Swedish, and 0.5 percent Russian. Finland has older immigrant populations, such as Rom, Tatar Moslems, and Jews, and since the 1990s approximately 100,000 immigrants speaking more than 100 languages have arrived.

Recent development have brought new diversity to the religious life of Finland, which now has a population of around 20,000 Muslims, but the general picture has remained as monotonous as in other Nordic countries, with Evangelical Lutheranism serving as the state church and "ethnoreligion." Loyalty to the established church is characteristic of Finnish civil religion; the five main revivalist movements have remained within the Lutheran Church. Despite a certain loosening of the situation following the freedom of religion law of 2002, the position of the Evangelical Lutheran Church, to which around 85 percent of Finns belong, is strong. The position of the Orthodox Church of Finland, which is an independent national church with four bishops, is stronger than its 1.2 percent membership would suggest, due to Finland's long history of Karelian roots.

Historically, the concept of *Finland* is newer and less complicated than that of the *Finn.* From the Middle Ages, Finland (proper) was one of the three to seven provinces of the Kingdom of Sweden. It became a state in 1809 when, as a Grand Duchy of the Russian Empire, it was granted autonomy, with Helsinki as the new capital. This autonomy favored nation-building ambitions that had been impossible during Finland's long history of Swedish control. The resultant nineteenth-century nation-building process was fed by Finland's notion of the uniqueness of its history, by the celebration of the epics in the *Kalevala,* and by nationalist identification with the Finnish *(suomi)* language.

A new Finnish self-esteem expressed by the historian Yrjö Koskinen (1830–1903) was based on the notion of language as the property shared by Finnish-related peoples in Russia; Finland, Koskinen wrote, stepped "into the light of history quite late because of the country's extremely peripheral location beside the sea of the Russian peoples." Identification with national roots was strengthened by research. Matthias Alexander Castrén's fieldwork among the Finno-Ugric peoples during the 1840s became the cornerstone of Finno-Ugristics. At the same time, a scientific study of the paradigmatic forms of Finnish religion was initiated.

Castrén's fieldwork stressed Finnish nationalism over Finno-Ugric identity. Castrén returned from his second expedition in 1849, after Lönnrot published his longer version of the *Kalevala,* the *(New) Kalevala,* which became recognized as the only proper version of the Finnish epic. It soon replaced the *(Old) Kalevala* of 1835, which in 1841 had been translated into Swedish by Castrén. The influence of Romanticism and a surge of nationalism inspired by the French Revolution of 1848 led to a completely new interpretation of the *Kalevala.*

The *Old Kalevala* had been compiled by Lönnrot as a compendium of Finnish myths and was intended to replace and expand upon the *Mythologia Fennica* (1789) of Christfried Ganander. The *New Kalevala* was declared to be the sacred history of the Finns, in a foreshadowing of the later Finnicized National Romanticism. A new historical interpretation of the *Kalevala* projected on to it a linear conception of time tied to the development of Christianity. In this rereading, *Kalevala's* history began with biblical creation and ended with the voluntary death of its hero, Väinämöinen, after he had been humiliated by the son of Marjatta, the Virgin Mary—the son being none other than Jesus Christ, who now replaced the old hero. Thus, the pre-Christian Finnish worldview was displaced by the faith of the new era. In spite of the consequent linear structure of the epic, the shamanic, cyclic worldview of the rune singers, with its circulation of life and death, is found in the single runes of the *Kalevala* and in the oral poetry that inspired it.

In the new conceptualization of the *Kalevala,* the frightening land of Pohjola, the Northern Land, became the Underworld. In the preface of the *New Kalevala* by Lönnrot, its plot was explained as the war between "us," the Finns and the Karelians, and "them" in the North, the Lapps in Pohjola. This war of two related peoples filled the social need for a narrative of the heroic Finnish past, following the model of the Viking Age war epic. The war culminated in the robbery of the Sampo from Pohjola, from out of the hands of the evil Lapps. The singing competition of two shamans, Väinämöinen and Joukahainen, was reinterpreted as the battle between "our" *noita* who, of course, was mightier than that of the Lapps. The theory was even advanced that the Sami (Lapps) had no epic poetry, and that Anders Fjellner's narrative *The Son of the Sun's Courting Journey to the Land of the Giants* (1849) was inauthentic. Research in the 1990s has shown that this theory is false; there is indeed a Sami style of epic shamanic *juoiggat.*

The profound changes in the interpretation of the *Kalevala* are related to Romantic nationalist ambitions, which got the upper hand in Lönnrot's work. Lönnrot himself played an active role in the process of transforming the *Kalevala* into a nationalist symbol. For the new Finnish political establishment, the *Kalevala* became the symbol of a Finnish national religion, expressed in paintings, music, solemn national holidays, and so on.

The discipline of folklore was established under the sway of this nationalistic spirit, and did not achieve true academic acceptance until the 1960s. Uno Harva (formerly Holmberg), Martti Haavio, and Lauri Honko are the three Finnish scholars who did the most to establish comparative religion as a serious field of study in Finnish universities. Harva and Haavio both had broad expertise on Finnish folk belief and traditional oral genres. As Honko wrote in Haavio's 1973 obituary: "Folkloristics and comparative religion were always intertwined in Martti Haavio's scholarly work" (*Temenos* 9, p. 148). Harva, Haavio, Honko, and others emphasize the power of words in Finnish religion, at first recognized by Domenico Comparetti, an Italian scholar of the *Kalevala.* The general perspective of the Finnish phenomenology of religion school is regionally Finnish—or Finno-Ugric. Broad phenomenological comparisons over space and time are made between Finnish words and Finno-Ugric myths; at the same time, parallels are drawn with elements of other religious systems, placing Finnish myths into the framework of global religious traditions.

Finnish cosmology includes elements typical of the symbolic structures shared by northern cultures in general. The region inhabited by humans was regarded as an island surrounded by a stream. Above earth stood the mighty vault of the heavens, the celestial sphere around the Polar Star as its cosmic column, surrounded by Orion, the Great Bear, and Perseus. The cosmic mountain is located in the center of the universe, and is its pillar. The cosmos was divided into three zones: the upper world, the human middle world, and the underworld. This tripartite structure of the universe is one of the oldest north Eurasian folk beliefs. The role of the shaman is to act as a mediator between the three levels of the universe. The kingdom of the dead (Finnish, *Tuonela*) is sometimes thought of as being in the Northern (Pohjola) village, with its iron gate and powerful female figures, such as Louhi, mistress of Pohjola. Another conception is that of the nether world, with its underworld inhabitants *(manalaise),* or *vainajat,* the spirits of the ancestors.

SOURCE MATERIALS. The first evidence concerning Finnish religions is archaeological, such as the graves indicating ancestor worship and the approximately one hundred pictograph fields dating from between 4500 and 500 BCE. A new interpretation of these pictographs is provided by Juha Pentikäinen and Timo Miettinen in their *Pyhän merkkejä kivessä* (2002); the joint study of an archaeologist and a scholar of religion, this book deciphers the hidden messages painted or carved on rocks, and analyzes them in relation to shamanic systems of thought and oral poetry.

Mythologia Fennica, published in 1785 by Christfried Ganander, Vicar of Rantsila (1741–1790), was the pioneering study of comparative mythology in Finland. It consisted of a dictionary of Finnish and Lapp sacred and historical vocabulary, accompanied by oral poetry transcriptions and mythology texts. Typically enough, it was concerned with the mythology of both the Finns and the Lapps.

Fragments of Lappish Mythology, published by Lars Levi Laestadius (1800–1861), is a reconstruction of folk beliefs. An important distinction is made between the religious and cultural knowledge of the average person (today defined as collective tradition) and the esoteric secret wisdom of the experts, called *noaidis* ("shamans") in Sami. Laestadius strongly criticizes the nature mythology of Carl Axel Gottlund, a contemporary scholar who did his fieldwork among the Forest Finns throughout Scandinavia.

See Also Castrén, Matthias Alexander; Donner, Kai; Finno-Ugric Religions; Haavio, Martti; Harva, Uno; Honko, Lauri; Laestadius, Lars Levi; Reguly, Antal; Shamanism; Tuonela.

Bibliography

Alho, Olli, et al., eds. *Finland: A Cultural Encyclopedia.* Finnish Literature Society editions no. 684. Helsinki, 1987.

Haavio, Martti. *Väinämöinen, Eternal Sage.* Translated by Helen Goldthwait-Väänänen. Helsinki, 1952.

Haavio, Martti. *Essais folkloriques.* Edited by Lauri Honko. Studia Fennica no. 8. Helsinki, 1959.

Haavio, Martti. *Suomalainen mytologia.* Porvoo, Finland, 1967.

Haavio, Martti. *Mitologia fi'nska.* Preface by Jerzy Litwiniuk. Warsaw, 1979.

Kuusi, Matti, Keith Bosley, and Michael Branch, eds. *Finnish Folk Poetry: Epic: An Anthology in Finnish and English.* Helsinki, 1977.

Laestadius, L. L. *Fragments of Lappish Mythology.* Edited by Juha Pentikäinen. Beaverton, Ontario, 2002.

Oinas, Felix J. *Studies in Finnic Folklore: Homage to the Kalevala.* Suomalaisen Kirjallisuuden Seuran toimituksia no. 387. Mänttä, Finland, 1985.

Pentikäinen, Juha. *Oral Repertoire and World View: An Anthropological Study of Marina Takalo's Life History.* Folklore Fellows' Communications no. 219. Helsinki, 1987.

Pentikäinen, Juha. *Kalevala Mythology.* Translated and edited by Ritva Poom. Folklore Studies in Translation series. Bloomington and Indianapolis, 1989.

Pentikäinen, Juha. "Northern Ethnography: On the Foundations of a New Paradigm." In *Styles and Positions,* edited by Heikki Pesonen, et al. Comparative Religion no. 8. Helsinki, 2002.

Vilkuna, Asko. *Das Verhalten der Finnen in "heiligen" (pyhä) Situationen.* Folklore Fellows' Communications no. 164. Helsinki, 1956.

Juha Pentikäinen (2005)

FINNO-UGRIC RELIGIONS

This entry consists of the following articles:

AN OVERVIEW
HISTORY OF STUDY

FINNO-UGRIC RELIGIONS: AN OVERVIEW

The Finno-Ugric peoples constitute a family of scattered nations and populations in northern Eurasia in an area that reaches from northernmost Scandinavia and Finland to western Siberia and from the Volga-Kama Basin to Hungary. They speak approximately thirty cognate languages, which, with four Samoyed languages, form the Uralic family of languages. It is mainly the linguistic affinity that links these peoples and cultures; the cultural and religious affinities between them are more difficult to ascertain, spanning as they do considerable geographical distance from each other and over 5,000 years of only partly shared history through which each of them had contacts with different peoples. An "original" Finno-Ugric religion postulated by various scholars thus remains hypothetical, but the religious beliefs and practices of the Finno-Ugric peoples have provided an interesting case for comparative methodology in the history of religions, or rather regional phenomenology of religion masterly covered by experts on Finno-Ugric religions.

Genealogy of Languages, Peoples, and Cultures. Theories of linguistic descent are usually based on the concept of a protolanguage and its subsequent differentiation. The real development, however, probably consisted of complex processes of multiple integration into and differentiation from cognate languages, with the interpenetration of noncognate languages in a given region also playing a role. According to the generally accepted chronology, the Uralic protofamily of languages began to split up into Finno-Ugric and Samoyed protolanguages around 4000 BCE. In the twenty-first century the Samoyed languages are spoken by some thirty-five thousand people living on the shores of the Arctic Ocean and along the banks of rivers flowing into it between the Taymyr and Kanin Peninsulas. The early Uralic and Finno-Ugric settlements were presumably located in the south, somewhere between the Ural Mountains and the middle reaches of the Volga River. After the differentiation of the Ugric branch around 3000 BCE, and its subsequent division into the Ob-Ugric (Khanty and Mansi in the north) and into a more southerly ethnos that later became the Hungarian branch, the rest of the Finno-Ugrians either stayed near the Volga and developed into the Mari (Cheremis) and Mordvin peoples of today or moved to the north or the northwest. The northern group, the Permian settlement, persisted over two millennia and became divided only a little over one thousand years ago into the Komi (Zyrians), living in the region between the upper reaches of the western Dvina, the Kama, and the Pechora Rivers; and the Udmurts (Votiaks), living between the Kama and Vyatka Rivers. The northwestern group reached the eastern shores of the Baltic Sea, became intermingled with the former inhabitants in contemporarary Finland and Scandinavia, and linguistically developed into what we now know as Sami (Lapps), Finns, Karelians, Ingrians, Votes, Veps, Estonians, and Livonians. The development was far from unilinear and regular, as is shown by contemporary linguistic groups within the Ugric branch range from fourteen million Hungarians to small populations of Mansi (Voguls) and Khanty (Ostiaks) in the northern Ural Mountains and along the Ob River. Similarly, among five million Finns and one million Estonians traces of almost extinct Votes and Livonians have been found. The most recent censuses and maps on the numbers and distribution of the Finno-Ugric peoples indicate radical changes that have taken place in the former Soviet Union and Russia, where most Finno-Ugric people are at least bilingual, as well as among the five almost extinct Sami languages out of nine to ten altogether.

Finno-Ugrians once inhabited most of northeast Europe. It was relatively late that the Slavic expansion changed the picture from the medieval era, and in Siberia from the sixteenth century onward. Another impact was made by the Turco-Tatar tribes and by the Bulgar empire in the Middle Ages, which particularly affected the culture of the southeastern Mari and Udmurts. Western influence was strongest in the Baltic sphere, where early loanwords were adopted from the Baltic- and Germanic-speaking people from the third to the first millennium BCE. Some remote groups of Finno-Ugrians were able to preserve their autochthonous religious traditions fairly late, even until the nineteenth and early twentieth centuries, because the discipline of Eastern Christianity was rather ineffective or permissive and more tolerant toward folk belief than in western Finland, for instance, where Western Christianity, such as Roman Catholicism from the medieval era onward and, later, Lutheranism, abolished sacred groves (Finnish *hiisi*) and several other archaic expressions of religious phenomena that had survived in the Russian Orthodox east (eastern Finland, Karelia, and Ingria) the southeastern Finno-Ugrians the traditions of their Islamic neighbors left marks on the folk religion.

Since the history of Christian missions and crusades is fairly long—the first signs and words from Eastern Christianity in Finland are from around 800 CE and Catholic crusades began in the twelfth century among the western Finns and in the fourteenth century among the Komi, for example—and trade relations with Christianized cultures existed much earlier, it must be assumed that the survival of early folk belief, myth, and ritual among the Finno-Ugrians is partly an example of the coexistence of great and little traditions; that is, Eastern and Western Christianity or Islam versus ethnic religions. The same people who were devout Christians could also perform ancient rites and hold beliefs that did not necessarily contradict Christian doctrine because they were so skillfully adapted and integrated into each other. Indigenous religion began to adopt Christian elements before formal missionizing took place, and long after it had established its position as the official religion, the Christian religion found itself in a symbiosis with pagan belief and custom, at least at the level of folk religiosity.

METHODS OF COMPARISON. The development of and variation in the religions of the Finno-Ugrians must be seen as an interplay of phenomenological, ecological, and historical aspects. At the phenomenological level the question asked by Lauri Honko, for example, is: Are there any typically Finno-Ugric contributions to the phenomenology of religious universals? The answer is: The wide natural-geographical and cultural-historical scale, ranging from mobile hunting and fishing communities in the Arctic north to stable farming and cattle-breeding societies in the south and from remote pockets of religious tradition to the crossroads of Byzantine and Roman influence, permits one to examine the relative importance of linguistic continuity in cultural variation. To reconstruct a true proto-Finno-Ugric religion may be impossible, as the religious systems have changed so many times, but some structural or systematic elements may be discerned, irrespective of whether they belong to a vertical tradition. There are similarities in cosmological belief, in the system of spirits, and in ancestor worship that may not occur as frequently among non-Finno-Ugrians. From the phenomenological point of view, however, dissimilarities may turn out to be as important as similarities, and in the area of language we must remember the existence of the superstrate and substrate area of traditions; that is, the language of a population may change while the traditional content is retained. Under Slavic linguistic form we may find substrata of Finno-Ugric tradition, especially in the north of Russia.

Ecological comparisons may help to explain similarities that are not based on historical contact and interaction between cultures. Ecological comparison often turns out to be regional: Similar trends become discernible among all or most cultures in a given zone, regardless of linguistic affinities. There are different "ecologies" to be observed: those that are based on the natural environment, those that are dependent on the sociocultural development or stage of development in the societies to be compared, and those that refer to the morphology of the religious tradition itself. Finno-Ugric material provides interesting points of departure for attempts to understand the extent to which physical environment, the stage of societal development, and the morphology of the tradition may interact with each other or with linguistic or regional factors.

The third and most common level of comparison has been the historical one. Most recent findings on rock art, pictographs, and petroglyphs in Russia, Karelia, the Kola Peninsula, and Finland have revealed new materials found from the territories occupied by the Finno-Ugric populations or their genetic or maybe even linguistic ancestors. This means that early historical sources and archaeological findings in the field of Finno-Ugric religion are more abundant and illuminating than suggested by Honko in the first edition of this entry. Although the testimonial value of these sources may be rather scanty and problematic, they should be carefully studied in the long chain starting from the archaeology of the petrified language on rock, painted by red clay or carved with hammer by a Neoloithic man, regardless of the language he spoke. Comparison may be made of the shamanic paraphernalia (e.g., *sejd* and other anthro- and zoomorphic stones, drums, dress, and so on) found in the shamans' graves, such as in Karelia (Elk Island on Lake Onega) and northern Finland (Kuusamo).

Tradition-historical analysis shows how the historical assumptions may be based on the evidence of relatively late documents of oral tradition. The assumption usually is unidirectional: One people has borrowed beliefs or rituals from another. Interaction in cultural contact or dissimilar functions of similar traits (or similar functions of dissimilar traits) in different tradition systems are rarely discussed. In spite of this, interesting evidence of early historically connected strata in Finno-Ugric religious tradition has been dectected, as for instance in the case of bear killing and the bear feast of the Ob-Ugrians, Karelians, and Sami. There are also phenomena that can only be explained historically, such as the revival of dirge ceremonies in Russian and Karelian areas because of the sufferings caused by World War II.

MORPHOLOGY. One way to organize the Finno-Ugric religious traditions is by the occupations of hunting and fishing, cattle breeding and nomadism, and agriculture and subordinate handicraft industries. These forms of subsistence do not normally occur alone, however, but in various combinations. It is the skillful combination of many different sources of livelihood and the calendar cycle based on these that characterizes most Finno-Ugric groups and their religious tradition. Three calendar systems basically contribute to the formation of the cycle: the calendars of nature, of human work, and of the church (saints' days and so on). The cycle requires new roles of the individual and the re-creating of different social worlds of the community; specialists exist, but the division of labor rarely allows specialists of one domain only. The calendrical cycle expressed by calendar rites is crucial for the cohesion of society and its communal economic activity.

Another important organizing factor of ritual life is the human life cycle from birth to death and the accompanying rites of passage. Through these it is possible to express and legitimize changes of social status and reinforce the prevailing social structure. The early Finno-Ugric communities do not seem to have developed elaborate ceremonies of initiation—even the shamanic initiation did not involve large audiences—but the idea of initiation can be seen in small rituals such as the wrapping of a newborn child in his or her father's sweaty shirt, bringing "tooth money" to the new child (Karelia), dressing the bride, guiding the deceased to their relatives in the otherworld, and so on. Weddings and funerals, along with feasts of the agricultural year, comprise the most developed ritual dramas.

Religion of hunters and fishermen. True hunting communities have survived longest in the Arctic and sub-Arctic zones, but traces of their mythology and religious rites continue to survive in various combined economies where hunting or fishing has played a subsidiary role. Finno-Ugric materials demonstrate a special sensitivity to and knowledge of nature. In the world of the hunter, who generally works alone, animals, plants, and rocks possess a character of their own and must be addressed properly. The hunter sees himself as an interloper on someone else's territory; the animals and features of the forest communicate promises, warnings, and threats. It is not enough for the hunter to know about the best fishing and hunting places and seasons. He must also know about the being who rules over the forest and its inhabitants, the forest master or mistress; he must understand the ways of the "lord of the animals," who determines the movement and fate of all the living creatures in the forest, and of the special guardian spirits that watch over particular animal species. The territorial aspect is also important, in that different formations of nature possess their own local spirits. No less important is the annual cycle, especially the beginning and the end of a season, which later on came to be marked by Christian saints' days. The Lapp way of life meant an annual cycle: The Sami were called the People of the Eight Seasons (after Ernst Manker's 1975 book) because they patterned their lives after their knowledge of the resources of the environment on the annual migration of the wild deer and elk; the spawning and mating cycles of the salmon, trout, and other fish, ptarmigan, swan, goose and other birds; the harvest season for berry picking; and so on.

The most venerated animal in their Arctic and sub-Arctic territories was the bear, seen by the Sami and Ob-Ugrians as their totemic ancestor and as the son of the sky god Num torem. Several myths that recount either the marriage between the first bear and a human girl or the heavenly origin of the bear and its descent to earth and relate how it was slain and returned home to the celestial father after special ceremonies seem to be of common Finno-Ugric origin. These myths were recited in bear ceremonies, during both the killing and the feast itself, events that abound in dramatic and verbal elements. The Ob-Ugrian Khanty and Mansi still perform the complex bear ceremony lasting seven days—with each day pertaining to one of the seven stars in the Great Bear constellation—which has been developed into actual theater performances; hundreds of ritual and semiprofane plays and dances are performed during the feast. The totemic element is apparent in the Ob-Ugric moiety system, which consists of the *mós* (the heavenly people, who are hunters and eaters of raw meat) and the *por* (the underground people, who are wizards and eaters of cooked meat); these phratries observe different norms concerning bear hunting. Although the bear is the object of rites and veneration among most of the northern peoples of Asia and America, there are few ritual dramas comparable to the bear ceremonies of the Ob-Ugrians, Finns, and Sami. Even during the course of the more normal hunting of game, the verbal component—prayers, spells, and songs—is well developed among the Finno-Ugrians. The spirits are usually designated by compounds such as "forest-man," "forest-father," or "forest-master." The system of "fathers" and/or "mothers" of territories, places, buildings, and so on was common.

Religion of cattle breeders and nomads. Cattle breeding is an important subsidiary means of livelihood especially among the Finno-Ugrians of the north, where agriculture is constantly threatened by the climate. The religious profile of cattle breeders is not as clear-cut as that of the hunters and farmers; it also appears in symbiosis with the beliefs of those who practice agriculture. As a means of subsistence, nomadism is also subsidiary, not only to agriculture, but also to hunting. When the flocks of wild reindeer grew thin, the Arctic hunters of both Fennoscandia and the Kanin Peninsula developed reindeer herding, which in some places, such as Sweden, led to full domestication and a dairy economy. Only the reindeer was capable of finding its food even under the snow, and it soon became an indispensable draft and slaughter animal. Another area for wide-scale herding was the Hungarian plains, where the swampy land was unsuitable for farming but provided excellent pasture.

The yearly cycle of the cattle breeder is roughly divided into two halves: the indoor period and the outdoor period; only in Hungary is there some outdoor herding all year round. In the winter horses and cows are under the rule of the owner/cattle breeder and his or her supranormal counterpart, the stable or cowhouse spirit. In the summer the herdsman, often an employee, takes over and the supranormal guardianship is transferred to the forest spirit or other spirits in the landscape. The cattle owner and herdsman observe many rituals, which tend to accumulate at the beginning and the end of a season; minor prayers and offerings that relate to such events as imminent danger or bad weather are also performed during the season.

In the Balto-Finnic areas Saint George's Day (April 23) marks the sending of the cattle to pasture; the ritual has to be performed even if it was too cold for outdoor herding. The animals were encircled by people who walk around the flock carrying an icon of Saint George, an ax, burning coal, gunpowder, churchyard dirt, quicksilver, a hymnal, and a bear's tooth, among other items. Magic signs were drawn on the animals, doorposts, or the cattle's intended route. Food offerings were brought to the forest spirit, and an egg was thrown over the flock. The cattle owner asked the herdsman, the victorious dragon-slayer Saint George, and the forest mistress to join forces to protect the cattle against bears, wolves, and other dangers.

In October the cattle were taken indoors; the autumnal season was brought to an end by slaughtering a sheep or cow around Michaelmas (September 29) or All Saints' Day (November 1). This was the first "New Year" festival, during which dead relatives visited one's home, and, in northern Karelia, the myth of the slaying of the Great Ox was sung. Many southern Finno-Ugric peoples combine their cattle breeding cult with summer feasts and offerings organized primarily as part of the agricultural cycle. In long prayers presented on these occasions cow luck, horse luck, and so on is asked from many gods of the sky and the earth.

Religion of farmers. The society and religion of hunters and cattle breeders is competitive; among the latter, especially, the rites are directed against fellows and neighbors. Even if the principle of "limited good" (one's success means another's loss and vice versa, because the sum of good is constant) is valid in agriculture, the atmosphere is clearly more social and collective than in cattle husbandry. This social atmosphere is clearly expressed in the great rural ritual feasts of the southern Finno-Ugric peoples: the Mordvins, the Mari, and the Udmurts. The traditions of the last two groups derive to a large extent from their Turco-Tatar neighbors, whereas the Mordvins have adopted more from the Russians; regardless, all three have used Finno-Ugric and other traditions of their particular region in creating their agricultural cycles. A broad social approach, in which success is sought not only for the individual or his family, but also for the whole village or a larger population, especially the poor and disabled, prevails in the long prayer recitations performed in connection with animal and food offerings to dozens of gods and spirits. A Mari prayer from the Kazan area lists what is valued in the following order: family, cattle, corn, bees, money, long life, and great happiness. Another value often stressed in prayer is "harmony"; that is, avoidance of quarrels and disruptive feelings, which is seen as a condition to be met before addressing the gods.

The central mythologems of the farmer are the earth and the sky. These parts of the cosmos or their personifications alternately are manifest in the prayers and rites. Earth is above all the female progenitor, Mother Earth; as such, she is sometimes represented as the generic Corn Mother, and sometimes as the mother or guardian of a particular kind of grain or field. The sky god is closely associated with rain, wind, and other types of storms. Thought of as male, he begets the earth. The myth of *Hieros gamos,* the matrimony of heaven and earth, has been preserved in epic poetry and in connection with rainmaking rituals of the Balto-Finnic area. Importance is also attached to the patron saints of agriculture, among whom Elijah and the Saints Peter and Nicholas are the most central. Various feasts may be observed during midsummer, the period of growth, when the working routines are laid still and the crops are at the mercy of the weather, insects, forest animals, and other natural factors. The Finno-Ugric farmer's worldview is oriented toward peace and harmony, every kind of growth and fertility, personal health, social good, and avoidance of misfortune. The farmer enumerates all the gods to avoid offending any of them and bows to them all; a Mari or Udmurt bows "upward," sacrificing a white animal to the sky, and "downward," sacrificing a black animal to the ancestors, thus placing himself in the middle of a three-storied universe.

Cosmology. Two well-known myths of the origin of the world are found among Finno-Ugric peoples, those of the earth diver and of the world egg. In the diver myth, God orders the Devil (originally a water bird) to bring earth from the botton of the primeval sea; on the third attempt, he succeeds but tries to hide some of the earth in his mouth. When God scatters sand and the earth begins to grow, the deceit is unmasked; from the earth found in the cheek of the Devil the mountains and hills are formed. The myth is known from the Ob River to Finland and to the Mordvins in the Volga area. The eastern Finnish variant contains an interesting introduction: God stands on a golden statue in the sea and orders his reflection in the water to rise; this reflection becomes the Devil. The global distribution of the world-egg myth is equatorial, but its northernmost occurrence is found in Finland and Estonia. A water bird or an eagle makes a nest on the knee of the creator (Väinämöinen), who is floating in the sea. It lays an egg, which rolls into the water, and pieces of it become the earth, the sky, the moon, and the stars. Myths concerning the creation of humans are found in various forms among the Mansi, Volga Finns, and Karelians; the Karelian version typifies the basic scenario: A hummock rises from the sea, a tree stump on it splits open, and the first human couple steps forth.

Cosmogonic myths function as powerful protomyths: The origin of any phenomenon must be linked to the central cosmographic symbols, and various etiological continuations to these basic myths are therefore abundant. According to the cosmography of the Finno-Ugrians, a stream encircles the world, which is covered by the canopy of the heavens, the central point of which is the North Star (the "nail of the sky" on which the sky rotates); this star is sometimes associated with the world pole that supports the sky. A world tree—often the tree of life—and a world mountain rise at the center of the universe; there is a world omphalos deep in the center of the earth and a corresponding abyss of the sea that swallows ships. On the backs of three fish rest the foundations of the earth; the movements of these fish cause floods and earthquakes. Another possible cause of the destruction of the world is that the world pole collapses and the heavens—sometimes described as being seven- or nine-storied—tumble down.

Much of this symbolism is well known in other parts of the world, but some details may be exclusively Finno-Ugric. An example is the belief that the sun, moon, and stars are found on the branches of the world tree, usually a great oak. Cosmographic symbols also occur frequently in contexts outside the rituals, in folk poetry.

SANCTUARIES AND OFFERINGS. The home sanctuary of the Udmurts is called the *kuala.* It is a small log cabin in the corner of a square building formation that constitutes the house. In the back corner of the *kuala* is a shelf, on which are branches of deciduous trees and conifers, and above them is a *vorsud,* an empty box with a lid. This is a family shrine for weekly offerings, but if the master of the house is the head of a large family, children may come from afar on certain days to worship here. A new *kuala* can only be founded with earth and ashes from the father's *kuala.* It is believed that in former times the *vorsud* was not empty but contained effigies of spirits. This tradition still continues among Finno-Ugric peoples. Juha Pentikäinen's field research in North Eurasia (1989-2003) includes several examples on shamanic practices of the mobile Ob-Ugric hunters who still carry their spirit effigies in a special sleigh when migrating.

Another Udmurt sanctuary is the *lud*—a fenced-off area in an isolated place in the woods. In the middle is a table for offerings that are made by the family to dispel diseases, to mark calendric observances, and so on. In addition, there are fenced-off sanctuaries for the offerings of the village; these sanctuaries are sometimes situated near the cornfields. Somewhat similar arrangements are found among the Volga Finns (the *keremet* of the ancestors) and in the Balto-Finnic area where, when slash-and-burn agriculture spread into virgin land and distances grew between pioneering families, village groves were replaced by sacrificial stones (with gouged cups on the surface) and sacred family trees near the dwellings.

Among the nomadic, reindeer-breeding and fishing Sami, the *seita* was a place for sacrifices; it was a cave, a tree stump, or a stone, often clearly visible because of its peculiar (natural) shape, usually chosen near difficult places along a reindeer trail or at some good fishing spot. Offerings were made to enhance the safety of reindeer, good fishing, and so on. Many a sanctuary was only temporary, used for one or two offerings only, and founded mainly to mark a good hunting or fishing ground and to guarantee future luck by giving the first piece of game to the gods.

SHAMANS AND OTHER MEDIATORS. Religious professionalism manifested as priesthood is rare among the Finno-Ugrians. The cults and rites discussed earlier were conducted by those in occupational roles, in some instances as head of a family or working team. Ancestor worship as the predominant cultic form tends to support this kind of arrangement as well. A division of labor took place so that washing and dressing the body as well as lamenting throughout mortuary ceremonies is female work, but shamanic visits to lift up bodies from graves, for example, usually belong to the male ritual repertoire of the shamanic society. Religious performance then becomes part and parcel of working routines and role performance in general.

There is, however, one important exception: the *noita* (shaman or sage). Since *noita* is spoken only in Finnish, Sami, and Mansi, the word is hardly Finno-Ugric. According to scholarly opinions, expressed by Vilmos Diószegi, Honko, Mihály Hoppál, and so on, the early stratum of Finno-Ugric religion must have contained shamanism, although pure shamanism has been documented only in the far north among the Sami and Samoyeds. Indirect evidence supporting this hypothesis is based on the form of similar oral traditions and officiants (from the Finnish *tietäjä* to the Hungarian *taltós*), who experience a kind of "verbal ecstasy" and display comparable shamanic symbols in their outfits. Although scholars argue that the Finno-Ugric shamans were many things, including diviners, healers, priests, and experts in various technical skills, it may not be proper to deal with all divine or priestry roles as expressions of shamanim. Rather, there were different types of experts among different Finno-Ugric peoples who held the highest authority on crisis rites and defended the society against malevolent forces by exercising counter-magic and performing rites of propitiation. Their interpretation became the guideline in times of uncertainty.

Cult priests like the Udmurt *tuno* or the Mari *kart* have accordingly been dealt with as representations of relatively late specialization under the impact of foreign culture, whereas the designation for shaman that is found from Finland (Finnish *noita*; northern Sami *noaidi*) to the Ob River (Mansi *najt*) speaks for a more original stratum (the term has many interesting parallels in these languages). Ancient Finnish folk poetry, Hungarian fairy tales, and other such material have been interpreted as carriers of shamanic motifs, and even if some assumptions prove faulty, the general picture has been regared as likely to persist. Although the old Scandinavian *saga* and *Edda* traditions also include a similar stratum, other European parallels should be considered. Sami drum and jojk singing is a clear parallel to Siberian and Ob-Ugrian shamanhood. Even though no drums have been found from the Finns, the fact remains that until the late nineteenth and early twentieth centuries the Finnish and Karelian *tietäjä* still fulfilled many functions and used many techniques and expressions in his charms and vocabulary reminiscent of shamanic practiuces and folklore in Siberia.

To balance the picture, Honko introduces the female counterpart of the *tietäjä,* the lamenter (Finnish *itkijä*), who with her ecstatic performance was able to set the entire audience at a funeral or a memorial feast in the socially proper mood and prepared a catharsis from uncertainty and grief for her community. Lamenting was customary in the rites of departure (conscription, weddings, and funerals) and the lamenter became a kind of psychopomp who with her intensive empathy and metaphorical language guided the helpless object of the rite. This tradition lived with the indirect support of the Russian Orthodox Church much longer than most traditions discussed earlier and is still practiced in certain parts of Soviet Karelia.

SEE ALSO Castrén, Matthias Alexander; Dömötör, Tekla; Finnish Religions; Haavio, Martti; Harva, Uno; Honko, Lauri; Hungarian Religion; Khanty and Mansi Religion; Mari and Mordvin Religion; Sami Religion; Samoyed Religion.

BIBLIOGRAPHY

A comprehensive presentation of Finno-Ugric mythology by Uno Holmberg (later, Harva) can be found in *The Mythology of All Races*, vol. 4 (1927; reprint, New York, 1964). Many monographs on the religion of the Finno-Ugric peoples have been published in the series *Folklore Fellows' Communications* (Helsinki, 1910–). More recent works are Ivar Paulson's "Die Religionen der finnischen Völker," in *Die Religionen Nordeurasiens und der amerikanischen Arktis*, edited by Paulson, Åke Hultkrantz, and Karl Jettmar, pp. 145–303 (Stuttgart, 1962), and "Religionen der finnisch-ugrischen Völker," in *Handbuch der Religionsgeschichte*, witten by Honko, edited by Jes Peter Asmussen and Jørgen Laessøe, vol. 1, pp. 173–224 (Göttingen, Germany, 1971). Honko, with Senni Timonen, Keith Bosley, and Michael Branch, published an assemby of Finno-Ugric ritual texts in their original languages and in translation, with commentaries, in *The Great Bear: Folk Poetry in the Finno-Ugrian Languages* (Helsinki, 1993). *Komi Mythology* by Nikolay Konakov and others is the first volume in the *Encyclopaedia of Uralic Mythology*, edited by Siikala, Napolskih, and Hoppal, and will include compendia on various Finno-Ugric religions dating the classical series "Suomen suvun uskonnot" (Religions of the Finno-Ugrian Peoples) by Kaarle Krohn, Holmberg (Harva), and K. F. Karjalainen. For further reading on Estonian fok religion, see Ivar Paulson's *The Old Estonian Folk Religion* (Bloomington, Ind., 1971). Additional references to basic Finno-Ugric sources can be found in respective entries of this dictionary, as well as in the bibliographies of the above-cited works and the *Wörterbuch der Mythologie* series (Stuttgart, 1965).

LAURI HONKO (1987)
JUHA PENTIKÄINEN (2005)

FINNO-UGRIC RELIGIONS: HISTORY OF STUDY

The ways of life and customs of peoples inhabiting the northern regions of Europe concerned even the earliest historiographers, such as Herodotos (c. 484–between 430 and 420 BCE) and Tacitus (c. 55–120 CE). Nevertheless, the first genuinely valid data regarding peoples of the Finno-Ugric language family can be found only much later, in the works of writers living from the fifteenth to seventeenth centuries: Mathias de Miechow, Sigismundus Herberstein, Olaus Magnus (1490–1557), Michael Agricola (1508–1557), Alessandro Guagnino, Nicolaes Witsen (1641–1717), Johannes Schefferus (1621–1679), Nicolaie Spataru (1663–1708), and Adam Olearius (1603–1671), among others. The information conveyed by these writers in their religious, geographical, ethnographical, or historical texts has proved to be a valuable contribution not only to social history and ethnography, but to the history of their religion(s) as well.

FOUNDATIONS OF EIGHTEENTH-CENTURY STUDY. The eighteenth century was a time of great journeys and discoveries as well as the publication of travel literature based on eyewitness accounts on respective areas. At this time the peoples of northern Eurasia and Siberia among others became objects of genuine scientific interest. Several authors of travel accounts, namely Y. E. Ides, D. G. Messerschmidt, P. J. Strahlenberg, Johann Georg Gmelin (1709–1755), and J. G. Georgi, made interesting observations not only about the languages of northern Eurasian peoples, but also about their customs and religious cults. These writings also established the basis for the eventual recognition of Finno-Ugric as a language family. Two German scholars, Johann Eberhard Fischer (1697–1771), who was a member of the Russian tsar's academy, and August Ludwig von Schlözer (1735–1809) played especially important roles in this discovery by summarizing in their scholarly works the available information concerning Finno-Ugric peoples: Fischer in *Sibirische Geschichte* (1768) and von Schlözer in *Allgemeine Nordische Geschichte* (1771). In Hungary Finno-Ugric comparative linguistic research was initiated by the study *Demonstratio: Idioma Ungarorum et Lapponum idem esse* (Proof that the languages of the Hungarians and the Lapps are the same; 1770), by Janos Sajnovics (1733–1785), and the study *Affinitas linguae Hungaricae cum linguis fennicae originis* (Relationship of the Hungarian language to languages of Finnic origin; 1779), by Samuel Gyarmathi (1751–1830).

The first Finno-Ugric studies were thus written simultaneously with, and not independently of, respective studies in Indo-European comparative linguistics. Progress in Finno-Ugric studies was slower than that of Indo-European studies because of the more remote distance between peoples themselves as well as scholars studying them. In the same way as the three Finno-Ugric peoples of Europe—Finns, Estonians, and Hungarians, who later on became the only ones to be able to found the national states where Finno-Ugric languages are in majority—lived far from one another, so their scholars also lived in scientific isolation without knowing too much about each other's scientific works and results.

Nevertheless, both the Finns and the Hungarians were able to complete their first mythologies in the last decades of the eighteenth century. In Finland, Henrik Gabriel Porthan (1739–1804), learned professor of rhetorics at Turku Academy, was familiar with theories on Finno-Ugric peoples in Germany. He advocated the publication of Erik Christian Lencquist's doctoral dissertation, *De superstitione veterum Fennorum theoretica et practica* (Superstition in belief and practice among the ancient Finns; 1782), which was based on data collected from people. Another Finnish scholar, Christfried Ganander (1741–1790), a Lutheran pastor in Rantsila, northern Ostrobotnia, created a network of over one hundred ministers and officials around Finland while gathering data for his huge Finnish-Swedish dictionary—until 1997 available in three facsimile volumes only—and Finnish mythology (*Mythologia Fennica,* 1789). The latter is a kind of Finnish-Lappish comparative mythology since it provides an alphabetical listing of Finnish and Lappish (Sami) mythological terms and concepts with historical and other information related to entries. The work is a valuable source of the original runic poems of the eighteenth century and the foundation of the comparative mythology school in Finland. Since it worked as Elias Lönnrot's (1802–1884) model for his further collecting of poems in the field, it was the primary basis for the whole creation of the idea of the Finnish epics. Typically enough, the first editions of the Finnish-Karelian epics compiled by Lönnrot carried the title *The Mythology of the Finnish People edited by Old Poems* before the book was finally named as the *Kalevala* in 1835, with a geographical reference to a mythical dwelling place of Kaleva's gigantic sons—in Lönnrot's thinking, Kaleva was the king of Finland.

Hungarian mythology was introduced in Europe by Daniel Cornides (1732–1787), who lectured on ancient Hungarian religion at the University of Göttingen in 1785. Basing his arguments on medieval chronicles, he compared the remains of ancient pagan Hungarian religion with elements of the ancient Jewish, Greek, and Scythian religions. Later on, in his short study *Commentatio de religione veterum Hungarorum* (Comments on the ancient religion of the Hungarias; 1791), he compared ancient Hungarian religion to Persian religion.

NINETEENTH-CENTURY NATIONAL MYTHOLOGIES. During the first decades of the nineteenth century there was a romantic interest in folk tradition many parts of Europe, especially in Germany. Under stimuli of Indo-European comparative linguistics and mythological research, the collection of folk poetry and the exploration of narrative folk traditions began. Two seminal works of the period were published in 1835. The first was *Deutsche Mythologie* by Jacob Grimm (1785–1863), which subsequently served as a model for reconstructing mythologies of several peoples, among them the Finns, the Estonians, the Sami, and the Hungarians. The other, the *Kalevala* by Lönnrot, contributed to the study of Finnish mythology by compiling folk poetry on the basis of epical songs. In accordance with its initial names, this (Old) *Kalevala* with thirty-two songs was the mythology of the Finns on the basis of the epical poems. Its second, enlarged edition published in 1849 contained almost a double amount of verses, 50 songs with 22,759 lines in all. After Grimm's speech in 1845 at the Academy of Berlin, the (New) *Kalevala* was now offered by Lönnrot as the national epic of the Finns, not as their mythology any more, but as the sacred history of the new nation. The European readers at large only became acquainted with the (New) *Kalevala* through its German translation published in 1852.

The discovery that the Finns, a people small in number, had produced heroic epic poetry comparable with the Homeric epics profoundly impressed the scholars of other Finno-Ugric nations as well. Encouraged by Lönnrot as early as the 1840s, Reinhold Kreutzwald (1803–1882) began collecting Estonian narratives and epic songs about Kalevi-poeg, a gigantic folk hero of exceptional strength. While the first prototext of about twelve thousand lines was completed by 1853, the reconstructed epic itself, *Kalevi poeg: Üks ennemuistene Eesti jut: Kaheskümnes laulus* (Kalevi-poeg: An ancient Estonian legend in twenty songs), was published considerably later (in 1862), in Estonian, even though it appeared in Finland. Meanwhile, Kreutzwald worked on reconstructing Estonian national mythology and published the study "Über den Charakter der estnischen Mythologie" in the journal *Verhandlungen der Gelehrten Estnischen Gesellschaft zu Dorpat* (1850).

The romantic quest for Pan-Finnish identity, to find related peoples and an ancient, common land of origin (where the forebears of related peoples had lived together), prompted scholars of the mid-nineteenth century to undertake long journeys of exploration. For example, Matthias Alexander Castrén (1813–1852) collected valuable material during his repeated Siberian travels and described his research in *Reiseerinnerungen aus den Jahren 1838–1844: Nordische Reisen und Forschungen* (Travel recollections, 1838–1844: Nordic travel and research; 1833). Castrén's lectures on Altaic (i.e., Finnic) mythology, given during the last years of his life, were published in translation from Swedish under the title *Vorlesungen über die finnische Mythologie* (1853).

Meanwhile, Castrén's Hungarian contemporary Antal Reguly (1819–1859) went on a research trip among the Ob-Ugrians and presented the results of his research in *Ethnographisch-geographische Karte des nördlichen Ural-gebietes* (Ethno-geographical map of the northern Ural region; 1846). Only some two decades later did Pál Hunfalvy (1810–1891), one of the founders of Finno-Ugric comparative linguistics, publish Reguly's collection, which contained valuable folk literature—primarily texts of Mansi (Vogul) heroic epics—in *A vogul föld és nép* (The Vogul land and its people; 1864).

For the sake of proper chronology, one must mention here the first comprehensive collection of Hungarian mythology, *Magyar Mythologia* (1854), published during the romantic era of reform after the Hungarian revolt against Austria (1848–1849). Its author, Arnold Ipolyi (1823–1886), a learned Roman Catholic bishop, collected folk tales, legends, and folk beliefs of the region. At the same time he was intimately familiar with the contemporary scholarly literature dealing with comparative mythology. As he pointed out, his work was greatly influenced by the mythological studies of Jakob Grimm, Georg Friedrich Creuzer (1771–1858), and Joseph von Görres (1776–1848), but he also quoted the Finnish studies by Lencquist, Ganander, and Castrén. Ipolyi's study, more than five hundred pages long, is a genuine comparative-mythological survey, though its assertions should today be looked on from a critical distance. A few years later, Ferenc Kállay (1790–1861) compiled another work, though more modest, about the religion of the pre-Christian Hungarians (*A pogány magyarok vallása,* 1861), in which he described the major figures of ancient Hungarian mythology.

For the one-thousandth anniversary of the Magyar conquest of Hungary, Kabos Kandra (1843–1905) prepared the third edition of *Magyar Mythologia* (1897). Although Kandra was in a position to build on the findings of contemporary Finno-Ugric linguistics, his work is basically the last romantic attempt at reconstructing the system of Hungarian mythology. While the most important text among the materials used for purposes of comparison is the *Kalevala,* the *Mythologia* also depends on quotations from the studies and text collections of Bernát Munkácsi (1860–1937). Munkácsi's fieldwork among the Udmurt (Votyaks) and Mansi (Voguls) took place in the second half of the 1880s. He published his own and Antal Reguly's findings in four thick volumes, with copious notes on mythology, titled *Vogul Népköltési Gyüjtemény* (Vogul folklore collection; 1892–1902). He also published studies on comparative mythology in Hungarian and German.

While there are early and finely detailed descriptions concerning the ancient religion of the Sami, for example, Ioannus Schefferus's *Lapponica . . . de origine, superstitione, sacris magicis* (1673), the first real reconstruction and description of Sami mythology *(Lappisk Mythologi, Eventyr og Folkesagn)* was published in Christiania (later Oslo) as late as 1871 by Jens Andreas Friis (1821–1896). Lars Levi Laestadius's *Fragments on Lappish Mythology* were written earlier in 1840–1845, but remained unpublished until the 1990s.

As the national self-awareness of the ethnic minorities of tsarist Russia began to increase during the last decades of the nineteenth century, collecting texts of folklore also started among them. One should mention Serafim Patkanov (1856–1888), who did research among the southern groups of Khanty (Ostyaks), and Ivan Nikolaevich Smirnov (1856–1904), a professor of the University of Kazan, Russia, who collected valuable materials among the Finno-Ugric peoples of Perm and along the Volga. Smirnov published several books on his findings concerning the Cheremis (Mari), Votyak (Udmurt), and Komi Permyak: *Cheremisy* (1889), *Votiaki* (1890), and *Permiaki* (1891), respectively. Several chapters in these volumes are devoted to the gods and religious customs of the Finno-Ugric peoples living by the Volga, and they serve as useful source material for comparative research.

Early Twentieth-Century Comparative Research. Around the turn of the twentieth century, Finno-Ugric studies became strengthened by scientifically planned fieldwork. For the most part it was carried out by well-trained linguists, who in the process of their fieldwork also recorded materials valuable for folklorists and students of mythology. In this context one should mention the Hungarian József Pápay (1873–1931) as well as the Finns Heikki Paasonen (1869–1919), Yrjö Wichmann (1868–1932), Kai Donner (1888–1935), and Artturi Kannisto (1874–1943). Their authentic text collections made it possible to reconstruct the belief systems of certain Finno-Ugric peoples and consequently to prepare comprehensive comparative studies. Since, unlike research on Indo-European mythology, Finno-Ugric comparative mythological research is based almost entirely on folkloric material, it was logical to study it in this context and to describe the mythology of particular peoples as accurately as the circumstances would allow.

In 1908 Kaarle Krohn (1863–1933), the first professor of folklore at the University of Helsinki, and Aladár Bán (1871–1960), a Hungarian scholar, jointly published *A finnugor népek pogány istentisztelete* (Pre-Christian god worship of the Finno-Ugric peoples) in Hungarian; with Bán's supplement, this work essentially became the first Finno-Ugric study of comparative religion. The book is based on *Suomen suvun pakanallinen jumalanpalvelus* (The heathen worship of Finnish tribe; 1894), which included posthumously published lectures of Julius Krohn (1835–1888), Kaarle Krohn's father, who was a docent at the University of Helsinki in 1884. In the first chapter, the history of research, the sources, and the scholarly literature are reviewed, and in subsequent chapters sacred places of sacrifice, sacred images, activities of shamans, and actual sacrificial rituals are discussed. What renders this volume valuable even today is its rich use of contemporary Russian scientific literature that is now not readily available.

The second major summary of the religious beliefs of the Finno-Ugric peoples, *Die Religion der Jugra-Völker* (The religion of the Ob-Ugrians; 1922–1927), a three-volume study, was written by Kustaa Fredrik Karjalainen (1871–1919). This monumental work based on the complete literature available at the time was combined with the author's original field research at the turn of the twentieth century. It remains the most detailed overview of the religious beliefs of the Finno-Ugric peoples to date. At the end of the 1920s, Uno Holmberg (later Harva, 1882–1949) published yet another summary, "Finno-Ugric Mythology," in the fourth volume of *The Mythology of All Races* (1927). Here, Holmberg methodically reviews beliefs in the soul, the cult of the dead, hunting magic, and veneration of nature spirits (spirits of stones, water, forest, and fire), of home spirits, of the lord of the sky, and of heroes revered as gods. He devotes a separate chapter to the description of sacrifices and the examination of questions concerning shamanism he found to be characteristic of the Finno-Ugric peoples.

Study on Finno-Ugric Religions during the Soviet Era. During the two generations of researchers from World War I and the October 1917 Revolution until the brief period of openness in the spirit of glasnost and perestroika under Mikhail Gorbachov's era at the end of the 1980s, most Finno-Ugric territories inside the borders of the Soviet Union remained closed from scholars living in Finland. Studies on Finno-Ugric languages and religions, however, continued; the rich archival materials gathered by the scholars on the nineteenth and early twentieth centuries were now carefully analyzed and published as linguistically transcribed collections in the Memoirs and Journals of the Finno-Ugric Society in Finland (founded in 1883) by experts on respective Finno-Ugric languages.

The topic of religion, labelled the opium of the people by Karl Marx (1818–1883), was taboo in the Communist empire of the Soviet Union. In spite of this, research on religion to a certain extent went on under the umbrella of Soviet ethnography. In 1931 there appeared in the Soviet Union, where most Finno-Ugric peoples lived, a collection of texts about the religious beliefs of the Soviet peoples (*Religioznye verovaniia narodov SSSR*). The sole value of this two-volume collection is that it quotes passages from older Russian publications. In the 1930s particularly, and for many decades following its publication, the monopoly of Marxist critiques of religion practically halted all religio-scientific and mythological research in the Soviet Union.

As far as the position of the Finno-Ugric peoples and the research on their cultures and religions in particular are concerned, World War II meant radical changes to the period between the two world wars. Estonia was annexed (formally as a republic) to the Soviet Union until 1991, and Hungary, although still independent, was occupied by Soviet troops as a part of the Eastern block, which divided Europe during the Cold War. Throughout the Cold War, several prominent scholars escaped from Eastern Europe to conduct their research on Finno-Ugric themes in western Europe and in the United States. Gradually, the Finno-Ugric territories inside the Soviet Union became targets for fieldwork organized by Estonian and Hungarian universities and academic research institutes.

Encyclopedic handbooks began to be published elsewhere, and summaries of research appeared every ten years or so. Of these, the overview written by Ivar Paulson (1922–1966), an Estonian emigrant scholar of religion in Sweden, should be mentioned. It provides a phenomenological synthesis of the religions of northern Eurasian hunting nations and uses the new ethnographic and archaeological data. Paulson's study was published in the third volume of *Die Religion der Menschheit* (1962). A second modern overview, written by Lauri Honko, was published in the first volume of *Das Handbuch der Religionsgeschichte* (1971). In its shortened English version titled "Finno-Ugric Religion," written for the *Encyclopaedia Britannica* (1974), Honko made this kind of observation: "Today there is general agreement that a hypothetical reconstruction representing the 'original religion' of a single language family is virtually impossible."

The second volume of the encyclopedic undertaking of Soviet researchers on myths of the peoples of the world (*Mify narodov mira,* 1982) includes an entry by V. Ia. Petrukhin and E. A. Helimski, who do not even attempt to provide a comprehensive picture, but instead discuss the mythologies of different peoples separately. This is in accordance with the notion that Finno-Ugric languages are distantly related, as are their folklore and religions. Despite the difficulties on editing folkloric texts constituting the basic sources, a few exceptional monographs have been produced that, though not aiming at a reconstruction of the whole system, nevertheless enable us to engage in comparative studies of certain topics. These topics include, for example, lower-order spirits, totemism, and the cult of idols (Haekel, 1946), hunting rituals and the bear cult (Edsman, 1957), and concepts of the soul of the northern Eurasian peoples (Paulson, 1958).

Late Twentieth-Century Russian Research Trends. In the latter part of the twentieth century, some new results were gained in certain areas, especially in the Soviet Union as a result of an effort to involve other sciences in comparative mythological research and thus to revive its methodological tools. Soviet researchers turned to archaeology, which is "materialistic," and to the cataloging of decorative art objects, which were seen as products of the mythological consciousness of ancient peoples. A characteristic monograph of these times is S. V. Ivanov's work about the folk arts of the peoples of Siberia. This book reviews museum collections assembled around the turn of the twentieth century (*Materialy po izobrazitel'nomu iskusstvu narodov Sibiri XIX-nachalo XX. V.*, 1954). This study, which contains both Finno-Ugric and other material, becomes especially interesting when read with the study by Dmitrii K. Zelenin (1878–1954) of Siberian idol cults and beliefs in spirits (*Le culte des idoles en Siberie,* 1952).

Russian archaeologists have been able to contribute most significantly to the reconstruction of ancient beliefs, and thus of Finno-Ugric mythology, by interpreting the highly diverse physical evidence. A few of the valuable works containing such analyses are Vanda Moshinskai's *Drevniaia skulptura Urala i Zapadnoi Sibiri* (Ancient sculptures of the Ural and western Siberia; 1976); Leonilla A. Golubeva's *Zoomorfnye ukrasheniia finno-ugrov* (Finno-Ugric zoomorphic decorative art; 1979); and Liubov S. Gribova's *The Animal Style as One of the Components of Social-Ideological System of Totemism and Stage in the Development of Fine Arts* (1980).

Soviet archaeologists can be credited with the discovery of another important source group: petroglyphs, or rock art. During the last decades, remains of rock art have been extensively uncovered (mostly in the form of engravings) in northern Eurasia. In this discovery Aleksandr P. Okladnikov (1908–1981) had a particularly outstanding role; with his coworkers he has published a series of monographs that contain more than ten thousand Siberian rock drawings and include valuable notes on the history of religions. His major contribution to Finno-Ugric research, written with A. I. Martinov, is *Sokrovishcha tomskikh pisamits* (Treasures of petroglyphs around Tomsk; 1972).

Aleksandr Zolotarev (1907–1943) began his research in the 1930s, under the influence of Marxist conceptions of ancient history and society, but his study of the mythology of ancient society, *Rodovoi stroi i pervobytnaia mifologiia* (Tribal system and ancient mythology; 1964), could be published only after his death. In this study, Zolotarev bases his arguments on a large body of source materials and shows that the dualistic cosmological myths and the dualistic societies of Siberian peoples reflected one another; basically, this recognition resembles Georges Dumézil's position. Zolotarev arranged his materials within a firm theoretical framework. Because of his recognition of the system of dual oppositions, he can be considered a forerunner of structuralism, though his work remains unknown to the West.

COMPARATIVE FINNO-UGRIC MYTHOLOGY AND SHAMANHOOD RESEARCH TRADITIONS. The introduction by Soviet scholars of structuralist and semiotic methods to mythological analyses at the beginning of the 1970s proved to be a methodological turning point. These scholars were independent of the West European (primarily French) structuralists in that they formed their own theories, basing them on their structuralist predecessors—for example, Roman Jakobson (1896–1982), Ol'ga Freidenberg (1910–1954), Vladimir Propp (1895–1970), and Mikhail Bakhtin (1895–1975). Their most important contention was that mythology is explicable as a system of signs and that it is one of the texts or codes of a culture (Ivanov and Toporov, 1973; Meletinsky, 1973). In his description of the Finno-Ugric mythological system, Mihály Hoppál employs this method. The hierarchy of the gods is described with the aid of dual oppositions functioning as distinctive features (Hoppál, 1976), and consequently mythological structures clarified through semantic characteristics are compared more accurately than before (Toporov, 1974).

Another current trend is related to comparative mythology emphasized by such Finnish scholars of phenomenology of religion and folk belief in the Finno-Ugric context as Martti Haavio, Lauri Honko, and Juha Pentikäinen. The research is related to the fact that in studying certain topics, scholars have moved outside the narrow Finno-Ugric confines and are analyzing particular topics within a wider Uralian or even Eurasian context, as in, for example, the investigation of the question of a supposed ancient Eurasian mother cult, bear and other expressions of animal ceremonialism, as well as shamanism in a Finno-Ugric, Arctic, and comparative context. Pentikäinen's *Kalevala Mythology* (1999) emphasizes the significance of shamanic poetry as the basis of the epical singing. Instead of shamanism, a concept of shamanhood (Russian *samanstvo*) has been introduced by him since he believes that shamanism is not a dogmatic religion, but rather a way of life.

The examination of shamanism has an especially old tradition among Hungarian scholars. Géza Róheim (1891–1953), the founder of psychoanalytic anthropology, devoted an interesting chapter to the question of Ob-Ugrian shamanism in *Hungarian and Vogul Mythology* (1954). Another study of this subject was written by Vilmos Diószegi (1923–1972), who explored the residues of shamanism in Hungarian folklore in *A sámánhit emlékei a magyar népi müveltségben* (1958). Two further studies on the question of Siberian shamanism have been published: *The Rite Technique of the Siberian Shaman* (1978), by Anna-Leena Siikala, and *Obriad i fol'klor v sibirskom shamanizme* (Ritual and folklore in Siberian shamanism; 1984), by Elena S. Novik, who analyzes the syntagmatic structure of shamanic ritual and of narrative folklore.

In summary one could say that, because Finno-Ugric peoples are generally not numerous, and because most of them have constituted ethnic minorities within the Soviet Union and Russia, their search for common roots and mythology, expressed in the language of folklore, has been one way of establishing their own identity and of buttressing their national self-consciousness. Finno-Ugric mythology and folklore will remain as areas of interest for many years to come. Apart from sociopolitical considerations, naturally, the strictly scientific-philological aspects are no less compelling, a fact that renders the prospect of comparative Finno-Ugric mythological research in the future exceptionally interesting in terms of methodology as well, precisely because of the still insufficiently clarified relations among Finno-Ugric peoples, because of their divergent lines of cultural progress and because of their varied relations with neighboring peoples.

SEE ALSO Castrén, Matthias Alexander; Donner, Kai; Haavio, Martti; Honko, Lauri; Indo-European Religions, article on History of Study; Laestadius, Lars Levi; Lönnrot, Elias; Sami Religion; Study of Religion, article on the Academic Study of Religion in Eastern Europe and Russia.

BIBLIOGRAPHY

Chernetsov, V. N. "Concepts of the Soul among the Ob Ugrians." In *Studies in Siberian Shamanism*, edited by Henry N. Michael, pp. 3–45. Toronto, 1963. One of the basic studies by the father of Finno-Ugric archaeology that is based on his own collection.

Corradi, Carla. *Le divinita femminili nella mitologia ugro-finnica.* Parma, Italy, 1982. A modern summary on female divinity.

Diószegi, Vilmos. *A pogány magyarok hitvilága.* Budapest, 1967. A reconstruction of the old Hungarian pagan mythological worldview in terms of shamanism.

Diószegi, Vilmos. *Tracing Shamans in Siberia: The Story of an Ethnographic Research Expedition.* Oosterhout, Netherlands, 1968.

Diószegi, Vilmos, and Mihály Hoppál, eds. *Shamanism in Siberia.* Budapest, 1978. A collection of studies on different aspects of shamanism.

Dömötör, Tekla. *Hungarian Folk Beliefs.* Bloomington, Ind., 1982. The most up-to-date outline of the Hungarian folk belief system.

Edsman, Carl-Martin. *Bärenfest.* Tübingen, Germany, 1957.

Ferdinandy, Michael de. "Die Mythologie der Ungarn." In *Wörterbuch der Mythologie*, edited by H. W. Haussig, vol. 1, pp. 211–259. Stuttgart, 1965. Since this study lists historical legends from medieval chronicles as its mythological sources, it is somewhat romantic in its outlook. Regardless, it contains rich material.

Glavatskaia, Elena. "Religious and Ethnic Identity among the Khanty: Processes of Change." In *Identity and Gender in Hunting and Gathering Societies.* Senri Ethnological Studies 56. Osaka, Japan, 2001.

Goldthwait-Väänänen. Helsinki, 1952. In this book, an orpheic figure is introduced as a shaman on the basis of rich shamanic epical poetry in folklore behind the *Kalevala.*

Haavio, Martti. *Essais folkloriques: Par Martti Haavio.* Edited by Lauri Honko et al. Helsinki, 1959. Haavio's essays in both German and English cover such topics as haunting soul beings and cultic places in Finnish folk religion.

Haavio, Martti. *Suomalainen mytologia.* Porvoo, Finland, 1967. The most detailed account of Finnish mythology to date that lists the gods and provides much material for comparative purposes, but one should read it with critical distance.

Haekel, J. "Idolkult und Dualsystem bei den Ugriern." *Archiv für Völkerkunde* 1 (1946): 95–163.

Hajdú, Peter, ed. *Ancient Cultures of the Uralian Peoples.* Translated by György Déry. Budapest, 1976. This study discusses the history of Uralic languages and the folklore, mythology, and folk poetry of the Uralic peoples.

Harva, Uno. *Die Wassergottheiten der finnisch-ugrischen Völker.* Helsinki, 1913.

Harva, Uno. *Über die Jagdriten der Nördlichen Völker Asiens und Europas.* Helsinki, 1925.

Harva, Uno. *Die Religion der Tscheremissen.* Edited by Arno Bussenius. Helsinki, 1926.

Harva, Uno. "Finno-Ugric Mythology." In *Mythology of All Races.* Vol. 4. Boston, 1927. To date the most detailed summary of the ancient religious beliefs of the Finno-Ugric peoples.

Harva, Uno. *Die religiösen Vorstellungen der Mordwinen.* Helsinki, 1952.

Honko, Lauri, Senni Timonen, and Michael Branch, eds. *The Great Bear: A Thematic Anthology of Oral Poetry in the Finno-Ugrian Languages.* Helsinki, 1993. A large collection of text, both original and translated, that deals with, for example, cosmology, hunting, the soul, healing, and death. It provides a good introduction to every field.

Hoppál, Mihály. "Folk Beliefs and Shamanism among the Uralic Peoples." In *Ancient Cultures of the Uralian Peoples,* edited by Peter Hajdú and translated by György Déry, pp. 215–242. Budapest, 1976. An outline and a semiotic description of beliefs and mythological worldview of the Finno-Ugric peoples, with special references to the main features of shamanism.

Hoppál, Mihály, ed. *Shamanism in Eurasia.* 2 vols. Göttingen, Germany, 1984. Based on a symposium on various aspects of Eurasian shamanism.

Ivanov, V. V., and V. N. Toporov. "Towards the Description of Ket Semiotic Systems." *Semiotica* 9 (1973).

Kannisto, Artturi. *Materialen zur Mythologie der Wogulen: Gesammelt von Artturi Kannisto.* Helsinki, 1958. One of the best and most credible mythological text collections of the Ob-Ugrians.

Karsten, Rafael. *The Religion of the Samek: Ancient Beliefs and Cults of the Scandinavian and Finnish Lapps.* Leiden, 1955. An overview of the gods of Sami mythology, shamanism, religious sacrifices, and cult of the dead. Even though it is based on the emphasis of animism theory, it is a thorough work.

Kuusi, Matti, Keith Bosley, and Michael Branch, eds. *Finnish Folk Poetry—Epic: An Anthology in Finnish and English.* Helsinki, 1977. The volume contains the authentic texts of the original folksingers' versions of the *Kalevala,* with numerous and thorough notes.

Laestadius, Lars Levi. *Fragments in Lappish Mythology.* Edited by Juha Pentikäinen. Helsinki, 2000.

Lehtinen, Ildikó, ed. *Traces of Central Asian Culture in the North.* Translated by Elayne Antalffy, Márta Cserháti, and Péter Simoncsics. Helsinki, 1986.

Loorits, Oskar. *Grundzüge des Estnischen Volksglaubens.* Vols. 1–3. Lund, Sweden, 1949–1957. The most complete overview of Estonian folk superstitions to date with abundant original texts and details.

Meletinsky, E. M. "Typological Analysis of the Paleo-Asiatic Raven Myths." *Acta Ethnographica* 22 (1973): 107–155.

Paulson, Ivar. *Die primitiven Seelenvorstellungender nordeurasischen Völker: Eine religionsethnographische und religionsphänomenologische Untersuchung.* Stockholm, 1958.

Paulson, Ivar. *The Old Estonian Folk Religion.* Translated by Juta Kõvamees Kitching and H. Kõvamees. Bloomington, Ind., 1971. A system reconstructed on the basis of Estonian folk beliefs, published after Paulson's death, and probably unfinished.

Pentikäinen, Juha. *Shamanism and Culture.* 3d ed. Helsinki, 1998.

Pentikäinen, Juha. *Kalevala Mythology.* Translated and edited by Ritva Poom. Bloomington, Ind., 1999.

Siikala, Anna-Leena, ed. *Myth and Mentality: Studies in Folklore and Popular Thought.* Helsinki, 2002.

Toporov, V. N. "On the Typological Similarity of Mythological Structures among the Ket and Neighbouring Peoples." *Semiotica* 10 (1974): 19–42.

Vilkuna, Asko. *Das Verhalten der Finnen in "heiligen" (pyhä) Situationen.* Helsinki, 1956.

MIHÁLY HOPPÁL (1987)
JUHA PENTIKÄINEN (2005)
Translated from Hungarian by Timea Szell

FIQH SEE UṢŪL AL-FIQH

FIRE. In early stages of civilization, humans learned to create fire by striking flint, drilling wood, and focusing solar rays. Myths attributed this wondrous, crucial acquisition to the daring of a culture hero, theft from a primordial bird or animal, burglary of heaven and obstinate gods who withheld it, emanation from the vagina of an old woman, or sometimes the outright gift of a divine being. Recognized as ambiguously creative and destructive, life-giving and life-taking, fire appeared in multiple mysteries of transmutation: of environs from cold, dark, and dangerous to warm, light, and secure; of food from raw to cooked; of substance from putrid to pure; of fields from sterile brush to fertile earth; of earth from ore to metal; of human bodies from disease to health; of spirits from profane to sacred; and of speech from babble to wisdom. Fire was identified in animals, plants, earth, air, and water. The human body contained its own fires of digestion, sexuality, and wrath, with fires in the blood, breath, semen, mind, heart, and spleen.

As the alchemist liberated secret interior fires from certain minerals, so with fire the smith accelerated nature's process by cooking and molding minerals into precious goods. Fire was appropriated by the shaman in the sweat lodge, by the *yogin* meditating as a fifth fire between four others, by the Australian aboriginal novice symbolically roasted and purified over a pit-fire, by the hero whose fury incinerated enemy warriors. In ancient India the hearth was said to be a womb and a householder was not born until he and his wife established sacrificial fires. Chinese esoteric alchemists spurned the smelting fire of the exoteric alchemist because a quest for immortality demanded the superior fire in the mind. Certain Native American tribes believed their ritual fires regenerated the sun and their new fires rekindled the new year. In modern Scandinavia some farmers of the old school still drilled new fire by hand to cure sick cows. Many religious traditions, ancient and contemporary, foresee a celestial or cosmic fire that will destroy the world, as it has in the past.

Fire has been adopted as a metaphor—for some, the only metaphor—of sublime, ineffable, transformative experiences in the spiritual quests of specialists of the sacred, and in works by mystics, philosophers, and writers as disparate as Richard of Saint-Victor, Dante Alighieri, and Blaise Pascal. Understanding across times and cultures responds to an early fourteenth-century voice, that of Richard Rolle de Hampole: "when settled in devotion . . . my soul is set on fire." Western ascetics and saints gained renown as living flames, like legendary salamanders with miraculous immunity to fire, while different traditions of Asia produced similar handlers of fire, and walkers on fire, who demonstrated superhuman status in kinship and seeming unity with the powerful element.

The cultic dimensions of fire are varied and countless. Some societies chose to center tradition on domestic hearths and community fire altars, with extensive links to sacred oral or written texts, while others held fire in supporting mythic and ritual roles. The discussion that follows must of necessity be selective and illustrative, not comprehensive.

ANCIENT INDIA AND IRAN AND SUBSEQUENT TRADITIONS. The oldest and most coherent body of myths, rituals, and symbols of fire is found in the Vedas of ancient India and the remnant Avestan and Pahlavi texts of ancient Iran. There are parallels in both domestic and community cults of fire, and between Indic *soma* and Iranian *haoma* (Indo-Iranian **sauma*), both essential offerings to deities poured into sacrificial fires. These, along with other key names and rituals, indicate an Indo-Iranian tradition of fire maintained by nomadic pastoralists in West Asia several centuries before and after 2000 BCE. Oral mythologies and ritual references collected in the *Ṛgveda* and *Atharvaveda* from around 1400 to 1000 BCE include some 200 hymns addressed to the god of fire, Agni. The opening verse of the *Ṛgveda* addresses him as Purohita, a hearth deity who is domestic priest within every household as well as priest for all the gods. In other Vedic Saṃhitās such as the *Yajurveda,* there appeared elaborate ritual schedules based on the identity of fire and the householder-sacrificer. Subsequent Brāhmaṇa texts explored the nature and function of this fire cult, which remained a focus for both household and expanded cooperative ritual programs. The tenth book of the *Śatapatha Brāhmaṇa* is *Agni Rahasya,* the "mystery of the fire altar," an esoteric text that set a precedent for philosophical speculations in the Upaniṣads.

In turn, by around 700 BCE these Upaniṣads generated a new worldview for Vedic Hinduism. Each of the two earliest contains the same teaching on *saṃsāra* (transmigration). After death, one not released from rebirths returns from the moon and passes through five sacrificial fires, the fourth being a man who offers his semen into a woman; the fruit of this fifth sacrifice is a new embryo. In the same period compendia of manuals known as sūtras systematized schedules of cooperative *(Śrauta)* and then domestic *(Gṛhya)* fire sacrifices that have lasted to the present time. Also in this pivotal era various techniques of asceticism grew into prominence, including the production of inner heat *(tapas)* by means of various austerities. Cosmic-human bodily correspondences were explored in yet another way with these new expressions of fire and heat.

As the god Agni himself is a cosmic triad, so there should be three fires set in every household, and still in India today there are *āhitāgnis,* secluded maintainers of Agni in their houses as *āhavanīya* (offering fire), *gārhapatya* (preparatory fire), and *dakṣiṇāgni* (protective southern fire). The *agnihotra,* morning and evening offerings of hot milk, comprise the basic domestic sacrifice. These now-rare three-fire sacrificers are eligible, as in ancient Vedic practice, to advance to the sacrifice of *soma* and then selected other *śrauta* rituals. The *yajamāna* (sacrificer) carries a terra-cotta bowl of fire in identification with Agni and with another Vedic god, Prajāpati, as world-creator. Solemn rituals include the forty-day *pauṇḍarīka,* employing seventeen priests with both animal and *soma* offerings in a type of *agnicayana* fire sacrifice reintegrating time and space in a cosmic construction of Agni. Five layers of thousands of bricks shape a gigantic eagle with the *ātman,* the Self, at the center, indicating that the sacrificer and fire are one. A striking feature of these contemporary survivals of ancient practice is the generation of Agni by friction from *araṇis* (male and female wooden drilling sticks). These have a capacity to absorb all three fires into themselves for transport if the *āhitāgni* and *patnī* (wife) must travel away from the house and constant tending of fires.

Confirmation of a belief in the identity of householder and fire is found both in the Vedic cremation ritual, in which the sacrificer or his wife is burned with the three sacrificial fires, literally absorbed by them in *antyeṣṭi,* a "final sacrifice," and, in another direction, in the vow to become a *saṃnyāsin,* a renunciant ascetic. *Saṃnyāsa* calls for the interiorization of fires, ritual deposition of fires in the self, and therefore an end to the external sacrifices that have previously structured life. Since the *saṃnyāsin's* breaths are the five cosmic fires, his *agnihotra* becomes the constant offering of *prāṇa* (breath).

Great Vedic fire sacrifices such as the *agnicayana, aśvamedha* (royal horse sacrifice), or *rājasūya* (consecration of a king) have not been a prominent feature of Hinduism since the late medieval period, and the god Agni himself has been reduced to minor status since the emergence of the Sanskrit epics and Purāṇas. But the role of fire in Hinduism has never diminished. Life-cycle rites *(saṃskāras)* are an array of ceremonies from conception and birth to cremation, the last still defined by the final offering of the body to Agni Kravyād, consumer of the deceased, on the funeral pyre. *Saṃskāras* depend on ritually kindled fires with domestic priests or householders themselves reciting either Vedic mantras or Sanskrit verses. As a complement to household worship, which is usually focused on images or symbols of favorite goddesses and gods assembled close to the kitchen hearth, Hindus may go to neighborhood temples and shrines for *devapūjā,* public worship. Inside temples housing a form of Devī, Viṣṇu, Śiva, or another deity, priests conduct on behalf of the visitor a schedule of worship, invariably including *ārati,* the waving of a lighted lamp or burning incense before the sacred image.

There are numerous fire festivals with bonfires, lamps, and fireworks in Hinduism. Dīvālī (Dīpāvalī) is a popular occasion for setting out multitudes of burning lights *(dīpas)* in October–November. In honor of *pitṛs* (ancestors), tiny bamboo boats carry hundreds of burning lamps down the nearest river. Torches are carried in rural communities in circumambulation around the entire village for certain festivals, and passage of all residents under arches of burning straw may be practiced at harvest time. A favorite vow in villages and towns of South India and Sri Lanka is firewalking, at times featuring hundreds of people crossing in single file a thirty-foot-long pit of glowing embers to the sounds of thunderous drums and shrill flutes. At other times a single person, possessed by a deity or the deified dead, may walk on coals, "play" with fire, dance with burning skewers, swallow burning charcoal, or hold burning camphor on the palm of the hand, all as demonstrations of divine power and grace. Devotion to a fierce goddess such as Pattini, Draupadī, Mārīamma, Poleramma, or some other manifestation of Amma (Mother) is thereby tested, and the unscathed devotee gains the goddess's protection against epidemic diseases and other misfortunes. Firewalking is performed by Fiji Island migrant Hindus in the South Pacific, by Buddhist as well as Hindu devotees of the popular god Kataragama (Skanda) in Sri Lanka, and by Shīʿī Muslims in South Asia, particularly during the annual festival of Muḥarram.

This sketch of South Asia over four millennia may be paralleled in greater Iran, where spiritual identifications of humans with fire occur on similar levels: individual, family-household, village, and in the case of kingship rituals, state. However, by comparison with India's still enduring oral traditions and Vedic-Hindu historical continuity in ritual, evidence for ancient Iranian cults of fire is limited first by a break in oral traditions and loss of much of the early written record, then by dispersal of Zoroastrians themselves during the medieval advance of Islam. What survives, however, indicates the centrality of the household hearth *(ātash dādgāh),* along with extended community *(ātash ādarān)* and royal or primary fires *(ātash bahrām)* and sacrifices similar to the pattern of Vedic Indo-Aryans to the east. A cosmic five-fire worldview, again as in India, complemented this basic triad, all based on a system of correspondences between natural fire and ritual fire. Among several major differences, however, was the emergence in Iran of permanent temples, "houses of a fire" enthroned on raised pedestals, perhaps under the influence of surrounding temple-building cultures of urban West Asia. Although fireplaces have been excavated in Bactria and Margiana (northern Afghanistan and southern Turkmenistan), in sites in the path of Indo-Iranian migrations from around 2500 to 1500 BCE, other than traces of ephedra (possibly *haoma*) there is little evidence regarding the beliefs and rituals of those who used them. It was not until the fourth century BCE that Achaemenid rulers of greater Iran erected temples of perpetual fire. Barely surviving two millennia of political and religious warfare, temples with fire in metal containers still serve today as spiritual centers for remnant Zoroastrians in Iran and for Parsis in western India who maintain eight *bahrām* fires.

Fire emerged as the basic symbol of Zoroastrianism, the religion that developed in the first half of the first millennium BCE, probably from the teachings of Zarathushtra in the *Gāthās.* The ancient Indo-Iranian deities were submerged into a cult of one "Wise Lord," Ahura Mazdā, although they resurfaced as his entities or qualities in a set of six *Amesha Spentas* (Beneficent immortals). Most prominent among them is Asha, the equivalent of Vedic *ṛta* (cosmic order). Asha, a quality of Ahura Mazdā—at one point recognized as an independent deity, Asha Vahishta—symbolizes truth and justice, and was represented by fire. The sun and light are visible forms of Ahura Mazdā, but above all he is fire. An ethical dualism presented a clear opposition in which the symbols of *asha*—fire, light, purity, and goodness—are on the side of Ahura Mazdā against *druj* (the lie), associated with darkness, impurity, and evil. In meditation, personal piety, and sacrifice (*yasna,* Avestan parallel to Vedic *yajña*) a worshiper relates to fire and participates in this cosmic, but also immediately human conflict. The offering into fires of sacrificial animals, particularly their fat, and of pressed *haoma* juice was suppressed by Zarathushtra, but these age-old rituals resurfaced in a later period. Among Parsis today only *haoma* is sacrificed. A symbolic libation of fat occurs only in funerals.

Aside from permanent fire temples, other features distinguish the Iranian fire cult from its Vedic-Hindu counterpart. The sovereign Vedic god Varuṇa governs *ṛta* (cosmic order), while in the case of Varuṇa's Avestan complement, Ahura Mazdā, *asha* is itself the representation of fire. In Iran, disposal of the dead was not by cremation, as in India, but rather by exposure, as seen with the famous stone towers still used today by Parsis in India. Fire burns nearby, but birds and beasts of prey are allowed to clean flesh from bone, thus protecting sacred fire from the pollution of death. Even human breath is polluting, and mouth-veils are worn by sacrificing, fire-tending priests, the only persons who may approach the altars.

Regarding fire, yet another distinction from Indo-Aryan tradition pertains to time. Vedic sacrifices reveal a cyclic pattern, as in the Rājasūya sacrifice used to consecrate kings, in which one performance, when completed, is immediately followed by preparations for another. The Purāṇas continued this model with the *pralaya* principle, based on an endless repetition of dissolutions and re-creations of the cosmos, destructions being total incineration by one or another form of Agni. Zoroastrianism, on the other hand, introduced a sense of final time and divine judgment, with eschatological fire expected on the last day in a one-time cataclysm. In historic time, judgment occurs routinely, as in ordeals by fire to test veracity and loyalty, but the day of final judgment awaits the future after resolution of the conflict of *asha* and *druj,* the light of truth and darkness of the lie, in favor of Ahura Mazdā and his eternal flame.

The Ancient Mediterranean. A fire altar *(bomos)* in a sacred precinct *(temenos)* was an essential feature of ancient religious practice for Greeks. The cult depended, as in India and Iran, on sacrifice to deities with commensal sharing of victims. Hesiod and Homer speak of the fat-wrapped thighbones of an ox, cuts of meat, and wine offered on the altar fire. Open fire pits opposite a temple entrance were standard, although some older temples had interior hearths. Hestia burned perpetually in her temple at Delphi, as a flame and with no image necessary to represent her. And in every home the hearth was the sacred center, a site of offerings, and a space where none could be violated.

In Hesiod's *Theogony,* Prometheus deceives and angers Zeus during a sacrifice of ox bones by stealing an ember from the altar and kindling the first fire to burn on earth. The Homeric *Hymn to Demeter* preserves an archaic legend of Eleusinian mysteries, the goddess Demeter's attempt to deify the boy Demophoon by secretly holding him in the hearth fire at night. That ritual, interrupted by the terrified mother, Metaneira, fails and the boy remains mortal. Again, as in India and Iran, cosmic correspondences exist between fire, breath (*pneuma,* Latin *spiritus*), and mind. The worldview of Heraclitus of Ephesus (c. 540–480 BCE) began with fire, an uncreated, eternal substance, essence of the universe, and medium of creation, associated with logos, mind, reason, and wisdom. The Pythagoreans, Parmenides of Elea, and Empedocles were other philosophers placing elemental fire in prominence.

The bare patch of ground on the Palatine Hill may not be "the hearth of Romulus," as claimed by today's tour guides, but ancient Rome did have its dual fire cults of domestic hearth, which received part of the meal before the family dined, and public altar (*ara* or *altaria*) with its own adjoining hearth. Vesta, Roman parallel to Hestia, was in a uniquely round temple without an image, her eternal flame being sufficient representation on what was essentially the hearth of the city, tended—like any domestic hearth—by females, six appointed Vestal Virgins tasked with kindling a new fire by friction every New Year's Day, March 1. On April 21, Pales, goddess of herders and their animals, was honored through the staging of Parilia, a festival including the racing of men and animals through burning straw, similar to one occurring in India today. The temple of Volcanus stood outside the city walls, a reminder of other fires: the dangerously destructive one sleeping in the heights of Vesuvius and Aetna, and the summer fires of cropfields and granaries.

Two centuries after Heraclitus, Stoic philosophers, including Zeno, Cleanthes, and others, elaborated Heraclitus's belief in fire as a basic element associated with logos as universal reason and regulative principle. The doctrine of seminal logos *(logos spermatikos)* led to belief in individual beings as immortal sparks from a divine fiery unity, a view adopted with modifications by Jewish, Christian, Gnostic, and other philosophical traditions. In the new Hellenistic culture acquainted with the wider world of Asia, several elements derived from early Upaniṣads (c. 700 BCE) are evident, including the notion of the individual soul, destined eventually to rejoin that original fiery unity, departing this earth for the moon.

ANCIENT ISRAEL, JUDAISM, CHRISTIANITY, AND ISLAM. To a limited extent scriptures of the two biblical traditions and Islam consciously separated the supreme being from the natural phenomenon of fire. And yet all three employed numerous symbols, beliefs, and folklore concerning the element of fire and associated phenomena of light. Only ancient Israel had a cult of fire maintained for animal sacrifices on a temple or open-air altar in the pattern of West Asia and, to a lesser extent, Egypt. With the destruction of the Second Temple in Jerusalem in 70 CE, sacrificial fire—along with the Temple and the altar—became eschatological symbols. Early Christian churches with wooden tables as altars for the symbolic sacrifice known as Eucharist, and Islamic mosques as houses of prayer, like synagogues, had place for discreet lamps but not open fire. The Shabbat lamp and the altar candle still serve as fire in miniature.

To a degree, all three religions were influenced by Zoroastrianism, as is particularly evident in postexilic Judaism and in a widespread belief in opposing angels and demons. Most important were apocalyptic and other eschatological imprints in the notions of a fiery last day of judgment, of hell as a place of flaming torment, and of a God who pursues the unrighteous with punishing fire. On the other hand, all three faiths produced mystics of independent and solitary vision and experience, some associated with sublime expressions of fire, heat, and love.

When Solomon prayed before the bronze altar "fire came down from heaven and consumed the burnt offering and the sacrifice and the glory of the Lord filled the temple" (*2 Chron.* 7:1). In a striking theophany Moses saw the angel of the Lord in the midst of a burning bush that was not consumed (*Exod.* 3:2), and in the flight from Egypt through the wilderness the Lord led the people of Israel in a pillar of cloud by day, a pillar of fire by night (*Exod.* 13:21–22). Believers are protected from destructive fire: "When you walk through fire you shall not be burned, and the flame shall not consume you. For I am the Lord your God" (*Isa.* 43:2). Shadrach, Meshach, and Abednego were not harmed when thrown into a fiery furnace for refusing to worship an image of gold (*Dan.* 3:1–30). "A chariot of fire and horses of fire" took Elijah "up by a whirlwind into heaven" (*2 Kings* 2:11). "My heart grew hot within me," says David in Psalm 39.3, "as I meditated, the fire burned; then I spoke with my tongue."

In the New Testament the sound of a mighty wind accompanied the arrival of the Holy Spirit that appeared to the apostles of Jesus as "tongues of fire, distributed and resting on each one of them" (*Acts* 2:1–4). Peter's second letter instructs that heaven and earth will be burned up on the day of the Lord (3:10), and *Revelation,* the Apocalypse of John, warns sinners of an end "in the lake that burns with fire and brimstone, which is the second death" (21.8). Early Christian desert saints of Egypt such as Abba Joseph of Panephysis, continuing the imagery of the Holy Spirit, were witnessed as flaming fires. The third-century church "father," Origen, foresaw a purification on the last day: Jesus will stand in a fiery river to baptize by fire all who enter paradise.

Fire and light play prominent roles in the extracanonical literature of Judaism and Christianity, and in Gnostic texts, particularly in various apocalypses. Developing traditions of Jewish mysticism and collections of Jewish legend (Haggadah) were significant in this regard. In a Haggadah account of creation it is said that the preexistent Torah was written with black fire on white fire, as she (the Torah) was lying in the lap of God. The *Gospel of Thomas* quotes Jesus as saying, "He who is near me is near the fire" (82), but also "I have come to cast upon earth fire, sword and war" (16), and the *Apocalypse of Peter* reveals the day of God with cataracts of fire, "a fierce fire that shall not be put out and it flows for the judgment of wrath" (4). Given the influence of Iranian traditions, it is not surprising to find parallels to cosmic conflict in the Qumran scroll "The War of the Sons of Light with the Sons of Darkness" and in the Gnostic "Paraphrase of Shem," with its visions of chaotic fires.

Elijah's chariot of fire, reminiscent of both Vedic and ancient Iranian chariots of fire-sacrificers, and Daniel's vision of "a throne of fiery flames with wheels of burning fire" (7:9) became foundational images of the divine throne-chariot *(merkabah)* for many centuries of mystical texts and schools. Enoch's vision, similar to Daniel's, records a heavenly throne of fire in a blazing mansion, with the Lord speaking to him from streams of fire. He is also given a tour of Hell with its rivers of fire *(I Enoch)*. The thirteenth-century Zohar, the seminal text for Qabbalah, identifies the ten *sefirot,* primordial numbers and emanations of light and power from the divine unity, a process later believed by qabbalists to include dissemination of sparks from that one source.

Inspirational to generations of Ḥasidim are stories of charismatic *rebbes* such as Baʿal Shem Tov (c. 1700–1760), known as the BeSHT. Once an overnight guest in his house, awakened at midnight in terror by a great flame rising from the hearth, fainted upon realizing it was the BeSHT. Another Hasidic *rebbe,* the Maggid of Mezeritch (1704–1772), sent his followers fleeing in panic by appearing suddenly as a being of fire.

The mystics of European Christianity often spoke and wrote of being consumed in ecstasy by *incendium amoris,* "the fire of love." Saints Augustine of Hippo (354–430), Gregory I (the Great) (c. 540–604), John of the Cross (Juan de la Cruz, 1542–1591), Catherine of Genoa (1447–1510), and Teresa of Ávila (d. 1582), the hermit Richard Rolle de Hampole (c. 1290–1349), and the philosopher Jakob Boehme (1575–1624) all used a language of fire and heat to convey the impact of mystical transformations or unitive states. Rolle speaks for many: "[T]he heart that truly receives the fire of the Holy Ghost is burned wholly and turns as it were into fire; and it leads it into that form that is likest to God" (*Incendium amoris,* ch. 17).

In some Greek villages today, devotees of Saint Constantine (the Great) and his mother Saint Helena believe they are protected by the pair when performing a firewalk after sacrificing a bull and sharing the feast of Anestanaria. Brought to the United States by immigrants, this ritual was soon swept into the 1970s New Age practice of firewalking, with its goals of self-realization and experimentation rather than ritual or worship. Today the American firewalking movement holds workshops in scores of states and some universities offer courses on firewalking.

Several times the Qurʾān recounts Moses' theophany of fire, but most references are warnings to those who reject the truth and deserve horrendous flame and molten brass on the day of judgment. Anecdotes of the Prophet preserved in popular bazaar tracts include such miracles as the moment when Muḥammad halted the sun in its course. A rich hagiographical literature, particularly in association with the Ṣūfīs, details the experiences of *awliyāʿ* (friends) of Allāh, saints, and mystics included in collections from the eleventh and following centuries. Examples of Ṣūfīs handling fire or using a language of fire bring to mind the mystics of Christianity. Ḥasan al-Baṣrī (642–728) caused a "fire-worshiping" Zoroastrian to convert to Islam by thrusting his own hand into a fire and leaving it there unburned. Rābiʿah al-ʿAdawīyah (d. 810), Abū Yazīd al-Bisṭāmī (d. 874), Jalāl al-Dīn Rūmī (d. 1273), and Najm Dāyā Rāzī (thirteenth century) all broke restraints of law, theology and proper behavior to identify Allāh and fire, and at times themselves with both. Union with fire readily lent itself to the contested notion of *fānaʾ,* mystical annihilation. One Ṣūfī complained that he could not sleep because of his fear of hell-fire. Rābiʿah was said to have carried a torch and a pail of water, explaining that she intended to burn Paradise and douse Hell in order to eliminate both hindrances to a pure vision of Allāh. One dark night in Basra she had several visitors. Having no lantern, she blew upon her finger, which then lighted the room until sun-up. In the famous account of his "ascension" according to the Tadhkirat al-Auliya', Abū Yazīd, founder of the "drunken" school of mystics, spoke from his dark night of the soul: "In my intoxication . . . I melted my body in every crucible in the fire of jealousy." And Rūmī, ecstatic poet of Persian odes and originator of the Mevlevi (Mawlawīyah) whirling dervish dance, sang to his divine beloved, Shams al-Dīn: "Face like fire, wine like fire, love afire . . . soul . . . lamenting 'Whither shall I flee?'" (136.6).

SEE ALSO Light and Darkness.

BIBLIOGRAPHY

On fire in general, see four works by Mircea Eliade: *A History of Religious Ideas,* 3 vols., translated by Willard R. Trask et al. (Chicago, 1978–1985), *The Forge and the Crucible,* translated by Stephen Corrin (New York, 1962), *Shamanism: Archaic Techniques of Ecstasy,* translated by Willard R. Trask (New York, 1964), and *Mephistopheles and the Androgyne,* translated by J. M. Cohen (New York, 1965); also see Gaston Bachelard, *The Psychoanalysis of Fire,* translated by Alan C. M. Ross (Boston, 1964); Carl-Martin Edsman, *Ignis Divinus* (Lund, Sweden, 1949); and David M. Knipe, *In the Image of Fire: Vedic Experiences of Heat* (Delhi, 1975).

On fire in Indo-European cosmogony and eschatology, see Bruce Lincoln, *Myth, Cosmos, and Society: Indo-European Themes of Creation and Destruction* (Cambridge, Mass., 1986). On Indo-European, Indo-Iranian, and Eurasian steppe backgrounds to historic India and Iran, see Asko Parpola, "Pre-Proto-Iranians of Afghanistan as Initiators of Sākta Tantrism," *Iranica Antiqua* 37 (2002): 233–324, and his "From the Dialects of Old Indo-Aryan to Proto-Indo-Aryan and Proto-Iranian," in *Indo-Iranian Languages and Peoples,* edited by Nicholas Sims-Williams, pp.43–102 (Oxford, 2002). Also useful are J. P. Mallory, *In Search of the Indo-Europeans* (London, 1989) and Richard B. Onians, *The Origins of European Thought about the Body, the Mind, the Soul, the World, Time, and Fate,* 2d ed. (Cambridge, U.K., 1954).

On the Vedic fire cult, see Frits Staal, *Agni: The Vedic Ritual of the Fire Altar,* 2 vols. (Berkeley, Calif., 1983); Musashi Tachikawa, Shrikant Bahulkar, and Madhavi Kolhatkar, *Indian Fire Ritual* (Delhi, 2001); H. W. Bodewitz, *The Daily Evening and Morning Offering (Agnihotra)* (Leiden, Netherlands, 1976); and David M. Knipe, *In the Image of Fire* (Delhi, 1975).

On Hinduism, see Wendy Doniger [O'Flaherty], *Asceticism and Eroticism in the Mythology of Śiva* (London, 1973) and David G. White, *The Alchemical Body: Siddha Traditions in Medieval India* (Chicago, 1996).

On ancient Iran and Zoroastrianism, compare two books by Mary Boyce, *A History of Zoroastrianism,* 3 vols. (Leiden, 1975–91; vol. 3 by Mary Boyce and Frantz Grenet) and *Zoroastrians: Their Beliefs and Practices* (London, 1979), with two by Jacques Duchesne-Guillemin, *Symbols and Values in Zoroastrianism: Their Survival and Renewal* (New York, 1966) and *Religion of Ancient Iran,* translated by K. M. Jamasp Asa (Bombay, 1973). Other standard works include Stig Wikander, *Feuerpriester in Kleinasien und Iran* (Lund, Sweden, 1946) and Klaus Schippmann, *Die iranischen Feuerheiligtumer* (Berlin and New York, 1971). Still authoritative is Jivanji Jamshedji Modi, *The Religious Ceremonies and Customs of the Parsees,* 2d ed. (Bombay, 1937).

On fire cults in Java, Bali, Tibet, China, and Japan, see essays by C. Hooykaas, Tadeusz Skorupski, and Michel Strickmann in

Agni: The Vedic Ritual of the Fire Altar, vol. 2, edited by Frits Staal, pp. 382–455.

On the yin-yang school of ancient China, see Fung Yu-lan, *A History of Chinese Philosophy,* 2d ed., vol. 1, translated by Derk Bodde (Princeton, N.J., 1952) and Joseph Needham, *Science and Civilization in China,* vol. 2: *History of Scientific Thought* (Cambridge, U.K., 1956).

On ancient Greece, compare Walter Burkert, *Greek Religion,* translated by John Raffan (Cambridge, Mass., 1985) with *Le sacrifice dans l'antiquité,* edited by Jean-Pierre Vernant and Olivier Reverdin (Geneva, 1981); Marie Delcourt, *Pyrrhos et Pyrrha: Recherches sur les valeurs du feu dans les légendes helléniques* (Paris: 1965); Carl-Martin Edsman, *Ignis Divinus* (Lund, Sweden, 1949); and William D. Furley, *Studies in the Use of Fire in Ancient Greek Religion* (New York, 1981). On firewalking in modern Greece and the United States, see Loring M. Danforth, *Firewalking and Religious Healing: The Anastenaria of Greece and the American Firewalking Movement* (Princeton, N.J., 1989), Anna Gault-Antoniades, *The Anastenaria: Thracian Fire-walking Festival* (Athens, 1954), and William D. Furley, *Studies in the Use of Fire in Ancient Greek Religion* (New York, 1981).

On ancient Rome, see Georges Dumézil, *Archaic Roman Religion,* translated by Philip Krapp, 2 vols. (Chicago, 1970) and Robert Schilling, *Rites, cultes, dieux de Rome* (Paris, 1979).

On ancient Israel and Judaism, see Menahem Haran, *Temples and Temple-Service in Ancient Israel* (Oxford, 1978); two works written by Gershom G. Scholem, *Major Trends in Jewish Mysticism,* 3d rev. ed. (New York, 1954) and *On the Kabbalah and Its Symbolism,* translated by Ralph Manheim (New York, 1965), and one edited by him, *The Zohar: The Book of Splendor* (New York, 1949); Ithamar Gruenwald, *Apocalyptic and Merkavah Mysticism* (Leiden, 1980); Willis Barnstone, ed., *The Other Bible* (San Francisco, 1984); and Elie Wiesel, *Souls on Fire: Portraits and Legends of Hasidic Masters,* translated by Marion Wiesel (New York, 1972).

On Christianity, see Carl-Martin Edsman, *Le Baptême de feu* (Uppsala, Sweden, 1940); Richard Rolle de Hampole, *The Fire of Love,* translated by Richard Misyn and edited by F. M. M. Comper, 2d ed. (London, 1920); E. Allison Peers, *The Complete Works of Saint John of the Cross,* 3 vols. (London, 1934–1935); *The Letters of Saint Teresa,* translated by the Benedictines of Stanbrook Abbey, 4 vols. (London, 1921–1926); Jakob Boehme, *Aurora,* translated by John Sparrow (London, 1960); Evelyn Underhill, *Mysticism* (1911; reprint, New York, 1955); and a book edited by Walter H. Capps and Wendy M. Wright, *Silent Fire: An Invitation to Western Mysticism* (San Francisco, 1978.)

On Islamic saints and mystics, see Farīd al-Dīn ʿAṭṭār, *Muslim Saints and Mystics: Episodes from the Tadhkirat al-Auliyaʿ ("Memorial of the Saints"),* translated by A. J. Arberry (Chicago, 1966); *Mystical Poems of Rūmī,* translated by A. J. Arberry (Chicago, 1968); Annemarie Schimmel, *Mystical Dimensions of Islam* (Chapel Hill, N.C., 1975); and R. C. Zaehner, *Hindu and Muslim Mysticism* (New York, 1960).

On shamanism, in addition to Eliade, *Shamanism* (New York, 1964), see Jean-Paul Roux, "Fonctions chamaniques et valeurs du feu chez lex peuples altaiques," *Revue de l'histoire des religions* 189 (1976): 67–101.

On Native Americans, see Claude Lévi-Strauss, *The Raw and the Cooked,* translated by John and Doreen Weightman (New York, 1969); Lawrence E. Sullivan, *Icanchu's Drum: An Orientation to Meaning in South American Religions* (New York, 1988); Åke Hultkrantz, *The Religions of the American Indians,* translated by Monica Setterwall (Berkeley, Calif., 1967); and Reinhilde Freise, *Studie zum Feuer in Vorstellungswelt und Praktiken der Indianer des südwestlichen Nordamerika* (Tübingen, Germany, 1969).

For a penetrating structural study of a fire ritual among the Ndembu of Zambia, see Victor Turner, *The Ritual Process: Structure and Anti-Structure* (Chicago, 1969).

On Australian aboriginals, see Ronald M. Berndt and Catherine H. Berndt, *The World of the First Australians: An Introduction to the Traditional Life of the Australian Aborigines* (Chicago, 1964).

David M. Knipe (2005)

FIRTH, RAYMOND. Raymond Firth (1901–2002) was born in New Zealand and grew up in a rural area on the edge of Auckland. He attended Auckland Grammar School, where, at the age of fourteen, he found a copy of F. E. Maning's *Old New Zealand,* which, he said, laid a foundation for his interest in the indigenous Polynesian people of New Zealand, the Maori. As a schoolboy he also discovered the *Journal of the Polynesian Society* in the Auckland Public Library, became a reader, and later a contributor. In 1925 he published an article in the journal on a Maori *pa* site, and seventy-six years later, at the age of one hundred, an article by him on Tikopia dreams was published in the same journal.

Growing up in New Zealand, Firth had Maori friends and learned their language, which helped him acquire fluency in the cognate language of Tikopia, where he later carried out anthropological fieldwork. His interest in Maori ritual and belief laid a foundation for his later work on religion in Tikopia.

In 1921 Firth graduated in economics from what was then Auckland University College, and in 1924 he wrote a masters thesis on the kauri gum industry. He arrived at the London School of Economics in 1924 to work towards a doctorate in economics, intending to focus his work on the frozen meat industry in New Zealand. However, he came under the influence of the then professor of social anthropology Bronislaw Malinowski and changed the direction of his work. His thesis, *Primitive Economics of the New Zealand Maori,* was published in 1929.

In 1928 Firth set out for Tikopia, a small Polynesian outlier in the Solomon Islands, where he would carry out his first truly anthropological fieldwork. He would return to the island several times. His publications about Tikopia provide a corpus of work about a small preliterate society that is probably unrivaled, comprising nine books and some one hundred articles. His ethnography of the island, *We, the Tikopia* (1936), has been reprinted many times. It introduces Firth's analysis of traditional Polynesian religion, which he developed in later publications, including *The Work of the Gods in Tikopia* (1940), *History and Traditions of Tikopia* (1960), *Tikopia Ritual and Belief* (1967), and *Rank and Religion in Tikopia* (1970).

Firth has provided a unique record of traditional Polynesian religious thought and practice. In general, missionization of the Pacific had been successfully carried out on the majority of island groups, beginning in the early 1800s. Therefore, a record of traditional beliefs often remained only in the journals of early missionaries, who regarded as benighted or inferior the religions they were replacing with Christianity. Tikopia escaped the earliest onslaught of missionaries because of its isolation. The Tikopia themselves were also extremely resistant to outside intrusion and successfully kept both missionaries and colonial government at bay until the early 1900s.

The first missionary to settle on the island in the 1920s was not European; he was a man from the Banks Islands working for the Melanesian Mission (Church of England). This man, Pa Pangisi, later married a Tikopia woman, and his more sympathetic view of traditional beliefs probably contributed to the fact that by the time Firth carried out his first fieldwork in Tikopia, fewer than half the inhabitants of the island had converted to Christianity, and only one of the four chiefs had done so. Firth, therefore, had the opportunity to record ritual practices firsthand, and his excellent knowledge of the language allowed him to translate the allusive and complex words of the various rituals.

Firth himself had been brought up a Methodist and taught Sunday school as a young man, but at the London School of Economics his opinions changed to a humanistic rationalism and he regretted the proselytization of Tikopia. In *We, the Tikopia* he wrote, "what justification can be found for this steady pressure to break down the customs of a people against whom the main charge is that their gods are different from ours?" (1936, p. 50). His sympathy and respect for the customs of Tikopia persuaded the chiefs of the island to share their ritual knowledge with him, and they later recalled Firth's distaste for the missionary habit of referring to traditional beliefs and paraphernalia as "things of darkness."

On return visits to the island in 1952 and 1966, Firth was able to record Tikopia's final conversion to Christianity. *Social Change in Tikopia* (1958) records the pragmatic decisions taken by the remaining three pagan chiefs, which led to all non-Christian Tikopia (with the exception of one old woman) converting to Melanesian Mission practice.

After Firth's initial period of fieldwork, he served as acting professor at Sydney University from 1930 to 1932, after which he returned to the London School of Economics, where he became a lecturer (1932–1935), reader (1935), and professor (in 1944). He remained there, with brief interruptions, until his retirement in 1968. While Tikopia remained central to his publications, he also carried out fieldwork in Malaya and in London, as well as writing more generally on topics of theoretical and anthropological interest. He received many honors during his long and distinguished career: he was knighted in 1973 and appointed Companion, New Zealand Order of Merit, in 2001. In 2002 the British Academy announced it was awarding him the first Leverhulme medal to be given to scholars of exceptional distinction in recognition of his "outstanding and internationally acknowledged contributions to 20th century anthropology." Raymond Firth died in February 2002.

BIBLIOGRAPHY

Firth, Raymond. *We, the Tikopia: A Sociological Study of Kinship in Primitive Polynesia.* London, 1936.

Firth, Raymond. *The Work of the Gods in Tikopia.* London, 1940; 2d ed., 1967.

Firth, Raymond. *The Fate of the Soul: An Interpretation of Some Primitive Concepts.* Cambridge, UK, 1956.

Firth, Raymond. *Social Change in Tikopia: Re-study of a Polynesian Community after a Generation.* London, 1958.

Firth, Raymond. *History and Traditions of Tikopia.* Wellington, New Zealand, 1960.

Firth, Raymond. "The Spirits Depart." *New Society* 11 (1966): 683–685.

Firth, Raymond. *Tikopia Ritual and Belief.* London, 1967.

Firth, Raymond. *Rank and Religion in Tikopia: A Study in Polynesian Paganism and Conversion to Christianity.* London, 1970.

JUDITH MACDONALD (2005)

FISH. Inherent in fish symbolism is the sacred power of the abyss, the reciprocities of life and death. Paleolithic fish figurines have been found with the spiral of creativity carved on one side and the labyrinth of death on the other, evincing the spiritual world of early humankind in which fish represented propagating and perishing, killing and consuming, life renewed and sustained.

In the ancient Near East and the Mediterranean world, fish were associated with the great goddesses, archetypal images of femininity, love, and fertility. Astarte was worshiped in the form of a fish; Atargatis named her son Ichthys, Sacred Fish. In ancient Greece, Rome, and Scandinavia, the goddesses Aphrodite, Venus, and Frigg were assimilated to fish, and on Friday, the day sacred to them, fish were eaten as a way of participating in their fecundity. In many parts of the world—India, Greenland, Samoa, and Brazil—virgins were thought to be made pregnant by the gift of a fish, while a "fishing dance" was a common fertility rite in the women's societies of Africa. The dual nature of the symbol was manifested, and fish were regarded as unclean, wherever the goddess was characterized as libidinous and devouring. Fish gods were venerated as creators and vivifiers among Sumero-Semitic peoples and represented phallic power. An Assyrian seal of about 700 BCE depicts "Fish Gods Fertilizing the Tree of Life." Babylonian seals bear the image of a great fish with a vase from which fish stream.

A ubiquitous food in much of the world, fish are a universal motif of plenty. They are an emblem of abundance and good augury on Buddhist altars and are cited as one of the five boons in the Tantric text *Vāmācāris.*

At ritual meals in the temples of Babylon, fish was the sacred food of the priests. In Judaism, fish was regarded as the food of the blessed in paradise and was eaten at the Sabbath meal. The old Jewish Passover was in the month of Adar, the Fish, and the traditional symbol of the national restoration that is to come with the advent of the Messiah is the great fish on which the righteous will feast. Sabbath utensils and the chalice of benediction are often decorated with images of fish.

Sacred fish occur in Syrian and Iranian myths. Throughout the dynastic period in Egypt, they were regarded as the manifestation or abode of a god. Hapi, father of the gods, was "Lord of the Fishes," and a fish denoted the phallus of the dismembered god Osiris. An attribute of the sea god Poseidon (or Neptune), fish were associated with lunar power, and when represented with an ax, as in Crete, designated both lunar and solar power. Pisces, the twelfth sign of the Zodiac, is a pair of parallel fishes pointing in opposite directions, symbolizing spiritual and temporal power, the upper and lower worlds, past and future, involution and evolution, the ending of one cycle and the beginning of another. A pair of fishes on Chinese Bronze Age vessels signifies creative power. The Japanese believed that the world was supported by a mighty fish. Among the primitive societies of Oceania, Africa, and North and South America, fish were sacred totemic figures, emblematic of the power of the clan. Peruvian Indians believed that the original fish had engendered all others; they worshiped the species that was caught in the greatest numbers. Sea gods riding on a fish signified freedom; shown on the footprint of the Buddha, a fish meant emancipation from attachment and desire.

A corollary of the fish as blessing is its assimilation to a savior. The alchemical sign for *Salvator mundi* is a fish. The Hindu god Viṣṇu, transformed into a fish by Brahma, recovered the Vedas from the flood, saved humankind, and started a new race. Christ was symbolized by the fish, as seen in carved inscriptions in the catacombs of Rome; in Greek, the initial letters of "Jesus Christ, Son of God, Savior" form the Greek word *ichthus* ("fish"). The depiction of Jesus standing in water confirms the metaphor of a fish drawn from the deep to bring salvation to humanity. The feeding of the multitude by the miraculous multiplication of the loaves and fishes is the prototype of the Eucharist; the fish, like the bread, symbolizes the body of the Lord. The concept of Christ as both sacrificed and sacrificer is inherent in the Mass. Three fish with one head, or three intertwined fish—found in the iconography of ancient Mesopotamia, Egypt, India, and Persia, and even down to modern times—is a universal symbol for unity in trinity, and came to represent Christian baptism. Christ's disciples and the newly baptized were denoted by the sign of a fish, and a neophyte in fish garb is depicted on early Christian lamps. In Christian mortuary painting, on pagan sarcophagi, and in representations of Chinese feasts of the dead, fish relate to resurrection and regeneration.

The experience of entering the belly of a whale or big fish, as in the Jonah story, is equated to a religious idea that informed the initiatory mysteries and rituals of death and of rebirth through newfound wisdom. Variants of this transition symbol are found worldwide, from the initiation rites of Oceania, West Africa, Lapland, and Finland to the North American Indian tale of Hiawatha, who was swallowed by the King of Fishes.

Fishing symbolizes both looking for souls and looking into the soul, that is, drawing the treasure of wisdom from the sea of the unknown. The Babylonians considered the sea the source of wisdom, and a mystic fisherman called "Warden of the Fish" is represented on a seal of the second millennium BCE. The mythical hero Ea-Oannes, half man, half fish, rose from the waters to bring culture and wisdom to mankind. The figure evolved into a fish god, Lord of the Deeps, whose priests wore fish skins and a fish headdress and whose image was ultimately transmuted into the miter of Christian bishops. The name *Orpheus* derives from a term for "fish," and one of the figures on an Orphic sacramental bowl of the third or fourth century BCE shows Orpheus as a fisher of men, with a fish and pole at his feet. The Celtic god Nodon was a fisher-god, and the Welsh god Bran the Blessed was called "Fisher of Men." His counterpart is the Grail King whom Parsifal found fishing as he waited for his deliverer. According to Augustine, Christ's exhortation "Follow me, and I will make you fishers of men" implied that the world is a sea of fish to be converted. For the tenth-century Ṣūfī mystic Niffari, the sea of spiritual experience through which the mystic passes on his journey to God is full of strange and frightening fish.

Many forms of sea life embody specific religious symbols. The dolphin was regarded as a divine intermediary between the upper and lower worlds; as a guide to departed souls, he was depicted on Greek vases bearing warriors to the Isles of the Blest. The dolphin as psychopomp, or guide of the souls of the dead, is also represented in Christian art. The octupus was a favorite motif in the ceramic arts of ancient Crete, allied to the spiritual in symbolizing the mystic center and the unfolding of creation. In the Celtic legend of Finn, the hero eats the Salmon of Wisdom, which endows him with the foreknowledge of the gods. The European Stella Maris, or starfish, is a symbol of the Virgin Mary and the Holy Spirit.

BIBLIOGRAPHY

Baum, Julius. "Symbolic Representations of the Eucharist." In *The Mysteries,* vol. 2 of *Papers from the Eranos Yearbooks,* edited by Joseph Campbell. New York, 1956. A close analysis of the symbolic acts of Christ represented in the rite of the Eucharist, based on fish iconography on sarcophagi and artifacts in sacramental chapels.

Campbell, Joseph. *The Masks of God,* vol. 4, *Creative Mythology,* New York, 1968. A survey of the mystic fisherman symbolism in Orphic, Babylonian, and Christian artifacts, correlating the symbols of the mystagogue, Orpheus the Fisherman, and the Fisher King of the Grail legend.

Lengyel, Lancelot. *Le secret des Celtes.* Paris, 1969. The fish as symbol of wisdom in the Celtic legend of the hero Finn and his acquisition of supernatural knowledge by consuming the Salmon of Wisdom.

Neumann, Erich. *The Origins and History of Consciousness.* New York, 1954. Includes an account of the predominance of female deities in early fish cults and of culture heroes that rise from the waters, half fish, half man, to bring revelation and wisdom to humankind.

Zimmer, Heinrich. *Philosophies of India* (1951). Edited by Joseph Campbell. Reprint, Princeton, 1969. In his summary of the *sastra* of the Science of Wealth, the author examines the Indian doctrine of *Matsya-nyāya,* or the law of the fishes, in which fish symbolize the breeding force of the sea—life abundant, self-sustaining, and self-consuming.

New Sources

Baird, Merrily. "Land and Sea Animals." In *Symbols of Japan: Thematic Motifs in Art and Design.* New York, 2001.

Lawrence, Raymond J., Jr. "The Fish: A Lost Symbol of Sexual Liberation?" *Journal of Religion and Health* 30 (Winter 1991): 311–319.

Slater, Candace. *Dance of the Dolphin: Transformation and Disenchantment in the Amazonian Imagination.* Chicago, 1994.

ANN DUNNIGAN (1987)
Revised Bibliography

FLACIUS, MATTHIAS

FLACIUS, MATTHIAS (1520–1575), known as Matthias Flacius Illyricus, was an Italo-Croatian scholar and polemicist; a creative, fiery theological leader of the late Lutheran Reformation. Born in Albona, Istria, Flacius was trained in the humanist schools of Venice under the influence of his uncle, the Franciscan provincial Baldo Luperino, who was sympathetic to Lutheranism. Flacius studied at Tübingen before moving to Wittenberg, where Luther's intervention in a personal religious crisis confirmed Flacius as his passionately committed disciple. The defeat of Lutheran princes in the Smalcald War ended Flacius's career as a Hebrew instructor at Wittenberg and propelled him into the leadership of the Gnesio-Lutheran party, formed by Luther's more radical disciples in opposition to the imposition of the Augsburg Interim (1548) and the compromise settlement worked out by other Lutheran leaders, the Leipzig Interim (1548). Flacius's historical and liturgical research, as well as his biblical, lay-oriented argumentation, led him to criticize both settlements, attacking the Leipzig Interim as a betrayal of Luther's Reformation. As a private scholar at the center of resistance to both interims, Magdeburg (1548–1557); as a professor and counselor at Jena (1557–1561); and later as a consultant and private scholar in Regensburg, Antwerp, and Strassburg, Flacius provided theological leadership and inspired controversy.

Among his major contributions are his pioneering work in Protestant biblical hermeneutics, which climaxed in *Clavis scripturae sacrae* (1567), and in Protestant historiography, which culminated in his own *Catalogus testium veritatis* (1556) and in the *Magdeburg Centuries,* composed by members of a research team that he helped organize and manage.

According to his modern biographer, Oliver K. Olson, Flacius's theology can be described negatively as a program of "de-hellenization," that is, a turning away from Platonism and Aristotle, and positively as an insistent prophetic witness to correct biblical teaching *(pura doctrina).* That witness led him to fight for the independence of the church from the state and to reject many aspects of medieval ecclesiastical custom and polity. Above all, it led him to defend Luther's doctrine of salvation by God's grace through faith in Christ in controversies with other Protestant theologians, especially his formidable antagonist Philipp Melanchthon. These controversies concerned, most importantly, the role of good works in salvation and the role of the human will in conversion. In the controversy over human will Flacius defined original sin as the formal substance of the fallen sinner, who, he argued, is the image of Satan. This position was misinterpreted even by some fellow Gnesio-Lutherans and contributed to his alienation from most of his contemporaries at the end of his life, when agents of leading Lutheran princes prevented him from finding a permanent home.

Flacius's ardent polemics in defense of Luther's message at a time when it was seriously menaced by political and ideological forces contributed much to its preservation, and his intellectual contributions in liturgics, hermeneutics, church history, and dogmatics greatly enriched Protestant orthodoxy.

BIBLIOGRAPHY

Oliver K. Olson provides a superb overview of Flacius's thought and life and a sketch of his two-volume biography, as well as an extensive bibliography, in his essay "Matthias Flacius Illyricus, 1520–1575," in *Shapers of Religious Traditions in Germany, Switzerland, and Poland, 1560–1600,* edited by Jill Raitt (New Haven, Conn., 1981), pp. 1–17. The classic treatment of the subject to date is Wilhelm Preger's *Matthias Flacius Illyricus und seine Zeit,* 2 vols. in 1 (Erlangen, 1859–1861). In addition to Olson's articles and dissertation, contemporary studies of Flacius include Günter Moldaenke's *Schriftverständnis und Schriftdeutung im Zeitalter der Reformation,* vol. 1, *Matthias Flacius Illyricus* (Stuttgart, 1936), and Lauri Haikola's *Gesetz und Evangelium bei Matthias Flacius Illyricus* (Lund, 1952).

ROBERT KOLB (1987)

FLAMEN

FLAMEN. The city of Rome presented itself as a community of people and gods, and the institution of the priesthood was necessary to mediate between those two spaces, to interpret the will of the gods and to ensure accuracy in the performance of rites. The *flamines*—etymologically, the "dispensers of the sacred" (Isidorus, *Etymologiae* 7.12.17)—were the *sacerdotes* of a particular deity (Cicero, *De legibus* 2.20). They stood in contrast to the pontiffs, who were learned men and men of law, and to other colleges of priests that acted in the name of the community.

The etymology of the word *flamen* is not clear. Based on the common etymology of the words *flamen* and *brahman* established by Georges Dumézil, Henri Le Bourdellès (1970) pointed out that the term—also recorded in the Messapic and Persian languages—designated the priest as invocator or minister of the word. But the functional duties of the Latin *flamen* and those of the Sanskrit *brahman* are far from similar, and the explanation that the Romans themselves offered for the term, relating it to the band of wool (*filum*) that wrapped around the *flamen's* cap (Varro, *De lingua Latina* 5.84), has been defended by Jens H. Vanggaard (1988).

The literature speaks of fifteen *flamines:* three major ones (*maiores*) and twelve minor ones (*minores*). Several authors, such as Vanggaard (1988, pp. 105ff) and Domenico Fasciano and Pierre Séguin (1993, pp. 22–23), have challenged the traditional thesis that the *flamines* were the specific priests of a certain deity. Fasciano and Séguin point out that the term *flamen* was applied to the *flamen* of the Arvals (*flamen Arvalium*) and to the priests of the thirty curiae into which archaic Rome was divided (*flamines curiales*), suggesting that the twelve *flamines minores* represented, in some way, certain sectors of the population, while the three *flamines maiores* represented the people as a whole, as the common sacrifices to the goddess *Fides* (a symbol of Rome's "faith"), mentioned by Livy (1.21.4), would illustrate. Such a thesis would also be supported by the common invocation in the conclusion of a treaty by the college of the *fetiales* (Pol. 3.25.6) and in the formula of the *devotio,* the oath taken by a Roman general vowing his life to the gods of the underworld (Livy 8.9).

The differences between the *flamines maiores* (instituted by King Numa) and the *flamines minores* would be due, according to the traditional interpretation (after Georg Wissowa), to the various levels of importance of the gods each *flamen* served. Thus, the *flamines maiores* were in the service of Jupiter, Mars, and Quirinus, the archaic triad that, according to Dumézil, represented the trifunctional Indo-European ideology of sovereignty, war, and production (with parallels to a similar triad among the Umbrian peoples: Jovius, Mars, and Vofionus). But such an explanation was challenged by Vanggaard (1988, pp. 46ff), for whom this distinction should be understood in terms of social differences along patrician-plebeian lines. He also rejects the possibility that the *flamines minores* could be patricians. Vanggaard has pointed at the relationship between the *flamines* and certain family groups (*gentes*), showing the predominance of the *gens* Cornelia and, in a secondary way, of the Postumius Albinus and the Valerius Flaccus families (Vanggaard, 1988, pp. 70ff).

Of the three *flamines maiores,* we know especially well the duties of the *flamen Dialis* thanks to the taboos (*caerimoniae, castus*) to which he was subject. These were cataloged in the pontifical books at the end of the third century or the first half of the second century BCE, and collected by the poet Aulus Gellius in the second century CE (*Noctes Atticae,* 10.15). One text from the Augustan antiquarian Verrius Flaccus, transmitted by Festus (198–200 L) in the second century CE places the priest of Jupiter at the head of the Roman priestly hierarchy, below the *rex sacrorum* and above the priests of Mars and Quirinus, who also outranked the *pontifex maximus.* The positions of *rex* (who is *potentissimus*) and *flamen Dialis* (said to be the priest of the entire world: "*universi mundi sacerdos*") represent the two types of sovereignty—warring and priestly—characteristic of Rome's "magical-religious" horizon. In the republican era, the more "political" figures of the magistrate and the pontiff replaced that pair (Marco Simón, 1996).

The cultic functions of the priest of Jupiter are well known: participating in the *confarreatio* marriage ceremonies (offering the couple the spelt bread that it would share), sacrificing a lamb to Jupiter on the day of the full moon (*Idus*), introducing the yearly wine harvest (*Vinalia*), and participating in the feast of *Lupercalia* on February 15. Together with the other two *flamines maiores* (the *flamen Martialis* and the *flamen Quirinalis*), he partook in the sacrifice to the goddess Fides. The *flamen Martialis* supposedly partook of the holiday of the October Horse, and the *flamen Quirinalis* in several rituals—*Quirinalia, Robigalia, Consualia,* and *Larentalia.*

The restrictions imposed on the *flamen* (*caerimoniae, castus*) defined his position. For the *flamen Dialis*—as for the virgins consecrated to Vesta—every day was holy (*cotidie feriatus*) because he symbolized the "stability" of the city itself. Four types of prescriptions insured that stability (Marco Simón, 1996): (1) restrictions that ensured his basic freedoms, including the prohibition to swear oaths or to wear symbolic constrictions such as rings or knots on his clothes; (2) restrictions aimed at ensuring his constant presence in Rome (*adsiduitas*), such as the prohibition from leaving his bed, which had to be in contact with the soil of the city, for more than three consecutive nights; (3) rules that established the symbolic role of the *flamen Dialis* in his double relationship with Jupiter (of whom he was a living image) and with society as a whole; and (4) restrictions that, because of the third category of rules, aimed at preventing contamination (*pollutio*) of the *flamen Dialis* by animals or any elements associated with the underworld or the world of the dead.

The wife of the *flamen Dialis* (*flaminica Dialis*) formed with him a sacred union that was an example to all Romans; it was unbreakable except by death, and she was under the same restrictions as her husband, according to Aulus Gellius (10.15.26), since she was the symbol for the fertility of Rome. She could not wash or comb her hair on certain dates that were associated with the Salian and Argean rites and with the cleaning of the Vestal temple.

One consequence of the taboos applied to the Jupiter priesthood (which prevented the priest from leaving Rome) was that the flaminate had little political appeal in comparison to other priesthoods, such as the augurate or the pontificate, which later served as stepping stones for political gain achieved through war. This led to a relaxation of the rules for the other two *flamines*, to whom, originally, the same restrictions had applied. This explains why the flaminate of Jupiter was vacant for seventy-five years after the suicide of Cornelius Merula in 87 BCE (Appian, *Bellum civile* 1.74; Velleius Paterculus, *Historiae Romanae* 2.22.2). Young G. Julius Caesar apparently was nominated for the post in 86 BCE, but he was never installed to it.

Only ten of the names of the twelve *flamines minores* are known. The first four were named after the most prominent gods: the *flamen Carmentalis* (Carmenta is a goddess associated with water and the human birthing process, destiny, and prophecy); the *flamen Volcanalis* (Volcanus is the god of celestial fire); the *flamen Portunalis* (Portunus is god of harbors and entrance ways), and the *flamen Cerialis* (Ceres is the goddess of growth and agriculture). The names of the last six *flamines* are known thanks to Ennius (in Varro, *De lingua Latina* 5.84); they served less eminent deities, associated especially with agriculture. They included the *flamen Volturnalis* (Volturnus is a deity associated with rivers and the wind); the *flamen Palatualis* (Palatua is probably the goddess of the Palatine and is identified with Pales); the *flamen Furrinalis* (Furrina is a goddess of wells and underground water), and the *flamen Floralis* (Flora is the goddess of the blossoming of wheat and orchards). The *flamen Falacer* was the only one bearing the same name as his god, not the adjective epithet. Finally, there was the *flamen Pomonalis* (Pomona is a goddess that protects orchards). Fasciano and Séguin (1993, pp. 141–146) suggest that the names of the two missing *flamines minores* were the *flamen Neptunalis* (Neptunus is the god of fresh water and humidity) and the *flamen Fontinalis* (Fons, or Fontanus, was the god of springs), whose deities were assimilated into Poseidon and the nymphs during the Hellenization of Roman religion.

In imperial times, the *flamines* were in charge of maintaining the cult of the emperor. The law that defined provincial priesthood in the Narbonensis province suggests that the statutes and prerogatives of the *flamines* were drafted following the model of the *flamen Dialis* (*CIL* XII 6038). These Augustal, municipal, and provincial *flamines* played an important role, since the imperial cult was a first-rate symbolic element in maintaining the political unity and cohesion of the vast and heterogeneous Roman Empire. The priests of the imperial cult received the title of *flamines* in the Hispanic provinces (Hispania Citerior, Lusitania, and Betica), in Gallia Narbonensis, the Maritime and Cottian Alps, Numidia, and the two Mauritanias (Caesarean and Tingitana), while the title *sacerdotes* (which is characteristic of the Flavian era,) prevails in the inscriptions of the altar of the Temple of the Three Gauls in Lugdunum (Lyons), and in the African provinces, Sardinia, and the Danubian region (Fishwick, 1987–2002).

SEE ALSO Roman Religion, article on the Early Period.

BIBLIOGRAPHY

Dumézil, Georges. *Archaic Roman Religión.* 2 vols. Translated by Philip Krapp. Chicago, 1970.

Fasciano, Domenico, and Pierre Séguin. *Les flamines et leurs dieux.* Montreal, 1993.

Fishwick, Duncan. *The Imperial Cult in the Latin West: Studies in the Ruler Cult of the Western Provinces of the Roman Empire.* 3 vols. Leiden, 1987–2002.

Le Bourdellès, Henri. "Le flamine et le brahmane: Nature de la fonction; étymologie." *Révue des Études Latines* 57 (1970): 69–84.

Liou-Gille, Bernadette. "César: 'Flamen Dialis destinatus.'" *Révue des Études Anciennes* 101, nos. 3–4 (1999): 433–499.

Marco Simón, Francisco. *Flamen Dialis: El sacerdote de Júpiter en la religión romana.* Madrid, 1996.

Porte, Danielle. *Les donneurs de sacré: Le prêtre à Rome.* Paris, 1989.

Vanggaard, Jens H. *The Flamen: A Study in the History and Sociology of Roman Religion.* Copenhagen, 1988.

Wissowa, Georg. *Religion und Kultus der Römer.* 2d ed. Munich, 1912. See especially pages 504–507.

FRANCISCO MARCO SIMÓN (2005)
Translated from Spanish by Fernando Feliu-Moggi

FLAVIUS JOSEPHUS SEE JOSEPHUS FLAVIUS

FLIGHT.

The image of a human being escaping the bonds of earthly life to float and soar about the skies unencumbered and free appears in religious myths, mystical tracts, ritual dramas, and imaginative expressions around the world, from the most archaic to the most contemporary of cultures. While of course their specific historical circumstances and motivations vary, one still feels that in some ways the imagination of the Paleolithic cave dweller who painted the figure of a man with a bird's head on the walls of the caves at Lascaux is not so different from the imagination that created the ancient Greek story of Icarus yearning to fly to the sun or that of the poets of Vedic India who sang praises of the long-haired ascetic who "flies through the air, looking on all shapes below, the friend to all the gods" (*Ṛgveda* 10.136.4). Perhaps, too, this imagination is not so different in the end from that which helped lift the Wright brothers into the air above Kitty Hawk.

Accounts of human flight are at times quite dramatic, as in the neo-Hebraic text the *Apocalypse of Moses,* which tells of Moses' ascension into the various heavens, each one inhabited by frightening and dreadful angels who breathe fire and lightning and whose sweat flows into a mighty burning river. Other tales of flight convey a mood of peacefulness, as in the nineteenth-century accounts of Sister Mary of Jesus Crucified, a Carmelite nun who floated about the yard of her nunnery for hours at a time, sometimes perching softly in the treetops like a bird. Some accounts are quite charming, like the medieval Sanskrit text that tells neophyte yogins that a person trying to master the art of levitation may have some difficulty at first and so will bounce across the ground like a jumping frog, but after increased practice will fly about with ease (see *Yogatattva Upaniṣad* 53–55).

Rituals as well as myths also frequently include references to or enactment of aerial travel. Alchemists and Daoist priests in ancient China, for example, clothed themselves with feathered wings while performing various religious ceremonies so that they might fly about the skies with the immortals. Similarly, at one point in the Vedic Vajapeya rite the priest and the ritual's patron are instructed to climb the sacrificial pillar, at the top of which they spread their arms as if flapping their wings and proclaim, "We have come to the heavens, to the gods we have come! We have become immortal" (*Taittīriya Saṃhitā* 1.7.9). The Vedic ritual system as a whole is often described in ornithological terms. The performance of the Agnicayana (fire ritual), for example, revolves around the construction of an altar in the shape of a bird, suggesting that the ritual transports its oblations to the heavens the way a bird soars through the skies.

DIMENSIONS OF MAGICAL FLIGHT. Scholars have offered a variety of theories regarding the origin and meaning of humanity's fascination with magical flight. Some, such as Arthur Maurice Hocart, an anthropologist, have seen in this theme remnants of an archaic solar worship and reverence for the king (who was felt to be the sun, or the son of the sun), who was always carried about on the shoulders of his subjects and thus "flew" everywhere he went. Others, such as Geo Widengren, a scholar of Near Eastern religions, have seen in myths and rituals involving flight distinct elements of religious ideologies based on divine kingship; the protagonist exemplifying such ideologies (originally the king, but later also a prophet or savior) is said to ascend to the realm of the high god in order to receive the sanction to rule the earthly community below. Some theorists feel that the theme represents elements of initiation and rites of passage: The flight typifies the state of being in which the initiate stands between the old and the new modes of existence. Some psychologists, especially those influenced by the theories of Sigmund Freud, have argued that the desire to fly is really a subliminal desire for sexual power, and that the feelings accompanying such an experience are repressed aspects of sexual arousal. Students of other disciplines in the social sciences maintain that magical flight expresses a person's search for a legitimation of authority over other people, or a wish to be free of personal limitations.

There is no doubt that to fly is to have power, and some theorists have held that the search for power is the central motivation common to all religious experience and expression. Whether or not this means, however, that themes of magical flight in religious myths and rituals derive from specific modes of power (such as royal prestige, prophetic influence, personal gratification, or existential autonomy) will remain open to debate. The issue is complicated by the fact that many types of persons—sovereigns, saints, visionaries, magicians, priests, ascetics, mystics, lovers, philosophers—have been said to undergo such uplifting experiences. Since the 1950s Mircea Eliade has argued that it would be a mistake to conclude that the mythic theme of magical flight derives from only one source, or that it reflects only one stage in human cultural or personal development. According to Eliade, magical flight and its related symbolism (learning the language of birds, the cultivation of ecstasy, rapturous mystical images, and so on) reflect an experience of abolishing everyday ways of knowing the world, the desire for which is expressed in images of transcendence and freedom. Eliade further maintains that this desire is, in fact, constitutive of humanity itself. If this interpretation is correct, then symbols of magical flight not only derive from a moment in human history but also reveal a structure of human consciousness, an existential dimension to the human imagination that "must be ranked among the specific marks of man" (Eliade, 1960, p. 106).

The point is well taken. Studies in the history of religions have repeatedly emphasized that *Homo sapiens* is *homo symbolicus,* defined in part by the ability to make and be moved by symbols, especially symbols of various extraordinary modes of being. At the start of the twentieth century James G. Frazer and Julius von Negelein, among others, noted that religions from around the world have used the image of the bird to signify the human soul, suggesting that celestial and aerial symbols often represent sublime emotions and spiritual ideals. One might recognize such themes in Augustine's account in his *Confessions* of his experience at Ostia when he and his mother, both radiant with spiritual love, soar up to the heavens from where the celestial bodies shine onto the earth. One finds similar themes in traditional Islamic accounts of Muḥammad's *Miʿrāj,* in which the Prophet ascends through the seven heavens of the vertical cosmos to learn sacred lessons from his predecessors in the prophetic lineage who now live in each heaven and draw near to the throne of Allah. This ascension has become a mythic and poetic paradigm for the practices and ideals of Ṣūfī mysticism. Tales of a person's flight through the skies frequently include an emotional tone of longing to be free of the bonds that tie humanity to the ways of the world. A similar longing perhaps enlivened the imagination of the Hebrew psalmist who sang, "Oh that I had wings like a dove! for then I would fly away and be at rest" (*Ps.* 55:6).

Protagonists who fly through the air do so for more than emotional and mystical reasons. They may assert their ability to rise above the laws of the physical world and thus to gain control over what may be experienced as an oppressive universe. This may be inferred from the South Asian use of such Sanskrit terms as *kaivalya* ("autonomy") to describe one of the goals of yogic practice, which is marked by such autonomous acts as flying through the air (see Patañjali's *Yoga Sūtra,* chap. 4 and its commentaries). Similarly, the Theravāda Buddhist tradition teaches that an adept monk can fly cross-legged through the atmosphere "like a bird in flight" (see *Majjhima Nikāya* 1.33, etc.).

At other times, the world is understood to reflect the beauty and wisdom of the divine plan; to fly about it, then, is to see more of it than is normally possible. This may be part of what the Persian Ṣūfī Farīd al-Dīn ʿAṭṭar longed to do when, in his epic poem *The Conference of Birds,* he expresses a wish to fly through the air to all regions of the earth in order "to enjoy all beauties."

At other times, people may want to fly in order to see into the future (movement through vertical space is often associated with movement through time); to escort dead people to their new lives in the unknown world; to obtain valuable medicinal or cultic knowledge from various spiritual beings; or to locate souls that have become lost in the different layers of the universe. While the religious specialist most adept at such divination is the shaman of north-central Asia, the ecstatic experience characterized by such flights appears throughout the world.

The ability to fly through the air therefore often includes an ethical or normative dimension, for the protagonist who can travel to the future, as well as to other worlds, can see what kinds of lives people on earth can expect to have in other realms after they die. Subsequent to such a flight, the aerial traveler can return to earth to tell people how to act so that they may live in the more comfortable or prestigious afterworlds. Such is the case, for example, in the Zoroastrian tale told in the *Ardā Wirāz Nāmag,* in which the priest Virāf falls into an ecstatic sleep after drinking a cup of *mang* and travels through the heavens and hells that are the respective postmortal homes of the pious and the infidel members of the priestly community. Having gained this knowledge, he then returns to his colleagues on earth and tells them what he has learned so that they can adjust their religious practices accordingly.

TYPES OF MAGICAL FLIGHT. The various scenarios in the world's myths and rituals involving extraordinary aerial flight are so numerous that one could distinguish any number of forms and interpret their individual meanings in an equal number of ways. To arrive at a universal typology of flight, then, is to generalize in a way that might make even thoroughgoing structuralists somewhat wary. The following schema is intended to be comprehensive, but does not pretend to include all variations.

Autonomous this-worldly flight (levitation). Hagiographies from religious traditions around the world often include depictions of various saints, mediators, devotees, and other exemplary figures who are able at certain times to float up off the ground without visible assistance and without injury. Sometimes these experiences are intentional and desirable, as is implied in a lesson from the *Yogatattva Upaniṣad* (117): "Thrusting the tongue into the back of the throat and focusing one's eyes on the spot between the eyebrows, one sits in the posture in which one gains the power to float up into the air." At other times, these experiences seem to catch the community by surprise, as in a story about Alfonso Liguori, who, while giving a sermon one day, offered himself to an image of the Virgin and, stretching out his arms (like a bird?), floated several feet off the platform, whereupon the two thousand people listening were amazed and filled with admiration. While most traditional hagiographies express wonder at such events, many also include implicit or explicit criticism of people who willingly drift about in the air in front of others, since such behavior is either physically dangerous or distracting to the normal person's religious concentration or constitutes an arrogant display of spiritual authority. The Ṣūfī tradition, for example, criticizes those who undertake a magical levitation in order to enact a miracle or gain a vision, for to do so is comparable to making the pilgrimage to Mecca merely for the sake of business or pleasure.

The Bollandists' *Acta Sanctorum* uses such descriptive terms as *a terra levabatur* ("raised above the surface of the earth"), *corporalite elevatus est* ("he or she was elevated bodily"), and *raptus* ("taken up") to describe those events in Roman Catholic history in which a person is reported to have floated up off the ground while deep in prayer, during moments of deep emotion, or while performing devotions. Since the classical period in India, Sanskrit texts have used such technical terms as *laghuman* ("lightness"), *utkramaṇa* ("stepping upward"), and *gauravahīnatā* ("gravity destroying") to describe the power a yogin gains while learning to meditate properly. Islam distinguishes two types of mystics, those who are passively "drawn upward" (*majdhūb*) and those who actively stride (*sālik*) upward through the spheres by their own arduous reflection and effort. But such technical terms, among any number of others from the literatures of the world's religions, seem too specialized for comparative use. The English and French word *levitation* has been used since the nineteenth century by European hagiographers to describe such events in their respective traditions. While the term seems somewhat clumsy, it might suit the comparativist who has recognized such themes in other religions as well.

Levitations may be intentional or unintentional, repeated or unique, momentary or long-lasting. They may take the person over an extensive geography or they may involve rising just an inch or two above the ground. In any case, the adept remains independent of external assistance and, while he or she may be said to alter the physical laws of the world, never leaves the physical structure of the cosmos.

Although levitations are often depicted as strange and astounding events that arrest people's attention and thrill the storytellers, they are of themselves rarely if ever soteriologically transformative and do not constitute an ultimately valuable experience. Rather, tales of levitation mark the esteem that the particular tradition holds for the central figure, or they serve as a means by which the tradition recognizes those specific practices and attitudes (spiritual integrity, strength of will, loving purity and devotion, self-discipline, obedience to the divine, etc.) that it holds to be most valuable.

Dependent this-worldly flight. To the category of dependent magical flights belong those instances in which a person is lifted up off the ground by a flying animal, spirit, or divine creature of some sort and is escorted through the skies over a wide area of the earth and sometimes at great height. These flights are similar to autonomous levitations in that the protagonists never leave the realm of the atmosphere and thus remain within the worldly cosmos, the realm of human activity and community. They differ from levitations in that the protagonists are dependent on another being or outside agent to bring them into the skies.

Sometimes these flights allow a hero to escape in a horizontal direction and at great speed from a situation of great anxiety or terror, often from death personified. Accordingly, the emotional tone of such stories is fervent and fearful. Folklorists have used the German term *magische Flucht* to describe such a flight from a frightening predicament and have found the theme in cultures all over the world. Eliade has noted that "it is important to distinguish one essential element [in such horizontal high-speed flights]: the desperate effort to be rid of a monstrous presence, to free oneself" (Eliade, 1960, p. 104).

At other times, this-worldly flights escorted by a supernatural being reflect less frightening feelings and signify less anxious situations. Sometimes they bring the central character to a new and highly desirable land or a more satisfying life in a distant earthly paradise. Sometimes they free him or her from the drudgery of daily chores long enough to add new wonder to their understanding of the world. Sometimes they show the character the superiority of his or her religious tradition over another, for to fly over the heads of the followers of another tradition is to be better than they are.

In general, tales of escorted this-worldly flights either express a notion that escape or existential change is possible no matter how bleak things look, or help the members of the religious community reaffirm the worthiness of their tradition and encourage people from other traditions to become part of their own. As such, many tales of an escorted this-worldly flight serve conversion as well as self-affirming functions.

Otherworldly flights (ascensions). A third general category of magical flights involves a protagonist's journey to dimensions or levels of the sacred cosmos other than the earthly one. These journeys may be solitary and autonomous or they may be guided by supernatural beings. In either case, otherworldly flights, or ascensions, necessarily involve a radical transformation of one's being, a change in ontological status so powerful that one moves from one mode of existence to another. This transformation is typically depicted as being of ultimate value and is considered soteriologically efficacious. Such experiences reward specific people for their commitment to religious practices, their transformative state of mind, or their embodiment of respected personality traits. The central axis of these aerial journeys tends to be a vertical one, although there are instances of horizontal travels to other worlds as well. Whereas stories of the *magische Flucht* type of this-worldly flight evoke emotions of release, freedom, safety, or personal power, narratives of ascent evoke emotions arising from the transcendence of this world and a concurrent disjunction with normal reality and personal existential situations. If this-worldly flight gets one out of the grasp of something horrible or above the heads of everybody else in the world, ascension gets one out of the world altogether.

Myths of vertical travel to the heavens above the skies are often associated with the protagonist's previous or subsequent descent along the same axis to the hells or otherworlds below. Therefore, ascensions, like other religious forms of magical flight, often include divinatory and ethical elements. However, unlike levitations and this-worldly flights (which involve travel across the geographies of the terrestrial world), an ascension takes one beyond the dimensions of human space and history, since vertical movement is often synonymous with movement through, or the abolition of, time. Ascensions are typologically different from levitations and this-worldly flights in that ascensions often include apocalyptic or eschatological themes. Thus, although they appear in other traditions as well, it is in Zoroastrianism, apocalyptic Judaism, Christianity, and Islam that myths of ascension are most prevalent, for it is in these traditions that the end of history is most consistently associated with the ascension of a savior into the vertical heavens above the terrestrial realm.

Figures from the world's religions who ascend to other worlds—prophets, visionaries, saints, founders, perfected beings, and so on—sometimes return to earth with new power or knowledge that is of soteriological benefit to the community as a whole. Such an ascending and returning mediator might well function, then, as a shaman. In other instances, he or she remains in the sacred world above, never to return. Such a person might then serve as a model for others in their religious practices and attitudes, or as an example of a new and transformed being.

SEE ALSO Ascension; Birds; Shamanism.

BIBLIOGRAPHY

The best place to begin further reading on flight and flight symbolism is with three works by Mircea Eliade: *Myths, Dreams and Mysteries* (New York, 1960), pp. 99–122; *Patterns in Comparative Religion* (New York, 1958), pp. 102–108; and *Shamanism: Archaic Techniques of Ecstasy,* 2d ed., rev. & enl. (New York, 1964), pp. 190–198, 477–507, and elsewhere. As always, Eliade's works are useful for their extensive bibliographies as well as their typological insights.

Students interested in the varieties of magical flight (more specifically, varieties of the *magische Flucht* of this essay's typology) in the world's folktales should look to Stith Thompson's *Motif-Index of Folk Literature,* 2d ed., rev. & enl., 6 vols. (Bloomington, Ind., and Helsinki, 1955–1958). Sample motifs include the following: D670, Magic Flight; E372, Soul in Form of Bird; F61, Person Wafted to Sky; F62, Bird Carries Person to or from Upper World; F1021, Extraordinary Flights through the Air. Folklorists would also want to see Antti Aarne's *Verzeichnis der Märchentypen,* translated and enlarged by Stith Thompson as *The Types of the Folk-Tale* (1928; reprint, New York, 1971), entries 313–314, "The Magic Flight," or Aarne's *Die magische Flucht* (Helsinki, 1930).

Those who wish to find traditional accounts of levitations, magical flights, and ascensions in the lives of Christian saints have no better place to turn than the *Acta Sanctorum,* a mammoth collection (64 volumes) of hagiographies edited by the Bollandists in a project that was begun in the seventeenth century by Johannes Bollandus and was carried on by Godefridus Henschenius and subsequent editors from the Society of Jesus in Belgium (Brussels, 1643–1931). A less imposing collection, and one centering exclusively on aerial events in the lives of the saints, is Olivier LeRoy's pedantic yet still somewhat amused *Levitation: An Examination of the Evidence and Explanations* (London, 1928). For accounts of celestial travel, usually by the soul after death, in antiquity, see Josef Kroll's *Die Himmelfarht der Seele in der Antike* (Cologne, 1931). A recent work that in a way complements LeRoy and Kroll is Ioan P. Culianu's "Le vol magique dans l'antiquité tardive," *Revue de l'histoire des religions* 198 (January–March 1981): 57–66; a short study of instances in late antiquity when people who are supposed to be able to fly fail to do so.

For views of the soul as a bird, see James G. Frazer's *The Golden Bough,* part 2, *Taboo and the Perils of the Soul,* 3d ed., rev. & enl. (London, 1911), or Julius von Negelein's "Seele als Vogel," *Globus* 74 (1901): 357–361, 381–384. Arthur Maurice Hocart's notion that magical flight derives from an ancient solar worship appears in his "Flying through the Air," *Indian Quarterly* (1923): 28–31 (also in *Indian Antiquary* 52 [1923]: 80–82). Readers will find Geo Widengren's ideas on divine kingship and the aerial motif in his *The Ascension of the Apostle and the Heavenly Book* (*King and Savior III*) (Uppsala, 1950) and *Muḥammed, the Apostle of God, and His Ascension* (Uppsala, 1955).

For a study of Zoroastrian notions of ascension, see Martin Haug's *Über das Ardâi Virâf nameh* (Munich, 1879). For a collection and discussion of Jewish, Christian, Gnostic, Greek, Roman, and Persian apocalyptic tales of ascension, see *Apocalypse: The Morphology of a Genre,* edited by John J. Collins, special issue of *Semeia* 14 (1975).

New Sources

Luck-Huyse, Karin. *Der Traum von Fliegen in der Anticke: mit 12 Aildungen.* Stuttgart, 1997.

WILLIAM K. MAHONY (1987)
Revised Bibliography

FLOOD, THE.

Many peoples relate that floods accompany the end of a world. According to one Egyptian text, the world will disappear in the Nun, the divine water where the first god was formed (*The Book of Going Forth by Day* 175). For the Aztec and the Maya, the universe goes through several eras, separated from each other by the invasion of waves. India has successive creations, in which everything is abolished by a vast expanse of water; this water then constitutes the ocean from which the next creation will arise (*Mahābhārata* 3.188.80, 3.189.42).

Several tales associate humans with this universal drama. The god Faro of the Bambara holds back the waters that will one day submerge the earth, to make way for the future world; warned of this occurrence, people must arm themselves with objects that will ensure their salvation. Iranian texts evoke the snows and floods that will cover the world at the end of a cosmic millennium; in anticipation of this crisis, Yima brings together a number of men in a hidden domain; they will survive and ensure the rebirth of humanity in the next millennium (*Vendidad* 2.22–41). A famous tale from the *Mahābhārata* makes Manu, the very symbol of man, the sole survivor of the flood; it is he who, through his spiritual austerities, will become the author of the new creation (*Śathapatha Brāhmaṇa* 1.8.1–6; *Mahābhārata* 3.190.2–56; *Bhāgavata Purāṇa* 8.24).

The most numerous narratives, however, deal with another sort of flood. They are more limited and find the full sense of their meaning in the history of mankind. They constitute one of its major expressions; for mankind, there is an antediluvian and a postdiluvian world.

THE ANTECEDENTS OF THE FLOOD; ITS CAUSES. Blunders sometimes characterize the beginning of a cosmogony, for example, the first union and first births of the Japanese deities Izanagi and Izanami, in the *Kojiki.* In an Indonesian myth, divine patriarchs came down one day from the heavens to the earth that was emerging from the waters. The first of them perched himself on the southern extremity and unbalanced it, so that it was inundated by the waves. The second placed himself at the other extremity as a counterbalance, but it folded up; the northern part plunged into the waves while the middle rose up. It was not until the last two patriarchs settled down in the central region that the earth recovered its flatness and stability.

In an equally awkward way, the gods began several times to create humanity on several occasions; floods are one of the means that they used to destroy the unfortunate results of their initial endeavors. After creating the heavens and the earth in darkness, say the Quechua peoples of South America, the god Viracocha made human beings too big; he turned some into statues and destroyed the rest with a flood. In the *Popul Vuh,* the sacred book of the Maya, formative or progenitor spirits create the first animated mannequins. These lived and procreated, but "this was only a trial, an attempt at humanity." They disappeared in the course of a complex series of events, in a vast inundation (*Popol Vuh* 3–4). Instead of annihilating an imperfect humanity, sometimes the creator god tries to improve it; he eliminates the defective humans by use of a flood. When everything seemed to be complete, say the Desána of South America, a number of plagues overcame the world, and evil beings ravaged humankind. Seeing the suffering of those he had created, Sun brought on a flood that drowned all the living, and then a fire that burned everything. There were survivors, however, and the god had them brought up.

In most of the myths, the flood occurs after a more complex series of events in which human behavior plays a decisive role, although humans are not necessarily at fault. In one Philippine story, the god of the sky causes a flood to destroy humanity because it was becoming too numerous. In a Mesopotamian myth, the growth of humanity is accompanied by a perturbation that tires out the gods; to destroy it, they unleash several catastrophes, the last of which is a flood (Lambert and Millard, 1969). Usually, however, humans commit some characteristic error. They refuse to give a god what he asks of them, show almost no compassion for the unfortunate, take to evil, or disobey religious and moral laws. In *Genesis*, it is because of the evil in humans that God wished to wipe them out (*Gn.* 6:1–7, 6:17).

The Survivors. In myths where the flood is supposed to destroy the original, defective humankind, sometimes the latter disappears completely. In other cases, there are one or more survivors.

The existing tales do not state what all the qualities are that earned the survivors this privilege. The more explicit stories, however, attribute particular traits to them. The Greek Deukalion was a son of the god Prometheus (Lucian, *De dea Syria* 12ff.). A close relationship joins Atrahasis or Utanapishtim to the Mesopotamian god of waters, the sage Enki-Ea (*Epic of Gilgamesh*, tablet 11; Lambert and Millard, 1969). Furthermore, they themselves seem to possess an eminent wisdom. The merits of the survivors are more evident elsewhere. Alone among humans, they give the gods what they ask. In Hindu myth, Manu is a great *ṛṣi*. A lengthy practice of asceticism raises him above his fellow mortals; he is able to recognize and save the divine being who, in the form of a fish, requests his protection. The biblical Noah by contrast is the only just man in an evil humanity.

The Postdiluvian World. It has been seen that when the flood destroys a world and all of humanity, it sometimes precedes the creation of a new universe. It appears to separate two successive eras within a cyclical time. On this point, however, matters are not always clear. Although the Egyptian Nun, into which the world will disappear, is identical to the primordial waters, it is not clear that another world will ever emerge from it. A Carib myth says that humans will one day disappear with the entire universe, which does not seem to leave any hope of a new beginning; a flood that has already taken place to punish human evil simply warns them of the final catastrophe, for which humankind will also be to blame.

What happens when floods are linked more specifically to the fate of mortals? In some cases, the gods, after completely destroying the original human species, create another one; in other cases, the survivors themselves must ensure the survival of the human race.

This is not always a matter of course. When only one person escapes death, a miracle is needed to provide that person with offspring. In a Jivaroan myth, the solitary man plants a part of his own flesh in the earth; from this a woman is born, with whom he couples. Other South American Indians relate that the woman came from bamboo. After the destruction of the world in Hindu myth, Manu feels the desire for posterity. He gives himself over to ascetic practices and offers a sacrifice. In the year that follows, a woman is born, approaches him, and says, "I am your daughter." He begets upon her the race of his descendants by practicing more spiritual austerities.

Things are less unusual when either a couple or numerous individuals escape death; in this case the conditions of natural procreation are fulfilled. However, it may be observed that the salvation of the survivors is in itself a marvel; in many cases, they owe their survival to divine intervention. In Australian Aboriginal myth, only the ancestors survive the flood: By eliminating their evil descendants, the inundation permits a return to origins, from which humankind will be able to start anew. Many myths attribute qualities to the survivors that set them apart: Their descendants will be the products of a process of selection. In short, even when the present humanity issues from antediluvian mankind, it constitutes a second race.

Thus, in the history of humankind, just as it sometimes happens in the history of the cosmos, a destructive flood precedes a sort of new creation. The story of *Genesis* is a good example; Yahveh repeats to Noah's family the words he had spoken to Adam and Eve: "Be fecund, multiply on the earth and rule it" (*Gn.* 9:1ff.; cf. 1:28). But this new beginning is unique; when on the scale of humanity, there no longer cyclical time. This is evident in the biblical concept: The flood takes place within a linear history that goes from an absolute beginning to a definitive end.

The Position of Postdiluvian Humanity. When the flood is supposed to correct the effects of an initial blunder, it fulfills a positive function and is part of progress. In this case, however, it must be noted that the second race is imperfect; it commits errors and undergoes many vicissitudes. In Quechua myth, the new men ignore Viracocha and do not venerate him. This is why the god causes a fire to fall from the heavens, which burns the earth; only those who beg for mercy are spared. The position such myths ascribe to present-day humanity is similar to that found in the other types of stories.

The flood sometimes appears to be a part of a more general degradation. On the original earth, say the Guaraní of Paraguay, people lived close to the gods. Then incest unleashed a series of events, after which the flood wiped out humanity. A new earth was then created, the land of evil reserved for humans. This pessimistic viewpoint is not common. More typically the flood follows a period of degradation and puts an end to it.

In all types of the myth, the new humanity exhibits traits that distinguish it from the old. Not only is it civilized, but many tales associate the flood with the origins of civilization itself. Viracocha teaches the rudiments of civilization to the second Quechua race he has just created, and the *Popul Vuh* relates how Maya civilization developed during the second humanity. In a myth of the Desána of Colombia, the sun god sends his daughter among the survivors of the flood to teach them the rules of living. Similarly, after a flood and other catastrophes, in a myth of the Fali of Chad and Sudan, the high god makes an ark descend from the heavens with the rain. This ark contains the symbol of all plant species, of wild and domesticated animals, and of the metals and tools of the smithy. Even in the pessimistic Guaraní myth, the man who survives the flood makes manioc, maize, and sweet potatoes appear.

In other narratives, the culture hero and the being who saves humanity from the flood are one and the same. This dual role appearsin stories told among African peoples and among American Indians. In Greek myth, Prometheus is not only the hero who gives fire to humans and teaches them the arts of civilization; it is also he who teaches Deukalion how to escape the flood.

Several peoples undoubtedly knew of the existence of an antediluvian civilization. The Mesopotamians list the kings prior to the cataclysm, while the Hebrews tell the story of those who, compelled to work, have succeeded each other on the earth up to Noah. But in these cases too, the flood is associated with the history of civilization. Ea, the god who saves Utanapishtim, had been the protector of the wise men of old, to whom Utanapishtim himself could be related; Gilgamesh, who met him, transmitted an antediluvian wisdom to humanity. The survivor of the Sumerian flood, Atrahasis, takes "the master craftsmen" with him in his ark. Noah is "the farmer." After the flood, his family receives moral laws: This is when homicide is clearly prohibited, when meat as well as plants are offered as food to humankind, and when the rules of slaughter are prescribed.

In addition, humanity finds itself in a new position vis-à-vis the gods. According to the Guaraní myth, before the flood people lived with the gods on earth; on the second earth, they are alone. For many Australian peoples, the flood coincides with the withdrawal of the "*dema* deity," who abandons earth for a celestial dwelling. In the biblical tale itself, the flood is the culmination of events that begin with the expulsion of Adam and Eve from Paradise; it follows the murder by Cain and other occurrences. In mentioning these misfortunes Yahveh repents for having created humanity.

The Greek myths make a correlation between this rupture and the origin of civilization. The events that include the flood give rise to both of them. Prior to them, humans received everything that was necessary for their subsistence from the gods and did not have to work at all. Separated from the gods, they must now toil in order to live, but they have learned the arts that will let them provide for their own needs.

The separation that accompanies the flood is not absolute, however. At the end of the inundation, there is a new sort of relation flourishing between humans and gods. Those who beg mercy of Viracocha while he burns them acknowledge his divinity, whereas before they had neglected him. The procedures of the cult of the *dema* deities are defined after their separation, at the end of the Australian floods. Furthermore, the aurora borealis then becomes a sign for humankind of the *demas*' disposition. The daughter whose birth is brought about by Manu's spiritual austerities bears the name of a ritual offering and also symbolizes it. By committing the act that unleashes the entire process of separation between humans and gods—the unequal allotment of a bovine—Prometheus makes a gesture to which the ritual of the great Greek sacrifices will refer: By bringing fire to mortals he gives them the instrument necessary for the burning of victims. At the end of the flood, his surviving son, Deukalion, celebrates the first sacrifice, and several traditions see in him the founder of cults. When the Mesopotamian flood has ended, Utanapishtim makes a sacrifice whose ritual is described in detail by the myth. Similarly, "Noah built an altar to the Lord, and took of every clean animal and of every clean bird, and offered burnt offerings on the altar" (*Gn.* 8:20). In addition, Yahveh makes an agreement with him that encompasses all of humankind to come, and of which the rainbow will remain a sign visible to the eyes of humans.

THE FORMS OF THE FLOOD AND THE FUNCTION OF THE DILUVIAL WATERS. The flood is not the only catastrophe with which the gods threaten to wipe out humanity. As the Egyptian wise men supposedly told Solon, "Men were destroyed and will be destroyed again in many ways; fire and water were the instruments of the most serious destructions" (Plato, *Timaeus* 22c). In some tales the flood itself is associated with other scourges, especially the burning of the earth. In the epic of Atrahasis it follows a plague and terrible droughts. Nevertheless, the myths return to the image of destruction by water, with particular frequency.

The diluvial waters are not just any water. As has been seen, the water into which the world disappears at the end of its existence coincides with the primordial water. The earth that the Indonesian patriarch unbalanced is an insular earth, located in the original ocean whose waves invade it.

If the flood takes the form of rain, as is often the case, this rain comes from the heavenly waters and can be accompanied by a brutal ascent of underground waters as well. "Nergal tears the beams from the heaven, Ninurta makes it unlock its dams . . . the foundations of the earth are broken like a shattered jar," reads a passage in the *Epic of Gilgamesh*. *Genesis* continues: "All the fountains of the great deep burst forth and the windows of the heavens were opened" (*Gn.* 7:11). The Greek poet Nonnus (early fifth century CE) expresses the same notion. The world is thus submerged by the waters that surround it on all sides. According to some myths, these cosmic waters are the very same primordial waters that were thrown back to the periphery of the universe at the creation.

The diluvial waves thus possess the virtues of water in all their original vigor. It is not only that they can be destructive, as when at the end of the world they reduce everything to a state of original indifferentiation. They are also capable of fulfilling an amniotic function, when a new creation succeeds this annihilation. Perhaps their cathartic nature can be seen in their elimination of the bad elements of the human race. Their generative strength is manifested in the marvelous rebirth and proliferation of a purified humanity. They can, finally, play a role in the immortalization of heroes who have lived through the flood and survived. The brother and sister whose incestuous union provoked the flood of the Guaraní myth went into the water, in animal form, and were deified. The Mesopotamian survivors, Utanapishtim and his wife, also became immortal.

CONCLUSION. The influence peoples have exercised over each other in the course of history is not enough to explain why myths of the flood are present on every continent. In order to account for this, some authors have supposed that everywhere people preserve the memory of distant prehistoric catastrophes that destroyed the universe or vast regions of the earth. Such an explanation strikes this writer as misguided. For it to be pertinent, one would have to be able to explain in similar fashion the other mythic scourges that have imperiled humanity: the burning of the earth, for example, or the rage of a goddess in the form of a lion, as in an Egyptian myth about the destruction of humankind.

By resorting to this type of explanation, one also neglects the very thing that makes the flood so significant: the return of the world to its original state, in the case of cosmic destructions, and, in the case of destructions that have a special impact on humankind, the idea of an original intimacy between humans and gods, the idea of their separation, and, finally, the belief that a relationship unites them despite this separation. Mythic thought uses the narrative to express these basic intuitions and elaborate on them. Commonplace occurrences, such as epidemics, ravishing fires, droughts or floods, the fear of wild animals, furnish it with vehicles for this purpose. Among such vehicles, the symbolic richness of water confers a special status to the image of the flood.

SEE ALSO Water.

BIBLIOGRAPHY

Eliade, Mircea. "The Waters and Water Symbolism." In his *Patterns in Comparative Religion*, pp. 188–215. New York, 1958.

Gerland, Georg. *Der Mythus der Sintflut.* Bonn, 1912.

Ginzberg, Louis. *The Legends of the Jews*, vol. 1 (1909). Translated by Henrietta Szold et al. Reprint, Philadelphia, 1937. See pages 145–167.

Keeler, Clyde E. *Secrets of the Cuna Earthmother: A Comparative Study of Ancient Religion.* New York, 1960. See pages 59–82.

Lambert, W. G., and A. R. Millard. *Atra-Hasis: The Babylonian Story of the Flood.* Oxford, 1969.

Müller, Werner. "Die ältesten amerikanschen Sintfluterzählungen." Ph.D. diss., Rheinische Friedrich-Wilhelms-Universität Bonn, 1930.

Osborne, Harold. *South American Mythology.* Feltham, England, 1968. See pages 100–105.

Pratt, Jane Abbott. *Consciousness and Sacrifice: An Interpretation of Two Episodes in the Indian Myth of Manu.* New York, 1967. See pages 3–33.

Robinson, Roland, et al. *Aboriginal Myths and Legends.* Melbourne, 1966.

Usener, Hermann. *Die Sintflutsagen.* Bonn, 1899.

Villas Boas, Orlando, and Claudio Villas Boas. *Xingu: The Indians, Their Myths.* Edited by Kenneth S. Breecher. New York, 1970.

New Sources

Huggett, Richard J. *Cataclysms and Earth History: The Development of Diluvialism.* Oxford; New York, 1989.

Pleins, J. David. *When the Great Abyss Opened: Classic and Contemporary Readings of Noah's Flood.* Oxford; New York, 2003.

JEAN RUDHARDT (1987)
Translated from French by Erica Meltzer
Revised Bibliography

FLORENSKII, PAVEL

FLORENSKII, PAVEL (1882–1943/1950s?), was a Russian Orthodox priest and theologian. Florenskii was born in Evlakh, Azerbaijan, in Transcaucasian Russia. His engineer father was Russian, perhaps half-Georgian; his mother was Armenian. Religion did not play more than a cultural role in the Florenskii family. Young Florenskii was a child prodigy during his elementary school years in Tiflis (present-day Tbilisi), Georgia. He was sent to study mathematics at Moscow University, where he also became intensely interested in philosophy. At the university he studied with the famous Sergei Trubetskoi and L. M. Lopatin, falling under their religious influence. At this time, with his friends V. F. Ern and A. V. Elchaninov, who was to become a famous émigré Russian Orthodox priest in Western Europe after the Russian Revolution, Florenskii founded the utopian Christian Brotherhood of Battle, an organization that worked for social reforms in Russia and a new church-state policy that would give freedom to the church along the lines of the theocratic philosophy of the sophiologist Vladimir Solov'ev. Upon graduation from the university, Florenskii gave up a research fellowship in mathematics to enter the Moscow Theological Academy on the advice of his spiritual guide, Bishop Antonii Florensov. After completing his studies at the academy in 1908, Florenskii was elected to the academy's faculty of the history of philosophy. He married Anna Mikhailovna Giatsintova on August 17, 1910, and was ordained a priest of the Russian Orthodox church on April 24, 1911.

As a priest, Florenskii never held a formal pastorate, although he served in one of the chapels at the Saint Sergius Trinity Monastery (at present-day Sergiyev Posad), where the Moscow Theological Academy was located, and he was always eager for pastoral work. His good friend Sergei Bulgakov, who returned to Christianity through Florenskii's ministry and became a famous Russian Orthodox archpriest and theologian, testified in his memoirs to the pastoral zeal of his spiritual guide. So also did the renowned, although very different, philosophers N. O. Lossky and Vasilii Rozanov, who also recovered their religious faith through his ministry, both the latter, however, would come to express serious doubts about their mentor's philosophical vision.

Florenskii wrote only one book of theology, the highly debated and generally considered epoch-making collection of twelve essays on theodicy titled *Stolp i utverzhdenie istiny* (The pillar and bulwark of the truth). Published in 1914 in a special typeface selected especially by the author, the book consists of more than eight hundred pages, with more than four hundred footnotes and commentaries touching upon virtually every area of human study: theology, philosophy, philology, history, mathematics, medicine, art, the various sciences, and even the occult. It is written in the form of intimate letters to a friend which Nikolai Berdiaev, among others, criticized for its pretentious aesthetical and lyrical stylization. The chapters, each introduced by a literary vignette, bear such titles as "Doubt," "Friendship," "Triunity," "Sophia," "The Comforter," "Light of Truth," "Contradiction," "Sin," and "Gehenna."

Stolp i utverzhdenie istiny is not a systematic work. Its controlling intuition is expressed in its opening sentence: "Living religious experience [is] the sole legitimate method for understanding [religious, and certainly Christian] dogma." The author's fundamental claim is that ultimate truth, which is religious, comes from the liturgical, spiritual, and ecclesial experience of the whole person within the community of faith and worship of the Orthodox church; this experience fundamentally is the gracious realization by creatures of the indwelling divine life of the trinitarian godhead: Father, Son, and Holy Spirit. Following such thinkers as Solov'ev, Aleksei Khomiakov, and Ivan Kireevskii, and interpreting the theology of the Eastern Christian church fathers and the liturgical hymnography and iconography of the Orthodox tradition in their light, Florenskii forges a magnificent, and extremely complex, worldview. At the heart of Florenskii's worldview lies the experience of free and joyous communion in truth, love, and beauty. This communion is perfected by all creatures made in the image of the uncreated Trinity of divine persons. The eternal being and life of the Trinity provides the archetypal structure for human existence and fulfillment.

The work that formed the basis for *Stolp i utverzhdenie istiny* was accepted by the Moscow Theological Academy as an orthodox expression of the faith of the Russian church, albeit in highly individualistic and idiosyncratic form, and Florenskii was granted his doctoral degree after its presentation. However, careful analyses of the finished and published product, accomplished almost exclusively outside of Russia after the Revolution, have questioned the work on virtually every point. Classical Orthodox theologians and scholars such as Vladimir Lossky and Georges Florovsky have rejected it as an expression of church dogmatics, and philosophers such as Nikolai Berdiaev have faulted its philosophical argumentation. So also have philosophical interpreters such as Vasilii Zenkovskii and N. O. Lossky, the latter of whom, as has been seen, was greatly influenced in his return to Christianity by Florenskii. In all cases, however, the brilliance of the gifted thinker, the fundamental correctness of his guiding intuition, and his rejection of a rationalist approach to religious and specifically Christian thinking, indeed, to any truly metaphysical reflections on the ultimate nature of things, have been applauded by all who have had the courage to labor through his prodigious creation.

After the Bolshevik Revolution of 1917 Florenskii was inducted by the regime into scientific service, often embarrassing the new rulers by appearing at scientific conferences and classes in his priestly cassock, wearing the cross. He worked for the Highest State Technical-Artistic Studios and the Commission for the Electrification of Soviet Russia. A member of the Academy of Sciences and editor of the Soviet *Technical Encyclopedia,* he was honored for several important scientific discoveries, one of which had to do with the refining of oil. He also wrote standard textbooks for Soviet schools. At the same time, he preached against the excesses of the regime whose fundamental worldview was contrary to his own. It is believed that Florenskii was imprisoned permanently during the Stalinist terror in 1933. According to Soviet records, he died in 1943, but other sources indicate that he may have survived into the 1950s. In 1956 the Soviet government formally rehabilitated the memory of the man who was called by many critics of his work the "Russian Leonardo da Vinci."

BIBLIOGRAPHY

Pavel Florenskii's major work, *Stolp i utverzhdenie istiny,* was originally published in Moscow in 1914. A limited reprint was made in Berlin in 1929. Translations into French (Lausanne, 1975) and Italian (Milan, 1974) also exist. An English version of the fifth letter on the Holy Spirit, titled "The Comforter," appears in Alexander Schmemann's *Ultimate Questions: An Anthology of Modern Russian Religious Thought* (New York, 1965). Essays on the life and work of Florenskii may be found in N. O. Lossky's *History of Russian Philosophy* (New York, 1951) and Vasilii V. Zenkovskii's *A History of Russian Philosophy,* translated by George L. Kline (New York, 1953). The only book in English on Florenskii, which contains complete bibliographical information in all languages, is Robert Slesinski's *Pavel Florensky: A Metaphysics of Love* (Crestwood, N. Y., 1984).

THOMAS HOPKO (1987)

FLOWERS. The blossom, or reproductive part, of trees, shrubs, and other flora is known as the flower. This part of a growing plant takes on very special and often sacred meanings in every culture and religion of the world. The symbolism of flowers is often determined by a flower's natural properties: its color and smell, where it grows, and the length of its blooming period. While each kind of flower may be assigned a special meaning, flowers in general symbolize beauty and the transitory nature of life. Flowers are often used to represent the cycle of life and are an important part of rituals and ceremonies that celebrate birth, marriage, death, and the promise of regeneration. Flowers also serve as offerings or as a means of communicating with a deity or other sacred being. They are frequently sacred gifts bestowed as signs of welcome or in celebration of victory. Flowers represent certain deities and are associated with cultural beliefs regarding heaven or the afterlife.

It is not just the bloom of a plant that holds these special meanings. Several different plants may be combined to create a "flower" for sacred purposes. In some societies other parts of a living plant may be referred to as a "flower." In Japan, maple leaves are considered to be flowers even though they are not the bloom of the maple tree. And even sea coral was treated as a flower in nineteenth-century Christianity in the United States and was believed to represent heavenly love. Palms and evergreens are often included in the general category of flowers and are used in sacred contexts.

Flowers are used to teach general religious principles. The Japanese myth *Mr. Butterfly and His Flowers* teaches that all creatures are destined to become Buddhas. In this story a hermit is visited by a number of women who are actually the spirits of the flowers from his garden, which he had left behind in his search for enlightenment. These flowers, as spirits of women, had come to share his Buddhist attainment because flowers too are on the path to enlightenment.

The art of flower arrangement in Japan is called ikebana ("living flowers") and has spiritual significance. The word for flower is *hana* and includes blossoms, branches, foliage of trees, as well as individual flowers and grasses. The art of arranging these "flowers" expresses the Buddhist ideals of content, calm, and piety. Religious spirit, restraint, serene disposition, and respect for humankind are qualities the flower arranger must possess as he or she strives to portray the growth cycle of the plant from bud to maturity. The Daoist concepts of *in* (Chin., *yin:* female, passive, earth, moon, darkness, coolness, silence) and *yo* (Chin., *yang:* male, heaven, sun, action, power) must also be combined in the flower arrangement.

The lotus is used in many cultures to stand for the ideal of purity and perfection. The plant grows in muddy water and yet remains pure. The flower itself is most frequently believed to symbolize the oneness of Buddhist instruction and enlightenment.

FLOWERS AND DEITIES. Flowers are connected to the sacred realm through their association with gods and goddesses. Flora, the Roman goddess of springtime and flowers, brings beauty and fragrance to blossoms, sweetness to honey, and aroma to wine. The Aztec god Xochipilli Cinteotl was one of thirteen day lords. He was the prince of flowers—the god of beauty, love, happiness, and youth. His female twin Xochiquetzal ("flower feather") was also the goddess of love. The Hindu love god, Kāma, is represented riding a parrot with a bow and arrow made of flowers. Ko-no-hana-sa-kura-hime ("the lady who causes trees to bloom") is a supernatural being of Japan, a fairy represented by the cherry blossom. The Japanese *tennyo* (like the Indian *devatās*) are female deities of the sky. They play music and scatter flowers and the aroma of celestial perfume. The *tennyo* surround pious Buddhists like angels, they appear as decorations in Buddhist temples, and some have their own shrines. The *tennyo* may be identified with Shintō goddesses. In Zoroastrianism, thirty different species of flowers are associated with the thirty *yazatas*, or deities, that preside over the thirty days of the month.

Flowers may be created through the actions of gods. Almost every culture credits the presence of all forms of life, including flowers, to the sacred realm. The ancient Greek and Roman religions include several tales of creation. Jupiter, wishing to render Hercules immortal, placed him at the breast of the sleeping Juno. Some drops of her milk fell to the earth from which sprang the white lily.

The Muslims consider the rose a sacred plant that had sprung from the drops of perspiration that fell from the Prophet during his heavenly journey. Among the Indian cultures of Latin America the geranium is believed to have grown from drops of Christ's blood that fell as he ran from Satan. And the lily of the valley is called "Our Lady's Tears," because this plant grew from the tears the Virgin Mary shed at the cross of Christ.

Flowers are also associated with the birth or creation of deities. Ancient Egyptian religion described the fixed stars in the heavens as gods or souls, and also as fields of heavenly flowers and plants, believed to be the dwelling place of the blessed dead. It was from these fields of flowers and souls that the gods were created. Ancient Egyptians also believed that the sun was born every day from a blue lotus in the celestial ocean. In Asia the lotus is the flower on which Brahmā alighted when he sprang from the navel of Viṣṇu. From this beginning Brahmā ordered the existence of all worlds.

Flowers and deities together may protect human birth. In China the *bodhisattva* Guanyin is known as "the lady who brings children." Sitting on a lotus flower and holding a child in her arms, she is a goddess of fertility and aids in the treatment of all sickness. Her image is found in most homes. Kishimojin (Hariti) is a female divinity of Japan who was converted by the Buddha. She is the protector of children and women in childbirth. This goddess is portrayed standing with a baby at her breast and holding the flower of happiness.

Important symbolism is attached to flowers through their appearance with a sacred being. Many times this connection arises because of particular characteristics of the flower or the season of the year in which the bloom appears and the relation of this blossoming to the religious calendar of the culture. Artists have depicted the angel Gabriel coming to Mary with a spray of lilies in his hand to announce that she will be the mother of Christ. Many flowers are connected to Mary. These flowers all stand for virginity and purity: the annunciation lily, the flowering almond, the madonna lily, the gillyflower, the snow drop, and the rose. The thorns of the rose allude to the suffering of Mary as the mother of Christ. Christ's crown of thorns is believed to have been formed from the acanthus, bramble, or rose-briar. The hawthorn is also believed to be a symbol of Jesus, because it blooms at Christmastime. Because the Easter lily blooms at Eastertide, it is a symbol of Christ's resurrection.

Flowers and Rituals. Flowers as a link between humankind and the deities are presented as offerings to the sacred world, as food for the gods, or even as a reward from the gods. Deities may be appeased and worshiped through the singing of hymns, the anointing of images, the use of lights and incense, and through the offering of foods and flowers. In India flowers are said to have dropped from heaven to express the joy of the gods.

The religions of Latin America are a mixture of sixteenth-century Catholicism and native Indian religions. In many areas the seven most important saint's days are celebrated in festivals lasting three days. The first day of the festival is spent renewing flower decorations and offerings for house and church altars. The flowers used on this day, and throughout the year, are important offerings to the saints and to God. The last day of the festival falls on the saint's day as declared in the Roman Catholic calendar.

Among the Sherpas of Nepal, the high gods have achieved salvation and bliss and are utterly fulfilled and self-contained. Following traditional Buddhist beliefs, these gods have obtained enlightenment partly through conquering the delights of the senses. The high gods are unconcerned with humans and must be drawn down to aid humankind through a complex ritual involving sacred offerings. The god is "trapped" or seduced by the various offerings, each designed to appeal to one of the senses. The flower used in this ritual tempts the god to use his sense of smell.

Rites of passage. A rite of passage is a vehicle for transforming an individual, or a group of individuals, from one way of being to another through a series of culturally recognized stages. In most cultures, these transitions are marked or given meaning through the ritual use of flowers.

The earliest evidence for the use of flowers in a rite of passage is connected with a Neanderthal burial in the Shanidar Cave in Iraq. This burial site dates from sixty thousand years ago and reveals that the Neanderthals covered the body of the deceased with at least eight species of flowers.

The association of flowers with rituals of death occurs all over the world. The Greeks and Romans covered the dead and their graves with flowers. The souls of dying Buddhists in Japan are carried upward on a lotus, and the gravestones in cemeteries may rest on carved lotuses. Lotus leaves are also constructed out of gold or silver paper and are carried at Japanese funerals. Tahitians leave bouquets wrapped in ferns by the body after death and then pour floral perfume over the corpse to ease its passage into the sacred afterlife.

In Zorastrianism, the "rite of flowers" is performed by two priests; it invokes the blessings of the sacred and includes vows to the deceased. The priests conduct a complicated exchange of flowers accompanied by prayers and gestures. These flower exchanges symbolize the exchange of life between this world and the world after death. The ritual is also concerned with good and evil and the importance of good thoughts, words, and deeds.

Flowers are used in marriage rituals as an expression of fertility, virginity, purity, and to represent the sacred union of the bride and groom. Christian weddings in the United States include flowers for the altar, a bridal bouquet that represents the bride's fertility and the children that will result from the marriage, and flowers for virtually all the ritual participants. A Roman Catholic bride often lays her bridal bouquet at the foot of a statue of the Virgin Mary at the conclusion of the wedding ceremony as a dedication of her virginity to the mother of Christ.

The marriage ceremony of Java is a syncretism of Hinduism, Islam, and folk religion. This ceremony is completed only when the bride and groom exchange the *kembang majang* ("blossoming flowers") that represent their virginity. These "flowers" are large composite plants. The stems are from a banana tree trunk, the "blossom" consists of leaves, and the entire "flower" is wrapped in coconut branches.

Flowers and the afterlife or paradise. Not only are flowers used to express cultural beliefs about the changes in the life cycle, but they are also connected to ideas of life after death and paradise. Chinese Buddhists believe that at the hour of death the Buddha will appear to them, and their souls will be placed in a lotus. The souls will remain there until they are cleansed of all impurities, and then they will go to the Land of Extreme Felicity in the West, a paradise of all delights where showers of blossoms fall to the ground. The Aztec paradise was located above the ninth heaven and was called Xochitlicacan, the "place of flowers." The Huichol Indians of northwest Mexico call their paradise Wirikúta, a land of many flowers and much water. It is there that the ancient ones dwell, the ancestors and deities of the Huichol. These ancestor deities are called *neyeteurixa,* from *yeteurixa,* a thistle plant that flowers and then becomes the dry burrs found in the everyday world. Through the ingestion of peyote, or the five-petaled "flower," these Indians are able to journey to Wirikúta and to meet and join their ancestors amid the flowers of paradise.

Supernatural Powers of Flowers. Flowers are believed to possess powers that arise from their connection to the sacred realm. Greek and Roman religion held the amaranth as a sacred flower and associated it with immortality. In Switzerland it is believed that if this flower is worn on Ascension Day, it will render the wearer invisible. The peony is valued for medicinal properties and is named in celebration of Apollo, who as Paeon healed the wounds received by the gods in the Trojan War.

The Maya Indians of Zinacantan perform an illness-curing ceremony called "he enters in the flowers." This ritual includes visits to the ancestor/deity mountain shrines that surround the city of Zinacantan, as well as a ceremonial circuit of the sacred Roman Catholic churches within the town itself. This ceremonial circuit is called "great vision," referring to the number of gods visited during the ceremony, or "big flower," named for the large number of flowers necessary for the success of the procession. These flowers include not only the blooms of plants but also the sacred tips of evergreen trees. These tips are considered to be natural crosses, and two are erected alongside a permanent wooden cross to form the *calvario,* or calvary. This re-creation of the three crosses present at Christ's crucifixion is necessary for many rituals, including curing ceremonies.

PERFUME, THE ESSENCE OF FLOWERS. Flowers may also be present at sacred times in the form of incense or perfume. The aroma of the blooms is believed to reach into the sacred sphere.

The people of Mayotte in the Comoro Islands have two religious systems that exist side by side. The public and male religion is Islam, while the religion of the private domestic sphere of women is a complex system of possession by spirits. Flowers, and especially the perfume made from them, are used to celebrate the sacred in both realms. The flowers are selected for their fragrance, not for their color or form. The cologne made from these flowers is used to mark and give meaning to several occasions: the onset of puberty in women, rituals of curing, and the anointing of the bride and groom during and after their wedding, as well as of the other major participants in the marriage ceremony. Every household keeps a supply of cologne and generously sprinkles the fragrance on body and clothing on all major holidays and Fridays at the weekly mosque service. Cologne is also offered to the mullahs at family rituals, especially during *mawlid* celebrations of the month of the Prophet's birth. Perfume contacts and pleases the sacred and enables prayers to travel more quickly.

The Zoroastrian Dhup-sarvi ("ceremony of the perfumes") involves the use of fragrant flowers, flower water, and other perfumes. These are passed out to the people, who are assembled to honor the dead, and they symbolize the fragrance and joyful nature of the path that righteous souls take to the afterworld.

The meanings attached to flowers, indeed the definition of *flower* itself, vary from culture to culture. The religious significance of these blooms is a very important part of the definition of *flower* for most societies. There is power in all life, especially in this form of nature that almost universally stands for beauty, purity, and the transitory nature of life.

SEE ALSO Gardens; Incense; Lotus; Paradise; Rites of Passage.

BIBLIOGRAPHY

One of the best examples of the nineteenth-century use of flowers by Christians is Andrew Joseph Ambauen's *The Floral Apostles, or, What the Flowers Say to Thinking Man* (Milwaukee, Wis., 1900). The use and meaning of flowers in religious practices, especially the historical development of their role in ritual, is well described by Jacques Duchesne-Guillemin in *Symbols and Values in Zoroastrianism: Their Survival and Renewal* (New York, 1966). For an excellent description of the Nyingmawa (Rñiṅ-ma-pa) sect of Tibetan Buddhist beliefs and practices, see Sherry Ortner's *Sherpas through Their Rituals* (New York, 1978). This book is primarily concerned with the underlying beliefs of hospitality that shape the lives of the Sherpas of Nepal and includes a consideration of flowers and their religious significance. The use of flowers as offerings to Mayan gods and Catholic saints is explored by Evon Z. Vogt in *Zinacantan: A Maya Community in the Highlands of Chiapas* (Cambridge, Mass., 1969). This is an extensive study of the Tzotzil-speaking Indians of Guatemala and includes a thorough description of the importance of flowers in ritual. Clifford Geertz's seminal work *The Religion of Java* (New York, 1960) describes the syncretism of Hindu, Islamic, and folk beliefs that constitute Javanese religion. He includes in this work an excellent consideration of flowers as part of the life-cycle rituals and in other religious celebrations. Michael Lambek presents a fascinating account of the importance of flowers and perfume among the people of Mayotte in the Comoro Islands in his *Human Spirits: A Cultural Account of Trance in Mayotte* (New York, 1981). Flowers and the perfume made from flower petals are essential ingredients for the two religious belief systems among the Mayotte: Islam and a native folk religion that centers around trance and possession by spirits. Barbara G. Myerhoff describes two different types of "flowers" in her consideration of Huichol Indian culture. In her book *Peyote Hunt: The Sacred Journey of the Huichol Indians* (Ithaca, N.Y., 1974), flowers represent the Huichol ancestor/deities in paradise and refer to the peyote, the five-petaled flower that enables the contemporary Huichol to journey to this paradise.

New Sources

Coffey, Timothy. *The History and Folklore of North American Wildflowers.* Boston, 1994.

Hielmeyer, Marine. *The Language of Flowers: Symbols and Myths.* New York, 2001.

Innes, Miranda, and Clay Perry. *Medieval Flowers.* London, 1997.

Laufer, Geraldine Adamich. *Tussie-Mussies: The Language of Flowers.* New York, 2000.

Ward, Bobby. *A Contemplation upon Flowers: Garden Plants in Myth and Literature.* Portland, Ore., 1999.

Wells, Diana. *100 Flowers and How They Got Their Names.* New York, 1997.

PAMELA R. FRESE (1987)
Revised Bibliography

FLOW EXPERIENCE. All major world religions, as well as most sects and tribal cults, are said to produce on occasion, among their faithful, states of ecstasy or altered states of consciousness. Such experiences constitute for many believers one of the main attractions of religion, if not a proof of its ability to mediate the supernatural. In cults and sects such experiences are often induced by chemical substances ingested in ritual contexts; by fasting; by various hypnotic trances, or by what Émile Durkheim called "collective effervescence," a condition engineered by rhythmic music, dance, and ritual movements.

Remnants of such direct sensory means for inducing altered experiential states can still be found in the major religions. The use of music, chanting, lighting, and scent in liturgy and of fasting and ritual feasting clearly derive from earlier methods for producing ecstasy. But the great religious traditions have become gradually less dependent on sensory means, while at the same time they have developed the ability to induce ecstasy through cognitive disciplines. Prayer, meditation, *satori, samādhi,* despite the tremendous variety of cultural differences represented in their settings, are all mechanisms for providing a sense of mystic union with a sacred, transcendent force.

Is the ecstasy reported in religious practices and rituals unique to religion, or is it a species of a broader genus of experiential states? At least since the writings of William James, psychologists have supported the latter hypothesis. It is assumed that there is no qualitative difference between the unusual states of consciousness occasionally experienced in religious contexts and analogous states reported in a variety of secular contexts. The task for the scholar is to describe the experiential state precisely, and to explain why it occurs in the context of religious practice.

Perhaps the state of consciousness that most closely resembles accounts of religious ecstasy is the "flow experience," so named because many people have used the word *flow* in describing it. This subjective state has been reportedly experienced by creative artists when working, by athletes at the height of competition, by surgeons while performing difficult operations, and by ordinary people in the midst of their most satisfying activities. In other words, states of optimal experience in a wide variety of context, including meditation, prayer, and mystical union, are described in terms of very similar subjective parameters. The subsequent experience is "ecstatic" in that it is characterized by a sense of clarity and enjoyment that stands out from the blurred background of everyday routine.

The flow experience is characterized by the following phenomenological dimensions:

(1) a narrowing of the focus of consciousness on a clearly delimited stimulus field;

(2) exclusion from one's awareness of irrelevant immediate stimuli, memories of past events, and contemplation of the future; hence a focusing on the unfolding present;

(3) merging of action and awareness, also described as absence of doubt and critical reflection about one's current activity;

(4) awareness of clear goals and unambiguous feedback; so that one knows one's standing with reference to the goals;

(5) lack of concern regarding one's ability to control the situation;

(6) loss of self-consciousness, which in turn may lead to a sense of transcendence of ego boundaries and of union with a larger, transpersonal system.

When these conditions are present in consciousness, the experience is usually interpreted by the individual as being enjoyable and autotelic (worth seeking for its own sake). Activities available in everyday life form a continuum in terms of their capacity to induce flow. At the lowest level are "microflow" activities such as doodling, pacing, or smoking, which provide fleeting experiences of ordered existence. At the other extreme are "deep flow" activities that provide relatively lasting and totally absorbing experiences, as in creative endeavors, complex symbolic or religious thought, or the heights of physical performance.

Whether an activity is capable of providing flow depends in large part on the kind and degree of challenges (opportunities of action) that it makes available, and on the actor's skill (capacity to relate to them). When these two are in balance, flow occurs. If challenges overshadow skills, anxiety ensues; if skills are greater than the opportunities for using them, boredom follows. The complexity of a flow experience—or its ability to provide deep flow—is a function of the extent of challenges the activity presents and of the actor's skills. Games, spectacles, and rituals are structured so as to provide the maximum of flow experience.

Religious action-systems present a wide variety of opportunities for action, ranging from microflow-like repetitive physical rituals (e.g., the spinning of Tibetan prayer wheels) to the purely cognitive sequences of doctrinal exegesis. Religions occasionally are able to transform a person's entire life activity into a unified action-system with clear and congruent goals. It might be argued, for instance, that the religion of the early Puritans was an all-embracing flow activity that focused the consciousness of believers on the necessity of attaining salvation and prescribed a productive vocation as a means for attaining *certitudo salutis.* In this process Puritanism had to exclude many pleasurable experiences from the consciousness of the faithful, but within the limitations of its goals and rules it provided an all-embracing and enjoyable field of action.

In general, however, flow experiences—religious ones included—are liminal in terms of the dominant patterns of consciousness required by social existence. Prayer, ritual, meditation, or the reading of sacred texts establishes interludes of flow in a stream of consciousness that otherwise tends to be structured either too loosely or too rigidly. These activities are occasionally able to provide concrete experiences of a mode of existence more conducive to the expression of individual potentials than the socially restricted historical reality is capable of doing.

SEE ALSO Consciousness, States of; Ecstasy; Religious Experience.

BIBLIOGRAPHY

Crook, John H. *The Evolution of Human Consciousness.* London and New York, 1980.

Csikszentmihalyi, Mihaly. *Beyond Boredom and Anxiety: The Experience of Play in Work and Games.* San Francisco, 1975.

Csikszentmihalyi, Mihaly. "Toward a Psychology of Optimal Experience." In *Review of Personality and Social Psychology,* vol. 3, edited by Ladd Wheeler, pp. 13–36. Beverly Hills, Calif., 1982.

James, William. *The Varieties of Religious Experience* (1902). New York, 1963.

Laski, Marghanita. *Ecstasy: A Study of Some Secular and Religious Experiences* (1962). Reprint, Westport, Conn., 1968.

Turner, Victor. "Liminal to Liminoid, in Play, Flow, and Ritual: An Essay in Comparative Symbology." *Rice University Studies* 60 (Summer 1974): 53–92. Reprinted in Turner's collection of essays entitled *From Ritual to Theatre: The Human Seriousness of Play* (New York, 1982), pp. 20–60.

New Sources

Csikszentmihalyi, Mihaly. *Flow: The Psychology of Optimal Experience.* New York, 1990.

Csikszentmihalyi, Mihaly. *Creativity: Flow and the Psychology of Discovery and Invention.* New York, 1996.

Csikszentmihalyi, Mihaly. *Finding Flow: The Psychology of Engagement in Everyday Life.* The Masterminds Series. New York, 1997.

Hume, Lynne. "Accessing the Eternal: Dreaming 'The Dreaming' and Ceremonial Performance." *Zygon: Journal of Religion and Science* 39 (March 2004): 237–258.

Inghilleri, Paolo. *From Subjective Experience to Cultural Change.* New York, 1999.

MIHALY CSIKSZENTMIHALYI (1987)
Revised Bibliography

FOGUANGSHAN. Founded in 1967, Foguangshan (Buddha's Light Mountain) had by the beginning of the twenty-first century developed into one of the most influential Buddhist organizations in Taiwan (the Republic of China, ROC) and had opened more than 150 temples in nearly thirty countries around the world. Approximately 1,300 clerics were within the Foguang ranks in 2004, and the order's lay society, known as the Buddha's Light International Association (BLIA), had a membership in the hundreds of thousands. Activities sponsored by Foguangshan and BLIA draw more than three million participants annually.

The order's founder, Master Xingyun, was born in 1927 in Jiangsu province of mainland China. He took his vows of renunciation at age twelve in Qixia Temple, Nanjing. Ten years later he accompanied the Nationalist army as it retreated to Taiwan. Unlike most monks who had come from the mainland, Master Xingyun did not remain in Taipei (the province's capital), but instead took charge of a small temple in a more rural location and eventually established Foguangshan in Kaohsiung county. For his followers, the master symbolizes the transmission of a revitalized version of traditional Chinese culture from the mainland to Taiwan. He has kept tenuous ties with the mainland through the years, returning to his ancestral temple in 1989 and again in 2000.

Foguangshan is regarded as a leading exponent of Humanistic Buddhism (*renjian fojiao*), by which is meant a refocusing of daily practice to more directly deal with the challenges of contemporary life. The this-worldly pragmatism that serves as the focal point of Humanistic Buddhism significantly affects Master Xingyun's interpretations of Chan (Jap., Zen) and Pure Land practice. Although a forty-eighth generation holder of the Linji *dharma* scroll, only in recent years has the master encouraged devotees to make formal meditation an important part of their cultivation. Up through the 1980s, he considered Pure Land recitation a more suitable expedient means (Chin., *fangbian*; Skt., *upāya*) to attract lay followers, given their busy lives, low education level, and scant understanding of the *dharma.* Clerics were similarly dissuaded from spending too much time in the Chan hall, for to do so was regarded as contrary to the *bodhisattva* spirit of serving all beings, not just attending to one's own liberation. Only in the early 1990s, when many lay Buddhists (and even non-Buddhists) were turning to meditation as a means to relieve stress, did Master Xingyun more actively discuss the value of such practice, backing up his rhetoric by constructing Foguangshan's beautiful Chan hall.

The form of meditation that Master Xingyun considers to be most compatible with Humanistic Buddhism is "active Chan" (*dongzhong chan*). Master Baizhang's maxim "A day without work is a day without food" has been broadened radically so that, rather than only justifying farm work as suitable for monastic life, at Foguangshan it has become a paean exalting industriousness as an essential part of religious practice. "Work is nutrition," exclaims the master, while "the most miserable person in this world is one who does not have any work; the greatest privation in life is the loneliness of boredom." Foguang laity are therefore exhorted to maximize productivity in their occupation as a means to serve society and, through generously contributing the resulting wealth, to support Buddhism. For Foguang clergy, active Chan occurs through vigorously attending to the multitudinous projects initiated by monastery leadership to promote the *dharma.* In the view of Foguang monastics, it is they—and not those clerics who sit in absolute silence for hours on end in some isolated monastery—who practice in such a way as to attain the most profound level of Chan realization.

The Humanistic Buddhist perspective has led Master Xingyun to regard the teachings of the Pure Land school in a new way as well. Rather than exerting their energies toward being reborn in a pure land in a different dimension of the universe, as is usually advocated by the Pure Land school, people are urged to transform our own immediate world into a Pure Land and thereby personally embody the *bodhisattva* aspiration for universal enlightenment. Master Xingyun pronounces that advances in science, technology, and medicine, as well as the global trend toward democracy and human rights, all foster the conditions of security, peace, and well-being required for cultivation. The notion of humanity's steady progress through history to ever-higher levels of comfort, freedom, ethical consciousness, and rationality is a central feature of the master's philosophy. Master Xingyun believes that radical, confrontational reforms are not an effective method for achieving such progress, since such tactics create too much suffering and remain within dualistic thinking. Instead, he espouses gradual amelioration through each person engaging in a daily regimen of contemplation, meditation, and self-reflection, while simultaneously devoting his or her energy to improving the welfare of others. Hence, Foguangshan periodically leads large-scale campaigns aimed at societal regeneration through moral persuasion and sponsors a variety of civic enterprises, including an orphanage, a medical clinic, several preschools, a high school, and a liberal arts university.

Although improving people's material and societal conditions is seen as essential to establishing a Pure Land on earth, the key to realizing such a utopia nonetheless remains cultivating people's wisdom and compassion through exposure to the *dharma.* Naturally, the master sees Buddhism in general, and Humanistic Buddhism as propounded by Foguangshan in particular, as being at the forefront of this movement. Each Foguang temple is regarded as a miniature Pure Land whose wholesome influence will slowly radiate outward to positively influence its surroundings, until eventually the entire world can be transformed into a realm of bliss.

Master Xingyun asserts that the key to extending such purity—or as he would phrase it, "spreading the Buddha's light,"—is implementing effective educational programs, both for the clergy who guide the process and for the laity who assure its widespread dissemination. Foguangshan is therefore especially well known in Taiwan for its system of monastic colleges and its publishing empire. By 2000, Foguangshan had a dozen seminaries with more than five hundred students enrolled. While most of the students come from within the Foguang ranks, a variety of smaller temples around Taiwan also send their novices to these seminaries for training. Foguangshan's publications include an edition of the Buddhist canon (with punctuation added), a six-volume encyclopedia of Buddhism, and scores of books, cassettes, videos, and CD-ROMs explicating Master Xingyun's version of Humanistic Buddhism. The organization also devotes considerable resources to maintaining its many websites and television station.

Foguang projects are typically undertaken in cooperation with political and corporate leaders. Large-scale Foguang activities in Taiwan, which can attract tens of thousands of participants, often take place at government facilities and have as the guests of honor top political officials, military brass, and business elite. Because of this, Master Xingyun's detractors have saddled him with the pejorative labels of "political monk" and "commercial monk." The former epithet gained especial salience after the master publicly endorsed one of his disciples in 1996 in the Republic of China's first open election for the presidency and then, later that same year, hosted U.S. vice president Al Gore at a banquet at Hsi Lai Temple (Hacienda Heights, California) for what turned out to be a fund-raiser for the Democratic National Committee. The label "commercial monk" came about not only because of the master's many wealthy devotees, but also due to his penchant to create high-profile, glitzy facilities and events. Foguang headquarters' eight-story-high statue of Amitābha Buddha, its Pure Land Cave (which was modeled on Disney's "It's a Small, Small World"), and its annual New Year's Festival of a Myriad Lights have over the years attracted millions of pilgrims and tourists. Master Xingyun is of the firm opinion that attracting society's elite to Buddhism and providing wholesome entertainment with a Buddhist theme are both effective expedient means for spreading the *dharma.* Nonetheless, partially in response to adverse press concerning his organization's forays into more secular spheres, the master decided in 1997 to henceforth allow only groups of Foguang devotees participating in organized pilgrimages to enter the headquarters' compound. Since that time the general public has been welcome to visit Foguangshan's many branch temples, but the headquarters in Kaohsiung has largely remained off limits.

Master Xingyun and his organization are not only influential in Taiwan, but since the early 1990s have played an increasingly prominent role in providing religious instruction and a sense of cultural identity to overseas Chinese. The beginnings of Foguangshan's globalization are to be traced to the master's visit to the United States in 1976, at which point he recognized the great potential for serving the rapidly expanding Chinese-American population. Twelve years later, the master opened the doors of Hsi Lai Temple, the largest Buddhist monastery in the Western hemisphere. In less than a decade after founding that temple, Foguangshan opened ninety-five overseas branches: twenty-seven in Asia (excluding the sixty temples in the ROC), thirteen in Australia and the Pacific Islands, nineteen in Europe, seven in Africa, five in South and Central America, and twenty-four in North America (nineteen in the United States and five in Canada). By the close of the twentieth century, Master Xingyun had decided to hold off on constructing other centers, so the number of Foguang temples has remained fairly steady since that time. This network is supplemented by the Buddha's Light International Association, which in 2000 had some 110 chapters worldwide.

Foguang temples may be found virtually anywhere a relatively large expatriate population from the ROC has coalesced. The reach of BLIA is still farther, extending to areas with even small communities of Taiwan emigrants. The only Chinese Buddhist organization with a comparable overseas network is Ciji Hui, which at the beginning of the third millennium had offices in twenty-eight countries. The two organizations differ from one another in that Foguangshan has stationed clerics, and therefore opened temples, while Ciji Hui has relied upon its impressive array of lay leaders to establish "offices." Foguangshan's international network of temples exceeds not only that of other Chinese Buddhist institutions, but is one of the most extensive of any Buddhist group.

Although the vast majority of devotees in Foguang branch temples outside of Taiwan are overseas Chinese Buddhists (with most having emigrated from Taiwan, although small numbers have come from mainland China, Vietnam, and Hong Kong), the organization has also devoted considerable energy to bringing others into its fold. Hsi Lai Temple, Nan Tien Temple (Wollengong, Australia), and Nan Hua Temple (Bronkhorstspruit, South Africa) have been at the forefront of Foguangshan missionary endeavor. Hsi Lai Temple and Nan Tien Temple both maintain BLIA chapters serving several dozen non-Chinese members. Nan Hua Temple has undertaken the ambitious task of establishing a seminary and orphanage. In the early years, at least, Foguangshan's efforts to attract non-Chinese to its lay membership or monastic corps has had only limited success.

Foguangshan gave formal symbolic imprint to its self-avowed role as leader of the global Buddhist community in 1997, when it sponsored an international Triple Altar Ordination in Bodh Gayā, India (site of the Buddha's enlightenment). One hundred and fifty novices representing Theravādin, Tibetan, and Mahāyāna lineages flew in from countries around the world to take the three sets of vows. The vast majority of participants were women, a significant fact since neither Theravādin nor Tibetan Buddhism provides women with the opportunity to take the necessary precepts for full ordination as a *bhikṣuṇī* nun. In the following years, Foguangshan sponsored several other ceremonies in which dozens more such women underwent *bhikṣuṇī* ordination. Only time will tell whether this campaign will gain momentum and have a noticeable impact on Theravādin and Tibetan Buddhist communities.

Master Xingyun and Foguangshan remain highly influential in Taiwan, enjoy a significant following among overseas Chinese, and to a more limited extent have influenced non-Chinese Buddhists around the world.

Bibliography

Chandler, Stuart. *Establishing a Pure Land on Earth: The Foguang Buddhist Perspective on Modernization and Globalization.* Honolulu, 2004.

Jiang Canteng. *Taiwan Dangdai Fojiao.* Taipei, 1997.

Jiang Canteng. *Dangdai Taiwan Renjian Fojiao Sixiang Jia.* Taipei, 2001.

Jones, Charles Brewer. *Buddhism in Taiwan: Religion and the State, 1660–1990.* Honolulu, 1999.

Laliberte, Andre. "The Politics of Buddhist Organizations in Taiwan, 1989–1997." Ph.D. diss., University of British Columbia, 1999.

Pittman, Don Alvin. *Toward a Modern Chinese Buddhism: Taixu's Reforms.* Honolulu, 2001.

Stuart Chandler (2005)

FO KWAN SHAN See FOGUANGSHAN

FOLK DANCE See DANCE, *ARTICLE ON* POPULAR AND FOLK DANCE

FOLKLORE.

Folklorists have been interested in religion as an area of research since the beginnings of the discipline in the nineteenth century, although early folklorists often conceived the beliefs of folk cultures not as religion but as superstition or magic. Many folklore scholars were grounded in scientific rationalism to the extent that they dismissed the beliefs of the folk as ignorant superstition, even if these beliefs were part of systems that functioned in ways similar to organized religion. By the early twentieth century, folklorists and other social scientists recognized the link between religion and folk belief, but condescended toward both. From the positivist perspective of folklore studies as a "historical science," superstition and religion were both considered prescientific. In 1930 Alexander Krappe stated in *The Science of Folklore*: "Superstition, in common parlance, designates the sum of beliefs and practices shared by other people in so far as they differ from our own. What we believe and practice ourselves is, of course, Religion" (p. 203). Krappe implies the dichotomy that later folklorists called folk/elite, with the folk an invention of an intellectual elite who always defined *folk* as inferior because they were construed as rural, isolated, and uneducated.

On the other hand, folklorists were part of a larger intellectual tendency to romanticize the folk, including idealizing certain beliefs and practices associated with folk culture. Folklorists' attitudes towards the folk were similar to anthropologists' attitudes toward the primitive. According to George E. Marcus and Michael M. J. Fischer in *Anthropology as Cultural Critique: An Experimental Moment in the Human Sciences* (1986), anthropologists have idealized the primitive since the nineteenth century: "They—primitive man—have retained a respect for nature, and we have lost it . . . they have sustained close, intimate, satisfying communal lives, and we have lost this way of life . . . and they have retained a sense of the sacred in everyday life, and we have lost this [spiritual vision]" (p. 129). Folklorists were similarly nostalgic about the folk and their beliefs, imagining some folk beliefs as representing a spiritual connection to nature that civilized people had lost and perceiving the folk as leading more sacred lives than people in modern urban environments. This romanticized construction of folk belief was maintained simultaneously with the opposite academic construction of folk belief as pathological. For instance, in the United States folklorists represented Appalachian people as a folk in ways that sometimes reinforced the stereotype of the irrational superstitious hillbilly and at other times projected the image of the wise old mountain healer who was spiritually close to nature.

SUPERSTITION AND RELIGION. Most folklorists made a distinction between superstition and religion, even when evidence indicated a close connection between beliefs and practices assigned to different categories. The religious orientation and theoretical approach of the researcher were factors in making this distinction, as were issues of race and class. A comparison of the 1920s and 1930s research of white folklorist Newbell Niles Puckett and black folklorist Zora Neale Hurston illustrates the complexity of the cultural representation of folk belief and religion in folklore scholarship. Puckett and Hurston viewed the African American tradition of hoodoo or conjuration in very different ways: Hurston as a religion and Puckett as superstitious behavior. Puckett was still theoretically grounded in the outdated nineteenth-century concept of cultural evolution, while Hurston was trained in the then current school of cultural relativism. Puckett, in his extensive collection *Folk Beliefs of the Southern Negro* (1926), associates superstition with "uncultured and backward classes of society" (p. 6), people who had not advanced up the ladder of cultural evolution as far as the educated elite. He therefore saw such African American folk practices as midwifery as "murderous lore" that "should be replaced by modern scientific knowledge."

Hurston rejected Puckett's pathological view and saw hoodoo and conjuration as a systematic religion comparable to Christianity. In a 1929 letter to the poet Langston Hughes quoted by Robert Hemenway in his "Introduction" to Hurston's *Mules and Men* (1935), Hurston writes "I am convinced that Christianity as practiced is an attenuated form of nature worship" (pp. xix–xx). After citing several Christian rituals that contain nature symbolism, she proclaims, "Sympathetic magic pure and simple. *They have a nerve to laugh at conjure.*" She accepted the spiritual efficacy of hoodoo to the point that she studied with a hoodoo priest and was initiated into the practice and came to believe that conjuration worked in particular instances. She argued against the pathological perspective toward folk belief, but in order to present a more positive picture of African American folk belief, she tended to romanticize black southern folk culture as closer to nature and more spiritual than modern societies. Hurston's subjective position as an African American ethnographer caused her to see her own culture in a more positive light than Puckett as a white sociologist/folklorist born and brought up in a southern racist society could. Despite their differences, Hurston and Puckett confronted the same problem that scholars had encountered since the invention of the *folk* in the eighteenth century: how to differentiate folk religion from other forms of religion.

FOLK RELIGION. In his seminal 1974 essay "Toward a Definition of Folk Religion," Don Yoder points out that "the discovery of folk religion in Europe had come at the time of the eighteenth-century Enlightenment, when rationalist clergy attacked folk 'superstitions' in sermons and ministerial periodicals" (p. 3). By the nineteenth century, German scholars had included religion as an important component in the study of *Volkskunde* (folklife), and by 1901 a German Lutheran minister used the term *religiose Volkskunde* (religious folklife) for the first time. In the twentieth century, European folklorists conducted extensive research on the religious beliefs and practices of folk groups throughout Europe among both Roman Catholics and Protestants. To German and other European scholars, the folk were uneducated peasants living in isolated rural areas, so that folk religion could be differentiated from other forms of religion on the basis of the elite/folk hierarchy: folk religion was simpler, contaminated by superstition, and often at variance with official church dogma. Yoder used this long-standing dichotomy as the basis for his definition of folk religion as "unofficial" and "relatively unorganized" in opposition to official organized religion: "Folk religion is the totality of all those views and practices of religion that exist among the people apart from and alongside the strictly theological and liturgical forms of the official religion" (p. 4).

The same basic dichotomy worked for folklorists and anthropologists as they began to study the religious life of peoples in the New World. Folklorists especially were looking for the equivalent of the European peasant in new environments so that any isolated, rural, and relatively uneducated people were designated folk, and folklorists began to collect such religious expressions as hymns, sermons, customs, and rituals from them. The definition of folk religion as religious practices of peasants persisted well into the twentieth century; William A. Christian Jr., who wrote the entry on "Folk Religion" in the original 1987 edition of *The Encyclopedia of Religion*, directed his attention to "past and present-day sedentary cultivators and pastoralists of Asia, North Africa, southern Europe, and Latin America, and historically to sedentary cultivators in northern Europe and North America as well" (vol. 5, p. 370). His definition of folk as pastoral leads him to conclude that the folk had disappeared from North America and northern Europe as a result of urbanization and industrialization, in contrast to such folklorists as Richard M. Dorson, who answered "yes" to the question posed in the title of his 1970 article, "Is There a Folk in the City?" Many of Dorson's examples came from European immigrants and southern rural migrants in heavily industrialized Gary, Indiana, so that the peasant idea was still underlying the conceptualization of folk.

Folklorists and anthropologists also conducted field research on religious folklore in both urban and rural areas in

Central and South America, where their theoretical concern was with cultural syncretism. They examined the way native religions merged with official religions. Yoder cites the "example [of] the mélange of African primitivism and Roman Catholicism that is in Haiti called 'Voodoo,' or the syncretism between Catholicism and native Indian religious beliefs and practices in Central and South America" (1974, p. 2). The fieldwork of Hurston offers an example of how syncretism also influenced folklore field research in the southern United States, since she recognized the Catholic elements in hoodoo in New Orleans. Anthropologists and folklorists still considered religious folklore in socioeconomic class terms as associated with peasants, although some had migrated to cities bringing their religion with them.

Throughout the history of folklore scholarship on religion, the folk/elite dichotomy has been a basic underlying principle, whether in the study of European peasants, African Americans, Appalachian whites, or people whose religions merge native and European elements. This began to change for some folklorists in the 1960s when they started to study urban and suburban folklore and gradually expanded their research to include educated people of a higher socioeconomic class, recognizing that folklore had adapted to technology so that new genres such as "xerox lore" became the subject of scholarly books. Finally, Alan Dundes could answer the question asked in his 1980 article "Who Are the Folk?" by saying that, in essence, we all are: a folk group is any group with any one linking factor. Once the folk/elite dichotomy had been undermined, folklorists who conducted research on religion were freed to reconceptualize it in nonhierarchical ways.

In 1995, Leonard Norman Primiano, in an important essay entitled "Vernacular Religion and the Search for Method in Religious Folklife," challenged the assumption of folk as inferior: "Scholars within the discipline have consistently named religious people's beliefs in residualistic, derogatory ways as 'folk,' 'unofficial,' or 'popular' religion, and have then juxtaposed these terms on a two-tiered model with 'official' religion" (p. 38). This implies the existence of a "pure" religion that is "contaminated" by the folk in their everyday religious practices. In order to correct the problems inherent in this hierarchical dichotomy, Primiano suggests a new term and a new theoretical concept: "Vernacular religion is, by definition, religion as it is lived: as human beings encounter, understand, interpret, and practice it" (p. 44). There is no opposition here between folk and elite since all religious practitioners would be included no matter what their socioeconomic class: every individual interprets religion within the context of his or her everyday life (the vernacular dimension of life). Priests, rabbis, prophets, shamans—no matter how high in the hierarchy of their respective religions—would all practice vernacular religion in the sense that they make individual interpretations of religious meaning and practice in everyday circumstances. This approach avoids the condescension of the old elite/folk dichotomy and attempts to treat religious practices with respect by concentrating on the experiential aspects of religion. Primiano recognizes that *vernacular* contains some of the same pejorative connotations as *folk*, and some folklorists prefer to continue using *folk religion* as the scholarly term, but the theoretical concept of *vernacular religion* has been widely accepted in folklore studies.

FOLKLORISTIC APPROACHES TO THE STUDY OF RELIGION. Concepts of the folk and definitions of folk religion have had a basic influence on theoretical approaches folklorists have used in the study of religion, and as these concepts and definitions have changed, so have the approaches. Since most folklore studies are grounded in field research, the best way to understand theoretical approaches in folklore scholarship is by examining representative individual studies since the early 1900s. In the eighteenth and nineteenth centuries, antiquarians were interested in religious folk customs as survivals of previous savage or barbarian times; they thought collecting the beliefs and customs of peasants could provide an understanding of the past. The concept of cultural evolution that was the basis for the survivalist approach had been discredited by the late nineteenth century, but some anthropologists and folklorists continued to base their interpretations of folk beliefs and religion on it well into the twentieth century. Puckett clung to cultural evolution as an explanation of African American folk beliefs in the 1920s, and Ovidiu Birlia used cultural evolution as the basic approach for his entry on "Folklore" in the 1987 edition of *The Encyclopedia of Religion.* However, for most anthropology and folklore scholars, cultural relativism had replaced cultural evolution by early in the twentieth century. The history of anthropological and folkloristic studies of religion continued to overlap as the new paradigm of cultural relativism developed models that then became dominant influences on the study of religious folklore.

Especially important was the anthropological approach that came to be known as functionalism. Bronislaw Malinowski's fieldwork among Trobriand Islanders became the basis for the functional explanation of magic belief and related behavior that he articulated in a 1931 essay, "The Role of Magic and Religion." His "anxiety ritual theory" influenced the anthropological and folkloristic study of a wide range of behaviors, from primitive magic to everyday superstitions to rituals in religious settings. He invited this widespread application by suggesting that such behaviors were found in both primitive and modern life: wherever there is uncertainty in human endeavors, there will be magic and ritual to help relieve the anxiety that arises from that uncertainty. Rituals, whether they are as mundane as not walking under a ladder or as elaborate as Catholic priests blessing fishing fleets, function to give a psychological sense of control over uncertainties in life. The functional approach was grounded in scientific rationalism as a way of explaining what seemed to be irrational behaviors; a functionalist might say that when modern educated people base their actions on "magico-religious" beliefs, their behavior is analogous to primitives. As folklorist Bonnie Blair O'Connor pointed out in her 1995 book, *Healing Traditions: Alternative Medicines and the Health Professions*, the functionalist approach is implicitly condescending to the people whose beliefs are being studied; "they" are not capable of understanding their own behavior the way "we" educated researchers are. This was a submerged problem as long as the subjects were classified as "primitive" or "folk," but as the concept of folk expanded beyond rural, isolated, relatively uneducated groups, the issue emerged as politically significant.

In retrospect, present-day scholars can see that condescension toward research subjects was a theoretical problem all along for folklorists, including those conducting research on folk religion in the United States. Most American researchers in folk religion concentrated their field research on fundamentalist Christians in the rural South. These American versions of European peasants were conceived of as the folk, and if a researcher wanted to study the full range of their traditional life, then their religion had to be included—a circular way of defining folk religion, but it went uncontested throughout most of the twentieth century. Despite the fact that there were a range of religions to study in the South, folklorists concentrated on the most conservative fundamentalist and evangelical Christian denominations, undoubtedly because they were large in number but also because they fit preconceived notions about the folk. The very conservatism of their religion made it seem more traditional, and from the educated perspective of the folklorist, fundamentalists were seen as more exotic than mainstream religions that were in many cases closer to the folklorists' own religious background.

In the 1960s and 1970s, folklorists studying fundamentalist Christian conversion experiences began to use such theoretical approaches as the one Victor Turner described in his 1969 book, *The Ritual Process: Structure and Anti-Structure.* One of the first folklorists to use ritual process theory was William Clements in his 1976 article "Conversion and Communitas"; he identified Turner's ritual states of "liminality" and "communitas" in the experiences of fundamentalists he interviewed in Arkansas. Clements posits that since "many folk Christians are poor, uneducated, and without social prestige," their experience of communitas functions "in a compensatory manner" to make up for their lack of "social commodities" (pp. 44–45). Following Clements, Patrick B. Mullen discerned the same ritual pattern in conversion narratives among evangelicals in "Ritual and Sacred Narrative in the Blue Ridge Mountains" (1983), and Jeff Todd Titon applied Turner's theory to religious expression in *Powerhouse for God: Speech, Chant, and Song in an Appalachian Baptist Church* (1988).

Unfortunately, ritual process theory continued the tendency toward condescension in the study of folk religion by applying it mainly to lesser-educated religious groups. Although folklorists concentrated fieldwork on lower socioeconomic fundamentalist religious groups in the rural South, Turner's ritual pattern can be seen across a wide spectrum of religions among various socioeconomic classes and in rural, urban, and suburban contexts. There was also a residual effect of scientific rationalism in this approach in that ritual process suggests social and psychological explanations for religious conversion experiences, rather than considering the possibility that they are spiritual experiences. A valuable corrective to the tendency to condescend toward fundamentalists was the 1988 collection of essays *Diversities of Gifts: Field Studies in Southern Religion.* The editors, Ruel W. Tyson Jr., James L. Peacock, and Daniel W. Patterson, and the contributors self-consciously tried to counter stereotypes by depicting fundamentalist religion as complex beliefs and behaviors in closely observed cultural contexts.

Folklorists theoretically refined the ritual process approach by applying it to contexts that required multiple interpretations, recognizing that communitas and liminality have significance beyond their religious meanings. A good example of this is Sabra Webber's study of the Islamic tradition of Ramaḍān. In "Ramadan Observed" (1984) she synthesizes Turner's ritual theory with cultural politics, seeing Ramaḍān as a space for the negotiation of religious and political meanings. She bases her study on her own fieldwork in Tunisia and on other ethnographic accounts from North Africa, where Ramaḍān combines elements of ritual and festival. Ramaḍān is a lunar month-long fast in which the breaking of the fast at the end is an important element. Webber sees Ramaḍān as a local liminal event that must be examined within a larger "liminal period in North African and Arab-world history" (p. 187), a publicly recognized awareness of great change between more stable periods. "Ramadan at its most basic . . . has become a paradigm that various political and social groups, as well as individuals, are seeking to use to represent their values" (p. 188). This multivocality complicates the concept of communitas: "while at a community level a kind of *communitas* is achieved, at the individual level it provides, for some people, an opportunity for intensification of pious or recreational behavior" (p. 191), and for others an opportunity for coming of age, an expression of Muslim identity in opposition to other religions, a statement of acceptance or rejection of modernity, and even, for some, a declaration of revolution. Webber's field research indicates an ongoing negotiation by Muslims about the meaning of Ramaḍān. Unlike the research on ritual among fundamentalist Christians, where the interpretation comes from outside observers, Webber's use of ritual theory incorporates interpretations from within the group, thus avoiding condescension.

Webber's research is one indication of a broader shift in the study of folk religious behavior from the nineteenth century to the present: a movement away from considering the folk and their beliefs as inferior. Folklorists accepted the underlying elite/folk hierarchy for a very long time, but once that was questioned, resistance to it created an effort to remove pejorative judgments from the documentation and analysis of folk religion. One result of this movement is folklorist David J. Hufford's "experience-centered" theory, which tries to avoid prejudging religious experiences. In a book and a series of articles, Hufford has identified the condescension toward and dismissal of spiritual experiences as a major scholarly problem in folk belief and folk religion studies. He began to formulate his approach to such phenomena in his 1982 book, *The Terror That Comes in the Night: An Experience-Centered Study of Supernatural Assault Traditions*, by researching the cross-cultural "old hag" or "Mara" tradition in which people wake up paralyzed in the night thinking that some supernatural entity is pressing down on their chests. The experience transcends religious difference with reports from Jewish and Christian believers, as well as from Islamic sources, where the experience is related to the *jinn*, an evil or mischievous spirit that visits during the night.

Hufford has also applied his approach to other spiritual phenomena, such as out-of-body experiences and visitations from the dead, in his essay "Beings without Bodies: An Experience-Centered Study of the Belief in Spirits" (1995). His approach to these experiences is grounded in phenomenology: he is critical of preconceived assumptions that explain the behavior in psychological or cultural terms, as, for instance, having Freudian symbolic meaning. Rather, his approach concentrates on the experience itself as reported firsthand by the person involved, opening up the possibility that the experience was an actual contact with another dimension.

Many folklorists who study religion have accepted Hufford's theoretical model as a useful balance to the social construction of reality that might view all such spiritual experiences as "deconstructed 'situated hallucinations,'" a phrase used by Margaret Mills in a 1993 article in which she urges folklorists to strive for a sense of what "feels real" in the lives of the people that they study. On the other hand, Patrick B. Mullen in his 2000 essay, "Belief and the American Folk," points out that researchers can never determine the exact nature of the "core experience" itself, that the experience is always mediated by the person in the act of telling it to the researcher. Mullen argues that folklorists should not just be interested in the core experience but also in the "examination of *narrating*, the process of communicating a supernatural or spiritual experience in a specific cultural context" (p. 137). A folklorist does not have to accept or reject a spiritual experience as real in order to examine the cultural process whereby the experience was communicated to others. This suggests that the performance approach, which has been a major component of folklore studies since the 1960s, still has relevance for the study of the expressive dimension of folk religion today.

Performance Approaches. Performance theory was part of a 1960s and 1970s paradigm shift in folklore studies that incorporated the contextual analysis of anthropology with the ethnography-of-speaking approach of sociolinguistics and the Kenneth Burke rhetorical approach of literary critical theory in order to examine folklore not as static text but as part of a dynamic cultural process. The emphasis was on the specific situation in which the folklore was communicated, the performance context. Richard Bauman defined performance in 1992 as "an aesthetically marked and heightened mode of communication, framed in a special way and put on display for an audience" (p. 41). This certainly describes many cultural expressions that occur within a religious context, and although folklorists concentrated on verbal art in secular storytelling at first, it was not long before theoretical principles from the performance approach were being used to interpret narrating in religious contexts.

Kirin Narayan's 1989 book, *Storytellers, Saints, and Scoundrels: Folk Narrative in Hindu Religious Teaching*, is based on field research in India, where she observed and participated in storytelling sessions conducted by a Hindu holy man, Swamiji. Narayan employs performance and other approaches to analyze the way Swamiji uses storytelling to teach people who come to him seeking spiritual guidance. She focuses on eight folk narratives in specific performance situations, taking into account the personality and character of the storyteller and dynamic interactions with his audience in order to explain how religious "truths . . . are made comprehensible and persuasive . . . through the medium of stories" (p. 243). Swamiji's stories communicate general religious principles, "yet by telling a story instead of making a generalizing statement, Swamiji endows these principles with a vital immediacy" (p. 244). Narayan's study of Hindu storytelling has application to storytelling in a wide range of other religious settings.

The performance approach mainly concentrated on narratives, but it has been applied more broadly to sermons, hymns, rituals, and other religious expressions. One of the first studies of religious expression as performance was Bruce Rosenberg's *The Art of the American Folk Preacher* (1970), but he goes back to an earlier model, the oral-formulaic approach, for his primary theoretical focus. In many ways, the oral-formulaic approach of Albert B. Lord and Millman Parry was a precursor of performance theory because of its emphasis on oral performance. In *The Singer of Tales* (1960), Lord formulated the oral-formulaic thesis based on fieldwork he and Parry had conducted on performances by South Slav epic poets that provided the evidence of certain oral formulas that also occur in written poetry. Rosenberg identified similar themes and formulas in improvised oral sermon performances by American preachers. Gerald Davis later argued in *"I've Got the Word in Me and I Can Sing It, You Know": A Study of the Performed African American Sermon* (1985) that formulas are indeed part of the African American preacher's performance, but they are culture specific and related to rhythmic patterns that are not the same as those used by epic poets. In both studies, belief is not so much an issue as the artistic dimension of the performance, and this gets at one of the problems that folklorists have faced in using a performance approach to religious expression: such studies contextualize traditional religious communication in terms of the specific circumstances of performance, but tend to leave out the dimension of belief.

As Diane E. Goldstein states in her 1995 article, "The Secularization of Religious Ethnography and Narrative Competence in a Discourse of Faith," many researchers treat "belief issues as essentially external to the scope of research. The folklorist's concern with verbal artistry provides grist for such an approach in that it often lays stress on 'the verbal' and 'the art' to the neglect of the underlying cognitive aspects of culture" (p. 23). We are reminded of Mills's concern that folklorists are leaving out the felt experiential nature of belief and practice in ethnographic descriptions. Goldstein points out that scholars tend to separate language from religion in order to avoid belief as a factor, and consequently they have not fully understood the cultural meaning of religious experience. She says that the performance approach concentrates on art in a way that leaves out the performer's sense of the divine, thus secularizing religious communication and making the approach inadequate as a means of understanding the cultural process being examined. The term *performance* suggests a metaphor underlying the theory, which prompts Goldstein to ask, "Why would you use the dramatistic metaphors of stages and actors if you knew about religious experience?" (p. 29).

Some folklorists respond that no matter how divinely felt the experience itself is, it is communicated from one human to another in social contexts that sometimes require the speaker to engage a listener through artistic means. The specific context of communication must be taken into account; some contexts require performance techniques and others do not. As most performance scholars recognize today, an effective theoretical approach to folk religion would combine performance and culturally based theories. The "keys" that define performance in Bauman's *Verbal Art as Performance* (1977) are culturally relative, so that a specific religious performance situation must be examined within its larger cultural frame, including the role of belief. The researcher needs to be "fluent" in the keys of the particular culture being studied. Goldstein points out that this has not been the case in many performance studies of folk religion, but this is not the result of a flaw in the theory, but in its application.

Goldstein's example from her own fieldwork illustrates the importance of taking the group's beliefs into account when examining communication about religious experience. She compares testimonies by two different women in an evangelical worship service; one seems to the researcher to be more articulate and effective and the other halting and ineffective, but to people in the congregation the inarticulate testimony was deemed more sincere and ultimately more authentic and divinely inspired, at least partially because it was not a smooth performance. Their belief system privileged effect over style: "touching the hearts" of people in the congregation was thought to be a sign of divine inspiration. In Bauman's terms, the competency of performance was not evaluated on the basis of artistic keys, but on authenticity of belief. Performance theory still seems relevant here: even if the qualities of performance are lacking in one testimony, they are made apparent by the presence of performance keys in the other. The important thing is for the researcher to be familiar with the relationship between aesthetics and belief in the particular religious culture under scrutiny.

CULTURAL STUDIES APPROACHES. Performance approaches to folk religion concentrated so much on the aesthetic dimensions of a specific situation that they neglected larger cultural and ideological issues that informed the performance itself, as J. E. Limon and M. J. Young point out in their 1986 critique of performance studies in general, "Frontiers, Settlements, and Development in Folklore Studies, 1972–1985." Limon and Young also criticized folklorists doing performance studies for their concentration on verbal art and neglect of material culture. These imbalances were partially corrected by the growing influence of cultural studies on folklore scholarship in the 1970s and 1980s.

Folklorists using cultural studies approaches helped fill in the gaps by examining power relations within folk religion contexts, including numerous studies of both oral traditions and material culture. For instance, in the 1993 essay "Multivocality and Vernacular Architecture: The Our Lady of Mount Carmel Grotto in Rosebank, Staten Island," Joseph Sciorra traces the history of a neighborhood grotto built by a group of Italian-American men in New York. He interviewed some of the builders to situate the tradition within local culture, and he also placed his study in the larger context of the history of Catholic grottoes in Europe and elsewhere. His research indicates the social and political reality of the official/unofficial dichotomy in folk religion. This may be an imagined construct, but it was manifested in the exercise of power by local church authorities in an attempt to keep religious activities within the control of the priests after local parishioners started their own neighborhood processions and grottos. The struggle took place over many years, but the folk parishioners were able to maintain the Mount Carmel grotto that still stands today as an attraction for thousands of visitors to an out of the way neighborhood on Staten Island.

A similar study by Suzanne Seriff in 1991, "Homages in Clay: The Figural Ceramics of José Varela," focuses on a Mexican-American folk artist whose clay figures often depict religious themes. Like Sciorra, Seriff's theoretical approach to folk religion is grounded in cultural politics and ethnic identity, focusing on power relationships between dominant and minority cultures. Seriff, Sciorra, and other folklorists concerned with cultural politics see religious and spiritual issues not just in aesthetic terms, but also within ideological contexts. Varela's folk art can be understood best through his "concern for community and his passion for the past as a fortification against the spiritual and cultural isolation of being Mexican in an Anglo-dominated world" (p. 162). Varela worked for low pay at an Anglo-owned brick and tile factory in a small Texas town; he "surreptitiously" used clay from the factory to create his figures and fired them in the factory kiln. Some of these he gave or sold to friends, and later in life he sold them at markets in San Antonio. He also donated his time to the local Catholic Church in order to build an outdoor grotto to the Virgin of Guadalupe, who "symbolizes the sacred essence of the Mexican community" (pp. 148–149). Varela "has created a productive niche for himself and his fellow Mexicans . . . in part by creatively manipulating the conditions of his own oppression—that is, by transforming the materials of the factory in which he works into familiar and fantastic forms to be circulated . . . among members of his own community" (p. 163). Folklorists often assume the role of advocates for the people they study, and Seriff and Sciorra's research suggests that they have defined the folk as oppressed and disenfranchised within the context of their religious practices in order to argue for their rights.

FEMINIST APPROACHES. Feminist approaches to folk religion share the political perspective of cultural studies while providing a more specific ideological focus. Seriff and another folklorist, Kay Turner, conducted field research that produced the 1987 essay "'Giving an Altar': The Ideology of Reproduction in a St. Joseph's Day Feast." "This woman-centered altar tradition provides a splendid case in point for understanding folklore practice and performance through a feminist orientation" (p. 446). Their approach combines performance and feminist concerns by viewing the feast of Saint Joseph as a creative symbolic expression of women's power of reproduction. The feast "gives dramatic and aesthetic recognition to the sustaining values of nurturance, care, comfort, and support—the birthright of the mother," but it moves from the religious to the ideological in that "religious belief is specifically wedded with the ideology of reproduction. . .it is through the care and nurturance shown to the Holy Family on this day that the importance of women's daily caretaking of the earthly family is sacralized" (p. 458). This study indicates how folklorists have gone beyond performance in a narrow aesthetic sense by viewing religious artistic communication within a broader ideological frame including feminist principles, and beyond verbal art to consider foodways and other aspects of material folk culture. Turner expanded the scope of her research in folk religion to include a variety of women's altars across cultures in *Beautiful Necessity: The Art and Meaning of Women's Altars* (1999).

Susan Starr Sered uses a similar feminist perspective to examine an entirely different religious group in *Women as Ritual Experts: The Religious Lives of Elderly Jewish Women in Jerusalem* (1992), and the principle of women's empowerment underlies her research as well. She moves beyond the focus on one genre of religious expression to consider a range of expressions and behaviors including life stories, rituals, nonverbal gestures, and everyday experiences. As in other feminist folklore studies, Sered analyzes women's religious activities within the context of a dominant patriarchal culture and identifies strategies whereby these largely illiterate women become experts at rituals that are concerned with maintaining the wellbeing of their families. She traces their empowerment in terms of both gender and age: "The Jerusalem women describe a shift from relative ritual powerlessness when young, to intense ritual respect and involvement in old age and especially widowhood" (p. 138). By focusing on illiterate women, Sered may be reinforcing the old concept of the folk as an oral culture, but this reinforces her feminist ideological perspective by concentrating on a group that is socially marginalized in the modern world.

Like Sered, Elaine J. Lawless began her scholarly research by concentrating on subjugated women within an already marginalized culture in *Handmaidens of the Lord: Pentecostal Women Preachers and Traditional Religion* (1988), but then she switched to more middle-class religious cultures in *Holy Women, Wholly Women: Sharing Ministries of Wholeness through Life Stories and Reciprocal Ethnography* (1993). The development of her research over those years illustrates a broader shift in folk religious studies from rural, relatively uneducated, fundamentalist religions to urban and suburban, educated, "mainstream" religions. In *Handmaidens of the Lord*, Lawless examines the process whereby women in a religion that considered them inferior and submissive to men could become respected preachers and leaders in their congregations. She concentrates on their life stories and sermons using both feminist and performance approaches. She analyzes preaching styles in performance terms, but the keys to performance reveal images directly related to their experiences as women. These stylistic devices then become verbal strategies that work to secure leadership roles for women in the church; specifically, the reproductive images used in women preachers' sermons are seen as part of a "maternal strategy" to reinforce the role of preacher as "Mother" to the congregation. As with other cultural studies approaches to folk religion, power relationships are the focus within a religious setting.

Lawless used her research in fundamentalist churches to begin to formulate the concept of "reciprocal ethnography" in which the field-worker is obliged to share her research findings with the subject. This collaborative research process requires an ongoing relationship between the folklorist and the person providing information about his or her culture, including discussion between ethnographer and subject on possible scholarly interpretations, and then incorporating the consultant's response in the final report. This approach is complicated by differences in levels of education, socioeconomic class, and religious belief between researcher and subject. Lawless writes in a 1992 essay, "'I Was Afraid Someone Like You . . . An Outsider . . . Would Misunderstand': Negotiating Interpretive Differences Between Ethnographers and Subjects," that she failed to take her consultants' responses into account in the published version of *Handmaidens of the Lord*, but she began a dialogue with one of the preachers later. This woman felt that because Lawless was a religious outsider she had misinterpreted her sermons, and Lawless herself came to believe that the preacher's responses should have been included in the book in order to make the scholarly interpretation fuller and richer.

Holy Women, Wholly Women is a product of reciprocal ethnography, taking into account the detailed responses of the women preachers who were the subjects of the research. However, in this case, the women were closer to Lawless in terms of education and religious beliefs, making the reciprocal process less difficult and the results more collaborative. Lawless uses feminist and performance approaches, but this time with mainstream, more highly educated preachers, again interpreting figurative language in their sermons, especially metaphors of nurturing, as revealing particular views and strategies of women. Differences in class and education have been transcended by gender in her two studies, and in both cases Lawless has situated herself subjectively within the study of religion.

Reflexive Ethnography. Subjectivity has taken on increasing importance in folk religion studies, developing from the earlier "invisible ethnographer" of "objective" research to the visibly foregrounded first-person narrator of reflexive ethnography. David J. Hufford has made the most comprehensive statement of the significance of reflexivity in folklore studies of belief in his 1995 essay, "The Scholarly Voice and the Personal Voice: Reflexivity in Belief Studies." Hufford argues for the necessity of the researcher situating himself or herself subjectively within the ethnographic enterprise, saying that this is especially important in studies of belief and religion because of the need to make clear the influence of the researcher's assumptions on the representation of the religious belief system of an "other." He points out that all too often the "objective" stance masks a position of disbelief in religious ethnography. "A reflexive analysis of our scholarship enables us to distinguish among the beliefs of our informants, our scholarly knowledge, our personal beliefs and our occupational ideology. This permits coherent discourse and various warranted moral actions" (p. 71). Instead of hiding one's own beliefs, the scholar should make them clear, thereby allowing different interpretations, including moral or ideological ones, to be stated directly, rather than implied as subtext.

Reflexivity in religious ethnography also opens up the possibility of fieldwork and analysis by members of the religious group, and this is a growing approach in folk religion studies. The "native" perspective is another position among many subjectivities and is legitimate as long as it is recognized reflexively; no longer can the insider's position be seen as less objective than the outsider's since they are both subjective. A good illustration of this is Nikki Bado-Fralick's *Coming to the Edge of the Circle: A Wiccan Initiation Ritual*, in which she uses her dual perspectives as a Wiccan priestess and as a scholar trained in folklore and religious studies to examine a Wiccan religious ritual. Bado-Fralick frames her study in terms of her subjectivity, allowing her to explore such ethical problems as dealing with secrecy and to examine processes of identity formation from within. Her research also indicates how folklorists have blurred the line between folk and popular religion, recognizing that both are systems of belief and practice as complex and worthy of study as the more academically privileged mainstream organized religions, and thus resisting the dismissal of such religions often implied in terms such as *New Age*.

Another study of what might be classified as New Age religion is Roseanne Rini's 1997 dissertation, "Elizabeth Kelly: Contemporary Spiritual Teacher and Healer," which was based on extensive interviews with a healer and psychic, Elizabeth Kelly, who was widely respected and consulted by well-educated people in the small college town of Yellow Springs, Ohio. Rini initially contacted the woman healer for personal advice and came to know her as a friend and to consult with her on a regular basis. Their personal relationship gradually expanded to include a researcher/consultant dimension, and Rini was able to gain a greater understanding of Kelly's belief and practice from a perspective that included her roles as scholar and believer. Reflexive ethnography has legitimized this kind of research within one's own religious groups in ways that were unimaginable in the past.

These examples of research in New Age religion illustrate that the scholarship in folk religion has expanded well beyond the old paradigm of the folk as peasant, and these and other examples from folklore scholarship since the early twentieth century indicate that the theoretical approaches have grown from simple survivalism to a complex pluralism of choices. The folk are now conceived as any group of people with any linking factor, although approaches grounded in cultural politics tend to focus on disenfranchised and oppressed minority groups as the folk. Folkloristic approaches to the study of religion have developed along similar lines as the general shifts in postmodern theory, with a special emphasis on performance, cultural studies, and feminism. Underlying all the various definitions and approaches used by folklorists to study religion is the ongoing concern for individual experience within specific everyday situations and broader cultural contexts.

See Also Anthropology, Ethnology and Religion; Folk Religion, overview article; Popular Religion.

Bibliography

Badone, Ellen, ed. *Religious Orthodoxy and Popular Faith in European Society.* Princeton, N.J., 1990.

Bauman, Richard. *Verbal Art as Performance.* Prospect Heights, Ill., 1977.

Bauman, Richard. "Performance." In *Folklore, Cultural Performances, and Popular Entertainments: A Communication-Centered Handbook*, edited by Richard Bauman, pp. 41–49. New York, 1992.

Birlia, Ovidiu. "Folklore." In *The Encyclopedia of Religion*, 1st ed., edited by Mircea Eliade, vol. 5, pp. 363–370. New York, 1987.

Christian, William A., Jr. "Folk Religion: An Overview." In *The Encyclopedia of Religion,* 1st ed., edited by Mircea Eliade, vol. 5, pp. 370–374. New York, 1987.

Clements, William. "Conversion and Communitas." *Western Folklore* 35 (1976): 35–45.

Davis, Gerald L. *"I've Got the Word in Me and I Can Sing It, You Know": A Study of the Performed African American Sermon.* Philadelphia, 1985.

Dorson, Richard M. "Is There a Folk in the City?" *Journal of American Folklore* 83 (1970): 185–228.

Dundes, Alan. "Who Are the Folk?" In *Interpreting Folklore,* edited by Alan Dundes, pp. 1–19. Bloomington, Ind., 1980.

Goldstein, Diane E. "The Secularization of Religious Ethnography and Narrative Competence in a Discourse of Faith." *Western Folklore* 54 (1995): 23–36.

Hufford, David J. *The Terror That Comes in the Night: An Experience-Centered Study of Supernatural Assault Traditions.* Philadelphia, 1982.

Hufford, David J. "Beings without Bodies: An Experience-Centered Study of the Belief in Spirits." In *Out of the Ordinary: Folklore and the Supernatural,* edited by Barbara Walker, pp. 11–45. Logan, Utah, 1995.

Hufford, David J. "The Scholarly Voice and the Personal Voice: Reflexivity in Belief Studies." *Western Folklore* 54 (1995): 57–76.

Hurston, Zora Neale. *Mules and Men.* Philadelphia and London, 1935; reprint, Bloomington, Ind., 1978.

Isambert, François-André. *Le sens du sacré: Fête et religion populaire.* Paris, 1982.

Krappe, Alexander H. *The Science of Folklore.* New York, 1930; reprint, New York, 1964.

Lawless, Elaine J. *Handmaidens of the Lord: Pentecostal Women Preachers and Traditional Religion.* Philadelphia, 1988.

Lawless, Elaine J. "'I Was Afraid Someone Like You. . .An Outsider. . .Would Misunderstand': Negotiating Interpretive Differences Between Ethnographers and Subjects." *Journal of American Folklore* 105 (1992): 302–315.

Lawless, Elaine J. *Holy Women, Wholly Women: Sharing Ministries of Wholeness through Life Stories and Reciprocal Ethnography.* Philadelphia, 1993.

Limon, J. E., and M. J. Young. "Frontiers, Settlements, and Development in Folklore Studies, 1972–1985." *Annual Review of Anthropology* 15 (1986): 417–460.

Lombardi-Satriani, Luigi. "Attuale problematica della religione popolare." In *Questione meridionale, religione e classi subalterne,* edited by Francesco Saija. Naples, 1978.

Lord, Albert B. *The Singer of Tales.* Cambridge, Mass., 1960; 2d ed., 2000.

Malinowski, Bronislaw. "The Role of Magic and Religion" (1931). In *Reader in Comparative Religion: An Anthropological Approach,* edited by William A. Lessa and Evon Z. Vogt, 4th ed., pp. 37–46. New York, 1979.

Marcus, George E., and Michael M. J. Fischer. *Anthropology as Cultural Critique: An Experimental Moment in the Human Sciences.* Chicago, 1986; 2d ed., 1999.

Mills, Margaret. "Feminist Theory and the Study of Folklore: A Twenty-Year Trajectory." *Western Folklore* 52 (1993): 173–192.

Mullen, Patrick B. "Ritual and Sacred Narrative in the Blue Ridge Mountains." *Papers in Comparative Studies* 2 (1982–1983): 17–38.

Mullen, Patrick B. "Belief and the American Folk." *Journal of American Folklore* 113, no. 448 (2000): 119–143.

Narayan, Kirin. *Storytellers, Saints, and Scoundrels: Folk Narrative in Hindu Religious Teaching.* Philadelphia, 1989.

Noy, Dov. "Is There a Jewish Folk Religion?" In *Studies in Jewish Folklore,* edited by Frank Talmage. Cambridge, Mass., 1980.

O'Connor, Bonnie Blair. *Healing Traditions: Alternative Medicines and the Health Professions.* Philadelphia, 1995.

Primiano, Leonard Norman. "Vernacular Religion and the Search for Method in Religious Folklife." *Western Folklore* 54 (1995): 37–56.

Puckett, Newbell Niles. *Folk Beliefs of the Southern Negro.* Chapel Hill, N.C., 1926; reprint, Montclair, N.J., 1968.

Rini, Roseanne. "Elizabeth Kelly: Contemporary Spiritual Teacher and Healer." Ph.D. diss., Ohio State University, Columbus, 1997.

Rosenberg, Bruce. *The Art of the American Folk Preacher.* New York, 1970.

Sciorra, Joseph. "Multivocality and Vernacular Architecture: The Our Lady of Mount Carmel Grotto in Rosebank, Staten Island." In *Studies in Italian-American Folklore,* edited by Luisa Del Guidice, pp. 203–243. Logan, Utah, 1993.

Sered, Susan Starr. *Women as Ritual Experts: The Religious Lives of Elderly Jewish Women in Jerusalem.* New York, 1992.

Seriff, Suzanne. "Homages in Clay: The Figural Ceramics of José Varela." In *Hecho en Tejas: Texas-Mexican Folk Arts and Crafts,* edited by Joe S. Graham, pp. 146–171. Denton, Tex., 1991.

Titon, Jeff Todd. *Powerhouse for God: Speech, Chant, and Song in an Appalachian Baptist Church.* Austin, Tex., 1988.

Turner, Kay. *Beautiful Necessity: The Art and Meaning of Women's Altars.* New York, 1999.

Turner, Kay, and Suzanne Seriff. "'Giving an Altar': The Ideology of Reproduction in a St. Joseph's Day Feast." *Journal of American Folklore* 100 (1987): 446–460.

Turner, Victor. *The Ritual Process: Structure and Anti-Structure.* Ithaca, N.Y., 1969.

Tyson, Ruel W., Jr., James L. Peacock, and Daniel W. Patterson, eds. *Diversities of Gifts: Field Studies in Southern Religion.* Urbana, Ill., 1988.

Vrijhof, Pieter, and Jacques Waardenburg, eds. *Official and Popular Religion: Analysis of a Theme for Religious Studies.* The Hague, 1979.

Webber, Sabra. "Ramadan Observed." *Papers in Comparative Studies* 3 (1984): 183–192.

Williams, Peter W. *Popular Religion in America: Symbolic Change and the Modernization Process in Historical Perspective.* Englewood Cliffs, N.J., 1980; reprint, Urbana, Ill., 1989.

Wilson, William A. "Folklore, a Mirror for What? Reflections of a Mormon Folklorist." *Western Folklore* 54 (1995): 13–21.

Yoder, Don. "Toward a Definition of Folk Religion." *Western Folklore* 33 (1974): 2–15.

PATRICK B. MULLEN (2005)

FOLK RELIGION

This entry consists of the following articles:

AN OVERVIEW
FOLK BUDDHISM
FOLK JUDAISM
FOLK ISLAM

FOLK RELIGION: AN OVERVIEW

Peasant populations (i.e., sedentary agricultural groups forming part of larger, more complex societies) have probably existed since 6000 BCE in southwestern Asia, since 3100 BCE in Egypt, and since 1500 BCE in southeastern Mexico. Unlike agricultural entrepreneurs who are active economic agents or semisubsistence cultivators practicing ritual exchange and barter, peasants are farmers whose surpluses are redistributed to urban centers by more powerful groups. In practice it is not always easy to decide who actually is or is not a peasant, especially in the case of farmers who hold factory jobs, modern European family farmers, contemporary North American small farmers, or cash crop slash-and-burn cultivators of South America and Africa. For the purposes of this article, this term applies to past and present-day sedentary cultivators and pastoralists of Asia, North Africa, southern Europe, and Latin America, and historically to sedentary cultivators in northern Europe and North America as well.

Because sedentary farming emerged independently at different times and in different parts of the world, taking radically different forms (including short-term fallowing with animal-drawn plows, alpine pastoralism, and permanent cultivation by means of hydraulic systems), the search for an original, universal religion based on agriculture seems doomed to wishful speculation. Attempts nevertheless have been made, concentrating on such notions as matriarchy, Earth Mother goddesses, and moon worship.

Yet peasant societies do, by definition, have features in common that set the requirements and limits on the kinds of religion that will serve their members: (1) peasants depend on a particular ecosystem; (2) most live in similar social environments (household-based, on dispersed farms or in small settlements); and (3) they depend on the larger society for which they produce food. Their religion usually provides them with ways to deal with the local natural and social world, as well as the wider social, economic, and political network of which they are a part.

To manage the ecosystem, peasants, like other people, mark the cycles of nature, day and night, the lunar cycle, the solar year, the life cycles of animals and plants—all hold particular importance for cultivators. Many peasant cultures have rituals and routines for transitions relating to equinoxes, planting, germination, and harvest. And because landscape and climate vary widely, peasants tend to establish locally distinct sacred places, times, and divinities. Whether it is at a spring, cave, mountaintop, riverbank, or a special tree, peasants come to pay homage to their divinities according to the calendar, and in times of crisis to seek solutions to such major agricultural threats as drought, hail, and insect plagues.

In terms of social relationships, peasant life is characterized by endemic disputes among households over such matters as inheritance, property boundaries, and irrigation; and yet as cultivators, peasants must normally undertake a certain amount of cooperative work with their neighbors (such as harvesting, herding, and maintaining roads and irrigation ditches), as well as provide mutual aid in time of crisis. To a lesser extent, these tensions and dependencies apply also between adjacent settlements, particularly when pasture or water rights are involved. In this context, religious devotion can facilitate the unity of households within a settlement (mutual fealty to a common divinity) and solidarity between settlements (worship at common shrines). On the other hand, religions also provide the source, pretext, or rallying cry for chronic and intractable conflict between settlements. With regard to patterns of authority and division of labor, the role of religion (through divine models of hierarchy, justice, and emotion) appears to be much the same in peasant as in nonpeasant societies.

Because the household is the critical social and economic unit, peasants pay special attention to consecrating the identity of household members at birth, the alliance of household economic units through marriage, and the reorganization of the household at death. In many peasant societies, elaborate care for the souls of deceased household members corresponds to the idea that the social personality of the house or farm endures beyond the lives of any particular inhabitants. Consequently, there are reasons why this relationship of religion and identity should be stronger with peasants than with others.

As a local phenomenon, peasant religion only rarely can be studied well from a distance, or by relying on surveys or written sources (aside from the rare documents of oral testimony). The ways that it consecrates relationships with nature, society, and identity must be lived to be understood. Context is crucial, for it gives meaning, often of a particularly local variety, to religious behavior that might otherwise appear to be universal.

Indeed, for most people, not just peasants, beliefs are more acted out (in the sense of worship or ritual) than they are thought out. Only when challenged are such beliefs formulated or declared by any but the religious specialist or exceptional devotee. Much of the study of religion as lived, therefore, is the study of that which is taken for granted, that which goes without saying. As a result students of peasant religion have adopted some of the methods used by anthropologists in studying tribal societies; they have stayed for extended periods in rural communities, paying special attention to public religious acts, local interpretation, individual biography, and the range of opinion and doubt.

But the religion of peasants does not address only local agricultural and human concerns, for by definition peasants are only specialists in a wider network of trade and power in which, given the vulnerability of agricultural life, they generally find themselves in a subordinate position. One of the vital tasks of government is to ensure an adequate food supply for its cities; peasant societies are geared for this purpose, for which they are both protected and exploited. Not coincidentally, there is always a major component of religion in peasant society that is held in common with city dwellers and that generally extends to even wider intersocietal or international exchange systems as well. Such religions include divine beings, sacred sites, rituals, and usually church organizations, all of which are common to peasant and nonpeasant alike.

One therefore can no more speak of a radical separateness of peasant religion than one can speak of a radical separateness of peasant society. Peasant religion is an integral part of wider religions, which provides a common frame of reference in the cosmic and ethical sense, a framework that sets the terms for regular social and economic interaction. Indeed, since peasants often do not experience the specifically agricultural features of their religion as something distinctly different or apart, it is usually incorrect to speak of peasant "religion" in any sense other than religiosity, for peasants are almost always Christians, Muslims, Jews, Buddhists, Daoists, or of some other religion that transcends their immediate arena.

The presence in peasant society of religious specialists trained in a broader social context provides a never-ending source of new techniques, ideas, and images, which the peasant society may adapt for specifically local purposes. And much of what anthropologists following Robert Redfield have called the "little tradition" of the peasantry is what survived of a "great tradition" in the countryside long after it was rejected or forgotten by urban theologians and administrators.

Because of the long-term stability of the peasants' physical and social landscape, some aspects of their religions have had a remarkable and perhaps misleading permanence, although the peasants themselves and the greater political and religious systems affecting them have undergone many changes. For example, present-day cult paintings and statues throughout the world contain elements from earlier, now extinct religions; places of veneration are located at the same kinds of sites as earlier devotions; and in many areas, vows and votive offerings have not essentially changed in over two thousand years.

Such apparent permanence, however, is often superficial, masking major changes in attitude and identity. Say that one finds that a given group of peasants who are self-confessed, practicing Muslims also leave offerings to images of cows, contrary to the teachings of the Qurʾān. It would be a distortion to think of them as covert pagans. For empirical studies have broadened the notion of religion to include both what believers profess and what they actually do and feel. Thus Islamic religion, for instance, can only be fully understood as the sum of the religious acts and beliefs of Muslims. Or, put another way, major world religions are, in practice, coalitions or mosaics of widely differing local adaptations that share a common core of beliefs, rituals, and organization.

While peasant religion may be composed of what may appear to be different kinds of elements and survivals from different traditions, in practice these elements usually form an indivisible, functional whole for believers. Where the notion of survivals exists among peasants themselves, it is often the result of church efforts to stigmatize nonapproved behavior as superstitious, or because of the spread of findings of early folklorists bent on unraveling the different strands of peasant religion according to "high" or "low" origin. More recent scholarship has concentrated on seeing how these strands work together as a whole.

A problem facing students of peasant or folk religion has been finding something with which it can be compared. One tack has been to treat it as "popular" religion and to compare it with the prescribed norms of the larger church or doctrine, much as the "little" tradition is compared to the "great." But such comparisons have not always proved fruitful, for they involve comparing two very different things—on the one hand, a religion as lived and, on the other, a set of norms that hardly represents a way of life and that, in fact, may not be lived strictly by any kind of person, peasant or nonpeasant.

A refinement on this method has involved observation of the practical impingement of the institutions of a central religion on the religious life of peasants—the extent to which peasant religion is effectively regulated, updated, and revised from without. For Europe, this has been done through longitudinal studies using field-work, church visitation, and government records.

An alternate approach compares the peasant religion to that of lay nonpeasants in the larger society, as in Clifford Geertz's studies in Java and much of the recent work on China. As yet little is known about urban or nonpeasant lay religiosity, so it is difficult to be sure that the religion of peasants, apart from its attention to the natural landscape, was in a given time and society fundamentally different from that of urban laypersons. At least for some places and times, a distinction between peasant and nonpeasant religiosity has not proved particularly revealing.

For when studied with care and sufficient evidence, peasant religiosity has been found to share many of the characteristics hitherto considered the domain of the "civilized." For instance, peasant religion is not necessarily homogeneous. Even when there is a single religion practiced, there is likely to be a wide range of doubt, opinion, and speculation, whether in a thirteenth-century French village or a twentieth-century Chinese hamlet. Nor is peasant religion particularly fixed or stable. Throughout history peasants have converted, have been converted, or have attempted to convert from one religion to another. And peasants are not invariably and instinctively religious. There are areas where peasant religious indifference has long been common, and recently entire age and gender groups have been known to abandon religion enthusiastically under militantly atheist governments.

Indeed, radical changes in the world political economy since the mid-nineteenth century have affected the terms in which peasant religion can be studied. Urban and rural industrialization, as well as the growth of the service sector, has brought an increased homogeneity in peasant and urban lifestyles. As a result of socialist, communist, and anarchist movements, active, militant disbelief may be an overt or latent presence in rural areas. Seasonal migrations to the cities, increased visiting in the cities with relatives, peasant participation in the international workforce, and the tremendous growth in literacy, as well as the spread of radio and television, have all helped to diffuse new religious styles and cults more rapidly among the peasantry.

In most places this broadening of horizons has made peasants more aware of their "otherness" in religious matters, so that it is they themselves who internalize behavioral distinctions proposed by the dominant culture. Some scholars refer to this process as "biculturalism": acting in different ways at different levels (the local and the metropolitan), clearly distinguishing between the two, and segregating behavior appropriately.

As a corollary to this bicultural insecurity, there is intense religious and political competition for the allegiance of the peasants whose religion has been devalued or rendered impractical. There exists a global religious competition, in keeping with the global economy in which peasants are now involved, in which the competitors are missionaries, again both religious and political. Among Peru's Altiplano peasantry one finds several lifestyles based on models and aid from American and European religious organizations. Indeed, some of the class/clan factionalism that unitary religions once served to ease is now expressed with rival religions from the wider world.

Yet it is not that peasants must choose only from the great religions; on the contrary, as the anthropologist Eric Wolf pointed out, there have been many instances of peasant religious innovation, through creative imitation or the inspiration of visionaries and prophets. Some have taken the form of millenarian movements, others as radical purification sects. (Some religiously innovative groups, such as the Mormons and the Mennonites, created peasants as much as they were created by them.) And as tribespeople become peasants in African nation-states, new sects and cults spring up that speak to the new conditions, most of which, true to form, are not just local but national or international in scope.

In the context of the nation-state, peasant religion is quite easily politicized. Two overlapping factors are at work. First, human-divine relations serve to consecrate and are thereby tied up with personal identities in the family, village, and nation. Second, the year-in, year-out give-and-take that characterizes peasant devotions to divine figures accumulate great emotional power. Both the investment of identity and the emotional power are generally located in divinities with relatively bounded territories of grace, presenting a permanent temptation to governments, political parties, and to the churches themselves. And if effective channels of political action are blocked by authoritarian regimes the local religion, its shrines, divine protectors, and priests, can embody the entire peasant way of life. Thus through religion, peasant discontent finds a charismatic expression. By the same token, in the face of all-pervasive regimes such as China during the Cultural Revolution, early modern Spain, or Spanish-occupied Peru, private religious acts and beliefs provide some peasants with a margin of independent identity and action, a buffer against the politicization of private life.

Often peasant religion is mobilized or exploited by non-peasant leaders. In the nineteenth and twentieth centuries, literary romanticists, folklorists, and nationalists alike have seen in local peasant religion a source of indigenous virtue, the survival of an earlier local culture and identity in the face of foreign domination. In Ireland, Brittany, Poland, the Basque country, Greece, Yugoslavia, Armenia, the Baltic states, as well as in many of Europe's colonial empires worldwide, independence and autonomy movements have fed on an exaltation of peasant religion that on a superficial level involves a kind of ruralization of the urban elite. An extreme but symptomatic example is Mohandas Gandhi's religious transformation from lawyer to peasant. In response to this kind of demand, rural gurus and seers circulate from city to city and nation to nation servicing devotees; they also spread their messages by the internet.

This type of idealization represents the obverse of metropolitan religious doctrines that long held much of peasant religiosity to be pagan superstition, an attitude shared by enlightened secularizers as well. For both clergy and sophisticates, peasant religion has represented an "other" against which both orthodoxy and civilization could be measured.

These seemingly contradictory points of view, by their emphasis on tradition, survivals, and stability, all draw attention to peasant religion's past rather than its dynamics of change or its present roles. Idealization and stigmatization both tend to attribute an integrity and homogeneity to this religion that it rarely possesses, and simplify a more complex, perhaps less manageable reality.

SEE ALSO Agriculture; Anthropology, Ethnology, and Religion; Dance, article on Popular and Folk Dance; Indo-European Religions, article on History of Study; Popular Religion.

BIBLIOGRAPHY

The search for universal features of the religion of cultivators in keeping with the framework theory of religious evolution, as exemplified by the work of James G. Frazer and Wilhelm Schmidt, is reviewed by Mircea Eliade in his *Patterns in Comparative Religion* (New York, 1958).

A persuasive exposition of general characteristics of peasant life from an anthropological viewpoint is provided in Eric Wolf's *Peasants* (Englewood Cliffs, N.J., 1966), following on Robert Redfield's *Peasant Society and Culture* (Chicago, 1956). A model study by Clifford Geertz, *The Religion of Java* (Glencoe, Ill., 1960), compares the religion of peasants with that of merchants and nobles, all under the wide mantle of Islam. For Buddhism, Stanley J. Tambiah in *Buddhism and the Spirit Cults in North-East Thailand* (Cambridge, 1970) shows how in practice the elements of different religious traditions function as a whole in the religion of a village. A number of scholars have produced excellent work on folk religion in China. Thomas DuBois, using primary written and oral sources has made a particularly thorough study of the different religious alternatives on the North China Plain in "The Sacred World of Cang County: Religious Belief, Organization and Practice in Rural North China During the Late Nineteenth and Twentieth Centuries." (Ph.D. diss., University of California in Los Angeles, 2001). For the religion of European peasantry, I describe Catholicism in northern Spain in its relation to the landscape and social relations in *Person and God in a Spanish Valley* (rev. ed. Princeton, N. J.,1989), and Lucy Rushton admirably relates Greek Orthodox theology to personal life in "Religion and Identity in a Rural Greek Community" (Ph.D. diss., University of Sussex, 1983).

Much of the early work on popular religion in Europe is discussed in P. Bolgioni's "Religione Popolare," *Augustinianum* 21 (1981): 7–75, with ample bibliographic notes. Richard F. Gombrich in *Precept and Practice: Traditional Buddhism in the Rural Highlands of Ceylon* (Oxford, 1971) argues against the notion of popular religion, as does Jean-Claude Schmitt in "'Religion populaire' et culture folklorique," *Annales: Économies, sociétés, civilisations* 31 (September–October 1976): 941–953. Unusual ethnographic information about peasant religion in the Friuli region of northeast Italy, gathered in the context of diocesan investigations, is provided by Carlo Ginzburg in *I Benandanti: Richerche sulla stregoneria e culti agrari tra Cinquecento e Seicento* (Turin, 1966), translated by John Tedeschi and Anne C. Tedeschi as *The Night Battles: Witchcraft and Agrarian Cults in the Sixteenth and Seventeenth Centuries* (Baltimore, 1983). Emmanuel Le Roy Ladurie's *Montaillou: The Promised Land of Error* (New York, 1978) describes in detail village Catholicism in the Pyrenees and the villagers' conversion to Cathar beliefs. Similarly rich in detail, although not about a single community, is Keith Thomas's *Religion and the Decline of Magic: Studies in Popular Beliefs in Sixteenth and Seventeenth Century England* (New York, 1971). Campaigns to change peasant religion are described in Eamon Duffy, *The Stripping of the Altars: Traditional Religion in England 1400–1580* (New Haven, Conn., 1992), by the same author in *The Voices of Morebath: Reformation and Rebellion in an English Village* (New Haven, Conn., 2001), and for Peru, in Kenneth Mills, *Idolatry and its Enemies: Colonial Andean Religion and Extirpation, 1640–1750* (Princeton, N.J., 1997). Nancy M. Farriss's *Maya Society under Colonial Rule: The Collective Enterprise of Survival* (Princeton, 1984) and Victoria Reifler Bricker's *The Indian Christ, the Indian King: The Historical Substrate of Maya Myth and Ritual* (Austin, Tex., 1981) are historical studies of religious syncretism in the Yucatan, building on a long line of distinguished ethnographies. Peter Brown, in his elegant *The Cult of the Saints: Its Rise and Function in Latin Christianity* (Chicago, 1981), challenges a radical distinction between peasant and nonpeasant religion in the Mediterranean, as I do in *Local Religion in Sixteenth Century Spain* (Princeton, N.J., 1981).

Peasant millennial movements are studied in *Millennial Dreams in Action,* edited by Sylvia L. Thrupp (New York, 1970). Charles Tilly's *The Vendée* (Cambridge, Mass., 1964) asks important questions about the social and economic roots of a peasant uprising in the name of religion.

WILLIAM A. CHRISTIAN, JR. (1987 AND 2005)

FOLK RELIGION: FOLK BUDDHISM

Religious traditions are, by their very nature, complex. One the one hand, the symbolize the highest aspirations of the human mind and spirit; on the other, they sanctify and give meaning to the most ordinary and commonplace human needs and activities. The complexity of religion and its functions have been analyzed in various ways. There has been a tendency, however, to distinguish between those aspects created by and appropriate to the educated elites, for example, priests and rules, and those that help the uneducated, common folk cope with the uncertainities and exigencies of life. Scholars have sometimes referred to this distinction as obtaining between "great" and "little" traditions or between "elite" and "folk" traditions. It must be kept in mind that these formal distinctions do justice neither to the multiplexity of religious traditions nor to the organic unity that characterizes them, even though such categories may serve a useful function.

"Folk" Buddhism may be understood as a persistent, complex, and syncretic dimension of the Buddhist tradition characterized by beliefs and practices dominated by magical intent and fashioned with the purpose of helping people cope with the uncertainties and exigencies of life. Its varied expressions emerge along the wide spectrum between the normative Buddhist ideal represented quintessentially but not exclusively by the Buddha and the concept of *nirvāṇa,* and the indigenous magical-animistic and shamanistic traditions of the given culture in which Buddhism becomes institutionalized. Consequently, some aspects of folk Buddhism (e.g., the figure of the Buddha, the person of the monk, and the practice of meditation) appear to be closely affiliated with the normative ideals of Buddhism, while others are barely distinguishable from native, non-Buddhist religious forms. Folk Buddhist institutional structures, religious practices and practitioners, and oral and written literatures reflect this variation.

Buddhism has had a folk or popular dimension since its inception. Early Buddhist scriptures challenge the view of a "golden age" of pure monastic practice dedicated to the pursuit of *nirvāṇa* unencumbered and undisturbed by the needs and expectations of a simple, uneducated laity. That the

Buddha and his followers were supported by laypersons for reasons of material gain and magical protection, as well as for spiritual benefit, cannot be denied. Even meditation, the *sine qua non* of monastic practice, was perceived as leading not only to equanimity and enlightenment but also to the acquisition of magical power. The *Mahāvagga* of the Theravāda Vinaya Piṭaka depicts the Buddha not simply as an enlightened teacher, but as a yogin who wins followers through his magic. Moreover, although the source is later commentary, it is significant that the future Buddha, just prior to his enlightenment, was said to have been offered food by a woman who mistook him for a tree deity. In general, Buddhist scriptures readily intermesh doctrinal exposition with magical and animistic figures and elements ranging from *devas* (gods) to *mantras* (sacred utterances).

To be sure, folk Buddhism became a more dominant aspect of Buddhist institutional and cultural life as the religion grew in size and cultural significance throughout Asia. In India, Aśoka's strong support of the Buddhist monastic order in the third century BCE proved to be crucial to its growth and diffusion, and the appropriation of folk elements from different cultures was a means by which Buddhism spread and accommodated itself to the cultures of Asia from at least the beginning of the common era. Indigenous folk religions, therefore, were the major media through which Buddhism became a popular religion not only in India, but in Southeast, Central, and East Asia as well. The fact remains, nevertheless, that the folk element within Buddhism has been a part of the tradition since its inception, and has persisted in different forms to the present.

Folk Buddhism has several different facets that reflect various modes of interaction between normative, doctrinal-institutional Buddhism and native religio-cultural traditions. In some cases, the normative Buddhist tradition made only inconsequential adjustments; in others, Buddhism emerged as a thinly veiled animism. The major ingredient of folk Buddhism is usually referred to as animism or magical-animism, that is, the belief in benevolent and malevolent supernatural powers and the attempt to avoid them or to enlist their aid. These powers range from spirits of the living and the deceased to deities of regional or even national jurisdiction associated with non-Buddhist (e.g., Brahmanic) pantheons. The dialectical relationship between Buddhism and indigenous animism such as the Bon of Tibet led to the parochialization of Buddhism, but also changed the face of those native traditions encountered in Tibet, Korea, Japan, and elsewhere. For example, Shintō, rooted in an autochthonous animism, developed in Japan in competition with the more sophisticated traditions of Chinese Buddhism, just as religious Daoism in China institutionalized, at least in part, in response to Indian Buddhist influence.

The complex nature of folk Buddhism can be analyzed in various ways, but the method should do justice to its common or generic elements as well as the uniqueness of distinctive religio-cultural environments. Folk Buddhism as an essentially syncretistic phenomenon can be seen in terms of three types or modes of interaction between Buddhist and non-Buddhist elements: appropriation, adaptation, and transformation. These categories are intended to characterize particular historical instances as well as describe general types. Although they have overlapping qualities, they point to the variety within folk Buddhist belief and practice as well.

APPROPRIATION. In many cases, folk Buddhism merely appropriated and subordinated indigenous symbols, beliefs, and practices with very little change in meaning. This is particularly true in the incorporation of a wide range of supernatural beings and powers into the Buddhist system. Generally speaking, these supernaturals, whether gods or spirits, malevolent or benevolent, were subordinated to the dominant Buddhist symbols and motifs. Most often they played a protective role, standing guard at a sacred Buddhist precinct, be it temple or *maṇḍala,* or functioned in an appropriately subordinate way in relationship to the Buddha. In Sri Lanka, for example, a kind of divine pantheon evolved, a hierarchy of gods and spirits ranging from the most localized guardian spirits of village and field to the suzerainty of regional gods the likes of Skanda and Viṣṇu with the entire structure under the sway of the Buddha. In Tibet the gods of the everyday world (*'jig rten pa*) became protectors of the *dharma,* obeying the commands of the great teachers. While they are so numerous and indeterminate as to defy a fixed ordering, they generally are divided according to the traditional Indian tripartite cosmology of heaven, earth, and the intermediate realm. In Burma (Myanmar) the indigenous *nat* spirits are incorporated into Burmese Buddhism as *devas*. Thagya Min, for instance, is assimilated into Sakka (the Brahmanic Indra), and resides in Tāvatiṃsa Heaven as king of the *devas*, but is also said to be ruler of the "thirty-seven *nats*." In Thailand various supernaturals including *devata, cao,* and *phī* have a complex relationship to Thai Buddhism involving linkage, hierarchy, and instances of both opposition and complementarity. In Japan, Buddhism absorbed native Japanese deities or *kami.* In many cases the *kami* are taken as manifestations of Buddhas or *bodhisattvas* (the theory of *honjisuijaku*), although a uniform set correspondence did not develop. A similar story can be told for Buddhism in China, Korea, and other parts of Asia. While the specific list of supernaturals appropriated into the Buddhist system varies from culture to culture, these beings represent a hierarchy of powers and suzerainties dependent on, under the authority of, or even in tension with, Buddhist figures, symbols, and motifs.

These supernaturals have been assimilated into the Buddhist cultus as well as into Asian Buddhist worldviews; they are amalgamated into orthodox ritual activity or become a distinct ritual subset. Throughout Buddhist Asia the guardian spirits of a temple precinct, such as the *phī* in Thailand or the *kami* in Japan, may be propitiated prior to an auspicious ceremonial event. In Tibet, Tantric ritual has provided a framework for customary religious practices in which Tibetan deities exist side by side with Indian Buddhist ones.

In Sri Lanka, devout Sinhala Buddhists paying respects to the Buddha at the famous sanctuary of Lankatileke outside of Kandy will make offerings before images of the Hindu deities enshrined in *devales* around the perimeter of the building. In Thailand, Brahmanic deities (e.g., Viṣṇu) may be invoked during a customary Buddhist ritual, and offerings are made to the guardians of the four quarters as part of the New Year celebration at a Buddhist monastery (*wat*).

Of special significance in folk Buddhism have been the belief in the soul (the existence of which is scarcely maintained in scripture), or spirit element(s), of the individual, and various rituals associated with this belief, especially life-crisis or life-transition rites. The role of Buddhism in the conduct of mortuary and death anniversary rites for the souls of the dead in China, Korea, and Japan is well known. In Japan, the Obon festival celebrated in the seventh month honors the return of the souls of the dead. Graves at Buddhist temples will be cleaned in preparation for the spirits' return, and the household altar (*butsudan*) will be decorated with flowers, lanterns, and offerings of fruit. In Burma, mortuary rituals are performed to prevent the soul of the deceased from remaining in its former haunts and causing trouble. In Thailand, soul-calling (*riag khwan*) rites are performed at life-transition times such as weddings and even as part of ordination into the monkhood.

ADAPTATION. In assimilating indigenous magical-animistic and shamanistic religious beliefs and practices, Buddhism itself has changed. This process of adaptation and parochialization has been part of the Buddhist tradition from its outset: the Buddha as teacher but also miracle-worker, meditation as the vehicle for the attainment of insight and supernatural powers, the monk as *nirvāṇa*-seeker and magician. In the Theravāda traditions of Sri Lanka and Southeast Asia the miraculous power of the Buddha is attested to not only in supernatural feats of magical flight, prognostication, and the like, but also in the cult of Buddha relics and Buddha images that typifies ritual practice in this region. The Mahāyāna and Tantryāna traditions elaborated the salvific function of the Buddha through the proliferation of Buddhas and *bodhisattvas*. In China, Dao'an (312–385) popularized Buddhism by promoting Maitreya as a savior Buddha, the god of Tuṣita Heaven, an earthly paradise accessible to all. Huiyüan (334–416) did for Amitābha Buddha and his Pure Land (Sukhāvatī) what Dao'an did for Maitreya and Tuṣita Heaven. Both Maitreyism and Amidism became fundamental to folk Buddhism. In Japan, one of the specific adaptations was the assimilation of popular elements into the figure of the *bodhisattva* Jizō (Skt., Kṣitigarbha), who thereby came to occupy an even more important place than did his Chinese counterpart, Dizang. Not only does Jizō deliver souls from hell, but he also helps women in childbirth and, like Kannon (Chin., Guanyin), another popular savior, is seen as the giver of healthy children and a guide to the Western Paradise of Amida.

The supernormal powers associated with meditation adepts has a close association with shamanism. Monks have become famous for their skills as alchemists, for their ability to communicate with the spirit world, and for their prognostication of future events, activities that conflict with the Vinaya. The biographies of such Tantric adepts as Padmasambhava and Mi la ras pa attest to this type of parochialization, and even the lives of the Chan (Zen) patriarchs are not exempt from supernatural hagiographic elaboration. In Sri Lanka, ascetic monks are revered not only for their piety but for their magical prowess as well, and in Thailand a significant cult of monk-saints has developed. Popular magazines attest to their extraordinary deeds, their advice is sought for everything from lottery numbers to military ventures, and their amulets are worn for protection against danger and disease.

TRANSFORMATION. Buddhism appropriated magical-animistic and shamanistic religious forms and adapted its own beliefs and practices to this type of cultural milieu. The degree to which assimilation and adaptation has occurred has led to profound transformations of the tradition. While decisive turns in the development of Buddhism have taken various forms, popular sectarian movements have provided one of the most fruitful contexts for this kind of transmutation. Examples abound throughout Buddhist Asia. In Burma and Thailand messianic Buddhist groups emerged in the modern period centered around charismatic leaders often claiming to be Maitreya Buddha. In China, Buddhist sectarian groups led by "rebel monks" split off from monasteries in the Northern Wei kingdom (386–535) as early as the fifth century. The best known is the White Lotus movement, a complex of rebel eschatologies active from the twelfth to the nineteenth century. Other major sects include the Maitreya, White Cloud, and Lo, or Wuwei. These groups were lay-based, heterodox, and syncretistic, and were often politically militant. The White Lotus sect developed its own texts, a married clergy, hereditary leadership, and by the mid-fourteenth century a full-blown eschatology derived from both the Maitreyan tradition and Manichaeism. By the late sixteenth century the principal deity of the White Lotus groups was a mother goddess. Eventually, by the late nineteenth century, the Buddhist elements were so extenuated that they had become congregational folk religion rather than a distinctive form of folk Buddhism.

In Japan as early as the Heian period (794–1185) holy men (*hijiri*) developed a folk Buddhism outside the orthodox ecclesiastical system. In the tenth and eleventh centuries Amida *hijiri* and Nembutsu *hijiri,* preeminent among whom was Kōya, a layman of the Tendai sect, taught universal salvation through the repetition of the Nembutsu (the formulaic recitation of the name of Amida Buddha). The Nembutsu came to be seen as a powerful form of protection against the spirits of the dead and evil spirits (*goryō*) and a means to release them into Amida's paradise. While the founders of the orthodox Pure Land sects, Hōnen and Shinran, rejected the animistic and magical aspects of the Nembutsu, the attitudes of the common folk did not substantially change. The Amida *mantra* was considered a causally effective means to attain the

Pure Land after death as well as a magical spell for sending evil spirits to Amida. Popular sectarianism has continued to develop into the contemporary period. Some of the so-called new religions (*shinkō shūykō*) in Japan represent a unique form of folk Buddhism. Arising in the nineteenth and twentieth centuries in a period of political and social crisis, these religions, which developed around strong, charismatic leaders, are syncretistic and often utilize magical ritual practices. Two of the best known are Risshō Kōseikai and Sōka Gakkai. Both are indebted to the *Lotus Sūtra*-Nichiren tradition. Through its political wing, Sōka Gakkai has become a sometimes militant force in Japanese politics.

The Buddhist encounter with folk religion, which has taken the forms of appropriation, adaptation, and transformation, has not occurred without conflict. In Southeast Asia stories abound of the Buddha's encounter with indigenous supernatural beings who are only eventually subdued and made to vow their allegiance to the *dhamma.* Other heroic figures exemplify a similar pattern. Especially noteworthy is Padmasambhava's propagation of the *dharma* in Tibet. The key to his success, in contrast to the previous failure of the great teacher Śāntirakṣita, was Padmasambhava's magical prowess in subduing the powerful Tibetan deities. Such conflict may be mirrored in Buddhist ritual as well as in myth and legend. In northern Thailand, for example, offerings of buffalo meat to the guardian spirits *(phī)* of Chiang Mai are made as part of the New Year celebration; however, this ritual activity has no formal connection with the elaborate ceremonies occurring at Buddhist sanctuaries in the area.

The practitioners of folk Buddhism likewise present a great diversity. Those most closely tied to the autochthonous animism may be likened to shamans, for they function in a shamanlike manner. They have the power to enter into the realm of the supernaturals, an act often symbolized by magical flight; they may also become possessed by supernatural beings or function as a medium between the supernatural and human realms, and have the knowledge to enlist or ward off their power. In Tibet, *mdos* rituals are performed by wandering lamas (Tib., *bla mas*) or exorcists (*snyags pa*) for protection against dangers, hindrances, injuries, illness, and obstacles caused by evil powers. The person who carries out exorcistic rituals (*gto*) must be an expert in meditating on his *yi dam* or tutelary divinity. The *yamabushi* or mountain ascetics of Japan, while affiliated with the Tendai and Shingon sects, perform exorcisms and function as village magicians. The Chinese shaman (*wu*), who exorcised spirits of evil and illness and danced and chanted to ward off disasters, influenced the popular conception of the charismatic leadership of folk Buddhist sects in China. Often, lay Buddhists are the principal practitioners of the folk traditions, especially because many of the magical practices associated with folk Buddhism are either forbidden or discouraged by the orthodox Vinaya. In the Esoteric schools of Buddhism (e.g., Shingon), as well as in sectarian movements, the differentiation between mainstream beliefs and practices and those of the folk dimension are more difficult to perceive. Even in the Theravāda countries of Southeast Asia, however, actual monastic custom and practice may be far removed from the strict ideal of monastic discipline, which discourages fortune telling, alchemy, and the like.

The texts of folk Buddhism also reflect the ways in which the normative tradition has appropriated, adapted, and been transformed by indigenous folk religion. An important genre of folk literature is the miraculous tale, often purporting to be an episode from the life of the Buddha or a famous Buddhist figure such as Maudgalyāyana or Vimalakīrti. Included in this literary genre are the Jātakas, which are themselves examples of the appropriation of folktales, mythic accounts of heavens and hells (e.g., *Petavatthu*), legendary elements in chronicles, lives of the saints in various Buddhist traditions, and vernacular collections such as the Chinese *pien-wen* (texts of marvelous events). Other texts, such as the *paritta* (scriptural passages that, when chanted, are said to have apotropaic power) in the Theravāda tradition, function in a magical manner in Buddhist ritual, even though the content reflects the highest ethical and spiritual ideals of the normative tradition. The *Bar do thos grol* (Tibetan *Book of the Dead),* although at the center of the Tantric technique of liberation, certainly incorporates shamanistic elements. Another type of folk Buddhist literature includes those texts specifically related to the practice of astrology, fortune telling, and animistic rituals.

In the final analysis, folk Buddhism should not be seen as a later degeneration of the normative Buddhist ideal. Rather, it is a complex dimension of the tradition, present from its origin, that has provided the tradition with much of its vitality and variation from culture to culture.

See Also Arhat; Avalokiteśvara; Buddhas and Bodhisattvas, article on Celestial Buddhas and Bodhisattvas; Chinese Religion, article on Popular Religion; Hijiri; Honjisuijaku; Japanese Religions, article on Popular Religion; Kṣitigarbha; Mahāsiddhas; Millenarianism, article on Chinese Millenarian Movements; Nats; New Religious Movements, article on New Religious Movements in Japan; Nianfo; Popular Religion; Priesthood, article on Buddhist Priesthood; Worship and Devotional Life, articles on Buddhist Devotional Life.

Bibliography

In recent years studies of folk or popular Buddhism have been greatly enhanced by the work of anthropologists, especially those working in Southeast Asia. These descriptive and analytic studies provide an important complement to the work of cultural historians and historians of religion. Notable of mention for the Theravāda Buddhist cultures are the works of Stanley J. Tambiah, in particular his *Buddhism and the Spirit Cults in North-East Thailand* (Cambridge, 1970). While this work is a microstudy, like many anthropologists Tambiah offers a more comprehensive interpretation of the religious system in northeast Thailand. Tambiah's structuralist-functionalist approach contrasts with the social-psychological perspective (as found, for instance, in the works of Abram Kardiner) of Melford E. Spiro's *Buddhism and Society: A Great Tradition and Its Burmese Vicissitudes,* 2d ed. (Berkeley, Calif., 1982). A dominant theme in anthropological studies is the nature of the interrelationship between the folk or "little" tradition and the "great" tradition. In various ways this theme is addressed in Michael M. Ames's "Magical-Animism and Buddhism: A Structural Analysis of the Sinhalese Religious System," in *Religion in South Asia,* edited by Edward B. Harper (Seattle, 1964), pp. 21–52; Gananath Obeyesekere's "The Great Tradition and the Little in the Perspective of Sinhalese Buddhism," *Journal of Asian Studies* 22 (February 1963): 139–153; Manning Nash's *The Golden Road to Modernity: Village Life in Contemporary Burma* (New York, 1965); and A. Thomas Kirsch's "Complexity in the Thai Religious System: An Interpretation," *Journal of Asian Studies* 36 (February 1977): 241–266. This theme figures in studies of the religious systems in Central and East Asia as well. See, for example, J. H. Kamstra's *Encounter or Syncretism: The Initial Growth of Japanese Buddhism* (Leiden, 1967), Alicia Matsunaga's *The Buddhist Philosophy of Assimilation: The Historical Development of the Honji-Suijaku Theory* (Rutland, Vt., and Tokyo, 1969), and Christoph von Fürer-Haimendorf's *Morals and Merit: A Study of Values and Social Controls in South Asian Societies* (London, 1967).

Popular Buddhist millenarian movements constitute another theme addressed by recent studies of folk Buddhism. For Southeast Asia, E. Michael Mendelson's "The King of the Weaving Mountain," *Journal of the Royal Central Asian Society* 48 (July–October 1961): 229–237, and Charles F. Keyes's "Millennialism, Theravāda Buddhism, and Thai Society," *Journal of Asian Studies* 36 (February 1977): 283–302, are particularly noteworthy. For China, Daniel L. Overmeyer's *Folk Buddhist Religion: Dissenting Sects in Late Traditional China* (Cambridge, Mass., 1976) is definitive.

Studies dealing with folk Buddhism that do not take a particular thematic perspective abound. Francis L. K. Hsu's *Under the Ancestors' Shadow; Chinese Culture and Personality* (New York, 1948) treats Chinese popular religion and the ancestral cult. H. Byron Earhart's *A Religious Study of the Mount Haguro Sect of Shugendō* (Tokyo, 1970) deals with the Shugendō sect, a popular movement combining Esoteric Buddhism with Japanese folk religious beliefs. René de Nebesky-Wojkowitz's *Oracles and Demons of Tibet: The Cult and Iconography of the Tibetan Protective Deities* (The Hague, 1956) treats popular Tibetan protective deities. For folk Buddhism in Japan, see also Hori Ichirō's *Folk Religion in Japan; Continuity and Change,* edited and translated by Joseph M. Kitagawa and Alan L. Miller (Chicago, 1968).

New Sources

Gellner, David N. *Monk, Householder, and Tantric Priest: Newar Buddhism and Its Hierarchy of Ritual.* Cambridge, U.K., 1992.

Gombrich, Richard, and Gananath Obeyesekere. *Buddhism Transformed: Religious Change in Sri Lanka.* Princeton, 1988.

LaFleur, William R. *Liquid Life: Abortion and Buddhism in Japan.* Princeton, 1992.

Mumford, Stan Royal. *Himalayan Dialogue: Tibetan Lamas and Gurung Shamans in Nepal.* Madison, Wis., 1989.

Numrich, Paul David. *Old Wisdom in the New World: Americanization in Two Immigrant Theravada Buddhist Temples.* Knoxville, Tenn., 1996.

Ortner, Sherry B. *High Religion: A Cultural and Political History of Sherpa Buddhism.* Princeton, 1989.

Swearer, Donald K. "Folk Buddhism." In *Buddhism and Asian History,* edited by Joseph Mitsuo Kitagawa and Mark D. Cummings, pp. 351–357. New York, 1989.

Tannenbaum, Nicola. *Who Can Compete against the World? Power-Protection and Buddhism in Shan Worldview.* Ann Arbor, 1996.

DONALD K. SWEARER (1987)
Revised Bibliography

FOLK RELIGION: FOLK JUDAISM

In the course of its millennial history, biblical and Jewish folk religion has found its expression in beliefs in male and female deities other than God; in angels, devils, demons, ghosts, and spirits; in saints and holy men; in the "evil eye" and other baleful influences; and in rites and practices such as magic, witchcraft, divination, and the use of amulets, charms, and talismans. Manifestations of Jewish folk religion were found from earliest biblical times and continued to appear, until in the nineteenth century it waned in those European countries in which the Jews came under the influence of the Enlightenment. In the Middle Eastern Jewish communities folk religion retained its vitality until 1948, after which the people of these communities were largely transplanted to Israel.

BIBLICAL PERIOD. In a few cases the biblical authors refer to folk beliefs and rites without condemnation. These "naive" references pertain mostly to cosmic origins or to the early history of mankind, the Hebrew patriarchs, and the people of Israel. Thus *Genesis* 6:1–4 clearly reflects a folk belief in the existence of "sons of God"; *Isaiah* 14:12–15, in a rebellious angel who was cast down into the netherworld; and various passages in *Isaiah, Psalms,* and *Job,* in sea dragons and other monsters who dared to oppose God. *Terafim,* small household gods taken by Rachel from her father's house (*Gn.* 31:19, 31:30–35), and larger versions of the same kept by Saul's daughter Michal (the wife of David) in her chambers (*1 Sm.* 19:13, 19:16), are clear examples of folk belief.

In sharp contrast to these uncritical mentions of folk religion are the condemnatory references to the popular (as well as institutional) worship of gods other than Yahveh contained in the historical and prophetic writings of the Bible. But these scornful references are, at the same time, also testimonies to the popular worship in Israel of several male and female deities (such as Baal, Kemosh, Milcom, Asherah, Astarte, and the Queen of Heaven) from the time of the Judges to the destruction of Israel and Judah in 722 and 587/6 BCE and even later (see *Jer.* 44:15–19). These biblical data are supplemented by archaeological discoveries of small figurines of goddesses (Asherah, Astarte) in many excavated Israelite homes from the biblical period all over the country.

Demons. With reference to demons the biblical evidence shows a similar duality. On the one hand, there are prohibitions of witchcraft and all trafficking with, or consultation of, demons, ghosts, and spirits, which practices are considered capital sins punishable by death (*Ex.* 22:17, *Dt.* 18:10–12), and historical notes tell of the attempted extermination by royal decree of "those that divined by a ghost or familiar spirit" (*1 Sm.* 28:3). On the other, there is ample testimony to the belief, shared by the Yahvist historians and prophets with the common folk, in the existence of demons and their power to harm people's bodies and minds (*Gn.* 32:25ff.; *Lv.* 16:10; *Is.* 13:21, 34:14; *1 Sm.* 16:15, 16:23; *1 Kgs.* 22:22–23; *Ps.* 91:5–6). Israelite folk religion seems to have made room for species of demons (*shedim, seʿirim*), as well as individual demons, for example ʿAzʾazel. Most of the latter are known from the religions of the neighboring peoples as gods, thus, for example, Lilith, Mavet ("death"), and Reshef ("pestilence"). From the late biblical and apocryphal literature are known the devil-like demons called Saṭan, Masṭemah, Belial (Beliyyaʿal), Asmodeus (Ashmedʿai), while both in the New Testament and in rabbinic literature demons are referred to as "unclean" or "evil spirits." In the three synoptic gospels the prince of demons has the name Beelzebul (Baʿal Zebub). These demons, generic and individual, are all reflections of Jewish folk belief.

Magic and divination. The Bible repeatedly condemns action taken to influence the mysterious forces of nature and the spirits. *Deuteronomy* 18:10–11 decrees, "There shall not be found among you any one that . . . useth divination, a soothsayer, or an enchanter, or a sorcerer, or a charmer, or one that consulteth a ghost or a familiar spirit, or a necromancer." *Exodus* 22:17 rules explicitly, "Thou shalt not suffer a sorceress to live" (cf. *Lv.* 20:27). Passages such as these indicate that the biblical authors shared with the common people the belief in the reality and efficacy of magic, but, in contrast with the common folk, condemned it as an act of unfaithfulness to God (cf. *Dt.* 18:12–13).

Recognizing the assurance divination provided, biblical legislation, while outlawing it in the form practiced by the Canaanites, supplied a substitute for it in the mantic activity of prophets, whose legitimacy, it states, would be proven by subsequent events (*Dt.* 18:14–22). The people, it seems, turned to the prophets primarily in order to profit from their mantic powers (*1 Sm.* 9:6; *1 Kgs.* 14:1ff., 22:5ff.; *2 Kgs.* 3:11). Divination included the questioning of the Urim and Tummim (*1 Sm.* 23:9–12), consultation of the *terafim* (*Jgs.* 17:5, 18:14; *Hos.* 3:4; *Ez.* 21:26; *Zec.* 10:2), the use of goblets (*Gn.* 44:5), arrows (*Ez.* 21:26), spoken words (*Gn.* 24:14, *1 Sm.* 14:9–10, cf. v. 12), and the interpretation of the liver (*Ez.* 21:26), stars (*Is.* 47:13, *Jer.* 10:2), and dreams (*1 Sm.* 28:6). The hold diviners had over the people is best illustrated by the story about King Saul: he "cut them off the land," but when in trouble sought out one of those who remained (*1 Sm.* 28:3–25).

The persistence into the first century BCE of magic as a part of popular religion is attested by *2 Maccabees* 12:40, which tells about the Jewish warriors who wore under their tunics amulets (*hieromata*) taken from the idols of Yavneh. This practice was condemned by the author because of the pagan derivation of the amulets. On the other hand, in *Tobit*, an apocryphal book of the first century BCE, a method of exorcising a demon from a possessed person with the help of fumigation is described as having been taught by the angel Raphael, that is, as a religiously orthodox act.

TALMUDIC PERIOD. After the Babylonian exile, Jewish folk religion found its expression, partly under the impact of Babylonian, Persian, and, later, Hellenistic influences, in a proliferation of angels, demons (some of whom had figured already in the Bible), evil spirits, the evil eye, and so on, and in practices aiming at the invocation of beneficial superhuman powers and the propitiation of, or protection against, those with evil intentions. While in the Jerusalem (Palestinian) Talmud only three categories of demons (*mazziqim, shedim,* and *ruḥot*) are mentioned, demonology is more prominent in the Palestinian midrashim. However, it is the Babylonian Talmud (completed c. 500 CE) that is the richest source for Jewish folk religion in general and demonology in particular.

For Talmudic Judaism the number of demons was legion. Ashmedʾai was their king, while their queen, Iggrat the daughter of Mahalat, went about with a retinue of 180,000 "angels of destruction" (B.T., *Pes.* 112b). The Talmudic sages fought valiantly, not against the popular belief in demons, but against the demons themselves. Thus Ḥaninaʾ ben Dosaʾ and Abbaye succeeded in restricting the activities of Iggrat to certain times and places. Other sages conducted conversations with demons. Most dangerous was the female demon Lilith, who seduced men at night and strangled babes, and who could be kept away only by means of protective charms.

Since both Talmuds and the *midrashim* record the sayings, rulings, and acts of the sages, and not of the common folk, our knowledge of folk religion is largely confined to its reflection in the recorded words and deeds of the rabbis, and it is on them that we must base our conclusions as to the religious beliefs and acts of the simple people. Thus, for example, the Mishnah (*San.* 6.4) and the Jerusalem Talmud (*San.* 6.9, 23c) tell about the leading first century BCE Palestinian sage and head of the Sanhedrin, Shimʿon ben Sheṭaḥ, that he had eighty witches hanged in the port city of Ashqelon. Such a report is, of course, evidence of the existence of a belief in witches among both the people and their spiritual leaders.

Occasional references in the Mishnah and Talmud indicate that *kishshuf,* witchcraft, was widespread, especially among women (*Sot.* 9.13, *Avot.* 2.7; B.T., *San.* 67a), despite the fact that it was a capital offense (*San.* 7.4, 7.11; B.T., *San.* 67b), punishable by stoning. Persons accused of witchcraft were frequently brought before the judges, who therefore were required to have a thorough familiarity with the workings of magic (B.T., *San.* 17a). They also had certain criteria by which they were able to differentiate between witchcraft and mere trickery (B.T., *San.* 67b).

Of several sages it is reported that they themselves practiced and taught magic (B.T., *San.* 67b–68a), as did the daughters of at least one of them (B.T., *Git.* 45a). Some women engaged in faith healing (B.T., *Sot.* 22a, cf. Rashi). One of the pious men of the first century BCE, Honi the Circle Maker, practiced rain magic (*Ta'an.* 3.8). The use of incantations and the recitation of magic formulas for curative purposes was widespread (B.T., *Shab.* 67a).

As for amulets (sg., *qamei'a*), in Talmudic times two kinds were in vogue: those written on and those containing roots and leaves. They were dispensed by physicians to cure ailments, and also used by people for protection against the evil eye and demons, and to make women conceive (*Kel.* 23.1, *Shab.* 6.2; B.T., *Shab.* 61a–b, *Pes.* 111b; J. T., *Shab.* 6, 8b top; *Gn. Rab.* 45; *Nm. Rab.* 12; et al.). (Whether the biblical *duda'im* [mandrakes] found by Reuben in the field were ingested by the sterile Rachel or used by her as an amulet is not clear. See *Gn.* 30:14–15, 30:22–23.) An amulet was usually put around the neck of a child soon after its birth (B.T., *Qid.* 73b), which custom has remained alive until modern times in Middle Eastern Jewish communities. Amulets that had proven their efficacy were allowed to be worn outside the home even on the Sabbath, although on that rest day the carrying of all objects was prohibited (*Shab.* 6.2).

Divination (*niḥush*) continued in the Talmudic period as an integral part of popular religion, despite rabbinic prohibition and its punishment by flogging. The influence of Jewish and Babylonian folk religion on the Babylonian amoraim (Talmudic sages of the third to fifth centuries) can be seen in the permission they gave to use *simanim* (signs or omens) in trying to foretell the future. Very popular in Talmudic times was the divinatory use of biblical verses randomly recited by children (B.T., *Ḥag.* 15a–b, *Ḥul.* 95b). There were so few people who refrained from practicing some kind of divination that those who did were considered more meritorious than the ministering angels (B.T., *Ned.* 32a).

MIDDLE AGES AND LATER TIMES. The medieval development of Qabbalah constituted a favorable environment for the further proliferation of the belief in demons. Folk belief and the teachings of Qabbalah mutually reinforced each other. The sexual seduction of humans by demons was considered an imminent danger, resulting in the birth of additional demons. Many illnesses were believed to be the result of spirit possession, and consequently the exorcism of spirits (dybbuks) became an important method of popular medicine. While the exorcists seem to have been men only, the persons considered possessed were mostly women. Childlessness—generally considered the wife's "fault"—gave rise to a wide variety of folk cures, including the ingestion of substances of animal origin prohibited by *halakhah* (traditional Jewish law).

Much of medieval Jewish folk religion expressed itself in rites and ceremonies performed at the three major stages of human life: birth (including circumcision), marriage, and death. On these occasions the demons were believed to be especially aggressive and dangerous, and the protection of the principals as well as the attendants was a major concern that gave rise to numerous folk rites.

Features of folk religion are also present at the celebrations of the official Jewish holy days, despite repeated attempts by rabbinical authorities to suppress them. The Tashlikh rite (the symbolic casting of one's sins into water on Ro'sh ha-Shanah, the Jewish New Year) and the Kapparah (the symbolic transference of one's sins onto a hen or a cock on the eve of Yom Kippur) are two examples of practices that Jewish folk religion introduced into the High Holy Days celebrations over the objection of the rabbis.

Of special interest for the historian of religion is the extent to which Jewish folk religion succeeded in being accepted by the leading Jewish religious authorities, who, by including numerous folk beliefs and customs into their halakhic codes, made them part of official Judaism. The *Shulḥan 'arukh*, the law code that governs Jewish traditional life to this day, contains rulings that show that its author, the Sefardi Yosef Karo (1488–1575), and his chief annotator, the Ashkenazi Mosheh Isserles (1525–1572), believed in the power of the evil eye to harm a person even in the synagogue, in the efficacy of amulets, in the influence of the stars on human life, in omens, in incantations to subdue demons and dangerous animals, in the magic prevention or cure of illness, in consulting the dead and the demons, and so on.

The veneration of saintly men and, more rarely, women, expressed mainly in visits to their tombs with appropriate offerings in the hope of obtaining various benefits, has been an integral part of Jewish folk religion, especially in Islamic countries, for centuries. Occasionally the same Jewish or Muslim saint has been venerated by both Jews and Muslims.

Although several leading medieval rabbinical authorities (including Moses Maimonides, 1135/8–1204) objected to the use of amulets, charms, and magic remedies, their popularity could not be checked, and after the expulsion of the Jews from Spain in 1492 they spread to eastern Europe. Prepared by rabbis, healers, or holy men for a fee, they were believed to save the wearer or user from all types of harm; to cure his (or her) ailments; to protect him from demons; and to provide good luck, health, and many other kinds of benefits. The amulets, widely used especially in the Middle East down to recent times, whether written on paper or made of silver, brass, tin, or iron, are often decorated with magic triangles and squares, the Magen David (Shield of David), or menorahs. The metal amulets typically have the shape of a circle, a square, a rectangle, a shield, a hand (the most frequent shape), and, rarely, a foot. They are inscribed with divine and angelic names, brief quotations from the Bible, and magic combinations of letters or obscure words. Often the amulet states the name of the person for whom it was prepared and the name of his or her mother.

In the seventeenth and eighteenth centuries in central and eastern Europe a magician who prepared such amulets was called *Baʿal Shem*, that is, "Master of the Name," because he was an expert in the use of holy names for magico-religious purposes. The founder of Hasidism, Yisraʾel ben Eliʿezer, known as the Besht (acronym of Baʿal Shem Ṭov), was, in his early years, such a provider of amulets. The popular belief in the efficacy of amulets was so strong that numerous rabbis openly supported their use and wrote treatises in their defense. While practically all the Hasidic *rebeyim* (as the miracle-working saintly leaders were known) were men, at least occasionally women functioned in the same capacity.

Divination continued to be a widespread practice among the Jews down to modern times. More recent methods resorted to include the lighting of candles, the observation of shadows, opening the Bible at random, casting lots, gazing at a polished surface, incantations, and consulting with the dead. The interpretation of omens developed into a veritable folk science to which frequent references are found in medieval and later rabbinic literature. It also led to a literary genre of its own in Hebrew, *sifrei goralot*, "books of lots," which contain instructions and rules for the predictive use of names of animals, birds, the twelve tribes, the twelve signs of the Zodiac, cosmic phenomena, the twenty-two letters of the Hebrew alphabet, and so on. These books, which, as a rule, are of southern European or Middle Eastern origin, are the counterpart in the field of divination to the even richer assortment of books on charms and magic remedies, some of which were composed or reprinted as late as the twentieth century.

MODERN PERIOD. The spread of the Haskalah (Jewish Enlightenment) in the nineteenth century resulted in a decline of both Jewish folk religion and Jewish orthodoxy. By the second half of the twentieth century folk religion remained a significant element only in the culture of a diminishing sector of unsecularized ultraconservative Jews. Those of Middle Eastern extraction transplanted into Israel colorful customs connected with the life cycle and the ritual calendar, as well as features such as the Moroccan Maimuna feast that commemorates the death of Maimonides and the veneration of other saints, similar to the long-established Lag ba-ʿOmer festivities at the tomb of the second-century tanna Shimʿon bar Yoḥai in Meron. In Israeli *kibbutsim* and in some circles in the United States, attempts are being made to endow traditional religious ceremonies (such as the Passover Seder) with contemporary religious, social, and political relevance. In the United States, outside Orthodox circles, traditional Jewish folk religion is largely moribund, but the transformation of the synagogue into a "center" of social, educational, cultural, and charitable activities and the proliferation of men's clubs, sisterhoods, youth groups, and *ḥavurot* (egalitarian religious fellowships) can be interpreted as a new departure in the realm of folk Judaism. Manifestations such as these can be taken as indications that folk religion, which has always been a significant aspect of Jewish religious life, is still alive and can be expected to produce as yet unforeseeable developments.

SEE ALSO Alphabets; Hasidism, overview article; Pilgrimage, article on Contemporary Jewish Pilgrimage; Prophecy, article on Biblical Prophecy; Talmud.

BIBLIOGRAPHY

There is no single book dealing with the whole field of Jewish folk religion, or even with Jewish folk religion in one particular period. There are, however, numerous studies on specific aspects of Jewish folk religion in each of the major historical periods of Judaism.

Biblical Period

Several of the standard histories of biblical Hebrew religion discuss such elements in it as folk belief, folk custom, and magic. See also Reginald C. Thompson's *Semitic Magic: Its Origins and Development* (London, 1908); Alfred Guillaume's *Prophecy and Divination among the Hebrews and Other Semites* (London, 1938); James G. Frazer's *Folk-Lore in the Old Testament*, 3 vols. (London, 1919); and S. H. Hooke's *The Origins of Early Semitic Ritual* (Oxford, 1938).

Talmudic Period

There is no study on Talmudic folk religion in general, but several books deal with Talmudic magic and other aspects of Talmudic folk belief. See Gideon Brecher's *Das Transcendentale, Magie, und magische Heilarten im Talmud* (Vienna, 1850), mainly of historical interest as a pioneering study; Ludwig Blau's *Das altjüdische Zauberwesen* (Strasbourg, 1898), still very valuable; Samuel Daiches's *Babylonian Oil Magic in the Talmud and Later Jewish Literature* (Oxford, 1913); *Sefer ha-razim*, edited by Mordechai Margalioth (Jerusalem, 1969); and my *Man and Temple in Ancient Jewish Myth and Ritual* (1947; 2d ed., New York, 1967).

Middle Ages and Later Times

The subject most thoroughly researched within the general field of medieval and later Jewish folk religion is magic. See in particular *The Sword of Moses: An Ancient Book of Magic*, edited by Moses Gaster (London, 1896), and Gaster's *Studies and Texts in Folklore, Magic, Medieval Romance, Hebrew Apocrypha, and Samaritan Archaeology*, 3 vols. (1925–1928; reprint, New York, 1971); Hermann Gollancz's *Book of the Key of Solomon*, in Hebrew and English (Oxford, 1914); Joshua Trachtenberg's *Jewish Magic and Superstition* (1939; reprint, New York, 1982); H. J. Zimmels's *Magicians, Theologians and Doctors* (London, 1952).

Special Subjects

Among the books dealing with special subjects within the general field of Jewish folk religion the following should be mentioned: Michael L. Rodkinson's *History of Amulets, Charms, and Talismans* (New York, 1893); Theodore Schrire's *Hebrew Amulets* (London, 1966); reprinted as *Hebrew Magic Amulets* (New York, 1982); Angelo S. Rappoport's *The Folklore of the Jews* (London, 1937); my *On Jewish Folklore* (Detroit, 1983); and Michael Molho's *Usos y costumbres de los Sefardíes de Salónica* (Madrid, 1950).

Much material on Jewish folk religion is contained in the journals devoted to Jewish folklore and folk life: *Mitteilungen zur jüdischen Volkskunde* (Berlin, 1898–1929) and *Jahrbuch für jüdische Volkskunde* (Berlin, 1923–1925), both edited by Max Grunwald; *Edoth: A Quarterly for Folklore and Ethnology* (in Hebrew and English), edited by myself and Joseph J. Rivlin (Jerusalem, 1945–1948); and *Yedaʿ-ʿAm*, edited by Yom-Tov Levinsky (Tel Aviv, 1948–).

New Sources

Cohen, Shaye J. D., ed. *The Jewish Family in Antiquity.* Atlanta, 1993.

King, Philip J., and Laurence E. Stager. *Life in Biblical Israel.* Louisville, Ky., 2001.

Lowenstein, Steven M. *Frankfurt on the Hudson: The German-Jewish Community of Washington Heights, 1933-1983, Its Structure and Culture.* Detroit, Mich., 1989.

Lowenstein, Steven M. "The Shifting Boundary between Eastern and Western Jewry." *Journal of Social Studies,* 4 (Fall 1997): 60–79.

Lowenstein, Steven M. *The Jewish Cultural Tapestry: International Jewish Folk Traditions.* New York, 2000.

Malina, Bruce J. *The Social World of Jesus and the Gospels.* New York, 1996.

Niditich, Susan. *Ancient Israelite Tradition.* New York, 1997.

RAPHAEL PATAI (1987)
Revised Bibliography

FOLK RELIGION: FOLK ISLAM

The dichotomy implied by the terminology of "folk" or "little" versus "orthodox" or "high" religious traditions has been challenged in various ways by folklorists, sociologists, and historians of Islam and other world religions. In recent decades folklorists have argued that all religion, at the point of enacted belief, may be considered "vernacular" and "oral." Yet at the same time, both within and across religious traditions and academic disciplines, debates rage on about the viability of terms like "folk" and "orthodox." The manifest vitality of abundant local variations on religious practice, and the debates that ensue among believers about their authenticity or permissibility, continue to fuel concern beyond the academic.

South Asia, more particularly India, provides a poignant example. Imtiaz Ahmad in the 1970s and early 1980s produced a series of volumes documenting and arguing the indigenous "Indianness" of South Asian Islamic belief and practice. His ethnographic approach was criticized by the religious historian Francis Robinson for being unduly synchronic and thus missing an overall, gradual trajectory of "Islamicization" (also noted by anthropologist Clifford Geertz) from more localized or "syncretic" practices and beliefs toward "perfection" in the form of closer adherence to a "high" religion as articulated in the entexted and canonized law, *sharīʿah.* Robinson further argued that the eighteenth-century decline of Muslim states (for example, Mughal in India, Ottoman in southwest Asia and North Africa) itself inspired the major Islamic revival movements active down to the present, which moved the believing community away from local "folk" practice toward greater orthodoxy even in the face of the weakening of Islamic state institutions. Robinson in turn was engaged by Veena Das and Gail Minault, arguing against an overly monolithic model of religious practice. Though this debate took place in the 1980s, it deserves new attention in the face of Hindu religious nationalism, which like Robinson's vision of Islam, develops a concept of religious orthodoxy that would reject arguments like those of Imtiaz Ahmad for the indigenous nature of South Asian or other regional Islam(s). Robinson criticized Ahmad as harboring a political motive for arguing the indigenous nature of South Asian Islam, reflected in its abundant vernacular or "folk" practices, with their rapprochement to Hindu devotional forms. Robinson was concerned that Ahmad's vision of South Asian Islam, arguing for an equilibrium between transnational orthodoxy and local practice, was weak on history. In the ensuing twenty years, however, the emergence of the Hindu right wing in India has made abundantly clear the lethal potential for politicization of essentialist distinctions among religious traditions as well.

More recently, and also with specific reference to South Asian local religious practice, Tony Stewart and Carl Ernst (2003) have mounted a trenchant general criticism of the whole notion of syncretism in religious discourse. They reject the concept of syncretism (a pejorative view of borrowing, mixing, or hybridization across distinct religious traditions) as founded on an untenably essentialist concept of discrete religious traditions in general, for "on examination, every 'pure' tradition turns out to contain mixed elements" (p. 586). The idea of the canonical or orthodox, they argue, entails a historically untenable concept of a pristine, clearly bounded, originary or primordial form to which later enactments strive to conform. Local or folk practice and belief are then implicated in a pejorative concept of syncretism or "mixing" to the extent that the local deviates from this timeless and placeless ideal.

While academic debates continue to swirl around critiques of essentialism and relativism in studies of the "folk," vernacular, or local belief and practice over against the canonical or orthodox, it is fair to say that within believing communities, reform movements operate along parallel lines of debate over the pure and the mixed, the authentic and the "tainted." Insofar as religious thought is based on a mythic vision of an *illud tempus* in which the terms of human existence were established, whether by act of creation or by prophetic revelation, it is hard to avoid some form of originary or essentialist logic. Folklorists simply grant this sense of the ideal to all believers, holding that all who believe find their beliefs to be legitimate and orthodox. This is not to say, however, that beliefs are not malleable through experience or critique. In religious belief and practice, as for the general notion of tradition held by contemporary folklorists, tradition is not fixed but dynamic, consisting of the creative responses of individuals in communities to the preexisting culture-specific materials of their received knowledge base, in dynamic interaction with the emerging conditions of their physical lives. Thus, the same person, over the course of a lifetime, without necessarily experiencing a definitive crisis of faith, may radically change her interpretation of her own spiritual experience: "Mādar Ẓher," whom I met as a woman of twenty-eight in Afghanistan in the mid-1970s, attributed an earlier episode of severe psychological distress in her life to the interference of *jinn* who had seen her and become interested in her. Eighteen years later, she attributed the same period of mental illness (*divanegi* in Persian) to stress and at least in part to the stern constraints of purdah imposed on her by her husband at that period of her life. Nonetheless, while her idea of the etiology of her illness had changed, both at the time of her illness and more than two decades later she considered that the appropriate cure for such illnesses was religious, through the prayerful intervention of an effective local saint (*pir*). Islam, whether orthodox or mystical, recognizes that human understandings of religious truths are partial and emergent, such that intention (*niyat*) or sincerity is the touchstone of true religion and acceptability to God, over and above the state of knowledge (*ʿerfān*) one has attained.

Such an operating principle may in practice, if not in principle, admit of a wide variety of religious views and activities and facilitate a gradualist or accommodationist approach to missionary work, as has been observed in the adjustments to local and preexisting religious beliefs and social practices in the poetry and preaching of Ṣūfī mystics and other lead missionaries on the frontiers of Islam, from South Asia to sub-Saharan Africa (Eaton, 1974; Horvatich, 1994; Lambek, 1990; Robinson, 1984). Yet even in the absence of an active reform movement, diversity of practice may also be the focus for pejorative group identifications, for religious *blason populaire* and scandalous migratory legends. One example is the "murdered saint" legend, ascribed to at least two local shrines in Afghanistan and Pakistan, respectively, alleging that the local population, hearing that a saint who had arrived in their midst would confer great blessings on the community in which he died and was buried, hastened to secure that benefit to themselves by killing him and building him a shrine. Another story, told as a joke to this author in Pakistan, is that of the "Pashtun *sayyed*," in which a Pashtun who has come to town advertising himself as a *sayyed* (a descendant of the Prophet, whose prayers and other healing interventions may be regarded as especially efficacious) is asked to bring a witness to his *sayyed* status. The witness he produces says, "Of course I can attest that he's a *sayyed,* I remember the day he became a *sayyed.*" Thus, the ethnic slur takes the form of casting aspersions on the legitimacy of a Pashtun's religious status claim. A third, large class of such marginalizing discourses is anticlerical humor and folktales, in which clergy are alleged to be more avaricious, lustful, or stupid than the general run of humanity. The ambidexterous genre of Mullā Naṣr ud-Din jokes (Hodja Nasruddin in Turkish), in which the famous clergyman is a scapegrace, a greedy fool when interacting with those less powerful than himself, and a foolish-wise underdog and trickster when interacting with those more powerful, offers additional rich examples of popular ambivalence toward clerical and other authorities. However tenuously these humorous forms may seem to connect with serious matters of belief and religious practice, they articulate fault lines in both the concept of the ideal community of the *ummah* (the total community of believing Muslims) and the trustworthiness of others' religious views and practices.

Folk poetry may articulate differential or contested religious identity in more specifically theological terms. Hassan Poladi (1989, p. 134) quotes a folk rhyme in Dari (Afghan Persian) that is both a statement of orthodox Sunnī faith and directed against the Shīʿah Hazara, who are thought to deny the legitimacy of the first three caliphs who led the community after the Prophet's death and to see only Alī, the Prophet's cousin and son-in-law, as his legitimate successor:

> Saram khāk-e rāh-e Chahār Sarwar,
> ʿOmar, Abubakr, ʿOṣmān wa Ḥaidar,
> Abubakr Yār-e Ghār, ʿOmar Mir-e Durrah-dar
> ʿOṣmān Shāh-sawar ast, ʿAli Fatḥ-e lashkar ast.
> Har ki az in Chahār Yār-e Rāh khilāfa nadānad
> Kamtarin-e khers wa khuk wa Yahudān-e Khaybar ast.
>
> My head be in the dust of the path of the four Knights [the first four caliphs of Islam]
> ʿOmar, Abu Bakr, ʿOṣmān and Ḥaidar
> Abubakr, Friend of the Cave, the Prince who possesses the pearl,
> Oṣmān is the Royal Knight, ʿAli is the Victorious Warrior
> Whosoever denies the caliphate of the Four Friends [of the Way],
> He is less than a bear, a pig, or the Jews of Khaybar [who rejected the Prophet's revelation].

The Jews of Khaybar are cited as the archetypal recalcitrant skeptics but are nonetheless regarded by Muslims as "People of the Book," who received a revelation of their own in the legitimate line of prophecy. In a situation of Sunnī-Shīʿī tension in upland Afghanistan, where Jews were few and far between, the Shīʿah were portrayed as worse than the Jews for having rejected the worldly successors of the Prophet, but at another time, in urban Herāt, where both Sunnīs and Shīʿahs coexisted with an ancient Jewish community until the post-1948 migration of that population to Israel, Afghan Sunnīs and Shīʿahs may agree to portray Jews as trying to sow dissension between otherwise (notionally) solidary Sunnī and Shī'ī Muslims (Mills, 1990).

Yet in other instances, shared veneration of a religious personage may dramatically cut across sectarian lines, as in the case of the Bengali figure of Satya Pir, whose Muslim devotees regard him as a somewhat cantankerous saint while his Hindu devotees consider him a god. The competing origin stories for Satya Pir are copresent and available for comparison by his devotees, as is also the case for Skanda, the deity of the great Kataragama Buddhist shrine in Sri Lanka, who is revered as the Prophet Khizr by Muslims who can visit the mosque located on the site.

Parallel practices may be less obvious to practitioners, as is the case with votive activities distributed across Muslim and Hindu southwest and south Asia. The votive offering called *nāẓir* in Arabo-Persian has a complex history in Shīʿī Iran, apparently connected also with Zoroastrian (pre-Islamic Iranian) practice (Jamzadeh and Mills, 1984). In local women's practice, the votive activity may involve the ritual performance of various kinds of oral narrative from legends of Shīʿī saints (called *rowzeh*) to international folktale variants (Betteridge, 1980; Mills, 1982) and be seen as marginal by clergy and by orthodox-aspiring women alike. Not all Muslim *nāẓir* rituals entail narrative recitations; from the data at hand this seems more common among Shīʿī than Sunnī *nāẓir* offerants. Indian Hindus have parallel practices in votive rituals called *vrat katha* ("vow stories"), conducted by women as domestic rites or more formally by male Brāhmaṇ priests, which indeed require the ritual performance of origin stories articulating the rite's relationship to the deity addressed (Wadley, 2003). While Muslims and Hindus share certain shrines in South Asia (as do, or did, Muslims and Jews in North Africa; see Ben-Ami, 1983), it is not clear that either the practitioners or the scholars have dwelt on the specific parallels in narrative-based *nāẓir* and *vrat katha*. Within Islam, the veneration of saints and shrine pilgrimage, a pervasively popular practice that is not limited to women, though often attributed primarily to them as religiously marginal, comes in for criticism from some of the orthodox, specifically as a form of *shirk* (worshiping personages other than God, which violates a basic tenet of the faith), whereas in Hinduism, *vrat katha* is a staple of worship.

Both *nāẓir* (with or without narrative) and *vrat katha* also involve a food offering or charity food distribution. In foodways in particular, one can see regional or local practices most closely tied to local ecology. In a wide belt from Anatolia across Central Asia to northern Pakistan, the staple grain is wheat, and wheat products are featured as the blessed elements in ritual meals. In particular, sprouted wheat porridges or fudgelike *halva*s figure in Spring New Year rituals predating Islam on the Iranian plateau but now included as part of Muslim festival cycles from Kurdish Turkey across Iran to Central Asia and the Karakorum. For several of these dishes, wheat must first be ritually sprouted, then dried and ground into flour and cooked to make a naturally sweet (because malted) ritual food called *samanu* or *samanak* in Persian (and by other names, for example, *shoshp* in the Khowar language). In many *nāẓir* rituals outside the context of the Spring New Year, various kinds of wheat bread are the sanctified food, sanctified before it is cooked because the saint is believed to visit and touch wheat flour laid out in advance for the rite if the offerant's petition is acceptable. Among Thai and Javanese Muslims, for whom folk ritual feasts are prominent as part of death memorial ceremonies, and as such also to some extent contested by the orthodoxy, the central ritual food, not surprisingly, is rice (Burr, 1983; Woodward, 1988).

An overview of the vast topic of folk Islam or Muslim vernacular religion can at best offer snapshot views both of actual devotional activities and of articulations of perceived differences in practice and belief within the community, that is, of Islamic folk religion and of Muslim folklore, through which Muslims reflect on being Muslims by alleging practices and beliefs of others that may or may not actually occur. Such differences only partly fall along sectarian lines. Gender and ethnicity also figure in Muslims' perceptions of insider and outsider, orthodox and heterodox, and differences in religious practice within the confessional community that defy the doctrinal ideal of equality before God for all pious believers. Vernacular practice provides scope for personal devotionalism, some of it of a highly local nature, for members of the community who may be otherwise marginalized (for example, women, who are not expected or encouraged to be regular mosque attendees in some Muslim communities). Perceptions of solidarity, of difference, or even of apostasy may be cast in absolute and ideal terms, but they also can be observed to vary dramatically at different times and places and to reflect and in part constitute political relationships or rifts that are in turn susceptible to community critique. As with other forms of folklore, vigorously held "folk" beliefs and practices may not be perceived as local or idiosyncratic by their adherents, or, on the contrary, they may indeed be espoused as part of local identity work, as in the case of the many instantly recognizable, locally distinctive, elaborated versions of modest dress for both men and women. Further, this identity work, a staple of folk process, may be viewed as benign, or as antireligious if it divides the community in the face of some perceived external threat. Not only practices but also the interpretations put upon them are emergent in terms of consciousness as ties and schisms among Muslims or between Muslims and non-Muslims wax and wane. Academically speaking, the jury remains out as to the overall and longer-term trajectory of universal Islamization (the goal of Islamic reform movements) versus the elaboration of local practices. From the viewpoint of non-Muslim venues, the globalizing trends of a new orthodoxy appear more influential at present, but on closer inspection, local vernacular (also known as "folk") practices (such as conventions and styles of women's modest dress) appear to thrive, to be invented, reinvented, and often enough, contested, even in diaspora populations.

See Also Domestic Observances, article on Muslim Practices; Islamic Religious Year; Oral Tradition; Rites of Passage, article on Muslim Rites.

Bibliography

Ben-Ami, Issachar. "Relations Between Jews and Muslims in the Veneration of Folk-Saints in Morocco." *International Folklore Review* 3 (1983): 93–105.

Betteridge, Anne. "The Controversial Vows of Iranian Women." In *Unspoken Worlds: Women's Religious Lives in Non-Western Cultures,* edited by N. A. Falk and R. M. Gross, pp. 141–153. New York, 1980.

Burr, Angela. "The Relationship Between Muslim Peasant Religion and Urban Religion in Songkhla." *Asian Folklore Studies* 43 (1983): 71–83.

Das, Veena. "For a Folk-Theology and Theological Anthropology of Islam." *Contributions to Indian Sociology* (n.s.) 18, no. 2 (1984): 293–299.

Eaton, Richard M. "Ṣūfī Folk Literature and the Expansion of Indian Islam." *History of Religions* 14, no. 2 (1974): 117–127.

Horvatich, Patricia. "Ways of Knowing Islam." *American Ethnologist* 21, no. 4 (1994): 811–826.

Jamzadeh, Laal, and Margaret A. Mills. "Iranian *sofreh*: From Collective to Female Ritual." In *Gender and Religion: On the Complexity of Symbols,* edited C. W. Bynum, S. Harrell, and P. Richman, pp. 23–65. Boston, 1984.

Lambek, Michael. "Certain Knowledge, Contestible Authority: Power and Practice on the Islamic Periphery." *American Ethnologist* 17, no. 1 (1990): 23–40.

Mills, Margaret A. "A Cinderella Variant in the Context of a Muslim Women's Ritual." In *Cinderella: A Folklore Casebook,* edited by Alan Dundes, pp. 180–192. New York, 1982.

Mills, Margaret A. "'Fill a pipe for the Akhond!' The Akhond and the Rabbi of Herāt." In *Rhetorics and Politics in Afghan Traditional Storytelling,* pp. 255–262. Philadelphia, 1991.

Minault, Gail. "Some Reflections on Islamic Revivalism vs. Assimilation Among Muslims in India." *Contributions to Indian Sociology,* n.s. 18, no. 2 (1984): 301–305.

Poladi, Hassan. *The Hazaras.* Stockton, Calif., 1989.

Robinson, Francis. "Islam and Muslim Society in South Asia." *Contributions to Indian Sociology* (n.s.) 17, no. 2 (1983): 185–203.

Robinson, Francis. "Islam and Muslim Society in South Asia: A Reply to Das and Minault." *Contributions to Indian Sociology* (n.s.) 20, no. 1 (1984): 97–104.

Stewart, Tony K. "Satya Pir, Muslim Holy Man and Hindu God." In *The Religions of South Asia in Practice,* edited by Donald S. Lopez Jr., pp. 578–597. Princeton, N.J., 1994.

Stewart, Tony K., and Carl W. Ernst. "Syncretism." In *South Asian Folklore: An Encyclopedia,* edited by Margaret A. Mills, Peter J. Claus, and Sarah Diamond, pp. 586–588. New York, 2003.

Toelken, Barre. "Introduction." *The Dynamics of Folklore.* Boston, 1979.

Wadley, Susan S. "Vrat katha." In *South Asian Folklore: An Encyclopedia,* edited by Margaret A. Mills, Peter J. Claus, and Sarah Diamond, p. 631. New York, 2003.

Woodward, Mark R. "The *Slmetan*: Textual Knowledge and Ritual Performance in Central Javanese Islam." *History of Religions* 28, no. 1 (1988): 54–89.

MARGARET A. MILLS (2005)

FOMHOIRE

FOMHOIRE. The Fomhoire are a hostile supernatural race who warred for control of Ireland against both gods and men. Descriptions of the Fomhoire vary widely in different texts and apparently reflect several distinct traditions. The Fomhoire are sometimes depicted as misshapen or half-animal in form, disproportionately female in numbers, or having only one leg, one arm, and one eye. In other sources, the Fomhoire resemble and intermarry with the gods, the Tuatha Dé Danann (The Tribes or Peoples of the Goddess Danu). Later Irish and Scottish Gaelic folklore know the *fomhóir* (Scottish Gaelic, *famhair*) as raiders from the sea or marauding giants, and throughout Irish literature the Fomhoire manifest both sea connections and supernatural origins. For example, "the cattle of Tethra"—an early poetic kenning about the Fomhorian king Tethra—refers to the waves, and in an eighth-century tale the people of Tethra dwell in a timeless realm of peace and abundance across the sea. The name Fomhoire is of uncertain derivation, meaning perhaps "undersea people" or "sinister supernatural beings." Suggested etymologies include taking the word as comprising *fo* (under) and an element meaning *sea.* Alternatively, the second element may be related to the *mare* of the English word *nightmare.*

ORIGINS OF THE FOMHOIRE. References to the Fomhoire appear in *Leabhar Gabhála Éireann* (The book of the taking of Ireland), a pseudohistorical compendium of medieval prose and poetry linking pre-Christian Ireland to the chronology of the Hebrew Bible and presenting gods and mythical ancestors of the early Irish as mortals descended from Noah. In this system, the Fomhoire are identified as descendants of Cain or of Noah's unfilial son Ham. Other sources include mythic and epic tales, glossaries, and place-name lore. In *Leabhar Gabhála* the Fomhoire (sometimes in the form of misshapen demons) repeatedly attack Ireland's colonists. After defeating two groups of settlers, they reduce a third, the people of Nemhedh, to one boatload of refugees, who survive to become ancestors of two later groups, the Fir Bholg and the Tuatha Dé Danann.

The Fir Bholg rule Ireland successfully without Fomhorian interference but are eventually dispossessed by the Tuatha Dé Danann. According to *Cath Maige Tuired: The Second Battle of Mag Tuired,* which includes language as early as the ninth century, once established in Ireland, the Tuatha Dé contract a marriage alliance with the Fomhoire and offer kingship to the half-Fomhorian Bres, son of Elatha. However, Bres's reign proves disastrous: He is greedy, self-centered, and oppressive, enforcing demands for tribute from his Fomhorian relatives. When the Tuatha Dé restrain his behavior, he flees to his powerful Fomhorian kin to gather an army. Demands for tribute by Fomhorian kings outside of Ireland (including Tethra, Elatha, and Indech, son of Dé Domnann, who ruled islands off Ireland and Scotland) are reminiscent of Viking control of these peripheral areas and may reflect legends surrounding Viking claims to overlordship.

Lugh, who ultimately leads the Tuatha Dé to victory in the Second Battle of Magh Tuiredh, is the half-Fomhorian product of the marriage alliance between the two peoples. The unsuccessful king Bres (Fomhorian on his father's side) is the product of an acknowledged but less formal union.

The theme of Fomhorian kinship amidst hostilities recurs in epic, recalling widespread traditions in other cultures of ambivalent relations between distinct but intermarrying groups. Lugh's son, the epic hero Cú Chulainn, can only marry the daughter of Forgoll Monach (a nephew of the Fomhorian Tethra) by abducting her against her family's armed opposition.

MYTHICAL STRUGGLES. Theomachy—the mythic struggle between gods and their supernatural opponents—is another theme shaping the relationship between the Fomhoire and the Tuatha Dé Danann. In comparative Indo-European terms, as enemies of the gods, the Fomhoire resemble the Asuras (in relation to the Indic Devas)—often monstrous in form but nonetheless blood relations. The ultimate victory of the Tuatha Dé Danann follows Lugh's single combat with his maternal grandfather, the Fomhorian Balar, who has a baleful eye of monstrous size and power. The contest is famous in the popular folklore of Mayo and Donegal.

Another mythic theme that may influence the role of the Fomhoire in the Second Battle of Magh Tuiredh—especially the conflict between Bres and his Tuatha Dé kin—is the struggle between divine representatives of functional aspects of social order. These functions are identified as: (1) the sacred and sovereign, associated with kingship, priesthood, and magical power; (2) physical, especially martial, force; and (3) fertility and abundance. Each of the three is linked to a social class or stratum (i.e., the priestly class, including the king; the aristocratic warrior class, from which kings may be drawn; and the class of ordinary free landowners or farmers) represented within both human and divine societies. The mythic struggle between representatives of the first two functions and those of the third leads to a resolution in which the powers of all three functions are available to society as a whole, although the nature of that resolution varies. For example, Bres's powers evoke fertility and abundance, his name ("The Beautiful") becomes a byword for beauty, and he is the husband of the Tuatha Dé goddess Brígh (patroness of domestic animals). When suggesting possible ransoms for his life to Lugh after the Tuatha Dé Danann victory, Bres includes the well-being and growth of crops and herds. Lugh's acceptance of Bres's final offer integrates the power of fertility, bringing the Tuatha Dé perpetual success in plowing, sowing, and reaping.

SEE ALSO Celtic Religion, overview article.

BIBLIOGRAPHY

Gray, Elizabeth A. *Cath Maige Tuired: The Second Battle of Mag Tuired.* Irish Texts Society, Vol. 52. Leinster, Ireland, 1982. Provides text and translation, contains extensive indices of references to the Tuatha Dé Danann and Fomhoire in early and later medieval Irish literature.

Mac Cana, Proinsias. *Celtic Mythology.* New York, 1970; reprint, 1973. Succinct, authoritative and comprehensive survey, extensively illustrated with photographs of significant items of Celtic material culture, includes chapters on the Tuatha Dé Danann and on the Irish heroic tradition.

Mac Neill, Máire. *The Festival of Lughnasa.* 2 vols. 2d ed. Dublin, 1982. Provides an extensive discussion of literary sources and folk customs related to Lugh and Balar.

Rees, Alwyn, and Brinley Rees. *Celtic Heritage: Ancient Tradition in Ireland and Wales.* London, 1961. Far reaching and ahead of its time, *Celtic Heritage* explores the range of Celtic mythic tradition in the Indo-European context, including reference to the work of Georges Dumézil, with exhaustive notes that provide access to both specialist studies and more general works.

ELIZABETH A. GRAY (2005)

FON AND EWE RELIGION. The Ewe and Fon, related linguistically and culturally, live along the coast and in the hinterland of Benin (formerly Dahomey), Togo, and eastern Ghana in West Africa. They number some three million; depend on fishing, intensive farming, and crafts (especially weaving); and live mostly in towns and large villages.

Europeans in contact with the Fon of Dahomey late in the seventeenth century left an exotic and exaggerated picture of kings, wealth, women soldiers ("Amazons"), brutal human sacrifice, and slave trading; such a picture has fallen into disrepute. Today the seat of the royal family is still centered in the towns of Abomey and Kana, which differ somewhat in both social organization and religion from the hinterland. The people today are organized into dispersed patrilineal clans in each of which the oldest living man is said to be "between the two worlds" of the living and the dead. There was traditionally a complex hierarchical organization from the compound to village chief to king. The kingdom has now lost its former political prerogatives but still retains many traditional ceremonies required by worship of the royal ancestors.

The Ewe of Togo and Ghana, historically representing the outposts of Fon civilization, share a sense of identity and history of migration (ultimately from Oyo in Nigeria) that is commemorated annually. The northern inland Ewe lack centralized political authority and have localized clans, while the coastal groups (known as Anlo Ewe) have a tradition of weak kingship, dispersed clans, and ancestral shrines that are of central importance in the religious life of the community. In each Ewe lineage there is a carved wooden stool, which is the locus of the cult of the lineage diety. During rituals this stool is the place to which ancestral spirits may temporarily be summoned.

FON. The ancestral cult, believed to be necessary for the perpetuation of the clan, is the focal point of Fon social organization and of much religious activity. Funeral ceremonies for dead adults are concluded three years after their death so that their souls are not lost to the clan. Every decade or so the ancestors are "established," that is, they are deified as *tovodu* (family gods) by a rite in which a local group head must name all the dead group members from the most recently dead back to the earliest. At this rite an ancestral shrine (*dex-*

oxo) is built. There, the *tovodu* are annually "fed" and honored with dancing and praise songs. The individual who is seen as the human founder of a clan is also a deified ancestor; because of this status, the founder is worshiped by a cult of priests and initiates who do not necessarily belong to that particular clan. Royal clan members, however, may worship only their own ancestral deities and cannot be cult-initiates of "public" pantheons of gods; ancestral worship is their only form of religious affiliation.

More powerful than the *tovodu* are the spirits of those who lived so long ago that their names are no longer known by their descendants: these ancestors, personified by Dambada Hwedo, are important because a "forgotten" ancestor is angry and dangerous. Also in the *tovodu* category are the spirits of twins, of children born after twins, and of malformed and aborted children. These last spirits are considered very powerful as they guard the rivers over which the spirits of the dead must pass to reach the other world. Furthermore, the world of the dead reflects that of the living, with local rank there being established by priority of birth in the land of the living.

The Fon have a number of variant cosmologies, and some disagreement exists concerning the identities of the various deities. Some say that the world was created by one god, Nana Buluku, both male and female, who gave birth to twins named Mawu and Lisa; the first, female, was given command of the night, and the second, male, was associated with the day. Opinion varies as to the identifying characteristics and even the relationship between the twins, whose names are often merged together in everyday speech as though they were a single deity, Mawu-Lisa. In addition to being siblings, Mawu and Lisa are also spouses. Other public gods who represent the forces of nature that affect all humans alike include Sagbata, the earth deity who watches over the fields and waters of the earth and punishes offenders with smallpox, and Sogbo, or Xevioso, the thunder and sea god who sends fertilizing rains but also punishes with his "ax," the thunderbolt. Under each of these is a pantheon of named deities (*vodu*) ranked according to their birth order, each with differing tasks. Worship of each pantheon of these gods is in the hands of an associated priesthood. None of these three pantheons of deities has universal worship.

No single god is all-powerful, not even Mawu who is the parent of the others and controls life and death. The "writing" of Mawu is called Fa, the destiny of the universe. A highly specialized system of divination (derived from the Yoruba), administered by officials known as *bokono,* permits humans to know what destiny has been decreed for them. Only the divine trickster Legba, who is the youngest son of Mawu, can change a person's destiny. His worship is universal (unlike that of the other major divinities) and individual, with neither priests nor cult houses. Other forms of divination are practiced, including mirror-gazing and the study of entrails. Finally, most widespread of all forms of divination are magical charms (*gbo*) of many and various kinds. These are said to be given to humans by Legba and Sagbata, and especially by the *aziza,* small hairy creatures who live in anthills and silk-cotton trees (*Eriondendron anfractuosum*).

Ewe. The Ewe share many aspects of culture, religion, and art with the Fon and indeed occasionally travel to Benin to obtain shrines and spiritual aid. They share many gods, including Mawu, the remote creator god associated with the sky, and Torgbi-nyigbla, the head of the nature gods (*tro*) associated with war and thunder (and thus with Xevioso). Similar, too, are the practice of Afa divination and the Legba cult, including both *dulegba* and *alegba* (town and individual protective deities). There is, however, ambiguous usage among the Ewe of such key terms as *vodu, dulegba, tro,* and *dzo* (amulets), which are often confused. Most of these deities come from outside Eweland and each is thought of as a discrete entity; this inconsistent usage probably reflects differences in the history of migration and introduction of the cults.

Religious Change. Vast numbers of slaves were taken from the Fon-Ewe coast to the New World and they took many aspects of their religion with them. Syncretized with Catholicism in Haiti, Brazil, Cuba, and Jamaica, Fon and Ewe religions contributed important influences to the formation of many cults in the New World, including Voodoo (*vodoun*) and the cult of Shango, among others.

Christian missionaries have worked among the Fon and Ewe since the mid-nineteenth century. Today the vast majority of people declare themselves to be Christian, although most Ewe are involved in both Christian and traditional religious practices. In the north, reportedly, many rites of passage are now abandoned; traditional funerals, especially in the south, however, are still very important.

See Also Mawu-Lisa.

Bibliography

The standard work on Fon religion is Melville J. Herskovits's *Dahomey: An Ancient West African Kingdom,* 2 vols. (New York, 1938); on the Ewe there are several early accounts, mostly very patchy and superficial, summarized by Madeline Manoukian in *The Ewe-Speaking People of Togoland and the Gold Coast* (London, 1952). More recent works include D. K. Fiawoo's "The Influence of Contemporary Social Changes on the Magico-Religious Concepts and Organization of the Southern Ewe-Speaking Peoples of Ghana" (Ph. D. diss., University of Edinburgh, 1958) and my "Mystical Protection among the Anlo Ewe," *African Arts* 15 (August 1982): 60–66, 90.

New Sources

Adler, Alfred. *Le Pouvoir et l'interdit: Royauté et religion en Afrique Noire: Essais d'Ethnologie Comparative.* Paris, 2000.

Meyer, Birgit. *Translating the Devil: Religion and Modernity Among the Ewe in Ghana.* Edinburgh,1999.

Riviere, Claude. *Anthropologie religieuse des Eve du Togo.* Paris, 1981.

Rosenthal, Judy. *Possession, Ecstasy and Law in Ewe Voodoo.* Charlottesville, Va., 1998.

Surgy, Albert de. *Le Système Religieux des Evhe.* Paris, 1988.

MICHELLE GILBERT (1987)
Revised Bibliography

FOOD. Historians of religion and cultural anthropologists face an extraordinarily difficult task when they attempt to analyze food customs on a worldwide basis. Dietary laws, food taboos, and the religious and social environments that have molded them are as varied as humanity itself.

Although there are no universal food customs or food taboos, such things are part of daily life in every society. Societies of every sort have restricted what their members may eat, specified the circumstances in which certain types of nourishment may be taken, and made use of food in religious ritual. Rules and practices regarding food constitute languages that express the values a culture teaches regarding nature, God, the sources of social authority, and the purposes or goals of life. In different religious systems, the same foods—milk, oil, blood, wheat, or rice, for example—may cleanse or defile, signify death or rebirth, give nourishment to gods or convey the power of gods to worshipers, depending on the contexts in which these foods are used.

FOOD TABOOS. Because food is a universal human need, the act of making some foods taboo is particularly revelatory of the values that distinguish one culture from another.

Judaism. No religion has such a complex set of food taboos as Judaism. Jewish dietary law begins with the Torah (also known as the Pentateuch, including the biblical books of *Genesis, Exodus, Leviticus, Numbers,* and *Deuteronomy*), which according to Orthodox Jews was given to Moses on Sinai; modern scholars date the final version of the Torah to the Babylonian exile, after 486 BCE. Since Roman times, rabbis have greatly expanded the food taboos of the Jews through commentary designed to show how the laws of the Torah may be kept.

Oldest among Jewish food taboos is the prohibition on eating blood, which forms part of the covenant between God and Noah in *Genesis* 9. From this prohibition grew the practice of kosher butchering, which emphasizes killing the animal with a quick cut of the neck and draining its blood. Jews also salt and boil meat to remove blood, broil organ meats in which the blood collects, and cook meat very thoroughly to eliminate blood. The taboo on blood and the laws of butchering mean that no animal killed by hunting can be eaten by an observant Jew.

Elaborating on a law repeated three times in the Torah, "Thou shalt not boil a kid in its mother's milk" (*Exod.* 23:19, 34:26; *Deut.* 14:21), the rabbis developed rules to prevent contact of meat and milk. Observant Jews not only abstain from cheeseburgers and avoid milk for some time after eating meat but also maintain two sets of dishes, pots, and utensils for meat and dairy meals. Restaurants observing *kashrut* (kosher) law limit themselves to serving either meat or dairy meals. Fish and vegetable oil fall into an intermediate class, known as pareve, that can be consumed with either milk or meat.

The Jewish taboo on pork has become famous because the pig is so popular as a source of protein in Europe and Asia, but Jews also abstain from a long list of animals found in *Leviticus* 11 and further defined by the rabbis. Only animals that have hooves (not claws) but also part the hoof (like cows and sheep, unlike horses) and chew the cud (ruminants, capable of eating grass) can be eaten. These restrictions eliminate such common food animals as rabbits, dogs, bears, horses, and camels as well as pigs, which divide the hoof but do not chew the cud. Predatory birds and swarming insects are also forbidden. Among sea creatures, only fish with fins and scales can be eaten; clams, lobsters, eels, squid, scallops, shark, sturgeon (with their caviar), porpoise, and whale are all forbidden, and swordfish are an object of dispute, since they are scaled only as juveniles.

During the eight days of Passover, the spring holiday commemorating the deliverance of ancient Israel from slavery in Egypt, Jews observe a taboo on leaven, which is ordinarily ubiquitous in bread and other products containing wheat. The observance of Passover can lead to a Jewish family owning a third and fourth set of dishes and pots for meat and dairy during Passover, or even a third kitchen, in order to avoid leaven. Not all prepared foods that are certified by rabbinical boards as kosher are also kosher for Passover, because some kosher foods may have been prepared with or in the presence of leaven. Even wine, which might have been thought to be exempt from laws regarding blood, milk, meat, forbidden animals, and leaven, must be certified as kosher or kosher for Passover depending on rabbinical supervision of the conditions of manufacture.

It should be noted that today, only about 10 percent of Jews keep the kosher laws strictly. Among Conservative, Reform, and Reconstructionist Jews, and among the large numbers unaffiliated with a synagogue, there was a strong movement away from keeping kosher during the nineteenth and twentieth centuries. Recently, a return to modified practice, sometimes called "kosher style," has gained ground among liberal Jews. Jewish food taboos have undoubtedly had one effect announced in the Torah: they have fostered solidarity among Jews by separating Jews from others, making "a distinction between the clean and the unclean" (*Lev.* 11:47) so that Israel may be "holy" (related to the word for "separate") as its God is holy.

Hinduism, Jainism, and Buddhism. Although the earliest Sanskrit scriptures indicate that the Aryan ancestors of modern Indians ate beef and sacrificed horses, Hinduism quickly (by about 1000 BCE) developed a taboo on meat for the three upper castes (the Brahmin or priestly, Kshatriya or warrior, and Vaisya or merchant). The cow became particularly sacred, so that only the outcaste or untouchable could work with leather or eat beef, but chicken and fish were also avoided by those who wished to maintain purity. Another powerful taboo involves saliva; a cook must not taste food during preparation because of the danger that saliva will come in contact with the food. Caste differences entailed general taboos on eating food prepared by someone of a lower caste, so that a demand arose for Brahmins willing to serve as cooks. Unlike in Judaism, where food taboos created solidarity among adherents of the religion, in Hinduism these taboos have emphasized difference. The purpose of abstaining from meat and avoiding impurity for Hindus is to avoid collecting *karma,* the attachment to the world that causes reincarnation after death. The same motive causes many Hindus to abstain from alcohol, although there is no absolute rule in the tradition against it, and ancient texts describe the ritual use of an intoxicating substance called soma, the identity of which is uncertain. Some traditions depict the Hindu god Śiva drinking a mixture of yogurt and *cannabis indica,* an Asian variety of marijuana.

During the sixth century BCE, the movements of Jainism and Buddhism gained adherents in India among those who sought freedom from castes and rituals and a more direct means of escape from reincarnation. Following their teacher Mahāvīra, Jains abstain both from meat and from plants that must be killed to be consumed. Their ideal diet consists of fruit that ripens on the tree and grains that dry of themselves; they avoid root vegetables that must be destroyed in the harvest.

Mahāvīra arose from the warrior caste to reject Brahmin rules, and so did Siddhārtha Gautama, who became known as the Buddha (the one who awoke). Not as strict as the Jains, Buddhists sought a middle way between indulgence and asceticism. The Buddha advised the monks whom he sent to spread his teaching not to allow anyone to kill an animal especially for them, but to eat if the animal had already been killed. In Buddhism the *karma* that binds humans to the wheel of rebirth has nothing to do with divine will, material pollution, or with the influence of matter on spirit, but depends entirely on attitude and can be dispelled by awareness. Buddhists have commonly counted the profession of a butcher as a forbidden means of livelihood, like that of gambler or prostitute, because a butcher causes suffering to sentient beings; yet Buddhism has adapted to many cultures in which meat eating is allowed. Some of the most traditional Buddhists, such as the Theravādan monks of Thailand, who go into the street to beg each day at dawn and eat nothing at all after noon, are not vegetarian. The Chan monks of China have normally followed a vegetarian diet themselves but only recently have begun to preach the virtues of vegetarianism to the laity. Tibet, where Buddhism has dominated for more than a thousand years, has never become vegetarian, although some of its religious leaders have. In Japan, the traditional diet of rice and seafood remained despite Buddhism, although the influence of Buddhist ideals of compassion helped to keep meat eating from gaining much favor until modern times. Although the Buddha forbade intoxication, Buddhists have disagreed as to whether this meant abstinence from all alcohol; with the exception of the Theravādan monks of South Asia (Sri Lanka, Burma [Myanmar], Thailand, Vietnam), most Buddhist cultures have not prohibited alcoholic drinks.

Christianity. The New Testament shows that early followers of Jesus struggled with questions of how far to continue Jewish food taboos and whether to compromise with Roman rituals of offering food to their ancestors and their gods. Although *Mark* 7:19 says that Jesus "declared all foods clean," it seems evident from the story of Peter and the Roman centurion Cornelius in *Acts* 10 that the disciples of Jesus had not begun to eat nonkosher food or to share meals with non-Jews even after taking up their mission of preaching the gospel. An argument between Peter and Paul mentioned in Paul's letter to the Galatians shows that the question of food taboos seemed very urgent two decades after the crucifixion. *Acts* 15 recalls a letter sent by agreement of the apostles to all non-Jewish Christians, telling them to abstain from blood, from anything strangled rather than butchered quickly, and from food consecrated to Roman ancestors or gods. In the *Book of Revelation,* Christians who have decided to eat at the same table where Roman food offerings were made are consigned to the pit of sulfur created for Satan and his angels. After the Roman Empire became Christian in the fourth century CE, this issue disappeared—until recently, that is, when it has demanded a decision by Christians who have friends or relatives who practice Chinese, Wiccan, Yoruba, or other traditions involving the offering of food to spirits. Except for the Coptic Christians of Egypt, who continue to follow some Jewish laws, and the mild restrictions on meat observed by Roman Catholics and Orthodox Christians during Lent and Advent, most Christians now observe no food taboos, and Christianity remains remarkable for its lack of such rules. In the nineteenth century, Adventists in the United States rediscovered the prohibition of *Acts* 15 on blood and went beyond it to vegetarianism; many Christians, especially Protestant evangelicals, Mormons, and Christian Scientists, adopted a taboo on alcohol; but most Roman Catholic, Eastern Orthodox, and Protestant Christians remained free, in theory, to eat and to drink anything.

Islam. The Qurʾān, the book of revelations to Prophet Muḥammad, explicitly forbids eating animals that have died of themselves, blood, pork, and food over which the name of a god other than Allah has been invoked (*sūrah* 2:173). Islamic slaughtering rules resemble those of Judaism with regard to cutting the neck and drawing the blood, but many Muslims also refuse any meat not killed by a Muslim, since only then can they be assured that an invocation of Allāh has accompanied the slaughter. Though abstinence from alcohol does not appear in the Qurʾān, the traditions (or *ḥadīth*) connecting such abstinence to the prophet Muḥammad are so strong that most Muslims believe that their religion forbids all alcohol, even if (as in Muslim countries like Morocco or Turkey) there are public places in which Muslims drink. Many Muslims avoid mozzarella cheese because of the ren-net, sometimes derived from the stomachs of pigs, involved in its manufacture.

Chinese traditions. It is part of the genius of China to make use of everything edible, if not as food then as medicine. However, Daoist wisdom does teach the avoidance of some combinations of foods because Daoist cosmology has led people to think that the combinations would be poisonous. Such combinations include garlic and honey, crab and persimmon, dog meat and green beans, and mackerel and plums.

Indigenous (or primal) traditions. Religions that remain limited to particular ethnic groups and places do not tend to develop general food taboos, such as the Jewish ban on pork or the Hindu reverence for the cow, which apply in all times and all places. Food taboos in these religions focus on specific times during which certain foods may not be eaten or specific people who may not eat certain foods. Even cannibalism, the strongest candidate for a universal food taboo, may be allowed or even encouraged or required at certain times; among the Hua of New Guinea, funerals involve children eating the parent of the same sex to recycle the limited supply of life force, or *nu.* Before death, Hua adults transmit *nu* to children by rubbing them with spit or other bodily secretions.

FOOD IN SYMBOL, MYTH, AND RITUAL. In some religious traditions, a particular food may stand for the whole identity of the group. The Hopi of southwestern North America say that their first act upon emerging into this world was to choose the short blue corn that expresses the hard but enduring life of their people. Since the purpose of Hopi ritual is to continue a cycle in which cloudlike ancestors (called *katsinas*) come from the mountains to nourish corn, which feeds the Hopi who eventually die and return to the mountains, the Hopi have sometimes said that "We are corn." Similarly, the Lakota of the northern Plains sometimes describe themselves as the descendants of "buffalo people" who emerged from under the Black Hills and gradually became human, never losing their kinship with the primary animal they hunted. This identification of food and people is not necessarily limited to small nations. Each year in Japan, the first planting of rice by the emperor, who is the living embodiment of Ninigo-no-mikoto, the god of the mature rice plant, is photographed for newspapers. When a bad harvest and World Trade Organization pressure caused the Japanese government to lower barriers against imported rice in 1993, the action caused a reaction that went beyond economics to the spiritual, and imported rice is still considered inferior and unclean by many Japanese.

Myths often associate death with the gift of food. The inhabitants of Ceram, an island in the Indonesian archipelago, tell the story of a quasi-divine young girl whose body produced tubers after it was cut up and buried. Among the Iroquois of northern New York, one variant of the creation story describes a girl who fell from the sky, then died and produced beans from her fingers and toes, squash from her stomach, corn from her breasts, and tobacco from her forehead. In Tongan mythology, Eel was condemned to death for allegedly causing the pregnancy of a virgin who shared his Samoan bathing pool. Villagers who planted Eel's severed head, as he had requested, testified that the coconut tree first appeared on that spot. Another Polynesian myth affirms that the breadfruit tree emerged from the plot where a woman buried the head of her husband.

As religions develop more philosophical perspectives, they distance themselves from myth, but food retains symbolic meanings and important roles in ritual and in healing.

Judaism. The story of Eden implicates a fruit in the beginning of death and of agricultural work (through the curse on Adam). According to *Genesis,* people were vegetarians in Eden but became carnivorous in the aftermath of the Flood; the offering of blood to God in the Temple remained as testimony that animal life still belonged to the creator. Jewish practice included a sacrificial lamb at Passover until the Temple was destroyed by the Romans. Even now, elements of the Passover include a bone to stand for the lamb and other elements such as an egg, salt water, and green herbs that point to a festival of rebirth with foods appropriate to the spring. Foods celebrated in Jewish stories include the manna, said to resemble coriander seed, that fell from heaven each day to feed Israel during its wandering in the wilderness and the cakes brought by ravens to feed the prophet Elijah when he fled into the desert from the wrath of Jezebel. According to Orthodox Jews, the coming of the Messiah will include the return of manna from heaven and a great banquet.

Daily Jewish practice includes a ritual blessing over bread and wine performed at home. On the Sabbath, it is a *mitzvah* (religious duty or good deed) to drink wine and to eat meat. Synagogue services now also commonly include a blessing and sharing of bread and wine. Holidays involve symbolic foods such as the *matzoh* (unleavened bread) of Passover and the round loaves of bread and apples with honey that are eaten to promote continuity and good fortune at the New Year.

Hinduism and Buddhism. Temple worship among Hindus involves large quantities of food because every statue of a god must be fed three times a day and bathed, not only in water but also in substances such as milk, sesame oil, coconut water, grain, and clarified butter. The bathing of a god with milk, oil, and colorful spices can make a striking visual impression. The primary duty of most temple priests is not to instruct but to perform this washing and feeding with correct prayer; people come to observe and to offer their own prayers as these ceremonies proceed, or they visit the gods at other times and make food offerings of their own. Food offerings include rice, curds, clarified butter, oil, many kinds of vegetables and fruits, almonds and other nuts, betel leaves, and combinations of spices including turmeric, salt, and pepper. Among Vaisnavites (worshipers of Viṣṇu and his avatars, such as Kṛṣṇa and Rāma), food offered to the gods is commonly shared by all worshippers under the name of *prasāda,* which may be taken home from the temple and eaten. Śaivites (worshipers of Śiva and his wife Parvati) consume only what has washed the *linga* and *yoni* statues that are his primary symbols, leaving the food offerings to the priests. On festivals (which often entail fasting), Hindus may bring large quantities of *prasāda* home and subsist on it for some days.

At home and in other areas outside the temples, Hindus hire Brahmin priests to perform fire sacrifices that also involve food. At a wedding or at the *brahmacharya* ritual that marks a son's beginning study of the scriptures, the priest will offer clarified butter, rice, and other foods in a fire while chanting appropriate prayers. In the temple, offerings of food enable worshipers to seek protection and favor from the gods, but in fire sacrifices, the food becomes fuel in the same economy of energy that created the gods and the universe itself; this cosmic energy is released by the fire and directed by the priest to the purpose for which he performs the ritual.

Although Buddhists do not hire priests for Brahmin rituals or bathe the Buddha's statues in food, they continue to leave offerings of fruit before these images. Food offered to the Buddha is not eaten by devotees but thrown away in compassion to animals or (in some cases, if there are large amounts) given to beggars. The tradition that the Buddha himself lived and taught as a beggar remains important in the Theravādan tradition that prevails in South Asia, where Thai monks usually receive food or flowers, not money, in the begging bowls they bring to the streets each morning.

Both Hindus and Buddhists sometimes use violations of food taboos as spiritual practices. For example, the *sannyasi,* or renunciates, of India always eat leftover (or symbolically leftover) food, violating the Hindu taboo on saliva; some yogis go so far to teach and to experience the reality of reincarnation as to eat their own excrement. Hindu ritual purification may entail eating a mixture of the cow's five products, which are milk, ghee (clarified butter), curds, urine, and dung. Tibetan Buddhists may remind themselves of emptiness and insubstantiality by drinking from cups made of the skulls of monks. Among those who practice the Tantric traditions of Hinduism and Buddhism, eating meat and drinking alcohol sometimes form part of secret rituals meant to teach that all things eventually contribute to deliverance.

Christianity. Building upon the blessing of bread and wine from Jewish mealtime, Sabbath, and Passover rituals, Christians have often made the sharing of bread and wine during Communion (or Eucharist) into the center of their ritual lives. During the Middle Ages, Roman Catholic theology defined this ritual meal as the miracle of transubstantiation, during which bread and wine are miraculously transformed into the actual body and blood of Jesus of Nazareth, who is the incarnation of God; Thomas Aquinas taught that the substance of Christ's body is then concealed under the appearance of bread and wine by another miracle in order to prevent disgust among the communicants. Although Protestants later rejected this doctrine, it still prevails among Catholics. One famous convert to Catholicism, the English writer Evelyn Waugh, was said to have converted because only Catholics offered the opportunity to "eat God."

Few symbolic foods are used by Christians today, but the Easter egg and its chocolate and candy variants are widely recognized; as in the Passover meal, the egg indicates the primordial roots of Easter in spring festivals of rebirth. Ethnic groups like the Italians, many of whom seek a meal of twelve types of seafood on Christmas Eve, often associate particular foods with Christian holidays. Some Protestants in the United States have substituted grape juice, which was invented for this purpose by a Methodist named Welch, for sacramental wine in many churches. Meanwhile, Protestants have made a virtual sacrament of coffee, with after-worship coffee hours following services at most churches. The coffeepot has become the unofficial symbol of Alcoholics Anonymous, a nondenominational spiritual group that grew from the Protestant ethos.

Chinese traditions. Daoist cosmology, and the traditional Chinese wisdom that precedes formal Daoism, sees all foods (and all things in the world) as composites of yin (dark, moist, soft, bland, feminine) and yang (bright, dry, hard, spicy, masculine), which in turn express the basic force of *qi* (breath, spirit) that inheres in all things. For Chinese tradition, every meal has symbolic and medical aspects, and every food establishes a direct and definable connection between the eater and the forces that move the stars. A typical Chinese menu seeks to balance yin and yang, cooling and heating properties, and so to have many ingredients offered in small portions over many courses. Folk traditions associate many symbolic foods, such as round cakes called mooncakes at the New Year, with holidays. Daily ancestor worship, the central practice of Chinese religion, involves offering food by placing it before tablets containing the names of ancestors, sometimes accompanied by pictures. Failure to perform this duty, which can only be done by the eldest son, will result in ancestors becoming hungry ghosts who cause disharmony in the home. For about three thousand years before 1911, the emperor of China offered animal sacrifice to the imperial ancestor and to the heavenly beings at least three times a year, on the Altar of Heaven at the capital; this ritual, which was also performed at times of crisis, was held to keep both the natural world and the nation in harmony.

Islam. Islam stands out among religions by involving no food or drink in its ordinary services of worship. Eating plays an important ritual and social role in the fasting month of Ramadān, when each day ends at sunset with an *iftar* meal that breaks the fast; these meals traditionally begin with figs, following the example of the Prophet. In Muslim countries like Egypt, *iftar* meals stretch into the night and create a festive atmosphere during the month. One of the main holidays of Islam, the ʿĪd al-Aḍḥā during the month of pilgrimage to Mecca, involves the sharing of food because each Muslim household is obligated to sacrifice a goat, sheep, ram, cow, or camel and distribute one-third of the meat to the poor.

In the United States, where many Muslims and others do not enjoy eating goat, it has sometimes been difficult to arrange for this meat to be used. The Muslim vision of Paradise involves both food and drink: the Qur'ān often pictures those in Paradise enjoying "fountains" and "fruits, any that they may select," with "flesh of fowls, any that they may desire" (*Sūrah* 56:18–21).

Yoruba (Vodou, Santeria, Condomble) traditions. The West African religion of the Yoruba and Fon peoples, native to such modern nations as Nigeria, Cameroon, Benin, and Dahomey, has spread through slavery and immigration throughout the Americas, becoming known as vodou in Haiti and Louisiana, as Santería in Cuba, and as Condomble in Brazil, bringing its own symbolic and ritual uses of food while integrating Christian elements into its African heritage. Here food is offered to the gods so that they descend into the community performing the ritual, taking possession of some participants and inducing trance, while communicating with and healing others. Each deity has favored foods and drinks and animals of sacrifice. For example, Elegba, the god of the crossroads who is invoked to begin any service, favors palm oil, fruits, nuts, roasted corn, and yams; he is drawn to the sacrifice of roosters and male goats; Oya, goddess of storms and cemeteries, enjoys red wine and purple grapes, eggplant and rice and beans; hens and female goats are sacrificed to her. Shango, companion of Oya, is a former human, a deified ruler of the Yoruba who has become the god of lightning and retribution; he is called upon with plantains, green bananas, and bitter kola nuts, and enjoys rum; rams and red roosters are sacrificed to him. The list of *orishas* (or *loa*, divinities) runs to the dozens, each with a set of preferences in food, drink, and sacrificial animal.

FOOD AND SACRIFICE. There is a vast body of literature on the origins and meaning of sacrifice and the role it has played in human history. With relation to food, farmers have often sacrificed the first fruits of the harvest, while shepherds have sacrificed the firstborn of each female in their flocks. Ancient Israelite tradition continued these sacrifices and added the substitution of a sacrifice or monetary gift for a firstborn son. Animals sacrificed at the Jerusalem Temple included bullocks, rams, lambs, pigeons, and doves; other foods included cooked and uncooked dough, prepared with oil and salt, and wine poured like blood at the foot of the altar.

After the destruction of the Jerusalem Temple, Jews gave up on sacrifice, but the Jewish and Gentile followers of Jesus, faced with the need to understand the crucifixion, gradually transmuted the traditional blessings of bread and wine into a sacrificial meal. Not only were the bread and wine understood as transubstantiated into the body and blood of Jesus, and hence of God, but the act of offering the bread and wine was held to have the effects of a sacrifice, releasing power that could gain favor for the living and shorten the punishment of souls in purgatory. Although the most dramatic examples of purely sacrificial worship—for example, the priests who did nothing but offer the sacrifice of the Mass in private—have been eliminated by reformers, Roman Catholics today still buy Mass Cards and give money so that Jesus may again be offered to God the Father, under the appearances of bread and wine, for the intentions of those who make the donations.

The most prevalent form of food sacrifice is the offering of food to ancestors, which takes place daily at millions of home altars in China, Korea, and Japan, under the influence of Confucian and Shintō traditions. Practitioners of the Yoruba and other African traditions also give food and drink to ancestors, as the ancient Greeks, Romans, and Egyptians did in their time. The Shintō priests of Japan offer food sacrifices—clean, fresh whole foods, fish, and fruits and rice—to the *kami,* or divinities who are said to inhabit eight million places in the islands of Japan. Regular worship takes place at striking waterfalls, impressive rocks, and dignified trees where the *kami* are believed to dwell; along with presentations of food, petitions from local people are read to the *kami.* At the center of the Shintō system are offerings of rice planted by the emperor to Amaterasu, the goddess of the sun and ancestor of the imperial house.

FASTING AND DIETING. One of the most universal of religious practices, fasting can be done for reasons that range from repentance for sins to the cultivation of mystical experience. For Muslims, fasting during the month of Ramaḍān stands as the fourth among five pillars of Islam. Muslims may not eat, drink, smoke, or engage in sex between sunrise and sunset during the month of Ramaḍān; those who are sick or traveling are supposed to fast an equal number of days at another time. The fast commemorates the month in which the first revelations of the Qur'ān were given to Muḥammad; Muslims often teach that the hunger and thirst of this month makes them more sensitive to the needs of the poor and more aware of their dependence on God.

Jews undertake two briefer, but more intense fasts, also abstaining from drink and sex as well as from food: from sunset to the next sunset on the Day of Atonement, Yom Kippur, which completes the New Year's holiday in the fall, and during the summer on Tisha B'Av, to commemorate the destruction of the Temple. Roman Catholics and Orthodox Christians fast for forty days called Lent, between Ash Wednesday and Easter, every spring; among Catholics, the rules of this fast have been relaxed in recent years. Lent involves no periods of complete denial of food and drink, but only abstinence from meat on certain days and a commitment to eat less every day. Among the devout, there is a tradition of voluntarily giving up a favorite food or drink, both to repent for sin and to provide money for charity. A celebration called Mardi Gras (French for "fat Tuesday") or Carnival often precedes the beginning of Lent, especially in Latin countries.

In many religions, monks and nuns and ascetics use restricted diets as a means to heighten awareness in prayer or meditation and to lessen the passions of the body. Under the Christian Rule of St. Benedict, each monk was allowed one pound of bread per day and a pint of wine, but meat was not recommended except for the sick. Monks in Thailand do not eat after noon, in imitation of the Buddha.

Many holidays that involve fasting from grain and beans for periods of two or three days punctuate the Hindu calendar. On those days, Hindus may subsist on milk and fruits that have become *prasāda* by being offering at a temple. In the twentieth century, Mahatma Gandhi added a political dimension to the Hindu tradition of fasting by his hunger strikes, which Gandhi employed both in order to convince the British to set India free and to convince the people of India to stop a religious war between Hindus and Muslims. Going beyond politics to spirituality, Gandhi taught that people should always eat according to a standard of "meagerness," keeping a perpetual fast in which they took food as medicine, in the interests of promoting clear thinking. Calling a "full" meal "a crime against God and man," Gandhi urged his followers not to allow food to make them sensual.

Late in the twentieth century, the rise of industrialized food production and marketing led to an epidemic of obesity, especially in the United States, which led in turn to a proliferation of diet plans and programs. Many of these programs take on spiritual connotations. Compulsions to diet, in the forms of anorexia and bulimia, have killed many young women and attracted attention from historians of culture. A historian of Christianity, Caroline Walker Bynum, pointed out that medieval ascetics like Catherine of Siena, though she may have killed herself with fasting, did so in order to gain power and control, while modern anorexics are driven by social pressure to their unhealthy behavior.

THEORETICAL PERSPECTIVES. In an attempt to make sense out of the array of food customs that have been documented in both ancient and modern societies at all stages of their development, scholars have traveled many different roads seeking common elements that would justify the organization of food customs into intelligible categories. For example, writers since Moses Maimonides (d. 1204) have suggested that hygiene motivated the Jewish food taboos. Maimonides said that pork contained too much moisture and so caused indigestion and denounced the filthiness of pigs; moderns have pointed to the danger of trichinosis from undercooked pork. The facts that parasitic diseases were not recognized until the nineteenth century and that permitted foods may also bear disease work against this perspective, though the experience of consequences as a factor in food taboos also forms part of an evolutionary perspective that could have some validity.

On the other hand, China developed a system of food wisdom even more elaborate than that of the Jews, and just as concerned with health and with spiritual well-being, without any taboos at all. As anthropologist Marvin Harris has said, the Jewish law could have completely eliminated trichinosis by outlawing undercooked pork. Clearly, the social structure and circumstances of each society need to be considered in understanding how the world's religions regulate food.

In *Purity and Danger* (1966), Mary Douglas focused on spiritual pollution as a common element in food taboos. Following the perspective of Émile Durkheim, Douglas argued that religions provide their adherents with a sense of identity. Identity is constructed through patterns of social behavior, such as those involved in the production, preparation, and consumption of food. Cleanliness, in this context, becomes an attribute of anything that strengthens group identity by contributing to the order of the universe. Applying this perspective to Judaism, Douglas saw the law of Moses as dividing the world into three types of creatures: those whose natural environment is either land, sea, or sky (see *Lev.* 12 and the creation story of *Genesis).* Creatures that seem "mixed," such as flightless birds or animals that live in the sea without fins (or with legs, like lobsters and crabs), are taboo.

Following this reasoning, pork becomes "unclean" because it violates another category, that dividing Israel from its neighbors. Douglas noted the command to be holy that surrounded the passages on food in the Torah, and she observed that the root meaning of the Hebrew *kadosh*, translated "holiness," is "to set apart or to cut off." According to the Torah, holiness is an attribute of God, and God wants Israel to be holy; therefore, Israelites must not eat the pork (or many other foods) that their Canaanite and Egyptian neighbors ate. The prohibition of pork would then be one of many laws, such as those prohibiting intermarriage with Canaanites or prohibiting any image of Israel's God, that were meant to keep the identity of Israel cleanly defined, or "holy." Though this argument has some force, it remains true that Israel borrowed many things, such as the architecture of the Temple and the words of many Psalms, from Canaanite models. The modern sense of ancient Israel's uniqueness may reveal as much about the work of later rabbis and the need of Christians to find heroic origins for their own religion as it does about the reasons for ancient Israelite law.

Observing that Muslims also do not eat pork, though they do eat camels and other animals prohibited by the Torah, Marvin Harris offered an evolutionary perspective on this law, contending that religions tend to promote behaviors that help their followers to survive. At first this would seem paradoxical with regard to a pork taboo, because the pig is a very efficient source of protein, converting food to meat much more quickly than other animals. However, Harris noted, in arid climates the pig becomes very expensive with regard to water; he finds that the Christian-Muslim divide in the Balkans corresponds to a divide between heavily forested land, friendly to pigs, and dry regions. Harris used the same reasoning to explain why the Aryans, who ate cattle before entering the dry Indian subcontinent, came to revere "mother cow" and to use her only for plowing and hauling and for milk as Hinduism developed.

Psychoanalytic explanations for food customs have begun from the infant–mother bond in nursing and the instinctual relations that this may establish between eating and sex. Many cultures, from the Lele of West Africa to modern

Orthodox Jews, have forbidden women from cooking during menstruation; the Bemba of central Africa keep children from eating food prepared by those who have not purified themselves by a ritual after sex. Perhaps the command of the Torah not to boil a kid in its mother's milk arose in order to forbid a kind of culinary incest that Canaanites practiced to promote fertility. Japanese menus still offer a "mother-child udon," or bowl of noodles that contains both chicken and egg, and the title still makes some diners cringe.

Seeking a psychological root for food rules in the realms of cognition and linguistics, Claude Lévi-Strauss proposed that all thought and language begins with binary oppositions such as self/other, human/animal, and nature/culture. In the domain of food, objects are classified according to the binary of cooked/rotten, between which the midpoint is raw. Lévi-Strauss classified the processes of food preparation, beginning with roasting, boiling, and smoking, along the continuum between cooked and rotten. He concluded that roasted food remained most similar to the raw and therefore was understood as possessing the most natural strength and prestige, while boiled food stood closer to rotten, weaker but more civilized, because boiling required a pot rather than a spit, and also more closely associated with rebirth (as in the cauldron of immortality that appears in many cultures). Lévi-Strauss thought that processes like frying, baking, and smoking, with variation depending on oils and spices, could be located along the same continuum between cooked and rotten in every civilization.

Abandoning the quest for universal systems, such functional anthropologists as A. R. Radcliffe-Brown, Bronislaw Malinowski, and Franz Boas have emphasized that every social group must be understood on its own terms, and that food forms part of a system that both expresses and reinforces the roles people play in helping the group to function. For example, they would say, women who contribute large dowries and exercise authority tend to eat with men of the same social status and to eat the same foods, while women in polygamous families who exercise no authority eat with the children and eat different foods. From this perspective, taboos on menstruating women preparing food arise from the definition of women by their availability for sex and for childbirth. Taboos on specific foods may reflect the low status (or the status as enemies) of people who possess that food.

Anthropologists have also observed symbolic uses of food that seem suitable to societies at various levels of social and technological development. Research has revealed, for example, that hunter-gatherer societies have much in common, whether they live in desert regions, the Arctic, India, or Africa. According to Joseph Campbell, one of the earliest analysts of world mythologies, hunter-gatherers tend to address prayer and sacrifice to a cosmic force (or a god) that stands apart, acting as master of the game animals. Campbell went on to say that when a group takes up agriculture, rituals and myths appear in which the cosmic force or god dwells within the object sacrificed, so that the sacrifice brings forth its own effects. The development of large communities with formal political authority brings another stage, at which large festivals and more serious sacrifice (often demanding human victims) begins to be seen as necessary to renew the supply of food each year. The human sacrifices of ancient China before the Shang dynasty, of ancient Rome in the arenas, and of the Incas and Aztecs in America lend some plausibility to this view.

Food in the Recent History of Religions. Since the worldwide distribution of foods that began with Columbus after 1492, and especially since the emergence of the empirical science of chemistry around 1650, a revolution has taken place with regard to the values placed upon food, at least in the Western world. Before then, both life and digestion were thought of as processes that resembled cooking, and the foods considered best were those that had cooked longest, with the most complex sets of ingredients, so that they could balance the humors of the body. The blancmange and the puddings of England and France, served with cooked drinks and spiced wines, the moles and sauces of Latin America, and the samosas and curries of India survive from those days. But after the seventeenth century, fermentation became the model of life, and high value was placed on fresh and roasted foods that could spoil quickly. Roasted meats, salads, fruits, and clear or sparkling wines came to dominate the tables of the West.

The goal of diet wisdom shifted from maintaining balance to returning to nature. Sometimes food became the means to a spiritual goal, expressed in terms of returning to nature or even regaining the innocence of Eden. Especially in the United States and in England, partisans of "diet reform," a program that advocated whole-grain flour, a minimum of cooking, and often vegetarianism, attempted to engage the conscience of the Christian world. Religious leaders like Sylvester Graham, a former minister and inventor of Graham flour, and John Harvey Kellogg, physician and inventor of the corn flake, profoundly influenced eating habits. Whole denominations, such as Kellogg's Seventh-day Adventists, emerged to embrace vegetarianism. Pledges against all use of alcohol prevailed among the Methodists, Baptists, Mormons, Presbyterians, Congregationalists, and even some Roman Catholics of the United States, until the nation passed a constitutional amendment prohibiting alcohol in 1919. The failure of Prohibition did not end the connection between diet and righteousness for American Christians. As Daniel Sack has documented, the menus of church suppers shifted from steak, brandy, and cigars in the 1890s to a mixture of ethnic foods in the 1950s to tofu and sprouts in the 1970s and then to starvation dinners, dramatizing the problem of world hunger, in the 1990s.

Food and Social Justice. In the twentieth century, many Christians, especially in the United States and England, began to see food as a primary field of social action and ethical responsibility. The Salvation Army, the Catholic Worker movement, the Universal House of Prayer, and many individual churches made soup kitchens and pantries for the poor into the center of their mission. Such organizations as CARE, Oxfam, and Bread for the World—a specifically Christian lobbying group, incorporated in Washington to influence U.S. policy—tried to ameliorate the unequal distribution of food in the world. Theorists including Arthur Simon of Bread for the World and Francis Moore Lappe, author of *Diet for a Small Planet,* argued that meat consumption stole grain from the starving and pointed out the inequities of a world market in which such food-exporting countries as the Philippines sent fruit to the United States while their own people starved. Several boycotts of food engaged religious groups and had clear effects: a boycott of California grapes in the 1960s helped to organize farmworkers; a boycott of Nestlé products in the 1980s modified the company's policy of promoting infant formula to women who could not get clean water; a boycott of Campbell's soup led to the company negotiating with its workers. Concern for animal rights led to a new kind of vegetarianism, in which people abstained from meat not because they were fasting or avoiding bad *karma,* but because industrial farm conditions seemed inhumane or because animals were seen as sentient beings whose right to live equaled that of a human.

GLOBALIZATION. The profusion of meat, potatoes, tomatoes, and corn from the Americas added new whole foods to the world's diet. Industrialization and modern transportation, refrigeration and freezing, petrochemical fertilizers, and hydrogenated fats and genetically modified crops have made vast resources available to the rich and the middle classes of all nations, while the world market in food has sometimes exacerbated inequities and hunger. Millions who once lived in stable, subsistence economies now work in industry for more money but run the risk of famine.

Resistance against and adaptation to globalization have sometimes taken religious forms. In 2003, U.S. military actions in the Muslim world sparked both a boycott of American products and the development of substitutes, such as Qibla Cola and Mecca Cola. Globalizing corporations have also shown a willingness to adapt to religious preferences: in India, McDonald's offered an extensive vegetarian menu, including the Maharaja Mac and eggless mayonnaise, prepared in separate kitchen areas by staff wearing green aprons. Even the nonvegetarian section served no beef but only chicken burgers and curry. Meanwhile in Israel, at the start of the twenty-first century, all 110 McDonald's guaranteed kosher beef, while seven were actually kosher restaurants, serving no dairy and closing on the Sabbath. Seventy-one McDonald's were operating in Saudi Arabia in the early twenty-first century, including two in Mecca, observing Muslim food laws. Both Detroit, Michigan, and Sydney, Australia, had *ḥalāl* McDonald's, where potatoes are fried without animal fat and all meat is slaughtered by Muslim butchers. Increasing numbers of immigrants and people exploring their heritage in every part of the world have given evidence that food customs often provide the most enduring forms of religious practice.

SEE ALSO Agriculture; Beverages; Bread; Cannibalism; Fasting; Kashrut; Leaven; Sacrifice; Salt; Taboo.

BIBLIOGRAPHY

Anderson, E. N. *The Food of China.* New Haven, Conn., 1988. A comprehensive treatment of the cosmological theories and the history linking Chinese religions and food.

Bynum, Caroline Walker. *Holy Feast and Holy Fast.* Berkeley, Calif., 1985. Explores the meaning of abstinence from food among medieval women mystics.

Campbell, Joseph. *The Masks of God,* vol. 1, *Primitive Mythology.* New York, 1959. Food myths of planters and hunters are discussed in this important work.

Counihan, Carole, and Penny Van Esterik, eds, *Food and Culture: A Reader.* New York, 1997. Perspectives on food from Anna Freud and Margaret Mead to recent analyses of anorexia and globalization.

Douglas, Mary. *Purity and Danger: An Analysis of Concepts of Pollution and Taboo.* New York, 1966. An excellent study of how food customs mirror the patterning of a society. Douglas's approach applies equally to secular and to religious life, ancient and modern.

Eliade, Mircea. *Patterns in Comparative Religion.* New York, 1958. Chapter 8 of this classic deals with "Vegetation: Rites and Symbols of Regeneration" and chapter 9 with "Agriculture and Fertility Cults."

Engs, Ruth Clifford. *Clean Living Movements: American Cycles of Health Reform.* Westport, Conn., 2000. Provides background on the religions of health that have shaped American attitudes toward food.

Fernandez-Armento, Felipe. *Near a Thousand Tables: A History of Food.* New York, 2002. Readable, Western-oriented story of food in history.

Goody, Jack. *Cooking, Cuisine and Class: A Study in Comparative Sociology.* Cambridge, U.K., 1982. Begins with a summary of the advances made by anthropologists and sociologists in their study of food customs. Compares differences in African and Eurasian cuisine as reflections of their different social structures.

Greenberg, Blu. *How to Run a Traditional Jewish Household.* New York, 1985. Intelligent, inside account of running a kosher kitchen.

Harris, Marvin. *Good to Eat: Riddles of Food and Culture.* London, 1985. Food customs explained from a Darwinian, evolutionary perspective.

Khare, R. S., ed. *The Eternal Food: Gastronomic Ideas and Experiences of Hindus and Buddhists.* Albany, N.Y., 1992. Excellent selection of articles on the practical uses of food in worship and in diet advice by Hindus and Buddhists.

Lappe, Francis Moore. *Diet for a Small Planet.* New York, 1971; updated editions, 1991 and 2002. Classic statement of the modern vegetarian movement.

Laudan, Rachel. "Birth of the Modern Diet." *Scientific American* 283, no. 2 (August 2000): 76–81. Connects advances in chemistry with wisdom regarding health and food.

Lévi-Strauss, Claude. "The Culinary Triangle." In *The Origin of Table Manners: Introduction to a Science of Mythology,* vol. 3. New York, 1968. Seeks the structure of a universal grammar behind cooking techniques across cultures.

Meigs, Anna. *Food, Sex, and Pollution: A New Guinea Religion.* Piscataway, N.J., 1984.

Sack, Daniel. *Whitebread Protestants: Food and Religion in American Culture.* New York, 2001. An amusing and insightful account of the evolution of communion elements and church suppers in the United States.

JAMES E. LATHAM (1987)
PETER GARDELLA (2005)

FOOLS, HOLY SEE CLOWNS; DRAMA; HUMOR AND RELIGION

FORTUNA was the Latin (and perhaps also the Sabine) goddess of the incalculable element in life. Her name is derived from the Latin word *fors* ("luck"). Cults dedicated to various manifestations of Fortuna existed throughout Latium—attes ted atTusculum, Signia, Cora, Ostia, and especially at Praeneste—as well as in Rome and Antium. Etruscan civilization also included worshipers of Fortuna; the Etruscans placed a great deal of importance on the idea of fate.

In Rome, Fortuna did not belong to the oldest stratum of cults traditionally connected with King Numa Pompilius. She is one of the Sabine divinities listed by Varro in his *De lingua Latina.* King Servius Tullius considered Fortuna to be his special patron and friend; consequently, he built two of the oldest temples dedicated to her in Rome. One of these temples, in the Forum Boarium, was associated with the temple of Mater Matuta; the other, on the right side of the Tiber River, was specifically known as Fanum Fortis Fortunae.

Scholars believe the sanctuary of Fortuna in the Forum Boarium dates back to the very beginning of urban life in Rome. Recent excavations have shown that sacred life in the Forum Boarium began around 575 BCE, when the first floor of the forum was laid. The ancient house of worship consisted solely of an open area with an altar in the center; the first actual temples identified with the temples of Mater Matuta and Fortuna were not built until the end of the sixth century BCE and later reconstructed by Camillus in 395 BCE.

Fortuna was also related to the goddesses of childbirth and fecundity, the Matralia, whose feast day was celebrated on June 11. Two other temples were dedicated to her in 293 BCE and 17 CE. In general, Fortuna appealed to the lower classes of Roman society, particularly to slaves; they considered her a benefactor, rather than a menace. The cult often prayed for fertility or for success in certain endeavors.

Married women worshiped Fortuna Muliebris, whose sanctuary was located at the fourth milestone on the Via Latina. She also played a part in the legend of Coriolanus, which attributed the founding of the temple to Coriolanus's mother and wife. On April 1, all women worshiped Fortuna Virilis, associated with Venus, by praying and taking ritual baths in men's bathhouses. This goddess is known only from the *fasti* and literature, especially from accounts of the aforementioned particular rite; this custom must have occurred relatively recently, however, because public baths were built in Rome during the second century BCE. Originally, Fortuna Virilis probably was the guardian spirit of men, *viri.* In addition to protecting the sexuality of men, she was supposed to help women to obtain the men's love.

Most scholars doubt the existence of a special cult of Fortuna Virgo. According to Wissowa, the Fortuna of the Forum Boarium was indeed a women's deity, but Fortuna Virgo may be a later name. This goddess eventually came to be called *Virgo* or *Virginalis,* but only three ancient writers recorded the epithet.

Fortuna Equestris received a temple of her own in 173 BCE, after a victory of the Roman cavalry; similarly, a temple to "Fortune of this day" (Fortuna Huiusce Diei) celebrated the victory by Q. Lutatius Catulus at Vercellae in 101 BCE. Chapels and altars to Fortuna Bona, Fortuna Mala, Fortuna Dubia, Fortuna Publica, and others multiplied, along with dedications to the Fortuna of certain localities. These minor monuments took more notice of the negative aspects of Fortuna. Later imperial temples, constructed in Rome and elsewhere, connect Fortuna, always positively, with the emperors (Fortuna Augusta, Fortuna Redux).

The sanctuary of Fortuna Primigenia at Praeneste (modern-day Palestrina) presented Fortuna as *filia primigenia,* or "first daughter" (of Jupiter?), a most unusual notion in a Latin context. Scholars have speculated about a possible Indo-European, Etruscan, or Greek influence. In his *De divinatione,* Cicero adds to the confusion by describing the Fortuna of Praeneste as Jupiter's nurse. The building, excavated by Italian archaeologists, dates to approximately the second century BCE, but the cult itself, famous for its oracle, is certainly much older. After a period of friction with Roman authorities, the cult of Fortuna Primigenia was introduced from Praeneste to Rome toward the end of the Second Punic War, where it became very popular. The first temple to Fortuna Primigenia erected on the Quirinal was soon followed by two other temples built on the same hill. Another famous center of the cult of Fortuna with an oracle was located in Antium. Here, for unexplained reasons, people worshiped two Fortunas.

The diffusion of the cult of Fortuna throughout Italy and the Latin West was influenced by the corresponding Greek cult of Tyche. This connection is evident in the iconography of Fortuna, who is often represented, as was Tyche, as a standing woman with a rudder in her right hand and a cornucopia in her left hand. Furthermore, both Tyche and Fortuna were sometimes depicted as possessing several attributes of Isis. The influence of Tyche is also clear in literary texts (for instance, in works by Horace and Seneca) that try to clarify the nature of Fortuna. Whereas in cult, her most typical attributes—the cornucopia, the rudder, and the globe—symbolized Fortuna as the giver of material blessing and as the arbiter of human destiny, in literature, her symbols accentuated fickleness and unreliability. Thus, the wheel was a common literary attribute of Fortuna, a symbol of her ever-changing nature. Other ways authors alluded to Fortuna's fickleness in literature included: portraying her as standing upon a stone or upon a sphere; as possessing wings, with which she could easily fly away; as roaming in the world without settling anywhere; and as expressing her ever-shifting favor or disfavor by her countenance, her smile, and her thundering voice. Goddess Fortuna was occasionally identified with Nemesis and associated with Felicitas and Bonus Eventus.

Two varieties of Fortuna came to have a great importance during the Roman Empire: Fortuna Augusta or Augusti, the guardian spirit of the Emperor, an equivalent of his Genius; and Fortuna Redux, the power that guarded the return of the Emperor from dangerous foreign journeys. Both deities were recorded on numerous votive inscriptions and coins; the honor paid to Fortuna Augusta and Fortuna Redux expressed loyalty to the state and to the reigning emperor. Though Christianity as a doctrine was incompatible with the pagan idea of Fortuna, the entity did not quite disappear; rather, she evolved into both an inherited literary figure and a pagan deity.

SEE ALSO Chance; Fate; Roman Religion, article on the Early Period.

BIBLIOGRAPHY

Castagnoli, F. "Il culto della Mater Matuta e della Fortuna nel Foro Boario." *Studi Romani* 27 (1979): 145–152.

Coarelli, Filippo, "La Porta Trionfale e la Via dei Trionfi." *Dialoghi di Archeologia* 2 (1968): 55–103.

Champeaux, Jacqueline. *Fortuna, Recherches sur le culte de la Fortune à Rome et dans le monde romaindes origines à la mort de César.* 2 vols. Rome, 1982–1987. Reviewed by Gerhard Radke in *Gnomon* 56 (1984): 419–426.

Dumézil, Georges. *Servius et la Fortune. Essai sur la fonction sociale de Louange et de Blâme et sur les éléments indo-européens du cens romain.* Paris, 1943.

Dumézil, Georges. "Mythe et épopée." In *Histoires romaines,* pp. 116–141 and 306–330. Paris, 1973.

Gagé, Jean. *Matronalia. Essai sur les dévotions et les organisations cultuelles des femmes dans l'ancienne Rome.* Collection Latomus, vol. 60. Brussels, 1963.

Gagé, Jean. *La chute des Tarquins et les débuts de la république romaine.* Paris, 1976.

Fasolo, Furio, and Giorgio Gullini. *Il santuario della Fortuna Primigenia a Palestrina.* Rome, 1953.

Kajanto, Iiro. "Fortuna." In *Aufstieg und Niedergang der römischen Welt,* vol. 2.17.1, pp. 502–558. Berlin and New York, 1981.

Liou, Bernadette. "La statue cultuelle du Forum Boarium." *Revue des Etudes Latines* 42 (1969): 269-283.

"Lazio Arcaico e mondo greco." *La Parola del Passato,* vol. XXXII (1977): 7–128.

Otto, Walter F. "Fortuna." In *Real-Encyclopädie der classischen Altertumswissenschaft,* vol. 13, cols. 12–42. Stuttgart, 1910.

Radke, Gerhard. *Die Götter Altitaliens.* Münster, Germany, 1965.

Wissowa, Georg. *Religion und Kultus der Römer.* 2d ed. Munich, 1912.

ARNALDO MOMIGLIANO (1987)
CHARLES GUITTARD (2005)

FORTUNE SEE CHANCE; FATE

FOUCHER, ALFRED (1865–1952), was a French Indologist and specialist in Buddhist archaeology. Alfred C. A. Foucher studied in Paris, under the guidance of Sylvain Lévi, and in India (1895–1897), where he combined philosophical training at the Sanskrit College of Banaras with "militant" archaeology through extensive pilgrimages to several places of historical interest.

Foucher was a pioneer in the area of religious archaeology with his study of the relation between artistic representations and their doctrinal and literary background. His field of predilection was the area known as Gandhara (roughly, those portions of Afghanistan and Pakistan between the Hindu Kush mountains and the Indus River), where the Indian and Greek worlds had been in contact at around the beginning of the common era. The publication of Foucher's *L'art gréco-bouddhique du Gandhâra: Étude sur les origines de l'influence classique dans l'art bouddhique de l'Inde et de l'Extrême-Orient* extended over half a century and comprised three volumes: volume 1, *Introduction; Les édifices; Les bas-reliefs* (1905); volume 2, *Images* (1922); and volume 3, *Additions et corrections; index* (1951). Though criticized for some of its conclusions regarding chronology and style, this work remains the most accurate sourcebook on early Buddhist iconography.

Foucher's interest in Gandhara received a new impulse when Afghanistan opened its frontiers to archaeological investigation. Foucher, who was then working at the Archaeological Survey of India (1919–1921), was immediately *à pied d'œuvre* as the first director of the Délégation Archéologique Française en Afghanistan (1921–1925). In Afghanistan, as previously in Northwest India, his habit of methodically following the itinerary of Xuanzang, his natural gift for observation, and his archaeological insight led Foucher to remarkable discoveries in Haḍḍa, Kāpiśī-Bēgrām, Bāmiyān, Balkh, and the Lampaka-Laghmān region. The gist of these discoveries is expressed in a work accomplished with the collaboration of his wife, Eugénie Bazin-Foucher, *La vieille route de l'Inde de Bactres à Taxila* (2 vols., 1942–1947). Foucher also collaborated with John Marshall in editing the three huge volumes of *The Monuments of Sanchi* (1939), a work focused on the main Buddhist site of central India.

The clear-sightedness of Foucher as an archaeologist was no doubt the result of his deep penetration of the Indian tradition. Foucher, who used old texts as guides in his archaeological researches, in turn used monuments for a better understanding of Buddhism and especially of its founder, Śākyamuni Buddha. Foucher's best-known book, *La vie du Bouddha* (1949; English trans., 1963) is, significantly, subtitled *D'après les textes et les monuments de l'Inde.* Foucher was aware of all the difficulties of such a biography. In 1894 he had translated from German into French Hermann Oldenberg's study of the Buddha's life (*Le Bouddha, sa vie, sa doctrine, sa communauté,* 2d ed., 1903), which remains the best "positive" history of the Buddha following the Pali sources. At the same time, Foucher was much in contact with Émile Senart, who had proposed a mythical interpretation of the life of the Buddha. In the 1930s, Foucher had also witnessed the brilliant attempt at a new interpretation of Buddhism through archaeology and sociology made by his young contemporary Paul Mus. It was only at the end of his life that Foucher's own biography of the Buddha came to maturation. This book shows the geographical (centers of pilgrimages) and historical (superposition of hagiographical patterns) influences on the tales surrounding Śākyamuni. It remains the most satisfactory approach toward the personality of the historical Buddha as he has been seen through the Asian tradition.

Though deeply original in his method and his achievements, Foucher cannot be isolated from a golden age of French philological studies of which he is a typical representative. Even if different in spirit, his *La vie du Bouddha* recalls the much earlier *Vie de Jésus* (1863) by Foucher's fellow Breton, Ernest Renan. Foucher's systematic inventory of architectural remains and iconographical documents as an approach to an understanding of Buddhism has a parallel in the encyclopedic research on Christian symbolism done by his contemporary Émile Mâle.

Besides his already mentioned sojourns in India and Afghanistan, Foucher lived for a time in French Indochina (1901 and 1905–1907), where he succeeded his friend Louis Finot as the director of the École Française d'Extrême-Orient, and in Japan (1925–1926), where he established with Sylvain Lévi the Maison Franco-Japonaise.

Bibliography

In addition to the writings mentioned above, Foucher's *The Beginnings of Buddhist Art and Other Essays in Indian and Central-Asian Archaeology* (London, 1917) should be noted. Although outdated, it remains a testimony to his exactitude, clarity, and elegance. For bibliographic data, see Shinshō Hanayama's *Bibliography on Buddhism* (Tokyo, 1961); *Bibliographie bouddhique,* 32 vols., compiled by Marcelle Lalou (Paris, 1928–1967); and Henri Deydier's *Contribution à l'étude de l'art du Gandhâra* (Paris, 1950). A biographical sketch of Foucher can be found in Alfred Merlin's "Notice sur la vie et las travaux de M. Alfred Foucher," in *Académie des Inscriptions et Belles Lettres: Comptes rendus* (Paris, 1954), pp. 457–469.

Hubert Durt (1987)

FOUNTAIN. The word *fountain* derives from the Latin *fons,* meaning "source." As physical phenomena serving as the material basis of hierophanies (appearances of the divine), fountains may be described as the flowing of pressurized water up and out through an aperture from some hidden depth below the earth's surface. As hierophanies, they manifest locally the flowing of diverse creative, recreative, or transformative potentialities from depths beyond the ordinary or profane plane of existence. There is no single sort of potentiality attributed in common to all sacred fountains in the world's religions, but a number of potentialities are severally attributed to them, for example, healing powers, oracular powers, rejuvenating powers, and so forth. Likewise, no single divinity is regarded as a manifestation common to all fountains; the various named and nameless gods, spirits, and nymphs of fountains are particular to individual instances. Furthermore, sacred significance is attributed seemingly no less to artificial than to naturally occurring fountains.

The typical attributes of fountains reflect diverse metaphoric images expressive of the principal water potentiality, the cosmogonic; cosmogonic water is viewed as pristine, as formless, as eternal, as receptive, as living, as chaotic. For example, the creative power of fountains can be understood as one manifestation of the world-creating power itself, and the water of fountains as homologous to the cosmogonic water from which creation arises and into which it dissolves, like the Babylonian waters of Apsu or the Vedic watery source of all things and all existence.

Some fountains are sacred as sources of divine power. In times of drought, for example, the priest of the god Zeus Lykaios in Arcadia cast an oak branch into the mountainside spring, activating the spring's power to make rain.

Again, some fountains restore to an original or pristine condition those who bathe in them or drink from their waters. It was thought, for instance, that when the goddess Hera or the members of her cult bathed in the Nauplian spring, they became virginal again. The pristine state is homologous to the virginal aspect of the cosmogonic waters before the creative act. Thus, fountains of youth manifest a forever self-renewing potentiality for creation. In Brahmanic legend the fountain of youth typically renews power or vigor, but it does not bestow immortality. However, in other legends immortality is granted. In the Greek romance of Alexander by Pseudo-Callisthenes, Alexander's cook accidentally discovers a fountain that bestows immortal life. In Islamic folklore, the figure Khidr is mentioned as the only being who gained immortality by drinking from the fountain of life, which represents the principle of eternal existence.

Some fountains function as principles or causes of life itself. For example, in the prophet Ezekiel's vision of Yahveh's regenerated Temple, a spring flows out from under the Temple. Its waters cause perpetually bearing fruit trees to spring up at once along its banks. This water demonstrates two additional potentialities attributed to certain sacred fountains, namely, healing and fructifying powers. "Fish will be very plentiful, for wherever the water goes it brings health, and life teems wherever the river flows" (*Ez.* 47:1–12).

In Babylonian religious thought, Apsu, the water of creation, is called "house of wisdom," or the house of Ea, god of wisdom. Wisdom, supernatural insight, oracular vision, and poetic inspiration are other typical attributes of various sacred fountains. For example, the gods in Germanic mythology determine the world's fate beside the Spring of Mímir, and the Germanic tribes had "springs of justice" where justice was meted out. Among the Romans, the priestess of Carmentis sang of the newborn child's destiny after drinking from a spring, and likewise the Greek priestess of Apollo at Delphi delivered oracles after drinking from the Castalian Spring. The Greek muses, goddesses of inspiration, were originally nymphs connected with springs.

Finally, the dissolving power of a fountain's water, its chaotic quality, is the typical attribute manifested by both those fountains having the positive potential for sacred cleansing and also those bringing insanity or terrible loss. The Greek term *numpholēptos,* meaning "insane, senseless, beside oneself with fright," is related to the poetic word for water, *numphē.* Similarly, in Germanic folklore the female spirits of certain springs stole children or seduced their human lovers to destruction.

BIBLIOGRAPHY

Jones, Francis T. D. *The Holy Wells of Wales.* Cardiff, 1954.

Kristensen, W. Brede. *The Meaning of Religion.* The Hague, 1960.

New Sources

Angelini, Pietro. "La fontana della giovinezza." *Parolechiave* 27 (2002): 175–182.

Bouke van der Meer, L. "*Flere* sur un miroir et sur une pierre de Fonte alla Ripa (Arezzo). Réflexions sur le culte des eaux en Etrurie." In *L'eau et le feu dans les religions antiques,* edited bt Gérard Capdeville, pp. 133–147. Paris, 2004. Useful bibliography on the cult of water in ancient Tuscany.

Caulier, Br. *L'eau et le sacré. Les cultes thérapeutiques autour des fontaines de France du Moyen Age à nos jours.* Paris, 1990.

Cocchiara, Giuseppe. "La Fontana della vita. Echi del simbolismo acquatico nella novellistica popolare." In *Il paese di cuccagna e altri studi di folklore,* pp. 126–158. Turin, 1956.

Hopkins, E. W. "The Fountain of Youth." *Journal of the American Oriental Society* 26 (1905): 1–67.

Lurker, Manfred. "Brunnen und Quelle." In *Wörterbuch der Symbolik.* Stuttgart, 1983, pp. 106–107.

Vaillat, C. *Le culte des sources dans la Gaule antique.* Paris, 1932.

Wadell, M. B. *Fons pietatis.* Göteborg, Sweden, 1969.

RICHARD W. THURN (1987)
Revised Bibliography

FOUR NOBLE TRUTHS.

All strands of the Buddhist tradition recognize in the four noble truths (Skt., *catvāry āryasatyānī;* Pali, *cattāri ariyasaccāni*) one of the earliest formulations of the salvific insight gained by the Buddha on the occasion of his enlightenment. For the Theravāda tradition, the discourse on the four truths constitutes part of the first sermon of the Buddha, the *Dhammacakkappavattana Sutta,* delivered in the Deer Park near Banaras to his five original disciples. The standard formulaic enumeration of the four truths as found in this discourse is as follows:

> This, monks, is the noble truth of *dukkha* ["suffering"]: birth is *dukkha,* old age is *dukkha,* disease is *dukkha,* dying is *dukkha,* association with what is not dear is *dukkha,* separation from what is dear is *dukkha,* not getting that which is wished for is *dukkha;* in brief, the five groups of grasping [i. e., the five *khandhas*; Skt., *skandhas*] are *dukkha.* And this, monks, is the noble truth of the uprising [*samudaya*] of *dukkha:* this craving, which is characterized by repeated existence, accompanied by passion for joys, delighting in this and that; that is to say, craving for sensual desires, craving for existence, craving for cessation of existence. And this, monks, is the noble truth of the cessation [*nirodha*] of *dukkha:* complete dispassion and cessation of craving, abandonment, rejection, release of it, without attachment to it. And this, monks, is the noble truth of the path [*magga*] leading to the cessation of *dukkha;* just this Noble Eightfold Way; that is to say, proper view, proper intention, proper speech, proper action, proper livelihood, proper effort, proper mindfulness, proper concentration. (*Saṃyutta Nikāya* 5.420ff.)

These four noble truths (formulaically, *dukkha, samudaya, nirodha, magga*) constitute a "middle way" between rigorous asceticism and sensual indulgence. The twin foci of truths are craving (Skt., *tṛṣṇā;* Pali, *taṇhā*) and ignorance (*avidyā*), craving to hold that which is impermanent, grasping for substantiality where there is no abiding substance, and not knowing that this orientation inevitably yields unsatisfactoriness (Pali, *dukkha;* Skt., *duḥkha*). Hence the twin foci draw attention to the fundamental cause (*samudaya*) of *dukkha,* and meditation on *dukkha* leads to a discernment that craving and ignorance are its matrix.

The eightfold path, the fourth of the four noble truths, provides a means especially adapted to lead one into salvific insight, a way conforming completely to the Buddha's own salvific realization. In this sense, the eightfold path is the proper mode of religious living, one that subsumes ethics into soteriology.

Although some uncertainty remains among scholars as to whether the passage quoted above indeed represents the earliest formulation of the Buddha's teaching, in the early phase of the Buddhist tradition in India (the so-called Hīnayāna phase) the four noble truths played a major role in shaping the fundamental orientation to religious living on the part of Buddhists. Early Buddhist schools in India differed in their interpretations of the four noble truths, but uniformly regarded its underlying thematic structure as one informed by metaphors of healing: symptom-disease, diagnosis-cause, elimination of cause, treatment or remedy. With the rise of the Mahāyāna tradition the four noble truths became less central as a fundamental statement of the life situation and one's mode of engagement in a soteriological process, but continued to be revered as a fundamental part of the Buddha's early teachings.

THERAVĀDA INTERPRETATIONS. The Theravāda Buddhist tradition is prevalent in contemporary Sri Lanka, Myanmar, and Thailand. For at least two millennia it has regarded the four truths as constitutive of its central soteriological doctrine. As a result, considerable effort has been expended in the tradition on its exegesis. In an extended discussion on the four noble truths, Buddhaghosa, in his fifth century CE classic, *Visuddhimagga* (The path of purity), comments at one point on the meaning of the term *sacca* ("truth"):

> For those who examine [truth] closely with the eye of salvific wisdom [*paññā*], it is not distorted, like an illusion, equivocated, like a mirage, and of an undiscoverable inherent nature, like the self among sectarians, but, rather, it is the pasture of noble gnosis [*ñāṇa*] by means of its actual, undistorted, authentic condition. Just like [the characteristics of] fire, like the nature of the world, the actual undistorted, authentic condition is to be understood as the meaning of truth. (*Visuddhimagga* 16.24)

Among the many interpretations offered by Buddhaghosa for the existence of four, and only four, truths is the Buddha's realization that the evolution of suffering, its cause, the devolution of suffering, and *its* cause are fully comprehensive of an analysis of the human condition and the way to liberation through it. (See *Visuddhimagga* 16.27.) Other analyses of the four truths suggest that the first Truth relates to the basis of craving; the second, to craving itself; the third, to the cessation of craving; and the fourth, to the means to the cessation of craving. Similarly, the truths may be viewed as pertaining, respectively, to the sense of attachment, delight in attachment, removal of attachment, and the means to the removal of attachment. (See *Visuddhimagga* 16.27–28.) According to the *Dhammacakkappavattana Sutta,* the practitioner is to cultivate a fourfold awareness of the four truths in which *dukkha* is to be fully understood; the origin of *dukkha,* abandoned; *nirodha,* realized; and *magga,* cultivated. The Theravāda commentarial tradition has maintained that the soteriological moment arises in the simultaneity of this fourfold awareness. (See *Visuddhimagga* 22.92.)

Although the tradition continued to elaborate analyses of the four truths arranged according to various numerical configurations (most frequently with the number sixteen), it has held to the conviction that when the truths are fully penetrated and soteriologically known it is by one knowledge, through a single penetration, and at one instant. This knowledge of the four truths, they aver, is in and of itself salvific.

The Theravāda has continued to interpret the Eightfold Path as comprising three basic elements deemed integral to religious living at its fullest: *sīla* (Skt., *śīla*), or moral virtue; *samādhi,* or meditative concentration; and *paññā* (Skt., *prajṇā*), or salvific wisdom. Proper view and intention are classed as salvific wisdom; proper speech, action, and livelihood are classed as expressions of moral virtue; and proper effort, mindfulness, and concentration are classed as forms of meditative concentration.

Finally, the tradition has utilized the notion of "emptiness" (Pali, *suññatā;* Skt., *śūnyatā*) in the analysis of the four noble truths. Buddhaghosa wrote:

> In the highest sense, all the truths are to be understood as empty because of the absence of an experiencer, a doer, someone extinguished, and a goer. Hence this is said:
>
> For there is only suffering, no one who suffers,
> No doer, only the doing is found,
> Extinction there is, no extinguished man,
> There is the path, no goer is found.
>
> Or alternatively,
>
> The first pair are empty
> Of stableness, beauty, pleasure, self;
> Empty of self is the deathless state.
> Without stableness, pleasure, self is the path.
> Such, regarding them, is emptiness. (*Visuddhimagga* 16.90)

MAHĀYĀNA INTERPRETATIONS. Although the Theravāda tradition applied the notion of "emptiness" in negating permanence, abiding happiness, and substantiality as legitimate descriptions of sentient life, it is within the Mahāyāna that one finds emptiness as a designation of reality in the highest sense. As part of the general critique of "substantiality" carried out by the Prajṇāpāramitā literature, even the four truths are declared void of real existence. In this analysis, suffering, the origin of suffering, the cessation of suffering, and the path to the cessation of suffering are themselves "empty."

In the *Saddharmapuṇḍarika Sūtra (Lotus Sūtra),* the old standard formulas of the epithets of the Buddha and characteristics of *dharma* are repeated for the Tathāgata Candrasūryapradīpa and his preaching, but the four noble truths are only mentioned by title—there is no elaboration. The *Saddharmapuṇḍarika* proclaims that such teaching is taken up and absorbed into the one comprehensive and central soteriological message (i.e., the "single vehicle"; *ekayāna*) of the sūtra.

Although the four noble truths are not featured in their earlier formulation in many Mahāyāna texts, the basic theme nonetheless persists: Life is awry, craving and ignorance are the cause, one's life can be changed, and a way or means that brings this about is available. For example, the verse text of Śāntideva's *Bodhicaryāvatāra* does not contain the complete formula of the four noble truths. Prajṇākaramati, a commentator on this great text, even points to the one verse (chap. 9, verse 41) where he finds a contrast clearly presented between the four noble truths and the "teaching of emptiness." Yet even though a fundamental shift in the understanding of the path to liberation has taken place in this and other Mahāyāna texts, the underlying assessment as to the cause of suffering, that is, the basic thematic structure of the four truths, remains unchanged.

In the *Madhyamakakārikā,* Nāgārjuna provides an incisive, penetrating analysis of the four noble truths. He maintains that *duḥkha,* which evolves from the interplay of the constituents of individuality and the objects of perception, can no longer be seen as having any fundamental ontological status, even in *saṃsāra,* the fleeting "whirl" of repeated existence. The same is true, for that matter, of *saṃsāra* itself, or even of *nirvāṇa:* All is emptiness (*śūnyatā*).

Thus, the older-formulated Eightfold Path, which provided the remedy for the disease (*duḥkha*) of undisciplined and uninformed human existence, yielded with this shift in worldview to another formulation of the soteriological process, to another religious orientation that is also to be cultivated—the *bodhisattva* path. Although the ontological interpretation of the four noble truths underwent change in the cumulative development of the Buddhist tradition, as in the case of the great Chinese Buddhist thinker Zhiyi (538–597), the fundamental theme that the inadequacy of human life results from craving and ignorance, which can be eradicated by following the path to enlightenment taught by the Buddha, has continued.

SEE ALSO Eightfold Path; Soteriology.

BIBLIOGRAPHY

The text of the *Dhammacakkappavattana Sutta* is available in English translation in *Saṃyutta Nikāya: The Book of Kindred Sayings* (1917–1930), translated by C. A. F. Rhys Davids and F. L. Woodward (London, 1950–1956). For the *Visuddhimagga,* see the reliable translation by Bhikku Ñyāṇamoli, *The Path of Purification,* 2d ed. (Colombo, 1964). A related text, Upatissa's *Vimuttimagga,* has been translated from the Chinese as *The Path of Freedom* by N. R. M. Ehara, Soma Thera, and Kheminda Thera (Kandy, 1977). For an overview and analysis of the four truths from a Theravāda perspective, see Walpola Rahula's *What the Buddha Taught,* rev. ed. (New York, 1974).

New Sources

Anderson, Carol S. *Pain and Its Ending: The Four Noble Truths in the Theravāda Buddhist Canon.* Richmond, Va., 1999.

Eckel, Malcolm David, and John Thatamanil. "Beginningless Ignorance: A Buddhist View of the Human Condition." In *Human Condition,* edited by Robert Cummings Neville, pp. 50–71. Albany, 2001.

Norman, K. R. "Why are the Four Noble Truths called 'Noble'?" In *Ananda: Papers on Buddhism and Indology: A Felicitation Volume Presented to Ananda Weihena Palliya Guruge on his Sixtieth Birthday,* edited by Y. Karunadasa, pp. 11–13. Columbo, 1990.

Pereira, Jose. "The Four Noble Truths in Vasubandhu." *Buddhist Heritage in India and Abroad,* edited by G. Kuppuram and K. Kumudamani, pp. 129–142. Delhi, 1992.

Skilling, Peter. "A Buddhist Verse Inscription from Andhra Pradesh." *Indo-Iranian Journal* 34 (1991): 239–246.

JOHN ROSS CARTER (1987)
Revised Bibliography

FOX, GEORGE

FOX, GEORGE (1624–1691), was the chief founder and early leader of the Quakers, a popular movement without clergy, ritual, or sacraments, gathered from among English Puritan Separatists. Despite frequent imprisonments, he traveled throughout Britain, North America, and northern Europe, calling hearers to experience directly the Spirit of God, met as "the Light of Christ" or "Truth" within each person. Those who were open and obedient to the Light he called upon to gather as "Children of Light" and to bear witness to God's power, which was to conquer the world without outward violence in "the Lamb's War." Fox also gave structure to gatherings, or Meetings of Friends, and wrote 270 tracts and 400 "epistles."

Fox was the son of a Puritan weaver of Fenny Drayton in Leicestershire. As a young man he was apprenticed as a cobbler and shepherd; his sensitivity to temptations caused him intense strain, which in 1643 drove him away from his family and then from a series of prominent Puritan clergy and congregations whom he had sought out in the Midlands and in London. By contacts with Separatist and Baptist groups, and perhaps also among Ranters and Familists, he acquired beliefs about the inward nature of heaven, the Last Judgment, the sacraments, and Christ's "heavenly body." He experienced in 1646 and 1647 a series of "openings," or insights, into the Bible, much of which he knew by heart: namely, that true ministers are not made at universities; that Christ within "can speak to thy condition"; that Christ too experienced and conquered temptation; that the source of temptation is the evil within human hearts. Notably, Fox saw evil in his own heart, where "there was an ocean of darkness and death, but an infinite ocean of light and love, which flowed over the ocean of darkness."

Having faced his dark impulses, he called others to "the witness of God within them," which would "judge and guide them"—not into a vicarious righteousness but into a total purging and obedience. When he began preaching in the Midlands he was jailed at Derby in 1650–1651 for blasphemy, having glimpsed perfect holiness as he "was come up in spirit through the flaming sword into the paradise of God." He refused a captaincy in Oliver Cromwell's army, because he "lived in the virtue of that life and power that took away the occasion of all wars." In 1651 he preached through northern Yorkshire, winning his chief colleagues, Nayler, Dewsbury, Farnworth, and Aldam. In 1652 he went northwest by way of Pendle Hill, where he had a vision of "a great people to be gathered," and he went on to win to his cause several groups of Separatists who met on Firbank Fell and in villages around the English Lake District. Swarthmoor Hall, home of Margaret Fell and her family, became the center for a mass movement throughout the poorly served moorland parishes of Westmorland and Cumberland, despite jailings and mob violence in several towns. In 1654, a "valiant sixty" of the newly won Quaker men and women, mainly yeomen farmers, spread out on foot throughout Britain as "publishers of Truth," announcing "the Day of the Lord."

Fox recalled them that winter to plan their further work and to have them agree to report their travels to Swarthmoor. In 1655 Fox was sent as a prisoner to London, which had already become a Quaker center through casual contacts and earlier missions. Freed by Oliver Cromwell, Fox talked sympathetically with him, attempting without success to persuade him to end the parish system.

While traveling through southern England to Lands End, Fox was jailed in Launceston's "Doomsdale" dungeon for a harsh winter, during which his colleague James Nayler let some women disciples stir up a breach between the two leaders and stage in Nayler's honor a reenactment of Palm Sunday at Bristol. Nayler was tried for blasphemy before Parliament and savagely punished, but this episode, offending England's growing conservatism from 1656 through 1658, cast a shadow over the Quakers. To rally them, Fox encouraged older Quakers to visit the struggling meetings already gathered for weekly worship in silence, while younger Friends carried the Quaker message overseas to Ireland, continental Europe, and the American colonies. Fox was mainly near London as the Puritan Commonwealth fell apart, and he went through weeks of doubt and exhaustion when the Quakers were asked by a radical Puritan government to provide Commissioners of Militia to protect twenty years' gains in justice and freedom. Fox's warning against reliance on arms became a standard to which Quakers could point after the returning Royalists in 1660 accused Friends of plotting rebellion against Charles II. Fox also organized weekly meetings of Quaker men and women leaders in London and wrote piecemeal his only long theological book, *The Great Mistery* (1659). Between and after two more long imprisonments for refusing the Oath of Allegiance (and all oaths) and defying the 1664 Conventicle Act, Fox again visited Quaker meetings throughout England and Ireland to set up a network of men's and women's monthly and quarterly meetings for local groups and for counties. At Bristol on October 17, 1669, he married Margaret Fell, eleven years a widow; though his letters to her were curiously formal, he began to express to her the affection and humor others had loved in him.

After the 1670 Second Conventicle Act, when Fox and thousands of "Nonconformists" to the Anglican church were again arrested, the Indulgence of 1672 freed him to sail with twelve other Quakers to visit Quaker groups in the American colonies. They proclaimed their Christian orthodoxy to the governor of Barbados and gathered into regular meetings the Friends of Jamaica and Chesapeake Bay and later those in New England and Virginia. Guided by Indians through the forests of New Jersey, Fox would urge Quakers to colonize there in 1675. Returning to England in June 1673, Fox was again imprisoned and seriously ill at Worcester in December. Later, recovering his health slowly at Swarthmoor Hall, Fox dictated to Margaret's son-in-law Thomas Lower the text of his *Journal.* In 1677 Fox traveled with William Penn and Robert Barclay to visit small Quaker groups in Holland and northwestern Germany. Fox revisited Holland in 1684 but spent most of his last years in or near London, where he died on January 13, 1691. Penn witnessed that "abruptly and brokenly as sometimes his sentences would fall from him . . . it showed that God had sent him, that he had nothing of man's wit or wisdom, so that he was an original, being no man's copy. He had an extraordinary gift in opening the Scriptures. But above all the most awful, living, reverent frame was his in prayer."

Bibliography

Works by Fox

A Battle-Dor for Teachers and Professors to Learn Singular and Plural (1660). Written with John Stubs and Benjamin Furly. Reprint, Menston, England, 1968. Shows that "thee & thou," as used by Quakers to all individuals, was true grammar in forty languages.

Catechism. London, 1657. Lessons for children.

Doctrinals (originally, *Gospel Truth Demonstrated*). London, 1706. Ninety-nine of his 52 previously printed tracts.

Epistles. London, 1698. Four hundred letters, twenty-nine previously printed.

George Fox's Book of Miracles. Cambridge, U.K., 1973. Henry Cadbury's careful reconstruction of a lost Fox manuscript.

The Great Mistery of the Great Whore Unfolded. London, 1659. Refutes anti-Quaker tracts by Puritans, Baptists, and others.

Journal. Edited by Thomas Ellwood, with a preface by William Penn. London, 1694. Repeatedly reprinted in abridged form with prefaces by Rufus Jones, Henry Cadbury, et al.; currently available from Friends United Press (Richmond, Ind., 1983).

The Works of George Fox. 8 vols. Philadelphia, 1831. Reproduces first editions of Fox's works uncritically.

Works about Fox

Bensen, Lewis. *Catholic Quakerism.* Philadelphia, 1968. Presents Fox's ethic.

Braithwaite, William C. *The Beginnings of Quakerism* (1912). Rev. ed. Cambridge, U.K., 1955. Presents historical facts and settings of Fox's life.

Braithwaite, William C. *The Second Period of Quakerism* (1919). Revised by Henry Cadbury. Cambridge, U.K., 1961.

HUGH BARBOUR (1987)

FOXES. The fox has enjoyed immense popularity as a character in the fables of many cultures, from those of Aesop to those of "Uncle Remus" to Leoš Janáček's opera *The Cunning Little Vixen.* It was once believed in Wales and Germany that witches assume the form of foxes. In fact, foxes were sometimes burned in the midsummer fires.

In the mythology of the North American Indians the fox as a male animal character is well known for its craftiness and slyness. Especially among the California Indians the fox plays a prominent role in trickster and other tales. In many instances Fox is a trickster's companion, and at times he deceives Coyote and eats the food that Coyote has procured for himself. The fox also appears as a female animal in a cycle of fox tales widespread among the North American Indians. A poor man, living alone, comes home at night to find his house in order and his dinner on the fire. He discovers that every morning a vixen comes to his hut, sheds her skin, and becomes a woman. Having stolen the skin, he makes her his wife. They live in happiness for many years until she discovers the skin, puts it on, and runs away. This scenario of the "mysterious housekeeper" is also found among the Inuit (Eskimo) in Greenland and Labrador, as well as among the Koriak of northeastern Siberia.

In Inner Asia, among the Buriats, the fox is known as a guide to the land of the dead; when the hero Mumonto lifts up a large black stone and shouts "Come here," a fox appears in the opening under the stone and says, "Hold fast to my tail."

Chinese folklore is rich in the motif of the fox who transforms itself into an attractive woman and seduces young men. Foxes are capable of this transformation through the study of Chinese classics or through erotic tricks. Foxes who study the classics acquire first the power to become humans, then immortals, and finally gods. In many stories, young foxes are depicted as sitting in a circle, listening to an old white fox at the center expounding the classics. Foxes can assume human form, if at first only briefly, through the absorption and accumulation of the *semen virile* of a male sex partner; by seducing humans, usually young men, foxes steal life essence and add it to their own. For example, an ambitious young man who has retired to a deserted cottage or temple to prepare for the state examinations is visited at dusk by a beautiful young woman who becomes his mistress. Her erotic skill is such that he becomes exhausted and dies. Fox-women sometimes sincerely love their human paramours and help them with their studies, but they seldom return the life essence they have stolen. Occasionally, the parents or friends become aware of the situation in time and call in either a shaman or a Faoist specially trained in fox exorcism and drive her away.

Folk belief in the fox is still alive in Japan; the fox is considered to be most skillful of animals in transforming itself into human form, often female. It is feared as a wicked animal that haunts and possesses people. But, at the same time, the fox is respected as the messenger of *inari,* the beneficent rice goddess Uka no Mitama, of Shintō religion.

Bibliography

On the fox in the East Asian spiritual world, there is much useful material in Marinus W. de Visser's "The Fox and the Badger in Japanese Folklore," *Transactions of Asiatic Society of Japan* 36, pt. 3 (1908): 1–159. Gudmund Hatt discusses the fox as a mysterious housekeeper in his *Asiatic Influences in American Folklore* (Copenhagen, 1949), pp. 96ff.

New Sources

Baird, Merrily. "Land and Sea Animals." In *Symbols of Japan: Thematic Motifs in Art and Design.* New York, 2001.

Berlin, Isaiah. *The Hedgehog and the Fox: An Essay on Tolstoy's View of History.* New York, 1953; reprint, New York, 1993.

Blust, Robert. "The Fox's Wandering." *Anthropos* 94 (1999): 487–499.

Huntington, Rania. "Foxes and Sex in Late Imperial Chinese Narrative." *Nan Nü* 2 (2000): 78–128.

Manabu Waida (1987)
Revised Bibliography

FRANCISCANS is the common designation for a number of religious communities professing to live according to the ideals of Francis of Assisi (1181/1182–1226). In 1206 Francis withdrew to the margins of society to adopt the life of a penitent hermit. His vocation received a decisive focus in 1208, when others joined him and he was inspired to "live according to the pattern of the Holy Gospel," as he called it, "following the footsteps and teaching of our Lord Jesus Christ" (*Testament,* 14; *Earlier Rule,* 1.1 [*Francis of Assisi: Early Documents,* I: 63-64, 125]). Within Francis's lifetime his followers organized into three distinct but related orders: his own Lesser Brothers; communities of contemplative women under the leadership of Clare of Assisi (d. 1253), known now as Poor Clare nuns; and the Brothers and Sisters of Penance, laypersons who wished to remain in the midst of society, later commonly known as the Third Order. Although they differed in their manner of expression, all were based on Francis's vision of a gospel way of life. The concrete implications of this vision have often led to bitter internal dissension over the course of Franciscan history.

The Order of Lesser Brothers (the literal meaning of Ordo Fratrum Minorum, commonly translated as Friars Minor) began as a largely lay movement of hermits and itinerant preachers. They lived on a mere subsistence level, without any permanent residences, supporting themselves by whatever trade they knew or by begging. Despite the radical nature of this way of life, Francis and his companions received initial papal approbation in 1209/1210. However, the new order underwent a rapid transformation over the ensuing decades. First of all, its phenomenal growth—by 1221 there were about three thousand brothers—demanded greater internal discipline and organization. At the same time the papacy recognized in the movement a potent instrument of church reform and increasingly intervened to oversee and channel its growth. Cardinal Hugolino di Segni, later Pope Gregory IX, played an important role in these developments. Historians have long debated Francis's own attitude toward this process, already evident in the definitive 1223 version of his rule. In any event by midcentury the friars were primarily engaged in the official pastoral ministry of the church, especially preaching and hearing confessions. The friars increasingly abandoned their hermitages to settle down in urban residences attached to a church, where they adopted more traditional patterns of religious life and pursued theological studies. In light of the new demands placed upon them, the brothers' rigorous observance of poverty was relaxed by several papal interventions. The houses of the order at such academic centers as Paris and Oxford soon produced some of the greatest masters of Scholastic theology, such as Bonaventure, John Duns Scotus, and William of Ockham.

Within the order, however, there was a significant resistance to these new directions. Toward the end of the thirteenth century, various minority factions, known collectively as Spirituals, demanded a literal observance of the rule and refused to submit to the modifications accepted by the majority of friars. The increasingly bitter internal conflict eventually led to the outright persecution of the Spirituals, culminating in a decision by John XXII in 1323 to brand as heretical the opinion that Christ and his apostles had led a life of absolute poverty. The Friars Minor thus gradually conformed to the practice of common ownership of property that was standard among other religious orders.

During the latter part of the fourteenth century, however, a reaction set in, with small groups of friars receiving permission to retire to remote houses to observe a more primitive form of Franciscan life. This movement, known as the Observant reform, gained momentum in the next century under such leaders as Bernardino of Siena, ultimately achieving virtual autonomy within the order. Nevertheless, relations between those friars who accepted this reform and those who did not, known as Conventuals (from the *conventi,* or large houses, they favored), grew increasingly acrimonious, leading Leo X in 1517 to divide the order into two independent congregations.

Over the course of the sixteenth century, the contemporary zeal for church reform continued to spawn new movements within the order, motivated by the desire for even stricter forms of Franciscan life. The largest of these, the Capuchins, so called because of the distinctive hood (*cappuccino*) of their habit, played a prominent role during the Counter-Reformation as popular preachers; they achieved the status of an independent congregation in 1619. Other groups of stricter observance—Discalced, Recollect, and Reformed friars—attained a large measure of autonomy while remaining under the leadership of the Observant general. Despite this fragmentation, the Friars Minor prospered between 1500 and 1750, a period that also witnessed a vast missionary effort by Franciscans, who accompanied Spanish, Portuguese, and French colonial expansion. By 1760 the Friars Minor had reached their peak membership, totaling 135,000 in their three branches.

Franciscans, especially the Conventuals, suffered greatly during the years 1760–1880, when secularizing government policies in Europe and Latin America restricted traditional religious orders. However, in the latter part of the nineteenth century a revival took place, accompanied by critical research into early Franciscan sources. Also, under papal initiative, the various groups within the Observant branch were reunited in 1897 under the simple name of the Order of Friars Minor. After 1965, Franciscans experienced a period of profound renewal and transition in the wake of the Second Vatican Council, which emphasized a return to the founding vision of Francis. In 2002 there were 16,300 Friars Minor, 10,800 Capuchins, and 4,500 Conventuals. There is also a small community of friars, the Society of Saint Francis, in the Anglican Church.

The Poor Clares, sometimes referred to as the Second Order, date from 1212, when Clare, of a noble Assisi family, renounced her social status and received the habit from Francis. Under his direction, Clare and her companions followed a simple form of life, but Cardinal Hugolino intervened in 1219, prescribing regulations that emphasized monastic observances, such as a strict cloister. Clare managed to gain approval for her own rule embodying her vision of poverty in 1253. Because each monastery of Poor Clares is largely autonomous, practices have varied greatly. A reform, analogous to the Observance among the friars, was begun by Colette of Corbie in the fourteenth century. In 2002 there were more than eight hundred monasteries of Poor Clares with fourteen thousand nuns.

Francis can be called the founder of the Brothers and Sisters of Penance, or Third Order, only in an analogous sense. His preaching of gospel conversion moved many of his hearers to reform their lives, and so he sought to prescribe for these individuals a way of life appropriate to their respective social conditions. Some became hermits, whereas others continued to live in their own homes but formed confraternities for mutual support. Rules for these local groups were developed in 1221; the fraternities developed closer relations with the friars over the course of the century. This Order of Penance was characterized by a simple way of life, engaging in works of charity, and the refusal to bear arms. The tertiaries were a potent religious and social force in late medieval society. In the latter part of the thirteenth century, some of these Franciscan penitents began living together in communities, eventually binding themselves under religious vows. The rule of this Third Order Regular received definitive form in 1521. During the nineteenth century there was a veritable explosion of congregations of women following this rule devoted to teaching, nursing, and other charitable activities. In 2002 there were over 450 distinct congregations of Franciscan sisters, with approximately 100,000 members and about 1,500 male members of the Third Order Regular. Meanwhile, the secular Franciscan fraternities continued to expand, but their countercultural way of life increasingly conformed outwardly to general societal norms; they numbered over one million in 2002. After Vatican II both branches of the Third Order revised their rule of life, attempting to return more closely to their original inspiration.

See Also Francis of Assisi.

BIBLIOGRAPHY

A general survey of the entire Franciscan movement is Lázaro Iriarte de Aspurz, *Franciscan History: The Three Orders of St. Francis of Assisi* (Chicago, 1982). For the medieval period, John R. H. Moorman, *A History of the Franciscan Order: From Its Origins to the Year 1517* (Oxford, 1968) is valuable. However, research during the late twentieth century significantly nuanced the understanding of early Franciscan history. The biographical sources on Francis, valuable for the understanding of the early movement, have been gathered in *Francis of Assisi: Early Documents*, ed. Regis J. Armstrong, J. A. Wayne Hellmann, and William J. Short, three volumes (New York, 1999–2001. A good summary is Maria Pia Alberzoni et al., *Francesco d'Assisi e il primo secolo di storia francescana* (Turin, Italy, 1997). David Burr, *The Spiritual Franciscans: From Protest to Persecution in the Century after Saint Francis* (University Park, Pa., 2001), provides an excellent survey of that movement. Maurice Carmody, *The Leonine Union of the Order of Friars Minor, 1897* (St. Bonaventure, N.Y., 1994), presents the nineteenth-century revival. The best introduction to the Third Order Regular women's congregations is Raffaele Pazzelli, *The Franciscan Sisters: Outlines of History and Spirituality* (Steubenville, Ohio, 1993).

DOMINIC V. MONTI (1987 AND 2005)

FRANCIS OF ASSISI (Giovanni Francesco Bernardone, 1181/2–1226) was a Christian saint and the founder of the Franciscans. John was Francis's baptismal name, but a fondness for France on the part of his merchant father and an acknowledgment of the national origin of his mother prompted the parents to call him Francis. Endowed with a jovial disposition and the means to pamper it, Francis enjoyed the good life of his times; this life was, however, interrupted when his hometown warred with neighboring Perugia. Inducted, imprisoned, and then released, Francis returned home with his military ambitions dampened. A business career with his father held no attraction.

Francis's conversion was the culmination of a period of prayerful reflection in a local grotto, an encounter with a leper, an invitation from God to repair Assisi's abandoned chapel of San Damiano, and Francis's study of *Matthew* 10, which imparted to him a sense of irreversible dedication to the kingdom of God. Within a few months (by April 1208) others asked to share his life, and thus a brotherhood was born.

In 1209 Francis journeyed to Rome to seek papal approval for the brotherhood. After some hesitation, Innocent III gave verbal assent to the rule authored by Francis, who then returned to Assisi and remained at the chapel of the Portiuncula; from there the brothers, two by two, preached gospel renewal. Intent on extending this preaching, Francis departed for Syria, but bad weather hampered the venture. Later a more successful journey took him to meet the sultan in Damietta. In 1212 Francis offered the religious habit to the young noblewoman Clare, and quickly other young women from Assisi sought to share her way of life at San Damiano, forming the order known as the Poor Clares. In 1215 the Fourth Lateran Council promulgated reforms championed in his preaching.

In 1220 Francis resigned his post as head of the Franciscans. Still, with more than five thousand brothers, his involvement continued. After reworking his rule, Francis submitted it to Pope Honorius III in 1223, and it received written approval. That same year Francis presented a living Christmas crèche at Greccio, which encouraged the popularity of that custom in subsequent centuries. At Alverna he received the stigmata (the wounds of Christ crucified), thereby reflecting outwardly that which he interiorly imitated.

Though suffering serious illness in his last years, Francis composed his intensely joyful "Canticle of Brother Sun." The closing strophe addresses "Sister Death," whom he welcomed on October 3, 1226. Within two years Francis was proclaimed a saint. In 1939 he was officially offered to Italy as its patron; in 1979 he was recognized by Pope John Paul II as the patron saint of ecology.

As Francis's brotherhood increased in size, his work encompassed the nurturing of followers including the Poor Clares and the Secular Franciscans (laymen and -women who wished to follow Francis). Franciscans were not committed to one particular work but engaged in whatever labors their travel and presence brought them. Francis's work and thought indicate a living, ecclesial faith that seeks to be for and with the poor.

Central to every aspect of his life was Francis's experience of the trinitarian God. He wanted to reveal the Father to all by imitating the Son through the inspiration of the Holy Spirit. Like his Lord, he was eager to make his way back to the Father and to summon all creation to accompany him on that painful but peaceful journey. An adult innocence aided him in transcending the spirit-matter dichotomy, making him a sublime example of both the spirituality of matter and the materialization of spirit.

Francis embraced voluntary poverty because he wanted to imitate his Lord, who had made himself poor (*2 Cor.* 8:9). In this poverty Francis found a freedom that fostered fraternity. The poor, in their more evident dependence on God, reminded Francis of the mystery of divine sympathy and of each creature's intrinsic poverty. In the spirit of poverty he urged his brothers to renounce their desire to dominate, and though called to minister to all, to favor labor among the lepers and farmhands.

Aware that the Roman Catholic church was capable of taming the gospel, Francis persisted in the belief that Christ was to be found in this institution, especially in the Eucharist. He sought a cardinal protector for the Franciscan order and acknowledged the pontiff to be the final arbiter in spiritual matters. Although Francis's relations with the Curia Romana may have weakened his project, the majority of scholars submit that his relation to the hierarchy was loyal, challenging, and constructive.

Movements for peace and for the marginalized have in Francis a ready patron. He sent his brothers out, not against but among the Saracens, and he required that all his followers (lay included) not bear arms. His pursuit of Lady Poverty inspires those of every age who seek simplicity. His fondness for animals and nature has deepened humanity's understanding of the interrelatedness of all creation grounded in a creator whose richness it reflects.

Francis managed to steer a course that avoided the excesses of feudal authority and of the bourgeois pursuit of money. In his rule he taught his followers to use only that which was needed, to own nothing, and to renounce any desire to dominate; he insisted that authority for the *minores* (those who wished to lead a biblically inspired simple life) meant fraternal service. The church, although initially cautious, soon adopted some of his insights for its own apostolic strategy; between 1218 and 1226 six papal bulls were issued relating to aspects of his vision. The Holy See recognized that the manner of his preaching touched the lives of the people; it also gave the vernacular a new respectability and provided themes for artists such as Cimabue and Giotto. Though no intellectual, Francis's emphasis on humanity inspired the deeply incarnational systems of Bonaventure and of Duns Scotus.

Francis's legacy to the Christian tradition was a revitalized gospel that clearly perceived many forms of brotherhood: with superiors—once, having been denied by a bishop the right to preach in his diocese, Francis exited, paused, reentered, and resubmitted his petition successfully; with strangers—in his rule of 1221 he calls for a simple, nonpolemical style of missionary presence; with the underclass—when a brother asked if it were proper to feed some robbers, he responded affirmatively, for in every person he saw a possible thief and in every thief a possible brother or sister; with nature—he urged his brothers when establishing the boundaries of their shelters not to build walls but to plant hedges. The movement founded by Francis offered the church a new form of gospel commitment. It combined a contemplative life with an apostolic work that was mobile, diverse, and urban. Although it was a consecrated life, it was not removed from daily concerns.

See Also Franciscans.

Bibliography

Kajetan Esser, the scholar most responsible for the critical texts of Francis's writings, discusses 181 manuscripts in his *Opuscula Sancti Francisci Assisiensis* (Rome, 1978) and his *Rule and Testament of St. Francis* (Chicago, 1977). The excellent *Francis and Clare: The Complete Works* (New York, 1982), edited by Regis J. Armstrong and Ignatius Brady, offers a list for the first time in English of Francis's authentic writings (twenty-eight in all) and inauthentic writings (including the popular "Peace Prayer"). The most practical single volume for primary sources remains *St. Francis of Assisi: Writings and Early Biographies, English Omnibus of the Sources* (Chicago, 1973), edited by Marion A. Habig. It includes lives of Francis by Celano and by Bonaventure, *The Little Flowers of Saint Francis* (a treasure of fourteenth-century popular literature), and an extensive bibliography, though not always reliably translated. Classic biographies include Omer Englebert's astute *Saint Francis of Assisi* (Chicago, 1965), and Father Cuthbert of Brighton's accurate *Life of St. Francis of Assisi* (London, 1912). Paul Sabatier's *Life of St. Francis of Assisi* (London, 1894) is provocative. Of the more than sixty modern biographies, G. K. Chesterton in *St. Francis of Assisi* (London, 1923) captures his heart and Nikos Kazantzakis in *Saint Francis: A Novel* (New York, 1962) presents a poet. A former mayor of Assisi, Arnaldo Fortini, in his *Francis of Assisi* (New York, 1981), offers an invaluable historical appendix. Anglican bishop J. R. H. Moorman presents, in his new edition of *Saint Francis of Assisi* (London, 1976), a precise historical life. Leonardo Boff characterizes Francis, in *Saint Francis* (New York, 1982), as a model for human liberation.

Raymond J. Bucher (1987)

FRANCKE, AUGUST HERMANN (1663–1727),

was, after Spener, the major spokesman for early Lutheran Pietism. Francke was born in the Hanseatic city of Lübeck on March 22, 1663. Both his father and his maternal grandfather were prominent jurists, and young August was more or less expected to take up a learned career. Because the Francke household was pervaded by the piety of Johann Arndt (1555–1621), it was quite natural for August to prepare himself for the Lutheran ministry. Accordingly, he studied at Erfurt and Kiel, and finally received his master of arts degree from the University of Leipzig. For religious reasons he refused further academic preparation, though much of his time continued to be spent in private study. Thus he emerged from his student career superbly prepared not only in philosophy, theology, and biblical studies but with considerable competence in Latin, Greek, Hebrew, Italian, French, and English, besides his native German.

As the result of an experience of a conscious religious awakening (1687), Francke joined the circle of Spener's followers and eventually became the leader of the Spenerian renewal movement of continental Protestantism. The University of Halle, to the faculty of which he was appointed in 1691, quickly became the intellectual center of Lutheran Pietism. His pioneer work in establishing an imposing array of educational and charitable institutions attracted much attention in Europe. His extensive system of connections included a large segment of European nobility as well as several European courts. The periodic reports of his work, such as *Segensvolle Fußstapfen* (translated into English in 1706 under the title *Liber Pietatis Hallensis*), spurred educational, charitable, missionary, and ecumenical impulses not only on the continent but in England and in the English colonies of North America. Under Francke's guidance the Canstein Bible Institute, begun in 1710, satisfied the ever-increasing need for cheap Bibles and devotional aids. The theological works issuing from Francke's pen and from Halle were a major factor in substituting biblical for dogmatic theology and ethically oriented concerns for purely theological discourses in Protestant pulpits. At the zenith of his career Francke was widely respected as an innovative pastor, theologian, educator, organizer of charitable institutions, promoter of domestic and foreign missions, and advocate of a new vision of ecumenical cooperation.

Bibliography

Important for Francke study is still D. Gustav Kramer's *August Hermann Francke,* 2 vols. (Halle, 1880–1882), though dated in many respects. The best biography is the scholarly, very appreciative study by Erich Beyreuther, *August Hermann Francke, 1663–1727* (Marburg, 1956). For Francke's theology, Erhard Peschke's *Studien zur Theologie August Hermann Franckes,* 2 vols. (Berlin, 1964–1966) is indispensable. Peschke also edited a selection of Francke's works titled *Streitschriften* (New York, 1981). Available in English are Gary Stattler's *God's Glory and the Neighbor's Good: A Brief Introduction to the Life and Writings of August Hermann Francke* (Chicago, 1982) and a small selection of Francke's writings in Peter C. Erb's *The Pietists: Selected Writings* (Ramsey, N.J., 1983).

F. Ernest Stoeffler (1987)

FRANK, JACOB. Yakov ben Lev (1726–1791), cynosure of the last large Jewish messiah-event, took the surname Frank at his baptisms in Poland in 1759 and 1760, when he also added the name Joseph and became Jacob Joseph Frank. The surname had become attached to him as an epithet that in Yiddish denoted a Turkish Jew and in Turkish denoted a European Jew. He himself never explained which he was, contenting himself with the ambiguity of the reference. Frank acted out the role of a Jewish messiah in the territory of the Ottoman Empire in Poland and in Bohemia and Germany from about 1750 until he died in a fit in Offenbach, to be succeeded by his daughter, Ewa.

Though Frank presented himself as the inheritor of Shabbetai Tsevi (1626–1676) and Barukhya Russo (d. 1721), his forerunners in this tradition, he did not do so in their urban Turkish environment, nor was his doctrine theirs. Frank defined both of them to his inner circle of disciples, the twelve Brothers and fourteen Sisters, as predecessor messiahs in the tradition of failed messiahs, and he discarded the entire qabbalistic system associated with them and their messianic roles in favor of an original mythology and cult management whose major characteristics were duplicity and a tyrannical authority shrouded in mystery. To the false conversions to Islam of Tsevi and Barukhya in Turkey, Frank added a false conversion to Roman Catholicism in Christian lands. He gave his name to three separate movements known as *Frankist*—the first being a community of Polish Shabbateans who had been adherents of the Dönmeh sect in Salonika into which he inserted himself in Turkey and, thereafter, in Poland; the second, his personal following; and the third in Bohemia, in which he played no active part.

Shortly after his own conversion, the Inquisition had him imprisoned for thirteen years in the fortress shrine of Częstochowa under suspicion of perpetrating a hoax and an attempted insurrection. His closest followers remained faithful to him. While Frank promoted a combination of obedience to himself and disingenuous behavior towards those outside his circle, many of his followers either sought their way back to Judaism or became Christians within his own lifetime, excepting those who had been part of the original company of adherents or who were with him at his courts in Brno and Offenbach after he regained his freedom and left Poland at the time of the Russian invasion in 1773.

In Brno and especially in Offenbach, Frank played the part of a noble maintaining a large court and retinue, and he sought to interfere in European politics in the West and East. Before his conversion he had persuaded Turkish powers that he would bring the Jews to Islam and promote the interests of the Ottoman Empire in Europe, and he had gained government support. After his entry into western lands, he sought, with the same degree of sincerity, to serve the interests of Prussia and Austria. Here his performance achieved greater success. His daughter Ewa served as a social and sexual pawn to attract social prestige, and Frank gained for a time the backing of Joseph II of Austria, among others.

In the intellectual and political society of early modern Europe, Frank was a familiar figure. To enlightened Christians and proselytizing millennialists he was a Jew converted to Christianity and a freethinker typified by mysterious connections and magic and secret riches. He was also seen as a herald of liberation from the oppression of gender, class, regime, religion, and mores, including sexual ones. To some Jews, he augured assimilation, enlightenment, political power, and millennial redemption. To other Jews, especially rabbinic figures, Frank was not just one more in a colorful crew of anomians or antinomians, leaders of the gullible from the time of Jesus through the contemporary movement of Hasidism—he was a catastrophe; the ultimate false messiah; the ruin of hope, faith, and religion; the diabolic climax of that history.

Frank served anti-rabbinic belligerents as their figurehead in two debates (Kamieniec, 1757; Lwów, 1759), though he did not seek these opportunities out; the debates were produced by the Polish Catholic authorities together with the remnants of Shabbatean followings. The theses argued in these debates—the last great public Christian-Jewish disputations, the first concluding with the last major public burning of Jewish books before the modern period—included old themes, such as the falsity of the Hebrew Bible in its rabbinic interpretation, as well as the blood libel and some novelties. The Frankists sought to achieve a separate existence and maintain for themselves many elements of Jewish culture while converting to Christianity and proclaiming the truth of the *Zohar* and its ostensible Trinitarianism. Frank wanted to establish the anti-rabbinic disputants as his own followers and gain a separate and autonomous community. The neighboring village of Iwanie was actually granted to them by Augustus III following the first disputation. The history of Frankism as Polish Shabbateanism ends here and is well documented in the recent work of Pawel Maciejko.

From the time in Iwanie through the years of his imprisonment, the establishment of his court in Brno and then in the palaces of the prince of Isenburg in Offenbach, Frank taught his own doctrine to the circle of the Brothers and Sisters, and records of the history of the group were kept. A lot of these materials remain and have received some study. The conduct of the sect can be studied through entries in the internal history, the *Chronicle;* Frank's own doctrine is found in the *Collection of the Words of the Lord.* In these works one sees Frank's talent in adapting himself to changing circumstances and persuading his followers to remain steadfast. The *Collection* displays Frank's prowess as the innovator of several literary forms, including threefold (allegorical) tales. Other contemporary observers have left a large body of accounts of his peculiar activities and self-presentation during this period, and these have been employed by later scholars. There are clear connections between this Frankism and developments in Hasidism in terms of the configuration of its leadership, as well as its characteristic literary modalities.

The third branch of Frankism in Bohemia, especially Prague, before, during, and after the disputations was, like the first, rooted in the continuation of Shabbateanism and can be associated with modernizing movements in Judaism, including assimilation. This variety knows almost nothing of Frank, his deeds, or his teachings.

SEE ALSO Messianism, article on Jewish Messianism; Shabbetai Tsevi.

BIBLIOGRAPHY

Doktór, Jan. *Księga Słów Pańskich.* Warsaw, 1997. The only complete edition of the manuscript fragments of Frank's dicta from the collection of the library of Jagiellonian University in Kraków. Both these works contain a fairly large number of errors, especially in the notes.

Doktór, Jan, ed. *Rozmaite adnotacje, przypadki, czynności i anekdoty Pańskie.* Warsaw, 1996. The only complete edition of original materials from the Łopaciński Library in Lublin, containing the *Chronicle* and later dicta.

Kraushar, Alexandr. *Jacob Frank: The End to the Sabbataian Heresy.* Edited by Herbert Levy. Lanham, Md., 2001. A translation of the Polish study, *Frank i Frankiści Polscy: 1726–1816.* Kraków,1895. The classic study in Polish; Levy's presentation is particularly untrustworthy in the translation of the original dicta and his introduction is preposterous, but this is all there is in English.

Maciejko, Pawel. "The Development of the Religious Teachings of Jacob Frank." Ph.D. diss., Oxford University, 2003. Adds a great deal of new information and documentation to the work of earlier scholars. The result is a careful restatement of the movements and their histories, especially in relation to political interests and the Christian interface. Includes the only comprehensive and up-to-date bibliography.

Scholem, Gershom. "Frank, Jacob, and the Frankists." *Encyclopaedia Judaica,* vol. 7, cols. 55–71. Jerusalem, 1971.

Scholem, Gershom. "Redemption through Sin." Translated by Hillel Halkin. In *The Messianic Idea in Judaism and Other Essays on Jewish Spirituality,* pp. 37–48. New York, 1971.

HARRIS LENOWITZ (2005)

FRANKEL, ZACHARIAS (1801–1875), was the founder, in Germany, of Historical Judaism, the forerunner of Conservative Judaism in America. A member of the first generation of modern rabbis, Frankel fashioned a multifaceted career as pulpit rabbi, spokesman for political emancipation, critic of radical religious reform, editor, head of the first modern rabbinical seminary, and historian of Jewish law.

Frankel was born in Prague, then still the largest Jewish community in Europe, into a financially comfortable family with a distinguished lineage of rabbinic and communal leaders. His education combined traditional immersion in Jewish texts with systematic exposure to secular studies in a manner that was still far from typical. In 1830 he received his doctorate from the University of Pest and in 1831 acquired the post of district rabbi of Litoměřice, becoming the first Bohemian rabbi to hold a doctorate. His advocacy of changes in the synagogue service, the education of the young, and the training and role of the rabbi brought him, in 1836, an invitation from the government of Saxony to occupy the pulpit in Dresden as chief rabbi of the realm. Despite several subsequent offers from the much larger and rapidly growing Jewish community of Berlin, Frankel stayed in Dresden until 1854, when he was called to become the first director of the new rabbinical and teachers' seminary in Breslau. By 1879, four years after his death, the seminary had instructed some 272 students and had placed nearly 120 teachers, preachers, and rabbis in the most important Jewish communities in Europe.

A self-styled moderate reformer in matters of religion, Frankel formulated his program of "positive, historical Judaism" in the 1840s to stem the rising tide of radical religious reform. Against the Reform movement's unbounded rationalism, Frankel defended Judaism's legal character, the sanctity of historical experience, and the authority of current practice. The term *positive* pointed to prescribed ritual behavior (*halakhah*) as the dominant means for the expression of religious sentiment in Judaism, while the term *historical* designated its nonlegal realm, sanctified by time and suffering.

What gives Frankel's definition its dynamic quality is the role of the people. Genuine reform evolves organically from below and not by fiat from above. It is for this reason that Frankel repudiated the innovations of the three rabbinical conferences of the 1840s; whether dictated by political considerations or the canons of reason, their measures did violence to prevailing sentiment and practice.

On a popular level Frankel tried, as author and editor, to deepen Jews' loyalty to the past by offering them a brand of heroic history that stressed cultural achievement. As a scholar Frankel was the preeminent modern rabbinist of his generation, and he devoted a prolific career to introducing the concept of the development of Jewish law over time. Using the method as well as the ideology of Friedrich C. Savigny's *geschichtliche Rechtswissenschaft,* Frankel tried to recover and analyze the stages of legal evolution, from Alexandrian exegeses of scripture to medieval rabbinic *responsa.* In the process he left enduring contributions to the modern study of the Mishnah and the Palestinian Talmud.

Frankel's undogmatic research on the Mishnah challenged the traditional image of the ancient rabbis as transmitters rather than creators of the oral law and provoked a bitter assault in 1861 from the Neo-Orthodox camp of Samson Raphael Hirsch. Growing religious polarization served to clarify denominational lines and forced Frankel to occupy the middle ground.

Two institutions created by Frankel embodied, amplified, and disseminated his vision of Historical Judaism. *Die Monatsschrift für Geschichte und Wissenschaft des Judentums,* which he edited for eighteen taxing years (1851–1868), provided its readers with a balance of high-level popularization and critical scholarship, setting the standard for all later nineteenth-century journals of Jewish studies. Similarly, the Breslau seminary, which he led for twenty-one years, transformed rabbinic education by integrating modern scholarship with traditional piety and requiring its graduates to be both spiritual leaders and practitioners of *Wissenschaft.*

BIBLIOGRAPHY

Brann, Marcus, ed. *Zacharias Frankel: Gedenkblätter zu seinem hundertsten Geburtstage.* Breslau, 1901.

Heinemann, Isaac. "The Idea of the Jewish Theological Seminary Seventy-Five Years Ago and Today." In *Das Breslauer Seminar,* edited by Guido Kisch, pp. 85–100. Tübingen, 1963.

Rabinowitz, Saul Pinchas. *R. Zekharyah Frankel* (in Hebrew). Warsaw, 1898.

Schorsch, Ismar. "Zacharias Frankel and the European Origins of Conservative Judaism." *Judaism* 30 (Summer 1981): 344–354.

New Sources

Brämer, Andreas. *Rabbiner Zacharias Frankel: Wissenschaft des Judentums und konservative Reform im 19. Jahrhundert.* Hildesheim, 2000.

Goetschel, Roland. "Aux origines de la modernité juive: Zacharias Frankel (1801–1875) et l'école historico-critique." *Pardès* 19–20 (1994): 107–132.

Horwitz, Rivkah, ed. *Zachaia Frankel and the Beginnings of Positive-Historical Judaism* (in Hebrew). Jerusalem, 1984.

ISMAR SCHORSCH (1987)
Revised Bibliography

FRANKFORT, HENRI (1897–1954), was an archaeologist and historian of religion. Frankfort began his studies at the University of Amsterdam, where he studied history, but he transferred to the University of London in order to work under Flinders Petrie in Egyptian archaeology. He always preferred, however, to designate himself as a historian.

In 1922, Frankfort became a member of Petrie's expedition to Egypt, and from 1924 to 1925, he studied at the British School of Archaeology in Athens. He obtained his M.A. from the University of London in 1924 and his Ph.D. from the University of Leiden in 1927. From 1925 to 1929 he served as director of the excavations of the Egypt Exploration Society at Tell al-ʿAmarna, Abydos, and Erment. In 1929 he accepted the directorship of the Iraq expedition of the University of Chicago's Oriental Institute, which he held until 1937, when excavations were discontinued. In 1932, Frankfort was appointed research professor of Oriental archaeology at the Oriental Institute and associate professor of the ancient Near East at the University of Amsterdam. He served as acting chairman of the Department of Near Eastern Languages and Literatures at the University of Chicago during World War II. In 1949 he accepted the post of director of the Warburg Institute in London and was appointed professor of the history of preclassical antiquity at the University of London.

Frankfort's first major work, *Studies in Early Pottery in the Near East* (1924–1927), was of fundamental importance for Near Eastern archaeology. He was the first to classify and date ancient Near Eastern ceramics and thus to make it a basic means of periodization and relative dating. Of similarly fundamental importance was his later study of cylinder seals, for which he identified characteristic features for successive periods, thereby establishing a relative dating system for this important and very numerous class of objects. The resulting study, *Cylinder Seals: A Documentary Essay on the Art and Religion of the Ancient Near East* (1939), is not only important to archaeologists but also presents the student of religion with a wealth of data on mythology and ritual.

The results of the various expeditions directed by Frankfort in Egypt and Iraq were published in a series of preliminary and final reports, partly by Frankfort alone, and partly by him and members of the staff. Among the former, the valuable volumes *Sculpture of the Third Millennium* B.C. *from Tel Asmar and Khafajah* (1939), *More Sculpture from the Diyala Region* (1943), and *Stratified Cylinder Seals from the Diyala Region* (1955) should be mentioned. Of more general purview are the important studies *Archaeology and the Sumerian Problem* (1932) and *The Birth of Civilization in the Near East* (1951). An overview of ancient Near Eastern archaeology is given in his *The Art and Architecture of the Ancient Orient* (1954).

Of special interest to historians of religion is *The Intellectual Adventure of Ancient Man* (1946), which was later reissued under the title *Before Philosophy* (1963). The lecture series on which this book is based was organized by Frankfort, and he and his wife contributed the introductory and concluding chapters, "Myth and Reality," a penetrating and clear analysis of the logic of mythopoeic thought, and "The Emancipation of Thought from Myth," which traces the road from mythical to genuinely philosophical thought. During the time that Frankfort initiated and contributed to these lectures, he finished the two larger studies, *Ancient Egyptian Religion: An Interpretation* (2d ed., 1949), and the influential *Kingship and the Gods: A Study of Ancient Near Eastern Religion as the Integration of Society and Nature* (1948). Frankfort's method of approach is that of phenomenology of religion, which respects the religious commitment and values reflected in the data studied. The aim of the latter work is well expressed in the subtitle, and the treatment of both Egyptian and Mesopotamian materials, with attention both to their characteristic similarities and to their differences, lends depth to the study. Frankfort was deeply aware that an understanding of religious data can be gained only in terms of the general culture in which the religion in question is embedded and from which the specific meanings of its symbols are derived. This position is given its most complete methodological statement in his Frazer Lecture of 1951, published as *The Problem of Similarity in Ancient Near Eastern Religions* (1951), where he argues cogently against a comparative method that would emphasize general similarities and neglect specific differences, for it is the latter that hold the true clues to understanding: "Once again, then, our danger lies in the similarities themselves, for it is—as always—the cultural context which holds the secret of their significance."

BIBLIOGRAPHY

In addition to works cited in the text, see Frankfort's lectures published in the *Journal of the Warburg and Courtauld Institutes:* "State Festivals in Egypt and Mesopotamia" (vol. 15, 1952, pp. 1–12), "The Dying God" (vol. 21, 1958, pp. 141–151), "Heresy in a Theocratic State" (vol. 21, 1958, pp. 152–161), and "The Archetype in Analytical Psychology and the History of Religion" (vol. 21, 1958, pp. 166–178). For an obituary notice written by Pinhas Delongaz and me, see "Henri Frankfort, 24 II 1897–16 VII 1954," *Journal of Near Eastern Studies* 14 (1955): 1–3; this piece is followed by a bibliography compiled by J. Vindenaess.

New Sources

The three lectures mentioned above have had a seminal influence on the comparative study of Near Eastern religions. They have been collected together and published in a book, Henri Frankfort, *Il dio che muore. Mito e cultura nel mondo preclassico* (Florence, 1992), Italian translation by Gabriella Sacandone Matthiae, with an important introduction by the archeologist Paolo Matthiae.

THORKILD JACOBSEN (1987)
Revised Bibliography

FRASHŌKERETI. The Avestan term *Frashōkereti* ("making wonderful" or "rehabilitation" of existence) corresponds to *Frashgird,* the Middle Persian term for the Last Judgment, or final day of humanity's existence. The Avestan term derives from the expression "to make existence splendid." The concept is eschatological and soteriological and, already present in the *Gāthās,* is at the basis of Zoroastrian doctrine. With this concept Zarathushtra (Zoroaster) abolished the archaic ideology of the cosmic cycle and of the eternal return modeled on atemporal archetypes, proclaiming the expectation of, and hope for, an *eschaton.* He thus introduced a linear conception of cosmic time, an innovation in religious thought that had an enormous influence on humanity's subsequent spiritual history. According to his doctrine, the final event will be completed not because of a cosmogonic ritual but by the will of the creator: the resurrection of the body and last judgment are essential and significant aspects of the Frashōkereti.

In the *Gāthās* the Frashōkereti is felt to be near, but later Zoroastrianism developed an eschatological doctrine situating it further off in time, within the concept of a Great Year divided into three periods, each a millennium in length and each beginning with the coming of a Saoshyant, a savior born of the seed of Zarathushtra. The last of these will be the Saoshyant par excellence, the maker of the final Frashōkereti.

The Frashōkereti is described in one of the hymns of the Avesta (*Yashts* 19). It declares that *druj,* the "lie," the principle or deity of evil, will be brought down; the *daiva* Aēshma, "fury," will be destroyed by a bloody mace; the *daiva* Aka Manah ("bad thought") will be overcome; hunger and thirst will be defeated; and the great god of evil, Angra Mainyu, deprived of his power, will be driven to flight.

The Pahlavi literature of the ninth and tenth centuries CE furnishes further details. The Frashgird will be announced by positive signs: the abolition of meat as a food for humans and its gradual replacement by an increasingly spiritual diet, without milk, water, or plants; the progressive fading of concupiscence; and so forth. Finally, after the resurrection of the body and after a test by molten metal, through which all, both just and unjust, must pass, there will take place a great, eschatological sacrifice of a bull. Its fat, mixed with white *haoma,* will make the drink of immortality for all humankind.

BIBLIOGRAPHY

Bailey, H. W. *Zoroastrian Problems in the Ninth-Century Books* (1943). Reprint, Oxford, 1971.

Boyce, Mary. *A History of Zoroastrianism,* vol. 1. Leiden, 1975.

Duchesne-Guillemin, Jacques. *La religion de l'Iran ancien.* Paris, 1962.

Gnoli, Gherardo. "Questioni sull'interpretazione della dottrina gathica." *Annali dell'Instituto Universitario Orientale di Napoli,* n.s. 21 (1971): 341–370.

Humbach, Helmut, ed. and trans. *Die Gathas des Zarathustra.* Heidelberg, 1959.

Lommel, Herman. *Die Religion Zarathustras nach dem Awesta dargestellt.* Tübingen, 1930.

Molé, Marijan. *Culte, mythe et cosmologie dans l'Iran ancien.* Paris, 1963.

Nyberg, H. S. *Irans forntida religioner.* Stockholm, 1937. Translated as *Die Religionen des alten Iran* (1938; 2d ed., Osnabrück, 1966).

Widengren, Geo. "Leitende Ideen und Quellen der iranischen Apokalyptik." In *Apocalypticism in the Mediterranean World and the Near East,* edited by David Hellholm, pp. 77–162. Tübingen, 1989.

Zaehner, R. C. *The Dawn and Twilight of Zoroastrianism.* London, 1961.

GHERARDO GNOLI (1987)
Translated from Italian by Roger DeGaris

FRAVASHIS, beneficent and protective guardian spirits whose services must be secured by means of ritual offerings, are an essential element of the religious structure of Zoroastrianism. They play an important role in the frequency of rainfall and are responsible for guaranteeing the prosperity and preservation of the family. As the spirits of the dead, they are the protagonists in a great feast held on the last night of the year. They are thought to preexist human beings and to survive them.

The *fravashi*s do not appear in the *Gāthās.* In the Avesta, the first mention of them occurs in the *Yasna Haptanhāiti,* and an entire hymn (*Yashts* 13) is dedicated to them.

The conception of the *fravashi* has all the characteristics of an archaic, pre-Zoroastrian belief that was later absorbed and adapted by the tradition. Examples of these characteristics include their identification with the spirits of the dead (Söderblom, 1899, pp. 229–260, 373–418) and their warlike nature.

As the spirits of the dead the *fravashi*s have often been compared to the Roman *manes* or to the Indian *pitaraḥ;* as warlike beings, they have been compared with the Germanic valkyries or to the Indian Maruts, the company of celestial warriors. In particular, in the context of the Indo-European tripartite ideology, the *fravashi*s are seen as a Zoroastrian substitute for the Maruts (Dumézil, 1953); both are linked to the concepts and ethics of the Aryan *Männerbund.* Most likely, Zoroastrianism absorbed this ancient concept, typical of a warrior society, through its ties to the cult of the dead and reinterpreted the *fravashi*s as combatants for the rule of Ahura Mazdā. We find such a zoroastrianization in the myth told in the third chapter of the *Bundahishn* (Book of primordial creation), which relates that the *fravashi*s chose to be incarnated in material bodies in order to fight Ahriman and the evil powers instead of remaining peacefully in the celestial world.

The etymology of the word *fravashi* is uncertain. Originally it may have been used to designate the spirit of a deceased hero who was endowed with **vṛti,* "valor" (Bailey, 1943, pp. 107ff.); or it may have expressed the theological concept, fundamental to Zoroastrianism, of choice, **fra-vṛti* (Lommel, 1930, pp. 151, 159–163) or that of the profession of faith (Hoffmann, 1979, p. 91; Schlerath, 1980, pp. 207ff.).

BIBLIOGRAPHY

Bailey, H. W. *Zoroastrian Problems in the Ninth-Century Books* (1943). Reprint, Oxford, 1971.

Duchesne-Guillemin, Jacques. "L'homme dans la religion iranienne." In *Anthropologie religieuse,* edited by C. Jouco Bleeker, pp. 93–107. Leiden, 1955.

Dumézil, Georges. "Víṣṇu et les Marút à travers la réforme zoroastrienne." *Journal asiatique* 241 (1953): 1–25.

Gnoli, Gherardo. "Le fravaši e l'immortalità." In *La mort, les morts dans les sociétés anciennes,* edited by Gherardo Gnoli and Jean-Pierre Vernant, pp. 339–347. Paris, 1982.

Hoffmann, Karl. "Das Avesta in der Persis." In *Prolegomena to the Sources of the History of Pre-Islamic Central Asia,* edited by János Harmatta, pp. 89–93. Budapest, 1979.

Kellens, Jean. "Les fravaši." In *Anges et démons,* edited by Julien Ries, pp. 99–114. Louvain-la-Neuve, 1989.

Lommel, Herman. *Die Religion Zarathustras nach dem Awesta dargestellt.* Tübingen, 1930.

Malandra, William W. "The 'Fravaši Yašt.'" Ph.D. diss., University of Pennsylvania, 1971.

Narten, Johanna. "Avestisch frauuaṣ̌i-." *Indo-Iranian Journal* 28 (1985): 35–48.

Nyberg, H. S. *Irans forntida religioner.* Stockholm, 1937. Translated as *Die Religionen des alten Iran* (1938; 2d ed., Osnabrück, 1966).

Schlerath, Bernfried. "Indo-Iranisch **var-* 'wählen.'" *Studien zur Indologie und Iranistik (Festschrift Paul Thieme)* 5–6 (1980): 199–208.

Söderblom, Nathan. "Les Fravashis: Étude sur les traces dans le mazdéisme d'une ancienne conception sur la survivance des morts." *Revue de l'histoire des religions* 39 (1899): 229–260, 373–418.

GHERARDO GNOLI (1987)
Translated from Italian by Roger DeGaris

FRAZER, JAMES G. (1854–1941), was a British anthropologist and historian of religion. James George Frazer, the eldest of four children, was born in preindustrial Glasgow, the son of a successful pharmacist. His parents were devout members of the Free Church of Scotland, a conservative sect that in the 1840s had broken away from the (Established) Church of Scotland on matters of church governance. Accordingly Frazer was raised in an atmosphere of deep piety, which, be it noted, he later said that he did not find oppressive.

Frazer early showed academic promise and entered the University of Glasgow at the then not unusually early age of fifteen. There, he writes in a genial memoir composed at the end of his life, three important things occurred: He conceived his lifelong love of the classics, he came to see that the world is governed by a system of unvarying natural laws, and he painlessly lost the religious faith of his childhood.

Frazer did brilliantly at Glasgow but soon realized that although Scottish education gave him a broader background than an English one would have, its standards were not as high. After taking his degree at Glasgow he therefore matriculated at Trinity College, Cambridge, in 1874 for a second baccalaureate. He took second place in the classical tripos of 1878. A dissertation on Platonic epistemology gained him a fellowship at Trinity in 1879, which after three renewals was granted for life; he was a fellow of Trinity for more than sixty years.

In 1896 Frazer married Mrs. Elizabeth (Lilly) Grove, a French widow with two children who had become a writer out of economic necessity. She wrote an early and important volume on the history of the dance, along with many playlets in French for schoolroom use. She soon became convinced that the academic world was overlooking her husband's merits and strove mightily to advance his career (he was the stereotype of a research scholar, unworldly and shy). She also arranged for his work to be translated into French, which meant that Frazer was very well known in France after the war. Frazer was knighted in 1914, became a fellow of the Royal Society in 1920, and was awarded the Order of Merit in 1925.

Frazer's first scholarly writing, from which his interest in anthropology can be said to date, came about through his friendship with William Robertson Smith (1847–1894), the eminent Scottish theologian and comparative Semiticist. More than any other person, Smith was responsible for disseminating the results of German biblical scholarship in Great Britain at the end of the century. For his pains he became the defendant in the last significant heresy trials in Great Britain. Although he was exonerated, Smith had become too notorious for provincial Scotland and therefore accepted an appointment in Cambridge. Among his many other activities, he was editor of the ninth edition of the *Encyclopaedia Britannica* and as such was always looking for likely contributors. Meeting his countryman Frazer at Trinity, Smith soon set him to work. Because in those days encyclopedias were brought out a volume at a time, and because the volumes through the letter *O* had already appeared. Frazer was assigned articles beginning with *P* and subsequent letters. Thus it was that he came to write the important entries "Taboo" and "Totem," which launched him into the then sparsely populated field of anthropology.

In 1889 Frazer wrote to the publisher George Macmillan offering him a manuscript on magic, folklore, and religion in the ancient world. Macmillan accepted *The Golden Bough,* and it was published in two volumes in the following year. It was generally well received, the reviewers noting Frazer's impressive erudition and stylistic gifts. As soon as he had brought out the first edition, Frazer began preparing an enlarged second edition, which duly appeared in three volumes in 1900. The third and final edition, in twelve volumes, came out from 1911 to 1915. It is this massive version that Frazer himself abridged in 1922; he produced a thirteenth volume, *Aftermath,* in 1936.

The Golden Bough merits special attention because it remains Frazer's best-known work, but it hardly exhausts his contribution to the historical and anthropological study of ancient and "primitive" religion. In 1898 he published *Pausanias's Description of Greece*—a translation of Pausanias's report of his travels—accompanied by five volumes of commentary, maps, and plates, all of which represented fifteen years of work. Pausanias, who in the second century CE prepared this guidebook to his country, was especially curious about religion and inquired ceaselessly about artifacts and rituals that had survived in the countryside but were no longer extant in Athens. Pausanias's record is frequently the only surviving witness of many phenomena of ancient Greek folk religion. His travels constituted an ideal text for Frazer, permitting him to use his classical as well as his comparative anthropological knowledge.

Among Frazer's other major productions in the history of religion are *Lectures on the Early History of the Kingship* (1905); *Totemism and Exogamy* (1910), which gave Freud much data as well as the idea for a title (*Totem and Taboo,* 1911); *Folk-Lore in the Old Testament* (1918), which arose out of Frazer's study of Hebrew; and an edition of Ovid's *Fasti* (1929). The *Fasti* is a narrative poem organized around the cycle of the Roman holidays, and, like *Pausanias,* it gave Frazer an opportunity to employ the whole of his considerable scholarly equipment.

The Golden Bough was noteworthy because it offered something that had not been done before in English: a treatment from the philosophical, evolutionary point of view, delivered in sonorous and untechnical language, of the beliefs and behavior of the ancient Greeks and Romans as if they were those of "primitives." By the end of the nineteenth century, the classical world had lost much of the privileged status it had enjoyed since the Renaissance as the origin and repository of the greatest that had ever been thought and said. Indeed eighteenth- and nineteenth-century classical historiography was largely demythologizing in its impulse. But because of the centrality maintained by the classics in the educational curriculum and thus in the training and habit of mind of the governing classes in Great Britain, it came as a shock to a cultured reader when Frazer insisted on the ways in which life and thought in classical antiquity strongly resembled, overall and in detail, those of the "primitives" (or "savages") who had become well known to Europeans as a result of the imperialist expansion of the eighteenth and especially the nineteenth century.

Although many scholars have disagreed with some or all of it, the argument of *The Golden Bough* may fairly be said by now to have become part of the basis of modern culture (at least on the level of metaphor), and many educated people who employ its argument are unaware of its origins. Briefly, the work purports to be an explanation of a curious ritual combat that took place, according to ancient sources, in classical times in the town of Aricia outside Rome. In a grove at Nemi a "priest" stood guard at all times, awaiting a challenger to his supremacy. The rule of the place was that any runaway slave who managed to reach the grove would gain his freedom if he succeeded in killing its guardian; with such success, however, came the obligation to assume the role of priest, and to kill or be killed in turn. In Frazer's view, this combat cannot be understood solely or wholly in terms of Roman religion; instead its elements must be analyzed comparatively (by adducing examples of analogous behavior from other "primitive" societies). He asserts that the guardian of the grove was a priest-king, who, like all such in primitive societies, literally incarnated the well-being of the community and thus had to be kept alive and well at all costs. This leads to a discussion of the strategies, both actual and symbolic (such as taboo, magic, sacrifice, and scapegoats), that such communities undertook to keep the king from weakness or death. At the heart of the work is a lengthy analysis of the complex of myth and ritual in the religions of the ancient eastern Mediterranean, all of which turn on death and resurrection and whose themes are often played out in seasonal combats and other fertility ceremonies. The main rites discussed are those of Attis, Adonis, Osiris, and Dionysos, all of whom Frazer understands as divine protagonists in the same, ubiquitous, recurrent vegetational drama.

The actual goings-on in the grove at Nemi are, Frazer finally admits, merely pretexts, for he is in fact interested in something more important: nothing less than the laws that describe the workings of the "primitive mind," which by definition is less well developed than the norm. Although this mind is inaccessible directly, it may be studied nevertheless, by adopting (from the work of the pioneering German folklorist Wilhelm Mannhardt) "the law of similarity": when customs are similar in different societies, one may then infer that the motives of the people performing them are also similar. This follows from the then generally accepted idea (advanced by E. B. Tylor) that the human race has evolved in a uniform fashion, mentally as well as physically. Further, because in Frazer's view the mentality of the primitive "Aryan" was still extant in that of the modern European peasantry because the peasantry still participated in a mental universe untouched by modern thought, it was therefore appropriate to compare the behavior of these so-called modern primitives (peasants and underdeveloped tribal societies) with that of historical societies of the ancient world in order to extract laws of primitive mental functioning.

Finally, however, Frazer was interested in even bigger game than primitive epistemology. For although in his survey of the dying-and-reviving gods of the eastern Mediterranean Frazer never mentions the name of Jesus, only the slowest of his readers could have failed to make the comparison between the pagan rites that result from an imperfect (because irrational) understanding of the universe and contemporary Christianity. Frazer employed the "objective," scientific comparative method as a weapon to finally dispatch Christianity as an outworn relic of misunderstanding, credulity, and superstition. There can be no doubt that his subliminal message was successfully delivered: The many uses of Frazerian arguments and images in the literature and cultural analysis of the post-World War I period (the most well-known of which is T. S. Eliot's *The Waste Land*) are ample testimony to that. (In addition, the Frazer papers in the library of Trinity College, Cambridge, contain many unsolicited letters from readers, educated and otherwise, that thank Frazer for having finally dispelled the veil of illusion from before their eyes as to the "real" nature of Christianity.)

As time has passed, Frazer's affinities are increasingly seen to be with those polymath scholars who, periodically since the Renaissance, have had the vision and industry to attempt a description and interpretation of the entire phenomenon of religion. Living when and where he did conferred several advantages on him. First, only by the end of the nineteenth century had European imperialism gone far enough to open up virtually the entire tribal world. Thus Frazer's was the first generation for which the data existed to permit a credible, anthropologically based worldwide conspectus of religious behavior. Second, the triumph of Darwinism automatically promoted as self-evidently correct any explanatory model that was based on evolutionary premises. If mind had developed in a linear fashion, as Frazer (and Tylor) believed, then a rigid, uniform progression from magic through religion to positive science seemed a plausible description of the pathway toward understanding that humanity had in fact taken.

From a current point of view, however, viewing Frazer from the other side of a gulf produced by a nightmarish century and by many years of anthropological fieldwork and much greater philosophical and methodological sophistication, he seems himself to be a relic of a habit of thought that, if not exactly primitive, then is at least of long ago and far away. His extreme empiricism and antitheoretical inclination made him a victim, finally, of his mountains of data. At the same time, he could never have presented such a stirring picture of the long evolutionary struggle of humanity toward self-understanding had he not been so willing to use simple categories under which to organize his data.

Frazer's professional descendants are many and various, as are their evaluations of his work. For English-speaking anthropologists, he is seen mainly as a horrible example of the "armchair school" of anthropology that was swept away by the advent of fieldwork. Historians of religion hold him in higher esteem, probably because the comparative method (of which his work is the greatest exemplar) is still in guarded use in that discipline. Finally, his name stands highest among literary critics and cultural historians, to whose field he made no explicit contribution.

It may be most reasonable to situate Frazer in a grand tradition—one that understands religion humanistically and therefore regards it as a perennially appropriate subject for discourse with the educated reader—that has been eclipsed in the present day as a result of the aspirations to scientific status of anthropology. One may see him, then, despite his obvious limitations, as a scholar whose vision and literary gifts ensure him a permanent place in the ranks of those who have expanded the modern idea of the mysterious past of humanity.

SEE ALSO Smith, W. Robertson.

BIBLIOGRAPHY

For further biographical information see my *J. G. Frazer: His Life and Work* (Cambridge, 1987). Two memoirs by Robert Angus Downie, *James George Frazer* (London, 1940) and *Frazer and the Golden Bough* (London, 1970), are sketchy. Theodore Besterman's *A Bibliography of Sir James Frazer, O. M.* (London, 1934) offers a useful guide to Frazer's complex oeuvre. E. O. James's obituary notice in the *Dictionary of National Biography, 1941–1950* (supp. 3), R. R. Marett's in the *Proceedings of the British Academy* 27 (1941): 377–492, and H. J. Fleure's in the *Obituary Notices of Fellows of the Royal Society* 3 (1941): 897–914, are helpful. See also Bronislaw Malinowski's "Sir James George Frazer: A Biographical Appreciation," in his *A Scientific Theory of Culture and Other Essays* (Chapel Hill, N.C., 1944), pp. 177–221 combines lucid criticism with appreciation of Frazer as founder of modern scientific anthropology and great humanist.

New Sources

Robert Ackerman, see "J. G. Frazer and the Jews," in *Religion* 22 (1992): 135–150, and *The Myth and Ritual School: J. G. Frazer and the Cambridge Ritualists* (New York and London, 1991; 2d ed. 2002), esp. chapter four: a book very informative, despite some factual mistakes and the overall inadequacy from the viewpoint of history of religions. These shortcomings are neglected in the review by Michel Despland, *Numen* 50 (2003): 479–481. Scathing criticism in an article by another prominent representative of British social anthropology: Edmund R. Leach, "Golden Bough or Gilded Twig?," *Daedalus* 90 (1961): 371–387. Very important for the religious-historical perspective is Jonathan Zettel Smith, *The Glory, Jest and Riddle. James George Frazer and the Golden Bough* (Ph.D. diss, Yale, 1969). Smith's views are summarized in the seminal article "When the Bough Breaks," *History of Religions* 12, no. 4 (1973): 342–371, reprinted in J. Z. Smith, *Map is not Territory*, Leiden, 1978, pp. 208–239, and in the fourth chapter of *Drudgery Divine* (Chicago, 1990), pp. 85–115. Frazer is central in Smith's redescription of the field of comparative religious studies, a work characterized by painstaking erudition and unequaled acumen, although very controversial in its far-reaching conclusions. See also the profile "James George Frazer" by Hans Wissmann, in *Klassiker der Religionswissenschaft von Friedrich Schleiermacher bis Mircea Eliade*, Munich, 1997, pp. 77–89. For the literary aspects of Frazer's oeuvre see John B. Vickery, *The Literary Impact of "The Golden Bough"* (Princeton, 1973); Robert Fraser, *The Making of "The Golden Bough"* (London, 1990) and *Sir James Frazer and the Literary Imagination*, edited by Robert Fraser (London, 1990).

Ackerman Robert. *The Myth and Ritual School.* New York, 1991.

Beard, Mary. "Frazer et ses bois sacrés." In *Les bois sacrés: actes du colloque international organisé par le Centre Jean Bérard et l'École pratique des Hautes Études* (V Section), edited by Olivier de Cazanove and John Scheid, pp. 171–180. Naples, 1993.

Gee, Emma. "Some Thoughts about the 'Fasti' of James George Frazer." *Antichthon* 32 (1998): 64–90.

ROBERT ACKERMAN (1987)
Revised Bibliography

FREEMASONS. The name for members of Freemasonry, the largest fraternal organization in the world, Freemasons are linked to numerous other rites, degrees, and orders collectively termed *Masonic.* Originally two words, *Free Mason,* the compound *Freemason* became standard by the nineteenth century. The term stands for "free and accepted mason," an accepted or "honorary" mason who is both freeborn (not bonded in servitude) and "free" from the original "operative" definition of *masonry,* the trade of stonecraft used to build churches and cathedrals throughout medieval Europe. Although there are records of noncraftsmen or "nonoperatives" joining earlier operative guilds, such as that of Elias Ashmole and Christopher Wren of Oxford, purely nonoperative "lodges" where Freemasons met were not publicly disclosed until the formation of the Grand Lodge of England in London in 1717. A Freemason (or simply "Mason") from about this time, and as outlined in the official *Constitutions* (1723 and 1738), was basically a "speculative" mason who, having undergone three degrees of initiation, lived a moral life devoted both to teachings derived from a symbolic understanding of the stonemason's craft and to the three great Masonic principles of brotherly love, relief, and truth.

Secrecy—and a certain mystique—has surrounded and continues to surround the Freemason rituals of initiation and moral instruction, yet Freemasonry, or "the Craft," is not in principle a "secret society" in the subversive social or political sense, since respect for lawful authority is a hallmark of Masonic teachings. Though sometimes viewed as representing a specific or even "revolutionary" political agenda, Freemasons have been found on both sides of major political and social conflicts in modern times. Moreover, information regarding the history, rituals, and proceedings of Freemasonry is readily available in public libraries, in bookstores, and on the Internet. In certain instances, the names of members and even the existence of the order in some parts of the world where Freemasonry has spread were withheld from political authorities that were undemocratic, dictatorial, or generally inimical, such as those of Nazi Germany, Communist Russia, Fascist Italy, Catholic Spain, and most Islamic countries today. On the other hand, political groups, such as the nineteenth-century Grand Orients in Spain and Portugal, have sometimes masqueraded as Freemasons.

As modern fraternal orders in secular societies, Masonic lodges and related organizations are open to public scrutiny, and membership is publicly displayed in almost all cases. Secrecy aside, one of the most engaging contemporary issues is whether Freemasonry is a "religion" or not. Membership requires a belief in a supreme being and the immortality of the soul, and there are ample references, albeit symbolic, to religious symbols, personalities, and places in the rituals. Yet while the order testifies to its own archaic religious and even mythical roots, Freemasonry today resists the appellation of "religion" in the sectarian sense, encouraging only "that religion to which all men agree." Also, not claiming tax exemption as a religious body, the order aims to transcend individual religious differences and unite men of diverse backgrounds in common cause under a symbolic notion of God as the great architect of the universe. Religious tolerance and liberty of conscience have been among the principles of Freemasonry since its inception.

Despite the great importance of Freemasonry and other secretive societies in any accurate description of the rise of Western civilization, few historians of religion have undertaken a comprehensive study of the history and cultural significance of Freemasonry in its various dimensions. In recent years, social scientists and historians of ideas (Clawson, 1989; Carnes, 1989; Jacob, 1991) have sought to understand the significance of Masonry within the larger spheres of religious fraternalism, gendered cultural systems, and the rise of modern democracy and civil society. In addition, competent historians within the fraternity (Hamill, 1992 and 1994; Roberts, 1961) have maintained active lodges of research with accessible archives. And as a wider net of scholars begin to tap the formidable amount of archival material available on Freemasonry worldwide, its significance as a vital factor in Western cultural history will be further appreciated. In addition, the rich symbolism found in Masonic rites can provide a treasure trove for ritual specialists, semioticians, phenomenologists, and gender scholars.

HISTORY. Recent scholarship has placed the historical emergence of Freemasonry either in England or Scotland between 1600 and 1717. Yet the origin of Freemasonry is still perceived by the lay observer as a tangled web of mystery and opacity, due partly to the institution's use of ancient legendary history in its rituals and ceremonies, and to the fragmentariness of the early records of Masonic meetings, many of which may have been destroyed in the Great Fire of London in 1666. The confusion is heightened by a surfeit of origin theories—propounded by both Masons and non-Masons—that are largely untenable, such as proposals that the order has roots in the Druids, Gnostics, Egyptian pharaohs, the mysteries of Isis and Osiris, Phoenicians, Dionysiac Artificers, Vedic Aryans, Zoroastrians, Rosicrucians, the Jewish Qabbalah, Hermeticism, Essenes, or the Crusades. While aspects of these traditions permeate some Masonic rites and derivative orders, their direct influence during the seventeenth century is elusive and has been difficult to document. In fact, the precise historical circumstances of the transition from a medieval operative guild system, largely Catholic in orientation, to a nonoperative, gradually de-Christianized, nondenominational fraternity still remains to be adequately described and analyzed. Notwithstanding these conditions, it is perhaps most useful to divide Masonic history into two parts: legendary, the period for which there is virtually no authentic documents but only myths and legends; and historic, the period for which authentic documents appear (c. fourteenth century and after).

Legendary Masonic history. The legendary period of Masonic history as outlined within the tradition is founded upon a unique blend of biblical, Greco-Roman, and Afro-Asiatic personalities, places, symbols, and events. James Anderson's *Book of Constitutions* of 1723 and 1738, with nearly 150 pages of Masonic "history" tracing Freemasonry from Adam right up to Anderson's own time, was a benchmark in establishing and perpetuating the more influential aspects of the legendary histories, including the Temple of Solomon. Anderson, a Scottish Presbyterian minister, drew upon earlier manuscripts known as *Old Charges* that were associated with operative guilds from the fourteenth to seventeenth centuries. From the perspective of these sources, stonemasonry was viewed in ancient times as nearly synonymous with geometry and architecture, knowledge of which was a privileged or secret possession available only through direct transmission between craftsmen. The legendary origins of stonemasonry, or the "royal art," as it was called by Anderson and understood by medieval craftsmen, formed the basis upon which modern speculative Freemasonry was constructed. As such, the following may be construed as a linear account of the legendary history of Freemasonry as understood by members of the Craft in the eighteenth century. While also historically untenable, this scenario follows what the mainstream tradition had more-or-less accepted within its ranks as representing the most effective means to convey symbolic teachings pertaining to Masonic truths and virtues.

The almighty architect (God) created the universe according to the principles of geometry, and lastly created Adam in his own image. Possessing the divine knowledge of geometry as delivered to him, Adam built the first temple or place of worship in Eden, and lived in an innocent state. Then, despite his fall from grace, Adam retained this wisdom and taught his sons Cain, who built a city, and Seth, who taught his offspring. Later, the sons of Lamech perfected the arts of metallurgy, music, and tent construction; Enoch, anticipating a cataclysm (flood), built two pillars and engraved on them the sciences of geometry and masonry. According to the oldest manuscripts of the *Old Charges*, it was Hermes in Egypt who recovered one of the pillars and was able to restore the art of geometry by passing it on to the Egyptian pharaohs. But, according to Anderson, it was Noah who built the ark by the principles of geometry and, with his sons and their descendents, brought masonry into the postdiluvian world after settling on the plain of Shinar (Tigris and Euphrates). Anderson refers to a mason as a "true Noachite," since the universal religious principles taught to Noah by God in the Bible represented important Masonic teachings. The descendants of Shem built the Tower of Babel under the direction of Nimrod who allegedly presided over the first Masonic organization in Babylon. After the destruction of the tower and the confusion of languages, the masons were able to preserve their teachings by devising a system of signs and passwords, and Nimrod succeeded in building an empire in Assyria at Nineveh, and passing on the wisdom to the Chaldean Magis of Persia. The descendants of Ham brought masonry into Egypt and Canaan, and the descendants of Japheth brought it into Greece, Italy, Great Britain, and America. The names of Pythagoras and Euclid are also included in these legendary histories, as well as the role of the mysteries of Osiris and Isis as prototypes for the use of symbolism in initiatory rituals.

Abraham, schooled in the builders' art in ancient Mesopotamia, answered God's call and moved his family to Canaan, where he taught geometry to the Canaanites, as well as to his own offspring. Their descendants, the Hebrews, were eventually enslaved in Egypt but rose up under Moses, who was learned in Egyptian masonry. After leading his people into the wilderness accompanied by an ark that was designed by divine geometrical instruction, Joshua and the Israelites established the masonic arts once again in Canaan, where preparations were later begun under King David for a magnificent temple to their God.

The biblical aspects of Freemasonry that relate to King Solomon's Temple reflect a closer alliance with recorded history. Though Solomon is briefly mentioned as part of the Masonic chain in the earliest manuscripts of the *Old Charges*, Solomon and his Temple are central to Anderson's account in which the Masonic lodge itself becomes a symbolic replica of the Temple, influencing successive generations of Freemasons. Anderson portrays King Solomon as the Grand Master of Jerusalem who was assisted in the construction of the Temple by "masons" and carpenters sent by Hiram, King (or Grand Master) of Tyre. Among the workers is the chief architect, Hiram Abif, a stonemason. In the biblical books of *Kings* and *Chronicles* (*1 Kgs.* 7:13–50; *2 Chr.* 4), there is mention of a Hiram from Tyre who is "filled with wisdom and understanding" and is primarily a worker in brass and metals. Building upon the biblical story, the Masonic version portrays Hiram Abif as a master mason who was murdered before completion of the Temple by ruffians for not revealing the secret master's word (i.e., password and signs). The legend of Hiram Abif, including his murder and "resurrection," became a death-and-rebirth allegory that is dramatized within the third degree ritual of today's Craft. The initiated master mason is imparted with the master's word and continues the line of succession, protecting this "intellectual property" into the future.

After describing events surrounding the destruction of the Second Temple, and its rebuilding under Herod, Anderson continues in his narration with Jesus Christ as the Grand Master of the Christians who rose again from the dead. Then he focuses primarily on the architectural achievements of the Romans and how the Royal art was then preserved through the Middle Ages by the patronage of the British monarchy, right up until the time of the stonemasons and the first nonoperative lodges.

Historic period. The Historic period of Freemasonry has been traced by scholars (Clawson, 1989; Jacob, 1991; Hamill, 1992 and 1994) to these same periodic gatherings and confraternities of operative stonemasons engaged in the building of medieval churches and cathedrals in England and Europe. The earliest manuscripts associated with the work and moral symbolism of the stonemasons, the *Old Charges*, date from the late fourteenth century and are also called the "Gothic Constitutions." Besides tracing the legendary history of the Craft of masonry, as shown above, they contain specific moral instructions that are enjoined upon members as apprentices, fellow craftsmen (or journeymen), and master masons. It is probable that secrecy dates from this period, when knowledge of the building techniques of individual master masons was restricted to guild members.

Freemasonry as an official public institution is normally dated from the establishment of the first national Masonic organization, the Grand Lodge of England, a result of the combination of four smaller lodges of nonoperative (noncraftsmen) masons at the Goose and Gridiron Alehouse, London, on June 24, 1717. While nonoperatives were included in operative masons clubs or guilds, no cooperative network of nonoperative lodges had been formally announced. The history of Freemasonry during this period is documented primarily through publications, private diaries, journals, minutes, and newspaper accounts. The Craft attracted royal patronage by 1720, and many of its early members in London were also connected to the Royal Society and the circle surrounding Isaac Newton.

The Masonic lodge became a radically new blend of aristocrat, commoner, Catholic, Protestant, and Jew, by which new ideas of liberty, equality, and fraternity were celebrated. Many Masons in Europe at this time were distinguished figures of the Enlightenment, including Voltaire, Edward Gibbon, Goethe, Johann Herder, Johann Fichte, Wolfgang Amadeus Mozart, Joseph Haydn, Alexander Pope, Jonathan Swift, and John Theophilus Desaguliers, an Anglican priest of Huguenot ancestry who became the order's third elected Grand Master. Mozart wrote an entire set of Masonic musical works for his lodge, as well as *The Magic Flute* (1791), an opera rich in Masonic symbolism.

The introduction of Freemasonry into France by 1725 signified the transition from a largely nonpolitical organization into a body that was also identified with the Jacobite cause for the restoration of the Stuart monarchy in England (King James). The descendants and followers of the exiled James II, who had died in1701, found sympathizers on the continent, especially in Catholic France, who viewed Masonry as a means of infiltrating themselves back into English society. Though the Grand Lodge of France was nominally in control, there was a proliferation of new Masonic orders and exotic degrees that went beyond expectation. Under the direction of Chevalier Michael Ramsay, a Scottish pro-Stuart Catholic Freemason, the initial three-degree ritual of the English Craft tradition was enlarged into a system of *hautes grades,* or high degrees, which greatly influenced the nature of the fraternity. In order to align Freemasonry with Scotland and the Stuarts, Ramsay made the claim in a famous speech that Freemasonry really originated from the Knights Templar, a monastic order protecting the Crusades that had been disbanded and persecuted by the pope in the fourteenth century, but which had sought asylum in Scotland until it resurfaced as Freemasonry. The Templar origin theory continues today in the works of John Robinson and Michael Baigent, as well as in some recently popular novels and films. Appealing to the French taste for high-sounding titles and rituals, and the continental aversion toward building trades, Ramsay initially contrived a series of three chivalric degrees that initiated the candidates into a kind of knighthood unknown to the British lodges. Numerous degrees were later added that included Rosicrucian, Gnostic, qabbalistic, and Hermetic elements (Knight of the Sun, twenty-eighth degree in the Scottish Rite), so that by the end of the nineteenth century there were literally hundreds of degrees offered by various Masonic and quasi-Masonic organizations, many of which were open to women.

Regarding certain occult aspects of Freemasonry, recent scholarship has shed light on the Hermetic and possibly Rosicrucian influences on the historical founding of Freemasonry. Building upon the work of Francis Yates, David Stevenson has shown plausible connections between early Freemasonry in Scotland, Hermeticism, Rosicrucian "invisible" brotherhoods (Lutheran mystical groups), and the ancient art of memory in the sixteenth century. According to Stevenson, the art of memory, originally a technique for improving the memory by visualizing rooms in a building, became, under the influence of the sixteenth-century Hermeticist Giordano Bruno, a magico-religious art for the ascent of the soul, and it was adapted into Masonry to fix the mind on images and symbols in the Masonic temple. As such, late Renaissance fascinations with Egyptian hieroglyphics, alchemical searches for immortality, Neoplatonism, and architecture were all persuasive factors in the genesis of the fraternity.

The higher degrees that survived into mainstream Freemasonry were later grouped into two principal rites, or systems: the Scottish Rite of thirty-three degrees, which was originally derived from the French but flourished in America; and the York Rite, a system of advanced degrees said to originate in York, England. The Scottish Rite, built upon the earlier Rite of Perfection of twenty-five degrees, was brought to the West Indies by Stephen Morin and formally established in the United States by 1801 in Charleston, South Carolina, where it was enlarged to thirty-three degrees. Albert Pike (1809–1891) rewrote all of these degrees during his term as Supreme Commander of the Ancient and Accepted Scottish Rite.

British Freemasonry, organized into separate Irish, Scottish, and English grand lodges, remained nonpartisan during the political-religious disputes of the eighteenth century. While there were some Protestant Christian advocates among the members, the order removed any requirement that its initiates be Christians with the adoption of the *Constitutions* of 1723, revised in 1738 by James Anderson. Largely as a result of British imperial expansion, initially among the military, lodges of Freemasons were established in North America, India, the West Indies, and throughout the world.

During the latter half of the eighteenth century, a rival grand lodge was formed by disaffected Irish and Scottish Masons that divided English-speaking Freemasonry for sixty years. Calling themselves "Antients" and the others "Moderns," this schism was finally healed in 1813 with the formation of the United Grand Lodge of England under the leadership of the duke of Sussex, who had been Grand Master of the Moderns. This division had led to the addition of the Holy Royal Arch to the basic three-degree system. While not of the highly imaginative character of continental degrees, the York Rite or Royal Arch provided Freemasons with a set of degrees that proposed to impart the ineffable name of deity to the degree's recipient. This rite was incorporated into the British Masonic system and also included Knights Templar and Knights of Malta degrees. Initially an Antient invention, the York Rite won wide acceptance throughout the Masonic fraternity in the nineteenth century.

The vital contribution of Freemasonry toward the establishment of the United States is confirmed by modern scholarship. Founding fathers like George Washington, Benjamin Franklin, John Hancock, and James Monroe, as well as the Marquis de Lafayette and a host of others, played key roles in making the ideals of Freemasonry a reality by creating America as a kind of Masonic "Temple of Virtue" that produced model citizens. Many of the principles laid down in the United States Constitution are essentially Masonic principles: liberty, freedom of conscience, religious tolerance, pursuit of happiness, and separation of church and state. Most federal and state government buildings were consecrated with Masonic ceremonies. In addition, Freemasonry became almost synonymous with patriotism toward America's "civil religion." Famous patriotic Masons like Irving Berlin ("God Bless America") and John Philip Sousa ("Stars and Stripes Forever") wrote stirring songs and marches, while lesser-known Masons designed the capital city of Washington, D.C., created the Statue of Liberty, and sculpted the faces on Mount Rushmore.

Freemasonry in the nineteenth and twentieth centuries continued to develop along the lines established by the differing English and French models. English, Irish, and Scottish Freemasonry shaped the fraternity and its teachings in Canada, the United States, the West Indies, India, and much of Africa. The impact of the French tradition, with its rationalistic and politicized emphasis, was more deeply felt in Austro-Hungary, Spain, Portugal, Italy, and Latin America. By 1877, communication between these two groups had virtually ceased, when the Grand Orient of France removed the requirement that its initiates declare a belief in the existence of God as the "Great Architect of the Universe." In English-speaking areas, Freemasonry has in general prospered as a support to constitutional, democratic government.

One notable blemish on the Craft was the anti-Masonic episode in the United States. The abduction and suspected murder of William Morgan of Batavia, New York, in 1829 caused a widespread reaction against Freemasonry throughout the country. Morgan had published an exposé of its rituals and had brought considerable wrath upon himself from the fraternity, yet no solid evidence of his murder has been brought forward. Other secret societies, including Phi Beta Kappa and college social fraternities that are derived from the Freemasons, were also publicly affected, largely as a reaction against the perceived influence of political and social elites. This situation also precipitated the first American political party convention, that of the Anti-Masonic Party in 1832.

Masonic Teachings. Since 1717, Masonic teachings have retained a remarkable continuity and consistency. Membership in Freemasonry is comprised essentially of three steps or "degrees." The prospective candidate, after initial screening and interviewing, is initiated into the first degree as "entered apprentice," passed to second degree as "fellowcraft," and raised to the third degree as "master Mason," usually within a year. In place within Masonic ritual by 1730, the completion of all three degrees in succession made a man a full Mason, with all the rights and privileges of lodge fellowship, but also with expectations of participation in leadership succession, charitable work, and submission of dues. As part of the transformation from operative to speculative (initiated and living according to Masonic virtues) Masonry, each of the three degrees has employed within its structure "working tools" of the operative stonemasons, transformed from raw implements into symbols of Masonic teachings. The entered apprentice degree uses the 24-inch gauge and the common gavel, the former symbolic of dividing the hours of the day into three periods of service to God, charity, and rest, and the latter symbolic of removing vices and superfluities of life (i.e., forming the perfect ashlar out of the rough or imperfect stone, itself symbolic of the new candidate). The fellowcraft degree utilizes the plumb, square, and level to symbolize walking upright before God and fellow humans, honesty ("fair and square"), and equality ("on the level"). The third degree of master Mason utilizes the trowel in order to spread ("the cement of") brotherly love. In this degree, the legendary architect of King Solomon's Temple, Hiram Abif, is portrayed in a drama whereby he is symbolically slain by ruffians for not revealing Masonic secrets, and then "resurrected," thus serving as a paradigm for the rebirth of the candidates into a new life.

In addition to the above tools, there are three immovable "jewels" of the lodge, the rough ashlar (unpolished state of noninitiation), the perfect ashlar (ideal "polished" state of Masonic life), and the trestleboard (the rules and designs given by the "Great Architect of the Universe," the symbolic name for God). Each implement as used in the lodge both illustrates and confers specific Masonic teachings and obligations that are spoken as part of a "catechism" memorized by the candidate for each degree. All Masonic degrees are related to the transformation of the human personality from a state of darkness to light ("light in masonry"), symbolic of a higher level of human moral perfection destined to reach the "celestial lodge above," the term used for immortality beyond death.

Because Freemasonry has transposed a system of moral and noetic teaching upon a graded institutional structure, it has often been deemed a threat to confessional and orthodox religion. The basis for such assumptions is the fraternity's use of symbols that describe the change of personal moral character and human awareness by stages or degrees. These degrees have been interpreted as a plan for spiritual redemption without penance and forgiveness of sin. A study of the basic ceremonials and teachings, however, suggests that the goal of Masonic initiation is not actually redemption in the literal sense, but rather a shift in the initiate's perception toward the betterment of his personal moral character.

The lack of central authority and the multitude of Masonic degrees and ceremonials make it impossible to state unequivocally that Freemasonry is religious in any final or conclusive sense. Since Pope Clement XII's encyclical *In eminenti* in 1738, the Roman Catholic Church has proscribed Masonic affiliation for Catholics, with excommunication as the penalty. The emancipation of Jews was one of the by-products of the Enlightenment, and was ascribed to Masonic influence. As such, the free admission of Jews into lodges of equal fellowship with Christians evoked further condemnation by the Roman Catholic Church. Moreover, the identification of major southern European and Latin American revolutionary leaders, such as Giuseppe Mazzini, Giuseppe Garibaldi, Simón Bolívar, Bernardo O'Higgins, and José Julián Martí y Pérez, with Freemasonry created more tension by the end of the nineteenth century, especially during the First Vatican Council (1869–1870). More recently, the Lutheran Church-Missouri Synod and the Southern Baptist Convention in the United States and the General Conference of the Methodist Church in England and Wales have legislated claims that Freemasonry is a system of faith and morals outside of the Christian tradition.

Beside suspicions of philo-Semitism, including the fictional notion of a worldwide Jewish-Masonic conspiracy, Christian opposition to Freemasonry stems from the alleged elements of deism, natural religion, and Neoplatonism in Masonic rituals that suggest the perfectibility of humanity rather than its sinful nature and need of redemption in Christ (see Whalen, 1958). However, many churches that maintain a less exclusive understanding of revelation have been much more tolerant of Freemasonry's belief in a universal brotherhood of humanity under the fatherhood of God. Many Christians today continue to enjoy both Masonic and Christian fellowship. Moreover, in parts of the world where religions other than Christianity prevail, the volume of sacred law used in Masonic lodges corresponds to the prevalent book or scripture: in India, the Vedas or *Bhagavadgītā;* in Muslim countries where Masonry is permitted, the Qurʾān; and in Israel, the Torah. As such, Freemasonry does not advocate deism or any other specific religious doctrine, stressing that members pursue their religious life outside of the fraternity, yet live a moral life according to universal principles of brotherly love, relief, and truth.

At the beginning of the twenty-first century, Freemasonry has a worldwide membership of approximately seven million people. It is governed by independent national grand lodges, except in the United States, Canada, and Australia, where grand lodges are organized by state or province. All Freemasons maintain membership in a specific lodge, yet are welcomed as fellow Masons in most places of the world where Freemasonry thrives.

Freemasonry has also provided a working structure or model for secret organizations. During the nineteenth century, many new fraternal orders were created that in some way were derivative of Freemasonry. The Knights of Columbus is a Masonic-like order for Catholics only, and the Order of B'nai B'rith has a Jewish clientele. There is an endless list of these, including Odd Fellows, Elks, Moose, Rotary, Kiwanis, Lions, and Eagles. Even such occult groups as Gardnerian Witchcraft, the Theosophical Society, and the Hermetic Order of the Golden Dawn are not without Masonic influence.

More closely within the Masonic fold are the groups that require initiation into the three Craft degrees. Beside the Scottish and York Rites, there is the Ancient Arabic Order of the Nobles of the Mystic Shrine (Shriners), which has a visible Islamic theme to its rituals, and, along with the Grotto, provides a recreational dimension to fraternity life that is also strongly committed to charity in the form of burn clinics and hospitals for crippled children. The Order of DeMolay is designed for young men, and Acacia is the name for the Masonic college fraternity.

Freemasonry is by no means an exclusively male concern. Since ancient times, women have also bonded together into sisterhoods, both religious and secular. The Eleusinian Mysteries in ancient Greece, and the various women's orders in the Roman, medieval, and Renaissance periods, are precursors for what came to be referred to as adoptive Masonry, established in France about 1775. The Adoptive Rite, designed for wives, sisters, widows, and daughters of Freemasons, consisted of four degrees: apprentice, companion, mistress, and perfect mistress. Numerous Masonic rites and orders that included women proliferated in the nineteenth century, including Co-Masonry.

The most famous and successful of the adoptive or androgynous orders (orders that include both men and women) emerged in the United States in 1868 under the guidance of Robert Morris, an active Freemason. This group is called the Order of the Eastern Star, and it has over two million women members worldwide. Their rituals, utilizing a five-pointed star, consist of five degrees drawn from the examples of five biblical heroines: Adah (Jephtha's daughter; *Judges* 11:29–40), Ruth, Esther, Martha, and Electa (alluded to in *2 John*). Florence Nightingale was one of their famous patron members. Other Masonic orders for women include the White Shrine of Jerusalem and the Order of Amaranth, with Job's Daughters and Rainbow Girls for young women. Beside these, there are now several full-fledged women's grand lodges in the United States, which are independent of male Freemasonry. These groups, like most Masonic organizations, engage in various charitable activities. While Freemasonry is racially mixed, there are also independent, largely black, grand lodges. The largest of these African American lodges is Prince Hall, named after a freed slave in eighteenth-century Massachusetts who received a charter from London. Many notable African Americans, such as Booker T. Washington and W. E. B. Du Bois were Prince Hall Masons, as were jazz musicians Louis Armstrong, Duke Ellington, Count Basie, and Nat King Cole.

FAMOUS MASONS. Any assessment of the Masonic fraternity must acknowledge the wide range of membership that cuts across religious, ethnic, cultural, and racial lines. The list below includes names of some Masons who have distinguished themselves in service to both Masonry and the society in which they lived.

Stephen Austin, "Father of Texas"; Luther Burbank, American naturalist; Robert Burns, Scottish poet; Marc Chagall, Russian artist; Walter Chrysler, American car manufacturer; Winston Churchill, English statesman; Ty Cobb, American baseball legend; Davy Crockett, American frontiersman; Cecil B. De Mille, American filmmaker; Arthur Conan Doyle, English author; W. C. Fields, American comedic actor; John Glenn, American astronaut; Pasha Ismail, Egyptian viceroy and builder of the Suez Canal; Jerome Kern, American composer; Rudyard Kipling, English writer; Charles Lindbergh, American aviator; Charles H. Mayo, American physician and co-founder of the Mayo Clinic; Andrew Mellon, American industrialist; Motilal Nehru, Indian politician and father of Jawaharlal Nehru; Norman Vincent Peale, American Protestant clergyman; Pedro I, first king of Brazil; Paul Revere, American Revolutionary War hero; Sugar Ray Robinson, American boxing champion; Roy Rogers, American actor; Antoine Sax, Belgian inventor of the saxophone; Walter Scott, Scottish novelist and poet; Jean Sibelius, Finnish composer; Arthur Sullivan, English composer; Leo Tolstoy, Russian author; Swami Vivekananda, Hindu ascetic and philosopher; John Wayne, American actor; and Oscar Wilde, Anglo-Irish writer.

United States presidents who were Masons include George Washington, James Monroe, Andrew Jackson, James Polk, James Buchanan, Andrew Johnson, James Garfield, William McKinley, Theodore Roosevelt, William H. Taft, Warren G. Harding, Franklin D. Roosevelt, Harry S. Truman, Lyndon B. Johnson, Gerald R. Ford, and Ronald Reagan.

SEE ALSO Esotericism; Rosicrucians.

BIBLIOGRAPHY

Anderson, James. *The Constitutions of the Freemasons.* London, 1723; facs. reprint, London, 1976.

Anderson, James. *The New Book of Constitutions.* London, 1738; facs. reprint, London, 1976.

Ars Quatuor Coronatorum: Transactions of Quatuor Coronati Lodge No. 2076. London, 1888 onwards. Transactions of the premier lodge of Masonic research.

Baigent, Michael, and Richard Leigh. *The Temple and the Lodge.* New York, 1989.

Beck, Guy L. "Celestial Lodge Above: The Temple of Solomon in Jerusalem as a Religious Symbol in Freemasonry." *Nova Religio: The Journal of Alternative and Emergent Religions* 4, no. 1 (2000): 28–51.

Bullock, Steven C. *Revolutionary Brotherhood: Freemasonry and the Transformation of the American Social Order, 1730–1840.* Chapel Hill, N.C., 1996.

Cahill, Edward. *Freemasonry and the Anti-Christian Movement.* 2d ed. Dublin, 1930.

Carnes, Mark C. *Secret Ritual and Manhood in Victorian America.* New Haven, 1989.

Clawson, Mary Ann. *Constructing Brotherhood: Class, Gender, and Fraternalism.* Princeton, 1989.

Coil, Henry Wilson. *Coil's Masonic Cyclopedia.* Rev. ed. Richmond, Va., 1996.

Dumenil, Lynn. *Freemasonry and American Culture, 1880–1930.* Princeton, 1984.

Ferguson, Charles W. *Fifty Million Brothers: A Panorama of American Lodges and Clubs.* New York and Toronto, 1937.

Fox, William L. *Lodge of the Double-Headed Eagle: Two Centuries of Scottish Rite Freemasonry in America's Southern Jurisdiction.* Fayetteville, Ark., 1997.

Hamill, John. *World Freemasonry: An Illustrated History.* London, 1992.

Hamill, John. *The History of English Freemasonry.* London, 1994.

Henderson, Kent. *Masonic World Guide.* London, 1984.

Horne, Alex. *King Solomon's Temple in the Masonic Tradition.* Wellingborough, UK, 1972.

Jacob, Margaret C. *Living the Enlightenment: Freemasonry and Politics in Eighteenth-Century Europe.* New York, 1991.

Keith Schuchard, Marsha. *Restoring the Temple of Vision: Cabalistic Freemasonry and Stuart Culture.* Leiden, 2002.

Knoop, Douglas, and G. P. Jones. *The Mediaeval Mason: An Economic History of English Stone Building in the Late Middle Ages and Early Modern Times.* 3d ed. New York and Manchester, UK, 1967.

Knoop, Douglas, G. P. Jones, and Douglas Hamer. *The Early Masonic Catechisms.* 2d ed. Edited by Harry Carr. London, 1963.

Mackey, Albert G. *The History of Freemasonry: Its Legendary Origins.* New York, 1898; reprint, 1996.

Ovason, David. *The Secret Architecture of Our Nation's Capital: The Masons and the Building of Washington, D.C.* New York, 2000.

Pike, Albert. *Morals and Dogma of the Ancient and Accepted Scottish Rite of Freemasonry.* Charleston, S.C., 1871.

Ridley, Jasper. *The Freemasons: A History of the World's Most Powerful Secret Society.* New York, 2001.

Roberts, Allen E. *House Undivided: The Story of Freemasonry and the Civil War.* Richmond, Va., 1961.

Robinson, John J. *Born in Blood: The Lost Secrets of Freemasonry.* New York, 1990.

Robinson, John J. *A Pilgrim's Path: Freemasonry and the Religious Right: One Man's Road to the Masonic Temple.* New York, 1993.

Stevenson, David. *The First Freemasons: Scotland's Early Lodges and Their Members.* Aberdeen, UK, 1988.

Stevenson, David. *The Origins of Freemasonry: Scotland's Century, 1590–1710.* Cambridge, UK, 1988.

Walkes, Joseph A., Jr. *Black Square and Compass: 200 Years of Prince Hall Freemasonry.* Richmond, Va., 1979.

Weisberger, R. William, Wallace McLeod, S. Brent Morris, eds. *Freemasonry on Both Sides of the Atlantic: Essays concerning the Craft in the British Isles, Europe, the United States, and Mexico.* New York, 2002.

Whalen, William J. *Christianity and American Freemasonry.* Milwaukee, Wis., 1958.

Yates, Frances A. *The Rosicrucian Enlightenment.* London, 1972.

WILLIAM H. STEMPER, JR. (1987)
GUY L. BECK (2005)

FREE WILL AND DETERMINISM. Free will is a moral, religious, and social concept that is central to philosophy and most religions. It has been argued that the basis of freedom lies in the contingency of natural events. Though this line of reasoning has been by and large abandoned, for freedom to exist at all the concept of strict universal causality will have to be suspended, at least in the moral sphere. Another line of thought sees the foundation of freedom in spirituality: The soul, as immaterial, is not subject to the deterministic laws of nature. Whatever the explanation, belief in free will amounts to the conviction that, as individuals, human beings are endowed with the capacity for choice of action, for decision among alternatives, and specifically that, given an innate moral sense, humans can freely discern good and evil and choose the good, though they often do not. Determinism is the philosophical view that, given certain initial conditions, everything that ensues is bound to happen as it does and in no other possible way; thus nothing in nature is contingent, nor is there any room for human freedom. The partisans of a "hard" determinism hold that none of one's actions is free, but only appear to be so; consequently, moral responsibility is an illusion as well; "soft" determinists, or compatibilists, believe that while one's actions are indeed caused, one is nevertheless free, since causality does not compel one's will.

PHILOSOPHICAL INTERPRETATIONS. In Greek antiquity the idea of free will was clearly derived from the difference between free individuals and slaves, in modern times from the political structures of rising democratic electoral systems. A whole lineage of philosophers tried to reconcile the idea of determinism, the theological one in particular, with that of free will as uninhibited intentional action. Early Greek thought regarded free will as the denial of all intrinsic limitations upon the pursuit of voluntary goals. Plato shows in the *Republic* that social structures and moral conventions can be masterminded and manipulated at will. Both Socrates and Plato shifted the locus of freedom from the power to affect external events to the inner exercise of will and conviction. For Aristotle the power of free will lies in the capacity of thought to harmonize itself not only with God but with the good and the good life (*On Interpretation,* chap. 9). To be free meant to be rational. According to Augustine of Hippo *(On Free Will),* God's foreknowledge of events does not curtail the capacity to choose and indeed the necessity of doing so, since God's knowledge of eternity is somewhat akin to that of a ubiquitous present. The will is certainly free and there is no reason to believe that God's knowledge of the object of the will should impair its freedom in any way. Humanity's freedom is to love God and act upon its own will. In accordance with the same line of argument, Boethius (*On the Consolation of Philosophy*) defined eternity as "the simultaneous and complete possession of infinite life." Thomas Aquinas similarly held that God's eternal vision could in no way cause one's actions (*Summa theologiae* 1.14.13).

Modern philosophers struggled with the dilemma of divine foreknowledge and human freedom by redefining the latter, for instance, as "lack of constraint" (Hobbes); others, for example, Descartes, emphasized the infinity of the will in espousing the true and rejecting the false even though human understanding may be limited. Spinoza conceived of human free will as self-determination; Leibniz, as a form of uncaused spontaneity, which was later to be equated with "freedom from indifference." It followed from these views that God could never be blamed for human errors. Yet this concept of a mind causally undetermined, inexplicably free, was found unsatisfactory and was replaced by Locke's concept of preference as cause (opposed to the previous idea about the irrelevance of judgments to one's will), and by Hume's argument that a free action is one that could have been avoided. For Kant, determinism is phenomenal and freedom is noumenal, since the pure practical reason upon which one freely acts lies outside the realm of causation and makes up the essence and autonomy of moral life. Hegel and his left-wing followers looked upon freedom and necessity as two sides of the same coin, two ideas dialectically interconnected through "knowledge" or "understanding": Freedom is necessity understood. Other nineteenth-century idealists, called libertarians, tended to postulate a special entity, the "self," which uses the body as a causal instrument while being itself immune to causation. The materialists, to the contrary, had favored since antiquity an almost total subordination of freedom to the necessary or contingent play of natural and social forces outside of both individual and divine control.

Religious Interpretations. The essential presupposition of most major religions is that humans are born with freedom of choice. Free will is the capacity to choose among courses of action, objectives, things, desires, and so forth, and also to assume full moral responsibility for them. For the will to be free it is therefore necessary that there be no direct coercion, serious compulsion, or distortion of truth (for example, through propaganda or brainwashing) and also that alternatives for choice be at hand. A variety of conditions in society will allow for a variety of beliefs and the free exercise of human choice. Classically, this idea is defined as the absence of obstacles to the realization of various freedoms; it has a negative aspect, *freedom from* (want, fear, et al.), and a positive one, *freedom for* (worship, creativity, symbolic acts of speech, et al.). Religious freedom, including, but not reducible to, freedom of worship, illustrates the inseparability of these aspects, being at the same time freedom from spiritual coercion (for example, forcibly inculcated atheism, active proselytism) and freedom for the consciousness to believe, the individual to practice, and the community to exercise the rules of conduct and rituals of its own tradition.

The principle of determinism, which claims that the states of the universe, including human volition, are to be rigidly deduced from previous causes, and that nothing could be other than it is or was, is a negation of free will. To the extent that they involve moral responsibility, all religions must recognize that a human being is a free agent. However, the presupposition of monotheistic religions that the one God is not only omnipotent but also omniscient seems to annul the power of free decision in humanity, which leads to the contradiction of one being held responsible for some courses of action for which one is actually not responsible.

Most religions have sought a theological solution to this dilemma. In Hinduism, even though the blame for evil is usually cast upon the god who causes human imperfections and thus dooms humanity to downfall, people are still held morally responsible for their woes, as they are for corrupting other human beings; parents are considered morally responsible for their children's—even physical—constitution. A concept present across the board in Asian religions, from Jainism and Brahmanism to Buddhism, Sikkhism, Parsi, and animistic religions, is *karman,* which mainly points to action and reaction in the long series of reincarnations but is erroneously understood sometimes as rigid universal determinism, fate, or even retributive justice. Actually *karman* encompasses the unity and interrelatedness of all phenomena, their fundamental contingency, and the acts or rituals (*karman*) capable of destroying the bonds of transmigration. Under the law of *karman* an individual is essentially free to accept or to attempt to change the chain of cosmic events. There are many oscillations (from myth to myth and scripture to scripture) and ambiguities concerning the status of the individual in the cosmos: On the one hand, he or she might be considered as a passive entity subject to the laws of the universe, now weakened and contaminated, now strengthened and purified, by the flow of events; on the other hand, the individual enjoys a certain amount of spontaneous freedom. In any case, the goodness to which one should aspire is the integration and the harmony of ambivalent features rather than their dissociation. This is what makes the Hindu concept of free will radically different from the Judeo-Christian one.

There are two main concepts designating freedom in Indian philosophy: The one is *svāraj* (self-rule), which appears already in the *Chāndogya Upaniṣad* and has definite social, political, and moral connotations; the other is *mokṣa*, which has the psychological and metaphysical connotations of deliverance, emancipation, and release. There is both a tension and a synthesis between the two, out of which the real notion of freedom in Hinduism emerges. *Mokṣa* is, however, the ultimate goal of Hindu religion. It is freedom from *karman* and bondage, which in turn is freedom from ignorance, a freedom to be attained not after death but here and now through physical and mental discipline. Biological and social freedom is a necessary yet not sufficient condition for its achievement.

In Judaism, a person is born free because he or she is created in the image of God (who is free). Also, it is God's goodness that is reflected in human freedom. The faithful are to abolish completely their will in favor of God's. Yet, according to the teachings of the Bible, human obligations flow from two sources: divine law and the voice of inner conscience. In the Talmud, the *mitsvot* appear as absolute prescriptions, that is, decrees to be followed by man. Jewish philosophers, nevertheless, and particularly those influenced by Hellenism (e.g., Philo Judaeus and Josephus Flavius), insist on the heteronomous nature of the *mitsvot,* which are also an explicit expression of natural law. Judaism offers little evidence for the idea that events in the life of an individual might have been "fated" (in the Greek sense of *moira*); yet the major collective occurrences in the life of the people of Israel were commanded and predetermined by God. As lord of history and judge, God both rules over nature and determines the end result of human deeds and conflicts. God may sometimes be portrayed in the Hebrew scriptures (*Is.* 34:17) as a caster of lots. In the rabbinical period, the belief emerged that God did predetermine major events such as the dates of birth, death, and marriage in the individual's life. Outside of these, however, there was no predetermination. Nothing could abolish the free will and therefore the moral responsibility of the person.

Islam holds the belief that major events are fated and decreed by God; this allows one to affirm the underlying uniformity and rationality of the universe. The concept of fate, however, was borrowed from pre-Islamic Arabic literature, especially from poetry that was not necessarily religious. It became subordinated in Islam to a divine predestination that by itself does not preclude the actual freedom of the individual's will. More and more, Islamic theologians shun the attribute of fatalism bestowed upon the Muslim religion. "Fate" is often a label given after the fact; to say that something is fated is to give an easy and weak explanation to an otherwise inexplicable event. The argument is that while in God's mind everything is determined in advance, the active believer is wholly ignorant of this determination and therefore enjoys fully the freedom to choose.

Christianity is among the major religions that emphasize the freedom of humanity to the last consequence. Even the existence of evil in face of the omnipotence of God is justified in terms of the supremacy of humankind's essential freedom to adopt its own goals and to choose its own course of action. The controversy between Augustine of Hippo and Pelagius as early as the fifth century set the scene for what was to be an ongoing theological debate in Western Christianity. To Augustine's almost exclusive emphasis on indwelling grace, Pelagius, a British monk who lived in Africa and was condemned for heresy by two synods, opposed the notion that the human, unassisted free will acts in a sovereign way in bringing about or jeopardizing human salvation. In the sixteenth century, Erasmus of Rotterdam defended the church doctrine of free will against Martin Luther's aggressive denial of it and Luther's affirmation of humankind's complete dependence upon God's grace. Protestant theology with Zwingli, Wyclif, Calvin, and their followers steadily upheld the soteriological and metaphysical doctrine of predestination.

In Mādhyamika Buddhism, freedom from pain, which implies a complete, blissful regeneration of humankind, is achieved by the elimination of all conceptual constructions at their very roots: the duality between "is" and "is-not." The spiritual discipline of attaining enlightenment or achieving Buddhahood through the resolution of the painful conflict between the private and the social good is conducive to wisdom, *prajñā,* which is itself liberating. To achieve freedom is mainly a negative process consisting in the elimination of hindrances that obscure the real, such as attachment, aversion, and all mental fictional constructions. *Śūnyatā* as the intellectual intuition of voidness is equated with freedom.

Avowedly the relationship between free will and determinism is one of paradox, that is, of mutual implication and repulsion occurring simultaneously. This paradox can more or less be dissolved by relegating free will to the realms of spiritual awareness, psychologically lived reality, and practical (moral) action; whereas determinism and predestination would belong to the actual ontological and existential givenness of things and events in the world. Attempts at solving this paradox have led some theistic process philosophers and theologians (e.g., Charles Hartshorne) to want to weaken the divine attributes of omniscience and omnipotence. It is not God's unsurpassable power but his monopoly on it that is denied. This should allow for openness and indeterminacy in the future in which humanity's options can be exercised freely. The present stage of the philosophical discussion of free will and determinism in relation to both cosmology and individual existence involves sophisticated epistemological arguments from the theory of explanation, causality, the symmetry of past and future, and the theory of human action.

See Also Conscience; Existentialism; Fate; Free Will and Predestination; Israelite Law; Karman; Materialism; Mokṣa; Morality and Religion; Naturalism; Pelagianism; Prajñā; Soteriology; Śūnyam and Śūnyatā; Theodicy.

Bibliography

Campbell, Charles Arthur. *Selfhood and Godhood.* London, 1957.

Hartshorne, Charles. *A Natural Theology of Our Time.* LaSalle, Ill., 1967.

James, William. *The Will to Believe.* New York, 1921.

Kant, Immanuel. *Critique of Practical Reason.* Translated by Lewis Beek. Chicago, 1949.

Morgenbesser, Sidney and James Walsh, eds. *Free Will.* Englewood Cliffs, N.J., 1962.

Murti, T. R. V. *The Central Philosophy of Buddhism.* 2d ed. London, 1955. See especially pp. 261–269.

Ryle, Gilbert. *The Concept of Mind* (1949). Reprint, Chicago, 1984.

Schopenhauer, Arthur. *Essay on the Freedom of the Will.* Translated by Konstantin Kolenda. Indianapolis, 1960.

Spinoza, Barukh. *Ethics.* Translated by William Hale White. New York, 1949.

Winter, Ernst, ed. *Discourse on Free Will: Selections from Erasmus and Luther.* New York, 1961.

Zagzebski, Linda. "Divine Foreknowledge and Human Free Will." *Religious Studies* 3 (1985): 279–298.

New Sources

Barker, Eileen. "'And the Wisdom to Know the Difference?': Freedom, Control and the Sociology of Religion." *Sociology of Religion* 64 (fall 2003): 285–308.

Dennett, Daniel C. *Freedom Evolves.* New York, 2003.

Noble, Greg, and Megan Watkins. "So, How Did Bourdieu Learn to Play Tennis? Habitus, Consciousness and Habituation." *Cultural Studies* 17 (May 2003): 520–540.

O'Connor, Timothy. *Persons and Causes: The Metaphysics of Free Will.* New York, 2002.

Pollack, Robert. *The Faith of Biology and the Biology of Faith: Order, Meaning and Free Will in Modern Medical Science.* New York, 2000.

Wegner, Daniel. *The Illusion of Conscious Will.* Cambridge, Mass., 2002.

Ileana Marcoulesco (1987)
Revised Bibliography

FREE WILL AND PREDESTINATION

This entry consists of the following articles:

AN OVERVIEW
CHRISTIAN CONCEPTS
ISLAMIC CONCEPTS

FREE WILL AND PREDESTINATION: AN OVERVIEW

Free will and predestination constitute a polarity in many of the religions of the world: is salvation determined by a divine choice or is it a matter of personal self-determination? *Free will* in this article does not refer to the general philosophical problem of the will's freedom but to the specific meaning and function of willing and self-determination in the process of salvation. Some religious thinkers have sharply distinguished between the will's freedom in the material and civil affairs of life and its freedom or unfreedom with regard to the spiritual life, and it is with the latter that this article is concerned.

At least two ways of thinking about the freedom of the will in spiritual matters have been common: free will as a freedom of choice, whereby one does freely what one has also had the power to choose to do, and free will as the absence of compulsion, whereby one willingly does what one does without actively choosing what is done. The latter has been described as voluntary necessity. In the first of these meanings of freedom, freedom seems incompatible with divine determination; in the second, it does not, and is opposed not to causality but to constraint.

Predestination as it is treated in this article is separated from the general consideration of providence, determinism, and fate, and refers only to the voluntary divine choice of certain groups or individuals for salvation. Sometimes predestination is considered as a part of divine providence, namely, that aspect of the divine determination of all things that refers to the supernatural end of souls, as opposed to the determination of persons with regard to all else or of the natural order. But predestination is to be sharply distinguished from some forms of determinism and from fatalism, which do not necessarily involve the theistic concept of a personal deity making conscious choices. *Determinism* may mean any one of a number of systems claiming that all events cannot occur otherwise than they do, sometimes without reference to deity. *Fate* suggests an impersonal determining force that may even transcend the gods.

The terms *election* and *reprobation* have meanings related to predestination. One traditional use of these terms considers predestination the larger divine act, which encompasses the separate decrees of election (predestination to salvation) and reprobation (predestination to damnation). *Reprobation,* however, is seldom used now, and *election* is more commonly simply substituted for *predestination,* because it seems more positive in its connotations. In biblical studies, *election* has been the preferred term for referring to divine choice.

Predestination has been considered not inevitably contradictory to free will. Sometimes both are held together as paradoxical, yet complementary, aspects of truth; but more classically, free will is understood not as freedom of choice but as voluntary necessity. That is, where freedom means the absence of compulsion, necessary acts determined by God nonetheless can be freely done. Almost all predestinarian theologies have therefore maintained that the predestined will acts freely and with consequent responsibility for its actions, even though it lacks the power to choose its actions. In this sense of freedom, even the decree of reprobation has been seen as compatible with responsibility and not as entailing a divine compulsion to do evil. This compatibility of free will and predestination has historically been a commonplace of Augustinian and Calvinistic theology in Christianity, and of Islamic theology through its doctrine of acquisition. Even such a materialistic determinist as Thomas Hobbes thought that necessary acts were entirely voluntary and therefore responsible acts. It is this that sharply distinguishes predestination from fatalism, which may entail compulsion to act in a certain way. Roman Catholic theology refers to any predestinarian doctrine that proceeds without reference to the will's freedom as the error of predestinarianism. Only in rare cases in Christian and Islamic theology has that way of understanding predestination appeared.

Occurrence in the History of Religions. The issue of free will and predestination in relation to salvation arises in those religions that believe in a personal, omnipotent God, and thus has appeared mainly in Judaism, Christianity, and Islam. But it has also occurred in ancient Greece and India among certain groups that have had a similar religious understanding.

Ancient Greece. Ancient Greek monotheism, centering on the figure of Zeus, came near to personal theism in Stoicism, particularly among the later Stoics who believed in immortality. They considered Zeus a universal mind and will determining all things, including the virtue by which good persons resigned themselves to the inevitable; through this providence elect souls triumphed over the sufferings of earthly existence.

Judaism. In Judaism, the Deuteronomic tradition especially accents Yahveh's choice of Israel as his people. In the Hebrew scriptures, the stories of Moses, Samuel, Isaiah, and Jeremiah show God's choice of particular persons to fulfill special offices. But this election, whether of persons or of the group, is grounded by the Hebrew scriptures in the divine initiative, not in the chosen object, and involves special tasks and responsibilities more than special privileges. The will's freedom of choice in obeying God's commandments is clearly asserted in many passages of the Hebrew scriptures, as, for example, in *Deuteronomy* 30:15–20. The apocryphal book of *Ben Sira* asserts that God does not lead persons astray but created them with the freedom not to sin (15:11–17).

Josephus Flavius, in describing the Pharisees to his Hellenistic audience, said that they considered all events predetermined but still did not deprive the human will of involvement in decisions about virtue and vice. The Sadducees he described as rejecting determinism altogether (*Jewish Antiquities* 13.171–173; *Jewish War,* 2.162–166). The Essenes were the most predestinarian of the Jewish groups, if the Qumran texts are to be attributed to them. The Qumran literature teaches that God created the spirits of men to be cast in the lots of either good or evil and that salvation is divinely initiated and based on God's choice. Nonetheless, the Essenes also maintained human accountability for evil. Elsewhere in the Judaism of the Hellenistic age, Philo Judaeus upheld the will's complete freedom.

Rabbinic literature taught both God's foresight and providence directing all things and human freedom of choice with respect to the doing of good or evil. A saying of ʿAqivaʾ ben Yosef juxtaposes them: "All is foreseen and yet freedom is granted" (*Avot* 3:15). Some rabbinic sayings suggest that everything about a person's life is determined by God except for the soul's obedience to God (B. T., *Ber.* 33b, *Meg.* 25a, *Nid.* 16b). This matter did not become a serious question for Jewish thinkers until contact with Islamic speculations in the tenth century, when Saʿadyah Gaon took up the problem. He and all the medieval Jewish philosophers maintained the will's freedom of choice. But Maimonides alluded to the view of "uninformed" Jews that God decrees that an individual will be either good or evil when the infant is being formed in the womb (*Mishneh Torah,* Repentance 5.2).

Christianity. Predestination has had a more central place in Christian thought. The theme of predestination to salvation appears strongly in the Pauline literature, especially the *Letter to the Romans.* For Paul, predestination results from the divine initiative and is grounded in grace, so that no one may boast of being saved by his own efforts. Paul also speaks of God's hardening of the hearts of unbelievers (*Rom.* 9:18).

In spite of the numerous New Testament references to predestination, patristic writers, especially the Greek fathers, tended to ignore the theme before Augustine of Hippo. This was probably partly the result of the early church's struggle with the fatalistic determinism of the Gnostics. Augustine, writing against the Pelagians, taught that God predestined to salvation some out of the mass of sinners, passing by the rest and thus leaving them to just condemnation for the sins they willingly committed. Augustine thought that the will was unable to do the good that God commanded unless aided by grace. To do evil willingly was a slavery to sin from which grace rescued those whom God had chosen. Augustine had many medieval followers in this doctrine, including Gottschalk in the ninth century, who stated the doctrine in an extreme fashion, and Thomas Bradwardine in the fourteenth century, who opposed those he considered his Pelagian contemporaries. Thomas Aquinas was also a predestinarian, but he treated the doctrine in the context of God's providence as a whole. On the other hand, such medieval Scholastics as John Duns Scotus and William of Ockham sought to reconcile God's prescience with human freedom of choice.

In the Renaissance and Reformation there was a revival of predestinarian thinking. Lorenzo Valla was the main representative of determinism among Renaissance philosophers, while almost all of the major Protestant reformers found the doctrine of predestination useful in their insistence upon the primacy of divine grace in salvation. Luther (and Lutheranism, in the Formula of Concord) soon backed away from the extreme predestinarian teaching of his early *Bondage of the Will* and taught only election to life, with the possibility of falling from grace. The Reformed churches, following their teachers Huldrych Zwingli, Martin Bucer, John Calvin, and Peter Martyr Vermigli, gave the doctrine an important role in the defense of grace in salvation and also taught double predestination, but still insisted on the freedom of the will, which they understood in the Augustinian sense of voluntary necessity. Later Scholastic Reformed theologians, such as Theodore Beza, William Perkins, and Franciscus Turretinus, gave the doctrine of predestination a central role in their theological systems. An important eighteenth-century defense of the Reformed view of predestination and the freedom of the will came from Jonathan Edwards in colonial Massachusetts. The Church of England adopted the predestinarian theology of the Reformers in its Thirty-nine Articles and in the first century of its existence generally taught the Reformed view of the matter.

The Roman Catholic theology of the same period, especially that of the Jesuits, stressed human responsibility in the process of salvation, with Luis de Molina maintaining the position of "congruism," that is, of grace as efficacious according as the will cooperates with it. Countering this was a revival of Augustinian theology, represented by the Spanish Dominican Domingo Bañez and by Cornelis Jansen in the Netherlands. The Jansenists in France, including Blaise Pascal, considered the Jesuits Pelagian. Predestination has not been an important theme in more modern Roman Catholic theology, and Catholic treatments of Augustine tend to focus on other aspects of his thought.

In the later history of Protestantism, emphasis upon predestination has generally declined, and freedom of choice in salvation has frequently been asserted. From the beginning, few of the Anabaptists were predestinarian. Some of the early Protestant reformers, including Heinrich Bullinger and Theodor Bibliander, were cautious in their treatment of predestination, and the Dutch Reformed theologian Jacobus Arminius (1560–1609) asserted that God predestined to salvation those whom he foresaw would believe. This assertion of the will's freedom of choice in salvation came to be known as Arminianism and gained ground among English Protestants throughout the seventeenth century. In the next century John Wesley adopted it as the theology of Methodism, and it generally made headway among evangelicals who wanted to be able to make straightforward appeals for conversions. Thus its avowal by the nineteenth-century American evangelist Charles G. Finney influenced many in the formally Calvinistic Presbyterian and Congregationalist denominations, although his contemporary, the Princeton theologian Charles Hodge, continued to uphold double predestination in its Scholastic form. The liberal Protestant theology of the nineteenth and early twentieth century usually rejected any form of predestinarian theology. But in the twentieth century, two Reformed theologians, Emil Brunner and Karl Barth, have attempted reformulations of predestination while abandoning its more unpalatable features.

Islam. Free will and predestination have been important issues in Islamic thought. Basic to Muhammad's religious experience was a sense of God's power, majesty, and judgment. The Qurʾān exhorts submission before the divine sovereignty and declares even that "God leads astray whom he pleases and guides whom he pleases" (*sūrah* 74:34). But the Qurʾān also presupposes choice on the part of persons who have been summoned by revelation. Early in the history of Islam, the predestinarian emphasis was reinforced by a general Arab cultural belief in fate, and some Muslims thought that God permitted Satan's irresistible incitement to evil. But one of the first groups of Islamic philosophers, the Muʿtazilah, argued that, however much other events were determined beforehand, there was a free human choice of good or evil. Later Muslim theologians, emphatically teaching predestination, nonetheless tried to reconcile it with free will through varying interpretations of the doctrine of acquisition. According to this doctrine, man is regarded as voluntarily willing his actions and thus "acquiring" them, even though God has created these acts so that they occur by necessity. Such a viewpoint has many parallels with Augustinianism, and generally Islam is no more fatalistic than is Christianity.

Hinduism. The main traditions of Hinduism and Buddhism do not posit a personal deity with an omnipotent will, and thus the polarity of free will and predestination in relation to the salvation of souls has not been so prominent as in Judaism, Christianity, and Islam. The doctrine of *karman* can constitute a kind of determinism whereby an individual's lot in life is determined by his behavior in past lives, but the doctrine can also imply that a soul is in charge of its future destiny; its modern proponents therefore sometimes consider the doctrine to imply freedom more than fatalism. But in either case, *karman* is usually seen not as the willing of a personal deity but as the workings of an impersonal force.

However, some schools of Hinduism maintain personal theism and an omnipotent God and consequently wrestle with the problem of free will and predestination. For example, the Vaiṣṇava sect of Madhva (1238–1317) believed that Viṣṇu predestined some souls to blessedness and others to damnation, simply for his good pleasure and not because of the merits or demerits of the souls themselves. A more cautious theology of predestination appeared in the interpretation of the Vedanta by Rāmānuja (fl. c. 1100). He taught that the souls of some persons were led to repentance by a divine initiative, but he also held that the choice of good or evil nonetheless included personal acts performed by means of a God-given freedom. Rāmānuja's followers divided over the extent to which divine power controlled souls. The Teṅkalai, or "cat school," taught that God's irresistible grace saves some souls the way the mother cat carries her young by the nape of the neck, while the Vaṭakalai, or "monkey school," taught that God's grace and the human will cooperate in salvation the way the infant monkey clings to the mother.

As a Phenomenon of Religious Experience. The notion of the freedom of the will in relation to salvation arises out of the everyday experience of free choice and personal responsibility. There seems to be a human need to feel in control of one's life. Modern experience has been especially characterized by a sense of autonomy, and this has abetted the assumption of the will's freedom of choice with reference to salvation.

Belief in predestination, on the other hand, represents and abstracts from the experience of creatureliness before the majesty of the divine. It was Friedrich Schleiermacher (1768–1834) who first looked at predestination as a transcript of subjective piety, concluding that it was an element in the religious person's consciousness of dependence upon God. Following Schleiermacher, Rudolf Otto attempted a phenomenology of the "creature feeling" that he thought lay behind the doctrine of predestination. As Otto interpreted it, the idea of predestination was rooted not in speculative thought but in religious self-abasement, the "annulment of personal strength and claims and achievements in the presence of the transcendent," and thus was "an immediate and pure expression of the actual religious experience of grace." The one who receives grace feels that nothing has merited this favor, and that it is not a result of his own effort, resolve, or achievement. Rather, grace is a force that has grasped, impelled, and led him. Predestination is thus a numinous experience of awe in the face of the *mysterium tremendum.*

Besides being rooted in the human sense of createdness and of grace, predestination as a religious phenomenon also depends on a sense of trust and confidence in the reliability of the divine and in its power to complete what has been begun in the creature. Such belief in an ordered world and rejection of the sheer fortuitousness of things is an important element of much religious consciousness and leads to a sense of assurance about God's purpose and about one's own spiritual security. Ernst Troeltsch thought that it was in the interest of the assurance of salvation that predestination became such a central doctrine in Protestant theology.

Belief in predestination may also be regarded as arising from the search for a purely spiritual religion, for it has the effect of stripping away all concrete mediation and leaving the soul alone before God. It was this that led Max Weber to consider belief in predestination as functionally related to the process of the elimination of magic from the world. This aspect of predestinarian religion has been greatly attractive to religious reformers, for the doctrine can become a means to sweep away much accumulation of religiosity.

Another aspect of belief in predestination as a matter of religious experience is that it has had the effect, not (as might be supposed) of giving rise to fatalistic acquiescence, but of energizing the will for the fulfillment of divinely assigned tasks. Thus Calvinist theologians spoke of predestination as election to holiness.

As a Problem of Religious Thought. While beliefs concerning free will and predestination may be rooted in religious experience, they are also connected to certain intellectual concerns and puzzlements. One motive for such reflection has been the simple observation that some believe while others do not—is this fact the consequence of personal freedom of choice or of divine predetermination?

Reflection on divine omnipotence has led to the inference that the divine choice must be the determining factor in salvation. If some things were excepted from the general principle that all things occur by virtue of a divine causality, then God would seem to lack the efficacy to bring his purposes to fruition. Even the bare acknowledgment of divine foreknowledge seems to entail determinism, for if God knows what will happen from eternity, it must necessarily happen in that way or else his knowledge would be rendered erroneous. And though it may be argued that God foresees actual human choices, nonetheless when the time for those choices arrives, they cannot be other than they are; this is precisely what identifies an event as predetermined. Opponents of this viewpoint have maintained, however, that foresight is not a cause and that therefore a foreseen event need not be a determined one.

Still, the doctrine of predestination has probably been rooted primarily not in this kind of consideration but in the theological need to maintain the gratuitousness of salvation. To connect this with predestination effectively rules out any possibility of human merit.

Theologies that have asserted the will's freedom of choice in salvation have, on the other hand, focused on different theological needs, primarily those of preserving human responsibility in the process of salvation and God's goodness and justice in the governing of his creation. If salvation is entirely God's gift, how can those left out be held responsible? In the modern period, the Augustinian definition of freedom as absence of constraint has not been widely persuasive, in spite of the fact that many elements of contemporary thought, especially in relation to heredity, have provided some basis for considering human freedom in this way.

The problem of theodicy, in Christian thought in particular, seems almost inevitably to rely on the assumption of human freedom of choice in salvation. Even the Puritan poet John Milton, in seeking to "justify the ways of God to man," fell back upon an assertion of such freedom.

Several considerations may be brought forward in religious thought in order, if not exactly to solve, then at least to extenuate this problem. One approach is simply to acquiesce to the polarity of free will and predestination as a paradox. Another consideration is Augustine's argument that God exists not in time but in the qualitatively different state of eternity. Thus since for God there is no past or future, there is no priority of time for his foresight or decree in relation to the events of salvation; priority is implied only by our inadequate language. A further Augustinian consideration is that, since the evil of an evil act is a deficiency of being, it requires no divine causality at all. Evil is only a falling away from the good (and from freedom) and hence needs no positive causality.

SEE ALSO Election; Fate; Free Will and Determinism; Grace; Justification; Theodicy.

BIBLIOGRAPHY

There are several useful introductions to the subject: C. H. Ratschow, Erich Dinkler, E. Kähler, and Wolfhart Pannenberg's "Prädestination," in *Die Religion in Geschichte und Gegenwart,* 3d ed. (Tübingen, 1957–1965), and Henri Rondet and Karl Rahner's "Predestination," in *Sacramentum Mundi: An Encyclopedia of Theology,* edited by Karl Rahner (New York, 1968–1970), both of which give an extensive bibliography in several languages; Giorgio Tourn's *La predestinazione nella Bibbia e nella storia* (Turin, 1978); and Vernon J. Bourke's *Will in Western Thought: An Historico-Critical Survey* (New York, 1964).

Rudolf Otto's *The Idea of the Holy* (1923), 2d ed. (London, 1950), offers a classic phenomenological analysis of the problem. Discussion of the general historical significance of predestination appears in my *Puritans and Predestination* (Chapel Hill, N.C., 1982), pp. 191–196. For the Bible and ancient Judaism, see Harold H. Rowley's *The Biblical Doctrine of Election* (London, 1950), Eugene H. Merrill's *Qumran and Predestination* (Leiden, 1975), and George Foot Moore's "Fate and Free Will in the Jewish Philosophies according to Josephus," *Harvard Theological Review* 22 (October 1929): 371–389. Two rather traditional Christian theological investigations of the problem, the first Protestant and the second Roman Catholic, are Gaston Deluz's *Prédestination et liberté* (Paris, 1942) and M. John Farrelly's *Predestination, Grace, and Free Will* (Westminster, Md., 1964). A more recent Christian theological treatment is Paul K. Jewett, *Election and Predestination* (Grand Rapids, Mich., 1985). For Indian thought, see Sarvepalli Radhakrishnan's *Indian Philosophy,* 2d ed., 2 vols. (London, 1927–1931), pp. 659–721, 731–751, and Rudolf Otto's *Die Gnadenreligion Indiens und das Christentum* (Gotha, 1930), translated by Frank H. Foster as India's *Religion of Grace and Christianity* (New York, 1930). The standard work on this subject for Islam is W. Montgomery Watt's *Free Will and Predestination in Early Islam* (London, 1948).

DEWEY D. WALLACE, JR. (1987 AND 2005)

FREE WILL AND PREDESTINATION: CHRISTIAN CONCEPTS

In an effort to explain the roles of human and divine agency in the accomplishment of salvation, Christian theologians have formulated concepts of free will and predestination. The concepts entered the creeds of the churches. The notion of predestination introduces the matter of time-order in affirming that God made a decision or decree about who over the course of the ages would be saved by Christ *prior* to any decision or action that those who are saved might take during their lifetime in relation to their own salvation. Following Augustine and Paul, theologians and the creeds have usually maintained that God's decision occurred "before the foundation of the world." In the face of this emphasis on God's previous power of decision, the notion of free will affirms the human role that might appear to be overridden thereby, and acknowledges the power of human decision within the process of salvation. The two notions exist in a paradoxical relationship with each other, and they turn on an understanding of history.

A widely held but mistaken opinion identifies the notion of predestination as a concept peculiar to Calvinists since the sixteenth century, asserting that Calvinist traditions have denied or rendered irrelevant the notion of free will. On the contrary, all Christian traditions that honor the ancient creeds have in some way affirmed both free will and predestination. They have, however, meant very different things by these concepts and have given them different roles in relation to each other. In recent times, churches have tended to mute their references to predestination, allowing the discourse to continue in a new form outside of ecclesiastical and theological milieux as a debate about freedom and determinism.

THE ISSUES AND THE SCRIPTURES. That the question arises—and that it persists—may be attributed to the human experience of being able to choose responsibly among real options while at the same time being overwhelmed by forces apparently beyond human ability to choose. Christians have used the doctrines of free will and predestination as their means of expressing these contrary experiences—on the one hand, the certitude of salvation as God's act; on the other hand, the human responsibility to believe and do what is right.

Christians have related these two concepts to many others, including God's sovereignty and grace, divine foreknowledge of future human acts, divine election in relation to human merits, eternity and time, causation, and the process of salvation. They have raised periodic warnings against trying to penetrate the mystery of salvation, against impugning the justice or the mercy of God, and against making God the author of evil.

Advocates of all positions have appealed to the Bible, even though the biblical scriptures do not contain what one might call doctrines or concepts of free will and predestination, nor even these words. The Latin term *praedestinatione* derives from the creation of an abstract noun from the translation of the Greek verb *proorizo,* which refers to deciding or setting limits on something beforehand. The word occurs six times in four passages in the New Testament: *Acts of the Apostles* 4:28, *Romans* 8:28–30, *1 Corinthians* 2:7, and *Ephesians* 1:3–14. The King James translation of the Bible renders the *Romans* passage this way: "For whom he did foreknow, he also did predestinate to be conformed to the image of his Son. . . . Moreover whom he did predestinate, them he also called. . . ." In constructing the concept, theologians had to piece together the several passages in keeping of some sense of logic, and the ways they did this led to differences. Commonly they linked *proorizo* with a time metaphor from *Ephesians* 1 about God "choosing us" "before the foundation of the world." This they augmented with Paul's references in *Romans* 9 to one Old Testament passage about God's "hardening the heart of Pharaoh" and another about God choosing Jacob instead of Esau even before these twins were conceived. Over the ages, through this process of turning verbs into nouns and metaphors into concepts, theologians have built a logical edifice of considerable magnitude. The process has passed through four phases so far.

From Scripture to Early Augustine. Paul's writings in the Bible formed the basis of all future treatments. For three hundred years after Paul, theologians were content to produce commentaries on the pertinent passages. Following the lead of Clement of Alexandria (fl. c. 200 CE), however, they interpreted *proorizo* as depending upon *proginosko* (foreknow)—those whom God foreknew would believe, God decided upon beforehand to save. The chief concern was to combat the concept of fatalism and affirm that humans are free to do what is righteous. Thus Origen fought the Gnostics toward the middle of the third century, and Augustine wrote *On Free Will* against the Manichaeans (c. 397). Origen asserted that humans were created with free will in the sense "that it is our own doing whether we live rightly or not, and that we are not compelled, either by those causes which come to us from without, or, as some think, by the presence of fate."

Augustine through the 1400s. Augustine changed his emphasis as a result of a challenge from Pelagius, who sought to defend human free will against Augustine's apparent denial of it in his *Confessions* (400): "Grant us what you [God] command, and command us what you will." In numerous treatises written over the succeeding two decades against Pelagius and those later called semi-Pelagians, Augustine gradually created the doctrine of predestination and established the terms in which virtually all subsequent discussions have carried on. He stated that God created humans with the free will to choose between good and evil. By choosing evil they lost their free will fully to do God's will, and thereafter needed God's grace to be saved and to live righteously. In *On the Predestination of the Saints* (428–429) Augustine claimed that God's gift of grace is prepared for by God's prior decision from eternity to predestine some to salvation. On this view, grace then comes as the effect of that predestination. God supremely predestined Christ to be the Son of God and called all those predestined for salvation to become members of Christ's body. Those so elected do indeed choose by their free will to believe, but since they are the elect, their "will is prepared by the Lord." In Augustine's view, none of this depends on divine foreknowledge of future human merits. In the *City of God* (413–426) he claims that God has "a plan whereby he might complete the fixed number of citizens predestined in his wisdom, even out of the condemned human race." God decides on the plan in eternity (an everlasting present) and foreknows in one sweeping vision the whole of time (the course of the past, present, and future). In *Enchiridion* (421) Augustine taught what came to be called "double predestination," that God not only in his mercy predestines some to salvation but in his justice predestines the rest to damnation or reprobation.

A succession of church councils culminating in the Council of Orange (529) elevated Augustine's position to the status of orthodoxy. Thereafter the view not quite accurately attributed to the Pelagians—that original sin has no power to keep humans from using their free will to gain their own salvation—was deemed unacceptable. The Council of Quiercy (853), responding to the concept of double predestination as elaborated by Gottschalk (848), declared that view unacceptable as well. The council held that while God surely preelects some to salvation, he merely leaves the remainder of humanity in their freely chosen sin with its predestined consequence of eternal punishment.

Between roughly 1050 and 1450, numerous theologians worked in Augustine's lineage to construct logical definitions of free will or predestination. They included Anselm of Canterbury (d. 1109), Peter Lombard (d. 1160), Duns Scotus (d. 1308), William of Ockham (d. 1349?), John Wyclif (d. 1384), Lorenzo Valla (d. 1457), and others. In his *Summa theologiae* (1266–1273), Thomas Aquinas gathered and elaborated a great array of logical distinctions to explain the concepts of free will and predestination: sufficient and efficient grace, habitual and actual grace, operating and cooperating grace, unconditional and conditional necessity, antecedent and consequent will, primary and secondary cause, and so on. According to Thomas, predestination was "the planned sending of a rational creature to the end which is eternal life." It "presupposes election, and election [presupposes] love." Thomas believed that his logic would show that none of this impairs free will.

Reformation through the 1800s. The rupture of Latin Christendom called the Reformation led to a proliferation of positions roughly analogous to the pluralism of ecclesiastical traditions produced after the 1520s. A brief statement by Martin Luther (1520) that appeared to deny free will prompted Desiderius Erasmus to write *On the Freedom of the Will* (1524) in the hope of settling the matter simply. Instead of a resolution, however, the ensuing debate initiated a controversy lasting four hundred years. By the time it ended, theologians in virtually all traditions had attempted definitions of the concepts of free will and predestination, and every major church tradition had built some statement of the concepts into its creed.

Erasmus picked up a concept that Thomas and others had used about cooperating grace and brought the analogous concept of cooperating will or assisting will into the discussion. Erasmus asserted that the will of God "preveniently moves the [human] will to will." Yet, humans do indeed will and achieve something. He concluded that *Philippians* 2:12–16 "certainly teaches that both humans and God work." Luther retorted with *On the Bondage of the Will* (1525), denying any possibility of cooperation between God and human will. The term *free will,* he claimed, applies only to God or to the "lower choices" that humans make about everyday matters. All matters pertaining to salvation "depend on the work of God alone," the only power able to free the will from bondage to sin. Luther adopted Augustine's position on predestination. The Lutheran Formula of Concord (1576) stated: "The predestination or eternal election of God extends only to the good and beloved children of God, and this is the cause of their salvation." Concerning the nonelect, the formula urged caution when speaking of reprobation.

Caution had become necessary, the Lutherans thought, because of John Calvin's views. In his *Romans* (1540) and *Institutes of the Christian Religion,* Calvin adopted Augustine's views and followed Luther in rejecting the notion of divine and human cooperation in salvation. By the final edition of the *Institutes* (1559), however, he defined predestination expansively to include double predestination: "By predestination we mean the eternal decree of God, by which he determined with himself whatever he wished to happen with regard to every person. All are not created on equal terms, but some are preordained to eternal life, others to eternal damnation." A succession of Reformed creeds, including the French Reformed Confession (1559), the Scots Confession (1560), the Belgic Confession (1561), and the Second Helvetic Confession (1566), adopted Calvin's teachings, excepting the notion of the nonelect. On this point they urged caution or, as in the Belgic Confession, affirmed that God was "just, in leaving others in the fall and perdition wherein they have involved themselves." Of the Reformed creeds, only the Westminster Confession (1647) adopted double predestination. The Canons of Dordt (1619) condemned the formulation presented by Jacobus Arminius and the Remonstrants' creed (1610) concerning God's assisting or cooperating grace. Arminius had characterized predestination as God's eternal decree by which he determines to save through Christ "those who, through the grace of the Holy Spirit, shall believe on this his Son Jesus" and who by cooperating grace are enabled to persevere to the end. Many generations later Jonathan Edwards wrote his *Freedom of the Will* (1754) against the Arminians. The mainstream of the Baptist tradition sided with the Calvinists against the Arminians in adopting the New Hampshire Confession (1833) and the Louisville Abstract of Principle (1859).

In the Anglican tradition, the Thirty-Nine Articles of the Church of England (1563, 1571) followed Calvin on both free will (article 10) and predestination (article 17), but not on double predestination. The Irish Articles (1615), written by James Ussher, included double predestination. Anglican theologians, from Richard Hooker (1590s) to J. B. Mozley (author of *Predestination,* 1855) sought various ways to affirm both predestination and free will.

For the Roman Catholic tradition, the Council of Trent treated the matter in its Decree on Justification (1547). The decree spoke of God's prevenient grace and associated it with predestination. But the council took issue with Luther and Calvin, declaring that God disposes people "through his quickening and assisting grace, to convert themselves to their own justification, by freely assenting to and cooperating with that grace." Certitude about being among the predestined came only when salvation was complete for those who persevered to the end. The Jesuit Luis de Molina expanded upon Trent in his *Concordia* (1588), in which he presented the concept of the concurrence of assisting grace with free will. Predestination, for Molina, depends on a *scientia media* by which God, when preordaining some to salvation, takes into account how each person would use free will in all possible circumstances. Cornelis Jansen wrote *Augustinus* (1640) to combat Molina, Trent, and the logical distinctions devised by Thomas Aquinas and the Thomists. He proposed a revival of Augustine's views in order to defeat any suggestion of concurrence and cooperation between divine and human will. A papal bull condemned Jansenism in 1653.

Among Eastern Orthodox, the Russian Orthodox Confession (1643) and the Confession of Jerusalem (1673) responded to the Lutherans, Calvinists, and Trent by reaffirming the pre-Augustinian belief that God predestines some to glory and others to condemnation solely because "he foreknew the one would make a right use of their free will and the other a wrong." They affirmed synergism, the working together of God's prevenient grace and human free will throughout a lifetime of perseverance.

In 1784, John Wesley, founder of what became the Methodist tradition, prepared the Articles of Religion, a revision of the Anglican Thirty-nine Articles. In them he omitted reference to predestination but retained a notion of divine "prevenience," i.e., the human free will to believe depends on "the grace of God by Christ preventing [i.e., going before] us." In *Predestination Calmly Considered* (1752) and other writings, Wesley himself had affirmed predestination in the form of what he called conditional election, God's eternal choice of some to be saved, based on foreknowledge of their future belief. He contended that unconditional election not based on such foreknowledge is really the same thing as double predestination.

THE TWENTIETH AND TWENTY-FIRST CENTURIES. In 1920, Max Weber pronounced predestination to be the cardinal doctrine of Calvinism and gave impetus to the view that the attached the notion to Calvinists in particular. Throughout the twentieth century, however, theologians as diverse as William Temple (Anglican), Karl Rahner (Roman Catholic), Karl Barth and G. C. Berkouwer (Reformed), and Wolfhart Pannenberg (Lutheran) gave significant attention to the concepts of free will and predestination. Church statements from Vatican II and the Lutheran-Roman Catholic dialogue in the United States to the Synod of the Christian Reformed Church referred positively to both concepts. At the same time, many Christian thinkers let the subject drop, in keeping with the declaration by the World Conference on Faith and Order (1937) that theories about how the truths of

God's grace and human free will might be reconciled are not part of the Christian faith. In any case, over the ages the vast host of Christians, not being theologians, have apparently had little awareness of, or concern about, what the theologians said on the subject. As Christians have become more appreciative of metaphor and the nuances of history, and more wary of logical abstraction, philosophers not thinking as Christians have filled the void with their own concepts of freedom and necessity, free will and determinism.

See Also Atonement, article on Christian Concepts; Free Will and Determinism; Grace; Justification; Merit, article on Christian Concepts.

Bibliography

Most of the original writings by the thinkers mentioned herein are readily available. The texts of many of the church creeds are in Philip Schaff's *Creeds of Christendom,* 6th ed., 3 vols. (reprint edition, Grand Rapids, Mich., 1983); and *Creeds of the Churches,* 3d rev. ed., edited by John H. Leith (Atlanta, 1982). Worthy studies of the doctrines are Francis Ferrier's *La Pédestination* (Paris, 1990); M. John Farrelly's *Predestination, Grace, and Free Will* (Westminster, Md., 1964); and *Predestination and Free Will: Four Views of Divine Sovereignty and Human Freedom,* edited by David Basinger and Randall Basinger (Downers Grove, Ill., 1986). The many books on particular thinkers or traditions are easily located in subject indexes. Of these, especially good are Dennis R. Creswell's *St. Augustine's Dilemma: Grace and Eternal Law in the Major Works of Augustine of Hippo* (New York, 1997); John M. Rist's *Augustine on Free Will and Predestination* (Oxford, 1969); Fredrik Brosché's *Luther on Predestination: The Antinomy and the Unity between Love and Wrath in Luther's Concept of* God (Uppsala, 1978); and Richard A. Muller's *Christ and the Decree: Christology and Predestination in Reformed Theology from Calvin to Perkins* (Durham, N.C., 1984).

C. T. McIntire (1987 and 2005)

FREE WILL AND PREDESTINATION: ISLAMIC CONCEPTS

Free will and predestination has been a prominent topic in Islamic religious thinking. For Muslims, the basis of the discussion is found in the Qurʾān and to a lesser extent in *ḥadīth* (reports from and about Muḥammad often called "traditions"), some of which reflect pre-Islamic Arab beliefs.

Predestination in Pre-Islamic Arabia. Something is known of the outlook of the pre-Islamic Arabs from what has been preserved of their poetry. In this we find a strong belief that much of human life, especially misfortune, is determined by time (*dahr, zaman*). It has sometimes been thought that time here is the same as fate, but since the same determination of human life is sometimes attributed to "the days" or even "the nights," the idea of time must be uppermost. Time here is not something to be worshiped but rather a natural fact, not unlike "the course of events."

In particular, it was believed that a person's *ajal,* the term or the date of the person's death, was determined or predetermined. A person destined to die on a certain day would die then, no matter what he or she did. It was also believed that a person's *rizq,* "provision" or "sustenance," that is, food, was also determined. This fatalistic attitude helped the nomads to survive in the harsh conditions of desert life. In the Arabian deserts the regularities of nature experienced elsewhere tended to be replaced by irregularities. One who tried to take precautions against all eventualities would become a nervous wreck, but a readiness to accept whatever happened fatalistically reduced anxiety and thus was an aid to survival. It is to be noted, however, that in the belief of the nomads it is the outcome of human actions that is determined, not the actions themselves.

Predestination in the Qurʾān. The belief of the pre-Islamic Arabs in the control of events by time is described in the Qurʾān (*sūrah* 45:24): "There is only our present life; we die and we live, and time [*dahr*] alone destroys us." The conception of the *ajal,* or term of life, also occurs several times, but it is God who both fixes the *ajal* beforehand and then brings about the person's death: "He is the one who created you from clay, and then fixed an *ajal*" (6:2); "God will not defer [the death of] any person when his *ajal* comes" (63:11). There is thus a sense in which God takes over the functions of time; indeed, there is a *ḥadīth* that reports that the Messenger of God said that God said, "The sons of Adam insult *dahr,* but I am *dahr.*" There are also several passages in the Qurʾān in which it is stated or implied that humankind's fate is not merely determined by God beforehand but also written down: "No misfortune has happened either in respect of the land or of yourselves but it was in a book before we [God] brought it about" (57:22). A clear statement of the uselessness of trying to avoid what has been predetermined is given in a passage about those who criticized Muḥammad's decision, when attacked in Medina by the Meccans, to go out to Mount Uhud to fight: "If you had been in your houses, those for whom killing was written down would have sallied out to the places of their falling" (3:154). The Qurʾān also speaks of God as the source of man's *rizq,* or provision: "He lavishes *rizq* on whom He wills, or stints it" (30:37); this may be regarded as a reflection of the common experience in desert life that one tribe might have plenty while a neighboring tribe was starving.

Just as the pre-Islamic Arab did not believe that his acts were predetermined, but only their outcome, so this seems to be all that is implied by the Qurʾanic statements about *ajal* and similar matters. All Muslims hold that human freedom in some sense and human responsibility in acting are implied in the Qurʾanic teaching that God judges mortals on the Last Day and that their good and bad deeds are weighed in balances. Human freedom is not necessarily contradicted by such verses as: "Do not say of anything, I am doing that tomorrow, without [adding], If God wills" (18:23); ". . . to him of you who wills to go straight; but you will not [so] will, unless God wills" (81:28). Such verses may be understood as expressing God's control of the outcome of acts. But a number of verses also speak of God guiding and aiding people or of leading them astray and abandoning them: "If God wills to guide anyone, He enlarges his breast for Islam" (6:125); "He leads astray whom He wills and guides whom He wills" (16:93), so that those whom he guides become believers and those whom he leads astray become unbelievers.

Other verses, however, assert that this guiding or leading astray is, as it were, in recompense for what the people in question have done previously: "Those who do not believe in God's signs, God does not guide" (16:104); "He leads astray none but the wrongdoers" (2:26). The phrase "leading astray" might be compared with God's "hardening of the heart" of the pharaoh and others in the Bible. One verse (18:28) specifically points to the ability of humans to choose to believe or not. It states, "The truth is from your Lord, so let him who will, believe; and let him who will, disbelieve." Verses such as 90:9–10, "Have we not created for him two eyes and a tongue and two lips and guided him in the highways, but he will not attempt the steep," and 4:31, "God wishes to explain to you and to guide you into the ordinances of those who were before you," also suggest human choice in responding to God's guidance. The numerous verses in the Qurʾān that exhort humans to ponder the "signs" of nature around them that reflect God's majesty and power and to draw moral lessons from the fate of previous generations are also suggestive of human choice in and responsibility for their actions.

Umayyad Apologetic and Qādarī Opposition. Most modern students of Islamic history have tended to suppose that the Umayyad dynasty, which ruled from AH 41 to 132 (661–750 CE), was not very religious. This view is based, however, on the acceptance of pro-Abbasid, anti-Umayyad propaganda and is not borne out by documents of the Umayyad period such as the poems of Jarir and al-Farazdaq. In these it becomes clear that the Umayyads, besides justifying their rule on traditional Arab lines, had a theological defense of their legitimacy: they held that the caliphate had been bestowed on them by God in the same way as the Qurʾān (2:30) described the bestowing of a caliphate on Adam. This meant taking the word *Khalīfah,* or caliph, in the sense of "deputy" rather than of "successor," which it can also mean, and from this they argued that to oppose their decisions was to oppose God.

It was because of this theological position of the Umayyads that some of their opponents adopted what came to be known as the Qādarī heresy. This includes various slightly different formulations, all asserting human free will in some form. One version held that a person's good acts came from God and his bad acts from himself. From this it would follow that the bad acts of an Umayyad caliph were from himself and not from God, and thus good Muslims could oppose such acts without making themselves unbelievers. The first to subscribe to the Qādarī heresy is usually said to have been Maʿbad al-Juhani, who participated in an armed revolt that began in 701, and who was executed three years later upon the collapse of the revolt. Many of the participants in this revolt, however, were not among the Qādirīyya. Another person frequently mentioned as holding Qādarī views was Ghaylan al-Dimashqi. For a time he was a government official and was friendly with more than one caliph, but his political program, while including Qādarī ideas, went beyond it; in 730 the caliph Hisham became suspicious of the program and had Ghaylan executed. For the next twenty years there are many references to Qādarī opponents of the Umayyad regime, especially in Syria. After the replacement of the Umayyad dynasty by the Abbasid in 750, the Qādarī movement lost much of its political raison d'être and either faded out or was absorbed into the rationalist Muʿtazili movement.

Earlier scholars attributed the belief in free will to Christian influence; Ghaylan was indeed of Coptic origin, while Maʿbad was said to have derived his views from a Christian. From what has just been said, however, it would appear that the doctrine of free will was brought into Islamic discussions not primarily because it was held to be true but because it served a useful purpose in internal Islamic political discussions.

Al-Ḥasan al-Baṣrī. The most important name connected with these theological questions is that of al-Ḥasan al-Baṣrī (d. 728). From his own lifetime or shortly afterward scholars debated whether he was a Qādarī or not, and both views were vigorously asserted. Distinguished Western scholars early in the twentieth century continued the debate. In 1933, however, there was published a long *risāla,* or epistle, written for the caliph ʿAbd al-Malik by al-Ḥasan in defense of his views on this topic. From this treatise it is possible to give an account of what he believed. The Qurʾān is central for him and is the source of his arguments. Against the predestinarians who quoted verses about God's leading astray, he replies with other verses that imply that those led astray were already wrongdoers and had in some form chosen evil. He also contends that the fact that God knows that some people will disbelieve is only descriptive; that is, he knows that by their own free choice they will disbelieve, but his knowledge does not predetermine their unbelief. He holds that the verse quoted above about misfortunes being in a book (57:22) applies only to wealth and material things and not to belief or unbelief, obedience or disobedience. He further holds that when the Qurʾān speaks of people acting or willing, they really do so, and their acts are not predetermined. He takes verse 33:38 to mean, "God's command [*amr*] is a determination [*qadar*] determined," and then argues that God determines human behavior only by commanding certain acts and prohibiting others. In this way, he can maintain that God creates only good and that evil comes from human beings or from Satan.

Politically al-Ḥasan al-Baṣrī was critical of the Umayyads. The later scholar Ibn Qutaybah (d. 889) thought him a Qādarī in some respects and told how some of his friends would say to him, "These princes [the Umayyads] shed the blood of Muslims and seize their goods and then say, 'Our acts are only according to God's determination [*qadar*].'" To this Ḥasan would reply, "The enemies of God lie." Ḥasan's remark must be understood in the light of his identification of God's determination with his command, but the Umayyads were doubtless taking *qadar* in the traditional sense of prior effective determination. Despite his critical attitude al-Ḥasan resolutely refused to join any insurrection against the Umayyads and urged his friends and disciples to do likewise. In view of all these facts, al-Ḥasan's position might fairly be described as moderately Qādarī.

A more extreme form of Qādarī doctrine may be encountered in the positions adopted by the Khārijī group known as the Shabibiyya about two decades after al-Ḥasan's treatise. They went as far as to say that God has no foreknowledge whatsoever of the actions of humans and their destinies and humans are left entirely to their own will and discretion. This kind of extreme position was attacked by the Umayyad caliph Umar II (d. 720) in an epistle he composed against Qādarī beliefs.

PREDESTINATION IN THE *ḤADĪTH* (TRADITIONS). Western scholars formerly thought that all *ḥadīth* were predestinarian and saw in this the reason why al-Ḥasan al-Baṣrī based his arguments on the Qur'ān and not on *ḥadīth.* There are indeed a few *ḥadīth* that express an opposite view, but the most likely reason for the absence of *ḥadīth* from al-Ḥasan's arguments is that at the time he was writing they were not regarded as having the authority later ascribed to them and perhaps were not widely known and circulated. Had they been generally regarded as authoritative, he would surely have had some argument against them. It was the jurist al-Shāfiʿī, about a century after al-Ḥasan, who gave *ḥadīth* an assured place in Islamic thought as one of the "roots of law," and by his time, the study of *ḥadīth* had become much more extensive.

It will suffice here to mention some of the best-known predestinarian *ḥadīth.* One was the report that the Prophet had said, "The first thing God created was the pen; then he said to it, 'Write all that will happen until the Last Day.'" Another group of sayings of the Prophet speaks of an angel being entrusted with the child in the womb and asking God to determine whether it is male or female, whether it is to be fortunate or unfortunate, what is its *rizq* and what its *ajal.* Again, in connection with the act of a Muslim fighter at the Battle of Uhud, who took his own life when his battle wounds became unbearable, the Prophet is reported to have said, "One man will work the works of the people of Paradise until he is only an arm's length from it, and then the book will overtake him, and he will work the works of the people of Hell and enter it," while in the case of another man the reverse will happen. Associated with such *ḥadīth* were some reported remarks by early Muslims to the effect that, if one wants to avoid hell, one must believe that God determines both good and bad, and that what reaches one could not have missed one, and what misses one could not have reached one.

It will be noticed that these predestinarian *ḥadīth* to some extent reflect pre-Islamic attitudes.

THE MOVE AWAY FROM QĀDARĪ THOUGHT. In the last half-century of the Umayyad period it seems likely that many of the religious scholars who were critical of the rulers were also sympathetic with at least a moderately Qādarī view, while those who supported the rulers inclined to predestinarian views. Among such views, however, two levels may be distinguished: (1) the belief that what happens to people is predetermined, but not their own acts; (2) the belief that both what happens to them and their own acts are predetermined. At a later period emphasis came to be placed less on God's predetermination of happenings and acts than on his present control of them.

Although something of the old pre-Islamic Arab predestinarianism was still strong among many Muslims and, because associated with God, felt to be part of Islam, it was difficult to express this sentiment under the Umayyads without seeming to approve all their actions. With the coming of the Abbasids, however, all this was altered. Belief in human free will lost most of its political relevance, and the expression of predestinarian views no longer suggested approval of an unjust government. Although those Qādirīyya who were primarily political were located chiefly in Syria, the main academic discussions took place in Basra among the followers and disciples of al-Ḥasan al-Baṣrī, where two opposing trends can be discerned, one toward more libertarian views, the other toward predestinarianism. Just as in pre-Islamic times belief in a predetermined *ajal* and similar matters helped to reduce anxiety, so the belief that God was in control of all events and that no disaster could happen to one except by his will relieved anxiety and gave confidence. The trend toward predestinarianism grew stronger not only in Basra but throughout the Islamic world, and some form of belief in God's control of events became an article in Sunnī creeds.

As this happened and as Qādarī views came to be regarded as heretical, there was a rewriting of history. Those with strong predestinarian or determinist views were unhappy to think that many great earlier scholars, their intellectual predecessors, had been tainted with heresy. They therefore emphasized the role of Maʿbad al-Juhami and Ghaylan al-Dimashqi in the origination and spread of Qādarī ideas, since these were men who had been rebels and also under foreign influence. A little later stories were spread to discredit one particular member of al-Ḥasan's circle, ʿAmr ibn ʿUbayd, and to suggest that he was worse than his contemporaries: besides being the leader of the libertarians among al-Ḥasan's followers, he had been elevated to the position of a founding father of the Muʿtazilah.

The Arabic name of the sect, Qādirīyya, itself bears witness to the struggle between the two trends among religious scholars generally. Like most early names of sects it is a nickname, but the curious point is that it is those who hold that the *qadar* is man's and not God's who are called "*qadar-*

people." Texts now published show that there was a time when each side in the dispute called the other "Qādarī." In his book on sectarian views, al-Ashʿarī (d. 935) mentioned that his own party had been called "Qādarī," but continued, "the Qādarī is he who affirms that the *qadar* is his own and not his Lord's, and that he himself determines his acts and not his Creator." There was no Qādirīyya, properly speaking, after the Umayyad period, but some scholars used the name as an offensive nickname for the Muʿtazilah.

Even in the heyday of the Qādirīyya there was never a single clearly defined Qādarī sect. What made one a Qādarī was one article of belief, either that defined by al-Ashʿarī or something like it, but this belief could be combined with a variety of beliefs on other matters. When the Abbasids came to power, many continued to believe in human free will but at the same time had views on the new political problems, and it was chiefly on the basis of these other views that sectarian names were bestowed. As a result the name Qādarī gradually died out, and after the first half-century of the Abbasid period is hardly found except as an alternative to Muʿtazili.

MUʿTAZILAH AND ASHʿARĪYAH. By the time of the caliph al-Maʾmun (r. 813–833), the Muʿtazilah had defined their sect as based on five principles, of which free will was only one. At the same time, some of the leading Muʿtazilah had important positions at the caliphal court. Just after 847, however, official policy changed abruptly; the Muʿtazilah fell from favor, while the government abandoned their doctrine of the createdness of the Qurʾān and on that and other points supported the central Sunnī position. The Muʿtazilah are chiefly remembered as the group that first developed the discipline of *kalām,* that is, the use of Greek philosophical concepts and methods of argument. Gradually, however, some scholars realized that *kalām* could be used also to defend more generally acceptable doctrines than those of the Muʿtazilah. The creation of a nonheretical Sunnī *kalām* is traditionally attributed to al-Ashʿarī, but it is now realized that in this he had several predecessors. Most of our information, however, is about the debates between Muʿtazilah and Ashʿarīyah.

Within the discipline of *kalām* the discussions about free will took a new direction and were chiefly concerned with God's control of human acts in the present. This did not imply abandoning the belief that God had predetermined these acts, since it could be held that in controlling them in the present he was acting in accordance with his foreknowledge of what he had predetermined. The Ashʿarī view was that God created human acts by creating in the agent at the moment of action the power to do the particular act. The Muʿtazilah agreed that the act came about through a power created by God, but held that this power was created by God before the act and was a power to do either this act or its opposite. In this way they left a place for the agent's choice.

For the Muʿtazilah in general, God's justice (theodicy) was a main concern of their discussions on free will and determinism. The notion of divine justice, influenced by Greek logic, militated against the idea that God could create and condone evil or unjust acts. Such acts are rather to be attributed solely to human choice and will. This belief was further linked to God's role as judge in the afterlife when he will reward or punish humans for their commission of good and evil deeds. The Muʿtazilah argued that if God sent people to hell as punishment for predetermined acts for which they were not responsible, he would be acting unjustly, and this was unthinkable. Their position was rooted in Qurʾanic verses such as 3:104: "God does not wish injustice to the worlds;" 22:10, "God is not unjust to His servants;" and 4:81, "Whatever afflicts you of bad is from yourself."

The Ashʿarīyah met this argument with the formula that human acts are God's creation and the agent's "acquisition" (*kasb*); this term could also be translated as "making one's own" or "having credited to one." In effect the Ashʿarīyah were saying that, although the act is God's creation, it is also in some unspecified way the human agent's act. The term *kasb* and the derivative *iktisab* hark back to Qurʾān 2:286, which states, "God will not burden any soul beyond its capacity. It will enjoy the good which it has acquired and bear the evil for the acquirement of which it labored." The term's usage in the context of free will and predestination is attributed to an early figure, Dirar b. ʿAmr, one of the Muʿtazilah, who is somewhat of an obscure character. Other scholars, even Sunnī theologians like the Māturīdīyah, found the term *kasb* obscure and unsatisfactory and called the Ashʿarīyah "determinists" (*mujbirah*). The eponym of the Māturīdīyah, Abū Manṣūr al-Māturīdī (d. 944) from Samarkand, Transoxiana, steered a middle path between the total predestinarian stance of the Jabriyya and the total free will of the Muʿtazilah, a position that became better known and more influential in the later period. He was essentially in favor of the doctrine of free will, with the qualification that God as the sole creator of the universe creates all acts as well. However, according to his school of thought, humans possess the freedom to choose their actions before their commission, so that they "acquire" these actions by virtue of the choices they make. This notion of "acquisition" is different from al-Ashʿarī's, since the latter proposed that humans acquire the capacity to perform their actions at the very moment of their commission. *Kasb* continues to have its place in general Sunnī thought and fresh generations of scholars have introduced new subtleties.

SHĪʿĪ VIEWS. Early Shīʿī views tend to diverge considerably from later "orthodox" points of view on free will and determinism. The eighth-century Shīʿī theologian Hisham b. al-Hakam (d. 795–796) maintained that human acts are created by God. He also believed that God has no foreknowledge of human actions or of things because his knowledge does not exist until the object of it exists.

An early Shīʿī belief attributed changeability to God's will, referred to in Arabic as *bada*ʾ ("mutability"), which allowed for change in an earlier divine ruling. Such beliefs were considered by the later Imamiyya to be "extremist," particularly since the concept of *bada'* had to be squared with God's omniscience. Thus, to effect a reconciliation, mainstream Imāmī thought proposed the idea that God in his dealings with humans is motivated by considerations of what is most expedient (*al-aslah*) and the best for humankind. Therefore, bada' can be explained as pointing to the susceptibility of the divine will to change should circumstances change, requiring a different determination.

The Imāmīs, in general, subscribe to the doctrine of divine determination with a nod in the direction of free will; Ismā'īlī views are not dissimilar. The Zaydī Shī'ī are closer to the Mu'tazilah in their views.

Modernist Views. Modernist Muslim commentators insist that the Qur'ān should be read holistically. Taking certain verses out of context and interpreting them atomistically has been conducive to the view that the Qur'ān encourages belief in predestination. Read as a whole, the Qur'ān endorses, however, the concept of human freedom in choosing one's belief and of human responsibility for their actions. God has foreknowledge of human actions, but this divine knowledge does not compel humans to commit sin. Mu'tazili influence is detected in these positions, tempered by an acknowledgment of God's creative power over everything, including all human acts. Muḥammad 'Abduh (d. 1905), and Fazlur Rahman (d. 1988), for example, were prominent exponents of the modernist view.

See Also Ash'arīyah; Fate; Kalām.

Bibliography

A general account of the Qādarī thinkers and their opponents will be found in W. Montgomery Watt's book *The Formative Period of Islamic Thought* (Edinburgh, 1973)—in which see especially pages 82–118, 232–242, and 315—and more briefly in his *Islamic Philosophy and Theology,* 2d ed. (Edinburgh, 1985). His earlier *Free Will and Predestination in Early Islam* (London, 1948) has greater detail but requires correction in the light of later works. Since 1973 Josef van Ess has published several important documents and discussions, notably, *Zwischen Hadit und Theologie: Studien zum Entstehen prädestinatianischer Überlieferung* (Berlin, 1975), *Anfänge muslimischer Theologie: Zwei antiqadaritische Traktate aus dem ersten Jahrhundert der Higra* (Beirut, 1977), and the article "Kadariyya," in *The Encyclopaedia of Islam,* new ed., edited by H. A. R. Gibb et al. (Leiden, 1960–). His earlier *Traditionistische Polemik gegen 'Amr b. 'Ubaid* (Beirut, 1967) is also of interest. An idea of how al-Ash'arī argued against the Mu'tazilah may be gained from the translations in *The Theology of al-Ash'arī* by Richard J. McCarthy (Beirut, 1953) and *Al-As'arī's Al-Ibanah* by Walter C. Klein (New Haven, Conn., 1940). For recent discussions of free will and predestination in the modern context, see Sarfraz Khan's *Muslim Reformist Political Thought: Revivalists, Modernists, and Free Will* (London and New York, 2003) and Ulrich Schoen's *Gottes Allmacht und die Freiheit des Menschen: gemeinsames Problem von Islam und Christentum* (Münster, Germany, 2003).

W. Montgomery Watt (1987)
Asma Afsaruddin (2005)

FRENZY. The English word *frenzy* comes through the Latin *phrenesis* from the Greek *phren,* meaning the midriff, the heart, the upper part of the body, the diaphragm, the lungs or pericardium—that is, that part of the body held responsible for passions and thought. The ultimate derivation of the word is from the Indo-European **gwhren-,* meaning the diaphragm, the seat of intellect, understanding, and thought. The term will be used in this entry in its restricted sense, to refer not to mental derangement, madness, or folly generally but to a seizure of violent agitation or wild excitement, to uncontrollable rage or to delirious fury.

Although "frenzy" is not an established category in religious studies, the term occurs frequently in the description of a number of religious states and activities, and its occurrence is often interpreted in religious terms. It is related to such categories as "enthusiasm," "mania," "fury," "inspiration," "intoxication," "spirit possession," and "ecstasy," and, like these states, it is characterized by a certain spontaneity, an autonomy, as if beyond the control of the individual, as if coming from without or from deep within him. In the *Phaedrus* (244ff.), Plato distinguishes several types of frenzy (*mania*) that impart gifts to humans: the frenzy of the seer who reveals the future; that of the consecrated mystic who absolves one from sin; that of the poet possessed by the Muses; and that of the philosopher. In common parlance, however, *frenzy* usually has an aggressive connotation.

Three manifestations of frenzy will be considered here: frenzy as the result of combat (furor), frenzy as a symptom of certain culturally specific psychotic syndromes (amok), and frenzy as a stage of trance understood as spirit possession. The juxtaposition of these three manifestations of frenzy should not be considered synthetic. The term *frenzy* should, in my opinion, be used descriptively in specific contexts and not isolated as a separate and separable category of religious experience.

Furor. It has been reported in both legend and history that in the heat of battle certain warriors enter into a delirious fury, attacking anyone in their reach. Moroccan Arabs recount, for example, that Sīdinā 'Alī, the prophet Muḥammad's son-in-law, whom they regard as the ideal warrior, was once in combat with the Jews. Blood flowed up to his stirrups, so great was his prowess. When he had killed all of the Jews, he turned on his own people and would have slaughtered them too, had not one of them, a beggar, asked him for a crust of bread (*barakah,* lit., "blessing"). This request cooled down his frenzy (*ḥashimīyah*), for he knew that only an Arab was fool enough to beg from him in his state. Roman legend has it that after one of the Horatii had defeated three enemy brothers, the Curiatii, he turned in furor on his sister, who, in mourning for one of them, had revealed the "feminine" weakness of a lover's grief.

In an analogous Celtic tale, Cú Chulainn, the hero of the Ulster legend, while still a child defeated the three sons of Nechta, the enemy of his people, and returned to his capital still in a frenzy. There he spurned the queen, who tried to divert him by making crude sexual advances. As he was momentarily distracted, his men seized him and threw him into a vat of cold water to cool him down. From then on Cú Chulainn kept his furor in reserve for battle. Georges Dumézil suggests that this tale of initiatory combat relates to the domestication of savage frenzy—the ideal of prehistoric Italic, Celtic, and Germanic warriors—and its submission to legionary discipline. To the psychoanalytically oriented, the tale is concerned with the conversion into disciplined military aggression of the warrior's uncontrolled rage toward his mother, or toward women more generally, and, by extension, toward his own weakness symbolized by women.

AMOK. There are a number of culture-bound reactive syndromes, the so-called ethnopsychoses, that involve frenzied behavior. The best known of these "hypereridic rage reactions" is amok, which occurs primarily in Malaysia and Indonesia. The *pengamok,* the person who runs amok, usually suffers from neurasthenia, chronic illness, or a loss of a sense of social order and, with time, comes to experience an increasingly threatening external pressure that frightens or enrages him. Suddenly, as if to escape this pressure, he runs wild, attacking people, animals, and objects around him, even himself. He then falls into a stupor and awakes depressed and without any memory of his having run amok. Amok has occurred among warriors dedicated to self-sacrifice, and it has been explained as an escape from the pervasive Malay-Indonesian sense of fatalism and concern for propriety (*alus*). As the occurrence of amok peaked in the nineteenth century, with Western contact, it has been regarded as a transitional reaction to modernization.

Similar hypereridic reactions have been reported elsewhere, for example, in New Guinea (wild-man behavior, *negi negi, lulu*), in Malawi (*misala*), and in Puerto Rico (*mal de pelea*). Just as frenzied behavior occurs in certain hypermanic disorders, so it occurs in other culture-bound reactive syndromes. Ainu women of northern Japan afflicted with *imu* burst out aggressively or flee in panic after seeing a snake and then, within minutes, fall into catalepsy, echo those about them, and execute orders automatically. Inuit (Eskimos) suffering from *piblotko,* or Arctic hysteria, tear off their clothing, run around, throw things, and imitate animals. Northern Algonquian-speaking Indians of Canada who are possessed of a *windigo* spirit are overcome with a frenzied craving for human flesh and are said to pounce on men, women, and children and devour them ravenously. Frenzied behavior is often interpreted as spirit possession or as the result of sorcery.

SPIRIT POSSESSION. Frenzy has often been associated with spirit possession. The herdsman's description of the Bacchantes, worshiping Dionysos, in Euripides' *The Bacchae* (ll. 677–774) is a classic example. Having himself escaped attack, the herdsman watches as the possessed women attack the villagers' grazing cattle.

> And then
> you could have seen a single woman with bare hands
> tear a fat calf, still bellowing with fright,
> in two, while others clawed the heifers to pieces.
> There were ribs and cloven hooves scattered everywhere,
> and scraps smeared with blood hung from the fir trees.
> And bulls, their raging fury gathered in their horns,
> lowered their heads to charge, then fell, stumbling
> to the earth, pulled down by hordes of women
> and stripped of flesh and skin more quickly, sire,
> than you could blink your royal eyes. Then,
> carried by their own speed, they flew like birds
> across the spreading fields along Asopus' stream
> where most of all the ground is good for harvesting.
> Like invaders they swooped on Hysiae
> and on Erythrae in the foothills of Cithaeron.
> Everything in sight they pillaged and destroyed.
> They snatched the children from their homes. And when
> they piled their plunder on their backs, it stayed in place,
> untied. Nothing, neither bronze nor iron,
> fell to the dark earth. Flames flickered
> in their curls and did not burn them.
> (*The Bacchae,* trans. Arrowsmith, ll. 736–758)

Euripides' description has become a model in Western discourse for literary descriptions of Dionysian worship (e.g., Thomas Mann's in *Death in Venice*) and indeed for scientific description of the frenzy of the spirit possessed.

In many exorcistic rites the spirit-possessed moves from a gentle, "dreamy," somnambulistic trance into a frenzied one in which he or she loses all control of behavior. Thus, in Balinese folk dramas (*sanghyangs*) an entranced dancer will imitate, say, a pig, lumbering about on all fours, grunting and groveling, and then suddenly, often on provocation from the audience, he will fall into frenzy, darting, leaping, thrashing about, wallowing uncontrollably in the mud, shaking in convulsions, and struggling against those who try to pin him down. Doused with water, he grows quiet. The frenzied stage of trance possession is usually followed by torpor and exhaustion. Such frenzies, as in *The Bacchae,* seem to be facilitated by group participation and excitement.

SEE ALSO Berserkers; Ecstasy; Enthusiasm; Healing and Medicine; Omophagia; Spirit Possession.

BIBLIOGRAPHY

Belo, Jane. *Trance in Bali.* New York, 1960. A detailed description of trance (including frenzy) in Bali.

Crapanzano, Vincent. *The Hamadsha: An Essay in Moroccan Ethnopsychiatry.* Berkeley, 1973. Discusses the frenzied state of spirit possession among Moroccan Arabs.

Dumézil, Georges. *The Destiny of the Warrior.* Translated by Alf Hiltebeitel. Chicago, 1970. Discusses furor in Indo-European thought.

Euripides. *The Bacchae.* Translated by William Arrowsmith. In *The Complete Greek Tragedies,* edited by David Grene and Richmond Lattimore, vol. 4, *Euripedes,* pp. 543–608. Chicago, 1959. Contains an exemplary description of frenzy.

Murphy, H. B. M. "History and Evolution of Syndromes: The Striking Case of *Latah* and *Amok.*" In *Psychopathology: Con-*

tributions from the Social, Behavioral, and Biological Sciences, edited by Muriel Hammer et al., pp. 33–55. New York, 1973. One of the few historical studies of amok.

Pfeiffer, Wolfgang M. *Transkulturelle Psychiatrie.* Stuttgart, 1971. A good discussion of amok and other ethnic psychoses.

Yap, Pow Meng. "The Culture-Bound Reaction Syndromes." In *Mental Health Research in Asia and the Pacific,* edited by William Caudill and Zongyi Lin. Honolulu, 1969. General discussion of ethnopsychoses, including amok.

New Sources

Simons, Ronald C., and Charles C. Hughes, eds. *Culture-Bound Syndromes.* Dordrecht, Netherlands, 1985.

Spores, John C. *Running Amok: An Historical Inquiry.* Athens, Ohio, 1988.

VINCENT CRAPANZANO (1987)
Revised Bibliography

FREUD, SIGMUND (1856–1939), originator of psychoanalysis, a method of treating those mental disorders commonly designated as the neuroses. Psychoanalysis began as a method of healing, but became also a psychological theory of personality or mind and a general theory of culture—of morality, group life, society, history, art, and religion. When treating his patients, Freud found it necessary to emphasize their unconscious feelings and thoughts, which, precisely because they were unacknowledged, created symptoms. Freud believed that dreams and dream symbolism were keys to his patients' unconscious thinking, and also to their symptoms. It was therefore inevitable that his method of treatment would generate theoretical concepts important for understanding the human mind, and that these in turn would lead him to psychological conclusions about the cultural meanings of the symbols found in religious myths, beliefs, and rituals. Freud's psychoanalytic theory is widely accepted by scholars in many different fields, and Freud is commonly ranked with Karl Marx, Max Weber, Friedrich Nietzsche, and Émile Durkheim as one of the architects of the modern world. But scholars of religion also acknowledge that Freud has made a lasting contribution to their understanding of the religious thought and life of humankind.

LIFE AND PRINCIPAL WORKS. Freud's personal beginnings contain little to suggest his later achievements. Born into a large Jewish family of modest means in Freiberg, Moravia (now Pribor, Czech Republic), he was four when his father, a wool merchant, moved the family to Vienna, where Freud spent all but the last year of his life. As a youth, he received an excellent education that emphasized both classics and science. For a while he contemplated a career in law or in politics, but finally decided upon scientific work and attended medical school at the University of Vienna, from which he graduated in 1881. A year later he became engaged to Martha Bernays, whom he subsequently married.

Partly for financial reasons and partly on account of official anti-Semitism (it was customary for the university to pass over Jewish candidates for research positions), Freud shifted his career goals to the medical practice of psychiatry. He became interested in hysterical patients, and began to collaborate with the eminent Viennese physician Josef Breuer.

Freud and Breuer discovered that the symptoms of hysterical patients diminished as they were encouraged to talk about the intense feelings they held toward those close to them. Freud also noticed that dreams were included in these reports, and he began to evolve his theory that both dreams and hysterical symptoms disguised deeply felt and deeply feared thoughts and feelings. At the end of his period of collaboration with Breuer, Freud began to write his first and most famous book, *The Interpretation of Dreams* (1900). This work contained the essence of all his major ideas about the neuroses, about dreams, and about psychoanalytic treatment—and also the essence of his theory that religious symbols and myths are modeled upon dreams.

In the 1910s and 1920s, Freud's reputation grew. New patients came, and he continued to publish papers and to gather students about him. Many of these men and women underwent psychoanalysis with Freud, and studied his ideas. Among the more eminent were the Swiss psychiatrist Carl Gustav Jung and the socialist Alfred Adler. In 1908 the first international congress in psychoanalysis was held in Salzburg, and in 1909 Freud and Jung gave lectures at Clark University in Massachusetts. The most important of Freud's many publications during these decades were *Introductory Lectures on Psychoanalysis* (1915), which explained psychoanalytic theory and practice to a lay audience; *Group Psychology and the Analysis of the Ego* (1921), in which Freud analyzed the psychological forces beneath the group behavior of armies and churches; and *The Ego and the Id* (1923), a theoretical treatise on the fundamental psychological structures of the human mind.

Although Freud throughout his life created new works of psychological observation and interpretation, which brought him ever greater recognition, the 1920s produced a major shift in his person and thought, one whose effects persisted to his death. The aftermath of World War I, the death of a beloved daughter, and the discovery of a cancerous growth in his jaw, all forced upon him a reflective and resigned attitude, which in turn fueled his most profound studies of culture and religion. Taking up arms in the time-honored conflict between science and religion, Freud asserted (in *The Future of an Illusion,* 1927) that psychoanalysis was but the latest and most compelling scientific argument against the consolations of religion. Three years later, in *Civilization and Its Discontents,* he addressed the oppressive quality of contemporary social life, arguing that society itself carried within it the mechanisms that created neurotic conflict. In his last major work, *Moses and Monotheism* (1939), written in sections over the 1930s, Freud returned to his own Jewish origins and searched for a positive estimate of that religion, arguing—paradoxically—that Western monotheism was an ascetic force that supported the renunciations required by scientific endeavors.

When the Nazis persecuted the adherents of psychoanalysis and forced Freud to leave his home, he fled to London, where—aged, ill, persecuted, and famous—he died on the eve of World War II.

Psychoanalytic Theory. While Freud's psychoanalysis is really a threefold discipline—clinical treatment of neurotic conflict, general theory of personality, and theory of culture and religion—it is important to realize that he generalized from the first to the second and from both to the third. Therefore, all expositions of his thought about religion should begin with the psychoanalytic method and its clinical context, usually referred to as the analytic situation.

Two concepts form the foundation of the analytic situation, the unconscious and childhood. All deliberate, intentional, and conscious life, for the healthy adult and the neurotic alike, is constantly subject to influence by an unconscious dimension of feeling, willing, and intending. Freud often referred to the unconscious as a portion of mental life split off from, and existing alongside of, the system of conscious mental processes. This separation first occurs during the years of childhood. Because of the prolonged and at times virtually total dependency of the infant upon caretakers, some of the strong feelings of love, hate, envy, and jealousy—in short, portions of all the fundamental wishes and fears of living and being—are forgotten or forced out of awareness. These thoughts and feelings, which Freud described as repressed, live on in the normal activities of the adult, making their appearance symbolically in dreams, slips of the tongue, jokes, and love relationships. The normal adult is capable of introspection and self-analysis when unconscious wishes and thoughts press for attention.

However, under conditions of stress produced by the various tasks and responsibilities of living, even the healthy adult can falter. In such cases, the mental organization of the person returns to earlier patterns of regulation, a process known as regression, and neurotic symptoms (for example, phobias or irrational fears, obsessional ideas, or compulsive acts) serve to defend against the return. Because persons in this condition can no longer control portions of their behavior, psychoanalytic treatment is helpful for them. In the analytic situation the patient allows his or her thoughts and feelings, and especially dreams, to flow freely (in "free association") without moral or intellectual control and in doing so forms an intense, irrational, emotional bond with the doctor. Freud called this bond "transference." Because the transference relation embodies old and forgotten childhood memories, the doctor can interpret the bond in the light of dreams and fantasies, gradually bringing the repressed wishes back under the control of conscious life.

Theory of Culture and Religion. Contrary to much opinion on the subject, Freud recognized religion as a complex phenomenon, and his estimate of it was both appreciative and skeptical. He was more interested in religion than he was in any other manifestation of culture. He rarely approached religion in the abstract, instead always seeing it in the context of culture as a whole—the social arrangements and systems of symbols that integrate a community of people. Understood as a system of authoritative beliefs about the world, which includes moral guides and the consoling sense of specialness that authoritativeness confers, religion is the historical force that energizes the forms assumed by culture. Freud therefore wrote about art, humor, morality, fairy tales, legends, myths, and rituals, without always attempting to make sharp distinctions among them.

The key to Freud's appreciative stance toward religion lies in his psychology of myth and in particular in his theory that myths are to be understood after the fashion of dreams, although they are collective rather than individual dreams. By noting parallels between dreams and myths, Freud transformed the model of dream interpretation into a tool for research into the psychological character of culture. Both dreams and myths, he felt, are imaginative structures composed of symbols organized along a narrative line. Both are produced by unconscious forces, for myths as well as dreams are experienced as given to individuals, rather than as being created by them. As such, both display mechanisms of symbol formation, whereby figures in dreams and myths take on shifting roles and significances. Both are therefore creative activities of the human mind.

But Freud also observed that dreams expressed the wishes, desires, and fantasies of his patients and were closely related to their motives and intentions. He concluded that myths are collective or group fantasies. Behind the apparent diversity of human societies and cultures there persist certain primordial or typical human situations—the conflicts between parents and children and between the children themselves, conflicts surrounding perennial human issues such as sexuality, death, envy, gratitude, hate, and love. Because these psychological constants or universals are shared by all people, and because they are so pervasive, powerful, and threatening, they are repressed to some degree by everyone, but they reappear for all to see in the myths of each society. A myth, then, represents the shared unconscious wishes of a group, and the psychological interpretation of myth discloses the nature of these wishes.

For example, in fairy tales a king and queen can represent shared unconscious ideas and fears about fathers and mothers, just as princes and princesses represent those held by sons and daughters. A witch can symbolize a hateful, unempathic mother, and a savage monster may suggest aggressive wishes too powerful for individual consciousness or an individual dream to support. Of the world religions, Freud was especially interested in Judaism and Christianity. The idea of God the Father in Judaism represents shared unconscious wishes for a totally powerful and morally perfect group father. Christianity's devotion to Jesus Christ, the Son of God, expresses the Western preoccupation with the anxiety sons experience in relation to their fathers. Catholicism's adoration of the Virgin discloses an intense idealization of motherhood, which Protestant families subsequently rejected. The omnipresence of explicitly sexual themes in the myths of Indian religions contrasts with their absence in Western religious traditions, whose asceticism betrays anxiety over bodily desires.

Freud's skeptical attitude toward religion derived from his training in physiology, neurology, and medicine, which emphasized causality, energy, and rigorous objectivity. But these scientific ideas also served a moral purpose for Freud. He believed that the most profound unconscious human wish was for a grandiose sense of specialness, which he called "narcissism," and that both science and psychoanalysis could reduce or modify this narcissism, or self-love. On the other hand, religion indulged and encouraged self-love by conferring upon people the illusion that they were special or privileged by virtue of their relation to an all-powerful and all-loving god. Freud cited the Western discovery that the earth revolved around the sun. As a result of that scientific insight, people could no longer think of themselves as central points in a divine drama. The theory of evolution deprived people of the wish to see themselves as special beings created by an omnipotent god. And Freud believed that his own discovery of the unconscious shattered the grandiose belief in the supreme capacities of human reason. Each scientific discovery was a blow to human narcissism and to the religious doctrine that supported it. Freud concluded that belief in an all-powerful divine being with whom one had a special relationship forestalled, rather than facilitated, new knowledge about the world—for in each case religious leaders had mounted the strongest objections to these discoveries.

Contribution to the Study of Religion. Because of Freud's appreciation of the power of religious symbols, and despite his skeptical stance toward religion, his theories exercised an important influence upon the religious thought of post–World War II Europe and, especially, America. By this time his ideas had become widely acknowledged, and the leaders of religious communities wanted to use them and to respond to his challenge. In particular, Paul Tillich and Mircea Eliade deserve mention here.

Paul Tillich was convinced that an overly rational society had cut the Christian faith off from its historic depths and from its role as a shaper of culture. He hailed the secular Freud's concept of the unconscious roots of religious reality as an attempt to restore what he called a depth dimension to human reason and cultural life. Even Freud's skeptical side Tillich incorporated into theology, arguing that modern churches had become authoritarian and oppressive to human depth, and that Freud's objections to religion were in this sense well founded. Tillich likened Freud to a biblical prophet whose attacks on the idolatry of the faithful were mounted in the service of a deeper, more transcendent reality.

Alongside Tillich's theological analyses of culture, a second movement emerged, led by the renowned historian of religions Mircea Eliade. Like Tillich, Eliade believed that contemporary culture was excessively rational and technological and that a renewal of a religious kind was essential. But unlike Tillich, Eliade turned to primitive religions and to Eastern traditions and myths to renew the life of modern humans. Eliade wrote that Freud's view of myth as an unconscious imaginative structure and the links he had built between dreams and myths would enrich the dry, technical tones of modern life, and that both could be used to reinstate a religious view of humanity. In fact, Eliade described the history of religions as a metapsychoanalysis, by which he meant that religion added a dimension to the foundations supplied by Freud.

Yet neither Tillich nor Eliade could tolerate Freud's skepticism, his view that once the unconscious meaning of a religious myth was disclosed, then the consoling sense of specialness that belief conferred would necessarily be given up in the interest of a broader psychological self-understanding. The task of advancing this thought was left to the sociologist Philip Rieff, who devised the term *psychological man,* to describe a new type of person in modern society, one who had accepted Freud's interpretations and had accordingly adopted a psychological rather than a religious ethic. Rieff's view called attention to the roles of religion and psychoanalysis as competing social forces in Western history, a focus ignored by Tillich and Eliade, who had centered their efforts on the more speculative aspects of Freud's theories of religion.

However, Freud's contribution to the study of religion did not end here. A new generation of scholars working with post-modern understandings has advanced quite different readings of Freud and his contribution to the study of religion. These scholars teach and write in universities and colleges rather than in seminaries and theological facilities, as did Tillich and Eliade, and the topics and methods they choose belong to the humanities and the social sciences. But there is also irony in these new developments. As noted, neither Tillich nor Eliade could tolerate Freud's skepticism about religion—his theories of religion were helpful, but only up to a point. On the other hand, post-modern scholars of religion make no such distinction and instead submit all of his writings to a generalized cultural critique, sometimes finding that what was "skeptical" for the theologian may be meaningful to the scholar of religion.

Bibliography

Freud's psychological writings have been collected for the English-language reader in *The Standard Edition of the Complete Psychological Writings of Sigmund Freud,* 24 vols., translated from German under the general editorship of James Strachey (London, 1953–1974). Each of Freud's publications in this definitive edition is prefaced by valuable information regarding date of composition and of first publication, relevant biographical details, and a short discussion of its leading ideas in relation to Freud's thought as a whole.

The best single book on Freud's life, social circumstances, and major ideas is Peter Gay, *Freud: A Life for Our Time* (New York, 1988). Philip Rieff's careful, thorough, and clearly written book *Freud: The Mind of the Moralist* (1959; 3d ed.,

Chicago, 1979) remains the best overall discussion of Freud's social, philosophical, and religious ideas. Rieff also analyzes the impact of psychoanalysis upon both the Western religious heritage and contemporary society. An excellent illustration of the use of Freud's approach to dream symbolism to interpret social and cultural symbols is Bruno Bettelheim's *The Uses of Enchantment: The Meaning and Importance of Fairy Tales* (New York, 1977). The best theological discussion of Freud's theory of religious experience is to be found in Paul Tillich's *The Courage to Be* (New Haven, 1952). The many implications of psychoanalysis for the historical study of religious myths are clearly stated by Mircea Eliade in *Myths, Dreams and Mysteries* (New York, 1960). A postmodern reading of Freud's thought as a whole with an emphasis upon the interplay between his psychology of religious faith and his theory of femininity is Judith Van Herik's *Freud on Femininity and Faith* (Berkeley, Calif., 1982).

PETER HOMANS (1987 AND 2005)

FREYJA ("Lady"), the daughter of Njǫrðr (Njord) and sister of Freyr, is the main Scandinavian goddess of the group of gods known as the Vanir. Although no extant source tells how she came to the world of the Æsir—the dominant group of gods—allusions to her arrival in their citadel Ásgarðr (Ásgard) suggest that there was a myth about this that has since been lost. According to Snorri Sturluson (1179–1241), Freyja is the noblest of goddesses, equal in dignity to Óðinn (Odin)'s wife Frigg. She lives in a grand hall, shares dominion over the dead with Óðinn, and travels in a cart pulled by cats. People often invoke her in matters of love. Incestuous marriage was usual among the Vanir, and it is likely that Freyja was married to her brother. The Æsir frowned on this practice, and once Freyja becomes a member of their community, she takes a different husband, Óðr (Odr). The name of this obscure deity is related to *Óðinn,* and the pair Óðr/Freyja may be a doublet of Óðinn and his wife Frigg. Freyja bore Óðr two daughters, Hnoss ("jewel") and Gersimi ("treasure"). These names are synonyms and most likely are later poetic reflections of the goddess herself. Freyja and Óðr's marriage was apparently not a happy one, as Óðr disappeared on long journeys, and Freyja wept tears of red gold in his absence. She looked for him in many countries and assumed various names in her wanderings. She is said to have owned a garment that allowed its wearer to take the shape of a falcon. Like her brother Freyr, Freyja rides a boar; hers is named Hildisvíni ("battle swine"). It has shining golden bristles and was made for her by the dwarves. Pigs are sacred to her as they are to Freyr, and one of her names is Sýr ("sow").

Freyja is often in demand as a bride. The Æsir agree to give away Freyja, the sun, and the moon to the master builder of Ásgarðr if he finishes by the first day of summer, and when the giant Hrungnir becomes drunk at a feast at Ásgarðr, he threatens to destroy the citadel and all its inhabitants except for Freyja and Þórr's wife Sif, whom he will keep for himself. The giant Þrymr (Thrymr) steals Þórr's hammer Mjǫllnir in order to have something of enough value that the Æsir would exchange Freyja for it. The gods ask Freyja to go to Þrymr, but she indignantly refuses, saying that such a journey would make everyone think that she was eager for sex. Þórr retrieves Mjǫllnir himself by going to Þrymr dressed as a bride and taking his hammer when it is brought out as part of the wedding ceremony.

Freyja's personality is complex: she is said to enjoy "love poetry," an erotic genre that was forbidden in Iceland under threat of banishment (Ström, 1975, p. 151). Her lustfulness is often stressed, not only by Loki, who denounces her as incestuous and grossly promiscuous (*Lokasenna* sts. 30 and 32), but also in other eddic poems such as the *Hyndluljóð* (sts. 30–31), where she is described as "running through the night in heat like [the goat] Heiðrún [Heidrun]." Her unfaithfulness to her husband is accentuated as well: "Under your apron still others have crept" (Hollander, 1962, p. 135). *Sǫrla þáttr,* a story in a late fourteenth-century manuscript, tells how she slept with four dwarfs in order to obtain the famous necklace Brísingamen, which they had forged. Such behavior is in keeping with the personality of a fertility goddess, but the story as a whole is a Christian creation intended as a demonstration of the evils of paganism, and its depiction of Freyja as a malicious near-giantess and as Óðinn's mistress is much more likely to be the author's invention than a reflection of authentic pagan tradition. Freyja's association with the cat is another hint at her lasciviousness, since the cat was considered by Norsemen to be a most lascivious animal. In the case of Freyja, the feline is the equivalent of the lions and panthers associated with such ancient Near Eastern fertility goddesses as the Dea Syria or Cybele.

Freyja also goes under such other names as *Hǫrn,* a term often occurring in skaldic kennings for "woman" and related to the Old Norse term *hǫrr* ("flax" or "linen"); it also occurs in a few place-names and points to the worship of the goddess as deity of the flax harvest in eastern Sweden (Vries, 1967, p. 331). As *Mardǫll* she appears in poetic circumlocutions for "gold" such as *Mardallar tár* ("Mardǫll's tears"). She is also known as *Gefn,* a name derived from the verb *gefa* ("give") and referring to the concept of the fertility goddess as the generous dispenser of wealth, goods, and well-being. This term is also preserved in the name of the Matronae Gabiae and Dea Garmangabis, recorded in the Rhineland in Roman times. Freyja has therefore been connected with Gefjun, who plowed the island of Sjælland away from the Swedish mainland with the help of her four sons. There are indeed some striking parallels between Freyja and Gefjun, as suggested by Loki's reference (*Lokasenna,* st. 20) to Gefjun's seduction of a "fair-haired lad" (possibly Heimdallr) who gave her a necklace (presumably Brísingamen) in exchange for her favors. Though the Eddas treat them as separate deities, Gefjun can hardly be anything but a local incarnation of the omnipresent fertility goddess. Another possible hypostasis of Freyja is the beautiful Menglǫð ("necklace-glad"), who lives in the company of nine maidens on top of the Lyfjaberg (the "mount of [magical] healing herbs"), surrounded by a wall of flickering flames (Vries, 1967, pp. 328–329).

Freyja's association with the dead has been understood as an expression of the opposition between physical death and fertility. Together with her shape-changing garment, this association also suggests a connection with shamanism. Another connection with shamanism is *seiðr,* a special kind of sorcery Freyja practiced that allowed her to see the future and do harm to others. The possession by the spirits that this entailed was considered to be too much like sexual penetration to be appropriate to men, so Freyja taught *seiðr* only to the Æsir goddesses and to Óðinn, who was willing to risk shameful effeminacy for its power. Sagas describe *seiðr* rituals performed by women in a variety of Norse communities.

Although one might expect that the goddess of love would be worshiped in private ceremonies, in fact the cult of Freyja was a public one. According to the testimony of Nordic place-names, the cult was comparatively old and was widely dispersed over Scandinavia, though it is not always easy to determine whether the toponyms refer to Freyr or to Freyja (Vries, 1967, pp. 308–310). The greatest concentration seems to be along the west coast of Norway and in the Swedish Uppland, and the name of the deity is joined with terms meaning "lake," "grove," "hill," "field," and "meadow," as well as "sanctuary" and "temple." An anecdote about the tenth-century Icelandic poet Hjalti Skeggjason throws light on Freyja's important position in heathen religion: at the general assembly in 999 he composed this mocking verse, "I don't like barking gods; I consider Freyja to be a bitch," and was promptly outlawed for blasphemy.

See Also Germanic Religion; Óðinn; Sagas; Snorri Sturluson.

Bibliography

Hollander, Lee M., trans. and ed. *The Poetic Edda.* 2d rev. ed. Austin, Tex., 1962.

Lindow, John. *Scandinavian Mythology: An Annotated Bibliography.* New York, 1988.

Lindow, John. *Handbook of Norse Mythology.* Santa Barbara, Calif., 2001.

Pulsiano, Phillip, ed. *Medieval Scandinavia: An Encyclopedia.* New York, 1993.

Ross, Margaret Clunies. *Prolonged Echoes: Old Norse Myths in Medieval Northern Society,* vol. 1: *The Myths.* Odense, Denmark, 1994.

Rowe, Elizabeth Ashman. "*Sörla Þáttr:* The Literary Adaptation of Myth and Legend." *Saga-Book of the Viking Society* 26 (2002): 38–66.

Simek, Rudolf. *Lexikon der germanischen Mythologie.* Stuttgart, Germany, 1984. Translated by Angela Hall as *Dictionary of Northern Mythology* (Cambridge, U.K., 1993).

Ström, Åke V. "Germanische Religion." In *Germanische und baltische Religion,* edited by Ström and Haralds Biezais, 11–306. Mainz, Germany, 1975.

Turville-Petre, E. O. G. *Myth and Religion of the North: The Religion of Ancient Scandinavia.* New York, 1964.

Vries, Jan de. *Altgermanische Religionsgeschichte,* vol. 2. 2d rev. ed. Berlin, 1967.

Edgar C. Polomé (1987)
Elizabeth Ashman Rowe (2005)

FREYR (Lord), the son of Njǫrðr and the brother of Freyja, is one of the Vanir hostages in Ásgarðr and is the main fertility god of ancient Scandinavia. According to Snorri Sturluson (1179–1241), Freyr is said to be handsome and powerful. The noblest of the gods, he rules over rain, sunshine, and growing plants. People invoked him for peace, good crops, and wealth. He made women happy and freed captives (*Lokasenna,* st. 37). He is a courageous fighter, and his name occurs in poetic circumlocutions for *warrior,* such as "spear-Freyr." He is represented as the ancestor of the Swedish kings under the name *Yngvi-Freyr* (Yngvi is the eponym of the royal family of the Ynglings), a name also associated with *Ing* (Gmc. Ingw[az]) in the Old English *Runic Poem* and the eponym of the Germanic tribal group the Inguaeones, but the relationship between Freyr, Yngvi, and Ingwaz is not fully understood.

Among Freyr's prized possessions is the dwarf-made ship Skíðblaðnir (Built of Slats; *Grímnismál,* st. 44); according to Snorri, it can be folded up and carried in a pouch, but, when needed, it can carry the whole company of the Æsir, weapons and all, and always sails with a favorable wind. The motif of the wonderful boat is significant because of the close association of ships with fertility cults, from their representation on Scandinavian Bronze Age rock carvings to medieval rites. Another important present from the dwarfs is Freyr's golden boar, Gullinbyrsti (Golden Bristle) or Slíðrugtanni (Razor Tooth), who runs faster than a horse and shines brightly at night.

In Mythology. Freyr is involved in few myths. The best known is told in the eddic poem *Skírnismál* (The lay of Skírnir). Seeing the beautiful giantess Gerðr, daughter of Gymir, from a promontory overlooking all the world, Freyr falls deeply in love with her. Pining away, he sends his servant Skírnir (possibly a double of Freyr, who is elsewhere described as *skírr* [bright, shining, pure]) to woo her. The journey to Gymir's home is hazardous, and Skírnir reaches it only because Freyr's horse, which he is riding, can jump over the circles of flames protecting the property. At the gate, Skírnir finds savage dogs and a shepherd sitting on a mound, who tells him he must be either doomed or dead to have come so far. Skírnir is nevertheless greeted by Gerðr, who offers him mead. As he begins his plea for her love on behalf of Freyr, he tries to entice her with presents—the apples of eternal youth, a magic arm ring, and Freyr's invincible sword—but he meets with refusal. Switching from blandishments to threats, Skírnir ominously warns Gerðr that she will be exiled and will waste away, ugly and desolate and plagued by lust, for having incurred the wrath of the Æsir; worse still, he will deliver her by magic to a three-headed fiend from hell, to quench her thirst with "stalings of stinking goats" (Hollander, p. 72). Intimidated, Gerðr gives in and promises to meet Freyr after nine nights in a "trysting glade" called Barri.

This myth seems quite archaic, and even if one sets aside the interpretations associating the story with any fertility ritual, there can be no doubt that sex and fertility lie at its core. The myth has also been interpreted as reaffirming the patriarchal structure of Old Norse society, depicting a male-female struggle for power and providing a matrix for resolving conflict between different families through a system of exchange and intermarriage. One of the conditions imposed on the Vanir hostages was that they give up their custom of incest, which left only giantesses for Freyr and his father to marry, as the Æsir did not want the male Vanir to marry upward, into their own group. However, the incorporation of giantesses into Ásgarðr imposed strains on the Æsir's social hierarchy, and at the gods' last battle at Ragnarök, Freyr is killed by the giant Surtr because he did not have his sword, contributing to the defeat of the Æsir as a whole. The loss of the sword, with which Loki insults Freyr (*Lokasenna*, st. 42), emphasizes the separation of the fertility function from the warrior function and implies the weakening effects of sexual obsession. Snorri's *Ynglingasaga* calls Gerðr the wife of Freyr and mentions their son Fjölnir, but this may be a post-pagan development undertaken to create a coherent dynastic origin.

Besides Skírnir, Freyr has two other servants (*Lokasenna* sts. 43–46): Byggvir, meaning "grain of barley" (as suggested by the reference to the quern [a hand-turned grain mill] in stanza 44), and Beyla, whose name Georges Dumézil interpreted in 1973 as a diminutive of the Germanic word for "bee," in spite of insuperable phonological difficulties. Such names would make these figures symbolic of beer and mead, the inebriating beverages used in ceremonial activities. However, it may be more correct to connect Beyla with the Old Norse *baula* (cow) and to see the couple as representatives of the two aspects of Freyr's functional domain: agriculture and animal husbandry.

Freyr and Gerðr have been identified as the man and woman depicted on Viking Age gold plates from Jæderen, Norway. She holds an object that could be a branch with leaves and a flower, and the man touches her cheek or her breast with his hand in a gesture of endearment. The clear erotic elements in this depiction seem to be entirely in keeping with the sexual connotations of fertility cults.

FREYR WORSHIP. Little is known directly about the worship of Freyr, but it held a prominent place in Sweden, where he was the principal god as well as the divine ancestor of the royal house. Adam of Bremen (IV:26), writing around 1070 and using eyewitness accounts, describes the triad of gods worshiped at the time in the temple at Uppsala. He notes that the statue of Freyr is endowed with a huge sex organ and adds that all kinds of "lewd practices that remain better unmentioned" accompanied the ceremonies of Freyr's cult. One version of the king's saga about Olaf Tryggvason includes a tale about a fugitive Icelander who joins the priestess of Freyr as she travels from farm to farm in Sweden in a chariot with a statue of Freyr in a wagon; this was believed to bring good harvests. The young man soon takes the place of the statue, and when the priestess becomes pregnant, the people take it as a sign of divine favor. Although this episode is probably intended to mock paganism, the practice it describes is confirmed from other sources, such as Tacitus's account of the procession of Nerthus. A late Icelandic saga (*Vatnsdæla saga*, ch. 10) notes that one devotee of Freyr carried an amulet of the god around with him in a bag, a practice substantiated by the find in Rällinge, Sweden, of a small yet phallic Viking Age statuette.

Toponymy supplies strong evidence of the spread of his cult: place-names incorporating *Freyr* are numerous in Sweden, especially in the agricultural area of Svealand. Similarly, the god's name combines with words for fields, meadows, and so on in agricultural regions of Norway, and it appears in a few places in eastern and southeastern Iceland. Here the traditional elements preserved in the Icelandic saga about a chieftain named Hrafnkell attest to the veneration of Freyr; he was a "priest of Freyr" (Old Icelandic *Freysgoði*), to whom he had dedicated a stallion. When a servant desecrated the horse by riding it in spite of Hrafnkell's stern warnings, Hrafnkell killed him. However, Hrafnkell's enemies captured the stallion and pushed it over a cliff after covering its head with a bag, as if they were afraid of the power in its eyes. Desecration of horses belonging to Freyr is also attributed to the missionary king, Olaf Tryggvason, who destroyed a sanctuary of the god in Norway.

The horse is not the only animal closely associated with Freyr; several sources relate the offering of a bull or an ox to Freyr. The boar was also considered suitable for sacrifice to Freyr, particularly at Yuletide, a critical period when the forces of fertility needed to be stimulated. Adam of Bremen (IV: 27) reported that at times up to seventy-two bodies of men, horses, and dogs would hang together in a grove near the temple at Uppsala, but he did not say which victims were dedicated to which gods.

The rationale for these sacrifices was presumably concern for good crops; this is suggested by the story of the death of the euhemerized Freyr related in *Ynglingasaga* (ch. 10). When "King Freyr" succumbed to long illness he was secretly buried, and people were made to believe he was still alive. For three years, their tribute—first of gold, then of silver, and ultimately of copper coins—was poured into Freyr's funeral mound, and good seasons and peace endured. This story has often been compared to the occultation of the Thracian god Zalmoxis, but as Mircea Eliade showed in *Zalmoxis, the Vanishing God* (1972), this comparison is not valid.

SEE ALSO Boats; Eddas; Germanic Religion; Loki; Njǫrðr; Sagas; Snorri Sturluson.

BIBLIOGRAPHY

Dumézil, Georges. *Gods of the Ancient Northmen.* Berkeley, Calif., 1973.

Eliade, Mircea. *Zalmoxis, the Vanishing God: Comparative Studies in the Religion and Folklore of Dacia and Eastern Europe.* Chicago, 1972.

Grimm, Jakob. *Deutsche Mythologie* (1835). Translated from the 4th edition and edited by James Steven Stallybras as *Teutonic Mythology,* 4 vols. 1966; reprint, Gloucester, Mass., 1976.

Hollander, Lee M. *The Poetic Edda.* 2d rev. ed. Austin, Tex., 1962.

Lindow, John. *Scandinavian Mythology: An Annotated Bibliography.* New York, 1988.

Ross, Margaret Clunies. *Prolonged Echoes: Old Norse Myths in Medieval Northern Society,* vol. 1, *The Myths.* Odense, Denmark, 1994.

Vries, Jan de. *Altgermanische Religionsgeschichte,* vol. 2. 2d rev. ed. Berlin, 1967.

EDGAR C. POLOMÉ (1987)
ELIZABETH ASHMAN ROWE (2005)

FRICK, HEINRICH

FRICK, HEINRICH (1893–1952), German religious thinker. The term *religious thinker* characterizes Frick as a scholar who endeavors to combine two potentially conflicting attitudes: Christian theological piety and the ability to analyze in a religio-historical way his own religion and the religions of others.

Born in Darmstadt, Hesse, Frick during his childhood belonged to Bible youth groups. He studied Protestant theology and Arabic in Giessen and Tübingen. He received his licentiate in theology in 1917 from the University of Giessen and joined the Lutheran ministry in Darmstadt. In 1918 he earned his doctorate, also at Giessen; his thesis was *Ghazalis Selbstbiographie: Ein Vergleich mit Augustins Konfessionen* (Al-Ghazālī's *Autobiography:* A Comparison with Augustine's *Confessions;* 1919). Frick began his academic career in 1919 as privatdocent in *Religionswissenschaft* and missiology at the Technische Hochschule, Darmstadt. He moved to the University of Giessen in 1921, from which he was called to Marburg as successor to Rudolf Otto, whose professorship in systematic theology was, for Frick, extended to include *Religionswissenschaft* and missiology. In addition, he became director of the Religionskundliche Sammlung, a collection of religious materials from many religions of the world that had been founded by Otto in 1927.

Frick's bibliography contains more than 150 items, most of them articles, reports, prefaces, lectures, speeches, sermons, and statements. Of his few books, only one pertains to *Religionswissenschaft* proper, that is, *Vergleichende Religionswissenschaft* (Comparative study of religions; 1928). Here he lucidly develops his typology of religions, analyzing parallels between historical religions of different origin, as well as their respective "peculiarities." He concludes his argument by presenting three fundamental typological phenomena as essentially characteristic of religion: the Catholic-Protestant dissension (religio-historical); the polarity of mystical and believing piety (religio-psychological); and, crucial to the "quality" a religion has, the alternative of symbolization in space or time (religio-philosophical). The book aims at demonstrating that comparative religion is an "indispensable branch of effective theology" (p. 134), in that it proves the necessity of choice between several religious possibilities and offers empirical arguments for a "clear answer to the question why we cling to the gospel in spite of all the parallels and in spite of all the attractions in non-Christian religion" (p. 132).

This theological intention did not prevent Frick from developing, here and in other publications, points of comparison between religions that have since been generally accepted. It was an approach he had already adopted in his thesis comparing al-Ghazālī with Augustine, and again in his reviews and articles on special problems, for example, "Der Begriff des Prophetischen in Islamkunde und Theologie" (The concept of the prophetic in Islamic studies and theology), in *Festschrift P. Kahle* (1935); and in his programmatic writings, two examples: *Das Esvangelium und die Religionen* (The Gospel and religion, 1933); and in his article "Christliche Grundbegriffe in ihrer Besonderheit gegenueber Fremdreligionen" (Fundamental Christian ideas in comparison with other religions), *Evangelische Missionzeitschrift* (1944): 193–205, 233–255.

Motivated by a lifelong sensitivity to secularistic tendencies and the "crisis of religion," Frick summed up his views on *Religionswissenschaft* near the end of his life in two lectures on *Religionsphaenomenologie* (1950) and *Religionswissenschaft* (1951). Casting doubt on the moral right of neutrality in the field of *Religionswissenschaft* at a time when modern humanity had become more and more irreligious, Frick called upon his colleagues to search for a synthesis of the venerable religio-cultural traditions and modernity. In his opinion the "most important task of present *Religionswissenschaft* and related fields in all the scholarly faculties is to fulfill its modest but irremissible part in this."

BIBLIOGRAPHY

Neubauer, Reinhard. "Heinrich Frick, 1893–1952: Theologe." In *Marburger Gelehrte in der ersten Hälfte des 20. Jahrhunderts,* edited by Ingeborg Schnack, pp. 75–90. Marburg, 1977.

Neumann, Käthe. "Bibliographie Heinrich Frick." *Theologische Literaturzeitung* 78 (1953): 440–442. A complete list of his publications is available at Religionskundliche Sammlung, Philipps-Universität Marburg.

Röhr, Heinz. "Der Einfluss der Religionswissenschaft auf die Missionstheorie Heinrich Fricks." Ph.D. diss., Marburg University, 1959.

MARTIN KRAATZ (1987 AND 2005)

FRIENDS, SOCIETY OF SEE QUAKERS

FROBENIUS, LEO

FROBENIUS, LEO (1873–1938), was a German ethnologist and philosopher of culture. Leo Viktor Frobenius was born July 29, 1873, in Berlin, where he spent his early years. Even in his youth he devoted himself enthusiastically to the investigation of African cultures, collecting all available written and pictorial material that dealt with particular ethnological motifs. (Later, these materials became the matrix for an Africa archive that Frobenius assembled.) Despite the fact that he never received a high school diploma and did not complete a university program, Frobenius achieved extraordinary success in his scientific pursuits.

Stimulated by the work of Heinrich Schurtz (whom Frobenius claimed as his teacher), Friedrich Ratzel, and Richard Andree, Frobenius was responsible for introducing a new way of scientific thinking into the field of ethnology. His new concept, hinging on the term *Kulturkreis* ("culture circle"), first appeared in his 1898 work *Der Ursprung der afrikanischen Kulturen* (The origin of African civilization). Unlike other scholars, who put the term to one-dimensional uses, Frobenius developed the concept of *Kulturkreis* into an all-encompassing cultural morphology. His method involved the notion that individual elements of culture should be investigated according to their placement within the organic whole of which they are parts. According to Frobenius, this method provides a way for understanding the complex, historical nature of cultures.

Frobenius's primary concern was for the investigator's recognition of the essence of culture in general. Frobenius found that cultures display "biological" characteristics similar to those of living organisms. He drew parallels between a culture's stages and the elements of an organic life cycle, using terms such as *Ergriffenheit* ("emotion," by which Frobenius meant to signify a culture's youth), *Ausdruck* ("expression," or a culture's maturity), and *Anwendung* ("utilization," its old age). Every culture, argued Frobenius, possesses laws that determine its process independently of the individual human beings who participate in the culture. He labeled this inherent power with the Greek word *paideuma* ("what is acquired by learning") and devoted an entire book, *Paideuma: Umrisse einer Kultur- und Seelenlehre* (Outline of a theory of culture and spirit; 1921), to this theme. *Paideuma* is also the title of a periodical, established by Frobenius in 1938, devoted to the problem of cultural morphology. Although the philosophy of culture espoused by Frobenius has been disputed, he is still considered an ethnological field-researcher of the first order.

Frobenius went on twelve research expeditions to various parts of Africa to document the lives of tribal peoples. In addition, he studied the most important rock-painting sites of both northern and southern Africa. The results of his ethnological researches were presented in a work entitled *Und Afrika sprach,* 3 vols. (1912–1913; translated as *The Voice of Africa,* 2 vols., 1913). He also published a series of twelve volumes of folk tales and poems under the general title *Atlantis* between 1921 and 1928; these have proved to be particularly rich source materials for historians of religions. He summarized his research in *Kulturgeschichte Afrikas* (1933).

Frobenius's impact upon the world outside his professional field is demonstrated by the fact that the Senegalese politician and poet Léopold Senghor has credited Frobenius with helping to foster a revitalization of self-awareness among present-day Africans. The materials collected on Frobenius's many expeditions were brought together in 1922 to be housed at the newly founded Institute for Cultural Morphology in Munich. In 1925 the institute was removed to Frankfurt, where Frobenius received an honorary lectureship in the department of ethnology and cultural studies at the university. In 1934 he was appointed director of the Municipal Ethnological Museum in Frankfurt. Shortly after his sixty-fifth birthday, Frobenius died at his residence on Lake Maggiore in Italy.

SEE ALSO Kulturkreiselehre.

BIBLIOGRAPHY

For bibliographical data, see Heinz Wieschoff's article "Das Schrifttum von Leo Frobenius," in *Leo Frobenius, Ein Lebenswerk aus der Zeit der Kulturwende,* edited by Walter J. Otto (Leipzig, 1933), pp. 163–170; *Afrika Rundschau* (1938), pp. 119–121; Jacques Waardenburg's *Classical Approaches to the Study of Religion,* vol. 2 (The Hague, 1974), p. 82; and especially Hermann Niggemeyer, "Das wissenschaftliche Schrifttum von Leo Frobenius," *Paideuma* 4 (1950): 377–418. For biographical information, see Helmut Petri's article "Leo Frobenius und die historische Ethnologie," *Saeculum* 4 (1953): 45–60.

New Sources

A very useful collection of Frobenius's most important articles on African history, art and ethnography in English is *Leo Frobenius 1873–1973: An Anthology,* edited by Eike Haberland (Wiesbaden, 1973). It includes a foreword by Léopold Sédar Senghor, an informative "Editor's Postscript," a selected bibliography of works of and on Leo Frobenius and inspiring illustrations. For biographical information and appreciation by his disciples and colleagues, see Ewald Volhard, "Leo Frobenius," *Paideuma* 1 (1938): 41–44; Adolf E. Jensen, "Leo Frobenius: Leben und Werk," *Paideuma* 1 (1938): 45–58; Wilhelm Mühlmann, "Zum Gedächtnis von Leo Frobenius," *Archiv für Anthropologie* 25 (1939): 47–51. Hans-Jürgen Heinrichs, *Die fremde Welt, das bin ich. Leo Frobenius: Ethnologe, Forschungsreiseinder, Abenteurer,* Wuppertal, 1998, is a monograph that includes a bibliography. For Frobenius's virtual connections with Bachofen's legacy and his contribution to the theory of historical ethnology, see Giovanni Casadio, "Bachofen, o della rimozione," in *Agathe Elpis. Studi storico-religiosi in onore di Ugo Bianchi,* edited by G. S. Gasparro, Rome, 1994, pp. 63–78, 69–70.

OTTO ZERRIES (1987)
Translated from German by John Maressa
Revised Bibliography

FROGS AND TOADS.

The frog or toad is a lunar animal par excellence. Its shape or behavior is reminiscent of the moon; it swells and shrinks, submerges under water but emerges again, and hides under the ground in winter but reappears in spring. The frog lives according to the lunar rhythm. In fact, a great many myths speak of a frog in the moon. According to the Chinese, the moon has not only an evergreen cassia tree and a rabbit but also a frog inside it. Thus the *Tianwen* section of the *Chuzi* (fourth or third century BCE) asks: "What is the peculiar virtue of the moon, the brightness of the night, which causes it to grow once more after its death? What does it advantage to keep a frog in its belly?"

The frog, then, is naturally associated with all sorts of aquatic elements such as water, rain, ocean, and flood. Frogs are said to croak incessantly before it rains, or to announce or bring rain by croaking. They are usually mentioned in the innumerable rites for inducing rain. North American Indians see in the moon the primeval toad, which contained all the waters and caused the flood by discharging them over the earth. According to the Kurnai of southeastern Australia, once upon a time all the waters were swallowed by a huge frog; the other animals tried in vain to make him laugh until the eel danced about, twisting itself into the most ridiculous contortions, whereupon the frog burst into laughter and the waters rushed out of his mouth and produced the flood. The frog sometimes plays a part in the precosmogonic period when there is nothing but water. A Huron myth narrates how several animals descended in vain into the primeval waters, until the toad returned successfully with a little soil in its mouth; the soil was placed on the back of the tortoise, and the miraculous growth of the land then began.

Significantly, the frog is also associated with the principles of evil and death. According to Altaic beliefs, the creation of man and woman by the god Ülgen was marred by the devil Erlik. Consequently, the god decided to destroy them, but changed his mind when a frog proposed that humankind exist under the curse of mortality. In Iranian mythology the frog appears as a symbol or embodiment of the evil spirit or the most important of its creatures. In Inner Asian cosmogonic myths—apparently colored by Iranian influence—frogs are among those animals that, together with lizards, worms, and mice, come out of the hole made in the earth by the satanic figure. In Africa the frog emerges sometimes as the messenger of death. At the time of beginning, say the Ekoi of Nigeria, the duck was charged by God with a message of immortality to humankind, whereas the frog was given a message of death. The frog got to the earth first, delivered his message, and thus brought death to humankind.

BIBLIOGRAPHY

There is much useful material in volume 2 of Robert Briffault's *The Mothers: A Study of the Origins of Sentiments and Institutions,* 3 vols. (1927; reprint, New York, 1969), pp. 634ff. Mircea Eliade has discussed frog symbolism in *Patterns in Comparative Religion* (New York, 1958), pp. 160ff. See also Lutz Röhrich's "Hund, Pferd, Kröte und Schlange als symbolische Leitgestalten in Volksglauben und Sage," *Zeitschrift für Religions- und Geistesgeschichte* 3 (1951): 69–76.

New Sources

Ribouli, Patricia, and Maria Robbiani. *Frogs: Art, Legend, History,* translated by John Gilbert. Boston, 1991.

MANABU WAIDA (1987)
Revised Bibliography

FRYE, NORTHROP.

The reputation of Northrop Frye (1912–1991) as a literary theorist was originally based upon his *Anatomy of Criticism* (1957), a book that sought to provide a structural framework for the study of literature through an analysis of its various modes, symbols, myths, images, and genres. The *Anatomy,* heralded for a generation as a twentieth-century *Poetics,* had a large following in the 1960s and 1970s, and twenty years after its publication it was the most frequently cited book in the arts and humanities by a writer born in the twentieth century. Seventeen translations of the *Anatomy* into thirteen languages (as of 2003) attest to its international standing. But some thirty books followed in the wake of the *Anatomy,* and the scope of Frye's work as a whole has come into focus with the publication of his collected works. While *Anatomy of Criticism* will remain an important twentieth-century study of literary conventions, it seems likely that Frye's major contribution will be defined by the books that serve as bookends of his career: at the beginning, *Fearful Symmetry: A Study of William Blake* (1947), and at the end, his two books on the Bible and literature, *The Great Code* (1982) and *Words with Power* (1990)—as well as his posthumous *The Double Vision* (1991).

Frye grew up in a Methodist environment in Moncton, New Brunswick. Although he rejected at an early age what he saw as the constraining features of fundamentalism and the oppressive demands of Methodist moral piety, he never abandoned his Protestant roots, particularly its low-church, dissenting traditions and the Methodist emphasis on experience. In 1929, at age seventeen, he entered Victoria College in Toronto as a "church student," and on completing his undergraduate honors degree in philosophy, he enrolled at Emmanuel College, the theology school at Victoria University. The papers he wrote at Emmanuel, collected in *Northrop Frye's Student Essays* (1997), show how deeply he immersed himself in the comparative mythology of James Frazer (1854–1941), Oswald Spengler's (1880–1936) theory of the organic rhythms of cultural history, Reformation theology, and the Romantic cultural revolution. Several of these essays also addressed the relationship of religion and art. Frye's basic insights came to him early, and these student essays contain an embryonic form of many of the deductive frameworks he subsequently developed. At age twenty-two Frye wrote, "religion and art are the two most important phenomena in the world; or rather the most important phenomenon, for they are basically the same thing" (*Correspondence,* 1966, vol. 1, pp. 425–426). This was an insight that Frye spent the next fifty-six years exploring.

Frye's interest in religion is, therefore, in many ways obvious: he became an ordained minister in the United Church of Canada; early in his career he wrote an extraordinary essay on American civil religion and another one on the relation of the church to society; at Victoria College, where Frye spent his entire career, he taught a course on the Bible for forty-four years; and he addressed religious subjects on numerous occasions (*Northrop Frye on Religion* [2000] contains forty-three texts, including a number of eloquent sermons and prayers). But having an interest in religion would be not be unusual for any thinker who engaged as expansive a range of literary, social, and cultural issues as Frye did. That would be the weak claim. The strong claim would be that religion was absolutely central to practically everything he wrote, the base upon which he built the massive superstructure that was his life's work. The reasons for the strong claim have become more insistent and the argument more convincing with the publication of Frye's notebooks, diaries, and other manuscripts.

Frye remarked on several occasions that all of his ideas derived from William Blake (1757–1827), a deeply religious poet, the code of whose "prophecies" Frye was more responsible than anyone else for deciphering. The most important thing Blake taught Frye was the religious vision of radical immanence. Blake insists, says Frye, that "everything God does comes through man—the consciousness and imagination of man. . . .God becomes man in order that we may be as he is" (Cayley, 1992, p. 54). Theologically, this is the doctrine of the incarnation, though Frye was not inclined to speculate on such paradoxes in theological terms—in what he called the second-phase language of discursive thought with its emphasis on subjects and objects. His approach was through the first-phase language of metaphor. "The metaphorical approach," he said, "moves in the direction of the identity of God and man" (Cayley, 1992. p. 183). This means that the principle of identity, which makes the paradoxical claim that two different things are the same thing, lies behind Frye's speculation on both religion and art. Identity is also a principle of myth: in our earliest stories, which are stories about gods, the gods are themselves identified with forces in nature. In such hyphenated words as *sky-god* or *river-god* the hyphen really functions as an equal mark, identifying the sky or the river *with* the god. *Mythos* or narrative, moreover, has to do with the loss and regaining of identity, or recognition of self by both literary characters and readers, which is the general topic of *The Secular Scripture* (1976).

Metaphor and myth, then, lie behind Frye's imaginative approach to the Bible in *The Great Code* and *Words with Power* and in the lectures on the Bible that he gave at Victoria College, published in *Northrop Frye's Notebooks and Lectures on the Bible and Other Religious Texts* (2003). The Bible for Frye was the primary text in the Western literary imagination, becoming for him a touchstone for studying what he called "positive analogies" in nonbiblical stories and images. His approach always moved away from the historical and doctrinal toward the poetic. But although he was known primarily as a literary critic, his lifelong project took the form of a religious quest and the structures he built for containing his expansive vision were fundamentally religious. "I am an architect of the spiritual world," Frye wrote in his *Late Notebooks* (2000, vol. 1, p. 414).

The architecture of this world was formed by a number of key terms that appear throughout Frye's work—what he called his "verbal formulas." Chief among these are (1) *interpenetration,* an idea that developed from his reading of Spengler, Alfred North Whitehead (1861–1947), David Bohm (1917–1992), and the sūtras of Mahāyāna Buddhism, and that, like *identity,* represented the erasing of the subject-object duality; (2) the *participating apocalypse* or revelation, which was the final stage of the reading process, opening up "myths to live by and metaphors to live in" and the gospel of love; (3) *kerygma,* the voice of proclamation that comes from the other side of the poetic; (4) *purgatory,* which represents the pilgrimage that serves as a crucible for the purified mind and the emancipated vision; (5) *anagnorisis* or recognition, which Frye associates with rebirth and renewed visionary perception; and (6) the *dialectic of Word and Spirit,* the goal of which was to reach spiritual insight.

Frazer and other comparative mythographers, including Carl Jung (1875–1961) and Mircea Eliade (1907–1986), were important in Frye's early work in helping him define the principles of myth, archetype, and ritual. In his late work such thinkers are displaced by G. W. F. Hegel (1770–1831), whose *Phenomenology of Spirit* (1807) Frye saw as the great philosophic statement of *anabasis.* Both Frye and Hegel climb a spiraling ladder to a higher level of being, except Frye moves upward by way of the language of myth and metaphor. Frye said, "If Hegel had written his *Phenomenology* in *mythos*-language instead of in *logos*-language a lot of my work would be done for me" (*Late Notebooks,* 2000, vol. 1, p. 192). About the same time he wrote, "The rush of ideas I get from Hegel's *Phenomenology* is so tremendous I can hardly keep up with it" (*Late Notebooks,* 2000, vol. 2, p. 631). Blake remained Frye's guiding light throughout his career, but Stéphane Mallarmé (1842–1898) was another important presence in his visionary poetics. In Mallarmé, Frye discovered a completely metaphoric and symbolic world, a world where divinity can be expressed only by the poetic word but which ultimately moved beyond the poetic. In his various accounts of Mallarmé the distinction between literature and religion tended to collapse.

Frye never escaped from his Christian roots, nor did he want to: the words *Christian* and *Christianity* appear more 3,400 times in his work. But he had more than a passing interest in Eastern religious traditions, and his notebooks reveal that he was deeply engaged with esoteric and mystical religious traditions. His library contains more than 250 annotat-

SACRED SPACE

A sacred space is any place recognized for its ability to direct the mind and body to holy matters. The basis for this power varies considerably. Sometimes spaces act like reliquaries—enclosures that mark the deposit of a saint's remains, or the site of an unusual event such as a vision or manifestation of divine power, or the place where a holy person preached or lived. Alternatively, sacred spaces are often built environments that seek to shape human consciousness toward states of worship or mindfulness. For example, Father Paul Matthias Dobberstein, an immigrant Catholic priest, constructed the Grotto of the Redemption in West Bend, Iowa (**a** and **b**), as well as seven other shrines and grottos in the midwestern United States, as spaces meant to awe and fascinate, but also to claim attention for the purpose of reflection and devotion. The beauty the priest admired in stone was dedicated to the spiritual beauty of Mary. Sacred space is therefore in many instances intended as an aesthetic shaping of consciousness as an act of adoration, an attempt to segregate the worshiper from other forms of life for the sake of cultivating a special dedication to a saint or deity. To that end, many sacred spaces are grand in scale and expensively appointed, particularly those associated with mass pilgrimage, such as the Buddhist temple district of Ayutthyā, Bangkok (**c**); the many cathedrals and public churches of Europe (**d**); or the Kaʿbah (**e**), the central pilgrimage site among the world's Muslims, who go there to visit the site where Muḥammad established

(**a**) Grotto of the Redemption, West Bend, Iowa, begun 1912. *[©2003 Phillip Morgan]*

(**b**) Nativity, Grotto of the Redemption. *[©2003 Phillip Morgan]*

(c) Phra Sri Ratana Chedi, a nineteenth-century Buddhist stupa within the Grand Palace complex in Bangkok, Thailand. *[©Royalty-Free/Corbis]*

(**d**) The main apse of the Church of San Vitale, completed in the mid-sixth century, Ravenna, Italy. *[©Scala/Art Resource, N.Y.]*

(**e**) The Kaʿbah, draped in black velvet, is the focal point of Muslim pilgrimage to Mecca, Saudi Arabia. *[©Reuters/Corbis]*

the faith, a site believed to have been first consecrated by Abraham, and even by Adam. And when they are not at Mecca, Muslims pray each day in its direction, which is registered in every mosque's *miḥrāb* **(f)**, the niche in the wall that indicates the *qiblah*, Mecca's direction, and the place where the *imām* stands to address the assembled company of the prayerful. Although the ancient temple is completely gone, Jews visit the last trace of the installation, the wall in Jerusalem **(g)**, for prayer and devotion.

While many Protestants might feel uneasy about the idea of "sacred space" in their practice, the pride they take in building and maintaining their church buildings **(h)** suggests an enduring commitment to a place set apart, even if its sacredness consists more in the public statement the building makes. In addition to this, however, the interior space fashions a gathering site where the faithful experience a sense of community, which for many Protestants is the primary locus of the sacred. The material architecture, in other words, provides a shell in which the

(f) A *miḥrāb*, a niche in the wall of a mosque indicating the direction of Mecca, at the Friday Mosque in Kerman, Iran. *[©Roger Wood/Corbis]*

(g) An Orthodox Jew (right) and three Israeli soldiers pray at the Western Wall in Jerusalem. *[©David H. Wells/Corbis]*

(h) The St. James-Bond United Church in Toronto, Ontario. *[©2004 Photograph by Neil Graham]*

human architecture of ordered bodies performs the communal event of sacred assembly.

In addition to being built, sacred space is also found in the natural state of trees, rivers, mountains, canyons, or the ocean. The Ganges is the dominant symbol of Hindu piety and is the daily site of ablutions, prayer, burial, and offerings **(i)**. Tree shrines are also a familiar part of Hindu practice. The holy is not understood to be limited to one place or object, but pervades the entire locale, every aspect of the natural and built environment. But the divine may be addressed at one site, marked by a tree or sculpture or image, like the sacred tree reproduced here **(j)**, a station along the road where passersby stop to pray or make an offering or simply to remember the goodness of the deity honored there.

In other instances, sacred spaces are constructed from local materials, which allow for an international religious

(i) Hindu pilgrims gather along the Ganges River in Vārāṇasī, (Banaras) an important pilgrimage site in northern India. *[©Brian A. Vikander/Corbis]* **(j)** A Hindu tree shrine, marked by a wooden sculpture, in the Udaipur district in Rajasthan, India. *[©Photograph by Stephen P. Huyler]*

(k) An elaborate compound made from reeds by disciples of Serigne Omar Sy, a Sūfī holy man in Djourbel, Senegal. *[Photograph by Mary N. Roberts and Allen F. Roberts]*

tradition to assume indigenous roots. The elaborate reed construction of a compound **(k)** at Djourbel, Senegal, was built by the followers of a local Sūfī holy man, Serigne Omar Sy, from the same material used to make the pens that write the word of God. Serigne Sy explained that the reed appeared to him in a dream and asked to be honored. Like Father Dobberstein's grotto in Iowa, the reed compound proceeded as a labor of love, in which followers of the Sūfī *marabout* joined to bring the dream to realization.

Still other sacred spaces are designed to recall the natural state of their site or components, as in the Zen rock garden **(l)** at Ryōanji in Kyoto, Japan. The Japanese Zen aesthetic seeks to amplify the peculiar characteristics of objects such as trees, bushes, rocks, or streams by carefully cultivating their natural setting. By surrounding the rock garden with walls and raking the pebbles into long rows that caress the contours of island-like boulders, the garden evokes a kind of microcosm. Absorbed in meditation, Zen practitioners may experience many levels of reality in a stillness that undermines the mind-body and

(l) A Japanese Zen rock garden, constructed in the 1480s, at Ryōanji in Kyoto. *[©Archivo Iconographico, S.A./Corbis]*

human nature dualities that Buddhists believe condemn human beings to suffering and illusion. There is no intrinsic or autonomous power in this space. Its elements may be changed, but when they are, it is in accord with an aesthetic sensibility that recognizes the power of forms to serve as suggestive prompts to meditation.

A final source for sacred space is appropriation: the adoption of a nonreligious form of built environment for sacred purposes. This occurs in modern urban societies with great frequency when small congregations or charismatic religious leaders acquire an abandoned store and convert it to a church or temple **(m)**. Given the expense of building anew, storefront churches are an affordable alternative. But convenience is not all they are about as sacred spaces. They offer congregants a space of their own that they modify to suit their practical purposes but also to act as public signage. And the appropriated spaces situate the sacred not in elaborate, dedicated structures, but in small, adapted environments that do not lose in most instances their connection to the surrounding secular world. Many storefront Christian and Spiritual-

(m) Tabernáculo de Fe, Iglesia de Dios en Cristo (Tabernacle of Faith, Church of God in Christ), a storefront church in South-Central Los Angeles. Photograph by Camilo Vergara. *[©Camilo José Vergara. Reproduced by permission]*

ist churches in the United States operate ministries of outreach among the downtrodden and those who suffer from alcohol and drug abuse, broken homes, joblessness, poor health, and chronic poverty. While they might long for wealth, health, and homes in the suburbs, those who belong to or are served by storefront churches often find in them a supportive community organized around charismatic preachers and healers whose churches are outposts in a brutal and dangerous landscape. The sacred is not the space itself, but what happens there.

BIBLIOGRAPHY

Berthier, François. *Reading Zen in the Rocks: The Japanese Dry Landscape Garden.* Translated by Graham Parkes. Chicago, 2000.

Huyler, Stephen P. *Meeting God: Elements of Hindu Devotion.* New Haven, 1999.

Jones, Lindsay. *The Hermeneutics of Sacred Architecture: Experience, Interpretation, Comparison.* 2 vols. Cambridge, Mass., 2000.

Metcalf, Barbara Daly, ed. *Making Muslim Space in North America and Europe.* Berkeley, 1996.

Meyer, Jeffrey F. *Myths in Stone: Religious Dimensions of Washington, D.C.* Berkeley, 2001.

Roberts, Allen F., and Mary Nooter Roberts. *A Saint in the City: Sufi Arts of Urban Senegal.* Los Angeles, 2003.

DAVID MORGAN (2005)

ed books that can be labeled *esoterica*, ranging from Alexandrian hermeticism through the medieval mystics to various forms of the occult, including alchemy, astrology, Gnosticism, magic, mysticism, Rosicrucianism, channeling, the tarot, numerology, astral projection, New Age science, Theosophy, synchronicity, and qabbalism. Frye had no interest in these traditions as matters of belief, but they did confirm his contention that poetic thought is schematic, and they contained grammars of literary and religious symbolism. He was drawn to the esoteric traditions only to the extent that he could make imaginative use of them.

Frye was a schematic thinker (he could hardly put pen to paper without a diagram in mind), but he was also a dialectical thinker, his mind repeatedly moving back and forth between opposing poles of reference: knowledge and experience, space and time, stasis and movement, the individual and society, tradition and innovation, Platonic synthesis and Aristotelian analysis, engagement and detachment, freedom and concern, *mythos* and *dianoia*, the world and the grain of sand, immanence and transcendence, and hundreds of other oppositions. A second feature of Frye's expansive body of work was its drive toward unity—an effort to get beyond the oppositions that he repeatedly introduced. He always resisted the Kierkegaardian either/or solution. But unity was not achieved at the expense of variety, and he never tires of insisting that opposites are never resolved by reconciliation, harmony, or agreement. They are typically resolved, rather, by the process of the Hegelian *Aufhebung*, a dialectic in which oppositions are, in the triple meaning of the term, canceled, preserved, and raised. The movement of passing through negation to another level of vision is present in the conclusions of each of the eight chapters of *Words with Power*, and it is operative as well in the final pages of each of the four chapters of *The Double Vision.*

Frye's own purgatorial journey, as he called it, took the form of a quest romance. The goal of this quest—the existential vision that came from the other side of the poetic—was for Frye, the Everlasting Gospel, in Blake's phrase, or the gospel of love. Charity or *agapē* is the note that is sounded in the conclusions of Frye's last three books. But the structural poetics that Frye developed in *Anatomy of Criticism* remained with him to the end. Therefore, to see Frye as a religious visionary and architect of the spiritual world is to consider his work less in revisionary terms than in expanded ones.

See Also Literature, article on Literature and Religion.

Bibliography

The authoritative texts of Frye's published and previously unpublished writings are being issued in the Collected Works of Northrop Frye (Toronto, 1996–), under the editorship of Alvin A. Lee. As of 2003, thirteen of the more than thirty volumes had appeared: *The Correspondence of Northrop Frye and Helen Kemp, 1932–1939* (2 vols., 1996); *Northrop Frye's Student Essays, 1932–1938* (1997); *Northrop Frye on Religion,* (2000); *Northrop Frye's Late Notebooks, 1982–1990* (2000; 2 vols.); *Northrop Frye's Writings on Education* (2000); *The Diaries of Northrop Frye, 1942–1955* (2001); *The "Third Book" Notebooks of Northrop Frye, 1964–1972* (2001); *Northrop Frye on Literature and Society, 1936–1989* (2002); *Northrop Frye on Modern Culture* (2002); *Northrop Frye on Canada* (2003); and *Northrop Frye's Notebooks and Lectures on the Bible and Other Religious Texts* (2003). The remaining volumes are expected at the rate of two per year.

Frye's major books are *Fearful Symmetry* (Princeton, 1947), *Anatomy of Criticism* (Princeton, 1957), *The Great Code* (New York, 1982), and *Words with Power* (New York, 1990). His essays have been collected in *Fables of Identity* (New York, 1963), *The Stubborn Structure* (Ithaca, N.Y., 1971), *Spiritus Mundi* (Bloomington, Ind., 1976), *Northrop Frye on Culture and Literature* (Chicago, 1978), *On Education* (Markham, Ont., 1988), *Myth and Metaphor* (Charlottesville, Va., 1990), *Reading the World* (New York, 1991), and *The Eternal Act of Creation* (Bloomington, Ind., 1993). His essays on Canadian literature and culture are in *The Bush Garden* (Toronto, 1971) and *Divisions on a Ground* (Toronto, 1982). Other significant books include *The Educated Imagination* (Toronto, 1963), *T. S. Eliot* (Edinburgh, U.K., 1963), *The Well-Tempered Critic* (Bloomington, Ind., 1963), *The Return of Eden* (Toronto, 1965), *The Modern Century* (Toronto, 1967), *A Study of English Romanticism* (New York, 1968), *The Critical Path* (Bloomington, Ind., 1971), *The Secular Scripture* (Cambridge, Mass., 1976), *Creation and Recreation* (Toronto, 1980), and *The Double Vision* (Toronto, 1991). His books on Shakespeare are *A Natural Perspective* (New York, 1965), *Fools of Time* (Toronto, 1967), *The Myth of Deliverance* (Toronto, 1983), and *Northrop Frye on Shakespeare* (Markham, Ont., 1986). Twenty-two interviews with Frye are collected in *A World in a Grain of Sand* (New York, 1991).

Secondary Sources

Adamson, Joseph. *Northrop Frye: A Visionary Life.* Toronto, 1993.

Ayre, John. *Northrop Frye: A Biography.* Toronto, 1989.

Boyd, David, and Imre Salusinszky, eds. *Rereading Frye: The Published and Unpublished Works.* Toronto, 1999.

Cayley, David. *Northrop Frye in Conversation.* Concord, Ont., 1992.

Cook, David. *Northrop Frye: A Vision of the New World.* New York, 1985.

Cook, Eleanor, et al., eds. *Centre and Labyrinth: Essays in Honour of Northrop Frye.* Toronto, 1985.

Cotrupi, Caterina Nella. *Northrop Frye and the Poetics of Process.* Toronto, 2000.

Denham, Robert D. *Northrop Frye and Critical Method.* University Park, Pa., 1978.

Denham, Robert D. *Northrop Frye: An Annotated Bibliography of Primary and Secondary Sources.* Toronto, 1987.

Denham, Robert D., and Thomas Willard, eds. *Visionary Poetics: Essays on Northrop Frye's Criticism.* New York, 1991.

Donaldson, Jeffery, and Alan Mendelson, eds. *Frye and the Word: Religious Contexts in the Criticism of Northrop Frye.* Toronto, 2003.

Dyrkjøb, Jan Ulrik. *Northrop Frye's litteraturteori.* Copenhagen, 1979.

Gyalokay, Monique Anne. *Rousseau, Northrop Frye, et la Bible: Essai de mythocritique.* Paris, 1999.

Hamilton, A. C. *Northrop Frye: Anatomy of His Criticism.* Toronto, 1990.

Hart, Jonathan. *Northrop Frye: The Theoretical Imagination.* London, 1994.

Kee, James M., ed. *Northrop Frye and the Afterlife of the Word.* Semeia 89. Atlanta, 2002.

Krieger, Murray, ed. *Northrop Frye in Modern Criticism.* New York, 1966.

Lee, Alvin A., and Robert D. Denham, eds. *The Legacy of Northrop Frye.* Toronto, 1994.

Lombardo, Agostino, ed. *Ritratto de Northrop Frye.* Rome, 1989.

O'Grady, Jean, and Wang Ning, eds. *Northrop Frye: Eastern and Western Perspectives.* Toronto, 2002.

Ricciardi, Caterina. *Northrop Frye, o, delle finzioni supreme.* Rome, 1992.

Russell, Ford. *Northrop Frye on Myth: An Introduction.* New York, 1998.

Ziolkowski, Eric. "Between Religion and Literature: Eliade and Frye." *Journal of Religion* 71 (1991): 498–522.

ROBERT D. DENHAM (2005)

FUDŌ, the "Immovable One" (Skt. Acala, also Acalanātha Vidyārāja), is one of the most popular esoteric Buddhist deities in contemporary Japan. Fudō is most frequently colored black or dark blue and portrayed as sitting or standing on a large stone which, according to the commentary by Śubhākarasiṃha (637–735), represents both the heaviness of the obscurations (Skt. *kleśa*) and the immovability of the thought of awakening (Skt. *bodhicitta*). This ambiguity is typical of tantric thought in which the obscurations are nondually identical with awakening (Jpn. *bonnō soku bodai*).

Fudō is encircled by flames that are produced by his state of concentration. These flames themselves are described as being "garuda-headed," that is, shaped like the head of the mythic garuda bird, said to be able to eat snakes without harm. For this reason, the garuda is taken as a symbol of the power of Buddhist teachings to transform the three poisons of ignorance, greed, and hatred. Fudō's hair is braided and hangs down on one side of his face, his eyes are crossed or bulging from anger, and two fangs emerge from his mouth—usually one pointed up, the other down. He holds in his right hand a *vajra* (a ritual implement representing a thunderbolt) sword that cuts through the delusions of sentient beings. Sometimes a dragon is coiled around the sword. In his left hand he holds a noose which is used to pull sentient beings toward awakening. His *mantra* is "*naumaku sanmanda bazaradan senda makaroshada sowataya un tarata kan man*" (Skt. "*namaḥ samanta vajrāṇāṃ caṇḍa mahāroṣaṇa sphoṭaya hūṃ traṭ hāṃ māṃ*"), meaning "Praise all *vajras,* Violent and Exceedingly Wrathful One, destroy (all delusions)." The *mudrā* (yogic hand position) used in ritual for Fudō is formed by extending the fore- and middle fingers of both hands straight out, and curling the thumb, ring and little finger into the palm. The right hand is held palm down, and the left hand palm up. This represents Fudō's *vajra* sword and its scabbard, respectively.

He is considered to be the chief of the five Kings of Wisdom (Jpn. Godai Myōō, Skt. Vidyārāja, also translatable as "*Mantra* Kings" given the ambiguity of the Sanskrit *vidya,* meaning both wisdom and *mantra*), who appear wrathful in their function as protectors of the *buddhadharma.* The other four Kings of Wisdom are Trailokyavijaya (Jpn. Gōzanze), Kuṇḍalin (Jpn. Gundari), Yamāntaka (Jpn. Daiitoku), and Vajrayakṣa (Jpn. Kongoyasha). Fudō frequently appears accompanied by children, most commonly two (Jpn. Kongara and Seitaka), or eight children.

Fudō appears in both of the two *maṇḍalas* of the Shingon tradition, the Matrix Maṇḍala (Skt. *garbhakośadhātu maṇḍala,* Jpn. *taizōkai mandara*) described in the *Mahāvairocana sūtra,* and the Diamond World *Maṇḍala* (Skt. *vajradhātu maṇḍala,* Jpn. *kongōkai mandara*) described in the *Vajraśekhara sūtra.* In the former, below the central assembly is the "mansion of the mantra holders," within which Fudō is central.

The temple of Tōji ("Eastern Temple," Kyōtō) as redesigned by Kūkai beginning in 839 has as its altar a sculptural *maṇḍala.* One of the three groupings is that of the five Kings of Wisdom. Fudō is in the center, with Gōzanze to the east, Gundari to the south, Daiitoku to the west, and Kongōyasha to the north. These directions are symbolic, rather than literal, and are associated with specific colors according to the Chinese system of five elements.

Fudō also appears together with the other Kings of Wisdom at the center of the *maṇḍala* used in the *Ninnō-kyō Hō,* an elaborate esoteric rite centering on the recitation of the *Benevolent Kings Sūtra* (Jpn. *Ninnō-kyō*). In this *maṇḍala* he is shown seated, with a *vajra* sword in his right hand, and a *dharma* wheel (Jpn. *hōrin,* Skt. *dharmacakra*) in his left. Much more commonly performed today, however, is the protective fire ritual (Jpn. *sokusai goma*) with Fudō as the chief deity. In the training for Shingon priests this is the final ritual practiced.

Fudō is considered to be the wrathful manifestation of Mahāvairocana Buddha, the central cult figure of Shingon Buddhism. Under the theory of "original form, trace manifestation" (Jpn. *honji-suijaku*), Fudō is identified with Amaterasu, the sun goddess who is the ancestress of Japan's imperial family.

Fudō is linked with the widespread practice of cold water austerities, the practice of bathing in cold water, thought to stimulate internal energy, during which his mantra is commonly recited; the cult of Shugendō, mountain ascetics who engage in the practice (along with other austerities) are one vehicle for the spread of Fudō's popularity. Shugendō practitioners also construct large, outdoor fire rituals (Jpn. *saito goma*) in which Fudō plays a central role. Such rituals continue today, both in traditional Shugendō settings and in such new religions as Agon shū.

The association of cold water austerities with Fudō is found in the literary record. For example, the *Heike monogatari* tells of the cold water austerities of the warrior Mongaku, who vows to stand under the waterfall at Kumano in midwinter for twenty-one days, reciting the *mantra* of Fudō. After eight days, Mongaku collapses a second time and is revived by Kongara and Seitaku, who reassure him that Fudō, who is residing in Tuṣita heaven, has heard his invocations. Now reinspired, he returns to the waters which, because of the divine protection that has been extended to him, now feel warm, though winter gales blow around him. He is able to successfully complete the twenty-one days as he had vowed.

Whereas the iconography of Fudō became fairly standardized in Japan, his appearance is more varied in the Indian sources. In addition to the one-faced and two-armed form found, for example, in the *Sādhanamālā*, there is a one-faced and six-armed form and a three-faced and four-armed form (both found in the *Niṣpannayogāvalī)*, and a three-faced and six-armed form (found in the *Piṇḍīkrama-Sādhana*). In a painting from central Tibet (c. 1200), Fudō is the central figure, depicted kneeling in a position that has his right foot and left knee on the ground (Skt. *acalāsana*), and with three eyes.

Fudō is also named Caṇḍamahāroṣaṇa (the "fierce and greatly wrathful one"), the main figure of the *Caṇḍamahāroṣaṇa* tantra, classified in the Tibetan system as one of the *anuttarayoga* tantras. In this text he teaches his consort while they are in sexual union, and is identified as a manifestation of Akṣobhya, whose quality is an unshakable resolve to attain awakening. It has also been suggested that Fudō is related to Śiva, for whom Acala is an epithet. They share the attribute of immovability, and the iconographic detail of dark blue or black color.

BIBLIOGRAPHY

De Mallman, Marie-Thérèse. *Introduction a l'Iconographie du Tântrisme Bouddhique.* Paris, 1986.

Frank, Bernard. *Le panthéon bouddhique au Japon: Collections d'Emile Guimet.* Paris, 1991.

George, C. S. *The Caṇḍamahāroṣaṇatantra: Chapters I–VII.* New Haven, Conn., 1974.

Izutsu, Shinryu, and Shoryu Omori. *Sacred Treasures of Mount Kōya: The Art of Shingon Buddhism.* Honolulu, 2002.

McCullough, Helen Craig, trans. *The Tale of Heike.* Stanford, Calif., 1988.

Orzech, Charles. *Politics and Transcendent Wisdom: The Scripture for Humane Kinds in the Creation of Chinese Buddhism.* University Park, Penn., 1998. Presents translations of the *Benevolent Kings Sūtra* and the Benevolent Kings rite, and a discussion of the *vidyārājas* in Chinese esoteric Buddhism.

Payne, Richard K. "Standing Fast: Fudō Myōō in Japanese Literature." *Pacific World, The Journal of the Institute of Buddhist Studies* 3 (1987): 53—58.

Payne, Richard K. "Firmly Rooted: On Fudō Myōō's Origins." *Pacific World, The Journal of the Institute of Buddhist Studies* 4 (1988): pp. 6—14.

Teeuwen, Mark. "The Kami in Esoteric Buddhist Thought and Practice." In *Shintō and History: Ways of the Kami*, edited by John Breen and Mark Teeuwen, pp. 95–116. Honolulu, 2000. Shows the interplay between the Indic Buddhist category of *vidyārāja* as *dharma* protector and indigenous Japanese category of *kami* as local, territorial deities.

RICHARD K. PAYNE (2005)

FUJIWARA SEIKA (1561–1619) was a Japanese Confucian scholar of the early Tokugawa period. Once regarded as the founder of Tokugawa neo-Confucianism, Fujiwara Seika is today understood increasingly as a transitional figure in the development of an intellectually self-contained Confucianism out of the Zen-flavored Confucianism that flourished in the Gozan Zen temples of the Muromachi period.

Seika was a twelfth-generation descendant of the thirteenth-century court poet Fujiwara no Teika, but his immediate forebears were small local lords in the Harima area (present-day Hyōgo prefecture). A younger son, at the age of seven or eight he was sent to study at a Zen temple in the area where, it so happened, the priests were interested in Confucianism. When he was eighteen, his father and elder brother were killed in battle, and the family's ancestral lands were lost. Through the mediation of two uncles who were priests at important Zen temples in Kyoto, Seika, who had taken refuge in the capital, became a priest at the major Zen center of Shōkokuji. There, as was common practice, he pursued the study of Confucian texts as an adjunct to his training as a Zen priest. Gradually he formed a deeper commitment to Confucianism, and in his mid-thirties he left the temple and devoted himself to the study of Confucianism.

In 1596, at the age of thirty-five, Seika attempted to go to China to study Confucianism with an authentic master. The attempt was unsuccessful, but he was able to broaden and deepen his understanding of Confucianism through contact with Korean scholars captured by Japanese troops during Toyotomi Hideyoshi's invasion of Korea and brought back to Japan. At his urging, the captive scholars were set to copying out the Four Books and the Five Classics, while he punctuated the copied text in Japanese according to the Song and Ming neo-Confucian commentaries. Individual classics had been punctuated previously by Japanese scholars using the neo-Confucian interpretations, but this was the first instance in which one person systematically punctuated all the central texts of Confucianism. Seika's plan to make his punctuated edition available in published form went unrealized, but the plan itself and his comprehensive rather than piecemeal approach to the basic Confucian texts stand as landmarks in the history of Confucianism in Japan.

In other ways, too, Seika took steps to establish Confucianism as a self-sufficient intellectual tradition independent of Buddhism. For some time after leaving Shōkokuji Seika continued to dress as a priest, but in 1600 he formally manifested the shift in his intellectual allegiance by adopting a style of dress patterned after that of the Chinese scholar-official class. The same year he lectured on Chinese historical works before Tokugawa Ieyasu, founder of the Tokugawa shogunate, and engaged the Zen monks present in a debate over the respective merits of the Confucian and Buddhist approaches to life. Seika refused an invitation to serve Ieyasu on a permanent basis, but he maintained informal ties as a scholar with a number of daimyo.

Although Seika took action that contributed to the development of Confucianism as a public teaching (in contrast to the "secret transmission" tradition of medieval scholarship) institutionally independent of Buddhism, his writings on Confucianism reveal lingering traces of Zen ideas. Seika objected to the otherworldly orientation of Buddhism, but his emphasis on "stilling the mind" so as to allow it to return to its original state of good reflects the influence of the Zen concept of enlightenment and of the views of late Ming scholars such as Lin Chaoen, who had attempted a fusion of Zen, Confucian, and Daoist teachings. For this Seika was criticized by later Confucian scholars, including his disciple Hayashi Razan.

See Also Confucianism in Japan.

Bibliography

Abe Yoshio. *Nihon Shushigaku to Chōsen.* Tokyo, 1965. An important reevaluation of the formation of Tokugawa neo-Confucianism that treats major thinkers individually and stresses the connections between Korean Confucianism and early Tokugawa thought.

Ishida Ichirō. "Hayashi Razan: Muromachi jidai ni okeru Zenju itchi to Fujiwara Seika-Hayashi Razan no shisō." In *Edo no shisōka tachi,* edited by Sagara Toru et al., vol. 1. Tokyo, 1979. A recent study that challenges earlier assumptions about the discontinuity between medieval and Tokugawa thought and instead attempts to trace the stages of development from the Zen-oriented Confucianism of the Muromachi period to the independent Confucianism of the Tokugawa period.

New Sources

Turner, John Allen. "Art, the Ethical Self, and Political Eremitism: Fujiwara Seika's Essay on Landscape Painting." *Journal of Chinese Philosophy* 31 (March 2004): 47–63.

Kate Wildman Nakai (1987)
Revised Bibliography

FULANI RELIGION See FULBE RELIGION

FULBE RELIGION.

The Fulbe are groups of pastoralists, semipastoralists, farmers, and city dwellers who constitute large minorities in the Sahelian countries stretching from the Atlantic Ocean to the Red Sea (Mauritania, Senegal, Gambia, Guinea, Mali, Burkina Faso, Niger, Nigeria, Chad, Cameroon, and Sudan). Also called Fulani, Fellata, and Peul, these people (with an estimated population in the early twentieth century of around twenty-five million) have played a significant role in West African history and attracted the attention of European observers of African societies. While a majority had become Muslims from the eighteenth century, they possess a strong cattle-herding tradition that antedates their Islamic allegiance.

The Fulbe speak Fulfulde (also called Pulār), a language of the West Atlantic branch of Niger-Congo languages. The northern section of the West Atlantic branch includes Wolof, Serer, and Fulfulde, which are the dominant languages of Senegal but were in earlier times spoken farther north, in today's Mauritania. The early Fulbe probably left some of the rock paintings of cattle and herders in the area that gradually became the Sahara. In the last millennium largely nomadic Fulbe have progressively migrated from this location to the east, as far as Cameroon and Chad. In recent centuries they have spread into the Sudan. Until the eighteenth century most of these Fulbe maintained a pastoral lifestyle and had relatively little attachment to Islam.

The intensive Islamization of the Fulbe since the eighteenth century makes it difficult to recapture pre-Islamic Fulbe religion. However, the Malian Fulbe intellectual Amadou Hampaté Ba and the French ethnographer Germaine Dieterlen, who recorded an initiation text from a Senegalese informant and made a French translation and commentary titled *Koumen,* have provided a very suggestive statement. Koumen, the initiation ceremony, consists of twelve chapters, or clearings, in which the first human herder acquires knowledge of cattle and the world. The world is governed by the eternal and all-powerful God. God designates Canaba, who usually takes the form of a serpent, to be the guardian of cattle, and Koumen to be Canaba's herder. It is Koumen, often in the form of a child, and his wife Foroforondu who actually provide instruction to the novice Sile (a local variation of Sulayman or Solomon). At the end of the story Sile becomes the first *silatigi,* master of the bush and pastoral life. The story reveals the close ties among men, cattle, land, and vegetation—the trees, vines, and creeping plants that supply the staffs, cords, calabashes, and other vital instruments, as well as the shrines where Sile must demonstrate his attachment to God and the numerous spirits that populate the universe. A rich symbolism of color and number runs throughout the text. Yellow, red, black, and white correlate respectively with fire, air, water, and earth; with east, west, south, and north; and finally with the four original lineages of the Fulbe: Jal or Jallo, Bâ, Sō, and Bari. Sile gradually learns to read the symbolism and to use the configuration of cattle of different coats to divine the proper course of action.

While the Koumen ritual is quite specific to the Fulbe, many of its features recall the religious beliefs and practices of other people living in the region of Senegal and Mali. The *silatigi* resembles a priest-king. His progress in understanding parallels the learning process that takes place in other initiations. The serpent Canaba recalls the importance of serpents in Soninke and Mandinka symbolism, and his path down the Niger River repeats the trajectory of Mande creation myths. The story also suggests the importance of military leadership, the social stratification characteristic of the Western Sudan, and through the evocation of Solomon, the influence of the Jewish, Islamic, and Christian heritage. A blacksmith who is a member of an artisan caste aids Sile in his initiation. Sile is expected to demonstrate *pulaaku,* the Fulbe code of honor, shame, and restraint. This code is often defined in contrast to the behavior of slaves, who do not have an affinity for cattle and do not know how to act in general. The slave is seen to be crude, naive, irresponsible, and dark in color; he or she resembles the other black, non-Fulbe populations of West Africa. *Pulaaku* resembles the codes of a number of other stratified societies in West Africa who distinguish sharply between the conduct that one may expect of the noble and free strata and the behavior that one must tolerate from slaves and the people of caste—the hereditary corporations of blacksmiths and other trades. In general, *pulaaku* and the whole ritual of Koumen are consistent with pastoral Fulbe custom across the Sahelian zone. In the present state of knowledge they can be considered representative of pre-Islamic Fulbe beliefs and practices.

Until the eighteenth century the Fulbe were not in the forefront of forming states or practicing Islam in the western and central Sudanic region. The Timbuktu scholars who wrote the chronicles called the *Ta'rīkh al-Fattāsh* and *Ta'rīkh al-Sudān* in the sixteenth and seventeenth centuries regarded some Fulbe as the enemies of Islam, agriculture, commerce, and cities. Beginning in the eighteenth century Fulbe in several locations took the lead in establishing specifically Islamic states and societies. They used the process of *jihād,* or war against unbelievers, to reverse regimes that they considered pagan or nominally Muslim, appoint leaders who were knowledgeable in the faith, and erect educational and judicial systems in which Islamic law would be learned and practiced. While they failed to implement all of their ideal, they did spur, for the first time, the permanent development of an Islamic culture in the countryside outside of the capitals and commercial centers. The leaders in this process were scholars and sedentary Fulbe who were already at some distance from the predominantly pastoral pre-Islamic tradition. Over time they developed new genealogies where the four original Fulbe lineages were all descended from ʿUqba, usually identified with ʿUqba ibn Nāfiʿ, the Arab conqueror of much of North Africa in the seventh century CE. This origin is widely accepted by Fulbe of all persuasions today.

The first two of these Islamic revolutions occurred in the eighteenth century in the two Fūtas, regions fairly close to the Atlantic Ocean. The leaders in Fūta Jalon, the mountainous zone of Guinea, created an elaborate system of Islamic instruction in Fulfulde as well as Arabic. The Fulfulde system, based on a modified Arabic alphabet, was designed to reach the women, pastoralists, and others who were unlikely to acquire the ability to read and write for themselves. The people of Fūta Tōro, the middle valley of the Senegal River, became known as the Tokolor, a word that served to distinguish them from the Fulbe who were less committed to the establishment of an Islamic state and culture.

The most important revolution occurred in Hausaland, or northern Nigeria. In the early 1800s Usuman (also called Uthman or Usman) dan Fodio, his brother ʿAbdullāh, and his son Muhammadu Bello launched the *jihād* against the ruling class of the Hausa state of Gobir. Dan Fodio's students and allies then carried the campaign against other states and established new settlements beyond Hausaland. By 1812 a vast new confederation had emerged with its principal center at Sokoto, in northwest Nigeria. Dan Fodio and his associates wrote a large number of influential treatises that became the standard texts for the practice and spread of the faith in the western and central Sudan.The last revolution occurred in the middle delta of the Niger River, between the towns of Segu and Timbuktu and created the caliphate of Hamdullāhi around 1820. The movement led by ʿUmar Tāl put an end to this regime in 1862.

Fulbe scholars also played an important role in spreading the Qādirīyah and Tijānīyah Islamic orders, which could be practiced in the countryside, away from the large mosques, schools, and courts of the towns. One can say that the Fulbe supplied the most important agents of Islamization in West Africa in the nineteenth century.

Many Fulbe have remained relatively marginal to these processes of state formation and Islamization. Despite devastating droughts in the 1980s, they have tried to sustain their pastoral economy and lifestyle in the regions of West Africa that are more suited to grazing than to agriculture. For all public purposes they are Muslim; they observe the obligations incumbent on all members of the faith. In their family life and relationship to cattle, they observe the customs and values reflected in the Koumen ceremony.

SEE ALSO Dan Fodio, Usuman; ʿUmar Tāl.

BIBLIOGRAPHY

The classic statement of Fulbe values is in Amadou Hampaté Ba and Germaine Dieterlen's *Koumen: Texte initiatique des pasteur peul* (Paris, 1961). A useful English statement on the Fulbe is Paul Riesman's *Freedom in Fulani Social Life: An Introspective Ethnography* (Chicago, 1977). Marguerite Dupire provided a detailed study of the social organization of the pastoral Fulbe in *Organisation sociale des Peul: Étude d'ethnographie comparée* (Paris, 1970). The dualism of many contemporary Fulbe is well described in Derrick J. Stenning's *Savannah Nomads* (London, 1959), while the similarities of myth and ritual in the western Sudan are explicated in two articles by Germaine Dieterlen in the *Journal de la Société des Africanistes,* "Myth et organisation sociale au Soudan Français," vol. 25, nos. 1–2 (1955): 39–76, and "Mythe et organisation sociale en Afrique occidentale," vol. 29, nos.

1–2 (1959): 119–138. For a useful summary of the Fulbe's role in the state-formation process of recent centuries, see David Robinson's *The Holy War of Umar Tal: The Western Sudan in the Mid-Nineteenth Century* (Oxford, 1985), esp. chap. 2.

New Sources

Azaryá, Victor, ed. *Pastoralists under Pressure?: Fulbe Societies Confronting Change in West Africa.* Leiden, 1999.

DAVID ROBINSON (1987)
Revised Bibliography

FUNCTIONALISM is the analytical tendency within the social sciences—most notably, sociology and social anthropology—that exhibits a particular interest in the functions of social or cultural phenomena. In its most traditional form, functionalism has claimed that all items and activities in a system should be explained in reference to their objective consequences for the system as a whole. Thus the pivotal meaning of *function* is the objective consequence of an activity or phenomenon for the system of which it is a part. A secondary—but nonetheless significant—meaning of *function* in social science is similar to the use of the term in mathematics. When it is stated that *x* is a function of *y*, it is meant that *x* varies in direct proportion to variation in *y*. In social science this perspective on the concept of function has to do with interrelatedness. The dominant and the secondary meanings are linked as follows. The notion of function as consequence for the state of the system suggests that all phenomena in the system are considered, at least initially, as being relevant to the system's persistence. It is then but a small move to the postulate that all phenomena in a system are interrelated and that a change in one aspect will have implications for all others and for the system as a whole.

THE EARLY FRENCH SCHOOL. The functional analysis of religion played quite an important part in the development of the functional orientation in social science as a whole. Of more immediate relevance, however, is the fact that the functional analysis of religion has also played a very significant part in the development of the sociology and anthropology of religion. The functional orientation has a long history, but it was during the French Enlightenment of the eighteenth century that the seeds were fully sown for the explicit crystallization of sociological functionalism in the second half of the nineteenth century. Many eighteenth-century French philosophers and protosociologists were interested in the possibility of a form of society that would operate according to principles of rationality and enlightenment, without what they saw as the impediments of religious dogma and clerical predominance. On the other hand, many of these thinkers were also concerned with what could take the place of religious faith and practice in a prospective rational-secular society. Thus one of the earliest and most influential of the Enlightenment philosophers, Jean-Jacques Rousseau (1712–1778), maintained that a society needed a civil religion—a religion concerned not with the traditional matters of faith and practice in relation to a supernatural being or realm but rather with the generation and maintenance of involvement in, and respect for, the society as such. He, like a number of his contemporaries, was well aware that religion had, among other things, traditionally performed significant functions of legitimation. In fact, at the end of the eighteenth century the leaders of the French Revolution made a great effort to replace traditional Catholic symbols and rituals with "secular-religious" ones.

The awareness of crucial links between religion and politics grew in a period when, in many parts of Europe, there was a widespread challenge to the intrinsic validity of religious belief and the traditional church (above all in predominantly Catholic countries). Yet despite the conviction that traditional religion had had deleterious consequences for society, it was affirmed that the functions supposedly performed by religion still had to be met. One particularly significant version of that perspective was provided in France by Claude Henri, Comte de Saint-Simon (1760–1825), who maintained that religion was a society's most significant political institution. That idea was later developed by Alexis de Tocqueville (1805–1859), who studied the relationship between religion and democracy. Tocqueville's particular interest was in the prospects for democracy in France, given the predominance there of Catholicism and the conviction of many intellectuals that democracy and religion were incompatible. Tocqueville tried to show that American evangelical Protestantism fostered the American democratic spirit. In so doing, he sought to disprove the claim that religion necessarily inhibited or disrupted democracy, and subsequently argued that, with modification, Catholicism could support democracy in France.

While Tocqueville did not argue explicitly in terms of what came to be called functionalism, he helped crystallize the sociological view that religion performs vital social functions. In the case of Saint-Simon, however, the functional orientation had been somewhat more explicit. After having celebrated the emergent industrial order and noted its antipathy to religion, Saint-Simon concluded that a "New Christianity" was necessary to provide commitment and vitality to the new industrial type of society. With Saint-Simon's protégé, Auguste Comte (1798–1857), an even more calculated functional orientation appears. Often spoken of as the father of sociology, Comte advocated a secular science of society, to be based on a "positive" philosophy that had been made possible by the epochal demise of theological and metaphysical modes of thought. Sociology should become the cognitive keystone of modern societies. Sociology and sociology-based ethics were to take the place of religion. However, late in life Comte—in parallel with Saint-Simon—restructured his views and argued that a "religion of humanity" was required in order to guarantee commitment to and respect for society. In that regard Comte made elaborate proposals for France concerning festivals, rituals, functionaries, and symbols for the religion of humanity.

SPENCER. It was the work of the English philosopher Herbert Spencer (1820–1903) that gave the concept of function and the functional orientation in sociology their first fully explicit renderings. Spencer argued that societies are organisms and that one should conceive of the former in the same terms as the latter. Thus he articulated the two main principles outlined earlier: the interrelatedness of all items in a system (most importantly the whole society) and the referring of items within a system to the functioning of the system as a whole. Spencer was, moreover, an evolutionist, which at that time implied, among other things, a belief that as societies progressed to an advanced evolutionary condition, they relied less and less on religious thought and practice. For Spencer, the main institutions of an advanced society were incompatible with religion, while the society as a whole operated increasingly in terms of contractual relationships among individuals (although Spencer did believe that the evolutionary engine was driven by a mysterious force that gave purposeful direction to societal change).

DURKHEIM. Unlike Saint-Simon and Comte, Spencer never showed signs of retreating from his own views concerning the (unproblematic) demise of religion. And it is in terms of this difference between Spencer and Saint-Simon that the seminal work of the French sociologist Émile Durkheim (1858–1917) can best be approached. Durkheim's work was based partly on a rejection of Spencer's highly secular conception of modern societies, even though it maintained some features of Spencer's methodological functionalism. At the same time, Durkheim was taken with the ways in which Saint-Simon and Comte had come to appreciate the functional significance of religion. He believed, however, that they had erred in first seeing society as bereft of religion and then attempting to add religion to it. What Durkheim sought, most elaborately in *The Elementary Forms of the Religious Life* (1912), was a way in which to ground religion in society itself.

In his early methodological work Durkheim argued that the sociologist should work with two basic explanatory concepts: function and cause. *Function* had to do with the general needs of the societal organism that a social phenomenon served, while *cause* referred to those features of society that more directly facilitated a phenomenon. Durkheim was eager to dissociate himself from those who closely related function to ends or purposes. He insisted that there is no mysterious final cause of societal patterns or change and that one should not think of function as having to do with the intentions lying behind the establishment of institutions. (On the latter point Durkheim argued that social phenomena do not generally exist for the useful results that they produce.) In his early writing on the forms of social solidarity, Durkheim reacted to Spencer by maintaining that all contractual relationships must be based on *pre*contractual elements of society. His interest in religion developed largely in the attempt to comprehend precisely what those precontractual elements are. From the outset, Durkheim had been concerned with the issue of morality in modern societies. While seeking a sociological understanding of the foundations of morality, he endeavored to show that, for moral principles to have social weight, they must be more than logically persuasive. Durkheim contended that the principles of moral reason adumbrated by Immanuel Kant in the eighteenth century could be socially operative only insofar as they were socially imperative. He wanted to know, in other words, on what the obligatory character of morals rest.

Durkheim eventually reached the full-fledged conclusion that the primary function of religion lay in its distinction between the sacred and the profane. Religion, said Durkheim, has to do with sacred things. It is "the serious life." Religion is crucial in providing individuals with freedom from unchecked desire, in highlighting the moral character of the collectivity, and in binding individuals together within the latter. Durkheim is often interpreted as having simply emphasized the positive, integrative functions of religion. That was indeed a significant aspect of his theory of religion (which was at the same time a theory of society), yet Durkheim was also deeply concerned with the social sources, the causes, of religious belief and practice, as well as with the larger ramifications of religion in human life. Although Durkheim's work was almost certainly the most vital contribution to the functionalist orientation in sociology and to the functionalist analysis of religion in sociology and social anthropology, his ideas were developed in specific reference to what he perceived as a moral crisis in modern societies. This is true even though his major work on religion referred mostly to the primitive religious life of Australian Aborigines and even though he was greatly inspired by the writing of the French historian Fustel de Coulanges on religion in ancient Rome and Greece and by that of the Scotsman W. Robertson Smith on ancient Semitic religion.

Because, in terms of Durkheim's own definition of religion as involving the distinction between the sacred and the profane (rather than being defined, more narrowly, as belief in supernatural beings), religion had been ubiquitous in all civilizations, Durkheim concluded that it must have been functionally essential to all societies. Yet he was acutely aware that traditional religious faith had become increasingly fragile. In articulating his own theory of religion, Durkheim emphasized at the outset that religion, in contrast to magic, is fundamentally a collective phenomenon and that, in religion, ritual is as important as belief. In those terms he set about showing how, at least in primitive societies, the basic categories of religious belief are established and maintained through the collective experience of social structure. In religious ritual individuals experience acutely a dependence upon society; indeed, religious worship can be thought of as the celebration of that dependence. In his most radical terms, Durkheim suggested that the real object of religious worship is society, not God. His main point, however, was that it is from one's experience of society that one obtains the sense of something transcendent and authoritative. Yet Durkheim denied that he was making a judgment about the intrinsic validity of religious belief. Rather, he concentrated upon showing both the social conditions and the social functions of religion. As far as modern societies are concerned, Durkheim asserted that there is now a need for new religious forms that would perform the same kind of function as traditional religion but in a less spiritualistic way. In the tradition of Rousseau, Durkheim argued the need for new forms of civil religion and saw religion as critical in the periodic regeneration of societies.

Malinowski and Radcliffe-Brown. Durkheim's writing had a great effect on those social anthropologists of the 1920s and 1930s who sought to redirect anthropological inquiry away from speculatory evolutionism toward more analytically rigorous fieldwork. The two major figures in that regard were the Polish-born Bronislaw Malinowski (1884-1942) and the British-born Alfred Radcliffe-Brown (1881–1955), both of whom employed functional orientations in the study of primitive societies, including the religious aspects thereof. Malinowski's functionalism centered upon two claims: first, that any particular society is a unique, functioning whole, and, second, that the social arrangements and cultural forms obtaining in a society have functional significance in relation to the psychological needs of individuals. Thus in spite of his interest in the functional interrelatedness of social institutions and practices, Malinowski saw their most fundamental functional significance in their meeting the psychological needs of individuals. In contrast, Radcliffe-Brown took a more self-consciously Durkheimian position. He advocated a systematic science of society, involving comparative analysis of the structural patterns of societies with respect both to their overall cohesiveness and to the functional requirements of societies as systemic wholes. Both Malinowski and Radcliffe-Brown wrote about religion in their respective functional terms.

Parsons and His Critics. Among those sociologists and anthropologists of religion who have written entirely within the twentieth century, the most prolific analyst of religion was the American Talcott Parsons (1902–1979). Deeply, but by no means only, influenced by Durkheim, Parsons in the 1950s acquired the reputation of being the functionalist par excellence. From Durkheim, Parsons took the basic idea that religion is a universal feature of human life. However, he expressed strong reservations concerning Durkheim's attempt to talk not merely about the functional significance of religion but also about its social-structural bases. In the latter regard, said Parsons, Durkheim was often a reductionist, in the sense of reducing religion to society. In contrast, Parsons himself considered religion to be the pivotal aspect of the realm of cultural values, beliefs, and symbols. According to Parsons, patterns of culture operate in varying degrees of independence from social structure and certainly cannot be reduced to the latter. Culture provides meaning, general morality, expressive symbols, and basic beliefs to systems of social action and to individuals. Religion also relates systems of human action to what Parsons called "ultimate reality." He maintained that questions concerning the ultimate boundary of human action and interaction constitute a universal attribute of human life. Parsons's attempt to establish what for a long time he called a structural-functional form of general sociological theory has met with considerable criticism from the late 1940s onward. One of Parsons's most influential critics has been the American sociologist Robert Merton (1910–2003), who has attempted to systematize functional analysis so as to overcome what he has regarded as its weaknesses. Religion has figured strongly in his discussion.

Merton argues that many functionalists have singled out the integrative functions of religion—mainly in reference to certain primitive societies—while neglecting its potentially disintegrative consequences, or dysfunctions. They have also, he maintains, confused two issues: whether what is indispensable to society is the phenomenon, such as religious belief, or only the function supposedly met by such a phenomenon. Merton emphasizes the dangers of viewing the phenomenon itself as indispensable and suggests that sociologists develop a clear conception of functional alternatives. As an example of such an alternative, he proposes that the positive functions of religion might well be provided by something other than religion in its conventional sense (e.g., secular ideology).

Merton also raises the question as to whether functionalism is—as many of its critics have charged—inherently conservative. His conclusion is that it is not. Even though the main modern tradition of antireligion—Marxism—regards religion as a consequence of an economically exploitative society, it also looks upon religion as performing integrative functions in precommunist societies. Religion, in Marxist perspective, inhibits social change. Thus functional analysis can be used from both conservative and radical standpoints. Indeed, since the 1960s a clear strand of Marxist functionalism has concerned itself with the persistence of capitalist societies and the function religion plays in that persistence.

Issues arising from the long debate about the functional form of analysis have been central to the controversy concerning the degree to which the modern world is characterized by secularization. For the most part, functionalists have resisted the thesis of extensive secularization, on the grounds that the functions performed by religion are essential to all societies. Thus Parsons tended to argue that even though a society may manifest ostensibly atheistic sentiments, it is still subject to the functional imperative of relating to ultimate reality. It was the hallmark of Parsons's approach to religion (and here he followed Durkheim) that one should not be overly constrained by the particular, substantive forms that religion has taken historically. In contrast to Spencer, Parsons argued that religion does not lose significance as human society evolves; rather, religion takes on increasingly general forms as societies become more differentiated and complex.

Recent Functionalist Theoreticians. A particularly radical type of functionalism was proposed by the German sociologist Niklas Luhmann (1927–1998). Luhmann argued that religion can no longer provide an overarching set of integrative values to a society. Unlike Parsons, who maintained that religious values and beliefs become more general but still remain overarching as societal evolution proceeds, Luhmann insisted that the social differentiation central to societal evolution has now gone so far that religion is but one subsystem among many. Religion is now "free" to concentrate on its primary function of answering purely religious—as opposed to social, economic, political, and scientific—questions.

Some of Luhmann's ideas overlap with those of the British sociologist Bryan Wilson, an adamant proponent of the secularization thesis. Wilson's argument hinges upon his claim that the historically latent functions of religion—*latent* is Merton's term for hidden, unrecognized functions—have become increasingly manifest (i.e., consciously recognized) and are now fulfilled by other social agencies, while historically manifest functions of religion—those providing guidelines for salvation—have been undermined. The main process that has both undermined the manifest and made manifest the latent functions of religion is the supplanting of communities by rationally organized, impersonal, and functionally specialized societies.

CONCLUSION. Even though functional analysis has been a frequent target of hostile critique, it has been continuously pivotal in the sociological and anthropological analysis of religion. And while there have undoubtedly been phases of crude functionalism—expressed in bland statements concerning the universality of religion and its beneficial consequences, as well as attempts to reduce religion to its societal consequences—it is nonetheless impossible to address the topic of religion in social-scientific terms without careful attention to its functional significance vis-à-vis other aspects of human life. Indeed, that perspective has pervaded modern consciousness, in the sense that religion is increasingly discussed and assessed in relation to its consequences for individuals and societies.

BIBLIOGRAPHY

The classic work in the tradition of functionalism is Émile Durkheim's *The Elementary Forms of the Religious Life* (1915; reprint, New York, 1965). An important discussion of functional analysis, with particular reference to religion, appears in Robert K. Merton's *Social Theory and Social Structure* (New York, 1968), pp. 73–138. Anthony F. C. Wallace's *Religion: An Anthropological View* (New York, 1966) contains an extended discussion of the functions of religion in several types of society. A flexible functionalist theory of religion is offered in J. Milton Yinger's *The Scientific Study of Religion* (New York, 1970). Relevant discussions of the history of the sociology of religion and of functionalist approaches are contained in my book *The Sociological Interpretation of Religion* (New York, 1970). Much of Talcott Parsons's theory of religion is found in his study *The Evolution of Societies* (Englewood Cliffs, N.J., 1977). For a lengthy discussion of Parsons's work on religion, with an extensive bibliography, see *Sociological Analysis* 43 (Winter 1982), a special issue edited by me. A functionalist interpretation of religion in the modern world is provided by Bryan R. Wilson in his *Religion in Sociological Perspective* (Oxford, 1982), while the radically functionalist theory of Niklas Luhmann is presented in his *Funktion der Religion* (Frankfurt, 1982). Analyses of civil religion in the tradition initiated by Rousseau, with reference also to Tocqueville, are provided in neofunctionalist terms by Robert N. Bellah and Phillip E. Hammond in their *Varieties of Civil Religion* (San Francisco, 1980).

New Sources

Dawson, Shawn Dawson. "Proper Functionalism: A Better Alternative?" *Religious Studies* 34 (June 1998): 119–134.

Kippenberg, Hans G. "Religious History, Displaced by Modernity." *Numen: International Review for the History of Religions* 47 (2000): 221–224.

Krech, Volkhard. "From Historicism to Functionalism: The Rise of Scientific Approaches to Religions around 1900 and Their Socio-Cultural Context." *Numen: International Review for the History of Religions* 47 (2000): 244–266.

Lewis, D. *Psychophysicalism and Theoretical Identificants: Readings in the Philosophy of Psychology.* Cambridge, Mass., 1990.

Owens, D. Alfred, and Mark Wagner. *Progress in Modern Psychology: The Legacy of American Functionalism.* Westport, Conn., 1992.

Putnam, Hilary. *Representations and Reality.* Cambridge, Mass., 1988.

Putnam, Hilary. "The Nature of Mental States." In *Mind and Cognition,* edited by William G. Lycan, pp. 20–26. Malden, Mass., 1990.

Sober, Elliot. "Putting Function back into Fundamentalism." In *Mind and Cognition,* edited by William G. Lycan, pp. 63–70. Malden, Mass., 1990.

ROLAND ROBERTSON (1987)
Revised Bibliography

FUNDAMENTAL CHRISTIANITY SEE EVANGELICAL AND FUNDAMENTAL CHRISTIANITY

FUNERAL RITES

This entry consists of the following articles:

FUNERAL RITES: AN OVERVIEW

Death is not only a biological occurrence leaving the corpse as a residue that must be administered to; it is also, and more importantly, a sociocultural fundamental because of the beliefs and representations it gives rise to and the attitudes and rituals it brings about. It is of course understood that rites are the immediate extension of beliefs, and that funeral rites, in particular, are the conscious cultural forms of one of the most ancient, universal, and unconscious impulses: the need to overcome the distress of death and dying.

This article will take the word *rite* in its anthropological sense; that is, in a larger sense, quite apart from liturgical or theological concerns. A rite, then, is a ceremony in which behaviors, gestures and postures, words or songs uttered, and objects handled, manufactured, destroyed, or consumed are supposed to possess virtues or powers or to produce specific effects. Centered on the mortal remains or its substitute, then on whatever survives of those—material traces or souvenir relics—funeral rites may reveal three finalities. First, it is believed that they preside over the future of the departed, over both the metamorphosis of the corpse and the destiny of the person, whenever death is defined as transition, passage, or deliverance. Second, they attend to the surviving close kin, mourners who must be consoled and reassured. Finally, they participate in the revitalization of the group that has been disturbed by the death of one of its own. Very often in traditional societies, in Africa and more often in Asia (notably in China), the funeral rites are presented as a theater of renewal, with acted parts, mimes, dancers, musicians, and even clowns.

Funeral rites are so important that the presence of the participants becomes a strict obligation, particularly in traditional societies. In traditional Africa, funeral rites are the most resistant to the pressure of acculturation. A function of the rite essential to the social group is easily seen; after all, numerous psychiatrists affirm that many problems derive from the guilt arising when one hurries over obsequies or comes out of mourning too soon.

Chief Moments in Funeral Rites. Funeral rites may comprise numerous ceremonies. The Toraja of Sulawesi (Celebes) see four fundamental stages. During the first, the deceased is said to be ill: Washed, dressed, and adorned, he may be nurtured for as long as a year. Then comes the first festivity, lasting from five to seven days, with sacrifices, lamentations, songs, and dances; this marks the difficult passage from life to death and ends with a provisional interment inside the house. During the following intermediary period, these festivities increase. Finally the ultimate ceremony is performed, requiring several months of preparation during which winding-sheets, cenotaphs, and, most notably, an effigy (the famous *tau-tau*) are employed, not without ostentation; it concludes with the burial and the installation of the deceased in the beyond.

The succession of funerary acts sometimes takes on a bureaucratic tone, particularly in Chinese Daoism, where the main part of the rite is devoted to drawing up documents and contracts with the gods. Especially noteworthy are the consultation of cosmic forces in order to determine propitious days and places for the rites; the *gongde,* or acquisition of merits for the deceased; the *pudu,* or offerings for wandering souls; and the ritual for liberating the soul.

Nevertheless, to determine the chief moments of funerals, anthropologists use the formulation, however incorrect, of the double funeral, which implies rites of separation followed by intervals varying from a few weeks to several years, followed by rites of integration that put an end to the mourning.

Separation rites. In most traditional societies, the passage from decay to mineralization dictates the two chief moments in the funerary ritual. The first funeral, or separation rite, is for the purpose of "killing the dead," as the Mossi of Burkina Faso say—in other words, killing what remains alive in the dead person by breaking the emotional bonds that unite him to the community. While the corpse decays, simultaneously corrupt and corrupting, it is terribly vulnerable and dangerous. Two attitudes, contradictory yet complementary, orient the conduct of the living toward the dead: solicitude and rejection, shown in a symbolic or realistic manner according to points of view that vary with each ethnic group.

Solicitude begins immediately after death, tinged with commiseration and fear: The dead person is given food, gongs are sounded to scare away evil spirits, the corpse is washed and purified, and its evolutions are watched, especially if the body lies in state for a long time (from three to twelve days among the Miao of Southeast Asia). It is dressed, its natural orifices are stopped, and, most important, the wake is organized. This can be the occasion for big reunions and a large-scale ritual. For the Maori of New Zealand it is an intensely dramatic ceremony, the key moment of the funeral rite, accompanied by songs, cries, lamentations, elegies, and more or less generous meals, depending on the fortune of the deceased. To multiple meals the Inca of Peru added games of dice with very complex symbolism. The outcome of the game was supposed to orient the soul of the deceased so as to help him attain heaven. The dead person participated by influencing the manner in which the dice fell, thereby revealing whether he was well or ill disposed toward the player. The deceased's possessions were divided according to the results.

When respectful solicitude has soothed the dead, rejection asserts itself. Once the last homages are rendered, the deceased is invited to rejoin his ancestors or to prepare for his afterlife (metamorphoses, reincarnation, sojourn with God, etc.). To overcome his hesitation, a number of methods are used: One may tie him down securely or mutilate him (poke his eyes out, break his legs); lose him by returning suddenly from the cemetery by a detour; or arrange to deposit him at the foot of a mountain or on the far side of a river he cannot cross. In compensation, sometimes an effigy remains at home as a substitute for him, or he may be promised an annual invitation. Because the decaying of the corpse constitutes a risk that its double will prowl in the village, the relatives submit to the constraints of mourning, which puts them outside the social circuit. The specific purpose of these interdictions is to separate all those contaminated by the corpse's decay. Curiously enough, in India the Toda have a single term, *kedr,* which simultaneously designates the corpse, the state of mourning, and the interval between the first and second funerals. A statement made by a dying Maori chief to his son likewise clarifies the problem: "For three years your person must be sacred and you must remain separated from your tribe . . . for all this time my hands will be gathering the earth and my mouth will be constantly eating worms . . . then when my head falls on my body, awake me from my sleep, show my face the light of day, and you shall be *noa* [free]" (Hertz, 1970, p. 33). Therefore, when mineralization, whether natural or artifically accelerated, sets in, it is a sign that the deceased has fulfilled his posthumous destiny. He has passed the initiatory tests imposed on him; he has rejoined the ancestors or the gods; or perhaps he is ready for metempsychosis or reincarnation.

Rites of integration and the cessation of mourning. In almost all traditional societies, double funerals are held. After a delay varying from a few weeks to ten years, according to the ethnic group and the resources at the family's disposal, a final ceremony takes place that confirms the deceased in his new destiny and confers on his remains a definitive status. Like the integration of the dead person, this ritual consecrates the reintegration of the mourners into the group: Order is reestablished and interdictions are lifted. As a rule, the bones are exhumed and then treated in different ways according to local traditions: Washed, dried, sometimes covered with ocher, they are preserved as visible relics, placed in containers, buried again, or even pulverized and mixed with ritual beverages. In sub-Saharan Africa, the latter custom is quite prevalent, especially among Bantu-speaking peoples. Among the Bamileke of Cameroon, the inheritance of skulls according to rigorous rules symbolically secures the collective memory and the continuity of the clam. In Madagascar the Famadihana (which has been wrongly translated as "turning over the corpses") gives way to costly festivities: When a family decides to celebrate the cult of its dead, they proceed from opening the tombs and changing the winding-sheets to rewrapping and reburial with great ceremony, before an audience in a state of great jollity. For two days songs, dances, music, processions, and festivities punctuate the ritual manipulations.

In Borneo, the Olo Nyadju give themselves up to analogous states on the occasion of Tiwah. Along with some degree of fasting, the majority of Indonesian ethnic groups do the same thing. This bone cult, which is generally referred to as an ancestor cult, flourishes among the American Indians, in China, and elsewhere, and still has its equivalent in Europe. There is hardly any difference between the old Chinese who carefully brushes his ancestor's bones and the skeleton washer of Neapolitan cemeteries who, two years after the burial, when the corpse has dried out, washes the bones in front of the families before putting them in a marble urn. In the French provinces, the custom of the anniversary meal and mass is clearly a response to the same fantasies of reestablishing order.

Indeed, the ritual of secondary obsequies ending in definitive burial has a twofold justification in the imagination. First of all, the transfer of the bones to another place completes the purification process. It is as if the earth has been corrupted by the decaying body, necessitating the removal of the purified bones to an unsullied location. Second, although the provisional inhumation is always individual, the final burial is very often collective. Such is the custom of the Goajiro Indians in Venezuala: Three years after death, the bones are sorted and dried, then exposed during a funeral wake. They are then transferred into a large urn, where the remains of all the dead from the matriclan or the matrilineage are gathered together. Thus, communal reunion of the sublimated remains follows the isolation of impure decay.

On the other hand, Western ossuaries, by virtue of their anonymous character, have hardly any impact on an individualistic society. At the very most, as "display cases" they provide the "exposition of the bones" as an aid to meditation. "Let us come to the charnelhouse, Christians; let us see the skeletons of our brothers," says a Breton song. In any case, if inhumation in a common ditch is judged shocking and infamous by us, the collective ossuary does not scandalize anyone. In fact, it can be seen as a solution to the problem of cemetery space and an orientation for a new cult of the dead. The possibility has even been raised of reintegrating the sacred into cemeteries in the form of an "ossuary-necrology" that would reassemble the community of the dead and make the living sensitive to the bonds uniting them to the past.

With the second funeral, therefore, the fate of the deceased has been settled. To borrow the vivid language of the Mossi of Burkina Faso, the ritual of integration "makes the dead live again." From then on, grief no longer has reason to exist. The marginal period has permitted the mourning work to be finished. But, in any case, is not ritualization, like elegance, a way of charming anguish? At this stage, interdictions are always relaxed. After undergoing purifying baths and multiple reparation sacrifices, the mourners are reintegrated into the group. Thanks to the symbolic support of the bone, life on every level henceforth reasserts all its rights—both the life of the metamorphosed deceased and the life of the group from which he emerged. Once the decaying flesh and the signs of death have disappeared, the imperishable vestige is left with its charge of symbols. Funeral rites thus have the capacity "to reduce any object at all to significance, let it pass over to the other side of the gulf" (Maertens, 1979, p. 236). This can be clearly seen in the following set of processes: decay? mineralization; excluded mourners? reintegrated mourners; oversignificant corpse? hypersignificant remains.

In Vietnam, ritual constitutes what is called the "transfer of life": While the body is buried in a tomb defined according to the rules of geomancy, the soul, set on a tablet that itself is enclosed in a box covered with a red and gold case, becomes the protective ancestor that one venerates and prays to at the family altar.

A qualifying remark must be inserted: The conditions of death (place, moment, means) orient the meaning of the rite. The evil dead person, for example, can be deprived of a funeral, or may have the right to only a truncated or clandestine funeral; he will never become an ancestor or know happiness. Status, age, and sex also play a determining role in the elaboration of ceremonies.

Some Key Rites. Only a few fundamental rites concerning the good death will be considered, because of their quasi-universality and the depth of the fantasies that they express.

Attendance at death, certification of death, and interrogation. If to die far away from home or to die a violent death is usually equivalent to a bad death in traditional societies, it is not only because uncertainty is alarming but also, and more importantly, because the dying cannot be helped. Mothering, making secure, and taking charge of the dying person, who is consoled, caressed, and helped to die for the same reason he was helped to be born, is a universal constant. This attitude has a religious aspect. To take only one example, the importance to elderly and very sick people of the Christian last sacraments is known, including the purifying aspersion that evokes baptism and redemption through the passion and the resurrection, as well as the profession of faith and, when possible, the Eucharist. As for the anointing of the sick, recall that this new ritual, although it abandons the expiatory aspect and gives only a circumstantial role to the effacement of sin, nevertheless insists on help by grace.

It is important to make sure that the deceased is really dead. Besides interpreting tangible signs such as the stopping of the breath and the heart, one can call on the diviner, the priest, or the doctor. There are also other ways of making sure: Right after the death of a Chinese, one of his close kin climbs the roof of the house to "call back his soul"; if it does not return, there is no doubt about his death. While for the Toraja of Sulawesi the deceased is not dead but only ill (as noted), among the Tibetans and the Miao (Hmong) the deceased must be informed that he is really dead because he does not know that he is: "The illness fell on the rocks and the rocks could not bear it. Then it slid into the grass, but the grass could not carry it. And that is why, O Dead One, the illness has come to you. The earth could not bear the illness, so the illness reached your soul. That is why you have found death" (Georges, 1982, p. 183). Then, with great kindness and consideration, they explain to him what he needs for the great journey: bamboos to communicate with the survivors or the gods, the "wooden house" (coffin), the hemp shoes, alcohol, food, and the cock that will show him the way. The announcement of the death also obeys precise rules. Women's lamentations punctuated by cries, drums, and bells, as well as symbolic formulas and the sending of messengers, are the most frequent practices.

In traditional societies, another notable belief is that the corpse is simultaneously alive and dead. It no longer has a voice, but in its fashion it speaks. No one hesitates to question it in order to learn why it died or, sometimes, its desires concerning the transmission of its possessions; only little children and fools escape this rite, because "they don't know what they say." Among the Diola of Senegal, the dead person, tied to a bier, is supported by four men, and people take turns asking it questions. If the corpse moves forward when questioned, the response is positive; if it moves backward, it is negative; if it wavers in the same place, it is indicating hesitation. Among the Somba of Benin, "no" is expressed by a rocking from left to right, and "yes" by a rocking from back to front. For the Senufo of the Ivory Coast, leaning to the left indicates the deceased's agreement, and leaning to the right, his disagreement. It sometimes happens that the dead person bears down on one of those present in order to demand that questions be put to him (the Diola) or requires that the carriers be changed in order to pursue the rite (the Lobi of Burkina Faso). Substitute objects sometimes replace the corpse at the time of the interrogation, on condition that they participate in its vital forces. An assegai with the hair of the deceased is an adequate substitute for the Boni of Guyana, while a tree trunk containing his nails and body hairs suffices for the Bete of the Ivory Coast. If the death was willed by God or the ancestors, a frequent occurrence among the Ẹgba of Benin and the Orokaiva of New Guinea, the group feels reassured. But if it resulted from a crime, witchcraft, or violation of a taboo, the fault must be immediately atoned for and the guilty punished. In its way, by its voiceless word the corpse plays an important role in social regulation.

Laying out the dead: purification and mothering rituals. The funeral rite proper begins with the laying out of the corpse, which, in its essential aspect, is equivalent to an authentic purification, a symbolic prelude to rebirth. A holy task among the Jews and especially in Islam, it is a matter of divine obligation, thus of *ʿibādāt,* involving a relationship with God and not just a social function. Laying out the corpse is universal and rigorously codified in ancient societies. In the West Indies, especially in the Antilles and in Haiti, this ritual is reminiscent of that of the midwife. Death, like birth, demands a certain ceremonial that is no less than the "transitory reintegration in the indistinct," to borrow Mircea Eliade's expression. By placing, for example, a vat of water underneath the couch where the corpse is lying, one symbolically reestablishes the sources of life (amniotic fluid). One is again assured that the soul, which has just left the body, will not disappear into nothingness, and that the deceased, thus purified, will be reborn in another world.

Among the Agni-Bora of the Ivory Coast, there is a similarity between the grooming of the newborn baby and the grooming of the deceased: Holding the naked body on their knees, old women wash it with three successive rinses, perfume it, and dress it. For the baby, the rite is always accompanied by singing; the washing is done from the head to the feet with the right hand. In the case of the deceased, however, the rite is executed in silence with the left hand, and proceeds from the feet to the head. This is because birth is an arrival, and rebirth a departure. In the European countryside the laying out is still the work of the "woman who helps" (the midwife), who is also the "woman who does the dead." The laying out of the dead is again an act of mothering.

Among the Miao, the deceased is rubbed with a warm towel without being undressed; then is dressed in new clothing finished off with a richly decorated kimono. The head is wrapped in a turban, and—an important detail—the feet are shod in felt or leather shoes with curled tips, like those sold by the Chinese. Sometimes the duty of one of the relatives is to make these shoes. The dead must depart with good shoes for the trip about to be undertaken. A harquebusier comes up to the deceased and forewarns deferentially: "Now we are going to fire a few shots that will accompany and protect you for the whole length of your trip. Don't be afraid."

Display of the deceased: the corpse detained. Aside from punitive exhibition (desecration of the corpse) in the case of a bad death, when a devalued dead person is deprived of a funeral, the display of the corpse reflects the noblest intentions (valorization of the corpse).

In traditional societies, where death is a public affair involving the whole community, display of the corpse is almost a general rule. It is stretched out on a mat, on a funeral bed, or in a coffin, placed in the mortuary in a special case or in the open air, or suspended at the top of a tree or on a scaffold in the middle of the village square. Sometimes it even presides over its own funeral. The presentation varies according to places and beliefs, but most often it is done in state, with all the symbols that recall the deceased's social function. In Senegal, the dead Diola appears much as if he were alive, but with his most beautiful clothes, his bow and arrows if he was a good hunter, his farming implements and sheaves of rice if he was a good farmer. The horns of cows he sacrificed during his life and heads of cattle are exhibited to emphasize his wealth. The ostentatious display of belongings is frequent. Sometimes the dead person is displayed in the midst of his herd, as among the Karamojong of Uganda and certain Indians of North America. The length of time for displaying the dead and his goods may vary according to his wealth: Among the Dayak of Borneo, it ranges from one to six years. Another custom, peculiar to the Sioux, is to suspend the head and tail of the dead person's horse on the same scaffold on which he is exposed. Display of the dead seems to serve a double function: to show the dead that he is being rendered the homage due him by offering him to view in his best light, and to show him as a model of the role he played in the group. The dead person is glorified as having accomplished his mission, and the aura with which he is endowed is reflected on the collectivity, which thus reaffirms the identity and cohesion it so needs upon losing one of its members.

In southern Sulawesi, the Toraja still use the effigy, or *tau-tau,* especially for the deceased of high rank. This figure, made of breadfruit wood according to strict rules, must resemble the deceased as much as possible (same sex, height, face), though often with improvements. Dressed in the dead person's clothing and adorned with jewels, necklaces, and bracelets, it is the object of numerous rites whereby it is in turn animated and made to die, wept over and consecrated. At the end of a very long ceremony, the corpse, swathed in its winding-sheets, is raised on a platform below which is placed the *tau-tau.* Both then preside over the buffalo sacrifices and receive their part of the offerings. Finally, when the corpse goes back to the sepulcher for the last time, its representative is permanently exhibited as near as possible to the tomb. For the Toraja, the effigy becomes more than a ritual object associated with death; it is, if not the deceased, at least its visible double.

In the West today, the embalmed corpse lies in state in funeral homes. It is still a matter of rendering homage to one no longer alive, and of facilitating the mourning work by conserving a better image of the departed: The mortician's work spares the dead person the stigma of death for a time and gives the impression that the deceased is sleeping in peace. The essential thing is that the dead person should be present, recognizable to his or her family (to a certain extent, a disfigured corpse is tantamount to an absent one). The certainty of the person's death can be borne more easily than the uncertainty surrounding his or her absence and silence.

In this respect, wakes have a soothing value, supposedly for the departed and certainly for the survivors. The sacred and the profane are mixed. In Spain, rosaries and responses are recited. People speak of the deceased, because to speak of the deceased is to be with the deceased again. And if sometimes the conversation turns to funny stories, this does not imply a lack of respect for the dead but a pleasant relationship with the deceased. At one extreme, these wakes are almost feast days. Perhaps this is because in some villages, like the Aragonese village of Leciñena, the immediate neighbors cook the celebrated *tortas,* a kind of brioche made only on feast days (the Feast of the Virgin, a marriage) and for a death wake.

When there are mourners, especially female ones, display of the dead facilitates the sincere and organized expression of emotions through praise of the departed, invitations to return among the living (visits, possession, reincarnation), reproaches or invectives concerning his cruelty in leaving his close kin, and advice for his posthumous destiny. This is how the rhapsodist addresses the deceased Miao after the ritual offering of the cock: "Take it and eat. Henceforth you will have the cock's soul with you. Follow it. Hurry and look for the silk suit you wore at birth. You will find it hidden under the earth [an allusion to the placenta of the newborn, which is always carefully buried near the house in which he was born]. Now leave" (Georges, 1982, p. 187). Again dressed in his silk garment and guided by the cock, the soul of the dead person then sets out on the long journey the singer is chanting about. Finally, before the final farewells, the dead person may be transported into the village and the fields, visiting for the last time the places where he lived, and communing with himself before the altars where he made sacrifices.

Food given to the dead and in homage to the dead. This article will mention only briefly the offering of victuals to the dead, whether during the funeral or at the moment of burial. To help the deceased on the long journey, the Aztec burned food with the deceased—usually a fat little dog with a tawny coat—to help him or her cross the rivers on the infernal route. This rite, common to almost all cultures, corresponds to a widespread belief: The offerings are the indispensable viaticum that permits the dead to survive the transitory journey into the world of the ancestors. The sacrifices offered simultaneously play the same role, albeit symbolically.

Better yet is the common meal that accompanies funerals almost everywhere. A practical necessity justifies it: Those who have come to honor the dead and console the close kin must be fed. The importance of the feast is often such that it takes on the dimensions of a potlatch: In numerous ethnic groups, brief rites are initiated at the time of death, and the funeral services are deferred until sufficient reserves of rice, palm wine, and cattle have been set out. In the view of traditional mythologies, it is a communal event in which the dead person participates: A seat, plate, or part of the food (often the best) is reserved for the deceased, or a descendant represents the deceased, or the table is set in the presence of the corpse—diverse customs showing an intention to intensify the relationship with the deceased and to persuade the group that he or she is not completely dead. In Western societies, the funeral meal is a means of appeasing grief by reinforcing the bonds that unite the living in the absence of the dead. The meal following the death is like a birth for the talkative and hungry community of the living, which has been wounded, split up, and interrupted by the death.

But all these reasons are valid only on an obvious level. On the symbolic level, the funeral meal is a way of retaining the dead person, and on these grounds, it is a substitute for the cannibalistic meal. In Haiti, the funeral meal is appropriately termed a *mangé-mort,* just as in Quebec, where the expression *manger le mort* is still in use. In fact, the manducation of the corpse is connected to a universal fantasy that psychoanalysts neatly term "the exquisite corpse" (an expression borrowed from surrealist poetry). Obeying the pleasure principle, the fantasy mechanism of the exquisite corpse responds to the trauma of loss through the desire for incorporation of the lost object. Amorous fusion with the other is then achieved in an exaltation that, in the real world, would perhaps be secret. The dead person is fixed and assimilated in their best features; one who devours the deceased makes the deceased one's own in spite of all taboos. In this connection, there is a strange Mexican custom that does not even disguise the necrophagic intention. On the Day of the Dead, an extraordinary commercial activity mobilizes the whole population: Superb confections are sold that represent the skulls and skeletons of the dead, ravishing or burlesque in appearance, with first names engraved in order to help the customers make their choices.

CONTROLLING DECAY. Decay is the justification for all funeral rites. Everything is brought into play in order to tame it (display of the corpse), hide it (winding-sheets, the sarcophagus), forbid it absolutely (embalming and mummification, incineration, cannibalistic ingestion), retard it (corporal attentions), or accelerate it (towers of silence; see below). A profound need underlies all these approaches to decay: to stabilize the deceased in an indestructible medium—a stage marking the reconciliation of the community with his death. These remains—mummy, relic, ashes, or bones—all civilizations, without exception, persist in preserving.

Tamed or accelerated decay. Conditions of exposure may eventually accelerate the mineralization of the corpse. Sunlight and even moonlight, as well as a smoky fire, are believed to contribute, but the body is sometimes also offered to birds of prey and other carnivores, or to ants. In the Tibetan tradition, corpses were torn apart by the *ragyapas* ("dismemberers") and thrown to the dogs, so that the bones would be stripped much faster. But the most spectacular example is given by the towers of silence built in the seventeenth century, particularly in Iran by the Zoroastrians. According to the sacred texts of the *Zand,* the corpse is the essence of impurity. It is therefore out of the question to pollute "the things belonging to the good creation" by carrying out the final burial of a decomposing body. Hence the custom of exposing the body in a remote location known to be frequented by carnivorous animals. Vultures, in particular, are the purifiers that disencumber the dead person of rotting flesh, the medium of demonic infection. From this came the practice, which spread little by little, of building towers of rock especially designed to isolate corpses and avoid their contaminating presence during the purification process. The interior of the "tower of silence," or *dakhma,* consists of a platform inclined toward a central pit. Cells (*pāvis*) hollowed out in three concentric circles receive the corpses—men in the outer zone, women in the middle zone, and children toward the central pit. In this case, in which the custom of second obsequies no longer takes the symbolic form of the commemorative meal, the dried bones are thrown down twice a year into the depths of the pit. There, under the combined effect of the sun and the lime that is spread there, the bones are transformed into dust. The pit branches into four canals for the evacuation of rainwater, which is received and purified in four subterreanean pits where carbon and sand clarify it. Formerly, the remains were removed periodically, to be kept in an ossuary: Cleansed of all impurities, they testified that the soul was ready for the final ceremonies.

Decomposition accepted but hidden. Obviously, the cemetery is a place where remains are preserved and concealed. The feminine and maternal valence of the earth responds to a universal fantasy: "Naked I came out of the maternal womb; naked I shall return there" (*Jb.* 1:21). In African cosmogonic thought, burial in Mother Earth, the source of fertility and dwelling place of the ancestors, takes on a quasi-metaphysical significance. The same symbolism serves for other forms of interment, such as the deposit of the corpse in grottos or in funeral jars that evoke the uterine cavity. The earth is indeed the place *par excellence* for transformations. Not only does one plow seeds into it at the time of sowing, but it is also a mediator in all rites of passage: The corpse is entrusted to it at the time of the funeral, as are neophytes' nail clippings, hair, and other fleshly remains from initiation rites and the placenta and umbilical cord at birth. Burial can also, in a sense, transform the land. Thus the Hebrews did not begin to bury their dead until as a people they became sedentary; burial is always connected to the ownership of land, that is, to the appropriation of a "promised land," without doubt, a way of salvation.

One could go on forever describing the infinite variety of types of cemeteries (mass burial sites or scattered individual crypts, as in Madagascar; at the heart of the village or far-flung) and types of tombs (simple ditches to elaborate mausoleums to modern, efficient columbaria for cremated bodies). In many systems of burial the distinction between social classes is still, as it were, heavily felt.

The corpse's position in the tomb is no less variable: seated; stretched out on its back or side; in the fetal position; even on its stomach, as was once the case in Western cultures for adulterous women; or standing, in the manner of some military men or heroes of the American West. The orientation of the body can also be important. For some emigrant groups, it is toward the country of birth. For populations that traditionally ascribe birth to sunrise and death to sunset, the deceased must have the head to the east in order to be in position for rebirth. On the other hand, medieval Christians who wanted to be buried facing the direction from which salvation came placed the head toward the west so that the deceased could face Jerusalem. Similarly, Muslims are buried on their right side, turned toward Mecca.

The necropolis does not exist in India or Nepal because ashes are thrown into the sacred rivers, nor is it commonly of importance in sub-Saharan Africa. But where it does exist, the cemetery is still a symbol charged with emotion, sometimes arousing fear and melancholy, sometimes calm and reflection. In this regard one must praise Islamic wisdom, by which the very texture and functions of the cemetery maintain a state of relative osmosis between the living and the dead. The cemetery (*maqbarah*) is often designated by the more euphemistic term *rawḍah* ("garden"). Certainly, its ground has often been consecrated to that use by a pious tradition, but it is not closed. The dead rest there on the bare ground in a simple winding-sheet, thus returning to the elements. In both senses of the term, it is open to nature. But it is open to society, too. The belief prevails that bonds exist with the bodies of the deceased before the Last Judgment and that for the living to visit the tombs is a praiseworthy act and, what is more, a deed that will be considered in their favor then. The cemetery is also a traditional place to go for a walk: Women often meet there on Fridays.

Prohibited decay. Setting aside the still rare phenomenon of cryogenation (in which the deceased wait in liquid nitrogen until the time when people will know how to restore them to life), there are three common forms of prohibited decay.

Cannibalism, decay, and mineralization. Robert Hertz (1970) has emphasized the particular function of cannibalism that spares the dead person the horror of a slow and ignoble decomposition and brings the bones almost immediately to their final state. This is obviously true for endocannibalism, when it is practiced on revered dead persons. There is no doubt that the purpose of cannibalism is to prohibit rotting. On the one hand, consumption of the flesh occurs as soon as possible after death, and, because the flesh is usually cooked, putrefaction does not begin in the course of consumption. On the other hand, inquiries among populations with a tradition of cannibalism clearly reveal the finality of the act: "In this way, we knew where he [the dead] was and his flesh would not rot," said the Australian Turrbals (Hertz, 1970, p. 24, n. 1). This is also the view expressed by the Merina, according to a historical Malagasy document of the last century: "Our kinsman is dead; what shall we do with his body, for he was a man we loved?" Some answered, "Since he is dead, let us not bury him but let us eat him, because it would be sad to see him rotting in the ground." (ibid., p. 28).

Cannibalism promotes mineralization, but intentions toward the corpse in this regard differ according to whether endocannibalism or exocannibalism is involved.

Endocannibalism refers us back to the traditional scheme of the double funeral: On the first occasion, the dead person is buried in the earth or, similarly, in the belly, where human digestion prepares its accelerated passage to mineralization; on the second occasion, the remaining bones are handled with respect and receive the final obsequies. The destruction resulting from the manducation is only a mutation of forms that symbolically achieve a kind of conservation: incorporation. In a sense, ingestion could be interpreted as embalming transferred to the oral register. As for exocannibalism, however, the situation is different, at least concerning the treatment of the remains. The cannibal feast undoubtedly implies incorporation and, by its reference to myths of origin, it can take the form of a veritable primitive mass in which the bread and wine are really flesh and blood. But whereas the vital force animating the enemy's corpse is assimilated, his bones and uneaten parts may be abandoned or held up to ridicule. The Ocaina Indians of the Peruvian Amazon suspend the enemy's penis from a necklace worn by the victor's spouse; the mummified hands are used as spoons, the bones as flutes, and the painted and exposed skull serves as a ritual bell.

The cremated corpse. According to many mythologies, the purifying fire is above all liberating. In Bali, as long as the fire has not reduced the corpse to ashes, the dead person is impure; he continues to wait, his spirit not yet separated from his body. According to many beliefs, fire is the promise of regeneration and rebirth. Through fire, a superior level of existence can be attained. According to Greek mythology,

Herakles stretched himself out on the pyre of Mount Oeta, while Zeus announced to the other gods that Herakles was about to become their equal: The fire would relieve him of his human part, immortalize him, and make him divine. The same theme is found in the Upaniṣads, the classic texts of Hinduism. It is therefore not the impurity of the corpse that is implicated in the cremation ritual, but the impurity of the body and the human condition. Ashes are the proof of that impurity; if the body were perfect, it would burn without ashes.

The destiny of the remains varies. In Japan, the bones are traditionally divided between two containers, one of which is buried at the place of cremation and the other in the natal village of the deceased. In Thailand, part of the remains are collected in an urn kept at home, while the remainder is buried at the foot of the pyre, kept in a reliquary monument, or even thrown into a river. In India, custom formerly demanded that the ashes be deposited in a tomb. Later a rule was imposed that still persists today: Because fire is the son of the waters, funeral rites should summon first one and then the other. Also, the ashes and noncalcinated bones are sprinkled with water, and cow's milk and coconut milk as well, before being thrown into the Ganges, the sacred river that flows from Śiva's hair. The same procedure is followed in Nepal and in Thailand, where other sacred rivers conduct the deceased downstream toward his celestial residence. In Bali, the remains are thrown into the sea after having been meticulously sorted by the relatives, washed in sacred water, arranged on white linen, and inserted into a dried coconut adorned with flowers. Finally, there is the particular case of the Yanoama Indians of Venezuela, who crush the remaining bones after the incineration of their warriors, in order to consume them mixed with game dishes or beverages in the course of a communal meal.

Cremation can be assimilated to all other modes of provisional burial, and people who burn their dead conform in many respects to the classic scheme of the double funeral, but with different means and a shortened duration. The first funeral, corresponding to the ritual of the exclusion of the dead, soothes the corpse and leads it to a purification that can be accomplished only by the process of decay. Those who cremate the dead find the equivalent of the first funeral in the rites that accompany the handling of the body during the generally short period between death and combustion on the pyre. The second obsequies, which concern the charred and purified remains, correspond to the rites of integration of the dead in his status in the beyond, while mourning is lifted for the survivors.

Preservation of bodies. Egyptian embalming practices are famous. The long, difficult techniques only make sense, however, in the framework of the osirification ritual that makes the dead person a god through assimilation with Osiris. Before, during, and after the technical manipulations, an extremely complicated ceremony took place, which undoubtedly explains the long duration of the treatment and the great number of participants. Invocations, readings, and prayers punctuated each act of the embalmers, whose very gestures were strictly regulated. Afterlife was not possible unless the liturgy was observed in its minutest details. "You will not cease living; you will not cease to be young, for always and forever," cried the priest at the end of the embalming. Then the last ceremony could be performed: the opening of the mouth. In the purification tent or at the entrance to the tomb, the gestures of the officiating priest were accompanied by aspersions, offerings, and sacrifices, fumigations with incense, and magico-religious formulas. With the end of his adz the priest touched the dead person's face in order to reintroduce the vital energy.

In addition, mummies discovered in South America and the testimony of Spanish chroniclers affirm that the Inca, for example, embalmed their dead. The technical success of their mummies seems not to have been as spectacular as that of the Egyptian mummies, especially if one remembers that the Inca empire occurred relatively close to the current time (at the end of the Middle Ages). The body was treated with different ingredients (honey, resin, and herbs) and painted with *roucou* (a vegetable dye); the viscera, preliminarily removed, were prepared and kept separate in a receptacle. The dry climate and the burial methods (a hole in a rocky wall, or a funeral jar) were favorable for preservation. Like the pharaohs, the sovereigns were the objects of particular care. An illustrated story from the sixteenth century, whose author, Huaman Poma, was of Inca origin, recounts the royal funeral ritual: The embalmed Inca, adorned with his emblems, lay in state for a month; at his sides were placed women and servants, likewise embalmed, to serve him in the other world. Although the techniques were rudimentary, there is good reason to assume that a very precise ritual was used to increase efficacy. Thus, the funeral offerings deposited next to the body appeased the maleficent spirits that caused decomposition. Indeed, because the life principle (the *aya*) remained in all parts of the corpse, rotting involved the destruction of the individual. On the other hand, if the body was preserved, the spirit of the dead could be reincarnated in a descendant. This belief in a second birth appears to explain the fetal position of corpses found in tombs and funeral jars.

Whatever the modalities, one can agree with Robert Hertz that it is legitimate "to consider mummification as a particular case derived from provisional interment" (Hertz, 1970, p. 20). If the interval separating death from final burial corresponds to the duration necessary for mineralization or desiccation, then a symmetry exists between the Egyptian rite and that of certain archaic ethnic groups. It is only when the embalming is concluded "that the body, having become imperishable, will be conducted to the tomb, that the soul will leave for the country of Ialou, and that the mourning of the survivors will come to an end." The waiting period, that is, the time necessary to achieve mineralization, can be reduced only by a manipulative intervention; it has not changed meaning at all, even if in this case the corpse is the equivalent of the body in its apparent totality (a mummy) or in part (a trophy head), rather than the residue of bones and ashes.

CONCLUSION. This article has, as it were, painted a composite picture of funeral rites, in which it can be seen that they border on the *stricto sensu* sphere of the sacred. It may in fact be argued that, thanks to rites—those of former times especially, and to a lesser degree those of today—everything is brought into play in order to put death (even if accepted) at a distance, and eventually to make fun of it or tame it by permitting the community, when it feels concerned, to pull itself together. This is why funeral rites can shift the drama of dying from the plane of the real to that of the imaginary (by displacements and metonymy, symbols and metaphors), and it is in this that their efficacy resides. To reorganize the society disturbed by death and to console the survivors even while the deceased is being served and his or her destiny oriented—these are the two fundamental aims of funeral customs. In all regions, then, such rites are simultaneously defined first as liturgical drama with its places and scenes, its actors and their scripts, and also as individual or collective therapies (one might recall Nasser's moving funeral). In this respect, traditional cultures have inexhaustible resources of rich symbolism that the modern world has forgotten.

Indeed, modern life, especially in an urban milieu, entails multiple mutations that are probably irreversible on the level of ritual, and perhaps disquieting for the psychic equilibrium of one's contemporaries. Many practices are simplified or omitted: The wake is impossible at the hospital or in tiny apartments; condolences and corteges are practically eliminated. Consider, for example, today's laying out of the dead: For the impurity of former times, the pretext of hygiene is substituted; for respect for the corpse as subject, obsession with or horror of the corpse as object; for family deference, the anonymity of an indifferent wage. In the same way, the signs of mourning have fallen into disuse—society has passed from "mourning clothes in twenty-four hours" to twenty-four hours of mourning!—and it is unseemly to show one's sorrow. People care less and less about the deceased, who sink into the anonymity of the forgotten; fewer and fewer masses are said for the repose of their souls, while the scattering of ashes eliminates the only possible physical support for a cult of the dead. If, at least on the imaginary plane, rites once primarily concerned the deceased, today they primarily concern the survivors. Thus, to take only one example, the new Roman Catholic ritual of anointing the sick tends to deritualize and desacralize death itself as an essential mutation. It is truly the disappearance of death, considered as a passage, that is witnessed by others.

Without a doubt, humankind today is condemning itself to a dangerous cultural void concerning rites and their symbols. One may well ask if funerals, expedited in the "strictest intimacy," do not dangerously deprive people of a ritual that would help them to live.

SEE ALSO Ancestors; Ashes; Bones; Cannibalism; Dakhma; Death; Fire; Rites of Passage; Tombs.

BIBLIOGRAPHY

Ariès, Philippe. *Western Attitudes toward Death: From the Middle Ages to the Present.* Translated by Patricia Ranum. Baltimore, 1974.

Ariès, Philippe. *Essais sur l'histoire de la mort en Occident.* Paris, 1975.

Gennep, Arnold van. *Rites of Passage.* Translated by Monika B. Vizedom and Gabrielle L. Caffee. Chicago, 1960. See chapter 8.

Gennep, Arnold van. "Du berceau à la tombe." In *Manuel de folklore français contemporain,* edited by Arnold van Gennep, vol. 1, pp. 111–373. Paris, 1976.

Georges, Elaine. *Voyages de la mort.* Paris, 1982.

Guiart, Jean, ed. *Les hommes et la mort: Rituels funéraires à travers le monde.* Paris, 1979.

Hertz, Robert. "Contribution à une étude sur la représentation collective de la mort." In *Sociologie religieuse et folklore,* edited by Robert Hertz. Paris, 1970.

Maertens, Jean-Thierry. *Le masque et le miroir.* Paris, 1978.

Maertens, Jean-Thierry. *Le jeu du mort.* Paris, 1979.

Thomas, Louis-Vincent. *Anthropologie de la mort.* Paris, 1975.

Thomas, Louis-Vincent. *Le cadavre.* Brussels, 1980.

Thomas, Louis-Vincent. *La mort africaine.* Paris, 1982.

Thomas, Louis-Vincent. *Rites du mort: Pour la paix des vivants.* Paris, 1985.

Urbain, Jean-Didier. *La société de conservation.* Paris, 1978.

Walter, Jean-Jacques. *Psychanalyse des rites.* Paris, 1977.

New Sources

Cressy, David. *Birth, Marriage, and Death: Ritual, Religion, and the Life-Cycle in Tudor and Stuart England.* Oxford and New York, 1997.

Holloway, Karla F. C. *Passed On: African American Mourning Stories: A Memorial Collection.* Durham, N.C., 2002.

Merridale, Catherine. *Night of Stone: Death and Memory in Twentieth Century Russia.* New York, 2001.

Metcalf, Peter and Richard Huntington. *Celebrations of Death: The Anthropology of Mortuary Ritual.* Cambridge, U.K., and New York, 1991.

LOUIS-VINCENT THOMAS (1987)
Translated from French by Kristine Anderson
Revised Bibliography

FUNERAL RITES: MESOAMERICAN FUNERAL RITES

Mesoamerican peoples practiced a rich variety of funeral rites based on a fundamental and widely shared vision of death as a regenerative social and cosmic power. Several types of sacred practices associated with death existed from the Preclassic period (2500 BCE–200 CE) until the arrival of the Spanish. The discussion that follows will survey two general kinds of rites associated with the dead; *funerary rites* and *mortuary rites.* Funerary rites were those actions performed after the death of an individual. Their goal was to dispose of the body, ensure the arrival of the soul to the netherworld, and socialize the loss. *Mortuary rites,* on the other hand, equipped individuals with an *object* or *offering.* The more common examples are sacrificial offerings, which were performed since very early times.

A third type of death ritual appears in the archaeological and ethnohistorical evidence during the late Postclassic period (900–1521 CE). In this ritual practice the remains of the deceased were not actually present. These were divinatory rites aimed at either causing the death of an enemy or rival, as well as rites aimed at protecting someone from magical aggressions and bad omens. A large numbers of rites dedicated to deities associated with death and dying were also widely practiced throughout Mesoamerican history.

FUNERALS IN AGRICULTURAL SOCIETIES. The first agricultural settlements were consolidated during the Preclassic period. Archaeological representations of skeleton-like beings in motion and images that show the duality of life and death date from this period. These are the earliest references to a belief in life after death.

Tlatilco, in the central highlands, is one of the settlements showing the most complex funerary practices. In this site, which flourished around 1000 BCE, bodies were buried under inhabited rooms, a practice that has been interpreted as an attempt at preserving the force of the deceased in the domestic space. The bodies of the dead were accompanied by funerary goods of different qualities, and in some instances the remains of a dog were buried next to the deceased.

In western Mexico, funerary practices were unusually important; most interesting is the construction of "shaft tombs," which consisted of a vertical tunnel leading to one or more funerary chambers excavated in volcanic tuff. The region has been sacked by grave robbers, and only a few intact graves have been explored, such as the one found in Huitzilapa, Jalisco, dated to 65 CE. The excavation of that site revealed a seven-meter-deep shaft and two funerary chambers. Three individuals had been laid in each of them, together with extraordinary pottery. Researchers have speculated that this was the burial shaft of an important family.

Other findings in western Mexico are also important, such as those in Chupícuaro, in the Mexican state of Guanajuato, a settlement characterized by its funerary arrangements. The remains of dogs were found next to human skeletons in excavated burial sites, suggesting that, since earlier times, these animals were considered as companions in the journey to the netherworld. Similarly, various offerings consisting of garments and tools the deceased may have used while living were found next to adults, while necklaces and musical instruments were placed in the tombs of children.

In the Maya region, individuals were buried near domestic spaces or ceremonial buildings. The bodies were laid in graves or funerary chambers and in some cases placed inside pots. While some burial sites contain a single individual, others contain several, with articulated skeletal remains and disarticulated bones. This variety could be attributed to regional funerary variations and to the identity of the dead. Offerings of varying quality were usually placed in the sites, and on special occasions the bodies were covered with red paint or a green stone was placed in the mouth of the deceased. The latter custom lasted into later periods.

As for mortuary rites, the collection of "trophy skulls" seems to begin at this time, as evidenced in the Maya region, the Toluca Valley, and Tlatlico. Bone fragments found at the latter site present evidence of cuts, showing that bodies were also used for other purposes. With time, such practices would become fundamental throughout Mesoamerica.

FUNERARY RITES IN THE CLASSICAL CITIES (200–600 CE). Important cities were created during this period including the magnificent cosmopolitan center, Teotihuacan, which was built as a replica of the sacred universe. During an era of splendor, known as the Classic period, Teotihuacanos practiced elaborate funerary rituals. Archaeological records show the careful preparation of the deceased body, primarily in the form of funerary bundles and offerings. Typically, individuals were buried under the floor of homes of both commoners and elites, and the tombs included funerary offerings. Cremations took place in some areas of the city, a funerary practice associated with the élite.

Archaeological work in Teotihuacan has revealed that it had political and cultural relations with many others parts of Mesoamerica. For example, different funerary patterns existed in various parts of the city, especially in what is referred to as the Oaxaca barrio. Excavations have uncovered a number of tombs placed under the floor of domestic areas. The graves, in the style of the great Monte Albán culture that flourished far to the south of Teotihuacan, were characterized by the presence of an access with doorjambs and glyphs carved in the stone. Precious figurines and urns done in the Oaxacan style also accompanied the burials of human beings.

The tradition of the shaft tombs continued in the western regions of Mesoamerica, while new ritual forms also began to emerge. One example of such a change can be found in Loma Alta and Loma Guadalupe, funerary islands located in Michoacán. In the former, individual were buried, and in some instances the rites included the cremation and subsequent pulverization of the bones. Loma Guadalupe served as a sort of cemetery, and several central tombs were surrounded by a series of smaller ones. The sepulchers could be used several times, and in some instances bones were removed to be transported elsewhere. An area devoted to food preparation has also been identified in the complex, perhaps associated with a ceremony that complemented the burial.

Classic Maya culture developed the elaborate practice of constructing royal tombs. In Calakmul, in the Mexican state of Campeche, the tomb of the ruler known as Jaguar-Claw was explored by a multidisciplinary team that concluded that the funeral bundle had been set on a wooden frame and finely decorated with marine elements. The exploration was performed so carefully that it allowed for the recovery of residues of lime, canvas, palm, and resins that accompanied the body of the individual, which had been adorned with jadeite jewels and a funerary mask. Jaguar-Claw was buried with two companions, a male child and a woman wearing a headdress, a funerary treatment associated with the élite.

Two examples of luxurious tombs were found in Palenque: the tomb of King Pacal and that of the so-called Red Queen. In the first site, the remains of the ruler were set in a monolithic sarcophagus; the cover was carved with the image of a character from whose chest grew a maize plant. The king was dressed in a luxurious green stone mask and was accompanied by several offerings and by the remains of individuals sacrificed at his burial. The monumental funerary pyramid was built specifically to house his tomb. The Red Queen was also buried in a monolithic sarcophagus with treasures made of jade, pearls, and shells. Her body was covered with cinabrio, a red mineral that colored the grave. Access to the site was through a set of stairs, and several companions were also sacrificed in her honor. The identity of the Red Queen still remains unknown, and she could be related to King Pakal.

Oaxaca was another area where funerals played an important role. Monte Albán, one of the main sites in the region, is characterized by burial sites placed in yards or rooms. The quality of the burials was a function of the identity of the deceased, since tombs range from very simple ones to those showing complex funerary architecture, including underground structures. Offerings were of great quality and included urns with figurines representing the gods and remains of dogs. The tombs were reused, and each time a new body was placed in them the skeletal remains already there were piled up to make more room.

The lavish funerary architecture developed for the ruling Zapotec class seems to re-create the opulence of the palaces. A classic example is the tomb at the archaeological site known as Huijazoo, an important underground complex. Nine steps lead to a vestibule that opened into two chambers and a yard that culminated with the main funeral chamber. Mitla is another Oaxacan city famous for its lavish funerals and the cross-shaped tombs placed under its palaces. Centuries later, in the Postclassic period, Zapotec tombs were reused by the Mixtecs, who used them to inter their leaders with offerings that are veritable treasures. Such is the case of the famous "Tomb Seven" in Monte Albán.

Oaxacan evidence related to domestic settings is also interesting because human burials were placed under the floors of homes that continued to be inhabited by the descendants of the deceased. The living and the dead shared a daily common space linking generation with generation.

Regional Capitals and Funerary Rites. Upon the fall of Teotihuacan during what has become known as the Epiclassic period (650–900 CE) a process of decentralization in Mesoamerica led to the formation of potent, regional city-states such as Xochicalco, Cholula, and Tajin. Xochicalco, in the state of Morelos has yielded impressive sepulchers inside religious buildings and domestic settings. In the context of sacred architecture, the persons were buried with fine anthropomorphic plates and other green-stone jewelry, while domestic burials included ceramic offerings. The site is also known because of an artificial terrace called "the cemetery," where twenty-one burial sites and a "trophy skull" were found.

Cholula was another important city in the highlands where funerals had great importance. Archaeological findings have revealed that funerary practices were carried out in relation to age, gender, and possibly the social occupation of the deceased. The city showed an increment in cremation practices, as demonstrated by thirty urns filled with the remains of bones that had been exposed to the fire and placed on the southern end of the great pyramid.

Another majestic city of that time was Tajín, on the Gulf of Mexico. Besides funerary sites, the evidence from the city exemplifies the importance of sacrifice and postmortem treatment, especially decapitation, which played a fundamental role in ritual ball games.

Archaeology, Historical Sources, and Funerals. During the Postclassic period (1200–1521 CE) war became uncommonly important, as did expansionism and sacrificial practices. There is ample evidence of funerary practices from this period, such as the ample historical record devoted to describing the funerals of the ruling class. Just as there are coincidences in the beliefs in an afterlife throughout the Mesoamerican region, there are also some similarities in funerary practices among the three most powerful groups of the period: the Maya, Tarasc, and Mexica, or Aztec. For the three peoples, two variables determined the type of funerary rite to be followed: the cause of death and social position. In the case of the Mexica, the *teyolía,* or soul, of the deceased had four basic destinations. Mictlan, the underworld, was the destination of those who died of common illnesses or old age. Those who died for a reason associated with water traveled to Tlalocan, a place of plenty that was presided over by Tláloc, the god of rain. It was believed that the soul of nursing children traveled to the place known as Chichihuauhcuahco, where they were fed by a nursing tree. Warriors who fell in battle went to the Sun Heaven, as did women who died giving birth. It was believed that the former received the sun at dawn and drove it towards its zenith, where they handed it over to the latter. To each form of death there was a corresponding funerary geography and a special treatment for the corpse.

Those who died of common illness or old age were cremated or buried, depending on their place in the social hierarchy. Upon the death of an individual, the body was washed and a green stone was placed in its mouth to symbolize the heart of the deceased, where the soul was located. The body was covered with blankets that were tied, forming a funerary bundle that received offerings useful in the journey to the afterlife, while the geographic instructions that would allow the soul to complete its cosmic destiny were detailed. If the deceased was a member of the élite, the body was cremated and placed next to offerings in a wooden funerary pyre that included a red dog. If it was a ruler, companions were sacrificed next to him, and their hearts were cast into the fire. The ashes were collected and placed in a container that was to be buried. Archaeological evidence from the Great Temple in Tenochtitlan shows that cremated remains of the dignitaries could be divided into several urns and buried in different places. On the other hand, historical sources suggest that when the individual was a commoner, the body was buried with very simple offerings.

The bodies of those who died by water were clad with paper adornments and had seeds placed in their mouths. The body was buried directly into the earth, as if it were a seed. Apparently, nursing children were also buried. It was believed that the nursing tree that would care for them was located in Tlalocan.

When a woman died in labor, she received a particular funerary arrangement. Her body was washed, dressed in new garments, and taken to a special temple for burial. The body had to be cared for, since some of its parts were believed to have magical powers. The bodies of warriors fallen in battle were also treated differently, even though their soul journeyed to the sun just like those of laboring women. Warrior funerals were collective acts and included processions and dances performed by the relatives of the deceased. Usually, the corpses were left in the battlefield, while bundles of wood representing the deceased were built in Tenochtitlan; the bundles were cremated after receiving offerings and orations, and the ashes were buried in a special place. These effigies of the funerary bundle allowed for the socialization of the death.

Funerary goods offered to the deceased can be classified as follows: (1) objects that were part of the funerary dowry; these objects signified the sacred exchange of energies between the life and death of the individual and Mexicas believed that this items could help the soul in the journey; (2) offerings to be handed to the deities of the netherworld once the deceased arrived there; (3) goods that functioned to make the ritual work effectively, such as the wood used in cremation. In more elaborated funerals, sacred practices such as music and ritual dance were common. It is also evident that some élite funerals included the sacrifice and self-sacrifice of special companions of the deceased. Ethnohistorical documents relate that the immediate and extended aftermath of a funeral was regulated by ritual. There were impositions of specific periods of mourning as well as the crafting and delivery of elaborated speeches aimed at consoling the family of the deceased.

Several tombs found in the Maya area had been set in places of worship, temples, and under living spaces. Similarly to what transpired in the central highland, the historical record confirms the preparation of the body and the placing in the mouth of a stone or maize kernels. Also, some offerings seem to be associated with the needs of the deceased in the journey to the netherworld. Although individuals were usually buried, other treatments have also been documented depending on the identity, occupation, or cause of death. The tombs of commoners were usually dug under homes or behind them, and the dwellings were abandoned, unless they were inhabited by many people. The deceased could be buried with the tools they had used in life for their occupations; for example, priests were buried with their sacred books.

Among the Maya, cremation was a late practice that extended into colonial times and was reserved for the élites. Friar Diego de Landa, who made a vast historical record in Yucatan during his labor of evangelization, wrote about the cremation of the Lords of Izamal and how their ashes were placed in pots, with temples were built above them. He also tells how the ashes of dignitaries were kept as relics inside of statues. As for the Lords of Cocom, de Landa records an unusual treatment for the bodies, which were decapitated, cooked, and defleshed; the ritual culminated with the modeling, in bitumen, of the likeness of the deceased over its bones. The archaeological record shows variation in funeral practices, often associated with religion or the identity of the individual. Thus it is possible to find graves, caves, funeral constructions, funerary chambers, sarcophagi, and vessels, all used as graves for the inhabitants of the Maya region.

In the powerful western state of Michoacán, funerals were very similar to those of the Mexica. When a dignitary died, the body was prepared and richly clad. A second funerary bundle was prepared with blankets and placed over the deceased. According to the colonial account of Friar Jerónimo de Alcalá, during the funeral of the king some forty individuals were sacrificed to serve their lord in the netherworld. The body was cremated and the ashes collected in blankets and adorned with a turquoise mask and other jewelry. This bundle was buried at the foot of the most important temple. The ritual was very solemn, and on subsequent days a large portion of the population was in mourning. In contrast, commoners were buried with simple offerings that reflected their social status.

The great diversity and wealth of the Mesoamerican funerary rites contrasts with the standardization imposed by the Christian religion after the arrival of the Spanish. Death in war and epidemics, together with the imposition of funeral taxes and the prohibition of crematory practices, were difficult to assimilate for the indigenous population. With time, syncretism developed and new funerary practices emerged. Today, it is still possible to identify in some communities some elements associated with pre-Columbian beliefs, such as the notion of the dog as a companion to the underworld, the tradition of processions and ritual games, and the offering of food, copal, and other gifts. These elements, combined with some that are typically Spanish, and the new ritual forms represent the wealth of funerary customs of modern Mexico.

SEE ALSO Mesoamerican Religions, articles on Classic Cultures, Formative Cultures, Mythic Themes, Postclassic Cultures, Pre-Columbian Religions.

BIBLIOGRAPHY

Alcalá, Jerónimo. *La Relación de Michoacán.* Morelia, 1980.

Becker, Marshall Joseph. "Caches as Burials; Burials as Caches: The Meaning of Ritual Deposits among the Classic Period Lowland Maya." In *Recent Studies in Pre-Columbian Archaeology,* edited by Nicholas J. Saunders and Olivier de Montmollin, vol. 1, pp. 117–139. Oxford, 1988.

Cabrero, Teresa. *La muerte en el occidente del México prehispánico.* Mexico City, 1988.

Durán, Diego. *Historia de las Indias de la Nueva España e Islas de tierra firme,* vol. 1. Mexico City, 1995. The funerals of Mexica warriors and kings are fully described in this historical account.

García Moreno, Renata, and Josefina Granados. "Tumbas reales de Calakmul." *Arqueología Mexicana* 42 (2000): 28–33.

Lagunas, Zaíd, Carlos Serrano, and Sergio López Alonso. *Enterramientos humanos de la zona arqueológica de Cholula, Puebla.* Mexico City, 1976.

Landa, Diego. *Relación de las Cosas de Yucatán.* Mexico City, 1938. Historical record written in Yucatán after the Conquest.

López Alonso, Sergio. "Cremación y entierros en vasija en Cholula prehispánica." *Anales del INAH* (1973): 111–118.

López Luján, Leonardo, Robert Cobean, and Alba Guadalupe Mastache. *Xochicalco y Tula.* Mexico City, 1995.

López Mestas, Lorena, and Jorge Ramos de la Vega. "La tumba de Huitzilapa." *Arqueología Mexicana* 30 (1998): 70–71.

Malvido, Elsa, Gregory Pereira, and Vera Tiesler. *El cuerpo humano y su tratamiento mortuorio.* Mexico City, 1997. Topics such as death, the concept of the human body, funerary and mortuary rituals from pre-Hispanic times to contemporary Mexico are described in this compilation.

Manzanilla, Linda, and Carlos Serrano, eds. *Prácticas funerarias en la Ciudad de los Dioses los enterramientos humanos de la antigua Teotihuacan.* Mexico City, 1990. Remarkable compilation of Teotihuacan's funerary practices. Includes new archaeological findings and the analysis of human remains recovered in this sacred place.

Matos Moctezuma, Eduardo. *Muerte a filo de obsidiana.* Mexico City, 1980. A book extraordinarily written, focused on the afterlife notions and funerary rituals among the Mexicas.

McAnany, Patricia. *Living with the Ancestors: Kingship and Kinship in Ancient Maya Society.* Austin, Tex., 1995.

Murillo, Silvia. *La vida a través de la muerte.* Mexico City, 2002. The author skillfully brings together ethnohistorical and archaeological data on funerary customs from the Toluca Valley, Mexico.

Rattray, Evelyn. *Entierros y ofrendas en Teotihuacan. Excavaciones, inventario y patrones mortuorios.* Mexico City, 1997. Exhaustive inventory of Teotihuacan's burial and funerary offerings.

Romano, Arturo. "Sistema de enterramiento." In *Antropología física, época prehispánica,* edited by Javier Romero Molina, pp. 83–112. Mexico City, 1974.

Ruz Lhuillier, Alberto. *Costumbres funerarias de los antiguos mayas.* Mexico City, 1989. A classic book with an exceptional inventory of archaeological funerary findings, historical information, and contemporary data on the Maya culture.

Sahagún, Bernardino. *Historia General de las Cosas de la Nueva España.* Mexico City, 1997. Account written after the Conquest. This book is the most important testimony of the Nahua culture, including the afterlife notions and ritual life.

XIMENA CHÁVEZ BALDERAS (2005)
Translated from Spanish by Fernando Feliu-Moggi

FUSTEL DE COULANGES, N. D. (1830–1889),

was a French historian, best known as author of *La cité antique* (1864). Numa Denis Fustel de Coulanges would perhaps be surprised to find himself the subject of an entry in this encyclopedia. He entered the École Normale Supérieure in Paris in 1850, and chafed under the strictly conventional classical education imposed by the regime of Napoléon III; if the revolutionary movements of 1848 left him with a lasting fear of civil war and violence, as expressed above all in his thesis on Polybius's approval of the Roman conquest of Greece (1858), the counterreaction engendered his equally persistent anticlericalism.

Fustel taught in Strasbourg from 1861 to 1870, then in Paris at the Sorbonne and the École Normale, of which he was director from 1880 to 1883. He saw himself as a scientific historian, examining evidence systematically and without preconceptions. Throughout his life, the main target of his critical scrutiny was the belief that primitive society was democratic. In *La cité antique* Fustel criticized the view that the concept of personal liberty was born in the ancient city-state and that in early Greek and Roman society there was no private ownership of land. Later, in the first volume of his *Histoire des institutions politiques de l'ancienne France* (1875), Fustel asserted that the determining influence in French history did not come from the Frankish invaders but from the Roman legacy in Gaul; finally, in his book *Recherches sur quelques problèmes de l'histoire* (1885), he argued that the primitive, democratic village community, which held land in common, could not be found even in Germany.

Fustel's reputation as a founding father of the sociology of religion is based largely on his assertion that religious ideas could have a decisive effect in the formulation of a society's social and economic structure. In *La cité antique* Fustel argues that the practice of worshiping ancestors determined the form of the family and the patrilineal form of lineage (*gens*) that grew out of it. The private ownership of land was derived from ancestor worship. A man was buried in the fields he had farmed, and because his descendants were obliged to care for his tomb they could not allow the land that contained it to pass out of the family. Religion tied culture and social structure to nature. To care for family tombs was natural and needed no explanation (or so it seemed to Fustel and his contemporaries, though the cemetery had only recently become a place of pilgrimage in their own time). At more complex levels of social organization religion was linked to nature in a different way: People worshiped gods who were believed to control physical forces and whose rites could be shared by a wide circle.

Pagan religion thus followed the contours of social organization. The paganism of the Gauls merged easily into that of the Romans as the Gauls became latinized. Fustel dismisses druidism as a brief interlude; he viewed the druids as professional religious specialists whose doctrines and practices did not arise naturally from social life. The power of the druids had been based on a close alliance with the native political elite who turned away from them after the Roman conquest.

Fustel's treatment of Christianity is more complex. Early Christianity, he thought, was truly democratic in its organization. With its incorporation into the empire, the structure of the church became more hierarchical, mirroring the structure of political society. Fustel became somewhat torn between his dislike of priestly hierarchy and his desire to see the church as the vehicle by which Roman social organization was preserved and transmitted to medieval France. Because it was separate from the state and grew up initially without official recognition, the church constituted an alternative source of authority on which the conception of the individual's rights against the state could be based; but contraposition to the state also turned the church into a political organization. In his early *Mémoire sur l'île de Chio* (1856) Fustel showed how the opposition between the Roman Catholic and the Greek Orthodox churches became the focus of hostility between Greeks and Franks.

Émile Durkheim and the structural-functionalists followed and extended Fustel's insight into the relation between religion and social structure. Louis Dumont has revived his idea of a link between Christianity and individualism in his *Essais sur l'individualisme* (1983). Fustel's complex attitude toward the priesthood and his interest in the relation between church and state form part of a chapter of nineteenth-century intellectual history that has yet to be written.

BIBLIOGRAPHY

The English edition of *The Ancient City* (Baltimore, 1980) contains an introduction by Arnaldo Momigliano and myself. A new French edition, with an introduction by François Hartog, was published in Paris in 1984. Fustel's other work on religion is to be found in the *Histoire des institutions politiques de l'ancienne France,* 6 vols. (Paris, 1888–1893), *Nouvelles recherches sur quelques problèmes de l'histoire* (Paris, 1891), and *Questions historiques* (Paris, 1893); all were edited posthumously by Camille Jullian. Jane Herrick's *The Historical Thought of Fustel de Coulanges* (Washington, D.C., 1954) contains useful material on Fustel's attitude to religion. Further bibliography and information on Fustel's intellectual background can be found in Arnaldo Momigliano's "*The Ancient City* of Fustel de Coulanges," in his *Essays in Ancient and Modern Historiography* (Oxford, 1977), pp. 325–343.

New Sources

Various materials and subtle interpretations are provided by François Hartog, *Le XIX siècle et l'histoire. Le cas Fustel de Coulanges.* 2d ed. Paris, 2001. Fustel's contribution to ancient history and law history is still the object of historiographical debate. See Arnaldo Marcone, *Il colonato tardo antico nella storiografia moderna: da Foustel de Coulanges ai nostri giorni,* Como, Italy, 1988; and Andrea Galatello-Adamo, *L'antico e il positivo: per un commento a N. S. Fustel de Coulanges,* Naples, 1981.

S. C. HUMPHREYS (1987)
Revised Bibliography

FYLGJUR are fetches and guardian spirits in Old Norse literary tradition. The term apparently derives from the Old Norse verb *fylgja* (to accompany), but it is homonymous with, and perhaps identical to, the word for "afterbirth" or "placenta." The singular noun *fylgja* denotes two distinct groups: fetches in animal form and guardian spirits in female form.

Fylgjur in animal form are most often wolves or bears, but many other animals are attested, such as oxen, boars, and such birds as eagles, falcons, and hawks. These figures appear to people primarily in dreams and warn of impending death, danger, or some future event. Frequently the *fylgja* is that of the doomed or threatened man's enemy.

These conceptions appear to reflect notions, common in Norse and later Scandinavian tradition, of the soul operating out of the body. In their textual context they must be viewed as part of a broader tradition of portents and dreams, but the animal form of the *fylgjur* may relate to the phenomena of the werewolf and the man-bear. The emphasis on beasts of battle suggests the cult of Óðinn, the most important shape-changer of Scandinavian myth and religion. Óðinn was known for his ability to send his soul out from his body and for sending his companion ravens out into the world as scouts. The animal form of Óðinn's berserkers may also be relevant.

The female fylgjur share many features with *ídísir* and *hamingjur,* and more distantly with *landvættirœ,* Norns, and valkyries; there is little terminological consistency. Unlike the animal *fylgjur,* they are not the alter egos of individuals. Their actions are to some extent comparable to those of the animal *fylgjur* in that they sometimes appear in dreams and portend death or foretell the future, but they generally act in sympathy with a central individual rather than in enmity, giving counsel, good fortune, or aid in battle. These *fylgjur* may attach to a single individual or an entire family. They may be related to the cult of the *matronae,* attested from the Roman period in Germany.

BIBLIOGRAPHY

A full treatment of the literary evidence is provided in Else Mundal's *Fylgjemotiva i norrøn litteraturø* (Oslo, 1974). Helpful for the larger context are Dag Strömbäck"s *Tidrande och diserna* (Lund, Sweden, 1949) and Folke Ström's *Diser, norner, valkyrjor* (Stockholm, 1954). On the Indo-European background of the cult of Óðinn and the role of animals, especially dogs and wolves, see Kris Kershaw, *The One-eyed God: Odin and the (Indo-) Germanic Männerbündeäü* (Washington, D.C., 2000). E. O. G. Turville-Petre"s "Liggja fylgjur þínar til Íslands," originally published in 1940 and reprinted in his *Nine Norse Studies* (London, 1972), distinguishes between the primarily concrete *fylgja* and the primarily abstract *hamingja.*

JOHN LINDOW (1987 AND 2005)

GADJERI. The name *Gadjeri (Gadjari, Kadjeri)* is known over a wide area of northern Australia. It means "old woman," implying status and not necessarily age. Gadjeri is also the "sacred mother," or "mother of us all," and the theme of birth, death, and rebirth is pervasive throughout all of the myths concerning her. She symbolizes the productive qualities of the earth—of all natural resources, including human beings. But it is people, and not natural species, who came from her uterus in the creative era of the Dreaming. Among a number of language groups from the Roper River westward, she is called Kunapipi (or Gunabibi), which means "uterus," "penis incision" (and, by extension, "vagina"), and "emergence" (referring to rebirth). In that same area she is also called Mumuna or Mumunga, a bull-roarer that, when swung, is her voice. In the northwest, on the Daly River and at Port Keats, as in the central-west part of the Northern Territory, she is also a bull-roarer named Kalwadi, although the term *Gadjeri* is more generally used; at Port Keats her local name is Mutjingga ("old woman"). In the southeastern Kimberley and southward into the Western Desert, she is known as Ganabuda. Mostly the Mother is a single mythic being, but in some cultural areas she may be identified with two females of equivalent characteristics, while the term *Ganabuda* may refer to a mythic group of women.

Gadjeri is often associated with two or more of her daughters, the Munga-munga, or Manga-manga, who play an important role in the mythic constellations of men and women in both secret-sacred and open-sacred ritual activities. The Munga-munga are sometimes referred to as the Kaleri-kalering, a name also used for a group of mythic men. The Mother's husband is Lightning or Rainbow Snake.

Baldwin Spencer (1914, pp. 162, 164, 213–218) first mentioned the term *Kunapipi* as the name of a bull-roarer used by people living in the areas of the Katherine and Roper rivers. The myth he recorded relates to a "big man" named Kunapipi who carries about with him woven bags containing spirit children. At one place he removes male children and places them on grass in an enclosed area surrounded by a raised mound. After decorat-

---

CLOCKWISE FROM TOP LEFT CORNER. The Court of the Lions in the Alhambra in Granada, Spain. *[©E.O. Hoppé/Corbis]*; Sixth-century BCE marble relief of Aphrodite, Artemis, and Apollo from the east frieze of the Siphnian Treasury at Delphi, Greece. Archaeological Museum, Delphi. *[©Erich Lessing/Art Resource, N.Y.]*; Eleventh-century Byzantine mosaic of the Madonna and Child at Hosios Loukas Monastery in Boeotia, Greece. *[The Art Archive/Dagli Orti]*; Gaṇeśa, twelfth to thirteenth century, from Mysore, India. De Young Memorial Museum, San Francisco. *[©Werner Forman/Art Resource, N.Y.]*; The Parthenon on the Acropolis in Athens, Greece. *[©Bettmann/Corbis]* .

ing them as circumcision novices, he divides the children into two groups (moieties) and into subsection categories and gives them "totemic" affiliations—instituting present-day social organization. He also carries out circumcision and subincision rituals that attract visitors from outlying areas. When the rituals are over he kills and eats some of the visitors, then vomits their bones—not whole bodies, as he had expected. Two men who escape from him go in search of their relatives, and together they all return to kill Kunapipi. When they cut open his belly, they find two of his "own children," who are recovered alive. Spencer recounts an additional myth relating to a woman whose Dreaming is Kunapipi and who possesses a Kunapipi bull-roarer: She too is responsible for leaving spirit children at particular places. Together with a number of other women of the same mythic affiliation, she performs rituals. These are observed by a mythic man who sees that the women have a bull-roarer and takes it from them. As a result, the women lose their power to carry out this form of secret-sacred ritual.

Actually, Spencer seems not to have been referring to Kunapipi as a male at all, but as a female. In the Alawa language group, Gadjeri is said to have emerged from the sea to rest on a sandbank at the mouth of the Roper River (Berndt, 1951, p. 188) and then to have proceeded upstream. In one Mara version, Gadjeri, as Mumuna, eats men who were enticed to her camp by her daughters, the Mungamunga. She swallows them whole but vomits their bones; she had expected them to emerge whole and to be revived. This happens on a number of occasions with different men, each time without success. Eventually, she is killed by relatives of the men she has eaten (Berndt, 1951, pp. 148–152). A crucial point here is the one made by the Aborigines who told this myth: "They didn't come out like we do, they came out half and half." That is, in Kunapipi ritual men enter the sacred ground, which is the Mother's uterus, and leave it reborn. The myth here emphasizes not cannibalism but the dangerous nature of this ritual experience.

When the Kunapipi cycle entered eastern Arnhem Land, it was adapted to local mythology (see Warner, 1958, pp. 290–311; Berndt, 1951, pp. 18–32ff.). In western Arnhem Land, two mythic Nagugur men, smeared with blood and grease, are credited with bringing the Kunapipi ritual complex. As they travel about the country they carry with them a Rainbow Snake (Ngalyod, in female form) wrapped in paper bark. In the rituals carried out in this area, a trench (*ganala*) symbolizes the Mother's uterus and is identified with Ngalyod; snake designs are incised on its inner walls (Berndt and Berndt, 1970, pp. 122–123, 138–142).

W. E. H. Stanner (1960, pp. 249, 260–266) gives a Murinbata (Port Keats) version of the Old Woman, or Mutjingga, myth. She swallows children whose mothers have left them for her to look after. Once the mothers return, they find the children missing and search without success; two men, Left Hand and Right Hand, eventually find Mutjingga hidden under the water. When she emerges, they kill her, open her belly, and remove the children, still alive, from her womb. They clean them, rub them with red ocher, and give them headbands, which signify that an initiation ritual has taken place. Although the myth differs from the Mara account in content, it is symbolically the same. Stanner, however, interpreted it as pointing to a "wrongful turning of life"; to him, the killing of Mutjingga was a kind of "immemorial misdirection" which applied to human affairs, and living men were committed to its consequences (see Berndt and Berndt, 1970, pp. 229, 233–234). Evidence from other cultures does not support the contention that "a primordial tragedy" took place in the myth. On the contrary, its format is consistent with that of other Kunapipi versions: It concerns the symbolism of ritual death and rebirth. Mutjingga is also linked in myth, but not in ritual, with Kunmanggur (Rainbow Snake), whom Stanner (1961, pp. 240–258) regarded as "the Father," complementing Mutjingga as "the Mother." In Port Keats, Kunmanggur dies in order to ensure that fire is available to human beings.

This pervasive theme of birth, death, and rebirth receives constant emphasis in the central-western Northern Territory Gadjeri. In drawings, for instance, the Mother is depicted with men and women "flowing from" her into a "ring place" (the sacred ground). She may also be shown as a composite structure of poles and bushes, decorated with meandering designs of feather down and ocher and wearing a pearl-shell pubic covering suspended from a hair waistband (see Berndt and Berndt, 1946, pp. 71–73). Furthermore, unlike many other deities or mythic beings, she does not change shape: She is not manifested directly through a natural species. Human birth is transferred to the nonhuman dimension through divine intervention, made possible through human ritual; that is, human ritual releases the Mother's power to make species-renewal possible. The central-western Gadjeri complex is quite close to the mainstream Kunapipi cultic perspective of the Roper River, except that the Mother's death is mentioned only obliquely in the central-western interpretation. For example, in regard to subincision, which is an integral part of her ritual, it is said that the blood which results from the regular opening of the penis incision is symbolic of that shed by the Mother when she was killed. But blood is also life-giving, and through this the Mother lives on spiritually and physically in her daughters, the Mungamunga.

In the northern and central-west areas of the Northern Territory, Gadjeri is ritually dominant, with or without the presence of the Rainbow Snake. In the fringes of the Western Desert her rituals focus mainly on other mythic beings. The Walbiri are a case in point. Their major mythic beings are the male Mamandabari pair. While this mythic constellation is classified under a Gadjeri heading and called "Big Sunday" (Meggitt, 1966, pp. 3ff.), and its ritual paraphernalia and symbolism are specific to Gadjeri, there is no reference either to the Mother or to her daughters. She is treated almost as a presiding deity who stands some distance away from ritual performance. The Mamandabari are similar to the two mythic Nagugur (of western Arnhem Land) who act as intermediaries. But what the Nagugur do is carried out in the name of Kunapipi, and this is not the case with the Mamandabari. Nevertheless, an important clue to the relationship between the Walbiri and Mara Kunapipi versions is to be found in a number of songs they hold in common (Meggitt, 1966, pp. 26–27).

In the southeastern Kimberley, Gadjeri is represented by the Ganabuda group of women, who are included in several of the mythic and ritual Dingari cycles. These Dingari are made up of an accretion of myths that are not necessarily woven into an integrated pattern. In them, the Ganabuda move from one site to another, either following or preceding a group of Dingari men who are concerned with initiating novices (see Berndt, 1970, pp. 216–247). In one excerpt, the Munga-munga walk ahead of the Ganabuda women, who are burdened with sacred *daragu* boards. During the course of their travels, they encounter a mythic man, who is astonished to see not only what they are carrying but also that they are swinging bull-roarers—because the men had none of these things. At night he sneaks up and steals their power, which resides under the armpits of the Ganabuda. In that way, men obtained ritual power.

In another excerpt, Dingari men sit within their ring place while the Ganabuda remain some distance away in their own camp. The women discover that some young men (novices) are among the older men. They meet some of the young men and have intercourse with them. When the older men find out about this, they become angry. They light a bush fire, which sweeps across the countryside, burning many of the young men to death. The Ganabuda escape the fire by submerging themselves in a lake. When the fire has passed by, they discover what has happened. Overwhelmed by grief and anger, they go in search of the older men and kill some of them in revenge.

Again, this last mythic incident represents, symbolically, a typical initiatory sequence: removal of novices from the authority of their "mothers," their seclusion from women (that is, their ritual death, expressed in their mythic death by fire), and the grief of the women at the loss of the young men (the women take revenge on the older men). In short, the Mara myth provides a glimpse of the Kunapipi Mother who has not perfected the ritual process of death and rebirth. She must therefore die in order to live spiritually in the form of her emblematic representation. In the Mutjingga myth the process is taken a step further, with the removal of the children alive from her womb. The central-western Northern Territory example gives assurance that Gadjeri has perfected the ritual process of death and rebirth: She is the epitome of all physical and spiritual renewal.

The Ganabuda mythology, on the other hand, poses a paradox which is not so easily explained. The answer lies in the nature of Western Desert mythology and ritual, which, although it emphasizes seasonal renewal and the growth of all species, also underlines the essential unpredictability of natural phenomena and the vulnerability of human beings. Gadjeri's womb is still fertile, but there are still many dangers associated with the ritual (and human) implementation of her life-giving power.

See Also Djan'kawu; Rainbow Snake.

Bibliography

Berndt, Ronald M. *Kunapipi: A Study of an Australian Aboriginal Religious Cult.* Melbourne, 1951. A study of the Kunapipi cult and ritual, focusing especially on northeastern Arnhem Land; includes songs of some of the major cycles, with interpretations, and dreams reported by participants.

Berndt, Ronald M. "Traditional Morality as Expressed through the Medium of an Australian Aboriginal Religion." In *Australian Aboriginal Anthropology,* edited by Ronald M. Berndt, pp. 216–247. Nedlands, Australia, 1970. This article contains an analysis and interpretation of the Ganabuda mythology and ritual relating to the southeastern Kimberley.

Berndt, Ronald M., and Catherine H. Berndt. Review of *The Eternal Ones of the Dream,* by Géza Róheim. *Oceania* 17 (1946): 67–78. Includes material on Gadjeri, with some illustrations.

Berndt, Ronald M., and Catherine H. Berndt. *Man, Land and Myth in North Australia: The Gunwinggu People.* Sydney, 1970. A study of Gunwinggu society and culture, which covers material on religious myth and ritual, including the western Arnhem Land Kunapipi.

Meggitt, M. J. *Gadjari among the Walbiri Aborigines of Central Australia.* Sydney, 1966. A detailed study of the Gadjeri cult that has been adapted to a fringe desert sociocultural perspective.

Stanner, W. E. H. "On Aboriginal Religion." *Oceania* 30 (1960): 245–278 and 31 (1961): 233–258. Focuses on the Port Keats area, but in general terms is analytic and interpretative.

Spencer, Baldwin. *Native Tribes of the Northern Territory of Australia.* London, 1914. A classic sourcebook that, although unsystematic in the recording of Aboriginal material, provides clues to a number of features of religious belief.

Warner, William Lloyd. *A Black Civilization: A Study of an Australian Tribe* (1937). New York, 1958. This important study of north-central coastal Arnhem Land society and culture contains empirical material on the Kunapipi (Gunabibi) in that area, and an analysis in relation to other local religious constellations.

Ronald M. Berndt (1987)

GAGE, MATILDA JOSLYN. Matilda Joslyn Gage (1826–1898), suffragist, abolitionist, and religious radical, was born March 24, 1826, in Cicero, New York, and spent her entire life within a thirty-mile radius of nearby Syracuse, raising her family of four with her husband, the merchant Henry H. Gage. Gage was the youngest member of the National Woman Suffrage Association (NWSA) leadership triumvirate (with Elizabeth Cady Stanton and Susan B. Anthony), presiding over the Executive Committee of the NWSA for most of the 1870s and 1880s while heading the New York State Suffrage Association. The three women, editors of the first three volumes of the *History of Woman Suffrage* (1881–1887), "will ever hold a grateful place in the hearts of posterity," predicted the *Woman's Tribune* in 1888.

A prolific writer and thorough researcher, Gage edited a suffrage newspaper for four years (*The National Citizen and Ballot Box*, 1878–1881) and contributed as correspondent to newspapers across the country. She wrote about the superior position of Haudenosaunee (Iroquois) women while she supported native sovereignty and treaty rights. Gage was a chief architect of the campaign of nonviolent civil disobedience in the 1870s that saw NWSA women refusing to pay their taxes, voting illegally, and petitioning Congress for relief from their political disabilities. Gage dropped out of the suffrage cause after what she perceived as a conservative takeover of the woman's movement in 1889, which she unsuccessfully moved to prevent.

The greatest danger at the time, Gage believed, was an attempt by Christian fundamentalists to place God in the Constitution and prayer in the public schools. Turning to what she believed was her grandest, most courageous work, Gage formed the Woman's National Liberal Union (1890) to challenge the religious right's drive to merge church and state. The organization, which lasted only a year, also strove to free woman from the "bondage" of the church, which "enslaved her conscience and reason."

Gage published her magnum opus, *Woman, Church, and State* in 1893, and Anthony Comstock, the press censor of the United States Postal Service, immediately banned the book from public school libraries, threatening to arrest anyone who made the book available to children. A powerful indictment of the church's primary role in the oppression of women, the book also exposed the institutionalized sexual abuse of women and children by the priesthood and documented gynocidal witch-burnings (nine million European women, Gage estimated, murdered by the church and later the state over a 500-year period). Gage argued that the early church had accepted the equal feminine nature of the divine, and women served at the altar and administered the sacrament until 824, when the Council of Paris removed women from religious duty. Women were then slowly forced out of the priesthood and the female in the godhead was removed.

Beginning in the 1870s, Gage charged in her writing and speeches that the foundation of the Christian church became the theory that woman brought sin and death into the world. The result was idolatry, a worship of the masculine, Gage told the International Council of Women in 1888. God punished Eve's sin by putting woman in subordination and servitude to man; women's second-class position in all areas—political, legal, educational, industrial, and social—resulted from this mythological story, Gage explained. The church required women to pledge obedience to their husbands in the marriage ceremony. When canon law became the foundation for common law, married woman's subordinate position rendered her "dead in the law," without rights or even legal identity.

The great underlying creative principle is female, Gage reasoned, a fact recognized by all ancient nations, where goddesses were seated everywhere with gods, and often considered superior to them. Gage believed that returning the motherhood of God to the place of sacredness from which it had been removed by the patriarchal Christian overthrow was critical to elevating the position of women. Women were not the only victims of Christianity; the authority of the Bible had been used to justify slavery and oppose science, art, invention, and all reform movements. Considering religious belief tantamount to the death of the soul, Gage celebrated the greatest lesson of her life—to think for herself—given in childhood by her father. She embraced moral relativism, believing that no absolute moral standard exists, but that what is considered right changes over time and from culture to culture.

While nominally a church member throughout her life—she joined the Baptist Church in childhood and her name stayed on the church rolls until shortly before her death—Gage's religious journey took her through membership in the American Theosophical Society (1885) and a serious investigation of the paranormal.

A contributor to the *Woman's Bible*, which Elizabeth Cady Stanton edited (1895–1898), Gage moved from her interpretation of the Bible as history or mythology to a reading of it as an occult work of ancient mysteries written in symbolic language. She suggested that the *Book of Revelation*, understood from this perspective, may be read as a work about woman's spiritual powers.

Gage remained hopeful about the future of women who were rising up against the "tyranny of Church and State" in the most important revolution the world had yet seen. It "will shake the foundations of religious belief, tear into fragments and scatter to the winds the old dogmas upon which all forms of Christianity are based," she predicted at the conclusion of *Woman, Church, and State.* The result "will be a regenerated world."

Gage died March 18, 1898, and was buried in the Fayetteville, New York, cemetery under a tombstone blazing her motto: "There is a word sweeter than mother, home or heaven. That word is Liberty."

See Also Gender and Religion; Politics and Religion.

Bibliography

A full-length comprehensive biography of Gage's life and work has yet to be written. Sally Roesch Wagner's monograph, *Matilda Joslyn Gage: She Who Holds the Sky* (Aberdeen, S.Dak., 2002), and Leila R. Brammer's *Excluded from Suffrage History: Matilda Joslyn Gage, Nineteenth-Century American Feminist* (Westport, Conn., 2000) pave the way. Several reprint editions of Gage's magnum opus, *Woman, Church, and State*, are available, including one from Humanity Books (Amherst, N.Y., 2002); the Modern Reader's edition, published by Sky Carrier Press (Aberdeen, S.Dak., 1998) and edited by Sally Roesch Wagner, is the only one containing a bibliography documenting Gage's extensive research. Gage's papers are available on microfilm from the Schlesinger Library, and her woman's rights scrapbooks from the Library of Congress, Rare Books Division. With Elizabeth Cady Stanton and Susan B. Anthony, Gage edited the first three volumes (1881–1887) of *History of Woman Suffrage* (reprint, Salem, N.H., 1985). Gage's important address, "Woman in the Early Christian Church," was delivered at the International Council of Women's Religious Symposium (Report of the International Council of Women, Washington, D.C.: National Woman Suffrage Association, 1888, pp. 401–407). In addition to the newspaper she edited, the *National Citizen and Ballot Box* (1878–1881), Gage wrote extensively for *The Revolution* (1868–1871). Two good sources for her religious views are *The Index* ("The Church, Science, and Woman," April 29, 1886) and *The Woman's Tribune* ("The Foundation of Sovereignty," April 1887).

SALLY ROESCH WAGNER (2005)

GAIA theory was first proposed by the English scientist James Lovelock in 1979 to explain how and why, as life appeared on the planet and grew abundant, its evolution and the earth's evolution merged into a single dynamic system he called *Gaia.* Lovelock was aware that this was the Greek name for a primordial cosmic goddess who was also a primal earth deity. He used the name and has continued to use it, in spite of criticism from some scientists, because of its metaphoric power. It conveys, he says, the idea of a superorganism composed of all life tightly coupled with the air, the oceans, and the surface rocks. By the end of the 1980s there existed sufficient evidence, models, and mechanisms to develop the theory further through transdisciplinary scientific research in cooperative projects between those working in such apparently disparate fields as practical ecology, ocean science, evolutionary biology, biochemistry, geology, and climatology.

Continuing this research, Lovelock and others have shown that Gaia self-regulates at a global scale through life-environment interactions, and that as a result the earth has remained in a habitable state over billions of years. The theory suggests that its habitability results from three intrinsic properties and one extrinsic property of living organisms. First, all organisms alter their environment by taking in free energy and excreting high-entropy waste products in order to maintain a low internal entropy. Second, organisms grow and multiply, potentially exponentially, thus providing an intrinsic positive feedback to life (the more life there is, the more life it can beget). Third, for each environmental variable there is a level or range at which the growth of a particular organism is maximum. Extrinsically, the fact that organisms both alter and are constrained by their environments in these ways means that feedback between life and its environment is inevitable.

In 2001 more than one thousand scientists signed the Amsterdam Declaration on Global Change, which states: "The Earth System behaves as a single, self-regulating system comprised of physical, chemical, biological and human components." This view sees the earth as a unified whole and humans as organic members of the entire community of life on earth. There is no question of human life being external to or independent of the planetary system's self-regulatory functioning, or of its common environmental resources, climatic variables, or ecosystem constraints. That being so, we need to take account of how we rely on and use those resources and adapt to those constraints. As Lovelock himself says, perhaps the greatest value of Gaia theory lies in its metaphor of a living earth. This reminds us that we are part of it and that human rights are constrained by the needs of our planetary partners.

Some religious implications follow from perceiving the earth and ourselves in this way. First, whatever is deemed sacred or holy in life cannot be separated out in any absolute sense from whatever we understand as the whole of existence. It may instead be seen as the internal transcendence of every living being. But as that cannot be divorced from the environment that supports life or from the interactions in which each being is connected with all others, so we cannot reduce the sacred to any one manifestation of being but must extend the concept to the whole dynamic system of relationships between God and the world. Lovelock says that Gaia, like life, is an emergent phenomenon, one that is comprehensible intuitively but difficult or impossible to analyze by reduction. Similarly, sacredness is an emergent property of life, one that cannot be analyzed reductively by separating it out or cutting it off from the interactions of daily life.

Second, if we accept that our species evolved in the same way as every other species, we cannot assume that we were created at a particular moment in time outside the processes or flow of evolution. Neither can we claim absolute privileges for our species in respect of our use of the earth's material resources. Nor can we assert that we alone know, through some divine revelation extraneous to or cut off from daily life, how our species began or what will happen to us at the end of time. Practically, we cannot assume that the earth and its resources evolved and now exist solely for our use.

Gaia theory therefore raises critical questions about the anthropocentrism of major Christian doctrines where they infer that: (1) the earth was created solely for our sake, so that its creatures and resources exist primarily for our benefit; (2) the revelation of God is fully contained in human words addressed to and historically recorded by humans; (3) death was brought into the world as punishment for one man's sin rather than being an evolutionary necessity; or (4) the life and death of Jesus is solely "for" human salvation from sin and death.

It also puts in question the traditionally vertical nature of hierarchical Christian imagery. This places God above angels, men, and women in descending order of value and importance, so that the earth and its creatures are presumed created in a position of subservience to human beings because they are of less value to God. The metaphoric power of the religious language of dominance based on this valuation system authorizes human domination over the entire household of life and claims it in God's name. The intrinsic value and sacredness of the more-than-human world in the sight of God is implicitly negated or at best reduced.

The practical effects of such claims to human exceptionalism are now evident in the exploitation through industrialization and technologization of the earth's resources. The scale of their extraction and the extent of their use and consequent waste far outstrip that of their natural replacement or disposal. Seen within the context of a relational understanding of human interactions with the environment, and of human rights constrained by those of our planetary partners, the implications of this exploitation for social justice are far-reaching.

The implications are of particular concern to four classes of people singled out in the documents proceeding from the 1992 United Nations Conference on Environment and Development as being most at risk from environmental degradation, most vulnerable to its effects, and most powerless to do anything about it: women, children, indigenous peoples, and the poor. Yet the dominant free-market model of development and continuing growth presupposes that the resources needed to sustain it are and will be available, and that thanks to science and technology, together with the spread and improvement of education, we shall be able to hand on a better global situation than the one we inherited. The presupposition behind this expectation is, of course, that the global biophysical environment will sustain this growth. Numerous research projects into the health of that environment, however, show precisely the opposite. Decline in fish stocks and freshwater supplies are well-publicized examples. The fact too that many of the poorest human communities live in battle zones, or are refugees from territories devastated by war, offers them little hope of redress for the loss of their pastures and access to clean water.

Yet human interdependence within Gaia means that we are all in some way implicated in and diminished by the contemporary expansion of militarist regimes and the consequent destruction of biodiversity and loss of material resources. Arms industries today use the chemical, physical, and biological resources of the planet to produce sophisticated weapons through the expenditure of billions of dollars and massive amounts of human energy. In 1994 the amount of weapons available was computed at twenty thousand kilograms of explosive for every person on the planet. By the year 2000 the available weapons-grade plutonium was the equivalent of a million atomic bombs. This waste of planetary resources is compounded by the fact that such weapons exist solely to destroy life and its support systems within Gaia.

Commitment to as nonviolent a lifestyle as possible is, therefore, an obviously appropriate response to a deepening understanding of the single, self-regulating planetary system within which we belong. Religions such as Jainism and Buddhism have made a nonviolent ethic an inherent and coherent part of a religiously inspired worldview. Now, Gaia theory is reminding Christians that Jesus—believed by them to be the authentic revelation of God—taught love of enemies, forgiveness, and nonretaliation for insults. He claimed that God has a direct interest in sparrows and in each flower of the field, was renowned for healing bodies, and died on a cross erected by military power, his own body pierced and broken after death by military weapons.

If, therefore, as Lovelock asserts, we each contribute, according to our kind, to the continuous and consistent relationships between organisms and their environments that constitute the support system of all life on earth, the adoption of as nonviolent a lifestyle as possible is a positive contribution to Gaia from a religious, ethical, and scientific perspective. This nonviolence is more than the negation of violence. It is a rational and spiritually powerful commitment to living in a way that asserts the sacredness of Gaia.

See Also Ecology and Religion; Evolution; Goddess Worship; Nonviolence.

Bibliography

Bunyard, Peter, ed. *Gaia in Action: Science of the Living Earth.* Edinburgh, 1996. A collection of papers from leading scientists and authors, based on a series of international conferences on Gaia, that seeks to define what the theory means in terms of their own disciplines.

Lenton, Timothy M. "Gaia and Natural Selection" *Nature* 394 (1998): 439–447. Addresses the question of how organisms alter their material environments and how their environment constrains and naturally selects organisms.

Lovelock, James E. *Gaia: The Practical Science of Planetary Medicine.* London, 1991. Draws attention to the similarity between Gaian and physiological self-regulation.

Lovelock, James E. *Gaia: A New Look at Life on Earth.* Oxford, 1995. Second revised edition of the 1979 book in which Lovelock proposed the Gaia theory.

Lovelock, James E. *The Ages of Gaia: A Biography of Our Living Earth.* Oxford, 1995. Second revised version of the 1988 edition; gives the background to new fields of research in Gaia theory.

Lovelock, James E. "The Living Earth." *Nature* 426 (2003): 769–770. Reviews the development of Gaia theory from its beginnings as part of NASA's planetary exploration program.

Potts, Grant H. "Imagining Gaia: Perspectives and Prospects on Gaia, Science, and Religion." *Ecotheology: The Journal of Religion, Nature, and the Environment* 8, no. 1 (2003): 30–49. Analyzes Gaia in relation to the writings of James Lovelock, Anne Primavesi, and Oberon Zell.

Primavesi, Anne. *Sacred Gaia: Holistic Theology and Earth System Science.* London, 2000. Develops the scientific and religious implications of the theory and presents a coherent theology rooted in awe at the sacredness of the whole earth system.

Primavesi, Anne. "The Wisdom of Gaia." *Irish Journal of Feminist Studies* 4, no. 2 (2002): 16–31. Considers Gaia as a project of contemporary wisdom that embodies the body politic and planetary, human, and more-than-human, and therefore open to women's ways of knowing.

Primavesi, Anne. *Gaia's Gift: Earth, Ourselves, and God after Copernicus.* London, 2003. Continues the exploration of human relationships with the earth in the light of the ideological revolution set in motion by Copernicus, Darwin, and Lovelock.

Ruether, Rosemary. *Gaia and God: An Ecofeminist Theology of Earth Healing.* London, 1993. Reviews from an eco-feminist perspective three classical creation stories that shaped the biblical and Christian tradition: the Babylonian story, the Hebrew Story, and the Greek (Platonic) story.

Volk, Tyler. *Gaia's Body: Toward a Physiology of Earth.* New York, 1998. An introduction to the field of earth physiology that examines long-term trends in the earth's evolution and humanity's role in Gaia.

ANNE PRIMAVESI (2005)

GALEN (130?–200? CE, or later) was a Greek physician and philosopher. The last and greatest medical scientist of antiquity, Galen exercised an unparalleled influence on the development of medicine. Galen was born in Pergamum (modern Bergama, Turkey), an important city in western Asia Minor, the only son of Nikon, an architect and geometer. He was educated by his father until the age of fourteen, when he began to attend lectures in philosophy. When Galen was sixteen his father decided that he should become a physician and thereafter spared no expense in his education. After studying under prominent medical teachers in Pergamum, Galen traveled to Smyrna in western Asia Minor, Corinth in Greece, and Alexandria in Egypt, to study medicine.

At the age of twenty-eight he returned to Pergamum, where he was appointed physician to the school of gladiators. This position provided him with broad medical experience that laid the foundation of his later career. In 161 Galen left Pergamum for Rome, where he quickly established a reputation as a successful physician and made many prominent acquaintances. He returned to Pergamum in 166, claiming as the reason the envy of his colleagues, but more probably to escape a severe plague. Shortly after his return, however, he was summoned by the emperor Marcus Aurelius to Aquileia (at the head of the Adriatic), where he was engaged in preparations for war against the Germans. Galen followed the emperor to Rome in 169 and avoided further military service by gaining appointment as physician to the emperor's son Commodus. His position gave him the leisure to pursue medical research, writing, and lecturing, which he did with great success. Not much is known of Galen's later career. He continued to attend Commodus after he ascended the throne in 180 as well as Septimius Severus, who became emperor in 193. The date of Galen's death is uncertain. One source states that he died at the age of seventy, which would be about 200 CE. However, according to Arab biographers, he lived to be more than eighty, which would place his death later than 210.

Galen was one of the most prolific authors of classical antiquity. He wrote more than four hundred treatises. Many of his works have been lost, including a large number of his philosophical treatises that were destroyed in a fire in the Temple of Peace at Rome in 191. Nearly 140 works in Greek that have survived either in whole or in part are attributed to Galen. Some are of doubtful genuineness and others are spurious. Still other works, while lost in Greek, are extant in Latin and Arabic translations. His writings are extremely diverse and include works on anatomy, pathology, therapeutics, hygiene, dietetics, pharmacy, grammar, ethics, and logic, as well as commentaries on Hippocrates and Aristotle. Most of his extant works deal with medicine. Galen wrote clear Attic Greek, but he was prolix and diffuse and his works are not easy to read. Moreover, he was vain, tactless, and quarrelsome, and his writings are often characterized by a polemical tone.

Galen was a brilliant student of anatomy. His exactness in dissecting primates and other animals (from which he drew inferences for human anatomy) was unequaled in the ancient world. His understanding of the human body and medicine followed traditional lines. He admired Hippocrates, whom he regarded as the repository of medical wisdom, and he claimed merely to reproduce his doctrines. Thus he accepted humoral pathology, which viewed health as the product of an equilibrium of the four humors. The basic principle of life for Galen was the *pneuma* ("spirit"), which he thought responsible for many vital processes. Galen's medical theory is deeply indebted to philosophy, the study of which he believed was essential to the education of a physician. He did not follow exclusively the teachings of any one philosophical school, though he was deeply influenced by Aristotle. As an eclectic, he borrowed freely from most philosophical schools with the exception of the Skeptics and Epicureans, whose doctrines he opposed.

Galen's writings reveal a strong teleological emphasis. He believed that everything had been made by the Creator (or Demiurge) for a divine purpose and that the entire creation bears witness to his benevolence. In his treatise *On the Usefulness of the Parts of the Human Body* he expresses the belief that true piety lies in recognizing and explaining the wisdom, power, and excellence of the Creator rather than in offering a multitude of sacrifices. He accepted the Aristotelian principle that nature does nothing in vain and he attempted to show that every organ was designed to serve a particular function. In the minutest detail the human body exhibits its divine design.

Although Galen believed in one god, his depiction of him as a divine craftsman was drawn not from Judeo-Christian sources, but from Plato's *Timaeus,* as was his argument from design. He criticized Moses for holding (in the account of creation in *Genesis*) the doctrine of *creatio ex nihilo* and the belief that nature was created as an act of God's sovereign will. Galen was acquainted with both Jews and Christians and he refers several times in his philosophical and medical works to their beliefs. He was the first pagan writer to treat Christianity with respect as a philosophy rather than, like most educated Romans, as a superstitious sect. He admired Christians for their contempt of death, sexual purity, self-control in regard to food and drink, and their pursuit of justice: in all of which he regarded them as not inferior to pagan philosophers. He criticized Christians and Jews, however, for their refusal to base their doctrines on reason rather than solely on faith and revealed authority. A group of Roman Christians in Asia Minor, led by Theodotus of Byzantium, attempted in the late second century to present Christianity in philosophical terms. They are said to have admired Galen and it is likely that they were influenced by his philosophical works. They taught an adoptionist Christology, and for this and other heresies they were excommunicated by church authorities.

Galen enjoyed an enviable reputation in his own time both as a physician and as a philosopher. Soon after his death he came to be recognized as the greatest of all medical authorities. His eclecticism, which permitted him to take what was best from all medical sects, his claim to reproduce the ideas of Hippocrates, the encyclopedic comprehensiveness of his medical works, and his greatness as a scientist were largely responsible for his influence. Because his writings were voluminous they were summarized in handbooks, synopses, and medical encyclopedias. The pre-Galenic medical sects gradually disappeared and were replaced by an all-embracing Galenic system that united medicine and philosophy and came to dominate medicine for over a millennium. As anatomical and physiological research ceased in late antiquity, medicine became increasingly scholastic and was taught from a selection of Galen's works.

Galen's direct influence was initially greater in the Byzantine East, where his ideas were relayed by medical encyclopedias, than in the Latin West. In the ninth century many of his works were collected and translated into Arabic and Syriac by Hunayn ibn Ishaq, a Nestorian Arab physician, and his school. In the course of the eleventh century they were translated from Arabic into Latin and Hebrew and came to dominate medicine in the West just as they had dominated Byzantine and Arabic medicine. The authority of Galen was regarded as second only to that of Aristotle. Although a pagan, he appealed equally to Jews, Muslims, and Christians, who found his teleology and monotheism compatible with their own faiths. The appearance of his collected Greek works in the sixteenth century spurred new interest in Galen and led to a revival of medical experimentation. It was during the Renaissance that his reputation reached its apex, but it soon began to be challenged by new discoveries, particularly in the fields of anatomy and physiology. Nevertheless, ideas championed by Galen (particularly humoral pathology) continued to influence medical theory until the nineteenth century.

Bibliography

The only complete edition of Galen, with Latin translation, remains C. G. Kühn's *Claudii Galeni Opera Omnia,* 20 vols. (1821–1833; reprint, Hildesheim, 1964–1965). While the text is unreliable, Kühn's edition is still useful in the absence of critical editions of most of Galen's works. Several of Galen's treatises have been translated into English. See in particular *Galen on the Usefulness of the Parts of the Body,* 2 vols., translated and edited by Margaret T. May (Ithaca, N.Y., 1968). A representative selection of extracts from Galen's writings is found in *Greek Medicine,* edited and translated by Arthur John Brock (London, 1929), pp. 130–244.

Brief but reliable introductions to Galen and his background are D. E. Eichholz, "Galen and His Environment," *Greece and Rome* 20 (1951): 60–71; and G. W. Bowersock; *Greek Sophists in the Roman Empire* (Oxford, 1969): 59–75. Aspects of Galen's life and work are explored in the composite volume *Galen: Problems and Prospects,* edited by Vivian Nutton (London, 1981). Several of Nutton's essays that deal with Galen's career are reprinted in *From Democedes to Harvey: Studies in the History of Medicine,* edited by Nutton (London, 1988). On Galen's theology and his attitudes to Christians and Jews, see Richard Walzer's *Galen on Jews and Christians* (Oxford, 1949); and Fridolf Kudlien's "Galen's Religious Belief," in *Galen: Problems and Prospects* (cited above). On the influence of Galen on medical thought, see Owsei Temkin's *Galenism: Rise and Decline of a Medical Philosophy* (Ithaca, N.Y., 1973).

Gary B. Ferngren (1987 and 2005)

GALILEO GALILEI (1564–1642) is considered to be the father of modern science. Born at Pisa, Italy, Galileo received some of his early schooling there. He then was sent to the ancient Camaldolese monastery at Vallombroso, where, attracted by the quiet and studious life, he joined the order as a novice. His father, however, wished him to study medicine and took him to Florence, where Galileo continued his studies with the Camaldolese monks until he matriculated at the University of Pisa in 1581. During his student years at Pisa, Galileo is said to have made his celebrated observation of the sanctuary lamp swinging like a pendulum from the cathedral ceiling and to have thereby discovered that the time taken for a swing was independent of the size of the arc, a fact that he used later for measuring time in his astronomical studies.

Finding that his talents for mathematics and philosophy were increasingly being recognized, Galileo gave up his medical studies and left the university in 1585, without a degree, to begin lecturing at the Florentine academy. There he published an account of his invention of the hydrostatic balance (1586) and then an essay on the center of gravity in solid bodies (1588), which won him a lectureship at Pisa. In 1592 he was appointed professor of mathematics at the renowned University of Padua, where he remained for eighteen years. There, in 1604, he published his laws of motion of falling bodies in his book *De motu.*

In 1597 Galileo wrote to Johannes Kepler that he had been a Copernican "for several years." Having heard in Venice of the newly invented telescope, Galileo immediately constructed one of his own and in 1610 announced many astronomical discoveries. These included his discovery that the Milky Way is made up of innumerable stars and his observation of the satellites of Jupiter. He also made observations of sunspots and of the phases of Venus. Thus he vastly expanded astronomical knowledge and challenged the established natural philosophy, which was based on Aristotelian ideas that had been reconciled with Christian doctrine by Thomas Aquinas. Shortly after the publication of these discoveries, Galileo was appointed philosopher and mathematician to the grand duke of Tuscany.

In 1613, Galileo's *Letters on Sunspots* was published. Its preface claimed that Galileo had been the first to observe sunspots, an assertion that generated bitter resentment among some Jesuit scholars (who had an arguable claim to priority of observation) and that eventually had serious consequences for Galileo. In this book, he first stated in print his unequivocal acceptance of Copernican astronomy, challenging a basic postulate of the Aristotelian view by insisting that all celestial phenomena should be interpreted in terms of terrestrial analogies. Furthermore, Galileo wished to make science independent of philosophy by his assertions that the essence of things cannot be known and that science should concern itself only with the properties of things and with observed events. It was the philosophers rather than the theologians who were the early opponents of the Copernican system and, insofar as he supported it, of Galileo's work. No doubt they were also put off by Galileo's extremely high opinion of himself, and they exploited personal jealousies and resentments against him and tried to enlist the aid of theologians in condemning both Copernican ideas and Galileo's advocacy of them.

Not until 1616, seventy-three years after the publication of Copernicus's *De revolutionibus orbium coelestium* (On the revolution of the heavenly spheres), did the Theological Consultors of the Holy Office declare it "false and contrary to Holy Scripture" and recommend that Copernicus's book be "suspended until corrected." Cardinal Roberto Bellarmino had earlier written to Galileo warning him to confine himself to the realm of hypothesis until demonstrative proof could be produced. When Galileo went to Rome to defend his position, he was officially cautioned neither to hold nor to defend the Copernican ideas. And Galileo, good Catholic that he was (and remained), agreed.

Throughout, Galileo maintained that the purpose of scripture is not to teach natural philosophy and that issues of faith and issues of science should be kept separate and should be settled on different grounds. He quoted Tertullian approvingly: "We conclude that God is known first through nature, and then again, more particularly, by doctrine; by nature in his works, and by doctrine in his revealed word." He also cited Cardinal Cesare Baronius, a contemporary, who had quipped, "The Bible tells us how to go to Heaven, not how the heavens go."

The appearance of the great comets in 1618 stirred up much controversy, which Galileo joined by writing his *Discourse on Comets,* annoying the philosophers still further because of his anti-Aristotelian bias. In 1623, Galileo published *The Assayer,* which he dedicated to Urban VIII, the new pope, who was much more favorably disposed toward intellectuals and their work than his predecessor had been. In 1624, Galileo visited Rome and had six audiences with the pope. In 1632, Galileo published his *Dialogue on the Two Great World Systems.* Having intended this book to be "a most ample confirmation" of the Copernican opinion, Galileo in effect had ignored the spirit of the instructions given him by the church in 1616. Nevertheless, during the trial that followed the publication of the *Dialogue*, Galileo maintained that he had obeyed the instructions to the letter.

Galileo's trial in 1633 marked the beginning of what has since become a cliché—namely, the idea that science and religion must inevitably be in conflict. Also, Galileo is often seen as science's first martyr in the perennial battle between the church and the spirit of free inquiry. There is no question that the church took a wrong position (contrary to its own tradition in such matters as established by Augustine and Thomas Aquinas); this much was acknowledged by a statement made by John Paul II in 1979, and it was underscored by the Vatican's publication, in 1984, of all documents from its archives relating to Galileo's trial. However, a considerable amount of blame for Galileo's persecution must also fall on the philosophers. Indeed, the decree of sentence issued by the Holy Office was signed by only seven of the ten cardinal-judges.

Unlike innumerable martyrs who have accepted torture or even death for the sake of their convictions, Galileo chose, most unheroically, to abjure his beliefs. (The myth that he, on leaving the tribunal, stamped his foot and said, "Yet it [i.e., the earth] does move," was invented by Giuseppe Baretti in 1757 and has no basis in fact.) Galileo's sentence was then commuted; there was no formal imprisonment. He was allowed to move back to his country estate near Florence, where he resumed his writing. His *Discourses concerning Two New Sciences,* regarded by many as his greatest scientific contribution, was published in 1638.

See Also Bellarmino, Roberto; Copernicus, Nicolaus.

Bibliography

The best scientific biography of Galileo, tracing the historical development of his thought, is Stillman Drake's *Galileo at Work* (Chicago, 1978). A knowledgeable presentation of Galileo's philosophy is Ludovico Geymonat's *Galileo Galilei: A Biography and Inquiry into His Philosophy of Science* (New York, 1965). For Galileo's theological views and accounts of his trial, the following three books are indispensable: Giorgio de Santillana's *The Crime of Galileo* (New York, 1955), Jerome J. Langford's *Galileo, Science and the Church* (Ann

Arbor, Mich., 1971), and Stillman Drake's *Galileo* (New York, 1980). The play by Bertolt Brecht, *Galileo* (New York, 1966), is tendentious and historically unreliable. Galileo's own views and remarks concerning the relationship between science and religion are scattered throughout his many letters and other writings. Among these the most important are his *Letter to the Grand Duchess Christina* (1615) and *The Assayer* (1623); both of these have been translated by Stillman Drake and are published in his *Discoveries and Opinions of Galileo* (Garden City, N.Y., 1957). The latest, and perhaps the final, effort made by the Roman Catholic church to repair its wrong decision in the case of Galileo is represented by the publication, by the Pontifical Academy of Sciences, of *I documenti del processo di Galileo Galilei* (Rome, 1984), which contains transcriptions of documents relating to Galileo's trial that had been held in the Vatican archives.

New Sources

Drake, Stillman. *Essays on Galileo and the History and Philosophy of Science.* Toronto, 1999.

Feldhay, Rivka. *Galileo and the Church: Political Inquisition or Critical Dialogue?* Cambridge, U.K., 2003.

Gingerich, Owen. "How Galileo Changed the Rules of Science." *Sky and Telescope* 85 (March 1993): 32.

Shea, William, and Mariano Artigas. *Galileo in Rome: The Rise and Fall of a Troublesome Genius.* Oxford, 2003.

RAVI RAVINDRA (1987)
Revised Bibliography

GALLICANISM. The political dominance of the papacy during a period of the high Middle Ages was necessarily a temporary phenomenon. In central Europe the political fragmentation that followed Charlemagne's attempt at imperial restoration was not reversed by the efforts of successive German dynasties to establish hegemony and to extend their power beyond the Alps. But in western Europe, territories were consolidated that would ultimately become national states. Their growth in size and complexity, together with developments in secular education, favored the employment of laity rather than ecclesiastics in public office. As the opportunity to build larger state units increased, so did the state's determination to assert its power over agencies within its territory. On the international level this would limit the papacy's capacity to intervene in temporal conflicts; within states, it led to a tightening of lay control over the church's tangible assets.

These changes in the relations of power inevitably brought conflict. In England tensions between crown and church are visible in the twelfth century; in France the harangue of King Philip IV (the Fair) before the first meeting of the Estates General in 1302 is a dramatic statement of the rights of the crown over against the church. In the aftermath of the schism that split the papacy between popes and antipopes, Charles VI spoke of "the traditional liberties of the French church." The fifteenth- and sixteenth-century Spanish monarchy combined centralization with control of the church, and the popes surrendered many ancient prerogatives. In some countries the process of realignment of power culminated in the total control of the church during the Protestant Reformation; in other countries it could promote or retard Catholic reformation. In Roman Catholic countries the doctrine of the state's ascendancy over the church received a variety of names: Gallicanism in France, Febronianism in the German states, cameralism or Josephism in the Habsburg lands, and regalism in Mediterranean countries.

Generically, this swing back to lay dominance in public affairs was a corollary of the growth of modern state power. An early formulation in a decree of the French king Charles VII—the Pragmatic Sanction of Bourges, 1438—contains the major elements that subsequently would be emphasized first, the supremacy of the king over the pope in the temporal affairs of the French church, with a rejection of the pope's right to intervene in these matters; second, the supremacy of regularly convened general councils over the papacy; and third, the cooperation of the crown and the episcopacy in settling French ecclesiastical issues.

Because the boundary between temporal and spiritual is never unambiguous, and because various interest groups interpreted these "Gallican liberties" to meet their specific needs, it is proper to distinguish several Gallicanisms. Royal Gallicanism sought the extension of state power over ecclesiastical appointments and properties, generally through negotiation. Academic Gallicanism usually enlisted a majority of Sorbonne doctors, who strongly defended the independence of the church and the dignity of the papacy but saw the need for some limitations to papal power. The episcopal Gallicanism of the bishops insisted on the control of their dioceses while accepting the crown's full temporal sovereignty in church affairs and the pope's full sovereignty in spiritual matters. Finally, the parliamentary Gallicanism of the superior courts claimed that the Pragmatic Sanction represented the constitution of the French church and that they were its guardians and interpreters; hence no papal document or agent could enter France without prior approval of the Parlement of Paris, which could also declare its jurisdiction over all church issues (*appel comme d'abus*).

The classic statement of Gallicanism appeared in a conflict between King Louis XIV and Pope Innocent XI involving royal financial control over vacant dioceses. The assembly of the French clergy in 1682 sought to reestablish peace by clearly defining the respective powers of pope, king, and bishops. The Four Gallican Articles, drawn up by the very orthodox bishop Jacques-Bénigne Bossuet of Meaux, were intended to be conciliatory. In substance they declared that (1) kings are not subject to any ecclesiastical power in temporal matters; (2) the reservations of the Council of Constance (1414–1418) on the spiritual supremacy of the pope still apply; (3) the pope is obliged to heed the customs and canons of the Gallican church in the exercise of his functions; and (4) the pope is supreme in matters of faith, but his decisions are not final unless they are confirmed by the judgment of the episcopacy. Although the popes ignored these decrees, Gallicanism retained considerable influence in eighteenth-century France and was generally taught in the seminaries. The Civil Constitution of the Clergy (1790), so decisive in fixing the religious pattern of the French Revolution, had a strong Gallican flavor, as did the seventy-seven Organic Articles unilaterally appended to the Concordat of 1801 by Napoléon.

The clearest example of parliamentary Gallicanism was its use by the Jesuits' Jansenist enemies, who employed it skillfully in securing the suppression of the Society of Jesus in France in 1764. Although many factors contributed to this condemnation, it could not have happened without the strong Gallican—and hence anti-Jesuit—orientation of the judicial bodies.

Gallicanism reached the flood tide of its political influence in the Revolutionary and Napoleonic eras; thereafter its strength ebbed. The sufferings and occasionally the heroism of the popes during this prolonged crisis evoked wide sympathy, not exclusively among the Roman Catholic populations. The disappearance or weakening of the Old Regime monarchs, who had been friendly to Catholicism while striving to control it, created a new political atmosphere in which isolated or persecuted Catholics turned to the papacy for protection. Improvements in communications and other features of modernization assisted. Nearly everywhere in the nineteenth century, ultramontanism, the antithesis of Gallicanism, triumphed. It is ironic that during the century when European nationalism reached its culmination, official Catholicism moved toward greater accent on its international features. Although the early stages of the modern national state system favored the development of Gallicanism, the maturation of the national state saw its virtual disappearance.

See Also Ultramontanism.

Bibliography

Martimort, A.-G. *Le gallicanisme de Bossuet.* Paris, 1953. Traces the development of Gallican ideas among the bishops, the magistrates, and the ministers of the crown. The best account available of the Extraordinary Assembly of the Clergy of France, 1681–1682.

Martimort, A.-G. *Le gallicanisme.* Paris, 1973. The best introduction to this complicated topic, with the most up-to-date bibliography currently in print. Although brief, it covers an immense span, from Phillip II to the First Vatican Council, with particular attention to the late medieval period. Chapter 7 is useful for its distinctions among the types of Gallicanism.

Martin, Victor. *Les origines du gallicanisme.* 2 vols. Paris, 1939. Martin apparently intended to encompasss the whole movement but ended his work after reaching the Pragmatic Sanction of Bourges. It is an immense mobilization of sources for the earlier period, with an exhaustive index.

Rothkrug, Lionel. *Opposition to Louis XIV: The Political and Social Origins of the French Enlightenment.* Princeton, 1965. A broad perspective on seventeenth-century conflicts. Chapter 1, "The Intellectual and Religious Opposition to Reform," includes a useful sketch of Gallicanism.

Van Kley, Dale. *The Jansenists and the Expulsion of the Jesuits from France, 1757–1765.* New Haven, 1975. The best explanation in English of the use made by the Jansenists of the Gallican attitudes of the Parlements. Particularly helpful in distinguishing the varied forms Gallicanism assumed in the eighteenth century. And it makes an exciting story.

Joseph N. Moody (1987)

GAMALIEL OF YAVNEH See GAMLI'EL OF YAVNEH

GAMALIEL THE ELDER See GAMLI'EL THE ELDER

GAMBLING.

The religious significance of gambling is, in effect, twofold. Many religious traditions, especially the great religions, in their works of legislation and codification, promote as their orthodox norm a prohibition against, or at least discouragement of, gambling. On the other hand, in many cultures gambling takes on religious significance in connection with myths and rituals.

This twofold simplification, however, addresses gambling only insofar as it takes on overt religious significance. No discussion of gambling would be complete, however, without acknowledging its covert religious significance, particularly in cultures that prohibit it or, having adopted a secularized attitude, look upon it as something nonreligious or merely "cultural." Although beyond the main focus of this essay, it is evident that much of what goes on in the name of secular, cultural, or even legalized gambling is both enhanced by the flaunting or circumvention of traditional prohibitions and heightened by ritualized procedures too numerous to mention, by special "sacred" and "liminal" times (the American Superbowl) and places (casinos in remote or international spots), and by a cast of mythological characters and aspirations (the cool, passionate, roving, or desperate gambler; the jackpot winner).

In definitional terms, religious gambling is not easily separated from games and divination. Because gambling cannot be discussed without reference to games, this article shall deal with games only where they are the focus of wages and stakes. As for divination, the use in certain cases of similar implements (lots, bones, dice) and the occurrence of similar attitudes to unseen forces are not sufficient to support the frequently aired view that gambling derives from divination (Tylor, 1871). One does not, in fact, need implements or games at all to gamble. This article shall, however, refer to the drawing of lots and other forms of divination where their use is similar or related to that of gambling practices.

Gambling in Traditional Cultures. Unless one adopts a diffusionist perspective and attempts to derive all forms of gambling from ancient Near Eastern or other Asian prototypes, the prevalence of gambling rites and myths in archaic cultures strongly suggests that the origins of religious gambling are irretrievable. Archaeologists have suggested that the painted pebbles found in the Mas d'Azil caves in the Pyrenees, from the Mesolithic period, are gambling implements. The earliest known dice and board game is that found in the Sumerian royal tombs at Ur, from about 2600 BCE. Gambling can only be assumed here, as with Indus Valley dice from about 2000 BCE and Egyptian (1990–1780 BCE), Cretan (1800–1650 BCE), and Palestinian (c. sixteenth century BCE) finds, some of which resemble cribbage boards. Evidence of ball games and gaming boards from Mesoamerican cultures, of types that continue to be played in that area today, is also traceable to about 1500 BCE. And *Ṛgveda* 10.34 provides the first gambler's lament in its "Hymn to Gambling" (c. 1200 BCE). The games of ancient cultures appear not only to be similar to those found in recent and contemporary field contexts but to have had in some cases—such as the Mesoamerican—remarkable continuity from past to present. As the religious significance of gambling is clearly more in a state of living "expression" than belated "application" (Jensen, 1963, pp. 59-64) in contemporary tribal cultures, such cultures present the best evidence for understanding the religious dimensions of gambling in general.

Unfortunately, ethnographic discussion of "sacred" gambling is uneven. There is sufficient documentation to be confident that it is found on all continents and probably among most, if not all, tribal communities. Many games and implements have been described and collected from around the world, but few studies have examined the cultural and religious significance of gambling at the field level in any detailed way. The only thorough field research on gambling seems to be Geertz's study of the Balinese cockfight, and in that situation its rather covert religious significance is tied in with the Balinese version of popular Hinduism (Geertz, 1973). Nonetheless, Geertz's findings and insights are illuminating with respect to a wider view of religious gambling.

Generally, one finds two models for understanding the archaic religious significance of gambling: Geertz's notion of "deep play," a consuming passionate involvement drawing on deeply ingrained cultural codes and strategies, and the pervasively cited notion that gambling games draw on "cosmic symbolism," or have "cosmic significance." Because Geertz mentions calendrical and cosmological ideas that bear upon the choice and placement of cocks (p. 427), it is evident that the two approaches are not antithetical. In fact, the "cosmic significance" clearly lends itself to the "deepening" of the play.

The cosmological significance of gambling games was maintained by Culin, author of several monumental works on games. In his book on North American Indian games, he summarizes the common pattern of references to gambling games in the origin myths of numerous tribes:

> They usually consist of a series of contests in which the demiurge, the first man, the culture hero, overcomes some opponent, a foe of the human race, by exercise of superior cunning, skill, or magic. Comparison of these myths . . . discloses the primal gamblers as those curious children, the divine Twins, the miraculous offspring of the Sun. . . . They live in the east and the west; they rule night and day, winter and summer. They are the morning and evening stars. Their virgin mother, who appears also as their sister and wife, is constantly spoken of as their grandmother, and is the Moon, or the Earth, the Spider Woman, the embodiment of the feminine principle in nature. Always contending, they are the original patrons of play, and their games are now played by men. (Culin, 1907, p. 32)

In Culin's Zuni example, the emblems of the Twin War Gods, their weapons, are classified fourfold in accord with the four directions and are interchangeable with their gaming implements. Thus, for example, stick dice are arrows, shafts, or miniature bows (ibid., p. 33). A correlation between dice and weapons is also made in the Hindu *Mahābhārata* epic.

It is not, in fact, difficult to advance the principle that every game, ancient or modern, creates a miniature cosmos, its arena, rules, apparatus, and players comprising a unique spatiotemporal world that reflects and symbolizes aspects of known and accepted cosmological structures. This is as true of Monopoly, football, or cricket as it is of more traditional games such as snakes and ladders, which in its Indian context symbolized a difficult ascent to heaven (Grunfeld, 1975, pp. 131–133). There are many examples from American Indian cultures of counting boards, playing boards, and ball-game courts having "gateways" or quadrants that correspond to the four directions; to the alternating seasons; to the equinoctial points; to tribal divisions such as men versus women, married women versus single women, old men versus young men; and to moiety divisions identified with heaven and earth, changes in the seasons, or other cosmological referents (Culin, 1907, pp. 34–208 passim). In his careful study of the Mesoamerican ball game, Humphrey (1979) thus allows that "there seems to be no question" that it "was based on a kind of cosmic symbolism." He suggests that the movement of the ball represented the course of heavenly bodies through dualistically conceived upper and lower worlds, the two sides thus enacting the struggle between light and darkness, summer and winter, life and death. The ancient Chinese game of pitchpot (see Yang, 1969, pp. 138–165) may rely on cosmological notions of the pot (or, sometimes, the gourd) as a container of the world and symbol of primal chaos. Also striking in this connection is the ancient Aztec board game of *patolli*, which has evident formal similarities with the South Asian game of *pachisi*. Arguments over whether the similarities are due to diffusion or independent use of similar cosmological structures have remained unresolved since the late nineteenth century. In any case, Beck (1982, pp. 199–205) has argued cogently for the cosmological significance of *pachisi*. The pieces move around the four-armed board, representing the world quarters, in a way that follows the reverse (counterclockwise) movement of the sun through the houses of the zodiac. The four-sided dice are identified with the four Indian ages (*yugas*). The goal of returning to the center thus suggests a triumph over spatiotemporal conditions.

Geertz's discussion of the Balinese cockfight draws its concept of deep play from Jeremy Bentham (1748–1832), the English economist and philosopher, who uses the term to refer to situations in which stakes are so high that participation is irrational. At the cockfight, two kinds of bets are made: even-money center bets between the two cock owners and their allied supporters, and side bets on odds made among the assembled crowd. As a rule, the larger the center bets, the more even are the odds reached in the crowd. Interest and "depth" are thus enhanced by making the outcome appear as unpredictable as possible. But the size of the center bet also "deepens" the stakes for the cock owners. For the stakes here are not just material, but are matters of honor, esteem, status, and, also, delight in bringing oblique affront to the opponent. Except for addicted gamblers, who are drawn—usually to their ruin—to the small center bet and long odds matches, real status remains largely unaffected, because victories and losses tend to balance out. But the deep play at status reversals and reclamations of status is real enough in its psychological and social impact. Only men play, while on the periphery of the cockfight, roulette and other gambling games of sheer chance are operated by concessionaires for women, children, the poor, and others who find themselves excluded.

"Deep-play" cockfighting is thus for "the solid citizenry" and resembles an *"affaire d'honneur"* (Geertz, 1973, pp. 435–436). Moreover, it pits not merely individuals against each other, but corporate groups—most notably, whole villages and patriarchal descent groups. Support money for the central bet comes from other members of the group, and even side-betting against the cock of one's group is considered disloyal. The cock owners thus have not only their own status at stake, but their status within their respective groups and that of the groups themselves.

All of this is displayed "in a medium of feathers, blood, crowds, and money" (ibid., p. 444) that arouses the deepest passions but is rounded off with furtive payments that affirm a cultivated embarrassment at such personal identification with the world of demonic and animal violence. For the cockfight is also, fundamentally, an encounter with the demonic: "a blood sacrifice offered, with the appropriate chants and oblations, to the demons in order to pacify their ravenous, cannibal hunger" (ibid., p. 420). The fights are regularly performed in connection with temple festivals and as collective responses to such natural evils as illness, crop failure, and volcanic eruptions.

A correlation between status—in the largest sense—and deep-play gambling can certainly be found. The importance of status is reflected in the fact that gambling is frequently the province of kings, heroes, and aristocrats: the models of what comes down to the present as the genteel bettor. Humphrey (1979, pp. 141–146) has applied Geertz's categories to the aristocratic patronage of the Mesoamerican ball game. But still better confirmation for such an analysis comes from descriptions of the North American Huron Indian dice games collected by Culin (1907, pp. 105–110). Sacrificial offerings of tobacco to the spirits of the game precede the action. Sometimes whole townships and even tribes contend. In one eight-day game between townships, every inhabitant of each party threw the dice at least once. Players with lucky dreams were sought out for the casting:

> At this game they hazard all they possess, and many do not leave off till they are almost stripped quite naked and till they have lost all they have in their cabins. Some have been known to stake their liberty for a time. . . . The players appear like people possessed, and the spectators are not more calm. They all make a thousand contortions, talk to the bones [i. e., throw the dice], load the spirits of the adverse party with imprecations. . . . They quarrel and fight, which never happens among [them] but on these occasions and in drunkenness. (ibid., pp. 105–106)

Women and girls play the same game, but only separately and under inferior conditions: with different numbers of dice, and throwing by hand on a blanket rather than with a dice box or basket as the men do (ibid., p. 107).

Gambling on one's freedom is an ultimate status wager and is a type of bet instanced in many cultures. Another suggestive feature of deep play that emerges here is the significance of "stripping," for being willing to gamble all one possesses may both literally and figuratively involve such an outcome. Loss of status is thus potentially far more than just loss of face. As Geertz remarks, there is both a literal and a metaphoric significance—sustained by the Balinese language as in the English—to the Balinese cockfighter's identification with his cock (Geertz, 1973, pp. 417–418). I shall note important recurrences of this gambling-stripping correlation, which has a wide range of effects, from deep humiliation to eroticism. Obviously, strip poker is a "secular" example of the latter orientation.

Ritualized gambling thus seems to rely on both its cosmological significance and its character as deep play. The forces of chance draw the contestants into deep involvement in a context that allows for both the regulated breakdown and the creative redefinition of the structural roles by which society and cosmos operate—a context that the games reflect. The games thus have the character of liminal passage rites, or ordeals (Humphrey, 1979, p. 144), as well as of reiterations of the cosmogony, the reestablishment of cosmos out of chaos. Such initiatory and cosmogonic overtones have been detected in the dice match that concluded the ancient Indian sacrifice of royal consecration, or *rajasuya.* In playing dice on even terms with members of different castes, the king overcomes the forces of chance, chaos, and confusion by his triumph (Heesterman, 1957, pp. 140–157). As is often the case in ritual gambling, the game is rigged to assure the desired outcome. But the important point is that the participants submit to the principles of the game. Similar initiatory and cosmogonic overtones are found in contexts where gambling is performed for the sick, over the dead, or at turning points in the seasons (for examples, see Culin, 1907, pp. 108–115; Hartland, 1924–1927, pp. 168–169; Jensen, 1963, p. 60).

PROHIBITIONS ON GAMBLING. The principles by which different religions have denounced or prohibited gambling are revealing on two fronts. First, they reflect the axiomatic theological and cultural values operative in the respective traditions. Second, they often provide theologically and culturally attuned indications of what it is that is so appealing about what they seek to oppose. Not surprisingly, cosmological significance and deep-play involvement are among the condemned attractions.

In *Isaiah* 65:11–12, gambling is thus one of the ways by which Israel provokes the Lord: "[You] who set up a table for Fortune and fill cups of mixed wine for Destiny, I will destine you to the sword." Gad (Fortune) and Meni (Destiny) were gods of fortune, possibly of Syrian or Phoenician origin. The polemic against gambling is thus made in the same terms as that against idolatry, which in turn is a polemic against involvement in false cosmologies ruled by false gods. The context also suggests that such gambling was, at least to the mind of the prophet, one of the alluring vices of acculturation besetting Israel. This attitude persists in Talmudic and rabbinic prohibitions against a variety of games, from the Greek Olympics to cards and chess, which Jews regarded themselves as having adopted from their neighbors. But it is particularly those games that involve gambling that are singled out for condemnation. The Mishnah declares twice that dice players and pigeon racers are disqualified from appearing as witnesses in a court of justice (*R. ha-Sh.* 1.8; *San.* 3.3), and the medieval Sefardic philosopher Mosheh ben Maimon (Maimonides, 1135/8-1204) extends the ban to include those who play chess for money (Commentary on *Sanhedrin* 3.3). This disqualification rests on the principle that gamblers are guilty of facilitating acts of robbery and are thus, in effect, criminals. Curiously, gamblers are similarly disqualified in Hindu law books, joined to thieves, assassins, and other dangerous characters for being "incompetent on account of their depravity" and persons in whom no truth can be found (*Narada Smrti* 1.159, 1.178; *Bṛhaspati Dharmaśāstra* 7.30).

The passage from *Isaiah* also introduces another strain of condemnation: Using the same Hebrew root in two words, Yahveh "destines" to the sword those who tempt "Destiny." Such a scene is, in fact, played out in another passage from *Isaiah,* where the *rabshakeh* (field marshal) of the Assyrian king Sennacherib challenges Israel to a wager over horses, and to an additional (though implied) theological wager—expressed by boasts referring to Yahveh as a fallible god like those of the surrounding nations—that Yahveh cannot deliver Israel. The wager over the horses is ignored, but the arrogant theological presumption of the affront to the Lord results in the salvation of Jerusalem and Sennacherib's death by the sword (*Is.* 36–37).

If gambling was denounced in the Bible, however, the casting of lots was not. The throwing of lots with the Urim and Tummim (Yes and No), articles kept in the priest's apron, was accepted as a means of discerning the divine will. Thus Saul was chosen by lot to be king (*1 Sm.* 10:20–21); rural priests were chosen by lot to serve in Jerusalem (*1 Chr.* 24–25); and Matthias was selected by lot to become Judas's successor as the twelfth apostle (*Acts* 1:26). In these instances, the casting of lots cannot be called gambling. But it is also evident that Israel knew of the use of lots for gambling, though the references suggest that it was only other nations that so employed them. In *Joel* 3:1–3, Yahveh speaks of bringing judgment upon the nations for "having divided up my land" and "cast lots for my people." And in *Psalms* 22:16–18, the psalmist, seeing himself dead, describes the "company of evildoers" who "divide my garments among them, and for my raiment cast lots." It is this latter passage that is taken in *John* 19:23–24 as a prophecy of the scene at Jesus' crucifixion, where the Roman soldiers divide up the crucified Christ's garments and gamble for his seamless tunic. Here the symbolism of stripping and gambling accentuates the deepest humiliation and suffering (see *Mk.* 15:16–20, 25; *Mt.* 27:28–29, 36).

Early Christian canon law condemned gambling in no uncertain terms. Two of the so-called Apostolic Canons (41, 42) prohibited both laity and clergy, under pain of excommunication, from engaging in games of chance. And at the Council of Elvira (306 CE), the seventy-ninth canon decreed a year's banishment from communion for anyone guilty of gambling. But restrictions of later councils were directed toward the clergy, and only certain games (especially cards and dice) were forbidden (Slater, 1909, pp. 375–376). Such relaxing of restrictions on lay gambling has facilitated church sponsorship of bingo and lottery games in fund-raising efforts. The same is true in Orthodox churches.

Christian condemnations of gambling gather their fullest force in Puritan writings. According to the doctrine of predestination, because every action is foreordained, matters of so-called chance are in the hands of God alone. To invoke God in the name of fortune is to offend him "by making him the assistant in idle pleasures" (Knappen, 1939, p. 439). Similarly, man is but a steward of his goods, which ultimately belong to God. Thus he must not wager what is truly God's (Paton, 1924, p. 166). Furthermore, losers at gambling tend to express themselves in curses.

A rather practical Islamic stance is expressed in the Qurʾān when Muḥammad discourages wine and a form of gambling with arrows in which the loser pays for a young camel that is slaughtered and given to the poor: "In both there is sin and profit to men; but the sin of both is greater than the profit of the same" (Palmer, 1880, p. 32).

The Hindu law books are full of cautionary remarks on gambling. As noted already, gamblers are judged incompetent witnesses in matters of law. There are statements that gambling makes one impure, and that the wealth obtained by gambling is tainted. Most significant, however, is a passage from the *Laws of Manu* concerning the duties of kings: Of the royal vices, ten are born of pleasure and eight of anger, and all end in misery; of the ten that "spring from love of pleasure," the most pernicious are drinking, dice, women, and hunting (7.45–50). This list of four vices recurs in the *Mahābhārata* (3.14.7) in the mouth of the divine Kṛṣṇa when he denounces the epic's famous dice match. Kṛṣṇa adds that gambling is the worst "desire-born" vice of all. Thus one seems to have here a condemnation of gambling as deep play. This correlation between gambling and desire is at the very heart of the Indian meditation on gambling, for actions born of desire are binding to this world. Yet in Hindu terms it is also the things of desire—including the four just mentioned—that draw people to the divine. Thus, whereas Kṛṣṇa here warns of gambling's dangers, when he reveals his "supernal manifestations" in the *Bhagavadgītā* he claims to be identical with the game of dice itself: "I am the gambling of rogues" (10.36).

Buddhist tradition sustains the same critique of gambling without such accent on the ambiguity. In the sixteenth chapter of the *Parabhava Sutta,* the Buddha includes addiction to women, strong drink, and dice as one of eleven combinations of means whereby men are brought to loss. The text contrasts these eleven roads to ruin with the one path to victory: loving the *dhamma,* the Buddha's teaching. Elsewhere, monks are warned that numerous games and spectacles—including combats between elephants, horses, buffalo, bulls, goats, rams, and cocks; various board games; chariot racing; and dicing—are addictive distractions and detrimental to virtue (*Tevijja Sutta, Majjhima Sīlam* 2–4).

Gambling Gods, Demons, and Heroes. Yet even the gods—not to mention their demonic adversaries—are wont to gamble. Yahveh makes an implied wager with Satan that Job will remain blameless and upright when deprived of all he has (*Jb.* 1:6–12). In Christian traditions, the devil continues to gamble for the human soul, as in Stephen Vincent Benét's story *The Devil and Daniel Webster* (1937). In Tibet, an annual ceremony was performed in which a priest representing a grand lama played dice with a man dressed as a demonic ghost king. With fixed dice, the priest won, chasing the demon away and confirming the truth of the teaching (Waddell, 1895, p. 512). In India, the two lowest of the four dice throws are demonic. Thus in the epic story of Nala and Damayantī, one demon (Dvāpara) enters the dice, and the other (Kali) "possesses" the hero, dooming him to lose all he has won (*Mahābhārata* 3.55–56). But the Hindu gods play anyway, and are even, as we have seen, identified with gambling. This is true not only of Kṛṣṇa but, more decisively, of Śiva, who is from very early times the lord of gamblers, and who plays dice in classical myths with his wife Parvati.

As noted, Indian dice are named after the four ages (*yugas*), which "roll" four by four a thousand times within the larger time unit of the *kalpa.* The dice play of the divine couple thus represents the continuity of the universe and their absorption with and within it. This "deep play" is one expression of the theological concept of *līlā,* literally "divine play" or "divine sport." The game's disruption holds the implication of the end of the universe (the *mahāpralaya*), while its resumption holds the implication of the recreation (the cosmogony). But insofar as the game is associated with the rise and fall of the *yugas*, it is played ritually at liminal temporal junctures in which the continuity of the universe is imperiled. Śiva and Pārvatī thus provide the mythic model for those who play dice ritually at the festival of Dīvālī (Dīpāvalī), which marks a traditional new year. And it is at the mythic juncture of the Dvāparayuga and the Kaliyuga that the great dice match of the *Mahābhārata* occurs.

One of the most important themes that unites the dice play of Śiva and Pārvatī with the dice match of the *Mahābhārata* is that of stripping. The stakes for which Śiva and Pārvatī play are their clothes and ornaments. When Śiva loses his loincloth, he gets angry, goes off naked, or refuses to pay up. Pārvatī points out that he never wins, except by cheating (O'Flaherty, 1973, pp. 204, 223, 247). Thus it never comes to pass that both of them are reduced to nakedness, which would imply their merger as Śiva and Śakti, Puruṣa and Prakṛti, at the *mahāpralaya.* What is striking about the dice match in the *Mahābhārata* is that after the five Paṇḍava brothers have gambled away everything, even their freedom and their wife-in-common, Draupadī, the culminating act is the attempt by the winners (the Kauravas) to disrobe the heroine in front of her husbands and the whole assembly. As Draupadī is an incarnation of the Goddess, the miraculous intervention by Kṛṣṇa that prevents her stripping is a sign that the dissolution of the universe will not occur in untimely fashion during the intra-*yuga* period in which the story is set.

It is seen, then, that divine gambling involves persistent encounters with the demonic. Hindu materials carry this theme to great depths, accentuating a continuum between demonic possession and divine rapture. In South Indian *terukkūttu* ("street-drama") folk plays that enact the epic story, the attempts by the Kaurava Duḥśāsana to disrobe Draupadī result in his demonic possession, while Draupadī at the same time experiences the most sublime *bhakti* ("divine love"). On the divine-demonic turf of gambling, in fact, no hero can hope to win without recourse to the powers that hold the demonic in check. The hero is thus the one who is willing to take the risk, even against the seemingly highest odds. It is striking how many epics include episodes of gambling, and even more striking how frequently the "good" hero loses, awaiting final triumph or vindication elsewhere. This occurs not only in the *Mahābhārata* but in Indian folk epics as well. In the Tamil folk epic *The Elder Brother's Story,* the twin brothers play six games of dice with Viṣṇu at intervals preceding dramatic turns of fortune, the last of which is their death (Beck, 1982, p. 143). In the Telugu epic

The Heroes of Palnāḍu, a cockfight wager divides irreparably the two camps of half brothers, and a game of tops and a dice match between another set of younger brothers in the heroic camp foreshadow the events that lead to their death. In recent years, actual cockfights have been outlawed at the festivals at which these stories are recited (Roghair, 1982, pp. 30 and 62–295 passim). In the Tibetan epic of Gesar of Ling, the hero repeatedly plays *mōs* (see Waddell, 1895, pp. 465–474), a game of divination using colored pebbles, before his adventures. Here the lots fall out in the divine hero's favor. In the Mwindo epic of the Nyanga people of the Congo Republic, the hero Mwindo plays *wiki,* a gambling game with seeds. Mwindo plays in the underworld against the supreme divinity of fire, first losing everything and then winning it back, in an effort to reclaim his antagonistic father from the underworld with a view toward their reconciliation.

Yet there is another dimension to the stance of the heroic gambler that figures, at least metaphorically, in all the great religions of faith: that of the person who may lose everything, or be stripped like Job or Draupadī, but will not gamble away salvation. In positive terms, this is the wager that God exists, the famous wager that Pascal set forth with such precision in his *Pensées* (1670):

> But here there is an infinity of infinitely happy life to be won, one chance of winning against a finite number of chances of losing. That leaves no choice; wherever there is infinity, and where there are not infinite chances of losing against that of winning, there is no room for hesitation. You must give everything. And thus, since you are obliged to play, you must be renouncing reason if you hoard your life rather than risk it for an infinite gain, just as likely to occur as a loss amounting to nothing. (Krailsheimer, 1966, p. 151)

Pascal is thus at pains to show that the central bet, as in the Balinese cockfight, is for even money.

See Also Chance; Divination; Games.

Bibliography

A good bibliography, mainly on the history and legislation of European and American gambling, is found in Stephen Powell's *A Gambling Bibliography, Based on the Collection, University of Nevada, Las Vegas* (Las Vegas, 1972). Valuable encyclopedia articles include those by J. L. Paton on "Gambling," E. Sidney Hartland on "Games," and G. Margoulith on "Games (Hebrew and Jewish)," in the *Encyclopaedia of Religion and Ethics,* edited by James Hastings, vol. 6 (Edinburgh, 1913); T. Slater's "Gambling," in *Catholic Encyclopedia,* vol. 6 (New York, 1909); and R. F. Schnell's "Games OT," in *The Interpreter's Dictionary of the Bible,* edited by George Arthur Buttrick (New York, 1962).

For theoretical discussion, see Edward Burnett Tylor's *Primitive Culture,* vol. 1, *The Origins of Culture* (1871; reprint, New York, 1958), pp. 78–83, emphasizing diffusion and divination, and Charles John Erasmus's "Patolli, Pachisi, and the Limitation of Possibilities," *Southwestern Journal of Anthropology* 6 (1950): 369–387, which evaluates Tylor's views and various opposing views (including those of Robert Stewart Culin). On "play" in different aspects, see Adolf E. Jensen's *Myth and Cult among Primitive Peoples,* translated by Marianna Tax Choldin and Wolfgang Weissleder (Chicago, 1963), pp. 59–64, and, especially, Clifford Geertz's *The Interpretation of Cultures: Selected Essays* (New York, 1973), pp. 412–453, on the Balinese cockfight. Recent proceedings of the Association for the Anthropological Study of Play (ATASP) are worth consulting, especially for the following: Bernard Mergen's "Reisman Redux: Football as Work, Play, Ritual and Metaphor" and Robert L. Humphrey's "Suggestions for a Cognitive Study of the Mesoamerican Ball Game," in *Play as Context* (ATASP Proceedings, 1979), edited by Alyce Taylor Cheska (West Point, N.Y., 1981), and Pierre Ventur's "Mopan Maya Dice Games from the Southern Peten," in *Play and Culture* (ATASP Proceedings, 1980), edited by Helen B. Schwartzman (West Point, N.Y., 1980).

On documentation, see Frederic V. Grunfeld's *Games of the World* (New York, 1975), for informed discussion with illustrations. On American Indian games, see the classic study by Robert Stewart Culin, *Games of the North American Indians,* "Bureau of American Ethnology Report," no. 24 (1907; reprint, Washington, D. C., 1973). See also Rafael Karsten's "Ceremonial Games of the South American Indians" (in English), *Societas Scientarum Fennica: Commentationes Humanarum Litterarum,* vol. 3, pt. 2 (Helsinki, 1930); Jan C. Heesterman's *The Ancient Indian Royal Consecration* (The Hague, 1957); Liansheng Yang's *Excursions in Sinology* (Cambridge, Mass., 1969); L. Austune Waddell's *The Buddhism of Tibet, or Lamaism* (1895; reprint, Cambridge, 1958). On prohibitions of gambling, see the articles by Hartland, Paton, and Slater mentioned above; M. M. Knappen's *Tudor Puritanism* (Chicago, 1939); and *The Qur'ān,* translated by E. H. Palmer in "Sacred Books of the East," vol. 6 (1880; reprint, Delhi, 1970).

On gambling in myths and epics, see Wendy Doniger O'Flaherty's *Asceticism and Eroticism in the Mythology of Siva* (Oxford, 1973); Brenda E. F. Beck's *The Three Twins: The Telling of a South Indian Folk Epic* (Bloomington, Ind., 1982); Gene H. Roghair's *The Epic of Palnadu: A Study and Translation of Palnati Virula Katha* (Oxford, 1982); Alexandra David-Neel's *The Superhuman Life of Gesar of Ling,* translated by Violet Sydney, rev. ed. (London, 1959); and Daniel P. Biebuyck and Kohombo C. Mateene's *The Mwindo Epic* (Berkeley, Calif., 1969). On Pascal's wager, see Blaise Pascal's *Pensées,* translated by A. J. Krailsheimer (Harmondsworth, 1966).

New Sources

Handelman, Don, and David Shulman. *God Inside Out: Siva's Game of Dice.* New York, 1997.

Alf Hiltebeitel (1987)
Revised Bibliography

GAMES are analytically distinguished from other forms of contest by being framed as "play" and from other forms of play by their competitive format and the institutional—public, systematic, and jural—character of their rules. The

American anthropologist Gregory Bateson (1972, pp. 177–193) has described the universal semantic process by which behaviors are framed as play. Conventionalized signals create a "metamessage" that instructs players not to take the behaviors they engage in as denoting what those behaviors would denote in other, nonplay, contexts. In this sense, game actions are "untrue." A nip is not a bite, a bullfight is not a hunt, a checkmate is not a regicide, a soccer match is not a war, a wrestling bout or footrace is not a cosmogony or theogony, regardless of overt similarities in the words, objects, gestures, emotional states, or social categories of persons involved. The framing of contests as play makes them self-referential in several ways, shifting attributed motivation to intrinsic enjoyment and sociability, turning means into ends in themselves, and understanding extrinsic outcomes as "mere" contingencies.

Yet, paradoxically, as Bateson and many other theorists of play have noted, the prior and consensual assertion of untruth, in the sense of disconnection from standard meanings, makes assertions of truthful correspondences between the worlds of nonplay and play possible, likely, and even predominant over a discourse of "set-apartness." Like other play forms, games are about boundaries and the boundaries between boundaries. Games create, in the phrases of the English psychoanalyst D. W. Winnicott (1971), a world of "transitional objects," a realm of the "not-not-true." Freedom from denotation makes rich freedom for connotation, for human individuals and groups to re-represent their lives to themselves in "experimental" ways. Alternative or virtual realities, including those asserted by religion, can thus be tested against what the phenomenologist Alfred Schutz termed "the paramount realities of everyday life."

PLAY IN CULTURE: THE RELIGIOUS CHARACTER OF GAMES. Contest and representation are basic aspects of play, argued the Dutch historian Johan Huizinga in his manifesto *Homo Ludens,* and they may "unite in such a way that the game 'represents' a contest or else becomes a contest for the best representation of something" (1955, p. 13). The materials of games are drawn from the sociocultural world and at the same time stand in figurative relations—metaphoric, analogical, symbolic—with it. "The more profound, double sense of 'social game,'" said the German sociologist Georg Simmel, "is not only that the game is played in a society (as its external medium) but that, with its help, people actually 'play' 'society'," including the society of the gods (1950, p. 50). Particularly where enjoyment, competition, and gambling supply strong motivations to attend to the progress and outcome of games, this setting of the empirical world in juxtaposition with "another" world can lead to an interrogation of their relationship sufficient to involve ultimate epistemological questions and functional necessities of human existence. On this general ground, the appearance of game forms in the religious mythologies and cults of various peoples has been explained by writers and scholars, some of whom have gone on to find in the ludic process a mode of transcendence and, therefore, an essential aspect of the religious imagination itself.

Among Western humanists, Huizinga has perhaps been the boldest in this regard. In *Homo Ludens,* he argued for "the identity of play and ritual" and even claimed, on the authority of Plato, that the sacred can be comprised in the category of play (pp. 18–19). "God alone is worthy of supreme seriousness," so Huizinga translated Plato (*Laws* 7.803), "but man is made God's plaything, and that is the best part of him. . . . What then is the right way of living? Life must be lived as play, playing certain games, making sacrifices, singing and dancing, and then a man will be able to propitiate the gods, and defend himself against his enemies, and win the contest." Whether Plato really meant to identify "play and holiness" so thoroughly can be disputed. Moreover, as the final clause of Huizinga's reading of Plato suggests, classicists have found reason to doubt that the "for-their-own-sake" character Huizinga believed crucial to "true play and games" was really present or developed in classical Greek ideology.

From the famous stadium games to the isomorphic agonistic ethos and format in other cultural domains, elements that together comprise what historians and sociologists from Jakob Burckhardt (1898–1902) to Alvin W. Gouldner (1965) have styled the "Greek contest system," functional requirements, inextricably civic and religious, do not appear to have been culturally "bracketed off" as contingencies in the classical world, as they have been in that stream of European thought that Huizinga so well represented. In Greek mythology and theology, in notable contrast to Christianity, the gods themselves played games, chartered the games of human beings, and intervened in them as "co-players." In athletic games—as the poetry of Pindar makes evocatively plain—individual fate, the polity, and the divine world found a preferential idiom of communication in archaic and classical Greek culture, such that an *axis mundi,* in the sense discussed by Mircea Eliade, could be created in the person of the victorious athlete.

The Olympic games, the Delphic oracle, and Homeric poetry emerged together in the eighth century BCE as pan-Hellenic institutions, just as the segmentary and rivalrous city-state was arising as the dominant form of social organization within the Greek world. Relations among these key institutions are apparent in the traditions of the ancient Olympic games. Homeric theology and hero cults came to inform the charter myths of the games at Olympia, and a famous oracle at Delphi (where crown games were also celebrated) "renewed" the sanction from Zeus, to whose worship the Olympic festival was devoted. The great games gave rise to practices seeking to distinguish Greek from non-Greek (*barbaroi* were not to compete at Olympia) and to mediate between Greek mythic and human time. Though its significance is much debated, the reckoning of dates according to the formula "in the second year of the Olympiad in which so-and-so won the *stade*" provided Greece with her main calendar of historical time beyond city-state and regional limitations.

One mythic tradition ascribes the foundation of the Olympic games to Idean Herakles, another to Pelops's victory over King Oenomaus in a chariot race for the latter's daughter Hippodamia ("horse woman"). Here, as in the related story of Atalanta in the Greek corpus and in other Indo-European contexts, comparative mythologists such as James G. Frazer, Georges Dumézil, Eliade, and Bernard Jeu have recognized a repeated pattern associating sacred marriage (*hieros gamos*), an implicit theogony (often of newer gods over older ones), the acquisition of transforming technology (fire, the horse, metallurgy, the chariot), the domestication of invader kings ("Dorians" in the Greek case), and the athletic race that embodies, mediates, and "resolves" these generative contests between vigorous and dying god-kings, male and female, earth and heaven, nature and culture, cosmos and history.

Games transform ambiguous, perturbed, or disputed potentials and conditions into certain outcomes, and this is one reason for their widespread association, in myth or in practice, with such ritualized natural and social transitions as seasonal cycles, birth, initiation, marriage, funerals, and warfare. Furthermore, games necessarily incorporate a dialectic between hierarchy and equality, two central organizing principles of human social arrangements and cognitive functioning. From an (at least asserted or presumed) equality before the rules of the game results a ranked hierarchy of outcomes. Societies and theologies differ in the relative valuation placed on hierarchy and equality in human and divine affairs and, thus, differentially emphasize one or the other pole in games. Yet for all known social types, games appear, in the expression of the French anthropologist Claude Lévi-Strauss, to be "good to think with" and, as the present-day Olympic games forcefully illustrate, may permit highly diverse and rivalrous social formations to compete cooperatively. If games have been seen as "the moral equivalent of war," it is because warfare and other means of political and ideological domination, including religion, have their moral dimensions.

Ingomar Weiler (1981) finds the "contest system" not limited to Greece but widespread in the ancient Mediterranean world, and scholars like Huizinga emphasize parallels to the Greek and Roman materials in non-Western warrior-states. In the Hindu *Mahābhārata,* the world is conceived as a game of dice between Śiva and his queen (8.2368, 8.2381), and a dice match for the kingdom sets off the conflict between the Kauravas and the Pāṇḍavas that organizes the epic. "I am the dicing of tricksters," says Kṛṣṇa in the *Bhagavadgītā* (10.36), and forms of *līlā,* or sacred play, are widely associated with this god and his worship. According to Marcel Granet (1930), the Chinese cosmic duality of *yin* and *yang* replayed important social dualisms; festal, magical competitions of many sorts were both the central agencies for regenerating life in the early "tribal" period and a means by which the later transformation to state institutions was accomplished. The Spanish philosopher Ortega y Gasset likewise argued for the "sportive origin of the state" out of primitive institutions of ritual contest involving both cosmological and social sanctions.

The ethnology of nonliterate "primitive" societies provided further rich material for such humanistic speculations. In his elaborate compendium *Games of the North American Indians,* Stewart Culin observed the common occurrence of game motifs in the origin myths of a wide variety of linguistically and culturally unrelated tribes. The complementarity in rivalry of the "divine twins"—associated with oppositions between night and day, winter and summer, east and west, morning and evening stars, consanguinal and affinal kin—or of a demiurgic First Man or First Woman with monsters, nature, or each other is a widespread motif. In folklore, culture-creating heroes—Coyote, Raven, or Spider—are frequently trickster beings whose fondness for games, as with other supernaturals, is both a source of their power and a means by which they can be manipulated for human moral or material purposes. As to adult human games, which he divided into those of "chance" and those of "dexterity," Culin concluded that "In general, [they] appear to be played ceremonially, as pleasing to the gods, with the object of securing fertility, causing rain, giving and prolonging life, expelling demons, or curing sickness" (Culin, 1975, p. 34).

Theories Regarding the "Desacralization" of Games. This stress on the religious character of games in the cultures of exotic or prestigiously ancestral "others" was generated by and contributed to those broader evolutionist trends of European thought variously styled "rationalization," "modernization," and "secularization." Huizinga and other philosophers of history, while seeking to show the essential unity of humankind in play, nevertheless saw games as becoming progressively "secularized" through "universal cultural history." British classicists, most notably Jane E. Harrison, proposed the view that games—like such other forms of cultural expression as theater, dance, music, and poetry—had separated from an original religious ritual matrix in the primitive and ancient worlds. Where games were seen to retain magical or religious elements, such as peasant Shrovetide football matches in the "folk cultures" of early modern France and England or the grand *sumō* tournaments of Shintō Japan or the various martial arts competitions in monastic communities of the Near and Far East, these were interpreted as backward "survivals" of an archaic past in "fossil" social structures still partially attuned in cult to cosmological and agricultural rhythms. Such views fit well with the nineteenth-century development of Western social science, centered around a purported evolutionary passage—"of potentially universal significance," as Max Weber put it—from "traditional" to "modern" societies under the impact of the industrial revolution and modern science. From important means by which communities represented their ultimate concerns to themselves and engaged in imitative worship, games became associated, in such Western eyes, with the sphere of secular leisure, recreation, mass entertainment:

"mere games" of undoubted commercial or social value but of little sacred or spiritual significance.

While still very influential, the "modernization" point of view has been criticized as Eurocentric and imperialist. Moreover, social history has shown that in the West itself religion has not regularly and inevitably declined and that the cultural history of forms like games has not followed any simple unilinear pattern. As symbolized by the emperor Theodosius's suppression of the Olympic games as a "pagan rite," early Christianity did indeed oppose itself to Greek (and certainly Roman) traditions of public games, save in the appropriation of athletics as an ascetic metaphor by canonical writers like the apostle Paul. A centuries-long tradition culminating in continental and English "puritanism" did seek to suppress games, gambling, and other forms of folk amusement as "works of the devil" that turned the Christian away from sober religious duty, the social predominance of the churches, and disciplined labor. Through much of the twentieth century, religious leaders and sociologists alike have attributed declining church attendance, where it has occurred, in part to the increasing popularity of sports events and other kinds of mass recreation on the Sabbath.

Yet contrary trends are everywhere in evidence. In the Middle Ages, the church may have turned against the cult of the body in athletic games, but it attached itself to the medieval tournament. In the contemporary *palio* horse race of Siena, Italy, which dates back to the eleventh century, the cult of the Virgin Mary and priestly blessings of the rival *contrade* are central features of the ritual contest. In nineteenth-century England, devout Anglican schoolmasters and Christian socialists, like Thomas Hughes and Charles Kingsley, played the central role in elaborating the ideology of "muscular Christianity," that combination of athletic games, virility, fair play, courage, and defense of the weak associated with a new *imitatio Christi,* on the one side, and with English colonialism, on the other. Many contemporary English soccer clubs are descended from church organizations, and missionaries in the British Empire sought not only to suppress the indigenous games of conquered peoples, particularly those with overt sexual and magical content, but to replace them with cricket, soccer, hockey, and running as "schools of Christian character." Upon decolonization in "new nations"—as East African long-distance running, Trobriand and Caribbean cricket, and Indian field hockey indicate—these game forms have often been retained, but transformed to reaccommodate indigenous cultural values or to serve "civil" or "national" religion, whether in the form of an explicit cult of the state or a more diffuse "functional equivalent" of traditional religious institutions. In dialectical concert with enduring ludic forms bent to "nativist" purposes—West African wrestling, Native American running (see Nabokov, 1981), central Asian *buzkashi,* Japanese *sumō,* or the Balinese cockfight made famous by the anthropologist Clifford Geertz (1972)—such transformations of imposed forms illustrate the inadequacies of any unilineal or evolutionary theory of world history and the place of games within it. Again in the Judeo-Christian context, home of such theories, present-day developments—from a skiing pope, decorated with the Olympic Order, to the incipient interlock between the directorates of the World Council of Churches and the International Olympic Committee, to the widespread activity of Christian athletes in domestic and foreign missionizing—further illustrate the labile relations between religion and games. Nor are such relations limited to practical and institutional exigencies. The recent "theology of play" movement in Christian religious circles (see Moltmann, 1972), with its rebellious attempt to reshape the image of the deity and its arguments that in the freedom and joy of games and festivity humans achieve a foretaste of the kingdom of heaven, suggests how the potentials for transcendence in play must ever draw religion into a dialogue with ludic form and experience. Even religions whose orthodox or mainstream versions may find less explicit place for play in their theophanies, cults, and ethics—Judaism, Christianity, and Islam, perhaps in contrast to Hinduism, Buddhism, and many tribal religions—must preoccupy themselves with what comparative religionist David L. Miller (1970, p. 14) calls "the game game," that effort to discover, articulate, and conform to an "ultimate reality" that sets a limit to divine and human manipulation.

Games and Social Life. Dissatisfaction with evolutionist or modernization perspectives has led to closer attention by theorists to the types and internal properties of games. The French sociologist of religion Roger Caillois suggested in *Man, Play, and Games* (1961) that games can be usefully placed along a continuum from *paidia* (relatively unstructured, spontaneous, labile forms typified by many children's games) to those of *ludus* (more conventionalized, jural, and elaborated forms). All true games, however, minimally involve specification of a goal for action, delimitations of space and time, selection of some subset of possibilities in a total action field as relevant and permissible (the "moves" of the game), rules for the initial apportioning of resources and roles and their reapportioning in the course of play, and criteria for evaluating the outcomes (success or failure, winning or losing). By selectively emphasizing features of this core structure of games, a number of classification schemes have been generated to reveal dominant metaphysical assumptions and to model theoretically how individuals and groups "play society."

Like most continental game theorists, Caillois focused on the experiential aspects of game types. Seeking not merely a sociology of games but a "sociology derived from games," Caillois subsumed all games under four categories: agon (competition), *alea* (chance), mimicry (simulation), and *ilinx* (vertigo). This scheme is helpful in parsing the religious functions associated with types of games: cosmological, eschatological, moral contests; divination; imitative magic and ceremonial; altered states of consciousness. But it has generated little insight of a truly comparative nature. Actual games contain combinations of these aspects—all games are in some sense competitive, for example—and all religions accommodate these functions. The insights of psychoanalysis, which sees in play and games the disguised representation of unconscious conflicts and a compulsion to repeat "primitive" traumas so as to master them, have been limited by inattention to cultural context and to the complexity and variety of game forms. Continental structuralism of the psychological sort associated with Piaget finds an important place for children's games in characterizing mental development, and the anthropological sort associated with Lévi-Strauss (1966, pp. 30–33) has revealed much of the symbolic "logic of the concrete" that connects games to myth, ritual, and kinship. Yet in the search for universal structures of mind these theories also overlook social and historical context, and their contributions have been largely methodological.

British and North American social scientists, on the other hand, have largely focused on the strategic and role-playing aspects of games, exploring them from the functional standpoint of social integration, decision making, and value transmission. "Game theory" in the social and information sciences has produced taxonomies of rational calculation and strategic choice among individual actors seeking to maximize their payoffs in the face of uncertainty and limited resources. Critics, however, have found "game theory" to be a fundamental misnomer, since play, under its aspects of intrinsic motivation and Batesonian framing, is missing or unaccounted for in such understandings of social action. "Game theory" has contributed little to the analysis of specifically religious institutions.

Social psychologists have focused on the role playing and socialization features of games to construct fundamental questions about the organization of the self itself. George Herbert Mead pointed to the youngster's ability to play a single position in a baseball game while articulating that role with all of the others on the field as a sign of and a means toward development of a "reflexive self," incorporating the expectations of others in the context of the "generalized other" represented by the total game. Erving Goffman (1967, 1974) still further stressed the aspects of role-playing, mimicry, dissimulation, and the "rules for breaking the rules" in building an explicit theory from the now popular metaphorical utterance, "social life is a game." The human self is seen by Goffman to be endlessly preoccupied with "the arts of impression management," ludic yet ever-watchful to define situations so as to prevent embarrassment to oneself and others. Like formal "game theory," social psychologies built from the model of games have contributed less to the understanding of social institutions per se, including religious ones, than they have to understanding individual and small-group processes of negotiation. At the same time, such theories do implicitly challenge authoritative ontologies and conventional understandings of divine affairs in Western cultures.

While games undoubtedly serve to reproduce or to rebel against dominant social structures and ideologies, they have been seen by recent anthropologists as speculative enterprises as well, means by which human communities discover their dominant values in the first place and formulate alternatives to them. Victor Turner—who like Huizinga saw cultural life as a process of passage from institutional structure to ludic, "antistructural" recombination, to the incrustations of structure once again—extended analysis of religious ritual to understand play forms in this way (1974). Clifford Geertz (1972), who sees the interpretation of experiences as in and of itself a human necessity, argues that the Balinese cockfight is a form of "social metacommentary," a "story the Balinese tell about themselves," a function likewise ascribed to religious ritual. Other anthropologists (Don Handelman and I, for example) find it important to stress the differences between games and ritual as collective hermeneutics. On the Batesonian level of metacommunication, ritual does seem to be framed differently from play. Ritual asserts a priori that all statements within it are true and not untrue and creates a world of "let us believe" rather than of "let us make believe."

Such distinctions make it possible to recognize complex performance types that incorporate both rite and game, like the *palio* or the Olympics, and depend for their power on moving actors and audiences back and forth from frame to frame. Then too, activities are reframed through the course of a people's history. Alexander Lesser (1978) has shown how the Pawnee hand game passed from a form of amusement to a religious salvation ritual and back again between 1865 and 1930, a process reminiscent of athletics in nineteenth-century England. What is discovered as possible (or impossible) in play and given organized display in games may be asserted by ritual as undeniable. Whether this is the essential relation between games and religion we will not know until greater conceptual clarity and theoretical sophistication are brought to bear on the vast new findings in the ethnology and social history of games, such that a ludic equivalent to Max Weber's comparative "economic ethics of the world religions" is achieved.

SEE ALSO Gambling; Martial Arts; Play; Reflexivity.

BIBLIOGRAPHY

The charter discussion of the Greek "agonistic" system is found in Jakob Burckhardt's *Griechische Kulturgeschichte,* 4 vols. (Berlin, 1898–1902), translated by Palmer Hilty in abridged form as *History of Greek Culture* (New York, 1963). On the classical world, see also Alvin W. Gouldner's *Enter Plato* (New York, 1965). In the soundest scholarly guide to athletic games in the ancient Mediterranean world, *Sport bei den Völkern der alten Welt* (Darmstadt, 1981), Ingomar Weiler argues against the uniqueness of Greece in this area, a position taken by Johan Huizinga as well. Huizinga's *Homo Ludens* (Boston, 1955) remains the essential manifesto on the role of play in culture, including relationships between games and religion. Victor Turner extends his discussion of religious ritual to include the role of play in culture in "Liminal to Liminoid, in Play, Flow and Ritual," *Rice University Studies* 60 (Summer 1974): 53–92.

Roger Caillois presents a taxonomy of games, intended both to refine Huizinga's insights and to organize cross-cultural material in more useful fashion, in *Man, Play, and Games* (New York, 1961). Among ethnological compendia on games in "primitive" societies, Stewart Culin's *Games of the North American Indians* (1907; Washington, D.C., 1975) has been the most widely cited. On running as practiced by Native Americans, see Peter Nabokov's *Indian Running* (Santa Barbara, Calif., 1981). Anthropological case studies of special value include Alexander Lesser's *The Pawnee Ghost Dance Hand Game* (Madison, Wis., 1978) and Clifford Geertz's "Deep Play: Notes on the Balinese Cock Fight," *Daedalus* 101 (1972): 1–38. On China, see Marcel Granet's *Chinese Civilization* (London, 1930).

David L. Miller's *Gods and Games* (New York, 1970) is indicative of the Christian "theology of play" movement and contains valuable discussions of the role of games in contemporary existential, linguistic, and mathematical philosophy. Also see Jürgen Moltmann's *Theology of Play* (New York, 1972).

Gregory Bateson's fundamental contribution to understanding play and games as forms of metacommunication is contained in "A Theory of Play and Fantasy," in his *Steps to an Ecology of Mind* (New York, 1972). Erving Goffman develops the view of social life as a game in several works, including *Interaction Ritual* (Garden City, N.Y., 1967) and *Frame Analysis* (New York, 1974). Also see Georg Simmel's discussion on social reality as play in *The Sociology of Georg Simmel,* translated and edited by Kurt H. Wolff (Glencoe, Ill., 1950). On the role of play in human development, see D. W. Winnicott's *Playing and Reality* (London, 1971). Claude Lévi-Strauss's discussion of the different logics of games and rituals is found in his *The Savage Mind* (Chicago, 1966). Don Handelman considers related problems in his "Play and Ritual: Complementary Forms of Metacommunication" in *It's a Funny Thing, Humour,* edited by A. J. Chapman and H. Foot (London, 1977), pp. 135–192. Complex performance forms joining games and rites are the subject of my "Olympic Games and the Theory of Spectacle in Modern Societies," in *Rite, Drama, Festival, Spectacle* (Philadelphia, 1984), pp. 241–280.

JOHN J. MACALOON (1987)

GAMLIʾEL OF YAVNEH, also known as Gamliʾel II, was a Palestinian tanna, rabbi, patriarch (*nasiʾ*), and head of the academy at Yavneh in the late first and early second century. In contrast to contemporary authorities, who either bear no title or, more often, are referred to by the title *rabbi,* Gamliʾel was accorded the apparently honorific title *rabban,* which he shares with other leaders of the patriarchal house (see *Avot* 1.16, 1.18). His traditions are recorded in the Mishnah and related texts.

Gamliʾel bore major responsibility for the centralization of rabbinical authority at Yavneh following the war with the Romans in 66–70. Succeeding the apparent founder of that academy, Yoḥanan ben Zakkʾai, Gamliʾel was in a position to guide the rabbinical effort in the reconstruction of a nation that had seen its spiritual center in the Jerusalem Temple destroyed, a nation that lacked clear leadership. To address this challenge, Gamliʾel supported the religious ascendency of the Yavneh academy and the political and religious authority of a Sanhedrin reconstituted under his leadership. He was later believed to have had a hereditary claim on the patriarchate.

It it reported that Gamliʾel sometimes conducted this campaign in an undiplomatic manner, but he won the support of contemporary rabbinical authorities. To assure a centralized authority, he insisted on the power of his court to fix the calendar for all of Jewry, to ensure the consistency of observance. To similar ends he demanded that individuals bow to the decision of the collective rabbinate in disputes, an insistence that in one instance is believed to have led to the ban on Eliʿezer ben Hyrcanus (B.T., *B.M.* 59b) and in another caused Yehoshuʿa ben Ḥananyah to transgress what by his reckoning was Yom Kippur (*R. ha-Sh.* 2.8–9). Nevertheless, he is described as declaring that this demand was not to assure his own honor, but to assure that "disputes not be multiplied in Israel" (B.T., *B.M.* 59b).

In response to the vacuum left in the wake of the Temple's destruction, tradition bears witness to Gamliʾel's activity in establishing ritual and prayer norms. His academy formalized the eighteen-benediction prayer (Shemoneh ʿEsreh) that has been employed in various forms to this day. Perhaps to facilitate its acceptance as the core of Jewish daily worship, he allowed formal representatives to recite the prayer for untutored individuals. In addition, Gamliʾel contributed significantly to the formulation of a post-Temple Passover Seder.

Appropriately to the image of patriarch, Gamliʾel is described as having had extensive exchanges with "philosophers" and others outside the Judaic tradition. Gamliʾel's son Shimʿon reports that "in my father's house five hundred [children] studied Greek wisdom . . . because they were close to the authorities" (B.T., *Sot.* 49b; Tosefta, *Sot.* 15.8). Sources relate that Roman authorities were sympathetic to Gamliʾel and the Judaism that he taught, and that Gamliʾel occasionally reciprocated their sympathy.

Gamliʾel's status is enhanced by the stories of his extensive travels, including a trip to Rome. He is also described as wealthy and spoiled, and his relationship with his righteous slave, Tabi, is legendary.

Gamliʾel was apparently a person of great piety and sensitivity. He was strict with himself, even when lenient with others, and he refused to excuse himself from his responsibilities to heaven for even one moment. To alleviate the immense burden put upon surviving relatives who had to see to the burial of their deceased, Gamliʾel had himself buried in simple shrouds, a practice followed by Jews to this day.

Gamliʾel's traditions are outstanding for the relatively high proportion that are set down in narrative form. This is probably connected to his patriarchal authority at a crucial period in history. He came to serve as a model for the rabbinic community. Also notable is the absence of significant contributions to criminal statutes, reflecting perhaps the diminished authority of the early patriarchate in this area.

See Also Sanhedrin; Tannaim.

Bibliography

The most comprehensive review of Gamliʾel's traditions is Shammai Kanter's *Rabban Gamaliel II, the Legal Traditions* (Chico, Calif., 1980). On Gamliʾel's deposition from leadership of the Yavnean academy, an event central to his struggle for authority, see Robert Goldenberg's "The Deposition of Rabban Gamaliel II: An Examination of the Sources," *Journal of Jewish Studies* 23 (Autumn 1972): 167–190. For a biography that also examines the nonlegal traditions, see "Gamaliʾel ben Shimʿon ha-neherag" in Aaron Hyman's *Toledot tannaʾim ve-amoraʾim* (1910; reprint, Jerusalem, 1964).

New Sources

Habas-Rubin, Ephrat. "Rabban Gamaliel of Yavneh and His Sons: The Patriarchate before and after the Bar Kokhva Revolt." *Journal of Jewish Studies* 50 (1999): 21–37.

Hanna, Ralph, and David Lawton, eds. *The Siege of Jerusalem.* Oxford, 2003.

Neusner, Jacob. "Die Pharisäer vor und nach der Tempelzerstörung des Jahres 70 n.Chr." In *Tempelkult und Tempelzerstörung: Festschrift für Clemens Thoma zum 60 Geburtstag,* edited by Simon Laur and Hanspeter Ernst, pp. 71–104. Bern and New York, 1995.

David Kraemer (1987)
Revised Bibliography

GAMLIʾEL THE ELDER

GAMLIʾEL THE ELDER (fl. first half of the first century CE), properly Rabban ("our teacher") Gamliʾel the Elder; the first Jewish teacher with this title. Gamliʾel was a son or grandson of Hillel and likewise was regarded in rabbinic tradition as a *nasiʾ* (head of the court). He is designated "the Elder" in Talmudic literature apparently to distinguish him from Gamliʾel of Yavneh (Gamliʾel II) with whom he is often confused, and he is referred to as a Pharisee and "teacher of the Law" in *Acts of the Apostles* (5:34).

Gamliʾel appears frequently in tannaitic sources, where his various *taanot* (enactments) are recorded. The following examples from Mishnah *Giṭṭin* (4.2–3) were considered "for the general welfare":

1. A man who wishes to invalidate a divorce document that he has already sent to his wife must convene a court in her town rather than elsewhere. Otherwise she may mistakenly believe the document is still valid and remarry.
2. Both parties to a divorce are required to use all of the names by which they are known when signing the document.
3. All witnesses to the delivery of the document must sign it.

These *taanot* were especially intended to benefit women. Similarly, Gamliʾel permitted a woman to remarry based on the testimony of one witness to the death of her husband, rather than the two generally required by Jewish law (*Yev.* 16.7). Of special interest are the letters that Gamliʾel is reported to have dictated on the steps of the Temple (Tosefta *San.* 2.6 and parallels). Those sent to "our brethren" in the upper and lower south (Daroma) and in the upper and lower Galilee contained reminders pertaining to tithes. Another directed to "our brethren" in Babylonia and Media and to all other exiles of Israel announced the leap year. It was said (*Soṭ.* 9.15) that "when Rabban Gamliʾel the Elder died, the glory of the Torah ceased and purity and abstinence perished."

In *Acts* (5:34ff.), Gamliʾel (Gamaliel) pleads with fellow members of the Sanhedrin to free the apostles. Elsewhere in *Acts* (22:3), Paul states that he was brought up "at the feet of" Gamliʾel from whom he gained knowledge of the "ancestral law." The tendency has been to view these traditions in the context of Luke's apologetic. The later, apocryphal Christian tradition transformed Gamliʾel into a secret Christian (*Ps. Clement. Recog.* 1:65–67) and into a martyr who died in the process of trying to defend and protect Stephen (*Discourse of Gregory, Priest of Antioch*). There is also an apocryphal, *Gospel of Gamaliel,* which relates events pertaining to Good Friday.

See Also Jewish Religious Year; Pharisees.

Bibliography

The references to Rabban Gamliʾel the Elder in Talmudic literature are collected and analyzed in volumes 1 (pp. 341–376) and 3 (pp. 272f., 314f.) of Jacob Neusner's *The Rabbinic Traditions about the Pharisees before 70,* 3 vols. (Leiden, 1971). Neusner questions Gamliʾel's association with Beit Hillel and regards him as more of a "public official" and leader within the Pharisees than a "sectarian authority" of that party. A discussion of Gamliʾel and some of the earlier assessments of him appears in Alexander Guttmann's *Rabbinic Judaism in the Making: A Chapter in the History of the Halakhah from Ezra to Judah I* (Detroit, 1970), pp. 177–182. Information on Gamliʾel in the Christian tradition can be found in volume 2 (pp. 367ff.) of Emil Schürer's *The History of the Jewish People in the Age of Jesus Christ, 175 B.C.–A.D. 135* (1901–1909), a new English version revised and edited by Géza Vermès, Fergus Millar, and Matthew Black (Edinburgh, 1979). Morton S. Enslin questions whether Paul actually "sat at Gamaliel's feet" and the extent of his rabbinic training, in "Paul and Gamaliel," *Journal of Religion* 7 (July 1927): 360–375. On Gamliʾel and the apologetic of Luke, see Jeffrey A. Trumbower, "The Historical Jesus and the Speech of Gamaliel (*Acts* 5:35–39)," *New Testament Studies* 39.4 (1993): 500–517. For an in-depth discussion of the historical issues pertaining to Gamliʾel and Paul, see Bruce Chilton's dicussion in *The Anchor Bible Dictionary,* II (1992), 904–906.

Stuart S. Miller (1987 and 2005)

GĀṆAPATYAS

GĀṆAPATYAS are a sect of Hindus who regard Gaṇeśa (Ganapati) as their supreme object of devotion. They view

Gaṇeśa, the elephant-faced son of Śiva and Parvati, as the form of ultimate reality (*brahman*) that is accessible to the senses, the mind, and (through devotional practices) the heart. Most Hindus worship Gaṇeśa along with other deities because he is the god who overcomes obstacles and makes rites and other undertakings effective. Gāṇapatyas share this view but extend it to make Gaṇeśa their central deity, either as their family or clan patron-god (*kuladevatā*) or their personal lord (*iṣṭadevatā*). Devotion in the first case tends to be more formal and take place during specific ceremonies and festivals, while the second form of devotion is more likely to be personal, informal, and intense.

Although Gāṇapatyas may be found in many parts of India and from many castes, the sect has found its most articulated cultic expression in western India, in the Marathi-speaking region of Maharashtra, among high-caste Hindus. The sect rose to prominence in the region between the seventeenth and nineteenth centuries CE, during the rule of the Marathas. Gaṇeśa worship is also important in South India, where a number of temples are dedicated to him.

Gāṇapatya groups first appeared between the sixth and ninth centuries CE, and worshiped their deity in various forms according to the prevailing Brahmanic and Tantric practices. Two Sanskrit Purāṇas, the *Gaṇeśa* and the *Mudgala,* date from the twelfth and fourteenth centuries CE, respectively. These Purāṇas recount and celebrate the myths of Gaṇeśa's triumphs over demons on behalf of the gods and his devotees. They also include instructions for ritual performance and hymns of praise. Since the seventeenth century there has been a steady flow of devotional literature in both Sanskrit and Marathi.

In Maharashtra, devotion to Gaṇeśa has centered around eight shrines (*aṣṭavināyakas*) clustering around the city of Poona (Pune) and the nearby village of Cincvad, and associated with Gaṇeśa's most famous devotee, Morayā Gosāvi (d. 1651). For the past three centuries Cincvad has served as the administrative center for the sect in the region. The Gāṇapatya tradition enjoyed the patronage of Hindu, and at times Muslim, kings. The *brahman* Peshwas, the hereditary rulers of the Maratha empire after the death of its founder, Śivajī, contributed substantially to the construction of shrines and financing of rituals during the eighteenth and early nineteenth centuries. That patronage continued for a while under British rule, but gradually diminished and has been replaced by contributions from the faithful. As Gaṇeśa's popularity among the masses of Hindus has increased in contemporary times, the Gāṇapatya shrines have prospered.

The sect regards Morayā Gosāvī as its spiritual progenitor. Tradition holds that Morayā migrated from southern India to the Gaṇeśa shrine at Moragaon (70 kilometers southeast of Poona), where he experienced a series of visions of Gaṇeśa. In one vision Gaṇeśa told him that he would incarnate himself in his devotee and remain in his lineage for seven generations. Morayā Gosāvī's own religious charisma and the tradition of living deities in the shrine at Cincvad contributed largely to its religious significance in the region. In 1651 Morayā Gosāvī underwent *jīvansamādhi,* or entombment while alive, in a chamber beneath the shrine, and thereby passed out of visible existence. Devotees believe he attained release (*mokṣa*) from rebirth and that his presence continues to endow the shrine with sacred significance. Several of Morayā Gosāvī's descendants are likewise enshrined at Cincvad. Devotees come there both to honor the image of Gaṇeśa and receive its auspicious sight (*darśana*), and to worship the shrines of Morayā Gosāvī and his descendants.

Twice each year the priests at Cincvad, along with thousands of devotees, take an image of Gaṇeśa from this shrine to the temple at Moragaon, where Morayā Gosāvī received his visions, about a hundred kilometers to the southeast. The second annual pilgrimage coincides with the intensely popular Gaṇeśa festival that is celebrated particularly in the towns and cities of Maharashtra in August and September.

Many Gāṇapatyas make periodic pilgrimages to receive the auspicious viewing of Gaṇeśa at his eight shrines. Devotees maintain that it is particularly salutary to visit all eight shrines in a single pilgrimage.

SEE ALSO Gaṇeśa; Marathi Religions.

BIBLIOGRAPHY

The works by Gāṇapatyas remain almost entirely untranslated into Western languages. Part of the *Gaṇeśa Purāṇa* has been translated and edited by Kiyoshi Yoroi in *Gaṇeśagītā: A Study, Translation with Notes, and a Condensed Rendering of the Commentary of Nilakaṇṭha* (The Hague, 1968). The most complete collection of Gāṇapatya literature and lore in Marathi is Amarendra L. Gadgil's *Śrī Gaṇeś Koś* (Poona, India, 1968). A survey of the Gāṇapatyas in the context of the myth and ritual traditions of Gaṇeśa can be found in my book *Gaṇeśa: Lord of Obstacles, Lord of Beginnings* (New York, 1985). Excellent discussions of the sect and its political significance appear in G. S. Ghurye's *Gods and Men* (Bombay, 1962) and in Laurence W. Preston's "Subregional Religious Centres in the History of Maharashtra: The Sites Sacred to Ganesh," in *Images of Maharashtra: A Regional Profile of India,* edited by N. K. Wagle (Toronto, 1980).

PAUL B. COURTRIGHT (1987)

GANDHI, MOHANDAS

GANDHI, MOHANDAS (1869–1948), political leader, social reformer, and religious visionary of modern India. Although Gandhi initially achieved public notice as a leader of India's nationalist movement and as a champion of nonviolent techniques for resolving conflicts, he was also a religious innovator who did much to encourage the growth of a reformed, liberal Hinduism in India. In the West, Gandhi is venerated by many who seek an intercultural and socially conscious religion and see him as the representative of a universal faith.

RELIGIOUS INFLUENCES ON GANDHI. Mohandas Karamchand Gandhi was born into a *bania* (merchant caste) family in a religiously pluralistic area of western India—the Kathiawar Peninsula in the state of Gujarat. His parents were Vaiṣṇava Hindus who followed the Vallabhācārya tradition of loving devotion to Lord Kṛṣṇa. His father, Karamchand Uttamchand, the chief administrative officer of a princely state, was not a very religious man, but his mother, Putalibai, became a follower of the region's popular Prānāmi cult. This group was founded in the eighteenth century by Mehraj Thakore, known as Prānaṇāth ("master of the life force"), and was influenced by Islam. Prānaṇāth rejected all images of God and, like the famous fifteenth-century Hindu saint Narsinh Mehta, who came from the same region, advocated a direct link with the divine, unmediated by priests and ritual. This Protestant form of Hinduism seems to have been accepted by Gandhi as normative throughout his life.

Other enduring religious influences from Gandhi's childhood came from the Jains and Muslims who frequented the family household. Gandhi's closest childhood friend, Mehtab, was a Muslim, and his spiritual mentor, Raychandbhai, was a Jain. Early contacts with Christian street evangelists in his home town of Porbandar, however, left Gandhi unimpressed.

When Gandhi went to London to study law at the age of nineteen he encountered forms of Christianity of quite a different sort. Respecting vows made to his mother, Gandhi sought meatless fare at a vegetarian restaurant, where his fellow diners were a motly mix of Theosophists, Fabian Socialists, and Christian visionaries who were followers of Tolstoi. These esoteric and socialist forms of Western spirituality made a deep impression on Gandhi and encouraged him to look for parallels in the Hindu tradition.

When, in 1893, Gandhi settled in South Africa as a lawyer (initially serving in a Muslim firm), he was impressed by a Trappist monastery he visited near Durban. He soon set up a series of ashrams (religious retreat centers) supported by Hermann Kallenbach, a South African architect of Jewish background, whom Gandhi had met through Theosophical circles. Gandhi named one of his communities Tolstoi Farm in honor of the Christian utopian with whom he had developed a lively correspondence. While in South Africa Gandhi first met C. F. Andrews, the Anglican missionary to India who had become an emissary of Indian nationalist leaders and who eventually became Gandhi's lifelong friend and confidant. It was through Andrews that Gandhi met the Indian poet Rabindranath Tagore in 1915, after Gandhi had returned to India to join the growing nationalist movement. Tagore, following the practice of Theosophists in South Africa, designated Gandhi a mahatma, or "great soul."

GANDHI'S RELIGIOUS THOUGHT. Although the influences on Gandhi's religious thought are varied—from the Sermon on the Mount to the *Bhagavadgītā*—his ideas are surprisingly consistent. Gandhi considered them to be Hindu, and in fact, they are all firmly rooted in the Indian religious tradition. His main ideas include the following.

1. *Satya* ("truth"). Gandhi equated truth with God, implying that morality and spirituality are ultimately the same. This concept is the bedrock of Gandhi's approach to conflict, *satyāgraha,* which requires a fighter to "hold firmly to truth." While Gandhi did not further define the term, he regarded the rule of *ahiṃsā* as the litmus test that would determine where truth could be found.
2. *Ahiṃsa* ("nonviolence"). This ancient Indian concept prohibiting physical violence was broadened by Gandhi to include any form of coercion or denigration. For Gandhi, *ahiṃsa* was a moral stance involving love for and the affirmation of all life.
3. *Tapasya* ("renunciation"). Gandhi's asceticism was, in Max Weber's terms, "worldly" and not removed from social and political involvements. To Gandhi, *tapasya* meant not only the traditional requirements of simplicity and purity in personal habits but also the willingness of a fighter to shoulder the burden of suffering in a conflict.
4. *Swaraj* ("self-rule"). This term was often used during India's struggle for independence to signify freedom from the British, but Gandhi used it more broadly to refer to an ideal of personal integrity. He regarded *swaraj* as a worthy goal for the moral strivings of individuals and nations alike, linking it to the notion of finding one's inner self.

In addition to these concepts, Gandhi affirmed the traditional Hindu notions of *karman* and *dharma.* Even though Gandhi never systematized these ideas, when taken together they form a coherent theological position. Gandhi's copious writings are almost entirely in the form of letters and short essays in the newspapers and journals he published. These writings and the accounts of Gandhi's life show that he had very little interest in what is sometimes regarded as emblematic of Hinduism: its colorful anthropomorphic deities and its reliance upon the rituals performed by Brahmanic priests.

It is not his rejection of these elements of Hindu culture that makes Gandhi innovative, however, for they are also omitted by the leaders of many other sects and movements in modern India. What is distinctive about Gandhi's Hinduism is his emphasis on social ethics as an integral part of the faith, a shift of emphasis that carries with it many conceptual changes as well. Gandhi's innovations include the use of the concept of truth as a basis for moral and political action, the equation of nonviolence with the Christian notion of selfless love, the broadening of the concept of *karmayoga* to include social service and political action, the redefinition of untouchability and the elevation of untouchables' tasks, and the hope for a more perfect world even in this present age of darkness (*kaliyuga*).

Gandhi's religious practices, like his ideas, combined both social and spiritual elements. In addition to his daily prayers, consisting of a simple service of readings and silent contemplation, he regarded his daily practice of spinning cotton as a form of mediation and his campaigns for social reform as sacrifices more efficacious than those made by priests at the altar. After Gandhi retired from politics in 1933, he took as his central theme the campaign for the uplift of untouchables, whom he called *harijans* ("people of God"). Other concerns included the protection of cows, moral education, and the reconciliation of Hindus and Muslims. The latter was especially important to Gandhi during the turmoil precipitated by India's independence, when the subcontinent was divided along religious lines. It was opposition to Gandhi's cries for religious tolerance that led to his assassination, on January 30, 1948, by a fanatical member of the Hindu right wing.

GANDHI'S LEGACY. Since Gandhi's death, neither Indian society nor Hindu belief has been restructured along Gandhian lines, but the Gandhian approach has been kept alive in India through the Sarvodaya movement, for which Vinoba Bhave has provided the spiritual leadership, and Jaya Prakash Narayan the political. Gandhi has provided the inspiration for religious and social activists in other parts of the world as well. These include Martin Luther King, Jr., and Joan Baez in the United States, E. M. Schumacher in England, Danilo Dolci in Sicily, Albert Luthuli in South Africa, Lanza del Vasto in France, and A. T. Ariyaratna in Sri Lanka.

Over the years, the image of Gandhi has loomed larger than life, and he is popularly portrayed as an international saint. This canonization of Gandhi began in the West with the writings of an American Unitarian pastor, John Haynes Holmes, who in 1921 proclaimed Gandhi "the greatest man in the world today." It continues in an unabated flow of homiletic writings and films, including David Attenborough's *Gandhi,* one of the most widely seen motion pictures in history. At the core of this Gandhian hagiography lies the enduring and appealing image of a man who was able to achieve a significant religious goal: the ability to live simultaneously a life of moral action and spiritual fulfillment. For that reason Gandhi continues to serve as an inspiration for a humane and socially engaged form of religion in India and throughout the world.

SEE ALSO Ahiṃsa; Bhave, Vinoba; King, Martin Luther, Jr.; Tagore, Rabindranath.

BIBLIOGRAPHY

Gandhi's own writings are assembled in his *Collected Works,* 89 vols. (Delhi, 1958–1983). Many briefer anthologies are available, however, including *The Gandhi Reader,* edited by Homer Jack (New York, 1961). A reliable biography is Judith Brown's *Gandhi: Prisoner of Hope* (New Haven, Conn., 1989). The religious ideas of Gandhi are best explored in Margaret Chatterjee's *Gandhi's Religious Thought* (Notre Dame, Ind., 1983) and Raghavan Iyer's *The Moral and Political Thought of Mahatma Gandhi* (New York, 1973). The concept of *satyāgraha* is explicated and put into comparative perspective in Joan Bondurant's *Conquest of Violence: The Gandhian Philosophy of Conflict,* rev. ed. (Berkeley, 1965), and my *Gandhi's Way: A Handbook of Conflict Resolution* (Berkeley,Calif., 2003). Gandhi's saintly politics are described in Lloyd I. Rudolph and Susanne Hoeber Rudolph's *Gandhi: The Traditional Roots of Charisma* (Chicago, 1983), and his image as a universal saint is discussed in my essay "St. Gandhi," in *Saints and Virtues,* edited by John Stratton Hawley (Berkeley, 1986).

MARK JUERGENSMEYER (1987 AND 2005)

GAṆEŚA

GAṆEŚA ("lord of the group") is the elephant-headed Hindu deity. Also called Vināyaka ("leader"), Gajānana ("elephant-faced"), Gaṇādhipa ("lord of the group"), Ekadanta ("one-tusked"), Lambodara ("potbellied"), Vighnarāja ("lord of obstacles"), and Siddhadāta ("giver of success"), he is the son of Śiva and Pārvatī, and leader of Śiva's group of attendants (*gaṇas*). His special province within the Hindu pantheon is to remove and create obstacles to various undertakings. His images are found both in temples dedicated exclusively to him and, more frequently, as doorway guardians of temples to other deities, especially Śiva and Pārvatī. Gaṇeśa enjoys widespread devotion from Hindus of various sectarian affiliations and ranks. Hindus who regard him as their principal deity of devotion are called Gaṇapatyas; they are located primarily in southern and western India.

Gaṇeśa's historical origins are obscure. Early Vedic literatures refer to a Gaṇapati ("lord of the group") and to Hastimukha ("elephant-faced"), and devotees regard these references as evidence for Gaṇeśa's Vedic roots. It is more likely that these epithets refer to Bṛhaspati, Indra, or Śiva. Numismatic evidence suggests that Gaṇeśa originated in the first century CE. Sculptural evidence places his entry into the Hindu pantheon about four centuries later. Literarily and iconographically, Gaṇeśa is well established in myth and cult by the fifth century within the general framework of Saivism, although he receives worship by Hindus of various devotional and sectarian orientations for his general role as the overcomer of obstacles.

Gaṇeśa's mythology centers on several themes: his birth, beheading and restoration, lordship over the *gaṇas*, associations with demons, and powers as creator and remover of obstacles. Stories in the Purāṇas and vernacular folklore traditions tell of occasions when Pārvatī created Gaṇeśa out of the substance, sometimes called *mala* ("dirt") or *lepa* ("rubbing"), rubbed off the surface of her body and formed into the shape of a handsome youth. Once, while Śiva was absent and deep in meditation, Pārvatī commanded this young man to guard her private quarters from all intruders. When Śiva returned and sought entry into Pārvatī's presence, the young man barred the door. During the battle that followed, Śiva beheaded the youth. Pārvatī became angry and demanded that Śiva restore him at once. Śiva sent out his group of attendants (*gaṇas*) to find the first available head, which happened to belong to an elephant. Śiva restored the youth with the elephant's head and gave him command over his group of *gaṇas,* thus naming him Gaṇapati or Gaṇeśa, Lord of the Group. Śiva also told all gods and brahmans that Gaṇeśa must be worshiped first before all other undertakings, ritual or otherwise, or else their efforts would come to ruin.

Gaṇeśa is also called Vināyaka, meaning "leader." The early Dharmasūtra literature, predating the above-mentioned myths of Gaṇeśa, describes rituals prescribed to ward off *vināyakas*, evil demons who possess their victims and cause them to act in strange and inauspicious ways. Gaṇeśa's dwarfish torso resembles the iconography of these *vināyakas*. Some scholars have suggested that Gaṇeśa may originally have been a member of this class of demons but gradually achieved brahmanical recognition and gained admittance into its pantheon as the son of Śiva and Pārvatī.

In receiving the head of the elephant, Gaṇeśa also takes on some of the symbolism associated with elephants in Indian culture. Elephant motifs frequently are found at the bases of temples, appearing to hold up the massive edifices. Elephants guard the doors of temples and serve as the vehicles for deities and royalty. Gaṇeśa also serves in these protective capacities as the remover and placer of obstacles.

SEE ALSO Elephants; Gaṇapatyas.

BIBLIOGRAPHY

Courtright, Paul B. *Gaṇeśa: Lord of Obstacles, Lord of Beginnings.* New York, 1985. A detailed survey of the myths and rituals surrounding the figures of Gaṇeśa in classical Sanskrit sources and contemporary western India (Maharashtra).

Getty, Alice. *Gaṇeśa: A Monograph on the Elephant-Faced God.* Oxford, 1936. A study of the myth and iconography of Gaṇeśa in India, Southeast Asia, and East Asia.

New Sources

Ganesh: Studies of an Asian God. Robert L. Brown, editor. Albany, 1991.

Ganesh, the Benevolent. Edited by Pratapaditya Pal. Bombay, 1995.

Grewal, Royina. *The Book of Ganesh.* New Delhi; New York, 2001.

Grimes, John A. *Ganapati: Song of the Self.* Albany, 1995.

Karunakaran, Rankorath. *The Riddle of Ganesha.* Bombay, 1992.

Nagar, Shanti Lal. *The Cult of Vinayaka.* New Delhi, 1992.

Shakunthala Jagannathan. *Ganesha, the Auspicious, the Beginning.* 1992.

PAUL B. COURTRIGHT (1987)
Revised Bibliography

GANGES RIVER.

The Ganges (Gaṅgā), considered the holiest of India's rivers, is 1,560 miles long. Rising at Gangotri in the Himalayas, this great river flows through the North Indian plain and into the Bay of Bengal. To Hindus, the Ganges is the archetype of all sacred waters; she is a goddess, Mother Gaṅgā (Gaṅgā Mātā), representative of the life-giving maternal waters of the ancient Vedic hymns; above all, she is the symbol *par excellence* of purity and the purifying power of the sacred. These affective and symbolic values of the Ganges hold true for all Hindus, irrespective of sectarian differences.

CELEBRATION OF THE GODDESS-RIVER. According to Hindu belief, the Ganges purifies all that she touches. Her entire course is a pilgrimage route for the faithful. Millions of Hindus visit the preeminent *tīrthas* ("crossings," places of pilgrimage) that mark her path: the source at Gangotri; Hardwar (also called Gaṅgādvāra, "gateway of the Ganges"), where the river enters the plain; Prayāg (present-day Allahabad), where she joins both the holy Yamnuā (Jumna) and the mythical river Sarasvatī, thus earning the name Triveṇī ("river of three currents"); Kāśī (Banaras), abode of the god Śiva and the holiest city of the Hindus; and Gaṅgāsagar, where the Ganges enters the sea. Pilgrims go to these places to bathe in the Ganges, to drink her water, to worship the river, and to chant her holy name. Especially in Banaras, many come to cremate their kin, to deposit the ashes of the dead in the river, or to perform religious rites for their ancestors. Some come to spend their last days on the banks of the river, to die there and thus "cross over" the ocean of birth and death. Holy men, widows, and others who have dedicated themselves to the contemplative life live in numbers in the sacred places along the Ganges. They in turn attract millions who congregate at periodic festivals and fairs, the greatest of which is the Kumbha Melā, celebrated every twelve years in Prayāg. All who come to the Ganges come in the firm belief that bathing in this river, even the mere sight of Mother Gaṅgā, will cleanse them of their sins, taking them a step nearer to final release (*mokṣa*). Those who cannot make the trip can partake of the river's sacred water from the sealed jars that pilgrims carry home. Ganges water is given to participants and guests at weddings, as well as to the sick and the dying; it validates Hindu oaths; and in an ancient daily rite, every devout Hindu invokes the Ganges, along with the other sacred rivers, to be present in the water in which he bathes. The purifying powers of the Ganges are great indeed.

THE GANGES IN MYTHOLOGY AND ICONOGRAPHY. The Vedic Aryans celebrated the Indus, not the Ganges, and her tributaries as their "seven sacred rivers." It is in the epics *Mahābhārata* and *Rāmāyaṇa* (roughly fourth century BCE), which reflect Aryan settlement in the Ganges Plain, that the Ganges takes her place at the head of seven holy rivers that are now geographically spread over all of India. The principal myths of the Ganges are found in the epics and the Purāṇas (mythological texts that include the lore of sacred places), and in Sanskrit hymns of praise such as the *Gāṅgālaharī* (The waves of the Ganges) by the seventeenth-century poet Jagannātha. The central myth of the Ganges is the story of her descent (*avatāra, avataraṇa*) from heaven to earth, a story narrated with variations in several texts (*Rāmāyaṇa*, "Bāla Kāṇḍa" 38–44; *Mahābhārata* 3.104–108; *Skanda Purāṇa*, "Kāśī Khaṇḍa" 30). In response to the great and steadfast penance of King Bhagīratha, the sky-river Ganges agreed to descend to earth in order to purify the ashes of the sixty thousand sons of Bhagīratha's ancestor Sagara, who had been burned by the wrath of a sage (Kapila) whom they had offended. The great ascetic god Śiva caught the falling stream in his matted hair in order to soften the blow on earth; the Ganges followed Bhagīratha to the sea, whence she flowed into the netherworld to fulfill her mission. This myth explains several of the Ganges's names, including Bhāgīrathī ("she who descended at Bhagīratha's request") and Tripathagāminī ("she who flows through the three worlds"). The descent of the Ganges is the subject of a famous seventh-century rock sculpture at Mahabalipuram in South India.

In the Vaiṣṇava version of the descent myth, the Ganges is said to have descended when Viṣṇu, as Trivikrama who measured heaven and earth, pierced the vault of heaven with his upraised foot. The association of the river with both great gods of Hinduism points to the universality of the Ganges in Hinduism. In minor myths the river is portrayed as the mother of the *Mahābhārata* hero Bhīṣma and the mother of Skanda-Kārttikeya, who was born from Śiva's seed flung into the Ganges.

The Ganges' most sustained association is with the god Śiva himself. Not only does she flow through his hair, she is considered to be his wife, along with Pārvatī, the other daughter of the god of the Himalaya, Himavat. As powerful river and goddess-consort, the Ganges is *śakti,* the feminine energy of the universe, and the female aspect of the androgynous Śiva. Like Śiva and the ambrosial moon on his head, the Ganges—whose life-sustaining ambrosial waters flow from the realm of the moon—is connected with both life and death.

The themes of purification, life, and death that appear in the myths and rites associated with the Ganges are also expressed in her iconography, especially in the representation of the Gaṅgā and Yamnuā as goddesses carved on either side of the entrances of Hindu temples of the medieval period (roughly from the fifth to the eleventh century CE). Ancient symbols of fertility (trees, vegetation, overflowing pots, the female herself) appear in these images; yet the Ganges rides on a *makara* ("crocodile"), who represents the dangers of death as well as the abundance of life. As "goddess of the threshold" the Ganges no doubt initiates, purifies, and blesses with worldly prosperity the devotee who enters the sacred realm of the temple; at the same time, in the esoteric symbolism of Yoga and Tantra, the river-goddess is said to represent *iḍā,* one of the *nāḍīs* (subtle channels) through which one's energy is activated in order to achieve the supreme realization of the self—final release from worldly existence. However, in the last analysis, for the average Hindu it is not a matter of esoteric interpretation but of simple faith—reinforced by popular texts—that the goddess-river Ganges is the most accessible and powerful agent of salvation available to him or her in the *kaliyuga,* the present dark and degraded age of humankind.

SEE ALSO Banaras; Kumbha Melā; Śiva.

BIBLIOGRAPHY

Diana L. Eck's essay entitled "Gaṅgā: The Goddess in Hindu Sacred Geography," in *The Divine Consort: Rādhā and the Goddesses of India,* edited by John Stratton Hawley and Donna M. Wulff (Berkeley, Calif., 1982), pp. 166–183, is the best introduction to the religious significance of the Ganges in Hinduism. The same author has a good discussion of the Ganges in the context of Kāśī, the holy city of the Hindus, in chapter 5 of *Banaras: City of Light* (New York, 1982). Spectacular visual images of the Ganges and the life along her banks, accompanied by a highly informative and readable introductory text, may be found in *Gaṅgā: Sacred River of India,* photographs by Raghubir Singh, introduction by Eric Newby (Hong Kong, 1974). Steven G. Darian's *The Ganges in Myth and History* (Honolulu, 1978) is a solid, well-written, well-illustrated historical study of the many dimensions of the Ganges. Finally, Heinrich von Stietencron's *Gaṅgā und Yamnuā: Zur symbolischen Bedeutung der Flussgöttinnen an indischen Tempeln* (Wiesbaden, 1972) is an excellent scholarly work on the symbolism of the iconography of the great river-goddesses in Hinduism.

INDIRA VISWANATHAN PETERSON (1987)

GANJIN (Chin., Jianzhen; 688–763) was a Buddhist Vinaya master from China who introduced procedures for ordaining Buddhist clergy into Japan and who established the Risshu, or Vinaya school, of Buddhism there. Ganjin's birthplace was Yangzhou, a prosperous shipping town in eastern China. There he underwent tonsure at a local temple in 701. Four years later he received the *bodhisattva* precepts, a set of vows administered as a sign of devotion to Mahāyāna Buddhist principles.

At the age of nineteen, Ganjin traveled to China's traditional capitals of Luoyang and Chang'an to study at the major centers of Buddhist learning. His primary field of training was Vinaya, the ancient rules and procedures governing the life and behavior of Buddhist priests and nuns. Interest in the Vinaya had peaked in China a century earlier, and a formal school, the Lüzong, was established to preserve and promote clerical practices based on the *Sifenlü* (T.D. no. 1428), the version of the Vinaya inherited from the Dharmaguptaka school of India. This Vinaya, which lists 250 precepts for priests and 348 for nuns, was Hīnayāna in origin, but it became the basis for ordination and clerical discipline in the overwhelmingly Mahāyāna schools of China and Japan. Ganjin himself took the 250 precepts at the time of his full ordination in 708, a year after his arrival in Chang'an. In 713, at the age of twenty-five, he returned to Yangzhou and began his own career as a Vinaya master. Over the next thirty years Ganjin distinguished himself as one of the most eminent Buddhist teachers in central China. He is said to have ordained more than 40,000 priests during his career and to have conducted formal lectures on the Vinaya on 130 occasions.

In 733 the Japanese imperial court sent two Buddhist priests, Eiei and Fushō, to China to enlist Vinaya masters to administer ordinations in Japan. There was great concern in Japan that all the ordinations performed up to that time were not valid, because the requisite number of duly ordained priests prescribed by the Vinaya had never been present to officiate. The Japanese felt it important to rectify this breach. Authentic ordination, they believed, made the clergy legitimate heirs of the Buddha's teachings and endowed them with religious and worldly power to act in behalf of Buddhism. Eiei and Fushō first succeeded in recruiting a young Vinaya master named Daoxuan from Luoyang. He arrived in Japan in 736, but was hampered in conducting ordinations for lack of the required number of ordained participants. In 742 they went to Yangzhou to seek Ganjin's assistance. He too was sympathetic, and he resolved to travel to Japan himself to oversee ordinations. But the path leading Ganjin to Japan was long and treacherous, involving five unsuccessful voyages thwarted by pirates, shipwreck, and arrest by civil authorities. During the course of these events Ganjin lost his eyesight and Eiei lost his life. Finally, in 753, on his sixth attempt, Ganjin reached the shores of Japan accompanied by twenty-four disciples whose participation would validate ordination ceremonies. Ganjin was sixty-five years old at the time.

In early 754 Ganjin and his entourage were welcomed into the Japanese capital of Nara with great fanfare. Within weeks he set up a temporary ordination platform at the Tōdaiji, the imperial temple in the capital, and performed the first proper ordination on Japanese soil. The following year he established a permanent ordination platform at the Tōdaiji, all according to the meticulous specifications of the Vinaya tradition in China. The establishment of specific locations for ordination had the effect of tightening control over the clergy, because entrance into the priesthood could be regulated by those overseeing ordination. This centralizing of authority, as well as the Vinaya's emphasis on strict discipline, suited the government's desire to harness Buddhism for its own interests. Ganjin, as the preeminent figure in this ordination process, was named to the Sōgō council, the ecclesiastical body responsible to the government for Buddhism's activities. He served in this capacity from 756 until his resignation in 758. A year later Ganjin was granted land on which to build his own temple. He constructed the Tōshōdaiji and spent the remaining four years of his life there instructing priests in the intricacies of the Vinaya. These followers formed the core of the Risshu in Japan. Ganjin died at the Tōshōdaiji in 763 at the age of seventy-five. His great contribution to Japan was the institution of ordination procedures and the delineation of clerical discipline. This model of discipline was later challenged by Saichō, who sought to substitute the *bodhisattva* vows of Mahāyāna for the clerical precepts of Hīnayāna. Nonetheless, Ganjin's system persisted alongside Saichō's as the traditional path of ordination in early Japanese Buddhism.

See Also Saichō; Vinaya.

Bibliography

The most important work in Western languages on Ganjin is a French study by Takakusu Junjirō, "Le voyage de Kanshin en Orient, 742–754," *Bulletin de l'École Française d'Extrême-Orient* 28 (1928): 1–41 and 29 (1929): 47–62. This is a translation of a biography written in 779 by the Japanese scholar Mabito Genkai entitled *Tō Daiwajō Tōsei den* (T.D. no. 2089). In Japanese there are numerous studies of Ganjin, including Ishida Mizumaro's *Ganjin: Sono shisō to shōgai* (Tokyo, 1958) and Ando Kōsei's *Ganjin Wajō,* "Jinbutsu sosho," no. 146 (Tokyo, 1967).

James C. Dobbins (1987)

GARDENS

This entry consists of the following articles:

AN OVERVIEW
GARDENS IN INDIGENOUS TRADITIONS
ISLAMIC GARDENS

GARDENS: AN OVERVIEW

Gardens are enclosed spaces, distinguished from the fields where staple crops are grown and from the rocks, forests, marshes, and tundra of the wilderness. There are zoological gardens, and parks for animals, but plant gardens do not usually find room for more than a few colorful birds and fish. The transcendental feelings inspired by ornamental gardens may be divided into Western and Eastern categories, with "Western" understood broadly as encompassing traditions associated not only with Christianity but also with Islam, and with the geographical line dividing Western from Eastern running through the subcontinent of India. In the West, nature has traditionally been conceived of as something to be conquered, and religious thought runs to extremes: the Day of Judgment, the triumph of the good, and the annihilation of evil. In the East, many religious traditions have sought to accommodate human beings to the world around them and to comprehend dualisms within an overarching whole. These differences find expression in the formal gardening of the West and in the landscape gardening of the East, and perhaps also in the fact that Western gardens are made for walking in, while Eastern ones are for sitting in, with separate pavillions for painting, composing poetry, practicing one's calligraphy, and (in recent centuries) drinking tea.

Western Recreational Gardens. The religions that inherited the traditions of the Old Testament, namely, Islam and Christianity, were founded in the desert. Their scriptures dwelt on the life-giving properties of water, foliage that was refreshing to the eye, and shade that was restful for the body. A man was blessed by being told he would be "like a watered garden" (*Isa.* 58:11) and cursed with the prospect of becoming "as a garden that hath no water" (*Isa.* 1:30). Wells and fountains quickened plant growth, and the trees that water brought to life provided both nourishment and fuel. Christians valued green herbs for their medicinal properties, and in seventeenth-century England Andrew Marvell envisaged paradise as "a green thought in a green shade." Green became the color of Islam itself, and a just king, as the Mughal emperor Akbar said when he invaded Kashmir in 1585 BCE, enabled his subjects to sit in the shade of tranquillity. Above all, the influence of the desert environment appeared in the way in which, in the West, the garden was seen as an oasis, in stark contrast to the barren wastes outside. The sense of the faith, or of the church, as an enclosure, a refuge from a hostile environment, was paramount (though a missionary church might be described as a garden without walls). Confusingly, there was another more puritanical tradition in which the roles were reversed, and the garden, with its luxury, was condemned as the scene of temptation, while the wilderness was celebrated as the true garden.

Gardeners, inspired by the supposition of a Garden of Eden at the beginning of history, aimed to re-create the conditions thought to have existed in the original garden, with its mild climate and its never-failing supply of flowers and fruit. The gardener brought order out of chaos, and gardens were laid out in regular patterns, with right angles and straight lines to extend humankind's dominion over fallen nature. Both the Garden of Eden and the future Heaven were commonly conceived of as formal gardens. The tradition that Eden was watered by four rivers led Muslim gardeners from Persia to Spain tenaciously to reproduce the *chahar bagh,* a rectangular enclosure divided into four quarters by two streams crossing at right angles. It was an approach that combined easily with humanist ideas—derived from the classical civilizations of Persia, Greece, and Rome—of the regular pattern as the triumph of human intelligence and of abstract principles of mathematics and law. In Europe, plans of grounds attached to a Roman villa, to a medieval monastery, or to a Renaissance palace are not dissimilar, and it is not always easy to disentangle spiritual influences from secular ones, though it seems safe to say that the inspiration behind the greatest of all geometrical gardens, at Versailles, was at least half worldly.

Where religious influences predominated every plant was imbued with symbolic spiritual meaning. Trees opened their arms in the gesture of the prayer of supplication, and the branches of an orchard bowed toward God. The silver on the topside of the leaves of the poplar reflected the light of heaven, while the dark side beneath served as a reminder of earth—or hell. The cypress (represented in so many central Asian carpets) stood both for mortality, because it did not sprout when felled, and for everlasting life, because it was evergreen. The violet genuflected. The lily epitomized the purity and the pomegranate the fruitfulness of a woman. Muslims believed that the rose, which enjoys primacy of esteem among Western gardeners, had been created from a drop of perspiration that fell from the Prophet's forehead as he was carried up into Heaven. The rosebush prayed standing upright, and the fragrant flowers budding among its thorns were interpreted as tokens of God's mercy emerging from God's wrath. In both Islam and Christianity this kind of imagery led writers like Rābiʿah al-ʿAdawīyah (d. 801 CE) to speak of "the real gardens and flowers" being "within." It was only when people's stonelike nature had been broken down into dust by affliction that their hearts could become gardens blessed by rain and have roses grow out of them.

The early symbolism of the garden in Islam ran parallel to that in Christianity, though the Muslim Paradise, with its *ḥūrīs,* its green brocades, and its nonintoxicating wines, was painted in more literal detail than the Christian Heaven. Where Christian tradition diverged from Islam was in the identification of the garden with specific occasions in the life of Christ. The "garden enclosed" of the *Song of Songs* was interpreted to refer to the Virgin Mary, whose womb was an oasis so select that none but the Holy Spirit could enter in. Adam had been a gardener. Through Adam, death came into the world. Christ, who had conquered death, therefore made his first appearance after the resurrection dressed in a gardener's clothes.

EASTERN COSMIC GARDENS. In China and Japan, both the awesome mountains and the streams that issued from them were thought to be possessed by spirits, and they were considered to be alive, like plants, animals, and human beings themselves. Space was organized from the center outward, and gardens were designed by professional geomancers, who surveyed the spiritual contours of the sites according to the science of *feng-shui.* The selection of rocks was a matter for the connoisseur. Everything was conceived within a mindset that has been called *universisme,* and the primary objective of landscape gardening was to raise people's understanding to the level of the cosmos. This was achieved through the art of *shan shui.* Rocks, pools, and streams were said to represent the physical geography of a region, such as the mountains of Central Asia and the seas of the eastern coast, or (in Daoist philosophy) the skeleton of the whole earth and the arteries that nourished it. To the Buddhist, the garden furnished a lesson on time. The flowers opened and withered within in a month. The seasons revolved. But stone decayed on a far longer time scale that turned the present into a moving infinity. The symbolism was as varied and extensible as the clouds that gathered around the mountain peaks.

The garden contained both friendly and unfriendly spirits. But threatening spirits were not persecuted as they might have been in the West: they were either left undisturbed (for example, by not digging the ground too deeply) or frustrated (as in the case of the demons who traveled in straight lines, who were thwarted through the construction of zigzag bridges). The universe, like the garden, was influenced by rival but related forces. The Chinese spoke of the *yin* and the *yang,* the Japanese of the *in* and the *yo. Yin* was female, passive, and weak; *yang* was male, active, and virile. In China, mountains were male, pools female; hence a mountain stood for intelligence, a lake for feeling. In Japan the more stylized gardens sometimes contained both male and female rocks—five erect, four recumbent. In both countries, gardens expressed conceptions about youth and age, growth and decay. The trunk of the tree upon which the "youthful" plum blossom hung resembled an old person's body, crooked and bent. Flowers were esteemed for being "as lovely in their withering as in their first florescence," and the samurai were compared to the blossom of the cherry—having a short life and an exquisite end. The *Yuan Ye* (a treatise on gardening, dating from the end of the Ming period) records that "when a remarkable tree was about to bloom," people moved their beds outdoors in order that they might be able to observe how the flowers expanded "from childhood to maturity and finally faded and died."

Nowhere is the contrast between East and West more apparent than in their respective attitudes to night and moonlight. In the West, day was connected symbolically with good, night with evil. The creatures that moved by night, such as bats, owls, and foxes, were repellent, ominous, or crafty, and the moon was contemned as a second-rate luminary. In China, on the other hand, day and night were accorded equal status, and night was said to raise men and women to the stars. Pavilions were built and furnished for the contemplation of the moon, Chinese poets sang of the moonlight "washing its soul" in the garden pool, and the *Yuan Ye* encouraged its readers to look forward to the day when they might even "dig in the moon[light] on the top of a mountain."

In the East a miniature garden might be esteemed as highly as an estate, and (as in the West) it was sometimes said that it was not necessary to own a property at all. Fictive gardens were held in high regard, and the most perfect garden of all was "the garden that isn't really here"—the one that existed only in the imagination. Real or imaginary, the garden was recognized as a representation of people's own lives containing symbols of the qualities respected in a human being. The cedar, resisting the storm, represented the beholder's own struggle with adversity, and the chrysanthemum, which braved the autumn frosts, was admired for its courage. Death itself lost some of its terrors when understood in the context of a continuous cycle of decay and regrowth. Much of Chinese gardening sought to encourage acceptance of humanity's lot. But gardens in the East could also express a yearning for transcendence. Daoists spoke of the Blessed Isles of the Eastern Sea, and many Buddhists have believed in a land, presided over by the Amida (*Amitābha*) Buddha, where lotus flowers holding the souls of the faithful bloom upon the waters of a brilliant lake—paradisal concepts for which there have been parallels in the West. More often than not, however, Buddhists have thought in terms of *nirvāṇa,* or a release from the cycle of reincarnation, and for this there is no Western equivalent. The Indian youth of the *Matsya Purāṇa* (c. 500 CE), who had passed through lives by the thousand and who had in his time been a beast of prey, a domestic animal, grass, shrubs, creepers, and trees, looked forward not to a better world but to release from self. In China the highest aspiration open to a landscape gardener was to imitate the Hang painter Wu Daozi, who is said to have entered into the scene he had created, merged with his masterpiece, and been seen no more.

SUBSISTENCE GARDENS. In recreational and cosmic gardens, long-lived trees, graceful foliage, and fragrant flowers have provided abundant material for religious symbolism. Orchards and fruit gardens, in which beauty and utility are combined, have also inspired their share of spiritual imagery, and the Bible contains many allegories concerning vines, figs, olives, and palms. Herb gardens and physic (medicinal) gardens have contributed their quota. But the kitchen garden, which supplies so much, does not seem to feed the imagination, and the Bible includes only one reference to the cucumbers, melons, leeks, onions, and garlic that the Israelites remembered having eaten in Egypt (*Num.* 11:5). The planting at Villandry shows how even the dominant tradition of classical French parterre gardening can be reinterpreted in terms of the potager. But this is an exception. In both West and East, class values have prevailed. The norm among aristocracies, and even among the middle classes, has been to place the vegetable garden out of sight. Historically, priests of all religions have kept their hands clean and been supported from the surplus created by the population at large. Monastic communities, withdrawn from the world, are the only ones to have embraced manual labor as a providential discipline. In both West and East, Benedictine and Zen Buddhist monks have placed gardening upon a par with prayer and meditation and supported themselves by growing their own food. Much of the virtue lies in the humble nature of the work.

Real-life peasants and laborers, on the other hand, with families to feed, know that in temperate latitudes the skills involved in planning and maintaining a subsistence garden are greater than those called for in a recreational or cosmic garden, because most of the edible plants are annuals. There is little time to compensate for failures, and sowings must succeed or the family will go without. The labor is unremitting, and, understandably, the rewards are associated with the satisfaction of the stomach rather than the refinement of the soul. Things are different in parts of the tropics where three crops may be harvested in a year and the division between extensive fields and intensive gardens breaks down. There, the subsistence garden may assume an idealized form. All over Southeast Asia, where high levels of light, heat, and moisture; the rapid growth of plants; and recycling of vegetable and animal waste allow a family to produce all their own food and fuel upon a tiny holding, there are self-reliant peasants living in ecological harmony with a bountiful nature. In Melanesia a twentieth-century study of the Trobriand Islanders found that even their staples (yams and taro) were grown in aesthetically pleasing gardens, and that skill in gardening determined social rank. Every stage from the clearing of the land, through the sowing, weeding, and thinning, to the gathering and display of the produce was carried out with the aid of the appropriate magic, and the spirits of the dead were invited to attend the harvest feast.

ALTERNATIVES. Sensuality has always wrestled with spirituality for the soul of the garden. In the West, Priapus and Venus presided over Greek and Roman gardens, and remain better known, to this day, than Saint Phocas and Saint Fiacre, the patron saints of gardening. No amount of Marian imagery could conceal the erotic meaning of the *Song of Songs,* and in the thirteenth century the *Roman de la Rose* contraposed a garden of courtly manners and passionate love to the ecclesiastically approved one of lowered eyes and chaste thoughts. In the eighteenth and nineteenth centuries, Voltaire challenged and Darwin overthrew the concept of gardening as an innocent activity. The struggle for survival is every bit as wasteful, and as blind (or cruel), in a garden as it is in the wilderness. The difference is that there are more human interventions. Even these do not appear, since Freud, as blameless as they once did. Gardeners are autocrats who draw arbitrary distinctions between plants and weeds. Except, perhaps, in India, they wage chemical warfare and carry out mass exterminations. Many—like the Chinese mandarins who were encouraged, when they fell from favor, to retire and take up gardening—are in denial, working off their frustrations by philosophically rationalizing the pleasures of an enforced rural retreat.

In addition to its literal sense, the word *garden* has frequently been used as a literary term, to mean an anthology. More than one collection of improving stories or homilies has been titled *A Garden of Flowers,* and others in this vein have been titled gardens of "consolation," "repose," or "contentment." But the word has become detached from its religious context. Many people no longer agree with Dorothy Frances Gurney that they are "nearer God's Heart in a garden than anywhere else on earth." J. M. Brinnin, who began writing poetry when he was a student at Harvard in the 1930s, thought of "garden" as "tragedy up to its generous eyes." Faced with the rise of the Fascist dictators, "even the illiterate snake," he wrote, must know "the garden is political" (the title of a collection of his poems published in New York in 1942). Within the last half-century others have offered readers gardens of disorder, evil, ignorance, illusion, lies, malice, poisons, and scandal. At the beginning of the twenty-first century, the meanings and associations of the word are still being contested.

SEE ALSO Flowers; Geomancy; Paradise.

BIBLIOGRAPHY

Few books on gardening pay sufficient attention to the significance of religious symbolism. Among those that do, the best general history remains Marie Luise Gothein's *A History of Garden Art,* 2 vols. (1928; New York, 1966). Islamic gardens may be studied in Elizabeth B. Moynihan's *Paradise as a Garden in Persia and Mughal India* (New York, 1979) and in a collection edited by Elizabeth B. MacDougall and Richard Ettinghausen, *The Islamic Garden* (Washington, D.C., 1976), one of the publications arising out of the colloquia held annually at Dumbarton Oaks since 1971. For medieval European gardens see Marilyn Stokstad's essay "Gardens in Medieval Art," written for the Gardens of the Middle Ages exhibition organized by the Spencer Museum of Art, University of Kansas, Lawrence, in 1983, and Teresa McLean's *Medieval English Gardens* (London, 1981). The "garden enclosed" of the *Song of Songs* is the subject of Stanley N. Stewart's study *The Enclosed Garden: The Tradition and the Image in Seventeenth-Century Poetry* (Madison, Wis., 1966). Some effects of the discovery of America on European gardeners' attempts to re-create the Garden of Eden are outlined in John Prest's *The Garden of Eden: The Botanic Garden and the Re-Creation of Paradise* (New Haven, Conn., 1981). Osvald Sirén's *China and Gardens of Europe of the Eighteenth Century* (New York, 1950) traces the influence of Chinese garden design upon the adoption of the landscape garden in Europe, particularly in England. The distinctive features of the successive periods of Japanese gardening are best conveyed in Teiji Ito's *The Japanese Garden: An Approach to Nature* (New Haven, Conn., 1972), and Norris Brock Johnson's article "Geomancy, Sacred Geometry, and the Idea of a Garden; Tenryu-ji Temple, Kyoto, Japan," *Journal of Garden History* 9, no. 1 (1989): 1–19. One of the earliest works written in English about Chinese gardening ideals, Dorothy Graham's *Chinese Gardens* (London, 1938), still contains valuable insights. More recent studies include Jan Stuart's "Ming Dynasty [1368—1644] Gardens Reconstructed in Words and Images," *Journal of Garden History* 10, no. 3 (1990): 162–172, and David L. Hall and Roger T. Ames's "The Cosmological Setting of Chinese Gardens," *Studies in the History of Gardens and Designed Landscapes* 18, no. 3 (1998): 175–186. Rolf A. Stein's *The World in Miniature: Container Gardens and Dwellings in Far Eastern Religious Thought,* translated by Phyllis Brooks (Stanford, Calif., 1998), continues the great tradition of French Far Eastern studies. A special issue edited by Léon Vandermeersch, "L'Art des jardins dans les pays Sinisés: Chine, Japon, Corée, Vietnam," *Extreme-Orient, Extreme-Occident* 22 (2000), covers the whole region and is invaluable. Bronislaw Malinowski's *Coral Gardens and Their Magic. A Study of the Methods of Tilling the Soil and of Agricultural Rites in the Trobriand Islands,* 2 vols. (London, 1935), is a classic anthropological study. Michael Niedermeier's " 'Strolling under Palm Trees': Gardens—Love—Sexuality," *Journal of Garden History* 17, no. 3 (1997): 186–207, touches on the garden as a setting for erotic love.

JOHN PREST (1987 AND 2005)

GARDENS: GARDENS IN INDIGENOUS TRADITIONS

Gardens are of economic importance and also of aesthetic and social significance for indigenous peoples who sustain themselves by the cultivation of vegetables and grains. They may be the subject or locus of myth, and they are regularly the focus of ritual. Where subsistence gardening is the major economic activity, people usually have some food gardens close to their homes and others farther afield. In many societies, gardening is complemented with hunting and/or fishing.

Among the Iroquois (Haudenosaunee) of North America, cultivation of the "Three Sisters" (corn, beans, and squash) provided vegetables, while the hunting of deer and other animals provided meat. Moreover, the Iroquois grew sacred tobacco for use in ceremonies. Like the Three Sisters, sacred tobacco is said to have first grown from the body of the Corn Mother, the woman who died after giving birth to Right-Handed Twin (the Creator) and the Left-Handed Twin. Iroquois gardening and hunting were supported by and celebrated in an annual ritual cycle that attended to the sun and moon and seasonal changes and gave thanks for both wild and domesticated fruits. These calendrical ceremonies included Bush Dance, Maple, Seed Planting, Moon, Sun, After Planting, Strawberry, Blackberry, Bean, Thunder, Little Corn, Green Corn, Our Sustenance, Harvest, End of Summer, and Midwinter (Sturtevant, 1985, p. 147). (Some of these ceremonies continue to be celebrated in Iroquois communities.) Iroquois ceremonies acknowledged the thunder spirits. In the American Southwest, among the Hopi, Zuni, and Navajo, the rain spirits were even more signficant. They were entertained in festivals and were encouraged to provide the moisture that the land and the people needed. Ceremonies for rain spirits remain an important focus in the agricultural cycles of the Southwest.

In colonial and postcolonial situations, subsistence economies have coexisted with cash economies, and gardening is no longer the only means of obtaining the food necessary for life. People may have income from wage labor or from an introduced form of gardening—cash cropping. Cash cropping often destroys traditional subsistence, because land once used for subsistence gardens may be taken over for the growing of crops such as coffee and tea to the detriment of a people's self-sufficiency. As well as being a primary source of food, the garden is also a metaphor for the meeting of life's needs. In Papua New Guinea, for example, a worker refers to his or her pay packet as *gaden bilong mi* (my garden). Similarly, gardening may be seen as homologous with other cultural domains such as marriage, exchange, speech, and weaving. Metaphors from gardening may be used to discuss sexual relations, and the maintenance of social alliances may be described in terms of planting and weeding.

Gardening includes not only practical endeavors such as clearing land, tilling soil, planting, and weeding, but also symbolic processes: rituals performed at crucial stages in the gardening process, spells or prayers recited to encourage plant growth and to ward off pestilence, and festivals to celebrate the harvest. Both the manual labor and the ritual activities are "work" for gardens. Rituals usually accompany the seasonal cycle of the crops, and ritual interventions to address crises such as disease or drought are made as warranted. Some societies employ garden specialists to carry out rituals; in others the gardeners themselves perform the necessary rituals or there may be a sharing of rituals. The practical side of gardening in indigenous societies has changed over time with the introduction of new crops, implements, and gardening techniques. Similarly, the spread of religious traditions such as Islam, Christianity, and Buddhism has occasioned changes in the ritual processes performed for the benefit of gardens. In many parts of Oceania and Africa, Christians include prayers for gardens in their church services, and they pray to God as they plant, weed, and harvest. The understanding that both practical work and religious work are necessary for successful outcomes continues to pervade the practice of subsistence gardeners around the world, whether they rely on their indigenous religion, on an introduced religion, or on both. Their welfare depends upon engaging the powers of garden fertility.

Probably the best-known ethnographic account of gardening is Bronislaw Malinowski's *Coral Gardens and Their Magic* (1935), which describes the gardening techniques and rituals of the matrilineal people of the Trobriand Islands, whose livelihood depends on gardening and fishing. In the communities Malinowski studied from 1915 to 1918, the garden magician is an hereditary specialist who coordinates a series of rituals that parallel stages in the gardening cycle and encourages people in the communal labor necessary for the gardens. "Gardening," Malinowski writes, "is associated with an extremely complicated and important body of magic, which, in turn, has its mythology, traditional charters and privileges. Magic appears side by side with work, not accidentally or sporadically as occasion arises or as whim dictates, but as an essential part of the whole scheme" (vol. 1, p. 55). He continues, "Gardening, and effective gardening at that, with a large surplus produce, lies at the root of all tribal authority as well as of the kinship system and communal organization of the Islanders. The gardens of the community are not merely a means to food; they are a source of pride and the main object of collective ambition" (vol. 1, p. 66).

Throughout Oceania the vegetables that make up the daily diet are grown by the family. Gardens are devoted to yams, taro, bananas, green leafy vegetables, beans, corn, and other crops. Flowers, which are used for body decoration, as part of traditional rituals, and to decorate churches for Christian services, may be grown at the border of the vegetables or in separate plots. Tobacco is frequently grown at the edge of gardens. In general, agricultural labor is divided between the sexes so that a man does the work of clearing land (e.g., felling trees, breaking up the soil), making drainage ditches, and fencing, whereas his wife plants and weeds. In many places a woman uses a digging stick for planting, weeding, and harvesting. Before planting, the couple performs a ritual to ensure a good crop. For example, in parts of the Papua New Guinea highlands it is common to bury egg-shaped fertility stones in the garden and to rub digging sticks with pig fat. In some places a couple may have sex in a new garden before planting takes place, and for some communities the garden is the regular place for sexual activity. Generally, women plant, tend, and harvest the sweet potatoes and green leafy vegetables, and men care for trees that provide fruit and nuts and tend the sugarcane and corn. In some areas men are also responsible for taro and yams. Women need to work in their gardens every day and to harvest tubers each day to feed their families and pigs; men's crops require less attention. It is common for crops to be designated as male or female according to who cares for them and in relation to their physical characteristics.

Writing of the Kuma of the Wahgi Valley in the New Guinea highlands as they were in the 1950s, anthropologist Marie Reay describes how during preparations for a major ceremony, a small rite is performed with the overt intention of promoting garden fertility. The men and boys carry toy bows and arrows, of the kind used in rites expressing traditional hostilities, and give them to a sorcerer, who holds them against a bundle of fresh leaves from the sweet potato vine. An orator announces that the fathers and grandfathers of all who are present are to be honored in the dance about to begin. Then the sorcerer returns the bows and arrows to the owners, each with a piece of sweet potato vine, which is later planted. Garden fertility is expressed both verbally and in the handling of sweet potato leaves. Traditional hostilities are implied in the use of toy bows and by the presence of the sorcerer. Thus, the rite for garden fertility is linked not only to the physical environment but also to the social situation. The Kuma expect their clan to prosper if they continue their fathers' and grandfathers' hostilities (Reay, 1959, p. 158).

In much of sub-Saharan Africa, gardens are dedicated to staple grain crops and tubers. Flowers may be grown either within the vegetable or grain garden or in separate plots. Flowers are cultivated for medicinal or culinary use or, less often, for decoration. Depending upon the particular culture and its contemporary religious patterns, prayers for gardens may be addressed to God, to nature spirits, or to spirits of the dead. In southern Africa among the Nguni, the myth of *Inkosazana yase zulweni* (the Princess of the Sky) describes a mythological figure who personifies vegetation and fertility. She is goddess of the corn and presides over the growth of the grain. It is said that from her the people learned how to brew beer. Moreover, she has the power to bring rain. She is said to visit the earth in the spring, and her visit is celebrated with festivals. People appeal to her for alleviation of misfortune and for protection from disease. In the summer (December) the Nguni hold a first fruits ceremony when the corn and other vegetables are ready to eat (Krige, 1950, pp. 197–200).

Rain-making specialists are common in Africa, where so much of the country is dry and the lives of people and crops depends upon rain (Mbiti, 1991, p. 134). As in Oceania, there are rituals for making new fields, for planting and weeding, for first fruits and for harvest (Mbiti, 1991, pp. 135–136). African gardening, like Oceanian gardening, is part of a total way of life and is related to other cultural processes. The Dogon cultivate land in squares following the pattern of the flat roof of the celestial granary of Dogon myth. Traditional cultivation, according to Ogotemmêli, the wise man who related his understanding of the Dogon world to the French anthropologist Marcel Griaule, "is like weaving; one begins on the north side, moving from east to west and then back from west to east. On each line eight feet are planted and the square has eight lines recalling the eight ancestors and the eight seeds" (Griaule, 1965, p. 77). "Moreover," says Griaule, "weaving is a form of speech, which is imparted to the fabric by the to-and-fro movement of the shuttle on the warp; and in the same way the to-and-fro movement of the peasant on his plot imparts the Word of the ancestors, that is to say, moisture, to the ground on which he works, and thus rids the earth of impurity and extends the area of cultivation round inhabited places" (p. 77). The original French title of Griaule's work, *Dieu d'Eau: entretiens avec Ogotemmêli* (Water god: Conversations with Ogotemmêli), points to the central importance of moisture in the world of Dogon gardeners.

Food and fertility are foci of all religions. Supplicants ask for their daily bread and pray for the fruitfulness of the land, the fecundity of flocks, and the flourishing of human beings. The emphasis on food and fertility is most obvious among those who tend gardens for their livelihood. Their myths and their rituals tell of their dependence on the powers of fertility, and through practical work and symbolic work they assert what control they can over their garden-world.

SEE ALSO Agriculture; Ecology and Religion, overview article; Food.

BIBLIOGRAPHY

Dieter, Michael, and Brian Hayden, eds. *Feasts: Archaeological and Ethnographic Perspectives on Food, Politics, and Power.* Washington, D.C., and London, 2001.

Griaule, Marcel. *Conversations with Ogotemmêli: An Introduction to Dogon Religious Ideas.* Introduction by Germaine Dieterlen. Translated by Ralph Butler. Oxford, 1965.

Kahn, Miriam. *Always Hungry, Never Greedy.* Cambridge, U.K., 1986.

Krige, Eileen Jensen. *The Social System of the Zulus.* (1950) Pietermaritzburg, South Africa, 1988.

Malinowski, Bronislaw. *Coral Gardens and Their Magic.* 2 vols. London, 1935.

Mbiti, John S. *Introduction to African Religion.* 2d ed. London, 1991.

Meigs, Anna S. *Food, Sex, and Pollution: A New Guinea Religion.* New Brunswick, N.J., 1984.

Reay, Marie. *The Kuma: Freedom and Conformity in the New Guinea Highlands.* Melbourne, Australia, 1959.

Sillitoe, Paul. *Roots of the Earth.* Kensington, Australia, 1983.

Sturtevant, William C. "A Structural Sketch of Iroquois Ritual." In *Extending the Rafters: Interdisciplinary Approaches to Iroquoian Studies,* edited by Michael K. Foster, et al., pp. 133–152. Albany, N.Y., 1985.

Young, Michael. *Magicians of Manumanua: Living Myth in Kalauna.* Berkeley, Calif., 1983.

MARY N. MACDONALD (2005)

GARDENS: ISLAMIC GARDENS

Islamic gardens represent cultivated spaces across the diverse span of Muslim history and geography, created and set apart from wilderness of various kinds. They were designed to enhance the humanly constructed environment, to ornament the landscape, and to symbolize cultural and religious values and aspirations. As such, they are together with architecture and the arts among the most significant and enduring of Muslim expressions of the role and relationship of nature in its broader sense to human beings. Gardens and landscape architecture in Muslim societies have been an important expression of ethical assumptions about stewardship, ecology, and beauty. This heritage of spaces and values has in recent times come under increasing pressure because of very high levels of demographic change, desertification (the degradation of formerly cultivated land), burgeoning urban growth, and general neglect.

Gardens in the Qur'ān. The Arabic word for garden (*jannah*) is used in the Qur'ān for paradise, the reward of the hereafter. There are a number of other references to the notion of the garden in the Qur'ān: *al-firdaws* (Q 23:11) originating from the Old Persian (*paridaiza*), and *al-rawda* (Q 30:15 and 42:22), with reference to the lush greenery of the garden. One of the settings in the Qur'anic narrative of creation (Q 2:34, 7:19) is the primordial garden where the first-created pair of human beings is placed. The garden is therefore also among God's creations and the theater in which the initial human drama unfolds. On one level it represents the ideal environment in which the first humans can subsist, close to God and in balance and harmony with nature. In an Arabic term referring to a Qur'anic verse, the word *ayah* also signifies a sign from nature. The human trespass, the act of disobeying God's command, results in dismissal from the garden and a sojourn on earth. The promise of the return to the garden—that is, the promised abode of the hereafter—is held out as the goal of human life; but until the return, the garden remains an aspiration and expectation, even a memory, that human imagination might be able to recreate on earth. Among the main features of the garden in paradise is water, an oft-repeated reference. The Qur'ān refers to the four rivers that flow in paradise (47:15)—rivers of water, milk, honey, and wine. Springs are mentioned and named, the best-known being *kawthar* (108:1) and *tasnīm* (83:27), from which the righteous may drink. Trees with fruit are to be found in abundance. Among the trees specifically designated is the lote-tree, a symbolic reference, which in Muslim tradition signifies the tree of life and knowledge marking the boundary of the "garden of refuge" (53:14–15); the *tūbā,* the tree of blessing; and fruit-bearing trees producing grapes, pomegranates, and other fruits.

This evocative, subtle, and richly symbolic historicized garden is the promised home of the righteous; in it the once-living share eternal joy among beings of great beauty, male and female. The latter, which are called houris, are compared to pearls and are eternally virgins, providing companionship, solace and love. The dominant themes that mark the lives of the garden's inhabitants are peace, reunion with families and communities, security, intimacy, luxury—and overwhelmingly, the joy of knowing that they have pleased God and that he is pleased with them. According to the Qur'ān, the return to God is the supreme joy of the righteous.

Islamic Gardens in History. Muslim rule and territorial control expanded rapidly during Islam's first two centuries, eventually encompassing significant areas around the Mediterranean Sea as well as former Byzantine and Sassanian-ruled territories in North Africa, Spain, the Middle East and Central Asia. This diversity of landscapes, climates, and geographical settings influenced the utilization and development of land. Patterns of existing use and the availability of water were major factors in transforming the landscape to mirror the changes in control, settlement, and cultural values.

Persia had a long history of gardens that predated Islam, a tradition that Muslims adopted and continued. Many of the earlier examples of Persian gardens have not survived; recent excavations, however, provide evidence of the extensive development of gardens under successive dynasties. The original Persian garden (*bāgh*) was irrigated by canals diverted from a river or stream. The new towns and cities under Muslim rule, including capital cities like the Baghdad of the Abbasids, contained several gardens influenced by the Persian pattern. Rulers continued to build gardens in newly established population centers, using existing water installations or creating new channels for irrigation. Muslim travelers' accounts from the medieval period describe a profusion of richly endowed gardens, public and private, with fountains and pavilions. One of the patterns that came to dominate the design of these gardens, though not exclusively, was the *chahār-bāgh*—the foursquare garden, often linked to the Qur'anic allusion to the four rivers of paradise. The Safavid gardens, particularly in Isfahan, are a fine example and extension of this foursquare style.

The Muslim Umayyad rulers of Andalusia continued Roman and local Spanish traditions in order to develop exquisite gardens, some of which survive in the early twenty-first century, as in the Alhambra. The excavations of the Umayyad palace city, Madīnat al-Zahra, destroyed in the eleventh century, reveal the presence of gardens, fountains, and pavilions. Most of these structures were created to reflect a symmetrical design, organized to present dramatic vistas, and also to afford a sense of privacy, intimacy, and leisure. It has been suggested that these gardens were framed within a geometrical pattern intended to reflect order, authority, and symmetry in nature as well as in society, thus simultaneously evoking religious, aesthetic, and political meanings. Another historical example of extensive garden construction is that of the Mughal period in Central and South Asia. Several of these gardens have survived in Afghanistan, India, and Pakistan. They illustrate connections with new landscapes combined with visions of spaces that mark transitions to the afterlife and the rich imagery of the Qur'ān.

The Qur'anic image of the garden and the rich enhancement of landscape throughout Muslim history have made these concepts a fertile source for Muslim poetry and literature. Two of the classics of Persian literature, Sa'di's *Rose Garden*, or *Gulistân* (c. 1256 CE), and his *Fruit Orchard*, or *Bustan* (c. 1257), are inspired in their form as well as their imagery by garden motifs. Much of Muslim mystical poetry builds on the symbolic meanings of the garden, its geometrical design, water, profusion, greenery, the budding of the rose, the bee among the flowers, the harmony of form and essence, and the transient and created nature of the earthly garden. The archetypal space is the site of the meaning of human life, its exalted destiny as well as the focus of its memory. The garden may represent both the place of transition as well as arrival, and of ultimate repose in the world or an anticipation of the hereafter.

ISLAMIC GARDENS IN MODERN TIMES. Pressures resulting from population growth, urbanization, climate change, and economic underdevelopment have led to the neglect, degradation and even extinction of public and private green spaces across the Muslim world. Many of the emerging Muslim nation-states and societies have sought to restore and revive their gardens through local initiatives or assistance from global organizations committed to preservation, restoration, and recreation. The erosion of the heritage is now balanced by such new efforts as the landscaping around the airport in Jakarta, the Bagh-e-Ferdowsi in Tehran, the reforestation project on the campus of a university in Ankara, and the Al-Azhar Park project in Cairo. There are many other cases that need to be addressed to repair both natural and human-made disasters. The heritage of gardens is inseparable from the vitality of culture in the Muslim world and the ecological aspirations of human beings that transcend time and space.

SEE ALSO Architecture; Geometry; Islam, overview article; Paradise.

BIBLIOGRAPHY

The following studies provide useful resources for the study of Islamic gardens and their broader relationship with Muslim architecture and cultures: John Brookes, *Gardens of Paradise: The History and Design of the Great Islamic Gardens* (London, 1987); Richard Ettinghausen and Elisabeth Macdougall, eds., *The Islamic Garden* (Washington, D.C., 1970); Valérie Gonzalez, *Beauty and Islam: Aesthetics in Islamic Art and Architecture* (London, 2002); and D. Fairchild Ruggles, *Gardens, Landscapes and Visions in the Palaces of Islamic Spain* (University Park, Pa., 2000). On architecture in particular, the reader is referred to Azim Nanji, ed., *Building for Tomorrow* (London, 1994), and *Modernity and Community: Architecture in the Islamic World* (London, 2001), a publication of the Aga Khan Award for Architecture. For visual resources on gardens see the web-site, http://archnet.org, developed by the Harvard MIT School of Architecture and Planning in cooperation with the Aga Khan Trust for Culture.

AZIM NANJI (2005)

GARIFUNA RELIGION.

The Garifuna are an ethnic group numbering roughly 300,000 with communities in some 40 villages dotting the Caribbean coasts of Nicaragua, Honduras, Guatemala, and Belize. Their traditional ancestor-focused religion presents a multilayered confluence of Amerindian, African, and Roman Catholic influences.

HISTORY. The Garifuna are descendants of Africans and Amerindians (Carib and Arawak) who shared the island of Saint Vincent beginning in the second half of the seventeenth century. *Garifuna* is properly the name of their language, which is affiliated with the Arawak linguistic family. The term is derived from *Kalinago*, the ethnic title used by Island Carib Amerindians to describe themselves but misrecognized by Christopher Columbus as "Carib." Europeans called the Garifuna "Black Caribs" because of the group's apparent African ancestry. That appellation was in common usage until the shift to Garifuna as a standard ethnic name after the middle of the twentieth century.

The African presence on Saint Vincent derived in part from survivors of a slaver shipwreck near the island dated to 1635. Most probably, then, their African origins derived from the slave trade out of the ports of west central Africa. The African presence also derived from Carib raids that carried slaves from European colonies and from the arrival of fleeing African maroons from neighboring Barbados and elsewhere. By 1674, according to accounts from the Jesuit missions, the "Black Carib" numbered as many as the "Red" Island Carib on Saint Vincent. Reports from 1700 indicate that they had already founded settlements separated from the Island Carib Amerindians.

After 1783 Saint Vincent became a permanent British colony and was slotted for sugar production. Following a period of military resistance in the Second Carib War (1795–1797), a British naval convoy deported approximately five thousand Garifuna to Roatan, an island just off the coast of Central America. Though half of those deported died in transit, their survivors settled the Central American coast early in the 1800s. This became the new homeland, the site of their reconstitution as a distinct ethnic group with its own specific set of religious practices.

RELIGIOUS TRANSCULTURATION. Garifuna religion provides a stunning example of the religious transculturation that occurred throughout the Caribbean Basin during the colonial period. Seventeenth-century missionary accounts of the Island Carib Amerindians describe religious leaders known as *piaye* or *boyé*. These were shamans who used gourd rattles and tobacco to cure patients of illnesses attributed to malignant spirits through their mastery and mediation of tutelary ancestral spirits. They are also recorded as performing divination. The "Black Caribs" adopted this religious office and techniques from their Saint Vincent hosts. Garifuna religion continues to rely upon the leadership of such shamans, still called by the similar title of *buyei*. They orchestrate and direct sophisticated ritual performances under the influence of the helping spirits of benevolent ancestors *(hiuruha)*. Other aspects of early Island Carib Amerindian religion, like the belief that a person is constituted by multiple souls, including the "heart-soul" (*uwani*) as the seat of agency and will and the "spirit double" *(afurugu)* that may wander during dreams and after death, remain a vital part of contemporary Garifuna religion as well. These bear witness to the legacy of Island Carib Amerindian societies, many of them now nearly assimilated or extinct, in Garifuna religious life.

Traditional west central African religious practices also left their mark on Garifuna religion. The most elaborate ritual performances, called *dügü*, utilize three drums to guide dances that culminate in spirit possession by returning ancestors, called *gubida*, who are feted as they dance and consult with the living. Drummers' use of polyrhythmic meter for dances like the *punta*, once a funerary dance, and the *junkunnu*, a mask dance, punctuate and offset the use of monorhythms like the *amalihani*. These complex drumming patterns recall in music and dance the west central African legacy.

Catholicism also played a key role in Garifuna religion as it assumed its current form after 1797. All traditional Garifuna religious actors also consider themselves to be Catholic, and Catholicism provides the overall mythic structure within which the ancestor religion is maintained. Malignant *(mafia)* spirits, for example, typically associated spatially with "the bush" *(el monte)*, are considered manifestations of the devil, while positive spirits are regarded as agents of the high God *(Bungiu)*. Postmortem rituals (see below) begin with "masses" *(lemesi)* adapted from official Roman Catholic liturgy and continue with novenas (ninth-night masses) and anniversary masses performed to remember and appease the dead. Catholic saints are prominent on Garifuna altars, and specific saints like Esquipula and Anthony are called upon as sources of solace and assistance.

SMALL-SCALE RITUAL EVENTS. Since the overall mythic and ethical structure of Garifuna religion is provided by Roman Catholic Christianity, the distinguishing characteristics of Garifuna religion are found in its sophisticated complex of ritual practices. Moreover since specific beliefs and ethical postures vary widely in relation to popular adaptations of Catholicism, correct ritual practice is particularly crucial to Garifuna religious identity. Myths and belief remain largely implicit, embedded in ritual performance.

In general, rituals are focused on the problem of death and the transfer in status from living human being to exalted ancestor *(gubida)*. Though the dead remain a source of power for the living, they must also be helped by living family members as they take the steps from this world to their status as recently departed spirits *(ahari)* and then to one of finally becoming *gubida* in the otherworld. The otherworld is called *Sairi*, the home of the ancestors, and is often physically located on Saint Vincent. The postmortem journey is simultaneously one of progressive spiritual advance and one of geographic traverse, or return, to the lost homeland. The ritualization of death is therefore in part an expression of diasporic consciousness, a means of looking back to a paradise lost.

Insofar as the ritual obligations to the dead are not adequately performed by the living, ancestors register their complaints through signs experienced by the living as nightmares, bad luck, accidents, and unexplained illnesses. Garifuna religion is in this sense rigorously this-worldly. It is concerned with alleviating concrete material problems by contemplating them and acting upon them as ruptures in the relations between of the living and the ancestors. These crises are addressed through a sequence of ritual interventions that demand progressively more serious investments. The ability to prosper in the material world is therefore understood as directly related to and contingent upon the attention devoted to the family ancestors' "advance" through the spirit world.

Veluria. When a member of the community dies, the corpse of the deceased is placed in a coffin and laid out in his or her house for public viewing. Candles are lit and placed at each corner, and near the coffin a simple altar is erected on a low table, including holy water and statues of Catholic saints. Crepe-paper streamers are hung in a canopy over the body. Friends and relatives arrive at the wake and hold vigil through the night, drinking coffee and rum (*aguardiente* or *guaro*), playing cards, and talking. At dawn the corpse is interred in a graveyard that is nearby yet spatially removed from the village. The burial is accompanied by wailing laments and the pouring of rum into the grave by family members and friends.

Amuidahani. Between six months and several years after the death, the family "bathes" the deceased. A small pit is dug immediately adjacent to the home, and a fresh change of clothes for the departed is suspended above it. Family members and intimate friends pour liquids into the pit, variously including freshwater, saltwater, strained cassava water, herbal infusions, and favored beverages like coffee and rum. Tobacco and favorite foods may be offered as well. Following the "bathing" of the deceased, the pit is closed. The ritual is small and intimate in nature, of short duration, and does not require the presence of the *buyei* as officiant.

Lemesi. Around a year following death, as well as later if called for by the ancestor through divination by the *buyei*, a "mass" is held for the spirit of the deceased *(ahari)*, who is viewed as still present in the village. The occasion marks the end of a period of mourning for the spouse who survives the dead and, as an occasion marking the return to everyday life, is conspicuously festive. Food and beverages are served, and the celebrative *punta* dance is drummed and danced in the yard. The *punta* is typically comprised of a circle into which a man and a woman enter in pairs, two at a time. The dance entails the rhythmic oscillation of the hips while holding the upper body perfectly still and the facial expression calm. It celebrates both the life of the deceased and the ongoing force of the community despite the loss of one of its members.

Women gathered for the purpose sing "women's songs" *(abaimahani),* standing in a line with little fingers linked and thrusting the arms forward in rhythmic concert, a gesture suggestive of shared labor. The song lyrics recall the struggles of family life and loyalty and sometimes speak from the perspective of the ancestors, pleading to not be forgotten. Men's songs *(arumahani)* are ideally presented in similar fashion, though since the twentieth century it has become increasingly challenging to find a choir of males able and willing to perform the old songs. This is because of a common male pattern of leaving the village for long durations in order to find work. The lyrics of men's songs often recall the necessity and dangers of travel for labor far from home and the longing to return.

In addition traditional tales *(úruga)* may be told, often humorous trickster-like narratives. The festivities continue until dawn.

MAJOR RITUAL EVENTS. While the foregoing are required in all cases, the most elaborate postmortem rituals, the *chugu* and the *dügü,* are called for only when specifically requested by an ancestral spirit. When a family member suffers unusual misfortune, recurring nightmares, or unexplained illnesses or pains, he or she may consult a shaman *(buyei).* With the patient seated before the *buyei's* altar *(gule),* the *buyei* lights a candle, smokes his or her pipe, and summons his or her tutelary spirits *(hiuruha)* by blowing the vapor of rum from the mouth over the altar. This activates it. Blowing smoke over the head of the patient, he or she consults with his or her spirits to "read" the nature of the problem at hand, depending on the movement of the smoke and the insights granted by tutelary spirits *(hiuruha).* This ritual act is called *arairaguni,* "bringing down the spirits." If the problem is one caused by the ancestors *(hasandigubida),* he or she negotiates with the afflicting spirit to decipher what it requires. This may be a *misa,* a *chugu,* or in the most serious of cases, a *dügü.* Together with the patient, and taking account of the family's financial resources, the shaman then plots the course of action.

Chugu. The *chugu,* literally the "feeding" of the dead, is a one- to two-day ceremony officiated by a *buyei.* In addition to all of the elements included in a "mass," it entails the assembly of a greater number of relatives and the preparation of large quantities of food offerings, including roosters *(gayu)* offered for sacrifice. Since a more intimate communication with the dead is required than in a "mass," the *buyei* erects his or her personal altar *(gule)* in the house where the *chugu* will take place. There he or she places the symbols of his or her key helping spirits as well as the implements of the shaman's vocation: the maracas *(sirisi)* used to call the spirit, the wand *(murewa)* used to communicate with and control the spirit should possession trance occur, and bottles of rum and tobacco used to purify the room and to activate, or "heat," the altar. Traditional foods are prepared, including most importantly the sacrificed roosters *(gayu)* and cassava bread *(ereba),* to present an abundant table to the dead. Women's and men's songs are performed at length, and the spirit may also be celebrated with *punta* dancing. Much rum is consumed to create the atmosphere of exuberance and generous abundance believed to be favored by the ancestors.

At the conclusion of the day's events, the *buyei* concocts a nog of beaten eggs and hot rum *(furunsu).* Each participant places his or her full cup upon the altar while making requests of the ancestor before exchanging the cup with another participant. The exchanged communal drink unites the group. Finally, the *buyei* "burns the table," pouring rum over its surface and igniting it in flame. A strong blue flame reveals the ancestor's approval of the offering and indicates that the precipitating symptoms of bad luck or illness that evoked the *chugu* should subside.

Dügü. Just as the *chugu* contains all the elements of the "mass," the *dügü* contains all the elements of the *chugu,* such that the larger ritual encompasses the smaller in the style of Chinese boxes. *Dügü* is short for *adugurahani,* "mashing down the earth," perhaps referring to the long periods of dance that are required of participants. It is regarded as the fullest expression of Garifuna religion and is a major ritual event that is prepared for a full year and performed over a week's duration. It typically occurs many years after the death of a family member and only when mandated by a *buyei* and his or her spirit helpers. Announcements about the *dügü* circulate for at least a year to insure that sufficient funds can be raised for sacrifices of roosters, pigs, and sometimes a cow and to feed a crowd of participants that may number in the hundreds for a week's time. All family members, even those residing in the United States, are obligated to attend. Indeed the ritual's efficacy depends on a complete demonstration of family unity to resolve the perceived crisis. It is arguably the emotional dramatization of family unity itself that provides in part the experience of the ritual as a healing cure.

First, a ceremonial house (*gayunere* or *dabuyaba*) must be constructed in "traditional" palm-thatch style on the beach. The *dügü* formally begins with the "return of the fishermen," a group sent three days prior to catch fish in the "traditional" way in the offshore cays. They arrive at dawn, attired as Garifuna ancestors wearing helmets of woven palm, and are greeted with exuberant songs by family members attired in matching red-dyed uniforms. They are given rum and cigarettes and are laid in hammocks, just as the ancestors will be later in the ritual when they are incorporated in living bodies of dancers through spirit possession.

Over the next two days follows a sequence of dances both to honor the ancestors and create the conditions for their arrival in possession. First are the *amalahani,* dances to honor the ancestors. These continue for up to four hours at a time, brought to crescendo by the shaman, who exhorts the large group until some are possessed by ancestors. Transformed into known figures from the past, they make requests and are soothed with rum and food. Living family members may ask questions, in response to which the ancestors give counsel.

Throughout the second and third day, the food offering *(chugu)* is prepared. Roosters—one required from each attending nuclear family—are sacrificed, massive amounts of rum assembled, and tables loaded with the most traditional Garifuna foods. The food is piled high on a wooden table and left for the ancestors' consumption. After the spirits "eat," the assembled participants also take their fill, rejoicing in the luxurious abundance far exceeding that of everyday life. At the close of the day, what remains of the spirits' food is buried in the ground or returned to the sea, taken by canoe and deposited in the deeps.

Finally, the shaman guarantees the ancestors' acceptance of the offerings. Pouring rum on the table, he or she feeds the flame and tips the table to all sides, as in the *chugu.* There is great joy, and all rush to wipe the sacralized liquor on their bodies as a balm for all pains. Reunited family groups run to enter the sea together in a temporary moment of *communitas.*

As the *dügü* summons and placates ancestors, it also reinforces family bonds among the living. This has become increasingly important as a third of the Garifuna have emigrated to the United States since the middle of the twentieth century. The *dügü* takes on new import and meaning for those residing abroad, serving the purpose of communicating the experience of home through the dense, compact form of ritual performance. Territoriality, or consciousness of place, is fortified above all in this central ritual performance. With increased migration, the *dügü* appears to be gaining in the frequency of its performance rather than suffering a decline.

NEW DEVELOPMENTS. Migration to cities like New York has sparked a new identity consciousness of the Garifuna's African roots. Religious leaders in New York have begun to conceive of their traditional practices within the purview of other African diaspora religions like Cuban Santería and Haitian vodou. This new form of indigenous syncretism justifies a view of the Garifuna as a dramatically innovative religion, especially as it is reshaped in the new contexts of U.S. urban centers. As Garifuna religious leaders in the United States return periodically to perform rituals in Honduras, Belize, and Guatemala, they carry with them a new identity consciousness. This will likely have transformative effects on homeland religious performance as well.

The second key contemporary issue of Garifuna religion is the rise of evangelical Christian sects since around 1980 in homeland villages. Converts to the new churches disavow all connections to traditional practices, which are regarded as diabolical. The use of dance, tobacco, rum, and altars are vehemently rejected, leading to the dismissal not only of Catholicism but of virtually all traditional rites. This creates friction within families and between village factions and generates new conundrums for traditional practices like the *dügü,* since in that ritual all members of the family are required to be present. When evangelicals refuse to attend such events, they are accused of jeopardizing the rituals' efficacy and therefore also the physical safety of everyone in their kin group. While such disputes are divisive, they also serve as explanations of future accidents, bad luck, and illnesses. The disputes therefore incite ritual as much they compromise it.

BIBLIOGRAPHY

Bianchi, Cynthia Chamberlain. "Gubida Illness and Religious Ritual Among the Garifuna of Santa Fe, Honduras: An Ethnopsychiatric Analysis." Ph.D. diss., Ohio State University, 1988. This dissertation goes to great lengths to show the rich detail of Garifuna postmortem rituals framed by an ethnopsychiatric approach to healing.

Coelho, Ruy. "The Black Carib of Honduras: A Study in Acculturation." Ph.D. diss., Northwestern University, 1955. Chapter 5 provides an important mid-century look at Garifuna religion in Honduras. Much of the literature gives attention to English-speaking Belize, giving added distinction to this source.

Conzemius, Eduard. "Ethnographical Notes on the Black Carib (Garif)." *American Anthropologist* 30, no. 2 (1928): 183–205. Possibly the earliest "modern" ethnographic description of Garifuna ritual.

Flores, Barbara. "The Garifuna Dugu Ritual in Belize: A Celebration of Relationships." In *Gender, Ethnicity, and Religion,* edited by Rosemary Radford Ruether, pp. 144–170. Minneapolis, 2002. A sympathetic and accomplished essay on the *dügü* ritual with special attention to the issue of gender.

Gonzalez, Nancie L. *Sojourners of the Caribbean: Ethnogenesis and Ethnohistory of the Garifuna.* Urbana, Ill., and Chicago, 1988. This is an important resource on Garifuna history and archaeology written by the preeminent Garifuna ethnographer.

Hulme, Peter, and Neil L. Whitehead, eds. *Wild Majesty: Encounters with Caribs from Columbus to the Present Day.* Oxford, 1992. This is a selection of descriptions of the Caribs, both Island Carib Amerindians and the "Black Carib," as represented by Europeans since the seventeenth century.

Jenkins, Carol L. "Ritual and Resource Flow: The Garifuna Dugu." *American Ethnologist* 10 (1983): 429–442. An important interpretation of the relationship between economic resources and ritual performance.

Johnson, Paul Christopher. "Migrating Bodies, Circulating Signs: Brazilian Candomblé, the Garífuna of the Caribbean, and the Category of 'Indigenous Religions.'" *History of Religions* 41, no. 4 (2002): 301–328. The essay compares types of religious dislocations and creative responses for the cases of Brazilian Candomblé and the Garifuna of Honduras and in New York City. The essay begins to elaborate and theorize the relation between migration and contemporary religious change.

Kerns, Virginia. *Women and the Ancestors: Black Carib Kinship and Ritual.* 2d ed. Urbana, Ill., and Chicago, 1997. A valuable text on Garifuna religion and ritual performance for its attention to women as the primary carriers and transmitters of tradition.

Melendez, Armando Crisanto. "Religious Elements of the Garifuna Culture and Their Connotations in the Americas." In

African Creative Expressions of the Divine, edited by Kortright Davis and Elias Farajajé-Jones, translated by Dorothea Lowe Bryce, pp. 121–128. Washington, D.C., 1991. A short, descriptive account of Garifuna beliefs from an important Garifuna choreographer, historian, and cultural activist.

Sanford, Margaret. "Revitalization Movements as Indicators of Completed Acculturation." *Comparative Studies in Society and History* 16 (1974): 504–518. A provocative essay arguing that religious revitalization, including the Garifuna case, is correlated with general acculturation or assimilation such that revivals are possible indicators of cultural distress.

Suazo, Eusebio Salvador. *Irufumali: La doctrina esotérica garífuna.* Tegucigalpa, 2000. A bilingual (Spanish and Garifuna) account of the *buyei's* knowledge from a Garifuna writer, acquired through interviews with practicing shamans.

Taylor, Douglas. *The Black Carib of British Honduras.* New York, 1951. The text offers several important chapters on Garifuna beliefs in relation to the soul and Garifuna ritual practices. Taylor brought rare linguistic depth to his descriptive task.

PAUL CHRISTOPHER JOHNSON (2005)

GARVEY, MARCUS. Marcus Mosiah Garvey (August 17, 1887–June 10, 1940), the founder of the Universal Negro Improvement Association (UNIA), led the largest mass movement among African Americans and can be regarded as one of the founding fathers of Pan-Africanism and the Black Consciousness movement.

Garvey was born in Saint Ann's Bay, Jamaica. During the first decade of the twentieth century, he was involved in the labor movement and advocated for labor reforms in his paper, the *Watchman.* But he quickly became disillusioned and grew skeptical about the ability of unions to bring about meaningful improvements in the lives of blacks, and about the willingness of whites to cooperate in achieving such a goal. After a brief stint working for the United Fruit banana plantation in Costa Rica, he moved to London, where he came under the influence of Duse Muhammad Ali and wrote articles for his paper, *Africa Times and Orient Review.* While he was in London, Garvey was inspired with a new vision after reading Booker T. Washington's *Up from Slavery.* When he returned to Jamaica in 1914, Garvey quickly formed the UNIA, whose purpose was to unite Africans from all over the world in a common purpose of uplift.

Following Washington's Tuskegee model, Garvey's first program was the establishment of a trade school. This effort never enjoyed success, however, due primarily to lack of financial resources. Washington invited Garvey to visit Tuskegee but died a few months before Garvey arrived in New York City in March 1916. Garvey began introducing himself at different churches and sharing his vision. By 1918 he had started a weekly, the *Negro World* that grew in circulation to fifty thousand. By 1919 Garvey had raised enough funds to purchase an auditorium on West 138th Street in Harlem called Liberty Hall, where throngs came to hear his spellbinding oratory. The popularity of Garvey and his movement grew exponentially after he launched his project to purchase ocean steamers to trade with Africa and take black people back to Africa. Blacks purchased stocks in his company, the Black Star Line, at five dollars per share. Over half a million dollars was raised, and the first ship was purchased in the first year. The UNIA's first international convention, attended by thousands of delegates from every part of the world, was held at Liberty Hall and Madison Square Garden in August 1920. The convention proclaimed Garvey the provisional president of the Republic of Africa and adopted a Declaration of the Rights of the Negro Peoples of the World.

Garvey's movement also had a religious component. Garvey did not think blacks could ever acquire a strong sense of self-esteem while worshipping a white God and a white Savior. He argued that God, Christ, and Mary were black. In 1921 the UNIA's chaplain general, George Alexander McGuire, formed the Good Shepherd Independent Episcopal Church and authored *The Universal Negro Catechism* and *The Universal Negro Ritual.* McGuire and Garvey disagreed over forming a separate denomination, and McGuire then formed the African Orthodox Church.

The Black Star Line's financial difficulties contributed significantly to Garvey's demise and the decline of his movement. The ships purchased were unsound, and the organization lacked the resources to repair them after two disastrous ventures. By 1921 two of Garvey's ships were inoperable. African American critics of Garvey's movement, including the leader of the National Association for the Advancement of Colored People, W. E. B. Du Bois, instigated Garvey's arrest for mail fraud. Garvey was tried and convicted in 1923; he was sentenced to five years in prison and fined $1,000.

Garvey was pardoned by President Calvin Coolidge in 1927 and was deported to Jamaica, where he tried unsuccessfully to rebuild his movement. In 1935 he moved to London and published a periodical, the *Black Man.* He died of a stroke in June 1940. Even though he achieved few of his goals, Garvey's name is still revered among black nationalists.

BIBLIOGRAPHY

Burkett, Randall K. *Garveyism as a Religious Movement.* Metuchen, N.J., 1978.

Garvey, Amy Jacques, ed. *The Philosophy and Opinions of Marcus Garvey.* 2 vols. New York, 1923–1925; reprint, Dover, Mass., 1986.

Hill, Robert A., ed. *The Marcus Garvey and Universal Negro Improvement Association Papers.* 9 vols. Berkeley, Calif., 1983–.

Martin, Tony. *Race First: The Ideological and Organizational Struggles of Marcus Garvey and the Universal Negro Improvement Association.* Westport, Conn., 1976; reprint, Dover, Mass., 1986.

Martin, Tony. *Marcus Garvey, Hero: A First Biography.* Dover, Mass, 1983. Published by the Majority Press as part of the New Marcus Garvey Library.

JAMES ANTHONY NOEL (2005)

GASTER, THEODOR H. Theodor H. Gaster (1906–1992) was a renowned Semiticist and follower of James G. Frazer. He was born in England, the son of the folklorist Moses Gaster, who was Romanian by birth and a legendary linguist and scholar of Judaica. When the family immigrated to England, Moses Gaster became chief rabbi of the Sephardic Jewish community in London. He was also a leading Zionist, and Theodor "recalled that the first draft of the Balfour Declaration [which announced the British aim of creating a homeland for Jews] was prepared in his father's home. For a time, Theodor, along with his young friends Abba Eban and Isaiah Berlin, would go from door to door in London soliciting donations on behalf of this future homeland" (Hiers and Stahmer, 1995, p. 64).

Theodor Gaster was educated in private schools in London. He received an undergraduate degree in classics from the University of London in 1928 and a master's degree in Near Eastern archaeology, also from the University of London, in 1936. His master's thesis, a preview of his key work, was titled "The Ras Shamra Texts and the Origins of Drama." His mastery of languages was extraordinary, and he was "one of the last generation of scholars equally at home in Classical, Ancient Near Eastern, and multiple modern languages" (Hiers and Stahmer, 1995, p. 65).

With few academic positions open to Jewish scholars, Gaster held a series of museum and library appointments for the first part of his professional life. His first major appointment came in 1928, as curator in the Department of Egyptian and Semitic Antiquities at the Wellcome Research Institution and Museum in London. He served there until 1932 and again from 1936 to 1939. In 1935 he became literary editor of the *Jewish Daily Post,* contributing an array of scholarly and popular articles almost daily during the nine months of its existence.

In 1937 Gaster became lecturer on biblical and Near Eastern archaeology at New College and Institute of Archeology of the University of London, where he served until 1939. In the 1930s he published innumerable scholarly articles on Ras Shamra and the Bible.

In 1939 or 1940 Gaster moved from London to New York and began work on a Ph.D. at Columbia University. While pursuing his doctorate he continued to publish prolifically. In 1941 and 1942 he was editorial secretary for the Institute of Jewish Affairs of the American Jewish Congress, and in 1943 he was executive secretary for the Conference on Jewish Relations. From 1943 to 1945 he was managing editor of *Jewish Social Studies* and frequently contributed articles on Judaica, the Bible, and the ancient and modern Near East. In the mid-1940s he also began contributing to *Commentary,* and in the mid- to late 1940s he published articles on the Bible in the *Jewish Quarterly Review.*

In the early 1940s Gaster apparently missed securing a professorship in Jewish learning at Duke University because his comparativist bent was considered insufficiently traditional. In 1942 he began teaching part time in the graduate school at Columbia University, and in 1945 he also began teaching part time at Dropsie College, in Philadelphia. From 1946 to 1950 he was a lecturer on Semitic civilization at New York University. From the mid-1940s until the mid-1960s, he was a visiting professor at many colleges and universities in the United States and three times at the University of Leeds.

Gaster's first full-time American post came in 1945, when he served for a year and a half as chief of the Hebraic Section of the Library of Congress in Washington, D.C. In 1951 and 1952, he was a Fulbright Professor in the history of religions at the University of Rome, and in 1961 he was a Fulbright Professor in biblical studies and history of religions at the University of Melbourne.

Most of the books for which Gaster is best known were published in the 1950s, including his translation of the Dead Sea Scrolls, widely admired for its felicitousness; *Thespis,* his application of the Frazerian myth-and-ritual theory to the ancient Near East and beyond; and his abridgment and updating of James Frazer's *The Golden Bough* (*The New Golden Bough* [1959]), in which he retained the theory but updated the data. This abridgment was of Frazer's third twelve-volume edition of his opus, which Frazer himself had abridged into one volume in 1922. Gaster's final major work, the two-volume tome *Myth, Legend, and Custom in the Old Testament* (1969). was similarly an abridgment and updating of Frazer's *Folk-lore in the Old Testament.*

Only in 1966, at the age of sixty, did Gaster secure a permanent full-time academic post, as professor of religion at Barnard College, the women's undergraduate division of Columbia University. He helped revamp the curriculum and served a term as chair. He continued to lecture widely, and from 1971 to 1981 he was professor of religion and director of ancient Near Eastern studies at Dropsie College, by then renamed Dropsie University. Upon his retirement from Barnard, he was once again a visiting professor at many American universities. He relocated to Florida to teach for several years at the University of Florida. He died in Philadelphia, where he had moved in 1988.

As a theorist, Gaster's main contribution was his distinctive brand of myth-ritualism—the theory that connects myth to ritual. Gaster assumed that existing versions of the theory downplayed myth in favor of ritual, and he strove to accord myth the same importance as ritual. Certainly the original version of myth-ritualism, that formulated by William Robertson Smith, made myth secondary to ritual, but it is debatable whether succeeding versions of the theory did.

Gaster's myth-ritualist scenario, which he painstakingly sought to reconstruct for the ancient Near East, derives from Frazer, whose dual and ultimately incompatible versions of myth-ritualism Gaster sought to combine. In Frazer's first version, the king is human and merely plays the role of the god of vegetation, who dies and, through the imitation of his rebirth, is magically reborn. In Frazer's second version the king is himself divine and is killed outright and replaced, with the soul of the god of vegetation thereby automatically transferred from the incumbent to his successor. For Gaster, the king either is god or merely represents god. It is simply not clear which he is asserting. On the one hand, according to Gaster, the king is literally or symbolically killed and replaced annually. Here Gaster is using Frazer's second version. On the other hand, according to Gaster, the killing and replacing of the king parallels the death and rebirth of the god of vegetation and, by magical imitation, causes the rebirth of the god. Here Gaster is using Frazer's first version. Followers of Frazer other than Gaster have also become confused in trying to reconcile actual regicide (king as divine) with magical imitation (king as human).

For Frazer, the myth of the death and rebirth of the god of vegetation explains the ritual. It is the script of the ritual. For Gaster, the myth does more than explain the ritual. By itself, the ritual operates on only the human plane. Myth connects ritual to the divine plane. The renewal sought thereby becomes spiritual and not merely physical. Rather than simply explicating the inherent, physical meaning of ritual, as Frazer did, Gaster saw myth as giving ritual its spiritual meaning. In this sense he accords myth a status at least equal to that of ritual. To do so, he must in fact be confining himself to Frazer's first myth-ritualist scenario, for only here is the myth of the god to be found.

SEE ALSO Frazer, James G.; Myth; Myth and Ritual School; Ritual.

BIBLIOGRAPHY

Gaster, Theodor H. "Divine Kingship in the Ancient Near East: A Review Article." *Review of Religion* 9 (1945): 267–281.

Gaster, Theodor H. *Passover: Its History and Traditions.* New York, 1949.

Gaster, Theodor H. "Semitic Mythology." In *Funk & Wagnalls Standard Dictionary of Folklore, Mythology, and Legend,* edited by Maria Leach, vol. 2, pp. 989–996. New York, 1949–1950.

Gaster, Theoodor H. *Thespis: Ritual, Myth and Drama in the Ancient Near East.* New York, 1950; rev. ed., Garden City, N.Y., 1961.

Gaster, Theodor H. *Purim and Hanukkah in Custom and Tradition: Feast of Lots, Feast of Lights.* New York, 1950.

Gaster, Theodor H. "Errors of Method in the Study of Religion." In *Freedom and Reason: Studies in Philosophy and Jewish Culture, in Memory of Morris Raphael Cohen,* edited by Salo W. Baron et al., pp. 372–382. Glencoe, Ill., 1951.

Gaster, Theodor H. *The Oldest Stories in the World.* New York, 1952.

Gaster, Theodor H. *Festivals of the Jewish Year: A Modern Interpretation and Guide.* New York, 1953.

Gaster, Theodor H. "Myth and Story." *Numen* 1 (1954): 184–212.

Gaster, Theodor H. *The Holy and the Profane: The Evolution of Jewish Folkways.* New York, 1955; 2d ed., New York, 1980.

Gaster, Theodor H. "Mythic Thought in the Ancient Near East." *Journal of the History of Ideas* 16 (1955): 422–426.

Gaster, Theodor H. *New Year: Its History, Customs and Superstitions.* New York, 1955.

Gaster, Theodor H. *The New Golden Bough.* New York, 1959.

Gaster, Theodor H. "Myth, Mythology." In *Interpreter's Dictionary of the Bible,* edited by George A. Buttrick, vol. 2, pp. 481–487. New York and Nashville, 1962.

Gaster, Theodor H. *Myth, Legend, and Custom in the Old Testament.* 2 vols. New York, 1969.

Grimes, Ronald L. "Ritual Studies: A Comparative Review of Theodor Gaster and Victor Turner." *Religious Studies Review* 2 (1976): 13–25.

Hiers, Richard H., with Harold M. Stahmer. "Theodor H. Gaster, 1906–1992: A Biographical Sketch and a Bibliographical Listing of Identified Published Writings." *Ugarit-Forschungen* 27 (1995): 59–114. The key source on Gaster's life and much relied on for this entry.

Hiers, Richard H., with Harold M. Stahmer. "Theodor H. Gaster: Biographical Sketch and a Bibliography: A Supplemental Note." *Ugarit-Forschungen* 28 (1996): 277–285.

Journal of the Ancient Near Eastern Society of Columbia University 5 (1973). Festschrift to Gaster with essays by 46 contributors. Includes a select bibliography.

ROBERT A. SEGAL (2005)

GATEWAYS SEE PORTALS

GAUḌAPĀDA,

Indian philosopher, was the reputed *para-ma-guru* ("teacher's teacher") of Śaṅkara. Information about Gauḍapāda is scant and has been subject to scholarly controversy. In what is now regarded as a fantastic thesis, Max von Walleser professed in his *Der ältere Vedanta: Geschichte, Kritik und Lehre* (Heidelberg, 1910) that Gauḍapāda never existed at all. However, both V. Bhattacharya (1943) and T. M. P. Mahadevan (1969) have argued convincingly that Gauḍapāda was a real person, the author of what is called *Āgama Śāstra* or *Gauḍapādīyakārikā,* or simply *Māṇḍūkyakārikā.*

The name *Gauḍa* indicates that he must have come from Gauḍadeśá ("Gauḍa country"), or Bengal. On the authority of the *Śārīrakamīmāṃsābhāṣya-vārttika* of Bālakṛṣṇananda Sarasvatī (seventeenth century CE), it is known that in the country of Kurukṣetra (north of present-day Delhi), near the Hīravatī River, there lived a group of people who had migrated from Bengal (and hence were called Gauḍas); the most eminent among them was one Gauḍapāda. Exactly when Gauḍapāda lived has also been a matter of controversy. Some scholars place him in the fifth century CE, but this theory contradicts the traditional belief that he was Śaṅkara's teacher's teacher, for Śaṅkara is generally assumed to have flourished somewhere between 788 and

820 CE. Another assumption is that Gauḍapāda was a contemporary of Apollonius of Tyana, who traveled to India in the first century CE. This, however, is highly conjectural, and would place Gauḍapāda at an earlier, and even less likely date.

According to Ānandagiri (a pupil of Śaṅkara), Gauḍapāda lived the final part of his life in Badarikāśrama, the holy residence of Nara-Nārāyaṇa, and spent his time in deep meditation on the lord (Nārāyaṇa-Kṛṣṇa). Greatly pleased with Gauḍapāda, the lord thus revealed to him an insight into the quintessence of Upaniṣadic wisdom, which he recorded in his *Māṇḍūkyakārikā.* Commenting on Gauḍapāda's *Āgama-Śāstra,* a certain Śaṅkara (perhaps identical with the great Śaṅkara) remarked that nondualism had been recovered from the Vedas by Gauḍapāda in order to refute the dualism of the Sāṃkhya masters.

The *Āgama Śāstra* is divided into four *prakaraṇa*s, or chapters. It is regarded as a commentary on the brief, enigmatic Upaniṣad called *Maṇḍūkya.* Only in the first chapter are the *mantras* of the *Maṇḍūkya* discussed. Then the author goes on to establish the Advaita ("nondual") doctrine by arguing against the dualists, such as the Sāṃkhya philosophers, and the pluralists, such as the Nyāya philosophers. His doctrine is called the *ajātivāda,* or the "theory of nonorigination." The paradox of permanence and change is invoked to show that causation or origination of new things is unintelligible. The Sāṃkhya philosophers who say that the cause persists in, and is identical with, the effect (*satkāryavāda*), and the Nyāya philosophers who say that the cause creates the effect, which was nonexistent before (*asatkāryavāda*), oppose each other and both, thereby, are refuted; this then points toward the truth of the view of nonorigination, that is, that nothing can originate. Creation is only an illusion; the diversity of the world has only a dreamlike existence, for the ultimate reality is a nondifferential unity.

It is believed that Gauḍapāda was strongly influenced by Buddhism, especially by the Yogācāra school. It has even been suggested that the *Āgama Śāstra* is actually a Buddhist text. But while the influence of Buddhist doctrines and arguments upon Gauḍapāda is undeniable, it would be wrong to conclude that he was a Buddhist. The fourth chapter of the *Āgama Śāstra* undoubtedly includes much Buddhist material. But it is still safe to conclude that Gauḍapāda was an early Vedāntin who must have influenced Śaṅkara in the development of his celebrated nondualism.

SEE ALSO Nyāya; Sāṃkhya; Śaṅkara.

BIBLIOGRAPHY

Bhattacharya, Vidhushekhara. *The Āgamaśāstra of Gauḍapāda.* Calcutta, 1943. An indispensable sourcebook containing edited text, annotated translation, and introduction.

Mahadevan, T. M. P. *Gauḍapāda: A Study in Early Advaita.* Madras, 1969.

New Sources

King, Richard. *Early Advaita Vedanta and Buddhism: The Mahayfana Context of the Gaudapadya-karika.* Albany, 1995.

BIMAL KRISHNA MATILAL (1987)
Revised Bibliography

GAUTAMA SEE BUDDHA

GE HONG

GE HONG (283–343) was a Chinese writer on alchemy and Daoism. Although a number of works have been attributed to Ge Hong, the only incontestable source for his thought is his *Baopuzi* (The master who embraces simplicity). This consists today of twenty "inner chapters" on Daoist themes, fifty "outer chapters" on more Confucian topics, and an account of his own life. In both portions of his work Ge demonstrates an encyclopedic eclecticism that has caused later scholars a certain amount of difficulty in assessing his ideas.

To understand Ge Hong's intellectual orientation, it is necessary to know his cultural situation. Ge was a member of the old aristocracy that had lived in the lands south of the Yangtze since the Han dynasty and had served in the separatist kingdom of Wu that in 222 succeeded the Han in South China. The Wu state was conquered from the north by the Jin in 280, but the expulsion of the Jin court from North China by barbarian invasions in the early fourth century forced this new regime to transfer its capital to present-day Nanjing. This demoralizing cultural invasion further accentuated the southern aristocrats' loss of independent political power, for the southerners saw themselves as the true heirs of Han civilization, unlike the northern immigrants, who had abandoned much of the Han heritage. Ge at first had some hopes of a political career under the Jin, but the premature death of his patron forced him to turn increasingly to a life of scholarship. As a consequence, his writings manifest an urge to collect the various strands of the old culture of pre-Jin times and make from them a compendium of southern intellectual conservatism. Dominant in this is a defense of local occult traditions against introduced religious and philosophical ideas.

To what degree Ge, the political outsider, managed to compensate for his disappointments by becoming a master of the occult is not clear. Recent scholarship has preferred to see him as an enthusiast who derived his knowledge from written sources more than from initiation into secret lore. But Ge used this knowledge to the full to defend his thesis that any person may become a genuine immortal. In arguing against those who interpreted immortality as a symbol of liberation from human limitations and against those who believed that immortals where born, not made, Ge provides a treasure trove of information on ancient techniques for achieving immortality. Ge's references to the alchemical preparation of elixirs of immortality have attracted the attention of modern historians of science, but he provides information on much else besides: sexual and other physiological practices, the use of talismans, herbal aids to longevity, lists of occult texts, and heterodox cults to be avoided. Because by the end of the fourth century, the religious situation in south China had been transformed totally by outside influences and internal developments, the *Baopuzi* constitutes virtually the only source for this type of lore at an earlier period.

Although the exact date of the *Baopuzi* is unknown, it would appear to have been substantially completed by 317. The Jin court bestowed on Ge honorary, politically powerless appointments in the following decade, but thereafter Ge seems to have sought to distance himself from court life in favor of alchemical pursuits. He managed eventually to obtain a posting to the far south (present-day North Vietnam) in order to search for the ingredients of the elixir of immortality. He was detained en route in present-day Guangdong and remained there, on Mount Luofu, until his death. His contemporaries readily believed that this was a feigned death and that he had in fact reached his goal of immortality.

Despite the philosophical Daoist underpinnings that he provides for his repertory of techniques, Ge Hong's contributions to the development of Daoism were in a sense negligible. His approach to the beliefs that he recorded remained a purely individual one, and his writings, in all their contradictory richness, can in no way be taken as representative of the religion of any particular body of believers. Indeed, the group religious practices of his day seem to have fallen largely outside the scope of his research. Nonetheless he may be seen as the first of a number of southern aristocrats with similar concerns. Such later figures as Lu Xiujing (406–477) and, especially, Tao Hongjing (456–536), though priests in the mainstream of Daoist belief, maintained Ge's emphasis on broad erudition and surpassed him in critical scholarship. But for Daoists and non-Daoists alike, the *Baopuzi* remained one of the most widely cited apologies for the pursuit of immortality.

See Also Alchemy, article on Chinese Alchemy; Daoism, article on Daoist Literature.

Bibliography

James R. Ware's *Alchemy, Medicine, and Religion in the China of A.D. 320: The Neipian of Ge Hong* (Cambridge, Mass., 1967), provides a complete translation of the "inner chapters" of the *Baopuzi* and of Ge's autobiography. Jay Sailey's *The Master Who Embraces Simplicity: A Study of the Philosopher Ge Hong, A.D. 283–343* (San Francisco, 1978) translates the autobiography, plus twenty more of the "outer chapters"; a lengthy study of Ge Hong and his thought is also appended. Neither volume is beyond criticism, but taken together they give a good picture of the diversity of Ge Hong's work.

New Sources

Lai, Chi-tim. "Ko Hung's Discourse of Hsien-Immortality: A Taoist Configuration of an Alternative Ideal Self-Identity." *Numen* 45, no. 2 (1998): 183–220.

Lopez, D. S. *Religions of China in Practice.* Princeton, 1996.

T. H. Barrett (1987)
Revised Bibliography

GEIGER, ABRAHAM

GEIGER, ABRAHAM (1810–1874), rabbi, foremost exponent and idealogue of Reform Judaism in nineteenth-century Germany and outstanding scholar of *Wissenschaft des Judentums* (the modern scholarly study of Judaism). Geiger was born in Frankfurt, where he received a distinguished, traditional Talmudic education. He was also attracted to secular studies and in 1833 received his doctorate from the University of Bonn for a work entitled *Was hat Mohammed aus dem Judenthume aufgenommen* (What did Muḥammad take from Judaism?), a study that measured Judaism's influence on early Islam. In 1832 Geiger became rabbi in Wiesbaden, and there he set out to rescue Judaism from medieval rabbinic forms that he regarded as rigid, unaesthetic, and unappealing to Jews of contemporary cultural sensibilities. He did this by initiating reforms in the synagogue service and by calling, in 1837, for a conference of Reform rabbis in Wiesbaden. Moreover, he hoped to show how the academic study of the Jewish past could be enlisted as an aid in the causes of Jewish political emancipation and religious reform through the publication of the *Wissenschaftliche Zeitschrift für jüdische Theologie* (1835–1847).

Geiger became embroiled in controversy in 1838 when the Breslau Jewish community selected him as *dayyan* (religious judge) and assistant rabbi over the strong protests of the Breslau Orthodox rabbi, Solomon Tiktin. Indeed, because of this opposition, Geiger could not accept the position until 1840. Upon Tiktin's death in 1843 Geiger became rabbi of the city. There he continued his activities on behalf of Reform, playing an active role in the Reform rabbinical conferences of 1845 and 1846, held respectively in Frankfurt and Breslau.

Geiger's undiminished commitment to the academic study of Judaism and his belief in the need for a modern rabbinical seminary to train rabbis in the spirit of modern Western culture and *Wissenschaft des Judentums* led, in 1854, to the creation of the Jüdisch-Theologisches Seminar in Breslau. Geiger was bitterly disappointed, though, when the board of the seminary decided to appoint as principal the more conservative Zacharias Frankel instead of himself. It was not until 1872, two years after Geiger had come to Berlin as a Reform rabbi to the community, that his dream of directing a modern rabbinical seminary came to fruition. For in that year the Hochschule für die Wissenschaft des Judentums was established, with Geiger at its head. He remained director of this center for the training of Liberal rabbis until his death.

Geiger's scholarship was prodigious and profound. His most influential work, *Urschrift und Uebersetzungen der Bibel* (The original text and translations of the Bible; 1857), advocated the methodology of biblical criticism, and a host of other scholarly and polemical articles and books displays his broad knowledge of all facets of Jewish history and culture. These publications reveal his determination to make Judaism an integral part of Western culture and indicate both his theological bent and his ability to employ historical and philological studies in the cause of religious reform.

Geiger's work, carried out in the context of *Religionswissenschaft,* pointed to the evolutionary nature of the Jewish religion and, under the influence of Schleiermacher, allowed him to focus on the inwardness of the Jewish religious spirit. Having thereby mitigated the force of tradition, Geiger was able, in terms borrowed from Hegel, to view Judaism as a universal religion identified with the self-actualization of the Absolute. He therefore downplayed nationalistic elements in the Jewish past, denied them any validity in the present, and justified Jewish separateness in the modern world by speaking of Judaism's theological uniqueness and spiritual mission. Nevertheless, Geiger, unlike his more radical colleague Samuel Holdheim, represented a moderate approach to Reform. He refused to serve a Reform congregation that separated itself from the general Jewish community, he observed Jewish dietary laws, and he urged the retention of traditional Jewish laws of marriage and divorce. In addition, he favored the observance of the second day of the festivals and, like his more conservative peer Frankel, spoke of "positive-historical" elements in Judaism.

Bibliography

The best English introduction to Geiger's life and writings appears in *Abraham Geiger and Liberal Judaism,* compiled and edited by Max Wiener and translated by Ernst J. Schlochauer (Philadelphia, 1962). David Philipson's *The Reform Movement in Judaism* (New York, 1967) also contains a great deal of information about Geiger's career and thought. Geiger's own views of Judaism are summarized in a series of lectures he delivered in Frankfurt that have been translated by Charles Newburgh as *Judaism and Its History* (New York, 1911). Jakob J. Petuchowski provides interesting insights into Geiger's approach to Judaism and contrasts him with Samuel Holdheim in the article "Abraham Geiger and Samuel Holdheim: Their Differences in Germany and Repercussions in America," *Leo Baeck Institute Yearbook* 22 (1977): 139–159. Finally, Petuchowski has edited a series of essays by several eminent scholars on the meaning and significance of Geiger's career and scholarship in a work entitled *New Perspectives on Abraham Geiger* (Cincinnati, 1975).

New Sources

Heschel, Susannah. *Abraham Geiger and the Jewish Jesus.* Chicago, 1998.

Koltun-Fromm, Kenneth. "Historical Memory in Abraham Geiger's Account of Modern Jewish Identity." *Jewish Social Studies* 7 (2000): 109–126.

Mack, Michael. *German Idealism and the Jew: The Inner Anti-Semitism of Philosophy and German Jewish Responses.* Chicago, 2003.

David Ellenson (1987)
Revised Bibliography

GELUGPA See DGE LUGS PA

GE MYTHOLOGY.

Before Brazilian expansion diminished their territories, the widely scattered, generally independent and isolated groups that speak languages of the Ge family occupied a large expanse of the Brazilian interior, from approximately 2° to 28° south latitude, and from 42° to 58° west longitude. They are usually grouped into three branches on the basis of linguistic similarities: the northern Ge (the Kayapó, Suyá, Apinagé, and the various Timbirá groups in the Brazilian states of Pará, Mato Grosso, Goiás, and Maranhão), the central Ge (the Xavante and Xerente, in the states of Mato Grosso and Goiás), and the southern Ge (the Kaingán and Xokleng, in the states of São Paulo, Santa Catarina, and Rio Grande do Sul).

In addition to their language affiliation, the Ge-speaking groups share a tendency to occupy savanna or upland regions away from rivers, to live in relatively large semi-permanent villages, and to subsist on extensive hunting and collecting and some degree of horticulture. Compared with other lowland groups in South America, the Ge have a fairly simple material culture and very complex forms of social organization involving moieties, clans, and name-based groups. Their rites of passage are long and elaborate. Several non-Ge-speaking groups on the Brazilian central plateau also have some of these traits. Among the most important of these are the Boróro and Karajá.

The French anthropologist Claude Lévi-Strauss has convincingly demonstrated that similarities among the myths of the Americas do exist. Ge mythology is, however, significantly different in content and emphasis from that of other large language families in lowland South America (the Tupi, Arawak, Carib, and Tucanoan). The complexity of Ge and Boróro social organization, the elaborateness of their rites of passage, and the apparently secular nature of many of their narratives have challenged scholars to explain the importance of their myths. Lévi-Strauss uses Ge and Boróro myths as a point of departure in his four-volume *Mythologiques* (1964–1971; translated as *Introduction to a Science of Mythology,* 1969–1981), and some of his most careful critics have used those myths to discuss his work or to investigate the sociological context of myths in general. Ge mythology thus occupies an important place in the study of South American mythology both because of the challenges the narratives themselves present and because of the ways a number of distinguished scholars have confronted them.

Narrative Styles. Most anthropologists who write about lowland South American mythology use the word *myth* to refer to any narrative, be it cosmogonic, historical, or apparently anecdotal, because genre distinctions are difficult to establish for cosmologies that have no deities. The Ge have many different styles of oratory, formal speech, and song; the narration of myths constitutes only a small part of this repertoire. The word *myth* covers a number of distinct narrative styles, which vary from the relatively fixed chanted texts of some Xokleng myths to fairly flexible narrative forms that closely resemble the European folktale in style and content. The definitions of genre differ from group to group. Among the Xavante, story, history, and dreams are apparently equated; other groups separate events of the distant past from those of the more recent past and again from the experience of dreams.

With the exception of some ritualized performances among the southern Ge, myths are neither secret nor restricted as to the time or place they may be told. They are often recounted at night, by men or women, to children or adults, and mix adventure, humor, ethics, and cosmogony in a way that delights the audience regardless of its age. The narrator imitates sounds and the voices of the characters with considerable musicality, and his or her gestures often add dramatic impact. Many myths have parts that are sung. Questions are often interjected by the audience, and in response the narrator may expand upon some point or another.

Ge myths published in collections are almost exclusively in the third person, but in performance they are not restricted to that format. Performance style varies greatly, which reflects the difference between an oral narrative and a written text. Many performances are almost entirely in dialogue form with a minimum of narrative explanation; the context is largely implicit, and the narrator presumes the audience has previous knowledge of the story. Members of the society have heard the stories from birth, and any given performance is an ephemeral event and so not preserved.

CONTENT AND SETTING. Compared with the mythology of the other major language groups in Brazil, Ge mythology exhibits in its subject matter little elaboration of the spirit world, an absence of genealogical myths about ancestors, and little cosmological complexity. Here Ge cosmology must be distinguished from Ge mythology. Ethnographies of the Ge societies report beliefs in several types of spirits, in an afterlife in a village of the dead, and in shamans who travel to the sky. Ge mythology, however, rarely describes either these beliefs or their origins.

One of the difficulties scholars have had in interpreting Ge myths is their apparent unrelatedness to other aspects of society, including the elaborate Ge ceremonial life. Some South American societies explain the present by referring to the way the ancestors behaved; but among Ge speakers myths rarely make direct reference to the present in their description of events that involve ethical dilemmas and social processes central to the society. No detailed native exegesis of the stories has been reported; the Ge rarely use a myth to interpret anything other than the narrative itself.

Ge mythology generally focuses on the relationships between the social world of human beings and the natural domain of the animal and the monstrous. The main actors are humans, animals, and beings that are both human and animal. The setting is usually the village and surrounding jungle, although some myths relate a visit to the sky or to a level below the surface of the earth. Because the subject of the myths is the tension between correct social behavior and incorrect or animal-like behavior, rather than the establishment of a given character as a deity or ancestor, the actors of one myth very rarely appear in another. Recurrent features are not individuals but rather relationships (brothers-in-law, siblings, parents and children, formal friends), settings (the villages or the forest), and animals (deer, jaguars, tapirs, wild pigs). All these appear regularly in the myths. An exception to this singularity of character is a series of stories about Sun and Moon found among the northern and central Ge.

TRANSFORMATION MYTHS. The central event in a Ge myth is usually a transformation, involving, for example, the change of a continuity into discontinuity, as in the origin of night and death; or the acquisition of an object that transforms society, such as fire, garden crops, and ceremonies that humans are said to have obtained from animals.

The origin of fire. A good example of a transformation myth is that of the origin of fire, versions of which have been collected from most Ge communities. Lévi-Strauss (1969) and Turner (1980) have analyzed it extensively. The following version was recorded among the Suyá; for the complete version, see Wilbert (1984).

> A long time ago the Suyá ate meat warmed in the sun because they had no fire. One day a man takes his young brother-in-law into the forest to look for fledgling macaws to take back to the village, where they will be raised for their feathers. The two walk a long way. The man sets a pole against a rock ledge, and the boy climbs up to look at a nest. When the man asks the boy what the young birds in the nest look like (i.e., whether they have enough feathers to survive in the village), the boy shouts down, "They look like your wife's pubic hair." (This insulting response is a very funny moment for Suyá audiences, who always laugh heartily and repeat the question and response several times for effect. The exact incident that results in the boy's being left in the nest varies among the different Ge groups.) Angered, the man throws aside the pole and leaves the boy up in the nest, where he grows very thin and is gradually covered with bird excrement. After some time a jaguar comes walking by. Seeing the boy's shadow, the animal pounces on it several times, then looks up and sees the boy. The boy tells the jaguar of his difficulty, and the jaguar asks him to throw down the fledglings. The boy does so, and the jaguar gobbles them up. Then it puts the pole against the cliff and tells the boy to descend. Although terrified, the boy finally climbs down and goes with the jaguar to its house. When they arrive, the boy sees a fire for the first time. It is burning on a single huge log. The jaguar gives the boy roasted meat to eat. A threatening female jaguar arrives. (The degree of threat varies among the different Ge groups.) The jaguar gives the boy more meat and shows him the way home. When he arrives at the village, he tells the men that the jaguar has fire. They decide to take it from the jaguar. Taking the form of different animal species, the

> men go to the jaguars' camp where they find the jaguars asleep. They place hot beeswax on the eyes and paws of the jaguars, which then run screaming into the jungle. The men-animals pick up the fire log and run with it back to the village, in the style of a burity-palm log relay race. First a rhea carries the fire log, then a deer, then a wild pig, then a tapir. The frog wants to carry the log and in spite of objections is allowed to do so. The log is so hot the frog runs with it to the water and drops it in. The fire goes out. "The fire is dead!" everyone shouts in consternation. Then the toucan, the curassow, and other birds run up, their head and neck feathers bright red because they have been swallowing the live coals that have fallen from the log. They vomit the coals onto the ashes, and the fire starts up again. The tapir picks up the log again and runs with it all the way to the village. When they arrive, the men return to human form and divide the fire among all the houses. Ever since then the Suyá have eaten roasted meat.

The origin of the Savanna Deer ceremony. The myth of the man who is turned into a savanna deer by a jealous rival, representative of another type of transformation story, is cited as the origin myth of a ceremony still performed today by the Suyá; for the complete version, see Wilbert (1984).

> Once, before the Suyá had learned the Savanna Deer ceremony, they were painting and preparing for a Mouse ceremony. In this ceremony the adult men take a few young women for collective sexual relations. While some of the men leap, dance, and sing, others choose the women who will take part in this activity, and take them to the men's ceremonial camp. One man is very possessive about his young wife. To prevent her from being taken as a sex partner for the ceremony, he sings standing next to her in the house. He does not leave her to sing in the men's house. Another man wants to have sexual relations with the woman and is angered by the husband's attentiveness. The angry man is a witch who can transform people or kill them. He decides to transform the woman's husband. The husband begins to sweat as he dances. His dance cape sticks to his head and will not come off. He tries to pull it off, but it has grown on and has begun to stick to his neck and back as well. "Hey!" he shouts, "I am being transformed into something bad!" He leaves his wife and goes to the men's house, where he sings all night along with the other caped singers. The next morning the singers' sisters strip them of their capes, and so the men stop dancing and singing, but the husband keeps on (he cannot stop, for his cape will not come off). The men shout at him to stop singing. He keeps dancing and singing. Suddenly he rushes off into the forest, still singing. Later his relatives go off to find him, and after several days they find him near a lake, his body bent over. The rattles tied to his legs have begun to turn into hooves. Antlers fan out above his head. He is singing. (Here the narrator usually sings the song the man-deer is supposed to have been singing.) The men who find him listen to his song. One man tells the others, "Listen and learn our companion's song," and they sit and listen. (Here the narrator usually sings the rest of the man-deer's song.) Then the husband becomes a forest deer. He still lives there at the lake. People have seen him there recently. Today the Suyá sing his songs in the Savanna Deer ceremony.

THE ANALYSIS OF GE MYTHOLOGY. Early collections of Ge myths were usually appended to ethnographic accounts of the societies, with little commentary. With the appearance of Lévi-Strauss's *Mythologiques,* however, scholarly interest in Ge mythology increased dramatically. These four volumes have engendered tremendous controversy, but they nonetheless provide an entirely new perspective on the mythology and cosmology of the Americas.

Lévi-Strauss argues that certain empirical categories, such as raw and cooked, fresh and decayed, and noisy and silent, are conceptual tools that the native populations of the Americas use to elaborate abstract ideas and to combine these ideas in the form of propositions. Amerindian mythology is thus a kind of philosophical speculation about the universe and its processes, but one that uses principles quite foreign to Western philosophy. These propositions are best discovered through an analysis that treats myths as elements of a nearly infinite body of partial statements, rather than through an analysis that isolates individual narratives. According to Lévi-Strauss, myths should be interpreted only through other myths, to establish similarities or differences. He further argues that the myths of one society can be interpreted through the myths of surrounding societies, or even through those of distant societies on the same or another continent.

Lévi-Strauss's work must be evaluated in two distinct ways. First, one must consider his comparative method. While the debate on structural analysis in anthropology and literature is extensive, much of the criticism of *Mythologiques* has centered on Lévi-Strauss's removal of myths from the contexts of the societies in which they are told, and on his preferring instead to compare them with the myths of very different societies. Lévi-Strauss (1981), writing in defense of his method of analyzing the native cosmologies of the Americas as a whole (rather than what he claims are individual manifestations, i.e., the myths of a particular society), defines his objective as being that of attempting to understand the workings of the human mind in general.

Second, one must consider whether those categories that Lévi-Strauss highlights as central to cosmologies across the Americas actually are important to specific societies. There is general agreement that they are, and some of the categories delineated by Lévi-Strauss have even proved to be keys to the analyses of the cosmologies of groups about which Lévi-Strauss had no information whatsoever. There is no doubt that the study of South American societies has been revolutionized by Lévi-Strauss's analyses of myth.

Although Lévi-Strauss's work is highly suggestive, his analyses do not answer the questions social anthropologists usually pose about myths: Why is it that a given people tells a given story and how does the mythology relate to other aspects of the society? Few anthropologists are satisfied with analyses that treat myth, religion, and cosmology as isolated phenomena. An alternative tradition of interpreting Ge myths derives from the founders of sociological and anthropological theory: Karl Marx, Max Weber, Émile Durkheim, and their followers. A number of important works have examined the relationship between Ge myths and other features of Ge-speaking societies. These authors often use some version of a structural method derived from Lévi-Strauss, but they employ it to quite different ends. They either analyze a myth of a single Ge society or compare a myth found in different groups to show how variations in the myth are paralleled by variations in specific features of the social organization. In this way they support the argument that myths and social processes are related in particular ways.

The most systematic and challenging of these alternative analyses is the work of the American anthropologist Terence Turner (1977, 1980), who combines his reanalysis of a Kayapó myth of the origin of fire with an extensive critique of Lévi-Straussian structuralism. Turner shows that every event, object, and relationship in the fire myth has particular relevance to specific features of Kayapó social organization, social processes, and cosmology. He argues that, for the Kayapó, the telling of myths plays an important part in their understanding of their lives.

Other analysts have related myth to general ethical propositions (Lukesch, 1976), to issues of domestic authority (DaMatta, 1973), to messianic movements, and to the ways in which the Ge societies have confronted conflict and contact with Brazilian society. All these analyses take into account the social, political, and ethical contexts of which Ge myths are always a part, and they have considerably advanced the understanding of the role of myths in tribal societies.

The two very different traditions of scholarship this article has described—the study of myths as logical propositions using categories found throughout the Americas and the study of myths within their specific social context—have stimulated the study of Ge narrative itself and have also resulted in the increasingly careful collection and greater availability of adequate texts. With improved recording technology, greater interest in the performative aspects of verbal art, and the contributions of missionaries who are themselves specialists in textual exegesis, there has been a vast improvement in the accuracy of published narratives. While early collections of myths were usually narrative summaries derived from dictation in Portuguese, more recent works have included exact transcriptions of longer Portuguese versions, careful transcriptions of recordings made in the native languages, collections recorded and translated by the Indians themselves, and bilingual publications designed for use as primers by the groups who tell the myths. These improved collections will allow specialists and nonspecialists alike to better understand the myths and evaluate analyses of them.

Bibliography

The outstanding English source for Ge myths is Johannes Wilbert's *Folk Literature of the Gê Indians*, 2 vols. (Los Angeles, 1979, 1984). In addition to assembling and translating the major published collections, Wilbert has indexed the 362 narratives using the Stith Thompson folk-literature motif index, which may aid comparative work. Texts collected and translated by Indians at a Salesian mission appear in Bartolomeu Giaccaria and Adalberto Heide's *Jeronomo Xavante conta mitos e lendas* and *Jeronomo Xavante sonha contos e sonhos* (both, Campo Grande, Brazil, 1975). Anton Lukesch presents an analysis of the major propositions of Kayapó mythology in *Mythos und Leben der Kayapo* (Vienna, 1968), translated as *Mito e vida dos índios Caiapós* (São Paulo, 1976). For ethnographic background on the Ge, see Curt Nimuendajú's *The Eastern Timbira* (Berkeley, Calif., 1946) and David Maybury-Lewis's edited volume *Dialectical Societies: The Gê and Bororo of Central Brazil* (Cambridge, Mass., 1979). Nimuendajú gives a detailed description of a single society, and Maybury-Lewis provides a good background on the sociological issues among the northern and central Ge. Claude Lévi-Strauss's four volumes on Amerindian mythology, published originally in French (Paris, 1964–1971), have been translated into English as *The Raw and the Cooked* (1969), *From Honey to Ashes* (1973), *The Origin of Table Manners* (1978), and *The Naked Man* (1981). My own *Nature and Society in Central Brazil: The Suya Indians of Mato Grosso* (Cambridge, Mass., 1981) demonstrates that many of the ideas and categories Lévi-Strauss discovered through the analysis of Ge mythology are indeed to be found in other aspects of the cosmology, social organization, and values of the Suyá, one of the northern Ge groups. For a critique of Lévi-Straussian structuralism and a reanalysis of one of the Ge myths, see Terence S. Turner's "Narrative Structure and Mythopoesis: A Critique and Reformulation of Structuralist Concepts of Myth, Narrative and Poetics," *Arethusa* 10 (Spring 1977): 103–163; and "Le dénicheur d'oiseaux en contexte," *Anthropologie et sociétés* 4 (1980): 85–115. Roberto DaMatta's "Mito e autoridade domestica," in his *Ensaios de antropologia estrutural* (Petrópolis, Brazil, 1973), is an excellent example of how the analysis of a single myth common to two societies can reveal differences in their social organization.

Anthony Seeger (1987)

GENDER AND RELIGION

This entry consists of the following articles:

GENDER AND AUSTRALIAN INDIGENOUS RELIGIONS
GENDER AND OCEANIC RELIGIONS
GENDER AND AFRICAN RELIGIOUS TRADITIONS
GENDER AND NORTH AMERICAN INDIAN RELIGIOUS TRADITION
GENDER AND MESOAMERICAN RELIGIONS
GENDER AND SOUTH AMERICAN RELIGIONS

GENDER AND RELIGION: AN OVERVIEW

The subtle patterns and dynamic of gender pervade all areas of religion, both explicitly and implicitly, whether fully recognized or unacknowledged. Widely debated and often misunderstood, gender concerns have immense significance in contemporary culture as they are part of the international political and social agenda of most countries in the world. The Gender Development Index has recorded the global monitoring of existing gender gaps since 1996, and it provides clear evidence of how much still needs to be done before a truly equitable gender balance is reached. Critical gender perspectives have made a significant difference to most academic fields, including the study of religion. Yet many scholarly publications on religion still seem to give little or no recognition to the profound epistemological, methodological, and substantive changes that contemporary gender studies, especially women's scholarship and feminist theories but also the growing field of men's studies in religion, have produced over the last thirty years. Sometimes seen as profoundly threatening, or disdainfully dismissed because of ignorance, misunderstanding, or other factors of personal and institutional resistance, the engendering of religions and their study provides a great challenge to contemporary scholarship.

The symbolic order and institutional structures created by religions have deeply affected and inspired human existence over millennia; they continue to do so for countless people in today's postmodern world. Their abiding importance is too great not to be affected by the transformations caused by the emergence of critical gender awareness as a genuinely new development in the history of human consciousness. This entry provides a general introduction to the most frequently debated issues and complex patterns that pertain between gender and religion, followed by a series of articles dealing with area- or tradition-specific discussions of gender.

WHAT GENDER MEANS AND DOES NOT MEAN. It needs to be made clear right at the start that "gender" is not a synonym for "women," although it is often mistaken as such for two reasons: first, gender studies originally developed out of women's studies and draw to a large extent on feminist scholarship in different disciplines; second, gender studies in practice remain necessarily more concerned with women than men because of the need to overcome the deeply entrenched, traditional invisibility and marginalization of women in history, society, and culture. It is essential, however, to recognize that gender studies always concern men as well as women, their respective identities, representations, and individual subjectivities, as well as their mutually interrelated social worlds and the unequal power relations between them. Although there exists a growing movement of "men's studies," inspired by the theoretical and practical developments of women's and feminist studies, it has as yet less momentum and commands less urgency to pursue profound political and social changes, given continuing widespread male dominance and the almost universal privileging of males in most societies of the world. Thus, there often exists a considerable cognitive dissonance between women's and men's understanding of "gender studies."

Equally widespread is the failure to problematize gender and recognize its radical, multidimensional potency. Although "gender" is now a widely used term, its complex and changing meanings are seldom fully grasped or critically reflected upon. Religion and gender are highly contested fields, and both need careful mapping to bring their manifold interactions into people's awareness and into the practices of scholarship. This does not happen spontaneously but involves decisive effort and agency, requiring what has been aptly called "making the gender-critical turn" (Warne, 2000b), since gender-critical thinking is neither "natural" in the current social context nor has it been historically available before the modern era. Thus, gender awareness is grounded in a self-reflexive, critical consciousness that has to be acquired.

Gender studies first developed in the social sciences during the late 1960s and 1970s through the investigation of human sexual differences and roles. A new binary distinction came into existence in which "sex" was associated with the biological differences between women and men, whereas "gender," previously used a grammatical term for distinguishing nouns, was transferred from a linguistic to a social context in order to distinguish the historically and culturally developed interpretations of what it means to be a man or a woman in different societies and cultures. Biological sex was seen as naturally given, whereas gender was understood to have been historically and socially constructed, often influenced by dominant religious teachings.

From then on the word *gender* has been fiercely debated and given multiple meanings, leading to a plethora of theoretical positions. From gender being taken as a sociobiological category to being completely deconstructed or simply understood performatively and discursively, the transformation of gender from its former merely grammatical application to nouns into a major analytical category in the study of history and society has spurred so many analyses and specialized studies that a newcomer can get thoroughly confused. Numerous rhetorical stances of great abstraction and abstruseness have been adopted, often appearing to obfuscate more than help, with the result that the distinction between sex and gender is now less clear than first assumed. Not only is gender a "useful category of historical analysis," as Joan Wallach Scott (1996) has so persuasively argued, but it is now also a category beset by pitfalls and problems, as Judith Butler's *Gender Trouble* (1990) and many others have clearly demonstrated. "Gender" is the title of one of twenty-two conceptual essays in *Critical Terms for Religious Studies* (ed. Mark Taylor, 1998). In this essay Daniel Boyarin states that now,

> when we study gender within a given historical or existing culture, we understand that we are investigating the praxis and process by which people are interpellated into a two- (or for some cultures more) sex system that is made to seem as if it were nature, that is, something that has always existed. The perception of sex as a natural, given set of binarily constructed differences between human beings, then, is now seen as the specific work of gender, and the production of sex as "natural" signifies the success of gender as a system imposing its power. (p. 117)

A lucid discussion of different subsets within the category of gender, and of different frameworks and strategies affecting its interpretation, is found in Randi R. Warne's article "Gender" in *Guide to the Study of Religion* (2000a, pp. 140–154; see also Juschka, 1999, 2001), describing the relationship between sex and gender as either homologous, analogous, or heterogeneous. What emerges from all these discussions is that the sex-gender distinction, however understood, is linked to binary oppositions, hierarchical ordering, and unequal access to power and resources, so that one can speak of a rigid "gender system" that has operated in most societies in the past and still exists in many in the present. The different roles and images associated with both sexes, and gender-differentiated patterns of power, status, and authority, vary enormously in different cultures, but if these have been created as well as changed in the past because of changing material and ideological conditions, it must also be possible to transform gender inequalities and gender relations in the present (Bonvillain, 1998; see chap. 8, "Gender and Religion"). This is a powerful argument for individual and societal gender transformation within a new global context of pluralism and diversity. It is this alternative—some may say utopian—vision of a different kind of reality, of greater justice and equality for all human beings of whatever sex, that has inspired social reformers and women campaigners since the onset of modernity, and some individuals much earlier than that.

Gender Studies and Religion. Gender studies have arrived rather later in the study of religion than in most other fields. At present there still obtains a harmful "double blindness" in which most contemporary gender studies, whether in the humanities, social sciences, or natural sciences, remain extraordinarily "religion blind," whereas far too many studies in religion are still quite "gender blind." It can be legitimately asked, however, what relevance contemporary gender insights may possibly have for the age-old beliefs of religion? To what extent can the study of religion benefit from the nuanced and highly sophisticated theoretical arguments of current gender debates? To give a satisfactory answer to such questions requires much conscious effort and many practical changes. Neither gender nor religion are stable, transhistorical categories; both function within specific sociohistorical contexts and large semantic fields. The complex controversies surrounding the meaning of both prove that we are dealing here not only with definitional minefields or merely academic matters but with issues of advocacy, personal commitment, ethical engagement, and fundamental choices about the nature of one's life and society.

Many religious teachings and practices, especially scriptural statements, religious rites, beliefs, theological doctrines, institutional offices, and authority structures, are closely intertwined with and patterned by gender differences, even when gender remains officially unacknowledged and is deemed invisible (to untrained eyes). The existing social and religious arrangements are considered "natural" or normatively prescribed by sacred scriptures and other religious teachings, handed down by tradition from the ancestors or "God-given," and thus unalterable. It is only since the Enlightenment and the onset of modernity that the existing gender arrangements of traditional societies and religious institutions have been radically called into question, leading to the emergence of the modern women's movement.

The first wave of this women's movement, from the late eighteenth through the nineteenth and early twentieth centuries, forms an essential part of the great transformations of modernity. Increasingly, historical studies provide new evidence that the motivation for women seeking greater freedom, equality, and participation in all areas of society, including religion, did not stem from secular philosophical and political developments alone but was also rooted in biblical teaching, shared by Jews and Christians, that women and men are created in the image of God. This was reinterpreted in a new, strongly egalitarian way, never understood in this manner in the past (Børresen, 1995). Theological ideas impacted women reformers far more than has hitherto been acknowledged; that applies even to so radical a thinker as Mary Wollstonecraft (Taylor, 2003), and similarly radical theological reflections can be found in the writings of Florence Nightingale (Webb, 2002). Nineteenth-century Europe and America witnessed the parallel development of women's organized social and political movements and, at the same time, the expansion of their religious activities, opening up new religious roles for women. The religious roots of the struggle for women's rights (Morgan, 2002; Zink-Sawyer, 2003) and the complex historical dynamic operating between religious faith and feminist consciousness are increasingly receiving more attention. Existing studies have so far focused mainly on women in Christianity and Judaism, with a growing focus on Islam as well. But a great deal more comparative research is needed to show the strength of motivation arising from concurrent secular and religious commitments of women from many different religious traditions engaged in working to abolish the traditional social and religious constraints of women's lives.

The second wave of the women's movement, which emerged during the latter part of the twentieth century, took a strongly self-reflexive, theoretical, and critical turn, expressing itself in militant feminist theory and politics and celebrating "global sisterhood." Feminism aims to overcome the universal oppression of women and to achieve their full humanity, so that women can speak with their own voices, from their own experience, their own subjectivity, agency, and autonomy—all terms that by now have become thoroughly theorized but also further problematized. Some argue that these concepts of autonomous subjectivity are themselves derived from the inherently androcentric, liberal worldview of post-Enlightenment Western thought and that they cannot be applied universally across boundaries of gender, culture, race, and class, but always function pluralistically.

There also exists a third wave feminism, sometimes referred to as "postfeminism," not meaning the end of feminism but accepting a multiplicity of feminisms, linked to theoretical reflections on femininities as well as masculinities. A more self-critical theorizing developed under the influence of psychoanalysis, poststructuralism, postmodernism, and postcolonialism, which also affected the development of gender studies that, in turn, had evolved out of women's and feminist studies. Feminist epistemology and theory as well as practical feminist strategies have opened up new experiences and questions that bear on gender relations in terms of both women and men. To work for greater gender justice, however understood, requires profound social, political, economic, religious, and cultural transformation for both sexes. At a practical level, therefore, gender studies impact on education and politics, on social work and care, on development work, on ecological and peace issues, on the media, and on academic scholarship. Like religious studies, gender studies are characterized by a pluralistic methodology and complex multidisciplinarity. It might even be more appropriate to speak of *transdisciplinarity,* because gender patterns are so pervasive in their potential implications that they transcend traditional disciplinary boundaries. Gender studies have also a strong international orientation, and while recognizing existing social, racial, ethnic, and sexual diversities as well as many individual nuances, their central insights are immensely important and relevant across traditional national, cultural, and religious boundaries. The basic ideas of women, feminist, and gender studies first emerged in Western societies; by now they have become globally diffused and have also been considerably transformed in their intellectual and practical applications to a wide range of social and religious issues within very diverse local contexts around the world.

Central Concepts and Concerns. Much of the feminist critique of society and culture focuses on patriarchy and androcentrism. Although the word *patriarchy* often refers to diverse theories of history and society, now often discredited, in the widest sense patriarchy means an all-male power structure that privileges men over women. Most religions still conform to this pattern in terms of their institutional organization and official representation. Moreover, most religions were founded by men, although there also exist a few women-led religions, especially among marginal, small-scale, and tribal groups (Sered, 1994). In most religions male religious figures (whether ascetics, monastics or yogins) and male religious communities are normally given more public recognition, respect, authority, and power than women's religious groups, however numerous and large. Similarly, traditional religious texts are almost exclusively the creation of men, and male interpretations of these texts hold authoritative status. The experience of men has been taken as normative without taking into account the experiences and thoughts of women, who are relegated to subordinate roles or, at worst, are completely suppressed in many foundational religious texts and excluded from significant religious rites. It is worth mentioning that the word *patriarchy* itself is of religious provenance, since it originally described "the dignity, see, or jurisdiction of an ecclesiastical patriarch" and "the government of the church by a patriarch or patriarchs" before it came to mean "a patriarchal system of society or government by the father or the eldest male of the family; a family, a tribe or community so organized" (*Oxford English Dictionary*). Patriarchy can also be understood as the structuring of society around descending hierarchies of fatherhood, whether understood as Father God, the supreme authority of a king, a lord, or *paterfamilias.* In recent theoretical debates, especially those influenced by Freudian psychoanalysis and French feminist theorists, much use is made of the concept of "phallocentrism," referring to the structuring of society around the values of the phallus as the ultimate symbol of power and activity, so that women represent absence, lack, and passivity. Another term is "phallogocentrism," that is to say the *logos,* word and thought, is centered on phallic male categories. Other debates have contrasted the historically dominant patriarchies across the world with earlier social structures of matriarchies, probably largely hypothetical, symbolizing alternative values and power structures linked to the authority of the mother rather than that of the father and centered on the worship of the Goddess. Today's feminist scholars generally regard the term *matriarchy* as misleading while discussing with renewed interest whether *prepatriarchal* societies ever existed and to what extent Goddess worship correlates with women's religious and social leadership (Gross, 1996; Raphael, 1996).

Religious beliefs, thoughts, and practices are not only profoundly patriarchal but often also thoroughly *androcentric,* that is to say predominantly, if not exclusively, shaped by male perspectives and experiences. Androcentrism, a term first introduced by the American sociologist Lester F. Ward in 1903, not only refers to the privileging of the human male, especially in language and thought, but also means that male experience has been one-sidedly equated with all human experience and taken as a universal norm by men and women alike, without giving full and equal recognition to women's knowledge and experience. The use of *man,* the male and masculine, as a universal category for the generically "human," is exclusionary since it erases women as subjects. The opposite of androcentrism is *gynocentrism,* the privileging of female experience and perspective, which is comparatively rare. Another widely used term is *sexism,* referring to the organization of social life and attitudes that not only sharply differentiates between different gender roles but also privileges and values one sex over the other. Juschka (2001, pp. 2–3) makes a helpful distinction between *androcentrism* as a falsifying male perspective and actual *misogyny* as an active negative attitude toward women as *female*. The inherent androcentrism of the study of religions was pointed out early in the pioneering collection of essays *Beyond Androcentrism* (Gross, ed., 1977).

Whereas sex is usually understood in a binary way, as consisting of two mutually exclusive categories of male and female, feminists have used gender in association with difference and diversity, in terms of multiple, rather than single, versions of femininities and masculinities that call into question general claims about women and men. Thus "the concept of gender has served as a flexible container for difference. . . . Lacking any stable content, the categories 'women' and 'men' acquire meaning through their use in particular contexts" (Bondi and Davidson, 2002, p. 336). As gender is not a stable essence but a fluid category linked to identity creation, world building, and boundary maintenance of social roles, it may be preferable to use an active, dynamic verb rather than a noun. "Engendering" is an action linked to perceiving, performing, reflecting, and enacting, and it is therefore more appropriate to speak about "(en)gendering religion" (Warne, 2001) or "doing gender in religion" than to speak about gender *and* religion in an additive manner. Religion and gender are not simply two parallel categories that function independently of each other; they are mutually *embedded* within each other in all religions, suffusing all religious worlds and experiences. It is because of this deep hidden embeddedness that gender is sometimes so difficult to identify and separate out from other aspects of religion until one's consciousness is trained into making a "gender-critical turn."

In terms of intellectual developments, a double paradigm shift has occurred. The first happened when women's studies—descriptive, phenomenologically and empirically oriented—developed into more critical, self-reflexive, and theoretically oriented feminist studies. The second paradigm shift has taken place with the further development of feminist studies into gender studies. But "paradigm shift" is too tame an expression for what is really happening, which is a shaking of foundations, a radical remapping of our intellectual, academic, and social landscapes. It has become increasingly obvious that it is not simply a question of bringing women's experience and knowledge into view but of radically restructuring the existing balance between genders. As in many other fields, we are not simply dealing with a reinterpretation of texts and traditions but with a complete repositioning of bodies of knowledge, a rearrangement and remapping of everything that relates to religion, society, and culture. As women's studies and feminist studies of religion have gained more institutional recognition over recent decades, some women scholars feel resistant toward gender studies because their development may mean the loss of some of the recent gains made. But feminist separatism apart, many female, and some male, scholars now work within a gender-critical framework and use gender-inclusive rather than exclusive models in their thinking. Strongly articulated gender theories possess considerable explanatory power and potential for the study of religion. Gender studies can of course be appropriated for conservative ends, even fundamentalist purposes (Hawley, 1994; Jeffery and Basu, 1998), or they can be used to reinforce androcentric bias through focusing on the analysis of masculinity without taking feminist theoretical insights into account. Gender studies in religion thus represent a complex field of many contradictory parts still in need of much further development, but they also hold much promise for new creative perspectives and approaches in religious scholarship.

NEW METHODOLOGIES AND SCHOLARSHIP. The introduction of feminist perspectives into the study of religion has been celebrated as an epistemological as well as a spiritual revolution. The rise of feminism relates both to an academic method and a new social vision (Gross, 1993, pp. 291–304). Female religion scholars have developed a practical "participatory hermeneutics," involving advocacy and personal engagement, as well as a theoretically sophisticated "hermeneutics of suspicion," which critically examines all traditional knowledge and practices of religion. These have to be thoroughly analyzed and deconstructed so that unequally weighted gender differences become clearly visible and reconstructed in a different way. June O'Connor (1989) has defined this task as "rereading, reconceiving and reconstructing religious traditions." By "rereading" she means that religious phenomena have to be examined with regard to women's presence and absence, their words and silences; "reconceiving" requires the retrieval and recovery of lost sources and suppressed visions, the reclaiming of "women's heritage"; "reconstructing" the past draws on new paradigms for thinking, understanding, and evaluating it differently. These expressions point to a dynamic of transformation, indicating that a profound change in thought and social structures is deliberately sought and worked for.

The development of women's studies in religion thus counteracts the deficiency and partiality of scholarship by retrieving women's forgotten histories and buried voices, their unacknowledged experiences hidden in the official histories of the past. Critical feminist theories were developed, based on the specificity and difference of women's experience, leading to endless debates, especially as some forms of "cultural feminism" claimed that women's experience is not only different from men's but morally and perhaps even spiritually superior to that of men, a theme that goes back at least as far as the Romantics.

Critical gender studies in religion have conclusively demonstrated that there are no gender-neutral phenomena. Everything is subtly, and often invisibly, patterned by a gender dynamic operating in language, thought, experience, and institutions. Traditional religiously defined and socially prescribed gender roles, if rigidly enforced, can become dehumanizing prisons, even though anthropological, historical, and comparative studies provide overwhelming evidence that gender roles are also remarkably fluid across different religions and cultures. At the present stage of humanity's global experience it is no longer possible to work with exclusive, hegemonic models of language, thought, or anything else, derived from only one gender. Historical descriptions, analyses, and theories need to take all genders and their differences into account, whether shaped by race, class, culture, religion, sexuality, or other identity markers. The theorization of multiple voices, of subjectivity and agency, of difference and identity, of standpoints and positionality, of liberation and transformation, is central to feminist thought. Its debates have anticipated several of the critical stances of postmodernism in destabilizing categories and in arguing against essentialist and universalist stances. Feminists have pioneered new epistemological insights, not only in terms of *what* we know but *how* we come to know, how knowledge is constructed, psychologically as well as socially. These theoretical advances of feminist theory have deeply influenced men's studies, leading to a new understanding of the construction of maleness, manhood, and masculinities. Both women's studies and men's studies, although approached from different gender perspectives, have to work in a gender-inclusive rather than gender-exclusive way in order to achieve further intellectual and social breakthroughs. At present, however, maleness has not yet been theorized to the same extent as femaleness.

Women's and men's studies in religion are both marked by critical and constructive approaches. There is the question of what remains *usable* of the past when religious texts and histories are reread from a critical gender perspective. The impact of gender analysis, coupled with an ethical commitment to gender justice, will lead to a deconstruction as well as a reconstruction of religious traditions and practices. At present this process has barely begun, and setbacks are unavoidable. Moreover, the deconstruction of an essentialist understanding of masculinity is only in its early stages (Doty, 1993; Berger, Wallis, and Watson, 1995). "Men doing feminism" (Digby, 1998), though still a largely Western project, is bound to gain momentum and widespread diffusion across contemporary cultures. More inclusive, critical "gender thinking" will therefore dislocate individual and social identities, creating the possibility for new social arrangements and new religious developments across the globe. Men's studies in religion have produced innovative research on religion and masculinities, male sexuality and spirituality, and male identities and bodies in relation to the gender-sensitive understanding of God and divinities (Eilberg-Schwartz, 1994; Boyd, Longwood, and Muesse, 1996; Krondorfer, 1996; Bradstock, Gill, Hogan, and Morgan, 2000), but there is still a long way to go before these developments catch up with women's studies in religion.

Yet further thinking is represented by queer theories, primarily debated within gay, lesbian, and feminist theologies dealing with sexuality and the production of raced and gendered bodies, much influenced by Michel Foucault's influential work on the history of sexuality. Such theories call into question how what counts as "normal" heterosexuality comes into existence, is legitimated and maintained as well as transgressed and subverted, so that concepts of identity, power, and resistance have to be critically reexamined. The "queering" of religion raises many ethical and theological questions, not fully discussed at present, so that it is still too early to predict whether queer thinking will have the same influence as feminist theories on what is a complex new field of scholarship in the study of religion (sometimes also called LGBT studies, relating to lesbian, gay, bisexual, and transgendered people) with far more resources on the web than in existing gender studies on religion. For an introduction to these discussions see *Fear of a Queer Planet* (Warner, 1993) and *Religion Is a Queer Thing* (Stuart, 1997).

Such studies from radically different perspectives highlight in a new way how monotheistic systems are male dominated and heterosexually structured (Boyarin, 1997) and how the "queering" of the body relates to wider issues of ordering gender relations, society, and configurations of power linked to ambiguous religious histories and teachings. It is therefore to be welcomed that new body theologies are being developed from both male and female perspectives (Nelson, 1992; Raphael, 1996; Isherwood and Stuart, 1998). These have their roots mainly in Christian thinking, but many other religious traditions possess rich resources for constructing alternative approaches to the body and its religious significance. For Asian perspectives see the SUNY (Albany) series on "Body in Culture, History, and Religion" edited by Thomas P. Kasulis and his colleagues. Contemporary Western discussions, marked by fluid postmodern instabilities and much experimentation, are continuously evolving in this area, so that new concepts such as "transgender" and "omnigender" are created to illuminate, and perhaps even to overcome, the multiple but still oppositional meanings of gender (Mollenkott, 2001).

Women's religious lives and roles in different religious traditions across the world, previously rarely examined at all, have now been studied from many different perspectives. A pioneering publication was *Unspoken Worlds: Women's Religious Lives* (Falk and Gross, eds., 2001, originally published in 1980 and subtitled Women's Religious Lives in Non-Western Cultures), followed by many others on women's roles and rituals in different religions, the records and writings left by women, and their exclusion or participation in religious rites and institutions. *An Anthology of Sacred Texts By and About Women* (Young, ed., 1994) was another milestone, presenting important scriptural sources on women in the major religious traditions, including women's own voices. Several recurring themes reveal the ambiguities affecting the image of women cross-culturally, such as the widespread association of women with both evil (through their body, sexuality, menstruation taboos, and death) and wisdom; sex role reversals in mythical and other stories of gender conflict; the figure of the ideal and exceptional woman; and the existence of many female religious experts, recognized for their charismatic authority without, in most cases, holding official institutional roles. Further evidence of casting women into particular stereotypes and make them submit to the moral rules of male-dominated society, often enforced by the teachings of religion, is provided by *Female Stereotypes in Religious Traditions* (Kloppenborg and Hanegraaff, eds, 1995). An absolutely indispensable reference work, and pioneering achievement, is the two-volume *Encyclopedia of Women and World Religion* (Young, ed., 1999), reflecting the diversity and richness of current theoretical debates and empirical data in contemporary scholarship on women's, and to some extent also men's, studies in religion. There exists no comparable reference work yet that offers a similar summation of gender studies and men's studies in religion.

Several feminist scholars have attempted feminist reconstructions of religious traditions as different as Judaism, Buddhism, and Sikhism, as well as Christianity, and the number of gender-critical studies on Islam and other traditions is also steadily growing. Some essay collections reflect constructive efforts in reinterpreting several religious traditions (Cooey, Eakin, and McDaniel, 1991), but most feminist challenges have been addressed to Judaism and Christianity, especially in North America and Europe. The rise of ever newer forms of feminist theologies has spawned remarkable voices of difference, from womanist to *mujerista* and Asian-American theologies, which have given birth to women doing Christian theology around the whole world, from Asia to Africa, Australia to Latin America, Europe to North America. The most challenging theoretical questions facing feminism and gender studies, admittedly from a largely Western point of view, are discussed in *Feminism in the Study of Religion: A Reader* (Juschka, ed., 2001). The pluralism of methods and interpretive strategies in current gender thinking on different religious experiences, texts, histories, and practices is evident from *Gender, Religion and Diversity: Cross-Cultural Perspectives* (King and Beattie, eds., 2004). By taking up a self-reflexive, critical position, several contributors to this volume, both female and male, show that these debates are more than sophisticated academic arguments; in practical terms they involve a strong commitment to gender justice and social transformation, whether in Judaism, Buddhism, Hinduism, Christianity, or Islam in different parts of the world.

This is not the place to pursue a trenchant critique of the androcentrism and defectiveness of previous scholarship, but the above examples provide ample evidence that now, when women are no longer merely occasional objects of male inquiry but have acquired the necessary academic education, professional training, and expertise to pursue the study of religion at all levels, they have increasingly become scholars in their own right who critically examine themselves as objects of analysis and debate. This historically recent development has led to new questions in the study of religion, which in turn have produced masses of new data and theories, opening up yet more new research fields. With the arrival of gender studies, this process has crossed yet another threshold of complexity that will contribute to an eventual thorough re-mapping of the entire field of religion and radically alter some of its underlying research presuppositions. The influential paradigm established by Mircea Eliade, reflected in the very existence of this encyclopedia, has received much scholarly comment and criticism, but these have not yet thoroughly addressed the hidden gender imbalances and implicit androcentrism of his entire *oeuvre.* Except for some brief essays (King, 1990; Christ, 1991, 1997: pp. 80–86), the defective construction of his *homo religiosus,* who remains quite literally "religious man" without including the religious worlds of *femina religiosa,* has not been sufficiently critiqued, and the specific dynamic of gender relations underlying his *Patterns in Comparative Religion* also awaits further deconstruction.

Significant Research Themes. A critical analysis of religious texts, histories, and historiographies in terms of their embedded "lenses of gender" (whether androcentrism, essentialism, or gender polarization) raises some intriguing issues. These can be grouped into three systematic clusters of research themes that contemporary scholars pursue from historical, phenomenological, philosophical, and comparative perspectives. Related to external and internal aspects of religion, these topics reveal the interstructured personal and institutional dynamics of power, authority, and gendered hierarchies that have patterned religious life in many different and often subtly invisible ways throughout history.

The first cluster concerns primarily, though not exclusively, the social and institutional aspects of religion with regard to the respective roles and status that different religious traditions accord to men and women. What access do women have to full participation in religious life, to religious authority and leadership, when compared with that of men? Have women formed distinct religious communities and rites of their own where their independent authority is acknowledged and not abrogated by male hierarchical structures? Are specific religious rites gender inclusive or exclusive, and which are the ones that exclude either women or men? Do both sexes have the authority to teach and interpret the foundational texts and central practices of the tradition? Comparative historical studies show that generally women hold higher positions in archaic, tribal, and noninstitutionalized religions than in highly differentiated traditions that have evolved complex structures and hierarchical organizations over a long period of time. Women magicians, shamans, healers, visionaries, prophetesses, and priestesses are found in primal and ancient religions, and in tribal and folk religions today. Comparative studies also provide much evidence that, during the formative period of a religion, at the time of a new religious founder or prophet when a "discipleship of equals" (Schüssler-Fiorenza) may exist, women often have a more egalitarian position, greater influence, and even leadership, whereas subsequently they are often relegated to secondary roles, losing much of their independent agency. Examples are found among women in early Buddhism, in the Jesus movement and early Christianity, or among the women associated with Muḥammad's work, or with nineteenth-century Christian missionary movements. Women religious founders and leaders are comparatively rare. They are more prominent in new religious movements that have come into existence in quite different religious and cultural contexts since the nineteenth century (e.g., Miki Oyasama and Mary Baker Eddy, founders of Tenrikyō and Christian Science, respectively; other examples are women leaders in African and South American new religions). Women can rise to religious leadership more easily within small religious groups outside the mainstream tradition, but modernity has also created space for many new religious roles within the mainstream (Wessinger, 1996). The charismatic, rather than institutional, authority of women is recognized in both traditional and new religions, but today a greater number of women religious leaders and teachers exist than in the past (Puttick, 1997; Puttick and Clarke, 1993). Several Christian denominations now ordain women as priests, and modern Hinduism knows of many women gurus, such as Ananda Mayi Ma and others.

The second cluster of research themes centers on the fluid area of religious language and thought, raising challenging questions about the entire symbolic order and the role of the imaginary in religion. How are male and female gender differences discursively constructed, culturally inscribed, and socially reproduced? Do different sacred scriptures and religious traditions project images of women as strong and powerful as those of men? Or does their language remain exclusive and androcentric, subordinating, disempowering, excluding, and oppressing women? What are the gendered patterns and symbols of their language of creation and salvation? How are the sacred, ultimate reality and the divine conceptualized, and how is feminine and masculine sacrality understood and valued? The evaluative gender hierarchy of religious language is equally inscribed in religious attitudes to the body, sexuality, and spirituality (for Jewish perspectives on body, sexuality, and gender see Eilberg-Schwartz, 1994; for Christian perspectives see Brown, 1988; Thatcher and Stuart, 1996; the gendered patterns of relations between sexuality and the sacred are richly documented by Nelson and Longfellow, 1994; Raphael, 1996). The widespread sacralization of virginity, and the spiritually privileged position accorded to asceticism and monasticism in many religions, especially in Jainism, Buddhism, and Catholic Christianity, have fueled profoundly misogynist views in the gender dynamics of numerous religious traditions, but a comparative-critical study of these phenomena from a self-reflexive gender perspective still remains to be written.

The narrow prison of gender symbols encloses the historically and socially located human perceptions of divine immanence and transcendence. Dominant androcentric images of God have been symbols of power and oppression not only for many women but also for many colonial people. Now recognized as limiting rather than liberating, they are radically called into question by contemporary theologians of both sexes, especially Jewish and Christian feminists. Where are the symbols and images of a feminine Divine, the female figures of wisdom, of the Spirit? Analyzing religious texts and teachings from a female gender perspective can lead to surprising new insights into human experience of the Divine, whether in gendered patterns of mystical experience or in the intimate presence of the Spirit within our bodies and in the natural world, as recognized by contemporary ecofeminism and the new ecofeminist spirituality (Adams, 1993; Cuomo, 1998). Discussions about the possibility and necessity of a divine feminine, accompanied by a revalorization of the body and the maternal, take central place in the lively debates of contemporary critical philosophers and theologians (Jantzen, 1998). These have been much influenced by the linguistic turn of postmodernism and the rise of psycholinguistics, especially its revolutionary use by French feminist theorists (Irigaray, Kristeva, Cixous, and others), which has strongly impacted Western philosophers of religion (Anderson, 1998; Jantzen, 1998; Joy, O'Grady, and Poxon, 2002, 2003). Feminist philosophers of religion are now engaged in sharply critiquing a traditionally almost exclusively male discipline shaped by problematic biases of gender, race, class, and sexual orientation. Different feminist theologians and biblical scholars have also taken up the topic of gender with much vigor (see Sawyer, *God, Gender and the Bible,* 2002).

A third cluster of research questions relates to the usually least visible (except for outward religious practices, and perhaps also spirit possession), the most internal, personal aspects of religion, that is to say religious and mystical experiences. How far are these differently engendered? To what extent are their occurrences, descriptions, images, and symbols gender specific? Are men's perception and pursuit of spirituality often quite different from women's spirituality? These questions can be applied to both the continuing and cumulative experience of ordinary day-to-day religious practice and to the extraordinary experiences of religious virtuosi, such as saints and mystics. Most religions seem to validate the ordinary lives of women in terms of domestic observances and family duties rather than encourage their search for religious knowledge and spiritual perfection. How far do different traditions prohibit or encourage women to seek a spiritual space of their own and follow demanding spiritual disciplines in the same way as men? By rejecting traditional sociobiological gender roles through becoming ascetics, yoginis, *sannyasinis,* or nuns, Jaina, Buddhist, and Christian women have pursued nontraditional, and sometimes extraordinary, paths of spiritual devotion and attainment, although the gendering of Hindu renunciation is a mostly modern phenomenon (Khandelwal, 2004). Women had to struggle to create their own religious communities; their gender always provoked male resistance to their claim to autonomy and power, so that their activities remained controlled and constrained by male hierarchies. Nowhere is this more evident than in the rich lives of Christian nuns in whose cloisters and convents appeared outstanding women scholars, mystics, artists, political activists, healers, and teachers over many centuries, whose biographies often reflect intensive gender struggles over power and authority (McNamara, 1996), also evident from the critical study of Christian mysticism (Jantzen, 1995).

It is especially the area of women's religious experience, in both the ordinary sense of religious devotions and duties and the special sense of a particular religious calling, that provides a rich field for contemporary research. It is important to investigate also the strongly affirmative and life-sustaining resources that countless women have found through the ages, and still find today, in a faith transmitted to them through the beliefs, practices, and spiritual heritage of a specific religious tradition. Such research provides a counterbalance to the more restrictive and oppressive role that religion has played in many women's lives.

Moving from religious experience and practice to the systematic articulations of faith that produced a wealth of philosophical and theological learning in all religious traditions, we largely meet worlds *without* women, as is all too evident from sacred and scholarly literatures, official histories of religious institutions, and more recently the historiographies and research monographs of Western scholars of religion (King, 1993). Women's religious worlds, experiences, and thought have on the whole made few contributions to these developments until the modern period. Gender studies and other intellectual advances have awakened us to such important themes as self and subjectivity; human identity and representation; authority and power relations; masculinity and femininity; body, sexuality and spirituality; and how to think and speak of ultimate reality and human destiny, of individuals and community, in a newly gendered, and sometimes transgendering, way. Feminist theologians and thealogians have reimaged God and Goddess or explored affinities with process thought (Christ, 2003); they have suggested alternative conceptualizations using androgynous and monistic models for ultimate reality; they have reshaped religious rites and invented new ones through creating either separate women's rituals or more inclusive liturgies. Many contemporary changes in religious practice are the result of an altered gender awareness, but many further social and institutional transformations of a more substantial kind are still needed. Discussions about the relationship between immanent, contingent gender experiences and perceptions of transcendence and divine otherness, or the nature of the sacred and numinous, continue unabated. However, too often these are still predicated on an essentialist dualism between the spirit as masculine and the body, whether female or male, as feminine, and they often perpetuate the traditional appropriation of the realm of transcendence and the spirit by men.

The above discussion of a wide range of research themes shows that a rereading of religions from a critical gender perspective reveals the existence of gendered texts and traditions, gendered hierarchies of power, gendered symbols of the sacred, gendered bodies and minds. The analysis of this wealth of new material is a truly daunting task and remains an ongoing one. There also arises the central question of whether gender studies in religion will be able to make a significant contribution to creating a postpatriarchal world by moving from dualistic and exclusive gender constructions to new social projects of gender reconciliation, implying profound personal and social transformations.

PROMINENT CONTEMPORARY DEBATES AND NEW DIRECTIONS. The relationship between gender and religion is still made more complex through debates about diversity and difference, a concept much hyped by postmodernism ever since Derrida's "*differance*" highlighted the disjuncture between objects of perception and their meanings as symbols or representations. Difference can mean many things; among others it can stand for a multiplicity of voices and meanings, for varied subject positions of the same individual, or it can negate the possibility of any particular authoritative account. It thus undercuts any essentialist position in debates about race, gender, and ethnicity. "Diversity" is sometimes used interchangeably with "difference," but they are conceptually distinct:

> Difference carries negative value baggage, while diversity differentials are captured by difference. The trick is to recognize difference as a fragmentation into insignificant units of resistance. By holding onto a concept of difference nuanced by a concept of diversity, significant political and intellectual action against oppression remains effective. (Juschka, 2001, p. 430).

The recognition of diversity has led to the realization that everywhere pluralities abound whereas singularity is rare. Thus, gender studies, feminisms, feminist theologies, sexualities, spiritualities, and many other categories are now more often expressed in the plural rather than the singular.

Difference is also correlated with "otherness," not only that of different experiences and social locations, of gender orientations and identities, but the multiple "otherness" of religious differences within and across specific cultures; there is the diversity of methods and approaches in understanding such differences; there is the "otherness" of one gender to another, especially the "otherness" of women for men, as traditionally understood. The social and political violence exercised by the West toward the "otherness" of "non-Western" cultures, whether through imperialism, orientalism, or neocolonialism, has come under fierce criticism that also impacts the gender and religion debate (Armour, 1999; Donaldson and Kwok, 2002). The history and concerns of feminist theory have to some extent paralleled those of postcolonial theory. Writing from the perspective of postcoloniality, feminist researchers perceive woman as a "colonized" subject relegated, like subject people of former colonies, to the position of "other" under various forms of patriarchal domination. The "epistemological violence" of Western religious and theological discourse toward other cultures and religions has come under fierce critique, as have debates about racial differences, which are being subverted through critiquing whiteness and its false neutrality, theorizing white also as "race" or de-emphasizing the importance of the category of "race" altogether. The essentialist understanding of race characterizes what is now called Whitefeminism, and new critiques of limited, essentialist perspectives of Whitefeminist theory and Whitefeminist theology, as well as religious studies theory, are being developed (Armour, 1999; Keller, 2004). One can argue, especially from the universalist, inclusive vision inherent in many religions, that there exists only one race, and that is the human race. One of the most significant issues is who has been counted as "human" in the past and who was marginalized as "other," "outsider," "barbarian," and "nonhuman." This raises the burning question of what it really means to be a human person today in the light of critical gender thinking (Nelson, 1992; Smith, 1992) and when taking into account all the other differentiations that pattern our multicultural, multiracial, and religiously plural global world.

Contemporary discussions are deeply affected by the processes of globalization, which produce transformative resources for religious worldviews, interreligious contacts and communication, and the international study of religions. Many of these depend on the globally diffused use of English, criticized by some as neocolonial form of dominance. These arguments are also present in gender debates, since more writings and scholarly communications about gender and its relevance for religion take place in English than in any other language. In postcolonial writing the "alchemy of English" (Kachru, 1986) is widely debated. Its usefulness as a non-native medium of communication is its perceived "neutrality" in that it cannot be automatically aligned with particular indigenous religious or ethnic factions, and therefore can be used just as much for imparting local, non-Western values as Western values. Thus, it is rather one-sided to see this hegemony of one Western language above others mainly negatively, for the global use of English can also be valued positively as an enabling means of wider communication and an empowering challenge for social and personal transformation. In the gender debate, people whose mother tongue is not English may initially feel at a disadvantage, but native English speakers are not necessarily better off, because a critical gender awareness always requires a new perception and the learning of a new vocabulary, linked to new attitudes and changed practices. Learning to make the "gender-critical turn" is an ongoing self-reflective process that everyone who embarks on the exciting journey of gender exploration must undergo, whatever their language.

These multiple new perspectives, now increasingly subsumed under "postcolonial studies," have spawned lively controversies on race, gender, ethnicity, nationalism, orientalism, discourse, body, and other topics, creating numerous formulations of hybridity rather than genuinely correlative or integral frameworks. These controversial ideas have also considerably influenced religious studies theory, although it is presently impossible to assess whether this tendency to identify ever more differences will have any lasting intellectual or practical impact on gender and race relations. Concepts of difference and diversity are also much discussed by feminist theologians seeking to account more appropriately for religious diversity and pluralism in feminist theological discourse.

Many further issues, whether theoretical or praxis-oriented, can only find brief mention. The influential critical theory of the Frankfurt School has itself been critiqued by feminists for its gender essentialism, although its male practitioners provide valuable insights into woman-as-object of masculine thought. Challenging the oversights of critical theory, Marsha Hewitt (1995) contends that it nonetheless possesses considerable emancipatory potential for feminist theology and religious theorists. Yet one can also argue that excessively complex theoretical elaborations remain ultimately barren and are just another example of the violence of abstraction. Faith-engaged activists in different religious groups and basic communities are consciously praxis-oriented in fighting the gendered pattern of violence against actual human beings, so starkly apparent in numerous contemporary conflict and war situations. The study of gender, religion, and violence has attracted increasing interest, and so has the topic of human rights and religion, including a growing awareness of women's human rights in relation to their religious traditions and cultures, whether Hindu, Buddhist, Muslim, or other (Jeffery and Basu, 1998; King, 2004; Svenson, 2000). The Malaysian scholar-activist Sharon Bong argues that although problematic in challenging the secularity of human rights discourse, it is essential, in fact "a moral and political imperative to negotiate women's human rights with cultures and religions," in order to complement other strategies for their empowerment (Bong, 2004, p. 241).

Also of great concern is the topic of religious fundamentalism, where research is only beginning to pay attention to gender differences, especially how women are affected by fundamentalist teachings and practices of different religions (Hawley, 1994; Howland, 1999) and the efforts made by conservative and Christian evangelical groups in redefining traditional gender roles in the light of changing social practices (DeBerg, 1990).

Randi Warne concludes one of her gender articles by saying:

> As long as we distinguish humans as "women" and "men," and as long as these distinctions carry symbolic meaning and cultural authority which shape human life possibilities, the concept of gender will be essential to any adequate analysis of religion. Gender as an analytical category, and gendering as a social practice, are central to religion, and the naturalization of these phenomena and their subsequent under-investigation have had a deleterious effect on the adequacy of the scholarship

> that the scientific study of religion has produced. Until the scientific study of religion becomes intentionally gender-critical in all of its operations, it will unwittingly reproduce, reify and valorize the nineteenth-century gender ideology which marks its origins, rendering suspect any claims to the scientific generation of reliable knowledge it seeks to make. (2000a, p. 153)

This is a bold statement, except that religion and gender do not concern the production of reliable knowledge alone. The reworking of language, thought, and theories, of knowledge and scholarship, are essential, but not sufficient, for creating a profoundly different, more gender-just and equitable world for all humans peopling this globe. To rethink sex, gender, and religion, we have to imagine that creative alternatives are available and that a nonhierarchical, more caring and participatory world can come into existence that is not aligned along a single, masculine model of sameness, but offers more spaces for rich cultural and religious differentiation. I agree with Christine Delphy that "perhaps we shall only really be able to think about gender on the day when we can imagine non-gender" (quoted in Juschka, 2001, p. 422).

The rich variety of gender entries on specific religious traditions that follow this article amply demonstrates that critical, transformative gender perspectives now affect the study of all religions and are consciously being taken up cross-culturally by scholars of both genders. Their research has created challenging perspectives of enquiry and produced a wealth of new scholarly work, as is evident from the following bibliography and those supplied on each religious tradition.

SEE ALSO Androcentrism; Domestic Observances; Ecology and Religion; Feminine Sacrality; Feminism, article on Feminism, Gender Studies, and Religion; Feminist Theology; Gaia; Gender Roles; Globalization and Religion; God; Goddess Worship; Gynocentrism; Homosexuality; Human Body, article on Human Bodies, Religion, and Gender; Human Rights and Religion; Mary; Masculine Sacrality; Men's Studies in Religion; Menstruation; Monasticism; Mysticism; Neopaganism; New Religious Movements; Nudity; Nuns; Ordination; Patriarchy and Matriarchy; Phallus and Vagina; Priesthood; Rites of Passage; Ritual; Sexuality; Shamanism; Shekhinah; Thealogy; Virgin Goddess; Virginity; Wicca; Wisdom; Witchcraft; Women's Studies in Religion.

BIBLIOGRAPHY

Gender as an Analytical Category

Nancy Bonvillain, *Women and Men: Cultural Constructs of Gender* (Upper Saddle River, N.J., 1998); Judith Butler, *Gender Trouble: Feminism and the Subversion of Identity* (New York and London, 1990); Joan Wallach Scott, "Gender: A Useful Category of Historical Analysis," *American Historical Review* 91, no. 5 (1986): 1053–1075; reprinted in *Feminism and History: Oxford Readings in Feminism,* edited by Joan Wallach Scott, pp. 152–180 (Oxford and New York, 1996). A very helpful, lucid account about locating and refiguring gender is provided by Liz Bondi and Joyce Davidson, "Troubling the Place of Gender," in *Handbook of Cultural Geography,* edited by Kay Anderson, Mona Domosh, Steve Pile, and Nigel Thrift, pp. 325–343 (London, Thousand Oaks, New Delhi, 2002); for the politics of interpretation regarding sex and gender see Terrell Carver, *Gender Is Not a Synonym for Women* (London and Boulder, Colo., 1996).

The problematic nature of masculine gender constructions is discussed in Maurice Berger, Brian Wallis, and Simon Watson, eds., *Constructing Masculinity* (New York and London, 1995) and William G. Doty, *Myths of Masculinity* (New York, 1993); see also Tom Digby, ed., *Men Doing Feminism* (New York and London, 1998). For a provocative philosophical enquiry into gender dualities and the gender system in relation to conceiving humanity and the communal project of democracy, see Steven G. Smith, *Gender Thinking* (Philadelphia, 1992).

Reference Works

Maggie Humm, *The Dictionary of Feminist Theory,* 2d ed. (Upper Saddle River, N.J., 1995) helps to clarify many basic concepts and theories of the social sciences that have impacted the study of religion. For historical and descriptive details on women in different religious traditions, see the series edited by Arvind Sharma and Katherine K. Young, *The Annual Review of Women in World Religions* (Albany, N.Y., from 1991 onwards). Theoretical and methodological issues are addressed in *Feminism and World Religions,* edited by Arvind Sharma and Katherine K. Young, (Albany, N.Y., 1999) and in *Methodology in Religious Studies: The Interface with Women's Studies,* edited by Arvind Sharma (Albany, N.Y., 2002). Much historical data on religion, women, and men are found in the five volumes of *A History of Women in the West,* edited by Georges Duby and Michelle Perrot (Cambridge, Mass., 1992–1994).

Often-cited readers that have assumed the status of classics, with mostly material on Judaism, Christianity, and new religions in the West, are *Womanspirit Rising: Feminist Reader in Religion,* 2d ed., edited by Carol P. Christ and Judith Plaskow (San Francisco, 1992); *Weaving the Visions: New Patterns in Feminist Spirituality,* edited by Judith Plaskow and Carol P. Christ (San Francisco, 1989); and *The Politics of Women's Spirituality. Essays by Founding Mothers of the Movement,* 2d ed., edited by Charlene Spretnak (New York, 1994).

Other Works

Darlene M. Juschka, ed., *Feminism in the Study of Religion: A Reader* (London and New York, 2001). An indispensable collection of articles dealing with wide theoretical issues, from women doing the study of religion to critical discourses, race, gender, sexuality, and class. Key texts from the last thirty years, grouped thematically, and introduced by excellent discussions on the impact of feminism on the study of religion. Serinity Young, ed., *An Anthology of Sacred Texts By and About Women* (New York and London, 1994). A wide-ranging selection of textual sources on women in different sacred writings. Serinity Young, ed. *Encyclopedia of Women and World Religion,* 2 vols. (New York, 1999). A superb reference work for first orientation; contains rich bibliographical sources on the fast-growing field of women's and feminist studies in religion. The premier journal disseminating feminist scholarship in religion is the *Journal of Feminist Studies in Religion,* published twice a year since spring 1985. It now invites "a variety of contributions that focus on women's experience or on gender as a category of analysis, and that further feminist theory, consciousness, and practice" (Spring 2003).

Individual Monographs and Multiauthor Volumes

Chosen from a large range of publications on gender studies in religion, the selection of the following titles was guided by several criteria: 1. use of theoretical and comparative gender discussions as well as reference to both genders; 2. cross-cultural and comparative examples from a wide range of religious and cultural traditions, by authors from different nationalities writing in English; 3. primary emphasis on the most significant works published since 1990, most of which include substantial bibliographies listing important earlier publications.

Adams, Carl J., ed. *Ecofeminism and the Sacred.* New York, 1993. The word *ecofeminism,* coined only in 1974, covers a wide, and sometimes contradictory, range of interests in the revaluation—and resacralization—of woman and nature, reflected in this collection of essays.

Ahmed, Durre S., ed. *Gendering the Spirit: Women, Religion, and the Post-Colonial Response.* London and New York, 2002. Fascinating postcolonial articles on feminism, religious traditions, and spirituality from South Asia. Includes section on violence against women in Hinduism, Christianity, and Islam.

Anderson, Pamela Sue. *A Feminist Philosophy of Religion: The Rationality and Myths of Religious Beliefs.* Oxford and Malden, Mass., 1998. Uses feminist psycholinguistics, standpoint epistemology, the idea of the philosophical imaginary, and a modified Kantianism to challenge the premises of Anglo-American analytical philosophy and to construct a daring, new feminist philosophy of religion.

Armour, Ellen T. *Deconstruction, Feminist Theology and the Problem of Difference: Subverting the Race/Gender Divide.* Chicago and London, 1999. Sophisticated deconstruction of "race" and "difference," critiquing Whitefeminist theology and theory.

Bong, Sharon A. "An Asian Postcolonial and Feminist Methodology: Ethics as a Recognition of Limits." In *Religion, Gender and Diversity: Cross-Cultural Perspectives,* edited by Ursula King and Tina Beattie, pp. 238–249. London and New York, 2004. Based on research into the standpoints of Malaysian female and male faith- and rights-based activists to change the lives of women. A fuller account of the same argument is found in Sharon Bong, "Partial Visions: Knowing through Doing Rights, Cultures and Religions from an Asian-Malaysian Feminist Standpoint Epistemology," Ph.D. diss., Lancaster University, 2002.

Børresen, Kari Elisabeth, ed. *The Image of God: Gender Models in Judaeo-Christian Tradition.* Minneapolis, 1995. Provides rich historical evidence from early Jewish, Christian, medieval, and modern writers to show that the understanding of God is closely interrelated with and dependent on dominant gender models prevalent during specific historical periods.

Boyarin, Daniel. *Unheroic Conduct: The Rise of Heterosexuality and the Invention of the Jewish Man.* Berkeley, Calif., 1997. In contrast to the prevailing warrior and patriarch image, this book offers a valuable alternative model of masculinity in terms of the ideal of a gentle, receptive male. Originating from the Talmud and further developed in other Jewish texts, this model provides helpful resources for constructing alternative gender norms.

Boyarin, Daniel. "Gender." In *Critical Terms for Religious Studies,* edited by Mark C. Taylor, pp. 117–135. Chicago and London, 1998. Succinct summary of some leading gender theoreticians, with discussion of some biblical texts and their rabbinic and Christian interpretations of gender differences.

Boyd, Stephen B., W. Merle Longwood, and Mark W. Muesse, eds. *Redeeming Men: Religion and Masculinities.* Louisville, Ky., 1996. Hailed as a groundbreaking book at publication, this book examines the dynamics of power and the role of religion in shaping masculine identities. It established men's studies in religion as a serious scholarly field.

Bradstock, Andrew, Sean Gill, Anne Hogan, and Sue Morgan, eds. *Masculinity and Spirituality in Victorian Culture.* Basingstoke, U.K., and New York, 2000. Contemporary Western gender relations still owe much to norms set down by Victorians, so far mainly studied in terms of their construction of femininities. Written by historians, these essays explore the alternative construction of masculinities, drawing on Christian (and one Jewish) examples from nineteenth-century England. Particularly fascinating is the concept of the "Christian soldier," a man fighting for his nation as well as his God.

Brown, Peter. *The Body and Society: Men, Women, and Sexual Renunciation in Early Christianity.* New York, 1988. A magisterial work on attitudes to sexuality and the body, and on sexual renunciation, in early Christianity.

Christ, Carol P. "Mircea Eliade and the Feminist Paradigm Shift." *Journal of Feminist Studies in Religion,* vol. 7, no. 2 (1991): pp. 75–94. Through examining Eliade's *A History of Religious Ideas,* Christ shows the androcentric bias of its author and the lack of recognition given to the importance of women and Goddesses in the history of religion.

Christ, Carol P. *Rebirth of the Goddess. Finding Meaning in Feminist Spirituality.* New York, 1997; repr. 1998. Drawing on feminist Christian and Jewish sources this book articulates a feminist thealogy and ethics. It includes a discussion of the resistance to Goddess history and a critical analysis of Eliade's work (pp. 80-86).

Christ, Carol P. *She Who Changes. Re-Imagining the Divine in the World.* New York and Basingstoke, U.K., 2003. A creative philosophical synthesis reflecting on Goddess/God in conversation with the process philosopher Charles Hartshorne, this book argues for the adoption of a "feminist process paradigm" in approaching the Divine.

Clark, Elizabeth A. "Engendering the Study of Religion." In *The Future of the Study of Religion: Proceedings of Congress 2000,* edited by Slavica Jakelić and Lori Pearson, pp. 217–242. Leiden and Boston, 2004. This article traces the development from women's studies in religion to gender studies and men's studies in religion. Profusely referenced, it provides clear evidence for the transformative impact of gender analysis on contemporary studies of religion, with the majority of examples drawn from Christianity.

Cohen, Jeffrey Jerome, and Bonnie Wheeler, eds. *Becoming Male in the Middle Ages.* New York and London, 2000. A title that breaks new ground in deconstructing male identities in the

Middle Ages. Drawing on gender, feminist and queer theories, the contributors to this volume examine how sexuality, society, and religious worldviews shaped the medieval Christian and Jewish understanding of different masculinities.

Cooey, Paula M., William R. Eakin, and Jay B. McDaniel, eds. *After Patriarchy: Feminist Transformations of the World Religions.* Maryknoll, N.Y., 1991. In looking for a postpatriarchal age, the female and male authors of this book reveal how far-reaching the transformations of world religions must be in order to find a liberating core that will be emancipatory for all.

Cuomo, Chris J. *Feminism and Ecological Communities: An Ethic of Flourishing.* London and New York, 1998. Argues persuasively for an ecological feminism that links theory and practice. Questioning traditional feminist analyses of gender and caring, the author asks whether women are essentially closer to nature than men, and how to link the oppression of women, people of color, and other subjugated groups to the degradation of nature.

DeBerg, Betty A. *Ungodly Women: Gender and the First Wave of American Fundamentalism.* Minneapolis, 1990. Shows how issues of sexual identity and gender-differentiated behavior are central to the emergence of American fundamentalism. Not only analyzes women and femininity but also sheds much light on how fundamentalist men understand their own masculinity in relation to shaping their families and church communities.

Donaldson, Laura E., and Kwok Pui-lan, eds. *Postcolonialism, Feminism and Religious Discourse.* London and New York, 2002. Cross-cultural perspectives that combine postcolonial thinking on religion, culture, and feminist discourse. Theoretical essays are supplemented by case studies from Hinduism, Islam, Judaism, and black American women's cultural and religious experience.

Eilberg-Schwartz, Howard. *God's Phallus and Other Problems for Men and Monotheism.* Boston, 1994. This study, which has been called a masterpiece, uncovers the inherent anxieties regarding male identity and sexuality in ancient Israelite religion and modern Judaism and provides a gender-sensitive critique of the God concept of monotheism.

Eilberg-Schwartz, Howard, and Wendy Doniger, eds. *Off with Her Head! The Denial of Women's Identity in Myth, Religion and Culture.* Berkeley, Calif., 1995. A fascinating collection of essays on women in Hinduism, Judaism, Buddhism, Christianity, and Islam based on the argument that the objectification of women as sexual and reproductive bodies results in their symbolic "beheading" and practical relegation to silence and anonymity.

Falk, Nancy Auer, and Rita M. Gross, eds. *Unspoken Worlds: Women's Religious Lives.* 3d ed. Belmont, Calif., 2001. First published in 1980, these essays deal with women's religious roles and experiences, their agency, power, and innovation, and their religious strategies in coping with male-dominated systems in a wide range of different religious traditions.

Gross, Rita M. *Buddhism after Patriarchy: A Feminist History, Analysis, and Reconstruction of Buddhism.* Albany, N.Y., 1993. The first feminist reconstruction of the Buddhist tradition, this book contains two theoretically challenging methodological appendices: a) "Here I stand: Feminism as Academic Method and as Social Vision"; b) "Religious Experience and the Study of Religion: The History of Religions."

Gross, Rita M. *Feminism and Religion: An Introduction.* Boston, 1996. Provides an excellent overview of the whole field of feminist research and women's studies in religion, using a large comparative framework rarely found in other publications.

Gross, Rita M., ed. *Beyond Androcentrism: New Essays on Women and Religion.* Missoula, Mont., 1977. Influential set of essays on methodology criticizing the prevailing androcentrism in the study of religions.

Hawley, John Stratton, ed. *Fundamentalism and Gender.* New York and Oxford, 1994. Extensive discussion of the meaning of fundamentalism, but no analysis of the concept of gender itself, which is, as so often, applied exclusively to women, with studies on American fundamentalism, Indian Islam, Hinduism, Japanese New Religions, and modern Judaism.

Hewitt, Marsha Aileen. *Critical Theory of Religion: A Feminist Analysis.* Minneapolis, 1995. A perceptive analysis of the theoreticians of the Frankfurt School, which highlights the androcentric and misogynistic aspects of their work while drawing on their new insights for developing a feminist critical theory of religion.

Howland, Courtney W. "Women and Religious Fundamentalism." In *Women and International Human Rights Law,* edited by Kelly D. Askin and Dorean M. Koenig, pp. 533–621. Ardsley, N.Y., 1999. Meticulously researched article on the challenge of different religious fundamentalisms to the liberty and equality rights of women. Includes a vast number of references to other publications on this important theme of great international relevance.

Isherwood, Lisa, and Elizabeth Stuart. *Introducing Body Theology.* Sheffield, U.K., 1998. Helpful survey on current discussions about embodiment, embodied theology, spirituality, and ecology, as well as the "queering of the body" and gender relations from a largely Christian perspective.

Jantzen, Grace M. *Power, Gender and Christian Mysticism.* Cambridge, U.K., 1995. Considered to be the first deconstructionist approach to Christian mysticism, analyzing the differently structured gendered rhetoric of male and female mystics. Argues for the plurality of Christian mysticisms and against its essentialist, experiential understanding, but sees mysticism rather as sets of social relations and representations informed by gender-differentiated power structures.

Jantzen, Grace M. *Becoming Divine: Towards a Feminist Philosophy of Religion.* Manchester, U.K., 1998. Drawing on Irigaray, Derrida, and Levinas, Jantzen explores the possibility of a new imaginary of religion that would replace a masculinist symbolic preoccupied with mortality and death by a feminist one based on natality and flourishing.

Jeffery, Patricia, and Amrita Basu, eds. *Appropriating Gender: Women's Activism and Politicized Religion in South Asia.* New York and London, 1998. Explores the paradoxical relationship of women to religious politics in India, Pakistan, Sri Lanka, and Bangladesh. Different gender identities emerge according to social, local, and political context in the struggle for national self-definition.

Joy, Morny, and Eva K. Neumaier-Dargyay, eds. *Gender, Genre and Religion: Feminist Reflections.* Waterloo, Ontario, 1995.

Challenging collection of gendered reflections on methodological perspectives, disciplinary discourses, and substantive issues of religious practice across different religious traditions.

Joy, Morny, Kathleen O'Grady, and Judith Poxon, eds. *French Feminists on Religion: A Reader.* London, 2002. Contains selections from the works of Irigaray, Kristeva, Clément, Cixous, and Wittig, with helpful introductions.

Joy, Morny, Kathleen O'Grady, and Judith Poxon, eds. *Religion in French Feminist Thought: Critical Perspectives.* London, 2003. This selection of articles by different authors complements *French Feminists on Religion* (2002). It deals with Irigaray, Kristeva, Cixous and Clément, and Wittig.

Juschka, Darlene M. "The Category of Gender in the Study of Religion." *Method and Theory in the Study of Religion* 11, no. 1 (1999): 77–105. Lucid discussion of some major feminist theorists, followed by reviews of Ursula King, ed., *Religion and Gender* (Cambridge, U.K., 1995) and J. Stratton Hawley, ed. *Fundamentalism and Gender* (New York,1994).

Kachru, Braj B. *The Alchemy of English: The Spread, Functions and Models of Non-Native Englishes.* Oxford, 1986. Examines the uses of English in postcolonial countries, showing how English is often still perceived as a language of prestige, power, and opportunity, without some of the limitations attributed to native languages, and with the additional potential for developing attitudes of neutrality and new forms of creativity.

Kasulis, Thomas P., Roger T. Ames., and Wimal Dissanayake, eds. *Self as Body in Asian Theory and Practice.* Albany, N.Y., 1993. Investigates the relationship between self and body in the Indian, Japanese, and Chinese philosophical traditions, with some attention given to gender differences.

Kawahashi, Noriko, and Masako Kuroki, eds. "Feminism and Religion in Contemporary Japan." *Japanese Journal of Religious Studies* 30, nos. 3–4 (Fall 2003). The articles provide an overview of feminist debates on religion in Japan; deal with women in Japanese new religious movements, but also in traditional Buddhism and Christianity. They also mention that women's studies research was introduced into Japanese universities from the 1980s onwards, but since the 1990s the emphasis has increasingly moved to gender studies. Volume 10, numbers 2–3 (1983) of the *Japanese Journal of Religious Studies* were devoted to "Women and Religion in Japan."

Khandelwal, Meena. *Women in Ochre Robes: Gendering Hindu Renunciation.* Albany, N.Y., 2004. A great contribution to the understudied topic of female renouncers in the Hindu tradition; through examining contemporary *sannyasinis* and women gurus, it reveals alternative models of Hindu femininity and sheds light on South Asian gender constructs.

King, Ursula. "Women Scholars and the *Encyclopedia of Religion.*" In *Method and Theory in the Study of Religion* 2, no.1 (1990): 91–97. Critique of the implicit (and sometimes explicit) androcentrism underlying some of the entries of the first edition of the *Encyclopedia* (1987) and the invisibility of past women scholars of religion.

King, Ursula. "Rediscovering Women's Voices at the World's Parliament of Religions." In *A Museum of Faiths: Histories and Legacies of the 1893 World's Parliament of Religions,* edited by Eric J. Ziolkowski, pp. 325–343. Atlanta, 1993. Highlights the historical contributions of women to the emergent interfaith movement. Discusses the nineteen women plenary speakers (out of a total of 190) and examines four of these in detail. More historical research is needed to recover women's considerable contributions to the historic World's Parliament and its impact on the development of the academic study of religion, and thereby make good a missing dimension in the historiography of the discipline.

King, Ursula. "Hinduism and Women: Uses and Abuses of Religious Freedom." In *Facilitating Freedom of Religion or Belief: A Deskbook,* edited by Tore Lindholm, W. Cole Durham, Jr., and Bahia G. Tahzib-Lie, pp. 523–543. The Hague, 2004. Published in a substantial reference work on religious freedom in relation to human rights, including the status and rights of women, this article highlights the tensions between the right to freedom to live a life of human dignity and worth and the freedom of an ancient religious tradition, sometimes practiced in denial of the human rights of Indian women.

King, Ursula, ed. *Religion and Gender.* Oxford and Cambridge, Mass., 1995. Based on the Religion and Gender Panel of the XVIth International Congress of the International Association for the History of Religions (Rome, 1990), this volume contains challenging theoretical reflections and empirical investigations on gender in the study of religion, as examined by an international group of women scholars.

King, Ursula, and Tina Beattie, eds. *Religion, Gender and Diversity: Cross-Cultural Perspectives.* London and New York, 2004. Discussion by an international group of scholars of a wide range of gender-sensitive issues in the contemporary study of religion. Includes among others postcolonial, race, gender, and class perspectives; gender archaeology; biblical gender strategies; feminist theological approaches to the Holocaust; the gendering of missionary imperialism; questions of Muslim women's identity; of Christian *Dalit* women; of male thealogical reflections; and debates about different sexual orientations.

Kloppenborg, Ria, and Wouter J. Hanegraaff, eds. *Female Stereotypes in Religious Traditions: Studies in the History of Religions.* Leiden, 1995. A fine discussion of remarkably widespread, ambiguous stereotypes used to control women in male-dominated societies, whether in the religions of ancient Israel and Mesopotamia, Zoroastrianism, Judaism, medieval Christianity, Islam, Indian Sufism, Hinduism, Buddhism, Tibetan religions, or even modern Neopaganism.

Krondorfer, Björn, ed. *Men's Bodies, Men's Gods: Male Identities in a (Post)Christian Culture.* New York, 1996. An excellent collection of essays that reflects the increasingly self-critical and theoretically sophisticated stances of the growing field of men's studies in religion.

Marcos, Sylvia, ed. *Gender, Bodies, Religions.* Adjunct Proceedings of the VIIth Congress for the History of Religions. Cuernavaca, Mexico, 2000. Contains a cross-cultural set of papers on methodological concerns in the study of gender and religion, approaches to bodies and reproductive issues in religion, and several case studies grouped under culture, religion, and gender.

McNamara, Jo Ann Kay. *Sisters in Arms: Catholic Nuns through Two Millennia.* Cambridge, Mass., and London, 1996. A highly acclaimed study of the history of Catholic nuns in the Western world. Women created their own space in religious communities where they could evolve spiritually, intellectually, and emotionally, but also continually had to struggle against male church hierarchies and the restrictions of their gender roles by society.

Mollenkott, Virginia Ramey. *Omnigender: A Trans-Religious Approach.* Berkeley, Calif., 2001. Carefully constructed gender boundaries are dismantled here, and sex-gender binaries are replaced by a new "omnigender" paradigm, a rainbow of varying degrees of genderedness among humanity. Written from a Christian perspective.

Morgan, Sue, ed. *Women, Religion, and Feminism in Britain.* Basingstoke, U.K., and New York, 2002. A collection of essays written from a variety of Christian and Unitarian approaches, which through their discussion of specific female figures highlight the complex interaction between religious belief and feminist activism.

Nelson, James B. *Body Theology.* Louisville, Ky., 1992. Discusses the theological and ethical authenticity of the human body as sexed body and deals with sexual theology, men's issues, and biomedical ethics. A masterful construction of what may well be a major shift in Western understanding of what it means to be a human person.

Nelson, James B., and Sandra P. Longfellow, eds. *Sexuality and the Sacred: Sources for Theological Reflection.* Louisville, Ky., 1994. Excellent essays from a Christian theological perspective that views sexuality as part of divine revelation and considers sex as integral to spirituality. Includes material on gender orientation, gender relations, and women's and men's experience, but also rare discussions of sexuality in relation to disability, aging, HIV, and AIDS.

O'Connor, June. "Rereading, Reconceiving and Reconstructing Traditions: Feminist Research in Religion." *Women's Studies* 17, no. 1 (1989): 101–123. A frequently cited article that discusses how religious texts, histories, and traditions have to be reinterpreted from a gender-critical perspective.

O'Grady, Kathleen, Ann L. Gilroy, and Janette Gray, eds. *Bodies, Lives, Voices: Gender in Theology.* Sheffield, 1998. Deals with women's voices rather than more inclusive gender theory, deemed as "modish" (p. 267) in this volume. Discusses representations of women in sacred texts and theologies; the need to recover the heritage of women; and the relevance of feminist theory for canonical texts. With the exception of Tamil Christian *Dalits,* this is an entirely Western, white-feminist study with no attention to cross-cultural issues or to religious diversity.

Puttick, Elizabeth. *Women in New Religions: In Search of Community, Sexuality and Spiritual Power.* Basingstoke, U.K., and New York, 1997. Challenges the view that women, who make up more than half the members of new religious movements, are exploited by charismatic male leaders; discusses interrelated issues of sexuality, spirituality, and power.

Puttick, Elizabeth, and Peter B. Clarke, eds. *Women as Teachers and Disciples in Traditional and New Religions.* Lewiston, Ky., 1993. Wide-ranging case studies of women's religious leadership, from early Christian Egypt to contemporary new religious groups in Hinduism, Buddhism, and Islam, to Bahian Candomblé, esoteric groups in Italy, and modern paganism.

Raphael, Melissa. *Thealogy and Embodiment: The Post-Patriarchal Reconstruction of Female Sacrality.* Sheffield, U.K., 1996. Important study of goddess feminism and female sacrality. Drawing on many feminist writers, it looks at the female body as a medium of divine creative activity and discusses the ethical implications of taking female sacrality seriously.

Sawyer, Deborah F. *God, Gender and the Bible.* London and New York, 2002. Illuminating discussion of Hebrew and Christian scriptural texts in the light of postmodern ideas about gender and power; shows that both maleness and femaleness are constructed in the light of divine omnipotence and that biblical writers use female characters strategically in order to undermine human masculinity and elevate the biblical God.

Schüssler Fiorenza, Elisabeth. *In Memory of Her: A Feminist Theological Reconstruction of Christian Origins.* New York and London, 1983. A classic of feminist biblical interpretation, which presents the history of Christian women in the early Jesus movement as a "discipleship of equals" with men.

Sered, Susan Starr. *Priestess, Mother, Sacred Sister: Religions Dominated by Women.* New York and Oxford, 1994. Looks at twelve cross-cultural examples of religions where women take a leadership role in religious practices and are often also the major participants, concluding that these occur mostly in matrifocal societies and that such practices focus especially on women's concerns as mothers.

Stuart, Elizabeth. *Religion Is a Queer Thing: A Guide to the Christian Faith for Lesbian, Gay, Bisexual and Transgendered People.* Sheffield, U.K., 1997. An example of a distinctive, radical Christian queer theology questioning the assumptions that underlie many doctrines and practices of the tradition.

Svenson, Jonas. *Women's Human Rights and Islam: A Study of Three Attempts at Accommodation.* Lund, Sweden, 2000. Examines Muslim participation in the international debate about women's human rights by analyzing the methods employed in interpreting religious sources in the works of the religious studies scholar Riffat Hassan, sociologist Fatima Mernissi, and legal studies and human rights scholar Abdullahi Ahmed an-Na'im. Different versions of Islam compete for recognition as the "true" representation of the divine will.

Taylor, Barbara. *Mary Wollstonecraft and the Feminist Imagination.* Cambridge, U.K., 2003. This scholarly study of Wollstonecraft's thought provides a fascinating account of her intellectual world and personal history and gives for the first time careful attention to the role that religion played in her work, thus opening a new chapter in feminist studies of this influential thinker.

Thatcher, Adrian, and Elizabeth Stuart, eds. *Christian Perspectives on Sexuality and* Gender. Grand Rapids, Mich., and Leominster, U.K., 1996. Contains a wide-ranging set of essays on Christian attitudes to the body, sexuality, and gender, with a primary focus on contemporary issues rather than historical discussions.

Warne, Randi R. "Gender." In *Guide to the Study of Religion,* edited by Willi Braun and Russell T. McCutcheon, pp. 140–154. London and New York, 2000a. Very accessible conceptual clarification of the key features, historical development, and associated subsets of the category of "gender," including a critical assessment of its contribution to the scientific study of religion.

Warne, Randi R. "Making the Gender-Critical Turn." In *Secular Theories on Religion: Current Perspectives,* edited by Tim Jensen and Mikael Rothstein, pp. 249–260. Copenhagen, 2000b. Illustrates brilliantly how gender thinking is neither natural nor neutral, and argues that a radical shift in thinking is required to make a "gender-critical" turn in all areas, including the study of religion.

Warne, Randi R. "(En)gendering Religious Studies." In *Feminism in the Study of Religion,* edited by Darlene M. Juschka, pp. 147–156. London and New York, 2001. A passionate, but measured and well-supported, plea to implement the radical implications of gender-critical thinking to all theoretical and practical areas of religious studies.

Warner, Michael. *Fear of a Queer Planet: Queer Politics and Social Theory.* New Brunswick, N.J., 1993. Anthology of essays described as pioneering in trying to push gay identity politics beyond its limitations in gay and lesbian studies, and highlighting the involvement of both political and religious figures in regulating sexual conduct.

Webb, Val. *Florence Nightingale: The Making of a Radical Theologian.* St. Louis, 2002. Carefully crafted study of Nightingale's little-known religious works that shows that her one aim in life was to organize religion, not hospitals. This analysis reveals her as an amazingly original woman thinker who anticipated feminist and process theological insights, applying gender criticisms far ahead of her time to Victorian society and the Christian churches.

Wessinger, Catherine, ed. *Religious Institutions and Women's Leadership: New Roles inside the Mainstream.* Columbia, S.C., 1996. Focused on the United States, the essays in this volume demonstrate how a growing number of new leadership roles have become available for Protestant, Catholic, and Jewish women. This is an ongoing process, slowed down by women hitting what has been called a "stained-glass ceiling." Contains a comprehensive chronological survey (pp. 347–401) of key events for women's religious leadership in the United States during the nineteenth and twentieth centuries.

Zink-Sawyer, Beverly. *From Preachers to Suffragists: Women's Rights and Religious Conviction in the Lives of Three Nineteenth-Century American Clergywomen.* Louisville, Ky., and London, 2003. By studying the religious rhetoric and theological ideas of Antoinette Brown Blackwell, Olympia Brown, and Anna Howard Shaw, three of the earliest women to be ordained in the United States, the author examines the religious roots of the women's rights movement, so often primarily understood as a secular movement.

URSULA KING (2005)

GENDER AND RELIGION: HISTORY OF STUDY

Any consideration of the historical development of gender and religion as a field of enquiry over the late twentieth century and the early twenty-first century must acknowledge the central role of feminism. From the beginning of the feminist movement a strong connection was made between the status of women and the authorizing function of religion (specifically Christianity) in maintaining gender inequalities. At the same time, however, attention was paid to its emancipatory potential. For example, campaigns for the abolition of slavery and extension of political rights to women were motivated by Christian ethical teachings. Furthermore moves to improve the status of women within ecclesiastical hierarchies were made: in 1853 the Congregational Church in New York ordained the first female minister, the Reverend Antoinette Brown (1825–1921), and in the early 1840s Oberlin College in the United States enrolled a small number of women into its theological school, having started admitting women to higher education in 1837. As Ursula King has noted, "Women's admission to theological studies [was] the most important contributory factor in making women theologically literate, thus enabling them to contribute to theological debates on their own terms" (Ursula King, 1990a, p. 278).

Despite these positive initiatives, a number of prominent suffragists highlighted the oppressive role of Christianity in maintaining the inferior status of women. For example, in 1893 Matilda Joslyn Gage (1826–1898) published *Woman, Church, and State,* which is generally accepted as the first attempt to offer a historical account of the subordination of women within the Christian tradition. She was, however, viewed by many within the suffrage movement as dangerously radical and was marginalized in historical accounts of the movement. Elizabeth Cady Stanton (1815–1902) suffered a similar fate following her publication of *The Woman's Bible* (1895–1898)—coedited by Gage and Susan B. Anthony (1820–1906)—a reworking of the Christian Bible in which all recognizably "antifeminist" passages were excised in order to demonstrate its marginalization of women. Despite the negative reception of her work among fellow suffragists, the significance of her contribution is seen by contemporary feminist theologians to lie in her initiation of a "long overdue process of biblical interpretation by and for women" (Isherwood and McEwan, 1993, p. 50). This work was taken up vigorously from the 1960s onward in the context of the women's liberation movement.

FEMINISM AND RELIGIOUS STUDIES: 1960–1990. The 1960s saw a number of rights-based movements emerge: black liberation and the Civil Rights movement, sexual liberation, gay liberation, the anti–Vietnam War movement, and the women's liberation movement or second wave feminism. Throughout the decade the women's liberation movement established itself as a major political force across Europe, North America, India, and elsewhere. Betty Friedan's *The Feminine Mystique* (1963) heralded the beginning of the women's liberation movement in the United States. Friedan identified what she called "the problem that has no name"—a "mystique" she defined as the sense of worthlessness that women experienced due to their financial, intellectual, and emotional dependence on men.

Context: The women's liberation movement. By 1970 women's liberation had come of age in North America. In the same year the first British conference on women's liberation was held in Oxford marking the founding of the British movement; Germaine Greer published *The Female Eu-*

nuch, arguing that sexual liberation was the key to women's liberation; Shulamith Firestone published *The Dialectic of Sex: The Case for Feminist Revolution,* in which she identified "sex class"—the condition of women as an oppressed class—and articulated a central tenet of radical feminism, that men's domination of women is the fundamental form of oppression; and Kate Millet published *Sexual Politics,* an analysis of patriarchy as a socially conditioned belief system that masquerades as the natural order.

The defining concerns of the feminist movement were quickly apparent. Firstly, feminists agreed that in every society that divided the sexes into bifurcated cultural, economic, or political spheres women were less valued than men. Secondly, key concepts like "patriarchy," "androcentrism," "sexism," and "misogyny" were formulated to explain the universal oppression of women. The idea of misogyny was a fundamental concept for the women's movement, seen as a lens through which all cultural and social practices, both historical and contemporary, could be viewed and explained, while patriarchy was viewed as the ubiquitous structure that enabled the elaborate expression of misogyny across a wide range of cultural, political, and intellectual systems. Thirdly, feminists critiqued the paradigms that placed men above women or represented them as the norm. Fourthly, feminists theorized an autonomous female identity where women's bodies and feminine activities were prioritized and represented as positive in contrast to the centuries-old portrayal of femininity as a source of danger, impurity, and evil. Finally, feminist activism was organized around the principle that women could collectively change their social position and identity by advocating equal employment and reproductive and sexual rights and by resisting all forms of gender-based discrimination.

However, despite broad agreement regarding the feminist assessment of the position of women, the women's movement was challenged by black feminists who experienced both sexual and racial discrimination (see Hull, Scott, and Smith, 1982; see also Ware, 1992, which shows that racism infected relations between white and black women even in the earliest stages of the feminist movement), and by lesbian feminists (see Myron and Bunch, 1975). Both groups argued that second wave feminism was overdominated by white, middle-class, and heterosexual agendas that were visibly unable (or even unwilling) to account for and challenge the multiple axes of oppression produced in the intersections between class, race, and sexuality. In other words, the plurality of women's material realities was mistakenly conflated with the universal and homogenous category "Woman," and this had the effect of erasing important differences between women. The failure of the leaders of the women's liberation movement to take the challenges of their fellow feminists seriously and to integrate their concerns resulted in the splintering of the movement.

If feminism was losing its way as a unified political movement, it was increasingly making its presence felt in universities as feminists recognized the powerful role of educational institutions in shaping cultural values and meanings. Women's studies departments and programs were established from the late 1960s onward as academic feminists sought to transform the androcentric basis of knowledge production and to challenge the omission of female perspectives. By the early 1980s women's studies had been an established field for over a decade, despite considerable hostility from those feminist activists who viewed it as a regrettable alliance with establishment values and a depoliticization of feminism. However, feminist theory did distinguish itself from mainstream academic scholarship by emphasizing its overtly political nature and its commitment to social, epistemological, and material change; feminist religious studies were no exception.

Content: Feminism and religious studies. Ursula King has noted the invisibility of religious studies within feminist and women's studies curricula and anthologies, and this can be attributed to the prevalent assumption among feminists that religion had little to offer women (Ursula King, 1990a, p. 275; 1995, pp. 219–220). Nonetheless some scholars working in the 1970s and 1980s, influenced by the insights of the women's liberation movement, began to examine religious traditions critically, at first in confessional contexts and then in the secular study of religions. June O'Connor has summarized their efforts as "rereading, reconceiving, and reconstruction" informed by questions regarding "women as subject," "sensitivity to and criticism of the manner in which [religious] traditions . . . have been studied and . . . formulated," and a concern with "our scholarly angles of vision, our research methods and approaches" (O'Connor, 1989, pp. 101–102). Accordingly four main preoccupations characterized work in the field during this period:

1. scholars exposed the androcentrism and misogyny of the Christian and, to a lesser extent, the Jewish traditions;
2. women were identified as a legitimate category of analysis as well as active agents of religious practice and study, with women's experiences being promoted as a credible and corrective hermeneutical tool;
3. new forms of female-centered religiosity were explored;
4. epistemological and methodological tools were developed in order to challenge the androcentric bias of mainstream scholarship in theology and religious studies.

Scholars began theological reflection from an engaged, although expressly critical, stance and initiated a movement away from the presentation of divinity as male within Christianity and Judaism. The quest was initially a personal and religious one: a question of finding, reshaping, and transforming symbols of divinity that would legitimize women's experiences and produce a positive sense of female identity.

Mary Daly's *The Church and the Second Sex* (1968) was a milestone, inaugurating a new era of feminist theological reflection marked by the systematic critique and reformulation of Christian doctrine from the perspective of women's experience. Following Daly, writers like Rosemary Radford Ruether (1983b, 1985), Elisabeth Schüssler Fiorenza (1983), and Judith Plaskow (1990) contributed to a lively and wide-ranging discourse based explicitly around the spiritual needs of contemporary women and the need to reform Christianity and Judaism from the standpoint of feminism.

However, Daly quickly moved to question whether or not Christianity was capable of reform or in fact irredeemably sexist. In 1971, as the first woman preacher at the Harvard Memorial Church, she spoke on the theme "The Women's Movement: An Exodus Community," inviting women in the congregation to leave the church together as a way of symbolically rejecting women's subordination within the church:

> We cannot really belong to institutional religion as it exists. It isn't good enough to be token preachers. It isn't good enough to have our energies drained and co-opted. Singing sexist hymns, praying to a male god breaks our spirit, makes us less than human. The crushing weight of this tradition, of this power structure, tells us that *we do not even exist.* Let us affirm our faith in ourselves and our will to transcendence by rising and walking out together. (Daly, 1972, p. 335)

Daly followed this up in 1973 with *Beyond God the Father,* marking the start of a protracted debate among feminist theologians regarding the extent to which religious commitment could be compatible with feminist goals and beliefs. Those who, like Daly, suggested that the only feasible option for Christian feminists was to abandon the tradition and create a new one based on women's contemporary religious experience were described as post-Christian feminists or as separatists (see Hampson, 1996). Other feminist theologians responded to Daly's work by offering their own critiques of the Christian tradition but, rather than rejecting it, affirmed that it was capable of reform (see Ruether 1974, 1981; Trible, 1978). They worked to produce new models that could act as correctives to oppressive ideologies and were broadly characterized as reformists. However, as with the broader women's movement, the issue of how to define women's experience became a contested area with the emergence of the distinctive voices of black and Womanist, Asian, Latin American *(mujerista),* and lesbian feminist theologians, which, while present from the beginning, began to find fuller expression in the 1980s.

The analysis of misogyny as well as the forms and conceptual underpinnings of patriarchy were related preoccupations in the area of feminist religious studies in the 1960s and 1970s. Feminist writers maintained that women had been deprived of their history (conceived of as originally matriarchal), that their unique religious contributions had been excised through a series of patriarchal interventions, and that the promotion of God as male in many religions had damaged women's relationships to both divinity and each other. A feminist project, known broadly as the Goddess movement or Feminist Spirituality, aimed to re-create and reimagine women's history and religious experience utilizing myth, folklore, and the archaeology of material culture. It was predicated on the conviction that what was lost in history could be recovered and would create a space for a feminine spirituality that centered on the Goddess and women's experience. Writers within the movement attempted to redefine the relationship between masculine and feminine aspects of deity by inverting their relative status so that the feminine was viewed as more originary and relevant to women's spiritual expression.

The Harvard archaeologist Marija Gimbutas's work provided a scholarly framework for the Goddess movement's account of matriarchal prehistory, giving it both an imprimatur of authenticity and a credible historical genealogy. She focused on the prehistoric cultures of Southeast Europe, featuring discoveries in "old Europe" of numerous "female" statues in stone, bone, ivory, and clay (some with pregnant bellies, large, exaggerated breasts, and stylized vulvae), as evidence for matriarchal societies in the Paleolithic and Neolithic eras (Gimbutas, 1982; 1989). The Goddess movement as well as Gimbutas's work have been severely critiqued from a variety of disciplinary perspectives, all of which have challenged the historical verifiability of its claims and have leveled charges of essentialism and reversed patriarchy (see Wood, 1996; Goodison and Morris, 1998; Eller, 2000).

In spite of the work highlighting women's historical subordination within religious traditions, feminist theologians as well as scholars of religions also drew attention to women as active agents and religious innovators in their own right. Within the context of feminist theology, this concern was a response to the contemporary controversy over the role of women in the church, particularly over the ordination of women. Much early scholarship was therefore concerned with women's leadership in the church in different historical periods. An important example was *Women of Spirit: Female Leadership in the Jewish and Christian Traditions* (Ruether and McLaughlin, 1979), which argued that although women had been excluded from institutional leadership roles, in the past they had held important positions. It was thus important to present women's involvement in the history of the Christian tradition as a way of contributing to its reformation. Studies exploring exceptional religious women, such as Clarissa Atkinson's *Mystic and Pilgrim: The Book and the World of Margery Kempe* (1983) and Elizabeth Dreyer's *Passionate Women: Two Medieval Mystics* (1989), also appeared.

Cross-cultural studies in the field of feminist religious studies also kept pace, investigating the relationship between the treatment of women within religious traditions and their position in wider social systems, demonstrating how women's strategies of resistance and innovation emerged within a multitude of religious traditions, and assessing the ambiguity of feminine symbolism within many religious systems. Notable among these were Carol P. Christ and Judith

Plaskow (1979), Yvonne Yazbeck Haddad and Ellison Banks Findly (1985), Clarissa W. Atkinson, Constance H. Buchanan, and Margaret R. Miles (1985), Caroline Walker Bynum (1987), Judith Plaskow and Carol P. Christ (1989), and Ursula King (1989).

A further trend was scholarship that addressed the neglect of women's perspectives and data within religious studies. The first of these—*Women and Religion*, edited by Judith Plaskow and Joan A. Romero—appeared in 1974, followed by Denise Lardner Carmody's *Women and World Religions* (1979). The first truly cross-cultural, nonconfessional volumes were published by Nancy Falk and Rita Gross (1980) and Ursula King (1987). Falk and Gross aimed to locate women's religious lives in a variety of traditions at the center of their study rather than the periphery, as was traditionally the case in religious studies. Numerous publications rendering women's participation in religious traditions more visible quickly followed (for example, Sharma, 1987). Studies focusing on the position and roles of women within single traditions were also produced (for example, Paul, 1979; Jacobson and Wadley, 1977; Al-Hibri, 1982).

The field of "Women and Religion" now gained limited recognition at the institutional level. Harvard Divinity School established a women's caucus in 1970, preparing the ground for the introduction of the Women's Studies in Religion program in 1973; the American Academy of Religion (AAR) introduced the "Woman and Religion" section to its annual conference; the Fourteenth International Association of the History of Religions (IAHR) Congress in Winnipeg in 1980 included a panel on "Femininity and Religion"; the British Association for the Study of Religion (BASR) titled its 1989 conference "Religion and Gender"; and Lancaster University established the first master's program in Women and Religion in the United Kingdom in the same year (Ursula King, 1990a, pp. 279–280). Although this work was vital for the recognition of female agency within religious traditions, it was generally ineffectual in challenging the androcentric bias of religious studies. Instead, a women-centered approach was seen within the field to be of concern only to women and with little to contribute to broader methodological debates. This was clear from the lack of integration of feminist perspectives in core syllabi, the comparatively low volume of publication in the area, the unsatisfactory profile of the subject at international conferences, the struggle to encourage university libraries to stock copies of relevant publications, and the underrepresentation of academics researching women in university departments (see Ursula King, 1990a; 1995a).

Feminist scholars in the study of religions thus began to offer methodological reflections in order to confront the androcentrism of the field. Rita Gross's pioneering article "Methodological Remarks on the Study of Women in Religion" (1974) and her book *Beyond Androcentrism: New Essays on Women and Religion* (1977) were the first to promote a feminist methodology in religious studies. Rosemary Ruether contributed her article "The Feminist Critique in Religious Studies" (1983a) to a volume on the impact of feminist studies in academia, and the *Encyclopedia of Religion* (Eliade, 1987) commissioned two articles on the topic: "Women's Studies" by Constance Buchanan and "Androcentrism" by Ruether (however, see King 1990b for a critique of the encyclopedia's failure to integrate feminist perspectives and for presenting an androcentric view of religion).

It was because of the entrenched marginalization of female perspectives at the empirical and institutional levels that the inclusion of feminist theory in the mainstream development of religious studies began to be framed in terms of offering a paradigm shift. Carol P. Christ (1987; see also 1989, 1991) was the first to suggest that the integration of feminist scholarship could ensure conceptual change and renewal within the discipline and would provide a necessary corrective to its androcentric foundations. Randi Warne (1989) also characterized the growth of women's studies in religious studies as "a brave new paradigm," drawing attention to the epistemological significance of the feminist challenge to the foundational premises of religious studies. Warne further made a connection between institutional structures, the feminist study of religions, and the status of women working within the field, suggesting that religious studies "must ensure that its departments are materially constructed in such a way that the presumption of male privilege is not maintained" (Warne, 1989, p. 43).

GENDER AND RELIGION FROM THE 1990S. The analysis of "male privilege" had of course been a central preoccupation of much feminist scholarship from the 1960s onward. However, a shift in emphasis emerged as scholars increasingly recognized the need to consider critically not only constructions of femininity and female identity but also the way they interacted with notions of maleness, especially insofar as they were articulated and promoted in social systems. The development of gender studies as an adjunct to women's studies was a result of this recognition. Feminist scholars from the 1970s onward thus theorized gender as a system of signs or signifiers assigned to sexually dimorphic bodies that acted to distinguish the social roles and meanings those bodies could have. They argued that gender was a social construct configured, enacted, and maintained in social systems and institutions rather than being biologically innate. Peggy Reeves Sanday and Ruth Gallagher Goodenough, for example, signaled discomfort with the decontextualized study of women found in much feminist work. They preferred instead to examine "gender meaning and gender representation" in order to draw out the "contradictory and variable views of maleness and femaleness" in different cultures (Sanday and Goodenough, 1990, p. 5). It also became problematic to discuss female and male relations and roles without taking into consideration the influence of cultural and social variables such as class, race and ethnicity, and sexuality as well as the colonialist distortion of knowledge production in the West.

Context: Gender theory. The emergence of gender studies in the 1990s as a separate field of enquiry was also the result of an increase in epistemological reflection informed by the critiques of poststructural, postcolonial, and queer theory, each of which problematized the dominant (European) humanist presentation of identity as homogenous, universal, and self-evident. Feminist scholarship was not exempt. For example, Chandra Talpade Mohanty, keen to develop a culturally contextualized "formulation of autonomous, geographically, historically, and culturally grounded feminist concerns and strategies," offered a powerful criticism of the "colonialist move" in some Western feminist scholarship on women in the third world, particularly insofar as it appropriated the "production of the 'third world woman' as a singular monolithic subject" (Mohanty, 1991, p. 51).

Another intervention in gender studies was signaled by Judith Butler, who sought to unmask the ways binarized gender categories supported inequitable gender hierarchies and compulsory heterosexuality. She asked, "What new shape of politics emerges when identity as a common ground no longer constrains the discourse on feminist politics? And to what extent does the effort to locate a common identity as the foundation for a feminist politics preclude a radical inquiry into the political construction and regulation of identity itself?" (Butler, 1999, p. xxix). Butler's work was instrumental in the foundation of a new area of inquiry, queer theory, that attended to the social construction of normative and deviant sexual behavior. Queer theory followed feminist and gay-lesbian studies in rejecting the idea that sexuality was determined solely by biology. Instead, sexuality was seen as a complex array of social codes and forces, individual activity, and institutional power-shaping ideas of sexual normativity or deviancy (see Sedgwick, 1990; Jagose, 1996; Warner, 1999).

Another significant shift that contributed to the move from women's studies to gender studies was the emergence of critical and self-reflexive masculinity studies that historicized and analyzed dominant constructions of maleness and was attentive to the differences among men. Pioneering studies were by Harry Brod (1987a, 1987b); Michael S. Kimmel (1987); David D. Gilmore (1990); William G. Doty (1993); and Roger Horrocks (1994).

Content: Gender theory and religion. The study of religions was certainly, if belatedly, influenced by the emergence of gender studies, and studies emerged that embraced the shift from a women-centered approach to the consideration of gender as a central category for critical reflection. The first scholars to acknowledge the potential of gender theory to illuminate the complex interrelationship of male and female roles within religious traditions were Caroline Walker Bynum, Stevan Harrell, and Paula Richman (1986). Studies exploring the connections between gender and religion, with a new theoretical sophistication, rapidly appeared, most notably by Bynum (1991), Leila Ahmed (1992), Grace M. Jantzen (1995), and Ursula King, whose groundbreaking edited volume *Religion and Gender* (1995) offered wide-ranging critiques of the gender-blindness of religious studies, reflections on the gendered nature of research, gender-critical perspectives on the empirical study of women in a variety of religious traditions, and reconsiderations of feminist spirituality.

Critical studies of masculinity and religion were inaugurated by Stephen B. Boyd, W. Merle Longwood, and Mark W. Muesse, who offered a comprehensive and provocative insight into masculinities and male experiences as specific and varying sociohistorical and cultural formations. The editors acknowledged their "tremendous debt to the influence of feminist theory," and the essays were built on the assumption that the construction of dominant forms of masculinity within religious traditions was problematic and in need of revision (Boyd, Longwood, and Muesse, 1996, p. xiii). Several other notable books in the area followed (Capps, 2002; Raines, 2001; Putney, 2001; Moore, 2001; Monti, 2002), and it is likely to prove an increasingly fruitful area of research in the coming years.

Issues regarding sexuality and religion also received attention, building on the earlier work of gay and lesbian theologians. Richard Hasbany's *Homosexuality and Religion* (1989) was a pioneering work exploring the dilemmas institutional religion posed for gays and lesbians. In the late 1990s studies of sexuality developed a new heuristic cogency as explorations were extended to issues of embodiment and corporeality (Coakley, 1997; Grovijahn, 1998; Carrette, 2000), the insights of gay-lesbian and queer theory (Schippert, 1999; Neitz, 2000), the place of homosexuality within religious traditions (Bouldrey, 1995; Stuart, 1997; Shallenberger, 1998; Rogers, 2002), gay-lesbian perspectives on the study of religions (Johnson, 2002; Althaus-Reid, 2001; Gill, 2004), and the intersections of race, sexuality, and gender (Carrette and Keller, 1999; Hayes, Porter, and Tombs, 1998).

Theoretical reflections on the conceptual underpinnings of the study of religions from the standpoint of gender theory were another influential trend. Marsha Aileen Hewitt (1995), Grace Jantzen (1998), and Pamela Sue Anderson (1998) offered impressive epistemological reflections on the discursive ideologies operating within the study of religions. Attention was also increasingly paid to the theories of the poststructural "feminist" scholars—Julia Kristeva, Hélène Cixous, and Luce Irigaray among others—as a means of reflecting on and critiquing the gendered nature of religious discourse (see Crownfield, 1992; Joy, O'Grady, and Poxon, 2002, 2003).

The most important and timely theoretical perspectives to emerge, however, were those of postcolonialist scholars critical of the ethnocentrism of the field of gender and religion. Their interventions have paralleled broader debates regarding the colonialist legacy of the study of religions (see McCutcheon, 1997; Flood, 1999; Richard King, 1999; Fitzgerald, 2000) and have led to accusations of the complicity of gender-theoretical scholars in the social, political, and epistemic violence exercised by the West toward non-Western cultures. Research challenging Western gender-critical scholars to reflect upon the relationship between scholarship and the ethics of representation from the perspective of non-Western "others" has proliferated (see Durre Ahmed, 2002), and Western scholars are beginning to respond to these critiques. Ursula King and Tina Beattie's volume *Gender, Religion, and Diversity* (2004) testifies to a new willingness to engage in dialogue, to challenge core assumptions, and to learn from the perspectives of non-Western gender-critical scholars. It is clear, however, that much work remains to be done. As Chandra Mohanty has suggested, "Western feminist writing on women in the third world must be considered in the context of the global hegemony of western scholarship—i.e., the production, publication, distribution and consumption of information and ideas" (Mohanty, 1991, p. 55).

Gender-critical scholars are therefore faced with the daunting task of dismantling and reforming the certainties of key feminist insights in order to ensure that the perspectives of postcolonial theorists are heard and acted upon. Given the scope and passionate engagement of gender scholarship in the late twentieth century and early twenty-first century, it is to be hoped that the task is taken up with the same commitment to social justice and transformation that has guided the field from its beginning.

SEE ALSO Androcentrism; Feminine Sacrality; Feminism, articles on Feminism, Gender Studies, and Religion, and French Feminists on Religion; Feminist Theology, overview article; Gage, Matilda Joslyn; Goddess Worship, article on Theoretical Perspectives; Gynocentrism; Human Body, article on Human Bodies, Religion, and Gender; Masculine Sacrality; Men's Studies in Religion; Patriarchy and Matriarchy; Stanton, Elizabeth Cady; Women's Studies in Religion.

BIBLIOGRAPHY

Ahmed, Durre S., ed. *Gendering the Spirit: Women, Religion, and the Post-Colonial Response.* London, 2002. This book discusses in detail the particular devotional subcultures of Asian women as well as postcolonial perspectives on the religious traditions of Hinduism, Buddhism, Islam, and Christianity.

Ahmed, Leila. *Women and Gender in Islam.* New Haven, Conn., and London, 1992. Offers a history of Islamic perspectives on women and gender, situating current debates within their historical frameworks. It is comprehensive, ranging from the ancient world to the present day, and examines the relationship of Middle Eastern women to discourses of imperialism, modernization, and feminism.

Al-Hibri, Azizah, ed. *Women and Islam.* Oxford and New York, 1982.

Althaus-Reid, Marcella. *Indecent Theology: Theological Perversions in Sex, Gender, and Politics.* London and New York, 2001. A remarkable and vigorous study that combines liberation theology, queer theory, post-Marxism, and postcolonial theory to examine the sexual experiences of the poor and to unmask the sexual ideologies of systematic theology.

Anderson, Pamela Sue. *A Feminist Philosophy of Religion: The Rationality and Myths of Religious Belief.* Oxford, 1998.

Atkinson, Clarissa W. *Mystic and Pilgrim: The Book and the World of Margery Kempe.* Ithaca, N.Y., and London, 1983.

Atkinson, Clarissa W., Constance H. Buchanan, and Margaret R. Miles, eds. *Immaculate and Powerful: The Female Sacred Image and Social Reality.* Boston, 1985.

Bouldrey, Brian, ed. *Wrestling with the Angel: Faith and Religion in the Lives of Gay Men.* New York, 1995. This collection examines the struggles of faith of twenty-one gay male writers. Each contributor reflects on the troubled relationship between spirituality and sexuality.

Boyd, Stephen B., W. Merle Longwood, and Mark W. Muesse, eds. *Redeeming Men: Religion and Masculinities.* Louisville, Ky., 1996.

Brod, Harry, ed. *The Making of Masculinities: The New Men's Studies.* Boston and London, 1987a.

Brod, Harry. "The New Men's Studies: From Feminist Theory to Gender Scholarship." *Hypatia* 2 (1987b): 179–196.

Buchanan, Constance. "Women's Studies." In *The Encyclopedia of Religion,* edited by Mircea Eliade, vol. 15, pp. 433–440. New York and London, 1987.

Butler, Judith. *Gender Trouble: Feminism and the Subversion of Identity* (1990). London and New York, 1999.

Bynum, Caroline Walker. *Holy Feast and Holy Fast: The Religious Significance of Food to Medieval Women.* Berkeley, Calif., and London, 1987. An original and provocative examination of women's ascetic practices, linking body, spirit, food, and the sacred together to demonstrate medieval women's creative appropriation and reemployment of religious symbolism.

Bynum, Caroline Walker. *Fragmentation and Redemption: Essays on Gender and the Human Body in Medieval Religion.* New York, 1991. An exemplary collection of essays exploring a number of medieval texts to draw out women's hidden voices and to demonstrate their strategies of resistance. Bynum offers an innovative interpretation of the role of asceticism and mysticism in Christianity.

Bynum, Caroline Walker, Stevan Harrell, and Paula Richman, eds. *Gender and Religion: On the Complexity of Symbols.* Boston, 1986.

Capps, Donald. *Men and Their Religion: Honor, Hope, and Humor.* Harrisburg, Pa., 2002. An insightful Freudian analysis of men's engagement with Jewish and Christian religious traditions that provides insights into the rapid rise of men's religious organizations such as the Promise Keepers.

Carmody, Denise Lardner. *Women and World Religions.* Englewood Cliffs, N.J., 1979.

Carrette, Jeremy R. *Foucault and Religion: Spiritual Corporality and Political Spirituality.* London, 2000. Carrette shows how Michel Foucault offers a twofold critique of Christianity by placing the body and sexuality at the center of religious practice and by offering a political spirituality of the self.

Carrette, Jeremy, and Mary Keller. "Religions, Orientation, and Critical Theory: Race, Gender, and Sexuality at the 1998 Lambeth Conference." *Theology and Sexuality: The Journal of the Institute for the Study of Christianity and Sexuality* 11 (1999): 21–43.

Chitgopekar, Nilima, ed. *Invoking Goddesses: Gender Politics in Indian Religion.* New Delhi, 2002.

Christ, Carol P. "Toward a Paradigm Shift in the Academy and in Religious Studies." In *The Impact of Feminist Research in the Academy,* edited by Christie Farnham, pp. 53–76. Bloomington, Ind., 1987.

Christ, Carol P. "Embodied Thinking: Reflections on Feminist Theological Method." *Journal of Feminist Studies in Religion* 5 (1989): 7–17.

Christ, Carol P. "Mircea Eliade and the Feminist Paradigm Shift," *Journal of Feminist Studies in Religion* 7 (1991): 75–94.

Christ, Carol P., and Judith Plaskow. *Womanspirit Rising: A Feminist Reader in Religion.* San Francisco, 1979. A classic anthology on feminist spirituality.

Coakley, Sarah, ed. *Religion and the Body.* Cambridge, U.K., 1997. A useful collection of essays on the ways diverse religious traditions understand and treat the "body" and problematize contemporary attitudes and assumptions.

Crownfield, David, ed. *Body/Text in Julia Kristeva: Religion, Women, and Psychoanalysis.* Albany, N.Y., 1992.

Daly, Mary. *The Church and the Second Sex.* New York, 1968.

Daly, Mary. "The Women's Movement: An Exodus Community." *Religious Education* 67 (1972): 327–335.

Daly, Mary. *Beyond God the Father: Toward a Philosophy of Women's Liberation.* Boston, 1973.

Doty, William G. *Myths of Masculinity.* New York, 1993.

Dreyer, Elizabeth. *Passionate Women: Two Medieval Mystics.* New York, 1989.

Eliade, Mircea, ed. *The Encyclopedia of Religion.* 16 vols. New York and London, 1987.

Eller, Cynthia. *Living in the Lap of the Goddess: The Feminist Spirituality Movement in America.* New York, 1993.

Eller, Cynthia. *The Myth of Matriarchal Prehistory: Why an Invented Past Won't Give Women a Future.* Boston, 2000.

Falk, Nancy Auer, and Rita M. Gross, eds. *Unspoken Worlds: Women's Religious Lives in Non-Western Cultures* (1980). San Francisco, 1999.

Firestone, Shulamith. *The Dialectic of Sex: The Case for Feminist Revolution.* New York, 1970.

Fitzgerald, Timothy. *The Ideology of Religious Studies.* New York and Oxford, 2000.

Flood, Gavin. *Beyond Phenomenology: Rethinking the Study of Religion.* London, 1999.

Friedan, Betty. *The Feminine Mystique.* New York, 1963.

Gage, Matilda Joslyn. *Woman, Church, and State* (1893). Watertown, Mass., 1980.

Gill, Sean. "Why Difference Matters: Lesbian and Gay Perspectives on Religion and Gender." In *Gender, Religion, and Diversity: Cross-Cultural Perspectives,* edited by Ursula King and Tina Beattie, pp. 201–211. London and New York, 2004.

Gilmore, David D. *Manhood in the Making: Cultural Concepts of Masculinity.* New Haven, Conn., and London, 1990. A useful cross-cultural survey of the culturally enforced norms of manhood.

Gimbutas, Marija. *The Goddesses and Gods of Old Europe, 6500–3500 BC: Myths and Cult Images.* London, 1982.

Gimbutas, Marija. *The Language of the Goddess.* San Francisco, 1989.

Goodison, Lucy, and Christine Morris, eds. *Ancient Goddesses: The Myths and the Evidence.* London, 1998.

Greer, Germaine. *The Female Eunuch.* London, 1970.

Gross, Rita M. "Methodological Remarks on the Study of Women in Religion: Review, Criticism, and Redefinition." In *Women and Religion,* rev. ed., edited by Judith Plaskow and Joan A. Romero, pp. 153–165. Missoula, Mont., 1974.

Gross, Rita M., ed. *Beyond Androcentrism: New Essays on Women and Religion.* Missoula, Mont., 1977.

Grovijahn, Jane M. "Theology as an Irruption into Embodiment: Our Need for God." *Theology, and Sexuality: The Journal of the Institute for the Study of Christianity and Sexuality* 9 (1998): 29–35.

Haddad, Yvonne Yazbeck, and Ellison Banks Findly, eds. *Women, Religion, and Social Change.* Albany, N.Y., 1985.

Hampson, Daphne. *After Christianity.* Valley Forge, Pa., 1996. Hampson examines the conception of God within the Christian tradition and the consequent production of woman as other and argues that the understandings of sin, salvation, sacrifice, and covenant are specifically masculinist. Hampson argues that Christianity is based on a myth that must be discarded if women are to achieve full humanity.

Hasbany, Richard, ed. *Homosexuality and Religion.* New York, 1989.

Hawthorne, Sîan. "Rethinking Subjectivity in the Gender-Oriented Study of Religions: Kristeva and the 'Subject-in-Process.'" In *Gender, Religion, and Diversity: Cross-Cultural Perspectives,* edited by Ursula King and Tina Beattie, pp. 40–50. London and New York, 2004.

Hayes, Michael A., Wendy Porter, and David Tombs, eds. *Religion and Sexuality.* Sheffield, U.K., 1998.

Hewitt, Marsha Aileen. *Critical Theory of Religion: A Feminist Analysis.* Minneapolis, 1995. This volume discusses key critical themes in the work of Elisabeth Schüssler Fiorenza, Mary Daly, and Rosemary Radford Ruether and shows how their work offers a point of departure for a feminist critical theory of religion.

Hiltebeitel, Alf, and Kathleen M. Erndl, eds. *Is the Goddess a Feminist? The Politics of South Asian Goddesses.* New York, 2000.

Horrocks, Roger. *Masculinity in Crisis: Myths, Fantasies, and Realities.* New York, 1994. This study provides a psychotherapeutic analysis of masculinity, arguing that many men feel devalued and fractured but are nonetheless expected by society to fulfill roles that require ruthless violence and self-reserve. He explores the consequences for men of these expectations and suggests a psychological approach to gender analysis as a way of resolving the crisis of identity that many men acknowledge they experience.

Hull, Gloria T., Patricia Bell Scott, and Barbara Smith, eds. *All the Women Are White, All the Blacks Are Men, But Some of Us Are Brave: Black Women's Studies.* Old Westbury, N.Y., 1982. A groundbreaking collection of essays that combines personal narrative, literary criticism, and empirical analysis to argue that black studies and women's studies do not sufficiently address the complex levels of discrimination faced by black women.

Isherwood, Lisa, and Dorothea McEwan. *Introducing Feminist Theology.* Sheffield, U.K., 1993.

Jacobson, Doranne, and Susan S. Wadley. *Women in India: Two Perspectives.* New Delhi, 1977.

Jagose, Annamarie. *Queer Theory.* Carlton, Australia, 1996. Offers a historical survey of attitudes toward same-sex sex and makes insightful connections to the AIDS epidemic and poststructuralism and other contemporary theoretical movements to argue for the relevance and importance of queer theory.

Jantzen, Grace M. *Power, Gender, and Christian Mysticism.* Cambridge, U.K., 1995. A brilliant deconstructive analysis of mysticism in Western Christianity showing the role of political and social power in determining the limits of the category "mystic" and the mechanisms through which women were excluded or marginalized as participants.

Jantzen, Grace M. *Becoming Divine: Towards a Feminist Philosophy of Religion.* Manchester, U.K., 1998.

Johnson, Jay E. "Searching for Religious Eroticism: The Solitary and the Ocular in Gay Religious Studies." *Theology and Sexuality: The Journal of the Institute for the Study of Christianity and Sexuality* 16 (2002): 45–53.

Joy, Morny, Kathleen O'Grady, and Judith L. Poxon, eds. *French Feminists on Religion: A Reader.* London and New York, 2002.

Joy, Morny, Kathleen O'Grady and Judith L. Poxon, eds. *Religion in French Feminist Thought: Critical Perspectives.* London and New York, 2003.

Kimmel, Michael S., ed. *Changing Men: New Directions in Research on Men and Masculinity.* Newbury Park, Calif., 1987. A useful collection of essays exploring what was once new research on men and masculinity within academic disciplines. It contributes to the demarcation of the new field of men's studies and to the analysis of masculinity within traditional academic disciplines. It addresses methodological issues and suggests future directions for men's studies.

King, Richard. *Orientalism and Religion: Post-Colonial Theory, India, and "the Mystic East."* London, 1999.

King, Ursula. *Women and Spirituality: Voices of Protest and Promise.* Basingstoke, U.K., and London, 1989. A wide-ranging account of women's contradictory and creative relationship with a broad range of religious traditions.

King, Ursula. "Religion and Gender." In *Turning Points in Religious Studies,* edited by Ursula King, pp. 275–286. Edinburgh, 1990a.

King, Ursula. "Women Scholars and the *Encyclopedia of Religion.*" *Method and Theory in the Study of Religion* 2 (1990b): 91–97.

King, Ursula, ed. *Women in the World's Religions, Past and Present.* New York, 1987.

King, Ursula, ed. *Religion and Gender.* Oxford and Cambridge, Mass., 1995.

King, Ursula, and Tina Beattie, eds. *Gender, Religion, and Diversity: Cross-Cultural Perspectives.* London and New York, 2004.

Langland, Elizabeth, and Walter Gove, eds. *A Feminist Perspective in the Academy: The Difference It Makes.* Chicago and London, 1983.

McCutcheon, Russell T. *Manufacturing Religion: The Discourse on Sui Generis Religion and the Politics of Nostalgia.* New York and Oxford, 1997.

Millet, Kate. *Sexual Politics.* Garden City, N.Y., 1970.

Mohanty, Chandra Talpade. "Under Western Eyes: Feminist Scholarship and Colonial Discourses." In *Third World Women and the Politics of Feminism,* edited by Chandra Talpade Mohanty, Ann Russo, and Lourdes Torres, pp. 51–80. Bloomington, Ind., 1991.

Monti, Alessandro, ed. *Hindu Masculinities across the Ages: Updating the Past.* Turin, Italy, 2002.

Moore, Stephen D. *God's Beauty Parlor: And Other Queer Spaces in and around the Bible.* Stanford, Calif., 2001. Examines themes of masculinity, beauty, homoeroticism, and violence in the Bible, particularly the *Song of Solomon,* the Gospels, *Romans,* and *Revelation.*

Myron, Nancy, and Charlotte Bunch, eds. *Lesbianism and the Women's Movement.* Baltimore, 1975.

Neitz, Mary Jo. "Queering the Dragonfest: Changing Sexualities in a Post-Patriarchal Religion." *Sociology of Religion* 61 (2000): 369–391.

O'Connor, June. "Rereading, Reconceiving, and Reconstructing Traditions: Feminist Research in Religion." *Women's Studies* 17 (1989): 101–123.

Paul, Diana Y. *Women in Buddhism: Images of the Feminine in the Mahāyāna Tradition.* Berkeley, Calif., 1979.

Plaskow, Judith. *Standing Again at Sinai: Judaism from a Feminist Perspective.* San Francisco, 1990. A feminist critique of Judaism and an examination of the increasing role of women in shaping Jewish tradition.

Plaskow, Judith, and Carol P. Christ. *Weaving the Visions: New Patterns in Feminist Spirituality.* San Francisco, 1989. Follows up the successful *Womenspirit Rising* with an impressive collection of essays that demonstrate the breadth of feminist theological scholarship.

Plaskow, Judith, and Joan A. Romero, eds. *Women and Religion.* Rev. ed. Missoula, 1974.

Putney, Clifford. *Muscular Christianity: Manhood and Sports in Protestant America, 1880–1920.* Cambridge, Mass., 2001. Charts the relationship between Protestantism and sports in the United States and surveys a variety of attempts to make Christianity seem more manly from 1880 to 1920.

Raines, John C. *Justice Men Owe Women: Positive Resources from World Religions.* Minneapolis, 2001. Examines ten purportedly patriarchal world religious traditions to reflect on gender injustices, showing that each of the traditions has a strong commitment to social justice, and argues that these used to advance equitable relations between the genders.

Rogers, Eugene F., Jr., ed. *Theology and Sexuality: Classical and Contemporary Readings.* Oxford, 2002. Draws on a wide range of resources and brings together a collection of essays by leading scholars to examine debates about theology and sexuality. Material is drawn from a variety of ancient, medieval, modern, and contemporary texts to provide readers with a broad perspective on sexuality in the Christian tradition.

Ruether, Rosemary Radford. *To Change the World: Christology and Cultural Criticism.* New York, 1981. Ruether offers reflections on Christology as a critical lens through which to view contemporary culture, viewing Christ as an iconoclastic prophet whose teachings elicit a commitment to the eradication of poverty, anti-Semitism, and gender-based oppression.

Ruether, Rosemary Radford. "The Feminist Critique in Religious Studies." In *A Feminist Perspective in the Academy: The Difference It Makes,* edited by Elizabeth Langland and Walter Gove, pp. 52–66. Chicago and London, 1983a.

Ruether, Rosemary Radford. *Sexism and God-Talk: Toward a Feminist Theology.* London, 1983b. Presents a revision of theological themes from a feminist perspective, including the use of male and female images of the divine in worship; the relationship between images of women, the body, and nature in Greek, Hebrew, and Christian thinking; and a new woman-centered look at images of both Christ and Mary.

Ruether, Rosemary Radford. "Androcentrism." In *The Encyclopedia of Religion*, edited by Mircea Eliade, vol. 1, pp. 272–276. New York and London, 1987.

Ruether, Rosemary Radford, ed. *Religion and Sexism: Images of Woman in the Jewish and Christian Traditions.* New York, 1974. A classic collection of essays that show the role of the Jewish and Christian traditions in shaping the social and cultural norms that have degraded and suppressed women.

Ruether, Rosemary Radford, comp. *Womanguides: Readings Toward a Feminist Theology.* Boston, 1985. A classic collection of readings from Jewish, Christian, Greek, Gnostic, Sumerian, Babylonian, and Egyptian religious literature that seeks to contextualize ideas about gender in the Christian tradition and to show alternative models that could empower women.

Ruether, Rosemary Radford, and Eleanor McLaughlin, eds. *Women of Spirit: Female Leadership in the Jewish and Christian Traditions.* New York, 1979.

Sanday, Peggy Reeves, and Ruth Gallagher Goodenough, eds. *Beyond the Second Sex: New Directions in the Anthropology of Gender.* Philadelphia, 1990.

Schippert, Claudia. "Too Much Trouble? Negotiating Feminist and Queer Approaches in Religion." *Theology and Sexuality: The Journal of the Institute for the Study of Christianity and Sexuality* 11 (1999): 44–63.

Schüssler Fiorenza, Elisabeth. *In Memory of Her: A Feminist Theological Reconstruction of Christian Origins.* New York, 1983. Traces the origins of Christianity through the lens of contemporary feminist assumptions and is aimed at challenging deeply embedded assumptions about biblical texts, and religious authority. Schüssler Fiorenza compares the letters of Peter and Paul, which insist on the submission of women, to the writers of the Gospels, who emphasize love and service as the essence of spiritual life. The picture that emerges is one in which women played active and important roles during the early stages of Christianity.

Sedgwick, Eve Kosofsky. *Epistemology of the Closet.* Berkeley, Calif., 1990. Offers a literary analysis of some of the classic texts of European and American literature, mapping the historical moment in which sexual identity became as important a marker of subjectivity as gender identity was. Sedgwick shows how the categories of "homosexual" and "heterosexual" continue to shape almost all aspects of contemporary thought.

Shallenberger, David. *Reclaiming the Spirit: Gay Men and Lesbians Come to Terms with Religion.* New Brunswick, N.J., and London, 1998. A useful study based on interviews with twenty-six gay men and lesbians from Chicago who discuss their family backgrounds, their early religious and spiritual experiences, and how identifying themselves as gay or lesbian impacted their spiritual lives.

Sharma, Arvind, ed. *Women in World Religions.* Albany, N.Y., 1987.

Stanton, Elizabeth Cady. *The Woman's Bible: The Original Feminist Attack on the Bible* (1895–1898). Edinburgh, 1986.

Stuart, Elizabeth. *Religion Is a Queer Thing: A Guide to the Christian Faith for Lesbian, Gay, Bisexual, and Transgendered People.* London, 1997. An accessible introduction to queer theology that is aimed at lesbian, gay, bisexual, and transgendered people who are either new to Christianity or who are interested in investigating theology from a queer perspective.

Trible, Phyllis. *God and the Rhetoric of Sexuality.* Philadelphia, 1978. A study of important biblical themes, through careful textual analysis of the Hebrew and Christian Scriptures, that are of special interest to feminists.

Ware, Vron. *Beyond the Pale: White Women, Racism, and History.* London and New York, 1992.

Warne, Randi R. "Toward a Brave New Paradigm: The Impact of Women's Studies on Religious Studies." *Religious Studies and Theology* 9 (1989): 35–46.

Warner, Michael. *The Trouble with Normal: Sex, Politics, and the Ethics of Queer Life.* New York, 1999. Warner argues against the heterosexual status quo that promotes marriage as the ideal, suggesting that gay marriage and other moves toward normalcy simply serve to reinforce social norms that ensure that gay and lesbian sexualities are marginalized. Instead, he offers a new model of sexual autonomy that seeks to change the way people think about sex, shame, and identity.

Wood, Juliette. "The Concept of the Goddess." In *The Concept of the Goddess*, edited by Sandra Billington and Miranda Green, pp. 8–25. London, 1996.

Sîan Hawthorne (2005)

GENDER AND RELIGION: GENDER AND HINDUISM

There are many ways to approach women's and gender studies in Hinduism. A more-descriptive, less-analytical approach usually deals with the traditional scriptural injunctions relating to women, the concept of *strīdharma*, feminine archetypes, symbolic structures, divine manifestations, and the ways these matters impact both male and female religious practices and identities. For example, the image of Hindu women (a supposedly homogeneous group essentially different from both Hindu men and non-Hindu women) is often derived from two categories of sacred texts: the Vedas, the oldest and most authoritative Indian texts (c. 1500–600 BCE) and *Manusmṛti*, the best-known prescriptive text and the most commonly cited source of Hindu *dharma* (c. second century BCE–second century CE).

Women in the Ancient Texts. The first group of texts confirms that there were women seers in the Vedic age (approximately 1 percent of the hymns of the *Ṛgveda* are attributed to women) and women philosophers capable of debating with men (Gārgī and *Maitreyī* in the Upaniṣads), that the sacrificer's wife played an instrumental (if far from equal) role in public rituals, and that a woman's primary function was to be the mother of sons. According to the much later text, *Manusmṛti*, women were denied access to learning altogether. Marriage for a woman was equated with religious initiation (*upanayana*) for a man, the service she offered her husband was equated with his religious studentship, and her performance of household duties was equated with his worship of the sacrificial fire (*Manusmṛti* 2.67); that is, her domestic duties constituted her religious life. The importance of procreation gave rise to the image of her womb as a field. The passivity of the field was assumed: The husband sowed the seed, which determined the crop, and because he was (ideally) the owner of both field and produce, it was essential to guard both from other men. The subordination of the wife was ensured by the criteria for choosing a bride. Men were advised to marry girls considerably younger than themselves (the ideal gap was sixteen to eighteen years) from families of the same or lower status and from families with which there were no existing kinship ties to soften her experience of isolation.

Whereas the religious life (*dharma*) of a man was usually described in terms of his class (*varṇa*; i.e., according to his membership of the priestly, ruling, mercantile, or servant class) and stage in life (*āśrama*; i.e., according to whether he was a religious student, a married householder, a hermit, or a renunciate), that of a woman focused solely on the cultural expectations of the good wife (*strīdharma*). Thus the narrative and prescriptive literature is full of glorifications of the ideal wife often startlingly juxtaposed with dire pronouncements regarding the inherently wicked nature of women (*strīsvabhāva*). That this was a strategy for the control of women is evidenced by the total lack of a parallel opposition between the ideal husband and the essential wickedness of all men. Cultural archetypes reinforce these patterns. In the *Rāmāyaṇa,* for example, male figures include Rāma (exemplar of the ruling class) and Hanumān (exemplar of the devoted servant). Conversely, for women, Sītā represents the perfect wife, and Kaikeyī stands for the inherent wickedness of women.

There are, however, other representations of the male–female relationship. According to Saṅkhya philosophy, for example, all existence is derived from two principles: *puruṣa* (the irreducible self—male, aloof, and perfect) and *prakṛti* (the manifest world, defined as female, needing attention, longing to serve, and the cause of the male self's entrapment in existence). The *puruṣa-prakṛti* dichotomy is clearly intended to apply to all existence and all individuals, including women. However, the cultural stereotypes underlying the philosophical message are undeniable, as is the implication that the truly religious man must abandon both women and the world if he is to attain his goal. In the context of devotional religion *(bhakti),* the male-female relationship receives a different emphasis: God is supreme, the only male in a world of devotees represented as feminine. In the worship of Kṛṣṇa, for example, male devotees imagine themselves as women in their devotion to their Lord, whereas female devotees have the advantage of being naturally subservient in their devotion.

Another twist is provided by the concept of the divine feminine *(śakti* or *pakti).* Although many goddesses are depicted as consorts rather than as independent deities, there is the widespread notion that divine power is feminine (*śakti,* meaning "power," is a feminine noun). According to this view, without *śakti,* the gods are powerless, and the ultimate power of the universe is that of Devī, the Great Goddess.

A more critical and reflective approach reveals that the very discussion of women and, more recently, gender in Hinduism has evolved within the context of and in specific response to complex historical developments from the early nineteenth century onward. Generally speaking, the history of women's studies and gender studies tends to follow a three-phase pattern. In the first phase, scholars look for and research sources and key individuals that can in some sense add women to a preexisting framework, the latter sometimes referred to as men's studies to emphasize the need for the missing component of women's studies. In the second phase, there is a movement away from the "men's studies plus women" approach toward finding ways to analyze and challenge the gender ideology inherent in the dominant discourses defining both women and men within the relevant patriarchal structures. In the third phase, the focus shifts once more, this time away from an exclusive focus on gender toward an articulation of more nuanced discourses that take into account issues of race, class, and ethnicity as well as gender.

This three-phase pattern may also be applied to the study of Indian religions and, more specifically, to the study of gender and Hinduism. In the Indian case, however, it is essential to realize that an acute interest in the role and position of women, at this point referred to as the *woman question,* predated the women's studies phase by more than one hundred years. The primary context of the woman question was political of course, but the relevance of these discussions to the study of religions is unambiguous. Indeed it is always important to view the debates on Indian and Hindu women against the background of the political paradigms dominant in India at the time: the discourses accompanying the British colonial enterprise, the narratives embedded in the Indian nationalist project, or the impassioned rhetoric of fundamentalism. A coherent history of the study of women and gender in relation to the study of Hinduism emerges only when these two models (i.e., the woman question and women's and gender studies) and these two disciplines (i.e., religion and politics) are made to work together.

THE WOMAN QUESTION. The woman question arose directly from India's encounter with colonialism. As Ashis Nandy noted in his groundbreaking work *The Intimate Enemy* (1983), colonial powers consistently viewed colonized peoples as weak and effeminate. Accordingly, to justify their particular colonial enterprise, the British portrayed the entire indigenous population of India as feminine, that is, as requiring protection. The need for vigorous intervention was further supported by what, in colonial discourse, was widely agreed to be the lamentable position of Indian (primarily Hindu) women. Whereas Hindu women were perceived to be in urgent need of social reform or uplift, Hindu men were believed to be innately incapable of providing it—hence the need for British intervention to achieve the necessary reforms. Examples of this type of discourse may be found in numerous publications ranging from James Peggs's *India's Cries to British Humanity* (rev. ed., 1830) to Katherine Mayo's polemical *Mother India*, a best seller in England and the United States from its publication in 1927.

The list of women-related social reforms advocated by the British is long: the eradication of child marriage, especially the marriage of child brides because of the high probability that they would become child widows; the remarriage of widows; the abolition of female infanticide, sati (the death of a woman on her husband's funeral pyre), and *kulīn* polygamy in Bengal (where the need for high-caste brahman girls to marry before they reached puberty and to marry only high-caste men had led to the practice of *kulīn* men of all ages being paid to marry large numbers of prepubertal *kulīn* girls without further economic obligation); and the education of women. Some of the reforms were counterproductive. For example, the regulations introduced in the Bengal presidency in 1812 distinguished between two categories of sati: voluntary sati (considered legal, perhaps even praiseworthy) and coerced sati (deemed illegal and to be condemned). Widely interpreted as a sign of government approval, this intended reform in fact led to a temporary increase in the incidence of sati in Bengal. What was less clear was how relevant these reforms were to most Hindu women, especially in the rural areas and among the urban lower classes. Most of the reforms involved only the urban middle classes, often substituting a restrictive British model of womanhood for traditional Hindu norms. The formation of the *bhadramahila* (gentlewoman), the concept of the ideal feminine as constructed by the Westernized male sections of the Bengali middle classes and largely internalized by their female counterparts, is paradigmatic in this respect.

It is significant that this early focus on women in India partly coincides with first-wave feminism in the West (c. 1850–1950) and shares many of the latter's attributes. In particular many Victorian feminists (e.g., Harriet Martineau [1802–1876], Annie Besant [1847–1933], and Josephine Butler [1828–1906]) constructed their own images both of British imperialism and of Indian Hindu womanhood, reserving a special place for what they believed was (British) women's essentially caring role in the imperial project. For most of these early feminists, the plight of Indian women was merely an extension of their own political campaigns for women's rights in the West. By stressing the Otherness and what they saw as the essential dependence of Indian women, Victorian feminists used the example of Indian women to bolster their own aspirations. At the other end of the spectrum of first-wave Western feminism stood the feminism of articulate, often Western-educated, Hindu women. Examples include Pandita Ramabai (1858–1922), author of *The High-Caste Hindu Woman* (1887) and herself a high-caste child widow; Cornelia Sorabji (1866–1954), who read law at Oxford before returning to Calcutta to work on behalf of women living in purdah (the confinement of women to the inner rooms of the home and to the invisibility of a palanquin when outside it); twenty-four-year-old Rukhmabai, whose determination not to live with a husband to whom she had been married at the age of eleven (case filed in 1884) sparked off a major political debate in both England and India; and the formidable Tarabai Shinde, who wrote a tract in Marathi in 1882 in response to the celebrated case of Vijaylakshmi, a young brahman widow condemned to death for the murder of her illegitimate baby. These remarkable individuals provided both a link between Western feminism and indigenous women's organizations and living models that resisted Victorian constructions of Indian women.

There was also the widespread idea, in Britain and among the emerging elites in India, that the position of women in a given culture was a mark of its degree of civilization, hence the significance attributed by both British colonizers and colonized Indians to social reforms relating to women. This idea has recurred throughout the history of the study of women and gender in India. As many scholars have argued, women figure in these public debates as symbols (or indeed as one monolithic symbol, "Woman") of the moral health of the Hindu tradition as discussed by men rather than as owners of views and voices in their own right. The battle between tradition and modernity continues to be fought over the bodies, minds, and images of women.

Unsurprisingly the Indian response was to produce positive historical accounts of the position of women. This was in part a defense of Indian masculinities (by distinguishing between the sexes) and in part a defense of Indian culture (by expounding the past or potential glories of Indian womanhood). The recovery of Indian culture, or tradition, from colonial slurs came to mean the construction of the "traditional woman" as adapted from a fixed eternal past encapsulated in religious texts. In the early stages of the nationalist movement, especially in early- and mid-nineteenth-century Bengal, the woman question sat center stage. For its reformist wing, accused by its opponents of being overly influenced by Western liberalism, the low status of women was seen as one of the two great evils of Hindu society (the other was caste).

Ram Mohan Roy campaigned against sati. Vidyasagar fought to promote widow remarriage (1855) and—as a *kulīn* brahman himself—the abolition of *kulīn* polygamy (1871, 1873). In the 1870s the Brahmo Samaj, a society dedicated to the reform of Hinduism, was twice divided on the marriage laws and the age of consent. In the ensuing debates on a range of issues relating to women, both sides sought their evidence within the textual sources of Hinduism, that is, in ancient Sanskrit religious texts composed and disseminated by the male brahman elite. Most of the works written during this period belong to the nationalist school. The prime example is A. S. Altekar's still influential and often reprinted overview, *The Position of Women in Hindu Civilisation* (1978/1938). A common starting point for such accounts was the conviction that Indian Hindu women had once enjoyed high status and that therefore contemporary problems must be the result of centuries of oppression by a series of invaders, notably the Muslims. These studies tended to glamorize the position of women in the supposedly glorious Vedic age, to focus on high-caste Hindu women within the family setting at the expense of other castes and other settings, and to exhibit a particular interest in sensational practices (now deemed essentially non-Hindu) such as female infanticide, child marriage, polygamy, seclusion, the deprivations of enforced widowhood, and sati. Particularly disturbing are the frequent overtones of both casteism (i.e., the denigration of low-caste women in favor of the higher castes) and communalism (i.e., anti-Muslim rhetoric). Although the simplistic explanatory framework of these early publications is flawed, the work that went into this phase constituted a useful foundation for the study of gender in Hinduism. Indeed scholars working in this area in the twenty-first century continue to respond to and critique discourses relating to the woman question.

WOMEN'S STUDIES. After Indian independence was achieved in 1947, the number of studies on women's roles within the family and on educated middle-class urban working women increased. Until the late 1960s, however, when the women's movement in the West gained momentum (known as second-wave feminism), there was little interest in rural or lower-caste women or in asking questions about the varieties of women's experiences and perspectives. Early examples of scholarly work in this phase include *Bengali Women* (1972), Manisha Roy's account of the lives of upper- and middle-class Hindu women in Calcutta, and *Women in India* (1977), the now-classic study by Doranne Jacobson and Susan S. Wadley of themes relating to Hindu women both in ancient tradition and in the lives of real women in contemporary India.

The term *women's studies,* borrowed from the West in the early 1970s, was used increasingly after the United Nations declaration of 1975 as International Women's Year and of the period 1975 to 1985 as International Women's Decade. The Committee on the Status of Women in India was appointed in 1972. The report on its findings revealed that "large masses of women in this country have remained unaffected by the rights guaranteed to them by the Constitution and laws enacted since Independence" (Committee on the Status of Women, 1974, preface). In 1979 the feminist journal *Manushi* began publishing articles on women in Indian society and culture, including items relating to religion. By the 1980s the link between women's studies and the women's movement, and thus its feminist agenda, was firmly established. Although the primary focus of women's studies was the rights of Indian women, there was a general consensus among scholars working in the field that religious ideology played a powerful role in maintaining the status quo. Madhu Kishwar, a prominent Indian activist and (with Ruth Vanita) one of the founders of *Manushi,* explained:

> The pervasive popular cultural ideal of womanhood has become a death trap for too many of us. It is woman as selfless giver, someone who gives and gives endlessly, gracefully, smilingly, whatever the demand, however unreasonable and however harmful to herself. She gives not just love, affection and ungrudging service but also, if need be, her health and ultimately her life at the altar of duty to her husband, children and the rest of her family. (Kishwar and Vanita, 1984, p. 6.)

The key to understanding the roles and images of both historical and contemporary Indian Hindu women was seen to lie in the precepts, rituals, myths, and narratives of a patriarchal religious tradition or complex of traditions: Hinduism in its broadest sense. This gave rise to a range of woman-centered studies of Hindu beliefs and practices in the 1980s. Examples include Susan Wadley's volume on the "powers" of Tamil women (1980); Lina Fruzzetti's study of the "gift of a virgin" in Bengali Hindu marriage rituals (1982); Lynn Bennett's work on the religious lives of high-caste Hindu women in Nepal (1983); Meredith Borthwick's exploration of the *bhadramahila* model of femininity in late-nineteenth-century and early-twentieth-century Bengal (1984); and Julia Leslie's analysis of the religious behavior of women (*strīdharma*) as prescribed in an eighteenth-century Sanskrit text (1989). The main aim of this phase was to make women more visible within Hinduism, both the experiences and perspectives of Hindu women themselves and what the various Hindu traditions said about them. Like the woman question before it, the women's studies approach remained an integral part of the study of gender and Hinduism (e.g., Leslie, 1991; Bose, 2000).

POSTCOLONIAL CRITICISM. The publication of Edward Said's celebrated *Orientalism* in 1978 is usually regarded as the start of postcolonial theory. Although Said himself was criticized for his lack of attention to women, postcolonial criticism in general may be seen to act as a bridge in the transition from Indian women's studies to the study of gender in Hinduism. A prime example of this phase is the work of Lata Mani on the colonial discourse on sati. Mani argued:

> Tradition is reconstituted under colonial rule and, in different ways, women and brahmanic scripture become interlocking grounds for this rearticulation. Women become emblematic of tradition, and the reworking of tradition is largely conducted through debating the rights and status of women in society. Despite this intimate connection between women and tradition, or perhaps because of it, these debates are in some sense not primarily about women but about what constitutes authentic cultural tradition. (Mani, 1989, p. 90)

This article was included in the groundbreaking volume *Recasting Women,* edited by Kumkum Sangari and Sudesh Vaid (1989). In seeking to reveal the relationship between colonial and indigenous patriarchies and between both patriarchies and feminism, these essays on Indian women in the context of the colonial history of India set the pattern for this phase.

The 1980s also saw the emergence of a school of history referred to as subaltern studies. Often regarded as the most significant achievement of South Asian cultural studies, the focus of this collective enterprise was to contest dominant modes of knowledge and knowledge production. What was previously regarded as a history of Indian elites was now construed as a history of subaltern groups. The inclusion of women among these subaltern groups gave rise to an unclear and uncomfortable relationship between subaltern studies and feminism. Kamala Visweswaran (1996), for example, distinguished between the figure of Woman (universalized and essentialized) as subaltern and "subaltern women," locating her own argument in the nonessentialized subject.

Alongside the feminist challenge to subaltern studies, feminist historiography focused on questions of voice, agency, and resistance with a particular interest in the oral histories of women. Examples include Malavika Karlekar's (1993) use of biographies, memoirs, and letters to present the "voices" of some remarkable women in nineteenth- and twentieth-century Bengal and Rosalind O'Hanlon's (1994) translation and analysis of Tarabai Shinde's 1882 diatribe on the ways men have silenced and disempowered Indian women.

This transitional phase was one of critique and revelation. Patriarchal constructions of Hindu women—whether those of the colonial British, those of Indian nationalists, or those of what may be termed Hindu "traditionalists"—were closely analyzed, whereas the perceptions of real Hindu women were brought into the foreground. This approach too became an integral part of the study of gender and Hinduism.

GENDER STUDIES. Overlapping with the initiatives already described, the study of gender rather than women dates from the end of the twentieth century and the beginning of the twenty-first century. In line with this shift in focus, *Samya Shakti*, the journal of women's studies edited by Malavika Karlekar and first published by the Centre for Women's Development Studies in Delhi in 1983, was in 1994 renamed the *Indian Journal of Gender Studies*. This phase was marked by a continuing concern with the explosive mix of religion and politics and an increasing interest in the gendered aspects of nationalist and communalist rhetoric (e.g., Sarkar and Butalia, 1995). In addition greater attention was paid to the diversities of women's religious and cultural experiences and to racial, ethnic, caste-related, regional, economic, and life-cycle differences (e.g., Malhotra, 2002). New research interests emerged too: women as subjects rather than as objects of study (e.g., Kumar, 1994); Hindu notions of masculinity (e.g., Sax, 1997); the androgyne, eunuch, or third sex (e.g., Zwilling and Sweet, 2000); Third World and Indian feminisms, usually defined in opposition to Western feminism (e.g., Gedalof, 1999); the vexed question of who speaks for whom (whether texts or informants for the subjects of study, researchers for texts and informants, men for women, higher castes for lower castes, Western women for Hindu women, or educated middle-class urban feminists for rural and low-caste Hindu women); and gender theory, especially in relation to the Other.

An interesting development in this phase was the publication of a particularly large number of edited volumes with gender as their focus. This type of publication made it possible to arrange a comprehensive collection of essays on a broad topic, taking advantage of the work of scholars in a wide range of disciplines and fields and giving rise to new levels of sophisticated thought. As some of these volumes demonstrated, there was also an increased contribution from male scholars researching aspects of gender and Hinduism.

THE IMPACT OF WOMEN'S AND GENDER STUDIES. The impact of women's and gender studies on the scholarly understanding of the Hindu tradition has been dramatic. Part of this change may be traced to the numbers of women scholars joining the ranks of the predominantly male disciplines of Indology, anthropology, and Indian studies generally. Textual and text-historical studies showed an increasing awareness of the implications of the (usually but—as became clear—not exclusively) high-caste male brahman authorship of the texts under discussion and allowed the subaltern perspectives of both women and lower castes to emerge. Strikingly different examples include Wendy Doniger's extensive work on gender and myth in ancient India (e.g., Doniger, 1973, 1980, 1999); a wealth of writing by women in thirteen Indian languages brought to the attention of the English-reading public for the first time by Susie Tharu and K. Lalita (Tharu and Lalita, 1991, 1993); and the application of the tools of feminist theory and those of the Hindu tradition to the study of women in the textual traditions of Hindu India (Patton, 2002). As a result of these and other works on women, men, and gender, scholarly interpretations of religious texts and ideas expanded to include more nuanced sociocultural and gendered understandings of prescriptive utterances, ritual implications, and soteriological paths.

In the fields of the anthropology and sociology of Indian religions, a new awareness of the significance of the sex of both scholar and informant, together with an increasing number of studies by women of women, radically altered understandings of the Hindu tradition. An earlier tendency to attribute a coherent group identity to Hindu women (and, to a lesser degree, Hindu men) was replaced by a greater awareness of individual, caste, class, and regional differences in the communities studied. North India was particularly well served. For example, *Listen to the Heron's Words*, an ethnographic study of some North Indian villages published in 1994 by Ann G. Gold and Gloria G. Raheja, challenged local ideologies of gender and kinship that routinely subordinate women to men. In Rajasthan, Lindsey Harlan (2003) examined narratives relating to Rajput masculinity, the hero as protector, sacrificial victim, and devoted "goddesses' henchman." In Maharasthra, Anne Feldhaus (1995) considered the feminine imagery associated with rivers and the special relationship between water and female divinity in the gendered religious meanings of Hinduism. Studies of South India include Anthony Good's (1991) focus on female puberty rituals in Tirunelveli, linking them with notions of female sexuality, myth, and religious tradition in southern India and Sri Lanka, and Karin Kapadia's (1995) analysis of the impact of caste and class on concepts of gender among so-called "untouchables" in a village in Tamil Nadu.

This new awareness of the implications of gender was also felt in specific subject areas. In relation to Hindu goddesses, for example, there was an outpouring of academic works. The earlier publications focused on descriptive material, locating sources, distinguishing the names and attributes of different goddesses, explaining the associated myths and symbols against a largely Pan-Indian background (e.g., Kinsley, 1986). Foundational text-historical studies focused on, for example, the *Devīmāhātmaya* (Coburn, 1984); the tension between the independent goddess Devī and what Lynn Gatwood (1985) calls the "spouse goddess"; the feminine principle and its relation to the rise of goddess worship (Pintchman, 1994); the South Indian folk goddess Draupadī as presented in oral and classical epics (Hiltebeitel, 1999); and Tantric goddesses (Kinsley, 1997). There were also several wide-ranging edited volumes on Hindu goddesses and female divinities (e.g., Hawley and Wulff, 1996; Pintchman, 2001). Although some of these authors did not focus on the implications of their work for Hindu women, some did. For example, William S. Sax's 1991 research on Nandādevī, a goddess worshipped in high-altitude Hindu villages in the central Himalayas of North India, revealed that her widespread popularity derived from the fact that her mythology paralleled—and therefore provided emotional, cultural, and religious support for—the daily lives of local women. Some studies were more gender-critical, even overtly feminist, than others. For example, Ellen Goldberg's (2002) analysis of the *ardhanārīśvara* form of the god Śiva, carefully defined as "the Lord who is half woman," combines both traditional Indian and contemporary feminist approaches. Finally, there was a new interest in the appropriation of Indian goddess mythology by the West. For example, a volume of essays exploring the ways in which the goddess Kālī is worshipped and understood in South Asian and Western settings and discourses (McDermott and Kripal, 2003) and another examining how far Hindu goddesses may be seen either to empower women ("Is the Goddess a Feminist?") or to serve the interests of patriarchal Hindu culture (Hiltebeitel and Erndl, 2000).

Early studies of ritual tended to favor the public or formal arena involving male priests and actors. As interest in women and gender issues increased, greater attention was paid both to the apparently marginal roles of women in ancient public rituals (e.g., Jamison, 1996) and to the changing religious roles of women in modern forms of Hinduism (e.g., Heller, 1999). Of particular interest were women's domestic rituals: their seasonal performance of vows (*vrat, vrata*) to maintain the health and well-being of their husbands and families, their periods of fasting, their special *pūjās* (e.g., Pearson, 1996). Accounts of sexuality in the context of Hinduism began with general explorations of Hindu culture (e.g., Kakar, 1989) and led in time to more in-depth studies such as the analysis of menstruation and female sexuality in early Indian texts (Leslie, 1996), an exploration of sexuality and mysticism in the life and work of the male saint, Ramakrishna Paramahamsa (1836–1886) (Kripal, 1998), and a collection of essays on same-sex sexuality and cultural identity in South Asia (Vanita, 2002). The implications of gender theory and postcolonial criticism for the study of dowry and dowry deaths allowed research in this area to move on from text-historical analysis and data collection to more sophisticated critical approaches (e.g., Oldenburg, 2002). Studies of sati continued apace, each generation of scholars adding a new angle or approach to the ongoing discussion. Similarly widowhood was studied by historians, text specialists, and anthropologists, resulting in both empirical data and conceptual insights. Whereas male saints, *ṛṣīs* (seers), ascetics, and gurus were already visible in scholarly research, their female counterparts now emerged in a range of accounts of women saints and female ascetics (e.g., Khandelwal, 2004) as well as in studies of key individuals, such as Lopāmudrā (Patton, 1996) and Ānandamayī Mā (Hallstrom, 1999). There was also a growing interest in the gender implications of male asceticism (e.g., Chowdhury-Sengupta, 1996). The changing, often conflicting, approaches of the emerging discipline of gender studies in relation to Hinduism was especially highlighted by the scholarly treatment of the temple woman or *devadāsī*. Blanket denunciations of what in colonial times was seen as a form of sexual slavery were replaced by explorations of ritual power, eternal auspiciousness, individual agency, and postcolonial presentations of *devadāsī* reform in colonial India (e.g., Marglin, 1985; Orr, 2000; Kannabiran and Kannabiran, 2003).

The increasing significance in the twenty-first century of nationalist politics in India, and of diaspora Hinduism generally, suggests that the study of gender in relation to both these topics will continue to develop. Other areas that will no doubt attract further research include the dominance of Western (especially American) metanarratives and the Othering of non-Western women in the scholarly writing of Western feminists; the impact on both Sanskrit studies and the study of Hinduism of the greater numbers of Hindu women entering these disciplines; the gendering of philosophical ideas; the representation of ambiguous sexualities; relationships between myth, text, or ritual on the one hand and historical or contemporary social realities on the other; and the integration of critical and gender theory into existing approaches to the study of Hinduism.

The study of gender in Hinduism has progressed through a series of overlapping yet transformative phases: the woman question, women's studies, postcolonial criticism, and a more full-fledged gender studies proper. Each phase emerged from and grafted itself onto what preceded it with the result that, although everything has changed, there is little that has been entirely lost. With such radical shifts in perspective accomplished, it is hard to anticipate where the next hundred years will lead in this particularly challenging aspect of Hindu studies.

SEE ALSO Bhakti; Dharma, article on Hindu Dharma; Goddess Worship, article on The Hindu Goddess; Hinduism; Ramabai, Pandita; Roy, Ram Mohan; Sati; Vedas; Women's Studies in Religion.

BIBLIOGRAPHY

Altekar, Anant Sadashiv. *The Position of Women in Hindu Civilisation: From Prehistoric Times to the Present Day* (1938). 3d ed. Delhi, 1978.

Bennett, Lynn. *Dangerous Wives and Sacred Sisters: Social and Symbolic Roles of High-Caste Women in Nepal.* New York, 1983.

Borthwick, Meredith. *The Changing Role of Women in Bengal, 1849–1905.* Princeton, N.J., 1984. This study of the lives of Bengali Hindu middle-class women (the *bhadramahila*) is drawn from personal accounts and Bengali written sources, such as women's journals, newspapers, biographies, autobiographies, and private papers. The author demonstrates that their models of femininity form a curious amalgam of brahmanic ideals and middle-class Victorian values.

Bose, Mandakranta, ed. *Faces of the Feminine in Ancient, Medieval, and Modern India.* New York, 2000. Bose offers twenty-five essays by Indian and Western women scholars specializing in the study of Indian culture. The essays are grouped into three sections: the lives and definitions of women in ancient India; issues relating to women and goddess worship in the medieval period, including an essay on Tantra; and colonial perceptions of women in the nineteenth century together with women's self-perceptions in the modern period.

Chowdhury-Sengupta, Indira. "Reconstructing Spiritual Heroism: The Evolution of the Swadeshi Sannyasi in Bengal." In *Myth and Mythmaking: Continuous Evolution in Indian Tradition,* edited by Julia Leslie, pp. 124–143. Richmond, Va., 1996.

Coburn, B. Thomas. *Devī Māhātmya: The Crystallization of the Goddess Tradition.* Delhi, 1984.

Committee on the Status of Women. *Towards Equality: Report of the Committee on the Status of Women.* Delhi, 1974.

Doniger O'Flaherty, Wendy. *Śiva: The Erotic Ascetic.* Oxford, 1973.

Doniger O'Flaherty, Wendy. *Women, Androgynes, and Other Mythical Beasts.* Chicago, 1980.

Doniger, Wendy. *Splitting the Difference: Gender and Myth in Ancient Greece and India.* Chicago, 1999.

Falk, Nancy Auer, ed. *Women and Religion in India: An Annotated Bibliography of Sources in English, 1975–1992.* Kalamazoo, Mich., 1994.

Feldhaus, Anne. *Water and Womanhood: The Religious Meanings of Rivers in Maharashtra.* New York, 1995.

Fruzzetti, Lina M. *The Gift of a Virgin: Women, Marriage, and Ritual in a Bengali Society.* New Brunswick, N.J., 1982; reprint, with a new introduction, Delhi, 1990.

Gatwood, Lynn E. *Devī and the Spouse Goddess: Women, Sexuality, and Marriages in India.* Riverdale, Md., 1985.

Gedalof, Irene. *Against Purity: Rethinking Identity with Indian and Western Feminisms.* London, 1999. The author introduces the work of a selected group of Indian feminists, arguing that their insights should be taken on board by white Western feminisms to develop more sophisticated models of identity.

Gold, Ann Grodzins, and Gloria Goodwin Deheja, eds. *Listen to the Heron's Word: Reimagining Gender and Kinship in North India.* Berkeley, Calif., 1994.

Goldberg, Ellen. *The Lord Who Is Half Woman: Ardhanārīśvara; In Indian and Feminist Perspective.* Albany, N.Y., 2002.

Good, Anthony. *The Female Bridegroom: A Comparative Study of Life-Crisis Rituals in South India and Sri Lanka.* Oxford, 1991.

Hallstrom, Lisa Lassell. *Mother of Bliss: Ānandamayī Mā (1896–1982).* New York, 1999.

Harlan, Lindsey. *The Goddesses' Henchmen: Gender in Indian Hero Worship.* New York, 2003.

Hawley, John Stratton, and Donna Marie Wulff, eds. *Devī, Goddesses of India.* Berkeley, Calif., 1996.

Heller, Birgit. *Heilige Mutter und Gottesbraut: Frauenemanzipation im modernen Hinduismus.* Vienna, 1999.

Hiltebeitel, Alf. *Rethinking India's Oral and Classical Epics: Draupadī among Rajputs, Muslims and Dalits.* Chicago, 1999.

Hiltebeitel, Alf, and Kathleen M. Erndl, eds. *Is the Goddess a Feminist? The Politics of South Asian Goddesses.* Sheffield, U.K., 2000.

Jacobson, Doranne, and Susan S. Wadley. *Women in India: Two Perspectives.* 2d ed., rev. and enlarged. Delhi, 1992. Four classic papers, first published in 1977, explore themes relating to Hindu women in the early textual tradition and in the lives of real women in contemporary India.

Jamison, Stephanie W. *Sacrificed Wife, Sacrificer's Wife: Women, Ritual, and Hospitality in Ancient India.* New York, 1996.

Kakar, Sudhir. *Intimate Relations: Exploring Indian Sexuality.* Delhi, 1989.

Kannabiran, Kalpana, and Vasanth Kannabiran, trans. *Muvalur Ramamirthammal's Web of Deceit: Davadasi Reform in Colonial India.* New Delhi, 2003. A new translation of Ramamirthammal's novel, written in Tamil in 1936, on the lives of *devadāsīs* at the time of the Self-Respect movement, together with a detailed editorial discussion of the political and social debates of the time.

Kapadia, Karin. *Siva and Her Sisters: Gender, Caste, and Class in Rural South India.* Boulder, Colo., 1995.

Karlekar, Malavika. *Voices from Within: Early Personal Narratives of Bengali Women.* Delhi, 1993.

Khandelwal, Meena. *Women in Ochre Robes: Gendering Hindu Renunciation.* Albany, N.Y., 2004. An intimate ethnography of female renouncers in Haridwar, North India, viewed within two disparate contexts, that of Hindu renunciation in general and that of the lives and emotions of Hindu women.

Kinsley, David R. *Hindu Goddesses: Visions of the Divine Feminine in the Hindu Religious Tradition.* Berkeley, Calif., 1986.

Kinsley, David. *Tantric Visions of the Divine Feminine: The Ten Mahāvidyās.* Berkeley, Calif., 1997.

Kishwar, Madhu, and Ruth Vanita, eds. *In Search of Answers: Indian Women's Voices from Manushi.* London, 1984. This volume brings together selected articles from the first five years of the publication of the Indian feminist journal *Manushi* (1979–1983).

Kripal, Jeffrey J. *Kālī's Child: The Mystical and the Erotic in the Life and Teachings of Ramakrishna.* Chicago, 1995; 2d ed., 1998. This controversial book focuses on the gender reversals implicit in the writings about Ramakrishna, giving rise to a sensitive analysis of the homosexuality of a man regarded as a saint by a largely homophobic Indian society.

Kumar, Nita, ed. *Women as Subjects: South Asian Histories.* Calcutta, 1994. The seven papers in this volume resist the fixed category of *woman* or even *women* in favor of a series of complex, often contradictory, always changing subjectivities. Viewing women as subjects reveals that they often deploy alternative discourses to manipulate the normative and create spaces for their own realities.

Leslie, I. Julia. *The Perfect Wife: The Orthodox Hindu Woman according to the Strīdharmapaddhati of Tryambakayajvan.* Delhi, 1989; reprinted as *Tryambakayajvan: The Perfect Wife (Strīdharmapaddhati),* Delhi, 1995.

Leslie, Julia. "Menstruation Myths." In *Myth and Mythmaking: Continuous Evolution in Indian Tradition,* edited by Julia Leslie, pp. 87–105. Richmond, U.K., 1996.

Leslie, Julia, ed. *Roles and Rituals for Hindu Women.* London, 1991.

Malhotra, Anshu. *Gender, Caste, and Religious Identities: Restructuring Class in Colonial Punjab.* Delhi, 2002. An important contribution to the social history of colonial Punjab, this monograph explores the ways concepts of gender, caste, and religion—including the tenuous link between women and caste and an emerging nationalistic notion of ideal femininity—led to the creation of new high-caste, middle-class structures of patriarchy among both Hindus and Sikhs.

Mani, Lata. "Contentious Traditions: The Debate on *Sati* in Colonial India." In *Recasting Women: Essays in Colonial History,* edited by Kumkum Sangari and Sudesh Vaid, pp. 88–126. Delhi, 1989.

Manushi: A Journal about Women and Society. Delhi, 1979.

Marglin, Frédérique Apffel. *Wives of the God-King: The Rituals of the Devadasis of Puri.* Delhi, 1985.

Mayo, Katherine. *Mother India.* London, 1927.

McDermott, Rachel Fell, and Jeffrey J. Kripal, eds. *Encountering Kālī: In the Margins, at the Center, in the West.* Berkeley, Calif., 2003.

Nandy, Ashis. *The Intimate Enemy: Loss and Recovery of Self under Colonialism.* Oxford, 1983.

O'Hanlon, Rosalind. *A Comparison between Women and Men: Tarabai Shinde and the Critique of Gender Relations in Colonial India.* Madras, India, 1994. A study of a tract by Tarabai Shinde, originally published in Marathi in 1882 in response to the celebrated case of Vijaylakshmi, a young brahman widow condemned to death (on appeal, changed to deportation) for the murder of her baby. It is an angry polemic against Indian men—whether priests, writers on religion, reformers, journalists, or politicians—who have consistently undermined their own culture and then blamed women for the result.

Oldenburg, Veena Talwar. *Dowry Murder: The Imperial Origins of a Cultural Crime.* New York, 2002.

Orr, Lesley C. *Donors, Devotees, and Daughters of God: Temple Women in Medieval Tamilnadu.* New York, 2000. This careful study of medieval temple inscriptions demonstrates the centrality and significance of temple women's activities as donors.

Patton, L. Laurie. "The Fate of the Female *ṛṣī*: Portraits of Lopāmudrā." In *Myth and Mythmaking: Continuous Evolution in Indian Tradition,* edited by Julia Leslie, pp. 21–38. Richmond, U.K., 1996.

Patton, L. Laurie, ed. *Jewels of Authority: Women and Textual Tradition in Hindu India.* New York, 2002.

Pearson, Anne Mackenzie. *"Because It Gives Me Peace of Mind": Ritual Fasts in the Religious Lives of Hindu Women.* Albany, N.Y., 1996.

Peggs, James. *India's Cries to British Humanity, Relative to the Suttee, Infanticide, British Connexion with Idolatry, Ghaut Murders, and Slavery in India; to Which Is Added Human Hints for the Melioration of the State of Society in British India.* 2d ed., rev. and enlarged. London, 1830.

Pintchman, Tracy. *The Rise of the Goddess in the Hindu Tradition.* Albany, N.Y., 1994.

Pintchman, Tracy, ed. *Seeking Mahādevī: Constructing the Identities of the Hindu Great Goddess.* Albany, N.Y., 2001.

Roy, Manisha. *Bengali Women.* Chicago, 1972.

Sangari, Kumkum, and Sudesh Vaid, eds. *Recasting Women: Essays in Colonial History.* Delhi, 1989. These eleven papers on feminist historiography (i.e., historiography that is feminist without focusing exclusively on women's history) are concerned with the "regulation and reproduction of patriarchy in the different class-caste formations within civil society" (p. 1).

Sarkar, Tanika, and Urvashi Butalia, eds. *Women and the Hindu Right: A Collection of Essays.* Delhi, 1995. An important collection that analyzes both the gendered imagery of the rhetoric of the Hindu Right and the roles of real women within the movement. These essays challenge the common identification of women's political activism with emancipatory politics, thereby posing difficult questions for the theory and practice of feminist politics.

Sax, William S. *Mountain Goddess: Gender and Politics in a Himalayan Pilgrimage.* New York, 1991.

Sax, William S. "Fathers, Sons, and Rhinoceroses: Masculinity and Violence in the Pāṇḍav Līlā." *Journal of the American Oriental Society* 117, no. 2 (1997): 278–294.

Tharu, Susie, and K. Lalita, eds. *Women Writing in India: 600 B.C. to the Present.* 2 vols. New York, 1991, 1993.

Vanita, Ruth, ed. *Queering India: Same-Sex Love and Eroticism in Indian Culture and Society.* London, 2002.

Visweswaran, Kamala. "Small Speeches, Subaltern Gender: Nationalist Ideology and Its Historiography." In *Subaltern*

Studies IX: Writings on South Asian History and Society, edited by Shahid Amin and Dipesh Chakrabarty, pp. 83–125. Delhi, 1996.

Wadley, Susan, ed. *The Powers of Tamil Women*. Syracuse, N.Y., 1980.

Zwilling, Leonard, and Michael J. Sweet. "The Evolution of Third-Sex Constructs in Ancient India: A Study in Ambiguity." In *Invented Identities: The Interplay of Gender, Religion, and Politics in India*, edited by Julia Leslie and Mary McGee, pp. 99–132. Delhi, 2000.

JULIA LESLIE (2005)

GENDER AND RELIGION: GENDER AND JAINISM

The birth act for the study of gender concerns in Jainism is undoubtedly the publication of Padmanabh S. Jaini's *Gender and Salvation: Jaina Debates on the Spiritual Liberation of Women* (1991). Jaini's monograph goes to the heart of the Jain tradition by dealing with a gender-based issue that is crucial to it and that marks one of the clearest differences between its two main ideological currents, the Śvetāmbara and the Digambara Jains (born from a split that probably took place in the beginning of the common era). Some of the other factors that encouraged reflecting on the place of women in the Jain tradition in the last 15 to 20 years, which run parallel to the general trend of developing reflection on the role of women in all traditions, are the following: an increasing interest in Jainism among female scholars (e.g., anthropologists, philologists) who, in the Indian context, have easier access to nuns or laywomen than their male colleagues; an interest for Jainism explicitly motivated by a gender-based approach; a growing consciousness of the immense wealth of tradition and issues represented by women in Jainism; and an increasing number of publications, especially in the United States, on the broad topic of women and religion. Before this, many of those who studied Jainism had noticed the numerical potential represented by women, especially in the monastic orders of the Śvetāmbara Jains, without really exploring the topic.

WOMEN AND SALVATION. The Jain religious discourse shares universal prejudices against women, who are viewed as temptresses and symbols of attachment, fickleness, and, above all, treacherousness. Acts of deception (*māyā*) are considered a woman's main characteristic, to the extent that deceitfulness comes to be adduced as an explanation for sex-differentiation: "As a result of manifesting deception a man in this world becomes a woman. As for a woman, if her heart is pure, she becomes a man in this world" (Maheśvarasūri, *Nānapancamīkahā* 3.17, tenth century).

However, the main question is whether the basic inequality between man and woman as such can be neutralized. The most original contribution of the Jains to world religions undoubtedly concerns the theological consequences of their image of woman and their vivid debates about women's ability to gain salvation. The position on this radically separates the Digambaras and the Śvetāmbara and is linked to the correlated question of nudity viewed, or not, as a prerequisite. For the former, whose name means "sky-clad," acceptance of nudity by the mendicants is a symbol of their perfect detachment from everything, whether material possession or any moral defilement.

Because the underlying idea is that a woman can by no means go naked because of her specific physiology and innate impurity due to the presence of numerous subtle microscopic beings in her body, she is not considered to be able to reach emancipation as a woman. She has to be reborn as a man first. This perspective may be one reason why nuns are less numerous than monks among the Digambaras. The "white-clads," on the other hand, focus on a more internal approach: Provided an individual is able to fulfill the right faith, right knowledge and right behavior, which are the only necessary conditions for attaining the ultimate goal, gender does not matter. From the beginning of the common era up to the twenty-first century, this debate about female religiosity has been continuously sustained in many texts—all written by male ascetics. Authors from the two groups have done their best to provide logical arguments and closely conducted discussions in favor of their respective opinions, trying to go beyond mere postulates. Some, for instance, have devised a fine analysis of the notion of *gender*, which they see as different from *sex*, through a Sanskrit term (*veda*) meaning, in fact, *libido*, thus transcending the physiological sex distinction.

WOMEN AND MYTHOLOGICAL CATEGORIES: THE JINAS. Theological debates on women and emancipation are mirrored in the construction of gender in myth. Basically atheistic, the mythology of the Jain tradition centers around the lives of its Ford-makers (*Tīrthaṃkaras*, or Jinas), who number twenty-four. Like other humans, the Jinas are beings who have gone through the world of transmigration and have been born under different shapes among gods, animals, or human beings. In their last incarnation, they are human beings who soon leave the worldly life and become religious mendicants to entirely devote themselves to the practice of asceticism, which results in perfect knowledge (*kevala-jñāna*) and finally emancipation. Accounts of the Jinas' biographies are an important part of the literary tradition. Both Śvetāmbaras and Digambaras agree that twenty-three out of these twenty-four Jinas are men, but they disagree about number nineteen, named Malli (linguistically an ambivalent form because *i* nominal stems can be masculine and/or feminine). The Digambaras unanimously tell that Malli (or Mallinātha) was a boy who lived the ordinary career of a Jina and occasionally consider the absence of any feminine image as a proof that Malli is masculine. The Śvetāmbaras, on the other hand, state that Malli became a Jina during her last birth as a woman. The Śvetāmbara narrative enhances the ambivalence of the woman status as seen by this religious group: Malli had to be a woman as a kind of atonement for some act of deception committed in a former existence, but, at the same time, she had earned a type of *karman* leading to become a Jina. The fact that the Śvetāmbaras include in their canon a specific text narrating the life of Malli, whereas all Jinas are not provided with a full-fledged individual biography, indicates their desire to stress their sectarian specificity regarding this point. However, there are linguistic and stylistic features that show that even Śvetāmbaras may not have wished to insist too much on Malli's femininity as such. Once she has decided to renounce the world because she was considered only as a sexual object by several young men who all wanted to marry her, she follows the same path as other Jinas and is given the same masculine titles (e.g., Mallijina, Mallinātha, *bhagavant, arahant, svāmin*). In other words, a woman can gain emancipation, but the nonemphasis on femininity is the way to reach it. This could explain that (except for a dubious case) no visual representation of Malli with any feminine sexual characteristic is available. This fact is, to some extent, in accordance with the idea that Jinas are pure emancipated souls who cannot be shown as human beings, but is in contradiction with the sexually marked sculptural representations of naked Jinas.

WOMEN IN THE LIFE OF MAHĀVĪRA. The fundamental theological difference between Śvetāmbaras and Digambaras—the latter having a basically negative view of women—explains their divergence of thought regarding the role of women in the life of their teacher, Mahāvīra, the twenty-fourth Jina. The Digambaras' position suffers no compromise: Mahāvīra cannot be conceived as subjected to women in any way. Albeit the young handsome son of a princely family, he renounces the world as perfectly chaste and never surrenders to the delights of love, thus embodying the perfect ascetic. On the contrary, several features underline the key role of women in this Jina's biography as told by the Śvetāmbaras: (1) although reluctant to do so, Vardhamāna (Mahāvīra) accepts his parents' command to get married; (2) he fathers a daughter; and (3) she becomes the wife of Vardhamāna's elder sister's son (instance of cross-cousin marriage documented in western India) and her husband is responsible for an important schism in the community. This probably intentional stress on feminine lineage may be a part of a strategy meant to underline sectarian identity against the Digambaras (and perhaps also against the Buddhists because Gotama is said to have fathered a son). The desire to describe Mahāvīra as a perfect householder before he renounces the world is perhaps a way to make the ideal he represents closer to the ordinary man and is a less extremist view more in accordance with the accepted current social patterns.

WOMEN IN WORSHIP: MYTHICAL FIGURES. In worship, female mythical figures, connected with grammatically feminine concepts, occupy a central place. Iconography testifies to a fairly ancient cult rendered to the mothers of the Jinas, and especially to Marudevī, the mother of the First One, who is said to have been the first emancipated soul. Knowledge, a cardinal concept in Jain doctrine, takes shape in figures that are all feminine. This applies to the goddess Sarasvatī, who is as important for the Jains as she is for other Indians, to the *vidyādevīs*, who are representations of various sciences (*vidyā*, a feminine noun), and to the "eight mothers" (*mātṛkās*; a group of eight basic notions of Jain ethics). The main feminine deities of the Jain tradition, however, are the female attendants (*Yakṣiṇīs*) attached to the main Jinas. Among them, Cakreśvarī, Padmāvatī and Ambikā (respectively connected with the twenty-second, twenty-third, and twenty-fourth Jina) have gradually become independent figures and occupy an outstanding place, being invoked by devotees who seek their protection on specific occasions of their daily lives. While the Jinas appear as distant spiritual ideals, these female deities are nearer to the human world and its difficulties and could have a role more prominent than their male counterparts (the *Yakṣas*).

HEROINES. Storytelling, an important pedagogical means of Jainism that takes various forms in various languages, functions significantly in the construction of gender. The lives of female legendary protagonists inform the minds of Jain women by providing identification patterns to be followed or avoided. In the virtually inexhaustible gallery of portraits, the Jinas' mothers and the sixteen *Mahāsatīs* are prominent. In short, the following key roles are illustrated by female characters: (1) willing or unwilling donor of alms (to be viewed in the light of the importance of food); (2) strong and faithful adherents to the basic principles of Jainism and propagators of the Jain faith to adverse members of the family; (3) virtuous and faithful wives despite dangerous situations putting life-safety at risk; and (4) renouncers of domestic life (e.g., the famous Rājimatī, dear to all Jain hearts; as her future husband renounced worldly life on the day of his marriage, she overcame her suffering, decided to become a nun, and later resisted the seductive attempts of her husband's elder brother).

WOMEN AND SOCIETY: RELIGIOUS ORDERS. Gender does not seem to have ever been an issue as far as the creation of a female order is concerned. When the community was structured by Mahāvīra, the main expounder of the doctrine (around the fifth century BCE), it was right away described as fourfold, including women as two of its components: laywomen (*śrāvikā*) and nuns (*sādhvī*), beside laymen and monks. This is recognized by all Jains, whether Śvetāmbara or Digambaras, and has not given rise to any discussion or embarrassment whatsoever (contrary to what happened in the beginnings of the Buddhist tradition).

Whether in ancient scriptures or in modern times (at least among Śvetāmbaras), statistics are clear: Nuns largely outnumber monks. However, higher number does not mean higher rank. In the specific texts devoted to the exposition of the monastic code developed by the Śvetāmbaras as a part of their canon, no explicit inequality between monks and nuns is recognized, but the patterns of redaction rest on the underlying thought that a woman, being unsteady by nature, needs more control. General rules applying to monks and nuns are largely similar, but there are additional and stricter rules that are meant to restrict options open to nuns in activities connected with their daily routine—especially food regulations. On the other hand, their independence and freedom are limited by a general subordination to the monks: (1) Even when having a long religious life, they may be under the authority of junior monks; (2) they need more years than their male colleagues to reach high positions in the religious hierarchy; and (3) nuns have their own religious titles that imply an inferior rank than those of monks.

NUNS AND LEADERSHIP. This last point is best exemplified in the organization of the Terāpantha movement, a modern subsect of the Śvetāmbaras mostly active in Rajasthan. When it originated in the eighteenth century, a single teacher (*ācārya*) was the head of both monks and nuns. The regular increase of nuns resulted in the institution of a female head (*pramukhā*) who commands smaller units. However, her role is that of a coordinator; she is not considered as the female counterpart of the *ācārya*, who is the decisional authority, and she remains subordinate to him. In fact, Jainism does not know of any female as a leader of a religious group of some significance. The only exception to this is very recent, rather marginal and locally based in Gujarat. It is represented by the case of Campābahen Mātājī (1918–1993) who became the leader of the Kānji Svāmī Panth, a twentieth century neo-Digambara movement, after the death of its founder in 1980 and who is credited with quasi-divine powers and knowledge of previous births.

NUNS AND SOCIETY. To some extent, monastic tasks are gender-based and tend to reproduce the distribution of domestic tasks in the secular world (e.g., sewing, mending of robes and other objects). Still, the fact that "religion serves as both a creative and conservative force in women's lives" (Vallely, 2002, pp. 21, 215.) accounts for the appeal that monastic life does have for young Jain women. In addition, "the value of chastity is one way concepts about women and renunciation combined in a manner favorable to female renunciation in Jainism. This connection between Jain wives and renouncers is strong enough, when combined with various other factors, to encourage more women than men to renounce in the Jain tradition" (Fohr, 2001, p. 1). The assymetries between nuns and monks in the communatarian hierarchy and the domestic roles assigned to nuns are not enough to alter this tendency.

In the modern context, the educational level of Jain nuns is a prominent issue. Theoretically, there is no avowed distinction between nuns and monks as regards access to sacred scriptures. Jainism (as well as Buddhism) basically admits access for all and differs, in this respect, from the orthodox Hindu tradition, in which women were traditionally refused access to the Vedas. However, in practice, all the orders within Jainism do not have the same position. Although some of them (e.g., Terāpanthins and Sthānakvāsins) claim that monks and nuns can study all texts, others (e.g., part of the Mūrtipūjaks) state that the nuns' abilities are less and prevent them from being in a position to study certain difficult or controversial canonical texts, especially those connected with the monastic code.

The efforts of some prominent nuns, who try to make use of their prestige and influence to promote women's education, must however be underlined. They profess that before getting religious initiation, the young girls must undergo a probational period during which they will be given at least basic knowledge not only in Jainism but also in grammar or literature. Promoting women's education is moreover an important point of the Terāpanthin subsect. It is being implemented through a special category of nuns who are officially free from certain rules restricting their movements and can visit distant institutions in India or abroad to pursue academic research. Although nuns are allowed to hold public sermons, not many of them do so. More often, they are seen surrounding the preaching monk and carefully listening to him: "*Sadhvis* are regarded first and foremost as 'devotees.' . . . The *sadhvi* is still evaluated according to the *pativrata* virtues of devotion, surrender, and self-sacrifice. These traditional virtues prescribed for women are not substituted for but rather supplemented with values more accordant with those of the ascetic ideal" (Vallely, 2002, pp. 215, 218).

Study of history also shows that in the past scriptural sources are essentially authored by or ascribed to male renouncers or are male-oriented. The few female religious figures whose names have come to us are sources of inspiration for men (e.g., Yākinī-mahattarā for Haribhadra, c. eighth century). In recent times, a few highly charismatic nuns have been able to express themselves through their autobiographies (e.g., Āryikā Jñānamati, 1990) or through the redaction of religious pamphlets, but no really breaking-through dogmatical treatise is known to have been composed by any woman of the tradition. A further dissymmetry appears in the field of worship. Worship of female deities or deified concepts is one thing; worship of human female teachers another one. Whereas images of male renouncers of some importance are common, at least in some groups, this is still an exceptional fact in the case of nuns.

ROLES FOR LAYWOMEN. As for Jain laywomen, their roles are mostly oriented toward the two areas in which the otherwise prevalent gender hierarchy is at least partly reversed: preparation of food and performance of rituals, for which the men are completely dependent on them. In a tradition such as Jainism, food is far from being a minor question. The observation of specific dietary rules is one of the clearest means to ensure sectarian identity. Thus the woman at home functions as a guardian or a modifier of the tradition through the various roles ascribed to her. She is the one who offers alms to the begging Jain mendicants who come at her door, which implies that she masters a minute sequence of actions and rules. She is also the one who prepares the meals for the family and decides whether a rule like the one that forbids eating after sunset will be observed or not, and she knows which type of food has to be cooked depending on the day (i.e., festival, ordinary). Finally, the woman is also the one who has a full command on the complicated calendar and typology of fasts that regulate the Jains' lives. Fasting is actually the true women's penance and a way for them to gain a high reputation of religiosity.

Reproduction of the community is in their hands through the handling of marriages and the imparting of basic teachings to young generations. This latter task is mainly done through the telling of Jain legends and stories, the old stock of which is continuously kept alive thanks to new versions, which the women mainly come to know in translations or rephrasing in modern languages, or by interaction with the religious order (e.g., sermons or personal conversations). Religious hymns form another category of literature in which women are quite proficient.

Creating such hymns, chanting, and reciting are manifestations of feminine religiosity at work in domestic as well as in temple rituals. Again, the risk of oversimplifying the situation is to be avoided: Differences exist among subsects as to whether women are to be allotted the same rights as men in worshiping the images. Fundamentalists hold that they should never be allowed to enter the innermost sanctuary and to touch the idols because they can never reach the indispensable degree of purity to do so, whereas others restrict direct contact to certain circumstances or temporary impurity only. The groups among the Jains who do not worship images, however, lay more stress on internal worship. Hence, their conceptions are more egalitarian. Recent studies have underlined that women have the real authority as far as conduct and performance of ritual itself are concerned, an area of religiosity in which they assess their power against the male sponsors.

Thus gender issues are indeed prominent both in Jain history and its contemporary realization. The construction of gender appears as a complicated process. In mythology and soteriology there is a clear and apparently irreconcilable divergence between the two main sects, although the woman-favoring tendency of Śvetāmbara Jainism should not be emphasized too much. Moreover, there is a true conception of gender that goes beyond physiological characteristics. At an institutional level, Jainism is basically man-centered, but there are signs to show that the numerical pressure of female renouncers may lead to an interesting evolution. Jain laywomen also have a key role both as reproducers of traditional values and as dynamic factors in Indian society in general.

SEE ALSO Asceticism; Jainism; Mahāvīra; Nuns, overview article; Sādhus and Sādhvīs; Sarasvatī; Soteriology.

BIBLIOGRAPHY

Please see the following works on Jainism in English: Walther Schubring, *The Doctrine of the Jains,* translated from the German, 2d ed., rev. (Delhi, 2000) and Helmuth von Glasenapp, *Jainism: An Indian Religion of Salvation,* translated from the German (Delhi, 1999), have a traditional approach which may not appeal to some but are extremely useful and should not be forgotten. Padmanabh S. Jaini's *The Jaina Path of Purification* (Delhi, 1979), with emphasis on the Digambara point of view, and Paul Dundas's *The Jains,* 2d ed. (London, 2002), with a vast bibliography, are indispensable.

An overview of various issues connected with the question of women in the frame of Jainism in history and in the contemporary world can be found in Nalini Balbir's "Women in Jainism," in *Women in Indian Religions,* edited by Arvind Sharma. (New Delhi, 2002) pp. 70–107; see also "Women in Jainism," in *Religion and Women,* edited by Arvind Sharma (New York, 1994), pp. 121–138. Padmanabh S. Jaini's *Gender and Salvation: Jaina Debates on the Spiritual Liberation of Women* (Berkeley, Calif., 1991) is a pioneering work. It is an in-depth study accompanied by translations and detailed discussions. The issue of gender and mythology is discussed in John E. Cort's article "Medieval Jain Goddess Traditions," *Numen* 34, no. 2 (December 1987): 235–255. As for the biography of the nineteenth Jina, Mallī, who, according to the Śvetāmbaras, was a female, see *Mallī-Jñāta. Das achte Kapitel des Nāyādhammakahāo im sechsten Aṅga des Śvetāmbara Jainakanons,* edited and translated into German by Gustav Roth (Wiesbaden, Germany, 1983) or Hemacandra's version in his *Triṣaṣṭiśalākāpuruṣacarita,* English translation by Helen W. Johnson, vol. 4 (Baroda, India, 1954). For monastic regulations as they are defined by the Śvetāmbara canon, see *Kalpasūtra,* English translation of Schubring's German translation by May S. Burgess, *The Indian Antiquary* 39 (1910): 257–267.

First-hand accounts by Jain nuns themselves are not numerous. Hence Āryikā Jñānamati's autobiography written in Hindi under the title *Merī smṛtiyāṃ* (My memories) (Hastinapur, India, 1990) deserves a mention as containing information about monastic daily life, commitments, and politics. Occasionally nuns' achievements or biographies come to the fore. For example, see the Felicitation Volume *Sādhvīratna Puṣpavatījī Abhinandan Granth,* edited by Dineś Muni (Udaipur, India, 1987) in honor of a Sthānakvāsī nun, and other such publications (in Hindi or Gujarati) locally available in India.

Four monographs, written by Western women, are valuable sources of information about encounters with Jain women: N. Shanta's *The Unknown Pilgrims. The Voices of the Sadhvis. The History, Spirituality, and Life of the Jaina Women Ascetics,* translated from the French [*La voie jaina*] by Mary Rogers (Delhi, 1997) is based on classical sources and on modern information; Anne Vallely's *Guardians of the Transcendent. An Ethnography of a Jain Ascetic Community* (Toronto, 2002) is based on fieldwork done in Ladnun (Rajasthan). M. Whitney Kelting's *Singing to the Jinas: Jain Laywomen Mandal Singing and the Negotiations of Jain Devotion* (Oxford, 2001) is a refreshing analysis of female roles as assumed by those who are not ascetics. Their lively presence is felt throughout the book through their songs of devotion. Sherry Elizabeth Fohr's "Gender and Chastity: Female Jain Renouncers" (Ph.D. diss., University of Virginia, 2001) shows, on the basis of extensive conversations with nuns, how the fundamental value of chastity is instrumental in renunciation and how Jainism provides an appropriate frame for its successful achievement. Josephine Reynell's articles—especially "Women and the Reproduction of the Jain Community," in *The Assembly of Listeners,* edited by Michael Carrithers and Caroline Humphrey (Oxford, 1991), pp. 41–65—are attempts at defining women's role in contradistinction to their male counterparts, whereas Marie-Claude Mahias's *Délivrance et convivialité. Le système culinaire des Jaina* (Paris, 1985), whose investigation is based on field-work conducted in Delhi, looks at the role of Jain women in connection with rules relating to food habits, which are so crucial for the definition of a Jain identity. Other valuable insights are found in Josephine Reynell, "Honour, Nurture, and Festivity: Aspects of Female Religiosity amongst Jain Women in Jaipur" (Ph.D. dissertation, University of Cambridge, 1985).

Scattered but valuable observations on the role of women are found in several ethnographic studies such as Lawrence A. Babb's *Absent Lord: Ascetics and Kings in a Jain Ritual Culture* (Berkeley, Calif., 1996), Ravindra K. Jain's *The Universe as Audience: Metaphor and Community among the Jains of North India* (Shimla, India, 1999), and James Laidlaw's *Riches and Renunciation: Religion, Economy, and Society among the Jains* (Oxford, 1995).

NALINI BALBIR (2005)

GENDER AND RELIGION: GENDER AND BUDDHISM

Early in the history of Western scholarship about Buddhism, several well-known women scholars wrote significant studies about the role of women in early Buddhism. C. A. F. Rhys Davids's translation of the *Therīgāthā* (The songs of the female elders) was published in 1909, and in 1930 I. B. Horner published the very significant book, *Women under Primitive Buddhism*. However, by the mid-twentieth century, these works had been largely forgotten and scholars almost never discussed how gender affects Buddhists' lives or the practice of their religion. Scholarship had become almost androcentric, giving us knowledge only about what men thought and did, proceeding as if women were not part of the religious community. Furthermore, these studies rarely discussed cultural and religious attitudes toward women, or the presence of female divine beings. Such omissions were typical of scholarship in general, not only Buddhist studies or religious studies.

When the second wave of feminism began in the mid-1960s, people did not immediately regard scholarship about religion as a feminist issue, but by the late 1970s a small group of scholars, mainly women, were keenly aware of the inadequacies of androcentric scholarship and its failure to provide a complete or accurate picture of whatever religion was being studied. In addition, many people were discussing the perceived injustices of male-dominated religions, including Buddhism. After a hiatus of almost fifty years during which no significant studies of gender and Buddhism had appeared, in 1979 Diana Y. Paul published her translation and commentary, *Women in Buddhism: Images of the Feminine in Mahāyāna Tradition*. In the following decade, interest in the topic of gender and Buddhism increased greatly, in keeping with scholarship in general and the culture at large. Many significant and provocative articles appeared, and in 1988 Sandy Boucher published *Turning the Wheel: American Women Creating the New Buddhism*, a semipopular account of American women Buddhist reformers of the tradition. By then concerns about gender and Buddhism had become an issue not only for scholars of Buddhism but also for Buddhist practitioners, who were, if anything, more aware of and more concerned about the issues than were the scholars. The first comprehensive book-length account of gender and Buddhism written by a scholar-practitioner appeared in 1993 when Rita Gross published *Buddhism after Patriarchy: A Feminist History, Analysis, and Reconstruction of Buddhism*. In the following ten years, a significant number of books, some scholarly, some more oriented to Buddhist practitioners, appeared. During that same period, scholars began to pay more attention to gender in their research and in general surveys of Buddhism and introductory textbooks.

AN OVERVIEW OF BUDDHISM AND GENDER. There is a certain ambiguity in the study of gender in general, not just in Buddhist studies. Do scholars genuinely mean *gender*, or do they, in effect, say *gender* but mean *women*? Writings on Buddhism and gender will always discuss women's roles and images of women, but they may have little to say about how the gender discriminations found in all religions affect men. And unless the term *gender* is in the title of a book or chapter, it usually does not contain much information about how gender practices affect either women or men.

In Buddhism's 2,500-year-long history, several generalizations about gender stand out. First, it could be argued that the most significant distinction within the Buddhist community is not between women and men, but between monastics and laypeople. In ancient India at the time of the Buddha, it was commonly believed that the householder lifestyle was simply too distracting and busy, filled with children and work, for a person to be able to make any significant progress toward deep understanding of reality and the consequent peace brought by such knowledge. The Buddha himself renounced his wealth, family, and social position for a life of religious seeking, and he ordained many followers as monks and nuns throughout his life. The prestige of the monastic lifestyle has never diminished in Buddhism, with the possible exceptions of Japanese Buddhism and newly converted Western Buddhists. Given the centrality of monasticism in Buddhist life, the presence or absence of a nuns' order is a significant gender issue in Buddhism. Though many Buddhist sources report the Buddha's initial hesitation to initiate a nuns' order, it did begin and has persisted, with many ups and downs, in most parts of the Buddhist world. Restoring the nuns' ordination in those parts of the Buddhist world where it has been lost, or to which it never was transmitted, is an important contemporary issue in Buddhism.

A second generalization is that there have been two radically different opinions about gender, and especially about the status of female rebirth in the Buddhist world, in all periods of Buddhist history, and in all forms of Buddhism. One opinion states that gender does not matter, that gender is irrelevant because both women and men can uncover the true nature of enlightened mind and that enlightened mind is not one iota different in women than it is in men. The other opinion states that gender does matter a great deal and that it is much more fortunate to be reborn as a man because of the social privileges that go with male rebirth. Monks always had more prestige than nuns and were better supported. The major institutions of Buddhism, including the nuns' order, have always been male dominated, though that is changing in contemporary times, especially among Western converts to Buddhism. Modern reformers have pointed out that these two well-entrenched traditional attitudes about gender are incompatible, for if gender is irrelevant, there can be little basis for awarding men social privilege and domination of Buddhist institutions.

Early Indian Buddhism and Developments in South Asia. Regarding gender, the most significant debate about early Buddhism, the Buddhism of the Buddha's day and the next three to five hundred years, is whether or not its basic view is misogynistic, that is, hating and fearing females and everything female. Male monasticism tends to produce literature, directed to monks, about the dangers of contact with women, and these are plentiful in the literature of this period. Some commentators interpret these passages as evidence that early Buddhism had strongly negative views of women. Others, however, argue that these remarks directed to monks are not the whole story, and that these passages about the dangers of contact with women are more about the weakness of men's discipline than about the inherent faults of women. The latter argument is bolstered by the existence of flourishing and highly accomplished nuns in early Buddhism, and by the high regard in which laywomen donors were held. Certainly nuns were not equal to monks in the modern sense of the term, but they nevertheless had a degree of freedom and independence that was rare in the ancient world. Their lifestyle is well represented in the *Therīgāthā.*

Almost every account of early Buddhism also tells the story of the Buddha's reluctance to allow women to ordain as nuns at all, along with that story's depressing coda about the eight special rules that subordinate all nuns to all monks, even the newest novice. Most also include the prediction that the Buddhist religion would only endure half as long as it otherwise would have because women had been admitted to the order. But scholars who have done textual analysis on these passages have expressed doubts about the origin of these stories and comments. Some suggest that they more likely came from a later period, some hundreds of years after the life of the Buddha when Buddhism was splitting apart into several mutually incompatible denominations, not from the Buddha himself or his times.

Buddhism first spread to Sri Lanka as a result of missionary efforts on the part of Emperor Aśoka of India in the third century BCE. It is said that Aśoka's daughter herself initiated the nuns' order there, and it was Sri Lankan nuns who went to China in the fifth century CE to initiate the nuns' order there. These Chinese nuns' ordination lineages are the source of most lineages for nuns' ordination in the contemporary world. However, after the eleventh century CE, Sri Lankan Buddhism saw the demise of the nun's order. The consensus of scholarship is that nuns' ordination never reached other Southeast Asian countries.

In the contemporary Theravāda world, reviving nuns' ordination is a hotly contested issue, though those in favor of reviving it may be slowly winning the battle. Conservatives argue that the Buddha did not want to ordain nuns in the first place and that the nuns' order can be revived only by the next Buddha—who is not expected to appear anytime soon. But women from Theravāda countries receive ordination from Chinese and Korean lineages and return to their Southeast Asian homes as fully ordained nuns. Though the nuns often face severe censure, especially in Thailand, gradually nunneries are being reestablished anyway. The first nuns' ordination to occur in a Theravāda country in over a thousand years took place in Sri Lanka in 1998.

Mahāyāna Buddhism. The origins of Mahāyāna Buddhism are still debated, but all would agree that it was present by five hundred years after the time of the Buddha, about the beginning of the common era. It is also often claimed that Mahāyāna Buddhism was more inclusive of laypeople and women than other forms of Buddhism found in India at that time, but there is little evidence for this claim in Buddhist institutional practices of the period and no historical women stand out in accounts of Mahāyāna Buddhist history. However, Mahāyāna literature sometimes also presents a very different picture of possible or ideal roles for laypeople, and especially for women. They are sometimes the heroes of Mahāyāna texts, and they are then portrayed as far more knowledgeable than their male opponents, who are representatives of the more established schools of Buddhism. Furthermore, texts that portray women as knowledgeable heroes are not minor, unimportant texts, but are among the most popular and influential texts. Such texts are also quite numerous.

Portrayals of accomplished women and girls range from those in which the woman changes her female body into a male body as a sign of her superior understanding, to portrayals in which she teaches unchallenged by anyone for taking on what is usually understood as a male role. The most famous episode in which a female transforms herself into a male occurs in the *Lotus Sūtra*, an Indian text that became especially important in East Asian Buddhism. The heroine is the eight-year-old daughter of the Nāga king, an improbable candidate for high spiritual attainment not only because of her gender but because of her age. Mañjuśrī, an important *bodhisattva* in the Mahāyāna pantheon vouches for her, and she proclaims that she will teach the *dharma* (Buddhist teachings), but Śariputra, one of the most important elders and disciples of the Buddha in the literature of older forms of Buddhism, objects that a female could not possibly be able to teach. After some debate with Śariputra, as the text delicately puts it, her "female organ disappeared and the male organ became visible."

This passage has been interpreted and commented upon many times. More conservative commentators have claimed that this passage indicates that women cannot become enlightened, but must first change into men, a rather common Asian Buddhist claim. If even the Nāga princess must change into a man, they would argue, surely all other women must become men before they can become enlightened. For most women, of course, this sex change will not happen until a future life, but the fact that "deserving women" will be reborn as men is claimed by some as proof that traditional Buddhism does not practice sex discrimination. However, more recent feminist commentators on this text have claimed that the problem pointed to by this text is not the Nāga princess's femaleness, but the obtuseness of Shariputra and the other male naysayers. Only something as abrupt and unlikely as an instantaneous sex change can convince these ideologically fixated, conservative men, who simply cannot hear true *dharma* when it comes out of a woman's mouth. The fact that the Nāga princess has the ability to magically change her sex as a last resort to demonstrate her skill to these men only enhances her claim to superior understanding. While Buddhist stories frequently include the motif of magical powers resulting from high meditative attainments, only the most advanced practitioners can accomplish such feats.

Another famous passage occurs in the *Vimalakīrti Nirdeśa Sūtra.* Śaripūtra is again debating with a highly accomplished woman, a so-called goddess who has been studying for twelve years in Vimalakīrti's palace. Śaripūtra is impressed with her knowledge and comments that someone who knows as much as she does should be a man. He then challenges her to change herself into a man. She replies that she had been looking for the innate characteristics of the female sex for twelve years, without success, so there was nothing that could be changed. When Śaripūtra persists with his objections, she suddenly changes him into a woman and herself into a man. The goddess, now a man, asks the female Śaripūtra if she (he) can find the essential nature of his newly female sex. A confused Śaripūtra replies that he cannot even figure out how he became a woman. Then the goddess changes Śaripūtra back into a man and herself back into a woman and asks Śaripūtra about the "female form and innate characteristics." A much chastened and wiser Śaripūtra replies, "The female form and innate characteristics neither exist nor do not exist," an answer much more in accord with Mahāyāna teachings on emptiness.

A final motif found in Mahāyāna texts portrays women teaching the *dharma*, but male challenges are defeated purely with logic, without recourse to sex changes. The logic is that, because emptiness of any essence is the only trait common to all things, no specific traits, such as maleness or femaleness, have true existence. They are only appearances. A woman named Jewel Brocade is challenged by a male elder who claims that supreme perfect enlightenment, which is very difficult to attain, cannot be attained in a woman's body. She replies that if enlightenment cannot be attained in a female body, then it cannot be attained in a male body either. Why? Because the thought of enlightenment is neither male nor female, and that which perceives through emptiness is neither male nor female. The text in which this story is embedded then concludes that "the *dharma* is neither male nor female."

It is difficult to assess the impact of these passages and ideas upon the actual lives of Buddhist women until we have more historical data and research. Although we know that monastic ordination lineages disappeared in many parts of the Buddhist world, it survived in China, one of the most important early sites for the development of Mahāyāna scriptures and ideology. Although androcentrism and misogyny continued to mark much of the Mahāyāna monastic world, exceptional women were, on occasion, able to found flourishing nunneries and to have influence in both religion and politics. Several collections recording the lives of nuns in East Asia survive, and recent work on nunneries in Japan has produced intriguing evidence of the multiplicity of contexts in which Buddhist women could thrive.

TANTRIC BUDDHISM IN TIBET. A late development in Buddhism, often called "Tantric Buddhism" or Vajrayāna, is of special interest to the question of the place of women, since it advocated sexual practice as a means to advance spiritually. Tantric Buddhism in India has only begun to be studied as a historical phenomenon, and there are many difficult interpretive questions for that study, given the often shockingly antinomian practices that the Buddhist tantric scriptures sometimes recommend. Scholarly knowledge is on somewhat firmer ground in its study of Tibetan Buddhism, and it is useful to consider that case in this context, since Vajrayāna Buddhist literature and practices had exceptional durability in Tibet throughout its Buddhist period.

Buddhism came first to Tibet from north India in the seventh century CE. A second dissemination gained momentum in the eleventh century. Women figure to some extent in both disseminations, and the Vajrayāna Buddhism that dominates Tibet often portrays female figures in art. There are also several important women in Tibetan Buddhist historical accounts.

Though there were many novice nuns in Tibet, most scholars think that full ordination for nuns never reached Tibet. In Tibetan Buddhism, however, a third, less well-known option of being a forest recluse, who has not taken monastic vows but who has taken on much more serious spiritual obligations than the average layperson, has always been prestigious and popular. Many women opted for this alternative, which gave them more freedom and prestige than they had in male-dominated monastic universities. (There were no equivalent educational institutions for women, and novice nuns were often trained only in chanting and other minor disciplines.) These people often lived alone in caves or retreat huts or with a small group of companions, both male and female, and women were much more likely to receive serious training in meditation as forest recluses than in the monastic universities. However, it would be inaccurate to claim that women and men were equal in the modern sense of the term.

A famous female figure in Tibetan Buddhism was Ye shes mtsho rgyal (Yeshe Tsogyel), who is thought to have lived in the seventh century CE. She became the partner and colleague of the Indian Padmasambhava, often considered to be the founder of Tibetan Buddhism, though he was not the first Indian to propagate Buddhism in Tibet. Though modern scholars are not convinced that Ye shes mtsho rgyal actually existed, she is given a prominent place in many Tibetan historical narratives, and liturgies that invoke Padmasambhava usually also invoke her. She is regarded as fully enlightened, no less realized than any of the great male teachers revered by Tibetan Buddhists. Another woman, Ma gcig lab sgron (Machig Labdron, c. 1055–1149), was important during the second transmission of Buddhism to Tibet. Her story is complex, but she is often credited with initiating *gcod (chöd)* practice, an important Vajrayāna practice designed to destroy clinging to one's selfhood, which is key to attaining enlightenment according to Buddhist teachings. It is also claimed that this is the only practice that went from Tibet to India, reversing the usual pattern.

The most controversial aspect of Vajrayāna Buddhism is its widespread use of sexual symbolism and its purported use of sexuality itself as a religious ritual. There is no doubt that sexuality is one of the central symbols of Vajrayāna Buddhism, which means that feminine symbolism is much more prominent in Vajrayāna Buddhism than in any other form of Buddhism. The basic meaning of this symbolism is nonduality or inseparability, one of the central teachings of Mahāyāna and Vajrayāna Buddhism. Within that dyadic unity, the female often symbolizes wisdom and the male often symbolizes compassion; their union symbolizes the inseparability and equality of wisdom and compassion. Likewise, the female symbolizes emptiness and the male symbolizes form. Their union symbolizes the inseparability of form and emptiness, or relative and absolute truth.

As for sexuality itself, both Ye shes mtsho rgyal and Ma gcig lab sgron are said to have had several sexual partners, and the stories of many great Tibetan teachers include accounts of their consorts. Their sexual experiences are considered part of the meditation practice rather than a purely secular or mundane activity. Evaluating the status of the female partners has been controversial. Many modern scholars think that the women were usually mere ritual implements used by male practitioners to enhance their meditative attainments, although some have argued that the women truly were partners and equals of the men. Despite great curiosity about these practices, they are closely guarded by Tibetans.

BUDDHIST FEMALE FIGURES. Several important females figure in the stories from the earliest period of Buddhism—the Buddha's mother, his wife, the woman who encouraged him to eat after severe fasting, the daughters of Māra who tempted him, the earth goddess who witnessed his generosity, Prajāpatī, the first nun, and other female disciples. Mahāyāna Buddhism developed a pantheon of deified figures, and in Vajrayāna Buddhism there are countless meditation deities whose status is often equal to that of a buddha. Many of these are female. In Mahāyāna Buddhism, there are also mythic *bodhisattvas* on the way to full enlightenment or enlightened buddhas of other eras and world systems. The mythic *bodhisattvas* are far more advanced than any human beings, but they are still on the path. Often they are models of key Buddhist virtues, such as wisdom and compassion. These too are sometimes female.

It is noteworthy that as soon as Buddhists began to imagine and pray to such Buddhist mythical figures, they began to invoke female as well as male figures. One of the first major female enlightened figures to develop was Prajñāpāramitā, the personification of wisdom and emptiness. She is cast as the "mother of all the buddhas," because to become enlightened, a buddha had to realize the wisdom she represented. Another important female *bodhisattva* is Tārā, a personification of compassion and one of the most popular figures in Tibetan Buddhism. She is frequently invoked by ordinary people. She is extremely compassionate and effective; she can save one from any kind of danger or provide any kind of benefit and is often called upon to do so.

In Vajrayāna Buddhism, mythic females are at least as numerous as male mythic figures, and they participate in all the same activities as their male counterparts. The importance of sexual symbolism, if nothing else, would translate into the presence of many mythic females. However, females also function independently as meditation deities and as *dharma* protectors, the two main functions of "deities" in Vajrayāna Buddhism. While they are often portrayed as beautiful and gentle, they are just as likely to be portrayed as wrathful and ugly, by conventional standards. If equality between male and female mythic figures is sought, Vajrayāna Buddhist iconography is perhaps one of the places where it is found.

It is important, however, to remember that high regard for mythic females does not necessarily translate into high status, freedom, or equality for human women. One of the most common mistakes in discussing gender and religion is to answer questions about gender with information about female deities and other mythic females. While such information is an important part of the topic of gender and religion, it is often used to gloss over and ignore inequality between women and men and the suppression of human females. This mistake is especially common in discussions of Vajrayāna Buddhism, probably because its intense regard for mythic females is so unusual.

MODERN BUDDHISM IN ASIA AND THE WEST. Two reform movements are especially significant in modern Buddhism—the increasing importance of lay meditation and the engaged Buddhist movement. Both are important in all forms of Buddhism, but Western Buddhism is almost entirely a lay movement, something very unusual in the history of Buddhism, and the engaged Buddhist movement is more prominent in Asia, though there are many Western counterparts.

Regarding attention to gender, the engaged Buddhist movement is somewhat disappointing, as it rarely engages in gender analysis or critiques male-dominant gender arrangements, whether within the Buddhist world or outside it. Every other major current social issue is discussed, and activists try to reform many economic and social injustices. But, like many reform movements throughout history, male dominance is exempted from such criticism. This is the case with both Asian and Western versions of the engaged Buddhist movement.

The lay meditation movement does not explicitly focus on gender either, but many laywomen do participate in meditation intensives, which would have been unusual in earlier forms of Buddhism. It would be expected that Western Buddhism, still in its infancy, would largely be a lay movement; the economic basis to support monastics and monasteries, so well developed in Asia, is completely lacking in the West. Extensive participation in meditation practices by laypeople in modern Asian Buddhism is also on the rise. Until recently, it was thought that laypeople did not have the time or the discipline to engage in meditation, but many Asian teachers are now willing to instruct laypeople, both women and men. In addition, there is a worldwide Buddhist women's movement. Several newsletters are devoted to this topic and one of the organizations, Sakyadhita, holds international conferences every two years. Central issues have included reinstating the nuns' order in countries where it has been lost and improving the education of nuns in other countries. Credit for the reintroduction of the nuns' order in Sri Lanka and support for nuns in other Theravāda countries goes to this movement. The education of Tibetan nuns has also been vastly improved, and nuns have begun to engage in practices that were never done by earlier nuns, such as debating and drawing sand *maṇḍalas.* Chinese and Korean nuns' orders are stronger than ever, and nuns usually outnumber monks.

The beginnings of large-scale conversion to Buddhism by Westerners coincided with the second wave of feminism, and many early converts also had feminist consciousness. Explicitly feminist loyalties were controversial for many Buddhists, but the way Western Buddhism has taken shape owes a great deal to feminism nevertheless. From the beginning of the movement in the 1970s, women participated in all aspects of Buddhist life and practice in equal numbers with men. This was a new experience for Asian male Buddhists who were teaching in the West, but they did nothing to discourage their women students and gradually began to empower them to teach, just as they empowered male students. As a result, by the mid-1990s almost half the Western *dharma* teachers were women, something totally unprecedented in the history of Buddhism.

SEE ALSO Ani Lochen; Buddhism, overview article; Feminism, article on Feminism, Gender Studies, and Religion; Magcig Lab sgron (Machig Labdron); Nuns, article on Buddhist Nuns; Tārā; Ye shes Mtsho rgyal (Yeshe Tsogyal).

BIBLIOGRAPHY

Allione, Tsultrim, trans. and ed. *Women of Wisdom.* London, 1984.

Bartholomeusz, Tessa. *Women under the Bo Tree: Buddhist Nuns in Sri Lanka.* Cambridge, U.K., 1994.

Blackstone, Kathryn R. *Women in the Footsteps of the Buddha: Struggle for Liberation in the Therīgāthā.* Surrey, U.K., 1998.

Boucher, Sandy. *Turning the Wheel: American Women Creating the New Buddhism.* Rev. ed. Boston, 1993. An interesting account of emerging women leaders of American convert women.

Cabezón, José Ignacio, ed. *Buddhism, Sexuality, and Gender.* Albany, N.Y., 1992. A useful collection of scholarly articles.

Dowman, Keith, trans. *Sky Dancer: The Secret Life and Songs of the Lady Yeshe Tsogyel.* London, 1984. A fascinating account of the life of Tibet's most famous woman practitioner and leader.

Dresser, Marianne, ed. *Buddhist Women on the Edge: Contemporary Perspectives from Western Frontier.* Berkeley, Calif., 1996.

Falk, Nancy Auer. "The Case of the Vanishing Nuns: The Fruits of Ambivalence in Ancient Indian Buddhism." In *Unspoken Worlds: Women's Religious Lives,* edited by Nancy Auer Falk and Rita M. Gross, pp. 196–206. Belmont, Calif., 2001. This is a classic article analyzing why the nuns' order declined and died out in India.

Faure, Bernard. *The Power of Denial: Buddhism, Purity, and Gender.* Princeton, 2003.

Friedman, Lenore, and Susan Moons, eds. *Being Bodies: Buddhist Women on the Paradox of Embodiment.* Boston and London, 1997.

Gross, Rita M. *Buddhism after Patriarchy: A Feminist History, Analysis, and Reconstruction of Buddhism.* Albany, N.Y., 1993. A comprehensive and challenging account of Buddhism and gender.

Gross, Rita M. *Soaring and Settling: Buddhist Perspectives on Contemporary Social and Religious Issues.* New York, 2000.

Gross Rita M., and Rosemary Radford Ruether. *Religious Feminism and the Future of the Planet: A Buddhist-Christian Conversation.* New York, 2001. Very useful for comparing feminist issues in Buddhism and Christianity.

Havnevik, Hanna. *Tibetan Buddhist Nuns: History, Cultural Norms, and Social Reality.* Oslo, 1989.

Horner, I. B. *Women under Primitive Buddhism: Laywomen and Alsmwomen.* London, 1930; reprints, Dehli, 1975 and 1990. A classic to be studied by all who wish to understand women's roles in early Indian Buddhism.

Kabilsingh, Chatsumarn. *Women in Thai Buddhism.* Berkeley, Calif., 1991.

Klein, Carolyn Anne. *Meeting the Great Bliss Queen: Buddhists, Feminists, and the Art of the Self.* Boston, 1995. An interesting book comparing postmodern feminism and some schools of Tibetan Buddhism.

Pao-Chang. *Lives of the Nuns: Biographies of Chinese Buddhist Nuns from the Fourth to Sixth Centuries.* Translated by Kathryn Ann Tsai. Honolulu, 1994.

Paul, Diana Y., trans. and ed. *Women in Buddhism: Images of the Feminine in Mahāyāna Tradition.* Berkeley, Calif., 1979. This collection of texts is a modern classic that is still very useful.

Rhys-Davids, C. A. F., and R. K. Norman, trans. *Poems of Early Buddhist Nuns (Therīgāthā).* Oxford, 1989. This joint publication of the two major scholarly translations of the *Songs of the Female Elders* is very useful.

Robinson, Paula Kane. *Women Living Zen: Japanese Soto Buddhist Nuns.* New York, 1999.

Sakyadhita: The International Association of Buddhist Women. *Sakyadhita Newsletter.* Available from http://www.sakyadhita.org/NewsLetters/newsindx.htm.

Schaeffer, Kurtis R. *Himalayan Hermitess: The Life of a Tibetan Buddhist Nun.* Oxford, 2004.

Shaw, Miranda. *Passionate Enlightenment: Women in Tantric Buddhism.* Princeton, 1994. A controversial book that argues that women played a far more central role in the development of Tantric Buddhism than earlier scholars had recognized.

Simmer-Brown, Judith. *Dakini's Warm Breath: The Feminine Principle in Tibetan Buddhism.* Boston, 2001. The most complete account of gender symbolism in Tibetan Buddhism.

Tsomo, Karma Lekshe, ed. *Sakyadhita: Daughters of the Buddha.* Ithaca, N.Y., 1988. A useful account of the status of nuns in most parts of the Buddhist world.

Tsomo, Karma Lekshe, ed. *Innovative Buddhist Women: Swimming against the Stream.* Richmond, U.K., 2000. Contains informative case studies of Buddhist women, especially nuns, in different parts of the world, including their social engagement with ethical issues.

Willis, Janice Dean, ed. *Feminine Ground: Essays on Women and Tibet.* Ithaca, N.Y., 1989.

Wilson, Liz. *Charming Cadavers: Horrific Figurations of the Feminine in Indian Buddhist Hagiographic Literature.* Chicago, 1996. An interesting scholarly discussion of monastic literature designed to impress upon monks that they should avoid women.

Rita M. Gross (2005)

GENDER AND RELIGION: GENDER AND SIKHISM

Although Sikh scripture offers valuable insights on gender, Sikh scholarship has not paid enough attention to this topic. The Sikh religion originated and developed within a "doubly" patriarchal milieu. Between the birth of the founder (Gurū Nānak in 1469) and the death of the tenth gurū (Gurū Gobind Singh in 1708), the Hindu society of North India succumbed to Muslim rulers from outside—Turks, Afghans, and Mughals. In the old Hindu caste society women were completely subjugated to their husbands, and under the new Muslim regime women had to stay in purdah. As a result all women, both Hindu and Muslim, ended up suffering from both forms of subjugation. Witnessing the multiple oppression of Indian women, the Sikh gurūs empathized with them and emphasized gender equality in sublime verse. They tried to open up a window of opportunity for women. But the ideals of the Sikh gurūs have been distorted because their lives and their words were recorded, interpreted, and taught primarily by male elites. And so gender becomes a complicated and convoluted issue for Sikhism.

Historical Context. Gurū Nānak's close association with his mother (Tripta), sister (Nānaki, after whom he was named), and wife (Sulakhni) was crucial in shaping his social and religious consciousness, which was then carried on by his nine successor gurūs. Though Sikh scholarship scarcely mentions these female figures, the simple *janamsākhī* narratives highlight the subtle awareness these women possessed. Mata Tripta is a noble woman who understands her son and can see into his unique personality—much more so than his father Kalu. Even the midwife Daultan is struck by the extraordinary qualities of the child she delivers. And like Mary Magdalene, who was the first woman to have witnessed the resurrection of Christ, Nānak's sister Nānaki is the first person to recognize Nānak's enlightenment. Sulakhni's role, however, is ambiguous, as if the *janamsākhī* authors did not quite know how to deal with Nānak's "wife."

Women became equal partners in the first Sikh community established by Gurū Nānak in Kartarpur. Both men and women participated in formulating the fundamental Sikh institutions of *sevā* (voluntary labor), *langar* (community meal), and *sangat* (congregation). Sikh men and women listened and recited sacred hymns. Together they cooked and ate *langar.* Together they formed a democratic congregation without priests or ordained ministers.

The pattern of inclusivity set up by Gurū Nānak in Kartarpur continued on, and women were not excluded by any of the Sikh gurūs from any aspect of religious life. In fact their vital participation in varied dimensions is deeply etched in popular memory. For example, Mata Khivi, wife of Gurū Angad (Nānak II), is fondly remembered for her liberal direction of *langar.* With Mata Khivi's generous supervision and her plentiful supply of *kheer* (rice pudding), *langar* became a real feast rather than just a symbolic meal. Gurū Amar Das (Nānak III) even assigned leadership roles to women. In order to consolidate the growing Sikh faith, he created a well-knit organization and set up twenty-two *manjis* (groups) covering different parts of India. Along with men, women served as supervisors of these communities.

Bibi Amaro, the daughter of Gurū Angad and Mata Khivi, became a liaison between the second and the third gurūs. A popular narrative recounts that a contemplative Amar Das was totally mesmerized by a verse of Gurū Nānak recited from the lips of Bibi Amaro. When he expressed his wish to meet the gurū who had been invested with such a rich legacy, Bibi Amaro enthusiastically escorted Amar Das to her father, Gurū Angad. Amar Das immediately became Gurū Angad's disciple and eventually succeeded him to the guruship, becoming Nānak III.

Gurū Amar Das's daughter Bibi Bhani had a tremendous impact on the historical development of Sikhism. Gurū Amar Das composed the Sikh wedding hymn (*lavan*) for her marriage with Ram Das and later chose Ram Das to be the fourth Sikh gurū. Bibi Bhani is also important because she donated the site of Amritsar to the Sikh community. She had been given this site by Emperor Akbar. It was on this land that her son Arjan, the fifth Sikh gurū, built the Harī Mandir and enshrined the sacred *Gurū Granth Sāhib.*

Mata Jitoji and Mata Sahib Devan are remembered as vital protagonists in the rite of *amrit* initiation. Mata Jitoji was Gurū Gobind Singh's first wife. When Gurū Gobind Singh was stirring water with his double-edged sword in the accompaniment of scriptural recitations at Anandpur during the 1699 spring festivities of Baisakhi (the first day of the Indian New Year), it was Mata Jitoji who added sugar puffs to the bowl. The *amrit* prepared by the gurū and Mata Jitoji fed the new family of the Khālsā and continues to nourish generations of Sikhs, physically and psychologically. When initiates sip the drink, they renounce their past with all its caste, class, and professional restrictions and claim their new identity with Gurū Gobind Singh and Mata Sahib Devan as their two equally important parents. Mata Sahib Devan was Gurū Gobind Singh's third wife. Tradition has it that their marriage was not physically consummated. Though she was not a biological mother, Sahib Devan became the spiritual mother of the Khālsā.

Gurū Gobind Singh's mother, Mata Gujari, and his second wife, Mata Sundari, are also important in Sikh history. The ninth gurū was often absent and was martyred when his son was only nine. So Mata Gujari had to raise Gurū Gobind Singh as a single parent. She imparted great wisdom and heroism not only to him but also to her grandsons. After the tenth gurū's death, it was Mata Sundari who provided guidance to the Sikhs. She appointed Bhai Mani Singh to manage the sacred shrines at Amritsar and commissioned him to collect the writings of Gurū Gobind Singh. Edicts issued under her seal and authority (*hukamnamas*) were sent out to Sikh congregations. Mata Sundari boldly rejected schismatic groups who tried to claim succession to guruship.

With Gurū Gobind Singh one also has the inspiring case of Mai Bhago. She was a courageous woman from the Amritsar district who rallied men to fight for the gurū against the imperial forces. She herself fought for the gurū in the battle at Muktsar in December 1705 and was injured. Thereafter she accompanied Gurū Gobind Singh as one of his personal bodyguards. Sikhs have built shrines in memory of her.

Sikh history is thus replete with excellent paradigms of women leading Sikh institutions of *sangat* and *langar*, reciting sacred poetry, fighting boldly against oppression and injustice, and generating liberating new rituals. But this feminizing process was not limited to the family members of gurūs; it was not just for women closely associated with them or for women of the elite. Rather, the Sikh faith opened up a wide horizon for all women, irrespective of caste, class, or marital status. They were all equal partners with men in Sikh practices and spiritual growth.

Scriptural Context. Sikh scripture, the *Gurū Granth Sāhib*, promotes gender equality in numerous ways. By designating the divine as numeral "One" at the very outset, it discards centuries-old images of male dominance and power and opens the way to experiencing the transcendent One in a female modality. The text offers a vast range of feminine symbols and imagery: the ontological ground of all existence is *mata,* the mother; the divine spark within all creatures is *joti*, the feminine light; the soul longing to unite with the transcendent One is *suhagan*, the beautiful young bride; the benevolent glance coming from the divine is the feminine *nadar,* grace. Sikh scripture continuously provides readers with a multivalent and complex feminine imagery. This variety in turn presents a host of options through which men and women can become who they choose to be.

Images of conception, gestation, childbirth, and lactation are unambiguously and powerfully present. Again and again scriptural verses remind Sikhs that they are created from the mother's blood, lodged in her womb, and first nurtured by her milk. The *Gurū Granth Sāhib* is unique in world scriptures in celebrating the centrality of menstrual blood (*Gurū Granth,* 1022, 706). Shunned as a private, shameful process, menstruation is acknowledged in Sikh scriptures as an essential, natural, creative process. Life itself begins with it. In fact Gurū Nānak reprimands those who stigmatize as polluted the garment stained with menstrual blood (*Gurū Granth,* 140). The *Gurū Granth Sāhib* also condemns pollution associated with childbirth and customs of purdah and sati.

The Sikh gurūs were men, but they expressed their love for the divine in the female gender. They do not repress or stunt themselves in male-female dualisms. Feeling the infinite intensely within, they openly identify with the female person, her psyche, her tone, her sentiments, and they trace the transcendent as both father and mother, male and female. Inspired by the infinite One, their verse spontaneously affirms woman's body, her activities, her dressing up, her tenacity, her longing. Throughout the *Gurū Granth Sāhib*, she is the model in forging a sensual and palpable union with the transcendent. In both praxis and poetry, the Sikh gurūs created an opening through which women could achieve liberty, equality, and sorority.

Contemporary Context. Unfortunately the empowering scriptural message has not been heeded. The radically uplifting female concepts, symbols, and images permeating the *Gurū Granth Sāhib* are simply neglected. The fundamentally patriarchal culture of the Punjab has continued to reproduce malestream interpretations, and other factors have produced androcentric attitudes in Sikh society. For instance, during the flamboyant regime of Māharājā Ranjit Singh, male dominance increased, and the practices of purdah and sati, which were condemned by the gurūs, found their way into the upper echelons of Sikh society. The British admiration for the "martial" character and the strong physique of the Sikh men (who were recruited into the British imperial army in disproportionately large numbers) generated a vigorous new patriarchal discourse—attaching patriotism and paternalism to the "brotherhood of the Khālsā." And twenty-first-century globalization is accelerating old patriarchal customs.

Sikh ethics is oriented toward this world. It affirms the body and the primacy of human relationships. There is no priesthood in Sikhism, so both men and women are free to read and recite the sacred verse at home or in public, and anybody from within the *sangat* (congregation) can be chosen to lead worship. The written laws of the Sikh religion grant full equality to men and women in all spheres—religious, political, domestic, and economic. But it is the unwritten laws that govern daily life, and these are quite different.

Public worship. Women play an active role in devotional practices at home, but leading pubic worship is a privilege restricted to men. Daily ceremonies like *prakash* (opening of the *Gurū Granth Sāhib*) and *sukhasan* (putting it to rest in the evening) in *gurdwaras*, the annual celebrations of Baiskahi and *gurpurabs* (birthdays or death anniversaries of the gurūs), and all rites of passage for Sikh men and women are conducted and administered almost exclusively by men. Gender distinctions do play a significant role because the superior role and privilege of men in public is unconsciously taken into the home, with the result that male domination is reproduced in the family, home, and Sikh society at large.

Rites of passage. In Sikhism there are four rites of passage: name giving, *amrit* initiation, marriage, and death. Though these rites are theoretically the same for both men and women, they end up being quite different in Sikh practice. For example, both male and female children are named in consultation with the holy book. Sikhs do not even have different names for boys and girls: the addition of the name *Kaur* (meaning "princess") for girls and *Singh* (meaning "lion") for boys indicates the gender of the child. This is another great feature traceable to Gurū Gobind Singh, for he freed women from the lineage of fathers and husbands. But this liberating phenomenon is buried under ancient discriminations against girls. The "same" name-giving ceremony ultimately depends on the "biology" of the child: the celebrations are more elaborate and joyous, with huge *langars*, for his name giving but not for hers.

Sikh initiation is also open to both men and women, and both are to wear the same five symbols. However, Sikh identity has been monopolized by masculinity, for it is the Sikh male, with his topknot or turban, who has come to represent all Sikhs. Boys are privileged in all spheres of Sikh life. Calendrical festivals, like the Punjabi winter ritual of Lohri, are celebrated only in Sikh homes where a boy is born. While parents and grandparents of a boy happily dole out money and gifts around crackling bonfires, the parents and grandparents of a girl remain sad during the cold dark nights of Lohri. Affluent Sikh families have also begun to celebrate the *dastar bandhan* (turban tying) with great pomp and show. This tying of the turban for the first time is becoming a popular rite of passage for boys.

The obsession for sons is so great among Sikhs that modern technology is abused to abort female fetuses. Ultrasound and other technologies are misused to preserve the legacy, business, property, and status of fathers and their sons. From the moment of birth the son and daughter are chartered out different roles and given a whole different set of obligations. Victims of false consciousness themselves, mothers and grandmothers continue to perpetuate double standards.

Sikh marriages are traditionally a simple and profound affair, but they have become extremely opulent, with extravagant dowries and exorbitant gifts to the daughter and her inlaws for every rite, ritual, and festival. The Sikh scriptural verse stating that "bride and groom are one spirit in two bodies" has no significance. It is taken for granted that the daughter leaves her natal home and joins her husband and his family. When there is a death in the family, it is the mother or wife's natal family that must offer a turban (in the case of a male) or a *dupatta* (in the case of a female)—and cash accompanies both modes of accoutrement. When a daughter dies, no matter what age or stage of life she may have been at, it is her natal family's responsibility to supply the meal following the cremation. From her birth till her death the daughter is a debit in the family economy.

Sikh *Rahit Maryada*. In its attempt to formalize the message of the gurūs, an ethical code called the *Rahit Maryada* was developed by Sikh reformers in the middle of the twentieth century. This code provides several rules to combat female oppression. Twice it makes the point that Sikh women should not veil their faces. It prohibits infanticide and even association with people who would practice it, although there is no prohibition against abortion. It allows widows to remarry and it underscores that the ceremony be the same as that of the first marriage. According to the Sikh *Rahit Maryada*, Sikhs should be free of all superstitions and not refuse to eat at the home of their married daughter. Dowry is prohibited.

Again many of these explicit rules are simply not followed. Out of "respect" for their daughters, Sikh parents will not accept a penny from their working daughter nor sip water in her married home. She is their prized "object," and so the ancient gender codes dating back to the Hindu *Manusmṛti* text continue to govern Sikh life.

Gender issues in global society. With their enterprising spirit and love of adventure, Sikhs travel to distant corners of the world. At first only men migrated, but after the elimination of U.S. national quotas in 1965, there has been a dramatic surge in the Sikh population, both male and female, all across North America. Sikh women arrive not only as wives, mothers, daughters, and sisters but also independently to pursue education or enter a variety of careers. Like their male counterparts, they are energetic and enterprising, but even in the New World the talents and potential of many Sikh women continue to be stifled by age-old societal norms. How to preserve Sikh identity in the contemporary world is a vital concern for Sikhs across the globe. Threatened by modernity and affluence, patriarchal formulations become even more stringent. Since women are literally the reproducers of the community, the preservation of "Sikhness" falls primarily on them. As a result Sikh women are subjected to manifold restrictions. Control over their reproductive rights leads to the reproduction of the family's identity and that of the Sikh community at large. "Honor" or *izzat,* which is identified with manliness and belongs to hierarchical and patriarchal systems, has come to be a central code of the Sikhs. Being a model community, Sikhs try to cover up female feticides, physical and psychological abuse, dowry deaths, and even "honor killings."

The economic and social demands of Sikh masculinity are so strong and pervasive that the teachings of the gurūs against objectionable treatment of women go unheeded. The egalitarian and liberating message of Sikh scripture has yet to be applied in daily lives and fully experienced by men and women alike.

See Also Ādi Granth; Gurū Granth Sāhib; Menstruation; Sati; Sikhism.

Bibliography

For a historical perspective, see Doris Jacobsh, *Relocating Gender in Sikh History: Transformation, Meaning, and Identity* (Delhi, 2003). For scriptural and theological analysis, see Nikky-Guninder Kaur Singh, *Feminine Principle in the Sikh Vision of the Transcendent* (Cambridge, U.K., 1993), "Why Did I Not Light up the Pyre? Refeminization of Ritual in Sikhism," *Journal of Feminist Studies in Religion* 16, no. 1 (2000): 63–85, and "Sacred Fabric and Sacred Stitches," *History of Religion* 43, no. 4 (2004): 284–302. For an ethnographic study on the renewed use of the turban among contemporary North American Sikh women, see Cynthia Mahmood and Stacy Brady, *The Guru's Gift: An Ethnography Exploring Gender Equality with North American Sikh Women* (Mountain View, Calif., 2000). For gender and identity in 3HO, the American Sikh community, see Constance Elsberg, *Graceful Women: Gender and Identity in an American Sikh Community* (Knoxville, Tenn., 2003). For a literary approach, see Shauna Singh Baldwin's novel, *What the Body Remembers* (New York, 1999). Diasporic issues relating to gender and Sikhism are taken up by Brian Keith Axel, *The Nation's Tortured Body: Violence, Representation, and the Formation of a Sikh "Diaspora"* (Durham, N.C., 2001); Parminder Bhachu, *Twice Migrants: East African Sikh Settlers in Britain* (London and New York, 1986) and *Dangerous Designs: Asian Women Fashion the Diaspora Economies* (New York, 2004); Christine Fair, "Female Feticide among Vancouver Sikhs," *International Journal of Punjab Studies* 3, no. 1 (1996): 1–44; and Gurpreet Bal, "Migration of Sikh Women to Canada: A Social Construction of Gender," *Guru Nanak Journal of Sociology* 18, no. 1 (1997): 97–112. Bhai Vir Singh, the Sikh renaissance writer, created many strong female protagonists in his popular fiction, including *Sundari,* which is also the title of the first novel written in the Punjabi language.

Nikky-Guninder Kaur Singh (2005)

GENDER AND RELIGION: GENDER AND CHINESE RELIGIONS

Chinese religious history opens with a shocking gender anomaly: a powerful priestess-class of shamanesses speaking the gods' own voices in the high court ritual of the Shang dynasty (c. 1766–1027 BCE) Through ritual performance these women conducted purifications, summoned the rain and healed the ills of the state, and, as one ancient dictionary, the *Shuowen jiezi,* stated, "caused the gods to descend into them through the medium of dance." Nor were these powerful mystics honorary men. By virtue of their female and sexual natures they served as the proper conduit for the divine. Through ritual exposure of their breasts to the sun they bought the rain, and, if later poetic recastings of the rites were true, they legitimized the king with a sexual encounter that mimicked a divine marriage with the goddess. They were, as E. H. Schafer phrased it, "the kingdom's rightful rainmakers" (1951, p. 137). Of course, it would seem as if little in the way of customary assumptions about Chinese religion would allow for such a class of women. Bureaucratic, imperial, hierarchical, canonically rigid, clerical, and masculine—these are the frequently named features of Chinese religion. But, if Mircea Eliade is right in his observations made on religion over 50 years ago (that religions encode not just one pattern of human-divine contact, but rather the "multiple modalities of being in the world" [1957, p. 15] and that religion reveals a world that is "transpersonal, significant and sacred" [1957, p. 18], whose sanctity can be revealed to the worshiper through the theurgic summons in "rites of ecstasy"), then the figure of the feminine ecstatic should not be impossible. And, indeed, this survey of gender in China's religions will reveal that the hierarchical, bureaucratic model is a limited paradigm, and that ecstatic communication by female officiants, as well a varied cast of women mystics, adepts, religious teachers, and goddesses all share the religious stage with the sober deities of a divine bureaucracy.

The major concerns of gender studies in China have been several: the excavation of lost voices within competing narratives (especially feminine voices), the methods of suppression of marginalized voices, cultural tautologies and the demonization of the feminine, the complicity of women in these tautologies, and, more recently, the theory of agency, whereby constructs of the feminine are not defined exclusively by larger power structures that victimize women, but as constructs that offered limited freedoms within the framework of masculine definition. The history of gender studies in the field begins explicitly with one of these issues, namely, suppressed narratives. Chinese philologists of the Republican Period (1911–1949), eager perhaps to overturn the radically conservative philological thrust of the Manchu, with its court-approved manipulation of the Confucian tradition, rigorously explored the counter-traditions and subtexts of Shang and Zhou (c. 1150–256 BCE) cultures. They hoped to establish the ways court-centered expositions of sanctity and legitimacy suppressed alternative constructs of the divine. They reconsidered epigraphy, the Confucian classics, and ancient poetry to retrieve the lost practices of popular and local cultures. Chen Mengjia, Wen Yido, Gu Jiegang, Marcel Granet, Edward Erkes, and Henri Maspero were among the first to uncover the significance of the goddesses Chang E, the lunar goddess; Nü Wa, the snail woman; and Xi He, the sun goddess, as well the authority of divine conduits called *wu* or shamanesses. A second generation of academics (e.g., E. H. Schafer, David Hawkes, Wolfram Eberhard, and Chang Kuang-chih) also retrieved the buried references to feminine sanctity in language, myth, and folklore.

The most important development in the field of gender studies, however, has come not from methodological innovation but from the exploitation of previously under-used materials. In some real sense, even into the 1950s, Qing dynasty (1644–1911) scholarly and political conservativism dominated much academic consideration of literary, cultural, and religious studies. The "little tradition," in all its manifestations, was considered beneath consideration, and consequently the vast issues of what shaped the culture beyond the walls of the court were neglected. But with the advent of research into uncensored documents with foci on regional, urban, and rural life—resources not winnowed, organized, and reproduced in the great Qing dynasty compendia—the construct of gender in religion has opened up. Recent scholars have exploited these sources, finding a canon of the counter-tradition and thereby remade the map of both male and female religious practice and ideation. They have, in particular, explored a plethora of sources that came with the expansion of the publication industry beginning in the Song dynasty (960–1279): mirabilia, Precious Scrolls, Goodness Books, ballads, pious tales, vernacular fiction, dramas, and popular songs as well as classical sources such as private journals (*biji*), classical fiction, hagiography of the sectarian cults, gazetteer accounts of regional practice, temple records, accounts of secret societies and lay organizations, hagiography, and poetry religious canon. All these sources are now used by scholars to open up the consideration of both masculine and feminine narratives in China's religious history.

Parsing China's religious life into the major religious traditions of Confucianism, Daoism, Buddhism, and popular religion has served bibliographers well. Worshipers and the worshiped, however, have found these neat divisions to be permeable. Popular religions have shaped Daoism, Indian Buddhism saw extraordinary shifts and elaborations as it became subject to the gravitational pull of local religions, and both sectarian and syncretic religions have thrived in complete ignorance of denominational categories; all, in fact, have given the lie to the neatness of the four categories. Considerations of gender further disturbs these categories for it is in looking at feminine and masculine icons of, for example, the sacred fool and the ecstatic, the divine marriage and ascetic, that we will find more of Eliade than the Qing bibliographer. But for the purposes of an overview we will yield to the familiar and exploit these four divisions as our method of organization.

POPULAR RELIGION. Popular religion—also referred to as folk religion, lay religion or diffused religion—is a vast aggregation of practices that includes shamanism, calendrical holiday festivals, ancestor worship, geomancy, ritual practices to assuage demonic influence, apotropaic practice tied to chronology and calendar, and prediction based on physical features of the human anatomy, the landscape, the detection of randomly heard voices, patterns of bird migration, and so on. Often this diffuse religion is defined by negatives: It lacks a centralized, clerical hierarchy, a large corpus of written, canonized texts, court affiliation, and an institutional identity. It is polytheistic to say the least, including door guardians, stove gods, a spirit of the privy, drought demons, avenging ghosts, a god of wealth, protectors of childbirth, drunken rebel-gods, astral spirits that cause disease or family strife, and ghosts, sprites, or demons of specific features of the landscape, whether mountain, roadside, river way, or neighborhood. There are many divine narratives: journeys to paradise or hell, supernatural visitations, and stern karmic principles of divine revenge. The connection to the divine can be through a class of mediums or through direct and personal discernment of the numinous. In the aggregate, popular religion is a kind of highly articulated and fully annotated animism. It mystifies the specific features of daily life and defines spirituality as a kind of esoteric knowledge of the divine signatures in nature, conveying, with a stunning degree of confidence, that life is, in some sense, sacramental.

Governing elites tend to favor a cooperative leadership class, the unimpeded collection of resources, and a religious practice that, in proving the connection of the state to the divine, legitimizes the state's efforts to perpetuate itself. Popular religions, however, reenact the powerful concerns and uncensored dramas of micro-cultures of individuals, families, clans, towns, regions, covenant affiliations, and ethnic groups. In the cults that thrive in such subcultures, views of sexuality, love, and lineage, of death and grief, of prosperity, production, and harvests, as well as of family continuities, community conflicts, and the connection (or lack of connection) between individual and state all find expression with some degree of autonomy from elite mandates. For women, who are excluded explicitly from the sites and definitions of power, as well as for men who may be rebels or misfits, it is in local religious practice that more complex and varied expressions of sanctity and identity are found than in centrally monitored religious practice. Thus, assessing these cults and practices, myths, and beliefs from the perspective of gender helps provide an astonishing illumination of the observer's field of vision, exposing a primordial soup of feminine archetypes and narratives and of feminine symbolic structures and thaumaturgic practices. Gender issues tend to reveal that official practice, although an efficient veneer, yet masks a powerful religious substrata.

Feminine sanctity and feminine religious power assert themselves vividly in popular religion, for however patriarchy may be lauded or reviled in elite tradition, in popular religion it is in some aspects blithely ignored. In popular religion, women are the domestic ritualists, the mediums, the warrior-saints, the magical adepts, and mystics. Female divinities benefit or terrify at every level, from the plethora of local ghosts appeased at uncountable numbers of riverside shrines to the great goddesses such as the Celestial Empress and the Eternal Mother. Yet this powerful aggregation of feminine practice and ideation has struggled as well, subjected to censorship and banishment. In the case of one of these practices—shamanism—we can see, in fact, a clear dialectic of the competing narratives of a vernacular feminine religious discourse eclipsed but never silenced by the orthodoxies of elite discourse. This dialectic, however, tells us much about how constructs of feminine sanctity survive without benefit of orthodox canon and centralized sponsorship, and proves not only the innate resiliency of the iconography of the feminine, but reveals as well the cultural mechanisms that help sustain the narratives.

Shamanism—condemned as heterodox and licentious, banned and declared illegal, denied the ample support accorded many religious cults—represents the prototypical suppressed feminine voice. Shamanism begins before either Daoism or Confucianism takes shape, in the Shang dynasty. It was central to court ritual, as the female—and to a lesser extent male—shamans constituted a class of divine conduits who revealed the voices of the gods through rituals of divine possession and the performance of ecstatic dance and speech. In the Shang dynasty shamanesses were the chief officiants in a court scapegoat drama, whereby the sins of the community were expiated through harsh sacrifice (often by maiming, drowning, or exposure to fire). Their ritual disfigurement or deaths purified the land in times crisis, especially times of drought and perceived astronomical anomalies. Nor were they mere ritual actors, but honored members of a ruling caste, serving as great officers of the court. During the Han dynasty (206 BCE–220 CE) through the Tang dynasty (618–907), due specifically to the influence of Confucianism, shamanism increasingly became a cultural outlaw, practiced in the breech. Wide-scale suppression of the cults relegated shamanic practice to the status of licentious rites, although literati noted that its "foolish rituals for healing the sick continued to delude the people" in more remote regions of the empire (Cass, 1999, p. 50).

The efforts of literati and court not withstanding, however, shamanism was consistently practiced and is known today throughout South China and in Taiwan and Hong Kong. In her research on the cult of the Medieval shamaness Chen Jinggu, titled "The Woman at the Water's Edge," Brigitte Baptandier found shamanic practice to be a solid feature of the local religious landscape. Like the shamanesses of the Shang period, the shamaness is "of the waters" (i.e., "the Woman at the Water's Edge"), and her help is sought times of drought, conception, and childbirth. She is a warrior-saint as well, pictured in statues and texts on horseback, armed with sword and whip, accompanied by her divine generals. Her current worshipers insist that her avatars have fought in many wars, including the Vietnam War and the Gulf War. Thus, despite banishment, shamanic practice has survived intact in local cultures. The survival of this regional voice has seemed surprising to some, as court orthodoxies, preserved in written instruments, should logically dominate regional cultures. Yet recent scholarship has proven that person-to-person, oral transmission is as effective as court methods of perpetuation; indeed, local religious practice thrives on the oral, the intimate, and the immediate. Popular rituals and vernacular entertainments preserve iconography faithfully, pilgrimage and religious teachers convey practice among temple networks, and merchant culture spreads folk traditions through merchant associations along expanding canal and sea routes. Thus, notwithstanding the efforts of the Tang court (618–906) to abolish shamanesses as heterodox, of the Qing court (1644–1911) to eliminate warrior-adepts as treasonous, of the courts of the People's Republic of China to eradicate local female mediums as feudal superstition, a multitude of feminine religious expression are surviving—if not thriving—at the local levels. In other words, as Baptandier has pointed out, if all the mediums in a town in Fujian were arrested, the practices would reassert themselves after the cadres left.

Shamanism has not, however, been limited to local practice, but has found re-expression in multiple features of the cultural landscape, surviving as one of the most powerful archetypes in Chinese mythology, The shamanic iconography of the feminine is explicitly concerned with the ambiguous power of the feminine, allying the feminine with the polarities of both fertility and danger. The iconic imagery of her mythos epitomizes her ambiguity; she is allied with water, blood, and the yin polarity. In religion, this elaboration of the feminine is often repeated, seeping through the boundaries that separate one religion from another. Shamanic constructs of the feminine inform as well the rhetorical streams that feed both the arts and cultural myths. In poetry, history, fiction, and drama, as well as in sex-based archetypes, the contours of shamanism are seen repeatedly. In fiction, in particular, this watery, lethal, and sexually powerful woman, often allied with snakes or water-borne creatures, thrives; she is seen in vernacular and classical stories, expatriate fiction from all over the globe, and finally recast in film and television.

CONFUCIANISM. Confucianism, allied with the imperial court, presents the greatest contrast with popular religions. It has a meticulously maintained written canon, an institutional hierarchy with a rigorously apprenticed and centrally selected membership consisting of officiants and practitioners, and speaks generally with a unified voice—thus, firmly occupying center stage in the official version of China's religious history. It evolved during the Zhou dynasty (c. 1150–256 BCE) from an aggregation of practices centered around the aristocratic cult of ancestor worship. Beginning in the Han dynasty (206 BCE–220 CE) Confucian beliefs were rigorously inculcated through the institution of what became the Examination System whereby entrance to political life required memorization of the Confucian canon. Confucianism was interlocked as well with the state cult, a set of theocratic practices sanctifying both the living family and the ancestral line of the emperor. Essential to Confucianism, especially in the late imperial periods—Song (960–1279) through Qing (1644–1911)—was the development of practices centered around the concept of the sacred lineage, or *zong*. A natural outgrowth of the cult of ancestor worship and the principles of piety, the practices of the sacred lineage formulated the family as a cult space. By this construct ancestors maintained active watch over the conduct of the living sending benefits or crises depending on the worth of the family's actions. In turn, individuals of the family lived consecrated lives, with all the myriad details of domestic life measured by the compass of family piety, examined carefully for ritual flaws.

The requirements of the sacred lineage created powerful resonances in constructs of both masculine and feminine sanctity. In Confucianism the ideal exemplar for both women and men was extreme self-sacrifice. For men, ideals of sanctity were rigorous. Men were idealized as lie, ardently heroic, or fiercely dedicated. The perceived magical connection to the ancestors required scarring personal sacrifice and an intense moral standard. Men realized the ideal through suicide in times of severe national crisis and through bold and dangerous challenges to corrupt power. Nor were these heroes of Confucianism simply icons of the state orthodoxy but exemplars told of in popular literature. Novels, drama, and short fiction lionized Confucian heroes who sacrificed their lives, configuring absolute dedication to the values of piety, loyalty, humaneness, or propriety as heroic feats of personal glory equal to the daring accomplishments of knights errant and warriors.

For women the pattern of divinity was extremely harsh; once a woman was engaged or married, her obligations to the sacred lineage (*zong*) of her fiancé or husband redefined her as a consecrated vessel dedicated to the continuation of the line. Women realized Confucian forms of sanctity through motherhood, through the role of the family matriarch, and through stern maintenance of the teachings of the *Ju*. Much has been made of the idealization of the masculine and the patriarchal in Confucianism; but, Confucianism also greatly mystified and idealized motherhood and the mother-son dyad. In fact, in novels and confessional journals women often appear as more powerful, more dedicated, and more memorable than men in a Confucian family. The apotheosis of the feminine ideal was achieved through the notion of martyrdom, whereby a daughter, fiancée, wife, daughter-in-law, or niece sacrificed herself to resolve the crisis occurring to the lineage. In the case of the death of the spouse, the martyred wife or fiancée committed suicide or dedicated her life to widow-solitude. If an elder in the family was ill, the cult required a woman to concoct from pieces of her own flesh a magically healing soup to be consumed by the ill patient. She thus became a *zhen nü*—literally, a sacred woman, often translated as filial, martyred, or chaste woman. Nor did these acts simply express moral ideals but were considered acts of transcendence that could serve the community as sources of divine efficacy. Locals worshiped at the shrines erected to commemorate the sacred woman, and it was believed the spirits of martyred women could relieve droughts or ward off disasters. This cult was of less significance in the ancient and medieval periods, but became highly influential in the late imperial periods, as the concept of the *zong*—or sacred lineage—became more fully articulated.

Despite the importance of these women as local cult figures, their worship was by no means purely a matter of local customs, however. As Katherine Carlitz (1997), Jonathan Chaves (1986), and Mark Elvin (1984) have pointed out these cults functioned in state worship. The female martyrs were publicly acknowledged as talismans of imperial legitimacy and as emblems of the state's connection to the ancestral line. They were recognized with imperial shrines and parades of local officials and immortalized in the historical canon. Nor was the state naïve about the pragmatic implications in these local cults. Martyred women cults functioned explicitly as vehicles for imposing centralized Confucian values on the local mores of distant localities. The court explicitly used the martyred women cult and the worship of the city-god to manipulate local worship and local loyalties. Fear of the power wielded by popular feminine cults may be a factor as well in state sponsorship. In some cases, it is clear that the government deliberately adapted local popular cults dedicated to female ghosts: the Bureau of Rites co-opted local worship of the waterside divinity and declared them to be *zhen nü* and a riverside ghost became, by imperial decree, a Confucian martyred woman. It may seem that the local river-ghost is a distant cousin of the harsh exemplar of family piety; yet. they share certain features. Drought relief, maiming and physical sacrifice, and the accretion of local worshipers were the patterns of feminine sanctity of both the martyred wife and the shaman.

DAOISM. Daoism, like Confucianism, arose out of Zhou-era (c. 1150–256 BCE) ritual and beliefs, centered possibly around rituals of healing, alchemy, and the arts of longevity. Early Daoism of the Zhou period was articulated first by the two elliptical and brilliant writers known as Master Lao and Master Zhuang. They emphasized nonpurposive action and rejected the worldly, the hierarchical, and the mundane, celebrating intuitive insight over reason and suggesting the existence of specific esoteric practices that lead to the state of transcendence. From the late Han (206 BCE–220 CE) and through the Six Dynasties period (220–589) Daoism sees elaborate articulations of practice and belief: the growth of large centers of worship centered around the teachings of the celestial master Zhang Daoling, the growth of a Daoist monastic movement, the development of a Daoist church with hierarchy and canon, the elaboration of the teachings of inner and outer alchemy, and the affiliations of secret societies and millenarian rebellious movements. Daoism is still practiced throughout Asia, especially in Taiwan, Southeast China, and Hong Kong. The celestial master in Taiwan is head of the Daoist church.

As with Confucianism, there is an elaborate hierarchical structure of officers and rigorously compiled and edited canon and codified ritual practice. Yet unlike Confucianism, Daoism has been pervasively shaped by the feminine discourse of the divine, for in the case of Daoism, a centralized hierarchical religion has not become a vehicle for masculine ideations of the divine. One reason for the richness of feminine narratives is precisely Daoism's long and profound connection to popular religion. Daoism has had a porous border with the rituals and beliefs of popular religion, especially shamanism. Exorcisms, purification rites, illness as punishment for ritual flaws, escorting the souls of the dead, and maimed mediums speaking in trance the words of the spirit world are all practices that have traveled from local practice to Daoist practice as easily as the skilled exorcist traveled to the realms of the dead. Daoism, in fact, mined popular practice, for, as Kenneth Dean noted, "Daoism seeks to channel the energies of the shamanic substratum" (1993, p. 9). Likewise, K. Schipper observed, with radical simplicity, "Daoism is the written tradition of local cults" (cited in Dean, 1993, p. 12).

Of course, many Daoist clerics have been eager to distinguish their practices from popular practice (especially blood sacrifices) but the liturgist's contempt for local practice reflected more a kind of sibling rivalry than structural distinctions between separate species. The implication for gender is obvious—popular religion is veined through and through with feminine narratives of the divine.

Even at the earliest stages of the formation of Daoism, in the earliest cosmological constructs, clear ideations of the feminine existed. Specifically the Zhou era texts of Laozi and Zhuangzi have multiple references to the great female, the dark valley, and, of course, the polarities of yin and yang. Analyses of these early texts to establish the significance of the feminine have, however, provided only limited satisfaction. The problem is not that such analyzes are groundless, because clearly the duality of yin and yang did profoundly shape the construct of Daoist iconography and beliefs, but that the texts are so terse, oracular, and elliptical, with little in the way of contemporaneous philological context, that the issue of the feminine in early Daoism is difficult.

The problem of inadequate context, however, is mitigated in the Han and Six Dynasties, in which texts are found presenting the pantheon, prayers, and ritual description, as well as texts recommending the religious, social, and domestic functions for both men and women. In these articulations of belief and practice, the role of the feminine becomes explicit, and feminine narratives are present in cosmology, myth, hagiography, and in descriptions of ritual practice and church leadership. Beginning with texts appearing in the third century, women appear alongside men as officers of the church, as female masters—both married and unmarried—who take on female disciples. Women in these texts have direct access to transcendence, govern in local parishes, and join religious organizations. Some women of the Dao are described in the domestic context as well. Wives and mothers are registered in the church as women dedicated to the Dao, proving that, even in the confines the family, "a woman could have a complete religious status of her own" (Overmyer, 1981, p. 100).

If women in the Daoist church had explicit importance, female saints and divinities ranked importantly in the Daoist pantheon. The Jade Girl, the Plain Girl, divine emissaries, immortals, and saints of the alchemical arts such as the Furry Woman and the Woman of the Great Polarities all had dedicated followers and temples throughout the empire. Daoist worshipers in the thousands gathered as well to worship the Goddess of the Azure Clouds, Bixiyuanjun, at her temple near the top of Mount Tai in Shandong. Indeed, a healthy portion of the Daoist pantheon was female. One of the most powerful goddesses was the Queen Mother of the West. Suzanne Cahill (1993) traced this cult of this goddess of kingship rites and of longevity. The Queen Mother of the West was patron saint of artists and of aristocratic women and was especially important to mystics and adepts who practiced astral travel. Many dedicated their lives to her at Daoist monasteries and abbeys.

As with the saintly women of Confucian practice, female mystics and divines were important to the court; many were brought to the capital to serve as "living auspicious omens," signs that the dynasty was blessed by the Dao. Some mystics gathered adherents in monasteries and hermitages in remote mountain sites; these teachers were maintained in monastic life by contributions from all classes of society from the poor to the aristocratic. Female religious leaders could gather worshipers even at their own homes in urban areas; the mystic Tan Yang Zi in the late Ming dynasty (1368–1644) gathered thousands of adherents in the city of Suzhou, and many of her followers were high-ranking members of the official class. Woman warriors were often allied as well with Daoist practice; the demon-quelling sword of the Daoist exorcist was her typical weapon. But these mystic-warriors summoned up dangerous political currents in her cult, and they were often allied with millenarian rebellions. As with popular practice Daoism has found drama, poetry, and fiction to be useful allies. From the medieval period come the Capeline Cantos, the songs of Daoist priestesses, as well as paens to goddesses. In the Late Imperial periods vernacular dramas, stories, and chantefables spread the mythoi of the goddesses and saints through urban areas. Daoism has provided one of the fullest possible articulations of feminine sanctity in China's religious history.

BUDDHISM. If Daoism opened its gates to the feminine, Buddhism, when it was first introduced to China, was less hospitable. The same groundswell of feminine archetypes that radiated through popular religion and Daoism, however, was no less active in Buddhism, and where Buddhism touched those ancient assumptions about the sanctity of the feminine, it found a feminine voice impossible to ignore. As Buddhism grew in China, it did not spread its influence like vat of dye spilled on the landscape, coloring all local practice and iconography in its path; rather, it transmogrified, changing and adapting to Chinese cultural assumptions, to local practices and native Chinese religious imperatives. And these changes in Buddhism tell, in turn, about the power of local religious narratives and, again, about the authority of native feminine ideations of the divine.

Buddhism entered China during the Han dynasty (206 BCE–220 CE) and dominated the religious landscape in the northern kingdoms of the Six Dynasties (220–589) period. Buddhist theocracies in northern China ensured that Indic Buddhism grew solid roots. Beginning in the Tang dynasty (618–906), Buddhism took firm hold empire-wide and, by the time of the Song dynasty (960–1279), had important centers in both the North and South. For both men and women, Buddhism presented problems specifically allied with gender. One debate centered on the configuration of feminine sanctity, or lack thereof. Women in Indic Buddhist doctrine were, as Diana Paul described it, "secular, powerless, profane and imperfect" (1985). Indian Buddhist construction of the divine was explicitly masculine; women's bodies were impure. "There are neither hell-beings, hungry ghosts, animals or women in the Pure Land," observed the Qing theorist Peng Shaosheng (cited in Grant, 1994, p. 77). Passage through karmic reincarnations—whereby a woman shed her female form—was required before a woman could, as a man, enter the Western Paradise. Both Indian Mahāyāna texts and Chinese Pure Land texts were explicit on the contaminated nature of the feminine.

If women were constructed as impure and incapable of divinity, however, the worshipers of popular Buddhist cults neglected to notice. Setting dogma aside, they implicitly reconfigured the feminine in Buddhism as sacred. The major example of this reconfiguration occurs in the change in the worship of the Indic god, the *bodhisattva* Avalokiteśvara. Chinese worshipers seized the notion of a god of mercy and, over time, over the course of the Tang and Song eras, recreated him as a goddess. Chün-fang Yü detailed brilliantly the change whereby Avalokiteśvara becomes the Goddess of Mercy, Guan Yin. Yü found that Buddhism was specifically changed through contact with native cults and, like Daoism, definitions of divinity were profoundly shaped by the gravitational pull of feminine narratives. Yü traces the transformation of god to goddess by "examining the relationship between Buddhism and indigenous cultural and religious traditions" (2001, p. 489), finding that the male god of mercy adapted to local beliefs, in which female divinities brought rain, watched over children, and relieved suffering. Thus, the male god of mercy became a white-robed goddess for Chan monks, a water-moon goddess for the literati, protectress of sailors for coastal worshipers, and finally a child-giving goddess for common folk. Orthodox monks of the monastic centers—like the disapproving clerics in the Daoist church—were quick to criticize the transformation of the god from male to female as heterodox practice, yet the pull of local belief proved too strong. The Goddess Guan Yin did, finally, redefine Buddhist sanctity as feminine; she became, in fact, one of the major Buddhist ideations of divinity. Ultimately, in the sectarian religions in late imperial China, she dominated in the pantheon, regarded as holding supreme position as creator and ruler of the universe. Ironically, it is just through such radical recalibrations of notions of the divine, attended by increased numbers of devotees to her cult, that Buddhism in Asia survived and still thrives. Her cult center on Putoshan Island, off the Yangzi Delta coast near Ningbo, was expensively and massively refurbished by donors from all over Asia at the beginning of the 1990s.

Chinese definitions of the domestic sanctity (i.e., idealized concepts of motherhood) also shaped Buddhist rituals and narratives. The Buddhist ritual drama of Mulian, one of the most popular ritual-narratives in China, reshaped Buddhist configurations of female impurity. Mulian was a saint whose chief work was the rescue of his mother from hell—a hell ordained for her by the doctrine of female corporeal corruption. Yet the ritual drama enacted to large audiences at temples and holiday congregations was, in effect, an enactment of the rituals of filial piety. Audiences seemed rather more interested in notions of the son's dedication than the mother's contamination. The tale of a mother's corporeal contamination was a weak shadow plot, inherently less interesting than the tale of piety for the mother. Thus Chinese concepts shaped the narrative which, in turn, helped resolve the inherent cultural conflict between Confucian piety toward motherhood and Buddhist revulsion for the female body. Elite Buddhist practice was no less subject to native reconfigurations. Chan (or Zen) Buddhism altered important aspects of gender-based sanctity. Beatta Grant (1996) has pointed out that although Pure Land Buddhism was explicit on feminine corporeal contamination, because Chan emphasized enlightenment, rather than passage to Paradise, Chan was more receptive to female students and masters. In fact, from the Chan *yulu* (discourse records of disciples) it is known that women served as teachers, pupils, and even "holders of the lineages" in Chan Buddhism.

In the late imperial period—Song through Qing—lay organizations contributed importantly to the expansion of feminine divine narratives and patterns of feminine worship. Beginning in the twelfth century, lay organizations began in affiliation with monastic organizations, but by the sixteenth century lay organizations were independent of monasteries, often located in urban areas of the South. These organizations had large numbers of female worshipers and an independent female leadership structure, they practiced economic support through tithing, and the members participated in a host of devotional activities: convocation and pilgrimage, large scale donation to build and sustain temples and monasteries, gathering at festivals to see ritual drama, reading or listening to vernacular tales and hagiography, and listening to teachers in public or in private. Whatever the regulations may have been for the cloistered woman—and many literati were at pains to remind women of these regulations—public congregation, study, religious dedication, travel, and even marriage-resistance societies were among the ideals for lay Buddhist worshipers. In addition to the practices allied with lay organizations, ritual dramas and vernacular hagiographies also expanded the constructs of feminine worship and sanctity, specifically offering women an ideal distinctly different from the ideal of domestic confinement. The immensely popular story of Miao Shan—celebrated in pilgrimage, ritual, and popular literature—articulates the conflict between family piety and devotion to Buddhist practice, offering an exemplar of Buddhist sainthood. Miao Shan converts her father before achieving apotheosis as the incarnation of Guan Yin.

In considering gender in Chinese religions the lines of two competing narratives can be clearly traced: the hierarchical, masculine, institutionalized, often state-sponsored paradigm and, in contrast, the regional paradigm that is, in varying degrees, charismatic, vernacular, and often feminine. Of course, these vernacular narratives are not fully transparent for court and state cultures do not typically condone variant constructs of sanctity. Indeed, the female narratives, in particular, often exist in competition with the hegemonic elaboration of sanctioned orthodoxies. The court and now the Communist Party regularly attack these micro-religions, measuring the competition they offer to mandarin pieties. But these religious narratives are linked to a thriving undercurrent of religious cultures and are a vigorous subcategory of the transpicuous in China, their cults summoning wide-scale support among both male and female worshipers and, in some cases, dominating regional subcultures. Thus the feminine and regional paradigm does not present a small voice in the religious chorus; rather, it is animated, energetic and forceful—able, in fact, to alter radically the orthodoxies of institutional religious traditions. Moreover, this dialectic between competing paradigms of sanctity unveils something useful about Chinese cultural history, revealing not only the elaborate and protean panorama that is Chinese religious history, but also enabling us as well to confront the bland assumptions made in ignorance of conflicts of interpretation that China is unchanging, monolithic, dynastic, imperial, and masculine.

SEE ALSO Ancestors, article on Ancestor Worship; Buddhism, article on Buddhism in China; Buddhism, Schools of, article on Chinese Buddhism; Chinese Religion, overview article and article on Popular Religion; Confucianism, overview article; Daoism, overview article; Folk Religion, article on Folk Buddhism; Gender Roles; Patriarchy and Matriarchy; Shamanism, overview article.

BIBLIOGRAPHY

Ahern, Emily. "Power and Pollution of Chinese Women." In *Women in Chinese Society*, edited by M. Wolf and R. Witke, pp. 169–191. Stanford, Calif., 1975.

Baptandier, Brigitte. "The Lady Linshui." In *Unruly Gods, Divinity, and Society in China*, edited by M. Shahar and R. Weller, pp. 105–149. Honolulu, 1996.

Baptandier, Brigitte. "Du bon usage des mythes en Chine, avant et après la revolution culturelle." *Cahiers de litterature orale* 26 (1989): 37–59.

Berg, Daria. *Carnival in China: A Reading of the Xingshi Yinyuan zhuan.* Leiden, 2002.

Cahill, Suzanne. *Transcendence and Divine Passion, the Cult of the Goddess Hsi Wangmu.* Stanford, Calif., 1993.

Carlitz, Katherine. "Shrines, Governing-Class Identity, and the Cult of Widow Fidelity in Mid-Ming Jiangnan." *Journal of Asian Studies* 56, no. 3 (1997): 612–640.

Cass, Victoria. *Dangerous Women, Warriors, Grannies, and Geishas of the Ming.* Lanham, Md., 1999.

Chang, K. C. *Art, Myth, and Ritual: The Path to Political Authority in Ancient China.* Cambridge, U.K., and London, 1983.

Chaves, Jonathan. "Moral Action in the Poetry of Wu Chia-chi (1618–84)." *Harvard Journal of Asiatic Studies* 46 (1986): 387–469.

Cleary, Thomas, trans. and ed. *Immortal Sisters: Secrets of Taoist Women.* Boston, 1989.

Dean, Kenneth. *Taoist Ritual and Popular Cults of Southeast China.* Princeton, N.J., 1993.

De Groot, Jan Jakob Marie. *The Religious System of China.* 6 vols. Leiden, 1882–1910.

Dudbridge, Glen. *The Legend of Miao-shan.* Oxford Oriental Monographs, no. 1. London, 1978.

Eberhard, Wolfram. *The Local Cultures of South and East China.* Translated from the German by Alide Eberhard. Leiden, 1968.

Eliade, Mircea. *Myths, Dreams and Mysteries: The Encounter between Contemporary Faiths and Archaic Realities.* Translated by Philip Mairet. New York, 1957.

Elvin, Mark. "Female Virtue and the State in China." *Past and Present* 104 (1984): 111–152.

Grant, Beata. "Who Is This I? Who Is That Other? The Poetry of an Eighteenth Century Laywoman." *Late Imperial China* 15, no. 1 (1994): 47–86.

Grant, Beata. "Female Holder of the Lineage: Lingji Chan Master Zhiyuan Xianggang (1597–1654)." *Late Imperial China* 17, no. 2 (1996): 51–76.

Hansen, Valerie. *Changing Gods in Medieval China, 1127–1276.* Princeton, N.J., 1990.

Hawkes, David. "The Quest of the Goddess." In *Studies in Chinese Literary Genres*, edited by Cyril Birch, pp. 42–68. Berkeley, Calif., 1962.

Hung Mei-hua. "Qingdai zhongji minjian mimi zongjiao zhong de funü" [Women in popular sectarian religions in the Qing period]. In *Chung-kuo fu-nü shih lun-chi,* edited by Pao Chia-lin, vol. 4, pp. 273–316. Taipei, 1995.

Johnson, David, ed. "Ritual Opera, Operatic Ritual: 'Mulian Rescues His Mother.'" In *Chinese Popular Culture.* Publication of the Chinese Popular Culture Project, 1. Berkeley, Calif., 1989.

Levering, Miriam. "Lin-chi (Renzai) Ch'an and Gender: The Rhetoric of Equality and the Rhetoric of Heroism." In *Buddhism, Sexuality and Gender,* edited by José Ignacio Cabezón, pp. 137–156. Albany, N.Y., 1992.

Li, Thomas Shiyu, and Susan Naquin. "The Baoming Temple: Religion and the Throne in Ming and Qing China." *Harvard Journal of Asiatic Studies* 48, no. 1 (1988): 131–188.

Mann, Susan. *Precious Records: Women in China's Long Eighteenth Century.* Stanford, Calif., 1997.

Maspero, Henri. "Legendes mythologiques dans le Chou King." *Journal Asiatique* 214 (1924): 1–100.

Overmyer, Daniel L. "Women in Chinese Religions: Submission, Struggle, Transcendence." In *From Benares to Beijing: Essays on Buddhism in Honour of Professor Jan Yun-hua,* edited by Koichi Shinohara and Gregory Schoper, pp. 91–129. Oakville, Ontario, 1981.

Paul, Diana. *Women in Buddhism: Images of the Feminine in Mahayana Tradition.* Reprint. Berkeley, Calif., 1985.

Pomeranz, Kenneth. "Power, Gender and Pluralism in the Cult of the Goddess of Taishan." In *Culture and State in Chinese History: Conventions, Accommodations, and Critiques,* edited by Theodore Huters, R. Bin Wong, and Pauline Yu. Stanford, Calif., 1997.

Potter, Jack. "Cantonese Shamanism." In *Religion and Ritual in Chinese Society,* edited by Arthur P. Wolf, pp. 207–231. Stanford, Calif., 1974.

Qu Dezai. *Taiwan Miao Shen zhuan* [Temples and their divinities in Taiwan]. Taipei, 1985.

Raphels, Lisa. *Sharing the Light: Representations of Women and Virtue in Early China.* Albany, N.Y., 1998.

Rowe, William T. "Women and the Family in Mid-Qing Social Thought: The Case of Ch'en Hung-mou." In *Family Process and Political Process in Modern Chinese History,* pp. 489–539. 2 vols. Taipei, 1992.

Sangren, Steven P. "Female Gender in Chinese Religious Symbols: Kuanyin, Ma Tsu, and the 'Eternal Mother.'" *Signs* 9, no. 1 (1983): 4–5.

Sawada Mizuho. *Chugoku no juho.* Tokyo, 1984.

Schafer, Edward. "Ritual Exposure in Ancient China." *Harvard Journal of Asiatic Studies* (1951): 130–184.

Schafer, Edward. *The Divine Woman Dragon Ladies and Rain Maidens in T'ang Literature.* Berkeley, Calif., 1973.

Schafer, Edward. "The Capeline Cantos, Verses on the Divine Loves of Taoist Priestesses." *Asiatische Studien* 32, no. 1 (1978): 5–65.

Shahar, Meir, and Robert P. Weller. "Introduction: Gods and Society in China." In *Unruly Gods, Divinity, and Society in China,* edited by M. Shahar and R. Weller, pp. 1–36. Honolulu, 1996.

Siu, Helen. "Recycling Rituals: Politics and Popular Culture in Contemporary Rural China." In *Unofficial Culture: Popular Culture and Thought in the People's Republic,* edited by Perry Link, R. Madsen, and P. Pickowicz, pp. 121–137. Boulder, Colo., 1990.

Smith, Richard J. "Ritual in Ch'ing Culture." In *Orthodoxy in Late Imperial China,* edited by K. C. Liu. Berkeley, Calif., 1990.

Stein, Rolf. "Religious Daoism and Popular Religion from the Second to Seventh Centuries." In *Facets of Taoism,* edited by Holmes Welch and Anna Seidel, pp. 53–58. New Haven, Conn., 1979.

T'ien Ju-k'ang. *Male Anxiety and Female Chastity, A Comparative Study of Chinese Ethical Values in Ming-Ch'ing Times.* Leiden, 1988.

Topley, Marjorie. "The Great Way of Former Heaven: A Group of Chinese Secret Religious Sects." *Bulletin of the School of Oriental and African Studies* 26 (1963): 362–392.

Van der Loon, Piet. "Les origines rituelles du theatre Chinois." *Journal Asiatique* 265 (1977): 141–168.

Waltner, Ann. "Tan-Yang-tzu and Wang Shih-chen: Visionary and Bureaucrat in the Late Ming." *Late Imperial China* 8, no. 1 (1987): 195–153.

Watson, James L. "Standardizing the Gods: the Promotion of T'ien Hou ('Empress of Heaven') along the South China Coast, 960–1960." In *Popular Culture in Late Imperial China,* edited by David Johnson, Andrew J. Nathan, and Evelyn Rawski, pp. 292–324. Berkeley, Calif., 1985.

Yü, Chün-fang. *Kuan-yin: The Chinese Transformation of Avalokitesvara.* New York, 2001.

Yu Songqing "Ming qing shiqi minjian nongjia jiaopai zhong de nüxing" [Women in popular religious cults of the Ming and Qing]. *Nankai xuebao* 5 (1982): 29–33.

Zhou Yiqun. "Mapping Female Religiosity in Late Imperial China, 1550–1900." *Late Imperial China* 24, no. 29 (2003): 109–155.

Zito, Angela R. "City Gods, Filiality, and Hegemony in Late Imperial China." *Modern China* 13, no. 3 (1987): 333–371.

VICTORIA CASS (2005)

GENDER AND RELIGION: GENDER AND JAPANESE RELIGIONS

The history of the study of gender in Japanese religion could be characterized by the observation made by Ursula King, concerning religious studies in general, that the field has remained resistant to important disciplinary changes brought about by gender studies and feminist thought (King, 2002, p. 372). This tendency seems stronger in the Japanese academic field, where introducing concepts of gender and feminism is often seen as insinuating a particular political agenda or a lack of scholarly neutrality. From an academic gender and feminist perspective, in turn, religion is seen as a tool of patriarchy that is still used to oppress and alienate women (see, e.g., Ōgoshi, 1997). In this sense, gender and feminist studies maintain an awkward relationship with religious studies in Japan.

One is, however, beginning to see the impact of gender and feminist studies on Japanese religions. Japanese religious circles have been informed by gender studies and feminism since the mid-twentieth century, and movements to reform religious organizations are taking root as a result. These movements have commonalities with feminist theology movements in Europe and the United States that use feminism for critical leverage to reform male-dominated Judeo-Christian religions (Kawahashi and Kuroki, 2003).

Space constraints prevent this entry from tracing women's roles and how they were perceived in Shintō, Buddhism, Confucianism, or other religious traditions. Rather, this overview of gender in Japanese religions will identify important debates and isolate points that deserve greater attention in terms of both methodology and empirical research.

Impact of Gender Studies. Barbara Ruch (2002) and Bernard Faure (2003) have written essential studies for considering the impact of gender studies on Japanese Buddhism. Studies of women and Buddhist history have shifted significantly away from a focus on institutions and activities of male priests. Questions are posed in ways that reveal this reversal. Instead of asking how the "Buddhism" of patriarchs, Buddhist orders, and doctrines viewed women, the approach informed by gender studies asks, from a woman's viewpoint, how women perceived Buddhism, how they were marginalized, and what roles women fulfilled and aspired to within their various social constraints and limitations. This signifies, above all, a project to consider how women's religious activities influenced the history of Japanese Buddhism (Katsuura, 2003, p. 2). Ruch presents the collaboration of Japanese and American scholars who examined women in premodern Japanese Buddhist history from that perspective.

Such research examines how gender has informed the world and history of Buddhism. Thus Faure aims to explicate Buddhist conceptions of women and gender in order "to see how the history and doctrine of Buddhism were changed because of its relationship with women" (Faure, 2003, p. 14). Such an approach, he finds, also reveals how "ascetic religion" and male-dominated Buddhist communities were feminized and domesticated.

As Faure attempts to demonstrate, Buddhist women's history does not progress teleologically from oppression to emancipation. Japanese Buddhist historians' rereadings of historical sources substantiate his point. The linear notion that elitist ancient Buddhism denied women salvation, which was later extended to them for the first time by more democratic Kamakura Buddhism, is mistaken (Yoshida, Katsuura, and Nishiguchi, 1999). The *Nihon ryōiki*, a ninth-century collection of didactic tales, already depicted a Buddhism that did not reject women and vividly described women living within that faith (Nakamura, 1973). The *henjō nanshi* doctrine that women experience five obstructions and cannot achieve salvation in a female body became widespread by the medieval period. However, women were not strictly constrained by the Buddhist view that women had to be taught by men (Katsuura, 2003, p. 61). Not just passive recipients of patriarchal Buddhist teachings, women also resisted and appropriated those teachings. There is a need to examine relationships between Buddhism and various types of women, including nuns, lay followers, the mothers and wives of priests, and folk shamanic practitioners, from this perspective.

Similarly, Confucian tradition was often generalized as an ideological and cultural force that made the women of Asia victims of patriarchy, but modern studies show that women resisted patriarchal norms. Dorothy Ko, Jahyun Kim Haboush, and Joan Piggott (2003) affirm that women in Confucian cultures should not be portrayed merely as suffering victims or heroic rebels but also as "agents of negotiations who embraced certain aspects of official norms while resisting others" (Ko, Haboush, and Piggott, 2003, p. 1).

This perspective also applies to the experiences of women in Japan's new religions. The new religions are sustained by their women memberships. These women are commonly represented as a troubled category, and new religions generally teach them to step back and humble themselves in order to achieve this-worldly benefits. Such strategies religiously sanction traditional, existing gender roles and therefore do not lead to an amendment of gender role assignments.

Helen Hardacre (1984) terms these "strategies of weakness" by women who are economically dependent upon male householders. Hardacre further asserts that features of gender ideology found in fundamentalist religion also exist in such Japanese new religions as Reiyūkai and Seichō-no-Ie. These religions take a "characteristically conservative stance in regard to family, gender, and interpersonal relations" that she finds analogous, in its sexual discrimination, to fundamentalist religion, which places women in positions subservient to men and forces them to be self-sacrificing (Hardacre, 1994, pp. 113, 119). However, this generalization is countered by newer studies. Women in the new religions have adopted a strategy of working from traditional domestic roles sanctioned by their religions and may also appear to lack critical attitudes toward the oppressed positions assigned them. Further studies, however, expose the error of concluding that these women simply accede to submissive positions in male-controlled institutions without taking any interest in criticizing or reforming their religious communities (Usui, 2000, 2003).

Usui Atsuko argues against a conventional view that sees women in new religions as a special category in modern society dealing with some kind of problem caused by their disadvantageous and relatively deprived social standing. To depict women in new religions as supporting male-dominance ideology in order to compensate for their feelings of deprivation, Usui says, leads to the experiences of these women being erased (Usui, 2003, pp. 221–222). She describes religious groups that emphasize the development of psychic or spiritual powers without essentializing gender categories, presenting these as instances of how, even in new religions, traditional gender ideology does not lead to the exclusion of women's religious experience.

As this implies, the experiences of women in the new religions are characterized by diversity. It may be difficult to claim agency by self-assertion in a context like religion, where self-transcendence is valued and emphasis is placed on new communal groups based on self-transcendent relationships. Nevertheless, future researchers would do well to conduct detailed fieldwork while attending to the agency of female believers. Theories relating to women's agency will no doubt require refinement. It is necessary to consider, for example, how women are able to enact values traditionally associated with femaleness without succumbing to their own subordination. This is not to counter the conventional model of victimized women by reifying exceptional, heroic figures in history, needless to say.

Throughout Japanese religious history, women's religious roles have been inextricable from belief in the "spiritual power of women." This was brought to light with the publication of *Imo no chikara* (Women's power) in 1940 by Yanagita Kunio, the founder of Japanese folklore studies. Yanagita viewed women as innately possessing a mystical spiritual power that originated in their reproductive capability. He believed that, by virtue of "female-specific physiology and emotional nature," women possessed various religious abilities. Carmen Blacker (1975) describes female shamanic practitioners who fit this view.

Critics point out, however, that Yanagita's view of women's spiritual endowment actually obscured discriminatory practices against them. They criticize Yanagita for imposing the view, based on biological essentialism, that women's spiritual power is inherent, natural, and universal in all women. In other words, Yanagita, who identified that mystical power with women's unique reproductive function, is indicted for essentialist views of female gender (Kawahashi, forthcoming [a]). Tanaka Takako shows how Yanagita excessively emphasizes women's reproductive power, which is linked with worship of female deities. Used uncritically, she states, this approach risks generating the facile fantasy that all women are worshipped as goddesses (Tanaka, 1996, p. 182).

Kuraishi Atsuko (1995) also criticizes Yanagita and other male folklorists for overemphasizing women's spiritual power. Although Yanagita writes that "in the past, the women in each household invariably served the deities, and it appears that the wisest among the women was the most superior priestess [*miko*]," he does not discuss specifically how ordinary housewives functioned as priestesses in their households (Yanagita, 1990, p. 25). According to Kuraishi, Yanagita's notion conveys his image of the ideal housewife. Citing Yanagita's statement that "women must make it their first precept to do everything possible to take care of the home, bear and rear good children, and never fail in performance of the memorial rituals for the ancestors," Kuraishi suggests that Yanagita's actual motive here was to turn women into the reservoir of Japanese traditions (Kuraishi, 1995, pp. 94–97).

The research done by Yoshie Akiko (1996) is important for understanding the ritual roles of women in Japanese religious history and their relationships to male ritual specialists. Contrary to Yanagita, who claimed that ritual observances were intrinsically the unique province of women, Yoshie points out that this cannot be verified throughout history and stresses that ancient rituals were performed by women and men acting together. Yoshie explains that the sexual union of women and men was considered an important aspect of ritual, and rituals for fertility were sustained by faith in the primal power of such sexual union (Yoshie, 1996, p. 20). Moreover, as she points out, women's ritual participation in this kind of sexual practice raises the possibility of a connection with the crucial role women played in agricultural labor. Consequently, as Yoshie suggests, the dramatic advances in farming technology and the structural changes in agriculture that took place toward the end of Japan's medieval period conclusively depreciated the significance of women's specific functions in the labor of farming and other such endeavors. At the same time, the practice of invoking fertility by means of sexual ritual also lost its importance (Yoshie, 1996, pp. 250–251).

It would, of course, be a mistake to think that Japan's folk religious tradition uniformly oppressed women, denying them opportunities to participate in religious activities or activate their spiritual nature. It would also be a mistake, however, to interpret the interaction between women and religion entirely within the framework of "women's power" or the "supernatural endowment of women," ignoring the locality and the particularized contexts of individual experience.

Okinawa, as one such context, has received increasing attention. Situated midway between Kyushu and Taiwan, Okinawa is Japan's southernmost prefecture, and Okinawan religion has been largely treated as a subset of Japanese religion. Yanagita, for example, derived his thesis of "women's power" from Okinawa. He actually borrowed this key term, which he used to describe indigenous Japanese beliefs, from the Okinawan context, thus fostering an illusory notion of Okinawa as representative of Japan's ancient past. Subsequent studies, however, have highlighted the distinctive gendered nature of Okinawan religious culture and its allocation of authority to females. These studies have also recognized Okinawa's value in world religious history. The fact is that in Okinawa, unlike the Japanese mainland, it is an everyday occurrence for housewives to act as priestesses, praying to the *hinukan* hearth deity enshrined in the kitchen to appeal for the family's well-being and happiness. Women nearly monopolized priest-like roles in village communities and kin groups and even at the state level during the time of the Ryukyu kingdom, which lasted until 1879. The Okinawan belief in *onarigami*, where sisters become the spiritual guardians of their brothers, is another characteristic distinguishing Okinawan from Japanese culture (Kawahashi, 2000; Wacker, 2003). Also unlike the Japanese mainland, Okinawa has almost no pollution beliefs associated with women, who are thus not excluded as unclean from ritual sites.

FEMALE GENDER AND RITUAL UNCLEANNESS IN JAPANESE RELIGIOUS CULTURE. While women were seen in Japanese religious history as possessors of spiritual power, there was also a view that women are polluted and must be kept apart from sacred things. Shintō notions of women's pollution, for example, are discussed in Yusa Michiko (1994). These are implicated in *nyonin kinsei* and *nyonin kekkai. Nyonin kinsei* is the practice of forbidding women to enter, reside, or perform religious practice in temples, shrines, sacred mountains, and ritual sites. *Nyonin kekkai* demarcates the boundary of a ritual space that women cannot enter. Some sacred mountains that traditionally upheld *nyonin kekkai* have been opened to women, while others, such as Mount Ōmine in Nara, maintain the exclusion. This is the subject of ongoing dispute, as demonstrated, for example, by a signature drive in 2004 demanding the lifting of *nyonin kinsei* at Mount Ōmine. Suzuki Masataka (2002) acknowledges criticism of *nyonin kinsei* as discriminatory, maintaining that his stance is not to condemn the practice but to clarify the processes whereby it came into being and to delineate its changes, if any (Suzuki, 2002, p. 4). Suzuki seems to be distancing himself from the polarization in accounts of *nyonin kinsei* as either discriminatory or religiously meaningful. Indeed, some suggest *nyonin kinsei* is an important ritual mechanism for male religious practitioners to acquire spiritual power. Yet the argument that sacred mountains had to be sealed off from women for the sake of male acquisition of spiritual power naturally raises the question of why men took priority over women. Ushiyama Yoshiyuki (1996), examining this problem as a Buddhist historian, identifies three basic reasons for the origination of *nyonin kinsei*: (1) the notion of women's blood pollution; (2) adherence to Buddhist precepts; and (3) the disdain shown to women in Buddhist scriptures. Ushiyama holds that while conventional accounts overemphasize pollution, the focus should instead be on the Buddhist precept against sexual indulgence, which is applicable to both genders, and suggests that the notion of blood pollution was a later development (Ushiyama, 1996, pp. 75–78).

In any event, researchers must attend not only to the logic and history underlying the practice but also to the perception of women themselves vis-à-vis the practice. It is necessary to examine how the perpetual or temporary exclusion of woman from a locus of cultural value is implicated in the situations of women in the early twenty-first century.

Another important issue in interactions between religion and gender in Japan is *mizuko kuyō* (memorial rituals for aborted fetuses and miscarried or stillborn babies), interpretation of which has occasioned various exchanges among researchers (Kawahashi, forthcoming [b]). The study of gender issues in Japanese religion, as in other traditions, must be positioned within a dialectic between research to refine existing theories of gender and feminism on the one hand and thoroughgoing fieldwork and rereading of historical texts on the other. It must also take into account contemporary maneuvers by Japanese women (and men) to reform religious communities as well as influences on Japanese society at large from religions that have been changed by feminist thought.

REFORM MOVEMENTS. One example is a women's movement that formed in Japanese Buddhist circles during the 1990s (Kawahashi, 2003). This is a diverse group that includes, among others, wives of male priests, female priests (nuns), women who are a combination of both, and women who do not belong to any particular Buddhist order. Their project is to amplify the voice of women in the Buddhist community by a variety of means, including workshops and the publication of workshop findings. They also aim to form networks across sectarian boundaries for information exchange. They seek, by means of women's participation, to transform present-day Buddhism to provide gender equality. The commitment of these women extends beyond the boundaries of any particular school. They envision a new Buddhism that empowers the women of the early twenty-first century, and their project necessitates reinterpretation of conventional, male-centered Buddhist history and doctrine in light of their own experiences.

These women, who find it natural to resist gender-discriminatory constructions, are building a fuller awareness of how patriarchal Buddhist orders have thwarted women's realization of their own religiosity. This is not to say that Buddhism is a primary cause of Japanese patriarchal structures, nor does their criticism make such a claim. This project seeks rather to find truths in Buddhism that point a way to freedom for women, and this is their rationale for redirecting Buddhism toward affirmation of women's experiences in their own life context.

The discipline of religious studies remains rather unaware of its habit of reducing other religious traditions to fit into Western categories. It is important to recognize, however, that the rise of non-Western feminism makes it necessary to consider feminisms in the plural. Researchers who categorize Japanese women as silenced victims of patriarchy and their religious experiences as strategies of the weak will be called on to be reflexively aware and critical of whether their own interpretations are imposing a Western (or some other) agenda on their subject. At the same time, the religious world in Japan must no longer dismiss the study of gender issues in Japanese religions as a problem for women, and therefore secondary, but instead improve the quality of researchers and raise the level of work in the field through institutional reform.

BIBLIOGRAPHY

Blacker, Carmen. *The Catalpa Bow: A Study of Shamanistic Practices in Japan.* London, 1975; 3d ed., Richmond, U.K., 1999. Classic wide-ranging description of shamanic practitioners in Japanese religious history.

Faure, Bernard. *The Power of Denial: Buddhism, Purity, and Gender.* Princeton, N.J., 2003. Multifaceted examination of whether Buddhism represents liberation for women or limitation, stressing diverse Buddhist notions of women's gender and sexuality.

Hardacre, Helen. *Lay Buddhism in Contemporary Japan: Reiyūkai Kyōdan.* Princeton, N.J., 1984. A study of Buddhist-based new religions by prominent Western researcher on Japanese new religions and women, based on fieldwork in the operation and organization of those religions.

Hardacre, Helen. "Japanese New Religions: Profiles in Gender." In *Fundamentalism and Gender*, edited by John Stratton Hawley. Oxford, 1994. An examination of gender in relation to Japanese new religions, proposing similarity between them and fundamentalist religions.

Katsuura Noriko. *Kodai-chūsei no josei to bukkyō.* Kyoto, Japan, 2003. General account of the roles of priests and nuns and men's and women's beliefs from ancient to medieval periods; essential reading on problems of convents in particular.

Kawahashi Noriko. "Review Article: Religion, Gender, and Okinawan Studies." *Asian Folklore Studies* 59 (2000): 301–311. This review of gender studies in Okinawan religious studies argues that Susan Sered's *Women of the Sacred Groves* (1999) has serious problems and so must be read critically.

Kawahashi Noriko. "Feminist Buddhism as Praxis: Women in Traditional Buddhism." *Japanese Journal of Religious Studies* 30, nos. 3–4 (2003): 291–313.

Kawahashi Noriko. "Japanese Folk Religion and Its Contemporary Issues." In *Companion to the Anthropology of Japan*, edited by Jennifer Robertson. Malden, Mass., forthcoming (a). An overview focusing on issues of folklore research and gender from postcolonialist perspectives.

Kawahashi Noriko. "Gender Issues in Japanese Religions." In *Nanzan Guide to Japanese Religions*, edited by Clark Chilson, Robert Kisala, Okuyama Michiaki, and Paul L. Swanson. Forthcoming (b). Review article that thematically discusses various gender issues in Japanese religious studies.

Kawahashi Noriko, and Kuroki Masako, eds. Special issue on Feminism and Religion in Contemporary Japan. *Japanese Journal of Religious Studies* 30, nos. 3–4 (2003). This special issue examines effects of gender studies and feminism on Japanese Buddhism, Christianity, and new religions and introduces feminist research on religion in Japan. Combined and contrasted with another *Japanese Journal of Religious Studies* special issue (Nakamura Kyoko, ed., *Women and Religion in Japan, Japanese Journal of Religious Studies* 10, nos. 2–3[1983]), it provides an overview of the two intervening decades of gender research in Japanese religion and represents a groundbreaking effort in this field.

King, Ursula. "Is There a Future for Religious Studies as We Know It? Some Postmodern, Feminist, and Spiritual Challenges." *Journal of the American Academy of Religion* 70, no. 2 (2002): 365–388. Argues for the importance of postmodernism and gender studies in the changing discipline of religious studies by a European pioneer of religion and gender studies.

Ko, Dorothy, Jahyun Kim Haboush, and Joan R. Piggott, eds. *Women and Confucian Cultures in Premodern China, Korea, and Japan.* Berkeley, Calif., 2003. An anthology that reassesses the position and significance of women and Confucian traditions and modifies former stereotypes of women.

Kuraishi Atsuko. *Yanagita Kunio to Joseikan.* Tokyo, 1995. Yanagita's views of women, especially studies of housewives, are critically examined from the perspective of a woman folklorist.

Kwon Yung-Hee. *Songs to Make the Dust Dance: The Ryōjin Hisho of Twelfth-Century Japan.* Berkeley, Calif., 1994.

Nakamura Kyoko. *Miraculous Stories from the Japanese Buddhist Tradition.* Cambridge, Mass., 1973. An examination of ancient Japanese Buddhist faith, centered on the classical *Nihon ryōiki* collection of didactic tales, by a pioneer of women's studies and religion in Japan.

Ōgoshi Aiko. *Josei to shūkyō.* Tokyo, 1997. An introductory work by a polemicist on Japanese feminism and religion; discusses subordination, abuse of women in religious history, and the need for feminism.

Ooms, Emily. *Women and Millenarian Protest in Meiji Japan: Deguchi Nao and Omotokyō.* Ithaca, N.Y., 1993.

Ruch, Barbara. *Engendering Faith: Women and Buddhism in Premodern Japan.* Ann Arbor, Mich., 2002. Groundbreaking collaborative collection of twenty studies by Japanese and Western scholars in this neglected area of Japanese cultural history.

Suzuki Masataka. *Nyonin kinsei.* Tokyo, 2002. An overview that provides the intellectual background for the origin and practice of *nyonin kinsei*, explicated in the broad context of Shugendō and Buddhism.

Tanaka Takako. *Seinaru onna.* Tokyo, 1996. A reexamination of former stereotypes of women in classical Japanese literature from a gender perspective.

Ushiyama Yoshiyuki. "Nyonin kinsei." In *Nihon no Bukkyō* 6, edited by Nihon Bukkyō Kenkyūkai. Tokyo, 1996. A study going beyond conventional views of *nyonin kinsei* by a scholar known for originality of research in Japanese Buddhism and women.

Usui Atsuko. "The Role of Women." In *Global Citizens: The Soka Gakkai Buddhist Movement in the World*, edited by David Machacek and Bryan Wilson. Oxford, 2000. A detailed discussion of religious experiences and activities in the women's organization of Sōka Gakkai.

Usui Atsuko. "Women's 'Experience' in New Religious Movements: The Case of Shinnyoen." *Japanese Journal of Religious Studies* 30, nos. 3–4 (2003): 217–241. A critical study of former views on women's position and significance in Japanese new religions, with a positive account of women's spiritual experience in Shinnyoen.

Wacker, Monika. *Onarigami: Die heilige Frau in Okinawa.* Frankfurt, Germany, 2000.

Wacker, Monika. "Onarigami—Holy Women in the Twentieth Century." *Japanese Journal of Religious Studies* 30, nos. 3–4 (2003): 339–359. A study tracing the history of the distinctive Okinawan belief in the spiritual superiority of women.

Yanagita Kunio. *Yanagita Kunio zenshū*, vols. 10–11. Tokyo, 1990. Includes *Imo no chikara*, *Fujo-kō*, and other core works of Yanagita folklore studies that attribute special spiritual power to women.

Yoshida Kazuhiko, Katsuura Noriko, and Nishiguchi Junko. *Nihonshi no naka no josei to bukkyō.* Tokyo, 1999. Foremost Japanese scholars examine issues of women and Buddhism from its arrival in Japan through the medieval period.

Yoshie Akiko. *Nihon kodai no saishi to josei.* Tokyo, 1996. Reevaluates previous research on women and ritual from a historical perspective.

Yusa Michiko. "Women in Shinto: Images Remembered." In *Religion and Women,* edited by Arvind Sharma, pp. 93–119. Albany, N.Y., 1994. A cogent, inclusive summary of women's position and significance in Shintō.

KAWAHASHI NORIKO (2005)
Translated from Japanese by Richard Peterson

GENDER AND RELIGION: GENDER AND JUDAISM

Feminist studies of gender and Judaism widely agree that, at least until the late 1970s, it is masculinity that has been almost exclusively generative of Judaism's authoritative religious and historical knowledge and leadership. Underpinning and perpetuating the secondary status of Jewish women are a male God, the male "founder," Abraham, and leader, Moses, a traditionally male rabbinical establishment historically subsequent to a hereditary male priesthood, and a male messiah in the times to come. Until the late twentieth century, most women (even those in relatively liberal circles) have known communal Judaism and Jewish thought from the perspective of the marginal other. Despite the existence of women of outstanding piety throughout Jewish history, and a very few instances of female scholars in the rabbinic and early modern periods particularly, women have not been the speaking subjects but the silent objects of Jewish discourse. They have not been the rabbinic commentators, decision makers, theologians, mystics, or philosophers. Matters concerning women have been discussed by male practitioners, usually in texts written by men and for men as problems or exceptions to what is normally the (masculine) case. The male Jew has been the normative Jew, and remains so in Orthodox communities. It is further arguable that recent change in the religious educational and devotional opportunities for Orthodox women is only to a degree and of a kind permitted by men within an essentially masculine dispensation.

JEWISH FEMINISM AND THE FEMINIST STUDY OF RELIGION. Judaism is founded on principles of justice and compassion that have driven social change through three millennia. It is therefore not surprising that the political impetus and methodological presupposition of the study of gender and Judaism have been loosely situated within the Jewish feminist movement and feminist criticism of intrareligious discrimination against Jewish women. The latter's foundational prophetic call that Judaism should institute an eleventh commandment—"Thou shalt not lessen the humanity of women"—that would be faithful to its own ethical judgment on the world remains as powerful a motivation today as it did when it was first articulated in 1979 by Cynthia Ozick.

Ozick's "eleventh commandment," which is intended more socially than theologically, nonetheless underpins all subsequent Jewish feminist theology. Jewish feminist theology is a critical theology that subjects Jewish texts, images, and practices to feminist analysis. In particular, it has been noted that biblical, rabbinic, and mystical Jewish theology includes images of the divine that are at least nominally feminine, such as Hochmah, Wisdom, and Shekhinah, the in-dwelling presence of God. The qabbalistic understanding of Shekhinah as a feminine element within God through whom God interacts with the world has recently been explored by Elliot Wolfson (1995). The mystical longing for a reunion of the male and the female elements within God has inspired Jewish feminists to envision the mending (*tikkun*) of history and of the cosmos itself. The more gender-neutral terms for God, such as *HaMakom* (the Place) and *HaShem* (the Name), also help to ground Jewish feminist theological reflection in the tradition. However, Judaism is a practical religion before it is a doctrinal religion, and therefore few Jewish women would ascribe a central place to theology in feminist Jewish Studies.

But Jewish feminism, like other feminisms, has a first as well as second wave period. After the rise of Jewish modernity in the early nineteenth century, the Reform movement's insistence on the freedom to choose the type and degree of one's Jewish commitment led to the creation of several types of Jewish feminism interconnected by their emphasis upon justice and relational values. Before the Holocaust, Jewish women's proto-feminist or first wave activism was channeled through political, educational, and welfare organizations that were often maternalist in character. The second wave Jewish feminism of the late 1960s was as much the result of disenchantment with early twentieth-century Jewish politics in the trade union, communist, and Zionist movements in Europe and North America and in the new settlements in Palestine, all of whose political radicalisms had largely failed to offer women the leadership roles their rhetoric of equality had seemed to promise them. By the end of the 1980s Jewish feminism had become a significant movement found across the spectrum of observance, bar that of the more closed communities of Ultra-Orthodoxy.

The different types of Jewish feminism fall into three categories. Jewish feminism within modern Orthodoxy seeks to adapt Jewish law to better serve women's interests, though only so far as Torah might permit; liberal Jewish feminism seeks equality with Jewish men through the ethical reform of tradition; and ultra-liberal or "postmodern" Jewish feminism offers a woman-centered approach (as in Gottlieb, 1995) that might include elements of the contemporary Goddess feminist spirituality considered to be historically continuous with ancient Israelite women's syncretistic practice. However, Judaism has tended to be a practical and social religion before it has been a speculative one and the view that Jewish feminist goals will be achieved by *halakhic* reform rather than through a revised or reformed theology has predominated.

By the end of the twentieth century, the study of gender and Judaism was no longer as politicized as it had been through the 1970s and 1980s by the Jewish feminist project. The question of whether Judaism either oppresses or liberates women had given way to the more nuanced study of gendered and intra-gendered difference. Two key insights have tempered the recent feminist study of gender and Judaism. The first of these is the recognition that Jewish women's experience is historically, socially, geographically and culturally diverse. Second is the observation that throughout the history of Judaism, women have led different types of authentically Jewish lives within and sometimes despite the constraints of their gender roles. Since what a young Jewish woman from London or New York may consider liberating may not be what an older Jewish woman from a Kurdish or Ethiopian Jewish community in Israel might consider liberating, the study of gender and Judaism has had to ask more nuanced questions of its subjects and no longer presumes to judge on behalf of other (non-academic) women whether Judaism is a source of fulfillment for them or not. Western religious detraditionalization also contextualizes the study of gender and Judaism. The spiritual "turn to the self" and the shift in late modern religious observance into what is effectively a lifestyle choice are reflected in feminist studies of Judaism that are concerned with decentralizing the position of canonical texts and studying the individual woman as an autonomous religious agent, defining and controlling the meanings of a Jewish life for herself.

Inevitably, studies in gender and Judaism have sought to correct Jewish scholarship's obliviousness to its own traditionally male perspective and have focused instead on the neglected particularities of women's experience of and representation in Judaism and Jewish culture. However, it is important to note, as Daniel Boyarin (1997) has done, that the interrelation between Jewish constructions of masculine and feminine roles, virtues, and symbols is a complex one, and it is not only popular anti-Semitic discourse that has "feminized" male Jews. Judaism in the post-biblical Diaspora presented an ideal Jewish male whose receptivity and orientation towards the family has challenged and continues to challenge Western assumptions of masculine dominance and aggression and which has made him an object of desire for Jewish women. The ideal male Ashkenazic Jew in the years before the establishment of the State of Israel and still in some Ultra-Orthodox circles today, while never effeminate, has been studious, otherworldly, and compassionate. Jewish masculinity is not traditionally defined economically by a man's being the main breadwinner or by macho physical prowess, but by the prestige of his religious scholarship. The people of Israel have also been feminized in being cast as God's (sometimes adulterous) wife. Conversely, it is widely argued that the Israeli establishment has legitimized its militarism by "feminizing" diasporic victims of persecution, especially survivors of Nazism, and defining the male Jew as the tough Israeli soldier—a secular reincarnation of the Israelite warrior of the biblical period.

JEWISH WOMEN'S HISTORY. Early Second Wave Jewish feminist historiography, in common with other such feminist historiographies, was something of an exercise in "contribution" history whose purpose was to rescue exceptional Jewish women's achievements from undeserved obscurity. Two such women who have become relatively well-known by these means are the nineteenth-century Hasidic female *tsaddiq* (a Hasidic leader noted for piety and learning) Hannah Rachel Verbermacher (also known as the Maid of Ludmir) and Regina Jonas, who in 1935, before her death in Auschwitz, was privately ordained as a Reform rabbi. Gradually, however, Jewish feminist historiography has yielded a sense not only of the contributions of women but also of the precedent and diversity of their experience, enabling scholars to question received periodizations of Jewish history and to redraw the boundaries of Jewish tradition.

The historiography of Jewish women begins with that of the biblical period. The picture that emerges from a wealth of popular and scholarly publications on the historical and literary roles of women in the Hebrew Bible is a mixed one of female vulnerability, oppression, rivalry, deceit, courage, loyalty, and wit. The picture changes over time as monarchical government replaces the political dispensation of ancient Israel around 1050 BCE. In some narratives, the Bible suggests that women in ancient Israel could, even if only exceptionally, enjoy the roles of prophet (such as Miriam in *Exodus* 15:20, Huldah in *2 Kings* 22:14, and Noadiah in *Nehemiah* 6:14); judge, prophet, and military leader (such as Deborah in *Judges* 4–5); and wise women (such as the "witch" of En-Dor in *1 Samuel* 28:3–25). The bonds of loyalty between women are poignantly expressed in *Ruth* 1:16–19, and the power of sisterly solidarity in the story of the daughters of Zelophehad (*Numbers* 27). Yet other narratives present highly sexualized images of female power as seductive rather than authoritative, as in the story of Jael in *Judges* 4:17–22 and in the stories of the matriarchs, where women are the biological rather than religio-political movers of Jewish redemption history and the narrative emphasis is on the birth and lineage of sons, not daughters.

Rather differently, scholars on the Jewish academic and spiritual left have used biblical texts and archaeological studies of the ancient Middle East to show that Israelite religious practice—especially that of women who were gradually excluded from the public cult of Yahweh during the monarchical period—was syncretistic and accommodated the local goddess cult of Asherah (see *2 Kings* 23:7). This body of research has funded feminist theological moves towards more gender-inclusive models of the Jewish God.

In its study of the post-biblical period, Jewish feminist historiography, like Jewish feminist anthropology, has challenged the normativity and centrality of *halakhic* Judaism in androcentric Jewish studies by noting the many local exceptions to its rule. Despite periods of intense persecution and ghettoization, Jewish women's lives have been led in complex interaction with non-Jewish religious and cultural communities. Ross Kraemer, for example, has argued that although Hellenization is generally regarded by Jewish historians in a negative light, diasporic Jewish communities in this era may have been less sexually segregated than later ones and may have offered (elite) women more access to public life than those more closely regulated by rabbinic law. Bernadette Brooten's now classic research into Greek and Latin inscriptions (1982) suggesting that women held leadership positions in late antiquity has also fuelled the argument that the legislation of gender roles in rabbinic law and custom has not necessarily prevailed in all parts and periods of the Jewish world. More generally, since Jewish studies has privileged the study of formal, communal masculine practice over female religious practice, feminist historians such as Chava Weissler (1998) have attended to how women have effectively integrated their ordinary relational and practical concerns with their spirituality and messianic hopes.

The study of gender and the Holocaust has been gaining momentum and prominence since the mid 1980s. Feminist historians have shown that the "Final Solution" was not gender-blind; women's gender-specific experience of the Holocaust cannot be subsumed into that of men. Without in any sense ranking women's suffering above men's, feminist historians such as Joan Ringelheim and Myrna Goldenberg were among the first to ask how Nazism placed Jewish women in "double jeopardy" as objects of both its anti-Semitism and its misogyny so that they endured, in Myrna Goldenberg's well-known phrase, "different horrors in the same hell." As mothers of future Jewish generations and less adaptable to the grueling physical requirements of slave labor than men, women and their children were the immediate targets of the Nazi genocide. Although women's chances of survival were generally greater in the early years of the Holocaust, by 1942 women were more likely than men to be deported to the death camps where, especially if pregnant or accompanied by children, women were also more likely than men to be selected for immediate death. Diverse recent studies (such as those of Nechama Tec [2003] and Melissa Raphael [2003]) have explored the ethical, spiritual, and theological dimensions of women's resistance to dehumanization through care of others during the Holocaust.

THE ROLE AND STATUS OF WOMEN IN RABBINIC JUDAISM. The corpus of rabbinic law and ethics in the Mishnah and, later, the Talmud, was complete by approximately 700 CE. This literature is not of merely antiquarian interest: through continual reinterpretation it has continued to provide a religious framework that regulates, if to widely varying degrees, the familial, economic, and social life of the whole Jewish community other than that of secular Jewry.

Rabbinic Judaism's understanding of the female role as one centered around the marital home can be summarized in the three positive commandments (sometimes regarded as punitive reminders of Eve's disobedience) that remain women's gender-specific obligations in Orthodox Judaism today. These are to light the Sabbath candles (*nerot*), to separate and burn a portion of the dough when baking the Sabbath loaf (*hallah*), and to observe the laws of menstrual or family purity that regulate physical contact between husbands and wives (*niddah*). Women are also obligated to observe the Sabbath, the dietary laws, and all other *halakhic* prohibitions.

There is no doubt that rabbinic literature contains misogynistic texts that enumerate women's supposed vices, derogate them as sources of sexual temptation and menstrual impurity, classify them as subordinated, immature, or defective others, and show a marked preference for the birth of sons over daughters. In rabbinic Judaism, women's testimony is generally inadmissible in a religious court as it is classed with, among others, that of minors, slaves, and the deaf and the blind. (Though since the 1951 Equality of Women's Rights Act in Israel, at least there has been some easing of the disqualification under Israeli civil law.)

Nonetheless, Judith Romney Wegner (1994) has shown that the late second-century Mishnah does not accord the same status to women throughout their lives, and it distinguishes between dependent girls and wives and relatively autonomous women, the latter being those divorcees, widows, and unmarried adult daughters who could control their property and arrange their own marriages, relatively free of male authority. While rabbinic patriarchy subordinates women to men and has on this and other grounds been rejected by liberal Jews as archaic, rabbinic Judaism is, then, more flexible than might be immediately apparent.

Admittedly on its own terms, rabbinic law respects the practical, emotional, and embodied interests of women and accords them rights to finance, medical care, and sexual satisfaction. Most notably, rabbinic law adjusted the more rudimentary biblical law so as to better protect women's interests. The classic case of a Western rabbinic ruling that broke with biblical and previous rabbinic law (a *takkanah*) was the ban on polygyny (actually already sharply in decline) ascribed to Rabbi Gershom ben Yehudah in the tenth century CE. (Orthodox feminism regards this *takkanah* as a precedent for sexually egalitarian proposals that appear to abrogate the law.) Other *takkanot* ascribed to Gershom ben Yehudah also tempered the inequalities of biblical marital practice, especially arbitrary divorce against a woman's will and without financial settlement. The rabbis were also generally opposed to wife-beating and permitted contraception to wives in certain medical circumstances. Although "acquired" from their fathers, wives are not, under rabbinic law, the purchased property of husbands; it is rather that marriage makes them unavailable to other men. Although, to this day, Orthodox Jewish law gives men alone the right to initiate divorce since it was they who have created the marriage bond, the *ketubah* or marriage "contract" describes a husband's financial and other duties to his wife. The case of the *agunah* or "anchored" woman who no longer lives with a husband who will not grant her a divorce is, however, an inequality to which some Orthodox rabbis have sought to provide solutions and against which feminists are still campaigning.

Generally speaking, the degree to which legal alleviation of sexual discrimination is permissible varies according to whether the community understands the whole Torah—written and oral—as the direct ordination and self-revelation of God (the Orthodox and especially Ultra-Orthodox view) or as divinely inspired but historically conditioned and of human authorship (the Reform perspective).

The Role and Status of Women in Orthodoxy. Orthodoxy—itself a spectrum of observance and cultural orientation—broadly continues to resist any construal of gender equality other than that summarized by the apologetic formulation "equal but different." Largely excluded from active participation in public ritual, women's traditional role is a supporting, enabling one (see BT Berakhot, 17a). Men and women's religious practice and orientation is considered complementary. Women are, by custom, not law, responsible for nurturing a sense of Jewishness in young children and for the infusion of a Jewish atmosphere and peace (*shalom bayit*) into the home. (Indeed, sociologists have sometimes argued that Jewish women's emotional and practical investment in family identity and continuity has made them rather less susceptible to secularization and assimilation than men.)

With certain important exceptions, such as eating unleavened bread at Pesach or reading the Megillah at the festival of Purim, Orthodoxy exempts women from those positive commandments whose observance is ordained for a specific time. So, for example, a woman is obligated to pray, but not at the times set for certain prayers and services. A woman's presence cannot be counted towards the quorum of ten men required for communal prayer. The classic rationale for such gendered exemptions or cultural prohibitions-in-effect can be either pragmatic or theological. Pragmatically, since women's first duties are to the welfare of husbands and children, the performance of religious duties cannot also be expected of them. Theologically, appeal may be made to the divine ordination of the gendered economy. Critics, however, have claimed that women's exemption from most time-bound positive commandments effectively privatizes a woman's religious life and subordinates her spirituality to the material needs of others. That women have also been strongly discouraged from the observance of certain commandments, such as those of religious study, that are not time-bound has also been questioned.

In response to such criticism, Orthodox commentators point out that after the destruction of the Second Temple in 70 CE, Jewish sacred space relocated from the Temple to the home, study house, and synagogue. As a locus of the holy, the post-biblical home has sacralized a woman's religio-domestic labor, namely the sustenance of relationships with her husband and children, her maintenance of a kosher kitchen, and her preparation for the Sabbath and other home-based religious festivals. Orthodox women's lives are, arguably, comprehensively spiritualized by their observance of *halakhah* (daily law) since this regulates rather than denigrates bodily needs and appetites.

Although regarded with skepticism by most feminists as a compensatory rhetorical strategy that safeguards male dominance and impoverishes Jewish women's religious lives, Ultra-Orthodox apologetics also consider women to be on a higher and more intuitive spiritual plane than men who must therefore shoulder a greater burden of religious duty in order to approach God. After the manner of the virtuous, tireless woman *(eshet chayil)* of *Proverbs* 31, wives are idealized or—from the Ultra-Orthodox perspective—esteemed as those whose "innate" spirituality needs no special training and allows them a more immediate relation to God.

While the requirements of feminine modesty (*tzniut*) may be interpreted by feminists as a means of controlling female sexuality, the traditional Jewish attitude toward sex is not prudish. While some periods of Jewish history have produced male devotional groups with ascetic tendencies, sexual abstinence plays no role in contemporary Jewish spirituality; celibacy is not considered vocational or meritorious, and men (not women) are commanded to procreate. In Hebrew, marriage (*kiddishin*) means sanctification, and marital sexuality is a sign and symbol of the covenant of love between God and Israel. Of course, Orthodox Judaism imposes clear moral restraints upon the sexual urge, and its satisfaction is exclusively heterosexual and marital. Nonetheless, pleasure is both legitimate and desirable. Men are obligated to satisfy the sexual needs of their wives. Indeed, the rabbinic laws of *onah* (women's sexual rights) schematize the husband's religious obligation to give regular sexual satisfaction to his wife. While he must never force himself upon her, she is entitled to sexual pleasure regardless of whether she is fertile, pregnant, or postmenopausal.

Only the most traditional of Orthodox Jewish women observe the laws of menstrual purity that require the physical separation, but not the seclusion, of women from men for roughly twelve days a month—as well as a period following the birth of a child (fourteen days followed by a further sixty-six days for a girl, and half of that—seven days plus thirty-three days—for a boy). While a boy child enters into the covenantal relation between God and the people of Israel by circumcision on the eighth day after birth, the birth of girl children is now usually celebrated in synagogue on her first Sabbath, though it is the father who recites the blessing of thanksgiving.

The laws of sexual segregation in worship intensified from the end of the third century of the common era and are still observed to varying degrees in Orthodox communities. Among the Ultra-Orthodox, there is also sexual segregation at communal celebrations that would involve the social mixing of men and women. While Judaism does not require the seclusion of women in the home (especially not in communities residing in non-Islamic countries), the vocation of Ultra-Orthodox women is largely confined to the rearing of large families and, in some cases, to paid work within the community where women may be employed to teach or care for young children. Orthodoxy does not necessarily confine women to the private sphere insofar as the customary equation of the private and domestic spheres does not straightforwardly apply to religious Jewish life. The domestic, familial sphere is not that of women alone: men practice Judaism in the domestic sphere, as well as in the public spheres of worship and study. In Judaism, the private sphere is essentially the secular sphere of the individual, while it is the religio-communal sphere of ritual, congregational, and legal leadership that is the public one. This means that Orthodox Jewish women have historically undertaken paid work and conducted business in the secular public sphere since this is classed as a private transaction.

Perhaps what is most significant to the study of gender and Judaism is the gendered inequality of power signaled by the language of male permission in relation to change; Orthodox women remain the dependent objects of male rulings. For the foreseeable future at least, it seems unlikely that Orthodoxy will permit systemic change as that would entail no less than a reconfiguration of divinely ordained gender roles in the Jewish home and family that would be considered inimical to the revelation and spirit of biblical and rabbinic tradition.

The matter can be summarized as follows. On the one hand, the revitalization of Orthodoxy in resistance to secular modernity has seen the reinforcement of an ideology of traditional sexual complementarity and an emphasis on the role of the Jewish family in rebuilding the worldwide Jewish community after the Holocaust. As Lyn Davidman points out (1991), this re-inscription of gender difference has been strongly supported by Orthodox women who can find stability, security, identity, continuity, authenticity, and respect for motherhood and homemaking in conservative ideologies of Jewish femininity. On the other hand, and irrespective of the conflict between traditional and progressive Jews over the role of women in Judaism, concerns for the survival of Judaism have focused Orthodox attention on giving women just some of the communal roles and responsibilities the contemporary Western sexual-political climate would lead them to expect.

Gender and Jewish Education. As itself an act of worship, the study of Torah is integral, not supplementary, to Jewish practice. In post-biblical Judaism, where study of the Torah replaced cultic worship as the means of knowing and observing God's commandments, it has been the father's obligation to teach his son Torah. Just as women were not priests, so too they were not to be scholars. By custom rather than law, women were and are urged to induct children, especially girls, into the ambience and domestic practicalities of the tradition. Women and girls are exempt from the study of Torah on the grounds that women are exempt from acts that a father is obligated to undertake for his son, namely teaching him Torah (BT Kiddushin 29a). In fact, the Talmud records some disagreement over Rabbi Eli'ezer's somewhat extreme opinion that the education of girls unravels the meaning of Torah into nonsense or obscenity, and it records the names of several learned rabbinical wives and daughters, best known of whom was Beruriah, wife of Rabbi Me'ir of the second century CE.

The religious educational opportunities for girls and women are clearly not equal to men's. Yet the degree of gendered inequality has differed according to women's class, economic standing, geographical location, and historical period. Scholarly Jewish women in the wealthy Sephardic families of the early modern period were, for example, more numerous than those of affluent Ashkenazic families in central and eastern Europe who, as the centuries progressed, were more inclined to offer girls a high level of secular rather than religious education.

It is not only feminist criticism that has produced a widespread change in attitudes toward women's religious education across the spectrum of Jewish Orthodoxy. It is also recognized by Orthodoxy that arresting the widespread contemporary decline in Jewish observance and population is in part at least dependent on women's informed commitment. To prevent the influence of secular values (especially those of Jewish feminism, which is widely misread as a secular project), the end of the twentieth century saw Orthodoxy making new provision of role-specific religious education for women—one that was both a product and cause of Jewish women's increased historical, textual, and linguistic competence in Judaism. (Note though, that like Ultra-Orthodox men, Ultra-Orthodox women do not normally participate in secular higher education.)

Orthodoxy is now seeking to redress some of the gendered inequalities of opportunity in Jewish religious education, though not to remove them entirely. In contemporary Israel, the cultural and economic influence of American Jewry has encouraged the establishment of religious educational establishments offering Jewish women from all over the world opportunities to study to ever higher levels of *halakhic* competence and to train as advocates for other women in religious courts, particularly in cases of divorce. A more advanced Jewish education has also enabled women to conduct prayer services even if modesty requires those to be conducted only for other women. However, such services are still not permitted in synagogues in Great Britain and parts of the American Orthodox community. Women in Orthodox communities are also not called up to recite the blessings accompanying the chanting of a portion of the Torah or to read from the Torah itself, since that might suggest that the men of the community are not proficient to do so.

Reform and Conservative Movements. The religious emancipation of Jewish women in liberal Jewish communities was subsequent to the humanistic ethic of Haskalah (Jewish Enlightenment) and to the civic emancipation of Western European Jewry. Over time, women in Reform communities have come to enjoy equal access to positions of educational and synagogal leadership and full participation in Jewish rites of passage. Since 1972 in the United States and 1975 in Britain, women have been ordained as rabbis. In the United States, the Conservative movement—a middle way between Orthodoxy and Reform—has also gradually instituted the equality of women and men and has given women access to rabbinical training since 1983. However, Conservative Judaism has a greater concern for maintaining continuities with Jewish law, and its congregations vary in their attitude to change. Other than in the most progressive communities on the liberal spectrum, marriage and ordination are still refused to Jewish lesbians and gay men.

Sexist language has been either tempered or eliminated from liberal liturgies, though the evocation of the divine as "God-She" remains controversial in all but the alternative quarters of progressive Judaism. As well as giving women equal access to the rituals marking religious maturity (bar mitzvah for boys, bat mitzvah for girls) new rituals have been devised in Britain and the United States by women rabbis and others to change the self-image and consciousness of women. Such rituals solemnize gender-distinctive life-changing events—whether these be traumas such as mastectomy or miscarriage or celebrations such as menarche and childbirth—to which the tradition, so often concerned with the ownership and control of women's sexuality and reproductivity, has not previously attended. Despite such attention to female difference there has been some feminist concern that in gaining equality with men, Reform and Conservative Jewish women have become, in effect, honorary men, while men have not become honorary women. The most prominent leadership roles are also still most commonly held by men, partly in ecumenical deference to the Orthodox community, with whom Reform and Conservative Judaism wishes to maintain cooperation and dialogue.

BIBLIOGRAPHY

Adler, Rachel. *Engendering Judaism: An Inclusive Theology and Ethics.* Philadelphia, 1998. Offers strategies for practical re-readings of traditional Jewish texts, with an emphasis on the theological reformulation of Jewish law, liturgy, and sexual ethics.

Baskin, Judith, ed. *Jewish Women in Historical Perspective.* 2d ed. Detroit, Mich., 1998. A collection of essays exploring Jewish women's history within Jewish and non-Jewish cultural and intellectual milieus from the biblical period through to twentieth-century North America.

Biale, Rachel. *Women and Jewish Law.* New York, 1995. A now classic study of *halakhic* views of issues relating to women.

Boyarin, Daniel. *Unheroic Conduct: The Rise of Heterosexuality and the Invention of the Jewish Man.* Berkeley, Calif., 1997. Shows how the construction of Jewish masculinity counters Western gender stereotypes.

Brooten, Bernadette, J. *Women Leaders in the Ancient Synagogue: Inscriptional Evidence and Background Issues.* Chico, Calif., 1982.

Davidman, Lyn. *Tradition in a Rootless World: Women Turn to Orthodox Judaism.* Berkeley, Calif., 1991. Examines the appeal of Orthodoxy to contemporary American Jewish women.

El-Or, Tamar. *Educated and Ignorant: Ultra-Orthodox Jewish Women and Their World.* Boulder, Colo., and London, 1994. Argues that Ultra-Orthodox women's education is designed not to liberate women but to perpetuate deference to male authority.

El-Or, Tamar. *Next Year I Will Know More: Literacy and Identity Among Young Orthodox Women in Israel.* Detroit, Mich., 2002. Explores the feminist dynamic and socioreligious effect of the sharp increase in Judaic study among young women in Orthodox Zionist communities.

Fuchs, Esther. *Sexual Politics in the Biblical Narrative: Reading the Hebrew Bible as a Woman.* Sheffield, U.K., 2000. Explores how the biblical text legislates and authorizes women's subordination and secures the power and interests of men.

Goldenberg, Myrna. "Different Horrors, Same Hell: Women Remembering the Holocaust." In *Thinking the Unthinkable: Meanings of the Holocaust,* edited by Roger S. Gottlieb pp. 150–166. New York, 1990.

Goldman, Karla. *Beyond the Synagogue Gallery: Finding a Place for Women in American Judaism.* Cambridge, Mass., 2000.

Gottlieb, Lynn. *She Who Dwells Within: A Feminist Vision of a Renewed Judaism.* San Francisco, 1995.

Greenberg, Blu. *On Women and Judaism: A View from Tradition.* Philadelphia, 1981. An early and influential reconciliation of feminism and traditional Judaism.

Hauptman, Judith. *Rereading the Rabbis: A Woman's Voice.* Boulder, Colo., 1998. Acknowledging the patriarchal nature of Bible and Talmud, Hauptman argues that the Talmudic rabbis significantly improved the rights and status of women, particularly with regard to marriage and inheritance.

Heschel, Susannah, ed. *On Being a Jewish Feminist: A Reader.* New York, 1983. Includes texts that were pivotal in establishing a framework for second wave Jewish feminism.

Kraemer, Ross. S. "Jewish Women in the Diaspora World of Late Antiquity." In *Jewish Women in Historical Perspective,* edited by Judith R. Baskin, pp. 46–72. Detroit, Mich., 1991.

Lentin, Ronit. *Israel and the Daughters of Shoah: Reoccupying the Territories of Silence.* New York and Oxford, 2000. Examines how the State of Israel has affirmed its construction of nationhood by "feminizing" Holocaust victims and survivors.

Neusner, Jacob. *Androgynous Judaism: Masculine and Feminine in the Dual Torah.* Macon, Ga., 1993. Argues that while Torah is not sexually egalitarian it nonetheless valorizes female virtues as proper not only to women but also to the male relationship of subordination and obedience to God.

Ofer, Dalia, and Lenore J. Weitzman, eds. *Women in the Holocaust.* New Haven, Conn., and London, 1998. Interdisciplinary scholarly essays examining the gendered particularities of women's Holocaust experience in a number of different contexts.

Ozick, Cynthia. "Notes Towards Finding the Right Question." In *On Being A Jewish Feminist: A Reader,* edited by Susannah Heschel, pp. 120–151. New York, 1983.

Peskowitz, Miriam, and Laura Levitt, eds. *Judaism Since Gender.* New York, 1997. Engages the postmodern turn in studies of gender and Judaism.

Plaskow, Judith. *Standing Again at Sinai: Judaism from a Feminist Perspective.* New York, 1990. A now classic revisioning of Judaism from a non-Orthodox feminist perspective.

Raphael, Melissa. *The Female Face of God in Auschwitz: A Jewish Feminist Theology of the Holocaust.* London and New York, 2003. Renders Jewish women's Holocaust witness theologically audible by correlating their memoirs with a feminist reading of the post-Holocaust theological corpus and the wider Jewish tradition.

Ringelheim, Joan. "The Unethical and the Unspeakable: Women and the Holocaust." *Simon Wiesenthal Center Annual* (1984): 69–87. Ringelheim later substantially revised the views she expressed in this foundational paper.

Rittner, Carol, and John Roth, eds. *Different Voices: Women and the Holocaust.* New York, 1993. Includes methodological reflection, editorial commentary, and excerpts from the women's Holocaust memoir literature.

Rothschild, Sylvia, and Sybil Sheridan, eds. *Taking Up the Timbrel: The Challenge of Creating Ritual for Jewish Women Today.* London, 2000. Women rabbis transpose traditional Jewish liturgies into new political, biological, and emotional contexts, marking the women's experiences that have not previously been engaged by traditional prayer and ritual.

Ruttenberg, Danya, ed. *Yentl's Revenge: The Next Wave of Jewish Feminism.* Seattle, Wash., 2001. Young writers engage contemporary ecological, cultural, political, and medical issues from a "third wave" Jewish feminist perspective.

Schely Newman, Esther. *Our Lives Are But Stories: Narratives of Tunisian-Israeli Women.* Detroit, Mich., 2002. Offers theoretical reflection on the life stories of four Tunisian-Israeli women, usefully correcting the Ashkenazic focus of much of the study in gender and Judaism.

Shokeid, Moshe. *A Gay Synagogue in New York.* Philadelphia, 2003. An ethnography of Beth Simchat Torah in New York, the largest gay and lesbian synagogue in the United States.

Tec, Nechama. *Resilience and Courage: Women, Men, and the Holocaust.* New Haven, Conn., and London, 2003. Uses oral and other sources to study how gender shaped patterns of resistance among Jews in the ghettos, camps, and partisan groups.

Umansky, Ellen, and Dianne Ashton, eds. *Four Centuries of Jewish Women's Spirituality: A Sourcebook.* Boston, 1992. An anthology of historic and contemporary texts including Jewish women's rituals, prayers, diary entries, poems, and other forms of spiritual reflection.

Wegner, Judith Romney. *Chattel or Person? The Status of Women in the Mishnah.* New York, 1988. Crucial to our understanding of early Jewish patriarchy, Wegner observes that in some circumstances second-century Mishnaic Judaism regards unmarried adult women, such as divorcees and most widows, as full legal persons. However, on account of their sexual reproductivity, girls and married women are the property of, and subject to the jurisdiction of, fathers and husbands respectively.

Weissler, Chava. *Voices of the Matriarchs: Listening to the Prayers of Early Modern Jewish Women.* Boston, 1998.

Wolfson, Elliot. *Circle in the Square: Studies in the Use of Gender in Kabbalistic Symbolism.* Albany, N.Y., 1995.

MELISSA RAPHAEL (2005)

GENDER AND RELIGION: GENDER AND CHRISTIANITY

Christianity has always been a gendered tradition—as indeed have most religions—insofar as sexual difference has formed an organizing focus for its doctrines, practices, and institutions. This has been more evident in Catholic and Orthodox forms of Christianity than in Protestantism, but the gendered hierarchies that have prevailed in Christian institutions from the time of Saint Paul persisted largely unchallenged until the middle of the twentieth century. Since then churches have faced a widespread intellectual challenge to their understanding of gender, arising partly out of the influence of feminism but primarily generated by a significant number of women becoming academic theologians and biblical scholars for the first time in history. Rosemary Radford Ruether's pioneering work of feminist theology, *Sexism and God-Talk,* first published in 1983, asks, "Can a male savior save women?" (Ruether, 1993, p. 116).

As a growing number of feminist theologians and, more recently, gender theorists have developed ever more refined forms of analysis in their studies of Christian doctrine, history, spirituality, and ethics, Ruether's question opens into a complex landscape in which the sexed human body occupies a central but often veiled position, inviting both redemptive and critical readings of tradition. Elizabeth Schüssler Fiorenza's (1983) advocacy of "a hermeneutics of suspicion" has influenced two generations of biblical scholars whose increasingly nuanced methods of interpretation are transforming the ways in which biblical texts are understood and applied with regard to gender constructs and sexual relationships. Although Western in origin, these intellectual revolutions have impacted non-Western cultures, so the question of Christianity and gender has become one of far-reaching significance for the doctrines and practices of the churches worldwide.

However, feminist and gender studies have so far been more thorough in their analyses of femininity and womanhood than of masculinity and manhood, so much of what still passes for normative humanity in Christian texts and practices is in fact male humanity, misleadingly represented as the generic human being. Until this masculine particularity is acknowledged, the Christian understanding of the human condition will continue to be shaped by implicitly androcentric perspectives. Despite forty years of feminist scholarship, the theological establishment remains, for the most part, highly conservative, and perspectives informed by feminism or gender theory are either ignored or marginalized in the majority of theological curricula.

If traditional Christian beliefs and practices have been problematized by feminism and gender studies, the question also arises as to how far these academic debates reflect the concerns of people's daily lives as they seek to live out their Christian faith in different contexts. For many, traditional forms of Christianity provide a bulwark against what are perceived to be the corrosive effects of secularization and materialism on religious values, and this generates considerable resistance to feminism. Given that a majority of women worldwide continue to regard the family as their most significant area of responsibility and commitment, the Christian defense of the family might in many situations be an important factor in the struggle for gender justice. In other situations, however, Christian beliefs associated with marriage, motherhood, fertility, and sexuality define women too narrowly in terms of domestic roles and responsibilities, so Christian family values can be experienced as repressive in terms of gender justice and human flourishing. Such questions feed into the larger question about what is meant by "the full humanity of woman" and what kind of transformations of belief and practice are necessary for Christianity to create a spiritual and social environment in which both sexes are able to live out the belief that human beings, male and female, are made in the image of God and are called to participate in the creative activity of God in sustaining, healing, and shaping the world (Ruether, 1993, p. 18).

The phrase *gender and Christianity* therefore opens into a kaleidoscopic range of insights that is constantly refigured as new perspectives come into view. As the scholarship of gender becomes more critically refined, early feminist critiques of religious traditions are being supplanted by methods that seek greater sensitivity to questions of historical, cultural, sexual, racial, and economic diversity. There is also a growing attentiveness to issues of gender at the more conservative end of the Christian theological spectrum, so the study of gender, sexuality, and embodiment is by no means the exclusive preserve of feminist scholars. What follows then is a brief overview of a picture that is in an ongoing state of development, so summarizing general trends necessarily risks some misrepresentation of the individual lives and communities that make up the gendered dimensions of the Christian story.

Doctrinal and Social Perspectives. The Christian tradition has been marked by deep ambivalences with regard to the significance of human embodiment and gender in terms of both sexual and social relationships. Christianity has always affirmed the goodness of the material world, including the human body, as having been created by God and redeemed by Jesus Christ. However, Christianity has also tended to adopt a negative attitude toward the body in recognition of its susceptibility to suffering and death, which are associated with sin. The original goodness of creation is believed to have been distorted by the effects of humanity's rebellion against God, and thus the body is a site of particular struggle and conflict in the Christian's desire to be reconciled to God. In terms of sexuality this has become deeply bound up with issues of temptation, sin, and fallenness, symbolically associated with Eve's temptation in the Garden of Eden, so a great deal of Christian anxiety has been focused on human sexuality in general and female sexuality in particular. Given the opaque and sometimes inscrutable relationship between gender constructs and sexual embodiment, this makes the task of unraveling Christian beliefs about gender particularly difficult, because embedded deep within these one often encounters a cluster of unacknowledged fears to do with the female body. In this Christianity may not be different from many other religions, but the Christian doctrines of the incarnation of Christ and the resurrection of the body mean that, in theory at least, this should be the most body-affirming of all religions. That its legacy has been more ambiguous is at least partly bound up with the ongoing failure of some parts of the Christian tradition to fully incorporate human sexuality into their vision of the goodness of creation.

The Christian understanding of human nature is premised on a belief in the dignity and equality of every human being in the eyes of God, and the Christian community of the baptized has been represented as one in which all divisions are overcome. Thus in his Letter to the Galatians, Paul writes, "There is no longer Jew or Greek, there is no longer slave or free, there is no longer male and female; for all of you are one in Christ Jesus" (*Gal.* 3:28). However, for most of Christian history women have occupied positions of subordination to men, being subject to restrictions that have precluded the full participation of both sexes in the formation of Christian faith and practice.

The New Testament texts and Apocryphal literature of the first three centuries attest to a struggle by male authority figures to control and delineate the role of women in Christian life and worship, suggesting a trend toward women holding positions of authority in some parts of the early church and a resistance to this trend in other parts. Whatever equality women may have enjoyed in these early centuries, however, their roles soon became circumscribed within authority structures modeled on the social order of imperial Rome. As a result, the institutions, beliefs, and practices of the Christian tradition have been constructed around the values of a patriarchal hierarchy, in which the authority of a Father-God is mediated through descending ranks of paternal leadership, from kings, princes, and bishops to lords, leaders, husbands, and fathers. Some feminist theologians argue that this patriarchal structure is consolidated and perpetuated in the centrality of the Father-Son relationship to the Christian understanding of Jesus as the Son of God.

However, this largely homogenous master narrative needs to be understood in relation to the diverse contexts that have allowed a plurality of beliefs, devotions, and relationships to flourish within Christian traditions. If gendered hierarchies have been carefully preserved in the texts and institutions of the church, attentiveness to the practices of Christianity suggests a more complex reality of shifting sexual relationships and values. For example, Christian men whose writings express misogynistic ideas have often enjoyed close relationships with women in the roles of spiritual director, confessor, and friend, suggesting a level of social and sexual interaction that may not be reflected in the textual legacy. Women such as Teresa of Ávila (1515–1582), whose writings suggest the internalization of sexual stereotypes, often used these as rhetorical devices to challenge male authority figures. Moreover, although the body has always been more determinative for women than for men and female embodiment continues to function as a basis for exclusion rather than inclusion, for example, with regard to ordination in the Roman Catholic and Orthodox Churches, gender was understood symbolically rather than biologically in the premodern church. So in different contexts maternal or feminine characteristics have been attributed to men and masculine characteristics to women to express certain social functions or personal characteristics. Moreover theological relationships between God, creation, Christ, the church, and Mary are described in a range of nuptial and familial metaphors and analogies, so it is impossible to identify any straightforward binary opposition between male and female when one analyzes the dynamics of Christian gender symbolism.

The separation between Eastern and Western Christianity since the eleventh century has also produced different concepts of the significance of gender. The Orthodox Church, influenced by thinkers such as Origen (c. 185–254) and Gregory of Nyssa (c. 335–c. 395), holds that matter, including the sexual human body, is a secondary feature of creation. Sexual embodiment is contingent upon the coming of death into the world and the need for procreation, so sexual difference does not have ontological significance and will not be a feature of the resurrected person. From the time of Augustine (345–430), the Roman Catholic tradition has understood the material world, including the sexed human body, as part of the original goodness of creation and therefore as ontologically significant. The resurrected body will be male or female, just as it was in the beginning. In the Orthodox Church, the Virgin Mary represents an iconic and mystical maternal presence at the heart of liturgy and prayer, symbolizing both awe and compassion but dissociated from later Western ideas of maternal femininity. Catholic representations of Mary have been influenced by cultural stereotypes associated with humanism, the Renaissance, and Romanticism, so that they have become heavily invested with changing ideals of motherhood and femininity. These symbolic representations both reflect and shape social values and meanings, so many different ways of seeing and relating are encoded within them in terms of gender, society, and doctrine. Since the Reformation, the increasing diversification of Christianity has led to multiple ways of understanding gender relations. Whereas the mainstream Protestant denominations have tended to uphold traditional gender distinctions and hierarchies, at least until the latter part of the twentieth century, movements such as Quakerism have been more egalitarian in their ideas and practices. Protestantism has by and large placed less emphasis on the symbolic or philosophical significance of sexuality, and therefore its representation of sexual difference has been expressed more in biblical and moral terms than in terms of eschatology, ontology, and symbolism.

The Bible and the Early Church. The Bible is a necessary but not a sufficient starting point for any study of Christianity and gender. From as early as the first century CE the Christian belief that God had become human in Jesus Christ was interpreted according to the symbolism of the *Genesis* narrative of creation and the Fall. This means that the story of Adam and Eve in *Genesis* 1–3 has had a formative influence on Christian beliefs about the divine image and the relationship between the sexes, understood both in terms of the original relationship among God, nature, woman, and man and in terms of the fall and its aftermath.

Christ is described as the Second Adam in the Pauline epistles, and by the end of the first century this imagery had been extended to include the Virgin Mary as the New Eve in the writings of Justin Martyr (c. 100–165 CE) and Irenaeus, bishop of Lyons (c. 130–200 CE). According to this interpretation, just as the first woman, Eve, brought death to the human race by disobeying God and eating the forbidden fruit, so the New Eve, first woman of the new creation in Christ, brought life to the human race by obeying God by agreeing to become the mother of the savior, Jesus Christ. This identification of Mary with Eve became invested with the language of sexuality, seduction, and sin associated with Eve and purity, obedience, and grace associated with Mary in a way that introduced a dualistic tendency into the Christian understanding of woman. In addition the Christian belief that patriarchal hierarchies are ordained by God for the good ordering of society has been justified through an appeal to the order of creation in *Genesis* 2, in which God created the woman after the man to be his helpmate.

The influential biblical scholar Phyllis Trible challenges this interpretation by offering a careful analysis of the language and meanings of the Hebrew text, and there is now widespread scholarly acceptance that a pervasive ideology of gender has shaped Christian readings of *Genesis.* Biblical writings about God, humankind, and sexual difference have also been interpreted by Christians through the lens of the Greek philosophical tradition, so the *Genesis* narrative has been overlaid with concepts about the essential nature of femininity and masculinity that are alien to the tradition of the Hebrew Scriptures. Thus Christianity has to a large extent constructed its understanding of gender not only around the Bible but around philosophical beliefs that associate masculinity with reason, transcendence, virtue, and divinity and femininity with emotion, immanence, moral weakness, and the body.

Although the interpretation of *Genesis* is crucial for an understanding of the symbolic construction of gender in Christianity, the New Testament offers numerous insights into the historical role of women as well as men in the ministry of Jesus and the early church. The Gospels, in particular the Gospels according to Luke and John, represent women as faithful disciples of Jesus, participating in his public ministry in a way that may have defied the sociosexual conventions of first-century Palestine. Figures such as Martha and Mary of Bethany, Mary Magdalene, the Samaritan woman at the well, and Mary the mother of Jesus feature at significant moments in the Gospel stories not as silent and submissive followers but as women who often appear to challenge or question Jesus and to contribute to a deeper understanding of his mission. Saint Paul's letters name a number of women who were leaders and patrons of early Christian communities. They include Prisca, Phoebe, and Junia, the latter two referred to as a deacon and an apostle respectively (*Rom.* 16). However, the Deutero-Pauline and Pastoral epistles represent a more complex picture with regard to gender relations. They include instructions to women to submit to men's authority in the church (compare *1 Tm.* 11–15) and to be subject to their husbands (compare *Col.* 3:18, *Eph.* 5:22) while enjoining husbands to love their wives as Christ loves the church (compare *Eph.* 5:25).

Studies of the early church suggest that women had considerable influence in the formative years of Christianity, with Apocryphal literature of the second century, such as the Acts of Thecla and the Gospel of Mary, providing rich additional sources to the biblical text. Whether these stories are rooted in history or legend, they are indicative of a complex process of negotiation and conflict around issues of gender and leadership in early Christianity.

The first four centuries after Christ saw the transition of Christianity from a marginal and persecuted minority to the official religion of the Roman Empire. In her study of patristic theology, Virginia Burrus argues that the conversion of the Roman Empire to Christianity created a crisis of identity for the church's male leaders, who found themselves having to occupy positions of authority defined according to imperial criteria of manliness. She suggests that this identity crisis had a lasting influence on Christian gender constructs in terms of masculine subjectivity, feminine alterity, and the fatherhood of God.

THE MIDDLE AGES. If women lost some of their early influence with the growing institutionalization of the church, they nevertheless continued to play a significant role in Christian leadership and theological reflection in late antiquity and the early Middle Ages. Although this was an era when the lives of the vast majority of men and women escape the historical record, evidence exists that women were included among the educated elite who ran the monasteries and religious institutions of the early medieval world. Abbesses such as Hilda of Whitby (d. 680), Lioba (700–780) and Hildegard of Bingen (1098–1179) were responsible for mixed monasteries in which women as well as men were educated in the context of religious life. The emergence of women's historians since the 1960s has seen a growing body of scholarship devoted to the recuperation of these neglected historical figures.

However, the eleventh-century Gregorian reforms marked the beginning of an era in which power in the church became more centralized and clericalized, which made it more difficult for women to gain access to theological education or positions of religious authority.

The establishment of the schools and universities in the twelfth and thirteenth centuries restricted theological education to celibate male scholars, and the institution of compulsory priestly celibacy intensified misogynistic attitudes toward women and female sexuality, assisted by the widespread dissemination of Aristotelian philosophy through the influence of Scholasticism. Women became more closely associated with the affective, devotional life of faith expressed in the vernacular, whereas male clerics became the custodians of theology and doctrine expressed in the highly stylized Latin of Scholasticism, signaling the beginning of a linguistic and conceptual division between Christian theology and spirituality that would have considerable implications for the understanding of gender.

Yet these changes also brought new opportunities for the expression of women's spirituality that appealed not to the authenticating norms of theology for its legitimacy but to a direct encounter with divine revelation. The next few centuries saw the emergence of women mystics, such as Julian of Norwich (1342–c. 1416) and Catherine of Siena (1347–1380), whose ideas have had an enduring influence on the Catholic tradition. The Beguines, a lay movement of women that flourished across northern Europe from the late twelfth century, produced a number of women spiritual writers, such as Mechthild of Magdeburg (c. 1212–1282), author of *The Flowing Light of the Godhead*, Hadewjich of Antwerp (thirteenth century), and Marguerite Porete (1280–1310), author of *The Mirror of Simple Souls*, who was burned at the stake for heresy. The Beguines were condemned at the Council of Vienne (1311–1312) and had virtually disappeared by the early fifteenth century, attesting perhaps to the vulnerability of women's religious visions and practices in male-dominated traditions. Their male counterparts, the Beghards, were numerically less significant, but they too fell under suspicion of heresy and immoral practices.

The twelfth century also saw the emergence of a new trend in Christian spirituality that affected both men's and women's devotional writings. From the time of Bernard of Clairvaux (1090–1153), the *Song of Songs* became a key text for the expression of the Christian longing for Christ, leading to forms of prayer and devotion in which the soul is represented as the feminine beloved and bride of Christ, expressing "herself" in sometimes highly eroticized metaphors of feminine desire. This constituted a significant change in the Christian understanding of gender, which had until then associated femininity unambiguously with frailty, moral weakness, and carnal susceptibility, with masculine virtue being the Christian ideal for both sexes. The emergence of a more positive understanding of femininity in Christian spirituality was partly due to the influence of the courtly love tradition, with the language of the troubadours being appropriated to express the feminine soul's desire for Christ or the celibate male's devotion to the Virgin Mary. Much work remains to be done on the ways in which this feminized language of prayer and mysticism bears the marks of sexual difference, but scholars such as Caroline Walker Bynum (1992) and Grace Jantzen (1995) see a tendency to focus more directly on the body and on physical manifestations of devotion associated with the Eucharist and with practices of asceticism and self-mortification in women's writings. Bynum suggests that the medieval belief that associated the soul with masculine divinity and the body with the female flesh coupled with belief in the virgin birth, which eliminated the male body's role in the conception of Christ, led women to identify Christ's humanity with their own female embodiment.

The medieval church was part of a complex social world that offered limited opportunities to women but that also celebrated motherhood as a flourishing social institution. The church itself was a Holy Mother whose sacraments were woven into the practices of everyday life, including women's domestic activities associated with pregnancy, childbirth, and motherhood. The image of the Virgin Mary as a solitary and unique example of womanhood, "Alone of All Her Sex," to quote the title of Marina Warner's (2000) influential book, is challenged by medieval art and devotion that suggest a more communal sense of female sainthood, with the Apocryphal figure of Saint Anne, mother of the Virgin Mary, occupying a position in fifteenth-century devotion second only to that of her illustrious daughter. Toward the end of the fifteenth century the cult of Saint Joseph, the putative father of Christ, began to eclipse that of Saint Anne, so the matriarchal groupings of medieval art and devotion were gradually replaced by the more modern grouping of the Holy Family comprising Mary, Joseph, and the infant Christ.

However, the fifteenth century also brought a new threat to women in the form of the witch hunts, which altogether spanned some four hundred years of Western history, from 1400 to 1800. It is impossible to calculate how many witch trials there were, but conservative estimates are in the range of 60,000 to 100,000 people killed, of whom two-thirds were women, including Joan of Arc (1412–1431). Recent scholarship suggests that these women were victims not primarily of medieval Catholicism, as has often been believed, but of the combined forces of science, rationalism, and religion in the sixteenth and seventeenth centuries, which recorded the greatest number of witch trials. It is impossible to calculate the impact of the witch hunts on the development of Christian thought and practice when one considers that the tens of thousands killed were probably among the most creative and independent-minded of Europe's Christian women, and the fate they suffered must have silenced many others who may otherwise have written and spoken out. It must, however, be borne in mind that this wave of destruction spanned the late medieval and early modern period, and therefore, from the historical perspective of women, to some extent it overshadows the Reformation.

The Reformation and the Enlightenment. The Reformation saw the emergence of new forms of Christianity, in which the sacramentality and symbolism of the medieval Catholic Church yielded to a more literate and moralistic form of Christianity based on the authority of Scripture and on individual faith in Jesus Christ. Although this did little to destabilize the gendered hierarchies of Christian theology and practice, it did provide limited opportunities for women to play an active role in the development of new Christian communities and churches. Reformers such as Martin Luther (1483–1546) and John Calvin (1509–1564) rejected the Catholic belief that celibacy was a higher ideal than married life, so marriage came to be understood in more positive terms as a partnership of love and mutual support. However, the vocation to religious life had provided medieval women with an alternative to the often oppressive demands of marriage and motherhood, and some scholars, including William Monter (1987) and Merry Wiesner (1990), argue that women after the Reformation became more narrowly identified with the domestic sphere, with a subsequent loss of public influence and visibility. Moreover the Reformation purged Protestant Christianity of maternal feminine imagery associated with the Virgin Mary, the women saints, and the maternal church, contributing to the emergence of a culture that was more vigorously patriarchal and masculine in its values, politics, and beliefs. With the transition to an increasingly scientific and rationalized worldview after the seventeenth century, the symbolic and spiritual significance of gender began to yield to a more literalistic understanding of human sexuality, so the sexed body increasingly became positioned not in terms of its sacramental and social significance but in terms of scientific definitions and moral prescriptions.

The Enlightenment constituted a change from a social order grounded in the appeal to divine revelation and scriptural authority to a vision of society informed by a belief in reason, personal liberty, and the social contract. This did not immediately change the status of women, and indeed its initial impact on women's lives may have been far from positive, but it laid the foundations for the liberal democracies in which women have ultimately gained a degree of social and political recognition that they were never able to achieve under the theocracies of the Christian tradition. Yet if the male philosophers of the Enlightenment saw a fundamental conflict between reason and faith (even though their ideas remained deeply rooted in Christian theology), it is by no means certain that women shared this perception. Gerda Lerner, in the introduction to the second volume of her study of *Women and History* (1993), describes how she discovered "the significance to women of their relationship to the Divine and the profound impact the severing of that relationship had on the history of women. . . . The insight that religion was the primary arena on which women fought for hundreds of years for feminist consciousness was not one I had previously had" (Lerner, 1993, pp. vii–viii). Mary Wollstonecraft (1759–1797), widely recognized as an early pioneer of the feminist movement, based her appeal for women's equality not only on Enlightenment values of reason, education, and the individual's right to political and social participation but on her faith in the compassion, wisdom, and mercy of God. If in the early twenty-first century those Enlightenment values are in their twilight years and new, as yet unpredictable, forms of social organization are appearing on the horizon, it remains to be seen to what extent Christianity may continue to offer women a language of divine wisdom to counter the political and social prejudices of powerful men.

The Nineteenth Century. The industrial revolution and the rise of capitalism in Protestant societies saw the establishment of what in the early twenty-first century some refer to as the traditional Christian family, although in reality this modern concept does not reflect the diverse social arrangements of the premodern family. Working-class life has rarely allowed men and women the luxury of playing out gendered stereotypes, but the image of Christian family life became identified in the nineteenth century with the clearly delineated gender roles and relationships of the middle classes. While the husband went out to work in commerce and industry where Christian ideals were inevitably compromised, the wife and mother, the "angel in the home," upheld Christian faith and values in the domestic realm. Thus nineteenth-century Protestant piety was to some extent associated with the sphere of femininity, with a gentle Jesus reflecting a domesticated ideal embodied in the good wife. Indeed during the nineteenth century church congregations were increasingly made up of more women than men, suggesting a gradual withdrawal of men from religion. The mid-1850s saw the emergence of "muscular Christianity," associated with writers such as Thomas Hughes and Charles Kingsley and later influencing American ministers such as Thomas Wentworth Higginson. This trend, which emphasized the masculinity of Christ and the manly virtues of the Christian faith, may have been a backlash against the perceived feminization of the churches and against the nascent women's movement.

However, these dominant social paradigms should not be allowed to eclipse the more radical opportunities that Christianity continued to offer to women. Josephine Butler (1828–1906) and Florence Nightingale (1820–1910) were activists whose work was rooted in a radical Christian theology and a profound personal piety. Butler's work with prostitutes exposed and challenged the trenchant hypocrisies of Victorian England, a society in which a rigid morality defined by Christian values masked the widespread exploitation and abuse of the poor and a flourishing sex trade in the cities. Evangelicalism afforded nineteenth-century Western women a public space from which to speak as missionaries, social reformers, and educators, even if their activities continued to be defined and restricted by men. The nineteenth century also saw the emergence of new women's religious communities in the Catholic Church, with the formation of religious orders committed to mission, education, and health care. Again these belonged within ecclesial and social structures governed by men, but they provided a means by which women could make a significant contribution to the public dimension of Christian life, extending their influence beyond the domestic sphere and allowing for considerable levels of social mobility and spiritual influence. In the United States the woman's suffragist Elizabeth Cady Stanton (1815–1902) pioneered what one day became feminist biblical criticism, and Harriet Tubman (1819/1820–1913) was one of many African American women whose triumphs over slavery inspired later generations of Christian theologians and writers. The emergence of independent African American churches in nineteenth-century America created a form of Protestant Christianity enlivened by the rhythms and gestures of African music, dance, and spirituality, which has afforded African American men and women a space in which to express their Christian faith free from the oppressive influences of racism and white domination. American feminist theologians and gender theorists in the twenty-first century work at a complex intersection of questions having to do with gender, race, and class in their explorations of the relationships among slavery, gender injustice, and Protestantism in the formation of modern American social values.

Christianity and Gender in Contemporary Culture. The twentieth century saw the widespread demise of the Christian faith across much of Western society, at least in its traditional and institutionalized forms, accompanied by a rapid growth in Christianity in some non-Western cultures, most notably in Africa and South Korea. The changed horizons opened by feminist and postcolonialist perspectives have brought new challenges and opportunities to Christian theology, as some of its most fundamental doctrinal and ethical claims have been called into question. The emergence of the contemporary women's movement in Western society coincided with the Second Vatican Council (1962–1965), an epoch-making event in the Catholic Church that opened the way to a much greater degree of participation by women and other previously excluded groups in theological reflection and formation. The result has been the ongoing transformation of Christian theology and practice, as theologically educated men and women address questions of doctrine, sexuality, social justice, and gender relations from an increasingly wide spectrum of cultural, economic, and intellectual localities. By the end of the twentieth century women were being ordained as priests and ministers in numerous Christian denominations, including the Church of England, with women bishops being ordained in some parts of the worldwide Anglican communion, and the issue of women's ordination became an increasingly divisive question in the Roman Catholic Church. According to the religioustolerance.org website, one in every eight American clergy is a woman, and in 1997 women constituted 30 percent of North American theology graduates (see http://www.religioustolerance.org/femclrg6.htm). Christian beliefs about marriage and sexuality have been challenged by the decline in marriage and rising divorce rates in Western societies. This has been accompanied by a growing desire for religious recognition and affirmation at all levels of church life by gays and lesbians in Western churches, to the consternation of many non-Western Christians who remain committed to a more conservative understanding of Christian sexual values.

These challenging new movements have provoked a backlash, with the reassertion of conservative values in both the Catholic and the Protestant churches and the emergence of fundamentalist Christian movements that tend to adopt a highly literalist approach to biblical teachings on questions of sexual ethics and gender relations. In the United States the organization Promise Keepers seeks to reestablish Christian family values by appealing to men to accept their responsibilities as husbands and fathers, with the concomitant expectation that women should perform their roles as dutiful wives and mothers. In Roman Catholicism the papacy of John Paul II has been remarkable in many ways, but it has seen the reassertion of traditional sexual values and gender stereotypes over some of the liberating tendencies of the postconciliar church. Perhaps the most traumatic event in this context was the publication of the papal encyclical, *Humanae Vitae*, by Pope Paul VI in 1968. This set out a vision of marriage that was revolutionary in its affirmation of the value of married love and sexuality but that, in its reiteration of the Catholic Church's opposition to artificial birth control, provoked an ongoing crisis of authority in the Catholic Church.

The social, demographic, and intellectual developments of the twentieth century mean that Christianity is undergoing a continuing crisis in its understanding of gender and sexuality, calling into question beliefs, practices, and authority structures that have prevailed almost unchallenged since the fourth century with regard to the different roles of men and women, the significance of human sexuality, and the ways in which these have been inspired and legitimated by the Christian understanding of God. It is impossible to predict what the church of the twenty-second century may look like or to what extent it will make sense to speak of the church at all. Some may see the future as a series of schisms, reformations, and revolutions that will lead to a global plurality of movements, sects, and cults loosely rooted in the Christian tradition, whereas others may have a more positive view of the Christian potential for unity and reconciliation after centuries of conflict and division. But it is likely that, whatever other changes take place, the Christian understanding of what it means to be male and female created in the image of God is one of the most urgent and complex questions of this age, and the ways in which Christians respond to that question will shape the churches of the future in profound and unforeseeable ways.

See Also Church; Enlightenment; Feminist Theology, article on Christian Feminist Theology; Heresy; Human Body; Incarnation; Mary; Mary Magdalene; Masculine Sacrality; Men's Studies in Religion; Mysticism; Nuns; Protestantism; Reformation; Resurrection; Sexuality; Teresa of Ávila.

Bibliography

Allen, Prudence. *The Concept of Woman: The Aristotelian Revolution, 750 BC– AD 1250.* Grand Rapids, Mich., 1985.

Allen, Prudence. *The Concept of Woman: The Early Humanist Reformation, 1250–1500.* Grand Rapids, Mich., 2002. Allen provides an excellent analysis of the ways the reception and dissemination of philosophical and theological ideas have shaped the role and representation of woman in the Christian tradition.

Anderson, Bonnie S., and Judith P. Zinsser. *A History of Their Own: Women in Europe from Prehistory to the Present.* Rev. ed., 2 vols. London, 1990. These two volumes offer a scholarly overview of women in European history from prehistory to the late twentieth century. They are invaluable for situating Christianity in its wider historical contexts with regard to the roles and positions of women.

Ashley, Kathleen, and Pamela Sheingorn, eds. *Interpreting Cultural Symbols: Saint Anne in Late Medieval Society.* Athens, Ga., 1994. A collection of essays that explores the symbolic and social significance of the medieval cult of Saint Anne.

Balthasar, Hans Urs von. *Theo-Drama III: The Dramatis Personae: The Person in Christ.* Translated by Graham Harrison. San Francisco, 1992. Balthasar's theology of sexual difference has had a formative influence on conservative Catholic theology since the Second Vatican Council. This is a developed account of his theory of the gendering of relationships in the Christian story.

Beattie, Tina. *Woman.* New Century Theology series. London, 2003. A theological analysis and reflection on the role and representation of women in Christianity and secular Western culture.

Børresen, Kari Elisabeth. *Subordination and Equivalence: The Nature and Role of Woman in Augustine and Thomas Aquinas* (1965). Kampen, Netherlands, 1995. Børresen's fine scholarly analysis of the writings of these two great Christian thinkers brings to light the complexity and also the contradictions inherent in the theological construction of gender.

Boswell, John. *Christianity, Social Tolerance, and Homosexuality.* Chicago, 1980. Boswell's study traces changing attitudes toward homosexuality in the Christian tradition from the early church to the Middle Ages.

Brown, Peter. *The Body and Society: Men, Women, and Sexual Renunciation in Early Christianity.* London, 1991. One of the most influential historical studies of early Christian ideas of gender and embodiment in their social contexts.

Burrus, Virginia. *"Begotten Not Made": Conceiving Manhood in Late Antiquity.* Stanford, Calif., 2000. Burrus uses contemporary critical theory, particularly the work of Luce Irigaray, to analyze the construction of gender in patristic theology.

Bynum, Caroline Walker. *Fragmentation and Redemption: Essays on Gender and the Human Body in Medieval Religion.* New York, 1992. Bynum remains one of the most significant and influential scholars writing about medieval attitudes toward gender and the body.

Coakley, Sarah. *Powers and Submissions: Spirituality, Philosophy, and Gender.* Oxford, 2002. In this collection of essays Coakley analyzes the ideas of philosophers, theologians, and gender theorists to explore the significance of gender in Christian thought.

Daly, Mary. *Beyond God the Father: Toward a Philosophy of Women's Liberation.* Boston, 1973; reprint, London, 1986. Although Daly's work seems somewhat dated, this book represents a dramatic shift in her thinking from Catholic feminist theology to radical post-Christian philosophy, and her work continues to have a widespread influence on feminist theory.

Ehrman, Bart D. *Lost Scriptures: Books That Did Not Make It into the New Testament.* Oxford, 2003. A comprehensive anthology of the extracanonical and Apocryphal writings of the early Christian era.

Elshtain, Jean Bethke. *Public Man, Private Woman: Women in Social and Political Thought.* 2d ed. Princeton, N.J., 1993. Elshtain's careful historical survey of theological, philosophical, and political attitudes to gender offers a feminist critique both of historical political values and of some feminist theories.

Fiorenza, Elisabeth Schüssler. *In Memory of Her: A Feminist Theological Reconstruction of Christian Origins.* New York, 1983. This pioneering feminist study argues that women occupied positions of equality in ministry and leadership in the early Christian Church.

Jantzen, Grace. *Power, Gender, and Christian Mysticism.* Cambridge, U.K., 1995. A feminist critique of the gendered constructs of Christian mysticism as these relate to the lives and practices of women mystics.

Jensen, Anne. *God's Self-Confident Daughters.* Louisville, Ky., 1996. Jensen explores the ways the status of women changed in the early church from having considerable influence to being increasingly marginalized and subordinated to men.

John Paul II, Pope. *Original Unity of Man and Woman—Catechesis on the Book of Genesis.* Boston, 1981. Audiences presented during 1979 and 1980, when Pope John Paul II considered the theology of male and female from the perspective of the *Genesis* account of Creation.

Kelly-Gadol, Joan. "Did Women Have a Renaissance?" In *Becoming Visible: Women in European History,* edited by Renate Bridenthal, Claudia Koonz, and Susan Stuard. 2d ed. Boston, 1987. Kelly-Gadol's highly influential argument, first published in 1977, calls into question the periodization of history by arguing that the Renaissance represented a time of diminished opportunities rather than intellectual and social awakening for European women.

Kienzle, Beverly, and Pamela Walker, eds. *Women Preachers and Prophets through Two Millennia of Christianity.* Berkeley, Calif., 1998. A collection of essays that explores the role of women in preaching and prophesy from the early church to the twentieth century.

King, Ursula, ed. *Feminist Theology from the Third World: A Reader.* London, 1994. This collection offers an insight into the diverse forms and methods of feminist theology that have flourished in critical engagement with Western feminism. It includes writings by African Americans, Asians, Africans, Latin Americans, and others, giving a sense of the global dimensions and international concerns of Christian feminism.

Küng, Hans. *Women in Christianity.* London, 2001. A critical appraisal of women's role in the Christian tradition by one of the Catholic Church's best-known theologians.

Laqueur, Thomas. *Making Sex: Body and Gender from the Greeks to Freud.* Cambridge, Mass., 2000. Laqueur analyzes the historical understanding of sex to argue that modern science and medicine were largely responsible for the idea of a fundamental biological and psychological difference between the sexes based not on scientific evidence but on changing social values and relationships.

Lees, Clare, ed. *Medieval Masculinities: Regarding Men in the Middle Ages.* Minneapolis, 1994. A collection of scholarly but accessible essays that explores concepts of manhood in the Middle Ages and how these have affected the historical understanding of masculinity.

Lerner, Gerda. *Women in History.* Vol. 1: *The Creation of Patriarchy.* Vol. 2, *The Creation of Feminist Consciousness: From the Middle Ages to Eighteen-Seventy.* New York, 1986, 1993. Lerner's two-volume work offers a carefully researched account of women in Western history. This is of particular value to those interested in Christianity and gender because of her attentive concern for the ways religion has influenced women's identities and roles and has been used in their struggles for self-expression and autonomy through the centuries.

Lloyd, Genevieve. *The Man of Reason: "Male" and "Female" in Western Philosophy.* London, 1984. Lloyd's survey of the philosophical construction of gender in Western culture remains one of the most accessible overviews of the subject.

Loades, Ann. *Feminist Theology: Voices from the Past.* Cambridge, U.K., 2001. A study of three different women (Mary Wollstonecraft, Josephine Butler, and Dorothy Sayers), showing how their ideas and activities were informed by their Christian faith and relating these to contemporary ethical issues concerning women in the churches.

Loades, Ann, ed. *Feminist Theology: A Reader.* London, 1990. This is a helpful resource for those seeking an introduction to feminist theology, although it does not cover significant developments in the field since the early 1990s.

Louth, Andrew. "The Body in Western Catholic Christianity." In *Religion and the Body,* edited by Sarah Coakley. Cambridge, U.K., 1997. Louth offers a careful scholarly analysis of the understanding of sexual difference and embodiment in the Western Church.

Malone, Mary T. *Women and Christianity.* Vol. 1: *The First Thousand Years.* Vol. 2: *The Medieval Period* AD*1000–1500.* Vol. 3: *From the Reformation to the Twenty-First Century.* Dublin, Ireland, 2000, 2001, 2003. Malone uses broad brushstrokes to offer a readable survey of women in Christianity from the time of Christ to the beginning of the twenty-first century.

Martin, Francis. *The Feminist Question: Feminist Theology in the Light of Christian Tradition.* Edinburgh, 1994. A critical analysis that poses a number of questions to the feminist theological enterprise while affirming some of its insights.

Merchant, Carolyn. *The Death of Nature: Women, Ecology, and the Scientific Revolution.* San Francisco, 1990. Merchant analyzes changing attitudes toward nature and the female body in the late medieval world and early modern world, arguing that the transition from a religious to a scientific worldview is associated with the emergence of a desire for dominance over the female body and nature, contributing to the witch hunts and to the exploitation of the natural environment.

Miller, Monica Migliorino. *Sexuality and Authority in the Catholic Church.* Scranton, Pa., 1995. A critique of feminist theology from the perspective of a conservative Catholic understanding of sexual difference.

Monter, William. "Protestant Wives, Catholic Saints, and the Devil's Handmaid: Women in the Age of Reformations." In

Becoming Visible: Women in European History, edited by Renate Bridenthal, Claudia Koonz, and Susan Stuard, 2d ed. Boston, 1987. First published in 1977, this is a balanced and carefully argued evaluation of the impact of the Reformation and Counter-Reformation on women.

Nelson, James. *The Intimate Connection: Male Sexuality, Masculine Spirituality.* London, 1992. One of the foremost Christian thinkers writing on issues of masculinity, Nelson adopts a liberal theological approach in his analysis of sexuality and gender.

Newman, Barbara. *From Virile Woman to WomanChrist: Studies in Medieval Religion and Literature.* Philadelphia, 1995. Newman considers changing perceptions of womanhood in Christianity through the literature of the early and medieval church.

Putney, Clifford. *Muscular Christianity: Manhood and Sports in Protestant America, 1880–1920.* Cambridge, Mass., 2001. Putney draws on cultural studies and historical analysis to offer a gendered reading of Protestant Christianity in the United States in the late nineteenth century and the early twentieth century. He argues that there was a strongly masculinist ideology in the churches that sought to counter the perceived feminization of Christianity.

Ranft, Patricia. *Women and Spiritual Equality in Christian Tradition.* New York, 1998; reprint, 2000. Ranft challenges accounts that present Christianity as exclusively misogynist by exploring an alternative historical tradition that has emphasized the spiritual equality of women in the Christian tradition.

Ruether, Rosemary Radford. *Sexism and God-Talk: Towards a Feminist Theology.* Boston, 1983; reprint, 1992. A groundbreaking book that was one of the earliest works of feminist theology. Although Ruether's liberal approach has been challenged by some later scholars, this remains a highly influential text in the development of feminist theology.

Schumacher, Michele M., ed. *Women in Christ: Toward a New Feminism.* Grand Rapids, Mich., 2004. A collection of essays that seeks to establish the contours of a "new feminism" inspired by the teachings of Pope John Paul II.

Soskice, Janet Martin, and Diana Lipton. *Feminism and Theology,* Oxford, 2003. A selection of textual extracts offering a survey of the work of key Christian and Jewish feminist thinkers.

Swanson, R. N., ed. *Gender and Christian Religion.* Woodbridge, U.K., 1998. A collection of papers read at meetings of the Ecclesiastical History Society, providing a wide-ranging scholarly analysis of Christian concepts of gender in different historical and cultural contexts.

Thatcher, Adrian, and Elizabeth Stuart, eds. *Christian Perspectives on Sexuality and Gender.* Leominster, U.K., 1996. Contributors offer a critical survey of traditional Christian attitudes toward issues such as gay and lesbian sexuality, sexuality and violence, the family, sexuality, and spirituality.

Trible, Phyllis. *God and the Rhetoric of Sexuality.* Philadelphia, 1978. Trible's careful exegetical readings of biblical texts has been highly influential in shaping feminist biblical scholarship.

Warner, Marina. *Alone of All Her Sex: The Myth and Cult of the Virgin Mary* (1976). New York, 2000. Warner's book was one of the earliest feminist critiques of the Marian tradition.

Webb, Val. *Florence Nightingale: The Making of a Radical Theologian.* Saint Louis, Mo., 2002. Webb's study reveals the extent to which the work of Nightingale was informed by a radical theological vision in protest against the cultural norms and values of her age.

West, Elizabeth A. *One Woman's Journey: Mary Potter—Founder—Little Company of Mary.* Richmond, Va., 2000. West draws on the insights and analyses of feminist theology for her careful biography of the founder of the Roman Catholic religious order Little Company of Mary. Her book gives an insight into the issues that shaped religion in Victorian England in terms of gender and denominational differences between Catholics and Protestants.

Wiesner, Merry. "Luther and Women: The Death of Two Marys." In *Feminist Theology: A Reader*, edited by Ann Loades. London, 1990. Wiesner argues that the Reformation was in many ways a retrogressive step for women, closing off opportunities previously afforded by religious life and restricting women's options to marriage and motherhood.

Williams, Delores J. *Sisters in the Wilderness: The Challenge of Womanist God-Talk.* Maryknoll, N.Y., 1993. Williams offers a critical evaluation and reinterpretation of Christian theology and biblical interpretation from the perspective of African American women.

Wollstonecraft, Mary. *A Vindication of the Rights of Woman* (1792). London, 1992. A pioneering feminist work that draws on philosophical, theological, and biblical perspectives in its spirited defence of women's rights.

TINA BEATTIE (2005)

GENDER AND RELIGION: GENDER AND ISLAM

During the twentieth century a new gender discourse focusing mostly on women's roles and rights in Islam emerged in various parts of the Muslim world. As is the case in the West, this gender discussion is not uniform, and it is greatly influenced by local cultures and conditions. The division between men and women pervades Muslim culture from the teachings of the Qurʾān to its language of Arabic, which carefully distinguishes between male and female. Based on the assumed asymmetry between the sexes, gender discourse in Islam concerns itself mainly with issues of power and inequality caused by patriarchal hierarchies that over time were strengthened by the religious, social, and cultural environment. Only recently and in a few places (e.g., in the writings of the American scholar Scott Siraj al-Haqq Kugle [2003]) has gender discourse started to include marginalized women and men, such as homosexuals. However, Muslim scholarship has always recognized the existence of hermaphrodites, who upset the division between the sexes.

Those involved in contemporary gender discourse operate from various ideologies. Their activities are manifold and include creating public awareness concerning gender issues, reforming laws and policies that are detrimental to women, and rediscovering women's histories. They find their inspiration in varying sources, from the United Nations' Universal Declaration of Human Rights to Islamic jurisprudence (*fiqh*). This movement has become wide-ranging, and it addresses, for example, women's health issues, domestic and public violence against women, the rights of women to education and work, democratic rights, children's rights, and human rights. In many Muslim countries some of these issues are still considered taboo.

The perceptions of Islam of those involved in gender activities are not monolithic. What binds most of them, however, is that their religion provides the core existential ground for their understanding of gender discourse. The theological reinterpretation of authoritative religious texts is in most cases fundamental to developing new understandings about gender in Islam. Revision of male-centered readings is unavoidable, since these were often influenced by the surrounding culture, which led to a gap between women's reality and the teachings of the Qurʾān that promote gender equality.

Since many Muslim countries continue to be governed by regimes that fail to provide basic needs for their citizens, those fighting for gender equality often face insurmountable difficulties. In spite of this reality, critical voices have come into existence that connect across the Muslim world, nowadays via the internet; they are developing a discourse on human rights, religious rights, and civil society that seeks social change for men and women, and empowerment of women in the public and religious sphere. The awarding of the 2003 Nobel Peace Prize to the Iranian Muslim human rights activist Shirin Ebadi (b. 1947) was a victory for all involved in this new gender discourse, for she is a living example of their agenda.

HISTORY OF THE STUDY OF GENDER CONCERNS. The process of rethinking the roles and rights of women in Islam first surfaced at the end of the nineteenth century in disparate places within the Muslim world. At that time, calls for changes in women's conditions emerged in countries ranging from Iran, to India (Bengal), Egypt, and Turkey. Women's voices (among others, Aisha Taymour [1840–1902], from Egypt) became heard via poems, stories, and essays, while women and men (e.g, Rokeya Sakhawat Hossein [1880–1932], from Bengal) started to demand education for girls and to question the practices of veiling, segregation, and polygyny. Qāsim Amīn's *Taḥrīr al-Marʾa* (The liberation of woman, 1899) stressed the need for women's education. As Leila Ahmad (1992) has pointed out, these objectives were not pursued for the sake of women, but served as a tool to resist colonialism and to transform society into modernity.

The Egyptian Muslim scholar Muḥammad ʿAbduh (1849–1905) entered the debate when he called for a correct understanding of Islam by returning to its original sources—the Qurʾān and *ḥadīth*. He interpreted these sources using the method of *ijtihād* (independent investigation of the religious sources), and when necessary he bypassed the teachings of the four legal schools of Islam, the *madhhabs*. Using this method, described as *modernist*, Muḥammad ʿAbduh placed Qurʾanic verses about women's comprehensive veiling and seclusion, polygyny, and the husband's unilateral divorce rights in their original social and cultural contexts, and he argued that because those contexts had changed, their application in modern times had to be adapted as well.

ʿAbduh's new hermeneutical methods presented an alternative to traditionalist scholars (*ʿulamāʾ*), and opened the way for equality between men and women based on Islamic teachings. The *ʿulamāʾ* used the method of *taqlid* (that is, to follow the opinions of established scholars of the Muslim past), and applied the teachings of jurisprudence (*fiqh*, the interpretation of the *sharīʿah*) via the four *madhhabs* of Islam. Traditionalist scholars are still prevalent in many Muslim countries, and their views on women often resemble those of Islamist or fundamentalist Muslims. They teach gender-polarized roles, male authority in the public realm, complementary roles for men and women, and equity but not equality in women's roles vis-à-vis men.

By the early twentieth century, the intellectual, educational, and philanthropic activities of upper- and middle-class Muslim women translated into organized associations, such as the Egyptian Feminist Union set up by Huda Shaʾrawi (1879–1947), who in 1923 publicly removed her veil upon her return from a gathering of the International Women's Alliance in Rome. Union members were the first women who wrote about women's rights based on the Qurʾān; they argued that veiling the face was not a Qurʾanic injunction.

In 1917, the Muḥammadīyah-related organization for women called ʿAisyiyah started in Indonesia, with efforts focusing on the religious and secular education of women. Education and journalism were women's most successful ways to advance their cause. Periodicals discussed the veil, women's segregation, Islamic rules, and issues of personal status law, including polygyny. Men welcomed these activities because they considered women to be actors in the national struggles for independence, and in many Muslim countries (Egypt, Turkey, Indonesia), the gender discourse on women remained connected to issues of secular nationalism and national advancement until these countries gained independence from colonial powers.

Around the 1960s, the focus of gender discourse changed. After independence, social reforms by the new nation-states provided education for all and a certain degree of legal protection for women via reformed legal codes. The 1979 revolution in Iran and the rapid transformation of economic and social structures in many Muslim countries triggered a process of redefining Muslim identities that led, among other things, to the ascendancy of Islamist groups. Saudi Arabia encouraged this development by using its oil wealth to spread the puritanical Wahābī interpretation of Islam. Gender discourse regressed in countries where Islamists took control of the government, such as Iran, Afghanistan, Pakistan, Bangladesh, and Sudan. For example, the government of Omar Hassan al-Bashir (who came to power in 1989) in Sudan dismissed women from public employment and limited their mobility by enforcing the rule that they must be accompanied by a *maḥram* (male guardian), and the Taliban in Afghanistan prevented women's access to education and healthcare altogether.

Concurrent with these new forces, the feminist movements that emerged in several countries started to take new directions, more or less becoming divided between secular and Muslim activism. Women benefiting from state-provided education acquired the intellectual tools to address issues, such as women's legal position, health, and work, without the assistance of men. In 1972, the Egyptian medical doctor Nawal El Saadawi published the book *Al-marʾa wa al-jins* (Women and sex), which dealt with sex, religion, and women's circumcision. The book raised awareness about women's sexual oppression across the Muslim world, unleashing intense reaction, especially from the conservative *ʿulamāʾ*.

Programs emerged that focused on local customs particularly detrimental to women. Women in such African countries as Egypt, Sudan, Ethiopia, Djibouti, Ghana, and Kenya started to question the practice of female genital mutilation, while honor killings became an important topic in the gender debate in Egypt, Jordan, Palestine, and Iraq. These practices were virtually unknown in Southeast Asia and most parts of sub-Saharan Africa. Other groups in Algeria, Nigeria, Iran, Sudan, Pakistan, and Malaysia started to fight the imposition of *sharīʿah* and research its consequences for women.

Awareness about gender issues was also raised by international initiatives such as the United Nations Convention on the Elimination of All Forms of Discrimination against Women (1979) and the United Nations Decade for Women (1975–1985). Later, the International Conference on Population and Development in Cairo (1994) and the World Conference on Women in Beijing (1995) helped boost networking among women activists all over the Muslim world.

Seminal works by Muslim scholars such as Fatima Mernissi and Leila Ahmed analyzed the conditions and mechanisms of women's oppression and exposed the ambiguity of interpretations of Islamic texts and jurisprudence. These writers called for just readings of those texts, readings that were sensitive to the point of view of women. Several women scholars of Islam took up this challenge and the phenomenon of Muslim feminism was born. The early modernist movement positioned women's rights within a program of renewal in Islamic society. It removed many roadblocks for women; however, as several scholars have observed, it did not fundamentally change unequal gender relations and left the system intact. Others argued that by ignoring jurisprudence, the modernist focus on the Qurʾān failed to address the underlying law system of the *fiqh* that directly ruled women's lives, for example, in matters of marriage and divorce. In order to bring about fundamental changes in the Muslim injunctions concerning women, they proposed a reinterpretation of the rules of the *fiqh,* which were formed in the ninth century and are susceptible to flaws caused by human intervention.

By the 1990s, broadly speaking, three approaches of feminism (*nisāʾīyyah*) shaped Muslim discourse: secular, Muslim, and Islamist.

Secular feminism. *Secular feminism* is an amorphous term in the Muslim world. It seldom indicates religious indifference (or atheism), although feminists such as Nawal El Saadawi have insisted on their secular identity. *Secular* refers to those whose activism is not directly based on the Islamic tradition but who struggle for women's rights within the framework of universal values and principles. To them, religion should be restricted to the private and spiritual domains. It also carries reference to the type of activities undertaken. Secular feminists do not have a unified, clear agenda, but in many Muslim countries their efforts to improve women's conditions are met with accusations that they are tarnishing local culture and religion with Western ideas.

To be secular does not necessarily mean "rejecting Islam." In order to underscore this reality, Margot Badran (2002) speaks of "feminism with Islam."

Most women's organizations in the Muslim world are secular in approach, and their agendas are manifold. For example, the Arab Women's Solidarity Association, formed in 1982, which gained headlines in 1992 when it had to move from Egypt under pressure from Islamists, focuses on eliminating honor killings. Egypt is also home to the FGM (female genital mutilation) Task Force, formed in 1994, as well as a coalition of about seventy organizations and individuals under the umbrella of the Egyptian Commission for Population and Development. Some movements congregate under the umbrella of human rights: for example, Women for Women's Human Rights in Turkey. There are too many such organizations to mention, but they form important sources of women's empowerment and civil resistance. For example, the Turkish Women's Movement against Sexual Assault was the first group in an Islamic country to offer legal assistance to victims of sexual assault. The Network of Women Living under Muslim Laws in southern France and the Pakistani Action Forum, founded in 1981, were formed in response to the introduction of the *sharīʿah* penal code in various countries. Apart from these grassroots activities, political parties often have women's branches that pursue a specific agenda to advance conditions for women in certain areas of life.

Muslim feminism. The term *Muslim feminism* emerged in the 1990s and was used in the writings of Muslims to describe a new gender paradigm. It refers to Muslim men and women who ground their methods and ideas in Islamic knowledge, and most of them articulate that the true spirit of the Qurʾān teaches gender equality and social justice. Some Muslim feminists, however, follow the view that women and men complement each other rather than being equal. Muslim feminists reinterpret the Qurʾān in a woman-centered fashion using the methodologies of *ijtihād* and *tafsīr* combined with the tools of social science, psychology, history, anthropology, medicine, and so on. In doing this, as Azza Karam (1998) has observed in Egypt, women who wish to engage in the official discourse of the *ʿulamāʾ* have met with great resistance.

Some scrutinize the various formulations of *sharīʿah* (Lebanese Aziza al-Hibri, Pakistani Shaheen Sardar Ali), or re-examine the *ḥadīth* and Qurʾān (Moroccan Fatima Mernissi, Turk Hidayet Tuksal, Riffat Hassan, and Asma Barlas, the latter two originally from Pakistan). In principle, these feminists follow modernist methodology. This has caused the pendulum to swing back to traditionalist methodologies that focus on *fiqh*. Muslim scholars such as Khaled Abou El Fadl argue that true gender equality has been obscured by the patriarchal thinking of Islamic jurisprudence as consolidated in the ninth century. A narrow modernist focus on the Qurʾān and *ḥadīth* only avoids the real problems that are inherent to the legal system. Hence the advice of Kecia Ali that "progressive Muslims cannot afford to ignore jurisprudence" (2003, p. 182). This approach requires extensive knowledge of the Islamic sources.

In Indonesia, the traditionalist organization Nahdlatul Ulama started to apply this method in the 1980s to promote an agenda of justice and social change. Inspired by Abdurrahman Wahid, religious leaders teamed up with feminists to organize the first Islam-based program in the world that advocated women's reproductive rights. Women's groups related to Nahdlatul Ulama, such as the Yayasan Kesejahteraan Fatayat, followed this method, focusing on other aspects of Islamic rights for women. This trend also emerged in Iran with representatives such as Hojjat al-Eslam Seyyed Mohsen Saʾidzadeh (who is prominent in Ziba Mir-Hosseini's *Islam and Gender,* 1999), and the journals *Farzanah* and *Zanan.*

These neo-traditionalists are especially interested in reinterpreting the regulations of Muslim personal status law, which is part of the *sharīʿah* and regulates marriage, divorce, and inheritance. They argue that, for example, in order to address the inherent inequalities within the marriage contract, one has to understand the mind frame of the jurists who interpreted the *sharīʿah* and saw it as a contract of ownership of the husband over the wife in exchange for a dower. This involved rights of the husband over the wife (he could, for example, forbid her to leave the house). Neo-traditionalists argue that it does not advance the cause of women to narrowly focus on the rights assigned to her by the Qurʾān and ignore the fact that, based on jurisprudence, the majority of Muslim men still see marriage as a modified contract of ownership.

Many Muslim feminists strive to align the Qurʾanic teachings about justice with those of universal human rights. The agenda of this philosophy includes such issues as women's reproductive rights, violence against women, domestic violence, homosexuality, prostitution, democratic rights, and the rights of children and of religious minorities in Muslim countries. Some of these issues still form unspeakable taboos in many parts of the Muslim world. Ironically, all groups discussing gender, from Islamists to progressive feminists, agree that the greatest challenge facing women in Islam is their lack of religious expertise. Where women have gained access to Islamic institutions of higher learning, they can participate in the rereading of the classical religious texts that traditionally were interpreted by men. Women with the required religious knowledge have moved into positions of religious authority, and they have become scholars of Islam and judges. This is still rare in most Muslim countries, and can mainly be witnessed in Indonesia and the United States, and increasingly in Iran.

Examples of Muslim feminist organizations are the Sisters in Islam in Malaysia; Rifka Annisa, Indonesia's first Islamic-based center for women suffering from domestic violence; the women's branches of Muḥammadīyah and Nahdlatul Ulama; and groups centered around the Iranian journals mentioned earlier.

Islamist feminism. Islamist feminism has grown with the onset of Islamist organizations; it stresses complementarity between men and women, rather than equality and male authority over women. This approach bases women's rights on the Islamic *sharīʿah* and favors an Islamic state. Islamists especially reject what they consider to be influences from the West. Both male and female Islamists extol a woman's role as mother and wife. They rely on the ideas of male ideologues, such as the Egyptian Sayyid Quṭb (1906–1966), who viewed the family, with a division of labor between husband and wife, as the basis of society. This philosophy led, for example, to women in secular Turkey demanding the right to wear the veil in universities and public offices, and to Muslim women in former Soviet republics calling for the application of polygyny as a tool for achieving women's protection and for allowing the surplus of women to give birth and fulfill their roles as mothers. This view, however, does not mean that all Islamists reject political roles for women.

Islamists claim a return to the fundamentals of faith and to a pure tradition unpolluted by modern influences. Islamists can be intolerant of other views and seek power to impose their ideology by, among other things, controlling women and their sexuality, especially their reproductive faculties. This is accomplished by, for example, denying them access to any form of birth control. Mernissi (1991a, pp. 98–99) has observed that since the 1980s Islamism has displayed a growing obsession with women's bodies and social roles, and has promoted texts by misogynist Islamic scholars from the thirteenth through nineteenth centuries. Some Islamists promote practices such as polygyny and early marriage as a means of preventing immorality. For the latter reasons the Shīʿī practice of *mutʿah* (temporary marriage) has increased in some Sunnī communities. In order to safeguard women's modesty, Islamism imposes dress codes that vary from the face veil of *ḥijāb* to the *chador* that covers a woman from head to toe.

Younger Islamists such as Heba Raouf (b. 1965) from Egypt argue that while being faithful to their roles as wives and mothers, women can occupy the highest public functions as long as they are qualified. Egypt produced the earliest and most prominent women Islamist activists: Zaynab al-Ghazālī (b. 1917), who in 1936 set up the Muslim Women's Association for Islamist women, lauding women's family duties and obligations; Safinaz Qazim (b. 1939), who vigorously campaigns for an Islamic society; and Heba Raouf, who is active in the Muslim Brotherhood–Labor Party Alliance, writes a woman's page in its newspaper, *Al-Sha'b,* and is one of the founders of the *Islam Online* website. These activists combat women's oppression and see Islam as the main tool of liberation. They publicize their views via writing, campaigning, and advising, while considering Western feminism as divisive and individualistic.

Gender Distinctions in the Qur'ān. The Qur'ān presents a double message concerning the status and rights of women. It considers women and men equal in their religious observance (Qur'ān 33:35); they can both, for example, lay claim to paradise (40:8). The Qur'ān also states that both males and females share the same origin because they were created from the same spirit (*nafs*) (4:1, 6:98, 7:189). The Qur'ān does not acknowledge original sin because both Eve and Adam were equally tempted by Satan (7:20–22). It refers to husband and wife as each others' "garments" (2:187), recognizes a mother's burden of childbirth (46:15), and comments on the age of weaning (2:233). In principle, the Qur'ān assigns to women considerable rights: they retain their financial independence after marriage and are entitled to maintenance, a dower, and inheritance.

However, these egalitarian texts have counterparts, such as verse 4:34, which some interpret as allowing men to beat their wives in cases of disloyalty, disobedience, or ill conduct. Prejudiced interpretation of this verse can lead to severe domestic violence. The same verse contains the much debated phrase that "men are in charge of [or the protectors of *qawwāmūn ʿalā*] women because God has given the one more than the other, and because they support them from their means." Traditionally this verse has been explained as referring to a man's superiority over women. However, feminist interpretation has pointed out that *qawwāmūn* refers to the fact that men should provide for their wives in their role as mothers. Apart from the Qur'ān there is an abundance of traditions, alleged to be from the Prophet, that confirm women's secondary position, stating, for example, that the majority of those entering hell are women.

The original interpreters of the Qur'ān were Middle Eastern men. Muslim feminists argue that these interpretations, as transmitted via the *fiqh,* are replete with instances where universal teachings from the Qur'ān were confused with local customs and values. Muslim feminists consider this to be most detrimental to women. Like the Qur'ān, most of the *fiqh* discussions are in principle ungendered; apart from distinctions with regard to menstrual purity, both men and women follow the same rules of purity, and there are no gender distinctions in the ritual obligations. The main gender differences concern the areas of marriage, divorce, inheritance, and child custody. Together these form the so-called personal status law, which is part of the *sharīʿah*-based Muslim family law that is widely debated in the Muslim world.

Muslim Family Law. Muslim family law is based on Islamic law, and in principle it is meant to improve the status of Muslim women. Early Egyptian reformers reinterpreted the law, trying to adhere to classical legal principles in the light of modern conditions, in an attempt to improve women's rights. The most widely followed code used to be based on the Hanafī school. Important contemporary changes in the legal code allow women to enter stipulations in the marriage contract and to protect their position in case of divorce. Tunisia's code (1957) provides the strongest rights for women; it bans polygyny, repudiation (*ṭalāq*), forced marriage, and the requirement that male guardians act on behalf of women. Many countries follow a middle course by including a minimum age for marriage, expanding women's rights to divorce, and restricting a man's right to polygyny. Because legal changes still comply with local patriarchal cultures and the demands of the conservative religious establishment, the rules of the personal code remain a central issue in the gender debate. For example, based on the Qur'ān (2:226–237; 65:1), many countries preserve the husband's unilateral right to divorce while Muslim women can only apply for a divorce on specific grounds.

With the rise of Islamism, there have been attempts to abandon family legal reforms under the banner of "return to the *sharīʿah.*" For example, after the revolution in 1979 in Iran, reforms introduced by the previous regime—increasing the minimum marriage age, restricting men's access to polygamy and unilateral divorce—were repealed. After Muslim activists protested that the new laws caused women great injustice and suffering, many of the abandoned reforms were brought back gradually. In 1992, the Iranian parliament amended the divorce laws to give women better protection in marriage, and in 2002 it increased the minimum age of marriage for girls from 9 to 13.

A few differences stand out between classical Sunnī and Shīʿī law. Divorce is more difficult under Shīʿī law because it requires the presence of two witnesses in pronouncing the divorce statement (*ṭalāq*). While Sunnī marriage only ends through death or divorce, Shīʿī law allows a man to contract an unrestricted number of temporary marriages. Activists consider this union detrimental to women because it leaves them without legal rights; for example, they are not entitled to the husband's inheritance.

Shīʿī inheritance law, however, is more favorable towards women. While Sunnī law in the absence of a son allows the daughter only half of the estate, or in some cases gives precedence to agnates, Shīʿī law allows a daughter to inherit the entire estate.

Religious and Domestic Observances in Sunnī and Shī'ī Islam. Domestic Muslim observances vary greatly depending on local cultures and traditions. Women are expected to fulfill the duties that are believed to form the basic obligations of all believers. They have to suspend these duties when ritually impure because of the flow of blood. Apart from that, the Qur'ān and *fiqh* do not differentiate male and female rules of worship. Depending on the country, a woman's state of impurity leads to restrictions in mosque attendance and recitation, learning, or touching of the Qur'ān.

The roles of women in religious or cultural-religious activities vary greatly over the Muslim world. Women's activities can include participating in religious vocations as preachers, specialists of the Qur'ān, or teachers of religion, or leading folk religious events such as the *zār*, a trance ceremony of healing for those who are possessed by spirits. Women also fulfill semi-religious roles in rituals connected with pregnancy, birth, and early childhood.

Although women live secluded in some places such as Bangladesh, northern Nigeria, and northern Sudan, this practice is virtually unknown in other regions. Ideas about seclusion shape women's public role in society, sometimes resulting in the denial to women of the most basic education.

Depending on the local culture, a certain code of conduct for women is identified with Islamic religion. Handbooks concerning duties and good manners instruct women, for example, on how to behave toward their family, neighbors, and other social contacts. Some teachings of such books gained a degree of religious authority after they were adopted into local *fiqh* texts. The moral code for women varies accordingly; while in the Middle East issues of honor and virginity are central to a family's reputation, they do not feature as such in public discussions in Southeast Asia.

Mosque Attendance. According to a *ḥadīth*, the prophet Muḥammad condemned those who sought to prevent women's attendance at the mosque. He also encouraged women to attend the liturgical events associated with the two main Islamic festivals: 'Īd al-Fiṭr after Ramaḍān, and 'Īd al-Aḍḥā after the *ḥājj*. In addition, women who were menstruating or unmarried and kept from public view were allowed to attend mosque (although menstruating women did not perform the prayer). Later scholars banned young women from mosques, eventually extending this rule to older women as well, fearing deleterious consequences and quoting a *ḥadīth* that a woman's prayer is more meritorious when performed at home.

Women's mosque attendance differs from country to country and may even differ between rural and urban areas. Although in the main mosque in Mecca men and women pray together, mosques mostly have separate women's sections, and few women attend the Friday prayers. In some cases, women have built their own houses of worship (Indonesian: *musholla; Arabic, muṣallan*); Indonesian Muḥammadīyah women built *musholla* as early as the 1920s. Nowadays, many mosques include women who preach (but not the Friday sermon) and teach Islamic lessons for other women. Islamic boarding schools for girls (in Indonesia, Pakistan, Iran, and Iraq) provide extensive religious education and opportunities for women to worship, with women leading daily ritual and *tarāwīḥ* prayers during Ramaḍān. Women preachers are gaining popularity due to information technology. Cassettes with their sermons are widely sold, and women preachers even appear on television. Some women who have memorized the Qur'ān are allowed to recite on television and in mosques during nonritual gatherings. For example, in Indonesia Maria Ulfa, who won the 1980 national Qur'ān reciting competition, regularly appears on television.

Women Ṣūfīs, Saints, and Sanctuaries. In the formative period of Islam, women had distinctive roles in Sufism as disciples of Ṣūfī masters or as masters themselves. The most famous of them was Rābi'ah al-'Adawīyah (d. c. 801) whose poems and sayings were published in 1928 by Margaret Smith (2001). While her legacy is well-known, many Ṣūfī women have vanished from history as their voices were incorporated into men's writings, but Muslim women scholars such as Rkia Elaroui Cornell have begun to rediscover them. In spite of their muffled voices, there have always been women who were regarded as saints, such as the Afghan mystic Hazrat Babajan (d. 1931) and Hagga Zakīyya of Cairo (1899–1982). Believers were healed through their prayers or consoled by their gift of clairvoyance.

Women's participation in Ṣūfī rituals diminished as public opinion accepted traditions about their spiritual and intellectual inferiority to men. Concurrent with the diminishing of their role in official Islamic discourse, with some exceptions, women were pushed to the margins of Ṣūfī rituals and ceremonies. At the same time, women have continued to play significant roles in rituals surrounding the graves of saints, and women have traditionally been the majority of those visiting shrines to seek blessing or help in solving such problems as infertility. But they do not participate in the *dhikrs*, and they confine their activities to seeking blessings or participating in public festivals (*maulids*). In some places in South Asia women can be itinerant singers or poets and keepers of saints' shrines. Some women saints remained famous after death; the shrines of Zaynab, the Prophet's daughter, in Cairo, Lalla Imma Tifellut in Algeria, and Mai Supran in Punjab continue to attract visitors.

The Impact of Gender Studies. The impact of gender studies in the Muslim world is undeniable and expresses itself in numerous ways. After gaining independence from colonial powers, Muslim nation-states strove to strengthen the public and private position of women by revising personal status law, improving women's education, and providing opportunities for work.

The modernist approach to interpreting the Qur'ān as proposed by Muḥammad 'Abduh influenced numerous scholars throughout the Muslim world. Interpretations sensitive to the needs of women forced the traditional *ʿulamāʾ* to reconsider their positions. Both sides defended their respective points of view in a plethora of books on gender and Islam. Muslims on all sides of the spectrum started to rediscover the social and historical contexts in which the interpretation of the Qurʾān and *fiqh* were developed. Some have proposed that the way to avoid the influence of negative human interference with the holy texts is to discern the divine, universal principles from within the human interpretations that arose from a cultural and geographic context.

Voices of women have penetrated the public domain and have influenced the academic study of Islam and general attitudes concerning women. On the Aljazeera television channel women are partners in debates about Islam. Women have also set up their own Qurʾān study groups and begun searching for their own histories. They have even started to participate in the reinterpretation of holy texts, the final bastion of male power.

In spite of the fact that gender debates remain controversial in many parts of the Muslim world, their influence reaches beyond issues of male and female. Muslim feminists such as Riffat Hassan, who wrote about equality and justice in Islam, are now engaged in studies on the compatibility between Islam and basic human rights. In some countries (e.g., Indonesia) advocates of women's rights also increase awareness of such issues as economic conditions and poverty, the plight of prostitutes, and debates on democratic rights. As women have become active agents in reflecting on the rules and guarantees granted by Islam, they have triggered a wave of self-reflection that can range from progressive Islam to Islamist expressions. Although in some countries women have had to cope with setbacks in the gender debates, their higher levels of education have opened doors that can never be closed. Women are not only recapturing their own history, they are also shaping it, now that they can read for themselves what the Qurʾān and the holy texts teach. This means that in spite of contrary images in some countries, gender discourse has changed and is still profoundly changing Muslim societies in all parts of the globe.

See Also Dhikr; Ḥadīth; Human Rights and Religion; Islam, overview article; Menstruation; Mosque, article on History and Tradition; Pilgrimage, article on Muslim Pilgrimage; Qurʾān, article on Its Role in Muslim Practice and Life; Spirit Possession, article on Women and Possession; Sufism.

Bibliography

Abou El Fadl, Khaled. *Speaking in God's Name: Islamic Law, Authority, and Women.* Oxford, 2001. The first neo-traditionalist writing analyzing *fiqh* teachings about women in English.

Afkhami, Mahnaz. *Faith and Freedom: Women's Human Rights in the Muslim World.* Syracuse, N.Y., 1995.

Ahmed, Leila. *Women and Gender in Islam: Historical Roots of a Modern Debate.* New Haven, 1992. One of the first analytical histories of women in Islam that dislodges preconceived notions.

Ali, Kecia. "Progressive Muslims and Islamic Jurisprudence: The Necessity for Critical Engagement with Marriage and Divorce Law." In *Progressive Muslims: On Justice, Gender, and Pluralism,* edited by Omid Safi, pp. 163–189. Oxford, 2003.

Badran, Margot. "Feminism and the Qurʾān." In *Encyclopeadia of the Qurʾan,* edited by Jane Dammen McAuliffe, pp. 199–203. Leiden, 2002.

Barlas, Asma. *Believing Women in Islam: Unreading Patriarchal Interpretations of the Qurʾān.* Austin, Tex., 2002.

Cornell, Rkia Elaroui, ed. and trans. *Early Sufi Women.* Louisville, Ky., 1999. Based on a manuscript about Ṣūfī women, this volume traces how they were edited out of the history of Islam. In connection with this topic see also Shemeem Burney Abbas, *The Female Voice in Sufi Ritual: Devotional Practices in Pakistan and India* (Austin, Tex., 2002), which argues that women are central to Ṣūfī Islam through their presence at shrines and their performances as musicians and singers of Ṣūfī poetry, and as a prominent narrative voice in Ṣūfī poetry itself.

Daly Metcalf, Barbara. *Perfecting Women: Maulana Ashraf Ali Thanawi's Bihishti Zewar.* Berkeley, 1990. One of the few translated handbooks that describe the duties of women and expectations concerning their behavior.

El Saadawi, Nawal. *The Hidden Face of Eve: Women in the Arab World.* Translated by Sherif Hetata. London, 1980. Her most famous book, covering women's reproductive rights and the chronic abuse of women.

Engineer, Ashgar Ali. *The Rights of Women in Islam.* New York, 1992; 2d ed., Chicago, 2004. A widely read example of modernist reading of the Qurʾān.

Esposito, John L., with Natana J. DeLong-Bas. *Women in Muslim Family Law.* Rev. ed. Syracuse, N.Y., 2001. A useful overview of Islamic rules concerning marriage.

Göle, Nilüfer. *The Forbidden Modern: Civilization and Veiling.* Ann Arbor, Mich., 1996. Studies the complex relationships between modernity, religion, and gender relations in the Middle East and the Western world.

Hassan, Riffat. "Equal before Allah? Woman-Man Equality in the Islamic Tradition." *Harvard Divinity Bulletin* 17 (1987): 2–4. Hassan has written numerous articles in which she rereads texts of the Qurʾān and the tradition that were foundational for misogynist views on women. She has also focused on Islam and human rights.

Ilkkaracan, Pinar, ed. *Women and Sexuality in Muslim Societies.* Istanbul, Turkey, 2000. One of the few books that addresses a wider range of gender issues, such as lesbian Muslims.

Kandiyoti, Deniz, ed. *Women, Islam, and the State.* Philadelphia, 1991.

Karam, Azza M. *Women, Islamisms, and the State: Contemporary Feminisms in Egypt.* New York, 1998. Analyzes the three levels of gender discourse in Egypt with a focus on Islamist ideologies.

Kugle, Scott Siraj al-Haqq. "Sexuality, Diversity, and Ethics in the Agenda of Progressive Muslims." In *Progressive Muslims: On Justice, Gender, and Pluralism,* edited by Omid Safi, pp. 190–234. Oxford, 2003. A detailed article that traces teachings about homosexuals and "men-who-behave-like-women" in the Qurʾān, the traditions (*ḥadīth*), and *fiqh.*

Lucas, Marie-Aimee Helle, and Harsh Kapoor, comps. *Fatwas against Women in Bangladesh.* Lahore, Pakistan, 1996. One of several publications published by the organization Women Living under Muslim Laws, analyzing the influence of Islamism on women's status.

Mayer, Ann Elizabeth. *Islam and Human Rights: Tradition and Politics.* 2d ed. London, 1995.

Mernissi, Fatima. *Beyond the Veil: Male Female Dynamics in a Modern Muslim Society.* Bloomington and Indianapolis, 1975.

Mernissi, Fatima. *The Veil and the Male Elite: A Feminist Interpretation of Women's Rights in Islam* (1987). Translated by Mary Jo Lakeland. Reading, Mass., 1991a.

Mernissi, Fatima. *Women and Islam: An Historical and Theological Enquiry.* Oxford, 1991b.

Mernissi, Fatima. *Women's Rebellion and Islamic Memory.* London, 1996. Mernissi's books have been seminal in Muslim gender discourse. She has exposed patriarchal influences on interpretation and formation of Islamic texts and discovered new meanings in the texts that allow for more equality in relations between men and women.

Mir-Hosseini, Ziba. *Islam and Gender: The Religious Debate in Contemporary Iran.* London and New York, 1999. The first book that discusses in detail emerging gender discourse in Iran, focusing on the importance of the *fiqh* perspective.

Roald, Anne Sofie. *Women in Islam: The Western Experience.* London and New York, 2001. Investigates the ways in which Islamic perceptions of women and gender relations tend to undergo significant changes in Western Muslim communities.

Safi, Omid, ed. *Progressive Muslims: On Justice, Gender, and Pluralism.* Oxford, 2003. Contains articles by Kecia Ali and Khaled Abou El Fadl that call for inclusion of *fiqh* studies to advance the gender discourse in Islam.

Samiuddin, Abida, and R. Khanam, eds. *Muslim Feminism and Feminist Movement.* Delhi, 2002. A series of nine volumes that attempts to chart feminist activities throughout the Muslim world. The contributions are uneven in quality, but its size testifies to the intensity of feminist activism.

Schimmel, Annemarie. *My Soul Is a Woman: The Feminine Is Islam.* Translated by Susan H. Ray. New York, 1997.

Smith, Margaret. *Muslim Women Mystics: The Life and Work of Rabi'a and Other Women Mystics in Islam.* Oxford, 2001.

Suad, Joseph, ed. *Encyclopedia of Women and Islamic Cultures.* Leiden, New York, and Cologne, 2004. The first volume of this continuing publication deals with "Methodologies, Paradigms, and Sources." This work testifies to the immensity of the developments that are taking place within the study of gender in Islam.

Svenson, Jonas. *Women's Human Rights and Islam: A Study of Three Attempts at Accommodation.* Lund, Sweden, 2000. Examines Muslim participation in the international debate about women's human rights by analyzing the methods employed in interpreting religious sources in the works of the religious studies scholar Riffat Hassan, sociologist Fatima Mernissi, and legal studies and human rights scholar Abdullahi Ahmed an-Na'im.

Toubia, Nahid, ed. *Women of the Arab World: The Coming Challenge.* Translated by Nahed El Gamal. London, 1988.

Tucker, Judith, ed. *Arab Women: Old Boundaries, New Frontiers.* Bloomington and Indianapolis, 1993.

Wadud, Amina. *Qur'an and Woman: Rereading the Sacred Text from a Woman's Perspective.* 2d ed. New York, 1999. One of the first systematic studies by a woman that tries to reread Qur'anic teachings on women.

Webb, Gisela, ed. *Windows of Faith: Muslim Women Scholar-Activists in North America.* Syracuse, N.Y., 2000. Contains writings by several Muslims, mostly modernist feminists residing in the United States, such as Riffat Hassan, Azizah al-Hibri, and Amina Wadud.

Yamani, Mai. *Feminism and Islam: Legal and Literary Perspectives.* New York, 1996. Mai Yamani was the first Saudi Arabian woman to earn a doctoral degree from Oxford.

NELLY VAN DOORN-HARDER (2005)

GENDER AND RELIGION: GENDER AND ZOROASTRIANISM

The extant documents produced by members of the faith and the nontextual materials influenced by Zoroastrian beliefs substantially represent religious manifestations of male discourses. Those writings and items helped contour feminine parameters within a society that was largely patriarchal. Yet, if the present is any guide to the past, religious issues must have been viewed and interpreted differently by members of each gender. Likewise, ritual acts must also have been practiced differentially by members of each gender because some female-specific rites still persist despite lack of sanction by the magi or male clergy who oversee most canonical ceremonies.

HISTORY OF THE STUDY. When gender issues were initially addressed in scholarly studies of Zoroastrianism, a picture quite different to societal realities was generated. Zoroastrianism was depicted as a faith embodying many Enlightenment and Protestant values, whose male and female followers had long been equal. The female gender was routinely held in a most dignified position, and any negative statements or imagery were deviations from orthodox tradition. So when women were discussed, directly or inter alia, the tone reflected laudation for gender equality. That conclusion became well entrenched in scholarship and continues in more recent studies. When it has come under question, there have been staunch defenses tinged with apologia. There are more traditional discussions of gender-related questions, as well. Some such works are broadly based. Others focus on narrower themes such as the Achaemenid period, the Sassanid dynasty, and modern times or on such issues as religious archetypes, rituals, iconography, incest, law, clothing, and art.

On the other hand, certain recent expansive examinations—on trends in Zoroastrianism, contemporary Parsis communities in India, and doctrines of purity and rites of purification—are informed by gender theory and methodology. Furthermore, studies on misogyny within scripture and theology, differential ritual requirements and actions, access and goals of education, and present-day demographic patterns are gradually reshaping the parameters for research on Zoroastrianism. So too are studies on classical stereotypes influencing views of ancient Iranian society.

Influence of Doctrine. Gender-based aspects in Zoroastrian doctrine are multifaceted, complex, and at times contradictory. Study of the religion's ancient history through its earliest texts is complicated by the Avestan language's root nouns being grammatically feminine. But the religion's earliest practitioners began anthropomorphizing abstract concepts and attributing biological or natural genders to those concepts. As a result, the divine and demonic spirits of Zoroastrianism display gender-specific characteristics that shaped how devotees viewed their societies and the roles of men and women.

The basic doctrinal dichotomy within Zoroastrianism is between *asha* (*arta, ardā*) or "order" equated to "righteousness," opposing *druj* or *drug* (*druz*) "confusion," equated to "evil" (*Gāthās* 30.3–6, 45.2). *Asha* is grammatically neuter, whereas *druj* is feminine. Two primordial eternal entities are believed to have chosen between order and confusion: Spenta Mainyu (Spēnāg Mēnōg) or the holy spirit, equated with Ahura Mazdā (Ōhrmazd), "the wise lord," or creator—now regarded as God—for making the religiously appropriate choice, and Angra Mainyu (Ahreman, Ahriman, Ganāg Mēnōg), "the angry spirit," or destroyer—now regarded as the devil—for not deciding rightly. The grammatical gender of Ahura Mazdā/Spenta Mainyu, and Angra Mainyu/Ganāg Mēnōg were transformed into biological gender as male during personification of the concepts that each represented—and depicted as such on rock reliefs commissioned by Sassanid monarchs.

Druj also became a designation for demonic creatures in general—that is, those spirits who had chosen to do harm—and for specific manifestations of evil. In its broadest sense, that word was utilized both in masculine and feminine grammatical gender; yet many of the *druj* were regarded as female. One specific materialization was supposed to be Drukhsh Nasush (Druz ī Nasush), or the ghoul of corpses and carrion. Zoroastrians in antiquity, the Middle Ages, and premodern times clearly viewed her as a demoness who preyed upon humans, polluted their bodies after death, and spread that pollution to the living. Grammatically feminine, Drukhsh Nasush would still be denounced in the late seventeenth century as "the most impudent, constantly polluting, and deceptive of all the demonic spirits" (New Persian *Farziyāt nāme, Book of Obligatory Duties,* p. 10). By the eighteenth century, the hold that *druj* had on Zoroastrian diabology had begun to decline in the wake of science. Yet even today, the notion of *druj* persists as a symbol of evil among Zoroastrian generally, while Drukhsh Nasush is still regarded as a potential source of impurity that vitiates rituals.

Another fundamental aspect of doctrine where gender dichotomies emerged was the heptad known as the *amesha spentas,* or holy immortal spirits linked to Ahura Mazdā. Among them, Haurvatāt (Hordād, Khordād), "integrity, wholeness," and Ameretāt (Amurdād, Awerdād), "immortality, rejuvenation," were the female spirits thought to counter thirst and hunger plus heal and restore all good creatures to order, through their personification of liquids and vegetation respectively (*Tishtar Yasht* 8.47, *Zamyād Yasht* 19.96). By medieval times their gender affiliation began shifting toward neuter entities whose function was society's "protection through wholeness and immortality" (*Dēnkard,* "Acts of the Religion," ninth century, pp. 415, 416). Spenta Ārmaiti (Spandarmad, Aspandarmad), who personified "holy devotion," serves as the spiritual mother of life and an ensurer of fertility. Veneration of all three—Haurvatāt, Ameretāt, and Spenta Ārmaiti—still remains central to both male and female Zoroastrians.

Opposing the *yazatas,* spirits worthy of worship in Zoroastrian belief, stand *daēvas* (*dēws*) or demonic spirits allied with Angra Mainyu. Prominent among those evil entities is thought to be Āzi (Āz), "concupiscence, lust." Although bearing a grammatically masculine epithet, "demon-spawned," in the *Avesta,* by medieval times Āzi had come to be regarded as the mistress of demonic hordes that ravage humanity. By then, she was firmly associated in Zoroastrian cosmogony with the downfall and demise of the primeval androgyne named Gayō Maretan (Gayōmard). She was denounced by medieval Zoroastrian writers as the "most malcontent and rapacious" and "most oppressive of demonic spirits" whose "covetous eye is limitless." Only with the advent of modern science has the Āzi's hold on Zoroastrian piety declined to simply a word for greed, paralleling use of the term *āz* in New Persian. Perceived as even more dangerous an embodiment of lust was a *daēva* known as Jahikā (Jēh). Mentioned only briefly in the *Avesta,* during the Sassanid period (third to seventh centuries) she was transformed by the magi into the mistress and assistant of Angra Mainyu. It was the Jēh who supposedly reinvigorated Angra Mainyu after the initial battle with Ahura Mazdā, then introduced lust to humanity. Therefore, this demoness came to be viewed as the primordial *jēh,* "whore."

Impact of Mythology. The dualism between order and confusion that shaped both doctrines and gender perceptions left its imprint on cosmogony, apocalyptic, and eschatology as well. The first human couple, Mashya, or man, and Mashyāna, or woman, who were born from Gayō Maretan's semen, are believed to have succumbed to lying and worshiping *daēvas,* resulting in their damnation. Mashyāna, in particular, was blamed for the act of demon worship. This tale, influenced in part by the biblical story of Adam and Eve, resulted in words of admonishment directed at all women—past, present, and future—attributed to Ahura Mazdā: "If I had found another vessel from which to produce man, I would never have created you." That rebuke also urged women to be wary of Jahikā because "sexual intercourse is for you [women] like the taste of the sweetest food." Jahikā was said to have mated with Angra Mainyu to "defile women so that they in turn could corrupt men and cause abandonment of appropriate duties."

Such ideas justified a medieval misogyny. Therefore, although men were enjoined that the ideal women were physically persons whose "head, buttocks, and neck are shapely, feet are small, waist is slender, breasts are like quinces, eyes are like almonds, and hair is black, shiny, and long," they were also urged to ensure that wives were "chaste, of solid faith, and modest" (*Pahlavi Texts* 117).

Negative attitudes toward women based on glorification of female physicality and denunciation of female sexuality shaped Zoroastrian ideas on the afterlife. According to one late Young Avestan text, the soul of a righteous Zoroastrian will be greeted by his religious *daēnā* (*dēn*), "conscience," in the form of "a beautiful girl, glorious, well-shaped, statuesque, with prominent breasts" who would lead him to paradise or heaven (*Hadōkht Nask* 2.9), a theme echoed in Middle Persian exegesis. The soul of an unrighteous Zoroastrian would encounter his *daēnā* "in the form of the naked Jahikā" who was described as a noxious creature. Beauty and sensuality became rewards, together with palaces, gardens, and fountains, for those men who upheld *asha* while alive. No premodern scriptural or exegetical passages refer directly to women encountering their *daēnās* after death. Only in modern Zoroastrian thought, with the breakdown of gender-particular ideas about the afterlife to more abstract notions, has it become acceptable to assume that women too encounter their consciences as manifestations of good or bad deeds.

Ancient Zoroastrian writings about the afterlife also included the idea of judgment after death preceding consignment to heaven, limbo, or hell. During medieval and premodern times, Middle Persian commentaries and miniature paintings on the inhabitants of heaven and hell presented a disproportionate number of women condemned to suffer at the hands of demons in hell until the final resurrection. Those images reinforced the notion that women were more prone to evil behaviors, including sexual profligacy, adultery, impurity, idolatry, sorcery, and strife. The popularity of such ideas began to attenuate only in the twentieth century, as part of a larger decline in diabology and religious-based misogyny among economically, educationally, and socially upward-mobile Parsis and Irani (or Iranian) Zoroastrians.

CONSEQUENTIAL REGULATIONS AND RITUALS. Owing to the impurity associated with corpses through the demoness Nasush, and because Zoroastrians regard earth, fire, water, and earth as holy creations by Ahura Mazdā, bodies would not be buried at land or sea nor cremated. So, the magi developed a disposal system in which human corpses would be given final rites, including purification, then exposed—initially in remote areas, subsequently in funerary towers open to the sky—until the flesh had been desiccated or consumed by wild animals (as first noted by Herodotos, the fifth-century BCE Greek historian). These practices continued among many Zoroastrian communities until the eighteenth century but have declined—except in large Indian cities like Mumbai and in the Pakistani city of Karāchi—in favor of inhumation because of an attenuation in diabology and an inability to practice exposure of corpses in Iran and Western countries.

The origin of a female biological process, menstruation, came to be explained by medieval diabology rather than physiology. Menstruation was said to have begun when Jahikā revived Angra Mainyu in hell after the devil had been initially defeated by Ahura Mazdā. Upon being comforted by Jahikā, the devil "arose from his stupor, kissed her face, and the pollution called menstruation appeared on her" (*Bundahishn* 4.5). Using lust as a tool, Jahikā supposedly transferred menstruation to Mashyāna and all subsequent generations of women. Consequently, menses became in religious terms a periodic sign of women's affliction by evil. Likewise, because blood and afterbirth tissue were also feared as falling under Drukhsh Nasush's control and becoming pollutants, procreation—which was otherwise regarded as a religiously meritorious function for bringing new devotees to life—took on negative aspects. To prevent women from ritually polluting men and precincts during menstruation and after childbirth, they were isolated, then underwent purificatory ablutions. These customs have largely fallen into disuse in modern times.

The most dramatic consequence of associating female physiology with demonology was the exclusion of women from all ranks of the magi or hereditary male clerical class. The barrier against ordination into the priesthood still remains firm worldwide. Texts have even suggested that married women fulfill obligatory prayers through daily service to their families. As a result, women's religiosity has been channeled into female-specific rites such as the ever-popular visiting of *pirs,* or shrines, and making of *sofres,* or votive offerings in Iran. Among the Parsis of modern India, women religious leaders have emerged within the Ilm-e Khshnum mystical movement and, further from the mainstream, in a Nag Rāni, or cobra queen, cult.

CHANGING GENDER RELATIONS WITHIN SOCIETY. In ancient times, authority within the home lay with the elder male of each household. It was prayed that a wife would give birth to illustrious sons, a practice continued by traditionalist Parsis and Irani women today through recitation of the *Hōm Yasht,* "Devotional Poem to Haoma." By the age of fifteen, all boys and girls would be initiated into the religion and regarded as adults for religious and legal purposes—still standard among all Zoroastrian communities worldwide. At that age, girls were also regarded as marriageable. Marriage involved obtaining the consent of a woman's parents. During the Achaemenid period (seventh to fourth centuries BCE), the *taumā,* or family, continued as the central focus of domestic life. Women's participation in Zoroastrian religious rites before fire altars is attested by very occasional images on seals. Yet women were not always required to follow the faith of their husbands. So non-Zoroastrian women married to Zoroastrian noblemen seem to have continued their own devotions. Private intergender relations in Parthian (third century BCE to third century CE) and Sassanid (third to seventh centuries) times seem to have conformed largely to previously established tenets. Women were expected to have remained virginal until marriage. Induced abortions were forbidden because children were regarded as new devotees. Sexual intercourse with a pregnant woman was forbidden in case harm occurred to the developing fetus.

In late antiquity and the early Middle Ages, Zoroastrian women were generally not required to veil themselves when venturing outside their residences. Nor did the art of the Sassanid period depict specific women with overt sensuality—they were usually depicted modestly wearing flowing robes. However, generic representations of women on metalwork and stonework in particular were highly sensual, with figures often partially clad or nude. Under the laws of Sassanid Iran, based on medieval Zoroastrian beliefs, each woman's consent had to be obtained at least technically prior to a marriage contract being entered into on her behalf by a male guardian. A wife's legal standing within her husband's household depended, among other factors, on her own social class prior to marriage, the stipulations of the marriage contract, and whether she gave birth to sons for her husband. Ranks among wives included those of *pādixshāy,* or "lawful, main wife"; *chagar,* or "dependent, levirate wife"; *xwasrāy,* or "self-sufficient, independent, wife" who had chosen her own husband; and *ayōkēn,* or "ancillary wife," specifically a woman whose male children through the marriage were legal successors to her father or brother. While polygyny as a religiously sanctioned practice was attested among Zoroastrians from ancient times, the evidence for polyandry, on the other hand, is so meager as to demonstrate its observance was highly unusual among Zoroastrians. Polygyny was phased out by the faith's leaders during the early 1900s as a practice no longer in conformity with modernity.

Most taxing on medieval Zoroastrian women were the beliefs equating menstruation with impurity, and the isolation practices involved. These seem to have been some factors that influenced Irani Zoroastrian women's conversion to Islam between the eighth and thirteenth centuries CE. Another factor was that of Zoroastrian women adopting the faith of their Muslim husbands.

Attitudinal change, spurred on by secularization and westernization, has produced new challenges for orthodox religious practices. One main issue of recent concern to Zoroastrians is the status of children born to women married to men of other faiths. The traditional, patriarchal structure of Zoroastrianism has generally accepted the children of a Zoroastrian father and non-Zoroastrian mother, but not vice versa. Many Zoroastrian women in the United States, Canada, England, and Australia have begun raising their children as Zoroastrians, taking them to religious classes and fire temples and having them initiated into the faith by liberal magi. Such initiations are not recognized by a majority of Zoroastrian clerics and laypersons in India, however, where the issue remains highly controversial.

The status of Zoroastrian women, first among the Parsis and then among the Iranis, began major reorientation through access to Western-style secular education in the nineteenth century. Initially, girls were educated at home by tutors. School-level education became widespread for both genders in India by the early 1900s and quickly extended to the university level. Among the Parsis in particular, English became the language of rapidly urbanizing and secularizing families. By 1931, 73 percent of Parsis women were literate. By the 1980s, 68 percent of Parsis women held university degrees. Educated Parsis women began entering the economic workforce, mingling with both Zoroastrians and non-Zoroastrians on a regular basis. Similar processes took place among Iranis in the twentieth century. These women have began choosing professional careers over marriage and domesticity, resulting in close to a quarter of them remaining unmarried by the 1980s. Both within the traditional homelands—Iran and India—of Zoroastrianism and within the new diaspora communities in the West that formed in the twentieth century, women remain the predominant sustainers and transmitters of religiosity from one generation to the next. More Zoroastrian women (75 percent) practice religious rites daily than do men (60 percent). Additionally, through prominent roles in the lay leadership at communal centers and through service as editors of the most widely read and influential Zoroastrian newsletters—such as *FEZANA Journal* in North America and *Parsiana* in the Indian subcontinent—they play a major function in directing attention to socioreligious issues impacting on both genders and in championing religious reform.

SEE ALSO Ahura Mazdā and Angra Mainyu; Eschatology, overview article; Indo-European Religions; Iranian Religions; Menstruation; Parsis; Purification; Zoroastrianism.

BIBLIOGRAPHY

Billimoria, H. M. *Attitude of Parsi Women to Marriage.* Bombay, 1991.

Boyce, Mary. *A History of Zoroastrianism,* 2d ed. Vol. 1. Leiden, 1989.

Brosius, Maria. *Women in Ancient Persia: 559–331 BC.* Oxford, 1996.

Choksy, Jamsheed K. *Purity and Pollution in Zoroastrianism: Triumph over Evil.* Austin, Tex., 1989.

Choksy, Jamsheed K. *Evil, Good, and Gender: Facets of the Feminine in Zoroastrian Religious History.* New York, 2002.

Choksy, Jamsheed K. "Women during the Transition from Sasanian to Early Islamic Times." In *Women in Iran from the Rise of Islam to 1800,* edited by G. Nashat and L. Beck, pp. 48–67. Urbana, Ill., 2003.

Culpepper, Emily E. "Zoroastrian Menstruation Taboos: A Women's Studies Perspective." In *Women and Religion: Papers of the Working Group on Women and Religion 1972–1973,* edited by J. Plaskow and J. A. Romero, pp. 199–210. Chambersburg, Pa., 1974.

Gould, Ketayun H. "Outside the Discipline, Inside the Experience: Women in Zoroastrianism." In *Religion and Women,* edited by A. Sharma, pp. 139–182. Albany, N.Y., 1994.

Gould, Ketayun H. "Zarathushti, Zoroastrian, Parsi: Women in Zarathushti Din, Zoroastrianism." In *Women in Indian Religions,* edited by A. Sharma, pp. 134–165. New Delhi, 2002.

Hjerrild, Bodil. *Studies in Zoroastrian Law: A Comparative Analysis.* Copenhagen, 2003.

Jamzadeh, Laal, and Margaret Mills. "Iranian Sofreh: From Collective to Female Ritual." In *Gender and Religion: On the Complexity of Symbols,* edited by C. W. Bynum, S. Harrell, and P. Richman, pp. 23–65. Boston, 1986.

Jong, Albert de. "Jēh the Primal Whore? Observations on Zoroastrian Misogyny." In *Female Stereotypes in Religious Traditions,* edited by R. Kloppenborg and W. J. Hanegraaff, pp. 15–41. Leiden, 1995.

Luhrmann, Tanya M. *The Good Parsi: The Fate of a Colonial Elite in a Postcolonial Society.* Cambridge, Mass., 1996.

Rose, Jenny. "The Traditional Role of Women in the Iranian and Indian (Parsi) Zoroastrian Communities from the Nineteenth to the Twentieth Century." *Journal of the K. R. Cama Oriental Institute* 56 (1989): 1–103.

Rose, Jenny. "Three Queens, Two Wives, and a Goddess: Roles and Images of Women in Sassanian Iran." In *Women in the Medieval Islamic World: Power, Patronage, and Piety,* edited by G. R. G. Hambly, pp. 29–54. New York, 1998.

Sancisi-Weerdenburg, Heleen. "Exit Atossa: Images of Women in Greek Historiography on Persia." In *Images of Women in Antiquity,* edited by A. Cameron and A. Kuhrt, pp. 20–33, 303. 2d ed. Detroit, 1993.

JAMSHEED K. CHOKSY (2005)

GENDER AND RELIGION: GENDER AND ANCIENT NEAR EASTERN RELIGIONS

The remarkable continuity of Mesopotamian civilization can be traced in its literature, public architecture, and city planning from the late fourth millennium BCE, when, almost simultaneously, urbanism and writing appeared, to 323 BCE and the death of Alexander the Great in Babylon. Mesopotamia's economic base was agricultural, but the social foundation was the city, embodied by the temple of the city god or goddess. Prosperity depended on a two-way relationship in which divine benevolence was encouraged by correct human ritual and ethical behavior. The largest temples owned much of the city's lands and employed thousands of people. From the end of the third millennium, kings asserted enough control over temples that important religious establishments became political extensions of the palace. The religious lives of common people, however, revolved around the patriarchal family's ancestral spirits and patron god or goddess.

The earliest writings from Mesopotamia are in Sumerian, a linguistic orphan unrelated to any known language. By the middle of the third millennium, however, Akkadian, a Semitic language related to Hebrew, began to displace Sumerian. Cuneiform, a wedge-shaped script written on clay tablets, was invented by the Sumerians but adapted for writing Akkadian. Some half-million cuneiform tablets recovered from ruined cities, supplemented by archaeological discoveries, have been the main sources of information about ancient Mesopotamia.

Ugarit on the northeastern Mediterranean coast is one of several Bronze Age cities in north Syria (also among them are Ebla, Emar, and Alalakh) with rich caches of cuneiform texts written in Akkadian or Ugaritic, a Semitic language related to Hebrew. Each Syrian city and its temples reflect a mix of Mesopotamian, Hittite, north Syrian, and local traditions. In Syria as in Mesopotamia, family religion centered on a patron deity and ancestral spirits.

GENDER IN ANCIENT NEAR EAST STUDIES. A systematic study of gender and religion in Mesopotamia or northern Syria has yet to be written. Assyriology, the technical (albeit imprecise) term for the study of ancient Mesopotamia, has been only minimally affected by gender analysis. Beyond innate conservatism, the abundance of available data, especially textual data, can daunt the most stouthearted of Assyriologists. The genealogy of gender studies in Assyriology begins in the 1970s with feminist scholars who focused on the retrieval of women's lives in textual and archaeological sources. Studies of women at Ugarit and other north Syrian cities have barely ventured beyond this level of inquiry largely because so much data is still lacking. Although only men are mentioned as praying at Ugarit, one cannot conclude women did not pray, for example.

Since the late 1980s a growing number of Assyriologists have demonstrated an awareness that gender and sexuality are human creations, or "constructions," operating within a social matrix of power relations, a matrix in which religion is an active ingredient. Assyriologists have begun to question their own scholarly assumptions, categories, and methodologies, acknowledging that even ostensibly objective works—the standard dictionary of Akkadian, for example—exhibit gender bias. As such, gender theory promises to open up new directions of inquiry. For example, gender is not marked in Sumerian; however, in literary Sumerian, goddesses use a distinct dialect called *Emesal* whose dynamics might be clarified by the application of gender theory. Archaeologists, too, have set aside their earlier confidence that artifacts are value-neutral, for they are aware that ideology and biases of many types inform the questions asked in the process of excavation and data analysis.

THE NATURE OF THE EVIDENCE. Textual sources for goddesses and the religious experience of women in Mesopotamia include traditional mythological texts, liturgical hymns and temple liturgies, god lists, offering lists, omen lists, votive dedications, seal inscriptions, and personal and place names. With far fewer texts from north Syrian cities such as Ugarit, Alalakh, or Emar, the application of gender theory there constitutes a greater challenge.

Writing was invented to manage and control economic records. However, almost simultaneously, writing became an instrument for managing and controlling society. Thus, texts preserve traditions about deities and kings, but they do not necessarily represent the experience or mindset of the average Mesopotamian or Ugaritian whose temples were run by the city's upper class. Cuneiform texts generally reflect the concerns of an exclusive group of male elites from royal, administrative, and/or land-holding circles who either could read themselves or employed scribes. Few women, even in the third millennium when the goddess Nisaba was the patron of scribes, were literate, and still fewer became scribes. Nevertheless, the same administrative system that produced the texts affected every level of society.

Archaeologists' interests have in the past mirrored the subjects of the texts they excavated: temples and palaces, city plans and fortifications, elite burials. However, beginning in the 1960s, archaeologists began to investigate the ecology of the cultivated countryside, diet, domestic architecture, and gendered space in the farmhouses, city neighborhoods, temples, and palaces. These new avenues of inquiry complement the data from cylinder seals, amulets, votive sculpture, and figurines that provide a visual record of gendered imagery in the ancient Near East. Mesopotamian grave goods, personal ornament, body image, and nudity have all been subjects of gender theory-based studies.

GODDESSES, WOMEN, AND POWER. Twentieth-century scholars under the influence of Sir James Frazer's *The Golden Bough* believed that ancient Near Eastern religion centered on a "cult of fertility" characterized by lurid sexuality, an impression informed more by the fantasies of male scholars than by the data, although, to be fair, this view derived ultimately from biblical discourse against non-Israelite religion and from Herodotos. Fertility is now considered to be one of many interwoven principles in ancient Near Eastern religion, just as scholars recognize three interconnected spheres of religious activity: temple/priest religion, royal religion, and folk/popular religion. Of the three, popular religion seems to have been the primary locus of female religious activity. Also untenable today are claims (uncritically endorsed by the contemporary "goddess movement") that ancient Near Eastern goddesses could be equated with one original divine "Mother," or that all goddesses' powers derived from their biology. Across the ancient Near East, both male and female deities bestowed fertility.

Four deities of one family consistently lead Mesopotamian god lists: An/Anu (father and sky god); Ellil/Enlil (god of kingship and executive action); Enki/Ea (god of wisdom and fresh water); and Inanna/Ishtar (goddess of sexual love and war). In the third millennium there were a multitude of prominent goddesses besides Inanna, some with family-based roles such as mother (e.g., Ninhursaga), spouse (e.g., Ninlil), or sister (e.g., Geshtinanna). Other goddesses supervised activities such as grain cultivation, sheep herding, writing, weaving, and pottery and jewelry making. Gula was one of several healing goddesses (male gods brought pestilence); divination, purification, and supplication all had patron goddesses. The queen of the underworld was Ereshkigal, Inanna's sister.

In the old Akkadian period (2350–2150 BCE) some 39 percent of city deities were female. Yet by the middle of the second millennium, most of the leading goddesses seem to have been eclipsed by male gods. The tradition of goddesses as creators did not disappear, but, except for Inanna/Ishtar, male deities came to dominate the world of the gods. The reasons for this are debated; a leading theory connected the transformation with the rising power of Semitic populations whose chief deity was the warrior storm god. More recently, scholars suspicious of ethnic arguments and aware of the role gender can play in the discourse of power have looked instead to changes in political structure with the rise of militarism. When Sargon of Akkad (2334–2279 BCE) united the Mesopotamian cities into the first empire, a new imperialist/royalist discourse, in which human women and goddesses had less influence, entered the Mesopotamian consciousness. The exclusion of women may relate to their exclusion from warfare; Inanna/Ishtar's continued prominence is explained by her association with war. It is unclear, however, whether the disappearance of goddesses from texts of this period reflects a change in popular perception, or a conscious attempt to shape a new "imperialist" ideology.

The three most prominent north Syrian goddesses in the second millennium texts—Asherah, Anat, and Astarte—are usually described as fertility goddesses. Asherah was consort of the high god, El; Anat, sister and consort of the storm god, Baal, was also goddess of war. Baal was also paired with Astarte. At Ugarit, unlike in Mesopotamia, the sun was a goddess, Shapshu, who was associated with wisdom and life and death transitions and also controlled human fate and ruled the world of lesser divinities. The goddess Usharaya supervised oaths, justice, and divination, the latter an exclusively male profession in the human realm. Ugaritic texts mention only royal women as sacrificing or otherwise officiating in the cult, reinforcing the impression, from a probably skewed text-base, that official religion reinforced the ideology of royal religion.

As the second millennium progressed in Mesopotamia, even royal women lost their former high positions in the cult, just as so many goddesses seem to have lost theirs. Inanna/Ishtar's ongoing popularity has been attributed not only to her martial qualities but also to her gender-transgressive nature; in her physical violence, insatiable sexual appetite, freedom from pregnancy, and flouting of patriarchal family mores, the divine Inanna defines by negative example the proper behavior of mortal women in a patriarchal society—a dynamic that also underlies the Greek Amazon tradition. In first-millennium Assyria, for example, Ishtar was preeminent, but women were not. In the visual record, too, women appear less often.

The Babylonian *Enuma elish*, the most famous Mesopotamian creation myth (dating to the second half of the second millennium), serves as a central witness to this so-called marginalization of the goddesses. This was an essentially political myth exalting Babylon, its god Marduk, and kingship.

In the myth the gods are created first, beginning with a sexual mingling between the goddess/matrix Tiamat (salt water) and the god Apsu (fresh water). In the second part of the myth, the active younger generation of gods disturbs the more passive Apsu and Tiamat and, roused to anger, Apsu tries unsuccessfully to destroy them. Tiamat marches out with her army to avenge her spouse's defeat. As the other younger gods quail, Marduk taunts them for fearing to fight a woman, and he becomes king by single-handedly battling Tiamat to the death. His victory is narrated in language reminiscent of rape, with phallic arrows flying into Tiamat's mouth to pierce her distended belly. Marduk creates the ordered universe from Tiamat's carcass and sets up a barrier to confine Tiamat's waters, now considered to be the embodiment of chaos. Goddesses are absent from all the creative activity that follows the killing of Tiamat. Tiamat, acknowledged at one point in the myth as "she who gave birth to them all," may represent the religious order of Mesopotamia's past when goddesses and women enjoyed more power.

Nevertheless, it is far from clear whether Mesopotamian worship of powerful female deities correlates with higher status for mortal women. On the one hand, in Sumer each city god or goddess was "married" to a human of the opposite sex called an *En* who administered the temple. There is also evidence for women (notably Enmebaragesi of Kish) ruling in their own name rather than as wife of a king. On the other hand, according to Sumerian and Akkadian royal ideology, the king ruled by virtue of being the chosen spouse of Inanna, a case of a man empowered by a female deity. A woman could achieve priestly power and status as *En* of a prominent male—not female—city god. Enheduanna, daughter of Sargon of Akkad and perhaps the first named author in history, was the *En* of Nanna, the moon god at Ur, and supervised his temple. On a contemporary votive disk from Ur she oversees a ritual, accompanied by a male priest and two male attendants. Yet Enheduanna's authority, like that of her *En* grandnieces, must also be assessed through the lens of her royal status and Sargon's political policies.

Sacred marriage (*Hieros gamos*), perhaps the most famous Mesopotamian religious ritual, represented an empowering union of the human and the divine. It served politically to demonstrate the king's leading role in mediating social and political harmony, of which fertility was one essential aspect. Into the early second millennium the ritual may have involved an actual act of sexual intercourse between the king and a human representative of the goddess Inanna. However, the failure of scholars, despite their best efforts, to determine the identity of Inanna's surrogate suggests the ritual may have been a poetic metaphor. In later centuries the sacred marriage rite flourished, but as an explicitly symbolic encounter centered on the cult statue.

Several Ugaritic ritual texts (all of the second millennium) hint at a symbolic sacred marriage between the king and Pidray, daughter of the royal family's patron deity, Baal. The marriage, as in Mesopotamia, served the political purpose of affirming an alliance between the human and divine royal families. In Emar, the Nin-Dingir priestess, chosen from a leading family, "married" the storm god, but only through symbolic ritual gestures, and here, too, the marriage ritual reinforced social integration among the elites of the city.

SEXUALITY, FERTILITY, AND CREATION. In Mesopotamian mythology creation comes about by procreation or by manufacture. The *Enuma elish* includes both techniques. In the earliest Sumerian sources of the third millennium, creation resulted when the god An (heaven) and the goddess Ki (earth) "talked" to each other; a slightly later text celebrates the goddess Nammu (subterranean waters) as the creator "who gave birth to the universe." Another story tells how Enki created the world by modeling bits of clay, the same technique used by mother goddesses Nammu and Aruru to create humans. Different Mesopotamian myths credit various male and female deities with the creation of humans; in the *Enuma elish* the god Ea (Sumerian Enki) fashions humans to free the gods from work. Two Sumerian myths, "Enki and Ninmah" and "Enki and Ninhursag," describe a fertility contest between Enki and a mother goddess. The first story ends by acknowledging the necessity for semen and womb alike, but Enki, the male principle, triumphs in the second.

In Syria, too, both goddesses and gods are associated with creation and fertility. Although no Ugaritic creation myth has yet been identified, El was creator of all and Asherah was progenitress of the gods. In mythic texts Baal and El rather than fertility goddesses bestow children on their human (male) protégés. Anat, like Inanna/Ishtar, transgressed gender conventions with her extravagant violence and exuberant sensuality.

Among gods and humans fertility depended upon male sperm and divine blessing, yet goddesses and female spirits ensured safe pregnancy and childbirth in both Mesopotamia and Ugarit. Mesopotamian divination texts and women's petitionary prayers for pregnancy—to deities of both sexes—express an anxiety that sin on the woman's part has caused her infertility. On the other hand, men were likely to blame their own sexual dysfunction on women, perceiving dangers from female power out of proportion to women's marginal status; the problem could be the Evil Eye, a female bird-like creature, or it could be gender-inappropriate behavior, such as the woman on top in sexual intercourse, or it could be witchcraft, a power associated with women as well as foreign men or other socially marginal groups.

A careful reading of mythological texts reveals distinctive sexualities for men and women. The lyrics of the Sumerian Love Songs celebrating the courtship of Inanna and her consort, Dumuzi, arguably speak in a "woman's voice," employing a feminine discourse of sexuality that exults in the pleasures of the vulva. Popular (male) expressions of sexuality are more evident. In Sumerian texts gods (notably Enki/Ea) satisfy their supercharged sex drives by raping goddesses. Therapeutic metaphors based on animal sexual behavior predominate in male potency incantations. Frustrated by love, a man could resort to sexually explicit love magic, and despite claims to the contrary in modern anthologies, no such texts can be interpreted unambiguously as expressions of female desire.

THE COMPLEXITIES OF "PATRIARCHAL" CULTURE. In Mesopotamia and Syria the patriarchal family (*bit abim*—"father's house") was the essential construct of social order, operative no less in the king's court or divine households. Families were patrilinear (descent traced through the father) and patrilocal (the wife lives with her husband's family). In contrast to the modern concept of the person as an independent individual, each man or woman shared a family group identity, a notable factor when considering gender and sexuality. The *paterfamilias* maintained and managed the family's property, which included the sexuality and fertility of its women as well as family honor, an essential, if intangible social currency. Although society condemned a wife who engaged in sex outside of marriage, married men could resort to prostitutes of both sexes without legal sanction.

Marriage, even the sacred marriage, was a social and economic contract between two families. Religion played a role in the wedding ceremonies, most visibly when the bride relinquished her own family gods and ancestors along with her family identity to realign herself with her husband's family and gods. The veilings that ritualized the bride's transformations demonstrate how gendered clothing (the veil) symbolized both identity and male-female dynamics within a marriage. Similarly, at Emar, the "marriage" of the Nin-Dingir priestess to Baal required a veil, shaving, and anointing.

Gender roles followed expected patriarchal trajectories, with women's lives centered on home and family. For most women, status and security depended on marriage and fertility, and in the Mesopotamian textual record, women's religiosity is most apparent in these contexts. Across the ancient Near East, women were particularly visible and active in connection with birth and death: as midwives skilled in magic, medicine, and purification; as birth goddesses and spirits; as female mourners, both familial and professional. By being "not-male" and thus possibly less "human," women possessed a liminality that could mediate between modes of being. They participated in but did not lead the domestic cult of the family god or goddess and spirits of foremothers and fathers. Yet these spirits and divinities required feeding with food prepared by family women, a phenomenon which points to complex interconnections between food, religion, and gender.

Public position and power were primarily male prerogatives, although in the third millennium and in the Old Babylonian period (early second millennium) women are more visible in the textual and visual record and seem to have enjoyed greater access to recognized positions of power. Only men inherited prominent priestly offices or owned a share in lucrative priestly prebendaries ("time-shares"). Nevertheless, women comprised a sizable portion of the workforce in vast temple and palace complexes that functioned essentially as wealthy extended households. These institutions were usually headed by men, but women—both enslaved and free—contributed as agricultural workers, craftspeople, and cultic functionaries, particularly dancers and singers. (At Ugarit, nonroyal women appear only as cult musicians.) Temples also supported destitute widows and the poor who had "given" themselves to the deity. How these women's "professional lives" should be understood in the context of the patriarchal family is unclear.

Whereas scholars formerly saw female "sacred prostitutes" all over the Near East, they now detect a complex range of female cultic offices whose exact nature remains elusive. Terms once thought to refer to "sacred" prostitution are now understood to describe women who worked in the cult establishment. Some may have been prostitutes not because the cult required ritual sex but because of monetary vows women, even married women, had made to the deity in exchange for a pregnancy, cure from illness, or other favor. Some female cult functionaries, such as the Sumerian female *Ens* or Old Babylonian *naditu* priestesses, were "dedicated to the god" and barred from childbearing.

In Mesopotamia and north Syria, only men were professional incantation priests, exorcists, or diviners, although there were female prophets at Mari. Male practitioners scorned the female diviners, necromancers, and other women skilled in magic arts to whom unsatisfied clients or the poor could turn. (Although the practice of folk religion by women at Ugarit or Emar is probable, no texts mention them.)

The dynamics of gender and sexuality in Mesopotamia often preclude simple binary oppositions such as male-female, wife-prostitute, or domestic-public. Categories for men and women might seem fixed in Mesopotamian legal texts, but they were more nuanced in real-life situations. For example, the stereotyped *harimtu* of literature (e.g., the harlot Shamhat in *Gilgamesh*) was in real life not a prostitute but a single woman independent of the patriarchal household and thus a person whose sexuality was not regulated. Her nonconformity to conventional gender expectations comes across in the primary texts as disturbing and problematic.

Gendered status fluctuated for men and women along a spectrum of innate and acquired characteristics including age, marital status, class, and race. At birth a Mesopotamian child's gender had to be ritually fixed by placing a spindle and hair ornament before a baby girl, a baton or axe before a baby boy. Besides male and female, Mesopotamian gender categories included also the castrated male and even a nonmale/nonfemale. Female homosexual activity is unrecorded, but male homosexual intercourse is well attested, although treated in omen and legal texts with ambivalence. Male functionaries in the cult of Inanna/Ishtar (goddess of love and war) practiced ritual transvestitism. Cross-gendering discourse makes a striking appearance in Assyrian treaty curses and war rhetoric: defeated soldiers are said to "turn into women"; from the male perspective, a man's gendered identity turns upon the public perception of his honor, itself a social construction.

IMAGERY. In Mesopotamian art, images of the male and female bodies—clothed or unclothed—reflected and reinforced concepts of gender. In the third millennium, somewhat squat-figured nude or seminude male priests pour libations or carry offerings while a clothed woman priestess/official (*viz.*, the Warka Vase; the Enheduanna disk) may preside but not visibly "act." The priests are gendered male by their genitalia or distinctive short skirt; the women not so much by the subtle swell of breasts as by clothing and hairstyle. For male priests, the shaved head and beard signal ritual purity, a state from which women were excluded by virtue of their biological "lack."

Depending on the context, male nudity could mean purity, quasi-divine heroism with a touch of the erotic, or humiliation and death. From the later third millennium on, the tall, nude, bearded male hero with rippling muscles who kills monsters is physically indistinguishable from male gods in "Battle of the Gods" scenes, hence the convention of clothed but godlike, "hypermasculine" kings who mediated between humans and the divine (e.g., the Naram Sin stele or Assyrian royal stelae). Across the ancient Near East, the only passive/submissive nude males are defeated, dead, and/or captive enemy soldiers whose bodies lack the careful definition of divine or "noble" males.

Votive portrait statues commissioned by elite Sumerian women to serve as substitute selves in the temple before the statue of the deity embody elite Sumerians' ideals of conventional womanhood. Like male votives, they are clothed with no emphasis on sexual attributes. Male votives are more plentiful, but access to the god seems to have been equally available to these male and female stand-ins. Only Inanna/Ishtar (or associated goddesses) was shown nude or semiclothed. Rather than fertility *per se*, female nudity seems to have represented the mysterious divine power (Sumerian: *me*) of eroticism and sexuality, arguably a female-gendered symbol of access to or proximity to the divine. Unfortunately, no one has yet satisfactorily determined whether the countless frontally nude female figurines of popular culture represent goddesses or mortals. Textual evidence confirms that images of female nudity could serve to stimulate male libido. By contrast, when a woman or goddess is clothed, her breasts and torso are hardly articulated at all. In the first millennium, clothed women appear only as captives on Assyrian reliefs, in whose gendered visual language "woman" signified humiliation.

Although Ugarit and north Syria shared close cultural affinities with Mesopotamia, their artistic repertoire was Egyptianizing. Ugaritic bronze figurines of the seminude "smiting god" (probably Baal) recall pharaonic images that shared Mesopotamia's visual discourse of heroic maleness. Kings, both human and divine, are clothed. Female imagery consists primarily of small pendants and plaques with a frontally nude female figure reminiscent of the Egyptian goddess Hathor but of uncertain identity, although she is often identified as Asherah.

CONCLUSION. Precisely because modern Western culture conceives itself as the direct heir of biblical and classical cultures, feminists and gender theorists in these fields have pursued an open agenda of exposing—"deconstructing"—ancient discourses of oppression in order to identify similarly unacknowledged discourses in the contemporary world. The perceived remoteness of Mesopotamia from modern culture (with the exception of the contemporary goddess movement) may diminish the urgency with which similar issues are addressed by assyriologists; nevertheless, representations of femaleness, maleness, and even transgenderedness within the complex cultures of Mesopotamia and north Syria have a role to play in the ongoing human quest for self-understanding.

SEE ALSO Astarte; Baal; El; Feminine Sacrality; Goddess Worship, article on Goddess Worship in the Ancient Near East; Hieros Gamos; Homosexuality; Human Body, article on Human Bodies, Religion, and Gender; Inanna; Marduk; Marriage; Masculine Sacrality; Mesopotamian Religions, overview articles; Nudity; Patriarchy and Matriarchy; Temple, article on Ancient Near Eastern and Mediterranean Temples; Thealogy; Witchcraft, article on Concepts of Witchcraft.

BIBLIOGRAPHY

Abusch, Tsvi. "The Demonic Image of the Witch in Standard Babylonian Literature." In *Religion, Science, and Magic*, edited by Jacob Neusner, Ernest S. Frerichs, and Paul Virgil McCracken Flesher, pp. 27–58. Oxford, 1989.

Asher-Greve, Julia M. "The Essential Body: Mesopotamian Conceptions of the Gendered Body." *Gender and History* 9, no. 3 (1997): 432–461. Discusses Sumerian body language and the gendered (sometimes ambiguously so) Mesopotamian visual coding of images and body parts.

Asher-Greve, Julia M. "Stepping into the Maelstrom: Women, Gender, and Ancient Near Eastern Scholarship." *Nin* 1 (2000): 1–22. Summary of the state of gender studies in the field.

Asher-Greve, Julia M. "Women and Gender in Ancient Near Eastern Cultures: Bibliography 1885–2001 AD." *Nin* 3 (2002): 33–114.

Assante, Julia. "The kar.kid/*harimtu*, Prostitute or Single Woman? A Reconsideration of the Evidence." *Ugaritische Forschungen* 30 (1998): 5–96. An exhaustive treatment of the subject.

Bahrani, Zainab. *Women of Babylon: Gender and Representation in Mesopotamia.* London, 2001. Summary of the history of feminist and gender studies including their place (and lack thereof) in Mesopotamian studies; applies gender theory to Mesopotamian art; useful bibliography on both feminist/gender issues and Mesopotamia.

Bottéro, Jean. *Religion in Ancient Mesopotamia.* Chicago, 2001. Useful recent survey often attuned to issues of gender and religion.

Cooper, Jerrold S. "Sacred Marriage and Popular Cult in Early Mesopotamia." In *Official Cult and Popular Religion in the Ancient Near East*, edited by Eiko Matsushima, pp. 81–96. Heidelberg, Germany, 1993.

Cooper, Jerrold S. "Gendered Sexuality in Sumerian Love Poetry." In *Sumerian Gods and Their Representations*, edited by Irving L. Finkel and Markham J. Geller, pp. 84–97. Groningen, Netherlands, 1997. Contends that the "female voice" can be partially retrieved by a sensitive reading of the Inanna-Dumuzi poetry cycle.

Dalley, Stephanie, ed. *Myths from Mesopotamia*. Oxford, 1989. Accessible collection of the most important myths; helpful introductions.

Fleming, Daniel. *The Installation of Baal's High Priestess at Emar*. Atlanta, 1992. The most comprehensive study of religion in the north Syrian city of Emar; gender issues come up by virtue of the topic.

Frymer-Kensky, Tikva. *In the Wake of the Goddesses*. New York, 1992. Lucid summary of Mesopotamian goddess traditions with full awareness of gender issues; considers what is lost and gained in the monotheistic, goddess-less tradition of the Bible.

Frymer-Kensky, Tikva. "The Marginalization of the Goddesses." In *Gilgamesh: A Reader*, edited by John Maier. Wauconda, Ill., 1997. Asserts that the plethora of Sumerian goddesses was eclipsed by male deities as a reflex of growing imperialism in the later third millennium. For a slightly different perspective, see Westenholz, below.

Goodison, Lucy, and Christine Morris, eds. *Ancient Goddesses: The Myths and the Evidence*. London, 1998. Temperate introduction and three articles focusing on goddesses of the ancient Near East.

Kessler Guinan, Ann. "Auguries of Hegemony: The Sex Omens of Mesopotamia." *Gender and History* 9, no. 3 (1997): 462–479. Insightful gender-theory-based analysis of early first millennium sex omens with regard to the "meaning and emotion attached to male erotic desires and the way they were located in a discourse of masculine hegemony" (p. 462); considers the construction of binary oppositions in terms of male and female sexual aggression, the role of animals and gender constructs; the male and female gaze; the ambiguous power constructs of sex between males.

Leick, Gwendolyn. *Sex and Eroticism in Mesopotamian Literature*. London and New York, 1994. Survey of Mesopotamian sexual social norms with particular attention to poetry/mythology.

Leick, Gwendolyn. *The Babylonians: An Introduction*. London, 2003. Short historical and cultural survey centered on but not limited to Babylon.

Maier, John, ed. *Gilgamesh: A Reader*. Wauconda, Ill., 1997. Many of the articles are sensitive to gender issues.

Marcus, Michelle I. "Art and Ideology in Ancient Western Asia." In *Civilizations of the Ancient Near East*, edited by Jack Sasson, et al. New York, 1995. Notably considers gender in her survey.

Marsman, Hennie. *Women in Ugarit and Israel: Their Social and Religious Position in the Context of the Ancient Near East*. Leiden, 2003. Long-needed, up-to-date survey; primarily interested in retrieving the facts of women's lives; minimal explicit incorporation of gender theory.

Michalowski, Piotr. "Sailing to Babylon, Reading the Dark Side of the Moon." In *The Study of the Ancient Near East in the Twenty-First Century*, edited by Jerrold S. Cooper and Glenn M. Schwartz. Winona Lake, Ind., 1996. Addresses a variety of current interpretive issues relating to Mesopotamian literature, including gender studies; illuminating examples add immeasurably to this short but comprehensive essay.

Pollock, Susan. "Women in a Men's World: Images of Sumerian Women." In *Engendering Archaeology*, edited by Joan M. Gero and Margaret W. Conkey. Oxford, 1991. Demonstrates the relevance of gender theory to Mesopotamian archaeology.

Rollin, Sue. "Women and Witchcraft in Ancient Assyria." In *Images of Women in Antiquity*, edited by Averil Cameron and Amelie Kuhrt. London, 1983. Cogent discussion of witchcraft and gender issues.

Roth, Martha T. *Babylonian Marriage Agreements, 7th–3rd Centuries BC*. Neukirchener-Vluyn, Germany, 1989.

Roth, Martha T. *Law Collections from Mesopotamia and Asia Minor*. Atlanta, 1995. Basic texts.

Roth, Martha T. "Gender and Law: A Case Study from Ancient Mesopotamia." In *Gender and Law in the Hebrew Bible and the Ancient Near East*, edited by Victor H. Matthews, Bernard M. Levinson, and Tikva Frymer-Kensky. Sheffield, U.K., 1998. Practical demonstration of gender-studies theory and the questions it generates.

Steinkeller, Piotr. "On Rulers, Priests, and Sacred Marriage: Tracing the Evolution of Early Sumerian Kingship." In *Priests and Officials in the Ancient Near East, Papers of the Second Colloquium on the Ancient Near East, The Middle Eastern Culture Center in Japan*, edited by Kazuko Watanabe. Heidelberg, Germany, 1999. More technical and more politically focused discussion of sacred marriage than Cooper (see above).

Sweet, R. F. G. "A New Look at 'Sacred Marriage' in Ancient Mesopotamia." In *Corolla Torontonensis: Studies in Honor of Ronald Morton Smith*, edited by E. Robbins and S. Sandahl. Toronto, 1994. Argues that sacred marriage was solely metaphorical.

Tringham, Ruth, and Margaret Conkey. "Rethinking Figurines: A Critical View from Archaeology of Gimbutas, the 'Goddess,' and Popular Culture." In *Ancient Goddesses: The Myths and the Evidence*, edited by Lucy Goodison and Christine Morris. London, 1998. Judicious presentation of evidence; sensitively addresses many axioms of the current goddess movement.

Van der Toorn, Karel. *From Her Cradle to Her Grave: The Role of Religion in the Life of the Israelite and the Babylonian Woman*. Sheffield, UK, 1994. Succinct survey of much that is known about religion in the lives of these ancient women.

Van der Toorn, Karel. *Family Religion in Babylonia, Ugarit, and Israel: Continuity and Change in the Forms of Religious Life*. Leiden, 1996. Helpful source on women at Ugarit.

Westenholz, Joan Goodnick. "Goddesses of the Ancient Near East, 3000–1000 BC." In *Ancient Goddesses: The Myths and the Evidence*, edited by Lucy Goodison and Christine Morris. London, 1998. Proposes that ancient Near Eastern goddesses cannot be reduced to biologically determined "mother goddess" functions, but must be seen in their complex variety and specific social contexts.

Winter, Irene J. "Women in Public: The Disk of Enheduanna, the Beginning of the Office of EN-Priestess, and the Weight of Visual Evidence." In *La femme dans le proche-orient antique (Compte rendu de la XXXIII rencontre assyriologique internationale)*, edited by Jean-Marie Durand. Paris, 1987.

Winter, Irene J. "Sex, Rhetoric, and the Public Monument: The Alluring Body of Naram-Sin of Agade." In *Sexuality in Ancient Art: Near East, Egypt, Greece, and Italy*, edited by Natalie Boymel Kampen. Cambridge, U.K., 1996. "Masculinist" study of the intersection of the male body, divinity, and royal rhetoric.

MARY JOAN WINN LEITH (2005)

GENDER AND RELIGION: GENDER AND ANCIENT MEDITERRANEAN RELIGIONS

Scholars reading ancient texts from a feminist stance have long identified the problematic of studying women's experience through men's records of history and male accounts of religious beliefs and practices. In naming the problem, or deconstructing how history has been presented, the way is made open to allow for reconstructions that are not necessarily inscribed with the "male gaze." Knowledge of the ancient world is fragmentary not only because it lacks a credible picture of women's lives but also because there is a void when it comes to those who belonged to anything other than an elite class or to specific geographical areas. In attempting to overcome these restraints, a variety of methodologies need to be employed to read the variety of ancient ethnographic evidence available to reconstruct women's experiences. The method of "reading against the grain," for example, can be employed to examine prohibitive legislation aimed at women's behavior and ask what were women actually doing that prompted such prohibitions. In addition certain types of evidence (e.g., epigraphic data from tombs, art, and artifacts; domestic archaeological finds) become central rather than peripheral. These can be studied as primary sources alongside written texts.

A pioneering classical scholar in the field of gender and religion and in the use of alternative methodologies for research was Jane Ellen Harrison (1850–1928). She argued, for example, in her original thesis (1882) that the evidence from ancient Greek vases offered commentaries on myth and ritual comparable with that of Homer's *Odyssey.* As second-wave feminism began to make inroads into the academic world from the late 1960s and to gain credence in the disciplines of the humanities and social sciences, studies of gender in the ancient Mediterranean world began to emerge. The publication in 1975 of Sarah B. Pomeroy's social history text *Goddesses, Whores, Wives, and Slaves: Women in Classical Antiquity* set a milestone for the subject and clearly demonstrated how religion cannot be separated out and studied in a vacuum apart from other matters, family, economics, politics, law, and so on. Religion in all its forms was an intrinsic part of life, intertwined with the seasons, birth, marriage, and death, and it resonated with the hopes and fears of men and women throughout their lives. *The Roman Mother* by Suzanne Dixon and *The Family in Ancient Rome: New Perspectives* by Beryl Rawson are examples of subsequent studies that demonstrate this intimate relationship among religion, family, and society. Mary Beard's work on Roman religion, particularly the cults of Magna Mater and Vesta, marks the convergence of the "third wave" in terms of gender study and classical studies. Informed by contemporary gender theory, Beard has uncovered the complexity of gender roles and how they were constructed, both male and female, in antiquity and demonstrated their divergence from the bipolarity of gender as played out or at least recounted in modernity.

In attempting to reconstruct women's lives in the ancient world in the light of sparse hard evidence, religious cults and their accompanying myths and rites represent a vital piece in the jigsaw. Religions reflect the experiences and expectations, fulfilled and unfulfilled, of their adherents and thus present mirror images of particular times and places, albeit on a cosmic scale. Religion thus can offer another insight into women's lives in the ancient world as the rich variety of beliefs and practices in effect act out society, politics, and legislation of the day.

The rich variety of beliefs and practices that make up the religions of the ancient Mediterranean reflects a long relationship of intermingling of the Egyptian, Hellenistic, and Roman worlds. This intermingling can be traced to the ascendancies of the great empires of the ancient world, beginning with Alexander the Great in the fourth century BCE and the engagement between Egyptian and Hellenistic cultures and seen to culminate in the rich tapestry of religion that was woven during the zenith of the Roman Empire. Some of the oldest beliefs and practices of the ancient Mediterranean stem from Egypt, and these reappear throughout ancient history as they are adopted and adapted for new contexts across the various empires.

GENDER IN THE ANCIENT WORLDS. When one examines Egypt itself, one discovers that the evidence is particularly scarce regarding the lives of women in ancient Egypt except for those at the pinnacle of this highly stratified society. In the time of the Middle Kingdom (2125–1650 BCE), for example, the wives and mothers of the pharaohs could wield significant influence and power, as witnessed by the evidence from their tombs. From the early dynastic period the pharaoh was identified with the sky god Horus and the son of the sun god Re. His Great Royal Wife was fully human, and her role of producing the royal heir was of supreme importance. The future king would be endowed with the unique divine–human nature that would enable him to act on behalf of both gods and human beings. In the time of the New Kingdom (1650–1069 BCE), Queen Hatshepshut succeeded in claiming the throne on the death of her husband and half brother. She based her claim to the throne on her own divine birth, which is detailed on the walls of her mortuary temple at Deir al-Bahri. The mural shows how the god Amun-Re, in the form of her father, Thutmose I, approaches her mother Ahmose, who conceives the goddess-king, the female Horus. Hatshepshut was depicted in the same manner as a male pharaoh, with a bare chest and short skirt (a guise used in the Hellenistic period to depict Cleopatra VII).

Less specifically, ancient Egypt was a rich resource for later empires that wished to broaden their religious as well as territorial boundaries, and the Roman Empire in particular was eager to import Egyptian religious practices into its cities across the empire and into the heart of Rome itself. Thus Egyptian myths with their accompanying cults offer windows into the lives and expectations of men and women not only in ancient Egypt but also throughout the ancient world. Their influence lasted until accession of Christianity as the dominant religion (but also beyond that time, when their influence on that religion is taken into account). A key example is the myth of Osiris and Isis, which can be traced back at least to the time of the first dynasty (beginning of the fourth century BCE).

Within the Hellenistic world, women in ancient Greek society led secluded lives, residing in the private domestic sphere and protected from the public arena. In the upper echelon of Greek society women who were not slaves and who were married to a head of a household led lives of seclusion away from male company, spending most of their time in the *gynaikonitis,* the women's quarters. However high their social ranks, women had no political voice or means of participation as citizens. Religious rituals, however, were an exception to the norm and provided a public function for women and a context in which they could contribute to the welfare of the city-state. Moving down the social ladder, one finds the sexes mingling more freely in the public arena, where female slaves, for example, worked alongside and served men. Foreign women worked as entertainers for male audiences, providing music, dancing, and escorts as well as sexual pleasures.

In contrast to at least the women of high social rank in Greek society, women living under the sociopolitical system of the Roman Empire enjoyed relative freedom. In the third century BCE the notion of "free marriage" as one of the legal forms of marriage was introduced. In this new system a woman remained attached to her former family, she retained her own property, and she had the freedom to divorce her husband. This is in contrast to earlier types of marriage in ancient Rome, *in manu,* for example, which literally means "in the hand of," that is, a wife was under the full control of her husband. A Roman wife could have a high profile not only in household management, where she had the task of overseeing male servants and slaves, but also in the education of her children. Prior to coming of age, sons and daughters of noble families were educated together, but as adulthood approached a sharp distinction was made between the sexes when boys were prepared for citizenship and a public career. Roman society remained patriarchal to the core, but in negotiating its boundaries, women within the nobility could realize a limited emancipation that blurred the distinction between domestic and public. A woman could develop a home-based industry in a larger household, for example, managing slaves in the production and distribution of cloth. Furthermore the Punic Wars of the third century BCE resulted in a huge death rate among men of the Roman Empire and left many women the sole heirs of the father's, brother's, or husband's estate. However, a noblewoman's power, wealth, education, and relative freedom were a world away from a slave woman's powerlessness, poverty, illiteracy, and servitude. For many women living in Roma society, life was little different from women in ancient Greek society, and thus the myths and rituals of the gods and goddesses resonated with their life experiences and their hopes and fears.

DEMETER AND PERSEPHONE. One goddess cult of ancient Greece that belonged to the great mystery religions and was particularly popular with women, although not exclusively so, was that of Demeter. Athenians celebrated the mysteries of this great cult at Eleusis as well as in the ancient Greek colonies of Sicily and southern Italy. This religion tended to remain limited to the religious experience of Greeks and Greek colonists possibly because the central myth and ritual of the cult reflected so closely the lives and expectations of women in Greek society. This feature is illustrated by the *Homeric Hymn to Demeter,* composed most probably in the late seventh century or early sixth century BCE at Eleusis, which describes a young girl's journey from puberty to womanhood. It describes how Demeter grieves for her daughter Persephone (also called Kore, "maiden"), who was first abducted by Hades and taken to the underworld and then given to him in marriage by Zeus. The stricken mother deserts Olympus, the sphere of the gods, for the world of mortals and goes to Eleusis, where she asks the people to build a temple for her. Unappeased, Demeter brings devastation to crops and cattle, ignoring the intercessory pleas from Zeus's divine envoys. She asks only for a glimpse of her daughter. Zeus has no choice but to agree to Demeter's terms, and he sends his messenger Hermes to the underworld to negotiate with Hades. Hades agrees to allow Persephone to see Demeter. Persephone pours out her heart to her mother and is consoled. Zeus decides to let mother and daughter remain together for two-thirds of each year, but Persephone must return to Hades for the remainder of the year. Content, Demeter allows the earth to be fertile once more, and the people of Eleusis continue their worship of her.

The importance of the Demeter and Persephone myth to Greek religion has been thought to stem from its connections with the seasons and the crucial issue of fertility. The centrality of female characters reflects the obvious links between women and birth. The depiction of marriage as beginning with rape is a common feature of Greek myth, as is the traumatic separation of young daughters from their mothers. The fathers are usually the instigators of this painful process, and although the anguish is well documented, marriage itself as the normative institution within society is not questioned.

THE ROMAN EMPIRE. The actual content of the Eleusinian mysteries remains hidden from the scrutiny of modern scholars, but there is evidence for many religious activities and devotions that focused on Demeter, some of which continued in popularity down into the Roman Empire. The Demeter myth reinforces traditional Greek practices regarding women's lives, in particular their rite of passage from daughter to wife, mirrored by the Demeter myth. The myth is a commentary on the way life is in Greek society, and by remembering it in the religious rites and devotions associated with it, the values of that society are reinforced.

Whereas the Demeter and Persephone devotions served the needs of women progressing from girlhood to womanhood, the devotions to Artemis and Hera focused on protection and success in childbirth and these cults were prohibited to slaves and foreigners. The third age of womanhood is represented by the goddess Hecate, regarded in negative terms as a haggish, cronelike demon and in positive terms as a goddess who could protect, grant success, and act as an advocate.

In contrast, the Greek myth of the Amazonian women seems then to contradict one general presumption concerning the lives of Greek women. It is about women who reject marriage and the confines of domesticity. It describes a society that prefers matrilineal descent to patrilineal and a society in which liberated women even engaged in active warfare. In its earliest forms the myth may have functioned as a mirror of a preclassical society. For instance, in the archaic epic of the sixth century the Amazons are described as female warriors who, with their Queen Penthesilea, who was killed by Achilles, battled against Bellerophon and Herakles. However, the status of the Amazon stories clearly changed by the fifth century as they began to fulfill a role within Athenian society of representing an inversion of the natural and preferred status of women. The Amazon women are now depicted as the female counterparts of the centaurs, the mythical, bestial, and violent rapists. Their representations in later centuries depict how alien such ideas would be to the patriarchal nature of Greek society. They are said to live in a totally female society, only venturing out for sex so they can conceive children. Only female babies are welcome, male offspring are offered for adoption or castrated or even killed. Diodorus Siculus, writing in the first century BCE, describes how Amazon men behave like women—tending home and children and cultivating women's skills, such as weaving. Thus the Amazonians are held up as the antithesis to Athenian society.

ADONIS AND DIONYSOS. The popularity of the Demeter and Persephone myth and the religious devotions associated with them as goddesses testifies both to the close bonds between women in Greek society and to how society sacrificed those bonds to the "higher" cause of marriages arranged by men. The participation of women in the male cults of Adonis and Dionysos could suggest a certain dissatisfaction among women with their given status and role. Neither Adonis nor Dionysos belongs to the essentially Greek hierarchy of gods, the Olympians; both have foreign pedigrees. Adonis has a Semitic name and is regularly associated with the dying and rising deities of the ancient Near East. In the male cults gods were closely associated with goddesses, Adonis with Aphrodite, his consort, Dionysos with Semele, his mother. Some of these cults had ceremonies designed to encourage women to be uninhibited. Dionysos, for instance, was the god of wine, and his worship naturally provided occasions for uninhibited behavior. Rituals associated with Dionysos range from the rather sedate Lenaia (from *lenai*, another name for Dionysos's devoted maenad), in which food and drink offerings accompany the ceremonial entry of the god's mask into the sanctuary for worship, to the more erotic Anthesteria, the winter wedding festival between Basilinna, the wife of the *archon basileus*, and Dionysos.

THE RITES OF *THE BACCHAE*. More extreme, however, were the rites recorded in *The Bacchae*, a play written as early as the late fifth century BCE by Euripides (c. 480–406 BCE). The Bacchae are the women followers of Dionysos, and they are also known by the more pejorative term *maenads*, from the verb *mainomai*, meaning "to be driven mad." The myth of Dionysos is recounted in many ancient sources, but Euripides drew the classic description of Dionysiac ecstasy, the source for accounts in later centuries.

According to Euripides' *Bacchae*, Dionysos introduced his rites in Thebes to avenge the injustices perpetrated against his mother Semele, who had been dishonored by the lies spread about by her sisters, Agave, Autonoe, and Ino. On hearing that Semele was pregnant, the sisters discounted her own truthful account that she had conceived through Zeus and instead told the story that she had been impregnated by a mortal. They said that her father, Cadmus, had persuaded her to lie and say it was Zeus. This, the sisters explained, was why Semele had been struck dead by one of Zeus's thunderbolts. However, Dionysos explains that his mother had in fact been the victim of the jealous Hera's thunderbolt. This was shot while his father Zeus grabbed him from his mother's womb, saving him from being a victim of Hera's jealous plot.

The revenge of Dionysos for his mother's honor is directed at his aunts. He induces insanity on them, and they and bands of women followers dance off to the countryside, wearing fawn skins with snakes around their necks, leaves and branches in their hair, and each with a wand (*thyrsos*) in her hand. They feed wild animals with their breast milk before they behave wildly—ripping animals apart, wrecking villages, abducting children. They are impervious to the missiles hurled at them by the men of the villages, who suffer terrible wounds from the women's wands. There are many such details recounting the anarchic behavior of the Bacchae as they maniacally devour the countryside.

Dionysos's revenge reaches its climax when his aunt Agave dismembers what she perceives to be a wild animal but is actually her own son Pentheus in disguise. She is allowed to regain her sanity in time to recognize the torn body of her son just as she brings it to her father. The outcome is that the dynasty of Cadmus is destroyed, Agave is exiled, and the city of Thebes becomes a center for the worship of Dionysos.

The account of Euripides implicitly details many of the features associated with Dionysiac rites known from artistic impressions on vases down the centuries—the lively dancing and dressing up in animal skins and various types of vegetation. The actual ceremonies remained the secret knowledge of initiates, and this secrecy motif was intensified by the rites being practiced at night, attracting many rumors and exaggerated imaginings from those outside the cult. The sexual nature of these rites seem to belong to the fantasies of external perception rather than the reality of the religion itself.

Classical scholars have had to weigh the evidence of the written accounts of the Dionysiac myths against what has been discovered from classical representations in various artworks. There is insufficient external evidence from Euripides' time to determine whether he based his account of the myth on the actual practices of the Dionysos cult as he knew it. It may be that his work actually provided the descriptions on which later rites were based. According to the myth, women are the main participants, the Bacchae. Pentheus is the only man mentioned, and he appears not as a man but disguised as a wild beast.

THE HELLENISTIC PERIOD. The evidence increases during the Hellenistic period. Plutarch (before 50–after 120 CE) refers to women's ecstatic rites associated with Dionysos, describing how some women got trapped in severe weather while they were celebrating winter rites for Dionysos. He also described how a group of maenads, in their ecstatic state, had strayed in to the territory of the enemy, but thanks to the protection of the women of that town, Amphissa, they survived. It is also at this time that the cult of Dionysos spread to Italy and then to Rome, noted later, in negative terms, by Livy (59 BCE–17 CE). Livy's account of one particular episode that occurred in 186 BCE gave Bacchae-type rites their debauched, orgiastic, and corrupt reputations. Livy recounts how a young man had to flee to avoid initiation into the cult at the shrine of Semele, which had introduced male participants. Livy's descriptions of the Dionysian Bacchae included the practice of male self-castration and gross ornamentation for its male priests. Livy wrote his account some 150 years after the events he described, and it is heavily dependent on the work of earlier Roman historians, conservative characters such as the elder Cato (234–149 BCE). Livy's later reconstruction of the bacchanalian scandal betrays many traces of the moral outrage of his historian forefathers.

ISIS. Isis was the focus of another Oriental cult imported into Roman culture. It had particular associations for women in terms of both its priesthood and its popularity. The Egyptian myth that lies at the heart of the rites of Isis is a familiar one of sibling rivalry. According to Plutarch's version, a king of Egypt, the god Osiris, has a brother, Typhon, and two sisters, Isis and Nephthys. Typhon conspires against his brother to gain power, luring him into an ornate treasure chest, which he then seals and throws into the Nile. Isis, who has been incestuously involved with Osiris since they shared the same womb, goes looking for her lost brother. In her search she discovers that Osiris has also been on sexual terms with their sister Nephthys, who has given birth to a son. Nephthys left this baby exposed to die because she was actually married to her other brother, the villain Typhon. Isis saves the child, named Anubis, who remains with her and becomes her attendant and protector. Continuing her search for Osiris, Isis finds the treasure chest on the river shore at Byblos, and she becomes pregnant, presumably by her dead brother, or she may have already been pregnant by him (Plutarch does not clarify this detail). Their child is Horus, a popular and significant figure in the rites associated with Isis and Osiris. Meanwhile Typhon comes across the treasure chest again, opens it, and cuts up his brother's body into fourteen pieces, which he scatters over the waters of the Nile. Distraught with news of this act, Isis combs the river marshes for the pieces and finds them all save for the penis, which some fish have eaten. Osiris then returns from the underworld and trains his son Horus to avenge Typhon on his behalf.

During the Hellenistic period, the Greeks identified Isis with Aphrodite, although she was much more than the goddess of love. Transported to Rome, the Isis and Osiris rites understandably lost their connections with the Nile. One dramatic rite in which the image of the river setting survived, however, was the March festival of Navigium Isidis, richly described by Apuleius (c. 123–c. 170 CE) toward the end of the second century CE. A great procession of women and men, mostly dressed in white linen, followed by priests carrying the sacred objects and the gods themselves (i.e., a person dressed as Anubis and a cow representing Isis) made their way to a nearby riverside (in Apuleius's account it was at the port of Cenchreae). A grand sailing boat was then purified by the high priest and launched by the devotees. Other rites (e.g., the Festival of Isia) retained the clear pattern of the myth, reenacting the death of Osiris and the mourning and searching of Isis, culminating in the joy of resurrection. In addition to the festivals there were daily rituals at the temple in which the figure of Isis was cleaned and dressed.

The Isis cult was not exclusive to women, but because two of the central characters, Isis and Nephthys, were female, women were given prominence in any ceremony that reenacted the myth. Apuleius's description from the second century CE makes it clear that the cult of Isis was popular among women of all classes in Italy and the western provinces: "Then followed a great crowd of the Goddess' initiates, men and women of all classes and every age, their pure white linen clothes shining brightly" (Apuleius, *Metamorphoses*, 18, in Graves, 1951). Pictorial evidence also exists. For example, in a first century CE wall painting from Pompeii, a ritual at a temple of Isis is depicted, and the popularity of this cult among women is reflected by the number of female figures represented.

The central focus of the cult of Isis is the relationship between a man and a woman. Its incestuous nature serves to intensify the bond. It embodies perfect heterosexual love that triumphs even over death, and as such it supports the Greco-

Roman ideal of the foundation of the family. It is tempting to interpret civic support of this cult as an attempt to endorse the family and the status quo of society and women's devotion to it as their acquiescence. Alternatively the cult so perfectly represented the expectations of Greco-Roman women that it provided sanction and sanctification for their lives. Another factor to explain the cult's popularity among women may have been linked to the countless military campaigns that characterized the years of the late republic and early empire, which left so many married women as widows. Living in that reality, rites that focused on a couple separated by death yet reunited by a love stronger than death would surely have special significance for women.

MAGNA MATER. The goddess Magna Mater, or Cybele, was imported into Rome from Pessinus in Asia Minor in 204 BCE and became one of Rome's foremost cults. It was equally popular among men and women, although its rituals, which revolved around the jealously of the goddess over her lover's infidelity, more explicitly reflect women's experiences. As was the practice in the case of foreign cults, it was given legal status in Rome through recourse to the Sibylline Books. It was a cult traditionally associated with the city of Troy, to which the origin of the Roman race was traced, and therefore could be regarded almost as an ancient Roman religion. In Rome an image of Magna Mater was set up in the heart of the city on the Palatine Hill. Although not her consort, Attis is the individual most closely associated with the goddess. The central theme of the many and varied legends describing Attis's relationship with Magna Mater focuses on the young mortal Attis, caught up in an ecstatic frenzy instigated by the goddess because she was jealous of his relationship with another woman. When in this frenzy Attis castrates himself and dies, the goddess brings him back to life.

One well-recounted aspect of the Magna Mater cult was the taurobolium, the killing of a bull. This was a particularly gory practice in which the animal was sacrificed in such a way to ensure the sacrificer was spattered with its blood. This messiness distinguishes the Magna Mater cult from the normal cultic practice of Roman religion in which the priest remained unstained throughout the sacrificial slaughter.

VESTAL VIRGINS. In the context of women's participation in religion in the Greco-Roman world, Vestal Virgins have furnished popular images and language down the centuries of Western culture, and this familiarity has tended to give them a prominence out of keeping with the religious situation of their time. Their numbers, for example, were minimal—six in total. They were a crucial factor, however, in Roman perceptions of the relationship between their city and the deities who protected it. The Vestal Virgins were chosen for their unique office before they had reached puberty, between the ages of six and ten. Once chosen they were celibate for thirty years and devoted to the task of tending the sacred fire of the round temple of Vesta at the center of the Forum. This shrine was the oldest of the Forum and—according to the account of Pliny the Elder (23–79 CE) who noted, however, that as a man he would have had no access to the shrine—it had no image of the goddess Vesta but contained a sacred phallus *(fascinum),* the Di Magni (i.e., household gods of Troy), and a sacred Trojan image of Athena known as the Palladion. The Vestal Virgins as a group are unique in social, political, and religious terms. Beard (1980), in recognizing their distinctive status, has noted similarities between them and aristocratic males as well as affinities with unmarried women and matrons. The celibacy of the Vestal Virgins was jealously guarded, and Plutarch described that if any of their number was discovered to have broken her vow, she was ceremonially buried alive.

The high priest of the cult was male. In fact the first emperor, Augustus (c. 27 BCE–14 CE), was elected high priest in 12 BCE, and when this happened he created a shrine to the goddess Vesta in his own home on the Palatine. Even the emperor, as high priest of the cult, could not enter the shrine—that privilege was reserved for its female virginal attendants. He could as high priest, however, carry out their execution. This office could be seen as yet another element in Augustus's search for infinite power and immortality.

The power of the Vestal Virgins was a visible reality in many aspects of the lives of these females, but these were in effect young women without any sexual autonomy. They were offered in the selection process for the Vestal Virgins at the age of six by their parents, and if chosen they were committed to that life for a minimum of thirty years. As noted, their sexuality was controlled or rather restricted by the state, and any independent act to exercise their own wills in this respect was met with execution by the hand of the male high priest. They did receive abundant privileges, such as attending senatorial dinner parties, going to the theater with the imperial women, and guarding precious documents of state. These privileges reflect the belief among Romans that these women were the true guardians of Rome, its purity and its potency.

BONA DEA. Another popular cult in Rome, associated with Roman matrons, was the cult of Bona Dea, the "good goddess." Her proper name was Fauna, understood as the daughter or sometimes the wife of Faunus, otherwise known as Pan. She was worshipped exclusively by women, and her official annual nocturnal rite was celebrated in early December in the house of the chief magistrate, led by his wife and assisted by the Vestals. This was a cult particularly associated with the *matronae,* who were distinguished as a group by their respectability; that is, they were legally married and therefore able to produce rightful heirs, and they were freeborn. They wore particular clothes: a long dress (stola) and a distinctive headband. They were involved in many religious festivals in Rome, but the Bona Dea cult was a particular focus for them. In fact the Bona Dea cult seems to have been elitist not only in terms of gender but also in terms of its popularity among the freed classes. Knowledge of the Bona Dea cult is, as so often, restricted to male descriptions, which are suspect because men were excluded from all the preparations and celebrations. One detailed account comes from Cicero (106–43 BCE), who was directly involved because his residence as magistrate was the venue for the December rite. His account is highly subjective because at the time (63 BCE) he was involved in a political struggle, and he interpreted particular happenings as signs to himself from the goddess. The next year a man tried to infiltrate the festival, this time at the house of Julius Caesar, who held the praetorship that year, by disguising himself as a female harp player. The infiltrator was recognized as Clodius, a prominent member of Roman elite society whose aim, it was alleged, was to seduce Caesar's wife during the celebrations. He denied the charge and was found not guilty, a result, according to Cicero, that came from a bribed jury.

This event formed the basis of Juvenal's (c. 55–130 CE) lively and erotic pastiche, which may be seen as a lurid undermining by male commentators of female religious practices (Juvenal, 1991, Satire 6). It would seem to be the case, however, that these rites did allow women an opportunity to behave in a more free and unrestrained manner than public events would normally allow. Hendrik H. J. Brouwer paints a convincing picture from all the available evidence of the December rites, at which women could drink undiluted wine, for example, and have boisterous songfests accompanied by female musicians. This party atmosphere developed when the ritual part of the evening—the sacrifice of a pregnant pig in front of the cult statue of Bona Dea brought from the temple—was completed.

Greco-Roman religious practices are filled with diversity and variety on a huge scale. It is impossible to make general observations about religions in the light of the extreme diversity, including a great number of variables, such as local political interest, geographical features, and fusion of residual culture with imported practices. It is clear, however, that religion expressed women's experiences—emotional and physical—from becoming young women to their lives as mature matrons. Religion is not only a reflection of those experiences but a prescriber and reinforcer of them.

INFLUENCE ON CONTEMPORARY WOMEN'S SPIRITUALITY. Religions of the ancient Mediterranean not only resounded with the experiences of men and women in the ancient world. In modern times the myths and cults of antiquity have furnished contemporary religious trends. In the context of the West, along with its colonial history, the monolithic religious system of Christianity was in the ascendancy from the time of Emperor Constantine in the early fourth century until modern times, and it gave shape and form to Western civilization and served as a means of defining tradition. In sum, religions of the ancient Mediterranean provide a "pretraditional" range of religious expression that is reflected in the contemporary period of the "posttraditional." This has been true especially in the context of feminist spirituality, where traditional religion, identified as patriarchal, has often been rejected or radically transformed. The goddess, who takes various forms in ancient Mediterranean religions, has been a particularly rich resource for women attempting to construct a spirituality with women's experience at its core. Key feminist scholars who have drawn on goddess mythology from ancient Mediterranean cultures for contemporary women's spirituality include Carol Christ, Starhawk, and Charlene Spretnak. These writers originally experienced traditional religion but use the resources of ancient goddess spirituality, that is, pretraditional religious experience, to take them beyond those traditions to posttraditional goddess spirituality.

SEE ALSO Cybele; Dionysos; Egyptian Religion, overview article; Goddess Worship, article on Goddess Worship in the Hellenistic World; Greek Religion; Hellenistic Religions; Isis; Thealogy.

BIBLIOGRAPHY

Beard, Mary. "The Sexual Status of Vestal Virgins." *Journal of Roman Studies* 70 (1980): 12–27.

Beard, Mary. "The Roman and the Foreign: The Cult of the Great Mother in Imperial Rome." In *Shamanism, History, and the State*, edited by Nicholas Thomas and Caroline Humphrey, pp. 168–169. Ann Arbor, Mich., 1994.

Beard, Mary, John North, and Simon Price. *Religions of Rome*, vol. 1: *A History*, vol. 2: *A Sourcebook*. Cambridge, U.K., 1998.

Beard, Mary, and John North, eds. *Pagan Priests: Religion and Power in the Ancient World*. London, 1990.

Blundell, Sue, and Margaret Williamson, eds. *The Sacred and the Feminine in Ancient Greece*. London, 1998.

Brouwer, Hendrik H. J. *Bona Dea: The Sources and a Description of the Cult*. EPRO 110. Leiden, Netherlands, 1989.

Christ, Carol P. *Laughter of Aphrodite: Reflections on a Journey to the Goddess*. San Francisco, 1987.

Christ, Carol P. *Rebirth of the Goddess: Finding Meaning in Feminist Spirituality*. New York and London, 1998.

Christ, Carol P., and Judith Plaskow, eds. *Womanspirit Rising: A Feminist Reader in Religion*. San Francisco, 1979.

Dowden, Ken. *Religion and the Romans*. London, 1992.

Fantham, Elaine, Helen Peet Foley, Natalie Boymel Kampen, Sarah B. Pomeroy, and H. Alan Shapiro. *Women in the Classical World: Image and Text*. Oxford, 1995.

Graves, Robert. *Apuleius: Transformations of Lucius*. New York, 1951.

Harrison, Jane Ellen. *Prolegomena to the Study of Greek Religion* (1903). Princeton, N.J., 1991.

Hawley, Richard, and Barbara Levick, eds. *Women in Antiquity: New Assessments*. New York and London, 1995.

Heyob, Sharon Kelly. *The Cult of Isis among Women in the Greco-Roman World*. Leiden, 1975.

Juvenal. *The Satires*. Translated by Niall Rudd. New York, 1991.

Just, Roger. *Women in Athenian Law and Life*. London, 1989.

Plaskow, Judith, and Carol P. Christ, eds. *Weaving the Visions: New Patterns in Feminist Spirituality*. New York, 1989.

Pomeroy, Sarah B. *Goddesses, Whores, Wives, and Slaves: Women in Classical Antiquity*. New York, 1975.

Robinson, Annabel. *The Life and Work of Jane Ellen Harrison.* New York, 2002.

Sawyer, Deborah F. *Women and Religion in the First Christian Centuries.* New York, 1996.

Snyder, Jane. *The Woman and the Lyre: Women Writers in Classical Greece and Rome.* Carbondale, Ill., 1989.

Spretnak, Charlene. *Lost Goddesses of Early Greece: A Collection of Pre-Hellenic Myths.* Boston, 1984.

Staples, Ariadne. *From Good Goddess to Vestal Virgins: Sex and Category in Roman Religion.* London, 1998.

Starhawk. *The Spiral Dance: A Rebirth of the Ancient Religion of the Great Goddess.* San Francisco, 1979.

Turcan, Robert. *The Cults of the Roman Empire.* Oxford, 1996.

Ward, Julie K. *Feminism and Ancient Philosophy.* New York and London, 1996.

DEBORAH F. SAWYER (2005)

GENDER AND RELIGION: GENDER AND CELTIC RELIGIONS

The ways in which gender identities are embedded in religious rituals, symbols, institutions, and language reflect changing social and political power structures, especially in relation to women. One effect of this wider debate has been to look to the past to provide paradigms in which access to power and influence in the institutions of religious life have been more equally balanced. Since ancient Greek writers first identified the Celts as *keltoi,* this group has provided a powerful symbol of otherness for the perception of women and their function in religious contexts in Celtic society. The issue of gender, and how this shaped concepts of sacredness in the religious behavior of the Celts, has been a topic of discussion since the late nineteenth century, and ideas of Celtic pagan and Christian spirituality have played a prominent role in alternative spirituality movements since the second half of the twentieth century.

HISTORICAL SOURCES. The main sources for information about Celtic religion come from archaeological evidence, the testimony of classical writers, and narrative material preserved by western Celtic groups, such as the Irish, Welsh, and Scots. Because much of the context has been lost or the commentary has come from outsiders, these sources present certain difficulties. Classical authors give information on religion and gender roles, but they often used Celtic behavior to comment on themselves. A number of mythological narratives are preserved as later written texts, but the time gap between them and a more ancient past means that themes in medieval texts cannot be assumed to reflect the survival of ancient religious practices. Another factor is the changed attitude to the nature of Celtic culture. Whereas once scholars assumed similarity and continuity between ancient Celts and later cultures in Britain, Ireland, and Brittany, since the 1980s there has been less emphasis on folk migrations and on supposed connections between continental and insular Celts and more emphasis on the effects of literacy and the introduction of Roman culture and Christianity. It is more difficult, therefore, to argue for Pan-Celtic deities or long-term continuance of religious behavior. The picture to emerge from this reassessment suggests that there was no centralized Celtic pantheon, although some deities had extensive spheres of influence. Participation in religious life also seems to have been more varied. The druids were an elite religious caste functioning in western areas of Gaul, Britain, and Ireland, and their role overlapped with that of bards and poets in the post-Roman world. The organization of religion in other areas such as Galatia or Celt-Iberia is less well known. However, despite these limitations, it is possible to consider some of the gender issues as they related to religion among groups of Celts in the ancient world and in the early cultures of insular groups such as Ireland and Wales.

The Roman geographer Strabo (64 BCE–24 CE) makes the tantalizing suggestion that gender tasks among the Celts were the reverse of those among Romans. In the context of religion, writers mention druids, and a few suggest the presence of female druids. According to the Roman historian Tacitus (c. 55–120 CE), black-robed, screaming women accompanied the druids during the Roman assault on their stronghold on Mona (Anglesey) in 60 CE. The fourth-century CE *Historia Augusta* has three references to female druids in Gaul. Two utter spontaneous prophecies to two emperors, whereas the emperor Aurelian (c. 215–275 CE) consults Gaulish druidesses directly. Even if these women were stereotyped figures of prophecy and magic, the links among druidry, power, and women are clear.

Women appear elsewhere in religious roles. The Greek writer Plutarch (before 50–after 120 CE) mentions Camma, wife of a Galatian ruler and priestess of a goddess identified with Artemis who shared a poisoned drink with a suitor to avenge her husband's death. Although the drink of milk and honey had underworld associations and the rite took place in the temple where Camma was a priestess, the passage emphasises her loyalty as a wife, rather than her religious role. Two Roman historians, Tacitus (c. 55–120 CE) and Dio Cassius (c. 155–235 CE) described the revolt led by the famous British queen Boudicca in 60 CE. Boudicca's comment that it was unusual for Britons to follow a woman war-leader may reflect Roman unease about women, rather than her actual words. The fact that she offered a hare to the tribal goddess before battle, combined with the after-battle atrocities such as cutting off the breasts of captured women, may indicate that Boudicca's leadership had a religious dimension.

The Roman geographer Strabo quoted a description from the Greek writer Posidonius (second–first century BCE) of an all-female cult among the Samnitae tribe. The women, identified as worshipers of Dionysos, inhabited an island off the western coast of France and only left to have sex to produce children. An annual rite of reroofing a temple occurred during daylight hours on a single day. Any woman who dropped roofing material was torn to pieces. The description hints that the sacrificial victim was chosen in this way, because the account notes that the victim was jostled. Pomponius Mela (first century CE) mentions an island on which a male deity sleeps while nine women priests attend a perpetual fire under a cauldron. There is a striking parallel between these early accounts and two later references. One occurs in a medieval Welsh poem, "The Spoils of Annwn," which describes a supernatural journey to a land where nine women keep a fire burning under a cauldron. The other, from medieval Ireland, claims that the site of Saint Brigid's Church at Kildare incorporated a pre-Christian sanctuary where women tended a sacred flame.

The archaeological evidence includes images of female deities and inscriptions addressed to them. Men, who controlled the wealth, dedicated most of these monuments, but women also feature as dedicatees. Most inscriptions date from the Romano-Celtic period (first century BCE–fourth century CE) and indicate the importance of female deities rather than the position of women in religion. Devotion to deities did not follow strict gender lines, and men and women alike left votives at shrines dedicated to both male and female deities. In so far as deities such as the *dea nutrix* were associated with childbirth or pregnancy, her devotees and perhaps officials were likely to be female, but the goddess Epona, associated with horses and horse craft, was popular among the Roman cavalry. A number of Romano-Celtic statuettes of women suggest female religious activity, although it is unclear, given the date of this material, whether the activity was specifically Celtic. However, a bronze statuette of a veiled woman from South Shields (Tyne and Wear), a naked bronze female dancer from Neuvy-en-Sullias (Loiret), and a wooden image of a veiled woman wearing a torc from Chaumelières (Puy-de-Dôme) are associated with Gaulish or British religious sites and could depict devotees or officials. Chaumelières was the site of the sanctuary of Sequana, goddess of the source of the Seine, and an important healing center with an extensive dormitory and hospital complex for those seeking cures. Women probably played a role in both religious and healing activities here and at similar shrines. Religion was an aspect of public life open to women in the ancient world, and other continental iconography depicts women, either as devotees or officials, worshipping at altars or in processions. The names of Gaulish and British women priests are recorded in connection with classical cults, and at least one Gaulish woman dedicated a temple altar to a native Gaulish goddess.

INTERPRETATION OF SOURCES AND LATER DEVELOPMENTS. Religion, particularly an aspect like gender, is difficult to reconstitute from archaeological evidence. However, it is possible to infer some ritual significance from the placement of burials, such as the woman interred within a ritual enclosure at Libeniçe in Bohemia (fourth century BCE) or two distinctive female burials from Wetwang Slack in Yorkshire (third century BCE)—one buried with an elaborate chariot and the other with a sealed bronze box. It has been suggested that native British rites continued as a countercultural religion designated as witchcraft after the introduction of Christianity and continue into the twenty-first century. There is no basis for such an extreme position, but possible negative gender roles are indicated from a small number of burials, mostly older women, in which the heads or jaws have been removed and placed beside the corpse. A striking occurrence of *bnas brictom* (Gaulish, meaning "women of magic") is inscribed on a lead curse tablet from Larzac in France (c. 90 CE). The exact meaning is unclear, but this, unlike other curses, indicates that the women themselves have power to harm.

Irish literature features female figures with supernatural powers such as the Morrígan, Eriu, and Danu, who may be late reflexes of Celtic land or sovereignty goddesses. In medieval Welsh literature, the character Rhiannon from a medieval Welsh tale, whose name means "Great queen" (Rigantona), has been linked with the Gaulish and British goddess Epona. Female druids and seers are mentioned in Irish sources and druidic imagery clusters significantly around some of them. Fedhelm from the Ulster cycle (seventh to eleventh centuries CE) studied in Alba, a reflection of the druid's long apprenticeship as mentioned in classical sources, and appears with the sole purpose of uttering prophesies. Although this material cannot directly reflect Celtic religion or women's roles in it, the pattern presented by the classical authors is one in which women participated in, rather than were excluded from, ritual activity. Taken as a whole, archaeological evidence and narrative texts support rather than contradict this.

Between the third and sixth century CE, Christianity was introduced to Gaul, Britain, and Ireland. The degree to which the new religion absorbed, subsumed, or coexisted with pagan culture is a complex topic linked to the controversial concept of a distinctive Celtic Church. The cult of the holy well has been the focus of much speculation on pre-Christian survival, but even here there is little direct archaeological evidence for continuity between pagan deities and later saints. Nevertheless, hagiographers endowed both male and female saints with pseudo-divine characteristics, and the complex cult of the Irish Saint Brigid of Kildare suggests that a pagan site was transferred to a holy woman, Brigid, who died in 524 CE. Women exercised considerable power and influence in early Christian foundations in Ireland and Wales, although here too it is not clear how much of this carried over from pagan structures and how much was the result of increased status introduced by the new religion.

MODERN REVIVAL. Issues of gender in Celtic religion and in early Christianity have been informed by the revival of interest in Celtic culture since the end of the nineteenth century. Romantic nationalism and Romantic feminism have undoubtedly over-interpreted the sources, but modern developments in paganism and Celtic spirituality draw crucial metaphors from images of a powerful goddess figure who embodied female power in a unified pre-Christian world and the idea that such a figure was intimately bound up with the cycle of nature. Since the middle of the twentieth century, women have become an important force in modern druidry and in the move toward a more inclusive spirituality. The popularity of modern paganism and Celtic spirituality is strengthened by the assumption that Celtic religion could survive domination by Roman culture and Christianity. Supposed survival, despite external domination, is an essential feature of countercultural rebellion, and the image of a united Celtic world in which women were given a voice in religion is powerful whatever the discontinuity between modern religious developments and historical sources.

SEE ALSO Celtic Religion, overview article.

BIBLIOGRAPHY

There is no overall scholarly study of gender in Celtic religion from the ancient to modern period; however, Philip Freeman's *WarWomen and Druids: Eyewitness Reports and Early Accounts of the Ancient Celts* (Austin, Tex., 2002) makes useful comments on the relevant classical references. A. Pelletier's *La Femme dans la societé gallo-romaine* (Paris, 1974) considers the position of women in Gaul, whereas Lindsey Allason-Jones's *Women in Roman Britain* (London, 1989) covers British society. Miranda Green's *Celtic Goddesses Warriors Virgins and Mothers* (London, 1995) surveys both society and mythology into the early Christian period. Christina Harrington's *Women in a Celtic Church: Ireland 450–1150* (Oxford, 2002) gives a detailed and authoritative view of religious life in Ireland, whereas Jane Cartwright's *Y Forwyn Fair, Santesau a Lleianod Agweddau a diweirdeb yng Nghymru'r Oesodd Canol* (Cardiff, 1999) examines images of the virgin, female saints, and nuns in medieval Wales. Elissa Henken's *Welsh Saints, A Study in Patterned Lives* (Woodbridge, U.K., 1991) examines the hagiography of gender, and Dorothy Bray's "The Image of Saint Brigit in the Early Irish Church," *Etudes Celtiques* 24 (1987): 209–215 considers the growth of this important cult, a theme developed by Elva Johnston's "The Pagan and Christian Identities of the Irish Female Saint," in *Celts and Christians New Approaches to Religious Traditions of Britain and Ireland*, edited by Mark Atherton, pp. 60–79 (Cardiff, 2002).

The study of gender in Celtic religion is linked to general attitudes to the Celts and to the concept of Celtic Christianity. Two articles by Wendy Davies, "Celtic Women in the Early Middle Ages," in *Images of Women in Antiquity*, edited by Averil Cameron and Amélie Kuhrt, pp. 145–66 (London, 1983) and "The Myth of the Celtic Church" in *The Early Church in Wales and the West*, edited by Nancy Edwards and Alan Lane, pp. 12–21 (Oxford, 1992), help to clarify the issues and define the parameters of the argument. Gearóid Ó Crualaoich's *The Book of the Cailleach* (Cork, 2003) surveys all aspects of the "divine female" motif in Irish. The Scottish journalist and folklorist Lewis Spence popularized the idea of Celtic religion as benevolent and magical nature worship in which women played an important role. Books such as *Boadicea, Warrior Queen of the Britons* (London, 1937) and *The Magic Arts in Celtic Britain* (London, 1945) have influenced popular approaches to the subject. Good surveys of modern Celtic paganism and Celtic spirituality are Ronald Hutton's *The Pagan Religions of the Ancient British Isles* (Oxford, 1990) and Marion Bowman's "Contemporary Celtic Spirituality," in *New Directions in Celtic Studies*, edited by Amy Hale and Philip Payton, pp. 69–91 (Exeter, U.K., 2000). Many Internet sites contain information drawn from secondary sources or personal experience. These sites attest to the enormous interest in women's spirituality and to the importance of Celtic images in providing metaphors for this to be expressed.

JULIETTE WOOD (2005)

GENDER AND RELIGION: GENDER AND AUSTRALIAN INDIGENOUS RELIGIONS

Indigenous Australian women's religious beliefs and practices and the nature of gender relations in Aboriginal societies continue to be the subject of considerable debate. Do women have ceremonies that are secret and sacred to them? Do their rituals implicate the entire society or only women? Should gender relations be represented as egalitarian, complementary, or hierarchical? What has been the impact of the colonization of traditional lands, the forced removal of children, and the policies of assimilation and self-determination on women and men's religious beliefs and relationships? Is it possible to generalize for the entire continent, or given that Indigenous people live in different situations across the country, is it only possible to document change for specific groups?

PROBLEMS WITH THE SOURCES. For a number of reasons, women's voices are barely heard, especially in nineteenth-century and early- to mid-twentieth-century sources. Indigenous women, women anthropologists, and historians women have contested the validity of the male-dominated record. Silences, cultural assumptions regarding the "proper role" of women, and paradigms locating women outside the religious domain have rendered women mute. Influential texts, such as Sigmund Freud's *Totem and Taboo* and Émile Durkheim's *The Elementary Forms of the Religious Life*, written by theorists with no direct fieldwork experience in Australia, cast women as the profane and "other." When women's experience, self-knowledge, and woman-focused activities are confined to the realm of the everyday, the mundane, and the hearth and home, the question does not arise as to whether the ceremonies women perform may have significance beyond the profane business of women's bodies. For these theorists, women have magic but nothing that could properly be called religion. Thus when Géza Róheim, heavily influenced by Freud's psychoanalytical approach, worked in the 1930s in Central Australia and addressed women's lives, he asked about their everyday preoccupations but not about religion.

In her 1979 article "Aboriginal Women and the Notion of 'The Marginal Man,'" Catherine Berndt traced the ways women in the records of nineteenth-century observers are routinely depicted as downtrodden slaves of their menfolk, objects for sexual barter, and the instigators of fights. In this schema women's politics are cast as squabbles, and the decision-making power they enjoy by virtue of being the economic mainstay for their hunting and gathering is rendered invisible. The trend continued well into the twentieth century. Denied agency, women are shadows in the landscape: they cannot and do not speak directly of their lives, beliefs, and practices. Women are "feeders, breeders and follow the leaders" (Cawte, 1974, p. 140).

The written record is further impoverished because most observers were men and, with the strict sex-division of labor, they faced practical difficulties in undertaking research among Indigenous women. Those who were accompanied by their wives sometimes recorded their wives' observations on Indigenous women or those of the wives of missionaries. But more often, where they make reference to women, male researchers have relied on Indigenous men for information regarding women's activities and status. These men, however, have been reluctant or unable to discuss what is sometimes referred to as "women's business."

Some insights are available from women who have set down their observations in fiction and diaries. Mrs. Aeneas Gunn, drawing on her experiences in the Roper River region of the Northern Territory, told the story of "Bett-Bett" in *The Black Princess* in 1905. For the most part the few trained women who undertook fieldwork in Australia did not focus on Indigenous women. Some ignored women, preferring to work on more "scholarly" prestigious topics. Some, like the journalist and self-taught anthropologist Daisy Bates (1863–1951), lived among and wrote about Indigenous peoples in Western and South Australia. Bates faithfully recorded aspects of women's ceremonial lives, had little time for women, and as a product of their times, assumed that male authority was part of the "natural order" of things.

Nancy Munn's careful documentation of Warlpiri women's ceremonies, sand drawings, and body paintings, published in 1973 in *Walbiri Iconography*, added to the richness of Central Australian desert ethnographies. But in pursuing her structural analysis, Munn focused more on the men's ceremonies, including the secret ones she was privileged to attend. She does not record having attended any secret women's ceremonies. Her conclusion that men held the keys to cosmic order echoed the 1972 opinion of Kenneth Maddock, in *Australian Aborigines*, that women's ceremonies are small and personal whereas men's ceremonies addressed broader societal concerns. On the basis of more explicitly feminist research and evidence in Aboriginal land claims, Maddock revised his position for the 1982 edition of that work.

In an effort to reclaim women from the sources and to explore why Indigenous women do not see themselves as the drudges of their society, women researchers began exploring the silences in the ethnographic and historical record. In the 1845 journal entries of the explorer and administrator Edward John Eyre, Fay Gale found evidence of women-only ceremonies among the people of the southern Murray River region of South Australia for her 1989 article "Roles Revisited." In rereading the 1901–1902 journal of Francis Gillen, who accompanied Baldwin Spencer on his travels through central and northern Australia, Diane Bell found data that did not appear in their ethnographies—it did not mesh with the evolutionary models of Spencer. But as she pointed out in her 1983 *Daughters of the Dreaming*, it did indicate that women's affiliations to the Dreaming were not mediated through men.

WOMEN SPEAK. The 1939 publication of Phyllis Kaberry's *Aboriginal Woman: Sacred and Profane* established that Indigenous women had secret ceremonies. This was work undertaken by a woman who went into the field to study women and who was prepared to interrogate Durkheim's sacred and profane dichotomy. Her portrait of independent women, rich in ritual knowledge and expertise, stands in stark contrast to the findings of W. Lloyd Warner that women were born profane and made little sacred progress through life. Kaberry worked in the Kimberley region of Western Australia and Warner in Arnhem Land in the north of Australia, but regional differences do not adequately explain the divergent portraits. Kaberry's monograph continues to be read as a book about women in the Kimberleys and Warner's as a text on religion.

Catherine Berndt's work in the 1940s and 1950s confirmed and extended Kaberry's findings to South Australia, the Northern Territory, and other parts of Western Australia. Likewise Annette Hamilton, working in the eastern Western Desert, documented the existence of women's secret ceremonies in her 1979 Ph.D. thesis. On the basis of her fieldwork and land claim experience in Central Australia in the 1970s and 1980s, Diane Bell detailed the breadth, depth, and power of women's religious lives; explored their control over women's residential and ceremonial spaces; and demonstrated that *yawulyu* (land-based ceremonies) and *yilpinji* (love magic or emotional management ceremonies) are structured along the same principles of ritual reciprocity as men's ceremonies.

Françoise Dussart, writing of her 1980s fieldwork with the Warlpiri of Central Australia, focused on the elements of competition and obligation of both men and women ritual leaders and revisited the centrality of kinship. Zohl Dé Ishtar, working at Wirrimanu (Balgo, Western Australia) where Catherine Berndt had spent many years, traced the internal struggles of this complex community in her 2003 Ph.D. dissertation. Accounts of women's art, music, and dance have further fleshed out dimensions of the dynamic and vibrant religious lives of Indigenous women. The ethnomusicologist Linda Barwick's 2000 recordings and accompanying texts are the first commercially available of the *yawulyu* style of Warumungu women from Tennant Creek, Central Australia. Jennifer Biddle's article "Inscribing Identity: Skin as Country in the Central Desert" offers a closer look at the significance of women's body painting.

In land claims brought under the Aboriginal Land Rights (Northern Territory) Act (1976), women offered testimony regarding their religious ties to land and their knowledge of myth through *yawulyu* performances. A 1979 report of Justice John Toohey, the then Aboriginal land commissioner, made special mention of the significance of women's ceremonies. In government-sponsored reports, Indigenous women across Australia have spoken out about their community, family, and individual concerns.

The portrait of women's religious lives that emerges from these accounts is that in the desert regions of central, western, and southern Australia and in the Kimberleys both men and women have ceremonies that are closed to the other. However, there are also ceremonial moments where each has a presence at the rituals of the other. Knowledge is earned. The sages of the society are the "old people." The nubile young wenches who caught the eye of some commentators were not repositories of the sacred and secret law.

Bringing women into active voice in the ceremonial domain has been the work of women. To explore what was going on in women-only domains required a woman researcher, one who could be trusted with women's secrets. Catherine Berndt worked with women while her husband worked with men. They provided gendered perspectives on the same communities, stories, and ceremonies, and their access deepened as they aged. Bell described taking her two children into the field in the mid-1970s and how she was instructed in the ceremonial responsibilities of a mother of a boy nearing the age of initiation and a girl approaching marriageable age.

By the 1980s Indigenous women were adding to an already extensive body of literature, but little of it addressed religious beliefs and practices directly. Rather, they presented autobiographical material, emphasized survival, and located women's strengths within families and communities. As she documented the ravages of dispossession on her people in New South Wales in her 1978 film *My Survival as an Aboriginal,* Essie Coffey highlighted the strength she derived from her family. Hyllus Maris and Sonia Borg told the history of two hundred years of occupation of Indigenous lands in *Women of the Sun,* the 1983 four-part television series with a woman as the central figure in each episode. Sally Morgan's 1987 international best seller, *My Place,* traced her quest for identity through a maze of secrets in her Western Australian family.

Many more stories of survival in the face of loss and trauma came to light in 1996 with the publication of *Bringing Them Home,* a report on the "stolen generations," children forcefully removed from their parents in the name of assimilation. Other women are now coming forward to share their stories. Doris Kartinyeri's *Kick the Tin* (2000) told her story for future generations.

Although women's ceremonial life was imperiled by missionary activity and government policies of assimilation, particularly in the heavily settled part of Australia, fragments of knowledge of the beliefs and practices of earlier generations have survived and are held dear by those who have earned the right to know. In the stories of survival, there are glimpses of the continued importance of family attendance at various ceremonies, including funerals. These gatherings serve to unite communities and celebrate kinship ties, as they did in the premissionary days.

Indigenous women continue to explore their relationship to feminism and the women's movement. For some, the women's movement offered new insights and opportunities. Others have explored distinctively indigenous modes of representing their struggles as Indigenous women and express ambivalence and sometimes hostility to what they see as a white women's movement.

GENDER RELATIONS. Here also the record is impoverished. Throughout the nineteenth century and much of the twentieth century, male dominance was accepted as an accurate depiction of gender relations, which were usually discussed in terms of role and status. Evidence of women's rituals constituted a challenge to this view, but it has not entirely dislodged the model of male dominance as universally applicable. Rather, from the 1970s onward there is greater nuance and complexity to the way gender relations are presented.

For Central Australia there is general agreement that women enjoy prestige and respect by virtue of their secret and sacred ceremonies, and this is apparent in their rights in and responsibilities for sacred sites and country. This contrasts with Arnhem Land, where polygyny is common, the separation of the sexes is not as dramatically marked, and women's ritual activity does not have the wide reach of women's ceremonies in the desert regions.

In *The Tiwi of North Australia* (1960) C. W. M. Hart and Arnold Pilling describe older women as toothless old hags. In *Tiwi Wives,* researched in the 1960s but not published until 1971, Jane Goodale found Tiwi women to be wise individuals. Unlike the practice throughout most of the Australia continent, Tiwi men and women of Melville and Bathurst Islands are initiated at the same ceremonies, but women are not expected to be innovators. That is men's work. Goodale characterized male-female relations as structurally unequal.

In their contributions to the 1970 landmark publication of *Woman's Role in Aboriginal Society,* Isobel White surveyed the literature and concluded that women were not pawns or chattels of men but "junior partners" (White, 1970, p. 26), whereas Catherine Berndt opted for a "two sex model, dependence and interdependence" (Berndt, 1970, pp. 39–48). Diane Barwick provided a nuanced account of Indigenous women's strategies in nineteenth-century Victoria as they took advantage of the opportunities afforded by mission and government stations to transform their roles within traditional patriarchal society and to enjoy the status of emancipated women (Barwick, 1970, pp. 31–38).

In 1979 John Bern, working in the Roper River area and echoing Warner's pronouncement on women's profane lives, argued that religion is the domain where status is conferred, and religion is a male domain. A year later Hamilton explored what might constitute a challenge to this ideology. She argued that in the eastern Western Desert women's matrilineal ties, autonomous religious lives, and lower polygyny rates than farther north in Arnhem Land constituted a structural impediment to the consolidation of male dominance. Fred Myers, working with the Pintupi of Central Australia, has conceded that women's ceremonies are of importance but, like Maddock's 1982 revised position, sees the scale of men's ceremonies, their elaborate nature of preparations, and their integrative scope as indicative of their greater importance.

Echoing the work of Kaberry and Hamilton, Diane Bell in 1983 wrote of female autonomy and the complementarity of the sexes in Central Australia. She argued that the life on settlements (reservations) provided many opportunities for women's ceremonies and indeed intensified the need for those ceremonies that concern resolution of conflict. Women on cattle stations (ranches) have fewer opportunities for large gatherings of women but often have been able to remain closer to their sacred places and country.

In her reconsiderations of women and anthropology in 1984, Kay Saunders called for a reintegration of male and female perspectives. Reviewing the last twenty-five years of the twentieth century, Francesca Merlan, in "Gender in Aboriginal Social Life: A Review" (1988), noted the difficulty presented by the range of views and claims that much of what purports to address gender relations too often focuses on women's position in the society. Lester Hiatt, in *Arguing about Aborigines,* recognizes that age and gender are critical factors in any conceptualization of gender relations but with his characterization, "double gendered gerontocracies," allows that the weight attached to either may or does vary across the continent (Hiatt, 1996, p. 77).

MYTH AND RITUAL. There are myths that explore themes of sexuality, sexualized power, and gender relations; myths that are known to women, and ones that are the domain of men; and gendered versions of the same myth wherein women and men emphasize aspects of ancestral activities that are relevant to their roles. From South Australia come men's stories of the whale, *kondoli,* and the theft of fire, his jealously guarded possession, and those of women about the old people riding whales and calling to whales, as if these large warm-blooded creatures were kin. Both women and men talk of the return of the whales to the waters of the Southern Ocean as a prophecy of the return of strength to their culture and communities.

Women feature in a number of Dreaming stories, some of which, like that of the Seven Sisters (the Pleiades) and the Mungamunga, traveling women who traverse the continent, interact with other Dreamings and establish rites of passage for women. In her 1965 article Catherine Berndt enumerated examples of present-day male ownership of myths that once belonged to women, the most well-known being the Djang'kawu sisters from northeastern Arnhem Land.

Myths are redolent with sexual imagery and make note of the aberrant and the taboo. Thus sex between mothers-in-law and sons-in-law leads to social disorder. Women's *yilbinji* songs of Central Australia may be used to attract or spurn a lover and to restore harmony.

In the central desert regions *yawulyu* ceremonies are the responsibility of senior women, and through their performance they make the country "come up green" and speak of "growing up" the country as one "grows up" children. In Warlpiri one is *kirda* for the country of one's father and *kurdungurla* for the country of one's mother's father. Other rights flow through mother's mother and father's mother, place of birth, and a number of idiosyncratic factors.

In the preparation of sacred objects for a ceremony, women may sing and speak of the significance of the stories that give meaning to their actions. Songs and designs painted on bodies, the ground, and ritual paraphernalia function as mnemonics and may be explored in greater detail in associated myths. Stories may be told when women are out hunting and gathering, and it is here that children first learn to name their country.

Adults tell myths, but the audience may be children, or it may be highly restricted on the basis of gender, age, family, and country affiliations. As one ages and grows in wisdom, the inside meanings of stories become available. This layering of knowledge may take one from a simple story told to scare children, such as the Mulyewongk (*bunyip*) of South Australia, to deeper and deeper meanings of significance to men and male initiation and to women and child rearing.

GENDER IN PUBLIC. Controversies regarding the value to be accorded to research findings by women working with women persist and extend beyond the walls of academe. Between 1994 and 2001 the weight accorded to the claim that a group of Ngarrindjeri women in the southeast of Australia had secret knowledge of sacred sites was contested in a number of legal cases. Diane Bell and Chris Kenny provide diametrically opposed readings of the Ngarrindjeri issues. Ultimately the women were vindicated in the decision by Justice John von Doussa in 2002 in the Federal Court, but the hearings, media coverage, and anthropological and community divisions generated by the matter illustrate how contentious "women's business" remains. The lives of the women pursuing protection for the sites had been profoundly altered by the missionary presence and assimilation policies—including the forced removal of children—and there was little in the ethnographic record to support their claims. However, the assertion of several Ngarrindjeri men and women that the Seven Sisters Dreaming traveled through their country could be substantiated from a number of sources. The politicized women of the so-called "settled south" were pitted against the traditional women of the "remote" communities and their authenticity as believers contested. Women-focused accounts were called biased, and the reflexive accounts where the researcher discussed the impact her presence has had on the collection of data were said to lack the objectivity of earlier positivist accounts.

Since the late 1980s the issue of violence against women has emerged as a highly emotive issue. Numerous reports have documented the increasing incidences of rape and physical abuse of women and children, and this has led to a lively debate concerning gender relations in traditional society and the weight to be accorded to the legacy of the gendered violence of the colonial frontier. Anthropologists and historians have debated the nature of the transformation of gender roles on the frontier. Berndt argued that women were advantaged by their privileged access to the hearth and home of the colonizers. Bell argued that women's lives were privatized by their domestication and that during the self-determination era men were groomed as leaders and negotiations were male to male. Assumptions regarding women's chattel-like status fueled the argument that violence against women was tolerated in "traditional" society. In response to Bell's call to all Australians to pay attention to intraracial rape, Indigenous women, such as Huggins, have argued that this is their business. This debate continues, as Bell documented in "White Women Can't Speak" and as "Tidda's Manifesto" illustrated.

Traditional religion is tied to place and firmly embedded in the kinship system. For a number of reasons, however, including dispossession of land, forceful removal of children, work requirements, and education, many people no longer live on their ancestral land. New spiritualities, in dialogue with different Christian modalities, formulations of social justice, environmentalism, and ecofeminism, have emerged. The hierarchical ordering of ancestral powers within these new theologies privilege male-identified beings, whereas some of the New Age romanticizations of the noble savage and the earth as mother articulate a female principle.

SEE ALSO Anthropology, Ethnology, and Religion; Australian Indigenous Religions, overview article; Durkheim, Émile; Ecology and Religion, overview article; Freud, Sigmund; Magic, article on Theories of Magic; Ritual; Totemism.

BIBLIOGRAPHY

Barwick, Diane. "And the Lubras Are Ladies Now." In *Woman's Role in Aboriginal Society*, edited by Fay Gale, pp. 31–38. Canberra, 1970. Ethnohistorical analysis of changes in women's role and status following the Board of Protection of Aborigines 1860 decision to settle tribes in Victoria on supervised government stations and missions, where they could farm and support themselves.

Barwick, Linda. *Yawulyu Mungamunga: Dreaming Songs of Warumungu Women, Tennant Creek, Central Australia.* Sydney, 2000. Women perform a cappella; songs relate travels of the Mungamunga Dreaming women; accompanying texts and explanation.

Bates, Daisy Mary. *The Passing of the Aborigines.* London, 1938. An edited and revised version of serialized articles that first appeared in the *Adelaide Advertiser;* a lament for a vanishing race.

Bell, Diane. "White Women Can't Speak?" *Feminism and Psychology* 6, no. 2 (1996): 197–203. Summary of the controversy over a 1988 paper by Bell concerning intraracial rape, the silence of feminists for fear of being called racist, and the male bias of the Australian legal system in advocating for Indigenous women victims of male violence and Jackie Huggins's insistence that this violence against women is not the business of white women.

Bell, Diane. *Ngarrindjeri Wurruwarrin: A World That Is, Was, and Will Be.* Melbourne, 1998. A historically grounded ethnography of the Ngarrindjeri of South Australia and the Hindmarsh Island affair.

Bell, Diane. *Daughters of the Dreaming.* Melbourne, 1983; 3d ed., 2002. An explicitly feminist ethnography of women's religion at Warrabri (Ali-curang) with Warlpiri, Kayetj, Alyawarr, and Warumungu women; based on doctoral research and land claim experience.

Bern, John. "Ideology and Domination: Toward a Reconstruction of Australian Aboriginal Social Formation." *Oceania* 50, no. 2 (1979): 118–132. Based on fieldwork in the Roper River region.

Berndt, Catherine H. "Women's Changing Ceremonies in Northern Australia." *L'Homme* 1 (1950): 1–88. M.A. thesis; documentation of the ceremonial lives and impact of cattle stations (ranches); song texts and body designs.

Berndt, Catherine H. "Women and the 'Secret Life.'" In *Aboriginal Man in Australia,* edited by Ronald M. Berndt and Catherine H. Berndt, pp. 238–282. Sydney, 1965. Examines song, ritual, and myth from women's perspective; locates within context of complementary relations between men and women in ritual and ceremonial spheres.

Berndt, Catherine H. "Digging Sticks and Spears; or, The Two-Sex Model." In *Women's Role in Aboriginal Society,* edited by Fay Gale, pp. 39–48. Canberra, 1970. A model of gender relations based on exploration of domestic, economic, and religious domains.

Berndt, Catherine H. "Aboriginal Women and the Notion of the 'Marginal Man.'" In *Aborigines of the West: Their Past and Their Present,* edited by Ronald M. Berndt and Catherine H. Berndt, pp. 28–38. Nedlands, Western Australia, 1979. Literature survey of historical and contemporary material primarily from Western Australia.

Berndt, Ronald M., and Catherine H. Berndt. *The Speaking Land: Myth and Story in Aboriginal Australia.* Ringwood, Australia, 1989. Anthology of two hundred myth stories drawn from around Australia as told to the Berndts.

Berndt, Ronald M., and Catherine H. Berndt, with John E. Stanton. *A World That Was: The Yaraldi of the Murray River and the Lakes, South Australia.* Melbourne, 1993. A reclamation of the traditions of the Yaraldi primarily based on fieldwork with two remarkable elders, Albert Karloan and Margaret "Pinkie" Mack, in the 1940s, revised in the 1990s, and published after the death of Ronald Berndt.

Biddle, Jennifer. "Inscribing Identity: Skin as Country in the Central Desert." In *Thinking Through the Skin,* edited by S. Ahmed and J. Stacey, pp. 177–193. London, 2001. A phenomenological analysis of Aboriginal women's paintings from the central desert of Australia.

Cawte, John. *Medicine Is the Law.* Honolulu, 1974. An examination of traditional Aboriginal society through the lens of psychiatric anthropology and an exploration of the possible alleviation of acculturation problems by sociomedical means.

Coffey, Essie. *My Survival as an Aboriginal.* 1978. Documentary film of the effects of dispossession, chronic depression, alcoholism, deaths in custody and poverty; filmed in Coffey's hometown, Brewarrina, in the far northwest of New South Wales.

Daylight, Phyliss, and Mary Johnstone. *Women's Business: Report of the Aboriginal Women's Task Force.* Canberra, Australia, 1986. An inquiry into Aboriginal women's involvement in critical social, political, and economic issues, including land rights; recommendations to the commonwealth government; based on an Australiawide, twelve-month consultative process by a team of thirteen Indigenous women.

Dé Ishtar, Zohl. "Holding *Yawulyu*: White Culture and Black Women's Law." Ph.D. diss., Deakin University, 2003. Research at Wirrimanu (Balgo), Western Australia; her role in establishing Kapululangu, a women's camp and cultural center; the politics of the community (including intra- and inter-black and white politics).

Durkheim, Émile. *The Elementary Form of the Religious Life.* New York, 1915. Classic account of religion, sacred and profane, draws on Australian material.

Dussart, Françoise. *The Politics of Ritual in an Aboriginal Settlement: Kinship, Gender, and the Currency of Knowledge.* Washington, D.C., 2000. Based on doctoral and subsequent research at Yuendumu in Central Australia; traces how ritual leaders function as individuals, women, Warlpiri, and members of residential kin groups.

Fergie, Deane. "Secret Envelopes and Inferential Tautologies." *Journal of Australian Studies* 48 (1996): 13–24. Account of the logic pursued in investigating the secrets of the Ngarrindjeri women in the Hindmarsh Island case.

Freud, Sigmund. *Totem and Taboo.* New York, 1950.

Gale, Fay. "Roles Revisited: The Women of Southern South Australia." In *Women Rites and Sites,* edited by Peggy Brock, pp. 120–135. Sydney, 1989. A reconciliation of the nineteenth-century literature on the role and status of Indigenous women—primarily those living at Point McLeay (Raukkan)—with perspectives of women in the twentieth century.

Gillen, Francis James. *Gillen's Diary: The Camp Jottings of F. J. Gillen on the Spencer and Gillen Expedition across Australia, 1901–1902.* Adelaide, 1968. Gillen, special magistrate and protector of the Aborigines, Alice Springs, worked with Baldwin Spencer, professor of biology at the University of Melbourne; Gillen spoke several of the local languages and recorded the daily activities of women.

Goodale, Jane C. *Tiwi: A Study of the Women of Melville Island, Northern Australia.* Washington, D.C., 1971. Based on doctoral research, traces woman's life cycle from birth to death; social structure of Tiwi society; importance of matrilineality and patrilineality.

Gunn, Mrs. Aeneas. *The Black Princess* (1905). Sydney, 1977. Jeannie Gunn (1870–1961) worked at Elsey Station, Northern Territory.

Hamilton, Annette. "Timeless Transformations: Women, Men, and History in the Western Australian Desert." Ph.D. diss., University of Sydney, 1979. Fieldwork at Everard Park Station (now Mimili), South Australia; argues the region is in flux; analysis of mode of production in relationship to reproduction and symbolic production.

Hamilton, Annette. "Dual Social Systems: Technology, Labour, and Women's Secret Rites in the Eastern Western Desert of Australia." *Oceania* 51, no. 1 (1980): 4–19. Separation of the sexes and consequences with special reference to women's secret religious lives.

Hart, C. W. M., and Arnold R. Pilling. *The Tiwi of North Australia.* New York, 1960. A study of a system of influence and power based on woman as currency and male competition for control of this "good."

Hiatt, Lester R. *Arguments about Aborigines: Australia and the Evolution of Social Anthropology.* New York, 1996. Explores major controversies in Australian anthropology; includes the chapter "The Woman Question."

Kaberry, Phyllis M. *Aboriginal Woman: Sacred and Profane.* London, 1939. Revised doctoral dissertation; based on fieldwork in early 1930s; portrays women as complex social personalities.

Kartinyeri, Doris E. *Kick the Tin.* Melbourne, 2000. Firsthand account of the struggles of a member of the "stolen generations" taken at birth and raised in the Colebrook Home in South Australia.

Kenny, Chris. *It Would Be Nice if There Was Some Women's Business.* Potts Point, Australia, 1996. An involved journalist's defense of the proposition that the Ngarrindjeri women fabricated their religious beliefs to thwart development of the Hindmarsh Island bridge.

Little, Janine. "'Tiddas in Struggle': A Consultative Project with Murri, Koori, and Nyoongah Women." *SPAN: Journal of the South Pacific Association for Commonwealth Literature and Language Studies,* no. 37, 1993. Includes discussion of Jackie Huggins and the development of the "Tiddas Manifesto," "white feminism," and the benefits that flow to white women from the dispossession and oppression of Koori people.

Maddock, Kenneth. *The Australian Aborigines: A Portrait of Their Society.* Ringwood, Australia, 1972; rev. ed., 1982. Revisits the claim that women's ceremonies centered on narrow, divisive, and personal interests and concedes that women may indeed celebrate their relationship to land and broad cohesive themes similar to men.

Maris, Hyllus, and Sonia Borg. *Women of the Sun.* Paddington, Australia, 1983. The book based on the award-winning television drama.

Merlan, Francesca. "Gender in Aboriginal Social Life: A Review." In *Social Anthropology and Australian Aboriginal Studies: A Contemporary Overview,* edited by Ronald M. Berndt and R. Tonkinson, pp. 15–76. Canberra, 1988. Detailed literature review; includes critique of reconstructions of "traditional" culture and calls for rereading the literature on sexuality and reproduction in a wider social context.

Moreton-Robinson, Aileen. *Talkin' up to the White Woman.* Saint Lucia, Australia, 2000. A critique of the exclusionary and racist practices of middle-class white feminism.

Morgan, Sally. *My Place.* Freemantle, Australia, 1987. Autobiography; a search for truth that implicates Morgan's whole family and frees her mother and grandmother to tell their stories.

Munn, Nancy D. *Walbiri Iconography: Graphic Representations and Cultural Symbolism in a Central Australian Society.* Chicago, 1973. An exploration of visual art and communications systems; examines the totemic designs as a representational structure and sociocultural symbolism; based on doctoral research at Yuendumu, Central Australia in the 1950s.

Myers, Fred R. *Pintipu Country, Pintupi Self: Sentiment, Place, and Politics among Western Desert Aborigines.* Washington, D.C., 1986. Based on doctoral research in Central Australia at Papunya, Yayayi, and beyond with senior Pintupi men.

Pattel-Gray, Anne, ed. *Aboriginal Spirituality: Past, Present, and Future.* Blackburn, Australia, 1996. Draws on papers from the First National Conference on Aboriginality and Perceptions of Christianity, South Australia, 1990, of explorations by Indigenous scholars and church and community leaders and theologians of their spirituality in relationship to Christianity.

Róheim, Géza. "Women and Their Life in Central Australia." *Royal Anthropological Institute Journal* 63 (1933): 207–265. Rich data, but assumes women's activities concern magic, not religion.

Saunders, Kay. "'The Old Order of Things': Women and Anthropology Reconsidered." *Hecate* 10, no. 1 (1984): 68–73. A historian's overview.

Toohey, John. *Land Claim by the Alyawarra and Kaititja.* Report by the Aboriginal Land Commissioner Toohey to the minister for Aboriginal affairs and to the administrator of the Northern Territory. Canberra, Australia, 1979. Makes reference to the performance of women's ceremonies as evidence of their rights and responsibilities in land.

Von Doussa, John. "Reasons for Decision." *Thomas Lincoln Chapman, Wendy Jennifer Chapman, and Binalong (Receivers and Managers Appointed) (in Liquidation) v. Lumins Pty Ltd, Deane Joanne Fergie, Cheryl Anne Saunders, Robert Edward Tickner, and Commonwealth of Australia.* Federal Court of Australia, No. SG 33 of 1997. The Federal Court decision of 2001 finding that the Ngarrindjeri women had not deliberately fabricated their religious beliefs to thwart development.

Warner, W. Lloyd. *A Black Civilization: A Social Study of an Australian Tribe.* New York, 1937. Based on doctoral research with the Murgin at Milingimbi in the Northern Territory; focus on kinship and social structure.

Watson, Lillian. "Sister, Black Is the Colour of My Skin." In *Different Lives: Reflections on the Women's Movement and Visions of Its Future,* edited by Jocelynne A. Scutt, pp. 45–52. Ringwood, Australia, 1987. Autobiographical account of life in Queensland; born in 1940; experienced searing racism; ambivalence toward and recognition of the importance of strong women's movements.

White, Isobel M. "Aboriginal Women's Status: A Paradox Resolved." In *Woman's Role in Aboriginal Society,* edited by Fay Gale, pp. 1–29. Canberra, 1970. A literature review; includes consideration of women's rights, the extent to which they are enforced, and consequences of breaching the rules of the society.

Wilson, Ronald. *Bringing Them Home: Report of the National Inquiry into the Separation of Aboriginal and Torres Strait Islander Children and Their Families.* Sydney, 1997. Report of the Human Rights and Equal Opportunity Commission on the "stolen generations."

DIANE BELL (2005)

GENDER AND RELIGION: GENDER AND OCEANIC RELIGIONS

Oceania, a vast area encompassing a variety of social and religious systems, is often divided into three regions: Polynesia, Melanesia, and Micronesia. In Polynesia, with its chiefs and ascribed ranks, a woman's position depends more on rank than on gender. The populations of Polynesia are historically related, and there are similarities in social patterning throughout the region, including the system of hereditary ranking. Sherry Ortner observes: "Sensualism, eroticism, and a high level of sexual activity are actively cultivated throughout the area. Homosexuality is unstigmatized. Relations between men and women are relatively harmonious and mutually respectful" (Ortner, 1981, p. 359). Melanesia, to the west, shows greater diversity in social organization, whereas Micronesia, to the north, is closer to the chiefly patterns of Polynesia. The Melanesian cultures of highlands New Guinea are often described as egalitarian, but the egalitarianism refers to relations among men and not to social relations across genders. Traditionally the peoples of Oceania have engaged in subsistence horticulture. People grew crops such as taro, sweet potato, breadfruit, bananas, coconuts, and various green vegetables. Gardening, supplemented with cash cropping and wage labor, remains the basis of their economies and is an important metaphor for life's work.

APPROACHES. Those who have studied gender and religion in Oceania have approached their subject from various perspectives. A male bias pervades the observations of early missionaries and colonial officials in the Pacific, and much early anthropological study was done by men who lacked access to the religious practices and ideas of Pacific women. At the beginning of the twenty-first century the large majority of the peoples of Oceania were Christian, and thus Christian understandings were reflected in their ideas and practices. At the same time, as many young people moved to urban centers for education and work, understandings of gender derived from ancestral traditions and from Christianity were changing.

Margaret Mead, the pioneering anthropologist who studied male and female identity in several societies in Oceania, also used her research as a basis for exploring "male" and "female" in the United States. For those who have followed her, there has been a convergence between interest in gender relations in their home cultures and in the cultures they study. In the last three decades of the twentieth century, as scholars worldwide turned their attention to the cultural construction of gender, a profusion of studies focused on Oceanian societies. Marilyn Strathern's doctoral dissertation, later published as *Women in Between* (1972), presented the mediating roles played by women of the Mount Hagen area of Papua New Guinea and foreshadowed the feminist anthropology that soon challenged the ways scholars studied Oceania. Strathern is remarkable not only for her feminist anthropology but also for her interrogation of the relations between feminism and anthropology. In *The Gender of the Gift* (1988) she suggested that the study of gender relations in Melanesia has been distorted by the assumptions of Western anthropologists who have imposed several Eurocentric binary oppositions—such as nature and culture, female and male, subject and object, domestic and public—on their Melanesian data. Her observation could be extended to all of Oceania.

Much of the post–World War II writing on the patrilineal societies of highlands New Guinea emphasized male domination, male cults, and male fears of menstrual pollution. Later studies gave more attention to understandings of women's roles and female spirits in fertility-oriented cults and rituals. In the early 2000s accounts of violence toward women in Papua New Guinea and other parts of the Pacific caused researchers to ask to what extent violence has a traditional mandate and to what extent it is the result of rapid and disorienting political and socioeconomic change. Some scholars of highlands New Guinea societies, among them Aletta Biersack and Lisette Josephides, have argued that men take advantage of women just as in capitalist societies those with means exploit the working classes. In analyzing the relationship between masculinity and motherhood in an Eastern Iatmul (Papua New Guinea) society, Eric Silverman drew on the distinction the literary theorist Mikhail Bakhtin makes between the "moral" and the "grotesque." Eastern Iatmul men, according to Silverman, "idealize an image of motherhood that is nurturing, sheltering, cleansing, fertile, and chaste, in a word, moral. But men also fear an equally compelling image of motherhood that is defiling, dangerous, orificial, aggressive, and carnal, hence, grotesque" (Silverman, 2001, p. 2). The ideology and ontology of Eastern Iatmul masculinity are established, he argued, through "an unresolvable dialogue with motherhood" (Silverman, 2001, p. 159).

Describing the situation on Vanatinai, literally "Motherland," a small island southeast of the main island of New Guinea in the Louisiade Archipelago, Maria Lepowsky depicted male-female relationships as markedly different from those of the highlands. Vanatinai, she says, is a place where "there are no ideologies of male superiority and female inferiority." In this matrilineal society, "Both women and men give and receive ceremonial valuables, foodstuffs, goods made by women such as clay cooking pots, sleeping mats, and coconut-leaf skirts, and goods made by men such as carved hardwood bowls and lime spatulas" (Lepowsky, 1993, p. viii). Women and men may both lead mortuary rituals and participate in a range of ritual activities, and women figure prominently in myth as shapers of the culture. From their mothers and their mothers' brothers, women and men equally inherit land, the use rights over forest and reef areas, and valuables. The postmarital residence pattern is bilocal. Women, Lepowsky maintained, "are construed as life-givers, nurturing children and yams, and feeding the heirs of the deceased in mortuary ritual" (Lepowsky, 1993, p. 302).

FERTILITY, SPIRITS, AND POWER. Food and fertility are major concerns of Oceanian communities and are the foci of ritual. It could be argued that the religions of Oceania consist of symbolic processes directed to the fertility of land and community. Throughout Oceania agricultural labor is divided between the sexes, with men clearing land and breaking up the soil for new gardens and women doing the planting and weeding. The actual distribution of tasks varies from place to place, and in many societies men take care of "male" crops, such as bananas, whereas women are responsible for staple "female" crops. Their cooperation is represented in the conjunction of male and female in garden rituals. In some places a couple will have sex in a new garden before planting takes place. In male cults of the New Guinea highlands there are "father" and "mother" officiants, both of whom are male. Thus gender is not only a social reality but also an idiom for thinking about the fruitfulness of vegetal and social life.

In Oceania economics and religion are not separate domains. Practical physical work and symbolic work (ritual) intersect in gardening, fishing, and exchange activities. Oceanian societies put a great emphasis on wealth exchanges. Men and women participate differently in these exchanges, with men taking the more public role in oratory and the transaction of valuables and women supporting their husbands and brothers by such activities as raising pigs, weaving mats, preparing tapa, providing food, and offering hospitality to guests. At the same time women also have exchange networks—mainly with other women—in which mats, baskets, net bags, and food products are transacted.

The religions of Oceania vary in their ideas about and practices concerning spirits and gods. Everywhere people interact with a variety of gods and spirits. Spirits of the dead are believed to have an ongoing relationship with the living. Following death, the spirit of the deceased is encouraged by gifts and entreaties to move on to its next destination. Many societies have practiced ancestor veneration, inviting the deceased members of the community to join in periodic festivals. In some areas people retain the skulls of the deceased for ritual presentation of food and dance. In chiefly societies cults honor the spirits of chiefs and high-ranking members of noble lineages. In highlands New Guinea the male cults typically honor the collective spirits of the patriline and in many societies provide for the initiation of males (Godelier, 1986; Herdt, 1982).

Where male cults flourish or once flourished, a female spirit may also be venerated. The Female Spirit, known as Payame Ima among the Duna of Papua New Guinea, is associated with parts of the environment, with other spirits, with human welfare, and with witchcraft (Stewart and Strathern, 2002, pp. 93–109). She dwells in the high forest where the wild pandanus nut trees grow and is regarded as an owner of these trees. She also dwells in forest pools, and people may cast pieces of pork into these pools as offerings to her. She can possess men and women and thereby endow them with abilities such as the power to heal, to divine, or to identify witches. She may endow ritual experts with the powers necessary to ensure the growth of boy initiates. These ritual experts must be bachelors at the time the relationship is established and remain so while they carry out their role in the initiation cult. Payame rewards her male devotees with shiny, healthy skin.

In her form as the Yuro Ima, the spirit of the Strickland River, she directs wild game, including wild pigs and cassowaries, so that hunters can catch them. She also gives inspiration to the singers of the *pikono* epic cycles that recount some of her own actions in helping humans. Payame Ima has a dangerous side, however. Gabrielle Stürzenhofecker points out that for the Duna, witchcraft is conceived of as a predominantly female power that men see as threatening their control over women. Witches are portrayed as mobile and attracted by valued foods, characteristics usually associated with men. The Female Spirit, she says, is "described as both originator of, and the protector against, female witchcraft" and "powerfully encapsulates the duality inherent in the relations between the sexes" (Stürzenhofecker, 1998, p. 10). Comparable understandings of witchcraft are found throughout Oceania. A rash of witch accusations and killing of witches in the Eastern Highlands Province of Papua New Guinea in the 1990s may well be a scapegoating response to social changes that have disempowered men.

In Polynesia and also in parts of Melanesia and Micronesia, sacred power is denoted by the related terms *mana* and *tapu*. *Mana* is understood as a state of being in which a person or object is temporarily or permanently under the influence of gods, spirits, or powers. The *mana*, or supernatural power, of chiefs is a largely innate and inherited quality. *Tapu*, often glossed as "forbidden," may, when used in reference to gods, chiefs, and temples, also be translated as "sacred." The "sacred maid" of western Polynesia is at the same time powerful and forbidden. In Samoa she is supposed to be a chief's sister's daughter but might in fact be his daughter (Mead, 1949). She leads a group of unmarried girls and untitled men's wives who are responsible for hosting visitors to the village. Unlike other unmarried young women, the sacred maid is under strict sexual constraint and is expected to retain her virginity until marriage. The prestige of the village is vested in her.

Myth and Ritual. In Oceania, as in other regions of the world, the identities and relationships of men and women are explored in myth and song. A myth widespread in Polynesia tells of a woman called Hina (in some places Sina or Ina) who lived long ago and who established women's activities, such as the making of tapa cloth. In one version of the myth Hina falls in love with a handsome chief, Tinirau (or Sinilau), who lives on a faraway island. She runs away from her family and swims across the sea (or rides on the back of a turtle or a shark) in order to marry him. In another version Hina is seduced by Tuna (Eel) while bathing. The trickster hero Maui realizes what is happening and kills the eel. Hina buries her lover's head, and it grows into the first coconut palm or, in a version narrated by the Maori of Aotearoa–New Zealand, the lover is chopped into many pieces that grow into the different species of eel. Some versions of the Hina myth tell that the heroine climbed up to the moon, where she can still be seen seated under a banyan tree beating tapa cloth. Maori narratives maintain that the moon is the true husband of all women, an idea found among many peoples of Oceania.

Whereas culture heroes and heroines may lay down patterns for human behavior, myths also explore the tensions between males and females. In many New Guinean cultures it is narrated that women were the trustees of ritual sacra such as bamboo flutes until they were stolen by men and came to be played in the male cult to impersonate the spirits (Silverman, 2001; Gillison, 1993). When men play the flutes in the context of the men's cult, they are doing something that originally, the narratives say, belonged to women. Moreover their ritual activities are held to produce on a social level what female reproduction does on a biological level. Gillian Gillison describes how, among the Gimi, men and women have their separate but complementary sets of myths that inform the understanding of kinship, marriage, and exchange relationships (Gillison, 1993).

Oceanian cultures understand that power resides in individual, social, and cosmic life. Ritual is the means to tap into power. Even in modern circumstances it is usual for women to carry out rituals for the "growing up" of children, for the fruitfulness of crops, for healing, and for success in attracting men. Similarly men carry out rituals for fishing and hunting, for success in exchanges, for healing and the overcoming of misfortune, and for finding and keeping sexual partners. Some, but not all, cultures in Oceania have rituals for the making of men (Godelier, 1986; Herdt, 1982; Langness, 1999) and the making of women (Lutkehaus and Roscoe, 1995).

Many societies in Oceania employ traditional processes for entry into marriage. These usually involve the exchange of wealth items between the families of the couple and, in the case of patrilineal societies, require a larger payment on the part of the man's supporters to compensate for the childbearing capacity and labor that are transferred from the woman's family to the man's family. Traditionally marriage in Oceania marked not only the union of a couple but the alliance of groups. Marriages that are entered into in traditional ways are usually also celebrated with Christian ceremonies, and indeed some people have only a Christian ceremony.

Periodic rituals to empower the land and to restore the collective good punctuate traditional Oceanian religious systems. If fertility is a major focus of ritual, the restoration of well-being through healing processes is its complement. Everyone knows some herbal remedies as well as spells and ritual actions for healing, but specialist healers, both male and female, command a larger repertoire. Some inherit their healing practice and are trained in it by a parent or other relative. Others may receive healing power through a religious experience. While overall there are more male than female healers, the situation differs from place to place, and even societies that once relied exclusively on male practitioners have seen women assume the practice of healing.

WOMEN'S LEADERSHIP. In the old Pacific, women of high rank in the chiefly societies exercised social and ritual roles, and throughout the area women participated in rituals concerned with land and garden fertility and with the growth and health of children and animals. Senior women initiated the young, and there were women who functioned as healers. Women priests are documented in the Solomon Islands (Burt, 1993, pp. 58, 138, 145, 271). Since the arrival of Christianity, which came first to the eastern parts of Oceania—to Tahiti in 1797 and to Hawai'i in 1820—and then made its way westward, women have also assumed roles of leadership in Christian communities. Some have become pastors in Protestant denominations, although not all denominations permit female ministers; some have served as catechists and evangelists; many have become Catholic and Anglican sisters. A missionary couple from the Cook Islands, Ruatoka and his wife Tungane, went to Papua in 1873 and served there for the rest of their lives. The first Papuan to be baptized, Aruadera, turned to Christ during a Sunday service in which Tungane was presenting the Christian message.

All the Christian denominations in the Pacific have fostered women's groups, and women's fellowships have frequently been a base for social activism. While Christianity provided some scope for women's agency, European missionaries tended to impose Western understandings of appropriate female behavior and family patterns on Pacific Islanders, resulting in changes in dress, housing, and domestic life (Jolly and Macintyre, 1989).

A variety of religious and social movements, some of which have been dubbed "cargo cults," emerged in Oceania in response to colonial and missionary activity. Women have played a role in these movements as mediums and diviners and sometimes as leaders. In Samoa a religious movement that came to be known as the Siovili Cult, after its male founder, arose about 1830 shortly after the introduction of Christianity by the London Missionary Society and lasted until about 1865. Siovili preached the imminent arrival of God's son, Sisu, with judgment to follow. God spoke through Sisu by way of Siovili and other mediums, many of whom were women. The leaders also carried out healings. It seems that this movement was a bridge between the old religion in which families and local communities paid homage to local gods and the Christian era with its universal God.

In Papua New Guinea too the transition from indigenous religions to Christianity gave rise to movements in which women functioned as mediums or prophets. In the early 1940s a Mekeo prophetess, Philo of Inawai'i, experienced dreams and revelations in which she understood that the mother of Jesus, "Our Mother Mary heavenly chief," was addressing her and asking her to work for the renewal of faith in her Catholic community (Fergie, 1977, p. 163). Part of Philo's message was that traditional values and Christianity are not incompatible. There were also male leaders in Philo's movement, some of whom took an anti-European and antimission stance. With the coming of World War II to Papua New Guinea, the Inawai'i movement faded. Philo married, and when she was interviewed by Deane Fergie in the 1970s, she was working as a healer in her village.

Philip Gibbs describes the leadership of women in the God Triwan movement, which started in the Catholic Pompabus parish in the Enga Province of Papua New Guinea in 1989 and spread to other parishes. The movement, which is characterized by divination and prophecy and, as in Philo's movement, devotion to Mary, was still active in the early twenty-first century. A number of scholars have described the emergence in Christian communities in Papua New Guinea of "spirit women," Christian spiritualists who share much in common with traditional male spiritualists embarking on soul journeys and acting as mediums (Lohmann, 2003, pp. 53–54).

Lorraine Sexton describes a women's movement known as Wok Meri (in Tok Pisin, "women's work") that began in the Eastern Highlands and Simbu Provinces of Papua New Guinea in the 1960s. Groups of women under the direction of senior women, called "big women," accumulated money and entered into exchange relationships with other groups. A mother group symbolically gave birth to daughter groups, with women tracing their Wok Meri ancestry through several generations. Members of the groups told Sexton that they were protesting against men's wastefulness in using money to buy beer and play cards and that they were showing their own competence and setting an example for both women and men to follow. Thus Wok Meri spoke to the responsibility women assume for their families and communities in a time of change. From the "sacred maids" of Samoa, to Christian evangelists, to spirit women and "big women," the agency of women in Oceania has been shaped both by social environments and by innovations in times of transition.

SEE ALSO Cargo Cults; Christianity, article on Christianity in the Pacific Islands; Gardens, article on Gardens in Indigenous Traditions; Melanesian Religions; Micronesian Religions; Polynesian Religions; Spirit Possession, article on Women and Possession; Taboo; Witchcraft, article on Concepts of Witchcraft.

BIBLIOGRAPHY

Biersack, Aletta. "Reproducing Inequality: The Gender Politics of Male Cults in the Papua New Guinea Highlands and Amazonia." In *Gender in Amazonia and Melanesia: An Exploration of the Comparative Method*, edited by Thomas A. Gregor and Donald Tuzin, pp. 69–90. Berkeley, Calif., 2001. A description of the male cult of the Paiela of the Papua New Guinea highlands that argues that it should be understood as a political act of reproduction in which women's capacity to reproduce is subordinated to men's claimed fertility.

Bolton, Lissant. *Unfolding the Moon: Enacting Women's Kastom in Vanuatu.* Honolulu, Hawaii, 2003. A study of the change that occurred between the early 1990s, when *kastom* in Vanuatu referred to men's knowledge and traditional practices, and 1992, when the Vanuatu Cultural Center extended the term *kastom* to include women's knowledge and practice with a particular focus on women's production of textiles as *kastom.*

Burt, Ben. *Tradition and Christianity: The Colonial Transformation of a Solomon Island Society.* Chur, Switzerland, 1993. A study of Kwara'ae religion that includes reference to women priests.

Fergie, Deane. "Prophecy and Leadership: Philo and the Inawai'a Movement." In *Prophets of Melanesia,* edited by Garry Trompf, pp. 147–173. Port Moresby, New Guinea, 1977. Discusses the role of the prophetess Philo in a renewal movement among the Mekeo of Papua New Guinea.

Gibbs, Philip. "The God Triwan Movement: Inculturation Enga Style." *Catalyst* 34, no. 1 (2004): 3–24. A missiological reflection on Christianity and culture in relation to a religious movement that discusses the complementary roles played by women and men.

Gillison, Gillian. *Between Culture and Fantasy: A New Guinea Highlands Mythology.* Chicago, 1993. An exploration of the complementarity of myths held by Gimi women and men.

Godelier, Maurice. *The Making of Great Men: Male Domination and Power among the New Guinea Baruya.* Cambridge, U.K., 1986. A study of the ritual making of men among the Baruya.

Herdt, Gilbert. *Guardians of the Flutes: Idioms of Masculinity* (1987). Chicago, 1994. A study of sex and sexual identity among the Sambia of Papua New Guinea that includes discussion of ritual insemination of boys as part of their initiation into adulthood.

Herdt, Gilbert H., ed. *Rituals of Manhood: Male Initiation in Papua New Guinea.* Berkeley, Calif., 1982. A set of eight essays exploring men's cults and initiatory rites in Papua New Guinea.

Hezel, Francis X. *The New Shape of Old Island Cultures: A Half Century of Social Change in Micronesia.* Honolulu, 2001. Includes chapters on gender roles, birth, marriage, and sexuality.

Jaarsma, Sjoerd R. "Women's Roles in Ritual: (Re)Constructing Gender Images in the Dutch Ethnography of the Southern New Guinea Lowlands." *Canberra Anthropology* 16, no. 1 (1993): 15–35. A survey of writings by administrative personnel, missionaries, and academic researchers on women's roles in ritual in Irian Jaya.

Jolly, Margaret, and Martha Macintyre, eds. *Family and Gender in the Pacific: Domestic Contradictions and the Colonial Impact.* Cambridge, U.K., 1989. A collection of twelve case studies examining changes in notions of gender following conversion to Christianity.

Josephides, Lisette. *The Production of Inequality: Gender and Exchange among the Kewa.* London, 1985. Examines men's control over women's labor and the resultant inequality of the sexes among the Kewa of the New Guinea highlands.

Langness, L. L. *Men and "Woman" in New Guinea.* Novato, Calif., 1999. A study of sex roles and initiation among the Benabena of Papua New Guinea.

Lepowsky, Maria. *Fruit of the Motherland: Gender in an Egalitarian Society.* New York, 1993. Describes egalitarian gender relations in the matrilineal society of Vanatinai, Papua New Guinea.

Lohmann, Roger. "Glass Men and Spirit Women in Papua New Guinea" *Cultural Survival* 27, no. 2 (2003): 52–55. A discussion of religious transformation among the Asabano since the arrival of missionaries in the 1970s.

Lutkehaus, Nancy C., and Paul B. Roscoe, eds. *Gender Rituals: Female Initiation in Melanesia.* New York, 1995. Eight case studies of female initiation rituals in Papua New Guinea.

MacKenzie, Maureen Anne. *Androgynous Objects: String Bags and Gender in Central New Guinea.* Chur, Switzerland, 1991. Considers the webs of gendered meanings woven into the looped net bags of New Guinea.

Mageo, Jeannette Marie. *Theorizing Self in Samoa: Emotions, Genders, and Sexualities.* Ann Arbor, Mich., 1998. A study of gender possibilities in Samoa.

Mageo, Jeannette Marie, and Alan Howard, eds. *Spirits in Culture, History, and Mind.* New York, 1996. A collection of case studies, most from Oceania, that examines the changing roles gods and spirits play in the construction of culture and in some cases in the construction of gender.

Mead, Margaret. *Coming of Age in Samoa.* New York, 1949. Mead's classic and much-debated psychological study of young women in Samoa in the 1920s.

Mead, Margaret. *Male and Female: A Study of the Sexes in a Changing World.* New York, 1949. A study of male-female relationships in seven Pacific societies is used as a basis for commenting on male-female relationships in the United States.

Meigs, Anna S. *Food, Sex, and Pollution: A New Guinea Religion.* New Brunswick, N.J., 1984. A study of the Hua of the Eastern Highlands of Papua New Guinea that discusses ideas about food, sexual activity, and relationships between the sexes, all of which have an effect on a person's vital essence or *nu.*

Ortner, Sherry B. "Gender and Sexuality in Hierarchical Societies: The Case of Polynesia and Some Comparative Implications." In *Sexual Meanings: The Cultural Construction of Gender and Sexuality,* edited by Sherry B. Ortner and Harriet Whitehead, pp. 359–409. Cambridge, U.K., 1981. Discussion of the sex-gender system in Polynesia that Ortner claims needs to be understood in relation to the "prestige system" that determines personal status.

Poole, Fitz John Porter. "Transforming 'Natural' Woman: Female Ritual Leaders and Gender Ideology among the Bimin-Kuskusmin." In *Sexual Meanings: The Cultural Construction of Gender and Sexuality,* edited by Sherry B. Ortner and Harriet Whitehead, pp. 116–165. Cambridge, U.K., 1981. Discusses the construction of gender and the role of female ritual leaders among the Bimin-Kuskusmin of the West Sepik Province of Papua New Guinea.

Sexton, Lorraine. *Mothers of Money, Daughters of Coffee: The Wok Meri Movement.* Ann Arbor, Mich., 1986. A study of the symbolism and economic import of a women's movement.

Shore, Bradd. "Sexuality and Gender in Samoa: Conceptions and Missed Conceptions." In *Sexual Meanings: The Cultural Construction of Gender and Sexuality,* edited by Sherry B. Ortner and Harriet Whitehead, pp. 192–215. Cambridge, U.K., 1981. A discussion of Samoan understandings of sex and gender using a distinction among biological, psychological, and sociocultural aspects.

Silverman, Eric Kline. *Masculinity, Motherhood, and Mockery: Psychoanalyzing Culture and the Iatmul Naven Rite in New Guinea.* Ann Arbor, Mich., 2001. A study of masculinity, ritual, and maternal representation among the people of Tambunum village in the Middle Sepik of Papua New Guinea.

Stewart, Pamela J., and Andrew Strathern. *Gender, Song, and Sensibility: Folktales and Folksongs in the Highlands of New Guinea.* Westport, Conn., 2002. An exploration of male-female relationships as expressed in songs, folktales, and spirit cults.

Stewart, Pamela J., and Andrew Strathern. *Remaking the World: Myth, Mining, and Ritual Change among the Duna of Papua New Guinea.* Westport, Conn., 2002. A discussion of how the Duna have remade their myths and rituals in response to influences of government, Christianity, and economic development. Includes a chapter on cults and a chapter on the Female Spirit.

Strathern, Marilyn. *Women in Between: Female Roles in a Male World, Mount Hagen, New Guinea.* London, 1972. A study of sex roles in Medlpa society.

Strathern, Marilyn. "Self-Interest and the Social Good: Some Implications of Hagen Gender Imagery." In *Sexual Meanings: The Cultural Construction of Gender and Sexuality,* edited by Sherry B. Ortner and Harriet Whitehead, pp. 166–191. Cambridge, U.K., 1981. Explores the contrast between personal and social goals as they are pursued by women and men in the Mount Hagen area of Papua New Guinea.

Strathern, Marilyn. *The Gender of the Gift: Problems with Women and Problems with Society in Melanesia.* Berkeley, Calif., 1988. Strathern asks what is involved in cross-cultural comparison and suggests that the study of gender relations has been distorted by the assumptions of Western anthropologists.

Strathern, Marilyn, ed. *Dealing with Inequality: Analysing Gender Relations in Melanesia and Beyond.* Cambridge, U.K., 1987. Ten essays, most based on Melanesian research, that explore the relations of equality and inequality between men and women and that grapple with the difficulties inherent in a Western observer's assessment of non-Western social relationships.

Stürzenhofecker, Gabrielle. *Times Enmeshed: Gender, Space, and History among the Duna of Papua New Guinea.* Stanford, Calif., 1998. Explores the fluidity of a social environment in which gendered personhood and agency develop in contexts of changing power relationships and spheres of cooperation between the sexes.

Tuzin, Donald. *The Cassowary's Revenge: The Life and Death of Masculinity in a New Guinea Society.* Chicago, 1997. A study of the abandonment of the male cult among the Ilahita Arapesh of Papua New Guinea and of the relationship of men and women in Ilahita culture.

Weiner, Annette B. *Women of Value, Men of Renown: New Perspectives in Trobriand Exchange.* Austin, Tex., 1976. A study of exchange in the Trobriand Islands that goes beyond the work of Malinowski and Powell to highlight the power of women in Trobriand society.

MARY N. MACDONALD (2005)

GENDER AND RELIGION: GENDER AND AFRICAN RELIGIOUS TRADITIONS

Gender has been variously defined in diverse contexts. For this entry, however, *gender* may be understood to refer to defined capacities and attributes assigned to persons based on their alleged sexual characteristics. Gender, then, is a construct within a people's living experience, embedded in the base of their philosophy and manifested at theoretical and pragmatic levels of their polity. Because gender is never independent of other social systems, it would be futile to consider it as a fixed and immutable construct; rather, it is a process. Further, gender classifications permeate a culture's cosmic perception and may be discernible in its language, storehouse of wisdom, rituals, and philosophy. Gender thus presents itself in every sector of a culture's experience of everyday life and philosophy of life. Gender classifications may be evident in perceptions of the ecosystem and supernatural forces.

HISTORICAL GENDER STUDIES IN AFRICAN RELIGIOUS TRADITIONS. History as a reference to past centuries will be misplaced if applied to the study of gender in African religious traditions, which include African indigenous religions, Christianity, and Islam. The latter two religions are classified as African religious traditions because of their influence on African culture. No longer can Islam and Christianity be described as foreign religions to Africa, as the people, through the prism of culture, have produced unique brands of Christianity and Islam (Olajubu, 2003). This misplacement of history may occur because basic assumptions concerning gender are conceptualized in Africa, rather than because of a deliberate attempt to ignore them (King, 1995) or as an indication of ignorance about gender studies in religion. African concepts of gender are integral to the people's religious experience and by implication their social life as well. Consequently, to perceive and pursue as a separate field the study of gender in African religious traditions would be misguided.

Possible reasons for granting cognizance to the study of gender in religion in Africa since the 1970s are multifarious. First, the global attention accorded to "women's issues" or the "female question" has influenced the need for scholars to delineate African gender construction within and outside of religion. Second, there arose the need to differentiate African conceptions and construction of gender from gender construction in other cultures. Third, interpretations given to gender construction in African ritual practice by some non-African scholars may be described as controversial, especially when compared to interpretations given by Africans participating in such rituals. Fourth, a good understanding of gender construction is essential to an understanding of African religious traditions. Religion is a belief system permeating all sectors of lived experiences. It exerts a profound influence on people's conception of gender. Indeed, in Africa religion is the basic principle from which gender construction is derived.

Works by scholars on gender in African religious traditions give a prime importance to ritual and the fluidity of African gender construction. Issues of cross-dressing, female cultic functionaries, and spirit possession are critically analyzed to substantiate the multidimensional complexities of gender construction in African religious traditions.

MYTHIC CONTEXTS IN CONSTRUCTING GENDER. The underlying basis of African gender issues could be located in the people's mythology, especially in cosmological myths. Myth, as a conveyor of meaning for that which history offers no explanation, provides a paradigm for gender construction and power relations. Myth supplies explanations for values and meanings in people's lives. As a model for human activity, myth elucidates the connections between the supernatural and the natural. Consequently, the roles played by the female and male personae in mythical narratives have profound implications for the expected roles of females and males in society. Some prominent attitudes on gender are signified in African mythological narratives, including, fertility, motherhood, cleansing, healing, deviance, and interdependent gender relations, as well as ambiguous perceptions of the body and of blood. These attitudes are reflected in narratives on traditions of the goddesses, sacred power, rituals, and cosmology.

African cosmological accounts often submit that God, the supreme being, created the world, nature, animals, and humans. Also, the consensus is that God created the first humans as male and female, "even if the exact methods of creating man differ according to the myths of different peoples" (Mbiti, 1969, p. 93). The Boshingo of Luanda's cosmological myth, for example, states that Bumba (God) was in terrible pain at the beginning of time, and retched and strained and vomited up the sun. After that, light spread over everything. Later, Bumba vomited the moon, stars, animals, and last of all, humans (Eliade, 1967). Moreover, some African creation myths record tension in gender relations and the sanction of God for mutual respect between male and female (Badejo, 1996; Olajubu, 2003). The Yoruba cosmological myth states that Olodumare (God) sent seventeen primordial divinities to earth at the beginning of time, Osun being the only female among them. The sixteen male divinities ignored Osun and excluded her from all decisions. In reaction to this, Osun gathered all women together and formed the Iya Mi group, which disrupted the smooth running of the universe with their powers, and the earth became ungovernable for the sixteen other primordial divinities. Olodumare advised them to make peace with Osun so that all might be well again. This they did, and everything returned to normal (Badejo, 1996, Olajubu, 2003). References to God's distribution of power to the female and the male in different areas may also be discerned from some of these accounts (Adediran, 1994).

Cosmological accounts in Africa thus prescribe and entrench complementary gender relations that find expression in the religious interactions of men and women, as well as in their relations in the polity. Consequently, female leadership roles and access to power in religion are anchored on divine provisions that are validated by these cosmological narratives. Again, these narratives confirm the African preference for areas of specialization for the female and the male. Whereas the obvious area of authority in the polity is in the custody of men, women control the base of men's public authority through mystical powers. An example of such power is demonstrated by the Iya Mi group of the Yoruba, where the women wield tremendous influence in an informal and often invisible but effectual way. Men are seen on the thrones and in official settings as rulers, yet perceived as unable to stand without the help of the invisible base. In general, interdependency and mutual sustenance mark African gender relations.

In African indigenous religions, deities who serve as lieutenants to the supreme being are both female and male. These gods and goddesses derive their authority and function from God. The conduct and interaction of goddesses in African religious narratives provide models for female roles at the religious and social levels. For instance, goddesses are usually represented as "givers" of children, as being in charge of bodies of water, and as possessing healing abilities for effecting physical and psychological well-being. Consequently, a study of goddesses would provide tools for evaluating and analyzing the status of women in African indigenous religions, as well as for assisting in analysis of the inherent gender dynamics in the traditions. For example, just as goddesses assume maternal roles to ensure fertility, motherhood and fertility are important features assumed for African women. Mystical dimensions of feminine empowerment reinforce roles that are linked to female procreative attributes.

Female religious alliances, such as the Iya Mi association among the Yoruba, wield tremendous cultural influence, and often link their powers to the women's access to fertility and motherhood (Olajubu, 2003, p. 17). Similarly, African indigenous religions often ascribe to women the ability to heal. This healing aptitude may be exhibited by women as individuals in their capacities as priestesses and healers, or in a collective as a religious group, such as the *zaar* cults of Ethiopia, Somalia, Egypt, and Eritrea. As wives to gods, goddesses are said to possess independent mystical powers, which they display independently or in conjunction with their husbands. Goddesses are sometimes perceived as wives in polygamous settings, just as polygamy often prevailed as a widespread social practice in Africa.

In addition, goddesses are presented as industrious beings who are often well off financially. In the same vein, African women are hardworking and prosperous, sometimes more so than their husbands. Similarly, African indigenous religions conceive of women as possessing mystical powers, which they are at liberty to use in the service of a personal agenda. Some refer to this mysticism as "witchcraft." Often, allegations of witchcraft indicate some level of fear or awe concerning women's lives and physiology, although these indications do not obliterate cases of witchcraft.

Goddesses are closely connected to the governance of some African communities. Osun, the goddesses of cool waters in Osogbo, Nigeria, is closely connected with the sovereignty of the town and the king. Osun is recognized as the owner of the land on which Osogbo stands. She is reported to have defended the people during wars, and provides for the people as well, including the provision of money, health, and peace. Appreciation for her care is demonstrated yearly in an elaborate festival that attracts devotees from within and outside Nigeria (Olupona, 2000). The king of Osogbo (Ataoja) rules in behalf of Osun; her support is crucial to the success of every endeavor in the land. Indeed, the state in which Osogbo is located is named after her. The relationship between Osun and the king and the indigenes of Osun State is that of mother and children.

Symbolic Construction of Gender Studies in African Religious Traditions. As a social category, gender appears to influence the work of many scholars; this influence is reflected by their research in African religious traditions, as well as in African economics, government, and the media. Many scholars offer tangential evidence of their interest in gender studies in their writings on subjects other than religion. Some of these scholars are Kemene Okonjo (1978), Filomena Steady (1987), Karin Barber (1991), Bolanle Awe (1992), Molara Ogundipe-Leslie (1994), Ifi Amadiume (1998), Mary Kolawole (1998), Anne Wynchank (1998), and Oyeronke Oyewumi (1999). Many other scholars focus their analysis of gender on African Christian, Islamic, and traditional religions: Judith Gleason (1987), Niara Sudarkasa (1987, 1996), Teresa Okure (1989), Rabiatu Ammah (1992), Deidre Crumbley (1992), Teresa Hinga (1992), Musimbi Kanyoro (1992), Anne Nasimiyu-Wasike (1992), Mercy Amba Oduyoye (1992, 1995), Sophie Oluwole (1993), J. Lorand Matory (1994), Amina Mama (1995), Diedre Badejo (1996), Flora Edouwaye S. Kaplan (1997), Dorcas Akintunde (2001), Mei-Mei Sanford and Joseph Murphy (2001), and Oyeronke Olajubu (2003).

Previously, gender studies in African indigenous religions have focused on rituals and symbols. Emanating from these studies are notions of fluidity in gender construction and the complexity attending gender as a social tool for religious analysis. This focus is especially true in light of other competing categories, such as seniority and lineage affiliation. African indigenous religions exhibit ritual features of transvestitism and interchangeable gender characteristics. Another feature is that women traditionally assume roles of leadership as priestesses, diviners, and healers. Furthermore, African religions view women as predominant participants in spirit possession. Scholars have propounded theories from different perspectives to explicate spirit possession and its implication for gender studies. Spirit possession in African indigenous religions bestows temporary respect and authority on women in some contexts, while in others it extends permanent benefits to the social status of women.

Symbols persistently reinforce the complexity of gender construction in African indigenous religions as conveyors of meaning in diverse contexts. Such symbols can occur as works of art, such as the sculpted birds that appear on elements of authority (e.g., crowns, staffs of office) among the Yoruba (Nigeria), or they can be hidden, such as the dance steps that are performed during the Nandi (Kenya) female initiation rites. An overriding principle for symbolism is interdependency in terms of gender relations. Symbols reinforce the authority of women who engage in their sphere of specializations (e.g., fertility), just as symbols reinforce the authority of men (master of the herd); neither could subsist without the other. Again, from these symbols, we may infer that the assumption of a total exclusion of females or males from any particular sphere in these indigenous religions is erroneous.

The introduction of Christianity to Africa began in the early centuries of the Christian era with the establishment of the Ethiopian and Coptic churches, though European missionary activities spanned (intermittently) the fourteenth to nineteenth centuries. Missionaries who introduced Christianity to Africa relegated women to the domestic domain, a division entrenched in biblical interpretations. However, with the emergence of the African independent, charismatic, and Zionist churches, the need to renegotiate gender relations became a relevant issue. Contributing to this need was the mass movement of worshipers from orthodox churches to the African independent, charismatic, and Zionist churches because African culture influenced the prevailing rituals in these churches. As examples of such influence, women assumed roles of leadership and symmetry of form in leadership cadres. Nearly all gender studies of African Christianity began because of these developments. Examples of such works include publications by J. Renita Weems (1991), Amba Mercy Oduyoye and Musimbi Kanyoro (1992), Musimbi Kanyoro and Nyambura Njoroge (1996), W. Musa Dube (2001), and M. Teresa Hinga (2002).

The history of gender studies in Islamic Africa is recent. On the one hand, there is the attempt to tease out feminist passages from the Qurʾān and strip away patriarchal interpretations that hindered previous appreciation. Such passages include the prophet Muḥammad's statements enjoining respect and appreciation for women and equity between the male and female. Emphasis in this regard has been on *taqwa* (piety), which is required of all adherents irrespective of sex by Allah (Mernissi, 1995 and Wadud, 1999).

There is the perspective that prioritizes the influence of African culture in paradigms concerning women, and this influences the women's understanding and practicing of Islam. A model is the leadership role of women in African culture, now manifested in various Islamic forms. This trend has manifested in two main ways. Some women following Islam in Nigeria claim divine calling to devote all their time to prayers and healing practices for clients who come to them. This has consequently elevated the status of such women in Islam. Second, because of the identified need to take the African culture seriously for the propagation of Islam, women are now installed as chiefs in the mosque's structures. Titles among the Yoruba of Nigeria include the Iya Addini (woman leader) and Otun Addini (assistant to the woman leader).

It may be surmised then that an understanding of gender constructions in Africa is significant to any meaningful analysis and evaluation of African religious traditions.

Rigidity and Flexibility in Gender Construction: The Ritual Sphere. The realm of ritual has proven versatile for displaying gender construction and deconstruction. Central to these attempts is the perception in African cultures of blood, especially menstrual blood. The presence or absence of menstrual blood contributes significantly to the construction of gender in religion. In its absence, the patriarchy views the female to be as pure as a virgin and fit for the habitation of the deity in the form of, for example, votary maids, adolescent girls dedicated to certain deities until the age of marriage. These girls are forbidden to engage in sexual relations and their upbringing is closely monitored. Votary maids bring messages to the adherent at worship or festival periods during spirit possession sessions, and observe diverse types of taboos to reinforce their separation unto the deity concerned. River goddesses are often known to have votary maids. In the presence of menstrual blood, the patriarchy views the female, usually a wife, as suspect, even though she is extolled as a mother. This ambiguous status of the female accommodates serious compromises for power relations between the genders. In addition, access to power and authority are consequences of these classifications. In African indigenous religions, then, menstrual blood evokes joy and yet instills limitation. However, among some Africans, limitations are not a consequence of contamination but a means of avoiding a clash of powers. The sacred domain is perceived as the abode of power, just as menstrual blood, which contains potential life, is considered a conveyor of power. Thus, there is a need to separate these two realms of power to avert a clash; this is particularly true of the Yoruba belief system.

African dual perspectives on blood restrict women's access to sacred space during menstruation. Often this restriction is temporary, but it could explain the prevalence of postmenstrual women in leadership cadres. However, current research shows increasing numbers of women of childbearing age in positions of leadership in African indigenous religions, and priestesses may be of any age. In addition, there are females who occupy important positions in male religious groups. Such women play symbolic roles, ranging from keepers of secrets, to the "mothers" of males, including the *iya magba* ("Magba's mother" of the Egúngún Yoruba religious group). These female roles exemplify the African notion of interdependency, mutuality, and compassion of gender relations. Furthermore, the ambivalence marking African expectations and assumptions for female status become evident. Whereas some myths may describe women as unable to keep secrets, women in certain domains are indeed the keepers of secrets.

Gender relations often manifest themselves as a cultural fluidity corresponding to a ritual domain of indigenous religions. This fluidity tends to reinforce complex gender constructions. For instance, legendary goddesses are known to possess "wives" (devotees, votary maids, and mediums), just as certain gods do. Some community rulers are considered to be "wives" of their affiliate deities, who may be perceived as male or female (Matory, 1994). Moreover, certain Yoruba priests of Ṣango are transvestites who take on the role of the male "wives" of the deities by wearing female costumes and plaiting their hair in a feminine style. Alternatively, when under the influence of certain deities, some female mediums of various religious groups exhibit characteristics generally associated with males. For example, while possessed by Ṣango (Elegun Ṣango), female mediums become "aggressive" under Ṣango's masculine authority.

African cultures often correlate group solidarity with gender construction. Group formations are expected of females in many sectors of the African polity, including economics, religion and social settings. While females practice group solidarity in many African religious traditions, males cannot be said to do the same. To explain this widespread practice of female solidarity, scholars of religion have propounded various theories. Whereas some perceive such solidarity as resistance against patriarchal suppression, others see it as an attempt to create an alternative space to empower women. In any case, clearly the motif of female group formation forms a salient feature of African religious traditions.

Contemporary Feminist Scholarship and African Religious Traditions. Available research and publications on gender and religions in Africa are few. Nonetheless, publications by African female scholars on gender are increasing, which explains the significant impact such works have had on the study of African religious traditions. Although their focuses vary, these works generally pursue the following set of goals (sometimes a single work may fulfill two or more of these conditions): (1) to offer analysis of gender constructions in African religious traditions from the feminine perspective by allowing women to tell their stories rather than imposing constructed meanings on data; (2) to seek paradigms and models from past African religious experiences, spanning history and mythology for the construction of gender relations in contemporary African religious life; (3) to offer new feminist interpretations and meanings for familiar but patriarchal narratives in African religious tradition and to utilize this for balanced gender relations; and (4) to correct assumed meanings for certain aspects of African rituals by taking serious cognizance of meanings ascribed to such rituals by the participants.

African scholars of religion are beginning to restructure the academic constructions of gender by exposing the biased implications proffered by colonial constructions of gender. The colonial experience in Africa instituted a disruption of gender structures by separating the integrated African domains of public and private space. This divisiveness, however, was attenuated in African religious traditions by an entrenched cultural recognition accorded female leadership prescribed in oral narratives. Viewed from a different perspective, the exposure of African religious traditions to the African diaspora since the 1970s has been tremendous. This exposure is particularly true of Yoruba religion, which can boast of adherents in every continent of the world. The movement of practitioners of Yoruba religion travels both ways between the continent and the diaspora. Priests and priestesses of Yoruba religion travel to the Americas and Europe to train and educate adherents, just as some adherents visit Africa regularly for training and renewal of energies. Consequently, this exposure has produced reliable research that compares and contrasts indigenous African religions with their variations in the Americas, especially Brazil, Cuba, and other parts of the Caribbean (Benard and Moon, 2000; Sanford and Murphy, 2001).

Such innovative research contributes to African scholarship by advocating cooperation among practitioners of diasporic and continental African religions. This cooperation has informed conferences, workshops, and symposia on the continent, as well as in the United States and Europe. The exchange of gender studies and religious traditions between the diaspora and Africa is producing fresh perspectives in understanding religious rituals.

Academic materials for investigating African religious traditions from a female perspective are now available in print and on the internet. Consequently, feminist scholars on gender and African religious traditions are establishing women's studies departments and gender institutes in African universities. Examples of such centers include the African Gender Institute at the University of Cape Town, South Africa, and the Institute of Women and Gender studies at the Makerere University in Kampala, Uganda.

See Also Gender Roles; Menstruation; Spirit Possession, article on Women and Possession.

Bibliography

Adediran, B., ed. *Cultural Studies in Ife.* Ile-Ife, Nigeria, 1994. A collection of articles on aspects of African culture, including rituals, ethics, aesthetics, and commerce.

Akintunde, Dorcas, ed. *African Culture and the Quest for Women's Rights.* Ibadan, Nigeria, 2001. Contains an array of articles on the rights of women and how the African culture can undermine these rights.

Amadiume, Ifi. *Male Daughters, Female Husbands: Gender and Sex in an African Society.* London, 1988. A consideration of the dynamics of gender construction in the Igbo society of Nigeria.

Ammah, Rabiatu. "Paradise Lies at the Feet of Muslim Women." In *The Will to Arise: Women, Tradition, and the Church in Africa,* edited by Mercy Amba Oduyoye and Musimbi R. A. Kanyoro, pp. 74–86. Maryknoll, N.Y., 1992.

Awe, Bolanle. *Nigerian Women in Historical Perspective.* Lagos, Nigeria, 1992. The author supplies information on some prominent women in Nigerian history to serve as role models for contemporary women and to place on record their achievements.

Badejo, Diedre. *Osun Seegesi: The Elegant Deity of Wealth, Power, and Femininity.* Trenton, N.J., 1996. Focuses on the Osun river goddess in Osogbo, Osun State, Nigeria by explicating the many sides of the goddess-economic dynamism, fecundity, and wisdom.

Barber, Karin. *I Could Speak Till Tomorrow: Oriki, Women, and the Past in a Yoruba Town.* Edinburgh, 1991. Analyses the Yoruba genre of praise names and poems for individuals and families. Oriki is an integral aspect of Yoruba identity construction and a storehouse of information on every aspect of the people's philosophy.

Benard, Elizabeth, and Beverly Moon, eds. *Goddesses Who Rule.* Oxford, 2000. A collection of essays on certain goddesses closely linked to governance across the globe.

Boddy, J. *Wombs and Alien Spirits: Women, Men and the Zaar Cult in Northern Sudan.* Madison, Wis., 1989. Examines the different connotations given to women's reproductive functions from a religious perspective.

Crumbley, Deidre. "Impurities and Power: Women in Aladura Churches" *Africa* 62 (1992).

Davis, Angela. "Sex—Egypt." in *Women: A World Report,* edited by Anita Desai, Toril Brekke, et al, pp. 325–348. London, 1985. Examines the conceptions in Egypt about sex and women and the consequences emanating from such positions.

Dube, W. Musa, ed. *Other Ways of Reading: African Women and the Bible.* Atlanta, 2001. A collection of essays that considers women in local churches and their participation in reading and interpretation of the Bible in Africa.

Eliade, Mircea. *From Primitive to Zen.* London, 1967. Displays an array of excerpts of some aspects of many indigenous religions worldwide, including Native American, African and Mesopotamian.

Gleason, Judith. *Oya: In Praise of an African Goddess.* Boston, 1987. An examination of Oya, the Yoruba goddess of winds and the river Niger. It attempts to show the dynamism in Yoruba gender construction.

Hinga, M. Teresa. "Jesus Christ and the Liberation of Women in Africa." In *The Will to Arise: Women, Tradition, and the Church in Africa,* edited by Mercy Amba Oduyoye and Musimbi R. A. Kanyoro, pp. 183–194. Maryknoll, N.Y., 1992. One work giving major consideration to the place of women in the interaction of Christianity and African culture in recent times. Articles therein present pertinent issues that proffer serious theoretical reviews for Christianity in Africa.

Hinga, M. Teresa. "African Feminist Theologies, the Global Village, and the Imperative of Solidarity Across Borders: The Case of the Circle of Concerned African Women Theologians." *Journal of Feminist Studies in Religion* 18, no. 1 (2002): 79–86.

Hollis, S. T. "Queens and Goddesses in Ancient Egypt." In *Women Goddess Traditions in Antiquity and Today,* edited by

K. L. King, pp. 210–238. Minneapolis, 1991. Considers the goddess tradition in Egypt and attempts to compare the present.

Kanyoro, Musimbi R. A. "Interpreting Old Testament Polygamy Through African Eyes." In *The Will to Arise: Women, Tradition, and the Church in Africa,* edited by Mercy Amba Oduyoye and Musimbi R. A. Kanyoro, pp. 87–100. Maryknoll, N.Y., 1992.

Kanyoro, Musimbi and Nyambura Njoroge, eds. *Groaning in Faith: African Women in the Household of God.* Nairobi, Kenya, 1996.

Kaplan, Flora Edouwaye S., ed. *Queens, Queen Mothers, Priestesses, and Power: Case Studies in African Gender.* New York, 1997. Considers the role of women in the different sectors of the polity and displays the dynamism of African gender construction.

King, Ursula, ed. *Religion and Gender.* Oxford, 1995. Examination of the connections between religion and gender, providing useful theoretical background.

Kolawole, Mary, ed. *Gender Perceptions and Development in Africa.* Lagos, Nigeria, 1998. Collection of essays focusing on African gender construction and developmental issues. Some of the essays employ literary studies to make their points.

Mama, Amina. "Women's Studies and Studies of Women in Africa during the 1990's." GWS Africa. *Feminist Knowledge: Review Essays.* 1995/1996. Available at: www.gwsafrica.org/knowledge/codesriabook.htm.

Matory, J. Lorand. *Sex and the Empire that Is No More: Gender and the Politics of Metaphor in Oyo Yoruba Religion.* Minneapolis, 1994. Considers embedded meanings of ritual in the worship of Sango in old Oyo, Nigeria and how they informed significant political considerations at the time.

Mbiti, John. *African Religions and Philosophy.* London, 1969; 2d ed., Oxford, 1990. A submission on the components of African philosophy and sense of time.

Mbiti, John. "The Role of Women in African Religion." In *African Traditional Religion in Contemporary Society,* edited by Jacob Kehinde Olupona, pp. 59–73. New York, 1991.

Mernissi, Fatima. *Women and Islam: An Historical and Theological Enquiry.* Translated by Mary Jo Lakeland. Oxford, 1995. An attempt to strip Islam of the label of patriarchy by exhibiting new interpretations of Qur'anic passages.

Nasimiyu-Wasike, Anne. "Christianity and the African Rituals of Birth and Naming." In *The Will to Arise: Women, Tradition, and the Church in Africa,* edited by Mercy Amba Oduyoye and Musimbi R. A. Kanyoro, pp. 40–54. Maryknoll, N.Y., 1992.

Oduyoye, Amba Mercy. *Daughters of Anowa: African Women and Patriarchy.* New York, 1995. A consideration of oppressions faced by women in Africa and the role of religion in this situation.

Oduyoye, Amba Mercy, and Musimbi R. A. Kanyoro, eds. *The Will to Arise: Women, Tradition, and the Church in Africa.* Maryknoll, N.Y., 1992.

Ogundipe-Leslie, Molara. *Re-Creating Ourselves: African Women and Critical Transformations.* Trenton, N.J., 1994.

Okonjo, Kemene. "The Dual Sex Political System in Operation: 1960 Women and Community Politics in Midwestern Nigeria." In *Women in Africa,* edited by J. Hafikin and Edna G. Bay, pp. 45–58. Stanford, Calif., 1976. Examines the role of women in governance at Nigeria's independence in 1960.

Okonjo, Kemene. "Women in Contemporary Africa." In *African Society, Culture, and Politics,* edited by Christopher Mojekwu. Washington, D.C., 1978.

Okure, Teresa. "A Theological View of Women's Role in Promoting Cultural/Human Development." *Ecclesiastical Review* 31 (1989).

Olajubu, Oyeronke. *Women in the Yoruba Religious Sphere.* Albany, N.Y., 2003. Considers the dynamism that attends women's roles in Yoruba religion and implications for the continuous reshaping of religious traditions among the Yoruba people.

Olupona, Jacob K. "Yoruba Goddesses and Sovereignty in Southwestern Nigeria." In *Goddesses Who Rule,* edited by Elizabeth Benard and Beverly Moon, pp. 119–132. Oxford, 2000. The essay focuses on some Yoruba goddesses and explicates their roles in governance through myth and rituals.

Oluwole, Sophie. *Womanhood in Yoruba Traditional Thought.* Bayreuth, Germany, 1993. Examination of the African worldview on women and their roles in society. Challenges faced by women in attaining or rejecting these ascribed roles are also considered.

Oyewumi, Oyeronke. *The Invention of Women: Making an African Sense of Western Gender Discourses.* Minneapolis, 1999. Submits that gender was imported into Yoruba Oyo philosophy from Western philosophy. It challenges the monolithic gender construction of some cultures by presenting the multidimensional construction of gender by the Yoruba.

Peel, J. D. Y. "Gender in Yoruba Religious Change." *Journal of Religion in Africa* 32, no. 2 (2002): 136–166. Considers the changing influence of Christianity on males and females from a historical perspective.

Sanford, Mei-Mei, and Joseph M. Murphy, eds. *Osun Across the Waters: A Yoruba Goddess in Africa and the Americas.* Bloomington, Ind., 2001. An attempt to forge a link on Yoruba religion between the diaspora and the African continent with a particular focus on Osun.

Steady, Filomena. "African Feminism." In *Women in Africa and in the African Diaspora,* edited by Rosalyn Terborg-Penn, Andrea Benton Rushing, and Sharon Harley, pp. 3–21. Washington, D.C., 1987. Identifies and explicates the brand of feminism that accommodates African culture and demands mutual respect.

Sudarkasa, Niara. "The Status of Women in Indigenous African Societies." In *Women in Africa and in the African Diaspora,* edited by Rosalyn Terborg-Penn, Andrea Benton Rushing, and Sharon Harley, pp. 73–87. Washington, D.C., 1987. Attempts to show that the issue of oppression between the male and female was alien in indigenous societies due to the interdependent modalities utilized in the community.

Sudarkasa, Niara. *The Strength of Our Mothers: African and African American Women and Families, Essays and Speeches.* Trenton, N.J., 1996.

Wadud, Amina. *Quran and Woman: Rereading the Sacred Text From a Woman's Perspective.* New York, 1999. An attempt to highlight the Qur'ān with serious consideration for the quest for women's empowerment.

Weems, J. Renita. "Reading Her Way through the Struggle: African Women and the Bible." In *Stony the Road We Trod: African American Biblical Interpretation*, edited by Cain Hope Felder, pp. 57–77. Minneapolis, 1991. Considers African women's attempt to relate the bible to daily experiences and to resolve challenges that arise in this process.

Wynchank, Anny. " 'The Sons Who Sell their Mothers' and 'The Devouring Calabash': Two Recurring Gender Myths in Western and Southern African Tales." In *Gender Perceptions and Development in Africa*, edited by Mary Kolawole, pp. 121–132. Lagos, Nigeria, 1998. Attempts to analyze African gender construction through the prism of tales, an important genre of literature in Africa.

OYERONKE OLAJUBU (2005)

GENDER AND RELIGION: GENDER AND NORTH AMERICAN INDIAN RELIGIOUS TRADITIONS

To pursue the theme of gender in North American Indian religious traditions is to bring the construction of gender, long in process, of ancient civilizations into dialogue with the concerns of the present. It necessarily involves a task of identifying carefully what gender means in traditional native cultures and defining the ways, past and present, that this aspect of culture can be assessed. Moreover it requires a critical appraisal of the propriety and accuracy of the conclusions made by those interpreters who were not inside the culture. Especially it demands a clear presentation of the relation of gender and religion, because this varies greatly from Western to traditional cultures.

THE CONSTRUCTION OF GENDER. The construction of gender—indeed even the understanding of it—always takes place in the wider project of imagining the shape of the cosmos as a whole. It is well known that the foundational insight of North American Indian traditions is that everything is dynamically alive, with relationships rather than rules as its laws. In such a world nothing and no one stands alone, but each is related to every other and the whole. Thus all is holy, sacred. The primary quality of each aspect is the spiritual nature of its being, which underlies the unique form that communicates its identity. This identity is not the external form but the complex reality of the inner life of that being. Gender as such is clearly related to this spiritual identity and is deeper than sexual marks of differentiation. These outer forms may change over a lifetime; the inner identity does not.

Significantly native peoples have a more diverse recognition of gender as it manifests itself in human life. Is it the early encounter with dualism that caused the western European world to see gender as only dual and complementary, male or female? Native peoples, over a long period of historical experience, recognized a third and even a fourth gender. Perhaps this cultural difference explains the cognitive dismay experienced by the European travelers as well as the curiosity of the early anthropologists and ethnologists. Among the distorted reactions were the harsh punishments dealt by the Spanish conquistadores and the Jesuits who were unable to distinguish sexual identity in native terms from unlawful sexual acts.

Proper recognition of the insights of earlier researchers should be given. The spectrum of those who studied Native American culture ranges from the onset of colonization into the twenty-first century and in manners as diverse as enlightened description (e.g., parts of the *Jesuit Relations*) to hostile rejection of cultural forms. In the broad phylum of objective scholars, ethnologists and anthropologists (male and female) have contributed significant portrayals. Worthy of note is the work of Ruth Landes among the Ojibwa and Ruth Densmore's ambitious project to record (and thus preserve) the ritual music of many diverse peoples. The presence of such women in the ranks of social scientists opened the door to appreciation of women's contribution to culture and its core of religious meaning.

Despite the criterion of scientific objectivity, however, each observer brings a structured view of particular reality to the efforts to encounter and understand a different people. Thus in the New World, as in Asia, the predominant frame of reference was that of the Western world. It could not have been avoided in fact. But this perspective has often clouded the view of native peoples. It is certainly the case that the strong influence of Christianity caused the perception of women, of native religion, and of the central place of women in society to be distorted in perception and description. There are of course some great exceptions to this, but they are not the predominant view.

FEMALE CONCEPTS OF SACREDNESS. A powerful example of cultural dissonance is reflected in the early views that native religious traditions were pagan and based on superstition. Scholars of the nineteenth and twentieth centuries (e.g., James Walker, Owen Dorsey, Ruth Benedict, and William Fenton), in their earnest efforts to portray and understand the meaning of the dense ritual complexes across the continent, rescued the great body of native religious insights from vanishing. The growing contributions of contemporary native scholars—women and men—have created a more realistic and profound view of indigenous native religious beliefs and practices.

One particular aspect that merits attention is the fascinating dialogue between native concepts of the sacred and those of Western Christianity. In concert with the emergent feminist movement, women scholars have emphasized the particularity and richness of native concepts of the sacred. This is a large subject; thus it is only possible to give a few examples.

In one of the earliest works on gender in native America, *The Sacred Hoop* (1986), Paula Gunn Allen offers a richness of description as she strives to recover the feminine in native traditions. From her own perspective as a Laguna Pueblo woman, she describes the overwhelming feminine aspect of the southwestern peoples but also reveals the parallels in other areas of the country. It is clear from her reflections and memories that there is the closest connection between a creatrix, Thought Woman, and the structure of reality as it proceeds from her sacred work.

> At the center of all is Woman, and nothing is sacred . . . without her blessing, her thinking. . . . She is a spirit who pervades all, who created all reality and languages. This originating power is female in her primacy and potency. She is the mother of all, and as her surrogate, Mother Earth enfolds and nurtures all creation. (Allen, 1986, pp. 13–14)

Thus the Keres people see her as the source of all life, bringer of corn, agriculture, weaving, social systems, religion, ritual, memory, and so on. In her vast presence she is honored as Mother and Father of all peoples and all creatures. Her power is manifest in generativity and so is much broader than maternity. Earth and women are linked as homologous parts of creation; their sacred role stems from their relation to Thought Woman.

The Constructs of Gynecocracy. Allen then demonstrates that this feminine aspect of the sacred is related to social structures of gynecocracy—a distinctive feature of native society that she sees as the predominant form of North American peoples before the coming of the Europeans. This is borne out by the current structures of Pueblo life, especially the Hopi, but also by the central role held by women in the confederacies of the Northwest and Southeast. Less obvious to the British was the powerful role of women among the Iroquois, but early records of encounter noted the high place of women among the Creek and Cherokee, because they were encountered in diplomatic missions.

There is a rich and growing literature on the subject of gender by native scholars and interested others. Credit should be given to one of the first pioneers, the Lakota anthropologist Beatrice Medicine. She initiated work by native women (e.g., Paula Gunn Allen, Patricia Albers, Marla Powers) who set about telling the stories of women in Native America. This is not to say that early students did not depict the life and development of native women. The shifting of history, however, ensured that what most caught their attention were the men who, throughout the nineteenth century, emblazoned across history the image of the heroic warriors and buffalo hunters who were fighting for the very survival of their culture.

In reality survival of a tribe depended on the full cooperation of all its members. Because biology makes women the bearers of children, they are also the keepers of the hearth. Yet in many native societies this was only one aspect of a much broader area of responsibility. All over the continent women have traditionally been associated with the earth. As previously noted, all reality is gendered, and the connection of women to the great source of nurture that is the earth reveals the enormous holiness and power with which she is endowed. This powerful connection appears in many nations in the great stories that preserve their heritage. Thus in the Iroquois origin story the Sky-Woman is the first of the People Above to begin the process of external creation. As she falls from the Sky World, she is supported by birds with their wings outstretched until at last a creature of the waters offers her a resting place. Her rescuer is Grandmother Turtle, and it is from the initial encounter of these persons that Iroquois life begins. The theme of women's power continues, as Sky-Woman's child gives birth to the twin sacred persons who will establish the full creation. Similarly in the Lakota story of the White Buffalo Calf Woman a Sacred Woman comes from Wakan Tanka and brings the great gift of the Sacred Pipe, then and now the symbol of the people's link to the Great Mystery. In the Cheyenne story of creation Maheo, the All-Father, makes man and woman from two ribs taken from his side (implying an equal origination). And among the Navajo, Changing Woman is crucial to the creation of the Navajo and their world. Her presence is believed to ensure cosmic balance, and each girl is initiated into her role and image during Kinaaldá, the female initiation rite.

These stories attest to the high regard for the feminine in creation. This respect traditionally had great influence in shaping the life roles of native women. It is well known that the Iroquois League valued the advice and wisdom of women so much that the representative sachems could not be named or selected without the consent of the women. Historically women had the power to temper the balance of power of the war chiefs by counterbalancing them with men who sought peace. Even in the early twenty-first century the proper protocol for Atatarho, the chief of the sachems, is to have a woman as his mediator. Thus the traditional customs witness to the essential balance of male and female to ensure right order.

Among the agricultural peoples (e.g., the Hopi), the women owned the fields and therefore the store of food that was the source of their people's lives. Women were also expected to have talents in craft making (beading, pottery), and often there is a mythic person who is considered to impart this gift (e.g., Spider-Woman, Double-Faced Woman). The power of female fertility received great respect; in fact periods of fertility necessitated that a woman stay away from ritual spaces as well as from hunters and warriors. Her power was viewed not as impurity but as a power capable of interfering with and subverting male power. A woman was viewed by many nations as the heart of her people. The Cheyenne say it well: "A nation is not conquered until the hearts of its women are on the ground."

A crucial part of any study of gender rests on the ways it is constructed in any society. Before the advent of sociology and psychology, this issue was considered a natural dimension of traditional education. As such it was taught in an imitative and exponential way, not as part of logical discourse (though this too had its place, specifically at puberty ceremonies, in which care was given to define sexual and gender roles). But traditional education involves a broader method than classroom learning. An entire clan group was responsible for imaging the roles adults have in contributing to the support of the whole group. Thus an intensive web of instruction accompanied a child from earliest years to the major threshold of adult initiation. This was true for girls and boys in a framework that allowed notice to be taken of those who did not quite fit the category.

Women in Rituals. The place of women in rituals, and the links perceived between them and the rationale and goal of the ritual, is perhaps most strikingly seen in rites of initiation. One strong example (representative of many others) can be found in the Navajo ceremony of Kinaaldá. In origin and purpose it illustrates the feminine aspect of ritual practice as well as the connection between such rites and the common good that ritual aims to support. The rite of Kinaaldá derives from the Navajo story of their creation or emergence. In it a powerful spirit, miraculously placed on the earth's surface, creates the first humans from her own flesh. She is called Changing Woman because she embodies all the seasons of life as well as of nature. She is unvaryingly benevolent and continues to nurture her people, especially through Blessingway, the chantway that is her gift, and through Kinaaldá.

What occurs in this Navajo ritual is a careful process intended to make the pubescent young girl a Navajo woman in potency and reality. This is accomplished by molding the girl into the image of Changing Woman and encouraging her to earnestly begin to emulate her model's qualities as woman through her contributions to the people. Thus physical strength, endurance, creativity, fruitfulness, and many skills and qualities are transferred to her during this special time when she is especially open to formative influences. The initiate is instructed to invite Changing Woman into her life, and in the realism of Navajo belief, this does happen. Thus the young woman is considered to be a special source of power for life and healing during this time. The rich ceremonial details of dress, painting, and ritual acts portray the transformation of the young girl into this powerful and benevolent spirit. Through this she is prepared to contribute to her people in life-giving ways throughout her life.

The remembered traditions of the peoples of North America reveal that the role of women in society and ritual is of utmost importance. Thus the varying ways of conducting the sun dance on the Plains insisted on the presence of the Sacred Woman at the heart of the ritual. This example demonstrates that, even in cultures that in historic times were seen as masculine (i.e., the warrior tradition that was so obvious to the invaders from the east), the whole could not be complete without the sacred presence of women. Any study of the elaborate ritual acts that made up the sun dance shows the profound understanding that the feminine is a necessary, constituent part of cosmic reality. Thus it is complementarity, rather than emphasis on a male or female hierarchy, that most accurately represents the religious understanding of native peoples of North America.

The sun dance represents not only thanksgiving for the gifts of life but also a primary moment to bring healing to the people. The role of healing is central to indigenous religions and in North America involved both genders. Because it was a uniquely important spiritual calling, this role was usually entered through a call in a dream or a vision and a period of specific instruction by an elder, experienced religious authority. This vocation was not restricted to men, but a different path was usual for women. In the many stories that exist of medicine women, it is clear that they could not exercise their full spiritual power until they were past menopause. Specifically, although they could offer herbs for healing, they were not to engage in the profound act of spiritual healing. Similar to the principle that menstrual blood could interfere with the exercise of power, in carrying out her role the medicine woman did not risk the conflict of sacred powers. Among the many tribes in which the medicine tradition was inherited (nonlinearly), women also served the people. In some places (e.g., California) only women became medicine people.

Women in Society. The role of males in traditional native societies varied with regard to geographical location, modes of subsistence, and the shape of major cultural myths. But seen against the broad background of the prehistoric past, all had internalized the primary occupation of ancestors—the endeavor to win survival through hunting. The skills and perceptual acuteness needed for successful hunting created an ideal that perhaps found its apex in the Plains Indian buffalo-hunting culture. But strong masculine images were noted in most cultures Europeans encountered, and these emerge in the accounts shared by the people themselves as they surveyed their oral histories. Here, as with the female gender, the essence of the male person was regarded as in process and as eventually completed in a spiritual encounter with sacred power. This reveals that the virtue associated with the strong male image were not merely natural but part of a complex relationship with the creative power that fills all life.

The myths tell of the first peoples looking for a homeland and sources of life. They are portrayed as knowing their weakness and welcoming the interventions by gods or spirits who come to assist them.

A paradigmatic story comes from the Navajo, who fall into error regarding the essential balance of men and women, male and female, in life on Mother Earth. They are gently led to reunite by the intervention of a spirit who manifests the vitality and rightness of that balance in himself. In the Lakota story of extended beginnings, the prototypical warrior, Stone Boy, works arduously to make the earth safe for the people, and in the story of the founding of the League of the Hodenosaunee, the prophet Deganawidah finds it necessary to temper the uncontrolled warlike nature of Atatarho, whom he defeats by skillful diplomacy. A powerful transformation takes place when the ferocious warrior chief surrenders his passions and agrees to be the servant of all—the chief of chiefs who holds the council fires together. The Iroquois honor this memory of the shift from uncontrolled aggression to diplomatic means to achieve harmony both within and around them.

Because the male was required to support not only his family but all those in need, much depended on developing a pattern of learning that relied on fostering certain verities. Courage was paramount, but skill in tracking, patience in waiting, and the will to endure privations—often for long periods of time—were also crucial. These skills, although important, are minor compared to the habits of mind and soul. Thus many people valued generosity and altercenteredness and viewed the whole as contributing to the attainment of honor. Much was expected of the man, and the burden this could impose was often felt as heavy. Anthony F. C. Wallace's study of the Seneca, based on a lifetime of work by others, such as William Fenton, illustrates how such pressure was in need of a means to release it without shaming the warrior. He notes the wisdom of a community that paid great attention to dreams, seen as early as the 1600s, as "wishes of the soul" and the acumen of soul that instituted a way private dreams could be enacted at the Midwinter (New Year's) Festival and answered in appropriate ways by the community. It is important to note here that the Iroquois, remembered by history as fearsome warriors, were actually part of a matriarchal society and that one of the most highly regarded warrior societies on the Plains was that of the Cheyenne, who were renowned for their courage and discipline and spirit of sacrifice. Their allies and friends the Lakota remarked that the Cheyenne women deserved as much honor as their men, being famed for their character and the extraordinary companionship, which they provided in peace and war.

The activities that occupied warriors concerned the support and defense of the people—both very serious responsibilities. They were also encouraged to hone their skills in sports and gaming and did so with relish, but the reality of their role was never far from their minds. Even though the level of aggression was magnified greatly by the dislocations and impact of colonization, raiding had a large part in life on the Plains and the severely impacted Northeast. One example shows what was really at stake in such skirmishes. Many peoples vied for honor by successfully getting away with horses or other goods by skillful stealth. The highest honor in fact was credited to the person who had the bravery to get close enough to a living enemy to touch him or her and escape with his or her own life intact.

More seriously, in the epic years of the final battles for freedom of the northern Plains Indians, the Lakota and Cheyenne each had a band of volunteers who joined sacred societies such as the Kit Fox Society or the Dog Soldiers. Each man had vowed to defend his people to the point of death. The Dog Soldiers wore a sash that, dismounting, they tied to the ground in the forefront of the battle. They understood the price and were willing to pay it. The descendants of the warrior societies of North American Indians have volunteered to fight in the major battles of the twentieth and twenty-first centuries. They have continued to distinguish the vital heritage from which they come.

Gender Recognition. Because sacred power is inextricably related to gendered living, it is not surprising that the freedom and creativity of that sacred power is ultimately the key to gender in Native America. Although the roles of women and men are clearly defined, they also are not strictly limited to sexual identity. It is not uncommon to find men, as among the Hopi, who do the weaving or to find women who are capable of excelling in manly arts. Apparently it is hard to limit the creative power of the sacred. Thus no one was surprised when a sister of a Cheyenne warrior, seeing him struck from his horse in battle, raced to take his place. Though Buffalo Calf Road Woman is vividly remembered, it was viewed as natural for her to assume that role.

More tellingly the recognition of other genders can be traced to a similar foundation. This aspect of gender has been captured in some early accounts, mostly in an objective way. Women such as Ruth Benedict (1887–1948), Alice Kehoe, Ruth Landes (1908–1991), Margaret Mead (1901–1978), and Ruth Underhill (1883–1994) actually strove to present sensitive descriptions based on intensive conversations in the field. But the real breakthrough occurred only in the last quarter of the twentieth century with the work of Walter Williams, Sabine Lang, and Paula Gunn Allen among others. What their contributions reveal is that a large range of gender issues have escaped the net of scholarship. The reasons are understandably many. So much of native culture has been interpreted by outsiders looking in that the deepest parts of sacred traditions have been carefully guarded. Part of that reality is the long-standing recognition of the existence of more than two genders, framed by the steady opposition of Christian Euro-Americans. Sadly some of these prejudices have crossed over during the difficult period of forced education that had assimilation as its goal. Traditional language, customs, and values were targeted for extinction. An inevitable part of this was the imposition of mores that are culturally alien to the native peoples. Thus the subject of diverse models of gender is often met with embarrassment, and some persons whose identity is neither male nor female have met with intolerance on their own reservations.

There is, however, a powerful lesson to learn from the traditional understanding (admittedly complex) of gender diversity. The kinship circle, which embraces all of life for a native person, includes a variety of gendered persons whose place in the community is determined by careful identification of recognized gender characteristics. Thus the designation of someone as a *winkte* among the Lakota or as a *nádleeh* among the Navajo rests on qualities that indicate a person's role in society rather than sexual identity. Growing contemporary research reveals a traditional past in which wide gender variety was regarded as part of the natural order. In some societies such persons were believed to possess special powers that could help the community flourish. The term *two-spirit,* in favor at the beginning of the twenty-first century, has been chosen to indicate the connection of such persons to the spiritual world, in particular their special place in ritual.

Early anthropological research brought the biases and categories of the Western worldview to the study of gender variances. Faced with a complex image of wide diversity in this area, the reports of these scholars could neither embrace nor appreciate the rich universe of meaning they had encountered. One example is the common use of the French term *berdache*, which is not only taken from a foreign context but is also burdened with a specific meaning (e.g., homosexuality, transvestism, hermaphrodism) unsuited to the broader universe that emerged at early encounters. Although this term was intended as a positive description of North American Indian customs, it could not begin to translate the rich diversity in balance with a view that all things are in dynamic process toward the cosmic purpose of everything that exists—*hozho*. The rich diversity in gender is not exceptional but rather a vital dimension of a multifaceted reality. The classification given by Wesley Thomas at the 1993 Wenner-Gren Conference in Washington, D.C., offered four main classifications known by the Navajo: feminine female, masculine male, masculine female (*nádleehí*), and feminine male (*nadleehí*). He notes that a crucial difference separates Western and traditional Navajo concepts relating to gender, sexuality, and sexual relationships. Thus a relationship between a female-bodied *nádleeh* (masculine female) and a woman or one between a male-bodied *nadleeh* (feminine male) and a man are not seen as homosexual in traditional Navajo culture.

That gender was distinguished from sex is clarified in a seminal paper (never published but widely circulated) by the highly regarded Lakota anthropologist Beatrice Medicine in 1979, revised as part of Patricia Alber and Beatrice Medicine's, *The Hidden Half: Studies of Plains Indian Women* (1983). Beatrice Medicine notes that the traditional vocation of the *winkte* included roles as ritualist, artist, specialist in production of women's crafts, herbalist, seer, namer of children, and (perhaps most interesting) rejection of the warrior's role. Among the highly disciplined Plains Indians, the warrior's place was greatly esteemed. To reject it required conviction and courage. Thus the *winkte* occupied a unique place in traditional Lakota society, as did the equivalent in many other cultures. It was Beatrice Medicine's intent to examine the changes wrought by urbanization imposed by the Bureau of Indian Affairs. For the young men and women transplanted to urban and intertribal settings, adaptation was a difficult process. One of the dimensions of native life that did not transfer well was the area of gender diversity. In a larger society unable to deal with ambiguities, labels were hastily applied. The distinction between gender and sex is perhaps too foreign for general acceptance, and certainly the circumstances of invasive cultural drifts onto the reservations complicated this area of culture. Thus the traditional context has been harder to retain, both on and off traditional lands. Medicine sadly notes that native *winkte* have experienced discrimination not only in the mainstream society but also at home. Thus a dimension of native spiritual understanding that has so much to offer the Western world has suffered a unique form of repression. The emerging voices and research in the twenty-first century of mainstream gay activists and their eagerness to lift from oppression victimized others holds a promise of a battle that could result in a better resolution.

Clearly, there is an innate link between gender and North American Indian religious traditions. Due to its limited scope, it can only be a summary of an exceedingly rich field. Through the early efforts of anthropologists and ethnologists to describe and understand them, through the great generosity of the people who were convinced of the need to speak, and now through the growing numbers of Native Americans who are speakers for themselves, a rich tapestry of variegated beauty is emerging. Their world is so much older than that of Euro-Americans, and their insights into the nature of reality enrich the story of the world's religions. They speak of wholeness, of complementarity, mutuality, and of harmony. Their image of difference is one that strives for unity yet preserves distinctness as the proper order of creation.

See Also Cosmology, overview article; Gender Roles; Gynocentrism; Lakota Religious Traditions; Mead, Margaret; Navajo Religious Traditions; North American Indian Religions, overview article; Shamanism, article on North American Shamanism.

Bibliography

Albers, Patricia, and Beatrice Medicine (Lakota). *The Hidden Half: Studies of Plains Indian Women.* Lanham, Md., 1983. An early sociological study of the life and culture of Native American women.

Allen, Paula Gunn. *The Sacred Hoop. Recovering the Feminine in Native American Traditions.* Boston, 1986. An engaging exposition of the depths of the feminine dimension in Native, American traditions, especially in the Southwest, by a Laguna Pueblo scholar.

Bataille, Gretchen M., and Kathleen Mullen Sands. *American Indian Women: Telling Their Lives.* Lincoln, Neb., 1984.

Beck, Peggy, and Anna Lee Walters. *The Sacred: Ways of Knowledge, Sources of Life.* Tsaile, Ariz., 1977.

Deloria, Vine, Jr. *God Is Red: A Native View of Religion.* New York, 1973. Revised edition, Golden, Colo., 2003.

DeMallie, Raymond, and Douglas Parks, eds. *Sioux Indian Religion: Tradition and Innovation.* Norman, Okla., 1987.

Irwin, Lee, ed. *To Hear the Eagles Cry: Contemporary Themes in Native American Spirituality. American Indian Quarterly* 20, nos. 3–4 (1996) and 21, no. 1 (1997).

Hall, Robert L. *An Archaeology of the Soul: North American Indian Belief and Ritual.* Urbana, Ill., 1997.

Hazen-Hammond, Susan. *Spider Woman's Web: Traditional Native American Tales about Women's Power.* New York, 1999.

Jacobs, Sue-Ellen, Wesley Thomas, and Sabine Lang. *Two-Spirit People: Native American Gender Identity, Sexuality, and Spirituality.* Urbana, Ill., 1997. An intriguing report of a conference designed to bring Native Americans into dialogue with scholars of the dominant society on gender issues in contemporary America.

Lang, Sabine. *Men as Women, Women as Men: Changing Gender in Native American Cultures.* Austin, Tex., 1998.

Powers, Marla N. *Oglala Women: Myth, Ritual, and Reality.* Chicago, 1986.

Schwarz, Maureen Trudelle. *Molded in the Image of Changing Woman: Navajo Views on the Human Body and Personhood.* Tucson, Ariz., 1997.

St. Pierre, Mark, and Tilda Long Soldier. *Walking in the Sacred Manner: Healers, Dreamers, and Pipe-Carriers—Medicine Women of the Plains Indians.* New York, 1995.

Vecsey, Christopher, ed. *Religion in Native North America.* Moscow, Idaho, 1990.

Wallace, Anthony F. C. *The Death and Rebirth of the Seneca.* New York, 1970.

Williams, Walter L. *The Spirit and the Flesh: Sexual Diversity in American Indian Culture.* Boston, 1986.

KATHLEEN DUGAN (2005)

GENDER AND RELIGION: GENDER AND MESOAMERICAN RELIGIONS

Religion forms an integral part of everyday life for indigenous peoples of Mesoamerica. Indeed, religious beliefs and practices cannot be separated from politics, healing, production, and other aspects of life. This article explores the relationship between religion and gender in Mesoamerica, or Middle America, a region extending from Central Mexico to Honduras. The area designates the territories where the ancient Aztec and Maya cultures flourished. Contemporary descendents of these cultures have retained core elements of the Mesoamerican cultural tradition despite a legacy of imperialist invasions. The sections below on the pre-Columbian and colonial periods focus on the Nahuatl-speaking ethnic groups of Central Mexico, including Mexicas, commonly referred to as Aztecs. The section on contemporary religions focuses on Mayas of Chiapas, Mexico.

RESEARCH ON GENDER IN MESOAMERICAN RELIGIONS. A gendered perspective on Mesoamerican religions began to emerge in the scholarly literature in the 1960s. Prior to this time scholars were mainly preoccupied with male forms of power in both the material and spiritual realms. The Spanish chroniclers who came to Mesomerica in the sixteenth century included Bernardino de Sahagún, Alonso de Zorita, Diego Durán, and Toribio Motolonía. They were influenced by Christian beliefs and practices and by their patriarchal ideology. Their writings give little attention to the important role women played in religion or in other aspects of life, although they do describe the gender dualities of Mesoamerican deities and the independence of women.

Ethnographers conducting research before the 1960s tended to generalize from data about men to communities at large, although they did note the gender specialization that characterized Mesoamerican life. They reported that involvement in religion was a daily aspect of life for women, complementing men's more formal roles in ritual events. Influenced by the women's movement in the 1970s, anthropologists, historians, and art historians brought a critique of Eurocentric assumptions about religion and gender to their research on Mesoamerican religions. Their studies indicate the significant economic, social, and spiritual roles women filled in Mesoamerica before and after the Spanish invasion. Subsequent scholarship has avoided sweeping generalizations by focusing on the local variations in gender arrangements and religious beliefs and practices across time and space. These studies have changed the way scholars view many traditional dichotomies, such as the domestic/public, sacred/secular, and natural/cultural spheres.

Feminist critiques of the marianismo/machismo dichotomy proposed by the political scientist Evelyn Stevens exemplify progress in refining understandings of gender in Mesoamerica. In a 1973 article, "Marianismo: The Other Face of Machismo," Stevens based marianismo on the Virgin Mary and defined it as "the cult of female spiritual superiority which teaches that women are semi-divine, morally superior to, and spiritually stronger than men" (Stevens, 1973, p. 91). Feminist scholars, such as Marysa Navarro, have criticized marianismo for labeling nonindigenous women throughout Latin America as passive, self-sacrificing, and dependent; for lack of grounding in any specific cultural, geographic, or historical context; and for ignoring the many ways that Latin American women have participated in political movements to challenge gender inequalities.

PRE-COLUMBIAN PERIOD. Gender roles are never static across time, geography, or social groups. Prior to the ascendancy of the Aztec state, gender roles in central Mexico had an egalitarian base, and gender was more fluid and negotiable than the first European chroniclers reported. In "Gendered Deities and the Survival of Culture," the anthropologist June Nash documents how changes in Aztec political structure transformed religious symbols and the position of women relative to that of men. Prior to the development of state-level societies, the core social unit in Mesoamerican societies was kinship-based, composed of clans. Later these clans became the basis for complex social stratification. During the formative period of what became the Aztec state (beginning around 800 CE), many deities were dual gender or androgynous figures. Coatlicue, Mother of the Gods, embodied opposites: life and death, night and day, light and dark, and male and female. But by the time of the reign of Itzacóatl (1429–1440), the Aztec empire was a military state with distinct class and gender stratification. During this period, Huitzilopochtli, the male sun god and war deity, replaced earlier androgynous deities.

Significant class distinctions within the Aztec state divided the nobles, who held political office and controlled the economic resources, from the *macehuales* (commoners) who paid rent and made up the majority of the population. Gender roles varied by class. The daughters of the nobles attended the *calmecac* (school for the elite) and could become priestesses. Commoners of both genders filled important ritual roles in their homes and fields.

Although the Aztec state denied women leadership roles, they had equal rights with men legally and economically. They were active producers, healers, and priestesses. A number of scholars describe gender parallelism among Aztec women, with males and females filling different but complementary roles. Most women's work was centered in the home and included weaving, spinning, sweeping, cooking, and caring for children. These tasks were highly valued and had a sacred significance; the home was a place of power. Aztecs compared women's work in childbirth to men's roles as warriors. While priests swept the temples, women swept their homes to defend them against danger and chaos. Wives of warriors swept not only at dawn but at noon and dusk, marking the sun god's path and assuring their husbands' success in battle. As further assurance, women placed their weaving shuttles, symbols of their husbands' weapons, on temple altars.

Colonial Period. The Spanish colonization of Mesoamerica in the sixteenth century led to dramatic changes in the social and spiritual lives of the locals. Millions of indigenous people were killed by disease, warfare, overwork, and murder. Whole villages were relocated and given new Christian names. By the early 1600s, Catholic churches had replaced Aztec ceremonial centers. Men and women were pressed into service and forced to pay tribute in the form of woven goods and agricultural products.

Spanish colonial priests and friars brought with them dualistic philosophical premises that profoundly contradicted those of the indigenous people. They emphasized free will, for example, while indigenous people tended to stress collective will, particularly at the household level, where marriages were tied to household production. In *Weaving the Past,* the ethnohistorian Susan Kellogg describes how the Spaniards focused on married couples rather than the extended family groupings that were so important in Mesoamerica. Friars exhorted young women to protect their virginity and to seek enclosure through acting modestly, covering their bodies fully, and staying home as much as possible. In some parts of Mesoamerica, priests constructed dwellings where young betrothed men and women came to stay until marriage. Yet priests gave no practical instructions to women and their daughters on how to sequester themselves when they were forced to work outside their home to provide tribute and to survive.

Physical intimidation of women became part of the fabric of life in colonial society. In indigenous communities, the tensions between native and colonial views of proper gender roles undoubtedly fueled the increasing violence toward native women. Men were forced into patriarchal roles in societies where gender equality and cooperation remained a strong principle, and in response to these stresses, many native men resorted to hitting their wives and sometimes to murder. Alcohol abuse was often a factor in the violence. The church encouraged native women to submit to their husbands' authority and to endure violent behavior, further undermining traditional complementary roles.

Native women were not passive in the face of these abuses. Kellogg explores the religious and spiritual roles women used to gain power and deal with the violence and stresses of colonial life. They served as midwives, *curanderas* (healers), sweepers of the church, and guardians of young women. As guardians, matrons escorted, advised, and protected young girls in schools run by the church. In both Nahua and Maya communities, women also became members of *cofradías,* religious cofraternities dedicated to the cult of a particular saint or aspect of the Christian deity. These offices allowed women some continuity in authority roles as priestesses and helped maintain a parallel gender structure in government.

During the sixteenth century, the Spanish attempted to enforce their belief system by linking the once-powerful female deities and women's roles as healers and midwives to evil and sorcery. In spite of these associations, some female-oriented beliefs, symbols, and practices persisted. Especially in central Mexico among the Nahuas, female deities were powerful symbols of fertility, sexuality, important foods, and other resources. Friars saw these deities as symbols of pagan beliefs that needed to be expunged. They were never entirely successful in eliminating them, however, due in part to their fear of entering native homes or places of worship, which they believed were tainted by the devil and would endanger their souls.

During the colonial era, the Virgin Mary was the only major sacred female figure Christianity had to offer to the indigenous people. Many women reported that they communicated with the Virgin as well as with Jesus, God, the saints, and demons. These women were viewed as mystics if they lived in convents, where they were tightly controlled. The Monastario of Corpus Cristi, the first convent for indigenous women, was established in Mexico City in 1724. Only the daughters of the indigenous nobles were accepted as novices in the convent. Most indigenous women did not live in convents, and they were often punished for their revelations. In or outside of convents, women's intimate communications with spiritual beings challenged the male church hierarchy's authority as the only legitimate mediators between human beings and spiritual beings.

Over the years native peoples infused the basic Catholic symbol of the Virgin Mary with new meanings. They found in her both an ally and a symbol of their empowerment and liberation. She is often associated with revitalization movements initiated by indigenous people during the colonial era. Several of these movements incorporated armed uprisings, which simultaneously resisted Spanish domination and reasserted indigenous beliefs and practices. A vision of the Virgin inspired the 1712 revolt in the Mayan community of Cancuc in Chiapas. A young woman named María de Candelaria reported that the Virgin Mary had appeared to her and asked that a chapel be built. When the local Spanish priests refused to recognize the visitation, thirty-two indigenous towns joined in a revolt against Spanish control. Their leaders claimed that Saint Peter, the Virgin Mary, and Jesus had called them to create an indigenous priesthood and to liberate themselves from Spanish power. Over a six-month period in 1712 and 1713, Spanish soldiers and their supporters suppressed the uprising. Subsequently, colonial officials instituted minor economic reforms to placate the indigenous population, however these reforms had little effect on reducing their impoverishment.

THE TWENTIETH CENTURY. Prior to the mid-twentieth century, most Mayan peoples of southern Mexico and Guatemala practiced a form of folk Catholicism commonly referred to as Traditionalism, which creatively combines beliefs about Mayan deities with local understandings of Catholicism. Central to Traditionalism are prayer, pilgrimages to places of sacred significance, and festivals carried out in honor of saints on important feast days. By the 1970s and 1980s thousands of indigenous peoples throughout Mesoamerica began to abandon Traditionalism in favor of Protestant churches and progressive Catholicism.

Traditionalism. In indigenous communities in Mexico and Guatemala, women play important roles that assure the physical as well as emotional, social, and spiritual well-being of both individuals and communities. For example, women take on important cargos, work on behalf of their communities, literally burdens or weights. Women's cargos include reciting prayers, preparing traditional foods, weaving ceremonial cloths and garments, and working alongside their husbands in a year-long series of obligations to a particular saint. Women often receive the call to serve a cargo from a saint in a dream or vision. After receiving the call, they request their husbands' assistance to fill the cargo. In many indigenous communities, cargo service underscores the complementarity and interdependence between males and females.

Women gain status and heat, a sign of spiritual strength, by working as midwives, healers, and cargo holders. Conceptions of human development among many Mesoamerican peoples see a person starting life in a cold state and then becoming hotter and hotter as he or she matures through serving his or her community. At death a person returns to a cold state. Women can acquire as much heat as men if they fulfill many duties for their communities. Women who communicate with powerful Christian and native deities on behalf of individuals and their communities are respected for their heat and knowledge. These women also enjoy significant independence, often traveling long distances in the night to visit people in need of their services.

Several key conceptions of deities from pre-Hispanic times survive in contemporary Mesoamerica. In highland Chiapas, earth, moon, caves, water, and the Virgin Mary are believed to embody powerful female spiritual forces. The sun is associated with a male god and Jesus Christ. A mother/father/ancestor/protector deity, called Totilme'il in Tzotzil-speaking towns and Me'tiktatik in Tzeltal-speaking towns, is important in daily life. Androgynous conceptions of deities exist as well. In San Pedro Chenalhó, Holy Cross, one of the three patron deities, is said to be androgynous and capable of both benevolent and malevolent acts. Dual and androgynous deities in contemporary Mesoamerican communities suggest that fluid and complementary symbols of gender exist alongside patriarchal ones.

Catholicism. Beginning in the 1960s, the Latin America Catholic Church underwent dramatic changes. The historic meetings of the Second Vatican Council between 1962 and 1965 and the Latin American bishops meeting in Medellín, Colombia, in 1968 emphasized the structural roots of poverty and called on the church to take concrete actions to end injustice. A progressive Catholicism began to spread in regions of Mexico, Guatemala, El Salvador, Honduras, and Nicaragua. It followed the "preferential option of the poor," placing marginalized peoples at the center of the church's work. Although class rather than gender was the primary concern, the Catholic Church attempted to involve women more fully in its work by training them as workshop leaders and catechists.

Since the 1970s in Mesoamerica, women have been particularly active in Christian base communities, small groups of men and women who meet to discuss their faith and interpret the conditions of their lives through the lens of Catholic doctrine. Through participation in base communities and in other lay roles, women perform important social, religious, and political work in their communities. They also question traditional gender roles, like the division of domestic tasks. Many women began their work in social activism in the Catholic Church. For example, Rigoberta Menchú, an indigenous woman of Guatemala and Nobel Peace laureate, first became involved in social activism as a catechist. In her 1984 autobiography, Menchú recalls the powerful experience of reading biblical stories of men and women who struggled to lead their people from oppression.

In the 1970s in Mexico's southeastern state of Chiapas, women throughout the Catholic diocese of San Cristóbal de Las Casas began to participate in local groups in which they read the Bible and discussed their problems. The most significant problems women face are poverty, racism, alcohol, and domestic violence. In 1992 these grassroots groups became formally linked through the Diocesan Coordination of Women (CODIMUJ). In hundreds of local groups throughout the diocese, the women of CODIMUJ meet to critique unequal gender relations and also to challenge structural forms of oppression, such as racism, political repression, and destructive economic policies.

Protestantism. Many indigenous people in southern Mexico and Guatemala began to convert to Protestantism beginning in the 1970s, with the Pentecostal and Presbyterian churches attracting the largest numbers of converts. (Studies estimate that 20 to 30 percent of the residents of

Guatemala and Chiapas are Protestant.) Through affiliation with Protestant churches, poor women find support in surviving dramatic social and economic changes and in some cases for challenging gender subordination.

The anthropologist Linda Green notes that evangelical churches in Guatemala provide a safe space where Mayan widows of the civil war create new forms of community and share emotional, psychological, and material support. Protestant congregations allow native people to reestablish a lost sense of community by creating fictive kin ties, calling one another *hermano* (brother) and *hermana* (sister). As people reconstruct their lives in times of social upheaval, they draw on past and present events, creatively blending indigenous worldviews with Christian ones. For example, it is not uncommon for Protestant converts to seek the assistance of traditional healers to treat grave illnesses. Through participation in new Christian churches, men and women redefine gender roles, relations, and ideologies by challenging social problems, such as alcoholism, domestic violence, and spousal abandonment. Women often initiate conversion within households, realizing the specific benefits they gain from ideologies that encourage men to stop drinking. Women's acts of conversion and activities in all-women's groups are part of a broader autonomy movement that sends a powerful message to outsiders that indigenous peoples can control their own affairs. Men have responded to women's new roles in a variety of ways, sometimes converting to new religions after their kinswomen convert, other times punishing their kinswomen for making major changes in their households.

RELIGION IN SECULAR MOVEMENTS. Religion is important even in secular movements in Mesoamerica. In contemporary Chiapas, the uprising of the Zapatista Army of National Liberation (EZLN) in 1994 was one aspect of a broad revitalization movement that began to build in the 1970s as a response by indigenous people to their waning control over their lives. Women have played a prominent role in the EZLN uprising, both as military insurgents and as members of civilian support bases who provide material aid to Zapatistas and implement Zapatista programs. The EZLN is a secular movement but includes people from a range of religious affiliations, including Catholics, Presbyterians, Pentecostals, Seventh-day Adventists, and Traditionalists among others. It differs from previous revolutionary models in respecting the religious choice of each member. Members of Zapatista base communities commonly pray before meetings, read the Bible together, and attend religious celebrations.

Women play central roles in base communities by reevaluating their ancestral traditions and bolstering those that serve their own and their households' well-being. The traditions women say they want to preserve are those that do not require centralized or hierarchically organized leadership and in which women have considerable authority. These include preparing altars to welcome back the souls of deceased loved ones on the Day of the Dead; preparing traditional foods daily and for special ceremonies; healing through herbs, prayer, and dream analysis; using a falsetto voice to show respect for elders who have held community cargos; contributing to pilgrimages three times a year to water holes and other sacred places; and weaving and wearing traditional clothing brocaded with ancestral cosmological motifs.

SEE ALSO Christianity, article on Christianity in Latin America; Gender Roles; Liberation Theology; Mesoamerican Religions, article on Contemporary Cultures.

BIBLIOGRAPHY

Burkhardt, Louise. "Mexica Women on the Home Front: Housework and Religion in Aztec Mexico." In *Indian Women in Early Mexico,* edited by Susan Schroeder, Stephanie Wood, and Robert Haskett. Norman, Okla., 1997. See pages 25–54. Burkhardt explores the religious significance of domestic occupations viewed as women's work among Mexicas.

Carrasco, Davíd. *Religions of Mesoamerica: Cosmovision and Ceremonial Centers.* San Francisco, 1990. Overview of Aztec and Mayan religions from the pre-Hispanic period through the colonial era.

Clendinnen, Inga. *Aztecs: An Interpretation.* New York, 1991. A study of Tenochtitlan on the eve of the Spanish Conquest; includes chapters on male and female roles.

Eber, Christine. *Women and Drinking in a Highland Maya Town: Water of Hope, Water of Sorrow.* Austin, Tex., 2000. Ethnographic study of alcohol use and abuse and religious change in San Pedro Chenalhó, Chiapas, Mexico, from indigenous women's viewpoints.

Eber, Christine, and Christine Kovic, eds. *Women of Chiapas: Making History in Times of Struggle and Hope.* New York, 2003. A compendium of ethnographic and humanistic works exploring issues that define women's modern struggles in Chiapas: structural violence and armed conflict, religion and empowerment, and women's organizing.

Gallagher, Ann Miriam. "The Indian Nuns of Mexico City's *Monasterio* of Corpus Christi, 1724–1821." In *Latin America Women: Historical Perspectives,* edited by Asunción Lavrin. Westport, Conn., 1978. See pages 150–172.

Green, Linda. *Fear as a Way of Life: Mayan Widows in Rural Guatemala.* New York, 1999. An ethnography describing the ways widows have been affected by and resisted structural and political violence; includes discussion of women's modern affiliation with Protestantism.

Joyce, Rosemary A. *Gender and Power in Pre-Hispanic Mesoamerica.* Austin, Tex., 2000. Comprehensive exploration of Mesoamerican gender and power relations from Olmec culture through the sixteenth century, applying Judith Butler's performance theory to suggest how Mesoamericans constructed more fluid and variable gender systems than previously assumed.

Kellogg, Susan. "From Parallel to Equivalent to Separate but Unequal: Tenochca Mexica Women, 1500–1700." In *Indian Women in Early Mexico,* edited by Susan Schroeder, Stephanie Wood, and Robert Haskett. Norman, Okla., 1997. See pages 123-143. An overview of the changing legal and social status of Mexica women from the late pre-Hispanic era to the early eighteenth century.

Lavrin, Asunción. "In Search of the Colonial Woman in Mexico: The Seventeenth and Eighteenth Centuries." In *Latin Ameri-*

can Women: Historical Perspectives, edited by Asunción Lavrin. Westport, Conn., 1978. See pages 23–59. An exploration of women's roles in colonial Mexican society. The study focuses on white urban women but also discusses other social and ethnic groups.

Lavrin, Asunción, ed. *Sexuality and Marriage in Colonial Latin America.* Lincoln, Neb., 1989. An edited book examining religion, sexuality, marriage, and divorce in Latin America from a historical perspective.

Menchú, Rigoberta. *I, Rigoberta Menchú: An Indian Woman in Guatemala.* Edited by Elizabeth Burgos-Debray. London, 1984. The life story of an indigenous woman of Guatemala. Includes discussion of the role of Catholicism in Guatemala and Menchú's work as a catechist in her efforts to combat social injustices.

Nash, June. *In the Eyes of the Ancestors: Belief and Behavior in a Mayan Community.* Prospect Heights, Ill., 1970. Ethnography of the relation between beliefs and behavior in the Tzeltal-speaking Maya township of Amatenango del Valle, highland Chiapas, Mexico. Provides detailed descriptions of the gendering of roles and social spaces and local adaptations to economic and political changes.

Nash, June. "Gendered Deities and the Survival of Culture." *History of Religions* 36 (1997): 333–356. A gendered historical analysis of the transformation in conceptions of female and male Mesoamerican deities from pre-Aztec to contemporary times.

Navarro, Marysa. "Against Marianismo." In *Gender's Place: Feminist Anthropologies of Latin America,* edited by Rosario Montoya, Lessie Jo Frazier, and Janise Hurtig. New York, 2002. See pages 257–272. Critique of marianismo, a term coined in 1973 by Evelyn P. Stevens to describe women's status in Latin America. Navarro argues that marianismo is an ahistorical and essentialist fabrication.

Rosenbaum, Brenda. *With Our Heads Bowed: The Dynamics of Gender in a Maya Community.* Albany, N.Y., 1993. Ethnography exploring gender ideologies, roles, and relations in San Juan Chamula, a highland Maya township of Chiapas, Mexico.

Rosenbaum, Brenda. "Women and Gender in Mesoamerica." In *Legacy of Mesoamerica: History and Culture of a Native American Civilization,* edited by Robert M. Carmack, Janine Gasco, and Gary H. Gossen. Englewood Cliffs, N.J., 1996. See pages 321–352. Survey of Mesoamerican gender roles, relationships, and ideologies from pre-Columbian to present times and an overview of current issues in the study of women and gender in Mesoamerica.

Sahagún, Fray Bernardino de. *Florentine Codex: General History of the Things of New Spain.* Translated by Arthur J. O. Anderson and Charles E. Dibble. 13 vols. Santa Fe, N. Mex., 1952–1983. A sixteenth-century treatise on Aztec culture with a detailed account of gender roles from the colonial period.

Schroeder, Susan, Stephanie Wood, and Robert Haskett, eds. *Indian Women in Early Mexico.* Norman, Okla., 1997. Edited volume of essays by ethnohistorians describing the lives of women in pre-Columbian and colonial Mexico.

Stephen, Lynn. *Women and Social Movements in Latin America: Power from Below.* Austin, Tex., 1997. Focuses on grassroots women's movements in Mexico, El Salvador, Brazil, and Chile.

Stevens, Evelyn. "Marianismo: The Other Face of Machismo." *Female and Male in Latin America: Essays,* edited by Ann Pescatello. Pittsburgh, Pa., 1973. See pages 89-101. Describes the concept of marianismo, or the cult of female superiority, which Stevens applies to mestizas throughout Latin America.

Tuñón Pablos, Julia. *Women in Mexico: A Past Unveiled.* Translated by Alan Hynds. Austin, Tex., 1998. An overview of Mexican women's lives from pre-Hispanic times through the 1980s. Explores the relationship between myths about women and the historical realities of their lives.

CHRISTINE EBER (2005)
CHRISTINE KOVIC (2005)

GENDER AND RELIGION: GENDER AND SOUTH AMERICAN RELIGIONS

Religion is central to South American society. Daily life and major events are marked, celebrated, and aided by the performance of religious rituals derived from a range of traditions, including Andean, Inca, shamanism, Catholicism, and Protestantism. In agricultural areas planting and harvesting are imbued with religious meaning. Marriage, healing, and even travel require celebration of religious rituals. Religion in South America also reflects and reproduces gender norms in the society. Forms of veneration, rituals of healing, rites of reconciliation, and specific religious cults follow gender lines.

RESEARCH ON GENDER AND RELIGION IN SOUTH AMERICA. The gender specificity of religious belief, practices, and rituals in pre-Colombian South America defied the logic of the Spanish who invaded the region in the sixteenth century. The principle characteristics of Andean and Inca religion are gender parallelism and complementarity, which reflect and reinforce social organization. By contrast, Spanish Mediterranean monotheistic religion in which a supreme male deity dominated supported a patriarchal model of the society in which men presided over the family and society. Spanish chroniclers misunderstood Andean and Inca religion and condemned religious practices that defied the patriarchal model by suggesting they were the work of the devil. Inca worship of a masculine Sun as the principle deity and of the feminine Moon as its counterpart seemed to the Spanish a result of diabolical intervention. Although they did not understand them, Spanish chroniclers recorded their observation of gendered practices of worship and of male and female deities. Their accounts provide researchers with insight into the gendered cosmology and practices of pre-Colombian South American society. Spanish clergy, including Pedro de Cieza de León, José de Acosta, Cristóbal Albornoz, Pablo José de Arriaga, Bernabé Cobo and Martin de Murua, whose goal was to eradicate local religion and establish Catholicism, also provide much of the available source material for understanding pre-Colombian South American religion. Andean and Inca manuscripts, including the Huarochirí Manuscript, and the accounts of Felipe Guaman Poma de Ayala and "El

Inca" Garcilaso de la Vega provide knowledge from an indigenous perspective. Researchers have examined these accounts using gendered categories of analysis to gain insight into the female, male, and androgynous components of Andean and Inca religion.

Archaeological evidence has also provided insight into the gender specificity of religion and ritual in South American society. Archaeological remains are subject to different interpretive challenges because analysis of them reflects contemporary assumptions about gender and worship. As a result, women's roles depicted in artifacts were sometimes ignored or misinterpreted. For example, in 1980 Anne-Marie Hocquenghem and Patricia J. Lyon identified a figure with long braids and feminine dress depicted in a Peruvian Moche "Sacrifice Scene" as a Moche priestess. Their interpretation was contested by researchers who identified this figure as male. Only in 1991 when the remains of a tomb where the ritual had been enacted in practice was found and the participant's bones were identified as female did researchers concur with Lyons and Hocquenghem that the image in the picture was that of a woman. Even with this recognition, the female figure was ascribed lower status than that of her male counterparts in the Sacrifice Scene. Two men depicted in the Sacrifice Scene often were identified as Moche warrior-priests and rulers, whereas the female figure was identified as a priestess rather than a ruler.

Irene Silverblatt's influential book, *Moon, Sun, and Witches* (1987), was among the first to provide a gendered analysis of Andean and Inca religion and the impact of Spanish Conquest. Using Spanish sources, Silverblatt concluded that gender parallelism and complementarity were core characteristics of Andean cosmology and of the organization of religious cults. She argued that the Incas used gender ideologies and religious practices to extend their control over Andean communities. Kathryn Burns's *Colonial Habits: Convents and the Spiritual Economy of Cuzco, Peru* (1999) carried a gendered analysis of religion into the colonial period. She demonstrated that the Spanish used religion and gender to assert control over the Incas and to establish a colonial order. Burns examines the Spanish foundation and development of two Catholic convents in the Inca capital of Cuzco. She argues that, by facilitating an inextricably linked exchange of prayer and material resources with the people of Cuzco, women religious played a central role in what she describes as the spiritual economy of colonial society. This research is complemented by ethnographic studies (e.g., Allen, 1988, Glass-Coffin, 1998) that illustrate the centrality of gendered practices of religion in contemporary Andean society, suggesting that elements of pre-Colombian religious ideals of Andean parallelism and complementarity survived Spanish conquest.

Andean Parallelism. Andean parallelism and complementarity are perhaps best illustrated by Pachamama and Pachatira. Pachamama, literally Mother Earth, is said to embody the generative forces of the earth and to sustain society by providing nourishment. She cannot, however, realize her procreative powers without a male celestial counterpart and is often paired with Illapa (or Rayo), the god of thunder and lightning, who dominates the heavens and provides the rain necessary for crop production. Pachamama is also inextricably linked with Pachatira, a temporal and material dimension of the earth associated with masculinity. Pachamama and Pachatira appear to represent different aspects of the pacha's nature as both a nurturing figure, yet also a potentially angry force that may punish people and requires their worship and sacrifice in exchange for sustaining them. Pachamama/Tirakuna may appear as distinct manifestations of Mother Earth with Tirakuna seen as sacred places identified as "Fathers" and Pachamama as the earth as a whole. Thus, rather than being completely separate, Pachamama/Tirakuna are distinct manifestations of a gendered Mother Earth.

Pierre Duviols observed that gender parallelism transcended life so that when elite Andean people died, they were transformed into two entities: a *mallqui*, the mummy of the live person and the feminine half that represented the seed of future generations, and the *huaca*, the masculine half, a phallic rock that represented the inseminating force. Thus like the Pachamama/Tirakuna the individual reflected a unified whole that was nonetheless gender distinct. Similarly Andean couples are known as the single composite word, *warmi-qhari* (woman-man), suggesting that couples represent a unified whole. This assumption is reflected in the mandate that only couples may perform religious cargos—elective offices held for a one-year term by male community members charged with responsibility for overseeing civil and religious activities crucial to indigenous communities' survival—like that of fiesta sponsors.

Religion, Gender, and State Expansion: Incas to Spanish. From 1200 to 1400 CE the Incas embarked on a program of expansion and conquest over surrounding Andean communities, which would lead them to control an area that spanned a third of the South American continent. Irene Silverblatt argues that the Incas, recognizing Andean religious practices and beliefs, used gender ideologies to mask their control. They sought to graft Inca divinities onto local Andean religious structures, thereby using them to establish legitimacy and authority. Central to this assertion was the Incas' establishment of a masculine Sun as the principal deity from whom all Inca men descended and who presided over the Inca kingdom, and a feminine Moon from whom all Inca queens descended and who presided over the earth and the sea. Thus the Inca kings were said to be sons of the Sun, and the Inca queens were the daughters of the complementary feminine Moon. The Incas made Mamacocha (Mother Sea) a descendant of the Moon and proclaimed her mother of all waters: streams, rivers, and mounting springs. Andean cosmology asserted that Pachamama's daughters embodied highland products and provided Andean people with knowledge of them and methods of cultivation. Saramama was associated with maize; Axomama, with potatoes; Cocamama, with coca; Coyamama with metals; and Sañumama, with clay. The Incas used this ideology by claiming that an Inca queen, Mama Huaco, had introduced the sowing of corn in the Andes, thus attributing to her the base for the survival of Andean communities and the Inca kingdom. The Incas thus used Andean cosmology to expand their empire.

The Incas also used gender and women to extend their control over communities through a system of female cults, marriage, and sacrifice. Chaste girls, *acllas,* were selected from Andean communities and they became virginal wives of the Sun. They were separated from their communities and sent to *acllawasis* (*aclla* houses) located in each province's state-run capital. After they were selected these virginal girls might become permanent servants to Inca divinities, or they might marry Incas or other men chosen by Incas. Those girls who served the deities were taught "women's tasks" including spinning, weaving, and the preparation of *chicha* and special foods that they provided for the service to the Inca king and gods. Although some Andean girls were selected as *acllas,* others were chosen for sacrifice. The number of human sacrifices appears to have increased during the Inca Empire and new ideals about human offerings developed. The Inca directed and controlled human sacrifice and used a variety of methods, including strangulation, burial, cremation, removal of heart and offering blood and heart while burning the body, and throat cutting in which the victims blood was offered. The Inca also buried victims alive or left them to die of exposure on mountains after they had been made insensible by drink or blows to the head.

These sacrifices were gender and age specific. Male sacrifices often involved bloodletting, whereas female sacrifices consisted of death by a nonblood-releasing means and burial. Most sacrifices were of prepubescent children who were selected by their communities for their beauty and brought to the Inca capital, Cuzco, where they were presented in a public ceremony. After the ceremony the children of the *capa cocha* ritual were returned to their communities where they were buried alive and then established as a local cult often overseen by their own family members. These sacrifices enhanced the community's privilege within the Inca kingdom and that of the girls' fathers and family members within their own communities. It provided a means of expanding Inca control.

The Spanish sought to establish patriarchal Catholicism in the Andes, and they introduced a distinct conception of sin. Although they did not understand Andean gender parallelism or complementarity, the Spanish nonetheless used gender to assert their authority and to expand their control. Because the Spanish did not share the same culture with the Andean and Inca people they sought to conquer, they relied on force and violence. Burns observes that during a brief respite in the violent conflict that threatened to destroy the nascent colonial society in Peru, the conquistadores established Santa Clara Catholic Convent in the Inca capital of Cuzco. Half a century later a second convent would be built in Cuzco atop the ruins of *acllawasi.* Santa Clara's purpose was to transform the daughters of Inca queens and Spanish conquistadores into culturally Spanish women who might either become nuns to serve God or marry Spanish men. Among the first entrants to the convent was the last Inca ruler's six-year-old daughter. These girls were wrested violently from their Inca mothers so they might be transformed. Although the purpose of Santa Clara convent was to create culturally Spanish girls of the mestiza women, the conquistadores' efforts were thwarted by the Spanish Abbess Francisca de Jesús and the small minority of Spanish nuns who distinguished themselves from their mestiza counterparts by donning a black veil. The black veils established the Spanish nuns as culturally superior to the mestiza nuns who were forced to wear white veils. Spanish nuns thereby reproduced the racial distinction the Spanish conquistadores sought to eradicate through religious training of mestiza girls. Both the Inca and the Spanish requisitioned daughters of the defeated to serve as participants in religious cults and as their spouses. Gender-specific religious imposition was central to the expansion of the Inca and Spanish states.

Whereas mestiza girls entered Santa Clara convent, Andean girls could enter *beatas* founded in Cuzco at the end of the seventeenth century, the Spanish golden age in the region. In contrast to Santa Clara convent where mestiza girls were subject to the authority of Spanish nuns and distinguished from them by a white veil marking their inferiority, Andean girls in *beatas* were autonomous. They redefined themselves and established themselves as honorable women by virtue of their religious faith, practice, and knowledge. Indigenous women became abbesses of the *beatas* and even defended themselves and their community against Spanish officials. They thus enjoyed greater autonomy than both their mestiza counterparts and Andean and mestizo men who were barred from becoming clergy or directing their own seminaries. Andean women who did not enjoy the formal protection of the church were subject to abuse, including rape, by Spanish clergy.

Rituals of Health and Healing. Gender parallelism and complementarity remain central to contemporary South American religion and are evident in rituals of marriage, health, and healing. The interdependence of men and women is considered a natural state of things and is reflected in the term *warmi-qhari* (woman-man) to refer to a couple. Formal marriage with a Catholic religious ceremony usually occurs many years after a couple has been established and has had children and often occurs in the context of a larger religious fiesta. Single adults are considered unnatural and cannot fulfill specific religious or civic cargoes in the community. Marriage also continues to serve as a means of allying distinct social groups with girls from less powerful families, who are considered "more Indian," marrying boys from more powerful families.

Religious fiestas, which mark specific points in the harvest and celebrate communities' founding saints, require sponsorship by couples within each community. Some fiestas require two sponsors because together they form a *warmi-qhari.* The junior sponsor in a fiesta is said to act like a woman, suggesting the fluidity of gender and its relation to specific roles. During fiestas, although men and women share the same physical space, they are separated within it to conform with the Andean ideals of a masculine and feminine.

Rituals of health and healing conform with the ideal of a gender division of labor and are infused with religious belief and practice. Joseph W. Bastien found, for example, that in Bolivia misfortune rituals designed to eliminate misfortune are usually carried out by a *warmi yachaj* (female diviner), whereas a *qari yachaj* (male diviner) performs good-fortune rituals to set in motion favorable events. The symbolic system of the Bolivian Aymara people avers to men stability and mountains and contrasts them with women associated with rivers and a natural cycle of dissolution and renewal. Women are seen to be especially appropriate for performing misfortune rites because their menstrual cycle enables them to experience a flow like that of rivers. The flow of blood cleanses them just as one needs to be cleansed of misfortune by returning it to a river so it can follow the natural cycle of dissolution and renewal. Male diviners, by contrast, help to fix good fortune by offering symbols of llama fat and fetus to the earth shrines of the region.

Men become shamans by encountering and surviving the masculine Illapa (Rayo), or lightning. The highest shamans survive this encounter three times. By contrast, women become midwives by recognizing their calling in dreams or giving birth to children seen as special or unusual. The dreams of midwives often include images of the Virgin Mary or Catholic saints who may appear among herbs in a garden, which become central to the women's curative role. There is a confluence of Andean and Catholic imagery in the calling of the midwife suggesting that conversion to Protestantism may be incompatible with the traditional practice of midwifery.

In Northern Peru men and women work as *curanderos,* participating in the same tradition of curing through a *mesa* and the ingestion of the San Pedro cactus. Men are, however, more openly associated with this tradition of healing, whereas women are often identified as *brujas,* sorceresses who transform themselves into black cats, ducks, pigs, and goats, engage in reunions with the devil, and cast spells. Bonnie Glass-Coffin attributes this distinction to a fiction created by Spanish clergy who identified female *curanderas* as witches—a perception that became popularized. One result of this perception is that it is more difficult to find female *curanderas* because they hide their practices.

Among the Warao in Venezuela, couples serve together as shamans. The wife of a male light shaman comes to be known as *shinakarani* (Mother of Seizure) because of her ability to save her husband from seizures resulting from ritualized nicotine consumption. The *shinakarani*'s role is modeled after that of the experience of the first light shaman, who suffers a nicotine seizure when he enters the celestial House of Tobacco Smoke and is saved by his wife who transforms into a frigate bird and covers the light shaman with her body and wings to save him from the seizure.

CATHOLICISM AND PROTESTANTISM. Until the 1960s most men and women in South America identified themselves as Catholic, although their practices might have included distinctly indigenous elements. In the 1950s and 1960s a new form of Catholicism strongly influenced by the Second Vatican Council and the rise of liberation theology was established in many South American countries. This Catholicism, which emphasized the transformative potential of this life rather than focusing on salvation in the next life, had an especially strong impact among women. In rural communities, indigenous women came to serve as Catholic catechists whose role was to discuss church doctrine and the bible with their communities. In urban communities, especially those composed of recent migrants from rural areas, Catholic women formed associations for prayer and community service. *Comedores populares* (community kitchens) were established by women with the assistance of lay and religious Catholic leaders. Through these associations women began to redefine their place in society and their relations with men.

During the same period of the 1960s and 1970s, a number of Protestant denominations, as well as Jehovah's Witnesses, Church of Latter-day Saints, and other religious groups, began to attract converts in South America. Protestants have, so far, received the greatest attention from researchers. Those who have focused on women's conversion emphasize the opportunity that Protestantism offered women to escape the system of fiestas, which was associated with alcohol consumption and costly expenditures. Lesley Gill suggests that Protestantism offered women migrants in new urban communities a means of explaining and coping with suffering. She also argues that Protestantism allows women to exert indirect control over abusive or neglectful spouses. Finally, Gill emphasizes that many women identify simultaneously as Protestant and Catholic or may go through a series of conversions rather than retaining a fixed religious identity. By converting to a new faith, women and men change their religious beliefs and practices and gain a means of transforming gender norms and thus their relations with each other and with society. Indeed, because religion is central to South America, where it reflects and reproduces gender norms, it is also central to understanding changes in gender and society.

SEE ALSO Inca Religion; Liberation Theology; Shamanism, article on South American Shamanism.

BIBLIOGRAPHY

Primary Sources

Cobo, Bernabé. *History of the Inca Empire* (1653). Translated by John Howland Rowe. Austin, Tex., 1979. Bernabé Cobo, a seventeenth-century Spanish Jesuit missionary, provides an overview of Andean customs and a treatise on Inca legends, history, and social institutions which offers insight into gender and religion in pre-Colombian society.

de Acosta, José. *The Natural and Moral History of the Indies* (1604). Translated by Clements R. Markham. New York, n.d. José de Acosta, a Spanish Jesuit missionary who traveled throughout the New World and worked extensively in Southern Peru, the heart of the Inca Empire, offers insight into Andean and Inca religion and society with reference to gender.

de Arriaga, Father Pablo José. *The Extirpation of Idolatry in Peru* (1621). Translated by L. Clark Keating. Lexington, Ky., 1968. Father Pablo José de Arriaga was responsible for imposing Catholic orthodoxy by violently destroying the last vestiges of Inca and Andean religion in Peru's indigenous communities in the seventeenth century. The account details the religious practices de Arriaga found and his efforts to destroy them with incidental references to gender.

de Betanzos, Juan. *Narrative of the Incas*. Translated and edited by Roland Hamilton and Dana Buchanan. Austin, Tex., 1996. Juan de Betanzos, a Spanish official who married an Inca woman and learned Quechua, provides one of the earliest accounts of Inca and Andean religion.

de Molina, Cristóbal. *Relacion de las fabulas y ritos de los Incas* (1573). Lima, Peru, 1943. Instruction to Spanish clergy and officials for discovering Inca sites of worship provides insight into Inca religious practices.

de Murua, Martin. *Historia del origin y geneologia real de los Incas* (1590). Madrid, 1946. Sixteenth-century Spanish Chronicle of the Incas by Fray Martin de Murua.

Duviols, Pierre. *Cultura andina y repression: Procesos y visitas de idolatries y hechicerias. Cajatambo. Siglo XVII.* Cusco, Peru, 1986. Compilation of documents from the extirpation of idolatries in seventeenth-century Peru.

Felipe Guaman Poma de Ayala, El Primero nueva cronica y buen gobierno (1631?). Edited by John Victor Murra and Rolena Adorno, Mexico City, 1980. Felipe Guaman Poma de Ayala, a native Quechua speaker from Peru, provides a unique account of Inca religion and society and prescriptions for creating a just society combining Spanish and Andean norms. The text combines a written history of the region with nearly four hundred drawn images depicting daily life under the Incas, the Spanish Conquest, and colonial society.

Garcilaso de la Vega, El Inca. *Royal Commentaries of the Incas and General History of Peru* (1609, 1616). Translated by H. V. Livermore. Austin, Tex., 1966. El Inca Garcilaso de la Vega was the son of an Inca princess and a Spanish conquistador who wrote his account of Inca society and history from Spain. Provides insight into the Inca elite family structure as well as into specific practices of worship.

The Huarochirí Manuscript. Translated by Frank Salomon and George L. Urioste with annotations and introductory essay by Frank Salomon. Austin, Tex., 1991. Seventeenth-century account written in Quechua of mythology and rituals of Andean people in the region of Huarochirí which provides insight into gender and has been used to suggest the centrality of an androgynous ideal in Andean gender relations.

Secondary Sources

Allen, Catherine J. *The Hold Life Has: Coca and Cultural Identity in an Andean Community.* Washington, D.C., 1988. Anthropological account of contemporary community life in the Southern Andes provides core insight into religion and gender by focusing on religious rituals and the structure of family and community.

Bastien, Joseph W. *Healers of the Andes: Kallawaya Herbalists and Their Medicinal Plants.* Salt Lake City, 1987. Anthropological account of healers, their methods, rituals, and medicines in the Andes of Bolivia with some specific insight into gendered practices of healing.

Bruhns, Karen Olsen, and Karen E. Stothert. *Women in Ancient America.* Norman, Okla., 1999. Broad overview of secondary literature in anthropology, archaeology, history, and art history which provides insight into women in ancient America with their role in religion providing one component of the overview.

Burns, Kathryn. *Colonial Habits: Convents and the Spiritual Economy of Cuzco, Peru.* Durham, N.C., 1999. Historical account of the establishment of two Catholic convents in the Inca capital of Cuzco during the Spanish colonial period and the role of women in the emerging colonial society. The author emphasizes the centrality of religion in transforming mestiza girls into culturally Spanish women who would worship the Spanish God, become conquistadores' wives, and participate in the spiritual economy of the society.

Burns, Kathryn. "Beatas, 'decencia' y poder: la formación de una elite indígena en el Cuzco colonial." In *Incas e indios cristianos. Elites indígenas e identidades cristianas en lso Andes colonials,* edited by Jean-Jacques Decoster. Lima, Peru, 2002. Brief article examining the foundation of Andean *beatas* as a counterpart to Spanish Catholic convents. Illustrates the role religion might play in granting Andean women a measure of autonomy.

Cadena, Marisol de la. "Matrimonio y etnicidad en comunidades andinas (Chitapampa, Cusco)." In *Más allá del Silencio: Las Fronteras de género en los Andes,* compiled by Denise J. Arnold. La Paz, Bolivia, 1997. Article uses an anthropological approach to examine the relationship between ethnicity and marriage strategies in contemporary southern Peru.

Castro Aguilar, Rosa. "Religion and Family: Catholic Experiences in Peru." In *Christianity and Social Change, and Globalization in the Americas,* edited by Anna L. Peterson, Manuel A. Vásquez, and Philip J. Williams. New Brunswick, N.J., 2001. Article examines the role that liberation theology and post–Vatican II Catholicism played among women in poor urban settlements in contemporary Peru.

Chávez Hualpa, Fabiola. "Mujeres que curan, mujeres que creen: un perfil de la medicina feminina." In "*Despierta, remedio, cuenta . . .*": *adivinos y medicos del Ande,* compiled by Mario Polia Meconi. Lima, Peru, 1996. Chapter focusing specifically on women as part of a larger compilation of work on traditional practices of health and healing in the Andean region.

Gill, Lesley. "Religious Mobility and the Many Words of God in La Paz, Bolivia." In *Rethinking Protestantism in Latin America,* edited by Virginia Garrard-Burnett and David Stoll. Philadelphia, 1993. Article examines the role that contemporary Protestantism plays in offering women a means of transforming gender relations and gaining a measure of autonomy in contemporary Andean society.

Glass-Coffin, Bonnie. *The Gift of Life: Female Spirituality and Healing in Northern Peru.* Albuquerque, 1998. Anthropological account focusing specifically on female *curanderas* in northern Peru, while also providing insight into the experience of a woman researcher who sought to become a *curandera.*

Harris, Olivia. "Complementarity and Conflict: An Andean View of Women and Men." In *Sex and Age as Principles of Social Differentiation,* edited by J. S. La Fontaine. London, 1978. Article provides key insight into gender complementarity in contemporary Andean society.

Matteson Langdon, E. Jean, and Gerhard Baer, eds. *Portals of Power: Shamanism in South America.* Albuquerque, 1992. Overview of Shamanism in South America with some specific details about gender.

Murra, John V. *The Economic Organization of the Inca State.* Greenwich, Conn., 1980. Analysis of the organization of the Inca state using Spanish chronicles to reconstruct the physical, political, and economic structure of society.

Rostworowski de Diez Canseco, María. *Estructuras Andinas del poder: Ideología religiosa y política.* Lima, Peru, 1983. Among the first works to include an analysis of the role of gender in Andean power structures.

Sánchez, Ana. "Pecados secretos, públicas virtudes: El acoso sexual en el confesionario." *Revista Andina* 14 (1996): 121–148. Article focuses specifically on the Catholic rite of confession and its association with clerical abuse of Andean, Spanish, and mestiza women.

Sikkink, Lyn. "El poder mediador del cambio de agues: género y el cuerpo politico condeño." In *Más allá del Silencio: Las Fronteras de género en los Andes,* compiled by Denise J. Arnold. La Paz, Bolivia, 1997. Analysis of gender and social and political structure in contemporary Andean Bolivian community.

Silverblatt, Irene. *Moon, Sun, and Witches: Gender Ideologies and Class in Inca and Colonial Peru.* Princeton, N.J., 1987. Among the first works to examine gender and religion. Provides key insight into gender parallelism and complementarity and the Inca's use of gender to extend control over Andean people.

Wilbert, Johannes. *Tobacco and Shamanism in South America.* New Haven, Conn., 1987. Overview of secondary literature detailing the practices, rituals, and beliefs of tobacco shamans in South America with some reference to gender specificity of practices.

SUSAN FITZPATRICK BEHRENS (2005)

GENDER ROLES. Gender roles are the culturally defined behaviors deemed appropriate for a man or a woman. A role is essentially performative. One learns how to play a masculine or feminine role, what is acceptable and what is not, how one should behave, think, evaluate oneself and others in a gendered manner. While age, ethnicity, class, and many other factors also have culturally prescribed norms, gender is the most universal and salient social organizing principle.

SEX AND GENDER. Following Margaret Mead's influential work *Sex and Temperament in Three Primitive Societies* (1935), feminist studies made a distinction between sex, regarded as biological, and gender, which is culturally constructed. Thus with few exceptions, one is born male or female according to chromosomal makeup and secondary sexual characteristics. One is socialized into masculine or feminine roles through culture. The link between maleness and masculinity and femaleness and femininity is made to appear natural and therefore unchangeable, constructing power and dominance hierarchies that generally leave men in control of women and children. Gender hierarchies are legitimized by recourse to ideology, ritual, and mythology.

Gayle Rubin coined the term *sex/gender systems* to describe the way in which kinship systems define roles and statuses in a manner that often contradicts genetic relationships. An example of this is woman-woman marriage among the Nuer of the Sudan. Fatherhood is defined through the payment of cattle as bride-price. Where a woman owns cattle, she can acquire a wife and will be regarded as the social father or pater of children born to her wife, regardless of the identity of the biological father or *genitor.* Rubin pointed out that every individual and each new generation has to learn to enact their sexual destinies and their statuses within the system. Sex and gender are not biological facts that emerge of and by themselves but are historical creations of specific societies. Oppression is experienced not only as a woman but as a result of having to be a woman, that is, by taking on feminine roles. Phyllis Chesler argued that psychological differences between the sexes are also the result of sex-role conditioning and that expectations of feminine roles are dysfunctional. To successfully conform to the stereotype of femininity in Western society is a prescription for failure or madness.

In contemporary Euro-American societies there is a tendency to regard genetics (and therefore biological sex) as essential and deterministic, with a gene to explain every aspect of behavior. Among social scientists, however, there is a move toward seeing sexuality as part of gender relations, theoretically inseparable from them rather than possessing an essential prior ontology. Sexual violence against women and violence against gay men are the result of institutional structures, ideologies, and practices that assign greater value to masculinity and to heterosexuality than to femininity and homosexuality. Governments and religious organizations are among those institutions that seek to maintain and reproduce the gender roles that permit such violence.

A theoretical focus on the body has also undermined the distinction between sex and gender. Judith Butler, in her influential work *Gender Trouble* (1999), argues, following a Lacanian perspective, that the loss of the maternal body leads to a perpetual displacement of the object of desire and that gender identity is a refusal of that loss "encrypted" on the body. Gender, described by Butler as a "literalizing fantasy," then appears as "natural fact." "Becoming" a gender involves "a laborious process of becoming *naturalized,* which requires a differentiation of bodily pleasures and parts on the basis of gendered meanings" (Butler, 1999, p. 89). Cultural norms, referred to by Butler as "the law," that prescribe heterosexuality and gender roles and proscribe homosexuality and incest, give the appearance of being subsequent to sexuality. In reality they are the effects, temporally and ontologically, of culture; the product of culture rather than prior to or outside culture (Butler, 1999, p. 94).

THE "NATURALNESS" OF GENDER ROLES. In the seminal article "Is Female to Male as Nature Is to Culture?" (1974) Sherry Ortner argued that a defining characteristic of human societies is that they are engaged in a process of generating and sustaining systems of meaning that enable them to transcend the most basic, natural limits of existence. Rituals, for instance, are a way of manipulating and regulating the relationship between natural forces and human life. Culture is seen as something that works on and transforms nature and in that sense is superior to it. According to Ortner, women are seen as closer to nature than men because of their biology and childbearing role. Women's more intimate form of relating can be seen simultaneously as a more natural and "lower" and as a morally superior "higher" position—as either ignoring or transcending social categories. Feminine symbols also demonstrate this polarized ambiguity. Women can be exalted (as goddesses, dispensers of justice, and occupants of the moral high ground) or debased (as witches, dispensers of the evil eye, castrating mothers). In either case the symbolic woman is "rarely within the normal range of human possibilities" (Ortner, 1974, p. 86). If culture is thought of as superior to nature, it is a small step to viewing men as superior to women.

Ortner later clarified her position, stating that while the distinction between "nature" and "culture" is not universal, the "*problem of the relationship* between what humanity can do, and that which sets limits upon those possibilities, must be a universal problem" (Ortner, 1996, p. 179). Gender is always situated at what Ortner refers to as the nature-culture border—the body. In most if not all societies the two sets of oppositions, nature and culture and female and male, "move into a relationship of mutual metaphorization" so that "gender becomes a powerful language for talking about the great existential questions of nature and culture" and vice versa (Ortner, 1996, p. 179). The asymmetry of these categories, in which the masculine and culture are valued above the feminine and nature, reflects the notion that culture is about the transcendence of nature.

NATURE, GENDER, AND MYTHOLOGY. In her book *Female Power and Male Dominance* (1981) Peggy Reeves Sanday contests Ortner's claim that because men are associated with culture and it is culture's job to control nature, men are universally regarded as having the right to control women. Sanday does admit to the "permeability between the categories of female and nature" in some societies but not all. She refers to such societies as having an inner orientation with a "reciprocal flow between the power of nature and the power inherent in women" (Sanday, 1981, p 5). In such societies the control and manipulation of these forces is left to women and to sacred natural symbols; men are largely extraneous to this domain and must be careful lest they antagonize earthly representatives of nature's power (namely women). Sanday argues that men are not unequivocally aligned with "culture" (defined as the transcendence of the natural givens of existence by means of systems of thought and technology). They are part of nature not only in their physicality but also in their need or desire to kill. "Men hunt animals, seek to kill other human beings, make weapons for these activities, and pursue power that is *out there*" (Sanday, 1981, p. 5). These more exterior life-taking activities of men are referred to as an outer orientation. Societies vary in the extent to which they value an inner or outer orientation, the powers of women and respect for reproduction versus the role of men and their more destructive externalized power. This is not a dichotomy between nature and culture, terms that are in fact hard to define and that arguably have no cross-cultural reference. Sanday's survey of "simpler societies" led her to conclude that there is a basic conceptual symmetry between the sexes in which "women give birth and grow children; men kill and make weapons. Men display their kills (be it an animal, a human head, or a scalp) with the same pride that women hold up the newly born" (Sanday, 1981, p. 5).

The variations in sex-role plans found in different societies show that they are cultural constructions rather than genetic. Historical and political factors as well as the environment in which people live affect the ways in which they interact. Sex-role plans in turn change the social and natural environment. Sanday identified four basic templates relating to the sexes. These can be segregated or merged, with decision-making powers vested in one sex or shared. These four types can be combined in various ways. Among the Mbuti of the Ituri Forest in central Africa, for example, the sexes are merged and decision-making powers shared. Among the Iroquois confederacy of North America, on the other hand, sexual differentiation was extreme, while decision making was still shared between the sexes. In both these societies the sex-role scripts give women both secular and religious power. Their cosmologies and rituals display a generally positive attitude to the world and the place of humans within it. In societies in which decision making is shared, female or paired deities are given prominence. In societies in which males dominate and women are relegated to a subordinate role in both sacred and secular domains, there is an emphasis on a male godhead. The sexes are also invariably segregated, as among the Hausa of northern Nigeria or Yanomamo of Venezuela and Brazil.

The environment appears to be a crucial variable in determining gender roles and the valuation given to men and male symbols or women and female symbols. Where large game is hunted, whether or not these animals are a nutritionally important part of the diet, Sanday argues that the major source of power is seen as a supreme being who resides in the sky or in animals. In fact any environmental tension, whether created by food scarcity, climactic unpredictability, warfare, or political uncertainty, tends to move a society in the direction of an outer orientation, male dominance, and androcentric mythology. Sanday suggests that there is transference of anxiety from the external world, which is beyond control, to women, who may be taken as symbolic representatives of the natural world. A lack of environmental security therefore correlates with control of women and male domination. If, on the other hand, the world is experienced as benign, an inner orientation develops in which both the environment and women are seen as partners rather than as sources of danger to men and to society as a whole.

TRANSCENDING, CONFOUNDING, AND SUBVERTING GENDER. There are many ways in which heterosexual masculine and feminine roles are challenged, undermined, reworked, and transformed in societies around the world. Such incidences reveal the ways normative gender roles based on biological sex require concerted social effort to construct and maintain and are far from "natural" and self-evident. One of the most widely reported examples of multiple genders is the berdache, "two spirits" or "man woman" found among more than 150 First Nation groups in the Americas. While sometimes described as an institutionalized form of gender reversal in which a person of one anatomical sex takes on the roles, attire, and status of the opposite sex, the variety of practices actually involved have led some scholars to use the term "third sex" or to think in terms of multiple genders. It is argued that Rubin's distinction between sex and gender (and sexuality) cannot be universally applied and that other societies conceive of the human person in ways that make no sense of such distinctions. In many cases North American "two spirits" have specific religious or occupational roles and may have a mythological account of origins distinct from that of men or women, so that it makes more sense to conceive of them as a third gender than as people who simply cross gender, according to Will Roscoe's book, *Changing Ones: Third and Fourth Genders in Native North America* (1998).

Another example of a group that transcends a binary gender classification is the *hijra* of India, anatomical males who identify and dress as females, forming a religious caste with their own mother goddess. Like the classical Galli of Greco-Roman mythology or eunuchs in much of the ancient world, the gender roles assigned to such a "third sex" are linked to specialist religious and administrative functions. They may be chosen by the individual or assigned by others. In Western religious tradition nuns have also been described as a "third sex" (Hastrup, 1978). They share many features of the *hijra* in the sense of forming a separate religious "caste" that both ignores (through celibacy) and transcends (by taking on some roles normally reserved for male priests) normative heterosexuality. Western gay and lesbian people have also utilized the notion of multiple genders as a way of overcoming the prescriptive binary gender roles associated with compulsory heterosexuality.

SEE ALSO Anthropology, Ethnology, and Religion; Culture; Feminism, article on Feminism, Gender Studies, and Religion; Gender and Religion, overview article, article on History of Study; Power.

BIBLIOGRAPHY

Butler, Judith. *Gender Trouble: Feminism and the Subversion of Identity.* New York and London, 1999.

Chesler, Phyllis. *Women and Madness.* Garden City, N.Y., 1972.

Connell, R. W. "Making Gendered People: Bodies, Identities, Sexualities." In *Revisioning Gender,* edited by Myra Marx Ferree, Judith Lorber, and Beth B. Hess, pp. 449–971. Thousand Oaks, Calif., 1999. A focus on gender often means in practice a focus on women (to redress the masculine bias in so much "ungendered" literature). That is largely true of this theoretically rich collection of essays.

Doniger, Wendy. *Splitting the Difference: Gender and Myth in Ancient Greece and India.* Chicago and London, 1999. The religious studies scholar has produced a fascinating account of gender.

Evans-Pritchard, E. E. *Kinship and Marriage among the Nuer.* London and Oxford, 1951.

Hastrup, Kirsten. "The Semantics of Biology: Virginity." In *Defining Females,* edited by Shirley Ardener, pp. 49–65. London 1978.

King, Ursula, ed. *Religion and Gender.* Oxford, and Cambridge, U.K., 1995. A specific focus on gender and religion that combines theoretical papers with case studies and specific examples.

Linn, Priscilla Rachun. "Gender Roles." *Encyclopedia of Religion,* 1st ed., Vol. 5, pp. 495–502. New York, 1987.

Low, Alaine, and Soraya Tremayne, eds. *Women as Sacred Custodians of the Earth? Women, Spirituality, and the Environment.* New York and Oxford, 2001. The editors bring spirituality into the equation with their interdisciplinary collection of essays.

Mead, Margaret. *Sex and Temperament in Three Primitive Societies.* New York, 1935.

Miller, Barbara Diane, ed. *Sex and Gender Hierarchies.* Cambridge, U.K., 1993. Another interesting comparative work that includes human and primate examples, evolutionary theory, and contemporary ethnographic studies of gender.

Ortner, Sherry B. "Is Female to Male as Nature Is to Culture?" In *Woman, Culture, and Society,* edited by Michelle Zimbalist Rosaldo and Louise Lamphere, pp. 67–88. Stanford, Calif., 1974.

Ortner, Sherry B. "So, *Is* Female to Male as Nature Is to Culture?" In *Making Gender: The Politics and Erotics of Culture,* by Sherry B. Ortner, pp. 173–180. Boston, 1996. A focus on gender often means in practice a focus on women (to redress the masculine bias in so much "ungendered" literature). That is largely true of this theoretically rich collection of essays.

Roscoe, Will. *Changing Ones: Third and Fourth Genders in Native North America.* New York, 1998.

Rubin, Gayle. "The Traffic in Women: Notes on the 'Political Economy' of Sex." In *Toward an Anthropology of Women,* edited by Rayna R. Reiter, pp. 157–210. New York and London, 1975. This is a rich collection of ethnographic and theoretical accounts of women's roles in various societies.

Sanday, Peggy Reeves. *Female Power and Male Dominance: On the Origins of Sexual Inequality.* Cambridge, U.K., and New York, 1981.

Sanday, Peggy Reeves, and Ruth Gallagher Goodenough, eds. *Beyond the Second Sex: New Directions in the Anthropology of Gender.* Philadelphia, 1990. An anthropological contribution to gender studies.

FIONA BOWIE (2005)

GENEALOGY. As formal structure, genealogy is foremost an intellectual discipline. Its concern is with recording and putting into systematic order the histories of families, differentiating them by rules of descent and allocating to each a share of those enduring human valuables that consist of privileges and honors, titles and powers. Although grounded in myth and circumscribed by tradition and, thus, seemingly a rote and rigid subject, genealogy is to be understood rather as a product of informed speculative reasoning about metaphysical, specifically ontological, matters. Its subject matter goes beyond the listing of pedigrees. It identifies and differentiates the forces and generative sources that give shape to and regulate the entire universe of life. From its cosmological concepts, it draws implications for human conduct and for the structure of the social order. Most directly, genealogies connect human families with their mythical origins, joining them as kinfolk within the universal community of gods, spirits, and other forms of life.

PRINCIPLES OF GENEALOGY. The genealogical discipline exercises a controlling influence upon everyday life, for it is the source of the morality and of the principles of systematic order that bind systems of descent into clans, lineages, and similar groupings. Among tribal societies especially, the genealogical order frequently dictates all social relations. In early and more complex traditional societies, where only royalty and related families come within its scope, the genealogical system acts as the focus of authority. In sum, for preindustrial societies the genealogical discipline is unitary and unifying, joining the social and the religious forms by demonstrating that society is an extension of the mythical era of original creations. From this unitary perspective, the gods, spirits, and ancestral beings who brought human beings into existence are themselves drawn into the human sphere. In more recent times, genealogical interest has been reduced. Stripped of its religious and cosmological associations, genealogy serves, at most, the general purpose of celebrating ethnicity.

The general model for making genealogical distinctions is drawn from nature. This is most clearly exemplified in totemic systems, whose family lines are represented as descended from animals or other distinctive natural forms. Each line of descent appears as a species and therefore stands as one among all the other natural varieties of life. In nontotemic systems, the special qualities attributed to particular human ancestors serve the same purpose of distinguishing the lines of descent. Thus, human founders of clans and lineages are held to be the primary sources of the vigor and continuity of their descendants, as are totemic ancestors. In both systems, the natural species exemplify the traits of continuity and social immortality that human societies seek through their own genealogies.

As a process, differentiation appears as the signifier of forces that promote growth and development. The natural evolution commonly depicted in creation myths begins with relatively amorphous beings and proceeds systematically to final stages of specificity. This understanding of the natural direction of life underlies the metaphoric assumption that takes the contrast between the chaotic and the structured in ritual and myth to be analogous to the contrast between the deathlike and the vigorous in social life. Accordingly, genealogical systems—the primary promulgators of differentiation—are impelled to drive toward singularity, to single out families and persons for special distinction as principal bearers of vital powers.

Essentially, all the systematic modes of differentiation upon which genealogical systems are constructed express some concept of generative powers. The rules of primogeniture and of relative seniority of descent generally concern the special nature of powers presumed to lie in primacy, that is, in the original conditions that generated forms and natural processes. The rules of descent by gender (matriliny, patriliny, bilaterality) stem from the distinctive generative powers of femininity and masculinity. The rules governing direct and collateral lines reflect closeness to the central sources, and those that differentiate between long and short genealogies involve issues of inherent longevity. Each mode of descent has the added significance of being the appropriate mode of transmission of powers, and each member of a genealogical chain has stature as a designated and graded conveyor.

In substance, the characteristic modes of genealogical transmission impose a powerful order upon social structures. They regulate marriage and other social relations, and they determine the formal lines of social divisions and the character of dependency in subordinate branches. In keeping with the general idea of a genealogical system as an organism that grows and branches, lineages are quite commonly envisioned as vegetative.

The social and cosmological implications of genealogical differentiation are realized most fully in lineage structures. In contrast to clans, which only imply and therefore generalize their putative connections to founders, lineages depend upon true pedigrees, upon the real chain of names and their sequences, and often upon the sequences of outstanding events that demonstrate the potency and special quality of the names. Genealogical traditions and related rituals evoke, reanimate, and, in some sense, reincarnate ancestors. Remembering the long line of ancestors by name (in Polynesia, as far back as ninety-nine generations) is an act of piety that, even in tribal societies, imposes the technical requirement of creating the scholarly and priestly craft of official genealogist for royal and noble lines.

Aristocracy, understood as a social system in which a singular descent line has come forward as the focus of generative powers, may take shape among clans as well as among lineages, drawing upon their common genealogical rules. But it is the specificity of the lineage and its greater adeptness for drawing fine distinctions that endow royalty with the extra degree of moral authority for governing. The lineage is so much the social instrument of royalty that it readily becomes its own characteristic form of organization. Even among tribal societies, among whom organic unities are the common norm, it is not exceptional for chiefly lines to be the exclusive protagonists of the lineage system, and for all others to fall into a binlike category of relatively generalized descent. The Kwakiutl and some Polynesians, who are discussed below, illustrate what are, in effect, the social fractures in a system of descent.

It may seem paradoxical that lineages, although they are buttressed by deeply held human convictions about the binding powers of common descent, should, in fact, promote, as a matter of principle, countertenets of antagonisms, oppositions, and structural divisions. Yet, these forms of divisiveness are not accidental but are the complements of systems that transmit singular powers. Powers must demonstrate efficacy; efficacy invites contention. As a consequence, aristocratic lineages must sustain themselves, not by their genealogical authority alone, but by the abilities of their actual rulers to balance sometimes conflicting claims of birth and force.

SYSTEMS OF GENEALOGY. Thus, their orderly premises notwithstanding, genealogical systems are variable. They are subject to the vicissitudes of history that ultimately erode the most formidable structures, as well as to the variability that is allowed by their rules and to the ambiguities of situation that disturb any social order. One cannot hope to describe the varieties of genealogical systems encyclopedically. The following examples from tribal societies and from ancient and more recent civilizations are not necessarily the most characteristic, but they call attention to special features that pertain to the general nature of genealogies.

The Cubeo. The Cubeo, tropical forest Indians of the Colombian Vaupés, exemplify genealogical aristocracy as developed within the constraints of a subsistence economy. Even within the meager material setting of slash-burn root horticulture, supplemented by fishing and hunting, the rudimentary form of aristocracy exhibited by the Cubeo resembles, in many formal respects, the hierarchical structures and the patterns of dominance and subordination of the more complex civilizations, indicating that aristocracy may be less a product of material than of genealogical factors. Cubeo society is an organization of ranked, exogamic, and patrilineal sibs (clans), who are joined together in a confraternity (phratry) for what are largely ritual purposes. The sibs exchange wives with those of similar rank in a corresponding phratry. The rank of the sibs was preordained and revealed in the order of birth from an underground dwelling that brought into being the first set of fraternal ancestors, the founders of sibs. The names of their descendants have entered into the genealogies of the sibs, to be inherited in alternate generations by the grandchildren. The personal names, like "souls," carry the immortality of the descent lines and, the Cubeo believe, promote the growth of the children who bear them.

The names are but one of four elements that enter into the substance of the genealogies. The others are sacred trumpets and flutes that bear the names and represent the original ancestors; the life souls that are apportioned to each of the sibs; and, finally, the figure of a sacred anaconda, in whose elongated form the sibs are imagined as ranked segments extending from the head to the tail. The anaconda symbolizes the animal nature of human beings and their kinship with the animal world. These four elements characterize the Cubeo genealogical structure as a complex conveyor of vital forces that ensure their ethnic continuity and are therefore central to their religious and ritual purposes, namely, to maintain connections with founding ancestors. "When we remember our ancestors," the Cubeo proclaim, "we bring them to life." For them, the act of re-creating the ancestors in memory is comparable to the original creation, when the Creator willed people into existence by means of his own imaginative thought.

The correspondence of the hierarchical order of the sibs to the order in which the first ancestors emerged is also, in essential respects, a memorial to the circumstances of their origins; they are designated by genealogical relations as older brother/younger brother, and as grandparent/grandchild; by an original distribution of ritual powers, as chiefs, priests, shamans, warriors, and servants; and, by their place as segments of the body of the sacred anaconda, they are assigned a fixed order of residence along the rivers they occupy. The highest ranks, corresponding to the head of the anaconda, live toward the mouth of the river; the servants, toward the source. Thus the genealogical system—recapitulating in each generation the generative conditions of origins as an action of creative remembering—encompasses the main areas of Cubeo social and religious existence.

The Kwakiutl. A similar genealogical system, but one notable for the unusual significance it attaches to hereditary personal names, prevails among the Kwakiutl Indians of Vancouver Island. The qualities commonly attributed to personal names imply the presence in them of spiritual or magical powers, a "name soul," as, for example, among the Inuit (Eskimo). The Kwakiutl seem to have elevated the concept of name soul to a high level of concreteness, thereby bringing to the surface a mystical attribute of names that in other cases exists only by implication. Their treatment of names suggests how pedigrees may indeed constitute a great chain of being.

In Kwakiutl genealogies, each personal name stands for a desirable attribute of being, ordinarily a special power, and the ensemble of ancestral names covers the range of attributes and powers that govern life and death and control valued possessions. Even as it is a specified segment of the patterned mosaic of life forces, each name also has existence as a being, as a spiritual personage who is attached to and yet may have an existence apart from its bearer. The bearer is no ordinary being either, having been set apart and sanctified in having met the genealogical qualifications of seniority. Among the Kwakiutl tribes, which once numbered in the tens of thousands, only a very small number of personal names are of this type; all others are scorned as "made-up." The real names are the exclusive property of a nobility of chiefs, the secular and religious leaders. The remainder are the names of commoners, people who cannot claim descent from mythical ancestors.

The chiefly or spiritual names possess an autonomy congruent with their character as ancestral incarnations, and, as such, they impose their natures upon those who bear them. Under certain circumstances they stand apart entirely. Thus, a chief who possesses several names, some belonging to different divisions of the tribe, might engage in ritual transactions with his distant name as though it were another person. He might present this name with gifts, or, under other circumstances, go through a sham marriage with a name attached for this purpose to his arm, for example. Kwakiutl genealogies are histories of the acquisition and descent of all such names and of their intrinsic properties. Chanted at all important ceremonial events, the family history is a repository of its accumulated powers and capacities.

Polynesian societies. Cubeo and Kwakiutl genealogical systems are noteworthy examples of aristocracy that is deeply enlaced in mythological and shamanistic conceptions and, therefore, politically undeveloped. Polynesian societies offer contrasting examples. Perhaps because their religions are more fully theistic and relatively free of these other associations, the Polynesians were able to move in another direction. Upon similar genealogical principles, and upon an equally undifferentiated economy, Polynesian societies produced such relatively modern institutions as socioeconomic stratification and centralized territorial states. Thus, the capability of a genealogical system to evolve or to elaborate a new social order is never a function of rules of descent alone. New patterns emerge when genealogical rules are joined to an appropriate religious doctrine. In Polynesia, that doctrine has been based upon a concept of *mana,* a force that animates all of nature and characterizes the energetic properties of all substance. In principle, *mana* descends from the gods to the human generations in measured proportions as defined by the genealogical rules. Senior lines are richly endowed with *mana* and are energized and hence ennobled by it; the junior descent lines are left behind as the weakly endowed commoners.

Conceptualized as an efficient force manifested objectively in results—on the battlefield, in the fields of production, in the perfection of craft skills, in personal charisma, in the efficacious management of religious rituals—*mana* is not automatically and indisputably the gift of inheritance. Its possessor has also to demonstrate worthiness by standing up to challenge. Nevertheless, although the conviction that the powers that animate and bestow efficacy move by the generative forces of genealogical rules may yield to the acid test of actual events, it is never abondoned. When lower ranks win royal power by force, as they occasionally do, from time to time, they are still obliged to discover genealogical authority for their new office. Genealogical guilds guard the sanctity of royal and noble pedigrees.

Polynesian societies differ in the way each has managed to sustain the shifting balances between the genealogical and the pragmatic. The Maori of New Zealand exemplify relatively close adherence to traditional genealogical criteria. The Samoans, the Easter Islanders, and the Mangaians demonstrate a greater flexibility in following the traditional rules of descent. The emergent states and stratified societies of Tonga, Tahiti, and Hawaii, for example, reveal a seemingly typical developmental cycle that moves from traditionalism to greater openness and, finally, to the consolidation of hereditary rule, but within the framework of a markedly restructured social order.

Major civilizations. The histories of major civilizations—those of classical Greece, Japan, or England, to take but three examples—show their genealogical life as comparable, in many respects, with that in tribal societies. Hesiod assembled from the body of Homeric mythology a genealogical order of the gods that allotted to each of them appropriate honors, titles, and cosmological functions, and described "how the gods and men sprang from one source." Theogony emerges as one aspect of cosmogony. The gods, humans, and the fully differentiated natural order evolve in these genealogical tales within a turbulent atmosphere, in a setting of disputes for power among contending forces, very much as they do in tribal creation myths. The patterns set by the gods, the immortals, in their evolution define the courses of human history.

The genealogists of archaic and preliterate Japan assembled from ancient myths a comparable cosmogony. Heaven and Earth, initially formed from Chaos, after several generations produced the god Izanagi and the goddess Izanami, who gave birth first to the islands of Japan, then to other gods, and, finally, after many generations and much social disorder, to humans. The first mikado was granted sovereignty by the sun goddess and, as a link in the succession of the gods, became the center of the national religious cult. Similarly, each distinguished family or clan also claimed its derived divinity from other gods and from ancestral association with emperors. The Japanese chronicles of hereditary titles authenticated the social and religious organization.

Christianity, in principle, breaks with the tenet of the traditional genealogical order that claims divine descent, but it leaves essentially untouched the issues of sanctity and an even deeper concern with singularity and inequality. Even the egalitarian Quakers in England succumbed to the temptation of differentiating major from minor family lines. As for English royalty, it had found in the Roman Catholic church, itself the heir to the political institutions of the Roman Empire, the questionable but powerful bases for claiming the "divine right of kings" as an authority for absolute power. The Glorious Revolution of 1688 set that thesis to rest, and later monarchs settled for the moderate option of divine approval.

Through the long course of English history, the constant principle of monarchy, starting with the Celtic rule of the fourth century BCE, is one of singular descent from divinely graced or otherwise extraordinary leaders. Except for kinship with the royal house, no other fixed principles for succession to the throne, as for example primogeniture, were established in England before the thirteenth century. As is common in such systems, genealogical authority fostered social unity when it was strong and wars for succession when it was weak. Social and cultural unity has been the aim and, to a considerable extent, the accomplishment of the genealogical order—which achieved its apotheosis in aristocracy—until relatively recent times.

NONGENEALOGICAL SUCCESSION. Tibetan Buddhism, or Lamaism, illustrates the contrary qualities of a dynastic order from which genealogical succession has been totally banished. In the fifteenth century, the monastery of Dge lugs pa (Geluk pa), a celibate order and the original seat of the Dalai Lama dynasty, promulgated a doctrine of successive reincarnations as the mode of accession to divine authority. They believed that the Dalai Lama would be reborn in some infant unrelated and unknown to him, and that through this reincarnation, he would continue his work of enlightenment. Discovered after an exhaustive search that brought to light his divine traits and evidence of an earlier existence, the new Dalai Lama was trained for his post during an interim regency. The Tibetan doctrine set aside traditional considerations of individuality and family distinction so that the divine presence, a manifestation of the Buddha, would appear directly, albeit in human form. However, whatever forcefulness this system gained through directness of access to the religious source was at least partly dissipated by the dispersal of its constituencies. Unaffiliated to a systematic line of succession, Lamaist adherents were free to join any one of numerous monasteries, each of which was headed by an abbot, himself the incarnation of a lesser lama.

SEE ALSO Dalai Lama; Names and Naming; Preanimism.

BIBLIOGRAPHY

Meyer Fortes was perhaps the most original and perceptive of anthropological authorities on genealogical issues. His *Kinship and the Social Order: The Legacy of Lewis Henry Morgan* (Chicago, 1969), a central work on the subject, is a most useful summary and refinement of his position with a rich bibliography of theoretical and ethnographic sources. For the Cubeo, the only work thus far is my *The Cubeo: Indians of the Northwest Amazon,* rev. ed. (Urbana, Ill., 1979), based on field work. Two exceptional studies on Barasana Indians, also of the Colombian Vaupés, that examine genealogical conceptions from structuralist and symbolist perspectives are Christine Hugh-Jones's *From the Milk River: Spatial and Temporal Processes in Northwest Amazonia* (Cambridge, U.K., 1979) and Stephen Hugh-Jones's *The Palm and the Pleiades: Initiation and Cosmology in Northwest Amazonia* (Cambridge, U.K., 1979). Taken together, the bibliographies in these three works are close to all-inclusive for this region. The best single-volume access to the very extensive literature on the Kwakiutl from the writings of Franz Boas and his native collaborator, George Hunt, is Boas's difficult but authoritative study, *The Social Organization and the Secret Societies of the Kwakiutl Indians* (1895; reprint, New York, 1970). A recent and useful interpretation of Kwakiutl culture and society that draws upon much of the Boas and Hunt texts is my *The Mouth of Heaven: An Introduction to Kwakiutl Religious Thought* (New York, 1975), which includes a bibliography of the published Boas field studies. There is no better introduction to the nature of Polynesian societies than the writings of one of Polynesia's native sons, Te Rangi Hiroa (Sir Peter Buck), of Maori descent and onetime director of the Bernice P. Bishop Museum at Honolulu. His greatest work is *The Coming of the Maori* (Wellington, 1952), an intimate yet anthropologically professional study. My *Ancient Polynesian Society* (Chicago, 1970) focuses more directly on genealogical issues because it is a study of variations in the forms of Polynesian aristocracy.

On the subject of the genealogies of the Greek gods, the principal sources are Hesiod's *Theogony* and *Works and Days,* conveniently available in the English translation by Hugh G. Evelyn-White in his *The Homeric Hymns and Homerica* (Cambridge, Mass., 1967). As background on the ancient period, M. I. Finley's *The Ancient Greeks* (New York, 1977) is both authoritative and succinct. For Japanese sources, the general work of choice is George B. Sansom's familiar classic, *Japan: A Short Cultural History,* rev. ed. (New York, 1962), to be used, however, in conjunction with the source book on the Japanese genealogical and historical chronicles, as compiled by Ryusaku Tsunoda, Wm. Theodore de Bary, and Donald Keene, *Sources of Japanese Tradition,* 2 vols. (New York, 1958). On the genealogies of the royal lines of England, G. M. Trevelyan's *History of England,* new illust. ed. (London, 1973), the *Oxford History of England,* especially volume 3, and Austin Lane Poole's *Domesday Book to Magna Carta, 1087–1216* (Oxford, 1955), are particularly noteworthy for their historical insights.

New Sources

Bakker, Egbert J., Irene J. F. de Jong, and Hans van Wees. *Brill's Companion to Herodotus.* Leiden and Boston, 2002.

Balsamo, Gian. *Pruning the Genealogical Tree: Procreation and Lineage in Literature, Law, and Religion.* London, 1999.

Detienne, Marcel. *Writing of Orpheus: Greek Myth in Cultural Contact.* Translated by Janet Lloyd. Baltimore, 2002.

Nanji, Azim. *Mapping Islamic Studies: Genealogy, Continuity, and Change.* Berlin, 1997.

Simons, D. Brenton, and Peter Benes. *Art of Family: Genealogical Artifacts in New England.* Boston, 2002.

Toullelan, Pierre-Yves, and Bernard Gille. *Mariage franco-tahitien: histoire de Tahiti du XVIIIe siècle à nos jours.* Tahiti, 1992.

Ulanov, Ann Belford. *Female Ancestors of Christ.* Boston, 1993.

Walens, Stanley. *Feasting with Cannibals: An Essay on Kwakiutl Cosmology.* Princeton, 1981.

IRVING GOLDMAN (1987)
Revised Bibliography

GENETICS AND RELIGION.

Science in general, and molecular genetics and the new science of genomics in particular, contest with claims of faith on the same terrain. Genetics is a complex, irreducible set of knowledge about the large molecule DNA, which by its structure and function transmits information about how proteins are made and folded in particular ways. DNA regulates the biochemical properties of all living cells. The unique feature of DNA is that it is the structure for the replication of coded information of the sort that can be transmitted across generations. This information is held in the DNA molecules in the cells of the human gametes—sperm and eggs that recombine to found a fertilized egg do so by recombining pieces of the DNA of each into a newly composed molecule with the codes from each genetic parent.

INTRODUCTION. The ability to recombine DNA is a feature of all living organisms and offers a defining and definitive set of norms and explanations for behaviors and biological processes that are highly conserved across many species. Genetic codes are so similar that much human genetic information is shared with other mammals, especially related primates. Mutations in these codes, often as small as a single allele difference, have been traced as causative to devastating diseases, and many more diseases are being identified as having genetic difference as their causation. It is likely that genetic causation in a more complex fashion will be found to be the cause for many diseases, including many long thought to be behavioral, such as depression, schizophrenia, and addictive behavior. This story is the largely acceptable story of modern molecular biology.

As such, genetic explanations for how the world functions, what can be known about the world, what one can hope for in the future, what a self is, what a family means, and the role of free will all challenge what has historically been the province of religion—a moral location in which what humans desire and what they can achieve have long been mediated. In large part, genetics and religion ask the same sort of questions: What does it mean to be human? What does it mean to be free? And what must I do about the suffering of others?

Further complicating the issue is that "genetics" refers to both the acquisition of the knowledge of how the molecules of DNA and RNA copy information and build programs within the cell—how the intricate "machineries" and pathways are reconstructed—as well as to how the molecules are interpreted, categorized, and cataloged. It has long been understood that how humans define, name, abstract, and group nature shapes how they see the world and provides a sense of self and possibility within the world. Finally, "genetic" also refers to the growing group of interventions into the code of the molecule itself, first by testing and then by attempting to alter the code into more auspicious variations.

Genetics in this last sense began with studies of plant and animal heredity. Working primarily with fruit flies, geneticists began creating—with exposure to radiation—the same sort of distinctive phenotypical variations observed in nature within species; through breeding the geneticists noted how the variation was transmitted and how it was expressed. This was a technique that followed biblical accounts of Jacob's goat herd, in which Jacob bred spotted goats to increase his portion of the herd, drawing on centuries of accumulated wisdom in agricultural societies. Gregor Mendel (1822–1884), an Austrian monk, also relied on the tradition of observing phenotypes, breeding, and noting hereditary traits. Fruit fly geneticists, then, drew on all of this material, and in the 1960s, after the invention of the electron microscope, were able to see the long chains of chromosomes along which the DNA was arranged in patterns. They were able to view how variations such as white and not red eyes, wrinkled or frizzled wings inside of smooth ones, or winglessness altogether could be predicted by linking trait to gene and therefore apply "forward genetics" (the breeding of a strain of model organisms from these variations).

Later advances allowed the gene itself to be diced and spliced (using chemicals to cut the gene at specified intervals) and then recombined to make new strains of mice or flies or worms entirely. These new strains would breed true because the trait spliced into the gene would persist. In fact, given the way that the genetic code is already highly conserved across species in nature, slices of DNA from one organism could be—and were—spliced into other species entirely, giving rise to a host of "created" organisms capable of enacting the DNA instructions of one species inside the body of another. Such knowledge led to an explosion of interest and capacity to understand many tricky problems in medicine, such as how addiction, mental illness, and cognition might function; how embryos develop; and how immune systems regulate response and apoptosis—all breakthrough insights that have already transformed clinical medicine.

Hence, the science itself suggested a use, much as the structure of DNA suggested a function. It is both the observation and notation of the world of molecular biology—its structure—and the alteration of the world at the molecular level—its function—that raise concerns about genetics in the communities of faith and in the scholarship of religion.

The issues can be grouped into several sorts of concerns, each of which has generated a considerable literature of commentary and response. Without exception, the articles of social and religious critiques of genetic science begin with the admission that genetic science holds enormous potential, yet their authors then write about their concerns and fears—rooted in the final analysis—that use of impermissible knowledge might lead to humans "playing God" (Peters, 2003).

ISSUES OF THE WORLD TO COME. For many commentators (such as Audrey Chapman, Leon Kass, and Francis Fukuyama) the problem of genetics is that humans have a particular telos. The ends of human life are shaped, in the view of these commentators, by both the finality of death and the sense of an afterlife. "The world to come" is the world in a resurrected body, in an afterlife, or in a messianic age. In this sense, then, the present moment, and the embodied life, is meant to be one of befallenness and affliction, not the source of perfection or the site for the final telos of human life. For many, including Stanley Hauerwas and Sondra Wheeler, the proper regard toward illness is one of witness and of comfort in the knowledge that "this story is not the end of the story for persons of faith." For medical researchers, the outcomes for which they strive are to provide a future based in a steady accumulation of advanced scientific knowledge that will lead to greater control over the outcome and the prevention of illness and injury. When researchers speak of curing genetic illness with heritable genetic interventions, and of cures both in this generation and in the next, many religious scholars and clergy with strong views of a heaven then fear a "post-human future." It is, for them, a future in which perfected humans are no longer subject to illness, disability, or even death. Is the "world to come" brought about by human creativity and effort? Or ought human yearning strive toward a divine reward? If aging and death are events to be mediated by religious faith, can such pivotal events be altered, either temporally or fundamentally, without destroying the fragility and vulnerability that makes one human? Genetic research, argues these scholars, is dangerous in its very structure, for its precise aim is to alter the future, to seek control over the ultimate causation.

To be sure, not all religious scholars take the position that the future is fundamentally sacred, nor that the particular condition of humanity in the early twenty-first century is the defining moment of humanity. For Jewish and Islamic scholars, among them Robert Gibbs, Laurie Zoloth, Elliot Dorff, and Abdul Aziz Sachedina, the duty to heal and the obligations embraced by medicine are a form of charity and debt restoration. In these traditions, as well as in some arguments advanced by Hindu and Buddhist scholars, the duty to the world to come entails medical research, healing, and an ongoing effort on behalf of one's progeny. For Jewish scholars—whose tradition has at best a muted set of texts about the afterlife—one's world to come is the world of the next generation. Hence, the idea that humanity is itself constituted in its morbidity and mortality is a weaker claim. Such scholars note that the condition of the human person, and most especially the human life span—which doubled in the last half of the twentieth century—is not fixed, but has in fact remarkably improved. These scholars are generally more supportive of genetic research, for they proceed from a model that suggests improved health, greater freedom from disease, and lessening infant and maternal mortality (the results of earlier research) have led to increasing capacities for human pursuits.

ISSUES OF PATERNITY AND HERITAGE. Linking the resistance about the genetic elimination of illness—and the pushing back of death and aging—is the idea that one's genetic self is the true self, the essential identity. This raises problems for religious scholars on the many fronts of the issue. For some, the idea that genetic identity is fixed supports the argument that the DNA, once created, is the self as an integrated system at conception. For others, issues of a DNA heritage are troubling if the DNA is "taken" from them, and the sample molecule used in any way. Additionally, ethical problems can arise when genetic knowledge is used to suggest that illness, behavior, or traits are traceable to ethnogeographic evolutionary narratives. It is true, finally, that for all religious scholars, the genome mapping and the haplotype grouping of human phenotypes raises issues of ethnicity, family, kinship, membership, and identity. Should genetic relatedness be privileged over other kinship ties? Is it proper to seek one's genetic origins, and to what purpose? Can valuations and status (such as the Cohen status for Jews) long understood to orally transmitted and trusted be challenged by genetic testing?

ISSUES OF ILLNESS AND SUFFERING. For early Christians, the act of healing was a core component of the liturgy (James Keenan). A central problem that religion sought to address was that of befallenness and the role of the healer, which manifested itself in two ways. First, religious faith and the act of prayer was seen, throughout much of antiquity, as at least as effective as a cure when medical and surgical interventions were largely futile. Second, illness was understood as predominately spiritual in nature, and causation for illness was linked in many traditions to a failure to understand—or to comply or properly enact—one's relationship to God, gods, or, for some Eastern religions, the path of spirituality itself. Hence addictive patterns, aggression, or schizophrenia, as well as tuberculosis, leprosy, and plague, were all linked to personal or larger social flaws. The response, therefore, that made sense to people in such cases was a proper regard for one's relationship to the divine world and word. Priests became the source of healing.

However, genetic causation reconfigures causality—especially if the disease can be modeled and studied in animals (the core method for understanding diseases genetically). If mice can be made more or less aggressive or more or less fearful by genetic alterations, as evidenced by the work of Lee Silver, then what is the role of moral activity and of religious training in the moral path? If addictive behavior (including sexual behavior) can be traced to genetic allelic variation, then what is the role of judgments in such cases? Further, because most genetic researchers understand the complexity of the gene-to/in-environment relationship, then if the malfunction of genes in particular environmental locations triggers diseases and disease susceptibility, what use is it to pray for reversal, or to hope that correct moral activity will result in a cure? What is to be made of claims that the "gene in my body makes me a glutton?" Does the search for a genetic predisposition to sexual orientation make behavior more or less acceptable to faith communities?

Here again, the responses vary. For many Christian scholars, including Stanley Hauerwas, Lisa Sowle Cahill, and Leon Kass, the activity of suffering calls forward a response that places Christianity at the center. For Jewish scholars, most notably Emmanuel Levinas, "suffering is nothingness . . . is evil itself" (Levinas, 1988). In this view, one must turn to any means—including genetic research and therapies—to address the suffering of the other. In direct contrast to the Christians who fear genetics as a gesture towards that which makes people "post-human," the response is that modernity and medicine is the basis of humanity.

ISSUES OF ENHANCEMENT OF CAPACITIES AND THE ISSUE OF JUSTICE AND EQUALITY. Religious scholars have been wary of a trajectory of healing both for its own sake as well as with a slippery slope potential in that genetic research intended for curing illness—such as muscle tissue repair in muscular dystrophy—could then lead to enhancement—for example, muscle tissue repair for athletic prowess. This enhanced world would be one of brutalized beings. These scholars believe it would be a world in which unenhanced "wild types"—likely to be the poor—would be even further disadvantaged as a result of class and ethnogeographic fates.

Because religion seeks to address fundamental issues of justice, the problem of difference is a primary concern. The project of genetic research (and the gene banking projects in particular), as well as the clinical translation of the genome project, brings to the forefront concerns of justice on a tangible, local level. It is here that the similarities and differences between humans can be found. This is not only true on a species level, at which regions are mapped in search of single nucleotide polymorphism (SNP) patterns to provide answers about population genetics, but also true at the cross-species level, where homologs and orthologs are used to define highly conserved regions of the human genome and to set up model organism systems to track genetic difference and diseases. It is the powerful combination of this data—this way of understanding biology and this new computational ability to use the data—that will allow humans a keener understanding of the ways in which they differ. Biological differences are, in fact, laden with variations in value that are at times instrumental, and, as well, symbolic. Humans value some differences more than others, however. For example, as rational actors, we value rationality; as embodied beings, we value strength, potency, and longevity.

Theories of justice, however, rely on insights that differ from those of science, which holds to the seventeenth-century ideas of natural reason, close observation, and objective methodology to study nature in its particulars. The basis for modern-day ideas of justice were created, in part, by discourses about freedom and liberty, and made possible by rationality and democracy: a self was able to make a clear social contract in a society governed by law. The emerging science of the twentieth century—both the social and the natural sciences—provided support for social contract theories by arguing that humans were largely alike, that skin color made no clinical difference of distinction. The issue of justice as shaped by human identities and differences has long been understood as a matter of human capacity shaped by both moral choice and by environment.

Genetic knowledge complicates this and makes it visible: in fact, it will warrant a confrontation of a serious problem, one noted by scholars in disabilities studies for decades. Genetic knowledge will reveal human differences and similarities in unexpected ways, and people will begin to understand not only single gene protein causation, but propensities for variation that underlie complex and common diseases and predispositions and propensities. These will suggest pathways to difference, diseases, traits, and behavior. Social relationships and social categories had long been assumed to match obvious phenotypical variation. However, in the post-genomic era, human understanding will become increasingly complicated.

Theories of justice based on the changing knowledge base are still in contention. What will the response be when it is found that humans are not precisely "equally endowed"? And, how will humans create theories of justice and just policy based on significant and fundamental inequality in propensities or in potential difference? How will social ethics be reconceptualized in a world that is, on a biological level, fundamentally unjust? Is it possible to go beyond the requirements of the law to protect privacy and confidentiality—problems that were first imagined in the early years of genetic research and that are now being enacted? Is it possible to achieve a creative and truly bold reflection on how these newly understood "selves" function as citizens in a world that is rent by robust difference in ability yet connected by relationships across previously understood categories? And what will the meaning of genomic relationships be for theories of justice and citizenship?

ISSUES OF IDENTITY, ETHNICITY AND CITIZENSHIP. When the Lemba of Southern Africa claimed to be Jews (Tudor Parfitt, Mark Thomas) or when the Melungians of Appalachia claimed to be Portuguese (Carl Elliott) the claims were widely considered dubious at best, and fanciful at worst. In the age of genetics, African Lemba and American Melungians are tested for variations on the Y chromosome, as well as in the mitochondrial DNA, to more fully investigate such claims. The claims of religion have long sought definitions along the call of nationalisms. Genetic knowledge in this area, as well, provides a powerful deconstruction of some narratives, while it reifies others.

ISSUE OF GENESIS NARRATIVE: HUMANITY AND FREEDOM. Of all the protuberance in the field of genetics and religion, none is as resonant as the claim that in seeking genetic knowledge, the very "book of life" itself (Watson, 2003) is revealed. By seeking such knowledge, the act of creation (the most godlike divine act) is challenged by hubristic scientists. If the reach toward the forbidden knowledge is completed, can catastrophe be far behind? In fact, the Abrahamic narrative of *Genesis* in the Hebrew Scripture—and echoed in other creation narratives in other sacred texts—is that of violation, fall, and redemption or escape. For Jewish thinkers like Rachel Adler, humanity's acts are rather more complex, as they are in some of the reconsideration of Christian narratives, such as those of Ted Peters.

The challenge to the essential narrative of genesis by genetics can be seen in at least two ways. First, genetic sciences deconstruct the boundaries of the nuclear family by allowing the separation of genetic heritage, gamete production, and the development of an embryo in a woman's womb. Gametes can be generated, but some detractors fear that gametes will also be commodified, sold, advertised, and fertilized outside the norms of a passionate embrace—and even more so outside the bounds of a nuclear family. The genesis drama of infertility and the promised fecundity has been similarly addressed by advanced reproductive techniques and sophisticated genetic screening. Additionally, embryos are the subject of discourse long before the birth in the debate of what is the moral status of embryos? Genetic knowledge allows humans to imagine the self in smaller, more atomized parts, rather than as an inevitable whole, and the genesis narrative of the singularity of the family has to now be reread in this new context. The second challenge to the essential narrative of genesis by genetics is that the genesis narrative questions the ability and limits of human naming, manipulation, and control of nature

ISSUES OF NATURE. Catholic moral theology and many native religious traditions, as studied by Mary Churchill, contend that nature itself has moral boundaries and moral limits. To violate them, suggests Leon Kass, is at the risk of "moral repugnance" (Kass, 2002), in that certain uses or even investigations in genetics or genomics threaten to undermine a moral universe at the most basic of foundations. Nature, in this argument, is normative. Its existence suggests moral authorities that predate human habitation, and thus humans (seen here as outside of nature and therefore a threat to it) can illegitimately befoul nature by radically altering it quickly or imprudently. Other theologians, including Laurie Zoloth and Ronald Green, have used terms such as *tikkun olom* (repair of the world) within Jewish thought. Additionally, Peters has argued strongly that human persons are "created co-creators" (Peters, 2003), and thus entitled to intervene across nature's boundaries. This leads to the question: Does human free will also include the free will to investigate in this way? Religious scholars vary in their answers.

CONCLUSION. Genomic and genetic research has transformed both humankind's fundamental knowledge of biology as well as its basic strategies for transforming the understanding of illness, aging, and disability. These historic developments offer extraordinary promise for the translation of basic knowledge into concrete clinical responses for the prevention and treatment of disease and the improvement of human health and welfare. Such knowledge offers hope not only for medicine but also for significant social discourse and thoughtful critical responses to personal and public health issues that potentiate poverty and despair.

The dramatic promise of genetics and genomic research offers an opportunity for the deepest and most reflective civic debate on the nature, meaning, and intent of human identity and difference. It poses questions of what is humanity, freedom, and free will, as well as illuminates the problems of what is to be done about the suffering of others. How will the engine of scientific knowledge drive policy, practice, and culture as people collectively confront the ethical, legal, and social implications of human genomic and genetic research? How does humanity attend to issues regarding access, human rights, the autonomous consent of subjects, and the fragile freedom of the research enterprise itself? What new languages, theories, and policies of ethics, theologies, philosophies, and law will need to be created along with the creation of genomic knowledge? And who should craft these new concepts? What policy should emerge to define the ethical boundaries for the use of genomics?

Now that the basic science of bioinformatics and genomics has allowed the sequencing of the human genome and several other animal models, the pace of application and use of DNA sequencing, haplotype mapping, proteinomics, and SNP patterning will accelerate. As new and more complex genomic data sets are made public, new research strategies envisioned, and biological processes at the heart of all medicine elucidated, this new data and analysis, as well as the translational research it allows and promotes, will engender new issues for the application and use of genetics.

The use of this information also engenders new challenges in a social understanding and use of genomic knowledge regarding the complex human relationships that make up a just human society. New theories of justice will be needed for the new persons and the new identities framed by the social and scientific knowledge of human and animal models of genomics. Genomics will reveal differences and unexpected similarities among us that will challenge long-held ideas about health, disability, and behavior, thus creating complex challenges in how a fair society is structured. Such differences and identities create new relationships, with new possibilities for alliances and divisions.

Such abilities and disabilities are also weighted differently—and not neutrally—in our society and this raises four challenges in genetic research. First, how will humans learn from such data and how will these create new and complex theories, languages, and practices of social justice? Second, how can humanists, lawyers, and social scientists understand the new science, methods, and cultures of basic biological research engendered by genomics? Third, how can the public understand and participate in genomic knowledge, and how can medical personnel guide this translation of basic science to the clinic? And, fourth, how can policy leaders shape new science and health care policy for a new era of genomic knowledge?

Religion in the late twentieth and early twenty-first centuries played a prudential role in this debate—often invoking the precautionary principle as their positions: avoid the action if there is doubt about its safety or consequence. Yet even this claim rests on a notion of fated inevitability—that a course is set in motion and will unfold unless humans intervene. However, inaction changes the future as surely as does action. As genetic knowledge increases, scholars will need to turn to the text of their faiths and reason and raise new questions. Can religions be another source of wisdom in guiding changes as they occur? Will the concerns of religion's voice be heard—and heard fairly—by the science community? And, furthermore, will all voices—including the religious voice in support of research science—be fairly heard?

Long before science began to shape the modern world, religious faith struggled to incorporate contemporary changes into its world—the theories of Galileo and Charles Darwin, for example, were first rejected, then widely accepted—and the centuries-long relationship between faith traditions and the world that surrounded them created religions of tremendous vigor, creativity, and energy. Further research is needed to track the relationship between science and religion as the field of genetics unfolds.

Bibliography

Adler, Rachel. *Engendering Judaism: An Inclusive Theology and Ethics.* Philadelphia, 1998.

Cahill, Lisa Sowle. *Sex, Gender, and Christian Ethics.* Cambridge, U.K., 1996.

Chapman, Audrey R., and Mark S. Frankel. *Designing Our Descendants: The Promises and Perils of Genetic Modifications.* Baltimore, 2003.

Churchill, Mary. "A Theology of Family." In *Sacred Rights: The Case for Contraception and Abortion in World Religions,* edited by Daniel C. McGuire. Oxford, 2003.

Dorff, Elliot N. *Testimony for the National Bioethics Advisory Committee.* Washington, D.C., 2000.

Dorff, Elliot N. *To Do the Right and the Good: A Jewish Approach to Modern Social Ethics.* Philadelphia, 2002.

Fukuyama, Francis. *Our Posthuman Future: Consequences of the Biotechnology Revolution.* New York, 2002.

Gibbs, Robert. *Why Ethics? Signs of Responsibilities.* Princeton, N.J., 2000.

Johnston, Josephine, and Carl Elliott. "From the Guest Editors." *Developing World Bioethics,* 3, no. 2. (2003): iii–iv.

Kass, Leon R. *Life, Liberty and the Defense of Dignity: The Challenge for Bioethics.* San Francisco, 2002.

Green, Ronald M. *The Human Embryo Research Debates: Bioethics in the Vortex of Controversy.* Oxford, 2001.

Harrington, Daniel J., and James F. Keenan. *Jesus and Virtue Ethics: Building Bridges Between New Testament Studies and Moral Theology.* Lanham, Md., 2002.

Hauerwas, Stanley. *Suffering Presence: Theological Reflections on Medicine, the Mentally Handicapped, and the Church.* Notre Dame, Ind., 1986.

Levinas, Emmanuel. "Useless Suffering." In *The Provocation of Levinas: Rethinking the Other,* edited by Robert Bernasconi and David Wood, pp. 156–167. London and New York, 1988.

Parfitt, Tudor. "Constructing Black Jews: Genetic Tests and the Lemba—The Black Jews of Southern Africa." *Developing World Bioethics,* 3, no. 2. (2003): 112–118.

Peters, Ted. *Playing God? Genetic Determinism and Human Freedom.* New York, 2003.

Sachedina, Abdul Aziz. *Testimony for the National Bioethics Advisory Committee.* Washington, D.C., 2000.

Silver, Lee M. *Remaking Eden: Cloning and Beyond in a Brave New World.* New York, 1997.

Thomas, Mark G., et al. "Y chromosomes Traveling South: The Cohen Modal Haplotype and the Origins of The Lemba—The 'Black Jews of Southern Africa.'" *American Journal of Human Genetics* 66 (2000): 674–686.

Watson, James D., with Andrew Berry. *DNA: The Secret of Life,* New York, 2003.

Wheeler, Sondra. "Parental Liberty and the Right of Access to Germ-Line Intervention: A Theological Appraisal of Parental Power." In *Designing Our Descendants: The Promises and Perils of Genetic Modifications,* edited by Audrey R. Chapman and Mark S. Frankel. Baltimore, 2003.

Zoloth, Laurie. "Uncountable as the Stars: Inheritable Genetic Intervention and the Human Future—A Jewish Perspective." In *Designing Our Descendants: The Promises and Perils of Genetic Modifications,* edited by Audrey R. Chapman and Mark S. Frankel. Baltimore, 2003.

Laurie Zoloth (2005)

GENGHIS KHAN See CHINGGIS KHAN

GENNEP, ARNOLD VAN (1873–1957), French anthropologist, was born in Ludwigsburg, Germany, his father a descendant of French emigrants. When van Gennep was six, his parents divorced, and his mother returned to France with him. Several years later she married a doctor who had a summer practice at a spa in the French province of Savoy. Van Gennep's attachment to this region, which he considered his adopted homeland, dates from these years. He was to travel through Savoy, village by village, collecting ethnographic and folkloric materials.

Van Gennep had a diversified and original university education at the École Pratique des Hautes Études and the École des Langues Orientales in Paris; his studies included general linguistics, ancient and modern Arabic, Egyptology, Islamic studies, and studies of the religions of primitive peoples. He possessed a rare gift for learning languages. For seven years he was in charge of translation at the Ministry of Agriculture in Paris, but he gave up this post, the only one that the French government ever offered him, in order to devote himself to his personal research. From 1912 to 1915, he taught ethnology at the University of Neuchâtel in Switzerland. After being expelled for having expressed doubts concerning Swiss claims to total neutrality during World War I, he made his living by the publication of numerous articles and periodic reports, lecturing, and commissioned translations.

His voluminous production can be divided into two periods separated by his most important work, *Les rites de passage* (1909). The concept that he discovered here permitted him, during the second part of his life, to devote himself entirely to the ethnography and folklore of France. In the first part he had been occupied with the problems posed by the English school of anthropology, concerning totemism, taboo, the original forms of religion and society, and the relationships between myth and rite. But he had approached these anthropological commonplaces with a certain originality. For example, in his study, based on documents collected in Madagascar, of the problems of taboo, he not only sees the expression of religious institutions and attitudes but also emphasizes the social effects of taboo, which creates, maintains, or transforms the order of nature, and which consolidates the bonds between a single clan's members, between animal and human members of a clan, between ancestors and descendants, and between humans and gods. Taboo, he believed, is both a social and religious institution. The appearance of his work *L'état actuel du problème totémique* (1920), which purported to be a provisory summation of works on totemism, was in reality, as Claude Lévi-Strauss says, the "swan song" of speculations on totemism. The personal theoretical position of van Gennep in this work is prefunctionalist: Totemism has as its function to maintain the existing cohesion of the social group and to assure its continuity, which the totem symbolically represents.

Van Gennep's main contribution remains the idea of "rites of passage," which he put forward and developed in the book of that title. By *rite of passage* he means any ceremony that accompanies the passage from one state to another and from one world, whether cosmic or social, to another. Each rite of passage includes three necessary stages: separation, boundary, and reaggregation (or the preliminal, the liminal, and the postliminal). Van Gennep also introduced other important ideas. By emphasizing "ceremonial sequence," van Gennep demonstrates the importance of the process of "unfolding" in rituals and in the relations that exist between rituals. He also introduces the concept of the "pivoting" of the sacred—that is, the idea that the sacred is not an absolute but rather an alternating value, an indication of the alternating situations in which an individual finds himself. Every individual, in the course of his life, passes through alternations of sacred and profane, and the rites of passage function to neutralize for the social group the harmful effects of the imbalances produced by these alternations.

Van Gennep was a nonconformist with regard to his ideas, which obliged him to live at the periphery of academic institutions. His most original contribution in the field of anthropology was to show profound connections between the social and religious spheres.

SEE ALSO Rites of Passage, overview article.

BIBLIOGRAPHY

Belmont, Nicole. *Arnold Van Gennep: The Creator of French Ethnography.* Translated by Derek Coltman. Chicago, 1978.

Gennep, Arnold van. *Manuel de folklore français contemporain.* 9 vols. Paris, 1937–1958.

Gennep, Arnold van. *The Rites of Passage.* Translated by Monika B. Vizedom and Gabrielle L. Caffee. Chicago, 1960.

Gennep, Ketty van. *Bibliographie des œuvres d'Arnold van Gennep.* Paris, 1964.

New Sources

Belier, Wouter W. "Arnold Van Gennep and the Rise of French Sociology of Religion." *Numen* 41 (May 1994): 141–162.

Schjødt, Jens Peter. "Initiation and the Classification of Rituals." *Temenos* 22 (1986): 93–108.

Zumwalt, Rosemary Lévy. *The Enigma of Arnold van Gennep (1873–1957): Master of French Folklore and Hermit of Bourg-la-Reine.* Helsinki: Suomalainen Tiedeakatemia, 1988.

NICOLE BELMONT (1987)
Translated from French by Roger Norton
Revised Bibliography

GENSHIN

GENSHIN (942–1017), also known by the title Eshin Sōzu, was a Japanese Buddhist priest of the Tendai sect and patriarch of Japanese Pure Land Buddhism. Genshin was born in the village of Taima in Yamato Province (modern Nara prefecture) to a family of provincial gentry named Urabe. By his mid-teens he had entered the Tendai priesthood and had become a disciple of Ryōgen (Jie Daishi, 912–985), one of the most eminent clerics of the age. Little is known of Genshin's early career except that he presided at an important Tendai ceremony in 973 and five years later, when he was thirty-six, wrote a learned treatise on Buddhist metaphysics (*abhidharma*), the *Immyōronsho shisōi ryakuchūshaku.*

Shortly thereafter, Genshin's interests seem to have changed. In 981 he wrote a work on a Pure Land Buddhist theme, the *Amida Butsu byakugō kambō* (Contemplation upon Amida Buddha's wisdom-eye), and in 985 he completed the work for which he is chiefly known, the *Ōjōyōshū* (Essentials of Pure Land rebirth). The *Ōjōyōshū* was one of the first works on a Pure Land theme to have been composed in Japan. It signaled not only a shift in Genshin's interests but also the beginning of a transition in the history of Japanese Buddhism. In this work Genshin quotes 654 passages from some 160 Buddhist scriptures on the most important themes of Pure Land Buddhism—on the sufferings of the six paths of transmigration and especially the torments of hell, on the pleasures and advantages of Amida (Skt., Amitābha) Buddha's Pure Land, and on the way to achieve transmigratory rebirth into Amida's Pure Land, the cultivation of *nembutsu* (reflection on the Buddha). This latter subject is treated in voluminous detail. There are descriptions of methods of difficult, meditative *nembutsu* (*kannen nembutsu,* envisualizing Amida's form and meditating on his essence), of easy, invocational *nembutsu* (*shōmyō nembutsu,* calling on the name of Amida Buddha in deep devotion), of *nembutsu* for ninety-day sessions, and of *nembutsu* for the hour of death. The faith that should accompany *nembutsu* and abundant confirmation of its efficacy and merits are set out as well. Throughout the work, Genshin repeatedly deplores the sufferings of this world and urges his readers, whether they be rich or poor, laity or clergy, to seek emancipation through reliance on the compassion of Amida Buddha. The *Ōjōyōshū* became one of the most popular works on a Buddhist theme in the history of Japanese literature.

In the year following the completion of the *Ōjōyōshū,* Genshin and other Pure Land devotees, both clergy and laymen, formed a devotional society called the Nujugo Zammai-e (Nembutsu Samadhi Society of Twenty-five). Genshin's *Ōjōyōshū* no doubt served as an inspiration and guide to the devotional exercises of this society.

In Genshin's life and works can be seen the beginning of a shift in Japan from elite, monastic Buddhism to popular, devotional Buddhism. The *Ōjōyōshū* itself is an attempt to reconcile these two types of faith. It teaches, for example, that meditative *nembutsu* is the highest form of spiritual cultivation, because it can bring about enlightenment in the present life, but that simple invocational *nembutsu* is excellent also, especially for laypeople and sinners, because it can result in rebirth in the next life into Amida Buddha's Pure Land and eventual enlightenment there. Thus Genshin's major significance lies in his contribution to the growth of a Pure Land movement in Japan.

For the common people, he vividly depicted the Pure Land Buddhist worldview of painful transmigration in this world versus the bliss of Amida's Western Pure Land, instilling a fear of the former and deep longing for the latter. To the intelligentsia and clergy, he introduced the vast literature of continental Pure Land Buddhism and an elaborate structure of Pure Land, especially *nembutsu,* theory and practice. For all Japanese, he offered the possibility of salvation based only on sincere devotion and simple *nembutsu* practice. Genshin's teachings were a major inspiration for Hōnen (1133–1212), founder of the Jōdoshū sect of Japanese Buddhism, and Genshin is considered one of the seven patriarchs of the Jodō Shinshū sect.

SEE ALSO Buddhism, article on Buddhism in Japan; Nianfo.

BIBLIOGRAPHY

Major works of Genshin, in addition to the *Ōjōyōshū,* include the *Ichijō yōketsu* (Essentials of the one vehicle) and *Kanjin ryakuyōshū* (Essentials of esoteric contemplation). For his complete works, see *Eshin Sōzu zenshū,* 5 vols. (Sakamoto, Japan, 1927–1928).

Works on Genshin in English are few. My study *The Teachings Essential for Rebirth: A Study of Genshin's Ōjōyōshū* (Tokyo, 1973) gives an outline of the development of Pure Land thought up to Genshin and an analysis of the *nembutsu* theory and practice of the *Ōjōyōshū.* In Japanese, Ishida Mizumaro's *Kanashiki mono no sukui: Ōjōyōshū* (Tokyo, 1967) summarizes Genshin's life and the Pure Land teachings of the *Ōjōyōshū.* Ishida has also edited the *Ōjōyōshū* and translated it into modern Japanese in his *Ōjōyōshū: Nihon Jōdokyō no yoake,* 2 vols. (Tokyo, 1963–1964).

ALLAN A. ANDREWS (1987)

GEOGRAPHY.

A deeply rooted aspect of human behavior, the ordering of space is an activity that consists of establishing differences between places in terms of varied functions and degrees of meaning. Among peoples of diverse religious traditions, the most significant places are identified with special spiritual presences, qualities that set certain locales apart from ordinary, profane space. Charged with supernatural power, sacred places function as fixed points of reference and positions of orientation in the surrounding world. With the passage of time, sacred places become invested with accumulations of mythical and historical meanings in complex layers of cultural memory. When joined by paths, processional ways, or great routes of pilgrimage, sacred places form networks that may embrace local village or tribal lands, large nations, or vast regions of the globe occupied by major civilizations. These networks form sacred geographies—webs of religious meaning imposed upon the land—where natural features and human-made symbols establish communication between the earthly and the spiritual, embodying collective values and shared norms of conduct. Sacred geographies form a unifying ground, a lasting source of remembrance and renewal for the most important aspects of individual and communal life in many cultural traditions.

The creation of sacred geographies is behavior partly anterior to the development of culture, for it stems from the marking, exploitation, and defense of territories that join humankind to the larger animal kingdom. But the articulation of landscapes with symbolic imagery and the way in which such landscapes are made to reflect layers of mythology and history also correspond to patterns of thought and complex ways of recording meaningful events that seem peculiar to humankind. The widely different ways in which sacred geographies have been organized show how humans have sought to grasp the perceived world and how they have explained their place within the cosmic schema. An examination of sacred geographies thus points to patterns of environmental cognition and ordering and to the wide range of spatial definitions that have evolved in response to different cultural needs, historical circumstances, and ecological possibilities.

This article focuses on four examples of sacred geography. They correspond to the symbolic landscapes of peoples of strikingly different social and cultural complexities who inhabit regions of varied ecologies. The first example is from the Australian Aborigines, whose gathering and hunting life in an austere desert environment was connected to systems of sacred places embedded within nature and unmarked by monumental art or architecture. These places, arranged in certain patterns within tribal territories, were thought to have been established by ancestral heroes in the Dreaming—the time of first creation. The second example is from the Maya Indian community of Zinacantan in southern Mexico, a farming people whose culture stems from an ancient native heritage. These Indians have evolved a pattern of centralization in their sacred geography that echoes similar structures among other peoples of sedentary farming life. The third example is from imperial China, where ancient beliefs concerning the worship of earth, water, and sky were expressed at great mountain shrines and in the sacred precincts of the imperial capital. In China is found the creation of a sacred geography closely tied to the concerns of a powerfully centralized state. The last example touches upon the sacred geography of medieval Europe. Though politically disunited, the peoples of Europe followed routes of pilgrimage to the periphery of Christendom and held Jerusalem, the Sacred City, to be the center of their world.

Aboriginal Australia. The Australian Aborigines are counted among the oldest human races. Their ancestors migrated from Southeast Asia perhaps thirty thousand years ago, when land bridges between New Guinea and Australia were almost certainly exposed. Throughout the millennia the Aborigines pursued an austere gathering and hunting life that was admirably adapted to their barren habitat. The Neolithic agricultural revolution never reached these isolated lands, where nomadic bands traveled within well-defined tribal territories, following seasonal rhythms in the unending search for food. But the inhabitants did not perceive the natural environment in economic terms alone; it was also seen as a storehouse of memory, replete with supernatural meanings. The flat, seemingly featureless terrain contained an invisible, magical domain in which hills, rocks, water holes, and groves were charged with sacred powers and mythical associations. Though apparently obeying the randomness of nature, such features were seen as well in terms of a specific order; people expressed their connection to them through pictographs, rock alignments, wooden sculptures, caches for totemic objects, and ceremonial places designed according to prescribed rules of organization.

The sacred sites of the Aborigines marked places where events in the Dreaming took place. This concept, which is central to Aboriginal cosmogony, concerns a time when heroes and heroines wandered over a land where there were no hills, water holes, or living things. The paths and camping places of these heroes are sacred places described in myths. The ancestral heroes also brought fire to the people as well as the laws by which people live; many such heroes eventually transformed themselves into trees, boulders, and other natural features, thus creating the landscape that exists at present. A symbolic order that related to the time of origins and the travels of creators, rather than the cardinal directions, was called into being. In these austere settings, no sharp divisions were made between animals, plants, inanimate objects, and humankind. The ancestral heroes were not distant entities but integral components of the land, and they were made part of the experience of daily life through religious reenactments of events of the Dreaming. Joined by a network of sacred places, the land itself became symbolic, affirming a coherence of the physical and mythological domains. Among the Aborigines, sacred geography was the source of authority as well as the source of tribal identity. The latter was based on a title to the land that went back to the time of first creation.

Zinacantan. Conquest, colonialism, and the advances of industrial civilization have often spelled destruction or major alteration for traditional religions. In North America, forcible removal of Indian populations from old homelands frequently meant social disintegration for those whose religious sense of belonging to a specific landscape had been destroyed. But colonial cultures have also often produced a range of creative adaptations, as subjected peoples evolved syncretistic religions in which ancient sacred geographies continued to play traditional functions. Latin America, among Indian communities in former Spanish possessions from the Rio Grande Valley in New Mexico to the Bolivian Andes of South America, is especially rich in such instances.

Among many examples that could be discussed, the community of Zinacantan in the high, forested mountain country of Chiapas, southern Mexico, is particularly well documented. The inhabitants are a Maya people, ultimately descended from those who built city-states in southern Mexico, Guatemala, and the Yucatán Peninsula during the first centuries CE. Today, these farming people live in hamlets dispersed throughout the hills, around a civic and religious center that consists of a church, school, and administrative buildings.

The visible sacred geography of Zinacantan incorporates mountains, caves, water holes, and human-made crosses erected at shrine sites at determined locations around the civic and religious center. Mountains have important economic meaning in the life of Zinacantan, but certain peaks are also considered to be homes of ancestral deities who live within. These ancestors control the mists and vapors that rise to form rain clouds on the peaks; they are able to direct the rain clouds over the community. Crosses, placed on pathways around the mountains surrounding the Zinacantan center, were borrowed by the Indians from the symbolic forms of Spanish Christianity. But the crosses are not seen in Christian terms; they are perceived as spiritual openings for communication with ancestral beings. Cave shrines are also places for communication with Yahval Balamil, the earth lord, who dwells beneath the surface of the land; he may also be reached through prayers in caves, at sinkholes, and at springs throughout the Zinacantan domain. Sacrificial offerings are regularly made, especially at the sites of cross shrines. They are most often performed by people walking on ceremonial circuits around the whole community. Shamans are the main ritualists, performing prayers and making offerings on behalf of patients. Processions of other worshipers may also follow ceremonial circuits, usually moving in counterclockwise direction. The village church and its Christian images are also frequently included in the processional itineraries. The circuits around Zinacantan are a way of establishing boundaries, a way of saying "This is our sacred center, through which the holy river flows and around which our ancestral gods are watching over us." Circuits are replicated on many levels around individual fields, houses, or other objects, symbolically establishing property rights as well as marking social spaces in the Zinacantan world. The community and land at Zinacantan are infused with the sense of being whole and sacred; sacred geography places the living community in an intimate religious bond with its natural setting and with the ancestors and gods that dwell within that setting.

Imperial China. The sacred geographies of tribes or small agrarian communities are usually encompassed by paths or roadways within relatively restricted zones. But the development of ancient empires embracing vast regions and diverse populations posed different problems of spatial symbolism. For rulers, the problem was to create symbolic orders that might tend to unify such disparate domains and polities. Great ritual centers were designed to communicate the religious and political concerns of state organizations. The symbolic structure of such places expressed the idea of a sacred geography in microcosm, through the use of monumental art and architecture.

In China, where continuity of religious themes has been maintained over millennia, imperial ritual was especially focused on two outstanding places. The first was a sacred mountain, Tai Shan, the central and most important of five sacred mountains associated with the cardinal directions and center. The worship of mountains has an ancient history in China, attested by early texts that describe peaks and the appropriate rites to be celebrated there. Some were local shrines affecting small areas, but others were majestic sovereigns that extended their influence over immense regions. These old beliefs surrounded Tai Shan, and the sacred place gradually was invested with imperial monuments throughout the centuries. In effect, the mountain became a symbol of the cosmos and the state. The mountain was given royal title during the Tang dynasty in 725, inaugurating a practice followed by successive emperors. These honorific names underlined the conception of the mountain as a producer of life forces. It was identified with rain clouds and fertility and figured as an object of worship in spring rites of planting and at the fall harvest season. It was also seen as a symbol of stability and permanence and as a preventer of droughts, floods, and earthquakes. Indeed, it was a divinity with a sacred force that could be touched by prayers and sacrifice.

Just as the mountain was a symbol of order in the natural environment, so did the emperor personify the social and moral order. A close relationship developed between ruler and mountain, for the emperor was the pivot between society and nature. But both the emperor and the mountain were subordinate to Heaven, for it was through the mandate of Heaven that all harmony and validation derived. These relationships were spelled out in the elaborate system of monuments with which Tai Shan was equipped. At the summit, an open circular platform was constructed for the Feng sacrifices, which consisted of burnt offerings to the heavens. Below, toward the base of the mountain, a polygonal open altar was constructed for the Shan sacrifices in honor of the earth. Between these key altars were a host of subsidiary temples dedicated to lesser nature divinities, ancestral heroes, and various miraculous saints and hermits. There were also commemorative monuments to various emperors, a school, a library, a Confucian temple, and many other sacred places scattered among the crags and groves. The whole site was simultaneously a symbol of the land, the empire, and the cosmos—a great unifying topographic icon.

The symbolic order that governed Tai Shan also informed the cosmic imagery of ritual centers within the imperial capital. In Beijing, sacred enclosures featured open platform altars to the sky and earth, with subordinate temples to the sun, moon, and agriculture, each with its own complement of satellite monuments, altars, and secondary buildings. The Chinese love of order, hierarchy, and classification governed the orientation and symbolic ornament of the temples, with their gleaming white marble and carved imagery of mountains, clouds, water, and earthly or celestial dragons. These cosmic figures expressed the notion of a sacred geography in abstract form, becoming universal symbols. The magnificent altars, with their surrounding concourses and processional paths, formed the setting for imperial rites where the emperor offered sacrificial covenants to heaven and earth. The sacrifices expressed a complementary relationship to one another. The mysterious, limitless heights of heaven and the regular movements of the celestial bodies symbolized Heaven's regulative power to keep the universe in stable order and to produce the proper succession of seasons. This power was especially important to an agricultural people, and through sacrificial acts the emperors expressed the harmony of a well-ordered society within the universal schema.

Medieval Europe. The sacred geographies of the Far East and among the Indian peoples of the Americas tend to express a correspondence between humanity and nature and to be arranged in patterns of centralization. By contrast, the sacred geography of medieval Europe did not focus on a single European capital but was cast instead as a vast network that ran through many lands, leading to pilgrimage cities at the extremities of Christendom. From central and southern France, pilgrimage routes ran south over the Pyrenees, converging on a road that led across northern Spain to Santiago de Compostela, the tomb of the apostle James. Another route threaded down the Italian Peninsula to Rome. There, amid the ruins of antiquity, the pilgrim might meditate upon the early saints and martyrs and visit the old Lateran—the Mother Church and seat of the earthly Vicar of Christ. But the most perilous of routes led farther south to the port of

Brindisi, and from there by ship across the Mediterranean, to the most distant, mysterious, and sacred of all goals, the city of Jerusalem.

The physical realities of this complex geography were translated in terms of a mythological hierarchy on thirteenth-century maps. These charts reveal a vision in which the horizontal surface of the earth was shown as a flat disc, with Jerusalem, the Holy City, marked clearly at the center. The outline of the Mediterranean Basin was summarily drawn, as were the features of Europe. Peripheral and unknown regions were shown to be the realms of bizarre or fabled races, sometimes held at bay behind great walled enclosures. On a vertical axis above Jerusalem, the Savior presided over the celestial sphere, while ferocious demons patrolled the infernal regions below. Such imagery was not primarily meant to illustrate an actual, material geography but rather a spiritual landscape whose central earthly icon, Jerusalem, could be interpreted on different levels. It was the Holy City of Palestine, the goal of pilgrims and crusaders; a symbol of the church; a metaphor for the Christian soul; and an analogy for the heavenly Jerusalem, the final Promised Land.

Such patterns were repeated in microcosm throughout Christendom in the art and architecture of cathedrals. In France, where these buildings reached their highest expression, sculpture, architecture, and stained glass formed a symbolic code to show the order of nature, to represent an abstract of history, and to summarize spiritual values. Within the soaring naves of the great cathedrals, at once mysterious and secure against the outside world, the assembled congregation saw the mirror of creation. Yet, like the maps, these buildings represented an essentially interior world, expressing the aims and aspirations of the innermost consciousness of the community. Such sacred places, joined in the larger network of routes to distant centers of faith, formed a sacred geography of a tradition that denied the physical world to emphasize instead theological, conceptual, and belief-oriented values that urged people to rise up, away from the earth, above animals, plants, and inanimate objects, toward a transcendent God.

CONCLUSION. This article summarizes the structure of four sacred geographies in societies that range from the level of tribal bands to complex civilizations. In all cases, sacred geographies have the functions of creating a sense of place and of creating a certain order in the world. Through the use of symbols, networks of meaning are imposed upon the land; such spatial orders clarify the difference between places by illustrating what is thought to be significant in the perceived world. These symbols may be natural features, such as mountains, lakes, or rivers; they may be pictographs or markings; or they may be elaborate works of art and architecture accompanied by writing. In the context of a landscape, such symbolic systems communicate the difference between sacred and profane space and answer the universal theme of establishing connections between a population and a time and place of origin.

Beyond such essential functions, sacred geographies are as varied as religions. These differences are the result of specific cultural and historical factors as well as geographical conditions. The circumstances of a wandering life in an isolated region; the need to form or unify a state organization; the pattern of an early chain of missions or military conquests; the lasting prestige and sacred quality of an ancient civic and religious center—these and countless other factors may determine how sacred geographies are shaped. By incorporating the imagery of history and related information, sacred geographies make visible a cultural or ethnic domain and signal territorial possession.

The study of sacred geography is especially important in understanding the processes of cultural history, particularly among peoples whose traditions are not documented in writing or whose traditions may be recorded in partly deciphered hieroglyphic texts and figural imagery. In Africa, Oceania, and the Americas, where the native spiritual and intellectual heritage was largely transmitted orally, major archaeological sites must be decoded without textual sources, and early European reports of contact are colored by an Indo-European outlook. Among these peoples, the broad patterns of sacred geography provide indispensable insight on the role of religious thought and symbolism in the evolution of civilization.

SEE ALSO Center of the World; Cosmology; Deserts; Gardens; Jerusalem; Lakes; Mountains; Oceans; Rivers; Sacred Space.

BIBLIOGRAPHY

Bastien, Joseph W. *Mountain of the Condor.* Saint Paul, 1978.

Berndt, Ronald M., and E. S. Phillips, eds. *The Australian Aboriginal Heritage.* Sydney, 1973.

Campbell, Tony. *Early Maps.* New York, 1981.

Chavannes, Édouard. *Le Tai Chan: Essai de monographie d'un culte chinois.* Paris, 1910.

Combaz, Gisbert. *Les temples impériaux de la Chine.* Brussels, 1912.

Harrington, John Peabody. *The Ethnogeography of the Tewa Indians.* Twenty-ninth Annual Report of the Bureau of American Ethnology, 1907–1908. Washington, D.C., 1908.

Hiatt, L. R. "Local Organization among the Australian Aborigines." *Oceania* 32 (June 1962): 267–286.

Hiatt, L. R. "Ownership and Use of Land among the Australian Aborigines." In *Man the Hunter,* edited by Richard B. Lee and Irven DeVore, pp. 99–102. Chicago, 1968.

Sirén, Osvald. *The Imperial Palaces of Peking.* 3 vols. Paris, 1926.

Stanner, William E. H. "Aboriginal Territorial Organization: Estate, Range, Domain and Regime." *Oceania* 36 (September 1965): 1–26.

Townsend, Richard F. "Pyramid and Sacred Mountain." In *Ethnoastronomy and Archaeoastronomy in the American Tropics,* edited by Anthony F. Aveni and Gary Urton, pp. 37–62. New York, 1982.

Turner, Victor, and Edith Turner. *Image and Pilgrimage in Christian Culture.* New York, 1978.

Vogt, Evon Z. *Zinacantan: A Maya Community in the Highlands of Chiapas.* Cambridge, Mass., 1969.

Wheatley, Paul. *The Pivot of the Four Quarters: A Preliminary Enquiry into the Origins and Character of the Ancient Chinese City.* Chicago, 1971.

New Sources

Gartner, William G. "Archaeoastronomy as a Sacred Geography." *Wisconsin Archaeologist* 77, no. 3–4 (1996): 128–150.

MacDonald, Mary N. *Experiences of Place.* Cambridge, Massachusetts, 2003.

Park, Chris C. *Sacred Worlds: An Introduction to Geography and Religion.* London; New York, 1994.

Richer, Jean. *Sacred Geography of the Ancient Greeks: Astrological Symbolism in Art, Architecture, and Landscape.* Albany, 1994.

Scott, Jamie S., and Paul Simpson-Housley. *Sacred Places and Profane Spaces: Essays in the Geographics of Judaism, Christianity, and Islam.* New York, 1991.

Scott, Jamie S., and Paul Simpson-Housley. *Mapping the Sacred: Religion, Geography and Postcolonial Literatures.* Amsterdam; Atlanta, GA, 2001.

Stoddard, Robert H., and E. Alan Morinis. *Sacred Places and Profane Spaces: The Geography of Pilgrimages.* Baton Rouge, 1997.

RICHARD F. TOWNSEND (1987)
Revised Bibliography

GEOMANCY is a form of divination based on the interpretation of figures or patterns drawn on the ground or other flat surface by means of sand or similar granular materials. The term is also used for the interpretation of geographic features. Among the Chinese, in particular, this practice of geomancy is rooted in traditional philosophic conceptions of the relationship that exists between human beings and the vital forces of their environment and the need to achieve a harmonious balance between the two to ensure well-being.

The Western form of geomancy, widespread in the Arab world, was also of importance in medieval Europe, where it was closely linked with alchemy and astrology. Geomancy of this kind is likely to have originated in the ancient Near East and may also have been developed further by Greek mathematical speculations. In the eighth and ninth centuries, during the period of Arab cultural florescence and expansion, it became systematized and was then widely distributed from its center to Byzantium and across North Africa and into Spain. From Spain it was also probably spread along a second route into Christian Europe. From Egypt and North Africa, geomancy was carried south with Islam and then even beyond, so that it is now found both in West Africa (for example, among the Yoruba of Nigeria) and in East Africa, including Madagascar.

The Arab system called *ram'l* ("sand") is based on complex mathematical calculations and involves conceptions of an orderly universe. Its numerical order provides the underlying framework for all other Western systems of geomancy. The fundamental common feature of geomancy is a pattern of binary oppositions of markings grouped into sixteen combinations of four positions. In both the Arab system and that of medieval Europe (*ars punctatoria*), points or lines were drawn on sand in a pattern based on chance. In the Yoruba system (Ifa), which has been particularly well described, markings are based on the casting of palm kernels or cowrie shells according to prescribed procedures. For each of the resulting figures, from among a total of 256 possible combinations and permutations there is a set of verses that the diviner (*babalawo*) will have memorized to interpret the pattern and to apply to the case at hand. In general, the aim of this practice is not to divine future events but to discover the supernatural causes of present situations and their remedies.

In the European system the sixteen figures are related to astronomical signs of the planets and the zodiac; the scheme also includes four elements and four qualities. Although various authors have offered divergent interpretations of this system, its basic structure is remarkably constant and has been integrated into different philosophical conceptions with striking flexibility.

The system of medieval European geomancy appears to have had a brief revival in the occultism of the nineteenth century. The African systems are still viable, and forms of the Yoruba practice, in particular, have even been discovered in the Americas, notably in Cuba and Brazil.

Less complex systems of geomancy, apparently unrelated to those of the West, are to be found in Tibet in the form of "stone divination" and "pebble divination." These systems each have their own sets of rules, recorded in manuals. They are quite distinct from those discussed above.

The term *geomancy* is also used to refer to *feng-shui* ("winds and waters"), the traditional Chinese technique for determining propitious locations for towns, dwellings, and tombs. This system, which is still in very widespread use, concerns the distribution over the earth, by winds and water currents, of various terrestrial and atmospheric emanations that are believed to exert important influences on people. In addition to being a system of calculations for establishing favorable sites, geomancy is also a method for discerning the causes of human illness and suffering. Geomancers may claim that these causes lie in the negative influences on people of badly placed residences or of the unfortunate positioning of the tombs of ancestors, who consequently send illness and misfortune to their descendants as expressions of anger. Moreover, a given dwelling or tomb, which was originally well placed, may, in time, have its geomantic position shifted as a result of changes in the area, such as new constructions that produce an alteration in the balance of positive and negative currents. A geomancer will not only divine such causes but will also seek to remedy the situation by recommending reburial at a better spot, changing the position of a tomb, or urging the building of a wall or other structure to modify the direction of the currents. Because of the belief that illness may be due to such influences, geomancers must be included in any list of traditional Chinese diagnosticians and medical practitioners.

See Also Divination.

Bibliography

Bascom, William R. *Ifa Divination.* Bloomington, Ind., 1969.

Bascom, William R. *Sixteen Cowries: Yoruba Divination from Africa to the New World.* Bloomington, Ind., 1980.

Caslant, Eugène. *Traité élémentaire de géomancie.* Paris, 1935.

Ekvall, Robert B. *Religious Observances in Tibet.* Chicago, 1964.

Granet, Marcel. *The Religion of the Chinese People.* Translated by Maurice Freedman. New York, 1975.

Jaulin, Robert. *La géomancie: Analyse formelle.* Paris, 1966.

New Sources

Ambelain, Robert. *La géomancie arabe et ses miroirs divinatoires.* Portes de l'étrange. Paris, 1984.

Asim, Ina. *Religiöse Landverträge aus der Song-Zeit.* Heidelberg, 1993.

Canova, Giovanni. *Scienza e Islam: atti della Giornata di studio.* Rome and Venice, 1999.

Erika Bourguignon (1987)
Revised Bibliography

GEOMETRY. During the last two millennia BCE, the period that produced most religious texts, geometry (lit., "earth measurement," from Greek *gaia, ge,* "the earth," and *metrein,* "to measure") was essentially a "geometrical algebra" with a focus on number. Problematic allusions to number and space, which abound in sacred texts, are presumably inspired by this early mathematical protoscience. During the much later development of Christianity and Islam, Euclidean geometry—based, so it seemed, on irrefutable deductive logic built from definitions, postulates, and theorems—became the rational paradigm for all sciences, including theology. The discovery of other geometries in the last two centuries has brought the realization that Euclidean geometry is merely a special case within a wider realm. Efforts to rid mathematics of its logical paradoxes have taught that perfect consistency and certainty are unattainable in rational thought. These developments, together with a new awareness of the complexity of physical space and a better understanding of how culture shapes perceptions, have dramatically altered philosophical dogmatism, making ancient and Eastern modes of thought more congenial to the modern West and contributing to the problems of contemporary religion.

Neolithic Cultures (6000–3500 BCE). In southeastern Europe and the Near East, Neolithic peoples decorated the surfaces of cult objects with geometric motifs—circles, ovals, parallel lines, chevrons, triangles, squares, meanders, and spirals. These abstract designs came to abound in the folk arts of most of the cultures of the globe, seemingly irrespective

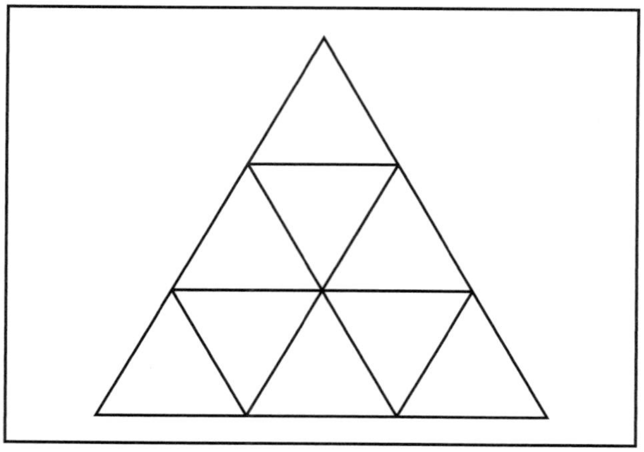

Figure 1. *Geometric Symmetry.* Simple design sequences, such as appear on Neolithic pottery, weaving, and basketry, suggest applied knowledge of propositions in geometry and arithmetic.

of time, of the degree of civilization attained, or of concomitant skill in the realistic depiction of natural objects such as animals, human faces, leaves, and landscapes. Creation myths inherited from Mesopotamia and Egypt of the third and second millennia BCE and later from Palestine, China, and Greece, as well as those recorded in modern times in the Americas, Africa, and Oceania show that the act of divine creation is universally conceived as an ordering, a shaping and selection that brings a world, a cosmos, into being. During the Neolithic period, the abstract geometrical motifs that ornament dress, vessels, walls, and other artifacts found in the earliest shrines and villages were expressions of an intuitive identification of order with the sacred and a consequent mobilization of aesthetic feeling in control of design.

In *A History of Mathematics* (1968), Carl B. Boyer observes that pottery, weaving, and basketry, from the time of their Neolithic origins, "show instances of congruences and symmetry, which are in essence parts of elementary geometry." To Boyer, "simple sequences in design"—such as translations, rotations, and reflections (see figure 1)—"suggest a sort of applied group theory, as well as propositions in geometry and arithmetic." Formal propositions did not appear, however, until the Greeks initiated them in the fifth and fourth centuries BCE. Group theory was not developed until the last two centuries; only recently has it been extended to cover the geometric symmetries in space that were already a concern in Palestinian stoneware, for instance, as early as 10,000 BCE. The oldest mathematical texts, dating from circa 1900 to 1600 BCE, show that geometry developed historically as "the science of dimensional order," in close alliance with arithmetic and algebra, although "the 'spaciness' of space and the 'numerosity' of number are essentially different things" (Alfred North Whitehead, *An Introduction to Mathematics,* 1911).

"There is a direct correlation between complexity of weaving and sophistication of arithmetic understanding,"

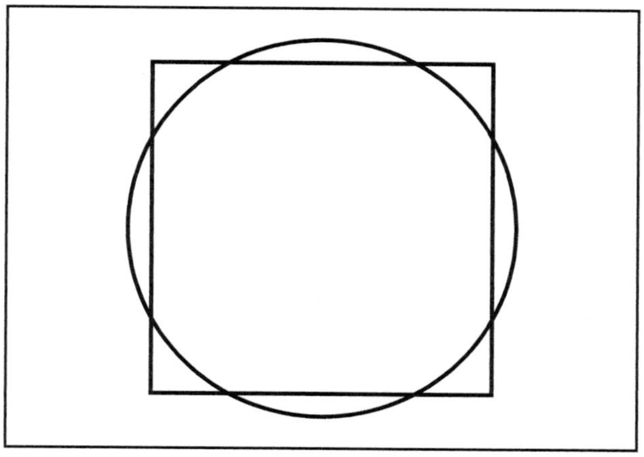

FIGURE 2. *Geometrical Algebra.* Ancient Egyptians approximated the area of a circle by a square with sides eight-ninths of its diameter. Attention is on the numerical answer.

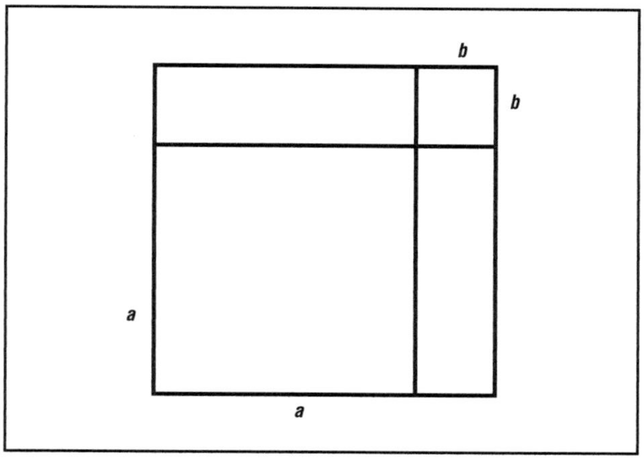

FIGURE 3. *Geometrical Algebra.* The binomial $(a + b^2) = a^2 + 2ab + b^2$ can be visualized as a problem in geometry.

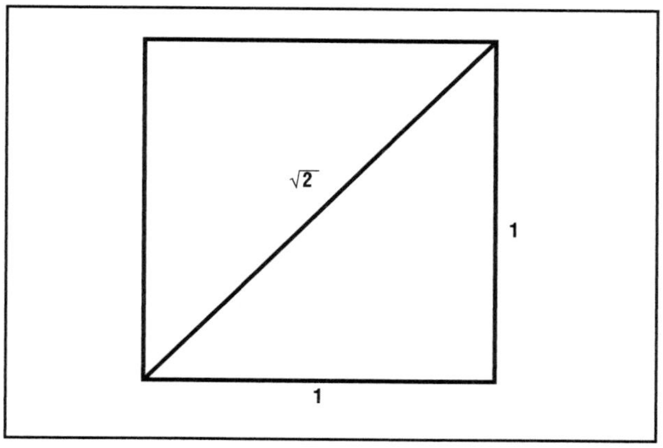

FIGURE 4. *Geometrical Algebra.* The square root of 2 can be visualized as the diagonal of a square.

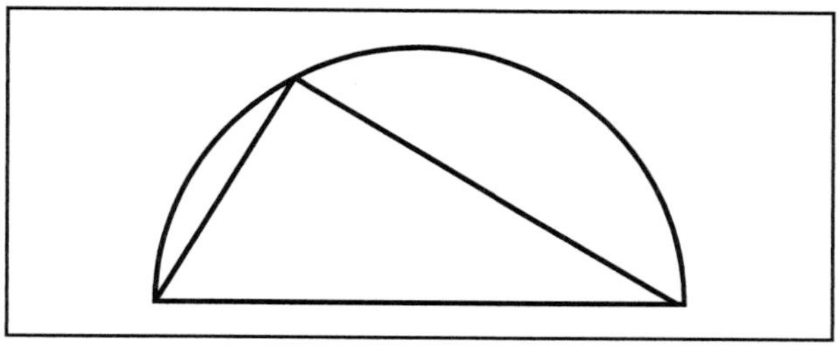

FIGURE 5. *Geometry of the Plane.* A triangle inscribed in a semicircle is a right triangle.

Walter A. Fairservis notes in *The Threshold of Civilization* (1975). In a settlement like that at Çatal Hüyük in central Turkey, occupied before 6500 BCE, the frame posts of the houses are filled in with sunbaked bricks made from molds, furnishing strong economic motivation for knowing precisely "how many bricks were necessary for each wall"; hence, "counting and notation were very much a part of the cultural scene." Far cruder artifacts—sequences of notches incised in bone, studied by Alexander Marshack (1972)—suggest "systems of lunar and other notation" that push the origins of arithmetic far back into Paleolithic times, twenty-five thousand and more years ago. Modern archaeologists and anthropologists are thus producing alternative theories to those of Herodotos (fifth century BCE), who believed geometry began in Egypt, motivated by the necessity of reestablishing boundaries after the annual Nile floods, and by Aristotle (fourth century BCE), who also assumed an origin in Egypt, but because "there the priestly caste was allowed to be at leisure."

ANCIENT EGYPT. Chief sources of knowledge of early Egyptian geometry are the Moscow Papyrus (c. 1890 BCE) and the Rhind Papyrus (c. 1650 BCE). The emphasis here is always on calculation, so that their geometry "turns out to have been mainly a branch of applied arithmetic" (Boyer, 1968). The concept of geometric similarity is applied to triangles, and there is a rudimentary trigonometry. There is a good approximation to π in the formula that computes the area of a circle by constructing a square on eight-ninths of its diameter (see figure 2). In addition, the Egyptians knew the formulas for elementary volumes and correctly calculated the volume of a truncated pyramid.

Modern scholars, however, are disappointed to find so little cause for the high estimation in which the Greeks later held Egyptian science. Respect for the organizational and engineering skills required for the building of palaces, canals, and pyramids, for example, is tempered by the realization that such civic projects entail little more then what Otto Neugebauer (1969) calls "elementary household arithmetic which no mathematician would call mathematics." Neugebauer concludes: "Ancient science was the product of a very few men; and these few happened not to be Egyptian." Of far greater interest is what was happening in Babylon.

Tetractys		Algebraic value	Arithmetic example
point	o	( )	1
line	o o	a b	2 3
plane	o o o	a^2 ab b^2	4 6 9
solid	o o o o	a^3 a^2b ab^2 b^3	8 12 18 27

FIGURE 6. *The Pythagorean Holy Tetractys.* Note the modern algebraic formula and the Pythagorean arithmetic example in smallest integers.

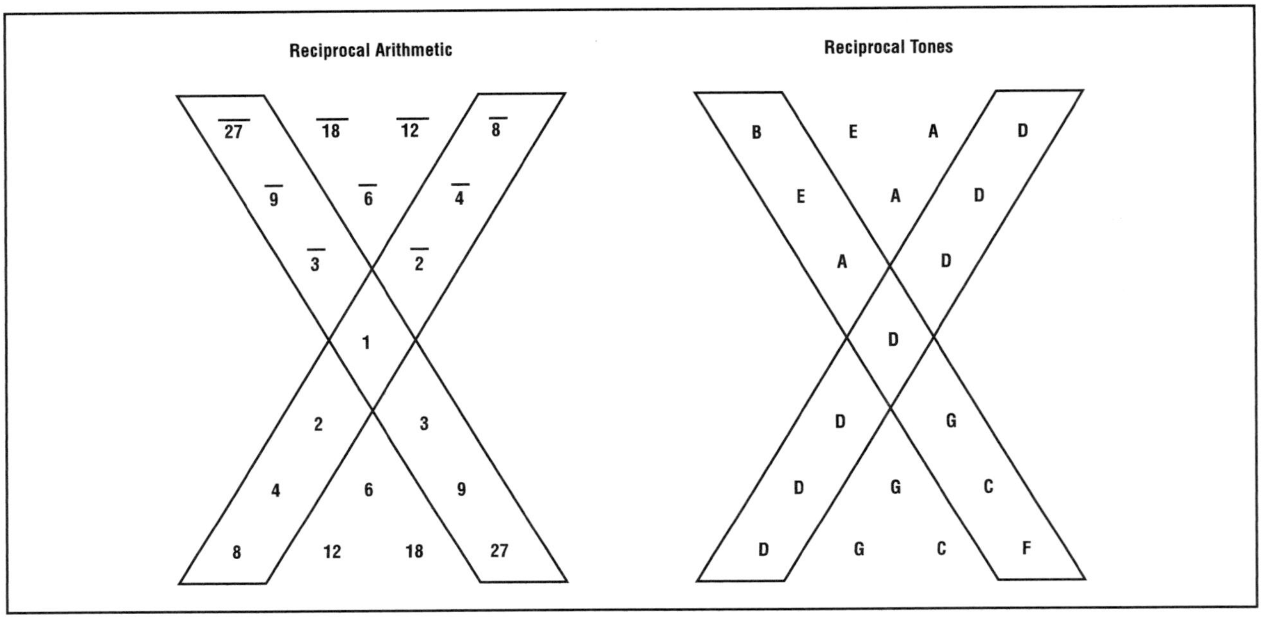

FIGURE 7. *Plato's Timaeus Cross* (X). This pattern reveals at a glance the Platonic theorem that between square numbers there is one geometric mean and between cube numbers there are two. The result is continuing geometric progression in every direction around the center. This construction is a stage in the process by which Plato develops the cubes of 2 and 3 into the model "world soul." Arithmetic doubles are known as octave equivalences to a musician and as modular identities to a mathematician.

BABYLON. Several hundred baked-clay tablets about the size of the palm of the hand, incised with neatly crowded rows of cuneiform inscriptions, provide more information about the mathematical sciences in Babylon circa 1900 to 1600 BCE than exists for any other place or time preceding the *Elements* of Euclid, circa 320 BCE. Standard tables of multiplication of reciprocals and a place value notation on base sixty facilitated computation at a level Neugebauer compares with that of Europe in the early Renaissance, more than three thousand years later.

Babylonian geometry, like that of Egypt, was still "applied algebra or arithmetic in which numbers are attached to figures" (see figure 3). The ratio between the side and diagonal of a square (i.e., the square root of two) was computed correctly to about one part in a million (see figure 4). Ratios between the areas of a pentagon, hexagon, and heptagon and those of squares built on one side were closely approximated, as was the value of π. A geometric concept of similarity is applied to circles, and perhaps also to triangles. An angle inscribed in a semicircle is known to be a right angle (see figure 5). The Pythagorean theorem (which holds that the square on the hypotenuse of a right triangle is equal to the sum of the squares on the other two sides) was understood in all its generality a thousand years before Pythagoras. One tablet, known as Plimpton 322, develops a set of fifteen "Pythagorean triplets" (three numbers defining right triangles, such as 3,4,5) in a sequence in which acute angles vary by approximately one degree. This "prototrigonometry," unsuspected until the tablet was translated, is one of the most astonishing mathematical achievements of the ancient world. It demonstrates empirical knowledge of a general formula:

Assuming integers p and q with $p > q$, and taking $p = 2$ and $q = 1$, the 3,4,5 triplet emerges as follows:

SIDE	SIDE	HYPOTENUSE
$2 pq$	$p2 - q2$	$p2 + q2$
2 (2 x 1) = 4	4 - 1 = 3	4 + 1 = 5

It was from the Babylonians, rather than from the Egyptians, that the Greeks inherited the fund of empirical insights that they transformed into an exact science. The example just cited—in which the ratio of the musical octave, 2:1, is transformed into the Pythagorean triplet 3,4,5—is the foundation of Plato's cosmogony, and it may turn out to be one of the most important clues to the numerology of the ancient world.

Greek Transformation of Egyptian and Babylonian Knowledge. Researchers are still trying to unravel the story of how the Greeks, in less than three centuries (600–300 BCE), transformed geometry—inherited essentially as an art of making arithmetical relations visible—into a science based on definitions, postulates, and theorems (and appealing therefore to an invisible *logos*). Material inherited from Egypt and Babylon through Thales (c. 585 BCE), and Pythagoras (c. 550 BCE) was riddled with confusion between exactness and approximation. A new "dialectical" spirit arose with Parmenides (c. 475 BCE) and his followers. Precise definition, always elusive, was the new goal that Socrates (d. 399 BCE) applied to moral and ethical questions by appealing to "harmonic" examples from the Pythagorean geometry of the vibrating string. Plato's affection for dialectics and his emphasis on abstraction bore unexpected fruit in Aristotle's rejection of his teacher's Pythagorean methods: "Dialectics is merely critical where philosophy claims to know" (*Metaphysics* 1004b). Aristotelian "first philosophy" developed a new syllogistic rigor in the generation after Theaetetus (c. 414–c. 369 BCE) and Eudoxus (c. 400–c. 350 BCE), who changed the method and enlarged the scope of mathematics. Another generation later, Euclid's *Elements* completed the mathematical transformation so successfully that the only traces of earlier Greek mathematics that survive must be gleaned from his work. Little else was deemed worth copying.

For current understanding of geometrical symbolism in ancient religions, the Greek transformation has almost no meaning. Although Christianity and Islam are historically young enough to have been affected by the transformation, their holy books show virtually no influence of the new Greek science. (A possible notable exception is the opening line of the *Gospel of John:* "In the beginning was the Logos.") Plato, the first author in history whose works have survived intact, made an extended commentary on the mathematical bias in his philosophy and offers the richest insight into the intentionality that inserted so many mathematical elements in ancient mythology. The musical geometry at the heart of his mathematics was common to both East and West; its simplest pragmatic formula is found in China.

Harmonic Cosmology in China and Greece. The natural, or counting, numbers (1, 2, 3, . . . , infinity) are a primordial image of order. Developed systematically into Pythagorean triplets, they lead to a prototrigonometry of the plane. Applied systematically to the geometry of a vibrating string, they link the magical realm of tone with the numbers that measure the world. To use economical modern concepts, the octave ratio 1:2 becomes the cyclic module (Plato's matrix, or "universal mother") in which the even numbers are "modular activities" (doubling and halving merely produce further "octave identities") and the odd numbers are "modular residues" (meaning that they define new pitches within the octave matrix). To build a scale, the simplest procedure is to follow the old Chinese rule of adding or subtracting one-third (from any reference pipe or string length). This is the geometrical analogue of the musical procedure of tuning by ear: A subtraction of one-third correlates with the musical interval of an ascending perfect fifth (3:2); an addition of one-third correlates with the descending perfect fourth (4:3). To avoid fractions in the arithmetic, the reference length must contain one factor of three for every "tone child" to be generated. The Chinese pentatonic (five-tone) scale must therefore be generated from 3;s4 = 81.

Tone	C	G	D	A	E
Number	81	54	72	48	64
Operation	-1/3	+1/3	-1/3	+1/3	

Rearranged into scale order, this number sequence has a reciprocal "twin" that defines frequency ratios:

Tone	C	D	E	G	A
Length ratio	81	72	64	54	48
Frequency	64	72	81	96	108

Both Chinese and Greek cosmology are projections from this tonal geometry, reducible to continued operations with the prime number 3. Note that the defining operation started on 34 = 92 = 81. Ancient China was conceived as 1/81 part of the whole world, that is, as 1/9 of one of the nine "great continents." China was also considered to be divided into nine provinces, so that each Chinese province was 1/729 of the whole world; now 36 = 93 = 729 is the base for the same tuning calculation when it is extended through seven tones for the complete diatonic scale, also standard in China in the fifth century BCE. At about the same time, Philolaus, a Greek Pythagorean philosopher, conceived the year as made up of "729 days and nights," a number that would seem to come from nowhere but such a musical cosmology. Plato linked the seven tones in this set to the sun, moon, and five planets; later, Ptolemy (second century CE) linked the scale to the zodiac.

The numbers 64 and 81, on which the alternate scale progressions commence, and the number 108, largest in the set of pentatonic frequency values, are immortalized in various ways. In China there are 64 hexagrams in the *Yi jing* divination text. The numbers 82 = 64 and 92 = 81 have been the favored squares on which to construct the Hindu fire altar since Vedic times (c. 1500 BCE). The number 108, upper limit in the set, is the number of beads in the Buddhist rosary. The tuning pattern itself has recently been discovered (but without numbers) on an Old Babylonian cuneiform tablet from circa 1800 BCE.

The set of twelve consecutive tones generated by the above procedure constitutes a chromatic scale. In ancient China each twelve tones in turn became the tonic of the standard pentatonic scale for a particular calendric period. Throughout Chinese history the bureau of standards remained wedded to a tonal geometry: The length of a pitch pipe (an end-blown hollow tube) sounding the reference tone determined the standard for both weights and volumes. Each new regime established a new reference pitch; today there is the record of dozens of succesives changes in the bureau of standards as the reference pitch oscillated over the range of about the interval of a sixth.

Unless one knows the musical procedure, the Daoist formula for the creation of the creation of the world sounds mystical: "The Dao [the Way] produced one, the one produced two, the two produced three, and three produced the ten thousand things [everything]." The creation myth related by Plato in the *Timaeus* similary develops the world's harmonical soul and body from the numbers 1,2, 3. Pythagoreans frankly announced that, to them, "All is number," and Aristotle quotes them as saying, "The world and all that is in it is determined by the number of three." Plutarch describes planetary ditances in the Philoaus system as "a geometrical progression with three as the common ratio." For eight hundred years Greek astronomers toyed with varations on this planetary motion (c. 1600 CE) while still looking for the right tones to associate with each celestial body. East and West, the "geometry" of heaven and earth was musical and profoundly trintarian while astronomy was being gestated.

The Greek view of this tonal-planetary geometry points in the direction of a more abstract mathematical system. The Pythagorean "holy tetractys" was a pebble pattern symbolizing continuing geometric progression from a point through a line and a plane to the "solid" dimension (see figure 6). Plato takes advantage of the double meanings of integers (both as whole numbers and as reciprocal fractions) to generate the material for a seven-tone scale at the cube dimension (33=27; see figure 7). Nicomachus (fl. c. 100 CE), writing an introduction to Plato, simplifies the double view of the multiplication table 2 x 3 up to the limit of 36 = 93 = 729 (see figure 8.) Stones, musical tones, planets, numbers, and geometry are all part of one vast Pythagorean synthesis, replete with symbolic cross-reference and a supporting mythology. An exasperated Aristotle mocked it; Euclid made it obsolete.

The problem of "excess and deficiency" with which a musician wrestles in adjusting the geometry of the string by ear had its arithmetical analogue in the ancient problem of making approximations between the areas of a circle and square and the volumes of a sphere and cube. Thus harmonics was a paradigm for an ethics of moderation; "nothing too much," the Greek ideal, had its counterpart in Confucian concepts of morality and behavior. Thousands of years earlier, the Egyptians had conceived the scales of Maat as the "great balance" on which the heart of the deceased was figuratively weighed to test its fitness for immortality. Thus the wisdom literature of the ancient world shows remarkable parallels between cultures.

The historical record is so fragmented, however, that interpretation of geometric symbols remains speculative. Modern studies in the neurophysiology of vision and in related psychological inferences suggest that schematic, geometric relations play decisive roles. The universal acceptance of the octave ratio 1:2 is further evidence of human psychophysical norms that could generate correspondence between cultures that were never in contact. While they can neither fully document the paths of cultural diffusion nor even claim that diffusion is necessary, researchers cannot entirely rid themselves of suspicion that there was a great deal more diffusion than can be proven.

PROBLEMS IN ANCIENT GEOMETRIC SYMBOLS. It is easy to imagine that the ancient stone circles that abound in Europe and America linked people to events in the sky—that the twenty-eight poles arranged in a circle for the lodge of the Arapaho Indians' Sun Dance, for instance, may correspond to twenty-eight lunar mansions; that the twelve sections of the Crow tribe's lodge for that ceremony may allude to the months of the year; and that other cultures possessed similar symbols of earth, sky, and calendar (Burckhardt, 1976). But many familiar symbols are more puzzling. Why, for instance, did the Pythagoreans take a five-pointed star (see figure 9) as their special symbol? Is it because each line cuts two others in "mean and extreme ratio" (meaning that the whole lines is to the longer segment as the longer is to the shorter) so that the figure symbolizes both "continuing geometric progression" (the world's "best bonds," for Plato) and a victory over the "darkness" of the irrational? Could the Hindu "drum of Śiva" (see figure 10)—with its inverted triangles and the interlocked triangles of the star-hexagon (see figure 11), prevalent in Indian and Semitic cultures—be related to the Pythagorean symbols in figures 6 and 7?

The so-called Pascal triangle (see figure 12), containing the coefficients for the expansion of the binomial (*a*+*b*)2,3,4,5,6 was known to Pingala (c. 200 BCE) as Mount Meru, the Hindu-Buddhist holy mountain. Pingala interpreted this triangle as showing the possible variations of meter built from monosyllables, disyllables, trisyllables, and so on. Could this "Mount Meru" be related to the holy mountains of other Eastern religions? Is the Pythagorean tetractys simply the Greek form of older holy mountains? Is it significant that the Sumerian symbol for mountain is a triangular pile of bricks (see figure 13), aligned in a pattern Pythagoreans found useful for numbers? Is the hourglass shape of the later Buddhist holy mountain simply a geometric variation of the "drum of Śiva"?

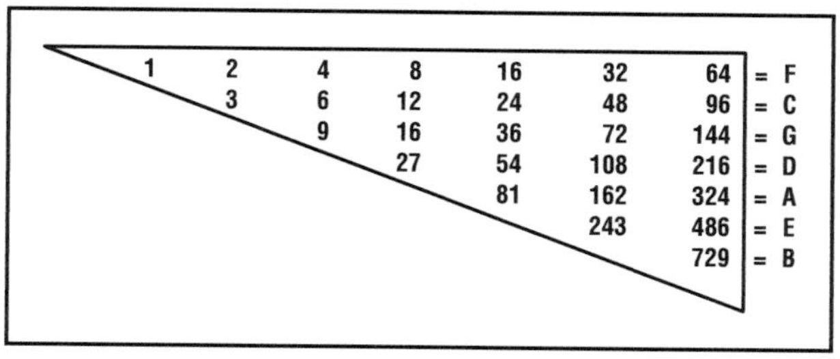
1 2 4 8 16 32 64 = F
3 6 12 24 48 96 = C
9 16 36 72 144 = G
27 54 108 216 = D
81 162 324 = A
243 486 = E
729 = B

FIGURE 8. *Nicomachus's Triangle.* Nicomachus presents Plato's reciprocal material in figure 7 in the form of a multiplication table for 2 x 3, extended to 36 = 93 = 729 to avoid fractions. Note that he describes the numbers written out from left to right rather than arranged in the form of the Greek letter chi (X) that Plato specified.

Translation of the ancient Babylonian mathematical texts now makes clear that the computational sophistication achieved four thousand years ago was so great that the sacred texts of all peoples must be studied with new alertness for evidence of rational—and not merely poetic—inspiration. The old Sumerian-Babylonian gods possessed straightforward numerical "nicknames" (used for scribal shorthand) in sexagesimal (base sixty) notation; the three great gods—Anu-An, whose numerical epithet was 60 (written as a large 1), Ea-Enki, associated with 40, and Enlil, associated with 50—are functional equivalents of Plato's 3,4,5 Pythagorean genetic triad. Could some of the ancient religious mythology turn out to be mathematical allegory?

It seems curious that the ancient Greek altar at Delphi is built on cubic dimensions, as are the chapel of the Egyptian goddess Leto that Herodotos saw in the city of Buto, the Vedic fire altar, the Holy of Holies in Solomon's temple, and the ancient Sumerian ark (first to "rescue a remnant of mankind from the flood"). The name of the most sacred Islamic shrine, the Kaʿbah at Mecca, literally means "cube," and the city of New Jerusalem in the *Book of Revelation* is also measured in such dimensions. All of these cubic consonances between various religions suggest that poetic religious imagination has had a geometrical, "protoscientific" component for a very long time.

GEOMETRY SINCE EUCLID. The thirteen books of Euclid's *Elements* culminate in a treatment of the five regular, or Platonic solids—tetrahedon, cube, octahedron, dodecahedron, and icosahedron—each with uniform sides and angles and all capable, when replicated, of closely packing three-dimensional, abstract space. Euclid mastered the transformational symmetries of these "rigid" bodies.

In the third century BCE Archimedes did important work on the area of the surface of a sphere and of a cylinder and on their respective volumes, and Apollonius carried the study of conic sections (ellipse, parabola, and hyperbola) to its highest development. Later Greek authors made further advances in geometry, but the great wave of development that had begun scarcely four hundred years earlier was spent.

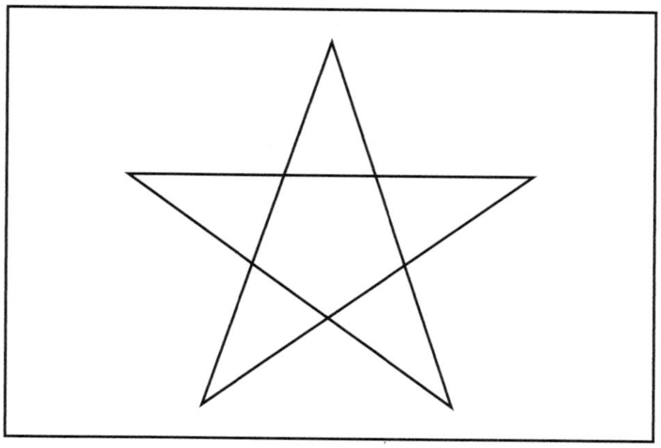

FIGURE 9. *Pythagorean Symbol.* Each line cuts two others in "mean and extreme" ratio.

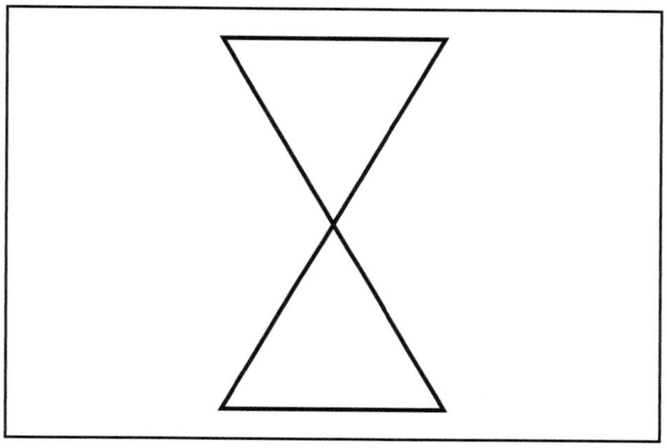

FIGURE 10. *The Drum of Śiva.* Note the hourglass shape attributed to Mount Meru, and compare with Plato's Timaeus pattern in figure 7.

Later Hindu talent has been mainly arithmetic and algebraic; theorems on the areas and diagonals of quadrilaterals in a circle were contributed by Brahmagupta (c. 628 CE). Important Arab contributions to the solution of cubic equations by the method of intersecting conics were summarized by ʿOmar Khayyam (c. 1100 CE). European development has been rapid since Kepler's time; it was Kepler who introduced the concepts of the infinitely great and the infinitely small, which Euclid had carefully excised from consideration. The invention of analytic geometry by Pierre de Fermat and René Descartes in the seventeenth century led to a new integration of geometry and algebra.

The contributions of Euclid's *Elements* to the invention and development of the physical sciences during all these centuries is inestimable. His kind of logical, geometrical argument is the basis for Archimedes' formalization of the laws

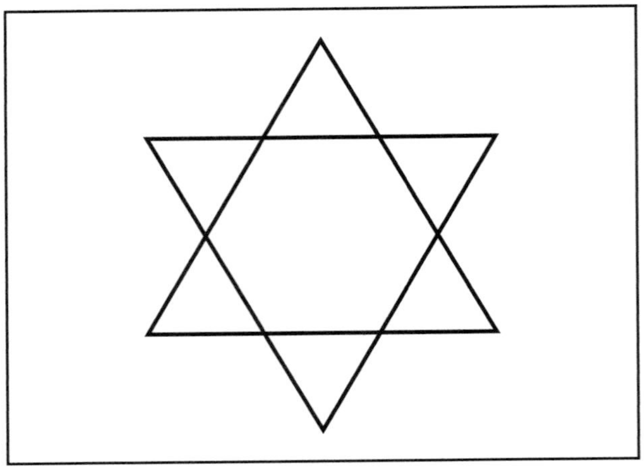

FIGURE 11. *Star Hexagon.* Indian and Semitic symbol.

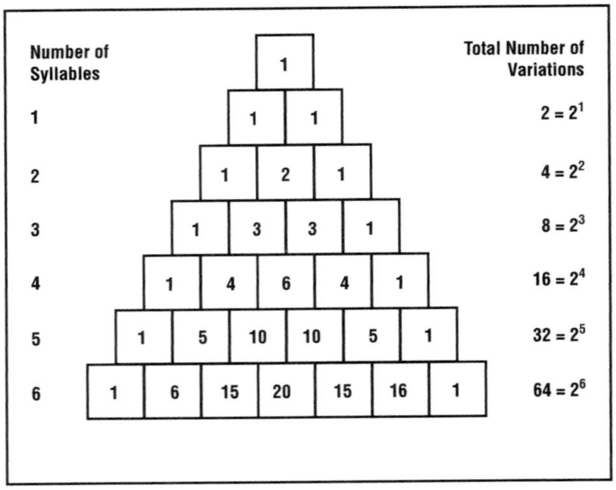

FIGURE 12. *Pascal's Triangle.* Known to Piṅgala (ca. 200 B.C.E.) as "Mount Meru," the Hindu and Buddhist holy mountain.

of the lever; for the Greek development of astronomy as a physical science (by Hipparchus, Ptolemy, and others); for Galileo's work on the dynamics of the inclined plane; for Kepler's laws of planetary motion; for Newton's laws of planetary gravitational dynamics; and for an endless host of related physical sciences. Euclidean geometry, still being improved today, has thus been one of the Western world's most powerful engines of progress. The *Elements* has been "the most influential textbook of all times" (Boyer, 1968), and it was long assumed to be as certain a guide to geometry as the Bible to absolute truth. God, it was confidently asserted, is a geometer.

During the nineteenth century, which Boyer calls the "golden age of geometry," this almost-perfected world of traditional, Euclidean-inspired mathematical physics exploded with a creative energy, leading to a crisis in the very foundations of mathematics. For example, one of the several new geometries that appeared, projective geometry, has nothing to do with measurement. Several "non-Euclidean" geometrics, by N. I. Lobachevskii, Wolfgang Bolyai, and G. F. B. Riemann, omit Euclid's famous sixth postulate concerning parallel lines, always somewhat suspect, to create equally logical geometries of even wider generality.

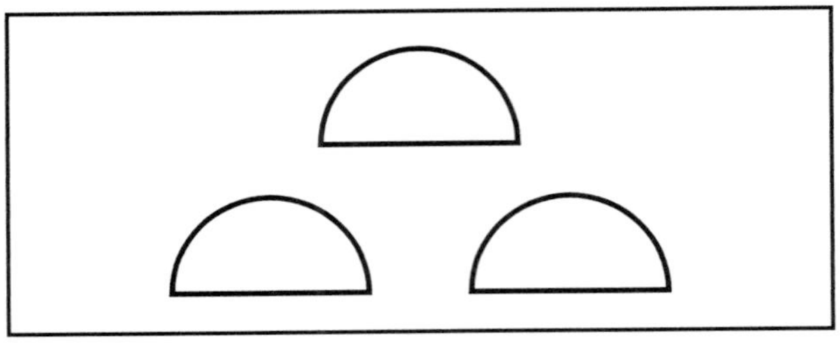

FIGURE 13. *Sumerian Symbol for a Mountain.* The triangular arrangement is the pattern that Pythagoreans found useful for numbers.

The favored status of Euclidean geometry has evaporated. There are no longer any assumptions that command universal assent, no systems of logic powerful enough to validate themselves even in mathematics. Mathematics has thus lost some of its certainty even while multiplying its powers. Einstein's notion of "space-time," with its curvatures and paradoxes, has relegated Euclidean geometry to the role of a convenient tool for certain modern intuitions within a severely limited local space. Space perception itself has been proved culturally biased; intuition can be taught new tricks. Space has also multiplied its hallowed three dimensions beyond any possibility of imagining; today the number of its dimensions is the number of independent variables in various formulas.

With the shattering of mathematical certainty and the ending of the idolatry of Euclidean rationalism, Western scientists in particular have felt a new attraction to the philosophical skepticism of Vedic poets and to Daoist and Buddhist feeling for how the world behaves. The ancient worldview was created in imagination; today imagination is still proving more powerful than logic. In the ferment of this present age, mathematics and physics are committed, perhaps more clearly than ever—but as an act of faith rather than of reason—to the primordial affection for symmetry, guided less by reason than by aesthetic feeling for elegance and beauty.

SEE ALSO Circle; Numbers; Quaternity; Sacred Space.

BIBLIOGRAPHY

For a basic textbook in Euclidean geometry and in the various non-Euclidean modern geometries, see H. S. M. Coxeter's *Introduction to Geometry* (1961; reprint, New York, 1969), notable for the elegant compression it achieves by rigorous pursuit of symmetry and of the "group" of transformations this includes. The history of geometry is set within the wider context of the whole of mathematics and the contributions of nations and individuals treated with great fairness in Carl B. Boyer's *A History of Mathematics* (New York, 1968). On the early period, Otto Neugebauer's *The Exact Sciences in Antiquity,* 2d ed. (New York, 1969), has become a classic. The transformation of Egyptian and Babylonian empirical knowledge into Greek science is studied in B. L. van der Waerden's *Science Awakening,* translated by Arnold Dresden (New York, 1963). Richard J. Gillings's *Mathematics in the Time of the Pharaohs* (Cambridge, Mass., 1972) is an effort to balance the somewhat negative views of mathematicians toward Egyptian science.

A splendidly illustrated study of Paleolithic stone and bone counting records is Alexander Marshack's *The Roots of Civilization* (New York, 1972). Neolithic symmetry in pottery and weaving designs is richly illustrated in Marija Gimbutas's *The Goddesses and Gods of Old Europe, 6500–3500 B.C.* (Berkeley, Calif., 1982). Modern concepts of symmetry are formalized, with great respect toward ancient craftsmen who explored it intuitively, in Hermann Weyl's *Symmetry* (Princeton, N.J., 1952).

Applications of traditional geometry to religious art and architecture can be found in Robert Lawlor's *Sacred Geometry: Philosophy and Practice* (New York, 1982) and Titus Burckhardt's *Art of Islam: Language and Meaning,* translated by J. Peter Hobson (London, 1976). A stone-by-stone analysis of the geometry employed by the several builders of a great cathedral is masterfully displayed in John James's *The Contractors of Chartres,* 2 vols. (Beckenham, U.K., 1980).

For a development of the tonal-geometrical symbolism hidden in ancient religious and philosophical texts, see my books *The Myth of Invariance* (New York, 1976), *The Pythagorean Plato* (Stony Brook, N.Y., 1978), and *Meditations through the Quran* (York Beach, Maine, 1981).

New Sources

Gray, Jeremy. *Ideas of Space: Euclidean, Non-Euclidean and Relativistic.* New York, 1989.

Lachterman, David Rapport. *The Ethics of Geometry: A Genealogy of Morality.* New York, 1989.

Magnani, Lorenzo. *Philosophy and Geometry: Theoretical and Historical Issues.* Boston, 2001.

Mlodinow, Leonard. *Euclid's Window: The Story of Geometry from Parallel Lines to Hyperspace.* New York, 2001.

Romano, David Gilman. *Athletics and Mathematics in Corinth: The Origins of the Greek Stadion.* Philadelphia, 1993.

Szulakowski, Urszula. *The Alchemy of Light: Geometry and Optics in Late Renaissance Alchemical Illustration.* Symbola and Emblemata Studies in Renaissance and Baroque Symbolism, vol. 10. Leiden, 2000.

Ernest G. McClain (1987)
Revised Bibliography

GERMANIC RELIGION

This entry consists of the following articles:

AN OVERVIEW
HISTORY OF STUDY

GERMANIC RELIGION: AN OVERVIEW

From the linguistic point of view, the Germanic people constitute an archaic branch of the Indo-European family. The earliest Germanic culture that archaeologists identify as such is the so-called Jastorf culture, a cultural province of northern Europe in the Early Iron Age (c. 600 BCE) covering present-day Holstein, Jutland, northeast Saxony, and western Mecklenburg. When Germanic tribes entered into written history in the works of classical authors such as Caesar and Tacitus, they had spread south towards the Rhine and the wooded hills of southern Germany, so that their closest neighbors were the Celts in Gaul. To the east their neighbors were the Balts and the Scythians and Sarmatians, Iranian tribes that roamed the plains of Russia. To the north they were in contact with the Sámi and the Finns. Although the Germanic people were primarily pastoralists, they also practiced agriculture and hunting. Their social organization was originally geared towards egalitarian communalism, but as contact with the Roman Empire changed economic conditions, a more diversified society developed in which wealth and rank tended to prevail, although nominally power still rested in the hands of the Thing, the assembly of all free men able to carry arms.

The post-Roman era saw the establishment of Germanic kingdoms in England and Scandinavia, some of which remained pagan for a surprisingly long time. The English adopted Christianity early in the seventh century, the Danes in the 960s, the Norwegians around 995 to 1000, and the Swedes not until the twelfth century. During the Viking age, pagan Scandinavian communities established themselves in Ireland, the Isle of Man, and northern and eastern England, and eventually accepted Christianity as they became assimilated. Iceland, which was settled in the late ninth century, was also a pagan Scandinavian country, although it was not a kingdom. Subject to the same missionary pressures as Norway, Iceland accepted Christianity in 999 or 1000. The pagan Scandinavian communities in Orkney, Shetland, and the Faroe Islands were converted at about the same time.

Sources. Our knowledge of Germanic religion comes from many different sources. A large number of Bronze Age rock carvings in southern Scandinavia are often referenced in descriptions of the religion's earliest phase, but these have to be interpreted with caution. For one thing, it is not certain that the creators of these carvings were Germanic. For another thing, the sets of pictures they present are particularly complex and mix many different kinds of symbols: ships, chariots, men plowing, people reveling to the sound of lurs and other musical instruments, worshipers carrying solar disks, and imprints of feet and hands. To call one figure among those the "spear god," for example, because of its larger size, and identify it as the spear-carrying Óðinn is conjectural at best. We cannot altogether dismiss the testimony of these petroglyphs, but quite possibly they are part of a kind of nature cult that cannot be fully connected with the pantheon later worshiped in the same places. Indisputably Germanic are gravesites and bog finds that provide information about funeral rites and sacrificial offerings. Monuments from the Roman period bear inscriptions with the names of Germanic deities, and classical writers refer to Germanic gods under their *interpretatio Romana.* The fourth- and fifth-century "Age of Migration" and the following period, when the Germanic kingdoms became established in western Europe, yield only meager documentation of the religion of the people who precipitated the downfall of the Roman Empire. However, place-name studies show the geographic extent of the cults of various gods, the antiquity of those cults, and the nature of a god's powers (for example, whether a god was worshiped by fishermen on the seacoast or by farmers in the interior), and the large number of runic inscriptions tell us something about pagan gods, priests, magic, and the remembrance of the dead. In literary sources such as chronicles, saints' lives, legal texts, and instructions to priests, Christian authors mention the pagan gods by name as they describe their cults and the actions taken by missionary kings and bishops and evangelizing saints against their worship. A considerable number of Scandinavian myths are transmitted in the lays of the *Poetic Edda,* some of which may date to the ninth century, but the bulk of our information about Scandinavian mythology comes from the thirteenth-century retellings and explanations compiled by Snorri Sturluson in his *Prose Edda.* The sagas describe life in pagan Iceland, Norway, and Sweden and contain numerous details on religious practices and specific forms of worship, as well as on the shift from paganism to Christianity. Like the other texts from the pens of Christian authors, the sagas have to be used with caution as a source of information on early Scandinavian belief and rites, but some of that information is certainly credible because it is confirmed by other kinds of evidence. Christian authors also copied a few charms and spells, which shed light on particular aspects of popular religion and superstition. One non-Christian source is the Arab diplomat Ibn Fadlan, who in 921 was on his way to the Bulgar court when he encountered a group of Scandinavian traders (Rūs') on the Volga. They had stopped to perform funeral rites for one of their companions who had died on the trip, and Ibn Fadlan's account of the cremation, accompanied by the drugging and killing of a woman to serve the deceased in the next world, is an amazing piece of early ethnography.

THE CREATION MYTH. In the *Prose Edda,* Snorri gives a complete description of creation that combines a number of older sources that are not always consistent with each other. The major Eddic poems used by Snorri are the *Lay of Vafþrúðnir* and and the *Lay of Grímnir,* which more or less duplicate each other, and *Vǫluspá* (Prophecy of the Seeress); but he also derives some details from sources lost to us and adds some deductions of his own. Quoting *Vǫluspá* (st. 3), Snorri stresses that at the beginning of time there was nothing but a great emptiness called Ginnungagap ("a void filled with magical forces"). According to the poem, "When Ymir lived, in earliest times, there was neither sand, nor sea, nor chill waves," whereas Snorri's prose explains, "In the beginning not anything existed; there was no sand, nor sea, nor cooling waves." Snorri's version probably reflects the older tradition, because the idea of an empty space and a world of mere potentiality preceding creation seems to belong to the ancestral heritage of the Germanic people (cf. the well-known cosmogonic hymn of the *Ṛgveda* [10.129]: "There was neither nonbeing nor being; nor was there space nor the sky above").

The first parts of the cosmos to emerge were Niflheimr ("dark world"), the sunless, misty world of death that lies in the north, and the blazing hot world of Muspell (the fire that would consume the earth) in the south. The antiquity of the association of death with the north is seen in Stone Age graves, which are oriented in this direction. Much later, the main or high seat in medieval Scandinavian houses—called *ondvegi* (way of the spirit) and supposed to be the seat of the ancestor—is located to the north. And in magical rites, water flowing northward is related to the kingdom of death. The antiquity of the concept of a fiery southern realm is seen in the occurrence of the Old High German word *muspilli* in a tenth-century Bavarian eschatological poem, where it designates the universal fire at the end of the world. In Niflheimr was a well called Hvergelmir ("resounding kettle"), from which eleven rivers flowed. According to Snorri, the showers pouring out of Niflheimr whipped up the rivers, and the spray froze, so that layer after layer of ice piled up in Ginnungagap. The sparks and glowing embers flying out of Muspell met the hoarfrost and the ice, and from the slush and heat, life emerged in the shape of an anthropomorphic being named Ymir or Aurgelmir. From this primal giant sprang the dreadful brood of the frost giants, whom he engendered by sweating out a male and a female from under his left arm. In addition, one of his legs begat a son with his other leg. Here Snorri has merged two traditions that the *Lay of Vafþrúðnir* keeps separate: in stanza 21 of the poem, Ymir is named as the giant involved in the formation of the world, but in stanzas 29–35, Vafþrúðnir, the oldest living giant, explains to Óðinn that the genealogy of the giants began with Aurgelmir, who fathered Þrúðgelmir, who fathered Bergelmir, who fathered Vafþrúðnir himself.

No direct source is available for the account of the origin of the gods that Snorri gives next: the melting rime has taken the shape of a cow, Auðumla, whose name contains the Old Norse word for "riches" and another term connected with the English dialect word *hummel* or *humble* (hornless cow), presumably designating a "rich hornless cow." This cow feeds Ymir with the milk flowing from her udders, a tradition paralleling that of the primeval cow in Indo-Iranian mythology. Auðumla gets her own food by licking the salty ice blocks, which she shapes into another primal being, Búri, who begets a son, Borr. Borr marries Bestla, the daughter of the giant Bölþorn ("evil thorn," a term still used in the Jutland dialect *[bøltorn]* to designate a "scrappy, violent person"). Borr and his wife have three sons: Óðinn, Vili, and Vé. The three divine brothers kill the giant Ymir, and the flow of blood gushing from his wounds drowns all the frost giants except Bergelmir, who escapes mysteriously with his family to continue the race. Now the three gods set about building the earth. The body of Ymir is carried into the middle of the great void; his blood forms the sea and the lakes, his flesh the earth, his skull the sky (with a dwarf at each corner, as if to hold it up), his hair the trees, his brain the clouds, his bones the mountains, and so on. Sparks flying from Muspell form the stars and heavenly bodies, and the gods order their movements, determining the divisions of time. The resulting world is circular, surrounded by a vast ocean. In the middle of the earth the gods establish Miðgarðr ("dwelling place in the middle"), a residence for mankind that is strengthened by a fence made from Ymir's eyebrows, and they provide land on the shore for the giants to settle down. The next task of the gods is the creation of man. Finally, they build Ásgarðr ("dwelling place of the Æsir"), their own residence.

A number of elements of the Eddic creation myth point to very old traditions. For example, the cow is a typical fertility symbol, and Auðumla reminds us of the celestial cow in Middle Eastern and South Asian myths. Further, in the myth of Ymir, two motifs have apparently merged: the engenderment of primeval beings and the creation of the world from parts of his body. The idea of an ancestral progenitor is already found in the classical sources about Germanic religion: Tacitus, in the second chapter of his *Germania*, tells of Tuisto, born from the earth, who begets Mannus, the common ancestor of the Germanic tribes. These names are quite revealing. *Tuisto* is related to the English word *two* and designates a bisexual being (cf. Ger. *Zwitter*). This androgynous ancestor resembles Ymir, who has other parallels in Indo-Iranian mythology, where the Old Indic *Yama* (cf. Av. *yima*, "twin") is supposed to have had incestuous relations with his twin sister. *Mannus* not only corresponds to the English word *man* but also has striking parallels in India, where Manu is the ancestor of man, and in ancient Phrygia, where the ancestor of the Phrygians is Mánes.

The three main Germanic tribes derive their names from the sons of Mannus, and in at least two cases show similar associations with deities. The Inguaeones, a tribe from the North Sea region, is linked with the minor god *Ingw[az], the male counterpart of the mother goddess. An Old English runic poem indicates that he was venerated in southern Scandinavia (indeed, the Danes are called Ingwine ["friend of Ing"] in the Old English poem *Beowulf*, lines 1044 and 1319), and his association with Freyr is illustrated by the Old Norse compound *Yngvifreyr* (Gmc. *Ingwja-fraujaz). Although little information is provided about his cult, he is undoubtedly associated with fertility, as is shown by the runic poem's reference to his wagon (cf. the sacred wagon kept in the grove of the Earth Mother, Nerthus. Yngvi is also considered the ancestor of the Yngling dynasty in Sweden. The tribe of the (H)erminones, whose territory extended from the lower Elbe southward into Bohemia, derive their name from Germanic **ermina-/*ermuna-* (mighty, lofty), a common divine epithet. (In Old Norse, Jörmunr is another name for Óðinn. In Saxon, [H]irmin is the god corresponding to Mars, and the name for the *axis mundi* is Irminsul. In Old High German, the compound *irmingot* [mighty god] occurs in the poem *Hildebrandslied*.) The tribe of the Istaevones of the Weser-Rhine area are not related to any specific deity, but their name is perhaps connected with Gothic *aistan*, meaning "honor" or "worship."

The idea of dismembering a giant to create the world is found also in Middle Eastern and other traditions. An Iranian myth preserved in Manichaeism is the closest to that of Ymir, as it equates a giant's skin with the sky, his flesh with the earth, his bones with the mountains, his hair with plants, and his blood with the sea. Here there can be no question of mutual influence, diffusion, or borrowing from a common source. Taking into consideration the Puruṣa myth in the *Ṛgveda* (10.90), which explains in a similar way the origin of the world and society through the sacrifice of primal man and the projection of his bodily parts into the macrocosm, it is clear than the Germanic creation story is a reflex of an old Indo-European myth. Bruce Lincoln (1986) has elaborated the complex data about creation in various Indo-European traditions into a coherent scenario in which the first priest, *Manu-, kills his twin brother, *Yemo-, the first king, thus performing the first sacrifice. As a result of this act the world is created, and *Manu- fashions the earth and heavens as well as the three social classes from his brother's body. The female bovine that appears in the European version of the myth originally fed and cared for the twins before the creative act. Against this background, many of the archaic elements in the Germanic tradition appear in a new and broader light.

THE GERMANIC COSMOS. After its creation, the Germanic cosmos consisted of nine worlds. Man lives in the center of the universe, and the major Germanic traditions concur in calling his dwelling place "the central abode" (Goth., *Midjungards;* OHG, *Mittilgart;* OE, *Middangeard;* ON, *Miðgarðr*). But the center is also where the gods built their residence, Ásgarðr. It is described as spacious, with numerous dwellings, surrounded by a beautiful green pasture, Iðavöllr, and by a palisade built by a giant. In addition to these places and Niflheimr and Muspell, there were also Álfheimr ("world of the [light] elves"), Svartálfheimr ("world of the dark elves"), Vanaheimr ("world of the Vanir"), Jötunheimr ("world of the giants"), and Útgarðr ("outer abode"), the dangerous world of demons, giants, and other frightening creatures.

Germanic myth evinces a real fear of this no-man's-land outside the settlement, and the idea of the frontier is there all the time, with the gods serving to ward off dangers from the wild. The islanders and the people along the shore believed that a universal ocean surrounds the earth, with an unfathomable abyss at the horizon and a huge snake curling at the edge to hold the world together. The serpent is called the Miðgarðr serpent or Jörmungandr; according to Snorri, this monstrous ophidian bit its tail—a concept that does not occur in the Eddic poems but that is quite common in Eastern religions and that was introduced in Scandinavia by medieval Christian scholarship. The symbol (similar to the *ouroboros* in Jungian psychology) may be borrowed, but the concept is old, as the name *Jörmungandr* shows. Connected with *jörmungrund* (meaning "earth" in st. 20 of the *Lay of Grímnir*), *jörmun-* (also a name of Óðinn) is an adjective meaning "great, powerful, lofty," and *gandr* means "magic wand." The compound *eormengrund* also appears in *Beowulf* (line 859).

When the gods go out into the world, it seems that the universal ocean does not exist for them, for in every direction they move on solid ground. The north and the east are particularly dangerous, being the abodes of demons, and the south will become so at the end of time, at Ragnarǫk, when the fire giant Surtr ("black," cf. English *swarthy*) will lead a host of monsters against the gods in their last battle. To the west lies the ocean. The old Germanic tradition of ship burials implies the concept of a world of the dead beyond the sea, a view perhaps borrowed from the Celts and manifested in the Irish legends about the "islands of the blessed." This concept is also reflected in the idea of a ship of death (made from the fingernails of corpses) that sails from the world of the demons at Ragnarǫk.

For the Germanic people in Norway, Útgarðr must have been represented by the high mountains and the arctic territories to the north. The road is over land; Skírnir (servant of the god Freyr) rides to Útgarðr on Freyr's horse (the *Lay of Skírnir*, st. 10), and the adventures of Þórr always take him eastward. There lie the realms of the giant Hymir, who lives at the "end of the world"; of the giants Þrymr and Hrymr (*Vǫluspá* 49); and the "iron forest" (ON, *járnviðr*), where the brood of demons is born (*Vǫluspá* 39). There is a great river at the border of Miðgarðr, with a boatman, Hárbarðr, to take people over. The frost giants live in the north, and Loki will seek refuge with them.

As has been mentioned, the world of the dead was thought to lie to the north. One concept of it was as a hall: the cold, dark, wet house of the witch Hel. In st. 43 of the *Lay of Vafþrúðnir*, the giant says that he has seen all the worlds, and Niflhel ("dark Hel") below them, which perhaps leads to Snorri's impression of it as being underground, for he says: "Helvegr liggr niðr ok norðr" ("The way to Hel lies downward and to the north"). The Old Norse term *Hel* (hiding) applies to both the place and its ruler. The belief in this underworld seems to be common to all Germanic cultures. In 915 a poet celebrating a victory of the Saxons over the Franks wonders whether there will be enough room in "hell" for all those who fell in the battle. Depite the later development of the name, Hel was not originally a place of punishment, but it was an unpleasant place to spend the afterlife. (Snorri, evidently influenced by the Christian concept of Hell, does describe Niflhel as "the lowest world where the wicked go.") An elaborate description is given in the Eddic sources: the approaches are protected by terribly noisy rivers, such as Valglaumir, Gjöll, and Sliðr, which, according to *Vǫluspá* (st. 35), "is filled with swords and knives." This picture is apparently influenced by Christian visionary literature; similar is st. 27 of the *Lay of Grímnir*, which also mentions the river Geirvimul ("swarming with spears"). There is a bridge over Gjöll, guarded by a giantess. The Greek hellhound Kerberos also has his parallel in Eddic tradition: the lay *Baldr's Dreams* (sts. 2 and 3) mentions a dog that comes out of Hel. The realm of Hel is also surrounded by a fence whose gates open only for the dead.

The sky is the abode of the gods in the later conception of the Germanic people, which transfers Ásgarðr to heaven. The changing views of Valhǫll are a typical example of the shift. Originally, it was a subterranean hall for warriors killed in combat. Later it was connected with Óðinn and became the heavenly residence of his heroic retinue. These are human warriors who die in battle and who will form Óðinn's army against the monsters at Ragnarǫk. According to Snorri, the warriors amuse themselves by fighting each other during the day and feasting every evening. (The contrast between Hel and Valhǫll was presumably meant to encourage men to fight to the death, for all other kinds of death would send the deceased to Hel.) Valhǫll is a huge palace with 540 doors so large that 800 warriors can exit through each (*Lay of Grímnir*, sts. 23–24). Over the gate and gable a wolf and an eagle are mounted, just as Charlemagne is said to have had an eagle nailed on his palace.

Like the netherworld, the sky is linked with the world by a bridge, this one guarded by the god Heimdallr; it is called Bilröst ("wavering road") or Bifröst ("shivering road"), names signifying the rainbow. In st. 29 of the *Lay of Grímnir*, the "bridge of the gods" is described as "ablaze with flames." Here the concept may represent the Milky Way, which the forces of evil from Muspell will walk at the twilight of the world, and which, in many religious systems, is described as the "path of the souls."

THE COSMIC TREE. The nine worlds are also linked by the ash tree Yggdrasill, which rises to the sky, its branches spreading over the entire world (*Vǫluspá*, st. 2). It is supported by three roots, which respectively stretch to the world of the dead (Hel), the world of the frost giants, and the world of men. At the foot of the tree are several springs: the spring of the goddess of fate, Urðr (*Vǫluspá*, st. 19) and the wells of Mímir (*Vǫluspá*, st. 28) and Hvergelmir (*Lay of Grímnir*, st. 26). Snorri tried to relate these three springs to the three roots, but it may be there was only one well, known under different names according to its symbolic functions as the source of wisdom (Mímir), of fate (Urðr), or of the rivers of the world (Hvergelmir). Yggdrasill has other characteristics and associations. For example, it is always green, and according to *Vǫluspá* (st. 19), a clear vivifying liquid called *aurr* drips down from the tree. Its branches are home to an eagle who carries between its eyes a hawk named Veðrfölnir ("faded by the weather"). A squirrel named Ratatoskr ("rat tooth") leaps up and down the tree, conveying words of abuse exchanged between the eagle and the monstrous Níðhoggr ("corpse-devourer"), one of the many snakes gnawing at the roots of the tree. Four deer gambol about the branches, eating the shoots. As well as being the location of the gods' daily council meeting, the cosmic tree is also an *axis mundi*; it props up the sky like the central pole of a tent holding up the roof. The idea of propping up the sky was part of the Germanic heritage, as is shown by the Irminsul, a Saxon "idol" destroyed by Charlemagne in 772 and described by the medieval historian Rudolf of Fulda as a huge tree trunk—*universalis columna, quasi sustinens omnia* (a universal column, as if holding up everything).

According to the contemporary testimony of Adam of Bremen in his history of the bishops of Hamburg, Yggdrasill was represented near the temple in Uppsala by a gigantic evergreen tree. What kind of tree is it? "Nobody knows," says Adam. *Vǫluspá* describes it as an ash, which definitely reflects the western Scandinavian tradition, but scholars have assumed that in eastern Scandinavia it could have been a yew. The yew was venerated in Gaul, and classical writers mention its importance in Germania as well. The name Yggdrasill itself is ambiguous. The second element, *drasill*, is a poetic word for "horse," but the first element might be either *Yggr*, a name for Óðinn (i.e., "Óðinn's horse"), or the adjective *yggr* ("frightening"). In either case, the dreadful mount appears to represent the gallows, thus implying a connection with Óðinn, who was known as "the god of the hanged." The identification of *ygg-* with the Old Norse term *ýr* ("yew") is less plausible on linguistic grounds.

The symbolism of the tree is extremely important, as it is mirrored in other traditions. In ancient Babylonia, for example, a cosmic tree, Kiskanu, grew in a holy place; radiant with shining lapis lazuli (symbolizing the starry night), it stretched towards the primeval waters. This was the dwelling place of Ea (the god of fertility and skills such as agriculture, arts and crafts, and writing), and his mother Bau (the goddess of plenty) rested there as well. Babylonian pictures of the tree sometimes show it surrounded by goats or with a bird poised on it. In ancient India, the universe is symbolized by an inverted tree, with its roots in the sky and its branches spreading over the earth, representing the downpouring of the sun's rays. Yggdrasill has sometimes been compared with the tree of life in the Hebrew scriptures, but there is no proof of any Judeo-Christian element in the concept of Yggdrasill. The presence of the eagle and the snake, however, reminds us of the cosmological motif found in Indian mythology, where the combat of Garuda with the reptile symbolizes the struggle between light and darkness (the eagle is a sun bird, whereas the snake belongs to the underworld). The liquid dripping from the tree can be compared with the streaming milk and honey in the Semitic myths of paradise, with *amrta* (the Old Indic beverage of immortality identified with mead), and with the honeydew spread by the Aśvins. In *Vǫluspá* (st. 27), the tree is described as secreting a clear liquid (*heiðr*) that must be the "sap of life." The element *heið-* also appears in the name of the magical goat Heiðrún, whose udders every day fill Valhǫll's cauldrons with mead for Óðinn's retinue.

The War of the Æsir and the Vanir. The Germanic gods are divided into two groups, the Æsir and the Vanir. Following the medieval practice of etymologizing, Snorri says that the Æsir's name shows that they came from Asia, but this interpretation does not appear to reflect any authentic tradition. Jordanes, the sixth-century historian of the Goths, cites a Gothic word *ansis* (or *anses*) that is glossed as "demigods." This element also occurs in men's names such as the Gothic *Ansila*, the Burgundian *Ansemundos* (cf. ON, *Ásmundr*), the Langobardic *Ansegranus*, and the Old High German *Ansgar* and *Anshelm*. Together with the Old Norse term *áss*, these words derive from the Germanic **ansuz*, designating some type of deity. The feminine form preserved in the southern Germanic divine name *Vihansa* might refer to a war goddess if **wih-* is an alternative form of **wig-* ("combat"; OHG and OE, *wig;* ON, *víg*). The Æsir, however, are ruling gods, which makes it more plausible to associate their name with the Hittite word *hashshush* (king) than with the Old Indic prefix *asu-* (breath of life), as is usually suggested.

The name *Vanir* has been connected with the Old Norse word *vinr* (friend), with *Venus* (the Latin name for the goddess of love), and with the Sanskrit *vánas-* (lust), an etymology very suitable for fertility gods. *Vanir* has also been related to the Sanskrit *vánam* (water; cf. the latinized Slavic ethnic name *Veneti*, meaning "people of the waters"), an interpretation made doubtful by the fact that the Vanir as a group are not aquatic deities, although one of them, Njǫrðr, is associated with the sea. Overall, the Vanir are fertility gods.

In the mythological "now," the Vanir live in peace with the Æsir, but this was not always the case. At the dawn of time, a bitter war was fought between the two groups, which Snorri reports (with varying details) in two different works, *Ynglinga Saga* (the first part of his history of the kings of Norway) and the *Edda*. The former is an euhemeristic narration of the early life of the Æsir in "Asia" (ON, *Ásaland, Ásaheimr*). Their neighbors, the Vanir, lived in Vanaland or Vanaheimr, in the vicinity of the Tanais (the classical name for the River Don). Óðinn leads his army against the Vanir, but they resist vigorously. The two sides are alternately victorious, and they loot each other's territory until they grow tired of fighting and conclude a peace that puts them on equal footing. They exchange hostages: the Vanir Njǫrðr and his son Freyr are transferred to the world of the Æsir, and the Æsir in turn deliver Mímir and Hœnir to the Vanir. As Mímir is very wise, the Vanir reciprocate by sending "the cleverest among them"—Kvasir—to the Æsir. In the *Edda*, however, Snorri claims that Kvasir was created from the saliva of the Vanir and the Æsir when they spat into the communal caldron at the conclusion of the peace. Other evidence linking Kvasir's blood to the mead of poetic inspiration suggests that this second version is closer to the original. In addition to the formal transfer of Njǫrðr and Freyr to Ásgarðr, the Vanir goddess Freyja (Njǫrðr's daughter and Freyr's sister) also ends up living with the Æsir. No extant myth explains how this came to pass, but hints in *Vǫluspá* suggest that Freyja went to Ásgarðr during the war, disguised as a witch named Gullveig, with the intention of corrupting the Æsir with greed, lust, and sorcery. Perhaps her visit was even the initial cause of the Æsir-Vanir conflict. This mythological war has been seen as a reflection of an actual religious war or the replacement of one cult with another, but it has also been taken as a symbolic explanation of the existence of different aspects of divinity.

THE PANTHEON. The earliest written testimony we have about the religion of the Germanic peoples is a statement by Julius Caesar in the sixth book of his account of the Gallic Wars indicating that they worshiped the sun, the moon, and Vulcan, which is generally taken to mean "fire." However, there is no trace of a moon cult in the Germanic territories, and the role of fire in cult and ritual seems to have been rather limited in historical times. Possibly Caesar was reporting an archaic version of Germanic religion, or perhaps his information was just inaccurate. Fortunately, the data supplied some 150 years later by Tacitus provide a fairly accurate picture of what must have been the structure of the Germanic pantheon in his time (end of the first century CE).

According to Tacitus, the main god is Mercury, whose Latin name, Mercurius, is a Roman interpretation of the Germanic name *Woðan[az]. This is confirmed by the translation of the Latin weekday-name *Mercurii dies* (Mercury's day) into the Germanic *Woðniz-dag[az] ("Woden's day"; cf. Eng., *Wednesday;* Du., *woensdag*). Mercury is flanked by Mars and Hercules. The former represents the Germanic god *Tiw[az], whose name is preserved in the English *Tuesday* (OE, *Tiwesdæg; cf. Lat., *Martis dies*). The latter is usually interpreted as representing the Germanic champion of the gods, *Þun[a]r[az], although, as thunder god, he was also equated by Latin writers with Jupiter, as is shown by the translation of the Latin weekday-name *Jovis dies* into "Thor's day" (Eng., *Thursday;* Ger., *Donnerstag;* Du., *donderdag*). As Mercury/*Woðan[az] is the only Germanic god credited by Tacitus with receiving human sacrifice, many scholars assume that the *regnator omnium deus* (god reigning over all) venerated by the Suevian tribe of the Semnones in their sacred grove and honored as their ethnic ancestor with regular human sacrifices must be the same deity, though perhaps Allan Lund (1990) is right in claiming that he must have been worshiped as an eponymous founder under the name *Semno.

Tacitus also refers to other locally worshiped Germanic deities such as Nerthus ("Mother Earth"), for whom the Inguaeonic people hold a yearly pageant during which they celebrate the powers of fertility that she incarnates, or the divine twins whom he calls Alcis (Gmc., *Alhiz) and equates with the Roman twins Castor and Pollux. In both cases he supplies a few details about cult and ritual, specifying, for example, that Nerthus shrouds herself in mystery. She remains hidden in a curtained chariot during her peregrinations among her worshipers, only her priest can approach her, and after the completion of her ceremonial journey she is bathed in a secret lake, but all those who officiate in this lustration rite are drowned afterward to maintain the "sacred ignorance" about her. Similarly, Tacitus indicates that the priests of the Dioscuri among the eastern Germanic Naharvales wear feminine attire, which presumably includes their long hair, a feature closely associated with the Germanic divine twins. Moreover, he points out that these deities are not represented by any image or statue, which corroborates his general statement about the aniconic character of Germanic religion—"[They] do not think it proper to portray gods with any kind of human countenance" (*Germania* 9)—but is at least partly contradicted by the archaeological finds of some roughly hewn stakes offering a rudimentary anthropomorphic representation of the gods.

In the *Annals,* Tacitus refers to other Germanic deities, such as Tamfana, whose sanctuary was an important center of cultural activities in the territory of the Marsi (between the Lippe and the Ruhr rivers). Her "temple" was allegedly leveled by the Romans during the celebration of an autumnal festival in 4 CE. Its very existence contradicts Tacitus's statement in the *Germania* that the Germanic people "refuse to confine their gods within walls" and the contention that worship generally took place outdoors and in the woods, as with the Frisian goddess Baduhenna, near whose sacred grove a Roman detachment was massacred.

In the Roman period, inscriptions provide further information about the deities venerated by the Germanic people within the boundaries of the empire, such as Nehalennia, whose sanctuary near Domburg on the Dutch island of Walcheren has yielded an abundance of altars and statues. She was worshiped mainly by seamen and traders, mostly natives of the northwestern provinces of the Empire, who dedicated the monuments to the goddess in return for the help received from her. Her attributes (cornucopias, specific fruits, dogs, etc.) characterize her as a fertility goddess with strong chthonic overtones, but she apparently also shares the patronage of navigation with Isis, whose presence Tacitus mentions "among part of the Suevians" (presumably the Hermunduri, who were in close contact with the Roman province of Noricum where the cult of Isis had been integrated with that of the national goddess Noreia).

Important also were the *matres* or *matronae* (mothers or matrons), whose worship is documented by votive stones with dedicatory inscriptions found mainly in the territory of the Ubii on the left side of the Rhine in the second and third centuries CE. Their worshipers belonged essentially to the lower classes but also included some high-office holders in the Roman administration and army. The *matres* were invoked for protection against danger and catastrophes or for the prosperity of the family, and were described as bestowing their blessings generously, as such epithets as *Gabiae* (givers),

Friagabis (generous donors), and *Arvagastiae* (hospitable ones) indicate. As they often appear in groups of three and seem to be associated with the fate and welfare of man, they have been compared with the Norns, especially as one stone carries the inscription "Matrib[us] Parc[is]," referring directly to the *interpretatio Romana* of the three deities of fate.

The picture that emerges from the data of the Roman period can be summarized as follows:

- The sovereign god *Woðan[az] (identified with Mercury) may have taken over the prominent place originally occupied by the old Indo-European sky god *Deiwos (Gmc., **Tiwaz;* Gk., *Zeus;* ON *Týr*), who has still preserved a sufficiently prominent position among certain tribes (e.g., the Chatti) for the spoils of the enemy to be dedicated to him and *Woðan[az] jointly.
- The divine champion Þun[a]r[az] is identified with the thunder god Jupiter or with Hercules.
- The divine twins, the *Alhiz, identified with Castor and Pollux, were venerated locally, especially among the eastern Germanic tribes.
- The fertility deities were worshiped regionally and had associated functions such as the protection of navigation or the determination of man's fate; they include Nehalennia, the *matres* or *matronae*, Nerthus, and *Ingw-[az].

Although poorly documented, the Germanic pantheon of the Migration and post-Migration periods shows an apparent continuity in this system:

- *Woðan[az] remains the supreme god and is honored as the ancestor of royal lineages; there is also some evidence of his connection with magic. *Tiw[az] recedes to the background but is perhaps to be identified with the tribal god of the Saxons, whose name occurs together with Woden and Thunaer in the abjuration formula the Saxons had to pronounce with their baptismal vows during the forcible conversion campaign conducted by Charlemagne. The third name in the abjuration formula, *Saxnote,* is ambiguous: it can either mean "sword companion" or denote a "sacrificial" god. Although the former interpretation fits in with the statement in the chronicles about the cult of "Mars" among the Saxons and could be connected with the presence of the cosmic pillar Irminsul in their main sanctuary (a reference to *Tiw[az]'s original function as sky god), the latter would make more plausible Dumézil's suggestion that the Saxon triad Thunaer-Woden-Saxnote corresponds to the Scandinavian trinity Þórr-Óðinn-Freyr in the Uppsala temple. Saxnote could indeed be a god of the tribal community, just as Freyr is *folkvaldi* (leader of the people). Saxnote would presumably have been sacrificed to, as was Freyr, the *blótgoð Svía* (sacrificial god of the Swedes).
- *Þun[a]r[az], the thunder god, progressively gains prominence as the divine representative of the warrior class.
- Although there is no direct evidence of a cult of the divine twins, their functional role is euhemerized in the figures of the twin founding heroes of various Germanic groups, such as Hengist and Horsa for the early Saxons in Great Britain, Raos and Raptos for the Vandalic Hasdingi, and Ibor and Aio for the Winnili (Lombards). The names Hengist and Horsa (related respectively to Ger. *Hengst,* "stallion," and Eng. *horse*) remind us of the association of the divine twins with horses. In Greek they are referred to as *leuko polo* ("with white horses") and in ancient India they are known as the Aśvinau ("possessors of horses"). The names Raos and Raptos (related respectively to Ger. *Rahe* [yard] and Eng. *rafter*) reflect the aniconic representation of the Dioscuri by beams, which occurred also in ancient Sparta, and in the shape of the Latin letter *H* or the Greek letter (pi). The Langobardic terms *ibor* (presumably from Gmc. **ebur-,* "boar") and *aio* (Gmc, **agjo,* "edge, sharp side of a blade") may refer to the sharp tusks of the wild boar, an animal also closely associated with the fertility deities Freyr and Freyja, with whose domain the divine twins also have direct links.
- Besides the already mentioned references to *Ingw[az], a number of names of deities associated with fertility occur, such as Erce, a name apparently borrowed from Celtic and used to designate Mother Earth in an Old English charm; Phol (OHG, *Vol*), appearing together with Woden and Balder in the Old High German Merseburg spell; Friia and Frig, the Old High German and Old English names, respectively, for the Germanic goddess identified with Venus, whose name survives in the German *Freitag* and the English *Friday.* The often assumed existence of a spring deity, *Austro, from whose name the word *Easter* (Ger, *Ostern*) is supposedly derived, is, however, doubtful: it rests on an interpretation of the Old English term *Eostrae* by Bede (672/3–735 CE) and has no backing either in cult or myth; it has recently been more convincingly explained as a Christian missionary term.
- There are also a few minor deities such as Fosite, to whom an island was consecrated at the juncture of the Frisian and Danish territories. He is known only from a reference in the life of Saint Willibrord, but his name shows a striking similarity to that of the Scandinavian god Forseti, whose specific function according to the *Lay of Grímnir* is to settle all disputes; he is the son of Baldr and lives in Glitnir, a hall "propped with gold and shingled with shining silver" (st. 15). Forseti's name is transparent: it means "presiding [over the Thing]," but no satisfactory explanation can be given for the loss of the [r] in Fosite, so that the connection between Fosite and Forseti remains conjectural.

Our knowledge of the Scandinavian development of the Germanic pantheon in the Viking age is much more detailed, for we have a fair amount of pagan poetry (copied in Christian times, but dating back to the ninth and tenth centuries) that mentions the gods and the myths about them. The blossoming of literature in medieval Iceland after the conversion also provides ample information about the pagan gods and cults of the Germanic North. Moreover, reports from various non-Scandinavian sources attest to the prevalence of the worship of Þórr among the Vikings. This is also confirmed by studies that show no people and very few places named after Óðinn, but many people and places named after Þórr. This situation should not be misinterpreted: Óðinn was the sovereign god, but he was the deity associated primarily with the warrior elite, whereas Þórr was worshiped by the majority of the people. The cult of Týr remained widespread only in Denmark, although his name appears frequently in West Norse poetry because it means simply "god" and was often used in synonyms for Óðinn.

The comparativist Georges Dumézil considered the common Indo-European "ideology" to have consisted of three principles or "functions" (the maintenance of cosmic and juridical order; the exercise of physical force; and the promotion of physical well-being, fertility, and wealth), and he interpreted the gods of the various groups of the Indo-Europeans' descendents as representing these "functions." Óðinn and Týr he saw as co-sovereigns, the former representing the magical aspect of the first "function" and the latter its juridical aspect. Þórr represented the second "function," including its manifestation in war, and Njǫrðr, Freyr, and Freyja represented the third "function." Such a presentation, however, oversimplifies the picture of the Scandinavian system, which fails to show the characteristic slant towards war in the second "function," as Dumézil himself acknowledges. All the deities supposedly representing different "functions" have some association with war. Óðinn intervenes in battles to give victory to his favorites, and Þórr frequently engages in hand-to-hand combat with giants of both sexes. Even the Vanir gods seem to acquire some of the Æsir's combative spirit when they move to Ásgarðr, as when the peaceful Freyr, who had given up his sword to obtain the favors of a beautiful giant maiden, faces the giant Beli without a weapon and kills him with a hart's horn. And while Óðinn collects half of the heroes who die on the battlefield to join his retinue in Valhǫll, it is certainly striking that Freyja gets the other half. Fertility is another area that is not easily compartmentalized as Dumézil would have it. The thunder god Þórr was the protector of the peasant class, which depended on the weather for its crops, but he shares control of the atmosphere with Njǫrðr, who controls the path of the wind and, as sea god, counteracts the effects of the thunderstorms, quieting the sea and smothering the lightning-sparked fires. Furthermore, some very important aspects of the major deities are not covered by Dumézil's labels. For example, Óðinn is as much the god of "inspired cerebral activity" as he is the god of sovereignty, but his role as the patron of the poets cannot be explained by Dumézil's system. And although Óðinn manifests his sovereign power through potent magical interventions, he is definitely not the only one to wield magical powers. The Vanir use *seiðr*, an effeminate form of sorcery that the Æsir deem despicable but which Óðinn nevertheless is keen to learn from Freyja. Finally, Óðinn's ability to change shape is more than matched by the metamorphoses of Loki. It is also shared by certain giants such as Suttungr, who pursues Óðinn in the shape of an eagle, or Þjazi, who also assumes the shape of an eagle to follow the trickster Loki. Indeed, complex figures such as Loki and Heimdallr do not fit into Dumézil's neat matrix at all.

Loki is extremely difficult to classify. Originally a giant, he nevertheless played an important part in the decisions and activities of the gods. Although primarily a mischievous trickster, Loki cannot be described as an "evil demon." He is restless and inventive, deceptive and unreliable. Frequently causing trouble for the gods, he usually redeems himself by solving the problem he created. Ultimately he goes too far when his delight in mischief leads to the death of Óðinn's son Baldr, utterly outraging the whole divine world and resulting in his being chained up until Ragnarǫk. Dumézil sees in him an incarnation of impulsive intelligence, but this interpretation is disputable. There is no trace of any cult devoted to Loki, nor are any people or places named for him.

Heimdallr occupies a similarly marginal position in the pantheon. It is not even clear to which group of gods he should be assigned. Apparently he offered up his *hljóð*, which was hidden as a pledge under the cosmic tree, Yggdrasill, as did Óðinn his eye. Óðinn appropriately received exceptional vision and Heimdallr was gifted with extraordinary aural perception: "He can hear the grass grow on the earth and the wool on sheep." It has therefore been assumed that the Old Norse term *hljóð*—generally translated "horn" in this context (*Vǫluspá*, st. 27) but usually meaning "silence, listening, hearing, what is heard"—must designate one of Heimdallr's ears. Offering up a body part in exchange for a major attribute is a characteristic feature of the most important Æsir, Óðinn and Týr. (The latter sacrificed his hand in order to guarantee a pledge that enabled the gods to fetter the monstrous wolf Fenrir, and in return assumed the role of protector of the Thing and patron of the law.) As guardian of the gods and watchman of Ásgarðr, Heimdallr assumes a military function, which would make him a second-function god in the Dumézilian system, like Þórr (with whom he shares the tendency to imbibe great quantities of mead). But the Eddic *Poem of Þrýmr* (*Þrýmskviða*, st. 15) describes him as one of the Vanir and able to "fathom the future." His affinity with the ram further complicates matters: was he originally a god of sheep breeders, as Freyr was a god of wheat growers and pig breeders?

The minor deities are also problematic. Some of them, such as Ullr, an archer god living in Ýdalir ("yew dales") in Ásgarðr, can be integrated into the tripartite functional scheme. His importance is made clear by Óðinn's statement in the *Lay of Grímnir* (st. 42) that among all the gods, Ullr especially will grant his blessing to him who "first quenches the fire." The most sacred oaths are sworn by Ullr's ring, and as a stepson of Þórr, he has close connections with the warriors. He is invoked by those engaged in single combat, and the poetic circumlocution an "Ullr of battle" means "a warrior." According to the evidence of place-names, he was the object of an extended cult in Norway and Sweden, where he was called Ullinn, but there he eventually seems to have been overshadowed by Þórr, Freyr, and Freyja. There is practically no trace of him in Denmark, which instead has many places named for Týr. This is rather significant in light of the story of Ullr's temporary usurpation of Óðinn's throne, as narrated by Saxo Grammaticus: Óðinn had committed a grievous breach of his royal majesty by assuming a feminine disguise, and as a result of this disgrace he was replaced by Ullr, who reigned for ten years. When Óðinn was restored, Ullr (whose name, latinized into *Ollerus*, means "glory, brilliance") fled to Sweden but was killed afterward by Danes. In view of Ullr's connection with oath-taking, Dumézil sees in this episode an illustration of the complementary nature of the two aspects of sovereignty, the inspired and the majestic. The latter, with its juridical connotations, is illustrated by Saxo's second story of Óðinn's temporary ouster from power. Óðinn's fall this time is brought about by the misconduct of his wife, Frigg, and he is replaced by a magician called Mithotyn, who introduces all kinds of innovations that the people dislike. As a result, Óðinn is welcomed back while Mithotyn flees and is eventually killed on the Danish island of Fyn. In this story, Dumézil has seen the contrast between the unitary and rather ill-defined religion of Óðinn and the analytic religion of Mithotyn (actually *Mitoðinn, from ON *mjötur*, "measurer," meaning "dispenser of fate"), who introduces rules where there were none. As Dumézil puts it, "The lawyer replaces the inspired, and his very precision makes him hatable!" (Dumézil, 1939, p. 224).

Bragi is another lesser god about whom little is known. His name seems to be related to the Old Norse word *bragr*, which designates "poetic form," and he is described as the "foremost of poets," being in this way in competition with Óðinn as patron of poetry. In the Eddic poem *Loki's Slanging Match* (*Lokasenna*, sts. 8–15) he bickers with Loki, who chides him for his lack of courage in combat. Obviously, his power is in speech, and his eloquence is strengthened by the magic of the runes carved on his tongue. Bragi is the husband of Iðunn, the guardian of the apples that ensure the eternal youth of the gods. The only myth relating to her tells that Loki delivered her and her apples to the giants. Catastrophe ensues when everyone in Ásgarðr grows old and infirm. They summon Loki before their council and compel him to retrieve Iðunn and her apples. The trickster flies to Jötunheimr in the shape of a falcon to recover Iðunn and her precious possessions from the clutches of the giant Þjazi. The latter pursues Loki in the form of an eagle and is killed when he tries to fly into Ásgarðr. Although apples were not cultivated in Scandinavia until late in the Middle Ages, the theme of this story must be quite old, as the Norwegian poet Þjóðólfr of Hvin refers to Iðunn and the "old-age medicine" of the gods in his composition *Haustlöng*, composed around the year 900. The desire of the giants for a goddess as well as for outrageous rewards from the Æsir is again illustrated by the story of the "master builder" of the divine stronghold, who requests Freyja as payment for his work and demands the sun and the moon to boot, obviously intending to plunge the world into darkness and sterility.

Very little information is given about the other goddesses, apart from Freyja:

- Frigg, Óðinn's wife, is the devoted mother of Baldr; she lives in Fensalir ("marshy halls"), attended by her confidant Fulla. Loki claims that she shared her sexual favors with her husband's brothers, Vili and Vé (*Lokasenna*, st. 26), and Saxo also refers to her loose morals, which trigger the episode with Mithotyn.
- Jörð ("earth"), the mother of Þórr, is also known under the name of Fjörgyn, which may mean "goddess of the furrow" (cf. Gmc., **furho;* OHG, *fur[u]h;* OE, *furh;* Fris., *furge;* Ger., *Furche;* Eng., *furrow*). Her male counterpart is Fjörgynn, who is believed to be either the father or the lover of Frigg, because the latter is called *Fjörgyns mær* (*Lokasenna*, st. 26: "Fjörgynn's maiden"). Fjörgynn's name, however, is related to the set of terms derived from the Indo-European term *perkw- and associated with thunder, craggy mountains, and the oak tree. Among them are the Lithuanian name *Perkunas* ("thunder"; cf. Slav., *Perunu), the Gothic word *fairguni* ("mountain"; cf. Lat., *Hercynia silva*, a wooded mountain range in ancient Germany), and the Latin word *quercus* (oak), as well as the Langobardic *fereha aesculus* and the Old High German *fereh-eih*, both of which designate a type of oak tree (cf. OE, *furh;* OHG, *for[a]ha*, "fir"). These etymological links rest on the age-old perception of the predilection of lightning for rocky spots and oak trees and reflect the correlations established between them in Indo-European myth and tradition.
- The goddess Gefjun is said to have torn away a sizable chunk of land from Sweden and dragged it away to form the Danish island of Sjælland. To perform this deed, she turned her four giant-begotten sons into oxen and yoked them to a plow. Although she is mentioned as a separate deity in *Lokasenna* (st. 20), she seems to be a hypostasis of Freyja, who is also known as Gefn ("giver"), a name befitting a fertility goddess. Loki, indeed, reproaches Gefjun for having "lured to lust" Heimdallr, who gave her a precious jewel—presumably the mysterious "sea kidney" (ON, *hafnyra*, probably referring to a piece of amber) he had won in an epic battle with Loki—even before she "threw [her] thighs about him" (a behavior paralleling that of Freyja for the possession of the valuable Brising Necklace). How Snorri can describe her as a virgin, served by women who die unmarried, remains unexplained.
- Sif, the wife of Þórr and the mother of Ullr by another

> male deity, plays a rather unobtrusive part in the society of the Æsir, but although she is shy and retiring, Loki claimed to have enjoyed her favors (*Loki's Slanging Match*, st. 54), and apparently Óðinn was aware of it, because he warns Þórr that "someone sleeps in her bower with Sif" (*Song of Hárbarðr*, st. 48). This explains why Loki dares to cut off Sif's hair, a punishment normally inflicted on adulteresses. But Þórr does not believe in the unfaithfulness of his wife and compels Loki to go to the dwarves to obtain hair made out of gold that will replace her lost locks. This story accounts for the poetic circumlocution "Sif's hair," which means "gold."

In many cases it is questionable whether some deities named by Snorri are anything more than local variants of major gods, used primarily to provide variation in poetic language. Thus we have no myths relating to goddesses such as Eir ("the best of physicians"), Sjöfn (who brings people to love), and Lofn ("permission," who brings together those who cannot marry).

The Creation of Man. The Germanic myth of the creation of man appears in two versions, that in *Völuspá* (sts. 17–18) and that in Snorri's *Edda.* In both cases, three deities are involved: the Æsir in the former and the sons of Borr in the latter. Walking along the shore, the gods find two tree trunks, which they animate and endow with various qualities. In the *Vǫluspá* account, Óðinn gives them breath and soul, Hœnir gives them feeling and sense, and Lóðurr gives them craft, bearing, and color. In Snorri's account, the first god gives them breath and life, the second god gives them consciousness and movement, and the third god gives them faces, speech, hearing, and sight. Close parallels to this myth are lacking. Hesiod mentions that Zeus created a race of men from ash trees, and indeed in the Old Norse name of the first man is *Askr* (ash tree). There is also some correspondence with an Indic tale in which a sculptor, a goldsmith, a weaver, and a priest whittle a piece of sandalwood into the shape of a pretty woman. The sculptor shapes it, the weaver dresses it, the goldsmith adorns it with jewels, and the priest breathes life into it through his incantations. The basic idea in these myths is the same—a human being is fashioned out of a piece of wood—but the elaboration of the theme is totally different. In the Indic tale, giving life is the crowning act of the long process of shaping a human being; in the Germanic myth, the triad of gods creates the primordial being right away. What characterizes the Eddic account is the unity of the creative act by direct divine intervention in spite of the distribution of the human qualities by three different gods. It is interesting, therefore, to examine how these gifts relate to the nature and function of the deities involved.

In Snorri's version, the gods in question are the sons of Borr: Óðinn, Vili, and Vé, the same group that created the world by dismembering the primal giant Ymir. As Vili and Vé are little more than hypostases of Óðinn, the whole process of creation is ascribed to that supreme god (perhaps a Christian-influenced effort to reduce the triad of gods to one). *Vǫluspá's* version of man's creation undoubtedly represents an older tradition. That man would receive the breath of life from Óðinn is in keeping with his position as the sovereign god, meting out life-giving power (ON, *önd*, "breath"; the translation "soul" has Christian implications that the Old Norse term acquires only later). Óðinn's name (Gmc.,*Wōðan[az]) derives from a root meaning "to blow" and includes the connotation "life-giving power" in some of its derivations; it is cognate to Old Irish *fáith* (seer, prophet) and Latin *vātes* (soothsayer). Óðinn is indeed the inspired god, the prince of the poets, the master of the divinatory runes, and the wielder of awesome magical powers. The Germanic stem of his name, **wōþ-*, also appears in German as *Wut* (rage). Adam of Bremen thus correctly interpreted Óðinn's name as "furor" in his description of the pagan gods worshiped at the temple at Uppsala. The Old Norse term *óðr*, usually translated "mind, reason, understanding," is the gift of Hœnir, according to *Vǫluspá* (st. 18). But *óðr* is also used as an adjective meaning "mad, furious, vehement; eager, impatient," all of which point to either strong emotional stress or lack of control over the power of reasoning. The inspired cerebral activity expressed by **wōþ-* can indeed verge on ecstasy; thus, the name of the mead of poetic inspiration, *óðrœrir*, literally means "rousing to the point of ecstasy." Stanza 18 of *Vǫluspá* is the only context in which *óðr* is assumed to have the meaning "mind, reason, understanding," and the main reason for ascribing this meaning to it here is the parallel text by Snorri, in which the second god endows man with *vit ok hrœring* (wit and movement), with special focus on *vit* (intelligence). However, *hrœring* need not apply only to physical movement. It occurs in compounds and phrases pointing clearly to emotions, so that Snorri's use of *vit* in association with *hrœring* may well indicate specifically the movements of the mind that *óðr* expresses in *Vǫluspá.*

This misinterpretation of *óðr* is also ascribable to the fact that Hœnir is often described as a wise god; his name is supposed to be derived from a root meaning "to make keen, to sharpen," so that he would be the god who sharpens the mind. Dumézil calls him "the patron of the deep, invisible part of intelligence" (Dumézil, 1986, p. 227). This view is based on two events. First, when the giant Þjazi, in the shape of an eagle, asks Hœnir for a full share of the meal the gods are cooking, Hœnir does not answer but cannot help breathing heavily with anger. Second, whenever he attends the assembly of the Vanir as a chief and fails to get Mímir's advice, Hœnir does not take a stand, but merely states "Let others decide!" Dumézil considers Hœnir's refusal to commit himself to be the only wise attitude under the circumstances, and contrasts it with Loki's rashness, which turns into disaster when he tries to beat Þjazi with a stick after the giant snatches four pieces of meat from the gods. In the case of the assembly, Dumézil suggests that Mímir and Hœnir represent complementary symbolizations of human thought processes: Mímir represents the "collective consciousness" on which we rely for decision making, and without which individual thought (i.e., Hœnir) is worthless. Dumézil's explanation is ingenious but far from convincing, for all the texts show Hœnir as unable to act on his own, and although that may not make him weak-minded, as various scholars have suggested, it hardly makes him a "god of reflective thought." Rather, he is the instrument of divine inspiration, the one who utters the message conveyed by another's wisdom. In the absence of Mímir (his source of inspiration), he remains silent at the assembly, and therefore he is described as the most fearful of all gods because he cannot act without being advised. After Ragnarǫk, he will function as priest, consulting the oracles (i.e., interpreting the signs given by an outside power, again as the vehicle of divine inspiration). It is in this capacity that he is instrumental in endowing man with "inspired mental activity" (*óðr*); thus some scholars have also considered him a hypostasis of Óðinn.

The third god in the divine triad, Lóðurr, is more difficult to define functionally, for he is hardly known outside this context. (Elsewhere he is described simply as a friend of Óðinn, an association he shares with quite a few gods in the Scandinavian pantheon.) Because in other contexts Óðinn and Hœnir are closely associated with Loki, scholars have also attempted to equate Lóðurr with Loki (as a god of fire) on the basis of etymological speculations, but the arguments advanced to back up this hypothesis have all proved untenable. The identification of Lóðurr with the term *logaþore*, which occurs with the name *Woðan* and *Wigiþonar* in the runic inscription on the Nordendorf Fibula (first half of the seventh century) is also disputable: *logaþore* is presumably cognate with the Old English *logor* or *logeer* (wily, crafty), applying to magicians. This connection with magic, with the connotation of plotting mischief, could fit the personality of Óðinn fairly well, so that Lóðurr might just be another hypostasis of this god. But before overriding the etymological difficulties connected with this view, it is advisable to examine more closely the gifts bestowed by Lóðurr upon the primal human couple: according to the text, he gives them *lá*, *læti*, and *litir góðir*. The last of these means "good colors," implying good health and also physical beauty, which was considered a sign of noble ancestry among the Germanic people. (Thus it is Beowulf's handsome appearance that distinguishes him from his companions, and the Anglo-Saxon poet uses for this peerless appearance the very same term that Snorri uses to qualify the gift of the third deity.) *Læti* means "noise, voice" or "gestures, attitude" and refers specifically to manners in other contexts. Since Snorri specifies speech, hearing, and sight as the gifts of the third deity to the first human couple, it is obvious that Snorri's account represents a different tradition from that of *Vǫluspá*. The term *lá* is problematic because its etymological connections are difficult to assess. The usual translation, "blood," rests on a disputable interpretation of a single line of poetry. In another poetic context the term is associated with the adjective *sölr* (pale, yellow), suggesting the interpretation "sallow-complexioned." This would imply that *lá* means "look, mien." Lóðurr would then have given man his mien and good complexion (i.e., his physical appearance). The only corroboration for this interpretation is provided by the Tocharian term *lek* (appearance, mien), derived from the same Indo-European root. An alternate solution would be to interpret *lá* as "hair" (from Gmc., **lawo,* "cutting"), showing the same semantic development as the Sanskrit cognate *lava-* (cutting, wool, hair). Thus the Eddic line could well be interpreted as "Lóðurr gave hair and fair complexion to man." If Óðinn and Hœnir bestow essentially spiritual qualities upon man, whereas Lóðurr provides him with his physical aspect, Lóðurr must be a god presiding over the physical aspects of life, closer to nature than the lofty Æsir. In other words, he must be one of the Vanir, part of the old Germanic fertility cult. His name may be connected with the Old Norse term *ló* (produce of the land). Swedish place-names indicate that there was a Germanic hypostasis of the great goddess of fertility named *Liuðgoða, and her male counterpart, *Loðverr, could survive in Lóðurr as a divinity of generation and growth and protector of the ethnic community.

THE MEAD OF POETIC INSPIRATION. The ability to compose poetry was highly valued by the Scandinavians, and it is not surprising that the patron god of poetry was the sovereign deity Óðinn himself. Moreover, the special language used in Norse poems made extensive use of allusions to the gods and supernatural beings such as giants and dwarves. For these reasons, the myth about the mead of poetic inspiration must have been of particular importance. It exists in several versions, but the gist is that malicious dwarves killed Kvasir (the being created in token of the accord between the Æsir and the Vanir) and brewed a mead from his blood that would bestow the ability to compose poetry. The dwarves were forced to relinquish this magical substance to the giants, who guarded it jealously, although they did not drink of it themselves. Óðinn obtains the mead by seducing its giantess guardian, swallowing it all, changing himself into an eagle, flying to Ásgarðr, and spewing it out into three crocks the Æsir had ready. This story illustrates the dichotomy between the gods, who are associated with culture and craft, and the giants, who are associated with the hostile natural environment. It also illustrates the dichotomy between the gods' ostensible motivation, which is the benevolent desire to make good use of a magical substance, and their behavior, which includes deceit, seduction, and theft. This myth must be part of the Indo-European heritage, for it has parallels with stories told about the Indian god Indra, who has an encounter with the monster Mada ("Drunkeness") and who is also the recipient of *soma*, the intoxicating sacrificial liquor that gives poetic ability, immortality, and knowledge of the divine. As with the mead of poetic inspiration, *soma* was brought to the gods by an eagle or possibly Indra in the form of an eagle.

THE DEATH OF BALDR. The story of Baldr's fate is probably the most moving and most controversial of all the Scandinavian myths. In this story, best known from Snorri's *Edda*, Óðinn's resplendent son Baldr is plagued by evil dreams of impending death. To protect against any danger, his mother, Frigg, exacts an oath from everything in the world not to harm him, but neglects the puny mistletoe. Jealous of the attention Baldr receives in the games of the gods, Loki, in the disguise of a woman, wheedles the secret of Baldr's invulnerability out of his mother. He then persuades Baldr's blind brother, Höðr, who has been prevented by his infirmity from any participation in the sportive tossing of objects at Baldr, to throw a dart of mistletoe. Under Loki's guidance the missile hits Baldr and kills him. The gods are stunned, and while preparations for Baldr's burial are in progress, they send out Hermóðr on Óðinn's horse to the kingdom of Hel to entreat the goddess of the netherworld for the release of the unfortunate god. Meanwhile, Baldr's wife, Nanna, dies of grief and her body is carried onto the ship Hringhorni ("curved prow"), where she joins her husband on the funeral pyre. As for Hermóðr, he returns with the message that Baldr will be released only on the condition that "everything in the world, both dead and alive, weeps for him." Immediately the Æsir dispatch messengers all over the universe to request everyone and everything to weep Baldr out of Hel's clutches. Even the stones and the metals participate in the universal grief, but a giantess called Þökk says she has no use for Baldr; as far as she is concerned, Hel can keep him! Þökk is actually Loki in disguise, and thus he succeeds in preventing the return of Baldr, who will only come back after Ragnarǫk. Scholarly interpretations of this myth are many and conflicting, but it worth mentioning that the story underscores the limitations of the Æsir, who for all their power essentially rule the universe for a single generation and are then destroyed.

The End of the World. The destruction of the world hangs over the gods and man as a permanent threat. *Ragnarǫk* (fate of the gods) or *aldar rök* (the fate of humankind) has been misinterpreted as *ragnarøkkr* (twilight of the gods). The Old Norse term *rök* means "course of events, destiny, fate." The Germanic apocalyptic vision of the end of time appears in *Vǫluspá*, presumably composed during the wane of paganism at the end of the ninth or the beginning of the tenth century. As Jan de Vries has indicated, the anonymous poet must have been a pious man, still convinced that sufficient faith in paganism persisted to promote a rebirth, but one who borrowed too much from Christianity to be considered a truly pagan seer (de Vries, 1956–1957, vol. 2, pp. 395–396). It is therefore difficult to assess how much of his worldview is genuinely Germanic and how much his vision of the future and his yearning for a "brave new world" free of strife and lies is shaped by Christian influences.

The prelude to the final catastrophe is the murder of Baldr, but the elements of decay appear to have been present in the world from the start. The *Lay of Grímnir* (st. 36) describes the cosmic tree Yggdrasill as having "the hart browsing above, its bole rotting, and Níðhǫggr gnawing beneath"; it is weakened more than humankind suspects. Initially the gods appear to enjoy an idyllic life in the shining plain of Iðavöllr, where they relax and play chess after building shrines and making gold jewels, until three giant maidens come to disturb the serenity of this garden of delight. These are the Norns, who bring uncontrollable fate into the Germanic world. From the moment of their arrival, events take their inescapable course. Tension grows between the Æsir and the Vanir, and the strife worsens into a war when the seeress Gullveig brings the corruption of greed, lust, and witchcraft into Ásgarðr. Peace is temporarily restored and hostages are exchanged, but the age of innocence is gone. The gods can no longer be trusted; they break their most solemn promises or resort to trickery to avoid fulfilling them. Then comes the worst, the treacherous killing of Baldr by the throwing of the mistletoe, the missile in the hand of his blind brother Höðr, guided by the perfidious Loki. Punishment follows for the criminal, but the fateful action has triggered the chain of events that will culminate in ultimate disaster, with one horrible scene following upon another.

In *Vǫluspá* the seeress describes the river of the netherworld, full of sharp blades, and the shore of death with Hel's hall, whose walls are "clad with coiling snakes." Through the river wade perjurers, murderers, and adulterers, and the serpent Níðhǫggr feeds on corpses along its banks. She also describes the evil brood of Fenrir in the Iron Woods to the east, the wolves that will devour the sun and the moon. The sun grows dim, the weather "woe-bringing"; a horribly long winter will bring famine, as described in the *Lay of Vafþrúðnir* (st. 44). The final doom is heralded by a couple of obscure stanzas in which three roosters crow to call up the fighters—giants, Óðinn's warriors in Valhǫll, and the dead in Hel's realm—for the last combat. Now the forces of evil break loose: the hellhound Garmr breaks its fetters, and in the world of men, fratricidal struggles erupt everywhere; the bonds of kinship are disregarded ("woe's in the world, much wantonness"), and no respect for human life remains. Heimdallr, the watchman of the gods, blows his horn, the cosmic tree Yggdrasill shakes in its roots, the world serpent "wallows in giant rage," and the ship of death breaks its moorings. All the forces of destruction move in. Loki leads the "witless hordes" of giants, and Surtr, the lord of Muspelheimr, arrives from the south with the fire demons that will set the world ablaze. The mountains totter, heaven is rent apart, and men tread the path of Hel. In the final clash the gods meet their fates: Óðinn is slaughtered by the wolf Fenrir but is avenged by his son Víðarr; Þórr meets his archfoe, the earth-girding serpent, and they kill each other; Freyr dies in single combat with Surtr. The sun turns dark, the stars fall from the sky, and the blazing earth sinks into the sea.

But this apocalypse does not mean that all is lost. The earth, which was originally lifted from the primeval waters by Óðinn and his brothers, reemerges purified and regenerated from the deep into which it had sunk. A new breed of gods meet again in the green pastures and find the chessmen left by the Æsir. Baldr and Höðr are reborn to dwell in perfect harmony in the divine halls, and henceforth guiltless men will live forever in a gold-roofed abode called Gimlé. A mighty unnamed deity will reign over all, but evil has not been completely eradicated, for Níðhöggr, the awful dragon carrying corpses in its pinions, is still roaming over the plains.

Vǫluspá, whose description of the fate of the gods has been presented here, does not constitute our only source about Ragnarǫk, nor does it strictly reflect popular beliefs about the end of time. The Eddic poems often contain divergent versions of certain episodes, and Snorri, who gave a detailed account of the same events in his *Edda*, quotes from all the sources available to him. Thus, describing Óðinn's tragic end and Víðarr's vengeance, Snorri prefers the cruder and more primitive version of the *Lay of Vafþrúðnir*, in which Víðarr, wearing a shoe made of all the leather pared off from men's shoes at the toes and heels since the beginning of time, pulls apart Fenrir's jaws. The strange similarity between the action of Víðarr and that of Lugh in the Irish tradition of the Second Battle of Magh Tuiredh, along with the association of the Celtic god Lug(us) with cobblers, may indicate that this strange reference to the origin of Víðarr's footwear reflects a very old, no longer well-understood tradition associating this Germanic deity with the shoemakers. Therefore, the *Vǫluspá* version, which states that Víðarr "hews the son of Hveðrungr to the heart," presumably represents a younger form of the story. In any event, there was a widespread intimation of the impending catastrophe affecting the gods in the Scandinavian world. This is widely demonstrated by numerous references in court poetry. For example, in a poem commissioned by the widow of the Norwegian king Eirik Bloodax (killed in England in 954), Eirik is assumed to have been called to Valhǫll by Óðinn, who needed him for the impending final conflict: "The grey wolf [Fenrir] is glaring at the dwellings of the gods, ready to jump." Similarly, Eyvindr the Plagiarist celebrated the Norwegian king Hákon the Good (d. 960) by saying: "Unfettered will fare the Fenrir-wolf and ravage the / realm of men ere that cometh a kingly prince as / good to stand in his stead" (Hollander, 1964, p. 127).

RELIGIOUS PRACTICES AND MORALITY. Apart from Ibn Fadlan's account of a Scandinavian funeral, there are few wholly reliable sources of information about pagan religious practices. Icelandic sagas contain characters who are pagan priests, seeresses, witches, and sorcerors, and they describe rituals such as fortune-telling, "baptism," funerals, sanctifications of land and temples, oath-taking, sacrifices, and feasts of sacrificial meat (in Iceland, often horse meat). The sagas are products of the Christian age, however, and for several reasons are liable to give inaccurate accounts of paganism. Nonetheless, we know that pagan Scandinavians had temples where sacrifices were conducted, and that the function of the priest was an important one. In addition, certain rites such as fortune-telling and sacrificing to the elves were conducted on individual farms.

Germanic and Scandinavian paganism was by no means a monolithic religion. Both the pantheon and religious practices evolved over time and were different in different places, facts of which medieval Scandinavians were dimly aware. For example, in his prologue to his history of the kings of Norway, Snorri discusses what he calls "The Age of Burning" (when the dead were cremated and memorial stones with runic inscriptions were erected in their memory) and "The Age of Barrows" (when the dead were inhumed and an artificial hill of earth was raised over their graves). Longships sometimes served as the coffins of kings and other people of rank, as in the Sutton Hoo burial in England and the Oseberg burial in Norway, and in Sweden the barrows were long, pointed ovals—the shape of the "footprint" of a longship. It is not clear whether this attests to a belief that the dead needed a ship to travel to the next world, or whether the ship (actual or symbolic) was considered something that would be useful in the afterlife, like the weapons or household tools that were sometimes placed in graves. There were also different beliefs regarding the afterworld. Norse mythology and court poetry focus on the life in Valhǫll of the warriors killed in battle, but the Icelandic sagas attest to beliefs that a dead person would spend the afterlife feasting with companions in his grave mound or would join his kin, who would be "living" in a nearby cliff or mountain. These beliefs were very likely to have originated in Norway, the homeland of many of the original settlers of Iceland. Finally, in addition to the geographic distribution of the cults of a particular god, Norse paganism seems to have involved no restrictions or requirements regarding an individual's beliefs. According to the sagas, at least, one person could be a devotee of Þórr, whereas his neighbor was a devotee of Freyr. From a very early period, Germanic and Scandinavian pagans were rarely wholly isolated from Christianity, and a certain amount of syncretism undoubtedly resulted. The sagas, for example, tell of one Icelander who prayed to Christ while he was ashore but to Þórr while he was at sea.

The value system of Germanic paganism had to do with people's actions rather than their thoughts, feelings, or beliefs. There was no religious moral code defining particular "virtues" or "sins"; instead, Germanic law, culture, and custom embodied a system in which certain actions would bring honor or dishonor to an individual. Shame might or might not be felt by someone who had brought dishonor upon himself, but a person's reputation was a product of his or her interaction with the community, not a matter between that person and a god. Generally speaking, showing bravery in battle, generosity in gift-giving and hospitality, and taking blood-vengeance in response to a killing or murder would enhance a man's honor. Generosity also enhanced a woman's honor, as did urging men to honorable actions and dying with them should their hall or farm be attacked. Cowardice and miserliness brought dishonor. There was no dishonor in amassing as much wealth as one could, only in not being generous with what one had. In the end, neither one's honor nor one's belief in a god or the gods seems to have been relevant to one's fate after death, despite the acceptance of the concepts of Valhǫll and Hel. Malicious people sometimes returned as destructive ghosts or revenants to harm the living, but there were ways of laying them to rest. The peaceful dead would be served in the afterlife by the things burned or buried with them (clothing, jewelry, weapons, tools, and household items, sometimes extending to food, dogs, horses, and servants), and in this world their reputations would live on after them "for as long as the northern part of the world is inhabited."

SEE ALSO Álfar; Axis Mundi; Baldr; Berserkers; Dismemberment; Dvergar; Eddas; Freyja; Freyr; Fylgjur; Heimdallr; Indo-European Religions, overview article; Jôtnar; Landvættir; Loki; Njǫrðr; Óðinn; Olaf the Holy; Paganism, Anglo-Saxon; Runes; Sagas; Saxo Grammaticus; Snorri Sturluson; Thor; Týr; Valhǫll; Valkyries.

BIBLIOGRAPHY

For the Indo-European creation myths, see Bruce Lincoln's *Myth, Cosmos, and Society: Indo-European Themes of Creation and Destruction* (Cambridge, Mass., 1986). On the Germanic pantheon, see E. O. G. Turville-Petre's general work *Myth and Religion of the North* (London, 1964) and Georges Dumézil's general study *Gods of the Ancient Northmen* (Berkeley, Calif., 1973). Other standard works on the topic include Jan de Vries's *Altgermanische Religionsgeschichte*, 2d ed., 2 vols. (Berlin, 1956–1957); R. L. M. Derolez's *Götter und Mythen der Germanen* (Darmstadt, Germany, 1959; Einsiedeln, Switzerland, 1963); and Régis Boyer's *La religion des Anciens Scandinaves* (Paris, 1981). Hilda R. Ellis Davidson's *Gods and Myths of Northern Europe* (Baltimore, 1964) is written for a wider public. A more controversial work is Åke V. Ström's *Germanische Religion*, vol. 19 of *Die Religionen der Menschheit* (Stuttgart, 1975). A better summary, strongly influenced by Georges Dumézil, is Werner Betz's "Die altgermanische Religion," in Wolfgang Stammler's *Deutsche Philologie im Aufriss*, vol. 3 (Berlin, 1957). Succinct presentations are found in Lennart Ejerfeldt's contribution to the *Handbuch der Religionsgeschichte*, vol. 1, edited by Jes P. Asmussen and Jørgen Laessøe (Göttingen, 1971), pp. 277–342; and in Eduard Neumann and Helmut Voigt's entry in *Wörterbuch der Mythologie*, vol. 2 of *Das alte Europa*, edited by H. W. Haussig (Stuttgart, 1972). On Tacitus, compare J. G. C. Anderson's *Cornelii Taciti De origine et situ Germanorum* (Oxford, 1961), Rudolf Much's *Die Germania des Tacitus erläutert*, edited by Wolfgang Lange and Herbert Jankuhn (Heidelberg, Germany, 1967), and Allan Lund's *Zum Germanenbild der Römer: eine Einführung in die antike Ethnographie* (Heidelberg, Germany, 1990). On the sovereign gods, consult Georges Dumézil's *Les dieux souverains des Indo-Européens* (Paris, 1977). On the divine twins, compare Donald Ward's *The Divine Twins: An Indo-European Myth in Germanic Tradition* (Berkeley, Calif., 1968) and Georges Dumézil's *From Myth to Fiction: The Saga of Hadingus* (Chicago, 1973), especially pp. 109–120. Dumézil's early views are found in *Mythes et dieux des Germains: Essai d'interprétation comparative* (Paris, 1939); a later comparative work is his *Loki* (Paris, 1986). Margaret Clunies Ross takes an anthropological approach in *Prolonged Echoes: Old Norse Myths in Medieval Northern Society*, vol. 1 (Odense, Denmark, 1994). John Lindow surveys the scholarship in *Scandinavian Mythology: An Annotated Bibliography* (New York, 1988) and also applies anthropological theory to the myth of Baldr in *Murder and Vengence among the Gods: Baldr in Scandinavian Mythology* (Helsinki, Finland, 1997). The encyclopedia-style entries of Phillip Pulsiano's *Medieval Scandinavia: An Encyclopedia* (New York, 1993), Rudolf Simek's *Dictionary of Northern Mythology* (Cambridge, U.K., 1993), and John Lindow's *Handbook of Norse Mythology* (Santa Barbara, Calif., 2001) are very detailed. For Germanic beliefs about the afterlife, see Hilda Roderick Ellis's *The Road to Hel: A Study of the Conception of the Dead in Old Norse Literature* (New York, 1968). Thomas A. DuBois examines the dynamic interrelationships of the various religions of pagan Scandinavia in *Nordic Religions in the Viking Age* (Philadelphia, 1999). An English translation of Snorri's euhemeristic history is provided by Lee M. Hollander, *Heimskringla: History of the Kings of Norway, by Snorri Sturluson* (Austin, Tex., 1964)

EDGAR C. POLOMÉ (1987)
ELIZABETH ASHMAN ROWE (2005)

GERMANIC RELIGION: HISTORY OF STUDY

This article concentrates on the most recent phase of the history of scholarship on Germanic religion. A 1956 study by Jan de Vries provides a detailed review of work up to the middle of the twentieth century, and 1985 reviews by Joseph Harris and John Lindow cover developments up to the early 1980s.

SCHOLARSHIP TO THE LATE NINETEENTH CENTURY. Medieval scholars of Germanic religion were divided into two camps. Euhemerists such as Snorri Sturluson (1179–1241) argued that the pagan gods were men who had migrated to Sweden from Troy but who were believed by the local inhabitants to be divine. In contrast, demonists such as the editors of the sagas about King Olaf Tryggvason (r. 995–1000) held that the pagan gods were manifestations of Satan. Knowledge of the pagan religion was never lost, as is shown by the existence of two versions of Snorri's *Edda* that were set down in seventeenth-century Iceland. However, the systematic study of Germanic mythology began with the publication in 1835 of Jacob Grimm's work on Teutonic mythology. Although his etymologies and interpretations are now largely rejected, his collection of materials was nonetheless a rich one and a monument to romanticism's interest in the Germanic past.

After Grimm, the nineteenth century witnessed various trends in the interpretation of myth. First were the nature interpretations, according to which the myths represented seasonal change and the gods represented phenomena such as storms, thunder, and fire. Among the general mythologists who worked with Germanic materials, Max Müller connected all myths with the cycle of the sun and Adalbert Kuhn offered meteorological interpretations. Among those specializing in Germanic religion, Wilhelm Mannhardt emphasized agricultural rites; some British scholars, such as Edward B. Tylor, postulated that the Germanic tribes were animists who believed in spirits and demons; and others, including Andrew Lang, interpreted myths as dreams. Scholars were also interested in using Germanic material to study still earlier societies: Müller, Kuhn, and Wilhelm Schwartz used comparative approaches to reconstruct proto-Germanic and Indo-European religions. This direction of research was superseded by the so-called folklore mythology, which began with Wilhelm Mannhardt's 1875 study of forest and field cults, and the use of folklore customs to interpret Germanic mythology continued for some seventy-five years. (Sir James Frazer's monumental *The Golden Bough* [1911–1915] is based on this line of research.)

Toward the end of the nineteenth century, monographs were devoted to major deities, including Rudolf Much's to the sky god and Vilhelm Grönbech's to religion and ethical and spiritual concepts. Germanic mythology also became of interest to philologists. Sophus Bugge questioned the originality of Germanic mythology with his revolutionary hypotheses about the origin of Germanic myths, which he held were derived entirely from Christian and classical thought. His theories were defended especially by Elard Hugo Meyer, who associated them also with the older natural-mythological interpretations, but all these views have lost acceptance. (Archaeological studies do hint at some Roman influence on the early development of the Scandinavian pantheon, and Christianity is now considered to have had an influence on Scandinavian paganism itself as well as on the textual sources, as Kaarle Krohn, Anne Holtsmark, and others have shown.) Eugen Mogk criticized the supposed reliability of Snorri's *Edda* and thus drew attention to the fundamental problem of the trustworthiness of Old Norse sources.

EARLY TWENTIETH CENTURY: FORMATIVE YEARS. The period from around 1900 to World War II saw a consolidation of the field, and the resulting view of Germanic religion, in its basics, is that still held at the turn of the twenty-first century. Walter Baetke described the Germanic peoples' concept of the holy, their ideas about fate, and their system of values; Magnus Olsen used place-names as a new source for the research of Germanic religion; and Grönbech examined the role of religion in the lives of the Germanic people and its influence on cult and custom. Ritual activity was the focus of the interpretations of Otto Höfler, who examined the links of mythology and cult and the significance of the cult in the lives of individuals. His argument for the existence of a cult group of warriors linked with Óðinn has found objections but no real refutation. Franz Rolf Schröder used both Germanic and non-Germanic parallels and relations in his study of the the religions of the Indo-European peoples, although not all his theories are still accepted. Axel Olrik, who from 1892 to 1894 had produced a study of Saxo Grammaticus (c. 1150—after 1216) that has never been superseded, was joined by Hans Ellekilde for a still largely respected study of Scandinavian mythology that made substantial use of comparative material.

Yet another comparativist, Georges Dumézil, arrived at a "three-function" theory of Indo-European mythology. He considered the common Indo-European ideology to have consisted of three principles—the maintenance of cosmic and juridical order, the exercise of physical force, and the promotion of physical well-being—and he interpreted the gods of the various groups of the Indo-Europeans' descendants as representing these "functions." He saw Óðinn and Týr as co-sovereigns, each dedicated to one of the elements of the first function; Þórr represented the second function, and Njǫrðr, Freyr, and Freyja the third. Despite some reservations, such as the objection to Dumézil's identification of Þórr as a war god, this theory has gained in importance since the 1950s. In 1956 and 1957, the second edition of de Vries's magisterial two volumes on the history of Germanic religion brought this newer work together with the older scholarship of historicists such as Karl Helm, who depended on philological and archaeological evidence. De Vries also presented findings from the study of folklore and place-names. His opus is the most extensive handbook of Germanic religion and is still useful, albeit insufficiently critical of the Nordic literary sources.

Studies of Old Norse mythology experimented with the functionalist and structuralist theories of the 1940s and 1950s, but in the main—except for Dumézil's brand of structuralism—the historicist (or literary-philological or positivist) approach of the nineteenth century is still in force. This line of thinking assumes that each myth had a single "original" form and meaning that can be reconstructed and that is the primary object of study. The neohistoricist or "new philological" approach of scholars such as Thomas A. DuBois, in contrast, assumes that myths may have had different meanings for different communities at different times. The latter approach is also seen in late-twentieth- and early twenty-first-century archaeologically based studies of Germanic religion. Archaeology also supplies new primary sources for the study of Germanic religion; for example, Karl Hauck argues that the human figures on Migration Age (late fourth century–early seventh century) bracteates represent Germanic divinities. (Bracteates are Germanic medallions, probably inspired by Roman coins, that depict figures and scenes that are still not fully understood.) Although not all of his identifications have been accepted, the evidence of the bracteates is considered relevant.

LATE TWENTIETH CENTURY. Despite some overinterpretation, place-name studies continue to be a productive field for the study of Scandinavian paganism. For example, in a 1999 paper, Alexandra Pesch searches the kings' sagas for interpretations of the ninth-century Oseberg (near Oslo) ship burial and then examines this information in light of the archaeological and place-name evidence. The former indicates that the burial is that of a pagan seeress or priestess rather than that of a queen, and the latter suggests that Oseberg (if from *Ásaberg*, meaning "mountain of the gods") may, like Uppsala, have been a center for the worship of several deities. The silence of the sagas regarding a heathen cult center or sacral landscape in this part of Norway reminds us that when it comes to early Scandinavian history, the sagas are far from preserving a full account of events.

Old Norse myth and Scandinavian society. One important development in the second half of the twentieth century was the idea that the well-documented Old Norse myths should be treated separately from the poorly documented

Scandinavian pagan rituals. Earlier, Frazer's view of ritual as the dramatization of myth had influenced pre–World War II scholars of Old Norse myth such as Magnus Olsen and Bertha Phillpotts and to some extent postwar scholars such as Holtsmark, Einar Haugen, and Anders Andrén. Scholars such as Margaret Clunies Ross, John Lindow, and Jens Peter Schjødt rely on the relationship between myth and ritual in non-Western societies to argue that myth and ritual are probably not as closely interrelated as Frazer and his followers thought. Following Victor Turner, such "anthropological" studies of Old Norse myth treat it as one symbolic form among the many that a society accesses during ritual performance, and following Émile Durkheim, they assume that myths express certain social and cultural realities for the people who create and use them. Drawing on semiology, these studies further consider mythology as a system of interrelated elements, and they avoid investigating myths on an individual basis.

Despite these common assumptions, scholars taking the anthropological approach have posited quite different aspects of society as central to Scandinavian mythology. Clunies Ross focuses on issues of exogamy as the source of tension between the Æsir, the Vanir, and the giants. She argues that the Æsir are unwilling to give their women in marriage to members of the other groups, as this would acknowledge that they are all of equal status, but the resulting unions between giantesses and Vanir and the various ploys to obtain Æsir women sow the seeds of the Æsir's own destruction. Lindow focuses on the social mechanism of the blood feud, which was the chief means of maintaining social stability both for the Æsir and for the Icelanders who worshiped them. The ongoing feud between the giants and the gods reflected a social reality that the Icelanders knew well, but the murder of the god Baldr, which sets brother against brother, is evidence of a fatal flaw in a strategy that is supposed to lead to resolution.

Germanic paganism and Christianity. The assumption that religions are not static but are changing and pluralistic is also productive for studies of the interaction of Germanic paganism with Christianity and other religions. For example, DuBois argues that the extensive and long-term intercultural contacts between the pagan Norse, the Sámi, and the Finns, and then between these groups and various kinds of Christianity, resulted in the continuous alteration of their religious traditions. DuBois shows that Christian notions of burial made inroads into the practices of Nordic pagans long before these people officially accepted the new religion. Concepts about the afterlife underwent transformations as well, with pagan communities adjusting their beliefs in line with Christian doctrines prior to their conversion. It is likely that Christian rites and beliefs affected traditions such as ship burial and Ragnarǫk, which rise in prominence during the late pagan era.

Lindow and John McKinnell have concentrated on the interaction of Christianity and Scandinavian paganism and on the question of Norse-Christian syncretism. Lindow argues that Norse mythology cannot be interpreted without reference to Christian influence, which may have been considerable, as the two cultures had ample opportunities to meet in an enormous number of contexts. Old myths may have been reworked in Christian forms; new versions may have emphasized certain aspects of the "original" myths for reasons related to Christian theology, or the new versions may have assimilated Christian modes of expression or imitated Christian forms. McKinnell sees the possibility of syncretism in tenth-century Norway, as archaeological and textual evidence points to an important Christian presence in Norway before the missionary efforts of King Olaf Tryggvason, and Peter Foote has pointed out the peculiarities of early Icelandic Christianity.

A different matter is the use of pagan iconography for a wholly Christian purpose, as when Christian sculptors in Viking Age England put scenes of Ragnarǫk on their crosses as a way of emphasizing the parallels between the two religions and simultaneously showing that the old religion had been replaced and surpassed by the new. Yet another aspect of the interaction between Scandinavian paganism and Christianity that has received recent scholarly attention is the learned, medieval context in which the myths are preserved. Such studies clarify the material and render less significant the gulf between pagan Scandinavia and the recording of the mythology centuries later in a Christian context.

With the exception of de Vries, whose history of the study of religion (translated into English in 1967) is widely cited, scholars of Germanic religion and Scandinavian mythology have been medievalists first and scholars of comparative religion and mythology a distant second, most likely because of the specialized skills necessary to study the primary sources. The anthropological studies of Norse myth are the most up-to-date with respect to theory, but of the internationally famous mythographers of the twentieth century, only Dumézil has had a major impact on the study of Scandinavian mythology. Claude Lévi-Strauss's ideas have been injected into Dumézil's system by Einar Haugen, and his principles have been applied to certain eddic poems, but he has not himself been concerned with Germanic materials. Similarly, the theoretical orientation of Joseph Campbell has been used by Loren Gruber to examine the role of rites of passage in the eddic poem *Hávamál,* but Campbell's own treatment of Germanic material has been incidental. Mircea Eliade, however, included many Norse references to Óðinn in his study of shamanism, and the Norse applications of his theories of the sacred and profane or myth of the eternal return are obvious.

See Also Eddas; Sagas; Saxo Grammaticus; Snorri Sturluson.

Bibliography

Translated excerpts from nineteenth-century German scholarship on Germanic religion are provided by T. A. Shippey and Andreas Haarder in *Beowulf: The Critical Heritage* (New York, 1998). Jan de Vries's survey is found in the first volume of the second edition of his *Altgermanische Religionsgeschichte* (Berlin, 1956–1957), and the reviews by Joseph Harris and John Lindow appear in *Old Norse—Icelandic Literature*, edited by Carol Clover and John Lindow (Ithaca, N.Y., 1985). Another bibliographic resource is Lindow's *Scandinavian Mythology: An Annotated Bibliography* (New York, 1988). Fine examples of his recent work are "Bloodfeud and Scandinavian Mythology," *Alvíssmál* 4 (1994): 51–68, and *Murder and Vengeance among the Gods: Baldr in Scandinavian Mythology* (Helsinki, 1997). Anthropological approaches are also pursued by Margaret Clunies Ross in the two volumes of *Prolonged Echoes: Old Norse Myths in Medieval Northern Society* (Odense, Denmark, 1994–1998) and in the essays she edits in *Old Norse Myths, Literature and Society* (Odense, Denmark, 2003) as well as by Thomas A. DuBois in *Nordic Religions in the Viking Age* (Philadelphia, 1999). An interdisciplinary approach was the focus of a conference whose proceedings are published in *Words and Objects: Towards a Dialogue between Archaeology and History of Religion* (Oslo, 1986), edited by Gro Steinsland; Steinsland's own study of Norse mythology is in *Det hellige bryllup og norrøn kongeideologi: En analyse av hieregami-myten i* Skírnismál, Ynglingatal, Háleygjatal, *og* Hyndluljóð (Oslo, 1991). The foremost modern scholar of Germanic ritual is Jens Peter Schjødt; for references to his work, see his essay "Myths as Sources for Rituals—Theoretical and Practical Implications" in Clunies Ross (2003). Peter Foote's study, "Secular Attitudes in Early Iceland," appeared in *Medieval Scandinavia* 7 (1974): 31–44, and Alexandra Pesch's paper on the Oseberg ship burial, "Die Oseberg-'Saga' in ihrer Vielschichtigkeit," is found in *Die Aktualität der Saga. Festschrift für Hans Schottmann*, edited by Stig Toftgaard Andersen (Berlin, 1999), pp. 177–199. Jan de Vries's general history of the study of religion was translated into English as *Perspectives in the History of Religions* (Berkeley, Calif., 1967), translated and with an introduction by Kees W. Bolle.

ELIZABETH ASHMAN ROWE (2005)

GERSHOM BEN YEHUDAH

GERSHOM BEN YEHUDAH (c. 965–1028), German halakhist and Jewish communal leader. Despite the many uncertainties surrounding Gershom's life and historical role, it is clear that he was the central figure in the crystallization of Ashkenazic learning and communal organization in pre-Crusade Europe. A generation or two after his death Gershom was already termed Ma'or ha-Golah ("light of the exile"), a title reflecting the perception of both his spiritual stature and his historical impact.

Gershom's origins are not known, but it is likely that his immediate ancestry was French. He spent his adult life in Mainz, where in addition to writing commentaries on the Talmud and some liturgical poetry, he trained the men who were to be the mentors of Rashi. Gershom's personal life reflected the most painful experiences of medieval Jewish life: his son (and, according to one report, his wife as well) converted to Christianity. His poetry expresses the reality of persecution and the yearning for redemption.

Gershom's major contribution is revealed in his *responsa* and in the enactments (*taqqanot*) attributed to him. The *responsa* on questions of Jewish law are of course rooted in Talmudic literature, but they expose an original, decisive legal mind grappling with the central problems of his day. Some of his *responsa* dealt with Jews who converted to Christianity under duress, encouraging their return to Judaism by smoothing their path back to the community; others relaxed prohibitive regulations on Jewish-gentile commerce and empowered the community to govern more effectively by transferring to local communal leadership powers of compulsion that in Talmudic law are granted to central rabbinical courts. Matters of communal governance as well as issues of general social import were at the heart of the enactments attributed to Gershom.

The actual relationship between Gershom and the communities in whose name the enactments are also recorded is shrouded in obscurity, but present scholarly consensus sees Gershom as the central, driving figure behind this legislation. The enactments provide, inter alia, that the minority in a community must accept the authority of the majority, that taxes in dispute are to be paid before they are litigated, and that a defendant in a civil suit may be brought before a court in any community. These *taqqanot* were of great historical significance in legitimating community governance. Other enactments, such as those that prohibit marriage with more than one wife at the same time (permitted by both biblical and Talmudic law) and that forbid a husband to divorce his wife against her will, remain decisive for modern Jewish law and society. Both enactments reflect the status achieved by women in Gershom's society. While originally designed for the German communities of the Rhineland, they were gradually accepted by world Jewry.

BIBLIOGRAPHY

The most comprehensive discussion of Gershom's life and achievement is in Abraham Grossman's *Ḥakhmei Ashkenaz hari'shonim* (Jerusalem, 1981), pp. 106–174. Louis Finkelstein, in *Jewish Self-Government in the Middle Ages* (1924; reprint, Westport, Conn., 1972), pp. 20–36, 111–139, presents the enactments attributed to Gershom in both the original Hebrew and in translation and discusses questions of authorship, provenance, and impact. Ze'ev W. Falk, in *Jewish Matrimonial Law in the Middle Ages* (Oxford, 1966), discusses the relationship between Gershom's enactments on monogamy and divorce and similar norms in Christian Europe.

GERALD J. BLIDSTEIN (1987)

GERSONIDES

GERSONIDES (1288–1344), French mathematician and philosopher, known also as Levi Ben Gershom and, in rabbinic texts, by the acronym RaLBaG (Rabbi Levi ben Gershom). Born in Bagnols, Gersonides lived most of his life in Orange and Avignon. Little else is known about him other than where he resided in Provence under the protection of the popes. Gersonides says almost nothing about his personal life, but some scholars have speculated that he may have functioned as a community rabbi, as a banker, or both. Given the nature of his writings and where he lived, it is not unreasonable to speculate that in addition to his involvement with the Jewish community, he may have taught astronomy/astrology in the papal university, medical school, or court. Gersonides is generally acknowledged to be the greatest and most independent medieval Jewish philosopher after the death of Moses Maimonides (Mosheh ben Maimon, 1135/8–1204). Of those rabbis who based their religious thought on the philosophy of Aristotle, Gersonides is the most thorough and rigorous; his major work in this area is *The Wars of the Lord* (1329). Gersonides also dealt with rabbinics, philosophy, mathematics, medicine, and astronomy.

In rabbinics Gersonides wrote commentaries on the Pentateuch, the Former Prophets, *Proverbs*, *Job*, *Song of Songs*, *Ruth*, *Ecclesiastes*, *Esther*, *Daniel*, *Ezra*, *Nehemiah*, and *1* and *2 Chronicles*, as well as a commentary on the thirteen hermeneutic rules of Yishmaʿeʾl ben Elishaʿ (a tanna of the first and second centuries) and a commentary on the tractate Berakhot of the Babylonian Talmud. In philosophy he published a treatise on direct syllogisms and supercommentaries on the middle commentaries and résumés of Ibn Rushd (1126–1198). In medicine he is known to have written a remedy for the gout. In mathematics he composed a treatise on algebra and a commentary on parts of Euclid's *Elements*.

Finally, Gersonides published a major treatise on astronomy (1340), which Moritz Steinschneider identified as *Sefer Tekhunah*, which consists of 136 chapters. (A summary of this more detailed work is contained in the second part of the fifth book of *The Wars of the Lord*.) What is of particular interest to historians of science is that the work contains significant modifications of the systems of Ptolemy and al-Bitruji, as well as useful astronomical tables. The work also includes a description of an instrument, which he calls a *megalleh ʿamuqqot* (detector of depths), which he invented for making precise astronomical observations. The work was praised and extensively quoted by Giovanni Pico della Mirandola in his *Disputationes adversus astrologiam divinatricem* (1495). In general Gersonides' instrument is considered the most useful tool developed to assist measurements in astronomy prior to the development of the telescope, and historians of science regard Gersonides as one of the most important European astronomers before Galileo.

The Wars of the Lord deals only with those questions that Maimonides either resolved in direct opposition to Aristotelian principles or explained so obscurely that Maimonides' own view cannot be determined. These questions are discussed in six treatises on, successively, the nature of the soul (i.e., psychology), prophecy (i.e., revelation), God's knowledge, divine providence, the nature of the celestial spheres (i.e., cosmology), and the eternity of matter (i.e., cosmogony).

In each treatise, every question is systematically discussed. First, Gersonides lists all of the different positions that had previously been taken on the issue in question. He then presents a critical analysis of each view, and in so doing lists every form of argument for each position and judges the extent to which each argument is and is not valid. Following this, he states his own view, and he then shows how each of the arguments given for other positions, to the extent to which they are valid, supports his own position. Finally, he demonstrates that his position is in agreement with the correct meaning of the Torah.

Gersonides' theory of divine knowledge was one of the most controversial parts of his work. In the subsequent history of philosophy it led some Jewish thinkers to condemn his work (e.g., Shem Tov ibn Shem Tov, c. 1390–1440) and others to follow him (e.g., Barukh Spinoza, 1632–1677). Gersonides argued that all terms correctly predicated of God and man are such that those terms apply primarily to God and derivatively to humans. Hence, the term-knower refers primarily to how God knows, and by reference to divine knowledge the term is applied to human beings. As their creator, God knows all things as they are essentially in and of themselves. In contrast, human beings, with the assistance of the Active Intellect, know these creations through their senses as effects. God knows everything, but he knows it in a single act of knowledge. The content of divine knowledge is expressible in human terms as an infinite conjunction of distinct universal, conditional propositions. Concerning a specific entity or fact, whereas human beings may know it accidentally, as a particular, through sense reports, God knows it essentially, as a unique individual, through his intellect. Gersonides' opponents interpreted this thesis to amount to a denial that God knows particulars, with the consequence that God is limited in knowledge and power.

Possibly the most original part of Gersonides' work was his cosmology. The concluding treatise of *The Wars of the Lord* consists of a detailed demonstration, based on astronomy and physics, of the existence of the different heavenly intelligences (angels) and the uniqueness of the ultimate intelligence (God). In terms of its philosophical and scientific elements, this treatise constitutes the most sophisticated work of theology in the history of Judaism. In it, Gersonides argues that this unending universe was created in time, not out of the remains of some previously existing universe but out of nothing. However, the "nothing" from which the world was created is not absolutely nothing; instead, it is an eternal, unformed matter, unlike any other matter of which we can conceive. Gersonides' account of this matter may be the most original part of the work. It is significantly different from the theory of prime matter found in any other work of Jewish, Muslim, or Christian philosophy. But to give an adequate account of it involves a technical discussion that goes beyond the confines of this essay. Suffice it to say that Gersonides' theory of prime matter bears some resemblance to the use by Hermann Cohen (1842–1918) of the term *ori-*

gin in his application of the infinitesimal calculus to ontology, and it may have parallels with the kind of high-energy radiation from which the universe originated, according to those astrophysicists who support the Big Bang theory.

SEE ALSO Jewish Thought and Philosophy, article on Premodern Philosophy.

BIBLIOGRAPHY

A full list of the published writings of Gersonides can be found in Bernhard Blumenkranz's *Auteurs juifs en France médiévale* (Toulouse, France, 1975), pp. 65–69. An extensive bibliography of secondary sources is given in Menachem M. Kellner's "Gersonides, Providence, and the Rabbinic Tradition," *Journal of the American Academy of Religion* 42 (1974): 673–685.

The best source for information about Gersonides' life are two essays by Joseph Shatzmiller, one in Hebrew (in *Studies in the History of the Jewish People and the Land of Israel* 2 [1972]: 111–126) and the other in French (in *Gersonide en son temps*, edited by Gilbert Dahan [Louvain, Belgium, and Paris, 1991], pp. 33–43). With reference to English translations of primary sources, Abraham Lassen has published an English translation of Gersonides' commentary on the Book of Job under the title *The Commentary of Levi ben Gerson (Gersonides) on the Book of Job* (New York, 1946). Furthermore, an English translation of the entire *Wars of the Lord* has been published by Seymour Feldman (Philadelphia, 1984–1999). In addition, there are three English translations of separate treatises, each of which contains valuable commentaries: on treatise 3, see Norbert M. Samuelson's *Gersonides' The War of the Lord, Treatise Three: On God's Knowledge* (Toronto, 1977); on treatise 4, see J. David Bleich's *Providence in the Philosophy of Gersonides* (New York, 1973); and on treatise 6, see Jacob J. Staub's *The Creation of the World according to Gersonides* (Chico, Calif., 1982).

Gersonides' positions on divine knowledge and providence, as well as his cosmogony, are inherently connected with his cosmology. As yet no one has undertaken the difficult task of translating his treatise on astronomy. However, considerable light on his cosmology is given in the many publications of Bernard R. Goldstein, especially *The Astronomy of Levi ben Gerson* (New York, 1985).

NORBERT M. SAMUELSON (1987 AND 2005)

GESAR.

GESAR. As is the case with most epic texts—*Rāmāyaṇa, Gilgamesh,* and *King Arthur,* for example—little is known of the historical and artistic genesis of the Gesar epic (Tibetan, *Gling Ge sar gyi sgrung*), a complex and lengthy narrative relating the heroic deeds of the divine king Gesar. The earliest known written version of the epic dates back to 1716, when it was translated—possibly from Tibetan—into Mongolian on the orders of the Manchu emperor. Different versions are attested: the Eastern Tibetan from Khams province (Eastern Tibet); the so-called Amdo Tibetan from a province in northeastern Tibet; the Western Tibetan from Ladakh, an oral version that has affinities with both the Eastern and Amdo versions, though it is shorter than the Eastern one; and the Mongolian one, which boasts a great number of episodes that cannot be found in the other versions. Hunza (northeast Pakistan), Lepcha (northeast Nepal), Buriat (North Mongolia), Khalkha (Mongolia), and Kalmuk (Siberia) versions are also recorded. Regardless of discrepancies among all versions, the core of the epic, which is made of six or seven episodes (sometimes called the proto-epic), has been extant since the seventeenth century at the latest.

THE EPIC: HISTORICAL BACKGROUND AND LINKS WITH BUDDHISM. Whether a real person lies behind the epic hero Gesar is still debated. One of the earliest written instances of his name (as Gesar, king of Phrom) appears in a ninth-century Tibetan manuscript, and the name also appears on a coin that may refer to the king of a Central Asian kingdom in the ninth or tenth century. For most Tibetans he is an eleventh-century historical figure who ruled Ling (Tibetan, *Gling*), a principality in Khams, that reached its peak in the thirteenth and fourteenth centuries. It has been suggested that Khrom (or Phrom, pronounced "Throm") could be a distant echo of Rome, via the Turkish word *Rûm* that designated Rome or Byzance, while Gesar would refer to *Kaisar*, the Turkish word for "king" or "emperor," derived from Caesar. But Gesar is also seen as a Buddhist character, since he is considered as an emanation of both Avalokiteśvara, the *bodhisattva* of compassion (also embodied in the Dalai Lamas of Tibet) and Padmasambhava (the semi-legendary introducer of Tantric Buddhism in Tibet in the eighth century). He fights in the name of the Buddhist doctrine and the well-being of all men—or, more precisely, Tibetans.

Whether the original epic (if ever there was such a thing) was devoid of references to Buddhism is hard to tell, but it came to pervade most of the narrative. For instance, between wars Gesar is described not as ruling his kingdom but as going into spiritual retreat until a vision summons him to fight another battle against another enemy. Most songs in the epic begin with an invocation of Buddhist or pre-Buddhist local deities and often include a sermon on important aspects of Buddhism. Although certain sects of the Tibetan clergy have shown hostility towards the epic, its content was gradually infused with Buddhist themes until famous Tibetan lamas of the nineteenth century assimilated Gesar to a Buddhist protective *dgra lha* (war deity). Moreover, the recitation of some episodes have come to acquire a ritualistic dimension: *Hor gling*—the battle against Hor—is associated with the fight against demons, and *Stag gzig nor 'gyed*—the battle for the wealth of Tagzig—with an increase of wealth. The Manchu emperors of China (1644–1911) identified Gesar with the Chinese god of war, and a cult to Gesar (Mongolian, Geser) has existed in Mongolia since the seventeenth century.

THE EPISODES. Most versions of the epic begin with three famous episodes: the decision of the assembly of gods to send a savior (the future Gesar) to defend the world, and more particularly Tibet, against the forces of evil (the episode called *Lha gling*); Gesar's childhood as the despised and ugly child Jo ru (the episode called *'Khrungs gling*); and Jo ru's unexpected victory at a horse race at the age of thirteen, whereby he becomes the respected and impressive Gesar, marries the beautiful princess' Brug mo (Drugmo) and becomes the king of the community of Ling (the episode called *Rta rgyug*). These are followed by a succession of narratives describing how, riding his supernatural horse and leading his thirty brave companions and his army, Gesar wages a series of wars against four foreign kingdoms and eighteen Tibetan principalities. The episodes always end with Gesar's victory and the pledge of the subdued armies to become his allies in conquests to come—as well as with the plundering of the enemies' wealth and its redistribution to the people of Ling. The last episode recounts how he rescues his mother from Hell. For Tibetan believers, Gesar is now residing in Shambala, a hidden realm from where he will come back to save humanity and Buddhism. A characteristic of this epic is its open ending; in the twentieth century at least two new episodes were added.

The total number of episodes is difficult to assess. The latest figures vary from 120 to 200, of which about 100 had been published by the early twenty-first century. Another peculiarity of the epic concerns its elaboration, which rarely resorts to literary creation, although a few episodes present themselves as rewritings of previously known versions. New episodes mostly appear through vision and revelation to either Buddhist masters or laypersons, who claim to be reincarnations of characters of the epic and whose previous life they recall, thereby "creating" a new episode. There also exist "treasure-bards" (Tibetan, *gter sgrung*) who "discover" episodes hidden in their mental continuum, in the same way as Buddhist "treasure-discoverers" (Tibetan, *gter ston*) discover Buddhist teachings or narratives thought to have been hidden in a previous time by Padmasambhava.

BARDS. Until the Chinese takeover of Tibet in the 1950s, most versions were passed on orally and few were committed to the written form, as manuscripts or, more rarely, xylographs (i.e., woodblock prints). Amateur performers would recite and sing it, and professional wandering bards (Tibetan, *sgrung mkhan* or *sgrung pa*) would roam the country narrating a few episodes in which they specialized. An estimate by Tibetan and Chinese researchers showed that the total number of bards in Tibet early in the twenty-first century varies between 100 and 140. Female bards are very rare, although women play an important part in the narrative (as mothers, wives, aunts, mistresses, etc.). A bard's performance usually alternates between short prose narrative parts and lengthy versified (often heptasyllabic) monologues in the form of songs. On average, one episode may contain between fifty and one hundred songs, the melody varying according to the character they represent. There are also melodies for certain types of songs (visions, prophecies, etc.). Bards would sometimes accompany their performance with painted prompts (Tibetan, *sgrung thang*) on which they would show the scenes referred to in their narrative.

In most cases, bards learn their craft from another bard or from a family member and rely on either a written text or their memory (Tibetan, *bshad sgrung*—literally, "narrating bard"—is a sub-category of the generic *sgrung mkhan* or *sgrung pa* category). But the most appreciated bards are those whose performance shares common characteristics with certain aspects of Tantric Buddhism and Tibetan "folk," pre-Buddhist religion. Called *'bab sgrung* (oracular or divine bards), they are often illiterate nomads who become bards after a serious illness and ensuing visions. They recite episodes of the epic in a state of trance during which they are said to be possessed by one character of the epic who retells the event from his or her point of view. In some instances, they begin their recitation as soon as they put on their "epic hat" (Tibetan, *sgrung zhwa*). One of the most famous of these bards, Grags pa (Drak pa) (1904?/6?–1986), could recite as many as twenty-five episodes of the epic (equivalent to fifteen thousand pages of a modern text). In the rarest cases, bards can "read" an episode by looking at the surface of a mirror (Tibetan, *spra sgrung*) or looking at an empty white page. In these cases, the bard has not memorized the episode, he is in a state of inspired trance.

APPROPRIATION OF THE EPIC. The widespread popularity of the epic and its protagonists in Tibet may be explained by the part everyday Tibetan life plays in its narrative—a rare instance in a literature usually dominated by Indian models aloof from the Tibetan world. This popularity may in turn explain why several authorities have vied for its appropriation. As mentioned already, some Buddhist clergy incorporated Gesar into the Buddhist pantheon; the Buddhist tone of a number of passages in the epic can thus be explained as an attempt at exploiting its popularity among the nomads and peasants of Tibet to spread the Buddhist doctrine further. At a more esoteric level, Gesar's battles are sometimes presented as a symbol of the Buddhist follower's struggle toward Enlightenment. Since the takeover of Tibet by China in the mid-twentieth century, the Chinese cultural authorities have supported research on the epic, which represents, in their eyes, a rare case of popular, secular culture within the Buddhist-dominated Tibetan civilization. In response, Tibetans have been quick to associate Gesar (either the divine king or the epic narrative) with Tibetan cultural revival and nationalism and to cherish it as a depository of distinct and authentic Tibetan culture.

BIBLIOGRAPHY

The Gesar epic has greatly benefited from support by Chinese authorities, and not a year passes without a new episode being published in China, where the publication of a forty-volume edition, based partly on the twentieth-century bard Drakpa's recitation, is in progress. In Bhutan, K. Tobgyal and M. Dorji edited *The Epic of Gesar* (Thimphu, Bhutan, 1979), a heterogenous and somehow haphazard compilation in thirty-one volumes. Episodes are also published in India under the auspices of the exiled Tibetan community.

Only parts of the Gesar epic have been translated into Western languages: A. H. Francke collected and published a translation of the Ladakhi version of the epic at the turn of the twentieth century; see his *A Lower Ladakhi Version of the Kesar Saga* (New Delhi, 2000). An edited synthesis of a version from Eastern Tibet can be found in A. David-Néel's *La vie surhumaine de Guésar de Ling, le héros thibétain* (Paris, 1931, 1995), translated into English as *The Superhuman Life of Gesar of Ling* (rev. ed., London, 1959). In his *L'Epopée tibétaine de Gesar dans sa version lamaïque de Ling* (Paris, 1956), R. A. Stein partly translated a nineteenth-century xylograph that contained three episodes of the core epic. *Gesar! The Epic Tale of Tibet's Great Warrior-King,* adapted by Zara Wallace (Berkeley, Calif., 1991) is the updated and rephrased prose edition of a 1927 English translation of the 1716 Mongolian version of the epic, via a 1839 German translation.

In the 1990s, D. J. Pennick used preexisting translations to rewrite the core epic for an opera libretto (*The Warrior Song of King Gesar,* Boston, 1996). This version has retained the alternance of prose and poetic passages and is clearly formulated for a Western audience. R. Kornman and a team of translators have undertaken the integral translation of the nineteenth-century version used by R. A. Stein for his 1956 summarized translation (cf. *supra*). It is due for publication in 2004. Some episodes were translated into German by M. Hermanns in *Das National-Epos der Tibeter Gling König Gesar* (Regensburg, Germany, 1965) and by R. Kaschewsky and P. Tsering in *Gesars Anwehrkampf gegen Kaschmir* (*Zentralasiatische Studien* 6 [1972]: 273–400) and *Die Eroberung der Burg von Sum-pa* (Wiesbaden, Germany, 1987). The most thorough study to date of the epic remains R. A. Stein's *Recherches sur l'épopée et le barde au Tibet* (Paris, 1959). An updated summary of R. A. Stein's views can be found in his "Introduction" to the 1979 Thimphu version (reprinted in *Tibet Journal* 6, no. 1 [1981]: 3–13).

S. Hummel's *Eurasian Mythology in the Tibetan Epic of Ge-sar* (Dharamsala, India, 1998) suggests the existence of German and Greek mythological influence in a restricted number of the epics's episodes. His views, although tentative and sometimes far-fetched, nevertheless present original mythical and literary openings to links between Central Asian and Tibetan cultures, and his lengthy bibliography includes many German-language sources. M. Helferr is the author of a musicological study of some songs of one episode of the epic, titled *Chants dans l'épopée tibétaine de Ge-sar d'après le livre de la Course de cheval* (Paris, 1977). In the 1990s, S. G. Karmay dedicated three interesting articles to the epic, which can all be found in *The Arrow and the Spindle: Studies in the History, Myths, Rituals and Beliefs in Tibet* (Kathmandu, Nepal, 1998): "Gesar: the Epic Tradition of the Tibetan People" is a good summary of the epic in a Tibetan context; "The Theoretical Basis for the Tibetan Epic" gives a clear chronological order of the epic and considers the kingdom of Gling in its relationship to its neighbors, taking into account both historical sources and episodes of the epic; and "The Social Organization of Gling and the Term *phu nu* in the Gesar Epic" shows how a study of kinship as presented in the epic can be used as a source for a political and social analysis of traditional Tibetan nomad society.

G. Samuel has also undertaken a study of Gesar and its relationship to anthropology, shamanism, music, and so on. For an overview of the epic and the state of the field, see for instance, his "Gesar of Ling: The Origins and Meaning of the East Tibetan Epic," in *Tibetan Studies: Proceedings of the 5th Seminar of the International Association for Tibetan Studies, Narita 1989* (Narita, Japan, 1992), edited by Shoren Ihara and Zuiho Yamaguchi; "Ge sar of gLing: Shamanic Power and Popular Religion," in *Tantra and Popular Religion in Tibet* (New Delhi, 1994), edited by G. Samuel, H. Gregor, and E. Stutchbury; "The Gesar Epic of East Tibet," in *Tibetan Literature: Studies in Genre* (Ithaca, N.Y., 1996), edited by José Ignacio Cabezón and Roger R. Jackson; and "The Epic and Nationalism in Tibet," in *Religion and Biography in China and Tibet* (Richmond, U.K., 2002), edited by Benjamin Penny.

For an early twenty-first century assessment of the appropriation of Gesar by China before and above all after 1950, see L. Maconi's "Gesar de Pékin? Le sort du Roi Gesar de Gling, héros épique tibétain, en Chine (post-)maoïste," in *Formes modernes de la poésie épique: nouvelles approches* (Brussels, 2004), edited by Judith Labarthe. Research on Gesar is also very active in China and Tibet: a number of episodes of the epic have been translated into Chinese, and a Chinese magazine is dedicated to the epic (*Gesaer yanjiu jikan* [Gesar studies]). See also Yang Enhong's *Minjian shishen: Gesaer yiren yanjiu* (Popular divine poets: Study on the singing tradition of "King Gesar"; Beijing, 1995), and her "The Study of Singing Tradition of the Tibetan Epic *King Gesar*" (*IIAS Newsletter* 18 [1999], p. 16), a short and documented article in English presenting a typology of bards. See also monographs and articles by 'Jam dpal rgya mtsho (Chinese, Jianbian Jiacuo) and Gcod pa don grub (Chinese, Jiaoba Dongzhu), two Tibetan specialists. For a study of Gesar in Mongolia and Tibet, see W. Heissig's *The Religions of Mongolia* (London, 1980), his *Ge-ser Studien: Untersuchungen zu den Erzählstoffen in den "neuen" Kapiteln des mongolischen Geser-Zyklus* (Opladen, Germany, 1983), and his *Fragen der mongolischen Heldendichtung* (Wiesbaden, Germany, 1982, 1985, and 1987), which he edited and which contains several contributions on Gesar as well as translations of some episodes. N. Poppe and Ts. Damdinsüren also dedicated many articles to the fate of the epic in Mongolia. See also Klaus Sagaster's article in the first edition of this encyclopedia for a short and synthetic presentation of Gesar, especially in the Mongolian context (*Encyclopedia of Religions* 1987: 536–537).

FRANÇOISE ROBIN (2005)

GESTURES SEE POSTURES AND GESTURES

GETO-DACIAN RELIGION. The Getae and the Dacians were ancient Thracian peoples who lived in Moesia, on the northern plain of the river Danube, and in the Carpathian Mountains, approximately in the territory of modern-day Romania and Moldova. Although the religion of the Getae and the Dacians escapes complete reconstruction, it forms, nevertheless, like the religion of the ancient Celts, one of the most interesting chapters in the history of Indo-European religions outside the Greco-Roman world. Despite the rationalistic tendency of some scholars to diminish the importance of religion among these peoples, evidence indicates that the foundation of the state consisting of the Getae and the Dacians was a result of theocratic ideas. These ideas stemmed from the worship of Zalmoxis, possibly an ancient religious reformer to whom the beginnings of Getic kingship are also related. Later on, Zalmoxis was divinized, a process that has frequent parallels in ancient Greece.

As for the Dacians, testimonies explicitly relate their name to the Phrygian word *daos* ("wolf"). Paul Kretschmer's etymology, which derives *dakoi* from the Indo-European **dhawo-s* ("wolf"), has been supported by Vladimir Georgiev and has received an exhaustive historico-religious comment from Mircea Eliade (1972). Eliade claims that the Dacians, like several other Indo-European peoples, formed a *Männerbund* based on the idea of ritual lycanthropy. Young Dacian warriors were probably trained to imitate the behavior of ferocious wolves. This has nothing to do with the Getae's legendary contempt for death, however, as that was based on the Zalmoxean promise of immortality. In all probability the message of Zalmoxis referred to a paradise in which valiant warriors would survive after death in a state of perpetual happiness.

Greek evidence, starting with Herodotos, establishes a close relationship between Zalmoxis and Pythagoras. The set of religious ideas whose origin is attributed to Zalmoxis indeed presents resemblances with Pythagoreanism. Besides immortality, Zalmoxis is said to have also taught a highly praised form of psychosomatic medicine based on charms, whose purpose was to heal the soul together with the body. Plato gives a vivid and enthusiastic account of Zalmoxean medicine in the dialogue *Charmides* (156d–157c). This medical tradition was apparently long-lived: Late in the third century CE forty-seven Dacian names of medicinal plants were inserted in the famous *Materia medica* of the Greek physician Dioscurides and in *De herbis,* attributed to Apuleius.

Zalmoxean Priesthood. The cult of Zalmoxis had strong connections with kingship. Plato, in fact, reports that Zalmoxis was king of the Getae (*Charmides* 156d), but Strabo (*Geography* 7.3–5) says that Zalmoxis was priest of the most important god of the Getae, that he became associated with kingship, and that he later was himself worshiped as a god; he was supposed to live in a cave on the sacred mountain Kogaionon, where only the king and his messengers could visit him. Sacred priesthood continued down to Strabo's time (first century BCE). The sacred cave must have been the most ancient place where the god was worshiped and his priests dwelled. In Herodotos's time (fifth century BCE) a sanctuary of Zalmoxis must have existed, for Herodotos (*Histories* 4.95) relates the legend that Zalmoxis had had an underground chamber built and that he hid himself there for three years, after which he reappeared. Such a sanctuary, with a vast underground complex, has been found at Sarmizegetusa Regia (modern-day Gradiştea Muncelului, Romania).

Jordanes, the historian of the Goths, born in Moesia in the sixth century, mingled the traditions of the Goths with those of the Getae in order to give the former the prestige of an ancient and superior population. He composed a list of Zalmoxean priests from the epoch of Burebista (c. 80–44 BCE) to the time of the Dacian king Decebalus (d. 106 CE). The series opens with the well-known Decaeneus (Dicineus), Burebista's counselor, who may have decisively contributed to the latter's power and to the origin of his kingship. Decaeneus taught the Getae philosophy, physics, ethics, logic, and astronomy. In particular he introduced them to the secrets of astrology, planetary revolutions, phases of the moon, measurement of the sun's size, and cosmic revolutions. Jordanes's testimony has been too lightly dismissed in the past. Decaeneus actually taught the Getae cosmology, astrology, and astronomy as well as introducing them to one of the most intriguing of ancient calendars, whose mystery has not been yet convincingly explained. Decaeneus's successors were the priests Comosicus and Coryllus, both of them kings, the latter in Dacia. Probably this Coryllus (sometimes called Cocrilus or Scorilus) was the immediate predecessor of Decebalus, who was the last king of the Daco-Getae and was finally defeated by the Roman emperor Trajan in 106 CE.

This list of Zalmoxean priests seems to contradict a second list also furnished by Jordanes (*De origine actibusque Getarum* 39), according to which the king Zalmoxis came after Decaeneus. In fact, Jordanes is obviously not referring here to chronology; he says only that among the Getae the most important thinkers were first (*prius*) a certain Zeutas, then (*post etiam*) Decaeneus, and then again (*tertium*) Zalmoxis. One should infer from this that the predecessor of Decaeneus was Zeutas, not that Decaeneus was followed by Zalmoxis, who is simply the legendary founder of the Geto-Dacian priesthood; in fact, Decaeneus was followed by Comosicus. The name *Zeutas* is related to the southern Thracian name *Seuthes* and further to the Avestan term *haotar,* signifying an Iranian priest. Therefore, *zeutas* may simply be a generic term signifying Thracian priests.

Pythagorean Patterns. The geographer Strabo, quoting the Stoic philosopher Posidonius, was the first to give precious, but confused, information about the *ktistai* living in continence and abstinence, and the *abioi* (lit., "lifeless," i.e., strangers to normal life conditions) of whom Homer tells (*Iliad* 8.5–7). Strabo (7.3.5) also reports that Zalmoxis introduced vegetarianism among the Getae.

The Jewish historian Josephus Flavius (first century) compares the life of the ascetic Essenes with that of "those among the Dacians who are called *pleistoi*" (*Jewish Antiquities* 18.22). It seems that this text should be left without emendation. Following Posidonius and Strabo, the deep religious concern of the Geto-Dacians (*spoude, theosebeia, pietas*) was a commonplace of antiquity.

The word *pleistoi* has received different interpretations, but it seems to be connected with the Thracian god Pleistoros (Herodotos, 9.119). Gheorghe Muşu has sought its etymology in the Indo-European root *$ple(is)$, meaning "to be full"; hence *pleistoi* would mean "bearers of fullness" (Muşu, in Vulpe, 1980). In a rather obscure article, Mihai Nasta has accepted the emendation *pleistois* in *polistais,* from *polizein,* meaning "to instruct in the spirit of the city [*polis*]; to polish" (Nasta, in Vulpe, 1980). The most probable etymology, however, is that proposed by Eugen Lozovan (1968), who reads *pleistoi* as a paronomasia of the Thracian **pleiskoi,* from the Indo-European **pleus-,* meaning "hair, lock." Hence, the *pleistoi* would be "hair bearers," that is, bearers, or wearers, of a woolen bonnet.

This explanation receives further confirmation from Jordanes (71), who reports that the headgear of the noble and wise priests of the Getae, called *pilleati,* was a tiara *(pilleus).* The rest of the people had no *pilleus;* thus they were *capillati,* or "bareheaded." Scholars have claimed that Jordanes's report was based on a misinterpretation of Dacian nobles as priests, because traditionally the *pilleus* was the distinctive sign of Geto-Dacian aristocracy. This observation is wholly irrelevant, however, because Geto-Dacian kingship had many of the characteristics of a theocracy, and the religious initiation of nobles was probably different from that of the common people. Thus, the *pilleati* could very well have been trained as priests. As often as not, Geto-Dacian high priesthood coincided with kingship.

THE CALENDAR TEMPLE AT SARMIZEGETUSA REGIA. In chapter 70 of his *De origine actibusque Getarum,* Jordanes presents a portrait of Getic warriors that has met only skepticism among modern scholars. According to Jordanes, the Getic warriors used the short time between battles to study the properties of plants and the secrets of the starry heavens. An astonishing confirmation of this picture has been provided by the decipherment of the meaning of the calendar temple discovered among the monumental ruins of Sarmizegetusa Regia, an impressive stronghold in the Carpathian Mountains that was the center of the Daco-Getic priesthood before the Roman conquest. The first hypotheses, put forward by D. M. Teodorescu, Constantin Daicoviciu, G. Charrière, and Hadrian Daicoviciu, have been recently replaced by an improved interpretation based on algorithms, proposed by Serban Bobancu, Cornel Samoilă, and Emil Poenaru (1980).

The calendar temple is composed of two circular sanctuaries made of pillars and slabs of stone and andesite and of wooden pillars plated with terra-cotta, disposed in regular patterns. The forms and materials correspond to different units of the Dacian calendar. According to the demonstration of Bobancu, Samoilă, and Poenaru, the Dacians used as their principal time measure a fluctuating week consisting of from 6 to 8 solar days. A Dacian year was composed of 47 such measures and had, accordingly, from 364 to 367 days. After one 13-year cycle the calendar needed a one-day correction, which was marked separately on a series of pillars indicating such cycles. After one "century" of 104 years, or 8 cycles of 13 years each, a new one-day correction was needed and marked. On a larger rectangular calendar, a 520-year time quantum could be measured, that is, a cycle of five Dacian centuries, after which a one-day correction was needed again. Besides the 104-year "centuries," the Dacian calendar also worked with 91-year "centuries," that is, 7 cycles of 13 years each.

Besides this "civilian" calendar, the Dacians also used a religious calendar, composed of 60 weeks of six days each. A 68-day correction, marked on a circle composed of 68 pillars, was exactly the astronomical operation needed after the passage of a 13-year cycle. Sophisticated and precise as it was, the Dacian calendar had a simple and effective method of use. After termination of each time quantum (week, year, 13-year cycle, 91-year and 104-year "centuries," 520-year period), a successive unit, represented by an architectural element (e.g., a pillar, a slab), was marked; this unit had another form and/or was made of a material different from that used for the preceding unit. The system of correspondences consists of distinguishing the different values of the circles of the sanctuaries and the different regular units of which each circle is composed. Once this is known, the whole pattern becomes predictable, and even a child or a modern scholar could be easily trained to keep the periodic marking.

Easy as it might seem in practice, such a calendar would be based on very complex mathematical principles. It would reach such a remarkable precision that after 2,275 years, corresponding to 175 cycles of 13 years, the time as given by the calendar would differ from the astronomical time by only 38.88 seconds. This is much too precise to be true.

The calendar temple at Sarmizegetusa Regia was not built before Decebalus, but it must have been based on a system discovered by Decaeneus. It provides perhaps a confirmation of Jordanes's characterization of the religious life of the Geto-Dacians.

SEE ALSO Zalmoxis.

BIBLIOGRAPHY

The written sources on the religion of the Geto-Dacians are contained in *Fontes historiae Dacoromanae,* 2 vols., edited by Virgil C. Popescu et al. (Bucharest, 1964–1970). On Thracian religion in general, Gawrill I. Kazarow's article, "Thrake (Religion)," in *Realencyclopädie der Altertumswissenschaft,* vol. 6 (Stuttgart, 1937), can still be profitably consulted, and an extensive bibliography can be found in Mircea Eliade's *Zalmoxis, the Vanishing God: Comparative Studies in the Religions and Folklore of Dacia and Eastern Europe* (Chicago, 1972).

For detailed study of the northern Thracians, the following works are recommended. In Romanian, Hadrian Daicoviciu's *Dacii,* 2d ed. (Bucharest, 1972), and I. I. Russu's article in *Anuarul Institutului de Studii Clasice* 5 (1944–1948): 61–137 are both essential works. Ion Horaţiu Crişan's *Burebista and His Time,* Bibliotheca Historica Romaniae Monographs, no. 20 (Bucharest, 1978), translated into English from his second edition, is useful for its description of the old sanctuary at Sarmizegetusa Regia. Radu Vulpe's *Studia Thracologi-*

ca, in French, contains important articles on Burebista and Decaeneus, and the *Actes du Deuxième Congrès International de Thracologie*, vol. 3, *Linguistique, ethnologie, anthropologie*, edited by Vulpe (Bucharest, 1980), contains several interesting articles by Ioan Coman, Gheorghe Muşu, Mihai Nasta, and others. A still useful survey of some problems connected with the religion of the Geto-Dacians is Eugen Lozovan's "Dacia Sacra," *History of Religions* 7 (February 1968): 209–243. The best interpretation of the calendar temple at Sarmizegetusa Regia and a discussion of earlier hypotheses are presented by Serban Bobancu, Cornel Samoilă, and Emil Poenaru in *Caldendarul de la Sarmizegetusa Regia* (Bucharest, 1980), which includes a useful English summary on pages 183–190.

New Sources

Alexandrescu, Petre. "Zalmoxis şi cercetările lui Mircea Eliade (Zalmoxis and Eliade researches)." *Pontica* 11 (1970): 51–58.

Avram, Alexandru. "Gadanken über den thrakisch-geto-dakischen Adel." *Studii clasice* 26 (1988): 11–25. Prudence concerning Eliade's hypothesis of Männerbunde in Dacia.

Barbulescu, Mihai. "La religione nella Dacia romana." *Atti Accademia Peloritana* 68 (1992): 145–159. A useful compendium.

Bianchi, Ugo. "Dualistic Aspects of Thracian Religion." *History of Religions.* 10, no. 3 (1971): 228–233. Concerning Zalmoxis and the notice by Posidonius.

Bodor, Andreas. "Die griechisch-römischen Kulte in der Provinz Dacia und das Nachwirken der einheimischen Traditionen." In *Aufstieg und Niedergang der Römischen Welt* 2, 18, 2. Berlin, New York, 1989, pp. 1078–1164. The most thorough survey, including eight plates, though the bibliography is outdated.

Casadio, Giovanni. "Non desiderare la donna d'altri: la famiglia secondo naura dei barbari." In *Civiltà classica e mondo dei barbari*, edited by Lidia de Finis. Trento, Italy, 1991, pp. 103–135. Dealing with the ascetic and mystic traditions of the Dacian tribes mentioned by Posidonius.

Dorcey Peter F. "The Cult of Silvanus in Dacia." *Athenaeum* 66 (1988): 131–140.

Hampartümian, Nicolae. "Child-Burials and Superstition in the Roman Cemetery of Sucidava (Dacia)." In *Hommages à M. J. Vermaseren.* Leiden, 1978, pp. 473–477.

Marghitan, L., and C. C. Petolescu. "Les cultes orientaux à Micia (Dacia superior). " In *Hommages à M. J. Vermaseren.* Leiden, 1978, pp. 718–731.

Nemeti, Sorin. "Eine donauländische ikonographische Variante der Göttin Nantosuelta." *Latomus* 60 (2001): 160–166.

Nemeti, Sorin. "Le dieu à l'anguipède dans la Dacie romaine." *Ollodagos* 17 (2003): 201–211. A study of magic gems.

Ramon Carbó, Juan. "El culto imperial en la Dacia romana. Consideraciones sobre la presencia de aspectos análogos en la religiosidad de los pueblos daco-getas." *Ilu* 6 (2001): 7–32. A comparison between the indigenous religion and the Roman acculturation.

Sirbu, Valeriu. "Rituels et pratiques funéraires des Géto-Daces, 2e siècle av. n. è-1er siècle de n. è." *Dacia* 30 (1986): 91–108. Incineration is the dominating funerary practice. In the case of inhumation, there is evidence for human sacrifices, a custom which is supported by literary tradition and comparison with Celtic data.

IOAN PETRU CULIANU (1987)
CICERONE POGHIRC (1987)
Revised Bibliography

GHAYBAH, the Arabic word for "concealment," in the sense of absence from human sight, is applied by various Shīʿī Muslim groups to the condition of one or another imam who disappeared rather than died and whose life is believed to have been prolonged (in a paradisial state or in God's presence) until his foreordained return as *mahdī* (the Expected Deliverer) to initiate the eschatological drama concluding history.

EARLY HISTORY. The Qurʾān contrasts the invisible or hidden spiritual realm (*al-ghayb*) with the observable world of human experience. Drawing upon prototypes of such eschatological prophet figures as Moses and Jesus, the first generations of Muslims embraced the view that certain prophets were withdrawn by God from the eyes of mortals, among them Jesus, Idrīs (Enoch/Hermes), Ilyās (Elijah), and Khiḍr. The Qurʾanic description of the crucifixion of Jesus (4:157–159) and legends of the bodily incorruptibility and the ascension and future return of a Mosaic-type prophet contributed to the focusing of such expectations on various members of the prophet Muḥammad's family. ʿAlī ibn Abī Ṭālib, the prophet's cousin and son-in-law, may have been the first given this honor by a small group of extremists among his partisans, the Sabʾīyah, who refused to admit his death after his assassination in 661. After the martyrdom of Ḥusayn ibn ʿAlī at Karbala in 680, another son of ʿAlī, Muḥammad ibn al-Ḥanafīyah (d. 700?) became the center of millenarian hopes in the revolt of al-Mukhtār and the Kaysānīyah that occurred in 686 at Kufa in lower Iraq.

The Kaysānīyah drew an explicit parallel between a "docetic" understanding of the passion of Christ and the concealment and eventual return of their imam. Speculation about the concealment of the imam was tied to the doctrine of return (*al-rajʿah*) in terms of a this-worldly, bodily resurrection before the end time to accomplish eschatological vengeance upon the wicked and victory and justice for the righteous.

THE LATER SHĪʿAH. The early tendency of "stopping" at a certain claimant to the imamate who was seen to be in concealment and awaiting his near-return helped fragment the energies of the original Shīʿah. Historical circumstances determined the continuity of the Imamiyah or Twelver Shīʿī line of imams until the death in 874 of the eleventh imam, al-Ḥasan al-ʿAskarī, whom tradition holds to have secretly fathered a son four years before his death, namely the twelfth or Hidden Imam, Muḥammad al-Mahdī. During the minor *ghaybah* from 874 to 941 this person's earthly existence and near-return was accepted by the Twelver communities, whose allegiance was given to at least four successive *safīrs*, or agents, the direct deputies of the Mahdi, especially in his juristic and financial functions. After 941 comes the era of the major *ghaybah,* in which the Twelver scholar-lawyers (*mujtahids* or *faqīhs*) collectively fulfill the functions of the imam's agents as an independently learned body of religious authorities. In the major *ghaybah* the Mahdi's concealment is seen as total and, though in earthly occultation, he is held to communicate to the faithful by virtue of his participation in the hierarchy of the invisible worlds.

The early Ismāʿīlī Shīʿah eschewed the notion of a miraculous prolongation of life for the imam and emphasized a continuing line of succession to the imamate that included temporary or cyclical periods of concealment termed *satr.* They centralized the spiritual and cosmic role of the imam developed earlier by the radical Shīʿah. The Druze, however, maintain belief in the *ghaybah* of their founders, the Fatimid caliph al-Ḥākim and Hamzah. The two major branches of the Fatimid Ismāʿīlīyah both revere a living line of successive imams: For the Nizārī Ismāʿīlīyah he is the present Aga Khan, while the Mustaʿlī Ismāʿīlīyah or Bohoras hold that the present imams are in earthly concealment and are represented by a continuing line of *dāʿīs*, or agents acting as heads of the community.

For the Twelver Shīʿah, the need for a visible stand-in for the Hidden Imam, or Mahdi, has been assuaged by belief in his continuing efficacy and necessary suprahistorical role. Dream visions and transcendent appearances were occasions for the imam to momentarily break his concealment, while popular eschatology dwelt on the apocalyptic scenario of his triumphant return or the miraculous nature of his concealment. Shīʿī theosophical treatments expanded the cosmic role of the concealed imam and his presence in the spiritual realm of prophets and saints. Ṣūfī treatments of *ghaybah* have interiorized it by focusing on the complementary experience of *hadrah,* "presence" with the divine. Ṣūfīs revered the popular figures of prophetic longevity such as Khiḍr as well as the invisible yet active hierarchy of saints headed by the *qutb,* or spiritual axis.

SEE ALSO Aga Khan; Druze; Imamate; Messianism, article on Messianism in the Muslim Tradition; Shiism, articles on Ismāʿīlīyah, Ithnā ʿAsharīyah.

BIBLIOGRAPHY

For descriptions of the early views on *ghaybah,* consult Israel Friedlaender's "The Heterodoxies of the Shiites in the Presentation of Ibn Hazm," *Journal of the American Oriental Society* 28 (1907): 1–80 and 29 (1908): 1–183. The Twelver doctrine of the concealment is well depicted by A. A. Sachedina in *Islamic Messianism* (Albany, N.Y., 1981), while the period of the minor *ghaybah* is treated in apologetic fashion by Jassim M. Hussain in *The Occultation of the Twelfth Imam* (London, 1982). Wilferd Madelung's articles, "Authority in the Twelver Shiism in the Absence of the Imam," in *La notion d'autorité au Moyen-Âge,* edited by George Makdisi et al. (Paris, 1982), pp. 163–174, and "Shiite Discussion on the Legality of the *kharāj,*" in *Proceedings of the Ninth Congress of Arabic and Islamic Studies* (Leiden, 1981), pp. 193–202, deal with the claim of the Shīʿī scholars to deputyship of the Hidden Imam. The esoteric Shīʿī approach can be sampled in Henry Corbin's study, "Divine Epiphany and Spiritual Birth in Ismailian Gnosis," in *Man and Transformation,* vol. 5 of *Papers from the Eranos Yearbooks,* edited by Joseph Campbell (New York, 1964), pp. 69–160, first published in the *Eranos-Jahrbuch* 23 (1954): 141–249.

DOUGLAS S. CROW (1987)

GHAZĀLI, ABŪ ḤĀMID AL-

(AH 450–505/1058–1111 CE), named Muḥammad ibn Muḥammad ibn Muḥammad, was the distinguished Islamic jurist, theologian, and mystic who was given the honorific title Ḥujjat al-Islām (Arab., "the proof of Islam").

LIFE. Al-Ghazālī was born in the town of Ṭūs, near modern Mashhad (eastern Iran), and received his early education there. When he was about fifteen he went to the region of Gorgān (at the southeast corner of the Caspian Sea) to continue his studies. On the return journey, so the story goes, his notebooks were taken from him by robbers, and when he pleaded for their return they taunted him that he claimed to know what was in fact only in his notebooks; as a result of this incident he spent three years memorizing the material.

At the age of nineteen he went to Nishapur (about fifty miles to the west) to study at the important Niẓāmīyah college under ʿAbd al-Malik al-Juwaynī (d. 1085), known as Imam al-Ḥaramayn, one of the leading religious scholars of the period. Jurisprudence would be central in his studies, as in all Islamic higher education, but he was also initiated into Ashʿarī theology and perhaps encouraged to read the philosophy of al-Fārābi and Ibn Sīnā (Avicenna). He later helped with teaching and was recognized as a rising scholar. When al-Juwaynī died, the powerful vizier of the Seljuk sultans, Niẓām al-Mulk, invited him to join his court, which was in fact a camp that moved about, giving al-Ghazālī the opportunity to engage in discussions with other scholars.

In 1091, when he was about thirty-three, he was appointed to the main professorship at the Niẓāmīyah college in Baghdad, one of the leading positions in the Sunnī world; it can be assumed that the appointment was made by Niẓām al-Mulk, the founder of the colleges bearing his name. After just over four years, however, al-Ghazālī abandoned his professorship and adopted the life of an ascetic and mystic.

Something of al-Ghazālī's personal history during these years in Baghdad may be gleaned from the autobiographical work he wrote when he was about fifty, entitled *Al-munqidh min al-ḍalāl* (The deliverer from error). This work is not conceived as an autobiography, however, but as a defense of his abandonment of the Baghdad professorship and of his subsequent return to teaching in Nishapur about a decade later. It is also not strictly chronological but was given a schematic form. In it, he describes his intellectual journey after the earliest years as containing a period of skepticism lasting "almost two months," when he doubted the possibility of attaining truth. Once he ceased to be completely skeptical, he set out on a search for truth among four "classes of seekers [of truth]," namely, the Ashʿarī theologians, the Neoplatonic philosophers, the Ismāʿīlīyah (whom he calls the party of *taʿlīm*, or authoritative instruction), and finally the Ṣūfīs, or mystics. He writes as if these were four successive stages in his journey, but in fact they must have overlapped; it is virtually certain that he gained some knowledge of mysticism during his early studies at Ṭūs and Nishapur. The period of skepticism, too, could only have come after he had some acquaintance with philosophy, because philosophical considerations were involved.

The first encounter, according to this scheme, was with the *mutakallimūn,* or rational theologians. These were, of course, the Ashʿarīyah, by whom he had been trained and among whom he is reckoned. In the *Munqidh* he complains that their reasoning is based on certain presuppositions and assumptions that they never try to justify, but which he cannot accept without some justification. In effect what happened was that he found in philosophy a way of justifying some of the bases of Ashʿarī theology. This can be seen in his principal work of Ashʿarī theology, *Al-iatiṣād fī al-iʿtiqad* (The golden mean in belief), where he introduces many philosophical arguments, including one for the existence of God. Until the end of his life he seems to have held that Ashʿarī theology was true so far as it went, and in his chief mystical work, *Iḥyāʾ ʿulūm al-dīn* (The revival of the religious sciences), he includes an Ashʿarī creed of moderate length; this is known as *Al-risālah al-qudsīyah* (The Jerusalem epistle) and was probably composed before his extensive study of philosophy.

The second encounter of his intellectual journey was with Greek philosophy and, in particular, the Arabic Neoplatonism of al-Fārābi and Ibn Sīnā. He had probably been introduced to philosophy by al-Juwaynī, but he began the intensive study of it early in his Baghdad professorship. Because philosophy, with other Greek sciences, was cultivated in institutions distinct from the colleges for Islamic jurisprudence and theology and was looked on with disapproval, al-Ghazālī had to study the books of the philosophers by himself. He describes how he devoted to this activity all the free time he had after lecturing to three hundred students and doing some writing. In less than two years he managed to gain such a thorough understanding of the various philosophical disciplines that his book, *Maqāṣid al-falāsifah* (The views of the philosophers), gives a clearer account of the teaching of Ibn Sīnā on logic, metaphysics, and physics than the works of the philosopher himself. After another year's reflection on these matters, al-Ghazālī wrote a powerful critique of the metaphysics or theology of the philosophers entitled *Tahāfut al-falāsifah* (The inconsistency of the philosophers). His argument against the philosophers is based on seventeen points on which he attacks their views as heretical and on three others on which he regards the philosophers as infidels. In discussing the seventeen points al-Ghazālī demonstrates the weaknesses of the philosophers' arguments for the existence of God, his unicity, and his incorporeality, and he rejects their view that God is a simple existent without quiddity and without attributes, their conception of his knowledge, and some of their assertions about the heavens and the human soul. The three points contrary to Islam are that there is no resurrection of bodies but only of spirits, that God knows universals but not particulars, and that the world has existed from eternity. Underlying the detailed arguments is his conviction that the philosophers are unable to give strict logical proofs of their metaphysical views. He therefore turned away from them also in his search for truth.

His third encounter was with a section of the Ismāʿīlīyah who held that true knowledge was to be gained from an infallible imam. It seems doubtful whether he seriously expected to gain much from such people. He did, however, study their views carefully, partly because the caliph of the day commanded him to write a refutation of them. He had little difficulty in showing that there were serious inadequacies in their teaching.

His final encounter was with Sufism; he had already realized that this mysticism entailed not only intellectual doctrines but also a way of life. After four years in Baghdad he felt himself so involved in the worldliness of his milieu that he was in danger of going to hell. The profound inner struggle he experienced led in 1095 to a psychosomatic illness. Dryness of the tongue prevented him from lecturing and even from eating, and the doctors could do nothing to alleviate the symptoms. After about six months he resolved to leave his professorship and adopt the life of a Ṣūfī. To avoid any attempts to stop him, he let it be known that he was setting out on the pilgrimage to Mecca. Actually he went only to Damascus, living there as a Ṣūfī for more than a year, and then made the pilgrimage to Mecca in 1096. Some six months after that he was back in Baghdad and then seems to have made his way by stages back to his native Ṭūs. There he established a *khānāqāh* (hostel or convent), where some young disciples joined him in leading a communal Ṣūfī life. The genuineness of his conversion to Ṣūfism has sometimes been questioned by Muslim scholars, and it has been suggested that he left his professorship because he was afraid his life was in danger on account of political involvements. To judge from his own account, however, religious considerations were uppermost in his mind.

The Muslim year 500 (which began on September 2, 1106 CE) marked the beginning of a new century. Muḥammad was reported to have said that God would send a "renewer" *(mujaddid)* of his religion at the beginning of each century, and various friends assured al-Ghazālī that he was the "renewer" for the sixth century. This induced him to take up an invitation from the vizier of the provincial governor in Nishapur to become the main professor in the Niẓāmīyah college there. He continued in this position for three or possibly four years and then returned to Ṭūs, probably because of ill health; he died there in 1111. His brother Aḥmad, himself a distinguished scholar, describes how on his last day, after ablutions. Abū Ḥāmid performed the dawn prayer and then, lying down on his bed facing Mecca, kissed his shroud, pressed it to his eyes with the words, "Obediently I enter into the presence of the King," and was dead before sunrise.

WORKS. More than four hundred titles of works ascribed to al-Ghazālī have been preserved, though some of these are different titles for the same work. At least seventy works are extant in manuscript; it is clear, however, that some of these, chiefly works of a mystical character, have been falsely attributed to al-Ghazālī, though in the case of one or two the inauthenticity is not universally admitted. Certain of these works are written from a standpoint close to that of the philosophers, and earlier scholars, regarding them as authentic, were led to suppose that before his death al-Ghazālī came to adopt the views he had previously attacked, or else that in addition to his publicly expressed views, he held esoteric views which he communicated only to a select few. Since about 1960, however, scholars have been aware of a manuscript written four years after his death, which bears a colophon stating that the short work it contains was completed by al-Ghazālī about a fortnight before he died. This work is *Iljām al-ʿawāmm ʿan ʿilm al-kalām* (The restraining of the common people from the science of theology), and in it he writes as a Shāfiʿī jurist who, at least up to a point, accepts Ashʿarī theology. It is also known that just over two years earlier he had completed a long and important work on the principles of jurisprudence, *Al-mustasfā* (The choice part, or essentials); this was presumably one of the subjects on which he lectured at Nishapur. These facts make it inconceivable that at the end of his life al-Ghazālī adopted the heretical views he had previously denounced, and thus they strengthen the case for regarding as inauthentic works containing views that cannot be harmonized with what is expressed in books such as the *Munqidh* and the *Iḥyāʾ*.

The genuine works of al-Ghazālī range over several fields. One of these is jurisprudence, which is dealt with in several early works, as well as in the much later *Mustasfā* mentioned above. These are the works most often referred to in connection with al-Ghazālī during the two centuries after his death. Most of these legal works were presumably written before he went to Baghdad. At Baghdad he turned to philosophy, producing the *Maqāṣid* and the *Tahāfut,* the exposition and critique of the Neoplatonic philosophers. About the same time, he wrote two small books on Aristotelian logic and a semi-philosophical work on ethics (which may, however, contain some interpolations). He also relates that it was in Baghdad that he composed for the caliph al-Mustaẓhir the refutation of Ismāʿīlī thought known after the patron as the *Mustaẓhirī*. His exposition and philosophical defense of Ashʿarī doctrine in the *Iqtiṣād* must have been written either shortly before or shortly after leaving Baghdad.

For some time after that, al-Ghazālī's literary occupation seems to have been the composition of his greatest work, the *Iḥyāʾ ʿulūm al-dīn.* It consists of four "quarters," each divided into "books" or chapters; a complete English translation would probably contain at least two million words. The first quarter, entitled "the service of God," has books dealing with the creed, ritual purity, formal prayer (*ṣalāt*), other types of prayer and devotion, almsgiving, fasting, and the pilgrimage. The second quarter deals with social customs as prescribed in the *sharīʿah* and has books on eating habits, marriage, acquiring goods, traveling, and the like; it concludes with a book presenting Muḥammad as an exemplar in social matters. The third quarter is about "things destructive," or vices, and, after two general books on "the mysteries of the heart" and how to control and educate it, gives counsel with regard to the various vices. The fourth quarter on "things leading to salvation" deals with the stages and aspects of the mystical life, such as penitence, patience, gratitude, renunciation, trust in God, and love for him. In most of the books al-Ghazālī begins with relevant quotations from the Qurʾān and the *ḥadīth* (anecdotes about Muḥammad, sometimes called traditions) and then proceeds to his own exposition. His overriding aim seems to be to show how the scrupulous observance of all the external acts prescribed by the *sharīʿah* contributes to the inner mystical life.

Al-Ghazālī presents a simpler version of the way of life to which the *Iḥyāʾ* points in *Bidāyat al-hidāyah* (The beginning of guidance). Other works of interest from his mystical period are an exposition of the ninety-nine names of God with the short title *Al-maqṣad al-asnā* (The noblest aim) and a discussion of light symbolism centered on the "light verse" of the Qurʾān (24:35) and entitled *Mishkāt al-anwār* (The niche for lights). There is also a Persian work, *Kīmiyāʾ al-saʿādah* (The alchemy of happiness), covering the same ground as the *Iḥyāʾ* but in about half the compass.

Among the works of doubtful authenticity is a refutation of Christianity with the title *Al-radd al-jamīl ʿalā ṣarīḥ al-injīl* (The beautiful refutation of the evidence of the gospel). Even if this is not by al-Ghazālī, it is of course an interesting document of roughly his period, and the same is true of the spurious mystical works.

THE ACHIEVEMENTS OF AL-GHAZĀLĪ: PHILOSOPHY, THEOLOGY, AND MYSTICISM. At the present time it is still difficult to reach a balanced judgment on the achievement of al-Ghazālī. After the first translation of the *Munqidh* into a European language (French) was published in 1842, many European scholars found al-Ghazālī such an attractive figure that they paid much more attention to him than to any other Muslim thinker, and this fashion has been followed by Muslim scholars as well. His importance has thus tended to be exaggerated because of relative Western ignorance of other writers. This ignorance is now rapidly decreasing, but care is still needed in making an assessment of al-Ghazālī.

Part of al-Ghazālī's aim in studying the various philosophical disciplines was to discover how far they were compatible with Islamic doctrine. He gave separate consideration to mathematics, logic, physics, metaphysics or theology (*ilāhīyāt*), politics, and ethics. Metaphysics he criticized very severely in his *Tahāfut,* but most of the others he regarded as neutral in themselves, though liable to give less scholarly persons an unduly favorable opinion of the competence of the philosophers in every field of thought. He himself was very impressed by Aristotelian logic, especially the syllogism. He not only made use of logic in his own defense of doctrine but also wrote several books about it, in which he managed to commend it to his fellow-theologians as well as to expound its principles. From his time on, many theological treatises devote much space to philosophical preliminaries, and works on logic are written by theologians. The great positive achievement of al-Ghazālī here was to provide Islamic theology with a philosophical foundation.

It is more difficult to know how far his critique of philosophy led to its disappearance. Arabic Neoplatonic philosophy ceased to be cultivated in the East, though there was an important Persian tradition of theosophical philosophy, but there had been no philosopher of weight in the East since the death of Ibn Sīnā twenty years before al-Ghazālī was born. In the Islamic West philosophy following the Greek tradition continued until about 1200 and included a refutation of al-Ghazālī's *Tahāfut* by Ibn Rushd (Averroës), so that the decline in the West cannot be attributed to al-Ghazālī.

Sufism had been flourishing in the Islamic world for more than two centuries. Many of the earliest Ṣūfīs had been chiefly interested in asceticism, but others had cultivated ecstatic experiences, and a few had become so "intoxicated" that they seemed to outsiders to claim unity with God. Such persons often also held that their mystical attainments freed them from duties such as ritual prayer. In al-Ghazālī's time, too, yet other Ṣūfīs were becoming interested in gnostic knowledge and developing theosophical doctrines. For these reasons many of the *ʿulamāʾ*, or religious scholars, were suspicious of all Sufism, despite the fact that some of their number practiced it in a moderate fashion without becoming either heretical in doctrine or antinomian in practice. Al-Ghazālī adopted the position of this latter group and, after his retirement from the professorship in Baghdad, spent much of his time in ascetical and mystical practices. The *khānāqāh* that he established at Ṭūs was probably not unlike a monastery of contemplatives. His great work the *Iḥyāʾ* provides both a theoretical justification of his position and a highly detailed elucidation of it which emphasized the deeper meaning of the external acts. In this way both by his writing and by his own life al-Ghazālī showed how a profound inner life can be combined with full observance of the shariʿah and sound theological doctrine. The consequence of the life and work of al-Ghazālī was that religious scholars in the main stream of Sunnism had to look more favorably on the Ṣūfī movement, and this made it possible for ordinary Muslims to adopt moderate Ṣūfī practices.

Bibliography

Two older books still have much of value, though they make use of works probably falsely attributed to al-Ghazālī: A. J. Wensinck's *La pensée de Ghazzālī* (Paris, 1940) and Margaret Smith's *Al-Ghazālī the Mystic* (London, 1944); the latter includes a full account of his life. My *Muslim Intellectual: A Study of al-Ghazali* (Edinburgh, 1963) looks at his life and thought in its intellectual context. In La *politique de Ghazālī* (Paris, 1970), Henri Laoust gives some account of his life as well as of his political thought. Hava Lazarus-Yafeh's *Studies in al-Ghazzali* (Jerusalem, 1975) includes among other things discussions of authenticity on the basis of linguistic criteria. The fullest account of all works ascribed to him, with extensive consideration of questions of authenticity, is Maurice Bouyges's *Essai de chronologie des œuves de al-Ghazālī,* edited by Michel Allard (Beirut 1956). The following are a few of the numerous translations available: my *The Faith and Practice of al-Ghazālī* (London, 1953) has translations of the *Munqidh* and *Bidāyat al-hidāyah*; Richard J. McCarthy's *Freedom and Fulfillment* (Boston, 1980) has translations of the *Munqidh* and "other relevant works" with introduction and notes; William H. T. Gairdner's *Al-Ghazzālī's Mishkāt al-anwār* (The Niche for Lights; 1924; reprint, Lahore, 1952) is a translation with introduction of a mystical text; Muḥammad A. Quasem's *The Jewels of the Qurʾān: al Ghazali's Theory* (Bangi, Malaysia, 1977), a translation of *Jawāhir al-Qurʾān,* shows how the Qurʾān was understood and used by Ṣūfīs; Robert C. Stade's *Ninety-nine Names of God in Islam* (Ibadan, 1970) is the descriptive part of *Al-maqṣad al-asnā.*

A general overview of the *Iḥyāʾ* is given in G.-H. Bousquet's *Ghazālī, Ih'ya ʿOuloum ed-dîn, ou vivification des sciences de la foi; analyse et index* (Paris, 1955). Translations of separate books include Nabih Amin Faris's *The Book of Knowledge* (book 1; Lahore, 1962); *The Foundations of the Articles of Faith* (book 2; Lahore, 1963); *The Mysteries of Purity* (book 3; Lahore, 1966); *The Mysteries of Almsgiving* (book 5; Lahore, 1974); *The Mysteries of Fasting* (book 6; Lahore, 1968); E. E. Calverley's *Worship in Islam* (book 4; 1925; reprint, Westport, Conn., 1981); Muḥammad A. Quasem's *The Recitation and Interpretation of the Qurʾān* (book 8; Selangor, Malaysia, 1979); D. B. Macdonald's "Emotional Religion in Islam as Affected by Music and Singing" (book 18), *Journal of the Royal Asiatic Society* (1901): 195–252, 705–748; and (1902): 1–28; Leon Zolondek's *Book XX of al-Ghazālī's Iḥyāʾ* (Leiden, 1963); and William McKane's *Al-Ghazali's Book of Fear and Hope* (book 33; Leiden, 1965).

W. Montgomery Watt (1987)

GHOSE, AUROBINDO See AUROBINDO GHOSE

GHOST DANCE.

The Ghost Dance was the major revivalist movement among nineteenth-century North American Indians. Dating from about 1870, it had its culmination in the 1890–1891 "messiah craze" of the Plains, which caused the last Indian war in the Dakotas. The name *Ghost*

Dance refers to the ritual round-dances that were thought to imitate the dances of the dead and were performed to precipitate the renewal of the world and the return of the dead. There were other American Indian ceremonial dances that were called ghost dances—for instance, a ritual dance among the Iroquois. However, it was the messianic Ghost Dance of 1890 that attracted general attention because of its message and consequences. It has been considered prototypical of other revivalist movements among North American Indians, so much so that most later movements have been classified as "ghost dances" (La Barre, 1970).

HISTORY. Strictly speaking, there have been two Ghost Dances, closely connected with each other and almost identical in form and cultic performance.

The 1870 Ghost Dance. The Ghost Dance movement of 1870 was introduced on the Walker Lake Reservation in Nevada by a Northern Paiute Indian, Wodziwob ("gray hair," 1844–1918?). During a trance he was conveyed to the otherworld, where he learned that the dead were soon to return, that the disappearing game animals were to be restored, and that the old tribal life would come back again. In order to hasten this change, people had to perform round dances at night, without fires. This Ghost Dance lasted some few years among the Paiute, several middle and northern California tribes, and some Oregon Indians.

Wovoka and the Ghost Dance of 1890. One of Wodziwob's inspired adherents was Tävibo ("white man"), who despite his name was a full-blooded Northern Paiute. He had a son, Wovoka ("the cutter," 1856–1932). Wovoka lived in Mason Valley, Nevada, where he served as a farmhand to a white family named Wilson, and because of this association he went under the name of Jack Wilson. During an eclipse of the sun, probably in January 1889, he fell into a trance and was transported to the supreme being in the sky. In this vision the supreme being showed him the land of the dead and the happy life there, and promised that the living would have a reunion with the deceased, providing a series of rules were followed.

At this point the information divides. To the whites, Wovoka said that the reunion would take place in the otherworld if people behaved correctly (i.e., did not lie, steal, or fight) and performed the round dance. To the Indians, he announced the speedy coming of the dead (who would be guided by a cloudlike spirit that was interpreted as Jesus) as well as the return of game and a lasting peace with the whites. The round dance would more quickly bring about this change. The scene was to be on earth, not in the otherworld. It is obvious that, to the Indians, Wovoka presented the same message, in many ways, as Wodziwob.

The round dance was the same as well. It was conducted on four or five consecutive nights. Men and women danced together in a circle, interlacing their fingers and dancing round with shuffling side steps. The dance was exhausting, although not continuous, and no fainting spells or visions were reported.

This second Ghost Dance appeared when the Plains tribes had been subjugated and their old style of living was on the wane. The freedom-loving Plains Indians looked for an escape, and in their desperation they found it in the Ghost Dance. Emissaries were sent over to the "Messiah," Wovoka (who in fact had claimed only to be a prophet, not a messiah), and were instructed in his doctrine. However, the Plains delegates misinterpreted the message to mean that the whites would be driven off or exterminated. The Ghost Dance spread like fire among the Plains Indians, and in particular the Arapaho, Cheyenne, Lakota, Kiowa, and Caddo became staunch believers. Dancing songs expressed the wishes of the arrival of the dead and praised the Father above.

The Lakota added several new traits that were in line with their visionary and militant ethos: they became entranced while dancing; they pondered military action against the whites; and they covered their upper bodies with white "ghost shirts," decorated with spiritual emblems. The ghost shirt was supposed to protect the wearer magically against enemy bullets. It was probably patterned on Mormon garments worn by the Paiute for protection from bodily harm.

Although the Lakota plans for action were very vague, their frenetic dancing in the summer and fall of 1890 released countermeasures from the suspicious white authorities in the Dakotas, resulting in the so-called Ghost Dance Uprising. Highpoints of this development were the arrest and assassination of the famous Lakota leader Sitting Bull and the massacre at Wounded Knee at the end of December 1890, when Hotchkiss guns indiscriminately killed men, women, and children in Big Foot's camp.

After these catastrophic events, enthusiasm for the Ghost Dance ebbed. Some groups continued dancing, but their expectations of the coming of the dead were projected to a distant future. The last Ghost Dances were held in the 1950s, among Canadian Dakota and Wind River Shoshoni.

THREE MAIN ROOTS. It is possible to find three main roots of the Ghost Dance: earlier religious movements stimulated by Christian missions, shamanic experiences, and indigenous rituals. Of these sources, the impact of earlier syncretic movements has been thoroughly analyzed, beginning with James Mooney's famous study (1896). The import of native religious development has been properly studied only relatively recently. Scholars have, of course, been aware of changes in the Indian's spiritual, cultural, and military background that may have triggered the outbreak of the Ghost Dance. There is no unanimity of opinion, however, as to whether readjustment to a new sociopolitical situation or predominantly religious drives steered the development. The overwhelming majority of scholars, all of them anthropologists, favor the first view, whereas historians of religions prefer the latter.

The impetus for the Ghost Dance revivalism was the Indians' enforced contact with an expanding white civilization beginning in the 1860s. Because of growing white settlements, the white military takeover, and the introduction of white jurisdiction, there was no more room for the continuation of the old native existence, in particular for the hunters and gatherers of the West. Their independent cultures ceased rapidly, sometimes even abruptly, as on the Plains: the whole culture of the northern Plains tribes, built on hunting buffalo, collapsed when in 1883 the last herd of buffalo was exterminated. The Indians had to adjust to white people's culture and, in part, to their values, in order to survive. At the same time the Indians drew on their past to mobilize a desperate spiritual resistance against the overwhelming white influence. In this reactive effort they combined Christian or Christian-derived elements with indigenous ideas and rituals to form a resistance ideology.

Earlier religious movements. The formation of mixed ("acculturated") ideologies is part of American Indian religious history since the beginning of European colonization: The restitutional ("nativistic") doctrines launched by the Tewa Indian Popé (1680–1692) and by Neolin, the so-called Delaware Prophet (around 1760), are among the better-known early instances. These prophets proposed an ethical and religious program. In many respects Neolin set the pattern for subsequent prophets, including those of the Ghost Dance: an inspired person who suffers from the ways of the white people enforced upon the Indian people, who long for a return to the good old Indian ways, and who experiences an ecstasy or similar state. In his vision the prophet is brought to the Master of Life, from whom is obtained instructions about a right life. Provided this road is followed, the prophet is told, the game will return, the whites will be driven away, and the old life will be restored. No wonder that such enchanting messages fostered Indian wars, like Pontiac's uprising, which was inspired by Neolin's prophecies.

While the messages of the prophets reflected a yearning for old value patterns, they were in fact deeply dependent on Christian missionary teachings. Exhortations to believers to refrain from liquor, adultery, lying, and murder and to show brotherly friendliness, even beyond tribal boundaries, reveal more or less Christian ethical precepts. Where the abandonment of traditional fetishes and rituals was propagated, as by the Shawnee prophet Tenskwatawa, Christian value judgments are easily recognizable. The very idea that the Supreme Being had to introduce the new religious program through revelation to a prophet also speaks of Christian influence. The hope for the day of salvation, or the coming liberation, implies a linear view of history and an eschatological goal, ideas that were never American Indian, but are thoroughly Christian.

Shamanic experiences. The second root of the Ghost Dance is shamanic experience. Although the instigators of the revivalist movements were prophets (i.e., ecstatics who had received their calling from God) and not shamans (i.e., vocational ecstatics acting on behalf of their fellowmen), the difference is a minor one, for shamans often receive their calling from spirits. There was definitely a Christian background to the Indian conception of the prophet, his reception of an eschatological message after a comatose experience, and his direct contact with a more or less christianized God. However, the pattern of spiritual communication is very much shamanic. Wovoka, for instance, was himself a medicine man, and fell repeatedly into self-induced trances. It was during these séances that he visited the otherworld and received his messages. Of course, the destination of his soul was the heaven of God, not the spirit land of the dead; these were two different realms in most Native American beliefs.

The Ghost Dance had its precursors in movements that crystallized around shamans. Leslie Spier (1935) retraced the Ghost Dance ideology to an older "Prophet Dance" founded on the intense relations of the living with the dead on the Northwest Coast and the Plateau. The Prophet Dance ideology contained such elements as a world cataclysm, renewal of the world, and the return of the dead. World renewal and the return of the dead could be hastened by the performance of the "dance of the dead." The Prophet Dance had its basis, according to Spier, in the periodic cataclysms (earthquakes) to which the region is subject and in the shamanic visits to the dead.

Round-dance ritual. The third main root of the Ghost Dance is, as Michael Hittman (1973) has observed, the indigenous round dance. The latter has been interpreted by some scholars as simply a dance for entertainment, but there is much evidence that the Basin round dance, performed around a pole or cedar tree, was a religious ceremony—the Father Dance, offered with thanksgivings to the Master of Life for food, rain, and health. In the Ghost Dance this old ceremony was given a new, eschatological meaning.

See Also Neolin; North American Indian Religions, article on Modern Movements; Shamanism, article on North American Shamanism; Wovoka.

Bibliography

The classic in the field is still James Mooney's *The Ghost-Dance Religion and the Sioux Outbreak of 1890* (1896; reprint, Chicago, 1965). It is a reliable account of Mooney's field visits, just after the Lakota conflict, to a number of tribes that performed the Ghost Dance. Other general works, but less professional, are Paul Bailey's *Wovoka: The Indian Messiah* (Los Angeles, 1957) and David H. Miller's *Ghost Dance* (New York, 1959). In a wider setting of so-called crisis cults, the Ghost Dance religion has been discussed in, among other works, Weston La Barre's *The Ghost Dance* (Garden City, N.Y., 1970).

The discussion of the Ghost Dance has, in comparative works on prophetism, messianism, and millenarianism, concentrated on terminological, psychological, and acculturation problems, whereas the specialized works on the Ghost Dance have paid attention primarily to its origins. Pathbreaking has been Leslie Spier's *The Prophet Dance of the Northwest and Its Derivatives: The Source of the Ghost Dance* (Menasha, Wis., 1935). Spier's idea of an exclusively aboriginal origin of the Ghost Dance religion is today in doubt, but much of his work remains extremely useful.

The grounding of the 1890 Ghost Dance in Wodziwob's movement of the same name twenty years earlier has directed scholars' attention to the latter. The details of the 1870 movement have been excellently clarified in Cora Dubois's *The 1870 Ghost Dance* (Berkeley, Calif., 1939). A new orientation, which argues for the mutual independence of the 1870 and 1890 movements, is represented in Michael Hittman's "The 1870 Ghost Dance at the Walker River Reservation: A Reconstruction," *Ethnohistory* 20 (1973): 247–278.

The connection of the Ghost Dance with the Father Dance has been worked out in my book, *Belief and Worship in Native North America,* edited by Christopher Vessey (Syracuse, N.Y., 1981); see especially "The Changing Meaning of the Ghost Dance as Evidenced by the Wind River Shoshoni," pp. 264–281.

Åke Hultkrantz (1987)

GHOSTS.

GHOSTS. In western Germanic languages words similar to the modern English *ghost* and the German *Geist* seem to be derived from roots indicating fury, wounding, or tearing in pieces. The spelling with *gh* in English appeared first in a work printed by William Caxton in the fifteenth century, influenced probably by a similar Flemish form. The term *ghost* has been used in various ways, to mean soul, spirit, breath, the immaterial part of man, moral nature, a good spirit, an evil spirit, and, in liturgical and dogmatic language, to designate the spirit of God as the "Holy Ghost." It has chiefly signified the soul of a deceased person appearing in a visible form, and hence has given rise to such phrases as *a ghost walking, raising a ghost,* or *laying a ghost.* It may be called "an apparition" or "a specter." In any case, the prevailing modern sense is that of a dead person manifesting its presence visibly to the living.

Other words are used to describe comparable phenomena, but with some differences. A fetch is, like the German *Doppelgänger,* the apparition of a living person. A wraith is an apparition or specter of a dead person or an immaterial appearance of someone living forewarning his own death. The Irish often speak of fetches, and the Scottish of wraiths. More generally, a phantom, from the Greek *phantasma,* is sometimes unreal or immaterial, an illusion or dream-image, a specter or ghost. A phantasm may be the same thing, but Edmund Gurney and others in *Phantasms of the Living* (1886) discussed as phantasms "all classes of cases where . . . the mind of one human being has affected the mind of another . . . by other means than through the recognized channels of sense" (vol. 1, p. 35). A poltergeist, from the German *poltern* ("to make noise") and *Geist* ("spirit") is regarded as a noisy spirit remarkable for throwing things about. Since the nineteenth century the French world *revenant* (lit., "one who comes back"), has been used in English to describe a being who returns from the dead.

The word *ghost* most commonly refers to a dead person who haunts or simply appears before the living, sometimes with a message or warning. The notion has been popular in literature. While Shakespeare wrote one play involving fairies and another involving witches, ghosts were an important feature in several of his works: Hamlet's father, Caesar, and Banquo all appear as ghosts. Hamlet's father—called a ghost, a spirit, an apparition, an illusion, and more than fantasy—expresses a belief in the activities of ghosts: "I am thy father's spirit; / Doom'd for a certain term to walk the night, / And for the day confin'd to fast in fires, / Till the foul crimes done in my days of nature / Are burnt and purg'd away" (1.5.9–13).

The Bible and the Qur'ān. The Hebrew scriptures have few references to ghosts. Isaiah attacked the practice of consulting "the mediums and the wizards who chirp and mutter" (*Is.* 8:19). This refers to the spiritualistic séance, forbidden but vividly illustrated in the story of the medium of Endor, consulted by Saul. She was said to raise up the dead prophet Samuel out of the earth, saying "An old man comes up, and he is covered with a robe" (*1 Sm.* 28:14). Samuel was not a haunting ghost, although he brought a fatal warning for Saul.

In *Psalm* 88:12 the grave is called the land of forgetfulness, and later Judas Maccabaeus makes sacrifices to free the dead from their sins (*2 Mc.* 12:45). In the apocryphal *Wisdom of Solomon* (17:15) lawless men are said to be troubled in their sleep by specters, apparitions, and phantoms. Otherwise ghosts are not mentioned except in the older translations where death is described as surrendering the spirit, "giving up the ghost."

In the New Testament there are also few references. When the disciples saw Jesus by night, on or by the sea, they were afraid, thinking him an apparition or ghost (*phantasma; Mark* 6:49; this is the only occurrence of this word in the New Testament). In one of Luke's accounts of the resurrection the disciples were terrified, supposing that they had seen a spirit (*pneuma*), but Jesus assured them that this could not be so, for he had flesh and bones that a spirit had not (*Lk.* 24:37–39). Lazarus might be called a revenant, but he was not, strictly speaking, a ghost, since he came out of the grave alive (*Jn.* 11:44). Later Christian insistence upon the "resurrection of the flesh" (*sarx*), as in the Apostles' Creed, also precluded "ghostly" survival and postulated instead a restoration of the full personality.

In developing Christian doctrine theologians discussed the nature of angels, good spirits, bad spirits, the resurrection of the dead, heaven, hell, and purgatory. But belief in ghosts and their possible return to earth was left indeterminate, neither accepted nor rejected. All Souls' Day, the commemoration of the faithful departed, has been universally celebrated in the Western church since the tenth century, and prayers at Mass request "to the souls of all thy servants a place of cool repose, the blessedness of quiet, the brightness of light . . . forgiveness and everlasting rest."

In practice many Christians have believed in ghosts and in haunted places, and this is said to have been particularly true among Germanic peoples. The survivors owed numerous duties to the departed, and unless honor and rituals were accorded, it was thought that the dead might return to take vengeance or reclaim their former property. Those who had died untimely or unnatural deaths, such as women in childbirth, might become wandering spirits. To this day stories are related in Europe about old monasteries or rectories where restless spirits are said to appear. Rituals of exorcism have been practiced, with restrictions, both to cast out evil spirits and to lay wandering ghosts to rest.

In the Islamic world the soul or self (Arab., *nafs;* cf. Heb. *nefesh*) was at first distinguished from the breath or wind (Arab., *rūḥ;* cf. Heb. *ruaḥ*), but the words came to be used interchangeably and are applied to the human spirit, angels, and genii (*jinn*). Theologians teach that at death the soul goes to a first judgment and then remains in the grave until the final resurrection. Edward A. Westermarck stated in *Ritual and Belief in Morocco* (1926, vol. 2, p. 246) that while it was believed that dead saints might appear to the living and the dead might come to see their friends but remain invisible, "as to ordinary dead people I have been assured over and over again that the dead do not walk, and I remember how heartily my friends . . . laughed when I told them that many Christians believe in ghosts." However, the Moroccans believed that the dead would be angry if they were offended by anyone and would punish him, and if children did not visit the graves of their parents they would be cursed by them. The voices of some of the dead were thought to be audible in cemeteries, though only good people, children, and animals could hear them. If a person had been killed, the spot would be regarded as haunted, and passersby might hear him groan.

Among Berber-speaking tribes there were said to be more traces of the belief in apparitions of the dead than among Arabic-speaking Moroccans. Some of the Tuareg of the Sahara claimed that ghosts had been seen at night near cemeteries. In Egypt many stories have been told of apparitions of dead people, and Arabian bedouin believe that spirits of the wicked haunt the places of their burial and that the living should avoid passing cemeteries in the dark.

The jinn may be thought to haunt burial grounds and many other places, but they are fiery spirits and not dead people. Ghouls (Arab., *ghūl)* are monsters thought to haunt cemeteries and feed on dead bodies. An *ʿifrit* is mentioned in the Qurʾān (27:39) as "one of the jinn," and in the *Thousand and One Nights,* in the story of the second shaykh, it is said that a benevolent Muslim woman "turned into an *ʿifritah,* a *jinniyah.*" She changed her shape, saved her husband from drowning by carrying him on her shoulders, and told him that she had delivered him from death by the grace of God, since she believed in him and in his Prophet. In Egypt the word *ʿifrit* came to mean the ghost of a man who had been murdered or suffered a violent death.

AFRICA. In many parts of Africa ghosts are thought to appear to give warning or seek vengeance. Among the Ashanti of Ghana, a man who has committed suicide is called a wandering spirit, unable to find rest and refused entry into the land of spirits, roaming between this world and the next until his appointed time of death. If such a suicide is reborn, he will come back as a cruel man who might again suffer a bad end. At one time criminals who were executed had powerful charms tied on them to prevent their ghosts returning to harm the executioners. Some of the dead had their heads shaved and painted red, white, and black so that they would be recognized if they walked as ghosts.

The Ga of the Ghana coastline think that the spirit of one who dies violently or prematurely wanders about for forty days as a ghost, angry at his early death and jealous of other people's pleasures. Those who go out late at night pursuing such pleasures may be pursued in turn by ghosts until they die of heart failure. Ghosts are said to be recognizable by their fiery breath and red mouths: red is the color of witches, fairies, and ghosts, but ghosts dislike white and may be kept away if one throws white cloths on the ground.

A common belief in the Ivory Coast is that the dead may return to their homes at night to steal children from their mothers' arms. Here and elsewhere widows must keep in mourning for months or years, often in rags, lest their dead husbands return and have sexual intercourse with them, which would have fatal results. Fishermen drowned at sea, hunters lost in the forest, people struck by lightning or burnt in fires, and others who die of diseases like smallpox or leprosy may not receive burial rites and so become ghosts, living in the "bad bush." Months after the death or disappearance, the family performs mourning ceremonies and lays the ghost to rest.

When infant mortality is high, a succession of dying children may be thought to be incarnations of the same child over and over again. The Yoruba of Nigeria call such babies "born to die" (*abiku*), and if one comes a third time and dies it is said that "there is no hoe" to bury it with. Marks are made on the body of the stillborn or dying baby to prevent the ghost from returning or to make the ghost recognizable.

In central Africa the Ila of Zambia think that some spirits are captured by witches and become their ghost-slaves, causing disease and sometimes possessing people. Like poltergeists, such ghosts reputedly attack people, knock burdens off their heads, or break axes and hoes. Ghosts are often thought to speak in unnatural ways, in guttural voices or twittering like birds, and some are said to be very small, with bodies reversed so that their faces are at the back of their heads. They appear in dreams, show anger at neglect, demand sacrifice, or cause sickness. Although stories are told that seem to imply that ghosts have objective or even physical existence, they are regarded as spiritual entities who only take the essence or heart of sacrifices.

In the region of Zaire the word *zumbi* is used for spirits of the dead and ghosts, and in Haiti it becomes *zombie,* a *revenant,* or one of the "living dead," whose soul has been eaten by a witch or whose corpse has been revived by a sorcerer for evil purposes.

South and East Asia. In popular Indian belief various words may be used for ghosts. The term *bhūta,* something that has been or has become, refers to the ghost of a dead person, one who has died a violent death or has not had a proper funeral ceremony, or it may apply generally to a good or evil spirit. In the *Bhagavadgītā* (9.25) the *bhūta* is a ghost or goblin, an inferior but not necessarily an evil being. A *preta* ("departed") is the spirit of a dead person before the obsequies are performed or an evil ghost; it also may be the spirit of a deformed person or of a child that died prematurely. A *yakṣa* is generally a benevolent spirit although sometimes classed with *piśācas* and other malignant spirits and ghosts; such terms are used loosely and often overlap.

Ghosts and demons in India are believed to haunt cemeteries or live in trees, appearing in ugly or beautiful forms and requiring food and blood. The special guardian against ghosts is the monkey god Hanuman, the "large-jawed"; his worshipers offer coconuts to him and pour oil and red lead over his images, taking some of the oil that drips off to mark their eyes as a protection. The lighting of lamps at the Dīvālī or Dīpavālī festival at the new year is also said to drive away ghosts and evil spirits.

Performance of Śraddha funeral ceremonies is essential in India for the rest of the departed spirit, in order to provide food for it and to prevent it from becoming an evil spirit. Special Śraddha is performed for those who died violently, as they would be likely to become haunting ghosts. Infants who die do not receive ordinary Śraddha, but presents are given to brahmans on their behalf.

Buddhist dialogues discuss various states after death. In the *Milindapañha* (294) there are said to be four classes of ancestors (*peta*), only one of which lives on offerings from benefactors; the others feed on vomit, are tormented by hunger and thirst, or are consumed by craving. Any of these may be ghosts. In Sinhala another word (*holman*) indicates similar dangerous beings. These appear at night as naked white figures, especially in cemeteries, and sunset, midnight, and dawn are the most dangerous times for their activities. One of them, Mahasōnā, perhaps meaning "great cemetery," puts his hand on the backs of wanderers in graveyards at midnight, marks them with his imprint, and kills them with shock. *Peta* may be offered inferior food, as well as drugs or excrement, and if they act as troublesome poltergeists they are exorcized. Another term for ghostly creatures, *bhūtayā* ("has been") may be substituted for *peta* and other words for demons and harmful spirits.

Burmese Buddhists believe that although all beings pass on to rebirth, most go first to one of four "states of woe" as an animal, demon, ghost, or inhabitant of hell. Rebirth as a human being is an exception, one of "five rarities." Monks may be reborn as ghosts. One account of five heads of a monastery who died in quick succession attributed the premature deaths to the ghost of the original incumbent, who had owned the monastery personally and died before appointing a successor. Those who followed were usurpers, and as a ghost he caused their deaths. As a consequence the villagers decided to abandon that monastery and build a new one for the next abbot.

In Thailand the Indian word *preta* is used for the ghosts of the recently dead, who may have been condemned to hell or to wander the earth. Although not harmful to humans they may be disgusting and gigantic in appearance. Because of their tiny mouths they suffer from constant hunger and thirst. Relatives may transfer merit to the *pretas* by extra gifts to monks; some writers consider *pretas* to be the inversion of the Buddhist monk. Mural paintings in Buddhist temples of South Asia often depict both the joys of paradise and the sufferings of unhappy spirits.

In China a ghost (*kuei;* f., *yao*) was the spirit of someone who had died an unusual death, often as the result of crime. Ghosts of bandits were thought to linger near the place of their execution, and if a woman had a difficult labor it was attributed to her having passed near such a place during pregnancy and having offended one of the bandit ghosts. The ghost might try to oust the rightful soul during labor and be born as the woman's son.

Under Buddhist influence souls were thought to live in zones of formlessness until the time of rebirth. They were fed by surviving relatives, and if nobody cared for them they would haunt people. In the seventh month after death there was a great festival for "hungry souls," when the priests would recite texts not only for relatives but for the souls of strangers and those without anyone to care for them. Meals, models of houses, and paper money were dedicated to the dead and burned as offerings. Especially in southern China, paper boats, often with a host of deities aboard or with lanterns in the shape of lotus flowers, were set drifting down rivers to light the way for spirits and ghosts to cross the river of transmigration. If sickness or calamity afflicted the community, however, it was attributed to inadequate propitiation of ghosts.

In Japanese belief one category of the ancestral dead is that of wandering angry ghosts. Neglected ancestors may quickly change from benevolent beings to vicious, cursing tyrants, attacking their families in painful ways until proper food and potent texts are offered to them. There are also spirits with no particular affinity (*muenbotoke*), those who die childless or without kin to worship them, and they may attack any stranger whose weakness lays him open to spiritual possession.

The most dangerous ghosts are those of people who die violently, are murdered, or die in disgrace. They become angry spirits *(onryō)* requiring rituals for appeasement. In the literature of the eighth to the tenth century there are striking examples of these furious ghosts, such as the story of Prince Sawara. After horrifying starvation, exile, and death by poison, he was said to have brought a whole series of calamities on the country. And a minister who died in 903 in disgrace and exile was credited with a succession of natural disasters thanks to his furious ghost. In early times discontented ghosts were depicted in animal or natural form, but in later *nō* plays they appear as ordinary men and women who are finally revealed as ghosts in horned masks and long red wigs.

Notions of ghosts and spirits as restless, perhaps unburied or unavenged, beings with a message to convey or a task to fulfill abound in popular belief in many countries, although there may be little formal doctrine or orthodox teaching in the scriptures to support these ideas.

See Also Afterlife; Soul.

Bibliography

The larger dictionaries provide examples of the ways in which *ghost* and similar words have been used, especially the complete or the "compact" edition of the *Oxford English Dictionary,* 2 vols. (Oxford, 1971). Biblical and ecclesiastical dictionaries rarely discuss ghosts, but the *Shorter Encyclopaedia of Islam* (1953; reprint, Leiden, 1974) has a useful article on the soul *(nafs).* Edward A. Westermarck's *Ritual and Belief in Morocco,* 2 vols. (1926; reprint, New Hyde Park, N. Y., 1968), is a treasury of popular beliefs. African beliefs have been collected in my *West African Psychology* (London, 1951). For Indian rituals Margaret S. Stevenson's *The Rites of the Twice-Born* (1920; reprint, New Delhi, 1971) is still valuable. There have been more recent studies of Buddhist countries: Richard F. Gombrich's *Precept and Practice* (Oxford, 1971) on Sri Lanka; Melford E. Spiro's *Buddhism and Society,* 2d ed. (Berkeley, Calif., 1982) on Burma; Stanley J. Tambiah's *Buddhism and the Spirit Cults in North-East Thailand* (Cambridge, 1970) on Thailand; and Carmen Blacker's *The Catalpa Bow* (London, 1975) on Japan.

Geoffrey Parrinder (1987)

GHOST THEORY See MANISM

GIBBONS, JAMES

GIBBONS, JAMES (1834–1921), American Roman Catholic churchman, archbishop of Baltimore, cardinal. The fourth child and eldest son of immigrant parents, James Gibbons was born in Baltimore on July 23, 1834. After a sixteen-year (1837–1853) sojourn in Ballinrobe, County Mayo, Ireland, where he received his early education, Gibbons returned to the United States and settled in New Orleans. Acting on a long-held desire to seek ordination, he studied for the priesthood at Saint Charles College in Ellicott City, Maryland, and at Saint Mary's Seminary in Baltimore. He was ordained a priest for the archdiocese of Baltimore in 1861.

Gibbons's career in the parish ministry ended in 1865 when Archbishop Martin Spalding made him his secretary. Thereafter, Gibbons experienced a swift rise through the ranks of the hierarchy. In 1868 he was named the first vicar apostolic of North Carolina and elevated to the rank of bishop; in 1872 he became the bishop of Richmond, Virginia; in May 1877 he was named coadjutor archbishop of Baltimore with right of succession; and in October 1877 he became the archbishop of Baltimore upon the death of James R. Bayley.

In assuming leadership of the archdiocese of Baltimore, Gibbons found himself in a position of great importance and high visibility in the American Catholic church. As the oldest diocese in the United States and the see within whose boundaries the national capital fell, Baltimore and its bishops enjoyed a degree of ecclesiastical and political prestige that other dioceses and bishops did not possess. These factors, together with Gibbons's longevity, his elevation to the cardinalate (1886), his accessibility to public officials and his personal friendship with every president from Cleveland to Harding, his tactful and conciliatory mode of governing, his irenic attitude toward non-Catholics, and the phenomenal success of his catechetical *Faith of Our Fathers* (1876), combined to make him the outstanding American Catholic churchman of his time.

Although he is justly famous for his contributions to such intramural Catholic projects as the founding of the Catholic University of America (1889) and the establishment of the National Catholic War/Welfare Council (1917), Gibbons's place in American Catholic history is really the result of the use he made of the prestige of his office and his personal talents in addressing four major problems that confronted the American church between 1877 and 1921: immigration, industrialization, nativism (the xenophobic reaction of Americans to immigrants), and Vatican apprehensions concerning American religious pluralism. Gibbons clearly saw that these four problems were interrelated, for all were concerned with the underlying problem of effecting some rapprochement between the Catholicism he loved and the American political and cultural life he revered. With his fellow americanizing bishops, John Ireland and John Keane, he sought both to assuage the fears of nervous nativists and to insure the internal unity of the church by advocating a pragmatic policy of assimilation that urged immigrant Catholics to adopt the language and mores of the host culture. His program did not endear him to German-American Catholics, but, combined with his conspicuous patriotism during the Spanish-American War and World War I, and his writings in praise of the American political system, it did much to enhance both his and his church's reputation as bulwarks of patriotism.

The same desires to demonstrate the social utility of the chuch to the nation, to insure the internal health of the church, and to protect the church from detractors animated Gibbons's defense of the Knights of Labor before the Roman Curia. His advocacy of the Knights as well as his work to reconcile New York's socially minded Father Edward McGlynn to the church earned him the reputation of a labor advocate comparable to Pope Leo XIII (1878–1903) and Cardinal Manning of Westminster in the universal church, and of a force for social peace at home.

While Gibbons enjoyed some measure of success in his attempts to demonstrate the compatibility of Catholicism and American life to non-Catholic Americans, the signal failure of his career was his inability to demonstrate the same either to conservative members of the American hierarchy or to Roman authorities who saw only a dangerous and corrosive indifferentism in the americanizers' praise of and accommodation to American mores. Leo XIII's condemnation of Americanism in 1899 *(Testem benevolentiae)* came as a stunning blow to Gibbons and his colleagues at the same time that it heartened the conservative followers of Archbishop Michael A. Corrigan of New York. In time, however, Gibbons's reputation in Rome was rehabilitated, and when he died in 1921 he was acknowledged by both his co-religionists and his fellow citizens to have been the dominant force in the American Catholic church.

BIBLIOGRAPHY

Browne, Henry J. *The Catholic Church and the Knights of Labor.* Washington, D.C., 1949. A narrative history of Catholicism's recognition of the rights of labor, with special attention to Gibbons's efforts to avert a papal condemnation of the Knights.

Cross, Robert D. *The Emergence of Liberal Catholicism in America.* Cambridge, Mass., 1958. Outlines the ideological position of the americanizers and the conservatives involved in the so-called battle of the prelates in the late nineteenth century.

Ellis, John Tracy. *The Life of James Cardinal Gibbons, Archbishop of Baltimore 1834–1921.* 2 vols. Milwaukee, 1952. The definitive biography of Gibbons.

Fogarty, Gerald P. *The Vatican and the American Hierarchy from 1870 to 1965.* Stuttgart, 1982. Examines the troubles encountered by the American hierarchy in dealing with a Curia that did not fully understand the American political system.

Gibbons, James. *A Retrospect of Fifty Years.* 2 vols. Baltimore, 1916. A collection of diary entries and articles written during Gibbons's episcopal career. Selections concerning the relationship of Catholicism and American life are especially helpful in understanding the man.

Joseph M. McShane (1987)

GIFT GIVING.

The exchange of gifts is one of the most telling characteristics of human culture and, according to some authorities, may form the original basis of economics. From a religious perspective, gift giving has two primary aspects with many variations. First, gift giving is incorporated in a variety of ways within the religious customs and sanctions that regulate social behavior. Second, in the sense of offering, gift giving is an essential aspect of sacrifices ritually presented to a deity or deities. In both aspects the process of gift giving may involve distribution of the gift within the selected social group to which it is appropriate; it may also entail the destruction of all or part of the thing given, to signify its disappearance into the metaphysical realm.

The Potlatch as a Model for Gift Giving. With regard to the social aspect of gift giving, Marcel Mauss's *Essai sur le don* (1925), translated as *The Gift* (1954), shows gift giving to be the very means by which value can be taught and understood in a society, provoking humans to productivity but at the same time inspiring a sense of an intangible presence in the things distributed. Mauss seems to regard the potlatch—an elaborate celebration entailing the lavish display and distribution of the host's possessions—as the most significant form of gift giving, possessing both religious significance and profound consequences for the development of economic systems. The gifts associated with the potlatch, as practiced by the Kwakiutl Indians, include both tangible, useful materials (such as blankets, boats, and food), and an entirely symbolic article—the most valuable *prestation* of all (Mauss's term, signifying the repayment of an obligation)—namely, a hatchet-shaped copper plaque.

The potlatch originated along the rich coast of northwestern North America. Many tribes in these regions adopted the potlatch, but the system appears in its most elaborate and well-recorded form among the Kwakiutl. It has been greatly modified as native peoples have become increasingly assimilated into the dominant white culture. Historically, the Kwakiutl were among the most thoroughly stratified tribes imaginable; they were fundamentally divided into two large groups, the *naqsala,* or nobility, and the *xamala,* or commoners. Every person, noble or common, belonged to further-interrelated subgroups within the overall structure of tribes and to *numina,* or subdivisions, within the particular tribe. The nobles, and even the commoners, were identified within all the interlocking groups by discrete honorific titles and by a system of seating according to rank. In the formalized feasting that was the ritual setting for the act of prestation, this seating system had much to do with the way in which goods were distributed.

In one respect, the potlatch system might be thought of as a means of increasing one's capital through interest on loans. One's status in the community was linked to the munificence with which one disposed of one's capital in the feasts. The capital consisted of what was regarded as valuable during a particular period: blankets, fish oil, food, shells, and slaves were such goods in premodern times. To cite an example, the list of gifts given in a potlatch in 1921 included the following items: Hudson Bay blankets, canoes, pool tables, bracelets, gaslights, violins, gasoline-powered boats, guitars, dresses, shawls, sweaters, shirts, oaken trunks, sewing machines, basins, glasses, washtubs, teapots, cups, bedsteads, bureaus, and sacks of flour and sugar (Rohner, 1970, p. 97). All of the items on this list were given to differentially ranked individuals. The pool tables, regarded as equivalent to the copper plaque (or "copper"), went to men of very high status. Glasses, washtubs, teapots, and cups went to women of various ranks. Thus, the distributor invested capital that gave him high status in the community and that was loaned, in a sense, in the expectation that all the items would be returned with interest at a future potlatch. Indeed, the interest was very precisely calculated; in the case of blankets, the return due at the end of one year was double the number of blankets given. The return of these loans (which were not solicited but had to be accepted, according to the system) was the occasion for the giving of new loans, much as it was the occasion for the potlatch feast. The purpose of the potlatch among the Kwakiutl was not to accumulate goods but to show one's ranked status in the community by the level of munificence one displayed. Some writers have compared the gift giving at the potlatch to a kind of warfare or war game in which the bestowal of extravagant gifts could inflict serious "wounds" on other participants.

Although it has not been commented on by leading writers, an analysis of the potlatch system reveals more than a few traits in common with the Hindu caste system, which likewise assigns rank during feasting in communal settings, and which includes a large element of redistribution of economic resources. Indeed, those who ranked highest on the curve of potlatch status owned not only goods in quantity but sacred names that could be distributed only during the communal feast; moreover, the highest-ranking regarded themselves as an exclusive group and had only limited contact with those lower in the system. Similar elements can be found in the caste system, wherein the caste name, sometimes irrelevant to the actual work performed, is understood to define an inescapable social status—indeed, the bestowal of magical and sacred names is an almost universal phenomenon throughout the Hindu religious system. Of course, this does not mean that the potlatch gift-giving system is the same as the caste system. But if Mauss's original insight is true, then the socially sanctioned distribution of gifts and other tokens of relationship, fraught with historical and structural significance as these things are, may be an irreducible element in human culture. The potlatch and caste systems are perhaps instances of a general principle. The universal relevance of these systems is clear, even in the apparent particularity of this description:

> The potlatch is more than a legal phenomenon; it is one of those phenomena we propose to call "total." It is religious, mythological and shamanistic because the chiefs taking part are incarnations of gods and ancestors, whose names they bear, whose dances they dance and whose spirits possess them. It is economic; and one has to assess the value, importance, causes and effects of transactions which are enormous even when reckoned by European standards. The potlatch is also a phenomenon of social morphology; the reunion of tribes, clans, families and nations produces great excitement. People fraternize but at the same time remain strangers; community of interest and opposition are revealed constantly in a great whirl of business. Finally, from the jural point of view, we have already noted the contractual forms and what we might call the human element of the contract, and the legal status of the contracting parties—as clans or families or with reference to rank or marital condition; and to this we now add that the material objects of the contracts have a virtue of their own which causes them to be given and compels the making of counter-gifts. (Mauss, 1967, pp. 36–37)

Caste relations in traditionalist Hindu society are problematic even today because of the threat of "pollution through contact." Mauss's idea is that such "pollution" is a sort of inversion of gift giving, for no matter what the degree of contact, there is some sort of giving involved, even if limited to the exchange of services. Mauss asserted that things given were still perceived to have links with the persons giving them. This characteristic of gifts would seem to be inescapable even in modern perceptions of their ultimate value, whether or not they are overtly sanctified by religion (as, for example, the blessed rings exchanged in a Christian wedding ceremony). After all, the caste system would have no power if it were not understood that everyone in the society exists of necessity in an intrinsic relation with everyone else. What is the basis of that relationship if not the exchange of goods and services, even if this must lead, at times, to measures to avoid the perceived consequences of pollution through contact?

Mauss Revisionists. Although the interesting interpretation of the potlatch by Mauss will certainly remain a point of reference for understanding gift giving, other authors have investigated the phenomenon from different theoretical perspectives and on the basis of other field research. Annette B. Weiner, in *Inalienable Possessions: The Paradox of Keeping-While-Giving* (1992), is concerned that in the Trobriand Islands, New Zealand, Samoa, and Hawai'i (Oceania) the special role of women in the creation of value through their reproductive and cultural productivity has been slighted in the history of the interpretation of gift giving, not just in the work of Mauss, but also in later works by Bronislaw Malinowski, Émile Durkheim, Claude Lévi-Strauss, and others. She bases her analysis upon a factor that is present in the exchange of gifts in these societies and that can also be found in the Kwakiutl potlatch system. As the title of her work suggests, the issue is that gift giving, or other connected bestowals, such as the granting of titles and sacred names, involves a heroic effort to maintain in one's own possession the most prestigious potential gifts while giving away quantities of other gifts that enhance or maintain the giver's prestige. Such a mandate is based upon a cosmological imperative from the imaginary other world. Status, as among the Kwakiutl, is of paramount importance in the social systems of Oceania and is not linked solely or even primarily to the roles of men in the hierarchy.

Weiner makes her most telling distinctions in describing the differences between *alienable* and *inalienable* possessions. It is the former that the society manufactures in sufficient quantities, often primarily through the production by women of fine woven mats, leaf skirts, and other commodities, to meet the requirements of gift giving in the particular social context. On the other hand, women also produce especially desirable mats and other types of "cloth" that are imbued with *mana* (a kind of sacrality). These items are linked to the reproductive power of female sexuality and cultural productivity, and they are inalienable. Other objects, such as shell arm bracelets (*mwali*) and necklaces (*soulava*), are also in this category. The ceremonial exchange of such goods is called *kula.* Somewhat like the system of the Kwakiutl, and found almost universally in the human world, gift giving is mandatory under certain ritual conditions, including, for example, when selecting a marriage partner (engagement), at weddings, at births, on recognized festivals, at the accession to high status of individuals in the society, at burials, and the like. For Weiner, what other anthropologists have failed to recognize is the essential role that women play in these systems, not only as cultural producers, but also as the recipients of the status connected with particular, inalienable possessions. Throughout Oceania there are numerous examples of women of high status—even chiefs, or, in Hawai'i, queens—who possess by right the inalienable items that it is their duty to maintain for the prestige of family and lineage. The greatest anxiety, underlying the alienable-inalienable dialectic, is that, however entrenched the inalienable potential gift may seem to be in one's own possession, occasions may arise when—because of defeat in warfare or as compensation for crimes such as murder, or due to other nearly catastrophic events—the gift must be surrendered to someone else. The requirements of gift giving under the social mandate of the group may demand such surrender when, through failure to produce substitutes in sufficient quantity, the inalienable possession itself must be surrendered to meet the social requirement.

According to Weiner, one of the ways that these societies maintain the integrity of particular lineages and their most valued possessions (titles and commodities) is through their extreme emphasis upon the brother-sister relationship. It is this factor that contributes substantially to the high status of women in these societies. The sister, even after her marriage, is in constant communication and relationship with her brother, even though he is married to another woman. Their relationship is often sanctified by a myth of a primordial incestuous sibling marriage that was the foundation of their lineage. The intensity of the link, which seems in part to be created to avoid the possible loss of familial, inalienable possessions, is carried to such lengths in the Trobriand Islands that the mother's brother, rather than the natural father, has "jural authority" over his sister's children (Weiner, 1992, p. 71). In Hawai'i the highest ranking families were actually the result of sibling marriages (p. 82), and, thus, brother-sister incest was not taboo—although it was taboo, in spite of the emphasis upon the brother-sister relationship, in most other areas of Oceania.

Maurice Godelier, in *The Enigma of the Gift* (1999), undertakes an exhaustive review, particularly of Mauss, with whom he agrees in many respects, and of Lévi-Strauss, with whom he agrees less, but also of Malinowski, Durkheim, and Weiner. Even though originally trained as a philosopher, Godelier claims the prerogative to comment on their work because he became an anthropologist and did fieldwork among the Baruya, a tribe that lives in the Eastern Highlands of New Guinea. He wishes to change Weiner's formula of "keeping-while-giving" to "keeping-for-giving," which he believes is a clearer way of stating the situation. Godelier goes on to say, subjecting Lévi-Strauss to criticism in the process, that "although Annette Weiner does not make the distinction between the imaginary and the symbolic, I would point out in passing that it is highly likely that the valuables, treasures and talismans which are not given but are kept are those which concentrate the greatest imaginary power and, as a consequence, the greatest symbolic value" (p. 33). What he means in particular is that Lévi-Strauss is wrong when he insists that *mana* and similar terms for the sacred are merely empty signifiers to make up for a lack of adequate language to refer to the intangible. Rather, Godelier thinks the whole of gift giving is wrapped up in the imaginary background of the social construct, which in itself can be thought of as "the total gift." In language that suggests the exquisite, even ineffable, way that gift giving plays this role—essentially of a religious nature, although Godelier does not believe that the human imaginary has any real links to a transcendent reality—he says something like the following in several places:

> From the moment most social relations in a society exist as and through the creation of personal bonds, as relations between persons, and from the moment these bonds are established by means of exchanging gifts which themselves entail the transfer and shifting of "realities," which can be of any kind (women, children, precious objects, services) as long as they lend themselves to being shared, all of the objective social relations which form the basis of a society (the kinship system, political system, and so forth), together with the intersubjective personal relations which embody them, can be expressed and "materialized" by the exchange of gifts and countergifts and by the movements, the trajectories followed by the "objects" of these gift-exchanges. (Godelier, 1999, p. 104)

Godelier makes a greater distinction than either Mauss or Weiner between *agonistic* and *non-agonistic* gift exchanges (1999, p. 48 et passim). The former, of which the potlatch is the exemplary type, implies the sometimes nearly warlike level of competition and is more absorbed in the transfer of the inalienable property, which may be an almost ineluctable goal that can lead to violence. The *non-agonistic* gift exchange, on the other hand, is much less fraught with tension.

The theoretical positions outlined above are drawn from field research among social groups whose imaginary construction of the gift-giving totality has been largely emptied of meaning in the economy of industrial nations and of its symbolic value in the modern Western way of life. Indeed, these studies give us great insight into the origins of the processes of exchange; but now, despite the preponderance of state-regulated or encouraged transfers to the most needy of the means to live, there may be a hankering after some unrealizable past state of human history. Godelier says very trenchantly, "When idealized, the 'uncalculating' gift operates in the imaginary as the last refuge of a solidarity, of an openhandedness which is supposed to have characterized other eras in the evolution of humankind. Gift-giving becomes the bearer of a utopia (a utopia which can be projected into the past as well as into the future)" (1999, p. 208). The major religions of the world, with their immense literary and cultural heritages, must be understood to have evolved their own rich complexities in the realm of gift giving, and these can only be indicated briefly and selectively in what follows.

GIFTS FOR THE GODS. In light of the foregoing conceptual frameworks and their implied universal applicability to social systems, it may be said that the characteristics of ritual gift giving provide a central element in religious life. What transpires at the social level, in the continuing drama of human relations, is reflected in the structure of the relationship between the human and the divine, as conceived in a particular group or religion. Much of the ritual in world religions symbolically connects hierarchy with the distribution of gifts, an act that is so powerful in the social relationship itself. Through Weiner's insight we might also theorize that most ritual behavior, religious charity, and religiously sanctioned social norms and behaviors participate in the alienable-inalienable tension of "keeping while giving" to the extent that these enhance status in the community and, also, imply an inalienable gift, such as a particularized salvation.

Hinduism. In the way that gifts were offered to the gods, Hinduism divides into two periods, characterized by the offerings presented in the so-called Vedic sacrifice and by the apparently endless variety of offerings of the later Hindu temple cult with its corollaries in household and sectarian worship. The gifts given to the gods in the Vedic sacrifice had relation to the organically perceived universe, which was, as the *Upaniṣad* says, "all food" (*Taittirīya Upaniṣad* 2.2), It appeared to the Vedic sacrificer that if the universe were to have the strength to keep running, certain foods had to be immolated on the Vedic fire altar. The ritual, as it has come down to us today, appears in several different forms. Great public rituals are now less common than before, although they are still performed on occasion. The numerous Brahmanic rituals, including the Saṇdhyā Vandanā (the daily service) and those connected with domestic life, and others oriented toward the welfare of departed spirits, involved simple offerings of ghee (clarified butter), water, grains, coconuts, and the like. In the Śrāddha ceremony for the dead, *piṇḍa* (rice balls) were believed to assuage the spirits. The more elaborate ceremonies in ancient times included animal sacrifices and the pressing of the *soma*, a type of intoxicant that was notably given to the god Indra to enable him to perform vigorously in his battle with Vṛtra, a cosmic monster. Horses and humans were slain in the sacrifices. The deities of the Vedic period had negative as well as positive traits; as in the context of other ritual systems, the offerings to the higher powers could bring benefits in reciprocation or ward off dangerous interventions. These are sometimes called the *do ut des* (I give that you may give) and *do ut abeas* (I give that you may go away) aspects of a ritual transaction.

In the period following 600 BCE, in the aftermath of the growing anthropomorphization of the deity (perhaps stimulated by the art and ritual of Buddhism and Jainism), the characteristic offerings in worship were likened to the food and gifts given to exalted human beings. Thus, it has often been mentioned that the style of Hindu temple worship is patterned after the court life of ancient India. The deity is considered to be the most respectable and powerful associate of humanity, a visitor from another realm who condescends to dwell for a time within images in temples, and who can be approached with gifts, services, art, music, and literature. In fact, gifts from the whole realm of human creativity can be offered to him. Two examples will be illustrative. It has been observed that among the later Kṛṣṇaite sects of North India, that of the Vallabha Sampradāy (founded by Vallabhācārya, 1479–1531), whose fervent love of the child Kṛṣṇa results in a daylong ceremonial offering of food, is the most lavish in "ritualistic materialism," if one may call it that. On special holidays, such as Kṛṣṇa's birthday, a mountain of food is prepared by the devotees and brought to the shrine to be offered to the image. Whenever offered, the food becomes *prasāda*, a kind of sacrament imbued with the power of the deity (because touched by him in a spiritual sense) and given back to the worshipers for their own consumption. Money offerings are given for the *prasāda*, which is, in effect, sold. The receipts are used to maintain the temple property, the priestly class, and the like. On the other hand, some gift-giving ceremonies are not at all lavish; a simple ceremony performed in the household for family members and guests or for a ladies' association that meets regularly by turn in members' homes for worship may entail the preparation of a simple meal or sweets, first offered to the deity and then given to the participants in the ceremony.

On holidays, it is common throughout India to provide new clothing for family members, servants, and other dependents during the feast of Dīvālī (October to November). This is the time when merchant castes close out their books and the goddess Lakṣmī is implored for an abundance of profit in the coming year. Sweets are exchanged between close friends and business associates. As for other special occasions, perhaps the most oppressive practice of gift giving in Hinduism, likewise representative of an aspect of caste or subcaste behavior, is the system of exchanges between a bride's family and a groom's family, sometimes observed for a number of years both before and after the marriage proper. The prevailing custom places the burden upon the bride's family, and the demands are so excessive that responsible parents in the poorer classes are frequently forced into penury to provide a daughter with a husband. It is not unheard of for a father to commit suicide so that his insurance money can be used to pay off the resulting indebtedness.

Buddhism. There is a type of gift giving that is explicitly meant to relieve the needs of the poor and the destitute.

Almsgiving, as this is called, likewise has a role to play in the economy of ascetic life, wherein monks and nuns live under some kind of vow of poverty and must therefore be supported by the actively working laity. Since Buddhism is a religion in which the monastic community (in its maintenance and perfecting of life in the *dharma*) is the main focus, it follows that almsgiving will be a general practice among Buddhists.

Apart from this necessary form of gift giving, Buddhism teaches generosity, self-giving, and even gift giving as illustrative of different aspects of the way toward *nirvāṇa*. For example, the *jātaka* stories that began to circulate early in the Buddhist period but were not completed before the fifth century CE demonstrate how the Buddha exemplified certain great lessons of life prior to his final emancipation. In his previous lives he was a *bodhisattva* and appeared in various embodiments. One of the *jātaka* tales tells how the Buddha-to-be practiced the virtues leading to emancipation while in the body of a hare. He taught the other animals—the jackal, the otter, and the monkey—to give alms, keep the precepts, and observe fast days. In observing their rule, the hare instructed his disciples on a certain fast day to give as alms to any stranger who might visit them food that they had obtained in the course of their usual ways. He himself vowed—since hares live on vegetation alone—to offer his own body as food to any meat-eating stranger who might approach him on the fast day. A heavenly being, made aware of the hare's vow, came to earth disguised as a *brahman* and tested each of the animals in turn as to the sincerity of its vow to offer hospitality after its own kind. The hare in due course threw himself into the fire to provide the *brahman's* supper; but the heavenly being prevented the hare's being burned and, to commemorate his magnanimity, drew a likeness of his face on the moon to be admired thenceforth by all on earth.

Gift giving is also mentioned in one of the most famous works of the Mahāyāna tradition, the *Saddharmapuṇḍarīka Sūtra.* Therein, the *bodhisattva* illustrates in numerous ways his vocation as savior of humanity, suffering in the endlessly repetitive world of *saṃsāra.* The *bodhisattva* offers to deluded humanity the gift of a paradisiacal afterlife as an inducement to abandon the gross physical world. The paradises of the *bodhisattva*, particularly that of Amida Buddha in the West, are filled with jeweled trees; sparkling, diamantine sands; and enchanting birds and flowers; together with fountains and the like. This paradise is meant to provide a mediating position between the world of *saṃsāra* and the absolute state of *nirvāṇa.* The *bodhisattva* vows to take all beings together into that emancipated state. The Buddhist parables of the burning house and the prodigal son are parallel tales illustrating the means by which one might, through gifts, relieve one's obsession with the material world in favor of the higher world. Thus, the children in the burning house are offered gifts to induce them to leave the house and come outside. The kindly, concerned father is the figure of the *bodhisattva*, likewise offering an escape from the material world into paradise. In the story of the prodigal son, deluded humanity is represented by a wealthy father who finds his lost son after many years; the father tries to change his son's attitude toward himself by giving him gifts and positions of responsibility. This can be understood to refer to the training in spiritual life through which, with the *bodhisattva's* help, the aspirant is brought into a state of awareness regarding the true nature of the world and the need for emancipation from it. Works in the Pali canon, such as the *Dakkhiṇāvi-bhaṅga Sutta* and the *Sigālovāda Sutta*, give precise instructions for the giving of gifts to monks and the giving of gifts between the laity and in connection with the Buddhist holidays.

Chinese religions. Reading the colorful sixteenth-century novel *The Golden Lotus*, which reflects life in China in the twelfth century, one gathers that in that period in China the well-positioned gift was an absolute essential for the improvement of one's social and economic position, for gaining preference at the court of the emperor, or for placating judges in the courts of law (see Egerton, 1972). Indeed, the novel affords a vivid object lesson on the ways in which bribes not only can move one up the ladder but also, as the companions of other vices, can bring one to one's doom, as is the case with the novel's hero Ximen Qing (or Ch'ing Hsimen). It has sometimes been said of the Confucian doctrine that it not only attempted to inculcate a reasonable morality on the basis of equity between human beings, as expressed in the so-called silver rule ("Do not do unto others what you would not have them do unto you"), but it also came to terms with what was perceived to be the natural inequality between persons. Giving and receiving gifts within the hierarchical Chinese society was an inevitable aspect of rank differentiation. Those highest in rank received the most expensive and most numerous gifts. Analogously, the ceremonial life of the public cult involved the emperor's presenting gifts at the altar of heaven within the so-called Forbidden City in Beijing, both at the winter solstice and at other times. Precious stones and costly cloth were among the offerings. Lower-ranking officials throughout the empire offered their respective gifts to the gods—to the city god, for example. This activity was consonant with the custom of making offerings at the shrines of family ancestors. Gifts of incense and fruits were regularly presented before the ancestral tablets.

The rites offered to the spirits of Confucius and other sages included sacrifices of pigs and oxen; the great deities of the Daoist pantheon were given wine, cakes, and meat offerings. Indeed, it is not too farfetched to see the development of Chinese cuisine in part as an outgrowth of ritual life. Feasts were regularly a part of the offerings made by individuals in the Daoist and Buddhist temples. In the latter case, vegetarianism required the development of a special cuisine so that the proper foods could be offered to monks and others under similar vows.

Rituals for the departed often included the burning of effigies of material objects, such as imitation money or a tomb made of paper. In contemporary rituals even such modern accoutrements of life as refrigerators and cars may be constructed of paper and burned in the temple furnace with appropriate reverence under the axiom that the thing itself is less important than the thought behind it.

As already noted in the discussion of the potlatch and the Hindu caste system, sociological theory lends credence to the applicability of the potlatch as an analogue to many systems of social organization. Marcel Granet, in *Danse et légendes de la Chine ancienne* (1926), proposed a relationship between the potlatch and the prefeudal (early or pre-Shang dynasty) system of China, which was influential in the formation of Confucius's ideas of the ideal social order. This position has been examined in the work of Eugene Cooper (1982), who argues convincingly for its validity.

Judaism. Diaspora Judaism's theory of almsgiving and charity was built on a thoroughgoing moral system. The record of sacrifices in the Hebrew scriptures—offerings given to God according to the seasons and particular festivals and the day-to-day demands of ritual—has been preserved by some Jews in synagogue worship through recitations from *Exodus*, *Leviticus*, and *Numbers* in the Orthodox preliminary morning service contained in *Ha-siddur ha-shalem* (see Birnbaum, 1949). With the destruction of the Temple in 70 CE it was no longer possible to maintain the offerings in the prescribed setting; the Jewish community's concern with the purity of food, however, dictated that there be a class of specialists in the ritual slaughter of animals (for food purposes if not for offering to God). With the establishment of the State of Israel, various groups, both Jewish and Christian (although there is considerable disagreement on the issue in Judaism), are making preparations for the rebuilding of the Temple in Jerusalem and for the reestablishment of ritual sacrifices. Of course, other offerings besides animals were made as well; these included grain, oil, incense, and wine, and some vestige of them remains both in Sabbath observances in the Jewish home and in the Passover meal.

Of the popular holidays, two in particular are connected with gift giving within the family or among friends. The better known, perhaps, is the custom at Ḥanukkah of giving gifts (money and other things) to children on each of the eight nights of the festival. Much is made in contemporary Jewish discussion of the need to maintain some kind of distinction between this Jewish observance and the Christmas festival of Christians, particularly since both occur at approximately the same time of year. The playing of games of chance, which of course relate to the potential of gift giving for the redistribution of valuables within the social community, is also a part of the Ḥanukkah observance.

Purim, which commemorates the rescue of the Jews from the evil minister Hamman in the court of the king of Persia, is an occasion for exchanging food. The legend itself is told in the *Book of Esther*, which is read in the synagogue on the holiday in a mood of revelry compared sometimes to that of Carnival in Latin Christian countries. *Shalaḥ Manos* is the custom of sending gifts of food from house to house on Purim; the type of food given is that which can be eaten and drunk on the same day.

Christianity. As with the history of Buddhism, the history of Christianity reveals the development of an elaborate system of gift giving for the maintenance of the institutions of the church, the clergy, and the monastic communities. During the earliest centuries of the church, persecutions were a constant threat, and the Christian community had to develop its own system of finances, since its survival was outside the concern of the state. From the time of Constantine (early fourth century) onward, the church received state recognition and was able to capitalize on its status to attract enormous endowments; with the advent of Muslim rulers in many Eastern Christian lands, however, the church was once again reduced to tense relations with the state. It survived in part through the generosity of the laity, and in part through official support, for even in Islamic lands the church was to a certain extent and at certain times patronized by the rulers. Gifts of lands and other wealth were given to the Church of the East (sometimes called Nestorian), which before the thirteenth century had spread into China and India. The Christian church of Kerala in South India received, until modern times, regular patronage from the Hindu rulers of the region. The right of the Christian community (and other religious communities) to receive gifts unencumbered by excessive government interference is an issue in the modern world. Specific exemptions from taxes and benefits for giving gifts are written into the laws to encourage the support of religious institutions.

The ritual life of Christianity is permeated with the idea of the gift and gift giving. The elements of the Eucharist—the bread and the wine, which are widely called the Holy Gifts—are offered to God as a "sacrifice," and according to some theologies they become the body and blood of Christ in an unbloody reproduction of the crucifixion. Other theologies describe these gifts as being received by God and sanctified to become the body and blood of Christ through the power of the Holy Spirit. The custom whereby the laity prepare and offer the bread and the wine of the Eucharist has been revived in some Christian bodies. In addition to the elements of the Eucharist and the paraphernalia that accompany it, such as chalices, monstrances, tabernacles of precious metal, and the like, the Christian churches have received uncountable offerings in the form not only of money but also of vestments, paintings, architecture, and sculpture—gifts representing the full range of human creativity. These gifts still constitute a principal part of the heritage of Western civilization. Although sometimes limited by theological constraints, Protestant churches have likewise encouraged gift giving through the arts. With the modern secularization of public life, however, the impetus to artistic creativity in connection with the religious gift-giving impulse seems to have been diverted.

Caught somewhere between the sacred and the profane is the gift-giving extravaganza carried out, now virtually around the world, in the name of the infant Christ, who was born in Bethlehem and whose birth is widely celebrated on December 25. The precedent for exchanging gifts on the Christian festival is based on the visit of the wise men from the East to the Christ child, even though their time of arrival at Bethlehem is commemorated on January 6. The date of Christmas was chosen, it is said, in order to attract the interest of the non-Christian masses of Europe who celebrated the winter solstice.

Islam. At least from what one gathers in reading the *ḥadīth* (traditions of Muḥammad, the Prophet of Islam), the Islamic idea of gift giving is but an extension of the underlying concept of alms, expressed in the two Arabic words *zakāt* and *ṣadaqah.* Perhaps because there are no sacrifices or sacraments in the usual religious sense in Islam—in other words, no way of transmuting a material object through a religious ceremony from the merely physical plane to a "new mode of being"—all events in Islamic religious practice tend to take on a moral overtone; righteousness is the primary goal of religious life. In general, it appears that goodness in Islam is thought of as consequent upon obedience to the command of God to act in certain ways. Generosity may be expressed in a great number of actions that reflect the moral earnestness of a discipline enjoined by a higher power. The myriad customs and observances of Islamic law and tradition are further extensions of the original act of submission, which is a call to acknowledge faith in the one God. The prophet Muḥammad represents the ultimate degree of perfection in answering the call. Meditation on the minutiae of his life remains the source of the moral earnestness that is the characteristic of Islamic ethics.

In the realm of gift giving, the so-called poor tax, or *zakāt,* can be understood as a practical example for all types of giving. Both in the Qurʾān and in the traditions of Muḥammad, the believer is constantly reminded that his days on earth are but a brief interlude, beyond which lies the state of bliss in paradise, provided the believer has merited a reward in the afterlife. In the prostration of prayer, believers are reminded that they are gazing into the pit of the grave where the two angels of paradise or hell will come to direct the soul to its intermediate state prior to the Last Judgment. The poor tax, especially as it impinges on human possessions, reflects this ascetic attitude toward the term of human existence; it is meant to make the Muslim believer deliver from his possessions a fixed amount annually—at the feasts of the end of Ramaḍān (the lunar month of fasting) and during the *ḥājj* (the pilgrimage to Mecca)—for the relief of certain classes in Muslim society.

In the larger sense of sharing what one possesses, the term *ṣadaqah* is used—for example, in the *Mishkāt al-maṣābīḥ* (see Robson, 1963–1965). In book 12, *On Business Transactions,* several chapters are devoted to gifts. The Prophet encouraged the setting aside in "life tenancy" of lands whose produce would maintain certain charitable activities, such as the provision of food for travelers. There are several references to gift giving within the family context in order to assure evenhandedness.

The problem of reciprocity in gift giving is also addressed in chapter 17, part 2, of the *Mishkāt,* wherein the Prophet is asked whether one must return equally for any gift received. His advice is to return equally if possible; if it is not possible, then an expression of sincere thanks and prayerful intercession will suffice. In general, the Prophet encouraged gift giving between neighbors and among members of the community in order to stimulate mutual good feelings. Perfume was one of the Prophet's favorite gifts in this connection. Even today, when Muslims gather for prayer in the mosque, it is counted a righteous act for them to offer perfume from a small container to their fellow worshipers. To be clean and sweet-smelling is a gift to those with whom one associates, particularly at the time of prayer. It is also considered an act of gift giving to offer a smile rather than a dour look to a fellow human.

SEE ALSO Almsgiving; Hospitality; Potlatch; Sacrifice; Tithes.

BIBLIOGRAPHY

Berking, Helmuth. *Sociology of Giving.* Translated by Patrick Camiller. London, 1999. Traces the origin of gift giving to the historical past but also analyzes the underlying moral issues as they affect modern life.

Birnbaum, Philip, ed. and trans. *Ha-Sidur ha-Shalem.* New York, 1949.

Burtt, Edwin A., ed. *The Teachings of the Compassionate Buddha.* New York, 1955; rev. ed., 1982.

Cooper, Eugene. "The Potlatch in Ancient China." *History of Religions* 22, no. 3 (1982): 103–128.

Dumont, Louis. *Homo Hierarchicus: An Essay on the Caste System.* Translated by Mark Sainsbury. Chicago, 1970; rev. English ed. (with the subtitle T*he Caste System and its Implications*), 1980.

Egerton, Clement, trans. *The Golden Lotus: A Translation, from the Chinese Original, of the Novel* Chin P'ing Mei. 4 vols. London, 1972; reprint, London and New York. 1995.

Ferdon, Edwin N. *Early Tahiti as the Explorers Saw It, 1767–1797.* Tucson, 1981.

Godbout, Jacques T., with Alain Caille. *The World of the Gift.* Translated by Donald Winkler. Montreal, 1998. An effort to rehabilitate the concept of gift giving with reference to recent intellectual trends, mainly in France.

Godelier, Maurice. *L'Enigme du don.* Paris, 1996. Translated by Nora Scott as *The Enigma of the Gift.* Chicago, 1999.

Granet, Marcel. *Danse et légendes de la Chine ancienne.* Paris, 1926; 3d ed., corrected and augmented by Rémi Mathieu, Paris, 1994.

Kolenda, Pauline. *Caste in Contemporary India: Beyond Organic Solidarity.* Menlo Park, Calif., 1978; reprint, 1985.

Krause, Aurel. *The Tlingit Indians: Results of a Trip to the Northwest Coast of America and the Bering Straits.* Translated by Erna Gunther. Seattle, 1956. Originally published in German in 1885.

Mauss, Marcel. *The Gift: Forms and Functions of Exchange in Archaic Societies.* Translated by Ian Cunnison. Glencoe, Ill., 1954; reprint, New York, 1967.

Mayer, Adrian C. *Caste and Kinship in Central India.* Berkeley, 1960.

Otnes, Cele, and Richard F. Beltramini, eds. *Gift Giving: A Research Anthology.* Bowling Green, Ohio, 1996. This is a combined effort, which, among other things, asserts the thesis "that gift giving has not diminished in importance, but rather has become one of the primary exemplars of symbolic consumer behavior in postindustrial societies" (p. 3).

Robson, James, trans. *Mishkāt al-maṣābīḥ.* 4 vols. Lahore, Pakistan, 1963–1965.

Rohner, Ronald P., and Evelyn C. Rohner. *The Kwakiutl: Indians of British Columbia.* New York, 1970; reprint, Prospect Heights, Ill., 1986.

Rosman, Abraham, and Paula G. Rubel. *Feasting with Mine Enemy: Rank and Exchange among Northwest Coast Societies.* New York, 1971.

Siegel, Richard, Michael Strassfeld, and Sharon Strassfeld, eds. *The Jewish Catalog: A Do-It-Yourself Kit.* Philadelphia, 1973.

Stryk, Lucien, ed. *World of the Buddha: A Reader.* Garden City, N.Y., 1968.

Weiner, Annette B. *Inalienable Possessions: The Paradox of Keeping-While-Giving.* Berkeley and Los Angeles, 1992.

Wouk, Herman. *This Is My God.* Garden City, N.Y., 1959.

Wu Cheng-en. *Monkey Subdues the White-Bone Demon.* Translated and adapted by Wang Hsing-Pei. Beijing, 1973.

Yan, Yunxiang. *The Flow of Gifts: Reciprocity and Social Networks in a Chinese Village.* Stanford, Calif., 1996. This is "an ethnographic account of the system of gift exchange and the patterns of interpersonal relations in a north China village" (p. 1).

CHARLES S. J. WHITE (1987 AND 2005)

GILGAMESH

GILGAMESH, a Sumerian hero, god, and ruler of the city-state Uruk, is the subject of a classic epic poem that Mesopotamian tradition attributes to the priest-exorcist and scribe Sin-leqi-unnini. The poem was the product of a lengthy compilation effort, which resulted in the composition of the national poem of Babylon. Until the 1990s there were five known Sumerian works that described the deeds of Gilgamesh, king of Uruk. The Sumerologist Samuel Noah Kramer identified them as: "Gilgamesh and Agga," "Gilgamesh and Hubaba," "Gilgamesh and the Bull of Heaven," "Gilgamesh, Enkidu, and the Underworld," and "The Death of Gilgamesh." The environment in which they were conceived and composed has been generally regarded as the court of the third dynasty of Ur (c. 2100–2000 BCE), whose sovereigns sought to trace a direct link between the figure of Gilgamesh and the royalty of Uruk. Giovanni Pettinato has suggested that a 107-line text found in 1975 at Tell Mardikh-Ebla is related to the Gilgamesh saga. This text, and the entire library from which it comes, can be dated to 2500 to 2400 BCE. The events described in this text concern relations between the king of Uruk and the city of Aratta. The narrative fits well with the tradition of epic wars between the royal dynasty of Uruk and the colony founded in an indeterminate location in Iran: both King Enmerkar and Lugalbanda, the supposed divine father of Gilgamesh, waged war against Aratta according to the four epics that concern these figures.

A new version of "The Death of Gilgamesh," rediscovered at Me-Turan in 1979, serves to confirm the narrative translated by Kramer, while also, because it is more complete, opening up new avenues of understanding concerning the complex nature of Sumerian civilization. This version verifies for the first time the Sumerian custom of collective burial, something for which there is archaeological evidence at Ur and Kish, but which had not been previously confirmed by epigraphic sources. This text also includes confirmation of the legend of Urlugal, the son of Gilgamesh, specifically named in the Sumerian King List as Gilgamesh's son and successor to the throne of Uruk. Similarly, a new version of "Gilgamesh and the Bull of Heaven" was found there in 1979.

Unfortunately the authors of Sumerian narratives featuring Gilgamesh are unknown to us, and scholars are not certain whether it is pure chance that the series of Gilgamesh poems is attributed to a single author. According to a catalog of authors and texts from the neo-Assyrian period, rediscovered in the library of Assurbanipal and published by W. G. Lambert (1962), the series of Gilgamesh was conceived by Sin-leqi-unnini, who according to Lambert lived between the thirteenth and twelfth centuries BCE, at the end of Kassite power in Babylon, and more precisely at the moment when Babylon, under Nebuchadrezzar I, managed to obtain its independence from foreign rule.

CONTENTS OF THE EPIC. The classic epic, while consisting of a reconstruction of a literary work conceived and composed in the Old Babylonian period, should be considered as a single unified composition. Sin-leqi-unnini was not simply responsible for a brief summary in twelve tablets of the story from earlier times; it can be said with some certainty that he, in a sense, reconsidered and re-created the entire story from scratch.

An important piece of evidence for the unity of the classical epic is the presence of a prologue, as well as an epilogue found at the end of Tablet XI, where part of the prologue is repeated. Tablet XII is generally considered by scholars to be an appendix to the epic. Its contents consist of a literal translation of part of the Sumerian story known as "Gilgamesh, Enkidu, and the Underworld."

The epic may be divided as follows:

1. Prologue: The hero Gilgamesh (Tab. I.1–51).
2. Enkidu, the alter ego of Gilgamesh (Tab. I.52–II.155ff.).
3. Gilgamesh, Enkidu, and the monster Hubaba (Tab. II.184–V.266).

4. Gilgamesh, Enkidu, and the Bull of Heaven (Tab. VI.1–182).
5. Death of Enkidu and despair of Gilgamesh (Tab. VI.183–VIII.207ff.).
6. Gilgamesh in the quest for immortality (Tab. IX.1–X.325).
7. Only the gods have the gift of life (Tab. XI.1–302).
8. Epilogue (Tab. XI.302–308).
9. Fate of humankind in the afterlife (Tab. XII.1–154).

INTERPRETATION OF THE EPIC. No interpretation of the epic should be separated from an analysis of the work of Sin-leqi-unnini. Closely connected to this is another investigation concerning the identity of the two main characters as divine or human. Thus far, we have spoken of the "epic" or "saga," putting into this category both the Sumerian stories and the various poetic versions that have Gilgamesh as their main hero, regarding them as *res gestae*, whether of a historical or legendary figure. A review of various scholarly interpretations indicates that the second problem cannot be decisively resolved. Although the majority of scholars are convinced that the king of Uruk is a historical figure, Pettinato and others think that Gilgamesh did not exist in a historical sense, but is instead a god who has been made into a historical figure.

The first interpreters of the work of Sin-leqi-unnini, which was discovered in 1872 by George Smith among the thousands of fragments of the library of Assurbanipal at Nineveh, were concerned with defining its nature. Apart from its real or supposed parallels with stories told in the Bible—the example of the universal flood on Tablet XI marks the beginning of an argument so heated that it has been called "the war between the Bible and Babel"—scholars have sought to explain the deeper meaning of the work centered upon Gilgamesh.

Hugo Winckler and Heinrich Zimmern came to the conclusion that the Gilgamesh poem was a myth concerning the sun god and in particular was constructed like the myth of the Dioscuri. Otto Weber confirmed this view, and pointed out that the twelve tablets contain clear reference to the signs of the zodiac. For Weber, the poem's basic theme is the journey of the sun through its twelve phases over the course of the year, with the figure of Gilgamesh functioning as an allusion to the sun god and Enkidu representing the moon. For these scholars, there are clear antecedents of the adventures of Odysseus in the *Epic of Gilgamesh*, as well as of the labors of Herakles and the later voyages of Alexander the Great.

Heinrich Schneider claimed that all the characters in the epic were either powerful gods or second-rate divine beings who, like Gilgamesh, had been made into human figures. Schneider also argues that the friendship between Gilgamesh and Enkidu corresponds to the medieval ideal of chivalry, and he defines the Old Babylonian story as heroic and the Ninevite story as chivalrous.

Meanwhile Peter Jensen's lengthy *Das Gilgamesch-Epos in der Weltliteratur* (The *Epic of Gilgamesh* in world literature, 1906) attempted to show the astral and mythological nature of the work. For Jensen, the epic was a description of the events that took place in the heavens during the course of the year, especially the heliacal rising of the stars. Notwithstanding Jensen's passion and deep convictions, important biblical scholars, such as Hermann Gunkel and Hugh Gressmann, not only categorically refuted alleged biblical parallels, but denied the mythical nature of the *Epic of Gilgamesh*, considering it rather as pure saga, clearly parallel to the romance of Alexander.

In 1923 the German scholar Arthur Ungnad, completely abandoning any mythical interpretation, argued that the epic was an ethical work and the forerunner of Homer's *Odyssey*. Although Ungnad does not propose that the Greek author copied the work of Sin-leqi-unnini, he has no doubts that the Greeks adapted and retold sagas from the East to suit their own temperament. A year later Hermann Häfker argued that the Gilgamesh epic was an entirely historical work, with its guiding theme being the problem of life and death. In 1937 there appeared an important contribution by the Swedish scholar Sigmund Mowinckel, in which he defends the divine nature of Gilgamesh and interprets the entire work as the description of a god who dies and rises again, a commonplace in the context of history of religions.

A completely different view was proposed by Benno Landsberger. For him the work is the national epic of the Babylonians and Gilgamesh is the personification of the ideal human being for the Babylonians. The predominant theme in the epic then is the problem of the eternal life, discussed using the familiar example of *Faust*.

Mythological interpretations were not completely abandoned however. Beginning in 1958 scholars such as Franz Marius Theodor Bohl and Igor M. Diakonov continued to hold this position, with Bohl stating that what lay behind the epic was a religious war between the followers of the cults of Ishtar and those of Shamash and Marduk, while for Diakonov the figures of Gilgamesh and Enkidu are personifications of the sun god and moon god.

Geoffrey S. Kirk argued that the *Epic of Gilgamesh* has as its theme the contrast between nature, represented by Enkidu, and culture, represented by Gilgamesh. For Thorkild Jacobsen, on the other hand, the poem contains a description of the process by which human beings become mature, moving from innocent and reckless adolescence to the awareness of values that are more real, though less apparent. This leads to a psychoanalytical interpretation: the love of Gilgamesh for Enkidu is the love of an adolescent boy for one of his peers, before discovering love for women.

Giorgio Buccellati interprets Gilgamesh in terms of wisdom. After analyzing the epic's various themes, such as impurity, fear, the wanderer's life as opposed to family life, and the uncertainty between dreams and reality, Buccellati concludes:

> The emphasis is shifted from the object of the search, life, to the actual effort of the search as such, to the assumptions upon which it is based, and to the consequences for the person who carries it out: these consequences are not external, as in the pursuit of a particular benefit, perhaps even physical life itself, but rather they are internal, deeply psychological and are concentrated upon the spiritual change of the person who is undertaking the search. (Buccellati, 1972, p. 34)

One of the first scholars to stress the central nature of the theme of friendship in the *Epic of Gilgamesh* was Landsberger, who wrote that one of the fundamental motifs of Sin-leqi-unnini's work is the ideal of a noble friendship between Gilgamesh and Enkidu, which not even death can erase. Indeed, from their first meeting after their battle in the streets of Uruk and then later in the dreams Gilgamesh has, the deep bond between these two characters is emphasized, to the extent that it has been compared to love for a woman. The troubled quest for eternal life also shows how much Enkidu means to Gilgamesh. However, the rejection of the love offered by Ishtar is not to be read as the repudiation of love for women, as Landsberger has it, but rather in a much more profound manner, as concerning the future destiny of the king of Uruk.

Other scholars have considered friendship to be the central theme of the epic, including Lubor Matouš, but in particular Giuseppe Furlani, who in an article titled "L'Epopea di Gilgameš come inno all'amicizia" (The *Epic of Gilgamesh* as a hymn to friendship) and then in the introduction to his 1946 translation of the epic, asserts that he is obliged to "revise the fundamental, central theme of the epic" in that "the epic of Gilgamesh is truly a hymn to friendship, a long-lasting friendship enduring even beyond the grave, between Gilgamesh of Uruk and Enkidu, shining, eternal examples of faithful friends" (Furlani, 1946, p. 587). Furlani further states that "the central and underlying idea of our poem has been thought of as a discussion of the problem of life and death. . .it seems to me instead that this idea should now be abandoned and we should recognize that the epic is in reality a hymn to friendship" (Furlani, 1946, p. 589).

Following Landsberger, who sets the problem of human existence at the heart of the epic, Alexander Heidel considered its central theme to be a meditation on death in the form of a tragedy. Heidel argues that the epic confronts the bitter truth that death is inevitable: all human beings must die. Matouš and A. Leo Oppenheim also stressed that the underlying theme of the work is the search for eternal life.

Readers of the epic of Sin-leqi-unnini should first take full account of the prologue: in the first eight lines, the author repeatedly identifies knowledge with wisdom. For him the adventures of Gilgamesh consist of a series of important staging points, necessary to reach a final end, which the author correctly identifies as the wisdom of his hero. The author advises the reader that this is the key to the text. As Buccellati emphasizes, seeing other motives or themes means considering the staging points and methods of approach to this ideal as ends in themselves. Therefore, an accurate reading of the poem cannot ignore the fundamental motifs proposed by its author. The fact that the author then mentions the troubled quest for eternal life as an essential part of the hero's personal journey, and that Gilgamesh, in attaining wisdom, has experienced all kinds of suffering, only serves to confirm the critical nature of wisdom in interpreting the work.

Scholars are in general agreement that the epic may be divided into two parts: the first narrates the marvelous adventures of the two heroes and their epic deeds, the killing of the monster Hubaba and the Bull of Heaven; the second part describes how Gilgamesh, who is two-thirds god and one-third human, is forced to deal with the eternal human problem of death. Gilgamesh tries to overcome death, and he hopes that he will receive a conclusive answer from the hero of the flood, but as we learn from Tablet XI, even this semidivine being does not succeed, and it is perhaps in this failure that Sin-leqi-unnini sees the logical ending of his work. This would be surprising however, since the author opens his work by praising the wisdom of Gilgamesh, so this must mean that he does not consider these events to be a failure as such. The treatment of the figure of Gilgamesh throughout the epic could not allow for such a dismal ending: the king of Uruk, besides being two-thirds god, is the paradigm of a true king. If the interpretation proposed below regarding the "plant of life" is correct, Gilgamesh is showing himself to be a true king at the very moment of his failure.

The real answer to all the problems of Gilgamesh has been seen in the final gift of Utanapishtim to the king, when he reveals to Gilgamesh the existence of a special plant. This interpretation is based upon an insertion accepted by the majority of scholars at line 270 in Tablet XI, which says: "You will obtain life." But nothing in the text justifies an insertion of this kind. The gift of Utanapishtim is defined as "a plant of restlessness," and Gilgamesh explains the nature of the plant: "It is reputed to turn an old man back into a man in his prime. So I want to eat the plant and become young again." This leads to the conclusion that Gilgamesh, by eating the plant, would be returned to a youthful state, with all its anxiety and restlessness. Hence the interpretation of the plant as an elixir of youth: by eating the plant, Gilgamesh would have been returned to the position he was in during the first part of the epic. The fact that he lost the plant is a further sign of the greatness of this king. Gilgamesh had not forgotten that a king is responsible for the fate of his subjects and he loses the plant precisely because he wanted to share it with his fellow citizens. His first thought when he is given the plant is to take it back to Uruk and feed it to the old.

However, the gift of Utanapishtim was not available for the whole of humanity, but reserved for Gilgamesh alone, perhaps as a reward for all his travels and his tenacious quest in pursuit of the unattainable ideal of eternal life. When Gilgamesh wanted to share this with other people, the serpent became its sole beneficiary: "Gilgamesh on that day sat down and wept / and the tears rolled down his cheeks." In these two lines the scribe expresses the diverse emotions of the hero, the first being his inability to fulfill his royal duty. Yet this admission itself marks the attainment of complete wisdom, of a maturity that is the legacy of a true king of Mesopotamia.

SEE ALSO Death; Heroes.

BIBLIOGRAPHY

Abusch, Tsvi. "Ishtar's Proposal and Gilgamesh's Refusal: An Interpretation of the Gilgamesh Epic, Tablet VI, Lines 1–79." *History of Religions* 26 (1986): 143–187.

Buccellati, Giorgio. "Gilgamesh in chiave sapienziale." *Oriens Antiquus* 11 (1972): 2–36.

Cavigneaux, Antoine, and Farouk N. H. Al-Rawi. "Gilgamesh et Taureau de ciel (*shul-mè-kam*) (Textes de Tell Haddad IV)." *Revue d'Assyriologie* 87 (1993): 97–129.

Cavigneaux, Antoine, and Farouk N. H. Al-Rawi. "New Sumerian Literary Texts from Tell Haddad (Ancient Meturan): A First Survey." *Iraq* 55 (1993): 91–105.

Cavigneaux, Antoine, and Farouk N. H. Al-Rawi. *Gilgamesh et la mort: Textes de Tell Haddad VI.* Groningen, Netherlands, 2000.

Cavigneaux, Antoine, and Farouk N. H. Al-Rawi. "La fin de Gilgamesh: Enkidu et les enfers d'après les manuscrits d'Ur et de Metura (Textes de Tell Haddad VIII)." *Iraq* 52 (2000): 1–19.

Furlani, Giuseppe. "L'epopea di Gilgamesh come inno all'amicizia." *Belfagor* 1 (1946): 577–589.

Furlani, Giuseppe. *Miti babilonesi e assiri.* Florence, 1958.

George, Andrew, trans. and ed. *The Epic of Gilgamesh.* London, 1999.

Heidel, Alexander, *The Gilgamesh Epic and Old Testament Parallels*, Chicago, 1967.

Kirk, Geoffrey Stephen. *Myth: Its Meaning and Functions in Ancient and Other Cultures.* Berkeley, 1970. See pages 132–152.

Matouš, Lubor. "Die Entstehung des Gilgamesh-Epos." *Altertum* 4 (1958): 195–221.

Oberhuber, Karl. *Das Gilgamesch-Epos.* Darmstadt, Germany, 1977.

Oppenheim, A. Leo. *Ancient Mesopotamia. Portrait of a Dead Civilization.* Chicago, 1964.

Pettinato, Giovanni. *La saga di Gilgamesh* (in collaboration with S. M. Chiodi and G. Del Monte). Milan, 1992.

Thompson, R. Campbell, trans. and ed. *The Epic of Gilgamesh.* Oxford, 1930.

Tigay, Jeffrey H. *The Evolution of the Gilgamesh Epic.* Philadelphia, 1982.

GIOVANNI PETTINATO (2005)
Translated from Italian by Paul Ellis

GILLEN, FRANCIS JAMES, AND BALDWIN SPENCER.

Baldwin Spencer and Frank Gillen both came to Australia in the latter half of the nineteenth century. Gillen arrived in Adelaide from Ireland, still in his mother's womb, in 1855 and was born later that year, while Spencer, born in England in 1860, migrated to Melbourne as a young man in 1887. Their backgrounds and careers were very different, yet they formed a remarkable ethnological partnership after first meeting in 1894. Gillen, the son of a laborer, received minimal formal education and chose a career in the postal service, eventually going to work on the Overland Telegraph Line that connected Adelaide and Darwin after 1872. Spencer, the son of bourgeois parents, was educated at a private school and at the University of Oxford, where he later became a fellow.

Spencer came to Australia to take up a chair in biology at the University of Melbourne, and it was in his capacity as biologist on the Horn Scientific Expedition to central Australia that he met Gillen in Alice Springs. By that time Gillen had long been an enthusiastic amateur ethnographer, and he was also the local magistrate and sub-protector of Aborigines. Spencer and Gillen became close friends, with Gillen's ethnographic enthusiasm firing Spencer's preexisting but tangential anthropological interests. When Spencer returned to Melbourne, he and Gillen corresponded feverishly about anthropological and other matters, and Spencer invited Gillen to contribute to the anthropological report of the expedition. In 1896 Gillen helped some local Arrernte (Arunta, Aranda) groups to stage a large-scale ceremony in Alice Springs, which Spencer attended. The records of this ceremony were added to those that Spencer and Gillen had conspired to produce mainly through long-distance correspondence, culminating in their 1899 landmark ethnography, *The Native Tribes of Central Australia.*

In 1901 Spencer and Gillen were both given leave to undertake ethnographic research in remote South Australia and the Northern Territory. The material generated from this trip considerably broadened their ethnographic base, resulting in a second major monograph, *The Northern Tribes of Central Australia*, published in 1904. Gillen's health declined dramatically after this and he died in 1912. Spencer, however, went on to cement his reputation as Australia's foremost expert on Australian Aborigines, undertaking further ethnographic research in the far north of the Northern Territory from 1911 to 1912 and in central Australia in 1923 and 1926, and producing further volumes. Among other things, he updated his and Gillen's 1899 study by publishing the two-volume *The Arunta: A Study of a Stone Age People* in 1927. Spencer died two years later on Tierra del Fuego, during an ethnographic expedition to the Yahgan Indians.

Gillen published very little by himself, mainly acting as a remote field-worker sending information to Spencer in Melbourne. It was Spencer who penned their jointly authored monographs, although Gillen's contribution went beyond the mere provision of data. Reflecting a not uncommon contemporary pattern, the formally educated Spencer acted as a kind of hinge between the metropolitan centers of Europe, where there were furious debates about the origins of religion and society, and the remote outpost of Alice Springs, where Gillen allegedly dwelt cheek by jowl with living representatives of the Stone Age. Spencer's evolutionist outlook was most specifically informed by his biologist's commitment to Darwinian principles, but it was also influenced at various stages by debates initiated by commentators such as Edward Tylor and James Frazer and ethnographers such as Lorimer Fison and Alfred Howitt. For his part, Gillen's outlook was informed partly by Spencer's prompts and questions, partly by his own reading of contemporary ethnography, and partly by inspiration derived from his life experiences. While Gillen deferred to Spencer as a trained scientist and sought to emulate the objectivity of the scientific establishment in general, his letters to Spencer indicate that his appreciation of Aboriginal religion was also inspired by a somewhat mischievous gift for comparing "Stone Age" myths and rituals with biblical tenets and solemn Christian practices.

Spencer and Gillen's detailed ethnographic descriptions provided material out of which many of the best-known general accounts of "primitive" religion were partly constructed. Émile Durkheim's *The Elementary Forms of the Religious Life* (1912) relied heavily on Spencer and Gillen's ethnography, as did some of the work of James Frazer (particularly *Totemism and Exogamy* [1910]) and Sigmund Freud (including parts of *Totem and Taboo* [1913]). The 1899 and 1904 ethnographies were widely acclaimed and taken up by the academic establishment as setting new standards in ethnographic reporting. They also excited the popular imagination, with Spencer eventually compiling volumes (*Across Australia* [1912] and *Wanderings in Wild Australia* [1928]) to meet the demand from the nonacademic market, in the process turning "the Arunta" and many aspects of their culture into household names.

All of Spencer and Gillen's books heavily reflect contemporary primitivist concerns with totemism, magic, kinship, and marriage, but the question of totemic religion is always most central. In 1899 the authors devoted no less than nine consecutive chapters to Arrernte totemism and its attendant mythology, ritual, and sacred paraphernalia. The 1904 book was similar and also popularized the term *dream times,* a translation of the Arrernte word *alcheringa* (*altyerrenge*). This term later evolved into *Dreamtime* or *Dreaming,* both of which are now widely used by Aborigines and non-Aborigines alike to describe indigenous Australian cosmology. The 1899 and 1904 books also popularized the Arrernte term *churinga* (*tywerrenge*), which, in its original context, refers to wooden or stone sacred objects and other things associated with totemic ancestors. As a result of the recent worldwide rush to embrace Aboriginal art and spirituality, *churinga* is now best known as a designer clothing label, whose shirts, sweaters, and other items carry totemic designs.

Spencer and Gillen's reputation is primarily based on their detailed descriptions of Arrernte and other Aboriginal people's lives. But while their apparently "raw" ethnography was an important way station on the road to contemporary anthropological fieldwork practice, they also provided muted conceptual insights into "primitive" religion, a fact that has often been obscured by their work's appropriation into more famous and explicit theoretical frameworks put forward by the likes of Durkheim, Frazer, and Freud. At a time when European scholars such as Frazer were questioning whether Aborigines had anything that could genuinely be labeled religion, Spencer and Gillen never balked at describing certain Aboriginal ceremonies and beliefs as "sacred." Indeed, detailed comparisons of passages from Spencer and Gillen with related ones from Durkheim's *Elementary Forms of Religious Life* suggest that Durkheim developed certain aspects of his sacred–profane dichotomy, at least insofar as it applied to totemism, from the descriptive language employed by Spencer and Gillen. On the other hand, Durkheim, like Frazer and others, also tended to simultaneously overtheorize and oversimplify the complex dimensions of Aboriginal totemism described by Spencer and Gillen. In that respect, Spencer and Gillen's intermediary position between the sometimes wild European theorizing about "primitive" religion and the little understood empirical complexities of Aboriginal ritual and belief remains critically important. That importance is measured by the extent to which the ethnographers' descriptions have stood the test of time in relation to the more radical revision of the theoretical systems that were allegedly confirmed or discredited by Spencer and Gillen's data. Of particular note in this regard was their conclusive demonstration that Aboriginal totemism was not in any simple or singular way connected to clans or group exogamy.

Howard Morphy argues that Spencer and Gillen's detailed accounts of Arrernte myth and ritual have a phenomenological character. Spencer and Gillen most certainly did not have phenomenological sensibilities in any formal sense, but their ethnographic accounts were firmly based on experience and attention to detail in the observation of ritual action and, to a lesser extent, the expression of religious sentiment. But the work of Spencer and Gillen's ethnographic and intellectual rival, the Lutheran missionary Carl Strehlow in *Die Aranda- und Loritja-Stämme in Zentral Australien* (1907–1920), truly was phenomenological, and the balance Strehlow provided in this respect made it regrettable that his work was not used nearly as extensively as Spencer and Gillen's in many European circles. Géza Róheim suggests in "Psycho-analysis of Primitive Cultural Types" that, while Spencer and Gillen's approach to Aboriginal religion was essentially "behaviorist," being based on observation but lacking in the kinds of insights that emerge from an intimate knowledge of Aboriginal languages, Strehlow's approach, premised firmly on fluency in Arrernte and painstaking translation work, was that of lifeless exegesis ("lifeless" because of Strehlow's self-imposed ban on attending "heathen" ceremonies). In that sense, Spencer and Gillen's ethnographic descriptions of Arrernte religion are best appreciated in conjunction with Strehlow's parallel contemporary account.

A more singular appreciation of the mutual interpenetration of "word" and "flesh" in Arrernte religion did not occur until the next generation of ethnographers, particularly with the psychoanalytic approach of Róheim and with the intensive ethnographic work of Carl Strehlow's son, Theodore (T. G. H.) Strehlow (for example, in *Aranda Traditions* [1947] and *Songs of Central Australia* [1971]).

Although Spencer and Gillen had firm evolutionist sensibilities, these were hardly reflected in their actual descriptions of sacred myths and ceremonies. These accounts stand out today as authoritative treatises on Aboriginal, especially Arrernte, religion, marking them off from the grander theoretical systems that were built on them and which have wearied with time. On the other hand, the accounts reveal a partiality of their own and are best treated as part of a larger corpus that gives a more rounded and intelligible picture of classical religion in central Australia. That religion persists in a recognizable form today, with Spencer and Gillen's books and collections sometimes making a significant contribution to the ongoing vitality of ancestral law. Books such *The Native Tribes of Central Australia* are treated with considerable fear or reverence by contemporary Aborigines because of the sacred material that they contain, and they may even be stored in secret places alongside other sacred objects, some of which are being repatriated to Aboriginal custodians from Spencer and Gillen's museum collections. The fate of these objects, and of the totemic religion connected with them, could not have been foreseen by either Spencer or Gillen, but it is certainly ironic that the two ethnographic pioneers should be posthumously playing the role of totemic ancestors in this "primitive" religious revival.

BIBLIOGRAPHY

Cantrill, Arthur, and Corinne Cantrill. "The 1901 Cinematography of Walter Baldwin Spencer." *Cantrill's Film Notes* 37–38 (1982): 25–56. A discussion of Spencer's pioneering cinematography. Spencer's ethnographic films include a number of religious ceremonies, including secret/sacred footage.

Morphy, Howard. "Empiricism to Metaphysics: In Defence of the Concept of the Dreamtime." In *Prehistory to Politics: John Mulvaney, the Humanities, and the Public Intellectual*, edited by Tim Bonyhady and Tom Griffiths, pp. 163–189. Melbourne, 1996. Partly a defense of Spencer and Gillen in relation to a postcolonial critique of their use of the term *dream times*.

Morphy, Howard. "Spencer and Gillen in Durkheim: The Theoretical Constructions of Ethnography." In *On Durkheim's Elementary Forms of Religious Life*, edited by N. J. Allen, W. S. F. Pickering, and W. Watts Miller, pp. 13–28. London, 1998. A detailed examination of the relationship between Spencer and Gillen's ethnography and Durkheim's most important work on religion.

Morton, John. "Sustaining Desire: A Structuralist Interpretation of Myth and Male Cult in Central Australia." Ph.D. diss., Australian National University, Canberra, 1985. The most comprehensive synthesis of Arrernte ethnography in relation to religion, amongst other things clearly placing Spencer and Gillen's work in its broader ethnographic context in the twentieth century.

Mulvaney, D. J., and J. H. Calaby. *"So Much That Is New": Baldwin Spencer, 1860–1929.* Melbourne, 1985. Magisterial, comprehensive biography of Spencer.

Mulvaney, John, Howard Morphy, and Alison Petch, eds. *My Dear Spencer: The Letters of F. J. Gillen to Baldwin Spencer.* Melbourne, 1997. These letters to Spencer illustrate Gillen's own particular thoughts about Aboriginal religion. The book carries a biographical essay on Gillen by John Mulvaney and an assessment of Gillen's work by Howard Morphy.

Spencer, Baldwin. *Native Tribes of the Northern Territory of Australia.* London, 1914. Spencer's lesser known ethnographic account of Aboriginal life in parts of the northern portion of the Northern Territory. Contains a great deal of material on local totemic religions.

Spencer, Baldwin, ed. *Report on the Work of the Horn Scientific Expedition to Central Australia.* 4 vols. Melbourne, 1896. Volume 4 contains an important early ethnographic report by Gillen.

Spencer, Baldwin, and F. J. Gillen. *The Native Tribes of Central Australia.* London, 1899. Spencer and Gillen's most famous account of central Australian religion and social life. Regarded as a benchmark in ethnographic reporting.

Spencer, Baldwin, and F. J. Gillen. *The Northern Tribes of Central Australia.* London, 1904. Greatly extends the insights and ethnographic range of the 1899 book.

Spencer, Baldwin, and F. J. Gillen. *The Arunta: A Study of a Stone Age People.* 2 vols. London, 1927. Spencer's late update of the 1899 classic.

Strehlow, T. G. H. *Songs of Central Australia.* Sydney, 1971. Detailed study of Aboriginal song poetry. The introduction contains a lengthy critique of Spencer and Gillen's work from a broadly phenomenological perspective.

Wolfe, Patrick. "On Being Woken Up: The Dreamtime in Anthropology and in Australian Settler Culture." *Comparative Studies in Society and History* 32, no. 2 (1991): 197–224. Critical discussion of the genesis and legacy of Spencer and Gillen's use of the term *dream times.*

Wolfe, Patrick. *Settler Colonialism and the Transformation of Anthropology: The Politics and Poetics of an Ethnographic Event.* London, 1999. Broad postcolonial critique of early Aboriginal anthropology and its legacy. Contains many discussions of Spencer and Gillen's work in relation to totemism.

JOHN MORTON (2005)

GILSON, ÉTIENNE (1884–1978), was an educator, lecturer, author, and historian of medieval philosophy. Born in Paris, Gilson was a Christian believer and lifelong promoter and defender of the intellectual life of the church. He treasured his Roman Catholic schooling but discovered his love for philosophy in a secular lycée and at the positivistic Sorbonne. Convinced that before doing philosophy one had to learn what philosophy already existed, he entered upon a career of exact historical study, following the principled method that would mark all his work: to study the original writings of the great thinkers, to understand their thought within its historical context, and to present their teaching objectively.

Under competent Cartesian scholars Gilson concentrated on the modern classics but did his research on the medieval sources used by Descartes. While teaching in the lycées (1907–1913), he completed his dissertation on the scholastic texts utilized by Descartes for his doctrine of freedom. Following his doctorate (1913) he was appointed to teach at Lille, then (after World War I) at Strasbourg, and from 1921 on at Paris. In these national universities Gilson introduced regular study of the medieval theologian-philosophers. His courses on Thomas Aquinas, Augustine of Hippo, and Bonaventure were published and became standard tools for medieval scholars. Studies of other medieval authors provided the substance of his teaching for fifty years in Paris and at Toronto (in the research institute he founded there in 1929) and of his masterwork, *History of Christian Philosophy in the Middle Ages* (1955).

What is more significant, these studies led him to hold firmly to two controversial positions:

(1) A distinct Christian philosophy is a matter of historical fact: It is the speculations of theologians about questions in principle accessible to natural reason.

(2) The Thomism of Thomas Aquinas, rather than that of his interpreters, is the unique instance of a Christian philosophy that best mirrors Catholic thinking and that grounds the truths achieved by all other Christian philosophies. Thomism is the philosophy of a theologian and is characterized both by its metaphysics of being, which holds that what is real and intelligible is so by virtue of its act of existing, and by its theses on the integrity of human intelligence and on the realism and evidentiality of knowledge.

Although these are controversial theses, Gilson was so sure of his own position that in more than forty books and countless articles he rarely engaged in argument about them.

Gilson the historian brought the thought of the Middle Ages to the attention of twentieth-century scholars. Gilson the philosopher sparked in his European and North American audiences an active engagement in philosophical and theological issues that had long been dormant. In 1949 the French philosopher Jacques Maritain, remarking on the apostolic quality of Gilson's career, asserted that his championship of Christian intellectual issues in France had lent courage to and secured a hearing for the less hardy. There is little doubt that his promotion of the study of medieval thought and his outspoken defense of his convictions have been of lasting benefit not only to academic scholars but also to religious believers.

Bibliography

Gilson's numerous works and the extensive writings about him are cited in Margaret McGrath's 1,210-item *Étienne Gilson: A Bibliography* (Toronto, 1982). Some major works by Gilson available in English are *The Spirit of Medieval Philosophy* (New York, 1936), an abridged version of *L'esprit de la philosophie médiévale,* 2 vols. (Paris, 1932); *The Christian Philosophy of St. Thomas Aquinas,* 5th ed. (New York, 1956); and *History of Christian Philosophy in the Middle Ages* (New York, 1955). The first of a number of appreciative symposia was that by Jacques Maritain and others, *Étienne Gilson: Philosophe de la Chrétienté* (Paris, 1949). The official biography was produced by a former student and colleague, Laurence K. Shook, *Étienne Gilson* (Toronto, 1984).

Linus J. Thro (1987)

GIMBUTAS, MARIJA (1921–1994) was an archaeologist, prehistorian, and influential interpreter of Stone Age religion. Born January 23, 1921, in Vilnius, the capital of Lithuania, Gimbutas grew up in a progressive and well-educated family. Her parents were both physicians who founded the first hospital in Lithuania. The family belonged to a circle of the best-known intellectuals and artists of their time in Eastern Europe. Even as a young girl, Marija developed a wide range of interests and talents; among other interests, she proved to be a highly gifted musician. In 1937–1938 she participated in an ethnographic expedition to southeastern Lithuania. This trip was the beginning of her lifelong attraction to folklore, an interest that had a prominent influence on her work in archaeology and her studies of prehistoric civilizations and cultures. In 1938 Gimbutas began to study linguistics at the University of Kaunas. The next year, after Vilnius had been freed from Polish occupation, Gimbutas returned to the Lithuanian capital. There she resumed her studies of folklore and began to collect materials from various regions of Eastern Europe.

Academic Career. Following the invasions of Lithuania, first by the Soviet Union and then by Nazi Germany, Gimbutas joined the underground resistance movement. Nonetheless she still completed her graduate studies in archaeology in 1942. She immediately began to publish articles on Baltic archaeology, mythology, and folklore. By now she was married and a mother. Together with her husband and daughter, she went to Tübingen, a German university where she completed her doctorate on prehistoric burials in Lithuania.

Gimbutas did not want to return to Lithuania after the end of World War II because her country had been integrated into the Soviet Union. She immigrated instead to the United States in 1949. The following year, she started working at Harvard University; in 1955 she was appointed a research fellow at Harvard's Peabody Museum. After 1964 she accepted a position at the University of California, Los Angeles. Gimbutas became involved in a wide range of projects concerning archaeological excavations in southeastern Europe and began to interpret her findings synthetically in light of her knowledge of folk art, folk tales, and Baltic mythology. This synthetic approach formed the core of her work and made Gimbutas's descriptions of Stone Age culture and religion vividly three-dimensional. At the same time, however, her synthetic approach is also what made her work so problematic.

Gimbutas's hypotheses assumed a distinctive shape over time. By the end of her life she was able to present a congruent picture of Neolithic civilization in her late publications, *The Language of the Goddess* (1989) and *The Civilization of the Goddess* (1991). She introduced one of her most important theories as early as 1956 at an international conference in Philadelphia. She claimed that the early and, as she believed, highly unified agricultural civilization of southeastern Europe was destroyed by mounted herdsmen and warriors, whom she named "Kurgan people" after the Russian word *kurgan*, meaning "hillock." Gimbutas hypothesized that the Kurgan people were Indo-Europeans who entered Europe from 4000 BCE onward and brought their patriarchal hierarchies with them—a type of social structure that had previously been unknown in southern Europe but soon gained ascendence there.

EVALUATIONS OF GIMBUTAS'S WORK. The Kurgan theory plays a crucial role in Gimbutas's large-scale ideas about European prehistory, for it provides an explanation for the disappearance of what she called "Old Europe"— a presumably matriarchal and goddess-worshipping civilization that was overcome by newer forms of social structure dominated by patriarchal structures and beliefs. It is not easy, however, to reconstruct the evolution of her ideas about the organization of a civilization called "Old Europe."

The main criticism of Gimbutas's work concerns her methodological inaccuracies. Nowhere did she ever inform her readers about the ideas she drew on or the tools she used for her reconstruction of cultural and religious meaning in prehistory—a period for which there are virtually no extant written historical sources. Gimbutas seems to have been aquainted with G. W. F. Hegel's philosophy of history and certainly with J. J. Bachofen's ideas but cites them nowhere in her work. Moreover she never once addressed the obvious similarities between her own work and the concepts of these two cultural theorists. Instead, she insisted that she gained her insights solely from archaeological materials that revealed to her an inherent "archaeomythology" —although she constantly referred to folklore from much later periods for parallels to supposedly prehistoric ideas. In addition Gimbutas's belief that cultural change can only have been brought about through military invasions by the Kurgan people—while at the same time ignoring other possible explanations—point to an oversimplified Darwinian view of history. Consequently the byways of Gimbutas's epistemological journeys seem to have been completely unclear to her throughout her career. In various interviews she claimed intuition as an important source of her information but did not offer the interviewers any further explanation of the connections between her intuitive ideas and the archaeological materials.

Gimbutas had initially been interested in determining the origins of culture in the Baltic area, but as she worked her archaeological investigations widened into an exploration of the general origins of a Pan-European prehistoric culture. In the course of her research she reached out far over the East and later the whole of Europe, where she detected an antagonism between the kind of Bronze Age culture imported by the assumed Indo-Europeans, or Kurgan people, and the previous Stone Age culture of "Old Europe." The latter term was meant to designate a homogeneous culture of Neolithic agricultural societies that emerged in eastern and central Europe in the seventh millennium BCE and in western Europe during the fifth millennium BCE. Gimbutas assumed the existence of important connections between these European societies and parallel developments in Asia Minor.

Gimbutas thought that her theories about archaeomythology allowed her to explain the symbolism of a vast amount of archaeological materials from different periods and different regions of prehistoric Europe. Archaeomythology as a scholarly methodology, however, is viewed as highly problematic by most contemporary archaeologists and prehistorians. Gimbutas drew together numerous unconnected discoveries and interpreted the finds in the light of much later written sources and folkloric artifacts. Neither her concept of a Kurgan people nor her belief in a unified and coherent Stone Age culture in "Old Europe" has been accepted by mainstream academia. Nevertheless Gimbutas herself had a firm interest in Neopaganism, and her ideas are extremely popular in certain feminist circles in the early twenty-first century. They have made substantial contributions to contemporary beliefs about goddess-centered cultures. In the early 2000s Gimbutas's most prominent successor, Joan Marler, teaches archaeomythology at the California Institute of Integral Studies in San Francisco.

As an inspiration for alternative religions in the early twenty-first century, Gimbutas's books are also of special interest to students of contemporary belief. Gimbutas seemed to project recent ideas and ideals into a remote past insofar as she detected primary religious concerns for peace and ecology in Stone Age culture. According to her interpretation, the religion of Stone Age people revered a monotheistic goddess who could appear in many forms. Gimbutas understood "the Goddess" as a representation of the generative as well as the destructive forces of nature. Her entire research focused almost exclusively on statuettes and figurines that she had detached from their archaeological contexts and interpreted in light of her goddess theory.

Gimbutas constructed an ingenious picture of the Stone Age religious mind-set that will probably never be proven entirely right or wrong as a result of the lack of written sources that could explain the meanings of Neolithic figurines, symbols, and icons. The application of later testimonies to these artifacts is certainly questionable. In favor of Gimbutas's approach, however, such testimonies often offer the only possibility for the researcher to make some sense of prehistoric archaeological materials. In any case Gimbutas's lifework provides a wealth of materials and provocative stimuli for readings of Stone Age religions. One particular problem that arises in assessing Gimbutas's work is that Gimbutas herself remained unaware of her own inclinations toward nineteenth-century theories about the history of culture and the inner dynamics of cultural developments. Shorn of this important background, her ideas may seem to be simply quixotic. Equally importantly her work tends to be either defended or rejected out of hand with little attention to the support that subsequent scholarship might offer. An appropriate challenge for the future would be a careful review of Gimbutas's ideas in the light of contemporary discussions of cultural theory.

SEE ALSO Archaeology and Religion; Bachofen, J. J.; Gender and Religion, article on History of Study; Goddess Worship, article on Theoretical Perspectives; Neopaganism.

BIBLIOGRAPHY

Gimbutas's lifework is summarized in her two late and highly influential books, *The Language of the Goddess* (San Francisco, 1989) and *The Civilization of the Goddess* (San Francisco, 1991). An important earlier monograph is *The Gods and Goddesses of Old Europe 7000 to 3500 BC: Myths, Legends and Cult Images* (San Francisco, 1974). The title was changed in the second edition to *The Goddesses and Gods of Old Europe* (San Francisco, 1982). Appreciations of her approach are included in Joan Marler, ed., *From the Realm of the Ancestors: An Anthology in Honor of Marija Gimbutas* (Manchester, Conn., 1997), and in a collection of articles in the *Journal of Feminist Studies in Religion* 12, no. 2 (1996). Substantial criticism from mainstream archaeology is summarized in Brigitte Röder, Juliane Hummel, and Brigitta Kunz, *Göttinnendämmerung: Das Matriarchat aus archäologischer Sicht* (Munich, Germany, 1996).

JULIA IWERSEN (2005)

GINĀN. A popularization of the Sanskrit word *jñan* ("contemplative knowledge"), the term *ginān* is used by the Nizārī Ismāʿīlīyah of Indo-Pakistan to refer to any one of the approximately eight hundred poems believed to have been composed by the Ismāʿīlī *pirs* or *dāʿīs* ("missionaries") between the thirteenth and early twentieth centuries. Composed in several Indian dialects and employing popular folk meters and indigenous musical modes, the *gināns* vary considerably in length. The shortest ones consist of four to five verses, while longer ones, called *granths* and distinguished by specific titles, may have well more than a thousand verses. The *gināns* are still sung and recited today as an integral part of religious ceremonies. Usually all members of the community who are present at such ceremonies participate in the recitation of the *gināns*.

The *gināns*, which often have several themes, may be classified into five major types according to the theme of greatest importance:

(1) "Conversion" *gināns* portraying Islam and specifically

its Ismāʿīlī form as the completion of the Vaiṣṇava Hindu tradition, and also including accounts that give Ismāʿīlī dimensions to traditional figures of Hindu mythology as well as hagiographic accounts of the great Ismāʿīlī *pirs* (the *Das Avatar,* for example).

(2) *Gināns* dealing with a wide variety of eschatological and cosmological themes (such as *Brahmā Gāyatrī*).

(3) Didactic *gināns* imparting ethical and moral instruction for the conduct of worldly and religious life (such as *Moman Chetāmaṇi*).

(4) *Gināns* connected with mysticism, including guides for an individual's spiritual progress, literary expressions of the composers' mystical experiences, and petitions for spiritual union or vision (*Anant Akhādo* and *Satveṇī,* for example).

(5) *Gināns* for recitation at certain religious rituals or at specific festivals such as the birthday of the Prophet or the Ismāʿīlī imam, Nawrūz (New Year), and so forth (*Nawrūznā din sohāmaṇā,* for example).

BIBLIOGRAPHY

Asani, Ali S. "The Ismāʿīlī *Ginān* Literature: Its Structure and Love Symbolism." In *Facets of Ismaili Studies.* Edited by Hermann Landolt. London, 1985.

Ivanov, Vladimir A. "Satpanth." In *Collectanea,* vol. 1, edited by Vladimir A. Ivanov, pp. 1–54. Leiden, 1948.

Nanji, Azim. *The Nizāri Ismāʿīlī Tradition in the Indo-Pakistan Subcontinent.* Delmar, N.Y., 1978.

ALI S. ASANI (1987)

GINZA. Among their many books, the Gnostic Mandaeans of Iraq and Iran rank the voluminous *Ginza* ("treasure"), their "holy book," as the most important. It is studied by priests, and its presence is required at the performance of the major Mandaean rituals. In the seventh century of the common era, during the Islamic conquest, the Mandaeans assembled the *Ginza* in order to gain status as a "people of the book," allowed to resist conversion to Islam. The work, separated into *Right Ginza* and *Left Ginza*, contains a number of myths concerning the creation of the world and of human beings, descriptions of the human lot on earth, moral teachings, polemics against other faiths, and hymns. In Mandaeism generally, "right" and "left" are connected to the otherworldly and the earthly realms, respectively. However, in the case of the two parts of *Ginza*, the designations seem to contradict this pattern, for *Right Ginza* contains a great deal of cosmogonic and anthropogonic material, while the left part deals with the otherworldly fate of the soul.

Left Ginza, which has been called a "book of the dead," falls into three parts. *Left Ginza* 1.1–2 describe the death of Adam, who is reluctant to leave behind his body as well as his wife and children. Part 1.4 portrays the soul's journey through the purgatories (*matarata*) between the earth and the Lightworld, the pristine upper world. The last two parts are composed of hymns for the soul rising to the Lightworld after the death of the body. The hymns of the twenty-eight sections of *Left Ginza* 2 concentrate on the complaints of the soul (here, *mana,* "vessel") in the earthly world. A helper is sent from the Lightworld to aid the soul. Some of the sixty-two *Left Ginza* 3 hymns are among the ritually used death-mass (*masiqta*) hymns, the oldest datable texts in Mandaeism (c. third century CE). Thus, these cultic texts testify to the antiquity of the *masiqta,* the "raising up" ceremony for the soul and the spirit at the death of the body.

In *Right Ginza,* helper figures command a central position. Two main envoys are Manda d-Hiia and Hibil, although a large tractate, *Right Ginza* 15, portrays several other messengers. In *Right Ginza* 5.1, Hibil descends to the underworld prior to the creation of the earth, in order to prevent an attack on the Lightworld by the powers of the underworld. He returns with Ruha, the spirit, the vital element necessary for human and earthly life. Extensive stories about the creation of the world and the human lot are found in *Right Ginza* 3 and 10. John the Baptist, the Mandaean prophet, expounds his teachings in *Right Ginza* 7. In view of the use of the Arabic form *Yaḥya* for John in this text, it was probably written in the seventh century. Polemics against Judaism, Christianity, Islam, and other religions characterize *Right Ginza* 9.1, and moral instructions and warnings against surrender to evil powers recur in *Right* Ginza 1, 2, 8, 13, 16, and 17. *Right Ginza* 18, written in the seventh century, is a Mandaean "history of the world" that ends in an apocalypse. This tractate closes *Right Ginza.*

Several European libraries possess *Ginza* manuscripts. The oldest, in the Bibliothèque Nationale in Paris, dates from 1560. In 1867, Heinrich Petermann published a largely useless edition and translation of *Ginza.* Mark Lidzbarski's 1925 version remains thus far the classical edition and translation. The new translation of *Ginza* undertaken by Kurt Rudolph will take into account the many discoveries of Mandaean texts and the advances made in studies on Mandaeism since Lidzbarski's time.

SEE ALSO Manda d'Hiia; Mandaean Religion.

BIBLIOGRAPHY

The most reliable edition and translation of the Mandaean "holy book" was published in German under the editorship of Mark Lidzbarski as *Ginza: Der Schatz; oder, Das grosse Buch der Mandäer* (Göttingen, 1925; new edition in preparation by Kurt Rudolph). Representative *Ginza* material is included in *Gnosis: A Selection of Gnostic Texts,* vol. 2, *Coptic and Mandean Sources* (Oxford, 1974), edited by Werner Foerster. Kurt Rudolph's *Theogonie, Kosmogonie und Anthropogonie in den mandäischen Schriften* (Göttingen, 1965) offers a historical analysis of the traditions portrayed in the *Ginza* tractates. For his most recent view on *Ginza,* one may consult Rudolph's "Die mandäische Literatur," in *Zur Sprache und Literatur der Mandäer: Studia Mandaica I* (Berlin, 1976), edited by Rudolf Macuch.

New Sources

Buckley, Jorunn Jacobsen. *The Mandaeans. Ancient texts and Modern People.* Oxford, 2002. The most refreshing and comprehensive book on the Mandaeans, including an overview of Mandaean literature. For the *Ginza* see pp. 10–11, mentioning the 1998 first-ever printed edition of the Mandaean holy book

JORUNN JACOBSEN BUCKLEY (1987)
Revised Bibliography

GINZBERG, ASHER.

Asher Ginzberg (1856–1927), best known by his pen-name Ahad Haʾam (meaning, literally, "One of the People") was the most influential intellectual in the Zionist movement in its formative years in the late nineteenth and early twentieth centuries. He produced, in the form of many highly influential Hebrew-language essays, a thorough-going reassessment of Judaism that deemphasized the centrality of religion and saw culture, writ large, as the true basis for Jewish life in the past and present. Born in Skvira, Ukraine, he was raised on a rural estate as a Hasidic prodigy, but by his early thirties he was able to read Russian, English, French, and German and was a Jewish nationalist devotee of Herbert Spencer and John Locke. His life was spent mostly in Odessa, London, and Tel Aviv (where he died), and he worked as a businessman, an editor, and, eventually, as a tea company manager. He served on the executive committee of the proto-Zionist Hovevei Zion, founded in the mid-1880s. He was also the founding editor of the influential Hebrew-language journal *Ha-Shiloach* and a close advisor to Chaim Weizmann (1874–1952) in the negotiations leading to the Balfour Declaration of 1917. He vigorously denied an interest in political leadership, insisting that his public activity—even his extensive journalistic work—had been thrust upon him unwillingly. But his aspirations were considerable, and at their core was the desire to reconstruct the spiritual and political foundations of contemporary Jewish life.

For several decades after the publication in 1889 of his first significant published article, "Lo zeh ha-derekh" (This is not the way), Ginzberg was Hebrew's most important essayist. His spare, ironic prose set new standards, and his Jewish nationalist teachings were vigorously promoted and debated, lacerated, and celebrated. He communicated a program that drew at one and the same time on the modernist presumptions of the Jewish enlightenment and the social optimism of European liberalism, and that managed to promise Jewish authenticity shorn of theology but inspired by aspects still more basic and enduring as taught, as he saw it, by history. At its core his was an extended, if eclectic philosophy of history.

It was culture, he argued, that had held the Jews together, with their faith in the paramount importance of intellect and an uncompromising belief in justice. These features of Jewish culture permitted it to accommodate itself to outside influences without losing itself. Hence, Jewish history was a tale of principled, dexterous accommodation to cultures that Jews made their own, but this ability was, increasingly, lost to them in modernity.

Overwhelmed already in the West by political emancipation and concomitant assimilation (which, he believed, was beginning to make substantial inroads in Eastern Europe, too), Jews had to deflect this onslaught without rejecting modernity. Hence, a Jewish homecoming was essential, with Jews returning to their original, creative site in the land of Israel. There, in a Hebrew-speaking milieu they would build a "spiritual center" (as he came to call it) that would grow into a self-sufficient economic and political entity. Its influence would recast Judaism elsewhere, transforming it from an increasingly moribund faith into a vibrant national culture.

Zionism as promoted by Theodor Herzl (its leader—and Ahad Ha'am's chief nemesis—from 1896 to his death in 1904) was shortsighted in its stress on diplomacy and tone deaf to Jewry's paramount cultural needs. Not anti-Semitism, as Herzl argued, but the prospect of Jewish cultural absorption in a larger, dangerously open society was the most critical prospect facing the Jewish people.

A key to Ginzberg's abiding reputation is his having been the first Zionist of stature to highlight the darker side of Arab-Jewish relations in Palestine. He insisted that what others saw at the time as merely skirmishes between Jews and Arabs were, in fact, threats to the Jewish nationalist enterprise and that this resistance must dampen Jewry's more ambitious and unrealistic claims. As early as his 1891 essay "Emet me-eretz yisarel" (Truth from the land of israel), he argued that the brutal treatment of Arabs by some Jews was itself a tragic, potentially disastrous response to Jewish subjugation; if left unchecked, such behavior could devastate Zionism. The weight he gave to this issue—especially in the last decade of his life—placed it, albeit tenuously, on the Zionist agenda.

Ginzberg's impact was extensive but also equivocal. He sought at first to build a political movement in the form of a semi-secret group called the Bnei Moshe (The Sons of Moses) that would recast the priorities of Jewish nationalism as a whole. This exercise failed in its political aspirations but left a considerable imprint on the thinking of many of Zionism's most influential figures, including Chaim Weizmann and Martin Buber.

Ahad Ha'am had a major impact on others, too, especially on those who shaped modern Judaism's cultural priorities. Devotees included Hayyim Nahman Bialik (1873–1934), the most important Hebrew poet in Zionism's classical period; the founder of Qabbalah studies, Gershom Scholem (1897–1982); and the first chancellor of Hebrew University, Judah Magnes. Ahad Ha'am was embraced as a primary inspiration by prestate bi-nationalists (who at their most radical phase eschewed the prospect of Jewish majority rule for Jews), and the American Reconstructionist religious movement of Mordecai Kaplan (1881–1983). In Israel, Ginzberg became best known, arguably, as an exemplary craftsman of Hebrew whose prime clientele, for many years, was schoolchildren taught to emulate his style.

Ginzberg raised many more questions than he answered. He was best as a critic, and while he sought to write a full-length book encapsulating his understanding of Jewish ethics, it was never written. Still, his many essays provide a framework for an ethically informed, self-consciously Jewish, modern political terminology. His insights continue to influence political debates over Zionism, Jewish theology, and conceptions of Jewish culture, its boundaries, and its prospects.

See Also Jewish Studies; Zionism.

Bibliography

Goldstein, Yosef. *Ahad Ha'am: Biografiah.* Tel Aviv, 1992.

Gorny, Yosef. *Zionism and the Arabs, 1882–1948.* Oxford, 1987.

Hertzberg, Arthur, ed. *The Zionist Idea: A Historical Analysis and Reader.* New York, 1997.

Zipperstein, Steven J. *Elusive Prophet: Ahad Ha'am and the Origins of Zionism.* Berkeley, Calif., 1993.

Steven J. Zipperstein (2005)

GLASENAPP, HELMUTH VON

GLASENAPP, HELMUTH VON (1891–1963), was a German Indologist. Von Glasenapp was born in Berlin to a "cheerful and gregarious" father who, though a lawyer and banker, was known as an expert on Goethe, and an art-loving mother who "tended to take everything in life seriously" (Glasenapp, 1964, pp. 11–12). As a scholar of Indian religions, Otto Max Helmuth von Glasenapp would come to embody these same traits of communicativeness, broadmindedness, and care, and, indeed, to prescribe them as necessary features of Indological research.

An event of such "decisive significance" that he recalled the exact date—June 30, 1908—occurred when von Glasenapp was not yet seventeen years old (Glasenapp, 1964, p. 28). He walked into a bookstore in Berlin and purchased the works of the German philosopher, Arthur Schopenhauer (1788–1860). The impressionable young scholar was so taken by Schopenhauer's high regard for Indian philosophy and religion, especially Buddhism, that he began reading widely in those fields. Although, two years later, von Glasenapp would enroll as a law student at Tübingen, he continued to pursue his interest in Indology, and beyond. In addition to his coursework in law, he visited seminars in Western philosophy and, under the Indologist Richard Garbe, the history of religions (*Allgemeine Religionsgeschichte*). Continuing his studies at Munich, von Glasenapp took courses in Sanskrit and Pali, as well as in psychology, economics, literature, classics, and theology. Von

Glasenapp's studies culminated in what he called "Benares on the Rhein" (Bonn) in 1914 with a doctoral dissertation under Hermann Jacobi, "Die Lehre vom Karman in der Philosophie der Jainas nach den Karmagranthas dargestellt," and finally, a *Habilitationsschrift* in 1918, also under Jacobi, entitled *Madhvas Philosophie des Vishnu-Glaubens.*

Von Glasenapp's subsequent career commenced in Berlin in 1920 as *Privatdozent.* During this period, he published *Der Hinduismus* (1922), *Der Jainismus* (1925), and *Brahma un Buddha: Die Religionen Indiens in ihrer geschichtlichen Entwicklung* (1926). In 1928 he was called to the professorship of Indology at Königsberg. This productive period saw the publication of nearly a dozen books, including the influential *Der Buddhismus in Indien und im Fernen Osten* (1936) and a pioneering study of esoteric or Vajrayāna Buddhism, *Buddhistische Mysterien* (1940). Although the *Rektor* of the university at Königsberg, one Professor von Grünberg, was an avid Nazi, von Glasenapp was spared the fate of his Jewish colleagues and many others who, like himself, refused to join the party. Von Glasenapp subscribes this good fortune to his "calm demeanor and isolated discipline" (i.e., Indology), as well as to his reputation as an abstracted and "unworldly" (*weltfremd*) scholar (Glasenapp, 1964, p. 155).

In 1946 von Glasenapp was called back to where he had begun, the university at Tübingen, for the final phase of his career. By the time he retired in 1959, he had published numerous additional books, including *Die Philosophie der Inder* (1949), *Vedānta und Buddhismus* (1950), and *Buddhismus und Gottesidee* (1954). In all, von Glasenapp's publication record includes a staggering output of 692 books, articles, book reviews, book chapters, *Festschrift* contributions, editions, and newspaper features. Helmuth von Glasenapp died in June 1963 from injuries sustained in an automobile accident.

The greatest legacy of von Glasenapp remains unfulfilled. In his posthumously published autobiography, *Meine Lebensreise: Menschen, Länder und Dinge, die ich sah* (literally, "My Life's Journey: People, Countries, and Things that I Saw"), von Glasenapp articulates a vision of Indology that combines the talents of "those who can read the texts, but don't know what they say" and those who "understand the contents, but can't translate them" (Glasenapp, 1964, p. 294). Von Glasenapp saw this as an unfortunate rift in the way that Indology was practiced. On the one side are those scholars for whom the linguistic structure (*sprachliche Form*) of a text is the most important matter; on the other side are those for whom the sole matter of scholarly interest is the intellectual-cultural content (*geistig-kulturelle Inhalt*). Aware of German Indology's origin in comparative linguistics, von Glasenapp discouraged the philologists of his day from living up to their reputation as practitioners of "the science of the trivial" (*die Wissenschaft des Nicht-Wissenswerten*) (p. 298). This reputation, he argued, stemmed from their "preference for things that do not contribute to the realization of the intellectual content" of a work (p. 298). A rich and stimulating Indology, by contrast, is one in which the scholar cultivates various methods of research culled from a variety of disciplines, and then skillfully transmits the results to his readers. As examples of this craft, von Glasenapp cites the "great Indologists" of an earlier generation: Max Müller, Albrecht Weber, Richard Pischel, Hermann Jacobi, and Heinrich Lüders. As these examples indicate, von Glasenapp envisioned an Indology that indeed valued linguistic rigor, but placed it in the service of "the great goal—of making comprehensible an alien way of thinking" (p. 302).

Bibliography

In his autobiography, *Meine Lebensreise: Menschen, Länder und Dinge, die ich sah* (Wiesbaden, Germany, 1964), the interested reader will find a multilayered account of von Glasenapp's extensive travels, studies, career, and personal observations on numerous social and intellectual topics. Zoltán Károlyi's *Helmuth von Glasenapp: Bibliographie* (Wiesbaden, Germany, 1968) provides an exhaustive list of von Glasenapp's writings, as well as literature, newspaper articles, magazine pieces, and other items, on von Glasenapp. For a summary of von Glasenapp's most important works, see Jacques Waardenburg's *Classical Approaches to the Study of Religion: Aims, Methods, and Theories of Research*, vol. 2: *Bibliography* (The Hague, 1974), pp. 89–91. Virtually all of von Glasenapp's works are exclusively in German. The English-speaking reader may refer to von Glasenapp's *Buddhism and Comparative Religion and Other Essays* (Kandy, Sri Lanka, 1967).

Glenn Wallis (2005)

GLOBALIZATION AND RELIGION.

Globalization refers to the historical process by which all the world's people increasingly come to live in a single social unit. It implicates religion and religions in several ways. From religious or theological perspectives, globalization calls forth religious response and interpretation. Yet religion and religions have also played important roles in bringing about and characterizing globalization. Among the consequences of this implication for religion have been that globalization encourages religious pluralism. Religions identify themselves in relation to one another, and they become less rooted in particular places because of diasporas and transnational ties. Globalization further provides fertile ground for a variety of noninstitutionalized religious manifestations and for the development of religion as a political and cultural resource.

Globalization. The term *globalization* is of quite recent provenance. It first appeared in the business and sociological literature of the 1980s, but by the end of the century it had become a broadly invoked expression in both academic and popular discourse around the world. Along the way, it has acquired a variety of meanings that it is well to understand at the outset. They share the common element implied in the word: all parts of the world are becoming increasingly tied into a single, globally extended social unit. Among the variants, however, by far the most widespread sees globalization primarily in economic terms, referring mostly to more recent developments in the operation of global markets, capital, and multinational corporations. A related view adds mass media and cultural components to the economic dimension, stressing the degree to which primarily Western, and especially American, firms have been spreading their products and way of life to all corners of the world. Economic globalization therefore focuses on the ways that global capitalism incorporates the world's regions into a single system. The role of states informs a further perspective, one that concentrates on global or international political relations, usually with a parallel emphasis on the hegemonic power of Western countries. Individual states, in this frame of analysis, appear as the primary actors in a globally extended system of such states.

In all of these versions, there are those variants that regard the process as a quite recent development and others that locate its beginnings decades and sometimes centuries in the past. There are also differences of opinion as to whether the process is generally good or mostly bad. Much of the literature is in fact quite critical, seeing the global as a kind of homogenizing imposition on the local, a development in which the strong, overtly or insidiously, presume their ways upon the comparatively weak, dominating or excluding the latter. A further approach to globalization, however, looks at this contrast of the global and the local differently, laying less stress on homogenizing economic and political institutions that impose themselves from above and rather more on local and global movements, networks, and organizations that also contribute to making the world more of a single place, sometimes parallel to the more hegemonic institutions, sometimes in consonance with them, sometimes even in express opposition them. This sort of globalization from below focuses on a wide variety of phenomena, from international nongovernmental organizations and networks among global migrants to antiglobalization, women's, and environmental movements. In part to distinguish this sort of globalization from the economic and political kind, some literature speaks in this regard of the development of a transnational civil society. Moreover, perspectives of this sort stress the renewed importance of cultural differences under conditions of globalization. The world is not just becoming the same; it is also becoming more pluralistic. It is almost exclusively under this meaning of globalization that religion appears as part of the process rather than as either irrelevant bystander or victim.

Various scholars have offered interpretative theories of globalization. Often these theories correspond closely to one of the dominant meanings of the term. One finds, for instance, theories of the global capitalist economic system or of the global state political system. Several efforts, however, seek to incorporate the various meanings as different aspects of a single process, often thereby setting the global and the local in dialogical relation rather than in opposition to one another. These approaches argue that local adaptations of globalized structures like capitalism, nationalism, or mass media are actually constitutive of the global; that globalization is not properly understood if we think of it only as a kind of imperialistic spread from one region to the rest of the world. In other words, the particular ways that people in different parts of the world—including those in rich Western countries—have responded to the context of globalization are what globalization is all about. Global factors become global by being localized or particularized around the world, and the local thereby takes on potentially global or universal significance. Among the many implications of such a perspective is that what are sometimes called?global flows? (of people, ideas, information, products, and other forms) do not go just in one direction, say from America and Europe out to the rest of the world. They also move the other way (reverse flows) and among regions other than the powerful Western ones (cross-flows). Thus, for example, African musical styles and Asian martial arts have a significant effect on North American and European art and culture; and migrants from Indonesia and Bangladesh seek work in the Middle East, all the while maintaining links and sending remittances to their home countries. These relations also contribute to globalization—are in their own way just as constitutive of it as Coca-Cola and the World Bank.

Religion and Globalization. The dialogical approaches to globalization, in conjunction with those that stress globalization from below, are of special significance when it comes to the topic of religion. By far the greatest portion of the by now vast literature on globalization completely or almost completely ignores religion, the partial exception being the attention that Islamicist political extremism receives. This absence can perhaps be attributed to the dominance of economic and political understandings of globalization, including among those observers who look at the phenomenon from within religious traditions. Yet even though a great many of the works that focus on globalization from below—for instance, much of the literature on global migration and ethnicity—also gives religion scant attention, it is among these approaches that one finds almost all the exceptions to this general pattern, probably because these are the only ones that, in principle, allow non-economic or nonpolitical structures like religion a significant role in globalization.

Consideration of the relation between religion and globalization involves two basic possibilities. There are, on the one hand, religious responses to globalization and religious interpretations of globalization. These are, as it were, part of doing religion in a globalizing context. On the other hand, there are those analyses of globalization that seek to understand the role of religion in globalization and the effects of globalization on religion. They focus on observing religion in a global society. By far the largest portion of the literature that relates religion and globalization is of the former sort, and therefore it is well to begin there.

Religious Perspectives on Globalization. A great many religious commentators understand globalization as at once a largely economic, imperialistic, and homogenizing process. They share the economic/mass cultural/political perspective, evaluating globalization as anywhere from a threatening challenge to the manifestation of evil in our world. In many respects globalization in this segment of the literature is a successor term for what used to be censured as the capitalist system or cognate terms. Accordingly, globalization results in violence and the unjust oppression of the majority of people around the world. It threatens local and indigenous cultures, imposing a particularly heavy burden on women. It is the chief cause of global and local environmental degradation, again to the principal detriment of the mass of marginalized humanity. Such theologically inspired positions are not restricted to the representatives of a particular religious tradition. Thus, for example, Christians, Buddhists, Muslims, Jews, and those speaking from indigenous traditions all arrive at similar critical assessments of globalization. And far from being a characteristically religious perspective, such arguments are quite common in the overall literature, whether recognizably religious or not. What they imply, among other consequences, is that religion and religious sensibilities are at root outside of and contrary to globalization, that globalization and religion are fundamentally incommensurate. Another segment of both the religiously inspired and the secular literature, while often sharing many of the negative judgments, nonetheless sees a much closer relation between the two. As noted, these observers almost invariably share the broader meanings of globalization, especially the dialogical and from below perspectives.

Religious insider perspectives do not necessarily limit themselves to opposition, however. Some theologically oriented observers argue that religion has an essential role in shaping globalization; that the negative outcomes of globalization point to the need for a positive global ethic, which religions can provide. The efforts led by Hans Küng in this direction are perhaps the most well known. For Küng, not only does the globalized world require a guiding global ethic, but key to the development of that ethic is harmonious relations and dialogue among the world's religions. The combination signals a dialogical understanding of globalization that Küng shares with many other observers. Here it applies to religion: the globalized whole depends for its viability on the contribution of religion, yet this contribution presupposes a plurality of particular religions that come to understand themselves in positive relation to one another. Unity and diversity are both constitutive of the global. This core assumption of Küng's Global Ethic Project points to general features of how those contributions to the globalization debate that do not ignore religion have sought to understand its role in the process: as an important dimension of globalization that exhibits the characteristic dynamic tension between global and local, between homogeneity and heterogeneity, between the universal and the particular.

Religion and Religions in Globalization. Globalization perspectives seeking to include religion have taken several directions of which the following are likely the most significant. Certain approaches analyze religion as a global or transnational institution, whose diverse manifestations operate to a large extent independently of economic and political structures and that bind diverse regions of the world together in ways comparable to global trade, international relations, mass media, sport, communications media, or tourism. A second but related focus of observation is the role that religious systems play as powerful cultural resources for asserting identity and seeking inclusion in global society, especially among less powerful and marginalized populations. It is in this context that religio-political movements, including so-called fundamentalisms, receive the most focused attention. A third strategy goes even further, attempting to show how the formation, reformation, and spread of religions have been an integral dimension of globalization as such. From this angle, what we today conceive as the most typical forms of religion and even the typical understandings that we have of religion are themselves outcomes and reflections of the historical process of globalization. Although these three directions are by no means mutually exclusive, for the sake of presentation they can be treated separately. Each implies a somewhat different theoretical emphasis, and each also tends to focus on different empirical manifestations of religion in our world.

Religion as Transnational Institution. The relative absence of religion from many globalization perspectives and theories is in some respects quite surprising, especially when one looks at the issue historically. Of the forces that have in the past been instrumental in binding different regions of the world together, in creating a larger if not exactly a geographically global system, economic trade and political empire have certainly been the most obvious; but in conjunction with these, it is equally clear that what we today call religions have also at times played a significant role. Hindu civilization at one time spread throughout South and Southeast Asia. Buddhist teaching and monastic traditions linked together the vast territories from Sri Lanka and the Indian subcontinent, through Afghanistan and China to Korea, Japan, and most of Southeast Asia. In the early Middle Ages the Christian church was the only institution that overarched and even defined as a single social unit that northwestern portion of the Eurasian landmass known as Europe. And this largely over against its neighbor, Islam, which by the twelfth century CE had succeeded in weaving a socio-religious tapestry that extended from Europe and sub-Saharan Africa through all of Asia into the far reaches of Southeast Asia. It informed without doubt the largest world system before the arrival of the modern era.

Yet perhaps most important in this regard is that, as the European powers expanded their influence around the globe between the sixteenth and twentieth centuries, thus setting the conditions for contemporary truly worldwide globalization, Christian religion and Christian institutions were throughout that entire period key contributors to the process. The churches accompanied European colonizers in Africa, the Americas, and Australasia; Christian missions, whether independently or in conjunction with secular authorities, sought conversions in all corners of the globe. In consequence, today the vast majority of globally extended religious institutions are in fact Christian organizations and movements. A wide variety of these include, for instance, the Roman Catholic Church (along with many of its religious orders), several Protestant and Eastern Orthodox churches, the World Council of Churches, Seventh-day Adventists, the worldwide Pentecostal movement, and Jehovah's Witnesses. Christian missions still crisscross the world: American missionaries are to be found in Latin America, Africa, and Asia; African and Latin American Christians conduct missions in Europe and the United States; Australians serve in India; South Koreans are a major presence in southern Africa; and everyone is trying to spread the word in the countries of the former Communist bloc.

Although Christian establishments thus dominate numerically, they are far from being alone among transnational religious institutions. Muslim movements and organizations such as the Ṣūfī and neo-Ṣūfī *ṭarīqah*, or brotherhoods (for example, Naqshbandīyah, Murīdīya, Qādirīyah), reform movements like the Pakistani Tablighi Jamaat and the Turkish Milli Görüş, and unity foundations like the World Muslim Congress or the World Muslim League are broadly established in different regions. They are far from negligible in importance. Buddhist organizations such as the Foguangshan or the Sōka Gakkai have a worldwide presence as do Hindu movements like the Ramakrishna Math and Mission, the Vishwa Hindu Parishad, and the Sai Baba movement. Parallel examples could be mentioned for other both major and minor religions ranging from Judaism, Sikhism, and Bahā'ī to Mormonism, Scientology, and the Brahmā Kumaris.

The specific literature on any of these is fairly substantial. Yet with some exceptions, notably Christian manifestations like the Roman Catholic Church and Pentecostalism, globalization perspectives have not concentrated on these perhaps most obvious of global religious forms as a characteristic dimension of the globalization process. Instead, a growing literature has been focusing on religion in the context of global migration. The more or less permanent displacement of large numbers of people from diverse regions and cultural backgrounds to many other parts of the world, but notably from non-Western to Western countries, has like few other phenomena brought home to an increasing range of observers just how much humanity is now living in a single world where identity and difference have to be renegotiated and reconstructed. Dialogical theories of globalization and those that stress globalization from below have been particularly apt to analyze the consequences of global migration, but the issue is not missing from many that understand globalization primarily in economic or political terms. Like global capitalism or international relations, this question is not susceptible to easy understanding on the basis of theories that take a more limited territory, above all a nation-state or a region like Europe, as their primary unit of analysis. In the context of the various other structures that make the world a smaller place, global migrants in recent times maintain far stronger and more lasting and consequential links with their countries of origin. Globalization approaches allow a better understanding of why they have migrated, what they do once they migrate, and the dynamics of their integration or lack thereof into their new regions.

Given that religious institutions, religiously informed worldviews, and religious practice are so often instrumental in these processes, the growing number of efforts to understand religion's role among global migrants is not surprising. Such contributions have focused on the concrete religious institutions of the migrants in their new homes, the immigration and integration policies and attitudes of the host countries, the transnational links and flows that the migrants maintain, and the influence of these diasporic communities on the global religions that are usually involved. Not infrequently in such analyses, the sorts of transnational religious organizations and movements just mentioned are salient topics, since the migrant communities are often instrumental in bringing about, developing, and maintaining their global character. Thus, for instance, we have consideration of Senegalese *murīd* presence in the United States, Taiwanese Foguangshan establishments in Canada, Turkish Süleymanli communities in Germany, Tablighi Jamaat mosques in Great Britain, Japanese Buddhist temples in Brazil, as well as African or Latin American Pentecostal churches in North America and Europe. As this illustrative list demonstrates, the bulk of this literature reflects the fact that it is people in Western countries that carry out most of such globalization analyses. This imbalance needs yet to be corrected. Nonetheless, the examples do demonstrate one of the important ways that globalization perspectives are being applied to religion, and conversely how the analysis of religion is coming to inform theories of globalization themselves. Moreover, the consideration of the role of transnational religious institutions in the context of global migration already implicates the second way that religion has been understood as a significant contributor to globalization processes, and that is as a cultural, but especially political resource.

Religion as Cultural and Political Resource. People who migrate from one part of the world to another in search of a better life often depend on their religions and their religious institutions to address an array of attendant problems. Religion can furnish them with a strong sense of identity and integrity in a situation where they may be strangers. Churches, temples, mosques, *gurdwaras*, and synagogues can serve as a home away from home where one can speak one's language, eat one's food, congregate with people who share one's situation, and even attain a measure of status that one is denied in the new host society. For many poorer migrants, religious institutions offer vital social services that make survival and establishment in the new land even possible. They may also provide a principal conduit for maintaining ties with the places of origin. In these circumstances religion both is the means for global connectivity and makes up important content of global flows. Globalization affords conditions for the elaboration of new and expanded transnational establishments whose primary reason for existence is religious but that also serve an array of other purposes. They are at the same time, however, important local institutions, places where people go in their everyday lives for everyday reasons. Thus, to take but one example, a Christian church founded by Mexican migrants in Atlanta is an important community resource for its participants, but it may also have ties with the church back in the Mexican village from which most of them originate, providing financial and other resources for that village church as well. The religious institution properly speaking includes both localities and is not properly understood unless one takes both into consideration. Globalization perspectives afford that inclusive view.

The role of religion in providing, broadly speaking, cultural resources in a global context is not limited to the situation of migrants, however. Globalization, irrespective of which meaning one favors, implies a kind of compression of space in which the upheaval and uprooting characteristic of the migratory experience are the lot of a great many of the world's people, whether they leave their homes or not. Parallel circumstances in Africa and Latin America can serve to make this similarity clear. Both these continents have large regions and large populations that are effectively excluded from the main globalized power structures, yet their lives are nonetheless profoundly affected by them. Religion and religious institutions are important resources for responding to the situation. In Latin America, for instance, one reason for the rapid rise of Pentecostal Christian churches along with significant growth among Afro-Brazilian religions like Candomblé and certain Roman Catholic movements is that these institutional religious forms provide people with ways of understanding themselves and coping in a world where their situation is changing and often precarious. They afford people narratives with attendant life practices by which they can give themselves a meaningful and dignified place in this world. Religion lends them a measure of power. Even more clearly, in sub-Saharan Africa above all Christian and Islamic organizations, centers, networks, and movements offer large numbers of people at least some access to an institution that actually functions reasonably to their benefit. Although they are localized institutions and largely in the control of local people, a far from insignificant part of the appeal of these religious establishments is that they have links to and represent access to the wider globalized world. This has always been one of the attractions of both Christianity and Islam; they have in effect been global religions for many centuries. In today's world they continue to fill that role. The degree to which religions contribute to the globalized circumstance as well as their character as globalized institutions becomes evident in these cases.

As noted earlier, the one phenomenon that has attracted the most attention to the global significance of religions is the proliferation of effective religio-political movements in almost all regions of the world. From the rise of Hindu nationalism in India and the heavy political involvement of certain Buddhist organizations in Japan to the many highly politicized Islamicist movements in countries as diverse as Iran, Indonesia, and Nigeria, politicized religion has been a constant feature of the global world since at least the 1960s and in many respects well back into the nineteenth century. Although the literature often analyzes them under the somewhat tendentious label of fundamentalisms, two of their most basic features illustrate quite clearly how relevant they are for theories of globalization and how they manifest the global nature of so much contemporary religion.

The first is simply that they have arisen in so many different countries, and almost always on the basis of the traditions and institutions of one of the globally recognized religions such as Islam, Christianity, Judaism, Hinduism, Sikhism, or Buddhism. Religions that are very different from one another provide the resources for remarkably similar political movements. The fact that one of the broadly homologous modern states is invariably implicated by such movements is one reason for this similarity, but so is the explicitly global view that they typically represent. Whether one takes the Islamic revolution in Iran, the religious Zionists of Israel, the Christian Right in the United States, liberation theological movements in Latin America, Sōka Gakkai in Japan, the Hindu nationalism of the Rashtriya Svayamsevak Sangh in India, or a host of other examples, most of these movements have justified themselves explicitly in global terms, in addition to local or national ones. Even the Islamicist Taliban in Afghanistan, a movement with hardly any global consciousness when it formed in the early 1990s, very much saw itself in global terms by the time the American-led invasion ousted its government in 2001. What these religio-political movements therefore also demonstrate once again is how localized religion does not have to be globally extended, let alone positive toward the process of globalization, for it to be globally relevant and therefore for globalization theories to be useful in understanding them.

Religion and Religions as Globalizing System. A further theoretical approach to the role of religion and religions in globalization goes beyond the idea that religious worldviews and institutions have participated in the process. It focuses on the degree to which both modern institutional forms and modern understandings of religion are themselves manifestations of globalization. With the centuries-long development of what is today a globally extended society, religion came to inform what is today a globally extended religious system consisting primarily of a series of mutually identified and broadly recognized religions. These religions, in virtually every region of the globe, include Christianity, Islam, Hinduism, and Buddhism, but a variable list of other religions receives almost as broad legitimacy. Among these are Judaism, Sikhism, Daoism, and Jainism, followed again by another set of less consistently or more regionally accepted ones such as Bahā'ī, Shintō, Candomblé, African Traditional Religions (ATR), Scientology, and so forth. The idea that religion manifests itself through a series of distinct religions may seem self-evident to many people, including a great many of their adherents. Yet that notion is historically of quite recent provenance. In Europe, where this understanding first gained purchase, it dates back at the earliest to the seventeenth century. Elsewhere, such as in most regions of Asia, one must wait until at least the nineteenth century. Its development and spread is entirely coterminous with the period most theories identify as the prime centuries of globalization.

For this approach to religion and globalization, the construction of the religious system is not only recent. It is also quite selective; not every possible religion, not everything possibly religious counts. Symptomatic of both aspects are ongoing and recent debates among scholars of religion concerning the meaning of the concept and its supposed Eurocentrism. One perspective in these controversies has it that religion is at best an abstract term, useful for certain kinds of analysis but not something real that is actually out there in the world. A prime argument in support of this position is how the ideas of religion as a separate domain of life and of the distinct religions are so demonstrably products of relatively recent history and so clearly attendant upon and implicated in the concomitant spread of Christian and European influence around the world. Another is that religions is empirically too narrow, as what is meant by them does not cover nearly everything in our world that is manifestly religious using slightly different notions of religion. Cogent as such arguments are, however, they point exactly to what the theory under review states: a peculiar way of understanding religion and institutionally embodying religion has developed in conjunction with and as an expression of the process of globalization. It is accepted and contested right around the world. Similar to global capitalism and the global system of sovereign states, the idea and its putting into practice exclude as well as include. It also involves power and imposition, as do all human institutions. And just as antiglobalization movements are themselves important manifestations of that which they seemingly oppose, so too is contestation—whether academic, theological, or broadly political—with reference to religion and the religions symptomatic of the social and cultural reality that it contests.

A strict corollary of this theory, a consequence of the selective nature of this religious system, is that new religions will constantly try to form and that much religiosity will escape the system. The existence of this global religious system, simultaneously at the global and local levels, therefore spawns its constant development and the constant challenging of the way it operates. That idea leads logically to consideration of the religiousness of the global system itself.

Religion, Globalization, and the Human Condition. More than a few theories of globalization explicitly address what one might call its ideal dimension, the way it shapes how people understand the nature and purpose of the world and their place in it. Given that such questions of ultimate concern or purpose often appear as defining features of religion, this ideal dimension can also be conceived as its religious dimension, although thereby not necessarily referring to the role of religious traditions and institutions in it. One can divide the analyses of this dimension of globalization according to whether it is seen as a positive or negative feature, and whether unity or diversity of vision dominates.

Positive and unitary interpretations come in a number of variants. There are still a few that see globalization as inevitably moving the world toward a future of ever greater material prosperity, political democracy, and technological progress shared equitably among all peoples. Far more numerous are those that share ideals such as equality and inclusion of all people in the benefits of global society, perhaps under the rubric of universal human rights; but they consider that at the very least human society has a long way to go before these are realizable, and that certain features of globalization actually stand in the way of their realization. Several perspectives grounded in institutionalized religion fall under this heading, for instance, the already discussed Global Ethic Project led by Hans Küng, or the Justice, Peace and Integrity of Creation program of the World Council of Churches. Typically, these and other examples consider such values as equality among peoples, religions, classes, and genders to be completely unquestionable. With equal self-evidence they exhibit strong ecological sensibility and valorize the natural environment. Into this category also belong those social-scientific approaches that stress the global preponderance of idealized models, especially models of progressive economy, the nation-state, education, legal structures, mass media, art, and culture.

Unitary but negative visions share most of these characteristics but reject the idea that any of these developments can have a positive outcome. Sometimes these take world-rejecting communitarian directions, advocating retreat from the globalized world. Ironically perhaps, it is not uncommon for these visions to espouse precisely the sort of egalitarian values typical of the positive versions but insist that this is only possible in a separated—and usually quite small-scale—society. Some subdivisions of environmental and back-to-nature movements exemplify this possibility. In many respects they are mirror images of globalized society, and in that respect reflections of it. By contrast, there are those rejections of a unitary globalization that insist on the unique validity of a particular culture or society. Some so-called fundamentalist visions fall in this category, but it must be stressed how comparatively rare they are. The Afghan Pashtun Taliban, in contrast to most Islamicist perspectives, may have been one of the few.

Pluralist visions of the world are variations on the unitary ones, putting greater stress on, respectively, the difference or the irreconcilability of diverse worldviews. The clash of civilizations model made famous by Samuel Huntington is representative of a negative version, dependent as it is on the idea—not to say ideal—that quasi-essential civilizations with particular characteristics actually exist logically prior to the globalized context in which mutually identifying them might make sense. Pluralist positive perspectives, by contrast, are even more mere variations on the unitary variety: the value of pluralist and egalitarian inclusion here is simply more strongly emphasized.

What is therefore especially noteworthy of all these representations of globalization's ideal dimension is just how close they are to one another. Without in the least underplaying the degree to which globalization entails vast differences in power and influence among different regions and different people; without denying the significant contestation, even conflict, between different visions of what the global world is or should be; this seeming narrowing of alternative world visions may in the end be one of the most powerful symptoms of the social reality which the idea of globalization seeks to name.

SEE ALSO Economics and Religion; Politics and Religion; Transculturation and Religion.

BIBLIOGRAPHY

Ahmed, Akbar S. *Islam, Globalization and Postmodernity.* London, 1994. An earlier work that deals well with the challenges that globalization presents for one of the major religions that is not Christianity. It explodes the myth that Islam is somehow fundamentally antiglobal or incapable of responding positively.

Appadurai, Arjun. *Modernity at Large: Cultural Dimensions of Globalization.* Minneapolis, 1996. A much cited and influential work that presents globalization from below and stresses the contested, pluralistic, and even chaotic character of globalization. It pays little attention to religion in any form.

Bauman, Zygmunt. *Globalization: The Human Consequences.* London, 1998. An excellent work not only in terms of the problematic outcomes of globalization but also in the way that it clearly shows how globalization involves a dialogical simultaneity of the global and the local.

Beck, Ulrich. *World Risk Society.* London, 1999. In focusing on the idea of risk among other concepts, this work presents a perspective on global society that stresses its somewhat unique features. It is in this way good for understanding how global society is different from nonglobal ones.

Berger, Peter L., and Samuel P. Huntington, eds. *Many Globalizations: Cultural Diversity in the Contemporary World.* Oxford, 2002. A compendium of chapters written by people in a wide variety of different countries, it is valuable for appreciating how globalization is constituted as much by local response and appropriation as by homogenizing imposition.

Beyer, Peter. *Religion and Globalization.* London, 1994. The first work entirely dedicated to the topic from the perspective of a theory of globalization, it focuses primarily on religion as a political resource in the context of global society.

Beyer, Peter, ed. *Religion im Prozeß der Globalisierung* (*Religion in the Process of Globalization*). Würzburg, 2001. A collection of theoretical and empirical articles about globalization and the possible place of religion in it. Contains a chapter in which the editor outlines key aspects of his theory of a global religious system.

Braman, Sandra, and Annabelle Sreberny-Mohammedi, eds. *Globalization, Communication and Transnational Civil Society.* Cresskill, N.J., 1996. A good representative sample of contributions that stress globalization from below and thereby the dimensions of globalization not subsumed under economic and political perspectives.

Castles, Stephen. *Ethnicity and Globalization: From Migrant Worker to Transnational Citizen.* London, 2000. A work that focuses on the important process of transnational migration and its consequences, it is representative of much such work that, while important, tends to ignore religion almost completely.

Chidester, David. *Savage Systems: Colonialism and Comparative Religion in Southern Africa.* Charlottesville, Va., 1996. A fine analysis of the modern development and use of the idea of religion as exemplified in the colonial history of South Africa. It demonstrates both the selectivity and the recentness of this development.

Coleman, Simon. *The Globalisation of Charismatic Christianity: Spreading the Gospel of Prosperity.* Cambridge, U.K., 2000. Although largely an analysis of the Pentecostalism of one Swedish church, this work simultaneously shows how understanding this important Christian phenomenon benefits from a globalization perspective.

Ebaugh, Helen Rose, and Janet Saltzman Chafetz, eds. *Religion across Borders: Transnational Migrant Networks.* Walnut Creek, Calif., 2002. The outcome of research on immigrant religious communities in Houston, Texas, this work shows graphically how migrant religion is at the same time very local and very global in its connections and meanings.

Haynes, Jeff. *Religion in Global Politics.* London and New York, 1998. An excellent survey of religio-political movements and implications around the world.

Held, David, and Anthony McGrew, eds. *The Global Transformations Reader: An Introduction to the Globalization Debate.* Cambridge, U.K., 2003. A good compendium of most aspects of the globalization debate, including the many and contested meanings of the term. Religion, however, is not well covered.

Hopkins, Dwight N., Lois Ann Lorentzen, Eduardo Mendieta, and David Batstone, eds. *Religions/Globalizations: Theories and Cases.* Durham, N.C., 2001. A collection of case studies, some theoretical, some empirical. Articles on Africa, Southeast Asia, and Latin America are particularly valuable.

Huntington, Samuel P. *The Clash of Civilizations and the Remaking of World Order.* New Delhi, 1996. The classic statement of the thesis. A notable aspect of the work is that Western civilization in particular is called to take note.

Juergensmeyer, Mark, ed. *Global Religions: An Introduction.* Oxford, 2003. A collection of articles, mostly about each of the major world religions, with overview articles attached. Good for getting a sense of some of the issues involved in each of the five majors along with African and indigenous traditions.

Küng, Hans. *A Global Ethic for Global Politics and Economics.* Translated by John Bowden. New York, 1998. A critical examination of what this influential Catholic theologian believes is needed for a healthier globalization.

Levitt, Peggy. *The Transnational Villagers.* Berkeley, Calif., 2001. An excellent work that shows just how difficult it is to understand the lives of contemporary global migrants if one does not take the global into perspective. The author also appreciates the importance of religion.

Martin, David. *Pentecostalism: The World Their Parish.* Oxford, 2002. To some extent a comparison of Latin America and Europe, the book emphasizes the simultaneously local and global character of this Christian movement. Also contains excellent theoretical reflections on the issue from a sociological perspective.

Meyer, Birgit, and Peter Geschiere, eds. *Globalization and Identity: Dialectics of Flow and Closure.* Oxford, 1999. A collection of works on Africa, another region where the local and global occur simultaneously. Good attention to religious dimensions.

Meyer, John W., John Boli, George M. Thomas, and Francisco O. Ramirez. "World Society and the Nation-State." *American Journal of Sociology* 103, no. 1 (1997): 144–181. A succinct statement of an important theory of globalization that posits the existence of a world polity in which globalized models inform what people do in all parts of the world. Also stresses the ideal or religious dimension of globalization overall.

Nederveen Pieterse, Jan. *Globalization and Culture: Global Mélange.* Lanham, Md., 2003. A good statement of globalization as what the author calls hybridization, not the juxtaposing of preexisting cultural identities so much as the re-creation of these identities and thereby their creative mixing and reinvention.

Prazniak, Roxann, and Arif Dirlik, eds. *Places and Politics in an Age of Globalization.* Lanham, Md., 2001. Another work that stresses the simultaneity of global and local with special attention to marginalized groups, women, and environmental issues.

Robertson, Roland. *Globalization: Social Theory and Global Culture.* London, 1992. The thus far classic statement of a highly influential and dialogical theory of globalization by the sociologist who first used the term technically and consistently in the 1980s. Sensitive to the importance of religion in the process.

Rothstein, Mikael, ed. *New Age Religion and Globalization.* Aarhus, 2001. A collection that debates an important domain of noninstitutionalized religiosity, with special emphasis on the question of whether New Age is basically Western or by now also global.

Rudolph, Susanne Hoeber, and James Piscatori, eds. *Transnational Religion and Fading States.* Boulder, Colo., 1997. A collection of articles primarily on Islam and Christianity. Contains a fine chapter by José Casanova on the Roman Catholic Church.

Scholte, Jan Aart. *Globalization: A Critical Introduction.* London, 2000. A very good introductory work on the entire question with some sensitivity to the role of religion.

Stackhouse, Max L., and Peter J. Paris, eds. *God and Globalization: Religion and the Powers of the Common Life.* Harrisburg, Pa., 2000. A collection of different perspectives including good theological reflections on the globalization process.

van Binsbergen, Wim, and Rijk van Dijk, eds. *Situating Globality: African Agency in the Appropriation of Global Culture.* Leiden, 2004. A further work on the important region of Africa. Well-balanced, with good emphasis on religion, both Islam and Christianity, and on women.

Van der Veer, Peter, ed. *Conversion to Modernities: The Globalization of Christianity.* London, 1996. A collection of articles on the particularization of Christianity in diverse parts of the world that demonstrates the degree to which this has also become a non-Western religion.

Vásquez, Manuel A., and Marie Friedmann Marquardt. *Globalizing the Sacred: Religion across the Americas.* New Brunswick, N.J., 2003. A very fine work that demonstrates in ethnographic detail, focusing on Latin America and the United States, how the highly localized religions of migrants and marginalized peoples have a global dimension. A good example of globalization from below.

Wallerstein, Immanuel. *The Modern World System.* 3 vols. New York, 1974–1980. An early and classic work on the historical development of the global capitalist system, it presents an excellent theoretical and empirical analysis of economic globalization.

PETER BEYER (2005)

GLOSSOLALIA (from the Greek *glōssa,* "tongue, language," and *lalein,* "to talk") is a nonordinary speech behavior that is institutionalized as a religious ritual in numerous Western and non-Western religious communities. Its worldwide distribution attests to its antiquity, as does its mention in ancient documents. It is alluded to in the Hebrew scriptures and in the New Testament, as in the well-known narration in the *Acts of the Apostles* about events on the Day of the Pentecost. There are references to it in the Vedas (c. 1000 BCE), in Patañjali's *Yoga Sutras,* and in Tibetan Tantric writings. Traces of it can be found in the litanies (*dhikrs*) of some orders of the Islamic Sufi mystics.

Early ethnographic reports of glossolalia treated it with contempt, calling it "absurd nonsense, gibberish scarce worth recording," while Christian theologians tended to think of it as an exclusively Christian phenomenon, peculiar, according to some, to apostolic times. Modern-day forms of glossolalia were classed as abnormal psychological occurrences, possible evidence of schizophrenia or hysteria, because researchers observed it only in mental patients. The situation started to change when, as the result of interest renewed by the upsurge of the Pentecostal movement, field-workers began to examine glossolalia as a part of religious ritual.

In an article published in 1969, for instance, Virginia H. Hine reported on a comparative anthropological investigation of the Pentecostal movement in the United States, Mexico, Haiti, and Colombia, combining the use of questionnaires, interviews, and participant observation (*Journal for the Scientific Study of Religion* 8: 212–226). Her functional analysis showed glossolalia to be a component in the process of commitment to a movement, with implications for both personal and social change. This conclusion agrees in substance with numerous ethnographic reports from non-Western societies, where glossolalia often appears before or during the initiation of religious practitioners.

A few years before Hine's study, the pathology model of glossolalia was refuted by L. M. Vivier-van Etveldt (M. D. diss., University of the Witwatersrand, Johannesburg, 1960). He tested two carefully matched groups, one made up of members of a church that practiced glossolalia and the other made up of members of a traditional orthodox reformed church where such behavior was not accepted. A number of psychological tests, such as the Thematic Apperception Test (TAT) and the Personality Factor Test developed by James Cattell, indicated no inherent weakness in the neural organization of the glossolalists. On the contrary, they appeared to be less subject to suggestion and better adjusted than their conservative counterparts. By implication, this finding should put to rest the numerous allegations that shamans, who frequently utter glossolalia, are psychotic. The salient difference between a religious practitioner and a mental patient lies in the fact that the latter is unable to control his behavior ritually.

As to formal properties, glossolalia is a nonordinary speech event in the sense that it consists of nonsense syllables. In contrast with natural languages, its syllables and segments are not words; that is, they do not exhibit the attribution of meaning, and they are not strung together according to rules of grammar. For this reason, linguists reject the interpretation of glossolalia as xenoglossia (from the Greek *xenox,* "stranger," and *glōssa,* "language"), which claims that glossolalia is some foreign language that could be understood by another person who spoke it. William J. Samarin, a linguist working with English-speaking Christian groups, regards glossolalia instead as a type of pseudolanguage. In his 1972 article "Variation and Variables in Religious Glossolalia" (*Language in Society* 1: 121–130), he defines it as "unintelligible post-babbling speech that exhibits superficial phonological similarity to language without having consistent syntagmatic structure and that is not systematically derived from or related to known languages." He notes that glossolalia is repetitious and can be subdivided into macrosegments, which are comparable to sentences; microsegments, which are reminiscent of words; and sounds. There is also a pattern of stress and pitch. According to Samarin, speakers of English have an "English accent" in glossolalia; that is, their sounds are English speech sounds. He attributes these regularities to a particular style of discourse that practitioners assume by imitating certain preaching styles.

This writer's own fieldwork and laboratory research have led to somewhat different conclusions. As a psychological anthropologist and linguist, the author of this article conducted participant observation in various English-, Spanish-, and Maya-speaking Pentecostal communities in the United States and Mexico as well as with the founder of a new religion in Japan. In addition, tape recordings of non-Christian rituals from Africa, Borneo, Indonesia, and Japan were compared. The results indicated that when all features of glossolalia were taken into consideration—that is, its segmental structure (such as sounds, syllables, and phrases) and its suprasegmental elements (namely, rhythm, accent, and especially overall intonation)—they seemed cross-linguistically and cross-culturally identical. Laboratory tracings that used a level recorder, which registers changes in pressure density (in this case, intonation), confirmed these impressions at least in the case of intonation. This method is also suitable for distinguishing glossolalia from such other nonordinary speech events as sleep talking and talking during hypnotic regression (see this writer's 1981 article "States of Consciousness: A Study of Soundtracks," *Journal of Mind and Behavior* 2: 209–219). The latter finding is important, because many ethnographic observers consider the behavior of which glossolalia is a part to be hypnotically induced, which in view of these results is in error.

Self-reporting by ethnographic consultants and observation of their behavior indicate the presence of a changed state of consciousness during glossolalia, ranging from minimal to quite intense. This author therefore attributes the cross-cultural agreements in the features of glossolalia to these neurophysiological changes, collectively and popularly called trance, and defines glossolalia as a vocalization pattern, a speech automatism that is produced in the substratum of the trance and that reflects directly, in its segmental and suprasegmental structures, the neurophysiological processes present in this changed state of consciousness.

Put more simply, whatever takes place in the nervous system during a trance causes utterance to break down into phrases of equal length, provided the pauses are also included. That is, using a concept taken from music rather than linguistics, it causes the phrases to be divided into bars, each of which is accented on the first syllable, and it causes the bars to pulsate, to throb rhythmically in a sequence of consonant-vowel, consonant-vowel. And it is this writer's belief that the trance state is responsible for the haunting intonation of glossolalia; never varying, it rises to a peak at the end of the first third of the unit utterance and drops to a level much lower than that at the onset as it comes to a close.

The sounds of glossolalia do not necessarily reflect the inventory of the speaker's language, for they frequently include phones not found in a speaker's native tongue. English speakers, for instance, often use /a/ as a high central, unrounded vowel, the so-called continental sound, which does not occur in English, and Spanish speakers in Mexico may use /ö/ (the long, closed *o,* as in the German word *Öse*), which is not a Spanish vowel. In addition, shrieks as well as barking, whistling, grunting, growling, and many other so-called animal sounds have also been reported.

Although glossolalia is often described as a spontaneous outburst, it is, actually, a learned behavior, learned either unawarely or, sometimes, consciously. The fact that individual congregations with a stable membership tend to develop their own characteristic glossolalia "dialect" indicates that learning has occurred, and the many traditional forms in which glossolalia appears in non-Western societies are obviously taught. These include such conventions as speaking individually, in groups, and in the form of a dialogue, often heard in the Japanese new religions, and singing.

As the foregoing characterization of glossolalia indicates, one probably needs to view trance as the primary behavior, on which vocalization is superimposed and into which the practitioner switches with the help of a large variety of stimuli, such as singing, dancing, clapping, and drumming. Present research suggests that this trance—a frenzy, rapture, ecstasy, or, in more neutral terms, an altered state of consciousness—involves a single, generalized neurophysiological process. Barbara W. Lex, a medical anthropologist, holds that what is involved is an alternation between two different arousals of the nervous system. This tunes the nervous system and releases tension, thus accounting for the beneficial effects of the experience. Observations of Christian and non-Western religious communities alike indicate that apparently anybody with a normal physical endowment is able to initiate this process and to switch into a trance. Differences in personality, treated extensively by early researchers, apparently do not enter into the picture.

An association between trance and glossolalia is now accepted by many researchers as a correct assumption (see, for instance, Williams, 1981). Thus, if one recognizes trance as the primary, generating process of the features of glossolalia, one could then conclude that a vocalization consisting only of nonsense syllables, no matter how varied, may in fact represent a cultural convention and that other types of speech could also be uttered while the practitioner is in a trance, with the trance, of course, still expressing itself in some form or other. Field observation shows that this is indeed true. Nonsense syllables may occur in combination with words from the vernacular and/or a foreign language—such as "Come, Jesus" and "Hallelujah," which are often heard from American Pentecostals—without disturbing the accent pattern or intonation of the utterance, its trance features. In the circumpolar region, many shamans, among the Inuit (Eskimo), the Saami (Lapps), Chukchi, the Khanty (Ostiaks), the Yakuts, and the Evenki, use in their religious rituals secret languages that consist of a mixture of nonsense syllables and the vernacular. Just like a natural language, these secret trance dialects are taught by the master shamans to their neophytes.

From Africa, there are reports of a secret religious trance language used exclusively by women. Bakweri women living on the slopes of Mount Cameroon speak a "mermaid language" in ritual context, which is taught to adolescent girls when they are ready for initiation. A girl's readiness is indicated by her "fainting," that is, experiencing a trance, and by her ability, while in this altered state of consciousness, to understand some of the mermaid language as it is spoken to her by a mature woman. No details of this language are known outside the tribe, for the male ethnographer was barred from learning it. (See Edwin Ardener, "Belief and the Problem of Women," in *The Interpretation of Ritual,* edited by J. S. La Fontaine, London, 1972, pp. 135–201.) It is probably a mixed form, for he mentions that scraps of the mermaid language are common currency even among Christian, educated, urban Bakweri women. This suggests that these "scraps" may have turned into words or that they were not originally nonsense syllables but had specific, assigned meanings.

When speaking in a trance, a practitioner may use no nonsense syllables at all, employing instead only the vernacular. If the principal pronouncement is in nonsense syllables, however, as, for instance, among Christians speaking in tongues or among the nomadic, reindeer-hunting Chukchi of Siberia, an "interpretation" may be provided. Such interpretations exhibit a distinct, trance-based rhythm and an intonation whose exactness cannot be reproduced in the ordinary state of consciousness. This is the same phenomenon exhibited in the many forms of "inspired," prophetic speeches, heard around the world, in which a scanning rhythm imparts a poetic quality to the utterance. In such speeches words are sometimes truncated, and rules of grammar violated, overridden by the exigencies of the trance. Even communicative intent may have to be altered. Thus the demons who spoke through the trance of a German university student, Anneliese Michel, could ask no questions because in spoken German the tone of an interrogative must rise at the end, while all trance utterances have a pronounced drop. (See this author's book about this case, *The Exorcism of Anneliese Michel,* New York, 1981.)

The case of Anneliese Michel brings up the question of what kinds of religious experience are commonly expressed by glossolalia. In her case, the experience was that of possession, and glossolalia was the voice, the "language," of the demons that she reported were possessing her. Possession is one of the most frequent ritual occasions for the use of glossolalia. In possession, an entity from the sacred dimension of reality is experienced as penetrating the respective person. In Christian contexts, the entity is most usually the Holy Spirit, and glossolalia is then felt to be its language. The Holy Spirit is experienced as power, not as personality, but other spirits—for instance, those of the dead of the Trobriand Islanders, ancestral spirits in Africa, and various spirits in Haitian vodou—have pronounced personality traits that are expressed in glossolalia. Western observers of possession may speak of role playing, but the experience is more that of being in the presence of a discrete being. The voice of the possessing being differs from that of the possessed practitioner. Anneliese Michel's demons spoke with a deep, raspy, male voice, and each one—there were six all told—exhibited distinct characteristics; Judas was brutal, for instance, and Nero effeminate. In vodou, female mediums are often possessed by male *lwa* (spirits), in which case a similar change in voice and, of course, in comportment takes place. In Umbanda, an Afro-Brazilian healing cult, possession by the child spirit will bring about an equally dramatic voice modification. Siberian shamans may be possessed by helpers in the form of animal spirits, and their speech then consists of animal voices, or "animal language." A similar change in language takes place when the shaman turns into an animal, which is a different experience, however.

According to a generally held belief, illness will result if a noxious being of the sacred dimension of reality possesses a person. Therefore, the harmful entity needs to be expelled, or exorcised. The method by which this is done depends on the tradition prevailing in the religious community in question. The ritual specialist carrying out the exorcism may merely recite a required formula while remaining in the ordinary state of consciousness—as was done for Anneliese Michel by a Catholic priest who spoke the exorcistic prayers from the *Rituale romanum*—or he may enter a trance and utter glossolalia, usually a mixed version, which is thought to influence the actions of demons. This happens in Tantric exorcistic rituals in Tibet, for instance, and during healing sessions among Buddhists of northern Thailand.

Communication by glossolalia is instituted not only with unfriendly beings, of course. On a tape recording made in Borneo a female healer can be heard calling her helping spirit. In the *zār* cult of Ethiopia, the shamans talk to the *zārs* (spirits) in a "secret language." The shamans of the Semai of Malaysia use glossolalia to invite the "nephews of the gods" to a feast, and the Yanomamö Indians of Amazonia chant while in trance to their *hekura* demons, calling them to come live in their chests.

Quite generally, glossolalia cannot be considered a symbol. Rather, it is a medium of communication that directly informs both the participants and the onlookers of a ritual about the presence of and contact with the powers or the beings of the sacred dimension of reality—about the Holy Spirit who is baptizing a convert, perhaps, or about the appearance of any one of the multitude of entities that inhabit sacred realms.

See Also Chanting; Enthusiasm; Frenzy; Language, article on Sacred Language; Pentecostal and Charismatic Christianity; Spirit Possession.

Bibliography

Three books, published simultaneously in 1972, discuss glossolalia from different angles. My own work, *Speaking in Tongues: A Cross-Cultural Study of Glossolalia* (Chicago, 1972), provides a linguistic analysis of glossolalia and a descriptive study of the entire behavior; John P. Kildahl, in *The Psychology of Speaking in Tongues* (New York, 1972), takes up the relationship between personality variables and the practice of glossolalia; and William J. Samarin, in *Tongues of Men and Angels: The Religious Language of Pentecostalism* (New York, 1972), seeks to answer the question of why people speak in tongues by placing the behavior in social context. A comprehensive review of the research into glossolalia ten years later, including references to non-Western material, can be found in Cyril G. Williams's *Tongues of the Spirit: A Study of Pentecostal Glossolalia and Related Phenomena* (Cardiff, 1981). An anthology edited by Irving I. Zaretzky and Mark P. Leone, *Religious Movements in Contemporary America* (Princeton, N.J., 1974), gives a panoramic view of the multitude of religious movements in the United States, many of which use glossolalia. For a good description of glossolalia in a non-Western society, see Arkadii Federovich Anisimov's "The Shaman's Tent of the Evenks and the Origin of the Shamanistic Rite," translated from Russian by Dr. and Mrs. Stephen P. Dunn, in *Studies in Siberian Shamanism*, edited by Henry N. Michael (Toronto, 1963).

New Sources

Holm, Nils G. "Ecstasy Research in the 20th century. An Introduction." In *Religious Ecstasy*, edited by Nils G. Holm, pp. 7–26. Stockholm, 1982.

Holm, Nils G. "Glossolalia as a Transition Rite." In *Transition Rites: Cosmic, Social and Individual Order*, edited by Ugo Bianchi, pp. 143–149. Rome, 1986. The theoretical conclusions of this essay and the preceding one are based on research on glossolalia within the Swedish-speaking Pentecostal movement in Finland.

Hutch, R. A. "The Personal Ritual of Glossolalia." *Journal for the Scientific Study of Religion* 19 (1980).

Williams, Cyril G. "Glossolalia." In *Concise Encyclopedia of Language and Religion*, edited by John F. A. Sawyer and J. M. Y. Simpson, pp. 249–250. Amsterdam, 2001.

Felicitas D. Goodman (1987)
Revised Bibliography

GNOSTICISM

This entry consists of the following articles:

GNOSTICISM FROM ITS ORIGINS TO THE MIDDLE AGES [FIRST EDITION]
GNOSTICISM FROM ITS ORIGINS TO THE MIDDLE AGES [FURTHER CONSIDERATIONS]
GNOSTICISM FROM THE MIDDLE AGES TO THE PRESENT
GNOSTICISM AS A CHRISTIAN HERESY
HISTORY OF STUDY

GNOSTICISM: GNOSTICISM FROM ITS ORIGINS TO THE MIDDLE AGES [FIRST EDITION]

Gnōsis ("knowledge") is a Greek word of Indo-European origin, related to the English *know* and the Sanskrit *jñāna*. The term has long been used in comparative religion to indicate a current of antiquity that stressed awareness of the divine mysteries. This was held to be obtained either by direct experience of a revelation or by initiation into the secret, esoteric tradition of such revelations.

Pre-Christian Gnosis. The experience of gnosis was highly esteemed at the beginning of our era in various religious and philosophical circles of Aramaic and Greco-Roman civilization. It is a key word in the scrolls of the Jews of the Essene sect found at Qumran. In the canonical *Gospel of John*, Jesus is quoted as having said at the Last Supper: "This is [not 'will be'] eternal life, that they know [not 'believe in'] Thee [here and now], and know Jesus Christ, whom thou hast sent" (*Jn.* 17:3). Not even the prevailing philosophy of the time, so-called Middle Platonism, was completely beyond the influence of this general movement. Middle Platonism was primarily religious and otherworldly; it distinguished between discursive reasoning and intuition and taught the affinity of the soul with the godhead, basing these teachings on an oral tradition of the Platonic schools. The writings of Hermes Trismegistos ("thrice-greatest Hermes," identified with the Egyptian god Thoth) reflect the same atmosphere. These eighteen treatises, of which *Poimandres* and *Asclepius* are the most important, originate in the proverbial wisdom of ancient Egypt. A saying in a recently discovered Armenian collection attributed to Hermes Trismegistos is "He who knows himself, knows the All." The author of *Poimandres* expresses the same insight: "Let spiritual man know himself, then he will know that he is immortal and that Eros is the origin of death, and he will know the All." And to illustrate this saying the author tells the story of a divine being, Anthropos (Man), who becomes enamored of the world of (lower) nature and so falls into a material body. Most Hermetic treatises take up a short saying and expound on it in this manner. They also preserve the impact of Egyptian mythology. The ancient Egyptians spoke freely about sexual intercourse and about the homosexual behavior of their gods. The explicit sexual imagery of Egyptian mythology was adopted in a Hermetic prayer that addresses the spouse of God in the following words: "We know thee, womb pregnant by the phallus of the Father."

The idea of emanation was also prominent in Egyptian religion. Egyptian myth depicts the Nile as tears of the sun god Re. This concept too is found in Hermetic literature. On the other hand, the same writings show the influence of Greek philosophy; indeed, there was a Platonic school of Eudorus in Alexandria. And the impact of the biblical book of *Genesis* and that of Jewish mysticism are only too obvious. Christian influences, though, are completely absent from the so-called *Corpus Hermeticum.* The treatises in this group of works were all written around the beginning of the Christian era in Alexandria. They appear to be the scriptures of a school of mystics, a sort of lodge that practiced spiritualized sacraments such as "the bath of rebirth," a holy meal, and the kiss of peace.

GNOSTICISM. Ever since the congress on the origins of Gnosticism held at Messina, Italy, in 1966, scholars have made a distinction between gnosis and Gnosticism. *Gnosticism* is a modern term, not attested in antiquity. Even the substantive *Gnostic* (Gr., *gnōstikos,* "knower"), found in patristic writings, was never used to indicate a general spiritual movement but was applied only to a single, particular sect. Today Gnosticism is defined as a religion in its own right, whose myths state that the Unknown God is not the creator (demiurge, YHVH); that the world is an error, the consequence of a fall and split within the deity; and that man, spiritual man, is alien to the natural world and related to the deity and becomes conscious of his deepest Self when he hears the word of revelation. Not sin or guilt, but unconsciousness, is the cause of evil.

Until recent times the Gnostic religion was almost exclusively known by reports of its opponents, ecclesiastical heresiologists such as Irenaeus (c. 180 CE), Hippolytus (c. 200), and Epiphanius (c. 350). Not until the eighteenth century were two primary sources, the Codex Askewianus (named for the physician A. Askew) and the Codex Brucianus (named after the Scottish explorer James Bruce), discovered in Egypt. These contained several Coptic Gnostic writings: (1) *Two Books of Jeû* from the beginning of the third century; (2) book 4 of *Pistis Sophia* from about 225; and (3) *Pistis Sophia,* books 1, 2, and 3, from the second half of the third century. To these can now be added the writings found near Nag Hammadi in Upper Egypt in 1945. The stories told about the discovery are untrustworthy. The only certain fact is that, to date, about thirteen of the codices (books, not scrolls) comprising some fifty-two texts are preserved at the Coptic Museum in Old Cairo. They have been translated into English by a team under James M. Robinson (1977). Not all these writings are Gnostic: the *Gospel of Thomas* (114 sayings attributed to Jesus) is encratitic; the *Thunder, Whole Mind* is Jewish; the *Acts of Peter and the Twelve Apostles* is Jewish-Christian; the *Prayer of Thanksgiving* is Hermetic; and the *Authoritative Teaching* is early Catholic (characterized by a monarchic episcopacy, a canon of holy writings, and a confession of faith). But the *Epistle of Eugnostos* and the *Apocryphon of John* lead us back very far, close to the sources of Gnosticism in Alexandria.

Origins. The hypothesis once supported by Richard Reitzenstein, Geo Widengren, and Rudolf Bultmann that Gnosticism is of Iranian origin has been abandoned; the alleged Iranian mystery of the "saved savior" has been disproved. At present, many scholars are inclined to believe that Gnosticism is built upon Hellenistic-Jewish foundations and can be traced to centers like Alexandria, which had a large Jewish population, much as the city of New York does today. Polemics in the writings of the Jewish philosopher Philo, who himself was an opponent of local heresies, make it clear that he knew Jewish groups that had already formulated certain basic elements of Gnosticism, although a consistent system did not yet exist in pre-Christian times.

The divine Man. The prophet Ezekiel tells us in the first chapter of the biblical book that bears his name that in 593 BCE, dwelling in Babylonia, he beheld the personified Glory of the Lord, who would not abandon him even in exile. This figure, at once Light and Man, is described as having a form like the appearance of Adam, or "Man" (*Ez.* 1:26). This vision became a stock image of Jewish mysticism. As early as the second century BCE, the Jewish Alexandrian dramatist Ezekiel Tragicus alludes to the same figure in his Greek drama *Exodus,* fragmentarily preserved in the *Praeparatio evangelica* (9.29) of the Christian bishop Eusebius. In the play, Moses in a dream beholds a throne on top of Mount Sinai. Upon this throne sits Man (Gr., *ho phōs*) with a crown on his head and a scepter in his left hand. With his right hand he beckons Moses to the throne, presents him with a crown, and invites him to sit beside him on an adjacent throne. Thus is Moses enthroned at the right hand of God. A parallel passage is found in Palestinian Judaism: according to the founding father ʿAqivaʾ ben Yosef (early second century BCE), there are two thrones in heaven, one for God and one for David (B. T., *Ḥag.* 14a). This is the oldest extant reference to Adam Qadmon, who later became the central figure of qabbalistic literature. Somewhat later, in the *Book of Daniel*, written soon after 168 BCE, this same figure is called the Son of Man (i.e., "divine Man"). The same figure is found in the Gospels. In the Fourth Gospel, the Son of Man is referred to as the Glory of God, which comes from heaven, touches the earth for a moment, is incarnated in the man Jesus, and eventually returns to the heavenly realm. In the letters of Paul, the Glory is called the last Adam (comparable to Ezekiel's *kavod*), who is from heaven and should be distinguished from the first Adam of *Genesis* 1 and 2, who is from the earth. In the Hellenistic world this divine Man is identified with the Platonic idea of man.

Plato himself never says that there is such a thing as an "idea of man." In the dialogue *Parmenides* this philosopher ridicules the concept of an *eidos anthrōpou* (130c). Probably this passage reflects a debate of Platonists among themselves and with other schools. It would seem that the Skeptics denied the idea of man a separate existence because then empirical man and his idea would have something in common, and this would require a new idea, the "third man." In several Middle Platonic sources, however, the idea of man is supposed to exist. The translator of Ezekiel in the Septuagint identifies the figure of divine Man with the Platonic idea when he translates the phrase *demut ke-marʾeh adam* (*Ez.* 1:26) as *homoiōma hōs eidos anthrōpou*, a hellenizing quotation of Plato.

The same figure is to be found in the Hermetic *Poimandres*, clearly influenced by Alexandrian Jews. This writing relates how God generated a son to whom he delivered all creatures. The son is androgynous, equally Phos (Man, Adam, Light) and Zoe (Eve, Life). This being, who is still to be distinguished from the Logos, descends in order to create but falls in love with nature and assumes a material body. That is why human beings are both mortal and immortal. And yet the human body has the form of the original Man. This view is very Jewish and has parallels in rabbinical literature: not the soul but the human body was created after the image and likeness of God.

A next stage is reached in Philo's works. He never quotes *Ezekiel* 1:26 about the Glory of God resembling the form of a man, and yet he must have been familiar with mystical speculations about this divine figure. Philo calls *logos* "Man after his [God's] image" or "Man of God" and identifies the *logos* with the idea of man: incorporeal and neither male nor female. Yet he polemicizes against the concept that this heavenly Man was androgynous: "God made man," he says, "made him after the image of God. Male and female he made—now not 'him' but 'them'" (*Who Is the Heir* 164). Obviously, before Philo there must have been Jewish thinkers who claimed that the heavenly Man was androgynous. Such circles originated the Anthropos model of *gnōsis*, which is found in the doctrine of Saturninus (Antioch, c. 150). In his system, the female figure is completely absent. Our world is said to have been created by seven angels, the seven planets. Thereupon the Unknown God manifested his shining image, the Glory of the heavenly Man. The angels of creation tried to detain this Anthropos but were unable to do so; it returned to heaven at once. Thereupon the angels shaped a human body in the likeness of the heavenly Man. But this creature was unable to stand erect and slithered upon the earth like a worm. The heavenly Adam, having pity on the earthly Adam, sent to him the spark of life, the Spirit, which raised him up and made him live. It is this spark that at death hastens back to its spiritual home, whereas the body dissolves into its constituent elements.

Variations of the myth of Saturninus are found in quite a few of the writings from Nag Hammadi. Valentinus (c. 150) alludes to this myth when, in a preserved fragment, he states that the Adam of *Genesis* inspired awe in the angels who created him because he had been fashioned after the preexistent Anthropos. Mani (216–277) refers to the same story when he relates that in the beginning the Primal Man is sent out to combat the powers of darkness. This Archanthropos is overpowered and forced to leave "the Maiden who is his soul" embedded in matter. The entire world process is necessary to shape the Perfect Man so that the original state of androgyny (male and maiden at the same time) will be restored. All these speculations presuppose the god Man of *Ezekiel* 1:26. Moreover, it is possible that Paul was familiar with the same concept when he said that Christ was both the power (*dunamis*) and the wisdom (*sophia*) of God (*1 Cor.* 1:24).

Sophia. In the *Wisdom of Solomon*, part of the Greek and Roman Catholic Bible, written in Alexandria close to the beginning of the Christian era, personified wisdom, called Sophia, is said to be a holy spirit or the Holy Spirit, which penetrates the All. She is also referred to as the effluence of God's glory, an emanation of eternal light, and an immaculate mirror of God's activity. She is described as the beloved both of the wise man and of God, even more as the spouse of the Lord (*Wis.* 8:30).

In the *Thunder, Whole Mind*, from the same period and milieu, Sophia manifests herself as the wisdom of the Greeks and the *gnōsis* of the barbarians, the saint and the whore, the bridegroom and the bride. Over and over, she introduces these startling and paradoxical revelations with the formula "I am."

According to the eighth-century BCE inscriptions found near Hebron and in the Negev, the God of Israel had a foreign spouse, the Canaanite goddess Asherah. And in the fifth century BCE, Jewish soldiers garrisoned in Elephantine (near Aswān, Egypt) venerated another pagan fertility goddess called Anat Yahu, the wife of the Lord. Prophets and priests in Judea did all they could to represent Yahveh as exclusively male and to delete all traces of the primeval matriarchy. But Wisdom survived as Ḥokhmah, especially in Alexandria.

This is the basis of the Sophia model of *gnōsis*, which finds expression in the teaching of the famous Samaritan Simon, who was attracted to and yet rejected by incipient Christianity (*Acts* 8). The Samaritans, the last survivors of the ten tribes of northern Israel, were and are heterodox Jews who keep the Law while rejecting the rest of the Bible. They transmit a certain tradition about Wisdom as the personal creator of the world. According to Simon, Wisdom, the spouse of the Lord, was also called Holy Spirit and God's first idea, the mother of all. She descended to the lower regions and gave birth to the angels by whom the world was created. She was overwhelmed and detained by these world powers that she might not return to her abode. She was even incarnated and reincarnated in human bodies, such as that of the Helen of Greek myth and poetry. Finally, she came to dwell as a whore in a brothel of Tyre in Phoenicia, where Simon, "the great power" of God, found and redeemed her. In the *Apocryphon of John* as well as in the school of Valentinus, this Sophia model has been combined with the Anthropos model. Both are pre-Christian in origin.

The Unknown God and the demiurge. The rabbis of the first Christian centuries complain repeatedly of the heretics (*minim*) who taught the existence of two gods. Dissident Jewish teachers believed that God had a representative, bearing his name Jao (the abbreviation of YHVH), who was therefore called Jaoel. According to this view, Jaoel sat upon a throne next to God's throne and was therefore called Metatron (a Greek loanword). In reality, however, Jaoel is nothing but an angel, the most important angel, the one who is called the angel of the Lord in the Hebrew Bible. Some dissident Jews called Magharians said that all anthropomorphisms in the Old Testament applied not to God himself but to this angel, who is also said to have created the world. In a Samaritan (i.e., heterodox Jewish) source called *Malef*, which is late but transmits earlier traditions, it is stated that the angel of the Lord formed the body of Adam from dust of the earth and that God breathed the breath of life into him.

Such views must have been known already to Philo of Alexandria, who polemicizes against them yet at the same time calls the Logos, who is instrumental in creation, both "a second god" and "archangel" on the one hand and "Lord" (YHVH) and "Name" (i.e., YHVH) on the other. Jewish Gnostics such as Simon and Cerinthus affirm that the demiurge (identified with YHVH) was in fact this angel of the Lord, who had not yet rebelled against God. In the *Apocryphon of John* the angel is called Saklas (Aramaic for "fool") because he does not know that there is a God greater than he. Valentinus, Marcion, and Apelles, who were familiar with the myth contained in the *Apocryphon of John*, all held that the demiurge was an angel. This is a typically Jewish concept. A non-Jew, when suffering under the misery of the world, would simply have declared that the *Genesis* story was a myth without truth; he could not have cared less about the origin of Jewish law. Only those who had been brought up to believe every word of the Bible and to cling to the faith that God is one, and who yet found reason to rebel against their inheritance, would have inclined toward the Gnostic solution: God is one and the Bible reveals the truth, but anthropomorphisms such as the handicraft of a creative workman and personal lawgiving are to be attributed to a subordinate angel.

The god within. The biblical *Book of Genesis* relates that God blew the breath of life into the nose of Adam, transforming him into a living being (*Gn.* 2:7). Already in certain passages of the Old Testament (*Jb.* 34:13–15, *Ps.* 104:29–30), this breath is identified with the spirit of God. That is especially clear in the Dead Sea Scrolls: "I, the creature of dust, have known through the spirit, that Thou hast given me." The Alexandrian Jews have integrated and amplified this concept. They were familiar with Greek philosophy and knew that the Orphics, Plato, and the Stoics considered the human soul to be a part of the deity. They were influenced by the Stoic Posidonius (c. 100 BCE), according to whom "the daimon in us [the spirit] is akin to *and of the same nature* as the Daimon [God] who pervades the All." The oldest translators of the Septuagint rendered "breath" (Heb., *neshamah*) in *Genesis* 2:7 as "spirit" (Gr., *pneuma*). This variant is evidenced by the Old Latin Version (*spiritus*) translated from the Septuagint. Philo polemicizes against this particular translation because it deifies sinful man (*Allegorical Interpretation* 1; 13). And yet the Alexandrian *Wisdom of Solomon*, still included in every Roman Catholic Bible, declares explicitly that God's incorruptible *pneuma* is in all things (12:1). Most Gnostics preserved this tendentious translation and made it the basis for their mythological speculations. It enabled them to tell how it came to pass that the Spirit sleeps in man and how it can be made conscious. So it is with Valentinus and Mani. Few people nowadays are aware that these mythologems presuppose a consensus of virtually all Greek philosophers and have a biblical foundation.

JEWISH GNOSTICISM. The themes discussed above are the basic elements that contributed to the rise of a Jewish Gnosticism, whose myth is contained in the *Apocryphon of John* and other related writings found at Nag Hammadi. The church father Irenaeus attributed this doctrine to the *gnōstikoi*. With this name he indicates not all those whom modern scholars call "Gnostics" but only the adherents of a specific sect. It is misleading to call them Sethians (descendants of Seth, the son of Adam), as some scholars do nowadays. Notwithstanding its name, the *Apocryphon of John* (a disciple of Jesus) contains no Christian elements apart from the foreword and some minor interpolations. It can be summarized as follows: from the Unknown God (who exists beyond thought and name) and his spouse (who is his counterpart and mirror) issued the spiritual world. The last of the spiritual entities, Sophia, became wanton and brought forth a monster, the demiurge. He organized the zodiac and the seven planets. He proclaimed: "I am a jealous god, apart from me there is no other." Then a voice was heard, teaching him that above him existed the Unknown God and his spouse. Next, the "first Man in the form of a man" manifested himself to the lower angels. He is the Glory of *Ezekiel* 1:26. His reflection appears in the waters of chaos (cf. the mirror of the Anthropos in *Poimandres*). Thereupon the lower angels created the body of Adam after the image that they had seen, an imitation of the Man, who clearly serves as an ideal archetype for the human body. For a long time the body of Adam lay unable to move, for the seven planetary angels were unable to raise it up. Then Sophia caused the demiurge to breathe the *pneuma* he had inherited from her into the face of his creature. So begins a long struggle between the redeeming Sophia and the malicious demiurge, the struggle for and against the awakening of human spiritual consciousness.

Written in Alexandria about the beginning of the Christian era, the myth of the *Apocryphon of John*, a pivotal and seminal writing, combines the Anthropos model and the Sophia model. It is very complicated and confusing but had enormous influence in the Near East, where so many remnants of great religions survive today. (In the 1980s, for example, there were 420 Samaritans and 30,000 Nestorians.) Even today some 15,000 Mandaeans (the Aramaic term for Gnostics) live in Iraq and Iran. Their religion features ablutions in streaming water and a funerary mass. When a Mandaean has died, a priest performs a complicated rite in order to return the soul to its heavenly abode, where it will receive a spiritual body. In this way, it is believed, the deceased is integrated into the so-called Secret Adam, the Glory, the divine body of God. This name confirms that, along with the Anthropos of *Poimandres* and the Adam Qadmon of later Jewish mysticism, this divine and heavenly figure is ultimately derived from the vision of the prophet Ezekiel. In Mandaean lore Sophia appears in degraded form as a mean and lewd creature called the Holy Spirit. The creation of the world is attributed to a lower demiurge, Ptahil, a pseudonym for the angel Gabriel (who, according to both the Mandaeans and the Magharians, is the angel who created the world).

The apostle Paul (or one of his pupils) maintains that Christ, who is for him the second Adam, is "the head of his Church, which is his body" (*Eph.* 1:22–23). The Christian is integrated into this body through baptism. Mandaean speculations about the Secret Adam may elucidate what Paul meant. In defining his view of the church as the mystical body of Christ, the apostle may be reflecting a familiarity with comparable Jewish and Hellenistic speculations about the *kavod* as the body of God. As a matter of fact, it has become clear from the verses of Ezekiel Tragicus that such ideas circulated in Alexandria long before the beginning of our era. They surfaced in Palestine toward the end of the first century CE in strictly Pharisaic circles that transmitted secret, esoteric traditions about the mystical journey of the sage through the seven heavenly places to behold the god Man on the throne of God. The author of the writing *Shiʿur Qoma*, the "measurement of the Body" of God, reports the enormous dimensions of the members of the Glory. The Orphics had taught that the cosmos was actually a divine body. Already early in Hellenistic Egypt similar speculations arose; these were the origin of the remarkable speculations of Palestinian rabbis concerning the mystical body of God. (These speculations ultimately led to the *Zohar*.) It is no coincidence that the Glory is called Geradamas (Arch-Adam) in some Nag Hammadi writings, Adam Qadmaia in Mandaean sources, and Adam Qadmon in medieval Jewish Gnosticism.

In the ninth century several groups of Islamic Gnostics arose in southern Iraq, where several other Gnostic sects had found refuge during late antiquity and where the Mandaeans continue to live today. The best-known Islamic Gnostics are the Ismāʿīlīyah, of which the Aga Khan is the religious leader. Mythological themes central to their religion are (1) the cycles of the seven prophets; (2) the throne and the letters; (3) Kuni, the creative principle, who is feminine (a typical remythologizing of a monotheistic Father religion); (4) the higher Pentad; (5) the infatuation of the lower demiurge; (6) the seven planets and the twelve signs of the zodiac; (7) the divine Adam; and (8) the fall and ascent of the soul.

Since the discovery of the Nag Hammadi codices it has been established that these themes are best explained as transpositions into an Islamic terminology of the Gnostic mythemes that are found in the *Apocryphon of John* and kindred documents of Jewish Gnosticism.

CHRISTIAN GNOSIS. According to a reliable tradition, Barnabas, a missionary of the Jerusalem congregation, was the first to bring the gospel to Alexandria, a relatively easy journey. Egyptian Christianity is Judaic in origin, not gentile, and the great Egyptian Gnostics seem all to have been of Jewish birth. The adherents of Basilides claimed: "We are no longer Jews and not yet Christians." The followers of Valentinus reported: "When we were Hebrews, we were orphans." Basilides and Valentinus both proclaimed a God beyond the Old Testament God, and both were familiar with the myth of the *Apocryphon of John*, which they christianized. The case of Marcion is similar: he was so well-informed about the Hebrew Bible and its flaws that his father, a bishop, may well be presumed to have been Jewish. Through a certain Cerdo, Marcion came to know an already existing Gnostic system. Those who reject the god of the Old Testament obviously no longer hold to the Jewish faith, but nevertheless still belong ethnically to the Jewish people. Both Valentinus and Marcion went to Rome and were excommunicated there between 140 and 150. Basilides, who stayed in Alexandria, remained a respected schoolmaster there until his death. The Christians in Alexandria were divided among several synagogues and could afford to be tolerant, for a monarchic bishop did not yet exist and their faith was pluriform anyhow. Basilides, Valentinus, and Marcion were Christocentric and let themselves be influenced by the *Gospel of John* and the letters of Paul.

Marcion. When Marcion, a rich shipowner from Sinope in Pontus (on the Black Sea), was excommunicated, he organized an enormous alternative church that persisted for a long time, especially in the East (e.g., in Armenia). Marcion was a violin with one string, a religious genius with one overpowering idea: God, the Father of Jesus, was not the Hebrew YHVH. Like the Gnostics, he distinguished between the Unknown God (whom he felt to be the only genuine God) and a lower divinity, the demiurge, who is responsible for creation and interacts with man. Above all, Marcion was fascinated by Paul's *Letter to the Galatians.* Following Paul, he contrasted the Law of the Old Testament and Israelite religion with the "gospel of forgiveness," which revealed the goodness of God.

Like his hero Paul, Marcion was overwhelmed by the unconditional and unwarranted love of God for poor creatures. This led him to deny the Gnostic idea that man's inmost Self is related to the Godhead. For Marcion, man is nothing more than the creation of a cruel demiurge; the loving God who has rescued him, without any ulterior motive but simply out of a freely bestowed loving kindness, is totally alien to man, his nature, and his fate.

Until Augustine, no one understood Paul as well as Marcion; yet Marcion, the one genuine pupil, misunderstood Paul as well. Notwithstanding his dialectics, Paul never rejected the created world, sexuality, or the people of Israel, as did Marcion.

Basilides. Basilides was active as the leader of a school in Alexandria in the time of the emperors Hadrian (r. 117–138) and Antoninus Pius (r. 138–161). He seems to have been one of those many liberal Jews who had left behind the concept of a personal lord for belief in the Unknown God. Yet he was never excommunicated and remained a respected member of the church of Alexandria until his death.

Basilides must have known the earlier Alexandrian, pre-Christian myth contained in the *Apocryphon of John.* He too begins his cosmogony with the Unknown God, "the not-being God, who made a not-yet-being world out of nothing" by bringing forth a single germ of the All. This germ was the primeval chaos. From it in due time one element after another arose on high, while below there remained only the so-called third sonship, or the Spirit in the spiritual man.

When the time was right, Jesus was enlightened at his baptism in the river Jordan (a typically Jewish-Christian notion). He is considered to be the prototype of all spiritual men, who through his revealing word become conscious of their innermost being, the Spirit, and rise up to the spiritual realm.

When the entire third sonship has redeemed itself, God will take pity on the world, and he will allow the descent of "the great unconsciousness" upon the rest of mankind. Thereafter no one will have even an inkling that there was ever anything like the Spirit. Basilides foresees a godless and classless society.

Valentinus. The greatest Gnostic of all times was the poet Valentinus. Despite his Latin name, he was a Greek born in the Nile Delta around the year 100 and educated in Alexandria. He and his followers did not separate from the church of Alexandria but created an academy for free research, which in turn formed a loose network of local groups within the institutional religion. Even among his opponents Valentinus became renowned for his eloquence and genius.

According to his own words, his views originated in a visionary experience in which he saw a newborn child. This vision inspired a "tragic myth," expressed by Valentinus in a psalm that described how the All emanates from the ground of being, called Depth, and his spouse, called Womb or Silence. Together they bring forth the Christ, or Logos, upon whom all aeons (half ideas, half angels) depend and through whom the All is coherent and connected. Through the revelation of Christ, Valentinus experienced the wholeness of the All, the fullness of being, and the nonentity "I and Thou" (known in Hinduism as *advaita*). Not dualism but duality is the underlying principle of reality, according to Valentinus: God himself is the transcendental unity of Depth and Silence; the aeons of the pleroma (spiritual world) are a diametrical union of the masculine, or creative, and the feminine, or receptive, principles; Christ and Sophia (Wisdom) are a couple (separated for a while on account of the trespass and fall of Sophia but in the end happily reunited). Man and his guardian angel, or transcendental counterpart, celebrate the mystical marriage of bride and bridegroom (the Ego and the Self). Polarity (Gr., *suzugia*; Lat., *coniunctio*) is characteristic of all things spiritual. On the basis of this metaphysical view, Valentinus and his followers valued both sex and marriage, at least for the pneumatics. A preserved fragment from the school of Valentinus gives the following interpretation of Jesus' statement in the *Gospel of John* that the Christian lives in the world but is not from it (*Jn.* 17:14–16): "Whosoever is in the world and has not loved a woman so as to become one with her, is not out of the Truth and will not attain the Truth; but he who is *from* the world and unites with a woman, will not attain the Truth, because he made sex out of concupiscence alone." The Valentinians permitted intercourse only between men and women who were able to experience it as a mystery and a sacrament, namely, those who were pneumatics. They forbade it between those whom they called "psychics" (Jews and Catholics) or "hylics" (materialists), because these two lower classes knew nothing but libido. As the only early Christian on record who spoke lovingly about sexual intercourse and womanhood, Valentinus must have been a great lover.

The Jung Codex. On May 10, 1952, at the behest of the Jung Institute in Zurich, I acquired one of the thirteen codices found at Nag Hammadi in 1945. In honor of the great psychiatrist who helped to put this manuscript at the disposal of competent scholars, it is called the Jung Codex. It contains five Valentinian writings:

1. The *Prayer of the Apostle Paul.*

2. The *Apocryphon of James* is a letter purporting to contain revelations of the risen Jesus, written by James, his brother. In reality, it contains Valentinian speculations grafted onto the root and fatness of the olive tree planted beside the waters of the Nile by Hebrew missionaries from Jerusalem (c. 160).
3. The *Gospel of Truth* is a meditation on the true eternal gospel proclaimed by Christ to awaken man's innermost being, the unconscious Spirit, probably written by Valentinus himself in about 150.
4. The *Epistle to Rheginos concerning the Resurrection* is adequate explanation of Paul's view on the subject: already, here and now, man anticipates eternal life, and after death he will receive an ethereal body.
5. The so-called *Tripartite Treatise* is a systematic and consistent exposition of the history of the All. It describes how the Spirit evolves through the inferno of a materialistic (pagan or "hylic") phase and the purgatory of a moral (Jewish and Catholic or "psychic") phase to the coming of Christ, who inaugurates the *paradiso* of final consummation, in which spiritual man becomes conscious of himself and of his identity with the Unknown God. The author, a leader of the Italic (Roman) school of Valentinianism, was most likely Heracleon (c. 170). It was against this shade of Valentinian gnosis that Plotinus, the Neoplatonic philosopher, wrote his pamphlet *Against the Gnostics* (c. 250).

LATER DEVELOPMENTS. Scholars have always admitted that Origen (c. 180–254), the greatest dogmatician of the Greek church, had much in common with the Valentinians: the spirits fall away from God and become souls before the creation of the world; the world purifies the soul; Jesus brings not only redemption to the faithful but also gnosis to the pneumatics. But whereas Valentinus was said to have taught predestination physics (the teaching that spiritual man was saved by nature), Origen on the contrary allegedly stressed free will. The *Tripartite Treatise* has undermined this apologetic position. There evil is no longer a tragic neurosis that befell Sophia but a free decision. Moreover, this writing is thoroughly optimistic: all is for the best in the best of all possible worlds, and providence educates mankind toward the realization of complete consciousness, as in Origen's soteriology. Some path led from the tragic view of Valentinus to the optimism of Heracleon, and from Heracleon to Origen was only one step more.

The Valentinians of Carthage spoke Latin, whereas the Christians in Rome spoke Greek. Translating their technical terms from Greek, the Valentinians coined Latin equivalents of *infinite, consubstantial, trinity, person,* and *substance.* These terms were eventually adopted by the Roman Catholic church. If ever there was a community that created a special language, it was the school of Valentinus at Carthage.

Mani. Gnosticism became a world religion when Mani (216–277) founded his alternative Christian church, which existed for more than a thousand years with adherents in lands from the Atlantic Ocean to the Pacific. From his fourth until his twenty-fifth year Mani was raised in a Jewish-Christian community of Baptists, followers of the prophet Elxai (c. 100). There he heard, first, that Jesus was "the true prophet," a manifestation of God's glory *(kavod)* who was first embodied in Adam, then revealed himself to the Old Testament patriarchs and was ultimately incarnated in the Messiah, Jesus. He also heard, second, that baptisms and ablutions were necessary for salvation and, third, that God was the origin of evil since Satan was the left hand of God. He modified the first belief, identifying himself as the seal of the prophets, who included the Buddha and Zarathushtra in the East and Jesus in the West. The second belief he rejected; in fact, he admitted no sacraments at all. Against the third belief he, being a cripple, rebelled with all his might. Evil, in Mani's view, did not originate in the world of light but had its source in a different principle, the world of darkness, matter, and concupiscence.

Influenced by encratitic asceticism of the Aramaic Christians of Asia, Mani rejected marriage and the consumption of alcohol and meat, and he designated among his followers an upper class of the elect who lived according to the Sermon on the Mount and a lower class of auditors who were allowed to have wives or concubines and to practice birth control. But very much in the spirit of Valentinus was Mani's primary religious experience. The basis of his entire myth, the encounter with his "twin" or transcendental Self, is Gnostic, very much in the spirit of Valentinus: "I recognized him and understood that he was my Self from whom I had been separated." Mani encountered his spiritual Self at the age of twelve and encountered it a second time at the age of twenty-five. He felt constantly accompanied by his twin, and when he died a martyr in prison he was gazing at this familiar. The encounter with one's twin is central to the life of every Manichaean. The mystery of conjunction, the holy marriage of Ego and Self, is thereby democratized. To illustrate this process, Mani related a myth that is indebted to earlier Gnostic movements. For Mani the world is in truth created by the Living Spirit, a manifestation of God, and not by a lower demiurge. But a split within the deity takes place when the archetypal Man loses in the battle against darkness, is thus overwhelmed, and abandons his soul as sparks of light dispersed throughout the material world and mankind. Man is contaminated in this way by concupiscence, an evil force from the world of darkness. The entire world system is devised to save these light elements and to restore man as Perfect Man in his original purity and integrity.

Augustine (354–430) was a Manichaean auditor for more than nine years before he became a Father of the Roman Catholic church. During that period he wrote a treatise (since lost), *On Beauty and Harmony,* in which he stated that the asexual mind was linked with a completely alien element of ire and concupiscence. As a heresy-hunter he later maintained that concupiscence was not created by God but was instead a consequence of the Fall. The assertion that the reproductive instinct is not a part of human nature does certainly have Manichaean overtones.

The Middle Ages. Manichaeism disappeared completely in the West and had no successors there: the term *medieval Manichee* is a misnomer. And yet Christianity during the Middle Ages both in western and in eastern Europe was not monolithically orthodox. Gnosticism flourished at that time. Such books as *Montaillou* by Emmanuel Le Roy Ladurie and *The Name of the Rose* by Umberto Eco have drawn the attention of a large public of interested outsiders to the existence of dualistic sects such as the Cathari in southern France and northern Italy and the Bogomils (or "friends of God") in Yugoslavia and Bulgaria, because their views resemble those of the ancient Gnostics. Indeed, their affiliation with ancient Gnosticism, if somewhat complicated, is well established.

The Paulicians were typically Armenian sectarians who, persisting into modern times, turned up in 1837 in the village of Arh'wela (in Russian Armenia) with their holy book, the *Key of Truth* (eighth century). Two versions of their doctrine exist. According to one, Jesus was adopted to be the son of God. According to the second version, there are two gods; one is the Father in heaven, while the other is the creator of this world. This can be explained in the following way: Christianity was introduced to Armenia from Edessa at an early date, and Edessa owed its (adoptionist) Christology to Addai, the Jewish-Christian missionary from Jerusalem. When Roman Catholicism was established as the state church in 302 by Gregory the Illuminator, the Christians of Armenia were branded as heretics. Marcionites and Gnostics had taken refuge in these marginal and mountainous regions. They united with the adoptionists to become one sect, the Paulicians, soon a warlike group. The emperors of Byzantium deported quite a few of them to the Balkans, especially to Bulgaria. It was there that the sect of the Bogomils originated, characterized by the belief that the devil (Satanael) created and rules this world. Their influence spread to the West, and from the beginning of the eleventh century gave rise to the church of the Cathari, which was strong in southern France and northern Italy. Thus Gnosticism was never completely suppressed but survived into the Middle Ages.

Modern gnosis. The gnosis of modern times, launched by the shoemaker Jakob Boehme (c. 1600), was generated spontaneously as a result of direct experience. It differs from ancient Gnosticism in that it derives not only the light but also the darkness (not only good but also evil) from the ground of being. Inspired by Boehme is the influential gnosis of the English poet and artist William Blake (1757–1827), the only authentic Gnostic of the entire Anglo-Saxon world. It is in the school of Boehme that the scholarly study of Gnosticism has its roots, beginning with the *Impartial History of the Churches and Heresies* (1699) by Gottfried Arnold. In this extremely learned work all heretics, including all Gnostics, are represented as the true Christians—innocent and slandered lambs.

Ever since, the study of Gnosticism has been an accepted academic subject in Germany, but in Germany alone. In his youth Goethe read Arnold's book and conceived his own Gnostic system, as reported in his autobiography. Toward the end of his life Goethe recalled the love of his youth when he wrote the finale to *Faust*, the hierophany of "the Eternally Feminine," a version of the Gnostic Sophia, the exclusive manifestation of the deity. Johann Lorenz von Mosheim and other great historians also took gnosis quite seriously. The brilliant August Neander, who belonged to the conservative reaction to the Enlightenment called the Great Awakening Revivalism (*Erweckungsbewegung*), wrote his *Genetic Evolution of the Most Important Gnostic Systems* in 1818. Ferdinand Christian Baur, a prominent Hegelian, published his monumental *Christian Gnosis* in 1835, in which he defends the thesis that gnosis was a religious philosophy whose modern counterpart is the idealism of Schelling, Schleiermacher, and Hegel, all based upon the vision of Boehme. According to Baur, even German idealism was a form of gnosis. Yet when "the people of poets and thinkers" became, under Bismarck, a people of merchants and industrial workers, this wonderful empathy, this fantastic feel of gnosis, was almost completely lost.

Adolf von Harnack (1851–1930), the ideologue of Wilhelm's empire, defined Gnosticism as the acute, and orthodoxy as the chronic, hellenization (i.e., rationalization) and hence alienation of Christianity. At the time it was difficult to appreciate the experience behind the Gnostic symbols. Wilhelm Bousset, in his *Main Problems of Gnosis* (1907), described this religion as a museum of hoary and lifeless oriental (Indian, Iranian, Babylonian) fossils. The same unimaginative approach led Richard Reitzenstein, Geo Widengren, and Rudolf Bultmann to postulate an Iranian mystery of salvation that never existed but was supposed to explain Gnosticism, Manichaeism, and Christianity.

Existentialism and depth psychology were needed to rediscover the abysmal feelings that inspired the movement of gnosis. Hans Jonas (*The Gnostic Religion*, 1958) has depicted these feelings as dread, alienation, and an aversion to all worldly existence, as if the Gnostics were followers of Heidegger. In the same vein are the writings of Kurt Rudolph, the expert on Mandaeism.

Under the influence of Carl Gustav Jung, I and other scholars (e.g., Henri-Charles Puech and Károly Kerényi) have interpreted the Gnostic symbols as a mythical expression (i.e., projection) of self-experience. As a lone wolf, the Roman Catholic convert Erik Peterson suggested that the origins of Gnosticism were not Iranian or Greek but Jewish. The Gnostic writings from Nag Hammadi have shown Jung and Peterson to be in the right. At last the origins, development, and goal of this perennial philosophy have come to light.

SEE ALSO Aga Khan; Cathari; Demiurge; Hermes Trismegistos; Ḥokhmah; Mandaean Religion; Mani; Manichaeism; Marcion; Sophia; Theosophical Society.

BIBLIOGRAPHY

Jonas, Hans. *The Gnostic Religion: The Message of the Alien God and the Beginnings of Christianity.* 2d ed., rev. & enl. Boston, 1963.

Pagels, Elaine H. *The Gnostic Gospels.* New York, 1979.

Quispel, Gilles. *Gnostic Studies.* 2 vols. Istanbul, 1974–1975.

Robinson, James M., et al. *The Nag Hammadi Library in English.* San Francisco, 1977.

Rudolph, Kurt. *Gnosis.* San Francisco, 1983.

GILLES QUISPEL (1987)

GNOSTICISM: GNOSTICISM FROM ITS ORIGINS TO THE MIDDLE AGES [FURTHER CONSIDERATIONS]

The term *Gnosticism* was coined in the eighteenth century to designate a composite ensemble of sects that arose from the late first century to the fourth century CE. These sects were classified by the Church Fathers among the earlier Christian heresies. Their adepts, in contrast with common believers, claimed to be endowed through an extraordinary revelation with spiritual awareness (Gk. *gnōsis*) concerning both God's hidden nature and the true human self, and to have deduced from that a mythological or theosophical account of the universe, the origin of evil, and otherworldly salvation. But the Gnostic phenomenon as a whole deserves a more flexible approach. Inasmuch as these sects, for the most part, were building up an entire doctrinal system of their own rather than simply discussing existing Christian doctrine (unlike later Christological or Trinitarian heresies), Gnosticism could hardly be reduced to an odd variant of Christianity; it was something quite original, although its dependence on the Judeo-Christian background remains central. Moreover, since the Gnostic movement existed historically in many diversified forms and single perspectives, any attempt at a specific definition is unsuitable. According to the Messina Congress (Bianchi, 1967), the name *Gnosticism* should be limited to the "Gnostic systems of the second century" referred to by Church Fathers and contemporary original texts; otherwise one should rather speak of *Gnosis* with its generic meaning of "knowledge of the divine mysteries." This is, of course, a compromise formula, which cannot obscure the fact that the foregoing roots of the second-century systems belong fully to the complexity of the Gnostic phenomenon.

THE EVIDENCE. Until the mid-twentieth century, the major sources for Gnosticism were the Church Fathers who dealt with heretics, the heresiologists (mainly Irenaeus, Hippolytus, Clement of Alexandria, and Epiphanius); some New Testament apocryphal writings (*Acts of Thomas, Acts of John*); and the double (Greek and Latin) version of a didactic romance falsely ascribed to Clement of Rome (*Pseudo-Clementines*). The only available Gnostic texts in the Coptic language, dating to the fourth century, were the two *Books of Jeu* and the so-called *Scriptum sine titulo* (*Bruce Codex*, from the purchaser's name, 1769) and the *Pistis Sophia* (*Askew Codex*, 1772). The *Corpus Hermeticum*, composed between the second and the fourth centuries and known in Europe since the Renaissance, is also commonly considered to be a Gnostic document. The *Corpus Hermeticum* numbers sixteen treatises in Greek, followed by fragments reportedly by the Byzantine erudite John of Stobi, Macedonia (Stobaeus), in which the salvific role of *gnōsis* is stressed in a pagan Greek-Egyptian framework. A dramatic increase in scholarly knowledge on Gnosticism took place thanks to the discovery in 1945 of the thirteen codices of Nag Hammadi, Egypt, which contained the *Apocryphon of John* (in four versions) and the *Gospel of Thomas*, along with forty-eight other remarkable writings in Coptic. All Nag Hammadi texts are thought to have been translated from Greek originals of the second or third century.

HISTORICAL OUTLINE: THE EMERGENCE STAGE. The earliest forms of Gnosticism (c. 50–120 CE) originated within different religious milieus of the late-first-century Middle East, in which a sectarian nonrabbinical Judaism and a still fluid and creative Christian mission were unfolding, sometimes reacting upon one another.

Baptist Samaritan sects. The movement founded by John the Baptist split in several offshoots (Jesus' group included therein) after John's death around 27 CE. In one of these sects, headed in turn by three Samaritans (Dositheus, Simon, and Menander), there emerged for the first time the idea that the world was the creation of more or less depraved angels who "ignored" the existence of the highest God—a striking radicalization of the apocalyptic angelology that was widespread in contemporary Judaism. The baptismal ritual therefore accomplished not only the remission of sins but also a regeneration, by means of which the natural death allotted to humans by the ruling angels could be overcome.

Analogously to concurrent Christian preaching, the Samaritan baptist sect requested from its adherents a belief in the person of the founder, or actual leader, who was viewed as the embodiment of God's power, spirit, or wisdom, and as the redeemer and revealer of true "knowledge." But unlike Christianity, this knowledge was given a marked mythological aspect. Irenaeus reports (1.23) that Simon drew up a mythical theology according to which God's personified power and wisdom (Gk. *dunamis, ennoia*) had been seized or raped by the wicked angels, and imprisoned successively in many female bodies, at last appearing as Simon's own concubine Helen, a former prostitute. Simon himself would have been the incarnation of the supreme God descended on earth to release her.

While the Simonian myth still seemed to be a personal adaptation of the prophet Hosea's story (*Hos.* 3:1), a decisive step toward an anti-biblical and anti-Jewish attitude was made by Saturninus (or Satornil, possibly an Aramaic version of the Latin name) operating around 100 CE in Antioch, Syria, where the sect had moved under Menander. Working out a combined interpretation of *Genesis* 1:27 and 2:7, Saturninus taught that seven angelic powers (a plain allusion to the Jewish godhead) fashioned a puppy resembling the image of the higher God in the form of a man. The inanimate *gōlem* was given by God the spirit of life, through which he gained a higher-ranking status than his fabricators (Irenaeus 1.25). This narrative was variously echoed in later Gnostic mythology. Hippolytus (6.9–18) reports an abstract of an alleged Simonian writing, *Great Revelation,* in which nothing of the Ennoia-Helen myth is mentioned. It seems a qabbalistic Midrash of *Genesis* 1–2, enriched with philosophical references. The godly first principle, symbolized as "fire," has a double nature, a standing one (Gk. *estōs*) and a dynamic one; the latter includes seven "powers," of which the seventh represents the divinity as concealed inside every being. This book was presumably written in the late second century.

Jewish-Christianity. Other offspring of the former baptist movement joined the Christians. The outcome of such mingling was the so-called Jewish-Christianity prevailing in Palestine and Syria, which, besides the baptismal ritual, maintained the basic observances of the Mosaic Torah. The Jewish-Christians held the "Christ" (Messiah) to be an eternal aspect of God's hidden nature, his "spirit" and "truth," who revealed himself throughout sacred history wearing the flesh of elected men or prophets (this idea of a forthcoming revelation can be traced back to the Dead Sea Scrolls). Such a function of the "true prophet" had been performed in the past by Adam, Seth, Henoch, Melchizedek, Moses, and more recently by Jesus, an ordinary human being on whom the "Christ" would have been "poured" in the moment of his baptism. The *Pseudo-Clementines* and the heresiological accounts about Cerinthus, the Nazoraeans, and the Hebionites illustrate such an interpretation of the Jesus figure (Irenaeus 1.26; Hippolytus 7.33–34; Epiphanius 28–30).

Around 100 CE a dissident Babylonian Jew named (or nicknamed) Elcasai begun to preach about an ecstatic experience he would have had, in which the Christ, along with his "sister" (or spouse), the spirit, appeared to him in their eternal form as a male and a female figure of colossal size (Hippolytus 9.13; Epiphanius 19). Elcasai gathered a new baptist congregation (perhaps a proper religion more than a sect, somewhat similar to the Mandaeans of Iraq) with a foremost apocalyptic doctrine, in addition to a peculiar Christian ingredient: Christ was apparently both God's son and a divine substance scattered everywhere (*Cologne Codex,* p. 97), as is also said in the *Gospel of Thomas* (77, and cf. Epiphanius 26.3). The young Mani took over this topic, probably while growing up in the center of this congregation in lower Mesopotamia. From the Parthian territory Elcasaitic, the movement spread rapidly into Roman Syria and gained adherents among the Christians of the Roman capital.

Christian radicalism and theosophy. The early Christian communities that broke with Jewish national religion (though keeping much of Judaic lore and symbolism) became, in a different way, original settings of Gnostic ideas. The starting point seems to have been a radicalization of the teachings of the apostles Paul and John, particularly in the sharp antithesis between flesh and spirit, the stressing of charismatic faculties and performances, and the rejection of the Jewish Law, which was viewed as imposed by defective angelic powers called *archons.* Some Christian thinkers drew the assumption, which is found throughout the history of Gnosticism, that the spirit (or the soul) alone is both object and subject of salvation, since all flesh belongs to the evil realm of the archons. They consistently denied Jesus' real incarnation and bodily resurrection. The followers of Jesus should also have no concern for their bodies, because only souls can be saved, namely by faith. Two radical consequences were in keeping with this rationale: the "elects" could either abolish any socially acknowledged norm, pursuing asceticism instead (Encratites: Clement, *Stromateis* 3.6 and 13), or they could yield themselves to immorality, since they had no ethical requirement with which to comply during their earthly existence (Nicolaites: Clement 3.4; Epiphanius 25).

Most likely, such milieus diffused the word *gnōstikos* (rarely attested in Greek, maybe an adaptation of the Hebrew *maśkīl),* which usually designated the conscious, well-cultivated Christian believer, but was also used by Christian radicals to describe themselves, insofar as they presumed a deeper insight and felt they were allowed an unrestrained freedom. Only in a few cases, however, did the term serve as a self-definition for Gnostic sects.

The Christianity of Alexandria, Egypt, became a veritable cradle of Gnosticism. The local church had a Jewish-Christian origin, gaining its members from both the Hebrew minority and the Greek majority of the town. The latter became dominant after the collapse of the Jewish community with the revolt of 115 to 117, giving anti-Jewish attitudes the upper hand. The Alexandrian ambience encouraged theological inquiry, which was developing freely since no definite border between "orthodoxy" and "heresy" existed yet. Various cultural patterns were available for Christian intellectuals *(gnōstikoi)* in conformity with their different backgrounds: Judaic apocalypticism, speculation on divine wisdom (as it had been undertaken by Philo), Greek philosophy, and Hellenistic mystery religions.

The transition from the Christian radical meaning of *gnōstikos* to "Gnostic" in the modern sense is exemplified by Carpocrates, a Greek Alexandrine active in the first decades of the second century. Carpocrates taught that Jesus was an ordinary man whose soul had realized the existence of a higher unknown God; Carpocrates therefore despised Jewish customs as devotion to maleficent world-ruling angels. Carpocrates and his son Epiphanes led a libertine sect of self-named Gnostics that combined extreme Pauline antinomism with topics borrowed from ancient Greek sophists (e.g., the appreciation of "nature" against social convention) and Jesus worship with syncretistic cults (Irenaeus 1.25; Clement 3.2).

Similar views were held later by Prodicus, the Antitacti (Clement 3.4), and other sects hinting at re-evaluating the negative figures of the Old Testament, such as the Cainites (Irenaeus 1.31).

A different perspective is offered by what was possibly the earliest Gnostic document known to us (c. 100), a Nag Hammadi treatise in the form of a letter, titled by the alleged author's name, *Eugnostos the Blessed.* It is a theosophical account of the supreme godhead displayed as a fourfold structure that expands progressively: (1) the all-transcendent God; (2) his likeness, the Light Man or the Father; (3) the latter's son, the Son of Man; and (4) the Son of the Son of Man, or the Savior. Figures 2 to 4 each include a female partner named *Sophia* (wisdom). The fourth couple engenders 365 "magnitudes" or space-time dimensions (aeons) in the shape of angels, who typify the cosmic order. Such a revelation of a quadripartite godhead was rooted in Judaic mystical circles building on *Ezekiel* 1. Christianity is not mentioned in the text, but the references to *Father, Son,* and *Savior* can hardly be understood as other than Christian suggestions. Sometime later the *Eugnostos* treatise was more explicitly Christianized when its contents were recycled under the title *Sophia of Jesus Christ* (Nag Hammadi codex III).

MATURE GNOSTICISM (C. 120–200). The Gnostic movement reached its acme during the Antonine age. There was a proliferation of groups, each having a distinctive rationale, even if links existed among at least a few of them and some aspects might occasionally be shared. Little is known about the social composition of such groups. In the Syrian and Egyptian countryside the adepts were poor farmers, but in the towns the groups included wealthy citizens, merchants, and intellectuals. Members of these groups apparently had no interest in political issues. In this time of religious persecution, Catholics were blaming Gnostics for practicing dissimulation.

Sethite-Barbeloite *Gnosis.* One self-designated Gnostic School, according to Irenaeus (1.11, 30), introduced a female as a full member into the male scheme of the quadripartite godhead (*Eugnostos*) and made her the protagonist of a myth that explained the origin of evil by means of an accident that occurred in the divine "family." There are two versions of the myth. In one version the fourfold scheme is personified as an androgynous figure with prevailing female traits called Barbēlō ("God-[is]-in-the-Four" in Aramaic), the Daughter-Spouse of God, who generates the Son (Christ) and the chief of the lower angels or archons, Yaldabaoth (Aramaic *yalda',* "youth"), a caricature of the biblical creator. Barbēlō prostitutes herself to the archons willingly (unlike the Simonian Ennoia myth) and consequently some part of her divine *dunamis* falls in their hands, forming human souls to be rescued (Epiphanius 25.3, 26.10). In the second version a female member of the quaternary named Holy Spirit, Wisdom (Gk. *Sophia*), or "Harlot" (Gk. *Prounikos*) ventures to the outer darkness and gives birth there to Yaldabaoth, the minor God who creates the world along with a cohort of maleficent archons. Later she repents. An interpretation of the *Genesis* narrative, similar to that of Saturninus, follows. The elevation of the first human, created by the archons as their servant, is illustrated by an inverted exegesis of the biblical episode about the tree of knowledge: Yaldabaoth forbids eating from the tree, but Adam is induced to contradict him (antinomism) by Sophia, temporarily embodied in Eve (or in the serpent). So what the Bible explained as a sin becomes here advancement, through which Adam obtains the *gnōsis* and the divine *pneuma* inherited thereafter by his third son, Seth (Irenaeus 1.30, Epiphanius 37.3).

Both versions have been revised and amalgamated in the *Apocryphon of John,* composed in Egypt around 120, which gives the standard form of the story (Nag Hammadi codex II). In this text, Barbēlō and Sophia are two distinct figures. Barbēlō, the likeness of the absolute, produces a complicated structure of aeons (the *plērōma*) among which the heavenly Seth (linked to Christ) is exalted as the ancestor of the Gnostic "race," having as an earthly counterpart Adam's son. Sophia is a subordinate aeon who carries the responsibility for the rise of the evil powers, but who also brings about human salvation. Jesus plays a key role as an earthly apparition of the heavenly Seth. The Sethites believed in predestination, as usual in sectarian circles. Only the true "seed of Seth" is saved because it shares the divine "pneumatic" nature and ought to return to its "place" of belonging; the other humans, creatures of the archons, have nowhere to go after death, so their spiritless souls are recycled in the lower world through reincarnation. The main Sethite ritual was baptism.

Recent scholarship has labeled the doctrines contained in the *Apocryphon of John* and related Nag Hammadi texts as Sethian Gnosticism. This is confusing, considering that the only "Sethians" mentioned in ancient sources are two later sects (Hippolytus 5.19–22 and Epiphanius 39), whose views had nothing in common and who had nothing to do with so-called Sethian Gnosticism. Of course the symbolic figure of Seth (Klijn, 1977) could be applied in very different contexts.

Gospel of Thomas. This masterwork of Gnostic literature was composed in northern Syria around 120 CE—the final accomplishment of an alternative Jesus tradition based on the "Lord's sayings" (*logia*) and not on biographical narrative. There are 114 such *logia* collected in Nag Hammadi Codex II, many of them converging with or altering verses of the canonical Gospels, but presumably other compilations existed, as can be inferred from references in the sources (Hippolytus 5.7.20). Any mythological frame is absent. Jesus is portrayed as a teacher who spoke in riddles and symbols. The central Gnostic notion is that of the "inside Man" or "Light-Man"—that is, the divine self (not the human "soul") hidden in the "garment" of flesh (24, 37). Being the everlasting "image" of God, this "inside Man" precedes earthly life and will be encountered in glory after death (18, 19). The "Hymn of the Pearl" in the *Acts of Thomas* (108–112) reflects such an idea.

Basilides was a prominent Christian theologian of Alexandria in the mid-second century CE. Only a few fragments of his ponderous works are extant. His main issue was the notion of divine grace assuring the salvation of the elects, a theory the heresiologists interpreted as natural predestination (frag. 11). Deeply influenced by Platonism, Basilides imputed sin to the embodiment of souls (frags. 6, 7) and explained human suffering as the consequence of sins committed in a previous existence (thus admitting reincarnation) since God should by no means be the cause of evil (frags. 4, 5). Basilides' disciples gave to his teachings a distinct Gnostic mark, as evidenced by the divergent reports of Irenaeus (1.24) and Hippolytus (7.20–27). Irenaeus's report looks like *Eugnostos*: a divine quaternary (denominated by Greek philosophical concepts) followed by 365 angels; God's first-born Son descends assuming the likeness of Jesus in order to free souls from the cosmic powers, but he only seemingly suffers death on the cross (docetism). Hippolytus's report also includes a divine quadruplet comprising the transcendent God and three "sonships." The third sonship falls into the lower regions under the rule of the archons and becomes the human souls; the archons acknowledge, however, the primacy of the true God and are converted to Him. Finally, Jesus, a man of the archontic world enlightened by the Spirit, preaches the gospel to bring about the rise of the third sonship to its due place.

Valentinus was another famous Christian theologian, Egyptian by birth, who taught in Rome in about the same period, well cultivated both in Platonic-Pythagorean philosophy and in Judaic mysticism. Valentinus described in fascinating imagery the likeness between God and humans, the intelligible sphere and the worldly reality sphere (frags. 1, 5), and the struggle inside the human "heart" between demonic influences and the Father's grace through Jesus the savior, the latter being conceived in a docetic way (frags. 2, 3). Analogously to Basilides, his thought was given a major Gnostic facet by his disciples. Valentinianism thus became the most dangerous adversary for the heresiologists, who provide an extensive account of it (Irenaeus 1.1–15, Hippolytus 6.29–36).

Valentinianism shares many features with Sethite-Barbeloite systems, though omitting their nomenclature. The myth of the aeon Sophia's fall is the central event. It is motivated, however, not through the crude sexual symbolism of the "Harlot" but by her willful emulation of the Father's generative act. Her incapacity to do so brings about the material world with its Fabricator (Demiurge), a defective but righteous God. Adam is given flesh and soul by the Demiurge, and *pneuma* (the divine self) by the repentant Sophia, but only one of his three sons (Seth) inherits it (Theodotus 54). Consequently there are three "natures" of humans: the "material" ones (*hulikoi*), who end in perdition; the "morally endowed" ones (*psukhikoi*), capable of a lower-range salvation; and the "spiritual" ones (*pneumatikoi*), predestinated to return to their divine place, having been appropriately instructed by Jesus' revelation.

Leading representatives of Valentinianism were Heracleon (who wrote a famous commentary on the *Gospel of John*), and Ptolemy, both operating in Rome. Driven out of the Roman church, the Valentinians spread their congregations in Syria and Egypt. Another community was founded in southern Gaul by Marcus the Magician, a noteworthy thinker who interpreted the Valentinian *plērōma* on behalf of a symbolic speculation about numbers and alphabet letters. This reflects a Jewish esoteric background.

Marcion. Coming from Asia Minor, "Little Mark" (Gk. *Markiōn*) preached in Rome around 150 CE his original vision of Christianity, which was grounded upon the antithesis between the righteous but merciless God of the Old Testament, who is the Demiurge of the material world, and the higher God of love, who sent Jesus Christ in order to free believers from the yoke of the law. Whether Marcion's theology can be classified as Gnostic is a long-debated question, but a few links are indeed evident, at least with some Gnostic groups: the distinction between the transcendent, "foreign" God and the creator; the emphasized anti-Jewish tendency; the idea of a purely spiritual salvation that excludes resurrection; and the docetic interpretation of the Jesus figure, denying his natural birth and bodily reality. The Marcionites were following a rigidly ascetic morality.

Serpent Gnostics. A few sects assumed their denomination after the "snake" symbol: the Naassenes (Heb. *nāḥāš*), also self-designated "Gnostics"; the Ophites or Ophians (Gk. *ophis*); and the Serpentarians (Lat. *serpens*). Moreover, the snake symbol is given a certain role by the Perates (from the Greek "nomads," or maybe from the Aramaic name of the Euphrates River), the Sethians, and the followers of an otherwise unknown Justin. The common geographical setting was Syria-Mesopotamia. The Ophites shared the Prounikos myth with the so-called Gnostic school and stressed the revealer function of the serpent toward Adam and Eve. Ritual handling of snakes was reportedly performed (Epiphanius 37). The Serpentarians' doctrine had the widespread Gnostic scheme of seven devilish archons of the material world (the Jewish God among them), arisen by a transgression of one member of the upper divine quaternary. Curiously, not a word about serpents is reported in the source (Theodoretus 11.78).

Once more a very different face of the Gnostic phenomenon is offered in the sects reported by Hippolytus (5.7–27). The general frame in this case is a triadic system of principles: (1) the supreme God; (2) an intermediary divine entity, sometimes associated with the serpent; and (3) matter, chaos, or darkness. According to the Naassenes, the heavenly Man—God's primary self-revelation—is lured by an earthly *gōlem* that resembles him, and he pours his "spirit" into the *gōlem*. The spirit remains consequently caught within human souls, but will be delivered as a result of Jesus' descent to earth. The snake (but also the phallus) symbolizes the spirit's yearning toward the highness. The Naassenes were eager to collect a huge amount of evidence derived from the Hellenistic mystery cults in order to indicate that pagan religion was also pursuing similar tenets and had similar purposes.

For the Perates, the serpent represents God's Son, swinging between the mutually opposed Father and matter. His serpentine movements imprint the forms of the fatherly powers on shapeless matter, which thence produces the multiplicity of living beings in the natural world. However, this scheme, borrowed from Plato's *Timaeus,* assumes here a negative meaning because worldly becoming is mastered by malignant astral forces from which the divine forms need to be saved. The serpent, portrayed as *logos* or Christ, implements also a revealer and a redeemer function. The creed of the Sethians is very similar. Numberless powers contained in the three principles (light, spirit, and darkness) clash and the natural world is grounded on the resulting mixture, with an awful winged serpent symbolizing the force that rules it. Christ disguises himself as a serpent in order to assist incognito the salvation of the spiritual particles dispersed in nature. The *Paraphrasis of Šēem* (Nag Hammadi Codex VII) matches this doctrine, but the savior is named here *Derdekeas* instead of Christ. The Sethian myth anticipates Manichaeism in several features.

Another triadic system, but without snake symbolism, was held by the Docetes (Hippolytus 8.8–9), a Christian sect with an optimistic view analogous to that of Valentinus and Basilides. Christ is the common "fruit" generated by all the powers of the three principles. Being more of a comprehensive symbol than a real person, Christ is thought to assume as many faces as there are religious visions trying to grasp his mystery.

Hermetism. The opening *Corpus Hermeticum* treatise, *Poimandres* (the meaning of the title is unclear) is close to the Gnostic mythical narrative. The second-born God's Son, named Man (the former being the Demiurge), is lured down by his own luminous likeness, which he has cast on lower Nature, while Nature becomes enamored of him and embraces him warmly on his descent. This mutual misunderstanding grounds the conjunction of spiritual and material elements, which make up human reality. The revelation of Hermes, "the thrice most Great" (*trismegistos*), was an attempt to appraise pagan tradition on behalf of Platonic concepts, but Judaic influences were also involved (*Corpus Hermeticum* III). Unlike the Gnostics, Hermetism suggested a predominantly positive vision of the world as upholding divine providence, immortality of the soul, and free will. Only the earthly sphere is affected by evil, due to the presence of matter, astral powers, demons, and fate. Through philosophical reflection, the enlightened one releases himself from bodily bounds and awakens to the awareness of his divine self (*Corpus Hermeticum* X, XII, XIII).

LATER DEVELOPMENTS (C. 200–390). During the third century the increasing aversion of the Catholic Church toward heretics, along with a general setback in the cultural and economic conditions of the Roman Empire, led to a decline of the Gnostic movement. Rebuffed by official Christianity, Valentinian and Marcionite congregations survived for a time in Asia, keeping a low profile. The more cultivated Sethite-Barbeloite sectarians attempted instead to find a new haven within Platonic philosophy, but encountered disdain from Plotinus (*Enneads* 2.9), whose lectures some of them had been attending in Rome around 260. The last masterworks of Gnostic literature were composed in this circle: *Zostrianos, Allogenes,* and *Marsanes* (Nag Hammadi Codices VIII, X, XI). Unlike earlier Sethite writings, there is little interest in mythology or the destiny of humankind in these works; the *plērōma* with its hierarchy of divine beings is nothing but a figured frame in which the inner meditation of the elect takes place, like an ecstatic voyage, mounting stage by stage until the identification of the true self with the One.

In the Constantinian age many sects were still abiding in the Syrian-Palestinian countryside: Elcasaites, Sethians, Archontics, Severians, Audians (Epiphanius 19, 38, 40, 45, 70; Theodoretus 11.63). These were mostly tiny ascetic groups, the last one notably pro-Jewish, whose rationales repeated in narrower form the topic of the wicked archons and the struggle of the elects against them. This same struggle was also interpreted by some fanciful Egyptian antinomian sects (Epiphanius 26.3–4) in the form of free sex performed as a sacramental rite and representing the appropriate means for impoverishing the archons of the life-energy they would have snatched from Barbēlō and concealed in human bodies.

The writings of the *Bruce* and *Askew* codices belong to the devotional ascetic side of Egyptian late Gnosticism. They offer an abstruse and overwrought description (with Sethite nomenclature) of the full-scale *plērōma,* ranging from the Godfather down to the earth, with passwords allowing the souls of deceased Gnostics to cross the angelic boundaries and ascend safely to the upper levels. When Christianity became the state religion of the Roman Empire in 391, all these sects went underground or over to Manichaeism, which carried out in its own way the heritage of Gnostic thought.

GENERAL OVERVIEW. What we now call *Gnosticism* is actually nothing but a set of topics singly elaborated, sometimes with similarities, by multifarious sects, each of which had a different origin and a peculiar placing at the crossroads of Judaism, Christianity, and the Hellenistic religions. These sects had in common only a kind of insight—a hermeneutics—that aimed to grasp a deeper truth in the existing religious or philosophical tradition, a truth that professional clerics and philosophers would have been unaware of.

Three elements were amalgamated through the implementation of such a project. The first was the investigation of the supreme deity above all ethnically determinate gods, which comes from Judaic esotericism. This deity is not a single being but a structure, thus bearing in its own complexity—and consequent fragility—the premise for the occurrence of evil described in mythical language (the same topic will be found in the Qabbalah). God is moreover the inexhaustible life energy (Light) that all inferior aeons, angels, and demons are yearning to share or to seize. Light essentially shines out of itself, and thus brings about the hidden God's likeness, revealing itself in human form either as heavenly Man or as Light-Man inside earthly humans. Salvation, as an actual process, means the recovery of the divine substance fallen outwards and scattered in the material sphere under the rule of the cosmic powers; from a subjective viewpoint, the discovery of one's deepest self.

Secondly, there is the Christian element. Salvation cannot be accomplished by moral deeds or by philosophical learning unless God's grace intervenes through the descent and commitment of a savior—it does not matter if the savior is named *Christ* or has another name—who restores his "brothers" to the place to which they belong. The stress on the symbolic features of the redeemer figure forms the basic difference with respect to the more realistic Catholic Christology.

But Gnosticism is not only engaged in theological speculation, because awareness of "mysteries" implies a better knowledge of the natural and historical world. That is the third element—the acquaintance of most Gnostic groups with Hellenistic culture. Because this world, though degraded, displays somehow an "imitation" (*tupos*) of the divine realm, both natural phenomena and the achievements of human culture can be exploited in order to recognize therein traces and evidence of Gnostic truth.

See Also Hellenistic Religions; Hermetism; Mani; Manichaeism, overview article; Nag Hammadi; Platonism.

Bibliography

Sources

Anthologies include Werner Foerster, *Gnosis: A Selection of Gnostic Texts* (Oxford, 1972–1974); Bentley Layton, *The Gnostic Scriptures* (Southampton, UK, 1987), in English; and Josep Montserrat Torrents, *Los gnósticos* (Madrid, 1983), in Spanish.

The Nag Hammadi texts are available in James Robinson, ed., *The Nag Hammadi Library in English* (New York, 1977; rev. ed., San Francisco, 1988). The single treatises of the library have been edited separately with translation and commentary in the Nag Hammadi Studies series by Brill Academic Publishers (Leiden) and the Bibliothèque copte de Nag Hammadi, Section Textes, series from Presses de l'Université Laval (Québec, Canada) and Editions Peeters (Louvain, Belgium). Particularly useful is *The Apocryphon of John: Synopsis of Nag Hammadi Codices II, 1; III, 1; IV, 1; with BG 8502,2*, edited by Michael Waldstein and Frederick Wisse (Leiden, 1995); and *Biblioteca de Nag Hammadi,* Vol. 1, Spanish translation by Josep Montserrat Torrents, with Francisco García Bazán and Antonio Piñero Saenz, 2d rev. ed. (Madrid, 2000).

For other original Gnostic texts, see *Pistis Sophia* and *The Book of Jeu and the Untitled Text of the Bruce Codex*, Coptic texts edited by Carl Schmidt with an English translation (both Leiden, 1978). Standard editions of the heresiologists include Irenaeus of Lyon, *Contre les hérésies*, Greek text and French translation by Adelin Rousseau and Louis Doutreleau (Paris, 1979). Clement of Alexandria's extant writings in Greek were edited by Otto Stählin, 2d ed. by Ludwig Früchtel (Berlin, 1905–1970), vol. 2, *Stromata I–VI,* vol. 3, *Stromata VII–VIII,* translated into German as *Des Clemens von Alexandreia Teppiche* (Munich, 1937) and into Italian as *Stromati: Note di vera filosofia* (Milan, 1985). Clement's extracts of the Valentinian Theodotus, *Extraits de Théodote*, were edited and translated by François M. Sagnard (Paris, 1948). Hippolytus of Rome, *Refutatio omnium haeresium*; Greek text edited by Miroslav Marcovich (Berlin and New York, 1986). Epiphanius of Salamis, Cyprus, *Panarion*, bk. 1, sects 1–46, translated by Frank Williams (Leiden, 1987). Tertullian, *Adversus Marcionem*, edited and translated by Ernest Evans (Oxford, UK, 1972). *Adversus Valentinianos*, translated into French by Jean-Claude Fredouille, (Paris, 1981). Theodor Bar Koni, *Liber scholiorum*, translated into French by Robert Hespel (Louvain, Belgium, 1984). Pseudo-Clementines, *Die Pseudoklementinen*; vol. 1, *Homilien*, edited by Bernhard Rehm, 2d ed. edited by Franz Paschke (Berlin, 1969); vol. 2, *Recognitiones*, edited by Bernhard Rehm (Berlin, 1965); vol. 3, *Konkordanz zu den Pseudoklementinen*; vol. 3.1, Latin concordance; vol. 3.2, Greek concordance, edited by Georg Strecker (Berlin, 1986 and 1989). Also available are *Les homélies clémentines*, translated into French by André Siouville (Paris, 1933; reprint, Lagrasse, France, 1991); and *Recognitiones*, edited by André Schneider and Luigi Cirillo with French translation (Turnhout, Belgium, 1999).

For the Cologne Manichaean Codex as a source for Elcasaitism, see *Der Kölner Mani-Kodex*, edited by Albert Henrichs and Ludwig Koenen, with a German translation (Opladen, Germany, 1988). For apocryphal acts, letters, apocalypses, see *New Testament Apocrypha*, edited by Wilhelm Schneemelcher, English translation by Robert McLachlan Wilson (Louisville, Ky., 1991). For the *Corpus Hermeticum*, see *La révélation d'Hermès Trismégiste*, with Greek text and French translation by André-Jean Festugière (Paris, 1952–1954).

Many original Gnostic and heresiological documents are available in English on *The Gnosis Archive*, with related links, at *www.gnosis.org*. These translations are useful but not free of errors or misunderstandings, and they should be used with caution.

Literature

General literature includes David M. Scholer, *Nag Hammadi Bibliography 1948–1969* (Leiden, 1972) and *Nag Hammadi Bibliography 1970–1994* (Leiden, 1997). Older monographs include Ferdinand Christian Baur, *Die christliche Gnosis: Oder die christliche Religionsphilosophie in ihrer geschichtlichen Entwicklung* (Tübingen, Germany, 1835; reprint, Darmstadt, Germany, 1967); Hans Leisegang, *Die Gnosis* (1924), 5th ed. (Stuttgart, 1985); Hans Jonas, *Gnosis und spätantiker Geist*, vol. 1 (Göttingen, Germany, 1934), vol. 2 (Göttingen, Germany, 1954); and Hans Jonas, *The Gnostic Religion* (Boston, 1963; reprint, New York, 1970).

More recent comprehensive works include Charles-Henri Puech, *En quête de la gnose* (Paris, 1978); Elaine Pagels, *The Gnostic Gospels* (New York, 1978); Kurt Rudolph, *Gnosis: The Nature and History of Gnosticism* (San Francisco, 1983); Giovanni Filoramo, *A History of Gnosticism* (Oxford, and Cambridge, Mass., 1990); Aldo Magris, *La logica del pensiero gnostico* (Brescia, Italy, 1997); Christoph Markschies, *Die*

Gnosis (Munich, 2001); and Karen L. King, *What is Gnosticism?* (Cambridge, Mass., 2003).

Collected papers of famous scholars include Alexander Böhlig, *Mysterion und Wahrheit* (Leiden, 1968); Ugo Bianchi, *Selected Essays* (Leiden, 1978); Kurt Rudolph, *Gnosis und spätantike Religionsgeschiche* (Leiden, 1996); and Carsten Colpe, *Kleine Schriften* (Berlin, 2002). Miscellaneous works that have marked the history of scholarship on the issue include Ugo Bianchi, ed., *Le origini dello gnosticismo* (Leiden, 1967); Martin Krause, ed., *Essays on the Nag Hammadi Texts* (Leiden, 1975) and *Gnosis and Gnosticism,* vol. 1 (Leiden, 1977); Robert McLachlan Wilson, ed., *Nag Hammadi and Gnosis* (Leiden, Netherlands, 1978); Martin Krause, ed., *Gnosis and Gnosticism,* vol. 2 (Leiden, 1981); Bentley Layton, ed., *The Rediscovery of Gnosticism* (Leiden, 1980–1981); Charles W. Hedrik and Robert Hogdson, eds., *Nag Hammadi: Gnosticism and Early Christianity* (Peabody, Mass., 1986); Michel Tardieu and Jean-Daniel Dubois, *Introduction à la littérature gnostique,* vol. 1 (Paris, 1986); and John D. Turner, ed., *The Nag Hammadi Library after Fifty Years* (Leiden, 1996).

For the history of the term, see Kurt Rudolph, "Gnosis and Gnosticism," in Alastair H. Logan and James M. Wedderburn, eds. *The New Testament and Gnosis* (Edinburgh, 1983). See also Michael A. Williams, *Rethinking "Gnosticism": An Argument for Dismantling a Dubious Category* (Princeton, N.J., 1996).

For Gnosticism as originated from Hellenistic mystery religions, mainly influenced by Iranian religion, see Wilhelm Bousset, *Hauptprobleme der Gnosis* (1907; reprint, Göttingen, Germany, 1973); Richard Reitzenstein, *Hellenistic Mystery-Religions: Their Basic Ideas and Significance* (1910; reprint of the English translation, Pittsburgh, Pa., 1978); and Carsten Colpe, *Die religionsgeschichtliche Schule* (Göttingen, Germany, 1961).

For Gnosticism as originated from Judaism, see Robert M. Grant, *Gnosticism and Early Christianity* (New York, 1966); Gilles Quispel, *Gnostic Studies* (Istanbul, 1974); Birget A. Pearson, "Jewish Elements in Gnosticism and the Development of Gnostic Self-Definition," in Edward P. Sanders, ed., *Jewish and Christian Self-Definitions* (London, 1980); Birget A. Pearson, *Gnosticism, Judaism, and Aegyptian Christianity* (Minneapolis, 1990); Gedaliahu Stroumsa, *Another Seed: Studies in Gnostic Mythology* (Leiden, 1984); and Roelof van den Broek, *Studies in Gnosticism and Alexandrian Christianity* (Leiden, 1996).

For the Christian origin or Gnosticism as a Christian heresy, see Simone Petrément, *A Separate God: The Christian Origins of Gnosticism* (Paris, 1984; San Francisco, 1990); Manlio Simonetti, *Ortodossia ed eresia tra I e II secolo* (Cosenza, Italy, 1991); and Alastair H. Logan, *Gnostic Truth and Christian Heresy: A Study in the History of Gnosticism* (Edinburgh, 1996).

Single Authors and Groups

For Jewish-Christianity, see Georg Strecker, *Das Judenchristentum in den Pseudoklementinen,* 2d ed. (Berlin, 1981); Kurt Rudolph, *Antike Baptisten* (Berlin, 1981); Gerhard P. Luttikhuizen, *The Revelation of Elcasai* (Tübingen, Germany, 1985); and Aldo Magris, "Qumran e lo gnosticismo," in Romano Penna, ed., *Qumran e le origini cristiane,* pp. 231–264 (Bologna, Italy, 1997).

For the early Christian Gnostics, see Karlmann Beyschlag, *Simon Magus und die christliche Gnosis* (Tübingen, Germany, 1974); Roelof van den Broek, "Eugnostos and Aristides on the Ineffable God," in Theo Baarda and Jaap Mansfeld, eds., *Knowledge of God in the Graeco-Roman World* (Leiden, 1988); Morton Smith, *Clement of Alexandria and a Secret Gospel of Mark* (Cambridge, Mass., 1973); Winrich A. Löhr, "Karpokratianisches," *Vigiliae Christianae* 49 (1995): 23–48; and Christoph Markschies, "Kerinth—Wer war er und was lehrte er?" *Jahrbuch für Antike und Christentum* 41 (1998): 48–76.

For Sethian Gnosticism, see Albertus Frederik J. Klijn, *Seth in Jewish, Christian, and Gnostic Literature* (Leiden, 1977); Hans-Martin Schenke, "The Phenomenon and Significance of Sethian Gnosticism," in Bentley Layton, ed., *The Rediscovery of Gnosticism* (Leiden, 1980–1981); Jean-Marie Sevrin, *Le dossier baptismal séthien* (Québec City, 1986); John D. Turner, "Typologies of the Sethian Gnostic Treatises from Nag Hammadi," in Louis Painchaud and Anne Pasquier, eds., *Les textes de Nag Hammadi et le problème de leur classification* (Québec City, 1995); and Harold W. Attridge, "Valentinian and Sethian Apocalyptic Traditions," *Journal of Early Christian Studies* 8 (2000): 173–211.

For Basilides, see Winrich A. Löhr, *Basilides und seine Schule* (Tübingen, Germany, 1996). For Valentinus and the Valentinians, see François Sagnard, *La gnose valentinienne et le témoignage de Saint Irénée* (Paris, 1947); Antonio Orbe, *Estudios valentinianos* (Rome, 1955–1966); Giovanni Casadio, "La visione in Marco il Mago e nella gnosi di tipo sethiano," *Augustinianum* 29 (1989): 123–146; Christoph Markschies, *Valentinus Gnosticus?* (Tübingen, Germany, 1992); Niklas Förster, *Marcus Magus* (Tübingen, Germany, 1999); Harold W. Attridge, "Valentinian and Sethian Apocalyptik Traditions," *Journal of Early Christian Studies* 8 (2000): 173–211; and Peter Lampe, *From Paul to Valentinus* (London and New York, 2003). For Marcion, see Adolf von Harnack, *Markion: das Evangelium vom fremden Gott* (Leipzig, Germany, 1921); and Edwin C. Blackman, *Marcion and His Influence* (London, 1948).

For serpent Gnostics and triadic systems, see Giovanni Casadio, "Antropologia gnostica e antropologia orfica nella notizia di Ippolito sui Sethiani" (1989), in *Vie gnostiche all'immortalità,* pp. 19–66 (Brescia, Italy, 1997); and Maria Grazia Lancellotti, *The Naassenes: A Gnostic Identity among Judaism, Christianity, Classical and Ancient Near Eastern Traditions* (Münster, Germany, 2000). For Hermetism, see Jean-Pierre Mahé, *Hermès en Haute-Egypte* (Québec City and Louvain, Belgium, 1978–1982).

Works Dealing with Specific Issues

For alleged pre-Christian Gnosticism, see Walter Schmithals, *Gnosticism in Corinth* (1956; English translation, Nashville, 1971); and Edwin Masao Yamauchi, *Pre-Christian Gnosticism: A Survey of the Proposed Evidences* (London, 1973; 2d ed., Grand Rapids, Mich., 1983). For Gnostic docetism, see Dieter Voorgang, *Die Passion Jesu und Christi in der Gnosis* (Frankfurt am Main, Germany, 1992). For a feminist approach, see Jorunn Y. Jacobsen Buckley, *Female Fault and Fulfillment in Gnosticism* (London, 1986); and Karen L. King, ed., *Images of the Feminine in Gnosticism* (Philadelphia, 1988). For social and historical background and conflict with the Catholic Church, see Walter Schmithals, *Gnosticism in Corinth* (1956; English translation, Nashville, 1971); Klaus Koschorke, *Die Polemik der Gnostiker gegen das kirchliche Christentum* (Leiden, 1978); Pheme Perkins, *The Gnostic Dialogue: The Early Church and the Crisis of Gnosticism* (New York, 1980); Henry A. Green, *The Economic and Social Origin of Gnosticism* (Atlanta, 1985); and Gian Carlo Benelli, *La gnosi: Il volto oscuro della storia* (Milan, 1991).

For Gnosticism and Greek philosophy, see Hans-Joachim Krämer, *Der Ursprung der Geistmetaphysik*, pp. 223–264 (Amsterdam, 1974); Takashi Onuki, *Gnosis und Stoa: Eine Untersuchung zum Apokryphon des Johannes* (Göttingen, Germany, 1989); Richard T. Wallis and Jay Bergman, eds., *Neoplatonism and Gnosticism* (Albany, N.Y., 1992); and John D. Turner, *Sethian Gnosticism and the Platonic Tradition* (Louvain, Belgium, and Paris, 2001).

Aldo Magris (2005)

GNOSTICISM: GNOSTICISM FROM THE MIDDLE AGES TO THE PRESENT

To a large extent Gnosticism in antiquity and later is part of a discourse meant to determine "the other" as "heretic" for the sake of shaping an identity for the Jewish, Christian, and Islamic orthodoxies. Hence, when discussing Gnosticism in any period of the history of religions, it must be kept in mind that one is dealing with the construction of a worldview that always served to emphasize "difference" in order to exclude individuals and groups from the "legitimate." Since late antiquity, certain forms of thought and, in particular, combinations of certain forms of thought, have been perceived as undesirable and therefore heretical. The undesirable elements that made up Gnostic heresies were the division of the world and humankind into a realm of light and a realm of darkness, individual (i.e. not church-controlled) encratism, individual spiritual charisma, and sometimes a blurring of gender boundaries.

The Notion of Gnosticism in the Context of Western Culture. Although the emerging Christian orthodoxies succeeded in defeating the Gnostic trends inherent in their cultural and religious heritage, Gnosticism did survive and made considerable contributions to the European (including the Jewish component) as well as to the Islamic history of ideas.

Following the suppression of larger Gnostic movements from the second to the mid-fourth century CE, the earliest Gnostic-type heretic appears to be Priscillian of Ávila, consecrated as bishop in 380, done away with as a heretic in 385. The case of this very erudite Spanish nobleman shows how Christian orthodoxy confined itself by banishing from Christian thought and practice cosmological and anthropological dualism, unauthorized religious authority, non-institutional encratism, and the quest for class and gender equality. From this point, Gnostic patterns of thought and belief are particularly noticeable in subversive, counterculture movements. A number of historians of religions and philosophers share the opinion that Gnosticism as a form of thought ought not to be limited to the full-blown systems of later antiquity, but can also be applied to other currents. This opinion relies on a certain view of a mainstream Western culture. According to this view, Western culture is world-affirming in that, first, there is a link between the universe and a positively acknowledged God as its creator and second, divine providence has determined this world as the place for humankind. Against this background, Gnosticism is often defined as a *Weltanschauung* that rejects this basic affirmation, hence its countercultural character. Interpreted in this mode, Gnosticism appears as "foreignness of the world" (*Weltfremdheit*, according to the German philosopher Peter Sloterdijk) or "metaphysical revolt" (Sloterdijk and Macho, 1991).

The Dynamics of Monism and Dualism in Gnosticism. The impact of Gnostic thought on the Western history of ideas is most obvious in the appearance of dualistic heresies during the Middle Ages, but can by no means be limited to them. On the contrary, Gnosticism can only be understood fully when one gives weight to the dynamics of dualism and monism in this distinct type of world-view. This is particularly important in dealing with neo-Gnosticism, because most of the transmission of Gnostic themes from antiquity through the Middle Ages—including medieval Islam and early modern Europe—remains obscure. The subliminal but seemingly ever-present potential for new Gnostic uprisings may be explained by Gnosticism's basis in more acceptable mystical versions of Jewish, Christian, and Islamic faith.

The core of Gnostic theology appears to be an all-encompassing God who is described in negative terms (such as immeasurable, invisible, and ineffable) and who therefore must be completely detached from the cosmos. The concept of an anti-God—(often identified with the God of the Old Testament) evolves primarily out of a Gnostic group's identity struggle with its broader cultic milieu. This pattern can be detected throughout the history of Gnosticism and explains the sometimes sudden revivals of rebellious dualistic separatism. Whereas monism is usually expressed through philosophical speculation and theories, Gnostic dualism is communicated through myths—usually creation myths—that transform the rejection and persecution members experience into a vivid metaphysical drama. These myths relate the origins of the Gnostic people in purely spiritual realms of the silent god, the fall of one of his creatures, and the subsequent evolution of psychic and physical layers of existence, where orthodox opponents reside. The fallen figures—the Primal Man (in Jewish Gnosticism and in Manichaeism), Sophia or Lucifer (in Christian Gnosticism), Kūni or Iblīs (in Islamic Gnosticism)—deserve special attention, for according to Gnostic understanding they can also provide salvation. This concept of salvation obviously points to the monistic matrix from which Gnostic dualism develops.

The peculiar dynamics of dualistic myths and monistic mysticisms may explain why some world-friendly religious movements have been characterized as Gnostic. Although

Christian mysticism describes an internal path of the individual soul to God, the label "Gnosticism" has also been applied to attempts at knowing God and the spiritual through the world, emphasizing the word *through.* Actually, it would be more adequate to classify such efforts as "Hermetic." Gnosticism and Hermeticism were closely intertwined in late antiquity, and Manichaeism, as well as some texts found in Nag Hammadi (e.g. *Asclepius; On the Origin of the World; The Paraphrase of Shem*), reveal a generally pro-cosmic attitude. Interest in Hermeticism was renewed in the Renaissance and taken up by Christian heretics. In early modern times this led to a new fusion of Hermetic ideas with Christian Gnosis, which was called *Pansophy* (Overall Wisdom) or *Natural Philosophy.*

Developments of Jewish and Islamic Gnosis in the Early Middle Ages. Jewish speculative and apocalyptic thought provided a rich source of semi-Gnostic cosmologies during the Middle Ages. Gnostic thought was communicated through the circulation of the *Sefer Yetsira,* edited probably in the ninth century. The text is essentially non-dualistic, showing the earliest roots of the Qabbalistic systems, which appeared in fully developed systems some centuries later.

Gnostic, Manichaean, Jewish, and Christian messianic ideas are likely to have influenced the first representatives of Shīʿah Gnosis. Just as Simon Magus was the archheretic of Christian Gnosis, the archheretic of Islamic *ghulūw* ("exaggeration") was ʾAbdallāh ibn Sabaʾ al-Hamdānī. The only available biographical information about him says that he was of Jewish origin, a follower of the prophet Muḥammad's son, the martyr ʾAli. He taught in the Iraqi town Kūfa that ʾAli had not really died but would reappear as the Mahdi in order to establish the kingdom of God.

Shīʿah movements, such as the Ismāʿīlīs, tend to endow their inspired messengers and salvational figures with cosmological significance. The *Kitāb al-Kashf* (*Book of Disclosure*), for example, relates the Ismāʿīlīs doctrine of the seven *imāms* (interpreters of divine teachings and themselves of otherworldly origin) to a cosmology with Qabbalistic traits, according to which God first created the letters of the alphabet. He creates them initially in two heptads (lines of seven). The first one corresponds to the prophets acknowledged widely by Shīʿah movements: Adam, Noah, Abraham, Moses, Jesus, Muḥammad, and the Mahdi, who is still to come. The second heptad corresponds to the seven Ismāʿīlīs *imāms.* As in the Qabbalah, the cosmos is symbolized by script. Another early Ismāʿīlīs tractate, the *Book of the Heptad and the Shadows (Kitāb al-haft wa al-aẓilla),* describes how God creates seven heavens and paradises, which are also, although more vaguely, connected to the *imāms.*

Christian Dualistic Heresies during the Middle Ages. After the case of Priscillian in the fourth century, the Byzantine as well as the Catholic orthodoxy succeeded in suppressing features considered Gnostic, but when people started to question the socio-economic order and the religious and intellectual premises upholding it, interest in ancient alternative forms of Christianity was renewed, particularly in the major European cities.

In the fourth and fifth centuries, adherents of Gnostic ideas who were fleeing church persecution sought refuge in Armenia. By the end of the seventh century, the Paulician movement emerged in Armenia and the northern regions of Syria. The movement's name was probably derived from their high regard for the apostle Paul. The first Paulician known to us by name was Constantine of Mananalis; he was said to have received his teachings in Samosata on the upper Euphrates. The Paulicians combined radicalized Pauline ideas with strong, even militant, demands for the Byzantine church to act in accordance with the early Christian idealization of poverty. Persecuted by both Christians and Muslims, the Paulicians were nearly destroyed in the eighth century but managed to gain importance again under the reformer Sergius Tychikos (d. 835). A large number of them were killed during the reign of the Byzantine empress Theodora, but Paulicianism survived in remote areas of the Byzantine Empire. The last retreat for Paulicians was Thrace, where their presence was still recorded in 1116.

Another dualistic movement containing unequivocally Gnostic elements burst forth in medieval Bulgaria under the influence of the Paulician mission. This heresy was named after its founder Bogomil, who was a village priest in the region south of Skopje, today belonging to Macedonia. The Bogomilian uprising took place in the second half of the tenth century, when southern parts of Bulgaria (which during the Middle Ages included wide areas of the Balkan between the Black and the Adriatic Seas) were being reconquered by Byzantium. As in the case of Paulicianism, the struggle of the Bogomils was not only one of heresy against orthodoxy, but also involved politics and social concerns. Paulicians and Bogomils were mostly peasants, whereas the Byzantine orthodoxy represented the land-owning ruling classes.

Cosmological and anthropological dualism, antinomianism, docetism, anticlericalism, encratism, and dietary restrictions characterized Bogomilism. Its mythic repertory clearly shows a derivation from ancient sources. According to the Bogomilian story of creation, God brought forth the four elements of fire, water, earth, and air and established his divine kingdom, which consisted of seven heavens inhabited by the angels. The angels were supposed to serve God and to fight on his behalf. One of them, Satanael, rebelled against the creator and therefore was banished to Earth. As a result, Satanael created a world for himself, separating water and earth. Although sunlight was of divine origin, Satanael brought forth the other forces of nature, such as rain, wind, and thunderstorms. Then he created life-forms and human beings as his servants. In the process, he managed to confine a number of angels in material bodies. As a consequence, human beings partake of the divine as well as the satanic creation, so that the cosmic dualism of good and evil is inherent in each person. Like Gnostic movements of antiquity, the

Bogomils had their own Christology. Christ was one of the divine ambassadors sent out to humankind to promote its salvation. He took human shape through his mother Mary but was never human in his essence. In order to prevent Christ's mission, Satanael arranged for his crucifixion, but Christ's suffering was only superficial. Three days after the crucifixion, Christ appeared on Earth again, put Satanael in chains, and cast him into hell. Nevertheless, Satanael escaped and renewed his reign on earth, with the help of worldly rulers and orthodox theologians.

Gnostic or Manichaean mythology must have survived in the frontier districts of the Roman Empire and mixed with local religious traditions, particularly with a pagan belief in spirits, which appear as demons in the Bogomilian belief. It is impossible, however, to determine more precisely what forces shaped the Bogomilian world-view. From the Bulgarian regions, Bogomilism spread to Thrace and Asia Minor and reached the capital of the Byzantine Empire in the eleventh century as an underground movement. Here it changed its character and spread among members of the middle classes and even within monastic communities. Bogomilian missionaries had a great deal of success during the twelfth century, particularly in Serbia and Bosnia, where orthodox church structures were weak. The Bogomils began to develop a church-like hierarchy themselves, but as a consequence they lost their attractiveness for the peasantry, which had made up the core of the movement. Hence, in the thirteenth century it started to decline. However, the final extinction of Bogomilism in Southeastern Europe and Asia Minor only took place with the conquest of these areas by the emerging Ottoman Empire.

Meanwhile Bogomilism had also spread westwards, probably mainly through refugees from the Balkan areas, to northern Italy and the South of France and contributed to the emergence of the Cathar movement. Like Bogomilism in the East, Catharism in Western Europe was a reservoir of heretical and folkloristic currents, loosely bound up by Gnostic-type cosmological mythologies that located metaphysical evil on the side of the Catholic Church. However, a lot of eleventh-century sectarians continued to go to the official church and to take sacraments. Their somewhat ambiguous attitude has been called crypto-heretic. Cathars also strongly venerated parts of the scripture. Although they rejected most of the Old Testament, they used the *Gospel of John* and the *Apocalypse of John* for dualistic and allegorical exegesis. In addition, the Cathars used apocryphal texts.

Although the Cathar myths and theological creeds closely resembled those of the Bogomils, they were less opposed to organization and more inclined to form their own well-ordered, although decentralized, communities. Cathar churches were established in northern Italy and southern France. They consisted of two classes of people: the pure *perfecti,* who could not get involved in any worldly affairs, did not marry, and were strongly committed to a selective vegetarian diet. Even the permitted plants had to be prepared by the *credentes,* the ordinary adherents of Catharism, who were allowed to marry and work for the sake of the community.

Despite local persecutions during the eleventh century, the Cathar churches spread widely through the southern and central parts of Western Europe. A particular stronghold emerged in the area of Toulouse, where the popularity of Catharism coincided with a supportive political situation. Because of power shifts in France, a political vacuum developed in the area of Toulouse. A local ruler tried to fill the void and made Catharism the state religion of his territory. This situation provoked a massive response against the Cathars. A crusade was organized against them in 1208 and a second one in 1227. The latter resulted in the fall of Montségur in 1244, the last place of refuge for a large Cathar community. Small, scattered groups survived in the southern European mountain regions for about another century.

Medieval Qabbalah. Medieval Qabbalah, which reached its climax at the end of the thirteenth century with the Zohar (Book of Glow), clearly shows Gnostic tendencies but never resulted in a mature cosmological dualism. On the contrary, the Zohar presents the construction of the universe as a (however fragile) harmony of divine forces. No element was viewed as essentially evil or satanic, but there was an inherent danger within the system that one of the sefirot (aspects of God) might become independent. Gnosticism claimed that this had already happened in the creation process, but the Zohar did not.

The Qabbalist who came closest to Gnostic concepts was Isaac Luria (1534–1572). He taught a small circle of adherents in Safed. Lurianic Qabbalah was very influential for its doctrine of *tsimtsum.* According to this doctrine, God "contracts" within himself, thus creating a space that is deprived of God and can be filled up with creation. In his description of the further process of creation, Luria employed the Gnostic dualistic pattern of the fundamental opposition between light and darkness: The first human being (*Adam Kadmun*) emerges from the divine light that radiated into the space emptied by *tsimtsum.* Out of *Adam Kadmun's* face flashed the *sefirot*-lights, which were supposed to be collected in vessels prepared for them. Some of these vessels, however, broke and were then filled up with dark matter, while their fragments fell down, void of creation.

Pansophy and Natural Philosophy in Early Modern Times. Renaissance scholarship and philosophy in Western Europe was profoundly influenced by Qabbalah and Hermeticism but did not develop the world-denying and rebellious overtones typical of dualistic Gnostic mythologies.

Mythic, dualistic gnosis was once more recognizable in seventeenth- and eighteenth-century Germany. There the enormous influence of Paracelsus (c. 1493–1541) had created an intellectual climate that offered a fertile soil for Gnostic currents. Paracelsian Pansophy (Overall Wisdom) prepared the way for German natural philosophy, which was mainly concerned with integrating nature into Lutheran theology. To natural philosophers, it seemed obvious that not only humankind, but also nature as a whole, is incomplete when measured against the original divine plan for creation. In order to explain this gap and to develop a strategy of salvation for fallen nature, the philosophers drew upon Gnostic mythology. The most creative and impressive new version of Gnostic cosmogonic myth was put forward by Jakob Böhme (1575–1624) In his visionary exegesis of biblical texts, Böhme resembled ancient Gnostic authors. According to him, nature had been born out of the original abyss and developed in seven stages. These stages corresponded to the Qabbalistic *sefirot,* which Böhme also referred to as *Source-Spirits* (*Quellgeister*). The first Source-Spirit to emerge from the abyss of nothingness was Desire; followed by the goad of Sensibility (*Stachel der Empfindlichkeit*); then by Anxiety *(Angst)* or Feeling *(Gemüt);* by Fire or Spirit; by Light or Love; by Resonance *(Hall),* Word, or Mind *(Verstand);* and by Body, Being, or Material Nature. The Godhead, in this process of unfolding, shows itself as a dynamic, dramatic, and even dialectical primal aetherical substance from which the immaterial as well as the material world take form. However, God is not fully responsible for the existence of matter. Matter came into being as a result of the fall of the rebellious angel Lucifer, who refused subordination to a higher will, just as the primal androgynous human being would do later. In his theology, Böhme avoided cosmological dualism. The fall took place within the one and only essentially divine realm. Instead of making Lucifer and the primal androgyn genuinely evil forces, Böhme emphasizes the role of divine freedom that can be used in accordance with the will of the Godhead or against it.

Friedrich Christoph Oetinger (1702–1782), another important representative of German nature-philosophy, studied Böhme thoroughly and was also acquainted with Lurianic Qabbalah. For him, God represented life as a unity and interplay of different forces and possibilities. In the Godhead, the components of this complex interplay are indissolubly interwoven, whereas in nature they can be separated. The human fall, according to Oetinger, has no cosmological grounds but was rather a misperception. Oetinger's emphasis on insight as a prerequisite for salvation could be construed as Gnostic, Oetinger's definition of insight is different.. Oetinger's Gnosis is one of synopsis (*Zentralerkenntnis*) in order to perceive the inherent unity of nature and God. Gnosticism in the narrower, dualistic sense, on the contrary, means by Gnosis the recognition of the two fundamentally opposing realms of light and darkness.

THE THEME OF THE REVOLUTIONARY AGAINST GOD. The metaphysical revolt that is often ascribed to Gnosticism is a rebellion not against God's creation, but rather against the limitations of knowledge. In *Genesis,* God forbade Adam and Eve to eat fruit from the Tree of Knowledge in the Garden of Eden. The snake, who convinced Eve to violate this prohibition, was often interpreted as the devil or Satan in younger sources. In their typical mode of re-evaluating biblical traditions, some Gnostics interpreted Satan as a positive figure who wanted to bring human beings divine knowledge, which the Old Testament God maliciously withheld from them. In various biblical and apocryphal traditions, Satan is equated with Lucifer, or the Islamic Iblīs. Other despisers of God's law, Cain in particular, also evoked Gnostic sympathy.

The theme of the light-bringing revolutionary has inspired several prominent authors. John Milton (1608–1674) and Johann Wolfgang Goethe (1749–1832) both show a great fascination with the rebellious angel who become the devil. In his epic *Paradise Lost* (1667), Milton described with a great deal of empathy Satan's expulsion from the heavenly realm, his renewed advance toward it, and his seduction of Eve. Goethe, who throughout his life was dissatisfied with Christian doctrine, created a personal theology. At the end of the eighth book of his autobiographical work *Dichtung und Wahrheit* (1811–1833), he introduces a myth that is clearly an imitation of Gnostic models: A primal Godhead creates another Divine Being as a reflection of itself and then a third one as a reflection of the two. When the fourth being is created, it no longer resembles the three preceding ones, thus introducing difference and contradiction to the divine world. The fourth being is Lucifer, who then creates his own worlds and forgets his origin. His pride and conceit finally cause his fall. In Goethe's drama *Faust* (1790–1832), the figure of the devil, here named Mephisto, plays a crucial role and is considered important for humankind's search for knowledge and spiritual development, although in the end he shall not triumph by possessing the human soul completely.

The fallen angel appears again in Alphonse de Lamartine's *La Chute d'un ange* (1838). Here the angel Cédar asks God to let him become a human being, because he wants to win the love of a woman. The epic was conceived as the first part of a comprehensive account of the fate of humankind from its divine origins through the many failures recorded in history. Apart from *La chute d'un ange,* Lamartine wrote only the final part of this epic, *Jocelyn* (1836), about a woman who dies as a result of caring for those sick with the plague.

Victor Hugo (1802–1885) undertook a similar narrative of human history in his *La légende des siècles* (1859), but the story lacks the typically Gnostic idea of light before darkness. However, Hugo's interpretation of history as a mythic battle between two hostile principles and his empathy for the Cain may remind the reader of Gnostic attitudes.

GNOSTICISM AND ROMANTICISM. Natural philosophy was still of considerable importance in the age of European and North American Romanticism. Emphasis had shifted, however, from the concordance of God and nature to the power of the self, which could be equated with the human being, the divinity, or nature. By viewing the self as the creative source of everything, the Romantics transcended the traditional Christian boundaries separating the individual, God, and the world. Their aim was a new unity centered in the self, which led them to face yet another dichotomy, that of the personal and the all-self. The Romantic experience of a multifaceted, at times fragmented, human self gave rise to new dualistic concepts that could be extended to the whole cosmos. Again we see that dualistic Gnostic systems are products not only of speculative pessimistic minds, but also of social unrest. In London, the Gordon Riots of June 1780 were suppressed in an effort to avert a larger revolutionary movement such as that which soon followed in France. English authors took up Gnostic metaphors to serve as mouthpieces for revolutionary ideas. William Blake (1757–1827) developed a unique allegorical approach to biblical texts and rewrote various aspects of the creation story in a Gnostic fashion. Blake avoided cosmological dualism, but his esteem for the free and independent human spirit, which he shared with many other Romantic poets, let him take up the typical Gnostic motif of the Divine Man. The Divine Man was in essence God himself and provoked the envy of some of the angels. In Blake's works, this figure is named Albion (a symbol for England) Orc (another name for Lucifer), Jesus Christ, or Prometheus. Orc rebels against Urizen, who represents both George III and his rule in Britain and also the Father-god of the Old Testament. Orc brings the new social order that is expected to be established with the return and reign of Christ. In his most highly acclaimed poetic work, *Prometheus Unbound,* Percy Bysshe Shelley (1792–1822) presents Prometheus as a symbol of hope for the suppressed and wretched masses in English cities during the time of industrialization.

Many Romantics were engaged with the dark side of being—with night as the fold of existence, and with death and its various stages of fading and decay. In some cases this resulted in a semi-Gnostic denigration of nature and the conditions of human life, which became the typical features of Romantic *Weltschmerz* (pain or melancholy about the world). For example, in *Dialogue of Nature and an Icelander,* Giacomo Leopardi (1798–1837) depicts nature as a pitiless persecutor of desperate humans and concludes that it is impossible to discover the meaning of a universe that sustains itself by regularly killing its inhabitants. Because of this conclusion, Leopardi cannot be called a Gnostic. Gnostic pessimism typically features a refractory dualism: The good and meaningful exist in the realm of light and in souls that become aware of their divine origin. Leopardi, however, rejects not only the goodness of this-worldly creation, but the existence of goodness and meaningfulness anywhere. Lord Byron's (1788–1824) poetry, too, lacks the rebellious spirit of mythic Gnosticism that believes that a better world can be achieved. Byron's Cain is guided by Lucifer to see a meaningless world that is created not by demonic forces, but by the human self.

Other important representatives of Romantic *Weltschmerz* were Arthur Schopenhauer (1788–1860), whose philosophy was inspired more by Buddhism than by Gnosticism, and Mihai Eminescu (1850–1889), who praised the Romantic genius as the only possible surmounter of the weary world.

GNOSTICISM, ANTI-SEMITISM, AND RACISM. By the end of the nineteenth century, extreme nationalist and anti-Semitic groups emerging in Germany co-opted Romanticism for their own purposes. They reshaped the Romantic worldview so that the decisive force in the world was no longer the human self, but race. In the 1920s and 1930s various trends culminated in a mixture of racism and esotericism, called *Ariosophy* (Wisdom of the Aryans). The Aryan myth was very simple. In its various versions, it told a story about the original dwelling places of the Aryans—either Thule (an island in the North Sea close to the pole but also equated with Iceland) or Shambala (located in Central Asia, most often in the Tibetan mountains)—to which they had come as survivors of Atlantis. The Aryans were characterized only by their physical appearance: they were supposed to have light skin and blond hair, and their only "ethical" requirement was to keep their race pure. Their racial purity made them superior to all other races. Hence, the Aryans were called to fight the forces that could contaminate their pure race, which meant that they should fight other races. The Aryans considered the Jews, who, according to the myth, had begun to infiltrate the Aryan race with alien blood and spirit the race most hostile and dangerous to them. According to Artur Dinter (1876–1948), an author who wrote extensively about religious ideas coming out of the *Völkische Bewegung,* the Jews were the lowest incarnations of originally spiritual beings after the fall. Therefore, Dinter explained, the Jews were intensely inclined to the material world and bound up with it. Thus, the racial battle between Jews and Aryans was interpreted as a battle between matter (darkness) and spirit (light). The hijacking of a mythic pattern known from Gnosticsm for an ideological foundation of radical anti-Semitism is not as surprising as it may seem, for the Jews were shown as descendents of the demiurge, the Old Testament God and antagonist of the realm of light in Gnostic myths from the second and third centuries CE.

GNOSTICISM IN MODERN AND POSTMODERN PHILOSOPHY. A number of important currents and themes of nineteenth- and twentieth-century philosophy have been related to patterns of thought derived from Gnosticism: the Hegelian theory of consciousness and knowledge, the Marxist doctrine of dialectical rather than logical progress in history; the death of God proclaimed by nihilism, the epistemological arguments of phenomenology, the notion of the human self in existentialism, and several features of postmodernism.

Georg Friedrich Wilhelm Hegel (1770–1831) outlined a universal theory according to which history is a process of the Divine Spirit becoming conscious of itself. This process is executed in three steps: First the Spirit is enclosed in itself, second it separates from itself and recognizes itself as "other," and third of the Divine Spirit integrates his experience by means of a return of the formerly differentiated aspect, which leads to an affirmation at a higher level. The first step parallels the dwelling of purely intelligible beings in the Gnostic *pleroma,* the second parallels the alienation of the spirit as the psychic and material world, and the third parallels state of Gnosis, the spiritual knowledge of the self about itself.

Karl Marx (1818–1883) adopted the Hegelian idea about dialectical development but imbued it with a materialistic instead of an idealistic conception of the world. Moreover, Marx stated explicitly that the knowledge about dialectics was not to be promoted in order to analyze the world, but to change it. According to Hegel, knowledge as a concluding synthesis about dialectical progression was still possible for an individual mind, but for Marx and other intellectual leaders of the Communist movement it was only possible as a totality of social practice. Some interpreters (Eric Voegelin and Boris Groys, for example) view this practical knowledge or wisdom—as opposed to various competing forms of analytical knowledge—to be in congruence with salvational Gnosis.

Gnostic attitudes that shaped Soviet ideology have also been detected in Russian philosophies of religion, particularly in the writings of Vladimir Solov'ev (1853–1900) and in nihilism. Friedrich Nietzsche's (1844–1900) nihilistic statement that God is dead can be interpreted as a rejection of the transcendent God of Judaism and Christianity for the sake of a self-divinization of humankind. Interestingly, critics of nihilism such as Eric Voegelin (1901–1985) and René Girard (1923–) use religious terminology themselves when they label nihilism "demonic." Thus, their arguments against nihilism appear as the direct successors of those by the Christian heresiologists against ancient Gnosticism. Hans Blumenberg (1920–1996) claims that the philosophies of Hegel and Marx do not draw upon Gnosticism. For him, modernism has surmounted Gnosticism's world-rejection and replaced it with a world-affirming trust in a rational understanding of the cosmos and the human situation. Because postmodernism calls into question this trust in rationality, it has also been suspected of Gnostic tendencies. Peter Koslowski (1952–) has advocated a Gnostic approach to the world, which he defines as an awareness of its fundamental deficiency. By acknowledging the world's deficiency and its need for improvement, humankind can, according to Koslowski, proceed in wisdom.

Although little attention has been devoted to the analogies between Gnosticism and the phenomenology of Edmund Husserl (1859–1938), with its aim at overcoming the differences between consciousness and Being, the Gnostic inclinations of Heideggerian phenomenology (existentialism) are generally agreed on. Hans Jonas (1903–1993), in his seminal study *Gnosis und spätantiker Geist* (1964), pointed to Heidegger's use of Gnostic terminology when explaining the situation of humankind as "thrown into the world." According to Jonas, the demonization of the universe combined with the idea of a transcendent acosmic self led to close parallels between exisentialism and Gnosticism. Moreover, a thorough analysis by Barbara Merker (*Selbsttäuschung und Selbsterkenntnis—Zu Heideggers Transformation der Phänomenologie Husserls,* 1988) showed that Heidegger's main work *Sein und Zeit* (1927) relied on Gnostic myths.

THE VARIETY OF NEO-GNOSTICISMS IN THE TWENTIETH CENTURY. Other neo-Gnostic trends of the twentieth century grew out of the variety of Romantic conceptualizations of Gnosis. Optimistic outlooks focused on the sacralization of self that was prevalent in Romanticism, which grew out of the Gnostic belief in the divine origin of humankind. In Hermann Hesse's (1877–1962) novel *Demian* (1919) and the works of Carl G. Jung (1875–1961) the Gnostic path was reinterpreted as humanity's search its sacred origin. Insofar as recent esoteric currents, such as the New Age movement, have contained Gnostic themes and motifs, they were particularly attracted by the possibility of self-salvation, often coupled with a claim for self-fulfillment through an awareness of humankind's own divinity. An example of developed dualistic neo-Gnosticism in newer religious movements can be found in the teachings of Colombian Samael Aun Weor (1917–1977), whose ideas gained an audience outside his homeland. Not much is know about his life or the sources from which he drew his eclectic ideas. He obviously depended heavily on Theosophy and the "sexual magic" of Aleister Crowley and the OTO (Ordo Templi Orientis). But whereas Crowley had been an excessive libertine, Weor advocated sexual magic within "sacred matrimony," matrimony understood in its bourgeois sense. His dualism was not so much cosmological as directed against what he saw as flaws of modern societies, among them Communism, women's liberation, and homosexuality. Nevertheless, Weor believed in an "eternal battle between YHWH and Christ," which was reflected in occasional anti-Semitic utterances.

To counter the focus on human self-realization, some thinkers have proposed the idea of an unworldly, nonhuman, and remote God who resembles the God of Gnosticism. The late Max Horkheimer (1895–1973) wrote about God as "Completely Other"; Karl Barth (1886–1968) developed a paradoxical negative theology in which God was incomprehensible to human thought and religion; and Simone Weil (1909–1943) was convinced that God cannot be present in the realm of time.

In reaction to the more than 52 million who died in World War II, Theodor Adorno (1903–1969) wrote *Minima Moralia* (1951), which is in part a Gnostic work. Adorno criticizes the immorality, materialistic consumerism, and general corruption of the world and thereby resurrects several Gnostic myths (for example, the myth of the descent of Great Ignorance upon the world). But unlike Romantic representatives of *Weltschmerz,* Adorno still allows for hope. However, because his hope is for a Messiah rather than for self-salvation, it is not Gnostic. Romanian-French philosopher Émile Michel Cioran (1911–1995) presented a more pessimistic expression of Gnosticism. In his book *Le mauvais démiurge* (1969), he drew on fragments of Gnostic ideas in order to unfold his own post-Nietzschean nihilistic and perspectivist philosophy. However, it must be emphasized that Cioran's explicitly anti-systematic approach not only lacks the salvational hope of Gnosticism proper, but also the inner consistency of Gnostic myth. Fernando Pessoa (1888–1935) revived Romantic *Weltschmerz* and combined it with Gnostic motifs. His poem *No túmulo de Christian Rosencreutz* immediately reminds the reader of Gnostic myths of descent.

In such stories as *La révolte des Anges* (1914) by Anatole France (1844–1924) and *Doktor Faustus* (1947) by Thomas Mann (1875–1955), twentieth-century literature took up the themes of the rebellious angel, Satan, and the human seeker who follows his path. Mann's Doktor Faustus was meant to represent the situation of German intellectuals whose over-reflexivity had led to mental paralysis. To overcome the crisis, the lead character, Adrian Leverkühn, flees into irrational ecstasy—a gift from the devil, who takes him in the end. Mann criticizes Gnosticism by using Gnostic metaphors to describe Nazi Germany. In his controversial 1988 novel *The Satanic Verses,* Salman Rushdie (1947–) played with the theme of the fallen angel, blending motifs from the time of Muḥammad with those from contemporary London. Rushdie uses the images of archangel Gabriel and Satan (Iblīs in Islamic mythology) to draw attention to racist perceptions of immigrants in Great Britain.

Gnosticism in Fantasy Literature. Gnostic concepts are very often relevant in fantasy novels. J. R. R. Tolkien's (1892–1973) trilogy *The Lord of the Rings* (1954–1955) tells about a Manichaean-style battle against Darkness. Middle-earth, Tolkien's fictitious world, has to defend itself against a major attack from the army of Sauron the Great. Sauron resides in Mordor, a realm of shadows, and is called the Dark Lord. He is the chief henchman of the more abstract Dark Power threatening to absorb the light of Middle-earth. However, Tolkien also brings in other themes that are foreign and even opposed to Gnostic myths, such as the importance of compassion and the danger of power.

Philip Pullman (1946–) comes very close to Gnostic views and attitudes in the trilogy His Dark Materials (*The Golden Compass,* 1995; *The Subtle Knife,* 1997; *The Amber Spyglass,* 2000). Inspired particularly by the works of William Blake and Milton's *Paradise Lost,* Pullman takes up the Gnostic depiction of the Old Testament God who refuses to let human beings have a certain kind of knowledge. In contrast to historical Gnosticism, this knowledge is not about the origin and true nature of light-beings, but about the ultimate identity of spirit and matter. Lord Asriel plays the role of Satan, trying to gain access to the higher worlds. His daughter Lyra, who is called "the new Eve," disobeys God, as represented by the church.

Gnosticism in Recent Science and Scholarship. The term *gnosis* is often used to name an approach that refuses to exclude the spiritual dimensions of reality. Thus anti-positivistic methods in academic work are sometimes labeled Gnostic. Since some scholars in the sciences as well as the humanities concede only to so-called objective forms of knowledge, they try to stigmatize insights that are based on other methodologies. In the 1970s, for example, a circle of scientists in the United States who were concerned with "alternative" research methods that led to non-mainstream results were known as the Gnostics of Princeton. Arthur Young (1923–), the founder of the Berkeley Institute for the Study of Consciousness, referred explicitly to Gnostic views when explaining cosmic developments and the significance of the human self.

The research on Gnosticism, and even the discipline of the history of religions has come under suspicion of inherent Gnosticism. In an article from 1987, Manfred Sommer (1945–) characterized Hans Jonas's interpretation of gnosis as *Endgestalt der Gnosis* (the final shape of gnosis). The author observes a self-entangledness that is reflected no only in Gnostic thought, but even in research about Gnosticism. Similar observations can be made about the scholarship of Gilles Quispel (1916–), who is heavily influenced by Carl Gustav Jung. Steven Wasserstrom in his book *Religion after Religion: Gershom Scholem, Mircea Eliade and Henty Corbin at Eranos* (1999) has pointed out that three major founders of this discipline were phenomenologists and therefore heirs to Gnostic traditions. Again, the use of the term *gnosis* by these scholars, and particularly by their interpreter Wasserstrom, is highly inconsistent. It shows once more that the label *Gnostic* is used to label any kind of dissatisfaction with mainstream ideologies, whether orthodox theology or orthodox academia (as in Scholem's fear of a "professorial death," for example), as well as for attacks and counterattacks from either side.

See Also Cathari; Druze; Heresy, article on Christian Concepts; Manichaeism, article on Manichaeism and Christianity; New Age Movement; Qabbalah; Shiism, article on Ismāʿīlīyah.

Bibliography

There are very few one-volume works dealing explicitly with neo-Gnosticism. The most important attempt to comprehend the continuity of Gnostic motifs from medieval through modern times is Ioan P. Couliano, *The Tree of Gnosticism: Gnostic Mythology from Early Christianity to Modern Nihilism* (San Francisco, 1990). For the intertwinement of monism and dualism in Gnostic thought, see Julia Iwersen, *Gnosis zur Einführung* (Hamburg, 2001). An interesting anthology of Gnostic writing in the religions, philosophy, and literature throughout history is provided by Peter Sloterdijk and Thomas H. Macho, eds., *Weltrevolution der Seele: Ein Lese- und Arbeitsbuch der Gnosis von der Spätantike bis zur Gegenwart,* 2 vols. (Düsseldorf, 1991). Various scholarly articles on Gnosticism in ancient and modern intellectual currents are collected in Barbara Aland, ed., *Gnosis: Festschrift für Hans Jonas* (Göttingen, 1978). Articles in the volume of special interest include: Giulia Sfameni Gasparro, "Sur l'histoire des influences du gnosticisme" and Gilles Quispel, "Hermann Hesse und Gnosis." Other resources on the topic can be found in Peter Koslowski, ed., *Gnosis und Mystik in der Geschichte der Philosophie* (Zurich and Munich, 1988), which includes contributions on Paracelsus, Böhme, Oetinger and many other important thinkers, as well as a particularly interesting article by Boris Groys on Gnosticism in Soviet ideology. The classic study by Arthur O. Lovejoy, *The Great Chain of Being: A Study of the History of an Idea* (Cambridge, Mass., 1964) can be used as an introduction to the Gnostic theme of otherworldliness, although it treats only the philosophical side and excludes the mythic dimensions of Gnosticism. For all other issues raised in this article, the reader needs to consult specialized studies on movements, writers, and philosophers, such as Martin Erbstösser, *Ketzer im Mittelalter* (Leipzig, 1984), which is very good on the social and economic roots of medieval Gnostic heresies. Relations between Shīʿah movements and Gnosticism are discussed by Heinz Halm in *Kosmologie und Heilslehre der frühen Ismaʿiliya: Eine Studie zur islamischen Gnosis* (Wiesbaden, 1978) and *Die islamische Gnosis: Die extreme Schia und die ʿAlawiten* (Zurich and Munich, 1982). A very good source for Gnostic trends in early modern times, with special reference to Goethe, is Rolf Christian Zimmermann, *Das Weltbild des jungen Goethe* (2 vols., Munich, 1969–1979; first volume reprinted in 2002). Albrecht Schöne, *Götterzeichen, Liebeszauber, Satanskult: Neue Einblicke in alte Goethetexte* (Munich, 1982) is an interesting examination of Gnostic theology in Goethe's *Faust.* Regarding Gnosticism and Romanticism, see Ioan P. Coulianu, "The Gnostic Revenge. Gnosticism and Romantic Literature," in Jacob Taubes, ed., *Gnosis und Politik* (Munich and Paderborn, 1984). For an examination of the Gnostic aspects of certain Romantic poets, see Patrizia Girolami, *L'Antiteodicea: Dio, dei, religione nello "Zibaldone" di Giacomo Leopardi* (Florence, 1995) and David V. Erdman, *Blake: Prophet against Empire* (1954, 3d ed., New York, 1991). The best study of Gnosticism and Nazism is Ekkehard Hieronimus, "Dualismus und Gnosis in der völkischen Bewegung," in Jacob Taubes, ed., *Gnosis und Politik,* pp. 82–89 (Munich and Paderborn, 1984). Another good resource is Nicholas Goodrick-Clarke, *The Occult Roots of Nazism: Secret Aryan Cults and Their Influence on Nazi Ideology* (New York, 1985, 1992), which takes a broader, less specific approach. Gnostic anti-Semitism within the full scale of history is examined by Micha Brumlik, *Die Gnostiker: Der Traum von der Selbsterl ösung der Menschen* (Frankfurt, 1992). On Gnosticism in modern philosophies, see "Wissenschaft, Politik und Gnosis" (1959), in *The Collected Works of Eric Voegelin,* edited by Manfred Henningsen, Vol. 5, *Modernity without Restraint: Political Religions; the New Science of Politics; and Science, Politics, and Gnosticism,* (Columbia, Mo., and London, 1999). The opposing view is offered by Hans Blumenberg, *The Legitimacy of the Modern Age* (Cambridge, Mass., 1985). Interrelations between Gnosticism and postmodernism are extensively treated by Peter Koslowski, *Die Prüfungen der Neuzeit: Über Postmodernität, Philosophie der Geschichte, Metaphysik, Gnosis* (Wien, 1989). For Gnostic influence on Heidegger's philosophy, Barbara Merker's *Selbsttäuschung und Selbsterkenntnis—Zu Heideggers Transformation der Phänomenologie Husserls* (Frankfurt am Main, 1988) is of special importance. Hans Jonas's *Gnosis und spätantiker Geist: Erster Teil: Die mythologische Gnosis* (Göttingen, 1934; reprint, 1964) was the groundbreaking study of Gnosticism in the light of existentialism. The English edition of *The Gnostic Religion: The Message of the Alien God and the Beginnings of Christianity* 2d ed. (Boston, 1963) is considerably shorter and therefore an incomplete presentation of Jonas's approach. Thirty years later, Kurt Rudolph edited the continuation of Jonas's work on Gnosticism, *Gnosis und spätantiker Geist. Zweiter Teil: Von der Mythologie zur mystischen Philosophie* (Göttingen, 1993). It is of particular interest for connections Jonas made between Gnosticism and Christian mysticism, and for his explanation of the transformation of dualistic myths into a monistic worldview. This volume also includes Jonas's important article "Gnosis, Existentialismus und Nihilismus," which was first published in 1973. In *The Modern Revival of Gnosticism and Thomas Mann's Doktor Faustus* (New York, 2002), Kirsten J. Grimstad examines various intellectual trends at the end of the nineteenth and beginning of the twentieth century in their relation to Gnosticism. This work also includes remarkable chapters on Jung and Jonas, as well as a discussion of Gershom Scholem's treatment of Jewish mysticism. Grimstad's work shows a solid familiarity with relevant historical discussion. For Gnosticism in science, see Raymond Ruyer, *La Gnose de Princeton* (Paris, 1974) and Arthur Young, *The Reflexive Universe: Evolution of Consciousness* (New York, 1976). On Gnosticism within Hans Jonas's work, see Manfred Sommer, "Metaphysikkritik als Gnosis," in Willi Oelmüller, ed., *Metaphysik heute?* [=*Kolloquien zur Gegenwartsphilosophie* 10] (Paderborn, 1987). Gilles Quispel's important works are *Gnosis als Weltreligion* (Zurich, 1951); two volumes of *Gnostic Studies* (Leiden, 1973–1974) and *Gnosis: De derde component van de Europese cultuurtraditie* (Utrecht, 1988), which includes contributions by several authors on the meaning of Gnosticism in European culture. A condensed form of Quispel's views is found in "Gnosis and Psychology," in Bentley Layton,ed., *The Rediscovery of Gnosticism,* vol.1, *The School of Valentinus* (Leiden, 1980). Steven M. Wasserstrom's *Religion after Religion: Gershom Scholem, Mircea Eliade, and Henry Corbin at Eranos* (Princeton, 1999) is a highly stimulating investigation into supposedly Gnostic epistemologies in the history of religions, although it obscures in a typically heresiological way its own ideological bases in Kantian and positivist philosophy. Wouter Hanegraaff's "On the Construction of 'Esoteric Traditions,'" in Antoine Faivre and Wouter Hanegraaff, eds., *Western Esotericism and the Science of Religion: Selected Papers Presented at the 17th Congress of the International Association for the History of Religions, Mexico City 1995,* pp. 11–61 (Leuven, 1998) is valuable for its analysis of various interpretations of Gnosticism and esotericism, although the author seems unaware of the influence of Kantian metaphysics when proposing an "empirical method."

JULIA IWERSEN (2005)

GNOSTICISM: GNOSTICISM AS A CHRISTIAN HERESY

The pluralism of early Christianity in regional faith and praxis, as well as the shifting lines of authority within the first and second centuries, make it difficult to draw the sharp boundaries required to exclude a particular opinion or group as heretical. In *Against Heresies,* Irenaeus says that his predecessors were unable to refute the Gnostics because they had inadequate knowledge of Gnostic systems and because the Gnostics appeared to say the same things as other Christians. Christian Gnostics of the second century claimed to have the esoteric, spiritual interpretation of Christian scriptures, beliefs, and sacraments. Their orthodox opponents sought to prove that such persons were not Christians on the grounds that Gnostic rites were occasions of immoral behavior, that their myths and doctrines were absurd, and that their intentions were destructive to true worship of God. In short, it appears that Gnostics were defined as heretics by their opponents well before they stopped considering themselves to be spiritual members of the larger Christian community.

Three periods characterize the interaction of Gnosticism and Christianity: (1) the late first century and early second century, in which the foundations of Gnostic traditions were laid at the same time that the New Testament was being written; (2) the mid-second century to the early third century, the period of the great Gnostic teachers and systems; and (3) the end of the second century into the fourth century, the period of the heresiological reaction against Gnosticism.

The fluid boundaries of Christianity in the first period make it difficult to speak of Gnosticism at that time as a heresy. Four types of tradition used in the second-century Gnostic systems were developed in this period. First, there was a reinterpretation of *Genesis* that depicts the Jewish God as jealous and enslaving: freedom means escaping from bondage to that God. Second, there arose a tradition of Jesus' sayings as esoteric wisdom. Third, a soteriology of the soul's ascent to union with the divine from the popular forms of Platonism was adopted. And fourth, possibly, there was a mythical story of the descent of a divine being from the heavenly world to reveal that world as the true home of the soul. Each of the last three types of tradition lies behind conflicts or images in the New Testament writings.

Some scholars have argued that the incorporation of the sayings of Jesus into the gospel narrative of his life served to check the proliferation of sayings of the risen Lord uttered by Christian prophets. The soteriology of the soul's divinization through identification with wisdom has been seen behind the conflicts in *1 Corinthians.* Second-century Gnostic writings use the same traditions from Philo that scholars invoke as parallel to *1 Corinthians.* The question of a first-century redeemer myth is debated in connection with the Johannine material. While the image of Jesus in the *Gospel of John* could have been developed out of existing metaphorical traditions and the structure of a gospel life of Jesus, the Johannine letters show that Johannine Christians were split over interpretation of the gospel. Both *1 John* and *2 John* condemn other Christians as heretics. Heretics deny the death of Jesus and may have held a docetic Christology. Though perhaps not based on the myth of a descending redeemer, the Johannine images contributed to second-century Gnostic developments of that theme as applied to Jesus.

The second century brought fully developed Gnostic systems from teachers who claimed that their systems represented the inner truth revealed by Jesus. During this period, the Greek originals of the Coptic treatises were collected at Nag Hammadi. From the orthodox side, Irenaeus's five books refuting the Gnostics marked a decisive turn in Christian self-consciousness. These were followed by the anti-Gnostic writings of Hippolytus, Clement of Alexandria, Origen, Tertullian, and Epiphanius. Though Irenaeus may have drawn upon earlier anti-Gnostic writings, such as Justin's lost *Suntagma,* his work suggests a turn toward the systematic refutation of Gnosticism. Rather than catalog sects and errors, Irenaeus turned to the refutation of Gnostic systems using the rhetorical skills and *topoi* of philosophical debate. At the same time, he sought to provide a theoretical explication of orthodox Christian belief that would answer arguments advanced by Gnostic teachers. He apparently had considerable information about Valentinian speculation, as well as some of the earlier sources of Valentinian mythology.

Like the other heresiologists, Irenaeus attacked Marcion as well as Gnosticism. Marcion provided an easier target to identify as a "heresy" because he rejected the Old Testament and established a Christian canon consisting of edited versions of *Luke* and the Pauline letters. Marcion was concerned to set the boundaries between himself and the larger Christian community in a way that the Gnostic teachers who claimed to provide the spiritual interpretation of Christianity were not. Irenaeus provided two guidelines for drawing the boundary that would exclude Gnostic teachers from the Christian community. The first is reflected in the *regula fidei* of his *Against Heresies* (1.10.3), which gives topics about which legitimate theological speculation is possible and consequently rules out much of the cosmological speculation of the Gnostic teachers. The second guideline is Irenaeus's rejection of Gnostic allegorization of scripture. He insists that biblical passages must mean what they appear to mean and that they must be interpreted within their contexts. In book five, Irenaeus argues that the Gnostics failed to support their claims for a spiritual resurrection in *1 Corinthians* 1:50 because they ignored the eschatological dimensions of the verses that follow.

The heresiologist's concern to draw boundaries between orthodox Christianity and Gnostic teachings ran counter to the practice of second-century Gnostics. Several of the Nag Hammadi treatises were apparently composed with the opposite aim. Writings such as the *Gospel of Truth* and the *Tripartite Tractate* drew explicit connections between Gnostic teaching and both the teaching practice and the sacramental practice of the larger Christian community. Other Gnostic writings fell within the developing patterns of ascetic Christianity in Syria and Egypt (e.g., *Gospel of Thomas, Book of Thomas the Contender, Dialogue of the Savior*). The ascetic tradition tended to reject the common Christian assumption that baptism provides a quality of sinlessness adequate to salvation and to insist that only rigorous separation from the body and its passions will lead to salvation. Such ascetic groups did, of course, draw sharp boundaries between themselves and the larger world of believers, but the preservation of the Nag Hammadi codices among Egyptian monks suggests that the division between ascetic and nonascetic Christians may have been stronger than that between "heretic" and "orthodox," even into the fourth century in some areas.

Other Gnostic writings show that the efforts of heresiologists to draw boundaries against Gnostics resulted in repressive measures from the orthodox side and increasing separation by Gnostics (cf. *Apocalypse of Peter, Second Treatise of the Great Seth*). The *Testimony of Truth,* apparently written in third-century Alexandria, not only contains explicit attacks on the beliefs of orthodox Christians but also attacks other Gnostic sects and teachers like Valentinus, Isidore, and Basilides. The author of this Gnostic work considers other, nonascetic Gnostics as heretics. However, the author still holds to something of the nonpolemical stance that had characterized earlier Gnostic teachers, saying that the true teacher avoids disputes and makes himself equal to everyone. Another example of the effectiveness of the orthodox polemic in defining Gnostics as heretics is found in what appears to be a Gnostic community rule that calls for charity and love among the Gnostic brethren as a sign of the truth of their claims over against the disunity of the orthodox in *Interpretation of Knowledge.* This call reverses one of Irenaeus's polemical points that the multiplicity and disunity of Gnostic sects condemn their teaching when contrasted with the worldwide unity of the church.

Some scholars think that this third period, in which the Gnostics were effectively isolated as "heretic" by orthodox polemic, led to a significant shift within Gnostic circles. Gnosticism began to become dechristianized, to identify more with the non-Christian, esoteric, and hermetic elements within its traditions. Gnostics became members of an independent esoteric sect, moved toward the more congenial Mandaean or Manichaean circles, existed on the fringes of Alexandrian Neoplatonism in groups that emphasized thaumaturgy, or joined the monks in the Egyptian desert, where they found a kindred spirit in the combination of asceticism and Origenist mysticism. Those associated with Manichaeism or Origenism would continue to find themselves among the ranks of heretical Christians. The rest were no longer within the Christian sphere of influence.

SEE ALSO Clement of Alexandria; Irenaeus; Manichaeism; Marcionism; Neoplatonism; Origen; Philo Judaeus; Tertullian.

BIBLIOGRAPHY

Anyone interested in Gnosticism should obtain the English translation of the Nag Hammadi codices edited by James M. Robinson, *The Nag Hammadi Library in English* (San Francisco, 1977). Another book that studies the structure and the apologetics of the Gnostic dialogues from the Nag Hammadi collection is my *The Gnostic Dialogue: The Early Church and the Crisis of Gnosticism* (New York, 1980). The only other reliable treatments of the new material and its significance for the interaction of Gnosticism and early Christianity are scholarly writings. Three volumes, containing papers by leading scholars in German, French, and English, provide important treatments of the subject: *Gnosis: Festschrift für Hans Jonas,* edited by Barbara Aland (Göttingen, 1978); *The Rediscovery of Gnosticism,* vol. 1, *The School of Valentinus,* and vol. 2, *Sethian Gnosticism,* edited by Bentley Layton (Leiden, 1980–1981). The best study of the Gnostic polemic against orthodox Christianity is Klaus Koschorke's *Die Polemik der Gnostiker gegen das kirchliche Christentum* (Leiden, 1978).

PHEME PERKINS (1987)

GNOSTICISM: HISTORY OF STUDY

The problem of the origin of Gnosticism has been approached in Western culture with methods and results that are sometimes in clear disagreement. Perhaps the first to deal with the subject critically was Gottfried Arnold, who wrote in 1699 the *Unparteiische Kirchen und Ketzer Historie* (*Impartial History of the Church and of Heresy*)—a work that influenced the poetry of Goethe in a Gnostic sense—although the subject was previously mentioned in by G. P. Marcossius's *De Vitis Secretis et Dogmatibus omnium Haereticorum,* printed in Cologne in 1569.

However, it was only with Johann Lorenz von Mosheim (1694–1755) that the study of Gnosticism came to the fore as an independent discipline. In his degree thesis entitled "Institutiones christianae maiores" (Helmstadt, 1739) the future Protestant pastor and theologian described *gnōsis* as an Eastern philosophy that had rapidly expanded of its own accord from Greece and Chaldea (=Mesopotamia), and reached as far as Egypt. This doctrine, almost by a process of osmosis, would have taken certain elements from Jewish thinking. In its turn, the Jewish world would also have drawn themes from Gnostic thought, using them in its polemic against Greek philosophy. In the analysis of Mosheim we can already discern in a nutshell a substantial part of the themes developed by later historiography.

The works of J. Horn and Ernest Anton Lewald partly disagree with Mosheim. According to them, the sources of Gnosticism could be traced back to the land and teaching of Zoroaster, thus forming the basis for that successful interpretation which considered ancient Gnosticism a classic example of dualist philosophy. However, the works of Johann August Neander and Jacques Matter follow the same line of interpretation as Mosheim. The extensive work of Matter describes *gnōsis* as the emergence at the heart of Christianity of all the cosmological and theosophical speculation which formed the greater part of Eastern religions and which had been adopted in the West by the Neoplatonists. This doctrine therefore arose as a synthesis of themes drawn from the philosophical works of Plato, Aristotle, the Avesta, the Qabbalah, and the Eleusinian and Orphic mysteries. If the work of Matter provided Gnostic doctrine with a certain notoriety and cultural dignity on the one hand, it was nevertheless an interpretation based upon a particularly stereotyped view of the East, and very much a product of its time.

From the very beginning there has been an attempt to reconstruct the possible relationship between Gnosticism and Judaism: in 1846 Heinrich Graetz, in his book *Gnostizismus und Judentum,* tried to prove Gnostic influence on a number of rabbinical traditions. Decades later, Moritz Friedländer would reverse the methodological model of Graetz, stressing Jewish influence upon Gnosticism and thus giving rise to a fresh line of interpretation which has lasted to the present day.

INFLUENCE OF THE *RELIGIONSGESCHICHTLICHE SCHULE.* In 1851, study of Gnosticism was given a new impetus thanks to the discovery of the *Philosophumena* or, rather, *The Refutation of All Heresies,* a work attributed to Hippolytus of Rome, which over the years has seen numerous editions and translations, including those by Paul Wendland and Miroslav Marcovich, to mention two that are very different. In 1853 came the work of F. C. Baur, *Das Christentum und die christliche Kirche der drei ersten Jahrhunderte,* which assembled an impressive range of comparative material and formed the basis for the bold speculations of scholars of the *Religionsgeschichtliche Schule,* especially Johann Franz Wilhelm Bousset (1865–1920) and Richard Reitzenstein (1861–1931). In the years that followed the publication of the work of Baur, there were significant researches by Gustav Volkmar, Gerhard Uhlhorn, and particularly Richard Adelbert Lipsius (1830–1892), who was responsible for a critical study of the Ophite Gnostic system and a monumental article on Gnosticism in the *Allgemeine Enzyklopaedie.*

The fundamental idea of placing Gnosticism in the context of Greek philosophy and in particular Platonic philosophy dates from the 1880s and is restated in the work of Manuel Joel. Some of the interpretations that regard Gnosticism as a philosophical phenomenon originating from the very heart of Christianity are the thinking and researches of Adolph Hilgenfeld (1823–1907) and Adolf von Harnack (1851–1930), scholarly philologists belonging to the so-called School of the History of Dogma.

In a certain way prefigured by the studies of ancient syncretism by Albrecht Dieterich, the pan-Egyptian theories of M. A. Amelineau, and the pan-Babylonian theories of Wilhelm Anz and Konrad Kessler, the School of the History of Religions put forward the theory that Gnosticism was a phenomenon that predated Christianity, and that so-called Christian *gnōsis* represented merely a particular and at times even marginal aspect of this. The work of Bousset, *Hauptprobleme der Gnosis,* is central to these hermeneutics. Despite the critical review of Carsten Colpe, it is a text that is still of fundamental importance to today. Bousset studied the various Gnostic motifs such as dualism, the myth of the descent of the Savior, and the ascension to heaven and the figure of the Mother of Light, tracing their origins back in the form of Iranian/Mesopotamian syncretism. Another very important scholar, classical philologist, and religious historian who concerned himself with the origins of Gnosticism was Eduard Norden (1868–1941) in his work *Agnostos Theos.* Even if in this book the topic was not dealt with explicitly, Norden assumes the existence of a pre-Christian Gnosticism, basing this interpretation on material derived from hermetic literature.

The high point of the historical religious trend was undoubtedly the *Das iranische Erlösungsmysterium* of Reitzenstein. Preceded by a work on hermetic literature and by one on mystery religions, the "Iranian Salvation Mystery" is an analytical development of several of the themes already set out in the works of Bousset. The central motif for Reitzenstein is the event which he defines as "The Savior Saved," namely the Messenger, the primordial man who descends to matter to set free the Light Soul. If God is light and a part of that light remained trapped in the world, when God comes down into the world in the form of the envoy to free it, by saving it he also saves himself. Reitzenstein, in support of the Iranian nature of these themes, refers to a supposed "Fragment of Zarathushtra," a spurious text which later philological criticism would identify as being a Manichaean literary creation and thus not Zoroastrian.

Reactions to the works of the *Religionsgeschichtliche Schule* were not long in coming: in 1925 in Paris the second edition of Eugène de Faye's book, *Gnostiques et gnosticisme,* was published. In this it was possible to catch a glimpse of several approaches, including an analysis of sources aiming to prove the existence of the *Syntagma* of Justin—the first true list of heresies—hypothetically reconstructed from pseudo-Tertullian and Epiphanius; an analysis of the individual features of various Gnostic systems; and the forceful statement that Gnostic philosophy predated its mythology. In short, de Faye intended to describe a Christian Gnosticism that was independent from previous Iranian or Mesopotamian religious models.

The Iranian hypothesis of the *Religionsgeschichtliche Schule* was also the basis of the exegetic work by the Protestant theologian Rudolf Bultmann (1884–1976). Studies on Mandaeism by the philologist and Semitist Mark Lidzbarski had a decisive influence on Bultmann in his interpretation of John's Gospel: the passages where Jesus is considered a heavenly messenger who has come down to bring revelation to humanity had certain parallels in Mandaean literature. For Bultmann the fourth Gospel represents the outcome of and reaction to a pre-Christian myth deriving directly from a Gnostic Mandaean milieu.

Harnack had defined Gnosticism as a phenomenon involving the "acute Hellenization of Christianity" (Harnack, 1893–1904). In stark contrast with this definition were the claims of Bousset and Reitzenstein, according to whom Gnosticism was a pre-Christian religious movement of Iranian/Mesopotamian origin. The controversy also involved the Iranist Hans H. Schaeder, at first a supporter of Reitzenstein in the joint work *Studien zum antiken Synkretismus* (Leipzig, 1926). A follower of the philosopher Oswald Spengler, Schaeder went on to describe hermeneutics according to which Gnosticism is seen as a combination of elements that were Greek in form but Eastern in content. This trend was continued by Hans Leisegang in his work *Die Gnosis,* which confirmed the dual nature of the Gnostic phenomenon but nonetheless stated its single origin, developed from the amalgamation of those two religious elements.

The work of Hans Jonas (1903–1993), *Gnosis und spätantiker Geist*, occupies an intermediate position. It is a work which is set out as the first genuine synthesis on the Gnostic problem. Jonas's work uses two main interpretative sources: the comparative material assembled by the *Religionsgeschichtliche Schule* (in particular Bousset and Reizenstein), and the existentialist theological hermeneutics of Bultmann (which is in turn indebted to the philosophy of Martin Heidegger). For Jonas, the central kind of *gnōsis* is "Syro-Egyptian," as distinct from the "Iranian" sort: the first has an emanative "de-evolutive" structure which finally produces a rebellious Demiurge; in the second there is an absolute dualism of two principles, in which the cosmos arises from the dismemberment of an original being (a typical Indo-Iranian motif). Jonas, however, as subsequently noted by Ioan Petru Culianu and Giovanni Casadio, omits to take into account the so-called Triadic Gnostic Systems that are usually defined as "Sethian," in which there are three main principles involved: Light, the *pneuma* (spirit), and Darkness. Starting from what he calls *das Prinzip der Konstruktion*, Jonas traces in Syro-Egyptian *gnōsis*, in addition to a large number of influences derived from hermetic and mystery writings, a new factor, that of regarding the world (=*kosmos*) as an ontological evil from which it is necessary to be set free. From this point of view God is therefore the one who saves humans from the world. The relationship between God and the world is developed in a cosmological and anthropological antithesis: if on the one hand God is the opposite of the world, on the other hand the *pneuma*, which is hidden in the human body, is opposed to the *psyche* and *hyle* (soul and matter). The earthly world has a totally autonomous beginning: it is Darkness, a substance which is "real" only in contrast to its opposite, Life, the shining *pleroma* (fullness). God and the world are absolutely incompatible. Such an idea is an absurdity to the Greek mind, and the anti-Gnostic *Ennead* of Plotinus is a confirmation of this. It is thus impossible to ascribe the origins of the Gnostic phenomenon to Platonic speculation. The Fathers of the Church were no less unresponsive to this idea of denial of the world, and thus rejected the possibility that the origin of Gnosticism should be found in the heart of the Christian church. As regards the figure of the Demiurge, he should not be identified with the Devil: his portrayal comes both from Platonic doctrines and from Jewish beliefs on creation. For Jonas, the most distinctive form of Gnostic dualism is the Syro-Egyptian emanative system, in which the passage from the perfection of the world of light to the disorder of the earthly world is marked by the *hybris* (arrogance) of an intermediate creature, Sophia. On the other hand, according to Jonas, the Iranian kind of Gnosticism would represent an anticosmic adaptation of a preexisting, specifically Iranian dualism.

JUDEO-CHRISTIAN ORIGINS. A large number of scholars eventually supported the theory of the Jewish or Judeo-Christian origin of Gnosticism. As has been said, one of the first and main exponents of this tendency was Friedländer in his *Der vorchristliche jüdische Gnosticismus*. He insisted in particular that there existed a popular religious feeling in the heart of Judaism, within which apocalyptic and subsequently Gnostic speculation emerged. In this hermeneutic vein, according to the writings of Erik Peterson (1890–1960) and Jean Daniélou (1905–1974), the first Gnostic writers should be sought in Jewish apocalyptic. Hans Joachim Schoeps offers a similar interpretation, in which he stresses the presence of a "Gnostic Judaism" in the writings of the Qumran community. Another scholar, Robert McLachalan Wilson, has noted the relationship between post-Christian Gnosticism and the Judaism of the Diaspora in his book *The Gnostic Problem* (1958). His conclusions tend to define the Gnostic phenomenon as being strongly influenced by the religious representations of post-Diaspora Judaism. In discussion of the work of Wilson, a German scholar, Alfred Adam, has set out evidence of the clear presence of Aramaic borrowings in the *nomina numina* of Gnostic mythology, a line of interpretation also pursued by the Coptic scholar Alexander Böhlig (1912–1996). The works of the U.S. scholar Birger A. Pearson are also important with regard to the hypothesis concerning Judaism. He has studied the Gnostic texts of Nag Hammadi for evidence of their possible sources and interpolations in Jewish writings.

The most complete description of the existence of a genuine Gnosticism at the heart of Jewish tradition is, however, by two scholars of exceptional talent: Gershom G. Scholem (1897–1982) and Gilles Quispel (b. 1916). Scholem is responsible for the "discovery" of mystic Jewish *gnōsis*, found in the ecstatic vision of the merkavah, the "chariot" or "throne" on which God sits in *Ezekiel* 1:26. Analysis of merkavah literature led Scholem to redefine the problem of Gnostic origins. First of all, these merkavah texts in many regards go back to orthodox Judaism and some are datable to the beginning of the fourth century CE. With tremendous erudition Scholem demonstrates that Gnostic documents considered "Christian" assume certain fundamental connections with the mysticism of the merkavah. Thus when Saint Paul describes his ascension into paradise, to the "third heaven," he borrows words from Jewish mysticism; thus it is also probable that the visionary author of *The Shepherd of Hermas*, and Valentinus were aware of Jewish speculation on the name of God; the documents of the Valentinian Gnosis, especially the *Excerpta ex Theodoto*, reveal the influence of teaching imparted in Jewish esoteric circles. For Scholem, in the end, this mystic Gnosticism of the merkavah was not outside the sphere of Halakhic tradition: it would eventually develop motifs and attitudes already present in orthodox rabbinical teaching of the law, upon which apocalyptic eschatology had exerted a marginal influence, expressing in the first decades of the Christian era the restlessness and religious revival of a large part of the Jewish world. The coptologist and religious historian Gilles Quispel has a related viewpoint, but expresses it differently. "Gnosis minus Christentum ist Gnosis" (Quispel, 1951); with this assumption Quispel claims independence and originality for Gnosticism as regards the philosophical and religious currents of Hellenistic and Roman syncretism. On the one hand, in line with the Jungian psychology of which Quispel is an adherent, *gnōsis* is a unique religious self-contained experience, namely a mythical projection involving the search for the true essence of the human person (=the self); on the other hand, Quispel traces the origins of this original pattern of thinking to a specific branch of Alexandrian Judaism. From this cultural milieu—more recently defined as "The Hermetic Lodge of Alexandria"—originated the thinking on the cosmos and on the human race found in the highly developed visions of Valentinus, if not directly those of Origen (185–254). Quispel is indebted, albeit indirectly, to the method of the *Religionsgeschichtliche Schule;* Giovanni Casadio has indeed noted how the pan-Judaic hypothesis regarding the origin of Gnosticism expressed by Quispel reflects the method and conclusions of the pan-Iranian hypothesis of Reitzenstein and his followers: heterogeneous aims then!

In the wake of the works of Scholem and Quispel followed the researches of Guy Gedaliahu Stroumsa (Judaic and Gnostic origins of the Manichaean myths), Jarl Fossum (Samaritan origins of Gnostic myths), and Nathaniel Deutsch. Deutsch in particular took up the ideas of Scholem on the mysticism of the merkavah, going into more detail on the subject as regards the mythological description in the Mandaean Gnostic texts. J. C. Reeves studied the Jewish Gnostic contributions as the basis of Manichaean texts such as *The Book of Giants,* arriving at an original definition of Syrian-Mesopotamian *gnōsis* in which elements drawn from Iranian tradition also converged.

According to the study of the patrologist Robert M. Grant, *Gnosticism and Early Christianity,* Gnosticism originated from the remains of the apocalyptic eschatological expectations after the fall of Jerusalem. The hope that the kingdom of YHWH would come to pass on earth had guided and sustained the people of Israel. From the Maccabean revolt to the fall of Jerusalem in 70 CE, to the extreme revolt of Bar Kosebah under Hadrian, a bloody chain of events left a deep mark on the destiny of the "people of YHWH." The failure of the eschatological hope to be fulfilled on earth thus signified the outbreak of a tremendous spiritual crisis, which led to the appearance of new religious forms. From the belief that the God of this world has not managed to fulfill the hopes of his people comes rejection of the world, which, together with eschatological dualism, are the characteristic features of Gnosticism. The outer fringes of Judaism (e.g., the Essene community of Qumran, the Jewish circles influenced by the Iranian/Chaldaean "theology" of the "Hellenized Magi," the Judaism of the Diaspora in direct contact with the Aramaic Syro-Mesopotamian world) provided the materials which were united in the synthesis of the great Gnostic masters of the second century CE.

A hermeneutic work, which is somewhat similar to Grant's but which draws rather puzzling conclusions, is that by Ioan Petru Culianu (1950–1991), a Romanian scholar linked to the school of Ugo Bianchi (1922–1995). According to Culianu the origin of Gnostic nihilism can be found in the problem of the "Angels of the Nations": in ancient Judaism there existed a belief that every nation on earth had its own representative in the heavenly court, and the Jews expected direct political advantages because their heavenly representative was God himself, or the archangel Michael, who occupied the first place next to God. The fall of the Second Temple in 70 CE profoundly altered this vision. As Rome had conquered Palestine, and the occupation of the Holy Land had begun to seem unending, this seemed to indicate only one thing: Samael, the angel of Rome, had replaced God or Michael in the role of leader of the Angels of the Nations; like the power of Rome itself, Samael was an evil angel, the equivalent of Satan. To this hermeneutic hypothesis, Culianu added a precise, detailed phenomenology of Gnostic myths, studied in a diachronic manner. In the work of Culianu the interlinking of Gnosticism and modern nihilist thought is particularly important, a topic analyzed impartially and sometimes relentlessly, which has had a significant effect on the work of the Italian philosopher and scholar Elémire Zolla (1926–2002).

GREEK PLATONIC ORIGINS. In its theoretical layout the work of Culianu is certainly indebted to the research of another significant Italian scholar, Ugo Bianchi, who was responsible for organizing the important Congress of Messina in 1966 on the origin of Gnosticism. An ardent supporter of the Orphic and Platonic origins of the key themes of Gnosticism, Bianchi further maintained that Gnostic mythology reabsorbed and redeveloped archaic material, which can be identified by ethnological and folkloric research. To this last aspect of the question, he dedicated a specific volume (*Il dualismo religioso),* an important work which laid bare the analogies and possible relationships between Gnostic myths and the sphere of religious ethnography. The hypothesis of a purely Greek Platonic origin of Gnostic theodicy is also present in the works of Simone Pétrement, a French scholar and follower of the philosopher Simone Weil. Pétrement, following at times slavishly in the footsteps of Harnack, maintains that Gnosticism is a phenomenon involving the Hellenization of Christianity, in which religious elements give rise to a political theology of rebellion against every kind of social oppression; this is a hermeneutic concept that is definitely borrowed from the Marxist ideology of Weil. Consideration of social and political themes is also found in the research of the American scholar Elaine Pagels, who has made particular study of the balance of power as the basis of the contradiction between Gnostic thought and the church hierarchy. On the relations between the origins of Christianity and Gnosticism, the works of Manlio Simonetti (b. 1926) and Christoph Markschies (b. 1962) should also be considered.

A German religious historian, Carsten Colpe (b. 1929), in a famous early work critically revisited the ideas of the *Religionsgeschichtliche Schule,* demonstrating that many of the hypotheses proposed by Reitzenstein were without foundation. Over the years Colpe has produced a series of fundamental analyses that aim to untangle the various syncretic elements that are intertwined in the original Gnostic texts. Despite Colpe's criticisms, the Iranist interpretation of the Gnostic phenomenon has been articulately expounded in the work of another historian of religions, the Swedish scholar Geo Widengren (1907–1996). Widengren has improved upon the research of his predecessors, identifying the origin of Gnosticism in a particular esoteric and philosophical tendency in the Mazdean religion Zurvanism. According to Widengren, such wisdom traditions, along with the ideas of the Aramaic Mesopotamian world, gave rise to the *gnōsis* of the Mandaeans and consequently in a whole series of documents ascribed to what he has defined as "Parthian gnosis." The hybrid production based on Iranian and Mesopotamian materials in the context of the kingdom of Parthia is further at the root of a complex syncretism that runs through apocalyptic texts such as *The Book of Enoch* or more typical Qumran texts such as *The War Rule*, examples of an intertestamental Judaism that was beginning to interpret everything according to Gnostic canons. The research of Widengren and the fascinating work of the *Religionsgeschichtliche Schule* have found support in the work of the Italian Gherardo Gnoli (b. 1937), a scholar who has forcefully pointed out the Iranian roots of the Gnostic phenomenon. In Gnoli we also find Manichaeism redefined as an "Iranian Gnostic religion." An attempt to find a middle way between the extreme positions cited has been made by the German Kurt Rudolph (b. 1929), who as well as stressing the Hellenistic Greek and Judaic Aramaic substratum of the origins of Gnosticism also emphasizes the presence of Iranian material.

NAG HAMMADI. The discovery in the 1940s at Nag Hammadi, ancient Chenoboskion, of an entire library of Gnostic texts written in Coptic has given a new impetus to studies concerning the origins of Gnosticism. This literary corpus was discovered by Jean Doresse, a Coptologist whose fame has been eclipsed by that of Henri-Charles Puech (1902–1986). Puech was responsible for an outstanding series of works on Gnostic phenomenology; mention should be made of his work *La gnose et le temps*, which was inspired by the Swiss psychoanalyst Carl Gustav Jung (1875–1961) and dealt with the correspondence between the conceptions of space and time in Gnostic demiurgy. The school on Gnosticism and dualism begun by Puech has been continued in the work of his pupil Michel Tardieu, a keen supporter of historicophilological method but also the first to use the approach of structural anthropology in interpreting the Gnostic myths. We should also recall in the same context the work of Antoine Guillaumont on Semitic expressions in the Gnostic texts.

The disputes and controversies involving the rediscovery and publication of the Coptic corpus of Nag Hammadi have resulted in a large number of editions and versions of the Gnostic tracts. Between the 1950s and the 1970s various translations were circulated (published mainly in the pages of academic reviews) with parallel texts in Coptic. Mention should also be made of the pioneering works of Puech, Quispel, Pahor Labib, Walter Till, Guillaumont, Jan Zandee, Soren Giversen, Rudolf Kasser, Hans-Martin Schenke, Martin Krause, and Bentley Layton. Recently a critical edition and translation of the Gnostic texts of Nag Hammadi has been completed by a group of international scholars led by James M. Robinson, who is in charge of the Coptic Gnostic Library Project of the Institute for Antiquity and Christianity of Claremont (California). A series of predominantly but not exclusively French-speaking scholars (Jacques É. Ménard, Bernard Barc, Paul-Hubert Poirier, Michel Roberge, Louis Painchaud, Wolf-Peter Funk, Jean-Marie Sevrin, Einar Thomassen, John Turner, and others) at the University of Laval in Quebec in Canada are working on a French translation with critical text, equipped with monumental theological historical commentary on all the Nag Hammadi texts.

BIBLIOGRAPHY

Adam, Alfred. "Neuere Literatur zum Problem der Gnosis." *Göttingische Gelehrte Anzeigen* (1962): 22–46.

Baur, F. C. *Das Christentum und die christliche Kirche der drei ersten Jahrhunderte.* Tübingen, Germany, 1853, 1860.

Bianchi, Ugo. *Il dualismo religioso.* Rome, 1958.

Bianchi, Ugo. "Le problème des origines du gnosticisme et l'histoire des religions." *Numen* 12 (1965): 161–178.

Böhlig, Alexander. *Gnosis und Synkretismus.* Tübingen, Germany, 1989.

Bousset, Johann Franz Wilhelm. *Hauptprobleme der Gnosis.* Göttingen, Germany, 1907.

Bultmann, Rudolf. "Die Bedeutung der neuerschlossenen mandäischen und manichäischen Quellen für das Verstondnis des Johannesevangelium." *Zeitschrift für die neutestamentliche Wissenschaft* 24 (1925): 100–146.

Bultmann, Rudolf. *Das Evangelium des Johannes.* Göttingen, Germany, 1941.

Casadio, Giovanni. "Donna e simboli femminili nella gnosi del II secolo." In *La donna nel pensiero cristiano antico*, edited by U. Mattioli, pp. 305–306. Genoa, Italy, 1992.

Casadio, Giovanni, ed. *Ugo Bianchi. Una vita per la storia delle religioni.* Rome, 2002.

Colpe, Carsten. *Die religionsgeschichtliche Schule. Darstellung und Kritik ihres Bildes vom gnostischen Erlösermythus.* Göttingen, Germany, 1961.

Culianu, Ioan Petru. *Gnosticismo e pensiero moderno: Hans Jonas.* Rome, 1985.

Culianu, Ioan Petru. *I miti dei dualismi occidentali: dai sistemi gnostici al mondo moderno.* Milan, 1989.

Culianu, Ioan Petru. *The Tree of Gnosis.* San Francisco, 1992.

Daniélou, Jean. *Théologie du Judéo-Christianisme.* Tournai, Belgium, 1958.

De Faye, Eugène. *Gnostiques et gnosticisme.* 2d edition. Paris, 1925.

Deutsch, Nathaniel. *The Gnostic Imagination: Gnosticism, Mandaeism, and Merkabah Mysticism.* New York, 1995.

Drijvers, Han J. W. "The Origins of Gnosticism as a Religious and Historical Problem." In *East of Antioch: Studies in Early Syriac Christianity*, edited by Han J. W. Drijvers, pp. 321–351. London, 1984.

Farina, Raffaello. "Lo gnosticismo dopo Nag Hammadi." *Salesianum* 32 (1970): 425–454.

Fossum, Jarl. *The Name of God and the Angel of the Lord.* Tübingen, Germany, 1985.

Friedländer, Moritz. *Der vorchristliche jüdische Gnosticismus.* Göttingen, Germany, 1898.

Gnoli, Gherardo. "Un particolare aspetto del simbolismo della luce nel Mazdeismo e nel Manichiesmo." *Aion (Annali dell'Istituto Orientale di Napoli)* n.s. 12 (1962): 95–121.

Gnoli, Gherardo. "La gnosi iranica: per una impostazione nuova del problema." In *Le Origini dello Gnosticismo: Colloquio di Messina*, edited by Ugo Bianchi, pp. 281–290. Leiden, 1967.

Gnoli, Gherardo. "Manichaeismus und persiscle Religion." *Antaios* 11 (1969): 274–292.

Gnoli, Gherardo. "Universalismo e nazonalismo nell'Iran del III secolo." In *Incontro di Religioni in Asia tra il III e il X secolo dC*, edited by L. Lanciotti, pp. 31–54. Florence, 1984.

Gnoli, Gherardo. "L'evolution du dualisme iranien et le problème zurvanite." *Revue des Histoire des Religions Paris* 201 (1984): 115–118.

Gnoli, Gherardo. *De Zoroastre à Mani.* Paris, 1985.

Graetz, Heinrich. *Gnostizismus und Judentum.* Krotoschin, Germany, 1846.

Grant, Robert M. *Gnosticism and Early Christianity.* New York, 1959.

Guillaumont, Antoine. "Sémitisme dans les logia de Jesus retrouvés à Nag-Hammadi." *Journal Asiatique* 246 (1958): 113–123.

Haardt, Robert. "Bemerkungen zu den Methoden der Ursprungsbestimmung von Gnosis." In *Le Origini dello Gnosticismo. Colloquio di Messina*, edited by Ugo Bianchi, pp. 161–173. Leiden, 1967.

Harnack, Adolf von. *Geschichte der altchristlichen Literatur bis Eusebius.* 3 vols. Leipzig, Germany, 1893–1904.

Hippolytus. *Werke, III: Elenchos = Refutatio omnium haeresium*, edited by Paul Wendland. Leipzig, Germany, 1916.

Hippolytus. *Refutatio omnium haeresium*, edited by Miroslav Marcovich. Berlin and New York, 1986.

Horn, J. *Über die biblische Gnosis.* Hanover, Germany, 1805.

Joel, Manuel. *Blicke in die Religionsgeschichte zu Anfang des zweiten christlichen Jahrhunderts*, vols. 1–2. Breslau, Poland, 1880–1883.

Jonas, Hans. *Gnosis und spätantiker Geist.* Gottingen, Germany, 1934–1954.

Jonas, Hans. "A Retrospective View." In *Proceedings of the International Colloqium on Gnosticism*, edited by Geo Widengren, pp. 1–15. Stockholm, 1977.

Koester, Helmut. "The History-of-Religion School, Gnosis, and Gospel of John." *Studia Theologica* 40 (1986): 115–136.

Leisegang, Hans. *Die Gnosis.* Leipzig, Germany, 1924.

Lewald, Ernest Anton. *Commentatio ad historiam religionum veterum illustrandam pertinens de doctrina gnostica.* Heidelberg, Germany, 1818.

Lipsius, Richard Adelbert. "Gnostizismus." *Allgemeine Enzyklopaedie*, vol. 21, pp. 223–305. Leipzig, Germany, 1860.

Mantovani, Giancarlo. "Gnosticismo e Manicheismo." *Vetera Christianorum*, 1978–1982.

Matter, Jacques. *Histoire critique du Gnosticisme*, vols. 1–3. Paris, 1828.

Mazza, Mario. "Gnosticismo e sincretismo. Osservazioni in margine alla letteratura recente sulle origini gnostiche." *Helikon* 5 (1965): 570–587.

Michelini Tocci, Franco. "Review of G. Scholem, Jewish Gnosticism." *Rivista degli Studi Orientali* 37 (1962): 140–145.

Neander, Johann August. *Genetische Entwicklung der vornehmsten gnostische Systeme.* Berlin, 1818.

Nock, Arthur Darby. "Rev. of H. Jonas, *Gnosis und spätantiker Geist* I." *Gnomon* (1936): 605–612.

Norden, Eduard. *Agnostos Theos.* Leipzig, Germany, 1913.

Pagels, Elaine. *The Gnostic Gospels.* New York, 1979.

Pearson, Birger A. *Gnosticism, Judaism and Egyptian Christianity.* Minneapolis, 1990.

Peterson, Erik. *Frühkirche, Judentum und Gnosis.* Freiburg, Germany, 1959.

Pétrement, Simone. *Le Dieu séparé. Les origins du gnosticisme.* Paris, 1984.

Pokorný, Peter. "Der Ursprung der Gnosis." *Kairos* 9 (1967): 94–105.

Puech, Henri-Charles. *La gnose et le temps.* Paris, 1978.

Quispel, Gilles. *Gnosis als Weltreligion.* Zurich, 1951.

Quispel, Gilles. "Rev. of K. Rudolph (ed.), *Gnosis und Gnostizismus* (Darmstadt 1975)." *Vigiliae Christianae* 29 (1975): 235–238.

Reeves, J. C. *Jewish Love in Manichaean Cosmogony.* Cincinnati, Ohio, 1992.

Reitzenstein, Richard. *Poimandres.* Leipzig, Germany, 1904.

Reitzenstein, Richard. *Die hellenistischen Mysterienreligionen*, Leipzig, Germany, 1910.

Reitzenstein, Richard. *Das iranische Erlösungsmysterium.* Bonn, Germany, 1921.

Reitzenstein, Richard, and Hans H. Schaeder. *Studien zum antiken Synkretismus.* Leipzig, Germany, 1926.

Ries, Julien. *Les études gnostiques hier et aujourd'hui.* Louvain-la-Neue, Belgium, 1982.

Rollmann, Hans. "Gnōsis and Logos: The Contribution of Kurt Rudolph to the Scholarly Study of Religions." *Religious Studies Review* 8 (1982): 348–352.

Rudolph, Kurt. "Gnosis und Gnostizismus, ein Forschungbericht." *Theologische Rundschau* 34 (1969): 121–175; 181–231; 358–361; 36 (1971): 1–61; 89–124; 37 (1972): 289–360; 38 (1973): 1–25; 50 (1985): 1–40; 55 (1990): 113–152.

Rudolph, Kurt, ed. *Gnosis und Gnostizismus.* Darmstadt, Germany, 1975.

Schoeps, Hans Joachim. *Auf frühchristlicher Zeit.* Tübingen, Germany, 1950.

Scholem, Gershom G. *Jewish Gnosticism, Merkabah Mysticism, and Talmudic Tradition.* New York, 1960.

Scholer, David Martin. *Nag Hammadi Bibliography 1948–1969.* Leiden, 1971.

Scholer, David Martin. *Nag Hammadi Bibliography 1970–1994.* Leiden, 1997.

Simonetti, Manlio. *Ortodossia ed Edesia tra I e II secolo.* Messina, Italy, 1994.

Stroumsa, Gedaliahu. *Another Seed: Studies in Gnostic Mythology.* Leiden, 1984.

Tardieu, Michel. *Trois mythes gnostiques.* Paris, 1974.

Van den Broek, Roelof. "The Present State of Gnostic Studies." *Vigiliae Christianae* 37 (1983): 41–71.

Weiss, H.-F. "Einige Randbemerkungen zum Problem des Verhältnisses von 'Judentum' und 'Gnōsis.'" *Orientalische Literarturzeitung* 64 (1969): 550–551.

Widengren, Geo. *Iranisch-semitische Kulturbegegnung in parthischer Zeit.* Cologne, 1960.

Widengren, Geo. *Fenomenologia della religione.* Bologna, 1984. Translated as *Phenomenology of Religion.*

Williams, Michael Allen. *Rethinking "Gnosticism." An Argument for Dismantling a Dubious Category.* Princeton, N.J., 1996. In a postmodern vein he considers Gnosticism a modern construct, not justified by any ancient self-definition.

Wilson, Robert McLachalan. *The Gnostic Problem.* London, 1958.

Yamauchi, Edwin Martin. *Pre-Christian Gnosticism. A Survey of the Proposed Evidences.* Grand Rapids, Mich., 1983.

EZIO ALBRILE (2005)
Translated from Italian by Paul Ellis

GOATS SEE SHEEP AND GOATS

GOBLET D'ALVIELLA, EUGÈNE (1846–1925),

was a Belgian historian of religions, jurist, politician, and grand master of Freemasonry (which means, in Belgium, that one is anticlerical). Count Goblet d'Alviella was the first professor of history of religions at the Université Libre (i.e., "free thinking") of Brussels, of which he was rector from 1896 to 1898. He was militant as a freethinker in trying to have the teaching of religion in schools replaced by that of the science of religion.

Goblet d'Alviella divided the study of religions into three disciplines: "hierography," "hierology," and "hierosophy." Hierography describes the development of each of the known religions. Hierology, by comparing religions, tries to formulate laws of evolution of religious phenomena; it thus "makes up for the paucity of information, in any given race or society, about the history of a belief or an institution, by appealing to the environment or period." Hierology is purely factual, while hierosophy is a philosophical attempt at classifying the various conceptions of humanity's relations with "superhuman beings."

Although lacking special philological training, Goblet d'Alviella studied, in hierography, various domains: Egyptian religion, Mithraism, Greek religion, Christianity, and Hinduism. In hierology, his most notable work was *La migration des symboles* (1891), in which he studied the forms, meanings, and migrations of such religious symbols as the swastika, the sacred tree, and the winged disk. The winged disk, for instance, originated in Egypt as a symbol of the sun and was adopted by the Syrians, the Hittites, the Assyrians, and the Persians, with additions and transformations in both form and meaning. In hierosophy Goblet d'Alviella studied Rationalist churches, the belief in immortality, the Buddhist catechism, progress, syncretism, and the crisis of religion.

BIBLIOGRAPHY

A large number of Goblet d'Alviella's articles are reprinted in book form under the title *Croyances, rites, institutions,* 3 vols. (Paris, 1911). Three of his works exist in English translation: *Contemporary Evolution of Religious Thought in England, America, and India* (New York, 1886); *The Migration of Symbols* (London, 1894); and his Hibbert Lectures of 1891, *Lectures on the Origin and Growth of the Conception of God as Illustrated by Anthropology and History* (London, 1892). A good summary of Goblet d'Alviella's work can be found in the article by Julien Ries in the *Dictionnaire des religions* (Paris, 1984).

New Sources

Dierkens, Alain, ed. *Eugene Goblet d'Alviella, Historien et Franc-Maçon.* Brussels, 1995.

Mollier, Pierre. "La Réécriture du Grade Maçonnique de Chevalier du Soleil par Eugène Goblet d'Alviella: Sources, Enjeux et Sens." In *Eugene Goblet d'Alviella, Historien et Franc-Maçon.* Brussels, 1995.

JACQUES DUCHESNE-GUILLEMIN (1987)
Revised Bibliography

GOD

This entry consists of the following articles:

GOD IN THE HEBREW SCRIPTURES
GOD IN THE NEW TESTAMENT
GOD IN POSTBIBLICAL JUDAISM
GOD IN POSTBIBLICAL CHRISTIANITY
GOD IN ISLAM
AFRICAN SUPREME BEINGS

GOD: GOD IN THE HEBREW SCRIPTURES

The God of Israel is the major character in the Hebrew scriptures. Although he is not mentioned in the *Book of Esther* or in the *Song of Songs,* God appears in all the remaining twenty-two books of the Hebrew Bible. Within these books God is depicted as creator, provider, and lawgiver. Most of the writers assume that he is just, that he has a special relation with the people of Israel, and that he hearkens to prayer. But because the Bible is not a systematic theological treatise and because not all internal contradictions were removed by its editors, we find major disagreements among the writers about the crucial elements of Israelite faith, including concepts of God.

BIBLICAL TERMINOLOGY OF THE DIVINE. The proper name of the God whose exclusive worship is demanded by the biblical authors is written consonantally as *YHVH*. This tetragrammaton, attested more than 6,600 times in the Bible, also occurs on the Moabite Stone (ninth century BCE) and in several ancient Hebrew letters and inscriptions. Vocalized biblical texts do not preserve the actual pronunciation of *YHVH*. Instead, they direct the reader to pronounce the divine name as though it were the frequent epithet *adonai*, meaning "lord." (It was the misunderstanding of this scribal convention that gave rise to the English form *Jehovah*.) The original pronunciation of *YHVH* is generally reconstructed as "Yahveh" or "Yahweh," on the basis of early Greek transcriptions. A shorter form, *YH*, generally considered secondary, is found 24 times in the Hebrew scriptures. In proper names, the theophoric element is never written as *-yhvh* but as *-yh* or *-yhv*.

The name *YHVH* occurs frequently in the compound *yhvh tsv't* (*yahveh tseva'ot*). Usually translated as "lord of hosts," its exact significance is uncertain. Most likely it means either "creator of the [heavenly] hosts" or "Yahveh is the [armed] host of Israel." *YHVH* is also sometimes combined with *elohim*, the most common generic word for "god," in the form *Yahveh Elohim*. The term *elohim* appears some 2,600 times in the Hebrew scriptures, and, although in form the word is plural, it is often construed with a singular verb. Most commonly, *Elohim* refers to the God of Israel and is thus synonymous with or interchangeable with *Yahveh*. Certain writers, in particular the author of the so-called Elohist source of the Pentateuch and the composers of certain Psalms, preferred *Elohim* to *Yahveh* as the proper name of the God of Israel.

Even when *Elohim* refers to the God of Israel, it can be treated as a plural (*Gn.* 20:13). Most frequently, however, the plural references are to gods whose worship by Israelites is condemned by the biblical authors. These are referred to as *elohim aḥerim* ("other gods"; *Ex.* 20:3, *Dt.* 5:7) and *elohim ḥadashim* ("new gods"; *Jgs.* 5:8). Similar are expressions in which the plural construction is employed. Examples are *elohei ha-nekhar* ("foreign gods"; *Gn.* 35:2, *Jos.* 24:20) and *elohei nekhar ha-arets* ("foreign gods of the land"; *Dt.* 31:16). It must be noted that the Hebrew writers employ the singular sense of *elohim* even when illicit divinities such as Astarte, Milcom, and Chemosh are meant (*1 Kgs.* 11:5, 11:33).

Because *elohim* is antithetical to *anashim* ("people"; see *Jgs.* 9:13), it can include gradations between the two categories of divinity and humanity. Among these are ghosts (*1 Sm.* 28:13, *Is.* 8:19) and minor divinities (*Gn.* 32:29, 48:15–16). The term can also serve in adjectival expressions of might, power, and the like. Among such examples are *ruah elohim* ("mighty wind"; *Gn.* 1:2), *nesi' elohim* ("great prince"; *Gn.* 23:6), *naftulei elohim* ("violent struggles"; *Gn.* 30:8), *ḥittat elohim* ("terror"; *Gn.* 35:5), *ḥerdat elohim* ("panic"; *1 Sm.* 14:15), *kis'akha elohim* ("your eternal throne"; *Ps.* 45:7), and *har elohim* ("majestic mountain"; *Ps.* 68:16). In addition, *elohim* can mean "happenstance," as in *etsba'elohim* (*Ex.* 8:15), and, frequently approximates "nature" in the late book *Ecclesiastes*.

Related etymologically to *elohim* is the shorter form *eloah*, construed solely as a grammatical singular. Most of its occurrences are in the later books of the Hebrew scriptures, although it is found also in the archaic poem in *Deuteronomy* (32:15, 32:17). The word occurs almost exclusively in poetry and never with the definite article. With the exception of two passages in *Daniel* (11:38–39), *eloah*, in contrast to *elohim*, does not refer to foreign divinities but has the virtual status of a proper name for the God of Israel.

Another important scriptural designation of divinity is *el*, whose function corresponds generally to that of *elohim*. The word has numerous cognates in the classical Semitic languages and is attested some 230 times in the Hebrew scriptures in the singular as well as the plural, *elim*. Like *Elohim*, *El* can substitute for *Yahveh* as a proper name for the God of Israel, its most common use (*Nm.* 12:13, 23:8, 23:19; *Is.* 8:8, 8:10). The Hebrew word *el* can take the definite article and appear as *ha-'el*, "the god" (*Gn.* 46:3, *Ps.* 85:9). It can also refer to pagan deities in such forms as *el zar* ("strange god"; *Ps.* 44:21, 81:10), *el aḥer* ("other god"; *Ex.* 34:14), and *el nek-har* ("foreign god"; *Mal.* 2:11, *Ps.* 81:10).

Unlike *elohim*, *el* has clear antecedents in older Semitic languages. Early documents from Ebla (modern-day Tel Mardikh) in central Syria and from Mesopotamia show that the closely related *ilu* was used in Akkadian for "god" as well as for the proper name of a high god. Chronologically closer to first-millennium Israel are the texts from Ugarit in northern Syria, which employ *el* for "god" in general and also for the head of the Canaanite pantheon. El was known for wisdom and beneficence as well as for his exploits with sex and alcohol. He was a healer and creator god who was sometimes depicted as a bull. Some biblical passages that mention *el* refer to this god (*Is.* 14:13, *Ez.* 28:2, *Hos.* 12:6).

Because the Yahveh cult appropriated the name of El to its own object of worship, we cannot always tell whether an *el* reference in a biblical text is to the Canaanite El, to Yahveh, to a blend of both, or to another divinity entirely. Among the problematic occurrences is *el ro'i*, "the god who sees me" or "El who sees me" (*Gn.* 16:13). The name *El Bet-'El* (*Gn.* 31:13) is even more problematic, because a divinity named Beth'el, doubtless the hypostasis of a shrine, was worshiped in Samaria in the eighth century (*Hos.* 10:15, 12:5), in Tyre in the seventh century, and at Elephantine in Egypt in the fifth century. Similar difficulties attend the proper understanding of *el shaddai* (*Gn.* 17:1, 28:3; *Ex.* 6:3), which occurs as well in the form *shaddai* (*Nm.* 24:4, 24:16; *Ez.* 1:24; *Jb.*, *passim*). Earlier attempts to connect El Shaddai with the Amorite Bel Shade ("lord of the mountains") have been disproved. Recently published texts in Aramaic from Deir 'Alla in Jordan refer to *shaddayin*—divinities. Whether this discovery will shed some light on the biblical *el shaddai* remains to be seen. There has been a great deal of scholarly discussion of the name *El 'Elyon* (*Gn.* 14:18; *Ps.* 78:35). It is uncertain whether the name should be rendered "God most high" or "El most high" and whether the name itself is a blend of two originally distinct non-Israelite divinities. Finally, a divinity named El Berit had a temple at Shechem (modern-day Nablus). The name might be translated as "god of the covenant" or "El of the covenant."

BIBLICAL VIEW OF THE ORIGINS OF THE WORSHIP OF YHVH. The original meaning of the name *YHVH* is unknown to modern scholars. Only one biblical writer, the author of *Exodus* 3:14, attempted an explanation, by relating the name to the verb *hayah* ("be, exist"): "and YHVH said . . . say unto the children of Israel: 'I am' hath sent me unto you."

The biblical writers differ among themselves as to when the worship of Yahveh originated. According to *Genesis* 4, Eve knew God by the name *Yahveh*, and her two sons, Cain and Abel, brought him sacrifices. Verse 26 of that same chapter tells us that in the days of Enosh (Hebrew for "person"), grandson of Adam, the name *Yahveh* began to be invoked. In other words, God was worshiped as soon as there was a human community. In contrast, the author of *Exodus* 6, commonly identified as the Priestly writer (or the P source) denies that Israel's ancestors knew God by this name (*Ex.* 6:3). Instead, he asserts that Abraham, Isaac, and Jacob knew their God as El Shaddai and that the name *Yahveh* was only first revealed to Moses. Though most scholars regard the P source as one of the latest documents, there is something to be said here for its reliability. It is unlikely that the writer would have originated the claim that the ancestors did not know the proper name of the ancestral god. At the same time, the writer might have wished simply to glorify Moses.

Extrabiblical data have not resolved the question of the origin of Yahveh worship. Similarities in the cultures and languages of first-millennium Israel and third-millennium Ebla, as well as second-millennium Mari, have led some scholars to interpret elements of personal names in texts emanating from these areas as references to Yahveh. These interpretations have not won general acceptance. The same holds for the fragmentary mention of a god called Yv at late second-millennium Ugarit. Perhaps the most promising clue comes from a location named Yhv' in the Negev or the Sinai desert mentioned in Egyptian sources from the thirteenth and fourteenth centuries BCE. These references lend some support to the Midianite or Kenite hypothesis that makes much of the biblical traditions that Yahveh revealed himself to Moses in Midianite territory (*Ex.* 3) and that the father-in-law of Moses was a Midianite priest (*Ex.* 2) who taught Moses how to administer divine law (*Ex.* 18).

THE HISTORICAL PROBLEM OF ISRAELITE MONOTHEISM. Scholars are in agreement that Judaism was a monotheistic religion by the end of the Babylonian exile (c. 539 BCE). Most also agree that Jewish monotheism was greatly encouraged by the preachings of the preexilic prophets. The Hebrew scriptures in their present form are colored by the belief that Yahveh was the sole legitimate object of Israelite worship from earliest times. In consequence, the biblical depiction of Yahveh worship presents the unusual situation of a people who seem to have disregarded for centuries what is in retrospect said to have been their official religion. The German scholar Julius Wellhausen ([1885] 1957) argued that the official religion of Israel had been originally polytheistic and that Yahveh had been a national god to whom every Israelite owed allegiance. In this respect, Yahveh did not differ from the Moabite god Chemosh or the Assyrian Ashur. The Bible notes time and time again that Israelites worshiped other gods alongside Yahveh. According to Wellhausen, no one viewed this as problematic until the rise of classical prophecy in the eighth century BCE. Yahveh, proclaimed the prophets, would punish unethical behavior on Israel's part by bringing foreigners against them. In order to make this threat credible, Yahveh had to grow in power at the expense of all other divinities.

Only with the fall of Judah (in 587/6 BCE), in Wellhausen's analysis, did the contrite Jewish masses begin to accept that the prophets had been right. The dispersion of Yahveh's people all over the world proved that Yahveh was a universal God and, finally, the sole God in existence. The exilic prophet "Second Isaiah" was the most articulate representative of this thoroughgoing monotheism. Under the influence of his and similar teachings, the bulk of the Pentateuch was composed, and the early prophetic and historical writings were reshaped. In other words, what the Hebrew scriptures present is largely retrojection of monotheistic beliefs of the exilic and postexilic periods onto true early Israelite religion.

In contrast to Wellhausen, other scholars, such as William F. Albright (1957) and, especially, Yeḥezkel Kaufmann (1970), argued that monotheism was Mosaic in origin and was Israel's official religion. These scholars generally accept the Bible's judgment that much of Israelite attention to other gods was sinful. Kaufmann, however, departs from this consensus. He argues that the prophets, in condemning Israelite idolatry, were in fact polemicizing against vestigial fetishism. The fact that their opposition was more often directed against "idolatry," the worship of "wood and stone," rather than against real gods was for Kaufmann highly significant. According to his theory, the monotheistic revolution fomented by Moses had so thoroughly eradicated polytheism from Israel that most Israelites no longer understood the myth, ritual, and magic practiced by their pagan neighbors. Aside from some government-sponsored or -tolerated exceptions, the Israelites were never guilty of more than leftover superstition. To the zealous prophets, however, these venial sins warranted Yahveh's harshest punishments. The correctness of the prophetic position was demonstrated, at least to the prophets, by Israel's political defeats.

Israelite monolatry. We have seen that the biblical writers (as well as modern scholars) disagree about the period in which the explicit worship of the one God began. There is no disagreement, however, that the Bible requires that the people Israel serve God exclusively. Various early formulations of God's demand for exclusive worship connect it with the exodus from Egypt, an event that, if exaggerated in magnitude, clearly has some historical basis (*Ex.* 20:2–3, *Hos.* 13:4, *Ps.* 81:10–11). According to the Pentateuch, a covenant (*berit*) between God and Israel was concluded through the mediation of Moses at the mountain variously called "Sinai," "Horeb," and "the mountain of God." This covenant bound Israel to Yahveh's exclusive service and carried with it the obligations that were understood as the Law. (*Ex.* 19–24, 34; *Dt.* 5). An additional covenant to the same effect was made in the plains of Moab (*Dt.* 29–30). *Joshua* 24 describes how Joshua caused his people to conclude a covenant for God's exclusive worship at Shechem (without reference to any Mosaic precedent). None of these covenant traditions insists that Yahveh is the sole god in existence, yet each maintains that Israel is bound to serve him alone.

Some of the early prophets, such as Amos and Isaiah, do not employ the covenant theme explicitly, but they likewise insist on Yahveh's demand to be worshiped by Israel to the exclusion of all other gods. That demand is best described as *monolatry*, a form of worship in which only one god is served but the existence of others is not denied. Monolatrous worship is, in theory, compatible with polytheism.

Monolatry was not unknown in the ancient Near East. In the fourteenth century BCE, Akhenaten, King of Egypt, had inaugurated a solar monolatry in which the royal family worshiped the Aton, the sun disk, to the exclusion of Egypt's traditional gods. Mesopotamian mythology describes the temporary worship of a single god in an emergency. In addition, ancient Near Eastern prayer literature regularly employed monolatrous language. A worshiper would approach various gods in turn with the declaration that each one was the only proper object of worship. Sometimes the suppliant went as far as saying that the other gods were no more than attributes or bodily limbs of the god addressed. Undoubtedly at the moment of utterance, these pious statements were meant sincerely, although their intent was not to invalidate the worship of other gods.

Yet the fact that monolatry was found outside of Israel does not explain why it was deemed so important in Israel. The books of the Bible agree that Israel's tenure in its own land depended on the exclusive worship of Yahveh. In spite of Yahveh's reminders tendered by his servants the prophets, the people insisted on worshiping other gods (*2 Kgs.* 17:7–23, *Jer.* 25:3–11), with whom they were supposed to have no relation (*Ex.* 23:32; *Jer.* 7:9). The fall of Samaria in 720 BCE and the fall of Judah in 587/6 BCE were caused, according to the biblical writers, by failure to adhere to the covenant with Yahveh.

The covenant, it must be understood, was integral to the very identity of the Israelites as a political entity. It was the god Yahveh who was credited with bringing out from Egypt those descendants of Egyptian slaves and native dissidents who were to constitute the people Israel. Through Yahveh, this new group was to acquire its own land, independent of the Egypto-Canaanite political system. This granting of land by Yahveh to his people was also described by the metaphor of *berit*, or "covenant," and was modeled after the international treaty formulas of the second millennium BCE. In Israelite theory, all the land belonged to Yahveh, who assigned it to his people in terms similar to those found in Hittite suzerainty treaties, in which the "great king" demanded sole allegiance from his clients. In its religious adaptation, the covenant notion meant that Israel was to serve Yahveh alone. The Hittite kings demanded exclusive allegiance because they knew that their clients might turn to other kings. Yahveh's representatives, who acknowledged the existence of other gods with whom one might be tempted to make a similar covenant (*Ex.* 23:32), demanded analogous exclusive allegiance. In addition, the covenant with Yahveh served as the theological expression of the mundane political union between the Canaanite natives and the outsiders who together made up Israel, a process described in *Joshua* 24. It may be noted that the setting of this chapter is Shechem, the scene of successful and unsuccessful coalitions with Canaanites (see *Gn.* 34 and *Jgs.* 8–9).

God in covenant and history. Because it had emerged in historical circumstances, the covenant metaphor imparted to the Israelite cult a far greater concern with "history" than was found in the other cults of the ancient Near East. The "triumphs of Yahveh" (*Jgs.* 5:11), as they are called in the ancient Song of Deborah, were more focused on human life than were Baal's victories over death and aridity. It is not that the gods of the other nations were not concerned with history nor that Yahveh was not concerned with nature. Rather, the degree of emphasis was markedly different in Israel in that Israelite writers were more likely to produce tales of Yahveh's political triumphs than to produce tales of his cosmic ones.

The relative space given in the Bible to God's "mythical" and "historical" deeds is very instructive. Several poetic passages refer to divine combat with a sea monster in which Yahveh vanquishes his foes in the manner of the Babylonian Marduk, the Canaanite Baal, and the Hittite Iluyankas (*Is.* 27:1, 30:7, 51:9–10; *Hb.* 3:8; *Ps.* 74:13–14, 89:10–11, 93:1–4; *Jb.* 26:10–14). The first eleven chapters of *Genesis* contain accounts of God's creation of the world by fiat in the manner of the Egyptian Ptah, the expulsion of Adam and Eve from Eden, the descent of the ancient heroes from the fallen divinities, and the great flood. Most of the biblical text, however, concentrates on God's relation to humanity and, especially, to Israel. The Bible is unique among the preserved literature of the ancient Near East in the extent to which a god is involved in human institutions. Thus although there are references to ritual instructions in Egyptian divine books and Mesopotamian accounts of the divine revelation of exorcisms and incantations, these are the exception. The well-known Code of Hammurabi of Babylon (1792–1750 BCE) contains numerous parallels to biblical law, but it is the king, and not the god of justice, who claims credit for its composition.

The Bible claims divine jurisdiction over all areas of life in a more thorough and consistent manner than do all other extant ancient Near Eastern sources. Although Babylonian legal collections such as Hammurabi's Code or the Laws of Eshnunna, for example, show close parallels to laws in the Pentateuch, the context is different. Thus, Hammurabi claims that the gods had called on him to establish justice and so he, the king, enacted the laws. In contrast, in the Hebrew Bible the claim is made that all laws governing all Israelite institutions and all personal relations were divinely revealed to Moses at Yahveh's sacred mountain. Every human action, even when wickedly intended, such as the sale of Joseph by his brothers, is part of the divine plan (*Gn.* 45:5, 50:19–20). Unlike the Akkadian speaker who could describe actions performed *lā libbi ilāni* ("without divine consent"), the Hebrew could refer only to divine disapproval.

The exclusive worship of Yahveh was the religious expression of the political and social factors that had brought Israel into existence. The demand to serve Yahveh alone came to the fore in the settlement of the land, in the formation of the monarchy under Saul (eleventh century BCE), in the purge of the house of Omri under Jehu (r. 842–815 BCE), in the anti-Assyrianism of Hezekiah (r. 715–686 BCE), and in the expansionism of Josiah (r. 640–609 BCE). It reached its logical conclusion, monotheism, in the exilic preachments of "Second Isaiah" and in the reconstitution of the postexilic community of the fifth century BCE.

The persistence of polytheism. At the same time, a number of factors undermined Yahvistic monolatry from the beginning. First, the people who made up Israel were themselves of diverse origin and could not easily forsake their ancestral gods (see *Jos.* 24). Second, monolatry does not deny the existence of the many divinities. As normality set in, the old gods whose existence had never been denied reasserted themselves; the international interests of the monarchy and of commerce also encouraged tolerance of other gods.

It should also be recalled that polytheism made sense in the ancient world. It was not until long after the Babylonian exile that such concepts as "nature" and "universe," which Greek thinkers formulated, began to make an impact in the Middle East. Israelite worship of gods and goddesses reflects the difficulty that the average person must have had in assuming an underlying unity in what appears to be a collection of diverse forces often opposed one to another.

Many Israelites must have resisted monotheism because of its difficulty in accounting for unwarranted suffering. To be sure, the problem of theodicy had been raised by Mesopotamian thinkers long before the rise of Israel, but because polytheists could always blame divine injustice on rivalry among the gods, the problem never became so pointed as in the late biblical writings *Job* and *Ecclesiastes.* These postexilic works were written by authors who took for granted that Yahveh was the sole god in existence. If that sole God was all-powerful and just at the same time, how could injustice persist? The author of *Job* answered that God was not omnipotent. The writer of *Ecclesiastes* answered that injustice was built into the system that God had set in motion.

THEOCRASY. The blending of gods and their characteristics is the salvation of monolatry and surely of monotheism. As increasing numbers of Israelites began to become consistent monolaters and monotheists, a process that took centuries, the figure of Yahveh began to absorb many of the functions and attributes of the older gods. We have seen that Yahveh assumed El's name in addition to that god's reputation for beneficence and wisdom. Yahveh likewise acquired Baal's thunderous voice (*1 Sm.* 2:10), his fructifying abilities (*Hos.* 2:10), and his title of "cloud rider" (*Ps.* 68:5).

The biblical writers did not, however, tolerate Yahveh's absorption of the attributes of Near Eastern goddesses. Instead, they condemned the widespread royal and popular worship of female deities. The mother of the pious king Asa (c. 913–873 BCE) had constructed an image of Asherah, and another representation of this same Canaanite "creator of the gods" stood in Yahveh's Jerusalem Temple until Josiah's time (*2 Kgs.* 21:7). In ancient Israel, Astarte remained popular in her classical form as well as in her Aramean-Mesopotamian incarnation as "queen of heaven" (*Jer.* 7:18, 44:17ff.). The biblical depiction of the popularity of female divinities is corroborated by external evidence. Recent archaeological discoveries at Kuntillet 'Ajrud and Khirbet al-Qum have brought to light Hebrew inscriptions referring to "Yahveh of Teman and his Asherah." It is possible that *asherah* in these inscriptions had become a common noun meaning "consort." Finally, the Jews at Elephantine in the fifth century BCE knew a divinity called Anatyahu, an apparent androgynous blend of Yahveh with the ancient Canaanite goddess Anat.

Despite the popularity of female divinity, or perhaps because of it, biblical monolatry excluded the female presence. With rare exceptions (*Isa.* 42:14; 66:13), the biblical writers personify Yahveh with masculine traits, a reflection of the power structure in Israelite society. The northern kingdom of Israel never had a reigning queen. Athaliah, the only reigning queen of the southern kingdom of Judah (842–837 BCE), had come to power under highly irregular circumstances (*2 Kgs.* 11:1–3). There were some women prophets, among them Miriam, Deborah, Huldah and the anonymous wife of Isaiah (*Isa.* 8:3), but no female priests.

THE RISE OF MONOTHEISM. The present state of the evidence suggests that monolatry arose early in Israel but that monotheism was a late development. Throughout the early first millennium BCE, only a minority of Israelites were consistent in their exclusive worship of Yahveh. To this tenacious minority we are indebted for the henotheistic concept of Yahveh that informs the earlier biblical books. The narratives of *Joshua* 24 and *Genesis* 35 reflect what must have been the majority view: to engage in the cult of Yahveh while images of other gods were present was defiling. Jeremiah assailed his contemporaries for committing crimes and then proceeding to Yahveh's temple and declaring that "we have been saved" (*Jer.* 7:9–10). Baal worship is among the enumerated crimes. Presumably the priesthood required of all entrants to the sanctuary the declaration that they served Yahveh alone, which at the moment they did, fulfilling the Decalogue's demand that "you shall have no other gods in my presence" (*Ex.* 20:3). The Temple priesthood was generally consistently monolatrous, although royal toleration and active support of other cults would have applied pressure on Yahveh priests to be flexible at times (*2 Kgs.* 1–8).

Some biblical writers took the existence of other gods for granted, though all agreed that Yahveh was superior to the other gods (*Gn.* 1:26, 3:22, 6:2; *Ex.* 12:12, 15:11; *Ps.* 82:1–8). Other writers, such as the prophets Amos, Isaiah, and Jeremiah, spoke of Yahveh as the only proper object of Israelite worship, as the only divinity in control of earthly and heavenly events. Among the prophets, Second Isaiah was the most consistent monotheist, insisting that Yahveh was the sole god in existence (*Is.* 43:10–12, 44:6–8, 45:5–7, 45:18–22, 46:9). In general, the biblical monolaters believed the worship of Yahveh alone to be both an Israelite obligation and privilege. Others might worship their own gods (*Dt.* 4:19; *Mi.* 4:5–6). The monotheists required all peoples to forsake their ancestral gods and to worship Yahveh alone (*2 Kgs.* 5:17–18; *Is.* 44:6–20, 45:22; *Jer.* 10:12–16; *Zep.* 3:9; *Zec.* 14:9).

Biblical Imagery of God. Although many verbal images of Yahveh are found in the texts, the Bible in God's name prohibits the physical depiction of all divine images (*Ex.* 20:4, 34:17; *Dt.* 4:15–17, 5:8), even for use in the cult. Clearly, this prohibition was not universally observed (*Jgs.* 17:35). Some verbal divine imagery echoed Israel's roots in the Canaanite past. Yahveh was spoken of as a bull (*Gn.* 49:24; *Is.* 1:24; *Ps.* 132:2, 132:5), a further legacy from the Canaanite El, and was represented sculpturally as a bull or calf (*Ex.* 32:4–5, *1 Kgs.* 12:28, *Hos.* 8:6, *Ps.* 106:20).

According to one theory, no one could see Yahveh and remain alive (*Ex.* 32:23), but there were exceptions (*Ex.* 24:10–11; *Nm.* 12:8; *Is.* 6:1, 6:5). God is often described as humanlike (*Gn.* 1:27, 18:2) and with a face (*Ex.* 33:20), a back (*Ex.* 33:23), arms (*Dt.* 32:40), and legs (*Na.* 1:3, *Zec.* 14:4; in *Exodus* 4:25, *legs* is a euphemism for Yahveh's genitals). As a warrior (*Ex.* 15:3, *Ps.* 24:8), God carries a bow (*Gn.* 9:13), arrows (*1 Sm.* 22:15), and a sword (*Dt.* 32:42). Second Isaiah says that Yahveh is indescribable (*Is.* 40:18, 40:25, 46:5) but dresses him in armor and a helmet (*Is.* 59:17). According to *Daniel* 7:9, God is old and has white hair. Other depictions refer to fire and smoke emanating from Yahveh's mouth and nose (*1 Sm.* 22:15) and to his thunderous voice (*Ex.* 20:18–19, *Ps.* 29:3–9, *Jb.* 40:9), images borrowed from the figure of Baal, the thunder god.

God's kingship. In many passages of the Hebrew scriptures, God is spoken of as king. We may distinguish two basic usages, Yahveh as king of the gods and Yahveh as king of Israel. The first meaning is rare but is attested in the verse "For YHVH is a great god, a great king over all the gods" (*Ps.* 95:3). More common is the notion of Yahveh's kingship over Israel (*Jgs.* 8:23; *1 Sm.* 8:7; *Is.* 41:21, 45:6) and over the world (*Ps.* 47:3, 93:1, 97:1). The gods of Assyria and Mesopotamia such as Marduk and Ashur were regularly spoken of as kings in relation to their own peoples and to the rest of the world. Like these gods, Yahveh as king was the divine enforcer of justice and equity, guardian of the rights of the defenseless widow and orphan. Like them as well, he controlled the nations of the world and regulated their movements for the benefit of the people to whom he was closest.

God's presence. Though God was generally not visible, he might manifest himself publicly in the *kavod*, a word usually translated "glory" but best rendered "person," or "self." The *kavod* of Yahveh showed Israel that Yahveh was present among them. Often this presence could be invited by cultic procedures (*Lv.* 9:6, 9:23). Frequently the *kavod* of Yahveh is associated with the wilderness tabernacle (*Ex.* 16:7, 16:10, 29:43, 40:34–35) and with the Jerusalem Temple (*1 Kgs.* 8:11; *Ez.* 43:2). Among Yahveh's cultic titles were *melekh ha-kavod* ("the king himself"; *Ps.* 24:7, 24:10) and *el ha-kavod* ("the god himself"; *Ps.* 29:3). Like its Akkadian counterpart *melammu* ("sheen"), the *kavod* of Yahveh is of intense luminosity (*Is.* 60:1–2, *Ez.* 43:2) and is often shielded by a cloud (*Ex.* 24:16, 40:34; *Ez.* 1:27–28). The *kavod* is sometimes spoken of as filling the entire earth (*Nm.* 14:21, *Is.* 6:3, *Ps.* 72:19).

God's transcendence. Yahveh is often described as *qadosh*. Similar terms are used to describe divinities a term Ugaritic, Aramaic Phoenician. Although scholars often ascribe to *qadosh* a basic meaning "set apart," it is best understood as a primary emotive category "holy," in the manner of its antonyms "profane," and "impure God is not bound by time, space, or form, nor by moral or ethical categories (*2 Sm.* 6:5–8). Yet because God serves as the guarantor of justice (*Jer.* 11:20), his divine justice could be questioned (*Gn.* 18:25, *Jer.* 12:1, and most of *Jb.*) and even denied (*Eccl.* 8:15).

Yahveh is frequently referred to as a jealous god (*Ex.* 20:5, 35:14; *Dt.* 4:24, 5:9, 6:15; *Jos.* 24:19; *Na.* 1:2). In these instances, the term employed is a derivative of the verb root *qn'*. In a Babylonian text, the goddess Sarpanitum is described by the identical term. What is unique to the description of Yahveh is the action that activates Yahveh's jealousy (*qinn'ah*) most often—the worship of other gods. Sometimes Yahveh's jealousy results in unbridled punishment (*Dt.* 4:24, 6:15). At other times, it results in strict retributive justice and would better be translated as "zeal" (*Na.* 1:2–3). At still other times, "passion" or "ardor" would be better choices (*Is.* 9:6; *Zec.* 1:14, 8:2).

God's emotions. At the same time, God is also spoken of as being slow to anger (*Ex.* 34:6, *Nm.* 14:18, *Jl.* 2:13, *Na.* 1:3), forgiving of sin (*Jon.* 4:1), and the receiver of the penitent (*Hos.* 14:2; *Jer.* 3:12, 35:3; *Jl.* 2:12; *Zec.* 1:3; *Mal.* 3:7). The different views of Yahveh reflect not only the temperaments of the individual writers but the vicissitudes of Israel's history as well. Because Yahveh was so embedded in Israel's political and social life and institutions, the changes in Israel's fortune provoked different aspects of the divine character. Paradoxically, Yahveh is at once the most transcendent god of the ancient Near East and the most human. This is expressed most sharply in the prophetic writings of Hosea and Jeremiah. God's love for Israel is like that of a husband for a wife (*Hos.* 3:11). Unlike God's love, which is constant, Israel's is fickle (*Hos.* 3:1, *Jer.* 2:25). Yet both Hosea and Jeremiah emphasize that God's love will be great enough to overcome Israel's inconstancy and that God's relation to his people is eternal (*Hos.* 2:21, *Jer.* 32:40).

SEE ALSO Biblical Literature, article on Hebrew Scriptures; El; Henotheism; Israelite Religion.

BIBLIOGRAPHY

Alberz, Rainer, *A History of Israelite Religion in the Old Testament Period.* Philadelphia, 1994.

Albrektson, Bertil. *History and the Gods.* Lund, 1967. A demonstration that the gods of the ancient Near East were concerned with history.

Albright, William F. *From the Stone Age to Christianity.* 2d ed. Garden City, N.Y., 1957. A classic synthesis of archaeology and biblical studies.

Freedman, David N., and David F. Graf, eds. *Palestine in Transition: The Emergence of Ancient Israel.* Sheffield, 1981. Essays that pursue various approaches to the "revolt model" of the formation of Israel.

Gottwald, Norman K. *The Tribes of Yahweh.* Maryknoll, N.Y., 1979. An attempt to apply sociological models in support of George E. Mendenhall's "peasant revolt" theory. Mendenhall, however, writing in the Freedman and Graf volume, listed above, distances his views from Gottwald's.

Gruber, Mayer. *The Motherhood of God and Other Essays.* Atlanta, 1992.

Hillers, Delbert R. *Covenant: The History of a Biblical Idea.* Baltimore, 1969. A readable distillation of ancient Near Eastern and biblical covenant notions.

Hoftijzer, Josef, and G. van der Kooij. *Aramaic Texts from Deir 'Alla.* Leiden, 1976.

Kaufmann, Yeḥezkel. *The Religion of Israel.* Translated and abridged by Moshe Greenberg. Chicago, 1970. An abridgment of an eight-volume attempt to show that monotheism was Mosaic in origin and the religion of Israel from earliest times.

Knauf, Axel E. "Shadday." In *Dictionary of Deities and Demons in the Bible,* pp. 749–753. Leiden, 1999. A good survey of the relevant material, but somewhat speculative in its conclusions.

McCarthy, Dennis J. *Treaty and Covenant.* Rome, 1963. The authoritative treatment of the concept of covenant in the Bible against its Near Eastern background. Contains an exhaustive bibliography.

Mendenhall, George E. "Covenant Forms in Israelite Tradition" and "The Hebrew Conquest of Palestine." In *Biblical Archaeologist Reader,* vol. 3, edited by Edward F. Campbell and David N. Freedman. Garden City, N.Y., 1970. The first article was the first study to utilize Near Eastern treaty formulas in an attempt to show the origins of early Israelite covenant theology. The second article is the first study to refer to the settlement of the Israelite tribes as an peasants' revolt.

Porter, Barbara N., ed. *One God or Many?* Casco Bay, Maine, 2000.

Selms, Adriaane van. "Temporary Henotheism." In *Symbolae biblicae Mesopotamicae Francisco Mario Theodoro de Liagre Böhl dedicatae,* edited by Martinus A. Beck et al., pp. 8–20. Leiden, 1973.

Smith, Mark. *The Origins of Biblical Monotheism.* NewYork, 2001.

Smith, Morton. "The Common Theology of the Ancient Near East." *Journal of Biblical Literature* 71 (1952): 135–147.

Smith, Morton. *Palestinian Parties and Politics That Shaped the Old Testament.* New York, 1971.

Sperling, S. David. "Mount, Mountain." In *The Interpreter's Dictionary of the Bible. Supplementary Volume.* Nashville, 1976. See pages 608–609 for discussion of El Shaddai.

Sperling, S. David. *The Original Torah: The Political Intent of the Bible's Writers.* New York, 1998. See pp. 61–74 for a discussion of covenant.

Toorn, Karel van der. "Yahweh" In *Dictionary of Deities and Demons in the Bible,* pp. 910–919 Leiden, 1999. A balanced presentation of the evidence.

Trible, Phyllis. *God and the Rhetoric of Sexuality.* Philadelphia, 1978.

Wellhausen, Julius. *Prolegomena to the History of Israel.* Translated by J. S. Black. Edinburgh, 1885. Reissued as *Prolegomena to the History of Ancient Israel* (New York, 1957). The classic statement of biblical criticism and its use in reconstructing the religious history of ancient Israel.

Wyatt, Nicholas. "Asherah." In *Dictionary of Deities and Demons in the Bible,* pp. 99–105. Leiden, 1999.

S. DAVID SPERLING (1987 AND 2005)

GOD: GOD IN THE NEW TESTAMENT

The New Testament enunciates no new God and no new doctrine of God. It proclaims that the God and Father of Jesus Christ is the God of Abraham, Isaac, and Jacob, the God of earlier covenants. What the New Testament announces is that this God has acted anew in inaugurating God's final reign and covenant through the career and fate of Jesus of Nazareth.

THE PRE-EASTER JESUS. Jesus inherited the Old Testament Jewish faith in Yahveh, which held that God was the creator of the world (*Mk.* 10:6 and parallel) and the one God who elected Israel as his people and gave them his law (*Mk.* 12:29 and parallels). Moreover, God promised the Israelites final salvation (*Is.* 35, 61). At the same time, the sense in the New Testament that God is now realizing ancient promises and is acting anew (cf. *Mt.* 11:4–5, an indubitably authentic saying of Jesus) gives Jesus' image of God a sense of immediacy.

God was not merely creator some thousands (or billions) of years ago; he is creator now, feeding the birds and clothing the flowers (*Mt.* 6:26–30, *Lk.* 12:24 and Q, the purported common source of *Matthew* and *Luke*). Not only did God give the law through Moses, but God now demands radical obedience in each concrete situation (cf. the antitheses of the sermon on the mount in *Mt.* 5:27–48). Above all, God is now offering in the proclamation and activity of Jesus a foretaste of final salvation. Jesus' announcement of the inbreaking of God's reign (*Mk.* 1:15, *Mt.* 10:7, *Lk.* 9:2, Q) is not an abstract concept detached from Jesus' own word and work. Jesus' word and work are the occasions through which God acts definitively and savingly. The same is true of Jesus' exorcisms: "If I by the Spirit [finger, *Lk.* 11:20] of God cast out demons, then the kingdom [i. e., reign] of God has come upon you" (*Mt.* 12:28, *Lk.* 11:20 Q).

Jesus issues a call, "Follow me" (*Mk.* 1:17, 2:14; cf. *Mt.* 8:22, *Lk.* 9:59, Q?), not because he advances any claim for himself as such, but only because in that call, as in his word and work in the world, God is issuing the call to end-time salvation. To confess Jesus (*Mt.* 10:32, *Lk.* 12:8, Q, *Mk.* 8:38) or to deny him before others is to determine one's ultimate fate on the last day—whether it be judgment or salvation. The verdict of the "Son of man" on that day will be determined by whether men and women confess Jesus now. Thus, in Jesus' call God is proleptically active as judge and savior. The Fourth Gospel puts it more thematically: God's salvation and judgment are already meted out here and now in the word of Jesus and people's response to it (*Jn.* 3:18, 5:22–27).

Jesus' conduct. Jesus eats with outcasts, and he defends his conduct by telling the parables of the lost (*Lk.* 15). These parables interpret Jesus' action as God's action in seeking and saving the lost and celebrating with them here and now the joy of the reign of God. Ernst Fuchs points out in *Studies of the Historical Jesus* (Naperville, Ill., 1964) that "Jesus . . . dares to affirm the will of God as though he himself stood in God's place" (p. 21).

God as Abba. Jesus' word and work are God's word and work because Jesus has responded to God's call in complete faith and obedience. This is brought out in the baptism, temptation, transfiguration, and Gethsemane narratives of the synoptists (*Mk.* 1:9–11 and parallels, *Mt.* 4:1–11, *Lk.* 4:1–13, Q, *Mk.* 9:2–8 and parallels, *Mk.* 14:32–42 and parallels), and once again it is thematically treated in the discourses of the Fourth Gospel (e.g., *Jn.* 8:28–29). This relation of call and obedience is summarized in Jesus' intimate address to God as Abba ("father"). This is no new doctrine, for the Old Testament and Judaism knew God as Father (e.g., *Is.* 63:16), nor does it imply a claim to metaphysical identity with the being of God or with an aspect of that being, as in later New Testament traditions. Again, Jesus does not pass the Abba appellation on to others as a way of defining God. Rather, he invites those who have responded in faith to his message of God's salvation to call God "Abba" with him. "Abba" is a familial mode of address that presupposes a new relationship with God. Because Jesus first made the response and enables others to make the same response, they too may call God "Abba" (cf. the Lukan version of the Lord's Prayer, *Lk.* 11:2).

Jesus' death. The saving activity in word and deed that fills the whole career of Jesus culminates in his journey to Jerusalem in order to make the last offer of salvation or judgment to his people at the very center of their national life. As a prophet, Jesus is convinced that he will be rejected and put to death and that this death will be the culmination of Israel's constant rejection of God's word as known through the prophets: "It cannot be that a prophet should perish away from Jerusalem" (*Lk.* 13:33; cf. the parable of the vineyard, *Mk.* 12:1–9 and parallels). Since it is the culmination of his obedience, his death, like all his other activity, is seen by Jesus as the saving act of God. The most primitive form of the suffering-Son-of-man sayings, namely, "The Son of man will be delivered into the hands of men" (cf. *Mk.* 9:31), if authentic, expresses this by using the divine passive: God will deliver the Son of man to death. It is God's prerogative to inaugurate covenants. Therefore, at the last supper, Jesus speaks of his impending death as a supreme act of service (*Lk.* 22:27; cf. the foot washing in *Jn.* 13:2–15), which inaugurates the final covenant and reign of God (*Lk.* 22:29; cf. *Mk.* 14:24, 25 and parallels). In the references to service, covenant, and kingdom (reign) at the last supper lies the historical basis for the post-Easter message of atonement.

Easter. The Easter experiences created in the disciples the faith that, despite the apparent debacle of the crucifixion, God had vindicated Jesus and taken him into his own eternal presence. The early community expressed this conviction chiefly through testimony about Jesus' resurrection: "God raised Jesus from the dead" (*Rom.* 4:24, 10:9; *1 Thes.* 1:10) or "Christ was raised" (*Rom.* 4:25, 6:9; *1 Cor.* 15:4—a divine passive). After Easter, for the believing community, God is preeminently the God who raised Jesus from the dead. Insofar as there is any specific New Testament definition of God, this is it (e.g., again, *Rom.* 10:9). This results in the ascription of titles of majesty to Jesus. At the resurrection, God made him Lord and Christ (Messiah) (*Acts* 2:36) and even Son of God, originally a royal title (*Rom.* 1:4). Jesus is exalted to a position as close as possible to God, to God's "right hand." That means God continues to act savingly, even after Easter, toward the community and toward the world through the proclamation of Jesus as the Christ. In saving activity, God and Christ become interchangeable subjects: what God does, Christ does at the same time. However, Christ does not replace God. All the titles of majesty declare that Christ is God's agent, not God's surrogate.

The Message of the Post-Easter Church. Like Jesus in his pre-Easter life, the early church did not approach Israel with a new doctrine of God. Its message was that God had decisively inaugurated the fulfillment of his promises in the career and fate of Jesus of Nazareth, and above all in his resurrection. This is the burden of the sermons in the early chapters of the *Acts of the Apostles:* "Jesus of Nazareth, a man attested to you by God with mighty works and signs which God did through him . . . this Jesus, delivered up according to the definite plan and foreknowledge of God . . . God raised him" (*Acts* 2:22–24).

The Hellenistic-Jewish mission. Members of the Greek-speaking Jewish community, initially led by Stephen (*Acts* 6, 7), first found themselves preaching the Christian message to Greek-speaking non-Jews (*Acts* 11:20). In approaching them, it was found necessary to change tactics. Instead of launching straight in with the Christ event as God's act of salvation, they had to start further back, with belief in God. Because these non-Jewish Greeks came from a pagan and often polytheistic environment, it was necessary first to establish belief in the one God before speaking about what this God had done in Christ and was now doing salvifically. In other words, the Hellenistic-Jewish Christians needed an apologetic for monotheism, arguments for the existence of the one God, in their mission to non-Jews. They were able to draw upon the apologetic that had earlier been worked out by Greek-speaking Jews in their approach to the pagan world. One of the earliest references to such an apologetic for monotheism is attested to by Paul when he reminds the Thessalonians of his original preaching to them before their conversion to Christianity: "You turned from idols to serve a living and true God" (*1 Thes.* 1:9). Note how this precedes the second part of the message: "and to wait for this Son from heaven, whom he raised from the dead" (*1 Thes.* 1:10). A further example of Pauline apologetic for monotheism, and a claim that creation contains a natural revelation of God and his moral demands, occurs in *Romans* 1:18–32 and 2:14–15. Humanity has, however, frequently rejected this revelation and disobeyed God's moral demands, and Paul seeks to recall pagans to such knowledge and obedience. He sees a close connection between idolatry and immorality: "They . . . exchanged the glory of the immortal God for images resembling mortal man or birds or animals or reptiles. . . . Therefore God gave them up in the lust of their hearts to impurity" (*Rom.* 1:23–24). Later examples of an apologetic for monotheism are to be found in *Acts* 14:15–17, addressed to an unsophisticated audience, and in *Acts* 17:24–29, addressed to a cultured one.

Pauline theology. Paul's theology is entirely occasional, that is, it was worked out in response to concrete problems in the Christian communities he knew. The focus of his theology is the death and resurrection of Jesus Christ and its saving consequences. He inherited from the liturgical tradition an understanding of Christ's death as a sacrifice. It was the blood that inaugurated the new covenant (*1 Cor.* 11:25). Christ was the paschal lamb (*1 Cor.* 5:7). But Paul did not develop these sacrificial images in his reflection on Christ's death, perhaps because such language tended to drive a wedge between Jesus and the Father, as though the sacrifice was offered in order to propitiate or appease an angry deity. The language of the (probably pre-Pauline) hymn in *Romans* 3:25–26, especially the word translated in the King James Version as "propitiation" (Gr., *hilastērion*), might be taken in that way. But God is the initiator in the atoning death of Christ ("whom God set forth"), and the word is better translated "expiation," as in the Revised Standard Version. This means that the crucifixion was an act of God dealing with and removing sin, the barrier between God and humanity, rather than an act of Christ directed toward God. It is an act of God's reconciling love, directed toward sinful humanity (*Rom.* 5:8). Through it God justifies the ungodly (*Rom.* 4:5). *Reconciliation,* like *expiation,* is a word denoting God's activity toward us, rather than Christ's activity toward God. Christ does not reconcile the Father to humanity, as traditional theology has often asserted (see, e.g., article 2 of the 1563 Thirty-nine Articles), rather, "God in Christ was [or, was in Christ] reconciling the world to himself" (*2 Cor.* 5:19). Justification and reconciliation (two slightly different images for the same reality) are expressions of the righteousness of God, a central concept in Paul's thinking about God. Righteousness is both an attribute and an activity of God; it is God's action of judging and saving.

A writing on the fringe of the Pauline corpus, not by Paul himself, is the *Letter to the Hebrews,* which interprets the saving act of God in Christ in terms of Christ as the high priest. Once again, this author is careful not to drive a wedge between God and Christ. As high priest, Christ does not offer a sacrifice to God for the purpose of propitiation. Rather, the Son offers his life in perfect obedience to the Father (*Heb.* 10:5–10) in order to make purification for sin. As in Paul, the object of Christ's deed is not God, but sin.

The Incarnation and the Being of Christ. All levels of tradition in the New Testament examined thus far speak of Christ's relation to God in functional terms. He is commissioned, called, and sent as divine agent. God is present with and in him and active through him. These biblical traditions do not raise the question about Jesus' personal identity in relation to God. There is no discussion of Jesus' "divinity" or of his "divine nature" in the earliest sources; these are Greek rather than Hebrew concepts. But given the exalted status of Jesus, which the Christian community believed him to have received at Easter, it was inevitable that the question of Jesus' identity would eventually be raised, especially in the Greek-speaking world. Such reflection initially employed the concept of the divine wisdom to elucidate the revelatory work of Jesus. Historically, Jesus had appeared as a spokesman for the divine wisdom, using the speech forms of the wisdom tradition as these are seen, for example, in *Proverbs.* The content of Jesus' wisdom utterances contained an implicit claim that he was wisdom's last and definitive spokesman; this view is drawn out explicitly in the Q material (*Mt.* 11:25–27, *Lk* 10:21–22, Q). Matthew himself even identifies Jesus with wisdom, although in a functional rather than ontological sense (*Mt.* 11:28–30; cf. *Sir.* 24:29, 51:23–26).

In first-century Judaism, however, the concept of God's wisdom was advancing beyond the stage of poetical personification of an aspect of God's activity, toward a hypostatization (i.e., an attribution of distinct, concrete existence) of an aspect of the being of God. As such, the wisdom of God was an outflow of his being, through which he created the world, became self-revelatory to humanity, called Israel, gave the law, and came to dwell with Israel's notables, such as Abraham, Moses, and the prophets, but this wisdom was constantly rejected by most of the people. In certain hymns in the New Testament (*Phil.* 2:6–11, *1 Cor.* 8:6, *Col.* 1:15–20, *Heb.* 1:1–3) the career and fate of Jesus are linked to this earlier activity of wisdom (though the term *wisdom* itself is not used); a single, continuous subject covers the preincarnate activity of wisdom and the earthly career of Jesus. The result is that Jesus becomes personally identified with the hypostatized wisdom of God. The agent of creation, revelation, and saving activity finally becomes incarnate in Jesus. But this development occurs only in hymnic materials and at this stage is hardly the subject of theological reflection.

Johannine incarnation Christology. The final step toward an incarnation Christology is taken in the Johannine literature, especially in the Fourth Gospel. This gospel is prefaced by the Logos hymn (*Jn.* 1:1–18). *Logos* ("word") was used as a synonym for the divine wisdom in the later wisdom literature. In this hymn *logos* is equated with, yet distinguishable from, the being of God: "In the beginning was the word [*logos*] and the word was with God and the word was God" (*Jn.* 1:1), which may be paraphrased as "God is essentially a self-communicating God. This self-communication was a distinct aspect within God's being, related to him, and partaking in his divine being."

The hymn goes on to speak of the activity of the Logos as the agent of creation, revelation, and redemption and finally states that the Logos became flesh, that is, incarnate (*Jn.* 1:14). There could be no clearer statement of the identity of Jesus of Nazareth with an aspect of the very being of God. In the rest of this gospel, the evangelist sets forth the life of Jesus as the incarnation of the divine wisdom, or Logos. (After *John* 1:14 neither *wisdom* nor *logos* is used in the Fourth Gospel, but imagery from the wisdom/Logos tradition is appropriated, especially in the "I am" sayings.) Jesus speaks as one fully conscious of personal preincarnate existence within the being of God. It is significant, however, that this new "high" Christological language does not replace the "lower" Christology, which speaks in terms of call, commission, and the response of obedience. Apparently John understands his "higher" Christology to be an interpretation of the "lower," refraining from abandoning the terms in which the pre-Easter Jesus spoke and acted. Much of later traditional church Christology has ignored the presence of these two levels in *John* and has rewritten the earthly life of Jesus exclusively in terms of the "higher" Christology.

Is Jesus God? Only very cautiously and gradually does the New Testament use the predicate *God* for Jesus. First, there are possible examples in some Pauline doxologies (e.g., *Rom.* 9:5), although there are problems of text, punctuation, and grammar that make it difficult to decide whether in such passages Paul actually does equate Jesus with God. Then the *Letter to the Hebrews* transfers Old Testament passages that speak of Yahveh-Kurios (Lord) to Christos-Kurios (e.g., *Heb.* 1:10). Only the Johannine writings directly and unquestionably predicate the deity of Christ. First, he is the incarnation of the Logos that was God. Then, according to the now generally accepted reading, he is the "only-begotten God" during his incarnate life (*Jn.* 1:18). Finally, Thomas greets the risen Christ as "my Lord and my God" (*Jn.* 20:28). Then *1 John* sums it up by predicating God as the preexistent, incarnate, and exalted one in a summary formula: "in his Son Jesus Christ. This is the true God and eternal life" (*1 Jn.* 5:20). Thus the New Testament can occasionally speak of Jesus as God, but always in a carefully nuanced way: he is not God-as-God-is-in-himself, but the incarnation of that aspect of the being of God which is God-going-out-of-himself-in-self-communication.

The Trinity. There is a triadic structure in the Christian experience of God. Through the power of the Holy Spirit, believers know Jesus Christ as the revelation of God the Father. This experience becomes crystallized in triadic formulas (*2 Cor.* 13:13, *Mt.* 28:19) or in unreflected theological statements (*1 Cor.* 12:4–6). But there is no attempt to work out a doctrine of the Trinity, or to integrate the Old Testament Jewish faith in the oneness of God with the Christian threefold experience. Like the doctrine of the incarnation, this was left to the post–New Testament church.

SEE ALSO Apologetics; Atonement, article on Christian Concepts; Incarnation; Jesus; Justification; Paul the Apostle; Theology; Trinity; Wisdom; Wisdom Literature.

BIBLIOGRAPHY

Ashton, John. *Understanding the Fourth Gospel.* Oxford, 1991. Shows how agents of God's revelation and action could be called "god" in pre-Christian Judaism. These agents include Moses, the angels, Wisdom, and Logos. This provides background for Jesus to be called "God" in a carefully nuanced sense occasionally in the Johannine writings.

Bornkamm, Günther. *Jesus of Nazareth.* New York, 1960. Not a life of Jesus, but a presentation of those dimensions of his message and career that can be critically reconstructed. The chapter entitled "The Will of God" (pp. 96–152) draws out Jesus' teaching on God.

Bultmann, Rudolf. *Theology of the New Testament.* 2 vols. in 1. New York, 1951–1955. The classic work of the leading New Testament scholar of the twentieth century. Especially serviceable in reconstructing the monotheistic preaching of the Hellenistic Jewish-Christian community aside from Paul; see vol. 1, pp. 63–92.

Das, A. Andrew, and Frank J. Matera, eds. *The Forgotten God: Perspectives in Biblical Theology.* Louisville, Ky., 2003). A collection of essays in honor of Paul Achtemeier, this work relates the biblical conceptions of God in their unity and diversity to the major themes of biblical theology such as Christology, pneumatology, and anthropology.

Dunn, James D. G. *Christology in the Making: A New Testament Inquiry into the Origins of the Doctrine of the Incarnation.* Philadelphia, 1980. An investigation of all possible lines of development of preexistence-incarnation Christology in the New Testament. Dunn finds this type of Christology exclusively in the Johannine writings. In keeping with the more usual scholarly view I have located such Christology in those earlier Christological hymns that indentify Christ as the incarnation of preexistent wisdom.

Hamerton-Kelly, Robert. *God the Father: Theology and Patriarchy in the Teaching of Jesus.* Philadelphia, 1979. Particularly concerned with the viability of the Father image in a postpatriarchal culture.

Lampe, G. W. H. *God as Spirit: The Bampton Lectures of 1976.* Oxford, 1977. The last work of this major British biblical scholar and theologian. Lampe finds the distinctively biblical view of God in the concept of God as Spirit. Jesus is for him the final human bearer of the Spirit but is not ontologically identical with an aspect of the divine being.

Martin, Ralph P., and Peter Toon, eds. *Reconciliation: A Study of Paul's Theology.* Atlanta, 1981. Investigates the leading themes of Paul's doctrine of salvation with special concentration on the passages dealing with reconciliation. Martin stresses that atonement is something done by God in Christ for humanity, not by Christ to God.

Wright, N. T. *Jesus and the Victory of God.* Minneapolis, 1996. A major thesis of this work is that Jesus' preaching of the kingdom of God (eschatology) was not an announcement of the end of history as such, but the inauguration of Israel's renewal, a return from exile, the end of history as Israel has known it. Some other scholars, such as E. P. Sanders and J. P. Meier, have advanced similar views.

REGINALD H. FULLER (1987 AND 2005)

GOD: GOD IN POSTBIBLICAL JUDAISM

Postbiblical Jewish thought concerning God can be divided into four distinct periods: the rabbinic or Talmudic (from the first century BCE to the sixth century CE), the philosophical or theological (represented chiefly by the medieval thinkers), the qabbalistic or mystical, and the modern (from the eighteenth century down to the present). While each of these periods has developed independently of the others, there is still a considerable overlapping of ideas from one period to another. Both the rabbinic and the philosophical approaches have had an influence on the mystical, and all three have served in modern attempts at reconstruction of Jewish theology. These four periods will be discussed in turn.

THE RABBINIC APPROACH. Rabbinic thought as contained in the Talmud and the Midrash is unsystematic in presentation. While there is an abundance of references in these sources to the nature of God and his relationship to man and the world, the statements are general responses to particular stimuli, not precise, theological formulations. It is consequently imprecise to speak of the rabbinic doctrine of God, even though the expression is used by some scholars. The Talmud and Midrash are the record of the teachings of many hundreds of individuals, each with his own temperament and disposition, as these individuals reflected on God's dealings with the Jewish people. Even in their edited forms, the rabbinic sources constitute more an anthology of diverse views than an official consensus by an assembly of elected or inspired teachers. Nevertheless, on the basic ideas about God there is total agreement. All of the rabbis are committed to the propositions that God is One, creator of heaven and earth; that he wishes all men to pursue justice and righteousness; that he rewards those who obey his will and punishes those who disobey; and that he has chosen the Jewish people from all the nations to give them his most precious gift, the Torah. The debates, discussions, and contradictory statements in rabbinic literature are about the detailed meaning and application of these basic concepts. In this section of the article, then, material is taken from the whole, vast range of rabbinic/Talmudic literature, avoiding unwarranted generalizations. A serious attempt is made to distinguish between sober theological reflection and poetic fancy; between individual opinions and broader and more categorical views; between a kind of rabbinic consensus, even where the topic was never put to the vote, and fiercely debated arguments and sheer contradictions. It is only in the very flexible form that one can speak at all of the rabbinic approach.

From an early period, the tetragrammaton, *YHVH*, was never pronounced by Jews as it is written because it is God's own, special name, too holy to be uttered by human mouth. The name *Adonai* ("my lord") was substituted as a euphemism with regard to which a degree of familiarity was allowed. On the other hand, the rabbinic doctrine of the imitation of God suggests a close point of contact between God and man following the scriptural teaching that man is created in God's image. This doctrine is formulated as follows: "Just as he is merciful, be thou merciful. Just as he is compassionate, be thou compassionate. Just as he feeds the hungry, clothes the naked, and comforts the mourners, do thou these things" (*Sifrei Dt.* 11.22; B.T., *Shab.* 133b, *Sot.* 14a).

The two most frequently found names for God in the Talmud are *Ribbono shel ʿolam* ("Lord of the universe"), used when addressing God in the second person, and *ha-Qadosh barukh huʾ* ("the Holy One, blessed be he"), used when speaking of God in the third person (B.T., *Ber.* 4a, 7a, and very frequently). The implication of this change of person is that while God can be addressed directly in prayer, his true nature is beyond human comprehension. He is the wholly other, totally distinct from any of his creatures, and of him it is permitted to say only that he is the Holy One.

Nevertheless, there are numerous passages in the Talmud and the Midrash in which human terms are applied to God. The rabbis were as little bothered by the problem of anthropomorphism as the biblical authors, though the more human metaphors, when used of God by the rabbis, are generally qualified implicitly, sometimes explicitly, by the expression *ki-ve-yakhol*, "if it were really possible [to say such a thing]." Occasionally the anthropomorphisms are startling, as when God is said to have requested Ishmael, the high priest, to bless him, or when it is said that God prays to himself, his prayer being "May it be my will that my quality of mercy prevail over my quality of judgment that I might behave with respect to my children beyond the letter of the law and pardon them" (B.T., *Ber.* 7a).

Other rabbinic names for God were intended to suggest either his distance from man or his nearness. The name *ha-Maqom* ("the place"), defined as "He is the place of the world but the world is not his place" (*Gn. Rab.* 68.9), suggests, if this is the original meaning of the term, God's nearness. The name *Shamayim* ("heaven," B.T., *Ber.* 31a, 33b, and frequently) suggests his remoteness. In the rabbinic expression "our father in heaven" (*Yoma'* 8.9, *Sot.* 9.15), both ideas are combined. The name *Shekhinah* (*San.* 6.5, and frequently), a feminine form from the root meaning "to dwell," denotes God's indwelling presence.

It is incorrect, however, to think of these names as implying the transcendence and immanence of God. Abstract terms of this nature are entirely foreign to rabbinic thinking. The description of God as king is ubiquitous in the rabbinic literature with antecedents in the Bible. This metaphor is also founded on the rabbis' experiences of earthly rulers. God is the divine king whose laws must be obeyed. When he is stern to punish evildoers, he is said to be seated on his throne of judgment. When he is gracious to pardon, he is said to be seated on his throne of mercy (B.T., *'A.Z.* 3b). The rabbis urge man to stand in prayer as if he were in the awesome presence of a king (*Ber.* 5.1), first uttering the king's praises and then offering him supplications (B.T., *Ber.* 31a). Yet there are numerous instances in which the rabbis declare that God is different from a human king. God obeys his own laws, unlike a human king, who is beyond the law (J.T., *R. ha-Sh.* 3a-b, 57a). God commands man not to steal, and he himself refuses to accept the sacrifice of an animal that has been stolen. To steal food and offer God thanks for the food is to be guilty of blasphemy (B.T., *B.Q.* 94a).

Especially after the dispersal of many Jews from the Holy Land and the destruction of the Temple in 70 CE, the idea, found only sporadically in the Bible, that God shares human suffering, grieving with the victims of oppression, was deepened by the rabbis. Whenever Israel is in exile, they taught, the *Shekhinah* is in exile with them (B.T., *Meg.* 29a). The idea that God is affected by human degradation is applied even to a criminal executed for his crimes. The *Shekhinah* is said to be distressed at such a person's downfall (*San.* 6.5).

A severe problem for the rabbis was the apparent conflict between the favoritism shown to Israel by God and God's concern for the whole of humankind. In one Talmudic passage, the ministering angels are made to ask God why he shows special favor to Israel, God replying that it is right for him to do so, since Israel is extraordinarily diligent in worshiping him (B.T., *Ber.* 20b). The ministering angels are a device used by the rabbis to express the problem of theodicy that they themselves were compelled by their sense of integrity to face. When, in the rabbinic account, the second-century rabbi 'Aqiva' ben Yosef is tortured to death by the Romans for teaching the Torah, the ministering angels similarly protest: "Is this the reward for teaching the Torah?" (B.T., *Ber.* 61b). In the same vein, the second-century rabbi Yann'ai declared: "We are unable to understand why the righteous suffer and the wicked prosper" (*Avot* 4.15). Despite such awareness of the illusive nature of any solution to the problem of suffering, there are rabbinic suggestions that such suffering is the outcome of sin or the misdeeds of parents and ancestors. There is also to be found the idea of "sufferings of love," of God visiting sufferings on a man in order to demonstrate that man's faith and trust in him come what may.

Both idolatry and dualism were strongly condemned by the rabbis. The twice-daily reading of the *Shema'* ("Hear O Israel, the Lord our God, the Lord is One," *Dt.* 6:4), Israel's declaration of faith in God's unity, was introduced at least as early as the first century BCE, probably in order to constantly reject the dualistic ideas prevalent in the Near East. The third-century Palestinian teacher Abbahu, in a polemic evidently directed against both Christian beliefs and dualism, expounded the verse: "I am the first, and I am the last, and beside Me there is no God" (*Is.* 44:6). His interpretation is "'I am the first,' for I have no father; 'and I am the last,' for I have no son; 'and beside me there is no God,' for I have no brother" (*Ex. Rab.* 29.5).

In rabbinic Judaism there is little denial that the legitimate pleasures of the world are God's gift to man, who must give thanks to God when they are enjoyed. In one passage it is even said that a man will have to give an account to God for his rejection of what he is allowed to enjoy (J.T., *Qid.* 4.12, 66d). Yet the emphasis is on spiritual bliss in the hereafter, when man, as a reward for his efforts in this life, will enjoy the nearness of God forever. Although the first-century teacher Eli'ezer sought to limit to Jews the blissful state of the world to come, his contemporary Yehoshu'a, whose view was later accepted, held that the righteous of all peoples have a share in the world to come (Tosefta, *San.* 13.2). That this bliss consists of the proximity of the righteous to God was given expression by the third-century Babylonian teacher Rav, who said: "In the world to come there is neither eating nor drinking, neither procreation nor business activity, neither hatred nor competition, but the righteous sit with their crowns on their heads and bask in the radiance of the *Shekhinah*" (B.T., *Ber.* 17a).

THE PHILOSOPHICAL APPROACH. The medieval Jewish theologians, influenced by Greek philosophy in its Arabic garb, had as one of their main aims the refinement of the concept of God. Unlike the Talmudic rabbis, the medieval thinkers presented their ideas on God in a systematic way. Pascal's distinction between the God of Abraham, Isaac, and Jacob and the God of the philosophers generally holds true for the distinction between the rabbinic mode of thinking and that of the medieval theologians. For these theologians, the doctrine that God is One means not only that there is no multiplicity of gods but that God is unique, utterly beyond all human comprehension, and totally different from his creatures, not only in degree but in kind. Moses Maimonides (Mosheh ben Maimon, 1135/8–1204), the most distinguished of the medieval thinkers and the most influential in subsequent Jewish thought, adapts for his purpose the rabbinic saying (B.T., *Ber.* 33b) that to over praise God is akin to praising a human king for possessing myriads of silver pieces when, in reality, he possesses myriads of gold pieces. Maimonides (*Guide of the Perplexed* 1.59) observes that, in the illustration, the king is not falsely praised for possessing thousands of gold pieces when in reality he has myriads. The distinction is between silver and gold. The very coinage of praise suitable for a human king is entirely inapplicable to God. Only the standard liturgical praises of God are permitted and these only because they are formal and so not a real attempt to describe the divine nature.

The medieval thinkers insisted that all of the anthropomorphic expressions used in the Bible about God must be understood in a nonliteral fashion. Maimonides codified thirteen principles of the Jewish faith, one of which is the belief that God is incorporeal. Anyone who believes that God can assume a corporeal form is a heretic to be read out of the community of believers, and he has no share in the world to come, according to Maimonides in his *Mishneh Torah* (*Repentance* 3.7). In his stricture to this passage in Maimonides, Avraham ben David of Posquières (d. 1198) vehemently refuses to read a believer in God's corporeality out of Judaism. Such a person cannot be dubbed a heretic simply because he is not a philosopher and takes biblical and rabbinic anthropomorphisms literally.

For the medieval thinkers God was both omniscient and omnipotent. A major problem for them was how to reconcile God's foreknowledge, seemingly implied in the doctrine of his omniscience, with human freedom to choose. If God knows beforehand how a man will choose, how can he be free to choose? Unwilling to compromise man's freedom of choice, essential to Judaism, both Avraham ibn Daud in his *Emunah ramah* (ed. S. Weil, Frankfurt, 1852, pp. 93–98) and Levi ben Gershom (Gersonides, 1288–1344) in his *Milhamot ha-Shem* (2.6) could see no solution to the problem and were led to qualify the doctrine of God's foreknowledge. God does know all the possible choices open to man, but he does not know beforehand the particular choice a man will make in a given situation. This qualification does not constitute a denial of God's omniscience. God knows all that can be known, whereas human choice, because it is free, is only possible, and the possible, the contingent, must be uncertain by definition. Such radical qualification failed utterly to convince other thinkers. Ḥasdai Crescas (1340–1410) felt obliged to conclude that since God does have complete foreknowledge this must, indeed, involve a denial that man is free to choose. For Crescas, man's freedom is an illusion (*Or ha-Shem* 2.4.5). Maimonides had earlier seized both horns of the dilemma: man is free, and yet God has complete foreknowledge (Mishneh Torah, *Repentance* 5.5). This is not an admission of defeat by Maimonides. His view is that for the solution of the problem it would be necessary for humans to grasp the nature of God's knowledge, and, since God's knowledge is not something outside of him but is God himself, such a grasp on the part of humans is quite impossible. In God the Knower, the Knowledge and the Knowing are one.

In addition to their discussions regarding God's nature, the medieval thinkers examined God's activity in the finite world, that is, his role as creator and the scope of his providence. That God is the creator of the universe is accepted as axiomatic by all the medieval thinkers, although Gersonides (*Milhamot ha-Shem* 6) is radical here, too, in accepting the Platonic view of a hylic substance, coeternal with God, upon which God imposes form but does not create. Maimonides (*Guide of the Perplexed* 2.13–15), while at first toying with the Aristotelian idea of the material universe as having the same relation to God as the shadow of a tree to the tree, eventually accepts the traditional Jewish view that God created the world out of nothing. Maimonides' motivation is not only to preserve tradition but to emphasize the otherness of God, whose existence is necessary, whereas that of all created things is contingent. As Maimonides remarks in his *Mishneh Torah*:

> The foundation of all foundations and the pillar of wisdom is to know that there is a First Being. He it is who brought all things into being, and all creatures in heaven and earth and in between only enjoy existence by virtue of his true Being. If it could be imagined that he does not exist, nothing else could have existed. But if it could be imagined that no other beings, apart from him, enjoyed existence, he alone would still exist and he could not cease because they have ceased. For all beings need him, but he, blessed be he, does not need them, any of them. Consequently, his true nature is different from the truth regarding the nature of any of them. (*Fundamental Principles of the Torah* 1.1–3)

Like the God of the biblical authors and the rabbis, the God of the medieval thinkers is a caring God whose providence extends over all of his creatures. Both Maimonides (*Guide of the Perplexed* 3.17–18) and Gersonides (*Milhamot ha-Shem* 4) limit, however, God's special providence to humans. For animals there is only a general providence that guarantees the continued existence of animal species, but whether, for instance, this spider catches that fly is not ordained by God but is by pure chance. Yehudah ha-Levi (Judah Halevy, c. 1075–1141) in his *Kuzari* (3.11) refuses to allow chance to play any role in creation: God's special providence extends to animals as well as to humans.

Saʿadyah Gaon (882–942) anticipated Thomas Aquinas's statement that "nothing that implies a contradiction falls under the scope of God's omnipotence" (*Summa theologiae* 1.25.4). Saʿadyah (*Book of Beliefs and Opinions* 2.13) observes that the soul will not praise God for being able to cause five to be more than ten without adding anything to the former, nor for being able to bring back the day gone by to its original condition. Centuries after Saʿadyah, Yosef Albo (d. 1444) similarly distinguishes that which seems impossible but imaginable from that which is impossible because it cannot be imagined. The latter as a logical impossibility does not fall under the scope of the divine omnipotence (*Book of Principles* 1.22).

THE QABBALISTIC APPROACH. The pre-Qabbalistic tendency in Jewish mysticism is that of the "Riders of the Chariot" which extended over the first ten centuries CE. These adepts would perform certain spiritual exercises and delve deeply in the recesses of the psyche on the mysteries of the merkavah, the divine chariot seen by the prophet Ezekiel (chapter one). The journey of the "Riders" would take them into the Heavenly Halls where God sits on his throne surrounded by the angelic hosts. Some of the descriptions of the visions they saw have come down to modern readers. Often these are so bizarre, such as the account of the Divine Body (*Shiur Komah*), in impossibly immense measurements that they can hardly have been taken literally. In the account of the Four Who Entered Paradise (*Ḥagigah* 14b), one dies, one goes mad, one becomes an apostate, and only one, Rabbi Akiba, emerges in peace. On the basis of this merkavah tendency, the later Qabbalah became known as "The Work of the Merkavah."

The mystical movement or tendency in Jewish thought known as Qabbalah arose in twelfth-century Provence, reaching its culmination, in Spain, in the Zohar, the greatest classical work of Jewish mystical speculation. The qabbalists accepted the arguments of the philosophers in favor of extreme negation of divine attributes. Yet they felt the need, as mystics, to have a relationship with the God of living religion, not with a cold abstraction. In the theosophical scheme worked out by the qabbalists, a distinction is drawn between God as he is in himself and God in manifestation. God as he is in himself is Ein Sof ("no end," i.e., "the limitless"), the impersonal ground of being who emerges from concealment in order to become manifest in the universe. From Ein Sof there is an emanation of ten *sefirot* ("spheres"; sg., *sefirah*), the powers or potencies of the godhead in manifestation, conceived of as a dynamic organism. Of Ein Sof nothing whatsoever can be said. More extreme than the philosophers in this respect, the qabbalists refuse to allow even negative attributes to be used of Ein Sof, but God in his aspect of manifestation in the *sefirot* can be thought of in terms of positive attributes. The living God of the Bible and of religion is the godhead as manifested in the *sefirot*. Ein Sof, on the other hand, is only hinted at in the Bible since complete silence alone is permissible of this aspect of deity. A later qabbalist went further to hold that, strictly speaking, even to use such a negative term as Ein Sof is improper (see I. S. Ratner, *Le-or ha-Qabbalah*, Tel Aviv, 1961, p. 39, n. 40). When the Zohar does refer obliquely to Ein Sof, the expression used is "No thought can grasp thee at all" (*Tiqqunei Zohar*, second introduction).

The *sefirot* represent various aspects in the life of the godhead, for instance, wisdom, justice, and mercy. These are combined in a very complex order, and through them the worlds beneath, including the finite, material universe, are controlled, the whole order conceived as a great chain of being from the highest to the lowest reaching back to Ein Sof. There is a male principle in the realm of *sefirot* and a female principle, a highly charged mythological concept that opponents of Qabbalah, medieval and modern, considered to be a foreign, verging on the idolatrous, importation into Judaism (see *responsa* of Yitshaq ben Sheshet Perfet, *Rivash*, edited by I. H. Daiches, New York, 1964, no. 157, and S. Rubin, *Heidenthum und Kabbala*, Vienna, 1893). The male principle is represented by the *sefirah* called *Tif'eret* ("beauty"), the female principle by the *sefirah* called *Malkhut* ("sovereignty"). The sacred marriage between these two means that there is complete harmony on high, and the divine grace can flow through all creation. But the flow of the divine grace depends upon the deeds of man, since he is marvelously fashioned in God's image. Thus, in the qabbalistic scheme, God has made his purposes depend for their fulfillment on human conduct; in this sense it is not only man who needs God but God who needs man.

The *sefirah* called *Malkhut*, the female element, is also known as the Shekhinah. A rabbinic term in origin (meaning the indwelling of God, from a root meaning "to dwell"), the *shekhinah* comes to denote for the qabbalists a person in the godhead. The rabbinic idea of the exile of the Shekhinah, originally meaning no more than that God is with Israel in its exile, means for the qabbalists that until the advent of the Messiah there is incomplete balance, the female element exiled from the male, and part of God exiled, as it were, from God. The task of restoration, of redeeming the Shekhinah from her exile, is man's task on earth. Again, the rabbinic name "the Holy One, blessed be he" is now a name for *Tif'eret*, the male principle. The latter-day qabbalists introduced a mystical formula before the performance of every good deed and religious act in which the worshiper declares: "I do this for the sake of the unification of the Holy One, blessed be he, and his Shekhinah."

In qabbalistic literature produced in the school of Isaac Luria (1534–1572), the mythological elements become even more pronounced. In Lurianic Qabbalah, the process by means of which Ein Sof emerges from concealment is traced back beyond the emergence of the *sefirot*. The first act of Ein Sof (although the qabbalists stress that these divine processes take place beyond time) is one of *tsimtsum* ("withdrawal, contraction"). Ein Sof first "withdraws from himself into himself" in order to leave an "empty space" into which the *sefirot* can emerge in their separateness; the Infinite becomes self-limiting so as to become revealed as a multiplicity of powers. The whole process is conceived of in terms of a flow of the light of Ein Sof and then its recoil, as if the Infinite can only produce limitation and ultimately a finite world by God allowing himself gradually, one might say painfully, to produce that which is outside of himself. In one version, current in some Lurianic circles but suppressed in others, the purpose of *tsimtsum,* producing that which is not God, is for God to purge himself of the evil that is latent in his being (see I. Tishby, *Torat ha-raʿ ve-ha-qelippah be-qabbalat ha-Ari,* Jerusalem, 1984). It is not surprising that such an astonishingly unconventional notion came to occupy a very peripheral role in the thinking of the qabbalists.

The eighteenth-century mystical movement of Hasidism, particularly the more speculative branch of the movement known as Habad, tended toward a panentheistic understanding of the idea of *tsimtsum. Tsimtsum* does not really take place, since the Infinite is incapable of suffering limitation, but *tsimtsum* represents no more than a screening of the divine light so that finite creatures might appear to enjoy separate existence. The only true reality is God. There is a basic difference between this panentheistic ("all is in God") or acosmic view and that of pantheism ("all is God"). In the pantheistic thought of Barukh Spinoza (1632–1677), God is the name given to the totality of things. God is the universe and the universe is God. In Habad thought, without God there could be no universe, but without the universe God would still be the unchanging same; in fact, God is the unchanging same even after the creation of the universe, since from God's point of view there is no universe. The traditionalist rabbis and communal leaders, the *mitnaggedim* ("opponents"), saw the Hasidic view as rank heresy. For them the verse that states that the whole earth is filled with God's glory (*Is.* 6:3) means only that God's providence extends over all and that his glory can be discerned through its manifestation in the world. Speculative Hasidism understands the verse to mean that there is only God's glory as an ultimate.

In the classic work *Tanyaʿ* (*Shaʾar ha-yihud ve-ha-emunah 1*) by the founder of the Habad school, Shneʾur Zalman of Lyady (1745–1813), God is described as a sun and a shield. The sun's rays are essential to life, but the sun must be screened from view to some extent if creatures on earth are to endure its splendor. In the sun itself, however, the rays are lost in its great light. Similarly, finite creatures can only enjoy existence because the divine light is screened. They are like the rays of the sun separated from the sun itself. Yet, in reality, the analogy is very inexact, says Shneʾur Zalman, since the divine light pervades all. From God's point of view, finite creatures are like the rays of the sun in the sun itself. They enjoy no separate existence at all. The verse "Know this day, and lay it to thy heart, that the Lord, he is God in heaven above and upon the earth beneath, there is none else" (*Dt.* 4:39) is taken by Shneʾur Zalman to mean not only that there are other gods but that there is no ultimate reality apart from God himself. The unity of God, understood by medieval thinkers in the sense of his uniqueness, is here interpreted to mean that there is no real multiplicity of beings but only one true being.

MODERN APPROACHES. Modern Jewish thinkers have been obliged to face the challenges to traditional theism provided by modern thought. From the Renaissance onward, the emphasis in the West has shifted from a God-centered to a human-centered universe. The inerrancy of the Bible was questioned. The idea of revelation as conveying infallible information about God appeared less convincing. Immanuel Kant and his followers questioned whether human reasoning is capable of proving the existence of God. The rise of modern science tended to favor mechanistic philosophies of existence and, in more recent years, both linguistic philosophy and existentialism, in their different ways, cast suspicion on all metaphysics. Although the Jew did not begin to participate fully in Western society and to assimilate Western patterns of thought until the end of the eighteenth century, modern Jewish thinkers have been influenced by all of these trends in Western thought, compelling them to rethink the traditional views concerning God. The result has been an espousal of differing attitudes toward theism, from a reaffirmation of the traditional to a radical transformation in naturalistic terms. In any event, the vocabulary used since, by both the traditionalists and the nonconformists, is that of modern thought, even when it is used to interpret the tradition.

Among twentieth-century Jewish thinkers, Mordecai M. Kaplan (1881–1983) is the most determined of the naturalists. For Kaplan and his disciples, God is not a supernatural, personal being but the power in the universe that makes for righteousness. Kaplan maintains that people really were referring to this power when they spoke of God, even though, in the prescientific age, they expressed their belief in terms of a supreme being, the creator of the world who exercises care over it. Faith in God does not involve belief in being outside the universe but is an affirmation that the universe itself is so constituted that the pursuit of righteousness will triumph. God is the power that guarantees salvation, in terms not of an otherworldly existence but of the enrichment of the human personality to its highest stage of evolution.

Martin Buber (1878–1965), the best-known of Jewish religious existentialists, stresses, on the contrary, the personal aspect of deity. In Buber's thought, when man has an I-Thou relationship to his fellows and to the world in general, he meets in dialogue the Thou of God. While the medieval thinkers devoted a significant part of their thought to reasoning about God's nature, Buber rejects such speculations as futile, cosmic talk, irrelevant to the life of faith. God cannot be spoken about, but he can be met as a person by persons. Franz Rosenzweig (1886–1929) has a similar existentialist approach. For Rosenzweig there are three elements in the universe: God, the world, and man. Religion, specifically Judaism, binds these three together through the processes of revelation, creation, and redemption.

Avraham Yitsḥaq Kook (1865–1935), the first chief rabbi of Palestine, is completely traditional in his concept of God but accepts the theory of evolution, which, as a qabbalist, he believed to be in full accord with the qabbalistic view. The whole of the universe is on the move, and man is rising to ever-greater heights ultimately to meet God. Abraham Joshua Heschel (1907–1972), strongly influenced by Hasidism, stresses the sense of wonder as the way to God. Because the universe is shot through with wonder, it points to the wondrous glory of its maker, who, in the title of Heschel's book, is "God in search of man." Heschel's God shares in man's tribulations. He is the God of the Hebrew prophets, involved intimately in human affairs, not a cold abstraction without power to save.

More than any other event, the Holocaust, in which six million Jews perished, compelled Jewish religious thinkers to examine again the doctrine that God is at work in human history. Efforts of medieval thinkers like Yehudah ha-Levi and Maimonides to account for evil in God's creation were, for many, totally inadequate to explain away the enormity of the catastrophe. Some contemporary thinkers invoke the idea found in the ancient sources that there are times when the face of God is hidden, when God surrenders his universe to chance if not to chaos and conceals himself because humankind has abandoned him. There is a reluctance, however, to explore such ideas, since they appear to condemn those who were destroyed, laying the blame, to some extent, at the door of the victims. The free-will defense has also been invoked by contemporary thinkers, both Jewish (e.g., Avraham Yitsḥaq Kook, Milton Steinberg) and non-Jewish (e.g., John Hick). For man to be free and exercise his choice in freedom to meet his God, the world must be a place in which naked evil is possible, even though the price might seem too high.

None of these theories has provided contemporary Jewry with an adequate response to the problem of evil. The widespread tendency among believers in God is to rely on faith rather than on reason; man finds it hard to believe in God but harder still to accept a mindless universe. The only Jewish thinker of note who has accepted, in part at least, the "death of God" theology is Richard Rubenstein. The others reaffirm, in their different ways, the traditional picture of God as existing and caring, even though, like Kaplan, their understanding of what this can mean departs from that picture. Orthodox thinkers accept the traditional idea in its totality, including the belief that the Torah, given by God, is the path to eternal life and that, even on earth, God will eventually intervene directly, bringing the Messiah to redeem the Jewish people and the whole of humankind. Thinkers belonging to the Reform movement also accept the idea that human history is moving toward its culmination in the acknowledgment of God with the establishment of God's kingdom; however, they speak not of a personal Messiah but of the dawning of a messianic age.

See Also Attributes of God, article on Jewish Concepts; Holocaust, article on Jewish Theological Responses; Jewish Thought and Philosophy, article on Modern Thought; Reconstructionist Judaism; Reform Judaism.

Bibliography

There are three works of general Jewish theology in which the Jewish doctrine of God is discussed with full bibliographical references for further study. *Jewish Theology Systematically and Historically Considered* (1918) by Kaufmann Kohler, with new material by Joseph L. Blau (New York, 1968), is a pioneering work but now dated and heavily influenced by Protestant thought of the first decades of the twentieth century. *Jewish Theology: A Historical and Systematic Interpretation of Judaism and Its Foundations* by Samuel S. Cohon (Assen, Netherlands, 1971) and my *A Jewish Theology* (New York, 1973) are more adequate in that they consider more recent trends in theological thought. The same applies to my *God, Torah, Israel: Traditionalism without Fundamentalism* (Cincinnati, Ohio, 1990) and to Neil Gillman, *Sacred Fragments: Recovering Theology for the Modern Jew* (Philadelphia and New York, 1990).

On the rabbinic views, *The Old Rabbinic Doctrine of God* by Arthur Marmorstein (1927; reprint, New York, 1968) is a detailed examination of the names of God in rabbinic literature by an expert in this literature. George Foot Moore's *Judaism in the First Centuries of the Christian Era, the Age of Tannaim,* 3 vols. in 2 (1927–1930; reprint, Cambridge, Mass., 1970), contains much information, by a non-Jewish scholar, on early rabbinic discussions of God and his relationship to Israel. *Aspects of Rabbinic Theology* by Solomon Schechter (New York, 1961) is a well-written and scholarly treatment of the subject. There is also a good deal of material in *A Rabbinic Anthology,* edited by C. G. Montefiore and Herbert Loewe (1938; reprint, Philadelphia, 1960), in which a Reform and an Orthodox Jew also debate their differing attitudes to the rabbinic formulations. Occasionally this discussion tends to shade off into apologetics and must be used with a degree of caution.

No work exists devoted specifically to God in medieval Jewish philosophy, but the subject is treated extensively in two histories: *A History of Mediaeval Jewish Philosophy* by Isaac Husik (New York, 1916) and *Philosophies of Judaism: The History of Jewish Philosophy from Biblical Times to Franz Rosenzweig* by Julius Guttmann, translated by David W. Silverman (New York, 1964). For Maimonides' thought on the subject, the indispensable work is his *Guide of the Perplexed,* translated with an introduction by Shlomo Pines (Chicago, 1963). On the doctrine of God in the merkavah, qabbalistic, and Hasidic literatures, the essential work is the classic *Major Trends in Jewish Mysticism* by Gershom Scholem (1941; reprint, New York, 1961). Scholem's *Jewish Gnosticism, Merkavah Mysticism, and Talmudic Tradition* (New York, 1965) is an important work on the subject in its title. There is a good deal of material on the personal approach in my *Jewish Mystical Testimonies* (London, 1996).

For useful summaries of modern thinkers on God, three works can be recommended. *Anatomy of Faith* by Milton Steinberg, edited by Arthur A. Cohen (New York, 1960), compares Jewish thought on God with Christian thought. *Modern Philosophies of Judaism* by Jacob B. Agus (New York, 1941) is an excellent examination of the thought of Buber, Rosenzweig, Kaplan, and other modern Jewish thinkers. My *Jewish Thought Today* (New York, 1970) is an annotated anthology with a section on God. *Judaism Faces the Twentieth Century: A Biography of Mordecai M. Kaplan* (Detroit, 1993) is a useful introduction to Kaplan's naturalistic view of God.

Louis Jacobs (1987 and 2005)

GOD: GOD IN POSTBIBLICAL CHRISTIANITY

Both New Testament writers and postbiblical Christians sharply opposed the God of their faith to the many gods of popular religion. In doing so they joined not only Jews but also most thoughtful pagans, who believed in one God beyond the many. Because the reality of the one God was not in doubt, arguments for God's existence in that era were unimportant.

There was, however, during the early centuries of the Christian era a great divide. On one side were those classical religious thinkers who continued to reflect on God in strictly philosophical ways, trusting their reason to suffice. This tradition reached its apex in Neoplatonism. On the other side were those who accepted the authority of Jewish (supplemented later by Christian or Islamic) scriptures, correlating the ideas found there with the fruits of reason. The great Alexandrian Jew Philo, a contemporary of the apostle Paul, gave classical expression to this second approach, which gradually won out in the Mediterranean world.

Justin Martyr provides an early picture of how Christians understood the relation of their doctrine of God to the wider culture. He reports that he sought knowledge of God from philosophy with little success. A Christian then persuaded him that the human mind lacks the power to grasp the truth of God and that one must begin with what God has revealed. Accordingly, Justin turned to the Hebrew scriptures, read now through Christian eyes, and found there what he wanted. His success did not lead him to a total rejection of Greek philosophy, however; he continued to admire Plato, but to avoid attributing Plato's wisdom to human reason, he claimed that Plato had learned from Moses.

The authority of scripture ensured that for Christians as for Jews, the God who sometimes appears as an impersonal deity in the philosophical writings would be understood as personal. On the other hand, under the influence of existing philosophical concepts, biblical ideas came to be set in a new key. For example, God's changelessness, which in the Bible means God's faithfulness and dependability, was generally understood to be God's freedom from transiency and perishing. Subsequently this concept was transformed by some into metaphysical immutability. Likewise, God's everlastingness (beginningless and endless life) was sometimes transformed into a nontemporal eternality.

The matter primarily in dispute was the content of divine activity in relation to humankind, what God had done, was doing, and would do. To be a Christian was to affirm that the God of whom the Hebrew scriptures speak had acted in Jesus for the redemption of the world. This conviction expressed itself in the doctrine of incarnation, and it was this doctrine that most distinguished Christian thought from Jewish and philosophical ideas. Yet even incarnation could find various points of contact in the wider religious context, and these analogies were used by some commentators to understand and interpret it. On the one hand, God was known to have spoken through prophets and sibylline oracles; the theologians of Antioch taught that the Word of God was present to and in Jesus even more fully than in the prophets and oracles. On the other hand, the idea that God sent heavenly messengers, or angels, was widespread; Arius taught that he who was sent to earth as Jesus was not just one angel among others but the one supreme creature through whom all other creatures, including the angels, were made. But the Christian conviction that in Jesus it was God who was incarnate opposed the latter theory, and the former still left God too separate from Jesus to be truly incarnational. Under the leadership of Athanasius the church determined at the Council of Nicaea (325) that what was incarnate in Jesus was truly God, and at the Council of Chalcedon (451) it maintained that while Jesus was fully God, his divinity left his humanity unimpaired.

While the church insisted that what was incarnate was truly God, it did not simply identify what was incarnate with the one whom Jesus called "Father." Instead, following the prologue in the *Gospel of John,* the Word (or Son) who was with God and who was God was the incarnated one. This required a distinction within the one God. Even so, the church lacked a conceptuality that could show how the Word could both be one with God and become incarnate in Jesus without diminution of Jesus' humanity; and so the assertion, unsupported by intelligible conceptuality, became a "mystery." Similarly, the doctrine of the Trinity, which grew out of these debates with the addition of the Holy Spirit, could not be conceptually clarified. Thus faith became assent to mysteries on the basis of the authority of the church.

Although the doctrines of incarnation and Trinity are inescapable and central to Christian theology, their character as mystery reduced their role in shaping early Christian thinking about God. For example, whereas one would expect thinking about God's attributes to be deeply influenced by the gospel accounts of Jesus, such an influence has in fact been uncommon. On the whole, God's attributes were understood much as they were affirmed in Jewish and philosophical thought of the time: God is incorruptible, unsusceptible of harm or decay; God is incorporeal and invisible, a purely spiritual being. An early Christian statement about God's attributes is to be found in the apocryphal *Preaching of Peter,* which describes God as

> the invisible, who sees all things,
> uncontained, who contains all things,
> without needs, of whom all are in need and because of whom they exist,
> incomprehensible, eternal, imperishable,
> unmade, who made all by the word of his power.

In the Middle Platonism of the second century there was a strong tendency to emphasize the radical difference of God from the world, and so the incomprehensibility of God, just mentioned in the *Preaching of Peter,* was accented. This note was strong among the Gnostics, but it became prominent also among Christian writers who were increasingly willing to draw consistent consequences from the idea that God was incomprehensible. For example, Clement of Alexandria wrote that God cannot properly be called "one or the good or the one itself or Father or God or Demiurge or Lord" (*Stromateis* 5.82.1).

The patristic writer Origen made still more explicit the tension between the increasingly negative theology, which the church assimilated largely from the surrounding culture, and the positive language of scripture. Earlier, in arguing against anthropomorphic myths of the gods, Christians had denied that God feels fear or anger or sexual passion and had sometimes generalized this to speak of the divine *apatheia;* Origen systematized this doctrine and drew the conclusion that all passages describing divine emotions such as joy or grief must be read allegorically.

In a late homily on *Ezekiel,* Origen seems to have reversed his position on this point, explicitly denying that the Father is impassible. But the weight of his influence, along with the general logic of the idea of metaphysical immutability, carried the day. The idea that God the Father could have feelings such as pity was called "patripassianism," and it has been generally regarded as unacceptable at least until the late twentieth century, when Dietrich Bonhoeffer, Jürgen Moltmann, Kazoh Kitamori, and many others, including process theologians generally, began to emphasize God's suffering.

Although there was broad consensus that all things derive from God, there were alternative images of the relationship between God and the world. One image emphasized creation as an external act of will. The world is envisaged as coming into being by divine fiat out of nothing. Another image, which envisioned the world as the outworking of the dynamism of the divine life, found its clearest expression in Plotinus's doctrine of emanation. Insofar as this image implied that the world was made of divine substance, it was rejected by the church, but some of its language remained influential. A third image was that of participation, wherein God is seen as perfect being, and creatures are thought to exist as they participate in this being in a creaturely way. This image was supported especially by God's self-revelation to Moses. God is understood to have said: "I am who I am. . . . Thus shalt thou say to the children of Israel: He Who Is, hath sent me to you." A fourth image was that of inclusion, according to which God is the "uncontained, who contains all things" *(Preaching of Peter).* This follows from the words attributed to Paul in *Acts:* "In God we live and move and have our being" (17:28).

The Platonic influence on developing Christian beliefs encouraged a correlation between the human intellect and God. Thus Gnosticism held that knowledge of God is superior to faith, and this idea was taken over also by some of the more orthodox Christians. A related concept held that the human soul or mind possessed a kinship with God that was lacking to the body. Such ideas encouraged intellectualistic mysticism and bodily asceticism. The Christian struggle to overcome this dualism can be traced from the fourth-century Cappadocians through the fourteenth-century Greek-speaking church. It required both the denial that God is of the order of thought or idea and the rejection of a further development in the thought of Plotinus, which located God as the One beyond thought who could be reached only through thought. At the same time it required the clarification of how human beings could have real communion with God by grace.

Basil of Caesarea made a distinction between the essence or substance of God, which is radically and eternally inaccessible, and the divine energies. These energies, he taught, are God's actual working in the world and are, therefore, fully God and wholly uncreated. Basil associated these energies especially with the Holy Spirit. "Through him the ascent of the emotions, the deification of the weak, the fulfillment of that which is in progress is accomplished. It is he who, shining brightly in those who are being purified of all uncleanness, makes them spiritual persons through communion with himself" (*On the Holy Spirit* 9.23).

The writings of Pseudo-Dionysius (Dionysius the Areopagite) shared much with the Neoplatonism of Plotinus. They served later in the West to encourage a Plotinian form of mysticism. But in the East, where their influence has been pervasive and their orthodoxy unquestioned, they have provided the basis for a Christian spirituality that overcomes a Platonic dualism.

These writings reaffirm the total inaccessibility of the divine essence while stressing the divine energies, powers, or processions. Created beings participate in the divine energy in the way proper to each. Thus the movement of God into the world of creatures enables the creatures to rise toward God. In this process both positive and negative theology are needed. Positive theology finds symbols for God everywhere in the created world. Negative theology points out that these are indeed symbols and that there is no name for God's essence. In neither process is there any priority of the intellectual over the physical.

In the eighth century, John of Damascus, the most authoritative theologian of the Eastern church, included these elements in his exposition *The Orthodox Faith,* thus ensuring their continued role. This role was most important in monastic practice, which sought to realize the presence of the Holy Spirit. Symeon, called the New Theologian, gave expression to this practice in the early part of the eleventh century. He wrote of the experience of the uncreated light that is neither sensory nor intellectual. This light illumines the human heart, judging, purifying, and forgiving. It is the foretaste of the Parousia.

This current of Eastern spirituality came to its fullest expression in Gregory Palamas in the fourteenth century. He wrote: "Illumination or divine and deifying grace is not the essence but the energy of God" (*Theophanes,* in *Patrologia Graeca* 150.932d). Essence and energy are the two modes of the one divine existence.

This basic structure of Eastern thought of God was the context also for the defense of icons. The Iconoclasts held that the use of icons in worship was idolatrous because it assumed that the icons shared the substance of God. The victorious defenders thought of divine energies as imparted to the icons without any loss of their creatureliness, while the divine substance remained radically transcendent and unknowable.

The impact of Platonic philosophy in Western thought of God took a different turn chiefly because of Augustine of Hippo. Augustine made fully explicit the theological issues raised for the Christian by dominant philosophical ideas. For example, the church taught the doctrine of creation of the world out of nothing. This seemed to imply that God first was alone and then, subsequently, created the world. But this notion of a temporal sequence of events in the divine life seemed in conflict with the perfection of God. If there was good reason to create a world, why would God delay? In any case, would this sequence not necessarily imply a change in God from precreating to creating? And would not the existence of the world introduce something new into the divine omniscience?

Augustine undertook to reconcile the doctrines of creation and immutability by radical reflection on time. Time, he held, is a function of the mutable, created order. It has, therefore, no reality for God. For humans there is past, present, and future; but from the perspective of eternity, the contents of time exist timelessly. This became standard theological teaching, often ignored in the rhetoric of the church, but rarely directly denied before the twentieth century.

Unlike the author of the pseudo-Dionysian writings, Augustine understood the essence of God to be all that which is common to the persons of the Trinity. God is truth itself, which is at once goodness itself. As the sun is the source of light by which one's eyes see the visible world, so God is the source of illumination of the mind by which it sees eternal truths. And just as it is possible, though difficult, to see the sun itself, so also it is possible, though difficult, to contemplate God.

Truth, according to Augustine, draws the mind to itself, but the mind is distracted by the sinful will, which directs itself toward inferior things. What is known is not different, therefore, from natural knowledge, but because of sin natural knowledge is always distorted. Hence the mind cannot attain to truth apart from the healing of the will. This is the work of grace through Jesus Christ, in whom God accepted humiliation in order to overcome human pride.

This basic pattern, reflective of Plato's influence, dominated early medieval thought of God. It came into conflict with thinking affected by a new, firsthand encounter with the writings of Aristotle, which were mediated to Christian theologians in the West chiefly through Islamic Spain. The Aristotelian influence in theology was long viewed with suspicion, but eventually it gained a strong foothold in Western Christianity through the acceptance of Thomas Aquinas, who, as the most authoritative teacher of the Roman Catholic Church, synthesized aspects of Aristotle with much of the Augustinian tradition.

Thomas found in Aristotle an achievement of natural reason that moved from sense experience to the demonstration of the existence of God. This he called natural theology. He recognized that reason based on sense experience cannot arrive at all the truths taught by the church; so he affirmed also that there are truths attainable only by revelation. In addition he saw that much that the philosopher can attain by reason is also revealed so that all may know.

The Augustinian tradition argues that knowledge of God's existence is already implicitly given in thought. Anselm's formulation of the ontological argument is the most thoroughgoing expression of this tendency. Thomas, on the other hand, seeks to lead the mind by inference from what is known through the senses to the affirmation of God as the supreme cause of the world. The emphasis in Thomas's idea of God shifts, accordingly, from that of the illuminator of the mind to the cause of the existence and motion of all creaturely things.

The Thomistic argument that has best stood the test of time is the argument that proceeds from the contingency of all creaturely things to a necessary existent. By itself, an infinite series of contingent causes cannot explain the actual existence of anything. This dependence of contingent being on necessary being is closely related to Thomas's most original metaphysical work, his analysis of *esse,* or the act of being in its distinction from essence. The broad outlines of this argument already existed in the patristic consideration of God's self-revelation to Moses interpreted as "He Who Is." But whereas Augustine understood it to mean that God is he who never changes, Thomas taught that God is *ipsum esse,* being itself, that is, the act of being. This is pure act, free from all potency, apart from which there can be nothing at all. As pure act it is necessary existence, that on which all contingent existence wholly depends. French neo-Thomists in the twentieth century, such as Étienne Gilson, highlighted these features of Thomas's thought, which had been partly obscured in the interim.

Being itself is radically different from any creaturely being, and because one's ideas are formed in the creaturely world, one cannot speak of God univocally. Nevertheless, the language about God is not merely equivocal. There is justification in using analogies that move from creaturely effect to divine cause, attributing to the supreme cause the perfect form of the excellences found in the effects.

Thomas thought of God not simply as *ipsum esse* but as *ipsum esse subsistens,* that is, as the one who is being itself. The unity of the idea of being itself with the idea of the supreme being has been characteristic of the Thomistic tradition. However, Meister Eckhart, the great fourteenth-century mystic, distinguished God as supreme being from godhead as being itself, and he sought the latter in the depths of his own being. Through this distinction and his experiential realization of being, Eckhart provided a Western Christian analog for the thought and practice of Hindus and Buddhists, who had long distinguished the transpersonal ultimate from the personal God.

Thomas subordinated the divine will to the divine wisdom. That is, God wills what is good. In this doctrine, his thought followed that of the church fathers, including Augustine. God remains for Thomas, as for them, the One, the True, and the Good. But there were others for whom this Platonic way of thinking ceased to be convincing, for whom there were no truth and goodness existing in themselves and attracting the human mind and will; they asserted that God is much more the efficient cause of natural motion, that God is free agent, bound to nothing, and, in short, that God is almighty will, determining thereby what is true and good. This voluntaristic emphasis is associated with the rise of medieval nominalism, influenced especially by William of Ockham. Nominalism is the doctrine that universals are names given to certain things. These universals have no existence in themselves. Furthermore, because there is an element of arbitrariness in how things are named, human choice and decision are accented instead of discernment of what is objectively there for the mind to discover. This doctrine entails the theory that God alone chooses what to require of human beings and what to do for them. What God has chosen cannot be learned by human reason; it can only be revealed by God.

This voluntaristic theology prepared a context for the Protestant Reformation. With the reformers the emphasis was not on philosophical limitations to human knowledge of God but on the radical corruption of the human mind by sin. This impairment does not eradicate all knowledge of God, but it does lead to distortion of every human effort to say who God is. For knowledge of God one is totally dependent on God's gracious and redeeming act in Jesus Christ.

In Calvin's systematic formulation, for example, God's reality is fully manifest objectively in the order of nature; but because of sin those who have tried to interpret nature by reason have been led astray. The truth of God's objective manifestation in nature is properly grasped only through scripture. But, once again, although the truth about God is perfectly clear in scripture, the sinful mind distorts that as well. Hence scripture is properly understood only through the illumination of the Holy Spirit, bestowed by God as God pleases and not according to human merit.

The problem of theodicy is present wherever God is affirmed to be both omnipotent and good, because to deny sin and evil would contradict both scripture and experience. The problem is heightened when, as among Calvinists, God's election is emphasized to be independent of human desert. For the voluntaristic tradition, however, the answer is also given: What is good is finally determined by the divine will. The human mind has no independent access to criteria by which to judge the goodness of God.

Most theologians, however, have attempted to mitigate the starkness of this answer. Calvin himself attempted to demonstrate that the reprobate fully deserves damnation, and he attempted also to display the justice and mercy of what God has chosen to do as humanly intelligible. Others have argued more systematically that any alternative ordering of things would reduce the goodness of the world; usually the necessity or inevitability of evil in a world where there are free creatures has been emphasized. Although the phrase has not been popular, because it seems to minimize sin and evil, most theodicy has undertaken finally to show, in Leibniz's words, that this is "the best of all possible worlds."

During the Renaissance a new wave of Platonic influence gave rise to the Hermetic tradition, which emphasized the mathematical character of the world, the power of movement immanent in things, and the interrelatedness of human thought with these things. The divine was perceived as indwelling power rather than as transcendent will. The voluntaristic tradition had earlier separated revelation from the support of reason and encouraged an authoritarian spirit; the Hermetic tradition, too, separated reason from revelation, but encouraged instead a critique of hierarchical structures in church and society. Together they paved the way for modern philosophy in the seventeenth century, whereupon there ended definitively the unity of theology and philosophy that had dominated Western thought for more than a thousand years.

The early development of modern science was chiefly in the Hermetic context. But partly for theological reasons, René Descartes and Robert Boyle argued for a mechanical nature of passive objects to which the human mind is essentially alien. This left the sovereign will of God as the source of all order. Newton vacillated between these two worldviews, but eventually he gave his great prestige to the mechanical alternative, and this came to be known as the Newtonian worldview.

The church meanwhile kept alive older modes of thinking of God. Many of the theological debates, such as the Socinian, Arminian, Wesleyan, Universalist, and Unitarian objections to strict Calvinism, paid little attention to the issues raised by modern science. Their concern was to recover the emphasis on human freedom and to make more intelligible the idea of God's love for all people.

Nevertheless, the Newtonian, or mechanical, worldview came to be accepted as the only legitimate one in a scientific age. When the church expressed its faith in ways that were not consistent with this worldview, it became increasingly ghettoized in relation to the intellectual community. Among the intelligentsia thought of God accommodated itself rapidly to the new vision, and popular thought gradually followed. God was conceived, accordingly, as sovereign will, the omnipotent creator and lawgiver. As lawgiver God imposed laws on nature whose mathematical character physicists were disclosing. Parallel to physical laws were moral laws imposed upon human beings. Because human beings are free, these laws functioned more like those of the state, except for the omniscience and omnipotence of the lawgiver. Thus, it was held, people can disobey, but their disobedience is punished—in part in this life, but fully and appropriately in the next.

This developing idea of God was fully personal in the sense that God was conceived to be a supreme mind and will. But human relations to God were mediated through impersonal laws. The term *deist* was applied to this position; originally synonymous with *theist,* it came later to imply the lack of any immediacy of inwardness of relationship. Deism pictured God as the maker of the machine, which then runs according to the principles built into it.

In the eighteenth century the chief issue was whether God, having established natural laws, ever acted contrary to them. All agreed that God was supernatural. The issue was whether God caused supernatural events in the created world, that is, whether miracles occurred. Orthodox Christians held that the biblical accounts of miracles were true, whereas the Deists held that natural law was perfect and that therefore God did not violate it.

The eighteenth century witnessed also the rise of religious skepticism. There had been skeptics all along, but their numbers and prestige were greatly increased during the Renaissance, as well as by the multiple divisions of Christianity and accompanying religious wars following the Reformation. Also, the increasing autonomy and success of natural science suggested that scientific explanation is sufficient by itself and does not require metaphysical and theological grounding. By the end of the eighteenth century belief in God had become radically problematic. The philosophy of David Hume brought the skeptical spirit to expression in ways that continue to influence contemporary thought. By insisting that causality must be an empirically observable relationship, Hume undercut every argument that begins with the world or with aspects of the world and reasons that there must be a cause that transcends the world.

Reflection about God on the European continent in the nineteenth and early twentieth centuries was shaped by the critical philosophy of Immanuel Kant. Influenced by Hume, Kant saw that empirical evidence alone could not ultimately serve as a sufficient ground for the Newtonian worldview. This perception led him to ground that worldview in necessary structures of thought wherein Newtonian space and time, as well as causality, are ways in which the mind necessarily orders phenomena.

Kant's conclusion was by no means atheistic. Even in relation to the exercise of theoretical reason, the idea of God has a beneficial effect, though it must not be introduced as an explanatory principle. More important, Kant points out that in addition to the sphere of theoretical reason there is another sphere of practical reason, which deals with how people should act. In this sphere, too, the fundamental moral principle is independent of theology. People should act always according to maxims that they can will to be universal principles. For example, if one cannot will that people in general lie, cheat, or steal whenever it is to their personal advantage to do so, then one ought not to lie, cheat, or steal for one's own advantage. This principle—the "categorical imperative"—holds whether or not God exists.

But Kant also affirmed that it would be fitting if the will that conforms to this imperative were happy. Indeed, the *summum bonum,* that whose realization all must desire, is the union of virtue and happiness. Such a state is not attained in this life, but one has the right to posit that it is not an illusion, that is, that this life is not the whole, and that in the larger sphere the *summum bonum* may be realized. This argument assumes that God exists as the guarantor of ultimate fittingness.

Although few have followed the exact way in which Kant correlated God with ethics, many have agreed that belief in God belongs with ethics rather than with science. Later in the nineteenth century Albrecht Ritschl was to found a neo-Kantian school, which interpreted theology as statements about values rather than about facts. God is that which is supremely valuable, not a being about whose existence it is suitable to argue.

Kant's philosophy opened up a particular idea of God of which he did not approve. Kant had given an elaborate account of the *a priori* structures of experience and thought, specifying that these structures apply to thought or mind as such; they are not accounts of contingent features of particular minds, but rather "transcendentals," and individual minds exist by participation in them. Mind as such—in German, *Geist*—has a reality of its own, transcending that of individuals. In developments subsequent to Kant much nineteenth-century German theology associated *Geist* with God.

The most influential thinker who made this association was Hegel, who believed that the structure of *Geist* was not static, as Kant thought, but dynamic. Hegel studied this dynamism in the process of thinking as such and also traced it through the great cultures of universal history. He saw it as directed toward a final completion or realization, which he called absolute *Geist.* This Hegelian effort to discern the working of *Geist* in the whole of human cultural and intellectual history has since been characteristic of such theologians as Ernst Troeltsch and Wolfhart Pannenberg.

Kant's philosophy can also be used to support the idea of a religious *a priori.* Theologians can argue that just as space, time, and causality are *a priori* structures of experience, so also is the sense of the divine. Friedrich Schleiermacher held that in all people there is to be found a "feeling of absolute dependence," and he built his theology around this feeling. Later, Nathan Söderblom and Rudolf Otto identified the feeling of the holy or the numinous as the essentially religious element in experience. Paul Tillich subsequently spoke of "ultimate concern."

This approach to the divine leaves somewhat ambiguous the reality of God as such. Its normal rhetoric implies that there is One on whom all are absolutely dependent, that there is One who is numinous, or that everyone's ultimate concern is correlated with that which in truth concerns them ultimately. In this way it crosses beyond the boundaries of strict Kantian thought. Even within the Kantian framework, it follows that because one cannot but experience the world in this way, the question of truth or falsity is irrelevant. In some such way as this there has been a widespread tendency in twentieth-century theology to avoid the need for arguments for the objective reality of God, without relapsing into subjectivism or giving up realistic language about God.

In the twentieth century an important segment of Roman Catholic Thomistic thought followed Kant in still another way by taking the "transcendental turn." Transcendental Thomists, such as Karl Rahner and Bernard Lonergan, probe with Kant within the human mind for the conditions of all thought and knowledge. But unlike Kant they discover not the categorical requirements for the Newtonian worldview but the horizon of being as such, which is God.

In the English-speaking world, in spite of Hume's skepticism on the matter, William Paley's arguments from the order of nature to a transcendent creator were convincing to many, and for many, therefore, Charles Darwin's theory of evolution generated a major crisis of faith. If one thinks of the world as having come into being with something like its present order, it is indeed difficult not to posit a supremely intelligent and powerful creator. But if one supposes that the complex forms of life now to be observed were produced by chance and necessity out of much simpler forms, the role of such a creator declines, eventually to the vanishing point. Hence Darwinism appeared to be a profound threat to theism, and out of the controversy was born fundamentalism as a self-conscious movement, holding to the literal accuracy of biblical teaching against dominant scientific and historical study. Its teaching, of course, had roots in the whole of conservative Protestant history, especially Calvinist, but its defensive stance against science was new.

Those who wished to accept the evolutionary perspective while remaining theists were compelled to reconceive the way God works in the world. Such thinkers, instead of conceiving of God deistically as one who produced the world, gave it its laws, and left it to run its course, found it possible to imagine God as working with creatures in the development of new patterns of order. To do so, however, required the introduction of the notion of purpose into evolution. Debate continues as to whether this modification is justifiable. Thus Teilhard de Chardin argued that the whole evolutionary process moves toward a final destiny, an Omega Point. Jacques Monod replied that science has now established that chance and necessity reign supreme. Yet Monod seems to attribute intelligent purpose to human beings and even to other animals. There is in fact considerable evidence that purposive behavior is an important factor in the evolutionary process, and defenders of theism can argue from it that God is the source of this purposiveness.

The most influential theologian of the twentieth century, Karl Barth, was shaped in much of his thought by Kant's critical philosophy, but he rejected all adaptations of the doctrine of God to philosophical requirements. He denied, more radically than the Protestant reformers, that God can be known by human reason. Humankind is entirely dependent, Barth maintained, on God's self-revelation, who is Jesus Christ. This revelation is known only in the scriptural witness to him. Central to what is revealed of God is radical, sovereign, dynamic freedom. Humans can lay no claims on God and make no judgments about how God will act except as they lay hold on the divine promises and the divine self-disclosure. In Germany this radically Christocentric theology provided a rallying point against compromise with the quasi-religious claims of Nazism.

Barth strove mightily to let his thought of God be shaped by scripture through and through. He wished to avoid dependence on the philosophical ideas that had been so influential throughout Christian history. He also wanted to avoid reaction against uncongenial or hostile modes of thought in contemporary society. His intellectual honesty and openness commanded the respect of many modernists, despite their discomfort with his conclusions; his radical faithfulness to scripture commanded the respect of many fundamentalists, despite his refusal to endorse their teachings about biblical inerrancy and despite his rejection of their quarrel with modern science and philosophy. In the English-speaking world, aided by the popularity of the supportive writings of Emil Brunner, Barth provided an alternative to modernism and fundamentalism, thus making possible an ecumenical center for theological discussion from the 1930s into the 1960s.

The dominance of a positivistically inclined linguistic analysis in English-language philosophy raised problems for the English-speaking Barthian consensus, as illustrated by the work of a North American student of Barth, Paul Van Buren, who called for a nontheistic interpretation of Barth's theology. Meanwhile opposition to Christian teaching about God continued, inherited from nineteenth-century skeptics and also from those who had found belief in God oppressive: Ludwig Feuerbach, who complained that humanity treated its own goodness as something alien, and projected this as "God"; Friedrich Nietzsche, who thought that human beings could not assert their own freedom until they "killed" God. Barth's reassertion of God as free and sovereign will did little to respond to these challenges, and the work of Thomas Altizer renewed this challenge in the mid-1960s. The "death-of-God" theology contributed further to weakening Barth's influence.

The appearance soon after World War II of the writings of Dietrich Bonhoeffer from a Nazi jail struck a responsive chord in those already uncomfortable with Barth's theology. The ideas sketched in these writings indicate a quite different way of thinking of God. "Only a powerless God," Bonhoeffer wrote, "can help." It is the Crucified One rather than the all-determining Lord who can speak to suffering humanity "come of age." Bonhoeffer thus helped gain a hearing for a current of thought that directly challenged God's impassibility and affirmed patripassianism. This position had been formulated philosophically in the United States by Alfred North Whitehead and was systematically developed by Charles Hartshorne; it was forcefully expressed theologically in Germany by Jürgen Moltmann.

Although few have followed Bonhoeffer's rhetoric of divine powerlessness, there has been considerable new reflection on the nature of God's power. Whitehead held that God's power is persuasive rather than coercive. That this was true with respect to human beings had long been taught—for example, by Augustine. But in Whitehead's view, to exist at all is to have some measure of self-determination. Hence God's relation to all creatures is persuasive. Wolfhart Pannenberg argues that God is to be thought of as the Power of the Future. God is not now extant as one being alongside others making up the given reality, but rather that which will be all in all. Pannenberg argues that all creative realization in the present comes into being from this divine future. Hence God remains all-determinative, but the mode of this determination is quite different from that against which people have protested for the sake of human freedom. Instead it is God's determination of the present that makes humanity free.

The association of God with the future, building on the eschatological language of the New Testament, has had other supporters. Whereas for Pannenberg it has ontological meaning, for J.-B. Metz and Jürgen Moltmann it is associated with a "political theology," which locates salvation primarily in the public historical realm. It is also central to the "liberation theology" of Rubem Alves, Gustavo Gutierrez, Juan Segundo, and other Latin Americans. These German and Latin American theologians argue that God's will is not expressed in the present structures of society or in some romanticized past, but rather in the promise of something quite different. Hence, the overwhelming tendency of religion to justify and even sanctify existing patterns, or to encourage nostalgia for a lost paradise, is opposed by the prophetic challenge in view of the hoped-for future.

Among these theologians, the image of God has been more important than the concept. Indeed, recognition of the difference between image and concept and of the great importance of image has played a large role in recent thought about God. Blacks in the United States, led by James H. Cone, have pointed out that God has been imaged as white. The fact that theological concepts about God make the notion of skin color absurd has not reduced the power of this image. Blacks then need to image God as black to claim their human and religious identity. They can go on to say that the biblical witness to God's self-identification with the poor and oppressed gives special justification to this image. Black theology has also provided stimulus for fuller indigenization of images of God in many non-Western cultures.

Similarly, although theologians have insisted that God is beyond gender, feminists have had no difficulty showing that the Christian image of God is overwhelmingly male: Whereas God's whiteness is clearly not biblical and is rightly rejected in the name of the Bible, God's maleness is biblical. Hence the denial of maleness to God requires a radical approach to scripture. Furthermore, the characteristics attributed to God by even those theologians who have rejected anthropomorphism have usually been stereotypically masculine ideals: omnipotence, impassibility, self-sufficiency. Feminists challenge this whole theological tradition. They divide between those, such as Mary Daly, who believe that the Christian God is inherently and necessarily patriarchal, and hence incompatible with women's liberation, and those, such as Rosemary Ruether and Letty Russell, who believe that the Christian deity is a liberator who can free humankind also from patriarchalism.

For a century now there has been a slow decline of the mechanistic worldview. Because the rise of that worldview had so marked an impact on Christian thinking about God, its decline would seem to be important as well. However, the change in theology has not been dramatic. Because of Kant's influence, theology in central Europe has been largely separated from questions of worldview. The effect of Barth's theology has been to reinforce this separation. Ironically, the separation has led to the continued acceptance of the mechanistic worldview by some theologians despite its loss of prestige among physicists. Rudolf Bultmann, for example, accepted this worldview unquestioningly and argued from it with respect to what is credible to modern people.

Nevertheless, others, such as Karl Heim, worked to adapt Christian theology to new developments in science; this approach was especially common in the French- and English-language worlds. Scientific developments abounded. After the controversy over evolution, more fundamental challenges to mechanism came from physics with the rise of quantum theory. Newtonian laws gave way to statistical probabilities, and self-contained atoms were replaced by fields. Substances gave way to events. But the lack of a fully articulated, generally accepted new worldview, correlated with the whole range of the sciences, has reduced the impact on theology of the decay of the older worldview. Meanwhile there has emerged largely outside the churches a popular religious culture that correlates religious beliefs with what it takes to be the new science.

The most impressive effort to propose a conceptually rigorous worldview or cosmology appropriate to postmechanistic science is that of Whitehead. Whitehead also spelled out what he saw as the implications of this new cosmology for belief in God. Because the new cosmology replaces atomism with a field of interrelated events, it calls for understanding God as also fully interrelated with the world. God is not a cosmic lawgiver but an intimate participant in every event. Similarly, every event enters forever into the inner life of God.

Whitehead's ideas have been systematically modified, developed, and defended by Charles Hartshorne. In light of the new ways of thinking of God Hartshorne reformulated classical arguments for God's existence, including the ontological argument, and he called his theism neoclassical. This neoclassical theism is a pan-entheism based on a doctrine of God as dipolar, absolute in essence but relational in actuality. Hartshorne's thought has played a central role in the emergence of "process theology."

Another context for Christian reflection on God in recent times is dialogue with representatives of other religious traditions. These dialogues intensify the question whether the Christian God is also worshiped in other traditions. In relation to Jews and Muslims, who share much scripture with Christians, there has rarely been serious doubt. It has also been usual missional strategy in countries previously unacquainted with these scriptures to use terms already present in their languages to speak of the Christian God. It has been widely assumed that, whatever the misunderstanding or distortion, every people has some notion of the one true God who is revealed in the Bible.

Such dialogue also usually leads to greater appreciation of the faith of the dialogue partner and increases the sense that the one true God is known also by the partner. This perception results in an effort to distinguish God from Christian ideas and images of God, so that Christians may respect ideas and images quite different from those to which they have been accustomed. H. Richard Niebuhr has provided a confessional model for dialogue in which the partners tell their story to one another in ways that celebrate the understanding to which their own story has brought them, without disparaging or closing themselves off from what others have learned from their own very different histories.

Reflection on the deep differences between dialogue partners can also lead to the conclusion that the reality of which the partner speaks is different from the biblical God. Meister Eckhart's distinction of godhead from God, Paul Tillich's language about being itself as the God beyond the God of theism, and Whitehead's distinction of creativity from God offer bases for fresh reflection on the relation of the mystical ultimate in Indian and Chinese religions to the Christian God.

The diversity of interests that lead to reflection on God witnesses to the continuing importance of the topic. It also produces great confusion. It is not clear that different statements using the word *God* have, any longer, a common topic. In the Christian context, however, one can almost always understand that, despite all the diversity of concepts and imagery, *God* refers to what Christians worship and trust. Further—with a few exceptions, such as Edgar S. Brightman and William James—God is associated with perfection. Part of the confusion lies in the changing ideal. Whereas for many centuries it seemed self-evident to most Christians that the perfect must be all-determining, affected by nothing external to itself, timeless, and completely self-sufficient, that supposition is no longer so evident today. Much of the debate about God is a debate about what people most admire and most desire to emulate.

SEE ALSO Androcentrism; Anthropomorphism; Apologetics; Councils, article on Christian Councils; Deism; Enlightenment, The; Evangelical and Fundamental Christianity; Gender Roles; Heresy, article on Christian Concepts; Hermetism; Iconoclasm; Icons; Incarnation; Modernism, article on Christian Modernism; Naturalism; Neoorthodoxy; Nominalism; Philosophy; Political Theology; Skeptics and Skepticism; Theodicy; Theology, article on Christian Theology; Trinity.

BIBLIOGRAPHY

Collins, James D. *God in Modern Philosophy* (1959). Westport, Conn., 1978.

Gilson, Étienne. *History of Christian Philosophy in the Middle Ages.* New York, 1955.

Grant, Robert M. *The Early Christian Doctrine of God.* Charlottesville, Va., 1966.

Hartshorne, Charles, and William L. Reese. *Philosophers Speak of God.* Chicago, 1953.

Lossky, Vladimir. *The Vision of God.* Clayton, Wis., 1963.

Prestige, George L. *God in Patristic Thought* (1936). London, 1952.

Wolfson, Harry A. *From Philo to Spinoza: Two Studies in Religious Philosophy.* New York, 1977.

Zahrnt, Heinz. *The Question of God.* New York, 1969.

New Sources

La Due, William. *Jesus among the Theologians.* Harrisburg, Pa., 2001.

Pattison, George. *The End of Theology and the Task of Thinking about God.* London, 1998.

Polkinghorne, John. *Faith, Science and Understanding.* New Haven, Conn., 2000.

Snedeker, Donald R. *Our Heavenly Father Has No Equals: Unitarianism, Trinitarianism, and the Necessity of Biblical Proof.* San Francisco, 1998.

Sölle, Dorothee. *Thinking about God.* London, 1990.

Twesigye, Emmanuel K. *Religion and Ethics for a New Age.* Lanham, Md., 2001.

Wierenga, Edward R. *The Nature of God: An Inquiry into Divine Attributes.* Cornell Studies in the Philosophy of Religion. Ithaca, N.Y., 1989.

JOHN B. COBB, JR. (1987)
Revised Bibliography

GOD: GOD IN ISLAM

The Qur'ān, Islam's holy scripture, states, "Verily, the religion of God (Allāh) is Islam" (3:19). According to medieval Muslim lexicographers, there are twenty to thirty opinions on the origin, etymology, and meaning of the term *Allāh.*

Some say that it should be read as a proper name, as in the English "God." Others claim that it is a contraction of *al-ilāh,* meaning "The God" or "The Divinity." Medieval Muslim manuscripts from North Africa and Islamic Spain often use al-Ilāh as a synonym for Allāh. Modern philologists relate the term to the Hebrew El or Elohim, used in the Bible. In Arabic, the verb *alaha* means, "he worshiped, served, or adored." In this sense, Allāh could be translated as "the One who is worshiped or adored." Similarly, the past participle *ma'luh,* taken from the same root as Allāh, is a synonym of *ma'būd,* "worshiped" or "adored." In the Qur'ān, the terms *ilāh* ("god" or "divinity") and *ilāha* ("goddess") are often used in contrast with Allāh, the former representing false gods or false objects of worship when compared with the One True God.

Every *sūrah* of the Qur'ān but one begins with the phrase *Bismillāh al-Raḥmān al-Raḥīm* (By the name of Allāh, the Beneficent, the Merciful). This phrase, known as the *basmalah,* is also used for oaths and at the beginning of important or sacred acts. Islamic prayers and supplications often begin with the expression *Allāhumma,* which is understood as meaning "Oh God!" (*yā Allāh*). The doubled letter *mīm* in this expression stands for the suppressed vocative particle *Yā* (Oh). Such uses of the term *Allāh* recall the practices of pre-Islamic Arabia, where Allāh was called upon as the creator god, the god of the heavens, the bringer of rain, and Lord of the Ka'bah in Mecca. Although this rather remote divinity was personified by the pagan Arabs, he was unique among other Arabian gods because images were not made of him. According to Toshihiko Isutzu, a Japanese scholar of Islam, Allāh was seldom worshiped as part of a cult in pre-Islamic Arabia. Instead, he was the object of what Isutzu called "temporary monotheism," the last recourse of prayer when all the other gods had failed (Isutzu, 1980, p. 101).

The Qur'ān provides evidence for Isutzu's conclusions. In certain passages it rebukes the pagan Meccans for asking the Prophet Muḥammad, "Who is *al-Raḥmān?*" when he invoked this "name" of God (25:60). Implied in the Qur'ān's rebuke of the Meccans is the idea that Allāh and many of his attributes were already known to those who denied Muḥammad's message (29:65). In this view, the Qur'ān introduced the new term *al-Raḥmān* (the Beneficent) into Arabia, but it did not introduce a new god. Rather, the Qur'ān brought the Arabian sky and creator god closer to human experience by stressing that Allāh was both transcendent and immanently near: "And when my servants question you concerning me, I am truly near. I answer the prayer of the supplicant when he calls on me. So let them heed my call and believe in me, so that they might be guided rightly" (2:186).

The Qur'anic Doctrine of Divine Unity. The Qur'ān uses a variety of arguments to demonstrate that knowledge of God as the creator of all things makes all other ideas of divinity superfluous. If Allāh created everything in the universe, then the lesser gods and powers worshiped by human beings must be created as well, and hence are not truly divine. Theologically, the religion of Islam replaced the pagan Allāh with a divinity of greater complexity. God in Islam is more than just a name; Allāh is both a theological concept and an active deity that creates and maintains the universe. Both immanent and transcendent, the full nature of God appears as a paradox to the human mind. Allāh is the One True God, as in the Greek phrase *ho theos* (The God). However, the oneness of God is not self-evident, nor is it self-evident that God is the ultimate cause of all things. The secondary causes and contingent realities of things in the world veil the nature of God from human understanding. The Qur'ān acknowledges this paradox by equating belief in God with "belief in the unseen" (2:3). Because the full reality of God is not self-evident, a book of revelation is needed to educate human beings about the existence and nature of divinity.

The intellectual quest for the understanding of God is depicted mythologically in the Qur'ān by the story of Abraham, who progressed from worshiping the stars, the moon, and the sun to acknowledging that Allāh is the sole cause of heavenly phenomena (6:75–79). However, simply understanding that God is the Cause of Causes only solves part of the divine mystery. There is still the problem of knowing how God, as the transcendent Truth (*al-Ḥaqq,* 22:6), may be discerned in the vast multiplicity of created things and events. This key problem of Islamic theology is expressed in the following poem by the sixteenth-century Moroccan Ṣūfī 'Abdallāh al-Ghazwānī (d. 1528) of Marrakech:

> Oh, he who is one of all! Oh, he for whom all is one! Mortal beings count you by number, oh one. You appear in the all such that one cannot be hidden, And you disappear in the all such that one cannot be seen. (al-Ghazwani, folio 5)

This paradox of divine unity was not only a problem for Ṣūfīs. It also appears in Shī'ī Islam, as in the following statement of Imām 'Alī (d. 661):

> To know God is to know his oneness. To say that God is one has four meanings: two of them are false and two are correct. As for the two false meanings, one is that a person should say "God is one" and be thinking of number and counting. This is false because that which has no second cannot enter into the category of number. Do you not see that those who say that God is the third of a trinity fall into this infidelity? Another meaning is to say, "So-and-so is one of his people," namely, a species of this genus or a member of this species. This meaning is also false when applied to God, because it implies likening something to God, whereas God is above all likeness. As to the two meanings that are correct when applied to God, one is that it should be said that "God is one" in the sense that there is no likeness to him among things. Another is to say that "God is one" in the sense that there is no multiplicity or division conceivable in Him, neither outwardly, nor in the mind, nor in the imagination. God alone possesses such a unity. (Tabatabai, 1979, pp. 127–128)

Theologically, the Qur'ān is an extended argument for the existence of the One God. As a revelation both from Allāh and about Allāh, it guides humanity toward a single, absolute Truth that transcends the world: "Say: He is Allāh the Only; Allāh the Indivisible; He gives not birth, nor is He begotten, and He is, in Himself, not dependent on anything" (112:1–4). These verses summarize the Qurʾanic definition of *tawḥīd,* the Islamic doctrine of divine unity. Most simply, *tawḥīd* means that God is one, unique, and not divisible into hypostatic entities or incarnated manifestations. He gives birth to no "son" or demiurge, nor is he begotten from another, for he is independent of his creation: "Your Lord is utterly independent, All-Engendering. If he wills, he can expel you and replace you with others, just as he multiplied you from the seed of others" (5:133). Along with this strictly monotheistic image of God, the Qurʾān also provides a more monistic image of a deity that is immanent in the world of creation: "He is the First and the Last, the Outward and the Inward; He is the Knower of every thing" (57:3). This complementary focus on the immanence of God implies that a full understanding of divine unity must somehow include the transcendence of number. This is the paradox addressed by al-Ghazwānī and Imām ʿAlī above, and the attempt to resolve it delineates the conceptual limits of theological inquiry in Islam.

As an aid in understanding the complexity of *tawḥīd,* the Qurʾān uses ninety-nine terms that convey various aspects of the divine nature. These terms are referred to as the "Excellent Names of Allāh" (77:180) and are tokens of God's presence in the world. Many of the divine names are incorporated into Muslim personal names, such as ʿAbd al-Raḥmān (Slave of the Beneficent), ʿAbd al-Jabbār (Slave of the Overpowering), or ʿAbd al-ʿAzīz (Slave of the Glorious). The fact that such names describe attributes of human beings is another reminder of God's immanence. With the exception of the supreme name Allāh and the Arabic neologism al-Raḥmān, which refers to the divine beneficence that creates and maintains the universe, all of the other divine names may be shared by both God and human beings. However, this sharing of attributes should not lead a person to believe that he or she is divine or that the sharing of attributes puts any limitation on God's transcendent nature. Such attitudes lead to the sin of *shirk,* associating things with God, or relying on contingent, created entities as if they were divine in themselves. *Shirk* is a major sin in Islam because it is the basis of *kufr,* literally "covering up" or denying the truth of God and of the Islamic religion.

DIVINE POWER. A constant concern of Islamic theology has been to maintain God's absolute power and agency. Divine agency is expressed in the Qurʾān by the name al-Qadīr (The All-Powerful or All-Potent), and by verses such as, "When [Allāh] decrees a matter, he merely says to it 'Be!' and it is" (2:117), or "You do not will, unless Allāh wills" (76:30). The desire to maintain the limitlessness of divine power was particularly important in theological discussions of free will and human agency. One of the earliest theological schools in Islam was the Jabrīyah (literally, "Compulsionists"), who conceived of power as a limited quantity and felt that any amount of choice or agency delegated to human beings reduced the amount of power available to God. This zero-sum approach led to a theology of fatalism and predestination, which was exploited by the Umayyad caliphs (r. 662–750) to justify their rule.

The Umayyads used the doctrine of predestination to claim that their opponents were unbelievers. Since God predetermined the affairs of the world, God's will was that the Umayyads should rule over Islam. To reject the Umayyads was thus to reject God's will, and the rejection of God's will is unbelief. This put their political opponents in a difficult theological situation. To say that the Umayyads were unfit to rule implied either that God's will was imperfect or that God created evil by creating corrupt rulers. The easiest way out of this dilemma was to cede the power of moral choice to human beings by saying that God creates good but humans create evil. This position is clearly supported by the Qurʾān: "Whatever good befalls you, it is from Allāh, and whatever evil befalls you it is from yourself" (4:79). Blaming human beings for their own faults and weaknesses prevents God from being accused of willing injustice.

The moral separation of God from the actions of created beings characterized the second theological school of Islam, the Qadarīyah (literally, "Determinists"), whose name refers to the power (*qudrah*) of human beings to partially determine their own fate. Just as the theology of predeterminism was used to justify the status quo, Qadarīyah theology was often advocated by opponents of the status quo and was combined with a strong moral imperative to oppose injustice. Qadarīyah tenets form the basis of Shīʿī theology, which stresses the responsibility to fight against injustice and the freedom to choose the Shīʿī *imām* as the rightful ruler of the Muslims. Qadarīyah doctrines make for good moral theology. After all, how could a just God punish human beings for their actions if they were not free to choose them? The theological choice between Islam and polytheism or the moral choice between good and evil would have no significance if a person's actions were predetermined. If a Muslim judge cannot punish a person for a crime that he or she was forced to commit, how could God do such a thing?

DIVINE EXCEPTIONALISM AND DIVINE JUSTICE. The most influential proponents of Qadarīyah theology were the Muʿtazilah (literally, "Withdrawers"), who called themselves The People of Divine Justice and Unity (*Ahl al-ʿAdl wa al-Tawḥīd*). Muʿtazilism was prominent in Islam for approximately four hundred years and has recently resurfaced as one of the theological positions of Islamic liberalism. From 833 to 850, it was the official theology of the Abbasid caliphate (750–1258) and had a significant influence on Shiism. As a movement of theological rationalism, it attracted the attention of Western scholars of Islam, who mistakenly believed that it foreshadowed the doctrines of the European Enlightenment. The Muʿtazilah believed in a doctrine of extreme exceptionalism with regard to God. One of their fundamental beliefs was that divine unity could be expressed only in terms of divine simplicity. According to this understanding, the statement "There is no god but Allāh" meant that nothing but God is equal to God or is even a part of God, including God's own actions and attributes. The attributes of God cannot be eternal because only God-in-himself is eternal. Thus, the "names" of God mentioned in the Qurʾān are not attributes. They are only metaphors, figures of speech, or created modes of divine action. The Muʿtazilah accused those who believed in divine attributes of falling into anthropomorphism (the belief that God has human attributes) or corporealism (the belief that God's attributes are corporeal entities that exist within Him).

For the Muʿtazilah, knowledge of God's unity is based on reason, which is a responsibility imposed by God on all human beings. This knowledge depends on four types of evidence: dialectical reason, the Qurʾān, the *sunnah* of the Prophet Muḥammad, and the consensus of the Muslim community. Of these, reason is the most important. This is because the validity of scripture, tradition, and consensus are based on the rational knowledge that God exists, that he is truthful, and that he is just. The existence of God can be proven by the argument from contingency. Experience tells us that we cannot live forever and that we are limited in our powers and abilities. Thus, we are contingent beings: we must depend on something outside of ourselves for our creation and support. This noncontingent, necessary being is God, who is unlike us in every way. Because God is exalted above all forms of resemblance, statements in the Qurʾān such as "What prevents you from prostrating yourself before what I have created with my two hands?" (38:75) can only be metaphorical. The "hands" of God must stand for something other than real hands, such as God's ability to create and maintain the world. Metaphors such as these should be understood as partial and approximate descriptions of a divine reality that is ultimately indescribable.

The Muʿtazilite principle of divine justice was derived directly from their view of divine agency and was based on two premises: (1) God desires good for human beings; thus, he does not will or create evil. (2) God provides guidance for human beings in the form of divine revelation; thus, he does not want people to go astray. According to these premises, it would be absurd to believe that God's voluntarism would lead him to predestine people to commit sinful acts. If God punished people for acts that they performed against their will, he would deny the justice that is his nature. Whatever God wills is objectively good, and his justice can be proved by reasoned arguments. Reason demonstrates that the *sharīʿah,* the Law of God, is good for humanity. God's justice, expressed in the *sharīʿah,* is like a rope thrown to a drowning man. God provides the opportunity for salvation, but it is up to the human being to accept it or reject it.

The Muʿtazilah believed that divine revelation, as the embodiment of God's law, was a created entity. For them, the Qurʾanic reference to a "Glorious Qurʾān on a Preserved Tablet" (85:21–22) meant that God created the Qurʾān as a model or template of divine scripture before the creation of the world. The Qurʾān that was revealed to the Prophet Muḥammad was a copy of this preexistent Qurʾān. The Muʿtazilite doctrine of the created Qurʾān was similar to the Jewish doctrine of the preexistent Torah. In Judaism, the Torah, as the source of divine law, is both preexistent and created: God created his law before he created the world. The Qurʾān also had to be created before the world because the world was created in conformity with the law, as is expressed in the Qurʾanic concept of "God's Way" (*Sunnat Allāh,* 48:23).

Sunnī Muslims rejected the doctrine of the created Qurʾān. In the first century of Islam, ʿAbdallāh ibn ʿAbbās (d. 687), a cousin of the Prophet Muḥammad, asserted that God's speech was uncreated and coeternal with God. According to this doctrine, the Qurʾān was also uncreated and eternal because it contained the word of God. Aḥmad ibn Ḥanbal (d. 855), a staunch opponent of the Muʿtazilah, claimed that the word of God is equivalent to God's knowledge. Since the Qurʾān is part of God's knowledge, the words and letters that are found in the Qurʾān must be regarded as the word of God. Because the word of God is uncreated, the Qurʾān must also be uncreated. Ibn Ḥanbal realized that the doctrine of the created Qurʾān contained a potential theological problem. If the Qurʾān were created, this might be construed to mean that the text of the Qurʾān was fixed in historical time; thus, its relevance would be limited primarily to the era in which it was revealed. This would imply that certain Qurʾanic injunctions might be superseded if the social or historical conditions that gave rise to them changed. However, an uncreated Qurʾān, not being fixed in historical time, would have no such limitations. Since it was coeternal with God's knowledge, it would be truly universal. Being free of the limitations of culture and history, its injunctions would be valid for all peoples and all times.

Divine Determinism. Until the modern revival of the teachings of Ibn Ḥanbal, the most important Sunnī theology of divine voluntarism was Ashʿarism. Named after Abū al-Ḥasan al-Ashʿarī (d. 935), Ashʿarite theology sought to recuperate an unrestricted sense of divine agency by promoting a new theory of predestination and a view of the universe that denied the empirical understanding of cause and effect. For the Ashʿarites, all power belongs to God. If God granted people the power of free choice as the Muʿtazilah believed, this would mean that God relinquished some of his power to determine the fate of his creatures. It was absurd to imagine that an all-powerful God would give up his power for any reason. For the Muʿtazilah, God endowed people with choice because human beings, alone among God's creatures, possessed reason. Since God endowed people with reason, he could not prevent them from using this gift to make their own decisions. For the Ashʿarites, it was absurd to consider anything impossible for God, even if it appeared to be illogical. If God's power were truly infinite, then even theoretical limitations on divine power were unacceptable.

According to Ashʿarism, the Qurʾanic verse "[God is the] doer of what he wills" (11:109) means that God is the creator of everything, including the actions of human beings. Al-Ashʿarī distinguished between "necessary" and "acquired" actions. Necessary actions, such as shivering from a fever or trembling with emotion, are involuntary. Acquired actions, such as walking, thinking, and making moral choices, are voluntary. In both cases God is the creator and the agent of all human acts; the human being only "acquires" the capacity to carry them out. This is the meaning of the Qurʾanic statement "God created you and that which you do" (37:96). A person's acquired capacity (*kasb*) is created by God at the time of the act itself. The human being acquires the capacity to either do or not do an action, like the "yes" or "no" binary switches on a computer chip. However, even these limited choices are not really one's to make. "Acquiring the power to do something" only means acquiring the capacity to do what God has already created one to do. The human being cannot produce anything he was not predestined to make. For Ashʿarism, to say that God is all-powerful is to say that human beings are essentially powerless.

The critics of Ashʿarism responded that this was merely a reconfiguration of the outmoded doctrines of the Jabrīyah, who believed that human beings had no freedom of choice whatsoever. The philosopher Ibn Rushd (Averroës) of Córdoba (d. 1198) rejected Ashʿarite theology as illogical. If both the ability to act in a certain way and the act itself are created by God, then, to all intents and purposes, the human being is compelled to behave in only one way. If the acquisition of an act created by God enables a person neither to "own" the act nor to create it, the act cannot really be described as a "power" possessed by the human being. It would therefore be unjust for a person to be judged by God for committing a sin that did not, in reality, "belong" to him. Despite such inconsistencies, Ashʿarite theology became dominant in Sunnī Islam because it provided a relatively simple solution to the problems of divine power and divine knowledge. By basing their arguments on Qurʾanic concepts, the Ashʿarites could create a Qurʾān-based theology more successfully than their opponents could. Muʿtazilite theology also resorted to the Qurʾān, but its emphasis on the use of human reasoning in attaining knowledge of God led to the criticism that revelation was either unnecessary or was reserved for those who were unable to think for themselves. Ashʿarite theologians also stressed the importance of reason. However, they considered divine revelation and prophetic tradition to be more essential because they provided the guidance necessary for reason to function properly. The Ashʿarites saw themselves as taking a middle path between reason and revelation. According to the great Ashʿarite theologian Abū Ḥāmid al-Ghazālī (d. 1111), revelation is understood through tradition, but its underlying truth is understood through reason.

The Ashʿarite theology of divine determinism operated in an atomistic and occasionalistic universe in which nothing was truly real except God. According to the Ashʿarite theory of atomism, the universe is divided into unbounded particles of matter, quality, space, and time. The related theory of occasionalism asserts that every action or event may be broken down into a series of discrete moments, which are completely independent of each other. Such moments are joined together solely through the agency of God's will. No logical continuity or order connects a series of events. To Ashʿarite theologians, the act of hitting a ball with a polo mallet was not perceived as a single motion. Instead, swinging the mallet and striking the ball were seen as a series of separate events, in which the mallet is brought closer and closer to the ball, until it finally strikes it. This illusory view of reality can be compared to a strip of movie film, in which what appears to be a single action is in reality a series of images of different events, which only seem to be continuous because of the speed at which they pass through the projector. In Ashʿarite occasionalism, objects, actions, and events exist only for a single moment. They appear to have continuity only because they are re-created by God in a series of instantaneous creations. This view of reality rejects the notion of "nature" or even of a natural order. Everything is possible for God, who can change reality at any time. No limitations of divine power are allowed to exist.

Ashʿarite occasionalism accepted neither the reality of continuity nor the law of cause and effect. Instead, the regularity of natural occurrences was explained by "habit" or "custom" (*ʿādah*), which God may change at any time. A miracle was simply a paranormal event (*kharq al-ʿādah*), literally, a "ripping" of the fabric of custom. A miracle seems impossible because it goes against normal expectations. However, from the point of view of Ashʿarism, a miracle is essentially normal. Because God creates and re-creates everything at every moment in time, all creation is a miracle. What we think of as a "miracle" is simply an example of God changing his *sunnah*, his customary way of doing things. Ṣūfīs adopted this concept of paranormality to explain their own doctrine of the miracles of saints. Most Ṣūfīs were proponents of Ashʿarite theology, and most Ashʿarite theologians accepted Sufism as a legitimate expression of Islam. The Ashʿarite doctrines of divine voluntarism, divine omniscience, predestination, and occasionalism can all be seen in the following verses, taken from an ode by the Spanish Ṣūfī Abū Madyan (d. 1198). The reference to the Arabic letters *kāf* and *nūn* in the poem recalls the divine command *Kun!* ("Be!"), through which God continually brings things into existence (Qurʾān, 2:117):

> All praise is yours! There is no granting what you forbid,
> And no forbidding what you abundantly bestow.
> Your will is preordained and your judgment is piercing,
> Your knowledge encompasses the seven heavens and the Earth.
>
> Your command subsists between the [letters] *Kaf* and *Nun,* [And is executed] more swiftly and easily than the blink of an eye.
>
> When you say, "Be!" what you say has already been, And your enunciation of it is never repeated.

You were, and nothing was before you; you were, and nothing was Other than you, yet you remain when mortal beings die.

You determined the fate of creatures before creating them, And what you determined was a predestined command. (Cornell, 1996, p. 150)

CREATIVITY AND INTENTIONALITY. Abū al-Ḥasan al-Māturīdī (d. 944) of Samarkand, a contemporary of al-Ashʿarī, developed a theology that split the difference between the Ashʿarite doctrine of divine determinism and the Muʿtazilite doctrine of reasoned choice. Although his ideas are often taken as a critique of Ashʿarism, they were developed independently. Maturidism became influential under the Ottoman Empire (1342–1924), and today it is accepted as a variant of Ashʿarism. The most important difference between the two theologies lies in the balance between divine voluntarism and human agency. According to al-Māturīdī, actions are shared between God and the human being. When an action is attributed to God, it is called "creation" (*khalq*), and when an action is attributed to a person, it is called "acquisition" (*kasb*). God's actions are essentially creative. They include miracles and other phenomena that the human mind cannot fully comprehend. God also creates the potential for human actions, but human beings are responsible for what they actually do. By being responsible, they "acquire" the act for themselves. Reward or punishment is the moral consequence of a person's intention (*nīyah*) to act in a certain way. Since Maturidism separated intentions from actual behaviors, it was better able than Ashʿarism to account for apparent paradoxes of the divine will, such as when an otherwise good person inexplicably commits a crime.

Another contribution of Maturidism was a theory of knowledge that balanced the dictates of reason and revelation. Al-Māturīdī was highly critical of blind traditionalism. This was particularly important with respect to notions about God, because the Qurʾān admonishes believers not to blindly follow their forefathers (43:23). Knowledge is of three types: knowledge from the senses, knowledge from testimony, and knowledge from reason. Knowledge from the senses includes knowledge from experience. One who denies the truth of empirical knowledge is unreasonable because he denies what he observes with his own eyes. Knowledge from testimony is what we would today call "history." This includes the testimony of the Qurʾān and the *sunnah*. Such testimony is believable because God stands behind the teachings of the prophets. However, the most important type of knowledge is from reason. Reason is the critical faculty by which we assess empirical and historical forms of knowledge. Reason enables us to understand the divine wisdom in creation. Without submitting the testimony of the prophets to reason and experience, the human being falls into traditionalism. Without submitting empirical knowledge to reason and revelation, the human being falls into materialism *(illḥād)*, which medieval Muslims likened to atheism.

THE ONE IN THE ALL. Today's limits of Islamic theology are marked by Wahhabism and Sufism. The elimination of the *falsafa* tradition of Islamic philosophy by the end of the thirteenth century and the decline of formal Sunnī theology during the Ottoman Empire led to the legalistic fideism that dominates Sunnī theology today. Most of what is left of these traditions has been subsumed into Shiism, as represented by the writings of Mullā Ṣadrā of Shiraz (d. 1641). Wahabbism, which was founded in the eighteenth century by Muḥammad ibn ʿAbd al-Wahhāb (d. 1787), goes beyond normal Sunnī fideism by advocating an extreme form of traditionalism. Its approach to divine unity relies on a literal reading of Qurʾān and *ḥadīth* that avoids rational speculation on the nature of God and his attributes. It also avoids the interpretation of ambiguities in the Qurʾān and even denies the metaphorical nature of certain Qurʾanic verses. Instead, Aḥmad ibn Ḥanbal's theological formula of *bilā kayf* (literally, "without how") is employed to assert that God has "hands unlike other hands," or "a face unlike other faces." Questions left unanswered by traditional sources are not to be investigated at all. The Wahhābī abandonment of rational interpretation has led their critics to accuse them of theological simple-mindedness and of anthropomorphizing God and his attributes.

Ṣūfī theology stands at the opposite pole from Wahhabism in that it does not reject hermeneutical inquiry. It confronts the paradox of divine transcendence and divine immanence by recognizing that the concept of divine unity must allow for the transcendence of number. Ṣūfī theology has been neglected in modern scholarship, especially in the Islamic world. In part, this has been the result of a Western emphasis on the concept of mysticism, which tends to overlook the use of reasoned arguments in Ṣūfī treatises and focuses instead on "ineffable" spiritual experiences. The identification of Sufism with mysticism has, in turn, affected the image of Sufism in Muslim countries, where it is often dismissed as nonrational or inauthentic. It particular, it is accused of incorporating ideas from Hinduism or Buddhism into Islam. In premodern Islam, however, Ṣūfī theology was the subject of lively debates, and the onus was on the opponents of Sufism to prove why this tradition was not authentic, rather than the other way around.

Abū al-Qāsim al-Junayd (d. 910) of Baghdad was one of the founders of Ṣūfī theology. Like other Sunnī theologians, he sought to combine Qurʾān and *ḥadīth* with a reasoned approach to interpretation. Unlike non-Ṣūfī theologians, however, he accepted mystical experience as epistemologically equivalent to reason. When combined with reason and revelation, mystical experience, which was known as "unveiling" *(kashf)*, led to a direct knowledge of God (*maʿrifah*) that was superior to the intellectual knowledge (*ʿilm*) of the theologians. The Ṣūfī reliance on mystical perception, however, did not mean that they ignored other approaches to theology. On the contrary, Ṣūfī treatises are full of discussions of theological issues. Al-Junayd was the founder of the "Baghdad school" of Sufism, which set the standards for Ṣūfī thought and practice. Maʿrūf al-Karkhī

(d. 816), a close associate of Shīʿī Imām ʿAlī al-Riḍā (d. 818), was an important forerunner of this tradition. Thus, it may be no coincidence that both Sufism and Shiism shared an interest in the paradoxical nature of divine unity.

For al-Junayd, the creedal pillar of *tawḥīd* meant "singling out the eternal from that which is created in time" (Abdel-Kader, 1976, p. 70). A later Ṣūfī, ʿAlī al-Hujwīrī (d. after 1072), glossed this definition in the following way: "You must not regard the eternal as a locus of phenomena, or phenomena as a locus of the eternal. You must know that God is eternal and that you are phenomenal, and that nothing of your genus is connected with him, and that nothing of his attributes is mingled in you, and that there is no homogeneity between the eternal and the phenomenal" (al-Hujwīrī, 1976, p. 281). Understood this way, there is nothing distinctively "Ṣūfī" about al-Junayd's definition. It even earned the approval of the Ḥanbalī theologian Ibn Taymīyah (d. 1328), who was one of the most influential opponents of the Ṣūfīs.

However, another possible interpretation of al-Junayd's definition is more problematical. "Singling out" the eternal from that which is created might be understood to mean that God could be found, or at least identified, within his creation. Al-Hujwīrī alludes to this when he warns: "When the eternal is believed to descend into phenomena, or phenomena to be attached to the eternal, no proof remains of the eternity of God and the origination of the universe; this leads to materialism. In all the actions of phenomena, there are proofs of unification and evidences of the divine omnipotence and signs, which establish the eternity of God, but men are too heedless to desire only him or to be content only with keeping him in remembrance. Ḥusayn ibn Mansur [al-Ḥallāj, d. 922] said: 'The first step in *tawḥīd* is the annihilation of separation'" (al-Hujwīrī, 1976, p. 281).

Muḥammad "Muhyiddin" ibn al-ʿArabī (d. 1240), arguably the most influential Ṣūfī theologian, agreed more with al-Ḥallāj's statement than with al-Hujwīrī's warning. Many of Ibn al-ʿArabī's writings discuss the issues of separating the eternal from the temporal and finding the one in the many. In the chapter on Noah in Fuṣūṣ al-Ḥikam (*Ring-Settings of Wisdom*), he summarizes the theological paradox of divine unity in the following poem:

> If you speak of transcendence, you are restricted. If you speak of immanence, you are limited.
>
> If you speak of both matters, you are complete. You are an Imam and a master of spiritual knowledge.
>
> He who speaks of joining is a polytheist. He who speaks of separating affirms unity.
>
> Beware of immanence if you are a dualist! Beware of transcendence if you are a Unitarian!
>
> You are not he; yet, you are he and you see him in The essences of things both boundless and limited! (Ibn al-ʿArabī, 1980, p. 70)

For Ibn al-ʿArabī, divine immanence means that God can be "found" in worldly phenomena. In Arabic, the verb "to find" is *wajada.* The experience of finding is *wijdān.* Most works on Sufism translate *wijdān* as "ecstasy." This obscures the theological importance of the term for Ibn al-ʿArabī. One "finds" ecstasy in *wijdān* because he or she perceives, or "finds" God in the essences of things. Ibn al-ʿArabī extends the metaphor of "finding" to all of existence, which in Arabic is denoted by the term *wujūd.* Existence is where the perceptive believer "finds" God. In other words, the world is a theater for the manifestation of the Absolute. Before creation, while possible things are in a state of nonexistence, God is the only existent. At their creation, things "acquire" existence, much as human beings "acquire" moral responsibility in Ashʿarite theology. The Qurʾān states: "We did not create the heavens and the Earth and all that is between them but in Truth" (15:85). For Ibn al-ʿArabī, this verse holds the key to the paradox of divine unity. Things and their effects "find" their way into physical existence through the divine names: "Since the effects belong to the divine names, and the name is the named, there is nothing in existence but God" (Ibn al-ʿArabī, 2002, p. 138).

In *al-Fūtuḥāt al-Makkīyah* (*Meccan Revelations*), Ibn al-ʿArabī states that no theological subject is more resistant to human reason than the transcendence of number. Because numbers are usually conceived as serial integers and are believed to bestow qualities on the things they designate, it is difficult to understand how the many are dependent on the one. Commenting on the anti-Trinitarian verse of the Qurʾān: "They disbelieve who say 'Verily, Allāh is the third of three'" (5:73), Ibn al-ʿArabī notes that the person who says "Allāh is the fourth of three" is not an unbeliever. If God were the third of three, he would be of the same genus (*jins*) as the other two. This is the theological sin of *shirk,* associating partners with God. However, as the "fourth of three," God would not be of the same genus as the three, so he is not one of them. Therefore, God is one for any group or plurality, but without becoming one of its kind: "He is the fourth of three, so he is one; the fifth of four, so he is one; and so on indefinitely" (Ibn al-ʿArabī, 2002, p. 137).

Ibn al-ʿArabī explains this theological principle in terms of algebra or set theory. Medieval Muslims called algebra *al-jabr wa al-muqābalah* (literally, "determination and juxtaposition"). God is the fourth of three as in the algebraic expression $(x + y + z)\ a$. The letter a is part of the expression because it is juxtaposed with the terms in parentheses, but it is not part of the set $(x + y + z)$. In the same way, Allāh can be "found" in the expression of his creation, but he is not part of the same set, or genus. This principle is also a key to the paradox of divine unity because it demonstrates how God can be transcendently separate and immanently involved with his creation at the same time. "This is what is called Allāh," observes Ibn al-ʿArabī. God is the existence manifest in the forms associated with the sites of his manifestation, but he is not of their kind. In his essence, he is Necessary Being, whereas created possibilities are "necessary nonexistence" in their essences eternally (Ibn al-ʿArabī, 2002, p. 136).

SEE ALSO Attributes of God, article on Christian Concepts; Creeds, article on Islamic Creeds; Free Will and Predestination, article on Islamic Concepts; Kalám.

BIBLIOGRAPHY

Abdel-Kader, Ali Hassan. *The Life, Personality, and Writings of Al-Junayd.* London, 1976. The most thorough study of this important Ṣūfī thinker, by a scholar from Egypt's Al-Azhar University.

Austin, R. W. J., trans. *Ibn al-ʿArabī: The Bezels of Wisdom.* New York, 1980. This is the most popular English translation of *Fuṣūṣ al-Ḥikam.*

Cornell, Vincent J. *The Way of Abū Madyan: Doctrinal and Poetic Works of Abū Madyan Shuʿayb ibn al-Ḥusayn al-Anṣārī (c. 509/115–16—594/1198).* Cambridge, 1996. The translation of Abū Madyan's ode above has been revised slightly from the original version.

Crone, Patricia, and Martin Hinds. *God's Caliph: Religious Authority in the First Centuries of Islam* (Cambridge, 1986). "The Letter of al-Walīd II," pp. 116–126, provides a good illustration of the Umayyad use of Jabrīyah theology.

Al-Ghāzwanī, Abū Muḥammad ʿAbdallāh. *Al-Nuqṭah al-azaliyah fi sirr al-dhāt al-Muhammadīyah* (The Eternal Point in the Secret of the Muhammadan Essence). Rabat, Bibliothèque Générale manuscript 4400D.

Al-Ḥujwīrī, ʿAlī B. ʿUthmān al-Jullābī. *The Kashf al-Mahjub: The Oldest Persian Treatise on Sufiism.* Edited by Reynold A. Nicholson. London, 1976; reprint of 1936 edition.

Ibn al-ʿArabī, Muhyiddin. *The Meccan Revelations,* vol. 1. Edited by Michel Chodkiewicz, translated by William C. Chittick and James W. Morris. New York, 2002.

Ibn al-ʿArabī, Muhyiddin. *Fuṣūṣ al-Ḥikam.* Edited by Abū al-ʿAlā ʿAfīfī. Beirut, 1980.

Isutzu, Toshihiko. *God and Man in the Koran: Semantics of the Koranic Weltanschaaung.* New York, 1980; reprint of 1964 original. See especially pp. 95–119.

Al-Juwaynī, Imam al- Ḥaramayn ʿAbd al-Malik. *Kitāb al-irshād ilā qawāṭīʿ al-adilla fī uṣūl al-Iʿtiqād* (A Guide to Conclusive Proofs for the Principles of Belief). Translated by Paul E. Walker. Reading, U.K., 2000. An English translation of one of the definitive Ashʿarite theological treatises, written by al-Ghazālī's teacher.

Lane, Edward William. *Arabic-English Lexicon.* Cambridge, 1984; reprint in one volume of 1863 original. See especially, pp. 82–83 for the section on Allāh. Although this work was not completed at the time of Lane's death, it remains the most thorough Arabic-English lexicon, and is especially useful for premodern uses of terminology.

Martin, Richard C., and Mark R. Woodward, with Atmaja, Dwi S. *Defenders of Reason in Islam: Muʿtazilism from Medieval School to Modern Symbol.* Oxford, 1997. *Kitāb al- uṣūl al-khamsah* (Book of the Five Principles), a famous summary of Muʿtazilite doctrine by Qādī ʿAbd al-Jabbār (d. 1024), is translated on pp. 90–115.

Al-Māturīdī al-Samarqandi, Abū Manṣūr Muḥammad. *Kitāb al-Tawḥīd* (Book of divine unity). Edited by Fathalla Kholeif. Beirut, 1982. Introduction in English.

Pines, Shlomo. *Studies in Islamic Atomism.* Jerusalem, 1997. This work, a reprint of Pines's doctoral dissertation, is the definitive work in English on this subject.

Tabatabai, Sayyid Muhammad Husayn. *Shiʿite Islam.* Translated by Sayyid Husayn Nasr. Houston, Tex., 1979.

Watt, W. Montogomery. *The Formative Period of Islamic Thought.* Oxford, 1998; reprint of 1973 original. The classic work is still the best introduction to early Islamic theology.

Wolfson, Harry Austryn. *The Philosophy of the Kalam.* Cambridge, Mass., and London, 1976. This work remains the most definitive study of Islamic theology in English.

VINCENT J. CORNELL (2005)

GOD: AFRICAN SUPREME BEINGS

African supreme beings are spiritual beings or divinities who are as varied as the peoples of sub-Saharan Africa, the world's second largest continent after Asia. Belief in a supreme being is universal among most of the over sixty peoples of Africa. Supreme beings carry a distinct and unique quality in African cosmology as creators with all other supreme attributes in the theocentric universe. The nature, characters, and attributes of the African supreme being reflect indigenous religious orthodoxy prior to the introduction of, and in spite of, the influence of Christianity and Islam, and these qualities reflect the continuing diversity of the African peoples' traditional sociopolitical structures and languages within the current modern nation-states. The African supreme being is usually associated symbolically with the varieties of indigenous cultures of the peoples. The indigenous concepts and conceptions of most African supreme beings have been retained by the adherents of the religions that were introduced into Africa in the ritual practices and the translations of the sacred texts (Bible and Qurʾān) of those religious traditions.

BASIC COMMON VIEWS. The diversity of cultural forms and linguistic differences of Africans, notwithstanding the relationships of African supreme beings to the created order (including the human, spiritual, and other entities), reveal to a great extent a certain uniformity and similarity in the nature, attributes, and powers of the supreme beings.

Mythologies: creation and existence. The different groups of Africa have developed myths around their supreme beings' transcendence and immanence. Africans' perceptions towards supreme beings, though varying from one people to the other, express certain basic patterns that reflect African social organization and hierarchical structures, including relationships between elders and youths and humans' interconnections with natural phenomena. The three interrelated elemental dimensions—the sky, the earth, and the underworld (beneath the earth)—are believed to be peopled by different categories of spiritual and physical beings, and all are connected in certain relational ways to the supreme being.

Most mythic narratives of African peoples hold the supreme being responsible for the creation of their universe, including the earth and sky, human beings, and spiritual beings. In some sense, cosmogenic and cosmological myths serve the social and political functions in the diverse traditional political groups of African communities, particularly the ways in which different ethnic groups came into existence. Most of the myths affirm that the supreme being delegated to lesser spiritual beings the responsibility of creating the local universes of Africa, and the supreme being is always credited with the creation and allotting of what each community considers to be the essence of human beings (including destiny and predestination). Thus, the entire creation is held to be dependent upon the supreme being, who is acknowledged to be at the apex of the cosmic structure. This is the general notion on which rests the concept of an intermediary in African religion, which is also reflected in African social and political setting. Many of the myths are handed down through many generations. They are often told in traditional language by priests of indigenous religious traditions and by elders.

Names: ancient and descriptive. The names of African supreme beings reflect the different African language groups. Within some nation states there are more than 250 languages, as in Nigeria, within others more than one hundred, as in Tanzania, and within some others more than forty, as in Kenya. Most of these names are encoded in etymologies which describe the qualities and functions of such supreme beings. Generally, the names used for the supreme being of every African people are classifiable into two groups: the ancient or primary local names, and the descriptive or secondary names. Ancient or primary names are those that are generally used by older and elderly members of the communities. Examples are Olódùmarè of the Yoruba of Nigeria and Mulungu of the Bantu-speaking peoples of East Africa. Ancient names express the inexplicable nature, character, essence, and attributes of a being who is an almighty, all-powerful, ever-present creator, and who is supreme in all senses of supremacy. The unknowable character of gods' names illustrates power and secrecy beyond human imagination or conception. Although the meanings of the ancient names are not easily explained by common sense or etymological interpretation, due to nonusage over a long period of time, descriptive names have etymologies that express the perceived knowledge and living experiences of peoples in their mundane situations. Furthermore, the etymologies of the descriptive names divulge intrinsic and functional meanings and functional spatial locations which identify supreme beings with the nature of such locations.

The names of the supreme being generally reflect the nature of African universe and sociopolitical structure, and they describe the people's perception of their conditioned environment and the polarity of the supreme being. The names describe the benevolence and activities of the supreme being on the people's life experiences. Both the ancient and descriptive names of the supreme being, however, express an intrinsic reality of the supreme being. It is important to note that each African people also have local names, from which one is adopted for common use by the general public.

Attributes: being and expression. There is a close relationship between the conception of the traditional claims of historic religions and those of Africans concerning the attributes of the supreme being. The conceptions of African supreme beings are similar to those of most Western and Eastern religions with regards to Godly characteristics, which include omnipotence, omniscience, omnipresence, transcendence, immanence, benevolence, and so on. These attributes express a complex relationship between the supreme being and other entities, human and nonhuman, animate and inanimate, visible and invisible, material, and spiritual. However, the degrees by which each African people express their supreme being differ in intensity and quality, and these are expressed in the indigenous names which each African group gives their supreme being. Some supreme beings, and particularly divinities who serve as intermediaries of supreme beings, also exhibit certain human negative behavioral attributes such as anger and fury. These attributes are manifested in such natural occurrences as thunder, storm, wind, whirlwind, thick cloud, running streams, beaming oceans, and so on.

Relationship to spiritual and human beings and other cosmic entities. Cosmogenic and cosmological myths detail different levels of relationship between a supreme being and other entities. The relationship with other spiritual beings or deities is expressed in stories about the creation and maintenance of the universe. These deities in most cases play the role of intermediaries between the supreme being and human beings. As guardian agents of morality, they function to maintain an ontological equilibrium on behalf of the supreme being. Thus, in ritual practices, these spiritual beings who populate the physical universe are popular and influential among human beings but are limited in power. Some of the deities bear the ritual sacrifices to the supreme being as sacred meals of appeasement and restoration. The supreme being has a close relationship with natural phenomena such as trees, oceans and seas, mountains and hills, the sun and moon, rainbows, and so on. Nature and the natural as well as physical locations of these phenomena are generally noted to have an effect on the people's conception and description of the supreme being. Natural phenomena provide avenues for hierophanic appearances (manifestation of the divine) by the deities who manifest aspects of the supreme beings. Some natural phenomena also serve as altars on which sacred meals are displayed as sacrifices for the deities to feed on, and they possibly carry some of the sacrifices to the supreme being. Africans' attitude to natural phenomena and their recognition of the deities as intermediaries between them and the supreme being have strongly influenced the derogatory description of African religious traditions as polytheism and fetishism by early anthropologists as well as missionaries.

The moral aspect of the relationship of the supreme being to the African universe reveals the polarity of the being who is essentially good, and yet whose works of creation directly or indirectly lead to misfortunes, chaos, and crises. The polarity is often explained by the concepts of free will and determinism, by which the supreme being operates in the theocentric universe. This idea is variously expressed in African mythologies that the supreme being creates certain spiritual beings and deities to whom he delegates responsibility for creating other universal entities, including human beings.

In African cosmology, the relationship of the supreme being to human beings is crucial because it has moral implications for human and universal harmony. This is a continual relationship in the interminable process of creation, particularly as it provides for reincarnation, which depends upon the quality of life which an individual person lives as a human being in the universe. As in some Eastern religions, a person who lives a worthy life on earth is accepted into ancestral status, and a person who lives a degenerate life reincarnates into a lesser being such as an animal and plant. Africans do not hold their supreme beings directly responsible for imperfectness in creation, but they do attribute fault and imperfectness in creation to the deities who are involved in the process. African myths attempt to justify deities on the grounds that each represents an aspect of the supreme being, and as such they only serve to check human excesses, bring order to chaos, and maintain an ontological equilibrium in the universe, which has been desecrated by human beings. Thus, human beings are liable for their actions and must accept responsibility for the consequences of the choices they make in their lives.

Anthropomorphic descriptions. The African supreme being is described in anthropomorphic terms which reflect to great extent human biological and social functions such as fatherhood and motherhood, and human physical and domestic activities and cares. In all, the role of the supreme being is conceived as encompassing both masculine and feminine roles in a gendered African universe. Most African myths reveal that the African supreme being, after the first order of creation, either retreated or traveled to the high heavens where he resides. Such retreat or withdrawal is claimed to be a consequence of human beings' misbehavior or disobedience. It can be argued that, contrary to the unduly negative assessments of Western writers, the withdrawl of the supreme being does not indicate that Africans hold their supreme being as distant and unreachable, for they always acknowledge him, not only through the intermediaries but directly as well.

SUPREME BEINGS IN LOCAL GEOGRAPHICAL CONTEXTS. The supreme beings selected here for specific discussion do not represent the totality of the conceptions and imaginations of the numerous African groups; instead, they have been chosen because of the popularity that has been accorded them in academic study and scholarly writings and analysis. Secondly, most of them represent large populations of people who have regarded themselves as kingdoms, especially before the colonial partitioning efforts that led to the current modern states. The supreme beings that are discussed here are selected from various parts of Africa—East, West, Central, and southern Africa—where indigenous cultures still flourish as regards the notion of indigenous African supreme beings: Amma, Nyame, Ngewo, Olódùmarè, Osanobwa, Chukwu, Kwoth, Mulungu, Nzambi, Nhialic, Ndjambi, Ngai, and uNkulunkulu.

Amma. Amma is the supreme being of the Dogon people of Mali. The Dogon attributed the creation of everything in the world, including human beings, earth, stars and so on to Amma, the supreme being. However, the myth of these creations is complex and profound. The myth "serves to demonstrate the rich system of correspondences between the natural order, the social realm, and personal life" (Sproul 1979, p. 49).

According to Dogon mythology, Amma created the heavens and the earth. The creation is envisaged in several stages with the use of sacred "word" by Amma. The first stage was the creation of nature, the second was an attempt to redeem human beings. The third creation included the sacred granary (including the world order of creation) and the rum which is a primary method of communication and symbolic of verbal language and culture. Amma exists in the shape of an oval egg with four collarbones joined together to form four quarters. These quarters contain the four elements of earth, air, fire, and water.

The creation of human beings, summarized by James Thayer, came when Amma placed a seed within himself and spoke seven creative words which caused the seed to vibrate and to extend itself into the image of man. Amma produced a set of male and female twins by dividing the egg into a double placenta that he placed in each of the twins. The twins emanated directly from Amma, and are thus his children. Yurugu, the male twin, due to impatience, broke through the placenta in need of a female. Yurugu did this to replicate Amma's creation. As the placenta tore away, a piece of it became the earth. Yurugu could not find a mate and instead mated with the earth, thereby defiling the earth, which was actually his mother. Amma tried to restore the creation. He made another male twin, Nommo, and then created four other spirits from Nommo. These were the ancestors of the Dogon. Nommo and the ancestors came down to earth on an ark. The ark was filled with those materials that they would need for proper restoration and successful abode in the world. There came light and rain that would purify the earth. It was through Nommo and the ancestors that human beings, animals, and plants were created. The four other Nommo spirits who were created by Amma gave birth to the four divisions of the Dogon and to their social life. Amma transformed Yurugu into an animal, known as "pale fox," that wanders the earth in search of his female counterpart. The diviners use the signs of the "pale fox" that are left on the earth to interpret important events in the life of the Dogon people.

The effect of Yurugu's "incestuous behavior" resulted in darkness, sterility, and death. This was balanced, however, by partial restoration by Nommo who produced light, rain and fertility. Yurugu personifies the night and all those places that are uninhabitable, including dry lands.

Other sets of creation first invented by Amma included the sun and the moon, made through the process of pottery. Dogon myth states that the sun is a pot raised to white heat and surrounded by a spiral of red copper with eight turns. The moon is the same shape, but the copper is white. The moon was heated one quarter at a time. Amma "took a lump of clay, squeezed it in his hand and flung it from him just as he did with the stars. The clay spread and fell on the north, which is the top, and from there stretched out to the south, which is the bottom, of the world, . . . the earth lies flat, but the north is at the top. It extends east and west with separate members like a foetus in the womb. . . . Its sexual organ is an anthill, and its clitoris a termite hill. Amma being lonely and desirous of intercourse with this creature, approached it. That was the occasion of the first breach of the order of the universe" (Sproul, 1979, 50–51).

However, the termite hill did not allow the passage, and intercourse could not take place. But Amma is all-powerful. He cut down the termite hill and had intercourse with the excised earth. Subsequent intercourse with his earth-wife was easy. Water, the divine seed, was able to enter the womb of the earth, allowing a normal reproductive cycle that resulted in the birth of twins, two beings. The two beings were green in color, half human beings and half serpents who were called Nummo, two homogenous products of Amma, of divine essence like himself. These beings also produced the pair which were present in all water. The pair became the source of all human actions.

Nyame (Onyankopon, Onyame). Nyame is the most common and the principal name for the supreme deity of the Akan people of Ghana. The variations of this name among the Ga of Ghana are Nyonmo, Nyama, and Nyam, which have the same basic connotation and meaning. Other common names among the Akan that are related in etymological interpretation are Nyankopon and Onyankopon. *Nyame* derives from two Akan words, *nya,* meaning "to get," and *me,* meaning "to be full" or "to be satisfied." *Nyame* is thus interpreted to mean "if you possess or get him, you are satisfied." That is, Nyame can be interpreted as the god of fullness or god of satisfaction. The name is also said to be derivable from the root word *nyam,* which can mean "shining," "brightness," or "glory." In the Akans' worldview, all of these are attributes of the supreme being, but how the idea of the supreme being itself originated is unknown.

The Akan do not possess any systematic account of the process of creation of the universe. There is, however, a strong belief indicated in variants of myths that the creation is credited solely to the supreme being, whatever name it is called. Various accounts specify that the sky was created first, followed by the earth, rivers, waters, plants, and trees. After this came the creation of the first man, called Okane, and the first woman, called Kyeiwaa, as one myth tells. Okane and Kyeiwaa live in a cave. Nyame teaches the couple the names of all things he creates. In all the accounts, Nyame is acknowledged as the author, the creator of all things, hence his praise name Odomankoma and his title Borebore, which means "excavator," "hewer," "carver," "creator," "originator," "inventor," or "architect." The next stage is the creation of the animals. Nyame orders and provides a structure in the hierarchies for and utilities of the human, animal, and plant species. Nyame is also said to have some divinities who are called his children because they derive their essential origin from him. There are many proverbs, songs, and other oratures which support the Akans' belief in Nyame as the creator and author of all that exists, including those essential aspects of human life. In *The Akan Doctrine of God,* J. B. Danquah records a stanza from the Akan songs (which are usually played with a talking drum) that praises Nyame as the creator: "Odomankoma, / He created the Thing, / Hewer-out Creator, / He created the Thing, / What did he create? / He created Order, / He created Knowledge, / He created Death, / As its quintessence!" (Danquah, 1944, p. 70).

Ngewo. Ngewo is the name for the supreme being of the Mende people of Sierra Leone in West Africa. The derivative of the name Ngewo is vague. The probable etymology claims that the name derives from Ngele-woo, a combination of *ngele* (sky) and *woo* (long ago), which suggests "in the sky, from long ago." Another name for the supreme being among the Mende is Leve, which is said to be the much older name that is used almost exclusively by very old people. Leve means "the giver of chicken" or "high one."

As in some other African communities, Ngewo, the supreme being of the Mende is claimed to be the creator of the universe. The Mende conceive of Ngewo in masculine terms, that is, they regard him as their father. He is also described as being "high up," and at the same time ubiquitous. As the controller of the universe, whose ultimate authority is affirmed, the Mende attribute their well-being, victory over their enemies, retribution, and defense to Ngewo.

In their book *The Springs of Mende Belief and Conduct* (1968), William T. Harris and Harry Sawyerr present the myth of the creative power and activities of Ngewo. The myth tells of a long ago when Ngewo made the earth and all things in it, after which he made a man and a woman. The myth of the creation of the animals that populate the world is a fascinating one. It is claimed that before Ngewo was called by that name, he was once a very big or great spirit, living in a cave that had a door. His power and authority was so immense that all he said would come to pass. There came a day when he said to himself, "I have all this power, why don't I use it? I have lived alone for a long time with no one to talk to and no one to play with." He went to the entrance of the cave and said, "I want all kinds of animals to live with me in this cave." The animals came in pairs. He closed the door of the cave. After some time he called the animals together and gave them the rules that would continue to guide them, the violation of which would lead them to a terrible consequence. The first item of the law was on food. He said, "I will give you anything you want, food and everything else, but you must not touch my own food." The spirit looked at himself, the animals, and the cave, and he said "This cave is too small." As he turned himself around, the cave became very, very big. The animals became happy as their food also increased to the size of the room. Also, the spirit was happy as he had neighbors to talk to and play with.

The spirit and the animals usually had a very intimate rapport. The animals usually came to greet him. One day, one of the animals came to greet him. As the animal was approaching him, it smelled some sweet-smelling food, saw the food and took some and ate it. The spirit is very knowledgeable, very strict about his rules, and powerful. The animal mysteriously found itself in front of the spirit. The spirit then said, "What brought you here? You have violated my law." The spirit threw the animal from the cave and said, "You! From now on, your name is cow." Later another animal also ate the food and was thrown out. This animal the spirit named monkey. This continued until all the animals were given different names and were thrown out of the cave. This was the genesis of why and how all animals and men wander around the world to look for this sweet-smelling food.

The first man and woman who were created by the great spirit usually referred to him as Maada-le ("He is grandfather"). One day Ngewo addressed the two, saying, "Everything you ask me for, if you want it, you shall have it." Whenever they needed anything, including food, they went to him requesting, "*Maada*, give us this, or *Maada*, give us that." As he gave it, he would say, "*In ngee*" (Yes, take it.). However, Ngewo saw their constant coming and requesting from him as wearisome and troubling. This made him decide to leave them. He said to himself, "If I stay near these people they will wear me with their requests; I will make another living place for myself far above them." The people went to sleep one night. They woke up the next morning and looked about, but could not see him. As they lifted up their heads, they saw him Ngawongo waa, (spread out very big) which forms another possible etymology of the word for Ngewo, the supreme being.

The spirit decided to go up far above men and animals, where he is sitting, watching to see who will eat his food. This spirit was later called Ngewo. Although this myth does not reveal the beginning of human beings, the Mende hold Ngewo as their creator and controller of their universe. They pray to him. They regard ancestors as intermediaries between them and the supreme being.

Olódùmarè and Ọlọ́run. Olódùmarè is the supreme god of the Yoruba people, a highly urbanized society with large city-state kingdoms in southwestern Nigeria. The origin of the name has been difficult to decipher through etymologies, but Yoruba mythology and conception of this being describe the supreme being as almighty, the first being, and the creator of the world. Olódùmarè is the ancient name of the Yoruba supreme being. The other name that is commonly used and which etymologically identifies the supreme being with the creation and ownership of the universe and close relationship with the sky is Ọlọ́run (one who owns or resides in the sky).

Although Olódùmarè is the creator, he works through hundreds of *òrìṣà* (divinities or deities)—some myths say 201, some say 401, and some say 601. These *òrìṣà* are said to share of the essence of Olódùmarè. After creating the *òrìṣà*, Olódùmarè delegates some *òrìṣà* to create certain aspects of the universe and some to maintain the universe. This networking by Olódùmarè through the *òrìṣà* stabilizes the social and psychological spaces of the human life. Each *òrìṣà* has a different elemental province. Prominent among the *òrìṣà* who were delegated to create are Ọbàtáálà, Ọ̀rúnmìlà, Odùduwà, Ọ̀ṣun, and Ògún. There are others who manifest aspects of Olódùmarè in the maintenance of morality and orderliness in the world. Èṣù is regarded as the neutral force who supervises sacrifices; that is, the sacrifices that are prescribed to clients through divination. Èṣù carries the sacrifices to *Olódùmarè*.

To create the world, Olódùmarè supplies some dry soil, a five-toed hen, and a chameleon. Olódùmarè gives the dry soil to Obàtáálá to drop on the primordial watery surface in the world. The five-toed hen then spreads the soil on the watery surface. Another version of the myth states that Odùduwà has to complete the creation of the earth because Obàtáálá gets drunk on the way to the world. The five-toed hen does the work. The chameleon tests and confirms the habitability of the now-solid space, and the report pleases Olódùmarè. Obàtáálá is also assigned to mold the human being with clay, and Olódùmarè breathes life into the figure. Ọ̀rúnmìlà is the deputy of Olódùmarè on matters of knowledge and wisdom, which are understood in Yorùbá mythology to be intertwined with the concept of destiny. Destiny is said to be enclosed in the "inner spiritual head," which is molded by another divinity called Àjàlá. Every human being is given or chooses from the many molded heads when coming from heaven. In these heads are contained all that a human being will experience in life. This further illustrates the Yoruba concept of free will and determinism, which holds that God is not responsible for human calamities. Olódùmarè also commands sacrifices to alleviate human sufferings. The way that the interactions of human beings with Olódùmarè and deities are explained is that the deities that are involved in the processes of controlling human beings moderate the activities of human beings in the world. The ordering of sacrifices by Olódùmarè and his deities, and the performance or nonperformance of the sacrifices by human beings, explains the resolution of the complexities and paradoxes of human responsibility in the cosmos. The relationship of Olódùmarè to human beings is a continuous one, as a well-lived life qualifies a human being to enter into the ancestral world.

The nature, character, and emotions of Olódùmarè are manifested through such divinities as Ògún, Sàngó, Ọ̀ṣun, Ọya, and several others. The divinities express the fury and anger of Olódùmarè, as Sàngó does when he draws on thunder and lightning. They also give provision, providence, and protection, as the people demonstrate in thanksgiving with votive offerings in times of plenty and bountiful harvest, and in their prayers and petitions in times of adversity and need.

Osanobwa, or Osanobua. Osanobwa, or Osanobua, is the name of the supreme being of the Edo people of western Nigeria. The name is a contraction of four components: *Osa,* meaning "the source of all beings"; *N'o,* meaning "who" or "which"; *B',* meaning "carries" or "sustains"; and *Wa* or *Uwa,* meaning "the world" or "the universe." Taken together, the name means "the source of all beings who carries and sustains the whole world or universe." To the Edo people, their god is the creator of the world and the absolute sustainer.

The creation account of the Edo people states that Osanobwa commissions two divinities who share some part of his essence as the "source being" to perform the creation of the earth. Osanowa is commissioned to create human beings and to continue to control the house or the township, whereas Osanoha is delegated to create animals of the bush and to rule over the place. Osanoha soon becomes jealous of Osanowa and plans to destroy his work. He builds a house and stores all kinds of diseases therein. When the creations of Osanowa, men and women, come from heaven down to earth, Osanoha causes a downpour of rain. The people look for shelter from the rain, and the only available place they find is the house built by Osanoha in which diseases are concealed. Unaware of the consequences (unfortunately for them), the people take shelter in the "disease" house of Osanoha, and this is how people carried various diseases into the world. This myth traces the origin of humans and animals to the supreme being as the source being.

Chukwu, or Chineke (Igbo of eastern Nigeria). Chukwu is the supreme being of the Igbo people in the eastern Nigeria. He is also called Chineke. The two names are commonly and interchangeably used in all parts of Igboland, although it is asserted that the names stem from different areas. Etymologically, *chi* in Igbo language can mean "source being" or "the source of being." It can also mean "spirit." Both *Chineke* and *Chukwu* are composed of *chi,* which has been accepted as the generic word for god; *Chineke* is *Chi + na + eke,* the "source being" + "that/who" + "creates," and *Chukwu* is *Chi + Ukwu,* the "source being" + "great," "immense," or "superlative." *Chukwu,* then, means "the great source being." Obasi is another, ancient name of the supreme being of the Igbo, but it is no longer in common use.

Chukwu is said to live away in the depths of the sky, but he is not really so distant, as he takes much interest in the affairs of human being. He is the creator and organizer of the universe. The Igbo people do not have any systematic account of the creation of the world, though the Igbo myth of creation states that Chukwu created the nature deities such as Anyanwu (Sun), Igwe or Amadioha (Sky), Ala (Earth), and so on. These deities are considered to be essential descendant powers of Chukwu; for instance, Anyanwu (Sun) is considered to be the son of emanation of Chukwu. Deities serve as messengers of Chukwu and usually are delegated to supervise different parts of the universe. The deities serve as the mediators between Chukwu and human beings. Chukwu creates a human spirit and gives him a *chi* (spirit that creates), which determines and dispenses the destiny of a person and protects and guards him. Chukwu controls the material world, offers the world new crops, and organizes the universe through the deities. For instance, it is Igwe who comes in the form of rain to fertilize Ala, his wife, to produce crops for human beings. Igwe also manifests the power and anger of Chukwu in thunderbolts and lightning to discover and punish undetected criminals.

It is important to note that there exist personal, family, and public altars of the supreme being among the Igbo, in contrast to most other African societies. People offer direct and regular sacrifices to Chukwu, as well as to deities in his behalf. Chukwu has several cult symbols, such as a tree planted in front of one's house. At the base of this tree is left broken pots and plates. P. Amaury Talbot succinctly describes the shrine of Chukwu thus: "The most common symbol of Chukwu is *Ogbu,* cotton, or *Awha* (or chi) tree, or sapling or a post, some four to six inches high, usually accompanied by round or flat stones, and a pot or pots, containing water and sometimes yellowwood, eggs, phallic chalk-cones round stones and palm-wine" (Talbot, 1926, p. 41).

Mulungu (Bantu and Sudanese of East Africa). Mulungu is the chief god of most Bantu-speaking peoples of East Africa: the Yao and Zimba of Malawi and Mozambique, the Kamba of Kenya, and the Gogo of Tanzania all recognize Mulungu as their supreme being. Also, the Swahili-speaking peoples of East and Central Africa use *Mungu* as the name of the supreme being. Variations of this name are *Muungu, Mungu, Murungu,* and *Mvungu. Mulungu* and its variations are claimed to be found in more than forty Bantu languages. It is said that *Mumbi,* which derives from a verb meaning "to create" or "to bring into existence," is an old name among the Bantu. These variations, which supposedly are due to different intonations by the several peoples, could be seen as insignificant in terms of the meanings and conceptions of the supreme being. *Mulungu* is a word of unknown origin, but it indicates the almighty and ever-present creator.

Mulungu is strongly associated with celestial phenomena, as the sky is said to be his abode, the thunder his voice, and the lightning his power. He rewards the good and punishes the wicked. As an instrument of displeasure and punishment, he uses drought. The common myth revolving around Mulungu relates to the creation of the world, the origins of death, the separation of heaven and earth, and the origin of man. Like most African creation myths, the Yao myth states that only Mulungu and the animals existed in the beginning. There was a day when chameleon, one of the animals, was fishing. He suddenly found in his net a pair of human beings, whom he referred to as unknown. He took the man and the woman to Mulungu, who instructed him (the chameleon) to take them out of the trap and put them down on the earth to grow. This was the first pair of human beings. Mulungu commanded the chameleon to raise the people and teach them the things they would begin to do including the ability to create fire. However, these human beings could not control the fire, and it raged across the earth and drove Mulungu away into the heavens through the rope which Spider spun for Mulungu. Mulungu still interacts with human being in their day-to-day affairs, however, particularly when human beings violate moral order. Mulungu is by nature benevolent. Although no formal cult is made for Mulungu and prayers are rarely directed to him, he is ruler and judge, omnipotent and omnipresent. Prayers are directed to lesser spirits who dwell on the earth to solicit and ensure their benevolence.

Nzambi. Nzambi (whose nickname is Mpungu) is the supreme being of the Bakongo people, a native tribe of the lower Congo River area. According to the Bakongo, Nzambi is the creator of men and all other things, including traditional medicine, which the people believe was given to the first inhabitants at the time of creation and passed on from generation to generation. The medicine is to be used for good, as expressed in their common saying that "if he had not given us our fetishes (*sic*), we should all be dead long ago." Nzambi is the sovereign master. He is inaccessible and unapproachable. He is believed by the people to have placed human beings here on earth, and he can take them away. As the creator, he is involved in the birth of every child.

Nzambi is invisible and very powerful. He watches a human being, searches him or her out everywhere, and takes him or her away, inexorably, whether young or old. Among the laws of the Bakongo are *nkondo mi Nzambi* (God's prohibitions), the violation of which constitutes a *sumu ku Nzambi* (sin against Nzambi), and an ordinary sanction of this is a *lufwa lumbi* (bad death). Thus, at the moral level, Nzambi is responsible for punishing violators of his prohibitions.

Nhialic. Nhialic, otherwise known as Jok ("spirit" or "power") is the supreme god of the Dinka people, a group numbering nearly four million in the southern Sudan region. Nhialic, which means "that which is above [in the sky]," is regarded as the greatest of the powerful and unseen superhuman forces and powers. He is referred to as creator and father. He is the giver of rain from the sky, where he resides. He is also described as the first ancestor of the people.

According to the Dinka myth of creation, Nhialic created the first people, whom he placed in a world of darkness. Nhialic was originally close to human beings, for the earth and the sky were very close to each other. Human beings could ascend to Nhialic freely by climbing a rope that connected them. Nhialic gave Garang and Abuk, the first humans, all the things that they wanted. Nhialic, however, gave instructions on how they should conduct themselves, including how much they could eat, where they could go, and the nature of human interpersonal relationships.

But one day, Abuk, the first woman, took a pestle to pound millet. Unfortunately, as she raised up the pestle she struck Nhialic, who then withdrew from the people by cutting the rope that connected him with them. This is what caused the separation of heaven and earth, and it marked the end of the golden age of Nhialic's direct protection of man, thus introducing work, suffering, and death.

Another version of Dinka myth states that the separation of heaven and earth was caused by Nhialic's refusal to yield to Aruu (Dawn), one of the ancestors, to make an opening in the world for people to see, so Aruu split the world in two with an ax, and the sky and the earth were divided to allow light to appear.

The influence of Nhialic on human lives is immense and noticeable, always affecting them for good or ill. Nhialic dispenses punishment to the wicked. Life and health are thought of as gifts attributable to Nhialic. The Dinka, who are mostly hunters, fishers, and subsistence farmers, make regular votive offerings to Nhialic in appreciation for recovery from illness, relief from famine, and success in hunting.

Kwoth. Kwoth, the supreme being of the Nuer of Republic of Sudan, is the concept on which the people's religion and worldview is centered. The etymology of Kwoth is taken from such actions as "blowing the embers of a fire; blowing into the uterus of a cow, while a *tulchan* is propped up before it, to make it give milk; the blowing out of air by the *bulyak* or puff fish . . . to blow on fire, to blow the nose, etc." (Evans-Pritchard, 1967, pp. 134–135). Evans-Pritchard claims that the Nuer conceive of Kwoth as being a pure spirit, a creative spirit. Basically, he is identified as Kwoth *nhial,* or *Kwoth a nhial,* meaning the spirit of the heavens or the spirit (who is) in the heavens. As the creator of material and nonmaterial entities, including custom and tradition, Kwoth is the first cause who provides the final explanation as an expression of ultimate rationality. That is, the meanings and origins of all that exist in the world are traced to him. Kwoth is both remote and far. He is both within and above the world. Although his exact nature is difficult to explain, he is said to be ubiquitous, and this is explained from the point of view of wind or air being present everywhere. He is comonly addressed as *gwandong,* a word that has been translated as "grandfather" or "ancestor," but which literally means "old father."

Kwoth plays a part in social and personal life. He judges human conduct, sanctioning right conduct and condemning wrong behaviors. Kwoth does this by rewarding a "righteous" person—one who does not violate the taboos of the land—with the good things of life. On the other hand, those who violate the taboos are inflicted with sickness. The gravity of the sickness is said to be the consequence of the seriousness of the taboo on the social order.

It is noted, as Evans-Pritchard remarks (1956, pp. 48–49), that the influence of Christianity and Islam on the Nuer does not affect their conception and perception of

Kwoth. The Nuer hold the view that Kwoth is the same supreme being as the Christian and Muslim God, only called by different names and communicated with in different manners. But the Nuer have a different attitude toward Kwoth when compared with believers in the Christian and Muslim God. They regard Kwoth as their father and friend, even though he punishes human beings.

The Nuer offer both public and private prayers. Apart from the corporate expression of belief in the reality of this supreme being, particularly in ritual prayers, individual dependence on God is expressed in spontaneous prayers, sometimes spoken aloud and sometimes unspoken. Evans-Pritchard's perception of the people's dependence on Kwoth is that of an "intimate, personal, relationship between man and God. This is apparent . . . in their habit of making short supplications at any time. This is a very noticeable trait of Nuer piety." (Evans-Pritchard, 1956, p. 317).

Ndjambi. Ndjambi is the supreme being of the Herero of the Bantu tribe of southwest Africa. He is also known as Karunga by the Ovambo, the neighboring tribe of the Herero. Ndjambi is said to reside in heaven. He is principally regarded as the giver of rain, and his voice is claimed to be clearly heard at the rising of the clouds. There is a great reverence for the name *Ndjambi,* which is not expected to be uttered. His most striking attribute is kindness, and human successes, achievements, and blessings are attributed to him. However, the worship of Ndjambi is not given any cultic form.

Ngai. Ngai, sometimes written as Mogai, is regarded as the supreme being, the Creator, and the giver of all things to the Kikuyu îGikuyuï, Masaai, and Kamba peoples of the Kenya Highlands of East Africa. Ngai's abode is the sky, but his special dwelling place on earth is Mount Kenya, called Kere-Nyaga (mountain of brightness). People face the mount whenever they pray, asking their ancestors for any kind of help. He also visits several places on earth where he makes a temporarily abode. These places are regarded as resting places of Ngai whenever he comes to carry out a "general inspection" among his people. During such inspection tours, he brings blessings and punishment to people, according to their behavior.

Unlike the supreme being of many other African communities, Ngai is approached with prayers and sacrifices that are traditionally offered to him on those special places where he is said to dwell. Certain big and large trees, which are regarded as sacred, are often chosen as places of prayer and sacrifice to Ngai. There are also four sacred mountains at the four cardinal directions of Kenya. Prayers and sacrifices are offered, particularly in moments of communal crisis and disaster, such as drought and epidemic, and for communal needs, such as planting, harvesting, and rites of passage. Prayers are usually accompanied by offering and animal sacrifice. Home-brewed beer and milk are offered to Ngai. These are consumed by the elders, prepubescent children, and postmenopausal women who attend the sacrifice, and a portion is burned on the fire for Ngai.

Ngai is invoked by chiefs or elders on behalf of the community or, in extreme cases, for personal need or distress. Ngai is approached only after lesser spiritual powers, including the ancestors, have been tried and found wanting. This level of relationship reflects the traditional social and political hierarchical structure and pattern of the Kikuyu society when societal problems or disputes are being resolved.

UNkulunkulu. The development of uNkulunkulu as a supreme deity among the Zulu people, a large ethnic group in South Africa, is shrouded in mystery. The name *uNkulunkulu,* from the Zulu language, is a contraction of words in which a superlative adjective is repeated: *uNkulunkulu* translates as "great, great one" or "old, old one." However, from what one can infer from the Zulu traditional myth on the development of the name, uNkulunklulu appears as a mystical figure. He is also called *Mvelinqangi,* meaning "the first outcomer." The Zulu regard Mvelinqangi as the ancestor of all. Although one oral tradition identifies uNkulunkulu with uThlanga, who is at the same time a man and a woman, the most common myth among the people holds that he is the first man. This myth suggests that uNkulunkulu appears from, or is created by, the breaking off of reeds, or that he comes out of, or breaks off from, a bed of reeds.

UNkulunkulu is "the first outcomer" human being, "the first man," and "the ancestor of all," and all humans are said to be derived from him. His status as the supreme deity and creator among the Zulu may have been occasioned by the influence of Christian missionaries' search for an equivalent of their biblical God; otherwise, uNkulunkulu is merely an early ancestral figure of the Zulu. However, there have been no known descendants from oral histories, narratives, and communal or corporate rituals from which uNkulunkulu could be traced. The Zulu believe that uNkulunkulu is the creator of human beings, that he gives them their social institutions such as marriage and chieftainship, and that he gives them spirits, diviners who would reveal the hidden things of the past and future, and doctors who would treat various diseases among the people.

WORSHIP. Although there is universality of belief in a supreme being among most African peoples, it is correctly asserted that there is no formal worship accorded the being and no organized cults or great temples built for him in most African communities. However, most popular myths about the supreme being express that he is a reality to many people. Most of the myths state that the sky is his dwelling place, which was once much nearer to the earth. Generally speaking, the worship of the supreme being is done through his many intermediaries, who bear aspects of his nature and characters.

Because the supreme being of most African communities is claimed to have his abode or seat in the sky, individual

Names of Notable Supreme Beings in Africa

Names of Supreme Being(s)	Meanings/Identity	Peoples	Location(s)
Morimo	Creator	Ndebele	Botswana
Naawum	Heaven; Creator of the world; Ultimate cause of everything that happens	Tallensi	Burkina Faso
Imana	Maker of all things	Hutu	Burundi
Kalumba		Luba	Congo
*Mulungu (Muungu, Murungu)	Supreme Deity, Judge, Ruler; Creator, god of storms and rain,;formless	Bantu-speaking	East Africa
		Karimojong	Ethiopia
Mawu, Nyame, Onyankopon	Supreme Deity	Ewe, Fon	Ghana
Nyonmo, Nyama, Nyam	Creator	Ga	Ghana
Odomankoma	That which is uninterruptedly, infinitely and exclusively full of grace." His capacity as creator is called *Odomankoma*	Akan and Ga	Ghana
Nana Buluku	Great Ancient Deity, Creator	Ewe-speaking people of Ghana; Fon of Dahomey	Ghana and Dahomey
**Nyame, Onyankopon, Onyame*	The great being of fullness or of satisfaction; the bright, glorious God of the heaven and earth who is before and gabo ve all things	Akan	Ghana, Ivory Coast, Twi and Ashanti
**Ngai*	Creator, Giver of all things	Kikuyu (Gikuyu), Masaai, and Kamba peoples of Kenya highlands of East Africa	Kenya
Molimo (Modimo)	Light, Protector, Father	Basuto	Lesotho
Nzambi	The Sovereign Master, unapproachable, sustainer of the universe and human beings	Bakongo	Lower Congo River area
**Amma*	Supreme god	Dogon	Mali
Mulungu		Swazi	Mozambique
Ndjambi, Karunga,	Heavenly Being	Herero (Bantu)	Namibia (South-West Africa)
Soko	Great or Supreme Deity that resides in heaven	Nupe	Nigeria
Aondo	The great unknown above, or the power above (skyey heaven) that creates and rules all things	Tiv	Nigeria
Temearau	She who creates and sustains all things	Ijo	Nigeria
Ọbasẹ wạ odeen		Yakurr	Nigeria (Cross River State)
Abasi Ibom	Creator, Greatest God who lives above the earth, governor of all	Ibibio	Nigeria (East)
Osanobwa, Osanobua	Creator and absolute sustainer of the universe	Edo	Nigeria (Mid-west)
*Olodumare; Olorun	Almighty Being; Owner of heaven	Yoruba	Nigeria (West)
Chukwu, Chineke	Great Spirit that creates	Igbo	Nigeria (East)
Akongo	Supreme spirit, the creator of the universe, the moulder of human beings like a potter; Beginner, Unending, Almighty, Inexplicable	Ngombe	Republic of Congo
Unkulunkulu, Mwali (Mwari)			Rhodesia (Zimbabwe)
Imana	Maker of all things, creator	Tusi	Rwanda
Ngewo, Leve	Creator, Eternal one who rules from the above. Leve is used by old people. This suggests that Leve is an ancient name of their Supreme Being.	Mende	Sierra Leone
Meketa, Yataa	One who was in existence long ago before anyone met him or before he was revealed to men; the great one. Meketa is the ancient name, not used in everyday language	Kono	Sierra Leone

(continued)

TABLE 1.

Names of Notable Supreme Beings in Africa (continued)

Names of Supreme Being(s)	Meanings/Identity	Peoples	Location(s)
**uNkulunkulu*	Great, Great One, Old, Old One; Ancient of days, creator of all things, ancestor of men	Zulu	South Africa
Kalunga	Supreme Spirit	Ovambo	South Africa
**Kwoth*	Creator, Spirit of the sky	Nuer	Sudan
**Nhialic, or Jok (Juok, Juong),*	Creator, father	Dinka	Sudan (Southern Sudan)
Mkulumncandi, Umkhulumncandi			Swaziland
Engai		Arusha	Tanzania
Katonda	Greater of all things in existence, creator and moulder of human beings	Baganda	Uganda
Adronga	Creator, Spirit in the sky and in the stream	Lugbara	Uganda and Belgian Congo
Dondari		Fulani	West Africa
Muluku (Vidye Muluku)	Great Lord, first ancestor	Baluba	Zaire
Chiuta, Lesa, Mulungu, Nyambe	The Great One of the bow (rainbow), Controller, Organiser	Tumbuka	Zambia
Bumba		Bashongo	Zambia
Leza	First Cause, creator of all, heat and cold, famine and disease, Moulder, Constructor	Tonga	Zambia, Tanzania, Upper Congo

Table courtesy of the author

and communal prayers are offered to him facing the sky or a special place considered to possess his divine presence—usually "high up." Generally, no temples are built or priests specifically initiated to serve in the worship of the supreme being. Ubiquitous in nature, no permanent settlement is constructed for him, nor is he localized. Thus, to the Africans, the sky is the face of God. However, among the Ashanti of Ghana there are temples of Nyame where priests serve as attendants, and the Dogon have group altars for Amma, at which the village chief officiates. A few other African peoples have cults for their supreme beings where they organize special and communal ceremonies. At crucial moments and times of crisis when deities or ancestors who serve as intermediaries fail, appeal is made to the supreme being, who is regarded as the highest authority. Certain symbols are also used to depict the characters of God and to express the people's need for such symbolic intervention at moments of need.

Early Studies and Contemporary Appropriation/Adoption. Much has been documented and cited of the impressions of explorers, anthropologists, and Christian missionaries of Africans' conceptions and perceptions of their supreme beings. Notable among early non-African commentators and writers on African religions include David Livingstone (1813–1873), Henry M. Stanley (1841–1904), Emil Ludwig, and Leo Frobenius (1873–1938). Their works represent the wide range of misconceptions about African religious worldviews, particularly the idea of the supreme being. These misconceptions later formed the basis for, and were propagated in, the scholarly works of Sir James Frazer (1854–1941), Émile Durkheim (1858–1917), and Lucien Lévy-Bruhl (1857–1939). The effect of the misconceptions on early African converts to Christianity were immense, for the Africans internalized the obnoxious labels of *paganism* and *heathenism.* The labeling came from Christian evangelists who demonized aspects of African indigenous cultures and practices (e.g., food and fruit items, music and drums, dress and dressing patterns, indigenous rites of passage) that were associated and connected with the Africans' ideas, beliefs, and worship, particularly regarding the worship of a supreme being.

Sir Samuel Baker, in his lecture to the Ethnological Society of London in 1866 (as cited in Eric O. Ayisi's *An Introduction to the Study of African Culture*), said that "without any exception, they [the Northern Nilotes, and indeed Africans in general] are without a belief in a supreme being. Neither have they any form of worship nor idolatry nor is the darkness of their minds enlightened by even a ray of superstition" (Ayisi, 1980, p. 72). Leo Frobenius, in *The Voice of Africa* (1913) made a similar submission, while giving credence to Islamic civilization in Africa: "Before the introduction of a genuine faith and a higher standard of culture by the Arabs, the natives had neither political organization, nor, strictly spoken, any religion, nor any industrial development" (p. 1f). The often and popularly cited questions of Emil Ludwig (cited by Edward Geoffrey Parrinder in *African Traditional Religion*) strongly expressed the same negative impression when he exclaimed "How can the untutored African conceive of God? How can this be? Deity is a philosophical concept which savages are incapable of forming" (Parrinder, 1962, p. 9).

However, African indigenous scholars and a few non-African scholars of African religions who have taken painstaking steps to study African traditional religion have challenged the misleading and erroneous assertions of the early scholars. The symposium *African Ideas of God* was an excellent exploration and breakthrough exercise that established the fact that most African peoples have had a belief in a supreme being as part of their worldview and religious praxis. Since 1950, when the symposium was published into a volume, many books and several articles have been written by African authors in support of the African belief in a spiritual being. Most prominent among these scholars are E. Bolaji Idowu, John S. Mbiti, Edward Geoffrey Parrinder, J. Omosade Awolalu and P. Adelumo Dopamu, and Jacob K. Olupona. They observed that long before their contact with Europeans and Arabs, Africans had developed a variety of distinct social institutions, political structures, cultures, and languages that were a product of their indigenous religious worldview, which had its basis in the belief in a supreme being. Understandably, however, the uncodified form of religious doctrines as well as the practical expression of religious life of the Africans (which developed from the respect and humility with which African sociopolitical and civil life is built) did not allow the early observers to objectively assess Africans' perception of the supreme being.

Conversion to Christianity and Islam, and the civilizing and proselytizing effects of this conversion, contributed to the demonizing process of African concepts of the supreme being, though it also strongly supported the view that Africans had, and still have, a belief in one supreme being, as can be seen in indigenous translations of the Bible and the Holy Qur'ān. These sacred texts use any or all of the indigenous names of African supreme beings described earlier as ancient or descriptive. For instance, among the Yoruba people of Nigeria, the Bible uses the word "Olórun" for God, "Olúwa" for Lord, and "Olódùmarè" for Almighty; the Yoruba version of the Qur'ān uses "Olórun" for Allah, and Olórun is found in day-to-day usage. Despite the deep-rooted seating of Islam among the Swahili people, Mulungu and its dialectal variations (Murungu, Mluku, Mulunguo, Muunguo) are used, and the indigenous names for the supreme being are mostly used instead of Allah. Mulungu is also adopted as the Christian equivalent for God.

With the emergence of the group of independent churches in Africa, there has been a heightened level of appropriation and adoption of indigenous belief systems and Christian tradition. The reason for this is that these churches operate within the indigenous worldview and religious sensibility, using indigenous languages that are full of metaphors and colors that appeal to people's imagination and sensitivity.

Scholars' use of the incorrect nomenclature to describe and define African supreme beings can be seen as a consequence of a lack of adequate knowledge of Africans' worldviews and languages. Early scholars had described these supreme beings as *deus absconditus* (withdrawn god) and *deus otiosus* (lazy god), both of which leave the world of human beings after creating the world. Polytheism—another term used by early Western scholars and early scholars on African religious traditions—is obvious in African religion, but it does not erode the position of the supreme being or African belief in it, because the supreme being is regarded as the finality of their life in thought and expression. Most African peoples regard their supreme being as the source being, creator, preserver, sustainer, and chief—as a sort of creative energy, the first ancestor who supervises all human and spiritual affairs and who operates a systematic structure. The supreme being is associated with lesser deities, ancestors, spirits, human beings, and natural phenomena. He involves all in the creation, maintenance, and administration of the universe. The African supreme being's association with other spiritual beings, human beings, and natural phenomena, and his involving them in the maintenance and administration of the universe, provides a complexity in the comparative analysis of the definitions and attributes of the African supreme being with the Christian-Muslim God. While Africans have a strong conception of the supreme being, they use a different definition and different attributes, which are directed toward finding meanings to, and explanations of, events, and toward seeking control over human affairs. The processes through which explanation, prediction, and control of human affairs are sought and achieved are explained by the practical involvement of human beings and spiritual agents responsible to the supreme being, who has the ultimate control of the universe.

The current shift in African beliefs and religious conceptions about the supreme being shows the dynamic nature, resilience, and integrative capability of African religion and culture to adapt, adopt, and appropriate other traditions. This ability is found both within and outside Africa, in places like Europe and many parts of the Americas, such as Cuba and Brazil, where African religious traditions have made inroads and are flourishing.

SEE ALSO African Religions, overview article; Cosmology, article on African Cosmologies.

BIBLIOGRAPHY

Awolalu, J. Omosade, and P. Ade Dopamu. *West African Traditional Religion.* Ibadan, Nigeria, 1979.

Ayisi, Eric O. *An Introduction to the Study of African Culture.* London, 1980.

Bascom, William. *The Yoruba of Southwestern Nigeria.* New York, 1969.

Berglund, Axel-Ivar. *Zulu Thought-Patterns and Symbolism.* London, 1976.

Booth, Newell S. Jr. "God and the Gods in West Africa." In *African Religions,* edited by Newell S. Booth, Jr., pp. 159–181. New York, London, and Lagos, Nigeria, 1977.

Callaway, Henry. *The Religious System of the Amazulu.* 1870; reprint, Cape Town, 1970.

Courlander, Harold. *Tales of Yoruba Gods and Heroes.* New York, 1973.

Danquah, J. B. *Akan Doctrine of God.* London, 1944.

Deng, Francis Mading. *Dinka Cosmology.* London, 1980.

Dickson, Kwesi A., and Paul Ellingworth, eds. *Biblical Revelation and African Beliefs.* Maryknoll, N.Y., 1969.

Downes, R. M., *Tiv Religion.* Ibadan, Nigeria, 1970.

Ellis, Alfred Burdon. *The Yoruba-Speaking Peoples.* London, 1894.

Evans-Pritchard, E.E. *Nuer Religion.* Oxford, 1956.

Evans-Pritchard, E.E. "Some Features of Nuer Religion." In *Gods and Rituals,* edited by J. Middleton. Austin, Tex. 1967.

Ezeanya, Stephen N. "God, Spirits, and the Spirit World." In *Biblical Revelation and African Beliefs,* edited by Kwesi Dickson and Paul Ellingworth, pp. 30–46. Maryknoll, N.Y., 1969.

Forde, Cyril Daryll, ed. *African Worlds: Studies in the Cosmological Ideas and Social Values of African Peoples.* Oxford, 1954.

Forde, Daryll, and G.I. Jones. *The Ibo and Ibibio-Speaking Peoples of South-eastern Nigeria.* London, 1950.

Fortes, M., and G. Dieterlen, ed. *African Systems of Thought.* London, 1965.

Frobenius, Leo. *The Voice of Africa,* vol. 1. London, 1913.

Gibbs, James L., ed. *Peoples of Africa.* New York, 1965.

Greene, Sandra E. "Religion, History and the Supreme Gods of Africa: A Contribution to the Debate." *Journal of Religion in Africa* 26, no. 2 (May 1996): 122–138.

Griaule, Marcel. *Conversations with Ogotemmêli.* Translated by Robert Redfield. London, 1965.

Harris, W.T. and Harry Sawyerr. *The Springs of Mende Belief and Conduct.* Sierra Leone, 1968.

Herskovits, Melville J. *Dahomey: An Ancient West African Kingdom,* vol. 2. New York, 1938.

Horton, Robin. *Patterns of Thought in Africa and the West: Essays in Magic, Religion and Science.* Cambridge, U.K., 1993.

Idowu, E. Bolaji. *Olodumare: God in Yoruba Belief.* London, 1962.

Idowu, E. Bolaji. "God." *Biblical Revelation and African Beliefs,* edited by Kwesi Dickson and Paul Ellingworth, pp. 17–29. Maryknoll, N.Y., 1969.

Idowu, E. Bolaji. *African Traditional Religion: A Definition.* London, 1973.

Ikenga-Metuh, Emefie. *African Religions in Western Conceptual Schemes: The Problem of Interpretation.* Ibadan, Nigeria, 1985.

Jahn, Janheinz. *Muntu: An Outline of the Neo-African Culture.* New York, 1961.

Kenyatta, Jomo. *Facing Mount Kenya.* New York, 1965. An impressive and concise introduction to the traditional life of the Kikuyu.

King, N. Q. *Religions of Africa.* New York, 1970.

Lawson, E. Thomas. *Religions of Africa: Traditions in Transformation.* San Francisco, 1985. A very brief textbook that focuses on Zulu and Yoruba religious systems.

Lienhardt, Godfrey. *Divinity and Experience: The Religion of the Dinka.* Oxford, 1961.

Lucas, J. Olumide. *The Religions of the Yorubas.* Lagos, Nigeria, 1948.

Mbiti, John S. *Concepts of God in Africa.* London, 1970. Topics include the nature and attributes of God, the problem of evil, anthropomorphism, the creation of man, worship, ethics, and death.

Mbiti, John S. *Introduction to African Religion.* London, 1975.

Mbiti, John S. *African Religions and Philosophy.* Oxford, 1990.

Mbiti, John S. "Divinities, Spirits, and the Living Dead." In *The Ways of Religion: An Introduction to the Major Traditions,* edited by Roger Eastman, pp. 442–450. New York and Oxford, 1993.

M'Timkulu, Donald. "Some Aspects of Zulu Religion." In *African Religions,* edited by Newell S. Booth, Jr., pp. 13–30. New York, London, and Lagos, Nigeria, 1977.

Nadel, S. F. *Nupe Religion.* London, 1954.

Olupona, Jacob K., ed. *African Traditional Religions in Contemporary Society.* Saint Paul, Minn., 1991.

Olupona, Jacob K., ed. *African Spirituality: Forms, Meaning, and Expressions.* New York, 2000.

Parrinder, Edward Geoffrey. *West African Religion.* London, 1949.

Parrinder, Edward Geoffrey. *African Traditional Religion.* London, 1962, 1975.

P'Bitek, Okot, *African Religions in Western Scholarship.* Nairobi, 1971.

Rattray, R. S. *The Ashanti.* Oxford, 1923.

Ray, Benjamin C. *African Religions: Symbol, Ritual, and Community.* Englewood Cliffs, N.J., 1976.

Sawyerr, Harry. *God: Ancestor or Creator?: Aspects of Traditional Beliefs in Ghana, Nigeria, and Sierra Leone.* London, 1970.

Shorter, Aylward. *African Christian Theology: Adaptation or Incarnation?* London, 1977. See especially "God and the Sun in the Religious Thought of East Africa," pp. 61–78.

Smith, Edwin W., ed. *African Ideas of God: A Symposium.* 2d ed. London, 1950.

Sproul, Barbara C. *Primal Myths: Creating the World.* New York and London, 1979.

Steward, Julian H., ed. *Contemporary Change in Traditional Societies,* vol. 1. Urbana, Ill., 1967.

Talbot, P. Amaury. *The Peoples of Southern Nigeria.* London, 1926.

Taylor, J. V. *The Primal Vision.* Ibadan, Nigeria, 1963.

Thayer, James S. "Amma" (vol. 1, pp. 237–238); "Kwoth" (vol. 8, pp. 409–410); "Mulungu" (vol. 10, pp. 155–156); "Ngai" (vol. 10, p. 420); "Nhialic" (vol. 10, pp. 424–425); "Nyame" (vol. 11, p. 29). In Mircea Eliade, ed. *The Encyclopedia of Religion.* New York, 1987.

Vedder, Heinrich. *The Native Tribes of South-West Africa.* Capetown, South Africa, 1928.

Williamson, S. G. *Akan Religion and the Christian Faith.* Accra, Ghana, 1965.

Zahan, Dominique. *The Religion, Spirituality, and Thought of Traditional Africa.* Chicago, 1970.

Zuesse, Evan M. *Ritual Cosmos: The Sanctification of Life in African Religions.* Athens, Ohio, 1979.

David Ògúngbilé (2005)

ISBN 0-02-865738-1
90000
9 780028 657387